D0467625

RV

Chambers

Dictionary
of Music

CHAMBERS

CHAMBERS
An imprint of Chambers Harrap Publishers Ltd
7 Hopetoun Crescent
Edinburgh, EH7 4AY

www.chambers.co.uk

This edition published by Chambers Harrap Publishers Ltd 2006

From the *Hutchinson Concise Dictionary of Music*, © Research Machines plc
(2005), all rights reserved. Helicon Publishing is a division of Research
Machines.

A CIP catalogue record for this book is available from the British Library.

ISBN-13: 978 0550 10322 2
ISBN-10: 0550 10322 8

Chambers Editor: Katie Brooks
Managing Editor: Camilla Rockwood
Publishing Manager: Patrick White
Prepress: David Reid

Designed and typeset by Chambers Harrap Publishers Ltd, Edinburgh
Printed in Great Britain by Clays Ltd, St. Ives plc

Contents

Introduction

Chambers Dictionary of Music was previously published as *The Hutchinson Concise Dictionary of Music*, which in turn was abridged from the acclaimed single-volume *Hutchinson Encyclopedia of Music*. It therefore draws on the accumulated musical expertise of those who were involved in editing or revising its 'family' volumes (notably Eric Blom, Sir Jack Westrup, David Fallows, David Cummings and Tallis Barker). The contents have been thoroughly revised, ensuring that it is an up-to-date as well as authoritative resource. *Chambers Dictionary of Music* now comprises approximately 6,500 entries and over 100 musical examples. It uses clear, accessible language and features ample cross-references for further explanation, ensuring ease of use.

The production of this type of compact reference work requires a particular focus and a strict policy of selection. The technical and theoretical aspects of music are central to the *Chambers Dictionary of Music*; it therefore contains extensive coverage of various musical genres and forms as well as the many instructions annotated in musical scores. The repertory is another essential aspect of music; many significant works are covered and biographies of composers, including lists of their principal compositions, are supplied. Information about librettists is included, as well as details of the writers on whose works notable compositions are based. Coverage of musical instruments, their makers and their mainstream repertory is provided; theorists, musicologists, patrons and some famous conductors in history are also described. The chronology provided at the end of the book allows the historical context of composers and works to be appreciated.

With this sharp focus, *Chambers Dictionary of Music* addresses the needs of a wide range of users. Although professional musicians often have access to much larger reference works, many also find it valuable to possess one compact book – to locate information quickly, to read a succinct yet accurate summary of a topic, or to have to hand when on the move. Avid concert-goers, enthusiastic CD collectors and regular radio-listeners will equally welcome a music dictionary that will inform without being beyond either the scope of their pockets or the depth of their understanding. Music students, whether at school, studying for graded music examinations or in further and higher education, will also find it an invaluable information resource.

The dictionary has been endorsed by the Open University as a recommended reference work for some of its music courses – it is a set text for *A214: Understanding Music: Elements, Techniques and Styles* – and it is fitting that two distinguished scholars of the Open University's Music Department, Professor Donald Burrows and Dr Barrie Jones, have been associated with the careful selection and editing of its contents. The result of their labours is a balanced and coherent dictionary that provides an accurate and concise reference source for the core information vital to the understanding and enjoyment of music.

A in music, the first note of the diatonic scale A–G, or A above middle C; orchestral ➤ **concert pitch**.

The note A in the treble clef.

Aaron or **Aron, Pietro (c.1480–c.1550)** Italian monk and contrapuntist. He wrote on history and science of music; his *Toscanello* (1523) gives advice on musical practice. He worked in Imola and Venice, and entered the monastery of San Leonardo, Bergamo, in 1536.

ABA form in musical analysis, a compositional structure comprising three basic parts, in which the first section (A) is followed by a second, often contrasting section (B), before the original section (A) returns in the same or a varied state. It is a simple kind of ➤ **ternary form**.

a battuta (Italian 'at the beat, with the beat') musical direction indicating that after a free passage the strict time is to be resumed.

Abbà-Cornaglia, Pietro (1851–1894) Italian composer. He studied at the Milan Conservatory and later became a teacher and music historian.
Works OPERA *Isabella Spinola* (1877), *Maria di Warden* (1884), *Una partita di scacchi* (1892).
OTHER Requiem; chamber music.

Abbado, Marcello (1926–) Italian composer and pianist, brother of the conductor Claudio Abbado. He studied with the composer Giorgio Ghedini at the Milan Conservatory, and from 1951 held teaching posts in Venice, Piacenza, Pesaro, and Milan; he was director of the Milan Conservatory from 1972.
Works ORCHESTRAL *Costruziono* for five small orchestras (1964); concerto for violin, piano, and two chamber orchestras (1967), concerto for piano, quartet, and orchestra (1969).
VOCAL *Ciapo*, cantata (1945).
CHAMBER three string quartets (1947, 1953, 1969).

abbellimenti (Italian 'embellishments') ornaments, especially florid passages introduced into vocal music.

Abbey, John (1785–1859) English organ builder. He worked in Paris from 1826 and built many organs in France and South America.

Abe, Komei (1911–) Japanese composer and conductor. He studied in Tokyo and with Joseph Rosenstock in Germany. He was professor of composition at Kyoto University 1969–74. His music is in a diatonic style.
Works ORCHESTRAL two symphonies (1957, 1960); sinfonietta (1965).
CONCERTOS cello concerto (1942), piano concerto (1945).
CHAMBER eleven string quartets (1935–82); piano sextet (1964); serenade (1963).

Abegg Variations Schumann's Op. 1, for piano, a set of variations on a theme constructed on the notes A, B flat, E, and G, and bearing the dedication 'à Mlle Pauline, comtesse d'Abegg', who did not exist, though there was a family of that name. The existence of Meta Abegg has yet to be proved. The work was composed in 1830 and published in 1832.

Abel, Carl Friedrich (1723–1787) German musician and composer. He played the harpsichord and viola da gamba, and was a member of the court band at Dresden 1743–58. From 1759 he lived in London, where he was appointed chamber musician to Queen Charlotte.
Abel was joint promoter, with Johann Christian Bach, of the Bach-Abel Concerts (1765–81). He wrote a large quantity of instrumental music, of which the works for viola da gamba are perhaps the most notable. His 40 symphonies and overtures are notable for their advanced harmonic style.

Abélard, Pierre (1079–1142) French scholar and musician. He composed songs for his beloved, Héloïse, Latin Lamentations, and a planctus (after 1130). He was castrated after secretly marrying Héloïse in 1118.

Abencérages, Les, ou L'Étendard de Grenade, **The Abencerrages, or The Standard of Granada** opera by Luigi Cherubini (libretto by V J E de Jouy, based on a novel by Jean-Pierre de Florian), first produced at the Paris Opéra, France, on 6 April 1813. The story deals with Moorish adventures in Spain.

Abendmusik or **Abendmusiken (German 'evening music')** evening performances of music of a semi-sacred character established by the German organist and composer Franz Tunder (1614–1667) in Lübeck in the 1640s and becoming so famous there that they were imitated by other north German towns, especially Hamburg. They were held mainly during Advent.

Abert, Hermann (1871–1927) German musicologist of Czech descent. He was professor of music at Leipzig University in succession to Hugo Riemann from 1920 and at Berlin from 1923. He wrote many historical works, including a greatly enlarged edition of Otto Jahn's *Mozart*.

Abos, Girolamo (1715–1760) Maltese composer, especially of Italian opera and church music; several of his operas were also produced in London, England.

Abraham, Gerald (1904–1988) English musicologist, a specialist in Russian music. He was professor of music at Liverpool University 1947–62, and Assistant Controller, Music, at the British Broadcasting Corporation (BBC) 1962–67. He edited volumes iv, vii, and ix of the *New Oxford History of Music* and coedited volume iii; he also wrote the *Concise Oxford History of Music* (1979).

Abraham and Isaac title of two musical works. The first is a sacred ballad for baritone and chamber orchestra by Stravinsky (Hebrew text), composed 1962–64 and first performed in Jerusalem, Israel, on 23 August 1964. The second is *Canticle II* by Benjamin Britten for alto, tenor, and piano, composed in 1952 for Kathleen Ferrier and Peter Pears and performed by them in Nottingham, England, on 21 January 1952.

Abramsky, Aleksandr (1898–1985) Russian composer. He studied at the Moscow Conservatory, and turned to Soviet ideology by writing an opera on the subject of life on a collective farm (*Laylikhon and Anarkhon*, 1943). His other works include a piano concerto (1941) and cantata, *Land of the Silent Lake* (1971).

Abreise, Die opera by Eugen d'Albert (libretto by F von Sporck, based on a play by August von Steigentesch), first produced in Frankfurt, Germany, on 20 October 1898. The plot concerns a husband's early return from a journey to test his wife's fidelity.

Absil, Jean (1893–1974) Belgian composer. He studied at the Brussels Conservatory, where he became professor in 1931, after being appointed director of Etterbeek Music Academy in 1923. Among his influences were Hindemith, Milhaud, and Bartók.

Works OPERA *Peau d'âne* (1937).
BALLET *Le Miracle de Pan* (1949).
RADIO OPERA *Ulysse et les Sirennes* (1939).
ORCHESTRAL five symphonies (1920–70).
CHAMBER four string quartets (1929–41), three string trios, and other chamber music.

absolute music music that refers to nothing apart from itself. It is intended to be enjoyed purely for its sound, as opposed to ➤ **programme music**, which is descriptive and has representational meaning.

absolute pitch or **perfect pitch** in music, the ability to sing or to recognize by sound the pitch of a note, without any prior reference point with which to determine the particular note.

Abstrakte Oper No. 1 opera by Boris Blacher (libretto by Werner Egk), first performed (as a concert) in Frankfurt, Germany, on 28 June 1953; the opera was first produced in Mannheim, Germany, on 17 October 1953. The text consists largely of nonsense words.

Abu Hassan Singspiel in one act by Carl Maria von Weber (libretto by F C Hiemer), first produced in Munich, Germany, on 4 June 1811. The story tells of Abu and his wife who attempt to feign death in order to gain a fortune.

Academic Festival Overture, German **Akademische Fest-Ouvertüre** Brahms's Op. 80, composed in 1880 and first performed at Breslau (Wrocław in modern-day Poland), on 4 January 1881, in acknowledgement of the honorary degree of doctor of philosophy, conferred on him by Breslau University in 1879. The thematic material is taken from German students' songs. The *Tragic Overture* (1880–81) was written as a companion piece.

Academie or **Akademie** 18th-century German term for a concert.

Acante et Céphise *pastorale-héroïque* by Jean-Philippe Rameau (libretto by J-F Marmontel), first produced at the Paris Opéra, France, on 18 November 1751. In the work, lovers are granted telepathic powers as protection against an evil character.

a cappella (Italian 'in the style of the chapel') choral music sung without instrumental accompaniment. In modern music it is characteristic of gospel music, doo-wop, and the evangelical Christian church movement.

Accademia (Italian 'academy' from Plato's Academia) Italian society for the encouragement and furtherance of science and/or the arts. An 'Accademia di Platone' was founded, on Plato's model, at the Medici court of Florence in 1470. The earliest academy of any importance devoted primarily to music was the 'Accademia Filarmonica' of Verona (1543); later ones included the 'Accademia di Santa Cecilia' in Rome (1584) and the 'Accademia Filarmonica' in Bologna (1666). In France the movement began with the foundation of the 'Académie de poésie et de musique' by Baïf and Thibaut in Paris in 1570, with the aim of promoting the ideals of ➤ *musique mesurée*.

accelerando (Italian 'quickening') in music, a tempo marking indicating a gradual increase in speed.

accent in music, the stress or emphasis on individual notes or passages. Accents may occur naturally in the music. For example, in 4/4 the main accent falls on the first beat, and a secondary accent, less strongly stressed, falls on the third beat. This is known as **metrical accent**. Adding loudness to a note is known as **dynamic accent** and is marked by symbols such as ‹ or with letters such as *sf* (*sforzando*) or *fz* (*forzando*).

acciaccatura (Italian 'crushed') in music, an ornamental ➤ **grace note** played simultaneously with, or just before, a normal note. It is released almost instantaneously. The notation is a ➤ **quaver** in small type with a line through the stem.

An acciaccatura in Bach's Partita no. 3.

accidental in music notation, a sharp (♯), flat (♭), or natural (♮) sign preceding a note which changes the pitch of the note by a semitone up (♯), down (♭), or back to normal (♮).

Less common are the double sharp (𝄪 or ♯♯), which raises a note by two semitones, and the double flat (♭♭), which lowers a note by two semitones (there is an example of a triple flat in one of French composer Alkan's piano works).

Once an accidental appears in a bar, it applies to all the other notes of the same pitch that follow until the end of the bar.

accolade in music, a brace used to join several staves.

accompaniment music and players providing a bass line, chord structure, and beat to support a solo performer. For example, a singer or instrumentalist may be accompanied by a piano or orchestra.

The accompaniment may provide harmonic support (as in the continuo playing of the 17th and 18th centuries), melodic imitation and continuation of the solo part (as in many 19th-century songs), atmospheric background (as in orchestral accompaniments to operatic arias), and so on. The art of the piano accompanist was raised to a high level in the 20th century by figures such as English pianist Gerald Moore.

In piano music, accompaniment can also refer to the chords in the bass supporting the melody in the treble.

Accompaniment to a Film Scene, German *Begleitungsmusik zu einer Lichtspielszene* orchestral work by Arnold Schoenberg, Op. 34. It was composed 1929–30 and first performed in Berlin, Germany, on 6 November 1930, conducted by Otto Klemperer. The three movements are for imaginary scenes.

accordatura (Italian 'at pleasure') the notes to which a string instrument is tuned.

accordion musical instrument of the free-reed organ type, comprising left and right wind chests connected by flexible, pleated bellows. The accordionist's right hand plays the melody on a piano-style keyboard of 26–34 keys, while the left hand has a system of push buttons for selecting single notes or chord harmonies.

It was patented under the name of Handäoline by Friedrich Buschmann in Berlin, Germany, in 1822, and by Cyrill Damien under the name Akkordion (German 'harmony') in Vienna, Austria, in 1829. The accordion spread throughout the world and can be heard in the popular music of Germany, France, China, Russia, and the USA.

Achille opera by Ferdinando Paër (libretto by G di Gamera), first produced at the Vienna Kärntnertortheater, Austria, on 6 June 1801. The plot concerns Achilles and Agamemnon who are allies in war but rivals during the siege of Troy. The opera contains a funeral march said to have been admired by Beethoven.

Achille et Polyxène opera by Jean-Baptiste Lully and Pascal Colasse (libretto by J G de Campistron), first produced at the Paris Opéra, France, on 7 November 1687. The opera was left unfinished at Lully's death and completed by his pupil Colasse.

Achille in Sciro, **Achilles in Scyros** opera by Antonio Caldara (libretto by Pietro Metastasio), first produced at the Vienna Burgtheater, Austria, on 13 February 1739. The story describes how Achilles is delayed by love on his way to Troy.

There are also settings with the same title by Niccolò Jommelli (Vienna, 1749), Johann Hasse

(Naples, 1759), Johann Gottlieb Naumann (Palermo, 1767), Giovanni Paisiello (St Petersburg, 1778), and Gaetano Pugnani (Turin, 1785).

Acide ➤ festa teatrale by Haydn (librettist G A Migliavacca), first produced in Eisenstadt, Austria, on 11 November 1763. Only fragments survive.

Aci, Galatea e Polifemo Italian serenata by Handel, composed in Naples, Italy, in 1708.

Acis and Galatea masque for soloists, chorus, and orchestra by Handel (libretto by John Gay, with additions by Hughes, Pope, and Dryden), composed about 1718 and first performed at Cannons, near Edgware, London; its first public performance was at the King's Theatre, London, on 10 June 1732. A composite, bilingual version of this and Handel's Italian serenata *Aci, Galatea e Polifemo* (1708) received several performances in 1732. The story tells of Galatea transforming Acis into a fountain, after he has been killed by the jealous Polyphemus.

Acis et Galatée, **Acis and Galatea** opera by Jean-Baptiste Lully (libretto by J G de Campistron), first produced at Anet at an entertainment given for the Dauphin by the Duke of Vendôme on 6 September 1686, and first performed in Paris on 17 September 1686.

acousmatic music term that is almost synonymous with ➤ electro-acoustic music.

acoustic term describing a musical instrument played without electrical amplification or assistance, for example an acoustic guitar or acoustic piano. It is also a term used by musicians to characterize room response, an important factor in performance. A so-called 'bright' acoustic provides a lively reverberation while a 'dry' or 'muddy' acoustic is lacking in response.

The Royal Festival Hall, London, designed with a neoclassical dry acoustic, had electrically assisted reverberation installed shortly after opening, in response to objections from musicians who performed there.

acoustics in music, the science of sound generation and propagation, embracing psychoacoustics, a branch of communications science.

acronym in music, any coded reference to a name using the letter names of notes to form a motif. The most widely quoted is B-A-C-H, playing on the German note names B (B♭)-A-C-H (B♮); Schumann's *Abegg Variations* (1830) is dedicated to a Meta Abegg; Berg's *Chamber Concerto* (1923–25) includes motivic references to himself and Schoenberg.

D-S-C-H is the acronym for Dimitri SCHostakowitsch (German spelling, S being 'Es' or E♭), the basis of a monumental *Passacaglia on DSCH*

(1961–62) by Ronald Stevenson. Boulez's tribute to Paul Sacher in *Messagesquisse* (1977) incorporates the French 'Re' for R.

action in music, the internal mechanism of a keyboard instrument, such as the piano, harpsichord, or organ, which links the keys to the strings or pipes when the keys are depressed. On a string instrument, it refers to the space between the strings and the ➤ fingerboard.

action musicale (French 'musical action') term used by Vincent ➤ d'Indy for some of his operas, evidently on the model of Wagner's 'Handlung für Musik'.

act tune term used in 17th-century England for a musical intermezzo or entr'acte performance between the acts of a play.

Actus Tragicus name often given to Johann Sebastian Bach's church cantata no. 106, *Gottes Zeit ist die allerbeste Zeit*. It was composed about 1707 for a funeral.

adagietto (Italian, diminutive of *adagio*, 'at ease', 'leisurely') in musical notation, indicating a pace slightly quicker than adagio. The best-known example is the fourth movement of Mahler's 5th symphony.

adagio (Italian 'at ease', 'leisurely') in music, a tempo marking indicating a slow pace, slightly faster than or approximately the same as ➤ lento (slow), depending on the historical period in which the music was written. It is also used as the title of a piece of music, or as the distinguishing title of a single movement.

Adam, Adolphe Charles (1803–1856) French composer of light operas and founder of the Théâtre National, Paris, in 1847. His stage works include *Le Postillon de Longjumeau/The Coachman of Lonjumeau* (1836) and *Si j'étais roi/If I Were King* (1852), but he is best remembered for his ballet score for *Giselle* (1841). Around 80 of his works were staged.

He wrote about 20 vaudeville pieces for three Paris theatres, 1824–29, then an operetta, *Pierre et Catherine*, for the Opéra-Comique in 1829, and his first opera, *Danilowa*, in 1830. He was allowed to study at the Paris Conservatory only as an amateur, but eventually became professor of composition there in 1849. His autobiographical *Souvenirs d'un musicien/A Musician's Memories* and *Derniers Souvenirs d'un musicien/Last Memories of a Musician* were published 1857–59.

Works OPERA *Le Châlet* (1834), *Le Postillon de Longjumeau* (1836), *Richard en Palestine* (after Scott; 1844), *La Poupée de Nuremberg* (1852), *Si j'étais roi* (1852), *Falstaff* (1856).

BALLET *Faust* (1833), *Giselle* (1841).

Adam de la Halle (c.1240–c.1290) French lyric poet, dramatist, and composer. His *Jeu de la feuillée* (c.1277) is one of the earliest French comedies. His *Le Jeu de Robin et Marion*, written in Italy about 1282, is a theatrical work with dialogue and songs set to what were apparently popular tunes of the day. It is sometimes called the forerunner of comic opera.

Adams, John Coolidge (1947–   ) US composer and conductor. He was director of the New Music Ensemble 1972–81, artistic adviser to the San Francisco Symphony Orchestra 1978–85, and Creative Chair of the St Paul Chamber Orchestra 1987–90. His minimalist techniques are displayed in *Electric Wake* (1968), *Heavy Metal* (1971), *Light over Water* (1983), *Harmonielehre* (1984–85), *My Father knew Charles Ives* (2003), and the operas *Nixon in China* (1987), *The Death of Klinghoffer* (1991), and *El Niño* (1999). His work *On the Transmigration of Souls* (2002, Pulitzer Prize) was written to commemorate the loss of life in the 11 September 2001 terrorist attacks on New York City.

He was elected to the American Academy of Arts and Letters in 1997.

Adam und Eva opera by Johann Theile (libretto by C Richter), first produced in Hamburg, Germany, at the opening of the first established German opera house, the Theater beim Gänsemarkt, on 12 January 1678.

Adam Zero ballet by Arthur Bliss (scenario by M Benthall, choreography by Robert Helpmann), first produced at Covent Garden, London, England, on 8 April 1946.

adaptation (Latin *adaptare*, 'to fit to') in literature and music, a term used to denote the modification of a particular art form to allow its suitable expression in another form, for example the adaptation of a play from a novel or the adaptation of a piece of music for a different type of instrument.

added sixth musical term invented by the French composer Jean-Philippe Rameau (*sixte ajoutée*) to describe the addition of a sixth from the bass to a subdominant chord when it is followed by the tonic chord.

An added sixth in the key of C major.

additional accompaniments in music, additional orchestral parts added to old oratorios and other works left by the composers in an incomplete state; to be played originally by the continuo player at the organ or harpsichord.

The most familiar examples are Mozart's additional accompaniments for Handel's *Messiah*.

'Adelaide' song by Beethoven to words by Friedrich von Matthisson, composed 1795–96 and dedicated to the poet.

'Adélaïde' Concerto violin concerto edited by Marius Casadesus in the early 1930s from a sketch supposedly written by Mozart and dedicated to Princess Adélaïde of France in 1766. It was in fact composed by Casadesus.

Adelson e Salvini opera by Bellini (his first) with libretto by A L Tottola. It was first produced at the San Sebastiano Conservatory in Naples in early 1825, and was revised in 1826 with recitative replacing dialogue. The story tells how Salvini, infatuated by Adelson's fiancée Nelly, recovers his senses after believing he has killed her.

Adieux, l'absence et le retour, Les, Farewell, Absence and Return title given by Beethoven's publisher for his piano sonata in E flat major, Op. 81a, composed 1809–10 and dedicated to the Archduke Rudolph to commemorate his absence from Vienna during the occupation by the French.

Adler, Guido (1855–1941) Czech-German musicologist and editor. He studied in Vienna, and was appointed professor of musicology at Prague University in 1885, becoming professor in Vienna in 1898, in succession to Eduard Hanslick. He wrote many books on music including studies of Wagner (1904) and Mahler (1916), and edited *Handbuch der Musikgeschichte/Handbook of the History of Music* (1924).

Adler, Samuel (1928–   ) German-born US composer. He moved to the USA at the age of 11 and studied with Walter Piston and Randall Thompson at Harvard, and with Aaron Copland and Serge Koussevitzky at Tanglewood. He was professor of composition at Eastman School of Music, New York, from 1966.

Works OPERA *The Outcasts of Poker Flat* (1962), *The Wrestler* (1972); *The Disappointment*, reconstruction of an American ballad opera of 1767.

ORCHESTRAL six symphonies (1953–83); organ concerto (1970); concerto for orchestra (1977), flute concerto (1977), piano concerto (1983).

CHAMBER seven string quartets (1945–81); four violin sonatas (1948–65).

VOCAL *From out of Bondage*, cantata (1969); *The Vision of Isaiah* for bass, chorus, and orchestra (1963).

ad lib(itum) (Latin 'freely') musical direction indicating that a passage may be played freely according to the performer's invention. The term also applies to an instrumental part that may be added or omitted in the performance of a work.

Adlung, Jakob (1699–1762) German organist and scholar. He was organist at Erfurt from 1727, and professor at the Gymnasium there from 1741. He wrote important music treatises.

Admeto rè di Tessaglia, Admetus, King of Thessaly opera by Handel (librettist Nicola Francesco Haym or Paolo Rolli), first produced at the King's Theatre, Haymarket, London, on 31 January 1727. In the plot, Alcestis promises to sacrifice herself to save Admetus. The opera was a vehicle for the rival sopranos Francesca Cuzzoni and Faustina Bordoni.

Adorno, Theodor Wiesengrund (1903–1969) German philosopher, social theorist, and musicologist. Deeply influenced by the thought of Karl Marx, Adorno joined the influential Institut für Sozialforschung (Institute for Social Research) in Frankfurt in 1931, becoming known as a member of the 'Frankfurt School' of sociologists. At the rise of fascism he fled first to Oxford (1935–38) and then to the USA, acquiring US citizenship, eventually returning to Frankfurt as professor of philosophy in 1949. With Max Horkheimer, the director of the Institute, he published the *Dialectic of Enlightenment* (1947), which argued that rationality had not been an emancipatory force, but that modern science was an instrument of dehumanization. He was also the main contributor to *The Authoritarian Personality* (1950), which analysed the psychological origins of fascism within a broadly Freudian framework.

As a young man, Adorno studied composition with Alban Berg, and he remained a great defender of the New Music of the Second Viennese School, which he saw as the 'authentic voice' of 20th-century music. He wrote prolifically on music, combining a practitioner's knowledge of compositional technique with his philosophical training, producing writings of forbidding intellectual complexity, but also of undoubted and profound insight. He is particularly known for his studies of individual composers, such as *Philosophy of Modern Music* (1948, on Schoenberg and Stravinsky), *In Search of Wagner* (1952), and *Mahler: A Musical Physiognomy* (1960).

Adorno was the main contributor to *The Authoritarian Personality* (1950), a psychoanalytical and social research project stemming partly from Erich Fromm's ideas, in which the F-scale (F standing for fascism) was constructed. His early writings show the influence of the Marxist thinking of Georg Lukács and Ernst Bloch, as well as considerable interest in Sigmund Freud.

Adorno's *Minima Moralia: Reflections from a Damaged Life* (1951) is a series of aphorisms in the style of Friedrich Nietzsche, many of which are concerned with the problems of exile. In *Negative Dialects* (1966) he is critical of all philosophers because they believed in some nonexistent absolute or ultimate entity that would explain everything else. This was dangerous, he argued, because it led to totalitarian and oppressive thinking that turned the individual into an object to be manipulated. Adorno also wrote extensively on the aesthetics and sociology of music and art, including *Die Philosophie der neuen Musik/The Philosophy of Modern Music* (1947).

Adrastus (lived 4th century BC) Greek philosopher. He was a pupil of Aristotle, and wrote a treatise on acoustics, *Harmonicon biblia tria*.

Adriana Lecouvreur opera by Francesco Cilèa (libretto by A Colautti, based on the play *Adrienne Lecouvreur* by Augustin Scribe and E Legouvé), first produced at the Teatro Lirico, Milan, Italy, on 6 November 1902. In the story Adriana meets a violent death from poisoned violets, given by a rival in love.

Adriano in Siria, Hadrian in Syria opera by Giovanni Battista Pergolesi (libretto by Pietro Metastasio), first produced at the Teatro San Bartolommeo in Naples, Italy, with the intermezzi *Livietta e Tracollo*, on 25 October 1734.

There are also settings with the same title by Antonio Caldara (Vienna, 1732), Baldassare Galuppi (Turin, 1740), Johann Hasse (Dresden, 1752), Johann Christian Bach (London, 1765), Ignaz Holzbauer (Mannheim, 1768), Pasquale Anfossi (Padua, 1777), Luigi Cherubini (Livorno, 1782), and Johann Mayr (Venice, 1798).

a due (Italian 'in two parts') musical term, generally written 'a 2'. The term is also used in the opposite sense in orchestral scores where pairs of instruments are to play in unison.

Aegyptische Helena, Die opera by Richard Strauss; see ➔ *Ägyptische Helena, Die*.

Aenéas ballet with chorus by the French composer Albert Roussel. It was composed in 1935 and first performed in Brussels, Belgium, on 31 July 1935.

Aeneas i Carthago opera by J M Kraus (libretto by J H Kellgren), first produced in Stockholm, Sweden, on 18 November 1799 and revived in concert form in Stockholm and New York in 1980.

Aeolian harp wind-blown musical instrument consisting of a shallow soundbox supporting gut strings at low tension and tuned to the same pitch. It produces an eerie harmony that rises and falls with the changing pressure of the wind. It originated in India and China, becoming popular in parts of central Europe during the 19th century. The instrument is named after Aeolus, the god of the winds in Greek mythology.

Aeolian mode in music, the mode or scale A–G, centred around and beginning on A, which uses only the notes of the C major scale.

aerophone one of the four main classes of musical instrument used in the original ➤ **Sachs–Hornbostel system**, the others being ➤ **idiophone**, ➤ **membranophone**, and ➤ **chordophone**. In instruments that are aerophones, the air itself is the primary vibrating agent. Subdivisions of aerophones distinguish between a wide range of types of instrument, but the class as a whole accommodates flutes and instruments of the orchestral brass family.

Aeschylus (525 BC–456 BC) Greek dramatist. His tragedies, based on mythical history, inspired generations of composers. Amongst works based on Aeschylus' themes are: **Fauré** (*Prométhée*), ➤ **Halévy** (*Prometheus*), **Hauer** (ditto), **Honegger** (*Prometheus* and *Les Suppliantes*), **Meyerbeer** (*Eumenides*), **Milhaud** (*Agamemnon, Choéphares*, and *Eumenides*), **Orff** (*Prometheus*), **Parry** (*Agamemnon*), ditto), **Pizzetti** (ditto), **Taneiev** (*Orestein*), and **Weingartner** (*Orestes*).

aetherophone electrophonic musical instrument that produces notes from the air. The transitions between the notes produce a sliding wail like that of a siren. It was invented by Lev Theremin of Leningrad in 1924.

The pitch of the note is determined by the position of the player's hand, but skill and judgement are needed to find the notes of the chromatic scale. See also ➤ **theremin**.

Affektenlehre (German 'doctrine of affections') 18th-century aesthetic theory, associated particularly with J J Quantz and C P E Bach, according to which music should be directly expressive of particular emotions. See ➤ *Empfindsamer Stil*.

affettuoso (Italian 'affectionate, feeling') in musical direction, 'with tenderness'.

affrettando (Italian 'urging, hastening') in music, a term often used to indicate emotional pressure as well as increase in speed.

Afranio Albonese (c.1480–c.1560) Italian priest. He was canon at Ferrara, and invented the phagotus, a type of bagpipes blown by bellows.

Africaine, L', The African Girl, original title **Vasco da Gama** opera by Giacomo Meyerbeer (libretto by Augustin Scribe), first produced at the Paris Opéra, France, on 28 April 1865, after Meyerbeer's death. The plot tells of the explorer Vasco da Gama who sails away from his native Portugal and is rescued by the tropical queen Sélika, whom he marries according to local custom. She later kills herself when he is seen with his former love Inés.

African music generally, traditional music from the area of Africa south of the Sahara desert. The continent of Africa is the home of thousands of different musical styles, but these divide roughly into two regional traditions: North African music, which is strongly influenced by Islam and Arab music; and the music of sub-Saharan Africa (sometimes called 'Black Africa'), which many people consider to be 'true' African music. The music of western, central, and southern Africa is based on ➤ **rhythm** much more than ➤ **melody** or ➤ **harmony**, and so percussion instruments, especially drums, almost always play a prominent part.

Within these two categories there are naturally many subdivisions, and some African music falls outside either classification. For example, Madagascar and parts of East Africa have been influenced by the music of Southeast Asia, and music in Egypt and Ethiopia has been influenced by Coptic Christianity. Used loosely, however, the term 'African music' is generally taken to mean the traditional music of western, central, and southern Africa.

music in sub-Saharan Africa The main feature of practically all traditional music south of the Sahara is the importance of rhythm, rather than melody or harmony, and of percussion instruments. Music is almost always a group activity with an emphasis on polyphonic forms resulting from group improvisation on short, simple themes, and ➤ **cross rhythms** formed by playing different rhythmic patterns together. These rhythmic ➤ **ostinatos** appear complex to the Western ear, partly because of their relationship with one another, and partly because of their frequent use of irregular subdivisions of the beat – for example, grouping a sequence of 12 beats as 4 + 3 + 5 (this technique, known as additive rhythms, has found much use in 20th-century European classical music, such as the music of György Ligeti). The melodies in most African music are comparatively simple, being based on a ➤ **diatonic** or ➤ **pentatonic** scale, often only using a few notes, with a static underlying harmony. Because of this, tuned instruments have remained few and simple, in contrast to the vast range of percussion instruments.

vocal music The same basic principles apply as much to vocal music as to instrumental music: unlike the monodic folk music of many other cultures, traditional African music is primarily polyphonic and rhythmic. It is also very much a group activity, so there are few solo songs, except in areas with some Islamic influence, such as Nigeria, where the griot (travelling musician/storyteller) intones or sings traditional stories. The commonest form of vocal polyphony is the call-and-response pattern, with a soloist improvising a melody between choruses, but there are several other forms of group improvisation in as many as eight different voices. Much instrumental music also imitates the tone patterns of speech, and many musical instruments are able to 'talk': the so-called talking drums in particular are often used to communicate with one another, or to address the dancers, either praising them or giving instructions.

drums The ➤ **drum** is the most common of all instruments in African music, and also the most varied. It has been suggested that it is widely used because of its dual role as a means of communication as well as being a musical instrument. This is certainly the case with the talking drums of Nigeria, but the reason is probably just due to the mainly rhythmical nature of the music. African drums take many forms, from the simple hollowed-out tree trunk to the hourglass-shaped, double-headed talking drums capable of instantly varying pitch. Drum-making is a respected occupation and the maker is usually a highly skilled worker.

The simplest form is the slit drum, made from a hollowed-out log with a slit running lengthways, either side of which the wood is carved to give two distinct pitches, but the most variety is found in drums with membrane heads. Drumheads are made of a variety of animal skins, including goat, leopard, cowhide, sheepskin, and deer, and are stretched over a resonant body, which is usually either cylindrical or bowl-shaped. Drums are made in a variety of shapes and sizes: single-headed, either open or closed at the other end; or double-headed. Although drums are often played by hand, variously shaped sticks of hardwood are also used. Talking drums are tuned and capable of producing a number of different notes; the 'language' they speak is not merely rhythmic, but also depends on the relative pitches of the notes.

other musical instruments It is not only the drums that are used to imitate language; almost all instruments in African music mimic speech patterns to a certain extent. Other percussion instruments include metallophones such as the gong-gong (a double bell) and various other gongs and bells; several versions of the ➤ **xylophone**, such as the balafon, which are made of a series of hard wooden strips arranged on a frame above gourd resonators; and the mbira or sanza (sometimes called the thumb piano or hand piano), made from a resonant board on which a set of metal tongues is plucked with the thumb and fingers.

There are also a number of string instruments, the most common of which is the **musical bow**. This is similar to the hunting bow, but is attached to any of a number of resonators such as gourds, or a covered hole in the ground, as in the case of the Ugandan ground bow. Lute- and harp-like instruments are also found, particularly in central and western Africa, and include the **kora**, a 21-string instrument. Less common in sub-Saharan countries are bowed string instruments, although varieties of fiddle are found in countries where there has been Islamic influence.

Wind instruments, although widespread, tend to be simple in comparison. There are rudimentary horns and trumpets, and many examples of flute or whistle, and in the north of the region forms of the Arab oboe, but the melodic range of these instruments is limited.

music in northern Africa Much of northern Africa has a basically Islamic culture, and the music of these countries is much more 'Arabic' than 'African'. Unlike sub-Saharan African music, it is mainly monophonic and melodic in structure, very often performed by solo performers or soloists with simple accompaniment, and there is much less emphasis on rhythm. As a consequence, it uses only a few percussion instruments in a secondary role to the many sophisticated string and wind instruments, which are usually Arabic in origin.

influence of African music African music and its rhythms have influenced much of the ethnic music of other continents, including the distinctive rhythms of much Latin American popular music, and have formed the principal component of ➤ **jazz**. The move towards more complex rhythmic structures, and indeed a rhythmic rather than harmonic basis, in Western classical music is found in an increased use of percussion instruments – many of them African in origin – and has prompted many composers to study traditional African music. This influence is most clearly seen in the work of the ➤ **minimalist** composers such as Philip ➤ **Glass** and Steve ➤ **Reich**, but has had an effect on the whole spectrum of Western art music.

modern African music Due to the colonization of Africa, and particularly as communication improves worldwide, the spread of Western culture has increased: the process of influence now works both ways, as music from the West – especially pop and rock music – can be heard in all but the remotest parts of Africa. Although this has meant the virtual disappearance of traditional music in some urban areas, it has also given rise to hybrid forms: highlife was one of the first of these, appearing in the early 20th century in West Africa, followed by the now-familiar southern African kwela in the 1950s, juju in Nigeria, and congolese in the Democratic Republic of Congo.

Age of Anxiety, The second symphony by Leonard Bernstein (after the poem by W H Auden), first performed in Boston, USA, on 8 April 1949, conducted by Serge Koussevitzky.

A plainsong setting of the Agnus Dei.

Age of Gold, The, Russian **Zolotyi vek** ballet by Shostakovich, Op. 22. It was first produced in Leningrad (now St Petersburg), Russia, on 26 October 1930, choreographed by E Kaplan and V Vaynonen. It takes as its subject the activities of a Stalinist football team.

agitato (Italian 'agitated') in musical notation, indicating energetic, excited expression. If not part of the initial tempo designation (for example, *allegro agitato*), it implies a faster tempo than the preceding material.

Agnes von Hohenstaufen opera by Gasparo Spontini (libretto by E Raupach), first produced at the Berlin, Opera, Berlin, Germany, on 12 June 1829, and revived in Florence, Italy, in 1954. In the story, Heinrich rescues Agnes from the evil King Philip of France.

Agnus Dei (Latin 'Lamb of God') the fifth and last item of the Ordinary of the Mass. Originally a part of the Litany, it was first introduced into the Roman Mass towards the end of the 7th century. It is not present in the Ambrosian rite. Its text is tripartite in structure, and its music in its simplest form consists of three statements of the same melody.

More complex ➤ **plainsong** settings exist and in the later Middle Ages numerous additional melodies were written. The Agnus Dei is naturally included in polyphonic settings of the Mass Ordinary, and in later settings of the same series of texts.

agogic a musical accent, affecting pulse and rhythm rather than dynamics, increasing the duration of a particular note. 'Agogic' also applies more broadly to all types of rhythm-related expression, such as ➤ **rubato** and ➤ **rallentando**.

Agon (Greek 'contest') ballet for twelve dancers by Stravinsky, composed 1953–57. It was first performed (as a concert) in Los Angeles, USA, on 17 June 1957, and first produced as a ballet in New York, USA, on 1 December 1957, choreographed by George Balanchine. It is one of Stravinsky's first compositions using the ➤ **twelve-tone system**.

agréments ➤ **ornamentation** of 17th-century French music, adopted as standard notation throughout Europe later in the baroque period.

Agricola, Alexander (1446–1506), adopted name of **Alexander Ackerman** Flemish composer. He is one of the most florid continental composers of the late 15th century, writing in a contrapuntal and decorative style. He served at the court of Galeazzo Maria Sforza, Duke of Milan, during the early 1470s, as well as with Lorenzo di Medici (the Magnificent) in Florence.

After a brief period at Mantua he returned to the Low Countries, and his name appears in the accounts of Cambrai Cathedral for 1475–76. After a second visit to Italy, in 1500 he entered the service of Philip the Handsome, Duke of Burgundy, whom he accompanied on journeys to Paris and Spain. During his second visit to Spain, Philip died of fever and Agricola apparently died at the same time. Agricola's epitaph (printed by Georg Rhaw in 1538) states that he died at the age of 60, the date of death being established by his disappearance from Philip's court rolls.

Works CHURCH MUSIC eight Masses, two Credos, 25 motets.

SECULAR MUSIC 93 secular pieces.

Agricola, Martin (1486–1556), adopted name of Martin Sore German music theorist and composer. His most important treatise was a work in verse on musical instruments, *Musica instrumentalis deudsch* (1528, based on Sebastian Virdung's *Musica getutscht*, 1511), and he contributed three pieces to Georg Rhaw's *Newe deudsche geistliche Gesenge* (1544).

Agrippina opera by Handel (libretto by V Grimani), first produced at the Teatro San Giovanni Crisostomo, Venice, Italy, on 26 December 1709. The plot concerns Agrippina, the wife of the Roman emperor, who has Poppea as a rival in the promotion of her son, Nero.

Ägyptische Helena, Die, *The Egyptian Helen* opera by Richard Strauss (libretto by Hugo von Hofmannsthal), first produced in Dresden, Germany, on 6 June 1928. The story tells of the errant Helen who is forgiven by her cuckolded husband.

Aho, Kalevi (1949–) Finnish composer. His music has developed from Russian symphonic influences, through atonality to postmodernism. He studied with Einojuhani Rautavaara in Helsinki and Boris Blacher in Berlin.

Works ORCHESTRAL seven symphonies (1969–88); concertos for violin, cello, and piano (1981–89).

CHAMBER three string quartets, oboe quintet

(1973), solo violin sonata (1973), accordion sonata (1984).

OPERA *Insect Life* (1985–87).

Aïda opera by Verdi (libretto by A Ghislanzoni, based on a scenario by F A F Mariette and outlined in French by C Du Locle), first produced in Cairo, Egypt, on 24 December 1871, and first performed in Italy at La Scala, Milan, on 8 February 1872. The plot describes a love triangle among (and eventually under) the pyramids.

Aiglon, L', The Eaglet opera by Arthur Honegger and Jacques Ibert (libretto by H Cain, based on Edmond Rostand's play), first produced at Monte Carlo on 11 March 1937.

air see ➤ ayre.

Airborne Symphony choral work by Marc Blitzstein in praise of the US Air Force Corps, in which the composer served during World War II; it was first performed in New York, New York, on 23 March 1946.

ajo nell'imbarazzo, L', The Tutor in a Fix opera by Donizetti (libretto by J Ferretti), first produced at the Teatro Valle, Rome, Italy, on 4 February 1824.

Akeroyde, Samuel (lived 17th century) English composer. He was Musician in Ordinary to James II in 1687 and later to William and Mary. He contributed many songs to various collections and to the third part of D'Urfey's play *Don Quixote* in 1696, the music to the first two of which had been written by Purcell the year before his death.

Akhnaten opera by Philip Glass (libretto by the composer with S Goldman, R Israel, and R Riddell), first produced in Stuttgart, Germany, on 24 March 1984. The story is based on the hermaphrodite, monotheist Egyptian Pharaoh of the 18th dynasty.

Akimenko, Feodor Stepanovich (1876–1945) Ukrainian composer. He was a pupil of Mily Balakirev and Nikolai Rimsky-Korsakov in St Petersburg, Russia. He taught in the court choir, where he had been a chorister, but lived in France 1903–06 and settled there after the Russian Revolution. He was Stravinsky's first composition teacher.

Works OPERA *The Queen of the Alps* (1914).

OTHER orchestral works, sonatas, and numerous piano works including *Sonate fantastique*.

Akutagawa, Yasushi (1925–1989) Japanese composer. He was active in Tokyo as a conductor and in promoting new music.

Works OPERA *L'Orphée in Hiroshima* (1967).

BALLET four ballets, including *Paradise Lost* (1951).

ORCHESTRAL *Ostinato Sinfonica* (1967), *Rhapsody* (1971).

al (Italian 'at the, to the') in music, word used in various combinations with nouns, such as al fine, 'to the end'.

Alain, Jehan (Ariste) (1911–1940) French composer. At the Paris Conservatory he studied organ with Marcel Dupré and composition with Paul Dukas and Jean Roger-Ducasse. He became a church organist in Paris in 1935, but served in World War II and was killed in action.

Works numerous choral compositions, mainly sacred; three dances for orchestra; chamber music; piano and organ works; songs.

À la manière de …, French '**In the manner of …**' two sets of piano pieces by Alfredo ➤ Casella (1911), and Casella and Maurice ➤ Ravel (1913) imitating the styles of Richard Wagner, Gabriel Fauré, Johannes Brahms, Claude Debussy, Richard Strauss, César Franck, Aleksandr Borodin, Vincent d'Indy, and Emmanuel Chabrier.

alba type of ➤ troubadour-➤ trouvère song, in which the singer watches for daybreak on behalf of two lovers (for example *Reis glorios*, by Guiraut de Bornelh). As used by the ➤ Minnesinger it was called *Tagelied*.

Albéniz, Isaac (1860–1909) Spanish nationalist composer and pianist. His works include numerous ➤ zarzuelas and operas, the orchestral suites *Española* (1886) and *Catalonia* (1899–1908) (with the assistance of Paul Dukas), and 250 piano works including the *Iberia* suite (1906–09), which helped to establish a distinctive national flavour, based on folk idioms.

Born in Cataluña, Albéniz appeared in public as a pianist at the age of four.

Works operas *The Magic Opal* (London, 1893), *Henry Clifford* (Barcelona, 1895), *Pepita Jiménez*, *San Antonio de la Florida*, *Merlin* (unfinished first part of Arthurian cycle); zarzuelas *Cuanto más viejo*, *Los Catalanes en Grecia*; contribution to Millöcker's operetta *Der arme Jonathan* for the London production in 1893, *Catalonia*, orchestrated with the aid of Dukas; c.250 piano pieces, including *Catalonia*, *La Vega*, *Navarra*, *Azulejos* and the cycle of twelve entitled *Iberia*; 13 songs.

Albéniz, Mateo Pérez de (c. 1755–1831) Spanish composer of church and keyboard music. He was *maestro de capilla* (music director) at Logroño and San Sebastián.

Albéniz, Pedro (1795–1855) Spanish pianist and composer, son of Mateo Pérez de Albéniz. He was organist at various towns from the age of 13. In 1830 he became professor of piano at Madrid Conservatory and then first organist at the royal chapel in 1834. He was appointed piano tea-

Alberti bass as used in the opening of Mozart's Sonata in C major, K.545.

cher to Queen Isabella and the Infanta Maria Luisa in 1841. He wrote a method for piano, about 70 piano works, and some songs.

Albert, Eugen (Eugène Francis Charles) d' (1864–1932) French-English (later Germanized) composer and pianist, son of C L N d'Albert. He appeared with great success as a pianist, notably performing the works of Bach, Liszt, and Beethoven, and later went to Vienna for further study under Hans Richter, finishing with a course under Liszt. During World War I he repudiated his British birth, declaring himself to be entirely German. Of his 20 operas, only *Tiefland* (1903) has had any real success. The rest of his considerable output has largely fallen into neglect.

Although born in Scotland, he came from Newcastle upon Tyne, and after being taught by his father as a precociously gifted child, he went as Newcastle scholar to the National Training School in London (later the Royal College of Music). In 1892 he married Teresa Carreño, but they were divorced in 1895 (d'Albert married six times). In 1907 he succeeded Joseph Joachim as director of the Hochschule für Musik in Berlin.

Works OPERA *Der Rubin* (after Hebbel; Karlsruhe, 1893), *Ghismonda* (Dresden, 1895), *Gernot* (Mannheim, 1897), *Die Abreise* (Frankfurt, 1898), *Kain* (Berlin, 1900), *Der Improvisator* (Berlin, 1902), *Tiefland* (Prague, 1903), *Flauto solo* (Prague, 1905), *Tragaldabas (Der geborgte Ehemann)* (Hamburg, 1907), *Izeÿl* (Hamburg, 1909), *Die verschenkte Frau* (Vienna, 1912), *Liebesketten* (Vienna, 1912), *Die toten Augen* (Dresden, 1916), *Der Stier von Olivera* (Leipzig, 1918), *Revolutionshochzeit* (Leipzig, 1919), *Scirocco* (Darmstadt, 1921), *Mareika von Nymwegen* (Hamburg, 1923), *Der Golem* (Frankfurt, 1926), *Die schwarze Orchidee* (Leipzig, 1928), *Die Witwe von Ephesus, Mister Wu* (unfinished, completed by L Blech).

OTHER *Der Mensch und das Leben,* choral work in six parts (1893); symphony in F; overtures *Esther* and *Hyperion*; two string quartets; piano suite and sonata.

Albert, Heinrich (1604–1651) German poet, organist, and composer. He studied music at Dresden with Heinrich Schütz, who was his uncle. His parents, however, compelled him to read law at Leipzig University; but in 1626 he set out for Königsberg, was taken prisoner by the Swedes, and at last reached that city in 1628, resuming music studies with Johann Stobäus. In 1631 he was appointed organist at the Old Church there, and became member of the Königsberg school of poets.

Works Te Deum; many hymns to words of his own; secular songs.

Albert, Stephen (1941–1992) US composer. His music embraces a variety of styles, including electronic. He won a Pulitzer Prize in 1985 for his symphony *Riverrun* (after James Joyce). A second symphony was posthumously premiered by the New York Philharmonic Orchestra in 1995.

He studied with Darius Milhaud, Roy Harris, and George Rochberg.

Works ORCHESTRAL *Cathedral Music* (1972), *Voices Within* (1975), *Riverrun* (1984), *Processionals* (1987); violin concerto (1988); cello concerto (1990).

VOCAL *Supernatural Songs* for soprano and chamber orchestra (1963); *Winter Songs* for tenor and orchestra (1965); *Bacchae* for narrator, chorus, and orchestra (1968); *Into Eclipse* for tenor and orchestra (1981); *Flower on the Mountain* for soprano and chamber orchestra (1985); *Distant Hills Coming Nigh* for soprano, baritone, and chamber ensemble (1991).

CHAMBER *Imitations* for string quartet (1964); *Winterfire* for seven players (1979); *Wind Canticle* for clarinet and ensemble (1992).

Albert Herring opera by Benjamin Britten (libretto by E Crozier, based on Guy de Maupassant's story *Le Rosier de Madame Husson*), first produced at Glyndebourne, Sussex, England, on 20 June 1947. The work focuses on events at a village fête.

Alberti, Domenico (c.1710–1746) Italian singer, harpsichordist, and composer, a pupil of Antonio Lotti. The characteristic left-hand accompaniment figuration in his keyboard music has given his name to the Alberti bass.

Alberti, Gasparo (c.1480–c.1560) Italian composer, a singer at the Church of Sta Maria Maggiore, Bergamo, from 1508. He was one of the earliest exponents of the compositional technique known as *cori spezzati* (Italian 'broken choir'), where a body of singers is divided into smaller groups performing alternately and all together.

Works CHURCH MUSIC five Masses, three Passions, and other church music.

Alberti bass a conventional broken-chord accompaniment common in 18th-century keyboard music, taking its name from Domenico Alberti, who made much use of it. Many familiar examples of the device can be found in the works of Haydn, Mozart, and Beethoven.

Albertus, Magister (lived early 12th century) French composer. A 'Benedicamus Domino' trope, *Congaudeant catholici*, is ascribed to him in the *Codex Calixtinus* of Compostela, around 1125, and is the earliest known three-part composition.

Albinoni, Tomaso (1671–1751) Italian baroque composer and violinist. He wrote over 50 operas and numerous sonatas and *concerti a cinque* (concertos in five parts) for oboe, trumpet, bassoon, violin, organ, and strings, which helped to establish baroque orchestral style. His work was studied and adapted by Johann Sebastian Bach.

He was wealthy and never held a musical appointment, but was a fully trained musician. His concertos were among the first to be in three movements, and the oboe concertos Op. 7 were the first published in Italy. The popular *Adagio*, often described as being by Albinoni, was actually composed from a fragment of original manuscript by his biographer, the Italian musicologist Remo Giazotto (1910–).

Works OPERA 55 operas, including *Radamisto* (Venice, 1698), *Griselda* (Florence, 1703), *Pimpinone* (Venice, 1708), and *L'impresario delle Canarie* (Venice, 1725).

CHAMBER nine Op. nos for instrumental chamber combinations, including five sets of twelve concertos, 30 other concertos, 42 trio sonatas, and 29 violin sonatas.

Albion and Albanius opera by Louis Grabu (libretto by John Dryden), first produced at the Duke's Theatre, London, England, on 3 June 1685. It is an allegory of the Restoration of Charles II.

alborada (Spanish *alba* 'dawn') 'morning song', in the same sense that a serenade is an evening song; compare French ➤ aubade. Originally the alborada was a popular instrumental piece of northwestern Spain, usually played on bagpipes.

Alborada del gracioso, The Jester's Morning Song a piano piece by Maurice Ravel, No. 4 of the set entitled *Miroirs*, composed in 1905. A version for orchestra was performed in Paris, France, on 17 May 1919.

Albrechtsberger, Johann Georg (1736–1809) Austrian music theorist, composer, and teacher. He was a prolific composer of church music and instrumental music, much of it in a contrapuntal style, and was for a short time Beethoven's teacher. He held the post of court organist in Vienna and Kapellmeister of St Stephen's Cathedral, Vienna.

Albrici, Vincenzo (1631–1696) Italian composer and organist, brother of Bartolomeo Albrici. He was a pupil of Giacomo Carissimi, and director of the Queen of Sweden's Italian musicians 1652–53; Kapellmeister at Dresden, Germany, from 1654; and in the service of Charles II in London, England, 1664–67. He returned to Dresden in 1667, and was organist of St Thomas's, Leipzig, 1681–82, and Kapellmeister at St Augustin, Prague (in the modern Czech Republic), from 1682 until his death.

Works Masses, psalms, concertos, and madrigals.

Albright, William (1944–1998) US composer, pianist, and organist. He studied at the Juilliard School of Music, New York, and in Paris, France, with Olivier Messiaen. He was a teacher of composition at Michigan University, USA, and director of the electronic music studio there.

Works multimedia and stage pieces (*Cross of Gold*, 1975); orchestral music (*Bacchanal*, 1981); chamber music and pieces for organ and piano, with jazz ensemble.

Albumblatt (German 'album leaf, page') in music, the title often given to a short piece, usually for piano, suggesting that the piece is one of many, forming a gathered album of unrelated pieces. Examples are by Schumann and Wagner.

Alceste opera by Christoph Willibald von Gluck (libretto by Raniero de Calzabigi after Euripides), first produced in Italian at the Burgtheater, Vienna, Austria, on 26 December 1767. The French version, revised by the composer (libretto by C L G L du Roullet after Raniero de Calzabigi) was first produced at the Paris Opéra, France, on 23 April 1776. The work tells the story of Alceste and her husband Admète who are saved from Hades by Hercules as Alceste prepares to sacrifice herself for the dying Admète.

There are other operas with the same title. The one by Nicolaus Strungk (libretto by P Thiemich, based on Aurelio Aureli's *Antigona delusa da Alceste*) was written for the opening of the Leipzig opera house, Germany, and was produced there on 18 May 1693. A further opera by Anton Schweitzer (libretto by Christoph Wieland) was produced at the court in Weimar, Germany, on 28 May 1773. It was the first German opera in the manner of Pietro Metastasio.

Handel also composed incidental music (later

used for *The Choice of Hercules*) to a play entitled *Alceste* by Tobias Smollett. It was to be produced at Covent Garden, London, England, in 1750, but did not take place.

See also ➤ *Alkestis*.

Alceste ou Le Triomphe d'Alcide opera by Jean-Baptiste Lully (libretto by Philippe Quinault), produced at the Paris Opéra, France, on 19 January 1674.

Alchemist, The incidental music by Handel, partly adapted from *Rodrigo*, for a revival of Ben Jonson's play *The Alchemist*, produced at the Drury Lane Theatre, London, England, on 7 March 1732.

Alchymist, Der opera by Ludwig Spohr (libretto by K Pfeiffer, based on W A Irving's story *The Student of Salamanca*), first produced in Kassel, Germany, on 28 July 1830. The story tells how the alchemist Tarnow refuses to let his daughter Louise marry until he has discovered the philosopher's stone. He releases her after her lover impersonates the devil, demanding a young woman as payment.

Alcidor opera by Gasparo Spontini (libretto by G M Théaulon de Lambert), first produced in Berlin, Germany, on 23 May 1825. Designated a 'Zauber-Oper mit Ballet', it begins with a chorus of gnomes accompanied by anvils (anticipating Wagner's *Rheingold*).

Alcina opera by Handel (libretto by A Marchi), first produced at Covent Garden, London, England, on 16 April 1735. In the story the sorceress Alcina loses her magic powers on an enchanted island, as Bradamante comes in search of the bewitched Ruggiero.

Alcione opera by Marin Marais (libretto by A H de la Motte), first produced at the Paris, Opéra, France, on 18 February 1706. The story tells how Neptune rescues young lovers after a shipwreck.

Aldeburgh Festival annual festival of operas and other concerts, established in 1948 at Aldeburgh, Suffolk. The events have centred on the works of Benjamin Britten, who lived at Aldeburgh, and take place at The Maltings, a concert hall at nearby Snape. First performances of Britten's works to be given here include the operas *A Midsummer Night's Dream* (1960) and *Death in Venice* (1973).

aleatoric composition music whose content is to some extent undetermined by the composer. Those who have used aleatory features in their works include John ➤ Cage, Pierre ➤ Boulez, and Cornelius ➤ Cardew.

aleatory music (Latin *alea* 'dice') method of composition practised by post-war avant-garde composers in which the performer or conductor chooses the order of succession of the composed pieces. Examples of aleatory music include Pierre Boulez's *Piano Sonata No. 3* (1956–57), Earle Brown's *Available Forms I* (1961), and Stockhausen's *Momente/Moments* (1961–72). Another term for aleatory music is 'mobile form'.

Aleatory music is distantly related to the 18th-century 'musical dice game' and to the freely assembled music for silent movies using theme catalogues by Giuseppe Becce and others. The use by John ➤ Cage of dice and the I Ching differs in that it intervenes in the actual process of composition.

Aleko opera by Rachmaninov (libretto by V I Nemirovich-Danchenko, based on Aleksandr Pushkin's poem *The Gypsies*), first produced in Moscow, Russia, on 9 May 1893. The plot tells how Zemfira is killed by Aleko after she tries to join the gypsies.

Aleksandrov, Anatol Nikolaevich (1888–1982) Russian composer. He studied under Alexandr Taneiev and at the Moscow Conservatory, where he later became professor.

Works OPERA *Two Worlds, The Forty-First, Bela* (Moscow, 1946), *The Wild Girl* (1957).

INCIDENTAL MUSIC incidental music for Maurice Maeterlinck's play *Ariane et Barbe-bleue* and Augustin Scribe's *Adrienne Lecouvreur*; music for the film *Thirteen*.

ORCHESTRAL overture on popular Russian themes and two suites for orchestra.

CHAMBER four string quartets (1921–53).

PIANO 14 piano sonatas, piano pieces.

VOCAL *Three Goblets*, for baritone and orchestra; songs, folksong arrangements.

Alembert, Jean Le Rond d' (1717–1783) French author, philosopher, and mathematician. His books included many studies of musical subjects, including acoustics, opera, and the theories of Jean-Philippe Rameau; as a musical author, he is best known for his articles to the *Encyclopédie*. He was one of the adherents of Christoph Willibald von Gluck (French opera style) against Niccolò Piccinni (Italian opera style).

Alessandri, Felice (1747–1798) Italian conductor and composer. He studied in Naples and first worked in Turin, Italy, and Paris, France; he produced his first opera in Venice, Italy, in 1767, went to London, England, the following year, and in 1786 to St Petersburg, Russia, in search of a court appointment, which he failed to secure. From 1789 to 1792 he was second Kapellmeister at the Berlin Opera, Germany.

Works OPERA about 35 operas, including *Ezio* (Verona, 1767), *Alcina* (Turin, 1775), *Artaserse* (Naples, 1783), *Il ritorno d'Ulisse* (Potsdam, 1790), *Armida* (Padua, 1794).

OTHER an oratorio; several symphonies; sonatas.

Alessandro opera by Handel (libretto by Paolo Rolli), first produced at the King's Theatre, Haymarket, London, on 5 May 1726. Its eponymous hero is Alexander the Great.

Alessandro della Viola (1530–after 1594) Italian tenor-bass, violist, and composer; see Alessandro ➤ **Merlo.**

Alessandro nell'Indie, Alexander in India opera by Johann Christian Bach (libretto by Pietro Metastasio), first produced at the Teatro San Carlo in Naples, Italy, on 20 January 1762. The plot tells how, defeated by Alexander the Great, the Indian king Porus resolves to rescue Queen Cleophis.

The first setting was by Leonardo Vinci (Rome, 1729); others were by Baldassare Galuppi (Mantua, 1738), David Perez (Genoa, 1745), Antonio Sacchini (Venice, 1763), and Niccolò Piccinni (Naples, 1774).

See also ➤ *Cleofide* and ➤ *Poro, rè dell'Indie.*

Alessandro Stradella opera by Friedrich von Flotow (libretto, in German, by F W Riese, pseudonym 'W Friedrich'), first produced in Hamburg, Germany, on 30 December 1844. It deals with doubtful incidents in the scandalous life of Stradella, and is based on a play with music, some by Flotow, P A A P de Forges, and P Dupert. Stradella deflects would-be assassins by singing to them of mercy and kindness.

Alessandro vincitor di se stesso, Alexander, Victor over Himself opera by Pietro Francesco Cavalli (libretto by F Sbarra), first produced at the Teatro Santi Giovanni e Paolo in Venice, Italy, probably on 20 January 1651.

Alexander Balus oratorio by Handel (libretto by T Morell), first produced at Covent Garden, London, England, on 23 March 1748.

Alexander Nevsky or **Aleksandr Nevski** film music by Sergey Prokofiev, composed in 1938 for the film by Sergei Eisenstein. It was later arranged as a cantata, Op. 78, for mezzo-soprano, chorus, and orchestra. The work was first performed in Moscow, Russia, on 17 May 1939.

Alexander's Feast oratorio by George Frideric Handel, a setting of the ode by the English poet John Dryden with words arranged and added to by Newburgh Hamilton. It was first produced at Covent Garden, London, England, on 19 February 1736. Handel's *Concerto Grosso* in C major, HWV 318 was also premiered in the same concert and is consequently sometimes referred to as 'Alexander's Feast'.

Alfano, Franco (1876–1954) Italian composer. He is best known for his twelve operas, including *Risurrezione/Resurrection* (1904), *The Shade of*

Don Juan (performed 1914), *Sakuntala* (1922), *The Last Lord* (1930), and *Cyrano de Bergerac* (1936). He completed Puccini's unfinished opera, *Turandot.*

He studied first at the Naples Conservatory and afterwards at that of Leipzig, under Salomon Jadassohn (1831–1902). He had some piano pieces published in Germany before the end of the century and in 1896 wrote his first opera, *Miranda*, on a subject from Fogazzaro. The ballet *Napoli*, produced in Paris in 1900, was his first big success, and was followed by the still greater success of his third opera, *Risurrezione/Resurrection*, a work in the *verismo* tradition. His most successful work was the colourful opera *La leggenda di Sakuntala*. His first symphony was performed at San Remo in 1910. In 1919 he was appointed director of the Liceo Musicale Rossini in Bologna and in 1923 of the Conservatory in Turin. After Puccini's death in 1924 he completed the unfinished *Turandot*, finishing the final scenes from Puccini's sketches; his work was not heard complete until 1982.

Works OPERA *Miranda, La fonte di Enschir* (Breslau, 1898), *Risurrezione/Resurrection* (based on Tolstoy; Turin, 1904), *Il principe Zilah* (1907), *L'ombra di Don Giovanni* (Naples, 1930), *Sakuntala* (after Kalidasa; 1922), *L'ultimo lord* (1930), *Cyrano de Bergerac* (after Rostand; Rome, 1936), *Il dottor Antonio* (begun 1941).

OTHER ballet *Napoli* (1900); two symphonies, *Suite romantica* for orchestra (1907–09); piano quartet, three string quartets; sonata for cello and piano; songs including three settings of poems by Tagore and a cycle *Dormiveglia.*

al fine (Italian 'to the end') musical term used in cases where an earlier portion of a composition is to be repeated (*da capo*) and indicates that it is to be played over again to the end, not to some earlier place, which would otherwise be marked with a special sign, the appropriate direction being then *al segno.*

Alfonso X (1221–1284), called **'El Sabio' (the Wise)** King of Castile and León. He assembled a collection of 400 songs in Galician-Portuguese, known as the *Cantigas de Santa Maria*, and founded a chair of music at Salamanca University in 1254.

Alfonso und Estrella opera by Schubert (libretto by F von Schober), composed 1821–22, but never performed in Schubert's lifetime. It was first produced by Liszt at Weimar, Germany, on 24 June 1854, with an overture by Anton Rubinstein. Schubert's original version was premiered at Graz, Austria, on 28 September 1991. The story tells how Alfonso gains the throne and marries Estrella, the daughter of his father's enemy.

Alfred masque by Thomas Arne (words by J Thomson and D Mallet), first performed at Cliveden in Buckinghamshire, England, the residence of Frederick, Prince of Wales, on 1 August 1740. It contains the song 'Rule, Britannia!'.

Alfred is also the title of an opera by Dvořák (his first; libretto by K T Korner). It was composed in 1870 and first produced at Olomouc, Czechoslovakia (now the Czech Republic), on 10 December 1938. It tells how King Alfred defeats the Danes and frees his bride.

Alfred, König der Angelsachsen, Alfred, King of the Anglo-Saxons incidental music by Joseph Haydn for a drama by J W Cowmeadow. It was first performed at Eisenstadt, Austria, in September 1796.

Algarotti, Francesco, Count (1712–1764) Italian scholar. His libretto *Iphigénie en Aulide* influenced the text set by Christoph Willibald von Gluck. Among many learned works he wrote a treatise on the reform of opera, *Saggio sopra l'opera in musica*, criticizing the practices of opera seria ('serious opera', treating classical subjects in a formal style), published in 1755.

Alghisi, Paris Francesco (1666–1743) Italian composer. He studied under Orazio Polarolo, organist of Brescia cathedral, and was engaged for some time at the Polish court. Two of his operas were produced in Venice: *Amor di Curzio per la patria* (1690) and *Il trionfo della continenza* (1691). He also wrote several oratorios and other works.

Ali Baba, ou Les Quarante Voleurs, Ali Baba, or The Forty Thieves opera by Luigi Cherubini (libretto by Augustin Scribe and A H J Mélesville), first produced at the Paris Opéra, France, on 22 July 1833. It was a new version of *Koukourgi*, composed in 1793 but not performed.

Alina, Regina di Golconda opera by Donizetti (libretto by F Romani), first produced in Genoa, Italy, on 12 May 1828. The story tells how Alina is courted by a rival but is eventually reunited with her lost husband.

aliquot parts (from Latin *aliquot* 'some') parts contained by the whole, integral factors; in music, the parts of a fundamental note vibrating separately as overtones.

aliquot scaling or **aliquot strings** additional strings introduced into the upper registers of pianos manufactured by the firm of Blüthner. These vibrate with those struck by the hammers, on the same principle as the ➤ **sympathetic strings** in bowed string instruments.

Alkan (1813–1888), pseudonym of **Charles Valentin Morhange** French piano virtuoso and composer. His formidably difficult piano pieces were neglected until the 1970s. Works include *Grande Sonate: Les Quatre Ages* (1848) and twelve *Etudes* in every minor key (1857), of which numbers 4–7 constitute a symphony for piano solo and numbers 8–10 a concert for piano solo.

Born in Paris, he was so precocious as a player that he was admitted to the Paris Conservatory at the age of six. After a visit to London in 1833, he settled in Paris as a piano teacher. In his works he cultivated an advanced, immensely difficult, and often very modern technique. As a performer he was ranked with Chopin (a close friend) and Liszt, but became a recluse after 1849. He is alleged to have been killed by a collapsing bookcase.

Works PIANO two piano concertos; piano trio; piano sonatas, numerous piano studies (including one for the right hand and one for the left), character pieces; four Op. nos of pieces for pedal piano.

Alkestis opera by Rutland Boughton (libretto taken from Gilbert Murray's English translation of the tragedy by Euripides), first produced at Glastonbury, England, on 26 August 1922.

It is also the title of an opera by Egon Wellesz (libretto by Hugo von Hofmannsthal, after Euripides), first produced in Mannheim, Germany, on 20 March 1924.

alla (Italian 'at the, in the manner of'; French à la) word used in various ways in combination with nouns to give musical directions, for example *alla marcia* ('march-like'), *alla francese* ('in the French manner'). It is abbreviated to *all'* before nouns beginning with a vowel.

alla breve or **cut time** of musical tempo, indicating that the minim rather than the crotchet is the basic unit of the beat in a bar of two beats.

allargando (Italian 'broadening') in musical notation, indicating a gradual slowing down while still maintaining a full tone quality.

allegretto (Italian, diminutive of *allegro*, 'merry, lively') in music, a tempo marking indicating moderately quick, but not as fast as ➤ **allegro**.

Allegri, Domenico (1585–1629) Italian composer. He was maestro di cappella at Santa Maria Maggiore in Rome 1610–29. His works include motets and music for voices and strings.

Allegri, Gregorio (1582–1652) Italian baroque composer. He was maestro di cappella of the Sistine Chapel, Rome, 1610–29. His output of sacred music includes Magnificats, a cappella Masses, motets, and the celebrated *Miserere mei* (Psalm 51) for nine voices. This was reserved for performance by the chapel choir until Mozart, at the age of 14, wrote out the music from memory.

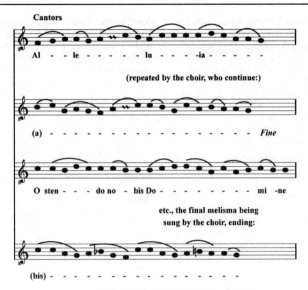

Alleluia. *The exact form as sung since the Middle Ages may be illustrated from the alleluia for the First Sunday of Advent.*

allegro (Italian 'merry, lively') in music, a tempo marking indicating lively or quick. It can be used as the title for a movement or composition.

Allegro Barbaro work for solo piano by Bartók, composed in 1911 but not performed until 27 February 1921, in Budapest, Hungary.

allegro, il penseroso ed il moderato, L', The Cheerful, the Thoughtful and the Moderate oratorio by Handel (libretto Parts i and ii by Milton, Part iii by Charles Jennens), first produced at the Lincoln's Inn Fields Theatre, London, England, on 27 February 1740.

Alleluia (Hebrew 'praise ye Jehova') the third chant of the Proper of the Mass, sung immediately after the Gradual. The word is Hebrew ('praise ye Jehova'), and was sung in many contexts in Jewish life, but especially in connection with the singing of the Psalms. It was taken over unchanged by the Christian church and sung both alone and as an addition to chants of various kinds, especially during the Easter season. As a Mass-chant of the Roman rite it was originally sung alone, at first during Eastertide only and, after the time of Gregory I, during the whole year except from Septuagesima (the third Sunday before Lent) to Easter. At some time before 750 one or more verses were added, in which form it became a responsorial chant, the choir singing the alleluia at the beginning and end, and the soloists the verse or verses in between.

The alleluia of the Ambrosian chant, possibly retaining more of its original oriental characteristics, is even more florid in character.

allemande medium-paced dance in four time, with an upbeat, in two symmetrical sections; the music forms part of a classical ➤ **suite.**

Allen, Hugh Percy (1869–1946) English professor of music. He was conductor of the Bach Choir, London, 1901–20; professor of music at Oxford University from 1918; and director of the Royal College of Music, London, until 1937. He was knighted in 1920.

As professor of music at Oxford, Allen did valuable work in widening the scope and practicality of the courses there. He was a fine choral conductor.

Allison or **Alison** or **Alyson, Richard (lived 16th–17th century)** English composer. He first appeared as a contributor to East's *Whole Book of Psalms* in 1592 and published a collection of church melodies set for voices and instruments, *The Psalmes of David in Meter*, in 1599. Other works include lute music and 24 songs for voices and instruments, *An Howres Recreation ...*, published in 1606.

all'ottava (Italian 'at the octave') in musical notation, a direction that a passage, so far as it is marked by a dotted line over it, is to be played an octave higher than it is written; it is usually represented by the symbol 8*va*. If the dotted line is below, it means an octave lower.

Almahide opera by Giovanni Bononcini (libretto after John Dryden's *Almanzor and Almahide*), first produced at the Queen's Theatre, Haymarket, London, on 10 January 1710. According to the music historian Charles Burney, it was the first opera to be performed in England wholly in Italian.

alme or **almeh** or **al-mai ('the learned')** name given by modern Egyptians and Arabs to the Egyptian singing girls who attend festivals, marriages, funerals, and other ceremonies. They are also found in Syria and other parts of the former Ottoman Empire.

almérie musical instrument, a kind of ➤ lute. It was invented in the 18th century by Jean Lemaire, and its name is an anagram of his.

Almira opera by Handel (libretto by F C Feustking), first produced at the Theater beim Gänsemarkt, Hamburg, Germany, on 8 January 1705. It is Handel's first opera, and tells the story of Almira who loves Fernando but must marry Osman.

Alpensinfonie, Eine, An Alpine Symphony symphony by Richard Strauss, Op. 64, first performed in Berlin, Germany, on 28 October 1915.

alphorn wind instrument consisting of a straight, usually wooden tube terminating in a conical endpiece with an upturned bell, sometimes up to 4 m/12 ft in length. It is used to summon cattle and serenade tourists in the highlands of central Europe.

The wood is split lengthways and hollowed out, then reunited and covered with bark or split cane to seal against leakage. In some areas the alphorn is made of metal.

al rovescio (Italian 'backwards') see ➤ cancrizans.

Also sprach Zarathustra, Thus Spake Zoroaster symphonic poem by Richard Strauss, Op. 30, based on Friedrich Nietzsche's prose poem. It was composed in 1896 and first performed in Frankfurt, Germany, on 27 November 1896. It became extremely well-known through its use in Stanley Kubrick's *2001: A Space Odyssey*.

Altenberglieder five songs for voice and orchestra to picture-postcard texts by 'Peter Altenberg' (pseudonym of Richard Englander, 1862–1919), by Alban Berg. At the first performance of two of the songs in Vienna, Austria, in 1913, a riot caused the concert to be abandoned. The first complete performance was given in Rome, Italy, on 24 January 1953, conducted by Jascha Horenstein.

altered chord in music, a chord in which one of the notes is raised or lowered by a semitone. The chord then includes augmented (enlarged) or diminished (contracted) intervals. Altered chords are often used to modulate keys (see ➤ modulation).

alternatim a manner of performance in which singers or players are heard in alternation, as in between two sides of a choir or between choir and organ. It can also be applied to alternation between music styles, as in plainsong and polyphony.

alternativo (Italian 'alternative') a contrasting section, much the same as the trio in a minuet or scherzo, but often in a piece of a different character, and there may be more than one alternativo in a single piece. Familiar examples appear in Schumann.

alto (Italian 'high') voice or musical instrument between tenor and soprano, of approximate range G3–D5. It is also used before the name of an instrument, for example alto saxophone, and indicates a size larger than soprano.

The traditional male alto voice of early opera, Anglican church choirs, male voice quartets, and choral societies is also known as **countertenor**. Trumpetlike and penetrating, it is an extension of the high (alto) male voice register, produced by ➤ falsetto. The term is also used as an abbreviation of 'contralto', the low register ('contra-alto') female voice, which is rich and mellow in tone; for example, the voice of the English singer Kathleen Ferrier. Alto is also the French name for the ➤ viola.

alto clef in musical notation, the C ➤ clef in which middle C is represented by the 3rd line of a five-line stave. It was used by musicians and singers until the 18th century and is now used most commonly by viola players.

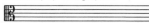

The alto clef.

alto flute ➤ flute in G with a range a fourth lower than that of the ordinary instrument. The instrument is sometimes mistakenly called a bass flute.

alto recorder US term for the treble ➤ recorder.

Alto Rhapsody English name for Brahms's ➤ Rhapsodie (1869).

Alwyn, William (1905–1985) English composer. He was professor of composition at the Royal Academy of Music, London, 1926–55; he wrote film music (*Desert Victory, The Way Ahead*), and composed symphonies and chamber music.

He was born in Northampton, and entered the

Royal Academy of Music as a student of flute, piano, and composition, studying the last under John Blackwood McEwen (1868–1948) and obtaining the Costa Scholarship. He played the flute in the London Symphony Orchestra and his first work for orchestra, *Five Preludes*, was given at a 1927 Prom concert. His music includes an unperformed opera *The Libertine*. He also published *The Technique of Film Music* (1957).

Works OPERA *Miss Julie* (1961–76).

FILM MUSIC *Our Country, The Lost Illusion*, and many others.

ORCHESTRAL five preludes, concerto grosso, overture to a masque, and five symphonies for orchestra (1949–73); piano concerto, violin concerto.

CHAMBER *Pastoral Fantasia* for viola and strings; two string quartets, Rhapsody for piano quartet; Sonata-Impromptu for violin and viola, sonatina for viola and piano; piano pieces; Divertimento for solo flute.

Alyabyev, Alexander Alexandrovich (1787–1851) Russian composer. He was an army officer who fought as a hussar against Napoleon, and cultivated music as an amateur from 1823.

Works OPERA two operas after Shakespeare: *Burya* (*The Tempest*, 1835) and *The Enchanted Night* (*A Midsummer Night's Dream*, 1839).

SONG his song 'The Nightingale' was used by Patti and Viardot for the letter scene in *Il barbiere di Siviglia*.

Alypios (lived 4th century) Greek theorist to whom our knowledge of ancient Greek notation is due.

Alzira opera by Verdi (libretto by S Cammarano, based on Voltaire's play *Alzire*), first produced at the Teatro San Carlo, Naples, Italy, on 12 August 1845. The plot relates how the Inca chief Zamoro stabs Gusmano, governor of Peru, as the Spaniard attempts to wed Zamoro's intended bride.

Amadigi di Gaula, Amadis of Gaul opera by Handel (libretto adapted from A H de la Motte's *Amadis de Grèce*, set by André Destouches, 1699), first produced at the King's Theatre, Haymarket, London, England, on 25 May 1715. The story tells how Amadigi and Oriana are united when the interfering infatuated sorceress Melissa abandons her deceptions.

Amadis opera by Jean-Baptiste Lully (libretto by Philippe Quinault, based on the old Iberian romance *Amadis de Gaula*), first produced at the Paris Opéra, France, on 18 January 1684. The plot describes the adventures of Amadis in his attempt to win the doubting heart of Oriane.

Also an opera by Massenet (libretto by J Claretie), composed about 1895 and performed posthumously in Monte Carlo on 1 April 1922.

Amadori, Giuseppe (c. 1670–after 1730) Italian composer. He was maestro di cappella in Rome, where his oratorio, *Il martirio di Sant' Adriano*, was produced in 1702. He also wrote Masses and other church music.

Amahl and the Night Visitors opera in one act by Gian Carlo Menotti (libretto by the composer, after Hieronymus Bosch's painting *The Adoration of the Magi*), produced on NBC Television on 24 December 1951. It is the first opera especially written for television.

Amarus lyric cantata by Janáček for soprano, tenor, baritone, chorus, and orchestra; composed about 1897, revised in 1901 and 1906. It was first performed in Kroměříž, now in the Czech Republic, on 2 December 1900.

Amat, Juan Carlos (1572–1642) Spanish scientist and author. He wrote the earliest-known treatise on playing the guitar, *Guitarra española* …, published probably in 1586.

Amati (lived 16th–17th centuries) Italian family of violinmakers working in Cremona. **Nicolò Amati** (1596–1684) taught Andrea Guarneri and Antonio ➔ **Stradivari**. Nicolò's grandfather **Andrea Amati** (c. 1511–c. 1580) brought the violin to its classic form.

Andrea Amati's earliest known violins were made with only three strings and it may have been he who first fitted the fourth string. He is known to have made small and large (the 'grand' model) violins and violas and to have made cellos, a set of which were commissioned by Charles IX of France after 1560 and some of which survive. The sound of his instruments is mellow and beautiful but less powerful than those of his successors of the Cremonese school, perhaps due to the highly arched belly which was a characteristic of his violins and violas.

Andrea was succeeded by two sons, **Antonio** (1550–1638) and **Girolamo (Hieronymus)** (1561–1630), who continued in the same tradition as their father, often signing their instruments jointly as 'the brothers Amati, sons of Andrea'. Nicolò Amati, the son of Girolamo, is the most illustrious member of the family. His violins produced a great intensity and richness of sound, which he achieved by using thicker wood and reducing the elevation of the belly. By this time Cremona violins had won the reputation, which they still hold today, of being the best in the world. The fame of Nicolò and of his pupils, Guarneri and Stradivari, has somewhat eclipsed the renown of Andrea and his sons, but they are remembered for their pioneer work in the introduction of a new craft into Italy.

Ambiela, Miguel (1666–1733) Spanish priest and composer. He was music director of the new cathedral at Saragossa, 1700–07, and maestro di cappella at Toledo, 1710–33.

Works CHURCH MUSIC Masses, *Stabat Mater*, and other church music.

Ambleto, Hamlet opera by Francesco Gasparini (libretto by A Zeno and P Pariati), first produced at the Teatro San Cassiano, Venice, Italy, during Carnival 1705.

It is also the title of an opera by Domenico Scarlatti (libretto again by A Zeno and P Pariati), first produced at the Teatro Capranica, Rome, Italy, during Carnival 1715.

Ambros, August Wilhelm (1816–1876) Czech-born German musicologist. He studied at Prague University. His life's work was a history of music which at his death reached only the fourth volume and the early 17th century. He also composed a Czech opera, *Bratislav and Jitka*, and overtures to Shakespeare's *Othello* and Calderón's *Mágico prodigioso*.

Ambrosian chant in Christian church music, reformed chant introduced by St Ambrose in the 4th century. It retains many features of Middle Eastern religious chant.

The number of available modes (scales) was reduced to four; the interval of the fifth was established as the basis of tonal music, having a lower key note, from which the chant rose and to which it returned; and a higher dominant was established at the fifth, around which the chant was elaborated.

amener (French *mener* 'to lead') French dance of the 17th century in triple time and moderate pace, with characteristic six-bar phrases. It occurs in French baroque instrumental suites and thence passed to some extent into German and Italian music.

America epic rhapsody by Ernest Bloch in three movements (1. 1620; 2. 1861–65; 3. 1926), composed 1926–27. It was first performed on 20 December 1928 and then on 21 December 1928 simultaneously in seven US cities. It won the prize offered by *Musical America* for the best US symphonic work.

American musical terminology the main differences from British usage are nearly all direct translations from German. Whole note, half note, quarter note, (for semibreve, minim, crotchet) are used, as well as concert master for leader, and so on. The most potentially confusing is the word 'tone' meaning British 'pitch': hence Americans tend to use 'tone row' for British 'note row', 'neighbor tone' for 'auxiliary note', 'whole step' and 'half step' for British 'tone' and 'semitone'. Other details in which usage tends to cross the Atlantic in both directions include 'flutist' (flautist), and 'measure' (bar).

American organ keyboard reed organ similar to the ➔ harmonium, differing from the latter in some details, particularly in sucking in the wind through its reeds instead of expelling it.

Its principle was discovered by a workman attached to Jacob Alexandre (1804–1876), an instrument maker in Paris, France, but he took it to the USA and the first important instruments of the kind were made by Mason & Hamlin of Boston around 1860.

Amériques work for orchestra by Edgard Varèse; instruments include sleighbells, a steamboat whistle, and a hand siren as used by the New York Fire Department. It was composed 1918–22 and first performed in Philadelphia, USA, on 9 April 1926, conducted by Leopold Stokowski.

Amfiparnaso, L', The Amphi-Parnassus madrigal opera by Orazio Vecchi, first produced in Modena, Italy, in 1594, and published in Venice in 1597, described as a *commedia harmonica*. It consists of three acts and a prologue, and the characters are the stock figures of the *commedia dell'arte*, but the musical setting of their speech is in the form of madrigals for mixed voices. It has been supposed that 'the action was produced in dumb-show while the madrigals were sung behind the scenes, but a passage in the text which says that 'the spectacle is to enter by the ear, not by the eye' gives good reason to doubt this. The same subject was treated earlier in a smaller form by the Flemish composer Roland de Lassus.

amico Fritz, L' opera by Mascagni (libretto by P Suardon, based on Erckmann-Chatrian's novel *L'Ami Fritz*), first produced at the Teatro Costanzi, Rome, Italy, on 31 October 1891. The plot tells how Bachelor Fritz falls for Suzel after encouragement from the matchmaker Rabbi David.

Amid Nature or **In Nature's Realm** concert overture by Dvořák, Op. 91, composed in 1891 and forming, with *Carnival* and *Othello*, a cycle with thematic connections, originally called *Nature, Life and Love*.

Amirov, Fikret Dzhamil (1922–1984) Azerbaijani composer. His music is influenced by local folk tunes.

Works OPERA *Sevil* (1953).

ORCHESTRAL double concerto for violin, piano, and orchestra (1948); piano concerto (1957).

VOCAL *The Pledge of the Korean Guerrilla Fighter* for voice and orchestra (1951).

Amleto, Hamlet opera by Franco Faccio (libretto by Arrigo Boito, after Shakespeare), first produced at the Teatro Carlo Felice, Genoa, Italy, on 30 May 1865.

It is also the title of an opera by Giuseppe Mercadante (libretto by Felice Romani, after Shakespeare), first produced at La Scala, Milan, Italy, on 26 December 1822.

Ammerbach or **Amerbach, Elias Nikolaus (1530–1597)** German organist and composer. He was organist at St Thomas, Leipzig, from 1560 and published two books of music in organ tablature, containing important explanations of ornaments and modes of performance.

amor brujo, El, *Love, the Magician* ballet by Manuel de Falla, composed 1913–14 and first performed at the Teatro de Lara, Madrid, Spain, on 15 April 1915.

amor coniugale, L' opera by Johann Mayr (librettist Giacomo Rossi, after Bouilly), first produced in Padua, Italy, on 26 July 1805 (four months before *Fidelio*, which is based on the same source). Condensed into one act, Leonore/Fidelio becomes Zeliska/Malvino, Pizarro is Moroski, and Rocco is Peters.

amore dei tre re, L', The Love of the Three Kings opera by Italo Montemezzi (libretto by S Benelli, from his play of the same title), first produced at La Scala, Milan, Italy, on 10 April 1913. In the story the king strangles his daughter-in-law and spreads poison on her lips; her lover and husband also die after kissing her.

amoroso (Italian 'amorous') musical direction indicating an emotional and tender manner of performance.

Amour médecin, L' comédie-ballet by Jean-Baptiste Lully (libretto by Molière), first produced at Versailles, France, on 16 September 1665.

Amours d'Antoine et de Cléopâtre, Les, *The Loves of Antony and Cleopatra* ballet by Rodolphe Kreutzer (choreography by J P Aumer, based on Shakespeare), first produced at the Paris Opéra, France, on 8 March 1808.

Amram, David (1930–) US composer and horn player. He studied at the Manhattan School of Music and with Charles Mills. He has written incidental music for Shakespeare's plays, films, and jazz bands. He received a Commission from the Library of Congress in 1995.

Works OPERA *The Final Ingredient* (ABC TV, 1965), *Twelfth Night* (1968).

ORCHESTRAL *Shakespearean Concerto* (1960), *King Lear Variations* for wind, percussion, and piano (1967), concertos for horn, jazz quintet, bassoon, and violin (1968–80).

CHAMBER string quartet (1961), sonata for solo violin (1964), wind quintet (1968).

VOCAL cantatas *The American Bell*, *A Year in our Land*, and *Let us Remember* (1962–65).

Amy, Gilbert (1936–) French composer of advanced tendencies. His compositions show the influence of oriental music, total ➤ **serialism**, and aleatory techniques.

He studied with Darius Milhaud, Olivier Messiaen, and Pierre Boulez. He was director of the Concerts du Domaine Musical, specializing in new music.

Works ORCHESTRAL *Mouvements* for chamber orchestra (1958), *Adagio et Stretto* for orchestra (1978), *Chant pour orchestre* (1980), *Orchestral* (1987).

CHAMBER *Alpha-Beth* for six wind instruments (1964); *Epigrammes* for piano (1961), *Obliques* I–III for piano (1987–89); *Mémoire* for cello and piano (1989).

VOCAL *Messe* for soloists, chorus, and orchestra (1983); *Écrits sur toile* for reciter and ensemble (1983); *Choros* for male vocalists, chorus, and orchestra (1989).

OTHER *Cycle* for percussion (1964–66); *La Variation ajoutée* for tape and instruments (1986).

Ana, Francesco d' (1460–1503) Italian composer. His works include frottole (songs) and lamentations. He is known to have been active at St Mark's, Venice, in 1490.

Anacréon acte de ballet by Jean-Philippe Rameau (libretto by P-J Bernard), first produced at Fontainebleau, France, on 23 October 1754; it was revised and produced at the Paris Opéra on 10 October 1758.

Anacréon, ou L'Amour fugitif opéra-ballet by Luigi Cherubini (libretto by R Mendouze), first produced at the Paris Opéra, France, on 4 October 1803. The story tells of the poet Anacréon's love for his protégée Chloë.

anacrusis in music, alternative term for ➤ upbeat.

Anakreontika Greek songs for mezzo and instrumental ensemble by Peter Maxwell Davies; first performed in London, England, on 17 September 1976.

analysis, musical as recently as the 1950s, the analysis of music was widely understood to denote any kind of description with some technical component. But for more than a century there has been a growing academic discipline that attempts to explain musical phenomena by means as rigorous and logical as possible, to approach formal models of how music works, or to break down the organism of musical structures into smaller components. Pure musical analysis often eschews value judgement, which is more the province of the critic or aesthetician. See Hans ➤ Keller, Leonard ➤ Meyer, Jean-Jacques ➤ Nattiez, Rudolf ➤ Réti, and Heinrich ➤ Schenker.

Ančerl, Karel (1908–1973) Czech conductor. Imprisoned during World War II, he resumed his career in 1945, becoming professor at the Academy of Musical Arts, Prague, in 1950. He conducted the Czech Philharmonic Orchestra 1950–68, and was music director of the Toronto Symphony Orchestra from 1969.

He studied with Jaroslav Křička and Alois Hába at the Prague Conservatory 1925–29, and was assistant to Scherchen in Berlin 1929–31. His public career began in 1931 as a theatre conductor and with Czech radio. He conducted at festivals of the International Society for Contemporary Music 1933–37.

Anda, Géza (1921–1976) Hungarian-born Swiss pianist and conductor. He excelled at Brahms, Bartók, and Mozart, whose piano concertos he conducted from the keyboard, inserting his own ➤ **cadenzas.** His playing was noted for its clarity and subtle nuances.

andamento (Italian 'proceeding', 'advancement') in music, a ➤ **fugue** subject of more than usual length and often in two contrasted sections.

andante (Italian 'going, walking') in music, a tempo marking indicating the music to be performed at a walking pace; that is, at a moderately slow tempo.

andantino (Italian, diminutive of *andante*, 'going', 'walking') in musical notation, a modification of ➤ **andante.** Interpretation of the term has varied; it is not clear whether it denotes a faster or slower tempo than andante. Beethoven himself was unsure as to the meaning. Most recent composers intend a faster tempo.

Anderson, Beth (1950–) US composer and performance artist. Her compositions involve freedom of improvisation and employ a wide range of resources.

She studied with the composers John Cage, Larry Austin, and Terry Riley at Mills College, Oakland, California; she also studied at the University of California.

Works OPERA *Queen Christina* (1973).

ORCHESTRAL *Revel* for orchestra (1985); *Music for Charlemagne Palestine* (1973).

ORATORIO *Joan* (1974).

CHAMBER *Rosemary Swale* for string quartet (1986).

OTHER text-sound piece *Riot Rot* (1984); music theatre *Soap Tuning* (1976) and *Elizabeth Rex* (1983).

Anderson, Emily (1891–1962) English musicologist. Although employed in the Foreign Office, she edited and translated the complete letters of Mozart and his family (two volumes, 1938) and those of Beethoven (three volumes, 1962).

Anderson, Laurie (1947–) US composer and performance artist. She trained as a violinist and minimalist painter and in 1974 began making her own instruments, including a violin with an internal speaker. She has appeared widely in Europe and the USA, notably in multi-media, cyberpunk shows which employ a voice-activated synthesizer; contact microphones have turned her body into a percussion set.

In 1973 she staged the 12-hour audio-visual show *The Life and Times of Josef Stalin* at Brooklyn Academy, USA. Her show *Songs and Stories from Moby Dick* premiered in Dallas, Texas, in April 1999 and went to the Barbican Arts Centre, London, England, in May 2000.

Works *Americans on the Move* (1979, developed into *United States Live*, 1983); *New York Social Life*; *Time to Go* (portraying a museum attendant at closing time); *Empty Places* (1989); the autobiographical *Stories from the Nerve Bible* (1993); album *Bright Red* (1994).

An die ferne Geliebte, To the Distant Beloved song cycle by Beethoven (six songs), Op. 98, to poems by Alois Jeitteles, composed in 1816. It is the first German set of songs intended to form a connected cycle.

Andrea Chénier opera by Umberto Giordano (libretto by Luigi Illica), first produced at La Scala, Milan, Italy, on 28 March 1896. The story tells how Chénier and Madeleine are guillotined after the French Revolution, after Chénier has been denounced by Gérard, a rival in love.

Andricu, Michel (1895–1974) Romanian composer. He studied at the Bucharest Conservatory and later became professor at the Royal Academy there, gaining the Enescu Prize for composition in 1924. From 1926 to 1959 he was professor at the Bucharest Conservatory.

Works BALLET *Taina* (1933).

ORCHESTRAL eleven symphonies (1944–70); 13 sinfoniettas (1945–73); nine orchestral suites (1924–58); serenade; three *Tableaux symphoniques*; *Suite pittoresque*; *Suite brève*; *Poem* (1923), and other pieces for orchestra.

CHAMBER string quartet (1931); *Novellettes* for piano quintet (1925) and other chamber music; sonatina; *Suite lyrique* and other piano works.

Andriessen, Hendrik (1892–1981) Dutch organist and composer. He studied under Bernard Zweers at the Amsterdam Conservatory, and later became director of the Utrecht Conservatory and choirmaster at the Roman Catholic cathedral there.

Works OPERA *Philomela* (1950), *The Mirror from Venice* (1964).

CHURCH MUSIC eight Masses and Te Deum (1943).

ORCHESTRAL four symphonies (1930–54), variations for orchestra.

VOCAL songs for voice and orchestra.

CHAMBER chamber music; cello and piano sonata; organ works.

Andriessen, Louis (1939–) Dutch composer. His earlier work was influenced by John Cage, Charles Ives, and Igor Stravinsky; he later preferred the simplicities of minimalism.

He studied with his father, Hendrik Andriessen, and with Luciano Berio in Milan, Italy.

Works ORCHESTRAL *Anachronie*, in memory of Ives, for orchestra (1966); *Velocity* for orchestra (1983).

THEATRE PIECES *Reconstructie* (anti-imperialist theatre piece, 1969), *Orpheus* (1977), *George Sand* (1980), *De Materie* (1985–88).

VOCAL *Dances* for soprano and chamber orchestra (1991).

OTHER *What it's Like* for electronics and 52 strings (1970); *Uproar* for 16 wind, six percussion, and electronics (1970); *The Nine Symphonies of Beethoven* for ensemble and ice-cream bell (1970); *Il Principe*, after Machiavelli (1974); *Matthew Passion* (1977); *Facing Death* for four amplified strings (1991); *M is for Man, Music, Mozart* (TV show for the bicentenary); *Rosa* ('a horse drama', with Peter Greenaway, 1994).

Andrieu, F (lived late 14th century) French composer. He set a double *ballade* by Eustace Deschamps on the death of Guillaume de Machaut (1377).

Andromaque, Andromache opera by André Grétry (libretto by L G Pitra, based on Racine's tragedy), first produced at the Paris Opéra, France, on 6 June 1780.

Anerio, Felice (c.1560–1614) Italian composer. He was a chorister in the papal chapel as a boy, later maestro di cappella at the English College in Rome, which he left for the service of Cardinal Aldobrandini. He was appointed composer to the papal chapel on the death of Palestrina in 1594, and commissioned to reform the Roman Gradual in 1611.

Works CHURCH MUSIC Masses, motets, hymns and other church music.

OTHER madrigals, canzonets.

Anerio, Giovanni Francesco (c.1567–1630) Italian composer, brother of Felice Anerio. He was maestro di cappella at the cathedral of Verona in 1609, and from 1613 to 1620 was music instructor at the Seminario Romano and maestro di cappella of the church of the Madonna de' Monti in Rome. He was in the service of Sigismund III of Poland 1624–28. His secular music, including madrigals and canzonettas, is more progressive than that of many of his contemporaries.

Works CHURCH MUSIC Masses, Requiem, Te Deum, and other church music.

OTHER madrigals, canzonettas.

Anet, Jean-Jacques-Baptiste (1676–1755) French violinist and composer. He wrote sonatas and other works for violin. He travelled in France and Italy, studying with Corelli in Rome, and made a great reputation in Paris 1701–35, at the Concert Spirituel with the Violons du Roy. He retired to the court of the ex-king of Poland, Stanislas (Stanisław) Leszczyński, at Lunéville in 1738.

Anfossi, Pasquale (1727–1797) Italian composer, a pupil of Niccolò Piccinni at Naples. He wrote operas from 1763, but had his first real success with *L'incognita perseguitata* (Rome, 1773). He later produced operas in Paris, London (he was a music director of the King's Theatre 1782–86), Berlin, and Prague. In 1762 he became maestro di cappella of St John Lateran in Rome. Mozart wrote insertion arias for two of his operas.

Works OPERA *Armida* (Turin, 1770), *L'incognita perseguitata* (Rome, 1773), *La finta giardiniera* (Rome, 1774), *Il geloso in cimento* (Vienna, 1774), *L'avaro* (Venice, 1775), *La vera costanza* (Rome, 1776), *Gengis-Kan* (Turin, 1777), *Il curioso indiscreto* (Rome, 1777), *I viaggiatori felici* (Venice, 1780), *Le gelosie fortunate* (Turin, Carignano, 1783).

OTHER church music.

Angélique opera in one act by Jacques Ibert (libretto by Nino), first produced at the Théâtre Fémina, Paris, France, on 28 January 1927.

Angiolina, ossia Il matrimonio per susurro, Angiolina, or The Marriage by Noise opera by Antonio Salieri (libretto by C P Defranceschi, based on Ben Jonson's *Epicoene*), first produced at the Vienna Kärntnertortheater, Austria, on 22 October 1800. See also ➤ **Schweigsame Frau** (Strauss).

anglaise (French 'English') dance form similar to that of the country dance, which in France became the *contredanse* in the 18th century, when the name of anglaise was sometimes given to it instead to show its English origin unmistakably.

Anglican chant form of ➤ **plainsong** used by the Anglican Church to set psalms, canticles (when they are not sung in a more elaborate setting), or other religious texts to music. It is usually sung in unison and with a free rhythm, based upon the inherent rhythm of the language. It may be accompanied by an organ, establishing a harmonic framework.

ängstlich (German 'anxiously, apprehensively') musical term used by Beethoven as a direction for the singing of the recitative in the 'Agnus Dei' section of his *Missa solemnis* (1819–23).

An answer as found in the top voice of Bach's Fugue in C major, Well-tempered Clavier, Book 1, No. 1.

Aniara opera by Karl-Birger Blomdahl (libretto by E Lindegren, after Harry Martinson's epic poem *Revue about Men in Time and Space*), first produced in Stockholm, Sweden, on 31 May 1959. The action is set on board a spaceship.

anima (Italian 'soul') in musical notation, as in 'con anima', meaning that the music should be played 'with soul'. It is often confused with ➤ **animato**, which is concerned primarily with a faster tempo.

Anima del filosofo, ossia Orfeo ed Euridice, The Philosopher's Stone, or Orpheus and Eurydice Haydn's last opera; it was composed in 1791 in London, England, but not performed. The first known production was in Florence, Italy, on 10 June 1951, conducted by Erich Kleiber, with Maria Callas and Boris Christoff in the leading roles.

animando (Italian 'animating') in musical notation, indicating a gradual increase of tempo, in the manner of ➤ **accelerando**.

animato (Italian 'animated') in musical notation, indicating an immediate increase of tempo, not a gradual one as in ➤ **animando**.

Anna Bolena, **Anne Boleyn** opera by Donizetti (libretto by Felice Romani), first produced at the Teatro Carcano, Milan, Italy, on 26 December 1830. It describes the events leading to the execution of Anne Boleyn, the second wife of Henry VIII of England.

Anna Karenina opera by Jenö Hubay (libretto, in Hungarian, by S Góth, based on Tolstoy's novel), first produced in Budapest, Hungary, on 10 November 1923.

It is also the title of an opera by Iain Hamilton (libretto by composer), first produced at the London Coliseum, England, on 7 May 1981.

Années de pèlerinage, **Years of Pilgrimage** four sets of piano pieces by Liszt, mainly recording his travels in Switzerland and Italy, composed between 1835 and 1877.

1ʳᵉ Année: En Suisse was composed 1835–36 and published in 1855. It comprises: 1. *Chapelle de Guillaume Tell*. 2. *Au Lac de Wallenstadt*. 3. *Pastorale*. 4. *Au Bord d'une source*. 5. *Orage*. 6. *Vallée d'Obermann* (inspired by Étienne Sénancour's

Obermann; the valley is an imaginary or unidentified one in the canton of Valais). 7. *Eglogue*. 8. *Le Mal du pays*. 9. *Les Cloches de Genève*. (Nos. 1, 2, 4, 6, and 9 originally formed part of an *Album d'un voyageur* for piano published in 1836; they were revised for the publication of the *Années de pèlerinage* in 1855).

2ᵐᵉ Année: En Italie was composed 1838–39 and published in 1846. It comprises: 1. *Sposalizio* (after Raphael's painting in the Brera at Milan). 2. *Il pensieroso* (after Michelangelo's statue of Giuliano dei Medici in the Medici mausoleum at San Lorenzo, Florence). 3. *Canzonetta del Salvator Rosa*. 4. *Sonetto No. 47 del Petrarca*. 5. *Sonetto No. 104 del Petrarca*. 6. *Sonetto No. 123 del Petrarca* (Nos. 4–6 are transcriptions of settings of these Petrarch sonnets for voice and piano). 7. *D'Après une lecture du Dante: Fantasia quasi Sonata* ('Dante Sonata').

3ᵐᵉ Année was composed 1872–77 and published in 1883. It comprises: 1. *Angelus: Prière aux anges gardiens*. 2. *Aux Cyprès de la Villa d'Este*. 3. ditto: *Thrénodie*. 4. *Les Jeux d'eau de la Villa d'Este*. 5. *Sunt lacrymae rerum en mode hongrois*. 6. *Marche funèbre* (in memory of the Emperor Maximilian I of Mexico, who died on 19 June 1867). 7. *Sursum corda*.

The Supplement to Vol. II, *Venezia e Napoli*, was composed in 1859 and published in 1861. It comprises: 1. *Gondoliera* (on a canzona by Cavaliere Peruchini). 2. *Canzone* (on the gondolier's song in Rossini's *Otello*). 3. *Tarantella* (on some canzoni by Guillaume Louis Cottrau). (This set is partly a revision of an earlier one of the same title composed in 1840, but not published.)

Ansermet, Ernest Alexandre (1883–1969) Swiss conductor. He worked with Diaghilev's Russian Ballet 1915–23. In 1918 he founded the Orchestre de la Suisse Romande, which he conducted until 1967. He was known for his accurate and well-balanced performances of Stravinsky's earlier music and gave the first performances of *The Soldier's Tale* (1918), *Pulcinella* (1920), and *Renard* (1922).

Originally a professor of mathematics 1906–10, he studied music with Ernest Bloch, Felix Mottl, and Arthur Nikisch. In 1961 he published a book criticizing certain aspects of modern, especially serial, music.

answer in a ➤ **fugue**, the second entry of the subject, brought in while the first entry continues with a counterpoint to it.

Antar programme symphony by Rimsky-Korsakov, Op. 9, based on Osip Senkovsky's oriental story of that name. It was composed in 1868 as '2nd Symphony', revised in 1875, first performed at the St Petersburg, Russian Music Society in January 1876, and republished in 1903 as 'symphonic suite'. The titles of the movements are I. Introduction; II. 'Joy of Revenge'; III. 'Joy of Power'; IV. 'Joy of Love'.

antecedent in musical analysis, a phrase or passage that is followed by a complementary ➤ **consequent** phrase. Antecedent/consequent phrases are also known as 'question/answer' phrases. Compositions favouring this technique are associated most closely with the classical period.

Antechrist work for chamber ensemble by Peter Maxwell Davies, composed in 1967 and first performed in London, England, on 30 May 1967.

Antegnati, Costanzo (1549–1624) Italian composer and member of a family of organ-builders famous in northern Italy from 1470 to 1642. They built about 400 organs, including instruments used by Frescobaldi, the Gabrieli, and other Renaissance composers. He wrote Masses, motets and madrigals, and organ and other instrumental music.

Antheil, George (1900–1959) US composer and pianist. He is known for his *Ballet mécanique* (1923–25, first performed in 1926, and revised 1952–53) scored for anvils, aeroplane propellers, electric bells, car horns, and pianos.

anthem in music, a short, usually elaborate, religious choral composition, sometimes accompanied by the organ; also a song of loyalty or devotion.

Composers of anthems include William ➤ **Byrd**, Orlando ➤ **Gibbons**, Henry ➤ **Purcell**, John ➤ **Blow**, and George Frideric ➤ **Handel**.

anticipation in music, the occurrence of a note or notes from a chord before the rest of the chord is sounded.

An example of 'anticipation' from Beethoven's Piano Sonata, Op. 27, No. 2.

Antico, Andrea de (c.1480–after 1539) Italian composer and music publisher who worked mainly in Rome and then in Venice during the first half of the 16th century. His publications include *Frottole intabulate da sonar organi* (Rome, 1517), the earliest-known printed edition of keyboard music in Italy.

Antifone work for orchestra by Hans Werner Henze, composed in 1960 and first performed in Berlin, Germany, on 20 January 1962, conducted by Herbert von Karajan.

Antigonae play with music by Carl Orff (text by Johann Hölderlin, after Sophocles), first produced in Salzburg, Austria, on 9 August 1949.

Antigone incidental music to Sophocles' tragedy by Mendelssohn, first produced at the New Palace, Potsdam, Germany, on 28 October 1841, and repeated at the Berlin Opera on 13 April 1842. The plot describes how the daughter of Oedipus attempts to bury her brother, against the wishes of King Creon.

It is also the title of an opera by Arthur Honegger (libretto by Jean Cocteau, after Sophocles), first produced at the Théâtre de la Monnaie, Brussels, Belgium, on 28 December 1927. There is an earlier opera on the same subject by Niccolò Zingarelli (libretto by J-F Marmontel), first produced at the Paris Opéra, France, on 30 April 1790.

Antigono opera by Christoph Willibald von Gluck (libretto by Pietro Metastasio), first produced at the Teatro Argentina, Rome, Italy, on 9 February 1756. The story describes how Antigonus, King of Macedonia, is rivalled in love by his son.

It is also the title of an opera on the same subject by Johann Hasse (libretto by Metastasio), first produced at Hubertusburg near Dresden, Germany, on 10 October 1743.

antiphon (Greek *anti*, 'against'; *phone*, 'voice') choral music in Greek or Roman liturgy involving the exchange of responses between solo voice and choir, or between choral groups, hence antiphony.

antiphony music exploiting directional and canonic opposition of widely spaced choirs or groups of instruments to create perspectives in sound. It was developed in 17th-century Venice by Giovanni Gabrieli and in Germany by his pupil Heinrich Schütz and Roland de Lassus; an example is the double-choir motet *Alma Redemptoris Mater* (1604). The practice was revived in the 20th century by Béla Bartók, Karlheinz Stockhausen, and Luciano Berio.

Antiquis, Giovanni de (lived 16th century) Italian composer. He was music director at the church of San Niccolo at Bari, and edited two books of *Villanelle alla napolitana* by musicians of Bari, including himself, published in Venice in 1574.

Antonio e Cleopatra opera by Riccardo Malipiero (libretto by composer, based on Shakespeare), first produced at the Teatro Comunale, Florence, Italy, on 4 May 1938.

Antony and Cleopatra opera by Samuel Barber (libretto by composer, based on Shakespeare), first performed on the opening night of the New York Metropolitan Opera in the Lincoln Center, on 16 September 1966. It was revised and produced at the Juilliard School of Music, New York, on 6 February 1975.

anvil orchestral percussion instrument that imitates the sound of a blacksmith's anvil, but is constructed of small steel bars struck by a mallet of wood or metal. It can be so made as to produce notes of definite pitch, as in Wagner's opera *Das Rheingold*, but is usually indeterminate in pitch.

Apel, Nikolaus (c.1475–1537) Compiler of a large manuscript in choirbook form (published in Leipzig, by the University Bibliothek in 1494) containing sacred and secular music of the late 15th and early 16th centuries. It has been published in full by Rudolf Gerber (as *Das Erbe deutscher Musik*, 32–34).

Apel, Willi (1893–1988) German-born US musicologist. He studied mathematics at Bonn, Munich, and Berlin Universities, and also piano under Edwin Fischer, Martienssen, and others. He settled in the USA in 1936 and taught at the Longy School of Music, Cambridge, Massachusetts, 1936–43, and Harvard University, 1938–42. He was professor at Indiana University 1950–63. His publications include *The Notation of Polyphonic Music* (fifth edition 1961), *Harvard Dictionary of Music* (revised edition, 1969), *Gregorian Chant* (1958), and *A History of Keyboard Music* (1972). He also published a joint edition, with A T Davison, of *Historical Anthology of Music* (2 volumes, 1946 and 1960).

aperto (Italian 'open, frank, straightforward') musical term used by Mozart in conjunction with *allegro* in some early works, such as the A major violin concerto, K219. The meaning is not clear, but may be taken to suggest an energetic delivery strictly in time.

a piacere (Italian 'at pleasure') musical direction indicating that a passage may be played or sung in any way the performer desires, especially in regard to tempo.

Aplvor, Denis (1916–2004) Irish composer of Welsh origin. He was chorister at Hereford Cathedral, later at Christ Church, Oxford, and studied composition with Patrick Hadley and Alan Rawsthorne; later influences included serialism.

Works OPERA *She Stoops to Conquer* (libretto by composer after Goldsmith; 1947), *Yerma* (1959), *Ubu Roi* (1966).

ORCHESTRAL two symphonies; two violin concertos, piano concerto; clarinet concertante (1981); sonata for clarinet, piano, and percussion, violin and piano sonata; clarinet quintet (1981); wind quintet (1981).

VOCAL *The Hollow Men* (T S Eliot) for baritone, chorus, and orchestra (1939); Chaucer songs with string quartet (1936); songs with words by Federico García Lorca and others.

Apollo e Dafne Italian cantata by Handel, for soprano, baritone, and chamber ensemble; it was composed about 1708.

Apollo et Hyacinthus Latin intermezzo by Mozart K38 (libretto by Rufinus Widl), first produced at Salzburg University, Austria, on 13 May 1767. In the story Hyacinthus is murdered by the jealous Zephyrus but Apollo transforms him into a flower.

Apollo Musagetes, Apollo, Leader of the Muses ballet for string orchestra by Stravinsky (choreography Adolph Bolm); it was composed 1927–28 and first produced in Washington, DC, USA, on 27 April 1928.

apollonicon large organ playable both by hand and mechanically by barrels, built by Flight & Robson in London, England, and exhibited by them in 1817.

Apostel, Hans Erich (1901–1972) German-born Austrian composer. He entered Karlsruhe Conservatory in 1916, and later studied with Arnold Schoenberg and Alban Berg in Vienna, where he lived from 1921. In 1937 his *Requiem* won the Hertzka Prize.

Works ORCHESTRAL *Variations on a Theme of Haydn* (1949); piano concerto.

CHAMBER two string quartets.

VOCAL *Requiem* (text by Rilke) for eight-part chorus and orchestra; songs with piano or orchestra on texts by Trakl and Hölderlin.

Apostles, The oratorio by Edward Elgar, Op. 49 (libretto compiled from the Bible by the composer), Part I of a trilogy. Part II is *The Kingdom* and Part III was never completed. The work was first performed at the Birmingham Festival, England, on 14 October 1903.

Appalachia variations for orchestra with chorus by Delius, composed in 1902, first performed at Elberfeld, on 15 October 1904; its first London performance was on 22 November 1907. The title is the old American Indian name for North

America; the theme is an African-American folk-song.

Appalachian Spring ballet by Aaron Copland (choreographer Martha Graham), first produced in Washington, DC, USA, on 30 October 1944. The orchestral suite from the ballet was first performed in New York, New York, on 4 October 1945, conducted by Artur Rodziński.

Appassionata Sonata (Italian 'impassioned') name commonly used for Beethoven's F minor piano sonata of 1804–05, Op. 57, but not authorized by himself.

Appenzeller, Benedictus (c.1485–after 1558) Flemish composer. A pupil of → Josquin Desprez, he was in the service of Mary of Hungary, dowager regent of the Netherlands.

Works chansons, church music, a *Nenia* on the death of Josquin, and other pieces.

Applausus Latin allegorical oratorio by Haydn for soloists, chorus, and orchestra, first performed in Zwettl, Austria, on 17 April 1768.

Appleby, Thomas (1488– c. 1562) English organist and composer of church music. He was appointed organist of Lincoln Cathedral in 1538, and the next year organist at Magdalen College, Oxford. He returned to Lincoln in 1541, and William → Byrd succeeded him there in 1563.

appoggiatura or **leaning note (Italian, from appoggiata, 'supporting', 'leaning')** in musical notation, a type of → grace note, of varying length, occurring on a strong beat. It creates a → dissonance which is resolved by the melody moving a note lower. It was a form of → ornamentation used in the 17th and 18th centuries, and to a more limited extent in the 19th century.

Various symbols have been used in the past to indicate an appoggiatura, the commonest of which is a note in smaller type (top); beneath that is an approximation of how these are played.

Apprenti sorcier, L', The Sorcerer's Apprentice scherzo for orchestra by Paul Dukas on Goethe's ballad *Der Zauberlehrling*. It was first performed for the Société Nationale de Musique in Paris, France, on 18 May 1897.

Arabella opera by Richard Strauss (libretto by Hugo von Hofmannsthal, based on his story *Lucidor*), first produced in Dresden, Germany, on 1

July 1933. This was Hofmannsthal's last libretto for Strauss.

Arabesk, An work by Delius for baritone, chorus, and orchestra (text by J P Jacobsen); it was composed in 1911 and first performed in Newport in 1920. The first London performance was given on 18 October 1929.

arabesque in music, a piece characterized by florid or ornamental melody. Claude Debussy and Robert Schumann wrote famous arabesques.

Aragonaise Spanish dance of Aragon, known as the *Jota aragonesa*.

Araia or **Araja, Francesco (1709–c.1770)** Italian composer. He produced his first opera in 1729. From 1735 he was for 24 years opera director to the Russian court in St Petersburg, where he produced several of his own works, *Il finto Nino* (1737), *Artaserse* (1738), *Scipione* (1745), *Mitridate* (1747), and *Bellerofonte* (1750). Another was *Cephalus and Procris* (1755), the first opera given in Russia known to have been sung in Russian and not in Italian.

Arbeau, Thoinot (1520–1595), born **Jehan Tabourot** French priest and author. He wrote a book on dancing, *Orchésographie* (1589), which contains a large number of dance tunes current in 16th-century France.

Arbore di Diana, L', Diana's Tree opera by Vicente Martín y Soler (libretto by Lorenzo da Ponte), first produced at the Burgtheater, Vienna, Austria, on 1 October 1787.

Arbre enchanté, L', ou Le Tuteur dupé, The Enchanted Tree, or The Tutor Duped comic opera by Christoph Willibald von Gluck (libretto by P L Moline, after J J Vadé), first produced before the court at the Schönbrunn Palace, Vienna, Austria, on 3 October 1759.

Arcadelt, Jacob (c.1505–c.1567) Netherlandish or French composer. He wrote Masses and motets, but is particularly noted for his Italian madrigals.

He entered the papal chapel in Rome in 1540, and received prebends in 1545 at St Barthélemy and St Pierre, Liège, from Pope Paul III. In 1551 he left papal service to go to France and, in 1554, entered the service of Charles, Duke of Guise, who was eventually appointed archbishop of Rheims. Arcadelt may also have been associated with the royal chapel of France for a time, for he was described as a musician of the king in 1557.

Arcadia in Brenta, L' opera by Baldassare Galuppi (libretto by Carlo Goldoni), first produced at the Teatro Sant' Angelo, Venice, Italy, on 14 May 1749. It was the first comic opera by Galuppi written in collaboration with Goldoni, and presents

Fabrizio welcoming guests to his new villa by the River Brenta.

Arcana work for large orchestra by Edgard Varèse; it was composed 1925–27 and first performed in Philadelphia, USA, on 8 April 1927, conducted by Leopold Stokowski.

'Archduke' Trio the name sometimes given to Beethoven's piano trio in B flat major, Op. 97, composed in 1811 and dedicated to the Archduke Rudolph of Austria.

archlute large lute, such as the ➤ **chitarrone** or ➤ **theorbo**, with two sets of strings, the pegs of which are set at different distances in the double neck; the longer bass strings have no fingerboard and can therefore not be altered in pitch during performance, but are used as the bass notes of the chords.

arco (Italian 'with the bow') in music, a direction to play with the bow, or to resume playing with the bow after playing pizzicato (plucked string).

Unusual instruments played with the bow include musical glasses, the suspended cymbal, and the musical saw.

Arden muss sterben, **Arden Must Die** opera by Alexander Goehr (libretto by E Fried, after the anonymous Elizabethan play *Arden of Faversham*), first produced in Hamburg, Germany, on 5 March 1967.

Arensky, Anton Stepanovich (1861–1906) Russian composer. His works include the opera *Nal and Damayanti* (1904), the ballet *Egyptian Nights* (composed in 1900, first performed in 1908), and the cantata *The Fountain of Bakhchisarai* (1899). He also composed church music, songs, symphonies, a set of variations for strings on a theme of Tchaikovsky, some chamber music, and many elegant piano works. His music is eclectic, but reflects the influence of Tchaikovsky.

Arensky was born in Novgorod, and studied under Karl Karlovich Zikke (1850–90) and, later (1879–82), under Julius Ivanovich Johannsen (1826–1904) and Rimsky-Korsakov at St Petersburg Conservatory. He was appointed professor at the Moscow Conservatory in 1882.

Works OPERA *A Dream on the Volga* (based on Ostrovsky's *Voyevoda*; 1891), *Raphael* (1894), *Nal and Damayanti* (1904).

BALLET *Egyptian Nights* (performed 1908).

ORCHESTRAL two symphonies (1883 and 1889); piano concerto.

OTHER incidental music for Shakespeare's *The Tempest*; chamber music, including piano trio in D minor; numerous piano pieces; choruses, songs, church music.

Argento, Dominick (1927–) US composer. He studied with Alan Hovhaness and Howard Hanson at the Eastman School of Music, New York, and with Luigi Dallapiccola in Italy. His music is in an agreeably tonal idiom.

Works OPERA *Sicilian Limes* (1954), *The Boor* (1957), *Christopher Sly* (1963), *The Masque of Angels* (1964), *The Shoemaker's Holiday* (1967), *The Voyage of Edgar Allan Poe* (1976), *Miss Havisham's Fire* (1978), *Casanova's Homecoming* (1985), *The Aspern Papers* (1988), *The Dream of Valentino* (1993).

ORCHESTRAL *A Ring of Time* (1972), *Five Variations* (1982); *Capriccio: Rossini in Paris*, for clarinet and orchestra (1985).

ORATORIO *Jonah and the Whale* (1973).

OTHER choral music and song-cycles, including *Six Elizabethan Songs* for voice and ensemble (1958); *In Praise of Music* (1977); *Casa Guidi*, five songs for mezzo and orchestra (1983); *Le Tombeau d'Edgar Poe* (1985).

aria (Italian 'air') melodic solo song of reflective character, often with a contrasting middle section. It is used to express a moment of importance in the action of an opera or oratorio. Already to be found in Jacopo Peri's *Euridice* (1600) and Claudio ➤ **Monteverdi's** *Orfeo* (1607), it reached its more elaborate form in the work of Alessandro ➤ **Scarlatti** and George Frideric ➤ **Handel**, becoming a set piece for virtuoso opera singers. An example is Handel's 'Where'er you walk' from the secular oratorio *Semele* (1744) to words by William Congreve. In instrumental music, an aria may be the title of a songlike piece, or a theme suitable for variations.

By the early 18th century an aria was a song in three sections, of which the third repeated the first, while the second introduced variety of subject matter, key, and mood. This is known more exactly as the 'da capo aria'.

After Handel's death (1759) and ➤ **Mozart's** youth (1760s) less rigid forms developed, sometimes based on sonata form (Mozart), and later shaped by the dramatic action of an opera (➤ **Beethoven**, ➤ **Weber**) or oratorio (➤ **Mendelssohn**).

Ariadne opera in one act by Bohuslav Martinů (libretto by composer after G Neveux), first produced in Gelsenkirchen, Germany, on 2 March 1961.

Ariadne auf Náxos play with music (melodrama) by Georg Benda (text by J C Brandes), first produced in Gotha, Germany, on 27 January 1775.

It is also the title of an opera by Richard Strauss (libretto by Hugo von Hofmannsthal), originally a one-act opera played after a shortened version of Molière's play *Le Bourgeois Gentilhomme*, with incidental music by Strauss. It was first produced in Stuttgart, Germany, on 25 October 1912; a second version, with a new operatic first act, was produced at the Vienna Opera, Austria, on 4 October 1916.

Ariane et Barbe-bleue, Ariane and Bluebeard opera by Paul Dukas (libretto from Maurice Maeterlinck's play with slight alterations), first at the Opéra-Comique, Paris, France, on 10 May 1907. The story tells of Ariane releasing Bluebeard's previous five wives from his castle.

Ariane, ou Le Mariage de Bacchus opera by Louis Grabu (libretto by P Perrin, previously set by Robert Cambert), first produced at the Drury Lane Theatre, London, England, on 30 March 1674.

Arianna opera by Benedetto Marcello (libretto by V Cassani), composed in 1727 but never performed in Marcello's lifetime. It was edited by O Chilesotti in 1885 and first produced at the Liceo Benedetto Marcello, Venice, Italy, on 27 April 1913.

Also an opera by Handel (*Arianna in Creta*, libretto adapted from P Pariati's *Arianna e Teseo*), first produced at the King's Theatre, Haymarket, London, England, on 26 January 1734. It concerns Theseus and the Minotaur, with a love subplot.

Arianna a Náxos, Ariadne on Náxos cantata by Haydn for soprano and keyboard, composed in 1790.

Arianna e Teseo, Ariadne and Theseus opera by Nicola Porpora (libretto by P Pariati), first produced in Vienna, Austria, on 1 October 1714.

Arianna, L' opera by Monteverdi (libretto by Ottavio Rinuccini), first produced at the ducal court of Mantua, Italy, for the wedding of the Hereditary Prince Francesco Gonzaga with Margherita, Princess of Savoy, on 28 May 1608. Most of the music is lost; only the *Lamento d'Arianna* (Ariadne's Lament) survives.

Aribo Scholasticus (lived 11th century) Flemish monk and music theorist. His treatise *De Musica* is important in the development of modal theory in the West, with its emphasis on melodic formulae as well as scales in the definition of mode.

arietta (diminutive of Italian *aria*, 'air') in music, a short, simple ➤ aria.

ariette (French 'little aria or air') now the same as an *arietta*, but in early 18th-century French opera an elaborate aria (sometimes with Italian words) and in late 18th-century *opéra comique* a song introduced into a scene in dialogue. See ➤ **Debussy** (*Ariettes oubliées*).

Ariodant opera by Étienne Méhul (libretto by F-B Hoffman, after Ariosto's poem *Orlando furioso*, 1516), first produced at the Théâtre Favart, Paris, France, on 11 October 1799. The plot describes how Othon attempts to make Ina leave her lover Ariodant.

Ariodante opera by Handel (libretto by A Salvi, based on Ariosto's *Orlando furioso*, 1516), first produced at Covent Garden, London, England, on 8 January 1735. The plot describes how the lovers Ginevra and Ariodante are threatened by the evil Polinesso, who would have Ginevra for himself.

Ariosi work by Hans Werner Henze for soprano, violin, and orchestra, to poems by Torquato Tasso. It was composed for Wolfgang Schneiderhan and Irmgard Seefried and first performed by them in Edinburgh, Scotland, on 23 August 1964.

arioso (Italian 'melodious') in music, a type of ➤ recitative (sung narration), of more lyrical than speechlike quality. Some composers use the arioso to initiate or conclude a recitative, such as Bach in his cantata *Ein feste Burg/A Safe Stronghold* (1724). It can also refer to a section or passage in an instrumental work, which imitates recitative, as in Beethoven's Piano Sonata No. 31 (1821).

Ariosti, Attilo (1666–c.1729) Italian composer. He produced his first opera in Venice in 1696, and was court composer in Berlin 1697–1703. Later, he visited Vienna, London, and Bologna, and wrote six operas for the Royal Academy of Music, London.

Works OPERA *La più gloriosa fatica d'Ercole* (Vienna, 1703), *La fede ne' tradimenti* (Berlin, 1701), *Amor tra nemici* (Vienna, 1708), *Coriolano* (London, 1723), *Vespasiano* (London, 1724), *Artaserse* (London, 1724), *Dario* (London, 1725), *Lucio Vero* (London, 1727), and others.

OTHER oratorio *Nabucodonosor*, Passion oratorio and others; cantatas; lessons for viola d'amore.

Ariosto, Lodovico (1474–1533) Italian poet. His works inspired numerous musical settings by composers such as Étienne Méhul (➤ *Ariodant*, based on *Orlando furioso*), Handel (➤ *Ariodante* and *Orlando*), Augusta ➤ **Holmès** (*Orlando furioso*), Albert Roussel (*Les Enchantements d'Alcine*), and Vivaldi (➤ *Orlando furioso*).

Aristoxenus of Tarentum (lived 4th century BC) Greek philosopher. His treatise *Harmonics* (on acoustics and music theory) is based on the music practice of his day rather than being purely speculative.

Arlecchino opera in one act by Ferruccio Busoni (libretto by the composer), first produced in Zurich, Switzerland, on 11 May 1917. It relates the adventures of Harlequin in a *Commedia dell'arte* setting.

Arlesiana, L', The Girl from Arles opera by Francesco Ciléa (libretto by L Marenco, based on Alphonse Daudet's play *L'Arlésienne*), first produced at the Teatro Lirico, Milan, Italy, on 27 November 1897.

Arlésienne, L', The Girl from Arles incidental music by Georges Bizet for Alphonse Daudet's play *L'Arlésienne*, first produced in Paris, France, on 1 October 1872. Bizet afterwards extracted an orchestral suite from it. (The second suite was arranged by Ernest Guiraud.)

Arme Heinrich, Der, Poor Heinrich opera by Hans Pfitzner (libretto by J Grun), first produced in Mainz, Germany, on 2 April 1895. It was Pfitzner's first opera. The plot concerns a singer and knight who can only be saved by the sacrifice of a virgin.

Armenian chant the music of the Church in Armenia from its establishment in 303. It pursued an independent path after the separation from the Greek Church in 536. Its original, alphabetical notation was replaced in the 12th century by a neumic system (in which the only manuscripts have survived), which cannot now be deciphered.

The Church's collection of hymns (the *Sharakan*) is arranged according to the eight modes or *echoi*, apparently defined by melodic formulae rather than by scale.

Armida opera by Haydn (libretto by J Durandi), first produced at Eszterháza, Hungary, on 26 February 1784. The plot describes how the sorceress Armida attempts to seduce the crusader knight Rinaldo.

It is also the title of an opera by Rossini (libretto by G Schmidt, after Torquato Tasso), first produced at the Teatro San Carlo, Naples, Italy, on 11 November 1817. A further opera on the same theme was composed by Dvořák (libretto by J Vrchlický, based on his Czech translation of Tasso), first produced at the Czech Theatre, Prague (now in the Czech Republic), on 25 March 1904.

There are also settings by Tommaso Traetta (Vienna, 1761), Pasquale Anfossi (Turin, 1770), Antonio Salieri (Vienna, 1771), and Antonio Sacchini (Milan, 1772).

Armida abbandonata Italian cantata by Handel for soprano, two violins, and continuo, composed in 1707.

Armide opera by Christoph Willibald von Gluck (libretto by Philippe Quinault, based on Torquato Tasso's *Gerusalemme liberata*), first produced at the Paris Opéra, France, on 23 September 1777.

The plot recounts that Armide's intended victim is Renaud, but he escapes her traps.

An earlier version of the opera by Jean-Baptiste Lully (libretto by Philippe Quinault) was first produced at the Paris Opéra on 15 February 1686.

Arminio opera by Handel (libretto by A Salvi), first produced at Covent Garden, London, England, on 12 January 1737. The story describes how the rebel chieftain Arminius defeats the Romans in spite of a love subplot.

It is also the title of two operas by Johann Hasse: I. (libretto by G C Pasquini), first produced before the court in Dresden, Germany, on 7 October 1745; II. (libretto by Salvi), first produced in Milan, Italy, on 28 August 1730.

A further opera on the same theme by Alessandro Scarlatti (libretto by Salvi) was first produced at the Villa Medici, Pratolino, Italy, in September 1703.

armonica alternative name for the ➤ **glass harmonica**, a musical instrument.

Armourer of Nantes, The opera by Michael Balfe (libretto by G V Bridgeman, based on Victor Hugo's *Marie Tudor*), first produced at Covent Garden, London, England, on 12 February 1863.

Arne, Michael (c.1741–1786) English singer and composer, son of Thomas Augustine Arne (probably illegitimate). He made his first appearance as a singer in 1750, and a collection of songs, *The Flow'ret*, was published the same year. In 1761 he produced his first opera, *Edgar and Emmeline*. He also collaborated with other composers in the production of works for the stage, *A Midsummer Night's Dream* (with Burney and others, 1763) and *Almena* (with Jonathan Battishill, 1764). He married the singer Elizabeth Wright in 1766, and the next year wrote the music for David Garrick's *Cymon*, his most successful work. In 1771–72 he toured Germany, where he conducted the first German performance of *Messiah*. He was also interested in alchemy; his search for the 'philosopher's stone' twice ruined him. He is still known today for the song 'The lass with a delicate air'.

Arne, Thomas Augustine (1710–1778) English composer. He wrote incidental music for the theatre and introduced opera in the Italian manner to the London stage with works such as *Artaxerxes* (1762, revised 1777). He is remembered for the songs 'Where the bee sucks' from *The Tempest* (1746), 'Blow, blow thou winter wind' from *As You Like It* (1740), and 'Rule, Britannia!' from the masque *Alfred* (1740).

Arne was educated at Eton and intended for the law, but practised secretly on a muffled harpsichord and learnt the violin from Michael Festing, until his father allowed him to make music his career. He also taught his sister Susanna singing, and she appeared in his first opera, a setting of Addison's *Rosamond*, in 1733. He wrote music for Henry Fielding's *Tom Thumb* (1733), John Milton's *Comus* (1738), and William Congreve's *The Judgement of Paris* (1740). He had married the singer Cecilia Young in 1736, and he and his wife worked successfully 1742–44 in Dublin, which they twice revisited in the 1750s. The masque *Alfred* was produced in 1740, at the residence of Frederick, Prince of Wales, at Cliveden. In 1744 he was appointed composer to the Drury Lane Theatre, and in 1745 composer to the Vauxhall Gardens. In 1746 he supplied music for the masque *Neptune and Amphitrite* and the songs in *The Tempest*. He composed two oratorios, *The Death of Abel* (1744) and *Judith* (1761). In 1760, after a quarrel with the actor-manager David Garrick, he gave up his post as composer to Drury Lane Theatre and became composer to the Covent Garden Theatre, where his popular dramatic pastoral *Thomas and Sally* was produced in 1760. In 1762 he produced his opera *Artaxerxes*, translated by himself from Pietro Metastasio and composed in the Italian manner. He was buried at St Paul's, Covent Garden. His son Michael (c. 1741–1786) was also a composer, mainly for the stage.

Works OPERA AND PLAYS WITH MUSIC *Thomas and Sally* (1760), *Artaxerxes* (1762), *Love in a Village* (1762), *May Day* (1775).

MASQUES *Comus* (Milton adapted by Dalton; 1738), *The Judgment of Paris*, *Alfred* (1740).

INCIDENTAL MUSIC Shakespeare's *As You Like It* (1740), *Twelfth Night* (1741), *The Merchant of Venice* (1741), *The Tempest* (1746).

OTHER oratorio *Judith* (1761); about 25 books of songs; eight overtures for orchestra.

Arnell, Richard (Anthony Sayer) (1917–) English composer. He studied with John Ireland at the Royal College of Music in London and took the Farra Prize in 1938. From 1939 to 1947 he lived in New York, where he was consultant to the British Broadcasting Corporation's (BBC) US service.

Works OPERA *Love in Transit* (1958), *The Petrified Princess* (1959).

BALLET *Punch and the Child* (1947), *Harlequin in April* (1951), *The Great Detective* (after Conan Doyle; 1953).

ORCHESTRAL seven symphonies; symphonic poem *Lord Byron* (1952) and other orchestral music; violin concerto.

CHAMBER five string quartets.

OTHER piano and organ music; film music.

Arnold, Malcolm Henry (1921–) English composer. His work is tonal and includes a large amount of orchestral, chamber, ballet, and vocal music. His best-known overtures include *Beckus*

the Dandipratt (1948), *A Sussex Overture* (1951), and *Tam O'Shanter* (1955). His operas include *The Dancing Master* (1951), and he has written music for more than 80 films, including *The Bridge on the River Kwai* (1957), for which he won an Academy Award.

Arnold was born in Northampton and studied at the Royal College of Music in London. He began his career as a trumpeter, becoming principal trumpet in the London Philharmonic Orchestra in 1942. He later took up the career of a full-time composer, writing much orchestral and film music in an agreeably diatonic style. He soon became known for his witty, high-spirited, and well- designed compositions. He was knighted in 1993.

Works BALLET *Homage to the Queen* (1953), *Rinaldo and Armida* (1955), *Solitaire* (1956), *Elektra* (1963).

FILM AND INCIDENTAL MUSIC more than 80 film scores, including *The Bridge on the River Kwai* (1957); incidental music for Shakespeare's *The Tempest*.

ORCHESTRAL overture *Beckus the Dandipratt* (1948) for orchestra; symphony for strings; nine symphonies (1951–87); concertos for horn, clarinet (2), flute (2), oboe, piano duet, and mouth organ; concertos for trumpet, recorder, and cello (1988–89).

CHAMBER two string quartets (1951, 1975); violin and piano sonata, viola and piano sonata; piano works.

Arnold, Samuel (1740–1802) English composer. In 1765 he became composer to Covent Garden Theatre, London, and produced the pasticcio *The Maid of the Mill* (1765). He was appointed organist of the Chapel Royal in 1783 and Westminster Abbey in 1793. He composed or arranged many works for the stage, including *The Spanish Barber* (1777), *Gretna Green* (1783), and *Turk and No Turk* (1784). He also wrote oratorios and church music.

Works OPERA AND PLAYS WITH MUSIC *The Maid of the Mill* (1765), *Dr Faustus* (1766), *The Portrait* (1770), *The Castle of Andalusia* (1782), *Gretna Green* (1783), *Peeping Tom of Coventry* (1784), *Inkle and Yarico* (1787), *The Surrender of Calais* (1791), *The Mountaineers* (1793), *The Shipwreck* (1796), *The Enraged Musician* (on Hogarth's picture; 1798), *Obi, or Three-fingered Jack* (1800) and many others.

ORATORIOS *The Cure of Saul* (1767), *The Resurrection* (1770), *The Prodigal Son* (1773), *Elisha* (1801).

OTHER church music; overture for orchestra; odes for chorus; harpsichord music; songs.

Aroldo opera by Verdi (libretto by Francesco Maria Piave), first produced at the Teatro Nuovo, Rimini, Italy, on 16 August 1857. It was a revision of *Stiffelio* (1850).

arpeggio (Italian 'like a harp') in music, the sounding of a chord in a way that its notes are spread out and thus heard one after the other, usually from the bottom to the top.

An example of arpeggios in early keyboard music can be found in Johann Sebastian Bach's *Chromatic Fantasia and Fugue* (1720, revised 1730), though they are much more commonly used in later music such as the *Etudes* of Frédéric Chopin.

The arpeggio sign indicates that the notes should be rolled upwards, starting from the lowest note.

arpeggione six-stringed musical instrument invented by G Staufer of Vienna, Austria, in 1823. A hybrid between a cello and a guitar, it has a fretted fingerboard and is played with a bow.

Schubert wrote a sonata for it in 1824, which today is usually played in transcription for cello, viola, or clarinet.

arpicordo alternative and much rarer name for the ➤ harpsichord.

arrangement or **transcription** in music, the adaptation of a piece to an instrument or instruments other than those for which it was originally composed.

For example, orchestral compositions can be 'arranged' for the pianoforte (or vice versa). In some cases the 'recreation' of a work in a new instrumental medium virtually qualifies as original composition, as, for instance, in the pianoforte arrangements of Liszt and Busoni.

arranger in music, a person who adapts or assists in orchestrating the music of another composer at the composer's request. The use of an arranger became established in Hollywood; Sergei ➤ Rachmaninov, George ➤ Gershwin, and Leonard ➤ Bernstein, among others, composed concert works employing such assistance.

Arrangers are also common in jazz: the more notable examples include Gil Evans (1912–1988), who arranged music for Miles Davis and others; and Billy Strayhorn (1915–1967) for Duke Ellington. Composers of unauthorized arrangements include Johann Sebastian Bach (Vivaldi), Mozart (Handel's *Messiah*), and Stravinsky (Tchaikovsky and Pergolesi).

Arrieta y Corera, (Pascual Juan) Emilio (1823–1894) Spanish composer. He studied under Nicola Vaccai at the Milan Conservatory, Italy, and produced his first opera there in 1845, returning to Spain the following year. He was professor of composition at the Madrid Conservatory from 1857 and director from 1868.

Works OPERA *Ildegonda* (Milan, 1825), *La conquista di Granada* (1850, revised as *Isabella la Católica*, 1855).

OTHER zarzuelas *El dómino azul*, *El grumete*, *La estrella de Madrid*, *Marina*, and about 50 others.

ars antiqua (Latin 'old art') music of the Middle Ages, generally lacking ➤ counterpoint. It includes ➤ plainsong and ➤ organum composed in France during the 12th and 13th centuries.

arsis (Greek 'lifting') in music, an alternative term, borrowed from Greek poetry, for ➤ upbeat. It is the opposite of thesis (Greek 'lowering') or ➤ downbeat. In German usage, however, 'arsis' and 'thesis' have opposite meanings to the original Greek and English words.

ars nova (Latin 'new art') music composed in France and Italy during the 14th century. Originally introduced by Philippe de ➤ Vitry, it is distinguished by rhythmic and harmonic variety, and the increased importance of duple time (two beats in a bar) and independent voice parts. Guillaume de ➤ Machaut mastered the style in France. In Italy the ➤ madrigal grew out of ars nova.

ars subtilior (Latin 'the more refined art') term found in the writings of Philipottus de Caserta to describe a late-14th-century style of great notational and rhythmic complexity. Certain works by composers such as Philipottus, Senleches, Ciconia, and Asproys include cross-rhythms of a baffling complexity that has no parallels until the 20th century.

Artamene opera by Tommaso Albinoni (libretto by B Vitturi), first produced at the Teatro di Sant' Angelo, Venice, Italy, on 26 December 1740.

It is also the title of an opera by Christoph Willibald von Gluck (libretto by B Vitturi), first produced at the King's Theatre, Haymarket, London, on 4 March 1746. This was the second of Gluck's two operas for London; he performed an aria from it before Charles Burney in 1770.

Artaserse, **Artaxerxes** opera by Girolamo Abos (libretto by Pietro Metastasio), first produced at the Teatro di San Giovanni Grisostomo, Venice, Italy, during Carnival in 1746. The plot describes an attempt by Artabano to poison Artaserse, which is prevented by his own son.

It is also the title of the first opera by Christoph Willibald von Gluck (libretto by Metastasio), first produced at the Teatro Regio Ducal, Milan, Italy, on 26 December 1741. There are other settings by Johann Hasse (Venice, 1730), Karl Graun

(Berlin, 1743), and Niccolò Jommelli (Rome, 1749).

Artaxerxes opera by Thomas Arne (libretto by composer, translated from Pietro Metastasio's *Artaserse*), first produced at Covent Garden, London, England, on 2 February 1762. It was revived in London on 16 March 1995, in an edition by Peter Holman.

Arteaga, Esteban (1747–1799) Spanish scholar. He was a Jesuit priest, but after the suppression of the Order went to Italy, where he worked for many years with Padre Martini in Bologna. Five treatises on music survive, the most important of them being that on opera, *Rivoluzioni del teatro musicale italiano*, published 1733–38.

Art of Fugue, The see ➔ *Kunst der Fuge*.

arts festival programme of events and performances either promoting a single or a combination of art forms. Arts festivals vary in size, content, and duration, but all share the general objectives of staging and promoting artistic output within a clearly defined and structured programme. Examples include the Salzburg Festival in Austria (music), the Spoleto Festival in Italy (music, drama, art), and the Edinburgh International Festival in Scotland (performing arts).

Stemming from the traditional community-based festival, marking a time of celebration and rejuvenation, arts festivals became a prominent feature of European culture after 1945, and enjoyed huge popularity in the 1980s.

Over 500 arts festivals take place annually in the UK. These include the Notting Hill Carnival, which attracts an estimated 1.5 million visitors, and the Glyndebourne opera festival.

Artusi, Giovanni Maria (c.1540–1613) Italian composer and theorist. His four-part canzonets appeared in 1598, and his *L'arte del contrapunto* in 1586–89. Apart from his polemical works against Zarlino, Galilei, and Bottrigari, his *L'artusi, overo delle imperfettioni della musica moderna* (1600) singles out nine as yet unpublished madrigals by Monteverdi for special attack, to which the composer replied in the preface to his fifth book of madrigals (1605). Here he promised a treatise, never completed, to be entitled *Seconda prattica overo delle perfettioni della moderna musica*, in contradistinction to the 'Prima prattica' of the conservatives. The controversy was continued in two more works by Artusi, published under a pseudonym (1606 and 1608), and by Monteverdi's brother Giulio Cesare in the preface to the *Scherzi musicali* of 1607.

Ascanio opera by Saint-Saëns (libretto by G Gallet, after P Meurice), first produced at the Paris Opéra, France, on 21 March 1890. In the plot a character from Berlioz's opera *Benvenuto Cellini* (1838) resurfaces in an episode from Cellini's life at the court of Francis I at Fontainebleau.

Ascanio in Alba opera by Mozart (libretto by G Parini), first produced at the Teatro Regio Ducal, Milan, Italy, on 17 October 1771. It describes how Venus orders her grandson Ascanius to marry the nymph Silvia.

Ascension, L' work for orchestra in four movements by Olivier Messiaen, composed in 1933 followed by a version for organ in 1934. The orchestral version was first performed in Paris, France, in February 1935.

Ashkenazy, Vladimir (1937–) Russian-born pianist and conductor. He was music director of the Royal Philharmonic, London, 1987–94 and of the Berlin Radio Symphony Orchestra from 1989. In 1998 he became chief conductor of the Czech Philharmonic Orchestra. He excels in his interpretations of pieces by Rachmaninov, Prokofiev, and Liszt.

After studying in Moscow, he toured the USA in 1958. In 1962 he was joint winner of the Tchaikovsky Competition with John Ogdon. He defected to the West in 1963, settling in London, England. He moved to Iceland in 1968, where he organized the biannual music festival in Reykjavik. He moved to Switzerland in 1982.

Ashkenazy was born in Gorky, Russia, and graduated from the Moscow Conservatory in 1960. Since moving to the West, he has given recitals all over the world and made more than 150 recordings. He has been a guest conductor with many of the world's major orchestra, including the Berlin Philharmonic, Boston Symphony, Los Angeles Philharmonic, San Francisco Symphony, Philadelphia, Cleveland, and Concertgebouw orchestras.

Ashley, Robert (1930–) US composer. He studied with Ross Lee Finney and Roberto Gerhard at the University of Michigan and was later influenced by Gordon Mumma and John Cage. With Mumma he cofounded the ONCE Festival for Experimental Music, 1961–68. He was also involved with the Sonic Arts Union, for the use of electronic music.

Works TV AND VIDEO OPERAS *In Memoriam … Kit Carson* (1963), *That Morning Thing* (1967), *Music with Roots in Aether* (1976), *Perfect Lives* (1980), *The Lessons* (1981), *Atalanta, Acts of God* (1982), *Atalanta strategy* (1984), *Foreign Experiences* (1984), *El Aficionado* (1987), *My Brother Called* (1989).

OTHER electronic music theatre *Night Train* (1966), *The Wolfman Motorcity Revue* (1968), *What She Thinks* (1976), *Title Withdrawn* (1976); film music, chamber pieces, and electronic works.

Ashwell or **Ashewell** or **Hashewell, Thomas (c.1478–after 1513)** English composer. In 1508 he was *informator choristarum* (choirmaster) at Lincoln Cathedral, and in 1513 held the equivalent post in Durham. His surviving works include four Masses, two (*God save King Harry* and *Sancte Cuthberte*) in a fragmentary state and two (*Ave Maria* and *Jesu Christe*) complete.

Asioli, Bonifazio (1769–1832) Italian music scholar and composer. He worked in his native town at the beginning and end of his career, but in between was at Turin, Venice, Milan, and Paris. He wrote much church, stage, vocal, and instrumental music, and several theoretical treatises.

Asola, Giammateo (c.1532–1609) Italian priest and composer. He was maestro di cappella successively at Treviso (from 1577) and Vincenza (from 1578). He wrote church music (including twelve books of Masses) and madrigals.

Aspern Papers, The opera in two acts by Dominick Argento (libretto by the composer, after Henry James); it was first produced in Dallas, Texas, USA, on 19 November 1988.

Asrael symphony by Josef Suk (his second), written in memory of his wife and of Dvořák, his father-in-law. It was first performed in Prague (now in the Czech Republic) on 3 February 1907.

Assafiev, Boris Vladimirovich (1884–1949) Russian composer and critic. He studied philosophy at St Petersburg University and music at the Conservatory, where he later became professor. He wrote numerous books on composers, including Glinka, Tchaikovsky, Skriabin, and Stravinsky, and on Russian and Czech music, under the pseudonym of Igor Glebov.

   Works OPERA *Cinderella* (1906), *The Bronze Horseman* (Pushkin, 1940).

   BALLET 27 ballets, including *The Fountain of Bakhchisserai* (after Pushkin, 1933), *Lost Illusions* (after Balzac, 1935).

   ORCHESTRAL five symphonies (1938–42); piano concerto.

   CHAMBER string quartet and other chamber works.

   OTHER incidental music to plays by writers including Shakespeare, Tirso de Molina, Sophocles, and Schiller; many piano works, choruses, and songs.

assai (Italian 'much, very') adjective used in music terminology, for example *allegro assai*, 'very fast'.

assassinio nella cattedrale, L', Murder in the Cathedral opera by Ildebrando Pizzetti (libretto by composer after T S Eliot's dramatic poem), first produced at La Scala, Milan, Italy, on 1 March 1958. It deals with the murder of the arch-bishop Thomas à Beckett in Canterbury Cathedral.

Astaritta, Gennaro (c.1745–after 1803) Italian composer of around 40 operas, 1765–93, including the popular *Circe ed Ulisse*, *L'isola disabitata* (Florence, 1773), *Armida* (Venice, 1777), and *Rinaldo d'Asti* (St Petersburg, 1796).

Aston, Hugh (c.1480–1558) English composer. He completed his studies at Oxford in 1510, and was choirmaster at Newarke College, Leicester, 1525–48. His works include six votive antiphons, two Masses, and a 'Hornepype' for keyboard. There are works on a ground bass of his by Whytbroke (for viols) and Byrd (for keyboard).

Astorga, Emanuele (Gioacchino Cesare Rincón), Baron d' (1680–1757) Italian nobleman and composer of Spanish descent. His opera *Dafni* was produced in Genoa and Barcelona in 1709. His most famous work is a *Stabat Mater* (c.1707). He also wrote a number of chamber cantatas in the manner of Alessandro Scarlatti. From around 1721 he seems to have lived mainly in Spain and Portugal.

astuzie femminili, Le, Women's Wiles opera by Domenico Cimarosa (libretto by G Palomba), first produced at the Teatro del Fondo, Naples, Italy, on 16 August 1794. The plot tells how the orphan Bellina wishes to marry Filandro, but faces competition from Don Lasagna.

Atalanta opera by Handel (libretto adapted from *La caccia in Etolia* by B Valeriani), first produced at Covent Garden, London, England, on 12 May 1736. It tells the story of the nymph Atalanta who is united with the shepherd king Meleager, in spite of her initial preference for the hunt and life in the woods.

Atem gibt das Leben, Breathing gives Life work for chorus by Karlheinz Stockhausen; it was performed in Hamburg, Germany, on 16 May 1975.

a tempo (Italian 'in time') in music, a direction to return to the original tempo. It is often found after ➜ **accelerando** or ➜ **ritardando**.

Athalia oratorio by Handel (words by S Humphreys), first produced in Oxford, England, on 10 July 1733.

Athalie incidental music for Racine's tragedy by Fanny Mendelssohn, Op. 74; the choruses were composed in 1843 and the overture between 1844 and 1845, and the work was first produced in Charlottenburg, Germany, on 1 December 1845.

   The choruses were also set by Jean Baptiste Moreau (Saint-Cyr, 5 January 1691), François Gossec (1785), Georg Vogler (1786), J A P Schulz

An example of expressionist atonal music in which the composer avoids any clear key; from Schoenberg's 3 Piano Pieces, Op. 11 *(1909).*

(1786), and François Boieldieu (1836).

Atlántida, L' scenic oratorio by Manuel de Falla (text by composer, after J Verdaguer), sketched 1926–46 and completed by E Halffter. It was first produced at La Scala, Milan, Italy, on 18 June 1962. It is a Spanish saga, from the flooding of Atlantis to Columbus and the New World.

Atmosphères work for orchestra by Györgi Ligeti. It was first performed in Donaueschingen, Germany, on 22 October 1961, conducted by Hans Rosbaud.

atonality music that has no sense of ➔ **tonality** and no obvious key. Atonal music uses the notes of the ➔ **chromatic** scale and, depending on the system employed, uses all twelve pitch classes in hierarchies other than triadic harmony. This means that there is no pull towards any particular tonic note.

Arnold ➔ **Schoenberg** was one of the first composers to explore atonality, from 1909, although Gustav ➔ **Mahler** experimented with it in many passages of his later symphonies. Schoenberg's aim was to extend tonal expression and not just

to disturb. He rejected the term as he felt it was misleading. Other important composers of atonality include Alban Berg, Anton Webern, Karlheinz Stockhausen, and Pierre Boulez. It has since become the main paradigm of all serious mid- to late-20th-century composers, due to the fact that the use of tonality now sounds clichéd due to all the possibilities of tonality having been exhausted.

Populist use of atonality can be found in film and television scores as background music for scenes of mystery or horror, although here it is only the ➔ **dissonance** (a small aspect of atonality) exploited for its ability to disturb.

attacca (Italian imperative 'attack, begin') musical direction placed at the end of a movement indicating that the next movement is to be started without a pause.

attacco (Italian 'attack') a short musical figure or phrase treated by imitation.

Atterberg, Kurt (Magnus) (1887–1974) Swedish composer and conductor. He composed in an undemanding style, and conducted much in

Europe.

After training as a civil engineer, he studied music at the Royal Academy of Music in Stockholm under Anders Hallén, and later at Munich, Berlin, and Stuttgart. He was music critic of the newspaper *Stockholms Tidningen* from 1919.

Works OPERA AND THEATRE five operas; pantomime-ballets; incidental music for plays.

ORCHESTRAL nine symphonies (one in memory of Schubert); nine suites; *Swedish Rhapsody*; symphonic poem *Le Fleuve*; *Rondeau rétrospectif* and *The Song* for orchestra; symphonic poem for baritone and orchestra; concertos for violin, cello, piano, and horn.

CHAMBER three string quartets; cello and piano sonata.

OTHER Requiem (1914); *Järnbäraland/The Land of Iron-Carriers*, for chorus and orchestra (1919).

At the Boar's Head opera by Gustav Holst (libretto by composer, drawn from Shakespeare's *Henry IV*), first produced in Manchester, England, on 3 April 1925.

Attila opera by Verdi (libretto by T Solera), first produced at the Teatro La Fenice, Venice, Italy, on 17 March 1846. It describes how Odabella avenges herself on Attila after her father has been murdered.

Attwood, Thomas (1765–1838) English organist and composer. Organist of St Paul's Cathedral, London, and composer to the Chapel Royal from 1796 to his death, he was one of the original members of the Philharmonic Society in 1813, and a professor at the Royal Academy of Music on its foundation in 1823. He was also a friend of Mendelssohn, whose three Preludes and Fugues for organ, Op. 37, were dedicated to him.

He was a chorister at the Chapel Royal and later studied in Naples and Vienna, where he was a pupil of Mozart 1785–87. His harmony and counterpoint exercises for Mozart still survive, with Mozart's corrections.

Works over 30 dramatic compositions; coronation anthems for George IV and William IV, service settings, anthems and other church music, and songs.

Atys opera by Jean-Baptiste Lully (libretto by Philippe Quinault), first produced at Saint-Germain, France, on 10 January 1676 and first performed in Paris in April 1676. It describes how Atys stabs himself for love and is transformed into a pine tree by Cybele.

The opera of the same title by Niccolò Piccinni (libretto by Quinault, altered by J-F Marmontel), was first produced at the Paris Opéra, France, on 22 February 1780.

Atzmon, Moshe (1931–) Israeli conductor. He won the Liverpool International Competition in 1964 and conducted in Sydney and Hamburg 1969–76. He made his opera debut in Berlin in 1969. He was principal conductor of the Basle Symphony Orchestra from 1972, and became director of the Dortmund Opera in 1991.

aubade (French from *aube*, 'dawn') 'morning song', in the same sense that a serenade is an evening song; compare Spanish ➤ **alborada**.

It was used as the title of a choreographic concerto for piano and 18 instruments by Poulenc, first performed in Paris, France, on 18 June 1929.

Auber, Daniel François Esprit (1782–1871) French operatic composer. He studied under the Italian composer and teacher Luigi Cherubini and wrote nearly 50 operas, including *La Muette de Portici/The Mute Girl of Portici* (1828) and the comic opera *Fra Diavolo* (1830). He wrote *Manon Lescaut* in 1856, 37 years before Puccini wrote his version.

Born at Caen in Normandy, he began to compose early, but as a young man was sent to London by his father, to follow a commercial career. His songs attracted attention, however, and on his return to Paris in 1804 he wrote cello concertos for the cellist Lamarre and a violin concerto for Mazas. In 1805 he appeared with a comic opera, *L'Erreur d'un moment*, the libretto of which had previously been set by Dezède, but he did not produce an opera in public until 1813 (*Le Séjour militaire*). It failed miserably, and he had no real success until his father's death in 1819 compelled him to make music his means of livelihood. *La Bergère châtelaine* (1820) was a brilliant success, and in 1822 he began his association with the librettist Augustin Scribe, and the two began a series of popular and successful productions, including *Fra Diavolo* (1830), *Le Cheval de bronze* (1835), *Le Domino noir* (1837), *Les Diamants de la couronne* (1841), and *Manon Lescaut* (after Prévost). *La Muette de Portici* was a precursor of French Grand Opera. In 1842 Auber became director of the Paris Conservatory and in 1857 of the Imperial chapel.

Works OPERA nearly 50, including *Emma* (1821), *Leicester* (1823), *Le Maçon* (1825), *La Muette de Portici (Masaniello)* (1828), *La Fiancée* (1829), *Fra Diavolo* (1830), *Le Dieu et la bayadère* (1830), *Le Philtre* (1831), *Le Serment* (1832), *Gustave III, ou Le Bal masqué* (1833), *Le Cheval de bronze* (two versions, 1835 and 1857), *Actéon* (1836), *L'Ambassadrice* (1836), *Le Domino noir* (1837), *Les Diamants de la couronne* (1841), *La Part du diable* (1843), *Haydée* (1847), *Marco Spada* (1852, with a later ballet version, 1857), *Jenny Bell* (1855), *Manon Lescaut* (1856), *La Circassienne* (1861).

Aubert, Jacques (1689–1753) French violinist and composer. A pupil of Jean Baptiste Senaillé, he was a member of the king's 24 violins from

1727 and of the Paris Opéra orchestra from 1728. He wrote numerous violin concertos, concert suites, and other instrumental works.

Aubin, Tony (Louis Alexandre) (1907–1981) French composer. He studied at the Paris Conservatory, where Paul Dukas was his composition master. He took the Prix de Rome in 1930; he was appointed head of the music department of the Paris-Mondial radio station in 1939 and professor at the Paris Conservatory in 1946.

Works ORCHESTRAL *Symphonie romantique* (1937), *Le Sommeil d'Iskander.*

VOCAL *Cressida* for solo voices, chorus, and orchestra (1935); cantata *Actéon* (1930).

CHAMBER string quartet; sonata; *Prélude, Récitatif et Final* for piano (1930).

OTHER six Verlaine songs.

Aubry, Pierre (1874–1910) French musicologist and orientalist. He lectured on music history at the École des Hautes Études Sociales in Paris, and did important research on French medieval music.

Aucassin et Nicolette 13th-century French narrative in prose and verse. Its verse sections show a technique similar to that employed in the *chanson de geste*, in that each pair of lines is sung to the same tune constantly repeated, each section being rounded off by a single line sung to a different tune. Its alternation between prose and verse, however, classifies it as a *chante-fable*.

Aucassin et Nicolette, ou Les Mœurs du bon vieux temps opera by André Grétry (libretto by J M Sedaine, based on the French 13th-century tale), first produced for the court at Versailles, France, on 30 December 1779 and given its first Paris performance at the Comédie-Italienne on 3 January 1780.

Auden, W(ystan) H(ugh) (1907–1973) English-born US poet and librettist. From 1935 he collaborated with Benjamin Britten on *Our Hunting Fathers* (1936), *Paul Bunyan* (1940–41), and *Hymn to St Cecilia* (1942). His close relationship with Chester Kallman from 1948 resulted in librettos for Stravinsky's *Rake's Progress* (1953) and Henze's *Elegy for Young Lovers* (1961) and *The Bassarids* (1966). Their work has been judged theatrically effective, but was also at times criticized as being somewhat contrived (the intermezzo in *The Bassarids*).

Audran, Edmond (1840–1901) French composer. He studied at Louis Niedermeyer's school in Paris and first made his mark as a church organist and composer in Marseille and Paris, producing a Mass, but later with operettas, the first of which, *L'Ours et le Pacha*, was produced at Marseille in 1862. His first production in Paris (1879) was *Les Noces d'Olivette*. Others included

La Mascotte (1880), *Gillette de Narbonne* (based on Boccaccio; 1882), *La Cigale et la fourmi* (based on La Fontaine; 1886), *La Poupée* (1896), and *Monsieur Lohengrin.*

Aufforderung zum Tanz, Invitation to the Dance piano piece by Carl Maria von Weber, Op. 65, which he calls a *rondeau brillant*, in waltz form with a slow introduction and epilogue, composed in 1819. It is usually heard today in the orchestral version by Hector Berlioz.

Aufstieg und Fall der Stadt Mahagonny, Rise and Fall of the City of Mahagonny opera by Kurt Weill (libretto by Bertolt Brecht), first produced in Leipzig, Germany, on 9 March 1930. It describes the experiences of Jenny and Jim in the city of Mahagonny.

Auftakt (German 'upbeat') see ➤ upbeat.

Auftrittslied (German 'entry song') a song or air in a musical play or opera, especially a German *Singspiel*, by which a character introduces and describes him- or herself to the audience, either directly or by addressing another character or characters, such as Papageno's first song in Mozart's *The Magic Flute.*

Augenarzt, Der, The Oculist opera by Adalbert Gyrowetz (libretto by J E Veith), first produced at the Kärntnertortheater, Vienna, Austria, on 1 October 1811. The story describes how Dr Berg restores sight to Wilhelmine, who turns out to be his long-lost sister.

Augenlicht, Das, Eyesight work for chorus and orchestra by Anton Webern (text by H Jone), composed in 1935. It was first performed in London, England, on 17 June 1938, conducted by Hermann Scherchen.

augmentation in music, notation of a musical figure in larger time values, used in counterpoint in order to combine it with the same figure in smaller time values.

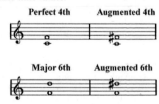

Perfect and augmented intervals.

augmented 6th chords in music, a group of chords that stand as the springboard for much of the more colourful harmonic style of the 19th century. They depend for their effect on the interval of an augmented 6th between the flattened 6th degree and the sharpened 4th degree of the

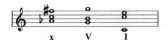

1. Italian

2. German

3. French

4. 'Tristan 6th'

1. Italian; 2. German; 3. French; 4. 'Tristan 6th'. The earliest augmented 6th chord, occasionally found even in the 17th c., is the Italian 6th, a three-note chord (in C major). Since the structure of the German 6th (in equal temperament) is identical with that of the dominant 7th, it is extremely useful for modulation to distant keys. The famous opening chord of Wagner's Tristan und Isolde may be interpreted as an augmented 6th like the French 6th but with the 3rd flattened, thus sometimes called the 'Tristan 6th' (here transposed from A minor to C minor for comparison).

diatonic scale. Almost invariably their logical progression is to the dominant (V) or to a second inversion triad on the dominant (I_4^6) which in turn leads to the dominant.

Of the four-note forms, the 'German 6th' first became a firm favourite at the end of the 18th century and was used with particular force by Beethoven. Less common is the 'French 6th', with its two middle notes a major 2nd apart. Finally, it may be noted that from the middle of the 19th century many other variants of the principle appear.

'Auld Lang Syne' song written by the Scottish poet Robert Burns about 1789, which is often sung at New Year's Eve gatherings. The title means 'old long since' or 'long ago'.

Auletta, Pietro (1698–1771) Italian composer. He made his debut as an opera composer at Naples in 1725 with *Il trionfo d'amore*, in which year he also received the title of maestro di cappella to the Prince of Belvedere. Several comic and then some serious operas followed. His most popular work, *Orazio* (1737), eventually became debased into a pasticcio by the addition of music by other composers, and was published in Paris as *Il maestro di musica* in 1753 under the name of Pergolesi.

aulos ancient Greek double-reed musical instrument, the equivalent of the Latin *tibia* and akin to the modern ➤ oboe.

The double aulos often seen in paintings and sculpture would have enabled the melody to be accompanied by a drone, both sets of reeds being blown simultaneously by one player.

Aureliano in Palmira opera by Rossini (libretto by F Romani), first produced at La Scala, Milan, Italy, on 26 December 1813. The overture was afterwards used for *Elisabetta regina d'Inghilterra*, and later for *Il barbiere di Siviglia*. Other parts of the music also appear in the latter work. The plot tells of how the Roman emperor Aurelianus allows Arsace and Zenobia to marry.

Auric, Georges (1899–1983) French composer. His works include a comic opera, several ballets, and incidental music to films including Jean Cocteau's *Orphée/Orpheus* (1950). He was one of the musical group called ➤ Les Six, who were influenced by Erik ➤ Satie.

Auric was born at Lodève, Hérault, and studied both at the Conservatoire and the Schola Cantorum in Paris. His first success was incidental music for Molière's play *Les Fâcheux* (1923), which he turned into a ballet. After his music for René Clair's film *À nous la liberté* (1932) he was much sought after by both French and English film studios. He also wrote a few choral, orchestral, and chamber works, and numerous piano pieces and songs.

Works COMIC OPERA *Sous le masque* (libretto by L Laloy, 1907).

BALLET *Les Noces de Gamache* (from *Don Quixote*), *Les Matelots* (1925), *La Pastorale* (1925), *La Concurrence* (1931), *Les Imaginaires* (1933).

INCIDENTAL MUSIC plays *Les Fâcheux* (Molière; 1923), *The Birds* (Aristophanes; 1928), *Volpone* (Ben Jonson; 1927), *Le Mariage de Figaro* (Beaumarchais), *Le 14 Juillet* (Rolland; 1931), and nine others; film music *À nous la liberté* (René Clair; 1932), *Caesar and Cleopatra* (after Bernard Shaw).

ORCHESTRAL symphony; suite; overture; *Fox-trot* and *Nocturne* for orchestra; piano concerto.

CHAMBER piano sonata and sonatina; *Three Pastorales* for piano (1920); *Chandelles romaines* for piano duet; trio for oboe, clarinet, and bassoon; violin and piano sonata.

OTHER several song cycles.

'Aus Italien' ('from Italy') symphony by Richard Strauss, Op. 16, composed 1885–86 during and after a visit to Italy in March 1887. The four movements are entitled *On the Campagna*, *The Ruins of Rome*, *On the Shore of Sorrento*, and *Neapolitan Folk Life*; the last contains a quotation of Luigi Denza's *Funiculì funiculà*, which Strauss took for a folksong.

Aus meinem Leben, From my Life subtitle of Bedřich Smetana's string quartet in E minor (1876). Slow movement depicts Smetana's love of his wife, and a sustained high note on the violin in the finale suggests his tinnitus.

Austin, Larry (1930–) US composer. He studied in California with Darius Milhaud and Seymour Shifrin and taught at the University of South Florida and North Texas State University (from 1978). His works employ a full range of electronic effects and are cast for a variety of theatrical media.

Works ORCHESTRAL *Improvisations*, for orchestra and jazz soloists (1961); *Phantasmagoria*, after Ives's unfinished *Universe* symphony (1982); *Sinfonia Concertante: A Mozartean Episode* (1986); *Concertante Cybernetica* (1987).

THEATRE PIECES *The Maze* (1967), *Agape* (1970), *Walter* (1971).

OTHER *Plastic Surgery* for tape and film (1970).

authentic cadence or **perfect cadence** or **full close** in music, a harmonic progression or modulation ending with a ➤ **dominant** harmony followed by the ➤ **tonic**.

authenticity in music, a trend initiated in Austria and the Netherlands in the 1950s and 1960s aiming to reproduce the original conditions of early music performance and instrumentation as a means of rediscovering aesthetic terms of reference. It was pioneered by performers like Nikolaus Harnoncourt and Gustav Leonhardt. Authenticity stimulated important practical research in manuscript editing and transcription, instrument making, dance, architectural acoustics, and vocal techniques and encouraged performance of vocal works in the original language. The interest in authenticity grew rapidly; there are a number of flourishing and highly regarded 'authentic' ensembles in the USA and in every major West European country as well as in certain Central European centres.

Notable exponents include the conductors Christopher Hogwood, Andrew Parrott, Roger Norrington, John Eliot Gardiner, Trevor Pinnock, William Christie, Nicholas McGegan, Reinhardt Goebel, Frans Brüggen, and the musicians Ton Koopman, David Munrow (woodwind), Anthony Rooley (lute), Jaap Schröder (violin), Emma Kirkby (soprano), and Frans Brüggen (flute).

Avison, Charles (1709–1770) English organist and composer. He was a pupil of Francesco Geminiani and organist at St Nicholas's Church, Newcastle, 1736–70. He is chiefly remembered for his treatise *An Essay on Musical Expression* (1752), but also wrote a quantity of instrumental music, including 48 concertos for chamber orchestra. He edited (with fellow composer John Garth, 1722–1810) 50 of Benedetto Marcello's Psalms in 1757. He is recognized as the foremost English concerto composer of his time.

Axman, Emil (1887–1949) Czech composer who studied at Prague University and was a composition student of Vítezslav Novák.

Works ORCHESTRAL six symphonies, symphonic poem *Sorrow and Hope*, sinfonietta, suite *From the Beskides*, Moravian dances for orchestra; violin concerto.

CHAMBER four string quartets (1924–46), piano trio, violin and piano sonata, cello and piano sonata; three piano sonatas, sonatina, and other piano works.

OTHER melodrama *Just Once*; cantatas and other choral works.

Axur, re d'Ormus see ➤ *Tarare*.

Aylward, Theodore (c. 1730–1801) English organist and composer. He was organist at several London churches. He received a doctorate in music from Oxford, and was appointed professor of music at Gresham College, London, in 1771.

Works INCIDENTAL MUSIC for Shakespeare's *Cymbeline* and *Midsummer Night's Dream* (with M Arne, Battishill, and Burney) (1765).

OTHER lessons for organ; canzonets for two voices; glees, catches, and songs.

ayre or **air** 16th-century verse song with lute or guitar accompaniment, as in 'It was a lover and his lass' (1600) by Thomas Morley.

azione sacra (Italian 'sacred action') 17th–18th-century term for a sacred drama with music or acted oratorio, such as Mozart's *La Betulia liberata*.

azione teatrale (Italian 'theatrical action') 17th-century term for an opera or musical festival play.

Azzaiolo, Filippo (lived 16th century) Italian composer of *villotte*, popular madrigal-like part songs. William Byrd wrote a keyboard piece on the bass of his popular 'Chi passa'.

B in music, the seventh note, or leading note, of the scale of C major. In Germany, B corresponds to B♭, and B♮ is represented by H.

Baal opera by Friedrich Cerha (libretto by the composer after Bertolt Brecht), first produced in Salzburg, Austria, on 7 August 1981. It portrays the poet Baal as a victim of society.

Baal Shem, *Three Pictures of Chassidic Life* suite for violin and piano by Ernest Bloch, composed in 1923. A version for violin and orchestra was completed in 1939; it was first performed in New York on 19 October 1941, with the violinist Josef Szigeti.

Baaren, Kees van (1906–1970) Dutch composer. He studied with Willem Pijper, and was a leading Dutch exponent of serial music, exploiting both tonal and 12-note varieties of this kind of composition, and also very active as a teacher. From 1957 he was director of the Royal Conservatory in The Hague.

Works *The Hollow Men* (words by T S Eliot), cantata for chorus and orchestra (1948); *Variazioni per Orchestra* (1959); a string quartet and a wind quintet (*Sovraposizione I and II*) (1963).

Babbitt, Milton (Byron) (1916–) US composer and theorist. A leading proponent of ➤ serialism, he pioneered the application of information theory to music in the 1950s, introducing set theory to series manipulations and the term 'pitch class' to define every octave identity of a note name. His works include four string quartets, works for orchestra, *Philomel* for soprano and electronic tape (1963–64), and *Ensembles for Synthesizer* (1967), both composed using the 1960 RCA Princeton-Columbia Mark II Synthesizer, which he helped to design.

Babbitt was born in Philadelphia, Pennsylvania. He studied music and mathematics at New York University under Marion Bauer (composer and writer, 1887–1955) and Philip James (composer and conductor, 1890–1975), and Princeton University, where one of his composition teachers was Roger Sessions. From 1948 he taught at Princeton University.

Babi-Yar subtitle of symphony no. 13 in B flat minor, for bass, male chorus, and orchestra by Shostakovich (text by Yevgeny Yevtushenko). It was composed in 1961 and first performed in Moscow, USSR, on 18 December 1962. Babi-Yar is the site of a World War II massacre of Russian Jews by the Germans.

Bacchus et Ariane ballet in two acts by Albert Roussel, with scenario by A Hermant; it was first produced at the Paris Opéra, France, on 22 May 1931. Suite no. 1 for orchestra was first performed in Paris on 2 April 1933, conducted by Charles Munch; Suite no. 2 was first performed in Paris on 2 February 1934, conducted by Pierre Monteux.

Bacewicz, Grażyna (1909–1969) Polish composer and violinist. She taught at Łódź Conservatory 1934–35, moving to Paris in 1945. Although most of her work has been described as neoclassical, her later music also uses avant-garde techniques.

She studied composition at the Warsaw Conservatory under Sikorski and later in Paris with Nadia Boulanger. Her fourth string quartet won first prize at the International Competition, Liège, in 1951.

Works ORCHESTRAL four symphonies (1945–53); seven violin concertos (1937–65); cello concerto; piano concerto; concerto for string orchestra.

CHAMBER seven string quartets; two piano quintets; six violin sonatas and various violin pieces.

B–A–C–H a musical theme formed of the notes B flat–A–C–B natural, which in German nomenclature are written B–A–C–H, and used by various composers as a reference to Johann Sebastian Bach, who was himself the first to use it.

Some examples of its use are found in the following works:

➤ **Bach**, Johann Sebastian, one of the subjects of the final fugue (unfinished) in *Die Kunst der Fugue* (four organ fugues are probably spurious).

➤ **Busoni**, *Fantasia contrappuntistica* for piano and for two pianos.

➤ **Eisler**, *Trio on a 12-note row.*

➤ **Honegger**, *Prélude, Ariso et Fughette* for piano.

➔ **D'Indy,** *Beuron* in *Tableaux de voyage* for piano.

➔ **Liszt,** Fantasy and Fugue for organ.

➔ **Nielsen,** *Riccardo, Ricercare, Chorale, and Toccata* for piano.

➔ **Rimsky-Korsakov,** Fugue in *Chopsticks* Variations for piano by various composers; six variations for piano, Op. 10.

➔ **Schoenberg,** *Variations for orchestra,* Op. 31.

➔ **Schumann,** *Six Fugues* for organ or pedal piano.

Bach, Carl Philipp Emanuel (1714–1788) German composer. He was the third son of Johann Sebastian Bach. He introduced a new 'homophonic' style, light and easy to follow, which influenced Mozart, Haydn, and Beethoven.

In the service of Frederick the Great 1740–67, he left to become master of church music at Hamburg in 1768. He wrote over 200 pieces for keyboard instruments, and published a guide to playing the piano. Through his music and concert performances he helped to establish a leading solo role for the piano in Western music.

He was educated at St Thomas's School, Leipzig, and at the universities of Leipzig (1731–34) and Frankfurt an der Oder (1734–38), where he studied law. He claimed to have received his musical training entirely from his father. He was connected with the household of the Crown Prince of Prussia from 1738, and in 1740, on the latter's accession as King Frederick II, he was appointed harpsichordist to the court at Berlin and Potsdam. In 1744 he married Johanna Maria Dannemann, and in 1747 his father visited him at court. His most important works at this time were keyboard pieces, which contributed much to the development of a more homophonic style and modern formal procedures. His treatise on keyboard playing (*Versuch über die wahre Art das Clavier zu spielen* 1753 and 1762) is a valuable guide to contemporary practice. Bach found Berlin restricting, partly because his duties involved only harpsichord playing, and partly because of the king's conservatism, and in 1768 he moved to Hamburg as municipal director of music at the five principal churches. Charles Burney visited him there in 1772, and commented on his remarkable talent for improvising. In Hamburg Bach had wider scope, directing concerts with great success, and there he wrote most of his music for large forces, such as oratorios.

Works ORATORIOS *Die Israeliten in der Wüste* (1769), *Die Auferstehung und Himmelfahrt Jesu* (1780).

CHURCH MUSIC Magnificat (1749), *Heilig/Sanctus* for double choir, Passions, and other church music.

ORCHESTRAL 19 symphonies; 50 keyboard concertos.

OTHER about 200 keyboard pieces (including sonatas, fantasias, and rondos), odes, and songs.

Bach, Jan (1937–) US composer. He studied with Aaron Copland and Donald Martino and has taught at Northern Illinois University from 1966. His works are based on traditional means.

Works OPERA *The System* (1974), *The Student from Salamanca* (1980).

ORCHESTRAL piano concerto (1975); horn concerto (1983); harp concerto (1986).

OTHER *The Happy Prince* for narrator, violin, and orchestra (1978); chamber and vocal music.

Bach, Johann Ambrosius (1645–1695) German organist and composer. He was taught by his father, Christoph Bach. He was town musician at Erfurt from 1667, and at Eisenach from 1671.

He was the twin brother of Johann Christoph Bach. He married Elisabeth Lämmerhirt at Erfurt in 1668. In 1671 he was appointed town musician at Eisenach. His wife died in May 1694 and he married Barbara Margaretha Keul in November, but died himself three months later.

Bach, Johann Christian (1735–1782) German composer. The eleventh son of Johann Sebastian Bach, he became celebrated in Italy as a composer of operas. In 1762 he was invited to London, where he became music master to the royal family. He remained in England until his death; his great popularity both as a composer and a performer declined in his last years for political and medical reasons.

Bach, Johann Christoph (1642–1703) German organist and composer. He became organist at Eisenach in 1665 and remained there to the end of his life. He composed motets, church cantatas, chorale preludes for organ, and harpsichord music.

He was Johann Sebastian Bach's father's cousin.

Bach, Johann Christoph Friedrich (1732–1795) German composer. Among his most notable works are the oratorios on words by Johann Gottfried Herder (attached to the court at Bückeburg 1771–74), *Die Kindheit Jesu* and *Die Auferweckung Lazarus*; a third oratorio and an opera, *Brutus*, both on words by the same poet, are lost.

The ninth son of Johann Sebastian Bach, he was educated at St Thomas's School and Leipzig University, where he studied law. He received his music training from his father, and in 1750 was appointed chamber musician to Count Wilhelm of Schaumburg-Lippe in Bückeburg, where he remained for the rest of his life, becoming Konzertmeister in 1759. He married the court singer Elisabeth Münchhausen in 1755. In 1778 he visited his brother Johann Christian in London.

Other works include the Passion oratorio *Der*

Tod Jesu (words by Ramler); cantatas (some with Herder); 20 symphonies; keyboard concertos and sonatas; chamber music.

Bach, Johann Michael (1648–1694) German organist, instrument maker, and composer. He was organist and parish clerk at Gehren from 1673, and composed motets, sacred arias, and other pieces.

Bach, Johann Sebastian (1685–1750) German composer. A master of ➤ counterpoint, his music represents the final stage of the baroque polyphonic style. His orchestral music includes the six *Brandenburg Concertos* (1721), other concertos for keyboard instrument and violin, four orchestral suites, sonatas for various instruments, three partitas and three sonatas for violin solo, and six unaccompanied cello suites. Bach's keyboard music, for clavier and organ, his fugues, and his choral music are of equal importance.

His appointments included positions at the courts of Weimar and Anhalt-Cöthen, and from 1723 until his death he was musical director at St Thomas's choir school in Leipzig.

He married twice and had over 20 children (although several died in infancy). His second wife, Anna Magdalena Wilcken, was a soprano; she also worked for him when his sight failed in later years.

Although he was not always appreciated by other musicians of his day, Bach's place in music history was aptly summed up by his first major biographer, Johann Nikolaus Forkel (1749–1818), in his book *Über Johann Sebastian Bachs Leben, Kunst, und Kunstwerke* (1802; English translation 1820 and 1920): 'He is the river, to which all other composers are tributaries'.

Born at Eisenach, Thuringia, Bach came from a musical family. After his father's death in 1695 he went to Ohrdruf and studied under his brother Johann Christoph. At 15 he became a chorister at Lüneburg, and at 19 he was appointed violinist in the court orchestra of the Duke of Weimar, but left the same year to become organist in Arnstadt. In 1705 he took leave to travel to Lübeck, to hear Dietrich Buxtehude play the organ.

In 1707 he moved to Mühlhausen, where he married his cousin Maria Barbara Bach; among their seven children were Wilhelm Friedemann and Carl Philip Emanuel. A year later he returned to Weimar as court organist, and remained there for nine years; during this time he wrote such famous cantatas as *Christ lag in Todesbanden*, *Weinen, Klagen, Sorgen, Zagen*, and *Ich hatte viel Bekümmernis*.

In 1717 Bach was appointed Kapellmeister (director) to the court of Prince Leopold of Anhalt-Cöthen. His wife died in 1720, and he married Anna Magdalena Wilcken in 1721. They had 13 children together. At Cöthen Bach had little opportunity for composing church music and there he wrote mainly instrumental works, including the *Brandenburg Concertos*, *Orchestral Suites*, and works for solo cello and violin. In these works instrumental music seems for the first time to emerge from private use into the public domain.

In 1723 he returned to church work when he succeeded Johann Kühnau as cantor of St Thomas's in Leipzig. He remained there for the rest of his life and wrote some of his greatest compositions there, including the B minor Mass, *St Matthew Passion*, and *Goldberg Variations*. In 1747, with his eldest son, Wilhelm Friedemann, he visited the court of Frederick the Great at Potsdam, where his second son, Carl Philip Emanuel, was court harpsichordist. Two years later his eyesight failed; an operation in 1750 was unsuccessful, and he spent his last months totally blind.

Although Bach did not make huge changes to musical forms, he invested contemporary models with a unique brand of creative polyphony and intense spirituality: all his works were dedicated 'To the Greater Glory of God'.

Works CHURCH CANTATAS 200 are extant. Among those most frequently performed are: no. 12 *Weinen, Klagen, Sorgen, Zagen* (1714), no. 20 *O Ewigkeit, du Donnerwort* (1724), no. 21 *Ich hatte viel Bekümmernis* (about 1714), no. 51 *Jauchzet Gott in allen Landen* (1730), no. 56 *Ich will den Kreuzstab gerne tragen* (1726), no. 61 *Nun komm der Heiden Heiland* (1714), no. 80 *Ein feste Burg ist unser Gott* (1724), no. 82 *Ich habe genug* (1727), no. 106 *Gottes Zeit ist die allerbeste Zeit* (about 1707), no. 140 *Wachet auf, ruft uns die Stimme* (1731), no. 147 *Herz und Mund und Tat und Leben* (1723).

SECULAR CANTATAS no. 202 *Weichet nur, betrübte Schatten* (about 1720), no. 211 *Schweigt stille, plaudert nicht/Coffee Cantata* (1734).

OTHER CHURCH MUSIC Mass in B minor, BWV 232, assembled about 1748 from previously composed music; *Magnificat* in E flat, BWV 243 (1723, including four Christmas texts; revised about 1730, in D, without Christmas texts); *St Matthew Passion* (1729); *St John Passion* (1724, later revised); *Christmas Oratorio*, six cantatas for Christmas to Epiphany (performed 1734–35) BWV 248; six motets BWV 225–30; *Easter Oratorio* (1725) BWV 249.

ORGAN 19 preludes and fugues, including E♭, ('St Anne', 1739) BWV 548; six trio sonatas BWV 525–530; Toccata and Fugue in D minor ('Dorian') BWV 538 and D minor BWV 565 (now doubtful); Fantasia and Fugue in C minor BWV 562 and G minor BWV 542; Toccata, Adagio, and Fugue in C BWV 564; Passacaglia in C minor BWV 582; *Pastorale* in F BWV 590 (about 1710); 134 chorale preludes BWV 599–768, some of the best known being *An Wasserflüssen Babylon*

BWV 653, *Ein feste Burg* BWV 720, *In dulci jubilo* BWV 729, *Jesu, meine Freude* BWV 713, *Vom Himmel hoch* BWV 700, *Wachet auf* BWV 645.

OTHER KEYBOARD *The Well-tempered Clavier*, Books 1 (1722) and 2 (about 1740), 24 preludes and fugues in each, BWV 846–893; Capriccio in B♭, on the departure of a beloved brother BWV 992; Chromatic Fantasia and Fugue in D minor BWV 903 (1720); six English Suites BWV 806–811; six French Suites BWV 812–817; *Goldberg Variations* BWV 988; 15 Inventions BWV 772–786; 15 Sinfonias BWV 787–801; *Italian Concerto* BWV 971; six partitas BWV 825–830; seven toccatas BWV 910–916.

CHAMBER three Partitas for solo violin, in B minor, D minor, and E, and three Sonatas for solo violin, in G minor, A minor, and C BWV 1001–1006 (about 1720); six Sonatas for violin and harpsichord BWV 1014–1019; six Suites for solo cello BWV 1007–1012 (about 1720); three Sonatas for viola da gamba and clavier BWV 1027–1029 (about 1720); Partita in A minor for solo flute BWV 1013 (early 1720s); *The Musical Offering* BWV 1079 (1747) for flute, violin, and continuo; *The Art of Fugue* BWV 1080 (about 1745–50; published 1751), for keyboard.

ORCHESTRAL concertos, six Brandenburg, in F, F, G, G, D, and B♭ BWV 1046–1051 (1721), for violin in A minor and E, for two violins in D minor, for flute, violin, and harpsichord in A minor, seven for harpsichord and strings BWV 1052–1058, three for two harpsichords, two for three, and one for four; four orchestral suites in C, B minor, D, and D BWV 1066–1069.

Bach, Wilhelm Friedemann (1710–1784) German composer. The eldest son of Johann Sebastian Bach, he was also an organist, improviser, and master of ✦ counterpoint.

He was educated at St Thomas's School and Leipzig University, and received his musical training from his father. He was appointed organist of St Sophia's, Dresden, in 1723, and in 1746 succeeded Friedrich Zachau as organist of St Mary's, Halle. He married Dorothea Elisabeth Georgi in 1751. He resigned in 1764, and never held another permanent position, living an unsettled life and attempting to support his family mainly by teaching. In 1770 he moved to Brunswick, and in 1774 to Berlin. There his remarkable organ playing could still arouse astonishment, but his last years were spent in increasing poverty.

Works cantatas and other church music; nine symphonies; keyboard concertos; nine sonatas, twelve fantasias, and other works for keyboard; organ music.

Bachianas Brasileiras nine pieces for various instrumental combinations by Heitor Villa-Lobos, in which Brazilian rhythms are treated in the spirit of Bach's counterpoint (1930–44).

Bachofen, Johann Caspar (1695–1755) Swiss composer. He was cantor of the grammar school in Zurich, 1720, and of the *Grossmünster*, 1742. He compiled and partly composed several books of hymns and sacred songs, collected in *Musikalisches Hallejulah* (1727), and in 1759 wrote a setting of the Passion oratorio by Brockes.

'Bach' trumpet special brass wind instrument of the trumpet type invented by Kosleck of Berlin and improved by Walter Morrow of London, so devised as to be capable of playing the high trumpet parts in the works of Johann Sebastian Bach and his contemporaries and forerunners. It was first heard at Eisenach, Germany, in 1884.

backfall in musical terminology, taken from the note above. See ✦ appoggiatura.

background see ✦ structural level.

background music accompanying music for a stage or film production which serves to establish a mood or stimulate appropriate audience responses. It differs from ✦ incidental music in not being part of the action, and in working on the listener subliminally.

The use of music as a media for psychological conditioning is prefigured in the 19th-century song without words, with Mendelssohn defending the view that music expressed a reality more definite than a poetic text. Magic lantern (early slide projector) entertainments accompanied by fragments of well-known works established a basis for the ✦ film score. Today, the use of piped music in shopping malls extends the principle to real life.

badinerie (French 'teasing, frivolity, playfulness') title given, sometimes as *badinage*, by French and German composers of the 18th century to light, playful pieces in quick 2/4 time (such as the final movement of J S Bach's B minor Orchestral Suite for flute and strings).

Badings, Henk (Hendrik Herman) (1907–1987) Dutch composer. Originally a mining engineer, he studied music with Willem Pijper and in 1935 abandoned science entirely for music. He was professor at the Music Lyceum, Amsterdam, and the Rotterdam Conservatory. In 1941 he was appointed director of the Royal Conservatory at The Hague. From 1956 he composed electronic music.

Works OPERA *The Night Watch* (after Rembrandt; 1942); *Salto mortale* (electronic, 1959).

BALLET AND INCIDENTAL MUSIC ballets including the electronic ballet *Kain* (1956); incidental music for plays.

ORCHESTRAL 14 symphonies (1932–68); symphonic variations; *Heroic Overture;* violin concerto, cello concerto, concerto for two violins and orchestra; recitations with orchestra.

CHAMBER four string quartets; violin and cello sonatas; piano pieces.

OTHER a cantata.

bagatelle (French 'trifle') in music, a short character piece, often for piano.

bagpipes any of an ancient family of double-reed folk woodwind instruments employing a bladder, filled by the player through a mouthpiece, or bellows as an air reservoir to a 'chanter' or fingered melody pipe, and two or three optional drone pipes providing a continuous accompanying harmony.

Examples include the old French musette, Scottish and Irish pipes, smaller Northumbrian pipes, Breton *biniou*, Spanish *gaita*, and numerous variants in Eastern Europe, the Middle East, and North Africa. The Highland bagpipes are the national instrument of Scotland.

Bainbridge, Simon (1952–) English composer and conductor. He studied at the Royal College of Music and has taught there and at the Guildhall School of Music and Drama. As a composer he has been commissioned by the BBC and the London Sinfonietta (among others), and as a conductor has worked with the BBC Symphony Orchestra and the Scottish Sinfonia. In April 1997 he was awarded the Grawemeyer Award for musical composition.

Works ORCHESTRAL *Music to Oedipus Rex* (1969); *Heterophony* (1970); *Spirogyra* for chamber orchestra (1970); viola concerto (1977).

CHAMBER wind quintet (1971); string quartet; *Landscape and Magic Words* for soprano and chamber ensemble (1981); *A cappella* for six voices (1985); *Metamorphosis* for ensemble (1988); *Cantus contra cantum* (1989); Double Concerto for oboe and clarinet (1990); *Caliban Fragments* for mezzo and ensemble (1991); Clarinet quintet (1993).

Baird, Tadeusz (1928–1981) Polish composer. His music was influenced by ➤ **serialism**, especially by Alban Berg. He studied at Łódź Conservatory, and was imprisoned during World War II.

Works OPERA *Jutro* (*Tomorrow*, after Conrad; 1966).

ORCHESTRAL three symphonies; *Cassation for Orchestra*; *Four Essays for Orchestra*; *Expressions* for violin and orchestra (1959); piano concerto; other orchestral music.

VOCAL *Goethe Letters*, for baritone, chorus, and orchestra (1970).

Bairstow, Edward C(uthbert) (1874–1946) English organist, conductor, and composer. After various posts as organist he took the DMus at Durham University in 1901 and became organist and choirmaster at York Minster in 1913. He edited *The English Psalter* and wrote *The Evolution of Musical Form* and (with Plunket Greene) *Singing Learnt from Speech*. He was professor of music at Durham University 1929–46.

Works services, anthems; organ music; variations for two pianos.

Baiser de la fée, Le ballet by Stravinsky. See ➤ **Fairy's Kiss**.

Bakchantinnen, Die, The Bacchantes opera by Egon Wellesz (libretto by the composer) based on Euripides; it was produced at the Vienna Staatsoper, Austria, on 20 January 1931. Set in ancient Greece, the plot sets Dionysus against Pentheus.

Baker, Theodore (1851–1934) US writer on music. He took his PhD at Leipzig, Germany, with the first major study of US Indian music. He became literary editor of G Schirmer Inc., New York, in 1892, and published *A Dictionary of Musical Terms* in 1895. His *Biographical Dictionary of Musicians* was issued in 1900 and remains the leading US music reference book (fifth and sixth editions by Nicolas Slonimsky, 1978; seventh and eighth by Slonimsky and Dennis McIntire, 1984 and 1992).

Bakfark, Balint (Valentin Greff) (1507–1576) Hungarian-born Polish lutenist and composer. He was a great virtuoso, as is reflected by the technical difficulty of his extant works. He published a lute book with Jacques Moderne of Lyon in 1552 (*Intabulatura ... transilvani coroniensis liber primus*) and a second with Andreae of Kraków (Andrzej z Krakowa) in 1565 (*Pannonii harmonicarum musicarum in usum testudinis factarum tomus primus*).

He learnt to play the lute while in royal service. He later lived in France, Vienna, and Padua, and was at the Polish court 1549–66.

Balakirev, Mily Alexeyevich (1837–1910) Russian composer. He wrote piano music, including the fantasy *Islamey* (1869), orchestral works, songs, and a symphonic poem *Tamara* (1867–82), all imbued with the Russian national character and spirit. He was the leader of the group known as 'The ➤ **Five**' and taught its members, Modest Mussorgsky, César Cui, Aleksandr Borodin, and Nikolai Rimsky-Korsakov.

Born in Nizhniy-Novgorod, he was taught music by his mother, but learnt most of what he knew as a youth in the house of Alexander Ulïbishev, on whose estate he was able to use the music library and gain experience with the private orchestra. At 18 he went to St Petersburg, full of enthusiasm for national music, and won the approval of Mikhail Glinka. In 1861 he became the leader of a group of nationalist musicians. Cui was his first disciple; Mussorgsky, Rimsky-

Korsakov, and Borodin followed later, and he even influenced Tchaikovsky to some extent at first. In 1862 he helped to establish the Free School of Music with the choral conductor Lomakin, and conducted some of its progressive symphonic concerts. In 1867 he became conductor of the Russian Musical Society.

In 1871 he had a serious nervous breakdown and withdrew from public life, feeling that he had been defeated by the 'official' musicians. He was forced to become a minor railway official to earn a modest living and turned to religious mysticism. Not until 1876 did he begin to take some interest in composition again, and only in 1883, when he was appointed director of the Imperial Chapel, did he fully return to music once more. He retired in 1895 with a pension and took up composition anew. He again lived in seclusion and was almost completed forgotten by his former friends. He died in St Petersburg.

As a composer, Balakirev is original, even though his music was influenced not only by Glinka, but also by Frédéric Chopin, Franz Liszt, Robert Schumann and, to a lesser degree, by Hector Berlioz.

Works ORCHESTRAL two symphonies, symphonic poems *Russia* and *Tamara*, overtures on a Spanish march, on three Russian themes, to *King Lear*, and on Czech themes; piano concerto (finished by Liapunov).

CHAMBER many piano works, including sonata in B♭ minor, *Islamey* fantasy (1869).

VOCAL 43 songs; two books of folk songs; six anthems for unaccompanied chorus; cantata for the unveiling of the Glinka monument.

OTHER incidental music for Shakespeare's *King Lear* (1860); scherzos, mazurkas, nocturnes, waltzes, and other pieces.

balalaika Russian musical instrument, resembling a guitar. It has a triangular soundbox, frets, and two, three, or four strings played by strumming with the fingers. A range of instruments is made, from treble to bass, and orchestras of balalaikas are popular in Russia.

Balfe, Michael William (1808–1870) Irish composer and singer. He was a violinist and baritone at Drury Lane, London, when only 16. In 1825 he went to Italy, where he sang in Palermo and at La Scala, Milan, and in 1846 he was appointed conductor at Her Majesty's Theatre, London.

Balfe was the son of a dancing master. On the death of his father in 1823, he was sent to London as a pupil of Charles Edward Horn (1786–1849). He studied composition with Karl Friedrich Horn and appeared as a singer in Weber's *Der Freischütz* at Norwich. In 1825 Count Mazzara became his patron and took him to Italy, where he introduced him to Luigi Cherubini. He then

went to Paris, met Rossini, and in 1827 appeared as Figaro in his opera *The Barber of Seville* at the Théâtre Italien.

Three years later he sang at Palermo and produced his first opera there, *I rivali di se stessi*. At Milan he sang with the soprano Maria Malibran and at Bergamo he met the Hungarian singer Lina Rosa, whom he married. Early in 1833 he returned to London and appeared in concerts. His first English opera, *The Siege of Rochelle*, was produced at Drury Lane, London, in 1835 and the next year Malibran sang in *The Maid of Artois*. In 1842 he went to live in Paris for some years and worked there with great success, though in 1843 he returned for a time to produce the opera *The Bohemian Girl* in London, for which he is most famous today. Triumphant visits to Berlin in 1849 and St Petersburg in 1852 followed, and in 1854 he produced *Pittore e Duca* at Trieste. That year he finally returned to England, having bought property in Hertfordshire, where he took to farming.

Works OPERA 29, among which are *Un avvertimento ai gelosi* (Pavia, 1830), *The Siege of Rochelle* (1835), *The Maid of Artois, Joan of Arc* (1837), *Falstaff* (1838), *Le Puits d'amour, The Bohemian Girl* (1843), *Les Quatre Fils Aymon* (Paris, 1844), *The Bondman, The Maid of Honour, The Sicilian Bride, The Rose of Castile, Satanella* (1858), *The Armourer of Nantes* (1863), *Il Talismano*.

OTHER operetta *The Sleeping Queen*; ballet *La Pérouse*; three cantatas, including *Mazeppa*; and many songs.

Ballabene, Gregorio (1720–c.1803) Italian composer. One of the latest adherents of the *stile antico* ('old style'), he wrote unaccompanied church music, often of considerable complexity, including a 48-part Mass.

ballabile (Italian 'in a dancing manner') term applicable to any piece in the form or character of a dance.

ballad in music, originally a dancing song or the music for a dancing song. By the 14th century the term had lost its connection to dance and by the 16th century it designated a simple, narrative song. In the 19th century a ballad described a popular song, often of romantic nature.

ballade in literature, a poetic form developed in France in the later Middle Ages from the ballad, generally consisting of one or more groups of three stanzas of seven or eight lines each, followed by a shorter stanza or envoy, the last line being repeated as a chorus. In music, a ballade is an instrumental piece based on a story; a form used in piano works by Chopin and Liszt.

Ballad of Baby Doe, The opera in two acts by Douglas Moore (libretto by J Latouche), first produced in Central City, Colorado, USA, on 7 July 1956.

Ballad of Blanik, The, *Balada blanická* symphonic poem by Janáček after a poem by J Vrchický; it was first performed in Brno (now in the Czech Republic), on 21 March 1920.

ballad opera an English light operatic entertainment, the fashion for which was set by John Gay's ➔ **The Beggar's Opera** in 1728 and continuing its vogue until the 1760s. The most distinctive feature of its music is that it consists mainly of short songs interspersed with dialogue and that they are not specially composed for the piece, but chosen from popular songs of the day.

Ballard (lived 16th–18th centuries) French family of music printers. The founders were Robert Ballard (c.1525–1588) and Adrien Le Roy, who became music printers to Henry II in 1553, issuing chanson collections. The brothers Pierre and Robert ii (c.1575–1650) continued the business, while Pierre's son Robert iii (c.1610–1673) published orchestral scores; his son Christophe (1641–1715) published works by Campra, Charpentier, the Couperins, and Lully. The firm declined from 1722, when Rameau's *Traité* was published.

Ballard, Louis (1931–) American Indian composer. He studied at Oklahoma University and had private lessons with Darius Milhaud and Carlos Surinach. He was program director of Indian Affairs at Washington, DC, 1971–79, and has published *Music of North American Indians* (1975). His works are indebted to the rhythms and tunes of his native music.

Works BALLET *Koshare* (1966), *The Four Moons* (1967).

ORCHESTRAL *Incident at Wounded Knee* (1974), *Xactce'oyan/Companion of Talking God* (1982), *Fantasy Aborigine* (1984).

CHAMBER *Ritmo Indio* for woodwind quintet and Sioux flute (1968).

ballata 14th-century verse form, often set to music, in which the refrain precedes and follows each stanza. The term implies an association with dancing.

ballet (Italian *balletto* 'a little dance') theatrical representation in dance form in which music also plays a major part in telling a story or conveying a mood. Some such form of entertainment existed in ancient Greece, but Western ballet as we know it today first appeared in Renaissance Italy, where it was a court entertainment. From there it was brought by Catherine de' Medici to France in the form of a spectacle combining singing, dancing, and declamation. During the 18th century there were major developments in technique and ballet gradually became divorced from opera, emerging as an art form in its own right.

In the 20th century Russian ballet had a vital influence on the classical tradition in the West, and ballet developed further in the USA through the work of George Balanchine and the American Ballet Theater, and in the UK through the influence of Marie Rambert.

Modern dance is a separate development.

history The first important dramatic ballet, the *Ballet comique de la reine*, was produced in 1581 by the Italian Balthasar de Beaujoyeux at the French court and was performed by male courtiers, with ladies of the court forming the *corps de ballet*. In 1661 Louis XIV founded the Académie Royale de Danse, to which all subsequent ballet activities throughout the world can be traced. Long, flowing court dress was worn by the dancers until the 1720s when Marie-Anne Camargo, the first great ballerina, shortened her skirt to reveal her ankles, thus allowing greater movement *à terre* and the development of dancing *en l'air*.

During the 18th century ballet spread to virtually every major capital in Europe. Vienna became an important centre and was instrumental in developing the dramatic aspect of the art as opposed to the athletic qualities, which also evolved considerably during this century, particularly among male dancers. In the early 19th century a Paris costumier, Maillot, invented tights, which allowed complete muscular freedom. The first of the great ballet masters was Jean-Georges Noverre, and great contemporary dancers were Teresa Vestris, Anna Friedrike Heinel, Jean Dauberval, and Maximilien Gardel.

Carlo Blasis is regarded as the founder of classical ballet, since he defined the standard conventional steps and accompanying gestures.

Romantic ballet The great Romantic era of the dancers Marie Taglioni, Fanny Elssler, Carlotta Grisi, Lucile Grahn, and Fanny Cerrito began about 1830 but survives today only in the ballets *Giselle* (1841) and *Les Sylphides* (1832). Characteristics of this era were the new calf-length white dress and the introduction of dancing on the toes, *sur les pointes*. The technique of the female dancer was developed, but the role of the male dancer was reduced to that of being her partner. Important choreographers of the period were Jules Joseph Perrot, Arthur Saint-Léon, and August Bournonville. From 1860 ballet declined rapidly in popular favour in Europe, but its importance was maintained in St Petersburg under Marius Petipa.

Russian ballet Russian ballet was introduced to the West by Sergei Diaghilev, who set out for Paris in 1909 and founded the Ballets Russes (Russian Ballet), at about the same time that Isadora Duncan, a fervent opponent of classical ballet, was touring Europe. Associated with Diaghilev were Mikhail Fokine, Enrico Cecchetti, Vaslav Nijinsky, Anna Pavlova, Tamara Karsavina, Léonide Massine, Bronislava Nijinska, George Balanchine, and Serge Lifar. Ballets presented by his company, before its break-up after his death in 1929, included *Les Sylphides, Schéhérazade, Petrouchka, Le Sacre du printemps/The Rite of Spring*, and *Les Noces*.

Diaghilev and Fokine pioneered a new and exciting combination of the perfect technique of imperial Russian dancers and the appealing naturalism favoured by Isadora Duncan. In Russia ballet continues to flourish, the two chief companies being the Kirov and the Bolshoi. Best-known ballerinas have been Galina Ulanova and Maya Plisetskaya, and male dancers have included Mikhail Baryshnikov, Irek Mukhamedov, and Alexander Godunov, now dancing in the West.

American ballet American ballet was firmly established by the founding of Balanchine's School of American Ballet in 1934, and by de Basil and René Blum's Ballets Russes de Monte Carlo and Massine's Ballets Russes de Monte Carlo, which also carried on the Diaghilev tradition. In 1939 the dancer Lucia Chase and ballet director Richard Pleasant founded the American Ballet Theater. From 1948 the New York City Ballet, under the guiding influence of Balanchine, developed a genuine American neoclassic style.

British ballet Marie Rambert initiated in 1926 the company that developed into the Ballet Rambert, and launched the careers of choreographers such as Frederick Ashton and Anthony Tudor. The national company, the Royal Ballet (so named in 1956), grew from foundations laid by Ninette de Valois and Frederick Ashton in 1928. British dancers include Alicia Markova, Anton Dolin, Margot Fonteyn, Antoinette Sibley, Lynn Seymour, Beryl Grey, Anthony Dowell, David Wall, Merle Park, and Lesley Collier; choreographers include Kenneth MacMillan. Fonteyn's partners included Robert Helpmann and Rudolf Nureyev.

ballet music During the 16th and 17th centuries there was not always a clear distinction between opera and ballet, since ballet during this period often included singing, and operas often included dance. The influence of the court composer Jean-Baptiste Lully on the development of ballet under Louis XIV in France was significant (Lully was a dancer himself, as was the king). During this period many courtly dances originated, including the ➔ **gavotte**, ➔ **passepied**, ➔ **bourrée**, and ➔ **minuet**. In the 19th century, as public interest in ballet increased, Russia produced composers of international reputation such as Pyotr Il'yich Tchaikovsky, whose ballet scores include

Swan Lake (1876), *Sleeping Beauty* (1890), and *The Nutcracker* (1892).

With the modern era of ballet which began in 1909 with the founding of the Ballets Russes, innovative choreography transformed the visual aspects of ballet and striking new compositions by Achille Claude Debussy, Maurice Ravel, and especially Igor Stravinsky (in, for example, *The Rite of Spring*, 1913) left their mark not only on the ballet composers who followed, but on the course of music history itself. Later in the century, the formal tradition of ballet was upset by the influence of jazz, jazz rhythms, and modern dance originating in the USA, which introduced greater freedom of bodily expression.

Today there exists a wide range of musical and choreographic styles, ranging from the classical to the popular. Many full ballet scores have been reduced by composers to ballet ➔ **suites** or purely orchestral works, which incorporate the essential musical elements, tending to omit musically nonthematic and transitional passages which may be, nevertheless, essential to the choreography and visual narration. Examples include Stravinsky's *The Firebird* (1910) and Ravel's *Boléro* (1928).

Ballet comique de la reine stage entertainment performed in Paris, France, on 15 October 1581, at the marriage of the duc de Joyeux and Mlle de Vaudemont, under the supervision of Balthasar de Beaujoyeux. The verse was by the Sieur de la Chesnaye, the scenery by Patin, and the music by the bass singer Lambert de Beaulieu, Jacques Salmon, and others. It was in effect the first *ballet de cour*.

ballet de cour (French 'court dance') an entertainment combining music, spectacle, dancing, song, and drama, developed at the French court during the second half of the 16th century. Light-hearted allegories based on classical mythology, *ballets de cour* played an important role in the evolution of ballet. One of the best known is the *Ballet comique de la reine* (1581), commissioned by Catherine de' Medici.

It was the patronage of Catherine de' Medici, who would have seen similar entertainments at the Florentine court in her youth, that encouraged the development of lavish *ballets de cour*. As in a ➔ **masque**, a closely related court entertainment, the parts were often played by members of the court – in the *Ballet comique de la reine*, commissioned by Catherine de' Medici to celebrate the marriage of her daughter Marguerite de Lorraine, both she and her daughter had roles.

The costume designs surviving from the early 17th century, especially those by Daniel Rabel (1578–1637), indicate the grotesque and humorous, as well as the opulent, aspects of these entertainments.

The fashion for hugely expensive and spectacular *ballets de cour* continued in the reigns of Henry IV and Louis XIII.

ballet-pantomime see ➤ **ballet**.

ballett or **ballet** a type of 16th–17th-century composition for several voices, resembling a ➤ **madrigal**, but in a lighter, more dance-like style.

balletti pieces of music intended for dancing, especially on the stage.

ballo (Italian 'dance') in music, a term referring to dance, or dancing. It is usually used in combination, for example *tempo di ballo* ('in dance time').

ballo delle ingrate, Il ballet-opera in one act by Monteverdi (libretto by Ottavio Rinuccini), first produced in Mantua, Italy, in 1608. The work was published in *Madrigali guerrieri et amorosi* in 1638. The 'ingrate' of the title are ladies who have declined the attentions of their suitors. The ungrateful spirits are summoned from Hades and perform a melancholy dance.

ballo in maschera, Un, *A Masked Ball* opera by Verdi (libretto by A Somma, based on Augustin Scribe's libretto for *Gustave III* set by Daniel Auber), first produced at the Teatro Apollo, Rome, Italy, on 17 February 1859. In the story King Gustav is stabbed by the jealous husband of Amelia.

Bamert, Matthias (1942–　) Swiss conductor and composer. He studied in Paris with Pierre Boulez and worked with the Cleveland Orchestra and the US Symphony Orchestra. He was music director of the Basel Radio Symphony Orchestra 1977–83 and principal guest with the Scottish National Orchestra from 1985. He has also led the Ulster Orchestra (Sibelius and Saariaho), BBC Symphony Orchestra (first performance of Martin Butler's *O Rio!*, 1991), the National Youth Orchestra at the 1993 London Proms (*Gawain's Journey* by Harrison Birtwistle), and the London Mozart Players from 1993.

Banchieri, Adriano (1568–1634) Italian organist, theorist, and composer. He was a Benedictine monk, and helped to found the Accademia dei Floridi in Bologna in 1615. He wrote theoretical works, especially on ➤ **figured bass** (*L'organo suonarino*, 1605). *Cartella musicale* (1614) advises on vocal ornamentation. His sequence of madrigals *La pazzia senile* (1595) has been described as the first comic opera.

A pupil of Gioseffo Guami, in 1596 he became organist at the monastery of San Michele in Bosco (Monte Oliveto) near Bologna, to which he returned in 1609, remaining there until shortly before his death; from 1600 to 1604 he was organist at Santa Maria in Regola at Imola.

Works Masses; sacred symphonies and concertos; comic intermezzi for the stage; organ works.

banda (Italian 'band') a military band, in particular a band used on the stage or behind the scene in an opera, as in Verdi's *Macbeth*.

bandurria or **Pandora** string instrument of the ➤ **cittern** type, with six double strings which are plucked with the fingers or with a plectrum.

banjo resonant stringed musical instrument with a long fretted neck and circular drum-type soundbox covered on the topside only by stretched skin (now usually plastic). It is played with a plectrum. Modern banjos normally have five strings.

The banjo originated in the American South among black slaves (based on a similar instrument of African origin).

It was introduced to Britain in 1846.

Bánk-Bán opera by Ferenc Erkel (libretto by B Egressy, based on a play by József Katona), first produced in Budapest, Hungary, on 9 March 1861. The story, set in 12th-century Hungary, tells how Bánk-Bán defends his wife, but both perish in the end.

Banks, Don (1923–1980) Australian composer. After studying at Melbourne Conservatory he went to London, England, in 1950, where he studied with Mátyás Seiber. In 1953 he went on to study with Luigi Dallapiccola in Florence, Italy, and finally settled in London.

Works CHAMBER horn concerto (1960); divertimento for flute and string trio; duo for violin and cello; violin sonata; three studies for cello and piano; Three Episodes for flute and piano. OTHER film music.

Bantock, Granville Ransome (1868–1946) English composer and conductor; professor of music at the University of Birmingham 1908–34. He is chiefly known today for his colourful *Pierrot of the Minute* overture (1908). Also notable amongst his vast output in all genres, much of it inspired by the East, are the *Hebridean Symphony* (1915), the oratorio *Omar Khayyám* (1906–09) for chorus and orchestra, *Atalanta in Calydon* (1911), a symphony for unaccompanied chorus, and *Sappho* (1906), an orchestral song cycle.

Born in London, the son of a doctor, he was educated for the civil service, but entered the Royal Academy of Music in 1889, where some of his earliest works were performed, and Lago produced the opera *Cædmar* at the Olympic Theatre in 1892. After some experience in theatrical conducting, he gave a concert of modern English music in 1896. The next year he was appointed conductor at the Tower, New Brighton, where he introduced much contemporary music. In February 1900 he gave a concert of new English music in Antwerp and in September was appointed principal of the Birmingham and Midland Institute School of Music. He remained in Birmingham until 1933, where he succeeded Edward Elgar as professor of music at the university in 1908.

Works STAGE operas, including *Sappho* (1906), *The Seal Woman* (1924).

ORCHESTRAL comedy overture *The Pierrot of the Minute* (1908), symphonic poem *Dante and Beatrice* (1911), *Fifine at the Fair* (1901), *Hebridean Symphony* (1915), *A Pagan Symphony* (1926), Symphony no. 3 (*The Cyprian Goddess*), Celtic Symphony.

CHORUS AND ORCHESTRA (with or without solo voices) *Omar Khayyám* (setting of FitzGerald's translation in three parts; 1909).

UNACCOMPANIED CHORUS choral symphony *Atalanta in Calydon* (Swinburne; 1911), *Vanity of Vanities* (Ecclesiastes).

SONGS including cycles *Songs from the Chinese Poets* (eight sets).

CHAMBER Viola sonata (1919), three cello sonatas (1924, 1940, 1945), three violin sonatas (1929, 1932, 1940).

bar modular segment of music incorporating a fixed number of beats, as in the phrase 'two/three/four beats to the bar'. It is shown in notation by vertical 'barring' of the musical continuum. The US term is **measure**.

Barbé, Anton (died 1564) Flemish composer and first of a line of Antwerp musicians. He was Kapellmeister at Antwerp Cathedral 1527–62. He published Masses, motets, and chansons, and contributed a Dutch song to Tielman Susato's *Het ierste musyck boexken/The First Music Book* (1551), one of eleven volumes of pieces by composers of the time.

Barbe-bleue, Bluebeard operetta by Jacques Offenbach (libretto by H Meilhac and L Halévy), first produced at the Théâtre des Variétés, Paris, France, on 5 February 1866. It is a satirical version of the original 'Bluebeard' story.

Barber, Samuel (1910–1981) US composer. He worked in a neoclassical, astringent style. Compositions include *Adagio for Strings* (1936) and the opera *Vanessa* (1958), which won one of his two Pulitzer Prizes. Another opera, *Antony and Cleopatra* (1966), was commissioned for the opening of the new Metropolitan Opera House at the Lincoln Center, New York City. Owing to an over-elaborate staging the opera was a failure at its premiere, although it had some success in a revised version in 1974. Barber's music is lyrical and fastidiously worked. His later works include *The Lovers* (1971).

He entered the Curtis Institute of Music in 1924, winning a prize with a violin sonata in 1928. In

the following years he won several more prizes, including the American Prix de Rome in 1935.

Works OPERA *Vanessa* (1958), *Antony and Cleopatra* (after Shakespeare, 1966, revised 1974).

ORCHESTRAL two essays for orchestra; overture to Sheridan's *School for Scandal* (1933); music for a scene from Shelley for orchestra; violin concerto (1940), cello concerto (1945), piano concerto (1962).

CHAMBER *Adagio for Strings* (from string quartet of 1936); *Capricorn Concerto* for flute, oboe, trumpet, and strings (1944); piano sonata.

VOCAL *Dover Beach* (Matthew Arnold) for baritone and string quartet (1933); *Knoxville, Summer of 1915* for soprano and orchestra (1948); works for unaccompanied chorus; many songs.

Barber of Baghdad, The comedy-opera by Peter Cornelius. See ➤ *Barbier von Bagdad, Der*.

Barber of Seville, The opera buffa by Rossini and an opera by Giovanni Paisiello. See ➤ *barbiere di Siviglia, Il*.

barbershop in music, a style of unaccompanied close-harmony singing of sentimental ballads, revived in the USA during the 19th century. Traditionally sung by four male voices, since the 1970s it has developed as a style of ➤ a cappella choral singing for both male and female voices.

Barbershop originated in 17th-century European barbers' shops, which also offered dental and medical services; making music was encouraged among waiting customers.

Barbier, Jules see Michel ➤ Carré.

barbiere di Siviglia, Il, ossia La precauzione inutile, The Barber of Seville, or Vain Precaution (original title *Almaviva, ossia L'inutile precauzione*) opera by Rossini (libretto by C Sterbini, based on Beaumarchais's comedy *Le Barbier de Séville*), first produced at the Teatro Argentina, Rome, Italy, on 20 February 1816.

barbiere di Siviglia, Il, ovvero La precauzione inutile, The Barber of Seville, or Vain Precaution opera by Giovanni Paisiello (libretto by G Petrosellini, based on Beaumarchais's comedy *Le Barbier de Séville*), first produced before the court at the Hermitage, St Petersburg, Russia, on 26 September 1782.

Barbier von Bagdad, Der, The Barber of Baghdad opera by Peter Cornelius (libretto by composer), first produced in Weimar, Germany, on 15 December 1858. The plot describes how Nureddin is helped by Abul Hassan in meeting Margiana.

Barbirolli, John (Giovanni Battista) (1899–1970) English conductor. He excelled in the Romantic repertory, especially the symphonies of Elgar, Sibelius, Mahler, and Vaughan Williams. Trained as a cellist, he was conductor of the New York Philharmonic Orchestra from 1937 to 1943, and of the Hallé Orchestra, Manchester, from 1943 to 1970.

Born in London, of French and Italian descent, he studied at Trinity College, London, 1911–12 and at the Royal Academy of Music, London, 1912–17. He made his debut as a cellist aged 11, and joined the Queen's Hall Orchestra in that capacity in 1915. He achieved recognition as a conductor in 1926, and later succeeded Arturo Toscanini as chief conductor of the New York Philharmonic Orchestra in 1937. He married the oboist Evelyn Rothwell in 1939. He returned to England in 1943, where he took over the Hallé Orchestra. In 1949 he was knighted and in 1950 received the Royal Philharmonic Society's gold medal. With the Hallé he gave the first performances of Vaughan Williams's seventh and eighth symphonies. He was guest conductor of the Berlin Philharmonic Orchestra, Boston Symphony Orchestra, and Chicago Symphony Orchestra.

Barcarola work for orchestra by Hans Werner Henze; it depicts a journey across the River Styx and quotes the Eton Boating Song. It was first performed in Zurich, Switzerland, on 22 April 1980, conducted by Gerd Albrecht.

barcarole song of the type sung by Venetian gondoliers. The barcarole is always in moderate duple time (6/8 or 12/8), with a swaying rhythm. Instrumental barcaroles also exist, for example Chopin's *Barcarolle* (1846).

bard Celtic minstrel who, in addition to composing songs, usually at a court, often held important political posts. Originating in the pre-Christian era, bards were persecuted in Wales during the 13th century on political grounds. Since the 19th century annual meetings and competitions in Wales – known as eisteddfods – have attempted to revive the musical tradition of the bard.

Barenboim, Daniel (1942–) Argentinian-born Israeli pianist and conductor. Pianist and conductor with the English Chamber Orchestra from 1964, he became conductor of the New York Philharmonic Orchestra in 1970, musical director of the Orchestre de Paris in 1975, and director of the Chicago Symphony Orchestra in 1991.

As a pianist Barenboim specialized in the German classic and romantic repertoire; as a conductor he extended into 19th- and 20th-century French music, including the work of French composer Pierre ➔ **Boulez**. He was married to the English cellist Jacqueline Du Pré.

Bärenhäuter, Der, The Bear Skinner opera by Siegfried Wagner (libretto by composer) first produced in Munich, Germany, on 21 January 1899.

bariolage in music, the alteration on a string instrument of the same note on an open string and a stopped string. Also the playing of high notes on a string instrument in high positions on the lower strings to obtain a different tone-colour or to facilitate the performance of rapid high passages without changing to lower positions.

baritone male voice pitched between bass and tenor, of approximate range G2–F4. It is also used before the name of an instrument, for example baritone saxophone, and indicates that the instrument sounds in approximately the same range.

Dietrich Fischer-Dieskau and Hermann Prey are well-known German baritone singers. 'Baritone' is also the name of a valved brass instrument of the saxhorn family, similar in pitch to the euphonium.

The approximate range of a baritone voice.

Barkin, Elaine (1932–) US composer and writer on music. She studied with Leo Kraft, Irving Fine, and Boris Blacher; edited the journal *Perspectives of New Music* 1963–85, and is on the faculty of University of California in Los Angeles. Her music is influenced by serialism, graphic notation, and interactive performance techniques.

Works CHAMBER string quartet (1969); *Inward and Outward Bound* for 13 instruments (1974); *Ebb Tide* for two vibraphones (1977); *Encore* for gamelan ensemble (1989).

VOCAL *De Amore*, chamber opera (1980); *Women's Voices* for four female reciters, tape, and slides (1983).

OTHER *Quilt Piece*, graphic score (1983).

Barlow, David (1927–1975) English composer. He studied with Gordon Jacob at the Royal College of Music, London, and with Nadia Boulanger in France. His early music was Romantic in style; from 1963 he adopted serial technique.

Works CHURCH OPERA *David and Bathsheba* (1969), *Judas Iscariot* (1975).

ORCHESTRAL two symphonies (1950 and 1959); variations for cello and orchestra (1969); Sinfonietta concertante for clarinet and orchestra (1972); *The Lambton Worm* for narrator and orchestra (1969).

CHAMBER string trio, string quartet (1969), brass quintet (1972).

CHURCH MUSIC *Passion Music* for organ.

Barlow, Samuel (1892–1982) US composer. He studied at Harvard and in Paris and Rome, becoming active on behalf of liberal causes. His opera *Mon Ami Pierrot* (1935) is based on the life of Jean-Baptiste Lully and was the first by a US composer to be given at the Paris Opéra Comique. Other operas were *Amanda* (1936) and *Eugénie*. His symphonic concerto *Babar* (1935) uses slide projections but this, a piano concerto (1931), and *Biedermeier Waltzes* (1935) are in a conservative idiom.

Barlow, Wayne Brewster (1912–1995) US composer. He studied with Howard Hanson at the Eastman School of Music, New York, and with Schoenberg at the University of Southern California in 1935. He was director of the electronic music studio at Eastman 1968–78.

Works ORCHESTRAL *Images* for harp and orchestra (1961), *Vistas* for orchestra (1963).

CHAMBER *Nocturne* for 18 instruments (1946), piano quintet (1951), *Divertissement* for flute and chamber orchestra (1980); *Sonatine for Four* (1984).

VOCAL cantatas *Zion in Exile* (1937), *Voices of Faith* (1976).

OTHER ballet *Three Moods for Dancing* (1940), *Moonflight* for tape (1970), *Soundprints in Concrete* (1972), *Frontiers* for band (1982).

Barnby, Joseph (1838–1896) English conductor, organist and composer. He held various organist's posts in London, was precentor at Eton College 1875–92, then principal of the Guildhall School of Music and Drama. Distinguished as a choral conductor, he gave oratorios by Johann Sebastian Bach and Antonín Dvořák and the first English performance of *Parsifal* (as a concert, 1884).

baroque music music of the period following the Renaissance and before the classical period, lasting from about 1600 to the deaths of Johann Sebastian ➤ Bach and George Frideric ➤ Handel in the 1750s. Baroque music is characterized by the contrapuntal use of voices and instrumental parts, for example in the ➤ fugue, which flourished during these years; the development of ➤ continuo writing, specifically the ➤ figured bass, for accompanying a melody line or orchestral parts; the ➤ concertante style of contrasting effects, both instrumental (as in the ➤ concerto grosso) and dynamic (for example, from forte (loud) to piano (soft), in the manner of an echo); the importance of melodic ➤ ornamentation; the use of ➤ tonic and ➤ dominant as primary harmonies; and the establishment of four-bar phrases as a compositional norm.

Baroque composers include Johann ➤ Pachelbel, Johann Sebastian ➤ Bach, George Frideric ➤ Handel, Antonio ➤ Vivaldi, Girolamo ➤ Frescobaldi, and Claudio ➤ Monteverdi's later works.

Barraqué, Jean (1928–1973) French composer. His disciplined technique was well suited to ➤ serialism, which formed a cornerstone of his composition. In 1955 he began work on his major composition, *La Mort de Virgile*, based on the book by Hermann Broch, but never completed it.

He studied with Jean Langlais and Olivier Messiaen, later working in the experimental laboratories of the Radiodiffusion Française in Paris. His first compositions were a piano sonata, begun in 1950, and *Sequence for Voice and Ensemble*, revised in 1955. In 1951 he wrote *Etude for Electronic Tape*. His last completed work was the clarinet concerto, 1962–68. He also wrote a short book on Debussy.

Works DRAMATIC CYCLE *La Mort de Virgile*, incomplete.

VOCAL AND ORCHESTRAL *Séquence* for soprano and chamber ensemble (after Nietzsche; 1955); *Au delà du hasard* (based on Hermann Broch) for voices and instrumental groups (1959); *Le Temps restitué* for voices and orchestra (1957).

CHAMBER *Chant après chant* for percussion (1966); piano sonata.

Barraud, Henry (1900–1997) French composer. He studied first at Bordeaux and later at the Paris Conservatory with Caussade, Dukas, and Aubert. He was expelled from the conservatory as a bad influence, but later in life turned to religion. In 1937 he was in charge of the music at the Paris World Fair; he then joined the radio service, where he rose to the post of head of the national programme in 1948.

Works OPERA *La Farce de Maître Pathelin* (1938), *Numance*, *Lavinia* (1959).

BALLET *La Kermesse* (1943), *L'Astrologue dans le puits*.

ORCHESTRAL three symphonies; piano concerto.

ORATORIO *Les Mystères des Saints Innocents* (1947).

CHORAL cantatas and other choral works, including *La Divine Comédie*, after Dante, for five solo voices and orchestra (1972).

CHAMBER woodwind trio, string trio, string quartet (1940), violin and piano sonata; piano music.

OTHER songs; film and radio music.

barré (French 'barred') in music, a chord on string instruments with fretted fingerboards, particularly the guitar, is said to be played barré when a finger is laid horizontally across the whole fingerboard, thus raising all the strings in pitch by the same interval's distance from the fundamental tuning.

barrel organ portable pipe organ, played by turning a handle, or occasionally by a clockwork mechanism. The handle works a pump and drives a replaceable cylinder upon which music is embossed as a pattern of ridges controlling the passage of air to the pipes. It is often confused with the barrel or street piano used by buskers, which employed a barrel-and-pin mechanism to control a piano hammer action.

The barrel organ was a common entertainment and parish church instrument in England during the 18th and 19th centuries.

Barry, Gerald (1952–) Irish composer from Newmarket-on-Fergus, County Clare. His major influences are the composers with whom he has studied: Peter Schat in the Netherlands, Stockhausen and Mauricio Kagel in Germany, and Friedrich Cerha in Austria. His *Cheveux-de-frise* caused a stir at the 1988 London Promenade Concerts. His opera *The Intelligence Park* (1987), commissioned by the Institute of Contemporary Arts in London, was first performed at the 1990 Almeida Festival and a second opera, *The Triumph of Beauty and Deceit* (1993), was written for Channel 4 Television. His music has been commercially recorded by the NMC, Largo, Black Box, Marco Polo, and Challenge labels.

Works OPERA *The Intelligence Park*, *The Triumph of Beauty and Deceit*.

ORCHESTRAL piano concerto (1977); *Cheveux-de-frises* (1988); *Reflections on Guinness* (1988); *Hard D* (1992).

CHAMBER *Handel's Favourite Song* for clarinet and ensemble (1981); *Cork* for string quartet (1985); *Sur les pointes* for chamber ensemble (1985); Sextet (1992); Octet (1995).

VOCAL *What the Frog Said* for soprano, bass, and ensemble (1985).

Barshai, Rudolf (1924–) Russian violist and conductor. He founded the Moscow Chamber Orchestra in 1956 and conducted it until he left Russia for Israel in 1976. He was principal conductor of the Bournemouth Symphony Orchestra 1983–88 and music director of the Vancouver Symphony Orchestra 1985–88. His transcriptions include Prokofiev's *Visions Fugitives*, for chamber orchestra, and Shostakovich's string quartet no. 8, for string orchestra.

Bart, Lionel (1930–1999) English composer and lyricist. His musical *Lock Up Your Daughters* (1959) ended the USA's domination of London's music theatre. Further acclaim followed with *Fings Ain't Wot They Used T'be* (1959), *Oliver* (1960), and *Blitz!* (1962).

Bart was born in London. His first success, *Lock Up Your Daughters*, was based on Henry Fielding's play *Rape upon Rape* (1730). *Maggie May*, a between-the-wars story of a Liverpool prostitute, was staged in 1964. His Robin Hood musical, *Twang!* (1965), and *La Strada* (1969) were box-office failures.

Bartered Bride, The, Czech **Prodaná Nevěsta** opera by Bedřich Smetana (libretto by K Sabina),

first produced at the Czech Theatre, Prague (now in the Czech Republic), on 30 May 1866; a revised version was produced on 29 January 1869, and the final version (with recitatives) was first produced on 25 September 1870. The story describes how Marchenka and Jeník wish to marry, but must first overcome a previously arranged marriage and each other's subterfuges.

Barth, Hans (1897–1956) German-born US pianist and composer. A meeting with Ferruccio Busoni encouraged him to experiment with new scales, and in 1928 he invented a quarter-tone piano, for which he composed a number of works. He also composed quarter-tone chamber and instrumental music, as well as more conventional pieces.

Barthélémon, François Hippolyte (1741–1808) French violinist and composer. An exponent of the 'galant' style, he produced *Pelopida*, the first of several successful dramatic works, in 1766.

He settled in London, England, in 1765. A year later he married the singer Mary Young, daughter of Charles Young and niece of Mrs Arne and Mrs Lampe. He composed stage pieces for the actor-manager David Garrick and visited France, Germany, and Italy with his wife, who sang there. He was a friend of Haydn during the latter's visits to London, and is said to have suggested the subject of *The Creation*.

Works STAGE WORKS *Pelopida* (1766), *The Judgement of Paris* (1768), *The Maid of the Oaks* (1774), *Belphegor* (1778).

ORATORIO *Jefte in Masfa*.

ORCHESTRAL symphonies; concertos.

CHAMBER sonatas, duets for violin.

Bartlet, John (lived 16th–17th centuries) English lutenist and composer. He published a *Booke of Ayres* for voices and instruments in 1606.

Bartók, Béla (1881–1945) Hungarian composer. His works are influenced by folk music and often use modality. His music is highly dissonant and contrapuntal, but not atonal (see → atonality). His large output includes six string quartets, a *Divertimento* for string orchestra (1939), concertos for piano, violin, and viola, the *Concerto for Orchestra* (1943–44), a one-act opera *Duke Bluebeard's Castle* (1911), and graded teaching pieces for piano.

A child prodigy, Bartók studied music at the Budapest Conservatory, later working with Zoltán → Kodály in recording and transcribing the folk music of Hungary and adjoining countries. His ballet *The Miraculous Mandarin* (1918–19) was banned because of its subject matter (it was set in a brothel). Bartók died in the USA, having fled from Hungary in 1940.

Bartók's father was a director of agriculture; his

mother, a schoolteacher, was a musician and taught him from an early age. He appeared in public as a pianist at the age of ten. He studied under László Erkel at Porzsony (now Bratislava) until 1899; he then went to the Budapest Conservatory, where he studied piano under István Thomán and composition under Hans Koessler (1853–1926).

Under the influence of Richard Strauss, Bartók wrote the symphonic poem *Kossuth* (1903), which was conducted by Hans Richter at Manchester, England, in 1904. His first string quartet (1908) begins with some similarity to late Beethoven but soon settles into a characteristic national style. About 1905 he began to collect folk tunes, often with Zoltán Kodály, and showed that the true Magyar music differed greatly from that of the Hungarian gypsies, which was popularly regarded as the only Hungarian folk music. Bartók was appointed professor of piano at Budapest Conservatory in 1907. The powerful opera *Duke Bluebeard's Castle* was composed in 1911 but not performed until 1918. After World War I he became known in Europe and the USA, and in 1922 was made an honorary member of the International Society for Contemporary Music. Some of his most demanding music was written in the years 1917–34: *The Miraculous Mandarin* (1918–19), his first two piano concertos (1926, 1930–31), string quartets nos. 2–5 (1917–34), and *Cantata Profana* (1930). The sensational *Miraculous Mandarin* ballet was written under the influence of Igor Stravinsky and the expressionist Arnold Schoenberg; it was banned after a single performance in Cologne, Germany.

Increasing political isolation in his homeland (Hungary became fascist before Germany) encouraged Bartók to pursue a career abroad. The first two piano concertos were premiered by him in Frankfurt, Germany, and demonstrate a full range of percussive effects. Bartók's own keyboard style was not appreciated by all – Percy Scholes reported that he had a touch 'like a paving stone'. Both concertos and the fourth and fifth quartets (1928, 1934) used palindrome patterns (reading the same backwards as forwards) to some extent, which with their formal repetition help to give a unity to chromatically complex music. A more easily accessible idiom, with longer melodic lines and less harsh harmony, was in evidence by 1938, with the *Music for Strings, Percussion and Celesta* (1936; one of many masterworks commissioned by the Swiss conductor Paul Sacher) and the second violin concerto (1937–38). The sixth quartet (1939) was the last music he wrote in Budapest, and seems to find the composer in mourning for the world he was about to leave behind; each movement begins with a long, melancholy viola solo.

In 1940 Bartók emigrated to the USA, where he taught briefly at Columbia University and Harvard. He was already suffering from leukaemia and was not in demand as a pianist or, initially, as a composer. A 1943 commission from the Koussevitzky Foundation, for the *Concerto for Orchestra*, helped to improve his financial difficulties. The third piano concerto was written when Bartók was mortally ill; the central adagio religioso pays direct tribute to Beethoven's 'Song of Thanksgiving' from the A minor quartet, although Bartók must have known that in his case there was to be no recovery from illness.

Bartók was one of the foremost composers of the 20th century and his influence can be clearly heard in later Hungarian composers such as György Ligeti. Much influenced by Hungarian folk music, he incorporated its rhythms and melodic characteristics into complex, subtle, and effective forms. Bartók's orchestral music has become relatively popular, although his genius is more fully seen in his innovative approach to the keyboard and especially the string quartets, which are widely regarded as the best since Beethoven.

Works STAGE *Duke Bluebeard's Castle*, one-act opera (1911); *The Wooden Prince*, one-act ballet (1914–17); *The Miraculous Mandarin*, one-act pantomime (1918–19; revised 1924 and 1935).

ORCHESTRAL *Dance Suite* (1923), piano concerto no. 1 (1926), piano concerto no. 2 (1930–31), *Music for Strings, Percussion and Celesta* (1936), violin concerto no. 2 (1937–38), *Divertimento* for strings (1939), *Concerto for Orchestra* (1943–44), piano concerto no. 3 (1945), viola concerto (completed by T Serly, 1945).

VOCAL *Cantata Profana* for tenor, baritone, chorus, and orchestra (1930), choruses on Hungarian and Slovak folk songs; many solo songs, including five to words by Endre Ady.

CHAMBER six string quartets (1908, 1917, 1927, 1928, 1934, 1939), two piano and violin sonatas (1921, 1922), sonata for two pianos and two percussion (1937, version with orchestra 1940), *Contrasts* for violin, clarinet, and piano (1938), sonata for solo violin (1944).

PIANO *14 Bagatelles*, Op. 6 (1908), Sonatina (1915), Suite, Op. 14 (1916), sonata (1926), *Out of Doors* (1926), *Mikrokosmos*, 153 'progressive pieces' in six volumes (1926, 1932–39).

baryton complex, bowed, stringed musical instrument producing an intense singing tone. It is based on an 18th-century ➤ **viol** and modified by the addition of sympathetic (freely vibrating) strings which are plucked by hand.

The baryton was a favourite instrument of Prince Nicholas Esterházy, patron of the Austrian composer Franz Joseph Haydn, who, to please him, wrote over 120 trios for violin, baryton, and cello, and many other works for the instrument.

Basili or **Basily, Francesco (1767–1850)** Italian singer and composer. He became director of the Milan Conservatory in 1827, and was maestro di cappella at St Peter's in Rome from 1837.

Works OPERA *La locandiera* (1789), *Achille nell'assedio di Troia*, *Ritorno d'Ulisse* (1798), *Antigona* (1799), *Achille*, *L'orfana egiziana* (1818).

ORATORIO *Sansone* (1824).

CHURCH MUSIC Requiem for Jannaconi; several settings of *Miserere*.

ORCHESTRAL symphony.

Basilius, Der königliche Schäfer, oder Basilius in Arcadien, The Royal Shepherd, or Basil in Arcady opera by Reinhard Keiser (libretto by F C Bressand), first produced in Brunswick, Germany, in about 1693. It was the first of more than 100 operas by Keiser.

bass lowest male voice, of approximate range C2–D4. It is also used before the name of an instrument and indicates that the instrument sounds in approximately the same range.

Well-known bass singers include the Russian Fyodor Chaliapin and the Bulgarian Boris Christoff. The term also covers the bass instrument of a consort or family, for example the ➤ bass clarinet, bass tuba, and ➤ bassoon, which all have a similar range. An instrument an octave lower than bass is a contrabass.

The approximate range of a bass voice.

Bassani, Giovanni Battista (c.1647–1716) Italian violinist and composer of the generation between Monteverdi and Vivaldi. He was organist at Ferrara from 1667 and was later in charge of the cathedral music at Bologna; he returned to Ferrara as maestro di cappella in 1683. He composed twelve oratorios, produced nine operas, and brought out a large amount of church and instrumental music.

Bassano, Giovanni (c.1558–c.1617) Venetian composer and cornet player. He led the instrumental ensemble at St Mark's, Venice, and wrote instrumental music including ornamented transcriptions of vocal works by Gabrieli, Marenzio, and others.

Bassarids, The one-act opera with intermezzo by Hans Werner Henze (libretto by W H Auden and Chester Kallman after *The Bacchae* of Euripides), first produced in Salzburg, Austria, on 6 August 1966. It had its first British stage performance at the London Coliseum on 10 October 1974, conducted by Henze. The plot describes how Pentheus, in attempting to establish monothe-ism, incurs the wrath of Dionysus and his followers, who eventually kill him.

bass chantante (French 'singing bass') bass voice especially suited to melodic delivery and lyrical parts.

bass clarinet single-reed woodwind instrument in B flat. It is twice the length of the 'ordinary' B flat ➤ clarinet with a range an octave lower. It has a rich and resonant sound. An example of the bass clarinet can be heard in the 'Dance of the Sugar-Plum Fairy' from Tchaikovsky's *The Nutcracker Suite* (1891–92).

bass clef in musical notation, the F ➤ clef in which the F below middle C is represented as the second line from the top of the five-line stave. Instruments with a range below middle C use the bass clef, including double bass, tuba, and piano (left hand).

The bass clef.

bass drum the largest drum of the orchestra or military band, with notes of indeterminate pitch, consisting of a cylindrical wooden body with two drumming surfaces (of hide or plastic). It is usually placed upright and drummed from one side.

In the military band, the bass drum is played together with the cymbals, one of which is placed on it, while the other is held in the player's non-drumming hand.

basse-contre low ➤ bass, whether a voice, an instrument, or an organ stop.

basse danse (French 'low dance') French dance of the 15th–16th century, so called because the feet were kept low, not thrown up in the air as in some other dances.

basset horn musical woodwind instrument, a wide-bore alto clarinet pitched in F, invented about 1765 and used by Mozart in his *Masonic Funeral Music* (1785), for example, and by Richard Strauss. It was revived in 1981 by Karlheinz Stockhausen and features prominently as a solo in his opera cycle *Licht*. Performers include Alan Hacker and Suzanne Stephens.

Bassett, Leslie (1923–) US composer. He studied with Ross Lee Finney, Nadia Boulanger, and Mario Davidovsky (electronic music); from 1952 he has taught at the University of Michigan, as professor since 1977. His works are clearly constructed and convey a strong spiritual content.

Works ORCHESTRAL variations for orchestra (Pulitzer Prize 1966); *Echoes from an Invisible World*, for the Bicentennial (1976); concerto for two pianos and orchestra (1976); trombone concerto (1983); *From a Source Evolving* for orchestra (1986).

CHAMBER four string quartets (1951, 1957, 1962, 1978); Sextet (1979);

DUO-INVENTIONS for two cellos (1988).

OTHER wind band music (Concerto grosso, 1982); choral works, songs, keyboard, and electronic music.

bass flute ➤ flute in C with a range an octave lower than that of the ordinary instrument. The term is also sometimes mistakenly applied to the ➤ alto flute.

basso cantante (Italian 'singing bass') in music, a ➤ bass voice especially suited to melodic delivery and lyrical parts.

basso continuo (Italian 'continuous bass') musical term, the original Italian term for ➤ continuo.

bassoon double-reed woodwind instrument in C. It is the bass of the oboe family and lowest sounding of the four main orchestral woodwinds (the flute, clarinet, oboe, and bassoon). It doubles back on itself in a conical tube about 2.5 m/7.5 ft long and has a rich, deep tone. The bassoon concert repertoire extends from the early Baroque via Antonio Vivaldi, Wolfgang Amadeus Mozart, and Paul Dukas, to Karlheinz Stockhausen.

The bassoon was developed from the Renaissance ➤ curtal about 1660 as a continuo instrument to provide bassline support. Further development in the 18th century led to the **double bassoon** or **contrabassoon**, an octave lower. Both instruments have an unexpected agility considering their low pitch range and rich, glowing tone. They are also capable of dignified solos at high register, a famous example for bassoon being the eerie opening bars of Igor Stravinsky's ballet *The Rite of Spring* (1913).

The normal compass of a bassoon, though a few higher notes are possible.

basso ostinato (Italian 'persistent bass', 'ground bass') in music, a bass part in a composition continually tracing the same melodic outline.

bass trumpet ➤ trumpet invented by Wagner, with a written compass an octave below that of the normal orchestral instrument.

Its range is more correctly described as tenor.

bass viol alternative name for the ➤ viola da gamba, a musical instrument.

Bastien und Bastienne Singspiel by Mozart, K50 (libretto by F W Weiskern and A Schachtner,

based on Charles-Simon Favart's parody of Rousseau's pastoral opera *Le Devin du Village*), It was first produced in Vienna, Austria, at the house of Anton Mesmer (the hypnotist) in September 1768. In the story Bastienne seeks the advice of a magician to win back the heart of the inattentive Bastien.

Bataille, Gabriel (1575–1630) French lutenist and composer. He contributed music to ballets danced at the court of Louis XIII. Between 1608 and 1623 he published many lute pieces and songs.

Bateson, Thomas (c.1570–1630) English organist and composer. He was probably organist at Chester Cathedral until 1609, when he became vicar-choral and organist at Christ Church Cathedral, Dublin. Two books of madrigals by him were published in 1604 and 1618.

Bathe, William (1564–1614) Irish priest and music scholar. In state service at first, he went to Spain and became a Jesuit priest in 1599. He wrote *Briefe Introductions to the True Art of Music and the Skill of Song* and *Janua linguarum*.

baton stick used by a conductor to control an orchestra. Typically, the baton is held in the right hand and is used in order to make the conductor's signals more apparent. Generally, conductors do not use a baton when working with choirs or small instrumental ensembles.

Earliest records of the baton date to the Sistine Chapel during the 15th century, when the conductor used a roll of paper to beat time. Jean-Baptiste Lully used a large cane. During the 19th century the first violinist waved his bow to conduct. The modern baton seems to have originated in the early 19th century, with its use by Beethoven and Mendelssohn.

battaglia di Legnano, La, **The Battle of Legnano** opera by Verdi (libretto by S Cammarano), first produced at the Teatro Argentina, Rome, Italy, on 27 January 1849. The plot describes how Rolando and Arrigo battle against the Germans, but Rolando must also fight when he discovers his wife Lida loves Arrigo. Later, the mortally wounded Arrigo proclaims Lida's innocence and the three are reconciled.

battement see ➤ mordent.

Batten, Adrian (1591–1637) English organist and composer. He was a chorister at Winchester Cathedral as a boy. In 1614 he went to London as vicar-choral at Westminster Abbey and in 1626 became organist at St Paul's Cathedral. He was probably the copyist of the Batten Organbook.

Works CHURCH MUSIC eleven services, about 50 anthems, and other church music.

batterie (French 'battery', 'collection') in music, an 18th-century term for rapid broken accompaniment figures. It is also a collective term for the group of percussion instruments in the orchestra.

Battishill, Jonathan (1738–1801) English harpsichordist, organist, and composer. He was a chorister at St Paul's Cathedral. In about 1762 he became harpsichordist to Covent Garden Theatre, where he produced in 1764 the opera *Almena*, written jointly with Michael Arne. About the same time he became organist of three city churches, and began to write church music. His best-known pieces are the anthems *Call to Remembrance* and *O Lord, look down from heaven*. Other works include music for the stage, glees, catches, and songs.

Battle of Prague, The a descriptive piano piece with violin, cello, and drum *ad lib* by Franz Koczwara, composed in 1788, of little musical value, but very popular in the early 19th century.

Battle of Vittoria, The Beethoven's 'Battle Symphony', Op. 91, originally entitled *Wellingtons Sieg oder die Schlacht bei Vittoria*, first performed on 8 December 1813. An extravagantly descriptive piece, originally intended for a mechanical instrument, it contains quotations from national songs, including 'Rule, Britannia!'.

battuta (Italian 'beat') in music, a term to mean the beat or tempo of a composition. It is often used loosely in the plural (for example *ritmo di 3 battute*) to indicate a change in the metrical scheme of bars grouped in unexpected numbers.

Baudo, Serge (1927–) French conductor. He made his debut in 1950 with the Concerts Lamoureux. He had engagements at the Paris Opéra from 1962, La Scala in Milan, and New York Metropolitan Opera, and was chief conductor of the Orchestre de Paris 1967–69. He gave the first performances of Olivier Messiaen's *Et exspecto resurrectionem mortuorum* (Chartres, 1965) and *La Transfiguration* (Lisbon, 1969). He founded the Berlioz Festival in Lyon, France, in 1979.

Baudrier, Yves (1906–1988) French composer. Originally a law student, in 1936 he formed the group La Jeune France with his fellow composers André Jolivet, Daniel Lesur, and Olivier Messiaen.

Works ORCHESTRAL symphonies, symphonic poem *Le Grand Voilier* (1939).
CHAMBER string quartet (1944); piano pieces.
CHURCH MUSIC Agnus Dei for soprano, chorus and orchestra.

Bauer, Marion (1887–1955) US composer and teacher. She studied with Nadia Boulanger in Paris and taught at New York University 1926–51. Her works are often in smaller forms and are neoclassical in spirit. Her books include *20th-Century Music* (1933) and *How Opera Grew* (1955).

Works PIANO piano pieces *New Hampshire Woods* (1921), *Sun Splendour* (1926, also for orchestra), and *Dance Sonata* (1932); piano concerto 'American Youth' (1943).
CHAMBER string quartet (1928); viola sonata (1936); oboe sonata (1940).
VOCAL *China* for chorus and orchestra (1945).

Bauldeweyn, Noel (died c.1530) Flemish composer. Maître de chapelle of Notre Dame at Antwerp 1513–18, he composed sacred and secular music including the Mass *Da Pacem* formerly thought to be by Josquin Desprez.

Bavarian Highlands, Scenes from the six Choral Songs with piano, Op. 27, by Edward Elgar; they were composed in 1895 and first performed in Worcester, England, on 21 April 1896. A version with orchestra was completed in 1896. Nos 1, 3, and 6 were arranged for orchestra alone as *Three Bavarian Dances*, first performed at Crystal Palace, London, on 23 October 1897, conducted by August Manns.

Bavicchi, John (1922–) US composer. He studied with Walter Piston at Harvard and after war service was active in Boston as a conductor and teacher (Arlington Philharmonic, 1968–82). His music often employs classical forms.

Works ORCHESTRAL concertante for oboe, bassoon, and strings (1961); *There is Sweet Music Here* for soprano and orchestra (1985).
CHAMBER string quartet (1961); music for chamber orchestra (1981); *Triptych* for horns (1987).

Bax, Arnold Edward Trevor (1883–1953) English composer. His works, often based on Celtic legends, include seven symphonies as well as the two tone poems *The Garden of Fand* (1913–16) and *Tintagel* (1917–19). He was Master of the King's Musick 1942–53.

Bayreuth town in Bavaria, south Germany, on the Red Main River, 65 km/40 mi northeast of Nuremberg; population (1995) 72,700. There are cotton textile, porcelain, cigarette, and optical industries. Bayreuth was the home of the composer Richard Wagner, and the Wagner theatre was established in 1876 as a performing centre for his operas. Opera festivals are held here every summer.

The theatre introduced new concepts of opera house design, including provision of an enlarged orchestra pit extending below the stage and projecting the sound outwards and upwards. Bayreuth has a university (founded in 1975).

Bayreuth's baroque buildings and rococo palaces recall its former status as residence of the margraves of Brandenburg-Kulmbach. Wagner himself designed the theatre, the Festspielhaus. There is also a baroque opera house (1748), as well as fine old churches, and a notable 18th-century castle (now a museum). The Eremitage, a rococo castle, was often visited by Frederick the Great, whose sister was margravine of Bayreuth. Wagner is buried in the garden of his former villa.

Bazelon, Irwin (Allen) (1922–1995) US composer. He studied with Hindemith, Milhaud, and Bloch and composed much film music and incidental music for Shakespeare's plays.

Works ORCHESTRAL seven symphonies (1963–80), *Symphonie Concertante* (1963), *Excursions* for orchestra (1966), *Early American Suite* (1970), *Spirits of the Night* for orchestra (1976), *Spires* for trumpet and orchestra (1981), *Trajectories* for piano and orchestra (1984), *Motivations* for trombone and orchestra (1985), *Fourscore 2* for percussion quartet and orchestra (1988).

CHAMBER *Chamber Symphony* for seven instruments (1957), *Sound Dreams* for six instruments (1977), two string quartets, three piano sonatas.

VOCAL *Legends and Love Letters* for soprano and chamber orchestra (1987).

BBC orchestras the British Broadcasting Corporation (BBC) sponsors a number of orchestras. They are:

BBC Symphony Orchestra founded in 1930 and based in London. Andrew Davis became its chief conductor in 1989. The orchestra specializes in new music; it has a regular concert programme at the Royal Festival Hall and provides the backbone to the annual season of the BBC Proms.

BBC Philharmonic founded as the BBC Northern Orchestra in 1933, taking its present name in 1982. It is based in Manchester, performing many of its concerts in the Bridgewater Hall and known especially for its Blue Peter Family Concerts. Its principal conductor is Yan Pascal Tortelier.

BBC Concert Orchestra founded in 1952 and based in London. Its repertoire ranges from classical works to popular songs and it makes frequent broadcasts on BBC Radio 2, Radio 3, and BBC Television. Barry Wordsworth became its principal conductor in 1989.

BBC Scottish Symphony Orchestra founded in 1935 and based in Glasgow. Its principal conductor is Osmo Vanska.

BBC National Orchestra of Wales based in Cardiff. Its musical director is Mark Wigglesworth.

Beach, Amy Marcy (1867–1944), born **Amy Cheney** US pianist and composer, also known as Mrs Henry Beach. She was one of the leading international composers of her day, influenced by Brahms, Debussy, and her US contemporaries writing in a romantic vein.

Works ORCHESTRAL *Gaelic Symphony* (1896, the first symphonic work by an American woman); *Christ in the Universe* for chorus and orchestra (1931); piano concerto.

CHAMBER string quartet, piano trio.

OTHER Mass in E; numerous songs.

beak flute, German **Schnabelflöte** alternative name for the ➔ **recorder**, a musical instrument.

Beamish, Sally (1956–   ) English composer and viola player. She studied at the Royal Northern College of Music and with Lennox Berkeley. She played viola in various London ensembles. In 1989 she became resident in Scotland, cofounding the Chamber Group of Scotland, after which she received a steady stream of commissions; she often writes for non-professional forces. Recent works include a cello concerto (1997) and *The Flight of the Eagle*, a children's introduction to the woodwind instruments of the orchestra.

Works ORCHESTRAL Symphony No. 1 (1992); *Tam Lin*, oboe concerto (1992); Concerto Grosso for strings (1993); viola concerto (1995); cello concerto (1997); Symphony No. 2 (1998).

MUSIC THEATRE *Ease* (1993); *Monster*, a 'psychodrama' produced in collaboration with writer Janice Galloway.

CHAMBER *The Caledonian Road* for chamber orchestra (1998) and other chamber music.

OTHER *Magnificat* for soprano, mezzo, and ensemble (1992).

Bearbeitung (German 'arrangement') in music, an arrangement of a piece, particularly the adaptation of a work for a different performing medium.

'Bear, The' nickname (*L'Ours*) of the first of Haydn's 'Paris' symphonies, no. 82 in C, composed in 1786.

It is also the title of an opera by William Walton (libretto by P Dehn and the composer, based on Chekhov), first produced at Aldeburgh, England, on 3 June 1967. The story tells how Widow Popova falls for her husband's creditor.

beat in music, a pulsation giving the tempo, for example a conductor's beat, or a unit of tempo, as in four beats to the bar. 'Beat music' is a general term for popular music having a strong and unvarying beat.

beat frequency in musical acoustics, fluctuation produced when two notes of nearly equal pitch or frequency are heard together. Beats result from the interference between the sound waves of the notes. The frequency of the beats equals the difference in frequency of the notes.

Musicians use the effect when tuning their instruments. A similar effect can occur in electrical circuits when two alternating currents are present, producing regular variations in the overall current.

Béatitudes, Les oratorio by César Franck for solo voices, chorus, and orchestra (words from the Bible), composed 1869–79 and first performed privately by Franck's pupils at his house on 20 February 1879 (piano accompaniment), and in public after his death, in Dijon, France, on 15 June 1891.

Beatrice di Tenda opera by Bellini (libretto by F Romani), first produced at the Teatro La Fenice, Venice, Italy, on 16 March 1833. The eponymous Beatrice is married to the greedy Duke Filippo but loves Orombello. She is executed on account of infidelity and treason by the Duke, who loves only the power acquired through her lands and her lady-in-waiting, Agnese.

Béatrice et Bénédict, Beatrice and Benedick opera by Hector Berlioz (libretto by composer, based on Shakespeare's *Much Ado about Nothing*), first produced in Baden-Baden, Germany, on 9 August 1862.

Beatrix Cenci opera in two acts by Ginastera (libretto by W Shand and A Girri after Shelley's *The Cenci*, 1819, and Stendhal's *Chroniques Italiennes*, 1837), first produced in Washington, DC, on 10 September 1971. The plot recounts how Beatrix kills her incestuous father and is herself executed.

beats in acoustics, the clashing of soundwaves of slightly different frequencies produced, for example, by two piano strings for the same note not perfectly in tune with each other, or certain organ stops using two pipes for each note purposely kept slightly out of tune to produce that wavering effect. Sensitive ears perceive beats as slight periodical swellings of the tone on sustained notes, and piano tuners rely on beats to tell them whether the strings of any one note are in tune or not.

Beaulieu, Eustorg de (c. 1500–1552) French poet and musician. He wrote a few *chansons*, but is better known for his verse, including a collection of early Protestant song texts.

Beaumarchais, Pierre Augustin Caron de (1732–1799) French author and musician. He sang and played the flute and harp, teaching the latter to the daughters of Louis XV. His great trilogy of pre-revolutionary plays is perfectly structured for musical adaptation. *Le Barbier de Séville* (1775) was set by Giovanni Paisiello in 1782 and performed all over Europe before Rossini's version of 1816. *La Folle Journée, ou Le Mariage de Figaro* (1784) had socially significant

implications that are still present in Mozart's setting (1786). *La Mère coupable* (1792) forms the basis of John Corigliano's *The Ghosts of Versailles*, successfully performed at the New York Metropolitan Opera in 1991 and featuring Beaumarchais himself as a kindly spirit who attempts to change history by writing a play that would save Marie Antoinette from the guillotine.

bebung (German 'trembling') musical vibrato achieved on the ➤ clavichord by a fluctuation of key pressure impinging on the metal tangent pressing on the string.

Bechstein, (Friedrich Wilhelm) Carl (1826–1900) German piano maker. He founded his own firm in 1856, after having worked as an employee of several other companies. It expanded rapidly, taking advantage of new technological developments, some of which were invented by ➤ Steinway. The company was bankrupt in 1993, but was saved by the intervention of the German government. Bechstein pianos are noted for their smooth but not particularly brilliant tone.

Beck, Conrad (1901–1989) Swiss composer. After studying engineering, he became a student at the Zürich Conservatory under Volkmar Andreae and others; later he studied in Berlin, Germany, and Paris, France, where he lived 1923–32 and was closely in touch with Albert Roussel and Arthur Honegger. He was awarded important prizes for composition in 1954, 1956, and 1964.

Works OPERA *La Grande Ourse* (1936).

THEATRE incidental music for Goethe's *Pandora* (1945) and other plays.

ORATORIOS *Angelus Silesius*, *Der Tod zu Basel*.

VOCAL Requiem; *Der Tod des Oedipus* for chorus and orchestra (1928); *Lyric Cantata* (Rilke) for female voices and orchestra; chamber cantata (sonnets by Louise Labé).

ORCHESTRAL five symphonies (1925–30), *Sinfonietta*, *Innominata*, and *Ostinato* for orchestra; concerto for string quartet and orchestra; concerto, concertino, and rhapsody for piano and orchestra; cello concerto.

CHAMBER *Konzertmusik* for oboe and strings; five string quartets (1922–52).

Beck, Franz (1734–1809) German violinist and composer. He was a member of the ➤ Mannheim School of Symphonists and a pupil of Johann Stamitz. He is said to have fled from Mannheim as the result of a duel; he went to Italy and later settled in France.

Works OPERA *La Belle Jardinière* (Bordeaux, 1767), *Pandore* (Paris, 1789).

OTHER about 30 symphonies; *Stabat Mater*; keyboard music.

Becker, John (1886–1961) US composer. After studying at the Cincinnati Conservatory, he taught at Notre Dame 1917–27. From 1930 he was associated with Carl Ruggles, Wallingford Riegger, Henry Cowell, and other avant-garde US composers. His series of *Soundscapes* create novel effects of instrumentation, while his theatre pieces anticipate later mixed-media works.

Works STAGE PIECES *A Marriage with Space* (1935), *Nostalgic Songs of Earth* (1938), *Rain Down Death* (1939), *When the Willow Nods* (1940), *Faust: a Television Opera* (1951).

ORCHESTRAL seven symphonies (1912–54); two piano concertos and concertos for viola (1937) and violin (1948); *Moments from the Passion* (1945).

OTHER film music and songs.

Bedford, David (1937–) English composer, teacher, and one-time member of the pop group The Whole World. He studied at the Royal Academy of Music in London with Lennox Berkeley and in Venice, Italy, with Luigi Nono.

Works OPERA school operas *The Rime of the Ancient Mariner* (1976) and *The Ragnarok* (1983); *The Camlann Game* (1987), *The Return of Odysseus* (1988), *Anna* (1993).

ORCHESTRAL symphony for twelve players, *Sun Paints Rainbows on the Vast Waves* (1982), *Seascapes* (1986), *The Transfiguration* (1988), *Frameworks* (1990), *Plymouth Town* (1992).

VOCAL *Star Clusters, Nebulae and Places in Devon* for chorus and brass (1971); *I am Going Home with Thee* for six women's voices and strings (1993).

OTHER *Toccata for Tristan* for brass (1989); *Allison's Concerto* for trumpet and strings (1993); many pieces for instrumental ensemble and voices and instruments.

Bedyngham, John (died c.1460) English composer. He wrote Masses, motets, and chansons, possibly including *O rosa bella*, often ascribed to John Dunstable. His music was widely known in continental Europe; one of his two Mass cycles is derived from a ballade by Gilles ➔ **Binchois.**

Beecham, Thomas (1879–1961) English conductor and impresario. He established the Royal Philharmonic Orchestra in 1946 and fostered the works of composers such as Delius, Sibelius, and Richard Strauss. He was knighted and succeeded to the baronetcy in 1916.

Beeson, Jack (Hamilton) (1921–) US composer. He studied with Howard Hanson at Rochester and with Béla Bartók in New York in 1945, and was professor at Columbia University 1965–88.

Works OPERA *Jonah* (1950), *Hello Out There* (1954), *The Sweet Bye and Bye* (1957), *Lizzie Bor-*

den (1965), *Dr Heidegger's Fountain of Youth* (after Hawthorne; 1978).

ORCHESTRAL symphony in A (1959), *Transformations* for orchestra (1959).

CHAMBER five piano sonatas.

OTHER TV opera *My Heart's in the Highlands* (after Sorayan; 1970).

'Bee's Wedding, The' the English nickname of Mendelssohn's *Song without Words* in C major Op. 67 no. 4, the German being *Spinnerlied* 'spinning-song'.

Beethoven, Ludwig van (1770–1827) German composer. His mastery of musical expression in every type of music made him the dominant influence on 19th-century music. Beethoven's repertoire includes concert overtures; the opera *Fidelio* (1805, revised 1806 and 1814); five piano concertos and one for violin; 32 piano sonatas, including the *Moonlight* (1801) and *Appassionata* (1804–05); 17 string quartets; the Mass in D (*Missa solemnis*) (1819–22); and nine symphonies, as well as many youthful works. He usually played his own piano pieces and conducted his orchestral works until he became deaf in 1801; nevertheless he continued to compose.

Beethoven was born in Bonn. His family were musicians in the service of the Elector of Cologne. He became deputy organist at the court of the Elector of Cologne when he was 13; later he studied under Joseph Haydn, who influenced his early work. From 1808 he received a small allowance from aristocratic patrons.

Beethoven's career spanned the change from Classicism to Romanticism, and he himself contributed to this change through his expansion of classical form, harmony, and thematic development. He was aware of the problems his music created for listeners and performers alike (part of the slow movement of the Choral Symphony had to be cut at its premiere), but although audiences of the day found his visionary late music difficult, Beethoven's reputation was well established throughout Europe. His best-known symphonies are the Third (*Eroica*) (1803), originally intended to be dedicated to Napoleon, with whom Beethoven became disillusioned, the Fifth (1807–08), the Sixth (*Pastoral*) (1808), and the Ninth (*Choral*) (1817–24), which includes the passage from Friedrich Schiller's 'Ode to Joy' chosen as the anthem of Europe.

Beethoven became a pupil of Christian Gottlob Neefe in 1781. In 1783 he was a harpsichordist in the court orchestra, and in the same year published three piano sonatas. He was second organist at court in 1784, and in 1789 also a viola player. A visit to Vienna in 1787 to study with Wolfgang Amadeus Mozart was cut short after only a few weeks as his mother was dying. He continued as a court musician in Bonn, and met Count Waldstein in 1788. In 1792 he returned to Vienna to be a pupil of Joseph Haydn, whom he had met in Bonn. He remained in Vienna for the rest of his life. Beethoven found Haydn too easy going, and instead took lessons from Johann Baptist Schenk, Johann Albrechtsberger, and Antonio Salieri (although his early music is full of Haydn's influence). In 1795 he published his Op. 1, three piano trios, and made his first public appearance in Vienna as a pianist and composer. He lived by playing and teaching, and later increasingly by the publication of his works.

The set of six string quartets Op. 18 (1798–1800), though classical in form, are strongly expressive in content: according to Beethoven the slow movement of the first work portrays the tomb scene in *Romeo and Juliet*. The First Symphony, written in 1800, was easily understood as it was similar to recent works by Haydn and Mozart. The deafness that had threatened from about 1795 increased, and his despair gave rise to the suicidal 'Heiligenstadt Testament' in 1802; Beethoven's musical response was the radiant and untroubled Second Symphony of 1802. His Third Symphony (*Eroica*) was dedicated to Napoleon, but Beethoven changed the dedication when Napoleon proclaimed himself Emperor. The symphony was important in moving music towards the Romantic style that developed later in the century; symphonic form was also hugely extended.

Beethoven conducted his only opera, *Fidelio*, in 1805. He faced many difficulties in reaching a final version, which is typical of his painstaking working methods. Beethoven's compositional process is summed up in *Fidelio*'s development from old-fashioned *Singspiel* in the first scene to a convincing drama.

He refused to accept regular employment under the old system of patronage, but received support from the aristocracy: in 1808, for instance, Archduke Rudolph, Prince Kinsky, and Prince Lobkowitz agreed to pay him an unconditional annuity; the Fifth symphony dates from the same year, and seems to proclaim the individual's sense of worth and identity. By 1806 he was forced to abandon public performance altogether. More time was now available for composition: there followed the fourth piano concerto, the Rasumovsky quartets, the violin concerto, Sixth (*Pastoral*), Seventh, and Eighth symphonies and the *Emperor* concerto. By turns lyrical, expansive, serene, and dynamic, the music of this middle period gained Beethoven further public recognition as the leading composer of the day.

In 1815, after his brother's death, he temporarily became guardian to his nephew Karl, a task he took very seriously and which caused him constant worry. Composition of the last five great piano works (four sonatas and the Diabelli Varia-

tions) started in 1818, with the *Hammerklavier* sonata being the first. These works pushed piano technique to new limits. By 1819 Beethoven was totally deaf, and communication with him was possible only in writing. He had begun work on the Choral Symphony in 1817 and this was followed by the Missa solemnis in 1819–22 and the last five quartets in 1822–26. In 1826 he caught an infection from which he never recovered, and died the following year. The cause of his death is still uncertain, although analyses of his hair in 2001 suggested that it was due to lead poisoning.

Works STAGE opera, *Fidelio* (1805, revised 1806 and 1814), incidental music for *Egmont* (Johann Wolfgang von Goethe, 1810), *The Creatures of Prometheus*, overture, introduction and 16 nos for a ballet produced at the Burgtheater, Vienna, 1801.

CHORAL WITH ORCHESTRA Mass in C, Op. 86 (1807), *Choral Fantasia*, for piano, chorus, and orchestra, Op. 80 (1808), Mass in D (*Missa solemnis*), Op. 123 (1819–22).

SYMPHONIES no. 1 in C, Op. 21 (1800), no. 2 in D, Op. 36 (1802), no. 3 in E♭ (*Eroica*), Op. 55 (1804), no. 4 in B♭, Op. 60 (1806), no. 5 in C minor, Op. 67 (1807–08), no. 6 in F (*Pastoral*), Op. 68 (1808), no. 7 in A, Op. 92 (1812), no. 8 in F, Op. 93 (1812), no. 9 in D minor (*Choral*), Op. 125 (1817–24).

CONCERTOS piano, no. 1 in C, Op. 15 (1795), no. 2 in B♭, Op. 19 (before 1793, revised 1794–95, 1798), no. 3 in C minor, Op. 37 (?1800), no. 4 in G, Op. 58 (1806), no. 5 in E♭ (*Emperor*), Op. 73 (1809); violin concerto, Op. 61 (1806), triple concerto for piano, violin, and cello, Op. 56 (1804).

OVERTURES *Leonora* 1–3 (1805, 1806), *Coriolan*, Op. 62 (1807).

CHAMBER Trio in B♭ for clarinet, cello, and piano, Op. 11 (1797); Variations for piano trio on *Ich bin der Schneider Kakadu*, Op. 121a (1798); Serenade for flute, violin, and viola in D, Op. 25 (1800); Septet in E♭, Op. 20 (1800); two quintets, for piano and wind in E♭ (1796), for strings in C, Op. 29 (1801); 17 string quartets, Op. 18 nos. 1–6, in F, G, D, C minor, A, and B♭ (1798–1800), Op. 59 nos. 1–3 (*Rasumovsky*) in F, E minor, and C (1806), Op. 74 in E♭ (*Harp*) (1809), Op. 95 in F minor (1810), Op. 127 in E♭ (1825), Op. 130 in B♭ (1826; present rondo finale replaces original *Grosse Fuge*, Op. 133), Op. 131 in C♯ minor (1826), Op. 132 in A minor (1825), Op. 135 in F (1826); five string trios (1794–98); six piano trios, Op. 1 nos. 1–3 (1794), Op. 70 nos. 1 and 2, in D (*Ghost*), and E♭ (1808), Op. 97 in B♭ (*Archduke*) (1811); ten violin sonatas (1798–1812); five cello sonatas (1796–1815).

PIANO 32 sonatas, Op. 2 nos. 1–3, in F minor, A, and C (1795), Op. 7 in E♭ (1796), Op. 10 nos. 1–3, in C minor, F, and D (1798), Op. 13 in C minor (*Pathétique*) (1799), Op. 14 nos. 1 and 2 in E and G (1799), Op. 22 in B♭ (1800), Op. 26 in A♭

(1801), Op. 27 nos. 1 and 2, in E♭ and C♯ minor (*Moonlight*) (1801), Op. 28 in D (*Pastoral*) (1801), Op. 31 nos. 1–3, in G, D minor, and E♭ (1802), Op. 49 nos. 1 and 2, in G minor and G (1802), Op. 53 in C (*Waldstein*) (1804), Op. 54 in F (1804), Op. 57 in F minor (*Appassionata*) (1804–05), Op. 78 in F♯ (1809), Op. 79 in G (1809), Op. 81a in E♭ (*Les Adieux*) (1801), Op. 90 in E minor (1814), Op. 101 in A (1816), Op. 106 in B♭ (*Hammerklavier*) (1818), Op. 109 in E (1820), Op. 110 in A♭ (1821), Op. 111 in C minor (1822); 15 Variations and Fugue on a theme from Prometheus (*Eroica Variations*) in E♭ (1802); 33 *Variations on a Waltz by Diabelli*, Op. 120 (1819–23).

SOLO VOICE Scena and aria *Ah! Perfido!* for soprano and orchestra (1796), *Adelaide* for tenor and piano (1795–96), *An die ferne Geliebte* for tenor and piano (1816).

Beffroy de Reigny, Louis Abel (1757–1811) French playwright and composer, known as 'Cousin Jacques'. Under this name he wrote satirical operettas popular during the Revolution, including *Nicodème dans la lune*, *Nicodème aux enfers*, and *La Petite Nanette*.

Beggar's Opera, The ballad opera, first produced at the Theatre in Lincoln's Inn Fields, London, England, on 29 January 1728, consisting of a play by John Gay interspersed with songs. The music, popular tunes of the day but for the most part not folksongs, was arranged by John Christopher Pepusch, who also composed the overture. There have been several modern realizations, including one by Benjamin Britten (1948).

Beginning of a Romance, The , Czech ***Počátek románu*** opera in one act by Leoš Janáček (libretto by J Tichý, after a story by G Preissová), composed in 1891 and first produced in Brno (Czech Republic) on 10 February 1894. The story concerns Tonek and the village beauty, Poluška.

Beglarian, Grant (1927–2002) Georgian-born US composer. He was influenced by Aaron Copland and Ross Lee Finney. He emigrated to the USA in 1947 and studied with Finney at the University of Michigan. He taught at the University of Southern California, Los Angeles, 1969–82.

Works ORCHESTRAL string quartet (1948), *Symphony in Two Movements* (1950), *Divertimento* for orchestra (1957), *Diversions* for viola, cello, and orchestra (1972), *To Manitou* for soprano and orchestra (1976), *Partita for Orchestra* (1986).

CHAMBER woodwind quintet (1966), *Sinfonia* for strings (1974).

Begleitungsmusik work by Schoenberg. See ➤ *Accompaniment to a Film Scene*.

Behrman, David (1937–   ) Austrian-born US composer of electronic music. He studied at Harvard and with Henri Pousseur and Karlheinz Stockhausen in Europe. He worked with John Cage and David Tudor in the 1970s, notably for the Merce Cunningham Dance Company.

Works *Pools of Phase-Locked Loops* (1972); *Cloud Music* (1979); *Indoor Geyser* (1981); *Orchestral Construction Set* (1984); *Inter-Species Smalltalk* (1984); *Installation for La Villett* (1985); many albums of experimental music for CBS.

Being Beauteous cantata by Hans Werner Henze for soprano, harp, and four cellos (text from Rimbaud), first performed in Berlin, Germany, on 12 April 1964.

Beinum, Eduard van (1901–1959) Dutch conductor. He was best known for his performances of Beethoven and was a champion of contemporary Dutch music. He toured Europe and America, and in 1956 became conductor of the Los Angeles Philharmonic Orchestra, but resigned and returned to Europe, where he died.

He studied with his brother and composition with Sem Dresden. After a post in Haarlem in 1926, he became second conductor of the Concertgebouw Orchestra of Amsterdam 1931–38, an associate to Willem Mengelberg in 1938, and his successor in 1945.

beklemmt (German 'oppressed') a term used by Beethoven in the Cavatina of the string quartet Op. 130.

bel canto (Italian 'beautiful song') in music, an 18th-century Italian style of singing with emphasis on perfect technique and beautiful tone. The style reached its peak in the operas of Gioacchino ➤ Rossini, Gaetano ➤ Donizetti, and Vincenzo ➤ Bellini.

Beldemandis, Prosdocimus de (c. 1375–1428) Italian music scholar. He wrote treatises on music, published between 1404 and 1413, and was professor of mathematics and astronomy at Padua in 1422.

Belfagor opera by Ottorino Respighi (libretto by C Guastalla, based on a comedy by E L Morselli), first produced at La Scala, Milan, on 26 April 1923. The plot tells how Candida is made to marry Belfagor, the Devil in disguise.

Belisario opera by Donizetti (libretto by S Cammarano), first produced at the Teatro La Fenice, Venice, Italy, on 4 February 1836. The story concerns the Roman general Belisario who is blinded and exiled after being accused of his son's murder.

bell musical instrument, made in many sizes, comprising a suspended resonating vessel swung by a handle or from a pivoted frame to make contact with a beater which hangs inside the bell.

Church bells are among the most massive structures to be cast in bronze in one piece; from high up in a steeple they can be heard for many miles. Their shape, a flared bowl with a thickened rim, is engineered to produce a clangorous mixture of tones. Miniature **handbells** are tuned to resonate harmoniously. Orchestral **tubular bells**, of brass or steel, are tuned to a chromatic scale of pitches and are played by striking with a wooden mallet. A set of steeple bells played from a keyboard is called a **carillon**.

The world's largest bell is the 'Tsar Kolokol' or 'King of Bells', cast in 1734; it weighs 220 tonnes, and stands on the ground at the Kremlin, Moscow, Russia, where it fell when being hung. The 'Peace Bell' at the United Nations headquarters, New York, USA, was cast in 1952 from coins presented by 64 countries.

bell in a wind instrument, the flat disc or flare at the opposite end of the tube from the mouthpiece.

In woodwind instruments, it acts as a shaped baffle controlling the expanding pressure wave emitted from the bell when all the finger holes are closed (at higher pitches pressure escapes from the highest open hole). In brass instruments, it also acts as a directional radiator, the thin metal vibrating with the variation between the escaping sound and atmospheric pressure.

'Bell Anthem' the name once given to Purcell's anthem *Rejoice in the Lord always*, composed about 1682–85. The instrumental introduction contains descending scales resembling the ringing of church bells.

Belle Hélène, La, The Fair Helen operetta by Jacques Offenbach (libretto by H Meilhac and L Halévy), first produced at the Théâtre des Variétés, Paris, France, on 17 December 1864. It is a satirical version of the myth.

Bellérophon opera by Jean-Baptiste Lully (libretto by T Corneille with B de Fontenelle and Boileau), first produced at the Paris Opéra, France, on 31 January 1679. The story concerns Bellérophon who is threatened by the monster Chimaera after he rejects the wife of King Proteus.

Belli, Girolamo (1552–c.1620) Italian composer. After studying with Luzzasco Luzzaschi, he was a singer at the Gonzaga court at Mantua, and was in Rome in 1582. He published several books of madrigals, of which six survive, as well as psalms, *Sacrae Cantiones*, and other church music including Masses.

Bellini, Vincenzo (1801–1835) Italian composer of operas. He worked with the tenor Giovanni Battista Rubini (1794–1854) to develop lyrical melodic lines, and his operas contain superbly crafted dramatic tension often with poten-

tially tragic themes, as in *La sonnambula/The Sleepwalker* and *Norma* (both 1831). In *I puritani/The Puritans* (1835), his last work, he discovered a new boldness and vigour of orchestral effect.

His popularity after his death was enormous, but his operas later fell into neglect. Since World War II, however, singers including Maria Callas, Joan Sutherland, and Montserrat Caballé, have helped to restore their popularity.

Bellini was born in Catania, Sicily. A Sicilian nobleman helped his father, an organist, to send him to study with Niccolò Zingarelli at the Naples Conservatory, where he met Gaetano Donizetti and Saverio Mercadante. His first opera, *Adelson e Salvini*, was produced in 1825, while he was still a student; it attracted the attention of Domenico Barbaia, who commissioned him to write a second, *Bianca e Gernando*, produced at the Teatro San Carlo in 1826. Its success induced Barbaia to ask for another opera (*Il pirata/The Pirate*) for La Scala, Milan. It was produced there in 1827 with Giovanni Battista Rubini in the cast. It was also successfully performed in Paris, and three other operas followed, at Milan, Parma, and Venice, before Bellini attained full maturity in *La sonnambula/The Sleepwalker*, brought out at Milan in 1831, with Maria Malibran as the heroine. *Norma* followed in December of the same year, with Giuditta Pasta in the title role. This opera marks Bellini's style at its best, with its long and lyrical melodic line and superbly crafted dramatic tension.

In 1833 Bellini went to London and Paris, where Gioacchino Antonio Rossini advised him to write a work for the Théâtre Italien. This was *I puritani/The Puritans*, produced there in 1835, with Giulia Grisi, Rubini, Antonio Tamburini, and Luigi Lablache in the cast; it was brought to London the same year for Grisi's benefit performance. Bellini went to stay with an English friend at Puteaux, at whose house he was taken ill and died.

Works OPERA *Adelson e Salvini* (1825), *Bianca e Gernando* (1826), *Il pirata/The Pirate* (1827), *La straniera/The Stranger* (1829), *Zaira* (1829), *I Capuleti e i Montecchi/The Capulets and the Montagues* (1830, based on Shakespeare's sources for *Romeo and Juliet*), *La sonnambula/The Sleepwalker* (1831), *Norma* (1831), *Beatrice di Tenda* (1833), *I puritani/The Puritans* (1835).

OTHER church music; songs; symphonies.

bell ringing or **campanology** the art of ringing church bells individually or in sequence by rhythmically drawing on a rope fastened to a wheel rotating the bell, so that it falls back and strikes in time. **Change ringing** is an English art, dating from the 17th century, of ringing a patterned sequence of permutations of between five and twelve church bells, using one player to each bell. See also ➤ **carillon**.

'Bells of Zlonice, The' symphony no. 1 in C minor by Antonín Dvořák; it was composed in 1865 as Op. 3 but lost until 1923. It was first performed in Prague (now the Czech Republic), on 4 October 1936.

Bells, The poem for orchestra, chorus, and soloists by Rachmaninov, Op. 35 (text by Edgar Allan Poe, translation by K Balmont); it was composed in 1913 and first performed in St Petersburg, Russia, on 30 November 1913. The work was revived in 1936 and performed in Sheffield, England, on 21 October 1936, conducted by Henry Wood.

belly in music, the surface of string instruments, which lies directly beneath the strings; also sometimes the soundboard of the piano.

Belshazzar oratorio by Handel (words by Charles Jennens), first produced at the King's Theatre, Haymarket, London, England, on 27 March 1745.

Belshazzar's Feast cantata by William Walton (words from the Bible arranged by Osbert Sitwell), first produced at the Leeds Festival, England, on 8 October 1931.

It is also the title of incidental music by Sibelius for a play by H Procopé, first performed in Helsinki, Finland, on 7 November 1906. The orchestral Suite Op. 51 in four movements was first performed in Helsinki on 25 September 1907.

bémol (French 'flat') in music, the sign for ➤ **flat**.

Benedicite work by Vaughan Williams for soprano, chorus, and orchestra; it was composed in 1929 and first performed in Dorking, England, on 2 May 1930, conducted by Vaughan Williams.

Benedict, Julius (1804–1885) German-born English conductor and composer. In 1835 he went to Paris and to London, where he remained for the rest of his life. He conducted a great deal in London, both opera and concerts.

He was a pupil of Johann Hummel and Carl Maria von Weber, and met Beethoven in Vienna in 1823, when he was appointed conductor at the Kärntnertortheater. Next he went to Naples, where he produced his first Italian opera in 1829. He was conductor of the Norwich Festival 1845–78 and of the Liverpool Philharmonic Society 1876–80.

Works OPERA *Giacinta ed Ernesto*, *I portoghesi in Goa* (1830), *Un anno ed un giorno* (1836), *The Gypsy's Warning*, *The Brides of Venice* (1844), *The Crusaders*, *The Lily of Killarney* (1862), *The Bride of Song* (1864).

OTHER two symphonies; two piano concertos; five cantatas; and other pieces.

Benevoli, Orazio (1605–1672) Italian composer. He held appointments at the churches of San Luigi de' Francesi and Santa Maria Maggiore in Rome, the former with an interruption 1644–46, when he was at the Austrian court in Vienna. In 1646 he became maestro di cappella at the Vatican.

Works Masses, motets, and other church music, much of it for several choirs in a large number of parts. The celebrated 53-part *Missa salisburgensis* formerly attributed to him, is probably by Biber.

Beni Mora Oriental Suite in E minor, Op. 29 no. 1 for orchestra by Gustav Holst. It was composed in 1910 after a visit to Algeria: the last of three movements is titled 'In the Street of the Ouled Naïls'. The work was first performed in London, England, on 1 May 1912, conducted by Holst.

Benjamin, Arthur (1893–1960) Australian pianist and composer. The influence of Latin American dance rhythms was important throughout his life. He was educated at Brisbane and studied at the Royal College of Music in London, England, where he later became professor. After fighting in World War I he returned to Australia to teach piano at the Sydney Conservatory 1919–20, but having developed as a composer, settled in London. He taught composition at the Royal College of Music from 1925, where Benjamin Britten was one of his pupils. From 1930 to 1936 he lived in Vancouver, Canada.

Works OPERA *The Devil Take Her* (1931), *Prima Donna* (1933), *A Tale of Two Cities* (after Dickens; 1950), *Tartuffe* (produced 1964).

ORCHESTRAL symphonic suite *Light Music* and *Overture to an Italian Comedy* for orchestra; *Romantic Fantasy* for violin, viola and orchestra; violin concerto (1932), concertino for piano and orchestra.

OTHER chamber music; songs; film music including *An Ideal Husband* (after Oscar Wilde).

Benjamin, George William John (1960–) English composer, conductor, and pianist. He was a pupil of Olivier ➤ **Messiaen**, and his colourful and sonorous works include *Ringed by the Flat Horizon* (1980), *A Mind of Winter* (1981), *At First Light* (1982), *Antara* (1985–7), and *Cascade* (1990).

He studied with Messiaen in Paris from 1974, at the Paris Conservatory in 1977, and with Alexander ➤ **Goehr** at Cambridge. At the 1983 Aldeburgh Festival he gave the first performance of Benjamin Britten's *Sonatina Romantica* (1940). Returning to France, he worked 1984–87 at the electronic music studios at the Institut de Recherche et de Co-ordination Acoustique / Musique (IRCAM).

Works ORCHESTRAL *Jubilation* for orchestra and

groups of children (1985), *Antara* for orchestra with electronics, *Cascade, Helix* (1992), *Sudden Time* (1993).

CHAMBER *At First Light*, for chamber orchestra; violin sonata (1977), octet (1978), duo for cello and piano (1980), *Meditations on Haydn's Name*, for piano (1982).

VOCAL *A Mind of Winter*, for soprano and ensemble; *Upon Silence* for mezzo and five viols (1990).

Bennett, Richard Rodney (1936–   ) English composer of jazz, film music, symphonies, and operas. His film scores for *Far from the Madding Crowd* (1967), *Nicholas and Alexandra* (1971), and *Murder on the Orient Express* (1974) all received Academy Award nominations. His operas include *The Mines of Sulphur* (1963) and *Victory* (1970).

He studied at the Royal Academy of Music in London, England, and in Paris, France, with Pierre ➤ Boulez. Influenced by Béla ➤ Bartók, he has used serial techniques but also writes in a lighter vein.

Works OPERA *The Ledge* (1961), *The Mines of Sulphur*, *A Penny for a Song* (1966), *Victory* (after Conrad).

BALLET *Isadora* (1981).

ORCHESTRAL three symphonies (1965, 1967, 1987); *Anniversaries* for orchestra (1982); Sinfonietta (1984); *Dream Dancing* (1986), *Celebration* (1992), *Aubade*; piano concerto (1968), oboe concerto; concertos for harpsichord (1980) and clarinet (1987).

CHAMBER four string quartets (1952–64); *Calendar* for chamber ensemble; *Memento* for flute and strings (1983).

OTHER *Love Songs* for tenor and orchestra (texts by E E Cummings) (1985); concertos for saxophone (for Stan Getz, 1990) and for trumpet and wind band (1993); vocal music; film, radio, and television music.

Bennett, William Sterndale (1816–1875) English pianist and composer. He was a chorister at King's College, Cambridge, and a student at the Royal Academy of Music in London. He then went to Leipzig, Germany, where he made friends with Mendelssohn. Schumann dedicated his *Études symphoniques* for piano to him. He conducted the first English performance of Bach's *St Matthew Passion* in 1854. He was professor of music at Cambridge University 1856–75 and principal of the Royal Academy of Music 1866–75.

Works ORCHESTRAL six symphonies (1832–64); overtures *The Naiads* and *The Wood-Nymphs*; fantasy-overture on Moore's *Paradise and the Peri*; five piano concertos (1832–38).

OTHER cantata *The May Queen* (1858); incidental music to Sophocles' *Ajax* (1872); odes for the International Exhibition (Tennyson) and the Cam-

bridge Installation of a Chancellor (Kingsley); anthems; piano pieces; songs.

Benoît, Peter (Léonard Léopold) (1834–1901) Belgian composer. He was a pupil of François Fétis at the Brussels Conservatory. He became conductor at a Flemish theatre and was keenly interested in Flemish national music as distinct from that influenced by French composers. He travelled in Germany and visited Paris, but tended more and more towards an indigenous type of music. His first opera was produced in 1857.

Works OPERA French opera *Le Roi des aulnes* (on Goethe's 'Erl-King'; 1859); Flemish operas *The Mountain Village, Isa, Pompeja*.

CHURCH MUSIC Te Deum, *Messe solennelle*, Requiem.

ORATORIOS *Lucifer* (1865), *The Scheldt* (1868).

CANTATAS *Petite Cantate de Noël* and many Flemish cantatas.

OTHER incidental music to Flemish plays.

Bentzon, Nils Viggo (1919–2000) Danish composer. He studied piano with his mother and composition with Knud Christian Jeppesen (1892–1974).

Works OPERA four operas, including *Faust III* (after Goethe, Kafka, and Joyce; 1964).

ORCHESTRAL 15 symphonies (1942–80); eight piano concertos, four violin concertos.

CHAMBER much chamber music, including a chamber concerto for eleven instruments, chamber symphony, nine string quartets (1940–76), sonata for solo cello, eleven piano sonatas, *Propostae Novae* for two pianos.

VOCAL *Bonjour Max Ernst*, cantata for chorus and orchestra (1961), and other vocal music.

Benvenuto Cellini opera by Hector Berlioz (libretto by L de Wailly and A Barbier, based on Cellini's autobiography), first produced at the Paris Opéra, France, on 10 September 1838.

berceuse lullaby, usually in the form of an instrumental piece in moderately relaxed duple time (6/8). The most famous example is Chopin's *Berceuse* (1844).

Berceuse élégiaque piano piece by Ferruccio Busoni, composed in 1909 and added to the *Elegien* of 1907. The orchestral version of 1909 is subtitled *Des Mannes Wiegenlied am Sarge seine Mutter/The Man's Lullaby at his Mother's Coffin* – Busoni's mother died on 3 October 1909. The work was first performed under the baton of Mahler, at his last concert, in New York on 21 February 1911.

Berchem, Jachet de (c.1505–c.1565) Flemish composer, not to be confused with Jachet of Mantua. Probably organist at the ducal court at Ferrara in 1555, he wrote church music, madrigals for four and five voices, and French chansons. He is credited with being the first to compose a madrigal cycle; his *Capriccio* is a setting of stories from Ariosto's *Orlando furioso*.

Berenice opera by Handel (libretto by A Salvi), first produced at Covent Garden, London, England, on 18 May 1737. The complex plot concerns the love problems of the Egyptian queen Berenice before her marriage to Alexander; politics, jealousy, and anger are happily resolved in the end.

There is also an earlier opera on the same subject by Giacomo Perti (libretto by A Salvi), first produced at the Villa Pratolino near Florence, Italy, in September 1709.

Berenice, che fai? Italian cantata by Haydn for soprano and orchestra (text from Pietro Metastasio's *Antigono*), composed in May 1795.

Berezovsky, Maksim Sosnovich (1745–1777) Ukrainian composer. He was a pupil at the academy in Kiev, later a singer in the service of the court. In 1765 he went to Italy to study under Giovanni Martini. On his return to the Ukraine, unable to secure an appointment, he finally committed suicide. His most important contribution was to church music; he also wrote an opera, *Demofoonte* (1773), and other works.

Berg, Alban (1885–1935) Austrian composer. He studied under Arnold Schoenberg and developed a personal 12-tone idiom of great emotional and stylistic versatility. His relatively small output includes two operas – *Wozzeck* (1914–20), a grim story of working-class life, and the unfinished *Lulu* (1929–35) – and chamber music incorporating coded references to friends and family.

His music is emotionally expressive, and sometimes anguished, but it can also be lyrical, as in the violin concerto (1935).

Berg was self-taught from the age of 15, and a pupil of Arnold ➤ Schoenberg in 1904–10. Schoenberg's influence on him was profound, and may be measured as Berg moved from the extended tonality of his early works to atonality and, later, serialism. He uses serial technique differently to other composers in that he does not avoid tonal references (as, for example, in the violin concerto). As a result, he is the most accessible member of the Second Viennese School. In 1911 he married Helene Nahowski. His first major work, the string quartet Op. 3, dates from the same year.

His music was known only to a small circle until the 1925 production of *Wozzeck*. The Chamber Concerto and Lyric Suite, written in 1923–24, use complex formal patterns, numerical puzzles, and autobiographical references. He was a friend of Alma Mahler and the death of her daughter, Manon, inspired his last completed work, the violin concerto. Dedicated 'To the Memory of an Angel', Berg wrote the concerto as a Requiem for Manon, yet in its passionate lyricism, quoting the Bach chorale *Es ist Genug/It is Enough*, it is the composer's own last testament. His second opera, *Lulu*, was begun in 1929 but left unfinished after his death and not performed in the full, three-act version until 1979.

Works OPERA *Wozzeck* (after Georg Büchner; 1914–20, produced Berlin, 1925), *Lulu* (after Frank Wedekind; 1929–35, two acts produced Zürich, 1937, act 3 realized by F Cerha, first performance Paris, 1979).

SONGS AND VOICE WITH ORCHESTRA 70 early Lieder; *Seven Early Songs* for voice and piano (1905–08, orchestral version 1928); *Five Altenberglieder* for voice and orchestra (1912, first performance Rome, 1953); *Lulu-Symphonie* for soprano and orchestra (1934).

ORCHESTRAL *Three Pieces*, Op. 6 (1914–15, revised 1929); Chamber Concerto for piano, violin, and 13 wind instruments (1923–24; first performance Berlin, 1927); violin concerto (1935; first performance Barcelona, 1936).

CHAMBER piano sonata Op. 1 (1907–08); *Four Pieces* for clarinet and piano (1913); *Lyric Suite* for string quartet (1925–26); adagio from Chamber Concerto arranged for violin, clarinet, and piano (1935).

Berg, (Carl) Natanael (1879–1957) Swedish composer. He studied at the Stockholm Conservatory and in Paris and Vienna.

Works OPERA *Leila* (after Byron's *Giaour*; 1910), *Engelbrekt* (1928), *Judith* (after Hebbel's drama; 1935), *Birgitta*, *Genoveva* (1946).

ORCHESTRAL five symphonies; symphonic poems; violin concerto; piano concerto.

CHAMBER two string quartets, piano quintet.

bergamasca Italian dance from Bergamo at least as old as the 16th century; it was called 'bergomask' by Shakespeare.

Berger, Arthur (1912–2003) US composer. He studied with Walter Piston at Harvard University, with Pirro, Pierre Lalo, and Paul Valéry at the Sorbonne in Paris, and composition with Nadia Boulanger; later influences included Milton Babbitt and Anton Webern. He became music editor of the New York *Sun*.

Works CHAMBER *Slow Dance* for strings; serenade for chamber orchestra (1944); three pieces for string quartet; wind quartet; two movements for violin and cello.

OTHER ballet *Entertainment Piece* and other works for piano; *Words for Music Perhaps* (Yeats) and other songs.

Berger, Theodor (1905–1992) Austrian composer. He studied at the Vienna Academy, and was much influenced by his teachers, Korngold and Franz Schmidt.

Works ORCHESTRAL *Malincolia* for strings (1938);

Homerische Symphonie (1948); *La Parola* for orchestra (1955); *Symphonischer Triglyph* on themes by Schubert (1957); violin concerto (1963); *Divertimento* for chorus, wind, and percussion (1968).

CHAMBER two string quartets (1930–31).

Bergknappen, Die, The Miners one-act *Singspiel* by Umlauf (libretto by P Weidmann), first produced at the Burgtheater, Vienna, Austria on the opening of its career as a national German opera on 17 February 1778. The plot recounts how the old Walcher competes with the young Fritz for the affections of Sophie but yields after Fritz rescues him in a mine.

Berglund, Paavo (1929–) Finnish conductor. After an early career as a violinist, he co-founded the Helsinki Chamber Orchestra in 1953. He was principal conductor of the Helsinki Radio Symphony Orchestra from 1962 and the Helsinki Philharmonic Orchestra 1975–79. He has conducted the Bournemouth Symphony Orchestra from 1964 and was music director 1972–79; he is associated with the revival of Sibelius's early *Kullervo* Symphony. He has been principal guest conductor of the Scottish National Orchestra from 1981. Recordings include symphonies by Dmitri Shostakovich.

Bergonzi (lived 17th–18th centuries) Italian family of violin makers who worked in Cremona. **Carlo Bergonzi** (c.1683–1747) began to work independently about 1716 and created his best instruments in the 1730s, rivalling Guarnieri and Stradivari. His son was **Michelangelo Bergonzi** (1722–1758).

Bergsma, William (1921–1994) US composer. He studied at Stanford University and the Eastman School of Music under Howard Hanson and Bernard Rogers, and after winning many awards he became a teacher of composition at the Juilliard School, New York .

Works OPERA *The Wife of Martin Guerre* (1956).

BALLET *Paul Bunyan* (1938), *Gold and the Señor Commandante* (1941).

CHORAL choral symphony; choral works.

CHAMBER symphony for chamber orchestra; four string quartets (1942–70).

OTHER songs.

Berio, Luciano (1925–2003) Italian composer. His work, usually involving electronic sound, combines serial techniques with commedia dell'arte and antiphonal practices, as in *Alleluiah II* (1958) for five instrumental groups. His large output includes eleven *Sequenzas/Sequences* (1958–85) for various solo instruments or voice, *Sinfonia* (1968) for voices and orchestra, *Formazioni/Formations* (1987) for orchestra, and the opera *Un re in ascolto/A King Listens* (1984).

Although Berio's compositional techniques are severe, the effect is softened by wit and theatricality. He was one of the most active composers of electronic music and worked with Boulez at the Institut de Recherche et de Co-ordination Acoustique/Musique (IRCAM). He also used graphic notation, and many of his works leave the performer with a wide range of choices. He was particularly interested in exploring the possibilities of language as developed in musical performance.

Berio was born in Oneglia, Italy. After studying with Giorgio Ghedini in Milan and with Luigi Dallapiccola in the USA, he met members of the European avant-garde such as Karlheinz ➔ **Stockhausen**, Pierre ➔ **Boulez**, and Bruno ➔ **Maderna**. With Maderna he founded an electronic studio, the Studio di Fonologia Musicale, at Milan Radio in 1953–60. He lived in the USA from 1963 to 1972, teaching at the Juilliard School, New York, in 1965–72. He was married 1950–65 to the US soprano Cathy Berberian, who gave the first performances of many of his works.

Works DRAMATIC *Laborintus II* (Paris, 1970), *Recital I (for Cathy)* (Lisbon, 1972), *La vera storia/The True Story*, opera (Milan, 1982), *Un Re in ascolto*, opera (Salzburg, 1984).

ORCHESTRAL *Chemins 1–IV*, after *Sequenze/Sequences* for instruments (1965–75), Concerto for two pianos and orchestra (1973), *Points on the curve to find ...* for piano and 20 instruments (1974), *Concerto II (Echoing Curves)* for piano and ensemble (1988).

VOCAL *Chamber Music* (texts by James Joyce; 1953), *Circles* for female voice, harp, and two percussion (texts by e e cummings; 1960), *Epifanie* for female voice and orchestra (texts by Marcel Proust, James Joyce, Bertolt Brecht, and others; 1961), *Sinfonia* for eight solo voices and orchestra (1968), *Ora* (text after Virgil; 1971), *Cries of London*, for eight solo voices (1973–75), *11 Folk Songs* for mezzo and orchestra (1975), *Coro* for 40 voices and orchestra (1976).

CHAMBER AND INSTRUMENTAL the important series of *Sequenze* (I–XI) for solo instruments: flute, harp, voice, piano, trombone, viola, oboe, violin, clarinet, trumpet, and guitar (1958–85), *Wasserklavier/Waterpiano* for piano (1964), and a second string quartet (1986–90).

Berkeley, Lennox Randal Francis (1903–1989) English composer. His works for the voice include *The Hill of the Graces* (1975), verses from Spenser's *Faerie Queene* set for eight-part unaccompanied chorus; and his operas *Nelson* (1954) and *Ruth* (1956).

Berkeley was born in Oxford, where he studied at Merton College until 1926. He then went to Paris until 1933 as a pupil of Nadia Boulanger. Much of his work is distinguished by a French elegance and neatness, but he also developed a more powerful style, especially in his opera *Nelson*. Works of his were heard at the International Society for Contemporary Music festivals at Barcelona and London in 1936 and 1938, and at the Leeds and Worcester festivals 1937–38.

Works OPERA *Nelson, A Dinner Engagement, Ruth*.

BALLET *The Judgement of Paris* (1938).

INCIDENTAL MUSIC for Shakespeare's *The Tempest*, the film *Hotel Reserve*.

ORATORIO *Jonah* (1935).

CHURCH MUSIC psalm *Domini est terra* for chorus and orchestra; *Missa brevis*.

ORCHESTRAL four symphonies (1940–78); *Nocturne* and divertimento for orchestra; piano concerto (1947); violin concerto.

CHAMBER three string quartets (1935–70); two violin and piano sonatas; sonata and pieces for piano; *Polka* for two pianos.

Berkeley, Michael (1948–) English composer, son of Lennox Berkeley. He studied at the Royal Academy of Music, London, with his father, and with Richard Rodney Bennett. In 1982 his oratorio *Or Shall We Die?* was performed in London: it contains a vivid protest at the threat of nuclear war. He was composer in residence at the London College of Music 1987–88.

Works OPERA *Baa-baa Black Sheep* (after Kipling; 1993).

ORCHESTRAL *Meditations*, for strings (1976), oboe concerto (1977), symphonies *Uprising* (1980), *Gregorian Variations*, for orchestra (1982); cello concerto (1982).

CHAMBER *Elegy* for flute and strings (1993); *Fantasia Concertante*, for chamber orchestra; string trio (1978); violin sonata; string quartet (1981); clarinet quintet (1983).

VOCAL *The Wild Winds*, for soprano and chamber orchestra (1978), *At the Round Earth's Imagin'd Corners* (text by Donne) for soloists, chorus, and organ (1980).

Berlin, Irving (1888–1989), adopted name of **Israel Baline** Belorussian-born US songwriter. His songs include hits such as 'Alexander's Ragtime Band' (1911), 'Always' (1925), 'God Bless America' (1917, published 1939), and 'White Christmas' (1942), and the musicals *Top Hat* (1935), *Annie Get Your Gun* (1946), and *Call Me Madam* (1950). He also provided songs for films like *Blue Skies* (1946) and *Easter Parade* (1948). 'White Christmas' has been the most performed Christmas song in history, with more than 500 versions recorded.

Berlin grew up in New York and had his first song published in 1907. He began providing songs for vaudeville and revues and went on to own a theatre, the Music Box, where he appeared in his own revues in 1921 and 1923. Generally writing both lyrics and music, he was instrumental in the development of the popular song, taking it from jazz and ragtime to swing and romantic ballads.

Berlioz, (Louis) Hector (1803–1869) French Romantic composer. He is regarded as the founder of modern orchestration. Much of his music was inspired by drama and literature and has a theatrical quality. He wrote symphonic works, such as *Symphonie fantastique/Fantasy Symphony* (1830) and *Roméo et Juliette/Romeo and Juliet* (1839); dramatic cantatas including *La Damnation de Faust/The Damnation of Faust* (1846) and *L'Enfance du Christ/The Childhood of Christ* (1850–54); sacred music; and three operas: *Benvenuto Cellini* (1838), *Les Troyens/The Trojans* (1856–58), and *Béatrice et Bénédict/Beatrice and Benedict* (1860–62).

Berlioz studied music at the Paris Conservatory. He won the Prix de Rome in 1830, and spent two years in Italy. In 1833 he married Harriet Smithson, an Irish actress playing Shakespearean parts in Paris, but they separated in 1842. After some years of poverty and public neglect, he went to Germany in 1842, where he conducted his own works. He later visited Russia and England. In 1854 he married Marie Recio, a singer.

Berlioz was born at La Côte-Saint-André, Isère, France, the son of a doctor who taught him the flute, but wished him to study medicine. As a boy he also learnt the guitar and picked up theoretical knowledge from books. Sent to the École de Médecine in Paris in 1821, he found the studies so distasteful that he decided to give them up for music. His parents opposed this, but Jean Lesueur accepted him as a pupil in 1823, when he at once set to work on an opera and an oratorio. The following year he wrote a Mass, which was lost for many years and was given its first modern performance in 1993. He entered the Conservatory in 1826, but failed several times to gain the Prix de Rome, winning it at last with the cantata *La mort de Sardanapale/The Death of Sardanapale* (1830). In the meantime he had fallen in love with Harriet Smithson and expressed his feelings for her in the *Symphonie fantastique* (1830). On the point of going to Rome, he became engaged to the pianist, Marie Moke, who during his absence married Camille Pleyel.

He wrote much in Rome, notably the overtures *King Lear* and *Rob Roy*, and returned to Paris in 1832, this time meeting Harriet and marrying her in October 1833. To supplement his income he became a music critic, writing witty and brilliant dissections of the follies of Parisian musical life. His *Grande messe des morts/High Mass of the Dead*, commissioned by the French Government in 1836, was performed the following year at a memorial service for soldiers who had fallen in

Algeria. In 1838 the violinist Niccolò Paganini sent him 20,000 francs so that he could devote all his time to composition; the Paganini-inspired *Harold en Italie/Harold in Italy* had been written in 1834 and was followed by *Roméo et Juliette* and *Benvenuto Cellini*. He separated from Harriet in 1842 and started a liaison with Marie Recio. He travelled much with her during the next few years, and conducted in Germany, Vienna, Prague, Budapest, Russia, and London. His brilliant légende dramatique *La Damnation de Faust* was premiered in 1846 and the massive Te Deum in 1855, but Berlioz continued to suffer throughout his life from lack of public recognition, particularly in his own country. After Harriet's death he married Marie in 1854; meanwhile he had resumed his journalistic work. He composed his masterpiece, the vast opera *Les Troyens*, in the late 1850s. The practicalities of staging such a work in the Paris of his time were forgotten as he entered the world of Virgil's epic poem.

Berlioz completed his last opera, *Béatrice et Bénédict* in 1862, and Marie died the same year; he later abandoned composition. He suffered much ill health during the 1860s and was greatly depressed by the death of his son Louis in 1867. After another visit to Russia he had a bad fall at Nice, where he had gone for his health in 1868, and he grew gradually more infirm.

For many years Berlioz's reputation rested on his *Symphonie fantastique*. It was not until his operas and other large-scale works were widely performed in the 1960s, that his true genius was fully revealed. He wrote seven books, including *Traité de l'instrumentation/Treatise on Orchestration* (1844) and his endearing but not always reliable *Mémoires*.

Works OPERA *Benvenuto Cellini* (1838), *Les Troyens* (two parts, 1856–58) and *Béatrice et Bénédict* (after Shakespeare's *Much Ado about Nothing*, (1860–62).

ORCHESTRAL *Symphonie fantastique* (1830), *Harold en Italie* (with solo viola) (1834), *Roméo et Juliette* (with voices) (1839), and *Symphonie funèbre et triomphale/Funeral and Triumphant Symphony* (for military band, strings, and chorus) (1840), concert overtures *Carnaval Romain/Roman Carnival* (1844), *Le Corsaire/The Corsair* (1844).

CHORAL AND SONGS Mass (1824), *Grande messe des morts* (Requiem, 1837), *La Damnation de Faust* (1846), Te Deum (1849–50), and *L'Enfance du Christ* (1850–54); 6 smaller vocal works with orchestra or piano, including *La mort de Cléopâtre/The Death of Cleopatra* (1829) and *La mort d'Ophélie/The Death of Ophelia* (1847); 28 songs including the cycle *Nuits d'été/Summer Nights*.

Bermudo, Juan (c.1510–c.1565) Spanish friar and music theorist. He wrote three music treatises, published 1549–55, including the *Declaración* (1555), with the first organ music printed locally.

Bernard de Ventadour (lived late-12th century) Provençal ➔ **troubadour**, probably born at the château of Ventadour. His father is said to have been a soldier and his mother a kitchen maid. He is known to have attended the coronation of Henry II of England and Eleanor of Aquitaine in 1154. Some 40 of his poems remain, notable for their freshness and lack of artifice.

Bernardi, Steffano (c.1585–1636) Italian priest and composer. Chaplain at Verona Cathedral, he studied in Rome later and became maestro di cappella of the church of the Madonna dei Monti. In 1611 he became maestro di cappella at Verona Cathedral, and in 1622 went into the service of the Archduke Karl Josef, Bishop of Breslau, and soon afterwards to Salzburg Cathedral, which he helped to consecrate in 1628. He wrote a Te Deum for twelve choirs (now lost), and many Masses, motets, psalms, madrigals, and instrumental works. His *Salmi concertati* deploy voices in different groups, as in the music of Heinrich Schütz and Giovanni Gabrieli.

Berners, Lord (Gerald Hugh Tyrwhitt-Wilson) (1883–1950) English composer, painter, and author. In the diplomatic service at first, he studied music at Dresden and Vienna, and also sought the advice of Stravinsky and Alfredo Casella. His operatic setting of Prosper Mérimée's comedy *Le Carrosse du Saint-Sacrement* was produced in Paris in 1924, and the ballet *The Triumph of Neptune* in London in 1926; another, with words by Gertrude Stein, *The Wedding Bouquet*, was produced at Sadler's Wells, London, in 1937 with settings designed by himself. He was famed for such eccentricities as dyeing the pigeons on his lawns different colours to match his moods.

Born at Arley Park, near Bridgnorth, Shropshire, and educated at Eton, he was in the diplomatic service 1909–24. His novels include *The Camel* (1936), *Far from the Madding War* (1941), and *The Romance of a Nose* (1942), and he also published two popular autobiographical works, *First Childhood* (1934) and *A Distant Prospect* (1945).

Works OPERA *Le Carrosse du Saint-Sacrement* (1924).

BALLET *The Triumph of Neptune* (1926), *Luna Park* (1930), *The Wedding Bouquet* (words by Gertrude Stein; 1937), *Cupid and Psyche* (1939).

ORCHESTRAL three pieces (*Chinoiserie, Valse sentimentale, Kasatchok*), *Fantaisie espagnole* (1920), and *Fugue* for orchestra (1928); *Variations, Ada-*

gio and Hornpipe for string orchestra.

PIANO *Le Poisson d'or, Trois Petites Marches funèbres* and *Fragments psychologiques* for piano; *Valses bourgeoises* for piano duet.

SONGS including three sets in the German, French, and English manners.

Bernstein, Leonard (1918–1990) US composer, conductor, and pianist. He was one of the most energetic and versatile 20th-century US musicians. His works, which established a vogue for realistic, contemporary themes, include symphonies such as *The Age of Anxiety* (1949), ballets such as *Fancy Free* (1944), and scores for musicals, including *Wonderful Town* (1953), *West Side Story* (1957), and *Mass* (1971) in memory of President J F Kennedy.

Born in Lawrence, Massachusetts, he was educated at Harvard University and the Curtis Institute of Music. In 1943 he made his debut as a conductor, beginning a highly successful international career. From 1958 to 1970 he was musical director of the New York Philharmonic. Among his other works are *Jeremiah* (1944), *Facsimile* (1946), *Candide* (1956), and the *Chichester Psalms* (1965).

Bertoni, Ferdinando Giuseppe (1725–1813) Italian composer. He was a pupil of Giovanni Martini at Bologna. Organist at St Mark's, Venice, from 1752 and choirmaster at the Conservatorio dei Mendicanti from 1757, he wrote many works for the female musicians there. He produced his first opera in Florence in 1745. In 1776 he produced his *Orfeo*, on the libretto by Raniero de Calzabigi already set by Christoph Willibald von Gluck in 1762; it contains many echoes of Gluck's music. He visited London to produce operas in 1778–80 and 1781–83. In 1785 he succeeded Baldassare Galuppi as maestro di cappella at St Mark's, Venice.

Works OPERA *Cajetto* (1746), *Orazio Curiazo*, *Tancredi* (1766), *Orfeo ed Euridice* (1776), *Quinto Fabio* (1778), and over 40 others.

OTHER oratorios and Latin cantatas; string quartets; keyboard music.

Bertrand, Antoine de (c.1535–c.1581) French composer. In some of his settings of Ronsard's *Amours* he experimented with quarter-tones. Altogether he published three volumes of chansons, and a volume of *Airs spirituels* appeared posthumously in 1582.

Berutti, Arturo (1862–1938) Argentine composer. He studied at the Leipzig Conservatory and in Paris and Milan, settling in Buenos Aires in 1896.

Works OPERA *Vendetta* (1892), *Pampa* (1892), *Evangelina* (1893), *Taras Bulba* (after Gogol; 1895), *Yupanki*, *Khrysé*, *Horrida nox* (1908), and *Los heroes*.

Berwald, Franz Adolf (1796–1868) Swedish violinist and composer. His best-known music is in the four symphonies of the 1840s: the titles *Capricieuse* and *Singulière* suggest their originality. He also wrote operas, a piano concerto, symphonic poems, and some distinguished chamber music. His music is an individual product of the early Romantic period, and shows a fertile and unusual harmonic imagination as well as an original approach to questions of form, though much of it remained unplayed in his lifetime.

He was born in Stockholm, and composed several works before studying in Berlin. He twice visited Vienna, where he had more success than at home, and was admired by Liszt and Schumann. His septet of 1828 was influenced by Ludwig Spohr and Beethoven. Jenny Lind sang in his operetta *A Rustic Betrothal in Sweden* (1847). Later stage works were less successful and *The Queen of Golconda* (1864) was not premiered until 1968. He settled in Stockholm in 1849 as director of music at the university and court *kapellmästare*; later he managed a sawmill and glassworks.

Works OPERA *Leonida* (1829), *The Traitor, Estrella di Soria* (1848, revised 1862), *The Queen of Golconda* (1864, performed 1968); operettas *I Enter a Convent, The Milliner, A Rustic Betrothal in Sweden* (1847).

ORCHESTRAL four symphonies, no. 1 *Sérieuse* (1842), no. 2 *Capricieuse* (1842), no. 3 *Singulière* (1845), no. 4 (1845); violin concerto (1820); piano concerto (1855); orchestral works include *Recollections of the Norwegian Alps*.

CHAMBER Septet (1828); three string quartets, two piano quintets, and other chamber music.

OTHER songs; incidental music to plays.

Besard, Jean-Baptiste (c.1567–after 1617), Latin **Johannes Baptista Besardus** French lutenist and composer. He first studied law at the University of Dôle, then the lute with Lorenzini in Rome. Later, he lived in Cologne and Augsburg, Germany. He published theoretical works and collections of lute music including his own. His *Thesaurus harmonicus* of 1603 contains more than 400 pieces by various composers and includes a manual on lute playing.

Besseler, Heinrich (1900–1969) German musicologist. He studied at Freiburg im Breisgau, Vienna, and Göttingen, where later he became lecturer at the university. He was professor at Jena, 1949, and at Leipzig from 1956. He wrote on medieval and Renaissance music, notably in *Die Musik des Mittelalters und der Renaissance* (1951).

Besuch der Alten Dame, Der, *The Visit of the Old Lady* opera by Gottfried von Einem (libretto by Friedrich Dürrenmatt after his own drama), first produced at the Staatsoper, Vienna, Austria, on 23 May 1971. The plot tells how a long-jilted lady pays people of her home town for killing her lover.

Betrothal in a Monastery, The, Russian **Obruchenie v monastyre** opera by Prokofiev (libretto by the composer and M Mendelssohn, after Sheridan's play *The Duenna*); it was composed 1940–41 and first performed at the Kirov Theatre, Leningrad (now St Petersburg), Russia, on 3 November 1946. The story tells how, after initial opposition from their father, Louisa and Ferdinando are allowed to choose their partners in marriage.

Betulia liberata, La, **Betulia Liberated** oratorio in two acts by Mozart to a text by Pietro Metastasio, based on the story of Judith and Holofernes. The work was commissioned by a Paduan nobleman, Giuseppe Ximenes, Prince of Aragon, and composed in 1771 in Italy and Salzburg but not performed in Mozart's lifetime. The first British performance was given in London on 6 November 1968, by Opera Viva. Metastasio's text was first set by Reutter (performed in Vienna, Austria, on 8 April 1734). There are later settings by Niccolò Jommelli (Venice, 1734), Ignaz Holzbauer (Mannheim, 1760), Florian Gassmann (Vienna, 1772), and Schuster (Dresden, 1796).

Bevis of Hampton or **Beves of Hamtoun** Anglo-Norman 13th-century romance. See ➤ *Buovo d'Antona*, the opera by Traetta.

Bialas, Günter (1907–1995) German composer. He studied in Berlin 1927–33, and taught in Breslau, Weimar, and Munich. His music shows a wide range of influences, including neoclassicism, twelve-tone technique, and medieval polyphony.

Works OPERA *Hero und Leander* (1966), *Die Geschichte von Aucassin und Nicolette* (1969), *Der gestiefelte Kater* (1974).

ORCHESTRAL viola concerto (1940), violin concerto (1949), cello concerto (1962), *Sinfonia piccola*.

CHAMBER three string quartets (1936, 1949, 1969).

OTHER sacred and secular choral music; *Erwartung*, for organ (1972).

Bianca e Falliero, ossia Il consiglio di tre, **Bianca and Falliero, or The Council of Three** opera by Rossini (libretto by F Romani, from Manzoni's tragedy *Il conte di Carmagnola*), first produced at La Scala, Milan, Italy, on 26 December 1819. The story tells how Bianca loves Falliero but is told to marry Capiello. Falliero is accused of treachery by the Council but is absolved in time to marry Bianca.

Bianca e Fernando opera by Bellini (libretto by D Gilardoni), first produced at the Teatro San Carlo, Naples, Italy, on 30 May 1826. It was Bellini's first opera to be heard in public. The story tells how Fernando rescues his father and sister Bianca from the ducal usurper Filippo.

Bianca und Giuseppe, oder Die Franzosen vor Nizza, Bianca and Giuseppe, or The French before Nice opera by Johann Friedrich Kittl (libretto by Wagner), first produced in Prague (Czech Republic) on 19 February 1848. Wagner had written the libretto for himself in 1836; it is based on a novel by Heinrich König.

Bianchi, Francesco (c.1752–1810) Italian composer. He was maestro al cembalo at the Comédie Italienne in Paris, France, in 1775, where he worked under Niccolò Piccinni and produced two operas. In 1778 he went to Florence, Italy, and in 1783 was appointed second maestro di cappella at Milan Cathedral. His most successful opera, *La villanella rapita*, was produced the same year in Venice. In 1795 he went to London, England, as composer to the King's Theatre, and three years later to Dublin, Ireland. He wrote popular *opéras-comiques* in Paris, 1802–07, but returned to London, where he remained until his death by suicide.

Works 60 operas, oratorios, church music, trio sonatas.

Biber, Heinrich Ignaz Franz von (1644–1704) Bohemian composer, virtuoso violinist, and Kapellmeister at the Archbishop of Salzburg's court. His brilliant violin technique is best heard in the solo sonatas with continuo of 1681 and the 16 *Mystery* or *Rosary* sonatas of 1676. Spatial effects are created in the *Vesperae* (1693), the *Missa Sancti Henrici* (1701), and Mass in F minor. He also wrote an opera, *Chi la dura, la vince* (1687), and the *Nightwatchman's Serenade*.

Works OPERA *Chi la dura, la vince* (1687).

CHAMBER several sets of violin sonatas, *Battalia* with violin, *Nightwatchman's Serenade*, partitas for three instruments.

CHURCH MUSIC vespers for voices, strings, and trombones; possibly the 53-part *Missa salisburgensis*, performed in Salzburg Cathedral in 1682 and formerly attributed to Benevoli.

Biches, Les ballet in one act with chorus by Poulenc; it was composed in 1923 and first produced at Monte Carlo on 6 January 1924, with choreography by Nijinska. The Orchestral Suite in five movements was rescored 1939–40. The title is hard to render from the French, but can be roughly translated as 'The Little Darlings'.

Billy Budd opera by Benjamin Britten (libretto by E M Forster and Eric Crozier, on Herman Melville's story), first produced at Covent Garden, London, England, on 1 December 1951. It was revised in 1960 and broadcast on BBC radio on 13

November that year; the new version was first produced at Covent Garden on 9 January 1964. The story tells how Billy Budd, accused of mutiny, kills the master-at-arms Claggart and is hanged by Captain Vere.

Billy the Kid ballet by Aaron Copland, first produced in New York on 24 May 1939.

binary form basic musical form in two sections (AB). Section A makes a musical statement but it sounds incomplete on its own. It is answered by section B, which creates the balance. In most binary pieces using the tonal language, the music modulates to the ➜ **dominant** key at the end of section A. Section B begins in the dominant and modulates back to the starting ➜ **tonic** key.

Binchois, Gilles de Bins (c.1400–1460) Franco-Flemish composer. Along with the composers Guillaume Dufay (whom he knew) and John Dunstable, Binchois was a major figure in 15th-century music. He composed 28 Mass-movements, six Magnificats, and around 30 other liturgical works (motets and hymns) in a severely functional style. His most characteristic works, however, are his chansons.

Binchois was probably born in Binche, near Mons, and was organist at the church of Ste Waldetrude, Mons, 1419–23. He was chaplain to Philip, Duke of Burgundy, from about 1430 until 1453, when he became provost of Saint-Vincent, Soignies.

He wrote around 55 chansons, mostly in three parts and in the form of *rondeaux* or *ballades*, with texts relating to courtly love. They are written in a more pleasing style than his sacred music; most are symmetrical and are set to graceful melodies for one voice and two instruments; they follow closely the form of the poetic text.

Binet, Jean (1893–1960) Swiss composer. He studied at the Jaques-Dalcroze Institute in Geneva and with Barblan, Templeton Strong, André Bloch, and others. He lived in the USA and Brussels for a time. Several of his works were premiered by Ernest Ansermet.

Works BALLET *L'Ile enchantée* and *Le Printemps* (1950).

ORCHESTRAL suites on Swiss and English themes and dances for orchestra.

CHAMBER concertino for chamber orchestra; string quartet (1927) and other chamber music.

VOCAL three psalms for chorus and orchestra; *Cantate de Noël* for chorus and organ; songs and part songs.

Bingham, Judith (1952–) English composer. She studied at the Royal Academy of Music, London, and with Hans Keller, and has appeared as a singer with the Taverner Consort and Combattimento.

Works ORCHESTRAL *Chartres* (1987).

VOCAL songs for mezzo, baritone, and choruses (*A Hymn before Sunrise in the Vale of Chamonix*, 1982); Mass setting and *A Winter Walk at Noon* (1984); *The Uttermost* for tenor, chorus, and orchestra (1992).

OTHER *A Divine Image* for harpsichord (1976).

Binkerd, Gordon (1916–2003) US composer. After study at the Eastman School of Music, New York, and Harvard, he was professor at the University of Illinois 1947–71. His music is tonally chromatic and contrapuntal in scope, and includes four symphonies (1955, 1957, 1961, 1963), two string quartets (1956, 1961), a string trio (1979), four piano sonatas (1955–83), and choruses.

Birthday Odes works for solo, chorus, and orchestra written by English composers from the Restoration onwards to commemorate royal birthdays. Purcell wrote six for Queen Mary, consort of William III, as follows: 1. *Now does the Glorious Day Appear* (1689), 2. *Arise my Muse* (1690), 3. *Welcome, Welcome, Glorious Morn* (1691), 4. *Love's Goddess Sure was Blind* (1692), 5. *Celebrate this Festival* (1693), 6. *Come Ye Sons of Art Away* (1694).

Birtwistle, Harrison (1934–) English avant-garde composer. In his early career he wrote much for chamber ensemble, for example, his chamber opera *Punch and Judy* (1967) and *Down by the Greenwood Side* (1969). Birtwistle's early music was influenced by the Russian-born composer Igor ➜ **Stravinsky**, by the medieval and Renaissance masters, and particularly by the book *On Growth and Form* by the biologist D'Arcy Wentworth Thompson (1860–1948). For many years he worked alongside Peter Maxwell ➜ **Davies**.

His operas include *The Mask of Orpheus* (1986, with electronic music realized by Barry Anderson (1935–1987)) and *Gawain* (1991), a reworking of the medieval English poem *Sir Gawain and the Green Knight*. This was followed by *The Second Mrs Kong* (1994), in which the composer returned to the myths of Orpheus, and *The Last Supper* (2000), inspired by the Bible story.

He studied at the Royal Manchester College of Music and later at the Royal Academy of Music, London.

His orchestral works include *The Triumph of Time* (1972) and *Silbury Air* (1977). His tape composition *Chronometer* (1971, assisted by Peter Zinovieff (1934–)) is based on clock sounds.

Works STAGE *Punch and Judy*, opera in one act (1967), *Monodrama* for soprano, speaker, and instrumental ensemble (1967), *Down by the Greenwood Side*, dramatic pastoral (1969), incidental

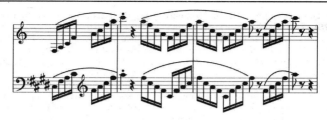

F major and F sharp minor appear simultaneously in Ravel's bitonal passage from L'Enfant et les sorti-lèges.

music for National Theatre production of *Hamlet* (1975) and *The Oresteia* (1981), *Frames, Pulses and Interruptions*, ballet (1977), *Bow Down*, music-theatre (1977), *The Mask of Orpheus*, opera (1973–75, 1981–84; produced 1986), *Yan Tan Tethera*, TV opera (1986), *Gawain* (1991), *The Second Mrs Kong* (1994).

ORCHESTRAL *Chorales* (1960–63), *Three Movements with Fanfares* (1964), *Nomos* (1968), *An Imaginary Landscape* (1971), *The Triumph of Time* (1972), *Grimethorpe Aria* for brass band (1973), *Melencolia 1* (1976), *Silbury Air* for small orchestra (1977), *Still Movement* for 13 solo strings (1984), *Earth Dances* (1985), *Endless Parade* for trumpet and strings (1987), *Ritual Fragment* (1990), *Gawain's Journey* (1991), *Antiphonies* for piano and orchestra (1993), *The Cry of Anubis* (1995), *Panic* for saxophone, drums, and orchestra (1995).

VOCAL *Monody for Corpus Christi* for soprano and ensemble (1959), *Narration: a Description of the Passing Year* for chorus (1963), *Entr'actes and Sappho Fragments* for soprano and ensemble (1964), *Carmen paschale* for chorus and organ (1965), *Ring a Dumb Clarion* for soprano, clarinet, and percussion (1965), *Cantata* for soprano and ensemble (1969), *Nenia on the Death of Orpheus* for soprano and ensemble (1970), *The Fields of Sorrow* for two sopranos, chorus, and ensemble (1971–72), *Meridian* for mezzo, chorus, and ensemble (1970–71), *Epilogue: Full Fathom Five* for baritone and ensemble (1972), *... agm ...* for 16 solo voices and three instrumental ensembles (1979), *On the Sheer Threshold of the Night* for four solo voices and 12-part chorus (1980), *Songs by Myself* for soprano and ensemble (1984), *Words Overheard* for soprano, flute, oboe, and strings (1985), *Four Songs of Autumn* for soprano and string quartet (1987); *An die Musik* (1988), *White and Light* (1989), and *Four Poems by Jaan Kaplinski* (1991), all for soprano and ensemble.

INSTRUMENTAL *Refrains and Choruses* for wind quintet (1957), *The World is Discovered* for chamber ensemble (1960), *Tragoedia* for ensemble (1965), *Verses for Ensembles* (1969), *Ut heremita solus*, arrangement of Jean d'Okeghem (1969),

Hoquetus David, arrangement of Guillaume de Machaut (1969), *Medusa* for ensemble (1970, revised 1980), *Chronometer* for eight-track tape (1971), *Chorales from a Toyshop* (1967–74), *Carmen Arcadiae Mechanicae Perpetuum* for ensemble (1977), *For O for O, the Hobby Horse is Forgot* for six percussion (1976), clarinet quintet (1980), *Pulse Sampler* for oboe and claves (1981), *Duets for Storab* for two flutes (1983), *Secret Theatre* for string quartet and ensemble (1984), and *Pulse Shadows* for string quartet and soprano (1993).

Bishop, Henry (Rowley) (1786–1855) English conductor and composer. He produced *Angelina* (composed with Francesco Lanza (1783–1862)) at Margate in 1804 and the ballet *Tamerlan et Bajazet* at the King's Theatre in London in 1806. From that time on he brought out one or more stage pieces almost each year until 1840.

Born in London, he studied under Francesco Bianchi. In 1813 he was one of the founders of the Philharmonic Society and became one of its conductors. He was appointed professor of music at Oxford in 1848. He was married twice; both his wives were singers: Sarah Lyon in 1809 and Anna Riviere in 1831.

Works STAGE over 100 pieces for the stage, including *The Corsair*, *The Circassian Bride* (1809), *Guy Mannering* (after Scott; 1816), *The Burgomaster of Saardam*, *The Heart of Midlothian* (after Scott; 1819), *Montrose* (after Scott), *The Law of Java*, *Maid Marian*, *Clari*, *Cortez*, *Faustus* (1825), *Aladdin*, *The Fortunate Isles* (1840); incidental music for three tragedies, for adaptations of Scott, Byron, and Shakespeare.

OTHER oratorio *The Fallen Angel*; cantata *The Seventh Day*; three volumes of national melodies with words by Moore and other collections of arrangements.

bisser (French, *bis* 'twice') in music, a term meaning to repeat as an ➔ **encore** a piece of music or performance.

bitonality in music, a combination of two parts in different keys, as in Stravinsky's *Duo Concertante* (1931–32) for violin and piano. Music of more than two simultaneous keys is called ➔ **polytonality**.

Bizet, Georges (Alexandre César Léopold) (1838–1875) French composer of operas. Among his works are *Les Pêcheurs de perles/The Pearl Fishers* (1863) and *La Jolie Fille de Perth/The Fair Maid of Perth* (1866). He also wrote the concert overture *Patrie* and incidental music to Alphonse Daudet's play *L'Arlésienne* (1872), which has remained a standard work in the form of two suites for orchestra. His operatic masterpiece *Carmen* was produced a few months before his death. His Symphony in C, written when he was 17, is now frequently performed.

Bizet was born near Paris. His father, a teacher of singing, gave him his first instruction in music and at the age of nine, being exceptionally gifted, he was admitted to the Paris Conservatory, studying piano under Marmontel, organ under François Benoist (1794–1878), and composition under Pierre Joseph Guillaume Zimmermann (1785–1853). In 1853, when Zimmermann died, he became a pupil of his future father-in-law, Jacques Halévy, having already taken a first prize for piano. His Symphony in C of 1855 is the least known of his earlier works, and one of the finest pieces written by an adolescent; the score, however, was not performed until 1935. In 1857 he won the Prix de Rome, but before he went to Rome he had already gained a prize in a competition for an operetta, *Le Docteur Miracle* (1857), sponsored by Offenbach. He tied with Charles Lecocq, whose setting was produced alternately with his own at the Théâtre des Bouffes-Parisiens.

He wrote several works in Rome and on his return to Paris in 1860 he set out to capture the operatic stage; but although the Opéra-Comique accepted his one-act opera, *La Guzla de l'Emir*, he withdrew it, destroying it later. The Théâtre Lyrique produced his next work, *Les Pêcheurs de perles*, in 1863; *Ivan le Terrible*, written in 1865, said to have been burnt by him, was recovered in 1944 and performed at Mühringen Castle, Württemberg, Germany. In 1869 the conductor Jules Pasdeloup gave him his first chance to appear with an orchestral work, *Souvenirs de Rome*, which he later entitled *Roma*. In the same year Bizet married Geneviève Halévy.

In 1872 he was commissioned to write incidental music for Daudet's play, *L'Arlésienne*, produced at the Vaudeville in October. In 1874 Pasdeloup produced his overture *Patrie* (unconnected with Victorien Sardou's play), but Bizet had set to work before that on *Carmen*, which was premiered at the Opéra-Comique, with spoken dialogue, in March 1875. At first it scandalized audiences by its realism, and did not achieve its great popularity until after Bizet's death. It received 37 performances; but Bizet died after about 30 performances, before the work had won through prejudice to a decided success.

Bizet is clearly influenced by Gounod but far transcends his model. In a sense, his reputation has become hostage to his best-loved work; the passion and melody of *Carmen* should not obscure the same qualities to be found in the Symphony in C, *Les Pêcheurs de perles*, and even *La Jolie Fille de Perth*.

Works OPERA five, including *Les Pêcheurs de perles* (1863), *La Jolie Fille de Perth* (after Scott; 1866), *Carmen* (after Mérimée, 1875).

STAGE incidental music to Daudet's *L'Arlésienne* (1872).

ORCHESTRAL works include symphony in C major (1855, first performed under Weingartner, 1935), suite *Roma* (1869), *Petite Suite* (*Jeux d'enfants*).

OTHER numerous songs and piano pieces.

Blacher, Boris (1903–1975) German avant-garde composer. After studying in Berlin, he began his career under great difficulties during the Nazi regime, but later became successful as a composer, developing a system of variable metres following arithmetical progressions, upon which many of his works are based. In 1953 he became director of the Berlin Hochschule für Musik.

Works OPERA *Fürstin Tarakanova* (1940), *Preussisches Märchen* (1949), *Abstrakte Oper No. 1* (1953), *200,000 Taler* (1969), *Das Geheimnis* (1975); chamber operas *Romeo und Julia* (1943, after Shakespeare) *Die Flut* (1946), *Die Nachtschwalbe* (1948).

BALLET several ballets including *Harlekinade* (1939), *Lysistrate* (1950), *Hamlet* (1949), *Der Mohr von Venedig* (1955).

ORATORIO scenic oratorio *Der Grossinquisitor* (after Dostoevsky; 1947).

ORCHESTRAL symphony; symphonic poem *Hamlet* (after Shakespeare); variations on theme by Paganini and other orchestral works; two piano concertos, viola concerto.

CHAMBER five string quartets (1930–67) and other chamber music.

OTHER piano music, songs.

'Black Key' Study Chopin's piano Study in G flat major, Op. 10 no. 5, written about 1831–32 and published in 1833. It is so called because the right hand plays only on the black keys throughout.

Black Knight, The cantata for chorus and orchestra by Edward Elgar, Op. 25, a setting of Longfellow's translation of Johann Uhland's ballad *Der schwarze Ritter*, first performed at the Worcester Festival, England, in 1893.

bladder pipe musical instrument, an early ➔ bagpipe with an animal's bladder used for the bag.

B-la-F Quartet a string quartet on the name of Belaiev by Rimsky-Korsakov, Liadov, Borodin, and Glazunov, performed on Mitrofan Belaiev's

50th birthday, 22 February 1886. It is constructed on the notes B flat, A, F.

Blaise le savetier, Blaise the Cobbler opera by Philidor (libretto by J M Sedaine, after La Fontaine), first produced at the Opéra-Comique, Paris, France, on 9 March 1759.

Blake, David (Leonard) (1936–) English composer. He studied at Cambridge, and with Hanns Eisler in Berlin, Germany, and taught at York University from 1964. He uses serial technique, and is influenced by the music of the Far East.

Works OPERA *Toussaint L'Ouverture* (1974–76, revised 1982), *The Plumber's Gift* (1985–88).

ORCHESTRAL two violin concertos (1976 and 1983); *Scherzi ed intermezzi* (1984); cello concerto (1989–93).

CHAMBER chamber symphony (1966), three string quartets (1962, 1973, 1982), Nonet for wind (1971), Capriccio, for wind, strings, and piano (1980); *Seasonal Variants* for seven players (1985).

VOCAL three choruses to poems by Frost (1964), *Lumina*, cantata for soprano, baritone, chorus, and orchestra, to text by Pound (1969), *From the Mattress Grave*, twelve Heine poems for soprano and eleven instruments (1978); *The Spear* for mezzo, speaker, and ensemble (1982); *Rise, Dove* for baritone and orchestra (1982); *Pastoral Paraphrase* for baritone and orchestra (1986).

Blake, William (1757–1827) English poet and artist. His works and thought inspired, among others, William ➔ **Bolcom** (*Songs of Innocence and Experience*), Benjamin Britten (*Songs and Proverbs*), Justin ➔ **Connolly** (*The Marriage of Heaven and Hell*), Alexander Goehr (*Five Poems and an Epigram*), Ralph Vaughan Williams (Job), Hubert ➔ **Parry** (*Jerusalem*), and Michael Tippett (*Song of Liberty*).

Blamont, François Colin de (1690–1760) French composer. He was a pupil of his father, who was in the royal band, and later of Michel-Richard Lalande. He became in 1719 superintendent of the royal music and, after Lalande's death in 1726, master of the chamber music.

Works STAGE PIECES (mostly ballets and ballet-operas) *Les Festes grecques et romaines* (1723), *Le Retour des dieux sur la terre* (for the marriage of Louis XV, 1725), *Le Caprice d'Erato* (1730), *Endymion* (1731), *Les Caractères de l'Amour, Les Amours du printemps, Jupiter vainqueur des Titans* (1745), *Les Festes de Thétis* (1750).

VOCAL cantata *Circé* and three books of *Cantates françaises* for solo voice; motets with orchestral accompaniment.

Blánik symphonic poem by Bedřich Smetana. See ➔ *Má Vlast.*

Blech (German 'brass') in music, an abbreviation often used in scores for *Blechinstrumente*, brass instruments.

Blessed Damozel, The cantata by Debussy. See ➔ *Damoiselle élue.*

Blind Man's Buff masque by Peter Maxwell Davies for high voice, mezzo, mime, and stage band (text by Davies from Büchner's *Leonce und Lena*, among others), first performed in London, England, on 29 May 1972, conducted by Pierre Boulez.

blind octaves a trick of piano writing: figures in octaves rapidly alternating between the two hands where the thumbs trace a continuous melodic line while the outer notes fly off at broken intervals.

Bliss, Arthur Edward Drummond (1891–1975) English composer and conductor. He became Master of the Queen's Musick in 1953. Among his works are *A Colour Symphony* (1922); music for the ballets *Checkmate* (1937), *Miracle in the Gorbals* (1944), and *Adam Zero* (1946); an opera *The Olympians* (1949); and dramatic film music, including *Things to Come* (1935). He conducted the first performance of US composer Igor Stravinsky's *Ragtime* for 11 instruments in 1918.

Bliss was educated at Rugby and Pembroke College, Cambridge, where he studied music under Charles Wood. He entered the Royal College of Music in London in 1913, studying with Charles Stanford, Ralph Vaughan Williams, and Gustav Holst, but joined the army in 1914, serving until 1918. He was appointed professor of composition at the Royal College of Music in 1921, but took wholly to composing the next year, never holding any official post until he was appointed music director of the BBC in 1941, an appointment he resigned to Victor Hely-Hutchinson in 1945. Early experiments with unusual musical media, as in a Concerto for tenor, piano, strings, and percussion and *Rout* for soprano and chamber orchestra to a text constructed of nonsense syllables, gained him a reputation as an *enfant terrible*. His early music was miniaturist in scope but he later embraced larger forms. With some success, Bliss sought to evoke comparisons with Edward Elgar in his *Colour Symphony, Introduction and Allegro*, and violin concerto. He published his memoirs, *As I Remember*, in 1970.

Works DRAMATIC operas *The Olympians* (libretto by J B Priestley; 1949) and *Tobias and the Angel* (C Hassall; 1960); ballets *Checkmate* (1937), *Miracle in the Gorbals* (1944), and *Adam Zero* (1946); incidental music for Shakespeare's *Tempest*; film music for *Things to Come* (H G Wells; 1935), *Conquest of the Air, Caesar and Cleopatra* (G B Shaw).

ORCHESTRAL *A Colour Symphony* (1922), *Intro-*

duction and Allegro (1926), *Hymn to Apollo, Meditations on a Theme by John Blow* (1955); concertos for piano and two pianos; march *Phoenix* for the liberation of France; *Music for Strings.*

VOCAL *Morning Heroes* for orator, chorus, and orchestra (1930), *Pastoral* for mezzo, chorus, flute, strings, and drums, cantata *Mary of Magdala* for contralto, bass, chorus, and orchestra (1963), *Serenade* for baritone and orchestra (1929), concerto for piano, tenor, and chamber orchestra, *Rout* for voice and chamber orchestra (1919), *Madam Noy* for voice and six instruments; several song cycles with various instruments or piano, including *Five American Songs* (Edna St Vincent Millay).

CHAMBER *Conversations* for flute, oboe, violin, viola, and cello; two string quartets (1941, 1950), oboe quintet, clarinet quintet; sonatas for violin and piano, and viola and piano.

Blitzstein, Marc (1905–1964) US composer. Born in Philadelphia, he was a child prodigy as a pianist at the age of six. He served with the US Army 8th Air Force 1942–45, for which he wrote *The Airborne* (1946), a choral symphony. His first great success was the opera *The Cradle Will Rock*, produced in New York in 1937 with piano accompaniment directed by Orson Welles, after a full performance was banned by the authorities. He was a political radical and was killed after an argument with American sailors.

Blitzstein appeared as solo pianist at the age of 15, and later studied composition with Rosario Scalero in New York, Nadia Boulanger in Paris, and Schoenberg in Vienna. He also studied piano with Alexander Siloti in the USA.

Works DRAMATIC operas *Triple Sec* (1929), *Parabola and Circula* (1929), *The Harpies, The Cradle Will Rock* (1937); ballet *Cain*; incidental music for Shakespeare's *Julius Caesar*; film music for *Surf and Seaweed, The Spanish Earth, No for an Answer* (1941), *Chesapeake Bay Retriever.*

VOCAL choral opera *The Condemned*; radio songplay *I've got the Tune*, Children's Cantata; *The Airborne* for orchestra, chorus, and narrator (1946).

ORCHESTRAL *Romantic Piece, Jigsaw* ballet suite, and variations for orchestra; piano concerto (1931).

CHAMBER string quartet and serenade for string quartet; piano sonata and *Percussion Music* for piano (1929).

Bloch, Ernest (1880–1959) Swiss-born US composer. His music is highly coloured in its orchestration and rhythms, often drawing on elements of Jewish folk music. Among his works are the lyrical drama *Macbeth* (1910), *Schelomo* for cello and orchestra (1916), five string quartets, and *Suite Hébraïque* for viola and orchestra (1953). He often used themes based on Jewish liturgical music and folk song.

Born in Geneva, Switzerland, he was a pupil of Émile Jaques-Dalcroze at first, then of Eugène Ysaÿe and Rasse at the Brussels Conservatory, and later at the Hoch Conservatory at Frankfurt, where Iwan Knorr was his composition master. His last teacher was Ludwig Thuille at Munich, and he then went to live in Paris, where he began the opera *Macbeth* on a French libretto by Edmond Fleg. It was produced in Paris in 1910, but he had in the meantime returned to Switzerland to conduct subscription concerts at Lausanne and Neuchâtel. He was professor of music aesthetics at the Geneva Conservatory 1911–15. In 1916 he went to the USA and settled in New York as professor at the David Mannes School of Music. A second opera, *Jézabel*, begun there in 1918, was unfinished.

From 1920 to 1925 Bloch was founder-director of the Cleveland Institute of Music, and in 1925 he was appointed head of the San Francisco Conservatory. In 1930 he retired to Switzerland to live quietly in remote places. Some interest was shown in his work in England and a good deal in Italy, where his *Sacred Service* was produced in Turin and *Macbeth* was revived in an Italian translation in Naples in 1938. But the anti-Semitic movement encouraged by the fascists put an end to this appreciation. As a US citizen he could no longer remain absent from the USA without losing his adopted nationality, and he returned there to live in retirement at the end of 1938.

Works OPERA *Macbeth* (1910).

ORCHESTRAL *Schelomo* for cello and orchestra (1916), *Voice in the Wilderness* for cello and orchestra (1926); violin concerto (1938); two violin and piano sonatas, viola and piano suite, *Concerto grosso* for piano and strings.

VOCAL *Sacred Service* (*Avodath Hakodesh*) for baritone solo, chorus, and orchestra.

CHAMBER piano quintet; *Baal Shem* three pieces for violin and piano; *From Jewish Life* (three pieces) and *Méditation hébraïque* for cello and piano.

Blockflöte (German 'block flute') alternative name for the ➔ **recorder**, a musical instrument of the fipple flute family.

block harmony in music, a term used for a type of harmonic accompaniment in which all the notes except the melody move together simultaneously in 'block' chords, without being made to depart from one another by means of figuration or counterpoint.

Blockx, Jan (1851–1912) Belgian composer. Most of his operas and all his cantatas for solo voices, chorus, and orchestra are set to Flemish words.

He learned music as a choirboy and went to the Antwerp School of Music, later to the Leipzig

Conservatory. In 1886 he became professor and in 1901 director of the Antwerp Conservatory, succeeding Peter Benoît, whom he followed as a Flemish music nationalist.

Works OPERA *Jets vergeten* (1877), *Maître Martin* (1892), *Herbergprinses* (1896), *Thyl Uilenspiegel* (1900), *De Bruid der Zee*, *De Kapel* (1903), *Baldie*.

BALLET *Milenka* (1887).

VOCAL cantatas *Op den Stroom*, *Een Droom van't Paradijs*, *Vredeszang*, *Klokke Roeland*, *De Scheldezang*.

ORCHESTRAL overture *Rubens*; Romance for violin and orchestra.

Blomdahl, Karl-Birger (1916–1968) Swedish composer. He wrote ballets and symphonies in expressionist style. His opera *Aniara* (1957–59) incorporates electronic music and is set in a spaceship fleeing Earth after nuclear war.

Blomdahl studied at Stockholm under various teachers, including Hilding Rosenberg and Mogens Wöldike. In 1960 he was appointed professor at the Stockholm Conservatory.

Works OPERA *Aniara* (a spaceship drama, 1957–59).

ORCHESTRAL three symphonies (1943, 1947, 1950), symphonic dances, concert overture, *Concerto grosso* for orchestra; violin concerto (1946), viola concerto.

CHAMBER chamber concerto for piano, wind, and percussion; two string quartets, string trio, woodwind trio, suites for cello and piano, and bassoon and piano; piano pieces.

OTHER trios for women's voices; incidental music.

Blow, John (1648–1708) English composer. He taught the English composer Henry Purcell and wrote church music, for example the anthem 'I Was Glad When They Said Unto Me' (1697). His masque *Venus and Adonis* (1685) is sometimes called the first English opera.

He became one of the children in the Chapel Royal in London as soon as it was re-established after the Restoration in 1660, and was taught by Henry Cooke. He wrote three anthems in 1663 and took a share with Pelham Humfrey and William Turner in the 'Club Anthem' about 1664. About the same time, at Charles II's request, he set Robert Herrick's 'Go, perjur'd man' in the style of Giacomo Carissimi. John Hingston and Christopher Gibbons also had a share in Blow's musical education. In 1668 he succeeded Albert Bryne as organist at Westminster Abbey; in March 1674 he was sworn a Gentleman of the Chapel Royal, and the following July he succeeded Humfrey as Master of the Children. In November he married Elizabeth Braddock. In 1679 he was followed in the Westminster organist's post by Purcell, but returned as organist after

Purcell's death in 1695. In 1687 he succeeded Michael Wise as almoner and choirmaster at St Paul's Cathedral (at that time unfinished). James II appointed him a member of the royal band and confirmed a previous appointment as Composer in Ordinary. Towards the end of the century he bought a property at Hampton, but still retained a house at Westminster, where he died.

Works MASQUE *Venus and Adonis* (1685).

CHURCH MUSIC AND ANTHEMS about twelve services; over 100 English anthems, nine Latin anthems; three coronation anthems for James II, one for William and Mary; anthem for the opening service at St Paul's Cathedral (1697);

SONGS AND ODES Act Songs for Oxford University; at least 16 Welcome Songs, five for St Cecilia's Day, odes on the death of Queen Mary (1695) and of Purcell (1696); song collection *Amphion Anglicus*, songs and catches, CHAMBER sonata for two violins and bass.

OTHER harpsichord lessons, suites, and pieces; some organ pieces.

Bluebeard see ➤ *Ariane et Barbe-bleue*; ➤ *Barbe-bleue*.

Bluebeard's Castle one-act opera by Béla Bartók. See ➤ *Duke Bluebeard's Castle*.

blue notes a device in blues, the playing of certain notes, especially the third and seventh of the scale, deliberately out of tune, between major and minor.

blues African-American music that originated in the work songs and Negro spirituals of the rural American South in the late 19th century. It is usually of a slow to moderate speed and characteristic features include a 12-bar (sometimes 8-bar or 16-bar) construction and a syncopated melody line that often includes 'blue notes' (quarter tones lying between the minor and major third of the scale – as found on some African five-note xylophones – or between the minor and major seventh). The lyrics are melancholy and tell tales of woe or unhappy love. The guitar is the main instrument, although the harmonica and piano are also common. Blues guitar and vocal styles have played a vital part in the development of jazz, rock, and pop music in general.

1920s–1930s The rural or delta blues was usually performed solo with guitar or harmonica, by such artists as Robert Johnson and Bukka White, but the earliest recorded style, classic blues, by such musicians as W C Handy and Bessie Smith, was sung with a small band.

1940s–1950s The urban blues, using electric amplification, emerged in the northern cities, chiefly Chicago. As exemplified by Howlin' Wolf, Muddy Waters, and John Lee Hooker, urban blues became rhythm and blues.

1960s The jazz-influenced guitar style of B B

King inspired many musicians of the **British blues boom**, including Eric Clapton.

1980s The 'blues *noir*' of Robert Cray contrasted with the rock-driven blues playing of Stevie Ray Vaughan.

In **classical music**, composers such as Maurice Ravel, Aaron Copland, and Michael Tippett have used aspects of the blues (especially the 'blue note') in various of their works, the Ravel piano trio in A minor (1914) being a notable example.

Blume, Friedrich (1893–1975) German musicologist. He studied at Munich, Leipzig, and Berlin. He was a prisoner in England for three years during World War I. After teaching in Berlin from 1921 he became professor at Kiel University from 1934 to 1958. He was editor-in-chief of the complete works of Michael Praetorius and the series *Das Chorwerk*, and was editor of the encyclopedia *Die Musik in Geschichte und Gegenwart* (known as *MGG*). His books include a history of Protestant church music.

Blumenfeld, Harold (1923–   ) US composer. He studied composition at Harvard and with Paul Hindemith at Yale, and conducting with Leonard Bernstein. He directed the Opera Theater of St Louis 1962–66 and the Washington University Opera Studio 1960–71, presenting works outside the standard repertory.

Works OPERA *Amphitryon* (1962), *Fritzi* (1979), *4-Score: An Opera of Opposites* (1985), *Season in Hell: A Life of Rimbaud* (1991–   ).

VOCAL *Eroscapes* for soprano and ensemble (1971); *Song of Innocence* for soloists, chorus, and orchestra (1973); *Voyages*, cantata after Hart Crane (1977); *La Face cendrée*, cantata after Rimbaud (1981).

ORCHESTRAL *Orchestral Evocations of Rimbaud* (1988).

Blumine original second movement of Mahler's first symphony, in D, and heard in the work's first performance in Budapest, Hungary, on 20 November 1889. The movement was discarded in 1894 and not performed again until 18 June 1976 at Aldeburgh, England, conducted by Benjamin Britten.

Blüthner, Julius Ferdinand (1824–1910) German piano manufacturer. He founded his firm at Leipzig in 1853.

Bluthochzeit opera by Wolfgang Fortner (libretto by E Beck after García Lorca's *Bodas de sangre*), composed for the opening of the new opera house in Cologne, Germany, and first performed there on 8 June 1957. The story concerns a bride who runs away with her former fiancé on her wedding day; the bridegroom follows and both men are killed in the ensuing fight.

An opera on the same subject by Sándor Szoko-lay (*Vérnász*, same source) was first produced in Budapest, Hungary, on 30 October 1964.

B Minor Mass setting of the Latin Mass by J S Bach; see ➔ **Mass in B minor**.

Boccherini, (Ridolfo) Luigi (1743–1805) Italian composer and cellist. He was a master of chamber music for string instruments, and was the most important Italian representative of the Viennese classical style, writing in his own distinctive manner. He studied in Rome, Italy, made his mark in Paris, France, in 1768, and was court composer in Prussia and Spain. He composed some 350 instrumental works, an opera, and oratorios.

Boccherini was born in Lucca. His father was a double-bass player, who began teaching his son himself, then sent him to Rome for further study in 1757. On his return to Lucca in 1761 he played cello in the theatre orchestra. With the violinist Manfredi he travelled widely on concert tours in Austria and France. He was particularly successful in Paris 1767–68, where he published his first chamber music. In 1769 he went to Madrid and settled there, being first in the service of the king's brother, the Infante Don Luis, until 1785, when the latter died. In 1787 Boccherini was appointed court composer to Frederick William II of Prussia, who had the exclusive right to his works, but he seems to have maintained his residence in Madrid. After the king's death in 1797 he was apparently without a permanent post, for he spent his last years in increasing poverty, largely owing to inconsiderate treatment by his publishers. He died in Madrid.

Works ORATORIOS *Giuseppe riconosciuto* and *Gioas, rè di Giuda* (about 1765).

CHURCH MUSIC *Stabat Mater* (1781), Mass (1800).

VOCAL cantatas, motets, and other pieces; zarzuela *La Clementina* (1780); concert arias.

ORCHESTRAL 26 symphonies; eleven cello concertos (including a pastiche by Grützmacher) and one each for flute, violin, and harpsichord.

CHAMBER 91 string quartets, 48 string trios, 125 string quintets, twelve piano quintets, 18 quintets for wind and strings, 16 sextets, two octets; 27 violin sonatas, six cello sonatas.

Bockstriller (German 'goat's trill') in music, a kind of vocal shake, produced by a rapid, bleating repetition of a single note. An example of this kind of shake occurs in the tailors' chorus in the third act of Richard Wagner's *Die Meistersinger von Nürnberg/The Mastersingers of Nuremberg*.

Boehm, Theobald (1794–1881) German flautist and composer. He invented the **Boehm system** of improvements to the flute in 1832. Using metalworking skills, he applied a series of levers and keypads to the instrument which improved performance and enabled the pitch holes to be drilled at optimum acoustical positions instead of, as formerly, to suit the player's fingers. His system was later applied to other woodwind instruments.

Boëllmann, Léon (1862–1897) French organist and composer. His *Gothic Suite* (1895) is well known.

He was born in Alsace and trained as an organist under Eugène Gigout, a teacher of church music in Paris. He was appointed organist of the church of St Vincent de Paul.

Works ORCHESTRAL symphony in F major; *Fantasie dialoguée* for organ and orchestra, *Variations symphoniques* for cello and orchestra (1893).

CHAMBER piano quartet, piano trio; cello and piano sonata.

CHURCH MUSIC AND ORGAN church music; organ works include two suites (first *Gothique*, 1895).

Boesmans, Philippe (1936–) Belgian composer. He studied with Henri Pousseur at Liège and worked with him at the electronic music studios there from 1971. His music has also been influenced by the French and Italian avant garde.

Works OPERA *La Passion de Gilles* (1983), *Reigen* (after Schnitzler's play; 1993).

ORCHESTRAL *Impromptu* for 23 instruments (1965); symphony for piano (1966); *Verticales* for orchestra (1969); *Intervalles* for orchestra (1973); *Multiples* for two pianos and orchestra (1974); piano and violin concertos (1978, 1979); *Conversions* for orchestra (1980).

VOCAL *Attitudes* for soprano and ensemble (1977).

OTHER *Ricercar* for organ (1983); realization of Monteverdi's *Poppea* with an array of modern instruments (1989).

Boethius, Anicius Manlius Severinus (c.480–524) Roman consul, senator, and philosopher. His most important work is the *De consolatione philosophiae* (some verses from which were set to music in Carolingian times), but he is also, in his *De institutione musica*, the interpreter of ancient musical theory to the Western world. In spite of some misconceptions, his work remained the fundamental basis of almost all medieval and Renaissance musical theory.

Boettcher, Wilfried (1929–1994) German conductor and cellist. He was conductor of the Hamburg Symphony Orchestra 1967–71 and guest conductor with other leading orchestras in Europe and the USA.

After studying in Hamburg and with Pierre Fournier in Paris, France, he founded the Vienna Soloists in Austria in 1959. He was principal guest conductor of the Northern Sinfonia, Newcastle, England, from 1986. He had opera engagements in Berlin, Vienna (State Opera), and Italy.

Bogatirev, Anatoly Vassilevich (1913–) Russian composer. He studied at the Minsk Conservatory under Zolotarev. Later he studied folksong and became deputy director of the Conservatory at Minsk.

Works DRAMA operas *The Two Foscari* (after Byron) and *In the Thick Woods of Polesye* (1939); incidental music for Romashev's *Stars Cannot be Dimmed*.

VOCAL *The Tale of a Bear* for solo voices, chorus, and orchestra, cantata *To the People of Leningrad*.

CHAMBER string quartet, piano trio; *Manfred* suite (after Byron) and variations for piano.

OTHER choruses, songs, folksong arrangements. In 1957 he made a performing version from the sketches of Tchaikovsky's seventh symphony.

Bohème, La, **Bohemian Life** opera by Ruggiero Leoncavallo (libretto by composer, based on Murger's novel *Scènes de la vie de Bohème*), first produced at the Teatro La Fenice, Venice, Italy, on 6 May 1897. The plot concerns Rodolfo and Mimi who face love and death. It was composed at the same time as Puccini's opera of the same title.

The opera by Puccini (libretto by G Giacosa and L Illica, also based on Murger), was first produced at the Teatro Regio, Turin, Italy, on 1 February 1896.

Bohemian Girl, The opera by Michael Balfe (libretto by A Bunn, based on a ballet-pantomime, *La Gypsy*, by J H V de Saint-Georges), first produced at the Drury Lane Theatre, London, England, on 27 November 1843.

Böhm, Georg (1661–1733) German composer. As a composer and organist he was an important forerunner of Johann Sebastian Bach. Before 1698 he was organist at Hamburg, then at St John's Church, Lüneburg. His works include a Passion, songs, and organ and harpsichord music.

Böhm, Karl (1894–1981) Austrian conductor. He is known for his stately interpretations of Beethoven, and of Mozart and Strauss operas.

Boieldieu, François Adrien (1775–1834) French composer. At 18 he composed his first opera, *La Fille coupable* (1793), which was produced at Rouen. In 1803 he occupied the post of maître de chapelle to Emperor Alexander at St Petersburg, Russia, but in 1811 returned to Paris to produce more operas, including the two most successful, *Jean de Paris* (1812) and *La Dame blanche* (1825).

Boieldieu was born in Rouen and studied under Broche, the organist of Rouen Cathedral. His first opera, *La Fille coupable*, was written to a libretto by his father, who was secretary to the archbishop. He also wrote many songs at that time, some of which were published in Paris. Having failed to establish a school of music at Rouen on the model of the Paris Conservatory, he left for the capital, where in 1797 he produced his first opera away from home, *La Famille Suisse*, which was so successful that he brought out four more within two years. He also became piano professor at the Conservatory in 1798. Being reproached by the composer Luigi Cherubini for having attained too easy a success on very slender gifts, he placed himself under that master for a course in counterpoint. In 1802 he married the dancer Clotilde Mafleuray, with disastrous results, and in 1803 he left for St Petersburg as conductor of the Imperial Opera. There he wrote nine operas 1804–10. In 1811 he returned to Paris, where he had greater success than previously; probably due to there being less competition and an improvement in his work.

He collaborated by turns with Cherubini, Charles Catel, Nicolò Isouard, Rodolphe Kreutzer, Ferdinand Hérold, Henri-Montan Berton, Ferdinando Paer, and Daniel Auber, also with some of these and Désiré Batton, Felice Blangini, and Michele Carafa in *La Marquise de Brinvilliers* (1831), but his best works were composed alone. In *La Dame blanche*, to match the libretto from Scott, he used some Scottish folk songs. His last years were troubled by illness and poverty: he began to suffer from tuberculosis contracted in Russia, and his fortune declined until he was granted a state pension. In 1827 he was married for the second time, to the singer Jenny Philis-Bertin, with whom he had long been living and by whom in 1815 he had a son, Adrien Louis Victor, who also became a composer. Boieldieu lived in Geneva, Switzerland, for a time not long before his death.

Works OPERA *Le Calife de Bagdad* (1800), *Ma Tante Aurore* (1803), *Aline, Reine de Golconde* (1804), *La Jeune Femme colère*, *Télémaque* (1807), *Rien de trop*, *Jean de Paris* (1812), *La Fête du village voisin*, *Le Petit Chaperon rouge*, *La Dame blanche* (1825), *Les Deux Nuits*, and others.

INCIDENTAL MUSIC incidental music for Racine's *Athalie*.

ORCHESTRAL piano concerto (1792), harp concerto (1801).

CHAMBER piano trio and other chamber music; duets for violin and piano, and harp and piano, six piano sonatas.

Boismortier, Joseph Bodin de (1689–1755) French composer. He is reputed to have written the first French concerto in 1729. He wrote three opera-ballets, *Les Voyages de l'amour* (1736), *Don Quichote* (1743), and *Daphnis et Chloé* (1747); eight cantatas, in two books (1724 and 1737), and over 50 instrumental works including many for musette and vielle.

Boito, Arrigo (1842–1918) Italian poet and composer. He wrote libretti for several composers as well as for himself, including those of Verdi's *Otello* (1887) and *Falstaff* (1893). Boito is most often heard today as Verdi's late librettist, although his own opera *Mefistofele* (1868) is one of the finest musical settings of the Faust legend.

Boito was born in Padua and studied at the Milan Conservatory. At first he worked as a journalist in Milan and Paris, and served under Garibaldi in Austria. He travelled much in France, Germany, and Poland, and produced his Faust opera, *Mefistofele*, at La Scala, Milan. It proved a failure but was more successful when played in shorter form in 1875. His only other opera, *Nerone*, was not produced until 1924, six years after his death. He also wrote the opera *Ero e Leandro*, but destroyed the music (the libretto was set by Giovanni Bottesini and later by Luigi Mancinelli) and he wrote a libretto on *Hamlet* for Franco Faccio. Boito published songs, novels, critiques, and dramas; of his verse the longest piece is *Re Orso*, a narrative poem describing the atrocities of the Minotaur.

Bolcom, William Elden (1938–) US composer and pianist. His works have been influenced by techniques of collage and microtonal electronics. As a pianist he has been heard in popular early American music, often with his wife, the mezzo Joan Morris.

Bolcom studied at Stanford University, USA, and the Paris Conservatory, France, and taught at the University of Michigan, USA, from 1973.

Works THEATRE PIECES *Dynamite Tonite* (1963), *Greatshot* (1969), *Theatre of the Absurd* (1970), *The Beggar's Opera* (adaptation of Gay, 1978), *McTeague* (1992).

ORCHESTRAL *Oracles*, symphony (1964), piano concerto (1976), violin concerto (1983), Concertante for viola, cello, and orchestra (1985), clarinet concerto (1989).

CHAMBER symphony for chamber orchestra (1979), octet for wind, strings, and piano (1962), piano quartet (1976), brass quintet (1980), *Spring Concerto* for oboe and chamber orchestra (1989), *Fantasy Suite* for piano (1989).

VOCAL *Songs of Innocence and Experience*, 48 Blake settings for solo voices and choruses (1958–81; version with orchestra performed Stuttgart 1984).

OTHER *Session*, works for various instrumental groups, with drum play (1965–67), 14 piano rags (1967–70).

bolero Spanish dance in moderate triple time (3/4), invented in the late 18th century. It is performed by a solo dancer or a couple, usually with castanet accompaniment, and is still a contemporary form of dance in Caribbean countries. In music, Maurice Ravel's one-act ballet score

➤ *Boléro* (1928) is the most famous example.

Boléro orchestral work by Maurice Ravel, commissioned as a ballet for Ida Rubinstein and first performed by her in Paris, France, on 22 November 1928. It consists entirely of a single theme of Spanish character, repeated over and over again with different orchestration and in a gradual taut *crescendo*.

Bologna, Jacopo da (Jacobus de Bononia) (1340–60) Italian composer. He belongs to the earliest generation of 14th-century composers – all his known works are madrigals, and nearly all are for two voices. He also wrote a short treatise, *L'arte del biscanto misurato*.

Bolt, The ballet in three acts by Dmitri Shostakovich (scenario by V Smirnov), first performed in Leningrad (now St Petersburg), Russia, on 8 April 1931. The ballet suite (no. 5) Op. 27a was first performed in 1933.

Bomarzo opera by Alberto Ginastera (libretto by M M Láinez, set in 16th-century Italy), first performed in Washington, DC, USA, on 19 May 1967. It was banned in Ginastera's own country, Argentina, owing to alleged obscenities in the ballet – Duke Francesco drinks a poisoned potion, believing it will bring immortality; as he dies, flashbacks of his tormented past and unfulfilled sexuality appear before him. The cantata *Bomarzo*, for baritone, speaker, chorus, and orchestra, was first performed in Washington on 1 November 1964.

bombard double-reed wind instrument, the bass instrument of the ➤ shawm family and a forerunner of the ➤ bassoon.

bombardon (French) brass instrument of the ➤ tuba variety. The name is derived from the bombard, and was previously applied to various instruments of the oboe and bassoon family. When used, the bombardon takes the lowest bass parts in military and brass bands. See ➤ saxhorn.

bongos small Cuban drums played in pairs by the fingers and thumbs. They consist of hollowed-out pieces of wood with a skin stretched over one end. Both drums are tuned, usually at least a fourth apart.

Bonini, Severo (1582–1663) Italian composer. He set Ottavio Rinuccini's poem 'Lamento d'Arianna' in recitative style in 1613, and wrote madrigals and spiritual canzonets for a single voice with ➤ continuo accompaniment. He was organist at Forli. His *Discorsi e Regole*, published about 1650, contains important information on early opera.

Bonne Chanson, La cycle of nine songs by Gabriel Fauré, set to poems from Paul Verlaine's volume of that name, composed 1891–92 and first performed in Paris, France, on 20 April 1895.

It it also the title of a symphonic poem by Charles Loeffler, based on the same source, composed in 1901 and first performed in Boston, USA, on 11 April 1902.

Bononcini or **Buononcini (lived 17th–18th centuries)** Italian family of musicians. **Giovanni Maria Bononcini** (1642–1678) was a pupil of Bendinelli, and maestro di cappella of Modena Cathedral. He wrote a treatise, *Musico prattico* (1673) and cantatas, sonatas, and suites.

His son, **Giovanni** (1670–1747), was a pupil of Giovanni Colonna and of his father, and maestro di cappella at San Giovanni in Monte at Modena. He produced his first opera in Rome in 1692. He lived in Vienna 1698–1711, in Italy 1711–20, in London, 1720–32 (where he had more success than Handel), and later in France and Vienna. He wrote the operas *Tullo Ostilio* (1694), *Il trionfo di Camilla* (1696), *Xerse*, *Endimione* (1706), *Astarto* (1715), *Crispo*, *Erminia* (1719), *Farnace*, *Calfurnia* (1724), *Astianatte*, *Griselda* (1733), and many others, including an act in *Muzio Scevola* with Handel and Amadei; seven oratorios; funeral anthem for Marlborough; music for the Peace of Aix-la-Chapelle; Masses, Te Deum, psalms, *Laudate pueri*; and chamber cantatas and duets.

Antonio Maria (1677–1726) was the second son of Giovanni. He became maestro di cappella to the Duke of Modena in 1721. He wrote about 20 operas and oratorios.

Bonporti, Francesco Antonio (1672–1749) Italian composer. He trained for the priesthood in Rome from 1691 and studied music with the composers Giuseppe Pitoni and Arcangelo Corelli. On his ordination he returned to Trento, and spent the next 40 years in hope of a canonry. He retired, disappointed, to Padua in 1740.

Works motets; trio sonatas; concertos; 'Inventions' for solo violin, which may have influenced Bach's works in the same form.

Bontempi, Giovanni Andrea (c.1624–1705) Italian castrato, theorist, and composer. He took the name of a patron, Cesare Bontempi, and sang in St Mark's, Venice, from 1643. At the end of the 1640s he went to Germany, where he became assistant conductor to Heinrich ➤ Schütz in Dresden in 1666, but devoted himself to science and architecture the next year. He returned to Italy in 1669 and after another visit to Dresden in 1671, settled down in his birthplace. He wrote three theoretical books.

Works OPERA *Paride* (1662), *Dafne* (1671), *Jupiter and Io* (1673).

Boosey & Hawkes London music publishers and instrument makers. They were originally two companies: Boosey, founded in 1816 as British agents for Rossini, Hummel, Mercadante, and others, and also manufacturing wind instruments from about 1850; and Hawkes, founded in 1865, handling brass and military band music. They merged in 1930.

Their catalogue includes many 20th-century composers, for example Richard Strauss, Sergey Prokofiev, Igor Stravinsky, Béla Bartók, Gustav Mahler, and Benjamin Britten. Contemporary composers include Elliott Carter, Leonard Bernstein, Steve Reich, György Kurtág, Robin Holloway and Peter Maxwell Davies.

bore in music, the internal diameter of tubing of a brass or woodwind instrument. The diameter of the bore affects the character of the instrument's tone.

Boréades, Les *tragédie-lyrique* in five acts by Jean-Philippe Rameau (libretto by L de Cahusac), written for the court of Louis XV in 1763 but not performed. Its first full performance (as a concert) was held in Paris, France, on 16 September 1964 and its first stage performance was in Aix-en-Provence, France, on 21 July 1982. In the story Queen Alphise wants to marry Abaris, but must marry a descendant of Boreas, god of the north wind. After she gives up the throne and suffers the wrath of Boreas, Abaris is revealed to be related to the god, and the couple marry.

boree one of the old English names for the ➔ **bourrée**, others being borea, bore, and borry.

Boretz, Benjamin (1934–   ) US composer and editor. He studied in New York with Lukas Foss, Darius Milhaud, and Roger Sessions. He has taught at Bard College from 1973 and was cofounder and editor of *Perspectives of New Music* 1961–84.

Works ORCHESTRAL *Group Variations I* (1967).

CHAMBER string quartet (1958), *Liebeslied* for piano (1974).

OTHER *Group Variations II* for computer (1971); *Language, as a Music* for speaker, piano, and tape (1980); other pieces involving sound on tape.

Borgomastro di Saardam, Il, The Burgomaster of Saardam comic opera by Donizetti (libretto by D Gilardoni, based on a French play by A H J Mélesville, J T Merle, and E C de Boirie), first produced at the Teatro del Fondo, Naples, Italy, on 19 August 1827. The subject was reworked in Gustav Lortzing's opera *Zar und Zimmermann* (1837).

Boris Godunov opera by Mussorgsky (libretto by composer, based on Aleksandr Pushkin's drama and N M Karamazin's *History of the Russian Empire*), composed 1868–69 and enlarged and revised 1871–72; this later version was cut and first produced at the Imperial Opera, St Petersburg,

Russia, on 8 February 1874, the original having been rejected in 1870. Rimsky-Korsakov's version was first produced at the St Petersburg Imperial Opera on 10 December 1896; this was further revised by Rimsky-Korsakov in 1908. The original work was first produced in Leningrad (St Petersburg) on 16 February 1928. The plot describes how Boris becomes tsar after having the heir to the throne murdered, but his guilt drives him insane and he eventually collapses and dies.

Borodin, Aleksandr Porfirevich (1833–1887) Russian composer. Born in St Petersburg, the illegitimate son of a Russian prince, he became an expert in medical chemistry, but enjoyed music and wrote it in his spare time. His main work is the opera *Prince Igor*, left unfinished; it was completed by Nikolai Rimsky-Korsakov and Aleksandr Glazunov and includes the Polovtsian Dances. His other works include symphonies, songs, and chamber music, using traditional Russian themes.

His father, Prince Gedeanov, registered Borodin as the son of one of his serfs. From childhood Borodin showed an equal liking for music and for science. He tried to compose at the age of nine and was given music lessons. In his studies at the Academy of Medicine he distinguished himself especially in chemistry, and while studying in Germany he met the pianist Ekaterina Protopopova, whom he married in 1863. The preceding year, having so far been self-taught in composition, he began to take lessons from Mily Balakirev, who conducted his first symphony in 1869. In the same year, he began his opera *Prince Igor*, working on it at irregular intervals; the score, completed posthumously by Rimsky-Korsakov and Glazunov, contains some of his finest music. He lectured on chemistry at the School of Medicine for Women from 1872 to his death and wrote important treatises on his subject. In spite of being best known for such 'highlights' as the Polovtsian Dances and even *Kismet/Fate*, Borodin's music is well worth much closer attention. His best work is highly charged and colourful, without being sensational or melancholy in the manner of some of his contemporaries.

Works OPERA *Prince Igor* (1869–87, unfinished).

ORCHESTRAL three symphonies (1867, 1876, third unfinished); *In the Steppes of Central Asia* for orchestra (1880).

CHAMBER two string quartets (1874–79, 1881); *Serenata alla spagnuola* for string quartet; *Petite Suite* for piano.

VOCAL *Serenade de quatre galants à une dame* for male voice quartet; songs.

borry English corruption of the French ➔ **bourrée** found in 17th-century music, such as that of Purcell.

Bortkievich, Sergei Eduardovich (1877–1952) Russian composer. He wrote a book about Tchaikovsky and Nadezhda von Meck in 1938.

He studied law at St Petersburg and composition under Liadov, later at Leipzig, Germany. He lived in Berlin until 1914, when he joined the Russian army, and at Constantinople (now Istanbul) after World War I. From 1922 until his death he lived in Vienna, Austria.

Works OPERA *Acrobats* (1938).

ORCHESTRAL two symphonies; symphonic poem *Othello*; four piano concertos (one for the left hand), two violin concertos, cello concerto.

OTHER piano sonatas and pieces; songs.

Bortniansky, Dimitri Stepanovich (1752– 1825) Ukrainian composer. He studied in Moscow and St Petersburg (Leningrad) under the Italian composer Baldassare Galuppi, whom he followed to Italy in 1768 with a grant from Catherine II. After further studies in Bologna, Rome, and Naples, he wrote motets and operas in Venice in 1776 and in Modena in 1778. In 1779 he returned to Russia and became director of the Imperial church choir, which he reformed and turned into the Imperial Chapel in 1796.

Works OPERA *Le Faucon* (1786), *Le Fils rival* (1787), *Creonte*, *Quinto Fabio* (1778).

OTHER 35 sacred concertos, 10 concertos for double choir, Mass, chants.

Börtz, Daniel (1943–) Swedish composer. He studied with Hilding Rosenberg and Karl-Birger Blomdahl, and also studied electronic music in Utrecht, the Netherlands. His opera *Backanterna* (after Euripides) was premiered in 1991 at the Stockholm Opera, directed by Ingmar Bergman.

Works OPERA two church operas; *Landscape with a River* (chamber opera after Hesse, 1974).

ORCHESTRAL eight symphonies (1973–88); two concerti grossi (1978, 1981); violin concerto (1985); oboe concerto (1986); *Parados* for orchestra (1987).

CHAMBER three string quartets (1966, 1971, 1987).

VOCAL *Josep K* for soloists, chorus, and orchestra (1969).

Böse, Hans-Jurgen von (1953–) German composer. He studied in Frankfurt and is best known for his stage compositions, both operas and ballets.

Works OPERA *Blutbund* (1974), *Das Diplom* (1974), *Die Leiden des jungen Werthers* (after Goethe; 1986), *Chimare* (1986), *63: Dream Palace* (1990, introducing some popular music elements), *Slaughterhouse Five* (1995).

BALLET *Die Nacht aus Blei* (1981), *Werther Szenen* (1989).

OTHER Symphony (1976), *Sappho-Gesänge* for mezzo and ensemble (1983), oboe concerto (1987), three string quartets (1973, 1977, 1987),

and variations for strings (1990).

Bösendorfer, Ignaz (1796–1859) Austrian piano manufacturer. He founded his firm in Vienna in 1828 and was succeeded in 1859 by his son Ludwig (1835–1919). In the 1980s the company developed an electronic pianola that sends details of the music played on it to a computer.

Boskovsky, Willi (1909–1991) Austrian violinist and conductor. He was with the Vienna Philharmonic Orchestra 1933–71, as coleader from 1939. He formed the Vienna Octet in 1948.

He conducted the New Year's Day concerts in Vienna, 1954–79.

Bossi, Marco Enrico (1861–1925) Italian organist and composer. He held various directorial posts, including that of the Royal Liceo of Santa Cecilia, Rome, 1916–23. His works include the *Canticum Canticorum* (biblical cantata, 1900), *Il paradiso perduto* (oratorio after John Milton, 1903), *Il cieco* (symphonic poem with voices), and church and organ music.

He studied at the Liceo Musicale of Bologna and at the Milan Conservatory. After various organist and teaching appointments he became director of the principal music schools at Venice, Bologna, and Rome in succession. Meanwhile he had become very famous as a concert organist. He died while returning from a tour in the USA.

Works OPERA *Paquita* (1881), *Il veggente* (1890), and *L'angelo della notte*.

CHORAL oratorios *Il Paradiso perduto* (after Milton) and *Giovanna d'Arco* (1914); Masses, motets, and sacred cantatas; secular choral works with orchestra or organ, including *Il cieco*, *Inno di gloria*, and *Cantico dei cantici* (1900).

ORCHESTRAL AND CHAMBER orchestral works; concerto for organ and orchestra; chamber music, 50 organ works, including suite *Res severa magnum gaudium*; piano pieces; songs.

Bossi, Renzo (1883–1965) Italian composer, son of the composer and organist Enrico Bossi. He studied under his father at the Liceo Benedetto Marcello in Venice and took a composition prize in 1902, when he went to Leipzig, Germany, to continue studying piano, organ, and conducting, the last under Artur Nikisch. He was conductor at several German opera houses before he went to Milan as assistant conductor at La Scala. He was professor of composition at Parma from 1913 and at Milan from 1916.

Works OPERA *Rosa rossa* (after Oscar Wilde; Parma, 1940), *Passa la ronda!* (Milan, 1919), *La notte del mille*, *Volpino il calderaio* (after Shakespeare's *The Taming of the Shrew*; Milan, 1925), *Proserpina*.

ORCHESTRAL AND CHAMBER symphonies, *Sinfoniale*, *Fantasia sinfonica*, and *Bianco e nero* for orchestra; violin concerto; chamber music.

Bottesini, Giovanni (1821–1889) Italian double bass player, conductor, and composer. His works include twelve operas and an oratorio. He wrote *Méthode complète de Contre-basse* and many pieces for double bass. As a virtuoso of his instrument he was compared with the violinist Niccolò Paganini.

Bottesini was born in Crema, Lombardy. In 1840 he went on an international concert tour which included engagements at Havana, Paris, Palermo, Barcelona, and Cairo, and established his fame as the greatest master of the double bass. He became director of the Conservatory in Parma.

Works OPERA *Marion Delorme* (after Victor Hugo; Palermo, 1862), *Ali Baba* (London, 1871), *Ero e Leandro* (Turin, 1879).

OTHER double bass concertos with orchestra; much music for double bass and piano.

Bottrigari (Bottrigaro), Ercole (1531–1612) Italian theorist. His *Il desiderio* (1594) deals with the problems of combining instruments of different families. From 1600 to 1604 he was involved in a controversy with Artusi.

Boucourechliev, André (1925–1997) French composer and musicologist of Bulgarian origin. He studied in Sofia, Bulgaria; Paris, France; and Darmstadt, Germany. He worked as a music critic and wrote on Schumann, Chopin, and Beethoven. His works are influenced by Pierre Boulez and include the series *Archipel* (from 1967) which allows the performer a wide range of interpretative choices.

Works ORCHESTRAL *Amers* for orchestra (1973), piano concerto (1976).

CHAMBER *Musiques Nocturnes* for clarinet, harp, and piano (1966), *Ombres* for eleven strings (based on themes from Beethoven's late quartets; first performance Brussels 1970, conductor Boulez).

VOCAL *Grodek* for soprano and ensemble (text by Trakl, 1963).

OTHER *Texte I* and *II* for tape (1959–60).

Boughton, Rutland (1878–1960) English composer. He idolized Wagner, and determined to found an English centre of opera on the same lines as Bayreuth. He began in a very modest way at Glastonbury with a series of music dramas on the Arthurian legends, producing *The Immortal Hour* in 1914. A special theatre was to be built in Glastonbury, but the project had to be abandoned.

Boughton was born in Aylesbury, England. He studied at the Royal College of Music in London under Charles Villiers Stanford and Walford Davies, but left after a short time and produced some early orchestral works, conducting for a time at the Haymarket Theatre, London. In 1914, in collaboration with Reginald Buckley, he founded the Glastonbury Festival School of Music Drama, where *The Immortal Hour* was produced; the festival was revived after World War I. In 1922 *The Immortal Hour* had a long run in London, and *Alkestis* was produced there by the British National Opera Company in 1924. From 1926 Boughton was an active member of the Communist Party.

Works MUSIC DRAMA *The Birth of Arthur* (1908–09), *Bethlehem* (1913), *The Immortal Hour* (1914), *The Round Table* (1916), *Alkestis* (1922), *The Queen of Cornwall* (1924), *The Lily Maid* (1934); dramatic scene *Agincourt* from Shakespeare's *Henry V*.

BALLET *Choral Dances*, *Snow White*, *The Moon Maiden*.

CHORUS AND ORCHESTRA *The Skeleton in Armour* (Longfellow), *The Invincible Armada* (Schiller), *Midnight* (E Carpenter), *Song of Liberty*; unaccompanied choral music.

CHAMBER two string quartets.

Bouilly, Jean-Nicolas (1763–1842) French writer. He was administrator of a department near Tours during the French Revolution. He wrote libretti for a number of operas (➤ **rescue opera**) for various composers, including Luigi Cherubini and Pierre Gaveaux. The libretto of Beethoven's *Fidelio* is based on his book for Gaveaux's *Léonore*.

Boulanger, Lili (Juliette Marie Olga) (1893–1918) French composer. She was the younger sister of Nadia Boulanger. At the age of 19, she won the Prix de Rome with the cantata *Faust et Hélène* for voices and orchestra.

She studied first as a pupil of her sister Nadia, then at the Paris Conservatory.

Works incidental music for Maeterlinck's *La Princesse Maleine* (1918); two poems for orchestra; cantata *Faust et Hélène* (after Goethe, 1913); psalms with orchestra.

Boulanger, Nadia Juliette (1887–1979) French music teacher and conductor. She studied under Gabriel Fauré at the Paris Conservatory, where she later taught, as well as at the École Normale de Musique and the American Conservatory at Fontainebleau. Many distinguished composers were her pupils, including her sister, Lili Boulanger, Lennox Berkeley, Aaron Copland, Jean Françaix, Roy Harris, Walter Piston, and Philip Glass.

She was the first woman to conduct the Royal Philharmonic, London, in 1937, and the Boston Symphony, the New York Philharmonic, and the Philadelphia Orchestra in 1938. After the outbreak of World War II in Europe in 1939, she went to the USA, returning in 1946.

Works incidental music to d'Annunzio's *La città morta* (with Pugno; 1911); cantata *La Sirène*

(1908); orchestral works; instrumental pieces, songs.

Boulevard Solitude opera by Hans Werner Henze (libretto by the composer and G Weil), first produced in Hanover, Germany, on 17 February 1952. The plot is a modern version of the Manon story: the lovers Manon and Armand are forced apart by poverty when she must take a rich admirer to support herself and her brother.

Boulez, Pierre (1925–) French composer and conductor. He is the founder and director of ➤ **IRCAM**, a music research studio at the Pompidou Centre in Paris, France, that opened in 1977. His music, strictly adhering to ideas of ➤ **serialism** and expressionistic in style, includes the cantatas *Le Visage nuptial* (1946–52) and *Le Marteau sans maître* (1953–55), both to texts by René Char; *Pli selon pli* (1962) for soprano and orchestra; and *Répons* (1981) for soloists, orchestra, tapes, and computer-generated sounds.

Boulez was born in Montbrison, France, on the River Loire. After abandoning studies in mathematics, he studied with Olivier ➤ **Messiaen** at the Paris Conservatory, and in 1946 took a course in serial technique with René Leibowitz. Also in 1946, he worked for the Renaud-Barrault theatre company and in 1953–54 founded the 'Domaine Musical' with Jean-Louis Barrault, which specialized in new music. As a composer he belongs to the avant garde, writing in a style which has its roots in ➤ **Debussy** and ➤ **Webern**, and also in the ideas of James Joyce and Stéphane Mallarmé. He is one of the pioneers of ➤ **integral serialism**, but later introduced freer elements into his music. Boulez is also a leading conductor of advanced new music. He was principal conductor of the BBC Symphony Orchestra 1971–75, and of the New York Philharmonic Orchestra 1971–77, giving notable performances of works by Berg, Bartók, Stravinsky, and members of the Second Viennese School, including Schoenberg's *Moses und Aron* in London, England, in 1974. He conducted Wagner's operas *Parsifal* at Bayreuth, Germany, in 1966, and *The Ring* in 1976, and gave the first complete performance of Berg's opera *Lulu* in Paris in 1979.

His early works (including *Flute Sonatina* (1946), *Le Visage Nuptial*, and the first two piano sonatas) are preoccupied with developments and extensions of Webern's serial technique. *Structures* (1952) for two pianos is a turning point in his development, taking account of the concepts of a series of durations, intensities, and timbres first proposed by Messiaen. Later works, such as *Le Marteau sans maître*, the third piano sonata, and *Pli selon pli* develop these ideas with greater flexibility, eventually leading to the use of open forms (as in the third piano sonata) in which the order of musical material may be deci-

ded by the performer. Since the 1960s he has become prominent as a conductor of international standing, and in 2001 he was named conductor of the year at the Royal Philharmonic Society awards in London. He wrote *Boulez on Music Today* (1971).

Works ORCHESTRAL ... *explosante fixe ...* (1971–73); *Rituel in memoriam Bruno Maderna* (1974–75); *Répons* for 24 players, six instrumental soloists, and computerized electronics (1981).

VOCAL *Le Soleil des eaux* for solo voices, chorus, and orchestra (after Char); *Le Marteau sans maître* for alto and six instruments (after Char; 1953–55); *Pli selon pli* for soprano and orchestra (after Mallarmé, 1962); *cummings ist der dichter* for 16 solo voices and 24 instruments (1970, revised 1986).

INSTRUMENTAL three piano sonatas (1946, 1948, 1957); *Livre* for string quartet (1948, revised for string orchestra 1968); *Eclat* for 15 instruments (1965, expanded as *Eclat/Multiples* for 27 instruments, 1966); *Dérive* for small ensemble (1984); *Dérive II* for eleven instruments (1988); *Message esquisse* for cello.

Boult, Adrian Cedric (1889–1983) English conductor. He conducted the BBC Symphony Orchestra 1930–50 and the London Philharmonic 1950–57. He promoted the work of Holst and Vaughan Williams, and was a celebrated interpreter of Elgar.

bourdon (French 'bumblebee') French musical term for the drone of an instrument such as the hurdy-gurdy or bagpipes, or for a piece of music imitating a drone accompaniment. The term is of particular relevance to the ➤ **musette**.

Bourgault-Ducoudray, Louis (Albert) (1840–1910) French composer. A lawyer at first, he entered the Paris Conservatory late and took a composition prize in 1862. In 1869 he founded a choral society in Paris with which he gave performances of unfamiliar works. He collected and published Greek and Breton folksongs, and lectured on history of music at the Conservatory from 1878.

Works OPERA *L'Atelier de Prague* (1858), *Michel Colomb* (1887), *Bretagne, Thamara* (1891), *Myrdhin* (1905).

STAGE satiric play *La Conjuration des fleurs*. CHURCH MUSIC *Stabat Mater*.

ORCHESTRAL *Fantaisie en Ut mineur, Carnaval d'Athènes, Rapsodie cambodgienne, L'Enterrement d'Ophélie* (after Shakespeare) for orchestra. VOCAL *Symphonie religieuse* for unaccompanied chorus.

Bourgeois, Derek (David) (1941–) English composer. He studied at Cambridge, and with Herbert Howells at the Royal College of Music, London, and was appointed lecturer at Bristol

The opening of Bach's famous Bourrée from his Cello Suite no.3.

University in 1971.

Works ORCHESTRAL two symphonies (1960, 1968), variations on a theme of Mozart, for double bass and orchestra (1967), symphonic fantasy *The Astronauts* (1969).

VOCAL *Jabberwocky-Extravaganza* for baritone, chorus, and orchestra (1963).

CHAMBER string quartet (1962), two brass quintets (1965, 1972).

Bourgeois Gentilhomme, Le, The Bourgeois as Gentleman comedy-ballet by the French dramatist Molière with music by Jean-Baptiste Lully, first produced at Chambord, France, on 14 October 1670.

Richard Strauss composed incidental music to a shortened version of Molière's comedy (translated by H von Hofmannsthal), preceding the one-act opera *Ariadne auf Náxos*, which was first produced in Stuttgart, Germany, on 25 October 1912. Strauss afterwards dropped it for a new operatic first act and made a concert suite for orchestra of the incidental music, adding a minuet by Lully (first performed in Vienna, Austria, on 31 January 1920, conducted by Strauss).

bourrée French dance form in fast double two time, accented on the second beat, and starting on the upbeat, the music for which is found in the classical ➤ suite.

boutade (French 'whim, frolic') 18th-century dance, or sometimes a whole ballet, in a whimsical style; also sometimes an instrumental piece of the same character.

Boutique fantasque, La, The Fantastic Toyshop ballet by Ottorino Respighi, arranged from music by Rossini (choreographed by Leonid Fedorovich Massin), first produced at the Alhambra Theatre, London, England, on 5 June 1919. The music consists mainly of small pieces written by Rossini in his retirement for the amusement of his friends.

bow in music, a stick holding lengths of stretched horsehair which is drawn across the strings of a member of the violin or viol family in order to produce sound vibrations in the string. Before the 17th century bows were convex, but changes in violin technique prompted the development of concave bows, perfected by François Tourte (1747–1835) at the end of the 18th century.

Unusual instruments that have been played with a bow include the ➤ glass harmonica and ➤ musical saw.

bowing in music, the art of using a bow, or the marking of scores and parts with indications about how to bow.

Bowles, Paul (1910–1999) US writer and composer. Born in New York City, he studied music composition with Aaron Copland and Virgil Thomson, writing scores for ballets, films, and an opera, *The Wind Remains* (1943), as well as incidental music for plays. He settled in Morocco, the setting of his novels *The Sheltering Sky* (1949, filmed 1990) and *Let It Come Down* (1952), which chillingly depict the existential breakdown of Westerners unable to survive self-exposure in an alien culture. Other works include *A Thousand Days for Mokhtar* (1989) and *Too Far from Home* (1994). His autobiography, *Without Stopping*, was published in 1972.

Bowles settled permanently in Tangier with his wife, the writer Jane Bowles (1917–1973), after World War II and became greatly influenced by Moroccan storytelling – he later turned to transcribing and translating tales by Muhammad Mrabet and others.

Boyarina Vera Sheloga work by the Russian composer Rimsky-Korsakov; see ➤ *Pskovitianka*.

Boyce, William (1710–1779) English composer and organist. He wrote church music, symphonies, and chamber music, but is best known for his song 'Heart of Oak' (1759). He was one of the most respected English composers of his time. Much of his music exhibits a fresh liveliness, particularly his many dance movements.

Boyce was a chorister at St Paul's Cathedral and a pupil of Maurice Greene, whom he succeeded as Master of the King's Musick in 1755. Meanwhile he held various organ posts in London, was appointed composer to the Chapel Royal in 1736, and conductor of the Three Choirs Festival the following year. From 1758 he was organist of the Chapel Royal. Deafness forced him to give up much of his work during his later years. Although his dance movements and fugues show much individuality, based on an idiom bequeathed by Handel, his numerous court odes are more easily forgotten. In recent years his music has been revived.

Works STAGE ENTERTAINMENTS *The Chaplet* (1749), *The Shepherd's Lottery* (1751); masques *Peleus and Thetis* (1740) and Dryden's *Secular Masque* (about 1746); incidental music for Shakespeare's *The Tempest*, *Cymbeline* (1746), and *Romeo and Juliet* (1750); pantomime *Harlequin's Invasion* (with M Arne and Aylward, and containing the song 'Heart of Oak', 1759).

ORCHESTRAL 20 symphonies and overtures.

CHAMBER 12 trio sonatas; keyboard music.

OTHER service settings and anthems; cantatas and odes; songs, and other pieces. He also completed a notable collection of earlier church music begun by Greene (published under the title *Cathedral Music* in three volumes (1760–73).

Boyd, Anne (1946–) Australian composer. She studied with Peter Sculthorpe in Sydney and with Bernard Rands in York, England, and was appointed head of the music department at Hong Kong University in 1980. Her music reflects oriental influences and includes some small-scale theatre pieces.

Works THEATRE PIECES *As Far as Crawls the Toad* (1970), *The Rose Garden* (1971); children's operas *The Little Mermaid* (1978), *The Beginning of the Day* (1980).

ORATORIO *The Death of Captain Cook* (1978).

ORCHESTRAL *Black Sun* (1989), flute concerto (1992), *Grathawai* (1993).

CHAMBER three string quartets (1968, 1973, 1991); *Wind across Bamboo* wind quintet (1984).

VOCAL choral and solo vocal music.

Boyhood's End cantata for tenor and piano by Michael Tippett (text by W H Hudson), composed in 1943 and first performed in London on 5 June 1943.

Bozay, Attila (1939–1999) Hungarian composer. He studied in Budapest at the Bartók Conservatory and with Ferenc Farkas. His music is influenced by serial technique and by Hungarian folksongs.

Works OPERA *Queen Kungisz* (1969), *Hamlet* (1984).

ORCHESTRAL *Pezzo concertato* for viola and orchestra, *Pezzo sinfonico* for orchestra (1967).

VOCAL *Trapeze and Bars*, cantata (1966).

CHAMBER two string quartets (1964, 1971).

CELLO *Formations* for solo cello (1969).

braccio, da (Italian 'on the arm') in music, a suffix originally used to distinguish violins, which are played resting on the arm, from viols, which are played da **→ gamba** (on the leg). The term

'viola da braccio' in 17th-century music signifies a violin or viola; today only the viola (German *Bratsche*) is so called.

brace in musical notation, a bracket connecting a number of simultaneously played staves, such as the two staves in piano and harp music, or a greater number of staves in a score.

Brack, Georg (Jörg) (lived 16th century) German composer. His part songs were published in collections printed by Schöffer in 1513, Arnt von Aich in 1519, and others.

Bradley, Scott (1891–1977) US composer of animation film music. Working for the US film-production company Metro-Goldwyn-Mayer (MGM), with Carl Stalling, he developed the **→ click-track** which enables a composer to write a music track to any desired tempo for a given length of film. He also introduced classical music to *Tom and Jerry* cartoons.

Examples of music for *Tom and Jerry* include Liszt's *Hungarian Rhapsody No. 2* for *Cat Concerto* (1947), and 12-tone row on piccolo to represent Jerry and the same row in reverse played by oboe to represent Tom for *The Cat that Hated People*.

Brahms, Johannes (1833–1897) German composer, pianist, and conductor. He is considered one of the greatest composers of symphonic music and songs. His works include four symphonies, lieder (songs), concertos for piano and for violin, chamber music, sonatas, and the choral *Ein Deutsches Requiem/A German Requiem* (1868). He performed and conducted his own works.

In 1853 the violinist Joseph Joachim introduced him to the composers Franz Liszt and Robert Schumann, who encouraged his work. From 1863 Brahms made his home in Vienna, Austria. Although his music belongs to a reflective type of **→ Romanticism**, similar to William Wordsworth in poetry, Brahms saw himself as continuing the classical tradition from where Beethoven had left it. To musicians of his day, he was a strict formalist, opposite to the arch-Romantic Wagner. His influence on Gustav Mahler and Arnold Schoenberg was profound.

Brahms was born in Hamburg, Germany. His father was a double bass player who taught him music as a child. Although he intended to be an orchestral player, he made so much progress on the piano that his parents decided to make him a prodigy performer when he was about 11. His teachers wisely opposed this. Soon afterwards he began to compose, but had to play in sailors' taverns and dancing-saloons at night to earn money for the family. He gave two concerts during 1848–49, but did not free himself from the drudgery of playing and teaching until he went on a concert tour with Eduard Reményi in 1853. It was then that he met Joachim, Liszt, and other important musicians, particularly Robert and Clara Schumann, who took much interest in him. He was engaged now and again at the court of Lippe-Detmold in 1857–60, travelled as a pianist, and worked in Hamburg, where he conducted a ladies' choir. In Hanover in 1859 he premiered his first piano concerto, which, although one of the great masterpieces of the genre, was poorly received by both audience and critics, probably as a result of inadequate rehearsal time.

He visited Vienna in 1862 and settled there the following year. From 1864 he devoted his time entirely to composition, except for some concert tours on which he played mainly his own works. In Bremen in 1868 he conducted the premiere of his most profound vocal work, *Ein Deutsches Requiem/A German Requiem*; one month later he added the movement *Ihr habt nun Traurigkeit/Though Ye Now be Sorrowful* in memory of his mother. His success as a composer was firmly established during the 1860s, and he became known abroad, but he did not complete his first symphony until 1876. It had taken him 15 years and was written in Beethoven's shadow, but after its premiere Brahms was established as the leading composer of instrumental music of his time. The symphony was soon followed by a more relaxed work in D major. He wrote much during summer holidays in Austria, Germany, and Switzerland, but hardly visited other countries except Italy. In 1877 he refused an honorary doctorate from Cambridge University, England, because he did not wish to travel to receive it in person, but he accepted a doctorate from the University of Breslau, Prussia, in 1879. In 1881 he was the soloist in the premiere of his second piano concerto. In 1896 he began to suffer seriously from cancer of the liver, the disease from which he died the following year. Brahms was the great compositional conservative of the 19th century. Musicians tended to be classified either as supporters of Brahms or of Wagner, the great innovator of the same period. However, what Brahms lacked in formal invention he more than compensated for in profundity and the perfection of contemporary models.

Works CHORUS AND ORCHESTRAL *Ein Deutsches Requiem/A German Requiem* (texts from Martin Luther's translation of the Bible), with baritone and soprano soloists (1857–68), *Rhapsody* for contralto, male chorus, and orchestra (1869), *Gesang der Parzen* (1882).

SYMPHONIES no. 1 in C minor, Op. 68 (1855–76), no. 2 in D, Op. 73 (1877), no. 3 in F, Op. 90 (1883), no. 4 in E minor, Op. 98 (1884–85).

CONCERTOS two for piano, no. 1 in D minor, Op. 15 (1854–58), no. 2 in B♭, Op. 83 (1878–81); violin in D, Op. 77 (1878); violin and cello in A minor,

Op. 102 (1887).

CHAMBER two string sextets, Op. 18 in B♭ (1860), Op. 36 in G (1865); three string quartets; two string quintets, Op. 88 in F (1882), Op. 111 in G (1890); three piano quartets, Op. 25 in G minor (1861), Op. 26 in A (1861), Op. 60 (1855–75); piano quintet Op. 34 in F minor (1864); clarinet quintet Op. 115 in B minor (1891); three piano trios, Op. 8 in B (1854, revised 1890), Op. 87 in C (1880–82), Op. 101 in C minor (1886); horn trio Op. 40 in E♭ (1865); two cello sonatas, Op. 38 in E minor (1862–65), Op. 99 in F (1886); three violin sonatas (1879–88); trio for clarinet, cello, piano (1891); two sonatas for clarinet or viola, Op. 120 in F minor and E♭ (1894).

SOLO PIANO includes three sonatas (1852–53); variations on themes by Schumann, Handel (Op. 24, 1861), Paganini (Op. 35, 1863), and Haydn (version for two pianos of work for orchestra, 1873); rhapsodies, intermezzos, and other pieces.

ORGAN includes eleven chorale preludes, Op. 122 (1896).

VOCAL numerous part songs; the song cycles *Die Schöne Magelone* Op. 33 and *Vier ernste Gesänge* for low voice and piano Op. 121; more than 200 lieder (1852–86).

Brand, Max (1896–1980) Polish-born Austrian composer. His opera *Maschinist Hopkins* (1929) is one of the outstanding works of the 'machinist' period of the 1920s; it was banned by the Nazis and not heard again complete until produced by the British Broadcasting Corporation (BBC) in 1986. He also experimented with electronic music and wrote *The Astronauts, an Epic in Electronics* (1962).

He studied in Vienna under Franz Schreker and Alois Hába. He settled in the USA in 1940 but returned to Austria in 1975.

Works opera; scenic oratorio *The Gate* (1944); symphonic poems, chamber music.

Brandenburg Concertos a series of six orchestral concertos in the ➔ concerto grosso style by Johann Sebastian ➔ Bach, dedicated in 1721 to the Margrave Christian Ludwig of Brandenburg.

They are: No. 1, in F, for three oboes, two horns, bassoon, *violino piccolo*, strings, and continuo; No. 2, in F, for recorder, oboe, trumpet, violin, strings, and continuo; No. 3, in G, for three violins, three violas, three cellos, bass, and continuo; No. 4, in G, for two recorders, violin, strings, and continuo; No. 5, in D, for flute, violin, harpsichord, strings, and continuo; and No. 6, in B flat, for two violas, two bass viols, cello, bass, and continuo.

Brandenburgers in Bohemia, The, Czech ***Braniboři v Čechách*** opera by Bedřich Smetana (libretto by K Sabina), first produced at the Czech Theatre, Prague, on 5 January 1866. The story tells of the Brandenburgers who invade Bohemia, and are thrown out.

Brandts-Buys, Jan (1868–1933) Dutch composer. He won a state prize as a youth and studied in Frankfurt, Germany. Most of his operatic successes were produced in Germany and Austria.

Works OPERA *Das Veilchenfest* (Berlin, 1909), *Le Carillon, Die Schneider von Schoenau* (Dresden, 1916), *Der Eroberer* (Dresden, 1918), *Mi-carême, Der Mann im Mond* (1922), *Traumland, Ulysses.*

ORCHESTRAL *Oberon Romancero* for orchestra; three piano concertos; suite for strings, harp and horn.

CHAMBER string quartets; quintet for flute and strings; piano trios; piano works.

OTHER songs.

branle a French dance in 2/2 or 3/2 time dating from the 15th century and cultivated until the 18th, called brawl in England.

brass band instrumental ensemble consisting of ➔ brass and sometimes ➔ percussion instruments. It differs from a military band, which would contain woodwind (although brass bands in Lancashire, England, also contain woodwind). The instruments of a brass band usually include (in descending order of pitch) the cornet, flugelhorn, tenor horn, B flat baritone, euphonium, trombone, and bombardon (bass tuba), as well as drums and other percussion as needed. It developed during the 19th century from the military band, and was particularly linked with the northern English manufacturing towns of Lancashire and Yorkshire. Some classical composers have written for the brass bands, including Edward Elgar in his *Severn Suite* (1930) and *Grimethorpe Aria* (1973) by Harrison Birtwistle.

brass instrument any of a group of musical instruments made of brass or other metal. It does not include woodwind instruments made of metal, such as the saxophone or flute. The sound is produced when the column of air inside the instrument is made to vibrate by the player's lips vibrating against the mouthpiece. Orchestral brass instruments are descended from signalling instruments (the 'natural horn', 'natural trumpet') consisting of a single tube with no extra mechanism. These instruments could only produce notes in their own harmonic series – the higher notes of the series being produced by the player increasing the lip tension. To achieve a variety of notes, a player used a set of crooks (several pieces of tubing of differing lengths). Early in the 19th century, the invention of the valve system meant that brass instruments could now play all the notes throughout their pitch range. They are powerful and efficient generators of sound, and produce tones of great depth and resonance.

The number and type of brass instruments needed in the symphony orchestra vary, but there are usually four French horns, two trumpets, three trombones, and one tuba. In the brass band they include the cornet, flugelhorn, tenor horn, B flat baritone, euphonium, trombone, and bombardon (bass tuba).

Brautwahl, Die, The Choice of a Bride opera by Ferruccio Busoni (libretto by composer based on a story by E T A Hoffmann), first produced in Hamburg, Germany, on 13 April 1912. The orchestral suite in five movements was first performed in Berlin on 2 January 1913. The story tells of Albertine who has two men over 300 years old among her suitors; she marries her favourite, the young painter Edmund, after he passes a test.

bravura (Italian 'bravery') musical term indicating that a passage demands brilliant virtuoso standards. It is associated especially with Romantic 19th-century music, such as many of Liszt's piano works.

break in music, the change in tone-quality between different registers of voices and of wind instruments, a natural defect which may be more or less successfully corrected by technical means.

breaking the 17th-century practice of varying a musical theme by dividing it into figurations of smaller note-values, as in divisions (variations). Breaking the ground was the same process if the theme was on a ground-bass.

Brecht, Bertolt (1898–1956) German poet and playwright. He was associated with the composer Kurt ➔ Weill from 1928 and has been credited with the text of the ➔ *Dreigroschenoper*; most of it is now known to be by Elisabeth Hauptmann, one of his several female collaborators. Brecht had more say in Weill's *Happy End* (1929), ➔ *Aufstieg und Fall der Stadt Mahagonny* (1930), and *Der Jasager*. From 1948 Brecht's Berliner Ensemble encouraged social realism and theatrical innovation, spawning a whole generation of original stage producers. See also ➔ Lehrstück.

Brehm, Alvin (1925–) US composer, conductor, and double bass player. He studied at the Juilliard School, New York, with Wallingford Riegger. As a soloist he performed with such groups as the Contemporary Chamber Ensemble (1969–73), the Group for Contemporary Music (1971–73), and the Chamber Music Society of Lincoln Center (1984–89); he has also led modern music as a conductor, from 1947.

Works concertina for violin and strings (1975), piano concerto (1977), sextet for piano and wind quintet (1984), tuba concerto (1982).

Brenet, Michel (1858–1918), pseudonym of Marie Bobillier French musicologist. She wrote studies of Okeghem, Palestrina, Handel, Haydn, P Grétry, and Berlioz.

Bretón, Tomás (1850–1923) Spanish composer. He was director of Madrid Conservatory from 1901.

Works OPERA *Guzman el Bueno* (1875), *Garin, Raquel* (1900), *Farinelli, El certamen de Cremona, Tabaré, Don Gil* (1914).

ZARZUELAS *Los amantes de Teruel, La Dolores, La verbena de la paloma* (1894), and about 30 others.

ORATORIO *Apocalipsia* (1882).

ORCHESTRAL *Las escenas andalazas, Salamanca, En la Alhambra*; violin concerto.

CHAMBER three string quartets, piano quintet, sextet for wind, piano trio.

breve (Latin 'short') the shortest note of 13th-century music. Since the subsequent addition of many other shorter notes, it is now the longest, equal in duration to eight ➜ crotchets. It is rarely used and is notated by an unfilled white notehead (often in the shape of a square) with two vertical lines attached to its left and right side.

Brian, (William) Havergal (1876–1972) English composer. His works (many unperformed, and most unpublished) include five operas (among them a *Faust* after Goethe), songs, and choral music (including settings of Blake and of Shelley's *Prometheus Unbound*). He wrote 32 symphonies in visionary Romantic style, including the *Gothic* (1919–27) for large choral and orchestral forces; he wrote the last 21 between the ages of 81 and 92.

Brian was born in Dresden, Staffordshire. The son of a potter, he was self-taught in composition but before World War I was regarded as a leading 'modern'. He became an organist and music teacher in Staffordshire and wrote criticism in Manchester from 1905. Later he moved to London, where he made a precarious living under great difficulties. Some of his early music was conducted by Henry Wood and Thomas Beecham, although he did not hear any of his 32 symphonies performed until 1954 at the age of 78, when his eighth symphony was produced by the British Broadcasting Corporation (BBC). The largest symphony, no. 1 *The Gothic*, was not performed until 1961. Despite the meagre prospects of hearing his own works performed during the early years – most of his symphonies are still unpublished – Brian continued to compose.

Works OPERA *The Tigers* (1916–29; first performance BBC, 1983), *Turandot* (1950), *The Cenci* (1952), *Faust* (1956), *Agamemnon* (1957).

ORCHESTRAL 32 symphonies (1919–68); three *English Suites, Hero and Leander*, overtures *For Valour* (Whitman) and *Dr Merryheart, Festal Dance, Fantastic Variations on Old Rhymes*, symphonic poem *In Memoriam* for orchestra.

VOCAL *By the Waters of Babylon, The Vision of Cleopatra*, and a setting from Shelley's *Prometheus* for chorus and orchestra (1937–44); Heine's *Pilgrimage to Kevlaar* for chorus and orchestra; songs; part songs.

Bride of Messina, The, Czech *Nevěsta Messinská* opera by Zdeněk Fibich (libretto by O Hostinský, based on Schiller's drama *Die Braut von Messina*), first produced at the Czech Theatre, Prague, on 28 March 1884.

bridge in music, a support for the strings of an instrument that determines its length and transmits vibration to the body. In violins, lutes, guitars, and other instruments the bridge is fixed, but in the Indian tambura (long lute) and Japanese koto (zither), bridges are movable to change the tuning. The ➜ monochord of music theory also has a movable bridge.

Bridge, Frank (1879–1941) English composer. His works include the orchestral suite *The Sea* (1911), and *Oration* (1930) for cello and orchestra. He taught the English composer Benjamin Britten.

Bridge was born in Brighton and studied at the Royal College of Music, London, where Charles Stanford was his composition master. He also learned the violin, viola, and conducting. He went on to play viola in various quartets and gained varied experience as an operatic and concert conductor, but later devoted his time to composition, under the patronage of Elizabeth Sprague Coolidge, though he also taught Britten privately. He won Cobbett Prizes for chamber music 1905–15 and honourable mention for his E minor string quartet at Bologna, Italy, in 1906. He won acclaim for such accessible works as *The Sea, Lament* (1915) for strings, and *There is a Willow* (1928). However, starting with the Piano Sonata (1924), his music explores dissonance to a greater degree, including bitonality. His third and fourth string quartets (1927, 1937) show an advanced harmonic idiom, not far removed from the music of Alban Berg. He was well known as a teacher; his pupil Britten's *Variations on a theme of Frank Bridge* (1937) are based on a theme from his master's Idyll no. 2 for string quartet (1906).

As a composer he possessed a formidably polished technique, and in his interwar compositions developed a radical cosmopolitan idiom, influenced by the atonality of Arnold Schoenberg. He is now recognized as one of the finest composers of his generation, particularly in the field of chamber music.

Works OPERA *The Christmas Rose* (1918–29; produced London, 1932).

ORCHESTRAL symphonic poem *Isabella* (1907), suite *The Sea* (1911), rhapsody *Enter Spring* (1927), tone poem *Summer* for orchestra; Lament for strings (1915); *There is a Willow Grows Aslant a Brook* (on a passage in *Hamlet*; 1928); *Phantasm* for piano and orchestra (1931), *Oration* for cello and orchestra (1930), *Rebus* overture (1940) and *Allegro moderato* for strings (1941).

CHAMBER four string quartets (1901–37), two piano trios, Fantasy quartet and several smaller pieces for string quartet, piano quintet, Fantasy Trio and quartet for piano and strings, string sextet, Rhapsody for two violins and viola, *Divertimenti* for wind instruments, violin and piano sonata, cello and piano sonata; numerous piano works including sonata, four *Characteristic Pieces*, suite *A Fairy Tale*, three Improvisations for the left hand; violin, viola, cello, and organ pieces.

VOCAL choruses; songs.

bridge passage in music, a transitional passage in a composition, usually the transition between first and second subjects in a ➤ sonata form movement.

Briegel, Wolfgang Carl (1626–1712) German composer. He was organist at Schweinfurt and Gotha and from 1671 to his death was music director at Darmstadt. He wrote operas and ballets, sacred works for several voices including seven cantatas, *Evangelische Gespräch* and *Evangelischer Blumengarten* (1660–81), pieces for three and four instruments, convivial and funeral songs for several voices, and hymns.

briganti, I, The Brigands opera by Giuseppe Mercadante (libretto by J Crescini, based on Schiller's drama *Die Räuber*), first produced at the Théâtre Italien, Paris, France, on 22 March 1836.

Brigg Fair rhapsody for orchestra by Delius on a Lincolnshire folksong, actually a set of variations, or a kind of passacaglia, composed in 1907 and first performed in Basel, Germany, in 1907. The first English performance was given in Liverpool on 18 January 1908.

brillant (French, *briller* 'to shine') in music, a word used either as an adjective in titles or as a direction showing how a particular passage is to be performed. It implies speed combined with clarity of tone.

brindisi (Italian 'a toast') drinking of someone's health, a drinking song, especially in opera, for example in Donizetti's *Lucrezia Borgia*, Verdi's *Macbeth*, *Traviata*, and *Otello*, or Mascagni's *Cavalleria rusticana*.

brio (Italian 'spirit, fire, brilliance') in music, a performance direction indicating that a piece or passage is to be played with energy and clarity; it is often used in the direction *con* ('with') *brio*.

brisé (French 'broken') in music, an arpeggio in keyboard or harp writing; détaché bowing in string music.

Britain, Radie (1903–1994) US composer. She studied in Chicago and with Marcel Dupré in Paris; piano with Leopold Godowsky, and taught privately in Hollywood. Much of her music is evocative of her native southwest scenery.

Works ORCHESTRAL *Heroic Poem* (1929), *Light* (1935), *Ononaga Sketches* (1939), *Serenata sorrentina* (1946), *Cactus Rhapsody* (1953), *Cosmic Mist*, symphony (1962).

VOCAL *Brothers of the Clouds*, for male voices and orchestra (1962); chamber and vocal music.

Britten, (Edward) Benjamin, Baron Britten (1913–1976) English composer. He often wrote for individual singers; for example, the role in the opera *Peter Grimes* (1945), based on verses by George Crabbe, was written for his life companion, the tenor Peter Pears. Among his many works are the *Young Person's Guide to the Orchestra* (1946); the chamber opera *The Rape of Lucretia* (1946); *Billy Budd* (1951); *A Midsummer Night's Dream* (Shakespeare; 1960); and *Death in Venice* (after Thomas Mann; 1973).

Born in Lowestoft, Suffolk, Britten was educated at Gresham's School, Holt, Norfolk. He studied piano with Harold Samuel and composition with Frank Bridge. Later, with a scholarship, he studied under Arthur Benjamin and John Ireland at the Royal College of Music, London. He worked in the USA in 1939–42, then returned to England and devoted himself to composing at his home in Aldeburgh, Suffolk, where he and Pears established an annual music festival in 1948. His oratorio *War Requiem* (1961) combines the liturgical text with poems by Wilfred Owen, and was written for the rededication of Coventry Cathedral in 1962.

Britten's earliest published work was a Sinfonietta for chamber orchestra (1932). His work was included at the International Society for Contemporary Music festivals of 1934, 1936, and 1938. He worked for the GPO Film Unit in 1935–37. His first international success was the *Variations on a Theme of Frank Bridge*, played at the Salzburg Festival in 1937. This was followed by a number of works which established him as the leading English composer of the day, especially the stark *Sinfonia da Requiem* (1940) and the *Serenade* (1943). He was also an excellent pianist and conductor. In 1945 his first major opera, *Peter Grimes*, established him as a dramatist; it was followed by further operas, including the chamber opera *The Turn of the Screw* (1954). Other large-scale operas are *The Rape of Lucretia*, *Albert Herring* (after Guy de Maupassant; 1947), *Billy Budd* (1951), *Gloriana* (1953), *Noyes Fludde* (1958), *The Little Sweep* for children (1949), *A*

Midsummer Night's Dream (1960), *Owen Win-grave* (after Henry James; 1971, commissioned for television), and *Death in Venice* (1993). Much of Britten's music is inspired by words, as shown by the many song cycles, the *Spring Symphony* (1949), and the *Nocturne* (1958); most of his tenor songs and roles were written for Pears. He had a close artistic association with Dmitri Shostako-vich and Mstislav Rostropovich from 1960.

Britten was something of an outsider; the themes of lost innocence, persecution, and isolation are constantly repeated in his music, especially the operas. Once treated with caution by both conservatives and the avant-garde, he is now more widely accepted.

Works STAGE operas *Peter Grimes* (M Slater, after George Crabbe, 1945), *The Rape of Lucretia* (R Duncan, 1946), *Billy Budd* (E M Forster and E Crozier, after Herman Melville, 1951, revised 1960), *Gloriana* (W Plomer, 1953), *The Turn of the Screw* (M Piper, after Henry James, 1954), *A Midsummer Night's Dream* (Shakespeare, 1960), and *Death in Venice* (M Piper, after Thomas Mann, 1973); ballet *The Prince of the Pagodas* (1957).

CHORAL including *A Ceremony of Carols* (1942), cantatas *Rejoice in the Lamb* (C Smart, 1943) and *Saint Nicolas* (Crozier, 1948), *Spring Symphony* (1949), *War Requiem* (1961).

ORCHESTRAL including *Variations on a theme of Frank Bridge* for strings (1937), *Sinfonia da Requiem* (1940), concertos for piano and for violin (1938–39), cello symphony (1963).

VOICE AND ORCHESTRA *Les Illuminations* (A Rimbaud, 1939) for high voice and strings, *Serenade* (various poets) for tenor, horn and strings, *Nocturne* (various poets, 1958), *Phaedra* for mezzo and orchestra (1975).

CHAMBER AND INSTRUMENTAL including four string quartets (1931 revised 1974; nos 1–3, 1941, 1945, 1975); cello sonata, three suites for solo cello; *Lachrymae* on song by Dowland for viola and piano (also with strings; 1950); *Six Metamorphoses after Ovid* for solo oboe.

SONG CYCLES *Seven Sonnets of Michelangelo* (1940), *The Holy Sonnets of John Donne* (1945), *Winter Words* (Hardy, 1953), Five Canticles (1947–74).

Brixi, Franz Xaver (1732–1771) Bohemian organist and composer. After various church posts he became Kapellmeister of Prague Cathedral in 1756.

Works largely church music; 105 Masses, including *Missa Pastoralis* (Christmas Mass); 263 of-fertories, hymns, and motets; eleven Requiems; 24 Vespers; Litanies, and other pieces; also music for organ, including three concertos, a sinfonia, and other pieces.

Broadwood, John (1732–1812) English piano manufacturer and music editor. He married Bar-bara, daughter of the Swiss-born harpsichord maker Burkat ➤ **Shudi**, in 1769, and was sole proprietor of Shudi & Broadwood from 1782. By 1781 he had built the first Broadwood grand piano, developed from the square pianos of Johannes Zumpe.

His son, **James Shudi Broadwood** (1772–1851), was taken into partnership in 1795, when the firm became John Broadwood & Son. James's brother, **Thomas Broadwood**, was taken into partnership in 1807, when the name became John Broadwood & Sons. By the middle of the 18th century, 2,500 pianos were manufactured per year, but the firm declined towards the 1880s. The present company was formed in 1951.

Brockes, (Barthold) Heinrich (1680–1747) German poet. His religious works inspired the Passions of ➤ **Handel** and ➤ **Telemann**. Part of his Passion oratorio libretto was used by Bach in the *St John Passion*.

broken consort in music, term for a mixed chamber ensemble of Renaissance and early baroque instruments.

Brook, Barry S(helley) (1918–1997) US musicologist. He took his PhD in Paris, France, in 1959 and taught there and in the USA (at the Juilliard School from 1977). He coordinated international bibliographical projects and was the joint editor of the complete works of Pergolesi (1986–). He also issued *The Symphony, 1720–1840* and *French Opera in the 17th and 18th Centuries*.

Bros, Juan (1776–1852) Spanish composer of church music. He was director by turns at the cathedrals of Málaga, León, and Oviedo.

Brossard, Sébastien de (1655–1730) French composer. He studied philosophy and theology at Caen and was self-taught in music. He lived in Caen until 1683, when he went to Paris and worked at Notre-Dame, later at Strasbourg. In 1687 he became *maître de chapelle* at the cathedral there and in 1698 music director at Meaux Cathedral. Although he was a prolific composer he is more famous for his dictionary of music (1703), the first in France).

Brown, Christopher (1943–) English composer. He studied with Lennox Berkeley and Boris Blacher. Much of his music has a spiritual content.

Works cantata *David* (1970), organ concerto (1979), Magnificat (1980), *The Vision of Saul* (1983), *Landscapes* for soprano, chorus, and orchestra (1987).

Brown, Earle (Appleton) (1926–2002) US composer. He pioneered ➜ **graph notation** (a method of notating controlled improvisation by graphical means) and mobile form during the 1950s, as in *Available Forms II* (1962) for ensemble and two conductors. He was an associate of John ➜ **Cage** and was influenced by the visual arts, especially the work of Alexander Calder and Jackson Pollock.

Works *Twenty-Five Pages* for 1 to 25 pianos (1953); *Available Forms I*, *Available Forms II* for 98 players and two conductors (1961–62); *Light Music* for electric lights, electronic equipment, and instruments (1961); *Sign Sounds* for chamber ensemble (1972), *Windsor Jambs* for soprano and orchestra (1979); *Folio II* for instruments (1970–93); *Sounder Rounds* for orchestra (1982); *Tracer* for ensemble and tape (1984).

Brown, Howard Mayer (1930–1993) US musicologist. He studied at Harvard and was professor at the University of Chicago from 1967. His writings include *Music in the French Secular Theater, 1400–1550* (1963), *Music in the Renaissance* (1976), and *Major Unpublished Works in a Central Baroque and Early Classical Tradition* (1977– ; planned in 60 volumes). He founded Collegium Musicum in Chicago, for the performance of medieval and Renaissance music.

Browne, John (lived c. 1490) English composer who contributed more pieces than anyone else to the Eton Choirbook and seems to have been the major English composer of his generation.

browning an English form of ➜ **fancy** for viols, similar to the ➜ **In Nomine**, but based on a folk-tune instead of a plainsong theme.

Bruce, (Frank) Neely (1944–) US composer and pianist. He studied at the University of Illinois and taught at the Wesleyan University from 1974. He founded the American Music/Theater Group 1977 and has also given premieres as a solo pianist. His music has progressed from serialism to American Indian influences.

Works *CHAMBER OPERA Pyramus and Thisbe* (1965), *The Trials of Psyche* (1971), *Americana* (1978–83). *ORCHESTRAL* concerto for percussion and orchestra (1967), violin concerto (1974), *Orion Rising* for orchestra (1988).

OTHER Eight Ghosts for four singers and electronics; keyboard music and songs; chamber pieces with voice.

Bruch, Max (1838–1920) German composer. He became professor at the Berlin Academy in 1891. He wrote three operas, including *Hermione* (1872). Among the most celebrated of his works are the *Kol Nidrei* (1881) for cello and orchestra, violin concertos, and many choral pieces.

Bruch learnt music as a child from his mother, who was a singer. Later, with a scholarship, he studied with Ferdinand Hiller (1811–85), Carl Reinecke, and Ferdinand Breunung. He visited Leipzig, Munich, and other musical centres to gain further experience and in 1863 produced his opera *Die Loreley* at Mannheim, having obtained permission from the poet Emmanuel von Geibel to use the libretto originally written for Mendelssohn. After two appointments at Koblenz and Sondershausen, he lived first in Berlin and then Bonn, wholly devoted to composition. From 1880 to 1883 he was conductor of the Liverpool Philharmonic Society, and in 1881 he married the singer Clara Tuczek. From 1883 to 1890 he conducted at Breslau and in 1891 became professor of composition at the Hochschule in Berlin, retiring to Friedenau in 1910. Until recently only the popular G minor violin concerto has allowed Bruch to emerge from the shadow of Brahms; revivals of such works as the oratorio *Odysseus* (1872), the opera *Loreley*, and chamber music such as the Septett have allowed a more balanced view of the composer.

Works *OPERA Die Loreley* (Mannheim, 1863).

VOICES AND ORCHESTRA works for solo voices, chorus, and orchestra: *Odysseus* (after Homer; 1872), *Das Lied von der Glocke* (Schiller; 1879), *Achilleus* (after Homer), *Das Feuerkreuz* (after Scott's 'Lay of the Last Minstrel'); three violin concertos (1868, 1878, 1891), *Scottish Fantasia* for violin, harp, and orchestra (1880); *Kol Nidrei* (1881) for cello and orchestra; Concerto in E minor for clarinet, violin, and orchestra, Op. 88; string quintet in A minor (1919), many choruses; instrumental pieces; piano music; songs.

Bruckner, (Josef) Anton (1824–1896) Austrian Romantic composer. He was cathedral organist at Linz 1856–68, and professor at the Vienna Conservatory from 1868. His works include many choral pieces and eleven symphonies, the last unfinished. His compositions were influenced by Richard Wagner and Ludwig van Beethoven.

Bruckner was the son of a country schoolmaster, and was intended to follow the same profession. On the early death of his father in 1837 he became a choirboy in the monastery of St Florian. There he learnt the organ and was appointed organist in 1845. By this time he had begun to compose, notably the Requiem in D minor (1849), but was dissatisfied with his poor technique and went to study counterpoint with Simon Sechter in Vienna in 1855. He was cathedral organist at Linz from 1856 to 1868, and wrote much in his spare time, including the first recognized symphony, *Linz*. On visiting Munich for the production of Richard Wagner's *Tristan und Isolde* in 1865, he became a supporter of Wagner. The early progress of his work was hindered by his association with the music of Wagner; Beethoven is probably a better comparison, particularly the Ninth Symphony. Bruckner's music typically contains a similar kind of spirituality; this is seen by the large amount of early religious works, and the late Te Deum (1881–84). In addition, Bruckner's orchestra tended not to be as massive as Wagner's.

He was appointed professor at the Vienna Conservatory in 1868, when his first symphony received its first performance at Linz, and remained in the capital for the rest of his life, but visited Nancy, Paris, and London as an organ virtuoso in 1869 and 1871. His third symphony, strongly influenced by Wagner, had its first performance at Vienna in 1873 but was a failure. Wide success came after the first performance of the seventh symphony in 1884. He was pensioned in 1891 and received an honorary doctorate from the University of Vienna. He was also Gustav Mahler's teacher.

Bruckner's symphonies went through several editions and revisions, first through well-meaning cuts and alterations made by Franz Schalk and the composer himself. The later editions by Robert Haas, followed by Leopold Novak, attempt to return to Bruckner's original thoughts.

Works SYMPHONIES F minor (1863), D minor ('no. 0', about 1863–64, revised 1869), no. 1 in C minor (1865, revised 1868–84), no. 2 in C minor (1871, revised 1873–77), no. 3 in D minor (1873, revised 1874–77), no. 4 in E♭ ('Romantic'; 1874, new scherzo 1878, new finale 1880), no. 5 in B♭ (1875–76), no. 6 in A (1879–81), no. 7 in E (1881–83), no. 8 in C minor (1884–87 and 1889–90), no. 9 in D minor (1891–94).

CHORAL Mass no. 1 in D minor (1864, revised 1876–82), no. 2 in E minor with woodwind accompaniment (1866, revised 1869–82), no. 3 in F minor (1867, revised 1876–93); also Te Deum in C for soloists, chorus, and orchestra (1881–84), five Psalm settings (1852–92), many motets.

INSTRUMENTAL string quintet in F (1879).

Bruhns, Nicolaus (1665–1697) German organist, string player, and composer. His elaborate preludes and fugues and sacred concertos form an important link between Dietrich Buxtehude and Johann Sebastian Bach.

He was first employed in Copenhagen, Denmark, and was then town organist at Husum, Slesvig-Holstein. He wrote cantatas, motets with orchestra, and organ music.

Brumel, Antoine (c.1460–c.1515) French composer. A contemporary of Josquin Desprez, he wrote 15 surviving Masses, including *Et ecce terrae motus* for twelve voices, and *L'homme armé* and *Missa pro defunctis*, both for four voices.

He also wrote sequences, antiphons, motets, chansons, and instrumental music based on popular melodies of the day. He was a singer at Chartres Cathedral in 1483, a canon at Laon in 1497, and from 1498 to 1501 choirmaster at Notre Dame in Paris. In 1506 he went to the court of the Duke of Ferrara, Italy, where he may have died.

Bruneau, (Louis Charles Bonaventure) Alfred (1857–1934) French composer and critic. The son of a painter, he learnt music including cello from his parents, who played violin and piano, and took a cello prize at the Paris Conservatory as a pupil of Auguste Franchomme. Afterwards he studied composition with Jules Massenet and played in Jules Pasdeloup's orchestra. In 1887 he produced his first opera; the next two were based on works by Émile Zola, who himself wrote the libretti for the next three stage works. The first of these, however, failed in 1897 because Bruneau and Zola were ardent supporters of Dreyfus. After Zola's death Bruneau wrote his own libretti, some still based on Zola's work. He wrote in a style indebted to Wagner, yet softened by the gentler lyricism of the French tradition, somewhat reminiscent of Charles Gounod and Massenet.

Works STAGE WORKS operas *Kérim* (1887), *Le Rêve* and *L'Attaque du moulin* (after Zola, 1893), *Messidor*, *L'Ouragan* (1901) and *L'Enfantroi* (libretti by Zola), *Lazare*, *Naïs Micoulin* and *Les Quatre Journées* (after Zola), *Le Tambour*, *Le Roi Candaule*, *Angélo, tyran de Padoue* (1928), *Virginie*; ballets *Les Bacchantes* (after Euripides; 1931) and *Le Jardin de Paradis*; incidental music to his adaptation of Zola's *La Faute de l'Abbé Mouret*.

VOCAL Requiem (1895), choral symphony *Léda*, *La Belle au bois dormant* and *Penthésilée*; cantata *Geneviève de Paris*; vocal duets; songs *Chansons à danser* and two books of *Lieds de France* (all words by Catulle Mendès).

ORCHESTRAL *Ouverture héroïque* for orchestra.

brunette (French 'a dark-haired girl') light love song of a type current in 17th–18th-century France, originally so called because of the association of the words with dark girls.

Brussilovsky, Evgeny (1905–1981) Russian composer. In 1933 he was commissioned to do research in Kazakh folk music and went to live at Alma-Ata, the capital of Kazakhstan. There he wrote operas in the national idiom.

Having lost both his parents, he joined the army at 16, but was released in 1922 in order to develop his talent at the Moscow Conservatory. He was expelled in 1924 for non-attendance, due to serious illness, but although very poor, managed to go to Leningrad and induced Maximilian Steinberg to teach him at the conservatory there.

Works OPERA *Kiz-Ji-Bek* (1934), *Er-Targhin* (1937), *Jalbir*.

ORCHESTRAL eight symphonies (1931–72).

OTHER instrumental pieces; piano pieces; songs.

Bruzdowicz, Joanna (1943–) Polish composer. She studied with Kazimierz Sikorski and with Olivier Messiaen and Pierre Schaeffer in Paris, France, and has founded electronic music studios in Paris and Brussels.

Works MUSICAL DRAMAS *The Penal Colony* (Tours, 1972), *The Trojan Women* (Paris, 1973), *The Gates of Paradise* (Warsaw, 1989), *Tides and Waves* (Barcelona, 1992), *Maison neuve* (Montréal, 1992).

ORCHESTRAL symphony (1974); concerto for piano (1974), violin (1975), double bass (1982).

OTHER cantatas, chamber and instrumental music.

Bryars, (Richard) Gavin (1943–) English composer. He studied music privately and has been professor of music at De Montfort University from 1985. His earlier compositions were influenced by the ideas of Erik Satie and John Cage; he later turned to Greek myth for inspiration.

Works OPERA *Medea*, (1984, after Euripides).

ORCHESTRAL *The Sinking of the Titanic* (1969), *My First Homage* (1978), *The English Mail-Coach* (1980), *Pico's Flight* (1986), *The Green Ray* for saxophone and orchestra (1991).

CHAMBER *Homage to Vivier* (1985) for small ensemble; two string quartets (1985, 1990).

OTHER *Cadman Requiem* (1989); *The Black River* for soprano and organ (1991).

Bucci, Mark (1924–2002) US composer. He studied at the Juilliard School, New York, and with Aaron Copland. His compositions, which include several operas and musicals, are noted for their energetic, diatonic style.

Works OPERA *The Boor* (1949, after Chekhov), *The Dress* (1953), *Sweet Betsy from Pike* (1953), *Tale for a Deaf Ear* (1957), *The Hero* (1965), *Midas* (1981).

MUSICALS *The Caucasian Chalk Circle* (1948), *The Adamses* (1956), *The Second Coming* (1976).

buccina musical instrument, the Roman bugle horn, used in the Roman army for signalling.

Bucenus, Paulus (1567–84) German composer. He worked as a church musician at Riga, where he may have died.

Works a *St Matthew Passion* (1578), Masses, motets, *Sacrae Cantiones*.

Buchardo, Carlos López (1881–1948) Argentine composer. He studied in Buenos Aires and with Albert Roussel in Paris, France. On returning to Argentina he became director of the National Conservatory in Buenos Aires.

Works the operas *El sueño de Alma* (1914), *Escenas argentinas* for orchestra (1920); piano pieces; songs.

Buch der hängenden Gärten, Das, The Book of the Hanging Gardens 15 songs for soprano and piano by Schoenberg, Op. 15 (texts by Stefan George), composed 1908–09 and first performed in Vienna, Austria, on 14 January 1910.

Buch mit sieben Siegeln, Das, The Book with Seven Seals oratorio by Franz Schmidt (text from the Apocalypse); composed 1935–37 and first performed in Vienna, Austria, on 15 June 1938.

Büchner, Georg (1813–1837) German poet and playwright whose works inspired Peter Maxwell Davies (➔ *Blind Man's Buff*), Gottfried von Einem (➔ *Dantons Tod*), Robert Müller-Hartmann, Franz Syberg, and Julius Weismann (*Leonce und Lena*), Rudolf Wagner-Régeny (*Günstling*), and Alban Berg and Manfred Gurlitt (➔ *Wozzeck*).

Buchner, Johann (Hans von Constantz) (1483–1538) German composer. He wrote sacred and secular songs, and organ pieces. His *Fundamentum* is a didactic (self-taught) work incorporating organ music for the liturgical year. He was probably a pupil of Paul Hofhaimer. He worked at Konstanz Cathedral, but left in 1526, because of its growing Protestantism, and went to Überlingen.

Budavari Te Deum work by Zoltán Kodály for soloists, chorus, and orchestra, first performed in Budapest Cathedral, Hungary, on 11 September 1936.

buffa (Italian 'comic') see ➔ opera buffa.

buffo (Italian 'comic', also 'comedian') in music, a singer of comic parts, used especially as adjective; *tenore buffo, basso buffo*.

bugle compact valveless treble brass instrument with a shorter tube and less flared bell than the trumpet. Constructed of copper plated with brass, it has long been used as a military instrument for giving a range of signals based on the tones of a harmonic series. The bugle has a conical bore whereas the trumpet is cylindrical.

Bühnenweihfestspiel (German, Bühne 'stage'; Weihe 'consecration'; Festspiel 'play') description given by Wagner to his *Parsifal*, which he did not wish to call an 'opera' or a 'music drama'.

Bukofzer, Manfred (1910–1955) German-born US musicologist. He studied at Heidelberg, Berlin, and Basel, and went to the USA in 1939, where after various appointments he became professor at University of California, Berkeley. He specialized in medieval, particularly English, music and edited the complete works of John Dunstable. His most important book is *Studies in Medieval* *and Renaissance Music* (1950).

Bull, John (c.1562–1628) English composer and keyboard virtuoso. He was a choirboy in the Chapel Royal in London under John Blitheman and became organist of Hereford Cathedral in 1582. On Blitheman's death in 1591 he became organist of the Chapel Royal. He gained his music doctorate at both Oxford (1592) and Cambridge (1589). In 1596 he was appointed first professor of music at Gresham College. In 1601 he travelled abroad when Thomas Byrd, son of William Byrd, acted as his deputy at Gresham College. He married Elizabeth Walter in 1607 and gave up his professorship, which could be held only by single men. In 1613 he left England, apparently to escape punishment for adultery, and became organist at the archducal chapel in Brussels. In 1617 he was appointed organist at Antwerp Cathedral, where he remained to his death. Much of his technically brilliant music for the virginals is in the collection *Parenthia* (1613).

Works anthems, including the 'Star' anthem *Almighty Lord*; secular vocal works for several voices; canons; a laud for the Blessed Virgin in Flemish; numerous organ and virginal pieces; some works for viols.

Bull, Ole (Borneman) (1810–1880) Norwegian violinist and composer. He wrote two concertos and many other works for the violin. He was largely self-taught, since his father insisted on his studying theology. In 1829 he visited Louis Spohr in Kassel, Germany, and in 1832 first made his mark as a public player in Paris, France. He founded the Norse Theatre in Bergen, Norway, in 1850.

While in Paris, he married a Frenchwoman, appeared with Chopin and Heinrich Ernst, and went on to visit Italy with great success. He went to England first in 1836 and to the USA in 1843. In 1870 he was married a second time, to an American.

Buller, John (1927–2004) English composer. From 1959 he studied with Anthony Milner and in the 1970s produced a series of works based on James Joyce's *Finnegan's Wake*. The opera *Bakxai* (after Euripides) was premiered by English National Opera in 1992.

Works OPERA *Bakxai* (1992).

ORCHESTRAL *The Theatre of Memory* (1981), *Bacchae Metres* (1993).

INSTRUMENTAL *The Cave* for flute, clarinet, trombone, cello, and tape (1970), *Le terrazze* for 14 instruments and tape (1974), *Familiar*, string quartet (1974), *Towards Aquarius* for ensemble (1983), *Mr Purcell's Maggot* (1994).

VOCAL AND INSTRUMENTAL two *Night Pieces* from *Finnegan's Wake* for soprano, clarinet, flute, piano, and cello (1971), *Finnegan's Floras* for chorus, percussion, and piano (1972), *Kommos* for chorus, soloists, and electronics (1981), *Of Three Shakespeare Sonnets* for mezzo and ensemble (1983).

bullroarer or **whizzer** or **whizzing stick** or **lightning stick** musical instrument used by Australian Aborigines for communication and during religious rites. It consists of a weighted aerofoil (a rectangular slat of wood about 15 cm/6 in to 60 cm/24 in long and about 1.25 cm/0.5 in to 5 cm/2 in wide) whirled rapidly about the head on a long cord to make a deep whirring noise. It is also used in many other parts of the world, including Britain.

American Indian peoples used it as an instrument of sympathetic magic, its noise representing the wind that accompanies rain, in order to induce, by mimicry, the rain itself. Some Australian Aborigines use it to frighten women away from tribal councils and rituals in which only men are allowed to participate. The women are told that the noise is the voice of the presiding god.

Bülow, Hans Guido Freiherr von (1830–1894) German conductor and pianist. He studied with Wagner and Liszt and in 1857 married Liszt's daughter Cosima. From 1864 he served Ludwig II of Bavaria, conducting first performances of Wagner's *Tristan und Isolde* and *Die Meistersinger*. His wife left him and married Wagner in 1870.

He studied law at Leipzig University and piano with Friedrich Wieck there. At first he was exclusively a Wagnerian as a conductor and gave the first performances of *Tristan und Isolde* (1865) and *Die Meistersinger* (1868), but after his wife went to live with Wagner became more enthusiastic about Brahms without abandoning Wagner. He conducted the first performance of Brahms's fourth symphony in 1885. He made many tours both as a conductor and as a pianist; as a soloist he gave the first performance of Tchaikovsky's first piano concerto in Boston, USA, in 1875.

buona figliuola, La, The Good Girl (also *La Cecchina*) opera by Niccolò Piccinni (libretto by Carlo Goldoni, based on Samuel Richardson's *Pamela*, first produced at the Teatro delle Dame, Rome, Italy, on 6 February 1760. The story tells how the Marchese della Conchiglia loves Cecchina, but his sister opposes their marriage because Cecchina is of a lower social class. Problems are resolved when the humble maid is revealed to be the daughter of a baron.

Buonamente, Giovanni Battista (died 1642) Italian violinist and composer. He was an imperial court musician from 1622, and maestro di cappella at the Franciscan monastery of Assisi from 1633. He wrote sonatas for two violins and bass, and music for mixed teams of instruments.

Buovo d'Antona, Bevis of Hampton opera by Tommaso Traetta (libretto by Carlo Goldoni, based on the Anglo-Norman 13th-century romance), first produced at the Teatro San Moisè, Venice, Italy, on 27 December 1758. It was revived in Venice in 1993, in edition by Alan Curtis. The plot describes how the knight Buovo returns from exile to unite with Druisina and drive out the evil Duke Maccabuono.

burbero di buon cuore, Il, The Good-hearted Grumbler opera by Vicente Martín y Soler (libretto by Lorenzo da Ponte, based on Carlo Goldoni's French comedy *Le Bourru bienfaisant*), first produced at the Burgtheater, Vienna, Austria, on 4 January 1786. Mozart wrote two extra arias for its revival in Vienna on 9 November 1789, and Haydn composed an additional duet for its production in London, England, in 1794. The plot concerns the bachelor Ferramondo in a complication with his bankrupt nephew and comely niece.

burden in old vocal music, the refrain sung at the end of each verse; in English medieval carols, the refrain or chorus.

Burgon, Geoffrey (1941–) English composer. He studied with Peter Wishart and Lennox Berkeley at the Guildhall School of Music. His music shows a range of influences, including jazz and medieval French music. He is best known for his themes for successful TV series, including *Brideshead Revisited* (1981).

Works STAGE opera *Hard Times* (1991, after Dickens); ballets *The Golden Fish* (1964), *Ophelia* (1964), *Persephone* (1979), *The Trial of Prometheus* (1988).

ORCHESTRAL *Brideshead Variations* (1981), *The World Again* (1983).

VOICES AND ORCHESTRA *Think on Dredful Domesday* (1969), *Magnificat* (1970), *Veni Spiritus*, *Orpheus* and *Revelations*, all for soloists, chorus, and orchestra (1979–84).

OTHER VOCAL *Songs of the Creation* for chorus and organ (1989), *A Vision* for tenor and strings (1991); other works for chorus, and for voice and piano or chamber ensemble.

Burian, Emil František (1904–1959) Czech singer, actor, author, stage manager, and composer. He studied at the Prague Conservatory, joined the Dada Theatre in Prague and was director of the dramatic studio of the Brno National Theatre 1929–30; he also founded a voice band, which sang to given rhythms without definite pitch, accompanied by percussion.

Works OPERA *Alladine and Palomides* (after Maeterlinck; 1923), *Before Sunrise* (1924), *Bubu de Montparnasse*, *Mr Ipokras*, *Fear*.

BALLET *The Bassoon and the Flute* (1925), *Manège*, *Autobus*.

OTHER choruses; chamber music, songs.

Burkhard, Willy (1900–1955) Swiss composer. He studied at the Bern School of Music, in Leipzig, Germany, with Sigfrid Karg-Elert (1877–1933) and Robert Teichmüller (1863–1939), at Munich with Walter Courvoisier (1875–1931), and later in Paris, France, with Max d'Olone (1875–1959). He became piano professor at Bern Conservatory, Switzerland, and conducted choirs and an amateur orchestra. In 1937 he settled at Davos to devote himself entirely to composition.

Works OPERA *Die schwarze Spinne* (after Gotthelf; 1948).

VOCAL oratorios *Musikalische Übung* (Luther; 1934) and *Das Gesicht Jesajas* (1933–35), Te Deum, choral suite *Neue Kraft*, festival cantata *Le Cantique de notre terre*, cantata *Das Jahr* and others, Psalm 93 for chorus and organ; *Christi Leidensverkündung* for tenor, chorus, and organ.

ORCHESTRAL two symphonies, *Ulenspiegel* variations for orchestra; Fantasy, Little Serenade, and concerto for string orchestra; two violin concertos, organ concerto (1945).

CHAMBER two string quartets, piano trio, two trio sonatas; Variations and Fantasy for organ.

SONGS numerous song cycles, including *Frage*, two on poems by Rilke, and one on poems by Morgenstern.

burla (Italian 'jest, trick, practical joke') in music, a humorous piece, rather more boisterous than a ➔ scherzo.

burlesca see ➔ burla.

burlesque another name sometimes used for the ➔ burletta in England.

burletta (Italian 'a little joke') a form of light comic opera or operetta in 18th- and 19th-century England.

Burmeister, Joachim (1564–1629) German music theorist. In treatises published in 1599, 1601, and 1606 he codified as *figurae* the various technical and expressive devices used by 16th-century composers.

'Burning Fiery Furnace, The' church parable by Benjamin Britten (libretto by W Plomer), first produced in Orford Church, Suffolk, England, on 9 June 1966. In honour of visiting Israelites, the Babylonian King Nebuchadnezzar organizes a feast, but throws the guests into a furnace when they do not worship his idols. Saved by an angel, they do not burn.

Burrell, Diana (1948–) English composer. She studied at Cambridge and has played the viola in various orchestras. Her music is skilfully crafted. Works include concertos for viola and clarinet; *Symphonies of Flocks, Herds and Shoals* (1995–96); and *Ave Verum Corpus* for chorus (1998).

Works OPERA *The Albatross* (1987).

ORCHESTRAL *Landscape* (1988), *Scene with Birds* (1989), *Resurrection* (1992).

VOCAL choral works *Missa Sancta Endeliente* (1980), *Creator of the Stars of Night* (1989), *You Spotted Snakes* (1991), *Night Songs* (1991).

CHAMBER *Concertante* (1985) and *Archangel* (1987) for ensemble; wind quintet (1990); *Arched Form with Bells* for organ (1990); *Sequence* for cello and tape (1993); *Anima* for strings (1993); viola concerto (1994); *Gulls and Angels* for string quartet (1993).

Burt, Francis (1926–) English composer. He studied at the Royal Academy of Music, London, and with Boris Blacher in Berlin, Germany. He was resident in Vienna, Austria, from 1957 and was professor of composition at the Hochschule für Musik from 1973.

Works OPERA *Volpone* (1960), *Barnstaple, or Someone in the Attic* (1969).

BALLET *The Golem* (1962).

ORCHESTRAL *Iambics* (1953), *Espressione orchestrale* (1959), *Fantasmagoria* (1963), *Morgana* (1986).

VOCAL *Und Gott der Herr sprach*, for soloists, chorus, and orchestra (1983).

CHAMBER string quartet (1953); *Echoes* for flute and ensemble (1989).

Burton, Avery (c.1470–c.1543) English composer. He is known as the composer of a Mass, *Ut re mi fa sol la*, in the Forrest-Heyther partbooks (this is probably not the Mass of 1494) and of a Te Deum for organ.

In November 1494 he was paid 20 shillings by Henry VII for composing a Mass; in 1509 he became a gentleman of the Chapel Royal. In 1513 he went to France with the Chapel Royal, a Te Deum of his being sung after Mass at Tournai in September; in June 1520 he was present at the historic meeting between Henry VIII of England and Francis I of France, known as the Field of the Cloth of Gold. His name disappears from the records of the Chapel Royal after 1542.

Burton, Stephen (Douglas) (1943–) US composer. He studied in Vienna and Salzburg, Austria, and with Hans Werner Henze, and taught at George Mason University, Virginia, from 1974. His music is eclectic in character.

Works OPERA *An American Triptych* (three one-act operas after Craine, Hawthorne, and Melville; 1974), *The Duchess of Malfi* (after Webster; 1978), *Aimée* (1983).

ORCHESTRAL *Stravinskiana* for flute and orchestra (1972), Variations on a Theme of Mahler, for

chamber orchestra (1982); violin concerto (1983). OTHER chamber and vocal music.

Busby, Thomas (1755–1838) English organist and composer. He sang at Vauxhall as a boy with great success, and later became a pupil of Battishill. He worked on a music dictionary with Samuel Arnold, and was appointed church organist at St Mary's, Newington, Surrey, around 1780. He gained a doctorate of music at Cambridge in 1801. He wrote several books on music, including a history (1825).

Works INCIDENTAL MUSIC for Cumberland's *Joanna of Montfaucon* (an English version of Kotzebue's *Johanna von Montfaucon*), Holcroft's *Tale of Mystery*, Anna Maria Porter's *Fair Fugitives*, and Lewis's *Rugantino*.

ORATORIOS *The Prophecy* (from Pope's *Messiah*; c.1784, performed Haymarket, London, 1799), *Britannia*.

OTHER settings of odes by Pope and Gay.

Busch, Fritz (1890–1951) German conductor. Like his brother Adolf Busch, he renounced German citizenship, and left Germany for Buenos Aires, Argentina, in 1933. He conducted the Glyndebourne Opera in England from 1934 to his death, giving the first performances there of *Figaro*, *Così fan tutte*, *Don Giovanni*, and *Macbeth*, and the British premiere of *Idomeneo*.

He studied at the Cologne Conservatory and after working with various German theatres and orchestras, became conductor of the Stuttgart Opera in 1918 and music director of the Dresden Staatsoper in 1922. He conducted there the first performances of Strauss's *Intermezzo* (1924) and *Die Ägyptische Helena* (1928), Busoni's *Doktor Faust* (1925), and Hindemith's *Cardillac* (1926).

Busenello, Gian Francesco (1598–1659) Italian librettist and poet who is best known for his libretto for Monteverdi's *L'incoronazione di Poppea* (1642); he also wrote the libretti for Cavalli's *Gli amori d'Apollo e di Dafne* (1640), *Didone* (1641), and *Statira* (1655).

Bush, Alan Dudley (1900–1995) English composer. He adopted a didactic simplicity in his compositions in line with his Marxist beliefs. He wrote a large number of works for orchestra, voice, and chamber groups. His operas include *Wat Tyler* (1948–51) and *Men of Blackmoor* (1955), both of which had their first performances in East Germany.

Bush studied composition with John Ireland and piano with Artur Schnabel. He became professor at the Royal Academy of Music in London, conductor of the London Labour Choral Union, and, in 1936, chair of the Workers' Music Association.

Works STAGE operas *The Press-Gang* (1946), *Wat Tyler* (1948–51), *The Spell Unbound* (1953), *Men* of *Blackmoor* (1955), *The Sugar Reapers* (1966), *Joe Hill: the Man who Never Died* (1970); incidental music for Shakespeare's *Macbeth*, Sean O'Casey's *The Star Turns Red*, and Patrick Hamilton's *The Duke in Darkness*.

VOCAL choral work *The Winter Journey* (Randall Swingler) and others.

ORCHESTRAL symphony no. 2 'Nottingham' (1949), no. 3 *Byron* (1960), no. 4 *Lascaux* (1983), and other orchestral music; piano concerto with chorus (Swingler), violin concerto, *Concert Suite* for cello and orchestra (1952).

CHAMBER AND INSTRUMENTAL string quartet, piano quartet, *Dialectic* for string quartet (1929); instrumental pieces with piano; piano and organ music, including 24 preludes for piano (1977).

Bush, Geoffrey (1920–1998) English composer. He was mainly self-taught in composition, but had much valuable advice from the composer John Ireland.

Bush became a choirboy at Salisbury Cathedral in 1928, went to Lancing College in 1933, and graduated from Balliol College, Oxford, in 1940. He received a PhD from Oxford in 1946. His studies were interrupted by war service at a hostel for evacuee children.

Works OPERA five operas including *Spanish Rivals* (1948).

ORCHESTRAL *Twelfth Night*, entertainment for chorus and orchestra; overtures *In Praise of Salisbury* and *The Rehearsal* for orchestra, Divertimento for string orchestra, two symphonies (1954, 1957); concerto for piano and strings, *Sinfonietta concertante* for cello and chamber orchestra, oboe concerto.

CHAMBER rhapsody for clarinet and string quartet; sonatas for violin and piano, and trumpet and piano; two piano sonatinas.

VOCAL *Portraits* and *La Belle Dame sans merci* (Keats) for unaccompanied chorus; songs.

Busnois, Antoine (c.1430–1492) French composer. He was a pupil of Jean de Okeghem and was in the service of the Burgundian court until 1482, when he became music director at the Church of Saint-Sauveur in Bruges.

Works two Masses, Magnificat, hymns, 61 songs for three or four voices; motets, including *Fortunata desperata*, used later by Josquin Des Prez.

Busoni, Ferruccio Dante Benvenuto (1866–1924) Italian pianist, composer, and music critic. Much of his music was for the piano, but he also composed several operas including *Doktor Faust*, completed by Philipp Jarnach after Busoni's death. His work shows the influence of Liszt and his ballet score for *Doktor Faust* shows his debt to Bizet. Specimens of his style at its best are to be found in his later sonatinas, *Sarabande*

und Cortège from *Faust*, and the monumental *Fantasia contrappuntistica* for piano. An apostle of Futurism, he encouraged the French composer Edgard Varèse.

Busoni was born in Empoli, near Florence. He appeared as a pianist in public at the age of seven, and later studied at Graz and Leipzig, Germany. He taught at the Helsinki Conservatory, Finland, in 1889, in Moscow, Russia, in 1890 (where he married the Swede Gerda Sjöstrand), and in Boston, USA, 1891–94. He settled in Berlin in 1894, but travelled widely as a pianist and during World War I lived first in Bologna, Italy, as director of the Conservatory and then in Zürich, Switzerland. In Bologna he hoped to influence Italian music, and to prove that he was himself an Italian composer, but was disappointed.

He rejected Wagnerian music-drama, and sought to re-establish links with great composers of the past, notably Johann Sebastian Bach and Mozart, and the commedia dell'arte. His opera *Doktor Faust* was first performed in 1925; missing sketches were located in 1974 and were used for a new edition by Antony Beaumont, which was performed in Bologna in 1985 and at the London Coliseum in 1986. His ideas on aesthetics, especially his *Sketch of a New Aesthetic of Music* (1907), were attacked by conservatives such as Hans Pfitzner.

As a pianist Busoni was considered to have the most powerful individuality and greatest technical mastery since Liszt and Rubinstein. As a composer he is sometimes regarded as a formidable intellect whose works rarely live up to his ambition; he was admired alike by Mahler and Schoenberg (one premiered his *Berceuse élégiaque* (1909), and the other arranged it) but it may be his Italianate pieces which are the most readily accessible.

Works STAGE *Die Brautwahl* (1908–11), *Arlecchino* and *Turandot* (1916–17), *Doktor Faust* (1916–24).

ORCHESTRAL violin concerto (1897), piano concerto, with male chorus in finale (1903–04), *Berceuse élégiaque* (1909), *Indianisches Tagebuch*, book two, 'Gesang vom Reigen der Geister' (1915), *Concertino* for clarinet and orchestra (1918), *Sarabande und Cortège*, studies for *Doktor Faust* (1919).

CHAMBER two string quartets (1881, 1887), two violin sonatas (1890, 1898).

PIANO *Elegien*, seven pieces (1907), *Indianisches Tagebuch*, book one (1915), *Fantasia contrappuntistica* (1910, as *Grosse Fuge*; revised 1910 and 1912; version for two pianos 1921), six sonatinas (1910–20). Also editions and arrangements of Bach for piano, including D minor Chaconne.

Büsser, (Paul-) Henri (1872–1973) French conductor and composer. He conducted Debussy's

Pelléas et Mélisande at its first production in 1902 and made an orchestral version of *Printemps.*

He was a pupil of Charles Widor and Félix Guilmant at the Paris Conservatory, and won the Prix de Rome in 1893. He was successively organist at Saint-Cloud, conductor of the choral class at the Conservatory, and director of Louis Niedermeyer's school. In 1921 he was appointed professor of composition at the conservatory.

Works OPERA *Daphnis et Chloé* (1897), *Colomba* (after Mérimée), *Les Noces corinthiennes* (1922), *La Pie borgne*, *Le Carrosse du Saint-Sacrement* (Mérimée; 1948).

OTHER Masses and motets; *Hercule au jardin des Hespérides*, *Suite funambulesque*, and other orchestral works; choruses, songs.

Bussotti, Sylvano (1931–) Italian composer. After producing some early works in a relatively traditional style, he turned to a graphical manner of composing, which is influenced by John Cage and attempts to suggest the type of improvisation required. His music can be very poetic and evocative; his chief work is the opera *Lorenzaccio* (1972).

Bussotti was born in Florence. He studied at the Florence Conservatory and with Max Deutsch in Paris, France. His interests lie equally in painting, music, and the theatre, and his scores often contain either considerable elements of graphic design (as in *Five Piano Pieces for David Tudor*, 1959) or are 'action scripts' (such as *Le Passion selon Sade*, 1969) which outline theatrical action and music.

Works OPERA *Lorenzaccio* (1972), *Nottetempo* (1976), *La Racine* (1980), *L'ispirazione* (1988), *Fedra* (1988).

VOCAL *Torso* for voice and orchestra; *Pearson Piece* for baritone and piano; cantata *Memoria* (1962); Requiem (1969).

INSTRUMENTAL *Fragmentations* for harp; *Five Piano Pieces for David Tudor* (1959); *Pour clavier* for piano; *Opus Cygne* for flute and orchestra (1979).

Bustini, Alessandro (1876–1970) Italian composer. He studied at the Accademia di Santa Cecilia in Rome, where he later became professor.

Works OPERA *Maria Dulcis* (based on a story in Berlioz's *Soirées de l'orchestre*; Rome, 1902), *La città quadrata*, and *L'incantesimo di Calandrino.*

ORCHESTAL two symphonies (1899, 1909), symphonic poem *Le tentazioni.*

CHAMBER two string quartets; sonatas for violin and piano and viola and piano.

OTHER funeral Mass for Victor Emmanuel II; piano pieces.

Buths, Julius (1851–1920) German pianist and conductor. He worked in Düsseldorf from 1890, and was director of the conservatory there and

conductor of the Lower Rhine Festival, where he introduced Elgar's *Dream of Gerontius* in 1901.

Butler, Martin (1960–) English composer. He studied at the Royal College of Music, London, and at Princeton, USA, and has attended Luciano Berio's electronic music studio in Florence, Italy. His music admits a variety of influences, including jazz.

Works OPERA *The Sirens' Song* (1986), *Craig's Progress* (1994).

ORCHESTRAL *The Flight of Coll* (1983), *Cavalcade* (1985), *Fixed Doubles* (1989), *O Rio!* (1990).

CHAMBER *From an Antique Land* for ensemble (1982); string quartet (1984); *Dance Fragments* for ensemble (1984); *Tin Pan Ballet* (1986); *Songs and Dances from a Haunted Place* for string quartet (1988); *Jazz Machines* for ensemble (1990); wind quintet (1991).

OTHER *Night Machines* for tape (1987); *To See the Beauties of the Earth* for chorus (1987).

Butterfly opera by Puccini. See ➤ *Madama Butterfly.*

'Butterfly' or **'Butterfly's Wing' Study** nickname sometimes given to Chopin's piano Study in G flat major Op. 25 no. 9.

Butterley, Nigel (Henry) (1935–) Australian composer. He studied at New South Wales Conservatory and with Priaulx Rainier in London, England. His music has progressed from a style influenced by Béla Bartók, Paul Hindemith, and Dmitri Shostakovich to the avant garde.

Works OPERA *Lawrence Hargrave Flying Alone* (1988).

ORCHESTRAL *Meditations of Thomas Traherne* for orchestra (1968), violin concerto (1970), symphony (1980), *From Sorrowing Earth* for orchestra (1990).

CHAMBER three string quartets (1965, 1974, 1979), clarinet trio (1979).

Butterworth, Arthur (1923–) English composer and conductor. In his compositions he has drawn primarily on local pastoral traditions, although he has also considered 12-note composition.

He was appointed conductor of the Huddersfield Philharmonic Orchestra in 1964.

Works three symphonies (1957, 1965, 1975) and an arrangement of Elgar's *Introduction and Allegro* for brass band (1976).

Butterworth, George (Sainton Kaye) (1885–1916) English composer. He collected folk songs, and cultivated folk dancing and composition, but enlisted on the outbreak of World War I and was killed in action. He suggested the idea for Vaughan Williams's *London Symphony* (1911–13), and the work is dedicated to his memory.

Butterworth was born in London. He was educated at Eton and Oxford, and studied music briefly at the Royal College of Music in London. His songs, 'A Shropshire Lad' and 'Bredon Hill', are regarded as among the finest in English music. He was killed at Pozières in the Battle of the Somme, shortly after being awarded the Military Cross.

Works Rhapsody *A Shropshire Lad* (1912) and Idyll *The Banks of Green Willow* (1913) for orchestra; *Bredon Hill* (1912); two song cycles on Housman's 'Shropshire Lad'; Sussex folk songs arranged; carols set for chorus; a few other choral pieces and songs.

Buus, Jachet (Jacques) (c. 1500–1565) Flemish organist and composer. He first published some work in France, but went to Italy and in 1541 became organist at St Mark's in Venice, succeeding Baldassare da Imola. He went to Vienna on leave in 1550 but never returned, and became organist at the court of Ferdinand I.

Works SACRED AND SECULAR MUSIC motets, madrigals; French *chansons*; *ricercari* for organ.

Buxheimer Orgelbuch large German manuscript of keyboard music (not all of it necessarily for organ) datable to about 1470. It contains mostly ornamented arrangements of sacred and secular vocal works; also several versions of the *Fundamentum organisandi* by Paumann and some liturgical organ music. The upper part is written on a staff of (usually) seven lines, the lower part(s) in letters. In some pieces the use of pedals is indicated.

Buxtehude, Dietrich (1637–1707) Danish composer. In 1668 he was appointed organist at the Marienkirche, Lübeck, Germany, where his fame attracted Johann Sebastian Bach and Handel. He is remembered for his organ works and cantatas, written for his evening concerts (*Abendmusiken*); he also wrote numerous trio sonatas for two violins, viola da gamba, and harpsichord.

From 1668 he was organist of St Mary's Church, Lübeck. From 1673 he gave pre-Christmas *Abendmusiken* at which his vivid and vocally elaborate cantatas were performed, for example *Das neugeborne Kindelein*. His vocal sacred concertos to Latin texts are in a style recalling Venetian models. He was the greatest organ composer of the period preceding Johann Sebastian Bach, who is alleged to have walked 320 km/200 mi to hear him play.

Works concerted works for chorus and orchestra (*Abendmusiken*); church cantatas, all with German texts, except a sequence of seven, *Membra Jesu nostri* (1680); sonatas for strings; organ music, including chorale preludes; suites for harpsichord.

buysine or **buzine** medieval musical instrument, a large horn dating from the 13th century. It originates from a long Saracen trumpet, which survived until the 16th century as a ceremonial instrument.

By an Overgrown Path, Czech **Po zarostlém chodníčka** work for piano in ten movements by Leoš Janáček (1901–11). The movements are titled: 1. Our evenings; 2. A blown-away leaf; 3. Come along with us; 4. The Virgin of Frýdek; 5. They chattered like swallows; 6. One cannot tell; 7. Good night; 8. In anguish; 9. In tears; 10. The little owl continues screeching.

Byrd, William (c.1543–1623) English composer. His sacred and secular choral music, including over 200 motets and Masses for three, four, and five voices, is typical of the English polyphonic style.

Probably born in Lincoln, Byrd studied under Thomas ➤ **Tallis** as one of the children of the Chapel Royal in London. He became organist at Lincoln Cathedral in 1563, and married Juliana Birley there in 1568. He was elected a Gentleman of the Chapel Royal in 1569, but continued his duties at Lincoln until 1572, when he became organist of Queen Elizabeth I's Chapel Royal jointly with Tallis. In 1575 Queen Elizabeth granted Byrd and Tallis an exclusive licence for printing and selling music and they dedicated to her their *Cantiones sacrae* published that year.

Byrd married for the second time in about 1587. In 1593 he bought Stondon Place near Stapleford-Abbott, Essex, where he remained for the rest of his life, as far as his duties in London would let him. He was frequently involved in litigation and was several times prosecuted for recusancy as a Roman Catholic, but remained in favour with the Queen.

Byrd's popular reputation rests with his three great Masses, in three, four, and five parts, which show his mastery of the contrapuntal style at its best, and with his much performed keyboard music. Other aspects of his genius are found in the ornate *Cantiones sacrae* and the large body of consort songs and instrumental music.

Works CHURCH MUSIC three Masses; 17 Latin motets in the *Cantiones sacrae* by Tallis and Byrd (1575); 61 Latin motets in two books of *Cantiones sacrae*; 99 Latin motets in two books of *Gradualia*; about 50 motets in manuscript form; four Anglican services; about 61 anthems; some miscellaneous English church music.

SECULAR *Songs of Sundrie Natures* (47 nos); four separate madrigals; consort songs, canons; rounds; fantasies for strings, seven *In Nomines* for strings, ten pieces for strings on plainsong tunes, some miscellaneous music for strings; about 100 pieces for the virginal, among them fantasias, preludes, grounds, variations, pavanes and galliards, and other dances.

SACRED AND SECULAR *Psalmes, Sonets and Songs* (18 nos); *Psalmes, Songs and Sonnets* (32 nos).

Byron, George Gordon (1788–1824) English poet. Hector Berlioz was inspired by *Childe Harold's Pilgrimage* (1812) and *The Corsair* (1814) to write *Harold en Italie* (1834) and the *Corsaire* overture (1831). Giuseppe Verdi wrote his opera *Il corsaro* in 1848. Schumann wrote incidental music to Byron's play in 1852 and he, Wolf, Mendelssohn, and Busoni set individual poems. Arguably one of the most compelling of all Byron settings is Schoenberg's *Ode to Napoleon* for reciter, string quartet, and piano (1942), which plays on the comparison between Bonaparte and Hitler.

Byzantine chant the name given to the Christian chant of the Greek-speaking Orthodox Church. In 330 Constantine the Great made Byzantium (henceforth Constantinople) capital of the Roman Empire; but only in 527, with the coronation of Justinian I as emperor, did Byzantine liturgy, art, and music gain supremacy throughout the empire. Other important dates are 726–843 (the iconoclastic age), 1054 (the final break from Roman Catholicism), and 1453 (the sack of Constantinople by the Turks). During the course of the 11th century the introduction of new hymns was forbidden, and the power of the Byzantine Empire was broken with the establishment of the Latin Empire (1204–61). However, the restoration of the Eastern Empire in 1261 led to a renaissance which lasted for a century, followed by a gradual deterioration until the end of the empire.

Byzantine music and liturgy were dominated by its hymns, which adorned the Offices rather than the Mass. The *troparion* (later *sticheron*) was an intercalation between the verses of a psalm. The *kontakion* was a sermon in verse, sung after the reading of the Gospel at the Morning Office. At the end of the 7th century it was replaced by the *kanon*, consisting of nine odes of nine stanzas each: each ode had its own melody. Finally acclamations to the emperor were sung throughout the period; unlike music actually sung in church, these were accompanied by instruments, especially the organ.

Byzantine music, notated in neumes, is based on a system of eight modes (*echoi*), defined by characteristic melodic formulas as well as by tonality. The verse itself it is Semitic in origin. The comparative simplicity of earlier and middle Byzantine music gave way, at the end of the period, to a highly embellished style in which the balance between verse and music tended to be destroyed.

C in music, the keynote, or tonic, of the scale of C major.

C.A. in music, abbreviation for **col arco**, meaning 'with the bow'.

cabaletta in music, a short aria with repeats which the singer could freely embellish as a display of virtuosity. In the 19th century the term came to be used for the final section of an elaborate aria.

Cabanilles, Juan (Bautista José) (1644–1712) Spanish organist and composer. In 1665 he was appointed organist of Valencia Cathedral, a post he held until his death. He was regarded as one of the great organ composers of his time, writing mostly *tientos*, pieces similar to the ➤ ricercare.

Cabezón, Antonio de (1510–1566) Spanish organist and composer. Although blind from early childhood, he studied with Tomás Gómez at Palencia and became chamber organist and harpsichordist to Charles V, remaining at court under Philip II, and accompanying him to England on his marriage to Mary I. He composed music for organ, vihuela, and other instruments.

cabrette (French dialect for *chevrette*, 'she-kid') musical instrument, a variety of ➤ musette from the Auvergnat region in France.

caccia, da (Italian 'hunting') in music, a suffix used to describe music or instruments associated with the hunt, for example the oboe da caccia, precursor of the ➤ cor anglais, and corno da caccia, or hunting horn.

Caccini, Francesca (1587–c.1640) Italian singer and composer. She was taught by her father, Giulio ➤ Caccini.
Works OPERA *La liberazione di Ruggiero* (1625).
BALLET *Il ballo delle zigane* (1615), *Rinaldo innamorato* (after Tasso).
VOCAL sacred and secular cantatas for one and two voices, and other pieces.

Caccini, Giulio (c.1545–1618) Italian singer, lutenist, and composer. He wrote short vocal pieces in recitative style and sang them to the the-
orbo, which led to larger essays of the kind, set to scenes by Count Giovanni Bardi, and eventually to Ottavio Rinuccini's libretto for the opera *Euridice*, first set by Jacopo Peri and immediately afterwards by Caccini in 1602. In 1604–05 he visited Paris, France, with his daughter, Francesca ➤ Caccini, who was herself a composer as well as a singer.

Caccini was born in Tivoli or Rome, and was taken to Florence by Cosimo I de' Medici around 1565. He was successful as a singer there, and became known throughout Italy. He used to attend Count Bardi's salon in Florence, and was credited with the invention of a new style of song, the *stile recitativo*, which developed there. The first mention of Caccini as a composer dates from 1589, when he composed music for the marriage of Grand Duke Ferdinando I. In 1600 he was appointed musical director at the court of the Medici family, and remained in their service until his death.

His two songbooks, *Le nuove musiche*, published in 1602 and 1614, contain pieces for solo voice and figured bass. The first has a preface on the new style of singing and composition adopted by Caccini, and embellishments in the music that were usually improvised are written out in full.

Works OPERA *Euridice* and *Il rapimento di Cefalo* (both 1602).
VOCAL *Le nuove musiche* containing madrigals and arias for voice and continuo (1602, 1614).

cachucha Andalusian dance in quick, energetic 3/4 time.

Cadéac, Pierre (lived 16th century) French composer. He was master of the choirboys at Auch (near Toulouse) in 1556. He composed Masses, motets, and chansons, including perhaps the 'Je suis déshéritée' ascribed to him by the music publisher Pierre Attaingnant in 1539 (but to 'Lupus' by the same publisher in 1533). This famous piece was used as the basis of numerous Masses in the 16th century, including one by Palestrina.

(a) perfect (US authentic): dominant to tonic

(b) plagal: subdominant to tonic

(c) imperfect: tonic to dominant

(d) deceptive (or interrupted): dominant to a chord other than the tonic (usually the submediant or subdominant)

(e) the so-called Phyrigan cadence, where the fall is in the lowest part (this derives its name from the Phrygian mode)

Cadence, from Latin cado = *'I fall'. Traditional forms are, in the key of C major: (a) perfect (US authentic): dominant to tonic; (b) plagal: subdominant to tonic; (c) imperfect: tonic to dominant; (d) deceptive (or interrupted): dominant to a chord other than the tonic (usually the submediant or subdominant); (e) the so-called Phrygian cadence, where the fall is in the lowest part (this derives its name from the Phrygian mode). Apart from these traditional forms any harmonic progression which suggests finality, if only temporarily, is technically a cadence.*

cadence in music, two chords that are specially chosen and arranged to give a logical end to a musical phrase or section. Music, like language, has a form of punctuation – with full stops, semicolons, and commas. This 'musical punctuation' is found at the end of phrases, which are natural resting points in music, and is called a cadence. Cadences have an important role in helping to establish the tonality of the music.

There are four main cadences in the tonal system: perfect, plagal, imperfect, and interrupted. The perfect cadence (or full close) uses chords V (dominant) and I (tonic). It gives the music a sense of completion or finality and is used when a full stop is needed, as at the end of a piece. The plagal cadence (or weak close) uses chords IV (subdominant) and I (tonic). It also creates a sense of finality and can be found at the end of a piece. It is sometimes called an 'Amen' cadence as it is often used at the end of hymns for the harmony of this word. The imperfect cadence (or half close) uses chords I (tonic) and V (dominant). This cadence is a temporary resting place and the music at this point sounds incomplete or unfinished. The interrupted cadence (or false close) uses chords V (dominant) and VI (submediant). As its name suggests, it falsely leads the listener to expect a perfect cadence (V–I) but this is 'interrupted' when chord V is followed by another chord. The second chord is usually chord VI although it can be almost any other chord except I (tonic).

Cadences in non-tonal music are achieved through various means. A popular method is where all the parts come to rest on one note (a pitch centre), this being the equivalent of the perfect cadence.

cadence-phrase in music, the final group in the exposition of a ➤ **sonata movement**, leading to the close in a key other than the tonic.

cadenza in music, an unaccompanied exhibition passage in the style of an improvisation, inserted by the soloist at the climax of a concerto movement.

The practice of improvising a cadenza largely ceased around 1780, composers thereafter supplying their own in written form. Recently, however, the practice of the interpreter composing a cadenza has re-emerged, with Stockhausen writing new cadenzas for Haydn and Mozart and Nigel Kennedy recording Beethoven's 1805 *Violin Concerto* with a cadenza of his own devising.

Cadi dupé, Le, The Cadi Duped opera by Christoph Willibald von Gluck (libretto by P R Lemonnier), first produced at the Burgtheater, Vienna, Austria, in December 1761. The story tells how the judge wants to divorce his wife Fatima and take the young Zelmira instead. She refuses him and he takes revenge by engaging her to an apparently destitute man, who turns out to be her lover, Nouradin.

Cadman, Charles Wakefield (1881–1946) US composer. He studied at Pittsburgh and became organist, chorus conductor, and critic there. He explored American Indian music and used it in some of his works. After a visit to Europe in 1910 he became organist in Denver, and later settled in Los Angeles.

Works OPERA *The Garden of Mystery* (1925), *The Land of Misty Water* (1909–12), *The Garden of Death, Shanewis/The Robin Woman* (1918), *A Witch of Salem* (1926), *The Willow Tree*.

ORCHESTRAL *Thunder-bird* suite (1914), *Oriental Rhapsody, Dark Dancers of the Mardi Gras* for orchestra; *American Suite* and *To a Vanishing Race* for string orchestra.

CHAMBER string quartet (1917), piano trio; violin and piano sonata, sonata and suite *Omar Khayyám* for piano.

VOCAL cantatas for mixed and male voices; songs.

Cadmus et Hermione opera by Jean-Baptiste Lully (libretto by Philippe Quinault), first produced at the Paris Opéra, France, on 27 April 1673. In the story, Cadmus loves Hermione but Mars has promised her to the giant Draco. Cadmus proves his bravery by killing a dragon. After complications introduced by the gods, all ends happily.

caduta de' giganti, La, The Fall of the Giants opera by Christoph Willibald von Gluck (libretto by F Vanneschi), first produced at the King's Theatre, Haymarket, London, England, on 7 January 1746.

Caffarelli (1710–1783), born **Gaetano Majorano** Italian castrato alto. A pupil of Nicola Porpora, he made his operatic debut in Rome, in 1726, in Sarro's *Valdemaro*. He sang for Handel in London, England, in 1738, creating the title roles in *Faramondo* and *Serse*.

Cage, John (1912–1992) US composer. His interest in Indian classical music led him to the view that the purpose of new music was to change the way people listen. From 1948 he experimented with instruments, graphics, and methods of random selection in an effort to generate a music of pure incident. For example, he used a number of radios, tuned to random stations, in *Imaginary Landscape IV* (1951). His ideas greatly influenced late 20th-century aesthetics.

Cage studied briefly with Arnold Schoenberg, also with Henry Cowell, and joined others in reacting against the European music tradition in favour of a freer style open to non-Western attitudes. Working in films during the 1930s, Cage assembled and toured a percussion orchestra using ethnic instruments and noisemakers, for which *Double Music* (1941) was composed (with Lou Harrison). He invented the ➤ **prepared piano**, in which different objects are inserted between the strings, altering the tone and the sound produced, to tour as accompanist with the dancer Merce Cunningham, a lifelong collaborator.

Cage was the most prominent pioneer and promoter of such 'experimental' ideas as indeterminacy, chance (➤ **aleatory music**), and silence. These ideas had a very considerable influence in both the USA and Europe. He worked to reduce the control of the composer over the music, introducing randomness and chance and allowing sounds to 'be themselves'. He was greatly influenced by oriental ideas. In a later work, *4'33"* (*Four Minutes and Thirty-three Seconds*) (1952), the pianist sits at the piano reading a score for that length of time but does not play, with whatever background sounds are occurring constituting the piece. He also explored electronic music.

Cage's essays and writings were collected in, for example, *Silence* (1961) and *For the Birds* (1981).

Works STAGE *Europeras I–IV* (1987–91), ballet *The Seasons* (1947).

ORCHESTRAL Concerto for prepared piano and chamber orchestra (1951); *Etcetera* (1973).

15

PERCUSSION AND ELECTRONICS *Construction 1 in Metal* for percussion sextet (1939); *Imaginary Landscape I* for turntables, frequency recordings, muted piano, and cymbal (1939); *Living Room Music* for percussion quartet (1940); *Construction II* and *III* and *Imaginary Landscape II* and *III*, all for percussion ensemble (1940–42); *Imaginary Landscape IV* (March no. 2) for twelve radios, 24 players, and conductor (1951); *Imaginary Landscape V* for tape (1952); *Fontana Mix* for tape or other instruments (1958).

CHAMBER string quartet (1950); *4'33" (Four Minutes and Thirty-three Seconds)* (no sound intentionally produced, 1952); *HARPSCHD* for seven harpsichords, or tape machines (1967–69); *Cheap Imitation* for violin (1977); 30 pieces for string quartet (1984).

PIANO AND PREPARED PIANO *Sonatas and Interludes* (1946–48); *Music of Changes* (1951); *Water Music* (1952); *One* (1988); *Swinging* (1989).

VOCAL many works, including Song Books, Solos for Voice 3–92 (1970); Hymns and Variations for twelve amplified voices (1978); *Litany for the Whale* for two voices (1980).

'Ça Ira' (French 'It will go on') song of the French Revolution, written by a street singer, Ladré, and set to an existing tune by Bécourt, a drummer of the Paris Opéra.

calando (Italian 'lowering') in musical notation, indicating a progressive softening, as in ➤ **diminuendo**, but also to an extent a progressive slowing down, as in ➤ **ritardando**.

calata an Italian lute dance of the early 16th century, similar to the French *basse danse*. It was written in duple time, but had a triple rhythm of three-bar groups.

Caldara, Antonio (1670–1736) Italian composer. He was a pupil of Giovanni Legrenzi in Venice, and after travelling much and working in Rome and Madrid, Spain, he settled in Vienna, Austria, as vice-conductor under Johann Fux in 1716, writing music for court celebrations there and in Salzburg. He was the first to set many of the libretti of Pietro Metastasio.

Works STAGE about 100 operas and other stage works, including *Ifigenia in Aulide* (1718), *Lucio Papirio, Gianguir* (1724), *Don Chisciotte* (1727), *La pazienza di Socrate con due moglie* (with Reutter, 1731), *Il Demetrio, Sancio Panza, Achille in Sciro* (1736).

OTHER church music, oratorios, cantatas, madrigals, canons; trio sonatas, quartets, septet.

Caldwell, Sarah (1924–2006) US conductor and producer. In 1976 she became the first woman conductor at the New York Metropolitan Opera House, conducting *La Traviata*. She staged her first opera while a student at Tanglewood, founded the Boston Opera Company in 1957, and gave the first US performances of *War and Peace, Moses und Aron* (as producer), *Benvenuto Cellini*, and the original versions of *Boris Godunov* and *Don Carlos*. She gave the first US performance of *The Ice Break* in 1979.

caledonica musical instrument, an alto ➤ **bassoon** invented by the Scottish bandmaster Meik around 1820. It was played with a clarinet reed mouthpiece.

Calife de Bagdad, Le one-act opera by François Boieldieu (libretto by C G de Saint-Just), first produced at the Opéra-Comique, Paris, France, on 16 September 1800. In the story, Isaoun loves Zétulbe, but wants her to love him for himself, not his riches. He courts her in disguise and wins her heart.

calinda or **calenda** an African-American dance introduced into the West Indies and later cultivated in the southern USA, originally an African ritual dance accompanied by drums, which remained a feature of its music. Delius makes use of it in his opera *Koanga*.

'Calino casturame' alternative spelling for the tune ➤ **'Callino casturame'**.

Calisto, La opera by Pietro Cavalli (libretto by G Faustini, after Ovid's *Metamorphoses*), first produced at the Teatro Sant'Apollinare, Venice, Italy, in 1651. It is known today in a free realization by Raymond Leppard (Glyndebourne, 26 May 1970), and in editions by Paul Daniel and René Jacobs. In the plot Jupiter assumes the identity of Diana in order to seduce the soprano Calisto.

Callcott, John Wall (1766–1821) English organist and composer. Having obtained a deputy organist's post, he found time to compose and in 1785 gained three of the four prizes offered by the Catch Club. Two years later he took part in founding the Glee Club. In 1809 he went insane, and died having reached letter P of a music dictionary, feeling unable to proceed further.

The son of a bricklayer, he had no regular music teaching, but picked up much knowledge from Samuel Arnold and Benjamin Cooke. When Haydn came to England, Callcott studied instrumental writing under him, but continued to write glees and catches with great success, and obtained a PhD from Oxford University in 1800.

Works the setting of Joseph Warton's *Ode to Fancy* (1785); anthem for Arnold's funeral; scena on the death of Nelson; a book of psalms edited with Arnold, with some new tunes; numerous glees, catches, and canons.

'Callino casturame' (probably corruption from Irish *Cailín ó chois Siúire mé* 'I am a girl from beside the [river] Suir') a tune mentioned in

Shakespeare's *Henry V* and set by 16th-century composers, including William Byrd.

Calm Sea and Prosperous Voyage works by Beethoven and Mendelssohn; see ➤ *Meeresstille und Glücklicke Fahrt.*

Calvisius, Seth (1556–1615) German scholar and musician. He was cantor of St Thomas's School, Leipzig, and music director of its church from 1594. In addition to writing several learned books on music, he compiled collections of vocal music and composed motets, hymns, and other pieces.

Calzabigi, Raniero da (1714–1795) Italian literary critic and author. From 1762 he collaborated with Christoph Willibald von Gluck in the more dramatically convincing 'reform' operas: *Orfeo ed Euridice* (1762), *Alceste* (1767), and *Paride ed Elena* (1770).

His first libretti were in the dry, formal style of Pietro Metastasio. After living in Paris and Vienna for a time, he returned to Italy in the 1770s. His last work, set by Giovanni Paisiello, returns to his earlier manner.

Cambert, Robert (c.1628–1677) French composer. His *Pomone* (1671) was the first French opera to be staged in public. Most of his music is lost. He was ousted by Jean-Baptiste Lully and went to live in London, England, in 1673.

He studied harpsichord with Jacques Chambonnières, was organist at the church of Saint-Honoré in Paris, and was appointed musical director at the court of Anne of Austria, mother of Louis XIV. He was associated with the poet Pierre Perrin, who in 1669 had obtained a grant of monopoly for the performance of musical stage works in the French language; their opera *Pomone* was performed in 1671. He also composed the music for Perrin's *Pastorale*, performed at the Château d'Issy in 1659; it was claimed, though erroneously, to be the earliest French comedy in music, or opera. Lully's intrigues transferred Perrin's monopoly into his own hands, and Cambert left Paris to settle in London.

Works STAGE a comedy with music *La Muette ingrate* (1658); a pastoral performed at Issy and another, *Les Peines et les plaisirs de l'amour* (1671); operas *Ariane, ou Le Mariage de Bacchus, Pomone* (1674); a trio for Brécourt's *Jaloux invisible; airs à boire.*

cambiale di matrimonio, La, *The Marriage Contract* opera by Rossini (libretto by Giacomo Rossi, based on a comedy by C Federici), first produced at the Teatro San Moisè, Venice, Italy, on 3 November 1810. It was Rossini's first opera to be performed. In the plot Tobias Mill is keen to sell off his daughter Fanny, but the young Milfort intervenes.

camera, concerto da or **sonata da camera (Italian 'chamber concerto or sonata')** secular work written for performance at home or at concerts, as distinct from a concerto or sonata *da chiesa*, 'for the church'.

camerata (Italian 'society') a group of intellectuals meeting for cultural exchanges, in particular one at Florence under Count Giovanni de' Bardi in about 1573–87 and strongly influenced by Girolamo Mei's research into ancient Greek music. The earliest operas seem to have emerged from their deliberations.

cameriera (Italian 'chambermaid') term used in Italian opera, especially of the 17th and 18th centuries, in the same way as *servetta/servant-girl* is used for soubrette parts.

Cameron, Basil (1884–1975) English conductor. He studied in Berlin, Germany, 1902–06, and as a conductor in Torquay adopted, but only up to the war, the name Basil Hindenburg in an attempt to negate the usual prejudice against conductors with English names. He was engaged with seaside orchestras 1912–30, then conducted orchestras in San Francisco and Seattle, USA, before returning to the UK in 1938. He assisted Henry Wood, then Adrian Boult, with the Prom Concerts from 1940; in September 1945 he conducted the first European performance of Arnold Schoenberg's piano concerto.

Camilla, *Trionfo di Camilla* opera by Giovanni ➤ **Bononcini.**

Cammarano, Salvatore (1801–1852) Italian librettist. He wrote various stage pieces before the libretto for Donizetti's *Lucia di Lammermoor* in 1835; his other libretti included *Roberto Devereux, Belisario,* and *Poliuto.* His first libretto for Giuseppe Verdi was *Alzira,* in 1841; later ones are *La battaglia di Legnano, Luisa Miller,* and most of *Il trovatore.* He also wrote the libretti for Giovanni Pacini's *Saffo* and Giuseppe Mercadante's *La vestale* and *Medea.*

Campagnoli, Bartolomeo (1751–1827) Italian violinist and composer. After studying with Pietro Nardini, he worked in Italy, Germany, and Paris, France. He wrote concertos, sonatas, duets, and other pieces for violin; flute music; caprices for viola; also an important work on violin playing, *Metodo per violino.*

campana sommersa, La, *The Sunken Bell* opera by Ottorino Respighi (libretto by C Guastalla, after G Hauptmann's *Die versunkene Glocke*), composed 1923–27 and first performed in Hamburg, Germany, on 24 November 1928. The story describes how the bell-maker Enrico falls for the elf Rautendelein and deserts his wife. At the news of his wife's suicide he rejects Rautendelein, but dies because he cannot live without her.

Campanella, La the third of Liszt's *Études d'exécution transcendante d'après Paganini* for piano, composed in 1838, already used by him 1831–32 for the *Grande Fantaisie de bravoure sur la clochette*. The theme is that of the finale of Paganini's violin concerto in B minor, Op. 7, a rondo in which harmonics are combined with a bell.

Campenhout, François van (1779–1848) Belgian tenor and composer. He sang in Belgium, Holland, and France until 1827. During the 1830 revolution he wrote the Belgian national anthem, 'La Brabançonne'.

Works OPERA *Grotius*, *Le Passepartout*, and *L'Heureux Mensonge*.

OTHER church music; choruses; songs.

Campian, Thomas alternative spelling of Thomas ➤ Campion.

campiello, Il, *The Square* opera by Ermanno Wolf-Ferrari (libretto by M Ghisalberti, after Carlo Goldoni), first produced at La Scala, Milan, Italy, on 12 February 1936. It portrays a slice of working-class Venetian life.

Campioli (lived 18th century), born **Antonio Gualandi** Italian castrato alto. He made his operatic debut in Berlin, Germany, in 1708, and sang in Handel's operas in London, England, 1731–32; he sang Argone in the first performance of *Sosarme* (1732).

Campion, Thomas (1567–1620) English poet and musician. He was the author of the critical *Art of English Poesie* (1602) and four books of *Ayres* (1601–17), for which he composed both words and music.

The *Art of English Poesie* is an attack on the use of rhyme and a plea for the adoption of unrhymed metres formed on classical models, such as are used in Campion's own 'Rose-cheeked Laura, Come'. He also wrote *Poemata* (1595), in Latin, containing poems, elegies, and epigrams.

Campion was born in Witham, Essex. Educated at Cambridge and other European universities, he then studied law, but left this profession and practised medicine in London.

He published a first collection of airs to the lute with Philip Rosseter in 1601 and four more followed between about 1613 and 1617, all the words of the songs being his own. He composed masques that are among the best of their kind, and produced many fine lyrics notable for their metrical finish. His songs are verbally delicate, and he composed most of his own settings for them; the balance between the lyrics and the music is sensitive and satisfying. The best known are 'There is a Garden in her Face' and 'My Sweetest Lesbia, Let Us Live and Love', a translation from Catullus.

In 1613 he published a book on counterpoint, and wrote the poetry for *Songs of Mourning* on the death of Prince Henry, set by Giovanni Coprario. His poem 'Neptune's Empire' was set for chorus and orchestra by Ernest Walker.

Works five books of airs to the lute (over 100) and three separate earlier songs; songs for the production of four masques, 1607–13, including *The Mask of Flowers*.

Campioni, Carlo Antonio (1720–1788) Italian composer. He was in the service of the Grand Duke of Tuscany, in Florence, and the King of Sardinia.

Works Requiem and other church music, trio sonatas, duets for two violins and for violin and cello; keyboard music.

Campra, André (1660–1744) French composer. He held various provincial organist's posts and settled in Paris in 1694, when he was appointed music director at Notre-Dame, where his motets soon attracted large congregations. He became equally famous as a stage composer, bringing out about 40 dramatic works which earned him great fame and made a link between the work of Jean-Baptiste Lully and Jean-Philippe Rameau. After many years of neglect, his works are now being revived and recorded.

He was born in Aix-en-Provence, where he learnt music at the church of Saint-Sauveur. His first stage work was the opera-ballet *L'Europe galante* (1697); his last was the opera *Achille et Déidamie*.

Works STAGE operas and opera-ballets *L'Europe galante* (1697), *Le Carnaval de Venise* (1699), *Hésione*, *Tancrède*, *Iphigénie en Tauride* (with Desmarets, 1704), *Alcine*, *Hippodamie* (1708), *Les Festes vénitiennes*, *Idoménée* (1712), *Le Jaloux trompé*, *Achille et Déidamie* (1735), and others; pasticcios *Fragments de Lully* and *Télémaque* (the latter with pieces by Charpentier, Colasse, Desmarets, Marais, and Rebel senior); entertainments *Amaryllis*, *Les Festes de Corinthe*, *Le Génie de la Bourgogne*, *Les Noces de Vénus* (1740), and others.

OTHER a Mass, cantatas, motets, and psalms.

canary or **canarie** or **canaries** a dance in quick triple time with a dotted rhythm, possibly originating from the Canary Islands.

cancan high-kicking stage dance in fast duple time (2/4) for women (solo or line of dancers), originating in Paris, France, about 1830. The music usually associated with the cancan is the *galop* from Jacques Offenbach's *Orphée aux enfers*/*Orpheus in the Underworld* (1858).

cancel US musical term for a natural (♮).

canción (Spanish, 'song') in music, a song, particularly in a Spanish or Latin American style.

(a) 'standard'

(b) by inversion

(c) by diminution

Canons: (a) 'standard'; (b) by inversion; and (c) by diminution. If the imitation is exact the canon is termed 'strict'; if it is modified by the addition or omission of accidentals it is 'free as to intervals'. A canon may proceed (1) by inversion, with one part going up where the other goes down and vice versa (illustration (b)); (2) by augmentation, with one part in notes twice or more the length of the other (illustration (c)); (3) by diminution, with one part in notes half or less the length of the other; (4) by retrograde motion (canon cancrizans), with one part going backwards while the other goes forwards. Various combinations of these forms are also possible. A canon may be accompanied by one or more independent parts. Two or more canons can occur simultaneously.

cancionero (Spanish, 'song book') collection of songs, usually Spanish. The term equally applies to the collection of the texts alone, without written music.

cancrizans (from Latin *cancer*, 'crab', 'crabwise') term used for the device of repeating a musical phrase or theme backwards, note for note. 'Canon cancrizans' is a canon in which one part or more proceed normally while another one or more go backwards. In ➤ twelve-tone music, the reversed form of the series is sometimes called cancrizans instead of the more usual retrograde.

Candide comic operetta by Leonard Bernstein (libretto by L Hellman, after Voltaire), first produced in Boston, USA, on 29 October 1956; it was revised in 1973 and produced at the New York City Opera on 13 October 1982. The story tells how, in spite of all the evidence to the contrary, Candide (tenor) believes everything in life is for the best. He eventually decides, after many adventures, that his philosophy was mistaken, and resolves to build a new life.

Canis, Corneille (c.1510/20–1561), also known as **Cornelis de Hond** Flemish composer. He was choirmaster of Charles V's imperial chapel in the Netherlands from 1548, and later became chaplain to the Holy Roman emperor Ferdinand in Prague. He wrote church music, chansons, and other pieces.

Cannabich, (Johann) Christian (1731–1798) German violinist, conductor, and composer. After studying with Johann Stamitz in Mannheim and Niccolò Jommelli in Rome, Italy, he became Konzertmeister of the Mannheim orchestra in 1758 and director of instrumental music in 1774. From 1778 he worked in Munich. His conducting was admired by Mozart, who taught Cannabich's daughter Rosa in 1777 and wrote a piano sonata for her.

Works operas, ballets, including *Renaud et Armide* (1768), symphonies, chamber music.

Cannon, Philip (1929–) English composer. He studied with Imogen Holst and later at the Royal College of Music, London, with Gordon

Jacob (composition) and Pierre Tas (violin). This was followed by some study with Paul Hindemith. After a period of lecturing at Sydney University, Australia, he returned to the Royal College of Music in 1952.

Works three operas; string quartet (1964) and other chamber music, vocal and choral music including *Lord of Light*, oratorio for soloists, chorus, and orchestra (1980), piano compositions; two symphonies, including *Son of Man*, for the UK's entry to the European Community.

canon piece or passage of contrapuntal music in which one voice repeats the part of another, like an echo. The first vocal or instrumental part begins with the melody and is followed soon after by the second part imitating that melody note for note (though often starting on a different note and keeping the intervallic distance throughout). This can go on up to five or six voices. The second part may follow at half a bar, one bar, two bars, or any other distance the composer chooses. Many examples of canon can be found in the fugues of Johann Sebastian Bach. Canon is called 'stretto' when used in a ➔ **fugue**.

Canonic variations may also introduce a difference in starting pitch between the voices. This can make it difficult to decide what key the music is in. The fugue is the most highly skilled of these variations. The main feature of the beginning (exposition) of a fugue is that all the parts or voices (so called whether the fugue is vocal or instrumental) enter one after the other, strictly imitating each other. The fugue has been written by composers since 1600. Johann Sebastian Bach is the undisputed master of the fugue and examples of his work are *The Art of Fugue* (published 1751) and *The Well-Tempered Clavier* (1722–40). Other major fugue composers include Dietrich Buxtehude, who Bach admired greatly.

cantabile (Italian 'singable') in musical notation, indicating a singing and lyrical style (of playing). It implies a full, rich tone and legato touch.

cantata in music, a work in three or more movements, using one or more vocal soloists, and sometimes a chorus. It is usually accompanied by an ensemble or small orchestra, and can be sacred or secular. The word comes from the Italian, meaning 'sung', as opposed to ➔ **sonata** ('sounded', 'played') for instruments. The first printed collection of sacred cantata texts dates from 1670. The most well-known composer of sacred cantatas was Johann Sebastian Bach, with Alessandro Scarlatti being a major master of the secular form.

Cantata Academica work by Benjamin Britten for soloists, chorus, and orchestra, composed in 1959 on Latin texts, for the 500th anniversary of Basel University, Germany; it was first performed in Basel on 1 July 1960.

Cantata Misericordium work by Benjamin Britten for tenor, baritone, small chorus, and chamber orchestra (text by P Wilkinson), composed for the centenary of the International Red Cross. It was first performed in Geneva, Switzerland, on 15 September 1963, conducted by Ernest Ansermet.

Cantata on the Death of the Emperor Joseph II work by Beethoven for soloists, chorus, and orchestra (text by S A Averdonk). It was commissioned from Beethoven in Bonn, Germany, after the death of the emperor on 20 February 1790, but was not performed until 1884. The manuscript was probably seen by Haydn on his return from his first visit to England, and led to his offering Beethoven lessons in Vienna, Austria. The cantata contains an anticipation of a theme from the last scene of Beethoven's opera *Fidelio*.

Cantata Profana or *A kilenc csodaszarvas/ The Nine Enchanted Stags* work by Béla Bartók for tenor, baritone, chorus, and orchestra, composed in 1930 and first performed in a BBC (British Broadcasting Corporation) concert on 25 May 1934.

Cantelli, Guido (1920–1956) Italian conductor. He quickly made his way in Italy and abroad as a conductor whose gifts were second only to Arturo Toscanini's. He conducted the National Broadcasting Company Symphony Orchestra from 1949 and the Philharmonia, London, from 1951.

He studied at the Milan Conservatory and, after escaping from a German prison camp and a fascist prison hospital in World War II, began to conduct concerts with the orchestra of La Scala in Milan. He was killed in an air accident.

Canteloube (de Malaret), (Marie) Joseph (1879–1957) French composer. In 1900 he began to collect and study French folk song, particularly of the Auvergne region, of which he published several collections. He is best known for his four volumes of folk-song arrangements *Chants d'Auvergne* (1923–30).

He studied with Vincent d'Indy at the Schola Cantorum in Paris, and lectured on French music and folk song from 1923.

Works OPERA *Le Mas* (1910–13), *Vercingetorix* (produced 1933).

ORCHESTRAL symphonic poems *Vers la princesse lointaine* and *Lauriers*; *Pièces françaises* for piano and orchestra; *Poème* for violin and orchestra.

CHAMBER *Dans la montagne* for violin and piano.

VOCAL songs with orchestra and with piano; many folk-song arrangements.

Canterbury Pilgrims, The opera by Charles Villiers Stanford (libretto by G A à Beckett, after Chaucer's *The Canterbury Tales*), first produced at the Drury Lane Theatre, London, England, on 28 April 1884.

canticle in the Roman Catholic or Anglican liturgies, a hymn or song of praise based on scripture and similar to a psalm, but whose text does not originate in the Book of Psalms. An example of a canticle is the ➤ **Magnificat** of Anglican evensong.

Canticles series of five works by Benjamin Britten: no. 1 *My beloved is mine* (text by F Quarles), for high voice and piano, first performed at Aldeburgh, England, on 1 November 1947; no. 2 *Abraham and Isaac* (text from Chester miracle play), for alto, tenor, and piano, first performed in Nottingham, England, on 21 January 1952; no. 3 *Still falls the rain* (text by Edith Sitwell), for tenor, horn, and piano, first performed in London on 28 January 1955; no. 4 *The Journey of the Magi* (text by T S Eliot), for countertenor, tenor, baritone, and piano, first performed at Aldeburgh on 26 June 1971; no. 5 *The Death of Narcissus* (text by Eliot), for tenor and harpsichord, first performed at Schloss Elmau on 15 January 1975.

Britten later quoted the music from the second canticle, *Abraham and Isaac* in his *War Requiem*, this time to set Wilfred Owen's anti-war metaphorical re-working of the story.

Canticum Sacrum (ad honorem Sancti Marci nominis) work by Stravinsky, in honour of St Mark's, Venice, for tenor, baritone, chorus, and orchestra; it was composed in 1955 and first performed in Venice on 13 September 1956.

Canti di prigionia, **Songs of Captivity** work by Luigi Dallapiccola for chorus, two pianos, two harps, and percussion (texts by Mary Stuart, Boethius, and Savonarola); it was composed 1938–41 in protest against Italian fascism and first performed in Rome, Italy, on 11 December 1941.

cantigas (Spanish 'canticles') Spanish sacred songs for single voice of the 13th century, mostly in honour of the Virgin Mary, allied in form to the French *virelai* and the Italian *lauda*.

cantilena in music, a sustained, flowing melodic line, especially when sung *legato* or played in the manner of such singing.

cantillation chanting in unison in the Jewish synagogue service.

cantino in music, the E (highest) string of the violin.

cantiones sacrae (Latin 'sacred songs') title often given to collections of Latin motets in the 16th and 17th centuries.

canto (Italian 'song') in music, the part of a composition, both instrumental and vocal, which has the chief melody. The direction *marcato il canto* indicates that such a melody is to be emphasized.

canto carnascialesco (Italian 'carnival song') a Florentine part song of the 15th–16th centuries with secular, often ribald, words, sung in carnival processions.

canto fermo another name for ➤ **cantus firmus**, a melody employed for reference in counterpoint.

cantometrics influential but controversial analytical system, developed by Alan Lomax and Victor Grauer in the late 1960s for a worldwide study of folk song. Musical factors relating to song style are submitted to statistical analysis and correlated with appropriate social and cultural data, with a view to delineating the role of song in its cultural context.

cantor or (Hebrew) **chazan (Latin *cantare*, 'to sing')** in Judaism and Roman Catholicism, the prayer leader and choirmaster, responsible for singing solo parts of the chant. The position can be held by any lay person. In Protestant churches, the music director is known as the cantor.

The Jewish cantor, or chazan, who leads the singing in synagogue has had a training not only in music and voice work, but in chanting the special prayers for different occasions. He may also assist the rabbi in leading services. Not all synagogues will have a chazan. In Liberal and Reform congregations the chazan may be a woman.

cantus firmus (Latin 'fixed song') in music, any familiar melody employed in counterpoint as a reference for the invention of an accompanying melody.

In early music, multiple parts were composed one at a time, each referring to the cantus firmus, but not to any other, with sometimes strange harmonic results, for example the final cadence E minor–G major–F major.

Canyons aux étoiles, Des, **From the Canyons to the Stars** work by Olivier Messiaen for piano, horn, and orchestra, composed 1970–74 and first performed in New York, USA, on 20 November 1974.

canzona (Italian 'song', 'ballad') 16th-century instrumental form modelled on vocal polyphony, adopted by Girolamo Frescobaldi, Johann Sebastian Bach, Andrea Gabrieli, and Giovanni Gabrieli.

canzonet (from Italian *canzonetta*, 'little song') light songs written in England round about 1600, either for several voices with or without instruments or for a single voice with lute accompaniment. Later it became simply a song in England, such as Haydn's English Canzonets.

canzonetta (Italian 'little song') term often synonymous with ➤ **canzona** in 16th–17th-century Italy; later it came to mean a light song or short and simple air in an opera.

canzoniere Italian, meaning 'song-book'.

Cape, Safford (1906–1973) US conductor and musicologist. In 1933 he founded the Pro Musica Antiqua, for the performance of medieval and Renaissance music, in Brussels, Belgium. He made many recordings for the Anthologie Sonore and History of European Music in Sound, and established the European Seminar on Early Music at Bruges, Belgium, and Lisbon, Portugal, in 1961.

Capella, Martianus Minneus Felix (lived 4th–5th centuries) Latin philosopher and writer on the liberal arts, active in Carthage. His *De musica*, widely read from the 9th century onwards, is the ninth and last book of his *De nuptiis Philologiae et Mercurii*. His treatise, deriving in part from Varro, had considerable influence on later medieval theorists. It was also largely based on *Peri mousikēs* by Aristedes Quintillianus, especially as concerns musical terminology, classification, and aesthetics of music.

Capirola, Vincenzo (1474–after 1548) Italian lutenist and composer. His collection of lute music, which dates from about 1517, is among the most important early manuscripts of the repertory.

Caplet, André (1878–1925) French conductor and composer. He was much influenced by Debussy, who allowed him to orchestrate a part of *Le Martyre de Saint Sebastien*, which Caplet premiered in 1911.

Works ORCHESTRAL symphonic study *Le Masque de la mort rouge* (after Poe, 1909); *Epiphanie* for cello and orchestra (1923). He orchestrated Debussy's *Children's Corner* and conducted the first performance of *Le Martyre de Saint Sébastien* (1911).

CHAMBER *Suite persane* for ten wind instruments; *Conte fantastique* (after Poe) for harp and string quartet (an arrangement of *Le Masque de la mort rouge*); *Sonata de chiesa* for violin and organ; children's suite for piano duet.

VOCAL Mass for unaccompanied voices; *Le Miroir de Jésus* for voices, string quintet, and harp (1924); *Le Pie Jésus* for voice and organ; song cycles *Prières*, *La Croix douloureuse*, *Trois Fables de La Fontaine*, *Cinq Ballades françaises*.

Capriccio opera by Richard Strauss (libretto by C Krauss and the composer), first produced at

the Munich Staatsoper, Germany, on 28 October 1942. An elegant 'conversation piece' in which the composer Flamand and poet Olivier compete for the affections of Countess Madeleine, it is also a deconstructionist opera about opera.

It is also the title of a work by Leoš Janáček in four movements for piano left hand and orchestra, composed in 1926 and first performed in Prague (now the Czech Republic) on 2 March 1928.

Stravinsky also composed a work with the same title for piano and orchestra in 1929; it was first performed in Paris, France, on 6 December 1929, conducted by Ernest Ansermet.

capriccio (Italian 'caprice') in music, an all-purpose name for a lightweight piece, often in the style of a ➤ **fugue**, combining technical virtuosity with entertainment.

Capriccio espagnol, **Spanish Caprice** orchestral work by Nikolai Rimsky-Korsakov, written as a display piece for the St Petersburg Orchestra; it was finished on 4 August and performed in St Petersburg, Russia, on 17 December 1887. It contains brilliant solo parts for most of the principal instruments and for the brass in groups. It was originally intended to be for violin and orchestra, a companion-piece to Rimsky-Korsakov's *Russian Fantasy* (1886).

Capriccio italien, **Italian Caprice** orchestral work by Tchaikovsky, composed during a visit to Rome, Italy, in 1880 and first performed in Moscow, Russia, on 18 December 1880.

caprichos, Los fantasia for orchestra by Hans Werner Henze; it was composed in 1963 and first performed in Duisburg, Germany, on 6 April 1967.

Capuleti e i Montecchi, I, **The Capulets and Montagues** opera by Vincenzo Bellini (libretto by Felice Romani, based on Shakespeare's sources for *Romeo and Juliet*). It was first produced at the Teatro La Fenice, Venice, Italy, on 11 March 1830. Bellini's example persuaded Hector Berlioz to set the play as an extended symphony with voices.

Caractacus cantata for solo voices, chorus, and orchestra by Edward Elgar, Op. 35 (libretto by H A Acworth), composed in 1898 and first produced at the Leeds Festival, England, on 5 October 1898. Its subject is the battles of the ancient Briton Caractacus against the Romans.

It is also the title of music by Thomas Arne for a dramatic poem by W Mason (published 1759), first performed at Covent Garden, London, on 6 December 1776.

Carafa (di Colobrano), Michele Enrico (1787–1872) Italian composer. On the failure of his first opera he enlisted in the bodyguard of

Murat, then king of Naples, took part in the Russian campaign in 1812, and was decorated by Napoleon, after whose fall he returned to music. He produced operas not only in Italy but in Vienna, Austria, and Paris, France, where he settled in 1827 and became very popular. He was professor of composition at the Paris Conservatory 1840–58.

Works OPERA about 35 operas, including *Il fantasma* (1805), *Il vascello d'occidente*, *Gabriella di Vergy* (1816), *Ifigenia*, *Berenice*, *Le Solitaire*, *La Violette* (1828), *La Fiancée de Lammermoor*, and *Elisabetta in Derbyshire* (after Scott, 1818), *Masaniello* (competing with Auber's *La Muette de Portici*, 1827), *La Prison d'Edimbourg* (after Scott's *The Heart of Midlothian*), *Jeanne d'Arc* (after Schiller, 1821).

Carattaco opera by Johann Christian Bach (libretto by G G Bottarelli), first performed at the King's Theatre, London, England, on 14 February 1767.

Cardew, Cornelius (1936–1981) English composer and pianist. He belonged at one time to the avant-garde school, whose ideas are much influenced by John Cage, but he later espoused Marxist principles and published a book, *Stockhausen Serves Imperialism* (1974). In 1969 he founded the Scratch Orchestra for non-performers, who are free to produce any sounds or no sounds on conventional or improvised instruments. His works have been widely performed in Europe.

Cardew was born in Winchcombe, Gloucestershire. He studied at the Royal Academy of Music, London, with, among others, Howard Ferguson. In 1958 he went to Cologne, Germany, to study electronic music, also working with Karlheinz Stockhausen until 1960.

Works *Octet 1959*; 193-page graphic score *Treatise* (1967); *The Great Learning* (1970); *Autumn 60* for orchestra; *A Bun* for orchestra; *The East is Red* for violin and piano (1972); *The Old and the New*, for soprano, chorus, and orchestra (1973); piano music.

Cardillac opera by Paul Hindemith (libretto by F Lion, based on E T A Hoffmann's story *Das Fräulein von Scudéri*), first produced in Dresden, Germany, on 9 November 1926; a revised version was produced in Zurich, Switzerland, on 20 June 1952. The story tells how the goldsmith Cardillac murders his clients to recover his handywork. After stabbing his daughter's fiancé, Cardillac reveals he is a murderer and is killed by a mob.

Carestini, Giovanni (c. 1705–c. 1760) Italian castrato alto. He first appeared in Rome in 1721, and sang in Handel's operas in London, England, 1733–35, creating roles in *Arianna in Creta*, *Ariodante*, and *Alcina*.

Carey, Henry (1687–1743) English poet and musician. He wrote the song 'Sally in Our Alley'. 'God Save the King' (both words and music) has also been attributed to him.

Carey was a pupil of Thomas Roseingrave and Francesco Geminiani. He wrote libretti for John Lampe's operas *The Dragon of Wantley*, *Margery*, and *Amelia*.

Works STAGE ballad operas *The Contrivances* (1729), *A Wonder, or the Honest Yorkshireman* (1735), *Nancy, or the Parting Lovers* (1739), and others; songs for Vanbrugh and Cibber's *The Provok'd Husband*.

OTHER cantatas and songs to his own words.

carillon bell-ringing mechanism in which a manual keyboard, and often pedals, played like an organ, are connected by wires to the beaters of up to 70 static bells. The bells are usually hung in a tower, often in a church. Carillons are found throughout Europe and the USA; mechanized carillons were the forerunners of musical clocks and boxes.

Carissimi, Giacomo (1605–1674) Italian composer. He was chapel master at the church of Sant' Apollinare in Rome, and is famous for his reform of the recitative, and for being practically the inventor of the cantata. He wrote sacred and secular cantatas and motets. His music is distinguished by its pure style and its exquisite melodies, and his followers included the elder Bononcini and Alessandro Scarlatti.

He was born in Marino, near Rome. He was maestro di cappella at Assisi 1628–29 and then went to Rome, where he held a similar post at the church of Sant' Apollinare attached to the German College, 1630–74. He pioneered the use of expressive solo aria as a commentary on the Latin biblical text. He wrote five oratorios, including *Jephtha* (c. 1650).

Works Masses, motets; *Lauda Sion* and *Nisi Dominus* for eight voices; oratorios *History of Job*, *Baltazar*, *Abraham and Isaac*, *Jephtha* (c. 1650), *The Last Judgement*, *Jonah*; sacred cantatas; vocal duets.

Carlton, Richard (c.1558–c.1638) English composer. He was educated at Cambridge, and later became vicar at St Stephen's Church, Norwich, and a minor canon at the cathedral. He published a book of madrigals in 1601 and contributed to the collection of English madrigals *The* ➔ *Triumphes of Oriana* (1603).

carmagnole (from Carmagnola in northern Italy) wild song and dance that accompanied the peasant costume of the same name, from Piedmont and the Midi, worn by southern French revolutionaries to Paris in 1793. The song and dance were very popular with the revolutionaries during the Terror in Paris.

The refrain of each verse was: 'Vive le son, vive le son / Dansons la Carmagnole / Vive le son du canon!'.

Carmen opera by Georges Bizet (libretto by H Meilhac and L Halévy, based on the story by Prosper Mérimée), first produced at the Opéra-Comique, Paris, France, on 3 March 1875. In the story, the bullfighter Don José is caught between the gypsy girl Carmen and his original love, Micaela. Obsessed by Carmen, who soon rejects him, he kills her outside a bullring.

Carmina Burana medieval Latin verse miscellany compiled from the work of wandering 13th-century scholars and including secular (love songs and drinking songs) as well as religious verse. The composer Carl ➤ Orff wrote a cantata based on the material in 1937.

Carnaval, Carnival suite of piano pieces on the notes ASCH by Robert Schumann, Op. 9. In German musical terminology, 'As' is A flat, S alone ('Es') is E flat, and H is B natural. The letters represent the only musical ones in Schumann's surname and the town of Asch in Bohemia, the home of Ernestine von Fricken, with whom he was in love in 1834–35, when he wrote the work. She is alluded to in the piece entitled *Estrella*; other persons referred to are Clara Wieck in *Chiarina*, Chopin and Paganini under their own names, and Schumann himself in his two different imaginary characters of *Florestan* and *Eusebius*.

A ballet on Schumann's music, orchestrated by Aleksandr Glazunov and others (choreographed by Mikhail Fokin), was first produced at the Paris Opéra, France, on 4 June 1910.

Carnaval des animaux, Le, The Carnival of the Animals suite ('grand zoological fantasy') by Camille Saint-Saëns for chamber orchestra with two pianos, privately performed and not intended by the composer to be published. It contains a number of humorous musical allusions.

Carnaval romain, Le, The Roman Carnival concert overture by Hector Berlioz, Op. 9, written in 1843 on material from the opera *Benvenuto Cellini* of 1834–38. It was first performed in Paris, France, on 3 February 1844.

Carnegie Hall largest concert hall in New York City, opened in 1891 and named after the millionaire philanthropist Andrew Carnegie. It has a distinctive rich ➤ acoustic.

The hall comprises three separate theatres. The main stage, the Isaac Stern Auditorium, seats 2,804; the Sanford I Weill Recital Hall seats 268, and the Arthur Zankel Hall (opened in 2003) seats 644.

Carnival concert overture by Antonín Dvořák, Op. 92, composed in 1891 and forming, with *Amid Nature* and *Othello*, a cycle with thematic connections originally called *Nature, Life and Love*.

It is also the title of a suite by Schumann; see ➤ Carnaval.

carol song that in medieval times was associated with a round dance; today carols are associated with festivals such as Christmas and Easter.

Christmas carols were common as early as the 15th century. The custom of singing carols from house to house, collecting gifts, was called 'wassailing'. Many carols, such as 'God Rest You Merry Gentlemen' and 'The First Noel', date from the 16th century or earlier.

Caron, Philippe Firmin(ius) (1450–80) Flemish or French composer, much praised by writers of the time. Four of his Masses and nearly 20 chansons survive. He may have had some connection with the Burgundian court, although it has proved impossible to identify him firmly with any surviving documentation. He is called 'Firminius Caron' in Tinctoris's *Liber de Arte Contrapuncti* (1477).

Carpani, Giuseppe (Antonio) (1752–1825) Italian poet and writer on music. He settled in Vienna, Austria, and was a friend and biographer of Franz Joseph Haydn. His book on the composer was plagiarized by the French writer Stendhal.

Carpenter, John Alden (1876–1951) US composer. He learnt music privately and studied with John Paine while a student at Harvard University, and (briefly) with Edward Elgar in Rome, Italy, in 1906, later at Chicago with Bernhard Ziehn. Although a businessman, he composed much in a varied style. His ballet *Skyscrapers* (1926) features red traffic lights operated by a keyboard.

Works BALLET *The Birthday of the Infanta* (after Wilde, 1919), *Krazy-Kat* (1921), *Skyscrapers* (1926).

ORCHESTRAL symphonies *Adventures in a Perambulator* (1915) and *Sea Drift* (after Whitman) for orchestra; concertino for piano and orchestra, violin concerto.

CHAMBER string quartet (1927), piano quintet.

VOCAL *Song of Faith* for chorus and orchestra; many songs including *Gitanjali* cycle (Tagore).

Carr, Benjamin (1768–1831) US composer and publisher. He was the first to publish the song 'Yankee Doodle' in the USA and his ballad opera *The Archers, or Mountaineers of Switzerland*, first performed in New York in 1796, is the first US opera of which music parts survive.

Arriving in Philadelphia in 1793, he founded a music publishing business there, becoming known as the Father of Philadelphia Music. He was a co-founder of the Musical Fund Society in 1820 and was also active in New York and Baltimore as a publisher, concert promoter, and organist.

Carré work by Karlheinz Stockhausen for four orchestras, four choruses, with four conductors, first performed in Hamburg, Germany, on 28 October 1960.

Carré, Michel (1819–1872) French librettist. He collaborated with Jules Barbier (1822–1901) on texts for most French opera composers of their time. They used works by Shakespeare, Goethe, Molière, and Corneille to provide material to suit the bourgeois tastes of contemporary audiences.

Carrillo, Julián (1875–1965) Mexican composer. He studied at the National Conservatory in Mexico City, won a violin prize, and made further studies at Leipzig and Ghent Conservatories in Europe. Returning to Mexico in 1905, he was active as a violinist and conductor as well as a composer. He experimented in his later works with music using small fractional divisions of the scale.

Works OPERA *Ossian* (1902), *Mexico in 1810* (1909), *Xulitl* (1920, revised 1947).

CHURCH MUSIC two Masses, Requiem.

ORCHESTRAL six symphonies (1901–48), three suites, overture *8 de Septiembre*, symphonic poem *Xochimilco* for orchestra; fantasy for piano and orchestra, concerto for flute, violin, and cello.

CHAMBER four string quartets, piano quintet, string sextet; four violin and piano sonatas.

OTHER 40 works in fractional scales, including *Ave Maria* for chorus, *Fantasía Sonido 13* for chamber orchestra, *Preludio a Cristóbal Colón* for soprano and ensemble.

Carrosse du Saint-Sacrement, Le, The Coach of the Holy Sacrament opera by Lord Berners (libretto from Prosper Mérimée's play), first produced at the Théâtre des Champs-Elysées, Paris, France, on 24 April 1924.

Carse, Adam (1878–1958) English music scholar and composer. He studied in Germany and at the Royal Academy of Music, London. He was assistant music master at Winchester College 1909–22 and professor at the Royal Academy of Music from 1923. He made a special study of instruments and the orchestra, and left a collection of early wind instruments to the Horniman Museum, London.

Carter, Elliott Cook (1908–   ) US composer. He created intricately structured works in Schoenbergian serial idiom, incorporating 'metrical modulation', an adaptation of standard notation allowing different instruments or groups

to remain synchronized while playing at changing speeds. This practice was first employed in his *String Quartet No. 1* (1950–51), and to dense effect in *Double Concerto* (1961) for harpsichord and piano. Other important works include the ballets *Pocahontas* (1939) and *Holiday Overture* (1944), his *Piano Sonata* (1946), and *A Symphony of Three Orchestras* (1976). His late music showed a new tautness and vitality, as in *Three Occasions for Orchestra* (1986–89).

Carter was educated at Harvard University, where he studied music with Walter Piston; later he was a pupil of Nadia Boulanger in Paris, France. From 1960 to 1962 he was professor of composition at Yale University and in 1960 was awarded a Pulitzer Prize. From 1972 he taught at the Juilliard School, New York. Carter's music is many layered and of extreme rhythmic complexity, sometimes recalling Charles Ives, with cross-rhythms and different rhythms played simultaneously.

Works STAGE opera *Tom and Lily* (1934), ballet *Pocahontas* (1939).

ORCHESTRAL symphony no. 1 (1942; first performance 1944), *Holiday Overture* (1944; first performance 1948), *Variations* (1953–55; first performance 1956), piano concerto (1965; first performance 1967), *Concerto for Orchestra* (1969; first performance 1970), *A Symphony of Three Orchestras* (1976; first performance 1977), *Penthode* for chamber orchestra (1985), *Partita* (1993), *Adagio tenebroso* (1995).

INSTRUMENTAL piano sonata (1946), cello sonata (1948), five string quartets (1951, 1959, 1971, 1986, 1995), *Night Fantasies* for piano (1980), *Triple Duo* for paired instruments: flute/clarinet, violin/cello, piano/percussion (1982), quintet for piano and wind (1992).

SOLO VOCAL *A Mirror on Which to Dwell* for soprano and nine players (six settings of Elizabeth Bishop, 1975), *In Sleep, in Thunder*, song cycle for tenor and 14 players (texts by Robert Lowell, 1981).

Carvalho, João de Sousa (1745–1798) Portuguese composer. He studied in Naples, Italy, and taught in Lisbon on his return to Portugal.

Works OPERA 15 Italian operas, including *Perseo* (1779), *Testoride Argonauta* (1780), *Penelope* (1782), *L'Endimione* (1783).

OTHER Masses and other church music with orchestra; harpsichord sonatas.

Carver, Robert (c.1490–after 1546) Scottish monk and composer. He was a canon of Scone Abbey. His work was influenced by such major Flemish contemporaries as ➤ Josquin Des Prez and Heinrich ➤ Isaac.

Works Masses (one in 10 parts), motets (one in 19 parts), and other church music.

Cary, Tristram (Ogilvie) (1925–) English composer. He has been a pioneer in the performance of electronic music in Britain and has experimented with the concept of environmental sound; he founded his own electronic studio and was an influential teacher at the Royal College of Music, London. He was appointed dean at Adelaide University, Australia, in 1982. His works include the cantata *Peccata mundi* (first performed in Cheltenham, England, 1972) and stage and film music.

Casals, Pablo (Pau) (1876–1973) Catalan cellist, composer, and conductor. He was largely self-taught. As a cellist, he was celebrated for his interpretations of Johann Sebastian Bach's unaccompanied suites. He wrote instrumental and choral works, including the Christmas oratorio *The Manger.*

He was an outspoken critic of fascism who openly defied Franco, and a tireless crusader for peace.

Casals was born in Tarragona. His pioneer recordings of Schubert and Beethoven trios in 1905, with the French violinist Jacques Thibaud and French pianist Alfred Cortot, launched his international career and established the popularity of the cello as a solo instrument, notably the solo suites of Johann Sebastian Bach recorded in 1916. In 1919 he founded the Casals Orchestra in Barcelona, which he conducted until leaving Spain in 1939 to live in Prades in the French Pyrenees, where he founded an annual music festival. In 1956 he moved to Puerto Rico, where he launched the Casals Festival in 1957. He toured extensively in the USA.

Casanova, André (1919–) French composer. He studied the 12-note technique with René Leibowitz. His works include trio for flute, viola, and horn, piano pieces, and songs.

Casella, Alfredo (1883–1947) Italian composer. He reacted strongly against the too exclusive and melodramatic operatic tendencies in the Italy of his time and aimed at reviving the classical Italian, predominantly instrumental music. His own work moved from the influence of Debussy and Mahler through atonality and towards neoclassicism. In 1924 he founded, with Gabriele d'Annunzio and Gian Francesco Malipiero, an association for the propagation of modern Italian music.

He was born in Turin, where his father was a teacher at the Liceo. In 1896 he went to the Paris Conservatory, France, to study piano under Diémer and composition under Gabriel Fauré. From 1912 he directed popular concerts at the Trocadero, Paris. At the start of World War I he went to Rome and taught piano at the Liceo di Santa Cecilia.

Works STAGE *La donna serpente* (after Gozzi; 1928–31), *La favola d'Orfeo* (1932), *Il deserto tentato*; ballets *Il convento veneziano* and *La giara* (after Pirandello).

ORCHESTRAL three symphonies, suite *Italia*, *Elegia eroica*, *Pagine di guerra*, *Introduzione*, *aria e toccata* (1933), concerto for orchestra; *A notte alta*, *Partita*, and *Scarlattiana* for piano and orchestra; concerto for violin, cello, organ, and orchestra.

CHAMBER concerto and five pieces for string quartet and other chamber music; cello and piano sonata; many piano works including sonatina and *Sinfonia, arioso e toccata*; two suites for piano duet.

VOCAL *Notte di maggio* for voice and orchestra (1914); numerous songs.

Caserta, Anthonello (Marotus) da (c.1365–after 1410) Italian composer. His works include eight French songs, several in the most complex three-voice style of the *ars subtilior*, and eight simpler Italian songs, mostly in two parts.

Caserta, Philipottus da (c.1350–after 1390) Italian composer and theorist. He composed works for the papal court of Clement VII (1378–94) and for the Milanese court of Bernabò Visconti (1354–85), and probably taught Johannes Ciconia. His works include one Credo, six French ballades (several in the most complex *ars subtilior* style), and three treatises on music.

Casken, John (1949–) English composer. His work has been influenced by Polish music and serialism.

He studied at Birmingham University with John Joubert and Peter Dickinson. He was a featured composer at the Bath Festival in 1980. In 1992 he was appointed lecturer at Manchester University.

Works OPERA *Golem* (1990).

INSTRUMENTAL piano concerto (1980), *Masque* for oboe, two horns, and strings (1982); *Erin* for double bass and small orchestra (1983), *Orion over Farne* (1984), *Maharal Dreaming* (1989), cello concerto (1991), *Darting the Skiff* for strings (1993); *Kagura* for 13 wind instruments (1973), *Amarantos* for nine players (1978), *Fonteyn Fanfares* for twelve brass instruments; string quartet (1982); *Ligatura* for organ; *Clarion Sea* for brass quintet (1985), piano quintet (1990).

Cassandra opera by Vittorio Gnecchi (libretto by L Illica), first produced at the Teatro Comunale, Bologna, Italy, on 5 December 1905. In 1909 the Italian critic Giovanni Tebaldini created a sensation by pointing out that Strauss's *Elektra*, which did not appear until that year, contained passages strikingly resembling Gnecchi's music.

cassation an 18th-century musical term, similar to divertimento and serenade, for a work in several movements suitable for open-air performance. The origin of the word is uncertain.

Casse-Noisette ballet score by Tchaikovsky; see
➤ *Nutcracker*.

**Cassiodorus, Flavius Magnus Aurelius
(c.487–c.580)** Roman senator, ecclesiastical
historian, and theologian. He wrote no specifically musical work, but the music theory contained in his *Institutiones* (about 560), deriving
largely from Aristoxenus, caused him to be regarded, with Boethius and Isidore of Seville, as one
of the three founders of medieval music theory.

castanets Spanish percussion instrument made
of two hollowed wooden shells, originally chestnut wood (Spanish *castaña*). They are held in the
palm and drummed together by the fingers to
produce a rhythmic accompaniment to dance.

Orchestral castanets or 'clappers', mounted on a
handle, were employed by silent-film effects musicians to imitate the sound of a galloping horse,
hence the phrase 'to run like the clappers'.

Castelnuovo-Tedesco, Mario (1895–1969)
Italian composer. He studied at the Istituto Musicale Cherubini in Florence and later with Ildebrando Pizzetti. At the age of 15 he wrote *Cielo di
settembre* for piano (later orchestra) and in 1925
he gained a prize for his opera *La mandragola*
(after Machiavelli). He settled in the USA in
1939, at first in Larchmont, New York, and then
Los Angeles.

Castelnuovo-Tedesco was born in Florence. In
1939, being a Jew, he was forced by Mussolini's
racial laws to leave Italy and settled in the USA,
later becoming a US citizen and establishing
himself as a film composer.

Works OPERA six operas, including *La mandragola* (1925) and *Bacco in Toscana* (1931).

ORCHESTRAL Shakespearean concert overtures,
twelve concertos for various instruments, including second guitar concerto (1953).

CHAMBER three string quartets (1929, 1948, 1964);
sonatas for many instruments; numerous piano
pieces, including *Questo fu il carro della morte*
(1913).

SONGS settings of all the songs in Shakespeare's
plays (in English) for voice and piano, and other
songs.

Castiglioni, Niccolò (1932–1996) Italian composer and pianist. His music is eclectic in style,
influenced by Debussy, Messiaen, Webern, and
John Cage, and remarkable for its frequently
delicate textures. He also pursued a career as a
concert pianist.

He studied with Giorgio Ghedini at the Milan
Conservatory.

Works ORCHESTRAL *Impromptus I–IV*, *Rondels*,
Sinfonia (1969).

INSTRUMENTAL *Movimento continuato* for piano

and small ensemble (1959), *Gymel* for flute and
piano; *Inizio di movimento* for piano.

VOCAL *A Solemn Music I* for soprano and chamber orchestra (after Milton; 1963).

Castore e Polluce, Castor and Pollux opera by
Georg Vogler (libretto based on one by C I Frugoni), first produced in Munich, Germany, on 12
January 1787. Weber wrote variations for piano
on an air from it, Op. 5.

Castor et Pollux opera by Jean-Philippe Rameau
(libretto by P J J Bernard), first produced at the
Paris Opéra, France, on 24 October 1737; a revised version was produced in June 1754. The plot
is based on the Greek myth: Pollux comes to the
rescue of his twin brother Castor, with help from
Jupiter.

castrato (Italian, 'castrated') in music, a high
male voice of unusual brilliance and power
achieved by castration before puberty, regarded
as the ideal timbre for heroic roles in opera by
composers from Monteverdi to Wagner. Castrati
were mainly, but not exclusively, active in 17th-
and 18th-century Italy, where they sang soprano
and alto parts in theatres and churches. Recordings preserve the voice of Alessandro Moreschi
(1858–1922), the last male soprano of the Sistine
Chapel.

Castration interrupts the normal growth of the
vocal folds in the larynx at puberty, preventing
the mature male voice from descending in pitch,
while allowing vocal prowess to benefit from
adult growth in all other respects.

Catalani, Alfredo (1854–1893) Italian composer. He studied first with his father, an organist, and produced a Mass at the age of 14. He went
on to study at the Paris Conservatory, France,
from 1871 and later taught at the Milan Conservatory.

Works OPERA *La Falce* (1875), *Elda* (1880), *Deja-
nice* (1883), *Edmea*, *Loreley* (1890), and *La Wally*
(1892).

OTHER Mass; symphonic poem *Ero e Leandro*,
and other pieces.

Catalogue d'oiseaux, Catalogue of Birds piano
work by Olivier Messiaen in seven books based
on his notations of birdsong, composed 1956–58
and first performed in Paris, France, on 15 April
1959.

catch a part song, in vogue in England from the
early 17th to the 19th centuries, in which the voices follow each other in the manner of a canon or
round, with the difference in the most characteristic examples that the words, thus mixed up, acquire new and ludicrous meanings, often of an
indecent nature in the 17th century.

Caterina Cornaro opera by Donizetti (libretto by G Sacchero), first produced at the Teatro San Carlo, Naples, Italy, on 12 January 1844; it was revived in 1972 with a concert performance in London and a production in Naples. The plot tells how the Venetian Caterina loves Gerardo but has been sworn to Lusignano, King of Cyprus. The competing wooers are reconciled when Lusignano saves Gerardo's life.

catgut strings term used to distinguish the strings of musical instruments from those made of metal or artificial material. Although still often so called, they are not made of the bowels of cats but of sheep. In general, they have a mellower sound and generate less volume than metal strings.

catline or **catling** or **catlin** or **catleen** in 16th-century music, a kind of roped and polished gut string, particularly for low pitches on viols and lutes; by the late 18th century it could refer to any high gut string.

Catone in Utica opera by Leonardo Vinci (libretto by Pietro Metastasio), first produced at the Teatro delle Dame, Rome, Italy, on 19 January 1728. In the story, Marcia, daughter of Cato (ruler of Utica) secretly loves Caesar, but Cato wants her to marry Arbace. When Caesar's armies overrun the Uticans and Cato commits suicide, Marcia is sworn to hatred against Caesar.

There are also versions by Johann Hasse (Turin, 1731), Vivaldi (Verona, 1737), Johann Christian Bach (Naples, 1761), and Giovanni Paisiello (Naples, 1789).

'Cat's Fugue, The' popular name for Domenico Scarlatti's G minor harpsichord sonata (no. 30 in his biographer Ralph Kirkpatrick's list). Its unusual theme has been suggested to resemble a cat picking its way along a keyboard.

Catulli Carmina scenic cantata by Carl Orff (text from poems by Catullus), the second of three works together called *Trionfi* (the other two are *Carmina Burana* and *Trionfo di Afrodite*), first produced in Leipzig, Germany, on 6 November 1943.

Causton, Thomas (c.1520–1569) English composer. He was a gentleman of the Chapel Royal in London. He wrote services, anthems, psalms, and contributed to Day's *Certaine Notes* and *Whole Psalmes* (1563).

Cavalieri, Emilio de' (c.1550–1602) Italian composer. He was long in the service of Ferdinando de' Medici in Florence. He was in close touch with the group of professional and amateur musicians known as the camerata, and with them worked towards the evolution of opera; in 1600 he produced *Euridice*, with text by Ottavio

Rinuccini and music by Giulio Caccini and Jacopo Peri, the first opera of which the music is extant.

Cavalieri was born in Rome, where he was organist at the Oratorio del Crocifisso 1578–84. In 1589 he oversaw the production of a lavish series of *intermedi* ('interludes'), to celebrate the marriage of Ferdinando to Christine of Lorraine. His own works were still dramatic pieces to be performed in concert form. They include the following, all set to words by Lelio Guidiccioni: *Il satiro*, *La disperazione di Fileno*, and *Il giuoco della cieca* (all lost), and *La rappresentazione di Anima, et di Corpo*, an allegory produced in 1600 and the first play set throughout to music.

Cavalleria rusticana, **Rustic Chivalry** opera by Pietro Mascagni (libretto by G Menasci and G Targioni-Tozzetti, based on Giovanni Verga's play), first produced at the Teatro Costanzi, Rome, Italy, on 17 May 1890. In the story, Turiddu loves Lola, now married to Alfio. His former love Santuzza tells Alfio of the infidelity; Alfio challenges Turiddu to a duel and kills him.

Cavalli, (Pietro) Francesco (1602–1676) Italian composer. He was organist at St Mark's, Venice, and the first to make opera a popular entertainment with such works as *Equisto* (1643) and *Xerxes* (1654), later performed in honour of Louis XIV's wedding in Paris. Twenty-seven of his operas survive.

cavata (Italian 'a thing carved or engraved') in music, a short ➔ **arioso** following a recitative, especially in the early 18th century.

cavatina short operatic aria, consisting of one section without repetition of text, unlike the aria's usual three-part division; for example 'Porgi amor' from Mozart's *Le nozze di Figaro/The Marriage of Figaro* (1786). It can also be an instrumental piece of songlike quality, for example a movement of Beethoven's String Quartet No. 13 (1826).

Cavazzoni, Marco Antonio (c.1490–c.1560) Italian composer, father of Girolamo Cavazzoni. The two *ricercari* from his *Recerchari, Motetti, Canzoni* for organ, published in Venice in 1523, are toccata-like pieces designed as preludes to the two motet arrangements; the *Canzoni* are arrangements of French chansons and the forerunners of the Italian instrumental canzone.

Cavendish, Michael (c.1565–1628) English composer. Born into a noble family, he seems to have held no appointments. He contributed to Michael East's *Whole Booke of Psalmes* in 1592 and published a volume of his own compositions in 1598, dedicated to Lady Arabella Stuart, his second cousin; the volume contained 20 airs to the lute, or with three other voices, and eight madri-

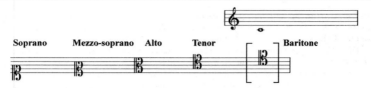

All five C clefs were formerly used; the baritone F clef is often substituted for the last.

gals. He also contributed a madrigal to *The* ➤ *Triumphes of Oriana* (1603).

Caverne, La, **The Cave** opera by Jean Lesueur (libretto by P Dercy, from an episode in Alain Lesage's *Gil Blas*), first produced at the Théâtre Feydeau, Paris, France, on 16 February 1793.

Cazden, Norman (1914–1980) US composer. He studied at the Juilliard School, New York, and with Walter Piston at Harvard. He worked as a pianist with dance groups, and collected folk music.

Works ballet *The Lonely Ones* (1944); symphony (1948); *Songs from the Catskills*, for band (1950); viola concerto (1972); wind quintet (1966) and other chamber music; songs.

C clef in music, the clef, derived from an ornamental letter C, which indicates that the line on which it is placed represents middle C. Only two C clefs are in use today: the alto, for the viola, and the tenor, for the tenor trombone and the upper register of the bassoon, cello, and double bass.

cebell a dance occurring in English 17th-century music, similar to the ➤ gavotte.

Cecilia, St (lived 2nd or 3rd century AD) Christian patron saint of music. She was martyred in Rome, Italy, and is said to have sung hymns while undergoing torture. Her feast day is 22 November.

There are many compositions in her honour; for example, Henry Purcell's *Ode on St Cecilia's Day* (1692) and Benjamin Britten's *Hymn to St Cecilia* (1942).

cédez (French imperative 'cede, give, surrender'; 'hold back') in music, a direction used by Claude Debussy and some other French composers to indicate a ➤ ritenuto.

celesta musical instrument, a keyboard ➤ glockenspiel producing high-pitched sounds of glistening purity. It was invented by Auguste Mustel of Paris in 1886 and first used to effect by Tchaikovsky in *The Nutcracker* ballet (1890).

Celestina, La opera by Felipe Pedrell (libretto based on an anonymous 15th–16th-century Spanish dialogue novel, *La comedia de Calisto y Melibia*, sometimes attributed to Fernando de

Rojas). It was not produced.

cello bowed, string instrument that is the third largest member of the violin family and one of the four instruments that make up the string quartet. Its full name is **violoncello** but the abbreviation cello is more commonly used today. Although similar in shape to the violin, it is more than twice the size and is played resting on the ground on an adjustable spike, being held in place lightly between the knees. It has a range of well over four octaves, with its four strings being tuned in fifths at C2, G2, D3, and A4. The solo potential of the cello was recognized by Johann Sebastian Bach (his five cello suites are still the instrument's most important repertoire), and its concerto repertoire extends from Joseph Haydn (who also gave the cello a leading role in his string quartets) and Luigi Boccherini to Antonín Dvořák, Edward Elgar, Benjamin Britten, György Ligeti, and Witold Lutosławski. The *Bachianas Brasilieras 1* (1930–44) by Heitor Villa-Lobos is scored for eight cellos, and Pierre Boulez's *Messagesquisse* (1977) for seven cellos. One of the best-known pieces for solo cello is 'The Swan' from Charles Saint-Saëns's *Carnival of the Animals* (1887).

cellone (Italian 'big cello') modern ➤ cello of large size made by Stelzner of Dresden, Germany, capable of being played seated and intended to supply a double bass instrument for chamber music. It has four strings tuned in perfect fifths two octaves below the violin.

Cello Symphony work by Benjamin Britten for cello and orchestra, Op. 68, composed in 1963 and first performed in Moscow, Russia, on 12 March 1964 by Mstislav Rostropovich.

Celos aun del ayre matan, **Jealousy, Even of the Air, is Deadly** opera on the subject of Cephalus and Procris by Juan Hidalgo (libretto by Pedro Calderón), first produced at the Buen Retiro, Madrid, Spain, on 5 December 1660. It is the first Spanish opera.

cembalo short form of clavicembalo, an accompanying ➤ harpsichord, a musical instrument.

Cendrillon, **Cinderella** opera by Nicolò Isouard (libretto by C G Etienne, after Charles Perrault), first produced at the Opéra-Comique, Paris, on 22 February 1810.

The opera of the same title by Jules Massenet (libretto by H Cain, after Perrault) was first produced at the Opéra-Comique in Paris on 24 May 1899. In this version prominence is given to Cinderella's father, the hen-pecked Pandolphe.

Cenerentola, Cinderella opera by Ermanno Wolf-Ferrari (libretto by M Pezzè-Pescolato, after Charles Perrault), first produced at the Teatro La Fenice, Venice, Italy, on 22 February 1900.

Cenerentola, La, ossia La bontà in trionfo, Cinderella, or The Triumph of Goodness opera by Rossini (libretto by J Ferretti, based on Etienne's text for Daniel Steibelt's opera), first produced at the Teatro Valle, Rome, Italy, on 25 January 1817.

cent in acoustics, unit by which musical intervals are measured, a cent being a hundredth part of a semitone in an equal-tempered scale.

Céphale et Procris opera by André Grétry (libretto by Marmontel), first produced for the court at Versailles, France, on 30 December 1773; the first Paris performance was at the Opéra on 2 May 1775. In the story, Cephalus tests his wife's fidelity by courting her in disguise.

Cephalus and Procris opera by Francesco Araia (libretto, in Russian, by A P Sumarokov), first produced for the court in St Petersburg, Russia, on 10 March 1755.

Ce qu'on entend sur la montagne, What is heard on the Mountain symphonic poem by Liszt, based on a poem by Victor Hugo; it was composed 1848–49 and first performed in Weimar, Germany, in February 1850.

Ceremony of Carols, A eleven settings by Benjamin Britten for treble voices and harp, composed in 1942 and first performed in Norwich, England, on 5 December 1942.

Cererols, Joan (1618–1676) Spanish composer and musician. He joined the monastery at Montserrat as a choirboy, became a novice in 1636, and remained there until his death as director of music. His works are often for double chorus and include *Missa de batalla*, for twelve voices, two Requiems, a Magnificat, and the antiphon *Alma redemptoris mater*.

Cerha, Friedrich (1926–) Austrian composer and violinist. In 1958, with Kurt Schwertsik, he founded Die Reihe, an organization devoted to the performance of new music. His completion of Act 3 of *Lulu* from Alban Berg's short score was performed in Paris, France, in 1979.

Cerha studied musicology at Vienna University and also composition with Alfred Uhl. He became director of the electronic studios of the Vienna Music Academy in 1960.

Works OPERA *Baal* (1974–79; first performance Salzburg, 1981), *Der Rattenfänger* (1987).

ORCHESTRAL *Espressioni fondamentali*; *Relazioni fragile* for harpsichord and chamber orchestra; *Intersecazioni* for violin and orchestra (1959–72); *Spiegel I–VII* (1960–68); concerto for violin, cello, and orchestra (1975), concerto for flute, bassoon, and orchestra (1982).

VOCAL *Baal-Gesänge* for baritone and orchestra (1982); *Requiem für Hollensteiner* (1983); *Keintate* for voice and eleven instruments (1983).

Cernohorský, Bohuslav Matěj (1684–1742) Bohemian composer, theorist, and friar. He travelled to Italy, where he was cathedral organist at Padua 1710–15 and at Assisi 1715–20 and 1731–41, and is believed to have taught Giuseppe Tartini and Christoph Willibald von Gluck. He was a highly valued composer of church and organ music, but most of his works were destroyed by fire in 1754.

Certon, Pierre (died 1572) French composer. He was in the Sainte-Chapelle in Paris in 1532, and became choirmaster there before 1542 and chaplain in 1548. As a canon of Notre Dame at Melun he founded an annual service there.

Works Masses, about 50 motets, psalms, canticles, about 200 chansons.

Cesaris, Johannes (lived c.1385–c.1420) French organist and composer. He is mentioned (with Johannes Carmen and Johannes Tapissier) by Martin le Franc in his poem 'Le Champion des dames' (1441–42) as having 'astonished all Paris' in the recent past. One motet and several chansons survive.

Cesti, (Pietro) Antonio (1623–1669) Italian composer. His work includes church music and sacred cantatas, but it was as an opera composer that he became most famous, his 15 operas being produced in Venice, Lucca, Innsbruck, Florence, and Vienna. *Il pomo d'oro*, first performed in Vienna in 1667, is the most elaborately spectacular baroque opera known to musical history.

After serving as a choirboy at Arezzo he became a Minorite friar in 1637. He was a pupil of Giacomo Carissimi in Rome, and in 1645 was appointed maestro di cappella at Volterra Cathedral. In 1653, having previously become a priest, he entered the service of the court at Innsbruck and remained there, with a brief interval as a tenor in the papal chapel, for 13 years. From 1666 to 1669 he was vice-Kapellmeister in Vienna.

Works OPERA *L'Orontea* (1649), *Il Cesare amante* (1651), *Alessandro il vincitor di se stesso*, *L'Argia*, *La Dori* (1657), *Tito*, *Nettuno e Fiora festeggianti* (1666), *Il pomo d'oro*, *Semiramide*, *Le disgrazie d'Amore* (1667).

OTHER motets; cantatas.

Chabrier, (Alexis) Emmanuel (1841–1894)
French composer. He wrote *España* (1883), an orchestral rhapsody, and the light opera *Le Roi malgré lui/The Reluctant King* (1887). His colourful orchestration inspired Debussy and Ravel.

Born in Ambert, Puy-de-Dome, he studied law and was employed at the Ministry of the Interior, but cultivated music as a gifted amateur. Having produced two operettas in 1877 and 1879, he devoted himself entirely to composition. From 1884 to 1885 he was chorus master at the Château d'Eau theatre, where he assisted Charles Lamoureux to produce two acts of Wagner's *Tristan und Isolde*. He also brought out selections from his opera *Gwendoline* (1885), which was performed as a whole in Brussels, Belgium, in 1886. After the production of *Le Roi malgré lui*, the run of which was interrupted by the fire of 25 May 1887 at the Opéra-Comique, he came under the influence of Wagner.

A colourful and ebullient figure (characteristics which were reflected in his music), Chabrier was one of the most entertaining letter-writers among French composers.

Works STAGE operas *Gwendoline* (1885), *Le Roi malgré lui* (1887), and *Briséis* (unfinished, one act performed Paris, 1897); operettas *L'Etoile* (1877) and *Une Education manquée* (1879).

ORCHESTRAL rhapsody *España* (1883) and *Joyeuse Marche* for orchestra (1888).

VOCAL *La Sulamite* for mezzo, chorus, and orchestra; songs.

PIANO ten *Pièces pittoresques*, *Habanera* and *Bourrée fantasque*, and other pieces for piano; three *Valses romantiques* for two pianos.

chace (Old French *chasse*; 'chase, hunt') 14th-century term for ➔ canon, because the parts 'chase' each other.

chaconne piece of music derived from a dance form, possibly of Spanish origin, in three time, constructed over a ➔ ground bass. An example is the aria 'Dido's Lament' from Purcell's opera *Dido and Aeneas* (1689), in which the inevitability of the bass line conveys a sense of Dido's inescapable fate.

chacony another name for a ➔ chaconne, a piece of music derived from a dance form.

Chadwick, George (Whitefield) (1854–1931)
US composer. He studied at Boston, Leipzig, and under Josef Rheinberger in Munich, Germany. He returned to the USA in 1880 and became organist at Boston, then professor at the New England Conservatory and its director in 1897.

Works OPERA *Tabasco* (1894), *Judith* (1900), *The Padrone* (1912), and others.

CHORUS AND ORCHESTRA *The Viking's Last Voyage*, *The Song of the Viking*, *Lovely Rosabelle*, *The Lily Nymph*, *Phoenix expirans*, and others.

ORCHESTRAL three symphonies (1882–94), symphonic poems *Cleopatra*, *Aphrodite*, *Angel of Death*, *Tam o'Shanter* (after Burns; 1911); overtures *Rip van Winkle*, *Thalia*, *Melpomene*, *Adonis* (after Shelley), *Euterpe*, and others; *Symphonic Sketches*; *Sinfonietta*; *Suite symphonique*.

CHAMBER five string quartets (1878–98), piano quintet.

OTHER songs with orchestra and with piano; piano and organ works; church music, part songs.

Chagrin, Francis (1905–1972) Anglo-Romanian composer. He studied at Zurich, Bucharest and, with Paul Dukas and Nadia Boulanger in Paris, and later with Mátyás Seiber in London, where he joined the French section of the BBC (British Broadcasting Corporation) Overseas Service in 1941. In 1943 he founded the Committee for the Promotion of New Music.

Works INCIDENTAL MUSIC for Shaw's *Heartbreak House* and Gozzi's *Re cervo*; music for films and broadcasts.

ORCHESTRAL Prelude and Fugue and suites for orchestra; two symphonies; piano concerto.

OTHER chamber music; piano pieces; over 100 songs.

Chailly, Luciano (1920–2002) Italian composer. He studied in Bologna and Milan, and with Paul Hindemith at Salzburg, Austria. He was artistic director at La Scala, Milan, 1968–71, and at the Milan Conservatory from 1969. His style is neoclassical, with some serial and electronic effects.

Works OPERA *Il canto del cigno* (Bologna, 1957), *Una demanda di matrimonio* (after Chekhov; Milan, 1957), *Procedura penale* (Como, 1959; English translation by A Jacobs as 'Trial by Tea-Party'), *Il mantello*, 'surrealist opera' (Florence, 1960), and *L'idiota* (after Dostoevsky; Rome, 1970).

Chalet, Le opera by Adolphe Adam (libretto by E Scribe and A H J Mélesville), first produced at the Opéra-Comique, Paris, France, on 25 September 1834.

chalumeau short, thickset double-reed wind instrument, ancestor of the ➔ clarinet. It is also the term used to describe the dark lowest register of clarinet tone.

chamber music music intended for performance in a small room or chamber, rather than in the concert hall, and usually written for instrumental combinations, played with one instrument to a part, as in the ➔ string quartet.

Chamber music developed as an instrumental alternative to earlier music for voices such as the madrigal, in which instruments only played an accompanying role and had little freedom for technical display. At first often played by wealthy amateurs who commissioned professional composers, it developed through Joseph Haydn and Ludwig van Beethoven into a private and often experimental medium, making unusual demands on players and audiences alike. During the 20th century, the limitations of recording and radio encouraged many composers to scale down their orchestras to chamber proportions, as in Alban Berg's *Chamber Concerto* (1923–24) and Igor Stravinsky's *Agon* (1953–57).

early developments The string quartet of Gregorio Allegri is believed to be the first example of its kind, while among English composers who wrote 'fantasy trios', or 'fancies', were William Byrd and Orlando Gibbons. In the 17th and early 18th centuries the harpsichord generally provided a harmonic background. The chamber sonata with a figured bass (improvised) accompaniment was established by the great Italian school of violinists – such as Vivaldi and Corelli. From the 18th century, a new type of chamber music was initiated by Haydn, in which members of a string quartet play on equal terms, with no additional keyboard instrument. Haydn also developed the classical ➔ sonata form in his chamber music. His quartets influenced those of Mozart, who in turn influenced Haydn's later works. The last quartets of Beethoven show many striking departures from the original classical framework and harmonic rules.

later developments In the 19th century chamber music found its way into the concert hall, sometimes taking on a quasi-orchestral quality, such as in the work of Brahms. The early 20th-century French school of Impressionists, such as Debussy and Ravel, experimented with chamber music forms, and, during the period which followed, developments such as ➔ atonality and ➔ polytonality have found expression in chamber music. Twentieth-century composers of chamber music include Berg, Webern, Hindemith, Stravinsky, Prokofiev, Shostakovich, Kodály, Bartók, Ireland, Bliss, Tippett, Rubbra, Copland, and Roy Harris.

chamber opera a type of opera written for few singers without chorus and a small orchestra often consisting entirely of solo instruments. Well-known examples are Strauss's *Ariadne auf Náxos* (1916) and Benjamin Britten's *The Turn of the Screw* (1954).

chamber orchestra small orchestra, consisting of about 25 players, made up of a small group of strings with a selection of woodwind, either single or in pairs. This was the size of a standard orchestra until the 19th century. When the wind sections expanded, followed by an increase in the number of string players to maintain a balanced sound, the orchestra grew to the size of

the modern symphony orchestra. In the 20th century, the chamber orchestra again became fashionable. This was partly as a reaction against the Romantic legacy of Richard Wagner (which included the use of large-scale instrumental groups), partly as a result of economic conditions, and partly as a result of the interest in ➔ early music. Famous chamber orchestras include the Academy of St Martin-in-the-Fields and the Orpheus Chamber Orchestra.

chamber organ small ➔ organ with one or two manuals (keyboards), suitable for playing figured-bass accompaniments or 18th-century solo concertos.

chamber pitch pitch to which orchestral instruments in Germany were tuned in the 17th and 18th centuries; see ➔ **Kammerton**.

Chamber Symphony title given by Arnold Schoenberg to his Op. 9 (1906) for 15 solo instruments and arranged by him for orchestra in 1922 and 1935. A second work with the same title was begun in 1906 and completed in 1939.

Chambonnières, Jacques Champion, Sieur de (c.1602–1672) French harpsichordist and composer. He was in the service of Louis XIII and XIV, and also worked for a time in Sweden. He taught several of the later harpsichordists, including François Couperin and Jean d'Anglebert, and published two books of harpsichord pieces, illustrating an important stage in the evolution of explicitly noted ornamentation.

Chaminade, Cécile (Louise Stéphanie) (1857–1944) French pianist and composer. She studied with various masters, including Benjamin Godard for composition. She began to compose at the age of eight, and at eighteen gave her first concert. She toured widely in France and England.

Works STAGE comic opera *La Sévillane*; ballet *Callirhoë* (1888).

VOCAL *Symphonie lyrique* for chorus and orchestra; songs.

ORCHESTRAL suites for orchestra; *Concertstück* for piano and orchestra (1896).

CHAMBER two piano trios; numerous light piano pieces.

Chandos Anthems twelve anthems by Handel, composed about 1717–20 for the Earl of Carnarvon, later Duke of Chandos, for performance in his private chapel at Canons, Edgware, near London.

chanson song type common in France and Italy, often based on a folk tune that originated with the ➔ troubadours. ➔ **Josquin Des Prez** was a chanson composer.

chanson de toile (French 'cloth song') French medieval song which tells its story or performs its actions with reference to a female, not a male, character. Hence the name, which refers to spinning or weaving.

Chansons de Bilitis, Trois songs for voice and piano by Debussy (texts by Pierre Louÿs) composed in 1892 and first performed in Paris, France, on 17 March 1897 (a version with orchestra was performed in Paris on 20 February 1926). The incidental music for two flutes, two harps, and celesta was composed in 1900 and first performed in Paris on 7 February 1901; this was arranged by Pierre Boulez with the addition of a reciter and performed in London, England, on 23 March 1965.

Chansons madécasses three songs by Maurice Ravel for voice, flute, cello, and piano (texts by E Parny), composed 1925–26 and first performed in Paris, France, on 13 June 1926.

chant ritual incantation by an individual or group, for confidence or mutual support. Chants can be secular (as, for example, sports supporters' chants) or religious, both Eastern and Western. Ambrosian and ➤ **Gregorian chants** are forms of ➤ **plainsong.**

Chant du rossignol, Le, The Song of the Nightingale symphonic poem in three movements by Igor Stravinsky, based on music from his opera *The Nightingale*, arranged in 1917 and first performed in Geneva, Switzerland, on 6 December 1919, conducted by Ernest Ansermet. The ballet version was first performed at the Paris Opéra, France, on 2 February 1920.

chanter in music, the pipe of the ➤ **bagpipes** on which the melody is played.

chanterelle (French 'the singing one') in music, the E string of the violin or (less often) the highest string of any stringed instrument.

chant-fable (French 'song-fable') a 13th-century narrative interspersed with songs.

Chapel Royal in the UK, a group of musicians and clergy serving the English monarch. Dating back at least to 1135, the Chapel Royal fostered some of England's greatest composers, especially prior to the 18th century, when many great musical works were religious in nature. Members of the Chapel Royal have included Thomas Tallis, William Byrd, and Henry Purcell.

There are chapels royal, in the sense of chapel buildings, at the former royal palaces of St James's, Hampton Court, the Tower of London (St John the Evangelist, and St Peter ad Vincula), and Windsor Castle (with a royal chapel also in Windsor Great Park), and a royal church at Sandringham, Norfolk.

Chaplet, The musical stage entertainment by William Boyce (libretto by M Mendez), first produced at the Drury Lane Theatre, London, England, on 2 December 1749.

Char, René (1907–1988) French poet. His works inspired Pierre ➤ **Boulez** (*Le Visage nuptial*, *Le Soleil des eaux*, *Le Marteau sans maître*).

Charakterstück (German 'character or characteristic piece') a short instrumental piece of music outlining some definite mood, human character, or literary conception.

Charpentier, Gustave (1860–1956) French composer. He went into business in Tourcoing at the age of 15, but a scholarship enabled him to study music at the Lille and Paris Conservatories. At the latter he was a pupil of Jules Massenet, and won the Prix de Rome for his cantata *Didon* in 1887. In 1902 he founded the Conservatoire Populaire Mimi Pinson, providing free instruction in music for working-class girls. His fame rests mainly on his opera about Paris working-class life, *Louise* (1900).

Works OPERA *Louise* (produced 1900) and *Julien* (1913).

ORCHESTRAL orchestral suite *Impressions d'Italie* (1889).

VOCAL cantatas *Didon* (1887) and *La Vie du poète* (1892; afterwards used in *Julien*); symphonic drama for solo voices, chorus, and orchestra; *Fête du couronnement de la Muse* (later used in *Louise*); *Impressions fausses* (Verlaine) and *Sérénade à Watteau* for voice and orchestra (1896); *Poèmes chantés* and five poems from Baudelaire's *Fleurs du mal* for voice and piano.

Charpentier, Marc-Antoine (c.1645–1704) French composer. He wrote incidental music in Italian style to plays by Molière, including *Le Malade imaginaire*/*The Hypochondriac* (1673). Later in life, as official composer to the Sainte Chapelle, Paris, he composed sacred music in French style and the opera *Médée* (1693).

Chartreuse de Parme, La, The Carthusian Monastery of Parma opera by Henri Sauguet (libretto by A Lunel, based on Stendhal's novel), first produced at the Paris Opéra, France, on 16 March 1939.

'Chasse, La', 'The Hunt' nickname of Haydn's symphony no. 73, in D major, composed in 1781; also of his string quartet in B flat major, Op. 1 no. 1, written about 1755.

Chasseur maudit, Le, The Accursed Huntsman symphonic poem by César Franck, based on a ballad by Bürger, composed in 1882. It was first performed for the Société Nationale, Paris, France, on 31 March 1883.

Chausson, Ernest (1855–1899) French composer. His early music was influenced by Jules Massenet and Wagner, and includes the symphonic poem *Viviane* (1882); he later turned to 18th-century French musical models. He was a pioneer of cyclic form. A fastidious, perhaps too self-critical artist, Chausson was one of the most important successors in the line of César Franck.

Chausson was born in Paris, where he attended the Conservatory for less than a year in 1880 and then became a pupil of Franck until 1883. Of independent means, he never held an official appointment, but helped to found the Société Nationale de Musique and was its secretary 1889–99. He died in a cycling accident, the first person to do so.

Works STAGE operas *Le Roi Arthus* (1886–95), *La Légende de Sainte Cécile* (1891), and others; incidental music to Shakespeare's *The Tempest*.

ORCHESTRAL symphonic poem *Viviane* (1882); symphony in B♭ major (1890).

VOCAL *Poème de l'amour et de la mer* for voice and orchestra (1882–90); *Chanson perpétuelle* for voice, string quartet and piano.

CHAMBER string quartet (unfinished), concerto for violin and piano with string quartet (1891), piano trio, piano quartet; piano and organ pieces.

SONGS 10 Op. nos of songs.

Chávez, Carlos Antonio de Padua (1899–1978) Mexican composer and pianist. His music incorporates national and pre-Columbian folk elements, for example *Chapultepec: Republican Overture* (1935). He composed a number of ballets, seven symphonies, and concertos for both violin and piano.

He was taught music as a child by his brother and two casual teachers, but later went to Europe and New York to gain experience. He was founder-director of the Mexico Symphony Orchestra 1928–48 (he later became its conductor), and director of the National Conservatory 1928–34. He held a post in the Department of Fine Arts, and was a leading figure in the cultural life of his country, doing much to explore Mexican folk music.

Works OPERA *Panfilo and Lauretta* (1953, produced in New York , 1957).

BALLET *El fuego nuevo*, *Los cuatro soles*, *Caballos de Vapor/Horse Power* (1926–27).

ORCHESTRAL *Sinfonía de Antígona*, *Sinfonía proletaria*, and *Sinfonía India* for orchestra; concertos for harp and for piano and orchestra.

CHAMBER *Energía* for instrumental ensemble; three string quartets (1921, 1932, 1944); sonata for four horns; piano pieces.

VOCAL *El sol* for chorus and orchestra.

Checkmate ballet by Arthur Bliss (choreographed by Ninette de Valois), first produced by the Sadler's Wells Ballet at the Théâtre des Champs-Élysées, Paris, France, on 15 June 1937; the first London performance was at Sadler's Wells on 5 October 1937.

chef d'attaque (French 'chief of attacks') in music, the ➤ leader of an orchestra, so called because great importance was always attached in France to unanimity of bowing and attack in orchestral string playing.

chekker 14th–16th-century keyboard instrument used in England, France, and Spain. In the latter countries it was called *échiquier*, *exaquir*, and similar names. The instrument is clearly a forerunner of the ➤ harpsichord and ➤ clavichord.

Chérubin opera (comédie chantée) in three acts by Jules Massenet (libretto by F de Croisset and H Cain, after the play by Croisset), first produced in Monte Carlo, Monaco, on 14 February 1904. It was not produced in the USA until 1989 (Santa Fe) and in England until 1993 (Covent Garden, London).

Cherubini, Luigi (Carlo Zanobi Salvadore Maria) (1760–1842) Italian composer. His first opera, *Quinto Fabio*, was produced in 1780. Following his appointment as court composer to King George III of England in 1784, he settled in Paris, France, where he produced a number of dramatic works including *Médée* (1797), *Les Deux Journées/The Water Carrier* (1800), and the ballet *Anacréon* (1803). After 1809 he devoted himself largely to church music.

Cherubini was born in Florence, where his father was a musician at the Teatro della Pergola. He studied first with his father, then under various masters, notably Alessandro and Bartolomeo Felici. At the age of 16 he had written an oratorio, Masses, and other pieces. About 1778, with a grant from the Grand Duke, he went to study with Giuseppe Sarti in Venice and in 1780 produced his first opera, *Quinto Fabio*, in Alessandria. His second opera *Lodoïska* (1791), set in Poland, was a huge success. In London he produced *La finta principessa* (1785) and *Giulio Sabino* (1786), and was appointed composer to George III, but left for Paris in 1786.

After a brief return to Italy he settled permanently in Paris in 1788. There he produced his first French opera, *Démophon* (1788), to a libretto by Marmontel. He soon became very busy conducting and writing operas, though without much success. In 1795 he married Cécile Tourette. In 1806 he produced *Faniska* in Vienna, Austria, where it had been specially commissioned, and met Beethoven, who admired his work and whose only opera *Fidelio* was influenced by it. On his return to France he lived, retired and embittered, at the Prince de Chimay's country residence and there wrote church music as well as more operas. In 1815 he composed an overture and a symphony for the Philharmonic Society, London. In 1816 he and Lesueur became attached to the royal chapel with large salaries and in 1822 he became director of the Conservatory, where he often confronted the precocious Berlioz. In 1833 he produced his last work for the theatre, *Ali Baba, ou les Quarante Voleurs*. Henceforward he devoted himself to church music, and his Requiem in D minor (1836) is one of his finest works. In his last years he was affected by depression and unsettled by an uneasy relationship with the authorities.

As a composer, he is, with Gluck, an austere representative of a nobler classical style in French opera; as a teacher his influence was harmful in restricting his pupils by the narrow rules of an earlier age. Beethoven greatly admired him, but Cherubini neither understood nor appreciated Beethoven. Mendelssohn was the only young contemporary whom he openly praised.

Works STAGE operas *Armida abbandonata* (1782), *Adriano in Siria* (1782), *Demetrio*, *Ifigenia in Aulide* (1788), *Lodoïska* (French; 1791), *Médée* (1797), *Les Deux Journées/The Water Carrier* (1800), *Anacréon, ou L'Amour fugitif* (1803), *Faniska* (1806), *Pimmalione*, *Les Abencérages* (1813), *Bayard à Mézières* (1814), *Ali Baba, ou Les Quarante Voleurs* (1833); ballet-pantomime *Achille à Scyros*.

CHORAL ten Masses and two coronation Masses, two Requiems (one for male voices) and other choral works.

ORCHESTRAL symphony in D major and overture for orchestra.

CHAMBER six string quartets (1834–37), string quintet.

OTHER songs.

chest of viols set of ✦ viols (usually six) of various sizes in a cupboard or chest, an article of furniture which was often found in well-to-do English households of the 16th and 17th centuries.

chest voice the lower register of the human voice, the chest being the source of sound production. It contrasts with the higher range available from the ✦ head voice. In the 19th century and earlier there was disagreement concerning the precise use of the term, some claiming that only head (high) and chest voices exist, others claiming that a third, middle register is also available. Today there is less concern about these distinctions.

Cheval de bronze, Le, The Bronze Horse opera by Daniel Auber (libretto by E Scribe), first produced at the Opéra-Comique, Paris, France, on 23 March 1835.

Chevreuille, Raymond (1901–1976) Belgian composer. He was mainly self-taught, although he took some courses at the Brussels Conservatory. His works are in a harmonically advanced idiom.

Works STAGE chamber opera *Atta Troll* (1952); three ballets.

VOICE AND ORCHESTRA symphony with vocal quartet, *Evasions* for soprano and chamber orchestra, *Saisons* for baritone and chamber orchestra; concerto for three woodwind instruments, cello concerto.

CHAMBER six string quartets (1930–45).

Chezy, Wilhelmine or **Helmina von (1783–1856)**, born **Wilhelmine von Klencke** German dramatist and novelist. He wrote the libretto of Carl Maria von Weber's *Euryanthe* and Franz Schubert's *Rosamunde*.

chiavette (Italian 'little keys') clefs other than those normal in 16th- and early 17th-century vocal music, used either to avoid leger-lines or to indicate transposition, for example the tenor clef might be used for a bass part, the treble clef for a soprano part, and so on.

Chihara, Paul (1938–) US composer. He studied with Nadi Boulanger in Paris, France, and Ernst Pepping in Berlin, Germany. He taught at University of California, Los Angeles, 1966–74, and was composer-in-residence with the San Francisco Ballet from 1980. His music has employed serial and aleatory techniques.

Works ORCHESTRAL viola concerto (1963); *Forest Music* for orchestra; symphony (1982).

CHAMBER string quartet (1965), *Redwood* for viola and percussion (1967), *Sequoia* for string quartet and tape (1984).

INSTRUMENTAL *Rain Music*, tape collage (1968), *Ceremony* series for various instrumental groups (I–V, 1971–75).

CHURCH MUSIC *Magnificat* (1966), *Missa Carminum* (1976).

BALLET *Mistletoe Bride* (1978), *The Tempest* (1980).

Child, William (c.1606–1697) English composer and organist. He was educated at Bristol Cathedral and was appointed one of the organists at St George's Chapel, Windsor, in 1632. At the Restoration he received a court appointment and in 1663 received a PhD from Oxford University.

Works CHURCH MUSIC about 25 services, about 50 anthems, motet *O bone Jesu*, 20 psalms for three voices with continuo, chants, Magnificat, 'in Gamut', Te Deum and Jubilate and other church music.

OTHER secular vocal pieces, catches and ayres; two suites of dances for viols.

Childhood of Christ dramatic cantata by Hector Berlioz. See ➤ ***Enfance du Christ, L'***.

Child of our Time, A oratorio by Michael Tippett for soloists, chorus, and orchestra composed 1939–41, inspired by the persecution of Jews following the assassination of a Nazi envoy in Paris, France. Tippett's own text includes African-American spirituals; it was first performed in London, England, on 19 March 1944.

Children's Corner a set of piano pieces, with English titles, by Claude Debussy, composed 1906–08 and dedicated to his daughter Claude-Emma Debussy (Chouchou). The pieces are: 1. *Doctor Gradus ad Parnassum*; 2. *Jimbo's Lullaby*; 3. *Serenade for the Doll*; 4. *The Snow is Dancing*; 5. *The Little Shepherd*; 6. *Golliwogg's Cake-Walk*. It was first perfomed in Paris, France, on 18 December 1908; the orchestral version by André Caplet was first performed in New York, USA, in 1910.

Childs, Barney (1926–2000) US composer and poet. He studied at Oxford and Stanford Universities, and with Elliott Carter and Aaron Copland. He was professor of composition at the University of Redlands, California, 1976–92. His music belongs to the avant garde, and allows the performer a large degree of freedom through improvisation and 'self-generating structures'.

Works ORCHESTRAL two symphonies (1954, 1956), concerto for timpani and orchestra (1989).

CHAMBER eight string quartets (1951–74), two violin sonatas (1950, 1956), *Sunshine Lunch and Like Matters* for bass clarinet and ensemble (1984), horn octet (1984).

INSTRUMENTAL *Interbalances*, six pieces for various groups (1941–64); *Couriers of the Crimson Dawn*, for any instruments (1977); *13 Classic Studies for the Contrabass* (1981).

VOCAL *When Lilacs Last in the Dooryard Bloom'd* (after Whitman, for soloists, chorus, and band, 1971).

Chinese block or **temple block** percussion instrument in the shape of a hollow wooden box. It produces a dry, rapping sound when struck. Whilst the sound is predominantly percussive, temple blocks do have approximate pitches, and in orchestral use often appear in groups of four or five different pitches, usually tuned to the pentatonic scale.

Chinese pavilion musical instrument shaped like a tree or pagoda and hung with brass plates and small bells, shaken to make a jingling noise and used in military bands, especially in the 18th century. It was popularly called 'Jingling Johnny' or 'Turkish Crescent'.

chitarrone (Italian 'big guitar') musical instrument, a long-necked bass ➤ lute (archlute) incor-porating freely vibrating bass strings which are twice the length (sounding an octave lower) of up to seven double courses of manually stopped strings, used in Renaissance and early baroque ensembles to provide a firm and resonant bass line.

Chlubna, Osvald (1893–1971) Czech composer. He was a pupil of Leoš Janáček and later professor at the Brno Conservatory. He scored the last act of Janáček's *Sarka* (staged 1925) and gave an upbeat ending to *From the House of the Dead* (1930).

Works OPERA *Catullus's Vengeance* (1917), *Alladine and Palomides* (after Maeterlinck; 1922), *Nura, The Day of Beginning*.

CANTATAS *Lord's Prayer, Minstrel's Child*, and others.

ORCHESTRAL *Symphony of Life and Love*, symphonic poems *Dreams, Before I Go Dumb, Two Fairy Tales, Song of my Longing*; overture *Fairy Land*; two suites for orchestra.

CHAMBER *Sinfonietta* for chamber orchestra; five string quartets, piano music.

OTHER songs.

choir group of singers with several performers or voices to a part. A **mixed voice choir** contains parts for both women and men; a **male voice choir** is usually men only, but may be boys and men; a **double choir** is two equal choirs often used in antiphonal singing (where the choirs sing alternately, one answering the other, creating a 'stereo' effect, heightened by their placement on either side of the church).

The choir was important for developing Renaissance polyphony, with instruments initially reading from vocal parts and only gradually developing distinct instrumental styles. The Venetian antiphonal style of Claudio Monteverdi and Giovanni Gabrieli treats voices and instruments as opposing choirs. During the 19th century, choir festivals became popular features of musical life, promoting mixed-voice choral singing by amateur groups.

choir organ third manual (keyboard) of an ➤ organ, characterized by quiet stops and pipes appropriate for accompanying a church choir. Often the pipes of the choir organ are housed separately from the rest, located behind the organist's back instead of being grouped together with the other pipes, usually in front of and above the player.

It was formerly often a small instrument set apart from the principal organ in a church, and used separately to accompany the choir.

Chopin, Frédéric François (1810–1849) Polish composer and pianist. He made his debut as a pianist at the age of eight. As a performer, Chopin revolutionized the technique of pianoforte-playing, turning the hands outward and favouring a light, responsive touch. His compositions, which include two piano concertos and other orchestral works, have great changes of mood, and flowing rhythms.

From 1831 he lived in Paris, France, where he became known in the fashionable salons, although he rarely performed in public. In 1836 the composer Franz Liszt introduced him to George Sand (Madame Dudevant), with whom he had a close relationship in 1838–46. During this time she nursed him in Mallorca for tuberculosis, while he composed intensively and for a time regained his health. His music was used as the basis of the ballet *Les Sylphides* by Mikhail Fokine in 1909 and orchestrated by Alexander Gretchaninov (1864–1956), a pupil of Mikhail Rimsky-Korsakov.

Chopin's father was professor of French at Warsaw University, Poland. Chopin began piano lessons at the age of six, played at a musical evening aged seven (when he first published a work, a Polonaise in G minor), and in public at eight. From 1822 he took composition lessons with Józef Elsner, and made great progress in both composition and improvisation. He left the Warsaw Conservatory in 1827 and played in Vienna, Austria, in 1829. On his return he fell in love with the singer Konstancja Gładkowska, who appeared at the third of his public concerts in 1830. He left Poland that year, played in Vienna and Munich and visited Stuttgart, where he heard of the taking of Warsaw by the Russians during the November Uprising. He went to Paris in October 1831 and decided to remain there. He appeared frequently in public and gave private lessons, especially in French and Polish aristocratic circles.

He met Maria Wodzińska at Dresden in 1835 and at Marienbad in 1836. They fell in love and became secretly engaged, but the engagement was broken off by her family. In 1838 he visited George Sand at Nohant, France, where she held house parties in the summer. Most summers were spent at Nohant until 1847, when a family quarrel between Sand and her children led to one with Chopin and they parted. The last ten years of his life were a continual struggle against illness, and he gave his last public concert in February 1848, but continued to teach and play at private houses. His pupil Jane Stirling took him to Scotland in August 1848 for a rest at the country house of her brother-in-law, Lord Torphichen. Chopin afterwards played at Manchester, Glasgow, and Edinburgh, and went to London in November. In January 1849 he was back in Paris in a critical state of health and finance, but was supported by wealthy friends until his death.

Chopin's music, written almost exclusively for solo piano, was the most important of the 19th century in the development and perfection of a Romantic style. It is entirely original, and although the melodies seem simple, the harmony, rhythm, and form can be complex. He was among the first to use the thumb freely on black keys. Many of his pieces, with eerie or echo effects or fairylike accompaniments, require the player to use a particularly subtle kind of finger technique and pedalling. They are a good test of the varied resources of the skilled pianist.

Works PIANO AND ORCHESTRA two concertos in E minor and F minor (1829–30); four other works with orchestra including *Andante Spianato* (1834).

SOLO PIANO 50 mazurkas in 13 sets (1830–49), 27 studies, 26 preludes (24 in all keys), Op. 28 (1836–39), 19 Nocturnes, 14 waltzes (1827–41), 16 polonaises, four ballades in G minor, F, A♭, F minor (1831–42), four impromptus, four scherzos in B minor, B♭ minor, C♯ minor, E (1831–39), three rondos, *Barcarolle* in F♯, *Berceuse*, *Boléro*, Fantasy in F minor, *Tarantella*, and other miscellaneous piano pieces.

CHAMBER three sonatas in C minor (1828), B♭ minor (1839), B minor (1844), piano trio (1829); cello and piano sonata (1832).

Chopsticks popular children's composition (anonymous) played on the piano with the forefingers of each hand, to which the name refers by analogy with the two sticks with which the Chinese eat their food.

'Chopsticks' Variations a set of variations for piano (three hands, the second player playing a variant in 2/4 time of the well-known tune with one hand) by Aleksandr Borodin, César Cui, Anatol Liadov, and Nikolai Rimsky-Korsakov, written before 1880, when a second edition appeared and Liszt contributed a new variation of his own.

Choral (German 'chorale') Lutheran hymn. The German word was originally used to mean the choral parts of Latin chant, and by extension plainsong in general, a meaning which it still bears today. At the Reformation, Lutheran reform required the congregation to take a greater part in the church service and the term also came to be used for simpler monophonic singing in the vernacular. Many of the melodies used were adaptations from the plainsong itself; hence the term *Choralbearbeitung/chorale arrangement* to denote any kind of setting of such melodies. The English word is simply an adaptation of the German in its Lutheran sense, the final 'e' being added to make the pronunciation clear and to avoid confusion with the adjective 'choral'.

German reformer Martin Luther himself wrote the words for many hymns. German composer Johann Sebastian Bach wrote a few original chorales, but mainly rewrote the harmony of traditional ones. Well-known chorales include 'Now Thank We All Our God' and 'Wake, O Wake, for Night is Flying'.

chorale traditional hymn tune of the German Protestant Church; see ➔ *Choral*.

chorale cantata term used for a form of church cantata, especially by Bach, which draws on the text and, usually, music of a Lutheran hymn. The chorale words and melody may (rarely) be present in each movement of the cantata (in *Christ lag in Todesbanden*), or some verses may be replaced by free paraphrases of the text or completely new material set as recitatives or arias. Treatment varies from the simple harmonizations found as the last movement of many cantatas to the complexity of the massive fantasia-like chorus which opens *Ein' feste Burg*.

chorale fantasy a type of organ composition in which a hymn tune is freely treated.

choral prelude a type of organ piece for church use by Bach; it introduces the tune of the hymn about to be sung by the congregation and artistically elaborates it by contrapuntal treatment or by the provision of an original accompaniment.

'Choral Symphony' popular name for Beethoven's Ninth Symphony in D minor, Op. 125, on account of its last movement, a setting of Schiller's ode *An die Freude/To Joy* for solo quartet, chorus, and orchestra. It was composed about 1817–24 and was first performed in Vienna, Austria, on 7 May 1824. It is the first symphony to include voices.

chord in music, a group of three or more notes sounded together. This 'vertical' combination of notes (of any number) is almost infinite in possibility, and yet is fundamental in determining a style of music. This goes some way to explaining the enormous variation of music in existence.

chording in music, a term used to designate either the spacing of the notes in a chord in composition or the performance of them strictly in tune in relation to each other.

chordophone one of the four main groups of musical instrument used in the original ➔ Sachs–Hornbostel system, the others being ➔ idiophone, ➔ aerophone, and ➔ membranophone. A chordophone describes any musical instrument whose sound is produced by vibrating stretched strings by plucking, bowing, or striking. This group includes harps, violins, pianos, guitars, and lutes.

Chorley, Henry F(othergill) (1808–1872) English music critic, librettist, and author. He contributed to the *Athenaeum* weekly magazine from 1830.

Choron, Alexandre (Etienne) (1771–1834) French music scholar and composer. Among his books are a music encyclopedia and treatises on music study, part-writing, and plainsong.

Works CHURCH MUSIC a Mass, a *Stabat Mater*, psalms, hymns.

Chorton (German 'choir-pitch') the pitch to which church organs in Germany were tuned in the 17th–18th centuries. It was higher, usually by a whole tone, than *Kammerton* ('chamber pitch'), and it is for this reason that J S Bach transposed the woodwind parts in his cantatas up, or alternatively transposed the organ parts down. The strings could, as necessary, play at either pitch.

chorus in opera or oratorio, a large group of singers providing an accompaniment in four or more parts to principal soloists. The term also describes a body of usually untrained male and female singers of secular unison songs, or providing the refrain element of solo verse songs.

Chout, The Buffoon ballet in six scenes, Op. 21, by Sergey Prokofiev (scenario by the composer, from a story by A Afansyev), composed in 1915 and revised in 1920. It was first produced at the Ballets Russes, Paris, France, on 17 May 1921. The Symphonic Suite from the ballet was arranged in 1920 and first performed in Brussels, Belgium, on 15 January 1924.

Chou Wen-chung (1923–) Chinese-born US composer. His music reflects oriental and avant-garde influences and includes *Nocturnal*, editions of *Ameriques* (1972), and *Octandre* (1980). He was appointed professor at Columbia University in 1972.

He studied in the USA from 1946, at first with Nicolas Slonimsky and Otto Luening, and with Edgard Varèse 1949–54.

Works ORCHESTRAL *Landscapes* for orchestra (1949); *Metaphors* for wind orchestra (1961); *Pien* for piano, percussion, and wind (1966).

CHAMBER *Beijing in the Mist* for chamber ensemble (1986); *Echoes from the Gorge* for percussion quartet (1989); *Windswept Peaks* for violin, cello, clarinet, and piano (1990).

OTHER choral and piano works, film music.

Christelflein, Das opera by Hans Pfitzner (libretto by I von Stach and the composer), first produced in Munich, Germany, on 11 December 1906, conducted by Felix Mottl. The story tells how a dying girl gets her Christmas tree before an elf takes her to heaven.

Christmas Concerto common name for Corelli's *Concerto grosso*, Op. 6. no. 8, for strings and continuo.

Christmas Eve, Russian *Notch Pered Rozhdestvom* opera by Nikolai Rimsky-Korsakov (libretto

An ascending and descending chromatic scale beginning on C.

by the composer, based on Gogol's story), first produced in St Petersburg, Russia, on 10 December 1895.

See also ➤ *Vakula the Smith*.

Christmas Oratorio, German **Weihnachtsoratorium** a series of six cantatas by Johann Sebastian Bach (1734) designed for separate performance between Christmas and Epiphany. They were not originally intended for performance as one composite work.

Christmas Symphony symphony by Franz Joseph Haydn; see ➤ *Lamentatione*.

Christophe Colomb opera by Darius Milhaud (libretto by P Claudel), first produced in at the Staatsoper, Berlin, Germany, on 5 May 1930, conducted by Carlos Kleiber. The work makes use of film. In the final scene, Queen Isabella rides to heaven on a mule provided by Columbus.

Christophorus, oder Die Vision einer Oper opera by Franz Schreker (libretto by the composer), composed 1925–29. The original production was banned by the Nazis and the opera was first performed in Freiburg, Germany, on 1 October 1978. The story is of a student who attempts to write an opera based on the life of St Christopher, but the characters of the legend become confused with his own friends.

Christus oratorio by Franz Liszt (words from the Bible and the Roman Catholic liturgy), composed 1855–66 and first performed in Weimar, Germany, on 29 May 1873.

It is also the title of an oratorio by Felix Mendelssohn (words by Chevalier Bunsen), begun in 1844 and resumed in 1847 but left unfinished.

Christus am Oelberg, Christ at the Mount of Olives oratorio by Beethoven, Op. 85 (libretto by F X Huber), first produced in Vienna, Austria, on 5 April 1803.

chromatic (from Greek *chrōmatikos*, 'coloured') scale proceeding entirely by semitones, that is, taking in all the notes available in traditional Western music. Chromatic harmony consists of chords using notes not included in the scale of the prevailing key and thus, in notation, involving the use of many accidentals.

Chromatic Fantasy and Fugue a keyboard work in D minor by Bach, written about 1720 and revised about 1730. The adjective refers to the harmonies of the fantasy and the subject of the fugue.

chromatic harp French ➤ harp which has strings for all the notes of the chromatic scale. They are not all strung parallel, but are slightly crossed, so that except where they actually intersect they stand away from each other in two ranges, one representing the diatonic scale of C major, the other the sharps or flats, like the white and black notes on the piano.

The normal harp has strings tuned to the scale of C flat major, but each string can be raised in pitch by a semitone or a whole tone with the aid of pedals. Whilst this limitation to seven notes within each octave is problematic for much 20th century music, most composers prefer in orchestral writing to use two or more ordinary harps rather than the chromatic harp; a fact which has contributed to the rarity of the instrument.

chromaticism in music, the use of enriched harmonies for added expression, practised by 19th-century composers mainly of French and Russian schools, for example Rimsky-Korsakov, Skriabin, Debussy, Ravel, Messiaen, Honegger, and Dutilleux.

Chromatic harmonies are ambiguous consonances rather than expressionist dissonances, influenced by the sounds of music imported from Indonesia and Japan and heard, for example, at the Paris Exposition of 1889, which influenced Debussy. Chromaticism is associated with the introduction of new timbres to the symphony orchestra including the celesta, glockenspiel, and xylophone.

chromatic madrigal a madrigal making free use of chromatic harmony; in 16th-century Italy, a *madrigale cromatico* was one using black notes as the basis of measurement and hence moving at a brisk speed.

chromatic scale musical scale consisting entirely of semitones. All the notes on a keyboard, black and white, are used for this scale. Dividing the octave into twelve equal steps of one semitone each makes this a neutral scale without a definite key.

Chronochromie*, *Time-colour work for orchestra in seven sections by Olivier Messiaen, composed in 1960 and first performed in Donaueschingen, Germany, on 16 October 1960, conducted by Hans Rosbaud.

Chrysander, (Karl Franz) Friedrich (1826–1901) German music scholar and editor. He lived in England for some time, researching material for his great biography of Handel, which was published 1858–67, though never completed. He also edited Handel's complete works. Other works of his on old music are valuable, but he was violently opposed to all of what he called 'modern' music (that is, music written after the time of Handel).

church mode or **authentic mode** in music, one of eight modes or scales developed by the medieval church, centring on the notes D, E, F, or G, and using the notes of the C major scale. See ➤ mode.

Chute de la Maison Usher, La*, *The Fall of the House of Usher opera by Claude Debussy (libretto by himself, based on Edgar Allen Poe's story), worked at between 1908 and 1918, but never completed. Realizations of Debussy's fragments were performed at Yale University, USA, and Frankfurt, Germany, in 1977.

ciaccona Italian spelling of ➤ chaconne, a piece of music.

Ciconia, Johannes (c.1335 or c.1373–1411 or 1412) Liègeois composer and music theorist. His only clearly documented activity is as choirmaster at Padua Cathedral from about 1401, though another man of the same name was born about 1335 and was active earlier in Avignon. He was perhaps the most important and influential composer of his generation. His works include Mass movements, motets, and secular works in both French and Italian. There is also a treatise, *Nova musica*.

He began to study music around 1385, as a choirboy at Saint-Jean l'Evangeliste, Liège. Before 1400 he went to Padua where he became choirmaster and a canon at the cathedral, posts which he retained until his death. His motets show an advanced approach to imitation; some of them are ceremonial works, and date largely from the time he spent in Padua. They include two isorhythmic pieces in honour of the city's bishop.

Cid, Der opera by Peter Cornelius (libretto by composer, based on Corneille's drama), first produced in Weimar, Germany, on 21 May 1865.

Cid, Le opera by Jules Massenet (libretto by A P d'Ennery, L Gallet, and E Blau, based on Corneille's drama), first produced at the Paris Opéra,

France, on 30 November 1885. In the story, Chimène loves Rodrigue; when Rodrigue's father is appointed guardian to the king's son, Chimène's father insults Rodrigue, who then kills him in a duel. Chimène seeks revenge against Rodrigue, but forgives him after he has saved Spain in battle.

Cilèa, Francesco (1866–1950) Italian composer. He produced his first opera in 1889, while still a student at Naples Conservatory. The publisher Sonzogno then commissioned a second, which was produced at Florence in 1892. Cilea was professor at the Reale Istituto Musicale, Florence, 1896–1904.

Works OPERA *Gina* (1889), *La tilda* (1892), *L'Arlesiana* (after Daudet; 1897), *Adriana Lecouvreur* (after Scribe; 1902), *Gloria* (1907).

CHAMBER cello and piano sonata; numerous piano works.

Cimadoro, Giovanni Battista (1761–1805) Italian composer. He successfully produced the dramatic works *Ati e Cibeli* (1789), *Il ratto di Proserpina* (Venice, 1791), and 'scena lirica' *Pimmalione* in Italy, but settled in London, England, in 1791. Other works include a concerto for double bass and vocal pieces.

Cimarosa, Domenico (1749–1801) Italian composer. He wrote more than 60 operas, including the witty *Il matrimonio segreto*/*The Secret Marriage* (1792). He also wrote orchestral and keyboard music.

He studied at Naples, where his masters included Antonio Sacchini and Niccolò Piccinni, and produced his first opera there in 1772. Later he lived by turns in Rome and Naples, became famous with several operas, travelled much, and in 1787 went to the court of Catherine II in St Petersburg, Russia. In 1791 the emperor Leopold II invited him to Vienna to succeed Antonio Salieri as court Kapellmeister. There he produced his most successful opera, *Il matrimonio segreto*, based on *The Clandestine Marriage* by George Colman and David Garrick; it was encored in its entirety at its premiere. His engagement in Vienna ended the same year, when, on the death of Leopold, Salieri was reappointed. Cimarosa returned to Naples, where he became maestro di cappella to the king. He was imprisoned because of his involvement in the Neapolitan rising of 1799. On his release he set out for St Petersburg, but died in Venice on the way, allegedly by poison.

Works OPERA over 60 operas, including *Le stravaganze del conte*, *L'Italiana in Londra* (1779), *Il pittore parigino*, *La ballerina amante* (1782), *L'Olimpiade*, *Artaserse* (1784), *L'impresario in augustie*, *Cleopatra* (1789), *Idalide*, *Il matrimonio segreto* (1792), *Le astuzie femminili* (1794), *Il mar-*

ito disperato, L'impegno superato, Gli Orazi ed i Curiazi, Penelope (1795), *Achille all' assedio di Troia.*

OTHER Masses, oratorios, cantatas.

Cimarrón, El work by Hans Werner Henze for baritone, flute, guitar, and percussion (text from *The Autobiography of a Runaway Slave,* by E Montejo), first performed at Aldeburgh, England, on 22 June 1970.

cimbalom musical instrument, a Hungarian pedestal ➔ **dulcimer** modernized during the 19th century from a gypsy instrument. It consists of a box-shaped resonator over which strings are stretched laterally, the performer playing front to back rather than across, using light beaters. The sound is brittle, not unlike a ➔ **fortepiano.** Composers include Stravinsky in *Renard* (1922) and Kodály in the orchestral suite *Háry János* (1927).

Cinderella English title of the operas ➔ **Cendrillon** and ➔ **Cenerentola.** Also, a ballet by Sergey Prokofiev.

cinesi, Le, The Chinese Ladies opera by Antonio Caldara (libretto by Pietro Metastasio), first produced at the court in Vienna, Austria, during Carnival in 1735. It presents four friends who while away the time acting out legends.

It is also the title of an opera by Christoph Willibald von Gluck (libretto by Metastasio), first produced for the court at Schlosshof, near Vienna, on 24 September 1754.

cinquepace (from French cinq pas,'five steps'; also colloquial 'sink-a-pace') a dance of the 16th century in quick 3/4 time and requiring movements in groups of five paces. The name was used both for the galliard following the pavana and for the tordion concluding the *basse danse.* Shakespeare makes a pun on it in *Much Ado about Nothing.*

ciphering in music, the escape of sound from organ pipes by a fault in or damage to the mechanism.

Circassian Bride, The opera by Henry Bishop (libretto by C Ward), first produced at the Drury Lane Theatre, London, England, on 23 February 1809.

Circe and Penelope two parts of a cyclic opera, *Ulysses,* by Reinhard Keiser (libretto by F C Bressand), first produced in Brunswick, Germany, in February 1696.

circular canon a canon whose tune, instead of coming to an end, returns to the beginning and may be repeated *ad infinitum.* The round *Three blind mice* is a familiar example.

Circus Polka work for piano by Igor Stravinsky, to accompany the elephants in the Ringling Bros' circus; it was scored for wind band by D Raksin in 1942, arranged by the composer for orchestra, and first performed in Cambridge, Massachusetts, USA, on 13 January 1944.

Ciro in Babilonia, o sia La caduta di Baldassarre, Cyrus in Babylon, or The Fall of Belshazzar opera by Gioacchino Rossini (libretto by F Aventi), first produced in Ferrara, Italy, on 14 March 1812. In the story, Belshazzar is 'found wanting' Amira, wife of King Cyrus, who has been defeated by the Babylonians. Cyrus faces execution, but his fate improves when his forces counterattack.

cithara ancient musical instrument resembling a ➔ **lyre** but with a flat back. It was strung with wire and plucked with a plectrum or (after the 16th century) with the fingers. The bandurria and laud, still popular in Spain, are instruments of the same type.

citole medieval plucked musical instrument, related to the ➔ **cittern** and once confused with the ➔ **gittern** by music historians. It became obsolete in the late 14th century.

cittern plucked stringed instrument, usually almond shaped, with a flat back and a fretted fingerboard. It originated about 1500, is easy to play, and was a popular alternative to the lute. Larger forms include the bandurria and the orpharion. It was superseded in the 19th century by the guitar.

The cittern usually had four pairs of wire strings tuned in either of two ways.

Clapp, Philip Greeley (1888–1954) US composer. After graduating from Harvard University he studied with Max von Schillings in Stuttgart, Germany, and in London, England. Following several academic appointments, he became professor of music at the University of Iowa.

Works ORCHESTRAL twelve symphonies (1908–44), piano concerto in B minor, *Fantasy on an Old Plainchant* for cello and orchestra, *Dramatic Poem* for trombone and orchestra.

VOCAL cantata *A Chant of Darkness* (H Keller); songs with orchestra.

OTHER string quartet and other pieces.

clarinet any of a family of single-reed woodwind instruments of cylindrical bore. It is one of the four main orchestral woodwinds, but did not join the orchestra until after the middle of the 18th century. In their concertos for clarinet, Wolfgang Amadeus Mozart and Carl Maria von Weber made good use of the instrument's wide range of tone from the rich, dark notes of the low register rising to brilliance in the high register, and its capacity for sustained dynamic control. The ability of the clarinet both to blend and to contrast with other instruments makes it popular for chamber music and as a solo instrument. It is also used in military and concert bands and widely as a jazz instrument.

The clarinet was developed from the double-reed ➔ chalumeau by the German instrument maker Johann Denner about 1700 and was occasionally used in the Baroque orchestra as an instrument of trumpetlike tone. In the 19th century, Theobald Boehm added a system of metal keys and levers to produce today's chromatic instrument. Hector Berlioz showed that the improved instrument had a raucous and shrill side to its character in the final 'Witches' Sabbath' movement of the *Symphonie fantastique/Fantastic Symphony* (1830). A broad range of clarinets are still in use, including soprano B flat and A (standard orchestral clarinets), alto F (military band), B flat bass, piccolo E flat and D, and curved contrabasses in E flat and B flat, the latter sounding two octaves lower than the soprano B flat, and virtually inaudible on its own.

The sounding compass of the A clarinet (top); of the B flat (centre); and of the E flat (bottom).

clarinette d'amour (French 'love clarinet') large ➔ clarinet made in continental Europe between the late 18th century and around 1820, usually a major third or fourth lower than the clarinet in C.

clarino (Italian 'clarion') name given to the trumpet in the 17th and 18th centuries, also the name of the highest register of the instrument, from C above middle C upwards, which was regularly used for florid passages in the works of Bach and his contemporaries. In the early 18th century the name was sometimes equivalent to clarinet, for which the normal Italian term was *clarinetto*.

Clari, or The Maid of Milan opera by Henry Bishop (libretto by J H Payne, based on Marmontel's story *Laurette*), first produced at Covent Garden, London, England, in May 1823. It contains the song 'Home, Sweet Home', not only as a song, but as a kind of *Leitmotiv* or theme song occurring in various forms.

Clarke, Jeremiah (c.1674–1707) English composer. He was organist at St Paul's Cathedral in London, and composed *The Prince of Denmark's March*, a harpsichord piece that was arranged by Henry Wood as a 'Trumpet Voluntary' and wrongly attributed to Purcell.

Clarke was a pupil of John Blow at the Chapel Royal, organist at Winchester College 1692–95, and in 1699 was appointed organist at St Paul's. He was sworn Gentleman-extraordinary of the Chapel Royal in 1700 and organist in 1704. He committed suicide, supposedly after an unhappy love affair.

Works STAGE operas *The Island Princess* (with D Purcell and Leveridge; 1699), *The World in the Moon* (Settle, with D Purcell; 1697); incidental music for Shakespeare's *Titus Andronicus*, Sedley's *Antony and Cleopatra*, and other plays.

HARPSICHORD harpsichord music, including *The Prince of Denmark's March* ('Trumpet Voluntary').

OTHER anthems; odes on the Assumption of the Blessed Virgin, in praise of Barbadoes, and *O Harmony*; setting of Dryden's *Alexander's Feast* (1697).

Clarke, Rebecca (1886–1979) English viola player and composer. In a competition in the USA in 1919 for a work for viola and piano she won the prize with a sonata, second only to Ernest Bloch's Suite. She settled in the USA at the outbreak of war in 1939 and married the pianist James Friskin (1886–1967) in 1944.

She studied at the Royal Academy of Music in London.

Works VOCAL Psalm for chorus; songs for voice and violin and for voice and piano.

CHAMBER piano trio (1921); viola and piano sonata, Rhapsody for cello and piano (1923), duets for viola and cello; instrumental pieces.

classical a term commonly used to denote the period of Haydn, Mozart, and Beethoven, as opposed to the later Romantic period and earlier baroque period.

classical music term used to distinguish 'serious' music from ➤ **pop music**, rock music, ➤ **jazz**, and folk music. It is generally used to refer to Western art music – that is, music for the concert hall or church written in the tradition that originated with European music of the Middle Ages and passed through the Renaissance, baroque, classical, and Romantic styles.

The term is also used (often with a capital C) for music of the classical period of music history, to distinguish it from ➤ **baroque music** and ➤ **Romantic** music. Music of the classical era emphasized elegance and formal logic over personal expression and emotion. The orchestra in this period expanded to include a full complement of woodwind instruments as well as some brass and percussion, and the piano replaced the harpsichord. The main musical form or structure to develop was the ➤ **sonata** form. The classical period lasted from about 1750 to about 1830, and included the music of composers such as Wolfgang Amadeus Mozart and Joseph Haydn, and the earlier works of Ludwig van Beethoven.

classical music term used specifically to refer to the period between approximately 1750 and 1830, in which composers' concerns for form and symmetry were analogous to those of the ideals of classical Greek and Roman art and philosophy. As epitomized by the Viennese classical school of Haydn, Mozart, and Beethoven, classical music is characterized by the growth of clear formal and sectional elements, especially ➤ **sonata form**; clear and often symmetrical harmonic and melodic relationships from phrase to phrase and section to section, influenced in part by the study of rhetoric (for example, the use of ➤ **antecedent/** ➤ **consequent** phrases); and the development from baroque ➤ **polyphony** and ➤ **counterpoint** to the melodic style of ➤ **homophony** with distinct and subordinate accompaniments.

'Classical Symphony' symphony no. 1 in D, Op. 25, by Sergey Prokofiev, written in emulation of Haydn, first performed in Petrograd (St Petersburg), Russia, on 21 April 1918.

Claudel, Paul (1868–1955) French poet and dramatist. His works and thought inspired the composers Darius ➤ **Milhaud** (➤ **Christophe Colomb**, ➤ **Homme et son désir**, *Protée*, *Annonce faite à Marie*, Aeschylus translations and songs) and Arthur ➤ **Honegger** (*Danse des morts*, *Soulier de satin*, ➤ **Jeanne d'Arc au bûcher**).

Claudine von Villa Bella play for music by Johann Wolfgang von Goethe. It is also the title of the music composed by Franz Schubert (libretto from Goethe's play); all three acts were composed in 1815 but the manuscripts of Acts 2 and 3 were used as firelighters by the servants of Josef Hüttenbrenner. The Overture and Act 1 were first performed at the Gemeindehaus Wieden, Vienna, Austria, on 26 April 1913.

clausula an interpolation in regular rhythm into 12th- and 13th-century ➤ **organum**, without words, but either sung to the syllable of the text immediately preceding it or played by instruments or both together. The lowest (tenor) part, which in the main portions of the music is in very long notes, here moves at a quicker speed, the notes being arranged in a rhythmical pattern. Numerous clausulae were also designed apparently as independent pieces. In later usage the term meant 'cadential formula'.

clavecin French term for ➤ **harpsichord**, a musical instrument popular in the 16th–18th centuries.

claves musical percussion instrument of Latin American origin, consisting of small hardwood batons struck together.

clavicembalo or **cembalo** alternative name for the ➤ **harpsichord**, a musical instrument.

clavichord small domestic keyboard instrument developed in the 16th century from the ➤ **monochord**. Its tone is soft and delicate and it is best suited for playing in small rooms. The notes are sounded by a metal blade striking the string, and a form of vibrato (➤ **bebung**) is possible by varying the finger pressure on the key. It dropped in popularity in the 18th century due to the arrival of the ➤ **fortepiano**.

In the 'fretted' clavichord each string is used for two adjacent notes, with the different pitches produced by striking the string at different points. The two adjacent notes cannot therefore be sounded at the same time. 'Fretless' clavichords have a separate string for each note. The first clavichords had few strings, using a keyboard-based array of metal tangents combining the function of plectrum and bridge to define and produce a range of pitches. Later instruments increased the number of strings.

clavicytherium musical instrument, a ➤ **harpsichord** whose wing-shaped body stands upright instead of being placed horizontally as in the grand piano.

clavier (German *Klavier*) in music, general term for an early ➤ **keyboard** instrument.

Clavierübung (German 'keyboard practice') a collection of keyboard music by Johann Sebastian Bach, published in four parts: I (1731), six partitas; II (1735), Italian concerto and French overture; III (1739), organ prelude and fugue in E flat major framing 21 chorale preludes on the catechism and four manual *duetti*; IV (1741 or 1742), 'Goldberg' variations.

claviorganum musical instrument that combines harpsichord and organ mechanisms. It dates from the late 16th century and was made in various forms until the 18th century.

Clay, Frédéric Emes (1838–1889) English composer. He wrote light operas and the cantata *Lalla Rookh* (1877), based on a poem by Thomas Moore.

He was born in Paris, France, and studied under Wilhelm Molique and Moritz Hauptmann in Leipzig, Germany. He began by writing light operas for amateurs 1859–60, but produced *Court and Cottage* at Covent Garden in London, England, in 1862.

Works STAGE light operas *Princess Toto*, *Don Quixote* (1876), *The Merry Duchess* (1883), *The Golden King*, and others; incidental music for Shakespeare's *Twelfth Night*.

CANTATAS *The Knights of the Cross* and *Lalla Rookh* (Moore; 1877), the latter including the song 'I'll Sing Thee Songs of Araby'.

SONGS 'She Wandered Down the Mountainside', 'The Sands of Dee'.

clef in music, a sign placed at the beginning of a ➤ stave to indicate the pitch of the written notes. It was introduced as a visual aid in plainchant notation, and takes the form of a stylized letter centred on a particular line to show the pitch of that line.

The standard clefs for most instruments are G (➤ treble) and F (➤ bass) clefs. The C clef is now comparatively rare, except for viola, high parts of the cello range, bassoon, and double bass.

Clemens non Papa (c.1510–c.1556), born **Jacques Clemens** or **Clément** Franco-Flemish composer. Clemens was a prolific composer known chiefly for his sacred works, especially his settings of *souterliedekens*, the Dutch psalms. He produced over 400 works, including Masses, motets, psalms in Flemish, and chansons.

The reason for the *non Papa* ('not the pope') in his name is uncertain, though it was probably coined as a joke, for Pope Clement VII died in 1534, and the name was not used in a publication until 1545.

He was succentor at Bruges Cathedral 1544–45, and in late 1550 was at 's-Hertogenbosch. He also spent some time in Ypres, and had links with Leyden and Dort. His three-voice psalms were the first polyphonic settings of the psalms in Dutch, with the use of popular song melodies as cantus firmi. All but one of his Mass settings are parody settings on chansons and motets by contemporary composers.

Clementi, Aldo (1925–) Italian composer. He studied with Goffredo Petrassi and Bruno Maderna, who influenced him towards 12-note serialism. His works are densely structured and

include *Informels* (1961–63); concerto for wind orchestra and two pianos (1967); stage series *Blitz* (1973); *Collage 4* (1979) and *Es* (1981); concerto for piano and eleven instruments (1986).

Clementi, Muzio (1752–1832) Italian pianist and composer. He settled in London, England, in 1782 as a teacher and then as proprietor of a successful piano and music business. He was the founder of the present-day technique of piano playing, and his series of studies, *Gradus ad Parnassum* (1817), is still in use.

Clementi was born in Rome, where he studied as a child, and at the age of nine was appointed to a post as organist. He afterwards studied under Santarelli and Carpani, and by the age of 14 had composed several contrapuntal works. He attracted the attention of Peter Beckford, member of Parliament, a cousin of the author of *Vathek*, who brought him to England, where Clementi continued to pursue his studies until the year 1773 when he published his first piano sonatas and appeared with spectacular success as a virtuoso pianist and composer. He was conductor of the Italian Opera in London 1777–80, after which he toured extensively in Europe, in 1781 playing before the Viennese court in competition with Mozart (who thought little of him). Back in London, Johann Baptist Cramer and John Field were his pupils. He was associated with the publishers and piano manufacturers Longman & Broderip, upon whose bankruptcy in 1798 he re-established the firm in partnership with Longman. His interest in the company (trading under a constantly changing variety of names) continued until his death. He was again on tour in Europe 1802–10, taking Field with him to St Petersburg, where the latter remained. In 1807 he met Beethoven in Vienna. From 1810, apart from occasional further travels, he remained in England.

On his return to England he founded a business as pianoforte-maker and musical publisher in London. John Field was his assistant and pupil there, and in 1802 Clementi took Field on a continental tour. In 1813 he assisted in forming the Philharmonic Society. He left about 70 sonatas, also symphonies and overtures, and was regarded as the founder of modern pianoforte technique.

His best-known work is the *Gradus ad Parnassum*, a collection of progressive studies, which have remained a valuable aid to piano technique. He died at Evesham and is buried in the cloisters of Westminster Abbey, London.

Works ORCHESTRAL four symphonies.

PIANO about 60 piano sonatas; 100 progressive piano studies entitled *Gradus ad Parnassum* (1817); capriccios and other piano pieces; sonatas for piano.

OTHER sonatas for various instruments; chamber music.

clemenza di Scipione, La, *The Clemency of Scipio* opera by Johann Christian Bach, first produced at the King'sTheatre, Haymarket, London, England, on 4 April 1778. In the story, Scipio holds prisoners after victory at Carthage. Luceius attempts to rescue his love, Arsinda, but is captured. Facing execution, he is saved when Arsinda threatens suicide and Scipio shows mercy.

clemenza di Tito, La, *The Clemency of Titus* opera by Christoph Willibald von Gluck (libretto by Pietro Metastasio), first produced at theTeatro San Carlo, Naples, Italy, on 4 November 1752.

It is also the title of an opera by Mozart (Metastasio's libretto, altered by Caterino Mazzolà), first produced in Prague, to celebrate the coronation of the emperor Leopold II as king of Bohemia, on 6 September 1791. The story tells how Titus forgives Vitellia and Sextus for plotting against him.

See also ➤ **Tito Vespasiano**.

Cleofide opera by Johann Hasse (libretto by M A Boccardi, based on Pietro Metastasio's *Alessandro nell'Indie*), first produced for the court in Dresden, Germany, on 13 September 1731. In the story Alexander the Great falls in love with Cleophis but she remains faithful to Porus.

Cleopatra, in full **Die betrogene Staats-Liebe, oder Die unglückselige Cleopatra, Königin von Egypten** opera by Johann Mattheson (libretto by F C Feustking), first produced at the Theater beim Gänsemarkt, Hamburg, Germany, on 20 October 1704. The story is based on Shakespeare's play and the events described in Plutarch's *Lives*.

Cleopatra e Cesare opera by Karl Graun (libretto by G C Bottarèlli, based on Corneille's *La Mort de Pompée*), written for the inauguration of the Berlin Opera, Germany, and first produced there on 7 December 1742. It was revived in Berlin in 1992 (250th anniversary).

Cléopâtre opera by Jules Massenet (libretto by L Payen), first produced in Monte Carlo, Monaco, on 23 February 1914.

click-track in film music, a technique to aid the coordination of music and film action invented by the composers Carl Stalling and Scott ➤ **Bradley**. Holes punched in the soundtrack of a composer's working print click at a desired tempo measured in frames, allowing a composer to construct a musical phrase to climax at a precise moment in the film action.

A metronome tempo of 144 beats per minute, for example, is equivalent to one hole every ten frames of film. A feature of cartoon films from 1937, the click-track was also employed by the composer Max ➤ **Steiner** for feature romance films, in which context it is called 'Mickey-Mousing'.

Clochette, La, *The Little Bell* opera by Egidio Duni (libretto by L Anseaume), first produced at the Comédie-Italienne, Paris, France, on 24 July 1766.

Clochette, La, ou Le Diable page, *The Little Bell, or The Devil as Page* opera by Ferdinand Hérold (libretto by E G T de Lambert), first produced at the Opéra-Comique, Paris, France, on 18 October 1817. Schubert wrote two songs for the Vienna production in 1821.

'Clock Symphony' the nickname of Haydn's symphony no. 101, in D major (no. 9 of the 'Salomon' symphonies), written for London in 1794. The name derives from the ticking motion of the accompanying figuration in the slow movement.

Clori, Tirsi, e Fileno large-scale Italian cantata for two sopranos, alto, and chamber ensemble by Handel, composed in 1707. Its first modern revival was in London, England, in 1984.

Club Anthem an anthem composed jointly by John Blow, Pelham Humfrey, and W Turner about 1664, when they were choirboys at the Chapel Royal. It is a setting of the words 'I will always give thanks'.

cluster in music, the effect of playing simultaneously and without emphasis all the notes within a chosen interval. It was introduced by the US composer Henry Cowell in the piano piece *The Banshee* (1925), for which using a ruler on the keys is recommended. Its use in film and radio incidental music symbolizes a hallucinatory or dreaming state, presumably because it resembles an internalized disturbance of normal hearing.

The cluster effect is also heard in *Ecuatorial* (1933–34) by Edgard Varèse, Karlheinz Stockhausen's *Piano Piece X* (1961), and György Ligeti's *Volumina* (1962) for organ, using the player's forearms. Cluster writing for strings features in Krzysztof Penderecki's *Threnody for the Victims of Hiroshima* (1960), and for voices in Ligeti's *Lux Aeterna*.

Cluytens, André (1905–1967) Belgian conductor. He studied piano at Antwerp Conservatory. He first worked for his father as a chorus trainer at the Théâtre Royal in Antwerp, where he later conducted opera. He then held numerous posts in France, including director of the Paris Opéra Comique, 1947–49. In 1955 he conducted Richard Wagner's *Tannhäuser* at Bayreuth. He made his US debut in 1956, with the Vienna Philharmonic

Orchestra, and conducted the Viennese Staatsoper from 1959.

Coates, Albert (1882–1953) English conductor and composer, born in Russia. He was sent to school in England and entered Liverpool University; he returned to Russia to enter his father's business but was sent to the Leipzig Conservatory. He studied conducting with Artur Nikisch and conducted opera at several German theatres before he was engaged at St Petersburg, where he conducted Wagner's dramas at the Mariinsky Theatre. He fled to England during the Revolution in 1919 and settled in London for good, conducting Wagner's *Tristan* and the *Ring* at Covent Garden; he led the first public performance of Holst's *The Planets* (1920).

Works OPERA *Assurbanipal*, *Samuel Pepys* (1929), *Pickwick* (Covent Garden, 1936), and *Gainsborough's Duchess*.

ORCHESTRAL symphonic poem *The Eagle*, Russian Suite for orchestra.

OTHER piano pieces.

Coates, Eric (1886–1957) English composer. He is remembered for the orchestral suites *London* (1933), including the 'Knightsbridge' march; *By the Sleepy Lagoon* (1939); *The Dam Busters March* (1942); and the songs 'Bird Songs at Eventide' and 'The Green Hills of Somerset'. He is best known as the composer of the signature tune for BBC Radio's *Desert Island Discs* (*By the Sleepy Lagoon*).

Coates was born at Hucknall, Nottinghamshire. He studied at the Royal Academy of Music in London and became a viola player in a quartet and in the Queen's Hall Orchestra, but later devoted himself to the composition of light and popular music. His autobiography, *Suite in Four Movements*, was published in 1953.

Cobbold, William (1560–1639) English organist and composer. He was organist at Norwich Cathedral 1599–1608, and was one of the ten musicians who harmonized the tunes in Thomas East's Psalter of 1592. In 1601 he contributed a madrigal to the collection *The* ➔ **Triumphes of Oriana**. Among his other few surviving works are eleven consort songs.

Coccia, Maria Rosa (1759–1833) Italian composer. At the age of 16 she passed a severe examination at the Accademia di Santa Cecilia in Rome and an account of her brilliant success was published. In 1780 another eulogy of her was issued with letters from the teacher Giovanni Battista Martini, the librettist Pietro Metastasio, and the castrato singer Farinelli.

Works Magnificat for voices and organ, written at 15, *Dixit Dominus* and a cantata, but most are lost.

Cochlaeus, Johannes (Johann Dobnek) (1479–1552) German cleric and music scholar. He was a Roman Catholic and an opponent of Luther, in office at Cologne, Worms, Mainz, and Frankfurt. He wrote a treatise on music, and composed odes.

Cockaigne (In London Town) concert overture by Edward Elgar, Op. 40, composed in 1900 and first performed for the Philharmonic Society, London, England, on 20 June 1901.

Coclico (Coclicus), Adrianus Petit (1499 or 1500–1592) Flemish composer. He became a Protestant and went to Wittenberg in 1545. After holding various posts in Germany he went to the Danish court in Copenhagen. He published a treatise entitled *Compendium musices* and a collection of psalm settings entitled *Consolationes piae*.

coda (Italian 'tail') in music, a concluding section of a movement added to emphasize the destination key.

codetta (Italian 'little tail') in music, a small form of ➔ **coda**, not appearing as a rule at the end of a movement, but rather rounding off a section of such a movement, or a theme or group of themes, thus assuming the function of a ➔ **bridge passage**.

Coelho, Rui (1892–1986) Portuguese composer. He studied in Lisbon and later with Engelbert Humperdinck, Max Bruch, and Arnold Schoenberg in Berlin, Germany. He became music critic of the *Diario de Noticias* in Lisbon and in 1924 won a prize with his second opera.

Works OPERA *Crisfal* (1919), *Belkiss* (1924), *Inés de Castro* (1925), *Tá-Mar* (1936), and *Entre giestas* (1946).

ORCHESTRAL symphonic poems 5 *Sinfonias camoneanas*, *Promenade d'été*.

OTHER chamber music; piano pieces; songs.

Coerne, Louis (Adolphe) (1870–1922) US conductor and composer. He studied in Europe and at Harvard University. After filling an organist's post at Buffalo and conducting there and at Columbus, he became associate professor at Smith College, Northampton, Massachusetts, and also taught at Harvard. Later he held other distinguished teaching posts and visited Germany, where some of his works were performed.

Works STAGE *A Woman of Marblehead*, *Zenobia* (1902; produced Bremen, 1905), *Sakuntala* (after Kalidasa); incidental music to Euripides' *Trojan Women*.

ORCHESTRAL symphonic poem *Hiawatha* (after Longfellow) and other works for orchestra; violin concerto.

CHAMBER string quartet in C minor, three piano trios in canon.

OTHER six-part Mass; songs.

Coffee Cantata name given to Johann Sebastian Bach's secular cantata BWV 211 (c. 1734–35), *Schweigt stille, plaudert nicht*. The libretto by Picanander deals in a humorous way with the then new vogue for drinking coffee.

Cohn, Arthur (1910–1998) US composer, conductor, and writer. He studied at the Juilliard School, New York, and conducted in Philadelphia 1942–65. His books include *Twentieth-Century Music in Western Europe* (1961) and *The Encyclopedia of Chamber Music* (1990). He wrote six string quartets (1928–45), a flute concerto (1941), and *Kaddisch* for orchestra (1965).

col (Italian 'with the') musical term, as in *col arco*, 'with the bow'.

Colas Breugnon opera by Dmitri Kabalevsky (libretto by V Bragin after R Rolland's novel), first produced in Leningrad (now St Petersburg), Russia, on 22 February 1938; it was revised in 1953 and 1969. In the story the carpenter Colas recalls his colourful life, in which he revenges himself on the Duke who has destroyed his creations.

Colasse, Pascal (1649–1709) French composer. In about 1677 he obtained an appointment at the Opéra from Jean-Baptiste Lully, in whose works he wrote some of the subordinate parts.

He studied at the Maîtrise de Saint-Paul and the Collège de Navarre in Paris. In 1683 he became one of the four superintendents of the royal chapel, each of whom had to direct the music for three months per year, and two years later he shared with Michel Lalande the appointment of royal chamber musician. In 1696 he was appointed maître de musique de chambre.

Works OPERA *Achille et Polyxène* (with Lully, 1687), *Thétis et Pélée* (1689), *Enée et Lavinie* (1690), *Jason, La Naissance de Vénus* (1696), *Polyxène et Pyrrhus*, and others.

CHURCH MUSIC motets, *Cantiques spirituels*, and other church music.

Coleman, Charles (died c.1664) English composer. He was chamber musician to Charles I and after the Civil War worked as a music teacher in London. He received a doctorate in music from Cambridge in 1651, and was appointed composer to Charles II in 1662. With Cooke, Hudson, H Lawes, and Locke he contributed music to William Davenant's *The Siege of Rhodes* (entertainment at Rutland House, 1656).

Coleman, Edward (died 1669) English singer, lutenist, and composer, son of Charles Coleman. He composed incidental music to James Shirley's play *Contention of Ajax and Achilles* in 1653, contributed songs to *Select Musicall Ayres and Dialogues* the same year, and pieces of his appeared in John Playford's *Musical Companion* in 1672.

Both he and his wife sang in *The Siege of Rhodes* in 1656. He became a Gentleman of the Chapel Royal on its re-establishment in 1660 and succeeded Lanier in the royal band in 1662.

Coleridge-Taylor, Samuel (1875–1912) English composer. He wrote the cantata *Hiawatha's Wedding Feast* (1898), a setting in three parts of Longfellow's poem. The son of a West African doctor and an English mother, he was a student and champion of traditional black music.

He sang at a church at Croydon as a boy, and entered the Royal College of Music as a violin student in 1890, but also studied composition under Charles Stanford. He had works performed while still at college and in 1899 he was represented at the North Staffordshire Festival at Hanley. He was appointed conductor of the Handel Society in 1904, and visited the USA that year, as well as in 1906 and 1910; but otherwise devoted all his time to composition and private teaching. In the last years of his life he did some teaching at the Guildhall School of Music, London.

Works STAGE *Thelma* (1907–09); incidental music for Shakespeare's *Othello* and Stephen Phillips's *Herod, Ulysses, Nero*, and *Faust* (after Goethe).

VOICES AND ORCHESTRA settings for solo voices, chorus, and orchestra of portions from Longfellow's 'Hiawatha' (three parts, 1898), Coleridge's 'Kubla Khan' (1905), Noyes's 'A Tale of Old Japan'; 'Five Choral Ballads' (Longfellow), 'Sea Drift' (Whitman) for chorus; oratorio *The Atonement*.

ORCHESTRAL symphony in A minor; violin concerto in G minor.

CHAMBER nonet for strings and wind, piano quintet, clarinet quintet, string quartet in D minor, and other chamber music.

OTHER piano music, songs.

colla parte (Italian 'with the part') in music, a direction indicating that the accompaniment to a vocal or instrumental solo part is to follow the soloist in a passage performed without strict adherence to the tempo.

collegium musicum (Latin 'musical fraternity') in 18th-century Germany, an association for the performance of chamber and orchestral music. Today the term is used in universities to refer specifically to an ensemble performing early music.

col legno (Italian 'with the wood') in music, a direction indicating that a passage for a string instrument or a group of such instruments is to be played by striking the strings with the stick of the bow.

It famously occurs to imitate the fluttering of bats' wings in the final movement of Hector Berlioz's *Symphonie fantastique*.

Collin, Heinrich Joseph von (1771–1811) Austrian poet. His chief connection with music is the drama *Coriolan* for which Beethoven wrote an overture. Stadler wrote incidental music for his tragedy *Polyxena*.

Collingwood, Lawrance (1887–1982) English conductor and composer. He was chorister at Westminster Abbey, London, and organ scholar at Exeter College, Oxford; he lived in Russia for a time and worked with Albert Coates at the St Petersburg Opera; he married there and returned to England during the Revolution. He was principal conductor at Sadler's Wells, London, 1931–46, and conducted the UK first performances of Rimsky-Korsakov's *Snow Maiden* (1933) and *The Tale of Tsar Saltan* (1937).

Works the opera *Macbeth* (1934), symphonic poem for orchestra, two piano sonatas.

Colombe, La, The Dove opera by Charles Gounod (libretto by J Barbier and Michel Carré, after La Fontaine), first produced in Baden-Baden, Germany, on 3 August 1860. The plot concerns Sylvie in rivalry with another Florentine lady.

Colonna, Giovanni Paolo (1637–1695) Italian composer. He studied in Rome with Giacomo Carissimi, Antonio Abbatini, and Orazio Benevoli. He became organist of San Petronio at Bologna in 1659 and maestro di cappella in 1674.

Works STAGE the opera *Amilcare di Cipro* (1692) and other dramatic works.

CHURCH MUSIC Masses, motets, psalms, litanies; oratorios.

Colonne, Edouard (actually Judas) (1838–1910) French violinist and conductor. He was the first to popularize Hector Berlioz and was well known for his performances of Wagner, Tchaikovsky, and other composers then unknown in France. He founded the Concerts Colonne.

coloratura in music, a rapid ornamental vocal passage with runs and trills. A **coloratura soprano** is a light, high voice suited to such music.

colour in music, the quality or timbre of an instrument or voice. A 'dark' sound denotes a thick, heavy sonority while a 'light' sound describes a thinner, more transparent sonority. The Russian composer and pianist Aleksandr Skriabin invented a keyboard which would project colours on to a screen in order to reflect the mood and character of the music.

colour music composers referring to or using colour (light):

Granville Bantock, *Atalanta in Calydon*, during the performance of which the concert-room is to be lighted in a different colour for each movement.

Arthur Bliss, *Colour Symphony*, each movement of which bears the name of a colour as title.

Arnold Schoenberg, *Die glückliche Hand*, in which coloured light plays a part, as noted in the score.

Aleksandr Skriabin, *Prometheus*, which contains an optional part for the *tastiera per luce*, designed to throw differently coloured lights.

Colporteur, Le, ou L'Enfant du bûcheron, The Pedlar, or The Woodcutter's Child opera by George Onslow (libretto by F A E de Planard), first produced at the Opéra-Comique, Paris, France, on 22 November 1827.

combattimento di Tancredi e Clorinda, Il, The Combat of Tancredi and Clorinda dramatic cantata by Monteverdi (text by Torquato Tasso, from Canto XII, *Gerusalemme liberata*), first performed at the Palazzo Mocenigo, Venice, Italy, in 1624. It was published in Monteverdi's *Madrigali guerrieri e amorosi* (1638).

combination tone in music, an acoustical phenomenon in which a third faint tone is heard when two notes are sounded loudly together. The frequency of the combination tone is the difference between the numerical frequencies of the two notes. For example, given note 1 = 500 Hz, and note 2 = 300 Hz, the combination tone is: 500 Hz − 300 Hz = 200 Hz. Combination tones are often used and manipulated in ➤ **electronic music**.

comédie lyrique an 18th-century French name for comic opera.

Comedy on a Bridge, Czech **Veselohra na moste** opera for radio in one act by Bohuslav Martinů (libretto by the composer, after V K Klicera), first produced on Prague Radio on 18 March 1937. The bridge in the story connects two feuding villages.

come prima (Italian 'as at first') in music, a direction indicating that the opening section of a movement is to be played again exactly as before, or that a passage is to be treated in the same manner as before.

come sopra (Italian 'as above') in music, a direction asking the player to repeat the manner of performance of a passage heard earlier.

'Come, Thou Monarch of the Vine' song by Franz Schubert, from Shakespeare's play *Antony and Cleopatra*, translated by F von Mayerhofer as *Trinklied*, 'Bacchus', and composed in Germany in 1826.

'Come, Ye Sons of Art, Away' ode by Henry Purcell for the birthday of Queen Mary II in 1694 (text probably by Nahum Tate).

commedia per musica (Italian 'comedy for music') Neapolitan term of the 18th century for comic opera.

common chord in music, a non-technical term for a major or minor ➤ **triad**.

common time in music, alternative name for 4/4 time. The symbol C which denotes common time originates in music of the Middle Ages in which triple time (three beats in a bar) was considered perfect (as it reflected the Holy Trinity) and notated by a circle (the perfect geometric shape), and duple time (two beats in a bar) was considered imperfect and notated by a broken circle.

Communion the last item of the Proper of the Roman Mass. Originally a psalm with antiphon before and after each verse, only the antiphon is now retained. In general style the Communion resembles the Introit.

comparative musicology the term used up to the middle of the 20th century to describe the branch of musicology which examines the music of different cultures – especially non-Western cultures (German *vergleichende Musikwissenschaft*). Since about 1950 the word ➤ **'ethnomusicology'** has replaced it in common usage.

compass in music, the range of notes covered by a voice or instrument.

Compenius, Heinrich (c.1525–1611), called **'the Elder'** German music theorist and composer, the eldest member of a family of organ builders who also worked in Denmark. His son **Esaias Compenius** (died 1617) built the organ at Frederiksborg Castle and was coauthor with Michael Praetorius of *Orgeln Verdingnis* (*Organographia*). Esaias's brother **Heinrich Compenius the Younger** (died 1631) built the organ at Magdeburg Cathedral. Heinrich's nephew **Johann Heinrich Compenius** (died 1642) built the organ at St Mauritius, Halle, for Samuel Scheidt.

Compère, Loyset (c.1445–1518) French composer. He started as a chorister at Saint-Quentin Cathedral, later became a canon, and was eventually appointed its chancellor.
    Works Masses, magnificats, and other church music; also many secular songs with French and Italian words.

composition art of combining sounds to create an original piece of music. It is also another word for the piece of music itself.

compound intervals in music, any intervals exceeding the compass of an octave, so called, as distinct from simple intervals, because they differ from the latter only in width, not in character; thus, a major tenth is essentially the same as a major third.

compound time in music, a metre in which each beat divides into three units. For example, 6/8 consists of two beats, each of three quavers.

computer-generated music music in which a computer has been used by the composer, generating or synthesizing the properties and timbre of sound; also, music which is generated by a computer's response to a series of commands, which are designed by a composer and fed to the machine on a computer program. A computer is often used in compositions which use elements of chance, as in a ➤ **stochastic** work.

Comte Ory, Le, Count Ory opera by Gioachino Rossini (libretto by Scribe and C G Delestre-Poirson), first produced at the Paris Opéra, France, on 20 August 1828. In the story the young Count Ory and his page Isolier pursue the Countess Adèle, dressed first as pilgrims, then as nuns. They must escape before Adèle's husband returns.

Comus masque by John Milton, with music by Henry ➤ **Lawes**, first produced at Ludlow Castle, Shropshire, England, on 29 September 1634. It was produced with alterations by Dalton and music by Thomas Arne at the Drury Lane Theatre, London, on 4 March 1738.

con (Italian 'with') musical term, as in *con espressione*, 'with expression'.

con amore (Italian 'with love, with affection') in music, indicating an enthusiastic manner of performance.

concento (Italian 'union, agreement') in music, the playing of the notes of a chord exactly together.

concert originally, as in the English 'consort', the singing or playing together under any conditions; now a public performance of music, except that of an opera or as a rule that given by a single performer, which is more often called a recital.

concertante term in music descriptive of an orchestral concerto in which a number of instruments perform solo, as in the sinfonia concertante works of Haydn and Mozart.

concertato (Italian 'concerted') a musical work or portion of a composition written for several persons to perform together.

concerted music any music written for several soloists to perform together. Any chamber music is concerted music, as are small groups of soloists featuring within a larger work, such as in opera or concerto grosso.

Concertgebouw (Dutch 'concert building') the principal concert hall in Amsterdam, the Netherlands, built in 1888. The Concertgebouw

Orchestra is in residence here.

concertina musical instrument, a portable reed organ related to the ➤ **accordion** but smaller in size and hexagonal in shape, with buttons for keys. Metal reeds are blown by wind from pleated bellows which are opened and closed by the player's hands. It was invented in England in the 19th century.

concertino (Italian 'little concert or little concerto') in music, originally a group of solo instruments playing alternately with the orchestra (ripieno) in a work of the ➤ **concerto grosso** type. The term has subsequently come to mean a small scale concerto for a solo instrument.

Examples include that by Leoš Janáček for piano, clarinet, horn, bassoon, two violins, viola, composed in 1925 and first performed in Brno (Czech Republic) on 16 February 1926; also that by Igor Stravinsky for string quartet, composed in 1920 and revised in 1952 for twelve instruments, first performed in Los Angeles, USA, on 11 November 1957.

concert master in music, the leader of an orchestra, usually the principal violinist.

concerto composition, traditionally in three movements, for solo instrument (or instruments) and orchestra. It developed during the 18th century from the ➤ **concerto grosso** form for orchestra, in which a group of solo instruments (concerto) is contrasted with a full orchestra (ripieno).

Arcangelo Corelli and Giuseppe Torelli were early concerto composers, followed by Antonio Vivaldi, George Handel, and Johann Sebastian Bach (*Brandenburg Concertos*). Mozart wrote about 40 concertos, mostly for piano. Recent concertos by György Ligeti (*Double Concerto*, 1972, for flute and oboe) and Luciano Berio (*Concerto for Two Pianos*, 1972–73), and Elliott Carter (*Violin Concerto*, 1990) have developed the concerto relationship along new lines.

Béla Bartók introduced a new concept in 1944 with his *Concerto for Orchestra*, in which there is no specific soloist, but rather a showcase for the virtuosity of the whole orchestra, both as an ensemble and with individual short solos. The form has also been used by Witold Lutosławski (1954), Elliott Carter (1929), and Peter Maxwell Davies (1994).

concerto grosso (Italian 'grand consort') composition that contrasts two groups of instruments: a group of solo instrumentalists called a concertino against a string orchestra called a ripieno. The concertino instruments sometimes play alone and sometimes are heard in combination with the ripieno group.

concert pitch in music, standard pitch to which concert ensembles tune up. In a symphony orchestra it is normally the pitch A4, which is common to instruments of the string orchestra. It is given by the oboe, otherwise by the concert master (principal violin) or deputy, or by the piano or organ if featured, as their tuning is fixed in advance.

In military and brass bands, concert pitch is B♭, for the reason that wind instruments in general are historically tuned to B♭ or a related dimension (the pitch of B♭ expressing a wavelength of specific measure).

The standard frequency associated with concert A4 pitch is 440 Hz (cycles per second) but this is subject to variation, some orchestras preferring 438 Hz, others tending towards 442 Hz, with slight but consequential effects on individual and ensemble tone. Prior to 1700 the pitch standard was local and set by the chapel organ, of which a number of Renaissance and baroque examples survive with values for A4 between a low extreme of 380 Hz and a high of 610 Hz. In 1862 Hermann ➤ **Helmholtz** gave a value for A4 of 431 Hz, an increase on 18th-century concert pitch. The revival of ➤ **authentic** early music practices after 1970 has led to agreement on standards of 460–465 Hz for High Renaissance music, 415 Hz for baroque and classical music, and 430 Hz for Romantic music.

Concertstück (German, also **Konzertstück, 'concerto piece')** in music, title sometimes given to works of the concerto type for solo instrument and orchestra which are not fully developed concertos. *Concertstücke* are often in one movement or in several connected sections. Although German, the title has been used by composers in other countries, for example Cécile Chaminade and Gabriel Pierné in France, and Frederic Cowen in England.

Conchita opera by Riccardo Zandonai (libretto, in French, by M Vaucaire, translated into Italian by C Zangarini, based on P Louÿs' novel *La Femme et le pantin*), first produced at the Teatro dal Verme, Milan, Italy, on 14 October 1911. The libretto was originally written for Puccini.

concord in music, the sounding together of notes in harmony that satisfies the ear as being final in itself and requiring no following chord to give the impression of resolution.

Concord Sonata work for piano by Charles Ives in four movements: *Emerson*, *Hawthorne*, *The Alcotts*, *Thoreau*, after the Concord, Massachusetts, group of writers admired by Ives. It was composed 1909–15 and the first complete performance was given in New York City on 20 January 1939, by John Kirkpatrick.

concrete music see ➔ musique concrète.

conducting in music, the direction of a performance by visual gestures. Groups of more than about six performers have nearly always needed someone to ensure ensemble and consistency of interpretation, and there is iconographic evidence of conductors in Egypt and Sumeria from the third millennium BC, just as there is for medieval chant choirs. With the rise of written polyphony, however, ensembles tended to be small and musical direction normally lay in the hands of a leading performer – in the baroque era often controlling the ensemble from an organ, harpsichord, or (particularly in classical music) from the violin. Conducting with a baton as an independent activity arose mainly in the 19th century, particularly with Gasparo Spontini, Ludwig Spohr, and Felix Mendelssohn; and the earliest professional career conductor seems to have been Otto Nicolai (1810–1849). Until the 20th century the most important conductors were usually primarily composers.

conductor in music, the director of an orchestra who beats time, cues entries, and controls the overall expression and balance of a performance.

Conductors of ballet and opera are normally resident, on a full-time contract, available for the ongoing preparation of new repertoire. Conductors for symphony orchestras are more often freelance, star performers in their own right, under temporary contract for concert or recording purposes and thus more reliant on the expertise of orchestras.

conductus a 12th–13th-century vocal composition originally processional in character and written for one or more voices. The basic melody of a conductus was generally a tune specially composed. A conductus cum cauda was a polyphonic composition ending with an elaborate tail-piece without words (*cauda*, Latin 'tail'). In the polyphonic conductus the parts normally move in the same rhythm.

conga Afro-Cuban barrel drum, long and narrow in shape, played with the fingers and palms; also an Afro-Cuban ballroom dance in duple time (2/4), with a syncopated rhythm.

Congreve, William (1670–1729) English dramatist and poet. His works inspired music by Frederic Austin (*The Way of the World*), John Eccles (*The Way of the World*, *Love for Love*, *Semele*, and *Ode for St Cecilia's Day*), Gottfried ➔ **Finger** (*Love for Love* and *The Mourning Bride*), Philidor (*Ode for St Cecilia's Day*), Henry ➔ **Purcell** (*The Double Dealer* and *The Old Bachelor*), and Egon ➔ **Wellesz** (*Incognita*); also the works *The* ➔ *Judgment of Paris* (by Eccles, Finger, Daniel Purcell, and John Weldon) and ➔ *Semele* (by Handel).

Connolly, Justin (Riveagh) (1933–) English composer. He studied at the Royal College of Music, London, with Peter Fricker, and was appointed professor there in 1966. He taught at Yale University, USA, in the early 1960s and his music has been influenced by Milton Babbitt and Elliott Carter.

Works ORCHESTRAL *Rebus* for orchestra (1970), *Diaphony* for organ and orchestra (1977), symphony (1991).

INSTRUMENTAL six sets of *Triads* (trios) for various instrumental ensembles (1964–74), five sets of *Obbligati* for various chamber ensembles (1965–81), *Antiphonies* for 36 instruments (1966), *Fourfold from the Garden Forking Path* for two pianos (1983).

VOCAL two sets of *Poems of Wallace Stevens* for soprano, clarinet, and piano (1967–70), *Sentences* for chorus, brass, and organ (to poems by Thomas Traherne, 1979), oratorio *The Marriage of Heaven and Hell* (text by Blake), *Spelt from Sibyl's Leaves* for six solo voices and ensemble (1989), *Cantata* for soprano and piano (1991).

OTHER *Chimaera* for dancer, alto, baritone, and ensemble (1979).

Conradi, Johann Georg (died 1699) German composer. He was one of the earliest composers of German operas, which include *Die schoene und getreue Ariadne* (1691), *Diogenes Cynicus*, *Numa Pompilius*, *Der tapffere Kayser Carolus Magnus* (1692), *Der Verstöhrung Jerusalem*, and *Der wunderbar-vergnügte Pygmalion*. He also wrote sacred music, and was music director at Ansbach 1683–86 and director of the Hamburg opera 1690–93.

Consecration of the House orchestral work by Beethoven. See ➔ *Weihe des Hauses, Die*.

consecutive in music, an adjective used to describe the progression of intervals of the same kind in similar motion.

consequent in music, the second phrase of a symmetrical two-phrase unit. Following the 'questioning' antecedent phrase, the consequent phrase often ends on a more stable harmony. Antecedent/consequent phrases are most typical of compositions from the classical period.

Conservatoire National Supérieur de Musique the chief school of music in Paris, France, opened in 1795 with Bernard Sarrette as director, having grown out of the École Royale du Chant, established in 1784 under the direction of François Gossec. Later directors were Luigi Cherubini, Daniel Auber, Ambroise Thomas, François Dubois, Gabriel Fauré, Henri Rabaud, Claude Delvincourt, Marcel Dupré, and Raymond Loucheur.

140

conservatory a school or college of music which specializes in preparing students for a career in performance or composition. The term originated in 16th-and 17th-century Italy with orphanages that taught music to a high standard. Famous conservatories include the ➔ **Juilliard School** in New York, the Conservatoire in Paris, and the ➔ **Royal College of Music** in London.

console in music, the part of an ➔ **organ** which is directly under the control of the player's hands and feet.

consonance in music, a combination of two or more notes that 'agree' with each other (due to their relationship within the naturally occurring harmonic series) and thus sound pleasing to the ear. It is the opposite of ➔ **dissonance**.

consort in music, a chamber ensemble of Renaissance or baroque instruments of uniform sonority, for example recorders or viols. A nonuniform ensemble, comprising mixed instruments, is called a broken consort.

Constant, Marius (1925–2004) Romanianborn French composer and conductor. He studied in Paris with Olivier Messiaen and Arthur Honegger, directed the Ballets de Paris 1956–66, and was music director of Ars Nova, an ensemble promoting new music, 1963–71. His early compositions were Impressionistic; in his later works he turned to serialism. He collaborated with Peter Brook in his reductions of *Carmen* and *Pelléas et Mélisande*.

Works STAGE operas *La Serrure* and *Le Souper* (both 1969), *La Tragédie de Carmen* (1981); ballets *Jouer de flute* (1952), *Haut Voltage* (1956), *Cyrano de Bergerac* (1960), *Paradise Lost* (1967), *Candide* (1970), *Le Jeu de Sainte Agnès* ('ecclesiastical action' for singers, dancers, actor, organ, electric guitar, trombone, and percussion; 1974). ORCHESTRAL piano concerto (1954); *Turner*, three essays for orchestra (1961); *103 Regards dans l'eau* for violin and orchestra (1981); *Pelléas and Mélisande Symphony* (1986). INSTRUMENTAL *Winds* for 13 wind instruments and double bass (1968), *14 Stations* for 92 percussion instruments and ensemble (1970). ORATORIO *Des droits de l'homme* (1989).

Consul, The opera by Gian Carlo Menotti (libretto by the composer), first produced in Philadelphia, USA, on 1 March 1950. The story tells how the freedom fighter John Sorel must emigrate to evade the secret police. His wife Magda tries to obtain a visa at the consulate, but fails. John is arrested and Magda commits suicide.

contano (Italian 'they count') musical direction in a vocal or instrumental part of a work where the performers have a prolonged rest, warning them to count bars in order to make sure of coming in again at the proper moment.

conte Caramella, Il opera by Baldassare Galuppi (libretto by Carlo Goldoni, partly based on Joseph Addison's comedy *The Drummer, or The Haunted House*), first produced in Verona, Italy, on 18 December 1749.

contesa dei numi, La, The Contest of the Gods opera by Christoph Willibald von Gluck (libretto by Pietro Metastasio), first produced for the court in Copenhagen, Denmark, on 9 April 1749, to celebrate the birth of Prince Christian, later Christian VII.

Contes d'Hoffmann, Les, The Tales of Hoffmann opera by Jacques Offenbach (libretto by J Barbier and Michel Carré, based on a play of their own and on stories by E T A Hoffmann), first produced at the Opéra-Comique, Paris, France, on 10 February 1881, after Offenbach's death. He did not finish it; the scoring is partly by Ernest Guiraud. In the story, Hoffmann tells of doomed love for Olympia, Antonia, and Giulietta.

Conti, Francesco Bartolomeo (1681–1732) Italian lutenist and composer. He was theorbo player to the Austrian court in Vienna 1701–05, and again from 1708. He was appointed court composer in 1713.

Works STAGE the operas *Alba Cornelia* (1714), *Clotilda, Il trionfo dell'Amore, I satiri in Arcadia, Don Chisciotte in Sierra Morena* (1719), *L'Issipile, Pallade trionfante* (1722), and others; stage serenades. VOCAL oratorios, cantatas.

Conti, Gioacchino (1714–1761) Italian soprano castrato. He was a rival of Caffarelli. He sang in Rome from 1730 and at Covent Garden, London, 1736–37, in the first performances of Handel's *Atalanta, Arminio, Giustino,* and *Berenice*. He sang in Italy and Spain until 1755 in operas by Johann Hasse, Niccolò Jommelli, and Baldassare Galuppi. He was praised for his expressive singing in a high range.

continental fingering in music, the fingering of piano music now in universal use, with the fingers marked 1–5 from the thumb. This system has displaced the so-called English fingering, marked + for the thumb and 1–4 for the other fingers, which however, was by no means in use throughout the whole history of English keyboard music.

continuo (Italian, *basso continuo* 'continuous bass') in music, the bass line on which a keyboard player, accompanied by a bass stringed instrument, builds up a harmonic accompaniment. In 17th-century baroque music, composers wrote figures under a bass part to indicate the chords to be played (also called figured bass) rather than write out each chord in detail. This continuo part was played as a single bass line by a bass stringed instrument, such as a cello or double bass. At the same time, another continuo player filled in the harmonies by playing the chords (broken into patterns) on lute or a keyboard instrument, such as a harpsichord or organ. The role of continuo is similar to the traditional role of the bass and piano or guitar in jazz music.

contra- in music, a prefix attached to the name of certain instruments or organ stops denoting a lower pitch (usually an octave below).

contrabass alternative name for the ➤ **double bass**, a musical instrument.

contrabassoon double-reed woodwind instrument, also known as the **double bassoon**. It is a larger version of the ➤ **bassoon**, sounding an octave lower.

contrafactum (Latin 'counterfeit') in music, a vocal composition in which the original words have been replaced by new ones, either secular words substituted for sacred, or vice versa. In the 16th century the Reformation was responsible for several changes of this kind, especially from Latin to vernacular words in the conversion of plainsong melodies to hymn-tunes.

contralto low-register female voice, a high (falsetto) male voice, or a low-register boy's voice; also called an ➤ **alto**.

contrapunctus in music, Latin term for ➤ **counterpoint**, the harmonious combination of different forms of a melody.

contrapuntal in music, a work employing ➤ **counterpoint**, multiple parts of imitative melody.

contrary motion in music, the movement of two voices in opposite directions from each other; the opposite of parallel motion. The strictest form of contrary motion is ➤ **inversion**, in which one voice plays the mirror image of the other. For example, two voices which sing simultaneously: C4–G4–F4 and C4–F3–G3.

contratenor (Latin 'against the tenor') in the 14th and 15th centuries, a singing voice in the same range as the tenor. It was used to embellish three-part vocal music; the other parts were the melody and the tenor. Later, when four-part songs became popular, the contratenor part was split into the *altus* 'high' and *bassus* 'low' parts, and these in turn developed into the modern contralto and bass parts.

Contredanse French name for English ➤ **country dance**.

convenzione ed inconvenienze teatrali, le one-act opera (*farsa*) by Gaetano Donizetti (libretto by the composer, after A S Sografi), first performed at the Teatro Nuovo, Naples, Italy, on 21 November 1827. It is sometimes given in modern revivals under the spurious title *Viva la Mama*. It is a satirical commentary on the 'conveniences', or agreed rules, concerning the rank of contemporary Italian singers.

Converse, Frederick Shepherd (1871–1940) US composer. In 1910 his *Pipe of Desire* became the first US opera to be performed at the New York Metropolitan Opera House. From 1917 to 1919 he served in the army and in 1930 became dean of the New England Conservatory, a post which he held until 1938.

Although intended for a commercial career, he studied music at Harvard University under John Paine. Later he studied piano with Carl Baermann and composition with George Chadwick at Boston, and took a finishing course in Munich. After his return to the USA he held teaching posts at Boston and Harvard until 1907.

Works OPERA *The Pipe of Desire* (1905), *The Sacrifice* (1910), *The Immigrants* (1914), *Sinbad the Sailor*.

ORCHESTRAL five symphonies (1920–40), orchestral tone poems *Endymion's Narrative* (1901), *The Mystic Trumpeter* (after Whitman, 1905), *Ormazd*, *Ave atque vale*, *Song of the Sea*, *Flivver Ten Million* (1927), romance *The Festival of Pan* for orchestra; *Night and Day* for piano and orchestra (after Whitman); concerto for violin and piano.

VOCAL *Job* for solo voices, chorus, and orchestra, *Laudate Dominum* for male voices, brass, and organ, *Hagar in the Desert* for contralto and orchestra, *La Belle Dame sans merci* for baritone and orchestra (Keats, 1902).

CHAMBER three string quartets; piano trio; sonata for violin and piano.

OTHER piano pieces; songs.

convitato di pietra, Il, The Stone Guest opera by Fabrizi (libretto by G B Lorenzi), first produced in Rome, Italy, in 1787.

convitato di pietra, Il, o sia Il dissoluto opera by Righini (librettist unknown), first produced in Prague (Czech Republic) in 1776. It is a setting of the Don Juan legend, produced 11 years before Mozart's version, *Don Giovanni*.

Conyngham, Barry (1944–) Australian composer. He studied with Peter Sculthorpe and Toru Takemitsu and taught at the University of Melbourne from 1975, and was a visiting scholar at Minnesota and Pennsylvania State universities, USA. His music reflects oriental and modern French influences.

Works STAGE operas *Ned* (1975–78), *The Apology of Bony Anderson* (1978), *Fly* (1984), and the puppet opera *Bennelong* (1988); *Crisis: Thoughts in a City* (1968), *Five Windows* (1969).

ORCHESTRAL concerto for orchestra (1981), *Vast I–IV* for orchestra (1987); concertos.

OTHER vocal and chamber music (string quartet, 1979).

Cooke, Arnold (1906–2005) English composer. He was educated at Repton School and Caius College, Cambridge, where he was awarded a music degree in 1929. From that year to 1932 he was a pupil of Paul Hindemith in Berlin, Germany, and in 1933 was appointed professor of harmony and composition at the Royal Manchester College of Music. In 1938 he settled in London, and was appointed professor of composition at Trinity College of Music, London, in 1947.

Works OPERA *Mary Barton* (1949–54), *The Invisible Duke* (1976).

VOCAL cantata *Holderneth* for baritone, chorus, and orchestra; four Shakespeare sonnets for voice and orchestra.

ORCHESTRAL six symphonies (1946–84), two clarinet concertos, concert overture for orchestra, *Passacaglia, Scherzo, and Finale* for string orchestra, piano concerto.

CHAMBER five string quartets (1933–78), and other chamber music.

Cooke, Benjamin (1734–1793) English organist and composer. He was a pupil of Johann Pepusch, whom he succeeded in 1752 as conductor to the Academy of Ancient Music. In 1757 he was appointed choirmaster at Westminster Abbey, London, in succession to Bernard Gates (c.1685–1773). He was awarded doctorates in music from Cambridge University in 1775, and from Oxford in 1782, when he became organist of St Martin-in-the-Fields, London.

Works CHURCH MUSIC services, anthems (some for special occasions), psalms, chants, and hymns.

ODES ode for Delap's tragedy *The Captives*, *Ode on the Passions* (Collins), odes for Christmas Day, on Handel, on Chatterton, and for the King's recovery, ode *The Syren's Song to Ulysses*.

OTHER glees, catches, and canons; orchestral concertos; organ pieces; harpsichord lessons.

Cooke, Deryck (1919–1976) English musicologist. His best-known works include the book *The Language of Music* (1959) and his performing version of Mahler's unfinished tenth symphony, heard in London, England, on 13 August 1964 (revised 1972).

He studied privately and at Cambridge University. From 1947 to 1959 he worked for the British Broadcasting Corporation, devoting much time to writing and broadcasting.

Coperario, Giovanni (c.1570–1626), adopted name of **John Cooper** English lutenist, viol player, and composer. He studied in Italy and on his return, about 1604, adopted the Italianized name of Coperario or Coprario. He taught the children of James I and was the master of William and Henry Lawes. In 1625 he was appointed composer-in-ordinary to Charles I.

Works *The Masque of the Inner Temple and Gray's Inn* (F Beaumont), *The Masque of Flowers*; *Funeral Teares* on the death of the Earl of Devonshire, *Songs of Mourning* on the death of Prince Henry (words by Campion); anthems; works for viols and for viols and organ; fancies for the organ based on Italian madrigals; lute music; songs and other pieces.

Copland, Aaron (1900–1990) US composer. His early works, such as his piano concerto (1926), were in the jazz style but he gradually developed a gentler style with a regional flavour drawn from American folk music. Among his works are the ballet scores *Billy the Kid* (1938), *Rodeo* (1942), and *Appalachian Spring* (1944; based on a poem by Hart Crane). Among his orchestral works is *Inscape* (1967).

Born in New York, Copland studied in France with Nadia Boulanger, and taught from 1940 at the Berkshire Music Center, now the Tanglewood Music Center, near Lenox, Massachusetts. He took avant-garde European styles and gave them a distinctive American feel. His eight film scores, including *The Heiress* (1949), set new standards for Hollywood.

He began to learn the piano at the age of 13 and studied theory with Rubin Goldmark. He later went to France and became a pupil of Boulanger at the American Conservatory at Fontainebleau. In 1924 a Guggenheim scholarship enabled him to spend two more years in Europe. He was represented for the first time at an International Society for Contemporary Music festival in Frankfurt, Germany, in 1927, and won a prize in American music with *A Dance Symphony* in 1930. He was first influenced by Igor Stravinsky and Boulanger but later used local American styles, notably in the ballets *Billy the Kid* and *Appalachian Spring*. His chamber music is more inward looking and complex in character. He did much to promote American music, and also wrote and lectured extensively. He also toured widely as a conductor of his own and other American music.

Works OPERA *The Tender Land* (1952–54); school opera *The Second Hurricane*.

BALLET *Billy the Kid* (1938), *Rodeo* (1942), *Appalachian Spring* (1944).

FILM *Of Mice and Men* (1939), *Our Town* (1940), *The Red Pony* (1948), *The Heiress* (1949).

ORCHESTRAL three symphonies (1925, 1933, 1946), *Music for the Theatre*, *Symphonic Ode*, *A Dance Symphony* (1925), *Statements*, *El Salón México*

(1936), *Music for the Radio, An Outdoor Overture, Quiet City* (1939), *Letter from Home, Danzón Cubano*; *Lincoln Portrait* for orator and orchestra (1942), piano concerto (1926), clarinet concerto (1948), *Connotations* for orchestra (1962), *Inscape* (1967), *Three Latin American Sketches* (1972).

VOCAL *The House on the Hill* and *An Immorality* for female chorus.

CHAMBER two pieces for string quartet; sextet for clarinet, strings, and piano; piano quartet; nonet; violin and piano sonata; piano sonata, piano pieces.

Coppélia, ou La Fille aux yeux d'émail, Coppelia, or The Girl with Enamel Eyes ballet by Léo Delibes (scenario by C Nuitter and A Saint-Léon; choreographed by L Mérante), first produced at the Paris Opéra, France, on 25 May 1870.

Coptic chant the music of the Christian church in Egypt, which from the middle of the 5th century has been Monophysite. There was a primitive system of notation by the 10th century, but nothing definite is known about the chant in its original form. It still flourishes today, and is characterized by the use of percussion instruments.

Coq d'or, Le opera by Nikolai Rimsky-Korsakov. See ➔ *Golden Cockerel, The*.

cor anglais or **English horn** musical instrument, an alto ➔ oboe, pitched a fifth lower (in F) than the oboe. It has a distinctive tulip-shaped bell and produces a warm nasal tone. It is heard in Rossini's overture to *William Tell* (1829), and portrays a plaintive Sasha the duck in Prokofiev's *Peter and the Wolf* (1936).

The cor anglais has many famous solos in the orchestral repertoire, including the César Franck symphony, Berlioz's *Symphonie fantastique* (1830), Dvořák's *New World* symphony (1893), Sibelius's tone poem *The Swan of Tuonela* (1895), and the famous tune in the slow movement of Rodrigo's *Concierto de Aranjuez* (1939).

corda (Italian 'string') in music, a term to indicate the string or strings of an instrument, as in **una corda** or **u.c.** ('one string') directing a pianist to depress the ➔ **soft pedal**, which moves the hammers so that they strike only one or two strings per key instead of the usual three. **Tre corde** ('three strings') or **tutte le corde** ('all the strings') reverses the marking.

cordatura (Italian 'crying together') in music, the notes to which a string instrument is tuned, such as G, D, A, E for the violin. Any change in the normal tuning made temporarily is called *scordatura*.

Cordier, Baude (lived 1400 or shortly before) French composer. Recent research makes it seem likely that he was the harpist Baude Fresnel (died 1397/98), who was employed at the court of Philip the Bold from 1384. Of his ten surviving chansons two are particularly famous because of their notation: 'Belle, bonne', written out in the form of a heart; and 'Tout par compas', written down in a circle.

Corelli, Arcangelo (1653–1713) Italian composer and violinist. Living at a time when the viol was being replaced by the violin, he was one of the first virtuoso players of the baroque violin, and his music, marked by graceful melody, includes a set of *concerti grossi* and five sets of chamber sonatas.

Born in Fusignano, near Milan, he studied in Bologna and in about 1685 settled in Rome, under the patronage of Cardinal Pietro Ottoboni, where he lived at the palace of his patron and published his first violin sonatas. He visited Modena and Naples, conducted at the Roman residence of Queen Christina of Sweden, collected pictures, and taught many violin pupils, including Francesco Geminiani and Pietro Locatelli. Corelli's music is richer in contrapuntal and harmonic interest than that of any other Italian baroque master, and has been admired for the poise, balance, and brilliance of its style.

Works a set of twelve *Concerti grossi* Op. 6, including no. 8 in G minor, 'fatto per la notte di Natale' (Christmas); five sets of chamber sonatas.

Corigliano, John (1938–   ) US composer. His brilliant and romantic extravaganza *The Ghosts of Versailles* was staged at the New York Metropolitan Opera House in 1991.

He studied with Otto Luening at Columbia University and privately with Paul Creston; and in 1973 began teaching at Lehmann College, New York.

Works ORCHESTRAL violin sonata (1963), *Elegy* for orchestra (1966), piano concerto (1968), clarinet concerto (1977), *Hallucinations* for orchestra (1981), *Echoes of Forgotten Rites* for orchestra (1982), Symphony (1990).

STAGE incidental music for plays by Sophocles, Molière, and Sheridan; opera *The Ghosts of Versailles* (1991).

OTHER *Naked Carmen*, arrangement of Bizet for singers, pop and rock groups, synthesizer, and instruments.

Coriolan Beethoven's overture, Op. 62, to the play of that name by Heinrich von Collin, composed in 1807 and produced with the play in March of that year. Apart from its subject the play has no connection with Shakespeare's *Coriolanus*.

cornamuse Renaissance capped double-reed woodwind musical instrument of straight bore and with a clear, reedy tone.

Corneille, Pierre (1608–1684) French poet and dramatist. His works inspired the composers Marc-Antoine ➔ **Charpentier** (*Polyeucte* and *Andromède*), Paul ➔ **Dukas** (*Polyeucte* overture), Jean-Baptiste ➔ **Lully** (*Œdipe*), Vittorio ➔ **Rieti** (*Illusion comique*), Antonio ➔ **Sacchini** (*Gran Cid*), and Johan ➔ **Wagenaar** (*Cid*); and the works ➔ *Der Cid* and ➔ *Le Cid* (Peter Cornelius and Jules Massenet), ➔ *Poliuto /* ➔ *Les Martyrs* (Donizetti), ➔ *Cleopatra e Cesare* (Karl Graun), ➔ *Flavio* (Handel), ➔ *Polyeucte* (Charles Gounod), ➔ *Roberto Devereux* (Donizetti, Giuseppe Mercadante), and ➔ *Tito Vespasiano* (Antonio Caldara and Johann Hasse).

Corneille, Thomas (1625–1709) French poet and dramatist, brother of Pierre ➔ **Corneille**. His works inspired the composers Jean-Baptiste Lully (➔ *Bellérophon* and ➔ *Psyché*) and Marc-Antoine ➔ **Charpentier** (*Pierre philosophale*, ➔ *Médée*, and two plays with Visé).

Cornelius, Peter (1824–1874) German composer and author. After failing as an actor, he began to study music, first with Siegfried Dehn in Berlin 1845–50, and from 1852 with Liszt in Weimar, where he joined the New German School of musicians and wrote eloquently about them in Schumann's *Neue Zeitschrift*, without however succumbing to Wagnerian influence in his own work. He sought out Wagner in Vienna in 1858 but declined to follow him to Munich in 1865 for the premiere of *Tristan und Isolde*.

Works OPERA *Der Barbier von Bagdad* (1855–58), *Der Cid* (1860–62), *Gunlöd* (unfinished).

VOCAL choral works *Trauerchöre* and *Vätergruft*; duets for soprano and baritone; songs including cycles *Liedercyclus*, *Brautlieder* (1856–58), and *Weihnachtslieder* (1859).

Corner, Philip (1933–) US composer. He studied in Paris, France, with Olivier Messiaen and in New York, USA, with Otto Luening and Henry Cowell, and taught at Rutgers University from 1972. His works show the influence of John Cage, minimalism, and Asian music.

Works THEATRE MUSIC *Carrot Chew Performance* (1963), *Rationalize Outside Sounds* (1966), *Metal Meditations* (1973), *Democracy in Action* (1979).

ORCHESTRAL *This Is It ... This Time* for orchestra (1959); ensemble works, including *Composition With or Without Beverly* (1962).

OTHER *Flares*, mixed media (1963); series '*Gamelan*' from 1975; piano music and works in graphic notation.

cornet soprano three-valved brass instrument, usually in B flat. It is similar in size to the ➔ **trumpet** but squatter in shape, and developed from the coiled post-horn in Austria and Germany between about 1820 and 1850 for military band use. Its cylindrical bore, compact shape, and deeper conical bell, give it greater speed and agility of intonation than the trumpet, at the expense of less tonal precision and brilliance. A small E flat cornet is standard in brass bands alongside a B flat cornet section.

The cornet is typically played with vibrato, and has its own repertoire of virtuoso pieces, heard in brass band concerts and contests, and consisting of voicelike airs, character pieces, Victorian dance forms, and sets of variations. A famous early player was the Frenchman Arban, for whom Hector Berlioz wrote an optional ➔ **obbligato** for the cornet in his *Symphonie fantastique* (1830) (often reinstated now in authentic performance). The cornet is a featured solo in Igor Stravinsky's ballet *Petrushka* (1911) and *The Soldier's Tale* (1918), though its part is now more usually played by the trumpet. It should not be confused with the ➔ **cornett**.

cornett musical instrument, the woodwind precursor of the orchestral brass cornet, of narrow conical bore and with finger holes and a cup mouthpiece. It was often made of wood, or of ivory covered with leather. Its clear, trumpetlike tone made it a favoured instrument of Renaissance ➔ **broken consorts** and baroque orchestras, and although superseded by brass instruments in the 18th century, the cornett remained popular with military and church bands until well into the 19th century.

Members of the cornett family include the straight soprano **mute cornett**, a curved alto **cornetto**, S-shaped tenor **lysarden**, and double S-shaped **serpent**.

corno di bassetto Italian name for the ➔ **basset horn**, a musical instrument.

In 1888–89 Bernard Shaw wrote music criticism for *The Star* under the pseudonym of C di B.

Cornyshe, William (died 1523) English composer. He was attached to the courts of Henry VII and Henry VIII, not only as a musician, but also as an actor and producer of interludes and pageants. He was made a Gentleman of the Chapel Royal in about 1496, and succeeded William Newark as Master of the Children in 1509. He wrote music for the court banquets and masques and officiated in France at the Field of the Cloth of Gold in 1520.

Several other musicians of the period also had the surname Cornyshe, including a **William Cornyshe senior** (died c.1502), who was the first recorded master of the choristers at Westminster Abbey, London, about 1480–90.

Works CHURCH MUSIC motets, Magnificats, *Ave Maria*.

SECULAR songs, some with satirical words, for instruments and voices, including a setting of Skelton's *Hoyda, Jolly Rutterkin*.

coronach (Gaelic 'crying together') a funeral cry or, in its more cultivated musical form, a dirge.

Coronation Anthems four anthems by Handel, composed for the coronation of George II and performed at the ceremony in Westminster Abbey, London, on 11 October 1727. 1. 'Zadok the Priest', 2. 'The King shall Rejoice', 3. 'My heart is Inditing', 4. 'Let Thy Hand be Strengthened'. A number of other composers, from Henry Cooke in the 17th century to Ralph Vaughan Williams in the 20th, have written anthems for coronations in England.

'Coronation' Concerto the nickname of Mozart's piano concerto in D, K537 (dated 24 February 1788), performed by him in Frankfurt, Germany, at the coronation festivities for Leopold II on 15 October 1790.

'Coronation' Mass popular name for Mozart's Mass in C K317 (dated 23 March 1779), so called because it is said to have been written to commemorate the crowning in 1751 of a miraculous image of the Virgin Mary.

Coronation Ode work by Edward Elgar in six sections for soloists, chorus, and orchestra, Op. 44; it was composed 1901–02 and first performed in Sheffield, England, on 2 October 1902. The finale is 'Land of Hope and Glory', based on the tune from his *Pomp and Circumstance* march no. 1.

Corregidor, Der, The Mayor opera by Hugo Wolf (libretto by R Mayreder, based on P A de Alarcón's story *El sombrero de tres picos/The Three-cornered Hat*), first produced in Mannheim, Germany, on 7 June 1896. In the story, Frasquita tries to avoid Don Eugenio's amorous advances while her husband Tio Lukas is detained by the Don's men. Incorrectly believing that Frasquita has been unfaithful, Lukas sets out to seduce the Don's wife, Donna Mercedes. After mistaken identities are resolved, Frasquita and Lukas are reunited.

corrente Italian name for a 17th-century French court dance; see ➔ **courante**.

Corrette, Michel (1709–1795) French organist, teacher, and composer. He held various organist's posts from 1737, and between 1737 and 1784 published 17 methods on performing practice; these included *L'École d'orphée* (1738), for violin, *Les Amusements du Parnasse* (1749), for harpsichord, *Le Parfait Maître à chanter* (1758), *Les Dons d'Apollon* (1762), for guitar, *Les Délices de la solitude* (1766), for cello, *Nouvelle Méthode pour apprendre la harpe* (1774), and *Le Berger galant* (1784), for flute.

Works BALLET *Les Ages* (1733) and *Le Lys* (1752).

SACRED MUSIC motets, Te Deum (1752), Laudate Dominum (1766), *Trois leçons de ténèbres* for low voice and organ (1784).

SECULAR MUSIC vocal pieces including ariettes and cantatas; concertos for musette, vielle, flute, and violin; sonatas; organ and harpsichord music.

Corri, Domenico (1746–1825) Italian conductor, publisher, and composer. He was a pupil of Nicola Porpora. He settled in Edinburgh, Scotland, in 1771 as conductor (of the Music Society), publisher, and singing-master. He failed in business and settled in London, England, around 1790, when he set up in partnership with Jan Dussek, who married his daughter Sophia in 1792. Apart from music, he also wrote theoretical works, including a music dictionary.

Works OPERA *Alessandro nell' Indie* (1774) and *The Travellers* (1806).

INSTRUMENTAL sonatas, rondos, and other pieces.

SONGS including *Six Canzones dedicated to Scots Ladies*.

Corsaire, Le overture by Hector Berlioz, Op. 21, composed in in Italy in 1831, rewritten in Paris, France, in 1844, and first performed there on 19 January 1845 as *La Tour de Nice*. The final version (*Le Corsaire*) was first performed in Brunswick, Germany, on 8 April 1854.

corsaro, Il, The Corsair opera by Giuseppe Verdi (libretto by Francesco Maria Piave, based on Byron's poem), first produced in Trieste, Italy, on 25 October 1848. In the story the Pasha of Coron captures the corsair Corrado, who falls in love with Gulnara, a slave in the harem. She frees him and kills her master, and together they return to Corrado's home, where they find his betrothed, Medora, dying.

Corsi, Jacopo (1561–1602) Italian nobleman and amateur composer. He was involved in the initiation of opera in Florence. Jacopo Peri's *Dafne* was produced at his house in 1598 and he took some share in its composition.

Corteccia, (Pier) Francesco di Bernardo (1502–1571) Italian organist and composer. He made a substantial contribution to the development of the madrigal; many of those he wrote were for particular occasions, the most famous being those composed for the wedding of Duke Cosimo I de' Medici to Eleonora of Toledo in 1539. He also wrote a considerable amount of liturgical music, though this is more conservative in style than his secular compositions.

From 1515 he served the Church of San Giovanni Battista, Florence, in various capacities and was organist there 1535–39. In 1531 he was appointed organist at the Church of San Lorenzo, Florence, and from 1539 was maestro di cappella to Duke Cosimo I. For the marriage of Cosimo's son Fran-

An example by Bach of double counterpoint. The second system reverses the position of each line.

cesco to Joanna of Austria in 1565 he collaborated with the elder Alessandro Striggio on music for Giovanni Battista Cini's intermezzo *Psiche ed Amore*. Corteccia also wrote a prologue, five *intermedii*, and an epilogue for Antonio Landi's comedy *Il comodo*, which was performed at the wedding banquet. The *intermedii* were written for solo singers, ensemble, and varying combinations of instruments to depict different times of the day; they were published in Corteccia's madrigal collection of 1547.

Works hymns in four parts, canticles and responses, madrigals; pieces for four to eight voices and instruments.

Cortot, Alfred (Denis) (1877–1962) French pianist and conductor. After serving as a *répétiteur* (tutor) in Bayreuth, Germany, he founded the Société des Festivals Lyriques in Paris, France, and conducted the first performance in France of Wagner's *Götterdämmerung* in 1902. In addition to his continuous activity as a pianist and conductor he gave many lectures on piano technique and interpretation and collected a valuable library of rare works.

He studied at the Paris Conservatory, where he gained the *premier prix* in 1896. In 1905 he formed a piano trio with Jacques Thibaud and Pablo Casals. From 1907 to 1917 he taught at the Paris Conservatory and in 1918 was joint founder of the École Normale de Musique. He was charged with Nazi collaboration in 1944.

cosa rara, Una opera by Vicente Martín y Soler. See ➔ *Una cosa rara*.

Così fan tutte, o sia La scuola degli amanti, All Women Do It, or The School for Lovers opera by Mozart (libretto by L da Ponte), first produced at the Burgtheater, Vienna, Austria, on 26 January 1790. In the story, Ferrando and Guglielmo test the fidelity of Dorabella and Fiordiligi by swapping partners and courting them in disguise.

Costa, Michael (Michele Andrea Agniello) (1808–1884) Italian-born English conductor and composer of Spanish descent. He studied in Naples and produced his first two operas at the Conservatory there 1826–27, and wrote a Mass, three symphonies, and other works. In 1829 he was sent to Birmingham, England, by Niccolò Zingarelli to conduct a work by that composer at the Festival, but by a mistake was made to sing tenor instead. He then settled in London, wrote many ballets and operas, and perfected the orchestra at the Opera; in 1846 he was appointed conductor of the Philharmonic Society and Covent Garden opera, and he became the most important festival conductor.

Works OPERA *Il delitto punito, Il sospetto funesto, Il carcere d'Ildegonda, Malvina, Malek Adhel* (1838), *Don Carlos* (1844).

BALLET *Kenilworth, Une Heure à Naples, Sir Huon*.

CHURCH MUSIC oratorios *La passione, Eli* (1855), *Naaman* (1864); Mass for four voices; *Dixit Dominus*.

OTHER three symphonies; vocal quartet *Ecco il fiero istante*.

costanza e fortezza, La, Constancy and Fortitude opera by Johann Fux (libretto by P Pariati), first produced at the Hradžin Palace, Prague, at the coronation of the emperor Charles VI as king of Bohemia and the birthday of the empress Elizabeth Christina on 28 August 1723. The plot concerns the Etruscans in a siege of Rome; the opera was composed in elaborate style and staged in great splendour.

Cotton, John (lived 12th century), also known as **John of Afflighem** English or Flemish music scholar. He was the author of a Latin treatise on music which seems to have been widely distributed in manuscript form; six copies are preserved in various European libraries.

Couleurs de la cité céleste work by Olivier Messiaen for piano, 13 wind, xylophone, marimba, and four percussion, composed in 1963. It was first performed in Donaueschingen, Germany, on 17 October 1964, conducted by Pierre Boulez.

counterpoint in music, two or more lines that are arranged so that they fit well together. Even though the combination of the melodies is the main aim, they must make a satisfactory harmony. Another word for this is ➤ **polyphony**. Giovanni Palestrina and Johann Sebastian Bach were masters of counterpoint.

It originated in ➤ **plainsong**, with two independent vocal lines sung simultaneously (Latin *punctus contra punctum* 'note against note').

counter-subject in music, a melody which follows the opening subject (principal melody) in a ➤ **fugue**. Typically, when the second voice enters with the subject, the first voice (which previously sang or played the subject) begins the counter-subject as a contrapuntal complement to the subject.

countertenor the highest natural male voice, as opposed to the ➤ **falsetto** of the male ➤ **alto**. It was favoured by the Elizabethans for its heroic brilliance of tone.

It was revived in the UK by Alfred Deller (1912–1979).

country dance an English dance which became very popular in France in the 18th century and was called *Contredanse* there, having appeared as *Contredanse anglaise* in publication as early as 1699. It spread to other countries, being called *Contratanz* or *Kontretanz* in Germany and Austria. It lost not only its rustic name but also its rustic nature in continental Europe, where it was used for ballroom dancing and cultivated by composers of distinction, including Mozart and Beethoven.

coup d'archet (French 'stroke of the bow') in music, the bow attack in string playing.

coup de glotte (French 'stroke of the glottis') in singing, a trick whereby vowel sounds are preceded by a kind of click in the throat produced by a momentary cutting off of the breath-stream.

It is effective as an inflection and insisted on as a point of good technique by many singing teachers, while others consider it harmful to the voice.

Couperin, François le Grand (1668–1733) French composer. He is the best-known member of a musical family that included his uncle Louis Couperin (c.1626–1661), composer for harpsichord and organ. He was a favourite composer of Louis XIV, and composed numerous chamber concertos and harpsichord suites, and published a standard keyboard tutor *L'Art de toucher le clavecin*/*The Art of Playing the Harpsichord* (1716) in which he laid down guidelines for fingering, phrasing, and ornamentation.

Couperin, Louis (c.1626–1661) French composer, harpsichordist, and organist. He is regarded as one of the finest keyboard composers of the 17th century; among his 215 surviving pieces are allemandes, courantes, sarabandes, chaconnes, and pascailles for harpsichord, preludes, fugues, and plainsong versets for organ, and fantaisies for chamber ensemble.

His father, Charles Couperin (c.1595–1654), was a musician. Louis was sponsored by Jacques Chambonnières, a court musician, and was active in Paris from at least 1651; in 1653 he became the first member of his family to hold the organist's post at Saint-Gervais. He was a treble viol player at court and took part in several ballet performances, including *Psyché* (1656).

coupler in music, an appliance whereby two manuals (keyboards) of an organ or a manual and the pedals can be so connected that while only one is being played the stops controlled by the other are brought into action. Special couplers can also be used to double the notes played automatically an octave above or below.

couplet a verse or stanza in a poem. In music, a strophic song, generally of a light and often of a humorous type, in which the same music recurs for each verse. Also the forerunner of the ➤ **episode** in the ➤ **rondo** form, occurring in the French rondeau as cultivated by Couperin and others, where a main theme returns again and again after statements of various couplets between.

courante (French 'running') 17th-century French court dance. Initially fast in tempo, with an emphasis on mime, it later became codified in a much slower and graver form. It was a favourite dance of Louis XIV. The music for the dance formed one of the standard movements of a baroque ➤ **suite**. The Italian courante, or 'corrente', is in quick triple time (3/8 or 3/4), with continuous 'running' figures in the melody. The French courante is in a more moderate triple time (3/2) or compound duple time (6/4), and often exploits the rhythmic disruption of changing from one metre to the other. J S Bach used this variety in the courantes of his famous *French Suites* (c.1722).

course on a musical instrument, a group of strings which are tuned to the same pitch and are played as one string. Lutes, some guitars, and mandolins have double courses, harpsichords have triple courses, and pianos range from heavy single courses in the bass to quadruple courses in the extreme treble. The 12-string guitar is a modern example of a double-course instrument, each pair tuned to the octave rather than to the unison.

While the original purpose of doubling of strings may have been to increase loudness, an additional factor is improved liveliness of tone caused by beat interference of near-unison strings, an important factor in the tuning of a modern concert grand piano.

Covent Garden popular name of the Royal Opera House at Covent Garden, London, England. The present building was completed in 1858 after two previous ones burnt down. The Royal Ballet is also in residence here.

Cowell, Henry Dixon (1897–1965) US composer and theorist. His pioneering *New Musical Resources* (1930) sought to establish a rationale for modern music. He worked with Percy Grainger in 1941 and alongside John Cage. Although remembered as a discoverer of piano effects such as strumming the strings in *Aeolian Harp* (1923), and for introducing tone-clusters, using a ruler on the keys in *The Banshee* (1925), he was also an astute observer and writer of new music developments.

Cowell also wrote chamber and orchestral music and was active as a critic and publisher of 20th-century music.

Works opera *O'Higgins of Chile* (1949); ballets *The Building of Bamba* (1917) and *Atlantis*; 21 symphonies (1916–65), *Synchrony, Reel, Hornpipe, Sinfonietta, Scherzo*, etc., for orchestra; ten 'tunes', 18 *Hymns and Fuguing Tunes, Exultation* and *Four Continuations* for strings; piano concerto; six string quartets (1915–62); Toccata for soprano (wordless), flute, cello, and piano; other chamber music; many piano works.

Cowen, Frederic (Hymen) (1852–1935) English composer and conductor. He was conductor by turns of the London Philharmonic Society, at Liverpool and Manchester.

He studied in London, Leipzig, and Berlin.

Works STAGE *Pauline* (1876), *Thorgrim, Signa* (1893), *Harold* (1895); operettas and incidental music.

ORATORIOS *The Deluge* (1878), *St Ursula, Ruth* (1887), *The Veil*, and others.

CANTATAS *The Corsair, The Sleeping Beauty, St John's Eve, Ode to the Passions* (Collins), *John Gilpin* (Cowper); cantatas for female voices.

ORCHESTRAL Six symphonies (1869–98: no. 3 *Scandinavian*, no. 4 *Welsh*, no. 6 *Idyllic*); four concert overtures, *Sinfonietta, Indian Rhapsody* and other works for orchestra; concerto and *Concertstück* for piano and orchestra.

CHAMBER string quartet (1866), piano trio.

OTHER jubilee (1897) and coronation (1902)

odes; anthems, part songs; many piano pieces; about 300 songs.

Cowie, Edward (1943–) English composer. Several of his works are based on the story of the Australian criminal Ned Kelly. His interest in painting is reflected in the *Choral Symphony* of 1982, subtitled *Symphonies of Rain, Sea and Speed*.

After studying with Alexander Goehr, Peter Fricker, and Witold Lutosławski, he taught in England, Germany, and Australia.

Works OPERA *Commedia* (1978) and *Kelly* (1980–82).

ORCHESTRAL *Concerto for Orchestra* (1980), two symphonies, *The American* and *The Australian* (1980–82), two clarinet concertos (1969, 1975), harp concerto (1982).

CHAMBER four string quartets (1973–83), *Kelly Passacaglia* for string quartet (1980).

VOCAL *Endymion Nocturnes* for tenor and string quartet (1973, revised 1981), *Kelly Choruses* for voices and harp (1981), *Kate Kelly's Roadshow* for mezzo and ensemble (1982); *Ancient Voices* for four voices (1983).

CHURCH MUSIC *Missa Brevis* (Mass for Peace, 1983).

Cowper, Robert (c.1474–between 1535 and 1540) English composer. He was clerk of King's College, Cambridge, 1493–95, and wrote sacred pieces and carols, notably those in *XX Songs* (1530).

Cradle will Rock, The 'play with music' in ten scenes by Marc Blitzstein. The Federal Theater banned the work because it depicted class warfare in Steeltown, USA. At the first performance on 16 June 1937 the cast sang from stalls seats, with the composer at a piano. Orson Welles directed.

Craft, Robert (1923–) US conductor and writer on music. From 1948 he was closely associated with Igor Stravinsky, and influenced his conversion to serial technique in the early 1950s. He collaborated with Stravinsky in recording his music, and was the first to record the complete works of Anton Webern. He also recorded much of Arnold Schoenberg's music.

He studied at the Juilliard School, New York. At Santa Fe in 1963 he conducted the first US performance of Alban Berg's opera *Lulu* (two-act version). With Stravinsky he compiled six volumes of 'conversations' (1959–69). Other books include *Stravinsky in Photographs and Documents* (1976).

Cramer, Johann Baptist (1771–1858) German-born composer, pianist, and teacher. He is most famous for his 84 studies for piano (1804, 1810), which are still used today. He composed in a con-

The example shows (i) the Mozarabic, (ii) the Gallican, and (iii) the Roman plainsong variants of the Credo.

servative style for his day, trying to emulate the music of Mozart. As a pianist he was admired for his technical command and ➜ **legato** touch. He was one of a group of composers known as the ➜ **London Pianoforte School**.

He was taken to London as a young child, and was taught by his father, Wilhelm Cramer (1746–1799), a violinist. He later went to Muzio Clementi for piano study, and first appeared in public in 1781. In 1824 he established a music publishing business. He lived abroad from 1835 to 1845.

Works nine piano concertos; two piano quartets and quintets; 124 piano sonatas, two volumes of 42 studies each, 16 later studies, 100 daily exercises, and other pieces.

Crawford (Seeger), Ruth (Porter) (1901–1953) US composer. She compiled many folk-song anthologies, including *American Folk Songs for Children* (1948), and wrote hundreds of her own piano accompaniments. Her own compositions are regarded as anticipating certain later developments in music.

She studied at the Chicago Conservatory and with Charles Seeger, whom she later married.

Works suite for piano and woodwind quintet (1927), nine piano preludes (1924–28), string quartet (1931), *Risselty, Rosselty* for small orchestra (1941), *2 Ricercari* for voice and piano (1932).

Creation Mass Mass by Haydn; see ➜ **Schöpfungsmesse**.

Creation, The, German *Die Schöpfung* oratorio by Haydn (libretto by Gottfried van Swieten after an English model, now lost, based on Genesis and John Milton's *Paradise Lost*, first produced at the Schwarzenberg Palace, Vienna, Austria, on 29 April 1798.

Credo (Latin 'I believe') the third item of the Ordinary of the Mass. Its text dates from the Council of Nicea (325), and its use was ordered in the

Mozarabic and Gallican liturgies in 589. It was not introduced into the Roman liturgy until 1071. Later medieval melodies are also known.

crescendo or **cresc. (Italian 'growing')** in music, a term indicating an increase in the loudness of a passage by constant degrees. *Crescendo poco a poco* ('growing little by little') means that the crescendo should progress more gradually. The opposite marking is 'decrescendo' or 'diminuendo'.

Crescentini, Girolamo (1762–1846) Italian male soprano. He made his first appearance in Rome in 1783, and sang in London, England, in 1785–87. In Italy he sang in the first performances of Rispoli's *Ipermestra* (1785), Cimarosa's *Gli Orazi* (1797), Zingarelli's *Meleagro* (1798), and Federici's *Ifigenia* (1809).

Creston, Paul (1906–1985), adopted name of **Joseph Guttovegio** US composer and teacher. His music uses jazzy rhythms and a rich orchestral palette.

He studied piano and organ, but was self-taught in harmony, theory, and composition. He also did research in music therapy, aesthetics, acoustics, and the history of music. In 1938 he was awarded a Guggenheim Fellowship.

Works six symphonies (1941–82), 15 concertos, including one for two violins, much orchestral music; choral works, many based on texts by Whitman; chamber music; songs.

Cristofori, Bartolommeo di Francesco (1665–1731) Italian harpsichord maker, inventor of the piano. In 1709 he constructed a *gravicembalo col piano e forte* ('harpsichord with softness and loudness'), consisting of a harpsichord frame with a new ➜ **action** mechanism: hammers hitting the strings instead of plucking them, allowing for the first time a gradation of soft to loud.

He worked first in Padua and then in Florence.

Three of his pianos survive, dated 1720, 1722, and 1726.

Critic, The, or An Opera Rehearsed opera by Charles Stanford (libretto by L C James, adapted from Richard Brinsley Sheridan's play), first produced at the Shaftesbury Theatre, London, England, on 14 January 1916.

Croce, Giovanni (1557–1609) Italian priest and composer. He was a pupil of Gioseffe Zarlino in Venice, where he worked at St Mark's and succeeded Baldassare Donati as maestro di cappella in 1603. He wrote motets, psalms, madrigals, and *capricci* for voices.

crociato in Egitto, II, The Crusader in Egypt opera by Giacomo Meyerbeer (libretto by Giacomo Rossi), first produced at the Teatro La Fenice, Venice, Italy, on 7 March 1824. The story tells how the crusader Armando, disguised as Elmireno, has secretly married the sultan's daughter, Palmide. In a struggle between Islam and Christianity, Sultan Aladino eventually allows Palmide to accompany Armando to Europe after the crusader saves Aladino's life.

Croesus, in full *Der hochmütige, gestürzte und wieder erhabne Croesus* opera by Reinhard Keiser (libretto by L von Bostel after the Italian of N Minato), first produced at the Theater beim Gänsemarkt, Hamburg, Germany, during Carnival in 1710. In the story, King Croesus battles against King Cyrus and loses. Croesus's mute son, Atis, now able to speak, returns to court and tests the fidelity of Elmira. About to execute Croesus, Cyrus has a change of heart. The happy ending is complete when Atis and Elmira are to marry.

Croft, William (1678–1727) English organist and composer. His most famous work is his setting of the Burial Service, which is still in use. Much other church music survives, including two volumes of anthems published under the title *Musica Sacra* in 1724. Other works include theatrical pieces and keyboard music.

He was a chorister of the Chapel Royal under John Blow. He later became organist of St Anne's, Soho, from 1700 and, with Jeremiah Clarke, of the Chapel Royal from 1704. He was Master of the Children there and organist of Westminster Abbey from 1708, succeeding Blow. He received a PhD in music from Oxford University in 1713.

crook in brass wind instruments, especially horns, a detachable piece of tubing that can be fitted to alter the length of the tube and thus change the tuning.

Crosse, Gordon (1937–) English composer. His works, sometimes showing the influence of Benjamin Britten, include the operas *The Grace*

of *Todd* (1969) and *The Story of Vasco* (1974). He has also written children's theatre pieces and the oratorio *Changes* (1966).

Born in Bury, Lancashire, he was educated at Oxford University and then undertook two years' research into 15th-century music. He studied under Egon Wellesz and later under Goffredo Petrassi in Rome. He has taught at Birmingham University, the University of Essex, and at King's College, Cambridge.

Works STAGE operas *Purgatory* and *The Grace of Todd* (both 1969); ballet *Young Apollo* (1984).

ORCHESTRAL two violin concertos (1962, 1969), two symphonies (1964 and 1976), *Dreamsongs* for orchestra (1979); *Array* for trumpet and strings (1986); *Quiet* for wind band (1987).

CHAMBER string quartet (1980); piano trio (1986).

PIECES FOR CHILDREN *Meet my Folks!* (poems by Ted Hughes; 1964), *Potter Thompson* and *Holly from the Bongs* (both 1974).

cross-fingering in music, a method of fingering woodwind instruments which omits some intermediate holes. It is often convenient, and may sometimes be necessary for high notes.

cross relation in music, an alternative name for ➤ false relation.

cross rhythms in music, either the simultaneous presentation of opposing rhythmic patterns within the same metre (for example one part playing two notes per beat while another part plays three notes per beat, '2 against 3'), or the superimposition of at least two different and unrelated metres (for example 3/4 in one part and 4/4 in another).

Crotch, William (1775–1847) English composer. He was a child prodigy who played the organ at the age of four, went to Cambridge at the age of 11 to assist Randall at the organs of Trinity and King's Colleges, and produced an oratorio *The Captivity of Judah* there in 1789. In 1788 he moved to Oxford to study theology. In 1790 he began to study music and was appointed organist at Christ Church, Oxford; he succeeded Philip Hayes as professor in 1798. On the establishment of the Royal Academy of Music in London in 1822 he became its first principal.

Works ORATORIOS *Palestine* (1805–11) and *The Captivity of Judah* (two settings).

ODES *Ode to Fancy* (J Warton) and ode for the installation of Lord Grenville as Chancellor of Oxford University, ode for the accession of George IV.

CHURCH MUSIC funeral anthem for the Duke of York; anthems and chants, motet *Methinks I hear*.

OTHER glees; concertos and fugues for organ.

crotchet, US **quarter note** in music, a note value one-quarter the duration of a ➤ semibreve. It is written as a filled black note-head with a stem. It is the basic unit of beat for the most frequently used time signatures (2/4, 3/4, 4/4, and so on).

Crozier, Eric (1914–1994) English librettist and stage director. He wrote the libretti for Benjamin Britten's *Albert Herring* (1946), *Saint Nicolas* (1948), *Let's Make an Opera* (1949), and *Billy Budd* (with E M Forster, 1951).

He studied in London and Paris and produced plays for British Broadcasting Corporation (BBC) television 1936–39. He was associated with Britten from 1945 and co-founded with him the English Opera Group in 1947 and the Aldeburgh Festival in 1948. He produced the premiere of *Peter Grimes* in 1945 and its US first performance, at Tanglewood, in 1946, and the premiere of *The Rape of Lucretia*, at Glyndebourne, England, in 1946. He also translated operas by Verdi, Mozart, and Richard Strauss.

Crucible, The opera in four acts by Robert Ward (libretto by composer and B Stambler after Arthur Miller's play), first produced at the New York City Opera on 26 October 1961. It depicts a 17th-century New England witchcraft trial as a precursor of Cold War anti-communist hysteria.

Crüger, Johann (1598–1662) German theorist and composer. He was cantor at St Nicholas's Church, Berlin, from 1622, and wrote several chorales which were later used by Johann Sebastian Bach. He also wrote manuals on singing and composition.

Works SACRED MUSIC *Praxis pietatis melica* containing hymn tunes with bass, *Geistliche Kirchen-Melodien* containing hymn tunes prescribed by Martin Luther, set for four voices with instruments (1649), *Magnificats*.

OTHER secular songs.

Crumb, George Henry (1929–) US composer of imagist works. His music employs unusual graphics and imaginative sonorities, such as the ➤ **musical saw** in *Ancient Voices of Children* (1970), settings of poems by the Spanish poet Federico García Lorca. He won a Pulitzer Prize in 1968 for his orchestral work *Echoes of Time and the River* (1967).

He studied in Berlin, Germany, and at the University of Michigan, Ann Arbor. His early work was influenced by Arnold ➤ **Schoenberg**, and he has also used improvisational techniques.

Works ORCHESTRAL *Variazoni* (1959), *Echoes of Time and the River* (1967).

INSTRUMENTAL *11 Echoes of Autumn* for violin, flute, clarinet, piano (1965), *Black Angels* for amplified string quartet, *13 Images from the Dark Land* (1970), *Voice of the Whale*, with electronics (1972), four books of *Makrokosmos* for ampli-

fied piano and percussion (1972–79), *Processional* for piano (1983), *A Haunted Landscape* for instrumental ensemble (1984), *An Idyll for the Misbegotten* for amplified flute and three percussionists (1985), *Zeitgeist* for two amplified pianos (1987).

VOCAL *Night Music* for soprano and ensemble (1963), four books of madrigals for soprano, with various instrumental ensembles (1965–69), *Ancient Voices of Children* for soprano and ensemble (1970), *Star-Child* for soprano, children's voices, male speaking choir, bell ringers, and orchestra, performed New York, 1977, conductor Boulez), *Federico's Little Songs* for soprano, flute, and percussion (1986).

crumhorn ('curved horn') any of a Renaissance woodwind family of musical instruments with a double reed enclosed in a cap, and with soprano, alto, tenor, and bass members. It has a narrow cylindrical bore and is curved upwards like a walking stick held upside down. It dates from the 15th century and emits a buzzing tone.

Crusell, Bernhard Henrik (1775–1838) Finnish composer and clarinettist. He was a member of the military band at Svaeborg Castle, Finland, before moving to Stockholm in 1791, where he studied with the Abbé Vogler. In 1798 he went to Berlin, Germany, and in 1803 studied with Henri-Montan Berton and François Gossec in Paris, France. A leading clarinet virtuoso of his day, he also worked at the Stockholm Opera, translating and conducting for the first time in Sweden operas by Beethoven, Rossini, Meyerbeer, and Auber.

Works OPERA *Den lilla slavinnan/The Little Slave Girl* (1824).

ORCHESTRAL three clarinet concertos (1811, 1818, 1828), Concertante for horn, bassoon, clarinet, and orchestra (1816), Concertino for bassoon and orchestra.

CHAMBER three quartets for clarinet and strings (1811, 1817, 1823), three clarinet duos (1821), Divertimento for oboe and strings (1823).

VOCAL 37 songs for four-part chorus.

crwth or **crot**, **crotta**, **crotte**, or **rotte (Welsh 'crowd')** early bowed string instrument, ancestor of the ➤ **violin family**.

Cry work by Giles Swayne for 28 amplified voices, depicting the creation of the world; it was composed in 1978 and first performed in London, England, on 23 July 1980.

csárdás a Hungarian dance consisting of a slow movement called *lassú* and a quick one called *friss*.

Cubana, La, oder Ein Leben für die Kunst, La Cubana, or a Life for the Arts vaudeville by Hans Werner Henze (text by M Enzensberger, after M Barnet); it was composed in 1973, first performed at the NET theatre, New York, on 4 March 1974, and given its stage premiere at the Theater am Gärtnerplatz, Munich, Germany, on 28 May 1975.

cue in music, a few notes printed in small type in instrumental or vocal parts of a work, serving as a guide to show where the performer is to come in after a lengthy rest.

Cui, César Antonovich (1835–1918) Russian composer and writer, of French parentage. An army engineer by profession, he became a member of 'The ➤ **Five**' group of composers and was an enthusiastic proponent of Russian nationalist music in the press. Despite this, his own musical tastes tended towards the France of Daniel Auber and Giacomo Meyerbeer in the operas *Angelo* (1876), based on Victor Hugo, and *Le Flibustier/ The Buccaneer* (1889), based on a play by Jean Richepin.

Cui composed some attractive vocal and piano miniatures, and ten operas, including *A Prisoner in the Caucasus* (1857–58), first performed in 1883, and *William Ratcliff* (1861–68), first performed in 1869. He also collaborated with Aleksandr Borodin, Modest Mussorgsky, Nikolai Rimsky-Korsakov, and Léon Minkus on the opera-ballet *Mlada*, and completed Mussorgsky's *Sorochintsy Fair*.

Cui was educated at the High School of Wilno, where his father, a French officer left behind in the retreat from Moscow in 1812, was professor of French. He had some lessons in music from Stanisław Moniuszko, but was sent to the School of Military Engineering in St Petersburg in 1850, where he became subprofessor in 1857. He became an authority on fortifications and remained an amateur in music, but he joined Mily Balakirev's circle of Russian nationalist composers and became one of 'The Five', though the least exclusively Russian among them. He became a critic in 1864 and did much literary work for the nationalist cause.

Works OPERA *A Prisoner in the Caucasus* (after Pushkin; 1857–58, produced 1883), *The Mandarin's Son* (1859, produced 1878), *William Ratcliff* (after Heine; 1861–68, produced 1869), *Angelo* (after Hugo; 1876), *Le Flibustier* (libretto by J Richepin; 1889), *The Saracen* (after Dumas senior; 1889), *A Feast in Time of Plague* (Pushkin; 1900), *Mam'zelle Fifi* (after Maupassant), *Matteo Falcone* (after Mérimée), and *The Captain's Daughter* (1911).

OTHER works for chorus with and without orchestra; four suites and other works for orchestra; string quartets in C minor (1890) and D (1907); 15 Op. nos of piano pieces, three pieces for two pianos; various instrumental pieces; about 25 Op. nos of songs including settings of

Pushkin, Lermontov, Nekrassov, Richepin, and Mickiewicz.

cuivré (French 'brassy') in music, term used to instruct brass players to play particularly forcefully, causing a brash, ringing tone. The effect is especially associated with the French horn.

Cummings, Conrad (1948–) US composer. He studied at Yale, Stanford, and Tanglewood, and has worked at the Columbia-Princeton Electronic Music Center and at the Institut de Recherche et de Co-ordination Acoustique-Musique (IRCAM) in Paris, France. He has been a teacher at the Oberlin Conservatory from 1980. His music draws on baroque models as well as electronic resources.

Works OPERA *Eros and Psyche* (1983), *Cassandra* (1985, revised as a dramatic scene), *Positions* (1956) (1988, after 1950s sex manuals), *Insertions* (1988), *Photo-Op* (1989), and *Tonkin* (after an incident in the Vietnam War, 1993).

OTHER *Subway Songs* for four-track tape (1974), *Movement* for orchestra (1975), *Skin Songs* for soprano and ensemble (1978), *Dinosaur Music* for ten-track tape and 14 loudspeakers (1981), *Music for Starlore* for stereo tape (1982).

cummings, e(dward) e(stlin) (1894–1962) US poet whose works inspired the musicians Richard R Bennett (*Love Songs*), Luciano ➤ **Berio** (*Circles*), Pierre ➤ **Boulez** (*cummings ist der Dichter*), Peter ➤ **Dickinson** (songs), Donald Erb (*Cummings Cycle*), Edward ➤ **Harper** (*Seven poems by e e cummings*), and Roger ➤ **Smalley** (septet for soprano and ensemble).

Cummings, W(illiam) H(ayman) (1831–1915) English organist, tenor, and scholar. He sang under Felix Mendelssohn's direction as a boy and later made an edition of 'Hark! the Herald Angels Sing' to music from Mendelssohn's *Festgesang*. He sang in Johann Sebastian Bach's Passions and conducted the Sacred Harmonic Society; co-founded the Purcell Society and edited three volumes for it; and wrote a biography of Henry Purcell (1881). He also wrote on John Blow, Thomas Arne, and Handel (biography, 1904). He was principal of the Guildhall School of Music and Drama 1896–1910.

cummings ist der Dichter, cummings is the poet work by Pierre Boulez for 16 voices and 24 instruments, composed in 1970 and first performed in Stuttgart, Germany, on 25 September 1970; it was revised in 1986. The title allegedly arose as the result of a misheard telephone conversation, concerning the name of the poet who provided the text for the work (e e cummings).

Cunning Little Vixen, The, Czech *Příhody lišky Bystroušky* opera by Leoš Janáček (libretto by the composer after R Těsnohlídek's verses for a comic strip published serially in a Brno newspaper during 1920). It was composed 1921–23 and first produced in Brno (Czech Republic) on 6 November 1924. The story tells how the vixen is captured but escapes, marries, and raises a litter. She is shot by a poacher, but her spirit survives in her cubs.

Cupid and Death masque by James Shirley with music by Matthew Locke and Christopher Gibbons, first performed at Leicester Fields, London, England, before the Portuguese ambassador on 26 March 1653.

curioso indiscreto, Il, Indiscreet Curiosity opera by Pasquale Anfossi (librettist unknown), first produced at the Teatro della Dame, Rome, Italy, in February 1777. Mozart wrote two extra soprano arias for it when it was produced in Vienna, Austria, on 30 June 1783. The story tells how the Marchese Calandrino tests the fidelity of Clorinda, who falls in love with the Contino, the Marchese's friend.

Curlew River church parable in one act by Benjamin Britten (libretto by W Plomer after the Japanese Nō play *Sumidagawa*), first produced in Orford Church, Suffolk, England, on 12 June 1964. It tells how a ferryman conveys a madwoman to her son's grave and how, during prayer, an angel restores her sanity.

Curran, Alvin (1938–) US composer. He studied with Elliott Carter at Yale, and in Rome, Italy, he co-founded the group Musica Electronica Viva in 1966; he has also given solo performances at festivals of new music.

Works *Songs and Views from the Magnetic Gardens* (1975); *Light Flowers, Dark Flowers* (1977); *The Works* (1980); *Maritime Rites* for foghorns, ships, and rowing boats full of singers (1984); *Crystal Psalms*, with six choruses (1988); *Electric Rags I* and *II* (1985, 1989).

curtain tune an old term sometimes used in the place of 'act tune' for an ➤ **intermezzo** or entr'acte in the incidental music for a play.

curtal capped double-reed Renaissance woodwind instrument, ancestor of the ➤ **bassoon**, of folded conical bore and mild reedy tone, also known as the **dulcian**.

Curtis, Alan (1934–) US conductor, harpsichordist, and musicologist. He is an authority on early keyboard music and has edited for recording and produced several 17th-century operas, including Monteverdi's *L'incoronazione di Poppea*, Pietro Cavalli's *L'Erismena*, and Pietro Cesti's *Il Tito* at Innsbruck, Switzerland, in 1983. He studied at Michigan and Illinois universities in the USA and with Gustav Leonhardt in Amsterdam, the Netherlands.

Curtis Institute of Music music school in Philadelphia, USA, founded by Mary Louise Bok in 1924 in memory of her father, Cyrus Curtis. Since 1928 students have not had to pay tuition fees. Directors have included Josef Hofmann (1926–38), Efrem Zimbalist (1941–68), Rudolf Serkin (1968–76), John de Lancie (1977–85), and Gary Graffman (from 1986).

Curwen English family of music educationists and publishers:

John (1816–1880), founded the Tonic Sol-fa method of music notation (originated in the 11th century by Guido d'Arezzo), in which the notes of the diatonic major scale are named by syllables (doh, ray, me, soh, lah, te) to simplify singing by sight; he established the Tonic Sol-fa Association in 1853 and the publishing firm in London in 1863.

John Spencer (1847–1916), son of John. He studied at the Royal Academy of Music, London, under Macfarren, Sullivan, and Prout, carried on his father's work, and began the competition festival movement in England with the Stratford (East London) Festival in 1882.

Annie (Jessy), born Gregg, later Matlock (1845–1932), wife of John Spencer. She studied at the Royal Irish Academy of Music, married in 1877, and wrote a number of books on a music-teaching method of her own.

cut time in music, an alternative term for ➤ **alla breve**.

cyclic form in musical analysis, a multi-movement work in which the same motif, theme, melody, or other notable compositional element is used throughout, at times in a different context or manifestation from its original form. Early examples include works by Handel and Vivaldi, but not until the 19th century did this technique reach its fruition, in works including Beethoven's Fifth Symphony (1808), Liszt's Piano Sonata in B Minor (1853), and compositions based on the theories of Wagner's ➤ **leitmotif** and Berlioz's 'idée fixe' (a repeated ➤ **theme**).

cyclic Mass a misleading term for a setting of the Ordinary of the Mass in which there is some kind of thematic connection between the movements.

cymbal ancient percussion instrument of indefinite pitch. It consists of a shallow, circular brass dish suspended from the centre. They are either used in pairs clashed together or singly, struck with a beater. Crashed cymbals can be heard in Dvořák's first and eighth *Slavonic Dances*. Extensive use of cymbals is found in much 20th-century orchestral music, often in conjunction with gongs and tam tams, such as in the The *Triumph of Time* (1972) by Harrison Birtwistle.

Smaller finger cymbals or **crotala**, of ancient origin but used in the 20th century by Claude Debussy and Karlheinz Stockhausen, are precise in pitch. Rivet or 'buzz' cymbals incorporate loose rivets to add a sizzle to the sound. This effect can also be achieved by draping small chains over the cymbal.

Cymon opera by Michael Arne (libretto by David Garrick, based on John Dryden's *Cymon and Iphigenia*), first produced at the Drury Lane Theatre, London, on 2 January 1767.

Cyrano opera by Walter Damrosch (libretto by W J Henderson, based on Edmond Rostand's play *Cyrano de Bergerac*), first produced at the New York Metropolitan Opera on 27 February 1913.

Cyrano de Bergerac opera by Franco Alfano (libretto by H Cain, based on Edmond Rostand's play), first produced in Italian translation at the Teatro Reale, Rome, Italy, on 22 January 1936.

Cythère assiégée, La, Cytherea Besieged opera by Christoph Willibald von Gluck (libretto by C S Favart, based on Longus' *Daphnis and Chloe*), first produced at the Burgtheater, Vienna, Austria, in the spring of 1759. In the story Scythian warriors lay siege to Cytherea but fall in love with her attendant nymphs.

Czaar und Zimmermann opera by Gustav Lortzing; see ➤ *Zar und Zimmermann*.

czakan woodwind instrument of the ➤ **flute** type, probably originating from Transylvania but very fashionable in Vienna, Austria, around 1830, made in the shape of a walking stick and often used as such.

Czernohorsky Bohemian composer, theorist, and friar; see Bohuslav ➤ **Cernohorský**.

Czerny, Carl (1791–1857) Austrian pianist, teacher, and composer. He was first taught the piano by his father, played brilliantly at the age of ten, and became a pupil of Beethoven about that time; he also took advice from Johann Hummel and Muzio Clementi. Not liking to appear in public, he took to teaching and soon had an enormous following of pupils, among which he chose only the most gifted. This left him enough leisure for composition, which he cultivated so assiduously as to produce almost 1,000 works. He is chiefly remembered for his books of graded studies and technical exercises used in piano teaching, including the *Complete Theoretical and Practical Pianoforte School* (1839) which is still in widespread use.

Works 24 Masses, four Requiems, 300 graduals and offertories; many symphonies, overtures, concertos, string quartets and trios; choruses, songs and much piano music, including studies, exercises, preludes, and fugues in all the keys and endless arrangements of other composers' works.

d in music, the tonic note in any key in tonic sol-fa notation, pronounced 'doh'.

D in music, the second note, or supertonic, of the scale of C major.

D in music, abbreviation for **Deutsch**; D followed by a number (for example, D956) indicates the listing of a work by Schubert in the thematic catalogue by Otto Erich Deutsch.

da capo (Italian 'from the top') term in written music instructing a player that the music at that point starts from the beginning. It is abbreviated to 'D.C.'. A companion instruction is dal segno ('from the sign').

da capo al fine (Italian 'from the beginning to the end') musical phrase in which the performer is asked to go back to the beginning; with the simple *da capo*, the composition is not to be repeated as a whole, but only to the point where the word *fine* ('end') appears.

da capo aria a distinctive type of vocal piece for a single voice (though duets and other ensemble pieces may be in the same form) consisting of three sections, the third of which is a repetition of the first, while the middle section is a contrast based sometimes on similar and sometimes on wholly different thematic material. The da capo aria was cultivated in the second half of the 17th and first half of the 18th century (up to the earlier works of Christoph Willibald von Gluck), notably by Alessandro Scarlatti, Handel, Johann Sebastian Bach, Johann Hasse, and Niccolò Jommelli.

Dafne opera by Heinrich Schütz (libretto by Martin Opitz, partly translated from Ottavio Rinuccini), first produced at Hartenfels Castle, Torgau, Germany, at the wedding of Georg, Landgrave of Hesse, and Sophia Eleonora, Princess of Saxony, on 23 April 1627. The music has not survived.

Dafne, La opera by Jacopo Peri (libretto by Ottavio Rinuccini), first produced in the Palazzo Corsi, Florence, Italy, during Carnival in 1597. It is the first Italian opera and the first opera on record anywhere. In the story, Apollo belittles Cupid but then falls victim to the arrows of love, pursuing an unyielding Daphne.

Marco da Gagliano's opera of the same name (libretto by Rinuccini) was first produced at the ducal court in Mantua, Italy, in January 1608.

Dafni opera by the Baron d'Astorga (libretto by E Manfredi), first produced at the Teatro Sant' Agostino, Genoa, Italy, on 21 April 1709.

Dahl, Ingolf (1912–1970) German-born US composer. After study in Cologne, Germany, and Zurich, Switzerland, he moved to the USA in 1935, teaching at the University of Southern California from 1945. His earlier work was dissonant and expressionistic; he later came under Stravinsky's influence.

Works ORCHESTRAL Concerto for saxophone and wind orchestra (1949), Symphony Concertante for two clarinets and orchestra (1953), *The Tower of St Barbara* for orchestra (1955), *Elegy Concerto* for violin and orchestra (1963), *Aria Sinfonica* (1965), *Intervals* for strings (1970).
CHAMBER piano quartet (his first serial work, 1957).

Dahlhaus, Carl (1928–1989) German musicologist. A prolific writer on music theory and history, his books and articles cover an enormous range of topics and periods; he is best known for his studies in 19th-century music and history. He was extremely influential in German-speaking musicology, and increasingly so in English-speaking circles from the early 1980s when his major works began to be translated. Dahlhaus believed that music cannot be divorced from the society and culture which produces it; therefore, an understanding of musical history can only flow from an understanding of history in a wider sense. He was influenced by the historical theories of Hegel and Marx, and by the philosophical approach to music taken by Theodor Adorno. His theoretical writings include *Esthetics of Music* (1967) and *Foundations of Music History* (1977); historical studies include *Nineteenth-Century Music* (1980), *Ludwig van Beethoven* (1987), and the articles collected as *Schoenberg and the New Music* (1987).

Dalayrac, Nicolas-Marie (1753–1809), born **Nicolas-Marie d'Alayrac** French composer. In 1777 he published six string quartets, and two small operas were performed privately in 1781. The following year he made his debut with *L'Eclipse totale/The Total Eclipse* at the Théâtre Italien. He changed his name from its aristocratic form during the Revolution, and adapted operatic airs to lyrics with Republican sentiments.

He first intended to study law, then in 1774 went to Versailles to embark on a military career, but his main interest was music and he took lessons in composition from Honoré Langlé (1741–1807).

Works OPERA about 60 operas, including *Nina ou La Folle par amour* (1786), *Les Deux Petits Savoyards*, *Camille*, *Adolphe et Clara* (1799), *Maison à vendre*.

OTHER 36 string quartets.

Dalby, Martin (1942–) Scottish composer. He studied at the Royal College of Music, London, with Herbert Howells (composition) and Frederick Riddle (viola). He has been influenced by jazz and by Spanish music; from 1965 he has held administrative posts in London and Glasgow.

Works ORCHESTRAL symphony (1970), *Concerto Martin Pescatore*, for strings (1971), viola concerto (1974), *Nozze di primavera* for orchestra (1984).

VOCAL *Keeper of the Pass* for soprano and instruments (1971), *Orpheus* for chorus, narrator, and eleven instruments (1972), *Call for the Hazel Tree*, for chorus and electronics (1979).

CHAMBER *Yet Still She is the Moon*, brass septet (1973), *Aleph* for eight instruments (1975), *Man Walking*, octet for wind and strings (1980); two piano sonatas (1985, 1989).

Dalcroze, Emile Jaques- Swiss composer and teacher; see Emile ➤ Jaques-Dalcroze.

Dale, Benjamin (1885–1943) English composer. He studied at the Royal Academy of Music in London, where he later became professor of composition and warden.

Works cantata *Before the Paling of the Stars* (1912), and *Song of Praise* for chorus and orchestra (1923); violin and piano sonata.

Dalibor opera by Bedřich Smetana (libretto in German by J Wenzig, translated into Czech by E Špindler), first produced at the Czech Theatre, Prague, on 16 May 1868. In the story Milada attempts to rescue the imprisoned Dalibor, but her plan is betrayed and both die in a final battle.

Dallam, Thomas (c.1570–after 1614) English organ builder. He built organs for King's College, Cambridge, and Worcester Cathedral. He travelled to Constantinople (Istanbul, Turkey) in 1599–1600 with a mechanical organ, a present from Queen Elizabeth I to the sultan.

Robert Dallam (1602–1665), Ralph Dallam (died 1673), and George Dallam, also organ builders, were probably members of the same family.

Dallapiccola, Luigi (1904–1975) Italian composer. Initially a neoclassicist, he adopted a lyrical 12-tone style after 1945. His works include the operas *Il prigioniero/The Prisoner* (1944–48) and *Ulisse/Ulysses* (1960–68), as well as many vocal and instrumental compositions.

Dallapiccola was born in Pisino, Istria. For political reasons his family was moved to Graz, Austria, in 1917, where his decisive first contacts with music (especially opera) were made. The family returned to Italy in 1921, where Dallapiccola studied at the Florence Conservatory and in 1931 became professor. In 1956 he was appointed professor at Queen's College, New York. His mature music, while using serial techniques, modified them to allow for a more lyrical style than is usual, not avoiding tonal references, thematic structures, and harmonic progressions.

He first attracted international attention at pre-1939 festivals of the International Society for Contemporary Music (ISCM). His *Canti di prigionia/Songs of Captivity* were prompted by the fascist racial laws of 1938, and represent the expression in music of an imprisonment that was as much mental as physical. This 'protest music', with its theme of mental persecution, was continued in his later opera *Il prigioniero* (after *La Torture par l'espérance* by Villiers de l'Isle Adam) and the choral *Canti di liberazione/Songs of Liberty* (1951–55). His early opera *Volo di notte* (1937–39; after Antoine de Saint-Exupéry) makes tentative use of serial techniques which were brought to fruition in his highly personal and poetic manner in the group of *Liriche greche/Greek Lyrics* (1942–45). In the 1950s Dallapiccola was much influenced by Anton Webern, and his own personal style gave way to a less poetic and more cerebral expression. Nevertheless his supremacy as a vocal writer was maintained on the large oratorio *Job* (1950) and *Requiescant* (1957–58), and small works such as *Goethe Lieder* (1953), *Cinque canti* (1956), *Preghiere* (1962), and *Parole di San Paolo* (1964). His large opera *Ulysses*, the fruit of ten years' work, reveals a return to his earlier poetic style. Dallapiccola was not successful with instrumentalism in spite of his excellence as an orchestrator. He had great influence in post-war Italy, and played a dominant part in the cultural renaissance of that country.

Works OPERA *Volo di notte* (1937–39), *Il prigioniero* (1944–48), *Ulisse* (1960–68).

BALLET ballet *Marsia* (1942–43).

VOICES AND ORCHESTRAL *Tre laudi* (1936–37) for solo voice and orchestra, *Canti di prigionia* (1941), *Canti di liberazione* (1951–55), *Concerto per la notte di natale* for soprano and orchestra (1957).

ORCHESTRAL *Piccolo concerto* for piano and orchestra (1941), *Tartiniana*, divertimento for violin and chamber orchestra (1951), *Piccola musica notturna* (1954; for chamber ensemble 1961).

OTHER music for three pianos; *Liriche anacreontiche Roncevals*, cycle of Greek and other songs; *Ciaccona, intermezzo e adagio* for solo cello (1945).

dal segno (Italian 'from the sign') term in written music instructing a player that the music at that point recommences from a place other than the beginning, indicated in the score by a crossed 'S' sign. The abbreviated form is 'D.S.'. To start from the beginning, the instruction is da capo ('from the top').

Dame blanche, La, **The White Lady** opera by François Boieldieu (libretto by Augustin Scribe, based on Walter Scott's *Guy Mannering* and *The Monastery*), first produced at the Opéra-Comique, Paris, France, on 10 December 1825. It contains some Scottish tunes. In the story, George Brown prevents the castle from falling into the wrong hands at an auction. With help from the orphan Anna, it is revealed that George is actually the missing heir, Julien Avenel.

Damett, Thomas (1389 or 1390–c.1437) English composer. He was at the Chapel Royal 1413–31, and was canon of Windsor from 1431 until his death. Works of his are included in the Old Hall manuscript.

Damnation de Faust, La dramatic cantata by Hector Berlioz (words by composer and A Gandonnière, based on Goethe's drama), composed in 1846, incorporating the *Huit Scènes de Faust* of 1828. It was first performed at the Opéra-Comique, Paris, France, on 6 December 1846, and first produced as an opera in Monte Carlo, Monaco, on 18 February 1893.

Damoiselle élue, La, **The Blessed Damozel** cantata for soprano, mezzo-soprano, and female chorus and orchestra by Claude Debussy, set to a French translation by Gabriel Sarrazin of Rossetti's poem in 1887–88. It was first performed at the Salle Erard, Paris, France, on 8 April 1893.

Dämon, Der, **The Demon** dance pantomime by Paul Hindemith (scenario by M Krell), composed in 1922 and first performed in Darmstadt, Germany, on 1 December 1923. The concert suite for small orchestra was arranged in 1923.

damper pedal on a piano, an alternative name for the → **sustaining pedal**. The tone is sustained because the pedal lifts the dampers off the strings. It should not be confused with the damping pedal.

damping pedal on a piano, the 'soft' pedal, which on a grand piano shifts the hammers of the instrument so that they touch only two

strings or a single string for each note, instead of three or two. For this reason its use is often indicated by the words *una corda* ('one string'). This outdated term should not be confused with the → **damper pedal**.

Damrosch, Walter (Johannes) (1862–1950) US conductor and composer, son of Leopold Damrosch. He studied in Germany and settled in the USA in 1871, and became conductor of the New York Oratorio and Symphonic Societies in 1885. He was director of the Damrosch Opera Company 1894–99, giving the first US performances of several operas by Wagner.

Works STAGE operas *The Scarlet Letter* (after Hawthorne; 1896), *Cyrano de Bergerac* (after Rostand; 1913), *The Dove of Peace*, *The Man without a Country* (1937); incidental music to Euripides' *Electra*, *Iphigenia in Aulis*, and *Medea*.

OTHER *Abraham Lincoln's Song* for baritone solo, chorus, and orchestra; Te Deum; violin and piano sonata; songs.

Danaïdes, Les opera by Antonio Salieri (libretto by F L du Roullet and L T de Tschudy, partly based on and translated from Raniero de Calzabigi's *Ipermestra* intended for Christoph Willibald von Gluck, composed by Millico), first produced at the Paris Opéra, France, on 26 April 1784. In the story, when Danaus orders his 50 daughters to kill their husbands, Hypermestra alone refuses for love of Lynceaus.

dance of death (German *Totentanz*; French *danse macabre*) popular theme in painting of the late medieval period, depicting an allegorical representation of death (usually a skeleton) leading the famous and the not-so-famous to the grave. One of the best-known representations is a series of woodcuts (1523–26) by Hans Holbein the Younger. It has also been exploited as a theme in music, for example the *Danse macabre* of Saint-Saëns (1874), an orchestral composition in which the xylophone was introduced to represent dancing skeletons.

Dance Rhapsody two works for orchestra by Frederick Delius: no. 1, composed in 1908 and first performed at the Hereford Festival, England, on 8 September 1909, conducted by Delius; and no. 2, composed in 1916 and first performed in London on 23 October 1923, conducted by Henry Wood.

Dances of Galánta orchestral work by Zoltán Kodály, composed for the 80th anniversary of the Budapest Philharmonic Society and first performed in Budapest, Hungary, on 11 December 1936.

Dances of Marchosszék work for piano by Zoltán Kodály, composed in 1927. The version for orchestra was first performed in Dresden,

Germany, on 28 November 1930, conducted by Fritz Busch.

Dance Suite work for orchestra in six movements by Béla Bartók, composed in 1923 for the 50th anniversary of the merging of Pest, Buda, and Obuda into Budapest. It was first performed in Budapest, Hungary, on 19 November 1925, conducted by Ernst von Dohnányi. A version for piano was arranged in 1925.

Dandrieu or **d'Andrieu, Jean François (1682–1738)** French organist and composer. He succeeded his uncle, Pierre Dandrieu, as organist of the church of Saint-Barthélemy in Paris, and in 1704 he became organist at Saint-Merry. He was appointed organist of the royal chapel in 1721. He wrote a book on harpsichord accompaniment.

Works a set of symphonies *Les Caractères de la guerre* (1718); trios for two violins and bass; violin sonatas; organ pieces; three volumes of harpsichord pieces.

Daniel-Lesur, adopted name of **Daniel Jean Yves Lesur (1908–2002)** French organist and composer. In 1938 he became professor of counterpoint at the Schola Cantorum in Paris. He was also appointed organist at the Benedictine abbey. With Yves Baudrier, André Jolivet, and Olivier Messiaen, he formed the group known as 'La Jeune France' in 1936.

His teachers included Charles Tournemire and George Caussade (1873–1936).

Works OPERA *Andrea del Sarto* (1969), *Ondine* (1982), *La Reine morte* (1987).

ORCHESTRAL *Suite française* for orchestra (1935), *Passacaille* for piano and orchestra (1937), *Fantasie concertante* for cello and orchestra (1993).

VOCAL *Le Voyage d'automne* for voices and orchestra (1990), three Heine songs for voice and string quartet, other songs.

CHAMBER suite for string trio and piano, *Noëls* and suite *Le Carillon* for piano.

OTHER *La Vie intérieure* for organ.

Daniel, The Play of, or Latin **Danielis Ludus** medieval liturgical music drama dealing with the story of Daniel in the lions' den. It was written by for Beauvais Cathedral, France, between 1227 and 1234 and intended almost certainly for performance after matins on the feast of the Circumcision (1 January).

Danse, La last of three entrées which make up Jean-Philippe Rameau's opéra-ballet *Les Fêtes d'Hébé* (libretto by A G de Montdorge), first produced at the Paris Opéra, France, on 21 May 1739. It is often heard as a separate item.

Danse sacrée et danse profane work by Claude Debussy for harp and strings, composed in 1903 and first performed in Paris, France, on 6 November 1904.

Danses Concertantes work for chamber orchestra by Igor Stravinsky, composed in 1942 in Hollywood, USA, and first performed in Los Angeles on 8 February 1942.

Dante Alighieri (1265–1321) Italian poet. His works and thought inspired musical compositions such as the ➤ *Dante Sonata* and ➤ *Dante Symphony* by Liszt. More specifically, his ➤ *Francesca da Rimini* inspired operas by Herman Goetz, Eduard Nápravník, Rachmaninov, Ambroise Thomas, and Riccardo Zandonai, as well as a symphonic fantasy by Tchaikovsky. The cantata *La vita nuova* by Ermanno ➤ **Wolf-Ferrari** was also based on Dante.

Dante and Beatrice symphonic poem by Granville Bantock, first performed at the London Music Festival in 1911.

Dante Sonata one-movement sonata by Franz Liszt, entitled *D'Après une lecture du Dante*, in the Italian volume of his *Années de pèlerinage*, composed 1837–39 and revised in 1849. Liszt called it a *sonata quasi fantasia*.

Dante Symphony symphony by Franz Liszt based on Dante's *La divina commedia*, composed 1855–56 and first performed in Dresden, Germany, on 7 November 1857. There are two movements, *Inferno* and *Purgatorio*.

Dantons Tod, Danton's Death opera by Gottfried von Einem (libretto by Boris Blacher and Einem, based on Georg Büchner's drama), first produced in Salzburg, Austria, on 6 August 1947. It is set during the French Revolution. The evil Robespierre spreads rumours that Danton is an aristocrat. After the trial Danton is guillotined; Lucile, the wife of his friend Desmoulins (also killed) longs for death.

danza, La opera in one act by Christoph Willibald von Gluck (libretto by Pietro Metastasio), first performed in Vienna, Austria, on 5 May 1755.

Danzi, Franz (1763–1826) German cellist and composer. He was a minor member of the Manheim school of symphonists. A pupil of Georg Vogler, he was a member of the court band in Mannheim and, from 1778, in Munich. He was Kapellmeister to the court of Württemberg in Stuttgart, and later in Karlsruhe.

Works the operas *Die Mitternachtsstunde* (1788), *Turandot* (after Gozzi; 1817); church music; symphonies, concertos and concertantes; chamber music.

Daphne opera in one act by Richard Strauss (libretto by Joseph Gregor), first produced in Dresden, Germany, on 15 October 1938. In the story Daphne spurns Apollo and is turned into a laurel tree.

Daphnis et Alcimadure pastoral by Jean de Mondonville (libretto, in the Languedoc dialect, by the composer), first produced before the court at Fontainebleau, France, on 4 November 1754; its first Paris performance was given at the Opéra on 29 December 1754.

Daphnis et Chloé ballet by Maurice Ravel (scenario after the Greek writer Longus, choreography by Mikhail Fokin), first produced at the Théâtre du Chatelet, Paris, France, on 8 June 1912. Ravel later arranged two orchestral suites for concert performance.

Da Ponte, Lorenzo (Conegliano Emmanuele) (1749–1838) Italian librettist. He is renowned for his collaboration with Mozart in *The Marriage of Figaro* (1786), *Don Giovanni* (1787), and *Così fan tutte* (1790). His adaptations of contemporary plays are deepened by a rich life experience and understanding of human nature.

Born in Ceneda (now Vittorio Veneto), he studied to take holy orders, proving a skilful versifier in both Italian and Latin. Appointed as a professor in literature at Treviso Seminary in 1773, his radical views and immoral behaviour led to his banishment from Venice in 1779. Travelling to Vienna, Austria, he was appointed as librettist to the New Italian Theatre in 1781 on the recommendation of Antonio Salieri. His first major success was in adapting Beaumarchais's comedy for Mozart's *The Marriage of Figaro*. *Don Giovanni* and *Così fan tutte* followed, together with libretti for other composers. In 1805 he emigrated to the USA, eventually becoming a teacher of Italian language and literature.

Daquin or **d'Aquin, Louis Claude (1694–1772)** French organist, harpsichordist, and composer. He studied under Louis Marchand and played before Louis XIV as a child prodigy at the age of six. At 12 he was appointed organist of Petit Saint-Antoine in Paris. In 1727 he was Jean-Philippe Rameau's successful rival for the post of organist at Saint-Paul, and in 1739 succeeded Jean Dandrieu at the Chapel Royal. He is especially remembered as one of the great French representatives of harpsichord music.

Works cantata *La Rose*; harpsichord pieces including *Le Coucou*; *Noëls* for organ or harpsichord.

Dardanus opera by Jean-Philippe Rameau (libretto by C A L de La Bruère), first produced at the Paris Opéra, France, on 19 November 1739. In the plot, Iphise loves her father's enemy Dardanus, but Teucer wants his daughter to marry Antenor. Captured by Antenor, Dardanus later escapes and slays an avenging sea monster, saving Antenor. Dardanus and Iphise are united.

The opera of the same title by Antonio Sacchini (libretto by de La Bruère, altered by N F Guillard), was first produced before the court at Versailles, France, on 18 September 1784 and was given its first Paris performance at the Opéra on 30 November 1784.

dargason an English country dance and folksong at least as old as the 16th century. Gustav Holst used it in his *St Paul's Suite*.

Dargillières (lived 16th century) Parisian family of instrument makers, including **Anthoine** (c. 1518–1572). He was 'faiseur d'orgues de la Chapelle du roi', and built various church organs in Paris. His son **Roch** (born 1559) built numerous organs in the Paris neighbourhood, including those at Rouen (St Michael) and Chartres (cathedral).

Dargomizhsky, Aleksandr Sergeievich (1813–1869) Russian composer. He studied music as an amateur at St Petersburg and led the life of a dilettante. After meeting Mikhail Glinka in 1833 he set to work on his first opera. After the next stage attempt he devoted himself mainly to songs between 1856 and 1860, including many of a satirical nature anticipating those of Modest Mussorgsky. In 1864 he visited Western Europe, but was able to gain a hearing only in Belgium, where he performed his orchestral fantasies. On his return he associated himself with Mily ➤ Balakirev's nationalist group, without actually joining it. He set Aleksandr Pushkin's poem 'The Stone Guest', based on the story of Don Juan, as an opera word for word. It was left unfinished at his death, but was completed, on his directions, by César Cui and orchestrated by Nikolai Rimsky-Korsakov in 1872.

Dargomizhsky was born in Tula. He showed musical talent at an early age and was taught to play the piano and violin; by the age of 11 he had made some attempt at composition. He entered the civil service in St Petersburg but retired in 1835 after four years and, moving in fashionable circles, became well known as an amateur pianist and a composer of dilettante drawing-room songs. It was his chance meeting with Glinka, who lent him his notes taken during his studies with Siegfried Dehn in Berlin, which gave his talents a more serious bias, and the two composers may be said together to have symbolized the pretensions of Russian musical genius at this period; but whereas Glinka's music was idealistic and lyrical, Dargomizhsky's was realistic and dramatic.

Though inferior to Glinka, Dargomizhsky is a figure of some importance in the history of Russian opera: his first opera was *Esmeralda* (1840), based on Victor Hugo's *Notre-Dame de Paris*; however, it was not accepted for the Imperial Opera until 1847. This was followed by a cantata on 'The Triumph of Bacchus', a dramatic poem by Pushkin, which he converted into a ballet-opera in 1867. Then came the opera *Rusalka or The Watersprite* (produced 1856), for the libretto of which Dargomizhsky again turned to Pushkin. This opera, superior to *Esmeralda*, gradually won a permanent place in the Russian repertory. Dargomizhsky's association with Balakirev and his circle gave him a leading part in the formation of a national and progressive school of Russian music. Dargomizhsky's own views on opera resembled those of Gluck and Wagner in the adaptation of the music to the dramatic import of the text.

Works STAGE operas *Esmeralda* (after Hugo; 1840, produced 1847), *Rusalka* (after Pushkin; 1856), *Rogdana* (unfinished), *The Stone Guest* (Pushkin, completed by Cui and Rimsky-Korsakov; produced posthumously 1872); ballet *Bacchus' Feast*.

ORCHESTRAL orchestral fantasies *Kazatchok*, *Baba-Yaga* and *Mummers' Dance*.

VOCAL a duet for an opera *Mazeppa*; about 90 songs, vocal duets, trios, quartets, choruses.

OTHER *Tarantelle Slave* for piano duet.

Dart, (Robert) Thurston (1921–1971) English harpsichordist and musicologist. His pioneer reinterpretations of baroque classics such as Johann Sebastian Bach's *Brandenburg Concertos* helped to launch the trend towards authenticity in early music.

dastgah melodic mode, used as a basis for improvisation or composition in Persian music.

Daughter of the Regiment opera by Donizetti; see ➤ *Fille du régiment, La*

Davenant (or D'Avenant), William (1606–1668) English poet and playwright. His works inspired the composers John Banister (*Circe*), William ➤ **Lawes** (*Triumph of the Prince d'Amour* and *Unfortunate Lovers*), and Matthew ➤ **Locke** (*Macbeth*), and the opera *The* ➤ **Siege of Rhodes** by Locke, Henry Lawes, Henry Cooke, C Coleman, and G Hudson.

David opera in five acts and twelve scenes by Darius Milhaud (libretto by A Lunel), written to celebrate the establishment of Jerusalem as the capital of Judea; it was first produced in Jerusalem, Israel, on 1 June 1954. It tells the story of the biblical David, founder of Jerusalem.

David, Félicien-(César) (1810–1876) French composer. He settled in Paris in 1841 and made a great success with his oriental descriptive symphony *Le Désert* (1844), inspired by his travels in Palestine. He was one of the first Western composers to introduce oriental scales and melodies into his music.

He was born in Cadenet, Vaucluse, and learnt music at the cathedral of Aix-en-Provence and from 1825 at a Jesuit college, and began to compose early. He entered the Paris Conservatoire in 1830, travelled in the East 1833–35, and after his return began to make a name as a composer of quasi-oriental music. He wrote symphonies, chamber music, and songs. Once highly popular, his music is now almost entirely forgotten.

Works OPERA *La Perle du Brésil* (1851), *Herculanum* (1859), *Lalla-Roukh* (after Moore; 1862), *Le Saphir* (1865), *La Captive* (withdrawn).

SACRED MUSIC oratorio *Moïse au Sinaï*; mystery *Eden*; motets and hymns.

ORCHESTRAL descriptive symphony *Le Désert* (1844) and *Christophe Colomb*; four symphonies.

CHAMBER four string quartets; 24 string quintets, two nonets for wind; *Mélodies orientales* for piano.

OTHER songs.

David, Johann Nepomuk (1895–1977) Austrian composer. He was a choirboy at St Florian and studied at the Vienna Academy. He taught composition successively at Leipzig, Salzburg, and Stuttgart, and published analytical studies of classical composers.

Works ORCHESTRAL eight symphonies (1936–65), two partitas for orchestra, two concertos for string orchestra; flute concertos; two violin concertos.

VOCAL *Requiem chorale* for soloists, chorus, and orchestra; chorale preludes.

CHAMBER three string quartets, four string trios, and other chamber music; three cello sonatas.

OTHER works for organ.

Davidde Penitente, The Penitent David cantata by Mozart, K469 (libretto probably by L da Ponte), made up in March 1785, mainly from portions of the unfinished C minor Mass, K427, of 1782–83. Only two arias are new.

Davidsbündlertänze, Dances of the League of David set of 18 piano pieces by Robert Schumann, Op. 6, composed in 1837. The title alludes to the *Davidsbund* (imaginary league of David) association, created to fight against the philistines of art.

Davie, Cedric Thorpe (1913–1983) Scottish composer and organist. He studied at the Scottish National Academy of Music in Glasgow, the Royal Academy of Music in London, and later the Royal College of Music there, where he was a pupil of Reginald Morris, Ralph Vaughan Williams, and Gordon Jacob, gaining the Cobbett and Sullivan Prizes in 1935. He also studied piano with Egon Petri in Germany, and composition with Zoltán Kodály in Budapest, Hungary, and Yrjö Kilpinen in Helsinki, Finland. He was head of music at St Andrews University from 1945.

Works STAGE opera *Gammer Gurton's Needle*, ballad opera *The Forrigan Reel* (James Bridie).

INSTRUMENTAL concerto for piano and strings; string quartet; violin and piano sonata, sonatinas for cello and piano and flute and piano.

VOCAL eight *Little Songs*.

Davies, Peter Maxwell (1934–) English composer and conductor. His music combines medieval and serial techniques with a heightened expressionism as in his opera *Taverner* (1970), based on the life and works of the 16th-century composer John ➤ Taverner. Other works include the chamber opera *The Lighthouse* (1980), the music-theatre piece *Miss Donnithorne's Maggot* (1974), and the orchestral piece *Mavis in Las Vegas* (1997).

He is the associate conductor/composer of the Royal Philharmonic Orchestra and the BBC Philharmonic, and the composer laureate of the Scottish Chamber Orchestra. He is currently Master of the Queen's Music (appointed 2004).

Davies was born in Manchester. After training at the Royal Manchester College of Music 1952–56 alongside the British composers Alexander Goehr and Harrison Birtwistle, he studied with the Italian composer Goffredo ➤ Petrassi 1957–59. From 1959 to 1962 he taught music at Cirencester Grammar School, and from 1962 to 1964 he studied with the US composer Roger Sessions at Princeton University. He co-founded the Pierrot Players ensemble in 1967 (renamed the Fires of London in 1970) with Birtwistle. Since 1970 he has been based in Orkney.

Works STAGE *Eight Songs for a Mad King*, music-theatre piece for voice and ensemble (1969), *Nocturnal Dances* (1970), *Taverner*, opera (1972), *Miss Donnithorne's Maggot*, music-theatre piece for mezzo and ensemble (1974), *The Martyrdom of St Magnus*, chamber opera (1977), *The Two Fiddlers*, opera for children (1978), *The Lighthouse*, chamber opera (1980), *Resurrection*, opera (1987), *Caroline Mathilde*, ballet (1990), *The Doctor of Myddfai*, opera (1996).

ORCHESTRAL *Worldes Blis* (1968), *Vesalii Icones* for dancer, cello, and ensemble (1969), *Ave Maris Stella*, for chamber ensemble (1975), six symphonies (1976, 1981, 1985, 1989, 1994, 1996), violin concerto (1986), ten Strathclyde concertos, for various instruments (1987–95).

VOCAL *O Magnum Mysterium*, four carols a cappella (1960), *Hymn to St Magnus* for mezzo and instruments (1972), *Fiddlers at the Wedding* for mezzo and instruments (1974), *Black Pentecost* for mezzo, baritone, and orchestra (1982), *Into the Labyrinth*, cantata (1983).

Davies, (Henry) Walford (1869–1941) English composer and broadcaster. His compositions include the cantata *Everyman* (1904), the 'Solemn Melody' (1908) for organ and strings, chamber music, and part songs. He also wrote sacred music and pieces for children. He was a popular radio broadcaster, particularly in his British Broadcasting Corporation (BBC) series *Music and the Ordinary Listener* (1926–30).

He was educated at St George's Chapel, Windsor, under Walter Parratt (1841–1924), and at the Royal College of Music in London, where Charles Stanford was his composition master. He held various organist's appointments, and graduated in music from Cambridge University in 1898, when he was appointed organist and choirmaster at the Temple Church. He was professor of music at the University of Wales, Aberystwyth, from 1919. He resigned from the Temple in 1923 and became organist at St George's, Windsor, in 1927. In 1934 he succeeded Edward Elgar as Master of the King's Musick.

Davis, Anthony (1951–) US composer and jazz pianist. He studied at Yale University and has been active in jazz ensembles in the USA and abroad; he was director of Episteme, and co-founded Advent in 1973. He has performed in New York with members of the Advancement of Creative Musicians.

Works OPERA *X: The Life and Times of Malcolm X* (premiered at New York City Opera, 1986) and *Under the Double Moon* (St Louis, 1989).

ORCHESTRAL piano concerto *Wayang V* (1985); *Notes from the Underground* for orchestra (1988); violin concerto (1988).

Davy, Richard (c.1467–c.1507) English composer. He was educated at Magdalen College, Oxford, where he was organist and choirmaster 1490–92. He later became chaplain to Anne Boleyn's grandfather and father 1501–15. He wrote motets, Passion music for Palm Sunday, part songs, and other pieces.

D.C. in music, abbreviation for **da capo** (Italian 'from the beginning').

'Death and the Maiden' Quartet Schubert's string quartet in D minor, D810, begun in March 1824, finished or revised in January 1826, and first performed in Vienna, Austria, on 1 February 1826. It is so called because the second movement is a set of variations on the introduction and the second half of his song 'Der Tod und das Mädchen' (D531, 1817, text by M Claudius), which consists of Death's quiet and reassuring answer to the girl's agitated plea to be spared. The work is sometimes heard today in an arrangement for string orchestra by Mahler.

Death and Transfiguration orchestral tone poem by Richard Strauss; see ➤ *Tod und Verklärung*.

Death in Venice opera by Benjamin Britten (libretto by Myfanwy Piper, after Thomas Mann), first produced at Snape Maltings, Suffolk, England, on 16 June 1973. The story tells how the writer Aschenbach, a believer in order, is seduced by the passion of Venice; his frustrated love of beauty and of the boy Tadzio destroys his ideals and finally himself.

Death of Klinghoffer, The opera in two acts by John Adams (libretto by Alice Goodman, based on the Palestinian hijacking of the *Achille Lauro*, 1985), first produced at the Théâtre de la Monnaie, Brussels, Belgium, on 19 March 1991.

Debora e Jaele, Deborah and Jael opera by Ildebrando Pizzetti (libretto by composer), first produced at the Teatro alla Scala, Milan, Italy, on 16 December 1922. It is loosely based on the biblical story; Sisera, here the king of Canaa, faces a conflict between his love for Jael and duty. Later Jael splits the sleeping Sisera's skull, rather than leave him to a worse death before the victorious Israelites.

Deborah oratorio by Handel (words by S Humphreys), first produced at the King's Theatre, Haymarket, London, England, on 17 March 1733.

Debussy, (Achille-) Claude (1862–1918) French composer. He broke with German Romanticism and introduced new qualities of melody and harmony based on the whole-tone scale. His work includes *Prélude à l'après-midi d'un faune/Prelude to the Afternoon of a Faun* (1894), illustrating a poem by Stéphane Mallarmé, and the opera *Pelléas et Mélisande* (1902).

Among his other works are numerous piano pieces, songs, orchestral pieces such as *La Mer/The Sea* (1905) and *Trois Nocturnes/Three Nocturnes* (1899), and the ballet *Jeux* (1913). Debussy also published witty and humorous critical writing about the music of his day, featuring the fictional character Monsieur Croche 'antidilettante' (professional debunker), a figure based on Erik
➔ **Satie.**

Debussy was the son of a shopkeeper. He took his first piano lessons at the age of seven, and from 1870 was taught for three years by Mme Mauté de Fleurville, a former pupil of Chopin. He entered the Paris Conservatory in 1873, studying with Albert Lavignac and Jean-Francois Marmontel, and later with Emile Durand. At 17 he failed to win a piano prize, but entered a composition class in 1880. For the next two summers he was domestic musician to Nadezhda von Meck, Tchaikovsky's former patroness. He taught her children, and she took him first to Switzerland and Italy and then to Russia the following year. He won the Prix de Rome in 1884 and went to Rome the next year, but left in 1887, before the required three years were completed.

During these years he began to reject the influence of Richard Wagner found in the music of the day, creating a new path towards what is often referred to as Impressionism. Debussy himself disliked this term, as he felt it implied vagueness; he was influenced by the Symbolist movement in art and literature, and preferred this interpretation of his work. Debussy's ideal was that music should have the effect of continuous improvisation. He began to compose seriously in the new manner for which he became known with a French translation of Dante Gabriel Rossetti's *Blessed Damozel* (1850), completed in 1888. He was influenced by Erik Satie in 1891 and performed his first important mature work, the prelude to Mallarmé's poem 'L'Après-midi d'un faune', in 1894. In 1899 he married a dressmaker, Rosalie (Lili) Texier, and in the same year he completed his *Nocturnes*. He became music critic for the *Revue blanche* in 1901, and the following year produced his only finished opera, a setting of Maurice Maeterlinck's *Pelléas et Mélisande*. The opera was described by its conductor, André Messager, as opening a window on the whole world of modern music; clear themes and strong contrasts are replaced by atmospheric depictions of mood. Debussy left his wife in 1904 for Emma Bardac, whom he married after divorcing his first wife in 1905. A private, depressive man of wide culture, Debussy was a friend of writers and painters, and himself a skilful critic. During his last decade he was generally acclaimed, but was also suffering from terminal cancer.

Debussy's approach to certain chords as 'sound-events' in themselves, important for their own colour and sensuous qualities even more than as stages in a harmonic progression, was a new way of thinking for Western music. His style is an inspired mixture of Jules Massenet and Modest Mussorgsky with a smattering of Franz Liszt and hints from his friend Satie. His influence affected composers as diverse as Maurice Ravel, Igor Stravinsky, Béla Bartók, Edgard Varèse, Olivier Messiaen, and Pierre Boulez, and continues to the present day in figures such as English composer George Benjamin.

Works STAGE opera *Pelléas et Mélisande* (1902); incidental music to d'Annunzio's *Le Martyre de Saint Sébastien* (1911); ballet *Jeux* (1913).

VOCAL three *Chansons de France* (Charles d'Orléans) for unaccompanied chorus; songs including sets *Ariettes oubliées* (Verlaine), two sets of *Fêtes galantes* (Verlaine), *Chansons de Bilitis* (Pierre Louÿs; 1898), *Trois Poèmes de Stéphane Mallarmé*.

ORCHESTRAL *Prélude à l'après-midi d'un faune/Prelude to the Afternoon of a Faun* (1894) *Trois Nocturnes/Three Nocturnes* (1899), *La Mer/The Sea* (1905) and *Trois Images* for orchestra (1912).

CHAMBER AND PIANO string quartet (1893); sonatas for cello and piano; flute, viola, and harp; and for violin and piano (1915–17); many piano pieces including *Suite bergamasque*, suite *Pour le piano* (1901), *Trois Estampes* (1903), *L'Île joyeuse*

(1904), two sets of three *Images*, suite *Children's Corner*, two sets of twelve *Préludes* (1910, 1913), and twelve *Etudes* (1915); *En blanc et noir* (1915) for two pianos.

Decius, Nikolaus (c.1485–after 1546)

German Lutheran pastor and theologian. He wrote the words and composed or adapted the music of three chorales, anticipating even Martin Luther in this field.

decrescendo or decresc.

(Italian 'decreasing') in musical notation, indicating a decrease in the loudness of a passage by constant degrees. *Decrescendo poco a poco* means that the decrescendo should progress more gradually. An alternative marking is 'diminuendo'. The opposite marking is 'crescendo'.

Dedekind, Constantin Christian (1628–1715)

German poet and composer. He studied at Dresden and in 1654 became a member of the Saxon court chapel and Konzertmeister in 1666. He arranged words for sacred music dramas.

Works psalms, sacred and secular vocal music, concertos for voices and instruments.

de Falla, Manuel

Spanish composer; see ➤ Falla, Manuel de.

degree

in music, the position of a note in a scale. The first degree of C major is therefore C, the second is D, the third is E, and so on. Alternative terms for the seven degrees of a scale are, starting with the first degree: tonic, supertonic, mediant, subdominant, dominant, submediant, and leading note.

Deidamia opera by Handel (libretto by P A Rolli), first produced at the Theatre Royal, Lincoln's Inn Fields, London, England, on 10 January 1741. It was Handel's last opera. In the story, Achilles dresses up as a girl but Deidamia discovers his secret; when Ulysses makes advances to Deidamia, Achilles reveals himself and joins Ulysses to fight at Troy.

Delage, Maurice (Charles) (1879–1961)

French composer. He travelled to the East and incorporated exotic elements into his music, which includes *Quatre poèmes hindous* (1913) for soprano and nonet.

He began to study music comparatively late in life, and was a pupil of Maurice Ravel.

Works overture to a ballet *Les Bâtisseurs de ponts* (after Kipling), symphonic poem *Conté par la mer* and other orchestral works; piano pieces; songs.

Delalande, Michel-Richard (1657–1726)

French organist and composer for the court of Louis XIV. His works include grand motets and numerous orchestral suites.

Delannoy, Marcel (François Georges) (1898–1962)

French composer. A painter and architect at first, he was mainly self-taught in music.

Works STAGE operas *Le Poirier de misère* (1925), *Philippine* (1937), *Fête de la danse*, *Ginevra* (1942); ballet-cantata *Le Fou de la dame*; ballets *La Pantoufle de vair* and *L'Eventail de Jeanne* (with others); incidental music for Aristophanes' *Peace* and other plays.

ORCHESTRAL symphonies and *Figures sonores* for orchestra, *Sérénade concertante* for violin and orchestra.

OTHER string quartets; many songs.

Delibes, (Clément Philibert) Léo (1836–1891)

French composer. His lightweight, perfectly judged works include the ballet scores *Coppélia* (1870) and *Sylvia* (1876), and the opera *Lakmé* (1883).

Delibes studied at the Paris Conservatory, where Adolphe Adam was his composition master. He became accompanist at the Théâtre Lyrique in 1853 and was organist successively at two churches. Later he became accompanist and chorus master at the Opéra and in 1881 professor of composition at the Conservatory.

Works OPERA *Maître Griffard* (1857), *Le Jardinier et son seigneur* (1863), *Le Roi l'a dit* (1873), *Jean de Nivelle* (1880), *Lakmé* (1883), *Kassya* (unfinished).

OPERETTAS *Deux Sous de charbon* (1856), *Deux Vielles Gardes*, *L'Omelette à la Follembûche* (1859), *Le Serpent à plumes* (1864), *L'Ecossais de Chatou*, and others.

BALLET *La Source* (with Minkus), *Coppélia* (on E T A Hoffmann's story *Olympia*; 1870), *Sylvia* (1876), *Le Pas des fleurs*; divertissement for Adam's ballet *Le Corsaire*.

OTHER incidental music for Hugo's *Le Roi s'amuse*; Mass; cantata *Alger*; dramatic scene *La Mort d'Orphée*; songs; children's choruses.

Delius, Frederick Theodore Albert (1862–1934)

English composer. His haunting, richly harmonious works include the opera *A Village Romeo and Juliet* (1901); the choral pieces *Appalachia* (1903), *Sea Drift* (1904), and *A Mass of Life* (1905); orchestral music such as *In a Summer Garden* (1908) and *A Song of the High Hills* (1911); chamber music; and songs.

Delius was born in Bradford. His father was a well-to-do businessman and wished him to follow a commercial career, but music was cultivated in the home and Delius worked steadily at music by himself, although he had little proper musical education. In 1884 he went to Florida, USA, as an orange planter and came under the influence of Thomas Ward, organist at Jacksonville. In 1886, after some teaching in the USA, he went to the Leipzig Conservatory, Germany, for a short time, but did not like its conservative teaching. While there, he met the Norwegian composer Edvard Grieg, who influenced Delius's romantic style of composition and persuaded his father to allow him to devote himself to composition. From 1889 Delius lived in France, mainly in Paris, and in 1897 he settled at Grez-sur-Loing, near Fontainebleau, with the German painter Jelka Rosen, whom he later married. A concert of his works was given in London in 1899 and he became known in both the UK and Germany. His early influences include Richard Wagner, Eduard Grieg, and Claude Debussy, but he found his own voice in *Koanga* (1904), *Paris: Song of a Great City* (1899), and *A Village Romeo and Juliet* (1901). From 1907 important first performances were given in England: Thomas Beecham conducted *Paris* in 1908 and *A Mass of Life* in 1909, and Henry Wood conducted *Sea Drift* in 1908. He contracted syphilis and in 1922 was attacked by paralysis, which gradually increased until, four years later, he was helpless and totally blind. However, he continued to compose with the assistance of Eric Fenby, to whom he dictated his music from 1928.

Works OPERA *A Village Romeo and Juliet* (1901; produced 1907), *Fennimore and Gerda* (1919).

CHORUS WITH ORCHESTRA *Sea Drift* (1904), *A Mass of Life* (1905), *A Song of the High Hills* (1911).

ORCHESTRAL *Paris: Song of a Great City* (1899), *Brigg Fair* (1907), *In a Summer Garden* (1908), *On Hearing the First Cuckoo in Spring* (1911), *Summer Night on the River* (1913), *North Country Sketches* (1913–14), *Eventyr* (after Asbjørnsen's fairy-tales; 1917); concertos for piano, violin, cello and violin and cello (1897, 1915, 1916, 1921).

OTHER chamber music: three violin and piano sonatas, cello sonatas, string quartet.

DelloJoio, Norman (1913–) US composer. His works combine the influences of jazz, Italian opera and the Catholic Church, and include three operas based on the story of Joan of Arc.

He studied at the Juilliard Graduate School in New York with Bernard Wagenaar, and later with Paul Hindemith at Yale School of Music. He was professor of music at Boston University 1972–79.

Works STAGE operas *The Ruby* (1953), *The Triumph of St Joan* (1959), and *Blood Moon* (1961); symphonic ballet *On Stage!* (1946); ballet suite *Duke of Sacramento* (1942).

ORCHESTRAL sinfonietta (1940), symphonic movement *Silvermine* for orchestra, *Colonial Variations* for orchestra (1976), concertos for piano, two pianos, harp, and flute; *Variations on a Bach Chorale* for orchestra (1985).

VOCAL *Western Star* for solo voices, narrator, chorus, and orchestra; *Mass* (1976).

CHAMBER quartet and trio for woodwind, trio for flute, cello, and piano; violin and piano sonata,

Duo concertante for cello and piano, sonatina for cello solo; suite and *Duo concertante* for two pianos; two sonatas, suite and two preludes for piano.

Del Mar, Norman René (1919–1994) English conductor, composer, and horn player. He founded the Chelsea Symphony Orchestra in 1944, and was a guest conductor with leading orchestras. He conducted an enormously wide range of music, but was especially known for Mahler, Elgar, and other late Romantics, above all Strauss, and was noted for his clear interpretations of complex scores. He also composed two symphonies, a string quartet, and a number of horn pieces.

He wrote three volumes on Richard Strauss (1960–72), as well as *Orchestral Variations* (1981) and *Companion to the Orchestra* (1987).

Del Mar was born in London and was educated at Marlborough public school. At the Royal College of Music, London, he studied violin, piano, and horn; conducting with Constant Lambert; and composition with Reginald Morris and Ralph Vaughan Williams. In World War II he played the horn in the RAF Central Band.

With the Chelsea Symphony Orchestra he performed what were then little-known modern works such as Mahler's Second and Ninth Symphonies. He became Thomas Beecham's assistant with the Royal Philharmonic Orchestra in 1947, conducting Strauss in the composer's presence. He was principal conductor of the English Opera Group 1949–56, and met Benjamin Britten and conducted his *Let's Make an Opera* and *The Rape of Lucretia* at the Aldeburgh Festival in 1949.

He was appointed chief conductor of several orchestras (including the British Broadcasting Corporation (BBC) Scottish Orchestra in 1960, the Göteborg Symphony Orchestra, Sweden, in 1968, the Academy of the BBC 1974–77, and the Århus Symphony Orchestra, Denmark, 1985–88) but not of any of the major London orchestras. He was also a professor of conducting at the Guildhall School of Music 1953–60 and the Royal Academy of Music 1974–77.

Delsarte, (François) Alexandre (Nicolas Chéri) (1811–1871) French music teacher and theoretician. Teaching at the Paris Conservatoire, he devised a system of body movements designed to develop coordination, grace, and expressiveness, which greatly inspired the pioneers of modern dance, such as Emile ➔ **Jaques-Dalcroze** and Ted Shawn.

He divided the movements of the human body into three categories: eccentric, concentric, and normal; and the expressions into three zones: head, torso, and limbs.

Del Tredici, David (1937–) US composer. His early music contains several settings of Joyce: *I Hear an Army* (1964) for soprano and string quartet, *Night Conjure-Verse* (1965) for voices and instruments, and *Syzygy* (1968) for soprano, horn, bells, and chamber orchestra. Since 1968 his music has been concerned with Lewis Carroll's 'Alice' stories.

He studied at Berkeley and with Roger Sessions at Princeton. His compositions on the 'Alice' theme include: *Pop-Pourri*, for voices, rock group, and orchestra (1968), *The Lobster Quadrille* for soprano, folk music ensemble, and orchestra (1969, revised 1974), *Vintage Alice* (1971; same forces), *An Alice Symphony* (1976), *Final Alice*, for orchestra (1976), *Child Alice*, for soprano and orchestra, in four parts: *In Memory of a Summer Day*, *Happy Voices*, *All in the Golden Afternoon*, and *Quaint Events* (1977–81; performed separately in St Louis, San Francisco, Philadelphia, and Rotterdam, 1980–83; first complete performance Aspen, 1984); *March to Tonality* for orchestra (1985); *Haddock's Eyes* for soprano and ensemble (1986); and *Steps* for orchestra (1990).

Demetrio, Demetrius libretto by Pietro Metastasio; also an opera by Antonio Caldara, first produced at the court in Vienna, Austria, on 4 November 1731. There are further settings by Johann Hasse (1732), Christoph Willibald von Gluck (1742), and Niccolò Jommelli (1749). In the story, Cleomice, new queen of Syria, must choose a husband. She loves Alcestis, a commoner, whom the rival Olinto orders to leave the country. When it is revealed that Alcestis is in fact Prince Demetrius, the marriage goes ahead.

Demetrio e Polibio opera by Gioachino Rossini (libretto by V Vigano-Mombelli). Rossini's first opera, it was written while he was a student at the Bologna Conservatory, from 1806, and was first produced at the Teatro Valle, Rome, Italy, on 18 May 1812. It describes how Demetrio, King of Syria, finds his long-lost son at the court of King Polibio.

demisemiquaver, US **32nd note** in music, a note value $\frac{1}{32}$ of the duration of a ➤ semibreve. It is written as a filled black note-head with a stem and three flags (tails).

Demofoonte, rè di Tracia, Demophoön, King of Thrace libretto by Pietro Metastasio; also an opera by Antonio Caldara, first produced on 4 November 1733. There are further settings by Christoph Willibald von Gluck (1743), Niccolò Jommelli (1743, the first of four), Karl Graun (1746), and Johann Hasse (1748). In the story, King Demophoön wants to sacrifice a virgin to appease Apollo, but the intended victim (Dirce) is secretly married to his son, Timanthes. There

are many twists in the plot, but a happy ending.

Demon, The opera by Arthur Rubinstein (libretto, in Russian, by P A Viskovatov, based on Mikhail Lermontov's poem), first produced in St Petersburg, Russia, on 25 January 1875. It was revived in Wexford, Ireland, in 1994. The story tells how the demon kills Tamara's lover but she is rescued by an angel.

Démophoon opera by Cherubini (libretto by Marmontel, based on Pietro Metastasio's *Demofoonte*), first produced at the Paris Opéra, France, on 5 December 1788. It is Cherubini's first French opera.

Demuth, Norman (1898–1968) English composer and author. He was educated as a choirboy at St George's Chapel, Windsor, and at Repton School. He studied music at the Royal College of Music in London and became professor of composition at the Royal Academy of Music there in 1930. His books include studies of César Franck, Maurice Ravel, and Albert Roussel.

Works five operas, including *Volpone* (after Jonson) and *The Oresteia* (Aeschylus); five ballets; four symphonies, two piano concertos; three sonatas for violin and piano, string trio, string quartet.

De natura sonoris two works by Krzysztof Penderecki: no. 1 for orchestra, first performed in Royan, France, on 7 April 1966; no. 2 for wind, percussion, and strings, first performed in New York, USA, on 3 December 1971.

Dench, Chris (1953–) English composer. He is self-taught and a leading member of the avant garde; his music has been performed by the London Sinfonietta, Ensemble InterContemporain, and the Arditti Quartet. He has appeared at Darmstadt, the Venice Biennale, and the International Society for Contemporary Music's World Music Days.

Works *Helical* for piano (1975), *Caught Breath of Time* for flute (1981), *Enonce* for 15 players (1984), *Strangeness* for string quartet (1985), *4 Darmstadter Aphorismen* (1986–89); *Sulle Scale della Fenice* for flute (1989), *Dark Neumes* for guitar, six brass, and amplified ensemble (1989).

Denisov, Edison (1929–1996) Russian composer. An early Soviet exponent of serial and electronic music, he studied at the Moscow Conservatory with Vissarion Shebalin and taught there from 1960.

Works STAGE operas *L'Écume des jours* (1981) and *The Four Girls* (after Picasso, 1986); ballet *Confession* (after de Musset, 1984).

ORCHESTRAL concertos for cello (1972), flute (1975), violin (1978), flute and oboe (1978), bassoon and cello (1982), oboe (1986), and clarinet (1989); symphony (1987).

CHAMBER string trio (1969), piano trio (1971), clarinet and piano quintets, with strings (1987), Octet (1992).

CHORAL Requiem (1980).

Density 21.5 work for solo flute by Edgard Varèse, first performed in New York, USA, on 16 February 1936. The piece was commissioned by the flautist George Barrère to inaugurate his new platinum flute; the title refers to the specific gravity of the metal.

Dent, Edward J(oseph) (1876–1957) English musicologist and composer. His books include works on Alessandro Scarlatti, Mozart's operas, English opera, Handel, and Ferruccio Busoni, and his compositions include polyphonic motets and a version of *The Beggar's Opera*. He was president of the International Society for Contemporary Music from its foundation in 1922 until 1938.

He was educated at Eton and at Cambridge University, where he was professor of music 1926–41. He was a governor of Sadler's Wells Opera, for which he translated many works, and was on the editorial board of the *New Oxford History of Music*.

Dering or **Deering, Richard (c.1580–1630)** English organist and composer. He became a Catholic and went to Brussels in 1617 as organist to the convent of English nuns, but returned to England to become organist to Henrietta Maria on her marriage to Charles I in 1625.

Works *Cantiones sacrae* for several voices, motets, anthems; canzonets for three and four voices, quodlibets on street cries; fancies and other pieces for viols.

De Sabata, Victor (1892–1967) Italian conductor and composer. He studied under his father, a chorus master at the Teatro alla Scala, Milan, and at the Milan Conservatory with Orefice and others. He later became conductor at La Scala and at the Royal Opera in Rome, and conducted at the Monte Carlo Opera from 1918 (including the first performance of *L'Enfant et les sortilèges* in 1925).

He visited the USA in 1938, conducted Wagner's *Tristan* at Bayreuth, Germany, in 1939, and visited London, England, with the Scala company in 1950, conducting Verdi's *Otello* and *Falstaff* at Covent Garden.

Works STAGE *Lisistrata* (after Aristophanes), *Il macigno, Mille e una notte* (1931); incidental music for Shakespeare's *The Merchant of Venice*.

ORCHESTRAL symphonic poems *Juventus, La notte di Platon, Gethsemani*, suite for orchestra.

descant in music, a high-pitched line for one or more sopranos, added above the normal soprano line (melody) of a hymn tune; a high-pitched instrument of a family, such as the descant recorder (known in the USA as soprano recorder); or an improvised melody sung against a written voice part, also known as faburden, fauxbourdon, or ➜ discant.

Older English writers used the term descant to mean ➜ counterpoint.

Descartes, René (1596–1650) French philosopher. He wrote a book on music, *Compendium musicae* (1618), in which he outlined the relationship between the physical aspect of sound and its perception by the listener.

Déserteur, Le opera by Pierre Monsigny (libretto by J M Sedaine), first produced at the Comédie-Italienne, Paris, France, on 6 March 1769.

Déserts work by Edgard Varèse for wind instruments, percussion, and magnetic tapes *ad lib*; it was composed 1953–54 and first performed in Paris, France, on 20 December 1954, conducted by Hermann Scherchen. Early use is made here of electronic sound.

Desmarets, Henri (1661–1741) French composer. He was educated at the court of Louis XIV. At the end of the 17th century he secretly married the daughter of a dignitary at Senlis and fled to Spain, becoming music superintendent to Philip V in 1700. In 1708 he became music director to the Duke of Lorraine at Lunéville.

Works OPERA AND BALLET *Didon* (1693), *Circé, Théagène et Chariclée* (on Heliodorus' *Aethiopica*, 1695), *Les Amours de Momus, Vénus et Adonis, Les Fêtes galantes* (1698), *Iphigénie en Tauride* (with Campra), and *Renaud ou La Suite d'Armide* (1722).

OTHER motet and Te Deum for the marriage of Princess Elisabeth Thérèse to the king of Sardinia; church music written early in his career under the name of Goupillier.

Des Prez, Josquin Franco-Flemish composer; see ➜ Josquin Des Prez.

Dessau, Paul (1894–1979) German composer. His work includes incidental music to Bertolt Brecht's theatre pieces; an opera, *Die Verurteilung des Lukullus/The Trial of Lucullus* (1949), also to a libretto by Brecht; and numerous choral works and songs.

From 1910 he studied at the Klindworth-Scharwenka Conservatory in Berlin and later in Hamburg, where in 1913 he became a coach at the opera. In 1933 he went to Paris, France, where he studied Schoenberg's serial method with René Leibowitz. He conducted all over Germany, but was forced to leave and in 1939 went to New York, USA. He collaborated with Brecht from 1942, when they met as political exiles in the USA, returning with him to East Berlin in 1948.

Works OPERA *Das Verhör des Lukullus* (1949; produced 1951), *Puntila* (1959; produced 1966), *Lanzelot* (1969), *Einstein* (1973), *Leonce und Lena* (1979); children's operas *Das Eisenbahnspiel, Tadel der Unzuverlässigkeit.*

OTHER concertino for solo flute, clarinet, horn, and violin; a piano sonata; much vocal and orchestral music, film and incidental music.

dessus (French 'top') the treble ➔ viol.

dessus (French 'top') in keyboard music, an instruction to place the specified hand above the other, used when both hands are playing in close proximity, or when crossing over hands.

Destouches, André(-Cardinal) (1672–1749) French composer. A sailor at first, and then a musketeer, he studied with Campra and produced his first stage work, *Issé*, in 1697. He held various court appointments and was director of the Opéra 1728–31.

Works operas *Amadis de Crèce* (1699), *Marthésie, Omphale, Callirhoé, Télémaque et Calypso* (1714), *Sémiramis* (1718), *Les Stratagèmes de l'Amour*; heroic pastoral *Issé*; comedy-ballet *Le Carnaval et la folie*; ballet *Les Eléments* (with Lalande, 1721), cantatas (*Enone*) and *Sémélé*.

détaché (French 'detached, separated') a bowing style in string playing. In quick passages the bow changes direction so that each note is clearly separated, but without the sound being perceptibly interrupted, as in *staccato*. The term is sometimes used for non-bowed instruments, indicating a similar effect is desired.

Dettingen Te Deum a Te Deum composed by Handel to celebrate the British victory of 26 June 1743 over the French at Dettingen, Germany. It was first performed in the Chapel Royal, London, on 27 November 1743.

Deuteromelia the second part of a collection of canons, rounds, and catches published by Thomas ➔ Ravenscroft in London, England, in 1609, the first part being ➔ Pammelia.

Deutsches Requiem, Ein, *A German Requiem* work for chorus, soprano, and baritone solo, and orchestra by Brahms, Op. 45, composed 1866–69 and first performed in Leipzig, Germany, on 18 February 1869, conducted by Carl Reinecke. The name refers to the fact that Brahms did not set the liturgical Latin text, but a choice of his own from Luther's translation of the Bible.

Deutsche Tänze (German 'German dances') type of country dance in 3/4 (slow waltz) time, cultivated by Mozart, Beethoven, Schubert, and others. The adjective 'Deutsche' was frequently used alone in titles.

Deux Avares, Les, *The Two Misers* opera by André Grétry (libretto by C G F de Falbère), first produced for the court at Fontainebleau, France, on 27 October 1770; the first Paris performance was given at the Comédie-Italienne on 6 December 1770.

Deux Chasseurs et la laitière, Les, *The Two Huntsmen and the Milkmaid* opera by Egidio Duni (libretto by L Anseaume, after La Fontaine), first produced at the Comédie-Italienne, Paris, France, on 21 July 1763.

Deux Journées, Les, *The Two Days*, better known as *The Water-Carrier* opera by Luigi Cherubini (libretto by J N Bouilly), first produced at the Théâtre Feydeau, Paris, France, on 16 January 1800. In the story, the fugitive Armand and his wife Constance are helped by the water-seller Mikéli. After several incidents Armand must reveal his identity to save Constance, but at that moment news arrives that the ban against the couple has been lifted.

Deux Petits Savoyards, Les, *The Two Little Savoyards* opera by Dalayrac (libretto by G J Marsollier), first produced at the Comédie-Italienne, Paris, France, on 13 January 1789.

developing variation in music, the technique of varying a musical motive so that each of its different occurrences remains identifiably related to the original form of the motive. The term was coined by Arnold Schoenberg, particularly in relation to the works of Brahms. See ➔ motivic analysis.

development in music, the compositional process of extending and developing material. In particular, the term refers to the central process of ➔ sonata form, following the ➔ exposition, where thematic material is subjected to various developments, and the harmony undergoes more adventurous modulation than in the exposition or ➔ recapitulation, generally avoiding the tonic key before its reappearance in the recapitulation. The usual procedure is to develop the first or second subjects or both, but the procedure is by no means fixed and new matter may be introduced at will.

Devil and Kate, The, Czech **Čert a Káča** opera by Antonín Dvořák (libretto by A Wenig), first produced at the Czech Theatre, Prague, on 23 November 1899. It tells how Kate is carried off to hell after announcing that she would dance even with the Devil, but her tongue gets her thrown out.

Devils of Loudun, The, Polish **Diabły z Loudun** opera by Krzysztof Penderecki (libretto by composer after John Whiting's play *The Devils*), based on a narrative by Aldous Huxley which describes a case of diabolic possession in a 17th-century convent of Ursuline nuns (Father Grandier is accused of bewitching them). It was first performed in Hamburg, Germany, on 20 June 1969.

Devil's Opera, The opera by George Macfarren (libretto by G Macfarren, the composer's father), a satire on the diabolic elements in works like Carl Maria von Weber's *Der Freischütz*, Giacomo Meyerbeer's *Robert le Diable*, and Heinrich Marschner's *Der Vampyr*. It was first produced at the Lyceum Theatre, London, England, on 10 September 1838.

Devil's Trill sonata by Giuseppe Tartini; see ➤ *Trillo del diavolo*.

Devil's Wall, The, Czech **Certova stena** opera by Bedřich Smetana (libretto by E Krasnohorska), first produced at the Czech Theatre, Prague, on 29 January 1882. It is Smetana's last completed opera. In it, Javek searches for a wife for Vok, but Beneš wants him to stay single and thereby receive Vok's inheritance. The Devil, in league with Beneš, tries to drown Vok in a monastery but the beautiful Hedvika warns Vok. Beneš repents, and Vok marries Hedvika.

Devin du village, Le, The Village Soothsayer opera by Jean-Jacques Rousseau (libretto by composer), first produced for the court at Fontainebleau, France, on 18 October 1752, with an overture and recitatives by Pierre de Jélyotte (1713–87) and Francœur. It was produced at the Paris Opéra on 1 March 1753, with music all by Rousseau. It describes how the soothsayer unites the discordant couple Colin and Colette.

Devisenarie (German 'device aria') type of ➤ aria of the 17th and 18th centuries in which the first word or words occur separately in the voice-part, as though the singer were announcing a title, before the first line of the text or more is sung continuously, often after a further instrumental passage.

de Vitry, Philippe French composer; see ➤ Vitry, Philippe de.

dhola musical instrument, a deep-toned Indian drum, barrel-shaped and played at both ends. It is played with the hands and, depending on how and where it is struck, produces a flexible tone that rises from bass to the tenor register.

dhrupad (Hindi 'fixed verse') vocal genre of north Indian (Hindustani) music, characterized by an extensive unmetred introduction (*alap*), a composed text setting of between two and four sections (*sthayi*, *antara*, and sometimes *sanchari* and *abhog*), and improvised development. Although less common than the ➤ *khyal*, it is considered to be the oldest variety of north Indian classical music still performed, and is highly prestigious.

Diabelli, Anton (1781–1858) Austrian publisher and composer. He was the original publisher of Beethoven, Haydn, and Schubert. He is most famous today for appearing in the title of Beethoven's *Diabelli Variations* (1823), which formed part of a contribution by 50 composers, each of whom was asked to compose a piece based on a waltz theme written by Diabelli himself.

He was educated for the priesthood, but studied music with Michael Haydn. He went to Vienna as piano and guitar teacher and joined Peter Cappi in his publishing firm in 1818; it became Diabelli & Co in 1824.

Works the operetta *Adam in der Klemme* (Vienna, 1809); Masses; many piano pieces, including the little waltz on which Beethoven wrote the 33 variations Op. 120, and other pieces.

Diabelli Variations Beethoven's variations on a waltz by Anton ➤ Diabelli; see also ➤ *Vaterländischer Künstlerverein*.

Diable à quatre, Le, ou La Double Métamorphose ballad opera with airs arranged by François André Danican Philidor (libretto by J M Sedaine, based on Coffey's *Devil to Pay*), first produced at the Opéra-Comique, Paris, on 19 August 1756.

Diable dans le beffroi, Le, The Devil in the Belfry opera by Claude Debussy (libretto by himself, based on Edgar Allan Poe's story), worked on in 1903 but not completed.

diabolus in musica (Latin 'the devil in music') in music, a medieval warning against the use of the tritone – the interval of the augmented fourth (such as C–F sharp or F–B) – which was considered unsuitable, both harmonically and melodically, for sacred compositions.

Dialogues des Carmélites, Les opera by Francis Poulenc (libretto by G Bernanos), first produced at La Scala, Milan, Italy, on 26 January 1957. It is set during the French Revolution, when the sisters of the Carmelite order are condemned to death. The opera follows the contrasting Blanche and Constance, who meet the same fate.

Diamants de la couronne, Les, The Crown Diamonds opera by Daniel Auber (libretto by Augustin Scribe and J H V de Saint-Georges), first produced at the Opéra-Comique, Paris, France, on 6 March 1841.

Diamond, David Leo (1915–2005) US composer. His works are written in a neoclassical style and include *Rounds* (1944) for string orchestra.

He studied at the Eastman School of Music at Rochester and later at the American Conservatory at Fontainebleau, France, with Nadia Bou-

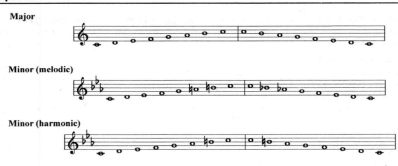

Major

Minor (melodic)

Minor (harmonic)

Three commonly used diatonic scales.

langer. After his return to the USA he was awarded several composition prizes.

Works ORCHESTRAL eleven symphonies (1941–89), sinfonietta, serenade, variations, *Psalm* for orchestra (1936), *Elegy in Memory of Ravel* (1938) and ballet suite *Tom* for orchestra; concerto and *Rounds* for string orchestra (1944); violin concerto (1936–67), *Hommage à Satie* and ballade for chamber orchestra, concertos for piano, cello, and violin (2) with chamber orchestra.

VOCAL *A Night Litany* (Ezra Pound) for chorus and three madrigals for unaccompanied chorus (James Joyce), *Choral Symphony: To Music* (1967); *A Secular Cantata* (1976).

CHAMBER ten string quartets (1943–76), string trio; sonatina for violin and piano, cello and piano sonata, partita for bassoon and piano; sonata and sonatina for piano; 52 preludes and fugues for piano.

diapason in music, the principal stop of an organ, which gives the instrument its characteristic tone quality. Diapasons may be 'open', producing a bright colour, or 'stopped', producing a muffled but sweet tone. The equivalent stop on a German-built instrument is the Prinzipal. In French usage, 'diapason' means tuning fork, hence 'diapason normal' is the equivalent of ➤ **concert pitch.**

diapente in music, the interval of the fifth. In old music canons at the fifth were called epidiapente when answered in the fifth above, and subdiapente when answered below.

diaphony, Latin **diaphonia** another term for ➤ **dissonance**, a displeasing combination of musical tones.

Diary of One Who Disappeared, Czech **Zápisník zmizelého** cycle of 22 songs by Leoš Janáček for tenor, alto, three-part women's chorus, and piano; it was composed 1917–21 and first performed in Brno (Czech Republic) on 18 April 1921.

diastole (from Greek 'distinction, differentiation') old term, in use to the middle of the 18th century, for the divisions of music into sections or phrases.

diatonic scale in music, a scale consisting of the seven notes of any major or minor ➤ **key.**

Dibdin, Charles (1745–1814) English singer, author, and composer. He began his career as a singing actor at Covent Garden, London, where his pastoral *The Shepherd's Artifice* was produced in 1764. Over 100 dramatic works followed. In 1789 he began his series of 'Table Entertainments', in which he was author, composer, narrator, singer, and accompanist. One of the most successful, *The Oddities* (1789), contained the song 'Tom Bowling'. Many other sea songs achieved great popularity.

He began singing as a chorister at Winchester Cathedral, went to London at the age of 15, and made his stage debut in 1762. In 1778 he was appointed composer to Covent Garden Theatre, and during the 1780s dabbled in theatrical management with variable success. A projected journey to India came to nothing, but the fundraising travels which were to have financed it provided material for his *Musical Tour* (1788). Towards the end of his life a publishing venture made him bankrupt, and he was saved from destitution by a public subscription. He wrote an account of his professional life and other literary works.

Works over 100 dramatic pieces, including *Lionel and Clarissa* (1768), *The Padlock*, *The Ephesian Matron*, *The Captive*, *The Ladle* (1773), *The Trip to Portsmouth*, *The Seraglio* (1776), *Rose and Colin*, *The Touchstone*, *The Milkmaid*, *Tom Thumb*, *Harvest Home* (1787); over 30 'Table Entertainments' containing innumerable songs.

Dibdin, Thomas John (1771–1841) English dramatist and songwriter. He is said to have written about 200 plays, including the pantomime *Mother Goose* (1807) and the patriotic *The Mouth of the Nile* (1798), and some 2,000 songs, many of them sea songs and ballads. He was the son of Charles Dibdin.

Dichterliebe, Poet's Love song cycle by Robert Schumann, Op. 48 (16 poems by Heinrich Heine), composed in 1840.

Dickinson, Peter (1934–) English composer and teacher. He was professor at Keele University 1974–84. He studied at Cambridge University and at the Juilliard School, New York. While in the USA he met John Cage and Edgard Varèse; other influences have been Erik Satie and Igor Stravinsky.

Works STAGE ballet *Vitalitas* (1959); music-theatre piece *The Judas Tree* (1965).

ORCHESTRAL *Monologue* for strings (1959), *Transformations, Homage to Satie* for orchestra (1970); piano concerto (1978–84), violin concerto (1986).

VOCAL settings of poems by W H Auden, Dylan Thomas, Alan Porter, e e cummings, and Emily Dickinson for voice and piano (1956–71); *Mass of the Apocalypse* for female chorus and four percussion (1984).

OTHER two string quartets; piano and organ music.

didgeridoo or **didjeridu** musical lip-reed wind instrument, made from a hollow eucalyptus branch 1.5 m/4 ft long and blown to produce rhythmic, booming notes of relatively constant pitch. It was first developed and played by Australian Aborigines.

Dido and Aeneas opera by Henry Purcell (libretto by N Tate, after the Roman poet Virgil), first produced ('by young gentlewomen') at Josias Priest's boarding school in Chelsea, London, England, in December 1689.

Dido, Königin von Carthago opera by Christoph Graupner (libretto by Heinrich Hinsch), first produced at the Theater beim Gänsemarkt in Hamburg, Germany, in the spring of 1707. It tells how Dido is pursued by the Numidian king Iarbas as Aeneas receives his sailing orders from Mercury and Venus.

Didon, Dido opera by Niccolò Piccinni (libretto by Marmontel), first produced for the court at Fontainebleau, France, on 16 October 1783 and given its first Paris performance at the Opéra on 1 December 1783.

Didone abbandonata, Dido Forsaken opera by Johann Hasse (libretto by Pietro Metastasio), first produced in Hubertusburg, near Dresden, Germany, on 7 October 1742. There are further settings by Niccolò Jommelli (1747) and Tommaso Traetta (1757).

Didone, La, Dido opera by Pietro Cavalli (libretto by G Busenello), first produced at the Teatro San Cassiano, Venice, Italy, during Carnival in 1641. It recounts how Dido accepts the love of Iarbas, as Aeneas departs for Italy.

Dienstag aus Licht, Tuesday from Light opera in two acts by Karlheinz Stockhausen, the fourth of a projected seven collectively known as *Licht* (libretto by composer); it was first performed in Lisbon, Portugal, on 10 May 1992. The day named after Mars depicts philosophical and martial battles between Michael and Lucifer.

Diepenbrock, Alphons (1862–1921) Dutch composer. At first a philologist, he was self-taught in music.

Works STAGE incidental music for Aristophanes' *The Birds*, Sophocles' *Electra* (1920), Goethe's *Faust*, Vondel's *Gysbrecht van Amstel*.

CHURCH MUSIC *Stabat Mater*, Te Deum for solo voices, chorus, and orchestra, Mass.

OTHER songs with orchestra; chamber music; songs.

Dieren, Bernard van (1887–1936) Dutch-born British composer. A scientist by training, he had little musical experience, apart from violin playing, before the age of 20, when he began to compose. In 1909 he settled in London as correspondent to foreign newspapers, after making serious music studies, which he continued in Germany in 1912, when his real creative career began. He wrote a book on the sculptor Jacob Epstein and a volume of musical essays, *Down among the Dead Men* (1935).

Works OPERA *The Tailor* (R Nichols, 1917).

ORCHESTRAL *Beatrice Cenci*, orchestral epilogue to Shelley's drama (1909), overture *Anjou*; serenade for small orchestra, overture for chamber orchestra.

VOCAL symphony on Chinese poems for solo voices, chorus, and orchestra; *Les Propous des beuveurs* (Rabelais) for chorus and orchestra; *Diafonia* for 17 instruments and baritone (Shakespeare sonnets, 1916), *Fayre eies* (Spenser) for baritone and chamber orchestra; three unaccompanied choruses.

CHAMBER six string quartets (1912–28); sonata and three studies for unaccompanied violin, and other pieces.

Dièse or **Dièze (French 'sharp')** in music, the sign for ✚ **sharp**.

Dies Irae (from Latin 'day of wrath') sequence from the Mass for the Dead dealing with the Day of Judgement. The text is lengthy and apocalyptic, and has inspired dramatic settings as part of a Requiem by composers including Wolfgang Amadeus Mozart, Giuseppe Verdi, Hector Berlioz, and Benjamin Britten.

The Dies Irae was originally associated with a distinctive ✚ **plainsong** theme, which has since been frequently quoted by composers as a kind of universal ✚ **leitmotif** to imply death or Hell. Examples of its use include:

Granville Bantock, 'Witches' Dance' in incidental music to *Macbeth*;

Hector Berlioz, 'Witches' Sabbath' in *Fantastic Symphony*;

Luigi Dallapiccola, *Canti di prigionia*;

Peter Maxwell Davies, *St Michael*;

Franz Liszt, *Totentanz* for piano and orchestra;

Sergei Rachmaninov, *Rhapsody on a Theme by Paganini* for piano and orchestra and *Symphonic Dances*, Op. 45;

Ottorino Respighi, *Impressioni brasiliane*;

Camille Saint-Saëns, *Danse macabre* for orchestra;

Ronald Stevenson, *Passacaglia on DSCH*;

Pyotr Tchaikovsky, *Theme and Variations* in Suite No. 3 for orchestra and song 'In Dark Hell';

Ralph Vaughan Williams, *Five Tudor Portraits* for chorus and orchestra (lament for Philip Sparrow).

A recent theory claims the Dies Irae as the 'hidden' theme of Edward Elgar's *'Enigma' Variations*.

diesis in ancient Greece, either the interval between a fourth and two 'major' musical tones or a quarter-tone. In modern acoustics, either the great diesis is the difference between four minor thirds and an octave, or the enharmonic diesis is the difference between an octave and three major thirds.

Dietrich, Albert (Hermann) (1829–1908) German composer and conductor. He wrote a violin and piano sonata jointly with Schumann and Brahms in 1853, though his most successful works were his songs. He was court music director at Oldenburg from 1861.

Works the opera *Robin Hood* (1879); incidental music to Shakespeare's *Cymbeline* (performed London, 1896); symphony in D minor; choral and orchestral works; horn concertos; chamber music.

digital in music, method of sound recording in which audio signals are converted into a series of electronically represented pulses, determined by the voltage of the sound. This information can be stored for reproduction or manipulation in the case of composition in the electronic medium.

Dillon, James (1950–) Scottish composer. His music has had Renaissance and non-Western influences and is densely composed. Works by him have been featured at the Bath, Darmstadt, Warsaw, and Paris festivals. His works include *Introitus* for strings (1990), *Vernal Showers* for solo violin and ensemble, and *Viriditas* for unaccompanied choir (1993).

Works INSTRUMENTAL *Cumha* for twelve strings (1978), *Once Upon a Time* for twelve instruments (1980), *Spleen* for piano (1980), string quartet (1983), *Le Rivage* for wind quintet (1984), *Windows and Canopies* (1985), *Helle Nacht* for or-

chestra (1987), *Shrouded Mirrors* (1988), *Blitzschlag* (1991), string quartet no. 2 (1991).

VOCAL *Babble* for 40 voices (1976), *Come Live With Me* for mezzo and four instruments (1981), *Viriditas* (1993).

diminished in music, a term used to describe intervals normally 'perfect' (fourths, fifth, octaves) or 'minor' (seconds, thirds, sixths, sevenths) which have been made a semitone narrower.

Perfect and diminished intervals.

diminished seventh in music, an interval consisting of a minor → **seventh** which is contracted (diminished) by one semitone, to create an interval of nine semitones (for example A–G♭); alternatively, a **chord** consisting of a minor seventh which is contracted (diminished) by one semitone. If every voice of the chord is filled in, there is also a minor third and a diminished fifth, for example A–C–E♭–G♭. This chord, which consists only of a series of minor thirds, is ambiguous harmonically and therefore useful in modulation (moving from one key to another).

The example illustrates two of the three possible diminished 7th chords.

diminuendo (Italian 'diminishing') in musical notation, indicating a decrease in the loudness of a passage by constant degrees. *Diminuendo poco a poco* means that the diminuendo should progress more gradually. An alternative marking is 'decrescendo'. The opposite marking is 'crescendo'.

diminution in music, a reduction of interval size, of chord, loudness level, or note values of a theme.

Dimitrij opera by Antonín Dvořák (libretto by M Červinková-Riegerová), first produced at the Czech Theatre, Prague, on 8 October 1882. The subject is the 'false Dimitri', the pretender who also figures in Mussorgsky's *Boris Godunov*. Having assumed the throne, Tsar Dmitrij marries Marina and then falls in love with Xenie. Jealous, Marina reveals that Dmitrij is in fact the son of a peasant. The opera ends when Prince Šujský shoots him.

d'Indy, Vincent French composer; see ➤ Indy, Vincent d'.

Dinorah opera by Giacomo Meyerbeer; see ➤ *Pardon de Ploërmel, Le*.

Dioclesian 'opera' by Henry Purcell; see ➤ *Prophetess, The*.

direct a sign used in plainsong notation and often in early music in staff notation, indicating at the end of the stave the position of the first note at the beginning of the following one.

dirge (Latin *Dirige Domine*, from the Office for the Dead, a funeral psalm) song of lamentation for the dead. A poem of mourning is usually called an elegy.

discant or **descant** in medieval music, a form of ➤ polyphony, originally an improvisation technique in which one voice had the ➤ cantus firmus (fixed melody) whilst another or several others extemporized a free accompanying part or parts. It is found in early medieval ➤ plainsong such as ➤ organum.

discord a combination of notes jarring to the ear. See ➤ dissonance.

disjunct motion in music, movement of a note to another note by a leap; see ➤ motion.

dissoluto punito, Il opera by Mozart; see ➤ *Don Giovanni*.

dissonance in music, a combination of two or more notes that 'disagree' with each other and so sound displeasing to the ear. It is the opposite of ➤ consonance.

Dissonance Quartet string quartet no. 19 in C, K465, by Mozart, composed in 1785. The dissonant introduction to the first movement gives the work its name.

dissonant counterpoint technique developed by the US composer Charles ➤ Seeger and espoused by, amongst others, Ruth ➤ Crawford and Carl ➤ Ruggles. In dissonant counterpoint, the traditional definitions of dissonant and consonant intervals are reversed, so that the composer deliberately avoids using traditionally consonant intervals (thirds, fourths, fifths, and sixths) except as passing harmonies. The technique seeks to replace the traditional rules of counterpoint, rather than extending them in the manner of Schoenberg's atonal works.

distratto, Il nickname of Haydn's symphony no. 60 in C major, so called on account of its being an adaptation of the incidental music to *Der Zerstreute* (1775), a German version of Jean Regnard's play *Le Distrait* (1697).

dital harp alternative name for the ➤ harp lute, a musical instrument.

Dittersdorf, Karl Ditters von (1739–1799), born **Karl Ditters** Austrian composer and violinist. He was educated in the household of Prince Hildburghausen in Vienna, and studied composition with Bonno. He played in the orchestra of the Imperial Opera in Vienna, 1761–63, during which time he travelled to Italy with Gluck, winning great success as a violinist. In 1765 he succeeded Michael Haydn as *Kapellmeister* to the Bishop of Grosswardein, and from 1769 to 1795 served the Prince Bishop of Breslau in the same capacity. Much of his time was spent in Vienna, where his most popular opera, *Doktor und Apotheker*, was produced in 1786. He was ennobled in 1773, henceforth calling himself von Dittersdorf. Kelly's *Reminiscences* contains an account of Dittersdorf playing string quartets with Haydn, Mozart, and Vanhal. During his last years he was in the service of Baron Stillfried at Rothlhotta. His autobiography, dictated shortly before his death, was published in 1801.

Works over 40 operas, for example *Amore in musica*, *Betrug durch Aberglauben*, *Doktor und Apotheker* (1786), *Hieronimus Knicker* (1789), *Das rothe Kaeppchen*, *Die Hochzeit des Figaro* (after Beaumarchais), etc.; oratorios *Isacco* (1766), *Davidde Penitente* (1771), *Esther*, *Giobbe* (1786); Masses and other church music; over 100 symphonies, including 21 on Ovid's *Metamorphoses*; concertos; divertimenti, chamber music.

Diversions work by Benjamin Britten for piano, left hand, and orchestra, composed in 1940 and revised 1954. It was first perfomed in Philadelphia, USA, on 16 January 1942, with Paul Wittgenstein as the soloist.

divertimento a suite of 18th-century music written for light entertainment, usually in four to nine movements, for a small string, wind, or mixed ensemble. Mozart wrote 25, entitling them, in addition to 'divertimento', 'serenades' and 'cassations'.

divertissement term mainly connected with ballet, where it means a set of varied dances with no particular plot. In music, it is a suite, particularly of arrangements or pieces based on familiar tunes, an entertaining piece of any kind, or a fantasy of a lighter sort, such as Schubert's *Divertissement à la hongroise*. In 18th-century French usage, a divertissement is a dance interlude, with or without songs, in a play or opera; also sometimes a short play with dances and songs.

Divine Poem, The title of symphony no. 3 in C minor, Op. 43 by Aleksandr Skriabin, first performed in Paris, France, on 29 May 1905, conducted by Artur Nikisch. The work's three movements, titled *Struggles*, *Delights*, and *Divine Play*, reflect Skriabin's mystic beliefs.

divisi or **div. (Italian 'divided')** in orchestral compositions, associated with passages of double notes, directing players reading one part (for example first violins) to divide into groups and play only one note per instrument, rather than trying to play both notes at once. It appears most often in orchestral string parts.

divisions in music, an old method of improvising ➤ variations by dividing the basic note values of a theme into smaller fractions representing higher tempi in proportion to the original time values (see ➤ diminution).

The medieval extension of harmonic ratios to tempo can be found in the keyboard variations of Mozart, Beethoven, and Brahms; in the late 20th century Karlheinz Stockhausen reinvented the concept by introducing a tempo scale equivalent to equal temperament, with metronomic values graduated within the 'tempo-octave' 60–120 beats per minute.

division viol musical instrument, a bass ➤ viol of moderate size on which ➤ divisions were often played in the 17th century.

Djamileh opera by Georges Bizet (libretto by L Gallet, based on Alfred de Musset's *Namouna*), first produced at the Opéra-Comique, Paris, France, on 22 May 1872. In the story, Haroun changes his mistress every month but Djamileh, who has fallen in love with him, returns in disguise, winning his heart.

djembe single-headed goblet-shaped drum from Senegambia in West Africa, with a high pitched tone. It is played with the hands.

Djinns, Les, **The Genii** symphonic poem by César Franck for piano and orchestra, based on verses from Victor Hugo's *Les Orientales*. It was composed in 1884 and first performed in Paris, France, on 15 March 1885.

DMus abbreviation for **Doctor of Music**.

do the old name for the note C (➤ solmization), still used in Latin countries. In tonic sol-fa notation the tonic note in any key, represented by the symbol **d**, pronounced doh.

Docteur Ox, Le opéra bouffe by Jacques Offenbach (libretto by P Gille and A Mortier, based on a Jules Verne story, first produced at the Théâtre des Variétés, Paris, France, on 26 January 1877.

dodecaphony music composed according to the ➤ twelve-tone system of composition.

Dodge, Charles (1942–) US composer. He specializes in electronic music. His work has been performed at the Tanglewood, Warsaw, and Stockholm festivals and by the New York and Los Angeles Philharmonic orchestras.

He studied with Gunther Schuller and Otto Luening at Columbia University, and studied computer music at Princeton.

Works *Changes* (1970), *Earth's Magnetic Field* (1970), *Extensions* (1973), *Palinode* with orchestra (1976), *The Waves* with soprano (1984), *Song Without Words* (1986), *The Voice of Binky* (1989).

Dodgson, Stephen (1924–) English composer and broadcaster. He is best known for his guitar concertos, but has also written for the clavichord and harpsichord.

Other works include a piano quartet, Symphony for wind (1974), *Epigrams from a Garden* for mezzo and clarinets (1977), concertos for bassoon (1969), clarinet (1983), and trombone (1986), a string quartet (1986), and songs.

doh the name for the tonic note in any key in tonic sol-fa, so pronounced, but in notation represented by the symbol **d**.

Dohnányi, Ernst (Ernö) von (1877–1960) Hungarian pianist, conductor, composer, and teacher. As a pianist his powers were prodigious, while as a composer he drew upon the classical German tradition, especially Brahms. His compositions include *Variations on a Nursery Song* (1913) and *Second Symphony for Orchestra* (1948).

Born in Bratislava, he studied under Carl Forstner, the cathedral organist in his native town, until 1893, when he went to the Hungarian Academy in Budapest, where he studied piano under Stephan Thomán and composition under Hans Koessler. In 1897 he had some lessons from Eugen d'Albert and appeared as a pianist in Berlin and Vienna. He visited England in 1898 and the USA in 1899, and made many more tours, but eventually became better known as a composer. From 1908 to 1915 he was professor of piano at the Hochschule in Berlin and in 1919 became conductor of the Budapest Philharmonic Orchestra and director of the city's conservatory. He premiered Béla Bartók's four orchestral pieces in Budapest 1922.

Rumoured to have been friendly with the Nazis during the 1930s and 1940s, he left Hungary in 1944 and subsequently settled in the USA.

Works OPERA *Aunt Simona* (Dresden, 1913), *The Tower of Voivod* (Budapest, 1922), *The Tenor* (1929).

BALLET *Pierrette's Veil*.

ORCHESTRAL symphonies in F minor, D minor, and E major, suite in F♯ minor and *Suite en valse* for orchestra; two piano concertos and *Variations on a Nursery Song* for piano and orchestra (1913);

two violin concertos, *Concertstück* for cello and orchestra.

CHAMBER three string quartets, piano quintet, sextet for violin, viola, cello, clarinet, horn, and piano, serenade for string trio; sonatas for violin and piano and cello and piano.

PIANO twelve Op. nos of piano music, including a passacaglia, four rhapsodies, *Humoresques in Form of a Suite*, *Ruralia hungarica*.

OTHER songs.

Doktor Faust opera by Ferruccio Busoni (libretto by composer) based on the Faust legend and Christopher Marlowe's play *Dr Faustus* (1589); it is not based on Goethe. The opera was left unfinished at Busoni's death; it was completed by Philipp Jarnach and first produced in Dresden, Germany, on 21 May 1925. The first production in Britain was at the London Coliseum on 25 April 1986, in a new edition by Antony Beaumont (first heard in Bologna, Italy, in 1985) in which the dying Faust transfers his soul to the corpse of a child.

Doktor und Apotheker, Doctor and Apothecary opera by Karl Ditters von Dittersdorf (libretto by G Stephanie, junior), first produced at the Burgtheater, Vienna, Austria, on 11 July 1786. The story tells how Gotthold and Leonore are forbidden to marry by their warring fathers, but after complications and disguises, the couple are united.

dolce (Italian 'sweet') in musical notation, indicating sweet, soft expression.

dolce stil nuovo (Italian 'sweet new style') a style of Italian lyric verse written between about 1250 and 1300. It was characterized by musicality, the spiritualization of courtly love, and a mystical and philosophical strain in the analysis of love. It was expressed in sonnets, *canzoni*, and ballads. The style was developed by Guido Guinizelli (c.1240–1276), Guido Cavalcanti, Gino da Pistoia (c.1265–c.1336), and above all Dante, whose lyrics in his *La vita nuova*, inspired by his love for Beatrice, are the finest examples of the *dolce stil nuovo*. It greatly influenced Petrarch and through him many later Italian poets.

The term was coined by Dante in *Purgatorio* XXIV 57.

dolcian musical instrument, an early form of ➔ bassoon.

Dolly suite of six children's pieces for piano duet by Gabriel Fauré, Op. 56, composed in 1893; an orchestral version for a ballet was arranged by Henri Rabaud in 1896 and it was first produced in Paris, France, on 23 January 1913. It is dedicated to the daughter of Mme Emma Bardac, later Claude Debussy's second wife. As in the case of Debussy's *Children's Corner*, the title and two of the sub-titles seem to suggest some English association: 1. *Berceuse*; 2. *Mi-a-ou*; 3. *Le Jardin de Dolly*; 4. *Kitty-Valse*; 5. *Tendresse*; 6. *Le Pas espagnol*.

Dolmetsch, (Eugène) Arnold (1858–1940) English musician and instrument maker, born into a Swiss family settled in France. Together with his family, including his son Carl (1911–1997), he revived interest in the practical performance of solo and consort music for lute, recorders, and viols, and established the baroque soprano (descant) recorder as an inexpensive musical instrument for schools.

He worked in Boston, USA, and Paris, France, as a restorer and maker of early musical instruments before establishing his workshop in Haslemere, England, in 1917.

Dolmetsch studied violin under Henry Vieuxtemps in Brussels, Belgium, but turned his interests to early music and instruments. He worked with the piano firm of Chickering in Boston 1902–09, and then with that of Gaveau in Paris until 1914, when he moved to England and set up his own workshop for harpsichords, viols, lutes, recorders, and other instruments in Haslemere. He arranged periodical festivals of early music and brought up a family to take part in them with various instruments. He edited early music and wrote a book on interpretation.

Domaines work by Pierre Boulez for solo clarinet and 21 instruments, composed in 1968 and first performed in Brussels, Belgium, on 20 December 1968.

Domestic Symphony orchestral work by Richard Strauss; see ➔ **Symphonia domestica**.

dominant in tonal music, the fifth note of a major or minor scale; for example, G in the C major scale. It is next in importance to the tonic and can be said to dominate because of its special relationship to the tonic (brass players will know it as the 'third harmonic' – the first being the 'fundamental' note produced by a length of tubing and the second being the octave above that).

Domino noir, Le, The Black Domino comic opera by Daniel Auber (libretto by Augustin Scribe), first produced at the Opéra-Comique, Paris, France, on 2 December 1837.

Dom Sébastien, Roi de Portugal, Dom Sebastian, King of Portugal opera by Gaetano Donizetti (libretto by Augustin Scribe), first produced at the Paris Opéra, France, on 13 November 1843. It tells the story of a crusade against the Moors led by the king of Portugal, Dom Sebastian. Although defeated by the Moors, Sebastian is saved by the amorous Zayda. Sebastian returns to Spain to find the throne has been usurped by his uncle, who throws the couple into prison; they are shot when they try to escape.

Donatoni, Franco (1927–2000) Italian composer. He studied in Rome with Ildebrando Pizzetti; he has been influenced by his teacher, and has used serial and, more recently, aleatory techniques.

Donatoni was born at Verona..He studied at the Accademia di Santa Cecilia in Rome with Pizzetti. At first his works were modelled on a Bartokian idiom, but after meeting the serialist composer Bruno Maderna in 1953 he took up integral serialism and produced his highly cerebral *For Grilly* (1960) as well as the *String Quartet II* (1958) and *Doubles* (1961). He tends to dense, heavily decorated writing, which has intensity but lacks clarity, especially in such concentrated orchestral scores as *Per orchestra* (1962), *Strophes*, and *Sezioni*. He is regarded as a leader of avant-garde music in Italy.

Works OPERA *Atem* (1985).

ORCHESTRAL Concerto for bassoon and strings (1952), Divertimento for violin and chamber orchestra (1954), *Black and White* for 37 strings (1964), *Doubles II* for orchestra (1970), *Portrait* for harpsichord and orchestra (1976), *In canda II* for orchestra (1994).

CHAMBER four string quartets (1950–63), *Etwas ruhiger in Ausdruck*, for chamber ensemble (1968; title from no. 2 of Schoenberg's piano pieces Op. 23); *Spiri* for string quartet and ensemble (1977), *Tema* for woodwind and strings (1981), *Refrain* for eight instruments (1986), *Flag* for 13 instruments (1987), *Chantal* for flute, clarinet, harp, and string quartet (1990), *Luci II* for bassoon and cornet (1996).

VOCAL *The Book with Seven Seals*, oratorio for soloists, chorus, and orchestra (1951), *Serenata* for soprano and 16 instruments (1959; text by Dylan Thomas), *Arias* for soprano and orchestra (1978).

Don Carlos opera by Giuseppe Verdi in five acts (libretto by F M Méry and C Du Locle, based on Schiller's drama), first produced at the Paris Opéra, France, on 11 March 1867. It is Verdi's second French opera. It was revised in four acts, in Italian, and produced at La Scala, Milan, Italy, on 10 January 1884. In the story, Don Carlos (heir to the throne) and Elisabeth love each other, but she has been promised to Carlos's father, King Philip. After the marriage, the lovers are discovered; Elisabeth withdraws to a monastery, where Carlos meets her. Philip arrives to hand his son over to the Inquisition, but Carlos is taken into the cloister by his grandfather's ghost.

Don Chisciotte della Mancia opera by Giovanni Paisiello (libretto by G B Lorenzi), first performed at the Teatro dei Fiorentini, Naples, Italy,

in the summer of 1769. A version by Hans Werner Henze was performed in Montepulciano, Italy, on 1 August 1976.

Don Chisciotte in corte della duchessa, Don Quixote at the Duchess's Court opera by Antonio Caldara (libretto by G C Pasquini, based on Cervantes), first produced in Vienna, Austria, on 6 February 1727.

Don Chisciotte in Sierra Morena, Don Quixote in the Sierra Morena opera by Francesco Conti (libretto by Zeno and P Pariati, based on Cervantes), first produced in Vienna, Austria, on 11 February 1719.

Don Giovanni, Don Juan opera by Mozart (originally *Il dissoluto punito, ossia Il Don Giovanni/The Rake Punished, or Don Juan*) (libretto by Lorenzo da Ponte). It was first produced in Prague (Czech Republic) on 29 October 1787; a new version with additions was produced at the Burgtheater, Vienna, Austria, on 7 May 1788. In the story, the dangerous Don Juan has a catalogue of conquests, but he fails to convince the Commendatore, murdered father of Donna Anna, who returns to drag him down to Hell.

Don Giovanni di Mañara opera by Franco Alfano; see ➔ *Ombra di Don Giovanni*.

Don Giovanni Tenorio, ossia Il convitato di pietra, Don Juan Tenorio, or The Stone Guest opera by Gazzaniga (libretto by G Bertati, based on the play by Tirso de Molina), first produced at the Teatro San Moisè, Venice, Italy, on 5 February 1787.

Donington, Robert (1907–1990) English instrumentalist and musicologist. He edited music, wrote learned articles, performed with various teams on early instruments, and produced books on instruments and ornaments, including *The Interpretation of Early Music* (1963).

He was educated at St Paul's School, London, and Oxford University, and studied early instruments and interpretation of music with Arnold Dolmetsch at Haslemere. He also published *Wagner's Ring and its Symbols* (1963) and *The Rise of Opera* (1981).

Donizetti, (Domenico) Gaetano (Maria) (1797–1848) Italian composer. He wrote more than 70 operas, including *Lucrezia Borgia* (1833), *Lucia di Lammermoor* (1835), *La Fille du régiment* (1840), *La Favorite* (1840), and *Don Pasquale* (1843). They show the influence of Gioacchino Rossini and Vincenzo Bellini, and his ability to create a good tune is heard in his expressive melodies.

Donizetti studied at Bergamo and at the Liceo Filarmonico in Bologna. He entered the army to avoid following his father's trade (caretaker of the municipal pawnshop), and while in Venice in 1818 produced his first opera, *Enrico di Borgogna*. *Anna Bolena* (1830) was the opera that brought him to fame. It was produced in 1830 in Milan, although by this time he had already written over 30 operas. His *Lucia di Lammermoor*, produced in Naples in 1835, was his greatest success. He excelled not only in serious operas, where he showed a gift for melody and mastery of dramatic ensembles, but also in comic operas, such as *La Fille du régiment/The Daughter of the Regiment* (1840), *L'elisir d'amore/The Elixir of Love* (1832), and *Don Pasquale* (1843). In 1839–40 and 1843 he visited Paris and produced operas there. At about this time his physical and mental health began to fail, and he became paralysed in 1845.

Donizetti's operas demanded capable singers, and first found favour through such great singers as Giuditta Grisi and Luigi Lablache. More recently, singers such as Maria Callas, Joan Sutherland, and Montserrat Caballé have helped find a new audience, in particular for the recently neglected serious works.

Works OPERA more than 70, including *Zoraida di Granata* (Rome, 1822), *L'ajo nell'imbarazzo* (Rome, 1824), *Emilia di Liverpool* (Naples, 1824), *Gabriella di Vergy* (composed 1826, performed Naples, 1869), *Il borgomastro di Saardam* (Naples, 1827), *Le convenienze ed inconvenienze teatrali* (Naples, 1827), *Il giovedi grasso* (Naples, 1828), *Alina, regina di Golconda* (1828), *Elisabetta, o Il castello di Kenilworth* (Naples, 1829), *Anna Bolena* (Milan, 1830), *Gianni di Parigi* (Milan, 1831), *Fausta* (Naples, 1832), *Ugo, conte di Parigi* (Milan, 1832), *L'elisir d'amore* (Milan 1832), *Il furioso all'isola di San Domingo* (Rome, 1833), *Torquato Tasso* (Rome, 1833), *Lucrezia Borgia* (Milan, 1833), *Rosmonda d'Inghilterra* (Florence, 1834), *Maria Stuarda* (Naples, 1834), *Gemma di Vergy* (Milan, 1834), *Marino Faliero* (Paris, 1835), *Lucia di Lammermoor* (Naples, 1835), *Belisario* (Venice, 1836), *Il campanello di notte* (Naples, 1836), *L'assedio di Calais* (1836), *Pia de' Tolomei* (Venice, 1837), *Roberto Devereux* (Naples, 1837), *Maria di Rudenz* (Venice, 1838), *La Fille du régiment* (Paris, 1840), *La Favorite* (Paris, 1840), *Maria Padilla* (Milan, 1841), *Linda di Chamounix* (Vienna, 1842), *Caterina Cornaro* (Naples, 1842), *Don Pasquale* (Paris, 1843), *Dom Sébastien* (Paris, 1843), *Poliuto* (Naples, 1848; originally composed in 1838 for Naples, it was banned and produced in Paris in 1840 as *Les Martyrs*), *Le Duc d'Albe* (written for Paris in 1840 but not produced; the score was completed by M Salvi and others and produced at the Teatro Apollo, Rome, on 22 March 1882).

Don Juan symphonic poem by Richard Strauss, Op. 20, based on Nikolaus Lenau's poem, composed 1887–88 and first performed in Weimar, Germany, on 11 November 1889.

Don Juan de Mañara opera by Eugene Goossens (libretto by Arnold Bennett), first produced at Covent Garden, London, England, on 24 June 1937.

Don Juan legend character of Spanish legend, Don Juan Tenorio, supposed to have lived in the 14th century and notorious for his debauchery. The story is that Don Juan, of the noble Tenorio family, is an abandoned profligate living in the days of Pedro the Cruel in Seville. When Ulloa thwarts Don Juan's schemes to seduce his daughter, he is stabbed by the dissolute lover. An atheist, Don Juan mockingly challenges a stone image of his victim to a banquet in his tomb. The outraged Ulloa comes to life, accepts, and then carries his murderer off to hell.

Well-known works based on the legend include ➔ *Don Giovanni* (➔ **Mozart**), ➔ *Don Giovanni Tenorio* (Giuseppe ➔ **Gazzaniga**), ➔ *Don Juan* (Richard ➔ **Strauss**), ➔ *Don Juan de Mañara* (Eugene ➔ **Goossens**), *Don Juan Mañara* (Enna, ➔ **Ferreira**), and ➔ *Ombra di Don Giovanni/Don Giovanni's Shade* (Franco ➔ **Alfano**). Other composers inspired by the story of Don Juan include Boris ➔ **Assafiev**, Ramón Carnicer, Vincenzo ➔ **Fabrizi**, Vincenzo Righini, Aleksandr ➔ **Dargomizhsky**, Paul ➔ **Graener**, Henry ➔ **Purcell**, Adolfo ➔ **Salazar**, Erwin ➔ **Schulhoff**, Vissarion ➔ **Shebalin**, and Henri ➔ **Tomasi**.

donna ancora è fedele, La, *The Lady is still Faithful* opera by Bernardo Pasquini (libretto by D F Contini), first produced at the Palazzo Colonna, Rome, Italy, on 19 April 1676.

donna del Lago, La, *The Lady of the Lake* opera by Gioachino Rossini (libretto by A L Tottola, based on Walter Scott's poem), first produced at the Teatro San Carlo, Naples, Italy, on 24 September 1819. The story, set in Scotland, tells how King James V loves Ellen, the daughter of the rebel Douglas. She in turn loves Malcolm, but must marry Douglas's ally Roderick. After Roderick is killed, James spares the captive Douglas and sanctions the marriage of Ellen and Malcolm.

Donna Diana opera by Emil von Reznicek (libretto by composer based on Moreto's comedy), first produced at the German Theatre, Prague (Czech Republic), on 16 December 1894. It describes how the haughty Diana is humbled by her persistent suitor.

donna serpente, La, *The Serpent-Woman* opera by Alfredo Casella (libretto by C Lodovici, based on Gozzi's comedy), first produced at the Teatro Reale, Rome, Italy, on 17 March 1932. In the story, the fairy Miranda marries Altidor against the wishes of her father, Demogorgòn, who forces her to test most cruelly Altidor's devotion. When eventually he fails the test she is turned into a snake, but thanks to the magic of wizard Geònca and Altidor's bravery, Miranda is restored.

donne curiose, Le, The Inquisitive Ladies opera by Ermanno Wolf-Ferrari (libretto by L Sugano, based on Carlo Goldoni's comedy), first produced in German in Munich, Germany, on 27 November 1903. It describes how a group of men are suspected of infidelities by their inquisitive womenfolk.

Donnerstag aus Licht, Thursday from Light first opera by Karlheinz ➔ **Stockhausen** from his projected opera cycle *Licht*. The work is semi-autobiographical: the three acts are titled *Michael's Youth*, *Michael's Journey around the Earth* (a huge concerto for trumpet and orchestra), and *Michael's Homecoming*. It was composed 1978–81 and first produced at La Scala, Milan, Italy, on 3 April 1981.

Don Pasquale comic opera by Gaetano Donizetti (libretto by composer and G Ruffini), based on Angelo Anelli's *Ser Marcantonio*, composed by Pavesi in 1810), first produced at the Théâtre Italien, Paris, France, on 3 January 1843. In the opera Pasquale disapproves of the match between his nephew Ernesto and Norina, but changes his mind after a mock marriage to 'Sofronia', Norina in disguise.

Don Quichotte opera in five acts by Jules Massenet (libretto by H Cain, based on Cervantes and Jacques Le Lorrain's comedy *Le Chevalier de la longue figure*), first produced in Monte Carlo, Monaco, on 19 February 1910. The story tells how Quichotte recovers Dulcinea's necklace from bandits, but she rejects him.

Don Quixote symphonic poem by Richard Strauss, Op. 35, based on Cervantes, composed in 1897 and first performed in Cologne, Germany, on 8 March 1898. The work is described as 'Fantastic Variations on a Theme of Knightly Character' and contains important solo parts for cello (Don Quixote) and viola (Sancho Panza).

Don Quixote, The Comical History of play by Thomas Durfey, based on Cervantes, with music by Henry Purcell and others. The music to parts i and ii was composed in 1694 by Purcell and John Eccles, and to part iii in 1695 by Akeroyde, Courteville, Pack, Morgan and Daniel Purcell. Part i was first produced at Dorset Gardens, London, England, in May 1694; part ii was produced at the same place in June 1694; and part iii at the Drury Lane Theatre, London, in November 1695.

Doppio Concerto work by Hans Werner ➔ **Henze** for oboe, harp, and strings, written for Heinz and

Ursula Holliger and performed by them in Zurich, Switzerland, on 2 December 1966.

doppio movimento (Italian 'double movement') in music, a direction indicating that a new tempo is to be exactly twice as fast as the one it displaces.

Dorati, Antál (1906–1988) US conductor, born in Hungary. He toured with ballet companies 1933–45 and went on to conduct orchestras in the USA and Europe in a career spanning more than half a century. Dorati gave many first performances of Béla Bartók's music and recorded all Haydn's symphonies with the Philharmonia Hungarica.

He studied at the Budapest Academy of Music with Bartók and Zoltán Kodály. He first conducted at the age of 18. In 1947 he became a US citizen and in 1948 conductor of the Minneapolis Symphony Orchestra. He was chief conductor of the British Broadcasting Corporation (BBC) Symphony Orchestra 1963–67, of the Royal Philharmonic Orchestra 1975–78, and of the Detroit Symphony Orchestra 1977–81. He also composed, and made a number of successful arrangements of pieces including Johann Strauss's *Graduation Ball*.

Dorfbarbier, Der, The Village Barber comic opera by Johann Schenk (libretto by J and P Weidmann), first produced at the Burgtheater, Vienna, Austria, on 30 October 1796.

Dori, La, ovvero La schiava fedele, Doris, or The Faithful Slave opera by Pietro Cesti (libretto by A Apolloni), first produced at Hof-Saales, Innsbruck, Switzerland, in 1657. In the work, Dori, disguised as a man, is sold as a slave to Arsinoe, her sister. The complicated plot ends happily with the sisters marrying Tolomeo and Oronte.

Dorian mode in music, one of the ➔ **church modes**, a scale D–C, centred around and beginning on D, which uses only the notes of the C major scale.

'Dorian' Toccata and Fugue organ work in D minor by Johann Sebastian ➔ **Bach**, so called on account of its notation without a key signature, the B flat being inserted where necessary as an accidental.

Dorn, Heinrich (Ludwig Egmont) (1804–1892) German composer, teacher, and conductor. He was a pupil of Carl Friedrich Zelter in Berlin, was taught by Robert Schumann at Leipzig, and was opera conductor at Hamburg and Riga, where he succeeded Richard Wagner in 1839. He later became conductor at the Royal Opera and professor in Berlin.

Works STAGE operas, *Die Rolandsknappen* (1826),

Die Nibelungen (1854); ballet *Amors Macht*.
OTHER Requiem; cantatas; orchestral works; piano music; songs.

Dostoevsky, Fyodor Mihailovich (1821–1881)
Russian novelist. His works and thought inspired the composers Riccardo ➤ Chailly (*L'Idiota*), Vladimir ➤ Rebikov (*The Christmas Tree*), Daniel ➤ Ruyneman (*The Brothers Karamazov*), and Heinrich ➤ Sutermeister (*Raskolnikov*), and the works ➤ *From the House of the Dead* (Janáček), ➤ The Gambler (Prokofiev), ➤ *Der Grossinquisitor* (Boris Blacher), and ➤ *Der Idiot* (Henze).

dot in music, a dot above or under a note normally indicates staccato. Uses other than this are: (*a*) in 18th-century violin music, a series of dots with a slur indicates notes to be detached without changing the bow; (*b*) in 18th-century clavichord music, a series of dots with a slur above or under a single note indicates repeated pressure on the key; (*c*) in older French music, dots above or under a succession of quavers or semi-quavers could mean the observance of equal note-values (*notes égales*), as opposed to the current fashion of lengthening or shortening such notes alternately (*notes inégales*).

A dot to the right of a note normally lengthens it by half. See ➤ dotted notes.

dotted notes notes with a dot placed on their right, with the effect of prolonging them by half their original value. A double dot has the effect of adding another half of the smaller value to the original note, which is thus lengthened by three-quarters of its value. Double dots were introduced by Leopold Mozart, before whose time their effect could not be precisely indicated in notation, though it was often produced at will by the interpreter, especially in slow movements written in singly dotted rhythm, such as the slow introductions in Lully's and Handel's overtures.

dot-way a 17th-century system of musical notation for recorders, with staves where each line represented a fingerhole, while dots placed over the lines showed which fingers were to be kept down for each note.

double the old French name for a type of musical variation that was merely a more highly ornamented version of a theme previously played in plainer notes.

double bar a pair of bar-lines placed very close together and marking off a principal section of a musical composition, such as the end of the exposition and beginning of the development in a sonata or symphony. It may be preceded or followed by repeat signs, or both, in which case the music before and/or after it must be repeated.

double bass largest and lowest-sounding instrument of the ➤ violin family. It is 1.85 m/6 ft high and is played resting on the ground with the performer either standing or sitting on a high stool. Its sloping shoulders and flatter back link it to the viol family, where it is descended from the bass viol or violone. Until 1950, after which it was increasingly replaced by the electric bass, it also provided bass support (plucked) in popular music, although it is still the main bass instrument used in jazz. Performers include Domenico Dragonetti, composer of eight concertos, the Russian-born US conductor Serge Koussevitsky (1874–1951), and the jazz player and composer Charles Mingus. The double bass features as a solo in 'The Elephants' from Charles Camille ➤ Saint-Saëns's *Carnival of the Animals* (1897).

The double bass has a range of just over three octaves and is tuned in fourths: E1, A1, D2, and G2.

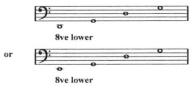

8ve lower

or

8ve lower

8ve lower

The double bass has four strings, formerly three, tuned (top or centre). The first of these is the one in general use. The range can be artificially extended either by tuning down the bottom string or by the addition of a fifth string. In the latter case the instrument is normally tuned as shown in the bottom illustration. If the C string is tuned down to B, this will continue the tuning in fourths.

double bassoon or **contrabassoon** musical instrument, a ➤ bassoon with a range an octave lower than that of the ordinary instrument.

double bass viol alternative name for the ➤ violone, a musical instrument.

double chant a chant in two sections used in the Anglican Church and covering two verses of a psalm.

double concerto a concerto for two solo instruments, such as Bach's D minor for two violins, Mozart's E flat major for two pianos, Brahms's A minor for violin and cello, and Elliott Carter's double concerto for piano and harpsichord.

double counterpoint see ➤ counterpoint.

double dots indication in musical notation that the value of a note is to be increased; see ➤ **dotted notes**.

double flat in music, an accidental, ♭♭, lowering the note before which it stands by a whole tone.

double fugue in music, a ➤ **fugue** consisting of two subjects (principal melodies). Of two types, one consists of three sections: a fugue on subject A, a fugue on subject B, and a fugue combining A and B. The other consists of a fugue in which both subjects are introduced at the beginning of the piece and combined throughout.

double sharp in music, an accidental, 𝄪 or ♯♯, raising the note before which it stands by a whole tone.

double stopping on a stringed musical instrument, the technique of producing two notes simultaneously by ➤ **stopping** two separate strings.

doucemelle keyboard instrument in use around the 15th century; a forerunner of the ➤ **piano**. It is also an alternative name for the ➤ **dulcimer**.

Dowland, John (c.1563–c.1626) English composer of lute songs. He become known as the greatest composer and finest performer of these 'ayres' and is considered the main pioneer in the development of the art song. For the first time the 'top' part became more important than the others and the lute was used to provide a real accompaniment. This was different to the previous style of the madrigal, where all voices are equally important. His work includes *Lachrymae* (1605).

Dowland, Robert (c.1591–1641) English lutenist and composer, son of John ➤ **Dowland**. He was appointed lutenist to Charles I on his father's death in 1626. He composed lessons for the lute, and published a book of airs by continental composers.

downbeat in music, the downward movement of a conductor's hand or baton, signifying the starting point or strong beat of a musical bar.

down bow in the playing of string instruments, the movement of the bow in the direction from the heel to the point. It is stronger than the up bow, and string technique usually places a down bow on important beats and accented notes, unless marked otherwise in the music.

Down by the Greenwood Side dramatic pastoral in one act by Harrison Birtwistle (libretto by M Nyman), for soprano, five actors, and chamber ensemble. It was first performed at the Pier Pavilion, Brighton, England, on 8 May 1969. It tells how St George is defeated by the Black Knight but revives under the vernal earth magic of the Green Man.

Draeseke, Felix (August Bernhard) (1835–1913) German composer. He studied at the Leipzig Conservatory and with Liszt at Weimar. He later taught at Dresden, Lausanne, Munich, and Geneva, and finally settled in Dresden in 1876, where he became professor of composition at the Conservatory in 1884.

Works OPERA *Gudrun* (1884), *Herrat*, *Merlin* (1903–05).

SACRED MUSIC Requiem; trilogy of oratorios *Christus*.

ORCHESTRAL five symphonies, overtures for orchestra, including *Penthesilea* (after Kleist); concerto for piano, violin, and cello.

VOCAL Easter scene from Goethe's *Faust* for solo voices, chorus, and orchestra (1907).

CHAMBER three string quartets, string quintet; many piano works including a sonata.

drag in playing the ➤ **snare drum**, a stroke preceded by a group of grace-notes, usually three or four.

Draghi, Antonio (c.1634–1700) Italian composer. He began his career as a singer in Venice. In 1658 he went to Vienna, Austria, to take up a court appointment, and was appointed Hofkapellmeister in 1682. He was also a librettist for other composers, including Bertali, Ziani, and the emperor Leopold I.

Works 67 operas, including *Timone misantropo*, after Shakespeare (1696), 116 smaller stage pieces, about 40 oratorios, cantatas, hymns, and other pieces.

drame lyrique a modern French term for a serious opera.

dramma (per musica) (Italian 'drama (for music)') 18th-century term for opera; in modern usage, plays written especially for the purpose of being set to music.

dramma giocoso (Italian 'jocular drama') name occasionally used for ➤ **opera buffa** in the later 18th century; Mozart's original designation of *Don Giovanni*.

Drátenik, The Tinker opera by Škroup (libretto by J K Chmelenský), first produced in Prague on 2 February 1826. It is the first Czech opera.

Dream of Gerontius, The oratorio by Edward Elgar, Op. 38 (words selected from Cardinal John Henry Newman's poem), first performed at the Birmingham Festival, England, on 3 October 1900.

Dreigroschenoper, Die*, *The Threepenny Opera operetta by Kurt Weill (libretto based on Elisabeth Hauptmann's German version of John Gay's *The Beggar's Opera*, with some additions by Brecht). It was first produced at the Theater am Schiffbauerdamm, Berlin, Germany, on 31 August 1928. It tells the story of how Mack the Knife escapes the gallows.

Drei Pintos, Die, The Three Pintos unfinished opera by Carl Maria von Weber (libretto by T Hell, based on Carl Ludwig Seidel's story *Der Brautkampf*), partly composed in 1821 and first produced in an edition completed by Mahler in Leipzig, Germany, on 20 January 1888. It concerns Don Pinto's misadventures on his way to wooing Clarissa. He is impersonated by her true love Don Gomez, who eventually marries her.

drone in music, a continuous accompanying note usually played in the bass. Its main feature is that it is sustained or persistently repeated throughout a piece or part of a piece of music. It is found in many classical and folk traditions, is common in the vocal music of the Russian, Greek, and Bulgarian Orthodox Churches, and is produced by many folk music instruments, including the Indian vina, bagpipes, and hurdy-gurdy. Drone effects in written music include the organ ➤ **pedal point** and the ➤ **musette** dance form.

Drone is also the name given to the three lower pipes of the bagpipes, which produce a fixed chord above which the melody is played on the ➤ **chanter**. It is also a bowed instrument with a single string stretched on a stick over a bladder, sometimes called a bumbass.

Among examples of drone in the concert repertoire are Wagner's overture to *Das Rheingold/ The Rhinegold* (1853–54) and the mystery chord of Schoenberg's third orchestral piece 'Farben'/ 'Chord Colours' from the *Five Pieces for Orchestra* (1909).

drone bass an unvaryingly sustained bass on any composition, resembling the drone of a bagpipe.

Druckman, Jacob (1928–1996) US composer. His earlier works were mainly chamber pieces; he later turned to writing orchestral music, including *Windows* (1972), for which he won a Pulitzer Prize.

He studied at the Juilliard School, New York, and in Paris, France. He directed electronic music centres at Princeton and Yale universities, USA.

Works ORCHESTRAL violin concerto (1956), *Windows* (1972), *Chiaroscuro* for orchestra (1976), viola concerto (1978), *Aureole* for orchestra (1979), *Prism*, three pieces for orchestra after music from operas by Marc-Antoine Charpentier, Cavalli, and Cherubini (1980), *Athenor* for orchestra (1985).

VOICES AND INSTRUMENTS *Dark upon the Harp* for mezzo, brass quintet, and percussion (1962), *The Sound of Time* for soprano and orchestra (1965), *Animus I–IV* for mezzo, instruments, and tape (1966–77), *Lamia* for soprano and orchestra (1974).

CHAMBER three string quartets (1948, 1961, 1981).

drum any of a class of percussion instruments consisting of a frame or hollow vessel of wood, metal, or earthenware with a membrane of hide or plastic stretched across one or both ends. Drums are usually sounded by striking the membrane with the hands, a stick, or pair of sticks. They are among the oldest instruments known and exist in a wide variety of shapes and sizes. They include **slit drums** made of wood, **steel drums** made from oil containers, and a majority group of **skin drums**.

tuned drums Most drums are of indeterminate low or high pitch and are used as rhythm instruments. The exceptions are steel drums, orchestral ➤ **timpani** (kettledrums), and Indian ➤ **tabla** which are tuned to precise pitches. Double-ended African kalungu ('talking drums') can be varied in pitch by the player squeezing on the tension cords; higher tension over the playing drumhead results in a higher pitch. Frame drums, including the Irish bodhrán and Basque tambour, are smaller and lighter in tone and may incorporate jingles or rattles.

orchestral and military drums Orchestral drums consist of timpani, tambourine, snare, side, and bass drums. The bass drum is either single-headed (with a single skin) and producing a ringing tone, called a gong drum, or double-headed (with two skins) and producing a dense booming noise of indeterminate pitch. Military bands of footsoldiers play snare and side drums, and cavalry regiments use a pair of kettledrums mounted on horseback for ceremonial occasions.

pop and jazz drums Drum kits have evolved from the 'traps' of Dixieland jazz into a range of percussion employing a variety of stick types. In addition to snare and foot-controlled bass drums, many feature a scale of pitched bongos and tom-toms, as well as suspended cymbals, hi-hat (foot-controlled double cymbals), cowbells, and temple blocks. Recent innovations include the rotary tuneable rototoms, electronic drums, and the drum machine, a percussion synthesizer.

Drum Mass popular name for Mass no. 7 in C major by Haydn; see ➤ **Paukenmesse**.

'Drum-Roll' Symphony, German **Symphonie mit dem Paukenwirbel** nickname of Haydn's symphony no. 103 in E flat major (composed for London, 1795), so called because it opens with a timpani roll.

Dryden, John (1631–1700) English poet, dramatist, and satirist. His works inspired numerous musical settings, such as ➤ **Acis and Galatea** and ➤ **Alexander's Feast** (Handel), ➤ **Albion and Albanius** (Louis Grabu), ➤ **Almahide** (Giovanni Bononcini), ➤ **Cymon** (Michael Arne), ➤ **Indian Queen** and ➤ **King Arthur** (Purcell), and ➤ **Ode for St Cecilia's Day** (Handel). Composers inspired by Dryden include William Boyce (*Secular Masque*), Jeremiah ➤ **Clarke** (*Alexander's Feast*), Giovanni Baptista Draghi (*Ode for St Cecilia's Day*), John Eccles (*Spanish Friar*), Pelham ➤ **Humfrey** (*Conquest of Granada* and *Indian Emperor*), Henry ➤ **Purcell** (*Amphitryon, Aureng-Zebe, Cleomenes, Love Triumphant, Spanish Friar, Tyrannic Love,* and *Oedipus*), and Nicholas ➤ **Staggins** (*Conquest of Granada* and *Marriage à la mode*).

D.S. in music, abbreviation for **dal segno** (Italian 'from the sign').

Dubois, (François Clément) Théodore (1837–1924) French composer. He studied at Rheims and then at the Paris Conservatory, where he won the Prix de Rome in 1861. Returning to Paris in 1866, he was active as an organist and teacher, and succeeded Camille Saint-Saëns as organist at the Madeleine in 1877. From 1896 to 1905 he was director of the Conservatory. His treatises on harmony, counterpoint, and fugue are still in use.

Works OPERA *La Guzla de l'Emir* (1873), *Le Pain bis* (1879), *Aben-Hamet, Xavière* (1895).

BALLET *La Farandole.*

SACRED MUSIC *Requiem, Messe de la Délivrance* and other Masses, motets and other church music; oratorios, *Les Sept Paroles du Christ* and *Paradis perdu.*

OTHER orchestral works.

due corde (Italian 'two strings') in music, direction to a pianist to depress the ➤ **soft pedal** halfway (as in Beethoven's Piano Sonata in A Flat, 1822) so that the hammer hits two of the three strings for each note, or directing a violinist to use two strings, which affects the timbre, even though the passage in question could be played on one string.

due Foscari, I, The Two Foscari opera by Giuseppe Verdi (libretto by Francesco Maria Piave, based on Lord Byron's drama), first produced at the Teatro Argentina, Rome, Italy, on 3 November 1844. In the story, the doge's son Jacopo has been accused of murder. He is first imprisoned, then exiled, against the pleas of his wife, Lucrezia. It is revealed too late that Jacopo is innocent: he dies upon leaving Venice.

due litiganti, Fra opera by Giuseppe Sarti; see ➤ **Fra due litiganti.**

Duenna, The, The Double Elopement opera by Thomas Linley, father and son (libretto by Richard Brinsley Sheridan), first produced at Covent Garden, London, England, on 21 November 1775. Sheridan was the son-in-law of Linley senior.

It is also the title of an opera by Roberto Gerhard (libretto by composer and C Hassall after Sheridan), first performed by the British Broad-

casting Corporation (BBC) and broadcast on 23 February 1949; it had its stage premiere in Madrid, Spain, on 21 January 1992. In the story, Luisa is inclined to Antonio but must marry Isaac Mendoza. After mistaken identities and twists in the plot, the opera ends with a triple wedding: Luisa marries Antonio, Luisa's brother Ferdinand marries Clara, and Isaac Mendoza marries Margaret, Luisa's duenna. See also ➤ **Betrothal in a Monastery.**

duet or **duo** music or ensemble of two voices or instruments. A piano duet is normally two players sharing a single instrument (also called 'piano four-hands'); a piano duo is two players on two pianos.

Dufay, Guillaume (c.1400–1474) Flemish composer. He wrote secular songs and sacred music, including 84 songs and eight masses. His work marks a transition from the style of the Middle Ages to the expressive melodies and rich harmonies of the Renaissance.

Dukas, Paul Abraham (1865–1935) French composer and teacher. His scrupulous orchestration and chromatically enriched harmonies were admired by Debussy. He wrote very little, composing slowly and with extreme care. His small output includes the opera *Ariane et Barbe-Bleue/Ariane and Bluebeard* (1907), the ballet *La Péri/The Peri* (1912), and the animated orchestral scherzo *L'Apprenti sorcier/The Sorcerer's Apprentice* (1897). *Ariane et Barbe-Bleue* is among the finest French operas of its day, premiered four years before Bartók wrote *Duke Bluebeard's Castle* (1918).

Dukas studied at the Paris Conservatory, where his teachers included Théodore Dubois and Ernest Guiraud. He taught the orchestral class there 1910–13 and was then appointed professor of composition; in 1926 he also began teaching at the École Normale, and held both posts until his death. Among his pupils at the Conservatory was Olivier Messiaen.

Works STAGE opera *Ariane et Barbe-Bleue* (Maeterlinck; 1907); ballet *La Péri* (1912).

ORCHESTRAL symphony in C major (1896), overture to Corneille's *Polyeucte, L'Apprenti sorcier* (on Goethe's poem 'Der Zauberlehrling'; 1897).

PIANO sonata in E♭ minor, *Variations on a theme by Rameau, Prélude élégiaque* on the name of Haydn (1909), *La Plainte, au loin, du faune* (in memory of Debussy; 1920).

VOICE AND PIANO *Sonnet de Ronsard* (1924) and *Vocalise* for voice and piano.

CHAMBER *Villanelle* for horn and piano.

OTHER unpublished overtures to Shakespeare's *King Lear* and Goethe's *Götz von Berlichingen.*

Duke Bluebeard's Castle, Hungarian **A kékszakállú hercegvára** opera in one act by Béla Bartók (libretto by B Balázs), composed in 1911 and first produced in Budapest, Hungary, on 24 May 1918, conducted by Egisto Tango. It recounts how the inquisitive bride Judith tours Bluebeard's blood-spattered castle and joins his former wives in eternal gloom.

Dukelsky, Vladimir (1903–1969) Russian-born US composer. Influenced by George Gershwin he wrote light music under the name of **Vernon Duke** and became well known for his stage and film scores. He also continued to write classical music, cultivating an advanced modern style under his own name. His concert music was promoted by Sergei ➤ **Koussevitsky.**

He studied at Moscow and Kiev, where his teachers included Reinhold Glière. He went to live in Constantinople, Turkey, in 1920 and settled in New York, USA, in 1922, where he wrote a piano concerto for Artur Rubenstein. In Paris, France, he wrote the ballet *Zéphir et Flore* for Sergei Diaghilev and he wrote stage music in London, England, 1926–29. From this point on he tended to use his original Russian name for his serious music and his adopted name for his more popular works. His best-known song was probably 'April in Paris' from the revue *Walk a Little Faster* (1932), while his best-known musical was *Cabin in the Sky* (1940).

Works STAGE operetta *Yvonne* (1926); ballets *Zéphir et Flore* and *Public Gardens.*
ORATORIO *The End of St Petersburg* (1937).
ORCHESTRAL four symphonies; piano concerto.
VOCAL *Dédicaces* for soprano, piano, and orchestra; song cycle *Triolets of the North* (Feodor Sologub); Three Chinese songs and other songs.
CHAMBER string quartet; violin sonata.

dulce melos (Latin 'sweet melody') keyboard instrument, also known as the ➤ **chekker.**

dulcian in music, an organ stop of reedy quality, usually of 16-foot pitch (sounding an octave lower than written); also an alternative name for the ➤ **curtal.**

dulciana an open ➤ **diapason** organ stop of delicate tone. It may embrace 1.2 m/4 ft, 2.4 m/8 ft, or 4.8 m/16 ft pipes.

dulcimer musical instrument, a form of ➤ **zither,** consisting of a shallow open trapezoidal soundbox across which strings are stretched laterally; they are horizontally struck by lightweight hammers or beaters. It produces clearly differentiated pitches of consistent quality and is more agile and wide-ranging in pitch than the harp or lyre. In Hungary the dulcimer is known as a cimbalom, and is a national instrument.

Of Middle Eastern origin, the dulcimer spread into Europe about 1100 and was introduced to China and Korea about 1800. Examples include the Iraqi *santir,* Chinese *yang shin,* Russian *chang,* Korean *yangum,* and Swiss *hackbrett.*

dulcitone keyboard instrument producing its sound on a set of tuning forks, similar to the ➤ **celesta.**

Dumanoir, Guillaume (1615–c. 1697) French violinist and composer. As the 'Roi des Violons' (the head of the guild of violin players) he came into conflict with the dancing-masters, whom he wished to compel to contribute to the violinists' guild of Saint-Julien. Being unsuccessful in this, he wrote the abusive pamphlet *Le Mariage de la musique avec la danse/The Marriage of Music and Dance* (1664). He composed dance music that was liked by Louis XIV, who appointed him ballet master of the royal pages.

He was the son of Guillaume Dumanoir, whom he succeeded as head of the Confrérie de Saint-Julien (the violinists' guild). He renewed his father's quarrel with the dancing masters, resigning in 1685. Before that he had quarrelled with Jean-Baptiste Lully over the privilege of training orchestra musicians and lost a lawsuit against him in 1673.

Dumbarton Oaks concerto in E flat for chamber orchestra by Igor Stravinsky, composed 1937–38 and first performed in Washington, DC, at Dumbarton Oaks, the private estate of R W Bliss, on 8 May 1938. The first public performance was given in Paris, France, on 4 June 1938.

dumka a lament, which in music takes the form of a slow piece alternating with more animated sections, as in Dvořák's 'Dumky' Trio.

'Dumky' Trio a piano trio by Antonín ➤ **Dvořák,** Op. 90, composed in 1891.

Dunhill, Thomas (Frederick) (1877–1946) English composer. He was assistant music master at Eton College 1899–1908, and organized concerts for chamber music and for the promotion of British music in London during the early years of the century. He entered the Royal College of Music, London, in 1893, where Charles Stanford was his composition master, and where he later became professor of composition.

Works OPERA *The Enchanted Garden* (1928), *Tantivy Towers* (A P Herbert, 1931), *Happy Families.*
BALLET *Dick Whittington, Gallimaufry.*
ORCHESTRAL symphony in A minor, *Elegiac Variations* in memory of Parry and overture *Maytime* for orchestra; *Triptych* for viola and orchestra.
CHAMBER piano quartet, two piano trios, five quintets.

Duni, Egidio Romoaldo (1708–1775) Italian composer. He wrote about ten serious operas in Italy, beginning with *Nerone* (1735), which was a great success. In 1757 he settled in Paris, France, where he became a leading composer of opéras comiques, notably *Le Peintre amoureux de son modèle* (1757).

He studied under Francesco Durante in Naples.

Works OPERA *Nerone* (1735), *Le Caprice amoureux*, *Le Peintre amoureux de son modèle* (1757), *L'Isle des fous*, *Le Milicien*, *Les Deux Chasseurs et la laitière* (1763), *La Fée Urgèle*, *La Clochette* (1766), *Les Moissonneurs*, *Les Sabots* (1768).

Dunstable or **Dunstaple, John (c.1385–1453)** English composer of songs and anthems. He is considered one of the founders of Renaissance harmony.

Duparc, (Marie Eugène) Henri Fouques (1848–1933) French composer. His songs are memorable for their lyric sensibility. Only 16 of them survive.

He was educated by Jesuits at the Collège de Vaugirard, where he learned piano from César Franck, and afterwards took private lessons in composition from him. His few works include the symphonic poem *Lénore* (1875), and a nocturne, *Aux étoiles*, but he is chiefly remembered for his songs, among them 'Invitation au voyage' and 'Phydilé'. He was a fierce critic of his own work and destroyed almost all his compositions. He never took any share in official musical life, but continued to compose at intervals until 1885, when he began to suffer from an incurable nervous complaint and retired to Switzerland.

Works ORCHESTRAL symphonic poem *Lénore* (on Bürger's poem, 1875) and nocturne *Aux étoiles*.

CHORAL motet *Benedicat vobis Dominus*.

SONGS 16 songs including 'Phydilé', 'Invitation au voyage', 'Soupir', 'La Vague et la cloche', 'Extase', 'Le Manoir de Rosemonde', and 'Lamento'; and several afterwards destroyed.

duplet group of two notes occupying the time of three.

duple time in music, a metre in which the bar may be divided into two beats, as in 2/4 and 6/8.

Dupré, Marcel (1886–1971) French organist and composer. He was appointed professor of organ at the Paris Conservatory in 1926 and organist at Saint-Sulpice in 1936, succeeding Charles Marie Widor. From 1954 to 1956 he was director of the Conservatory.

He played Bach from memory at the age of ten, and in 1898 was appointed organist of the church of Saint-Vivien in Rouen. He produced an oratorio in 1901. After that he studied piano, organ, and composition at the Paris Conservatory and won the Prix de Rome in 1914 as a pupil of Widor. He was organist at Notre-Dame 1916–22 during the illness of Louis Vierne. His pupils at the Conservatory included Jehan Alain and Olivier Messiaen.

Works the oratorio *Le Songe de Jacob*, motets and *De Profundis*; two symphonies; concerto for organ and orchestra (1934); violin and piano sonata; cello pieces; songs; many organ works including *Symphonie-Passion*, 79 chorales, *Le Chemin de la Croix*.

dur (German 'hard') in music, the German equivalent of 'major' when referring to a key, as in 'C *dur*' (C major). *Dur* is the opposite of *moll*.

Durand, Auguste Frédéric (1770–1834), born **Auguste Duranowski** Polish-born French violinist and composer. A virtuoso violinist, he was renowned for his technique and was a significant influence on Niccolò Paganini.

Duranowski, August Fryderyk Polish-born French violinist and composer; see Auguste ➔ **Durand**.

Durante, Francesco (1684–1755) Italian composer. His works consist largely of church music, also sonatas, toccatas, and other pieces for harpsichord. Unusually for a Neapolitan composer, he wrote no operas.

He was educated in Naples, where in 1742 he became maestro di cappella at the Conservatorio di S Maria and in 1745 at that of S Onofrio. His pupils included Tommaso Traetta, Giovanni Paisiello, Antonio Sacchini, Giovanni Pergolesi, and Niccolò Piccinni.

Durchführung (German 'through-leading') in music, term for the ➔ **development** or working-out section of a movement in sonata form.

durchkomponiert (German 'set throughout') in music, a descriptive term for a song in which the words are set to music continuously, not strophically with the same music repeated for each verse.

Durey, Louis (1888–1979) French composer. He did not study music until the age of 22, and in 1914 he enlisted on the outbreak of World War I. In 1916, during leave, he came under the influence of Erik Satie and joined the group known as Les Six, but was the first to secede from it in 1921. In 1923 he went to live in seclusion in southern France, writing very little.

Works STAGE opera on Mérimée's *L'Occasion* (1925); incidental music to Hebbel's *Judith* (1918).

CHAMBER three string quartets, piano trio, string trio.

SONGS song cycles with chamber music or piano.

durezza (Italian 'hardness') in music, term now used in the direction *con durezza* to indicate that a harsh or unyielding manner of performance is required. Up until the 17th century the term was used for discord.

Durfey or **D'Urfey, Thomas (1653–1723)** English playwright and poet. His works inspired the composers ➤ **Akeroyde** and Ralph Courteville (*Don Quixote*), Giovanni Baptista Draghi (*Wonders in the Sun*), John Eccles (*Don Quixote*), Mathew ➤ **Locke** (*Fool turned Critic*), Daniel ➤ **Purcell** (*Cynthia and Endymion*), Henry ➤ **Purcell** (*Fool's Preferment*, *Marriage-Hater Matched*, *Richmond Heiress*, *Sir Barnaby Whigg*, and *Virtuous Wife*), William ➤ **Turner** (*Fond Husband* and *Madam Fickle*), and ➤ **Don Quixote, The Comical History of** by Purcell and others.

Durkó, Zsolt (1934–1997) Hungarian composer. His music breaks away from local influences and favours the avant garde.

He studied in Budapest and with Goffredo Petrassi in Rome, Italy.

Works OPERA *Moses* (produced Budapest 1977).

ORCHESTRAL *Organismi* for violin and orchestra (1964), *Fioriture* for orchestra (1966), *Turner Illustrations* for orchestra (1976).

VOCAL *Dartmouth Concerto* for soprano and orchestra (1966), *Altimara* for chorus and orchestra (1968), *Funeral Oration*, oratorio (1972), *Ilmarinen* for chorus (1989).

CHAMBER two string quartets (1966, 1969), *Impromptus in F* for flute and ensemble (1984); wind octet (1988).

Durón, Sebastián (1660–1716) Spanish composer, an early exponent of Spanish opera. He was organist at Seville Cathedral 1680–85. In 1691 he became organist at the court of Madrid and was appointed maestro de capilla in 1702.

Not having supported the Bourbon succession, he seems to have gone into exile in 1706.

Works OPERA AND ZARZUELAS *Muerte en amor es la ausencia*, *Apolo y Dafne*, *Selva encantada de Amor*, *Las nuevas armas de Amor*, *La guerra de los gigantes*, *Salir el amor del mundo*.

OTHER incidental music for a comedy, *Jupiter*; two ballets.

Dürr, Alfred (1918–) German musicologist. He studied at the University of Göttingen. From 1953 he edited the *Bach-Jahrbuch* and has been principal contributor to the Bach *Neue Ausgabe* (complete works). Bach's cantatas are at the centre of his research.

Dürr, Walter (1932–) German musicologist. He studied at Tübingen University and taught there from 1962; from 1965 he was joint editor of the *Neue Schubert-Ausgabe* at Tübingen. Other fields of study are Mozart and the Italian madrigal.

Duruflé, Maurice (1902–1986) French organist and composer. He learnt music in the choir school of Rouen Cathedral 1912–18, and then studied at the Paris Conservatory under Louis Vierne, Charles Tournemire, and Paul Dukas. He was appointed organist at the church of Saint-Etienne-du-Mont in 1929.

Works Requiem for chorus and orchestra (1947); *Messe-cum jubilo* (1966); chorale on *Veni Creator*, suite and many other works for organ; *Prelude, Recitative and Variations* for flute, viola, and piano; three dances for orchestra.

Dušek, Franz (František Xaver) (1731–1799) Bohemian (Czech) pianist and composer. He wrote about 40 symphonies and 20 string quartets.

He was a pupil of Georg Wagenseil in Vienna, Austria. Dušek himself later taught in Prague, Bohemia, and was the master of many famous pupils. He and his wife Josefa (1754–1824) were friends of Mozart, and worked on his opera *Don Giovanni* at their home in Prague.

Dussek, Jan Ladislav (1760–1812) Bohemian (Czech) composer and pianist. A virtuoso pianist, his compositions, which include over 40 piano sonatas and about 18 piano concertos, often display technically challenging passages, by the standard of his day. Composing more fully textured (and often more harmonically adventurous) music than most of his contemporaries, Dussek foreshadowed many of the musical developments of the 19th century. He was one of a group of composers known as the ➤ **London Pianoforte School**.

Dussek was an accomplished pianist at the age of five and an organist at nine. He was educated at a Jesuit College and Prague University, where he read theology. He had shown early promise, and in about 1779 went to the Netherlands, where he held organ posts at Malines and Bergen-op-Zoom. He gave up his organist's career about 1782, and won great success in Amsterdam and The Hague as a pianist and composer. Concert tours took him to Hamburg (where he studied with C P E Bach), Berlin, and St Petersburg, where he entered the service of Prince Radziwill, spending the next two years on the latter's estate in Lithuania. He played before Marie Antoinette in Paris in 1786, and after a visit to Italy returned there in 1788. At the French Revolution he fled to London, where he first appeared at one of Salomon's concerts in 1790. In 1792 he married the singer and pianist Sophia Corri (1745–1847), and joined his father-in-law's firm of music publishers. The business failed, and in 1800 he went to Hamburg to escape his creditors. More travels followed. He was with Prince Louis Ferdinand of Prussia 1803–06, then in the service of the Prince of Isenburg and, finally, Talleyrand.

His piano music uses the instrument in a novel and congenial way. His sonatas show many striking anticipations of later composers; his influence on Beethoven was particularly important.

Works STAGE incidental music for *The Captive of*

Spilburg (London, 1798) and Sheridan's *Pizarro* (both with Kelly).

ORCHESTRAL three overtures and serenade for orchestra.

CHURCH MUSIC Mass (1811).

CHAMBER three string quartets; about 65 sonatas with violin or flute.

PIANO two piano quartets, piano quintet, about 20 piano trios; about twelve sonatas for piano duet, sonata for two pianos; about 18 piano concertos, about 32 sonatas, about 25 rondos, about 20 sets of variations, various miscellaneous pieces.

Dutilleux, Henri (1916–) French composer. He wrote instrumental music in elegant Neo-Romantic style. His works include *Métaboles* (1962–65) for orchestra, *Ainsi la nuit/Thus the Night* (1976) for string quartet, *Timbres, espaces, mouvement* (1978) for orchestra, *Le jeu des contraires* (1989) for piano; and *Diptyque: Les Citations* (1991) for oboe, harpsichord, double bass, and percussion. His music is regarded as being in the tradition of ➔ Ravel, ➔ Debussy, and ➔ Messiaen, although he has always strictly refused to join groups or musical schools, or even to be regarded as belonging to a particular group.

He studied at the Paris Conservatory and won the Prix de Rome in 1938; he was professor of composition at the Ecole Normale de Musique in Paris 1961–70, and also taught as an associate professor at the Conservatory in Paris 1970–71.

Works ORCHESTRAL two symphonies (performed Paris, 1950 and Boston, 1959), *Cinq Métaboles* for orchestra (first performance Cleveland, 1965), *Tout un monde lointain* for cello and orchestra (1970), *Timbres, espaces, mouvement* for orchestra (first performance Washington, 1978), *L'Arbre des songes* for violin and orchestra (1985).

BALLET *Le Loup* (1953), *Summer's End* (1981).

VOCAL *La giole* for voice and orchestra (1944).

CHAMBER AND INSTRUMENTAL *Ainsi la nuit* for string quartet (1976); *Mystère de l'instant* for 24 strings, cimbalom, and percussion (1989); *Le Jeu des contraires* for piano (1989); *Diptyque: Les Citations* for oboe, harpsichord, double bass, and percussion (1991).

Duval, François (c. 1673–1728) French violinist and composer. He was a member of Louis XIV's '24 violons du roi'. His violin sonatas are written in the Italian style and were published as the first of their kind in 1704. He wrote numerous books of sonatas for violin and bass and two violins and bass.

Dvořák, Antonín Leopold (1841–1904) Czech composer. His Romantic music extends the classical tradition of Ludwig van Beethoven and Johannes Brahms and displays the influence of Czech folk music. He wrote nine symphonies;

tone poems; operas, including *Rusalka* (1900); large-scale choral works; the *Carnival* (1891–92) and other overtures; violin and cello concertos; chamber music; piano pieces; and songs. International recognition came with two sets of *Slavonic Dances* (1878 and 1886). Works such as his *New World Symphony* (1893) reflect his interest in American folk themes, including black and American Indian music. He was director of the National Conservatory, New York, in 1892–95.

Dvořák was the son of a village innkeeper and butcher. He heard only popular and simple church music as a child, but developed remarkable gifts. He was sent to the organ school at Prague in 1857, began to compose two years later, and joined an orchestra as violinist. He played viola in the orchestra of the Bohemian Provisional Theatre at Prague, conducted by Richard Wagner from 1862, and from 1866 by Bedrich Smetana. Eleven years later he became organist of the church of St Adalbert, Prague. In 1865 he wrote the song cycle *Cypresses*, inspired by his hopeless love of his pupil, Josefina Čermaková. In 1873 he married Anna, Josefina's sister, and produced his first compositions to receive attention, including the 3rd symphony; earlier works had been strongly influenced by Wagner. During this period he wrote many songs, overtures, and symphonies, and in 1874 produced his opera *King and Charcoal-Burner*, which was not a success. The same year he received for the first time the Austrian state prize for composition. One member of the committee was the composer Johannes Brahms, who befriended Dvořák and introduced him to his publisher, Fritz Simrock. The *Slavonic Rhapsodies* and *Dances* of 1878 show a nationalist character to his music, and their publication brought him international fame. They were followed by the first of his great string quartets, the E♭ Op. 51, and the powerful 6th symphony (1880); the former work contains folk elements, and in the latter the influence of Brahms can be heard.

Dvořák first visited England in 1884 to conduct the *Stabat Mater* in London. In 1885 he bought the country estate of Vysoká, which remained his home. In 1891 he received an honorary doctorate from Cambridge University, and was appointed professor at Prague Conservatory, where he became director in 1901. In 1892–95 he was director of the new National Conservatory in New York, and spent some holidays at the Czech community of Spillville, Iowa. The premiere of the *New World Symphony* at Carnegie Hall in 1893 was one of his greatest successes.

In 1896 he paid the last of his many visits to England, where he had produced several works at the music festivals. The mighty and classically modelled 7th symphony was premiered in London in 1885, and the cello concerto followed ten years later; Josefina, his first love, died during its composition, and in memory of her the slow section of the finale quotes her favourite song from *Cypresses*.

Works OPERA ten operas, including *Dimitrij* (1882), *The Jacobin* (1889), *The Devil and Kate* (*Čert a Káča*, 1899), *Rusalka* (1900), *Armida* (1904).

CHORAL WITH ORCHESTRA (some with solo voices): *Stabat Mater* (1877), Requiem (1890); Te Deum; four sets of vocal duets; 68 songs.

ORCHESTRAL nine symphonies, including no. 5 in F, Op. 76 (1875); no. 6 in D, Op. 60 (1880); no. 7 in D minor, Op. 70 (1885); no. 8 in G, Op. 88 (1889); no. 9 in E minor, '*From the New World*', Op. 95 (1893). Five symphonic poems *The Water-Sprite* (1896), *The Noon-day Witch* (1896), *The Golden Spinning-Wheel* (1896), *The Wood-Dove* (1896), *Hero's Song* (1897); seven concert overtures; orchestral works including Serenade in D minor for wind, cello, and bass (1878); *Scherzo capriccioso* (1883), *Symphonic Variations* (1877); two sets of Slavonic Dances (1878, 1886); *Serenade* for string orchestra; concertos for piano, violin, and cello (1876, 1880, 1895).

CHAMBER MUSIC 14 string quartets, including no. 12 in F, Op. 96 (1893, *American*), no. 13 in G, Op. 105 (1895), no. 14 in A♭, Op. 106 (1895); two string quintets: in G, Op. 77, with double bass (1875), in E♭, Op. 97, with viola (1893); four piano trios, including F minor, Op. 65 (1883), in E minor, '*Dumky*', Op. 90 (1891); piano quintet in A, Op. 81 (1887); sonatina (1893) for violin and piano.

PIANO 14 Op. nos. of piano pieces, including Theme and Variations; six sets of piano duets, including *Slavonic Dances* (1878).

Dygon, John (c.1485–1541) English cleric and composer. He took his Bachelor of Music at Oxford in 1512, probably in 1521 went to Louvain to study with the Spanish humanist Juan Luis Vives, and became a prior at St Austin's Abbey, Canterbury. A motet of his is preserved and a treatise on

proportions in Trinity College library, Cambridge.

dynamics in music, markings added to show the varying degrees or changes in volume or loudness. They are written as words, abbreviations, letters, or signs. For example: dynamics for volume include **f** for forte (loud), **mf** for mezzo forte (medium loud), **mp** for mezzo piano (medium soft), and **p** for piano (soft); changes in volume include **crescendo** (becoming gradually louder), and **diminuendo** (becoming gradually softer); accents include **sf** for sforzando (meaning a sudden accent on a note or chord).

Dynamic expression developed slowly during the 18th century as improvements were made to instruments of the orchestra that increased their freedom of expression. The piano was also becoming a more important instrument at this time. Its name 'fortepiano' was used to advertise its greater expressive advantages over the fixed-register harpsichord. After 1950 many composers experimented with serialism (twelve-tone music) and attempted to bring dynamics under serial control.

Dyson, George (1883–1964) English composer. He wrote choral and orchestral music, including a setting of Chaucer's prologue to the *Canterbury Tales* (1931). In 1937 he was appointed director of the Royal College of Music, London, in succession to Hugh Allen, retiring in 1952.

He studied at the Royal College of Music and became music director at Winchester College in 1924, having already taught at Osborne, Marlborough, Rugby, and Wellington, serving in World War I between.

Works *The Canterbury Pilgrims* (setting of Chaucer's prologue, 1931) and other compositions for solo voices, chorus and orchestra; orchestral, chamber and piano music; songs.

E in music, the third note, or mediant, of the scale of C major.

early music music composed in previous periods. The meaning of the term has changed over the years: originally it referred to Western music composed from the early Middle Ages to the Renaissance. As the ➤ **authenticity** movement grew during the mid-20th century it came to include music of the baroque period as well. Today early music has no precise limit, but it is generally accepted to include music as late as the early 19th century. The journal *Early Music*, established in 1973, focuses on ➤ **performance practice** and other musicological issues concerning music prior to the Romantic period.

Early Reign of Oleg, The Russian 'opera' or play with music (libretto by Catherine II). The score was composed by Pashkeievich, Canobbio, and Sarti, and the 'opera' was first produced for the court at the Hermitage Theatre, St Petersburg, Russia, on 26 October 1790.

Earth Dances work for orchestra by Harrison Birtwistle, first performed in London, England, on 14 March 1986.

ear training in music, the development of the sense of pitch, involving elements such as ready distinction of intervals and identification of various types of chords.

Easdale, Brian (1909–1995) English composer. He wrote *Missa coventrensis* (1962) for the consecration of Coventry Cathedral.

He was educated at Westminster Abbey choir school and the Royal College of Music in London.

Works STAGE AND FILM *Rapunzel* (1927), *The Corn King* (1935), *The Sleeping Children* (1951); incidental music for Eugene O'Neill's *Mourning Becomes Electra*; film music *The Red Shoes*.

OTHER *Missa coventrensis* (1962), *Dead March*, *Tone Poem*, *Six Poems* for orchestra; piano concerto (1938); string trio; pieces for two pianos; song cycles.

East, Michael (c. 1580–1648) English composer. He was apparently in the service of Lady Hatton in London early in the 17th century and from 1618 was organist of Lichfield Cathedral.

Works Evening Service, anthems; six books of madrigals (some with anthems) and a madrigal contributed to the collection *The* ➤ ***Triumphes of Oriana*** (1603); music for viols.

Easter music-drama medieval church representation of the Easter story; see ➤ **liturgical drama**.

Easter Oratorio, German ***Kommt, Eilet und Laufet*** work by Johann Sebastian Bach performed as a church cantata in 1725 and revised 1732–35 as an oratorio.

Eastman School of Music US conservatory, in Rochester, New York, founded in 1912 and taken over in 1917 by George Eastman (1854–1932). It became part of the University of Rochester in 1921, with Howard Hanson as director 1924–64; he was succeeded by Walter Hendl, 1964–72, and Robert S Freeman from 1972. The Cleveland Quartet has been its quartet-in-residence.

Eaton, John (1935–) US composer. He studied with Roger Sessions and Milton Babbitt at Princeton, and taught at Indiana University from 1970. His works use microtones, serial techniques, and a synthesizer called the syn-ket; his operas include *Ma Barker* (1957), *Heracles* (1968), *Myshkin* (1973), *The Tempest* (1985), and *The Reverend Jim Jones* (1989).

Eben, Petr (1929–) Czech composer. His works are mostly chamber and vocal pieces, and reflect his interest in religion and myth.

He studied in Prague and has taught at the university there.

Works BALLET *Curses and Blessings* (1980).

INSTRUMENTAL piano concerto (1961); wind quintet (1965); *Faust* for organ (1980); string quartet (1981); organ concerto (1983); piano trio (1986); *Hommage à Dietrich Buxtehude* for organ (1987); two *Invocations* for trombone and organ (1989).

CHORAL oratorio *Apologia Sokrates* (1964); *Ubi caritas et amor* for chorus (1965).

Eberlin, Johann Ernst (1702–1762) German organist and composer. He was esteemed as a composer of church music.

He settled in Salzburg, Austria, in 1724, where he became organist to the court and cathedral in 1729, and Kapellmeister in 1749.

Works several operas, to texts by Metastasio, over 50 Masses; twelve Requiems; offertories and other pieces; several oratorios; organ music.

Ebony Concerto work by Igor Stravinsky for clarinet and orchestra, composed in 1945 for Woody Herman and his band and performed by them in New York, USA, on 25 March 1946.

Eccard, Johann (1553–1611) German composer. His works were chiefly choral pieces. As a Lutheran composer, Eccard made much use of the chorale melodies in his works. The collection of sacred pieces which he published in 1597 contains simple harmonizations, but in other volumes he developed the complex chorale motet, of which he was one of the major exponents.

He was a pupil of David Köler in the choir school attached to the Weimar court chapel, 1567–71, and then of Orlande de Lassus in the Hofkapelle in Munich. From the late 1570s he was in the service of Jacob Fugger in Augsburg, and in 1579 joined the Chapel of the Margrave of Brandenburg-Ansbach in Königsberg; he was assistant Kapellmeister there until 1604 when he succeeded to the senior post. In 1608 the new Elector Joachim Friedrich of Brandenburg in Berlin appointed Eccard Kapellmeister at his Berlin court, and Eccard continued to serve his successor, Johann Sigismund. His music was still printed 30 years after his death.

Works motets, chorales (some harmonized, some newly composed by him); sacred songs; secular German songs for several voices, wedding songs, odes, festival songs.

échappée (French, short for note échappée; 'escaped note') in music, the progression between two adjacent notes which deviates by at first taking a step in the opposite direction and then taking the second note aimed at by an interval of a third.

An échappée between the notes E and D in the top voice of this example.

Echelle de soie, L', The Silken Ladder opera by Pierre Gaveaux (libretto by F A E de Planard), first produced at the Opéra-Comique, Paris, France, on 22 August 1808. Rossini based his *Scala di seta* on it.

echo musical effect. In composition, various echo effects have been used in many ways; Roland de Lassus's madrigal *Olà, che buon eco*, the witches' chorus in Purcell's *Dido and Aeneas*, the *Echo* piece in Bach's B minor clavier partita, the *Scène aux champs* in Berlioz's *Symphonie Fantastique*, or the second act of Engelbert Humperdinck's *Hänsel und Gretel*.

Echo et Narcisse opera by Christoph Willibald von Gluck (libretto by L T de Tschudy), first produced at the Paris Opéra, France, on 24 September 1779. The story tells how Echo is in despair when Narcissus prefers his own reflection to her. She dies from grief, but when Narcissus recovers his senses she is restored to life.

Éclats work by Pierre Boulez for 15 instruments, first performed in Los Angeles, USA, on 26 March 1965. It was expanded as *Éclat/Multiples* and performed in London, England, on 21 October 1970.

écossaise (French 'Scottish one') dance long supposed to be of Scottish origin but no longer considered so. As a fashionable ballroom dance in the early 19th century, it was in fairly animated 2/4 time, about halfway between the polka and the galop in speed. Among the composers who cultivated it were Beethoven, Schubert, and Chopin. The German *Schottisch* (usually written *Schottische* in English) is the same thing.

Écuatorial work by Edgard ➔ **Varèse** for bass voice, eight brass, piano, organ, two ondes Martenots, and six percussion (the text is a Spanish translation of a prayer from the sacred book of the Maya Quiché, the *Popul Vuh*). It was first performed in New York, USA, on 15 April 1934, conducted by Nicolas Slonimsky.

Edelmann, Johann Friedrich (1749–1794) Alsatian pianist and composer. He became famous in Paris through the patronage of his pupil, Baron Dietrich. He was a friend of Gluck, and Mozart thought well of his piano compositions. He apparently played a discreditable part during the French Revolution, and died on the guillotine.

Works OPERA *Ariane dans l'île de Náxos* (1782), *La Bergère des Alpes* (1781), *Diane et l'Amour* (1802).

OTHER symphonies; keyboard concertos and sonatas.

Eder, Helmut (1916–2005) Austrian composer. He studied in Stuttgart and with Carl Orff in Munich, Germany. He co-founded the electronic music school at Linz Conservatory in 1959 and was professor at the Salzburg Mozarteum from 1967. His music progressed towards electronics from neoclassicism and serialism.

Works OPERA *Oedipus* (1960), *Der Kardinal* (1965), *Der Aufstand* (1975), *Georges Dandin* (1979), *Mozart in New York* (1991).

BALLET *Moderner Traum* (1957), *Anamorphose* (1963), *Die Irrfahrten des Odysseus* (1965).

ORCHESTRAL five symphonies (1950–80), three violin concertos (1963, 1964, 1982), cello concerto (1981), concertino for classical orchestra (1984).

CHAMBER string quartet (1948), clarinet quintet (1982).

Edgar opera by Giacomo Puccini (libretto by F Fontana, based on Alfred de Musset's *La Coupe et les lèvres*), first produced at La Scala, Milan, Italy, on 21 April 1889. In the story, Edgar loves Fidelia but runs away with the Moorish girl Tigrana when she is threatened by villagers. Regretting the loss of Fidelia, he decides to join the soldiers in battle. Later he is reunited with Fidelia, who stabs Tigrana.

Edipo Re, King Oedipus opera in one act by Ruggiero Leoncavallo (libretto by G Forzano, after Sophocles), first produced in Chicago, USA, on 13 December 1920.

Eduardo e Cristina opera in two acts by Gioachino Rossini (libretto by G Schmidt, written for Pavesi, altered by A L Tottola and G Bevilacqua-Aldovrandini), first produced at the Teatro San Benedetto, Venice, Italy, on 24 April 1819. It is a pastiche, assembled from *Ricciardo e Zoraide*, *Ermione*, and *Adelaide di Borgogna*.

Education manquée, Une operetta in one act by Emmanuel Chabrier (libretto by E Leterrier and A Vanloo), first produced privately in Paris, France, on 1 May 1879, and publicly at the Théâtre des Arts, Paris, on 9 January 1913. It describes how Count Gontran is educated in the facts of life.

Edwards, Richard (c.1522–1566) English poet, composer, and dramatist. He was highly regarded for his comedies, madrigals, and interludes. A pupil of the musician, physician, and Greek scholar George Etheridge of Thame, he entered Corpus Christi College, Oxford, in 1540, and transferred to Christ Church on its foundation in 1546. He was appointed Master of the Children of the Chapel Royal in London in 1561, and wrote two plays for them. He was also a playwright, producing *Palamon and Arcite* before Queen Elizabeth I in Oxford in 1566, and also writing *Damon and Pithias* (1564), and a poet, compiling and contributing to a book of verse *The Paradise of Dainty Devices* (1576).

Works music to his own *Damon and Pithias*; part songs *In Going to My Naked Bed* and *O the Silly Man*.

Edwards, Ross (1943–) Australian composer. He studied in Sydney and Adelaide, with Peter Sculthorpe and Peter Maxwell Davies. He was lecturer at the New South Wales conservatory from 1976.

Works STAGE *Quen Quaeritis*, children's nativity play (1967); *Christina's World*, theatre piece (1983).

ORCHESTRAL *Etude* for orchestra (1969); *Mountain Village in a Clearing Mist* for orchestra (1973); piano concerto (1982); *Maninyas* for violins and orchestra (1988); *Varregh* for solo percussion and orchestra (1989).

VOCAL series *Maninya I–V* for chamber ensemble with voices (1981–86); *Reflections* for piano and three percussion (1985); *Flower Songs* for chorus and percussion (1986).

CHAMBER string quartet (1982).

Egdon Heath work for orchestra by Gustav Holst, inspired by the Dorset landscape described by Thomas Hardy in *The Return of the Native* (1878). It was commissioned by the New York Symphony Orchestra and first performed on 12 February 1928 in New York.

Egisto, L', Aegisthus opera by Pietro Cavalli (libretto by G Faustini), first produced at the Teatro San Cassiano, Venice, Italy, in the autumn of 1643. Its first modern revival was in Santa Fe, USA, in 1974, in a free realization by Raymond Leppard. The story tells how Egisto and Clemene resolve to find their original lovers after being separated by pirates. They become involved in love triangles which eventually resolve happily.

Egk, Werner (1901–1983) German composer. He wrote music for the opening of the Berlin Olympics in 1936.

He was mainly self-taught and began to compose to broadcasting commissions. He settled near Munich and succeeded Paul Graener as head of the faculty of composition in the Nazi Reichsmusikkammer. From 1936 to 1940 he conducted at the Berlin Staatsoper and from 1950 to 1953 was director of the Hochschule für Musik in Berlin.

Works OPERA *Columbus* (1932; produced 1942), *Die Zaubergeige* (1935), *Peer Gynt* (1938), *Circe* (1945), *Irische Legende* (after Yeats; 1953), *Der Revisor* (after Gogol; 1957), *Die Verlobung in San Domingo* (1963).

BALLET *Joan von Zarissa* (1940), *Abraxas* (1948).

ORCHESTRAL dance suite *Georgica* for orchestra; violin concerto (*Geigenmusik*, 1936), *Französische Suite* (after Rameau; 1949), *Spiegelzeit* for orchestra (1979).

Egmont incidental music by Beethoven for Goethe's tragedy of that name, Op. 84, written 1809–10 for a revival at the Burgtheater in Vienna, Austria, on 15 June 1810.

Egyptian Helen, The opera by Richard Strauss; see ➤ *Ägyptische Helena, Die*.

Eichendorff, Joseph von (1788–1857) German poet and novelist. His works were used by the composers Robert ➤ Franz (songs), Mark ➤ Lothar (*Freier*), Hans ➤ Pfitzner (*Von deutscher Seele*), Othmar ➤ Schoeck (*Schloss Dürande*, *Wandersprüche*, and songs), Robert ➤ Schumann (*Liederkreis*), and in six songs by Johannes ➤ Brahms, 16 by Schumann, and 28 (including eight early songs) by Hugo Wolf.

Eighteen-Twelve Overture concert overture by Tchaikovsky; see ➤ *Year 1812*.

eilen (German 'to hurry') in music, a term indicating an increase in tempo; also sometimes used as the warning *nicht eilen*, 'do not hurry'.

Eimert, Herbert (1897–1972) German composer and critic. In 1951 he founded an electronic studio at the Cologne branch of West German Radio. He wrote extensively on modern music.

He studied music and musicology at Cologne Conservatory and University 1927–1933. He worked for German radio and edited the *Kölnische Zeitung* 1936–45 and from 1955 edited *Die Reihe*.

Works *Glockenspiel* (1953); *Etüden über Tongemische*; *Requiem für Aikichi Kuboyama* (1962); choral and chamber music and electronic pieces.

Eine kleine Nachtmusik composition by Mozart; see ➤ *kleine Nachtmusik, Eine*.

Einem, Gottfried von (1918–1996) Austrian composer. His opera *Der Besuch der alten Dame* (1971) was based on a stage vehicle for the actor Ingrid Bergman.

He worked at the Wagner theatre at Bayreuth, Germany, in 1938, and at the Staatsoper in Berlin; and studied further in London and Vienna. A plan to study with Paul Hindemith was frustrated when the latter was suspended by the Nazis in 1934, and Einem and his mother were themselves arrested by the Gestapo. After his release he studied with Boris Blacher, with whom he wrote the libretto for his first opera and secured a post at the Dresden Staatsoper. In 1948, after the success of *Dantons Tod*, he was invited to help to direct the festival in Salzburg, where he later lived.

Works OPERA *Dantons Tod* (on Büchner's drama; 1947), *Der Prozess/The Trial* (after Kafka; 1953), *Der Besuch der alten Dame* (after Dürrenmatt; 1971), *Kabale und Liebe* (after Schiller; 1976), *Jesu Hochzeit* (1980), *Prinz Chocolat* (1983), *Tuliphant* (1990).

BALLET *Prinzessin Turandot* (after Gozzi; 1944).

ORCHESTRAL *Capriccio* (1943), concerto for orchestra, 'Philadelphia' symphony (1960), piano concerto, *Bruckner Dialog* for orchestra (1971),

Wiener Symphonie (1976), *Ludi Leopoldini* (1980).

CHAMBER three string quartets (1975, 1977, 1980); wind quintet (1976).

OTHER piano pieces; Hafiz songs.

Einleitung (German 'introduction') musical term; see ➤ introduction.

Ein musikalischer Spass work for two horns and strings by Mozart; see ➤ *musikalischer Spass, Ein*.

Einstein, Alfred (1880–1952) German musicologist. He revised Hugo Riemann's *Musiklexicon* in 1912, 1922, and 1929, and Ludwig von Köchel's Mozart catalogue in 1937. He also wrote works on German viola da gamba music, on Gluck and Mozart, a short history of music, and in particular specialized in the study of the Italian madrigal, on which he wrote a monumental book in 1949. He also published *Schubert* (1951).

A pupil of Adolf Sandberger, he took his doctor's degree in 1903. He became editor of the *Zeitschrift für Musikwissenschaft* in 1918, and was music critic of the *Berliner Tageblatt* from 1929. In 1933 he went into exile from Germany, settling first in London, then Florence, and lastly in Northampton, Massachusetts, USA, where he was professor at Smith College.

Einstein on the Beach opera by Philip Glass (text by Robert Wilson), first produced in Avignon, France, on 25 July 1976 and then at the New York Metropolitan Opera House on 21 November 1976 (at the Lincoln Center but not with the Metropolitan Opera Company). The text includes poems by a mentally impaired man; references are made to Patty Hearst and pop idols David Cassidy and the Beatles. The audience is invited to come and go at will during the $4\frac{1}{2}$ hours of performance.

Eisler, Hanns (1898–1962) German composer. He collaborated with the playwright Bertolt Brecht, but their work displeased the Nazis, and both men fled Nazi Germany for the USA. Eisler returned to East Berlin in 1950. The music he wrote for the new communist state consisted chiefly of songs and music for stage and films.

He studied with Arnold Schoenberg in Vienna, Austria, and won a composition prize in 1924. He taught in Berlin 1925–33, but emigrated to the USA when a price was put on his head for his interest in music for the proletariat and in anti-Nazi activities. He was appointed professor at the New School of Social Research there, but left the USA in 1948, living first in Vienna and then returning to East Berlin.

Works STAGE operas *Galileo* (1947) and *Johannes Faustus* (1953); didactic plays *Mother* (after Gorky's novel; 1931), *Hangmen Also Die, For Whom*

the Bell Tolls, *The Roundheads and the Pointed-heads*, and others; *Die Massnahme* (1930), *Lenin-Requiem* (1937), *Solidaritätslied* (1930), *Kinderlieder* (1951), and *Schweyk im Zweiten Weltkrieg* (1957), all to texts by Brecht.

ORCHESTRAL orchestral suites on Russian and Jewish folk songs.

VOCAL German Symphony for solo voices, chorus, and orchestra (1935–39), cantatas, choral ballads, proletarian songs, and other pieces; chamber cantata *Palmström* for speech-song, flute, clarinet, violin, and cello; *Zeitungsausschnitte* for voice and piano; *Ernste Gesänge* for baritone and orchestra (1962).

CHAMBER string quartet (1937), nonet (1939), two septets (1941, 1947), piano quintet (1944).

OTHER music for numerous films.

Eitner, Robert (1832–1905) German musicologist and bibliographer. He was founder of the Gesellschaft für Musikforschung in 1868, editor of the *Monatshefte für Musikgeschichte*, and compiler of the *Quellen-Lexicon* (a catalogue of the contents of music libraries) and other bibliographical works.

Elder, Mark Phillip (1947–) English conductor. He studied at Cambridge and in 1970 was on the staff at Glyndebourne and at the Royal Opera House, Covent Garden, London. He made his debut there in 1976, with *Rigoletto*. He worked with the English National Opera Ensemble in London from 1974, and was principal conductor 1979–93; he led the first performance of David Blake's *Toussaint* in 1977. In 1980 he became principal guest conductor of the London Mozart Players and in 1981 gave *Die Meistersinger* at Bayreuth. In April 1986 he gave the British stage premiere of Busoni's *Dr Faust* (at the London Coliseum). He was appointed musical director of the Rochester Philharmonic Orchestra in 1989, and principal guest conductor at the City of Birmingham Symphony Orchestra in 1992. He conducted *Euryanthe* at the QEH, London, in 1994. He was awarded a CBE in 1989.

electro-acoustic music music in which the composer uses electronic or computer-based means to shape sounds directly, without the use of notation or performers. The original sounds may be recorded or synthesized, or both. It is more or less synonymous with acousmatic music.

electrochord electrophonic piano invented by Vierling of Berlin, Germany, 1929–33. It produces its notes by the conversion of electrical waves into audible sounds.

electronde electrophonic musical instrument that produces notes from the air. The notes it produces are graded according to the chromatic scale by means of a switch, and are not indeterminate in pitch like those of the aetherophone or ➤ theremin. It was invented by Martin Taubman of Berlin, Germany, in 1929.

electronic music music composed completely or partly of electronically generated and/or modified sounds. The term was first used in 1954 to describe music made up of synthesized sounds recorded on tape, to distinguish it from ➤ musique concrète ('concrete music'), but later included music for electronic sounds with traditional instruments or voices.

Karlheinz Stockhausen was a pioneer of electronic music, and his *Gesang der Jünglinge/Song of the Youths* (1955–56), for boys' voices and electronic sounds, was one of the first important pieces in this style. Luciano Berio also composed music using a mixture of electronic and traditional instruments, such as *Differences* (1957) for chamber ensemble and tape. Other composers working in the early years of electronic music were Milton Babbitt, Bruno Maderna, and Edgard Varèse, the latter being a very early pioneer.

The development of portable electronic instruments in the late 1950s meant that electronic music could be played live and no longer had to be created in a studio and recorded on tape. Computer technology has also greatly improved the range and versatility of electronic instruments. Composers such as Pierre Boulez and Iannis Xenakis have written electronic pieces using the latest computer technology, and many other composers now incorporate electronic instruments in their work.

early electronic music The synthesis (construction) of musical sounds was first made possible early in the 20th century by the invention of the thermionic valve. The first experiments in this field gave rise to various musical instruments such as the ➤ theremin, ➤ ondes martenot, and electronic organ, in which the sound is produced by means of oscillators, transformed by filters, and fed out of loudspeakers. The development of 'pure' electronic music only came about after the perfection of the tape recorder in 1950; before then electronic instruments tended to be used to augment traditional ensembles or as solo instruments mimicking or replacing acoustic ones, and no distinctive style for these new instruments had been developed.

the Cologne studio In 1951 a studio was set up at Cologne Radio under the direction of Herbert Eimert. Its aim was to use only sounds synthesized by electronic oscillators as the raw material for electronic manipulation. This differed from the musique concrète practised in Paris, which used only external sounds, both musical and unmusical, for its material. However, the methods of managing these two sorts of material were similar, making use of electronic filters, intensity control, reverberation, and tape manipulation. One of the most important composer pioneers in the field was Stockhausen, who was director of the Cologne studio from 1963. His later compositions, such as *Mikrophoponie I* (1964) and *Mikrophoponie II* (1965), and work by other composers in the Cologne studio went further in the direction of using external sounds as well as pure electronic sound, thus merging musique concrète and pure electronic music. In the late 1950s composers began to use prerecorded electronic music with 'live' instruments in pieces such as Stockhausen's *Kontakte* for piano, percussion, and tape (1959–60).

equipment A typical electronic music studio of that time would contain a number of oscillators or sound sources, producing basic wave forms and noise, and a number of devices for treating these sound sources: filters, to alter the tone quality of a sound by eliminating or emphasizing certain harmonics in its harmonic series; envelope shapers, to control the attack, duration, and intensity curve of a sound; reverberation units, to provide resonance; and ring modulators, by which one sound modulates another to produce dramatic changes in quality. In addition, very slow wave forms were used to control the ➤ **pitch**, intensity, duration, ➤ **timbre**, and other parameters of the sounds generated by the oscillators, allowing a certain amount of preprogramming of the studio without the aid of computer techniques.

computers and electronic music After 1960, with the arrival of the purpose-built synthesizer developed by Robert Moog, Peter Zinovieff, and others, a greater interest developed in computer-aided synthesis, which resulted in the installation of the 4X system at the Institut de Recherche et de Coordination Acoustique-Musique (➤ **IRCAM**) in Paris. The use of computers in electronic music has introduced greater flexibility, allowing whole compositions to be programmed and stored in memory banks. This, along with the arrival of digital recording techniques, has eliminated the need for laborious tape editing. The computer can be used to control and sequence the sounds and their characteristics, and also to synthesize any desired wave form. This has made it possible to produce complex electronic music live in the concert hall, without needing to record it on tape first, and even to manipulate the sounds of the various instruments during the performance, as in Boulez's ... *explosante fixe* ... (1971–73) and George Benjamin's *Antara* (1985–7).

electronics and popular music The electronic music of the 1960s, particularly the work of Stockhausen, had a profound influence on many jazz and rock musicians. Miles Davis in particular found inspiration for his jazz/rock fusion, and paved the way for future developments in the field. Groups such as Weather Report incorporated electronic instruments into their ensembles, and the expressive capabilities of the synthesizer were particularly suited to the style that had evolved from free jazz. In the world of rock and pop, more electronic instruments were being played from the early 1960s. At the more popular end of the spectrum, the Beach Boys used an ondes martenot in their hit 'Good Vibrations' (1966), while more progressive bands such as Emerson, Lake and Palmer, and Pink Floyd explored the possibilities of the newly invented ➤ **Moog synthesizer**. The use of electronically generated music continued throughout the 1970s and 1980s, especially in dance music, where in some cases it totally replaced conventional guitars and drums. For some rock musicians, notably Frank Zappa, the use of electronic instruments helped to bridge the gap between rock and 'serious' music; this trend has continued through to the present in the work of composers such as Brian Eno.

electrophone any of a class of musical instruments that generate their tone by electronic means.

elegy (from Greek *elegeia*, from *elegos* 'mournful poem') in poetry, a piece of sorrowful and usually commemorative character; in music either a vocal setting of such a poem or an instrumental piece suggesting the mood awakened by it.

Elegy for Young Lovers opera by Hans Werner Henze (libretto by W H Auden and Chester Kallman), first produced at the Schlosstheater, Schwetzingen, Germany, on 20 May 1961; the first British production was at Glyndebourne, Sussex, on 13 July 1961. It describes how a poet gains inspiration from the mountainside death of two lovers.

Elektra opera by Richard Strauss (libretto by Hugo von Hofmannsthal, a much modernized reinterpretation of Sophocles), first produced at the Royal Opera House in Dresden, Germany, on 25 January 1909. In the story, Clytemnestra kills the father of Elektra and Orestes, who decide to take revenge.

Elgar, Edward (William) (1857–1934) English composer. Although his celebrated oratorio *The Dream of Gerontius* (1900), based on the written work by the theologian John Henry Newman, was initially unpopular in Britain, its good reception in Düsseldorf, Germany, in 1902 led to a surge of interest in his earlier works, including the *Pomp and Circumstance Marches* (1901). His *Enigma Variations* (1899) brought him lasting fame.

Among his works are oratorios, two symphonies, a violin concerto, chamber music, songs, the symphonic poem *Falstaff* (1902–13), and the moving Cello Concerto of 1919. After this piece, Elgar did not publish any more important music. He concentrated on transcriptions and made some early gramophone recordings of his own work.

Elgar was the son of a music dealer who was also organist at St George's Roman Catholic church, Worcester. He was self-taught as a composer, and at the age of 12 wrote music for a little domestic play, *The Wand of Youth*. He was sent to work in a solicitor's office at 15, though he preferred to help at his father's shop. From the age of 16 he was employed locally as a teacher, played bassoon in a wind quintet, and joined the Worcester Glee Club. In 1879 he became a leader of the Worcester Philharmonic and was conductor of the Glee Club and of the band at the county lunatic asylum at Powick, for which he arranged much music. He also played organ at his father's church and became a member of W C Stockley's orchestra in Birmingham, which gave the first public performance of his *Sérénade mauresque*. In 1889 he married Caroline Alice Roberts and they lived in London until 1891.

In 1890 the Three Choirs Festival (held at Worcester that year) included for the first time a work of his, the *Froissart* overture (1890). This is the first work that shows Elgar's skill in orchestration. Choral works, including *Scenes from the Saga of King Olaf* (1896) and *Caractacus* (1898), were heard at festivals, and the *Enigma Variations* for orchestra were conducted by Hans Richter in 1899. *The Dream of Gerontius* was produced at the Birmingham Festival in 1900 and at the Lower Rhine Festival, Düsseldorf, in 1901 and 1902. An Elgar Festival at the Covent Garden Theatre, London, in 1904 brought him greater recognition, and he was knighted that year. He was professor of music at Birmingham University in 1905–06.

His first symphony was performed under Hans Richter in Manchester and London in 1908, and its immense success led to 100 further performances throughout Europe. Fritz Kreisler premiered the violin concerto in 1910. During World War I, Elgar wrote much topical music and afterwards the cello concerto and three chamber works. After the death of his wife in 1920 he wrote only some small pieces and incidental music. He was Master of the King's Music from 1924. At his death he left unfinished a third symphony and an opera, *The Spanish Lady*, based on Ben Jonson's play *The Devil is an Ass*.

Elgar's songs, chamber music, and smaller works are often poetic, but add nothing to a reputation founded on *Gerontius*, the symphonies, and the symphonic study *Falstaff*, which reveal a highly individual mastery of orchestration.

Works ORCHESTRAL two symphonies (1908, 1911); concert overtures *Cockaigne* (1901) and *In the South* (1904); many miscellaneous orchestral works, including *Enigma Variations* (1899), *Introduction and Allegro* for strings (1905), and the symphonic study *Falstaff* (1902–13); *Pomp and Circumstance Marches* (nos 1 and 2, 1901; no. 3, 1904; no. 4, 1907; no. 5, 1930); violin concerto (1910), cello concerto (1919).

VOCAL cantatas *Caractacus* (1898), *The Music Makers* (1902–12); oratorios *The Dream of Gerontius* (1900), *The Apostles* (1903), *The Kingdom* (1901–06).

CHAMBER string quartet, E minor, piano quintet, A minor (1919), violin and piano sonata, E minor (1918).

OTHER songs for solo voice, including cycle *Sea Pictures* with piano or orchestra (1897–99); *Severn Suite* for brass band (1930).

Elijah, German **Elias** oratorio by Felix Mendelssohn (words from the Old Testament), produced first in the English version at the Birmingham Festival, England, on 26 August 1846; the first German performance was given in Hamburg on 7 October 1847.

Elisa opera by Johann Fux (libretto, in Italian, by P Pariati), first produced for the court at Laxenburg Palace near Vienna, Austria, on 25 August 1719.

Elisabetta regina d'Inghilterra, **Elizabeth, Queen of England** opera by Gioachino Rossini (libretto by G Schmidt), first produced at the Teatro San Carlo, Naples, Italy, on 4 October 1815. The overture was taken from his earlier opera *Aureliano in Palmira* and afterwards used for his *Il barbiere di Siviglia*. It tells how Elizabeth I imprisons the Earl of Leicester when he marries Mathilde, daughter of Mary Queen of Scots. She later releases him and survives an assassination attempt by the treacherous Norfolk.

elisir d'amore, L', **The Love Potion** opera by Gaetano Donizetti (libretto by F Romani, based on Augustin Scribe's *Le Philtre*, composed by Daniel Auber), first produced at the Teatro della Canobbiana, Milan, Italy, on 12 May 1832. In the story, the simple Nemorino hopes to win the landowner Adina with a love potion from the fraud Dulcamara. At first she spurns him, ready to marry Belcore, but then falls genuinely in love with him, without the help of the potion.

Eliza, ou Le Voyage aux glaciers du Mont St Bernard opera by Luigi Cherubini (libretto by J A de R Saint-Cyr), first produced at the Théâtre Feydeau, Paris, France, on 13 December 1794.

Ellis, David (1933–) English composer. He studied at the Royal Manchester College of

Music and worked as an administrator with the British Broadcasting Corporation (BBC) from 1964. He was Head of Music for BBC North 1978–86, and artistic director of the Northern Chamber Orchestra from 1986.

Works OPERA *Crito* (1963).

ORCHESTRAL *Sinfonietta* (1953), violin concerto, piano concerto (1962), *Fanfares and Cadenzas* for orchestra (1968), *February Music* for cello and chamber orchestra (1977), *Circles* (1979); *Suite franglaise* for strings (1987).

CHORAL *Sequentia I–V* for soloists, chorus, and orchestra (1962–75).

CHAMBER string trio (1954), wind quintet (1956); piano sonata (1956); string quartet (1980).

Eloy, Jean-Claude (1938–   ) French composer. He studied with Darius Milhaud and Pierre Boulez; other influences include Edgard Varèse, Anton Webern, and oriental music. He worked at the electronic music studio in Cologne, Germany, with Karlheinz Stockhausen.

Works ORCHESTRAL *Etude III* (1962), *Fluctuante-Immuable* (1977).

OTHER INSTRUMENTAL *Equivalences* for wind and percussion (1963), *Polychronies* for chamber ensemble (1964), *Yo-In* (Reverberations) for four tapes and percussion (1980).

VOCAL *Kamakala* for chorus and three orchestral groups (1971), *Shanti* for six solo voices and electronics (1972–74); *Kshara-Akshara* for soprano, chorus, and three orchestral groups (1974).

El Salón México symphonic sketch by Aaron Copland, named after a Mexico City nightclub and including local colour and tunes. It was first performed in Mexico City on 27 August 1937, conducted by Carlos Chávez.

Elsner, (Ksawery) Józef (1769–1854) Polish composer of Swedish descent. Intended for a career in medicine, he had little music teaching in his youth but learnt the violin and some harmony at Breslau (Wrocław, Poland) and studied more assiduously on going to Vienna, Austria. In 1791 he became violinist at the Brno theatre, Moravia (Czech Republic), and the next year conductor at Lwów (Lviv, Ukraine). He went to Warsaw, Poland, as theatre conductor in 1799, establishing a music society there in 1815 and became the first director of the Conservatory opened in 1821. He was the formative teacher of Chopin.

Works 27 operas (22 in Polish), *Król Łokietek* (1818), ballets and melodramas; *Stabat Mater*, church music; eleven symphonies; six string quartets; instrumental pieces.

Elwell, Herbert (1898–1974) US composer. He studied with Ernest Bloch in New York and with Nadia Boulanger in Paris. He was head of composition at the Cleveland Institute 1928–45, and teacher at Oberlin Conservatory from 1946.

Works BALLET *The Happy Hypocrite* (1925).

ORCHESTRAL *Introduction and Allegro* for orchestra (1942).

VOCAL *I Was With Him*, cantata (1937); *Blue Symphony* for voice and string quartet (1944); *Lincoln: Requiem Aeternam* (1946).

CHAMBER two string quartets; piano sonata.

embellishment in music, an alternative name for ➔ ornamentation.

embouchure in music, the position of the lips and tension of the facial muscles required to produce a good tone on a brass or woodwind instrument.

Emerald Isle, The unfinished operetta by Arthur Sullivan, completed by Edward German (libretto by B Hood) and first produced at the Savoy Theatre, London, England, on 27 April 1901.

Emma di Resburgo, Emma of Roxburgh opera by Giacomo Meyerbeer (libretto by Giacomo Rossi), first produced at the Teatro San Benedetto, Venice, Italy, on 26 June 1819. It was Meyerbeer's first major success, but Anton Weber maintained that he had imitated Rossini.

Emmanuel, (Marie François) Maurice (1862–1938) French musicologist and composer. He wrote several learned books on the musical idiom, Greek music, modal accompaniment, Burgundian folk song, and other subjects.

He studied at the Paris Conservatory and was a pupil of François Gevaert in Brussels. After various appointments as a historian and musician he became professor of music history at the Conservatory in succession to Louis Bourgault-Ducoudray in 1907 and retained the post until 1936.

Works STAGE *Prométhée enchaîné* (1916–18) and *Salamino* (1921–28, both after Aeschylus); operetta *Pierrot peintre* (1886); incidental music for Plautus'*Amphitryon*.

ORCHESTRAL two symphonies, *Suite française*, *Ouverture pour un conte gai*, *Zingaresca* for orchestra.

VOCAL three *Odelettes anacréontiques* for voice, flute, and piano (1911); *In memoriam matris* and *Musiques* for voice and piano.

CHAMBER violin and piano and cello and piano sonatas; *Sonate bourguignonne* and six sonatinas for piano.

'Emperor' Concerto nickname for Beethoven's E flat major piano concerto, Op. 73.

Emperor Jones opera by Louis Gruenberg (libretto by K de Jaffa, based on Eugene O'Neill's play), first produced at the New York Metropolitan Opera House on 7 January 1933. It tells the story of an escaped convict, Brutus Jones, who rules a Caribbean island, exploiting the locals until they rebel against him and he commits suicide.

'Emperor' Quartet composition for string quartet by Haydn; see ➤ *Emperor's Hymn, The*.

Emperor's Hymn, The or **Gott erhalte Franz den Kaiser/God Preserve the Emperor Francis** hymn composed by Haydn (words by L L Haschka), and first sung to celebrate the emperor's birthday, 12 February 1797. It was also used by Haydn as a theme for variations in the string quartet Op. 76 no. 3 (known as the 'Emperor' Quartet). The tune was later adopted as the Austrian national anthem. It is well known in England as a hymn-tune.

Empfindsamer Stil (German 'sensitive style') term applied to music by some German 18th-century composers, especially Carl Philipp Emanuel Bach and Johann Quantz, who sought to make their music directly expressive of feeling. See ➤ *Affektenlehre*.

Encina, Juan del (1468–1529) Spanish poet, playwright, and composer. He cultivated especially the ➤ villancico, a form resembling the French ➤ virelai. Over 60 of his songs are contained in a manuscript in Madrid, the *Cancionero musical de palacio*.

Encina studied at Salamanca University and entered the service of the Duke of Alba in Toledo. His poems were published at Salamanca in 1496. In 1498 he went to Rome, Italy, where he held a post at the court of the Spanish pope. While there he produced the *Farsa de Placida e Vittoriano* and composed many songs for his own plays. He was archdeacon of Málaga Cathedral from 1508–19, and of León Cathedral from 1519 until his death.

encore (French 'again') in music, an unprogrammed extra item, usually short and well known, played at the end of a concert to please an enthusiastic audience.

Ende einer Welt, Das, **The End of a World** radio opera in two acts by Hans Werner Henze (libretto by W Hildesheimer), first performed in Hamburg, Germany, on 4 December 1953; it was revised for the stage in 1964 and produced in Frankfurt on 30 November 1965.

end pin alternative term for the ➤ tail pin of a cello or double bass.

Enée et Lavinie, **Aeneas and Lavinia** opera by Pascale Colasse (libretto by B de Fontenelle, after Virgil), first produced at the Paris Opéra, France, on 16 December 1690.

The opera of the same title by Antoine Dauvergne (libretto by de Fontenelle), first produced at the Paris Opéra on 14 February 1758.

Enescu, George (1881–1955) Romanian violinist and composer. In 1899 he began his career as a virtuoso violinist and teacher of the instrument; Yehudi Menuhin and Arthur Grumiaux were among his pupils.

He studied at the Vienna Conservatory, Austria, 1888–93, and then went to Paris, France, to finish his violin studies with Marsick and to study composition with Jules Massenet, André Gedalge, and Gabriel Fauré.

Works OPERA *Œdipe* (after Sophocles, 1921–31; produced 1936).

ORCHESTRAL five symphonies (1905, 1912–14, 1916–21, with chorus and piano solo, 1934 and 1944, with tenor and chorus); *Poème roumain/Romanian Rhapsodies*, suites and intermezzi, and other pieces for orchestra.

CHAMBER string octet (1900), wind dectet (1906), two piano quintets (1894, 1940), two piano quartets (1909, 1943), two string quartets (1920, 1953), two piano trios (1897, 1916); three violin and piano sonatas (1897, 1899, 1926), two cello sonatas (1898, 1935); suites and other works for piano.

OTHER songs.

Enfance du Christ, L', The Childhood of Christ oratorio by Hector Berlioz, Op. 25, for solo voices, chorus, and orchestra, composed 1850–54 and first performed in Paris, France, on 10 December 1854.

Enfant et les sortilèges, L', The Child and the Spells opera in one act by Maurice Ravel (libretto by Colette), first produced in Monte Carlo, Monaco, on 21 March 1925. It tells how a spoiled child faces all the animals he has tortured; he redeems himself by tending a wounded squirrel.

Enfant prodigue, L', The Prodigal Son lyric scene by Claude Debussy (libretto by E Guinand), written for the Prix de Rome and published in 1884; it was produced as an opera at the Royal Opera House, Covent Garden, London, on 28 February 1910 with Perceval Allen, conducted by Percy Pitt. See ➤ *Prodigal Son*.

Engel, Carl (1883–1944) US musicologist. He studied at Strasbourg and Munich, Germany, and settled in the USA in 1905. He was appointed chief of the music division of the Library of Congress, Washington, DC, in 1922, and succeeded Sonneck as editor of the *Musical Quarterly* in 1929. He was one of the organizers and president 1937–38 of the American Musicological Society. He published many articles and books on music, including essay collections *Alla Breve: from Bach to Debussy* (1921) and *Discords Mingled* (1931).

English Cat, The opera ('a story for singers and instrumentalists') in two acts by Hans Werner Henze (libretto by Edward Bond after Balzac's *Peines de coeur d'une chatte anglaise*), first produced in Schwetzingen, Germany, on 2 June 1983. All the characters are cats. The story concerns Minette, who must marry Lord Puff. She is seen with Tom, and is taken to divorce court for adultery. Minette is drowned, Tom is stabbed, and 'the lawyers will make a huge profit'.

English horn alternative name for the ➤ **cor anglais**, a musical instrument of the oboe family.

English Suites six keyboard suites by Johann Sebastian Bach, composed by 1724–25.

Englund, (Sven) Einar (1916–1999) Finnish composer. His music is influenced by Sibelius and Shostakovich. He taught at the Sibelius Academy, and was best known for his symphonic works.

He studied with Selim Palmgren in Helsinki and with Aaron Copland at Tanglewood.

Works ORCHESTRAL seven symphonies (1946–88), cello concerto (1954), two piano concertos (1955, 1974), concerto for twelve cellos (1981), violin concerto (1981), serenade for strings (1983), flute concerto (1985).

CHAMBER piano trio (1982), string quartet (1985), suite for cello, *The Last Island* (1986).

enharmonic in music, a harmony capable of alternative interpretations, used as a link between passages of normally unrelated keys. For example, an enharmonic modulation from C sharp to F major plays on the equivalence, in keyboard terms, of the notes E sharp and F.

enigma canon a canon written down in a single part with no indication where the subsequent entries of the other parts are to occur, the performers being left to guess how the music fits by solving a riddle.

'Enigma' Variations set of orchestral variations by Edward Elgar, Op. 36, entitled *Variations on an Original Theme*, composed in 1898 and first performed in London on 19 June 1899, conducted by Hans Richter. Each variation is a musical portrait of some person indicated only by initials or by a nickname, all of whom have, however, been identified. The word 'Enigma' appears over the theme. See Cipriani ➤ **Potter**.

Enoch Arden melodrama for reciter and piano by Richard ➤ **Strauss**, Op. 38 (a setting of Tennyson's poem in German translation by A Strodtmann), first performed in Munich, Germany, on 24 March 1897 (and performed in Vienna, Austria, on 13 January 1899 with Alexander von Zemlinsky at the piano).

En Saga symphonic poem by ➤ **Sibelius**, Op. 9, composed in 1891 and first performed in Helsinki on 16 February 1893. It depicts no particular incident, but has a distinctly narrative, ballad-like tone.

ensalada (Spanish 'salad') a kind of burlesque madrigal cultivated in Spain in the 16th century, in dramatic form, like Orazio Vecchi's *L'Amfiparnaso*, not intended for stage performance. Also a ➤ **quodlibet**.

ensemble (French 'together') group of singers or instrumentalists, usually made up of one per part, for example instrumentalists playing chamber music. In opera, the word often refers to a section where several solo singers perform together, for example in the final scene of an act where all the characters sing at once, giving their opinions on the current situation. It can also describe the quality of the teamwork in a performance, for example 'their ensemble was poor' or 'a good ensemble'.

Entflieht auf leichten Kähnen double canon for chorus *a cappella* by Anton Webern, Op. 2; it was composed in 1908 and first performed in Fürstenfeld, Austria, on 10 April 1927.

Entführung aus dem Serail, Die, *The Abduction from the Harem* opera by Mozart (libretto by C F Bretzner [*Belmont und Constanze*] altered by G Stephanie, junior), first produced at the Burgtheater, Vienna, Austria, on 16 July 1782. In the story, Constanze resists the amorous Pasha Selim, who keeps her locked up. Belmonte (her true lover) and Pedrillo attempt to rescue her but are caught. The Europeans expect execution but are shown mercy by the Pasha.

entr'acte (French 'between acts') orchestral music played between the acts of an opera or play.

entrée (French 'entrance', 'entry') in the 17th and 18th centuries, a piece of music in a stately rhythm accompanying the entry of processions in ballets and other stage pieces; also, more generally, an introduction or prelude to any work, but more especially a ballet or opera where it accompanies the rise of the curtain; an entrée could also be the beginning of each new scene in a ballet.

entries in music, the appearances of the subject in the different parts of a fugue.

entry a 17th- and 18th-century English term for ➤ **prelude**.

Éolides, Les symphonic poem for orchestra by César Franck, on a poem of the same name by Leconte de Lisle; it was composed in 1876 and first performed in Paris, France, on 13 May 1877.

Eötvös, Péter (1944–) Hungarian conductor and composer. He was music director of the Ensemble Intercontemporain, Paris, 1979–91. As principal guest conductor for the British Broadcasting Corporation (BBC) Symphony Orchestra from 1985, he conducted the first performance of Harrison Birtwistle's *Earth Dances* in 1986.

He studied at Budapest and Cologne. In 1981 he gave the first performance of Karlheinz Stockhausen's *Donnerstag aus Licht*, at La Scala, Milan, and premiered Steve Reich's *Desert Music* in 1984.

Works *Hochzeitmadrigal* for six soloists (1963/1976), and *Chinese Opera* for chamber orchestra (1984).

Ephesian Matron, The comic serenata by Charles Dibdin (libretto by I Bickerstaffe), first produced at Ranelagh House, London, England, on 12 May 1769.

Epic of Gilgamesh, The oratorio by Bohuslav Martinů for soloists, speaker, chorus, and orchestra; it was composed 1954–55 and first performed in Basel, Switzerland, on 24 January 1958, conducted by Paul Sacher. The work's three sections are titled *Gilgamesh*, *The Death of Enkidu*, and *Invocation*.

episode in music, a passage or section of a ➔ fugue linking appearances of the subject (principal melody), usually non-thematic in nature and often forming sequences in order to modulate (move from one key to another) before the subject establishes a new key; or in a ➔ rondo, one of a variety of sections appearing between and contrasting with the recurring principal theme.

equale (Italian, plural equali, 'equals') term used for instrumental pieces, especially trombones (for example, Beethoven's *equale*), written for a group of similar instruments.

equal temperament in music, a type of ➔ temperament (tuning of a scale) in which every semitone within an octave is exactly equal.

equivoci, Gli, The Doubles opera by Stephen Storace (libretto by L da Ponte, based on Shakespeare's *The Comedy of Errors*), first produced at the Burgtheater, Vienna, Austria, on 27 December 1786. In the story, comic confusion is caused by the activities of identical couples.

equivoci nel sembiante, Gli, Dissimilarity in Similarity opera by Alessandro Scarlatti (libretto by D F Contini), first produced at the Teatro Capranica, Rome, Italy, on 5 February 1679. It is Scarlatti's first opera. It tells the story of the nymph Lisetta and her sister, Clori, who are in love respectively with the shepherd Eurillo and Armindo; the latter causes confusion by being disguised as Eurillo.

Erard (lived 18th–19th centuries) Family of French piano and harp makers. Sébastien Erard (1752–1831) introduced mechanical improvements that enhanced key and pedal action.

His firm was established about 1777 and pro-

duced its first grand piano in 1796. He opened a shop in London, England, in 1792. He was joined in business by his nephew, Pierre Erard (1796–1855).

Erb, Donald (1929–) US composer. His works are influenced by jazz and neoclassical techniques, and also employ electronics. His early career was as a trumpeter in dance bands.

He studied at the Cleveland Institute and with Nadia Boulanger in Paris, France. He has taught in Cleveland, Bloomington, and at the Southern Methodist University in Dallas, USA.

Works ORCHESTRAL *Symphony of Overtures* (1964), *The Seventh Trumpet*, for orchestra (1969), cello concerto (1975), trumpet concerto (1980); *Fantasy for Cellist and Friends* (1983); clarinet concerto (1984); concerto for orchestra (1985); concerto for brass and orchestra (1986).

CHAMBER *The Last Quintet* for woodwind (1982).

VOCAL *Cummings Cycle* for mixed chorus and orchestra (1963), *New England's Prospect* for choruses and orchestra (1974).

ELECTRONIC *The Purple-roofed Ethical Suicide Parlor* (1972), *Autumnmusic* (1973).

Ercole amante, Hercules as Lover opera by Pietro Cavalli (libretto by F Buti), first produced at the Tuileries in Paris, France, on 7 February 1662. It was the only opera specially written for Paris by Cavalli. The ballet music was by Jean-Baptiste Lully. The title alludes to the marriage of Louis XIV. Hercules wants Iole, but she hates him for having killed her father, who consented to her marriage with Hercules' son, Hyllus. Hercules imprisons his son and is about to marry Iole when she saves herself by giving him a deadly shirt to wear.

Erickson, Robert (1917–1997) US composer. He studied at the Chicago Conservatory and with Ernst Krenek at Hamline University, St Paul. He was professor at the University of California, San Diego, from 1967. His music progressed from serialism, through electronic means, to musique concrète.

Works ORCHESTRAL concerto for siren and other flyers, for orchestra (1965), *East of the Beach* for small orchestra (1980), *Auroras* for orchestra (1982).

VOCAL cardenitas, for singer, seven musicians, and tape (1968), *Sierra* for voice and chamber orchestra (1984).

CHAMBER chamber concerto (1960), concerto for piano and seven instruments (1963), *Solstice* for string quartet (1985).

OTHER INSTRUMENTAL *Pacific Sirens* for instruments and tape (1969).

Erismena opera by Pietro Cavalli (libretto by A Aureli), first performed at the Teatro San Apollinare, Venice, Italy, in 1656. Modern editions have been arranged by Lionel Salter (BBC, 1967) and A Curtis (1974). The story tells how Erismena dresses as an Armenian soldier to pursue the seducer Idraspe.

Eritrea opera by Pietro Cavalli (libretto by G Faustini), first performed at the Teatro San Apollinare, Venice, Italy, in 1652. An edition by Jane Glover was conducted by her at the Wexford Festival in Ireland in 1975. The story tells how, disguised as her dead brother, the captured Eritrea falls for an Egyptian prince.

Erkel, Ferenc (1810–1892) Hungarian composer. In creating the Hungarian opera, he was responsible for its distinctive national style. His own most important operas are *Hunyadi László* (1844) and *Bánk Bán* (1861), both based on Hungarian historical events. He was important in all fields of Hungarian music and composed Hungary's national anthem in 1844.

Erkel was born in Bekesgyula and studied at Pozsony (now Bratislava). As a pianist and conductor, he organized musical life at Kolozsvar in his early days. In 1825 he became music director of the Hungarian theatre in Buda, in 1836 assistant conductor of the German theatre in Pest, and in 1838 conductor of the National Theatre. He founded the Budapest Philharmonic Society in 1853 and was director of the Academy of Music 1875–89.

Works OPERA *Bátori Mária* (1840), *Hunyadi László* (1844), *Bánk Bán* (1861), *Dózsa György*, *Brankovics György* (1874), *Névtelen Hösök*, *István Király/King Stephen* (1874).

OTHER piano music; songs, and other pieces.

Erlkönig, Erl King ballad by Goethe, set to music by Franz Schubert in 1815, at the age of 18, and first sung in public by Johann Michael Vogl in Vienna, Austria, on 7 March 1821 and published as Op. 1 that year.

Ernani opera by Giuseppe Verdi (libretto by Francesco Maria Piave, based on Victor Hugo's drama *Hernani*), first produced at the Teatro La Fenice, Venice, Italy, on 9 March 1844. It was the first of Verdi's operas to be produced outside Milan. It concerns the outlawed Ernani and Don Carlos, King of Spain, who are both in love with Elvira. Don Carlos becomes Holy Roman emperor, Ernani marries Elvira, and Silva (guardian and former fiancé of Elvira) gets revenge.

Ernelinde, Princesse de Norvège opera by Francois Philidor (libretto by A H H Poinsinet), first produced at the Paris Opéra, France, on 24 November 1767.

ernste Gesänge, Vier composition by Brahms; see ➔ *Vier ernste Gesänge*.

eroe cinese, L', The Chinese Hero opera by Giuseppe Bonno (libretto by Pietro Metastasio), first produced for the court at the Schönbrunn Palace, Vienna, Austria, on 13 May 1752.

Ero e Leandro, Hero and Leander opera by Giovanni Bottesini (libretto by Arrigo Boito, at first intended for himself), first produced at the Teatro Regio, Turin, Italy, on 11 January 1879.

The opera of the same title by Luigi Mancinelli (libretto by Boito) was first produced as a cantata at the Norwich Festival, England, on 8 October 1896; its first stage production was at the Teatro Real, Madrid, Spain, on 30 November 1897.

'Eroica' Symphony Beethoven's symphony No. 3 in E flat major, Op. 55, composed 1803–04. It was to have been entitled *Bonaparte*, but on hearing that Napoleon had declared himself emperor, Beethoven renamed it *Sinfonia Eroica, composta per festeggiare il souvenire di un grand'uomo/Heroic Symphony, Composed to Celebrate the Memory of a Great Man*.

'Eroica' Variations Beethoven's piano variations and fugue, Op. 35 (composed in 1802), so called because they used the same theme as the finale of the 'Eroica' symphony. The theme, however, was taken from one of Beethoven's dances, and the variations were written before the symphony.

Erreur d'un moment, L', ou La Suite de Julie, The Error of a Moment, or The Sequel to Julie opera by Nicolas Dezède (libretto by J M B de Monvel), first produced at the Comédie-Italienne, Paris, France, on 14 June 1773.

Erwartung, Expectation monodrama for soprano and orchestra by Arnold ➔ Schoenberg (libretto by Marie Pappenheim), composed in 1909 but first produced in Prague (Czech Republic) on 6 June 1924, conducted by Alexander von Zemlinsky, with Marie Gutheil-Schoder. It describes a solitary woman searching through a wood for her lover; she finds his murdered body, which prompts an array of stark emotions.

Esclarmonde opera by Jules Massenet (libretto by E Blau and L de Gramont), first produced at the Opéra-Comique, Paris, France, on 15 May 1889. In the story, Esclarmonde, daughter of the king of Byzantium, uses magic powers to seduce the knight Roland. She is later exorcized and forced to renounce him, but Roland wins her back at a tournament, becoming king.

Escobar, Pedro (c.1465–after 1535) Portuguese composer. He spent much of his life in Spain, where he was maestro de capilla in Seville early in the 16th century. He composed church music and secular pieces for three and four voices.

Esmeralda opera by Fabio Campana (1815–1882) (libretto by G T Cimino, based on Victor Hugo's novel *Notre-Dame de Paris*), first produced in St Petersburg, Russia, on 30 December 1869.

It is also the title of an opera by Aleksandr Dargomizhsky (libretto by composer translated from Victor Hugo's libretto based on his *Notre-Dame de Paris*, and written for Louise Angélique Bertin [1805–1877] for her opera produced in Paris in 1836), first produced in Moscow, Russia, on 17 December 1847.

España rhapsody for orchestra by Emmanuel Chabrier of Spanish tunes collected by the composer during a visit to Spain in 1882–83; it was composed in 1883 and first performed in Paris, France, on 4 November 1883. Emil Waldteufel later made a ballroom waltz of it.

espressione (Italian 'expression') term used in musical notation. It usually appears as *con espressione*, 'with expression'.

espressivo or **espr. (Italian 'expressive')** term used in musical notation to indicate the performer should play with the necessary technique to generate an expressive effect.

Esquivel Barahona, Juan de (c.1565–after 1613) Spanish composer. He was maestro de capilla at Salamanca Cathedral in 1608 and at Ciudad-Rodrigo 1611–13. His Masses and motets were published in two volumes in 1608, and a volume of miscellaneous sacred works in 1613. An *Officium pro defunctis/Mass for the dead* survives in manuscript form.

essential discord in music, a chord that is dissonant according to acoustic theory, but whose notes belong to the key in which a composition or passage is written and has become sufficiently current to be introduced without preparation.

Estampes, Engravings set of three piano pieces by Claude Debussy, composed in 1903; 1. *Pagodes*, 2. *Soirée dans Grenade*, 3. *Jardins sous la pluie*.

estampida (Provençal; French estampie) an instrumental dance form of the 13th and 14th centuries, related to the troubadour/trouvère repertory. Its form consisted of several *puncta* (sections), each played twice, with first- and second-time endings, called *ouvert* and *clos*. Frequently the *ouvert* and *clos* endings, which often comprised the greater part of each *punctum*, were the same throughout the piece, resulting in a great deal of repetition.

Esther oratorio by Handel. It was first performed as a masque entitled *Haman and Mordecai* (libretto probably by Pope and Arbuthnot, after Racine) at Canons, near Edgware, London, England, about 1720. It was subsequently recast,

with additional words by Samuel Humphreys, and performed as an oratorio in London, at first privately to celebrate Handel's birthday and then at King's Theatre, Haymarket, on 2 May 1732.

The oratorio of the same title by Karl Ditters von Dittersdorf (libretto by S I Pintus) was first performed in Vienna, Austria, on 21 December 1773. During the interval of a revival of the work, on 16 December 1785, Mozart's piano concerto no. 22, K482, received its first performance.

estinto (Italian 'extinct, dead') in music, a direction indicating that a passage is to be performed in a toneless manner.

estompé (French 'stumped, shaded off') in music, a direction indicating damped or muffled; frequently used by Claude Debussy in pieces requiring a veiled or dull tone.

Es war einmal, Once upon a time opera by Alexander von Zemlinsky (libretto by Drachmann), first produced at the Hofoper, Vienna, Austria, on 22 January 1900. The opera was conducted by Mahler, who assisted Zemlinsky in revising the work. It tells how a princess married to a gypsy fits the wedding dress offered by a mystery prince, her husband in disguise.

Eternal Gospel, The, Czech **Věčné evangelium** legend by Leoš Janáček for soprano, tenor, chorus, and orchestra (text by J Vrchlický), composed in 1914 and revised in 1924. It was first performed in Prague (Czech Republic) on 5 February 1917.

Et exspecto resurrectionem mortuorum work in five sections by Olivier Messiaen for 18 woodwind, 16 brass, and three percussion, composed in 1964 to commemorate the dead of the two world wars. It was first performed at the Sainte-Chapelle, Paris, France, on 7 May 1965, conducted by Baudo.

ethnomusicology expanding earlier definitions of the field as the study of non-Western musics, 'ethnic music' or 'world music', ethnomusicology is the anthropological study of music as a culture-specific phenomenon and a universal aspect of human social behaviour. It developed out of late 19th-century studies of 'exotic' Asian scales in Europe and studies of American Indian music in the USA. Since the 1950s there has been a gradual process of incorporation of the insights offered by **comparative musicology**, with its emphasis on collection, documentation, systematization, classification, transcription, and analysis with the **anthropology of music**, with its emphasis on extended periods of field work, participant observation, the learning of vocal and instrumental performance skills by researchers, and the search for the social functions of music.

Ethnomusicologists attempt to describe music

cultures as whole systems or 'music cultures' but the general trend has been towards studies focused on specific theoretical problems, such as the role of music in healing, the cultural role and symbolism of musical instruments, and the relationship of musical aesthetics, values, and social power. Ethnomusicologists find themselves increasingly concerned with the ethics of fieldwork and the politics of representation, the music of migrant populations, the relationship between music, ethnicity, and identity in the construction of place, and a study of popular musics worldwide.

See: ➤ comparative musicology, ➤ organology, ➤ cantometrics.

Etler, Alvin (1913–1973) US composer. His music is influenced by serialism and shows concern for textural elements.

He studied at the Cleveland Institute and with Paul Hindemith at Yale University, and he taught at Smith College 1949–73.

Works ORCHESTRAL two sinfoniettas (1940, 1941), concerto for orchestra (1957), concerto for wind quintet and orchestra (1962), concerto for string quartet and orchestra (1968).

CHAMBER concerto for cello and chamber group (1971), concerto for violin and wind quintet (1958), two string quartets (1963, 1965).

Étoile, L' opéra bouffe by Emmanuel Chabrier (libretto by E Leterrier and A Vanloo), first produced at the Théâtre Bouffes-Parisiens, Paris, France, on 28 November 1877. It tells how, on the advice of an astrologer, a superstitious king cancels the execution of Lazuli, a pedlar who has insulted him.

Étoile du Nord, L', The North Star opera by Giacomo Meyerbeer (libretto by Augustin Scribe), first produced at the Opéra-Comique, Paris, France, on 16 February 1854. In the story, the disguised Katherine joins the Russian army and warns Tsar Peter of a conspiracy.

étouffé (French 'stifled, smothered') in music, a direction to deaden the tone on instruments where it is liable to vibrate after being sounded, as on the harp or the kettledrums.

Étranger, L', The Stranger opera by Vincent d'Indy (libretto by composer), first produced at the Théâtre de la Monnaie, Brussels, Belgium, on 7 January 1903.

Ettinger, Max (1874–1951) German composer. He studied in Berlin and Munich and lived at both places until 1933, when he went into exile in Italian Switzerland.

Works OPERA *Clavigo* (after Goethe; 1926), *Judith* (after Hebbel), *Frühlingserwachen* (after Frank Wedekind; 1928), *Juana* (after Georg Kaiser), *Dorlores* (1931).

CHORAL oratorios *Königin Esther*, *Moses*, *Weisheit des Orients* (from Omar Khayyám) for solo voices, chorus, and orchestra.

CHAMBER string quartet (1945).

étude (French 'study') in music, an exercise designed to develop technique. Although originally intended for practice only, some composers, notably Frédéric Chopin, wrote études of such virtuosity that they are now used as concert showpieces.

Études symphoniques a set of twelve concert studies for piano by Robert Schumann, Op. 13, at first entitled *Études en forme de variations*, composed in 1834. They are variations on a theme by the father of Ernestine von Fricken, with whom Schumann was in love at that time, but they are dedicated to Sterndale Bennett, in whose honour Schumann introduced into the finale a theme from the opera *Ivanhoe* by Marschner, *Der Templer und die Jüdin*: a song in praise of England. Five further variations are sometimes now given.

etwas (German 'somewhat, rather') in music, term used in conjunction with an adjective denoting speed or character, such as *etwas langsam*, 'rather slowly'.

Eugene Onegin opera by Tchaikovsky (libretto by composer and K S Shilovsky, based on Aleksandr Pushkin's poem-novel), first produced by students of the Conservatory, Moscow, Russia, on 29 March 1879. Its first professional performance was at the Bolshoi Theatre, Moscow, on 23 January 1881. It tells how Onegin rejects Tatiana's proposal by letter, but realizes too late by Act III that he loves her after all; she is now married to Prince Gremin.

eunuch flute early woodwind instrument with a mouthpiece containing a membrane that vibrates when the player sings into it. It dates back to the 16th century at least, but was never much more than a toy.

eunuch singers singers who were formerly castrated to preserve their boyhood voices; see ➤ castrato.

euphonium tenor four-valved brass band instrument of the bugle type, often mistaken for a tuba. It is used chiefly in brass and military bands.

The compass of the euphonium.

euphony suavity and harmoniousness of sound, the opposite of cacophony.

eurhythmics practice of coordinated bodily movement as an aid to musical development. It was founded about 1900 by the Swiss musician Emile ➤ **Jaques-Dalcroze**, professor of harmony at the Geneva conservatoire. He devised a series of 'gesture' songs, to be sung simultaneously with certain bodily actions.

Euridice, L' opera by Giulio Caccini (libretto by Ottavio Rinuccini), first produced at the Palazzo Pitti, Florence, Italy, on 5 December 1602. It tells how Orfeo's bride, Euridice, dies from a snake bite, but is allowed to return from Hades after divine intervention.

The opera of the same title by Jacopo Peri (libretto by Rinuccini) was first produced at the Palazzo Pitti, Florence, on 6 October 1600.

Euripides (lived c.484–406 BC) Greek dramatist. His tragedies, based on mythology and early history, inspired the following musical settings: ➤ **Alkestis** (Rutland Boughton and Egon Wellesz), *Baccanti* (Giorgio ➤ **Ghedini**), *Bacchantes* (Ernst ➤ **Toch**), *Backantenna* (Daniel ➤ **Börtz**), ➤ **Bakchantinnen, Die** (Wellesz), *Bakxai* (Buller), ➤ **Bassarids, The** (Hans Werner Henze), *Electra* (Walter ➤ **Damrosch**), *Getreue Alceste* (Gerard ➤ **Schürmann**), *Hippolytus* (Vladimir ➤ **Senilov**), ➤ **Ifigenia in Aulide** (Antonio Caldara, Luigi Cherubini, Karl Graun, and Niccolò Zingarelli), *Iphigenia in Aulis* (Damrosch), ➤ **Iphigénie en Aulide** (Christoph Willibald von Gluck), ➤ **Ifigenia in Tauride** (Baldassare Galuppi, Ghedini, Giovanni Maio, and Tommaso Traetta), *Iphigenia in Tauris* (Charles ➤ **Wood**), ➤ **Iphigénie en Tauride** (André Campra, Gluck, and Niccolò Piccinni), *Medea* (Damrosch and Virgil ➤ **Thomson**), *Orestes* (Nicolas ➤ **Slonimsky**), ➤ **Troades** (Aribert Reimann), and *Trojan Women* (Louise ➤ **Coerne**, Cecil Gray, and John ➤ **Foulds**).

Europe Galante, L' opera-ballet by André Campra (libretto by A H de la Motte), first produced at the Paris Opéra, France, on 24 October 1697. The work's four entrées are entitled *La France*, *L'Espagne*, *L'Italie*, and *La Turquie*, and depict the amorous inclinations of each country.

Euryanthe opera by Carl Maria von Weber (libretto by H von Chézy), first produced at the Kärntnertortheater, Vienna, Austria, on 25 October 1823. It tells how Lysiart is in league with the evil Eglantine to prove Euryanthe, Adolar's bride, unfaithful. They trick her and Lysiart succeeds in winning a bet, thereby ruining Adolar. Later the innocent Euryanthe is vindicated.

evensong an evening service of the Anglican Communion in which most of the liturgy is sung in ➤ **Anglican chant**. It also contains hymns, psalms, and the canticles ➤ **Magnificat** and ➤ **Nunc Dimittis**.

Éventail de Jeanne, L', Joan's Fan ballet in ten numbers (leaves of the fan), with music composed by Georges Auric, Marcel Delannoy, Pierre Ferroud, Jacques Ibert, Darius Milhaud, Francis Poulenc, Maurice Ravel, Roland-Manuel, Albert Roussel, and Florent Schmitt (choreography by Alice Bourgat). It was first produced in private in Paris, France, on 16 June 1927, and in public at the Paris Opéra on 4 March 1929.

Eventyr, Once upon a time ballad for orchestra by Frederick Delius after fairy tales by P C Asbjørnsen (1812–1885), composed in 1917 and dedicated to Henry Wood, who gave the first performance in London, England, on 28 June 1919.

Everyman incidental music by Sibelius, Op. 83, for Hugo von Hofmannsthal's German version, *Jedermann*, of the 15th-century English morality play *Everyman*. It was composed in 1916 and first performed at the National Theatre, Helsinki, Finland, on 5 November 1916. Six monologues from *Everyman* were set by Frank Martin for baritone and piano in 1943; an orchestral version was arranged in 1949.

Evocations three symphonic poems by Albert Roussel, composed 1910–12: 1. *Les Dieux dans l'ombre des cavernes*; 2. *La Ville rose*; and 3. *Aux bords du fleuve sacré*. It was first performed for the Société Nationale in Paris, France, on 18 May 1912.

The symphonic suite with the same title by Ernest Bloch was composed in 1937 and first performed in San Francisco, USA, on 11 February 1938. It has the three movements *Contemplation*, *Houang/God of War*, and *Renouveau*.

Ewen, David (1907–1985) US writer on music. He moved to the USA in 1912 and studied in New York. He worked at the University of Miami from 1965. In 50 years he published more than 80 music reference books, notably *Dictators of the Baton* (1943), *Encyclopedia of the Opera* (1955, revised 1971), *The World of 20th-Century Music* (1968), *Composers Since 1900* (1969), *Musicians Since 1900* (1978), and *US Composers* (1982).

Excursions of Mr Brouček, The, Czech *Výlety pana Broučka* opera by Leoš Janáček (libretto by the composer with F Gellner, V Dyke, F S Procházka, and others, after two novels by S Čech), first produced in Prague, Czechoslovakia (now the Czech Republic), on 23 April 1920. It was first produced in Britain in Edinburgh, Scotland, on 5 September 1970, by the Prague National Theatre Company. Part I depicts sausage-eating Brouček amidst aesthetic, vegetarian moon-dwellers; part II concerns the 1420 Czech defence in battle of their Hussite faith. Brouček is almost punished for cowardice but returns to the present.

Expert, Henri (1863–1952) French musicologist. He studied, and later taught, at Louis Niedermeyer's school in Paris, and was also a pupil of César Franck and Eugène Gigout. He was professor of music at the École des Hautes Études Sociales and librarian of the Conservatory library. He edited a series of early French music, *Les Maîtres musiciens de la renaissance française* and *Monuments de la musique française*, of settings of Ronsard's poetry, early songs, church and harpsichord music.

'...explosante fixe...' work by Pierre Boulez for unspecified forces. It was first performed, with flute, clarinet, and trumpet, in London, England, on 17 June 1971, and was performed with the same forces, plus strings and computer-controlled electronics, by the New York Philharmonic Orchestra, conducted by Boulez, on 5 January 1973. A further revised version under Boulez was performed by the British Broadcasting Corporation (BBC) Symphony Orchestra in Rome, Italy, on 13 May 1973.

exposition in music, the opening statement of piece in ➤ **sonata form**, in which the principal themes are clearly outlined.

expression in music, signs or words providing a dramatic context for the interpretation of neutral performance indicators for tempo, dynamics, phrasing, and so on.

expressionism in music, use of melodic or harmonic distortion for expressive effect, associated with Arnold ➤ **Schoenberg**, Paul ➤ **Hindemith**, Ernst ➤ **Křenek**, and others.

expression marks in musical composition, all the indications by which composers indicate their wishes as to the manner of performance of a work, especially from the dynamic point of view (*forte*, *piano*, *crescendo*, *diminuendo*); they may extend also to matters of speed and rhythm (*rallentando*, *rubato*, or *accelerando*). Expression marks were little used before the 18th century and hardly at all before the 17th century.

extemporization another term for see ➤ **improvisation**.

extended technique in general, nontraditional methods of obtaining sounds from musical instruments. Many 20th-century composers experimented with extended techniques of various sorts, particularly for wind instruments. An early example is the use of percussive keystrokes in Edgard Varèse's *Density 21.5* for solo flute (1930), in which the performer makes an audible sound by hitting the keys of the flute hard when changing note. Other examples of extended technique for woodwind include multiphonics (splitting the note so that two separate harmonics are heard; a technique often achieved accidentally by beginners, but extremely difficult to control deliberately), humming into the mouthpiece, and so forth.

extravaganza (from Italian *estravaganza*) word sometimes used for a composition of an unusual nature, especially for a light and fantastic stage piece with music, such as Gilbert and Sullivan's *Trial by Jury* (1875).

Eybler, Joseph Leopold von (1765–1846) Austrian composer. He attempted to complete Mozart's Requiem (1791) and suffered a stroke while conducting it in 1833. After holding various appointments in Vienna, he was chief Kapellmeister to the Austrian court 1824–33.

He was a pupil of Johann Albrechtsberger.

Works OPERA *Das Zauberschwert* and others.

CHORAL Requiem in C minor (1803, for Empress Maria Theresa), oratorio *Die vier letzten Dinge* (1810), cantata *Die Hirten bei der Krippe*.

CHURCH MUSIC seven Te Deums, 32 Masses, offertories, graduals, and other church music.

ORCHESTRAL AND CHAMBER symphonies; chamber music, piano pieces, and other pieces.

Ezio, Aetius libretto by Pietro Metastasio, first set to music by Nicola Porpora (Venice, 1728); other settings are by Handel (1732), Niccolò Jommelli (1741), Gluck (1750), and Johann Hasse (1755). The story tells how the general Aetius and the emperor Valentinian both love Fulvia. Maximus, her father, plays them off against each other to try and gain the throne. After much complication, Aetius and Fulvia are united and Maximus is pardoned.

f in music, abbreviation for ➤ **forte** (loud).

fa the old name for the note F (see ➤ **solmization**), still used in Latin countries, and in tonic sol-fa notation the sub-dominant note in any key represented by the symbol f, pronounced fa.

Faber, Heinrich (before 1500–1552) German theorist and composer. He was the author of a music textbook for beginners, *Compendiolum musicae pro incipientibus*, which was first published at Brunswick in 1548 and ran into numerous editions. There is some church music to Latin and German texts.

fabliau (old French 'fable') ➤ **troubadour** ballad with narrative words, distinct from the love songs sung by the troubadours.

Fabricius, Werner (1633–1679) German organist and composer. After pursuing other studies at Leipzig University, including law, he became music director at St Paul's Church there in 1656 and, in addition, at St Nicolas' Church in 1658. He was also a public notary.

He studied under his father, Albert Fabricius, who was organist at Flensburg; his other teachers were Thomas Selle and Heinrich Schiedemann at the Hamburg Gymnasium.

Works motets; hymn tunes; sacred and secular songs for several voices; suites for viols and other instruments.

Fabrizi, Vincenzo (1764–after 1812) Italian composer. He had written 14 operas by the time he was 24; many of them were short comic pieces, performed all over Italy. His *Il convitato di pietra (Don Giovanni Tenorio)* was premiered in Rome in 1787, the same year as Mozart's *Don Giovanni* was given in Prague, and rivalled the success of Mozart's work for several years.

faburden musical term meaning 'false bass'; see ➤ **fauxbourdon**.

Façade diversion by William Walton (poems by Edith Sitwell), privately produced at the Chenil Gallery, Chelsea, London, in 1922. Its first public performance was at the Aeolian Hall, London, on 12 June 1923. Two concert suites were arranged

later for enlarged orchestra and for piano duet. The work was also produced as a ballet (choreography by Frederick Ashton) at the Cambridge Theatre, London, on 26 April 1931.

Fackeltanz (German 'torch dance') dance in which each performer carries a torch.

fadinho (Portuguese *fado*) type of popular song performed in Portuguese towns, in the streets and cafés, accompanied by the guitar and enlivened by dancing.

Fago, Nicola (1677–1745) Italian composer, nicknamed Il Tarantino after his birthplace. He was educated at the Conservatorio della Pietà dei Turchini in Naples. He was maestro di cappella at the Conservatorio di S Onofrio 1704–08 and at the Conservatorio della Pietà 1705–40. His works consist mainly of church music but he also wrote four or more operas including *Radamisto* (1707) and *Cassandra* (1711), oratorios, and other works.

Fagott German name for the ➤ **bassoon**, a musical instrument.

fagotto (Italian 'fagot or bundle') alternative name for the ➤ **bassoon**, a musical instrument.

Faidit, Gaucelme (c.1160–c.1215) Provençal ➤ **troubadour**. He was at first a jongleur, and travelled with his wife, Guilhelma Monja, to various European courts. In 1202 he accompanied Boniface III of Montserrat to the Fourth Crusade and several of his songs exhort the young and strong to take part in the holy war. Among his patrons were Richard the Lion-Heart (whose death he lamented in a beautiful *planh*), Raymond d'Agoult, and Geoffrey of Brittany.

Fairies, The opera by John Christopher Smith (libretto by composer, based on Shakespeare's *A Midsummer Night's Dream*), first produced at the Drury Lane Theatre, London, England, on 3 February 1755.

Fair Maid of Perth opera by Georges Bizet; see ➤ *Jolie Fille de Perth, La*.

Fair Maid of the Mill song-cycle by Franz Schubert; see ➤ **schöne Müllerin, Die.**

Fair Melusina overture by Felix Mendelssohn; see ➤ **schöne Melusine, Die.**

Fair of Sorotchintsy unfinished opera by Mussorgsky; see ➤ **Sorotchintsy Fair.**

Fairy Queen, The semi-opera by Purcell (libretto adapted from Shakespeare's *A Midsummer Night's Dream* by Elkanah Settle), first produced at the Dorset Gardens Theatre, London, England, in April 1692. The plot broadly follows that of Shakespeare's play, without setting any of the words. It was revived by the English National Opera for the Purcell tercentenary in 1995.

Fairy's Kiss, The, French **Le Baiser de la fée** ballet in four scenes by Stravinsky, based on songs and piano pieces by Tchaikovsky, first produced at the Paris Opéra, France, on 27 November 1927, choreographed by Bronislava Nijinska. A suite for orchestra, *Divertimento*, was arranged in 1934.

Fairy Tale, Pohádka work by Leoš Janáček for cello and piano, inspired by the tale *Czar Berendei* by Vasili Zhukovski, first performed in Brno, Czechoslovakia (now the Czech Republic), on 13 March 1910, and revised about 1923.

fa-la a light 16th–17th-century English composition for several voices of the ➤ **ballett** type. Its name derives from the syllables to which the refrain was sung.

Falconieri, Andrea (1586–1656) Italian composer. He lived successively in Parma, Florence, Rome, and Modena, and also visited Spain. He was maestro di cappella in Naples from 1650.
  Works motets, madrigals, instrumental pieces.

fall in music, a ➤ **cadence** (such as 'dying fall' in Shakespeare).

Fall, Leo(pold) (1873–1925) Austrian composer. He studied at the Vienna Conservatory and became conductor at Berlin, Hamburg, and Cologne in Germany. He wrote some 25 works for the stage, chiefly operettas, including *Die Dollarprinzessin* (1907), *Die geschiedene Frau* (1908; *The Girl in the Train*), *Eternal Waltz* (1912), *Der liebe Augustin* (1912; *Princess Caprice*), and *Madame Pompadour* (1922).

Falla, Manuel de (1876–1946), born Manuel Maria de Falla y Matheu Spanish composer. The folk music (flamenco) of southern Spain is a major part of his compositions. His opera *La vida breve*/*Brief Life* (1905; first performed 1913) was followed by the ballets *El amor brujo*/*Love the Magician* (first performed 1915) and *El sombrero de tres picos*/*The Three-Cornered Hat* (1919), and his most ambitious concert work,

Noches en los jardines de España/*Nights in the Gardens of Spain* (1916). He also wrote songs and pieces for piano and guitar.

  He was born in Cádiz, and began to study the piano in Madrid at the age of eight. In 1902 he produced a zarzuela (piece of musical theatre), *Los amores de Inés*, written with very little tuition in composition. This had no success, and he studied composition in 1902–04 at the Madrid Conservatory with Felipe Pedrell, the founder of the modern national Spanish school of composition. In 1905 he won two prizes for piano playing and for his opera *La vida breve*/*Brief Life*. He lived in Paris, France, 1907–14, where he was influenced by the Impressionist composers Claude Debussy, Maurice Ravel, and Paul Dukas, but returned to Spain and settled in Madrid on the outbreak of World War I. The production of *La vida breve* at Nice and Paris in 1913 and of the ballet *The Three-Cornered Hat* in London, England, in 1919 spread his reputation. In 1921 he moved to Granada, southern Spain, and became more of a nationalist composer again; but had later works performed in England, Paris, and New York. In 1939 he moved to Argentina, where he died at Alta Gracia, leaving unfinished his most ambitious work, the cantata *L'Atlántida*, on which he had worked since 1928.

  Works OPERA *La vida breve*/*Brief Life* (1905), *El retablo de maese Pedro* (for puppets after Cervantes's *Don Quixote*; 1923); ballets *El amor brujo*/*Love, the Magician* (1915), *El sombrero de tres picos*/*The Three-Cornered Hat* (1919).

  INSTRUMENTAL AND SOLO VOCAL *Noches en los jardines de España* for piano and orchestra (1916); *Fantasia baetica* for piano (1919); *Psyché* for mezzo-soprano, flute, violin, viola, cello, and harp (1924); concerto for harpsichord, flute, oboe, clarinet, violin, and cello (1926); *Homenaje: pour le tombeau de Debussy* for guitar; seven popular Spanish songs.

false relation or **cross relation** in musical harmony, the appearance of different voices (independent parts) of two notes which bear the same note name but not the same pitch, either simultaneously or in close succession; that is, where one is modified by a flat or sharp, and the other is a natural. For example, false relations occur if an E flat in the soprano voice is followed in the next chord by an E natural in the tenor voice. In traditional harmony and counterpoint, false relations are not encouraged because harmonic alterations in one voice, as represented by a modifying sharp or flat, are resolved most smoothly within the same voice.

falsetto in music, the tone-production of male singers resulting in notes above their normal pitch in the female (soprano or alto) register, and sounding like an unbroken voice. The notes are 'falsely', or artificially, produced by making the vocal cords vibrate at a length shorter than usual. Falsetto is the voice normally cultivated by male countertenors.

falsoborodone musical term meaning 'false bass'; see ➤ **fauxbourdon**.

Falstaff opera by Giuseppe Verdi (libretto by Arrigo Boito, based on Shakespeare's *The Merry Wives of Windsor* and *King Henry IV*), first produced at La Scala, Milan, Italy, on 9 February 1893. In the story, Falstaff hopes to solve his money problems by seducing Alice Ford and Meg Page; he realizes his folly when he is tipped into the River Thames.

It is also the title of a symphonic study by Edward Elgar, Op. 68 (based on Shakespeare's *King Henry IV* and references to Falstaff in *King Henry V*), composed in 1913 and first performed at the Leeds Festival, England, on 2 October 1913.

Other works based on the same sources and character of Falstaff include Gustav Holst's ➤ *At the Boar's Head*, Otto Nicolai's ➤ *Lustigen Weiber von Windsor*, and Ralph Vaughan Williams's ➤ *Sir John in Love*.

Falstaff, ossia Le tre burle, ***Falstaff, or The Three Jests*** opera by Antonio Salieri (libretto by C P Defranceschi, after Shakespeare), first produced at the Kärntnertortheater, Vienna, Austria, on 3 January 1799. Beethoven wrote an early set of piano variations on the opera.

fanciulla del West, La, ***The Girl of the [Golden] West*** opera by Giacomo Puccini (libretto by G Civinini and C Zangarini, based on David Belasco's play), first produced at the Metropolitan Opera House, New York, on 10 December 1910. In the story, Jack Rance the sheriff and Dick Johnson the bandit compete for Minnie's affections. Realizing that Dick is an outlaw, Jack hunts him down and prepares to lynch him, but Minnie arrives in time to save the day.

fancy in music, old English term equivalent to the Italian *fantasia*, that is, a polyphonic composition for a consort of viols, ➤ **broken consort**, or keyboard instrument. Fancies had no definitely determined form, but always made considerable use of counterpoint and were generally divided into a number of sections, played without a break but not thematically connected.

fandango an 18th-century Spanish dance in moderate to fast triple time (3/8 or 3/4), danced by a couple with the accompaniment of a guitar and castanets. Fandangos are found in Mozart's *Le nozze di Figaro/The Marriage of Figaro* (1786), Gluck's *Don Juan* (1761), and Rimsky-Korsakov's *Capriccio espagnol/Spanish Capriccio* (1887).

fanfare a short call or flourish for trumpets, or other instruments imitating the effect of trumpets. It is often used for the arrival of an important person, or to introduce a ceremony or important event. Traditionally fanfares were written for valveless (natural) instruments, and usually include notes of the major ➤ **triad** and ➤ **diatonic scale**. An example of a fanfare is the introduction to Act II of Richard Wagner's *Tristan und Isolde* (1865).

Faniska play with music by Luigi Cherubini (libretto, in German, by Josef Sonnleithner), first produced at the Kärntnertortheater, Vienna, Austria, on 25 February 1806.

fantaisie French term for ➤ **fantasia**.

Fantaisies symphoniques title for Bohuslav Martinů's sixth and last symphony, composed in 1953 to celebrate the 75th anniversary of the founding of the Boston Symphony Orchestra. It was first performed in Boston, USA, on 12 January 1955, conducted by Charles Munch.

fantasia or **fantasy** or **phantasy** or **fancy** in music, a free-form instrumental composition for keyboard or chamber ensemble, originating in the late Renaissance, and much favoured by the English composers John Dowland, Orlando Gibbons, and William Byrd.

It implies the free manipulation of musical figures without regard to models of form. Later composers include Georg Telemann, Johann Sebastian Bach, and Mozart.

Fantasia Concertante on a Theme of Corelli work for strings by Michael Tippett, based on Corelli's Concerto Grosso Op. 6 no. 2, composed in 1953 for the tercentenary of his birth. It was first performed in Edinburgh, Scotland, on 29 August 1953.

Fantasia contrappuntistica work for piano composed in 1910, with the sub-title 'Grosse Fuge', by Ferruccio Busoni. It is based on the Contrapunctus XVIII of Johann Sebastian Bach's *The Art of Fugue* and completes the last unfinished fugue, with extra subjects created by Busoni. Two more versions for solo piano were completed by 1912 and a version for two pianos by 1921, first performed in Berlin, Germany, on 16 November 1921.

Fantasia on a Theme by Thomas Tallis work for double string orchestra and string quartet by Ralph Vaughan Williams, based on no. 3 of nine psalm tunes (1567) by Thomas Tallis, first performed in Gloucester, England, on 6 September 1910.

Fantasia on a theme of Handel work by Michael Tippett for piano and orchestra, composed 1939–41, and first performed in London, England, on 7 March 1942. It was written while Tippett was in conflict with the wartime government as a conscientious objector; just over a year after the first performance he spent three months in Wormwood Scrubs prison.

Fantasiestück (German 'fantastic piece') short instrumental piece of a free or fantastic character, rather less extended as a rule than a fantasy and keeping to a single movement and mood, whereas the latter is usually in several connected sections.

Fantastic Symphony symphony by Hector Berlioz; see ➜ *Symphonie fantastique*.

Faramondo opera by Handel (libretto by A Zeno, altered), first produced at the King's Theatre, Haymarket, London, England, on 3 January 1738. It is set in medieval France and tells how King Gustaavo plots revenge against Faramondo, the alleged murderer of one of his sons. The unusually convoluted plot also deals with deceptions and love rivalries.

farandole a dance of Provence, probably of Greek origin. It is danced by large groups of people in procession through the streets and accompanied by pipe and tabor. The music is in 6/8 time, so that the example in Bizet's *Arlésienne* music is not traditionally correct, though very evocative.

farce (from Latin *farcire*, 'to stuff, to lard') in 18th-century opera, a comic scene introduced into a serious work. Hence a complete comic opera so interpolated, or simply a comic opera in one act (Italian *farsa*). The modern sense of the term in English (an absurdly comic play) is derived from this. In earlier English the verb had the meaning it still has in French of stuffing food with seasoning, and in music it was used for the practice of interpolating words in the *Kyrie eleison*.

Farewell, Absence and Return piano sonata by Beethoven; see ➜ *Adieux, l'absence et le retour, Les*.

'Farewell' Symphony nickname of Haydn's symphony no. 45 in F sharp minor, composed in 1772 as a hint to Prince Esterházy that the orchestra would welcome leave of absence. In the finale the players leave the stage one by one until only two violins remain.

Farinelli, real name **Carlo Broschi (1705–1782)** Italian castrato soprano. He was a pupil of Nicola Porpora, in whose *Eumene* he made his debut in Rome in 1721. He sang with great success in many European cities, including Vienna and London. He remained in the service of the European court 1737–59, singing every night in private for Philip V, then Ferdinand VI. He retired to Bologna, Italy.

Farkas, Ferenc (1905–2000) Hungarian composer. After travelling to enlarge his experience and holding two posts at provincial schools of music, he was professor of composition at the Academy of Dramatic Art in Budapest 1949–75.

He studied at the Budapest Conservatory and with Ottorino Respighi in Rome.

Works STAGE opera *The Magic Cupboard* (1942), *A Gentleman from Venice* (produced in Budapest, 1991); musical plays and operettas; ballet *Three Vagabonds*; incidental music (including Shakespeare's *Timon of Athens*, *As You Like It*, and *Romeo and Juliet*).

OTHER cantata *Fountain of St John*; symphonies and other orchestral works, chamber music, piano music, songs.

Farmer, John (born c. 1570) English composer. He wrote a treatise on the polyphonic setting of plainsong tunes.

He was organist of Christ Church Cathedral, Dublin, Ireland, 1595–99, and then went to London.

Works psalm tunes set for four voices contributed to Thomas East's Psalter; madrigals; instrumental pieces.

Farnaby, Giles (c.1563–1640) English composer. He wrote madrigals, psalms for the *Whole Booke of Psalms* (1621), edited by Thomas Ravenscroft (1582–1633), and music for the virginal (an early keyboard instrument), over 50 pieces being represented in the 17th-century manuscript collection the ➜ *Fitzwilliam Virginal Book*.

He lived in London, where he married in 1587, and took a degree in music at Oxford University in 1592.

Works 20 canzonets for four and one for eight voices, madrigals, psalm tunes set for four voices in Thomas East's Psalter; over 50 virginal pieces.

Farnaby, Richard (c.1594–1623) English composer, son of Giles ➜ **Farnaby**. In 1608 he became apprentice to Sir Nicholas Saunderson of Fillingham, Lincolnshire. He wrote 52 keyboard pieces which were included in the *Fitzwilliam Virginal Book*, compiled by Francis Tregian who died in 1619.

Farquhar, George (1678–1707) Irish dramatist. His works inspired the composers John Eccles (*Stage Coach*), Gottfried ➜ **Finger** (*Sir Harry Wildair*), Richard ➜ **Leveridge** (*The Constant Couple, The Recruiting Officer, Love and a Bottle*), and Daniel ➜ **Purcell** (*The Beaux's Stratagem, The Constant Couple, The Inconstant*).

Farrant, Richard (c.1530–1580) English organist and composer. He was a Gentleman of the Chapel Royal in London until 1564, when he became organist and choirmaster at St George's Chapel, Windsor. He also wrote music for the

Blackfriar's Theatre, London.

Works service in A minor (usually sung in G minor), anthems 'Call to Remembrance' and 'Hide not Thou Thy Face', and other church music, songs for plays produced by him with the choirboys before Queen Elizabeth I; keyboard pieces in the Mulliner Book.

farsa or **farsa per musica (Italian 'farce' or 'farce for music')** Italian term of the early 19th century for a type of comic opera in one act, such as Rossini's *La cambiale di matrimonio* (1810).

Farthyng, Thomas (died 1520) English composer. He worked at King's College, Cambridge, as a chorister, 1477–83, and as a clerk, 1493–99. He was appointed at the Chapel Royal, 1511–20. He wrote church music and secular songs.

Fasch, Carl Friedrich (Christian) (1736–1800) German harpsichordist and composer. He was appointed second harpsichordist (with C P E Bach) to the court of Frederick the Great in 1756, but the outbreak of the Seven Years' War (1756–63) cost him his position and forced him to live by teaching. In 1791 he founded the Berlin Singakademie, the choral society which he conducted until his death.

He was a pupil of his father, Johann Friedrich ➔ **Fasch**, and later of Johann Hertel in Strelitz. He was conductor of the court opera in Berlin 1774–76.

Works oratorio *Giuseppe riconosciuto* (1774), Mass for 16 voices, cantatas, psalms, and other church music; also some instrumental music.

Fasch, Johann Friedrich (1688–1758) German organist and composer; father of Carl Friedrich ➔ **Fasch**. He founded the Collegium Musicum in Leipzig, travelled after 1714, held various posts in Gera, Greitz, and in the service of Count Morzin in Lukaveč, Bohemia, and in 1722 was appointed Kapellmeister at Zerbst. He was famous as a composer in his day, though his works were not published until after his death.

He was a pupil of Johann Kuhnau at St Thomas's School, Leipzig.

Works four operas including *Die getreue Dido* (1712); Masses, a Requiem, church cantatas, motets, a Passion; about 90 orchestral suites, 60 concertos, trios, sonatas, and other pieces; many of his vocal pieces are now lost.

Faun and Shepherdess song-suite for mezzo-soprano and orchestra for Stravinsky (text by Aleksandr Pushkin), composed in 1906 and first performed in St Petersburg, Russia, on 4 February 1908. At the same concert the E♭ symphony, dedicated to Rimsky-Korsakov, was given its first performance.

Fauré, Gabriel (Urbain) (1845–1924) French composer. He wrote songs, chamber music, and a choral *Requiem* (1887–89). He was a pupil of Saint-Saëns, became professor of composition at the Paris Conservatoire in 1896, and was its director 1905–20.

Fauré studied at Louis Niedermeyer's school of music in Paris 1854–66, and became church organist at Rennes in the latter year. He returned to Paris in 1870, became organist first at Saint-Sulpice and then at Saint-Honoré, and choirmaster at the Madeleine in 1877, being appointed organist there in 1896, a post he held until 1905. He had many distinguished composition pupils, including Maurice Ravel, George Enescu, and Charles Koechlin.

His early music, notably the song cycle *La Bonne Chanson* (1892–93), 1st violin sonata, and 1st piano quartet, was lyrical and contemplative in nature. His best known work, the *Requiem*, also dates from this period. He adopted a terser, more rigorous style at the turn of the century, with the open-air lyric drama *Prométhée* (1900), and continued in this style with the piano quintets and cello sonatas.

Works STAGE opera *Pénélope* (1913); incidental music *Pelléas et Mélisande* (Maeterlinck; 1898).

ORCHESTRAL *Pavane* (1887), suite *Masques et bergamasques* (1919).

CHAMBER two piano quintets (D minor, C minor, 1906, 1921), two piano quartets (C minor, G minor, 1879, 1886); string quartet (1924); piano trio (1923); two sonatas for violin and piano (A major, E minor, 1876, 1926), two sonatas for cello and piano; pieces for violin and piano, cello and piano, and flute and piano.

VOCAL Requiem for solo voices, chorus, and orchestra (1887–89); *Messe basse* for female voices and organ; eleven miscellaneous religious vocal pieces.

SOLO PIANO 34 Op. nos of piano music, including five Impromptus, 13 Barcarolles, four Valses-caprices, eight Nocturnes, Theme and Variations, nine Preludes; *Dolly*, six pieces for piano duet (1893–96).

SOLO VOCAL 96 songs including cycles *Poème d'un jour*, *La Bonne Chanson* (Verlaine; 1892–93), *La Chanson d'Eve* (Charles van Lerberghe, 1906–10), *L'Horizon chimérique* (1921).

Faust legend of a magician who sold his soul to the devil. The legend has inspired many writers and, in turn, composers.

Episodes from Nikolaus Lenau's poem *Faust* inspired two orchestral pieces by Franz ➔ **Liszt**, *Night Procession* and *Dance in the Village Inn* (originally titled *Mephisto Waltz*), composed about 1860.

The opera of the same title by Charles ➔ **Gounod** (libretto by J Barbier and Michel Carré, based on Johann Goethe's drama *Faust*), was first produced at the Théâtre Lyrique, Paris, France, on 19

March 1859.

The opera by Ludwig ➤ **Spohr** (libretto by J K Bernard, founded on the Faust legend without reference to Goethe's work, which was not completed at that time), was first produced in Prague, Bohemia (now the Czech Republic), on 1 September 1816. It was revised without spoken dialogue in 1852 and produced at Covent Garden, London, England, on 4 April 1852.

The overture by Richard ➤ **Wagner**, not for Goethe's drama, but a kind of symphonic poem on it, was composed in Paris 1839–40, after Wagner heard Beethoven's symphony at the Conservatory. It was first performed in Dresden, Germany, on 22 July 1844; it was rewritten 1854–55 and performed in Zürich, Switzerland, on 23 January 1855.

Other works based on the Faust legend include those by Adolphe ➤ **Adam** (ballet), Samuel Arnold (*Dr Faustus*), Nils ➤ **Bentzon** (*Faust III*), Hector Berlioz (➤ **Damnation de Faust**), Arrigo Boito (➤ **Mefistofele**), Ferruccio Busoni (➤ **Doktor Faust**), Henri ➤ **Pousseur** (*Votre Faust*), Hermann ➤ **Reutter** (*Doktor Johannes Faust*), Alfred ➤ **Schnittke** (*Historia von D Johann Fausten*), and Robert Schumann (➤ **Szenen aus Goethes 'Faust'**).

Fausta, Empress Fausta, wife of Constantine I opera by Gaetano Donizetti (libretto by D Gilardoni), first produced at the Teatro San Carlo, Naples, Italy, on 12 January 1832. The story is not related to the Faust legend. It describes how Fausta, wife of the Roman emperor Constantine, loves her stepson, Crispo, who loves Beroe. Crispo rejects Fausta, but charges are nonetheless brought against him for supposedly loving the queen. He is condemned to death and Fausta poisons herself.

Fausto, Faust opera by Louise Angélique Bertin (1805–1877) (libretto, in Italian, by the composer, based on Goethe's drama), first produced at the Théâtre Italien, Paris, France, on 8 March 1831. It was the first *Faust* opera and the only one by a woman. Bertin was the sister of Hector Berlioz's editor of the *Journal des Débats*, and Berlioz may have had a hand in the work; he probably suggested the subject, at least.

Faust-Symphonie, Eine symphony by Franz Liszt, based on Goethe's drama, 'in three character pictures': 1. *Faust*; 2. *Gretchen*; 3. *Mephistopheles*; with a final chorus 'Alles Vergängliche ist nur ein Gleichnis'. It was finished, without the chorus, on 19 October 1854, the chorus was added in 1857 and revised in 1880; the work was first performed at the Court Theatre, Weimar, Germany, on 5 September 1857, on the occasion of the unveiling of the Goethe–Schiller monument. The symphony is dedicated to Hector Berlioz. It was performed at Bayreuth, conducted by Daniel Barenboim, on the centenary of Liszt's death, 31 July 1986.

fauxbourdon ('false bass') name given to a wide variety of technical procedures in the 15th–16th centuries, usually involving improvisation. As originally used by Guillaume Dufay and others, the term implied the use of chains of $\frac{6}{3}$ chords, the middle part being 'improvised' by doubling the top part a fourth lower throughout; later, different techniques were employed to achieve the same effect. The English used their version of the word for a similar process, the three parts being improvised straight from plainsong (at first in the middle, later in the top part). The fauxbourdon itself (that is, the lowest part) was also used as the basis of entirely new compositions.

In the later 15th and early 16th centuries, the use of the term in both France and England was enormously extended to include techniques in which the idea of $\frac{6}{3}$ chords was entirely lost. It is to this final stage in its history that the Italian use of the term belongs, meaning initially a kind of fauxbourdon in four parts with the 'true' bass supplied beneath the false one, and ultimately nothing more than simple declamatory composition in note-against-note style.

Faux Lord, Le, The False Lord opera by Niccolò Piccinni (libretto by G M Piccinni, the composer's son), first produced at the Comédie-Italienne, Paris, France, on 6 December 1783.

Favart, Charles Simon (1710–1792) French playwright and librettist. He made a reputation as a librettist of light operas. He wrote ➤ **Bastien und Bastienne** (Mozart), ➤ **Cythère assiégée** (Gluck), ➤ **Löttchen am Hofe** (J A Hiller), ➤ **Rosina** (Shield), and for Franz ➤ **Süssmayr** (*Soliman II*).

favola d'Orfeo, La, The Story of Orpheus opera by Claudio Monteverdi (libretto by A Striggio), first produced at the court of the hereditary prince Francesco Gonzaga in Mantua, Italy, during Carnival in 1607. It was revived in a version by Vincent d'Indy and given in concert performance in Paris, France, in 1904; it was staged in Oxford, England, in 1925, under Jack Westrup. There are also versions by Gian Malipiero, Carl Orff, Paul Hindemith, Raymond Leppard, and Nikolaus Harnoncourt.

The opera of the same title by Alfredo Casella (libretto by C Pavolini, after A Ambrogini [Poliziano (1454–1494)]), was first produced at the Teatro Goldoni, Venice, Italy, on 6 September 1932.

favola per musica (Italian 'story for music') early Italian term for opera of a legendary or mythological character; it now indicates a story of that kind in dramatic form written for the purpose of being set to music.

Favorite, La opera by Gaetano Donizetti (libretto, in French, by A Royer and G Vaëz, with Augustin Scribe's assistance), first produced at the Paris Opéra, France, on 2 December 1840. In the story, Fernand falls in love with King Alphonse's mistress, Léonor, without knowing her true identity. After their marriage he finds out and feels dishonoured, retreating to a monastery. Later Léonor contracts a fatal illness, and as she dies is reconciled with Fernand.

Fayrfax, Robert (1464–1521) English composer. He was a Gentleman of the Chapel Royal on the accession of Henry VIII, with whom he attended the Field of the Cloth of Gold in 1520.

He became organist and choirmaster at St Albans Cathedral before 1502. He gained a degree in music at Cambridge University in 1501 (for his Mass *O quam glorifica*) and a PhD in 1504; he received a PhD from Oxford in 1511.

Works six cyclic Masses, motets, two Magnificats, *Stabat Mater*; songs for several voices, and other pieces.

Feast at Solhaug, The incidental music for Henrik Ibsen's play composed by Hugo Wolf for a production of a German translation by Emma Klingenfeld, first performed in Vienna, Austria, on 21 November 1891.

Fedé, Jehen (c.1415–c.1477) French composer. He was well known in his day as a writer of sacred and secular music, but only six pieces believed to be by him have survived.

He was vicar of Douai 1439–40, a papal singer 1443–45, at the Sainte Chapelle in 1449, at the court of Charles VII 1452–53, at St Peter's, Rome in 1466, and a member of Louis XI's chapel 1473–74.

fedeltà premiata, La 'dramma pastorale giocoso' (comic opera) by Haydn (libretto by G Lorenzi), first performed at Eszterháza, Hungary, on 25 February 1781; it was successfully revived in recent years at the Camden and Glyndebourne festivals in England. The story tells how the goddess Diana demands a sacrifice of two faithful lovers unless one hero offers to take their place. Fileno and Celia face this danger, but when Fileno offers his life to save Celia's, Diana shows mercy.

Fedora opera by Umberto Giordano (libretto by A Colautti, based on Victorien Sardou's play), first produced at the Teatro Lirico, Milan, Italy, on 17 November 1898. In the story, Fedora's husband, Vladimir, is murdered. After tracking down the killer, Count Loris, Fedora learns that the motive was revenge for an affair Vladimir had had with Loris' wife. The two fall in love, but come to a bad end when Vladimir's father takes revenge.

Fedra, Phaedra opera by Ildebrando Pizzetti (libretto based on Gabriele d'Annunzio's tragedy), first produced at La Scala, Milan, Italy, on 20 March 1915. Phaedra, the wife of Theseus, loves her stepson, Hippolytus, who rejects her. She makes Theseus believe Hippolytus has raped her, and Hippolytus is then killed. Phaedra takes poison, but unlike the version in Greek myth, she remains defiant to the end.

Feen, Die, The Fairies opera by Wagner (libretto by the composer, based on Carlo Gozzi's comedy, *La donna serpente*), composed in 1833, when Wagner was aged 20, and not staged in his lifetime. It was first produced in Munich, Germany, on 29 June 1888, rehearsed by Richard Strauss, who was not allowed to conduct the performance. Dramatic ideas from *Die Feen* are developed in Strauss's opera *Die Frau ohne Schatten* (1919). In the story, Ada, a half fairy, marries King Arindal on the condition that he does not ask about her true identity. He fails, and she is turned to stone, but Arindal restores her and the two leave for fairyland.

Fée Urgèle, La, The Fairy Urgéle opera by Egidio Duni (libretto by C S Favart, based on a story by Voltaire, founded on Chaucer's *Tale of the Wife of Bath*), first produced before the court at Fontainebleau, France, on 26 October 1765, and given its first public performance at the Comédie-Italienne, Paris, on 4 December 1765. The story is set in 7th-century France. The knight Robert is imprisoned and can be released only when he successfully answers a riddle. To find the answer he agrees to marry the crone La Vieille, who turns out to be his lover, Marton.

Felciano, Richard (1930–) US composer. He studied with Darius Milhaud and Luigi Dallapiccola, and worked at the University of California at Berkeley.

Works OPERA *Sir Gawain and the Green Knight* (1964).

ORCHESTRAL *Mutations* (1966), *Galactic Rounds* (1972).

CHAMBER *Contractions* for woodwind quintet (1965), *Salvatore Allende* for ensemble (1983), *Palladio* for violin, piano and percussion (1989).

OTHER *Soundspace for Mozart* for flute and tape (1970); *In Celebration of Golden Rains* for organ and gamelan (1977).

Feldman, Morton (1926–1987) US composer. An associate of John Cage and Earle Brown in the 1950s, he devised an indeterminate notation based on high, middle, and low instrumental registers and time cells of fixed duration for his *Projection* series for various ensembles (1950–51), later exploiting the freedoms of classical notation in a succession of reflective studies in vertical tone mixtures including *Madame*

Press Died Last Week at 90 (1970).
He studied with Stefan Wolpe and Wallingford Rieger. Influenced by abstract expressionist painting, he introduced the element of chance into his music, indicating often only an approximation of what is to be played.

Works ORCHESTRAL AND INSTRUMENTAL *Extensions I–V* (1951–60); *Durations I–V* (1960–61); *Vertical Thoughts I–V* (1963); *Two Instruments* for cello and horn; *De Kooning* for piano, cello, violin, horn, and percussion (1963); ballet *Ixion*; series of works with orchestra, featuring cello, string quartet, piano, obeo, flute, and violin (1972–79); two string quartets (1979, 1983); Trio (1980); *The Turfan Fragments* for orchestra (1980); *Triadic Memories* for piano (1981); *For John Cage* (1982); violin concerto (1984).

VOCAL *For Franz Kline* for soprano, violin, cello, horn, chimes, and piano; *The Swallows of Salangan* for chorus and 76 instruments; *The Rothko Chapel* for viola, chorus, and percussion (1972); *The Viola in my Life I–IV* (1970–71); *Neither*, monodrama to text by Beckett for soprano and orchestra (1977); *Three Voices* for three sopranos, or voice and tape (1982).

Feldpartie or **Feldpartita (German 'field suite')** old German term for suites written for wind instruments and played in the open on military occasions.

Félix, ou L'Enfant trouvé, **Felix, or The Foundling** opera by Pierre Monsigny (libretto by J M Sedaine), first produced for the court at Fontainebleau, France, on 10 November 1777 and given its first public performance at the Comédie-Italienne, Paris, on 24 November 1777. It was Monsigny's last opera.

Fellowes, Edmund H(orace) (1870–1951) English clergyman and musicologist. He was educated at Winchester College and Oxford, and attached to St George's Chapel, Windsor, as a minor canon from 1900. He was awarded an honorary doctorate of music at Dublin, Ireland, in 1917 and Oxford in 1938. He wrote books on the English madrigal, William Byrd and Orlando Gibbons, edited *The English Madrigal School* (1913–24), English lutenist songs, and Byrd's works, and co-edited *Tudor Church Music*.

Felsztyński, Sebastian (c.1490–c.1544) Polish composer. He studied at Kraków University. He wrote church music, and compiled a hymnbook for Sigismund I in 1522.

Felton, William (1715–1769) English organist and composer. He became famous as a performer on the organ and harpsichord, for which he wrote concertos and lessons. The celebrated *Felton's Gavotte* was a set of variations in one of the concertos.

Felton was educated at Manchester and Cambridge. He became a clergyman, a vicar-choral, and later a minor canon at Hereford Cathedral.

feminine in music, adjective used to describe a ➔ cadence or phrase which ends on an unstressed beat of the bar, most typically the second beat.

Fenby, Eric William (1906–1997) English composer and writer on music. From 1928–34 he acted as amanuensis to Frederick Delius, who was living blind and paralysed at Grez-sur-Loing, France, and helped him to commit *Songs of Farewell*, *A Song of Summer*, *Fantastic Dance-Idyll*, and other late works to paper. He published a memoir, *Delius as I Knew Him* in 1936 (revised 1981).

Fenby became an organist at the age of 12 and studied music with A E Keeton. He was professor of harmony at the Royal Academy of Music, London, 1964–77.

Works symphonic, overture *Rossini on Ilkla Moor*, and other pieces.

Fennell, Frederick (1914–2004) US conductor. He founded the Eastman Wind Ensemble in 1952 and made many successful recordings with it. He was conductor-in-residence at the University of Miami School of Music, Florida, 1965–80, and conductor with the Kosei Wind Orchestra, Tokyo, Japan, from 1984.

He studied at the Eastman School and conducted the Little Symphony and Symphonic Band 1939–65.

Fennelly, Brian (1937–) US composer. He studied at Yale University and has been professor at New York University. His music draws on a wide range of sources.

Works ORCHESTRAL *In Wildness is the Preservation of the World*, fantasy for orchestra after Thoreau (1975); *Quintuplo* for brass quintet and orchestra (1978); *Scintilla* for cello and orchestra (1981); saxophone concerto (1984).

CHAMBER *Evanescences* for ensemble (1969); string quartet (1971); series *Tesserae*, for various instrumental groups (1971–81); brass quintet (1987); *On Civil Disobedience* (1992–93).

CHORAL *Winterkill* for chorus and piano (1981).

Fennimore und Gerda opera in eleven pictures by Frederick Delius (libretto, in German, by the composer, based on Peter Jacobsen's novel *Niels Lyhne*), first produced in Frankfurt, Germany, on 21 October 1919. In the story, Erik and Niels love Fennimore. She marries Erik and thier relationship sours. Later Erik is accidentally killed; the last two pictures concentrate on Niels's romance with Gerda.

Feo, Francesco (1691–1761) Italian composer. He was a pupil of Gizzi and Fago at the Conservatorio della Pietà della Turchini in Naples, and later of Pitoni in Rome. He produced his first opera, *L'amor tirannico*, in Naples in 1713. He was maestro di cappella of the Conservatorio St Onofrio 1723–28 and of the Conservatorio dei Poveri 1739–43. Niccolò Jommelli and Giovanni Pergolesi were among his pupils.

Works OPERA *Siface* (1723), *Ipermestra, Arianna* (1728), *Andromaca* (1730), *Arsace* (1740), and others.

OTHER Masses and other church music.

Feragut, Beltrame or **Bertrand (c.1385–c.1450)** French composer who travelled in France and Italy. His motet *Excelsa civitas Vincencia* was written in honour of a new bishop of Vicenza, Francesco Malipiero, in 1433. A few other sacred works survive.

Feramors opera by Anton Rubinstein (libretto, in German, by J Rodenberg, based on Thomas Moore's *Lalla Rookh*), first produced in Dresden, Germany, on 24 February 1863. It tells how the Kashmiri princess Tulipchuk loves Feramors but must marry the Khan of Bbukhara, but the two men turn out to be the same person.

Ferguson, Howard (1908–1999) Irish composer and pianist. Ferguson was a professor at the Royal Academy of Music, London, 1948–63. He made many editions of early keyboard works, and was active as an accompanist.

Ferguson was educated at Westminster School and the Royal College of Music in London as a pupil of Reginald Morris.

Works BALLET *Chaunteclear* (1948).

ORCHESTRAL partita and four *Diversions on Ulster Airs* for orchestra; concerto for piano and strings (1951).

CHAMBER Octet (1933); two violin and piano sonatas, four pieces for clarinet and piano; sonata and five bagatelles for piano.

VOCAL two ballads for baritone and orchestra; three *Medieval Carols* for voice and piano (1932–33); *The Dream of the Rood* for soprano or tenor, chorus, and orchestra (1958–59).

fermata (Italian 'pause') prolonging a note or rest beyond its normal length. For very short pauses a square sign was invented by Vincent d'Indy, but this device never found general acceptance. In *da capo* arias the fermata sign over the final chord of the first section indicates where the aria is to end after the repeat. In a chorale, or a chorale prelude, it indicates the end of a line.

Fernand Cortez, ou La Conquête de Mexique, Hernáen Cortés, or The Conquest of Mexico opera by Gasparo Spontini (libretto by J A Esménard and V J E de Jouy, based on a tragedy by Alexis Piron), first produced at the Paris Opéra, France, on 28 November 1809. In the work, Cortez's brother Alvar is a prisoner of the Aztecs;

Cortez's Aztec lover Amazily, seen as a traitor by her own people, offers her life to save Alvar, but Cortez rescues her just in time.

Fernando operetta by Franz Schubert (libretto by A Stadler), composed in 1815 but never performed in Schubert's lifetime; it was first produced in Magdeburg, Germany, on 18 August 1918 (the first concert performance was given in Vienna, Austria, in 1905). The story concerns Fernando who is rescued from a life as a hermit after killing his brother-in-law.

Ferne Klang, Der, The Distant Sound opera by Franz Schreker (libretto by the composer), first produced in Frankfurt, Germany, on 18 August 1912. It tells how the young couple Fritz and Greta separate to seek their fortunes: the 'Distant Sound'. Fritz becomes a composer and Greta a courtesan. They meet years later and he dies in her arms.

Ferneyhough, Brian John Peter (1943–) English composer. His uncompromising, detailed compositions include *Carceri d'invenzione* (1981–86), a cycle of seven works inspired by the engravings of Piranesi, *Time and Motion Studies* (1974–77), and string quartets.

He studied in Birmingham and with Lennox ➔ Berkeley at the Royal Academy of Music in London 1966–67, and undertook further study in Amsterdam, the Netherlands, and Germany. He has taught at the Freiburg Musikhochschule and at Darmstadt, Germany. His music is of the advanced avant garde, and includes electronic devices.

Works ORCHESTRAL *Firecycle Beta* for orchestra with five conductors (1971), *La Terre est un homme* for orchestra (1978).

CHAMBER *Prometheus* for wind sextet (1967), *Sonatas* for string quartet (1967), *Epicycle* for 20 strings (1969), third and fourth string quartets (1987, 1990).

VOCAL *Missa Brevis* for twelve voices (1971), *Transit* for six voices and chamber orchestra (1975), *Etudes Transcendantals* for voices and ensemble (1984).

OTHER INSTRUMENTAL *Sieben Sterne* for organ (1969–70); *Intermedio alla Ciaccona* for violin (1980); *Mnemosyne* for bass flute and tape (1986); *Kurze Schatten* for guitar (1983–89); *Trittico per G S* for double bass (1989).

Ferrabosco, Alfonso (1543–1588) Italian composer. He was the most important of the Italian musicians who lived in England in the 16th century. He wrote madrigals, lute pieces, and motets. Many of his works appear in *Musica Transalpina*.

He was born in Bologna, son of the singer and composer Domenico Ferrabosco (1513–1574). He settled in London before 1562; left the service of

Queen Elizabeth I in 1569, after becoming involved in a murder case, and returned to Italy on leave, which he extended until 1572. In 1578 he left England for good and entered the service of the Duke of Savoy in Turin, leaving his children in England.

Works motets, madrigals, and other pieces.

Ferrabosco, Alfonso (c.1575–1628) English composer of Italian descent. He was left behind, being probably illegitimate, when his father Alfonso Ferrabosco left England in 1578. He was trained in music at Queen Elizabeth I's expense, became one of James I's court musicians, and succeeded John Coprario as Composer of Music to the King in 1626.

Works MASQUES songs for masques by Ben Jonson, including *The Masque of Blackness*, *Hymenaei*, *The Masque of Beauty*, *The Hue and Cry after Cupid*, *The Masque of Queens*, *Love freed from Ignorance and Folly*.

OTHER fancies for viols; lessons for lyra viol; ayres with lute and bass viol; contributions to Leighton's *Teares or Lamentacions*.

Ferrari, Benedetto (c.1597–1681) Italian music theorist, playwright, and composer. The final duet of this opera *Il pastor regio* (Bologna, 1641) may have been used as the duet at the end of Monteverdi's *L'incoronazione di Poppea*.

He lived in Venice, where he began to produce music dramas with words and music of his own in 1637. In 1645 he went to the court of Modena, where he remained until 1662, except for a visit to Vienna 1651–53. He was then dismissed, but reappointed in 1674.

Works OPERA *Armida* (1639), *La ninfa avara* (1641), *Il pastor regio* (1641), *Proserpina rapita*, and others; oratorio *Sansone*; three books of *Musiche varie a voce sola*.

Ferreira, Manuel (died 1797) Spanish composer and conductor. He was attached to a Madrid theatre and wrote incidental music for plays and light operas which are early examples of tonadillas (short stage pieces, often of a satirical nature).

Works STAGE opera *El mayor triunfo de la mayor guerra*; numerous light operas; incidental music to plays by Calderón, Moreto, and others, including Antonio de Zamora's *Don Juan*.

Ferretti, Giovanni (c.1540–1609) Italian composer and priest. He was maestro di cappella at Ancona Cathedral from 1575, and later worked at the Santa Casa in Loreto. Apart from a few sacred works, he specialized in the lighter types of madrigal, publishing five books of *Canzoni alla Napolitana* (1573–85).

Fervaal opera by Vincent d'Indy (libretto by the composer, based on and altered from Elaias Tegnér's *Axel*), first produced at the Théâtre de la Monnaie, Brussels, Belgium, on 12 March 1897. In the story, Fervaal can save his people only if he renounces love, but he falls for Guilhen. Defeated by the Saracens, he carries Guilhen's body away, pledging a new age of Christianity.

festa teatrale (Italian 'theatrical feast or festival') 18th-century type of opera of a festive kind, especially one expressly written for an occasion, such as a royal or princely patron's wedding. The subject of the libretto was usually mythological and allegorical. Mozart's *Ascanio in Alba* (1771) is an example.

Festes vénitiennes, Les, The Venetian Feasts opera by André Campra (libretto by A Danchet), first produced at the Paris Opéra, France, on 17 June 1710. It was revived in Aix-en-Provence, France, in 1975. It consists of a prologue followed by five (originally three) acts, which are all independent love stories.

Festin de l'araignée, Le, The Spider's Banquet ballet by Albert Roussel (choreography by G de Voisins, based on Henri Fabre's *Souvenirs entomologiques*), first produced at the Théâtre des Arts, Paris, France, on 3 April 1913.

Festing, Michael (Christian) (c.1680–1752) English violinist and composer. He was music director of the King's Theatre, London, from 1737 and of Ranelagh Gardens from 1742.

He was a pupil of Francesco Geminiani in London. He made his first appearance there in 1724 and became Master of the King's Musick in 1735.

Works paraphrase of the third chapter of Habakkuk, Milton's *Song on May Morning* (1748), Addison's *Ode for St Cecilia's Day*, and other odes; cantatas; symphonies; concertos and sonatas for various instruments; songs.

Fêtes de l'Amour et de Bacchus, Les, The Feasts of Cupid and Bacchus pastorale by Jean-Baptiste Lully (libretto by Philippe Quinault, with Molière and I de Benserade), first produced at the Paris Opéra, France, on 15 November 1672. It is a pastiche derived from his and Molière's *comédies-ballets*.

Fêtes de Thalie, Les, Thalia's Feasts opera-ballet by Jean Mouret (libretto by J de Lafont), first produced at the Paris Opéra, France, on 19 August 1714. It comprises a prologue followed by three independent 'entrées' (acts) about love: *La Fille*, *La Veuve*, and *La Femme*.

Fêtes d'Hébé, Les, ou Les Talens lyriques, Hebe's Feasts, or The Lyrical Gifts opera-ballet by Jean-Philippe Rameau (libretto by A M de Montdorge), first produced at the Paris Opéra, France, on 21 May 1739. It describes how divinities gather on the banks of the River Seine to celebrate gifts to the lyric stage: *La Poésie*, *La*

Musique, and *La Danse*.

Fétis, François Joseph (1784–1871) Belgian musicologist. He wrote a *Biographie universelle des musiciens* (1835–44), an unfinished *Histoire générale de la musique* (1869–76), and many theoretical works. He also wrote several operas. He is seen as the founder of modern musical lexicography and probably the most prolific musicologist ever, though his work is often highly unreliable.

He was born in Mons, and was trained by his father and in Paris. He was appointed organist and professor of music at Douai in 1813, professor at the Paris Conservatory in 1821, and director of the Brussels Conservatory and chapel master to Leopold I in 1833. In 1827 he founded the *Revue musicale*.

Feuersnot, Fire Famine opera by Richard Strauss (libretto by Ernst von Wolzogen), first produced in Dresden, Germany, on 21 November 1901. As revenge against the mocking and chaste Diemut, Konrad casts a spell by which all the town's lights are extinguished until Diemut yields to Konrad's desires.

Février, Henri (1875–1957) French composer. He studied under Jules Massenet and Gabriel Fauré at the Paris Conservatory.

Works STAGE operas *Monna Vanna* (after Maeterlinck; 1909), *Ghismonda* (1918), *La Damnation de Blanchefleur*, *La Femme nue* (1932), and *L'Île désenchantée*; operetta *Sylvette* (with Delmas); comic operas *Le Roi aveugle*, *Agnès dame galante*, and *Carmosine* (after Musset).

OTHER songs .

ff in music, abbreviation for ➔ **fortissimo**, very loud.

f holes or **ff holes** the sound-holes of instruments of the ➔ **violin family**, so called because of their shape.

fiamma, La, The Flame opera by Ottorino Respighi (libretto by C Guastalla after H W Jenssen), first produced at the Teatro Reale, Rome, Italy, on 23 January 1934. It describes how Silvana, the wife of Basilio, falls in love with her stepson, Donello, using magic to seduce him. The two are found together; Basilio drops dead, and Silvana is tried for witchcraft. She realizes the futility of her passion and is condemned to death.

Fibich, Zdeněk (1850–1900) Czech composer. His music is personal rather than national, and was considerably advanced and daring for its time. After studying in France and Germany, and having taught in Poland for a time, he returned to Czechoslovakia in 1874 and conducted at the National Theatre in Prague. He retired in 1881 to devote himself entirely to composition, and wrote over 600 works of various kinds.

Fibich was born in Šerbořic, near Časlav. Very precociously gifted, he studied at the Leipzig Conservatory, Germany, under Carl Richter and Salomon Jadassohn (1831–1902), also piano under Ignaz Moscheles. He also studied in Paris, France, 1868–69 and Mannheim, Germany, 1869–70.

He wrote seven operas and a trilogy of melodramas (spoken text accompanied by music) entitled *Hippodamia* (1891), the most ambitious work of the kind ever produced; also choral works, three symphonies and other orchestral music, melodramas with orchestra and with piano, chamber and piano music, and songs.

Works STAGE operas *Bukovin* (1874), *Blaník* (1881), *The Bride of Messina* (after Schiller; 1884), *The Tempest* (after Shakespeare), *Hedy* (after Byron's *Don Juan*), *Šárka* (1897), *Pad Arkuna*; melodramas *Christmas Eve*, *Eternity*, *The Water-Sprite*, *Queen Emma*, *Haakon*, and the trilogy *Hippodamia* (1891); incidental music to Vrchlický's comedy *A Night at Karlstein*.

ORCHESTRAL three symphonies, overtures, symphonic poems *Othello* and *The Tempest* (both after Shakespeare), and four others.

CHAMBER two string quartets (1874, 1879), piano quartet, piano trio, quintet for piano, violin, cello, clarinet, and horn; piano sonata, 350 pieces *Moods, Impressions and Memories* for piano.

VOCAL songs, vocal duets.

fida ninfa, La, The Faithful Nymph opera by Antonio Vivaldi (libretto by S Maffei), first produced at the Teatro Filarmonico, Verona, Italy, on 6 January 1732. It was published in Cremona in 1964, in an edition by R Monterosso. The story tells how Licori is pursued by the pirate Oralto but remains true to Osmino.

fiddle any instrument from a widespread family of bowed lutes consisting of one or more strings stretched the full length of a fingerboard terminating in a soundbox. The timbre of a fiddle depends on the resonance of the soundbox, which depends on the frequency of the sound vibration. The lower the frequency (the lower the pitch of the note) the larger the soundbox needed to produce a full tone. 'Fiddle' is also the colloquial name given to instruments of the violin family.

Most fiddles are flat-backed; the 13th-century **rebec**, however, is tear-shaped and has a convex back like a lute. Many fiddles incorporate ➔ **sympathetic strings** which vibrate when the string next to them is sounded, enriching the overall effect.

The **American Apache fiddle** has a hollow tubular body, often made of cactus; the **Middle East spike fiddle** rests on the leg and has a dish-shaped soundbox; **African fiddles** take many forms, including the shoelike rebab; **Asian fiddles** include the Japanese *ko-kiu*, the Mongolian *morinchur*, and the Chinese *erh-hu*. **Medieval and Renaissance fiddles** held at the shoulder are the immediate predecessors of the violin.

In folk fiddle traditions, from the gypsy music of Eastern Europe to US country music, the violin was widely adopted as the successor to the fiddle. In Norway, four sympathetic strings were added to create the Hardanger fiddle.

Fiddler's Child, The, Czech **Šumařovo dítě** ballad for orchestra by Leoš Janáček, after a poem by S Čech, composed in 1912. It was first performed in Prague, Bohemia (Czech Republic), on 14 November 1917.

Fidelio, oder Die eheliche Liebe, **Fidelio, or Wedded Love** opera by Beethoven (libretto by J Sonnleithner, based on Bouilly's libretto of *Léonore, ou L'Amour conjugal* written for Pierre Gaveaux), first produced at the Theater an der Wien, Vienna, Austria, on 20 November 1805, conducted by Beethoven, with the overture *Leonora No. 2*. A revised version, with the overture *Leonora No. 3*, was performed at the same theatre on 29 March 1806, conducted by Ignaz Seyfried. The overture *Leonora No. 1* was written for the first performance but abandoned as unsuitable; a second revision was produced at the Vienna Kärntnertortheater on 23 May 1814, with the *Fidelio* overture in E major. The story of the opera concerns the political prisoner Florestan who is rescued by his disguised wife (Leonore/Fidelio) when the evil Pizarro arrives to kill him.

Field, John (1782–1837) Irish-born composer and pianist. He is often regarded as one of a group of composers known as the London Pianoforte School, and all of his works include the piano, reaching their peak artistically with his ➔ **nocturnes**, a genre he named and devised. These anticipate Chopin's nocturnes by 20 years, especially regarding their forward-looking textures and ➔ **passage work**.

As an apprentice to Muzio Clementi, Field travelled throughout Europe demonstrating instruments for the firm of piano makers established by his master. In 1803 he settled in St Petersburg, Russia, where he composed most of his mature music.

Field was the son of a violinist at the Dublin theatre. He was taught music and the piano by his grandfather, an organist. On moving to London he was apprenticed to Clementi, who taught him and at whose piano warehouse he was employed to show off the instruments by improvisation. He made his first public appearance at Giuseppe Giordani's concerts in Dublin in 1792 and in London in 1794. In 1802 Clementi took him to Paris, Germany, and Russia. He left him behind at St Petersburg in 1803, where he became a piano teacher and in 1808 married a Mlle Perch-

eron. In 1822 he settled in Moscow, where he had as great a success as he had had in the new capital. He travelled much as a pianist, visiting London in 1832, and afterwards Paris, Switzerland, and Italy. In Naples he was taken ill and lay in hospital for months until a Russian family took him back to Moscow, where he died soon after his return.

Works Seven piano concertos (1799–1822); 17 nocturnes, four sonatas, and many rondos, fantasies, variations, and other pieces for piano; piano quintet and other chamber music; works for piano duet.

Fielding, Henry (1707–1754) English novelist and dramatist, author of the ballad operas *The Intriguing Chambermaid*, *The Lottery*, *Miss Lucy in Town*, *Don Quixote in England*, and others. His works inspired the composers Thomas Arne, Monro (*Temple Beau*), and François Philidor (*Tom Jones*).

Field Mass work by Bohuslav Martinů for baritone, male chorus, and orchestra, composed in 1939 in Paris, France. It was first performed in Prague, Czechoslovakia (Czech Republic), on 28 February 1946, conducted by Rafael Kubelik.

Fierrabras, The Braggart opera by Franz Schubert (libretto by Kupelwieser, after Calderón, taken from A W von Schlegel's *Spanisches Theater*), composed in 1823, but not performed during Schubert's lifetime; it was first produced in Karlsruhe, Germany, on 9 February 1897. In the story, the French knight Roland loves the Moorish princess Florinda; her brother Fierrabras loves Charlemagne's daughter Emma, who in turn loves Eginhard. The Moorish leader Boland imprisons Roland and other knights, but Charlemagne arrives victorious to save the day.

Fiery Angel, The, Russian **Ogenny Angel** opera in five acts by Sergey Prokofiev (libretto by the composer after the novel by Valery Bryusov), composed 1919–27. It was first performed (as a concert) in Paris, France, on 25 November 1954, and first produced in Venice, Italy, on 29 September 1955. Themes from the opera are used in Prokofiev's third symphony, in C minor, Op. 33; composed in 1928 and first performed in Paris on 17 May 1929, conducted by Pierre Monteux. The story tells how Renata, possessed by the spirit of her former lover, Heinrich, fails to find release in the passion of her admirer Ruprecht. She is ordered to be burned when she enters a convent and involves the nuns in diabolic possession.

fifara 17th-century name for the transverse ➔ **flute**, a musical instrument.

fife (German Pfeife) small transverse ➔ **flute**, originally with finger holes, without keys, and of similar range to the ➤ **piccolo**. Of Swiss origin, the fife is a popular military band instrument, played with the side drums and associated with historic parades. The name is now used for a military flute in B flat, with six finger holes and several keys.

Fifine at the Fair orchestral fantasy by Granville Bantock on Robert Browning's poem, composed in 1901 and first performed at the Birmingham Music Festival, England, in 1912.

fifth in music, an interval of five diatonic notes, consisting of three whole tones and a semitone, for example C–G. A fifth is an example of a 'perfect interval' because it remains the same in both major and minor keys. A fifth may be augmented (by one semitone), for example C–G♯, or diminished (by one semitone), for example C–G♭.

Figaro character of dramatic fiction. He made his first appearance in Pierre de Beaumarchais's plays *The Barber of Seville* (1775), *The Marriage of Figaro* (1784), and *The Other Tartuffe* (1792). Since Beaumarchais's time Figaro has become the type of ingenious roguery, intrigue, and cunning, who displays the utmost sang-froid in all his daring deceptions. He appears conspicuously in Mozart's opera *The Marriage de Figaro* (1786) and Rossini's *The Barber of Seville* (1816), both operas being based on the plays of the same names.

Figaro see ➤ *nozze di Figaro, Le* and ➤ *barbiere di Siviglia, Il*.

figlia del reggimento, La Italian title of Donizetti's opera; see ➤ *Fille du régiment, La*.

figuration the persistent use of decorative or accompanying figures of similar type throughout a piece of music.

figure a short musical phrase, especially one that assumes a distinctive character in the course of a composition.

figured bass in 18th-century music, notation of a leading harpsichord or organ part indicating the bass line in standard notation, and the remaining music by numeric chord indications, allowing the player to fill in as necessary.

It arose because the keyboard player often doubled as conductor, and is still practised by session musicians.

figured chorale a hymn-tune setting, especially for organ, in which the plain notes of the melody are surrounded by more rapid patterns of notes, usually all of the same kind of formation.

Figures-Doubles-Prismes work for orchestra by Pierre Boulez, first performed in Strasbourg, France, on 10 January 1964; it is an expansion of his *Doubles* for orchestra, first performed in

Paris, France, on 16 March 1958.

filar la voce or **filar il tuono (Italian; French *filer la voix* 'spin the voice' or *filer le son* 'spin the tone')** in singing, to sustain the voice on a long-drawn soft note, without crescendo or diminuendo.

fileuse ('spinner', from *filer*, 'to spin') name of a type of instrumental piece with rapid figurations of various kinds suggesting the motion of a spinning-wheel and often, in its melody, a spinning-song. There are familiar examples by Joseph Raff and Gabriel Fauré (in the latter's incidental music for *Pelléas et Mélisande*), and Felix Mendelssohn's Song without Words, Op. 67 No. 4, although not so entitled, conforms to the type, being in fact nicknamed *Spinnerlied* in German, though called *The Bee's Wedding* in English. The prototype of the fileuse was vocal, for example the spinning-choruses in Haydn's *Seasons* (Winter) and Wagner's *The Flying Dutchman*, and Franz Schubert's song *Gretchen am Spinnrade*.

Fille du régiment, La, **The Daughter of the Regiment** opera by Gaetano Donizetti (libretto by J H V de Saint-Georges and J F A Bayard), first produced at the Opéra-Comique, Paris, France, on 11 February 1840. It was Donizetti's first French opera. It tells the story of Marie, who was found as an infant and has been brought up by the regiment. Tonio becomes a soldier in order to marry her. After complications by Marie's newly discovered relatives, all ends happily.

film score in contemporary usage, music specially written to accompany a film on the soundtrack. In the early days of cinema a symphonic poem was composed as a loosely aligned accompaniment to a major silent film, or background music was improvised or assembled by pit musicians with the aid of a Kinothek theme catalogue. With the arrival of optical sound on film came the fully synchronized Hollywood film score. Composers in the European Romantic tradition, including Erich Korngold, Max Steiner, and Franz Waxman, initially tried to adapt the symphonic style to the faster moving screen action; a more successful transition was made by animated film music specialists, such as Scott ➤ **Bradley**. After 1950 a younger generation including Alec North and Elmer Bernstein adopted simpler, jazz-oriented idioms.

Composers for silent films include Camille Saint-Saëns, Arthur Honegger, and Edmund Meisel, whose music for Sergei Eisenstein's *Battleship Potemkin* (1925) was banned by the authorities. Composers for sound film include Georges Auric, Aaron Copland, Sergey Prokofiev, William Walton, Bernard Herrmann, and Ennio Morricone.

filosofo di campagna, Il, **The Country Philosopher** opera by Baldassare Galuppi (libretto by
Carlo Goldoni), first produced at the Teatro San
Samuele, Venice, Italy, on 26 October 1754. It tells
how Eugenia loves Rinaldo but has been promised to Nardo, whom she has not yet met. Eugenia's sister, Lesbina, impersonates Eugenia and
falls in love with Nardo. Complications are followed by marriage.

final in music, the tonic note of the modes on
which the scales of the authentic modes begin
and end. In the plagal modes the final is on the
fourth above the starting-note. See ➔ **modes**.

final (French 'finale') musical term, an alternative spelling of ➔ **finale**.

finale in music, a normally fast final movement
of a classical four-movement work, or an elaborate conclusion of an opera incorporating a variety of ensembles.

Finck, Hermann (1527–1558) German composer and theorist. He wrote a theoretical book,
Practica Musica (1556), in five volumes. His
works include motets, sacred songs, and wedding songs for several voices.
He studied at the University of Wittenberg,
where he taught music from 1554. In 1557 he was
appointed organist in Wittenberg, but died the
following year at the age of 31.

Fine, Irving (1914–1962) US composer. His
music reflected two of the major trends of the
20th century – neoclassicism and atonality.
He studied at Harvard with Walter Piston and in
Paris, France, with Nadia Boulanger. He went on
to teach at Harvard 1939–50 and Brandeis University 1950–62.
Works ORCHESTRAL *Toccata concertante* (1948),
Blue Towers for orchestra (1959), *Diversions* for
orchestra (1958), *Symphony* (1962).
CHAMBER *Partita* for wind quintet; string quartet
(1952).
VOCAL *Alice in Wonderland*, suite for chorus and
orchestra (1949), *Mutability*, six songs for mezzo
and piano (1952), *Serious Song* (1955).

Fine, Vivian (1913–2000) US composer and pi-
anist. She studied in Chicago 1919–31 and with
Roger Sessions 1934–42. She began performing
contemporary piano works in 1931 and taught at
Bennington College, Vermont, 1964–87.
Works STAGE ballet *Alcestis* (1960); chamber
opera *The Woman in the Garden* (1978).
ORCHESTRAL *Drama for Orchestra* (1982), *Poetic
Fires* for piano and orchestra (1984); *After the Tra-
dition* for chamber orchestra (1988).
VOCAL *A Guide to the Life Expectancy of a Rose*,
for soprano, tenor, and chamber ensemble (1956);
Paen for narrator, women's voices, and brass en-
semble (1969).

Fingal's Cave or **'Hebrides' Overture** concert
overture by Felix Mendelssohn, Op. 26, composed in recollection of an 1829 visit to the Scottish Hebrides, in Rome, Italy, in December 1830;
the revised version was completed in London,
England, in the summer of 1832. (The first score
was entitled *Die einsame Insel/The Lonely Island*).

Finger, Gottfried or **Godfrey (c.1660–1730)**
Moravian composer. Nothing is known of his career until he went to London, England, about
1685, working under the patronage of James II.
He left in 1702, piqued at having gained only the
fourth prize after John Weldon, John Eccles, and
Daniel Purcell for the composition of William
Congreve's masque *The Judgement of Paris*.
On leaving London he went to Berlin, where he
entered the service of Sophia Charlotte, Queen
of Prussia. Later he lived in the Palatinate and
wrote some operas for Neuburg and Heidelberg.
Works STAGE operas *The Virgin Prophetess* (Settle), *Sieg der Schönheit über die Helden* (1706),
L'amicizia in terzo (in part); masques *The Loves
of Mars and Venus* (Motteux, with Eccles) and
The Judgement of Paris (Congreve, 1701); incidental music (some with D Purcell) for Lee's *The
Rival Queens*, *The Wive's Excuse*, *Love for Love*
and *The Mourning Bride* (both Congreve), *Love
at a Loss*, *Love makes a Man* (Cibber), *The Hu-
mours of the Age* (Southerne), *Sir Harry Wildair*
(Farquhar), and *The Pilgrim* (Vanbrugh).
OTHER concertos and sonatas for various instruments; pieces for violin and flute (with Banister),
and other pieces.

fingerboard in string instruments, the upper
surface and continuation of the neck, against
which the fingers press the strings to alter their
length and therefore their pitch.
Violins have smooth fingerboards, allowing the
player scope to alter the pitch continuously;
other instruments, such as the guitar and lute,
have ➔ **frets** attached or inlaid to regulate intonation.

fingered tremolo in music, a type of ➔ **tremolo**
created by fingerwork.

fingering in music, notation directing the player
to use specific fingers on specific notes. In keyboard music '1' represents the thumb, '2' the index finger, and so on. In orchestral string music
'1' represents the index finger, '2' the middle finger, and so on.

finite canon in music, a ➔ **canon** sung through
once, without repetition of its phrases.

Finke, Fidelio Friedrich (1891–1968) German
composer. He became inspector of the German
music schools in Czechoslovakia in 1920 and director of the German Academy of Music in

Prague in 1927.

He studied at the Prague Conservatory with his uncle Romeo Fidelio and with Vítězslav Novák for composition. He taught there from 1915.

Works the opera *Die Jacobsfahrt* (1936); *Pan* symphony, overture, and other works for orchestra; two string quartets.

Finlandia symphonic poem for orchestra by Jean Sibelius, Op. 26, composed in 1899 (revised 1900; first performed in Helsinki, Finland, on 2 July 1900). It has become a work for national celebrations in Finland, being based on material sounding like Finnish patriotic songs, the whole of which, however, is the composer's own invention, not folk music.

Finney, Ross Lee (1906–1997) US composer. His compositions have attempted a reconciliation between tonal and serial music.

He was educated at Carleton College, Minnesota, and studied music at Minnesota University and later in Paris, France, and Vienna, Austria, with Nadia Boulanger and Alban Berg; he also studied with Roger Sessions at Harvard University.

Works ORCHESTRAL Overture to a Social Drama for orchestra; four symphonies (1942–72); piano concerto, violin concerto.

CHAMBER eight string quartets (1935–60), piano trio, violin and piano sonata, four piano sonatas.

VOCAL *John Brown* for tenor, male chorus, and chamber orchestra; eight Poems for soprano, tenor, and piano.

Finnissy, Michael (1946–) English composer. He studied at the Royal College of Music, London, with Bernard Stevens and Humphrey Searle. He taught in the music department at the London School of Contemporary Dance 1969–74.

Works STAGE operas *The Undivine Comedy* (Paris, 1988), *Thérèse Raquin* (London, 1993); *Mysteries*, eight separately performable music theatre pieces with Latin texts from the Bible: 1. *The Parting of Darkness*, 2. *The Earthly Paradise*, 3. *Noah and the Great Flood*, 4. *The Prophecy of Daniel*, 5. *The Parliament of Heaven*, 6. *The Annunciation*, 7. *The Betrayal and Crucifixion*, 8. *The Deliverance of Souls*.

VOCAL *Jeanne d'Arc* for soprano, tenor, cello, and small orchestra (1971), *Babylon* for mezzo and ensemble (1971), *Orfeo* for soloists and instruments (1975), *Mr Punch* for voice and instruments (1977), *Sir Tristan* for soprano and ensemble (1979), *Vaudeville* for mezzo, baritone, instruments, and percussion (1983); *Ngano* for mezzo, tenor, chorus, flute, and percussion (1984); *Two Motets* for countertenor and guitar (1992).

ORCHESTRAL seven piano concertos (two for piano alone), *Offshore* for orchestra (1975–76), *Pathways of Sun and Stars* (1976), *Red Earth* (1988), and *Eph-phatha* (1989) for orchestra.

CHAMBER AND OTHER INSTRUMENTAL string trio (1986), string quartet (1986), *Obrecht Motetten* I–IV for various instrumental groups (1989–92), *In stiller Nacht* for violin, cello, and piano (1990), *Cambridge Codex* for flute, violin, cello, and two bells (1991), *Nine Romantics* for piano (1992).

finta giardiniera, La, The Pretended Garden-Girl opera by Pasquale Anfossi (libretto by Raniero de Calzabigi), first produced at the Teatro delle Dame, Rome, during Carnival in 1774.

It is also the title of an opera by Mozart (libretto by de Calzabigi), first produced in Munich, Germany, on 13 January 1775. In the story, Count Belfiore has fled, believing he has killed Countess Violante in a quarrel. However, she seeks him amorously, disguised as Sandrina, a gardener.

finta semplice, La, The Pretended Simpleton opera by Mozart (libretto by M Coltellini), composed for Vienna in 1768, but not performed there; it was first produced in Salzburg, Austria, on 1 May 1769. In the story, Fracasso and Simone marry Giacinta and Ninetta, as Giacinta's brothers fall for the Baroness Rosina, sister of Fracasso.

finte gemelle, Le, The Pretended Twins opera by Niccolò Piccinni (libretto by G Petrosellini), first produced at the Teatro Valle, Rome, Italy, on 2 January 1771.

finto Stanislao, Il, The False Stanislas opera by Adalbert Gyrowetz (libretto by Felice Romani), first produced at La Scala, Milan, Italy, on 5 August 1818. The libretto was used by Verdi in 1840 for *Un giorno di regno*.

Finzi, Gerald (1901–1956) English composer. He was professor of composition at the Royal Academy of Music, London, 1930–33, and afterwards went to live in the country to give his whole time to composition. His output includes concertos for clarinet and cello, and a wide range of vocal works, including settings of Milton and Shakespeare.

Finzi was born in London. He studied privately with Edward Bairstow and Reginald Morris.

Works ORCHESTRAL *Introit* for violin and small orchestra (1925), *New Year Music* for orchestra (1926), *Romance* for strings (1928), concerto for clarinet and strings (1949).

VOCAL festival anthem (Crashaw), Thomas Hardy song cycles *By Footpath and Stile* for baritone and string quartet (1922), *A Young Man's Exhortation* for voice and piano (1926–29), cantata *Dies Natalis* for high voice and orchestra (Traherne; 1926–39), two sonnets by Milton for tenor and small orchestra (c.1928), *Earth and Air and Rain*, songs (1936), *Intimations of Immortality* for chorus and orchestra (Wordsworth, about 1938, revised 1950), three Elegies (Drummond; 1926) and seven part songs (Robert Bridges; 1934–37) for unaccompanied chorus, *Let us Garlands Bring*, five Shakespeare songs (1942), *Farewell to Arms* for tenor and small orchestra (Ralph Knevet and George Peele; 1945), *For St Cecilia* for chorus and orchestra (Edmund Blunden; 1947), *Before and After Summer* (1949).

CHAMBER *Interlude* for oboe and string quartet (1933–36), prelude and fugue for string trio, five bagatelles for clarinet and piano.

OTHER incidental music for Shakespeare's *Love's Labour's Lost*.

Fioravanti, Valentino (1764–1837) Italian composer. He was a pupil of Sala at one of the Naples Conservatories. He produced his first opera in Rome in 1784, worked as conductor in Lisbon, Portugal, from 1803 and visited Paris, France, in 1807, returning to Italy to become maestro di cappella at St Peter's in Rome.

Works OPERA *Le avventure di Bertoldino* (1784), *Le cantatrici villane* (1799), *I virtuosi ambulanti* (1807), *Ogni eccesso è vizioso* and 66 others.

OTHER church music.

fioriture (Italian 'flowerings, flourishes, decorations') in music, ornamental figures elaborating a plainer melodic passage, either according to the composer's notation or improvised according to the performer's invention.

fipple flute in music, a term describing a whistle, such as the baroque ➤ recorder, that has a plug or 'fipple' inserted in the mouthpiece to direct the flow of air precisely at the aerofoil.

Firebird, The, Russian *Zhar Ptitsa* ballet by Igor Stravinsky (choreography by Mikhail Fokin), first produced at the Paris Opéra, France, on 25 June 1910, conducted by Gabriel Pierné.

'Fire Symphony' nickname of a symphony by Haydn, No. 59, in A major, composed about 1766–68.

Fireworks fantasy for large orchestra by Igor Stravinsky, composed in 1908 to celebrate the marriage of Nadezhda Rimsky-Korsakov, his teacher's daughter, to Maximilian Steinberg, in St Petersburg, Russia, on 17 June 1908. The score was revised for smaller forces and performed on 22 January 1910.

'Fireworks Music' Handel's *Music for the Royal Fireworks*, a suite of pieces originally for wind band, composed for the celebrations of the Peace of Aix-la-Chapelle and first performed in Green Park, London, England, on 27 April 1749.

Firsova, Elena (1950–) Russian composer. Her music is in a variety of instrumental forms, many of them small scale, and was first heard outside the USSR in Paris, France, and Venice, Italy, in 1979. She made her British debut in 1980 with *Petrarca's Sonnets* (1976).

She studied at the Moscow Conservatory, and has learned from Edison Denisov. One of several composers who chose to live in the West after the collapse of communism, she became professor and composer-in-residence at Keele University, Staffordshire, England, in 1993.

Works OPERA *Feast in Time of Plague* (1972), *The Nightingale and the Rose* (1991).

ORCHESTRAL cello concerto (1973), two violin concertos (1976, 1983), *Stanzas* (1975), *Autumn Music* (1988) and *Cassandra* (1993) for orchestra.

CHAMBER four string quartets (1970, 1974, 1980 – in memoriam Igor Stravinsky – and 1989), *Chamber Music* (1973), four chamber concertos (1978, 1982, 1985, 1988), *Spring Sonata* for flute and piano (1982), piano sonata (1986), *Music for 12* (1986) and *Odyssey* for ensemble (1990), *The Night Demons* for cello and piano (1993).

VOCAL *Petrarca's Sonnets* for voice and ensemble (1976) and settings of Pasternak, Mayakovsky, Mandelstam, and Shakespeare for voice and instruments; *Silentium* for mezzo and string quartet (1991), *Distance* for voice, clarinet, and string quartet (1992), concerto for violin and 13 strings (1993), *Before the Thunderstorm* for soprano and ten instruments (1995).

first-movement form in music, term sometimes used for ➤ sonata form. It avoids the confusion between the movement structure named sonata form and the composition genre of the ➤ sonata, but in doing so generates new confusion as, even in 17th-century classical works, not all first movements are in this form.

'First of May, The' symphony no. 3 in E flat, Op. 20, by Dmitri ➤ Shostakovich. The finale is a choral tribute to International Workers' Day (text by S Kirsanov) but the first performance in Leningrad (St Petersburg), Russia, on 21 January 1930 did not gain official approval. Shostakovich met with further trouble in his next work, *Lady Macbeth of the Mtsensk District*, denounced in *Pravda* and by Stalin.

Fischer, Edwin (1886–1960) Swiss pianist and conductor. In addition to his activities as a soloist he also conducted orchestras in Lübeck, Munich, and Berlin, Germany. He edited a number of early keyboard works and wrote books on Bach and on Beethoven's piano sonatas.

He studied at the Basel Conservatory, where he later taught for several years. He returned to Switzerland from Germany in 1942 and was a successful teacher in Lucerne and elsewhere.

Fischer, Johann Caspar Ferdinand (c.1665–1746) German composer. From 1692 he was Kapellmeister to the Margrave of Baden in Schlackenwerth (Bohemia) and Rastatt. His keyboard music includes *Ariadne Musica* (1715), a series of 20 preludes and fugues, each in a different key, and thus a precursor of Bach's *Das Wohltemperierte Clavier*.

Other works include *Musicalisches Blumen-Büschlein* (a collection of keyboard suites in the French style), *Musicalischer Parnassus* (nine suites named after the Muses), *Blumenstrauss* (organ preludes and fugues on the eight modes), *Le Journal de printemps* (suite for orchestra with trumpets *ad lib*), and church music.

Fischietti, Domenico (c.1720–c.1810) Italian composer. He was a pupil of Francesco Durante and Leonardo Leo in Naples, where he produced his first opera in 1742. He worked as a conductor in Prague, Bohemia (Czech Republic), then became Kapellmeister in Dresden, Germany, 1766–72, and at Salzburg Cathedral, Austria, 1772–79.

Works OPERA *Lo speziale* (with V Pallavicini, 1754), *Il signor dottore*, *Il mercato di Malmantile*, *La ritornata di Londra* (all on libretti by Goldoni), and about 20 others.

OTHER church music.

Fišer, Luboš (1935–1999) Czech composer. He studied in Prague, where his two operas, *Lancelot* and *The Good Soldier Schweik*, were produced in 1961 and 1962. He emigrated to the USA in 1971 and became composer-in-residence with the US Wind Symphony Orchestra at Pittsburgh. His music often returns to myth and religion for inspiration.

Works BALLET *Changing Game* (1972).

ORCHESTRAL two symphonies (1956, 1960), 15 *Prints after Dürer's Apocalypse* for orchestra (1965), *Kretzer Etude* for chamber orchestra (1974), *Serenade for Salzburg* (1977), *Albert Einstein* for organ and orchestra (1979), piano concerto (1980), *Centaurs* for orchestra (1983).

CHAMBER string quartet (1955), cello sonata (1975), piano trio (1978), and five piano sonatas (1955–78).

VOCAL *Requiem* (1968); *Lament over the Destruction of the City of Ur*, for soloists, narrators, chorus, and bells (1969).

Fitelberg, Jerzy (1903–1951) Polish-born US composer. He played percussion in his father's orchestra as a boy and studied composition at the Warsaw Conservatory and under Franz Schreker in Berlin, Germany. He settled in Paris, France, in 1933 and in New York, USA, in 1940. His fourth string quartet (1937) received an Elizabeth Sprague Coolidge award.

Works ORCHESTRAL Concert Pieces, *Sinfonietta* (1946), *Polish Pictures*, *Nocturne*, and two suites for orchestra, symphony for strings, piano, harp and percussion, concerto for strings; two piano concertos (1929, 1934), two violin concertos, cello concerto.

CHAMBER five string quartets (1926–45), string trio, woodwind quintet; suite for violin and piano, sonatina for two violins, duo for violin and cello, sonata for cello solo; piano sonata and pieces.

Fitzwilliam Virginal Book manuscript collection of 297 mainly English 17th-century compositions for keyboard instruments, copied by Francis Tregian and acquired by Richard Fitzwilliam (1745–1816) who bequeathed it to Cambridge University. Among composers represented are William Byrd, John Bull, and Giles Farnaby.

Five Movements for String Quartet work by Anton Webern, composed in 1909 and first performed in Vienna, Austria, on 8 February 1910. A version for string orchestra was arranged in 1929 and first performed in Philadelphia, USA, on 26 March 1930.

Five Orchestral Pieces, German **Fünf Orchesterstücke** work for large orchestra by Arnold Schoenberg, Op. 16, composed in 1909 revised in 1922, and first performed in London, England, on 3 September 1912, conducted by Henry Wood. Schoenberg gave the five pieces the titles *Premonitions*, *The Past*, *Chord-Colours*, *Peripetie*, and *Endless Recitative*.

Schoenberg's pupil, Anton Webern, wrote Five Pieces for orchestra 1911–13, first performed at the International Society for Contemporary Music (ISCM) concert in Zurich, Switzerland, on 22 June 1926 (four of the five pieces last for less than one minute). Webern's five posthumous pieces for orchestra (1913) were performed in Cologne, Germany, on 13 January 1969.

Five, The or **The Mighty Five** or **The Mighty Handful (Russian *Moguchaya kuchka*)** term initially applied by art critic Vladimir Stasov (1824–1906) to the St Petersburg group of five composers – Mily ➤ **Balakirev**, Aleksandr ➤ **Borodin**, César ➤ **Cui**, Modest ➤ **Mussorgsky**, and Nikolai ➤ **Rimsky-Korsakov** – whose establishment of a distinctively Russian nationalist idiom he promoted.

Five Tudor Portraits choral suite by Ralph Vaughan Williams on poems by John Skelton. It comprises 1. Ballad, *The Tunning of Elinor Rumming*; 2. Intermezzo, *My Pretty Bess*; 3. Burlesca, *Epitaph on John Jayberd of Diss*; 4. Romanza, *Jane Scroop: Her Lament for Philip Sparrow*; and 5. Scherzo, *Jolly Rutterkin*. It was written for mezzo-soprano, baritone, chorus, and orchestra, and was first performed at the Norwich Festival, England, on 25 September 1936.

Flackton, William (1709–1798) English organist and composer. He was a bookseller, but played the organ and violin, and also taught and composed harpsichord and string music, including works for viola.

flageolet musical instrument, a whistle flute of tapered bore popular in France and England as a town-band instrument during the 17th–19th centuries.

flam on the ➤ **side drum**, a double stroke, as distinct from a roll.

flamenco generic term applied to a particular body of *cante* (song), *baile* (dance), and *toque* (solo guitar music) from Andalusia in southern Spain. It has attracted worldwide interest and flamenco clubs can be found in places as far apart as the USA, Japan, and Germany, as well as all the major cities throughout Spain. It is also known as *cante gitano* (gypsy song) and *cante hondo* (deep song). Despite the varied conjectures concerning its origin, consensus points to the early history and development of *cante flamenco* to Andalusia.

flat, symbol ♭ in music, a sign that tells a player to lower the pitch of a note by one semitone. It can also describe the inaccurate intonation of players when they are playing lower in pitch than they should be.

flautando (Italian 'fluting') in music, a flutelike tone produced by drawing the bow lightly over the strings of a violin, near the end of the fingerboard.

flautino (Italian 'little flute') small ➤ **recorder**, either the descant recorder or the flageolet, also called *flauto piccolo* in the early 18th century (for example in Handel's *Rinaldo*).

flauto traverso the transverse ➤ **flute**, that is the modern flute held horizontally as distinct from the recorders and similar flutes played vertically.

Flavio, rè de' Longobardi, Flavius, King of the Lombards opera by Handel (libretto by N F Haym, partly based on Corneille's *Le Cid*), first produced at the King's Theatre, Haymarket, London, on 14 May 1723. It is set in a mythical Britain. Guido kills the father of his lover Emilia in a duel; King Flavio restores Guido to her after his execution is threatened.

Flavius Bertaridus, König der Longobarden, Flavius Bertaridus, King of the Lombards opera by Georg Telemann (libretto by C G Wendt), first produced at the Theater beim Gänsemarkt, Hamburg, Germany, on 23 November 1729.

flebile (Italian 'plaintive, mournful') in music, a direction used in notation indicating a mournful effect.

Flecha, Mateo (1481–c.1553) Spanish monk and composer. He was a pupil of Juan Castelló in Barcelona, and became maestro de capilla to the Infantas of Castile, the daughters of Charles V. He later became a Carmelite and settled in the monastery of Poblet.

Flecha, Mateo (1530–1604) Spanish monk and composer. He was taught by his uncle Mateo ➤ **Flecha**. Works by the two Flechas (not always distinguishable) include church music, madrigals, *ensaladas* (burlesque madrigals), and other pieces. A stage work of his, *El Parnaso*, is believed to have been performed in Madrid in 1561.

He was in the service of the emperor Charles V until 1558 and of Philip II. He then went to Prague in the service of the emperor Maximilian, and after the emperor's death in 1576 he remained there until 1599. After this he joined the abbey of Solsona as a Franciscan monk.

Fledermaus, Die, The Flittermouse, The Bat operetta by Johann Strauss, junior (libretto by C Haffner and R Genée, based on a French vaudeville, *Le Réveillon*, by H Meilhac and L Halévy, taken from a German comedy, *Das Gefängnis*, by R Benedix); it was first produced at the Theater an der Wien, Vienna, Austria, on 5 April 1874. It describes how Rosalinde, her husband Eisenstein, and her lover Alfred get mixed up in a practical joke at Prince Orlofsky's ball.

Flem, Paul Le French composer and critic; see ➤ **Le Flem**.

flicorno Italian brass instrument used in military bands, corresponding to the ➤ **saxhorn** and ➤ **flugelhorn**.

Fliegende Holländer, Der, The Flying Dutchman opera by Wagner (libretto by composer, based on Heinrich Heine's *Memoiren des Herrn von Schnabelewopski*, Frederick Marryat's novel *The Phantom Ship*, and other sources), first produced in Dresden, Germany, on 2 January 1843. The story tells how a Dutchman is condemned by blasphemy to sail his ship forever until redeemed by the love of a faithful woman; Senta, ready to die for him, is his saviour.

Flood, The musical play by Igor Stravinsky (text by Robert Craft from Genesis and the York and Chester miracle plays), composed 1961–62 and first performed on Colombia Broadcasting System (CBS) TV on 14 June 1962. Its first stage performance was given in Hamburg, Germany, on 30 April 1963, conducted by Robert Craft.

Florentinische Tragödie, Eine opera in one act by Alexander von Zemlinsky (text from the blank-verse drama *A Florentine Tragedy* by Wilde, in German translation by M Meyerfeld); it was composed 1915–16 and first produced in Stuttgart, Germany, on 30 January 1917, conducted by Max von Schillings. It was performed in a Hamburg Opera production in 1983 in Edinburgh, Scotland, and in 1985 at the Royal Opera House, Covent Garden, London. It recounts how the jealous husband Simone kills Guido in a duel and is reunited with his wife Bianca over the corpse.

Florida suite for orchestra by Frederick Delius, composed 1886–87 and dedicated to the people of Florida (it had been Delius's ambition to become an orange planter). It was performed privately in Leipzig, Germany, in 1888, and given its first public performance in London, England, on 1 April 1937, conducted by Thomas Beecham. The score was not published until 1963. The four movements are titled *Daybreak*, *By the River*, *Sunset*, and *At Night*.

Floridante, Il opera by Handel (libretto by R A Rolli), first produced at the King's Theatre, Haymarket, London, England, on 9 December 1721. In the story, Floridante loves Elmira, the adopted daughter of the usurper King Oronte. Oronte also loves Elmira, and threatens Floridante with death. At the last moment Oronte is overpowered, and Floridante and Elmira become king and queen.

Flos Campi, Flower of the Field work by Ralph Vaughan Williams in six movements for viola, wordless chorus, and small orchestra, first performed in London, England, on 10 October 1925, with Lionel Tertis, conducted by Henry Wood.

Floss der Medusa, Das, The Raft of the Medusa 'popular and military oratorio' by Hans Werner Henze (text by E Schnabel), for soloists, chorus, and orchestra, dedicated to the memory of Ché Guevara. The projected first performance in Hamburg, Germany, on 9 December 1968 had to be cancelled when members of the chorus, revolting students, and the police came into conflict. It was performed (as a concert) in Vienna, Austria, on 29 January 1971; its first stage production was given in Nuremberg, Germany, on 15 April 1972. The *Medusa* of the title was a French frigate abandoned at sea in 1816. The officers escaped in lifeboats and cut adrift the entire crew on a single raft.

Flothuis, Marius (1914–2001) Dutch composer. He was artistic director of the Concertgebouw Orchestra 1955–74, and was appointed professor of musicology at the University of Utrecht in 1974. He studied with Hans Brandts-Buys.

Works ORCHESTRAL concertos for flute, horn, violin, chamber orchestra; *Sinfonietta Concertante* for clarinet, saxophone, and chamber orchestra.

CHAMBER cello sonata, *Partita* for two violins (1966), *Romeo's Lament* for horn (1975), sonata for oboe, horn, and harpsichord (1986), *Preludio e Fughetta* for three trumpets (1986).

VOCAL *Hommage à Mallarmé* for voice, flute, cello, and piano (1980).

Flotow, Friedrich Adolf Ferdinand, Freiherr von (1812–1883) German composer. He wrote 18 operas, including *Martha* (1847).

Flotow was born in Teutendorf, the son of a nobleman. He went to Paris, France, in 1827 and studied music under Antonín Reicha and others. He began to produce operas at aristocratic houses and wrote incidental music for the play *Alessandro Stradella* at the Palais-Royal in 1837 (it was enlarged into an opera in 1844). Over the next two years he contributed musical numbers to Albert Grisar's operas *Lady Melvill* (1838) and *L'Eau merveilleuse* (1839), and in 1839 he made his first public stage success with *Le Naufrage de la Méduse*, based on an incident in 1816 involving a French ship whose crew were left adrift on a raft while the officers escaped in lifeboats.

His greatest success came with *Martha*, produced in Vienna, Austria, in 1847; its blend of German sentiment and Italian ardour made it popular for many years in Europe and at the New York Metropolitan Opera House. He was intendant of the court theatre at Schwerin, Germany, 1856–63. He then returned to Paris, but went to live near Vienna in 1868.

Works STAGE French, German, and Italian operas, including *Le Naufrage de la Méduse* (1839), *L'Esclave de Camoëns* (1843), *Stradella* (1844), *L'Ame en peine*, *Martha* (1847), *Rübezahl*, *L'Ombre*, *Il fior d'Harlem*, *Rob Roy* (after Scott); ballets *Lady Henriette* (with Burgmüller and Deldevez, on which *Martha* was based later), *Die Libelle*, and *Tannkönig*; incidental music to Shakespeare's *A Winter's Tale* (1859).

OTHER *Fackeltanz*, overtures, and other pieces for orchestra; chamber music, songs.

flourish in old English, a fanfare, but in modern music terminology a short figure used as an embellishment rather than as a theme.

Floyd, Carlisle (1926–) US composer. His first opera, *Susannah*, was produced at the University of Houston in 1955 and at New York City Opera in 1956; it has since become one of the most widely produced of all US operas.

He studied at Syracuse University and privately with Rudolf Firkušný.

Works STAGE *Wuthering Heights* (Santa Fe, 1958), *The Passion of Jonathan Wade* (New York, 1962), *The Sojourner and Mollie Sinclair* (Raleigh, South Carolina, 1963), *Markheim* (New Orleans, 1966), *Of Mice and Men* (after Steinbeck; Seattle, 1970), *Bilby's Doll* (Houston, 1976), *Willie Stark*

(Houston, 1981), *All the King's Men* (1981).

flue pipes in music, the majority of pipes in an ➤ organ, which generate sound by directing air over a narrow rigid edge (as when a person blows across the top of a bottle). The other pipes are known as reeds.

Flügel (German 'wing') German name for the grand ➤ piano, which is wing-shaped.

flugelhorn valved brass instrument of the ➤ bugle type. It is made in three sizes: soprano, alto, and tenor, and is used in military and brass bands. In Britain only the alto instrument, in B flat, is used, normally only in brass bands. The alto flugelhorn has a similar range to the ➤ cornet but is of mellower tone.

flute or **transverse flute** side-blown woodwind instrument with a long history, capable of intricate melodies and a wide range of expression. The player holds the flute horizontally, and to the right, and blows across an end hole. The air current is split by the opposite edge of the hole, causing the air column inside the instrument to vibrate and produce a sound. The fingers operate a system of keys to open and close holes in the side of the flute to create different notes. The standard soprano flute has a range of three octaves.

The instrument originated in Asia about 900 BC. European flutes can be traced back to about AD 1100, and include the military fife, developed by the Hotteterre family of instrument-makers into the single-key Baroque flute. Today's orchestral chromatic flutes with extensive keywork come from modifications in the 19th century by Theobald Boehm. Today members of the flute family are usually made of metal (even silver, gold, or platinum) rather than wood. They include the soprano flute in C4, the higher ➤ piccolo in C5, the alto in G3, and the bass flute in C3. The bass flute is a rarity in the orchestra but was much in fashion during the avant-garde 1950s as a concert instrument and an accompaniment to films of the **nouvelle vague** era.

The flute has an extensive concert repertoire, including familiar pieces by Johann Sebastian Bach, Wolfgang Amadeus Mozart, and the pastoral refrain of Claude Debussy's *Prélude à l'après-midi d'un faun/Prelude to the Afternoon of a Faun* (1894). Antonio Vivaldi wrote a number of concertos for piccolo, and Bruno Maderna has composed for alto and bass flutes. A noted current performer is James Galway.

flûte à bec (French 'beak flute') French name for the fipple flute, flageolet, or ➤ recorder, a musical instrument.

flûte douce (French 'sweet flute') alternative name for the ➤ recorder, a musical instrument.

The compass of the flute.

flutter-tonguing in music, a technique used mainly in playing woodwind and brass instruments, in which the player rolls an R while playing, creating a fluttering tone.

The technique is particularly effective on the ➤ flute, where can be used to create an ethereal effect. It is extremely hard on double-reed instruments such as the ➤ oboe.

Flying Dutchman, The English title of two musical works; see ➤ *Fliegende Holländer, Der* and ➤ *Vaisseau-fantôme*.

Foerster, Josef Bohuslav (1859–1951) Czech composer. He held various appointments as an organist, teacher, and critic. He wrote six operas, incidental music for plays, church and secular choral music, five symphonies and other orchestral works, two violin concertos and a cello concerto, chamber music, numerous piano pieces and songs, and about 30 recitations with piano accompaniment.

Foerster was born in Dětenice, Bohemia, and studied at the Prague Organ School. From 1893 he lived for ten years in Hamburg, Germany, where he worked as a music teacher and critic and his wife, Berta Foerster-Lauterer (1869–1936), sang at the opera. After 1903 they lived in Vienna, Austria, where he taught at the Conservatory, but from 1918 until his retirement in 1931 he was professor of composition in Prague.

Works STAGE operas *Deborah* (1893), *Eva*, *Jessica* (on Shakespeare's *The Merchant of Venice*, 1905), *The Invincibles*, *The Heart*, *The Fool*; incidental music for Vrchlický's *Samson*, Strindberg's *Lucky Peter's Journey*, Schiller's *Maria Stuart*, and other plays.

CHORUS AND ORCHESTRA *Stabat Mater* and other works for chorus and orchestra.

ORCHESTRAL five symphonies (1887–1929), six suites, four symphonic poems, and two overtures for orchestra; two violin concertos.

CHAMBER five string quartets, three piano trios, quintet for wind instruments; two violin and piano sonatas, cello and piano sonata; works for piano, organ, and harmonium.

VOCAL ten recitations with piano accompaniment; songs, part songs.

Fogliano, Ludovico (died after 1538) Italian music theorist and composer, brother of Giacomo Fogliano. He sang in the papal chapel and was choirmaster at Modena Cathedral. His *Mu-*

sica Theorica was published in 1529, and a single *frottola* was included in Ottaviano Petrucci's ninth book, published in 1508.

Folia, La or **The Folly** in music, term used for a specific melody found in popular dances and songs of the baroque period. First mentioned by Francisco de Salinas in 1577, the melody was first used as the basis for variations in 1604 and later variations have been by Arcangelo Corelli, Henrico Albicastro, and Marin Marais (c. 1700), Alessandro Scarlatti, and C P E Bach (1778). Liszt used the theme in his *Rhapsodie Espagnole*, Rachmaninov in his *Variations on a theme of Corelli* (dedicated to Fritz Kreisler, first performed in Montréal, Canada, on 12 October 1931), and Hans Werner Henze in *Aria de la folia española* (1977).

folk music traditional music, especially from rural areas, which is passed on by listening and repeating, and is usually performed by amateurs. The term is used to distinguish it from the ➤ **classical music** of a country, and from urban popular or commercial music. Most folk music exists in the form of songs, or instrumental music to accompany folk dancing, and is usually melodic and rhythmic rather than harmonic in style.

Each country has its own styles of folk music, based on distinctive ➤ **scales** and ➤ **modes**, and often played on instruments associated with that culture alone, such as the Scottish ➤ **bagpipes**, the Russian ➤ **balalaika**, or the Australian ➤ **didjeridu**. A number of composers of classical music have used folk music in their own pieces to give them a particular national character, and in the late 19th century the use of folk tunes was a prominent feature of ➤ **nationalism** in music.

In the 20th century a number of people, such as the composers Zoltán ➤ **Kodály** and Béla ➤ **Bartók** (who recorded over 1,000 East European folk songs in the early 20th century) and the musicologists Cecil ➤ **Sharp** and Alan Lomax, transcribed (wrote down) and recorded folk music to preserve it for the future. Since World War II, a renewed interest, especially among young people, led to a 'folk revival'. Traditional folk music was performed to a much wider audience, and songwriters such as Pete Seeger, Joan Baez, and Bob Dylan composed popular songs in a folk style.

Elements of folk music have also been combined with rock and ➤ **pop music**, and form an important part of world music.

folk music in the British Isles Interest in ballad poetry in the late 18th century led to the discovery of a rich body of folk song in Europe, but it was not until the late 19th century that there was any systematic collection of folk music. In England, this was seen in the transcription and preservation of folk tunes by such people as the Rev

Sabine Baring-Gould and Cecil ➤ **Sharp**. The Folk Song Society was founded in 1898 and became the English Folk Dance and Song Society in 1911. In true Victorian fashion, they bowdlerized much of the material they collected, and edited out much of the sophisticated ornamentation and rhythmic complexity, which they felt to be 'primitive', or simply poor performance. The collection of folk music continued through the first half of the 20th century, with important contributions made by Ralph ➤ **Vaughan Williams** (whose collections not only influenced his own music but have been a significant source to the present day), A L Lloyd, and Ewan MacColl; and a unique and invaluable collection gathered by several generations of the Copper family of Sussex.

Although recognizably different styles of folk music can be seen within the countries of the British Isles, a rough classification can be made by national boundaries: English, Scottish, Irish, and Welsh folk music all have their own characteristics.

In England, folk song is generally in the ballad tradition, either unaccompanied or with a simple concertina or melodeon accompaniment, and, typically for a maritime nation, there is also a large number of shanties. The two folk-dance traditions, Morris dancing and country dance and their many regional variations, each have their own associated tunes, usually played on a pipe and drum, fiddle, or concertina.

Scottish folk music can be divided roughly into two styles: Highland (associated with the Gaelic language), and Lowland. Unusually for a true oral folk tradition, most Scottish folk songs are by known composers and poets whose names have been passed down with their songs, which are mainly in the form of unaccompanied ballads. Instrumental music includes dance music for fiddle and concertina, and a uniquely Scottish genre, the pibroch, a form of theme and variations specifically for the bagpipes.

Irish folk song can similarly be divided according to language, with distinct musical traditions for both Irish and English lyrics. Dances such as the jig and the reel are typical in Irish instrumental music, and are played on the fiddle and pipe, and Irish versions of the harp and bagpipes, almost invariably with the rhythmic accompaniment of the bodhrán, a kind of drum. Much of the traditional repertoire has been preserved and played by groups such as the Chieftains.

Although there is a long tradition of musical culture in Wales, very little true folk music has survived. Welsh traditional music, like Scottish folk music, is mostly by known poets and composers, but because of its association with the Bardic culture, this is perhaps more accurately regarded as a classical rather than a folk culture.

folk revival in the UK The post-World War II folk

revival in the USA had a counterpart in the UK, with both a renewed interest in traditional folk music and a new generation of songwriters and performers in a folk style. The 1960s saw the appearance of performers in many different folk styles: the Watersons, who popularized traditional unaccompanied folk singing; groups such as Pentangle and the Incredible String Band, and the singer Donovan produced new music in a folk style; and folk-rock bands such as Fairport Convention and Steeleye Span brought some of the folk repertoire to a new audience by performing using the instruments of the rock band, as well as introducing new songs in a folk idiom. This folk revival continued through the 1980s, and was furthered by rock guitarist Richard Thompson and such Irish groups as the Pogues (formed in 1983), while the English singer/songwriter Billy Bragg continued in the tradition of the political protest song. In recent years, there has been a growing interest in roots, or world, music, encompassing traditional as well as modern music from many cultures.

folk v. classical The term 'folk music' is generally used to describe music of an aural/oral tradition performed by amateurs, particularly in rural areas, to distinguish it from the classical, urban, or commercial music of a particular country or culture. This definition, however, makes it only relevant to cultures that have a classical, art music tradition (such as China, India, Europe, and North America); other countries tend not to recognize the distinction. The influence of Western music around the world, and in particular Western popular music, has thrown the traditional music of many countries into sharp contrast; this non-Western music has recently been categorized with genuine folk music as world music or roots music.

origins All music is thought to have its beginnings in storytelling, worksongs, and ritual, and these are the basic forms still prevalent in folk music around the world. The ballad, often unaccompanied, is the most common genre of folk song, and probably evolved as a means of memorizing traditional stories to be passed on from generation to generation. The worksong was used to establish a regular rhythmic accompaniment to repetitive physical work, often in a call and response pattern. Instrumental folk music is usually restricted to accompaniment for folk dance, and has its roots in rituals – especially those associated with specific events in the rural calendar such as harvest, midwinter, and the beginning of spring.

the study of folk music In Europe at the end of the 19th century there was a resurgence of interest in folk music, partly because of a fear (since proved to be well-founded) that it might be lost to posterity in the face of increasing urbaniza-

tion, and partly to establish 'schools' of composition with some form of national identity to distinguish them from the mainstream (that is, Austro-Germanic) classical music of the time. There was also a wider interest in the music of other cultures, which led to the establishment of the new discipline of ethnomusicology. As the 20th century progressed, organizations began to form for the preservation and study of folk music, and musicologists transcribed and later recorded performances of traditional folk music from all over the world. In 1931, the first international folk festival was held in Copenhagen, Denmark. Many such festivals are now held in almost every country in the world. Internationally, folk songs and music are studied and published by the International Folk Music Council, founded in 1947, and the Society for Ethnomusicology, founded in 1956.

folksong a traditional song of often great but indeterminate antiquity, whose origins and composer are unknown, but which has been preserved by being handed down orally from generation to generation, often in several different versions or corruptions.

Folquet de Marseille (died 1231) Provençal ➔ troubadour. His output consists mainly of love songs, sober in tone and moralizing in content. The son of a wealthy merchant, he became a Cistercian monk and, in 1205, bishop of Toulouse, in which capacity he was a notorious persecutor of the Albigensian heretics.

Fomin, Evstigney Ipatovich (1761–1800) Russian composer. He studied under Giovanni Martini in Bologna, Italy, and later became conductor in St Petersburg, Russia. His opera *The Americans* (1800) is about the Spanish conquest of the Americas.

Works STAGE melodrama *Orfey i Evridika* (1792) and operas *Boyeslav* (1786), *Orpheus* (1792), *Clorinda and Milo*, *The Americans* (1800), *The Golden Apple*.

Foote, Arthur (William) (1853–1937) US organist and composer. He held organ appointments in Boston for many years. His compositions are chiefly chamber and choral pieces, and include *A Night Piece* for flute and strings (1922).

He studied at the New England Conservatory in Boston and later with John Paine at Harvard.

Works VOCAL cantatas on Longfellow's *The Farewell of Hiawatha* (1885), *The Wreck of the Hesperus* (1887), and *The Skeleton in Armour* (1891); choral works; songs.

ORCHESTRAL overture *In the Mountains*, prologue to *Francesca da Rimini*, and three suites for orchestra; cello concerto.

CHAMBER three string quartets (1883–1901),

piano quartet, piano quintet, two piano trios; organ and piano pieces.

Ford, Thomas (c.1580–1648) English lutenist and composer. He was in the service of Henry, Prince of Wales, in 1611, and was appointed one of the musicians to Charles I in 1626.

Works *Musick of Sundrie Kindes* (1607) with airs to the lute (also to be performed in four vocal parts), catches and rounds; two anthems contributed to Leighton's *Teares and Lamentacions* and others including *Miserere my Maker*, dances for lute.

forefall musical term; see ➤ **appoggiatura** ('from below').

foreground musical term; see ➤ **structural level**.

Forest (died c.1446) English composer, possibly the John Forest who was canon and later dean of Wells, dying there in 1446. His motet *Qualis est dilectus tuus* was included (together with the beginning of *Ascendit Christus*, ascribed to John Dunstable in a continental manuscript) among the latest additions to the Old Hall manuscript. Other sacred music survives in continental sources.

forlana or **furlana** an old Italian dance in 6/8 time. A classical example of its use is in Bach's Overture (Suite) in C for orchestra and a modern example is in Ravel's *Le Tombeau de Couperin*.

form the basic plan or temporal structure of a piece of music. The simplest forms are ➤ **binary form**, which consists of two sections often separated by a double bar (marking off a section), and simple ➤ **ternary form**, which consists of three sections – the first section, followed by a contrasting section, returning to the first section as in song form: ABA. Most larger-scale forms are an expanded and developed version of these two basic types. Examples include ➤ **sonata form** and ➤ **rondo** form. During the 19th century, Romantic composers such as Richard Wagner broke away from classical forms, using returning motifs (called ➤ **leitmotifs**) to unify the work. These composers tended to take more interest in literature.

In the 20th century form changed in order to accommodate new parameters in harmonic development and rhythm. Béla Bartók's string quartets use alternating sections of different length, and later the composer Witold Lutosławski invented 'chain form', where contrasting sections link over each other to provide large-scale development in the piece. Chance-based operations such as those of John Cage in *Music of Changes* (1951) often, paradoxically, produced clear and differentiated structures, although different each time.

Formé, Nicolas (1567–1638) French composer. He was a clerk and singer in the Sainte-Chapelle in Paris 1587–92, then became a countertenor in the royal chapel and succeeded Eustache du Caurroy as choirmaster and composer there in 1609. Although almost dismissed from the Sainte-Chapelle for not conforming to the ecclesiastical rules, he returned there in 1626 and, as a favourite musician of Louis XIII, enjoyed special privileges. Only his church music survives.

Works Masses, motets, Magnificat, and other church music.

Förster, (Emanuel) Aloys (1748–1823) German oboist and composer. He wrote a treatise on thorough bass. He was a prolific composer of piano and chamber pieces. Beethoven acknowledged his debt to Förster in the composition of string quartets.

After two years as a military bandsman, 1766–68, he lived as a freelance teacher and composer, first in Prague, Bohemia (Czech Republic), then from 1779 in Vienna, Austria.

Works 48 string quartets; four string quintets; six piano quartets, and other chamber music; piano concertos, sonatas, variations and other pieces.

Forster, Georg (c. 1510–1568) German music publisher and composer. He published five sets of German songs, the *Frische Teutsche Liedlein* (1539–56), some of which he wrote himself; he also composed sacred and Latin works.

forte or **f (Italian 'strong')** in musical notation, a direction to play loudly.

Forte, Allen (1926–) US music theorist. He is known for his formulation of set-series, particularly to explain atonal music. His major works are *The Structure of Atonal Music* (1973) and *The Harmonic Organization of The Rite of Spring* (1978).

fortepiano early 18th-century piano invented by Italian instrument maker Bartolommeo Cristofori in 1709. It has small, leather-bound hammers and harpsichord strings. Unlike the harpsichord, it can produce a varying intensity of tone, depending on the pressure of the player's touch, hence the name, which means 'loud-soft' in Italian.

It was rendered obsolete by technical developments, but has been revived by performers working with period instruments. Present-day performers include Trevor Pinnock, Gustav Leonhardt, and Jörg Demus.

forte piano or **fp (Italian 'loud soft')** in music, of dynamics, loud then immediately soft.

fortissimo or **ff (Italian 'very strong')** in musical notation, a direction to play very loudly.

Fortner, Wolfgang (1907–1987) German composer. He studied with Hermann Grabner. From 1931 to 1954 he taught theory and composition at the Evangelical Church Music Institute in Heidelberg, where he founded and conducted a chamber orchestra. In 1954 he became professor of composition at the German Music Academy in Detmold, and in 1957 succeeded Genzmer at the Musikhochschule in Freiburg im Breisgau. His music shows the influence of Max Reger and Paul Hindemith. He also used serial techniques in later years, approaching integral serialism.

Works STAGE operas *Bluthochzeit* (after Lorca, 1956; revised 1963), *Corinna* (1958), *In seinem Garten liebt Don Pimperlin Belison* (after Lorca, 1962), *Elisabeth Tudor* (1972); ballet *Die Weisse Rose* (after Wilde; 1950).

CHORAL *Deutsche Liedmesse, Marianische Antiphonen* for unaccompanied chorus.

ORCHESTRAL symphonies, *Sinfonia concertante* for chamber orchestra; concertos for various instruments and small orchestra.

CHAMBER four string quartets (1929–75), *Suite* for solo cello (1932), *Five Bagatelles* for wind quintet (1960).

Forty-Eight (Preludes and Fugues), The nickname for Johann Sebastian Bach's preludes and fugues for keyboard; see ➔ **Wohltemperierte Clavier, Das**.

forza d'amor paterno, La, The Force of Paternal Love opera by Alessandro Stradella (librettist unknown), first produced at the Teatro del Falcone, Genoa, Italy, during Carnival in 1678.

forza del destino, La, The Force of Destiny opera by Giuseppe Verdi (libretto by Francesco Maria Piave, based on the drama by A P de Saavedra, Duke of Rivas, *Don Alvaro, o La fuerza de sino*), first produced in St Petersburg, Russia, on 10 November 1862, and first performed in Italy at the Teatro Apollo, Rome, on 7 February 1863. In the story Leonora and Alvaro elope together, but he accidentally kills her father and the two are separated in their flight. Leonora's brother Carlo searches to find her 'seducer', to avenge the dishonour fallen upon the family. After a series of coincidences, Leonora and Alvaro die together.

forzando (Italian 'forced') in music, a direction which, placed against a note or chord, indicates that it should be strongly accentuated. The more usual word is *sforzando*, marked *sf*.

Foss, Lukas (1922–), born **Lukas Fuchs** US composer and conductor. His stylistically varied works, including the cantata *The Prairie* (1942) and *Time Cycle* for soprano and orchestra (1960), express an ironic view of tradition. A prolific composer, in the 1940s he wrote vocal music in neoclassical style; in the mid-1950s he began increasingly to employ improvisation; and he has also written chamber and orchestral music in which the players reproduce tape-recorded effects.

Born in Germany, Foss studied in Berlin and Paris. In 1937 he went with his parents to the USA, and studied at the Curtis Institute in Philadelphia. Later he studied with Paul ➔ **Hindemith** at Yale University; in 1944 he gave the first performance of Hindemith's *Four Temperaments* for piano and strings, in Boston. In 1945 he won a Guggenheim Fellowship and in 1950 a Fulbright Fellowship. He became professor of composition at the University of California Los Angeles (UCLA) in 1953. He was conductor of the Buffalo Philharmonic Orchestra 1963–71, music director of the Brooklyn Philharmonic 1971–90, and music director of the Milwaukee Symphony Orchestra 1981–86.

Works STAGE *The Jumping Frog of Calaveras County* (after Mark Twain; 1950), *Griffelkin* (television opera, 1955), *Introductions and Goodbyes* (libretto by Foss and Menotti; 1959); ballet *Gift of the Magi* (1945); incidental music to *The Tempest*.

VOCAL cantata *The Prairie* (after Carl Sandberg; 1942), oratorio *A Parable of Death* (Rilke, 1952); *Time Cycle* for soprano and ensemble (1960), *American Cantata* for tenor, chorus, and orchestra (1976), *Thirteen Ways of Looking at a Blackbird* for soprano, flute, piano, and percussion (1978), *Round a Common Centre* for voice and ensemble (1979), *De Profundis* (1983), *With Music Strong* for mixed chorus and ensemble (1988).

ORCHESTRAL two piano concertos (1944, 1951); three symphonies (no. 3 *Symphony of Sorrows*, 1988); *Solomon Rossi Suite* (1975), *Renaissance Concerto* for flute and orchestra (1986), *American Landscapes*, guitar concerto (1989).

CHAMBER *Orpheus* for cello, oboe, and clarinet; three string quartets (1947, 1973, 1975), brass quintet (1978), percussion quartet (1983), horn trio (1984), *Taski* for six instruments (1986), *Central Park Reel* for violin and piano (1989).

Fossa, Johannes de (c.1540–1603) German or Flemish composer. He wrote six Masses and other sacred works. He succeeded Roland de Lassus as Kapellmeister at the Munich court in 1594.

Foster, Stephen Collins (1826–1864) US songwriter. He wrote 175 sentimental popular songs including 'The Old Folks at Home' (1851), 'My Old Kentucky Home' (1853), and 'Beautiful Dreamer' (1864), and rhythmic minstrel songs such as 'Oh! Susanna' (1848) and 'Camptown Races' (1850).

Born in Lawrenceville, Pennsylvania, he had no formal training in music but began to write early, and published his first song as early as 1842. Although many of his songs became very popular and profitable, he mismanaged his career and spent the last years of his life in debt.

Foulds, John (Herbert) (1880–1939) English composer and conductor. He joined a theatre orchestra in Manchester at the age of 14 and the Hallé Orchestra in 1900. He worked at various opera houses abroad, gave concerts for the forces during World War I, and wrote *A World Requiem* (1919–21) for the war dead. He later conducted various music societies in London.

Works STAGE incidental music for Kalidasa's *Sakuntala*, Euripides' *Trojan Women*, and several others; *A Vision of Dante* (concert opera, 1905–08).

CHORAL *A World Requiem* for solo voices, chorus, and orchestra (1919–21).

ORCHESTRAL *Epithalamium*, *Keltic Suite* (1911), and *Suite Fantastique* for orchestra; *Holiday Sketches*, *Suite française*, and *Gaelic Dream Song* for small orchestra; *Idyll* for string orchestra.

CHAMBER *Mood Pictures* for violin and piano; *Variations* and *Essays in the Modes* for piano.

Fourier transform in music, the mathematical technique by which a complex sound wave can be broken down into its constituent simple waves or partials. It is essential to techniques of sound synthesis which produce or manipulate sounds identical to those produced by live instruments.

Four Last Songs, German **Vier letzte Lieder** sequence of songs for soprano and orchestra by Richard Strauss, composed in 1948, his last work. They were first performed in London, England, on 22 May 1950, with soloist Kirsten Flagstad, conducted by Wilhelm Furtwängler. The first three texts are by Hermann Hesse, *Frühling*, *September*, and *Beim Schlafengehen*; no. 4 is by Joseph von Eichendorff, *Im Abendrot*.

Four Saints in Three Acts opera in four acts by Virgil Thomson (libretto by Gertrude Stein), first produced in concert form at Ann Arbor, Michigan, USA, on 20 May 1933, and on the stage at Hartford, Connecticut, on 8 February 1934. It deals with the deeds of 16th-century Spanish saints.

Four Sea Interludes concert work by Benjamin Britten, derived from his opera *Peter Grimes* (first performed in London, 1945). The four sections are titled *Dawn*, *Sunday Morning*, *Moonlight*, and *Storm*; the work was first performed in Cheltenham, England, on 13 June 1945.

Four Seasons, The, Italian **Le quattro stagioni** four violin concertos by Antonio Vivaldi in E, G minor, F, and F minor, depicting the seasons. They are the first four of twelve violin concertos Op. 8 published in 1725 in Amsterdam, the Netherlands, as 'The contest between harmony and invention'.

Four Serious Songs song cycle by Brahms; see ➔ *Vier ernste Gesänge*.

Four Temperaments, The title for symphony no. 2, Op. 16, by Carl Nielsen; it was composed 1901–02 and first performed in Copenhagen, Denmark, on 1 December 1902.

Four Temperaments, Theme and Variations, The work for piano and string orchestra by Paul Hindemith, commissioned by the ballet choreographer George Balanchine and composed in 1940. It was first performed (concert) in Boston, USA, on 3 September 1944, with Lukas Foss as the soloist. The first stage production was given by the City Ballet, New York, on 20 November 1946. The four main sections are titled *Melancholy*, *Sanguine*, *Phlegmatic*, and *Choleric*.

fourth in music, an interval of four diatonic notes consisting of two whole tones and a semitone, for example C–F. A fourth is an example of a 'perfect interval' because it remains the same in both major and minor keys. A fourth may be augmented (increased by a semitone), for example C–F♯

A fourth may be perfect; it can also be augmented or diminished.

Fowler, Jennifer (1939–) Australian composer, resident in London, England, from 1969. She studied in Perth and at the electronic music studio in Utrecht, the Netherlands. Recent works include *Veni Sancte Spiritus* for chamber choir and *Blow Flute: Answer Echoes in Antique Lands Dying* for solo flute.

Works ORCHESTRAL *Look on this Oedipus* (1973), *Chant with Garlands* (1974), and *Ring out the Changes* for orchestra.

CHAMBER *Chimes, Fractured* for ensemble (1970), *Revelation* for string quintet (1971), *The Arrows of St Sebastian I and II* for ensemble (1981), *Line Spun with Stars* for piano trio (1983), *Echoes from an Antique Land* for ensemble (1983), *Threaded Stars* harp solo (1983), *Between Science and the World* for wind quintet (1987), *We Call it to You, Brother* for ensemble (1988), *Reeds, Reflections* for oboe and string trio (1990).

VOCAL *And Ever Shall Be* for mezzo and ensemble (1989).

Fox Strangways, A(rthur) H(enry) (1859–1948) English musicologist, critic, and editor. He was educated at Wellington College and Balliol College, Oxford, and also studied in Berlin, Germany. After teaching at Dulwich and Wellington Colleges until 1910, and visiting India, on the music of which he wrote a book (*The Music of Hindostan*), he became assistant critic of *The Times* in London in 1911 and chief critic of the *Observer* in 1925. He founded *Music and Letters* in 1920 and edited it until 1936. He also wrote a biography of Cecil Sharp and translated many songs (some with Steuart Wilson), by Schubert, Brahms, and Wolf.

fp in music, abbreviation for ➤ **forte piano**, loud then immediately soft.

Fra Diavolo, ou L'Hôtellerie de Terracine, Brother Devil, or the Inn at Terraccina opera by Daniel Auber (libretto by Augustin Scribe), first produced at the Opéra-Comique, Paris, France, on 28 January 1830. It tells the story of Lorenzo on the hunt for the bandit Fra Diavolo, who plans to kill Zerlina, Lorenzo's love. He catches the criminal and gets the girl.

Fra due litiganti il terzo gode, Between Two Litigants the Third Makes Profit opera by Giuseppe Sarti (libretto altered from Carlo Goldoni's *Le nozze*), first produced at La Scala, Milan, on 14 September 1782. Mozart quotes a tune from it in the second-act finale of *Don Giovanni*; it was first produced in Vienna, Austria, on 28 May 1783. Set against a background of feuding Count and Countess, the steward Masotto wins the heart of the serving maid Dorina after outmanoeuvring his rivals Titta and Mingone.

Françaix, Jean (1912–1997) French composer. His music was noted for its wit and brilliance, and showed the influence of Erik Satie and Les ➤ **Six**.

Françaix was born in Le Mans. He studied under his father, who was director of the Conservatory there, and with Nadia Boulanger in Paris. He showed great talent at an early age and a great facility in his writing.

Works OPERA *Le Diable boiteux* (1938), *La Main de gloire* (1950), *Paris à nous deux* (1954), *La Princesse de Clèves* (1965).

BALLET *Beach*, *Le Roi nu* (after Hans Christian Andersen).

ORCHESTRAL two symphonies (1932, 1953), *Suite concertante*, *L'Horloge de flore* for oboe and orchestra (1959), *Divertissement* for string trio and orchestra; piano concerto (1936) and concertino, flute concerto (1966), fantasy for cello and orchestra; concertos for violin (1970, 1979), double bass (1974), bassoon and strings (1979), guitar and strings (1983), trombone and wind (1984), flute and clarinet (1991); Cassazione for three or-

chestras (1975), *Mozart new-look* for double bass and ten wind instruments (1981), concerto for 15 soloists and orchestra (1988).

CHAMBER *Petit Quatuor* for strings, quintet for flute, harp, and strings, two wind quintets (1948, 1987), octet (1972), *Danses exotiques* for twelve players (1986), *Dixtuor* for wind and string quintet (1986), *Elegie* for wind instruments (1990), suite for four saxophones (1990).

OTHER songs and piano music.

Francesca da Rimini title of several operas and musical works, based on Dante.

The opera by Generali (libretto by P Pola, based on Dante), was first produced at the Teatro La Fenice, Venice, Italy, on 26 December 1829.

The opera by Eduard Nápravník (libretto by O O Paleček and E P Ponomarev, based on a play by Stephen Phillips, *Paolo and Francesca*, and farther back on Dante), was first produced in St Petersburg, Russia, on 9 December 1902. It is derived from a part of Dante's *Inferno*. Francesca must marry the crippled Gianciotto, but she falls in love with his brother, Paolo. After learning of her infidelity, Gianciotto sets a trap and kills the pair.

Rachmaninov's opera on the same subject (libretto taken from scenes of Aleksandr Pushkin's play, with additions by Modest Tchaikovsky, based on Dante), was first produced in Moscow, Russia, on 24 January 1906.

Riccardo Zandonai's opera (libretto by T Ricordi, based on d'Annunzio's tragedy, and farther back on Dante), was first produced at the Teatro Regio, Turin, Italy, on 19 February 1914.

Tchaikovsky's symphonic fantasy, Op. 32 (based on Dante), was composed in 1876 and first performed in Moscow, Russia, on 9 March 1877.

There is also an unfinished opera by Herman Goetz, completed by Ernst Frank (libretto by the composer), which was first produced in Mannheim, Germany, on 30 September 1877.

See also ➤ **Françoise de Rimini** and ➤ **Paolo e Francesca**.

Francesco Canova da Milano (1497–1543) Italian lutenist and composer. Known as *Il divino* ('the divine'), he was the finest composer of lute music before John Dowland. He was in the service first of the Duke of Mantua, about 1510, and then of Pope Paul III from 1535. He was a prolific composer, publishing and contributing to several books of lute pieces.

Franchetti, Alberto (1860–1942) Italian composer. He studied first in Italy, then with Draeseke at Dresden and at the Munich Conservatory, Germany, under Rheinberger. He was director of the Cherubini Conservatory, Florence, 1926–28.

Works OPERA *Asrael* (1888), *Cristoforo Colombo*

(1892), *Fior d'Alpe*, *Signor di Pourceaugnac* (after Molière, 1897), *Germania*, *La figlia di Jorio* (after d'Annunzio), *Notte di leggenda*, *Glauco*, and (with Giordano) *Giove a Pompeii* (1921).

ORCHESTRAL symphony in E minor.

Franck, César Auguste (1822–1890)

Belgian composer. He was a pioneer of cyclic form, and his harmonic style was influenced by his experience as a church organist. His music, mainly religious and Romantic in style, includes the *Symphony in D Minor* (1886–88), *Variations symphoniques* (1885) for piano and orchestra, the *Violin Sonata* (1886), the oratorio *Les Béatitudes/The Beatitudes* (1879), and many organ pieces.

Franck was born in Liège. A precociously gifted child, especially as a pianist, he made a concert tour in Belgium at the age of 11. Sent to Paris, France, in 1835 to study, he entered the Conservatory in 1837; there he won prizes each year until he left in 1842. He returned to Belgium, but settled permanently in Paris in 1844. In 1848 he married a young actor and was appointed organist at the church of Saint-Jean-Saint-François in 1851. In 1853 he became choirmaster and in 1858 organist at Sainte-Clotilde. He was particularly noted for his skill in improvisation. He was appointed professor of the organ at the Conservatory in 1872.

Franck gathered together a circle of young, eager students, including Vincent d'Indy, Ernest Chausson, Guillaume Lekeu, and Henri Duparc, and with them pursued the study of polyphonic and symphonic music; he was the founder of a special branch of modern French music, one which absorbed the innovations of Wagner without loss of individuality.

He became a Chevalier of the Legion of Honour in 1885 and two years later, in January 1887, a festival of his music was held.

Works ORCHESTRAL symphony in D minor (1886–88); symphonic poems, *Les Éolides* (1876), *Le Chasseur maudit* (after Burger; 1882), *Psyché* (with chorus; 1887–88); *Les Djinns* (1884) and *Variations symphoniques* for piano and orchestra (1885).

CHORAL WITH ORCHESTRA (some with solo voices): *Rédemption* (1874), *Les Béatitudes* (1879), *Rébecca* (1881), Psalm 101; *Paris: chant patriotique* for tenor and orchestra; *Messe solennelle* for bass and organ (1858); Mass for three voices, organ, harp, cello, and double bass (1860); three motets, three offertories, and other small sacred vocal works.

CHAMBER piano quintet (1879), string quartet; sonata for violin and piano (1886).

KEYBOARD AND SONGS about 16 works for piano, including *Prélude, Choral et Fugue* (1884) and *Prélude, Aria et Final* (1886–87); nine works for

organ, including six *Pièces pour grand orgue* (1862).

Franckenstein, Clemens von (1875–1942)

German composer. He studied in Vienna, Austria, and later in Munich, Germany, with Ludwig Thuille and Frankfurt with Iwan Knorr. After a visit to the USA he conducted the Moody–Manners Opera Company in England 1902–07, then worked at the court theatres of Wiesbaden and Berlin, and in 1912 became general intendant of the Munich court theatres.

Works STAGE operas *Griseldis* (1898), *Rahab* (1911), *Des Kaisers Dichter* (1920); ballet *Die Biene*.

ORCHESTRAL variations on a theme by Meyerbeer, dance suite, serenade, rhapsody, praeludium, symphonic suite, *Das alte Lied*, four dances, *Festival Prelude*.

OTHER chamber music; piano works; songs.

Franccœur, François (1698–1787)

French violinist and composer. He joined the Paris Opéra orchestra at the age of 15 and there met François Rebel, with whom he worked for the rest of his life. They collaborated on several operas, of which *Pyrame et Thisbé* (1726) was the first.

He was a pupil of his father, Joseph Francœur, who was a double bass player at the Opéra. In 1720 he published his first violin sonatas, and in 1723 went with Rebel to Prague, Bohemia (Czech Republic), for the coronation of Charles VI. After his return to Paris in 1726 he gradually rose to the highest positions in French music, being appointed composer to the court in 1727, member of the king's band in 1730, inspector of the Opéra in 1743 and director in 1757, and superintendent of the king's music in 1760 (he held the last three jointly with Rebel).

His nephew, Louis Joseph Francœur (1738–1804), was also a violinist and composer and was for a time director of the Opéra.

Works the operas, composed jointly with Rebel, beginning with *Pyrame et Thisbé* (1726), ballets, violin sonatas, and other pieces.

Françoise de Rimini, Francesca da Rimini

opera by Arthur Thomas (libretto by J Barbier and Michel Carré, based on Dante), first produced at the Paris Opéra, France, on 14 April 1882.

Franco of Cologne (lived mid-13th century)

French music theorist. He wrote an *Ars cantus mensurabilis* which survives in seven manuscripts. It expounds the system of notation in his day, now called 'Franconian'.

An anonymous monk of Bury St Edmunds, England, writing of Parisian music in the 13th century, refers to a 'Franco primus', apparently a Parisian, who also wrote on the same subject.

Francs-Juges, Les, *The Judges of the Secret Court* unfinished opera by Hector Berlioz (libretto by H Ferrand), composed 1827–28. The first performance of the overture was given in Paris, France, on 26 May 1828. The rest was discarded or used elsewhere, as in the *Symphonie fantastique* (1830–31).

Frankel, Benjamin (1906–1973) English composer and teacher. He studied the piano in Germany and continued his studies in London while playing jazz violin in nightclubs. His output includes chamber music and numerous film scores, notably *The Man in the White Suit* (1951) and *A Kid for Two Farthings* (1955).

He made a precarious living as a music teacher, café pianist, and jazz-band violinist while attending the Guildhall School of Music in the daytime. He gradually improved his living by working as an orchestrator and theatre conductor, finally succeeding as a conductor and composer of film music. In his published work he became an early English exponent of serial technique.

His reputation in the film world grew with music for *The Seventh Veil* (1945), *The Years Between* (1946), and *Dear Murderer* (1947). In his mature works, which include eight symphonies, an important violin concerto (1951), *The Aftermath* (Robert Nichols; 1947) for tenor and orchestra, four string quartets, and other chamber works, he successfully espoused serial methods in conjunction with a strong feeling for tonality.

Works ORCHESTRAL music for many films, *Pezzo sinfonico* for orchestra, *Solemn Speech and Discussion* and *Music for Young Comrades* for string orchestra, eight symphonies (1952–72), violin concerto.

VOCAL *The Aftermath* (Robert Nichols; 1947) for tenor, strings, trumpet, and drums.

CHAMBER five string quartets, *Three Sketches* for string quartet, string trio, trio for clarinet, cello, and piano, *Early Morning Pieces* for oboe, clarinet, and bassoon; violin and piano sonata, sonatas for unaccompanied violin and viola, *Sonata ebraica* for cello and harp, *Elégie juive* for cello and piano; passacaglia for two pianos; piano pieces.

Franz, Robert (1815–1892), born **Robert Knauth** German composer. He was one of the finest exponents of German songs, the first of which he published in 1843 and which attracted the attention of Schumann, Mendelssohn, Liszt, and others. His output of lieder (songs), though influenced by Schubert and Schumann, was characterized by its striving toward simplicity and the style of folk song.

After much parental opposition he became a pupil of Friedrich Schneider at Dessau in 1835, and after two years returned home, devoting himself to study and composition without being able to secure a musical post. He then became a church organist and choral conductor, also lecturer at Halle University. Much troubled by increasing deafness and a nervous complaint, he had to retire in 1868, but did much work in editing the older choral classics.

Works more than 350 songs to texts by Burns, Eichendorff, Lenau, Geibel, Heine, Müller, and Goethe; church music; part songs.

Frauenliebe und -Leben, *Woman's Love and Life* song cycle by Robert Schumann, Op. 42 (using eight poems by Adelbert von Chamisso), composed in 1840.

Frau ohne Schatten, Die, *The Woman without a Shadow* opera by Richard Strauss (libretto by Hugo von Hofmannsthal), first produced at the Vienna Opera House, Austria, on 10 October 1919. It tells how the empress searches for her shadow, the symbol of fertility, in order to save her husband from being turned to stone. In contrast, Barak's wife is willing to sell her shadow, but is eventually united with her husband, while the empress gains her own shadow.

Fredegunda opera by Reinhard Keiser (libretto by J U König, from the Italian by Francesco Silvani), first produced at the Theater beim Gänsemarkt, Hamburg, Germany, in March 1715.

Frederick II (the Great) (1712–1786) King of Prussia, flautist, and composer. He learnt music from Gottlob Hayne, the Berlin Cathedral organist, and in 1728 had flute lessons from Johann Quantz. In 1734 he established a private band at his castle at Rheinsberg and on his accession to the throne in 1740 established a court band at Berlin and Potsdam. Johann Graun, Quantz, and C P E Bach were in his service.

Works part of the opera *Il rè pastore* (Metastasio) and the libretti for several operas by Graun; over 120 instrumental works, many with prominent flute parts.

Fredigundis opera by Franz Schmidt (libretto by B Warden and I M Welleminsky, after F Dahn), composed 1916–21 and first produced in Berlin, Germany, on 19 December 1922. In the story, Fredigundis murders the wife of King Chilpenich and becomes queen, but a poison she prepares for a rival is drunk by her husband and daughter.

free-reed instrument musical wind instrument such as the ➤ **mouth organ**, ➤ **accordion**, or ➤ **harmonium**, that employs tuned metal tongues vibrating at a predetermined frequency as valves controlling the escape of air under pressure. Free reeds do not ➤ **overblow**, but the mouth organ can be made to 'bend' the pitch by varying the air pressure.

Freischütz, Der, The Freeshooter opera by Carl Maria von Weber (libretto by F Kind, based on a story in Apel and Laun's *Gespensterbuch*), first produced at the Berlin Schauspielhaus, Germany, on 18 June 1821. It tells how Max invokes the 'Black Huntsman' to help win a shooting competition and Agathe. He is banished for his use of the supernatural, but is allowed to return in a year to marry.

French horn brass instrument descended from the natural hunting horn. It is valved and curved into a circular loop, with a funnel-shaped mouthpiece and wide bell.

French overture in music, a type of ➤ overture.

French sixth musical term; see ➤ augmented 6th chords.

French Suites six keyboard suites by Johann Sebastian Bach, composed mainly in Cöthen, Germany, about 1722 and completed by about 1724. They differ from the *English Suites* in having no preludes.

Frescobaldi, Girolamo (1583–1643) Italian composer and virtuoso keyboard player. He was organist at St Peter's Cathedral, Rome, in 1608–28. His compositions included various forms of both instrumental and vocal music, and his fame rests on numerous keyboard toccatas, fugues, ricercari, and capriccios in which he advanced keyboard technique and used clever and daring modulations of key.

He studied in Ferrara under the cathedral organist Luzzasco Luzzaschi, and first gained a reputation as a singer. It was reported that 20,000 people came to hear his first recital at St Peter's in Rome. He was given leave of absence in 1628–33, during which time he served as organist to Ferdinand II, Duke of Tuscany. He also worked in Brussels, Mantua, and Florence. Johann Froberger was among his pupils. Bach owned a copy of his *Fiori musicali* (1635); it contains various pieces for use in the Mass.

Works two Masses, a Magnificat, motets and madrigals; ricercari, canzoni, toccatas, and other pieces for organ and for harpsichord; fantasies for instruments in four parts.

Frescoes of Piero della Francesca, The work for orchestra in three movements by Bohuslav Martinů, depicting three of the frescoes by Piero at Arezzo, Italy; it was composed in 1955 and first performed in Salzburg, Austria, on 28 August 1956, conducted by Rafael Kubelik.

fret on the fingerboard of a plucked or bowed string instrument, an inlaid ridge of a material such as gut, wood, ivory, or metal, or a circlet of nylon, against which a string is pressed to shorten its vibrating length and therefore change pitch.

Frets enable the player to play in tune with certainty, since the vibrating length of the string is fixed by the fret.

Freunde von Salamanka, Die, The Friends of Salamanca operetta by Franz Schubert (libretto by J Mayrhofer), composed in 1815 but never performed in Schubert's lifetime; it was first produced, with a new libretto by G Ziegler, in Halle, Germany, on 6 May 1928. The story describes how Don Alonso wins the Countess Olivia with the help of his friends.

Fricker, Peter Racine (1920–1990) English composer. His music avoided local pastoral influences and learned instead from continental neoclassical and serial models.

He studied at the Royal College of Music in London and later with Mátyás Seiber. His wind quintet won the Clements Prize in 1947 and his first symphony won the Koussevitsky Award. He became composer-in-residence at the University of California at Santa Barbara in 1964.

Works RADIO OPERAS *The Death of Vivien* and *My Brother Died* (1954).

BALLET *Canterbury Prologue* (after Chaucer).

CHORAL oratorio *A Vision of Judgment* (1957–58); *Whispers at the Curtains* for baritone, chorus, and orchestra (1984).

ORCHESTRAL five symphonies (1948–76), *Prelude, Elegy and Finale* for strings; violin and viola concertos, *Concertante* for three pianos and strings.

CHAMBER wind quintet, four string quartets (1947–76); violin and piano sonata; organ sonata.

Friede auf Erden, Peace on Earth work for chorus *a cappella* by Arnold Schoenberg (text by C F Mayer), composed in 1907. It was first performed in Vienna, Austria, on 9 December 1911, conducted by Franz Schreker.

Friedenstag, Peace Day opera by Richard Strauss (libretto by J Gregor, who first suggested it to Stefan Zweig, based on Calderón's play *La redención de Breda* and Velázquez's picture illustrating that), first produced in Munich, Germany, on 24 July 1938. It describes how a besieged town faces self-destruction rather than defeat. At the last moment a peace is declared and enemies meet as brothers.

Froberger, Johann Jacob (1616–1667) German organist and composer. He was court organist at Vienna, Austria, and travelled to England, France, Germany, and the Low Countries performing keyboard music.

He studied under his father, who was a singer, and later Kapellmeister, in Stuttgart. He was appointed court organist in Vienna on the accession of the emperor Ferdinand III in 1637, and remained there until 1657, but spent 1637–41 in Italy as a pupil of Girolamo Frescobaldi. In 1662 he went to London, where he is said to have arrived destitute, having been twice robbed on the way. In later years he lived in the house of Sibylla, Dowager Duchess of Württemberg, at her retreat at Héricourt.

Works harpsichord suites, many pieces for organ and harpsichord including toccatas, ricercari, and 30 suites.

'Frog' Quartet nickname of Haydn's string quartet in D major, Op. 50 no. 6, the finale of which is supposed to have a 'croaking' theme.

Froissart overture concert overture by Edward Elgar, Op. 19, composed in 1890 and first performed at the Worcester Festival, England, of that year on 9 September, conducted by Elgar. The title refers to the French historian Jean Froissart (1338–1404). Elgar prefaced the score with a quotation from Keats: 'When chivalry lifted up her lance on high'.

Fromm, Andreas (1621–1683) German composer. He was cantor at the Marienkirche and professor at the Pädagogium of Stettin in the middle of the 17th century.

Works the oratorios *Actus Musicus* (one of the earliest known in German), and *Vom reichen Mann und Lazarus* (1649); *Dialogus Pentecostalis.*

From My Life string quartet by Smetana; see ➤ *Aus meinem Leben.*

From the House of the Dead, Czech **Z Mrtvého Domu** opera in three acts by Leoš ➤ Janáček (libretto by the composer, after Fyodor Dostoevsky), first produced in Brno, Czechoslovakia (now the Czech Republic), on 12 April 1930. In the work, various prisoners in a Siberian gulag recall their earlier lives. The opera is framed by the incarceration and eventual release of the political prisoner, Alexandr.

'From the New World' symphony by Dvořák; see ➤ *'New World' Symphony.*

Frosch (German 'frog') in music, the heel of the violin bow. The direction *am Frosch* found in German scores means that a passage is to be bowed near the heel of the bow.

frottola an early 16th-century Italian song, originating in Milan, for several voices or for solo voice and instruments, forerunner of the madrigal but less polyphonically elaborate.

The term is used in a general sense to cover numerous different forms: *strambotto*, *oda*, or *capitolo*, and also in a particular sense, to mean a song in several stanzas with a refrain or burden (*ripresa*) sung complete at the beginning and (usually) curtailed, but often with a musical extension, after each stanza; the same music serves for both refrain and stanza.

Frye, Walter (lived c. 1450–75) English composer. His *Ave Regina Caelorum Mater Regis* was copied into 13 continental manuscripts and is found in three arrangements for keyboard in the *Buxheimer Orgelbuch*.

He is believed to have been a choral conductor at Ely Cathedral in the 1440s and later joined the London Guild of Parish Clerks. He wrote three Masses (*Flos Regalis*, *Nobilis et Pulchra*, and *Summa Trinitati*), chansons, and antiphons.

Fuchs, Robert (1847–1927) Austrian composer. He was professor at the Vienna Conservatory 1875–1912, where Mahler, Hugo Wolf, Alexander von Zemlinsky, and Franz Schreker were among his pupils. His serenades are still sometimes performed in Germany.

Works two operas, *Die Königsbraut* (1889) and *Die Teufelsglocke* (1893); Mass; symphony in C major, five serenades (four for strings); piano concerto; chamber music.

fuga (Italian 'flight') in music, an old Italian term for a ➤ **canon**, another being caccia.

fuga ricercata musical term; see ➤ **ricercare**.

fugato (Italian 'fugued') in music, a passage written in the manner of a ➤ **fugue**, occurring incidentally in a composition; or a piece in fugal style that cannot be considered to be in the form of a fugue.

fughetta (Italian 'little fugue') in music, unlike a ➤ **fugato**, a fughetta is formally a proper ➤ **fugue**, but much more condensed.

fugue (Latin 'flight'; Italian 'chase') in music, a contrapuntal form where two or more (usually four) parts or voices (principal melodies for voices or instruments) are woven together. The voices enter one after the other in strict imitation of each other. They may be transposed to a higher or lower key, or combined in augmented form (larger note values). The fugue is the highest form of contrapuntal composition as heard in works such as Johann Sebastian Bach's *Das musikalische Opfer/The Musical Offering* (1747), on a theme of Frederick II of Prussia, and *Die Kunst der Fuge/The Art of the Fugue* published in 1751, and Ludwig van Beethoven's *Grosse Fuge/Great Fugue* for string quartet (1825–26).

Fulda, Adam of (c.1445–1505) German monk, music theorist, and composer. He wrote a tract on music and composed motets and other pieces.

full close in music, alternative name for a perfect ➤ **cadence**, in which the ➤ **dominant** chord resolves to the ➤ **tonic**.

full organ in music, direction to an organist to couple the manuals (keyboards) together and use all the louder stops.

The exposition of Bach's fugue in A flat major, Well-tempered Clavier, Book II, no. 17.

full score all the lines of music for each instrument playing in a composition. The music is arranged on the page according to the four sections of the orchestra. From top to bottom this is: woodwind, brass, percussion, and strings. Within each section, the instruments are arranged with the highest-sounding instrument at the top to the lowest-sounding at the bottom. A full score is usually printed on large paper for easy reading, such as for a conductor's score.

functional harmony musical term; see ➤ **harmonic analysis**.

fundamental in musical acoustics, the lowest ➤ **harmonic** of a musical tone, corresponding to the audible pitch.

fundamental bass in music, an imaginary harmonic phenomenon expounded by Jean-Philippe Rameau. The fundamental bass is the root bass of any chord occurring in a composition, and according to Rameau no composition was aesthetically satisfying unless that bass, either actually present or implied, was in each chord used, proceeding from the one before it to the one after it in accordance with definite rules

of musical logic.

fundamental line, German **Urlinie** in voice-leading analysis, the fundamental line is the deepest level of melodic organization in a tonal work. It consists of a linear descent from a specific note of the tonic chord to the tonic note, written as 3–2–1 or 5–4–3–2–1, or (unusually) 8–7–6–5–4–3–2–1. According to Heinrich Schenker's theory of tonal structure, each note of the fundamental line must be supported by a structural harmony. The first note of the fundamental line is called the primary tone (*Kopfton* or head-note), and this is often prolonged for the bulk of the piece. A section of the piece before the primary tone appears is called the 'ascent', the section prolonging it is called the 'structure', the section prolonging the other notes of the fundamental line is the 'descent', and a section prolonging the last note is the 'peroration'.

fundamental structure, German **Ursatz** in voice-leading analysis, the fundamental structure is the deepest level of harmonic organization in a tonal work. It consists of a two-part contrapuntal figure, the bass line consisting of the progression I–V–I, and the upper line consisting of the fundamental line of the piece, where the first note and the last two notes coincide with the bass. According to Heinrich ➤ **Schenker's** theory of tonal harmony, it is the presence of the fundamental structure in all well-formed tonal pieces which gives their tonal structure coherence and organic unity. See ➤ **structural level.**

funeral march a type of ➤ **march.**

Funeral Ode ode by Bach; see ➤ **Trauer-Ode.**

furiant lively Czech dance in 3/4 time with a characteristic effect of cross-rhythm, often used in place of a scherzo by Antonín Dvořák and other Czech composers of the national school.

furlong in music, Old English name for the ➤ **forlana.**

Furrer, Beat (1954–) Swiss-born composer who studied with Roman Haubenstock-Ramati and formed the Société de l'Art Acoustique ensemble.

Works the music drama *Die Blinden* to texts by Rimbaud, Hölderlin, and Maeterlinck (Vienna, 1989); *Risonanze* for orchestra in three groups (1988); *Face de la Chaleur* for five instrumental groups (1991); two string quartets.

Furtwängler, (Gustav Heinrich Ernst Martin) Wilhelm (1886–1954) German conductor. He was leader of the Berlin Philharmonic Orchestra 1924–54. His interpretations of Wagner, Bruckner, and Beethoven were valued expressions of monumental national grandeur, but he also gave first performances of Bartók, Schoenberg's *Variations for Orchestra* (1928), and Hindemith's opera *Mathis der Maler/Mathis the Painter* (1934), a work implicitly critical of the Nazi regime. He ascended rapidly from theatre to opera orchestras in Mannheim 1915–20 and Vienna, Austria, 1919–24, then to major appointments in Leipzig and Vienna.

Furtwängler studied at Munich with Joseph Rheinberger and Max von Schillings, and early began gaining experience as conductor of concerts and opera at Zürich, Munich, Strasbourg (where he was a deputy to Hans Pfitzner), and Lübeck. After an engagement at Mannheim he followed Arthur Nikisch at the Leipzig Gewandhaus. He made his London debut in 1924, and his New York debut in 1925. He conducted the Vienna Philharmonic Orchestra from 1924 (and was principal conductor 1927–28 and 1933–54).

In 1928 he became conductor-in-chief of the Berlin Philharmonic. In 1934 he was obliged to resign his post, when he supported Hindemith against the attacks of Goebbels and other Nazis. He toured infrequently but with great success, visiting Bayreuth 1931–44 and the Royal Opera House, Covent Garden, London, 1935–38, performing Wagner's *Tristan* and *The Ring*. Furtwängler was also active as a composer, producing three symphonies, a piano concerto, a Te Deum, and some chamber music.

Fussell, Charles C(lement) (1938–) US composer and conductor. His music is largely traditional in scope and content. He founded the Group for New Music at the University of Massachusetts in 1974.

He studied at the Eastman School and with Boris Blacher in Berlin, Germany, and has taught at Boston University from 1981.

Works OPERA *Caligula* (1962).

ORCHESTRAL three symphonies (1963, 1964–67, 1978–81), *Northern Lights* for chamber orchestra (portraits of Janáček and Munch, 1979), *Virgil Thomson Sleeping* for chamber orchestra (1981).

VOCAL *Cymbeline*, romance for soprano, tenor, and ensemble (1983), *A Song of Return* for chorus and orchestra (1989), *Wilde* two monologues for baritone and orchestra (1990).

INSTRUMENTAL *Last Trombones* for five percussionists, two pianos, and six trombones (1990).

Fux, Johann Joseph (1660–1741) Austrian composer and theorist. His rules of ➤ **counterpoint**, compiled in his *Gradus ad Parnassum* (1725), were studied by Haydn and Beethoven, and are still used as a teaching formula by many music schools. He wrote a considerable quantity of sacred music, including 50 masses and 10 oratorios.

Fux was organist to the Schottenkirche in Vienna 1696–1702, became court composer in 1698, second Kapellmeister at St Stephen's Cathedral in 1705 and first in 1712, vice-Kapellmeister to the court in 1713, and Kapellmeister in 1715.

Works 18 operas, including *Costanza e fortezza* (1723); eleven oratorios including *Gesù Cristo negato da Pietro* (1719); around 80 Masses and quantities of other church music; 38 trio sonatas; partitas and other pieces for orchestra; keyboard music.

fz in music, abbreviation for Italian ➤ *forzando.*

G in music, the fifth note, or dominant, of the scale of C major.

Gabrieli, Andrea (c.1533–1585) Italian composer. He was organist at St Mark's, Venice, from 1566, and his music, for example *Concerti* (1587), makes much use of the spatial effects possible within St Mark's, with vocal and instrumental groups separated in contrasting ensembles.

He was a member of a Venetian school which cultivated an antiphonal style suited to the two choir galleries and two organs of St Mark's Church. He became second organist at St Mark's in 1566 and first organist in 1584. He was a famous teacher and had many distinguished pupils, Italian and foreign, including his nephew Giovanni ➤ **Gabrieli** and the Germans Hans Hassler and Gregor Aichinger.

Works Masses, motets, and other church music with instruments; spiritual songs; madrigals, and other pieces for several voices; choruses for Sophocles' *Oedipus Tyrannus*; ricercari for organ.

Gabrieli, Giovanni (c.1555–1612) Italian composer. He succeeded his uncle Andrea Gabrieli (c.1533–1585) as organist of St Mark's Cathedral, Venice. His sacred and secular works include numerous madrigals, motets, and the antiphonal *Sacrae Symphoniae* (1597), sacred canzoni and sonatas for brass choirs, strings, and organ.

Gaburo, Kenneth (1926–1993) US composer. He studied at the Eastman School and with Goffredo Petrassi in Rome. He was a professor at the University of Illinois 1955–68 and at San Diego 1968–75. He founded and directed the Studio for Cognitive Studies at San Diego 1975–83; his music was concerned with extending verbal limits within composition, and frequently employed electronics, as in his series of *Antiphonies* I–X (1958–89).

Works OPERA *The Snow Queen* (1952), *Blur* (1956), *The Widow* (1961).

ORCHESTRAL *Shapes and Sounds* (1960), *A Dot is no Small Thing* (1984), both for orchestra.

CHAMBER string quartet (1956).

Gade, Niels Vilhelm (1817–1890) Danish composer. He was a violinist with the royal orchestra in Copenhagen before going to Leipzig, Germany, where he was engaged as assistant conductor of the Gewandhaus Orchestra. After returning to Denmark he established a permanent orchestra and became co-director of Copenhagen's Academy of Music. He was the most important Danish composer of the 19th century.

His teachers included Andreas Berggreen and Christoph Weyse. Having won a composition prize for his *Ossian* overture in 1841, he was enabled to go to Leipzig for further study with a royal grant. There he came into contact with Mendelssohn, who produced his first symphony in 1843 and engaged him to conduct the Gewandhaus concerts in his absence. He returned to Copenhagen in 1848 and worked as organist, conductor, and teacher, becoming court music director in 1861.

Works OPERA *Mariotta* (1849).

CANTATAS *Baldurs Drom* (1858), *Comala, Erl King's Daughter, Zion, The Crusaders, Den Bjaergtagne* (1873), *Psyche*, and others.

ORCHESTRAL eight symphonies (1842–71); overtures *Echoes from Ossian, In the Highland, Hamlet* (after Shakespeare), *Michelangelo*, and others; suite *Holbergiana* for orchestra.

CHAMBER string quartet, quintet, string octet, piano trios, and other chamber music; four violin and piano sonatas; instrumental pieces; piano sonata in E minor and pieces for piano solo and duet.

OTHER songs, part songs.

Gafori, Franchino (1451–1522) Italian priest, theorist, and composer. He wrote several theoretical books, including *Theorica musicae* (1492) and *Practica musicae* (1496), and also composed Masses and other church music. Leonardo da Vinci was among his friends.

He was maestro di cappella at Monticello and Bergamo, and from 1484 was attached to Milan Cathedral.

gagaku traditional court music of Japan with origins in ancient China and 8th-century Japan.

The tonal systems, scales, and modes of gagaku are also derived from ancient Chinese theory and practice and each category of gagaku has a separate instrumentation (for example, the use of the 'wagon' zither in Shinto ritual music) and tonal system.

Gagliano, Giovanni Battista da (1584–1651), born Zenobi Italian composer. He was instructor at the church of San Lorenzo in Florence in 1613, in succession to his brother Marco da ➤ Gagliano, and later musician to the Grand Duke of Tuscany.

Works motets, psalms, and other church music.

Gagliano, Marco da (1582–1643) Italian composer, brother of Giovanni Battista da ➤ Gagliano. In 1607 he founded the Accademia dell' Elevati for the cultivation of music. His opera *Dafne* (1608), a setting of Ottavio Rinuccini's libretto, followed Monteverdi's epoch-making *Orfeo* by one year; it also developed early operatic form, to include airs and choruses as well as recitative.

He studied organ and theorbo under Luca Bati at the Church of San Lorenzo, Florence, where he was a priest. He became instructor there in 1602 and maestro di cappella in 1608. About 1610 he was appointed maestro di cappella to the Grand Duke of Tuscany. He was in touch with the ducal family of Gonzaga at Mantua, where *Dafne* was produced in 1608. He also wrote music for the wedding of the Duke's son.

Works OPERA *Dafne* (1608), *Il medoro* (1616; music lost), *La flora* (1628).

SACRED AND CHURCH MUSIC oratorio *La regina Santa Orsola* (1624, music lost); Masses, Offices for the Dead, *Sacrae cantiones*.

OTHER madrigals.

gagliarda Italian for ➤ galliard, a 16th-century dance.

gaillarde French for ➤ galliard, a 16th-century dance.

Gál, Hans (1890–1987) Austrian composer and musicologist. After the Anschluss (the annexation of Austria by Germany) he took refuge in Edinburgh, Scotland, where he was lecturer at the University 1945–57.

He was a pupil of Eusebius Mandyczewski in Vienna, Austria, and lectured at the university there from 1918; he later became director of the Music Academy in Mainz, Germany.

Works OPERA *Der Fischer, Der Arzt der Sobeide* (1919), *Ruth, Die heilige Ente* (1923), *Das Lied der Nacht* (1926), *Die beiden Klaus, Der Zauberspiegel.*

CHORAL *Requiem für Mignon* (from Goethe's *Wilhelm Meister*, 1923) for chorus and orchestra, and other choral works.

ORCHESTRAL *Sinfonietta, Ballet Suite, Pickwick-*

ian Overture (after Dickens), and other pieces for orchestra; serenade for strings; piano concerto, violin concerto.

CHAMBER four string quartets (1916–71), five intermezzi for string quartet, serenade for string trio; piano works.

galant (French and German 'courtly') in music, an adjective used to designate a special musical style of the 18th century, especially that of C P E Bach and the Mannheim school. Its main characteristics are elegance, a certain restraint of feeling, formality (often using sonata form), and the abandonment of baroque counterpoint in favour of a distinct division between melody and accompaniment.

galanteries (French 'courtesies'; German *Galanterien*) extra dances or other pieces added to those which were normal in the baroque suite or partita (➤ allemande, ➤ courante, ➤ sarabande, and ➤ gigue). The most frequently used galanteries were the ➤ bourrées, ➤ minuets, ➤ passepieds, ➤ chaconnes and, among pieces other than dances, airs.

Galatea, La opera by Schürer (libretto by Pietro Metastasio), first produced before the court in Dresden, Germany, on 8 November 1746.

Galilei, Vincenzo (c.1520–1591) Italian composer, theorist, and lutenist. He took part in the discussions which, after his death, helped transform the Florentine camerata into opera; he also wrote theoretical books. Galilei upheld Greek drama against the contemporary madrigal, becoming involved in controversy with his teacher, Gioseffo Zarlino. He was the father of the astronomer Galileo Galilei.

Works cantata *Il conte Ugolino* from Dante, a setting of the Lamentations of Jeremiah (both lost, and both among the earliest music for a single voice with accompaniment); two books of madrigals; pieces for two viols; a lute book in tablature; *Dialogo della musica antica et della moderna* (1581).

galimatias or **galimathias (French 'gallimaufry, farrago, gibberish')** term found in Mozart's *Galimathias musicum* (K32) written by him in The Hague in 1766, at the age of ten, for the coming of age of William of Orange. It contains the Dutch national air 'Wilhelmus van Nassouwe'.

galliard spirited 16th-century court dance in triple time, originating from Lombardy, Italy. It was a very athletic dance, full of complicated steps, mainly performed by couples and popular in the court of Elizabeth I of England. It became increasingly lascivious in the 17th century. The music for the galliard consists of compound duple time (6/8) with bars of simple triple time (3/4) intermingled to upset the pulse. The galliard is

This galliard by Byrd opens with a melody related to the pavane also shown here.

often coupled to a ➤ **pavane**, of contrasting common time (4/4).

Gallican chant Provençal ➤ **plainsong** in use in France until the introduction of the Roman ritual in the 8th century.

Galliculus or **Hähnel** or **Alectorius, Johannes (lived first half of the 16th century)** German theorist and composer. He taught at Leipzig 1520–50, wrote a theoretical work *Isagoge [later Libellus] de compositione cantus*, and composed a Passion according to St Mark, two Magnificats, a psalm, and liturgical works for Easter and Christmas.

galop (French 'gallop') quick ballroom dance in 2/4 time, a variant of the ➤ **polka**, first appearing under that name in Paris, France, in 1829, but of older German origin, its German name (now *Galopp*) having been *Hopser*, 'hopper', or *Rutscher*, 'glider'.

galoubet small wind instrument, the pipe used with the accompanying ➤ **tabor** (French *tambourin*).

Galuppi, Baldassare (1706–1785) Italian composer. His serious operas met with indifferent success, but his comic operas are notable, especially those on libretti by Carlo Goldoni, the most famous being *Il filosofo di campagna* (1754).

Galuppi was born on the island of Burano, near Venice. He studied with his father and later, after the failure of his first opera in 1722, with Antonio Lotti in Venice. His operatic career proper began in 1728, after which he composed a vast quantity of works. He visited London, England, 1741–43, and produced several operas there. He was appointed second maestro di cappella at St Mark's, Venice, in 1748, and first maestro and director of the Ospitale degl'Incurabili in 1762. He was di-

rector of Catherine the Great's chapel at St Petersburg, Russia, 1765–68, writing new operas and Russian sacred music. Thereafter he composed few operas and devoted himself chiefly to oratorios for the Incurabili.

Works OPERA *Alessandro nell' Indie* (1738), *L'Olympiade*, *L'Arcadia in Brenta* (1749), *Il conte Caramella*, *Il mondo della luna* (1750), *Il mondo alla roversa*, *La calamità de cuori*, *Il filosofo di campagna* (1754), *Le nozze* (1755), *L'amante di tutte*, *Le tre amanti ridicoli*, *Il marchese Villano* (1762), *Ifigenia in Tauride* (1768), and others (over 90 in all).

OTHER 27 oratorios; church music; instrumental music.

Galway, James (1939–) Irish flautist, born in Belfast. He played with the London Symphony Orchestra in 1966, the Royal Philharmonic Orchestra 1967–69, and was principal flautist with the Berlin Philharmonic Orchestra 1969–75 before taking up a solo career. He also has a profile outside classical music because of his popular recordings, such as the cover of John Denver's 'Annie's Song' in 1978. Recent popular recordings are *Celtic Legends* (1997), *Winter's Crossing* (1998) with Phil Coulter, *Music for my Little Friends* and *A Song of Home: An American Musical Journey* (both 2002). Galway has done much to popularize the flute in the 20th century. He was knighted in 2001.

gamba, da (Italian 'on the leg') in music, suffix used to distinguish viols, which are played resting on the leg, from members of the violin family, which are played under the chin, or 'on the arm' (viola da braccio).

Gambler, The, Russian **Igrok** opera in four acts by Sergey Prokofiev (libretto by the composer, after the story by Fyodor Dostoevsky), composed

1915–17, revised in 1928, and first produced in Brussels, Belgium, on 29 April 1929. It had been planned for performance in St Petersburg, Russia, in 1917, but was cancelled at the outbreak of the Revolution. The orchestral suite *Portraits*, Op. 49, in four movements, was first performed in Paris, France, on 12 March 1932. In the story, Alexey, in love with Pauline, ruins himself for her sake. He takes to gambling and makes a fortune, but she rejects him.

gamelan percussion ensemble of 15 to 20 players using mainly tuned knobbed gongs and keyed metallophones found in Indonesia (especially Java and Bali) and Malaysia. Most modern gamelan are tuned to a five-note or seven-note system. Gamelan music is performed as an accompaniment for dance and theatre.

gamma (Greek letter Γ) the name of the lowest note of the musical scale known to medieval theory, G on the bottom line of the bass stave. Where the hexachord was based on it, it received the name of 'gamma-ut' (hence ➔ 'gamut'), and in France the name of the scale is still *gamme*.

gamut (derived from 'gamma-ut') in medieval musical theory, the lowest note; see ➔ **gamma**. It is also a generic term for scale, or for the entire spectrum of pitches, from the lowest to the highest.

The lowest note of the gamut.

gamut-way 17th-century term for music written in ordinary notation, as distinct from tablature.

Ganne, (Gustave) Louis (1862–1923) French composer. He conducted the Opéra balls in Paris and orchestras at Royan and Monte Carlo, and became very popular as a composer of ballets and operettas.

He was a pupil of Théodore Dubois and César Franck.

Works OPERETTA *Rabelais*, *Les Colles des femmes*, *Les Saltimbanques* (1899), *Hans le joueur de flûte* (1906).

BALLET *La Source du Nil* and several others.

OTHER popular songs including 'La Marche Lorraine' and 'Le Père la Victoire'; dances *La Tsarine*.

gapped scales in music, any scale containing less than seven notes, such as the pentatonic scale, which has five. The name derives from the fact that the scale must contain at least one 'gap' of more than a tone.

Garcia, José Mauricio Nunes (1767–1830) Brazilian composer. He directed music at Rio de Janeiro Cathedral from 1798 and composed about 20 Masses, the later ones being influenced by Italian opera. His brilliant Requiem of 1816 established his reputation throughout South America.

Garden of Fand, The symphonic poem by Arnold Bax, composed in 1913 and first performed in Chicago, USA, on 29 October 1920. Fand is a heroine of Irish legend, but in this work the garden of Fand is simply the sea, charged with Irish legendry.

Gardiner, H(enry) Balfour (1877–1950) English composer. He was educated at Charterhouse School and Oxford, and studied music under Iwan Knorr at Frankfurt. He became music master at Winchester College for a short time, then devoted himself to composition. He financed and conducted series of concerts at Queen's Hall, London, 1912–13, including early performances of works by British contemporaries, including the first performance of Gustav Holst's *The Planets*.

Works CHORUS AND ORCHESTRA *News from Wydah* (Masefield; 1912).

ORCHESTRAL symphony in D, *English Dance*, Fantasy and *Shepherd Fennel's Dance* (after Hardy; 1910) for orchestra.

CHAMBER string quartet, string quintet (1905), and other chamber music.

OTHER *Noel*, five pieces for piano; part songs.

Gardiner, John Eliot (1943–) English conductor. He first made his mark establishing the Monteverdi Choir in 1966, which he continues to conduct. He is an authority on 17th- and 18th-century music, and an exponent of the ➔ **authenticity** movement. He has also recorded modern music. He was knighted in 1998.

Gardner, John (Linton) (1917–) English composer. Chamber music of his was heard in London and Paris in the 1930s, but his first great success was the performance of the first symphony at the Cheltenham Festival of 1951.

Gardner was educated at Wellington and Oxford, became music master at Repton School in 1939, and after doing war service was appointed coach at the Royal Opera House, Covent Garden, London. He taught at Morley College, London, 1952–76.

Works OPERA *The Moon and Sixpence* (after Somerset Maugham, 1957), *Tobermory* (1977).

ORCHESTRAL symphony (1951), *Variations on a Waltz by Nielsen* for orchestra (1952), piano concerto (1957), *An English Ballad* for orchestra (1969).

CHORAL Mass in C (1965), *Cantata for Easter* (1970).

CHAMBER string quartet (1939), oboe quintet; two piano sonatas.

OTHER *Intermezzo* for organ; songs.

Garland for the Queen set of songs for mixed voices dedicated to Queen Elizabeth II on her coronation in 1953, with contributions by Arnold Bax, Lennox Berkeley, Arthur Bliss, Gerald Finzi, Herbert Howells, John Ireland, Alan Rawsthorne, Edmund Rubbra, Michael Tippett, and Ralph Vaughan Williams.

Garlandia, Johannes de (lived 13th century) Scholar and writer on music. He taught at the University of Paris. His two treatises on plainsong (*De plana musica*) and mensural music (*De mensurabili musica*, about 1240), were among the most influential writings of their time.

Gaspard de la Nuit three poems for piano by Maurice Ravel after Aloysius Bertrand, composed in 1908 and first perfomed in Paris, France, on 9 January 1909. The movements are *Ondine*, *Le Gibet*, and *Scarbo*.

Gasparini, Francesco (1668–1727) Italian composer. He wrote over 60 operas, as well as choral and church music. He was also highly regarded as a teacher. His treatise *L'armonico pratico al cimbalo* was published in 1708.

He was a pupil of Arcangelo Corelli and Bernardo Pasquini. He later became choirmaster at the Ospedale della Pietà, Venice, and in 1725 was appointed maestro di cappella of the church of St John Lateran, Rome.

Works OPERA 61 operas, including *Il più fedel fra i vassalli*, *La fede tradita e vendicata* (1704), *Ambleto* (on Shakespeare's *Hamlet*, 1705).

CHORAL AND CHURCH MUSIC oratorios *Mosè liberato dal Nilo*, *La nascita di Cristo*, and *Le nozze di Tobia* (1724); church music; cantatas.

Gassenhauer (German 'street-beater') 16th-century term for a popular dance, which was very soon used to mean a popular song. It survived till the 20th century. The modern term is *Schlager*.

Gassmann, Florian Leopold (1729–1774) Bohemian composer. He settled in Vienna, Austria, as a ballet composer in 1763. In 1771 he was involved in founding Vienna's first music society, the Tonkünstler-Sozietät. He wrote 15 operas, most of them comic, including *L'opera seria* (1769), a satire on contemporary operatic practices, which was revived in Berlin, Germany, in 1994.

Gassmann studied with Padre Martini in Bologna, Italy. He was appointed court Kapellmeister in succession to the younger Georg Reutter in 1772.

Works OPERA 25 operas, including *Gli uccellatori* (1759), *L'amore artigiano*, *La notte critica* (1768), and *La contessina* (1770).

ORATORIO *La Betulia liberata* (1772).

ORCHESTRAL AND CHAMBER over 50 symphonies; chamber music.

OTHER much church music.

Gast, Peter (1854–1918), born **Johann Heinrich Köselitz** German composer. He studied at the Leipzig Conservatory and later went to Basel, Switzerland, as a friend and disciple of the philosopher Nietzsche, some of whose compositions he revised. Afterwards he lived in Venice, Italy, and Weimar, Germany.

Works STAGE operas *Wilbram* (1879), *Orpheus und Dionysos*, *König Wenzel*, *Die heimliche Ehe* (based on the libretto of Cimarosa's *Il matrimonio segreto* and farther back on Colman and Garrick's *The Clandestine Marriage*, 1891); festival play *Walpurgis* (1903).

CHORUS AND ORCHESTRA *Hosanna*.

ORCHESTRAL symphonies, symphonic poem *Helle Nächte*, and other orchestral works.

CHAMBER string quartet, septet.

OTHER songs.

'Gastein' Symphony symphony in C major, supposed to have been written by Franz Schubert during a visit to Gastein in the autumn of 1825, of which no trace is left. It has been suggested that it is identical with the Grand Duo for piano duet, Op. 140, but recent views identify it as the 'Great' C major symphony. It must therefore have been composed in 1825, not, as previously thought, in 1828.

Gastoldi, Giovanni Giacomo (c.1550–1622) Italian composer. He was maestro di cappella at the church of Santa Barbara, Mantua, 1592–1608; he was then appointed choirmaster at Milan Cathedral.

Works a Magnificat and other church music; madrigals; canzoni and balletti for voices and instruments (those of 1591 influenced Morley and Weelkes).

gat (Hindi 'movement', 'action') Hindustani composition type, usually played on plucked stringed instruments such as the ➔ sitar and ➔ sarod. Most are based on one of a limited number of stereotypical stroke patterns, and comprise two or three sections (*sthayi*, *antara*, and sometimes *manjha*). The most common type is the Masitkhani gat, named after the 19th-century sitarist Masit Khan in the 16-beat metric cycle *teental* at a slow tempo.

Gaudentios (lived 2nd century AD) Greek music theorist. He was the first to formulate a system of eight *tonoi* (modes in the scalic sense) based on the idea of joining the interval of a fourth to that of a fifth with one note common to both.

Gaveau, Etienne (1872–1943) French piano manufacturer. He followed his father **Joseph Gaveau** (1824–1903) and built a factory at Fontenay-sous-Bois in 1896, and a concert hall (Salle Gaveau) in Paris in 1907.

The opening of Bach's gavotte from his French Suite no. 5

Gavinès, Pierre (1728–1800) French violinist and composer. His compositions for the violin, including *Les Vingt-Quatre Matinées* (1800), were the most demanding pieces in the violin repertory before Paganini.

He made his first appearance in Paris in 1741, at the Concert Spirituel, of which he was conductor 1773–77. He was professor of violin at the Paris Conservatory from its foundation in 1795.

Works OPERA *Le Prétendu* (1760).

VIOLIN violin concertos; sonatas for violin and bass, violin and piano, two violins, and unaccompanied violin, violin studies *Les Vingt-Quatre Matinées* (1800), violin pieces including the *Romance de G.*

gavotte light-hearted dance in common time (4/4), originating from the Pays de Gap, France, whose inhabitants were called Gavots. Originally a folk dance, it was adopted by the court and continued to develop ever more complicated steps until it could only be performed by professional dancers. The music begins with an ➤ **upbeat** of two crotchets, and the phrases usually begin and end in the middle of each bar. It became popular at the court of Louis XIV (Jean-Baptiste Lully composed several gavottes), later becoming an optional movement of the baroque ➤ **suite**. The gavotte was revived by some 20th-century composers, including Prokofiev and Schoenberg, who used one in his *Suite* (1934).

Gawain opera in two acts by Harrison Birtwistle (libretto by D Harsent after the anonymous medieval poem *Sir Gawain and the Green Knight*), first produced at the Royal Opera House, Covent Garden, London, on 30 May 1991.

Gay, John (1685–1732) English poet and playwright. He wrote the libretti for Handel's ➤ *Acis and Galatea*, his own *The* ➤ *Beggar's Opera*, Kurt Weill's *Die* ➤ *Dreigroschenoper*, and *Polly*. His odes were set to music by Thomas ➤ **Busby**.

Gaztambide y Garbayo, Joaquín (Romualdo) (1822–1870) Spanish conductor and composer. He studied at Pamplona and the Madrid Conservatory. After a stay in Paris, France, he became a theatre manager and conducted in Madrid.

Works 44 zarzuelas, including *La mensajera, El estreno de una artista, El valle de Andorra, Cata-*

lina, Los Magyares, El juramento, and *La conquista de Madrid.*

gazza ladra, La, The Thieving Magpie opera by Rossini (libretto by G Gherardini, based on the French melodrama *La Pie voleuse* by J-M T B d'Aubigny and L C Caigniez), first produced at La Scala, Milan, Italy, on 31 May 1817. It tells how Ninetta is condemned to death for stealing silverware but is released when a magpie is identified as the culprit.

Gazzaniga, Giuseppe (1743–1818) Italian composer. Of his 44 operas, *Don Giovanni o sia Il convitato di pietra* (1787) was an immediate forerunner of Mozart's opera of the same title (which was produced later the same year in Prague); it has been revived in Wexford, Ireland, and elsewhere in recent years.

Gazzaniga was a pupil of Nicola Porpora and Niccolò Piccinni in Naples, where his first opera was produced in 1768. Later, he lived chiefly in Venice, until his appointment as maestro di cappella at Crema Cathedral in 1791. His works also include oratorios, a symphony, and three piano concertos.

Gebrauchsmusik (German 'utility music') term for a type of musical work written for practical use and best translated as 'workaday music'. It was common among German composers in the 1920s and 1930s, most closely associated with Paul ➤ **Hindemith**, who is usually credited with having coined the phrase, although he later disavowed this. Hindemith's published works of the kind (several are unpublished) are: *Spielmusik* for strings, flutes, and oboes (1927), four three-part *Songs for Singing Groups*, an educational work for concerted violins in first position (1927), *Music to Sing or Play* (five nos for various vocal or instrumental combinations), *Lesson* for two male voices, narrator, chorus, orchestra, a dancer, clowns, and community singing (1929), *Let's Build a Town*, a musical game for children (1930), and *Plöner Musiktag* (1932; four nos for various vocal and instrumental combinations). Some other composers, such as Darius Milhaud in France, Aaron Copland in the USA, and Kurt Weill and Carl Orff in Germany, have done similar work.

Geburtstag der Infantin, Der, The Birthday of the Infanta pantomime by Franz Schreker after the story by Oscar Wilde, composed in 1908 and first performed in Vienna, Austria, on 27 June 1908. It was orchestrated in 1923 as a suite for large orchestra and performed in Amsterdam, the Netherlands, on 18 October 1923, conducted by Willem Mengelberg. A new ballet scenario by Schreker was arranged in 1926, with the title *Spanisches Fest*, and was performed in Berlin, Germany, on 22 January 1927, conducted by Leo Blech. Wilde's story was set as an opera by Alexander von Zemlinsky in 1920–21, *Der* ➔ *Zwerg*.

gedackt or **gedact (from German gedeckt 'covered')** musical term meaning 'stopped'. It refers to ➔ **diapason** organ stops producing a muted 8-ft tone.

gedämpft (German 'damped') musical term meaning 'muted', 'muffled', usually used to refer to drums.

Geduldige Socrates, Der, The Patient Socrates opera by Georg Telemann (libretto by J U von König, after Minato), first produced in Hamburg, Germany, on 28 January 1721. It describes how Socrates has his patience tried by the squabbling of his two wives.

Geharnischte Suite (German Geharnischte, 'armoured man') second suite for orchestra by Ferruccio Busoni, composed in 1895, revised in 1903, and first performed in Berlin, Germany, on 1 December 1904.

Geheime Königreich, Das, The Secret Kingdom fairy-tale opera in one act by Ernst Krenek (libretto by the composer; 1926–27), first produced in a triple bill with *Der Diktator* and *Schwergewicht* in Wiesbaden, Germany, on 6 May 1928. It relates how the king and queen find the answer in the forest to the riddle 'What contains the whole world in itself?'.

Geheimnis des entwendeten Briefes, Das chamber opera by Boris Blacher (libretto by H Brauer after Edgar Allen Poe's story 'The Mystery of the Purloined Letter'). The first performance was planned for 2 February 1975 but was postponed after Blacher's death on 30 January; it was produced in Berlin, Germany, on 14 February 1975.

Geibel, Emanuel von (1815–1884) German poet. His works inspired the composers Adolph ➔ Jensen (*Spanisches Liederbuch*), Max Bruch and Felix Mendelssohn (➔ *Loreley*), Robert ➔ Schumann (*Vom Pagen und der Königstochter*), Hugo Wolf (➔ *Spanisches Liederbuch*), and Fritz Volbach (*Vom Pagen und der Königstochter*).

Geige (German 'fiddle') colloquial German name for the ➔ violin.

Geiringer, Karl (Johannes) (1899–1989) Austrian-born US musicologist. He studied in Berlin and Vienna and was librarian at the Vienna Gesellschaft der Musikfreunde, 1930–38. He was resident in the USA from 1940 and professor of music history and theory at Boston University, 1941–62. He became professor of music at the University of California, Santa Barbara, 1962–72. He edited Haydn's music and published a monograph *Haydn: A Creative Life in Music* in 1946. He also wrote on Brahms (1935), musical instruments (1943), and the Bach family (1954).

Geisslerlieder (German 'flagellants' songs') sacred German monophonic songs of the Middle Ages in the Italian *laude* tradition and particularly cultivated at the time of the Black Death in 1349. The chief manuscript source is the *Chronikon* of Hugo von Reutlingen, which also describes how the singing was accompanied by penitential rites performed by the *Geissler* ('flagellants').

Gellert Lieder six songs by Beethoven for voice and piano to texts by C F Gellert, Op. 48, composed about 1802. The titles are: 1. *Bitten*, 2. *Die Liebe des Nächsten*, 3. *Vom Tode*, 4. *Die Ehre Gottes aus der Natur*, 5. *Gottes Macht und Vorsehung*, and 6. *Busslied*.

gelosie fortunate, Le, The Fortunate Jealousies opera by Pasquale Anfossi (libretto by F Livigni), first produced at the Teatro San Samuele, Venice, in the autumn of 1786. Mozart added an aria to it on its production in Vienna, Austria, on 2 June 1788.

gelosie villane, Le, The Rustic Jealousies opera by Giuseppe Sarti (libretto by T Grandi, based on a comedy by Carlo Goldoni), first produced at the Teatro San Samuele, Venice, Italy, in November 1776.

gemel alternative spelling of ➔ gymel, vocal music in two parts.

Geminiani, Francesco (1687–1762) Italian violinist and composer. His treatise *The Art of Playing the Violin* (1751) was the first violin tutor ever published. His music was influenced by Arcangelo Corelli and is typically brilliant in fast movements and expressive in slow movements. He lived in London, Paris, and Dublin.

Geminiani was born in Lucca. He studied music under Alessandro Scarlatti and Corelli. In 1714 he visited England, where he very quickly became famous and decided to settle. A few years later he went to Dublin, and afterwards divided his time between England and Ireland. His teaching introduced modern violin technique to England, and he wrote several theoretical works.

Works concerti grossi, violin sonatas, cello sonatas, trio sonatas, keyboard pieces.

Gemma di Vergy opera by Donizetti (libretto by E Bidera, based on the elder Dumas's play *Charles VII chez ses grands vassaux*), first produced at La Scala, Milan, Italy, on 26 December 1834. The story tells how the Count of Vergy wants to annul his marriage with his infertile wife Gemma. Her slave Tamas stabs the new wife Ida, then kills himself; Gemma grieves.

gemshorn in music, an obsolete type of recorder made from an animal's horn (especially that of a cow or goat). It disappeared from use during the 16th century. The name is also used for an organ stop of light, sweet tone, with conical pipes and usually 4-foot pitch (one octave above that written).

Generalbass (German 'general bass') musical term; see ➤ **thorough bass**.

Generali, Pietro (1773–1832) Italian composer. He studied under Giovanni Masi in Rome and in 1802 produced his first opera there. In 1817–21 he conducted opera in Barcelona, Spain, and later became maestro di cappella at Novara Cathedral, Italy.

Works OPERA about 60 operas, including *Gli amanti ridicoli*, *Il duca Nottolone*, *La villana in cimento*, *Le gelosie di Giorgio*, *Pamela nubile* (after Richardson, via Goldoni's comedy, 1804), *La calzolaia*, *Misantropia e pentimento* (after Kotzebue), *Gli effetti della somiglianza*, *Don Chisciotte* (after Cervantes), *Orgoglio ed umiliazione*, *L'idolo cinese*, *Lo sposo in bersaglio*, *Le lagrime di una vedova* (1808), *Adelina* (1810), *La moglie giudice del marito*, *I baccanali di Roma* (1816), and *Francesca da Rimini* (after Dante).

OTHER Masses and other church music; cantata *Roma liberata*.

general MIDI, GM; acronym for general Musical Instrument Digital Interface standard set of 96 instrument and percussion 'voices' that can be used to encode musical tracks which can be reproduced on any GM-compatible synthesizer, or ➤ **MIDI**.

general pause or.**G.P.** in music, a rest in an orchestral work of at least one full bar for the entire orchestra, often appearing suddenly after a climax. It originated in 18th-century Germany.

Genet, Elzéar (Carpentras) (c.1470–1548) French composer. He wrote secular works to both Italian and French texts, and numerous Masses, motets, hymns, and Magnificats. He was a papal singer to Julius II in 1508 and maestro di cappella under Pope Leo X (1513–21), as well as being at the court of King Louis XII some time between those dates.

Genoveva opera by Robert Schumann (libretto by the composer, altered from one by R Reinick

based on the dramas of Tieck and Hebbel), first produced in Leipzig, Germany, on 25 June 1850. In the story, Genoveva's husband Siegfried departs for battle and entrusts his castle to Golo, who loves Genoveva. After being rejected, he frames her for adultery and is about to execute her, when Siegfried returns and the couple are reconciled.

Gentle Shepherd, The ballad opera (libretto by Allan Ramsay, using traditional tunes), first produced at the Taylor's Hall, Edinburgh, Scotland, on 29 January 1729. It was first published (1725) as a pastoral comedy, and is therefore not, as is sometimes said, the first ballad opera, since *The Beggar's Opera* (1728) was staged earlier. In the story, Patie, of noble birth but brought up as a shepherd, wants to marry humble Peggy, but he believes it would be socially impossible. Later it turns out that she too is of noble blood.

Genzmer, Harald (1909–   ) German composer. His compositions include choral, orchestral, and chamber pieces. He taught composition at the Hochschule für Musik at Freiburg im Breisgau 1946–57, and was appointed professor at the Munich Hochschule in 1957.

He studied first in Marburg and later with Paul Hindemith in Berlin.

Works the cantata *Racine* (1949); Mass in E; symphony no. 1, *Bremen* symphony; concertos for piano, cello, oboe, flute (2), trautonium (2); two string quartets; sonatas for violin, flute, and other chamber music.

George, Stefan (1868–1933) German poet. His works were used in Alban ➤ **Berg's** compositions (*Wein*, *Lyric Suite*), Arnold ➤ **Schoenberg's** *Buch der hängenden Gärten*, and Anton ➤ **Webern's** songs Op. 3 and Op. 4.

Gerber, Heinrich Nicolaus (1702–1775) German organist and composer. He was court organist at Sonderhausen from 1731. He improved and invented instruments, including the ➤ **Strohfiedel**. He was the father of Ernst Ludwig Gerber.

He studied at Leipzig University under Johann Sebastian Bach.

Works a hymn-book with figured basses; variations on chorales for organ; music for harpsichord, organ, harp.

Gerbert, Martin (1720–1793) German music historian. He entered the Benedictine monastery of St Blasien in 1737 and was ordained priest in 1744, and abbot in 1764. He published a history of church music in 1774 under the title *De cantu et musica sacra*, and a collection of medieval music treatises in 1784.

Gerhard, Roberto (1896–1970) Spanish-born British composer. He studied with Enrique Granados and Arnold Schoenberg and settled in England in 1939, where he composed twelve-tone works in Spanish style. He composed the *Symphony No. 1* (1952–55), followed by three more symphonies and chamber music incorporating advanced techniques.

His achievement was to unite atonal methods with the colours and rhythms of his native Spain; some of his later music, notably the Third Symphony (*Collages*, 1960) allows some avant-garde techniques. His opera *The Duenna* (1945–47) received its British premiere in 1992 (it was premiered in Wiesbaden, Germany, in 1957).

Gerhard was born in Valls, near Barcelona. Although a choirboy and a tentative pianist and composer from an early age, he began serious music studies late, owing to parental opposition. He studied piano with Granados and composition with Carlos Pedrell at Barcelona 1915–22 and then composition with Schoenberg in Vienna, Austria, 1923–28. He taught at Barcelona 1929–38, was in charge of the music department of the Catalan Library, for which he edited music by 18th-century Catalan composers, translated various music treatises into Spanish, and contributed to the literary weekly *Mirador*. Pedrell introduced him as a composer and he began to make his way in Spain and Latin America.

He settled in England after the Spanish Civil War in 1938, and lived in Cambridge, first on a research studentship at King's College, then for the rest of his life off his compositions, which included occasional, radio, and film music as well as more substantial works.

Works STAGE opera *The Duenna* (after Sheridan, 1945–47); ballets *Ariel* (1934), *Soirées de Barcelone* (1938), *Alegrias* (1942), *Pandora* (1944), *Don Quixote* (after Cervantes; 1950).

ORATORIO *The Plague* (after Camus, 1964).

MUSIC FOR RADIO PLAYS *Cristóbal Colón* (1943) and *Adventures of Don Quixote* (Eric Linklater after Cervantes, 1952).

ORCHESTRAL violin concerto (1943), four symphonies (1952–67, no. 3 *Collages* for orchestra and magnetic tape, 1960), *Hymnody* for 11 players (1963), concerto for orchestra (1965), *Epithalamion* for orchestra (1966).

VOCAL *Cancionero de Pedrell, Serranillas*, and *Cançons i Arietes* for voice and orchestra; cantata for solo voices, chorus, and orchestra; song cycle *L'infantament meravellós de Shaharazada* (1917), and other songs.

CHAMBER *Concert for Eight*, nonet (1956), two string quartets (1955, 1962), piano trio (1918), wind quintet, *Gemini* for violin and piano.

OTHER various arrangements of old Spanish music.

Gerle, Hans (c. 1500–1570) German lutenist, violist, and lute-maker. He was the son of Conrad Gerle (died 1521), also a lute-maker. He published a book on viol and lute playing and two collections of lute pieces in tablature.

German, Edward (1862–1936), born **Edward German Jones** English composer. He is remembered for his operettas *Merrie England* (1902) and *Tom Jones* (1907), and he wrote many other instrumental, orchestral, and vocal works.

He studied at Shrewsbury and the Royal Academy of Music in London, 1880–87. He became an orchestral violinist and in 1888 music director of the Globe Theatre, writing incidental music for various productions, including well-received music for Henry Irving's version of *Henry VIII* (1892). In 1901 he completed *The Emerald Isle*, left unfinished by Arthur Sullivan. He had his enduring success the following year, with *Merrie England*, often performed by amateur opera companies.

Works STAGE light operas *The Rival Poets* (1886, revised 1901), *Merrie England* (1902), *The Princess of Kensington* (1903), *Tom Jones* (after Fielding; 1907), *Fallen Fairies* (W S Gilbert; 1909); incidental music for Shakespeare's *Richard III* (1889), *Henry VIII* (1892), *Romeo and Juliet* (1895), *As You Like It*, *Much Ado about Nothing*, Anthony Hope's *Nell Gwyn* (1900), and others.

ORCHESTRAL two symphonies, symphonic suite in D minor, symphonic poem *Hamlet*, symphonic suite *The Seasons*, *Welsh Rhapsody* (1904), *Theme and Six Diversions* and other orchestral works.

OTHER Coronation March and Hymn for George V; chamber music and many songs.

German flute name for the transverse ➔ flute in England in the 18th century.

German Requiem, A Requiem by Brahms; see ➔ **Deutsches Requiem**.

German sixth musical term; see ➔ **augmented 6th chords**.

Gero, Jhan (1540–55) Franco-Flemish composer. He lived in Venice, Italy, and was connected with the music printers Antonio Gardane (Gardano; 1509–1569) and Girolamo Scotto (1505–1572). He composed motets, madrigals, and a highly successful book of duos, published in 1541.

Gershwin, George (1898–1937), born **Jacob Gershvin** US composer. His musical comedies, mostly to lyrics by his brother **Ira Gershwin** (1896–1983), were among Broadway's most successful in the 1920s and 1930s, including *Strike up the Band* (1927), *Funny Face* (1927), and *Girl Crazy* (1930). He also wrote concert works including the tone poems *Rhapsody in Blue* (1924) and *An American in Paris* (1928). His opera *Porgy and Bess* (1935) used jazz rhythms and popular song styles in an operatic format.

Successful songs from the Gershwin brothers'

musicals include 'I Got Rhythm', ''S Wonderful', and 'Embraceable You'.

Gershwin was born in Brooklyn, New York. He worked as a pianist in a music publisher's office in 1914–17, and wrote songs (his first was published in 1916) and a musical comedy, *La, La, Lucille* (1919). Although his scores to musicals made him famous, his 'serious' work, including *Rhapsody in Blue* (1924) and *Piano Concerto in F* (1925), earned him much critical acclaim. *Of Thee I Sing* (1931), a collaboration between the Gershwin brothers, was the first musical to win a Pulitzer Prize.

Although his melodic gift was long recognized, it took many years for his masterpiece, *Porgy and Bess* (1935), to reach a wide audience; it was not staged at the New York Metropolitan Opera House until 1985, and had to wait until 1986 for its premiere by a British company, at Glyndebourne. Interestingly, Gershwin was highly respected by Arnold Schoenberg.

Works STAGE opera *Porgy and Bess* (1935); many musical comedies including *Lady, Be Good* (1924) and *Of Thee I Sing* (1931).

ORCHESTRAL *Rhapsody in Blue* (1924), concerto for piano and orchestra (1925), *An American in Paris* (1928), *Cuban Overture* (1932).

SONGS a large number of popular songs, including 'Oh, Lady, Be Good', 'I Got Rhythm', 'The Man I Love', 'Embraceable You', and 'Love Walked In'.

OTHER music for several films, including *Delicious* (1931), *Shall We Dance* (1937), and *The Goldwyn Follies* (1938). The film *Rhapsody in Blue* (1945) was semibiographical.

Gervaise, Claude (lived 16th century) French arranger and composer. He composed a considerable amount of dance music for various instruments, and several books of chansons, 1541–57.

Gesang der Jünglinge, The Song of the Youths work by Karlheinz Stockhausen for sung and spoken boys' voices, electrically processed and relayed through five loudspeakers. The text is from the Book of Daniel in the Bible and concerns three Hebrew youths undergoing ordeal by fire in Babylon. The work was first performed in Cologne, Germany, on 30 May 1956.

Geschöpfe des Prometheus, Die, The Creatures of Prometheus ballet by Beethoven (choreographed by Salvatore Vigano), first produced at the Burgtheater, Vienna, Austria, on 28 March 1801.

Gese, Bartholomäus (1555 or 1562–1613), also known as **Barthel Göss** German theologian and composer whose works were important in the development of the Protestant Passion. He was cantor at the Marienkirche, Frankfurt, from 1593 until his death.

Works Masses (one on themes by Lassus), motets, psalms, hymns, sacred songs, and other pieces, all for the Lutheran Church; Passion according to St John; wedding and funeral music.

Gesius, Bartholomäus alternative spelling of Bartholomäus ➜ **Gese**.

Gestalt (German 'shape, formation') word that has gained currency as a musical term in German-speaking countries, used in music analysis and in philosophical or aesthetic discussions on music to designate a musical idea as it comes from the composer's mind in what is supposed to be a kind of primeval or pre-existing form.

gestopft (German 'stopped, obstructed') in music, notes played on the horn with the hand inserted into the bell to produce an altered sound. Formerly this technique enabled the player to obtain extra notes not in the series of natural harmonics, a device made unnecessary by the valve horn.

Gesualdo opera by Alfred ➜ **Schnittke** (libretto by Richard Bletschacher), first produced at the Staatsoper, Vienna, Austria, on 26 May 1995. It is based on the life of Carlo ➜ **Gesualdo**, Prince of Venosa.

Gesualdo, Carlo (c.1561–1613), Prince of Venosa Italian composer and lutenist. His compositions, which comprise sacred and secular vocal music and some instrumental pieces, are noted for their complex (modern-sounding) harmonic structure, most unlike the work of his contemporaries. His highly chromatic madrigals (in six books, 1594–1611), set to emotional, passionate texts, were admired in the 20th century by Igor Stravinsky, among others.

In 1590 he had his wife and her lover murdered; he married Leonora d'Este of Ferrara in 1593, and lived at the court in Ferrara until 1596.

Gesualdo took his music studies seriously in his youth and became a very accomplished lutenist. He married his first cousin Maria d'Avalos, a Neapolitan noblewoman, in 1586. Though only 21, she had already been married twice and had children. She bore him a son, but became the lover of Fabrizio Caraffa, 3rd Duke of Andria; Gesualdo had them both murdered on the night of 16 October 1590. In 1594 he went to the court of Ferrara and married Leonora d'Este there, but returned to his estate at Naples in 1596, where he spent the rest of his life in a state of profound depression.

His work is notable for its expressive power and chromatic harmony. In 1960 Stravinsky orchestrated three of Gesualdo's madrigals, to mark the 400th anniversary of his birth. He is the subject of Alfred ➜ **Schnittke**'s second opera, *Gesualdo*.

Works seven books of madrigals (the last posthumously published of pieces composed in 1594); two books of *Sacrae cantiones*, responds for six voices.

Getreue Alceste, Die, The Faithful Alcestis opera by Schürmann (libretto by J U König), first produced in Brunswick, Germany, in February 1719.

Gevaert, François Auguste (1828–1908) Belgian music historian, theorist, and composer. He studied in Ghent and worked as organist there; later he travelled in Spain, Italy, and Germany. He was director of music at the Paris Opéra 1867–70, and at the Brussels Conservatory from 1871. He wrote several treatises on history, plainsong, and theory.

Works OPERA *Hugues de Zomerghem* (1848), *La Comédie à la ville*, *Georgette* (1848), *Le Billet de Marguerite*, *Les Lavandières de Santarem* (1855), *Quentin Durward* (after Scott, 1858), *Le Diable au moulin*, *Château Trompette*, *La Poularde de Caux* (1861), *Les Deux Amours*, *Le Capitaine Henriot*.

CHORAL Requiem for male voices and orchestra (1853), Christmas cantata, psalm *Super flumina*, cantatas *De nationale verjaerdag* and *Le Retour de l'armée*.

ORCHESTRAL *Fantasia sobre motivos españoles*.

Gezeichneten, Die, The Stigmatized opera by Franz Schreker (libretto by the composer), composed 1913–15 and first produced in Frankfurt, Germany, on 25 April 1918. The crippled Alviano loves Carlotta, but loses her to the handsome Tamare. Carlotta dies as Alviano kills his rival.

Ghedini, Giorgio Federico (1892–1965) Italian composer. He made editions of music by Monteverdi, the Gabrielis, and Frescobaldi. He studied at Turin and Bologna, at first intending to be a conductor. He later taught at the conservatories of Turin, Parma, and Milan, but eventually devoted himself to composition.

Ghedini was born in Cuneo, Piedmont. He studied at Milan Conservatory, where he eventually became director. A follower of Alfredo Casella, his best orchestral pieces are among the neoclassical works which come closest to the spirit of the Italian instrumentalism of Vivaldi's lifetime. He wrote the opera, *Billy Budd* (after Melville), in 1949, but is most renowned for his orchestral pieces such as *Partita* (1926), *Architetture* (1940), and *Concerto dell'albatro* (1945).

Works STAGE eight operas, including *Le baccanti* (after Euripides, produced Milan, 1948) and *Billy Budd* (after Meville, produced Venice, 1949); incidental music for Euripides' *Iphigenia in Tauris*.

CHORAL two Masses and various choral works.

ORCHESTRAL *Partita* (1926), symphonies, *Concerto dell' albatro* (after Melville's *Moby Dick*; 1945) for orchestra; concertos for piano, two pianos, two cellos, and violin; concerto for violin and flute with chamber orchestra.

CHAMBER wind quintet, piano quartet; two string quartets and other chamber music; violin and piano sonata.

OTHER piano works; songs.

Gherardello da Firenze (c.1320/25–1362/63) Italian composer. He wrote sacred works, madrigals, and other pieces, but is famous especially for his caccia (canonic hunting song) 'Tosto che l'alba del bel giorno appare'.

Gherardeschi, Filippo Maria (1738–1808) Italian composer. He was a pupil of Padre Martini at Bologna 1756–61, and became maestro di cappella at the cathedrals of Volterra and Pistoia, and finally, from about 1766 to his death, at San Stefano in Pisa. He was also music director to the court of the Grand Duke of Tuscany.

Works seven operas; church music; keyboard music.

Ghiselin or **Ghiselin-Verbonnet, Jean (c.1455–c.1511)** Flemish composer. He was active especially in Ferrara, Italy. The music printer Ottaviano Petrucci of Venice published several of his works between 1501 and 1507. He composed Masses (a volume was published in 1503), motets, songs, and other pieces.

Ghislanzoni, Antonio (1824–1893) Italian baritone, novelist, music editor, and librettist. He edited the *Gazzetta musicale* of Milan and collaborated on the libretto for Verdi's *Aïda*, as well as writing some 85 libretti of his own.

Ghosts of Versailles, The opera in two acts by John Corigliano (libretto by W H Hoffmann, after Pierre de Beaumarchais), first produced at the New York Metropolitan Opera House on 19 December 1991. Beaumarchais himself makes a ghostly appearance, and attempts to rescue Marie Antoinette from the guillotine.

'Ghost' Trio nickname given to Beethoven's piano trio in D major, Op. 70 no. 1, on account of its slow movement in D minor, which has a mysterious, gloomy, and haunting theme, accompanied frequently by string tremolos. Sketches for the work appear on the same sheet as sketches for a projected opera on Macbeth.

Ghro or **Groh, Johann (c.1575–1627)** German organist and composer. He was organist at Meissen 1604–12 and later became music director at Wesenstein.

Works intradas, pavanas, galliards, and other pieces for several instruments; sacred music.

Giacobbi, Girolamo (1567–c.1629) Italian composer. He was maestro di cappella at the church of San Petronio in Bologna 1604–08.

Works OPERA AND INTERMEDI *Andromeda* (produced Salzburg, 1618; perhaps first opera outside Italy), *L'Aurora ingannata*, *Amor prigioniero*, *La selva dei mirti*, *Il Reno sacrificante*.

CHURCH MUSIC motets, psalms, and other church music.

Giacomelli, Geminiano (c.1692–1740) Italian composer. He was a pupil of Capelli at Parma, and possibly later of Alessandro Scarlatti. He was maestro di cappella at Parma 1719–27 and 1732–37, at Piacenza 1727–32, and at Loreto from 1738.

Works OPERA *Ipermestra* (1724), *Cesare in Egitto* (1735), and about 16 others.

OTHER two oratorios and other sacred works; concert arias.

Giannettini, Antonio (1648–1721) Italian composer. He sang at St Mark's, Venice, about 1674–86, and was maestro di cappella at the ducal court of Modena from 1686. He produced his first opera, *Medea in Atene*, in Venice in 1675.

Works OPERA *Temistocle* (1683), *Artaserse* (1705). SACRED MUSIC oratorios, cantatas, motets, psalms.

Giannini, Vittorio (1903–1966) US composer, brother of Dusolina Giannini. He studied at the Juilliard School, New York, with Rubin Goldmark and taught there from 1939; he taught at the Curtis Institute from 1956. His music reflects his Italian ancestry.

Works OPERA *Lucedia* (1934), *The Scarlet Letter* (1938), *Beauty and the Beast* (1938), *The Taming of the Shrew* (1953), *The Harvest* (1961), *The Servant of Two Masters* (1967).

ORCHESTRAL symphony *In Memoriam Theodore Roosevelt* (1935) and four numbered symphonies; three divertimenti; piano concerto (1937).

CHORAL *Stabat Mater* and Requiem (1937).

OTHER chamber music and songs.

Gianni Schicchi one-act opera forming part of Puccini's *Il ➔ trittico*.

'Giant's Fugue' nickname of Bach's fugal chorale prelude on 'Wir glauben all', in Part III of the *Clavierübung*, so named because of a striding figure in the pedals.

Giardini, Felice de (1716–1796) Italian violinist and composer. He played in the opera orchestras in Rome and Naples, visited Germany in 1748, and then settled in London, England, where he succeeded Michael Festing as leader of the Italian opera orchestra at the King's Theatre in 1752. He played and taught there until 1784, when he retired to Italy, but he reappeared in London in 1790 and died during a tour of Russia.

Giardini was born in Turin. He was a chorister at Milan Cathedral and later a pupil of Giovanni Battista Somis in Turin.

Works STAGE operas *Enea e Lavinia* (1764), *Il rè pastore* (1765), and others; incidental music for William Mason's *Elfrida*.

ORATORIO *Ruth* (with Avison).

ORCHESTRAL twelve violin concertos.

CHAMBER 21 string quartets, six string quintets, seven sets of string trios; sonatas for violin and piano; violin duets.

Giasone, Jason opera by Pietro Cavalli (libretto by G A Cicognini), after the Greek myth of Jason and the Argonauts; it was first produced at the Teatro San Cassiano, Venice, Italy, probably on 5 January 1649. It tells how Jason gets the golden fleece and falls in love with Medea, but in the end returns to his first love, Hypsipyle.

Gibbons, Orlando (1583–1625) English composer. He wrote sacred anthems, instrumental fantasias, and madrigals including *The Silver Swan* for five voices (1612). From a family of musicians, he became organist at Westminster Abbey, London, in 1623.

He was brought up in Cambridge, where he took a degree in music in 1606. He was a singer at the Chapel Royal from 1603 and organist there from about 1615 until his death. Oxford awarded him an honorary PhD in 1622, and the following year he was appointed organist at Westminster Abbey. He died suddenly in Canterbury while waiting to officiate at Charles I's marriage service, for which he had written music.

Works CHURCH MUSIC Anglican church music (five services, about 13 full anthems, and about 25 verse anthems).

VOCAL 20 madrigals; *Cries of London* for voices and strings.

STRINGS 30 fantasies for strings, four *In Nomine* for strings, two pavans and two galliards for strings.

KEYBOARD 16 keyboard fantasies, six sets of variations for keyboard, and other keyboard pieces.

Gibbs, C(ecil) Armstrong (1889–1960) English composer. He was educated at Winchester College and Trinity College, Cambridge, where he studied music with Edward Dent, and later at the Royal College of Music in London, where he became a professor of composition.

Works STAGE incidental music to Maeterlinck's *The Betrothal* (1921); comic opera *The Blue Peter* (A P Herbert, 1923); play with music *Midsummer Madness* (Clifford Bax); Nativity play *The Three Kings*.

CHORAL AND ORCHESTRAL cantata *The Birth of Christ* (1929), Passion according to St Luke, choral symphony *Odysseus*; *La Belle Dame sans merci* (Keats, 1928), *The Highwayman* (Alfred Noyes), and *Deborah and Barak* for chorus and orchestra.

ORCHESTRAL symphony in E major.

CHAMBER string quartet in A major.

OTHER songs.

Gibbs, Joseph (1699–1788) English organist and composer. He was an organist at various Essex churches, finally at St Mary-le-Tower, Ipswich, from 1748 until his death. His most important publication is a set of eight violin sonatas (dating from about 1746); six string quartets (from about 1777) and organ music also survive.

Gibson, Alexander (1926–1995) Scottish conductor. He co-founded Scottish Opera in 1962; *Les Troyens* (1969) and *Der Ring des Nibelungen* (1971) were notable achievements.

He studied in Scotland and London, and spent the 1950s with Sadlers Wells Opera and the British Broadcasting Corporation (BBC) Scottish Symphony Orchestra. He was principal conductor with the Scottish National Orchestra 1959–84. His US debut was with the Detroit Symphony Orchestra in 1970, and he was principal guest conductor with the Houston Symphony Orchestra from 1981. In 1990 he conducted *Tosca* with Scottish Opera, *Otello* for Kentucky Opera, and *Tristan* at the Bruckner Festival, Linz, Austria.

giga (Italian 'jig') Italian form of the 16th-century English jig; see ➤ **gigue**.

gigue lively dance form which developed in two directions, one French, one Italian (*giga*), probably from the 16th-century English jig. The French variety, popular in France during the early 1700s, is in a moderate or fast tempo (6/4 or 6/8) while the Italian variety is quicker (12/8).

In musical notation, the writing of the French form is characterized by wide leaps and dotted rhythms. It is more contrapuntal than most other dance forms of the period, similar in style to a ➤ **fugue** with an inverted subject (principal melody) for the second theme. The Italian variety is characterized by 'running' figures and few leaps. It is non-fugal with a more obvious harmonic framework. The gigue came to be used, more often than not, as the last movement of a baroque ➤ **suite**. Composers of the more common French form include Bach, Handel, and Johann Froberger.

Gilbert, Anthony (1934–) English composer. He studied at Morley College under Anthony Milner and Walter Goehr. He has taught in Manchester and London and has worked as a music editor.

Works OPERA *The Scene Machine*, one-act opera (produced Kassel, 1971).

ORCHESTRAL *Sinfonia* for chamber orchestra (1965), *Regions* for two chamber orchestras (1969), Symphony (1973), *Towards Asavari* for piano and small orchestra (1978), *Dream Carousels* for wind orchestra (1988).

VOCAL *Cantata* (1972), *The Chakravaka Bird* song drama for radio (1977), *Beastly Jingles* for soprano and ensemble (1984), *Certain Lights Reflect-*

ing for soprano and orchestra (1989), *Upstream River* for narrator and ensemble (1991).

CHAMBER *Vasanta with Dancing* for chamber ensemble (1981), two string quartets (1986–87), *Tree of Singing Names* for chamber orchestra (1989, revised 1993).

Gilbert, Henry (Franklin Belknap) (1868–1928) US composer. He studied at Boston and became a businessman, but later devoted himself to composition. He often used ragtime and African-American tunes for his thematic material.

Works STAGE symphonic prologue to Synge's *Riders to the Sea* (1913), ballet *The Dance in Place Congo* (after G W Cable; 1918).

VOICES AND ORCHESTRA *Salammbô's Invocation to Tanith* (after Flaubert) for soprano and orchestra; *Indian Sketches* and *Hymn to America* for chorus and orchestra.

ORCHESTRAL *Americanesque*, *Comedy Overture on Negro Themes* (1906), three *American Dances* (1911), *Negro Rhapsody* (1913), *Legend*, and *Negro Episode* for orchestra.

PIANO AND VOICE *The Island of Fay* (after Poe, 1923); *Indian Scenes* and *Negro Dances* for piano; *Pirate Song* (Stevenson) for voice and piano; edition of 100 folk songs.

Gilbert, W(illiam) S(chwenck) (1836–1911) English playwright and librettist. He wrote libretti for operettas with music by Arthur Sullivan, *The* ➤ **Gondoliers**, *The* ➤ **Grand Duke**, ➤ **HMS Pinafore**, ➤ **Iolanthe**, *The* ➤ **Mikado**, ➤ **Patience**, *The* ➤ **Pirates of Penzance**, ➤ **Princess Ida**, ➤ **Ruddigore**, *The* ➤ **Sorcerer**, ➤ **Thespis**, ➤ **Trial by Jury**, *Utopia Limited*, and *The* ➤ **Yeoman of the Guard**.

Giles, Nathaniel (c.1558–1634) English organist and composer. He was organist of Worcester Cathedral 1581–85, and then became organist and choirmaster of St George's Chapel, Windsor. In 1596 he became organist and choirmaster of the Chapel Royal in London, and took the official titles of Gentleman and Master of the Children on the death of William Hunnis in 1597. He collaborated with the playwright Ben Jonson at Blackfriars Theatre, London, from 1600.

He received a PhD in music from Oxford University in 1622.

Works services, anthems, motets; madrigal 'Cease Now, Vain Thoughts'.

Gilson, Paul (1865–1942) Belgian composer. He was appointed professor of harmony at the Brussels Conservatory in 1899 and at the Antwerp Conservatory in 1904. He was also music critic of the newspapers *Le Soir*, 1906–14, and then of *Le Midi*.

His teachers included François Gevaert. He won the Belgian Prix de Rome in 1889.

Works STAGE operas *Prinses Zonneschijn* and *Zeevolk* (1895); ballets *La Captive* and *Daphne*.

CHORAL oratorio *Le Démon* (after Lermontov); *Francesca da Rimini* (after Dante) for solo voices, chorus, and orchestra (1892).

VOCAL *La Mer* for reciter and orchestra (1892).

Ginastera, Alberto Evaristo (1916–1983) Argentine composer. His early works, including his *Pampeana No. 3* (1954), are mostly in a nationalistic style, but after 1958 he turned to modern techniques of ➤ **serialism**, aleatory rhythms (see ➤ **aleatory music**), and the use of microtones. He is best known for his operas, which renounce his earlier nationalist style for more advanced atonal techniques: *Don Rodrigo* (1964), *Bomarzo* (1967), and *Beatrix Cenci* (1971).

He studied with Athos Palma at the National Conservatory of Buenos Aires and graduated in 1938. He visited the USA 1945–47, and from 1948 taught in Buenos Aires, where he was director of the Centre for Advanced Musical Studies from 1963. After *Bomarzo* was banned in Argentina for alleged obscenities in the ballet, he left Buenos Aires and lived in the USA from 1968 and Europe from 1970.

Works STAGE operas *Don Rodrigo* (1964), *Bomarzo* (1967), *Beatrix Cenci* (1971); ballets *Panambi* (1940), *Estancia* (1941).

VOCAL psalms for chorus and orchestra, cantata *Bomarzo* for narrator, baritone, and orchestra (1964).

ORCHESTRAL *Variaciones concertantes* for orchestra (1953), *Concerto per corde* (1965), *Estudios sinfónicos* (1967), two piano concertos (1961, 1972), violin concerto (1963), two cello concertos (1968, 1980).

CHAMBER three string quartets (1948, 1953, 1973), three piano sonatas (1952, 1981, 1982), piano quintet (1963), cello sonata (1979).

Gines Pérez, Juan (1548–1612) Spanish composer. He held a church appointment in his native town at the age of 14. He was maestro di cappella and director of the choir school at Valencia 1581–95. In 1595 he returned home as canon at Orihuela Cathedral.

Works motets, psalms; secular Spanish songs; contributions to the Mystery play performed annually at Elche, near Alicante.

Gintzler, Simon (c.1500–after 1550) German composer. His collection of lute music was published in Venice, Italy, in 1547, and he also contributed to Hans Gerle's *Eyn Newes ... Lautenbuch*, published in Nuremberg in 1552.

Gioconda, La opera by Amilcare Ponchielli (libretto by Arrigo Boito, based on Victor Hugo's *Angelo*), first produced at La Scala, Milan, Italy, on 8 April 1876. In the story, Gioconda loves Enzo, but so does Laura. The evil Barnaba does his best to thwart everyone's happiness, eventually causing Gioconda's suicide.

giocoso (Italian 'jocose') in musical notation, merry, humorous.

gioielli della Madonna, I, The Jewels of the Madonna opera by Ermanno Wolf-Ferrari (libretto by E Golisciani and C Zangarini), first produced, in German, at the Kurfürsten-Oper, Berlin, Germany, on 23 December 1911. It tells how Gennaro wins Mariella by stealing the jewels of the Madonna, but the rival Raffaele intervenes and the lovers kill themselves.

Giordani, Tommaso (c.1730–1806) Italian composer. The son of a travelling opera impresario, he produced his first opera with his father's company in London, England, in 1756. He subsequently lived chiefly in London (he was director at the King's Theatre, Haymarket 1768–83) and Dublin, Ireland, and composed a large number of theatrical works for both cities. He was unrelated to either Carmine or Giuseppe Giordani.

Works STAGE operas *La comediante fatta cantatrice* (1756), *L'eroe cinese* (1766), *Love in Disguise* (1766), *Il padre e il figlio rivali, Artaserse, Il re pastore* (1778), *Phillis at Court*, and others, about 50 in all; songs for Sheridan's *The Critic*.

SACRED MUSIC oratorio, *Isaac*; church music.

INSTRUMENTAL concertos and sonatas for piano and other instruments; string quartets, trios.

OTHER songs.

Giordano, Umberto (1867–1948) Italian composer. He was a popular composer in the tradition of romantic realism that was the vogue at the end of the 19th century, and most of his themes were melodramatic. He is best known for the operas *Andrea Chénier* (1896), set in the French Revolution, *Fedora* (1898), and the comic *Il rè/The King* (1929).

Giordano was born in Foggia, the son of an artisan. He was allowed to learn music as best he could, but in the end studied at the Naples Conservatory under Paolo Serrao. He attracted the attention of the publisher Edoardo Sonzogno (1836–1920) with the opera *Marina* (1889), written while he was still a student, and soon became very successful with a series of stage works.

Works OPERA *Marina* (1889), *Mala vita* (1892), *Regina Diaz* (1894), *Andrea Chénier* (1896), *Fedora* (after Sardou, 1898), *Siberia* (1903), *Marcella, Mese Mariano, Madame Sans-Gêne* (after Sardou and Moreau, 1915), *Giove a Pompei* (with Franchetti), *La cena delle beffe* (1924), *Il rè* (1929).

giorno di regno, Un, ossia Il finto Stanislao, A Day's Reign, or The False Stanislas opera by Verdi (libretto by Felice Romani, used earlier by Adalbert Gyrowetz for his ➤ *Finto Stanislao*), first produced at La Scala, Milan, Italy, on 5 September 1840. It is Verdi's only comic opera apart from *Falstaff*. In the story, Belfiore is disguised as King Stanislaus to protect the sovereign and prevents his love, the widow Marchesa, from marrying another.

Giovanna d'Arco, Joan of Arc opera by Verdi (libretto by T Solera, based on Schiller's drama *Die Jungfrau von Orleans*), first produced at La Scala, Milan, Italy, on 15 February 1845. It describes how Joan rallies the troops of the defeated Charles VII of France. Although denounced as a follower of Satan by her father, Giacomo, she goes on to save the day, but falls in battle.

Giovanna di Guzman alternative name for *Les* ➔ *Vêpres siciliennes*, an opera by Verdi.

Giovannelli, Ruggiero (c.1560–1625) Italian composer. After holding various church apointments in Rome, he succeeded Giovanni Palestrina as maestro di cappella at St Peter's in 1594, and was maestro di cappella of the Sistine Chapel 1614–24. At the request of Pope Paul V he contributed to a new edition of the Gradual.

Works Masses, Miserere, and other church music; six books of madrigals, one of canzonette and villanelle.

Giovannini (died 1782) Italian composer. The customary identification of Giovannini with the comte de St Germain remains without proof. The only works extant under the name Giovannini are a handful of songs (including 'Willst du dein Herz mir schenken' in Bach's *Anna Magdalena Notebook*) and eight violin sonatas.

Giove in Argo, Jupiter in Argos opera by Antonio Lotti (libretto by A M Lucchini), first produced at the Redoutensaal, Dresden, Germany, on 25 October 1717, the new opera house not being ready. The latter was opened with the same work on 3 September 1719. (An English adaptation of the same libretto, under the title *Jupiter in Argos*, was set by Handel and first produced at the King's Theatre, London, England, on 1 May 1739.)

gioventù di Enrico V, La, The Youth of Henry V opera by Giovanni Pacini (libretto by J Ferretti, partly based on Shakespeare's *Henry IV*), first produced at the Teatro Valle, Rome, Italy, on 26 December 1820.

Gipps, Ruth (1921–1999) English composer, pianist, and oboist. In 1944–45 she played second oboe and English horn in the City of Birmingham Symphony Orchestra. She conducted the London Repertoire Orchestra 1955–86, and was a professor at the Royal College of Music, London, from 1967.

She studied under her mother at the Bexhill School of Music and later under Ralph Vaughan Williams at the Royal College of Music. MBE 1981.

Works BALLET *Sea Nymph*; five symphonies

(1942–80), other orchestral music, including six concertos, and chamber works.

Giraud de Borneil (1156–1200), also known as **Guiraut de Bornelh** Provençal ➔ troubadour. He was a professional poet who wrote in most of the lyric genres. His love songs, often complex in thought and expression despite his defence of a simple style, were praised by Dante for their moral seriousness.

Girdlestone, C(uthbert) M(orton) (1895–1975) English scholar. He was educated at the Sorbonne in Paris and at Cambridge, where he became lecturer in French. He was professor of French at King's College, Newcastle-upon-Tyne, 1926–61, and wrote the books *Mozart et ses concertos pour piano* and *Jean-Philippe Rameau*.

Girl of the [Golden] West opera by Puccini; see ➔ *fanciulla del West, La*.

Giselle, ou Les Wilis ballet by Adolphe Adam (choreography by Jean Coralli, on a story by Heinrich Heine, adapted by Théophile Gautier), first produced at the Paris Opéra, France, on 28 June 1841.

gittern medieval guitar with four strings, played with a plectrum. It survived in England until around 1400; the term was then applied to other members of the guitar family in the 16th–17th centuries.

Giuliano opera by Riccardo Zandonai (libretto by A Rossato, based on Flaubert's *Saint Julien l'Hospitalier*), first produced at the Teatro San Carlo, Naples, Italy, on 4 February 1928.

Giulietta e Romeo, Juliet and Romeo opera by Vaccai (libretto by Felice Romani, after Shakespeare's sources for *Romeo and Juliet*), first produced at the Teatro della Canobbiana, Milan, Italy, on 31 October 1825.

It is also the title of an opera by Riccardo Zandonai (libretto by A Rossato, after Shakespeare), first produced at the Teatro Costanzi, Rome, Italy, on 14 February 1922.

A further opera with the same title was composed by Niccolò Zingarelli (libretto by G M Foppa) and first produced at La Scala, Milan, on 30 January 1796.

Giulio Cesare opera by Gian Francesco Malipiero (libretto by the composer, based on Shakespeare's *Julius Caesar*), first produced at the Teatro Carlo Felice, Genoa, Italy, on 8 February 1936.

Giulio Cesare in Egitto, Julius Caesar in Egypt opera by Handel (libretto by Nicola Francesco Haym), first produced at the King's Theatre, Haymarket, London, England, on 20 February 1724. It tells how Julius Caesar beats off his rivals in love and war to marry Cleopatra.

Giulio Sabino opera by Giuseppe Sarti (libretto by P Giovannini), first produced at the Teatro San Benedetto, Venice, Italy, in January 1781.

giuramento, II, The Vow opera by Giuseppe Mercadante (libretto by Giacomo Rossi, based on Victor Hugo's *Angelo*), first produced at La Scala, Milan, Italy, on 10 March 1837. In the story, Manfredo commands Bianca to take poison after her adultery with Viscardo, but the envious Elaisa substitutes a sleeping potion.

Giustini, Lodovico (1685–1743) Italian composer and organist. In 1732 he published a book of sonatas, probably the first published music written specifically for the piano, as distinct from music for keyboard instruments in general.

Giustinian, Leonardo (1383–1446) Italian poet. He wrote love poems for musical settings, some of which he provided himself, which were called after him as late as the 16th century.

Giustino opera by Handel (altered libretto from Nicolo Beregani), first produced at Covent Garden, London, England, on 16 February 1737. In the story, Giustino joins Anastasius in battle against Vitalian. Later Giustino and Vitalian join forces to defeat the usurping Amantius, who has imprisoned Anastasius. The opera concludes with Giustino united with Leocasta, whom he has rescued earlier.

giusto (Italian 'just', 'strictly') term used in musical notation, as in *tempo giusto*.

Glagolitic Mass work by Leoš ➔ Janáček for soloists, chorus, organ, and orchestra (text by M Weingart from the Ordinary of the Mass in Old Church Slavonic). It was composed in 1926 and first performed in Brno, Czechoslovakia (Czech Republic), on 5 December 1927.

The piece was written to celebrate the independence of Czechoslovakia (now the Czech Republic); as part of this Janáček wished to use the oldest Slavonic version of the Ordinary that could be found. He believed that the 9th-century manuscript which was found and transcribed for him was in a language called 'Glagolitic', however he was mistaken: Glagolitic was the liturgical alphabet in which it was written. Janáček's score uses Cyrillic and Roman, but the distinctive name has remained.

Glanville-Hicks, Peggy (1912–1990) Australian composer. In 1938 her choral suite was performed at the International Society for Contemporary Music festival in London, England.

She studied at the Melbourne Conservatory and from the age of 19 under Ralph Vaughan Williams, Gordon Jacob, and Reginald Morris at

the Royal College of Music in London. She won a scholarship in 1932 and another in 1935, which enabled her to travel and to study further with Egon Wellesz in Vienna, Austria, and Nadia Boulanger in Paris, France. In 1939 she married the composer Stanley Bate, with whom she went to the USA, living in New York until 1958 and Greece from 1959.

Works OPERA *Caedmon* (1934), *The Transposed Heads* (1953), *The Glittering Gate* (1959), *Nausicaa* (1961), *Sappho* (1963).

ORCHESTRAL *Sinfonietta*, *Prelude*, and *Scherzo*, *Span*, *Suite*, and *Music for Robots* for orchestra; piano concerto, flute concerto.

VOCAL choral suite (Fletcher) for women's voices, oboe, and strings; six Housman songs.

CHAMBER *Concertino da camera* for flute, clarinet, bassoon, and piano.

Glareanus, Henricus (1488–1563), born **Heinrich Loris** Swiss music theorist. He studied the relationship between the Greek and the church modes and wrote treatises, notably *Isagoge in musicen* (1516) and *Dodecachordon* (1547), containing his new theory of twelve church modes.

He studied music at Berne and Cologne, Germany, and taught at Basel, Switzerland, from 1515 and again from 1522, after holding a professorship in Paris, France, from 1517 on the recommendation of Erasmus of Rotterdam. In 1529 he settled at Freiburg im Breislau, Germany.

Glass, Louis (Christian August) (1864–1936) Danish composer. He is best known for his symphonies, which include no. 3 *Skovsymfoni/Wood Symphony* (1901) and no. 5 *Svastica* (1911).

Glass studied at the Brussels Conservatory, Belgium, and came under the influence of César Franck. He was a contemporary of Carl Nielsen but his music more often recalls Austrian models of the same period. Some of his symphonies have been revived in recent years by Edward Downes.

Works ORCHESTRAL symphonies no. 1 (1893), no. 2 (1899), no. 3 *Skovsymfoni/Wood Symphony* (1901), no. 4 (1911), no. 5 *Svastica* (1911), no. 6 *Skjoldungeaet/Birth of the Scyldings* (1926); concertos for oboe, violin, and cello.

CHAMBER four string quartets (1890–1906); string sextet (1892); piano quintet (1896); cello sonata and two violin sonatas.

OTHER piano music and songs.

Glass, Philip (1937–) US composer. While a student of French music teacher Nadia ➔ Boulanger he became strongly influenced by Indian music; his work is characterized by repeated rhythmic figures that are continually expanded and modified. His compositions include the operas *Einstein on the Beach* (1976), *Akhnaten* (1984), *The Making of the Representative for Planet 8* (1988), and the *'Low' Symphony* (1992) on themes from English pop singer David Bowie's *Low* album.

He studied at the Juilliard School, New York, and with Boulanger in Paris, France. Under the influence of Indian and North African music he has developed a technique (minimalism) whereby melodic ideas are not developed but are placed side by side in 'timeless' repetitions. He achieved early fame in New York with the $4\frac{1}{2}$-hour *Einstein on the Beach*, and had further success with the Gandhi opera *Satyagraha* (1980), and *Akhnaten* (1984). Later works seemed to lack fresh musical ideas, but he was back on form with an opera for Columbus Day, given at the New York Metropolitan Opera House in 1992, and the musical work, *Symphony No 5* (2000), which brings together writings from different religions as well as a range of music and voice.

Works OPERA *Einstein on the Beach* (Avignon and New York Metropolitan Opera House, 1976), *Satyagraha* (Rotterdam, 1980), *The Photographer* (Amsterdam, 1982), *Civil Wars* (1982–84), *Akhnaten* (Stuttgart, 1984), *The Juniper Tree* (Cambridge, Massachusetts, 1985, with Robert Moran), *The Fall of the House of Usher* (Cambridge, 1988), *The Making of the Representative for Planet 8* (Houston, 1988), *1,000 Airplanes on the Roof* (Vienna Airport, 1988), *Hydrogen Jukebox* (Charleston, South Carolina, 1990), *The Voyage* (New York Metropolitan Opera, 1992), *Symphony No 5* (2000).

INSTRUMENTAL ENSEMBLE WORKS including *Music with Changing Parts* (1970), *Music in 12 Parts* (1971–74), violin concerto (1987), string quartet (1993).

glass harmonica or **armonica** musical instrument based on the principle of playing a wine glass with a wet finger. It consists of a graded series of glass bowls nested on a spindle and resting in a trough partly filled with water. Rotated by a foot pedal, it emits pure tones of unchanging intensity when touched either by the fingers or mechanically. It was devised by Benjamin Franklin; Mozart, Beethoven, and Schubert all wrote pieces for it.

Glazunov, Aleksandr Konstantinovich (1865–1936) Russian composer. He achieved fame with his first symphony, which was written when he was only 17. He absorbed a range of influences, from his teacher Rimsky-Korsakov's orchestrational skill to Tchaikovsky's lyricism. His own style fits between that of the Russian national school of The ➤ **Five** and that of the Western European 'cosmopolitan' composers. He made a significant impact as a teacher on the following generation of composers, including Prokofiev and Shostakovich.

Glazunov was born in St Petersburg. After being taught music at home as a child, he studied with Rimsky-Korsakov from 1880 and finished his course in 18 months, having a first symphony ready for performance early in 1882. Mitrofan Belaiev arranged a concert of his works in 1884 and began to publish them. He visited Western Europe in 1884, and his music thereafter reconciled current European musical trends with Russian influences from Tchaikovsky and Borodin. In 1897 he conducted the premiere of Rachmaninov's first symphony, allegedly while drunk. He was appointed director of the St Petersburg Conservatory in 1905, and wrote little after that to augment his enormous earlier output. He completed several of Borodin's unfinished works, notably the overture to *Prince Igor*. He left Russia in 1928 and settled in Paris, France.

Works STAGE ballets *Raymonda* (1897) and *The Seasons* (1899).

ORCHESTRAL eight symphonies (1881–1906), symphonic poem *Stenka Razin* (1885), violin concerto (1904), two piano concertos, concerto for saxophone.

CHAMBER seven string quartets (1881–1930), string quintet; many works for piano including two sonatas and *Theme and Variations*.

glee ➤ **part song**, usually for male voices, in not less than three parts, much cultivated by English composers in the 18th and early 19th centuries. The word is derived from the Anglo-Saxon *gliw* ('entertainment'), particularly musical entertainment. Samuel Webbe, Richard Stevens, John Callcott, William Horsley, Thomas ➤ **Attwood**, Jonathan ➤ **Battishill**, Benjamin ➤ **Cooke**, and others cultivated the glee.

Gleichnisarie German musical term; see ➤ **parable aria**.

gliding tone musical tone, continuously rising or falling in pitch between preset notes, produced by a synthesizer.

Glière, Reinhold Moritzovich (1875–1956) Russian composer. He made research into Azerbaijani, Uzbek, and Ukrainian folk song and based some of his later works on it. In 1939 he became chairman of the Organizing Committee of USSR composers.

He learnt the violin as a child, but soon began to compose and was sent to the Kiev School of Music and later to the Moscow Conservatory, where he was taught by Anton Arensky, Sergey Taneiev, and Mikhail Ippolitov-Ivanov. He taught at the Gnessin School of Music in Moscow and at the Kiev Conservatory, of which he became director in 1914, but settled in Moscow in 1920 (professor of composition at the Conservatory until 1941). Among his pupils was Prokofiev, who said of him 'Glière is fat and middle-aged, rather like a well-fed cat'.

Works STAGE *Shakh-Senem* (1926), *Leyli and Mej-*

nun (1937), *Rachel* (after Maupassant's *Mlle Fifi*; 1943), *Ghulsara* (1949); ballet *The Red Poppy* (1927); incidental music for Sophocles' *Oedipus Rex*, Aristophanes' *Lysistrata*, Beaumarchais's *Marriage of Figaro*, and others.

ORCHESTRAL three symphonies (No. 3, *Ilia Muromets*, 1909–11), three symphonic poems, concert overtures; harp concerto, fantasy for wind instruments.

VOCAL concerto for soprano and orchestra; 22 Op. nos of songs.

CHAMBER four string quartets (1900–48); three string sextets, string octet; many instrumental pieces; 18 Op. nos of piano music.

Glinka, Mikhail Ivanovich (1804–1857) Russian composer. He broke away from the prevailing Italian influence and turned to Russian folk music as the inspiration for his opera *A Life for the Tsar* (originally *Ivan Susanin*, 1836). His later works include the opera *Ruslan and Lyudmila* (1842) and the instrumental fantasia *Kamarinskaya* (1848). He is often regarded as the founder of Russian music, exerting a strong influence on two generations of composers, most notably Mussorgsky, Tchaikovsky, and Stravinsky.

The son of a wealthy landowner, Glinka was born on his father's estate at Novospasskoye. He was sent to school in St Petersburg 1817–22. He picked up lessons casually, including some piano lessons from John Field, and also studied violin and theory. At his father's wish he worked in the Ministry of Communications 1824–28, but he gave it up, not being obliged to earn a living and wishing to devote himself to music. He visited Italy 1830–33, where he had lessons from Francesco Basili in Milan, then Vienna, Austria, and lastly Berlin, Germany, where he studied under Siegfried Dehn. On his father's death he returned to Russia, settled in St Petersburg, and married in 1835. There he worked at *A Life for the Tsar* and succeeded in having it produced in 1836; it was an immediate success, combining nationalist musical elements with a patriotic tale composed at a time of unrest. *Ruslan and Lyudmila* was delayed by domestic troubles and the separation from his wife in 1841, and was produced in 1842. In 1844 he visited Paris, France, and Spain, in 1848 Warsaw, Poland, and France again in 1852–54. It was during a visit to Berlin, 1856–57, that he died.

Glinka freed Russian opera from German and Italian influences and at the same time introduced harmonic innovations that were to bear fruit in the work of nearly all the later nationalist Russian composers. He wrote a vast amount of music for one who was trained so late, including over 80 songs, and died comparatively early.

Works STAGE operas *A Life for the Tsar* (formerly *Ivan Susanin*, 1836) and *Ruslan and Lyudmila* (1842); incidental music to Count Kukolnik's *Prince Kholmsky*.

ORCHESTRAL *Jota aragonesa* (*Capriccio brillante*), *A Night in Madrid* (1851), *Kamarinskaya* (1848), *Valse-Fantaisie*.

CHAMBER string quartet in F major; trio for clarinet, bassoon, and piano; sextet for piano and strings.

OTHER about 40 piano pieces; Polish hymn and *Memorial Cantata* for chorus; about 85 songs; some vocal duets and quartets.

glissando in music, a rapid uninterrupted scale produced by sliding the finger across a keyboard or harp strings, or along the fingerboard of a violin or guitar. In wind instruments, it corresponds to a gliding tone, a famous example being the clarinet glissando at the start of George Gershwin's *Rhapsody in Blue* (1924).

As a direction in musical notation, it is frequently abbreviated to 'gliss'.

Globokar, Vinko (1934–   ) Yugoslav composer and trombonist. His avant-garde virtuosity encouraged Karlheinz Stockhausen, Mauricio Kagel, and Luciano Berio to write works for him.

He studied in Ljubljana and at the Paris Conservatory, France, and later with René Leibowitz and Berio. In 1968 he was appointed professor of trombone at the Cologne Musikhochschule, Germany. With Heinz Holliger he gave the UK first performance of Toru Takemitsu's *Gemeaux* at Edinburgh, Scotland, in 1989. He was the featured composer at Dartington, England, in 1992.

Works VOICES AND ORCHESTRA *Voie* for narrator, chorus, and orchestra (1965), *Traumdeutung* for four choruses and instruments (1967), *Concerto grosso* for five solo players, orchestra, and chorus (1970), *Carrousel* for four voices and 16 instruments (1977).

INSTRUMENTAL *Fluide* for twelve instruments (1967), *Ausstrahlungen* for soloists and 20 players (1971), *Discours I–IX* for various instruments (1967–93), *Les Emigrés* (1982–86), *L'Armonia Drammatica* (1986–89), *Labour* (1992), *Blinde Zeit* (1993).

glockenspiel tuned percussion instrument of light metal bars mounted on a carrying frame for use in military bands or on a standing frame for use in an orchestra (in which form it resembles a small xylophone or celesta). It is played with hammers or via a piano keyboard attachment.

Gloria (Latin *Gloria in excelsis Deo*, 'Glory to God in the highest') second item of the Ordinary of the Mass, following immediately after the ➔ Kyrie. Although the Ambrosian Gloria is sung to an even simpler tone, the melody printed with Mass XV of the Vatican edition is probably the oldest.

In addition to the original melody, the text has

Glo- ri - a .... in ex - cel- sis De - o
Et in ter - ra pax ho- mi- ni- bus bonae vo- lun- ta - tis
Lau - .... da- mus te
Be - ne - .... di - ci - mus te
Ad - o - .... -ra - mus te
Glo - ri - ...... fi - ca - mus te
Gra - ti - as a - gi- mus ti - bi propter magnam glo - ri- am tu - am

The plainsong melody of the Gloria found in Mass XV of the Vatican edition.

been set to music alone or as part of a complete mass by many composers including Antonio Vivaldi, Ludwig van Beethoven, and Francis Poulenc.

Gloriana opera by Benjamin Britten (libretto by William Plomer), first produced at the Royal Opera House, Covent Garden, London, on 8 June 1953. In the plot, Robert Devereux, Earl of Essex, and Lord Mountjoy compete for Queen Elizabeth I's attention. Essex is appointed to suppress an Irish rebellion but fails, himself becoming rebellious to the crown. Reluctantly the Queen has him beheaded.

Glover, Jane (1949–   ) English conductor and musicologist. She studied at Oxford University, where she wrote a doctoral thesis on Francesco Cavalli, which was later published as a book. She made her professional debut as a conductor at the Wexford Festival, Ireland, in 1975, with her own edition of Cavalli's *Eritrea*.

She started her Glyndebourne career as chorus mistress, then as conductor on tour 1982–85, conducting *Don Giovanni* at the Festival in 1982. She was artistic director of the London Mozart Players 1984–92, and made her Covent Garden debut in 1988 with Mozart's *Die Entführung*. In 1989 she conducted the English National Opera's production of *Don Giovanni*, and in 1992 Gilbert and Sullivan's *Princess Ida*.

Gluck, Christoph Willibald von (1714–1787) Bohemian-German composer. His series of 'reform' operas moved music away from the usual practices of the day, in which the interests of singers were the most important considerations. He felt that music should serve poetry by means of expression and follow the situations of the story without interrupting the action. He therefore replaced the endless recitatives with orchestral accompaniments, which helped improve the dramatic flow. In 1762 his *Orfeo ed Euridice/Orpheus and Eurydice* revolutionized the 18th-century idea of opera by paying more attention to the dramatic aspects of opera and less attention to the formal musical aspects. It was followed by *Alceste/Alcestis* (1767) and *Paride ed Elena/Paris and Helen* (1770).

In 1774 his *Iphigénie en Aulide/Iphigenia in Aulis*, produced in Paris, France, brought to a head the fierce debate over the future of opera in which Gluck's French style had the support of Marie Antoinette, while his Italian rival Niccolò Piccinni had the support of Madame du Barry. With *Armide* (1777) and *Iphigénie en Tauride/Iphigenia in Tauris* (1779), Gluck won a complete victory over Piccinni.

Born in Erasbach, Bavaria, the son of a forester, he left home in the face of his parents' opposition to music and entered Prague University in 1731. About 1735 in Vienna, Austria, he entered the service of Prince Melzi, with whom he went to Italy. He may have studied under Giovanni-Battista Sammartini in Milan, where he made his debut as an opera composer in 1741 with *Artaserse* (libretto by Pietro Metastasio). A number of operas followed, all in the conventional Italian form. He went to England, perhaps with Prince Lobkowitz, in 1745, possibly visiting Paris on the way. In London, he met George Frideric Handel, produced two operas, and appeared as a performer on the glass harmonica. In about 1747 he joined the Mingotti touring opera company, later becoming their Kapellmeister (director), and travelled widely.

Gluck married in 1750 and settled in Vienna two years later. He was connected with the court as Kapellmeister to Maria Theresa from 1754, though without official title (only in 1774 was he appointed court composer). Under the management of Count Durazzo the Viennese theatre moved away from conventional *opera seria* (treating classical subjects in a formal style), and Gluck wrote a number of French *opéras-comiques* (including spoken dialogue). The dramatic ballet *Don Juan*, using the choreographer Jean-Georges Noverre's ideas on modern dance, was produced in 1761.

In *Orfeo ed Euridice/Orpheus and Eurydice*, Gluck and his librettist Raniero de Calzabigi placed more importance on the drama of the opera rather than the musical side. The aims of this 'reform' were set out in the prefaces to *Alceste/Alcestis* and *Paride ed Elena/Paris and Helen*. In many ways, such as making the chorus and ballet more important, these works adopted features of French opera, and Gluck now turned to Paris, where *Iphigénie en Aulide/Iphegenia in Aulis* was produced in 1774, followed by French versions of *Orfeo* and *Alceste* in 1774 and 1776, and *Armide* in 1777. Gluck was reluctantly involved in a squabble between his supporters and the partisans of Piccinni, but this was settled by the triumph of his *Iphigénie en Tauride* (1779). His last opera for Paris, *Echo et Narcisse/Echo and Narcissus* (1779), was unsuccessful, and he returned to Vienna, where he remained until his death.

Gluck's idea of a drama in which music and stage action work together had a huge influence on later composers. Richard Wagner's idea of the *Gesamtkunstwerk* ('total art-work') is an obvious successor. Although *Orfeo ed Euridice* has remained popular, the rest of Gluck's output is still relatively neglected.

Works OPERA SERIA *Artaserse* (1741), *Demetrio*, *Demofoonte* (1743), *Il Tigrane*, *La Sofonisba* (1744), *Ipermestra*, *La caduta de' giganti* (1746), *Artamene* (1746), *Le nozze d'Ercole e d'Ebe*, *La Semiramide riconosciuta* (1748), *La contesa dei numi* (1749), *Ezio* (1750), *La clemenza di Tito* (1752), *Le cinesi*, *Antigono*, *Il rè pastore* (1756), *Telemaco* (1765).

FRENCH OPERAS-COMIQUES *L'Îsle de Merlin* (1758), *La Cythère assiégée* (1759), *L'Arbre enchanté* (1759), *L'Ivrogne corrigé*, *Le Cadi dupé* (1761), *La Rencontre imprévue* (1764).

'REFORM' OPERA *Orfeo ed Euridice* (1762), *Alceste* (1767), *Paride ed Elena* (1770).

FRENCH OPERA FOR PARIS *Iphigénie en Aulide* (1774), *Orphée et Euridice* (1774) and *Alceste* (1776; both French versions of the earlier Italian operas), *Armide* (1777), *Iphigénie en Tauride* (1779), *Echo et Narcisse* (1779).

BALLET *Don Juan* (1761), *Semiramide* (1765), and others.

OTHER a number of symphonies, eight trio sonatas, a setting of *De profundis* for chorus and orchestra (1787), and seven settings of Friedrich Klopstock's *Odes*.

Glückliche Hand, Die, The Lucky Hand

opera by Arnold Schoenberg (with libretto by Schoenberg), composed in 1913 and first produced at the Volksoper, Vienna, Austria, on 14 October 1924. It is a symbolic drama in which the artist/humanity is made to face a choice between worldly success and spiritual truth.

Glyndebourne

site of an opera house in East Sussex, England, established in 1934 by John Christie (1882–1962). Operas are staged at an annual summer festival and a touring company is also based there. It underwent extensive rebuilding work in the early 1990s.

Gnecchi, Vittorio (1876–1954)

Italian composer. He studied music in Milan. His first opera, given in Bologna in 1905, was at the centre of great controversy in 1909, when Richard Strauss's opera *Elektra* appeared and showed striking similarities to Gnecchi's music.

Works OPERA *Cassandra* (after Homer's *The Iliad*, 1905) and *La Rosiera* (1927).

ORCHESTRAL heroic poem for orchestra *Notte nel campo di Holoferne*.

Gnessin, Mikhail Fabianovich (1883–1957)

Russian composer and teacher. He studied with Rimsky-Korsakov and Anatol Liadov at the St Petersburg Conservatory and in Germany 1911–14. He settled in Rostov in 1914, in Moscow in 1923, and became professor at the Leningrad Conservatory in 1936; his pupils included Aram Khachaturian and Tikhon Khrennikov. His work is influenced by Jewish music.

Works STAGE operas *Youth of Abraham* (1921–23) and *The Maccabees*; incidental music for plays, including Sophocles' *Antigone* and *Oedipus Rex* (1915), Gogol's *The Revisor*, Blok's *The Rose and the Cross*.

VOICES AND ORCHESTRA *The Conqueror Worm* (after Poe) for solo voices, chorus, and orchestra (1913); songs with orchestra.

ORCHESTRAL *Symphonic Fragment* (after Shelley), *Song of Adonis*, and *Fantasia in the Jewish Style* for orchestra.

CHAMBER *Requiem* for piano quintet, *Variations on Jewish Themes* and *Azerbaijan Folksongs* for string quartet, sextet *Adygeya*; violin and piano sonata in G minor, *Sonata-Ballade* for cello and piano.

SONGS song cycles to words by Alexander Blok, Sologub; Jewish folk-song arrangements.

Godard, Benjamin (Louis Paul) (1849–1895)

French composer. In 1878 he tied with Théodore Dubois in gaining the prize in a competition organized by the municipality of Paris with the dramatic symphony *Le Tasse* for solo voices, chorus, and orchestra. In 1885 he established a series of 'modern concerts' without success.

He studied violin and composition at the Paris Conservatory, and became a viola player in chamber music.

Works STAGE operas *Pedro de Zalamea* (1884), *Jocelyn* (1888), *Le Dante* (1890), *La Vivandière*, *Les Guelfes*; incidental music to Shakespeare's *Much Ado about Nothing* and Fabre's *Jeanne d'Arc*.

ORCHESTRAL *Scènes poétiques* (1879), dramatic poem *Diane*, *Symphonie-Ballet*, *Symphonie gothique*, *Symphonie orientale*, and *Symphonie légendaire* for orchestra; two violin concertos, two piano concertos.

CHAMBER three string quartets (1883–93), two piano trios; five violin and piano sonatas.

OTHER piano pieces; over 100 songs.

God Save the King/Queen British national anthem. The melody resembles a composition by John Bull and similar words are found from the 16th century. It has also been attributed to Henry ➤ **Carey**. In its present form it dates from the Jacobite Rebellion of 1745, when it was used as an anti-Jacobite Party song.

In the USA the song 'America', with the first line 'My country, 'tis of thee', is sung to the same tune. Variations on the 'America' theme were composed by Charles Ives in 1891.

Goebel, Reinhard (1952–) German conductor and violinist. He studied in Cologne and with Gustav Leonhardt in Amsterdam, the Netherlands. He founded the Musica Antiqua Cologne in 1973 and has given many concerts of early music throughout Europe, the Americas, and the Far East.

He performed at York Festival, England, in 1989 with music by Giovanni Legrenzi, Johann Schmelzer, and Heinrich Biber. Recordings include Georg Telemann's *Tafelmusik*.

Goehr, (Peter) Alexander (1932–) German-born English composer. He was professor of music at Cambridge from 1976. A lyrical but often hard-edged serialist, he nevertheless usually remained within the forms of the symphony and traditional chamber works, and later turned to tonal and even neo-baroque models. His output includes four string quartets, the opera *Arianna* (1995), and *The Mouse Metamorphosed into a Maid* (1991) for solo soprano.

Goehr, Walter (1903–1960) German-born British conductor and composer. He gave the first performances of Benjamin Britten's *Serenade* and Michael Tippett's *A Child of our Time*. He also made editions of Monteverdi's *Vespers* of 1610 and *Poppea*.

He studied with Arnold Schoenberg in Berlin, conducting the Radio Orchestra there 1925–31. In 1933 he moved to London and was music director of the Columbia Graphophone Company until 1939. He conducted Morley College concerts from 1943. He was the father of Alexander Goehr.

Works symphony, radio opera, incidental, and chamber music.

Goethe, Johann Wolfgang von (1749–1832) German poet, novelist, dramatist, and philosopher. His most significant influence in the world of music has been through his drama ➤ **Faust**. Successful settings of other dramas have been made by Beethoven (*Egmont*), Mendelssohn (*Die erste Walpurgisnacht*), Brahms (*Rinaldo*), Ambroise Thomas (*Mignon*), and Massenet (*Werther*). Much of Goethe's poetry was created with musical setting in mind. Many of Schubert's greatest lieder (songs) are based on Goethe, although the poet failed to recognize his genius, preferring simple strophic settings.

Some of Schubert's Goethe lieder are *An den Mond*, *Erlkönig*, *Der Fischer*, *Ganymed*, *Gretchen am Spinnrade*, *Heidenröslein*, *Kennst du das Land?*, *Der Musensohn*, *Nähe des Geliebten*, *Prometheus*, and *Wanderers Nachtlied*.

Other composers and works inspired by Goethe include Johann André (*Erwin und Elmire*), Beethoven (*Meeresstille und Glückliche Fahrt*), Nils Bentzon (*Faust III*), Felice Blangini (*Die Letzten Augenblicke Werthers*), Brahms (*Gesang der Parzen*), Max Bruch (*Scherz, List und Rache*), Paul Dukas (*L'Apprenti sorcier* and *Götz von Berlichingen*), Hans Gál (*Requiem für Mignon*), Karoly Goldmark (*Götz von Berlichingen* and *Meeresstille und glückliche Fahrt*), E T A Hoffmann (*Scherz, List und Rache*), Anselm Hüttenbrenner (*Erlkönig*), Charles Koechlin (*Nuit de Walpurgis classique*), Ernst Křenek (*Triumph der Empfindsamkeit*), Liszt (*Tasso, lamento e trionfo*), Carl Loewe (*Erlkönig*), Mendelssohn (*Meeresstille und Glückliche Fahrt*), Johann Reichardt (*Claudine von Villa Bella*), Anton Rubinstein (*Wilhelm Meister*), Othmar Schoeck (*Erwin und Elmire*, *Dithyrambe*, and songs), Schubert (*Claudine von Villa Bella* and 20 lieder), Robert Schumann (*Requiem für Mignon*), Heinrich Stiehl (*Jery und Bätely*), Václav Tomášek (songs), Georg Vogler (*Erwin und Elmire*), Anton Webern (two choral songs), Egon Wellesz (*Scherz, List und Rache*), Peter Winter (*Scherz, List und Rache* and *Jery und Bätely*), Carl Zelter (songs), and Johann Zumsteeg (*Clavigo*).

Settings include five songs by Brahms, one by Mozart (*Das Veilchen*), 71 by Schubert, 19 by Schumann, and 60 (including nine early) by Hugo Wolf.

Gogol, Nikolai Vassilevich (1809–1852) Russian novelist. His works inspired the composers Boris ➤ **Assafiev** (*Christmas Eve*), Arturo ➤ **Berutti** (*Taras Bulba*), Werner Egk (*Der*➤ *Revisor*), Mikhail ➤ **Gnessin** (*Der Revisor*), Janáček (➤ *Taras Bulba*), Bohuslav Martinů (*The* ➤ *Marriage*), Mussorgsky (*The* ➤ *Marriage* and ➤ *Sorochintsy Fair*), Rimsky-Korsakov (➤ *Christmas Eve* and ➤ *May Night*), Humphrey ➤ **Searle** (*Diary of a Madman*), Alexander ➤ **Serov** (*Christmas Eve Revels*), Shostakovich (*The* ➤ *Nose*, Tchaikovsky (➤ *Vakula the Smith*), and Karel Weis (*Revisor*).

'Goldberg Variations' monumental set of 30 variations by Johann Sebastian Bach for two-manual harpsichord, BWV 998. A wide variety of keyboard technique is explored, in particular the canon, which is developed in each third variation.

Golden Age ballet by Shostakovich; see ➤ *Age of Gold, The*.

Golden Cockerel, The, Russian **Zolotoy Petushok** opera by Rimsky-Korsakov (libretto by V I Bielsky, based on Aleksandr Pushkin's satirical fairy tale), first produced in Moscow, Russia, on 7 October 1909, after Rimsky-Korsakov's death. It was his last opera. In the story, King Dodon's astrologer presents a golden cockerel, which can warn of trouble. The king falls in love with Queen Shemakha, whom the astrologer names as his price for the cockerel. The king refuses and the cockerel kills him.

Goldene Bock, Der chamber opera by Ernst Krenek (libretto by composer), first produced in Hamburg, Germany, on 16 June 1964. It tells how Jason time-travels to Route 66 in the USA, and divorces Medea when she serves him soup made from the flesh of a Greek shipping magnate.

Golden Legend, The oratorio by Arthur Sullivan (on Longfellow's poem), first produced at the Leeds Festival, England, in 1886. It was revived at Leeds on 15 March 1986, conducted by Charles Mackerras.

'Golden Sonata' nickname given to the ninth (F major) of Henry Purcell's ten *Sonatas of IV Parts* for two violins, cello, and continuo, published posthumously in 1697.

Goldmark, Karoly (Carl) (1830–1915) Austro-Hungarian composer. His best-known work today is the *Rustic Wedding Symphony*, although he established his reputation with the Wagner-influenced opera *Die Königin von Saba/The Queen of Sheba* (1875).

Goldmark was the son of a poor Jewish cantor, who managed to enter him at the Sopron school of music in 1842. He studied violin and made such rapid progress that he was sent to Vienna the next year and entered the conservatory in 1847. During the 1848 Revolution he played at the theatre at Györ in Hungary and was nearly shot as a rebel. In 1850 he returned to Vienna, where he eventually settled as a teacher.

Works OPERA *Die Königin von Saba* (1875), *Merlin* (1886), *Das Heimchen am Herd* (after Dickens's *The Cricket on the Hearth*, 1896), *Die Kriegsgefangene*, *Götz von Berlichingen* (after Goethe, 1902), and *Ein Wintermärchen* (after Shakespeare's *The Winter's Tale*, 1908).

ORCHESTRAL symphonic poem *Rustic Wedding* and two symphonies; two scherzos for orchestra and overtures *Sakuntala* (after Kalidasa), *Penthesilea* (after Kleist), *Im Frühling*, *Der gefesselte Prometheus*, *Sappho*, *In Italien*, and *Aus Jugendtagen*; symphonic poem *Zrinyi*; two violin concertos.

CHORAL *Meeresstille und glückliche Fahrt* (Goethe) for male chorus and horns, and other choral works.

CHAMBER string quartet (1860), piano quintet, three piano trios, and other chamber music; two suites and sonata for violin and piano, cello and piano sonata.

OTHER piano pieces; songs.

Goldmark, Rubin (1872–1936) US composer of Austro-Hungarian descent, nephew of Karoly ➔ **Goldmark**. He studied at the Vienna Conservatory and the National Conservatory in New York, where Antonín Dvořák was his composition master. He was director of the Colorado College Conservatory 1895–1901, but returned to New York in 1902 and settled as private piano and composition teacher, until, in 1924, he was appointed to the Juilliard Graduate School there.

Works ORCHESTRAL *Hiawatha* (after Longfellow, 1900), *Samson* (1914), *Requiem* (on Lincoln's address at Gettysburg), *Negro Rhapsody*, and *The Call of the Plains* for orchestra.

CHAMBER string quartet in A major; piano trio in D minor; violin and piano sonata.

OTHER violin pieces; piano music; songs; choruses.

Goldoni, Carlo (1707–1793) Italian playwright and librettist. His works were used in ➔ *Arcadia in Brenta* (Badassare Galuppi), ➔ *Buovo d'Antona* (Tommaso Traetta), *Il* ➔ *burbero di buon cuore* (Vicente Martín y Soler), *Ciarlone* (Giovanni ➔ **Paisiello**), *Le* ➔ *donne curiose* (Ermanno Wolf-Ferrari and Usiglio), *Dorfdeputierten* (E W Wolf), *Il* ➔ *filosofo di campagna* (Galuppi), four operas by Domenico ➔ **Fischietti**, ➔ *Fra due litiganti il terzo gode* (Giuseppe Sarti), Pietro ➔ **Generali's** *Pamela nubile* (after Richardson), *L'* ➔ *isola disabitata* (Giuseppe Scarlatti), ➔ *Lottchen am Hofe* (Johann Hiller), three operas by Gian Francesco ➔ **Malipiero**, *Il* ➔ *mondo alla roversa* (Galuppi), *Il* ➔ *mondo della luna* (Galuppi and Haydn), *Le* ➔ *pescatrici* (Bertoni and Haydn), *The Philosophical Princess* (Johan ➔ **Wagenaar**), *I portentosi effetti della Madre Natura* (Giuseppe Scarlatti), *I* ➔ *quattro rusteghi* (Ermanno Wolf-Ferrari), *Lo* ➔ *speziale* (Haydn), *Il* ➔ *Tigrane* (Gluck), *Vendemmia* (Giuseppe Gazzaniga), and *Vittorina* (Niccolò ➔ **Piccinni**).

Goldschmidt, Adalbert von (1848–1906) Austrian composer. He devoted himself as an amateur to the composition of large-scale works, the first of which, produced in Berlin, Germany, in 1876, showed remarkable affinities with Wagner's *Ring*, which was not heard until later the same year, at Bayreuth.

Works STAGE music-dramas *Die sieben Todsünden* (1876), *Helianthus*, *Gaea* (trilogy); opera *Die fromme Helene* (after Wilhelm Busch).

OTHER symphonic poem; about 100 songs, and other pieces.

Goldschmidt, Berthold (1903–1996) German-born English conductor and composer. He left Germany in 1935 and settled in England. He did not compose for many years, and the music he had written went through a long period of neglect. However, following a revival of his music in the mid-1980s, he returned to composing and produced several notable chamber works before his death.

He studied in Berlin, became assistant conductor of the Staatsoper there in 1926, and conducted at the Darmstadt Opera in 1927. In 1931–33 he conducted on Berlin Radio and was artistic adviser to the municipal opera there, but the Nazi régime drove him to England. In 1964 he conducted the first performance of Deryck Cooke's performing version of Mahler's tenth symphony. His clarinet quintet (1983) was premiered in Pasadena, California, in 1985.

Works STAGE operas *Der gewaltige Hahnrei* (after Crommelynck, produced Mannheim, 1932) and *Beatrice Cenci* (after Shelley, 1949–50); ballet *Chronica*; overture to Shakespeare's *Comedy of Errors*.

ORCHESTRAL symphonies and other orchestral works, including *Ciaconna Sinfonica* (1936, premiered in Vienna, 1960, performed under Simon Rattle in Berlin, 1987, and heard at the 1993 London Proms); violin, cello, and harp concertos.

CHAMBER four string quartets (1925, 1936, 1989, 1992), clarinet quintet (1983), piano trio (1985), string trio (*Retrospectum*, 1991), *Capriccio* for violin (1992), and others.

Goldschmidt, Otto (1829–1907) German pianist and composer. He studied at the Leipzig Conservatory under Felix Mendelssohn and in 1848 went to Paris, France, intending to study with Chopin. In 1849 he went to London, England, and settled there in 1858. He was accompanist to the singer Jenny Lind, whom he married in 1852. He was the founder of the Bach Choir in 1875.

Works CHORAL oratorio *Ruth* (1867), cantata *Music* for soprano and female voices (1898).

PIANO piano concerto; piano trio; two duets for two pianos; studies and pieces for piano.

OTHER songs.

Golgotha oratorio by Frank Martin for five soloists, chorus, and orchestra (text from the Bible and St Augustine); it was composed 1945–48 and first performed in Geneva, Switzerland, on 29 April 1949.

Gombert, Nicolas (c.1495–c.1556) Flemish composer. His music was admired for its sombre colours and close-knit textures.

Gombert was a pupil of ➤ **Josquin Des Prez**. He was in service at the emperor Charles V's chapel in Flanders from 1562 and became maître des enfants (master of the choirboys) in 1529; later he

became a canon at Tournai and in 1537 went to Spain with 20 singers and held a post in the imperial chapel in Madrid. He was exiled in 1540 for gross indecency with his choirboys.

Works 10 Masses, 160 motets, psalms; about 80 chansons.

Gomes, (Antônio) Carlos (1836–1896) Brazilian composer. He studied with Lauro Rossi in Milan, Italy, and in 1895 was appointed director of the Conservatory at Pará, Brazil, but was delayed in Lisbon by illness and died soon after his arrival. The once-popular opera *Il Guarany* (1870), based on a local Indian legend, has been revived in recent years with Placido Domingo.

Works STAGE operas *A noite do castello* (1861), *Joana di Flandres*, *Il Guarany* (1870), *Fosca*, *Salvator Rosa* (1874), *Maria Tudor* (on Victor Hugo's play, 1879), *Lo schiavo*, *Condor* (1891); revues *Se sa minga* and *Nella luna*.

OTHER ode *Il saluto del Brasil* (Philadelphia Exhibition, 1876) and cantata *Colombo* (Columbus Festival, 1892).

Gomis, José Melchor (1791–1836) Spanish composer. He was bandmaster in Barcelona, moved to Madrid about 1817, and in 1823 went to Paris, France, for political reasons. In 1826–29 he taught singing in London, England, where he published many Spanish songs, and then returned to Paris, where he produced comic operas.

Works STAGE Spanish monodrama *Sensibilidad y prudencia, ó La aldeana*; French comic operas *Le Diable à Séville* (1831), *Le Revenant* (after Scott, 1835), *Le Portefaix*, and *Rock le barbu* (1836).

VOICES AND ORCHESTRA *L'inverno* for four voices and orchestra; songs.

Gondoliers, The, or The King of Barataria operetta by Arthur Sullivan (libretto by W S Gilbert), produced at the Savoy Theatre, London, England, on 7 December 1889. In the story, the baby prince of Baratavia is brought up by gondoliers. Not knowing the heir's true identity, the Inquisitor later appoints Marco and Giuseppe as rulers, but it is eventually revealed that the servant Luiz is the true king.

gong percussion instrument originating in ancient China, consisting of a round sheet of metal with a turned-up rim. It is struck with a hammer, which may be covered with any of a range of materials, according to the quality of sound required. A large gong is also called a ➤ **tam-tam**.

Gonzaga, Guglielmo (1538–1587) Duke of Mantua. He succeeded to the duchy in 1556, became a great patron of music, and was himself a composer. He published anonymously a book of madrigals and one of *Sacrae cantiones*.

Goodall, Reginald (1901–1990) English conductor, known for his slow, expansive interpretations of Wagner. He conducted without a baton, and never took curtain calls.

Goodall studied at the Royal College of Music, London, and in Germany. His broad tempi and intensity of expression were regarded as belonging to the best traditions of German conductors. He conducted the first performance of *Peter Grimes* at Sadler's Wells, London, in 1945. In 1946 he joined the staff at the Royal Opera House, Covent Garden, London, but his gifts were not properly recognized until major success came with Wagner's *Die Meistersinger* at Sadler's Wells in 1968. He conducted *Parsifal* at Covent Garden in 1971; at the London Coliseum he conducted Wagner's *Ring* in 1973 and *Parsifal* in 1986; for Welsh National Opera he conducted *Tristan* in 1979 and *The Valkyrie* in 1984. He also conducted Bruckner's symphonies.

Good-Humoured Ladies, The ballet by Vincenzo Tommasini based on music by Domenico Scarlatti (choreography by Léonide Massine), first produced at the Teatro Costanzi, Rome, Italy, on 12 April 1917.

Goodman, Benny (1909–1986) US clarinettist, composer, and band-leader, nicknamed the 'King of Swing'. He played in various jazz and dance bands from 1921. In 1934 he founded a 12-piece band, which combined the expressive improvisation of black jazz with disciplined precision ensemble playing. He is associated with such numbers as 'Blue Skies' and 'Let's Dance'.

Born in Chicago, he studied classical clarinet with Franz Schoepp of the Chicago Symphony Orchestra before beginning a successful freelance solo career in 1921, influenced by the New Orleans style. He introduced jazz to New York's Carnegie Hall in 1938. In the same year he started a parallel classical career, recording the Mozart *Clarinet Quintet* with the Budapest String Quartet, and commissioning new works from Béla Bartók (including *Contrasts*, 1938), Aaron Copland, Igor Stravinsky (*Ebony Concerto*), Paul Hindemith, and others. He also recorded jazz with a sextet in 1939–41 that included the guitarist Charlie Christian (1916–1942). When swing lost popularity in the 1950s, Goodman took a series of smaller groups on world tours, the highlight of which was a US-government-sponsored visit to Moscow in 1962.

Goossens, (Aynsley) Eugene (1893–1962) English conductor and composer. As a composer he was prolific in most departments of music and progressive in technique. His works include two operas to libretti by Arnold Bennett: *Judith* (1929) and *Don Juan de Mañara* (1937), and much orchestral and chamber music. He was the grandson of Eugène Goossens (1845–1906) and son of Eugène Goossens (1867–1958), both conductors

of the Carl Rosa Opera Company. His brother Leon was a leading oboist, and his sisters Marie and Sidonie both renowned as harpists.

After study at Bruges, Belgium, and Liverpool, England, and under Charles Stanford at the Royal College of Music in London, he played the violin in the Queen's Hall Orchestra 1911–15. His first appearance as a conductor was in 1916, deputizing for Thomas Beecham (with whom he was closely associated for the next few years) in Stanford's *The Critic* (1916). After that he formed an orchestra of his own, giving early English performances of works by Stravinsky, and conducting the Russian Ballet. As a conductor he was afterwards associated with many famous orchestras in England and the USA, most notably the Cincinnati Symphony Orchestra, which he conducted 1931–46. In 1947 he was appointed director of the New South Wales Conservatory in Sydney, Australia, and conductor of the symphony orchestra; he returned to England in 1956.

Works STAGE operas *Judith* (1929) and *Don Juan de Mañara* (1937); ballet *L'Ecole en crinoline* (1938).

ORCHESTRAL sinfonietta (1922), two symphonies (1940, 1944), Fantasy Concerto for piano and orchestra, oboe concerto (1927), violin concerto.

CHORAL *Silence* for chorus and orchestra (1922).

CHAMBER two string quartets (1915, 1940).

Goovaerts, Alphonse (Jean Marie André) (1847–1922) Belgian composer and writer on music. He studied at the Jesuit College of Antwerp, and at the age of 15 was obliged by financial losses to take a commercial career; but he studied music thoroughly by himself and in 1866 obtained a post at the Antwerp town library. In 1869 his *Messe solennelle* was performed. In 1874 he was appointed music secretary to Antwerp Cathedral where he established a special choir, for which he copied a vast quantity of old motets of various schools. He began to write on the reform of church music, and in 1898 was appointed keeper of the royal archives in Brussels.

Works motets, *Petite Messe*, *Messe solennelle* and other church music; songs, part songs.

gopak or **hopak** a Russian folk dance with music of a lively character in quick 2/4 time.

Gorczycki, Grzegorz (c. 1664–1734) Polish composer. He was *Magister cappellae* at Kraków Cathedral from 1698. He wrote motets and other church music.

Gordigiani, Luigi (1806–1860) Italian composer. He was a pupil of his father, Antonio Gordigiani, who died when he was 14, and he had to make a living by writing piano pieces under German names. The Russian prince Nikolai Demidov and the Polish prince Józef Poniatowski discovered his great gifts and gave him their patronage, the latter providing him with the libretto for his opera *Filippo*, produced in Florence, Italy, in 1840.

Works ten operas; *Canzonette, Canti popolari* and other songs (about 300 in all); duets for female voices; Tuscan airs with piano accompaniment.

Górecki, Henryk Mikolaj (1933–) Polish composer. His study with Olivier ➤ **Messiaen** and exposure to avant-garde influences after 1956 led him to abandon a politically correct neoclassical style and seek out new sonorities. He later adopted a slow-moving tonal idiom appealing to revived religious tradition, often on tragic themes from Polish history, as in *Old Polish Music* for orchestra (1969), and his third symphony, *Sorrowful Songs* (1976), which propelled him to fame in the West in 1992.

He studied with Bolesław ➤ **Szabelski** at Katowice Conservatory 1955–60. He joined the faculty there in 1968 and was provost until 1979.

Works ORCHESTRAL, SOME WITH CHORUS AND/OR VOICES *Symphony no. 1* (1959), *No. 2* for soprano, baritone, chorus, and orchestra (1972), and *No. 3* for soprano and orchestra (1973); *Scontri* for orchestra (1960); *Canticum Graduum* for orchestra (1969); *Old Polish Music* for brass and strings (1969); *Beatus Vir* for baritone, chorus, and orchestra (1979); harpsichord concerto (1980); *Concerto-Cantata* for flute and orchestra (1992); *Genesis III: Monodrama* (1963); *Two Sacred Songs* for baritone and orchestra (1971).

CHORAL cantata *Epitafium*; *Epitaph* for mixed chorus and instruments (1956).

CHAMBER *Quartettino* for wind (1956); sonata for two violins (1957); series *Genesis I–IV* for various instrumental groups (1962–70); *Aria* for tuba and ensemble (1987); *Already it is Dusk* (string quartet no. 1, 1988); *Quasi una fantasia* for string quartet (1991); *Kleines Requiem für eine Polka* for piano and 13 instruments (1993).

Gorzanis, Giacomo (c. 1525–after 1575) Italian composer. He published four books of lute music, including numerous dance suites in two or three movements. One of these, consisting of a *passo e mezzo* and *padovana* (1561), provides an early example of 'sonata' used as a title. He was blind.

Göss, Barthel German theologian and composer; see Bartholomäus ➤ **Gesius**.

Gossec, FrançoisJoseph (1734–1829) Belgian-born French composer. On the foundation of the Paris Conservatory in 1795 he became one of its directors and professor of composition. As one of the leading composers of the French Revolution, he wrote many works for public ceremonies, often using vast forces. His works include over 30 symphonies, church and chamber music, ballets and theatre music, and 19 operas. He wrote little after 1800.

Gossec was a chorister at Antwerp Cathedral. In 1751 he went to Paris, where with Jean-Philippe Rameau's help he obtained a post writing symphonies for La Pouplinière's private orchestra in 1754. He later became music director to the Prince of Condé. He founded the Concert des Amateurs in 1770, and in 1773 took over the direction of the Concert Spirituel. He also produced much chamber music and in 1760 performed a Requiem in which, as in other works, he anticipated the experimental manner of Hector Berlioz. From 1795 to 1816 he was professor of composition at the Conservatory.

Works OPERA *Les Pêcheurs, Toinon et Toinette* (1767), *Thésée* (1782), *Rosine* (1786), and others.

BALLET *Les Scythes enchaînés*, added to Gluck's *Iphigénie en Tauride* (1779), *Mirsa*, and *Callisto*.

SACRED oratorio *La Nativité* (1774); Requiem (1760), *Dernière Messe des vivants*, motets and other pieces; funeral music for Mirabeau.

SECULAR *Le Chant du 14 juillet*, *L'Offrande à la liberté*, and other music for the Revolution.

OTHER about 50 symphonies (1756–1809), overtures, and other orchestral music; twelve string quartets, trios, and other chamber music.

Gossett, Philip (1941–) US musicologist. He studied at Princeton (PhD 1970) and taught at the University of Chicago from 1968 (professor and chair of the music department 1978–84). He was general editor of the critical edition of Verdi's works, joint editor of the Rossini edition from 1979, co-editor with Charles Rosen of *Early Romantic Operas* (New York, 1978–83, in 44 volumes), and editor of a facsimile edition of *Il barbiere di Siviglia* (Rome, 1993).

Gothic Symphony first symphony by Havergal Brian, for soloists, children's choruses, brass band, and orchestra of 180; the last of the four movements is a setting of the Te Deum. It was composed 1919–27 and first performed by amateur forces in London, England, on 24 June 1961; the first professional performance was given in London on 30 October 1966, to mark Brian's 90th birthday. It was broadcast live to the USA by satellite on 25 May 1980.

Götterdämmerung, Twilight of the Gods opera by Richard Wagner (libretto by composer), first produced at Bayreuth, Germany, on 17 August 1876. Following the conclusion of *Siegfried*, this fourth and final opera of the ➤ *Ring des Nibelungen* cycle opens with the awakening of Brünnhilde. Siegfried, having inadvertently drunk a magic potion, betrays her to Gunther; Gutrune hopes to acquire Siegfried. Meanwhile Hagen, Alberich's son, has conspired to try to gain power and the Ring. Hagen murders Siegfried, but Brünnhilde takes the Ring, returning it to the Rhinemaidens as Valhalla burns.

Gottschalk, Louis Moreau (1829–1869) US composer and pianist. His adoption of Creole and American folk music, Latin American rhythms and dance forms, and striking colouristic effects won the admiration of Hector Berlioz, Franz Liszt, Jacques Offenbach, and others. His compositions include *Souvenir d'Andalousie/Souvenir of Andalusia* (1851) for piano and orchestra and numerous piano pieces, among which are *La Gallina: danse cubaine/La Gallina: Cuban Dance* (c. 1868) and *Le Banjo – esquisse américaine/Banjo – American Sketch* (1854–55).

Gottschalk studied in Paris, France, and had much success there as a pianist from his debut in 1844. He toured throughout Europe and, from 1853, North and South America. He died of yellow fever while on tour in Brazil.

Works *Escenas campestres* for soprano, tenor, baritone, and orchestra (1860); two symphonic poems, *La nuit des tropiques* and *Montevideo*; numerous piano pieces including *The Dying Poet* and *Grand Fantasy on the Brazilian National Anthem*.

Götz, Hermann (1840–1876) German composer. At first he studied music only incidentally when a student at Königsberg University, but later went to the Stern Conservatory in Berlin. In 1863 he went to Switzerland as organist at Winterthur and in 1867 he settled in Zürich. From 1870 he devoted himself wholly to composition.

Works OPERA *Der Widerspänstigen Zähmung* (on Shakespeare's *The Taming of the Shrew*, 1874) and *Francesca da Rimini* (unfinished, produced Mannheim, 1877).

CHORAL *Nänie* (Schiller) and Psalm 137 for solo voices, chorus, and orchestra; cantata for male voices and orchestra.

ORCHESTRAL symphony in F major, *Spring* overture for orchestra; violin concerto in G major (1868), piano concerto in B♭ major.

CHAMBER piano quintet, piano quartet, piano trio; sonata for piano duet; sonatina, *Genrebilder* and other works for piano.

OTHER songs.

Goudimel, Claude (c.1514–1572) French composer. He contributed chansons for several voices to many collections, also four-part settings to a book of odes by the Roman poet Horace and to another of sacred songs (*chansons spirituelles*) by Marc-Antoine de Muret (1526–85) in 1555, and settings of French translations of the psalms, including a complete Protestant psalter.

After studying at Paris University, Goudimel then worked with the publisher Nicolas du Chemin as a proofreader and later as a business partner. He first appeared as a composer in Paris in 1549, when he contributed chansons to a book published by du Chemin. About 1557, having become a Huguenot, he went to live in Metz with the Protestant colony there, and composed his first complete psalter in 1564. About ten years later he left for Besançon, and afterwards for Lyon, where he died in the massacre of the Huguenots in August 1572.

Goudimel wrote Masses, motets, and chansons, but it is for his psalm settings that he is remembered. They range in style from motetlike works to simple harmonizations.

Works five Masses, three Magnificats, psalms in motet form and other works for the Catholic Church; psalms, including a complete psalter, for the Protestant Church; sacred songs and numerous secular chansons for several voices.

Gould, Morton (1913–1996) US composer and conductor. He studied at New York University, and later worked as a pianist at Radio City Music Hall and presented music programmes on radio. His works are much indebted to popular idioms.

Works BALLET *Interplay* (1945), *Fall River Legend* on Lizzie Borden – America's most famous orphan (1947), and *Fiesta* (1957).

ORCHESTRAL three *American Symphonettes* (1922, 1935, 1937), piano concerto (1937), violin concerto (1938), *Little Symphony* (1939), four symphonies (1942, 1944, 1947, 1952), *A Lincoln Legend* (1941), *Spirituals* (1941), viola concerto (1943), *Concerto for Orchestra* (1945), *Dance Variations* for two pianos and orchestra (1953), *Concerto for Tap Dancer* (1953), *Jekyll and Hyde Variations* (1957), *Festive Music* (1965), *Venice* for double orchestra and brass bands (1966), *Vivaldi Gallery* (1967), *Symphony of Spirituals* (1976), *American Ballads* (1976), *Housewarming* (1982), flute concerto (1984), *Chorales and Rags* (1988), *Concerto Grosso* (1988).

OTHER music for Broadway shows, films, and state occasions (including the Los Angeles Olympics, 1984).

Gounod, Charles François (1818–1893) French composer and organist. His operas, notably *Faust* (1859) and *Roméo et Juliette* (1867), and church music, including *Messe solennelle/Solemn Mass* (1849), combine graceful melody and elegant harmonization. His *Méditation sur le prélude de Bach/Meditation on Bach's 'Prelude'* (1889) for soprano and instruments, based on Prelude No. 1 of Bach's *Well-Tempered Clavier*, achieved popularity as 'Gounod's *Ave Maria*'.

Gounod was born in Paris, the son of a painter. His mother, a good pianist, taught him music from an early age and he was educated at the Lycée Saint-Louis and at the Paris Conservatory, where his masters included Jacques Halévy, Ferdinando Paër, and Jean Lesueur. In 1839 he won the Prix de Rome and spent the statutory three years in Rome, studying early Italian church music; his interest in this music culminated in the elaborate *Messe solennelle de Ste Cécile* (1855). After a tour in Austria and Germany he returned to Paris and was appointed organist at the church of the Missions Étrangères. Intending to become a priest, he did not produce any important music until his opera *Sapho* appeared in 1851. From 1852 to 1860 he conducted the united choral societies named Orphéon. His five-act setting of *Faust* for the Paris Opéra in 1859 brought his melodic gift before a huge public and Gounod became the most popular opera composer of his time; his success was consolidated by a saccharine but effective version of *Romeo and Juliet*. While living in London, England, in 1870–75, he founded what later became the Royal Choral Society.

Works STAGE operas *Sapho* (1851), *La Nonne sanglante* (1854), *Le Médecin malgré lui* (after Molière, 1858), *Faust* (after Goethe, 1859), *Philémon et Baucis* (1860), *La Reine de Saba* (1862), *Mireille* (after Mistral; 1864), *La Colombe*, *Roméo et Juliette* (after Shakespeare, 1867), *Cinq-Mars* (after Alfred de Vigny; 1877), *Polyeucte* (after Corneille, 1878), *Le Tribut de Zamora* (1881); incidental music for Ponsard's *Ulysse*, Legouvé's *Les Deux Reines*, and Barbier's *Jeanne d'Arc*.

SACRED MUSIC oratorios *La Rédemption* (1868–81), *Mors et Vita* (1885), *Tobie*; eight cantatas; 16 Masses, Requiem (1895), *Stabat Mater*, Te Deum, *De profundis*, *Ave verum corpus*, *Pater noster*, Magnificat and other sacred vocal pieces.

OTHER two symphonies (1855–56); some piano compositions including the *Funeral March for a Marionette*; *Méditation sur le prélude de Bach* for soprano, violin, piano, and organ (1889); some smaller choral works; many songs.

Goyescas opera by Enrique Granados (libretto, in Spanish, by F Periquet y Zuaznabar), first produced at the Metropolitan Opera House, New York, on 28 January 1916. Much of the material is taken from the piano work below. The story tells how Pacquito and Fernando duel over Rosario, and Fernando dies in her arms.

Granados composed two sets of piano pieces, inspired by paintings of Spanish scenes by Goya, first performed in Paris, France, on 4 April 1914. They comprise: I. *Los requiebros/The Compliments*, *Coloquio en la reja/Colloquy at the Grilled Window*, *El fandango del candil/The Fandango of the Lantern*, and *Quejas, ó La maja y el ruiseñor/Plaints, or The Maja and the Nightingale*; II. *El Amor y la Muerte/Love and Death*, and *Epilogo: la serenata del espectro/Epilogue: the Spectre's Serenade*. (A *maja* is the feminine counterpart of *majo*, 'a fop, a dandy'). Granados also wrote a separate *escena goyesca* for piano: *El pelele* (a puppet or straw-man tossed in a blanket).

Gozzi, Carlo (1722–1806) Italian dramatist. His works inspired the composers Alfredo Casella (*La ➤ donna serpente*), Francis ➤ Chagrin (*Il re cervo*), Franz ➤ Danzi (*Turandot*), Gottfried von ➤ Einem (*Prinzessin Turandot*), J P E Hartmann (*Ravnen*), Hans Werner Henze (➤ *König Hirsch*), F H ➤ Himmel (*Sylphen*), Adolf ➤ Jensen (*Turandot*), Prokofiev (➤ *Love for Three Oranges*, Roger Sessions (*Turandot*), Wilhelm ➤ Stenhammar (*Turandot*), the incidental music for ➤ *Turandot* by Carl Maria von Weber and the operas by Ferruccio Busoni and Puccini, and Wagner's ➤ *Feen*

G.P. in music, abbreviation for ➤ general pause, a moment where all players are silent.

Grabmusik, Funeral music cantata by Mozart for soloists, chorus, and small orchestra; it was composed in 1767 (when Mozart was ill) and first performed in Salzburg Cathedral, Austria, on 7 April 1767.

Grabu or **Grabut** or **Grebus, Louis (1665–94)** French violinist and composer. He was appointed composer to Charles II in 1665, and was Master of the King's Musick 1666–74.

Works the operas *Ariane, ou le mariage de Bacchus* (1674) and *Albion and Albanius* (libretto by Dryden; 1685).

grace in music, alternative name for embellishment or ➤ ornamentation.

grace note in music, an ornamental note written in small type to show that its duration is not counted as a part of the metre of the bar, but must be subtracted from either the following or the preceding full note. When appearing singly, written as a quaver or sometimes a crotchet, it can indicate an ➤ appoggiatura ('leaning' note), requiring up to half the value of the next note. If it appears as a semiquaver or as a quaver with a stroke through the stem, it generally appears just on or before the beat, in the manner of an appoggiatura or ➤ acciaccatura ('crushed' note). When appearing in a large group, as in a cadenza by Beethoven or a melody by Chopin, the grace notes usually fill in the duration of a single note in the melody, and may (if time permits) be played with greater rhythmic flexibility than in standard notation.

Gradus ad Parnassum (Latin 'Steps to Parnassus') treatise on counterpoint by Johann ➤ Fux, published in 1725.

It is also the title of a series of 100 instructive and progressive piano pieces by Muzio Clementi, published in 1817. The first piece in Claude Debussy's *Children's Corner* for piano alludes satirically to Clementi's collection.

Graener, Paul (1872–1944) German composer. His lieder (songs) and operas were popular in the

1920s, and he was one of a large number of composers who were successful during the Third Reich.

He was a choirboy in Berlin Cathedral and at the age of 16 entered the Veit Conservatory, but soon began to teach himself, and led a wandering life, conducting at various theatres and composing a number of immature works. He was in London, England, 1896–1908 as a teacher at the Royal Academy of Music and conductor at the Haymarket Theatre. He was then appointed director of the New Conservatory in Vienna, Austria, and in 1910 became director of the Mozarteum at Salzburg. After some years in Munich, Germany, he succeeded Max Reger as professor of composition at the Leipzig Conservatory, but resigned in 1924. In 1930 he became director of the Stern Conservatory in Berlin, and under the Nazi régime was vice-president of the Reichsmusikkammer, being succeeded by Werner Egk in 1941.

Works OPERA *Don Juans letztes Abenteuer* (1914), *Der vierjährige Posten* (Körner, 1918), *Theophano* (Byzanz, 1918), *Schirin und Gertraude, Hanneles Himmelfahrt* (after G Hauptmann, 1927), *Das Narrengericht* (1931), *Friedemann Bach* (1931), *Der Prinz von Homburg* (after Kleist, 1935).

ORCHESTRAL symphonies (*Schmied Schmerz*), *Romantic Fantasy, Variations on a Russian folk song*, and others.

CHAMBER six string quartets, three piano trios; sonata and suite for violin and piano, suite for cello and piano.

OTHER choral works; piano pieces; over 100 songs.

Grainger, Percy Aldridge (1882–1961)
Australian-born US experimental composer and pianist. He is remembered for piano transcriptions, songs, and short instrumental pieces drawing on folk idioms, including *Country Gardens* (1925), and for his settings of folk songs, such as *Molly on the Shore* (1921).

Grainger shared his friend Ferruccio Busoni's vision of a free music, devising a synthesizer and composing machine far ahead of its time.

Grainger was a pupil of his mother and of Louis Pabst in Melbourne. He later studied in Frankfurt, Germany, with James Kwast (1852–1949), Iwan Knorr, and Busoni. He lived in London in 1900–14 and became interested in folk music. He toured Scandinavia in 1909, and settled in the USA in 1914, later becoming naturalized. He made a successful New York debut in 1915, and in 1928 married Ella Viola Ström at the Hollywood Bowl, conducting his *To a Nordic Princess* in honour of the occasion. In 1938 he founded a museum in Melbourne, to house his manuscripts and souvenirs; his request for the museum to display his skeleton after his death was declined.

Works COMPOSITIONS FOR CHORUS AND ORCHESTRA, WITH AND WITHOUT SOLO VOICES *Marching Song of Democracy* (1901–17), *The Bride's Tragedy* (Swinburne; 1908), *Father and Daughter* (Faroe folk song; 1908–09), *Sir Eglamore* (1904, revised 1912–13), *We Have Fed our Seas* (Kipling; 1900–04, revised 1911), *Tribute to Foster* (1913–16, 1931, *Bridal Song*, and others; part songs including *Brigg Fair* (1906, revised 1911), *Morning Song in the Jungle* (Kipling; 1905); pieces for small orchestra: *Molly on the Shore* (1907), *Shepherd's Hey* (1908–09), *Mock Morris* (1910), *Irish Tune from County Derry* ('Londonderry Air', 1913), clog dance *Handel in the Strand* (1930).

PIANO, DANCES, AND SONGS *Walking Tune* (c.1905), suite *In a Nutshell* for two pianos (1916); four Irish dances on themes by Stanford, and other pieces for piano; songs. He edited and arranged hundreds of British and Scandinavian folk songs.

gramophone an instrument (invented by Thomas Edison in 1877) that reproduces recorded sound. The early version, known as a phonogram, recorded and reproduced sound by means of cylinders; music is now recorded on magnetic tape, afterwards transferred to a disc of vinylite. The sound waves of the music are reproduced thereon in a continuous groove. In performance the disc revolves, a static needle is brought into contact with the groove, and the 'frozen' sound waves are released and electronically amplified. From 1958 sounds were directed to the listener with greater realism by means of stereophonic recordings, followed in the 1970s by quadraphonic recordings.

A more recent development is the **compact disc**, on which the musical signal is digitally encoded so that it can be decoded by laser with absolutely no wear to the disc, with complete fidelity and with virtually no danger of destroying the disc through careless handling.

Granados, Enrique (1867–1916)
Spanish composer and pianist. His piano work *Goyescas* (1911), inspired by the work of the artist Goya, was converted to an opera in 1916.

Granados studied composition with Carlos Pedrell in Barcelona and piano in Paris, France. Returning to Spain in 1889, he became a well-known pianist and in 1900 he founded the Sociedad de Conciertos Clásicos in Madrid, which he conducted. After a visit to New York, USA, for the production the operatic version of *Goyescas* in January 1916, he went down in the *Sussex* when it was torpedoed by a German submarine in the English Channel. He had swum to rescue his wife, but was weighed down with the gold that the New York Metropolitan Opera had paid him for *Goyescas*.

Works STAGE operas and zarzuelas *Maria del Carmen* (1898), *Gaziel* (1906), *Goyescas* (1916, based on the piano work), *Petrarca, Picarol* (1901), *Follet* (1903), *Liliana* (1911).

ORCHESTRAL symphonic poem *La nit del mor*, four suites, *Escenas poéticas* (1926), and other pieces for orchestra; *Oriental* for oboe and strings.

CHORAL *Cant de las Estrelles* for chorus, organ, and piano.

PIANO *Goyescas* (two volumes; composed 1911, first performed 1914), ten Spanish Dances, six pieces on Spanish folk songs, six *Escenas poeticas* including *Libro de horas*, six *Escenas románticas*, Impromptus, piano trio, children's pieces for piano.

OTHER songs *Escritas en estilo antiguo*, and a collection of tonadillas.

gran cassa (Italian 'great case, great box') Italian name for the **➤ bass drum**.

grand chœur (French 'great choir', 'full organ') a musical direction that the organ is to be used with all the registers.

Grand Duke, The, or The Statutory Duel operetta by Arthur Sullivan (libretto by W S Gilbert), first produced at the Savoy Theatre, London, England, on 7 March 1896. It was Gilbert's last libretto for Sullivan.

Grande-Duchesse de Gérolstein, La operetta by Jacques Offenbach (libretto by H Meilhac and L Halévy), first produced at the Théâtre des Variétés, Paris, France, on 12 April 1867. It describes how the grand duchess has an eye for the recruit Fritz, promoting him eventually to the rank of general. When he still prefers to marry the peasant Wanda, she turns against him. After complications, there is a happy ending.

Grande Messe des Morts, High Mass for the Dead setting of the Requiem Mass by Hector Berlioz for tenor, chorus, and orchestra, composed in 1837 and revised in 1852 and 1867. It was first performed in Paris, France, on 5 December 1837. It called for orchestral forces of a size never previously heard of, including at least 16 timpani and four brass bands. Despite its explicitly French title (the original commission was for a piece to commemorate the Revolution), the piece is still frequently referred to as Berlioz's *Requiem*.

Grandi, Alessandro (c.1575–c.1630) Italian composer. His church music was in part inspired by the spacious architecture of St Mark's, Venice, and many of his motets are in the concertato style, with singers positioned in different parts of the church to give a 'stereophonic' effect. His later motets employ instrumental accompaniments and anticipate the sacred concertos of Heinrich Schütz and other north European masters.

Grandi may have studied under Giovanni Gabrieli in Venice. He was maestro di cappella at Santo Spirito, Ferrara, 1610–17, and then at St Mark's, where he sang under Monteverdi's direction and became his deputy in 1620. In 1627 he became choirmaster at the Church of Santa Maria Maggiore in Bergamo. He died of the plague.

Works five Masses, about 200 motets, psalms; madrigals; cantatas, arias for solo voice.

grand jeu (French 'great play') in music, an alternative term for *grand chœur*, 'full organ'; also the name of a harmonium stop that brings the whole instrument into play.

Grand Macabre, Le opera by György Ligeti (libretto by composer and M Meschke, after M de Ghelderode), first produced in Stockholm, Sweden, on 12 April 1978. It was performed at the London Coliseum on 2 December 1982, with the original roles of Spermando and Clitoria 'translated' by G Skelton as Amando and Miranda. In the story, Nekrotzar returns from the grave in an attempt to destroy the world, but is disappointed when a threatening comet passes by harmlessly.

grand opera type of opera without any spoken dialogue (unlike the *opéra-comique*), as performed at the Paris Opéra, France, in the 1820s to 1880s. Grand operas were extremely long (five acts), and included incidental music and a ballet.

Composers of grand opera include Daniel Auber, Giacomo Meyerbeer, and Ludovic Halévy; examples include Verdi's *Don Carlos* (1867) and Meyerbeer's *Les Huguenots* (1836).

grand piano large, wing-shaped form of the **➤ piano**, with horizontal stringing and soundboard.

Grange, Phillip (1956–) English composer. He studied at York University and with Peter Maxwell Davies. He became Head of Composition at Manchester University from 2000, and his music has been performed at most major UK festivals and the London Proms in 1983, also in Europe and the USA.

Works STAGE music theatre *The Kingdom of Bones* (1983).

ORCHESTRAL *Variations* (1986), *Concerto for Orchestra* (1988), *Changing Landscapes* (1990).

CHAMBER piano sonata (1978), *Cimmerian Nocturne* for ensemble (1979), sextet for wind quintet and piano (1980).

Gran Mass, French **Graner Messe** Mass by Franz **➤ Liszt** for solo voices, chorus, orchestra, and organ, composed in 1855 for the inauguration of a church at Gran (Esztergom) in Hungary and performed there on 31 August 1856.

graphic scores in music, scores by 20th-century composers which seek to convey musical ideas by means of nontraditional notation. Some scores are intended to symbolize particular sounds or textures, others allow the interpreter more latitude. Examples are by Morton Feldman, Karlheinz Stockhausen, John Cage, György Ligeti, Sylvano Bussotti, and Cornelius Cardew. Graphic scores have been admired as much for their visual as their musical qualities.

graph notation in music, an invented sign language representing unorthodox sounds objectively in pitch and time, or alternatively representing sounds of orthodox music in a visually unorthodox manner. A form of graph notation for speech patterns used in phonetics was adopted by Karlheinz Stockhausen in *Carré/Squared* (1959–60).

Graphic representation of sounds begins with medieval plainchant, which originally aimed at recording the real inflection of a singing voice. Its reappearance in modern times dates from 1856, with the invention by León Scott of the **phonautograph** for recording visual traces of speech sounds. The possibility of drawing sound for direct reproduction was raised by composer Ernest Toch in 1928; with the arrival of optical sound on film during the 1930s A M Avraamov and B A Yankovsky in Russia and Rudolf Pfenninger in Germany successfully devised methods of optical waveform synthesis for music production.

The artists László Moholy-Nagy in Berlin, Germany, and Jack Ellit in London, England, were experimenting at this time with freely drawn soundtracks incorporating found images, thumbprints, and so on, of predictable rhythm but noisy character, a technique later adopted by the Canadian film-maker Norman McLaren. In 1940 Heitor Villa-Lobos composed *New York Skyline* based on the outline of a photograph projected onto graph paper and thence to music manuscript. Percy Grainger's proposed Free Music Machine (1948), designed by Burnett Cross, applies optical sound principles on a larger scale, a technique continued in digital synthesizers such as the Fairlight. Development of the sound spectograph in 1944 by engineers at Bell Telephone Laboratories introduced a much improved projection of audio events in pitch and time, providing a model for Stockhausen's iconic score *Elektronische Studie II/Electronic Study II* (1953–54). John Cage's graphic scores of the 1950s revive memories of film experiments in the 1930s, as may be said of many European composers of graph scores from the period 1959–70.

Graupner, Christoph (1683–1760) German composer. He wrote more than 1,400 cantatas and over a hundred symphonies, as well as operas, chamber music, and keyboard pieces. He was Kapellmeister at Hesse-Darmstadt from 1712, and was elected cantor of St Thomas's, Leipzig, in 1723, but was unable to obtain his release from Darmstadt, so that the post fell to Johann Sebastian Bach.

He was a pupil of Johann Schelle and Johann Kuhnau at St Thomas's, Leipzig, and was harpsichordist at the Hamburg opera under Reinhard Keiser 1707–09, where he produced his first operas. In 1709 he entered the service of the Landgrave Ernst Ludwig of Hesse-Darmstadt as vice-Kapellmeister, becoming Kapellmeister in 1712 on the death of Wolfgang Briegel.

Works OPERA *Dido* (1707), *Antiochus und Stratonica* (1708), *La costanza vince l'inganno* (1715), and others.

CHORAL over 1,400 church cantatas.

ORCHESTRAL 113 symphonies; 87 overtures; about 50 concertos.

OTHER quantities of chamber music, keyboard music.

grave (Italian 'heavy, serious') musical direction indicating a slow tempo.

gravicembalo 17th-century name for the clavicembalo or ➤ **harpsichord**.

Gray, Cecil (1895–1951) Scottish writer on music and composer. In 1920 he became joint editor of the *Sackbut* with Philip Heseltine, with whom he also wrote a book on the composer Don Carlo Gesualdo (1926), and whose biography as a composer (Peter Warlock) he published. Other books are a *History of Music* (1928), essays 'Predicaments' (1936), and 'Contingencies' (1947), and two works on Sibelius (1931, 1935).

Works OPERA *Deirdre*, *The Temptation of St Anthony* (after Flaubert), and *The Trojan Women* (after Euripides).

grazia, con (Italian 'with grace') musical direction; 'with grace', Italian *grazioso*.

grazioso (Italian 'graceful') in music, term used to indicate a graceful manner of playing.

Great Fugue composition for string quartet by Beethoven; see ➤ **Grosse Fuge**.

great organ in music, the principal manual (keyboard) of an ➤ **organ**, characterized by the most powerful pipes and stops of the instrument. It often has the greatest number of stops, ranging from a wide variety of ➤ **flue pipes** to a selection of reeds.

great staff in music, a theoretical clarification of the relationship of the traditional clefs. On an 11-line stave with, for example, the treble clef four lines from the top and the bass clef four lines from the bottom, the middle line will represent middle C.

Greaves, Thomas (lived 1604) English lutenist and composer. He was in the service of Sir Henry Pierpoint, whose wife was a cousin of Michael

Cavendish. In 1604 he published the book *Songs of Sundrie Kindes*, containing seven songs to the lute, four songs for voice and viols, and four madrigals.

Grechaninov, Aleksandr Tikhonovich (1864–1956) Russian composer. He studied under Rimsky-Korsakov, and earned a living composing music for the Russian Orthodox Church. He left Russia after the Revolution and settled in Paris, France, in 1925. In 1929 he moved to the USA.

Although the son of semiliterate small shopkeepers, Grechaninov managed to study piano at the Moscow Conservatory under Vassily Safonov, but in 1890 he went to St Petersburg as a composition pupil of Rimsky-Korsakov.

Works STAGE operas *Dobrinya Nikitich* and *Sister Beatrice* (after Maeterlinck's play, 1910); incidental music for plays.

CHURCH MUSIC much music for the Russian Church, including 44 complete liturgies; Catholic Church music, including Masses and motets.

CHORAL *Music Pictures* for bass solo, chorus, and orchestra; other choral works.

ORCHESTRAL five symphonies (1894–1936), elegy for orchestra; concertos for cello, violin, and flute.

CHAMBER four string quartets.

Greek opera in two acts by Mark-Anthony Turnage (libretto by composer and J Moore, after Steven Berkoff's play), first produced at the Carl-Orff Saal, Munich, Germany, on 17 June 1988. It is an updated version of the Oedipus legend, in a troubled urban setting: Eddy kills a café manager and marries his wife, who later turns out to be his mother.

Greek Passion, The opera by Bohuslav Martinů (libretto by composer from the novel by Nikos Kazantzakis), composed 1955–58 in Nice, New York, Pratteln, and Rome. It was first produced in Zurich, Switzerland, on 9 June 1961, conducted by Paul Sacher. In the story, the villagers of Lyeovrissi prepare for their annual Passion play. Manolios, who is to play Christ, fights for some local refugees, but is killed by Panais, who was to play Judas.

Greene, Maurice (1696–1755) English organist and composer. By the time of his death, he had held all the major musical appointments in England, including organist at St Paul's Cathedral (1718), organist and composer of the Chapel Royal (1727), and Master of the King's Musick (1735). An inheritance in 1750 enabled him to devote time to a collection of English church music, which after his death was completed by William Boyce and published under the title *Cathedral Music*.

The son of a clergyman, Greene was a chorister at St Paul's Cathedral, studied the organ there under Richard Brind, and after holding church posts was appointed organist of St Paul's in 1718. On William Croft's death in 1727 he became organist and composer of the Chapel Royal, and in 1730 he succeeded Thomas Tudway as professor at Cambridge University. He was co-founder (with Michael Festing) of the Royal Society of Musicians in 1738.

Works SACRED AND CHORAL over 100 anthems, the most notable published in *Forty Select Anthems* (1743), and other church music; oratorios *The Song of Deborah and Barak* (1732) and *Jephtha* (1737).

SECULAR pastorals *Florimel, or Love's Revenge* (1734), *The Judgement of Hercules*, and *Phoebe* (1747); Odes for St Cecilia's Day and other occasions; miscellaneous songs and catches; overtures; organ voluntaries; harpsichord music.

Gregorian chant any of a body of ➔ plainsong choral chants associated with Pope Gregory the Great (540–604), which became standard in the Roman Catholic Church.

Gregorian tones chants of the Gregorian psalmody sung in groups corresponding to the eight church modes (four authentic and four plagal).

Grenon, Nicolas (c.1380–1456) French composer. He wrote sacred Latin music and chansons.

The earliest mention of Grenon is at Paris in 1399. He later worked at Laon and Cambrai cathedrals and at the Burgundian court chapel under Duke John the Fearless. He was master of the choirboys at the papal chapel 1425–27, and finally returned to Cambrai where he was for many years Guillaume Dufay's neighbour and was probably an influence on the younger composer.

Gresham, Thomas (c. 1519–1579) English merchant financier who founded and paid for the Royal Exchange and propounded **Gresham's law**: 'bad money tends to drive out good money from circulation'. He also founded Gresham College in London. The college was provided for by his will, and among the professorships was one for music, which has continued to the present day. Knighted in 1559.

Gretchen am Spinnrade, Margaret at the Spinning-Wheel Franz Schubert's setting of Gretchen's song in Goethe's *Faust*, Part I, composed in 1814 at the age of 17 and published as Op. 2 in 1821.

Grétry, André Ernest Modeste (1741–1813) Belgian-born French composer. He wrote about 40 operas, and was a leading figure in the development of *opéras-comiques*, which included spoken dialogue. He is best known through the arrangement of his *Zémire et Azor* (1771) made by the conductor Thomas Beecham.

Grétry was a chorister at the church of St Denis, Liège, and received his initial musical training from his father (a violinist) and local church musicians. By 1759 he had already composed some symphonies and church music, which won him a scholarship to study in Rome, Italy, where he remained until 1765, when he produced the intermezzo *La vendemmiatrice*. After a time in Geneva, Switzerland, he went to Paris, France, in 1767 to make his way as an opera composer. From 1768 he produced a continuous stream of *opéras-comiques*, the most popular being *Richard Cœur-de-Lion* (1784), an early example of a rescue opera. He was made an inspector of the Paris Conservatory on its foundation in 1795, and the same year became one of the original members of the Institut de France. He published his memoirs in three volumes 1789–97, and wrote other literary works.

Works OPERAS-COMIQUES *La vendemmiatrice* (1765), *Isabelle et Gertrude, Le Huron* (1768), *Lucile, Le Tableau parlant* (1769), *Silvain, Les Deux Avares, L'Amitié à l'épreuve, Zémire et Azor* (1771), *L'Ami de la maison, Le Magnifique, La Rosière de Salency, La Fausse Magie* (1775), *Les Mariages samnites* (several versions), *Matroco* (1777), *Le Jugement de Midas, Les Fausses Apparences, ou L'Amant jaloux* (1778), *Les Événements imprévus, Aucassin et Nicolette* (1779), *Thalie au Nouveau Théâtre, Théodore et Paulin* (later *L'Épreuve villageoise*), *Richard Cœur-de-Lion* (1784), *Les Méprises par ressemblance, Le Comte d'Albert* (1786), *Le Prisonnier anglais* (later *Clarice et Belton*), *Le Rival confident, Raoul Barbebleue* (1789), *Pierre le Grand, Guillaume Tell* (1791), *Basile, Les Deux Couvents, Joseph Barra, Callias* (1794), *Lisbeth, Le Barbier du village, Elisca*. Produced at the Paris Opéra: *Céphale et Procris* (1773), *Les Trois Ages de l'opéra* (1778), *Andromaque, La Double Épreuve, ou Colinette à la cour, L'Embarras des richesses* (1782), *La Caravane du Caire, Panurge dans l'île des lanternes* (after Rabelais, 1785), *Amphitryon, Aspasie, Denys le Tyran, La Fête de la raison, Anacréon chez Polycrate* (1797), *Le Casque et les colombes* (1801), *Delphis et Mopsa*, and others.

Grétry, Lucile (1772–1790) French composer, daughter of André ➤ **Grétry**. At the age of 13 she composed the opera *Le Mariage d'Antonio* which, scored by her father, was successfully produced in 1786 at the Comédie Italienne, followed by *Toinette et Louis* a year later.

Grieg, Edvard (Hagerup) (1843–1907) Norwegian nationalist composer. Much of his music is written on a small scale, particularly his songs, dances, sonatas, and piano works, and strongly identifies with Norwegian folk music. Among his orchestral works are the piano concerto in A

minor (1869) and the incidental music for Henrik Ibsen's drama *Peer Gynt* (1876), commissioned by Ibsen and the Norwegian government.

Grieg was born in Bergen, the son of a merchant. He was taught piano by his mother from 1849. In 1858 the Norwegian composer Ole Bull persuaded Grieg's parents to send him to study at Leipzig, Germany, and he entered the conservatory there. In 1863 he went to live in Copenhagen, Denmark, and studied with Niels Gade. In 1864 he met Rikard Nordaak, who fired his enthusiasm for Norwegian national music, and became engaged to his cousin Nina Hagerup, whom he married in 1867, settling as a teacher and conductor in Christiania (Oslo). He was a director of the Christiania Philharmonic Society in 1866 and played a part in the formation of the Norwegian Academy of Music. In 1869, in Copenhagen, he premiered his most lasting work, the piano concerto in A minor. The premiere of Henrik Ibsen's *Peer Gynt*, in February 1876, secured Grieg's reputation as the leading Scandinavian composer of the day and showed his talent at its best. In 1888–89 he and his wife appeared in London, Paris, and Vienna. He was awarded honorary doctorates by Cambridge University in 1894 and by Oxford University in 1906.

Once dismissed by Claude Debussy as 'a pink bonbon stuffed with snow', Grieg is now returning to critical favour. In his music he rapidly developed a style that included echoes of Norwegian folk song and his own harmonic experiments. This combination produced music of great strength and individuality. He was primarily a lyrical composer.

Works SOLO VOICES, CHORUS, AND ORCHESTRA *Landsighting, Olaf Trygvason; Bergliot* (Bjørnson) for declamation and orchestra.

CHAMBER AND SOLO VOCAL string quartet in G minor (1878); three sonatas for violin and piano; sonata for cello and piano; 24 Op. nos of piano pieces, including ten volumes of *Lyric Pieces*, sonata in E minor, *Slåtter, Norwegian Peasant Dances* (1903); 143 songs, including *Haugtussa* cycle (Garborg, 1895), settings of Ibsen and Bjørnson.

OTHER incidental music for Ibsen's *Peer Gynt* (1876) and Bjørnson's *Sigurd Jorsalfar* (1872); *Holberg Suite* for string orchestra (1884); piano concerto in A minor (1869).

Griffes, Charles T(omlinson) (1884–1920) US composer. He studied in Berlin, Germany, with Engelbert Humperdinck and taught there for a time. He returned to the USA in 1907, and became a music teacher at a boys' school in Tarrytown, New York. His early death was brought about by ill health and overwork.

Works STAGE Japanese mime play *Schojo* (1917); dance drama *The Kairn of Koridwen* (1916). ORCHESTRAL *The Pleasure Dome of Kubla Khan* (after Coleridge) for orchestra (1917); *Poem* for flute and orchestra (1918).

CHORUS *These Things Shall Be* (J A Symonds) for unison chorus.

CHAMBER Sketches on Indian themes for string quartet; piano sonata and pieces.

OTHER songs.

Grigny, Nicolas de (1672–1703) French organist and composer. He studied under his father – Louis de Grigny (c.1646–1709), organist at Notre-Dame of Rheims – and in Paris. He was organist of the abbey of Saint-Denis, Paris, 1693–95, and then of Rheims Cathedral. Organ music written by him and published in 1699 was known and copied by Johann Sebastian Bach in his early years.

Grillparzer, Franz (1791–1872) Austrian poet and dramatist. He was a friend of Ludwig van Beethoven and Franz Schubert. He wrote a funeral oration for the former and a sketched inscription for the latter's gravestone. For works used by composers, see Johann ➤ **Hummel** (*Ahnfrau*), C ➤ **Kreutzer** (*Libussa* and *Melusine*), ➤ **Sappho** (Hugo Kaun), ➤ **Schöne Melusine** (Mendelssohn and Conradin Kreutzer), ➤ **Schubert** (*Ständchen* and *Mirjams Siegesgesang*), Ignaz ➤ **Seyfried** (*Ahnfrau* and *König Ottokar*), and Oskar ➤ **Straus** (*Traum ein Leben*).

Grisar, Albert (1808–1869) Belgian composer. He was intended for a business career and was sent to Liverpool, England, but ran away to Paris, France, to study music in 1830. He became a pupil of Antonín Reicha, but was driven to Antwerp by the Revolution. He produced *Le Mariage impossible* in Brussels in 1833, and returned to Paris, where he had further operatic successes. He studied with Giuseppe Mercadante in Naples, Italy, in 1840 and returned to Paris in 1844.

Works OPERA *Sarah* (after Scott, 1836), *L'An 1000, Lady Melvill* (1838), and *L'Eau merveilleuse* (both with Flotow), *Le Naufrage de la Méduse* (with Flotow and Pilati), *Les Travestissements* (1839), *L'Opéra à la cour* (with Boïeldieu, junior), *Gille Ravisseur* (1848), *Les Porcherons* (1850), *Bonsoir M Pantalon, Le Carillonneur de Bruges* (1852), *Les Amours du diable, Le Chien du jardinier* (1855), *Voyage autour de ma chambre* (after Xavier de Maistre, 1859), *La Chatte merveilleuse* (1862), *Bégaiements d'amour, Douze Innocentes* (1865).

Griselda, La opera by Alessandro Scarlatti (libretto after A Zeno), first produced at the Teatro Capranica, Rome, Italy, in January 1721. It was the last of Scarlatti's 69 operas, beginning with *Gli equivoci* (1679). A modern edition was arranged by Lionel Salter. In the story, King Gualtiero tests his wife, Griselda. She must live as a peasant, is threatened with the loss of her son,

and is pursued by Ottone. She remains true and is restored as queen.

Grisélidis opera by Jules Massenet (libretto by A Silvestre and E Morand), first produced at the Opéra-Comique, Paris, France, on 20 November 1901. It was revived at the Wexford Festival, Ireland, in 1983. It tells how Grisélidis the shepherdess marries the Marquis de Saluces, who has the Devil test her fidelity.

Grocheio, Johannes de (lived 1300) Music theorist of uncertain nationality who worked in Paris, France, around 1300. His *De musica* survives in two manuscripts and is important for the light it throws on the secular music of his day and how it was performed.

Grofé, Ferde (1892–1972) US composer and arranger. He worked as an arranger for the Paul Whiteman band, and in 1924 arranged George Gershwin's *Rhapsody in Blue*. His own music includes *Mississippi Suite*, *Hollywood Suite*, and the well-known *Grand Canyon Suite*, which was premiered under Paul Whiteman in 1931.

grosse caisse (French 'great case or chest') French name for the ➤ **bass drum**.

Grosse Fuge, Great Fugue a work for string quartet by Beethoven, Op. 133, in a fugal form 'tantôt libre, tantôt recherchée', written in 1825 as the finale of the B flat major string quartet, Op. 130, and first performed with it in Vienna, Austria, on 21 March 1826. Beethoven was persuaded by his publisher that it was too long, difficult, and abstruse for that purpose and subsequently wrote the new finale, now part of Op. 130. There is also a version for two pianos, Op. 134.

It is also the title for the first version of Ferruccio Busoni's *Fantasia contrappuntistica* (1910).

Grossin or **Grossim, Estienne (lived c.1420)** French composer. He was chaplain at St Merry, Paris, in 1418, and *clerc de matines* at Notre Dame in 1421. He wrote church music and chansons, including a Mass (without *Agnus*) with a part labelled 'trombetta'.

Grossinquisitor, Der, The Grand Inquisitor oratorio by Boris Blacher (text by L Borchard, from Fyodor Dostoevsky's *The Brothers Karamazov*); it was composed in 1942 and first performed in Berlin, Germany, on 14 October 1947.

Grossvater-Tanz (German 'grandfather's dance') believed at one time to be a 17th-century German dance (with words referring to a grandfather's wooing), sung and danced at weddings, and later used as the final dance at balls and therefore called *Kehraus*, 'sweep-out'. Robert Schumann used it both in *Papillons*, Op. 2, and *Carnaval*, Op. 9, in the latter to stand for the 'Philistines' in the finale. The dance was actually written by Karl Gottlieb Hering (1765–1853).

Grosz, Wilhelm (1894–1939) Austrian composer. His music has become associated with Kurt Weill, and a concert of their music was given at the London Proms in 1993.

Grosz studied theory under Guido Adler and composition under Franz Schreker. In 1921 he was appointed conductor at Mannheim Opera, Germany, but returned to Vienna in 1922 to make a living as pianist and composer. From 1928 he worked with a gramophone company in Berlin, and conducted the Kammerspiele in Vienna 1933–34. He then left Germany and became a refugee in London and New York.

Works STAGE AND INCIDENTAL MUSIC operas *Sganarell* (1925) and *Achtung, Aufnahme* (1930); play with music *St Peters Regenschirm*; ballets *Der arme Reinhold* (1928) and *Baby in der Bar*; incidental music to Werfel's *Spiegelmensch* and Hauptmann's *Die versunkene Glocke*; music for films and radio.

ORCHESTRAL Symphonic Variations, serenade, suite, overture to an opera buffa and other pieces for orchestra; Symphonic Dance for piano and orchestra.

CHAMBER string quartet; two violin and piano sonatas; three piano sonatas.

ground in music, composition built on a ➤ ground bass, or the bass itself.

ground bass in music, a bass line that repeats cyclically, over which an evolving harmonic-melodic structure is laid. Examples are the ➤ chaconne and ➤ passacaglia.

Grout, Donald J(ay) (1902–1987) US musicologist. He studied at Syracuse and Harvard universities in the USA and in Strasbourg, France, and Vienna, Austria. He taught at Harvard 1936–42, and was professor of music at Cornell University, USA, 1945–70. Early opera and the works of Alessandro Scarlatti were at the centre of his research. His books include *A Short History of Opera* (1948, revised 1965), *A History of Western Music* (1960, revised 1973, 1980 and, with C V Palisca, 1988), and *Mozart in the History of Opera* (1972).

Grove, George (1820–1900) English scholar. He edited the original *Dictionary of Music and Musicians* (1889), which in its expanded and revised form is still one of the standard music reference sources. He was also the first director of the ➤ Royal College of Music. He was knighted in 1882.

Groves, Charles Barnard (1915–1992) English conductor. Known both as a choral and symphonic conductor, he is an outstanding interpreter of British music, especially the works of

Frederick Delius. He was knighted in 1973.

Gruber, H(einz) K(arl) (1943–) Austrian composer. He has played the double bass in various Viennese orchestras, and co-founded the avant-garde group **MOB Art and Tone ART**.

He studied at the Vienna Hochschule and with Gottfried von Einem.

Works STAGE melodrama *Die Vertreibung aus dem Paradies* for speakers and six instruments (1966); spectacle *Gomorrah* (1972); 'pandemonium' *Frankenstein!!* for baritone and orchestra (1977); stage work *Gloria von Jaxtberg* (1993).

ORCHESTRAL concerto for orchestra (1964), *Manhattan Broadcasts* for chamber orchestra, *Arien* for violin and orchestra, *Rough Music*, concerto for percussion and orchestra (1983); two violin concertos (1978, revised 1992, and 1988); cello concerto (1989).

VOICES AND INSTRUMENTS Mass for chorus, two trumpets, horn, double bass, and percussion (1960), *Reportage aus Gomorrah* for five singers and eight players (1976).

OTHER *Demilitarized Zones* for brass band (1979), *Bring Me the Head of Amadeus*, TV film for the Mozart bicentenary (1991).

Gruenberg, Louis (1884–1964) US pianist and composer. His most successful work was the opera *Emperor Jones*, premiered at the New York Metropolitan Opera House in 1933 with Lawrence Tibbett in the title role.

Gruenberg was born in Russia and was taken to the USA at the age of two. He studied in Berlin, Germany, and Vienna, Austria, where he was a piano pupil of Ferruccio Busoni. He first appeared as a pianist in Berlin in 1912 and then began to travel, but from 1919 remained in the USA to devote himself wholly to composition.

Works OPERA *The Bride of the Gods* (1913; libretto by Busoni), *The Dumb Wife*, *Jack and the Beanstalk* (after Eugene O'Neill, 1933), *Helena of Troy* (1936); children's opera *The Witch of Brocken*; radio opera *Green Mansions* (after W H Hudson; 1937).

ORCHESTRAL five symphonies, *The Hill of Dreams* (1921), *Enchanted Isle*, Serenade for orchestra; violin concerto.

VOICE AND ORCHESTRA *The Daniel Jazz* (V Lindsey), *Animals and Insects*, and *The Creation* for voice and chamber orchestra.

CHAMBER *Four Indiscretions* for string quartet, two string quartets, two sonatas for violin and piano; piano pieces.

Gruppen work by Karlheinz Stockhausen for three orchestras, placed in different parts of a hall and playing different music; it was composed 1955–57 and first performed in Cologne, Germany, on 24 March 1959.

gruppetto or **gruppo** or **groppo** in music, one of several similar Italian terms used in the 16th century for trills (rapid oscillation between adjacent notes), and later for the turn (a form of melodic pirouette around a note). As a turn, the gruppetto designates a four-note figure consisting of the note above the principal note, the note itself, the note below, and the note itself. It was often used as an extemporized embellishment, especially by singers.

gruppo in music, a trill or turn. See ➤ **gruppetto**.

GSMD abbreviation for ➤ **Guildhall School of Music and Drama**.

Guadagni, Gaetano (c. 1725–1792) Italian castrato alto, later soprano. He made his first appearance in Parma in 1747, and went to London, England, in 1748, where he sang in *Messiah*, *Samson*, and *Theodora* (first performance 1750). He later sang in Dublin, Paris, Lisbon, Italy, and Vienna, where he was the first Orpheus in Christoph Willibald von Gluck's *Orfeo* in 1762.

Guadagnini, Giovanni Battista (J B) (1711–1786) Italian violin maker. He worked in Piacenza, Milan, Cremona, Parma, and Turin. His father, **Lorenzo Guadagnini** (before 1695–c.1748), worked in Piacenza, and may have been a pupil of Stradivari. Giovanni Battista's son, **Giuseppe Guadagnini** (c.1736–1805), nicknamed *Il soldato* ('the soldier'), worked in Como, Pavia, and Turin.

Guarini, Giovanni Battista (1537–1612) Italian poet. He inspired musical works including *Il* ➤ *pastor fido* (Handel and E ➤ **Settle**) and *Idropica* (Salomone ➤ **Rossi**).

Guarnieri, (Mozart) Camargo (1907–1993) Brazilian composer. He was conductor of the Orquestra Sinfônica Municipal, São Paulo, and director of the Conservatory from 1960. He often visited the USA, where many of his works were performed.

He was a pupil of Charles Koechlin in Paris, France.

Works four symphonies; five piano concertos (1936–70), two violin concertos (1940, 1953); chamber music; cello and piano sonata; piano pieces; songs.

Gubaidulina, Sofia (1931–) Russian composer. In 1975 she co-founded the group Astreya, for improvisations on folk instruments from Russia and Caucasia. A leading member of the New Music generation of Russian composers, she has often turned to literature and religion for inspiration. She has been resident in Germany since 1991, the year in which her opera-oratorio-ballet *Prayer for the Age of Aquarius* was premiered.

She studied at the Moscow Conservatory

1954–59 and later with Vissarion Shebalin.

Works ORCHESTRAL *Offertorium* violin concerto (1980–86), *Seven Words* for cello, bayan, and strings (1982), *Stimmen ... verstummen* symphony in twelve movements (1986), *Pro et Contra* for large orchestra (1989).

VOCAL *Night in Memphis* cantata (1968–92), *Rubayat* cantata for baritone and orchestra (1969), *Perception* for soprano, baritone, and seven strings (1985), *Hommage à T S Eliot* for soprano and octet (1987), *Aus dem Stundenbuch/From the Book of Hours* for cello, orchestra, male chorus, and female speaker (1991).

CHAMBER piano sonata (1965), four string quartets (1971, 1987, 1987, 1990), *De Profundis* for bayan (1978), *Garten von Freuden und Traurigkeiten* for flute, harp, and viola (1988), string trio (1988), *Silenzio* five pieces for bayan, violin, and cello (1991), *Even and Uneven* for seven percussionists (1991).

Guerrero, Francisco (1528–1599) Spanish composer. He published a large number of works, both religious and secular, and earned himself a reputation in Spain second only to that of Tomás de Victoria as a composer of church music in the 16th century. His works include Masses, requiems, motets, psalms, and Passions in a flowing polyphonic style; they were much admired for their complex canonic devices and remained in use long after his death, especially in South America.

He studied under his brother Pedro Guerrero and Fernández de Castilleja at Seville Cathedral, where he was a chorister 1542–46; he also had some lessons from Cristóbal de Morales as a child. In 1546 he was appointed maestro de capilla at the Cathedral of Jaén, and after the death of Morales to that of Málaga, though he never lived there, but filled posts at Seville Cathedral from 1549 until he succeeded Castilleja as maestro de capilla in March 1574. He visited Lisbon, Rome (twice), Venice, and in 1588 went to the Holy Land. Many of his works were published in France and Italy.

Works 18 Masses, about 150 liturgical pieces, including motets, psalms, vespers, Magnificats, Te Deum; sacred and secular songs.

Guglielmi, Pietro Alessandro (1728–1804) Italian composer. He produced his first opera in Naples in 1757, and thereafter had great success throughout Italy and abroad. He was in England intermittently 1767–72, and also visited Brunswick and Dresden, Germany. In 1793 he was appointed maestro di cappella at St Peter's, Rome.

He studied under Francesco Durante in Naples.

Works OPERA about 100, including *Il ratto della sposa* (1765), *La sposa fedele* (1767), *La villanella ingentilita* (1779), *I finti amori*, *La virtuosa di Mergellina* (1785), *L'inganno amoroso*, *La pastor-*

ella nobile, and *La bella pescatrice* (1789).

ORATORIOS AND CHURCH MUSIC oratorios including *La morte d'Abele, La Betulia liberata*, and others; church music.

OTHER symphonies; chamber music, keyboard music.

Guglielmi, Pietro Carlo (c.1763–1817) Italian

composer, son of Pietro Alessandro ➤ **Guglielmi**. He studied at the Conservatorio di Santa Maria di Loreto in Naples, producing the first of many successful operas in 1794 in Madrid, Spain. He also visited London, Lisbon, and Paris.

Works almost 50 operas, *Amor tutto vince* (1805), *Guerra aperta* (1807); oratorio *La distruzione di Gerusalemme* (1803).

Guglielmo Ratcliff, William Ratcliff opera by

Pietro Mascagni (libretto by composer, based on Heinrich Heine's tragedy), first produced at La Scala, Milan, Italy, on 16 February 1895. It is an earlier work than his *Cavalleria rusticana*, although it was produced later. In the story, Mary and Count Douglas are to marry, but Ratcliff wants to kill Douglas to avenge his father, killed by Mary's father. In the end he kills Mary and himself as well.

Guido d'Arezzo (c.990–c.1050) Italian Bene-

dictine monk and music theorist. He greatly advanced solmization and mutation by adapting the syllables Ut, Re, Mi, Fa, Sol, and La to the hexachord and by demonstrating the hexachordal positions on the fingers by the use of the 'Guidonian hand'.

He lived in Pomposa and Arezzo, and visited Rome. He was once, rather doubtfully, credited with the invention of the music stave, the use of which he certainly encouraged. His chief theoretical work, written about 1026, is entitled *Micrologus de musica*.

Guildhall School of Music and Drama, GSMD

conservatoire established in 1880 as the first municipal music college in Great Britain. It now offers courses in music, acting, and technical theatre, and is owned, funded, and managed by the Corporation of London. Since 1977 it has been housed in the Barbican, London.

Guilelmus Monachus (lived 15th century)

Music theorist of uncertain nationality who lived in Italy but may possibly have been English. His treatise *De praeceptis artis musicae* contains references to the English use of 'fauxbourdon' and 'gymel'.

Guillaume Tell, William Tell opera by André

Grétry (libretto by J M Sedaine), first produced at the Comédie-Italienne, Paris, France, on 9 April 1791.

It is also the title of an opera by Rossini (libretto by V J E de Jouy and H L F Bis, based on Schiller's drama), first produced at the Paris Opéra, France, on 3 August 1829. It was Rossini's last opera. It tells the story of the Swiss patriot William Tell.

Guilmant, (Félix) Alexandre (1837–1911)

French organist and composer. He toured widely with great success and was professor of organ at the Schola Cantorum in Paris, which he had helped Charles Bordes and Vincent d'Indy to found, and at the Paris Conservatory.

He was a pupil of his father, an organist at Boulogne, where he afterwards held several church appointments, studying briefly in Brussels with Jaak Lemmens in 1860 and moving to Paris in 1871, where he was organist at the Trinité Church until 1901.

Works two symphonies for organ and orchestra; eight sonatas and 25 sets of pieces for organ, organ music for church use.

guimbarde French name for the ➤ Jew's harp.

Guiraud, Ernest (1837–1892) French com-

poser. He wrote operas, several cantatas, and overtures, and recitatives for Bizet's *Carmen* and Offenbach's *Contes d'Hoffmann*; he also finished the orchestration of the latter.

Guiraud was born in New Orleans, USA, the son of a French musician. He studied at the Paris Conservatory and won the Prix de Rome in 1859. He served in the Franco-Prussian War and in 1876 became professor of harmony and accompaniment at the Conservatory, following Victor Massé as the head of the advanced composition class in 1880. Debussy was one of his pupils.

Works OPERA *Sylvie* (1864), *En Prison* (1869), *Le Kobold* (1870), *Madame Turlupin, Piccolino* (1876), *Galante Aventure, Le Feu, Frédégonde* (unfinished, completed by Saint-Saëns).

BALLET *Gretna Green* (1873).

ORCHESTRAL overture *Arteveld, Chasse fantastique* (after Hugo's *Beau Pécopin*), and suite for orchestra; Caprice for violin and orchestra.

OTHER recitatives for Bizet's *Carmen* and orchestration of Offenbach's *Contes d'Hoffmann*.

Guiraut de Bornelh alternative spelling of ➤ Gir-

aud de Borneil, Provençal troubadour.

Guirlande, La, ou Les Fleurs enchantées acte

de ballet by Jean-Philippe Rameau (libretto by J-F Marmontel), first produced at the Paris Opéra, France, on 21 September 1751. In the story, the garlands exchanged by Myrtil and Zélide will only stay fresh as long as they remain faithful.

guitar plucked, fretted string instrument. It may

be called the classical guitar, the Spanish guitar (because of its origins), or the acoustic guitar (to differentiate it from the electric guitar). The fingerboard has ➤ frets (strips of metal showing where to place the finger to obtain different notes), and the six or twelve strings are plucked or strummed with the fingers or a plectrum. The strings are tuned to E2, A3, D3, G3, B4, and E4. The Hawaiian guitar is laid across the player's lap, and uses a metal bar to produce a distinctive gliding tone. The solid-bodied ➤ electric guitar, was developed in the 1950s by Les Paul and Leo Fender. It mixes and amplifies vibrations from electromagnetic pickups (microphones which 'pick up' the vibration of the strings and convert them to electrical impulses) at different points to produce a range of tone qualities.

The guitar is used widely in folk music, and its prominence in popular music can be traced from the traditions of the US Midwest; it played a supporting harmony role in jazz and dance bands during the 1920s and adapted quickly to electric amplification. It is also played as a classical instrument, and its 20th-century revival owes much to Andrés Segovia, Julian Bream, and John Williams. Important solo works have been written for the instrument by Luciano Berio. Concertos for guitar and orchestra have been written by Malcolm Arnold, Richard Rodney Bennett, and several by the Spanish composer Joaquín Rodrigo, including *Concierto de Aranjuez* (1940).

The open strings of the modern classical guitar.

guitar, electric amplified acoustic guitar employing optional electromagnetic pickups set under the strings to detect vibration, bypassing the soundbox. The solid-bodied instrument developed in the 1950s by Leo Fender and Les Paul has a cutaway body to extend fingering positions, and multiple pickups for harder and softer timbres that can be varied in balance while playing.

The technique of 'humbucking' uses feedback circuits to recycle guitar body reverberation to create indefinite sustain. This allowed the development in the 1970s of a distinctive singing tone by hard-rock lead guitarists.

Other forms include the **double-neck guitar** and the **electric bass**, a guitar version of the string bass.

Composers who have used the electric guitar include Frank Martin, Pierre Boulez, and Luciano Berio.

guitar violoncello alternative name for the ➤ arpeggione, a stringed musical instrument.

Gundry, Inglis (1905–2000) English composer. Educated at Oxford, he read classics and philosophy, then qualified as a barrister, but turned to literature, writing poems and a novel, *The Countess's Penny* (1934), and working as a teacher and a librarian. He studied at the Royal College of

Music, London, under Ralph Vaughan Williams, Gordon Jacob, and Reginald Morris. After war service in the navy, he became instructor lieutenant and music adviser to the Admiralty education department, for which he edited a *Naval Song Book*. He went on to write several operas, for which he also wrote the libretti, as well as composing and editing several other orchestral works.

Works OPERA *Naaman: the Leprosy of War* (1937), *The Return of Odysseus* (after Homer, 1938), *The Sleeping Beauty* and *Partisans* (1946).

BALLET *Sleep.*

ORCHESTRAL Variations on an Indian theme and overture *Per mare, per terram* for orchestra; Comedy Overture for small orchestra; *Sostenuto and Vivace* for strings.

CHAMBER Fantasy string quartet.

OTHER songs.

Günther von Schwarzburg opera by Ignaz Holzbauer (libretto by A Klein), first produced for the court in Mannheim, Gemany, on 5 January 1777. It tells how Günther battles with Karl for control of the Holy Roman Empire, finally being poisoned by Karl's mother. The opera was admired by Mozart.

Guntram opera by Richard Strauss (libretto by composer), first produced in Weimar, Germany, on 10 May 1894. It was Strauss's first opera. A revised version was produced in Weimar on 22 October 1940. In the story, Guntram kills Duke Robert after being attacked by him, but the idealistic minstrel realizes that his deed was caused by love for the Duke's wife, Freihild. Guntram seeks solitude for introspection.

Guridi, Jesús (1886–1961) Spanish composer of Basque descent. He studied at the Schola Cantorum in Paris, France, also at Liège and Cologne. His music is based on Basque themes.

Works STAGE operas *Mirentxu* (1915), *Amaya* (1920); zarzuela *El caserío* (1926).

OTHER orchestra and organ music; church music; four string quartets; settings of Basque folksongs.

Gurney, Ivor (Bertie) (1890–1937) English composer and poet. He was a choirboy at Gloucester Cathedral and later studied at the Royal College of Music in London with a scholarship. He suffered much from ill-health and during World War I was badly wounded and shell-shocked. He struggled for a time against poverty, but in 1922 lost his reason. He died of tuberculosis.

He published two volumes of poetry, *Severn and Somme* (1917) and *War's Embers* (1919).

Works *The Apple Orchard* and *Scherzo* for violin and piano; two sets of piano pieces; song cycles *Ludlow and Teme* (A E Housman) and *The Western*

Playland, over 200 songs, some to his own poems.

Gurrelieder, Songs of Gurra work by Arnold Schoenberg for five soloists, speaker, four choruses, and large orchestra, including iron chains (the text is a German translation of the Danish poems by J P Jacobsen). It was composed 1900–11 and first performed in Vienna, Austria, on 23 February 1913, conducted by Franz Schreker. Its first US performance was in Philadelphia on 8 April 1932, conducted by Leopold Stokowski.

Gustave III, ou Le Bal masqué, Gustavus III, or The Masked Ball opera by Daniel Auber (libretto by Augustin Scribe), first produced at the Paris Opéra, France, on 27 February 1833. In the story King Gustav is stabbed by the jealous husband of Amelia.

Gutiérrez, Antonio Garcia (1812–1884) Spanish dramatist. His works inspired the operas ➤ *Simon Boccanegra* and *Il* ➤ *Trovatore* by Verdi.

Guy, Barry (1947–) English composer and double bass player. His early interest was in jazz; he later studied at the Guildhall School of Music with Buxton Orr and Patric Standford. Since he formed the Jazz Composers' Orchestra in 1971 his works have combined improvisatory with more controlled avant-garde techniques.

Works *D* for 15 solo strings (1972); *Anna* for amplified double bass and orchestra (1974); *Statements III* and *IV* for jazz orchestra (1972–75); string quartet *III* (1973); *Songs from Tomorrow* for 13 instruments (1975); *Voyages of the Moon* for double bass and orchestra (1983); *Blitz*, septet (1984); *rondOH!* for piano, violin, and double bass (1985); *Video Life* for double bass and electronics (1986); ballet for London Contemporary Dance Theatre; *After the Rain* (1992); *Bird Gong Game* (1992); *Witch Gong Game* (1993); *Portraits* (1993).

Guy-Ropartz, Joseph Guy Marie Ropartz (1864–1955) French composer. After studying law, he went to the Paris Conservatory as a pupil of François Dubois, Jules Massenet, and César Franck. In 1894 he became director of the Nancy Conservatory and in 1919 of that of Strasbourg. Later he retired to Brittany, where he was born.

Works STAGE four operas, including *Le Pays* (1913); ballet *L'Indiscret*.

CHURCH MUSIC three Masses, motets, and other church music.

ORCHESTRAL five symphonies (1895–1945), *La Cloche des morts*, *La Chasse du Prince Arthur*.

CHAMBER six string quartets (1893–1951); three violin and piano sonatas, two cello and piano sonatas.

OTHER songs; organ music.

Gwendoline opera by Emmanuel Chabrier (libretto by C Mendès), first produced at the Théâtre de la Monnaie, Brussels, Belgium, on 10 April 1886. In the story, Gwendoline, daughter of the Saxon leader Armel, is to marry the Dane Harald. Armel plans to massacre the Danes during the festivities. Gwendoline tries to warn Harald, but it is too late and kills herself.

gymel (from Latin *gemellum*, 'a twinsong') vocal music in two parts, both of the same range. A characteristic feature is the use of parallel thirds. The term first occurs in the 15th century, when it usually refers to a divided voice-part in a polyphonic composition, but examples are found as early as the 14th century.

Gymnopédies three pieces for piano by Erik Satie, composed in 1888. Nos. 1 and 3 (*Lent et triste*, *Lent et grave*) were orchestrated by Claude Debussy and performed in Paris, on 20 February 1897.

Gymnopédies refers to Greek dances in honour of Apollo, performed by naked men and boys; Debussy's music has become a popular ballet.

Gyrowetz or **Jírovec, Adalbert (Vojcěch) (1763–1850)** Bohemian composer. He wrote about 40 operas and 100 chamber and piano pieces, mostly in a style resembling Haydn's. He knew Beethoven, and was a pall-bearer at his funeral in 1827.

He learnt music from his father, a choirmaster. He later went to Prague to study law, but continued to work at music. As private secretary to Count Franz von Fünfkirchen, he was expected to take part in the domestic music. He then went to Italy for study under Nicola Sala in Naples and later visited Paris, France, where symphonies of his had been performed under the name of Haydn. In 1789 the French Revolution drove him to London, England, where the score of his opera *Semiramis* was burnt in the fire of the Pantheon in 1792. He returned to Vienna, Austria, soon after, and in 1804 was appointed conductor at the court theatres, where he wrote many works until 1831.

Works STAGE Italian operas *Federica ed Adolfo* (1812) and *Il finto Stanislao* (1818); German operas *Agnes Sorel* (1806), *Ida die Büssende* (1807), *Der Augenarzt*, *Robert, oder Die Prüfung* (1815), *Helene*, *Felix und Adele*, *Hans Sachs*, *Die Junggesellen-Wirtschaft*, *Der Sammtrock*, *Aladin* (after Oehlenschläger), *Das Ständchen* (1823), and others; ballet *Die Hochzeit der Thetis* (1816) and others; melodramas *Mirina* and others.

VOCAL comic cantata *Die Dorfschule*.

ORCHESTRAL over 60 symphonies, serenades, overtures, and other orchestral works.

CHAMBER about 60 string quartets, quintets, numerous trios; about 40 violin and piano sonatas.

OTHER instrumental pieces, dances; songs.

H in music, the German equivalent of ➤ B natural.

Haas, Robert (Maria) (1886–1960) Austrian musicologist. He edited the original versions of Anton Bruckner's works 1932–42, and was succeeded in this task by Leopold Nowak. He wrote books on baroque music, musical performance, Mozart, and Bruckner.

Haas received a doctorate from Prague University and became assistant to the musicologist Guido Adler. He later became a lecturer at Vienna University and director of the music department of the State Library there.

Hába, Alois (1893–1973) Czech composer. Much of his work (after the suite for strings 1917) is based on the division of the scale into quarter-tones. He later employed sixth-tones (as in the fifth quartet, 1923), and fifth-tones (as in the 16th quartet, 1967). He also wrote some 12-tone music, for example *Fantasia* for nonet (1932).

He gained a knowledge of folk music before he began studying at the Prague Conservatory under Vitězslav Novák. He later became a pupil of Franz Schreker in Vienna, Austria, and Berlin, Germany. While working for Universal Edition in Vienna he gained a good knowledge of Arnold Schoenberg's music. He was appointed professor at the Prague Conservatory in 1924.

Works OPERA *Matka/Mother* (Munich, 1931).

ORCHESTRAL overture and symphonic music for orchestra; fantasy for piano and orchestra; violin concerto.

CHAMBER 16 string quartets (1919–67) and other chamber music.

INSTRUMENTAL piano sonata and other works (some for quarter-tone piano); works for string instruments.

habanera or **havanaise** Cuban dance named after the city of Havana. The most popular dance in Latin America during the 19th century, it was the ancestor of other dance forms, including the Argentine tango. The habanera is usually in slow duple time (2/4) and uses a variety of standard rhythms. There is a celebrated example in Bizet's opera *Carmen* (1875).

Habeneck, François Antoine (1781–1849) French violinist and conductor. He was the founder of the Société des Concerts du Conservatoire in Paris, conductor at the Opéra 1824–47, and gave the first performances of *Guillaume Tell*, *Les Huguenots*, *La Juive*, and *Benvenuto Cellini*. He was the first conductor to cultivate Beethoven's music in France. He was a pupil of Pierre Baillot.

Hacomblene or **Hacomplaynt, Robert (c.1456–1528)** English composer. He was a scholar at Eton 1469–72 and King's College, Cambridge, from 1472. He was a fellow at Cambridge 1475–93 and provost from 1509 until his death. A *Salve Regina* by him is in the Eton Choirbook.

Haddon Hall operetta by Arthur Sullivan (libretto by Sydney Grundy), first produced at the Savoy Theatre, London, England, on 24 September 1892.

Hadley, Henry (Kimball) (1871–1937) US conductor and composer. He studied with his father, George Chadwick in Boston, and Eusebius Mandyczewski in Vienna, Austria. He conducted opera in the USA and Germany, and was conductor of the Seattle Symphony Orchestra 1909–11 and the San Francisco Symphony Orchestra 1911–15. From 1920 he lived in New York.

Works OPERA *Safié* (1909), *Azora, Daughter of Montezuma* (1917), *Bianca, Cleopatra's Night* (1920), and *Mirtil in Arcadia*.

VOCAL AND ORCHESTRAL Music, *The New Earth*, and *Resurgam* for solo voices, chorus, and orchestra; five symphonies; overtures *In Bohemia*, *Herod*, and to Shakespeare's *Othello*; symphonic fantasy; tone poems *Salome*, *Lucifer*, and *The Ocean*.

Hadley, Patrick (Arthur Sheldon) (1899–1973) English composer. His musical output is small but distinguished, and includes incidental music for Greek plays, choral works *The Trees so High* (1931) and *The Hills* (1944), a rhapsody *One Morning in Spring* for small orchestra, vocal works, church music, and a string quartet.

He was educated at Winchester College and Cambridge University, and studied music at the Royal College of Music in London, where in 1925 he joined the teaching staff. He received a PhD from Cambridge in 1938, and was appointed lecturer at the university and professor of music 1946–62.

Works STAGE incidental music to Sophocles'*Antigone.*

VOICE, CHORUS, AND ORCHESTRA symphony for baritone and chorus *The Trees so High* (1931), *La Belle Dame sans merci* (Keats) for tenor, chorus, and orchestra, *My Beloved Spake* (Song of Solomon) for chorus and orchestra; cantatas *The Hills* for soprano, tenor, bass, chorus, and orchestra (1944), and *Travellers, Ephemera* (Yeats) and *Mariana* (Tennyson, 1937) for voice and chamber orchestra.

CHAMBER string quartet in C major, fantasy for two violins and piano.

OTHER songs; part songs.

Hadow, W(illiam) H(enry) (1859–1937) English educationist and music scholar. He was educated at Malvern College and Oxford, where later he lectured on music, having studied at Darmstadt, Germany, and under C H Lloyd. He was principal of Armstrong College, Newcastle-upon-Tyne, 1909–19, and vice-chancellor of Sheffield University 1919–30. He edited the *Oxford History of Music* and wrote volume v, *The Viennese Period* (1904); other books include *Studies in Modern Music* (1892, 1894, revised 1926) and *English Music* (1931). He also composed chamber music and songs.

'Haffner' Serenade Mozart's Serenade in D major, K250, written in Salzburg, Austria, in July 1776 for the marriage of Elisabeth Haffner, daughter of the late Bürgermeister Sigmund Haffner, celebrated on 22 July.

'Haffner' Symphony Mozart's Symphony in D major K385, composed in Vienna, Austria, in the summer of 1782 for the Haffner family, probably on the occasion of the ennoblement of Sigmund Haffner, junior, on 29 July 1782.

Hagith opera in one act by Karol Szymanowski (libretto by composer after F Dormann); it was composed 1912–13, while Szymanowski was living in Vienna, Austria, and first produced in Warsaw, Poland, on 13 May 1922. In the story, Hagith is stoned to death after she refuses to become a sacrifice for King David.

Hahn, Reynaldo (1874–1947) French composer and conductor. He was popular in Parisian salons as a performer of his own songs, and was admired by the French novelist Marcel Proust. In 1934 he was appointed music critic of *Le Figaro*,

and in 1945 became music director of the Paris Opéra. As a conductor he specialized in Mozart and as a composer he wrote much incidental music for plays, two ballets, operas, and operettas.

He was sent to the Paris Conservatory at the age of 11, where his teachers included Jules Massenet. He had his first work published at the age of 14 and his first opera produced at 23.

Works OPERA *L'Île du rêve* (1898), *La Carmélite* (1902), *La Colombe de Bouddha* (1921), *Nausicaa, Le Pauvre d'Assise, La Reine de Saba, Le Temps d'aimer, Brummel* (1931), *Le Marchand de Venise* (after Shakespeare, 1935), and many operettas including *Ciboulette* (1923).

OTHER ballets *La Fête chez Thérèse* (1907) and *Le Dieu bleu* (1912); incidental music for Shakespeare's *Much Ado about Nothing*, Rostand's *Le Bois sacré*, Sacha Guitry's *Mozart* (1925), and others; ode *Prométhée* for solo voices, chorus, and orchestra; symphonic poem *Nuit d'amour bergamasque*; string quartet and other chamber music; piano pieces; songs including cycles *Chansons grises, Chansons latines, Chansons espagnoles.*

hairpins in musical notation, colloquial term for *crescendo* and *diminuendo* marks.

Halévy, Jacques François Fromental (Elias) (1799–1862), born **Jacques Lévy** French composer. His music, which consists almost entirely of operas, is brilliant and charming, rather than profound. Halévy's daughter married Georges Bizet, who finished Halévy's last opera, *Noe*, as *Le Déluge.*

From 1809 he studied at the Paris Conservatory under Luigi Cherubini, who was both a friend and a strong musical influence. After twice taking a second prize, he won the Prix de Rome in 1819. He continued to study in Italy, and on his return to Paris tried to gain a foothold on the operatic stage, for which he had already written more than one work. He succeeded with *L'Artisan* in 1827, after which he wrote an enormous number of operas. In the same year he became professor of harmony and accompaniment at the Conservatory, of counterpoint and fugue in 1833, and of composition in 1840.

Works OPERA about 40, including *La Dilettante d'Avignon, Ludovic* (begun by Hérold), *La Juive* (1835), *L'Éclair, Guido et Ginevra, Le Shérif, Le Guitarréro, La Reine de Chypre, Charles VI* (1843), *Les Mousquetaires de la reine* (1846), *Le Val d'Andorre, La Fée aux roses, La tempestà* (in Italian, after Shakespeare, 1850), *La Dame de Pique* (after Mérimée), *Le Juif errant* (after Sue), *Jaguarita l'indienne* (1855), *La Magicienne*, and others.

BALLET *Yella, Manon Lescaut* (after Prévost).

OTHER incidental music to *Prométhée enchaîné*

(translated from Aeschylus); cantatas *Les der-niers moments du Tasse*, *La mort d'Adonis* and *Herminie*; funeral march and *De profundis* on the death of the duc de Berry.

Halévy, Ludovic (1834–1908) French novelist and librettist. He collaborated with Hector Cré-mieux in the libretto for Jacques Offenbach's *Or-pheus in the Underworld*, and with Henri Meilhac on librettos for Offenbach's *La Belle Hé-lène* and *La Vie parisienne*, as well as for Georges Bizet's *Carmen*.

half-close in music, an imperfect ➤ **cadence**, such as one in which the dominant chord is pre-ceded by the tonic.

A half-close from C to G major.

Halffter, Cristóbal (1930–) Spanish com-poser. His music tends towards total serialism. In 1962 he became professor of composition at Madrid Conservatory. He was a lecturer at the University of Navarra 1970–78, and was appoin-ted director of the electronic music studio at Frei-burg im Breislau, Germany, in 1978.

He is the nephew of the brothers Ernesto and Rodolfo Halffter. He studied with Conrado del Campo and Alexandre Tansman.

Works STAGE opera *Don Quichotte* (produced Düsseldorf, 1970); ballet *Saeta*.

CHORAL cantata *In expectatione resurrectionis Domini* (1962), *Antifona pascual* for soloists, chorus, and orchestra, *Dona nobis pacem* for mixed chorus and ensemble (1984).

ORCHESTRAL concertino for string orchestra, *Sin-fonia* for three instrumental groups (1963), *Cinco microformas* for orchestra, *Dos movimientos* for timpani and string orchestra, cello concerto (1974), violin concerto (1979), two cello concer-tos (1979, 1985), Sinfonia ricercata for organ and orchestra (1982), flute concerto (1982), concerto for violin, viola, and orchestra (1984), piano con-certo (1988).

OTHER INSTRUMENTAL *Espejos* for four percussio-nists and tape (1963), *Misa ducal*, *Tres piezas* for string quartet, *Formantes* for two pianos, *Tres piezas* for solo flute, sonata for solo violin.

half tone or **half step** in music, alternative terms for ➤ **semitone**.

Halka opera by Stanisław Moniuszko (libretto, in Polish, by W Wolski, based on a story by K W Wójcicki), first performed as a concert in Wilno

on 11 January 1848 and first produced as an opera in Wilno on 28 February 1854; a revised version was performed in Warsaw, Poland, on 1 January 1858. The Polish national opera, Wallek-Walewski's opera *Jontek's Revenge*, is a sequel to it. In the story, Halka commits suicide after she is seduced and abandoned by the nobleman Janusz.

Halle or **Hale, Adam de la** French poet and com-poser; see ➤ **La Halle**.

Hallé, Charles (Carl) (1819–1895) German conductor and pianist. Settling in England in 1848, he established and led Manchester's Hallé Orchestra from 1858 until his death. As a pianist, he was the first to play all 32 Beethoven piano so-natas in London (also in Manchester and Paris).

Halling Norwegian dance originating from the Hallingdal between Oslo and Bergen. It is usu-ally in 2/4 time and goes at a moderately quick pace. In its early form, as distinct from that culti-vated by Edvard ➤ **Grieg** and other composers, its music is played on the ➤ **Hardanger fiddle**.

Haman and Mordecai masque by Handel, later recast as the oratorio ➤ *Esther*.

Hambraeus, Bengt (1928–2000) Swedish composer and musicologist. He studied musicol-ogy at the University of Uppsala 1947–56, and from 1957 worked for Swedish Radio, at the same time teaching at Uppsala University. He partici-pated in courses at Darmstadt, Germany, being chiefly influenced by the work of Anton Webern, Karlheinz Stockhausen, and Pierre Boulez.

Works OPERA chamber opera *Experiment X* (1971), church opera *Se nännis kan* (1972).

ORCHESTRAL AND ELECTRONIC *Rota* for three orches-tras, percussion, and electronic tape (1964); *Con-stellation II* for recorded tape; *Constellation III* derived from nos I and II; *Doppelrohr II*, an elec-tronic piece; *Introduzione-Sequenze-Coda*.

OTHER *Constellation I* for organ.

Hamilton, Iain Ellis (1922–2000) Scottish composer. His intensely emotional and harmoni-cally rich works include the ballet *Clerk Saunders* (1951), the operas *Pharsalia* (1968) and *The Royal Hunt of the Sun* (1967–69), which renounced mel-ody for inventive chordal formations; and sym-phonies. He was one of the first British composers to exploit the serial method.

Born in Glasgow, he worked as an aircraft en-gineer from 1939 to 1946, and from 1947 to 1951 studied at the Royal Academy of Music in Lon-don, where various works of his were introduced. He won the Royal Philharmonic Society prize for his clarinet concerto and the Koussevitsky Award for his second symphony. He was professor at Duke University, North Carolina, USA, 1961–81.

Works OPERA *Agamemnon* (1969), *The Royal Hunt of the Sun* (1967–69; produced 1977), *The*

Catiline Conspiracy (after Jonson, 1974), *Tamburlaine* (1977), *Anna Karenina* (1981), *Lancelot* (1984), *The Tragedy of Macbeth* (1990), *London's Fair* (1992).

BALLET *Clerk Saunders* (1951).

ORCHESTRAL four symphonies (1950–81), two violin concertos (1952, 1971), two piano concertos (1949, 1967), Variations for strings, *Aurora* for orchestra (1975).

CHORAL *Requiem* (1979), Mass in A (1980), *St Mark Passion* (1982).

CHAMBER octet for strings (1984), clarinet quintet, string quartet, flute quartet; variations for solo violin; viola and piano sonata; pieces for wind instruments and piano; piano sonata; violin concerto.

Hamlet incidental music for Shakespeare's tragedy by Tchaikovsky, Op. 67a, including 16 numbers and an abridged version of the *Hamlet* fantasy-overture, Op. 67, first performed in St Petersburg, Russia, on 17 November 1888. The play was first performed with Tchaikovsky's music in St Petersburg on 21 February 1891.

See also ➤ *Ambleto*; ➤ *Amleto*; ➤ Shakespeare.

Hammerklavier (German 'hammer keyboard instrument') alternative name for the ➤ piano, used to distinguish it from the ➤ harpsichord, in which the strings are plucked. Beethoven designated his sonatas Op. 101 and 106 as 'für das Hammerclavier', and the word is now used as a nickname for the latter sonata.

Hammerschmidt, Andreas (1612–1675) Bohemian composer. He was taken to Freiberg, Saxony, in 1626 and became organist there in 1635, and in Zittau in 1639. He wrote much Lutheran church music, which was published in 14 collections 1639–71.

Works sacred concertos and madrigals for several voices, sacred dialogues for two voices, odes, motets, and hymns, 17 short Lutheran Masses; thanksgiving for eight voices for the Saxon victory at Liegnitz; dances for viols.

Hammerstein, Oscar, II (1895–1960) US lyricist and librettist. He collaborated with Richard ➤ Rodgers over a period of 16 years on some of the best-known US musicals, including *Oklahoma!* (1943, Pulitzer Prize), *Carousel* (1945), *South Pacific* (1949, Pulitzer Prize), *The King and I* (1951), and *The Sound of Music* (1959).

He was a grandson of the opera impresario Oscar Hammerstein (I) (1846–1919). He earned his first successes with *Rose Marie* (1924), with music by Rudolf Friml (1879–1972); *Desert Song* (1926), music by Sigmund Romberg (1887–1951); and *Show Boat* (1927), music by Jerome Kern. *Show Boat* represented a major step forward in integration of plot and character. After a period of moderate success in film music, he joined Rodgers and began their 16-year collaboration. His adaptation of *Carmen* as a musical (*Carmen Jones*) was premiered in 1943.

His grandfather established the Manhattan Opera House in 1906, in rivalry with the New York Metropolitan Opera House. US premieres of *Elektra* and *Pelléas et Mélisande* were given but in 1920 he was bought out by the New York Metropolitan and prevented from mounting opera in New York and other major US cities. A London Opera House, opened at Kingsway in 1911, lasted only two seasons.

Hammond organ electric ➤ organ invented in the USA by Laurens Hammond in 1934. It is widely used in gospel music. Hammond applied valve technology to miniaturize Thaddeus Cahill's original 'tone-wheel' concept, introduced drawslide registration to vary timbre, and added a distinctive tremulant using rotating speakers. The ➤ synthesizer was developed from the Hammond organ.

Hampton, John (c.1455–after 1522) English composer. He was master of the choristers at Worcester Priory 1484–1522. He is represented in the Eton Choirbook.

Hanboys, John (lived 15th century) English Franciscan friar and music theorist. His treatise *Summa ... super musicam* is a commentary on ➤ Franco of Cologne.

Handbassl (Austrian and South German dialect 'little hand bass') Leopold Mozart's name for the ➤ violoncello piccolo, a musical instrument.

hand bells small hand-held bells of various pitches that are rung by a group of performers. They provide a form of practice for 'change ringing' (a team method of ringing full-size church bells using hand ropes). Many pieces of music, including Christmas carols, are easily transcribed for hand bells.

Handel, George Frideric (1685–1759), born **Georg Friedrich Händel** German composer, a British subject from 1726. His first opera, *Almira*, was performed in Hamburg in 1705. In 1710 he was appointed Kapellmeister (director) to the Elector of Hanover (the future George I of England). In 1712 he settled in England, where he established his popularity with such works as the *Water Music* (1717), written for George I. His great choral works include the *Messiah* (1742) and the later oratorios *Samson* (1743), *Belshazzar* (1745), *Judas Maccabaeus* (1747), and *Jephtha* (1752).

Visits to Italy in 1706–10 inspired a number of operas and oratorios, and in 1711 his opera *Rinaldo* was performed in London. *Saul* and *Israel in Egypt* (both 1739) were unsuccessful, but his masterpiece, the oratorio *Messiah*, met with popular approval on its first performance in Dublin, Ireland, in 1742. Other works include the pastoral *Acis and Galatea* (1718) and a set of variations for harpsichord that were later nick-named *The Harmonious Blacksmith* (1720).

Handel was born in Halle, Germany. After some opposition from his father, a barber-surgeon, he studied music with Friedrich Zachau in Halle. In 1702 he enrolled at the university there to read law, while also holding the post of organist at the Domkirche (the Calvinist Church). The next year he abandoned law to become a violinist, and later a harpsichordist, at Keiser's Opera House in Hamburg, and had the operas *Almira* and *Nero* staged in 1705. He travelled in Italy in 1706–09, visiting the major cities and meeting the leading composers. *Agrippina* was success-fully produced in Venice in 1709, and he also made a great reputation as a harpsichordist. Other works composed in Italy include the ora-torios *La resurrezione* and *Il trionfo del tempo* (1707), solo cantatas, chamber duets, and other pieces. In 1710 he was appointed Kapellmeister to the Elector of Hanover who agreed that he should be allowed to visit London. *Rinaldo* was performed there the next year to great success. Again in London on leave in 1712, he settled there, never returning to his post in Hanover.

Between 1712 and 1715 Handel staged four op-eras, and in 1713 wrote a Te Deum and Jubilate to celebrate the Peace of Utrecht, receiving a life pension of £200 from Queen Anne. On her death in 1714 the Elector of Hanover succeeded to the throne as George I, and apparently forgave his former Kapellmeister's truancy and doubled his pension. In about 1717 Handel composed the *Water Music*, to accompany George I on his jour-ney down the River Thames. As music director to the Earl of Carnarvon (later Duke of Chandos) in 1717–20, he wrote the *Chandos Anthems* (1717–18), *Acis and Galatea* (1718), and the masque *Haman and Mordecai* (1720). From 1720 he directed the opera at the King's Theatre, Hay-market.

The founding of the Royal Academy of Music in 1720 began Handel's most prolific period as an opera composer, and over the next 20 years he wrote more than 30 works. Opera in Italian met with limited success (Dr Johnson called it 'an ex-otic and irrational entertainment'), and it was only in recent years that the beauties of *Giulio Cesare* (1724), *Orlando* (1733), *Ariodante* (1735), and *Alcina* (1735) have been appreciated. The ri-valry of the fashionable Italian composer Gio-vanni Bononcini, and John Gay's ridicule in *The Beggar's Opera* (1728), led him to abandon Italian opera for English oratorio.

Handel ran into difficulties with some of the people around him and also Bononcini. This was made worse by quarrels between his two leading ladies, Faustina Bordoni and Francesca Cuzzoni. The popular success of Gay's *The Beg-gar's Opera* made matters worse, and in that year the Royal Academy of Music went bankrupt. Handel continued to produce operas, acting as his own impresario in partnership with Johann Jakob Heidegger (1666–1749), a Swiss impresario active in London, but rival factions, now of a po-litical nature, again spoiled his success, and in the 1730s he increasingly turned to oratorio. *Es-ther* (1732), a revision of the masque *Haman and Mordecai*, was followed by *Deborah* (1733), *Saul* (1739), and *Israel in Egypt* (1739).

Handel's last opera was produced in 1741, after which he devoted his time chiefly to oratorio. *Messiah* summed up his life's work. It was com-posed in a matter of weeks but included some elements from earlier music. Its success encour-aged him to write twelve more oratorios, some on Old Testament texts (*Samson*, 1743; *Solomon*, 1749), others on classical mythology (*Semele*, 1743). He continued to appear in public as a con-ductor and organist, playing concertos between the parts of his oratorios, but his health declined. In 1751, despite receiving treatment for cataracts, he became totally blind. His last major public success came in 1749 with the suite for wind in-struments, to accompany the Royal Fireworks in Green Park.

Works OPERA *Agrippina* (1709), *Rinaldo* (1711), *Radamisto* (1720), *Giulio Cesare* (1724), *Tamerla-no* (1724), *Rodelinda* (1725), *Scipione* (1726), *Alessandro* (1726), *Orlando* (1733), *Ariodante* (1735), *Alcina* (1735), *Serse* (1735), *Giustino*, *Bere-nice* (1737), *Imeneo* (1740), *Deidamia* (1741).

ORATORIOS *Athalia* (1733), *Saul* (1739), *Israel in Egypt* (1739), *Messiah* (1742), *Samson* (1743), *Bel-shazzar* (1745), *Judas Maccabaeus* (1747), *Joshua* (1747), *Susanna* (1749), *Solomon* (1749), *Theodora* (1750), *Jephtha* (1752).

OTHER CHORAL WORKS *Acis and Galatea* (1718), *Alexander's Feast* (1736), *Ode for St Cecilia's Day* (1739), *L'allegro, il penseroso ed il moderato* (after John Milton; 1740), *Semele* (1743); eleven *Chan-dos Anthems* (1717–18); anthems for the coron-ation of George II in 1727: *Let Thy Hand be Strengthened*, *My Heart is Inditing*, *The King shall Rejoice*, and *Zadok the Priest*; dramatic can-tatas: *Apollo e Dafne* (1708) and *Aci, Galatea e Polifemo* (1708); numerous other solo and duo cantatas, including *Armida abandonata* (1707), *Silete venti* (1729); Utrecht Te Deum and Jubilate.

INSTRUMENTAL trio sonatas and other pieces, twelve *concerti grossi* for strings, oboe concertos, organ concertos, *Water Music* (1717), *Music for the Royal Fireworks* (1749), and other pieces; key-board music, including organ fugues and harpsi-chord suites.

Handford, Maurice (1929–1986) English conductor and horn player. He studied at the Royal Academy of Music, London. He was principal horn with the Hallé Orchestra 1949–61 and conducted the orchestra from 1966, notably in complex scores by Olivier Messiaen and Witold Lutosławski, but resigned in 1971. He was often heard with regional British Broadcasting Corporation (BBC) orchestras and was principal conductor of the Calgary Philharmonic Orchestra 1971–75.

Handl, Jacob (1550–1591), also known as **Jacobus Gallus** Slovene composer. He was a prolific composer of church music, and wrote 16 Masses, motets, a Te Deum, and a cycle of music for the liturgical year. He also wrote German songs and other secular works, many of which show the influence of Franco-Flemish composers. Contemporary critics complained about the complexity of his music – his four-volume *Opus Musicum* (1586–91) included two pieces scored for 24 voices.

Handl was born in Ribniča near Ljubljana, and went to Austria in the mid-1560s. He was a singer in the Chapel of Emperor Maximilian II in Vienna 1574–75. He then travelled through Austria, Bohemia, Silesia, and Moravia, and was choirmaster to the Bishop of Olomouc 1579–85. By mid-1586 he was cantor at the Church of St Jan na Brzehu in Prague, where he remained until his death.

Hansell, Kathleen (Amy Kuzmick) (1941–) US musicologist and organist. She studied at the University of Illinois and took her PhD at Berkeley in 1980. She was a teacher and organist in Illinois and Iowa from 1967, and archivist at the Swedish Music History Archive, Stockholm, from 1982. Publications include *Lucio Silla*, for the *Mozart Ausgabe*, editions of Berwald and Hindemith, and *Zelmira* for *Tutte le opere di G Rossini*. She made contributions to *Grove's Dictionary of Music and Musicians* and other lexicographical sources.

Hänsel und Gretel opera by Engelbert Humperdinck (libretto by A Wette, Humperdinck's sister, from a tale by the brothers Grimm), first produced in Weimar, Germany, on 23 December 1893. It is based on the fairy tale: using her gingerbread house as bait, the wicked witch preys on hungry children, but Hänsel and Gretel outwit her, saving themselves and all her previous victims.

Hans Heiling opera by Heinrich Marschner (libretto by E Devrient, originally written for Mendelssohn), first produced at the Berlin Opera, Germany, on 24 May 1833. It tells of the gnome Heiling who gives up his supernatural powers to live above ground with the peasant girl Anna; he returns to the caves after losing her affections.

Hanslick, Eduard (1825–1904) Austrian music critic. He wrote for the *Neue freie Presse* in Vienna and was a lecturer in music history at the university. A fierce opponent of Wagner's later music and an ardent partisan of Brahms, he argued that the true value of music lay within the formal aesthetics of music itself, not in the expression of extra-musical feelings. His books included *Vom Musikalisch-Schönen/Of the Beautiful in Music* (1891). In Wagner's original draft for the libretto of *Die Meistersinger von Nürnberg/ The Mastersingers of Nuremberg* the unsympathetic role of Beckmesser was given as Hans Lich.

Hanson, Howard (1896–1981) US composer. He studied music in New York and at Evanston University, Illinois. After various appointments, he gained the American Prix de Rome, and after his stay in Italy was director of the Eastman School of Music at Rochester, New York, 1924–64.

Works OPERA *Merry Mount* (after Hawthorne, 1934).

CHORAL *The Lament for Beowulf* for chorus and orchestra (1926).

ORCHESTRAL seven symphonies (1923–77), symphonic poems *North and West*, *Lux aeterna*, and *Pan and the Priest* for orchestra.

CHAMBER string quartet (1923), piano quintet, concerto for piano quintet.

OTHER piano pieces; songs.

Hans Sachs opera by Gustav Lortzing (libretto by composer and F Reger, based on a play by J L F Deinhardstein), first produced in Leipzig, Germany, on 23 June 1840. It is an earlier opera on the subject of Wagner's *Meistersinger*, which was also used before Wagner by Adalbert Gyrowetz. It recounts how Sachs loses his bride Kunigunde to Eoban in a rigged singing competition, but the emperor Maximilian intervenes.

Harawi, chant d'amour et de mort song cycle by Olivier Messiaen for soprano and piano (text by composer), first performed in Brussels, Belgium, in 1946. It is the first of a trilogy of works inspired by the Tristan legend: others are the *Turangalîla* symphony (1946–48) and *Cinq Rechants* for chorus *a cappella* (1949).

Harbison, John (1938–) US composer. He studied at Harvard and with Roger Sessions at Princeton, and taught at the Massachusetts Institute of Technology 1969–82; he was composer-in-residence for the Pittsburgh Symphony Orchestra 1982–84.

Works STAGE operas *The Winter's Tale* (1979) and *Full Moon in March* (after Yeats, 1979); ballets after Homer *Ulysses' Raft* and *Ulysses' Bow* (1983–84).

The harmonic minor scale on C.

ORCHESTRAL violin concerto (1980), two symphonies (1981, 1987), concerto for oboe, clarinet, and strings (1985), viola concerto (1990).

CHAMBER two string quartets (1985, 1987).

Hardanger fiddle, Norwegian **hardingfele** Norwegian musical instrument similar to the ➤ **violin**. It has four strings and four or five ➤ **sympathetic strings**, and is used for playing folk music.

Many of Edvard Grieg's piano pieces were inspired by the music of the Hardanger fiddle.

Hardy, Thomas (1840–1928) English novelist and poet. His works inspired ➤ **Egdon Heath** (Gustav Holst), Edward ➤ **Harper** (*Fanny Robin* and *The Mellstock Quire*), Alun ➤ **Hoddinott** (*Trumpet Major*), Dominic ➤ **Muldowney** (*Love Music for Bathsheba and Gabriel Oak*), Stephen ➤ **Paulus** (*The Woodlanders*), and *Tess* (Camille Erlanger), as well as poems set as songs by, among others, Arnold Bax, Benjamin Britten, Gerald Finzi, Holst, and John Ireland.

'Hark, Hark, the Lark' song by Franz Schubert from Shakespeare's *Cymbeline*, translated by A W Schlegel as *Ständchen aus 'Cymbeline'* and composed in Germany in 1826.

harmonic in music, the generation on a musical instrument of a pure tone from the ➤ **harmonic series**, rather than the fundamental.

In string playing the player lightly touches a ➤ **node** on a string, rather than pressing the string down onto the neck. This causes a high, clear, but thin tone, used to effect in the opening of Gustav Mahlers first symphony.

In woodwind and brass, harmonics are achieved by ➤ **overblowing** and form a basic part of playing technique.

It is also a prefix denoting organ pipes, producing harmonic notes from pipes of double, triple, or quadruple speaking length. See ➤ **harmonics**.

harmonica musical instrument, a pocket-sized reed organ blown directly from the mouth, invented by Charles Wheatstone in 1829; see ➤ **mouth organ**.

The ➤ **glass harmonica** (or armonica) is based on an entirely different principle.

harmonic analysis method of describing the chords and progressions used mainly in music of the 18th and 19th centuries. The principles rest on the identification of a chord by its root and by the position of the root within the scale. Thus, a root-position chord on the tonic is designated as I, its first inversion as Ib (or, using the parlance of ➤ **thorough bass**, I^6) and its second inversion as Ic (or I_4^6); further elaborations of the system are all based on figured bass notation. Within diatonic music with straightforward harmonies, the main chords are I, IV, and V; II and VI are also common, but III and VII are used more rarely. First inversions are important and used frequently except in structural cadences. Second inversions of triads are normally considered discords and can be used only in particular circumstances.

A further refinement of this system is 'functional harmony', first devised by Heinrich Riemann in his *Vereinfachte Harmonielehre* (1893). Here every chord was described as part of a tonic (I), dominant (V) or subdominant (IV) function. This system, still little practised outside Germany, makes the entire chordal vocabulary of the classical and romantic eras more comprehensible as a logical system; but at the same time many details need to be glossed over and this leads to the use of 'reduction' graphs which describe certain chords as passing chords within a broader progression. Hierarchical reductions of this kind led to the analytical techniques of Heinrich Schenker and his followers.

harmonic bass in music, another name for the acoustic bass organ ➤ **stop**.

harmonic minor scale in music, one of the minor scales where the seventh note of the scale is raised (sharpened) by a semitone. It is so called because its notes are used when creating chords or harmonies.

harmonic rhythm the rhythm of harmonic change. For most tonal music, the variety of harmonic rhythm is of considerable importance to the musical effect. Thus it may be noted, for instance, that in many simple melodies of the classical era the harmonic rhythm speeds up towards the cadence: the faster chord changes at that point help to clarify the end of the phrase. Another example might be the moment before the recapitulation in sonata-form movements (sometimes called the 'retransition'): here the harmonic rhythm often slows down to a standstill, normally on the dominant, thus not only increasing the tension but allowing for a sudden change in harmonic rhythm at the moment of recapitulation.

harmonics in music, a series (the 'harmonic series') of partial vibrations that combine to form a musical tone. When a stretched string or a column

The harmonic series. Those marked x are not in tune with the normal scale. The members of the series have a proportional relation to each other. Thus if the lowest note vibrates at 64 cycles per second, the octave above it will be at 128 cps, the G (no. 3) at 172 cps, middle C at 256 cps, and so on.

of air in a tube is made to vibrate, it does so as a whole, in two halves, three thirds, four quarters, etc., all at the same time. The easiest vibration to hear is that of the whole. It is the lowest note and is called the **fundamental**. The vibrations of the halves, thirds, quarters, etc., produce a series of fainter, higher pitches at the same time. These are known as the **harmonics**, or **upper partials**, or **overtones**. Instruments vary in their tone colour (or timbre) because of the different number and different intensity of the harmonics. An oboe has many harmonics, while a flute has few.

harmonic series the composite series of notes that can be produced by a vibrating substance or air column.

Harmonie der Welt, Die, The Harmony of the World opera by Paul Hindemith (libretto by the composer) in five acts, first produced in Munich, Germany, on 11 August 1957. The symphony from the opera was completed in 1951 and first performed in Basel, Switzerland, on 24 January 1952. The opera is based on the life of the astronomer Johannes Kepler (1571–1630), who maintained in *Harmonices mundi* that the planets emit musical sounds in their orbits round the Sun.

Harmoniemesse Mass in B flat by Haydn, composed in 1802 and first performed in Eisenstadt, Austria, on 8 September 1802. The title derives from the prominent use of wind instruments (German *Harmonie*, 'wind band'). It was Haydn's last Mass.

Harmoniemusik (German 'wind band music') music for a combination of woodwind and brass instruments with or without percussion, such as a military band.

Harmonious Blacksmith, The name given to the Air and Variations in Handel's E major harpsichord suite (Book I, no. 5, published in 1720). Despite the traditional story that Handel composed the piece after hearing a blacksmith singing at his work, the nickname is of 19th-century origin.

harmonium small 19th-century organ whose sound was produced by the vibration of free reeds (thin metal tongues). The vibrations were created by air flow from foot-operated bellows, and lever-action knee swells controlled dynamics. It was invented by Alexandre Debain in Paris, France, in about 1842.

It was widely adopted in Europe and the USA as a home and church instrument. In France and Germany the harmonium flourished as a concert solo and orchestral instrument, being written for by Sigfrid Karg-Elert, Arnold Schoenberg (*Herzgewächse*/*Heart's Bloom*, 1907), and Karlheinz Stockhausen (*Der Jahreslauf*/*The Course of the Years*, 1977).

harmony in music, the sounding together of notes to produce a chord. Although the term suggests a pleasant or agreeable sound, it is applied to any combination of notes and the chord can therefore be consonant or dissonant. The term also refers to the progression (flow) of chords in a piece of music and the way they relate to each other.

An important contributor to the theory of harmony was Jean-Philippe ➜ Rameau. In his *Traité de l'harmonie*/*Treatise on Harmony* (1722), he put forward a system of chord classification on which later methods of harmony have been based.

Harnasie ballet pantomime by Karol Szymanowski (scenario by J Iwaszkiewicz and J M Rytard); it was composed 1923–31 and first produced in Prague, Czechoslovakia (now the Czech Republic), on 11 May 1935.

Harold en Italie descriptive symphony by Hector Berlioz, Op. 16, for solo viola and orchestra, based on Lord Byron's *Childe Harold*, composed in 1834 and first performed in Paris, France, on 23 November of that year. It was suggested by Paganini, but not played by him.

harp plucked musical string instrument. It consists of a set of strings stretched vertically over a triangle-shaped frame. The strings rise from a sloping soundboard and are tensioned at the opposite end by pegs. The orchestral harp is the largest instrument of its type. It has 47 strings covering the range B0–C7 (seven octaves). At its base there are seven double-action pedals (one for each note of the octave) to alter pitch. Before the pedals are depressed, the strings sound the scale of C flat major, but each note can be raised a semitone or a whole tone by one of the pedals. Thus all the notes of the chromatic scale can be sounded.

It is one of the oldest of all musical instruments, with its ancestor the lyre being played in ancient Greece. It existed in the West as a harp as early as the 9th century, and was common among medieval minstrels. At that time it was quite small, and was normally placed on the knees. It grew in size because of a need for increased volume, following its introduction into the orchestra in the 19th century. Composers for the harp include Wolfgang Amadeus Mozart, Maurice Ravel, Carlos Salzedo, and Heinz Holliger. The harp has also been used in folk music, as both a solo and accompanying instrument, and is associated with Wales and Ireland.

Harper, Edward (1941–) English composer. He studied at Oxford and with Gordon Jacob, and also at the Royal College of Music, London, and lectured at Edinburgh University, Scotland, from 1964.

Works OPERA *Fanny Robin*, opera in one act from an episode in Hardy's *Far from the Madding Crowd* (1975), *Hedda Gabler* (after Ibsen; 1985), *The Mellstock Quire* (after Hardy; 1987).

ORCHESTRAL piano concerto (1969), *Bartók Games* for orchestra (1972), *Ricercari in memoriam Luigi Dallapiccola* for eleven instruments (1975), clarinet concerto (1982), *Intrada after Monteverdi* for chamber orchestra (1982).

VOCAL *Seven poems by e e cummings* for soprano and orchestra (1977), *Chester Mass* for chorus and orchestra (1979), *The Lamb* for soprano, chorus, and orchestra (1990), *Homage to Thomas Hardy* for baritone and chamber orchestra (1990).

CHAMBER string quartet (1986), *Double Variations* for oboe, bassoon, and wind (1989), *In Memoriam* for cello and piano (1990).

harp lute or **dital harp** stringed musical instrument invented early in the 19th century. It was derived from instruments of the lute type, but had a larger number of strings held by pegs in the harp-shaped head, about half of them changeable in pitch by a fingerboard, the others remaining open and thus capable of playing only a single fixed note.

'Harp' Quartet nickname given to Beethoven's string quartet in E flat major, Op. 74, composed in 1809, because it contains, in the first movement, several arpeggios divided between the instruments.

harpsicall or **harpsicon** old English terms, variations of ➤ harpsichord.

harpsichord largest and grandest of the 18th-century keyboard instruments, used in orchestras and as a solo instrument. The strings are plucked by 'jacks', made of leather or quill, when the keys are pressed. However, unlike the piano, the volume and tone cannot be varied by the player's touch. In the 18th century double-manual (two keyboard) harpsichords were developed (and later three-manuals), which offered greater variation in tone. The revival of the harpsichord repertoire in the 20th century owed much to Wanda ➤ Landowska and Ralph Kirkpatrick (1911–84).

In classical orchestral music, such as that of George Handel or Joseph Haydn, the harpsichord often has a continuo part improvised over a ➤ figured bass.

Harpsichords have to be tuned regularly, and may have their tuning system (temperament) adjusted according to the repertoire. Famous makers of harpsichords include the English Kirckman and the Flemish Ruckers families. A modern repertoire has developed for the concert harpsichord, with concertos by Elliott Carter (1961), Manuel de Falla (1926), Frank Martin (1952), Bohuslav Martinu (1935), and *Continuum* for solo harpsichord by György Ligeti (1968).

Harris, Roy (Leroy Ellsworth) (1898–1979) US composer. His works, which make use of American folk tunes, include the *Symphony No. 10* (1965, known as 'Abraham Lincoln') and the orchestral *When Johnny Comes Marching Home* (1935).

His father was a farmer who migrated to California during Harris's boyhood, and at 18 Harris had a farm of his own. In 1916 he enlisted to fight in World War I. In 1918 he returned to the USA and became a music student at the University of California, driving a dairy cart to earn a living. Next he studied under Arthur Farwell for two years and in 1926 produced an Andante for strings for the New York Philharmonic Orchestra. The next two years were spent in Paris, France, studying with Nadia Boulanger. He returned to the USA in 1929 and later held posts at the Westminster Choir school at Princeton, New Jersey, Cornell University, Colorado, Logan (Utah), Nashville, and Pittsburgh. His most successful work was his third symphony, declaring American ruggedness at the onset of war. It was premiered under Sergei Koussevitsky in Boston in 1939.

Works ORCHESTRAL 13 symphonies (1934–76), *Farewell to Pioneers* (1936), and others; concerto for violin and orchestra.

CHAMBER AND INSTRUMENTAL three string quartets (1930–39), sextet and quintet for wind and piano, piano quintet; pieces for violin and viola and piano; piano works, including sonatas and *Children's Suite*.

CHORAL *Symphony for Voices* for eight-part unaccompanied chorus.

Harrison, Frank Llewelyn (1905–1987) Irish musicologist and educationist. He studied in Ireland and later under Schrade and Paul Hindemith at Yale University, USA. He was music director at Queen's University, Kingston, Canada, 1935–46, and professor of music at Colgate University, Hamilton, New York, 1946–47 and at WA University, St Louis, 1947–52. From 1952 to 1970 he was a lecturer in music, subsequently reader, at Oxford University, England, and was professor of ethnomusicology at Amsterdam University, the Netherland, 1970–80. He specialized in the study of English medieval music, edited *The Eton Choirbook* (three volumes), and published *Music in Medieval Britain* (1958). He was general editor of the series *Early English Church Music*.

Harrison, Lou (1917–2003) US composer. He experimented with new sonorities, including novel scales and methods of tuning. He helped promote the music of Edgard Varèse, Carl Ruggles, and Henry Cowell, and conducted the first performance of Charles Ives's third symphony in 1946. A visit to the Far East in 1961 inspired much music for the gamelan.

Harrison studied with Cowell and Arnold Schoenberg 1937–40. He then taught at Mills College and at the University of California in 1942. From 1945 to 1948 he was a music critic for the *New York Herald-Tribune*. He taught at San José State University 1967–82, and at Mills College 1980–85.

Works STAGE opera *Rapunzel* (1959); ballets *Solstice*, *The Perilous Chapel* (1949), *Almanac of the Seasons*, *Johnny Appleseed*, *Changing World*, and others.

ORCHESTRAL Prelude and Saraband for orchestra, three symphonies, piano concerto (1985).

CHAMBER AND INSTRUMENTAL string quartet set (1979), *Ariadne* for flute and percussion (1987), *Recording Piece* for percussion, *Simfony I*, three suites, violin concerto with percussion orchestra, string trio, suite for cello and harp, piano music.

VOCAL *Four Strict Songs* for eight baritones and orchestra in pure intonation (1955).

Hartmann, Karl Amadeus (1905–1963) German composer. He began composing late in life, but destroyed his early works and turned to serialism under the influence of Anton Webern. After World War II he organized the important 'Musica Viva' concerts in Munich to propagate new music. In 1952 he was elected to the German Academy of Fine Arts and in 1953 became president of the German section of the International Society for Contemporary Music.

He studied with Josef Haas at the Munich Academy and later with Hermann Scherchen.

Works CHAMBER OPERA *Des Simplicius Simplicissimus Jugend* (1934–35; produced 1949).

ORCHESTRAL AND CHAMBER eight symphonies (1936–62), concerto for piano, wind, and percussion, *Musik der Trauer* for violin and strings (1939), two string quartets.

Harty, (Herbert) Hamilton (1879–1941) Irish conductor and composer. After much conducting experience in London he was appointed conductor to the Hallé Orchestra, Manchester, in 1920. He gave the first British performance of Mahler's ninth symphony in 1930.

He studied piano, viola, and composition under his father and became an organist at the age of 12. He later became organist in Belfast and Dublin, where he studied further under Michele Esposito. In 1900 he settled in London as an accompanist and composer and married the soprano Agnes Nicholls. He retired from the Hallé in 1933.

Works ORCHESTRAL arrangement of Handel's *Water Music* and *Fireworks Music*, Irish Symphony (1924), *Comedy Overture* (1907), symphonic poem *With the Wild Geese* for orchestra (1910); violin concerto.

VOCAL *Ode to a Nightingale* (Keats) for soprano and orchestra (1907); cantata *The Mystic Trumpeter* (Whitman; 1913); many songs.

Harvey, Jonathan Dean (1939–) English composer. His use of avant-garde and computer synthesis techniques is allied to a tradition of visionary Romanticism in works such as *Inner Light II* (1977) for voices, instruments, and ➔ **tape music** and *Mortuos plango, vivos voco/I Mourn the Dead, I Call the Living* (1980) for computer-manipulated concrete sounds, realized at ➔ **IRCAM**. Later works include the opera *Inquest of Love* (1993) and the orchestral work *Calling Across Time* (1998).

He studied at Cambridge and Glasgow universities, and was appointed professor at Sussex University in 1980. He has worked with Karlheinz ➔ **Stockhausen** and Milton ➔ **Babbitt**.

Works OPERA *Passion and Resurrection*, church opera (performed Winchester, 1981), opera *Inquest of Love* (1993).

ORCHESTRAL symphony (1966), *Persephone Dream* (1973), *Madonna of Winter and Spring* (1986), *Lightness and Weight* for tuba and orchestra (1986), cello concerto (1990), *Calling Across Time* (1998).

CHAMBER AND INSTRUMENTAL *Smiling Immortal* for chamber orchestra and tape (1977), *Easter Orisons* for strings (1983), *Mortuos plango, vivos voco* for computer-processed concrete sounds (performed Lille, 1980), *Modernsky Music* for two oboes, bassoon, and harpsichord (1981; title from one of Schoenberg's three satires Op. 28, in which Stravinsky is mocked as 'Modernsky', for apparently following musical fashion), *Curve with Plateaux* for cello (1982), *Valley of Aosta* for 13 players (1988), *Scena* for violin and ensemble

(1992), *Chant* for viola (1992).

VOCAL ten cantatas for soloists and various instrumental combinations (1965–76), *Hymn* for chorus and orchestra (composed 1979 for the 900th anniversary of Winchester Cathedral).

Háry János ballad opera by Zoltán Kodály (libretto by B Paulini and Z Harsányi, based on a poem by János Garay), first produced in Budapest, Hungary, on 16 October 1926. It contains popular Hungarian tunes and begins with an orchestral imitation of a sneeze. The orchestral suite was first performed in New York, USA, on 15 December 1927. In the work, János tells tall tales about his youth, spent defeating Napoleon and winning the heart of the emperor's wife; all along he remained true to his bride back in his native village.

Hassan, or The Golden Journey to Samarkand incidental music by Frederick Delius for the play by James Elroy Flecker; it was composed in 1920 and first produced at His Majesty's Theatre, London, England, on, 20 September 1923, with ballets arranged by Mikhail Fokine. The orchestral suite was arranged by Eric Fenby, with instruments including camel bells, and first performed on British Broadcasting Corporation (BBC) television on 1 August 1933.

Hasse, Johann Adolf (1699–1783) German composer. He began his career as a singer in Hamburg, and produced his first opera, *Antioco*, in 1721. He wrote about 70 operas, and became the most successful composer of *opera seria* (treating classical subjects in a formal style) of his generation.

Hasse was a tenor at the Hamburg Opera under Reinhard Keiser 1718–19, then at Brunswick, 1719–22, where *Antioco* was first produced. In 1922 he went to Italy and studied with Nicola Porpora and Alessandro Scarlatti. After many successful operas for Naples, he became maestro di cappella at the Conservatorio degli Incurabili in Venice in 1727. He married the singer Faustina Bordoni in 1730, and in 1734 went to Dresden as Kapellmeister to the Saxon Court, a post he held for 30 years. He was allowed generous leave of absence, however, and travelled widely, including a visit to London, England, in 1734. In 1764, after the death of the Saxon Elector, he moved to Vienna, then in 1773 to Venice, where he lived for the rest of his life.

Works OPERA *Antioco* (1721), *Il Sesostrate* (1726), *Tigrane* (1729), *Artaserse, Cleofide* (1731), *Cajo Fabricio* (1732), *Il Demetrio, Siroe, rè di Persia* (1733), *Tito Vespasiano* (1735), *Lucio Papirio* (1742), *Didone abbandonata, Antigono* (1743), *Semiramide riconosciuta* (1744), *Arminio, Leucippo, Demofoonte* (1748), *Attilio Regolo* (1750), *Il Ciro riconosciuto* (1751), *Solimano, Ezio, Olim-*

piade, Alcide al Bivio (1760), *Il trionfo di Clelia* (1762), *Partenope, Piramo e Tisbe* (1768), *Ruggiero* (1771), and many others.

OTHER oratorios *I pellegrini al sepolcro, Sant' Elena al calvario* (1746), *La conversione di Sant' Agostino* (1750); Masses and other church music; concertos for flute and for violin; solo sonatas, trio sonatas, harpsichord pieces.

Hassell, Jon (1937–) US composer and trumpeter. As a composer and performer he has been involved with minimalism, Balinese music, and electronics. He studied with Karlheinz Stockhausen and Henri Pousseur in Cologne, Germany, and at the Eastman School, New York.

Works INSTRUMENTAL *Music for Vibraphones* (1965), *Blackboard Piece with Girls and Loops* (1969), *Goodbye Music* (1969), *Solid State* for two synthesizers (1969), *Superball* (1969), *Landscape Series* (1969–72).

OTHER *Sulla strada*, theatre piece after Kerouac's *On the Road* (performed Venice, 1982). Recordings include music from the Far East (*Earthquake Island, Aka-Dhari-Java*).

Hassler, Hans Leo (1564–1612) German organist and composer. He wrote considerable quantities of church music in Latin and German, in addition to many secular songs in German and Italian, and other pieces. He was one of the first Germans to study in Italy, and the polychoral techniques and rich sonorities of his Masses and motets show the influence of the Venetians.

Hassler was born in Nuremberg and was taught by his father, Isaac Hassler (c. 1530–1591), who was himself an organist. After an appointment at Nuremberg he was sent to Venice for further study under Andrea Gabrieli. He was organist to Octavian Fugger at Augsburg 1585–1600; he published many works there and established a wide reputation. Having returned to Nuremberg as organist of the Church of Our Lady, he married and went to live at Ulm in 1604, but soon went into the service of the emperor Rudolph in Prague. In 1608 he became organist to Christian II, the Elector of Saxony at Dresden, but suffered from tuberculosis and died during a visit with the Elector to Frankfurt.

Although Hassler was a Protestant, his early works are all for the Catholic Church. His German church music is somewhat conservative, and though it often uses Lutheran melodies, it shows the influence of Roland de Lassus. He was famous for his Italian madrigals and canzonets, and his German songs were widely known: the tune of his love song, 'Mein G'müt ist mir verwirret' (1601), was used for the Lutheran hymn, 'O Haupt voll Blut und Wunden' which features in Bach's St Matthew Passion.

Works Masses, Magnificats, hymn tunes, motets (including two collections *Sacrae cantiones* and *Sacri concentus*), fugal psalms, and Christian songs; Italian canzonets for four voices, Italian and German madrigals, *Lustgarten neuer Teutscher Gesäng* (32 German songs for four to eight voices, 1601); ricercari, toccatas, and other pieces for organ.

Hatton, John (Liptrott) (1808–1886) English composer. He was almost wholly self-taught in music. He settled in London in 1832, became attached to Drury Lane Theatre as composer in 1842, and in 1844 visited Vienna, Austria, to produce his opera *Pascal Bruno*. In 1848 he went to the USA and later became music director of the Prince's Theatre, London, where he wrote much incidental music for Edmund Kean's productions.

Works STAGE operas *Pascal Bruno* (1844) and *Rose, or Love's Ransom* (1864); operetta *The Queen of the Thames*; incidental music for Shakespeare's *Macbeth*, *Henry VIII*, *Richard II*, *King Lear*, *The Merchant of Venice* and *Much Ado About Nothing*, Sheridan's *Pizarro*, an adaptation of Goethe's *Faust* and other plays.

OTHER Mass, two services, eight anthems; oratorio *Hezekiah*; cantata *Robin Hood*; over 150 songs, including *To Anthea* (Herrick); many part songs.

Haubenstock-Ramati, Roman (1919–1993) Polish-born Israeli composer. His first works are conservative in idiom; he later moved on to serial and aleatory techniques.

He studied composition in Kraków and Lwów (Lviv) from 1937 to 1940. From 1947 to 1950 he was music director of Radio Kraków and then emigrated to Israel, where he became director of the music library in Tel-Aviv. In 1957 he moved to Paris, France, living also in Vienna, Austria, where he worked for Universal Edition.

Works STAGE opera *Amerika* (after Kafka, 1964); ballet *Ulysses* (1977).

ORCHESTRAL *La Symphonie des timbres* for orchestra; *Vermutungen über ein dunkles Haus* for three orchestras; *Papageno's Pocket-size Concerto* for glockenspiel and orchestra (1955); *Recitativo and Aria* for cembalo and orchestra; *Sequences* for violin and orchestra; *Petite Musique de nuit*, mobile for orchestra (1958).

VOCAL AND INSTRUMENTAL *Blessings* for voice and nine players; *Mobile for Shakespeare* for voice and six players (1960); *Jeux* for six percussion groups; concerto for strings (1977); *Interpolation*, mobile for solo flute; *Ricercari* for string trio.

Hauer, Josef (Matthias) (1883–1959) Austrian composer. He published a series of pamphlets on composition according to his own 12-note system, which was different from that of Arnold Schoenberg. All his works use this system, which

is based on groups of notes he called *Tropen*, derived from the combinations of the twelve notes of the chromatic scale allowed by the agreement of their overtones.

Works STAGE opera *Salammbô* (after Flaubert, 1929; performed Vienna, 1983); play with music *Die schwarze Spinne* (after Jeremias Gotthelf, 1932; performed Vienna, 1966); music for Aeschylus' *Prometheus Bound* and tragedies by Sophocles.

VOCAL Mass for chorus, organ, and orchestra; cantata *Wandlungen*; *Vom Leben* recitation with singing voices and chamber orchestra for broadcasting; six song cycles to poems by Hölderlin and other songs.

ORCHESTRAL sinfonietta, eight suites, seven Dance Fantasies (1928), Concert Piece, *Apocalyptic Fantasy* (1913), *Kyrie* and other pieces for orchestra; symphony for strings, harmonium, and piano; violin concerto, piano concerto.

CHAMBER AND INSTRUMENTAL six string quartets (1924–26), quintet for clarinet, violin, viola, cello, and piano; many piano pieces including two sets of studies and pieces on Hölderlin titles; about 87 *Zwölftonspiele* for different instruments and instrumental combinations.

Haunted Tower, The opera by Stephen Storace (libretto by James Cobb), first produced at the Drury Lane Theatre, London, England, on 24 November 1789.

Hauptmann, Moritz (1792–1868) German theorist, writer on music, and composer. He studied in Dresden and began to work there, lived in Russia 1815–20, played violin in Ludwig Spohr's orchestra in Kassel from 1822, and was cantor at St Thomas's Church in Leipzig from 1842 to his death. He wrote on acoustics, harmony, and fugue.

Works the opera *Mathilde* (1826); two Masses, motets and psalms; choruses and part songs; three sonatas for violin and piano, violin duets; songs.

Hauptwerk in music, the German equivalent of the → great organ, the manual (keyboard) of the most powerful pipes and stops.

hautbois (French 'high-wood' or 'loud-wood') in music, term used for smaller members of the → shawm family, used in England and France after 1500. 'Hautboy' was the English term for → oboe (the shawm's descendant) in the 17th and 18th centuries. It is still the French name for the oboe.

haute-contre in music, alto or high tenor, whether voice or instrument. Hence an old name for the alto or tenor → viol and the → viola.

Hawkins, John (1719–1789) English music historian and antiquary. Devoted at first to architec-

ture and then to law, he gradually became interested in literature and music. Having married a wealthy woman in 1753, he was able to retire and to undertake, in addition to minor works, his *General History of the Science and Practice of Music*, published in five volumes in 1776, the same year as the first volume of Charles Burney's similar work.

Hawte, William (c.1430–1497) English composer. He wrote four settings of the *Benedicamus Domino* (Cambridge, Magdalene College, Pepys MS 1236) and a processional antiphon, *Stella caeli*.

Haydn, (Franz) Joseph (1732–1809) Austrian composer. He was instrumental in establishing and perfecting the classical sonata form, and wrote numerous chamber and orchestral works (he produced more than a hundred symphonies). He also composed choral music, including the oratorios *The Creation* (1798) and *The Seasons* (1801). He was the first great master of the string quartet, and was a teacher of Mozart and Beethoven.

Haydn was employed by the Hungarian Esterházy family from 1761, being responsible for all the musical entertainment at their palace. His work also includes operas, church music, and songs, and the 'Emperor's Hymn', adopted as the Austrian, and later the German, national anthem.

Born in Lower Austria, the son of a wheelwright, Haydn went at the age of eight as a chorister to St Stephen's Cathedral in Vienna under Georg Reutter (junior). On leaving the choir school in about 1749 he lived as a freelance, playing violin and organ, and teaching. He was for a time pupil-manservant to the Italian composer Nicola Porpora in Vienna, but in composition he was largely self-taught, studying the works of C P E Bach, Johann Fux's *Gradus ad Parnassum*, and others. His earliest compositions date from these years, especially church music, including two Masses. His first string quartets were written about 1755 for Baron Fürnberg, through whom he obtained the post of music director to Count Morzin in 1759. The next year he entered into what proved to be an unfortunate marriage, and in 1761 took employment with the Esterházy family. In 1766 he became Kapellmeister (music director), a post he held for the rest of his life.

At Eszterháza, the magnificent palace in the Hungarian marshes, completed in 1766, Haydn wrote the majority of his instrumental music and operas. At first he wrote symphonies and instrumental pieces for the prince, notably more than a hundred trios for the ➔ **baryton** over ten years. Beginning with symphony no. 22 (*The Philosopher*) in 1764 and continuing through the 1760s to no. 49 (*La passione*), Haydn gained his maturity as a composer, showing inventiveness

in each work. The first truly mature string quartets, the set of six Op. 20 (1772), continue this developing mastery and were followed by the six quartets Op. 33 (1781). These include *The Joke* and *The Bird*, and were claimed to be written 'in a quite new and special manner'. In the set of Op. 50 (1787), Haydn repays the debt which Mozart had acknowledged when dedicating his own quartets to the older composer.

Though Haydn was isolated in Eszterháza, his fame spread. His works were published abroad, and he received invitations to travel, which his duties obliged him to refuse. In 1786 he was commissioned to compose six symphonies for the Concert de la Loge Olympique in Paris; these works are full of splendid invention and brilliant orchestral effects, declaring for the first time Haydn's genius to the world at large.

On the death of Prince Nikolaus in 1790 the Esterházy musicians were disbanded. Haydn, though retaining his title and salary, was free to accept an invitation from the violinist and impresario J P Salomon to go to England. His first visit to London, in 1791–92, for which he composed an opera (not produced) and six symphonies, was a great success, and was followed by another in 1794–95, for which a further six symphonies were written. The twelve London symphonies confirmed his reputation as the most original composer of the genre during his time. The wit, melodic inventiveness, and densely woven developments of these works were matched in the great sets of string quartets written in 1791–97 (Op. 64, Op. 71, Op. 74, and Op. 76).

In 1792 he received an honorary doctorate from Oxford University. On the accession of Prince Nikolaus II in 1795 the Esterházy music establishment was in part revived; but Haydn's duties were light, chiefly involving the composition of a Mass each year for the princess's name day, and giving rise to the six great Masses of 1796–1802. Inspired by the works of Handel he had heard in London, he composed *The Creation* and *The Seasons*. From 1803 he composed little, living in retirement in Vienna.

In spite of huge advances made in the knowledge and performance of Haydn's music in recent years, the sheer range and quantity of his output is intimidating, and some of his works are still unpublished.

Works OPERA 20 works for the stage, of which seven are lost (all first performances at Eszterháza, unless otherwise stated): *Acide*, festa teatrale (Eisenstadt, 1763), *La cantarina*, intermezzo (Eisenstadt, 1766), *Lo speziale*, dramma giocosa (1768), *Le pescatrici*, dramma giocosa (1770), *L'infedeltà delusa*, burletta (1773), *L'incontro improvviso*, dramma giocosa (1775), *Il mondo della luna*, dramma giocosa (1777), *La vera costanza*, dramma giocosa (1779), *L'isola disabitata*, azione teatrale (1779), *La fedeltà premiata*, dramma pastorale giocosa (1781), *Orlando Paladino*, dramma eroicomico (1782), *Armida*, dramma eroico (1784), *L'anima del filosofo* (now known by its alternative title of *Orfeo ed Euridice*, written for London 1791 but not performed; first known production Florence, 10 June 1951, with Callas and Christoff); marionette operas *Philemon und Baucis* (1773), *Hexen-Schabbas* (1773, lost), *Dido* (1776, lost), *Die Feuerbrunst* (1776), *Die Bestrafte Rachbegierde* (1779).

MASSES 14: Missa 'Rorate coeli desuper' (1748), Missa brevis in F (1749), Missa Cellensis (Cäcelienmesse) in C (1766), Missa in honorem BVM (Grosse Orgelmesse) in E♭ (1771), Missa Sancti Nicolai in G (1772), Missa brevis (Kleine Orgelmesse) in B♭ (1778), Missa Cellensis (Mariazeller Messe) (1782), Missa Sancti Bernardi (Heiligmesse) in B♭ (1796), Missa in tempore belli (Paukenmesse) in C (Vienna, 1796), Mass in D minor (Nelson Mass) (Eisenstadt, 1798), Mass in B♭ (Theresienmesse) (1799), Mass in B♭, (Schöpfungsmesse) (Eisenstadt, 1801), Mass in B♭ (Harmoniemesse) (Eisenstadt, 1802). A fragment of the lost Mass *Sunt bona mixta malis* (about 1769) was discovered in Ireland in 1983.

CANTATAS AND ORATORIOS Stabat Mater (1767), *Applausus* (Zwettl, 17 April 1768), *Il ritorno di Tobia* (Vienna, 1775), *Die Sieben letzten Worte unseres Erlösers am Kreuze/Seven Last Words* (Vienna, 1796), *Die Schöpfung/The Creation*), (Vienna, 1798), *Die Jahreszeiten/The Seasons* (Vienna, 1801). Also Te Deum in C (1800).

SYMPHONIES 104: nos. 1–5 (1758–60); nos. 6–8, *Le Matin, Le Midi, Le Soir* (1761); nos. 9–21 (about 1762); no. 22 in E♭, *The Philosopher* (1764); nos. 23–25 (1764); no. 26 in D minor, *Lamentatione* (1770); nos. 27–29 (1765); no. 30 in C, *Alleluja* (1765); no. 31 in D, *Hornsignal* (1765); nos. 32–42 (about 1768), no. 43 in E♭, *Mercury* (1772); no. 44 in E minor, *Trauersinfonie* (1772); no. 45 in F♯ minor, *Farewell* (1772); no. 46 in B and no. 47 in G (1772); no. 48 in C, *Maria Theresa*, and no. 49 in F minor, *La passione* (about 1768); nos. 50–52 (1773); no. 53 in D, *The Imperial* (1778); nos. 54–59 (1774); no. 60 in C, *Il distratto* (1774); nos. 61–72 (about 1779); no. 73 in D, *La Chasse* (1782); nos. 74–81 (1781–84); nos. 82–87 *Paris Symphonies*; no. 82 in C, *The Bear*, no. 83 in G minor, *The Hen*, no. 84 in E♭, no. 85 in B♭, *La Reine*, no. 86 in D, no. 87 in A (1785–86); no. 88 in G, no. 89 in F, no. 90 in C, no. 91 in E♭ (1787–88); no. 92 in G, *The Oxford* (1789); nos. 93–104 *London Symphonies*, no. 93 in D, no. 94 in G, *The Surprise*, no. 95 in C minor, no. 96 in D, *The Miracle*, no. 97 in C, no. 98 in B♭, no. 99 in E♭, no. 100 in G, *The Military*, no. 101 in D, *The Clock*, no. 102 in B♭, no. 103 in E♭, *The Drumroll*, no. 104 in D, *The London* (1791–95).

CONCERTOS four for violin, in C, D, A, and G (1769–71); two for cello in C and D (1761 and 1783); organ concerto in C (1756); concerto for violin and harpsichord (1766); harpsichord concertos in F, G, and D (1771–84); for trumpet in E♭ (1796); Sinfonia concertante in B♭ for oboe, violin, cello, and bassoon (1792); five concertos for lire organizzate (about 1786); five concertos for oboe, flute, horn, and bassoon are either lost or spurious.

STRING QUARTETS The usually given number of 83 is incorrect: from this must be subtracted the set of six Op. 3, now known to be by Romanus Hoffstetter, and the arrangement of *The Seven Last Words*, hitherto counted as seven separate quartets. Op. 1 nos. 1–6 (about 1757); Op. 2 nos. 1, 2, 4, and 6 (about 1762); Op. 9 nos. 1–6 (about 1771); Op. 17 nos. 1–6 (about 1772), Op. 20, nos. 1–6, *Sun Quartets* in E♭, C, G minor, D, F minor, A (1772); Op. 33 nos. 1–6, *Russian Quartets* in B minor, E♭ (*The Joke*), C (*The Bird*), B♭, G, D (1781); Op. 42 in D minor (1785); Op. 50 nos. 1–6 in B♭, C, E♭, F♯ minor, F, and D (*The Frog*) (1787); Op. 54 nos. 1–3 in G, C, and E (1788); Op. 55 nos. 1–3 in A, F minor, and B♭ (1790); Op. 64 nos. 1–6 in C, B minor, B♭, G, D (*The Lark*), and E♭ (1791); Op. 71 nos. 1–3 in B♭, D, and E♭ (1795); Op. 74 nos. 1–3 in C, F, and G minor (*The Rider*) (1796); Op. 76 nos. 1–6 in G, D minor (*The Fifths*), C (*The Emperor*), B♭ (*The Sunrise*), D, E♭ (1797); Op. 77 nos. 1 and 2 in G and F (1802); Op. 103 in D minor (1803).

OTHER INSTRUMENTAL 32 piano trios, 126 baryton trios and other chamber music; 60 piano sonatas (1760–94), five sets of variations for piano including F minor (1793); solo songs, part songs, arrangements of Scottish and Welsh folk songs. Twelve canzonettas to English words for solo voice and piano including 'My Mother Bids Me Bind My Hair', 'Sailor's Song', and 'She Never Told Her Love' (1794–95); solo cantatas *Arianna a Náxos* (1789) and *Berenice che fai* (1795).

Haydn, (Johann) Michael (1737–1806) Austrian composer, brother of Joseph ➔ **Haydn**. As well as a great deal of church music, including over 30 Masses, he also wrote about 40 symphonies, some chamber music, and an opera.

He was a chorister at St Stephen's Cathedral in Vienna under Reutter from about 1745. In 1757 he was appointed Kapellmeister to the Archbishop of Grosswardein, Hungary, became Konzertmeister to the Archbishop of Salzburg in 1762, and was cathedral organist there from 1781. Apart from occasional visits to Vienna, he remained in Salzburg till his death, in 1801 refusing the post of vice-Kapellmeister (under his brother Joseph) to Prince Esterházy.

Works *CHURCH MUSIC* 32 Masses including *Missa Hispanica* (1786); two Requiem Masses, including C minor Requiem, for Archbishop Sigismund (1771), which influenced Mozart's Requiem; eight German Masses; six Te Deum settings; 117 Graduals; 45 Offertories; 27 Holy Week Responsories; and other pieces.

STAGE opera *Andromeda e Perseo* (1787); German *Singspiele*, and other music for the stage.

CHORAL oratorios; cantatas.

ORCHESTRAL 46 symphonies including one with a slow introduction by Mozart (K444: Mozart's '37th' symphony); five concertos.

CHAMBER AND INSTRUMENTAL six string quintets; eleven string quartets; keyboard music.

'Haydn' Quartets familiar name of Mozart's six string quartets dedicated to Joseph Haydn: G major, K387 (1782), D minor, K421 (1783), E flat major, K428 (1783), B flat major, K458 (1784), A major, K464 (1785), and C major, K465 (1785).

'Haydn' Variations set of variations by Johannes Brahms; see ➤ *Variations on a Theme by Haydn*.

Hayes, William (1708–1777) English organist and composer. He was organist at Worcester Cathedral from 1731 and organist and master of the choristers at Magdalen College, Oxford, from 1734; he was appointed professor in 1742. He introduced many of Handel's works to Oxford, Bath, and Winchester; his own works were indebted to Handel.

He was the father of Phillip Hayes.

Works SACRED oratorios *The Fall of Jericho* and *David* (about 1776), 16 psalms, Te Deum in D, 20 anthems.

MASQUES *Circe* (1742) and *Peleus and Thetis*.

ODES *When the Fair Consort* (1735), *Where Shall the Muse* (1751), *O that Some Pensive Muse* (Ode to the memory of Handel, about 1760), *Ode on the Passions* (about 1760), and *Daughters of Beauty* (1773).

OTHER six cantatas, concertos, and trios.

Haym, Nicola Francesco (1678–1729) Italian cellist, librettist, and composer of German descent. He went to London, England, in 1702, and with François Dieupart and Thomas Clayton was active in establishing Italian opera there. From 1713 he wrote several libretti for Handel, including *Teseo*, *Radamisto*, *Giulio Cesare*, and *Rodelinda*; he also wrote for Giovanni Bononcini and Attilio Ariosti. His own works include a Latin oratorio and a serenata, anthem *The Lord is King*, and two sets of trio sonatas.

Hayman, Richard (1951–) US composer. He studied at Columbia University, and later learned from John Cage and Pierre Boulez. Early employment included renovating church organ pipes. In 1975 he wrote *Dalí*, commissioned by the artist Salvador Dalí and inscribed on a toothpick. *It is not here* was realized in Morse Code at the Museum of Modern Art, New York, in 1974. His later works include *sleep whistle* (1975), which the composer performs while asleep in a store window, and *roll*, executed while lying down in the street and covered by Hindu bells. *Dreamsound* was performed at Berkeley, California, in 1976.

Hayne van Ghizeghem (c.1445–between 1472 and 1497) Franco-Flemish composer. His life is documented only for the years 1457–72, which he spent at the court of Burgundy. His entire surviving output is of French chansons, several of which were among the most successful of their age, including 'De tous biens plaine', 'Allez regretz', and 'Amours, amours'.

head voice the upper register of the human voice, referring to the head as the area of sound production. The head voice of a male singer is called ➤ falsetto. However, there has been disagreement (in the 19th century and earlier) concerning the precise use of the term, some claiming that only head voice and ➤ chest voice (the lower register) exist, others claiming that a third middle register is also important. Today, there is less concern about these distinctions.

Heart's Assurance, The the song cycle by Michael Tippett for high voice and piano (poems by Sidney Keyes and Alun Lewis); it was commissioned by Peter Pears and performed by him and Benjamin Britten in London, England, on 7 May 1951.

Heath, John (lived 16th century) English composer. His morning and communion services were printed by John Day in 1560, but had already been in use about 1548. There is also an anthem and a part song, and a keyboard piece in the Mulliner Book is almost certainly his.

He is not to be confused with the John Heath of Rochester, who wrote English church music and died in 1668; this may have been his grandson.

'Hebrides' Overture concert overture by Mendelssohn; see ➤ *Fingal's Cave*.

Heckel, Johann Adam (1812–1877) German instrument maker. He founded the family firm in Biebrich in 1831 and became the foremost German bassoon maker, making many improvements to the instrument.

Heckelclarina musical instrument specially created by the firm of Heckel in Biberich, Germany, for the playing of the shepherd's pipe part in Act III of Wagner's *Tristan und Isolde*.

heckelphone musical instrument, a wide-bore baritone ➤ oboe in B flat. It was introduced by the German maker Wilhelm Heckel (1856–1909) and adopted by Richard Strauss in the opera *Salome* (1905).

heel in stringed musical instruments, the end of the bow held by the player.

Heiligmesse, Holy Mass the *Missa Sancti Bernardi von Offida*, in B flat, composed in 1796 by Joseph → Haydn as a companion to the *Missa in tempore belli/Mass in Time of War* (1796).

Heimchen am Herd, Das, The Cricket on the Hearth opera by Karoly Goldmark (libretto by A M Willner, based on Charles Dickens's story), first produced at the Vienna Opera House, Austria, on 21 March 1896. In the story, May is to marry Tackleton, the owner of a doll factory, after her love Edward, a sailor, goes to sea. Edward returns and the two marry.

Heimkehr aus der Fremde, Die, The Return from Abroad, better known as **Son and Stranger** operetta by Felix Mendelssohn (libretto by K Klingemann), first produced in Leipzig, Germany, on 10 April 1851. In the story, Kauz has to leave town in a hurry after he tries to impersonate the son of a magistrate.

Heine, Heinrich (1797–1856) German poet. His works and thought inspired the following composers and works: Havergal → Brian (*Pilgrimage to Kevlaar*), → Dichterliebe (Robert Schumann), *Der* → Fliegende Holländer (Wagner), → Giselle (Adolphe Adam), *Guglielmo Ratcliff* (Pietro Mascagni), *Wallfahrt nach Kevlaar* (Engelbert → Humperdinck), → Liederkreis (Robert Schumann), → Schwanengesang (Franz Schubert), and → William Ratcliff (César Cui), as well as six songs by Brahms, six by Schubert, and 39 by Schumann.

Heinichen, Johann David (1683–1729) German composer and theorist. After training as a lawyer, he became a composer of operas and other pieces. He also wrote two important treatises on figured bass.

He studied under Schelle and Kuhnau in Leipzig, then practised law in Weissenfels, but in 1709 returned to Leipzig as an opera composer. The following year he went to Italy to study, and remained there until 1716. In 1717 he was appointed Kapellmeister to the Elector of Saxony in Dresden, where he lived until his death.

Works operas, numerous Masses, motets, and other church works, cantatas, symphonies, orchestral suites, solo and trio sonatas.

Heinö, Mikko (1958–) Finnish composer. He studied in Berlin, Germany, and at the Helsinki University, Finland, where he taught from 1977 until 1985, when he became professor of musicology at the University of Turku, Finland. His works include five piano concertos, horn concerto, concerto for orchestra, *Brass Mass*, and *Wind Pictures* for choir and orchestra. His books include *The Twelve Tone Age in Finnish Music*

(1986) and *Postmodern Features in New Finnish Music* (1988).

Heinrich, Anthony Philip (1781–1861) Bohemian-born US composer. Popular throughout the main US music centres of the time, New York, Boston, and Philadelphia, he became known as the 'Beethoven of America'. Heinrich's experiences of the frontier included a deep awareness of American Indian music, and in *The Jubilee* (1841), a work for soloists, chorus, and orchestra, he depicts the story of the British colonists in America.

He emigrated to the USA in 1810, settling first in Philadelphia then moving to Kentucky in 1817; in Lexington he conducted the first known performance of a Beethoven symphony in America. His first compositions date from 1818; they include the collection of songs and violin and piano pieces entitled *The Dawning of Music in Kentucky, or the Pleasures of Harmony in the Solitudes of Nature*. His orchestral music, often for huge forces and developing from models by Haydn and Beethoven, dates from 1831 with *Pushmataha, a venerable Chief of Western Tribe of Indians*; later such works include *The Treaty of William Penn with the Indians* (1834), *The Ornithological Combat of Kings* (1847), and *The Wildwood Troubadour* (1834–53). He visited Europe from 1827 and his *Ornithological* symphony was performed in Graz, Austria, in 1836. Other works include *The War of the Elements and the Thundering of Niagara* (c.1845), for orchestra, and *A Chromatic Ramble of the Peregrine Harmonist*, for piano. His status in the history of American music is suggested by his nickname, 'Father Heinrich'.

Heldenleben, Ein, A Hero's Life symphonic poem by Richard Strauss, composed in the autumn of 1898. It was first performed in Frankfurt, Germany, on 3 March 1899. The work is autobiographical.

Heliogabalus Imperator 'allegory for music' by Hans Werner Henze, after M Enzensberger; composed 1971–77 and first performed in Chicago, USA, on 16 November 1972, conducted by Georg Solti.

Heller, Stephen (1813 or 1814–1888) Hungarian pianist and composer. At the age of nine he caused some sensation as a boy pianist. He studied in Paris, France, and worked there as a pianist and teacher until his death, becoming one of the group which included Hector Berlioz, Chopin, Liszt, and Charles Hallé. He wrote entirely for the piano, except two works with violin entitled *Pensées fugitives*, in collaboration with Heinrich Ernst, and achieved an individual style of great lyrical charm.

Heller was born in Pest. He studied with Anton

Halm in Vienna, Austria, made his first public appearance at Pest in his teens, and later went on tour in Germany. He lived in Augsburg, Germany, 1830–38 after a long illness, working quietly at composition, and settled in Paris in 1838. In 1850 and 1862 he visited England.

Works PIANO four sonatas, a very large number of studies, variations, and fantasies on operatic tunes, five Tarantellas, Caprice on Schubert's *Trout*, several sets entitled *Im Walde*, *Promenades d'un solitaire* (after Rousseau's letters on botany), *Blumen-, Frucht- und Dornenstücke* (after Jean Paul, 1853), *Dans le bois*, *Nuits blanches*, and other pieces.

Helm, Everett (1913–1999) US composer and writer. He studied at Harvard with Walter Piston, and later with Gian Francesco Malipiero and Ralph Vaughan Williams. He appeared widely as teacher and lecturer and has written books on Béla Bartók (1965) and Franz Liszt (1972).

Works two piano concertos (1951, 1956); *Adam and Eve*, medieval adaptation (1951); *Le Roy fait battre tambour*, ballet (1956); *Sinfonia da camera* (1961); string quartets, woodwind quintet (1967).

Helmholtz, Hermann Ludwig Ferdinand von (1821–1894) German physiologist, physicist, and inventor of the ophthalmoscope for examining the inside of the eye. He was the first to measure the speed of nerve impulses and the first to explain how the cochlea of the inner ear works. He also specialized in the musical aspects of acoustics. In physics he formulated the law of conservation of energy, and worked in thermodynamics.

Helmholtz's scientific work in many fields was intended to prove that living things possess no innate vital force, and that their life processes are driven by the same forces and obey the same principles as nonliving systems. He arrived at the principle of conservation of energy in 1847, observing that the energy of life processes is derived entirely from oxidation of food, and that animal heat and muscle action are generated by chemical changes in the muscles.

Helmholtz was born in Potsdam and studied at the Friedrich Wilhelm Institute in Berlin. He first became professor at Bonn in 1855 and ended his career as director of the Physico-Technical Institute of Berlin from 1887.

Helmholtz invented the ophthalmoscope, which is used to examine the retina, 1851, and the ophthalmometer, which measures the curvature of the eye, 1855. He also revived the three-colour theory of vision first proposed 1801 by English physicist Thomas Young, by showing that a single primary colour (red, green, or violet) must also affect retinal structures sensitive to the other primary colours. This explained the colour of afterimages and the effects of colour blindness.

In acoustics, Helmholtz produced a comprehensive explanation of how the upper partials in sounds combine to give them a particular tone or timbre, and how resonance may cause this to happen. In 1863 he published his *Lehre von den Tonempfindungen als physiologische Grundlage für die Theorie der Musik* (translated by A J Ellis as *On the Sensations of Tone*).

Helmholtz resonator spherical vessel of metal or glass with an opening and an earpiece on opposite sides, from a harmonic series of 19 such vessels constructed for the German physicist Hermann Helmholtz (1821–1894) as an instrument of acoustic analysis. Placed in the ear, it acts as an acoustic filter, allowing only sounds of a particular pitch to be heard. Helmholtz also used resonators in series with tuning forks as sound sources in pioneering experiments in synthesizing instrumental timbres.

The ear canal acts in a similar way, enhancing frequencies in the range 1,000–4,000 Hz.

hemidemisemiquaver, US **64th note** in music, a note value $\frac{1}{64}$ of the duration of a ➔ semibreve. It is written as a filled black note-head with a stem and four flags (tails).

hemiola rhythmic device based on the ratio 3:2, in which two bars of triple time are articulated in the manner of three bars in duple time. It was much favoured by Brahms, and also by baroque composers for use in passages approaching a ➔ cadence.

Hemmel, Sigmund (died 1564) German composer. He composed the first complete polyphonic metrical psalter in Germany (published in Tübingen in 1569). He also wrote German and Latin sacred songs, and a Mass.

Henrici, Christian Friedrich (known as Picander) (1700–1764) German poet and cantata librettist. From 1726 he was involved in a collaboration with Johann Sebastian Bach, which resulted in the texts for the *St Matthew Passion*, *St Mark Passion*, and part of the *Christmas Oratorio*. He also furnished libretti for many of Bach's occasional vocal works and some of the church cantatas.

After study in Wittenberg he moved to Leipzig in 1720. He was well known as a playwright and published five volumes of poems, under the title *Ernst schertzhafte und satyrische Gedichte*.

Henry, Pierre (1927–) French composer. He worked with Pierre ➔ Schaeffer at the Groupe de Recherche de Musique Concrète 1950–58; their collaborations include *Symphonie pour un homme seul* (1950) and the opera *Orphée* (1953). After leaving Schaeffer's studio he founded a private electroacoustical studio at Apsome in 1958. He studied with Olivier Messiaen and Nadia Boulanger.

Works BALLET *Haut Voltage* (1956), *Le Voyage* (1962), *Messe pour le temps présent* (1967), and *Nijinsky, clown de Dieu* (1971).

OTHER *Messe de Liverpool* (1967), *Gymkhana* (1970), *Ceremony* (1970), *Futuriste I* (1975).

Henry VIII (1491–1547) King of England 1509–47. He composed or arranged several songs found in a manuscript (British Museum, Add 31,922) dating from his reign, and a three-part motet *Quam pulchra es*.

Henry VIII opera by Camille Saint-Saëns (libretto by L Détroyat and P A Silvestre), first produced at the Paris Opéra, France, on 5 March 1883. It tells how Henry defies the Pope to marry Anne Boleyn.

Henze, Hans Werner (1926–) German composer. His immense and stylistically restless output is marked by a keen literary sensibility and seductive use of orchestral coloration, as in the opera *Elegy for Young Lovers* (1961) and the cantata *Being Beauteous* (1963). Among later works are the opera *Das Verratene Meer/The Sea Betrayed* (1992), based on Yukio Mishima's novel *The Sailor who Fell from Grace with the Sea*, and *L'Upupa oder Der Triumph der Sohnesliebe/L'Upupa and the Triumph of Filial Love*, an opera commissioned by the 2003 Salzburg Festival and for which Henze also tried his hand for the first time as librettist. He also composed ten symphonies (1947–2002).

He studied with Wolfgang Fortner at Heidelberg, Switzerland, and René Leibowitz in Paris, France. He is influenced by Arnold Schoenberg, though not strictly a 12-note composer, and has also done much to further the ballet in Germany; from 1950 to 1952 he was ballet adviser to the Wiesbaden Opera. In 1953 he moved to Italy, where his music became more expansive, as in the opera *The Bassarids* (1966). Following the student unrest of 1968 he suddenly renounced the wealthy musical establishment in favour of a militantly socialist stance in works such as the abrasive *El Cimarrón* (1970) and *Voices* (1973), austere settings of 22 revolutionary texts in often magical sonorities. The opera *We Come to the River* (1976) and the ballet *Orpheus* (1979) were written in collaboration with Edward Bond. In subsequent years Henze returned to the musical past, becoming increasingly lyrical and elaborate: his reconstruction of Monteverdi's *Il ritorno di Ulisse* was staged in Salzburg, Austria, in 1985. In 1988 he founded the Munich Biennale, a festival for new music theatre, of which he has since been artistic director.

Works STAGE *Elegy for Young Lovers*, chamber

opera (Schwetzingen and Glyndebourne, 1961); *Der junge Lord*, comic opera (Berlin, 1965); *The Bassarids*, opera seria (Salzburg, 1966); *Orpheus*, ballet by Edward Bond (Stuttgart, 1979); *The English Cat*, chamber opera (Schwetzingen, 1983); *L'Upupa oder Der Triumph der Sohnesliebe/L'Upupa and the Triumph of Filial Love*, opera (Salzburg, 2003).

ORCHESTRAL ten symphonies (1947–2002); two violin concertos (1948, 1978); two piano concertos (1950, 1967); *Doppio Concerto* for oboe, harp, and strings (1966); *Requiem* (nine spiritual concertos) for piano, trumpet, and chamber orchestra (1992).

VOCAL five *Neapolitan Songs* for baritone and orchestra (1956); *Nocturnes and Arias* for soprano and orchestra (1957); *Kammermusik* for tenor, guitar, and chamber orchestra (1958); *Ariosi* for soprano, violin, and orchestra after Tasso (1963); *Das Floss der Medusa*, oratorio to the memory of Ché Guevara (1968); *Versuch über Schweine/Essay on Pigs* (1969); *El Cimarrón*, for baritone and ensemble (1970); *Voices*, for mezzo, tenor, and instruments (22 revolutionary texts; 1973).

CHAMBER MUSIC five string quartets (1947–77), *Royal Winter Music*, two sonatas for guitar on Shakespearean characters (1975–79).

heptachord in music, a scale of seven notes.

Herbert, Victor (1859–1924) Irish-born US conductor and composer. In 1893 he became conductor of the 22nd Regiment Band, also composing light operettas for the New York stage. He was conductor of the Pittsburgh Philharmonic 1898–1904, returning to New York to help found the American Society of Composers, Authors, and Publishers (ASCAP) in 1914.

The second of his two cello concertos, written in 1894, inspired Dvořák to write his own cello concerto.

Born in Dublin, Republic of Ireland, Herbert trained as a cellist at the Stuttgart Conservatory, and began his professional musical career in Vienna, Austria. He emigrated to the USA in 1886 and played with the New York Metropolitan Opera and Philharmonic Orchestra.

Works OPERA *Natoma* (1911), *Madeleine* (1914); operettas *The Wizard of the Nile* (1895), *Babes in Toyland* (1903), and over 30 others.

ORCHESTRAL symphonic poem *Hero and Leander* (1901) and three suites for orchestra.

CHAMBER Serenade for strings.

VOCAL dramatic cantata *The Captive* (1891); songs.

Hercules secular oratorio by Handel (libretto by T Broughton), first produced at the King's Theatre, Haymarket, London, England, on 5 January 1745.

Herder, Johann Gottfried von (1744–1803) German philosopher, philologist, and author, influential in the forming of the early-Romantic idea of music as an independent art. His poetic works inspired the composers J C F ➤ **Bach** (*Brutus*, oratorios and cantatas), Adolph ➤ **Jensen** (*Stimmen der Völker*), Franz Liszt (➤ *Prometheus*), and Johann ➤ **Reichardt** (*Morning Hymn*).

Hermannus Contractus (1013–1054), also known as **Hermann the Cripple** German music scholar and composer. He studied at the monastery of Reichenau in Switzerland and became a Benedictine monk. He wrote musical treatises and composed hymns, sequences, and other pieces.

Hermann von Salzburg (lived 14th century) Austrian monk and composer. He belonged to the tradition of the Minnesinger but also wrote a few polyphonic pieces and a love song addressed to a lady acquaintance of the archbishop of Salzburg.

Hermione opera by Max Bruch (libretto by E Hopffer, based on Shakespeare's *The Winter's Tale*), first produced at the Opera House, Berlin, Germany, on 21 March 1872.

Hernried, Robert (1883–1951) Austrian-born US scholar and composer. He studied in Vienna, and after a career as an opera conductor 1908–14 he held various teaching posts and professorships in Germany and the USA, where he emigrated in 1934. In 1946 he was appointed professor at Detroit University. He wrote several books and over 300 articles.

Works the operas *Francesca da Rimini* (after Dante) and *The Peasant Woman*; Mass; over 60 choral works; concert overture for orchestra; chamber music and songs.

Hero and Leander English translation of the opera ➤ *Ero e Leandro*.

Hérodiade, Herodias opera by Jules Massenet (libretto by P Milliet and 'Henri Grémont' (Georges Hartmann), based on a story by Gustave Flaubert), first produced at the Théâtre de la Monnaie, Brussels, Belgium, on 19 December 1881. In this version, Salome, the abandoned daughter of Hérodiade, loves John the Baptist and kills herself rather than yield to Herod.

Hérodiade orchestral recitation by Paul Hindemith, after Stéphane Mallarmé. It was composed in 1944 and first performed in Washington, DC, USA, on 30 October 1944, with the Martha Graham dance group.

Hérold, (Louis Joseph) Ferdinand (1791–1833) French composer. He had considerable success with the operas *Zampa* (1831) and *Le Pré aux clercs* (1832), but is best known today for the ballet *La Fille mal gardée* (1828).

Hérold was born in Paris and studied under his father, the pianist François Joseph Hérold (1755–1802). Later he was taught by François Fétis, Louis Adam, Charles-Simon Catel, and Étienne Méhul, and won the Prix de Rome in 1812. In Rome and Naples, where he became pianist to Queen Caroline, he wrote several instrumental works, and the comic opera *La Jeunesse de Henri V*. Returning to Paris in 1816, he collaborated with François Boieldieu in the opera *Charles de France*, and in 1817 began to produce operas of his own. He was accompanist at the Théâtre Italien from 1820 until 1827, when he married Adèle Elise Rollet and became choirmaster at the Opéra. About this time he began to suffer seriously from tuberculosis, from which he died.

Works OPERA *Les Rosières* (1817), *La Clochette* (1817), *Le Premier Venu*, *Les Troqueurs* (1819), *L'Amour platonique*, *L'Auteur mort et vivant* (1820), *Le Muletier* (1823), *Lasthénie*, *Le Lapin blanc*, *Vendôme en Espagne* (with Auber), *Le Roi René* (1824), *Marie*, *L'Illusion*, *Emmeline* (1829), *L'Auberge d'Auray* (with Carafa), *Zampa* (1831), *Le Pré aux clercs* (1832), *Ludovic* (unfinished, completed by Halévy).

BALLET *Astolphe et Joconde* (1827), *La Sonnambule* (1827), *Lydie*, *La Fille mal gardée* (1828), *La Belle au bois dormant* (after Perrault; 1829).

OTHER incidental music for Ozaneaux's *Dernier Jour de Missolonghi*; two symphonies; four piano concertos; cantata *Mlle de la Vallière*, *Hymne sur la Transfiguration*; three string quartets; two sonatas, variations, rondos, and other pieces for piano.

Heroldt, Johannes (c.1550–1603) German composer. His works include a setting of the *St Matthew Passion* for six voices, published at Graz in 1594.

Hero's Life, A symphonic poem by Richard Strauss; see ➤ *Heldenleben, Ein*.

Herrmann, Bernard (1911–1975) US film composer. His long career began with *Citizen Kane* (1941); besides Orson Welles, he collaborated with Alfred Hitchcock (*North by Northwest*, 1959, and *Psycho*, 1960), François Truffaut (*Fahrenheit 451*, 1966), and Martin Scorsese (*Taxi Driver*, 1976). He wrote his best scores for thrillers and mystery movies, and was a major influence in the establishment of a distinctively American musical imagery.

Born in New York, he won a composition prize at the age of 13 and began studying with Phillip James at New York University and later at the Juilliard Graduate School of Music. He joined CBS (Columbia Broadcasting System) in 1933 as a composer and conductor of music for drama and documentary programmes, and worked with

Orson Welles on a number of radio projects before making his film debut. An eclectic stylist, he made his own orchestrations and sought out many new and exotic instruments for special effects and authentic colour.

Works OPERA *Wuthering Heights* (1948–50; produced Portland, Oregon, 1982).

CANTATAS *Moby Dick* (1937), *Johnny Appleseed* (1940).

ORCHESTRAL AND CHAMBER symphonic poem *City of Brass*, *Fiddle Concerto*, symphony; string quartet.

FILM SCORES including *Citizen Kane* (1941), *Psycho* (1960), *The Birds* (1963), and *Taxi Driver* (1976).

Herschel, (Frederick) William (1738–1822) English astronomer and musician of German parentage. He played the oboe in the band of the Hanoverian Guards and in 1755 was posted to Durham. For the next eleven years he was active in Newcastle, Halifax, and Leeds as an organist, violinist, and composer of symphonies. He moved to Bath in 1766 and directed choral concerts. While earning his living as a musician he pursued a private interest in astronomy; his discovery of Uranus in 1781 led to his appointment as Astronomer Royal in 1782. From this point on he cultivated music only as an amateur. He was knighted in 1817 and became the first president of the Royal Astronomical Society in 1821. His works include 24 symphonies (1760–64), concertos for oboe, organ, and violin; six fugues, 24 sonatas, and 33 voluntaries for organ.

hertz (Hz) term for frequency in musical pitch, corresponding to cycles per second, and named after the German physicist Heinrich Hertz (1857–1894). For example, the phrase A 440 Hz means the note A (A4) of the frequency 440 cycles per second.

Hervé (1825–1892), born **Florimond Ronger** French composer. He studied music as a choirboy, then with Antoine Elwart and Daniel Auber. He was organist at various Paris churches, including Saint-Eustache, and later theatre manager, operetta singer, librettist, and conductor.

Works OPERA more than 80 operettas, including *Don Quixote et Sancho Pança* (after Cervantes, 1848), *Le Hussard persécuté*, *La Fanfare de Saint-Cloud*, *Les Chevaliers de la table ronde* (1866), *L'Œil crevé*, *Chilpéric*, *Le Petit Faust*, *Les Turcs* (parody of Racine's *Bajazet*, 1869), *La Belle Poule*, *Le Nouvel Aladin*, and *Frivoli* (1886).

BALLET *Dilara*, *Sport*, *La Rose d'amour*, *Cléopâtre*, *Les Bagatelles*.

OTHER symphony *The Ashanti War* for solo voices and orchestra (1874); many light songs.

Herz, Das, **The Heart** opera by Hans Pfitzner (libretto by H Mahner-Mons), composed 1930–31 and first produced in Berlin and Mu-

nich, Germany, on 12 November 1931. It was Pfitzner's last opera. It tells how Dr Athanasius attempts the diabolic resuscitation of the Duke's dead son, but the price is his wife's heart. He is condemned for sorcery, but atones.

Herzgewächse work by Arnold Schoenberg for high soprano, celesta, harmonium, and harp, Op. 20, composed in 1911. It first British performance was a BBC (British Broadcasting Corporation) concert on 1 December 1960.

Herzogenberg, Heinrich von (1843–1900), **Baron Heinrich Peccaduc** Austrian composer and conductor. He studied at the Vienna Conservatory and settled in Leipzig, Germany, in 1872. He conducted the Bach society there 1875–85, before becoming professor of composition at the Berlin Hochschule für Musik. His wife, Elisabeth von Herzogenberg (1842–1892), was a fine amateur pianist and pupil of Brahms.

Works SACRED MUSIC Mass (1895), Requiem (1891), psalms; oratorios *Die Geburt Christi* and *Die Passion*, cantata *Columbus*.

ORCHESTRAL three symphonies, no. 1 entitled *Odysseus*.

CHAMBER five string quartets (1876–90), two piano trios, two string trios; two violin and piano sonatas, cello and piano sonata; two sets of variations for two pianos, many piano pieces and duets.

OTHER fantasies for organ; songs, vocal duets, part songs.

Heseltine, Philip (Arnold) real name of the English composer Peter ➤ **Warlock**.

heterophony form of group music making found in folk music worldwide, in which the same melody line is presented simultaneously in plain and individually embellished forms.

Heuberger, Richard (Franz Josef) (1850–1914) Austrian music critic and composer. He studied engineering at first, but at the age of 26 devoted himself to music, becoming a choral conductor in 1878 and a critic in 1881. His best-known work is *Der Opernball/Ball at the Opera House* (1898).

Works OPERA *Manuel Venegas* (1889), *Miriam* (later *Das Maifest* 1894), *Abenteuer einer Neujahrsnacht* (1896), *Barfüssele*; operettas *Der Opernball* (1898), *Ihre Exzellenz*, *Der Sechsuhrzug*, *Das Baby*, *Der Fürst von Düsterstein*, *Don Quixotte* (after Cervantes).

BALLET *Die Lautenschlägerin* and *Struwwelpeter*.

Heure espagnole, L', **The Spanish Hour** opera in one act by Maurice Ravel (libretto by Franc-Nohain, based on his own comedy), first produced at the Opéra-Comique, Paris, France, on 19 May 1911. It describes how the mule-driver Ramiro and the poet Gonzalve keep good time with the clockmaker's wife Concepción.

hexachord in music, not a chord in the true sense, but a group of six individual notes. Introduced in the 11th century as a method of sight-singing, a series of overlapping scalar hexachords embraced the entire compass of notes. In the 20th century the term was redefined by composers using the ➤ **twelve-tone system**, particularly Arnold Schoenberg and Anton Webern, as being half of a twelve-tone (twelve-note) row, allowing further compositional manipulation.

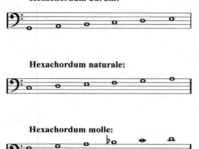

Hexachordum durum:

Hexachordum naturale:

Hexachordum molle:

The three hexachords on G, C, and F respectively.

---

hexachord fantasy a type of composition cultivated particularly by 16th–17th-century English composers, a piece based on the first six notes of the scale, ascending or descending. The pieces were often entitled 'Ut, re, mi, fa, sol, la'.

Hexameron a collective piano work, published in 1837, consisting of bravura variations on the March in Bellini's *I puritani* by Franz Liszt, Sigismond Thalberg, Johann Pixis, Henri Herz, Karl Czerny, and Frédéric Chopin, with an introduction, finale, and connecting passages by Liszt.

hey old country dance similar to the ➤ **reel**, and probably to the ➤ **canary**.

Heyden, Sebald (1499–1561) German theologian and music theorist. His explanations of the musical notation of his time are particularly valuable.

Heyns, Cornelius (lived 15th century) Flemish composer. He was succentor at St Donatian in Bruges 1452–53 and 1462–65. His Mass *Pour quelque paine* has also been attributed to Johannes Okeghem.

Heyse, Paul (Johann Ludwig) (1830–1914) German poet and novelist. His work inspired the ➤ *Italienisches Liederbuch* (Hugo Wolf) and ➤ *Spanisches Liederbuch* (Wolf and Adolph ➤ **Jensen**).

Hiawatha three cantatas for solo voices, chorus, and orchestra by Samuel Coleridge-Taylor, a set-ting of parts of Longfellow's poem: 1. *Hiawatha's Wedding Feast*, 2. *The Death of Minnehaha*, 3. *Hiawatha's Departure*. They were first performed as a whole in London, England, on 22 March 1900.

Hidalgo, Juan (c.1614–1685) Spanish composer. He was influential in the introduction of Italian-style operas to Spain, and collaborated with the playwright Pedro Calderón de la Barca in the composition of several operas, including *Celos aun del aire matan* (1660), the first known Spanish opera.

He was a harpist and harpsichordist in the royal chapel in Madrid, and is said to have invented an instrument called the *claviharpa*.

Works STAGE operas *Celos aun del aire matan* (libretto by Calderón, 1660) and *Los celos hacen estrellas* (libretto by Guevara); incidental music to various plays by Calderón including *Ni amor se libra de amor*.

hidden fifths, hidden octaves in music, the movement of two parts in the same direction to a fifth or an octave. In many contrapuntal styles this is to be avoided, especially when involving the top or bottom line. Textbooks in formal counterpoint gave them this title as having an effect similar to that of consecutives.

Highland fling Scottish dance step, rather than a dance itself, although it is often so called. The music is that of the ➤ **strathspey** and the step is a kick of the leg backwards and forwards.

Hignard, (Jean Louis) Aristide (1822–1898) French composer. He was a pupil of Jacques Halévy at the Paris Conservatory, where he gained the second Prix de Rome in 1850.

Works OPERA *Hamlet* (after Shakespeare; composed 1868 but not produced until 1888, owing to success of Thomas's *Hamlet*), *Le Colin-Maillard*, *Les Compagnons de la Marjolaine* and *L'Auberge des Ardennes* (all on libretti by Jules Verne and Michael Carrol) and eight others.

OTHER choruses; *Valses concertantes* and *Valses romantiques* for piano duet; songs.

Hildegard, Saint (1098–1179), also known as **Hildegard of Bingen** German abbess and musician. She was educated at the Benedictine nunnery of Disisbodenberg, where she became abbess in 1136. She wrote monophonic music for the church which shows some departures from traditional plainsong style. She wrote music to her own poetry from 1140, collected in the 1150s as *Symphonia armonie celestium revelationum* (77 poems based on the liturgical calendar). The morality play *Ordo virtutum* concerns the struggle of virtue against the devil and contains 82 melodies.

Hill, Alfred (1870–1960) Australian composer, conductor, and teacher. His early career was in Leipzig, Germany. He moved to New Zealand in 1902 and became influenced by Maori music. He was professor at New South Wales Conservatory 1915–35.

Works OPERA eight operas, including *Tapu* (1903), *A Moorish Maid* (1905), and *Giovanni, the Sculptor* (1914).

ORCHESTRAL AND CHAMBER ten symphonies (1896–1958); 17 string quartets, six sonatas for violin and piano.

Hillemacher, Paul (Joseph Wilhelm) (1852–1933) and Lucien (Joseph Edouard) (1860–1909) French composers, brothers who wrote all their works in collaboration. They studied at the Paris Conservatory, where Paul won the Prix de Rome in 1876 and Lucien in 1880.

Works STAGE operas *Saint-Mégrin* (1886), *La Légende de Sainte Geneviève*, *Une Aventure d'Arlequin* (1888), *Le Régiment qui passe* (1894), *Le Drac*, *Orsola*, *Circé* (1907); mimed dramas *One for Two* and *Fra Angelico*; incidental music for Haraucourt's *Héro et Léandre* and for George Sand's *Claudie*.

OTHER symphonic legend *Loreley* and other orchestral works; chamber music, songs, part songs.

Hiller, Ferdinand (1811–1885) German pianist, conductor, and composer. He succeeded Felix Mendelssohn as conductor of the Leipzig Gewandhaus 1843–44. From 1850 he lived in Cologne, where he founded the Conservatory.

He was taught music privately as a child and appeared as a pianist at the age of ten. In 1825 he went to Weimar to study under Johann Hummel. After a brief return to Frankfurt he lived in Paris, France, 1828–35, where he taught and gave concerts. He produced his first opera in Milan, Italy, in 1839 and his first oratorio in Leipzig in 1840, then studied with Giuseppe Baini in Rome, lived in Frankfurt, Leipzig, and Dresden, became conductor in Düsseldorf in 1847 and finally in Cologne in 1850, where he remained.

Works OPERA *Romilda* (1839), *Die Katakomben* (1862), *Der Deserteur* (1865).

ORATORIOS *Die Zerstörung Jerusalems* (1840) and *Saul*.

CANTATAS *Nala und Damajanti*, *Prometheus*, *Rebecca*, and others, including one from Byron's *Hebrew Melodies*.

ORCHESTRAL four symphonies, four overtures (including one to Schiller's *Demetrius*), and other works; two piano concertos (1835, 1861), violin concerto (1875).

CHAMBER three string quartets, three piano quartets, five piano trios; violin and cello sonata.

PIANO sonata, 24 studies, *Modern Suite*, and many other works for piano.

OTHER songs, part songs.

Hiller, Johann Adam (1728–1804) German composer. He spent the greater part of his life in Leipzig, where he was the central figure in the musical activity of the city. He founded subscription concerts and a musical weekly, and was one of the originators of the German *Singspiel* ('sung play', or opera), of which he wrote many successful examples 1766–82.

He was a chorister under Homilius in Dresden, and studied law at Leipzig University. After a short period in the service of Count Brühl, he returned to Leipzig, working as a flautist, singer, and conductor. In 1763 he founded subscription concerts on the model of the Paris Concert Spirituel, these becoming the Gewandhaus concerts in 1781. He also produced a musical weekly, *Wöchentliche Nachrichten*, 1766–70. He left Leipzig in 1785, but after some short-term posts returned to succeed Johann Doles as municipal music director and cantor of St Thomas's.

Works SINGSPIELE *Der Teufel ist los* (after Coffey's *The Devil to Pay*, 1766), *Lisuart und Dariolette*, *Lottchen am Hofe* (1767), *Die Muse*, *Die Liebe auf dem Lande* (1768), *Die Jagd*, *Der Dorfbalbier* (1771), *Der Aerndtekranz*, *Der Krieg* (1772), *Die Jubelhochzeit*, *Das Grab des Mufti*, *Das gerettete Troja*.

OTHER settings of Gellert's odes and other choral works; cantatas; 100th Psalm; instrumental music; also many theoretical and critical writings on music.

Hiller, Lejaren (1924–1994) US composer. He learned from Roger Sessions and Milton Babbitt and co-created the first computer composition, *Illiac Suite* (1957). He directed the experimental music studio at the University of Illinois 1958–68, and was appointed professor of music at the State University of New York, Buffalo, in 1968.

Works two symphonies (1953, 1960), piano concerto (1949), seven string quartets (1949–79), six piano sonatas (1946–72); *Computer Cantata* (1963), seven *Electronic Studies* (1963), *Rage over the Lost Beethoven* (1972); *The Fox Trots Again* for chamber orchestra (1985). He collaborated with Cage on *HPSCHD* for 1–7 harpsichords and 1–51 tapes (1968).

Hilton, John (1599–1657) English organist and composer. He took a degree in music at Cambridge University in 1626 and two years later became organist at St Margaret's Church, Westminster.

Works services and anthems; madrigals, *Ayres, or Fa La's* for three voices (published 1627; the last English madrigal publication); *Elegy on the death of Wm Lawes* for three voices and bass; collection of catches, rounds, and canons *Catch that Catch Can* (1652); songs, fantasies for viols, hymn 'Wilt Thou Forgive That Sin Where I Begun' from Donne's *Divine Poems*.

Himmel, Friedrich Heinrich (1765–1814) German harpsichordist, pianist, and composer. He read theology at Halle University, but later under the patronage of Frederick William II of Prussia studied music at Dresden under Johann Naumann and in Italy, where he produced two operas. Appointed court Kapellmeister in Berlin in 1795, he was still able to travel and visited Russia, Scandinavia, Paris, London, and Vienna.

Works OPERA *Il primo navigatore* (1794), *La morte di Semiramide* (1795), *Alessandro* (1799), *Vasco da Gama* (1801), *Frohsinn und Schwärmerei*, *Fauchon das Leyermädchen* (1804), *Die Sylphen*, *Der Kobold* (1813).

ORATORIO *Isacco*.

CHURCH MUSIC funeral cantata for the King of Prussia; Masses, Te Deum, motets, psalms and other church music.

OTHER instrumental music, songs.

Hindemith, Paul (1895–1963) German composer and teacher. His operas *Cardillac* (1926, revised 1952) and *Mathis der Maler/Mathis the Painter* (1933–35) are theatrically astute and politically aware; as a teacher in Berlin 1927–33 he encouraged the development of a functional modern repertoire ('Gebrauchsmusik'/'utility music') for home and school.

In 1939 he emigrated to the USA, where he taught at Yale University and was influential in promoting a measured neoclassical idiom of self-evident contrapuntal mastery but matter-of-fact tone, exemplified in *Ludus tonalis* for piano (1942) and the *Symphonic Metamorphosis of Themes by Carl Maria von Weber* (1943). In later life he revised many of his earlier compositions to conform with a personal theory of tonality.

He was taught the violin as a child and entered the Hoch Conservatory in Frankfurt, where he studied under Arnold Mendelssohn and Bernhard Sekles. Later he played in the Frankfurt Opera orchestra and was leader there 1915–23; in 1921 he founded a string quartet (the Amar-Hindemith quartet) with the Turkish violinist Licco Amar, in which he played viola. The quartet was disbanded in 1929, the year in which he premiered William Walton's viola concerto in London.

Works of his were heard at the Donaueschingen festival in 1921 and at the International Society for Contemporary Music festival at Salzburg, Austria, in 1922. His one-act operas of 1921–22 scandalized audiences and some musicians, and he had an early reputation as an iconoclast. His Kammermusik series, begun in 1922, sought to re-establish the musical values of the baroque concerto; *Cardillac* uses neoclassical forms, although its story of a goldsmith who murders his clients to regain his work recalls the savagery of Hindemith's early pieces for the stage.

From 1927 he taught composition at the Berlin Hochschule für Musik, and his music was conducted by Wilhelm Furtwängler and Otto Klemperer, but the Nazis proscribed his works as degenerate art. His opera *Mathis der Maler* was therefore produced in Zürich, Switzerland, in 1938; a three-movement symphony from the opera was premiered in Berlin in 1934 by Fürtwangler, prompting a temporary break with the Nazi authorities. For some years after 1933 he was in Ankara, Turkey, in an official capacity to reorganize Turkish music education. In 1939 he emigrated to the USA, where he taught at Yale University, but in 1946 he returned to Europe and was active for several years as a conductor.

In his late, largely orchestral works, Hindemith sought further to establish the values of tonality and classical restraint. The vision of the astronomer Johannes Kepler in his last opera, *Die Harmonie der Welt* (1957), suggests the composer himself striving to hear the sounds emitted by the planets as they circle the Sun, oblivious to the harsher musical realities around him.

Works OPERA *Cardillac* (after E T A Hoffmann, 1926), *Mathis der Maler* (1933–35), *Die Harmonie der Welt* (1957).

BALLET *Nobilissima Visione* (1938).

ORCHESTRAL *Kammermusik* nos. 1–7 (1922–27; see separate entry), *Mathis der Maler*, symphony from the opera (1934), *Der Schwanendreher*, concerto after folk songs, for viola and small orchestra (1935), *Trauermusik* for viola and strings (1936), *Nobilissima Visione*, suite from the ballet (1938), cello concerto (1940), Symphony in E♭ (1940), *Theme and Variations 'The Four Temperaments'* for piano and strings (1940), *Symphonic Metamorphosis of Themes by Carl Maria von Weber* (1943), *Symphonia Serena* (1946), clarinet concerto (1947), horn concerto (1949).

CHAMBER AND KEYBOARD six string quartets (1918–45); 16 sonatas for various instruments, including four for solo viola; *Ludus tonalis*: twelve fugues with prelude and postlude, and other works for piano; three organ sonatas.

CHORAL AND SOLO VOCAL *Das Marienleben*, 15 songs for soprano and piano (texts by Rilke, 1922–23); Requiem, after Walt Whitman's 'When Lilacs Last in the Dooryard Bloom'd' (1946).

Hin und Zurück, There and Back opera in one act by Paul Hindemith (libretto by M Schiffer after an English revue), first produced in Baden-Baden, Germany, on 17 July 1927. The plot, concerning a jealous husband, goes into reverse at half way. At the first performance the part of the errant, palindromic wife was sung by Otto Klemperer's wife, Johanna.

Hippolyte et Aricie, Hippolytus and Aricia opera in five acts by Jean-Philippe Rameau (libretto by S J de Pellegrin), first produced at the

Paris Opéra, France, on 1 October 1733. In the story, Hippolytus and Aricia are in love. Believing her husband Theseus to be dead, Phaedra confesses love for her stepson Hippolytus, who rejects her. Theseus returns and condemns his son for what appears to be an attack on Phaedra. Hippolytus is carried off by a sea monster, but survives and is reunited with Aricia.

See also ➤ *Ippolito ed Aricia.*

Hirt auf dem Felsen, Der, The Shepherd on the Rock song by Franz Schubert, D965, for piano and soprano with clarinet obbligato (text by W Müller and H von Chezy), composed in October 1828. It was commissioned by Anna Milder-Hauptmann (1785–1838), the first Leonore in *Fidelio* (1805). With *Die Taubenpost*, it was Schubert's last work.

Histoire du soldat, L', The Soldier's Tale theatre piece involving narration, dancing, and music by Igor Stravinsky (libretto by C F Ramuz), first produced in Lausanne, Switzerland, on 28 September 1918, conducted by Ernest Ansermet. Stravinsky later arranged the music for concert performance by various sizes of ensemble.

Histoires naturelles song cycle by Maurice Ravel for voice and piano, composed in 1906 and first performed in Paris, France, on 19 March 1907. The five animals depicted are *The Peacock*, *The Cricket*, *The Swan*, *The Kingfisher*, and *The Guinea Fowl*.

Hitchcock, (Hugh) Wiley (1932–) US musicologist. He studied in Michigan and Paris, France (with Nadia Boulanger), and was appointed professor of music at Brooklyn College in 1971. His research interests involve US music history and the music of the French baroque. He was editor for the Americas in the *New Grove Dictionary of Music and Musicians* and co-editor of the *Grove Dictionary of US Music*. Other publications include *Music in the United States* (1969, 1975, 1988), *Les Oeuvres de Marc-Antoine Charpentier* (1982), and editions of Giulio Caccini, Leonardo Leo, and Jean-Baptiste Lully.

HMS Pinafore operetta by Arthur Sullivan (libretto by W S Gilbert), first produced at the Opéra Comique, London, England, on 25 May 1878. It was the first work by Gilbert and Sullivan to be a worldwide success.

Hoboken, Anthony van (1887–1983) Dutch musicologist. He studied in Frankfurt, Germany, and Vienna, Austria, and in 1927 founded a manuscript archive in the National Library in Vienna; an almost complete thematic catalogue of Haydn's works was published in 1957 and 1971. Haydn's works are commonly designated 'Hob.' with a roman numeral denoting group classification (for example opera, symphony), followed by

an Arabic numeral for a work within a group.

Hobrecht, Jacob Flemish composer; see Jacob ➤ **Obrecht.**

Hochzeit des Camacho, Die, Camacho's Wedding opera by Felix Mendelssohn (libretto by C A L von Lichtenstein, based on Cervantes' *Don Quixote*), first produced at the Schauspielhaus, Berlin, Germany, on 29 April 1827. The story tells how Quiteria loves Basilio but must marry the rich Camacho. At the wedding Basilio feigns attempted suicide; Camacho allows him to marry Quiteria so that he may die a happy man. The subterfuge is revealed, but Camacho accepts the lovers' union.

hocket in music, a device in medieval vocal and instrumental music, consisting of phrases when broken up by rests, in such a way that when one part is silent another fills the gap. A hocket is also a piece written in this style.

The word is similar to 'hiccup' and derived from the French equivalent *hoquet.*

Hoddinott, Alun (1929–) Welsh composer. In addition to major works in standard genres (including nine symphonies, several concertos, and ten piano sonatas), Hoddinott has composed works in a lighter vein, including carols and *Quodlibet on Welsh Nursery Tunes* for brass quintet.

He studied at the University College of South Wales, Cardiff, where he was appointed professor of music in 1967. He was artistic director of the Cardiff Festival of 20th-Century Music 1966–89.

Works OPERA *The Beach of Falesá* (1974), *The Magician* (1976, first produced as *Murder the Magician* on television, 1976), *The Rajah's Diamond* (1979), *The Trumpet Major*, after Hardy (1981).

ORCHESTRAL eight symphonies (1954–92), four sinfoniettas (1968–71), *Variants* (1966), *Night Music* for orchestra, two clarinet concertos (1954, 1986), oboe concerto, three piano concertos, organ concerto (1967), *Doubles* for oboe, harpsichord, and strings (1982), Triple concerto for violin, cello, and piano (1986), *Noctis Equi* for cello and orchestra (1989).

OTHER choral music; clarinet quartet, three string quartets (1966, 1984, 1988), string trio; ten piano sonatas.

Hoffmann, E(rnst) T(heodor) A(madeus) (1776–1822) German composer and writer. He composed the opera *Undine* (1816), but is chiefly remembered as an author and librettist of fairy stories, including 'Nussknacker/Nutcracker' (1816). His stories inspired Jacques ➤ **Offenbach's** *Tales of Hoffmann.*

Hoffmeister, Franz Anton (1754–1812) Austrian music publisher and composer. Beethoven and Mozart were among his clients. The best known of his nine operas was *Der Königssohn aus Ithaka* (1803). Whether by accident or design, many of his works were ascribed to Haydn.

He started in Vienna as a law student but in 1783 established his publishing firm. With Kühnel in Leipzig he established a bureau which later became the publishing house C F Peters. He wrote 66 symphonies, about 60 concertos, including 25 for flute, 42 string quartets, and 18 string trios.

Hoffmeister Quartet string quartet no. 20, in D major, by Mozart (K499), composed in 1786 and published by F A ➤ **Hoffmeister.**

Hofmann, Leopold (1738–1793) Austrian composer. He was Kapellmeister at St Stephen's Cathedral in Vienna from 1772. He belongs to the Viennese school of symphonists.

Works church music, symphonies, concertos.

Hofmannsthal, Hugo von (1874–1929) Austrian poet and dramatist. He inspired the following works and composers: *Die* ➤ **Ägyptische Helena** (Richard Strauss), ➤ **Alkestis** (Egon Wellesz), ➤ **Arabella**, ➤ **Ariadne auf Náxos**, *Le* ➤ **Bourgeois Gentilhomme**, and ➤ **Elektra** (Richard Strauss), ➤ **Everyman** (Jean Sibelius), *Die* ➤ **Frau ohne Schatten** and ➤ **Josephslegende** (Richard Strauss), Frank ➤ **Martin** (*Jedermann*), ➤ **Oedipus und die Sphinx** (Edgard Varèse), August Reuss (*Der Tor und der Tod*), *Der* ➤ **Rosenkavalier** (Richard Strauss), Alexander ➤ **Tcherepnin** (*Hochzeit der Sobeide*), Heinz ➤ **Unger** (*Tor und der Tod*), Rudolf Wagner-Régeny (*Das Bergwerk zu Falun*), Egon ➤ **Wellesz** (*Lied der Welt* and *Leben, Traum und Tod*), and Alexander von ➤ **Zemlinsky** (*Das gläserne Herz*).

Holby, Lee (1926–) US composer. He studied at the Curtis Institute and in Rome, Italy, and Salzburg, Austria, and is best known for his operas, influenced by Gian Carlo Menotti: *The Scarf* (after Chekhov, produced in Spoleto, Italy, in 1958), *Beatrice* (after Maeterlinck, 1959), *Natalia Petrovna* (after Turgenev, 1964), and *Summer and Smoke* (after T N Williams, 1971); also incidental music to John Webster's *The Duchess of Malfi* (1957).

Holborne, Anthony (1584–1602) English composer. He was in the service of Queen Elizabeth I. His collection *The Cittharn Schoole* (1597) contains pieces for cittern and bass viol, as well as three-part songs by his brother William. A further collection, *Pavans, Galliards, Almains and Other Short Aeirs*, was published in 1599.

Holbrooke, Joseph or **Josef (1878–1958)** English composer. After a hard struggle as a pianist and conductor he came under the patronage of Lord Howard de Walden, who wrote the libretti for his dramatic trilogy *The Cauldron of Annwen* (1912–16). Other works (many on subjects from

Edgar Allan Poe) include ballets, symphonic poems, and a great deal of chamber music.

He studied at the Royal Academy of Music, London.

Works OPERA *Pierrot and Pierrette* (1909; revised 1924 as *The Stranger*), *The Snob*, *The Wizard*, and the trilogy *The Cauldron of Annwen* (*The Children of Don* (1912), *Dylan* (1914), and *Bronwen* (1916)).

BALLET *The Red Mask* (after Poe), *The Moth and the Flame*, *Coromanthe*, and others.

CHORUS AND ORCHESTRA *Dramatic Choral Symphony* and *The Bells* for chorus and orchestra (both after Poe, 1903).

ORCHESTRAL AND CHAMBER symphonic poems *The Raven* (1900), *Ulalume* (1904), and *The Masque of the Red Death* (all after Poe); violin concerto (1917); six string quartets (including *Pickwick Club* after Dickens).

OTHER piano music and songs.

Hölderlin, Johann Christian Friedrich (1770–1843) German poet. His works inspired the composers Hans Erich ➤ **Apostel** (songs), Benjamin Britten (*Hölderlin Fragmente*), Brahms ➤ **Schicksalslied**, and Richard ➤ **Strauss** (three hymns).

Höller, York (1944–) German composer. He studied at the Cologne Musikhochschule under Bernd Zimmermann and Alfons Kontarsky, and came under the influence of Pierre Boulez at Darmstadt. He has worked at the electronic studio in Cologne.

Works OPERA *Der Meister und Margarita* (1989) and *Caligula* (1992).

ORCHESTRAL *Topic* (1967), piano concerto (1970), *Chroma* (1974), *Arcus* (1978), *Mythos* (1980), *Traumspiel* for soprano, orchestra, and tape (1983), *Fanal* for trumpet and orchestra (1990), *Pensées* for piano, orchestra, and tape (1991), *Aura* (1992).

CHAMBER AND INSTRUMENTAL cello sonata (1969), *Antiphon* for string quartet (1977), *Moments musicaux* for flute and piano (1979), *Improvisation sur le nom de Pierre Boulez* for 17 instruments (1985), *Pas de deux* for cello and piano (1993).

ELECTRONIC *Horizont* (1972), *Tangens* (1973).

Holliger, Heinz (1939–) Swiss oboist and composer. He has created avant-garde works in a lyric expressionist style, including *Siebengesang/Sevensong* (1967) for amplified oboe, voices, and orchestra. He has given first performances of works written for him by Luciano Berio, Ernst Krenek, Hans Werner Henze, and Karlheinz Stockhausen.

His compositions include his *Scardanelli Cycle* for chorus, flute, and orchestra (1991); the opera *Snow White* (1998); *Partita* (2001); and the song cycle *Puneigä* (2002).

He studied oboe, piano, and composition in Bern, Switzerland, and Paris, France. He has won several prizes for his oboe playing.

Works OPERA *Snow White* (1998).

VOCAL cantata *Himmel und Erde* for tenor and chamber group (1961), *Studie* for soprano, oboe, and cello with harpsichord; chamber operas *Come and Go* (1977) and *What Where* (1988); song cycle *Puneigä* (2002).

INSTRUMENTAL AND CHAMBER *Improvisation* for oboe, harp, and twelve string instruments (1963), *Pneuma* for 34 wind instruments and percussion (1970), *Engführung* for chamber orchestra (1984), *Der ferne Klang* for ensemble (1984), *Tonscherben* for orchestra (1985), *Scardanelli-Zglus* 1–4 (1975–91); sonata for oboe and piano, sonata for oboe solo, string quartet (1975); *Scardanelli Cycle* for chorus, flute, and orchestra (1991).

Holloway, Robin (Greville) (1943–) English composer. His music, which shows a textural and harmonic eclecticism, has been influenced by German Romanticism.

He studied at Cambridge, and was later appointed lecturer there.

Works OPERA *Clarissa* (1968–76; first performance 1990).

ORCHESTRAL AND INSTRUMENTAL *Scenes from Schumann*, seven paraphrases for orchestra (1970), and the *Fantasy-Pieces*, on the Heine *Liederkreis* of Schumann, for 13 players (1971); two concertos for orchestra (1969, 1979), *Serenata Notturna* for four horns and orchestra (1982), *Serenade in G* (1986), *Inquietus* for chamber orchestra, in memory of Peter Pears (1986), concerto for clarinet and saxophone (1988), violin concerto (1989), *Wagner Nights* for orchestra (1989), *Serenade for Strings* (1990), *Summer Music* and *Winter Music* for ensemble (1991, 1992).

VOCAL *Clarissa Symphony*, for soprano, tenor, and orchestra (1981), *The Spacious Firmament* for chorus and orchestra (1989).

Holman, Peter (1946–) English harpsichordist, director, and writer. He studied at King's College, London, with Thurston Dart. He founded the early music group Ars Nova while still a student, co-founded with Roy Goodman the Parley of Instruments (1979), and gave many performances in the UK and Europe with Renaissance and early baroque string consort music. He was music director of Opera Restor'd from 1985, performing 18th-century English masques and operas in authentic style. He was professor at the Royal Academy of Music, London, and joint artistic director of the Boston Early Music Festival. Publications include *The Violin at the English Court, 1540–1690* (1993) and a book on Purcell for the tercentenary (1995). His edition of

Thomas Arne's *Artaxerxes* was performed in London under Roy Goodman in 1995.

Holmboe, Vagn (1909–1996) Danish composer. Denmark's most distinguished composer after Carl Nielsen, Holmboe published twelve symphonies, 13 chamber concertos, 20 string quartets, and many other pieces, including the *Requiem for Nietzsche* (1963–64). With his wife, the Romanian pianist Meta Graf, he explored Romanian folk music.

He studied with Knud Jeppesen (1892–1974) and Finn Høffding in Copenhagen, Denmark, and Ernst Toch in Berlin, Germany. From 1940 to 1949 he taught at the Institute for the Blind in Copenhagen, and thereafter at the Copenhagen Conservatory.

Works STAGE opera *Fanden og Borgmesteren* (1940), ballet *Den galsinde de Tyrk*.

ORCHESTRAL twelve symphonies (1935–88).

CHAMBER 13 chamber concertos (1939–56), 20 string quartets (1948–75), three violin sonatas.

Holmès, Augusta (Mary Anne) (1847–1903), born **Augusta Holmes** Irish naturalized French pianist and composer. Although her parents were against her taking up music, she played the piano and sang as a child prodigy and began to compose under the name of Hermann Zenta. Later she studied with César Franck.

Works OPERA *Héro et Léandre*, *La Montagne noire* (1895), *Astarté*, *Lancelot du Lac*.

CHORAL *Les Argonautes* (on Homer's *The Iliad*, 1881), psalm 'In exitu', odes *Ludus pro patria* and *Ode triomphale*.

ORCHESTRAL symphony on Ariosto's *Orlando furioso*, *Lutèce*, and *Pologne*, symphonic poem *Irlande* (1882).

OTHER song-cycle *Les Sept Ivresses*.

Holoman, D(allas) Kern (1947–) US musicologist and conductor. He studied in North Carolina and played the bassoon in an orchestra there before becoming the founding director of the Early Music Ensemble, 1973–79. He was chair of the music department at Davis, California, 1980–88. The music of Hector Berlioz formed the centre of his research, and he has published on the composer's creative process (1980), a catalogue (1987), and a biography (1989).

Holst, Gustav(us Theodore von) (1874–1934) English composer of distant Swedish descent. He wrote operas, including *Sávitri* (1908) and *At the Boar's Head* (1924); ballets; choral works, including *Choral Hymns from the Rig Veda* (1908–12) and *The Hymn of Jesus* (1917); orchestral suites, including *The Planets* (1914–16); and songs. He was a lifelong friend of Ralph ➤ Vaughan Williams, with whom he shared an enthusiasm for English folk music. His musical style, although tonal and drawing on folk song, tends to be severe. He was the father of Imogen Holst (1907–1984), musicologist and his biographer.

Holst's father was a music teacher and his mother a pianist, and he had early experience as an organist and choral and orchestral conductor in a small way. In 1892 he went to the Royal College of Music in London, but disliked the keyboard instruments and studied composition under Charles Stanford. Suffering from neuritis, he took up the trombone instead of the piano, and on leaving played in the orchestra of the Carl Rosa Opera Company, and later in the Scottish Orchestra. In 1903 he became music master at a school in south London, and in 1905 at St Paul's Girls' School, where he remained to his death. In 1907 he was appointed music director at Morley College for Working Men and Women; in 1912 he conducted there the first modern performance of Henry Purcell's *Fairy Queen*. From 1919 he taught composition at the Royal College of Music and in 1919–23 at Reading College. He had to wait a long time for recognition. It was not until the public premiere of *The Planets* in 1919 that Holst achieved the first real success of his career. In 1923 he conducted at the University of Michigan, USA, and his opera *The Perfect Fool* (a satire on Wagnerism) was given at the Royal Opera House, Covent Garden, London. The choral symphony after John Keats was given at the 1925 Leeds Festival and in 1928 his bleak tone poem after Thomas Hardy, *Egdon Heath*, was premiered by the New York Symphony Orchestra. The *Choral Fantasia* was first heard in 1931 and the *Brook Green Suite* in 1933.

Side by side with the influence of English folk music was that of Indian literature (*Sávitri* is the story from the *Mahābhārata*), and a number of choral hymns and songs are set to texts from the Rig-Veda, translated by Holst from the Sanskrit. He was also influenced by the early music of Thomas Weelkes and William Byrd.

Works OPERA *Sávitri* (1908; produced 1916), *At the Boar's Head* (on Shakespeare's *Henry IV*, 1924), *The Wandering Scholar* (1929–30).

CHORAL *Choral Hymns from the Rig Veda* with orchestra (1908–12), *The Hymn of Jesus* for chorus and orchestra (1917), choral symphony (John Keats) for soprano, chorus, and orchestra (1925).

ORCHESTRAL *A Somerset Rhapsody* (1907), *Beni Mora* suite (1910), *The Planets* (1914–16), *Egdon Heath* for orchestra (after Thomas Hardy, 1927); *St Paul's* suite for strings; *Fugal Concerto* for flute, oboe, and strings (1923), concerto for two violins and orchestra (1929).

OTHER *A Moorside Suite* for brass band; nine hymns from the *Rig-Veda* for voice and piano (1908).

Holt, Simon (1958–) English composer. He studied at the Royal Northern College of Music

with Anthony Gilbert and was featured composer at the 1985 Bath Festival. He has written pieces to commissions from the Nash Ensemble and London Sinfonietta.

Works ORCHESTRAL *Syrensong* (1987), *Walking with the River's Roar* (1991).

CHAMBER ensemble pieces *Mirrormaze* (1981), *Shadow Realm* (1983), *Burlesca obscura*, clarinet quintet (1985), *Danger of the Disappearance of Things* for string quartet (1989), *Sparrow Flight* (1989), *Icarus Lamentations* (1992).

VOCAL WORKS WITH ENSEMBLE *Wyrdchanging* (1980), *Canciones* (1986), *Ballad of the Black Sorrow* (1988), *A Song of Crocuses and Lightning* (1989), *Tangara* (1991), *A Knot of Time* (1992); *Lunas Zauberschein* for mezzo and bass flute (1979).

OTHER piano music.

Holzbauer, Ignaz (1711–1783) Austrian composer. Originally intended for a career in law, he was largely self-taught in music, and visited Italy to complete his studies. Director of the court opera in Vienna intermittently 1742–50, he was appointed Kapellmeister in Stuttgart, Germany, in 1751, and two years later to the court of the Elector Palatine in Mannheim, where the orchestra under Johann Stamitz was the most famous of the time. During visits to Italy on leave of absence he produced several operas, and in Mannheim produced the German opera *Günther von Schwarzburg* (1777). As a composer of symphonies he belongs to the Mannheim School.

Works OPERA *Il figlio delle selve* (1753), *L'isola disabitata* (1754), *Nitetti* (1758), *Alessandro nell' Indie*, *Tancredi*, *Günther von Schwarzburg* (1777).

ORATORIOS AND CHURCH MUSIC *La passione* (1754), *Isacco* (1757), *La Betulia liberata* (1760); Masses, motets and other church music.

ORCHESTRAL AND CHAMBER 65 symphonies; concertos; chamber music.

Holzbläser or **Holzblasinstrumente (German 'woodblowers', 'woodblown instruments')** German name for ➤ woodwind instruments.

Holztrompete (German 'wooden trumpet') musical instrument designed for use in the third act of Wagner's *Tristan und Isolde*, actually a revival of the ➤ cornett, but provided with a valve.

Homer Greek poet. His works *The Iliad* and *The Odyssey* inspired the composers Max ➤ Bruch (*Achilles* and *Odysseus*), August Bungert (➤ *Homerische Welt*), Luigi Dallapiccola (➤ *Ulisse*), Vittorio Gnecchi (*Cassandra*), Robert Heger (*Bettler Namenlos*), Hans Werner Henze and Monteverdi (*Il* ➤ *ritorno d'Ulisse in patria*), Heinrich von Herzogenberg (*Odysseus* symphony), and Augusta ➤ Holmès (*Argonautes*).

Homerische Welt, Homeric World operatic tetralogy by Bungert (libretto by the composer, based on Homer's *The Odyssey*). The four parts are: I. *Kirke/Circe*, first produced in Dresden, Germany, on 29 January 1898; II. *Nausikaa/Nausicaa*, produced in Dresden on 20 March 1901; III. *Odysseus Heimkehr/The Return of Ulysses*, produced in Dresden on 12 December 1896; and IV. *Odysseus Tod/The death of Ulysses*, produced in Dresden on 30 October 1903.

It was Bungert's attempt to create a Wagnerian cycle but based, like Hector Berlioz's *Troyens* and Sergey Taneiev's *Oresteia*, on classical Greek subjects.

'Homme armé, L'' (French 'the armed man') name of an old French secular song, the tune of which was often used by composers of the 15th and 16th centuries as ➤ **cantus firmus** for their Masses, which were then designated by that name.

Homme et son désir, L', Man and his Desire ballet by Darius Milhaud (words, 'plastic poem', by Paul Claudel, choreographed by Jean Borlin), first produced at the Théâtre des Champs-Élysées, Paris, France, on 6 June 1921.

homophonic (from Greek 'alike-sounding') term applied to music in which the individual lines making up the harmony have no independent significance, that is to say, for most purposes chordal.

homophony music comprising a melody lead and accompanying harmony, in contrast to ➤ **heterophony** and ➤ **polyphony** in which different melody lines of equal importance are combined.

Honegger, Arthur (1892–1955) Swiss composer. He was one of the group of composers known as ➤ **Les Six**. His work was varied in form, for example, the opera *Antigone* (1927), the ballet *Skating Rink* (1922), the dramatic oratorio *Le Roi David/King David* (1921), programme music (*Pacific 231*, 1923), and the *Symphonie liturgique/Liturgical Symphony* (1946). He also composed incidental music for Abel Gance's silent movie classics *La Roue/The Wheel* (1923) and *Napoléon* (1927).

Honegger was born in Le Havre, France, and was given his first music lessons there by the organist R C Martin. He then studied at the Zürich Conservatory, Switzerland, 1909–11, and at the Paris Conservatory 1911–13. After that he became a private pupil of Charles Widor and Vincent d'Indy and in 1914 began to compose. Though always in touch with Switzerland, he belonged mainly to the French school. He married the composer Andrée Vaurabourg, who was also attached to *Les Six*, though less closely.

Works STAGE stage oratorios *Le Roi David* (1921),

Judith (1925), *Jeanne d'Arc au bûcher* (Paul Claudel, 1938); incidental music for *Phædre* (d'Annunzio, 1926), *Oedipe-Roi* (Sophocles, 1948).

ORCHESTRAL AND VOCAL WITH ORCHESTRA *La Danse des morts* (Claudel) for solo voices, chorus, and orchestra (on Holbein), *Chant de joie*, prelude to Shakespeare's *The Tempest* (1923), *Mouvements symphoniques: Pacific 231, Rugby*, and No. 3 (1923–33), five symphonies (1930–51), *Prélude, Arioso et Fugue* on B.A.C.H., *Pastorale d'été* (1920); cello concerto; *Five Poems by Guillaume Apollinaire* for voice and orchestra (1910–17).

CHAMBER AND SOLO VOCAL two violin and piano sonatas, sonatas for viola and piano, cello and piano, clarinet and piano.

hopak Russian folk dance; see ➤ **gopak**.

Horenstein, Jascha (1898–1973) Russian-born conductor. He went with his family to Germany as a child, and studied with Max Bode in Königsberg, Adolph Busch in Vienna, Austria, and composition with Franz Schreker in Berlin. He was appointed conductor of the Düsseldorf Opera in 1926 and settled in the USA in 1941; he gave the first US performance of Ferruccio Busoni's *Doktor Faust* there in 1964. Well known for the works of Schubert, Bruckner, and Mahler, he conducted the first performances of Alban Berg's *Three Movements for strings* (Berlin, 1929) and *Altenberg Lieder* (Rome, 1953). He conducted Wagner's *Parsifal* at the Royal Opera House, Covent Garden, London, a few weeks before his death.

Horizon chimérique, L' song cycle by Gabriel Fauré, Op. 118 (texts by Jean de la Ville de Mirmont), composed in 1921. It was first performed in Paris, France, on 13 May 1922, with Charles Pinzéra.

horn member of a family of lip-reed wind instruments used for signalling and ritual, and sharing features of a generally conical bore (although the orchestral horn is of part conical and part straight bore) and curved shape, producing a pitch of rising or variable inflection.

Many horns are based on animal horns, for example the shofar of Hebrew ritual and the medieval oliphant and gemshorn, and shells, for example the conch shell of Pacific island peoples. Horns made of metal originated in South America and also Central Asia (Tibet, India, Nepal), and reached Europe along with the technology of metalwork in the Bronze Age. The familiar hunting horn, unchanged for many centuries, was adapted and enlarged in the 18th century to become an orchestral instrument, its limited range of natural harmonics extended by a combination of lip technique and hand stopping within the bell and the use of extension crooks for changes of key.

The modern valve horn is a 19th-century hybrid B flat/F instrument; the name **French horn** strictly applies to the earlier *cor à pistons* which uses lever-action rotary valves and produces a lighter tone. The **Wagner tuba** is a horn variant in tenor and bass versions devised by Wagner to provide a fuller horn tone in the lower range. Composers for horn include Mozart, Haydn, Richard Strauss, Weber, Schumann (*Konzertstück* for four horns, 1848), Ravel, and Benjamin Britten (*Serenade for Tenor, Horn, and Strings*, 1943).

The normal compass of the horn. One or two higher and lower notes are possible. The modern keyed horn is built in F and high B flat, with four valves, one of which transposes the instrument from the lower to the higher pitch.

Hornbostel, Erich (Moritz) von (1877–1935) Austrian musicologist. He is most famous (with Curt Sachs) for his part in the Sachs–Hornbostel classification of musical instruments, still employed by most scholars and museums.

He studied physics and philosophy at Vienna, Austria, and Heidelberg, Switzerland, and in 1906 became head of the gramophone archives in Berlin, Germany, for the recording of ethnic music, on which he wrote several learned works. In 1933 he left Germany and went to New York, USA; in the following year he went to London and Cambridge, England.

Horne, David (1970–) Scottish pianist and composer. He studied in Edinburgh and at the Curtis Institute, Philadelphia (1989), and Harvard in the USA. He has won prizes at the Huddersfield Festival, as composer, and British Broadcasting Corporation (BBC) Young Musician of the Year (piano section). He has performed as soloist with the City of Birmingham Symphony Orchestra, London Sinfonietta, and Scottish National Orchestra, and performed Prokofiev's Third Concerto at the 1990 Proms in London.

Works ORCHESTRAL *Light Emerging* (1989), *Northscape* for chamber orchestra (1992), piano concerto (1992).

CHAMBER string quartet (1988), *Splintered Unisons* and *Towards Dharma* for ensemble (1988–89).

hornpipe English dance popular between the 16th and 19th centuries, associated especially with sailors. During the 18th century it changed from triple time (3/4) to common time (4/4). Examples include those by Purcell and Handel.

hornpipe obsolete wind instrument, once common to Celtic cultures, consisting of a wooden pipe with a single-reed mouthpiece on one end, and a horn for the bell.

Horn Signal, Symphony with the nickname of Haydn's symphony no. 31 in D major, composed in 1765, so called because of the horn fanfares at the beginning and end.

'Horst-Wessel-Lied' song introduced by the Nazis as a second German national anthem. The text was written to a traditional tune by Horst Wessel (1907–1930), a Nazi 'martyr'.

Horvat, Milan (1919–) Croatian conductor. He studied at Zagreb and was conductor of the Zagreb Philharmonic Orchestra 1946–53 and 1958–69, and chief conductor of the Radio Telefis Éireann (RTE) Symphony Orchestra in Dublin, Ireland, 1953–58. He was principal conductor of the Zagreb Opera 1958–63, giving many Yugoslav first performances, and of the Austrian Radio Symphony Orchestra 1969–75. He gave many concerts as guest conductor elsewhere in Europe (including the Salzburg Festival 1970, Krzysztof Penderecki's *St Luke Passion*). He became principal conductor of the Zagreb Symphony Orchestra in 1975. Recordings include music by Shostakovich and Hindemith.

Horwood, William (died 1484) English composer. He became master of the choristers at Lincoln Cathedral in 1477. His music, consisting of Latin antiphons and a Magnificat, is included in the Eton Choirbook; a fragmentary *Kyrie* has also survived.

Hothby, John (c.1410–1487) English Carmelite, music scholar, composer, and doctor of theology. He graduated at Oxford and lectured there in 1435. He probably travelled in Spain, France, and Germany, and settled in Florence, Italy, around 1440; he possibly also lived in Ferrara. He was called Giovanni Ottobi in Italy, and was at Lucca from about 1468 to 1486. He taught there, but was recalled to England by Henry VII. He wrote a number of theoretical treatises. Some of his sacred and secular compositions were entered in the Faenza Codex.

Hotteterre, Jacques-Martin (1674–1763) French flautist, bassoonist, and instrument maker. He came from a family of woodwind instrument makers and composers responsible for developing the orchestral baroque flute and bassoon from folk antecedents. A respected performer and teacher, he wrote a tutor for the transverse flute and composed trio sonatas and suites for flute and bassoon.

Developments of the oboe from the shawm, the bassoon from the curtal, and the transverse flute from the cylindrical flute are often credited to members of the Hotteterre family.

Jacques Hotteterre called himself *Le Romain* after an early visit to Italy. From 1708 at the latest he was a bassoonist in the Grands Hautbois and was a flautist in the service of the king. His book *Principes de la flûte traversière* (1707) was the first such treatise to be published; it was followed by *L'Art de préluder sur la flûte traversière* and *Méthode pour la musette* (1737).

House of the Dead, From the opera by Janáček; see ➤ *From the House of the Dead*.

Housman, A(lfred) E(dward) (1859–1936) English poet and Latin scholar. His poems from *A Shropshire Lad* (1896) and *Last Poems* (1922) were set to music by many composers, including Samuel Barber, George Butterworth, Ivor Gurney, John Ireland, E J Moeran, Charles Orr, Arthur Somervell, and Ralph Vaughan Williams.

Hovhaness, Alan (1911–2000) US composer. Much of his work is influenced by Armenian religious music as well as elements from other musical cultures, including Indian and Japanese. A prolific composer, he destroyed a great deal of his work in 1940.

He studied piano with Heinrich Gebhard and composition with Frederick Converse and Bohuslav Martinů. One of his most original works is the orchestral piece *And God Created Great Whales* (1970), which incorporates the singing of whales.

Works OPERA ten operas.

ORCHESTRAL 63 symphonies (1939–88); *Arekeval*; concerto for orchestra; *Ad Lyram*.

INSTRUMENTAL AND CHAMBER *And God Created Great Whales* (1970) including taped part for humpbacked whale, two *Armenian Rhapsodies* for strings, 23 concertos (1936–80) including *Elibris* for flute and strings; *Lousadzak* for piano and strings; concerto for trumpet and strings; *Sosi* for violin piano, percussion, and strings; chamber music including five string quartets (1936–76).

Howard, Samuel (1710–1782) English organist and composer. He was a pupil of William Croft at the Chapel Royal and later of Johann Pepusch. He was organist at the churches of St Clement Danes and St Bride. He received a doctorate in music from Cambridge in 1769. He assisted William Boyce in compiling his *Cathedral Music* (1760–73).

Works anthems and other church music; pantomimes, *The Amorous Goddess*, or *Harlequin Married* and *Robin Goodfellow*; cantatas and songs.

Howells, Herbert Norman (1892–1983) English composer, organist, and teacher. His works are filled with an 'English' quality, as with those of Edward Elgar and Ralph Vaughan Williams. Often elegiac in expression, as in some of the *Six Pieces for Organ* (1940), much of his music after the mid-1930s reflects his mourning over the death of his son. He wrote choral and chamber music, as well as solo works, both sacred and secular.

Howells studied under Herbert Brewer at Gloucester Cathedral and later under Charles Stanford at the Royal College of Music in London, where he became professor of composition. Later, having been first sub-organist at Salisbury Cathedral, he lived a retired life 1917–20 owing to poor health. He succeeded Gustav Holst as music director at St Paul's Girls' School 1936–62, and was professor of music at London University 1952–62. His best-known work is the *Hymnus Paradisi* (1938), written in memory of his son, in which he escapes the influence of Vaughan Williams and other pastoralists.

Works ORCHESTRAL *Procession* (1922), *Paradise Rondel* (1925); concerto for strings (1939), two piano concertos (1913, 1924).

CHORAL *Hymnus Paradisi* for soloists, chorus, and orchestra (1938), *Collegium Regale*, for unaccompanied choir (1944), *Stabat Mater* (1963).

CHAMBER clarinet quintet; two organ sonatas; oboe sonata, clarinet sonata; *Lambert's Clavichord* (1926–27) and *Howells' Clavichord* (1951–61) for clavichord.

OTHER much church music; piano pieces; songs, especially to words by Walter de la Mare.

Hoyland, Vic(tor) (1945–   ) English composer. His music has been featured at the Bath, Aldeburgh, and California Contemporary Music Festivals. He is a senior lecturer at the Barber Institute of Fine Arts, and reader at the University of Birmingham. His output includes the music theatre piece *Crazy Rosa – La Madre* (1988) and a chamber concerto with piano (1993). He studied at York University with Bernard Rands and Robert Sherlaw-Johnson.

Works STAGE music theatre *Xingu* (1979), *Crazy Rosa – La Madre* (1988).

ORCHESTRAL *In Transit* (1987).

CHAMBER AND INSTRUMENTAL *Serenade* for 14 players (1979), *Quartet Movement* (1982), quintet for brass (1985), string quartet (1985), *Of Fantasy, Of Dreams and Ceremonies* for 13 strings (1989), piano trio (1989), piano quintet (1990), Chamber Concerto, with piano (1993).

VOCAL *Em* for 24 voices (1970), *Ariel* for voice and ensemble (1975), *Michelangiolo* for baritone and ensemble (1981).

Hubay, Jenö, originally **Eugen Huber (1858–1937)** Hungarian violinist and composer. He travelled much, edited and completed some of Henri Vieuxtemps' works, and became violin professor at the Brussels Conservatory, Belgium, in 1882 and at the Budapest Conservatory, Hungary, in 1886, of which he was director 1919–34.

A pupil of his father Karl Huber, he appeared as a prodigy at the age of 11, but later went to study with Joseph Joachim in Berlin, Germany.

Works OPERA *Alienor* (1891), *A Cremonai Hegedüs* (after Coppée's *Luther de Crémone*, 1894), *A Falu Rossza*, *Karenina Anna* (after Tolstoy, 1915), *Az álarc*, and others.

OTHER four symphonies; four violin concertos; *Sonate romantique* for violin and piano; many violin pieces, studies.

Huber, Hans (1852–1921) Swiss composer. After attending seminary at Solothurn, he studied music under Carl Munzinger there and later at the Leipzig Conservatory, Germany. After teaching in Alsace, Germany (now France), he settled in Basel, Switzerland, in 1877. In 1889 he became professor at the Conservatory there and succeeded Selmar Bagge as its director in 1896, retiring in 1918.

Works OPERA *Weltfrühling* (1894), *Kudrun* (1896), *Simplicius* (1912), *Die schöne Bellinde*, *Frutta di mare* (1918).

CHORAL Masses, cantatas.

ORCHESTRAL nine symphonies (No. 2 on pictures by Böcklin) and other orchestral works *Sommernächte*, *Serenade*, *Carneval*, and *Römischer Carneval*; four piano concertos, violin concerto.

OTHER much chamber music; piano music; songs, including Hafiz cycle.

Huber, Klaus (1924–) Swiss composer. His music combines avant-garde techniques with a strong religious awareness.

He studied with Willy Burkhard at the Zürich Conservatory and with Boris Blacher in Berlin, Germany. From 1950 he taught violin in Zürich and from 1960 music history at the Lucerne Conservatory.

Works OPERA *Jot, oder Wann kommt der Herr zürück* (1973).

VOICES, CHORUS, AND ORCHESTRA cantata for voices and four instruments *Des Engels Anredung an die Seele* (1957), oratorio *Mechthildis* for alto voice and chamber orchestra (1957), *Auf die ruhige Nacht-Zeit* for soprano and chamber group (1958), *Soliloquia* for soloists, chorus, and orchestra, *Spes contra spem* for voice, narrator, and orchestra (1988).

ORCHESTRAL AND INSTRUMENTAL *Sonata da chiesa* for violin and organ, *Concerto per la Camerata* (1955), *Tempora*, violin concerto (1970); *Turnus* for orchestra and tape (1974); *Litania instrumentalis* for orchestra (1975); *Von Zeit zu Zeit*, string quartet (1985); *Protuberanzen* for orchestra (1986).

Hughes, Anselm (actually Humphrey Vaughan) (1889–1974) English music scholar and Angli-

can Benedictine, prior of Nashdom Abbey. He was a member of the editorial board of the *New Oxford History of Music*, editor of volume ii, and joint editor of volume iii.

Hughes, Gervase (1905–) English composer. He studied at Oxford, and in 1926 joined the music staff of the British National Opera Company; he later conducted at various theatres. In 1933 he left the music profession, but after World War II took to composing again. He wrote books on Arthur Sullivan (1960) and Antonín Dvořák (1967).

Works STAGE opera *Imogen's Choice*; operettas *Castle Creevy* and *Venetian Fantasy*.

ORCHESTRAL symphony in F minor, *Overture for a Musical Comedy* for orchestra.

OTHER piano music, songs.

Hugh the Drover, or Love in the Stocks opera by Ralph Vaughan Williams (libretto by Harold Child), first produced at the Royal College of Music, London, on 4 July 1924. It tells how the itinerant Hugh wins Mary in a boxing contest and both are released from the stocks to lead a wandering life.

Hugo, Victor (1802–1885) French poet, novelist, and dramatist. His works inspired the following composers: Michael Balfe (*The ➤ Armourer of Nantes*), César ➤ Cui (*Angelo*), Aleksandr ➤ Dargomizhsky (➤ *Esmeralda* and *Notre-Dame de Paris*), Léo ➤ Delibes (*Le Roi s'amuse*), Donizetti (➤ *Lucrezia Borgia*), César Franck (➤ *Djinns*), Gabriel ➤ Fauré (songs), Carlos Gomes (➤ *Maria Tudor*), Franz ➤ Liszt (*Ce qu'on entend … and* ➤ *Mazeppa*), Giuseppe Mercadante (*Il* ➤ *giuramento*), Felix Mendelssohn (➤ *Ruy Blas*), Carlo Pedrotti (*Marion Delorme*), Amilcare ➤ Ponchielli (*La* ➤ *Gioconda* and *Marion Delorme*), Franz Schmidt (➤ *Notre Dame*), Verdi (➤ *Ernani* and ➤ *Rigoletto*), and Rudolf Wagner-Régeny (*Der Günstling*).

Huguenots, Les opera by Giacomo Meyerbeer (libretto by Augustin Scribe and Emile Deschamps), first produced at the Paris Opéra, France, on 29 February 1836. It tells the story of an amorous conflict set against 16th-century religious massacres.

Hulda opera by César Franck (libretto by C Grandmougin, based on a play by Bjørnstjerne Bjørnson), not performed in Franck's lifetime. It was first produced in Monte Carlo, Monaco, on 8 March 1894. Set in 11th-century Norway, the story tells how Hulda seeks revenge on Aslak and his clan, who killed her family. All the characters are killed in the end.

Humfrey, Pelham (1647–1674) English composer. At the Restoration in 1660 he entered the re-established Chapel Royal in London under Henry Cooke, joined John Blow and William

Turner in the composition of the so-called 'club anthem', and was sent abroad for study by Charles II in 1664. On his return from France and Italy in 1667 he became a Gentleman of the Chapel Royal, where in 1672 he succeeded Cooke as Master of the Children.

Works STAGE music to Shakespeare's *The Tempest* (1674), Dryden's *The Conquest of Granada* and *The Indian Emperor*, Crowne's *History of Charles VIII*, and Wycherley's *Love in a Wood*.

OTHER anthems; odes, sacred songs, airs for one and two voices.

Hummel, Ferdinand (1855–1928) German pianist, harpist, and composer. After playing piano and harp in public as a child, he studied at Theodor Kullak's Conservatory in Berlin and later had success with his realistic operas.

Works STAGE operas *Mara* (1893), *Angla* (1894), *Ein treuer Schelm* (1894), *Assarpai*, *Sophie von Brabant* (1899), *Die Beichte* (1899), *Die Gefilde der Seligen*; incidental music for 14 plays by Wildenbruch and others.

OTHER symphony, overture; piano concerto, fantasy for harp and orchestra; choral works; chamber music; piano pieces.

Hummel, Johann Nepomuk (1778–1837) Austrian pianist and composer. Following in the steps of Mozart (his teacher), his melodies are graceful if somewhat overly symmetrical and 'square'. He was known as a conservative in his lifetime, clinging to a decaying tradition in the face of growing Romanticism. In addition to his keyboard works, which include seven concertos, he wrote choral and chamber works and operas.

He learnt music at first from his father, the conductor Joseph Hummel, who had gone to Vienna in 1785 as conductor of the Theater auf der Wieden. By that time Johann was already a brilliant pianist and Mozart took him as a pupil for two years. In 1787 he went on tour in Germany, Holland, Scotland, and England and had further lessons from Muzio Clementi in London, where he stayed until 1792. In 1793 he was back in Vienna, studying composition with Johann Albrechtsberger, Haydn, and Antonio Salieri. In 1803 he visited Russia and was music director to Prince Esterházy 1804–11. In 1816–19 he held a similar post at the court of Württemberg in Stuttgart and was at the court of Weimar 1819–22 and from 1833 to his death, undertaking extensive concert tours in between and spending much time in London. He was a friend of Beethoven and was the original dedicatee of Schubert's last three piano sonatas. He married the singer Elisabeth Röckl (1793–1883).

Works STAGE operas *Die Rückfahrt des Kaisers* (1814) and *Mathilde von Guise* (1810); ballets *Hélène et Paris* (1807), *Das belebte Gemälde*, *Sappho*; pantomime *Der Zauberring* (1811),

incidental music to Grillparzer's *Die Ahnfrau*.

OTHER Masses and other church music; seven piano concertos; trumpet concerto (1803), chamber music; sonatas for piano with another instrument; piano sonatas, rondos, variations.

humoresque 19th-century French and English title (German *Humoreske*) for a short instrumental piece characterized by a lively and capricious nature. Famous examples include humoresques for piano by Robert Schumann (1839) and Antonín Dvořák (1894).

Humperdinck, Engelbert (1854–1921) German composer. He studied in Cologne and Munich and assisted Richard Wagner in the preparation of *Parsifal* at Bayreuth in 1882. He wrote the musical fairy operas *Hänsel und Gretel* (1893) and *Königskinder/King's Children* (1910).

He was born in Siegburg. He studied under Ferdinand Hiller at the Cologne Conservatory and later with Franz Lachner and Josef Rheinberger at Munich. In 1879 he met Wagner in Italy and acted as his assistant at Bayreuth 1881–82. Later he travelled in France, Italy, and Spain and taught at the Barcelona Conservatory 1885–87. In 1890–96 he taught at the Hoch Conservatory at Frankfurt and was for a time music critic of the newspaper *Frankfurter Zeitung*. His enduring success, *Hänsel und Gretel*, was premiered at Weimar in 1893 under Richard Strauss. In 1900 he became director of the Meisterschule for composition in Berlin.

Works STAGE operas *Hänsel und Gretel* (1893), *Dornröschen* (1902), *Die Heirat wider Willen* (1905), *Königskinder* (1910), *Die Marketenderin* (1914), *Gaudeamus* (1919); play with music *Königskinder* (an earlier version of the opera); spectacular pantomime *The Miracle*; incidental music to Shakespeare's *The Merchant of Venice* (1905), *The Winter's Tale* (1906), *The Tempest* (1906), and *Twelfth Night*, Maeterlinck's *The Blue Bird* (1912), Aristophanes' *Lysistrata*.

OTHER choral works *Das Glück von Edenhall* (Uhland), *Die Wallfahrt nach Kevlaar* (Heine); *Humoreske* and *Maurische Rhapsodie* for orchestra; part songs, songs.

Humphries, John (c.1707–c.1740) English composer. He published six solos for violin and bass and two sets of concertos. He may be the J S Humphries who published a set of sonatas for two violins in about 1733.

Hungarian Sketches work for orchestra by Béla Bartók, arranged from piano pieces including *Four Dirges* and *Three Burlesques* in 1931 and first performed in Budapest, Hungary, on 26 November 1934. The movements are titled *An Evening in the Village*, *Bear Dance*, *Melody*, *Slightly Tipsy*, and *Swineherd's Dance*.

Hunnenschlacht, Battle of the Huns symphonic poem by Franz Liszt inspired by the German painter Wilhelm von Kaulbach's fresco, composed in 1857. It was first performed in Weimar, Germany, on 29 December 1857.

'Hunt' Quartet familiar nickname of Mozart's B flat major string quartet, K458, because the opening suggests hunting horns.

Hunyady László opera by Ferenc Erkel (libretto by B Egressy), first produced in Budapest, Hungary, on 27 January 1844. It is the chief Hungarian national opera. After surviving one plot against him, the politician László is imprisoned by the palatine Gara, the father of László's fiancée Mária, who promises his daughter to the king in exchange for László's death. László survives three blows of the executioner's sword, but the fourth kills him.

Huon de Bordeaux medieval French romance. See ➔ *Oberon, König der Elfen* (Paul Wranitzky) and ➔ *Oberon, or The Elf King's Oath* (Carl Maria von Weber).

hurdy-gurdy musical instrument, usually with six strings, resembling a violin in tone but using a form of keyboard to play a melody on the top string, while drone strings provide a continuous harmony. An inbuilt wheel, turned by a handle, sets the strings vibrating.

Hurlstone, William (Yeates) (1876–1906) English pianist and composer. He studied at the Royal College of Music in London, having already published waltzes for piano at the age of nine. He was professor of counterpoint at the Royal College of Music from 1905 to his early death.

Works ORCHESTRAL Fantasy-Variations on a Swedish Air and suite *The Magic Mirror* for orchestra (1896); piano concerto (1896).

CHAMBER string quartet in E minor, piano and wind quintet, piano quartet, Fantasy string quartet (1906); sonatas for violin and piano, cello and piano, bassoon and piano, suite for clarinet and piano.

Husa, Karel (1921–) Czech-born US composer and conductor. He studied at Prague Conservatory and with Nadia Boulanger and Arthur Honegger in Paris, France. He emigrated to the USA in 1954, and was professor at Cornell University from 1961. He has been influenced by Czech folk music, neoclassicism, and serialism.

Works ORCHESTRAL AND INSTRUMENTAL Sinfonietta (1947), *Trois Fresques* (1949), Divertimento for strings (1949), Symphony (1954), *Fantasies* (1957), Mosaïques (1961), Concerto for brass quintet and orchestra (1970), trumpet concerto (1974), *Monodrama* (1976), *The Trojan Women*, ballet for orchestra (1981); *Symphonic Suite*

(1984), Concerto for Orchestra (1980), concertos for organ, trumpet, and cello (1987–88).

CHAMBER three string quartets (1948–68), *Variations* for piano quintet (1984).

OTHER *12 Moravian Songs*.

Husitská concert overture by Antonín Dvořák, Op. 67, composed in 1883 and first performed in Prague (Czech Republic) for the reopening of the National Theatre on 13 November 1883. It is based on the 10th-century St Vaclav chorale and the 15th-century Hussite hymn.

Huston, Scott (1916–1991) US composer. He studied with Howard Hanson at the Eastman School and taught at the Cincinnati Conservatory 1952–88. His works include the opera *Blind Girl* (New York, 1984), six symphonies (No. 6, *The Human Condition*, 1982), *Sounds of the Courtesans* for voice and ensemble (1985), and *The Unpredictable Pendulum of Temperaments* for dancers and ensemble (1988).

Huygens, Constantijn (1596–1687) Dutch official, physicist, poet, writer, linguist, and musician. He was military secretary at The Hague from 1625 until his death. He was a lutenist and also played viol and the keyboard instruments, paying three visits to England and others to Germany, Italy, and France. He collected a library and wrote on the use of the organ in church and other musical subjects. He composed nearly 900 pieces for lute, theorbo, guitar, etc. One of his sons, Christian (1629–95), was also a musician as well as a mathematician.

hymn song in praise of a deity. Examples include Akhenaton's hymn to the Aton in ancient Egypt, the ancient Greek Orphic hymns, Old Testament psalms, extracts from the New Testament (such as the 'Ave Maria'), and hymns by the English writers John Bunyan ('Who Would True Valour See') and Charles Wesley ('Hark! The Herald Angels Sing'). The earliest sources of modern hymn melodies can be traced to the 11th and 12th centuries, and the earliest polyphonic settings date from the late 14th century. Gospel music and ➔ carols are forms of Christian hymn-singing.

During the period between the Reformation and 1822, no singing was allowed in services of the Established Church apart from the reciting of the psalms. The Free Churches, however, included hymn-singing; the most important collection was *Collected Hymns for the Use of People Called Methodists* (1780), and these hymns were sung in Established Churches from 1822. Perhaps the most famous collection of hymns in the English language is *Hymns Ancient and Modern* (1860), which included both Methodist hymns and many new hymns by members of the Oxford Movement, including those by English writers J M Neale and John Henry Newman.

Notable Christian hymn writers include Reginald Heber (1783–1826) ('From Greenland's Icy Mountains'), Henry Francis Lyte (1793–1847) ('Abide with Me'), John S B Monsell (1811–1875) ('Fight the Good Fight'), and Sabine Baring-Gould (1834–1924) ('Onward Christian Soldiers'). The English poet and artist William Blake's 'Jerusalem' was set to music by Hubert Parry. Vaughan Williams edited the *English Hymnal* (1906), writing new hymns as well as giving new arrangements to many existing ones. Less conventional is Benjamin Britten's 'Hymn to St Cecilia' (1942).

Hymne au Saint Sacrément work for orchestra by Olivier Messiaen, composed in 1932 and first performed in Paris, France, on 23 March 1933. Its first US performance was given in New York on 13 March 1947, conducted by Leopold Stokowski.

Hymnen, Anthems work for electronic instruments by Karlheinz Stockhausen, which reprocesses a selection of the world's national anthems. It was composed in 1966 and first performed in Cologne, Germany, on 30 November 1967. There are versions with added soloists, and a shorter version with orchestra.

Hymn of Jesus, The work by Gustav Holst for three choruses and orchestra, Op. 37 (the text is Holst's, translated from the Apocryphal Acts of St John); it was composed in 1917 and dedicated to Ralph Vaughan Williams. The work was first performed in London, England, on 25 March 1920.

Hymn of Praise, German **Lobgesang** Felix Mendelssohn's symphonic cantata, Op. 52, in which three movements of a symphony precede the choral portion. It was composed in 1840 and first produced in St Thomas's Church, Leipzig, Germany, on 25 June 1840. The first performance in English was given at the Birmingham Festival, England, on 23 September 1840.

Hymn of the Nations cantata by Verdi; see ➤ *Inno delle nazioni*.

Hymnus Amoris, **Hymn of Love** work by Carl Nielsen for soloists, adult and children's choruses, and orchestra (text in Danish by A Olrik, in Latin by J L Heiberg); it was composed in 1896 and first performed in Copenhagen, Denmark, on 27 April 1897, conducted by Nielsen.

Hyperprism work by Edgard Varèse for wind and percussion; it was first performed in New York, USA, on 4 March 1923.

Iberia four sets of piano pieces by Isaac Albéniz, representing different parts of Spain, composed at various times before 1909. It comprises: I. *Evocación, El puerto, Fête-Dieu à Séville*; II. *Triana, Almeria, Rondeña*; III. *El albaicin, El polo, Lavapiés*; IV. *Málaga, Jérez, Eritaña*.

Ibéria symphonic pieces by Debussy; see ➔ *Images pour orchestre*.

Ibert, Jacques François Antoine (1890–1962) French composer. Although writing in a variety of genres and styles, his music is generally considered light, due in large part to his seven often witty operas. However, his music reflects its subject matter: in his ➔ symphonic poem *La Ballade de la geôle de Reading* (1922) he captures the horror of Oscar Wilde's poem, while in his Flute Concerto (1934) he involves the full technical range of the solo instrument.

He studied at the Paris Conservatory and won the Prix de Rome in 1919. He became director of the French Academy in Rome in 1937 and returned there after World War II. From 1955 to 1957 he was director of the Opéra-Comique in Paris.

Works STAGE AND FILM seven operas, two ballets, and contribution to *L'Eventail de Jeanne*; incidental music to Labiche's *Le Chapeau de paille d'Italie* and other plays; film music including *Don Quichotte*.

ORCHESTRAL suites *Escales* (1992) and *Paris*, Symphonie Concertante for oboe and strings (1949), *Divertissement* for chamber orchestra (1930); concertos for piano, for saxophone, and for cello and wind.

Ice Break, The opera by Michael Tippett (libretto by the composer), first produced at the Royal Opera House, Covent Garden, London, England, on 7 July 1977, conducted by Colin Davis. It tells how the Soviet dissident Juri joins his wife Nadia and son Juri in the USA, Nadia dies, the father and son fall out, the son is injured in a race riot, and they are reconciled in the end.

Ideale, Die, The Ideals symphonic poem by Franz Liszt, based on a poem by Schiller, composed in 1857. It was first performed in Weimar, Germany, on 5 September 1857 at the unveiling of the Goethe–Schiller monument.

idée fixe Hector Berlioz's term for a theme (in the ➔ *Symphonie Fantastique*) which recurs in varying forms in the course of a composition as an allusion to some definite idea.

idiophone one of the four main classes of musical instruments used in the original ➔ Sachs-Hornbostel system, the others being ➔ aerophone, ➔ membranophone, and ➔ chordophone. In instruments which are idiophones, the sound emanates from the vibration of 'the substance of the instrument itself'. Thus, bells and gongs are included, as are castanets and glass harmonicas.

Idiot, Der ballet-pantomime by Hans Werner Henze (scenario by I Bachmann after Fyodor Dostoevsky), first produced in Berlin, Germany, on 1 September 1952.

Idoménée, Idomeneus opera by André Campra (libretto by A Danchet), first produced at the Paris Opéra, France, on 12 January 1712.

Idomeneo, rè di Creta, ossia Ilia ed Idamante, Idomeneus, King of Crete, or Ilia and Idamantes opera by Mozart (libretto by G B Varesco, based on the French libretto by A Danchet), first produced in Munich, Germany, on 29 January 1781. It was not performed at the Royal Opera House, Covent Garden, London, until 1978, and was first performed at the Metropolitan Opera House, New York, in 1982. It tells how the returning Cretan king must sacrifice his son to fulfil his promise to the gods.

Idyll work for string orchestra in seven movements by Leoš Janáček, composed in 1878 and first performed in Brno, Moravia (modern Czech Republic), on 15 December 1878.

Idyll: Once I Passed Through a Populous City work by Frederick Delius for soprano, baritone, and orchestra (text from Walt Whitman); it was composed 1930–32, with reworkings from the then unperformed opera *Margot-la-Rouge*, (1901–02), and first performed in London, England, on 3 October 1933, conducted by Henry Wood. It was Delius's last work.

Ifigenia in Aulide, Iphigenia in Aulis title of several 18th-century operas with libretti based ultimately on Euripides. The opera by Antonio Caldara (libretto by A Zeno) was first produced in Vienna, Austria, on 4 November 1718. Karl Graun's opera (libretto by L de Villati, after Racine's *Iphigénie en Aulide*) was produced at the Royal Opera, Berlin, Germany, on 13 December 1748. Frederick II of Prussia probably collaborated. Niccolò Zingarelli's opera (libretto by F Moretti) was produced at La Scala, Milan, Italy, on 27 January 1787. Luigi Cherubini's opera (libretto by F Moretti) was first produced at the Teatro Regio, Turin, Italy, on 12 January 1788.

Ifigenia in Tauride, Iphigenia in Tauris opera by Baldassare Galuppi (libretto by M Coltellini, based on Euripides), first produced for the court at St Petersburg, Russia, on 2 May 1768. The opera of the same title by Tommaso Traetta (libretto by Coltellini) was first produced for the court at the Schönbrunn Palace, Vienna, Austria, on 4 October 1763. See ➤ *Iphigénie en Tauride* for plot synopsis.

Ifigenia, L' opera by Niccolò Jommelli (libretto by M Verazi), first produced at the Teatro Argentina, Rome, Italy, on 9 February 1751.

Île de Merlin, L', ou Le Monde renversé, Merlin's Island or the World Upside-Down opera by Christoph Willibald von Gluck (libretto by L Anseaume), first produced for the court at the Schönbrunn Palace, Vienna, Austria, on 3 October 1758. It tells how Pierrot and Scapin are rewarded with love and happiness on a miraculous island, courting Merlin's nieces Argentine and Diamantine.

Illica, Luigi (1857–1919) Italian playwright and librettist. He is best known for his libretti for Puccini's *Manon Lescaut, La Bohème* (with G Giacosa), *Tosca*, and *Madama Butterfly*.

The first of his 88 libretti was for Antonio Smareglia's *Il vassallo di Szigeth* (produced in Vienna, Austria, in 1889); he also collaborated with Alfredo Catalani, Umberto Giordano, Pietro Mascagni, and Baron Frédéric D'Erlanger.

Illuminations, Les song cycle by Benjamin Britten for high voice and strings (setting for nine prose poems by Arthur Rimbaud, 1872–73), composed 1938–39 and first performed in London, England, on 30 January 1940.

Images two sets of piano pieces by Claude Debussy. The first series was composed in 1905 and comprises *Reflets dans l'eau, Hommage à Rameau*, and *Mouvement*; it was first performed in Paris, France, on 3 March 1906. The second series was composed in 1907 and comprises *Cloches à travers les feuilles, Et la lune descend sur le temple qui fut*, and *Poissons d'or*; it was first performed in Paris on 21 February 1908.

Images pour orchestre three symphonic pieces by Claude Debussy: *Gigues* (originally *Gigues tristes*), composed 1906–11; *Rondes de printemps*, composed in 1909; *Ibéria (Par les rues et par les chemins, Les Parfums de la nuit*, and *Le Matin d'un jour de fête*), completed in 1908. *Ibéria* was first performed in Paris, France, on 20 February 1910, conducted by Gabriel Pierné; the three pieces were first performed together in Paris on 26 January 1913, under Pierné.

Imbrie, Andrew (Welsh) (1921–) US composer and pianist. He studied with Roger Sessions and at the University of California, at Berkeley; he was professor there from 1960. He writes in standard forms, with 12-note technique.

Works OPERA *Christmas in Peebles Town* (1964), *Angle of Repose* (1976).

ORCHESTRAL three symphonies (1966–70), concertos for violin (1954), cello (1972), piano (1973, 1974), and flute (1977).

CHAMBER five string quartets (1942–87), cello sonata (1969).

CHORAL *Requiem* for soprano, chorus and orchestra (1984).

Imeneo, Hymeneus opera by Handel (libretto adapted from S Stampiglia), composed in 1738 and first produced at Lincoln's Inn Fields, London, England, on 22 November 1740. It was Handel's penultimate opera. In the story, the Athenian Rosmene has promised her hand to Tirinto, but marries Imeneo, who has rescued her from pirates. The moral is that gratitude and reason should triumph over the passions.

imitation in music, a ➤ contrapuntal device in which a theme or motif is repeated in different vocal or instrumental parts. The strictest form of imitation is the ➤ canon, in which every voice has, in turn, exactly the same notes and rhythms as the one before it. In a ➤ fugue the subject (principal melody) is treated imitatively, before a greater degree of contrapuntal freedom occurs in a non-thematic episode (a passage linking appearances of the subject). The use of imitation in composition can be traced back to early forms of ➤ polyphony from about 1200.

Immortal Hour, The opera by Rutland Boughton (libretto by the composer, adapted from plays and poems by Fiona Macleod), first produced at Glastonbury, England, on 26 August 1914. It tells how King Eochaidh falls in love with the fairy princess Etain, who cannot remember her true identity. She is later reclaimed by Midir; the Lord of Shadows mercifully kills Eochaidh so that he will not suffer.

imperfect cadence musical term; see ➤ **half-close**.

Impériale, L' nickname of Haydn's symphony no. 53 in D major, composed about 1775.

impresario in angustie, L', The Impressario in Distress opera by Domenico Cimarosa (libretto by G M Diodati, similar to that of Mozart's *Schauspieldirektor*), first produced at the Teatro Nuovo, Naples, Italy, in October 1786.

Impresario, The comedy with music by Mozart; see ➤ *Schauspieldirektor, Der*.

Impressionism in music, a style of composition emphasizing instrumental colour and texture. The term was first applied to the music of Claude Debussy.

impromptu in music, a 19th-century character piece in the style of an improvisation. Composers of piano impromptus include Schubert and Chopin.

improvisation creating music 'on the spot' as it is being performed. It is a principal means of artistic expression among oral cultures, including popular music and jazz in the West. It is based on standard models, including song form (ABA), modes, ➤ **raga**, or scales of specific significance, and on standard rhythms, or familiar melodies combining modal and rhythmic components.

A composer/performer creates a fresh and personal interpretation of a model at each performance, one showing understanding of the stylistic history of the original, and bringing an experienced artistry to bear on expression and decoration. Successful improvisation relies on the awareness of an audience, knowing the prototype, and freely responding to refinements of artistic variation. Organists are taught improvisation as a technique and it was the norm amongst composers from the Renaissance to mid-Romantic period. Improvisation was also the principal technique of silent film accompaniment.

Improvisation sur Mallarmé two works by Pierre Boulez after the French poet Stéphane Mallarmé. No. 1.i, for soprano, harp, tubular bells, vibraphone, and four percussion, was composed in 1957 and first performed in Hamburg, Germany, on 13 January 1958, conducted by Hans Rosbaud. A version for soprano and orchestra (No. 1.ii) was first performed in Donaueschingen, Germany, on 20 October 1962, conducted by Boulez. No. 2, for the same forces as No. 1.i, with piano, was composed in 1957 and first performed on 13 January 1958.

incalzando (Italian 'persuading, urging forward') in musical direction, accelerating the pace.

incidental music accompanying music to stage or film drama that, in addition to setting a mood (see ➤ **background music**), is also part of the action, as in Thomas Arne's music (including songs) for the stage, music for ➤ **masques**, and so on.

Incognita opera by Egon Wellesz (libretto by E Mackenzie, on William Congreve's story), first produced in Oxford, England, on 5 December 1951. As the title suggests, it involves amorous intrigues and mistaken identities.

incontro improvviso, L', The Unforeseen Meeting opera by Haydn (libretto by K Friberth, translated into Italian from Florent Dancourt's *La Rencontre imprévue*, composed by Gluck), first produced at Eszterháza, Hungary, on 29 August 1775. In the story, Prince Ali and Princess Rezia were once lovers, but were captured by pirates and separated. Rezia, now the favourite of the Egyptian sultan, escapes with the newly found Ali, thanks to the help of slave Osmin.

incoronazione di Poppea, L', The Coronation of Poppaea opera by Claudio Monteverdi (libretto by Busenello, based on Tacitus), first produced at the Teatro S Giovanni e Paolo, Venice, Italy, in the autumn of 1643. Modern editions have been produced by Jack Westrup (first British production, Oxford, 1927), Ernst Krenek, Vincent d'Indy, Gian Francesco Malipiero, Giorgio Ghedini, Raymond Leppard, Roger Norrington, and Nikolaus Harnoncourt. It was the first opera not to be based on a mythical or religious theme, and tells how Poppea defeats her rivals and weds the Roman emperor Nero.

Indes galantes, Les, Love in the Indies opera-ballet by Jean-Philippe Rameau (libretto by L Fuzelier), first produced at the Paris Opéra, France, on 23 August 1735. The four entrées are *Le Turc généreux*, *Les Incas du Pérou*, *Les Fleurs*, and *Les Sauvages*. It was revived in New York in 1961 and London in 1972.

indeterminacy in music, the absence of specific instruction concerning a significant element of a composition. A mobile piece is unspecific in terms of the order of sections; a graphic score is indeterminate in notation or timing. All music is indeterminate to some degree, since no two live performances can be totally alike.

Indeterminacy as an aesthetic goal of the avant-garde around 1950–70 aims, by stripping away the means of achieving an exact performance, to re-establish extemporization as an element of virtuosity, and to provoke new discoveries. With the aid of multichannel tape recording, pop musicians in the 1970s developed an art of composing by experiment from taped initial ideas. Composers of indeterminate music include Luciano ➤ **Berio**, Karlheinz ➤ **Stockhausen**, and the Polish composer Roman Haubenstock-Ramati (1919–). After 1970 indeterminacy became a music education cause, aimed at releasing repressed creativity.

India, Sigismondo d' (c.1582–1629) Italian composer. His highly chromatic madrigals have been valued as second only to those of Claudio ➤ **Monteverdi**.

He left his native Sicily to work as director of music at the Turin court of the Duke of Savoy 1611–23. His madrigal collections were published in eight books (1606–24) in Milan and Venice. In 1625 his sacred drama *Sant' Eustachio* was produced in Cardinal Maurizio's palace at Rome. The following year he moved to Modena. Other important influences on his style came from Luca Marenzio and the chromaticism of Carlo Gesualdo.

Indianische Fantasie work by Ferruccio Busoni for piano and orchestra, Op. 44, based on American Indian themes (Busoni was professor at New England Conservatory 1891–94). It was composed in 1913 and first performed in Berlin, Germany, on 12 March 1914.

Indian music classical musical culture of the Hindustani tradition found in North India, Pakistan, Nepal, and Bangladesh, and of the Karnatic tradition in South India and Sri Lanka. An oral culture with a long history, it is linked to Muslim traditions of the Middle East and Central Asia. It resembles the medieval European troubadour tradition of composer-performer, being an art of skilful improvisation in a given mood (rasa), selecting from a range of melody patterns (ragas) and rhythmic patterns (talas), understood in the same way as in the West 'blues' defines a mood, a scale, and a form, and 'boogie-woogie' an associated rhythm.

Indian music is geared to the time of day, and a composition/performance does not have a fixed length. An ensemble consists of a melody section, featuring voice, sitar, sarod, surbahar, violins, shrill reed woodwinds, or harmonium, solo or in combination; a drone section featuring the vina or tambura, providing a resonant harmonic ground (repeated bass line); and a rhythm section of high and low tuned hand drums. The music has a natural buoyancy, the melody effortlessly rising, while the drone has the same function as a tonic or key chord in European tonal music, exerting a gravitational pull to provide tension and release in the music. The sounds of Indian music are rich in high frequencies, giving an impression of luminous radiance. Indian

music became more popular in the West after world tours in the 1950s by virtuosos Ravi ➤ **Shankar** (sitar) and Ali Akhbar Khan (sarod). In Britain, a tradition of both popular and classical music thrives among expatriate communities and in schools.

Indian Queen, The play by John Dryden and Robert Howard, first produced in 1664; it was adapted as a semiopera with music by Henry and Daniel Purcell and produced at the Drury Lane Theatre, London, in 1695. It tells how the Mexican queen Zempoalla fights invading Peruvian forces led by Montezuma. He discovers she has overthrown the legitimate queen, who is revealed to be Montezuma's long-lost mother.

Indigo und die vierzig Räuber, Indigo and the Forty Robbers operetta by Johann Strauss, junior (libretto by M Steiner), first produced at the Theater an der Wien, Vienna, Austria, on 10 February 1871. It was Strauss's first operetta.

Indy, (Paul Marie Théodore) Vincent d' (1851–1931) French composer. He studied under César Franck, and was one of the founders of the Schola Cantorum. His works include operas (*Fervaal*, 1897), symphonies, tone poems (*Istar*, 1896), and chamber music.

Although born in Paris, he belonged to a noble family of the Ardèche district in the Vivarais. His mother died at his birth and he was brought up by his paternal grandmother, a good musician. At the age of 11 he was sent to Louis Diémer for the piano and Albert Lavignac for theory, and later studied piano under Jean Marmontel. In 1870 he published his first works and served in the defence of Paris against the Prussian army. To please his family he studied law, but was determined to be a musician and went for advice to Franck, who offered to teach him. He also joined Edouard Colonne's orchestra as a timpanist to gain experience. Jules Pasdeloup gave the first performance of one of his works, the overture to Schiller's *Piccolomini*, afterwards part of his *Wallenstein* trilogy.

Next to Franck he admired Franz Liszt, with whom he spent two months at Weimar in 1873, and Richard Wagner, whose first *Ring* cycle he attended at Bayreuth in 1876. He helped the conductor Charles Lamoureux introduce Wagner's music to Paris (*Lohengrin*, 1887) and revived works by Jean-Philippe Rameau, Christoph Willibald von Gluck, and Claudio Monteverdi (*Poppea* in his own edition). In 1894 he joined Charles Bordes, together with Félix Guilmant, in founding the Schola Cantorum; he taught there until his death and had many pupils of the highest distinction, including Edgard Varèse. From 1912 he also directed the orchestral class at the Conservatory.

Works STAGE operas *Fervaal* (1897), *L'Étranger* (1898–1901).

ORCHESTRAL *Symphonie sur un chant montagnard français* (*Symphonie cévenole*) for piano and orchestra (1886); symphonic variations *Istar* (1896), *Jour d'été à la montagne* (1905).

CHAMBER three string quartets (1890, 1897, 1929), string sextet and piano quintet (1924), trios for piano, violin, and cello, suite for trumpet, two flutes and string quartet; sonata for cello and piano.

PIANO AND SONGS 18 Op. nos. of piano works, including sonata in E major, *Thème varié*; 90 *Chansons populaires du Vivarais* arrangements of twelve French folk songs for unaccompanied chorus.

Inextinguishable, The, Danish **Det Undslukke-lige** title of Carl Nielsen's fourth symphony; composed 1915–16 and first performed in Copenhagen, Denmark, on1 February 1916, conducted by Nielsen.

Inez de Castro opera by Giuseppe Persiani (libretto by S Cammarano) first produced at the Teatro San Carlo, Naples, Italy, on 28 January 1835. It was written for Maria Malibran.

Infantas, Fernando de las (1534–after 1609) Spanish composer, descendant of the Fernández family of Córdoba. He is known by the name Infantas because one of his ancestors conveyed the infantas Constanza and Isabella to Bayonne, occupied by the English in the 14th century, before their respective marriages to John of Gaunt and Edmund Langley. His compositions attracted the attention of the bishop of Córdoba, the archduke Charles of Austria. He settled in Rome, Italy, around 1559, but took holy orders in 1584 and went to Paris, France; he had returned to Spain by 1608.

Works motets, some for special occasions, such as the death of the emperor Charles V (1558) and the Battle of Lepanto (1571); a setting of Psalm 99.

infinite canon in music, a ➤ canon contrived to make the end overlap with the beginning, so that it can be repeated to infinity.

inganno felice, L', The Happy Deceit opera by Gioachino Rossini (libretto by G M Foppa), first produced at the Teatro San Moise, Venice, Italy, on 8 January 1812. Falsely accused of adultery, the abandoned Isabella is reunited with her husband.

Ingegneri, Marc Antonio (c.1545–1592) Italian composer. He learnt music from Vincenzo Ruffo at Verona Cathedral and, around 1570 became maestro di cappella at Cremona Cathedral. Monteverdi was his pupil there.

Works two books of Masses, three books of motets, one of hymns and eight of madrigals; also 27 responsories for Holy Week (long attributed to Palestrina).

Inghelbrecht, D(ésiré-) E(mile) (1880–1965) French conductor and composer. He conducted many concerts of modern music in Paris, also the Swedish Ballet in Paris and London. He conducted at the Paris Opéra 1945–50 and founded the French National Radio Orchestra in 1934, conducting it until 1944 and again 1951–58.

Works STAGE operas *La Nuit vénitienne* (after Musset, 1908) and *La Chêne et le tilleul* (1960); two operettas; ballets *El Greco* (1920) and *Le Diable dans le beffroi* (1921).

CHORUS AND ORCHESTRA Requiem; *Cantique des créatures de Saint François* for chorus and orchestra; *Sinfonia breve* (1930).

CHAMBER AND INSTRUMENTAL string quartet; sonata for flute and harp; quintet for strings and harp; *Suite Petite-Russienne* and other piano works; *La Nursery* for piano duet (three books).

OTHER songs.

In Nature's Realm concert overture by Dvořák; see ➤ **Amid Nature.**

inner part in ➤ polyphonic music, the voices (independent parts) whose registers (instrumental or vocal ranges) are neither the highest nor lowest. In a four-voice choir, for example, the alto and tenor sing inner parts, their registers falling between the soprano and bass. In a string quartet usually the second violin and viola are inner parts between the first violin and cello.

innig (German 'inward, intimate, heartfelt') term frequently used by German Romantic composers, especially Robert Schumann, where profound feeling is required in performance.

innocenza giustificata, L', Innocence Vindicated opera by Christoph Willibald von Gluck (libretto by G Durazzo, with words for the airs by Pietro Metastasio), first produced at the Burgtheater, Vienna, Austria, on 8 December 1755. In the story, Julia's innocence is proved by divine intervention.

Inno delle nazioni, Hymn of the Nations cantata by Giuseppe Verdi written for the International Exhibition in London, England, but first produced at Her Majesty's Theatre on 24 May 1862. It introduced national airs in contrapuntal combination.

in nomine instrumental piece of the later 16th century for viols or keyboard, similar to the fancy or fantasia, but based on a plainsong melody used as a *cantus firmus*. The melody is that of 'Gloria tibi Trinitas', an antiphon for Trinity Sunday, which was used by John Taverner as the *cantus firmus* of a Mass with the title *Gloria tibi Trinitas*. Part of the *Benedictus* of this Mass, beginning at the words 'In nomine Domini', was arranged as an instrumental piece, and this seems to have suggested to other composers the idea of writing original instrumental pieces on the same *cantus firmus*. The last composer to write *in no-mines* was Henry Purcell.

Inori, Adorations work for soloist(s) and orchestra by Karlheinz Stockhausen, first performed in Donaueschingen, Germany, on 20 October 1974.

In questa tomba oscura a collective work, of which only Beethoven's song remains known today. In 1808 composers were invited to set this poem by Giuseppe Carpani, probably at the invitation of Countess Rzewuska in Vienna. Among the 63 composers who responded were, apart from Beethoven, Bonifazio Asioli, Luigi Cherubini, Karl Czerny, Ferdinando Paër, Johann Reichardt, Antonio Salieri, Václav Tomášek, Karl Weigl, and Niccolò Zingarelli.

Insanguine, Giacomo (1728–1795) Italian composer. He studied at the Conservatorio di Sant' Onofrio in Naples, where he taught from 1767, eventually becoming maestro di cappella. Between 1756 and 1782 he produced 21 operas; other works include Masses and other church music, cantatas, and arias.

instrumentation in music, the art of composing for particular instruments in a manner appropriate to their range and sound. ➤ **Orchestration** is similar in meaning, usually referring specifically to instruments in an orchestral setting.

intavolatura (Italian 'tablature') a 16th- and 17th-century musical term used for publications issued for keyboard instruments and written on two staves, as distinct from instrumental music printed in score or in separate parts.

Intégrales work for small orchestra and percussion by Edgard Varèse, composed in 1923. It was first performed in New York, USA, on 1 March 1925, conducted by Leopold Stokowski.

integral serialism in music, a type of ➤ **serialism** pioneered by Pierre ➤ **Boulez** and Karlheinz ➤ **Stockhausen** in the early 1950s that brings as many musical elements as possible under serial control. This technique applies not only to pitch, but also to dynamics, duration, and timbre.

Intendant manager or director of an opera house or other theatre in Germany, especially one attached to a court in former times.

interdominant musical term used to describe temporary dominants in the keys in which episodes may appear in the course of a composition, other than the dominant of the prescribed key. It is the same as the German *Zwischendominante*.

interlude piece or passage of music played between two other works or sections. This may occur between scenes of an opera, for example, as in Benjamin Britten's *Sea Interludes* from *Peter*

Grimes (1945). In the 18th century, interludes were played between the verses of a hymn or psalm. In the latter case, the organist often improvised passages and so there are few remaining printed examples. Exceptions include certain organ chorales, such as Bach's *In dulci jubilo*.

intermède French musical term for ➤ **interlude**, or ➤ **intermezzo**.

intermedii or **intermezzi** in 15th- and 16th-century Italy, musical or dramatic interludes played between the acts of a play or during the intervals of a banquet. The musical *intermedii* consisted of instrumental pieces played out of sight of the audience. The dramatic *intermedii* were stage spectacles performed by singers, dancers, and actors in costume. These were broadly similar to the English interlude.

In their combination of music and drama, *intermedii* can be regarded as an important forerunner of opera.

Intermedii were first performed during the intervals of Renaissance plays – the court of 15th-century Ferrara was particularly important in their development. Sometimes the subject matter of the *intermedii* was connected with that of the play, though more often unrelated pastoral scenes with allegorical figures were presented. The Medici court in Florence was the scene of many lavish entertainments, the most spectacular being that performed in 1589 at the wedding of Christine of Lorraine and Ferdinando de' Medici, for which the music was provided by leading composers, including Luca Marenzio and Giulio ➤ **Caccini**.

intermedio another word for ➤ **intermezzo**.

intermezzo in music, initially a one-act comic opera, such as Giovanni Pergolesi's *La serva padrona/The Maid as Mistress* (1732); also a short orchestral interlude played between the acts of an opera to denote the passage of time. By extension, an intermezzo has come to mean a short piece to be played between other more substantial works, such as Brahms's *Three Intermezzos for Piano* (1892).

Intermezzo opera by Richard Strauss (libretto by the composer), first produced in Dresden, Germany, on 4 November 1924. The material of the libretto is autobiographical. The composer Robert Storch is in trouble when his wife Christine reads a misdirected love letter.

Internationale international revolutionary socialist anthem composed in 1870 and first sung in 1888. The words by Eugène Pottier (1816–1887) were written shortly after Napoleon III's surrender to Prussia; the music is by Pierre Degeyter. It was the Soviet national anthem 1917–44.

interpretation in music, the manner in which a performer plays a work. Except in the case of pre-recorded electronic music, which excludes the performer altogether, the limitations of notation mean that a composer cannot indicate the most subtle levels of dynamics, expression, articulation, and other details of ➤ **performance practice.** Inevitably the performer is responsible for these, although during some periods it has been the convention for the musician to take greater liberties than during others. For instance, the 18th-century performer had much greater freedom than the 20th-century performer, not only to alter a composer's dynamics and articulation without criticism, but also, to a degree, to change the notes themselves.

interval in music, the distance or difference in pitch between two notes. It is written in terms of the major or minor scale. To work out the number of the interval, the letter name of both notes is included. For example, C to D is a second, C to E is a third, C to F is a fourth, and so on. A complete description of an interval includes not only its number, but also its 'quality'. There are five descriptions used: perfect, major, minor, augmented, and diminished; for example, perfect fifth and major second. When the two notes are played together they form a **harmonic interval;** when one note follows the other, it is a **melodic interval.**

In the Mists, Czech **V mlhách** work by Leoš Janáček in four movements for piano, composed in 1912.

In the South, Alassio concert overture by Edward Elgar, Op. 50, composed during a visit to Italy in 1903 and published in 1904. It was first performed in London, England, on 16 March 1904, conducted by Elgar.

Intimate Letters, Czech **Listy důverné** subtitle of Leoš Janáček's second string quartet, composed in 1928 and inspired by his unrequited love for Kamilla Stoesslová, 38 years his junior, to whom he wrote almost daily letters during the last ten years of his life. It was first performed in Brno, Czechoslovakia (now the Czech Republic), on 11 September 1928, one month after Janáček's death.

intonation in music, the means by which a performer maintains correct tuning. Pitch accuracy requires continuous slight adjustments of pitch in those instruments for which it is feasible. For orchestral violins, violas, cellos, and double basses, pitch is adjustable by finger positioning (instruments losing pitch as a result of atmospheric conditions are retuned between movements). Woodwind instruments are of relatively fixed pitch, but a note may 'bend' using a combination of finger and breath technique, or be shifted mi-

crotonally by adopting a different fingering. Trumpets are equipped with a tuning slide, controlled by the little finger; horns can be modified in pitch by inserting the left hand into the bell.

intonazione (Italian 'intonation') 16th-century musical term for a ➤ **prelude,** especially one for organ used in church to precede a service.

Into the Labyrinth cantata for tenor and orchestra by Peter Maxwell Davies (text by G Mackay Brown), first performed in Kirkwall, Orkney, Scotland, on 22 June 1983.

intrada (Italian entrada 'entrance, entry') musical term; see ➤ **introduction,** ➤ **prelude.**

introduction in music, a section preceding the main body of a work. Many symphonies of the 18th century featured a slow introduction (including works by Haydn, Mozart, and Beethoven), and this practice was sometimes transferred to quartets and keyboard works, as in Beethoven's *Sonata Pathétique* (1799). The introduction may be related motivically or thematically to the rest of the work, as in the *Pathétique,* or it may be more independent, as in Edward Elgar's *Introduction and Allegro* (1905) for strings.

Introduction and Allegro work for string quartet and string orchestra by Edward Elgar, composed 1904–05 and first performed in London, England, on 8 March 1905, conducted by Elgar. It is also the title of Maurice Ravel's septet for harp, string quartet, flute, and clarinet, composed in 1906 and first performed in Paris, France, on 22 February 1907.

Introit (Latin introitus, 'entrance') the first item of the Proper of the Mass, accompanying the entry of the ministers. Originally a complete psalm with antiphon before and after each verse, it was reduced in the Middle Ages to its present form of antiphon, psalm-verse, *Gloria Patri* and repeat of antiphonorary. The antiphon is a freely composed melody, the psalm being sung to a slightly ornate psalm tone.

invention in music, a term not commonly used by composers, but made famous by Bach in his *15 Inventions* for keyboard (1720). In two parts, each composition is contrapuntal and highly imitative, based upon a short melodic motif or phrase. Bach's so-called 'three-part inventions' were not named as such by the composer, but rather the term 'sinfonia' was used instead (*15 Sinfonias,* 1723).

Inventions title given to Bach's two sets of short keyboard pieces written strictly in two and three parts respectively, and probably designed as technical studies. He called the three-part set 'symphonies', but there is no essential difference in character between them and the two-part inventions.

inversion in music, the mirror image of a melody used in counterpoint; alternatively a chord in which the natural order of notes is rearranged.

In classical counterpoint, melodic inversion usually includes a degree of flexibility to avoid dissonance or unwanted harmonic implications; in strict ✦ **twelve-tone** music the inversion is exact.

A root position triad on C with first and second inversions.

invertible counterpoint musical term; see ✦ **counterpoint**.

Invisible City of Kitezh, The Legend of the opera by Rimsky-Korsakov; see ✦ *Legend of the Invisible City of Kitezh and Maiden Fevronia.*

Invitation to the Dance piano piece by Carl Maria von Weber; see ✦ *Aufforderung zum Tanz.*

Iolanta opera in one act by Pyotr Tchaikovsky (libretto by Modest Tchaikovsky, Tchaikovsky's brother, based on Henrik Hertz's play *King René's Daughter*), first produced in St Petersburg, Russia, on 18 December 1892. It tells how the blind Iolanta's sight is restored in response to amorous interest from Vaudemont.

Iolanthe, or The Peer and the Peri operetta by Arthur Sullivan (libretto by W S Gilbert), first produced at the Savoy Theatre, London, England, on 25 November 1882, and at the Standard Theatre, New York, USA, on the same date. In the story, Phyllis loves Strephon, but his half-fairy parentage and the Lord Chancellor cause problems. The fairy mother Iolanthe intervenes and the couple are united.

Ione, old Italian spelling **Jone** opera by Enrico Petrella (libretto by G Peruzzini, based on Edward Bulwer-Lytton's novel *The Last Days of Pompeii*), first produced at La Scala, Milan, Italy, on 26 January 1858.

Ionian mode in music, a ✦ **mode** that is equivalent to the major scale. On a piano, it is the scale from C to B using only the white notes.

Ionisation work by Edgard ✦ **Varèse** for 13 percussionists. It was first performed in New York, USA, on 6 March 1933, and is probably the first work for percussion only. The majority of the work uses untuned percussion; it is only in the last section that a piano, glockenspiel, and tubular bells introduce pitched material.

Ipermestra, Hypermnestra opera by Christoph Willibald von Gluck (libretto by Pietro Metastasio), first produced at the Teatro San Giovanni Cristostomo, Venice, Italy, on 21 November 1744. Warned by an oracle, King Danaus orders his daughter to kill her betrothed, Lynceus, on their wedding night. She cannot do it, and instead separates from him. After complications, there is a happy ending.

Iphigénie en Aulide, Iphigenia in Aulis opera by Christoph Willibald von Gluck (libretto by F L L du Roullet, based on Racine and further back on Euripides), first produced at the Paris Opéra, France, on 19 April 1774. It was Gluck's first opera for the Paris stage, though not his first French work. In the story, Agamemnon must sacrifice his daughter, Iphigénie, in order to gain favourable winds to sail for Troy. At the last moment she is saved by the goddess Diana, who leaves a deer in her place.

Iphigénie en Tauride, Iphigenia in Tauris title of a number of operas based on Euripides. The story is a sequel to *Iphigénie en Aulide*; Iphigénie has been transported to Tauris from the sacrificial altar by Diana. Orestes, Iphigénie's brother, arrives in the barbaric kingdom to return a statue of Diana to Greece. He is captured, but there is a happy ending. The opera by Henri Desmarets and André Campra (libretto by J F Duché and A Danchet) was first produced at the Paris Opéra, France, on 6 May 1704. The opera by Christoph Willibald von Gluck (libretto by N F Guillard) was first produced at the Paris Opéra on 18 May 1779. Niccolò Piccinni's opera (libretto by A C Dubreuil) was first produced at the Paris Opéra on 23 January 1781. See also ✦ *Ifigenia, L'.*

Ippolito ed Aricia, Hippolytus and Aricia opera by Tommaso Traetta (libretto by C I Frugoni, translated from S J de Pellegrin's libretto for Jean-Philippe Rameau's *Hippolyte et Aricie*, 1733). It was first produced in Parma, Italy, on 9 May 1759.

Ippolitov-Ivanov, Mikhail Mikhailovich (1859–1935) Russian composer. His compositions show a strong influence from the Caucasus; he wrote a book on Georgian folk music, and his symphonic suite *Caucasian Sketches* (1894) is probably his most popular work. He orchestrated the rediscovered St Basil scene from Mussorgsky's *Boris Godunov* (1925) and added three acts to Mussorgsky's unfinished opera *The Marriage* (1931).

He studied under Nikolai Rimsky-Korsakov at the St Petersburg Conservatory. In 1884 he was appointed conductor of the Imperial Opera at Tiflis, and in 1893 professor at the Moscow Conservatory, of which he was director 1906–22. He composed seven operas, as well as cantatas, choral works, and orchestral, chamber, and instrumental music. His memoirs were published as *Fifty Years of Russian Music* (1934).

Works OPERA *Ruth* (1887), *Azra*, *Assia* (after Turgenev's story, 1900), *Treachery* (1910), *Ole from Norland* (1916), *The Last Barricade*, also completion of Mussorgsky's *The Marriage* (1931).

ORCHESTRAL two symphonies, *Caucasian Sketches* (1894), *Iberia*, *Armenian Rhapsody* (1895), *Mtsyri* (after Lermontov), *From Ossian, Episode from Schubert's Life*, *Turkish Fragments* (1930), *Musical Scenes from Uzbekistan*, *The Year 1917*, *Catalonian Suite*, and other pieces for orchestra.

CHORAL *Hymn to Labour* for chorus and orchestra (1934).

OTHER two string quartets; *An Evening in Georgia* for harp and wind instruments; violin and piano sonata; piano and other instrumental pieces; cantatas for chorus and piano; 116 songs.

IRCAM, abbreviation for **L'Institut pour la Recherche et Coordination Acoustique/Musique, 'Institute for Research and Coordination in Acoustics/Music'** research institute founded by the French government as part of the Georges Pompidou Centre in Paris, France, and opened in 1977 under the directorship of Pierre ➔ Boulez. IRCAM aims to combine scientific research into acoustics, psychology, and the development of computer applications in music with compositional activity and performance of contemporary works by its body of musicians, the Ensemble InterContemporain. Composers commissioned to work at IRCAM collaborate with computer programmers to produce their works. Notable examples of works produced at IRCAM include *Répons* by Boulez (1981–82), *Mortuos plango, vivos voco* by Jonathan ➔ Harvey (1980), and the mime interludes from *The Mask of Orpheus* by Harrison Birtwistle (1986).

Ireland, John Nicholson (1879–1962) English composer. His works include the mystic orchestral prelude *The Forgotten Rite* (1913), a piano concerto (1930), and several song cycles. His pupils include Benjamin Britten and E J Moeran.

He was born in Bowdon, Cheshire, and was educated at Leeds Grammar School and at the Royal College of Music in London, studying under Charles Stanford 1893–1901. Apart from organist's appointments, and his later composition professorship at the Royal College of Music, he devoted himself entirely to creative work. Other pupils included Humphrey Searle. In 1932 he received an honorary PhD from Durham University. His music is small-scale, and influenced by Debussy and early Stravinsky.

Ireland's first compositions were concerted chamber music and songs. Two violin sonatas followed, and these established his reputation at once. His best-known subsequent works are a pi-

anoforte sonata, a symphonic rhapsody *Mai-Dun* (1921), and a piano concerto (1930). He also wrote a large number of songs, one of the best known being the setting of John Masefield's 'Sea Fever'. Several song cycles are important, and all his songs are distinguished by his sensitive choice of words from the finest English poetry, and by the lyrical beauty and sincerity of their music, which is also found in the piano music.

Works CHORUS AND ORCHESTRA *These Things Shall Be* (John Addington Symonds) for chorus and orchestra (1936–37).

ORCHESTRAL prelude *The Forgotten Rite* (1913), *A London Overture* (1936); *Concertino pastorale* for string orchestra (1939); concerto in E flat for piano and orchestra.

CHAMBER two violin and piano sonatas, cello and piano sonata, fantasy-sonata for clarinet and piano; piano sonatina and many shorter pieces such as *Sarnia* (1941).

OTHER music for the film *The Overlanders* (1946–47); song settings including *Five Poems by Thomas Hardy* (1926); *A Downland Suite* for brass band (1933).

Iris opera by Pietro Mascagni (libretto by L Illica), first produced at the Teatro Costanzi, Rome, Italy, on 22 November 1898. Abducted by Osaka and Kyoto, Iris is thrown into Kyoto's brothel. She kills herself when her father finds out.

Irische Legende opera by Werner Egk (libretto by the composer) after W B Yeats's drama *The Countess Cathleen*, 1898), first produced at Salzburg, Austria, on 17 August 1955, conducted by Georg Szell. It was revised in 1970. In the story, the benevolent countess sells her soul to rescue the famine-stricken people.

Irish Symphony Charles Stanford's third symphony, in F minor, Op. 28, composed in 1887 and first performed in London, England, on 27 June 1887.

Irmelin opera in three acts by Frederick Delius (libretto by the composer), composed 1890–92 and first produced in Oxford, England, on 4 May 1953, conducted by Thomas Beecham. In the story, the much courted Irmelin is rescued from her suitors by Nils, a prince brought up as a swineherd.

Irrelohe opera by Franz Schreker (libretto by the composer), composed 1919–23 and first produced in Cologne, Germany, on 27 March 1924, conducted by Otto Klemperer. It tells how Count Henry of Irrelohe rises above the reputation of his rapist father, marrying Eva and defending her against Peter.

Isaac, Heinrich (Henricus) (c.1450–1517) Flemish composer. He was a prolific composer of songs and instrumental music, and wrote a

Choralis Constantinus consisting of 58 offices for the whole year, but he is popularly remembered for the song 'Innsbruck ich muss dich lassen', later harmonized by Johann Sebastian Bach. His wide travel is reflected in the various national influences in his music. He was a major contemporary of Josquin Des Prez, Jacob Obrecht, and Pierre de La Rue.

Isaac was born in Brabant. In about 1484, when he seems to have been in Innsbruck, Switzerland, and in touch with Paul Hofhaimer there, he went via Ferrara to Florence, Italy, as musician to the Medici family. He sang in the choir at the Chapel of San Giovanni at Florence, and was regularly employed at the cathedral from 1485. He visited Rome in 1489, and married Bartolomea Bello, the daughter of a wealthy butcher.

Lorenzo de' Medici died in 1492 and subsequently Isaac accepted an invitation from the emperor Maximilian, who visited Pisa in 1496, to join the imperial court, just then about to be transferred from Augsburg to Vienna. He seems to have visited Innsbruck again to be formally appointed and was possibly appointed in Augsburg too. His duties were not arduous, so that he was able to live by turns in Vienna, Innsbruck, Constance (all connected with the court), and Italy. He also spent much time at the court of Ercole d'Este, Duke of Ferrara. During his last years he remained in Florence.

Works CHURCH MUSIC many Masses, about 50 motets, sequences, Lamentation *Oratio Jeremiae*, 58 four-part settings of the offices under the title *Choralis Constantinus*, the first polyphonic cycle of liturgical works for the ecclesiastical year; four-part Monodia on the death of Lorenzo de' Medici (words by Poliziano).

OTHER many German, Italian, French, and Latin songs (including 'Innsbruck, ich muss dich lassen', which may not be his own tune), 58 instrumental pieces in three–five parts, 29 domestic pieces in two–five parts.

Isabeau *leggenda drammatica* by Pietro Mascagni (libretto by L Illica), first produced in Buenos Aires, Argentina, on 2 June 1911, conducted by Mascagni. It tells how the disobedient Isabeau is condemned by her father, King Raimondo, to ride naked before the populace. The townspeople pity her and do not watch. The only exception, Folco (with whom Isabeau falls in love) is killed.

Isidore of Seville (c.560–636) Spanish philosopher, theologian, writer, and missionary. His *Etymologiae* was the model for later medieval encyclopedias and helped to preserve classical thought during the Middle Ages. As archbishop of Seville from 600, he strengthened the church in Spain and converted many Jews and Aryan Visigoths. His *Chronica Maiora* remains an important source for the history of Visigothic Spain.

His contribution to music theory is contained in book III of his *Etymologiae* (largely a summary of Cassiodorus). He also deals with practical matters of church music in *De Ecclesiasticis Officiis*.

Isis opera by Jean-Baptiste Lully (libretto by Philippe Quinault), first produced at Saint-Germain, France, on 5 January 1677 and first performed in Paris, France, in April 1677.

Isle of the Dead, The symphonic poem by Sergei ➔ **Rachmaninov**, after a painting by Arnold Böcklin; it was composed in 1907 and first performed in Moscow, Russia, on 1 May 1909. Like many of Rachmaninov's works, it prominently features the ➔ **Dies Irae** melody.

isola disabitata, L', The Desert Island opera by Haydn (libretto by Pietro Metastasio), first produced at Eszterháza, Hungary, on 6 December 1779. It tells how the shipwrecked sisters Constanza and Silvia are rescued by husband Germando and lover Enricompany. There are also settings by Giuseppe Scarlatti (Venice, 1751) and Tommaso Traetta (Bologna, 1768).

isometric (from Greek 'equally metrical') a manner of writing vocal music in several parts mainly in block chords, that is, in the same rhythm.

isorhythm in music, a form in which a given rhythm cyclically repeats, although the corresponding melody notes may change. It was used in European medieval music, and is still practised in classical Indian music. The composers Alban Berg, John Cage, and Olivier Messiaen used isorhythmic procedures.

isorhythmic (from Greek 'equally rhythmic') modern term for a method of construction used by composers for polyphonic music in the 14th and 15th centuries. One or more of the parts were arranged in a rhythmic pattern several bars long, which was repeated throughout the piece, sometimes with changes of tempo (indicated by the use of smaller note-values, or different mensuration signs).

Isouard, Nicolò (1775–1818) Maltese composer of French descent. Educated at a military academy in Paris, he had to leave France at the Revolution, and after a time in Malta studied music in Palermo and in Naples, Italy, under Sala and Guglielmi. He made his debut as an opera composer in Florence with *L'avviso ai maritati* in 1794. The following year he was appointed organist to the Order of St John of Malta in Valetta, and later became maestro di cappella there. Leaving Malta in 1799 he settled in Paris, where he produced many operas and also appeared as a pianist.

Works OPERA over 40, including *L'avviso ai mari-tati* (1794), *Artaserse* (1794), *Le Tonnelier* (1801), *Michel-Ange* (1802), *Cendrillon* (1810), *Le Billet de loterie* (1811), *Joconde, Jeannot et Colin*, and *Aladin ou La Lampe merveilleuse* (1822).

OTHER Masses, motets, cantatas, and other vocal works.

Israel in Egypt oratorio by Handel (words from the Bible and the Prayer Book version of the psalms), composed in 1738 and first performed at the King's Theatre, Haymarket, London, England, on 4 April 1739.

'Israel' Symphony symphony by Ernest Bloch, composed 1912–16 and first performed in New York, USA, on 3 May 1916.

Issé opera by André-Cardinal Destouches (libretto by A H de la Motte), first produced before the court at Fontainebleau, France, on 7 October 1679; its first Paris performance was given at the Opéra on 30 December 1697. In the story, Apollo woos Issé, disguised as the shepherd Philemon.

-issimo Italian superlative ending denoting an extreme quality, as in *pianissimo* (softest) or *fortissimo* (loudest).

Istar symphonic variations by Vincent d'Indy, Op. 42, first performed in Brussels, Belgium, on 10 January 1897. The work is based on the Babylonian legend of Ishtar's descent into limbo, and illustrates her disrobing at the seven stations of her progress by the devices of presenting the variations first, in diminishing complexity, and stating the theme only at the end, in bare octave unison.

Istel, Edgar (1880–1948) German musicologist. He studied at Munich, and studied composition with Volbach and Thuille, and musicology with Sandberger. He lived and taught there until 1913, when he went to Berlin as lecturer in music. In 1920 he was in Madrid, Spain, and later moved to the USA. His books include works on Wagner, Peter Cornelius, Paganini, and especially on various aspects of opera.

istesso tempo, l' (Italian from lo stesso tempo, 'the same pace') a musical direction given where a change is indicated in the time-signature, but the composer wishes the music to continue at the same pace or beat in the new rhythm. The change is thus merely one of metre, not of movement.

italiana in Algeri, L', The Italian Girl in Algiers opera by Gioachino Rossini (libretto by A Anelli), first produced at the Teatro San Benedetto, Venice, Italy, on 22 May 1813. It describes how the captured Isabella outwits the amorous Mustafà and is reunited with Lindoro.

italiana in Londra, L', The Italian Girl in London opera by Domenico Cimarosa (libretto by G Petrosellini), first produced at the Teatro Valle, Rome, Italy, on 28 December 1778. In the story, Livia arrives in London to search for her lover Arespingh, who has abandoned her. Arespingh is torn between his arranged marriage and Livia, whom he still loves. In the end he chooses Livia.

Italian Concerto harpsichord work in three movements by Johann Sebastian Bach, published (together with the 'French Overture') in the second part of the *Clavierübung* in 1735. The two manuals of the harpsichord are used to reproduce the contrast between *concertino* and *ripieno* characteristic of the *concerto grosso*.

Italian overture in music, a type of ➤ overture.

Italian sixth musical term; see ➤ augmented sixth chords.

'Italian' Symphony Felix Mendelssohn's fourth symphony, Op. 90, in A major and minor, begun in Italy in 1831 and finished in Berlin, Germany, on 31 March 1833; it was first performed in London, England, on 13 May 1833, conducted by the composer.

Italienisches Liederbuch, Italian Song Book Hugo Wolf's settings of Italian poems in German translated by Paul Heyse, composed (22 nos) 1890–91 and (24 nos) 1896.

Ivanhoe opera by Arthur Sullivan (libretto by J R Sturgis, based on Walter Scott's novel), first produced at the Royal English Opera House (now the Palace Theatre), London, England, on 31 January 1891. It tells how Rowena and Rebecca compete for the errant knight Ivanhoe.

Ivan le terrible opera by Georges Bizet (libretto by A Leroy and H Trianon, first offered to Charles Gounod and abandoned by him), composed in 1865 and accepted for production by the Théâtre Lyrique in Paris, France, but withdrawn by the composer. The first performance (as a concert) took place at Mühringen (Württemberg, Germany) in 1946. The first stage performance was given in Bordeaux, France, on 12 October 1951. The story tells how the tsar Ivan defeats and assassination attempt and marries Princess Marie.

Ivan Susanin opera by Catterino Cavos (libretto by Prince A A Shakhovskoy), first produced in St Petersburg, Russia, on 31 October 1815. The subject is that on which Mikhail Glinka's *Life for the Tsar* was based in 1836. It is also the title given to Glinka's *Life for the Tsar* in Soviet Russia.

Ivan the Terrible opera by Rimsky-Korsakov; see ➤ Pskovitianka.

Ives, Charles Edward (1874–1954) US composer. He experimented with ➤ atonality, quarter tones, and clashing time signatures, decades before the avant-garde movement. Most of his music uses (simultaneous) quotations from popular tunes, military marches, patriotic songs, and hymns of the time. He wrote four symphonies, including the *Dvorakian Symphony No. 1* (1895–98); chamber music, including the *Concord Sonata* (piano sonata no. 2, 1909–15); and the orchestral works *Three Places in New England* (1903–14), *New England Holidays* (1904–13), and *The Unanswered Question* (1908).

Much of Ives's music is in a polytonal style, and occasionally employs ➤ microtones (intervals smaller than a semitone). In addition, he experimented with conflicting rhythms, dissonant harmony and counterpoint, chord clusters, and the spatial presentation of music. He also made frequent use of hymn and folk tunes. He composed alone, without much thought for the ease of performer or publisher, earning his living very successfully from his own insurance company. He stopped composing around 1920, but it was only after his death that his music was widely played and appreciated. He was a child prodigy on the piano and organ, and worked as an organist well into his adult life.

Born in Danbury, Connecticut, Ives studied at Yale University under Horatio Parker and Dudley Buck, and wrote his first symphony there in 1895–98 (the *Dvorakian Symphony No. 1*. His father was something of an inventor and eccentric, and encouraged Ives in his experiments. For example, he gave him early ear training by playing in one key while singing in another. He was already impatient with tradition and from an early age he was interested in different sounds occurring together; the occasion when he heard two bands playing different tunes made a lasting impression. He moved to New York in 1898, working as an insurance agent and setting up his own agency in 1907. A second symphony (1896–1902) was written in his spare time, and the third, *The Camp Meeting* (1904–11) impressed Gustav Mahler, who was then conductor at the New York Metropolitan Opera.

Much of his music was written from 1910, but by 1918 his health was suffering. He gradually retired from business and took to revising earlier works rather than writing new ones. The huge *Concord Sonata* was published in 1919, but not performed until 1939. Its first performance (by John Kirkpatrick) was well received, in spite of its complexities. His orchestral music was taken up first by Eugene Goossens at New York in 1927, then by Nicolas Slonimsky. The third symphony was premiered at New York under Lou Harrison in 1946 but the fourth was not performed until eleven years after Ives's death, under Leopold Stokowski. Leonard Bernstein was also a successful champion of the symphonies.

Works ORCHESTRAL four symphonies: no. 1 in D minor (the *Dvorakian Symphony*, 1895–98), no. 2 (1896–1902), no. 3 (1904–11, for chamber orchestra, *The Camp Meeting*), and no. 4 (1910–16); other orchestral works *New England Holidays* (*Washington's Birthday*, *Decoration Day*, *Fourth of July*, *Thanksgiving*; 1904–13); *Three Places in New England*/Orchestral Set no. 1: *The St Gaudens in Boston Common*, *Putnam's Camp, Redding, Connecticut*, and *The Housatonic* at Stockridge (1903–14); Orchestral Set no. 2: *An Elegy to our Forefathers*, *The Rockstrewn Hills Join in the People's Outdoor Meeting*, and *From Hanover Square North at the end of a Tragic Day* (1909–15); *Central Park in the Dark* (1898–1907); *The Unanswered Question* (1908).

CHORAL *Three Harvest Home Chorales* for chorus, brass, double bass, and organ (1898–1912), *General William Booth Enters into Heaven* for bass, chorus, and orchestra (1914); ten Psalm settings, including *Psalm 90* (1924).

CHAMBER string quartet no. 2 (1907–13); four sonatas for violin and piano (1902–15); *From the Steeples and the Mountains* for brass quintet (1901); *Concord Sonata* (piano sonata no. 2: *Concord, Massachusetts, 1840–1860: Emerson, Hawthorne, The Alcots, Thoreau*; 1909–15).

OTHER organ music; 114 songs (1884–1921).

Ivrogne corrigé, L', The Reformed Drunkard opera by Christoph Willibald von Gluck (libretto by L Anseaume on a fable by La Fontaine), first produced at the Burgtheater, Vienna, Austria, in April 1760. It tells how the drunkard Mathurin is reformed by a chorus of demons in disguise. In the process he allows his niece to marry the man of her choice.

Jachet da Mantova (died 1559) Flemish singer and composer. He was attached to San Pietro Cathedral in Mantua, Italy, 1527–58 and wrote Masses, Magnificats, motets, psalms, hymns, and other pieces.

jack in music, the mechanism in the virginal, harpsichord, and similar instruments by which the strings are plucked. In a piano the jack accommodates the fall of the hammer from the string.

Jackson, Francis (1917–) English organist and composer. He studied at Durham University and with Edward Bairstow, whom he succeeded as organist at York Minster in 1946. He is well known as a recitalist, most often heard performing Vierne and Franck. His own works include a Te Deum and Jubilate (1964), Symphony in D minor for orchestra, and *Sonata giocosa* for organ (1972).

Jackson, William (1730–1803) English organist and composer. He learnt music as a choirboy at Exeter Cathedral, then studied in London. He became music teacher at Exeter and from 1777 held various appointments at the cathedral there.

Works STAGE operas *The Lord of the Manor* (1780) and *The Metamorphosis* (1783); stage piece *Lycidas* (based on Milton, 1767).

CHURCH MUSIC Te Deum, services, anthems and other church music.

OTHER setting of Pope's ode *The Dying Christian*; various vocal pieces and songs; harpsichord sonatas.

Jacob, Gordon (Percival Septimus) (1895–1984) English composer and conductor. An eminent specialist in orchestration, as a composer he was prolific in music always ideally suited to the chosen medium. His works include ballet and film music, two symphonies, three suites, variations and other works for orchestra, concertos for various instruments, and chamber music.

Jacob was born in London. He studied under Charles Stanford and Charles Wood at the Royal College of Music, London, and became profes-

sor of orchestration there in 1926.

Works BALLET *The Jew in the Bush* and *Uncle Remus* (after J C Harris).

ORCHESTRAL variations on an air by Purcell and on an original theme for orchestra, *Passacaglia on a Well-known Theme* ('Oranges and Lemons') for orchestra (1931); two symphonies (1929, 1944), sinfonietta (1942), *Denbigh* suite for strings, Divertimento for small orchestra; concertos for piano, violin, viola, oboe, bassoon, and horn; clarinet concerto (1980).

CHAMBER AND INSTRUMENTAL quartets for oboe and strings, clarinet and strings, and other chamber music; instrumental pieces.

OTHER music for films; suite for military band.

Jacobin, The opera by Antonín Dvořák (libretto by M Cervinková-Riegrová), composed 1887–88 and first produced in Prague, Bohemia (Czech Republic), on 12 February 1889; it was revised in 1897. It tells how Bohuš returns to his father's favour after false accusations by his cousin Adolf.

Jacobsen, Jens Peter (1847–1885) Danish poet and novelist. Musical settings to his work include ➔ *Fennimore und Gerda* (Delius), ➔ *Gurrelieder* (Schoenberg), and *Marie Grubbe* (Ebbe Hamerik).

Jacques, Reginald (1894–1969) English organist and conductor. He studied at Oxford and held various posts there before founding the Bach Choir, London, in 1931, which he conducted until 1960. He founded the Jacques Orchestra in 1936 and gave many wartime concerts. He is well known for performances of the Bach passions with traditional forces and style.

Jacquet, Elizabeth French harpsichordist and composer; see ➔ La Guerre.

Jagd, Die, The Hunt opera by Johann Hiller (libretto by C F Weisse, based on J M Sedaine's libretto for Monsigny's *Le Roi et le fermier*), first produced at Weimar, Germany, on 29 January 1770. It tells how Röschen loves Töffel, but can only marry after her brother, Christal, has married his fiancée, who has been kidnapped by the evil count. She escapes, and the king arrives to bless the two marriages.

Jakobsleiter, Die, Jacob's Ladder oratorio by Arnold Schoenberg, composed 1917–22 but left unfinished. The scoring was completed by Winfried Zillig, and the works was first performed in Vienna, Austria, on 16 June 1961, conducted by Rafael Kubelik.

jaleo Spanish dance in moderate 3/8 time, accompanied by castanets.

Janáček, Leoš (1854–1928) Czech composer. He became director of the Conservatory at Brno in 1919 and professor at the Prague Conservatory in 1920. His music, highly original and influenced by Moravian folk music, includes arrangements of folk songs, operas (*Jenůfa*, (1904), *The Cunning Little Vixen* (1924)), and the choral *Glagolitic Mass* (1926).

Janáček was the son of a poor schoolmaster. He became a choirboy at the monastery of the Austin Friars in Brno and later earned his living as a music teacher and went to the Organ School in Prague to study. He conducted various choral societies, made some desultory studies at Leipzig, Germany, and Vienna, Austria, and in 1881 returned to Brno to found an organ school there. He had meanwhile become involved with Moravian folk music, collecting, harmonizing, and performing folk songs; their influence is heard in his first mature work, the opera *Jenůfa*, begun in 1894 and staged in Brno in 1904. Although it was a success, wider recognition did not come until the its production in Prague in 1916, which was followed by a production in Germany.

The last ten years of Janáček's life saw a great burst of creative activity, with the composition of many new works that are full of exuberance, expressive power, and characteristic jagged rhythms. The opera *The Excursions of Mr Brouček* was premiered in Prague in 1920, and the following year the rhapsody after Gogol, *Taras Bulba*, was given in Brno. Much of his astonishing later music, in particular the opera *Káta Kabanová* (1921) and the second string quartet *Intimate Letters* (1928), was inspired by his unrequited love for Kamila Stösslová, to whom he wrote constant letters during the last decade of his life. Many scenes in his operas, as well as the song cycle *The Diary of a Young Man Who Disappeared* (1921), seem to have an epistolatory basis; they are often brief vignettes in which the characters communicate with one another in a confiding, confessional manner.

He made close studies of folk song and speech, which he applied to his vocal music; speech rhythms were particularly important to Janáček in the portrayal of a character's mood. His vocal music often reflects this, and moves fluently between neutral speech-dominated patterns and moments of intense emotion and expressive power. Although he was not an orthodox religious believer, Janáček's music suggests an articulate pantheism, with a profound sympathy for the human condition and an ecstatic celebration of the natural world and the part of a creator in it.

Works OPERA nine, including *Jenůfa* (1904), *The Excursions of Mr Brouček* (1920), *Káta Kabanová* (1921), *The Cunning Little Vixen* (1924), *The Makropoulos Case* (1926), and *From the House of the Dead* (1930).

CHORAL *Glagolitic Mass* for solo voices, chorus, and orchestra (1926), numerous choral works, including *Rikadla* (1927).

ORCHESTRAL rhapsody *Taras Bulba* (on Gogol, 1918, performed 1921), Sinfonietta for orchestra (1926), concertino for piano and chamber orchestra (1925), *Capriccio* for piano left hand and ensemble (1926).

CHAMBER two string quartets (one on Tolstoy's *Kreutzer Sonata*, 1923, no. 2 *Intimate Letters*, 1928), wind sextet *Mládí/Youth* (1924); *By an Overgrown Path* (for piano, 1901–08); *The Diary of a Young Man who Disappeared* (1921) for voices and piano.

Janequin, Clément (c.1472–c.1560) French composer of chansons and psalms. He was choirmaster of Angers Cathedral 1534–37 and was based in Paris from 1549.

His songs of the 1520s–30s are witty and richly textured in imitative effects, for example 'Le Chant des oiseaux/Birdsong', 'La Chasse/The Hunt', and 'Les Cris de Paris/Street Cries of Paris'.

'La Bataille de Marignan/The Battle of Marignan' (1515) incorporates the sounds of warriors fighting.

Japanische Festmusik, Japanese Festival Music work for orchestra by Richard Strauss, Op. 84, composed for the 2,600th anniversary of the Japanese Empire and first performed in Tokyo, Japan, on 11 December 1940, less than a year before Pearl Harbor. See also ➔ **Sinfonia da Requiem**.

Jaques-Dalcroze, Emile (1865–1950) Swiss composer and teacher. He is remembered for his system of physical training by rhythmical movement to music (➔ **eurhythmics**), and founded the Institut Jaques-Dalcroze in Geneva, Switzerland, in 1915.

He studied with Léo Delibes in Paris, France, with Anton Bruckner and Robert Fuchs in Vienna, Austria, and at the Geneva Conservatory, where in 1892 he became professor of harmony. There he invented his system of teaching music by coordination with bodily movement.

Works STAGE operas *Le Violon maudit* (1893), *Janie* (1894), *Sancho Panza* (after Cervantes, 1897),

Le Bonhomme jadis (1906), *Les Jumeaux de Bergame*, *La Fille au vautour* (after W von Hillern's *Die Geier-Wally*); festival play *La Fête de la jeunesse et de la joie* (1932).

CHORAL *La Veillée*, *Festival vaudois*.

ORCHESTRAL suite for orchestra; two violin concertos (1902, 1911).

CHAMBER three string quartets.

OTHER piano music and songs.

Jarnach, Philipp (1892–1982) German composer of Catalan/French descent. He studied with the composer Ferruccio Busoni and completed his unfinished opera *Doktor Faust* (1925) from the material then available after Busoni's death. Further sketches were completed by Antony Beaumont for performance in 1985. Jarnach's own works, in Italianate neoclassical style, include orchestral and chamber music.

He studied piano with Edouard Risler (1873–1929) and composition with Albert Lavignac in Paris, France. In 1914 he went to Switzerland and taught counterpoint at the Zürich Conservatory 1918–21, he then settled in Berlin, Germany, and continued his studies with Busoni.

Works ORCHESTRAL prelude to *Prometheus*, suite *Winterbilder* (1915), *Prologue to a Tournament*, *Sinfonia brevis*, *Morgenklangspiel* (1925), Prelude No. 1, *Musik mit Mozart* for orchestra (1935).

CHAMBER string quartet and quintet (1916, 1920); violin and piano sonata, two sonatas for unaccompanied violin.

OTHER *Konzertstück* for organ; sonatina and other works for piano; songs with orchestra and with piano.

Järnefelt, (Edvard) Armas (1869–1958) Finnish composer. He is chiefly known for his 'Praeludium' (1907) and the lyrical 'Berceuse' (1909) for small orchestra, from music for the drama *The Promised Land*.

After studying under Martin Wegelius, Ferruccio Busoni, and Jules Massenet in Helsinki, Berlin, and Paris respectively, he conducted at various German theatres and in Helsinki, Finland, 1898–1903. He was appointed conductor of the Opera there in 1903 and was conductor in Stockholm, Sweden, 1907–32. He often conducted works by Sibelius and gave the first Swedish performances of works by Mahler and Schoenberg.

Works incidental music to *The Promised Land*; choral works; orchestral music including *Praeludium* (1907) and *Berceuse* (1909) for small orchestra; songs.

jazz important type of popular music featuring solo virtuosic ➤ **improvisation**. It developed in the southern USA at the turn of the 20th century. Initially music for dancing, often with a vocalist, it had its roots in African-American and other popular music, especially ragtime. Developing from ➤ **blues** and spirituals (religious folk songs) in the southern states, it first came to prominence in the early 20th century in New Orleans, St Louis, and Chicago, with a distinctive flavour in each city.

Typical features found in all types of jazz are the modified rhythms of West Africa; the emphasis on improvisation; western European harmony emphasizing the dominant seventh and the ambiguity between the major and minor third (the so-called 'blue note'); characteristic textures and ➤ **timbres**, first illustrated by a singer and rhythm section (consisting of a piano, bass, drums, and guitar, or a combination of these instruments), and later by the addition of the saxophone and various brass instruments, and later still by the adoption of electrically amplified instruments.

Major figures in the development of jazz include Louis Armstrong and Count Basie in swing music, Duke Ellington and Benny ➤ **Goodman** in big-band jazz, Charlie Parker, Thelonius Monk and Dizzy Gillespie in bebop, Miles Davis in cool jazz, and John Coltrane and Ornette Coleman in free jazz.

Jean de Paris opera by François Boieldieu (libretto by C G de Saint-Just), first produced at the Opéra-Comique, Paris, France, on 4 April 1812. In the story, the king has chosen the princess of Navarre as a bride for the dauphin. Disguised as simple Jean, the dauphin meets her and falls in love.

Jeanne d'Arc au bûcher, Joan of Arc at the Stake dramatic oratorio by Arthur Honegger (libretto by Paul Claudel), first produced in Basel, Switzerland, on 12 May 1938.

Jeffries, George (c.1610–1685) English composer. He was steward to Lord Hatton of Kirby, Northamptonshire, and was also a member of the Chapel Royal, and organist to Charles I at Oxford in 1643 during the English Civil War.

Works SACRED services, anthems, over 120 motets, sacred solos and duets, carols.

SECULAR music for masques and plays; secular songs, duets, and other pieces; fancies for strings and virginals.

Jemnitz, Alexander (1890–1963) Hungarian composer and critic. He studied at the Budapest Conservatory, then with Max Reger in Leipzig and lastly with Arnold Schoenberg in Berlin, Germany, where he also taught. Later he returned to Budapest.

Works the ballet *Divertimento* (1947); Prelude and Fugue, seven *Miniatures* for orchestra (1947); choral music; string quartet, two string trios (1924, 1927), trios for various other instruments, Partita for two violins, three violin and piano sonatas, sonata for viola and cello.

'Jena' Symphony symphony in C major discovered at Jena, Germany, in 1909 and attributed to Beethoven because it bears the inscription 'par L van Beethoven' in an unidentifiable hand; it is now known to be by Friedrich Witt (1771–1837). It was edited by Fritz Stein and first performed by him in Jena on 17 January 1910.

Jenkins, John (1592–1678) English composer, lutenist, and string player. He composed both in the traditional English style and in the new Italian fashion, and wrote a large quantity of music for consorts of viols, which was popular with amateur players.

He lived under the patronage of the gentry and nobility, especially Sir Hamon L'Estrange in Norfolk and Lord North, whose sons, including Roger, he taught music. His last patron was Sir Philip Wodehouse at Kimberley.

Works fancies and consorts for viols and violins with organ anthems and psalms; Elegy on the death of W Lawes, *Theophila, or Love's Sacrifice* (Benlowes), *A Divine Poem* for voices; rounds, songs.

Jenkins, Newell (1915–2000) US conductor and scholar. He studied in Germany, in Dresden, and with Carl Orff in Munich. He made his debut with *Dido and Aeneas* at Freiburg im Breisgau in 1935. He founded the Yale Opera Group in 1940 and conducted the Bologna Chamber Orchestra 1948–53. As music director of the Clarion Music Society, New York, from 1957, he gave performances of Joseph Kraus, Agostino Steffani, Monteverdi, and Pietro Cavalli. He worked as a lecturer at University of California at Irvine 1971–79, and made recordings of operas by Mayr and Rossini, Kraus's Funeral Ode, and Luigi Cherubini's Mass in D Minor.

Jensen, Adolph (1837–1879) German pianist and composer. He studied under various teachers and visited Russia and Copenhagen, Denmark, where he got to know Niels Gade. He was back at Königsberg 1860–66, taught the piano in Berlin for the next two years, and then lived in Dresden, Graz, and elsewhere for his health.

He was the grandson of the organist and composer Wilhelm Jensen (died 1842).

Works OPERA *Die Erbin von Montfort* (1858–65; adapted to a new libretto based on Gozzi's *Turandot* by Kienzl after his death).

CANTATAS *Jephthas Tochter* (1864), *Der Gang der Jünger nach Emmaus* (1865), *Donald Caird* (Scott, 1875), and *Adonisfeier*.

ORCHESTRAL concert overture and *Geistliches Tonstück* for orchestra.

OTHER about 25 Op. nos of piano music and settings of Heyse and Geibel (*Spanisches Liederbuch*) and Herder.

Jenůfa opera by Leoš Janáček (libretto by composer after G Preissova; known in Czech as *Jeji Pastorkyna/Her Foster-daughter*); it was composed 1894–1903 and first produced in Brno (Czech Republic), on 21 January 1904. It was revised 1906–16 and performed in Prague on 26 May 1916 with some reorchestration by the conductor Karel Kovařovic (1862–1920). In the story, Jenůfa is to marry Steva, but she is disfigured by Steva's half-brother Laca, who later wins her love. Her step-mother the Kostelnička hides her while she bears Steva's child. After Steva rejects Jenůfa the Kostelnička drowns the baby, but later must pay the price.

Jephtas Gelübde, **Jephtha's Vow** opera by Giacomo Meyerbeer (libretto by A Schreiber), first produced in Munich, Germany, on 23 December 1812. It was Meyerbeer's first opera.

Jephte oratorio by Giacomo Carissimi; composed by 1650 and published in several modern editions; the work was realized by Hans Werner Henze and first performed in London, England, on 14 July 1976.

Jephté, **Jephtha** opera by Michel de Montéclair (libretto by S J de Pellegrin), first produced at the Paris Opéra, France, on 28 February 1732. After making a vow to the gods, the Israelite general Jephtha must sacrifice his daughter Iphthé for success on the battlefield.

Jephtha oratorio by Handel (libretto by T Morell), first produced at Covent Garden, London, England, on 26 February 1752.

Jérusalem title of the French version of Verdi's opera *I lombardi alla prima crociata*.

Jessonda opera by Ludwig Spohr (libretto by E H Gehe, based on Lemierre's tragedy *La Veuve de Malabar*), first produced in Kassel, Germany, on 28 July 1823. In the story, the Portuguese general Tristan discovers his long-lost love Jessonda is to be killed as a sacrifice, but has sworn not to interfere in local ceremonies. He is free to rescue her, and does so, after the Indians break a ceasefire.

Jesus and the Traders, Hungarian **Jezus es a kufarok** motet by Zoltán Kodály for mixed voices a cappella, composed in 1934.

jeté (French 'thrown') in music, a style of bowing on string instruments. The upper part of the bow is made to fall lightly on the string so that it rebounds several times during the downward motion and repeats notes in a rapid ➤ staccato.

Jeu de cartes, **Card Game** ballet in three deals by Igor Stravinsky; composed in 1936 in Paris,

France, and first produced at the New York Metropolitan Opera House, USA, on 27 April 1937, with choreography by George Balanchine.

Jeune Henri, Le, The Young Henry opera by Étienne Méhul (libretto by J N Bouilly, originally intended for André Grétry and called *La Jeunesse de Henri IV*), first produced at the Opéra-Comique, Paris, France, on 1 May 1797. The overture called *La Chasse du jeune Henri* was known as a concert piece long after the opera was forgotten. The opera describes the worthy deeds of Henry, who kills a wolf and wins a race, magnanimously giving up his prize.

Jeune Sage et le vieux fou, Le, The Wise Youth and the Old Fool opera by Étienne Méhul (libretto by F B Hoffman), first produced at the Opéra-Comique, Paris, France, on 28 March 1793.

Jeux, Games ballet by Claude ➤ **Debussy** (choreography by Vaslav Nijinsky), composed in 1912 and first produced at the Théâtre du Châtelet, Paris, France, on 13 May 1913.

Jeux d'enfants suite for piano duet by Georges Bizet, Op. 22, composed in 1871. The *Petite Suite* for orchestra arranged from five pieces of it (1872) was first performed in Paris, France, on 2 March 1873.

Jewels of the Madonna opera by Ermanno Wolf-Ferrari; see ➤ *gioielli della Madonna, I.*

Jew's harp musical instrument consisting of a two-pronged metal frame inserted between the teeth, and a springlike tongue plucked with the finger. The resulting drone excites resonances in the mouth. Changes in the shape of the mouth cavity will vary the pitch of these resonances to produce a melody.

jig dance popular in the British Isles during the 16th century, which is thought to have developed into the ➤ **gigue**, later commonly used as the last movement of a baroque ➤ **suite**.

Joachim, Joseph (1831–1907) Hungarian-born German violinist, composer, and conductor. He visited England every year from 1862, and in 1877 conducted the first British performance of Brahms's first symphony; he took part in the first performance of the Double Concerto in 1887. He was the dedicatee of Dvořák's concerto, but refused to play it.

He made his first appearance at the age of seven. He studied at the Vienna Conservatory, Austria, and in Leipzig, Germany, where he came under the influence of Mendelssohn and played under him at the Gewandhaus concerts in 1843. In the following year he played Beethoven's violin concerto in London. He was leader of the orchestra at Weimar 1849–53 and at Hanover 1853–68. In

1868 he was appointed director of the Berlin Hochschule für Musik. He founded the Joachim quartet in 1869.

Works overtures for orchestra to Shakespeare's *Hamlet* and *Henry IV*, in commemoration of Kleist and on two comedies by Gozzi; three violin concertos (including 'Hungarian'), variations for violin and orchestra.

Joan of Arc see ➤ *Giovanna d'Arco,* ➤ *Jeanne d'Arc au bûcher,* and ➤ *Maid of Orleans, The.*

Job masque for dancing by Ralph Vaughan Williams (choreography by Ninette de Valois, settings by Gwendolen Raverat, based on Blake's illustrations to the Book of Job), first produced at the Cambridge Theatre, London, England, on 5 July 1931. It is also the title of an oratorio by Hubert Parry (words from the Book of Job), first produced at the Gloucester Festival, England, in 1892.

Jochum, Eugen (1902–1987) German conductor. He studied piano and organ at Augsburg Conservatory 1914–22 and composition at the Munich Academy of Music 1922–24. After some time as a *répétiteur* (tutor) in Munich and Kiel, he conducted at Mannheim and Duisburg, becoming music director of the Hamburg Staatsoper 1934–45. From 1949 he was conductor of the Munich Radio Orchestra. His US debut, with the Concertgebouw Orchestra, was in 1961. He conducted Bartók and Stravinsky during World War II in Hamburg and was well known for Bach and Bruckner.

Johannes de Garlandia scholar and writer on music; see Johannes de ➤ **Garlandia.**

Johnny Strikes Up opera by Ernst Krenek; see ➤ *Jonny spielt auf.*

Johnson, John (c.1540–1595) English lutenist and composer. He was attached to Queen Elizabeth I's court and possibly also to the household of Sir Thomas Kitson at Hengrave Hall, Suffolk, and in London 1572–74. He took part in the Earl of Leicester's entertainments at Kenilworth Castle in 1575. He wrote lute solos and duets.

Johnson, Robert (c.1583–1633) English lutenist and composer, presumed to be a son of John ➤ **Johnson.** He was taught music at the expense of Sir George Carey, husband of Sir Thomas Kitson's granddaughter, in whose household he was brought up, and was appointed lutenist to James I in 1604. He taught Prince Henry and remained in his post under Charles I.

Works songs for several voices; songs to the lute; catches; pieces for viols; also songs in Shakespeare's *The Tempest,* in Fletcher's *Valentinian,* and *The Mad Lover.*

Johnson, Robert (c.1500–1554) Scottish priest and composer. He fled to England as a heretic and settled in Windsor, where he may have been chaplain to Anne Boleyn. He wrote Latin motets, English services and prayers, In nomines for instruments, and songs.

Johnson, Robert Sherlaw (1932–2000) English composer and pianist. He studied at Durham University, the Royal Academy of Music in London, and in Paris, France. He taught at Leeds and York universities and, from 1970, Oxford. He was elected Fellow of the Royal Academy of Music in 1984. His works include *Where the Wild Things Are* for soprano and tape (1974) and a piano concerto (1983).

Works OPERA *The Lambton Worm* (produced Oxford, 1978).

VOICES AND INSTRUMENTS *Carmen Vernalia* for soprano and chamber orchestra (1972), *Where the Wild Things Are* for soprano and tape (1974), *Festival Mass of the Resurrection* for chorus and orchestra (1974), *Anglorum Feriae* for soprano, tenor, chorus, and orchestra (1977); *Veritas veritatis* for six voices (1980); piano concerto (1983), three piano sonatas, two string quartets (1966, 1969).

Joio, Norman dello US composer; see ➤ **Dello Joio.**

Jolas, Betsy (1926–   ) French composer. Most of her compositions are for small groups of instruments or voices, and she has experimented with substituting voices for instruments, as in *Quatuor II* (1964).

She studied at Bennington College, New York, USA, 1940–46, and at the Paris Conservatory with Darius Milhaud and Olivier Messiaen. She also taught at the Conservatory from 1974 and has taught widely in the USA.

Works OPERA *Le Pavillon au bord de la rivière* (1975), *Le Cyclope* (1986), *Schliemann* (1989).

ORCHESTRAL *Musique d'hiver* for organ and small orchestra (1971), *Trois Rencontres* for string trio and orchestra (1973), *Stances* for piano and orchestra (1978).

CHAMBER *D'un opéra de voyage* (1967), *États* (1969), *How Now* (1973), and *Préludes-Fanfares-Interludes-Sonneries* (1983) for ensemble; two string quartets (1973, 1989), string trio (1990).

OTHER keyboard music and songs.

Jolie Fille de Perth, La, The Fair Maid of Perth opera by Georges Bizet (libretto by J H V de Saint-Georges and J Adenis, based on Walter Scott's novel), first produced at the Théâtre Lyrique, Paris, France, on 26 December 1867. It tells how Catherine and Smith are united, despite competition from the Duke of Rothsay and a case of mistaken identity.

Jolivet, André (1905–1974) French composer. He was interested in primitive forms of religion, magic, and mysticism, and believed that music is a cosmic force endowed with magical properties. His music is intended to convey such magical qualities; it employs a wide range of rhythmic and dynamic effects to produce an appropriately receptive mood in the listener. His work includes symphonic works, ballets, and chamber pieces, as well as music for films and plays.

He was a pupil of Paul Le Flem and Edgard Varèse, and formed the group 'La Jeune France' with Yves Baudrier, Jean Yves Daniel-Lesur, and Olivier Messiaen in 1936. He became director of music at the Comédie Française, Paris, in 1945.

Works STAGE opera *Dolorès* (1947); two ballets.

ORATORIO *La Vérité de Jeanne* (1956).

ORCHESTRAL three symphonies (1953, 1959, 1964); concertos for trumpet (2), flute, piano, harp, bassoon, and ondes Martenot.

CHAMBER string quartet; sonata and suite *Mana* for piano.

OTHER songs.

Jommelli, Niccolò (1714–1774) Italian composer. During his lifetime he was famous as an opera composer throughout Italy and in Vienna, Austria, writing over 50 *opere serie* (treating classical subjects in a formal style) and more than 20 comic operas. He also wrote sacred cantatas, oratorios, and Masses.

He studied with Francesco Durante, Francesco Feo, and Leonardo Leo in Naples, made his debut as an opera composer there in 1737, and soon achieved widespread fame. He was Kapellmeister to the Duke of Württemberg at Stuttgart 1753–69. He then returned to Naples, but was unable to recapture his old success in Italy; he had developed the dry conventions of the Metastasian *opera seria*, but the Neapolitans were turning their attentions to comic opera.

Works OPERA *Ricimero* (1740), *Ezio* (three settings: 1741, 1748, 1758), *Semiramide* (1741), *Sofonisba* (1746), *Artaserse* (1749), *Ifigenia in Aulide* (1751), *Talestri, Attilio Regolo* (1753), *Fetonte, La clemenza di Tito* (two settings: 1753, 1765), *Pelope, Il matrimonio per concorso, La schiava liberata, Armida* (1770), *Ifigenia in Tauride* (1771).

CHORAL oratorios *Isacco, Betulia liberata* (1743), *Santa Elena al Calvario,* and others; cantatas.

CHURCH MUSIC Passion oratorio, *Miserere,* Masses and other church music.

OTHER symphonies and other instrumental music.

Jones, Daniel (Jenkyn) (1912–1993) Welsh composer. He began composing at a very early age and later produced a large quantity of music, including twelve symphonies, eight string quartets, and five string trios.

He studied at University College, Swansea,

where he read English, and later at the Royal Academy of Music in London. He studied conducting with Sir Henry Wood and composition with Harry Farjeon. He was awarded an OBE in 1968.

Works STAGE operas *The Knife* (1963) and *Orestes* (1967); incidental music for *Under Milk Wood* (Dylan Thomas).

ORCHESTRAL twelve symphonies (1944–90); symphonic poems *Cystuddiau Branwen, Cloud Messenger*; concertino for piano and orchestra.

CHAMBER eight string quartets, string quintet, five string trios, violin sonata, cello sonata, piano sonata, sonata for kettledrums, wind septet, wind nonet.

Jones, John (1728–1796) English organist and composer. He was appointed organist of the Middle Temple in 1749; in 1753 became organist of Charterhouse, succeeding Johann Pepusch; and was appointed organist of St Paul's Cathedral, London, in 1755. He wrote chants, harpsichord lessons, and other pieces.

Jones, Robert (c.1485–c.1536) English composer. He was a Gentleman of the Chapel Royal from 1513. He composed a song, 'Who Shall Have My Fair Lady', a Mass, *Spes nostra*, and a Magnificat.

Jones, Robert (c.1570–c.1617) English lutenist and composer. He worked for several patrons and took a degree in music at Oxford University in 1597. In 1610, with Philip Rosseter and others, he obtained a patent to train children for the Queen's revels, and in 1615 they were allowed to erect a theatre in Blackfriars, London, but its opening was subsequently prohibited.

Works madrigals, five books of *Songs and Ayres* to the lute, anthems.

Jongen, Joseph (1873–1953) Belgian composer. He taught at the conservatories of Liège and Brussels. Most of his compositions are orchestral or chamber pieces.

He studied at the Liège Conservatory. He was awarded a prize from the Académie Royale in 1893 and the Belgian Prix de Rome in 1897. After teaching for a short time at the Liège Conservatory, he went to Rome, Italy, and later travelled in Germany and France, taking up a professorship at Liège in 1903. In 1914–18 he was in England as a war refugee, but returned to Liège until 1920, when he became professor at the Brussels Conservatory, of which he was later appointed director.

Works BALLET *S'Arka*.

ORCHESTRAL *Fantaisie sur deux Noëls wallons* (1902), symphonic poem *Lalla Rookh* (after Thomas Moore, 1904), symphony (1910), *Impressions d'Ardennes* (1913), *Tableaux pittoresques* (1917), *Symphonie concertante* for organ

and orchestra (1926), *Passecaille et Gigue* for orchestra (1930), *Pièce symphonique* for piano and wind orchestra, violin concerto, harp concerto (1944), suite for viola and orchestra.

CHAMBER three string quartets (1894, 1916, 1921), concerto for wind quintet (1923), two serenades for string quartet, piano trio, two violin sonatas, cello sonata.

OTHER *Sonata eroica* for organ; songs.

Jongleur de Notre Dame, Le, Our Lady's Juggler opera by Jules Massenet (libretto by M Léna on a story by Anatole France in *L'Etui de nacre*, based on a medieval miracle play), first produced in Monte Carlo, Monaco, on 18 February 1902. It tells the story of the juggler Jean who, having given up street performances, enters a monastery. As a tribute, he performs before a statue of the Virgin, and expires amidst a sacred halo.

Jonny spielt auf, Johnny Strikes Up opera by Ernst Krenek (libretto by the composer), first produced in Leipzig, Germany, on 10 February 1927, and given its US premiere at the New York Metropolitan Opera House in 1929. It was the first opera to incorporate jazz music; Johnny is a black jazz musician.

Jonson, Ben(jamin) (1573–1637) English poet and dramatist. Musical settings of his works have been made by Handel (*The* ➤ **Alchemist**), Antonio Salieri (➤ **Angiolina, ossia Il matrimonio per susurro**), George ➤ **Auric** (*Volpone*), Alfonso ➤ **Ferrabosco** (masques), Henry Harington ('Drink to Me Only'), Nicholas ➤ **Lanier** (*Lovers made Men* and *Vision of Delight*), Mark ➤ **Lothar** (*Lord Spleen*), Arthur Bliss (➤ **Pastoral**), Richard Strauss (*Die* ➤ **Schweigsame Frau**), Edward Elgar (➤ **Spanish Lady**), and Ralph ➤ **Vaughan Williams** (*Pan's Anniversary*).

Joplin, Scott (1868–1917) US composer and pianist. He first came to attention as a pianist at brothels in St Louis and Chicago. He achieved fame with *Maple Leaf Rag* in 1899, and was considered the leading exponent of 'classic rag', in which the standard syncopated rhythm was treated with some sophistication. He published *The Entertainer* in 1902 and formed the Scott Joplin Opera Company in 1903, for the performance of his opera *A Guest of Honour* (music lost). *Treemonisha*, an opera about a black baby girl found under a tree by a woman called Monisha, was completed in 1911 and performed in concert in 1915.

Joplin's last years were ruined by syphilis. His posthumous fame was initiated with a revival of *Treemonisha* at Atlanta in 1972 and continued in 1974, when *The Entertainer* was one of the best-selling discs. Joplin was awarded a posthumous Pulitzer Prize in 1976.

Joseph opera by Étienne Méhul (libretto by A Duval), first produced at the Opéra-Comique, Paris, France, on 17 February 1807. Carl Maria von Weber wrote piano variations, Op. 28, on a romance from it. The opera recounts how Joseph, sold into slavery by his brothers, is successful in Egypt. He later meets them and tests their remorse.

Joseph and his Brethren oratorio by Handel (libretto by J Miller), first performed at Covent Garden, London, England, on 2 March 1744. It tells how the blind Jacob is reunited with his long-lost son.

Josephs, Wilfred (1927–1997) English composer. As well as film and television music, he wrote ten symphonies, concertos, and chamber music. His works include the *Jewish Requiem* (1969) and the opera *Rebecca* (1983).

He studied at the Guildhall School of Music and in Paris, France. His *Requiem* of 1963 won first prize in a competition at La Scala, Milan, Italy.

Works STAGE opera *Rebecca* (after Hollywood rather than du Maurier; produced Leeds, 1983); dramatic works for children and for TV; ballets *The Magic Being* (1961), *La Répétition de Phèdre* (1965), *Equus* (1978), and *Cyrano de Bergerac* (1985).

ORCHESTRAL ten symphonies (1955–85); two piano concertos, violin concerto, clarinet concerto (1975), concerto for viola and chamber orchestra (1983).

VOCAL *Mortales* for soloists, chorus, and orchestra (texts by Blake, Shelley, Nashe, and Luther; first performance Cincinnati, 1970).

CHAMBER four string quartets (1954–81), octet (1964), two violin sonatas, piano trio (1974).

Josephslegende ballet in one act by Richard Strauss (scenario by H Kessler and Hugo von Hofmannsthal); it was composed 1912–14 and first produced by Diaghilev's Ballets Russes at the Paris Opéra, France, on 14 February 1914.

Joshua oratorio by Handel (libretto by T Morell), first performed at Covent Garden, London, England, on 23 March 1748.

Josquin Des Prez or **Josquin des Prés (c.1440–1521)** Franco-Flemish composer. His combination of Flemish counterpoint and Italian harmony, learnt while in the service of the Rome papal chapel in 1484–1503, marks a peak in Renaissance vocal music. In addition to Masses on secular as well as sacred themes, including *Missa 'L'Homme armé'*/Mass on 'The Armed Man' (1504), he also wrote secular chansons such as 'El grillo'/'The Cricket' using vocal effects that imitate each other.

Josten, Werner (1885–1963) German-born US composer and conductor. He studied in Munich, Germany, Geneva, Switzerland (with Émile Jaques-Dalcroze), and Paris, France. In 1918 he became assistant conductor at the Munich Opera, but in 1920 emigrated to the USA. He was appointed professor at Smith College, Northampton, Massachusetts, in 1923. He conducted the first US performance of *L'incoronazione di Poppea* (1926), and led *Orfeo* (1929) and the US premieres of Handel's *Giulio Cesare* (1927), *Rodelinda* (1931), and *Serse* (1928). In 1938 he gave the first modern revival of Johann Fux's *Costanza e fortezza* (1723).

Works BALLET *Batouala* (1931), *Endymion* (1933), *Joseph and his Brethren* (1936).

VOICES, CHORUS, AND ORCHESTRA *Crucifixion* for bass solo and chorus, *Hymnus to the Quene of Paradys* for contralto solo, women's chorus, strings, and organ, *Ode for St Cecilia's Day* for solo voices, chorus, and orchestra (1925).

ORCHESTRAL symphony in F major, serenade, symphonic movement *Jungle* (on Henri Rousseau's picture *Forêt exotique*, 1929) for orchestra; symphony and two *Concerti sacri* for strings and piano.

jota Spanish dance, especially of Aragon and Navarre. It dates from the 12th century and is said to derive its name from the Moor Aben Jot. It is in quick 3/4 time. The music is played on instruments of the guitar type and often accompanied by castanets and other percussion.

Joubert, John (1927–　) South African composer. He studied at Cape Town University and the Royal Academy of Music in London. He was a lecturer at Hull University 1950–62, and at Birmingham University 1962–86.

Works OPERA *Antigone* (1954), *In the Drought* (1956), *Silas Marner* (1961), *Under Western Eyes* (1968).

CHORAL cantatas *The Leaves of Life* and *Urbs beata*; three motets; other choral works.

ORCHESTRAL symphonic prelude, two symphonies (1956, 1971), *In Memoriam, 1820* for orchestra; violin concerto (1954), piano concerto.

CHAMBER two string quartets (1950, 1977) and other chamber music.

OTHER songs.

Jour de fête collective work for string quartet, comprising: 1. *Les Chanteurs de Noël* (Aleksandr Glazunov); 2. *Glorification* (Anatol Liadov); and 3. *Chœur dansé russe* (Nikolai Rimsky-Korsakov).

Jubel-Ouvertüre, **Jubilee Overture** concert overture by Carl Maria von Weber, Op. 59, composed in 1818 as a companion piece to the *Jubel-Cantate* for the 50th anniversary of the accession of the king of Saxony, Frederick Augustus, and performed in Dresden, Saxony (Germany), on 20 September that year. It concludes with the tune of 'God save the King'.

Judas Maccabaeus oratorio by Handel (libretto by T Morell), composed 9 July–11 August 1746 and first produced at Covent Garden, London, England, on 1 April 1747.

Judgment of Paris, The masque by William Congreve, for the composition of which a prize was advertised in the *London Gazette* in 1700. The first four prizes were won by John Weldon, John Eccles, Daniel Purcell, and Gottfried Finger in 1701. Eccles's setting was first produced at the Dorset Gardens Theatre, London, on 21 March; Finger's setting was produced on 27 March. The libretto was later set by Giovanni-Battista Sammartini and produced at Cliveden, Buckinghamshire, on 1 August 1740, and by Thomas Arne, produced at Drury Lane, London, on 12 March 1742.

Judith opera by Natanael Berg (1879–1957) (libretto in Swedish, by the composer, based on Friedrich Hebbel's drama), first produced in Stockholm, Sweden, on 22 February 1936. It is a tale of biblical blood-letting, as Holofernes is decapitated. Oratorios with the same title were written by Thomas Arne (libretto by Isaac Bickerstaffe), first performed at the Drury Lane Theatre, London, England, on 27 February 1761; and by Hubert Parry (libretto from the Bible), performed at the Birmingham Festival, England, in 1888. The play with music by Arthur Honegger (libretto by R Morax) was first produced at the open-air Théâtre du Jorat, Mézières, France, on 13 June 1925; the operatic version was performed in Monte Carlo, Monaco, on 13 February 1926.

Juditha triumphans devicta Holofernes barbarie oratorio by Antonio Vivaldi (text by J Cassetti), first performed in Venice, Italy, in 1716. It is sometimes given in modern revivals as a stage work, as at Camden Festival, London, England, in 1984.

Juha opera in three acts by Aarre Merikanto (libretto by Aino Ackté), composed 1920–22 and first produced at the Music College, Lahti, Finland, on 28 October 1963. It tells how Juha drowns himself when the truth of his wife's infidelity is revealed.

Juif polonais, Le, **The Polish Jew** opera by Camille Erlanger (libretto by H Cain and P B Gheusi, based on Erckmann-Chatrian's novel), first produced at the Opéra-Comique, Paris, France, on 11 April 1900. The subject is that of the play *The Bells*, in which the actor Henry Irving had his greatest popular success.

Juilliard School music school and college founded in New York, USA, in 1924, financed by the will of Augustus D Juilliard, a cotton merchant. One of the world's leading conservatories, it moved in 1969 to its current location, the newly built Lincoln Center. The Juilliard Quartet was founded in 1946 by the school's president William Schumann, and became famous initially for its interpretation of Bartók's works.

Juive, La, **The Jewess** opera by Jacques Halévy (libretto by Augustin Scribe), first produced at the Paris Opéra, France, on 23 February 1835. Prince Leopold, posing as a Jew, woos Rachel, the apparent daughter of the Jewish goldsmith Eléazar. When Rachel discovers the deception, and that Leopold is married, she denounces him. All three face trial for inter-racial love, and Rachel and Eléazar are executed.

Julie opera by Nicolas Dezède (libretto by J M B de Monvel), first produced at the Comédie-Italienne, Paris, France, on 28 September 1772. Mozart wrote piano variations (K264) on the air 'Lison dormait' in 1778.

Julien, ou La Vie du poète, **Julian, or The Poet's Life** opera by Gustave Charpentier, a sequel to *Louise* (libretto by the composer). It was first produced at the Opéra-Comique, Paris, France, on 4 June 1913. It recounts Julien's artistic fantasies and peregrinations.

Julietta, or The Key to Dreams lyric opera by Bohuslav Martinů (libretto by the composer, after the play by G Neveux), composed 1936–37 and first produced at the National Theatre, Prague, Czechoslovakia (now the Czech Republic), on 16 March 1938. It tells how Michel and Julietta meet and part in a disturbing dream world where reality and fantasy mingle.

Julius Caesar operas by Gian Francesco Malipiero and Handel; see ➔ *Giulio Cesare* and ➔ *Giulio Cesare in Egitto*.

Junge Lord, Der, **The Young Lord** opera by Hans Werner Henze (libretto by Ingeborg Bachmann, after Wilhelm Hauff), first produced at the Deutsche Oper, Berlin, Germany, on 7 April 1965. It describes how Milord Edgar, a monkey in disguise, makes a fool of the German townspeople.

Junge Magd, Die, **The Young Girl** six songs for alto, flute, clarinet, and string quartet by Paul Hindemith (texts by Georg Trakl); they were first performed in Donaueschingen, Germany, on 31 July 1922.

Jungfernquartette (German 'maiden quartets') nickname for Haydn's six string quartets, Op. 33, also known as the 'Russian quartets' and more generally as 'Gli scherzi'.

Jungfrun i Tornet, **The Maiden in the Tower** opera in one act by Jean Sibelius (libretto by Hertzberg), composed in 1896 for Robert Kajanus's Helsinki Orchestra and orchestra school, and first performed on 7 November 1896. It tells the story of an imprisoned maiden who is released to join her lover.

Juon, Paul (1872–1940) Russian composer. He studied with Sergey Taneiev and Anton Arensky in Moscow and with Woldemar Bargiel in Berlin, Germany, where he settled and was later appointed professor at the Hochschule für Musik by Joseph Joachim.

Works BALLET *Psyche*.

ORCHESTRAL symphony in A, serenade, three violin concertos (1909, 1913, 1931), *Episodes concertantes* for violin, cello, piano, and orchestra, five pieces for string orchestra.

CHAMBER chamber symphony, three string quartets (1898, 1904, 1920), sextet for piano and strings, two piano quintets (1906, 1909), two piano quartets (1908, 1912), piano trios (1901, 1915), Divertimento for wind and piano, ditto for clarinet and two violas; instrumental pieces; *Satyrs and Nymphs*, *Preludes*, and *Capriccios* for piano.

'Jupiter' Symphony nickname (not the composer's own) given to Mozart's last symphony, K551, in C major, finished on 10 August 1788.

justiniana a type of 16th-century ➤ villanella for three voices, the words of which satirized the Venetian patricians. There is no connection between this and the *villanella* set to poetry of the type originated by Leonardo Giustinian.

just intonation in music, singing or instrumental playing in what is said to be the pure natural scale, not that artificially fixed on keyboard instruments by ➤ **equal temperament**.

Kabale und Liebe opera by Gottfried von Einem (libretto by the composer after Schiller's tragedy, 1784), first performed at the Staatsoper, Vienna, Austria, on 17 December 1976.

Kabalevsky, Dmitri Borisovich (1904–1987) Russian composer and pianist. While he was known in the West for his keyboard and instrumental works, his reputation in the USSR was based upon vocal works, including the opera *The Taras Family* (1947). Kabalevsky's work mirrored the Soviet authorities' policy of 'socialist realism' in his transparent neoclassical style.

As a result, his work is more immediately accessible than that of his contemporaries Prokofiev and Shostakovich, who were frequently criticized by the government. He helped guide the official course of music in the USSR after World War II.

He was born in St Petersburg, and entered the Skriabin School of Music in Moscow when his family settled there in 1918. He studied piano and became a composition pupil first of Sergey Vasilenko and Georgy Catoire, afterwards of Nikolai Myaskovsky. He later became professor of composition there.

Works STAGE operas *The Golden Spikes*, *Colas Breugnon* (after Romain Rolland's 1938 novel), *Before Moscow* (1943), and *Nikita Vershinin* (1955); incidental music for Shakespeare's *Measure for Measure*, Sheridan's *The School for Scandal*, and an adaptation of Flaubert's *Madame Bovary*.

FILM MUSIC *Poem of Struggle*, *Our Great Fatherland*, and *People's Avengers* for chorus and orchestra.

ORCHESTRAL four symphonies (no. 3 *Requiem for Lenin*); three piano concertos (1931–53), violin concerto, two cello concertos.

CHAMBER two string quartets (1928, 1945); three sonatas, two sonatinas, and other piano music.

OTHER Requiem; songs.

Kabeláč, Miloslav (1908–1979) Czech composer. He studied composition at the Prague Conservatory 1928–31 with Karel Jirák and later also the piano at the Master School. In 1932 he

joined the staff of Czech Radio.

Works eight symphonies (1941–70); cantatas *Mystery of Time*, *Do Not Retreat*; two overtures; wind sextet; suite for saxophone and piano; violin and piano pieces; choral music.

Kabuki Japanese theatrical form popular since the Edo period (1603–1868) and the source of many musical genres. There are two main kinds of Kabuki play: *jidaimono* or pseudo-historical pieces and *sewamono* or stories dealing with the cultural life of the Edo period. There are also modern plays. Musical instruments are played onstage (accompanying dance or providing narrative comment) or offstage (programmatic music) and Kabuki music uses percussion, flutes, shamisen (long-necked lutes), and vocals.

Kadosa, Pál (1903–1983) Hungarian composer and pianist. He studied with Zoltán Kodály at the Budapest Academy and taught piano at Fodor Conservatory 1927–43. He was professor at the Budapest Academy from 1945. His compositions are influenced by Béla Bartók.

Works OPERA *The Adventure of Huszt* (1951).

CANTATAS five cantatas (1939–50).

ORCHESTRAL eight symphonies (1941–68); four piano concertos (1931–66); two violin concertos (1931, 1941).

CHAMBER concerto for string quartet and chamber orchestra (1936); three string quartets (1934–57); two string trios (1930, 1955); two piano sonatas (1926–60).

Kagel, Mauricio (1931–) Argentine composer of advanced tendencies. He studied in Buenos Aires, and settled in Cologne, Germany, in 1957. He has evolved a very complex style, employing serial and aleatory techniques, permutations of different languages, light effects, and aural distortions.

Works STAGE *Sur scène*, theatrical piece in one act for speaker, mime, singer, and three instruments (1962); *The Women*, dramatic scene for three female voices, three actresses, a dancer, chorus of women, and electronic tapes; *Staatstheater*, 'ballet for nondancers', with instruments including chamber pot (1971); opera, *Die Erschöpfung der*

Welt (produced Stuttgart, 8 February 1980); ballet *Dance School* (1988).

VOICES, CHORUS, AND INSTRUMENTS *Anagrama* for four soloists, speaking chorus, and chamber ensemble (1958); *Match* for three players; *Diaphony* for chorus, orchestra, and two projectors (1964); *Transición I* for electronic sounds; *Transición II* for piano, percussion, and two tapes; *Hetrophonie* for an orchestra of solo instruments; string sextet; *Ludwig Van*, film score (1970); *Sankt–Bach–Passion* (1985); piano trio (1985); *A Letter* for mezzo and orchestra (1986); *Quodlibet* for women's voices and orchestra (1988); third string quartet (1988); *Fragende Ode* (1989).

Kaiser Quartett composition for string quartet by Haydn, better known as the ➤ *'Emperor' Quartet*.

Kajanus, Robert (1856–1933) Finnish conductor and composer. He studied at the Helsinki and Leipzig conservatories, and also studied composition with Johan Svendsen in Paris, France. He founded the orchestra of the Helsinki Philharmonic Society in 1882, with which later he paid several important visits to foreign countries, giving many early performances of works by Sibelius. He was director of music at Helsinki University 1897–1926.

Works symphony *Aino* (on an incident from the *Kalevala*), and other pieces.

Kalabis, Viktor (1923–) Czech composer. He studied at the Prague Academy and Charles University. He was manager of the music department at Prague Radio 1953–72.

Works ORCHESTRAL five symphonies (1956, 1961, 1971, 1972, 1976); concerto for orchestra (1966), and nine instrumental concertos.

CHAMBER two nonets, two wind quintets, seven string quartets; sonatas for violin, cello, clarinet, and trombone (1967–82); *Incantations* for 13 wind instruments (1988).

OTHER ballet on *Alice in Wonderland*, *Two Worlds* (1980).

Kalcher, Johann Nepomuk (1764–1827) German organist and composer. He studied at Munich, where he became court organist in 1798. Carl Maria von Weber was one of his pupils. He wrote Masses, symphonies, organ music, and songs.

Kalinnikov, Vassily Sergeyevich (1866–1901) Russian composer. He was educated at a seminary, where he conducted the choir. In 1884 he went to Moscow and, in spite of great poverty, obtained a musical education at the Philharmonic Society Music School. After conducting Italian opera for the 1893–94 season, he was found to suffer from tuberculosis and from that time lived mainly in the Crimea, devoted to composition.

Works incidental music to Alexey Tolstoy's *Tsar Boris* (1899); cantatas *St John Chrysostom* and *Russalka*; two symphonies, suite, two Intermezzi and two sketches for orchestra; string quartets; piano pieces; songs.

Kalkbrenner, Friedrich (Wilhelm Michael) (1785–1849) German pianist, teacher, and composer. He studied under his father, Christian Kalkbrenner (1755–1806), and at the Paris Conservatory, France. He made his first public appearance in Vienna, Austria, in 1803, returning to Paris in 1806. He lived in London, England, as a teacher and performer 1814–23 and then settled in Paris as a member of the piano firm of Pleyel, but continued to teach and perform.

Works PIANO four piano concertos (1823–35), concerto for two pianos; piano septet, sextet and quintet; piano school with studies appended, sonatas, variations and numerous other works for piano.

Kalliwoda, Johan Vaclav (1801–1866) Czech violinist and composer. He studied at the Prague Conservatory 1811–17 and played in the orchestra 1817–22. He then became music director to Prince Fürstenberg at Donaueschingen, Germany, until his retirement in 1866.

Works the opera *Blanka*; seven symphonies (1826–43); concertinos for violin, for clarinet, and other instruments; three string quartets; violin duets, violin pieces.

Kálmán, Imre (1882–1953) Hungarian composer. He had great success with the operetta *Tatárjárás* (1908; produced in New York and elsewhere as *The Gay Hussars*).

He studied in Budapest, then lived in Vienna, Austria, until 1938. He moved to Paris, France, in 1939, and in 1940 emigrated to the USA, where he lived in New York and Hollywood.

Works OPERA operettas *Der gute Kamerad* (1911), *Der Zigeunerprimas* (1912), *Die Csárdásfürstin* (1915), *Die Faschingsfee* (1917), *Gräfin Mariza* (1924), *Die Zirkusprinzessin* (1924), and *Der Teufelsreiter*.

Kalomiris, Manolis (1883–1962) Greek composer. He studied in Athens, Constantinople, and Vienna. He taught at Kharkov, Ukraine, 1906–10 and then settled in Athens as professor at the Conservatory. From 1919 he was director of the Hellenic Conservatory there until 1926, when he founded the National Conservatory and became its director.

Works OPERA *The Master Builder* (after N Kazantzakis, 1915), *The Mother's Ring* (after J Kambyssis, 1917), *Anatoli*, and *The Haunted Waters* (after Yeats, 1950–52).

OTHER incidental music; two symphonies, symphonic poems for orchestra; chamber music; piano works; songs.

Kamarinskaya fantasy for orchestra on two Russian themes by Mikhail Glinka, composed in 1848 and known only in an edition revised by Nikolai Rimsky-Korsakov and Aleksandr Glazunov.

Kamieński, Maciej (1734–1821) Hungarian-Polish composer. He studied in Vienna, Austria, and settled in Warsaw, Poland, in about 1760. He produced the first Polish opera there on 11 May 1778.

Works OPERA *Happiness in Unhappiness* and five others in Polish and two in German.

OTHER church music, cantata for the unveiling of the Jan III Sobieski monument.

Kammermusik German term for ➤ **chamber music.**

Kammermusik, Chamber Music seven works by Paul ➤ **Hindemith** composed 1922–27. The first, for small orchestra, was first performed in Donaueschingen, Germany, on 31 July 1922, conducted by Hermann Scherchen. It uses an unusual combination of instruments (including accordion). The subsequent six works all have a solo instrument, and are essentially small-scale concertos.

The remaining *Kammermusik* are: no. 2 for piano and twelve instruments, first performed in Frankfurt, Germany, on 31 October 1924, conducted by Clemens Krauss; no. 3 for cello and ten instruments, first performed in Bochum, Germany, on 30 April 1925, conducted by Hindemith; no. 4 for violin and chamber orchestra, first performed in Dessau, Germany, on 25 September 1925; no. 5 for viola and chamber orchestra, first performed in Berlin, Germany, on 3 November 1927, conducted by Otto Klemperer; no. 6 for ➤ **viola d'amore** and chamber orchestra, first performed in Cologne, Germany, on 29 March 1928; and no. 7 for organ and chamber orchestra, first performed in Frankfurt on 8 January 1928. Usually included with the set is an additional piece, *Kleine Kammermusik*, which was published alongside *Kammermusik No. 1*, and is for four wind instruments and percussion.

Kammerton (German 'chamber-pitch') pitch to which orchestral instruments in Germany were tuned in the 17th–18th centuries. It was lower, by a whole tone or more, than the *Chorton* (choir-pitch) used for church organs, and it was for this reason that Johann Sebastian Bach, in his Leipzig cantatas, transposed the organ parts down a tone in order to make them agree with the orchestra. The transposition applied only to the organ parts; the orchestral parts could be used as they stood.

kapellmeister (German 'chapel master') chief conductor and chorus master, in effect director of music; also resident composer for a private chapel, responsible for musical administration.

Kapellmeistermusik (German 'conductor's music') contemptuous term for a musical work which betrays creative weakness and has no merit but that of a knowledge of rules and glib craftsmanship.

Karajan, Herbert von (1908–1989) Austrian conductor. He dominated European classical music performance after 1947. He was principal conductor of the Berlin Philharmonic Orchestra 1955–89, and artistic director of the Vienna State Opera 1957–64 and of the Salzburg Festival 1956–60. A perfectionist, he cultivated an orchestral sound of notable smoothness and transparency; he also staged operas and directed his own video recordings. He recorded the complete Beethoven symphonies four times, and had a special affinity with Mozart and Bruckner, although his repertoire extended from Bach to Schoenberg.

Karel, Rudolf (1880–1945) Czech composer. He studied composition under Antonín Dvořák at the Prague Conservatory. In 1914, on holiday in Russia, he was interned as an Austrian subject, then taught at Taganrog and Rostov-on-Don, fled to Siberia, and eventually escaped to Czechoslovakia, where he became professor at the Prague Conservatory. He died tragically in a concentration camp.

Works STAGE operas *Ilsa's Heart* (1909) and *Godmother's Death* (1932); incidental music to Knud Hamsun's *The Game of Life*.

VOICES AND ORCHESTRAL *Awakening*, symphony for solo voices, chorus, and orchestra; two symphonies, *Renaissance* and *Spring*; symphonic poems *The Ideals* and *Demon*; suite, fantasy, Slavonic dances for orchestra; violin concerto.

CHAMBER three string quartets (1902–36).

Karelia incidental music in nine movements by Jean Sibelius, composed in 1893 and first performed in Viipuri, Karelia (Gulf of Finland), on 13 November 1893. The suite for orchestra in three movements, Op. 11, was also composed in 1893.

Karetnikov, Nikolai (1930–1994) Russian composer. From the time of his fourth symphony (1963), he was obliged to compose and publish in secrecy, owing to his political dissent. His opera *Til'Ulenshpigel* was written and recorded over five years with the cooperation of friends; it was dubbed the first *samizdat* (underground) opera and was premiered in Bielefeld, Germany, in 1993.

He studied with Vissarion Shebalin at the Moscow Conservatory.

Works *The Mystery of Apostle Paul*, opera oratorio (1972–87), chamber suite *From Shalom-*

Aleham (1986), quintet for piano and strings (1990), and *Six Spiritual Songs* (1992).

Karg-Elert, Sigfrid (1877–1933) German composer. After studying at Leipzig he devoted himself to the European harmonium. His numerous concert pieces and graded studies, including *66 Choral Improvisations* (1908–10), exploit a range of impressionistic effects such as the 'endless chord'.

He became professor at the conservatories of Magdeburg and Leipzig. He was a brilliant pianist, but was persuaded by the Norwegian composer Edvard Grieg to devote himself to composition.

Works ORCHESTRAL a symphony, two piano concertos (1901, 1913).

CHAMBER string quartet; violin and piano sonatas; sonata and other works for piano.

HARMONIUM AND ORGAN pieces for harmonium and many organ works, including *66 Chorale Improvisations* (1908–10), 24 preludes and postludes, Sonatina, passacaglia, fantasy and fugue in D major, *Chaconne, Fugue-Trilogy and Chorale*, ten characteristic pieces, three symphonic chorales, seven *Pastels from Lake Constance* (1919), six *Cathedral Windows* (1923), 54 variation-studies *Homage to Handel*.

OTHER over 100 songs.

Karłowicz, Mieczysław (1876–1909) Polish composer. The son of a noble family, he travelled much in Europe as a child and learnt the violin in Prague, Dresden, and Heidelberg, and soon played chamber music with his parents, a cellist and a pianist. He later studied at Warsaw, where his composition teacher was Zygmunt Noskowski, and afterwards with Heinrich Urban in Berlin, Germany. He also studied conducting with Arthur Nikisch at Leipzig. He settled at Zakopane in the Tatra Mountains in 1908 and was killed in a climbing accident.

Works STAGE incidental music to *Biała Gołąbka*.

ORCHESTRAL serenade (1897), symphony in E minor, symphonic poems *Returning Waves* (1907), *The Sad Story (Preludes to Eternity), Stanisław i Anna Oświęcimowie* (1912), *An Episode of the Masquerade, Lithuanian Rhapsody* for orchestra; violin concerto (1902).

OTHER songs.

Karl V opera by Ernst Křenek (libretto by the composer), first produced at the German Opera, Prague, Czechoslovakia (Czech Republic), on 15 June 1938; the revised version was produced in Vienna, Austria, in 1984. It offers reminiscences of the emperor Charles V, presented as an anti-Nazi parable; this was not appreciated by the Viennese authorities and it was cancelled in rehearsal in 1934.

Kashchei the Immortal, Russian **Kashchei Bessmertny** opera by Nikolai Rimsky-Korsakov (libretto by the composer), first produced in Moscow, Russia, on 25 December 1902. Kashchei is the wizard of Russian fairy lore who appears also in Igor Stravinsky's *Firebird* ballet.

Kastner, Jean Georges (Johann Georg) (1810–1867) Alsatian composer and theorist. He studied theology at home, but produced an opera, *Die Königin der Sarmaten*, and was sent by the Strasbourg town council to study with Henri Berton and Antonín Reicha at the Paris Conservatory, France. He wrote a treatise on orchestration, a manual on military music, and methods for various instruments.

Works operas, cantatas, and songs.

Káta Kabanová opera by Leoš Janáček (libretto by V Červinka, based on Alexander Ostrovsky's play *Groza*), first produced in Brno, Czechoslovakia (now the Czech Republic), on 23 November 1921. It tells the story of the adulterous Káta who is driven to suicide in the River Volga.

Katerina Izmailova opera by Shostakovich; see ➔ **Lady Macbeth of the Mtsensk District**.

Kauer, Ferdinand (1751–1831) Austrian composer. He studied at Znaim and Vienna, where he was appointed leader and second conductor at the Leopoldstadt Theatre, for which he wrote music for about 100 pantomimes and farces, as well as operettas and operas.

Works OPERA *Das Donauweibchen* (1798), *Das Waldweibchen.*

ORATORIO *Die Sündflut.*

CHAMBER trio *Nelsons grosse See-Schlacht.*

Kaun, Hugo (1863–1932) German composer. He had written over 150 works before he was 16 and studied with Kiel at the Berlin Academy of Arts. In 1884 he went to the USA as a pianist, but had to give up that career owing to an injury; in 1887 he settled in Milwaukee, but returned to Berlin in 1901, teaching composition first at the Academy and from 1922 at the Klindworth–Scharwenka Conservatory.

Works OPERA *Der Pietist, Sappho* (1917), *Der Fremde* (1920), *Menandra* (1925).

ORCHESTRAL three symphonies, *Minnehaha und Hiawatha* (after Longfellow), symphonic prologue *Marie Magdalene*, humoresque *Falstaff* (after Shakespeare), and other orchestral works.

CHAMBER four string quartets, piano quintet, two piano trios, octet; violin and piano sonata.

OTHER several choral works.

Kay, Ulysses Simpson (1917–1995) US composer. He studied with Howard Hanson at the Eastman School, New York, and with Paul Hindemith at Tanglewood. He was professor at the Lehman College, New York, 1968–88.

Works OPERA *The Boor* (after Chekhov; composed 1955, produced 1968), *The Juggler of our Lady* (composed 1956, produced 1962), *The Capitoline Venus* (1971), *Jubilee* (1976).

ORCHESTRAL suite for strings (1949), serenade for orchestra (1954), fantasy variations for orchestra (1963).

CHAMBER *Scherzi musicali* for chamber orchestra (1971); two string quartets (1953, 1956), piano quintet (1949).

VOCAL *Song of Jeremiah*, cantata (1954); choral pieces; songs.

kazoo simple wind instrument adding a buzzing quality to the singing voice on the principle of 'comb and paper' music.

Keats, Donald (Howard) (1929–) US composer. He studied at Yale and Columbia universities until 1953, and was professor of music at the University of Denver from 1975. His music is basically tonal, and includes settings of T S Eliot (*The Hollow Men*), e e cummings (*Anyone Loved in a Pretty How Town*), and W B Yeats (*A Love Triptych*).

Works ORCHESTRAL two symphonies (no. 2 Elegiac, 1960).

CHAMBER two string quartets (1951, 1965), piano sonata (1966), and *Musica Instrumentalis* for nine instruments (1980).

Keiser, Reinhard (1674–1739) German composer. As chief composer to the Hamburg Opera, he composed over 100 operas, making Hamburg the most distinguished operatic centre in Germany.

A pupil of Johann Schelle at St Thomas's School, Leipzig, he worked in Brunswick from 1692 under Johann Kusser, whom he succeeded as chief composer to the Hamburg Opera in 1695. He was appointed Kapellmeister to the Danish court in Copenhagen in 1723, and returned to Hamburg as cantor of the cathedral in 1728.

Works OPERA *Basilius, Circe* (1702), *Penelope* (1702), *Der geliebte Adonis, Augustus, Orpheus* (1702), *La forza della virtù, Stoertebecker und Joedge Michaels, Die verdammt Statt-Sucht* (1703), *Nebucadnezar* (1704), *Octavia, Masagniello furioso* (1706), *Desiderius* (1709), *Croesus* (1710), *Fredegunda* (1715), *Die grossmüthige Tomyris* (1717), *Ulysses, Der lächerliche Printz Jodelet* (1726), and others.

SACRED Passion oratorios *Der blutige und sterbende Jesus* (Hunold, 1704), *Der für die Sünde der Welt gemartete und sterbende Heiland Jesus* (text by Brockes, 1712); cantatas; motets.

OTHER instrumental music.

Kelemen, Milko (1924–) Croatian composer. His mature style employs serial and aleatory techniques.

He studied at the Zagreb Conservatory with

Štjepan Sulek (1914–1986).

Works OPERA *König Ubu* (1965), *State of Siege* (after Camus's *The Plague*, 1970), and *Apocalyptica* ballet-opera (1979).

ORCHESTRAL *Koncertantne Improvizacije* for strings (1955), *Concerto giocoso* for chamber orchestra, concertos for violin and bassoon, certino for double bass and strings, *Symphonic Music 57, Abecedarium* for strings (1973), *Mageia* for orchestra (1979), *Dramatico* for cello and orchestra (1985), *Fantasmas* for viola and orchestra (1986).

CHAMBER *Memoirs* for string trio (1987), *Sonnets* for string quartet (1988), nonet (1988), piano sonata.

OTHER *Games* song cycle.

Keller, Gottfried (1819–1890) Swiss poet and novelist. Six of his poems were set by Hugo Wolf. Other works and composers inspired by him include ➔ *Kleider Machen Leute* (Alexander von Zemlinsky), ➔ *Romeo und Julia auf dem Dorfe* (Delius), Othmar ➔ Schoeck (*Gesangfest im Frühling, Lebendig begraben, Gaselen, Unter Sternen, Sommernacht*, and songs), and Otto ➔ Vrieslander (songs).

Keller, Hans (1919–1985) Austrian-born British journalist and critic. In 1959 he joined the British Broadcasting Corporation (BBC) in London. He had much influence on broadcasting policy, and in his programmes of functional analysis he sought to elucidate structure and ideas by musical example, rather than verbal explanation.

After studying in Vienna he fled to England in 1938; he played the violin and viola in various ensembles before joining the BBC. An apparent mastery of his adopted language led to a prolific career as a journalist. He wrote the libretto for Benjamin Frankel's opera *Marching Song* (BBC, 1983) and published *The Great Haydn Quartets* (1986).

Kelley, Edgar Stillman (1857–1944) US composer and writer on music. He studied at Chicago and Stuttgart, Germany, and on his return to the USA became an organist and critic in California, where he also made a study of Chinese music. He then taught at Yale University, in Berlin, and, from 1910, at the Cincinnati Conservatory.

Works STAGE operetta *Puritania* (1892); incidental music for Shakespeare's *Macbeth*.

ORCHESTRAL orchestral suite on Chinese themes, *Aladdin, Gulliver* symphony (after Swift), *New England Symphony*, suite *Alice in Wonderland* (after Lewis Carroll, 1913).

CHORAL cantata *Pilgrim's Progress* (after Bunyan, 1918), *Wedding Ode* for tenor, male chorus, and orchestra; *My Captain* (Whitman) and *The Sleeper* (Poe) for chorus.

CHAMBER variations for string quartet, string

334

quartet, piano quintet; piano pieces.
OTHER songs.

Kelly, Bryan (1934–) English composer who studied with Gordon Jacob and Herbert Howells; he has written extensively for brass band and for educational use. He was professor of composition at Royal College of Music in London 1962–84; he then moved to Italy.

Works STAGE *Herod, Do Your Worst*, nativity opera (1968); *The Spider Monkey Uncle King*, opera pantomime (1971).

ORCHESTRAL *The Tempest Suite* for strings (1967); two symphonies (1982, 1986).

BRASS BAND *Edinburgh Dances* (1973), Concertante Music (1979) for brass band.

VOCAL *Stabat Mater* for soloists and orchestra (1970), *Latin Magnificat* for chorus and wind instruments (1979).

Kelly, Michael (1762–1826) Irish tenor, actor, and composer. Kelly made his operatic debut in Naples, Italy, in 1781. He began composing dramatic works in 1789, and produced over 60. His entertaining *Reminiscences* (1826), though not fully reliable, contain valuable information on his contemporaries, especially Mozart.

Kelly studied with Michael Arne and others, and went to Naples in 1779 to study with Fedele Fenaroli (1730–1818) and Giuseppe Aprile (1732–1813). At the Court Opera in Vienna, Austria, 1784–87, he was the first Basilio and Curzio in Mozart's *The Marriage of Figaro* (1786). He returned to London in 1787.

Works *A Friend in Need* (1797), *The Castle Spectre* (1797), *Blue Beard* (1798), *Pizarro* (Sheridan; 1799), *The Gipsy Prince* (1801), *Love Laughs at Locksmiths* (1803), *Cinderella* (1804), *Polly* (1813).

Kelterborn, Rudolf (1931–) Swiss composer. He studied with Jacques Handschin and Willy Burkhard, Boris Blacher, and Wolfgang Fortner. In 1960 he became an instructor at the Detmold Music Academy, and was director of the Basel Academy from 1983. In his music he tends towards integral serialism.

Works OPERA *Die Errettung Thebens* (1963), *Kaiser Jovian* (1967), *Ein Engel kommt nach Babylon* (1977), *Der Kirschgarten* (after Chekhov, 1984), *Julia* (1991).

ORCHESTRAL *Metamorphosen* for orchestra (1960); concertino for violin and chamber orchestra; concertino for piano and chamber orchestra; suite for woodwind, percussion, and strings; sonata for 16 solo strings (1955); cello concerto (1962).

VOCAL *Cantata Profana* for baritone, chorus, and 13 instruments (1960); cantata *Ewige Wiederkehr* for mezzo, flute, and string trio (1960).

CHAMBER chamber music for various instrumental groups including five string quartets (1954–70), *5 Fantasien* for flute, cello and harpsichord; *7 Bagatellen* for wind quintet; *Metamorphosen* for piano; *Meditation* for six wind instruments.

kemence heavy, short-necked fiddle of Rajasthan, northwestern India, played by the Manghaniyar caste of musicians and poets.

Kempe, Rudolf (1910–1976) German conductor. Renowned for the clarity and fidelity of his interpretations of the works of Richard Strauss and Wagner's *Ring* cycle, he conducted Britain's Royal Philharmonic Orchestra 1961–75 and was musical director of the Munich Philharmonic from 1967.

Kempff, Wilhelm Walter Friedrich (1895–1991) German pianist and composer. He studied piano with Hans Barth and composition with R Kahn. After winning both the Mendelssohn Prizes in 1917, he became a concert pianist. From 1924 to 1929 he was head of the Hochschule für Musik in Stuttgart. He made his London debut in 1951 and his New York debut in 1964. He was best known as one of the finest and most thoughtful interpreters of the classical piano repertory, especially the music of Beethoven.

Works operas *König Midas* (1930) and *Die Familie Gozzi* (1934); symphonies and ballets; concertos for piano and violin; string quartets; and many pieces for solo piano and organ.

Kendale, Richard (died 1431) English grammarian and music theorist. A short musical treatise by him is included in the manuscript written down by John Wylde, precentor of Waltham Holy Cross Abbey, in about 1460 (British Museum, Lansdowne 763).

Kepler, Johannes (1571–1630) German philosopher, astronomer, and writer on music. He was an early supporter of the Copernican view of the solar system, which placed the Sun at its centre, and was the first to propose that the orbits of the planets are eliptical. His *Harmonices Mundi* (1619) elaborates various music theories; book five elaborates on the ancient Greek doctrine of Pythagoras that the planets emit musical sounds in their orbits round the Sun. Kepler's theories form the basis of Paul ➔ **Hindemith's** opera *Die* ➔ **Harmonie der Welt** (1957).

Kerle, Jacob van (c.1531–1591) Flemish composer. He spent some time in Italy, partly in Rome in the service of Otto von Truchsess, cardinal-archbishop of Augsburg, in whose service he was 1562–75. He was with the cardinal in Augsburg at times, and may have attended the Council of Trent with him (1562–63). Later he became canon of Cambrai, but was often in Vienna and Prague attending on the emperor Rudolf.

Works *Preces*, commissioned by the cardinal of Augsburg in 1562, Masses, motets, Te Deums, Magnificats, hymns, *Sacrae cantiones*.

Kerll, Johann Caspar von (1627–1693) German organist and composer. He wrote eleven operas, all of which are now lost. Of his other compositions, 18 Masses and other church music survive, as well as secular pieces. He excelled in writing for the organ.

He settled early in Vienna, Austria, as a pupil of Giovanni Valentini; then studied in Rome, Italy, with Giacomo Carissimi and probably studied the organ with Girolamo Frescobaldi. He was in the service of the Elector of Bavaria in Munich 1656–74. He returned to Vienna as a private teacher, and was appointed court organist there in 1677, but went back to Munich in 1684.

Works OPERA *Oronte*, *Erinto*, *Le pretensioni del sole* (1667), *I colori geniali*.

CHURCH MUSIC Masses, motets, and other church music.

INSTRUMENTAL sonatas for two violins and bass; toccatas, ricercari, and other works for organ.

Kerman, Joseph (Wilfred) (1924–   ) US music scholar and critic. He studied in London, New York, and Princeton, and was professor at the University of California from 1960 and at Oxford 1971–74. He is an authority on William Byrd. His books include *Opera as Drama* (1956), *The Beethoven Quartets* (1967), and *Musicology* (1985).

Kern, Jerome (David) (1885–1945) US composer. A pupil of Paolo Gallico and Alexander Lambert in New York, he turned to the composition of musical comedy and other light music. His most successful musical was *Show Boat*, which included the number 'Ol' Man River'. He moved to Hollywood in 1939 and wrote film music and songs for the movies, including the Academy Award-winning 'The Last Time I Saw Paris', from the film *Lady be Good* (1941).

Works MUSICAL COMEDIES *Sunny* (1925), *Show Boat* (1927), *Music in the Air* (1932), *Roberta* (1933) and others.

Kertész, István (1929–1973) Hungarian conductor. Zoltan Kodály was among his teachers. After gaining experience at the Budapest Opera, he left Hungary during the 1956 uprising. He was musical director of the Cologne Opera, Germany, from 1964 until his death and brought the company to London, England, in 1969.

His UK debut was with the Royal Liverpool Philharmonic Orchestra in 1960; he was principal conductor of the London Symphony Orchestra 1965–68. He led Verdi's *Un ballo in maschera* at the Royal Opera House, Covent Garden, London, in 1966. He is noted for his interpretations of Mozart and Dvořák, and was also heard in

Benjamin Britten, Prokofiev, Bartók, Stravinsky, and Henze. He drowned while swimming near Tel Aviv, Israel.

kettledrum musical instrument; see ➤ **timpani**.

Keuris, Tristan (1946–1996) Dutch composer. He studied at Utrecht with Ton de Leeuw 1963–69. He was head of composition at the Sweelinck Conservatory, and lectured in the USA, Norway, and Berlin.

Works ORCHESTRAL quintet for orchestra (1967), *Choral Music* (1969), *Soundings* for orchestra (1970), alto saxophone concerto (1971), *Sinfonia* (1975), *Serenade* (1976), piano concerto (1980), *Movements* for orchestra (1982), violin concerto (1984), *Symphonic Transformations* (Houston Symphony Orchestra commission, 1987), *Catena: Refrains and Variations* for 31 wind instruments, percussion, and celesta (1989), organ concerto (1993).

CHAMBER two string quartets (1982, 1985), *Five Pieces* for brass quintet (1988).

VOCAL *To Brooklyn Bridge* for 24 voices and ensemble (1988).

key in music, describes any piece where the melodies and harmonies are based on the notes of a major or minor scale. For example, a piece in the key of C major uses mainly the notes of the C major scale, and the harmonies are made up of the notes of that scale. The first note of a scale is known as the ➤ **tonic** and is the note that tells us the name of the key.

Most music which uses this system (known as the key system or tonal system) does not remain in one key, but moves to related keys in a process known as ➤ **modulation**. This adds contrast and creates tension, which is relieved when the music returns to the 'home' or tonic key.

The term is also used for the lever on ➤ **keyboard** instruments, such as the piano or organ, which the player presses in order to produce a note; and for the levers on ➤ **woodwind** instruments which players press to cover the note holes beyond the reach of their fingers.

Key, Francis Scott (1779–1843) US lawyer and poet. He wrote the song 'The Star-Spangled Banner' while Fort McHenry, Baltimore, was besieged by British troops in 1814; since 1931 it has been the national anthem of the USA.

Key was born in Maryland. He served as US attorney for the District of Columbia 1833–41.

keyboard in music, a horizontal set of black and white levers, called keys, found on keyboard instruments. They are arranged in order of the pitch of the notes they control, and allow performers to play many more strings or reeds than they could have done otherwise, and jump between them very rapidly. The keyboard is a major innovation of Western music. It was used on medieval instruments of the organ type (including the portative organ and the reed organ), and then on Renaissance stringed instruments such as the ➤ **clavichord** and ➤ **hurdy-gurdy**. Keyboard instruments were designed so that musical intervals could always be reproduced accurately.

The early clavichord is sometimes thought of as a ➤ **monochord**. This was basically a soundbox with one stretched string. The pitch was changed by moving the bridge to different points on the string. Adding the keyboard to the clavichord gave the instrument a greater flexibility and reliability of pitch and was important in showing the relationship of string length to pitch. Instrument makers seized on the user-friendly keyboard mechanism to create new markets for amateur and domestic use, creating in the clavichord a mechanized plectrum guitar, in the harpsichord a mechanized lute, in the hurdy-gurdy a keyboard viol, and in the fortepiano a mechanized dulcimer.

key bugle or **Kent bugle** musical instrument, a type of ➤ **bugle** with side holes covered with keys similar to those used on woodwind instruments. It was invented in the early 19th century.

keynote in music, the ➤ **tonic**: the note on which the scale begins and ends, which determines the key of a piece of music in major or minor and after which that key is named.

key relationships in music, key relationships may be close or remote, based largely on the similarity of key signatures; for instance, in the key of C major the relation of the tonic chord (C) with the dominant (G) is close. The relation of C minor with E♭ major (its relative major) is also close, whereas the relation of C major with E♭ major is less close. Transference from one key to another may be abrupt or may be effected by modulation.

key signature in music, sharps or flats printed at the beginning of every line (or stave) of music after the ➤ **clef**. It tells a player what key the music is in. A key signature without any sharps or flats means the piece is in C major or A minor, or that the music is nontonal.

As shown above, each key signature is shared by two keys: a major key and its relative minor (the relative minor is found three semitones below the major key).

To change a key signature during a piece, all that is needed is to write the new key signature after a double-bar line.

Khachaturian, Aram Il'yich (1903–1978) Armenian composer. His use of folk themes is shown in the ballets *Gayaneh* (1942), which includes the 'Sabre Dance', and *Spartacus* (1956).

His father, a bookbinder, was able to send him

Tonic/dominant and relative major/minor relationships are close; C major and E flat major are not closely related.

to study in Moscow only after the Revolution. He entered the Gnesin School of Music there and studied under Mikhail Gnesin in 1923; from 1929 until 1937 he studied at the Moscow Conservatory under Sergey Vasilenko and Nikolay Myaskovsky. He studied the folk songs of Russian Armenia and other southern regions, which influenced his compositions. He was successful with a pre-war symphony and piano concerto, but was denounced in the composers' purge of 1948 and as a result turned to patriotic film and ballet music.

Works STAGE ballets *Happiness* (1939), *Gayaneh* (1942), *Spartacus* (1956); incidental music for Shakespeare's *Macbeth*, Lope de Vega's *The Widow of Valencia*, Pogodin's *Kremlin Chimes*, Kron's *Deep Drilling*, Lermontov's *Masquerade*, and others.

ORCHESTRAL three symphonies (1932–47), *Dance Suite* (1933), *Solemn Overture*, 'To the End of the War' for orchestra; *Song of Stalin* for chorus and orchestra (1938); marches and pieces on Uzbek and Armenian themes for wind band; concertos for piano, violin, cello, and violin and cello.

CHAMBER string quartet (1932), trio for clarinet, violin, and piano; sonata and pieces for violin and piano; piano music.

OTHER part songs; songs for the Russian army.

Khamma ballet-pantomime in two scenes by Claude Debussy (scenario by W L Courtney and M Allan), composed in short score 1911–12, orchestrated by Charles Koechlin 1912–13, and first

Maj.	Min.
C	A
G	E
D	B
A	F♯
E	C♯
B	G♯
F♯	D♯
C♯	A♯
C♭	A♭
G♭	E♭
D♭	B♭
A♭	F
E♭	C
B♭	G
F	D

The complete series of key signatures in order of increasing complexity by sharps, returning towards C major through the flat keys.

performed (as a concert) in Paris, France, on 15 November 1924, conducted by Gabriel Pierné. The first stage performance was given at the Opéra-Comique, Paris, on 26 March 1947.

khorovod a type of ancient Russian folksong sung in chorus of two or more parts in a primitive kind of counterpoint. It was sung mainly at religious and family festivals and on seasonal occasions.

Khovanshchina unfinished opera by Modest Mussorgsky (libretto by the composer and V V Stassov), first produced as completed and scored by Rimsky-Korsakov after Mussorgsky's death, in St Petersburg, Russia, on 21 February 1886. Shostakovich also added to Rimsky-Korsakov's work. The plot is based on historical events surrounding the opponents of Tsar Peter the Great: Prince Khovansky, head of the militia, the regent Sofia as represented by the actions of Prince Golitsin, the 'Old Believers' as personified by Marfa. All come to an unhappy end.

Khrennikov, Tikhon Nikolaievich (1913–) Russian composer. He was secretary of the Union of Soviet Composers from 1948, and was made a Hero of Socialist Labour in 1973. He played a prominent part in the Stalinist-inspired denunciations of Prokofiev and Shostakovich, and renewed his attacks with the emergence of the New Music generation of composers, Alfred Schnittke and Sofia Gubaidulina.

He was taught music at home, but entered the Gnesin School of Music, Moscow, in 1929 and the Conservatory in 1932 as a pupil of Vissarion Shebalin.

Works STAGE AND INCIDENTAL MUSIC operas *The Brothers* (*In the Storm*, 1939) and *Mother* (after Gogol, 1957); incidental music for Shakespeare's *Much Ado about Nothing*, an adaptation of Cervantes' *Don Quixote*, and others; film music for *The Pigs and the Shepherd*.

ORCHESTRAL three symphonies (1955–73); three piano concertos (1933–82).

OTHER piano pieces; songs to words by Pushkin and Burns; war songs.

khyal (Hindi 'thought', 'idea') vocal genre of north Indian (Hindustani) music. It is characterized by a text setting (usually in two sections, *sthayi* and *antara*) and a wide variety of improvisation techniques, most distinctively 'tan', melismatic flourishes which can be highly elaborate. Khyal is the most commonly heard vocal genre in the tradition.

Kielflügel (German 'quill-wing') German name for the → harpsichord, so named from the quills that pluck the strings and the wing shape of the instrument's body.

Kilpinen, Yrjö (1892–1959) Finnish composer. He had a few lessons in theory at the Helsinki Conservatory and in Berlin, Germany, and Vienna, Austria, but was otherwise self-taught. Like Sibelius, he was enabled by a government grant to devote himself to composition. He was one of the finest song composers of the 20th century, and wrote over 500 songs to Finnish, Swedish, and German texts.

Works cello sonata, viola da gamba sonata; piano sonatas; over 500 songs on Finnish, Swedish, and German poems.

Kim, Earl (1920–1998) US composer. In its precision and rhythmic subtlety, his music reflects his Korean origins. He was professor of music at Harvard 1967–90.

He studied at University College of Los Angeles with Arnold Schoenberg in 1939, and with Ernest Bloch and Roger Sessions at Berkeley.

Works OPERA *Footfalls* (1981).

ORCHESTRAL AND INSTRUMENTAL *Dialogues* for piano and orchestra (1959), violin concerto (1979), twelve caprices for violin (1980).

VOCAL AND INSTRUMENTAL *Now and Then* for soprano, flute, viola, and harp (1981), *Where Grief Slumbers* for soprano, harp, and strings (1982), *The 11th Dream* for soprano, baritone, piano, violin, and cello (1989), *Three Poems in French* for soprano and string quartet (1989), *Some thoughts on Keats and Coleridge* for chorus (1990).

Kindermann, Johann Erasmus (1616–1655) German composer and organist. He studied with Johann Staden and in common with other German composers of his time probably visited Venice, Italy, where he would have met Girolamo Frescobaldi and Pietro Cavalli. From 1640 he was organist at the Egidienkirche, Nuremberg.

Works VOCAL *Cantiones Jesu Christi* (1639), *Friedens Clag* (1640), *Concentus Salomonis* (1642), *Opitianischer Orpheus* (1642), *Musica catechetica* (1643), *Gottliche Liebesflamme* (1651); nine cantatas, and other pieces.

INSTRUMENTAL *Harmonia organica* (1645), 27 Canzoni, nine sonatas, 30 suite movements, and other pieces.

Kinderscenen, Scenes from Childhood 13 piano pieces by Robert Schumann, Op. 15; composed in 1838.

Kindertotenlieder, Songs of Dead Children cycle of five songs by Gustav ➤ **Mahler,** with orchestra or piano, to poems by Friedrich Rückert; they were composed in 1902 and first performed in Vienna, Austria, on 29 January 1905, conducted by Mahler.

King, Robert (lived 17th–18th centuries) English composer. He joined the royal band in 1680 on the death of John Banister, received a licence to give concerts in 1689, and took a degree in music at Cambridge University in 1696.

Works incidental music for Crowne's *Sir Courtly Nice* and many other plays; Shadwell's Ode on St Cecilia's Day, Motteux's Ode for John Cecil, Earl of Exeter; many songs for one and more voices.

King and Charcoal-Burner, Czech **Král a Uhlíř** opera by Antonín Dvořák (libretto by B Guldener), first produced at the Czech Theatre, Prague, in the modern Czech Republic, on 24 No-

vember 1874. It was Dvořák's first opera to be produced. In the story, King Matyáš, lost in the forest, talks to Liduška, daughter of charcoal burner Matěj. Young Jeník becomes jealous and embarks on a glorious military career before he is united with her.

King Arthur, or The British Worthy semi-opera by Henry Purcell (libretto by John Dryden), first produced at the Dorset Gardens Theatre, London, England, in 1691. It tells how Arthur and Merlin fight the Saxon leader Oswald to establish a united Britain and rescue the beloved Emmeline.

King Charles II opera by George Macfarren (libretto by M D Ryan, based on a play by J H Payne), first produced at the Princess's Theatre, London, England, on 27 October 1849.

King Christian II incidental music by Jean Sibelius for a play by Adolf Paul; it was composed in 1898 and first performed in Helsinki, Finland, on 28 February 1898, conducted by Sibelius. The suite for orchestra in six movements from it (1898) was his Op. 27. The first British performance was given in London on 26 October 1901, conducted by Henry Wood.

Kingdom, The oratorio by Edward Elgar, Op. 51 (libretto compiled from the Bible by the composer), Part II of a trilogy of which I is *The Apostles* and III was never completed. It was first performed at the Birmingham Festival, England, on 3 October 1906.

King Goes Forth to France, The, Finnish **Kuningas lahtee Ranskaan** opera in three acts by Aulis Sallinen (libretto by P Haavikko), first produced at the Savonlinna Festival, Finland, on 7 July 1984. It was also staged at Santa Fe, USA, in 1986, and the Royal Opera House, Covent Garden, London, England, in 1987. It tells how a future prince seizes power from the prime minister and, facing a new ice age, leads an army south into France.

King Lear title of several musical works inspired by Shakespeare's tragedy. Incidental music for the play was composed by Johann André and first produced in Berlin, Germany, on 30 November 1778; also by Mily Balakirev for production in St Petersburg, Russia, in 1861. A *King Lear* overture was written by Hector Berlioz, Op. 4; it was composed in Italy in 1831 and first performed in Paris, France, on 9 November 1834. An opera based on the play was composed by Vito Frazzi 1922–28, and first produced in Florence, Italy, in 1939. Verdi worked at the Shakespearean subject for many years, but never brought the opera anywhere near completion, and his sketches were destroyed after his death, at his own wish. See ➤ **Re Lear.** For the opera by Aribert Reimann, see ➤ **Lear.**

'King of Prussia' Quartets string quartets written by Mozart; see ➤ *'Prussian' Quartets*.

King Olaf cantata for solo voices, chorus, and orchestra by Edward Elgar, Op. 30, set to words by Henry Wadsworth Longfellow altered by H A Acworth; it was first produced at the North Staffordshire Festival, Hanley, England, on 30 October 1896.

King Priam opera in three acts by Michael Tippett (libretto by the composer), first produced by the company of the Royal Opera, Covent Garden, London, in Coventry, England, on 29 May 1962. It describes the judgement of Paris followed by the destruction of Troy.

King Roger opera by Karol Szymanowski (libretto by the composer and J Iwaszkiewicz), first produced in Warsaw, Poland, on 19 June 1926. It tells how Queen Roxane and her husband Roger are converted by a wandering shepherd-prophet, Dionysus in disguise.

King Stephen incidental music by Beethoven; see ➤ *König Stephan*.

Kinkeldey, Otto (1878–1966) US musicologist. After a general academic education in New York and Berlin, Germany, he studied music with Edward MacDowell 1900–02 while he was a schoolmaster and chapel organist. After further studies at the university and academy for church music in Berlin, he became organ teacher at a similar institution at Breslau (Wrocław in modern-day Poland), and later lecturer and professor of musicology. Returning to the USA in 1914 he was alternately chief of the music division of the New York Public Library and professor at Cornell University. He wrote a dissertation on 16th-century keyboard music and made many valuable contributions to periodicals.

Kinsky, Georg (1882–1951) German music scholar and editor. Self-taught in music, he worked at first at the Prussian State Library in Berlin and then became curator until 1927 of the Heyer Museum of musical instruments, of which he compiled a valuable catalogue. From 1921 he was also active at the Cologne Conservatory, from which he retired in 1932. His books include a *History of Music in Pictures*, works on instruments, and a catalogue of Beethoven's works.

Kirbye, George (c.1565–1634) English composer. He first appeared as the most copious contributor, except John Farmer, to Thomas East's psalter *The Whole Book of Psalmes* (1592). In 1598 he married Anne Saxye, and he seems to have lived at that time at Rushbrooke near Bury St Edmunds, Suffolk, as domestic musician at the residence of Sir Robert Jermyn. In 1597 he dedicated his book of 24 madrigals to Jermyn's daughters.

In 1601 he contributed a madrigal to The ➤ *Triumphes of Oriana*.

Works motets, a hymn; madrigals; pavana for viols.

Kircher, Athanasius (1601–1680) German mathematician, philosopher, and music scholar. He was professor at the Jesuit College of Würzburg, but was driven from Germany in 1633 by the Thirty Years' War. He travelled to Avignon, Vienna, and in 1637 to Rome, Italy, where he settled for the rest of his life. His chief theoretical work is *Musurgia universalis* (1650).

Kirckman, Jacob (1710–1792) German-born organist and composer. He settled in London, England, about 1730 and founded a family firm of harpsichord makers which dominated the British market during the late 18th century and moved into piano manufacture in 1809.

Kirkpatrick, John (1905–1991) US pianist and scholar. He studied at Princeton and with Nadia Boulanger in Paris, France, and performed works by many modern US composers, in particular Charles Ives. In 1939 he gave the first performance in New York of the *Concord Sonata*, vital in the wider recognition of the music of Ives; he also made a significant academic contribution in this respect.

Kirkpatrick, Ralph (1911–1984) US harpsichordist and musicologist. He published a number of scholarly editions, including Bach's *Goldberg Variations* and an important book on Domenico Scarlatti (published in 1953) which gives definitive listings for all the sonatas given 'Kk' numbers.

He studied piano at home and theory at Harvard, and went on to study with Nadia Boulanger in Paris, France. In Paris he took harpsichord lessons with Wanda Landowska, as well as working with Arnold Dolmetsch in Haslemere, Surrey, England. He received a Guggenheim Fellowship in 1937 and toured Europe studying early manuscripts. In 1940 he was appointed to Yale University.

Kirnberger, Johann Philipp (1721–1783) German theorist and composer. He was a pupil of Johann Sebastian Bach in Leipzig 1739–41. After various posts, he entered the service of Frederick the Great as a violinist in 1751. Appointed Kapellmeister and teacher of composition to Princess Amalia of Prussia in 1758, he increasingly abandoned performance and composition to devote his time to theoretical writings. Among many treatises the most important is *Die Kunst des reinen Satzes*, in which he promoted the conservative musical values of Bach. His compositions include cantatas, motets, and instrumental music.

Kiss, The, Czech *Hubička* opera by Bedřich Smetana (libretto by E Krásnohorská, based on a story by K Světlá), first produced in Prague, in the modern Czech Republic, on 7 November 1876. It tells how Vendulka declines a kiss from the widower Lukáš, for fear of offending the spirit of his dead wife. The pair are later united.

kit diminutive ➤ **violin**, formerly used by dancing masters who, on account of its small size and narrow shape, were able to carry it in the long pockets of their tail coats. It is therefore known in French as *pochette* and in German as *Taschengeige*.

Kitezh opera by Rimsky-Korsakov; see ➤ **Legend of the Invisible City of Kitezh and Maiden Fevronia**.

kithara plucked string instrument of ancient Greece. See ➤ **lyre**.

Kjerulf, Halfdan (1815–1868) Norwegian composer. He studied in Germany, and wrote a large number of songs that combine Norwegian folk tunes with German Romanticism.

At his father's wish, he studied law at Christiania (Oslo) University, but on the death of his father in 1840 he decided to devote himself to music. He taught, and published some songs even before he had done much in the way of theoretical study. In about 1850 he received a government grant to study at Leipzig, Germany, for a year, and on his return he tried to establish classical subscription concerts, with little success. He became a friend of Bjørnstjerne Bjørnson, who wrote many poems especially for him to set.

Works choruses and quartets for male voices; piano pieces; over 100 songs.

Klagende Lied, Das, The Song of Lamentation cantata by Gustav ➤ **Mahler** (text by composer) for soloists, chorus, and orchestra. The first version was composed in 1880 in three parts: *Waldmärchen*, *Der Spielmann*, and *Hochzeitstück*. It was revised in 1888 with part one omitted, and first performed in Vienna, Austria, on 17 February 1901, conducted by Mahler. The original version was first performed in Vienna on 8 April 1935, conducted by Arnold Rosé.

Klaviatur German name for a musical ➤ **keyboard**.

Klavier German name for the ➤ **piano**, but see also ➤ **clavier**.

Klavierübung collection of keyboard music by Johann Sebastian Bach; see ➤ **Clavierübung**.

Klebe, Giselher (1925–) German composer. He studied at the Berlin Conservatory with Kurt von Wohlfurt and later with Josef Rufer and Boris Blacher. From 1946 to 1949 he worked for Berlin Radio. His music follows the traditions of Arnold Schoenberg and Anton Webern.

Works OPERA *Die Räuber* (after Schiller, 1957), *Die tödlichen Wünsche* (1959), *Alkmene* (1961), *Figaro lässt sich scheiden* (1963), *Jacobowsky und der Oberst* (1965), *Ein wahrer Held* (after Synge, 1975), *Das Mädchen aus Domrémy* (1976), *Das Rendez-vous* (1977), *Der jüngste Tag* (1980), and *Die Fastnachtsbeichte* (1983).

BALLET *Pas de trois*.

ORCHESTRAL *Con moto* for orchestra, five symphonies (1951–77), *Divertissement joyeux* for chamber orchestra, *Zwitschermaschine* for orchestra (after Paul Klee); concerto for violin, cello, and orchestra (1954); concertos for cello, organ, clarinet, and harpsichord (1957, 1980, 1985, 1988).

VOCAL *Geschichte der lustigen Musikanten* for tenor, chorus, and five instruments.

CHAMBER wind quintet, three string quartets (1949, 1963, 1981); two sonatas for solo violin, viola sonata, double bass sonata (1971).

Kleiber, Erich (1890–1956) Austrian conductor. He was appointed music director of the Berlin Staatsoper, Germany, in 1923, and gave several important premieres, in particular that of *Wozzeck* (1925), of which he also conducted the first British stage performance in 1952. Differences with the Nazis over artistic policy obliged him to resign his Berlin post, and in 1937 he left Germany for Argentina, but returned to Europe in 1948. His son Carlos Kleiber is also a conductor.

After apprentice years in Darmstadt and Düsseldorf, he became music director of the Berlin Staatsoper, making his debut with *Fidelio*. He made his London concert debut in 1935, with the London Symphony Orchestra, and in 1938 conducted *Der Rosenkavalier* at the Royal Opera House, Covent Garden. He made his New York debut in 1930. From 1937 to 1949 he was active in Buenos Aires, becoming an Argentine citizen in 1938. On his return to Europe in 1948 he conducted the London Philharmonic Orchestra, and in Florence, Italy, in 1951 he gave the first known performance of Haydn's last opera, *Orfeo ed Euridice*, with Maria Callas.

Kleider Machen Leute opera by Alexander von Zemlinsky (libretto by L Feld after G Keller), first produced at the Volksoper, Vienna, Austria, on 2 December 1910. In the story, Nettchen and other villagers assume that the travelling tailor Strapinski is a count. Nettchen falls in love with him, and her feelings remain unchanged after his lowly origins are revealed.

kleine Nachtmusik, Eine (German 'A Little Serenade (Night-music)') Mozart's own title for his serenade in G major for strings, K525, finished on 10 August 1787.

Kleist, (Bernd) Heinrich (Wilhelm) von (1777–1811) German poet, novelist, and dramatist. He inspired several composers and musical works, including Felix ➤ Draeseke and Karoly ➤ Goldmark (*Penthesilea* overture), Paul ➤ Graener, Hans Werner Henze, and Heinrich ➤ Marschner (*Der* ➤ *Prinz von Homburg*), Joseph ➤ Joachim (commemoration overture), Othmar Schoeck and Hugo ➤ Wolf (➤ *Penthesilea*), Hans ➤ Pfitzner (*Käthchen von Heilbronn*), and Rudolf Wagner-Régeny (*Zerbrochene Krug*).

Klemperer, Otto (1885–1973) German conductor. He was celebrated for his interpretation of contemporary and classical music (especially Beethoven and Brahms). He conducted the Los Angeles Orchestra 1933–39 and the Philharmonia Orchestra, London, from 1959.

Klengel, Julius (1859–1933) German cellist and composer. He joined the Leipzig Gewandhaus orchestra at the age of 15, began to travel as a virtuoso in 1875, and in 1881 became leading cellist in the orchestra and professor of cello at the Leipzig Conservatory.

He studied cello with Emil Hegar and composition with Salomon Jadassohn (1831–1902).

Works four cello concertos, double concertos for violin and cello and two cellos, *Hymnus* for twelve cellos; *Caprice in form of a Chaconne* for cello solo; many cello pieces and studies.

Klindworth, Karl (1830–1916) German pianist and conductor. He was a pupil of Franz Liszt, and arranger of music for his instrument, including vocal scores of Richard Wagner's works. He lived in London as a pianist, conductor, and teacher 1854–68, then became piano professor at the Moscow Conservatory, Russia, but returned to Germany in 1884 and opened a school of music in Berlin in 1893. His adopted daughter Winifred Williams (1897–1980) married Siegfried Wagner.

Klingsor, Tristan (Léon Leclère) (1874–1966) French poet. See ➤ *Shéhérazade* by Maurice Ravel.

Klopstock, Friedrich (1724–1803) German poet. His works inspired the composers C P E ➤ Bach (*Morgengesang am Schöpfungstage*), Christoph Willibald von ➤ Gluck (odes), Jean François ➤ Lesueur (*Mort d'Adam*), Gustav Mahler (➤ *Resurrection Symphony*), Giacomo ➤ Meyerbeer (sacred cantatas), Corona Schröter (songs), Christian Friedrich Schwenke (odes), Ludwig ➤ Spohr (*Vater unser*), Maximilian ➤ Stadler (*Frühlingsfeier*), and Philipp Wolfrum (*Grosse Hallelujah*). Thirteen songs were set by Franz Schubert.

Klotz (lived 17th–18th centuries) German family of violin makers in Mittenwald, including Matthias (1653–1743), who worked for a time in Florence and Cremona, Italy, but returned to Mittenwald in about 1683; and three sons, Georg (1687–1737), Sebastian (1696–1775), and Johann Carl (1709–1769).

At least 18 members of succeeding generations are known.

Kluge, Die, *The Clever Girl* opera by Carl Orff (libretto by the composer, after Grimm), first produced in Frankfurt, Germany, on 20 February 1943.

Knaben Wunderhorn, Des, *The Youth's Magic Horn* German anthology of old folk poetry. The poems have been set to music by composers including Gustav ➤ Mahler and Otto ➤ Vrieslander.

The 13 poems which Gustav Mahler scored for voice and orchestra in 1900 are: (1) *Der Schildwache Nachtlied*; (2) *Verlor'ne Muh*; (3) *Trost im Ungluck*; (4) *Wer hat dies Liedlein erdacht?*; (5) *Das irdische Leben*; (6) *Des Antonius von Padua Fischpredigt*; (7) *Rheinlegendchen*; (8) *Lied des Verfolgten in Turm*; (9) *Wo die schönen Trompeten blasen*; (10) *Lob des hohen Verstandes*; (11) *Es sungen drei Engel*; (12) *Urlicht*; and (13) *Das himmlische Leben*.

Knappertsbusch, Hans (1888–1965) German conductor. He studied at the Cologne Conservatory with Fritz Steinbach and Otto Lohse 1909–12 and then took various positions as an opera conductor. In 1922 he became conductor at the Munich Staatsoper, where he remained until 1938, when he became director of the Vienna Staatsoper, Austria. In 1937 he made his Salzburg opera debut (with Richard Strauss's *Der Rosenkavalier*) and conducted his only opera in London, England (Richard Strauss's *Salome*, at Covent Garden). He was guest conductor at the Wiener Philharmoniker 1947–64. He was best known for his performances of Wagner, especially *Parsifal*, which he conducted at Bayreuth from 1951.

Knecht, Justin Heinrich (1752–1817) German organist and composer. He worked as an organist and conductor in Biberach from 1771, and was vice-Kapellmeister in Stuttgart 1806–08.

Works a symphony entitled *Le Portrait musical de la nature* (about 1784) which has a programme similar to that of Beethoven's 'Pastoral' Symphony.

Kniegeige (German 'knee fiddle') German name for the ➤ viola da gamba, a musical instrument.

Knipper, Lev Konstantinovich (1898–1974) Russian composer. His early work shows the influence of Stravinsky, but after 1932 he wrote in a more popular idiom, as in the symphony *Poem of Komsomol Fighters* (1933–34) with its mass battle songs. He is known in the West for his song 'Cavalry of the Steppes'.

knot alternative name for the ornamental fretwork sound hole of many flat-bellied string instruments and keyboard instruments, more generally called a rose.

Knot Garden, The opera by Michael Tippett (libretto by the composer), first produced at the Royal Opera House, Covent Garden, London, on 2 December 1970, conducted by Colin Davis. It tells how, under the auspices of the psychoanalyst Mangus, Faber and Thea overcome marital difficulties, and how the gay couple Mel and Dov separate when Mel's lust is directed towards Thea's sister, Denise.

Knussen, (Stuart) Oliver (1952–) English composer and conductor. An eclectic and prolific composer, his works include the operas *Where the Wild Things Are* (1983), based on the children's story by Maurice Sendak, and *Higglety Pigglety Pop!* (1984–90). He studied in the USA with Gunter Schuller.

Works OPERA *Where the Wild Things Are* (1983) and *Higglety Pigglety Pop!* (1984–90; produced at Glyndebourne).

ORCHESTRAL three symphonies (1966–79), concerto for orchestra (1970), *Coursing* for chamber orchestra (1979), *Chiara* for orchestra (1986).

VOCAL *Hums and Songs of Winnie-the-Pooh* for soprano and ensemble (1970–83), *Trumpets* for soprano and three clarinets (1975), *Late Poems and an Epigram of Rainer Maria Rilke* for soprano (1988),*Whitman Settings* for soprano and orchestra (1991).

PIANO AND INSTRUMENTAL *Sonya's Lullaby* for piano (1978),*Variations* for piano (1989); *Songs Without Voices* for eight instruments (1992).

Koanga opera by Frederick Delius (libretto by C F Keary, based on G W Cable's novel *The Grandissimes*), first produced in Elberfeld, Germany, on 30 March 1904. Uncle Joe tells the story of Koanga, a slave-prince who falls in love with slave-girl Palmyra. The plantation owner Perez prevents the wedding. Koanga kills him and is himself captured and killed. Palmyra commits suicide.

Koch, (Sigurd Christian) Erland von (1910–) Swedish composer. His compositions are chiefly instrumental and based on folk music. He studied at the Stockholm Conservatory and later in London, Paris, and Dresden.

Works ORCHESTRAL four symphonies (1938–53), symphonic poem *A Tale from the Wilderness*, *Symphonic Episode, Symphonic Dance*; three piano concertos (1936–72), violin concerto.

CHAMBER suite for chamber orchestra; six string quartets (1934–63), string trio; violin and piano sonata.

OTHER piano works; songs.

Köchel, Ludwig (Alois Ferdinand) Ritter von (1800–1877) Austrian naturalist and music bibliographer. He lived in Salzburg 1850–63 for the purpose of compiling his thematic catalogue of Mozart's works, published in 1862 (sixth edition 1964).

Kodály, Zoltán (1882–1967) Hungarian composer and educationalist.With Béla Bartók, he recorded and transcribed Magyar folk music, the scales and rhythm of which he incorporated in a deliberately nationalist style. His works include the cantata *Psalmus Hungaricus* (1923), a comic opera *Háry János* (1925–27), and orchestral dances and variations. His 'Kodály method' of school music education is widely practised.

Kodály learnt the violin as a child, sang in a cathedral choir, and tried to compose without systematic instruction. In 1900, after living in small provincial towns, he entered the University of Budapest to study science, but also became a pupil at the Conservatory. He studied Hungarian folk song and in 1906 wrote his university thesis on it; in the same year his *Summer Evening* was premiered in Budapest. He collected folk songs in collaboration with Bartók 1907–14. He was appointed professor at the Conservatory and deputy director in 1919.

His music was performed at the International Society for Contemporary Music festivals from their inception in 1923. Beatrice Harrison gave London performances in 1924 of his finest chamber work, the sonata for solo cello, and further recognition on the international stage came with the premieres of the *Háry János* suite in 1927 and the *Dances of Marosszék* in 1930. The popular *Psalmus Hungaricus* was performed in London and New York from 1927; Henry Wood programmed *Summer Evening* and *Dances from Galanta* at the London Promenade concerts in 1930 and 1931.

Variations on a Hungarian Folksong: The Peacock was composed for the Concertgebouw Orchestra in 1939 and the *Concert for Orchestra* for the Chicago Symphony Orchestra in 1941. His final work for orchestra was the symphony in C 'In memoriam Arturo Toscanini', which was premiered in Lucerne, Switzerland, under Ferenc Fricsay in 1961. In 1945 Kodály became president of the newly founded Hungarian Arts Council, and in 1967 was awarded the Gold Medal of the Royal Philharmonic Society. In 1960 he received an honorary doctorate in music from Oxford University.

Works OPERA *Háry János* (1925–27).

ORCHESTRAL *Summer Evening* (1906), *Ballet Music* and *Suite* for *Háry János* (1925–27), *Dances of Galánta* (1933), *Dances of Marosszék* (1930), *Variations on a Hungarian Folksong: The Peacock* (1939).

CHAMBER AND VOCAL two string quartets (1909, 1918); duo for violin and cello (1914); sonatas for cello solo (1915) and for cello and piano (1909); 21 works for chorus with and without orchestra, including *Psalmus Hungaricus* (1923), *Budavari Te Deum* (1936), *Missa brevis* (1944).

Koechlin, Charles (1867–1950) French composer. He never appeared as an executive musician or held any official appointment, but devoted himself largely to composition and the writing of some theoretical books as well as studies of Debussy and Fauré. Other influences on his music were Ravel, Poulenc, and Stravinsky.

He studied at the Paris Conservatory, where his teachers included Massenet and Fauré. He exercised a considerable influence on younger French composers, not least through his theoretical writings. His output is vast and leaves hardly any category of music unprovided, and although he sought no success and obtained little, his work is of high quality and lasting interest.

Works ORCHESTRAL seven pieces inspired by Kipling's *Jungle Book*, including *Trois Poèmes* for soloists, choir, and orchestra, Op. 18 (1899–1919), symphonic poems *La Course de printemps* (1925–27), *La Méditation de Parun Baghat* (1936), *La Loi de la Jungle* (1939), and *Les Bandar-Log* (1939–40); *Symphonie d'hymnes* (1910–33); *Seven Stars Symphony* (on film stars including Greta Garbo, Marlene Dietrich, and Charlie Chaplin; 1933); symphonic poem *Le Docteur fabricius* (1944).

CHAMBER three string quartets; sonatas for violin, viola, cello, flute, oboe, clarinet, bassoon, and horn, all with piano; 13 sonatinas for piano.

OTHER choruses, songs.

Koffler, Józef (1896–1943) Polish composer. After studying with Arnold Schoenberg, he began to cultivate the 12-note system, the first Polish composer to do so. Later he became professor at the Lviv State Conservatory, but was killed during a Nazi roundup of Jews near Kraków.

He studied composition with Hermann Theodor Otto Grädener (1844–1929) and musicology with Guido Adler (1855–1941) in Vienna, Austria.

Works BALLET *Alles durch M.O.W.*

ORCHESTRAL three symphonies (no. 3 performed London, 1938) and *Polish Suite* for orchestra; 15 variations for string orchestra.

CHAMBER string quartet, string trio (performed Oxford, 1931).

VOCAL cantata *Die Liebe* for voices, viola, cello, and clarinet; four poems for voice and piano.

PIANO *Musique de ballet* (1927), *Musique quasi una sonata*, sonatina, and other pieces; 40 *Polish Folksongs*.

Kokkonen, Joonas (1921–1996) Finnish composer. His early work was neoclassical in spirit; later influences were Bach, Sibelius, and Bartók. He was professor of composition at the Sibelius Academy, Helsinki, Finland, 1959–63.

He studied with Selim Palmgren and Tauno Hannikainen at the Sibelius Academy, Helsinki.

Works OPERA *Viimeiset Kiusauset/The Last Temptations* (produced Helsinki, 1975; London, 1979). ORCHESTRAL five symphonies (1960–82), *Music for Strings* (1957), cello concerto (1969). SACRED *Missa a cappella* (1963), Requiem (1983). CHAMBER piano trio (1948), three string quartets (1959, 1966, 1976), *Sinfonia da camera* for twelve strings (1962), ... *durch einen spiegel* for twelve strings and harpsichord (1977), *Improvvisazione* for violin and piano (1982), *Il paesaggio* for chamber orchestra (1987).

Kokoschka, Oskar (1886–1980) German poet, playwright, and painter. His works inspired the composers Paul Hindemith (➤ **Mörder, Hoffnung der Frauen**) and Ernst Křenek (➤ **Orpheus und Eurydike**).

Kolb, Barbara (1939–) US composer. She has taught theory and composition in New York and has directed the Third Street Music School Settlement from 1979. She was resident at the electronic studio ➤ **IRCAM** in Paris, France, 1983–84. She studied composition and clarinet at Hartt College and with Lukas Foss and Gunther Schuller at the Berkshire Music Center.

Works ORCHESTRAL *Millefoglie* for chamber orchestra (1988), *The Enchanted Loom* for orchestra (1989), *Voyants* for piano and chamber orchestra (1991), *All in Good Time* for orchestra (1993). INSTRUMENTAL *Trobar clus* for 13 instruments (1970), *Soundings* for eleven instruments and tape (1972), *Musique pour un vernissage* for ensemble (1977), *The Point that Divides the Wind* for organ and four percussionists (1981), *Clouds* for organ, piano, and tape (1992). VOCAL AND INSTRUMENTAL *Frailties* for tenor, tape, and orchestra (1971).

kolenda, modern **kolæda** a type of Polish folksong (carol) sung at Christmas; some specimens date back to the 13th century.

Kollmann, August Friedrich Christoph (1756–1829) German organist, theorist, and composer. He held a post at Lüne, near Lüneburg, but in 1782 went to London, England, where he was appointed sacristan and cantor of the German Chapel, St James's. He wrote many theoretical works, and also composed a piano concerto and chamber music.

Kol Nidre, All Vows work for cello and orchestra by Max ➤ **Bruch**, composed in 1881. There is also a version for cello and piano. Arnold ➤ **Schoen-**

berg's *Kol Nidre* for speaker (rabbi), chorus, and orchestra, Op. 39, was composed in the autumn of 1938, and was first performed in Los Angeles, USA, on 4 October 1938, conducted by Schoenberg.

kolo Siberian dance in quick 2/4 time. The 15th of Dvořák's *Slavonic Dances* for piano duet is a kolo.

Kondracki, Michał (1902–1984) Polish composer. He studied with Karol Szymanowski in Warsaw and with Paul Dukas and Nadia Boulanger in Paris, France, returning to Poland in 1931.
  Works STAGE opera *Popieliny* (1934); ballet *Legend of Kraków* (1937).
  CANTATAS *Cantata ecclesiastica* and humorous cantata *Krasula*.
  ORCHESTRAL *Little Mountain Symphony*, symphonic action *Metropolis* (1929), toccata and fugue, symphonic picture *Soldiers March Past*, *Match*, partita for small orchestra, nocturne for chamber orchestra; piano concerto.

Kondrashin, Kiril (1914–1981) Russian conductor. He conducted opera in Leningrad and Moscow 1936–56. He was principal conductor of the Moscow Philharmonic Orchestra 1960–75 and assistant conductor of the Concertgebouw Orchestra from 1975. He recorded the Shostakovich symphonies and gave the first performances of no. 13 (1962) and the second violin concerto (1967). He conducted at the Hollywood Bowl one month before his death.

König Hirsch, The Stag King opera by Hans Werner Henze (libretto by H von Cramer after Carlo Gozzi's *Re cervo*, 1762), first produced in Berlin, Germany, on 23 September 1956. It was revised as *Il re cervo* in 1962 and produced in Kassel, Germany, on 10 March 1963. The first staging of the complete score in the original version was given in Stuttgart, Germany, on 5 May 1985. The story tells how King Leandro assumes the shape of a stag and his treacherous chancellor, Tartaglia, magically transforms himself to the king's appearance, and orders a stag hunt. Tartaglia is killed by the assassin Coltellino who, under contract from Tartaglia himself, believes him to be the king. All rejoice.

Königin von Saba, Die, The Queen of Sheba opera by Karoly Goldmark (libretto by S H Mosenthal), first produced at the Vienna Opera House, Austria, on 10 March 1875. It tells how King Solomon's diplomat Assad forsakes his fiancée Sulamith for a secret affair with the queen of Sheba. Assad blasphemes publicly, placing the queen above the gods; he is banished to the desert, where he is reconciled with Sulamith and dies.

Königskinder, King's Children opera by Engelbert Humperdinck (libretto by E Rosmer), first produced as a play with accompanying music in Munich, Germany, on 23 January 1897; the operatic version was first produced at the New York Metropolitan Opera House on 28 December 1910. The story tells how a goose-girl escapes from the witch and is united with the king's son, but both are rejected by the townspeople, and die after eating the witch's poisoned bread.

König Stephan incidental music by Beethoven, Op. 117, for August von Kotzebue's play written for the opening of the new theatre at Pest (now Budapest), Hungary, and first performed there on 9 February 1812.

Kontakte work by Karlheinz ➜ **Stockhausen** for piano, percussion, and four-track tape, composed 1959–60 and first perfomed in Cologne, Germany, on 11 June 1960.

Kontrapunkte work by Karlheinz Stockhausen for six wind instruments, piano, harp, violin, and cello, composed 1952–53 and first performed in Cologne, Germany, on 26 May 1953.

Konzertmeister (German 'concert master') the ➜ **leader** of an orchestra.

Konzertstück German 'concerto piece'; see ➜ **Concertstück**.

Kopfton (German 'head note') musical term; see ➜ **fundamental line**.

kora plucked harp-lute with 21 strings, from West Africa. It is used by professional male musicians known as *jalolu* (singular *jali*) of the Mandinka people of Gambia and Senegal. The kora mainly accompanies narrations, recitations, and songs in honour of a patron.

Korn, Peter (Jona) (1920–) German-born US composer and conductor. After studies with Edmund Rubbra in London, England, he moved to the USA in 1941, continuing his studies with Ernst Toch and Arnold Schoenberg. He founded the Los Angeles New Orchestra in 1948 and was its conductor until 1956. In 1967 he was appointed director of the Strauss Conservatory in Munich, Germany.
  Works OPERA *Heidi* (1963, first performance 1978).
  ORCHESTRAL three symphonies (1946, 1952, 1956), violin concerto (1965), *Beckmesser* variations for orchestra (1977), trumpet concerto (1979).
  CHAMBER two string quartets (1950, 1963), wind quintet (1964), piano trio (1975), octet (1976), duo for viola and piano (1978).

Korngold, Erich (Wolfgang) (1897–1957) Austrian composer. Son of Julius Korngold (1860–1945), music critic of the *Neue Freie Presse* in Vienna. Through his father's influence, Korngold had his pantomime *Der Schneemann* (1910), orchestrated by Zemlinsky) produced at the Court Opera when he was 13. He studied with Fuchs, Grädener and Zemlinsky and was appointed conductor at the Hamburg Opera in 1919, and professor at the Vienna State Academy in 1927. After the *Anschluss* he emigrated to the USA, where he collaborated with Max Reinhardt at his Theatre School at Hollywood. He was successful as a writer of film music, which developed from his earlier late Romantic style.

Works VOCAL operas *Der Ring des Polycrates*, *Violanta* (1916), *Die tote Stadt* (1920), *Das Wunder der Heliane* (1927), *Die Katrin* (1939); songs.

ORCHESTRAL incidental music to Shakespeare's *Much Ado about Nothing* (1919); film music for *Sea Hawk*, *The Adventures of Robin Hood*, etc.; *Symphonietta*; *Symphony-overture*; *Overture to a play*; a piano concerto for the left hand (1923); a violin concerto (1946).

INSTRUMENTAL string quartet; piano trio; piano quintet; sextet; sonata for violin and piano; three piano sonatas and other works for piano.

Kossuth symphonic poem in ten tableaux by Béla Bartók; composed in 1903 and first performed in Budapest, Hungary, on 13 January 1904.

koto plucked Japanese string instrument; a long ✦ zither of ancient Chinese origin with 13 silk or nylon strings stretched over moveable bridges. It rests on the floor and the strings are plucked with ivory plectrums worn on the thumb and two fingers of the right hand. The left hand presses the strings behind the bridges to alter the tuning, add ornaments, and create effects such as vibrato and slide. The koto produces a brittle sound.

Kotzebue, August (Friedrich Ferdinand) von (1761–1819) German playwright. He inspired the following composers and works: Beethoven (✦ König Stephan and ✦ Ruins of Athens), Pietro ✦ Generali (*Misantropia e pentimento*), Albert ✦ Lortzing (*Wildschütz*), Johann ✦ Reichardt (*Kreuzfahrer*), Peter Ritter (*Eremit auf Formentara*), Antonio ✦ Salieri (*Hussiten vor Naumburg*), Franz Schubert (*Des* ✦ Teufels Lustschloss), Franz ✦ Süssmayr (*Wildfang*), and Paul ✦ Wranitzky (music for plays).

Koukourgi opera from which Luigi Cherubini derived his ✦ Ali Baba, ou Les Quarante Voleurs.

Koussevitsky, Sergei (1874–1951) Russian musician and conductor. He is well known for his work in the USA. He established his own orchestra in Moscow in 1909, introducing works by Prokofiev, Rachmaninov, and Stravinsky. Although named director of the State Symphony after the Bolshevik Revolution of 1917, Koussevitsky left the USSR for the USA, becoming direc-

tor of the Boston Symphony Orchestra in 1924.

Koussevitsky was trained at a conservatory in Moscow, becoming a recognized virtuoso on the double bass; he later specialized as a soloist on the instrument and toured Europe. He first appeared as a conductor in Berlin, Germany, in 1908. In 1924 he was appointed conductor of the Boston Symphony Orchestra, and in 1934 founded the annual Tanglewood summer music festival in western Massachusetts. He commissioned Stravinsky's *Symphony of Psalms* in 1931 and in 1943 Béla Bartók's Concerto for orchestra. Other works he premiered include the Mussorgsky/Ravel *Pictures* (1922), Prokofiev's first violin concerto (1923) and second symphony (1925), and Leonard Bernstein's second symphony (1949). The Koussevitsky Music Foundation, set up as a memorial to his wife, commissioned Benjamin Britten's *Peter Grimes* (1945), among other works.

Kozeluch (Kotzeluch, Koželuh), Leopold (1747–1818) Bohemian composer. He was a pupil of his cousin Johann Anton Kozeluch (1738–1814), and studied law at Prague University, but devoted himself entirely to composition from 1771. In 1778 he went to Vienna, Austria, and succeeded Mozart as imperial composer in 1792.

Works STAGE operas *Didone abbandonata*, *Judith*, *Deborah*, and others; 24 ballets and three pantomimes.

ORATORIO *Moisé in Egitto* (1787).

ORCHESTRAL eleven symphonies; 22 piano concertos and several for other instruments.

CHAMBER six string quartets, 63 trios; piano sonatas.

OTHER folk-song arrangements.

Kraft, Anton (1749–1820) Bohemian cellist and composer. Beethoven's Triple Concerto was composed for him, and he played in the first performance of Beethoven's seventh symphony in 1813. Haydn's D major cello concerto was once ascribed to Kraft.

Originally intended for a career in law, he was engaged by Prince Esterházy as principal cellist in 1778, remaining until 1790 and receiving tuition in composition from Haydn. He was subsequently in the service of Prince Grassalkovich and (from 1795) Prince Lobkowitz.

Works concertos, sonatas, and other pieces for cello, duets for two cellos.

Kraft, William (1923–) US composer and timpanist. He founded and directed the Los Angeles Percussion Ensemble, giving the US first performances of Karlheinz Stockhausen's *Zyklus* and Pierre Boulez's *Le Marteau sans maître*. He was principal with the Los Angeles Philharmonic Orchestra 1955–81 and composer-in-residence 1981–85.

He studied at University College of Los Angeles, then at Columbia University 1949–52, with Henry Brant and Otto Luening.

Works ORCHESTRAL AND INSTRUMENTAL *Concerto Grosso* (1961), Concerto for four percussion and orchestra (1966), *Triangles* for percussion and ten instruments (1969), piano concerto (1973), timpani concerto (1983), *Weavings* for string quartet and percussion (1984), horn concerto (1988).

VOCAL *Contextures II* for soprano, tenor, and chamber orchestra (1984), *A Kennedy Portrait* for narrator and orchestra (1988).

krakowiak a Polish dance from the region of Kraków, sometimes introduced into ballets and ballrooms in the 19th century under the name of *Cracovienne*. In its original form it was danced by all the assembled couples and sometimes words were sung to it. It is in quick 2/4 time. The best-known example is Chopin's concert rondo Op. 14 (1828).

Krämerspiegel, The Shopkeeper's Mirror cycle of twelve songs for voice and piano by Richard Strauss (texts by Alfred Kerr), composed in 1918. The work includes ironic references to German publishers: no. 2, *Einst kam der Bock als Bote*, refers to the Berlin publishing firm, Bote und Bock. The cycle was first performed in Berlin, Germany, on 1 November 1926.

Kraus, Joseph Martin (1756–1792) German composer. He settled in Sweden and became director of music to the king. His opera *Proserpina* (1781) was revived at the Drottningholm Theatre, near Stockholm, Sweden, in 1981.

He studied law and philosophy at Mainz, Erfurt, and Göttingen, and studied composition with Georg Vogler. He went to Stockholm and remained there as a theatre conductor, becoming music director in 1781. In 1782–87 he travelled widely with a grant from the king of Sweden. In 1788 he succeeded Francesco Uttini as Kapellmeister at Stockholm.

Works OPERA *Soliman II, Aeneas at Carthage* (produced 1799), *Proserpina* (1781).

SACRED church music; *Funeral Cantata for Gustavas III* (1792).

ORCHESTRAL AND CHAMBER symphonies and overtures; string quartets.

Krauss, Clemens (1893–1954) Austrian conductor. From 1912 he conducted at several opera houses in Germany and Austria, including Vienna and Berlin. He was closely associated with Richard Strauss, both as a conductor, and in the case of *Capriccio*, as joint librettist; he conducted the first performances of *Arabella, Friedenstag*, and *Die Liebe der Danae*.

Krauss studied with Hermann Theodor Otto Grädener (1844–1929) and Richard Heuberger at the Vienna Conservatory. In 1922 he became

conductor at the Vienna Staatsoper and in 1924 opera intendant and conductor of the Museum concerts in Frankfurt. He was director of the Vienna Staatsoper 1929–34 and the Berlin Staatsoper 1934–36, after which he directed the Opera at Munich. He married the singer Viorica Ursuleac (1894–1985).

Krebs, Johann Ludwig (1713–1780) German organist, harpsichordist, and composer. He was a pupil of Johann Sebastian Bach in Leipzig from 1726, and became organist at Zwickau, Zeitz, and Altenburg.

Works Magnificat, settings of the Sanctus; trios; sonatas, suites, fugues, choruses, with variations, and other pieces for clavier; flute sonatas, organ music.

Krehbiel, Henry (Edward) (1854–1923) US music critic and author. After studying law at Cincinnati, he became music critic to the *Cincinnati Gazette* in 1874 and to the *New York Tribune* in 1880. He edited Alexander Thayer's life of Beethoven, collected and wrote on African–American folksongs, and wrote many books including studies of opera, Richard Wagner's works, and US musical life.

Kreidekreis, Der, The Chalk Circle opera by Alexander von Zemlinsky (libretto by composer after Klabund), composed in 1932 and first produced in Zurich, Switzerland, on 14 October 1933. It was Zemlinsky's last completed opera. It tells the story of how the prostitute Haitang becomes empress of China after Prince Pao reveals he is the father of her child.

Kreisler, Fritz (1875–1962) Austrian violinist and composer. He was a US citizen from 1943. His prolific output of recordings in the early 20th century introduced a wider public to classical music from old masters such as Johann Sebastian Bach and François Couperin to moderns such as Manuel de Falla and Sergei Rachmaninov. He also composed and recorded romantic pieces in the style of the classics, often under a pseudonym. He gave the first performance of Edward Elgar's *Violin Concerto* in 1910, dedicated to him by the composer.

Kreisler appeared as an infant prodigy at the age of seven. He studied at the Vienna Conservatory under Joseph Hellmesberger and Jacques Auber, and at the Paris Conservatory under Joseph Massart and Léo Delibes, winning the gold medal at the age of 12. After touring in the USA in 1889 he returned to Austria to study medicine. After his military service and a period of intense study, he reappeared as a soloist in Berlin in 1899 and again toured in the USA. After three months' service in the Austrian army in 1914 he was discharged on account of wounds and returned to the USA, where he eventually made his home. He made frequent tours in Europe and gave the first performance of Elgar's violin concerto (10 November 1910). He was best known for his broad-toned and emotionally committed performances of the Brahms and Beethoven violin concertos. His compositions include a string quartet, the operetta *Apple Blossoms* (1919), and a number of violin solos, some of which he at first tried to present as the work of 18th-century composers.

Kreisleriana a cycle of piano pieces by Robert Schumann, Op. 16, composed in 1838 and dedicated to Chopin. The title is borrowed from the musician Kreisler in E T A Hoffmann's stories *Fantasiestücke in Callots Manier*.

Krejčí, Iša (1904–1968) Czech composer. He was a pupil of Vitězslav Novák and Karel Jirák. After working for some time in Bratislava, he returned to Prague and joined the radio service.

Works STAGE opera *Confusion at Ephesus* (on Shakespeare's *The Comedy of Errors*, 1946); operatic scene *Antigone* (after Sophocles, 1934).

ORCHESTRAL sinfonietta for orchestra.

CHAMBER *Little Ballet* for chamber orchestra; string quartet in D major, nonet, trios for oboe, clarinet, and bassoon and clarinet, double bass and piano; sonatina for clarinet and piano.

OTHER songs.

Křenek, Ernst (1900–1991) Austrian-born US composer and theorist. Following early popular success with the jazz-influenced operas *Jonny spielt auf/Johnny Strikes Up* (1926) and *Leben des Orest/Life of Orestes* (1930), he supported himself as a critic while working on the ambitious 12-tone opera *Karl V/Charles V* (1938). He moved to teaching posts in the USA in 1939 but remained in contact with post-war developments in extended serialism and aleatoric music with *Quaestio Temporis/In Search of Time* (1957), and with electronic music in *Spiritus intelligentiae sanctus* (1956).

His writings include the study *Johannes Ockeghem* (1953) and *Horizon Circled* (1974).

Křenek studied with Franz Schreker in Vienna, Austria, and Berlin, Germany. In the 1920s he appeared at several of the smaller festivals in Germany and 1925–27 was conductor at the operas of Kassel, Wiesbaden, and other smaller towns in order to gain experience in operatic stagecraft. His first wife was Gustav Mahler's daughter Anna. After the success of *Jonny spielt auf*, he worked in 12-note music as a disciple of Arnold Schoenberg. In 1933, when the Nazi régime gained the upper hand, he settled in Vienna and worked on behalf of progressive Austrian composers, but he was opposed by the fascists and his *Karl V* was banned from the Vienna Staatsoper. He left Austria for the USA in 1937, where he later became dean of the School of Fine Arts

and director of the music department at Hamline University, St Paul, 1942–47; he lived in California from 1948. His book *Über neue Musik*, first published in Vienna in 1937 and then translated and revised as *Music Here and Now* (New York, 1939), is a defence of the 12-note system.

Amends for the hostile treatment he received in Vienna were made with the 1990 first performance of his 1930 musical satire *Kehraus um St Stephan* – a revision of *Karl V* had been given at Vienna in 1984. Belated recognition in his homeland was also shown with the 1988 Salzburg Festival premiere of his 1935 oratorio *Symeon der Stylit*.

Works OPERA *Jonny spielt auf* (1926), *Leben des Orest* (1930), *Karl V* (1938), *Der goldene Bock* (1964).

CHORAL MUSIC *Lamentatio Jeremiae Prophetae* (1941).

ORCHESTRAL five symphonies (1921–50), two *Concerti grossi*; four piano concertos (1923–50), two violin concertos (1924, 1954), cello concerto; theme and 13 variations for orchestra (1931).

CHAMBER AND SOLO VOCAL eight string quartets (1921–52); 25 songs, song cycles *Reisebuch aus den österreichischen Alpen* (1929), *Gesänge des späten Jahres*.

Kreutzer, Conradin (1780–1849) German conductor and composer. He held the post of Kapellmeister in Stuttgart, Donaueschingen, Vienna, and Cologne. His most successful composition was the opera *Der Verschwender* (1834).

He first learnt music as a choirboy, then went to Freiburg im Breisgau to study law, but gave it up for music. He travelled in Switzerland as a pianist and singer and in 1804 went to Vienna to study composition with Johann Albrechtsberger. After conducting at the courts of Stuttgart and Donaueschingen, he returned to Vienna and became conductor at the Kärntnertortheater for three periods between 1822 and 1840 and of the Josefstadttheater 1833–40. Later he worked in Cologne and Paris, and again in Vienna.

Works STAGE operas *Conradin von Schwaben* (1812), *Die Alpenhütte* (1815), *Libussa* (libretto by Grillparzer, 1822), *Melusine* (libretto as above, 1833), *Das Nachtlager von Granada* (1834), *Cordelia*, and about 25 others; incidental music to plays including Raimund's *Der Verschwender* (1834).

SACRED oratorio *Sending Moses* (1814); church music.

OTHER chamber music; piano works; male-voice part songs and songs.

Kreutzer, Rodolphe (1766–1831) French violinist and composer of German descent. Beethoven dedicated his violin sonata Op. 47 to him, known as the *Kreutzer Sonata*.

Kreutzer was born at Versailles, and was taught

mainly by his father. When he was 16 the French queen Marie Antoinette appointed him first violin in the royal chapel, where he learnt much from hearing Nicola Mestrino (1748–1789) and Giovanni Battista Viotti. Later he became leader at the Théâtre Italien, where he began to write operas of his own. He toured much and became violin professor at the Paris Conservatory in 1795. In 1798 he went to Vienna, Austria, in the suite of Count Bernadotte and got to know Beethoven. He often played violin duets with Pierre Rode, and on the latter's departure to Russia in 1801, Kreutzer became leader at the Paris Opéra. He later held court appointments under both Napoleon I and Louis XVIII. He compiled a *Méthode de violon* with the violinist Pierre Baillot.

Works OPERA *Jeanne d'Arc à Orléans* (1790), *Paul et Virginie* (after Saint-Pierre), *Lodoïska* (1791), *Imogène, ou La Gageure indiscrète* (after Boccaccio, 1796), *Astyanax, Aristippe* (1808), *La Mort d'Abel* (1810), *Mathilde* and many others.

BALLET *Paul et Virginie*, *Le Carnaval de Venise*, *Clari*, and others.

ORCHESTRAL 19 violin concertos (1783–1810), four *Symphonies concertantes*.

CHAMBER 15 string quartets; 15 trios; sonatas, caprices, studies, airs with variations for violin.

'Kreutzer' Sonata nickname of Beethoven's A-major violin and piano sonata, Op. 47, composed in 1803 and dedicated to Rodolphe Kreutzer. The work is the subject of Leo Tolstoy's novel *The Kreutzer Sonata*, in which it has a disastrous effect on the morals of the characters. Beethoven and George Bridgetower gave the first performance of the work on 17 May 1803. It is also the subtitle of Janáček's first string quartet, composed 1923–24, based on a lost piano trio of 1908–09. This piece was inspired by the Tolstoy novel, and bears no thematic relation to Beethoven's original sonata. It was first performed in Prague, Czechoslovakia (modern Czech Republic), on 17 September 1924.

Křička, Jaroslav (1882–1969) Czech composer. He taught in Russia, and on his return to Prague in 1909 became conductor of the Glagol choral society. He was director of the Prague Conservatory 1942–45.

He studied at the Prague Conservatory 1902–05, and came under the influence of Vítězslav Novák, enlarged his experience in Berlin, and then went to Russia, teaching at the music school of Ekaterinoslav.

Works OPERA *Hypolita* (after one of Maurice Hewlett's *Little Novels of Italy*, 1916) and *The Gentleman in White* (after Wilde's *Canterville Ghost*, 1929); several operas for children.

CHORAL *The Temptation in the Wilderness* (1922) and many others, with and without orchestra.

ORCHESTRAL symphony in D minor, symphon-

ic poems *Faith*, overture to Maeterlinck's *Blue Bird* (1911), *Polonaise* and *Elegy on the Death of Rimsky-Korsakov*, *Children's Suite* for small orchestra (1907), *Nostalgia* for string orchestra.

CHAMBER three string quartets (1907–39), violin and piano sonata.

OTHER piano music and songs.

Krieger, Johann (1651–1735) German organist and composer. He was court organist at Bayreuth 1671–77, and later became organist and town music director at Zittau.

He was taught by his brother, Philipp ➤ Krieger.

Works plays with music; sacred and secular songs for several voices with instruments; organ works; six partitas, preludes and fugues for clavier.

Krieger, Johann Philipp (1649–1725) German organist and composer, brother of Johann ➤ Krieger. He travelled in Italy and studied under Johann Rosenmüller in Venice. He then entered the service of the Duke of Saxe-Weissenfels, and was chamber musician and organist at Halle from 1677 and music director at Weissenfels from 1712.

Works the opera *Der grossmütige Scipio* (1690) and others; plays with music; church music; arias for one to four voices with instruments; sonatas for violin and viola da gamba; *Partien* for wind instruments.

Krips, Josef (1902–1974) Austrian conductor. He studied in Vienna with Eusebius Mandyczewski and Felix Weingartner, and became a violinist in the Volksoper d   e. In 1924 he began his career as a conductor and from 1926 to 1933 was general music director at Karlsruhe. In 1933 he became a conductor at the Vienna Staatsoper and in 1935 professor at the Vienna Academy of Music.

He made his Salzburg Festival debut in 1935 with *Der Rosenkavalier*; he returned in 1946, with *Don Giovanni*. During World War II he lost these positions, but rejoined the Vienna Staatsoper in 1945; he took the company to the Royal Opera House, Covent Garden, London, England, in 1947, conducting Mozart's three Da Ponte operas. He returned with the Covent Garden company in 1963, with *Don Giovanni*. From 1950 to 1954 he was conductor at the London Symphony Orchestra, then with the San Francisco Symphony Orchestra 1963–70 and the New York Metropolitan Opera from 1967 (with *Zauberflöte*).

kriti (Telugu 'work', 'composition') an important genre of south Indian (Carnatic) music. Essentially a song in three sections (*pallavi, anupallavi, charanam*), it is often performed with the addition of improvised sections. Kritis also form an important part of the solo instrumental repertoire. Important composers include Tyagaraja (1767–1847) and Muttuswami Dikshitar (1775–1835).

Krommer, Franz, originally **Kramář, František Vincenc (1759–1831)** Moravian violinist, organist and composer. Having been an organist 1776–84, he went to Hungary and later became music director to Prince Grassalkovich in Vienna. In 1818 he succeeded Leopold Kozeluch as court music director.

Works two masses; music for wind band; symphonies; and 69 string quartets and quintets.

Krumhorn German spelling of ➤ crumhorn, a Renaissance double-reed woodwind instrument.

Krumpholz, Johann Baptist (1742–1790) Bohemian harpist and composer. He grew up in Paris, France, travelled as a virtuoso, and was in the service of Prince Esterházy 1773–76, receiving tuition in composition from Haydn. After further travels he settled in Paris, and was responsible for some notable improvements to his instrument. When his wife deserted him for the composer Jan Dussek, he drowned himself in the River Seine.

Works eight concertos, 32 sonatas for harp; two symphonies for harp and small orchestra; harp duets.

Kubelík, Jan (1880–1940) Czech violinist. He was taught by his father, a gardener and good amateur musician, and made his first public appearance in Prague in 1888. In 1892 he entered the Conservatory as a pupil of Ševčik and began his real career with a concert in Vienna in 1898. He made his London debut in 1900 and worked in the USA from 1902, retiring in 1940. Among his compositions are six violin concertos.

Kubelík, Rafael (1914–1996) Czech conductor and composer. Son of Jan Kubelík, he studied at the Prague Conservatory, making his debut with the Czech Symphony Orchestra in 1934. From 1939 to 1941 he was conductor of the National Theatre in Brno and from 1942 to 1948 of the Czech Philharmonic Orchestra. Between 1948 and 1950 he was often in England and in 1950 was appointed principal conductor of the Chicago Symphony Orchestra. He returned to Europe in 1953 and became music director at the Royal Opera House, Covent Garden, London (1955–58), conducting the first British *Jenůfa* there in 1956 and the first complete *Les Troyens* in 1957. In 1961 he became conductor of the Bavarian Radio Symphony Orchestra and in Vienna gave the first performance of Schoenberg's oratorio *Die Jakobsleiter*. He made his debut at the Metropolitan Opera House, New York in 1973 with *Les Troyens*. He returned to Czechoslovakia in 1990, after the Velvet Revolution, and conduc-

ted Smetana's *Ma Vlást* to wide acclaim. He has also composed, and his works include the operas *Veronika* (1947) and *Cornelia Faroli* (on the life of Titian, 1972); a choral symphony; concertos for violin and for cello; a Requiem; and some chamber music.

Kubik, Gail (1914–1984) US violinist and composer. She studied at the Eastman School of Music, Rochester, New York , and won several composition prizes.

Works BALLET *Frankie and Johnnie* for dance band and folk singer (1946).

VOCAL *In Praise of Johnny Appleseed* (Vachel Lindsay) for baritone, chorus, and orchestra.

ORCHESTRAL three symphonies (1949–57); suite for orchestra; two violin concertos, *American Caprice* for piano and 32 instruments.

CHAMBER two *Sketches* for string quartet, piano trio, wind quintet, *Trivialities* for flute, horn, and string quartet.

Kuhlau, (Daniel) Frederik (Rudolph) (1786–1832) German-born Danish composer. His music spans the end of the classical period and the beginning of the Romantic style. During the French occupation he went to Denmark to escape conscription and became a flautist in the court orchestra in Copenhagen. In 1825 he visited Vienna, Austria, and met Beethoven, who composed a punning canon on his name.

A child of poor parents, he picked up musical knowledge at Brunswick and Hamburg, Germany.

Works STAGE operas *Røverborgen* (1814), *Trylleharpen* (1817), *Lulu* (1824), and several others; incidental music for Heiberg's *Elverhøj* (1828).

OTHER piano works; flute pieces.

Kuhnau, Johann (1660–1722) German organist, harpsichordist, composer, and writer on music. He was Johann Sebastian Bach's predecessor in the post of cantor at St Thomas's Church, Leipzig. His biblical sonatas for harpsichord are early examples of ➤ programme music.

He was cantor at Zittau and went to Leipzig in 1682. In 1684 he became organist at St Thomas's, in 1700 was appointed music director of the university and the churches of St Nicholas and St Thomas, and in 1701 became cantor of St Thomas's.

Other works include motets on hymn tunes and other church music; partitas and other pieces for harpsichord, including seven sonatas entitled *Frische Clavier-Früchte*, and the six sonatas *Biblische Historien* (1700).

Kullak, Theodor (1818–1882) German pianist and composer. He was intended for a career in law and at some time studied medicine, but in 1842 decided definitely in favour of music and went to Vienna, Austria, to finish his piano stud-

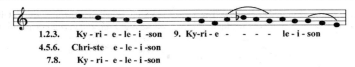

1.2.3.　Ky - ri - e - le - i -son　9. Ky-ri - e - - - - le - i - son
4.5.6.　Chri-ste　e - le - i -son
7.8.　Ky - ri - e - le - i -son

A kyrie in which the plainsong melody is varied only on the ninth and final time.

ies with Carl Czerny. In 1846 he became court pianist to the king of Prussia and settled in Berlin, founding a conservatory with Julius Stern and Adolph Marx there in 1850, and one of his own in 1855.

Works a piano concerto in C minor; piano trio; duets for piano and violin; a vast number of piano pieces, studies.

Kullervo symphonic poem by Jean Sibelius for soloists, chorus, and orchestra, based on legends from the *Kalevala*. It was withdrawn after its first performance in Helsinki, Finland, on 28 April 1892 and not heard again until after Sibelius's death in 1957. It is also the title of an opera in two acts by Aulis Sallinen (libretto by composer, after Aleksis Kivi), first produced at the Music Center, Los Angeles, USA, on 25 February 1992. It tells how Kullervo, raised in violence and alienation, commits violence on all around him, before his own suicide.

Kunst der Fuge, Die, The Art of Fugue Johann Sebastian Bach's last work, left unfinished at his death in 1750. It is a series of examples of the art of fugal and canonic writing, all based on the same theme.

Kupferman, Meyer (1926–2003) US composer and clarinettist. He made his debut as a soloist in New York in 1946. He taught at the Sarah Lawrence College from 1951. His music derives from jazz, electronics, and serialism.

Works OPERA *In a Garden* (1949) and *Doctor Faustus Lights the Lights* (1953), both after Gertrude Stein.

ORCHESTRAL two piano concertos (1948, 1978); eleven symphonies (1950–83); concerto for cello and jazz band (1962); violin and clarinet concertos (1976, 1984); *Savage Landscape* for orchestra (1989).

CHAMBER five string quartets; *Sound Phantoms*, ten pieces for chamber ensemble, no. 10 (1981); *Top Brass Five* for five trumpets (1989).

VOCAL *Wicke Combinations*, song cycle for mezzo and piano (1989); *A Crucible for the Moon* for soprano, alto saxophone, and percussion orchestra (1986).

Kurtág, György (1926–) Hungarian composer. Early influences were Béla Bartók and Zoltán Kodály; later he employed a post-Webern serial technique, in which mosaics of sound are used to build a larger compositional picture.

He studied in Budapest, Hungary, and Paris, France.

Works CHAMBER AND INSTRUMENTAL string quartet (1959); eight duets for violin and cimbalom (1961); string quintet (1971); *Splinters*, for solo cimbalom (1975); *Homage to Luigi Nono*, for chamber ensemble (1980); *Officium Breve*, for string quartet (1989); double concerto for piano, cello, and two chamber ensembles (1990).

VOCAL *In Memory of a Winter Sunset*, for soprano, violin, and cimbalom (1969); *Messages of the Late Miss R V Troussova* for soprano and chamber ensemble (1980); *Scenes from a Novel* for soprano and ensemble (1981); *Attila-József Fragments* for soprano (1981); *Kafka Fragmente* for soprano and violin (1986); *Requiem for the Beloved* for soprano and piano (1987); *Samuel Beckett: What is the Word* for alto voices and ensemble.

Kurzwellen, Shortwaves work by Karlheinz Stockhausen for electronics and four short-wave radios; first performed in Bremen, Germany, on 5 May 1968. It was developed as *Beethausen, Op. 1970, von Stockhoven*.

Kvapil, Jaroslav (1892–1958) Czech composer. He studied with Leoš Janáček at Brno and was later appointed professor of organ and counterpoint at the Organ School there. In 1911–13 he continued studying at the Leipzig Conservatory, Germany, and on his return to Brno became professor of piano and composition at the Conservatory and conductor of the Philharmonic Society.

Works ORCHESTRAL four symphonies, variations and fugue for orchestra.

VOCAL cantata for baritone solo, chorus and orchestra.

CHAMBER six string quartets, piano quintet, piano trio; two violin and piano sonatas, cello and piano sonata; piano sonata and pieces.

OTHER songs.

Kyrie Eleison (Greek 'Lord have mercy') the words spoken or sung at the beginning of the Mass in the Catholic, Orthodox, and Anglican churches. Following the Introit, it has three parts of text: 'Kyrie Eleison, Christe Eleison, Kyrie Eleison', each of which is repeated three times, reflecting the Holy Trinity.

In musical setting, it is the first item of the Ordinary of the Mass. Originally it was not part of the Mass but of various Litanies, at the head of which it still stands. In the Mass it has a nine-fold structure, and the simplest melodic form consisted of eight repetitions of a simple melody followed by a quite different melody for the ninth clause. This melody closely resembles that still used for the Litany Kyries for Rogationtide and Holy Saturday. Other musical forms in common use were: *aaa bbb aaa'*; *aaa bbb ccc'*; and *aba cdc efe'* (a stroke represents an extended form of the phrase concerned).

l in music, the submediant note in any key in tonic sol-fa notation, pronounced Lah.

La in music, the old name for the note A (see ➤ **solmization**), still used in Latin countries, and in tonic sol-fa notation the submediant note in any key, represented by the symbol l, pronounced Lah.

La Barbara, Joan (1947–   ) US composer and vocal performer. She was a vocalist with Steve Reich and Musicians 1971–74, and worked with Philip Glass 1973–76. Her performances involve novel techniques of sound production, rather than singing as such. She gave the first performances of works by John Cage, Morton Feldman, and her husband, Morton Subotnick.

She undertook vocal studies with Phyllis Curtin at Tanglewood and in New York, and studied composition at New York University.

Works *VOICES AND INSTRUMENTS Hear What I Feel* for amplified voice (1974), *Space Testing* for acoustic voice (1976), *Chandra* for amplified solo voice, men's voices, and chamber orchestra (1978), *Winds of the Canyon* for voice and tape (1982), *The Solar Wind I-III* for voice(s) and ensembles (1983–84), *Loose Tongues* for eight amplified solo voices and tape (1985), *Urban Tropics*, sound portrait (1988), *Conversations* for low voice (1988), *In the Dreamtime*, self-portrait sound collage (1990), *Awakenings*, for chamber ensemble (1991), *Klangbild Köln/Sound Portrait of Cologne* (1991).

Lac des cygnes, Le ballet score by Tchaikovsky; see ➤ **Swan Lake**.

Lächerliche Prinz Jodelet, Der, The Ridiculous Prince Jodelet opera by Reinhard Keiser (libretto by J P Praetorius, based on P Scarron's comedy *Jodelet, ou Le Maître valet*), first produced at the Theater beim Gänsemarkt, Hamburg, Germany, in 1726.

Lachrimae John Dowland's collection of 21 dances for five bowed instruments with lute (London, 1604). Its opening pavana, *Lachrimae antiquae*, is a version of his song *Flow My Teares* (first published in 1600), though in its original form it was probably a pavan for solo lute. In the early 17th century the piece appeared in many other arrangements for different ensembles and by different hands, usually with the title *Lachrimae*.

Lachrymae work for viola and piano by Benjamin Britten, '*Reflections on a Song of John Dowland*', composed in 1950 and first performed at Aldeburgh, England, on 20 June 1950. It was arranged for viola and string orchestra in 1976 and first performed in Recklinghausen, Germany, on 3 May 1977.

lacrimoso (Italian 'tearful') term used in musical notation.

A Lady Macbeth of the Mtsensk District, Russian **Lady Macbeth Mtsenskago Uyezda** opera by Dmitri Shostakovich (libretto by A Preis and the composer, based on a novel by N S Leskov), first produced in Moscow, Russia, on 22 January 1934. It was very successful at first, but was later discountenanced as decadent by the Soviet government; it was revised as *Katerina Izmaylova* and produced in 1963. It tells how, tormented by her father-in-law Boris, Katerina Izmaylova has an affair with a servant named Sergei while her ineffectual husband, Zinovy, is away. Boris discovers Sergei and brutally whips him, but Katerina has her revenge by poisoning Boris. Suspicious, Zinovy returns and beats her, but Sergei intervenes and kills him. The police are informed and the couple are led away. In a group of convicts, Sergei flirts with a young prisoner to provoke Katerina. She throws her rival off a bridge, and jumps into the rapids herself.

Lady of the Lake, The collection of songs by Franz Schubert set to German translations from Scott's poem by P A Storck (1825) and published in 1826 as Op. 52. They are: 1. Ellen's first song, 'Soldier, Rest!'; 2. Ellen's second song, 'Huntsman, Rest!'; 3. Ellen's third song, 'Ave Maria'; 4. Norman's song, 'The Heath this Night'; and 5. lay of the imprisoned huntsman, 'My Hawk is Tired'. Op. 52 contains two more poems from Scott's work, 'Boating Song' for male chorus and

'Coronach' for female chorus.

La Grotte, Nicolas de (c.1530–c.1600) French composer and keyboard player. He published settings of poems by Pierre de Ronsard in 1569 and examples of *musique mesurée à l'antique*. In 1583 he published with Claude Le Jeune pieces for the *Ballet comique de la Royne*.

La Guerre, Elisabeth-Claude Jacquet de (1666 or 1667–1729) French harpsichordist and composer from the Jacquet family of musicians and instrument-makers. A pupil of her father, Claude Jacquet (died 1702), she showed early promise and attracted the patronage of Louis XIV and later Mme de Montespan, being particularly gifted at improvisation. She married the organist and composer Marin La Guerre (1658–1704) before 1684.

Works the opera *Céphale et Procris* (1694); cantatas; Te Deum and other church music; violin sonatas, trio sonatas, harpsichord music.

Lah in music, the name for the submediant note in any key in Tonic Sol-fa, so pronounced, but in notation represented by the symbol l.

La Halle or **La Hale, Adam de (c.1230–c.1288)** French poet and composer. He was educated for the priesthood, but fell in love and married a young girl, whom he left to rejoin the Church at Douai around 1263. In 1282 he went to Naples with the comte d'Artois.

Works the stage pieces *Le Jeu d'Adam, ou de la feuillée* and *Le Jeu de Robin et de Marion* (1285); motets; chansons.

La Hèle or **La Helle, Georges de (1547–1586)** Flemish composer. He wrote Masses, motets, and chansons; some of his works were destroyed in a fire in Madrid, Spain, in 1734.

He was a chorister at the royal chapel in Madrid in his youth. In 1578 he was choirmaster at Tournai Cathedral, but was probably back in Spain by 1580. He won two prizes at the Puy de Musique at Evreux in 1576.

lai (French; later English *lay*) a medieval lyrical poem in pairs of stanzas in different metrical forms; also the music set to such poems.

Lajtha, László (1892–1963) Hungarian folksong expert and composer. He studied at the Music High School at Budapest, specializing in folk music, and joined the folklore department of the National Museum in 1913. He was professor at the Budapest Conservatory 1919–49.

Works BALLET three ballets including *Lysistrata* (1933) and *Capriccio* (1944).

CHORAL two Masses and other choral works.

ORCHESTRAL ten symphonies (1936–61); violin concerto.

CHAMBER ten string quartets and other chamber music; sonatas for violin, cello, and piano.

Lakmé opera by Léo Delibes (libretto by E Gondinet and P Gille), first produced at the Opéra-Comique, Paris, France, on 14 April 1883. It tells how the Brahmin priest Nilakantha opposes an affair between his daughter Lakmé and the English officer Gerald. After being stabbed, Gerald is nursed by Lakmé, who poisons herself when she realizes that Gerald must return to his duties.

Lalande, Michel-Richard de (1657–1726) French organist and composer. He taught himself to play the violin, bass viol, and harpsichord. On being refused admission to Jean-Baptiste Lully's orchestra, he took up the organ and secured organist's appointments at three churches. He failed to obtain the post of court organist, but was given charge of the princesses' musical education and became maître de chapelle in 1704.

He learnt music as a chorister at the church of Saint-Germain-l'Auxerrois in Paris. In 1683 he was appointed one of the superintendents of the royal chapel, and was appointed master of the royal chapel in 1704. In 1684 he married the court singer Anne Rebel, who died in 1722; his second wife, whom he married in 1723, was Mlle de Cury, daughter of one of the court surgeons.

Works BALLET AND OPERA-BALLET *Ballet de la jeunesse* (1686), *Le Palais de Flore* (1689), *Adonis* (1696), *Myrtil et Mélicerte* (1698), *Les Fées* (1699), *L'Amour fléchi par la constance*, *L'Hymen champêtre* (1700), *Ballet de la paix*, *Les Folies de Cardenio* (from Cervantes's *Don Quixote*, 1720), *Ballet de l'inconnu*, *Les Éléments* (with Destouches, 1725), *L'Amour berger*, *Eglogue, ou Pastorale en musique*, *Les Fontaines de Versailles*.

OTHER 70 motets with orchestral accompaniment; cantata *Le Concert d'Esculape*; *Trois Leçons des ténèbres*, Miserere for solo voice; music for the royal table, including *Sinfonias pour les soupers du Roi*.

Lalla-Roukh opera by Félicien David (libretto by H Lucas and Michel Carré, based on Thomas Moore's *Lalla Rookh*), first produced at the Opéra-Comique, Paris, France, on 12 May 1862.

Lallouette, Jean François (1651–1728) French violinist and composer. From 1668 to 1677 he was violinist and conductor at the Paris Opéra, but Jean-Baptiste Lully dismissed him for claiming collaboration in his *Isis*, which may have been true, for he was said to have often assisted Lully.

He studied violin with Guy Leclerc and composition with Lully. In 1693 he became maître de chapelle at Rouen Cathedral, in 1695 at Notre-Dame at Versailles, and in 1700 at Notre-Dame in Paris.

Works dramatic interludes and ballets; Masses, motets, Misereres.

Lalo, (Victor Antoine) Edouard (1823–1892) French composer. His Spanish ancestry and violin training are evident in the *Symphonie espagnole* (1873) for violin and orchestra, and *Concerto for Cello and Orchestra* (1877). He also wrote an opera, *Le Roi d'Ys/The King of Ys* (1887).

He first studied violin and cello at the Lille Conservatory and then violin in Paris, taking composition lessons privately at the same time. In 1855 he became viola player in the Armingaud-Jacquard quartet. He wrote little until 1865, the year of his marriage to Mlle Bernier de Maligny, who sang his songs in public. Gradually his success grew both in the opera house and the concert room.

His most popular works during his lifetime were the opera *Le Roi d'Ys* and the ballet *Namouna* (1882). He is best known today for the five-movement *Symphonie espagnole* for violin and orchestra, and the cello concerto.

Works STAGE operas *Fiesque* (after Schiller, composed 1866–67), *Le Roi d'Ys* (1887), *La Jacquerie* (unfinished, completed by Coquard, performed 1895); pantomime with choruses *Néron*; ballet *Namouna* (1882).

ORCHESTRAL *Symphonie espagnole* (1873), *Fantaisie norvégienne* (1878), *Romance-Sérénade* (1879) and *Concerto russe* (1879) for violin and orchestra, *Rhapsodie norvégienne* (1881), symphony in G minor (1886), *Divertissement*, scherzo for orchestra, two aubades for small orchestra, concerto, concertos for piano and for cello.

CHAMBER string quartet (later revised as No. 2), three piano trios; violin and piano sonata and a number of pieces, cello and piano sonata and pieces; *La Mère et l'enfant* for piano duet.

OTHER over 30 songs and two vocal duets; church music.

Lambe, Walter (c.1452–c.1500) English composer. His known music was all included in the Eton Choirbook: it consists of a Magnificat and five votive antiphons (a sixth can be completed from another manuscript; another is partially lost, and four more completely so).

He was King's Scholar at Eton in 1467 (aged 15), and clerk at St George's, Windsor, from 1479 to 1499, acting as master of the choristers 1480–84 (at first jointly with William Edmunds).

Lambert, Constant (1905–1951) English composer, conductor, and critic. His works include *The Rio Grande* (1929) and the ballet score *Horoscope* (1938), which react against contemporary English pastoralism and look to jazz and early Stravinsky for inspiration.

Lambert was born in London, the son of the painter George Washington Lambert. He studied at the Royal College of Music in London, under

Ralph Vaughan Williams. While he was still a student, Sergei Diaghilev commissioned the ballet *Romeo and Juliet* from him and produced it at Monte Carlo, Monaco, in 1926. It was followed by *Pomona* at Buenos Aires, Argentina, in 1927. He began to make his mark as a conductor of ballet with the Camargo Society and was later engaged to conduct ballet at the Sadler's Wells Theatre, London, with which he appeared in Paris, France, in 1937, having already conducted at the International Society for Contemporary Music Festival in Amsterdam, the Netherlands, in 1933. He also became a concert conductor, was for a time music critic to the journal *Referee*, and published a book of criticism, *Music Ho! A Study of Music in Decline* (1934).

Works STAGE AND INCIDENTAL MUSIC ballets *Romeo and Juliet* (Monte Carlo, 1926), *Pomona* (Buenos Aires, 1927), *Horoscope* (London, 1938); incidental music for Shakespeare's *Hamlet*; music for films *Merchant Seamen* and *Anna Karenina* (after Tolstoy).

VOCAL AND ORCHESTRAL *Summer's Last Will and Testament* (Nash), masque for baritone solo, chorus, and orchestra (1932–35); *The Rio Grande* for piano, orchestra, and chorus (1929); dirge in Shakespeare's *Cymbeline* for voices and orchestra; *Music for Orchestra*; *Aubade héroïque* for small orchestra; concerto for piano and chamber orchestra.

OTHER piano sonata; four poems by Li-Po for voice and piano.

Lamentatione name (apparently authentic) given to Joseph ➔ **Haydn**'s symphony no. 26 in D minor, composed about 1768, on account of the use it makes of a chant associated with the Lamentations of Jeremiah.

Lamentations the Lamentations of Jeremiah used in the Roman Catholic service at matins in Holy Week; originally sung in ➔ **plainsong** and still surviving in that form, but from the early 16th century also used in polyphonic settings.

lamento (Italian 'lament') plaintive aria in early 17th-century Italian opera conventionally placed before the tragic culmination of the plot. The best known example is the *Lamento d'Arianna*, the only surviving fragment from Monteverdi's *Arianna*.

Lamoureux, Charles (1834–1899) French violinist and conductor. In 1881 he founded the Concerts Lamoureux, at which he made a great deal of orchestral music, including that of Wagner, known to a wide public.

He studied violin and theory at the Paris Conservatory, joined a theatre orchestra, then played at the Paris Opéra. In 1860 he helped to found a chamber music society for the introduction of new works, and conducted choral works by Bach,

Handel, and others in the 1870s. He then became conductor at the Opéra. He toured Russia in 1893 and gave regular concerts in London, England, from 1896.

Lampe, John Frederick (Johann Friedrich) (1703–1751) German bassoonist and composer. He left Brunswick about 1725 and settled in London, England, but went to Dublin, Ireland, in 1748 and to Edinburgh, Scotland, in 1750. He married Isabella Young, sister of Thomas Arne's wife.

Works STAGE burlesque operas *The Dragon of Wantley* (1757) and *Margery, or A Worse Plague than the Dragon* (1738; libretti by Carey); mock opera *Pyramus and Thisbe* (from Shakespeare's *A Midsummer Night's Dream*, 1745); masque *The Sham Conjurer* (1741); music for Carey's *Amelia*; about ten other stage works.

OTHER cantata to celebrate the suppression of the Stuart rebellion; songs.

Lampugnani, Giovanni Battista (1706–1786) Italian composer. Successful throughout Italy as an opera composer, he went to London, England, in 1743 to take over the opera at the King's Theatre from Baldassare Galuppi, but later returned to Milan, where he wrote his five comic operas 1758–69.

He studied in Naples, and made his debut as an opera composer there in 1732. From 1779 he was maestro al cembalo at the Teatro alla Scala.

Works OPERA about 30, including *Semiramide* (1741), *Rossane*, *Tigrane* (1747), *Artaserse*, *Siroe* (1755), and *L'amor contadino* (1760).

OTHER trio sonatas, church music.

Lancelot and Elaine symphonic poem no. 2 by Edward MacDowell, Op. 25, based on the Arthurian legend; it was composed in 1888.

Landarzt, Ein, A Country Doctor radio opera by Hans Werner Henze after the story by Franz Kafka; it was broadcast in Hamburg, Germany, on 29 November 1951, revised for Dietrich Fischer-Dieskau as a monodrama in 1964, and first performed in Berlin, Germany, on 12 October 1965. The radio opera was revised for the stage in 1964 and first performed in Frankfurt, Germany, on 30 November 1965. It tells the story of a doctor's macabre night-call to a village boy.

Landi, Stefano (c.1586–1639) Italian singer and composer. He was maestro di cappella in Padua about 1620 and in Rome from 1624, and sang alto in the papal chapel from 1630. His sacred opera *Il Sant'Alessio* (1631) was successfully revived in Rome and Innsbruck, Austria, in 1981 and in Los Angeles, USA, in 1988.

Works OPERA *La morte d'Orfeo* (1619) and *Il Sant'Alessio* (1631).

OTHER Masses and psalms; madrigals and cantatas; arias for one voice.

Landini, Francesco (c.1325–1397) Italian organist, lutenist, composer, and poet. He was one of the chief exponents of the Italian ➤ ars nova. Although blind from early childhood, he became a skilled player of various instruments, in particular the portative organ, and was organist at the Church of San Lorenzo, Florence, 1369–96.

He was born in Florence and spent most of his life there, but also visited Venice, where he was highly acclaimed. As a composer he is remarkable for his madrigals and *caccie*, both forms that later underwent considerable development.

Works madrigals, *ballate*, and other pieces.

Landini sixth a ➤ cadence in music of the 14th and 15th centuries named after Francesco Landini, of whose vocal works it is a feature. The idiom is not confined to Italian music nor is there any evidence to suggest that Landini invented it.

The Landini sixth in C major.

ländler Austrian country dance in 3/4 or 3/8 time, in which couples spin and clap. It was very popular in the late 18th century and composers, such as Mozart, Beethoven, and Schubert, wrote music in the rhythm of the dance.

Landon, H(oward) C(handler) Robbins (1926–) US musicologist. He has devoted himself particularly to the study of late 18th-century music and has published a number of articles and books, including *The Symphonies of Joseph Haydn* (1955), *The Collected Correspondence and London Notebooks of Joseph Haydn*, and *Haydn: Chronicle and Works*, five volumes (1976–80).

He studied at Swarthmore College and Boston University. Since 1947 he has lived in Europe. He has also published *Haydn: His Life and Music* (1988), and editions of numerous works by Haydn, including several operas and the complete symphonies. He has published books on Beethoven (1970) and Mozart as a Mason (1983), and also in 1983 edited recently discovered material for Handel's Roman Vespers. Other works include *Mozart's Last Year* (1988), *Mozart: The Golden Years* (1989), *Mozart and Vienna* (1991), and *Vivaldi, Voice of the Baroque* (1993).

Landowska, Wanda Luiza (1877–1959) Polish harpsichordist and scholar. She founded a school near Paris, France, for the study of early music, and was for many years one of the few artists regularly performing on the harpsichord. In 1941 she moved to the USA.

She toured widely and settled in France, where in 1927 she opened a school for the study of early music at Saint-Leu-la-Forêt, near Paris. She wrote books and articles on aspects of early music. Falla's harpsichord concerto (1923–26) and Poulenc's *Concert Champêtre* (1927–28) were composed for her. In 1933 she gave the first public performance of Bach's *Goldberg Variations* and recorded Bach's *The Well-Tempered Clavier* 1949–56.

Lang, Paul Henry (1901–1991) Hungarian-born US musicologist. In 1924 he went to the University of Paris, France, and four years later to the USA. He became professor of musicology at Columbia University in New York in 1939. In 1945 he was appointed editor of the *Musical Quarterly*. Among his writings are *Music in Western Civilization* (1941) and *George Frideric Handel* (1966).

Langlais, Jean (1907–1991) French organist and composer. He held several organist's appointments at Paris churches, lastly at Sainte-Clotilde. Blind himself, he taught organ and composition to blind pupils at the Institut des Jeunes Aveugles. His best-known works are for organ, but he also wrote many others.

He was educated at an institute for the blind and studied organ under André Marchal, also blind, later with Marcel Dupré at the Paris Conservatory, where he also studied composition with Paul Dukas.

langsam (German 'slow'; langsamer 'slower') term used in musical notation.

Lanier or **Laniere, Nicholas (1588–1666)** English painter, flautist, singer, and composer of French descent. In 1613, with John Coperario and others, he composed a masque for the marriage of the Earl of Somerset and in 1617 he not only set Ben Jonson's *Lovers made Men*, but sang in it and painted the scenery.

He was probably taught by his father, John Lanier, a sackbut player. In 1625 he was sent to Italy to collect pictures for the royal collection, and in 1626 was appointed Master of the King's Musick. He lived in the Netherlands during the Commonwealth, but resumed his post at the Restoration. Several other members of his family were musicians in the royal service.

Works MASQUES *Lovers made Men* (1617) and *The Vision of Delight* (Jonson, 1617).

VOCAL cantata *Hero and Leander*, New Year's songs; vocal dialogues, songs.

Lanner, Joseph (Franz Karl) (1801–1843) Austrian violinist and composer. He composed country dances and waltzes, in which he was Jo-

hann Strauss's greatest rival.

He was born in Vienna, the son of a glove-maker, and taught himself to play the violin. Anxious to conduct an orchestra, he began by forming a string quartet, in which Strauss, senior, played viola. They performed at various taverns, playing his arrangements of selections from favourite operas. He was engaged to conduct the orchestra at dances, visited provincial cities with his own band, and finally conducted the court balls in turn with Strauss.

Works over 200 waltzes, country dances, quadrilles, polkas, galops, marches.

Lantins, Arnold de (died 1432) Flemish composer from the diocese of Liège. He was in Venice, Italy, in 1428 and was included (with Guillaume Dufay) in a list of papal singers in 1431. He composed chansons, motets and a Mass, *Verbum incarnatum*.

Lantins, Hugo de (lived early 15th century) Flemish composer, possibly the brother of Arnold de ➔ Lantins. Like Arnold, he visited Italy, and in 1420 wrote an epithalamium for Cleofe Malatesta di Pesaro. Two of his five motets connect him with Venice (1423) and Bari respectively. He also wrote numerous chansons.

Laparra, Raoul (1876–1943) French composer. He studied at the Paris Conservatory. His *Habanera* was given at the Royal Opera House, Covent Garden, London, in 1910 and at the New York Metropolitan Opera House in 1924. He was killed in an Allied air raid near Paris.

Works OPERA *Peau d'âne* (1899), *La Jota* (1899), *La Habanera* (1908), *Le Joueur de viole*, *Las Toreras* (1929), *L'Illustre Fregona*.

OTHER *Un Dimanche basque* for piano and orchestra; string quartet; songs.

La Pouplinière, Alexandre Jean Joseph le Riche de (1693–1762) French music patron. He was farmer-general of taxes and amassed a huge fortune. He kept a private orchestra, had Jean-Philippe Rameau living in his house for several years and studied under him, and patronized a number of other composers and performers, including Jean de Mondonville.

Lara, Isidore de (1858–1935), born **Isidore Cohen** English composer. He studied composition with Alberto Mazzucato and singing with Francesco Lamperti at the Milan Conservatory, and later went to Édouard Lalo in Paris. He returned to London and became well known in wealthy drawing rooms as a song composer and performer. Later he came under the patronage of the Princess of Monaco, which enabled him to have his operas staged in the Grand Manner.

Works OPERA *The Light of Asia* (1892), *Amy Robsart* (after Scott's *Kenilworth*, 1893), *Moïna*

(1897), *Messaline* (1899), *Soléa, Sanga, Naïl, Les Trois Masques* (1912), *The Three Musketeers* (after Dumas, 1921), and others.

OTHER cantata *The Light of Asia* (first version of the opera); many songs.

largamente (Italian 'broadly, spaciously') in music, an indication that a movement or phrase is to be played in a broad manner.

large the largest note value in the medieval system of measured musical notation. It was known in Latin as *duplex longa* or *maxima*, and was divisible into two longs.

larghetto musical tempo indication for a slow movement, less slow than a *largo*.

largo (Italian 'large, broad, wide, spacious') musical tempo indication for a slow movement denoting a broad style as much as a slow pace. See also ➔ **larghetto**.

'Largo' popular name for the aria 'Ombra mai fù/Shade never was' from Handel's opera *Serse* (1735; *Xerxes*), more generally known as an instrumental piece published in all kinds of arrangements. The familiar title is not even the original tempo indication, which is larghetto.

Lark Ascending, The romance for violin and orchestra by Ralph Vaughan Williams, composed in 1914 and first performed at the Queen's Hall, London, England, on 14 June 1921, conducted by Adrian Boult.

'Lark' Quartet nickname sometimes given to Haydn's string quartet in D, Op. 64 No. 5, on account of the exposed high first-violin passage at the opening.

Larsen, Jens Peter (1902–1988) Danish musicologist. He studied at Copenhagen University and taught there from 1928, becoming professor in 1945. He was organist at Vangede Church 1930–45. He edited several works by Haydn and other composers, and authored *Die Haydn-Überlieferung, Die Haydn Kataloge*, and *Handel's 'Messiah'*. He wrote an entry for Haydn in the *New Grove's Dictionary of Music and Musicians* (1980).

Larsen, Libby (1950–) US composer. She studied at the University of Minnesota with Dominick Argonto. In 1993 she became artistic director of the Hot Notes Series, giving performances with synthesized sound.

Works OPERA *Tumbledown Dick* (1980), *Frankenstein, the Modern Prometheus* (1990), *Mrs Dalloway* (1993).

ORCHESTRAL *Symphony: Water Music* (1985); piano concerto: 'Since Armstrong' (1990); *Ghosts of an Old Ceremony*, dance (1991); Third Symphony 'Lyric' (1991); *Marimba* concerto (1992).

ORATORIO *Coming Forth into Day* (1985).

VOCAL *Sonnets from the Portuguese*, song cycle for soprano and chamber ensemble (1989); *Mary Cassat*, for mezzo, trombone, and orchestra (1994).

CHAMBER *Quartet: Schoenberg, Schenker and Schillinger*, for string quartet (1991).

Larsson, Lars-Erik (1908–1986) Swedish composer, conductor, and critic. His works vary between traditional and more modern styles. For instance, the ten *Two-Part Piano Pieces* (1932) introduced the ➔ **twelve-tone system** to Swedish music, while his *Sinfonietta*, composed in the same year, is contrapuntal and neo-baroque in style. However, despite the dichotomy in his work, the characteristic that threads Larsson's music together is his gift of lyricism.

He studied at the Royal Academy of Music in Stockholm, and later in Leipzig, Germany, and Vienna, Austria, where he was a pupil of Alban Berg. He was a conductor for Swedish radio 1937–54; professor of composition at Stockholm Conservatory 1947–59; and director of music at Uppsala University 1961–66.

Works STAGE opera *The Princess of Cyprus* (1937); incidental music to Shakespeare's *The Winter's Tale*.

ORCHESTRAL three symphonies (1927–45), two concert overtures, lyric suite for orchestra; sinfonietta for strings (1932), divertimento for chamber orchestra; saxophone concerto.

La Rue, Jan (1918–2004) Indonesian-born US musicologist. He studied at Harvard and Princeton, and was at New York University from 1957. He wrote particularly about style analysis and 18th-century music, striving for objectively verifiable conclusions.

La Rue, Pierre de (c.1460–1518) Flemish composer. He was a pupil of Johannes Ockeghem, and was in the service by turns of the court of Burgundy, Charles V, and Margaret of Austria. He was appointed prebendary of Courtrai and later of Namur.

Works 31 Masses, seven Magnificats, Requiem, 38 motets; chansons.

Laserna, Blas (1751–1816) Spanish composer. He became official composer to several Madrid theatres in 1779.

Works STAGE comic opera *La gitanilla por amor* (1791); incidental music for plays by Calderón, Lope de Vega, Moreto, Ramón de la Cruz's *El café de Barcelona* (1788), and others.

OTHER lyric scene *Idomeneo* (1792), numerous tonadillas, and other pieces.

Lassen, Eduard (1830–1904) Danish-born conductor and composer. He was taken to Brussels, Belgium, at the age of two, later studied at the Conservatory there, and took the Belgian Prix de Rome in 1851. Unable to get his first opera staged in Brussels, he took it to Liszt in Weimar, Germany, who produced it in 1857. He was music director there from 1858 and conductor of the opera from 1860. He conducted the first performance of Saint-Saëns's *Samson et Dalila* (1877).

Works STAGE operas *Landgraf Ludwigs Brautfahrt* (1857), *Frauenlob* (1860), *Le Captif*; incidental music to Sophocles' *Oedipus*, Goethe's *Faust* and *Pandora*, Calderón's *Circe*, and Hebbel's *Nibelungen* (1876; the year of the first production of *The Ring*, at Bayreuth).

OTHER festival cantata, Te Deum; *Biblische Bilder* for voices and orchestra; two symphonies, *Beethoven* and *Festival* overtures.

Lassus, Orlande de or **Roland de (c.1532–1594)**, also known as **Orlando di Lasso** Flemish composer. The abundance, variety, and polyphonic ingenuity of his music make him one of the greatest composers of the Renaissance.

He seems to have gone to Italy as a boy, and he travelled there and served in various noble households, in Sicily, Naples, and Milan. In 1553–54 he was choirmaster at St John Lateran in Rome, after which he returned home and settled for two years in Antwerp, where in 1555–56 he began to publish his first works. In 1556 he went to Munich and entered the service of the Duke of Bavaria. There he married Regina Weckinger in 1558, and in 1563 became chief Kapellmeister in succession to Ludwig Daser. He made a visit to Venice in 1567 to find musicians for Munich, and to Ferrara. In 1570 he was ennobled by the emperor Maximilian.

After a visit to Paris, France, in 1571 Charles IX offered him a post as chamber musician, but he returned to Munich after the king's death in 1574. That year he went to Rome to present Pope Gregory XIII with a volume of Masses and received the order of the Golden Spur. In spite of an offer from Dresden, he remained attached to the Bavarian court to the end. His Latin motets were collected and published in 1604 by his sons Ferdinand and Rudolph under the title *Magnum opus musicum*.

Works more than 2,000 compositions: about 60 Masses, four Passions, 101 Magnificats, Requiem, about 500 motets, *Sacrae cantiones*, psalms (including seven penitential psalms); madrigals, Italian *canzoni*, French chansons, German songs for several voices.

Last Judgement, The English title of Ludwig Spohr's oratorio *Die letzten Dinge*, first produced in Kassel, Germany, on 25 March 1826.

Latrobe, Christian Ignatius (1757–1836) English clergyman and composer. He studied at the college of the Moravian Brethren at Niesky in Upper Lusatia and in 1795 became secretary of the English branch. He dedicated three sonatas to Haydn, with whom he made friends during the latter's visits to England. He edited Moravian hymn-tunes and six volumes of German and Italian church music.

Works *Dies irae* (1823), Te Deum, Miserere (1814), anthems and other church music; instrumental sonatas; airs to poems by Cowper and Hannah More.

Lauda Sion (from Latin Lauda Sion Salvatortem,'Zion, praise thy Saviour') a sequence sung at Mass on the Feast of Corpus Christ in the Roman Church, with words by St Thomas Aquinas written about 1264.

It is also the title of a cantata by Felix ➤ Mendelssohn written for a festival at Liège, Belgium, and first performed there on 11 June 1846.

laudi spirituali Italian sacred songs of the 13th century and later, with words in the vernacular, at first for single voice and later in parts. Their centre of origin was Florence.

Laudon Symphony nickname of Haydn's symphony no. 69 in C, composed about 1778 and dedicated to Field Marshal Baron Gideon Ernst von Loudon.

Lavignac, (Alexandre Jean) Albert (1846–1916) French musicologist. He studied at the Paris Conservatory, where he became professor in 1882. He was founder and first editor of the *Encyclopédie de la musique* (1913–16); he also wrote many technical treatises and a study on Richard Wagner.

lavolta, Italian **volta**; French **volte** an old dance in 3/2 time, probably of Italian origin, since the jump that was a feature of it retained the Italian word *volta*.

Lavotta, János (1764–1820) Hungarian violinist and composer. He was one of the outstanding exponents of *verbunkos* (national style) music.

He was of noble birth, but left home on his father's remarriage and became a professional musician, at the same time following a legal career. He became very fashionable in Vienna and Budapest, conducted at various theatres, but took to drink and ended in decay.

Lawes, Henry (1596–1662) English composer. His works include music for John Milton's masque *Comus* (1634). His brother **William Lawes** (1602–1645) was also a composer, notably for viol consort.

Lawes, William (1602–1645) English composer. Like his brother Henry ➤ Lawes, he studied with John Coperario and became a musician at Charles I's court. He joined the Royalist army during the Civil War and was killed by a shot during the siege of Chester.

Works MASQUES music for Shirley's masque *The Triumph of Peace* (with Ive, 1634) and Davenant's *The Triumph of the Prince d'Amour* and *The Unfortunate Lovers* (1638).

OTHER anthems and psalms; music for consorts of viols; airs for violin and bass; catches and canons; airs and dialogues for one and more voices.

Layolle, François de (1492–c.1540), born Francesco dell'Aiolle French organist and composer. He was Benvenuto Cellini's music teacher. He worked at the church of SS Annunziate, Florence, Italy, until 1518. His son Aleman Layolle afterwards taught Cellini's daughter and became organist at Lyon by 1521.

Works Masses, motets; canzoni, madrigals.

leader the usual English name for the principal first violin in an orchestra or of a string quartet or other chamber music team.

In the USA, especially in journalism, the conductor is often called a 'leader'; the usual US term for the leading first orchestral violin is Concertmaster, from German *Konzertmeister*.

leading motif (German *Leitmotiv*) musical term; see ➤ leitmotif.

leading note in music, the seventh note of an ascending ➤ diatonic scale, so called because it 'leads' inevitably to the upper tonic or key note. It is tuned ➤ sharp in minor keys to maintain its leading character.

The leading note is very dissonant in relation to the tonic, but consonant in relation to the chord of the fifth, or dominant. Typically the transition from leading note to tonic is expressed in the V–I 'perfect' ➤ cadence.

Lear opera by Aribert Reimann (libretto by C Henneberg after Shakespeare), first produced in Munich, Germany, on 9 July 1978. King Lear disowns his faithful daughter Cordelia after she is unable to express her love for him, dividing his kingdom between his treacherous daughters Goneril and Regan instead. Lear becomes insane and they all die.

Leben des Orest, The Life of Orestes opera by Ernst Křenek (libretto by composer), first produced in Leipzig, Germany, on 19 January 1930. It tells how Orestes travels from early matricide to eventual forgiveness.

Le Brun, Jean (lived 15th century) French priest and composer. He wrote motets and chansons.

Lechner, Leonhard (c.1553–1606) Austrian composer. He was music director to Count Eitel Friedrich of Hohenzollern at Hechingen 1584–85 and in 1595 was appointed to a similar post at the court of Württemberg at Stuttgart, Germany. After studying with Orlande de Lassus in the

court chapel at Munich, he became a schoolmaster at Nuremberg in 1570. In 1579 he began to publish a revised edition of Lassus's works.

Works Masses, motets, Magnificat, psalms, introits, wedding motet for the Elector Johann Georg I of Saxony; sacred and 160 secular German songs for two–five voices in seven published books; St John Passion (1594).

Leclair, Jean-Marie (1697–1764) French composer and violinist. Originally a dancer and ballet-master, he composed ballet music, an opera, *Scylla et Glaucus* (1746), and violin concertos.

Leclair was born in Lyon. He began his career as a dancer, and in 1722 was a ballet master in Turin, Italy, but while there turned to the violin, studying with Giovanni Battista Somis. In 1728 he settled in Paris, France, where he had great success as a player and composer. He was a member of the royal orchestra 1734–36, then went to Holland, returning to Paris after various travels in 1743. For a time he was in the service of Don Philip of Spain at Chambéry, and joined the orchestra of the Duke of Gramont in 1748. He met his death at the hand of an unknown murderer.

Works STAGE opera *Scylla et Glaucus* (1746; concert performance London, 1979); ballets and 'divertissements'.

OTHER twelve violin concertos; 48 violin sonatas; violin duets; trio sonatas.

Lecocq, (Alexandre) Charles (1832–1918) French composer. His first operetta, *Le Docteur Miracle* (1857), won joint first prize with a work by Georges Bizet in a competition organized by Jacques Offenbach. However, he had no great success until he produced *Fleur de Thé* in 1868, and until then supplemented his income by teaching and organ playing. After that he made a fortune with his many operettas.

Lecocq was born in Paris, where he studied at the Conservatory 1849–54.

Works OPERA *Plutus* (1886); operettas *Les Cent Vierges*, *La Fille de Madame Angot* (1872), *Giroflé-Giroflà* (1874), *La Petite Mariée* (1875), *Le Petit Duc* (1878), *Camargo* (1878), *Ninette*, *Barbe-bleue*, and about 40 others.

OTHER orchestral works; violin and piano sonata; sacred songs for women's voices *La Chapelle au couvent*; instrumental pieces; piano works; songs.

Leçons des ténèbres settings of the Lamentations of Jeremiah for performance at matins on the last three days of Holy Week. See also ➤ Lamentations.

ledger line or **leger line** in music, notation used to indicate exceptionally high or low notes, consisting of short lines added above or below the ➤ stave. In music prior to the classical period it was common to change clefs in order to avoid using ledger lines. For example, if a part reading bass clef became too high, the composer would notate tenor clef. This practice is continued for cello and bassoon writing but not for other instruments such as the keyboard. The first known example of a ledger line occurs in an organ book of 1523.

Lee, Nathaniel (c.1653–1692) English playwright. His works inspired the composers Gottfried ➔ **Finger** (*Rival Queens*, with Daniel Purcell), Henry ➔ **Purcell** (*Oedipus, Massacre of Paris, Sophonisba*, and *Theodosius*), and Nicholas ➔ **Staggins** (*Gloriana*).

Lees, Benjamin (1924–) Russian-born US composer. He was taken to the USA as a child, and studied piano in San Francisco and Los Angeles. After serving in the US Army 1942–45, he studied at University of California at Los Angeles, theory, harmony, and composition with Halsey Stevens, Ingolf Dahl, and Ernst Kanitz, also taking private lessons from George Antheil. In 1955 he won a Guggenheim Fellowship and in 1956 a Fulbright Fellowship.

Works OPERA *The Oracle* (1955), *The Gilded Cage* (1971).

ORCHESTRAL five symphonies (1953–86; no. 3 for string quartet and orchestra), *Profile* for orchestra, concerto for orchestra, two concertos for violin, oboe, and piano, *Declamations* for string orchestra and piano, concerto for brass and orchestra (1983), *Portrait of Rodin* for orchestra (1984), horn concerto (1992).

CANTATA *Visions of Poets*, a dramatic cantata (1961).

CHAMBER four string quartets (1951, 1955, 1982, 1989), three violin sonatas (1953, 1972, 1991), cello sonata (1981), piano trio (1983), four piano sonatas (1949, 1950, 1956, 1963), violin sonata, piano music.

Leeuw, Ton de (1926–1996) Dutch composer. His chief interest was experimental music, and he was influenced by *musique concrète* as well as serialism.

He studied composition in Paris, France, with Olivier Messiaen and Thomas de Hartmann. He became interested in musical folklore and in 1961 toured India to collect material.

Works OPERA TV opera *Alceste* (1963), opera *De Droom/The Dream* (1965).

CHORAL oratorio *Job* (1956), and other choral music.

ORCHESTRAL two symphonies, *Ombres* for orchestra and percussion, concertos for piano and string orchestra, *Spatial Music I–IV*, *Litany of Our Time* (1965–68), *Resonances* for orchestra (1985), concerto for guitar and strings (1989).

CHAMBER two string quartets (1958, 1964); *Appa-*

rences I for cello (1987); piano music.

OTHER electronic pieces.

LeFanu, Nicola (1947–) English composer, daughter of Elizabeth Maconchy. She studied at Oxford and with Egon Wellesz and Goffredo Petrassi. She lectured at Morley College, London, 1970–75, and in 1977 was appointed lecturer at King's College, London.

Works STAGE operas *Dawnpath* (1977), *Blood Wedding* (1992), and *Wild Man* (1995); ballet *The Last Laugh* for soprano, tape, and chamber orchestra (1972).

ORCHESTRAL *Preludio* for strings (1967; revised 1976), *The Hidden Landscape* for orchestra (1973), *Columbia Fall* for percussion, harp, and strings (1975), *Farne* for orchestra (1979), *Variations* for piano and orchestra (1982), concerto for alto saxophone and orchestra (1989).

VOCAL *The Valleys Shall Sing* for chorus and wind (1973), *For We are the Stars* for 16 voices (1978), *Like a Wave of the Sea* for chorus and ensemble of early instruments (1981), *Stranded on my Heart* for tenor, chorus, and strings (1984), *The Silver Strand* for chorus (1989).

CHAMBER clarinet quintet (1971), *Collana* for six instruments (1976), *Deva* for cello and seven instruments (1979), *Invisible Places* clarinet quintet (1986), *Nocturne* for cello and piano (1988).

Le Flem, Paul (1881–1984) French composer and critic. He was professor at the Schola Cantorum, Paris, chorus master at the Opéra-Comique, conductor of the Chanteurs de Saint-Gervais, and critic for *Comoedia*.

His teachers included Vincent d'Indy and Albert Roussel at the Schola Cantorum.

Works STAGE operas *Le Rossignol de Saint-Malo* (1942) and *Dahut*; choreographic drama on Shakespeare's *Macbeth*.

CHORAL cantata *Aucassin et Nicolette* (1908) and other choral music.

ORCHESTRAL AND CHAMBER four symphonies (1908–78), *Triptyque symphonique* for orchestra, fantasy for piano and orchestra; chamber music; violin and piano sonata, piano works.

Le Franc, Guillaume (died 1570) French composer. A Protestant, he fled to Switzerland, and settled in Geneva in 1541. He established a school of music there, becoming master of the children and singer at the cathedral the following year, and edited John Calvin's Genevan Psalter, in which Louis Bourgeois and Clément Marot also had a hand. In 1545 he left for the cathedral of Lausanne, and in 1565 issued a new Psalter there with some tunes of his own.

legato (Italian 'tied') term used to describe music that is to be played or sung smoothly.

Légende de Saint Christophe, La opera by Vincent d'Indy (libretto by the composer), first produced at the Paris Opéra, France, on 6 June 1920.

Legende von der heiligen Elizabeth, Die, *The Legend of St Elizabeth of Hungary* oratorio by Franz Liszt (words by Otto Roquette), first performed in Budapest, Hungary, on 15 August 1865; it was first produced as an opera in Weimar, Germany, on 23 October 1881.

Legend of Joseph, The ballet score by Richard Strauss; see ➤ *Josephslegende*.

Legend of the Invisible City of Kitezh and Maiden Fevronia, Russian **Skazhanie o nevidimom gradie Kitezh i dieve Fevronie** opera by Nikolai Rimsky-Korsakov (libretto by V I Bielsky), first produced in St Petersburg, Russia, on 20 February 1907. It was revived in St Petersburg and London, England, in 1994. In the story, a golden mist magically hides the city of Kitezh from the invading Tatars. Fevronia, captured by the barbarians, escapes to her slain groom, Prince Vsevolod, in eternal life in the Invisible City.

Legend of Tsar Saltan, The, Russian **Skazka o Tsarie Saltanie** opera by Nikolai Rimsky-Korsakov (libretto by V I Bielsky, after Aleksandr Pushkin), first produced in Moscow, Russia, on 3 November 1900. It tells how Prince Guidon transforms himself into a tree to rescue his mother and return her to the tsar.

leger line musical notation. See ➤ **ledger line**.

leggenda di Sakuntala, La opera by Franco Alfano (libretto by the composer, based on Kālidāsa's play), first produced at the Teatro Comunale, Bologna, Italy, on 10 December 1921. The manuscript was destroyed during World War II. Alfano reconstructed the opera for production in 1952, as *Sakuntala*. Sakuntala expires after meeting her lover king, but their child becomes a world hero.

leggiero (Italian 'light'; leggieramente 'lightly') in musical notation, term that often implies a detached articulation.

legno (Italian 'wood') in music, the wood of the bow. See ➤ **col legno**.

Legrant, Guillaume (1418–56) Franco-Flemish composer. Between 1419 and 1421 he was a member of the papal chapel. He wrote three chansons, a florid organ piece without a title, and a very chromatic *Gloria-Credo* pair.

Legrenzi, Giovanni (1626–1690) Italian composer. He was organist at Bergamo from 1645, then maestro di cappella at Ferrara 1656–65. In 1672 he became director of the Conservatorio dei Mendicanti in Venice and in 1685 maestro di cappella of St Mark's there.

Works OPERA *Achille in Sciro* (1663), *Eteocle e Polinice* (1675), *La divisione del mondo*, *Germanico sul Reno* (1676), *Totila*, *I due Cesari* (1683), *Il giustino*, *Pertinace* (1684), and about ten others.

OTHER Masses, motets, psalms, and other church music; orchestral works; church sonatas.

Lehár, Franz (1870–1948) Hungarian composer. He wrote many operettas, among them *The Merry Widow* (1905), *The Count of Luxembourg* (1909), *Gypsy Love* (1910), and *The Land of Smiles* (1929). He also composed songs, marches, and a violin concerto.

Born in Komárom, the son of a military bandmaster, he studied at the Prague Conservatory, in the modern-day Czech Republic, intending to become a violinist, but then became a military bandmaster. His music shows the influence of the southern Slavonic folk tunes and he first tried to win fame as a composer of serious opera as, for example, in *Kukuška* (1896; later renamed *Tatjana*), but it was in the field of operetta that he achieved real distinction. During his last years he lived in retirement in Ischl.

Works OPERA AND OPERETTA opera *Kukuška* (1896, later called *Tatjana*); operettas *The Merry Widow* (1905), *The Count of Luxembourg* (1909), *Gypsy Love* (1910), *The Three Graces*, *Pompadour*, *Springtime*, *Frasquita* (1922), *Clo Clo*, *The Blue Mazurka*, *Frederica* (1928), *The Land of Smiles* (1929), and many others.

ORCHESTRAL symphonic poem *Fieber*, three comedy scenes for orchestra.

Lehmann, Liza (Elizabetta Nina Mary Frederika) (1862–1918) English singer and composer. In 1885 she made her first appearance as a singer at St James's Hall, London, where she sang for the last time in 1894, when she married Herbert Bedford.

She was taught at first by her mother, Amelia Chambers, herself an accomplished amateur composer. She later studied in Rome, Italy, Wiesbaden, Germany, and at home with Hamish MacCunn, also singing with Alberto Randegger. The composer David Bedford is her grandson.

Works STAGE light opera *The Vicar of Wakefield* (after Goldsmith, 1906); musical comedy *Sergeant Brue* (L Housman); incidental music for *Everyman* and other plays.

VOCAL ballads for voice and orchestra; song cycles *In a Persian Garden* (Omar Khayyám) and *In Memoriam* (Tennyson).

Lehrstück (German 'didactic piece, educational play') small form of music drama cultivated in Germany in the 1920s and 1930s by Hanns ➤ Eisler, Paul ➤ Hindemith, Kurt ➤ Weill, and other composers, the chief literary exponent being Bertolt Brecht. It was cultivated mainly by the working classes in Germany at first as part of the

➤ **Gebrauchsmusik** ('useful music') movement, though later the influence spread to other European countries and to the USA. The Lehrstück makes use of historical material and dialectical discussion for the purpose of enlightening the masses, and it was for a time a counteragent to the Nazi movement until its exponents were forced to emigrate.

The first performance of Hindemith's *Lehrstück*, for soloists, chorus, and orchestra (texts by Brecht) was in Baden-Baden, Germany, on 28 July 1929.

Leibowitz, René (1913–1972) French-Polish composer. After studying with Arnold Schoenberg and Anton Webern, he destroyed all his works written before 1937, including six string quartets, and devoted himself entirely to 12-note music. He was known as a leading teacher of 12-note composition and published *Schoenberg et son école* and *Introduction à la musique de douze sons*.

Leibowitz settled in Paris, France, in 1926 and studied in Germany and Austria 1930–33 with Schoenberg and Webern. He conducted works of the 12-note school in the USA 1947–48.

Works STAGE music drama *La Nuit close* (1949).

VOCAL four unaccompanied choruses, *Tourist Death* for soprano and chamber orchestra (1943), *L'Explication des métaphores* for speaker, two pianos, harp, and percussion; songs.

ORCHESTRAL symphonies and variations for orchestra.

CHAMBER chamber symphony for twelve instruments, chamber concerto for violin, piano, and 17 instruments; string quartet, ten canons for oboe, clarinet, and bassoon, wind quintet; violin and piano sonata; sonata and pieces for piano.

Leicester, ou Le Château de Kenilworth opera by Daniel Auber (libretto by Augustin Scribe and A H Mélesville, based on Walter Scott's *Kenilworth*), first produced at the Opéra-Comique, Paris, France, on 25 January 1823. It describes the Earl of Leicester's friendship with Queen Elizabeth I, which makes his wife superfluous.

Leich (German 'lay') medieval type of German song similar to the French *lai*.

Leichtentritt, Hugo (1874–1951) German musicologist. He studied with John Paine at Harvard University, USA, and later at the Hochschule für Musik in Berlin, Germany, where he became professor at the Klindworth-Scharwenka Conservatory. In 1933 he left Germany as a refugee from the Nazi régime and returned to the USA to join the staff of Harvard University. His books include studies of Reinhard Keiser, Handel, Chopin, Ferruccio Busoni, and the motet.

Leigh, Walter (1905–1942) English composer. He studied at Cambridge and with Paul Hindemith in Berlin, Germany. In 1932 a work of his was performed at the International Society for Contemporary Music festival in Vienna, Austria. He enlisted during World War II and was killed in action.

Works STAGE comic operas *The Pride of the Regiment* (1932), *Jolly Roger* (1933); pantomime *Aladdin* (1931); revues *Nine Sharp* and *Little Revue* (1939); incidental music to Aristophanes' *Frogs*, Shakespeare's *A Midsummer Night's Dream*.

ORCHESTRAL overture *Agincourt*, *Music for String Orchestra*, *Three Pieces for Amateur Orchestra*; concertino for harpsichord and strings.

CHAMBER three movements for string quartet (1929), trio for flute, oboe, and piano, sonatina for viola and piano.

OTHER songs.

Leighton, Kenneth (1929–1988) English composer. He was lecturer at Edinburgh University, Scotland, 1956–68, and at Oxford University, England, 1968–70. From 1970 he was professor at Edinburgh University. His output includes three piano concertos and the fantasy octet 'Homage to Percy Grainger' (1982).

He studied at Queen's College, Oxford, and with Goffredo Petrassi in Rome, Italy. He won several prizes for composition.

Works OPERA *Columba* (1980).

ORCHESTRAL concerto for strings, two symphonies (1964, 1974), three piano concertos (1951–69), violin concerto, cello concerto.

CHAMBER string quartet, two violin sonatas, three piano sonatas, fantasy octet 'Homage to Percy Grainger' (1982).

OTHER choral works.

Leinsdorf, Erich (1912–1993) Austrian-born US conductor. He was music director with the Boston Symphony Orchestra 1962–69, and principal conductor with the West Berlin Radio Symphony Orchestra 1977–80.

Leinsdorf studied with Paul Emerich and Hedwig Kammer-Rosenthal at the Vienna Gymnasium. In 1934 he became assistant to Bruno Walter and Arturo Toscanini at the Salzburg Festival and later appeared as a conductor in Italy, France, and Belgium. In 1938 he was engaged as an assistant conductor at the New York Metropolitan Opera, making his debut with *Die Walküre*, and becoming chief conductor 1939–43. He served in the US Army from 1944 and returned to the New York Metropolitan Opera 1958–62.

leitmotif, German **Leitmotiv (German 'leading motive')** in music, a recurring theme or motive used to illustrate a character or idea. The term is strongly associated with Richard ➤ **Wagner**, who frequently employed this technique with great sophistication in his music dramas; it is also strongly prevalent in music for film.

Leitner, Ferdinand (1912–1996) German conductor. He studied in Berlin with Franz Schreker, Artur Schnabel, and Karl Muck, and conducted in Berlin, Hamburg, and Munich before moving to Stuttgart. He was music director until 1969 and led many productions of Wieland Wagner; he also gave first performances of Carl Orff's *Oedipus der Tyrann* (1959) and *Prometheus* (1968). He made his US debut in Chicago in 1969, with *Don Giovanni*. He was at the Zurich Opera, Switzerland, 1969–84 and was principal conductor of The Hague Philharmonic Orchestra, the Netherlands, 1976–80. He was a well-known conductor of Bruckner and Mozart, and gave operas by Berg and Busoni (the only recording of *Doktor Faust*). He conducted Mozart's C-minor Mass in Salzburg, Austria, in 1985, *Tannhäuser* in Chicago in 1988, and *Ariadne auf Náxos* for Radio Audizioni Italiane (RAI) in Turin, Italy, in 1989.

Le Jeune, Claude or **Claudin (c.1530–1600)** Franco-Flemish composer. He worked for most of his life in Paris, France. Having become a Huguenot, he tried to escape from Paris during the siege of 1588, and his manuscripts were saved from seizure by the Catholic soldiers by his colleague Jacques Mauduit, himself a Catholic. Later Le Jeune became chamber musician to the king. Like Jean-Antoine de Baïf (1532–1589) and Mauduit, he was an exponent of *musique mesurée*.

Works motets, psalms set to rhymed versions in measured music and also to tunes in the Genevan Psalter set for three voices; chansons, madrigals; instrumental fantasies, and other pieces.

Lekeu, Guillaume (1870–1894) Belgian composer. In 1891 he won second prize in the Belgian Prix de Rome with the lyric scene *Andromède*, and was thought likely to become the leading representative of the Belgian school had he not died at a very early age.

Lekeu was born in Heusy, Verviers. He studied with César Franck and Vincent d'Indy in Paris, France. His most memorable works are an adagio for strings, a string quartet, a piano trio, a piano quartet (finished by d'Indy), a violin sonata, and a piano sonata.

Works ORCHESTRAL symphonic study on Shakespeare's *Hamlet* (1887), *Fantasie sur deux airs populaires angevins* for orchestra, adagio for string quartet and orchestra, introduction and adagio for brass.

VOCAL *Chant lyrique* for chorus and orchestra, *Trois Poèmes* for voice and piano.

CHAMBER piano quartet (completed by d'Indy), piano trio, violin and piano sonata (1891), cello

and piano sonata (completed by d'Indy), three piano pieces.

Lélio, ou Le Retour à la vie, Lélio, or The Return to Life 'lyric monodrama' by Hector Berlioz for an actor, solo voices, chorus, piano, and orchestra, Op. 14 bis, composed in 1831 as a sequel to the *Symphonie fantastique* and first performed with the latter at the Paris Conservatory, France, on 9 December 1832.

Lemminkäinen's Return symphonic legend by Jean Sibelius, Op. 22, one of four on subjects from the *Kalevala*, composed 1893–95 and first performed in Helsinki, Finland, on 13 April 1896. The other three are *The Swan of Tuonela*, *Lemminkäinen and the Maidens of Saari*, and *Lemminkäinen in Tuonela*.

'Leningrad' Symphony Dmitri ➤ Shostakovich's seventh symphony, Op. 60, awarded the Stalin prize in 1942 and first performed in Kuibishev (present-day Samara, Russia) by the evacuated Bolshoi Theatre Orchestra of Moscow on 5 March 1942. The symphony was written during World War II, whilst Shostakovich was trapped in the besieged city of Leningrad.

The first movement is famous for its huge crescendo which is based around a single repeating melody, usually taken to be representative of the approach of the Nazi armies – the tune is a parody of a melody from *The Merry Widow*, one of Hitler's favourite operas. Shostakovich's march was subsequently parodied by Béla Bartók in his *Concerto for Orchestra* (1944).

lento (Italian 'slow') in musical notation, slightly slower than, or approximately the same tempo as ➤ adagio, depending on the historical period in which the music was written.

Leo, Leonardo (Lionardo Oronzo Salvatore de) (1694–1744) Italian composer. His comic operas (often in Neapolitan dialect) were ranked with those of Giovanni Pergolesi and had a great influence on later Italian masters of the genre. He also wrote much church music. Niccolò Piccinni and Niccolò Jommelli were among his pupils.

He was a pupil of Francesco Provenzale and Nicola Fago at the Conservatorio della Pietà dei Turchini, Naples, 1709–13, where his first oratorio was performed in 1712. Appointed supernumerary organist to the court at Naples in 1713, he rose to become maestro di cappella just before his death. He taught at the Conservatorio della Pietà from 1715 (appointed primo maestro in 1741) and the Conservatorio S Onofrio from 1725 (appointed primo maestro in 1739).

Works OPERA *Sofonisba* (1718), *Lucio Papirio*, *Caio Gracco* (1720), *La 'mpeca scoperta* (in Neapolitan dialect, 1723), *Timocrate*, *Il trionfo di Camilla*, *La semmeglianza di chi l'ha fatta*, *Il Cid*,

Catone in Utica (1729), *La clemenza di Tito* (1735), *Demofoonte*, *Farnace* (1736), *Siface*, *Ciro riconosciuto*, *L'amico traditore*, *La simpatia del sangue*, *L'Olimpiade* (1737), *Vologeso*, *Amor vuol sofferenza* (*La finta Frascatana*, 1739), *Achille in Sciro* (1740), *Scipione nelle Spagne* (1740), *Il fantastico* (*Il nuovo Don Chisciotte*, after Cervantes, 1743), and about 40 others.

OTHER oratorios *Il trionfo della castità di S Alessio* (1713), *Dalla morte alla vita* (1722), *La morte di Abele*, *S Elena al Calvario* (1734), *S Francesco di Paolo nel deserto*, and others; Masses, motets, psalms, and other church music; concerto for four violins, six cello concertos; harpsichord pieces.

Leoncavallo, Ruggero (1858–1919) Italian operatic composer. He played in restaurants, composing in his spare time, until the success of *I pagliacci/The Strolling Players* (1892). His other operas include *La Bohème/Bohemian Life* (1897) (contemporary with Puccini's version) and *Zaza* (1900).

He studied piano privately at first and then entered the Naples Conservatory, which he left in 1876 with a master diploma. He went to Bologna to attend Giosuè Carducci's lectures in literature, and was on the point of producing his first opera, *Chatterton* there, but was swindled and found himself penniless. He made a precarious living by giving lessons and playing the piano at cafés, but later managed to travel widely as a café pianist. He then began a trilogy on the Italian Renaissance, *Crepusculum*, with *I Medici*, but never produced the planned two following works, *Savonarola* and *Cesare Borgia*. In the meantime he enjoyed enormous success with *I pagliacci* in Milan in 1892 and soon all over Italy.

La Bohème in Venice in 1897 suffered from the appearance of Puccini's work on the same subject, and in spite of a commission for a German opera for Berlin, *Der Roland von Berlin*, in 1904, he never repeated the success of *I pagliacci*. He wrote all his own libretti and some for other composers.

Works OPERA operas *Chatterton* (after Alfred de Vigny, composed 1876, produced 1896), *I Medici*, *I pagliacci* (1892), *La Bohème* (after Murger, 1897), *Zaza* (1900), *Der Roland von Berlin* (after Willibald Alexis, 1904), *Maia* (1910), *Gli zingari*, *Goffredo Mameli*, *Edipo rè* (after Sophocles, 1920), *Tormenta* (unfinished); operettas *A chi la giarettiera* (1919), *Il primo bacio*, *Malbruk* (1910), *La reginetta delle rose* (1912), *Are You There?* (1913), *La candidata*, and *Prestami tua moglie*.

BALLET *La vita d'una marionetta*.

ORCHESTRAL symphonic poem *Serafita* (after Balzac's novel).

Leoni, Leone (c.1560–1627) Italian composer. He was maestro di cappella of Vicenza Cathedral from 1588.

Works Masses, motets (some in many parts with instruments), *Sacrae cantiones*, psalms, Magnificats and other church music, sacred and secular madrigals.

Leoninus (c.1163–1201), French **Léonin** French poet, theologian, and composer. First documented in 1179, he was active mainly at Notre-Dame, Paris, for which he is said to have composed the *Magnus liber organi* containing at least 42 settings of music for the Mass and Office in two voices. This formed the basis of the great Notre-Dame repertory later elaborated by Perotinus Magnus and others.

Leonora, ossia L'amore conjugale, *Leonora, or Wedded Love* opera by Ferdinando Paër (libretto by G Cinti, based on Bouilly's libretto for Pierre Gaveaux), first produced in Dresden, Germany, on 3 October 1804. It tells how the political prisoner Florestan is rescued by his disguised wife (Leonore/Fidelio) when the evil Pizarro arrives to kill him.

Leonora Overtures operatic overtures by Beethoven; see ➤ *Fidelio, oder Die eheliche Liebe*.

Léonore, ou L'Amour conjugal, *Leonora, or Wedded Love* opera by Pierre Gaveaux (libretto by J N Bouilly, based on a real event), first produced at the Théâtre Feydeau, Paris, France, on 19 February 1798. It was a forerunner of and model for Beethoven's ➤ *Fidelio, oder Die eheliche Liebe*.

Leopold I (1640–1705) Holy Roman emperor from 1658. He composed an opera, *Apollo deluso*, to a libretto by his court musician Antonio Draghi in 1669, and contributed to numerous other operas by the same composer. His oratorios include *Il sagrifizio d'Abramo* (1660), *Il figliuol prodigo* (1663), and *Il lutto dell'universo* (1668).

Leopolita, Martinus (c.1540–1589), also known as **Marcin Lwowczyk** Polish composer who might have studied under Sebastian z Felsztyna and Jan Jeleń of Tuchola. He was a member of the College of Roratists (Cappella Rorantistarum), established at the Royal Chapel at the Wawel royal residence in Kraków in 1543, and court composer there from 1560.

Works Masses, including *Missa Paschalis*, motets; secular songs for several voices, and other pieces.

Leppard, Raymond John (1927–) English conductor and musicologist. His imaginative reconstructions of Monteverdi and Cavalli operas did much to generate popular interest in early opera and to stimulate academic investigation of the performance implications of early music manuscript scores.

He studied at Cambridge and made his debut as a conductor in London in 1952. From 1960 he was a regular conductor of English Chamber Orchestra, and of the BBC Northern Symphony Orchestra 1973–80. He conducted *Solomon* at the Royal Opera House, Covent Garden, London, in 1959 and Monteverdi's *L'incoronazione di Poppea* at Glyndebourne, East Sussex, in 1964. This was the first of several realizations of Venetian opera, all of which attracted negative scholarly comment for making too many transpositions, having too much music from other sources, and instrumental parts realized in too lavish a manner. However, Leppard's versions of Monteverdi, and of Cavalli's *L'Ormindo*, *La Calisto*, *L'Egisto*, and *Orione* have been popular with the public. Leppard also produced Monteverdi's *Ballo delle ingrate* in 1958, and Cavalli's *Messa Concertata*. He made his US concert debut in New York in 1969, his opera debut in Santa Fe in 1974 with *Egisto*, and his New York Metropolitan Opera House debut in 1978 with *Billy Budd*. He has been based in the USA since 1976, being principal guest conductor of the St Louis Symphony Orchestra from 1984 and of the Indianapolis Symphony Orchestra from 1986.

Leroux, Xavier (Henri Napoléon) (1863–1919) Italian-born French composer. He studied at the Paris Conservatory, France, one of his masters being Jules Massenet, and gained the Prix de Rome in 1885. He became harmony professor there in 1896 and edited the periodical *Musica*.

Works OPERA *Evangéline* (1885), *Astarté*, *La Reine Fiammette* (after Catulle Mendès, 1903), *William Ratcliff* (after Heine, 1906), *Théodora*, *Le Chemineau* (1907), *Le Carillonneur* (1913), *La Fille de Figaro* (1914), *Les Cadeaux de Noël* (1914), *Nausithoé*, *La Plus Forte*, *L'Ingénu*.

OTHER incidental music to Sardou and Moreau's *Cléopâtre* (1890), Aeschylus' *The Persians*, and Richepin's *Xantho chez les courtisanes*; cantatas *Endymion* (1885) and *Vénus et Adonis* (1897); overture *Harald*; Mass with orchestra; motets; numerous songs.

L'Escurel, Jehannot de (died c.1303) French composer. His 34 secular works, all but one of which are monophonic, are included in the same manuscript as the *Roman de Fauvel*.

Lessel, Franz (Franciszek) (1780–1838) Polish-Austrian composer. He studied medicine in Vienna, but became a pupil of Haydn, whom he looked after until his death. He then returned to Poland and lived with Prince Czartoryski's family until they were driven away by the Revolution. The rest of his life was unsettled.

Works three Masses, Requiem and other church music; five symphonies; piano concerto; chamber music; piano sonatas and fantasies.

***Les Six* (French 'The Six')** group of French composers: Georges ➜ Auric, Louis ➜ Durey, Arthur ➜ Honegger, Darius ➜ Milhaud, Francis ➜ Poulenc, and Germaine ➜ Tailleferre. Formed in 1917, the group had Jean Cocteau as its spokesperson and adopted Erik ➜ Satie as its guru; it was dedicated to producing works free from foreign influences and reflecting contemporary attitudes. The group split up in the early 1920s.

lesson in music, a 17th–18th-century term for a keyboard piece, generally of an instructive character.

Lesueur, Jean François (1760–1837) French composer. He wrote operas and much church music and introduced some orchestral innovations anticipating Hector Berlioz, who was his pupil.

He was born in Drucat, near Abbeville, and first learnt music as a choirboy at Abbeville. He then held church appointments at Amiens and Paris. After 1781 he became musical director successively at Dijon Cathedral, Le Mans, Tours, and Saints Innocents, Paris, in 1784, and Notre-Dame, Paris, in 1786. He was allowed to use a full orchestra at Mass and to open the proceedings with an overture. This aroused a controversy which led to his resignation, and he spent the years 1788–92 in the country, devoted to the composition of operas. In 1793 he was appointed professor at the school of the National Guard and in 1795 one of the inspectors at the newly opened Conservatory. In 1804 he succeeded Giovanni Paisiello as maître de chapelle to Napoleon, after whose fall he was appointed superintendent and composer to the chapel of Louis XVIII. In 1818 he became professor of composition at the Conservatory, where his pupils included Berlioz and Charles Gounod.

Works OPERA *La Caverne* (1793), *Paulin et Virginie* (after Saint-Pierre, 1794), *Télémaque* (1796), *Ossian, ou Les Bardes* (1804), *Le Triomphe de Trajan* (with Persuis, 1807), *La Mort d'Adam* (after Klopstock, 1809), and some others.

CHURCH MUSIC Mass and Te Deum for Napoleon's coronation, three Solemn Masses, *Stabat Mater*, motets, psalms, and other church music.

CHORAL oratorios *Messe de Noël*, *Debora*, *Rachel*, *Ruth et Noémi*, *Ruth et Boaz*; cantatas.

letters, music based on composers have sometimes amused themselves by turning names or other words into notes representing in musical nomenclature the letters of which they are formed, or as many as can be thus used. In English the letters A to G can be thus represented; in German H (B natural) and S (Es is equivalent to E flat) can be added, and in French and Italian the syllables Do, Re, Mi, Fa, Sol, La, Si may be used. In France a system was devised for the works on the names of Gabriel Fauré and Haydn listed below, whereby the notes A to G were followed by further octaves named from H onwards. Examples include:

Abegg (supposed friends of Schumann's): Robert Schumann, *Variations on the Name of Abegg* for piano, Op. 1

Asch (the birthplace of Ernestine von Fricken): Schumann, *Carnaval* for piano Op. 9

Bach ➔ **B.A.C.H.**

Bamberg (the maiden name of Cui's wife): César Cui, scherzo for piano duet (on BABEG and CC = César Cui)

Belaiev: Aleksandr Borodin, Aleksandr Glazunov, Anatol Liadov, and Nikolai Rimsky-Korsakov, string quartet on 'B-la-F'

Faber: canon in seven parts by Bach, dated 1 March 1749, sung over a ground or *Pes* on the notes F. A. B flat. E. and marked 'F A B E Repetatur', thus forming the name Faber, which may be a Latin form of some German surname derived from some kind of manual labour. The canon also bears an inscription in Latin containing the following acrostics on the names of Faber and Bach: 'Fidelis Amici Beatum Esse Recordari' and 'Bonae Artis Cultorem Habeas'

Fauré: pieces by Daniel Aubert, George Enescu, Charles Koechlin, Paul Ladmirault, Maurice Ravel, Jean Roger-Ducasse, and Florent Schmitt contributed to a Fauré number of the *Revue musicale* in 1924

Gade: Schumann's piano piece so entitled in *Album für die Jugend*

Gedge: Edward Elgar, allegretto for violin and piano on GEDGE, dedicated to the Misses Gedge.

Haydn: Ravel, *Menuet sur le nom d'Haydn* for piano.

Sacha: Glazunov, *Suite sur le thème du nom diminutif russe* for piano, Op. 2.

Schumann (letters SCHA only): *Carnaval* (inversion of the letters ASCH).

Leveridge, Richard (c.1670–1758) English bass and composer. He appeared as a singer mainly in pantomimes, but also in Italian opera, his career extending from 1695 to 1751. As a composer he is remembered for his songs.

Works STAGE incidental music for Shakespeare's *Macbeth* (1702), Farquhar's *The Recruiting Officer, Love and a Bottle*, and (with D Purcell) *The Constant Couple*, Vanbrugh's *Aesop*, and other plays; masque *Pyramus and Thisbe* (after Shakespeare, 1716).

SONGS 'The Roast Beef of Old England' and others.

Levi, Hermann (1839–1900) German conductor. He conducted the first performance of Wagner's *Parsifal* at Bayreuth, Germany; at first, Wagner objected that a Jew should conduct what

was essentially a Christian opera, but nevertheless accepted him as 'the ideal Parsifal conductor'. He continued at Bayreuth until 1894, and conducted at Wagner's funeral.

He studied with Vinzenz Lachner in Munich and at the Leipzig Conservatory. After various appointments he became director of the Munich court theatre 1872–96, where he conducted his own editions of Mozart's operas.

Levin, Robert D (1947–) US pianist and musicologist. Mozart has been at the centre of his research and he has published completions of various works.

He studied with Nadia Boulanger 1960–64 and graduated from Harvard University in 1968. He has given solo and chamber concerts throughout the USA, Europe, and Japan from 1970; and was pianist with the New York Philomusica from 1971. His completions of works by Mozart include the D minor Requiem and a four wind concertante that was conjectural orchestration but retains the wind parts of the concerto known as K297b (with clarinet replaced by original flute). He has made recordings with Malcolm Bilson and Melvyn Tan.

Lewis, Anthony (Carey) (1915–1983) English musicologist, conductor, and composer. He edited and conducted operas by Purcell, Jean-Philippe Rameau, and Handel. He was professor of music at Birmingham University 1947–68 and principal of the Royal Academy of Music, London, 1968–82.

He was educated at Wellington College and Cambridge University, studying music at the latter, and went on to study at the Royal College of Music in London and with Nadia Boulanger in Paris, France. He was on the music staff of the BBC (British Broadcasting Corporation) 1935–47 (except during his war service 1939–45), where he organized various music series including the music for the Third Programme (later Radio Three).

Works *Choral Overture* for unaccompanied voices; *Elegy and Capriccio* for trumpet and orchestra; horn concerto.

L.H. in musical notation, abbreviation for **left hand**, directing a pianist to use the left hand. This is usually in order to facilitate a technically difficult passage, dividing the notes between both hands rather than playing the passage solely with the right hand. It can also be notated in French as M.G. (*main gauche*) or in Italian as M.S. (*mano sinistra*). The opposite is R.H. ('right hand').

L'Héritier, Jean (c.1480–after 1552) French composer. He wrote Masses, motets, and other pieces.

He was a pupil of Josquin Des Prez. In the 1520s he was in Rome, Italy, and was music director to the Cardinal de Vermont at Avignon 1540–41.

L'Homme armé French song; see ➤ **Homme armé, L'.**

Liadov, Anatol Konstantinovich (1855–1914) Russian composer. He wrote especially well for the piano, but also composed orchestral works which made him a distinguished member of the national Russian school.

Liadov was born in St Petersburg, where he studied under his father and later with Nikolai Rimsky-Korsakov at the St Petersburg Conservatory. He became a teacher there in 1878, and his pupils included Sergey Prokofiev and Nikolay Myaskovsky. The Imperial Geographical Society commissioned him, with Mily Balakirev and Sergey Liapunov, to collect folk songs in various parts of Russia. His gift was essentially reclusive and small-scale; Igor Stravinsky described Liadov's relief at not getting the commission for *The Rite of Spring* from Sergei Diaghilev.

Works ORCHESTRAL symphonic poems *Baba Yaga* (1904), *The Enchanted Lake* (1909), *Kikimora* (1909), two orchestral scherzos, *The Inn-Muzurka*, *Polonaise in Memory of Pushkin for orchestra*.

CHORAL choral settings from Schiller's *Bride of Messina* and Maeterlinck's *Sœur Béatrice*, three choral works for female voices.

OTHER about 40 Op. nos of piano pieces, including *Birulki/Spillikins*, ballads 'From Days of Old', 'Marionettes', 'Musical Snuff-Box', variations on a theme by Glinka and on a Polish song, 'From the Book of Revelation', studies, preludes, mazurkas, and other pieces; songs, folk-song settings (1903).

Liapunov, Sergey Mikhailovich (1859–1924) Russian pianist and composer. From 1891 to 1902 he was assistant director of the Imperial Chapel, and from 1910 professor at the St Petersburg Conservatory. He fled to Paris, France, to escape the Russian Revolution.

He studied at Nizhegorodsk and at the Moscow Conservatory. In 1893 the Imperial Geographical Society commissioned him, with Mily Balakirev and Anatol Liadov, to collect Russian folk songs.

Works ORCHESTRAL two symphonies (1887, 1910–17), *Ballad*, *Solemn Overture*, Polonaise and symphonic poem *Hashish* for orchestra; two piano concertos (1890, 1909), rhapsody on Ukrainian themes for piano and orchestra (1908).

PIANO AND OTHER numerous piano pieces, including suite *Christmas Songs*, and other pieces; folk-song settings.

Liberté or **14 tableaux inspirés par l'histoire du peuple de France** music by Marcel Delannoy, Arthur Honegger, Jacques Ibert, Daniel Lazarus, Darius Milhaud, Roland-Manuel, Manuel Rosenthal, Germaine Tailleferre, and others, first produced at the Théâtre des Champs-Élysées, Paris, France, in May 1937.

libretto (Italian 'little book') the text of an opera or other dramatic vocal work, or the scenario of a ballet.

Libuše opera by Bedřich Smetana (libretto in German, by J Wenzig, Czech translation by E Spindler), first produced at the Czech Theatre, Prague, in the modern-day Czech Republic, on 11 June 1881. It tells the story of Libuše, new queen of Bohemia, who must choose a husband to help her rule after her quarrelling brothers Chrudos and Šťáhlov refuse to obey her authority. She chooses the peasant Přemsyl.

licenza (Italian 'licence', 'freedom') in musical notation, from the term *con licenza* ('with freedom'), direction to the performer to take liberties with the tempo, using ➤ **rubato** and other forms of expression.

Lichnovsky, (Prince) Karl (1761–1814) Polish aristocrat, resident in Vienna, Austria. After early patronage of Mozart, he was introduced to Beethoven by Haydn. Beethoven's early chamber works were played at his house before publication, notably the string quartets Op. 18, with the Schuppanzigh quartet.

Licht*, *Light cycle of seven projected operas by Karlheinz Stockhausen, one for each day of the week. See ➤ **Dienstag aus Licht,** ➤ **Donnerstag aus Licht,** ➤ **Montag aus Licht,** ➤ **Samstag aus Licht.**

Lidarti, Christian Joseph (1730–after 1793) Austro-Italian composer. He was in the service of the Cavalieri di S Stefano in Pisa, Italy, 1757–84.

He was taught by his uncle, Giuseppe Bonno, in Vienna, Austria, and later by Niccolò Jommelli in Italy.

Works trio sonatas, catches, and glees.

Lidholm, Ingvar (1921–) Swedish composer. From 1947 to 1956 he was conductor of the Örebro Symphony Orchestra.

He studied at the Stockholm Conservatory with, among others, Hilding Rosenberg and Tor Mann. Later he studied in Italy and France, and also with Mátyás Seiber.

Works OPERA *The Dutchman* (after Strindberg, 1967).

ORCHESTRAL concerto for string orchestra, *Toccata e canto* for chamber orchestra (1944), *Ritornell* for orchestra (1956), concertino for flute, cor anglais, oboe, and bassoon, *Greetings from an Old World* for orchestra (1976), *Kontakion* for orchestra (1978).

VOCAL *De Profundis* for chorus, *Cantata* for baritone and orchestra.

CHAMBER string quartet, four pieces for cello and

piano, sonata for solo flute.

Liebe der Danae, Die, Danae's Love opera by Richard Strauss (libretto by Josef Gregor), intended for production at the Salzburg Festival, Austria, and given a public dress rehearsal on 16 August 1944. Production was postponed owing to war; it was finally produced in Salzburg on 14 August 1952. (The title was originally *Der Kuss der Danae/Danae's Kiss*.) In the story, Danae, who spurns all men, is pursued by King Midas and Jupiter, favouring the 'golden touch' of Midas. She then falls genuinely in love with him, and continues to love him after vengeful Jupiter makes him destitute.

Liebe im Narrenhaus, Die, Love in the Madhouse opera by Karl Ditters von Dittersdorf (libretto by G Stephanie, junior), first produced at the Kärntnertor-theater, Vienna, Austria, on 12 April 1787. Constanze has been promised to the lunatic asylum director Bast, so her lover Albert feigns insanity. When Albert inherits a fortune the lovers are allowed to marry.

Lieberson, Peter (1946–) US composer. He studied in New York with Milton Babbitt, Charles Wuorinen, and Donald Martino. He studied Buddhism 1976–81 and was inspired to write his piano concerto of 1983.

Works ORCHESTRAL *Drala* (1986), *Gesar Legend* (1988).

INSTRUMENTAL in a serial idiom *Tashi Quartet* (1979), *Lalita (Chamber Variations)* for ten instruments (1984), *Raising the Gaze* for seven instruments (1988), and *Wind Messengers* for 13 instruments (1990).

Liebert, Reginaldus (lived early 15th century) French composer. His main work is a complete Mass (Ordinary and Proper) of the Blessed Virgin Mary for three voices.

He probably succeeded Nicolas Grenon at Cambrai in 1424. A Gautier Liebert, composer of three *rondeaux*, was a singer in the papal chapel in 1428.

Liebeslieder, Love Songs a set of waltzes by Johannes Brahms for piano duet with solo vocal quartet *ad lib*, Op. 52, composed in 1869. There is a second set of *Neue Liebeslieder*, Op. 65, written in 1874.

Liebesverbot, Das, oder Die Novize von Palermo, The Love-Ban, or The Novice of Palermo opera by Richard Wagner (libretto by composer, based on Shakespeare's *Measure for Measure*), first produced in Magdeburg, Germany, on 29 March 1836. It tells how the viceroy Friedrich outlaws pleasure but desires Isabella. Friedrich having imprisoned her brother Claudio, Isabella is willing to sacrifice herself for Claudio's agreed release, but she sends Friedrich's wife to the rendezvous. Friedrich's hypocrisy is exposed and there is a happy ending.

lied (German 'song', plural lieder) musical dramatization of a poem, usually for solo voice and piano; referring especially to the Romantic songs of Franz Schubert, Robert Schumann, Johannes Brahms, and Hugo Wolf.

Lieder eines fahrenden Gesellen, Songs of a Wayfarer song-cycle by Gustav Mahler for low voice and piano (texts by Mahler), composed in 1884, orchestrated about 1895, and performed in this version in Berlin, Germany, on 16 March 1896, conducted by Mahler. The titles of the songs are: 1. *Wenn mein Schatz Hochzeit macht/When my Sweetheart Gets Married*, 2. *Ging heut' Morgen übers Feld/I Walked This Morning Through the Fields* (thematically related to the first movement of the contemporary first symphony), 3. *Ich hab ein glühend Messer in der Brust/I Have a Burning Knife in My Breast*, and 4. *Die zwei blauen Augen/The Two Blue Eyes*. The work is also heard in a version with a chamber ensemble by Arnold Schoenberg.

Liederkreis title used for two sets of songs by Robert Schumann: nine Heine settings Op. 24 and twelve Eichendorff settings Op. 39 (both composed in 1840). See also ➤ song cycle.

Lieder ohne Worte thirty-six piano pieces by Felix Mendelssohn in the form and character of songs exploiting the principle of accompanying melody rather than polyphonic textures. They are: Vol. I, Op. 19, nos. 1–6 (composed 1830–32); II, Op. 30, 7–12 (1833–7); III, Op. 38, 13–18 (1836–37); IV, Op. 53, 19–24 (1841); V. Op. 62, 25–30 (1842–43); and VI, Op. 67, 31–6 (1843–45). The only titles which are Mendelssohn's own are those of the three *Venezianische Gondellieder (Venetian Barcarolles)*, nos. 6, 12, and 29, the *Duetto*, no. 18, and the *Volkslied*, no. 23.

Liederspiel (German 'song-play') play with songs similar to the ➤ Singspiel. The term was first used by Johann Reichardt in 1800. It may also mean 'song cycle', as in Robert Schumann's *Spanisches Liederspiel*.

Lied von der Erde, Das, The Song of the Earth symphony for mezzo, tenor, and orchestra by Gustav ➤ Mahler. The words are from Hans Bethge's anthology of German translations of Chinese poetry, *Die chinesische Flöte*: 1. (Li-Tai-Po) *Das Trinklied vom Jammer der Erde/The Drinking-Song of Earth's Misery*; 2. (Tchang-Tsi) *Der Einsame im Herbst/The Lonely One in Autumn*; 3. (Li-Tai-Po) *Von der Jugend/Of Youth*: 4. (Li-Tai-Po) *Von der Schönheit/Of Beauty*; 5. (Li-Tai-Po) *Der Trunkene im Frühling/The Drunkard in Spring*; 6. (Mong-Kao-Yen and

Modern equivalent

Various ligatures (left), with literal and modern representations (right).

Wang-We) *Der Abschied/The Farewell*).The work was composed in 1908 and first performed in Munich, Germany, on 20 November 1911, after Mahler's death.

Mahler himself referred to the piece as a symphony, but named it differently, and refused to give it a number, as his previous symphony had been numbered 8. A highly superstitious man, he was terrified by the prospect of writing a Symphony no. 9, as Beethoven, Schubert, and Bruckner had all died after or during the composition of their ninth symphonies.

Lieutenant Kijé symphonic suite by Sergey ➤ Prokofiev, arranged in 1934 from film music composed in 1933. The five movements are *Birth of Kijé*, *Romance*, *Wedding*, *Troika*, and *Burial*. The work was first performed in Paris, France, on 20 February 1937, conducted by Prokofiev.

Life in the Times of the Tsar, A, Russian *Zhizn za Tsaria*; or **Ivan Susanin** opera by Mikhail Glinka (libretto by C F Rosen), first produced in St Petersburg, Russia, on 9 December 1836. In the story, Ivan Susanin delays the wedding of his daughter Antonida to Bogden Sobinin because of invading Poles who are hunting down the tsar. Knowing where the tsar is hiding, Susanin deliberately leads the Poles astray, knowing that he will be killed when the deception is discovered. Susanin willingly sacrifices his life for the tsar; his bravery is praised by all.

ligature in music, the adjustable metal brace used to attach the reed to the mouthpiece of an instrument of the clarinet family.

ligature in music, notation used in the 13th–16th centuries in which two or more notes are combined to form a single symbol. Depending on the shape of the ligature, the same group of notes could indicate different rhythms. In addition to its rhythmic implications, a ligature indicates that only one syllable is to be sung for the duration of its notes, similar in function to a modern slur marking in vocal works (also known as a ➤ tie).

Ligeti, Andras (1953–) Hungarian conductor. He studied violin at the Budapest Academy and was leader of the Hungarian State Opera House Orchestra 1976–80. He conducted concerts in Europe and Canada, and was associate conductor with the Budapest Symphony Orchestra from 1985 (tours of the UK and the USA). He made his UK debut with the BBC Symphony Orchestra in 1989, and with the BBC Philharmonic Orchestra in 1991 (Bartók's *Bluebeard's Castle* and Mahler's fifth symphony).

Ligeti, György Sándor (1923–) Hungarian-born Austrian composer. He developed a dense, highly chromatic, polyphonic style in which melody and rhythm are sometimes lost in shifting blocks of sound. He achieved international prominence with *Atmosphères* (1961) and

Requiem (1965), used as part of the score for Stanley Kubrick's film epic *2001: A Space Odyssey* (1968). Other works include an opera *Le Grand Macabre* (1978) and *Poème symphonique* (1962), for 100 metronomes.

Ligeti studied composition at the Budapest Music Academy 1945–49 and taught there 1950–56. In 1956 he went to the Studio for Electronic Music in Cologne, Germany, and in 1959 was appointed instructor at the International Courses for New Music at Darmstadt. In 1961 he was visiting professor of composition at the Stockholm Music Academy, and eventually settled in Vienna, Austria. His mature music is experimental in nature, featuring complex textures which he called 'micropolyphony', in which the individuality of a large number of separate parts is subsumed, giving the impression of a slowly changing single mass.

Works OPERA *Le Grand Macabre* (produced Stockholm, 1978).

ORCHESTRAL *Apparitions* (1959), *Atmosphères* for large orchestra (1961), cello concerto (1967), *Ramifications* for string orchestra (1969), *San Francisco Polyphony* (1974).

VOCAL *Aventures* for soprano, alto, and baritone with seven instruments (1962), *Nouvelles Aventures* for soprano and seven instruments (1965), Requiem for soloists, chorus, and orchestra (1965; Kyrie used in film *2001*), *Lux aeterna* for 16 solo voices (1966), *3 Phantasien* and *Hungarian Studies*, both for 16 voices (1983), *Nonsense Madrigals* for six voices (1988).

CHAMBER chamber concerto for 13 instruments (1970), trio for violin, horn, and piano (1982), *Études* for piano (1985), piano concerto (1985–88), violin concerto (1990), *L'Escalier du diable* for piano (1993).

OTHER *Artikulation* for electronic sounds (1958), *Poème symphonique* for 100 metronomes (1962).

Lighthouse, The chamber opera in one act by Peter Maxwell Davies (text by the composer, based on the 1900 disappearance of three Outer Hebridean lighthouse keepers); it was composed in 1979 and first performed in Edinburgh, Scotland, on 2 September 1980.

Light of Life, The or **Lux Christi** oratorio by Edward Elgar for soloists, chorus, and orchestra, Op. 29 (text by E Capel-Dure from the Scriptures); it was composed in 1896 and first performed in Worcester, England, on 10 September 1896, conducted by Elgar.

'Lilliburlero' a satirical song sung in Ireland after the appointment of General Talbot to the lord-lieutenant in 1687. It is not likely that the earlier attribution of the tune to Purcell is justified: it was probably a popular melody merely arranged by him, much as 'The Prince of Denmark's March'

was arranged by Jeremiah Clarke.

Lima, Jeronymo Francisco de (1743–1822) Portuguese composer and organist. He was elected to the Brotherhood of St Cecilia, visited Italy, and in 1798 became conductor of the Royal Opera in Lisbon.

Works the opera *Le nozze d'Ercole e d'Ebe* (1785) and five others (all Italian); church music; cantatas.

Limburgia, Johannes de (lived late 14th and early 15th century) French composer. He worked at churches in Liège 1408–19, and in Italy from about 1430. His 50 or so compositions (all church music) include a complete Mass (three and four voices) and 16 motets.

Lincoln Portrait, A work by Aaron Copland for orchestra and a speaker, who declaims portions of Abraham Lincoln's speeches. It was first performed by the Cincinnati Symphony Orchestra on 14 May 1942.

Linda di Chamounix opera by Gaetano Donizetti (libretto by Giacomo Rossi, after a vaudeville, *La Grâce de Dieu*), first produced at the Kärntnertortheater, Vienna, Austria, on 19 May 1842. In the story, the poor girl Linda loves the viscount Carlo, who has disguised himself as a destitute painter. She follows him to Paris and learns his true identity, but goes mad upon learning of his supposed marriage to another woman. Carlo reassures her and Linda recovers.

Lindblad, Adolf Fredrik (1801–1878) Swedish composer and singing teacher. He studied with Carl Zelter in Berlin, Germany, and in 1827 settled in Stockholm, Sweden, as a teacher of singing. Jenny Lind was among his pupils.

Works the opera *Frondörerna* (1835); two symphonies; seven string quartets; duo for violin and piano; vocal duets, trios and quartets; numerous songs.

linear counterpoint in music, a term for a kind of ➤ counterpoint in 20th-century music which regards the individuality of melodic lines as more important than the harmony they produce in combination.

Linley, Elizabeth Ann (1754–1792) English soprano, daughter and pupil of Thomas ➤ Linley. She first sang in her father's concerts in Bath. She made her London debut in 1770, but after her marriage to the dramatist Richard Brinsley Sheridan in 1773 she retired from singing. Her portrait was painted by Gainsborough and Reynolds.

Linley, Mary (1758–1787) English singer, daughter and pupil of Thomas ➤ Linley. She sang at festivals and gave oratorio performances, but retired on her marriage to Richard Rickell, commissioner of stamps and dramatist, who wrote *The Carnival of Venice* for his father-in-law and altered Ramsay's *Gentle Shepherd* for him.

Linley, Thomas (1733–1795) English singing master and composer. He studied with Thomas Chilcot, the organist of Bath Abbey, and with Domenico Paradies in London, and settled in Bath as a singing teacher and concert promoter. From 1774 he managed the oratorios at the Drury Lane Theatre in London jointly with John Stanley and from 1786 with Samuel Arnold. Richard Brinsley Sheridan became his son-in-law in 1773, and he and his son, also Thomas, wrote music for Sheridan's play *The Duenna* in 1775. In 1776 he moved to London and bought David Garrick's share in the Drury Lane Theatre, where he managed the music and wrote music for various pieces.

Works STAGE opera *The Royal Merchant* (1767); music for Sheridan's *The Duenna* (1781) and *The School for Scandal* (the song 'Here's to the Maiden'), *The Carnival of Venice* (1781), *The Gentle Shepherd*, *Robinson Crusoe* (pantomime by Sheridan, after Defoe), *The Triumph of Mirth*, *The Spanish Rivals* (1784), *The Strangers at Home* (1785), *Love in the East* (1788), and other plays; adaptations from Grétry: *Zelmire and Azor* and *Richard Cœur-de-Lion*; accompaniments for *The Beggar's Opera*; music for Sheridan's monody on the death of Garrick.

OTHER six elegies for three voices; twelve ballads; cantatas, madrigals.

Linley, Thomas (1756–1778) English violinist and composer, son and pupil of Thomas ➔ **Linley**. He was also a pupil of William Boyce, later of Pietro Nardini in Florence, Italy, where he struck up a friendship with the young Mozart in 1770. On his return to England he played in his father's concerts, and collaborated with him in the composition of *The Duenna* in 1775. He was drowned in a boating accident.

Works STAGE opera *The Cadi of Bagdad* (1778); music for Shakespeare's *The Tempest* (1777) and Sheridan's *The Duenna* (with his father).

OTHER oratorio *The Song of Moses* (1777); *Ode on the Witches and Fairies of Shakespeare*; anthem 'Let God Arise'; violin concerto, several elegies.

Linley, William (1771–1835) English composer and government official, son and pupil of Thomas ➔ **Linley**; also a pupil of Karl Abel. He held official posts in India, but in between was Richard Brinsley Sheridan's partner in the management of the Drury Lane Theatre, for which he composed some unsuccessful works. He settled in London in 1806 as a writer and composer.

Works pantomimes *Harlequin Captive*, *The Honey Moon*, *The Pavilion*; songs to Shakespeare's plays; glees.

'Linz' Symphony Mozart's symphony in C major, K425, composed at the house of Count Thun at Linz, where Mozart and his wife stayed on their return from Salzburg to Vienna, and first performed there on 4 November 1783.

Lioncourt, Guy de (1885–1961) French musicologist and composer. He studied under Vincent d'Indy at the Schola Cantorum in Paris and later taught there. In 1918 he gained a prize with a musical fairy tale, *La Belle au bois dormant* (after Charles Perrault).

Works the opera *Jean de la lune*, liturgical drama *Le Mystère d'Emmanuel* (1924); church music; cantata *Hyalis le petit faune* (Samain, 1909–11) and sacred cantatas; chamber music.

Lionel and Clarissa opera by Charles Dibdin (libretto by Isaac Bickerstaffe), first produced at Covent Garden, London, England, on 25 February 1768.

lira (Italian 'lyre') in music, a generic name given to various early bowed string instruments, such as the rebab, or ➔ **rebec**, and the ➔ **crwth** in earlier times.

lira da braccio (Italian 'arm lyre') bowed string instrument current in the 16th and early 17th centuries. It had seven strings, two or more of which served as drones. As the name implies, it was played on the arm.

lira da gamba (Italian 'leg lyre') musical instrument, a larger version of the ➔ **lira da braccio**, played between the legs. The number of strings, including drones, varied from 11 to 15.

lira organizzata Italian name for the ➔ **vielle organisée**, a musical instrument.

Lissenko, Nikolai Vitalievich (1842–1912) Ukrainian composer. He studied natural science, but while making researches in ethnography he became interested in Ukrainian folk song, specimens of which he began to collect. He then studied at the Leipzig Conservatory and later with Rimsky-Korsakov at St Petersburg. He settled in Kiev.

Works OPERA *Taras Bulba* (after Gogol, produced 1903), *Sappho*, *The Aeneid* (after Virgil), and others; operettas.

OTHER cantatas and other choral works; *Ukrainian Rhapsody* for violin and piano; piano pieces; songs, settings of Ukrainian folk songs.

l'istesso tempo (Italian 'the same tempo') in musical notation, direction given when a change is indicated in the time signature, the composer intending the music to remain at the same pace despite the new rhythm.

Liszt, Franz (1811–1886) Hungarian pianist and composer. An outstanding virtuoso of the piano, he was an established concert artist by the age of 12. His expressive, romantic, and frequently chromatic works include piano music (*Transcendental Studies*, 1851), Masses and oratorios, songs, organ music, and a symphony. Much of his music is programmatic; he also originated the symphonic poem. Liszt was taught by his father, then by Carl Czerny. He travelled widely in Europe, producing an operetta *Don Sanche* in Paris, France, at the age of 14. As musical director and conductor at Weimar, Germany, 1848–59, he championed the music of Hector Berlioz and Richard Wagner.

Retiring to Rome, Italy, he turned again to his early love of religion, and in 1865 became a secular priest (adopting the title abbé), while continuing to teach and give concert tours for which he also made virtuoso piano arrangements of orchestral works by Beethoven, Schubert, and Wagner. He died in Bayreuth, Germany.

Liszt's father, a steward of the Esterházy family's property, was Hungarian, his mother Austrian. At the age of nine he gave a concert at Sopron and in 1823 he had advanced so amazingly that his father took him to Vienna and Paris, where he had immense success. In 1824–25 he paid two visits to England and another in 1827. His father died that year, and he was taken to Paris by his paternal grandmother, who looked after his education there. He remained in Paris, and after a period of religious mysticism under the influence of Félicité de Lamennais, achieved great success and fame as a pianist, his flamboyant stage manner having almost as much to do with his success as his dazzling technique. In Paris he came into contact with the Romantics, including Berlioz, Chopin, Paganini, and George Sand, and in 1833 he began his liaison with the Countess d'Agoult. They went to live in Geneva, Switzerland, in 1835, where a daughter, Blandine, was born, followed by another, Cosima (who became first Hans von Bülow's and then Wagner's wife), at Como in 1837. A son, Daniel, was born in Rome in 1839. During this time Liszt wrote the *Album d'un voyageur*, first published complete in 1842 (several of the pieces reappeared in the first book of *Années de pèlerinage*, 1855).

He travelled widely as a pianist and made much money. In 1840 he collected funds for the Beethoven memorial in Bonn, and often played for charitable purposes organized on a large scale. He paid further visits to England 1840–41, playing before Queen Victoria, and toured Russia, Turkey, and Denmark 1842–44. He and the Countess separated in 1844, and the following year he visited Spain and Portugal; two years later, in Kiev, he met Princess Caroline Sayn-Wittgenstein, the wife of a wealthy Russian landowner, who fell in love with him and in 1848 left with him for Weimar, where he was engaged as conductor and music director to the grand-ducal court for certain periods of the year. He produced many new operas there, including Wagner's *Lohengrin* (1850) and Berlioz's *Béatrice et Bénédict* (1862), and settled down to write various works, some on a very large scale, having previously confined himself almost exclusively to piano music. His piano sonata of 1853, followed by the *Faust* and *Dante* symphonies (1854–57 and 1856), were revolutionary for their extension of sonata form in a cyclic process extending for several movements, and for their use of limited motifs that become transformed as a means of development. His chief orchestral writings are connected with his Weimar career, and the music of this period had a profound influence on his contemporaries: echoes of the opening theme of Liszt's *Faust* symphony appear in Sieglinde's solo scene at the end of *Die Walküre*, act II, by Wagner, while traces of the *Dante* symphony survive in *Parsifal* by the same composer.

He retired to Rome in 1861, and took minor orders in 1865, becoming an abbé, and henceforward many of his works were of a sacred character: *Missa solemnis* (1855), and other Masses, *Christus* (1862–66), Psalms, and the Requiem for male voices and organ. Becoming president of the Budapest Academy of Music in 1875, he lived in Budapest, Weimar, and Rome from this date. In his last years he often visited his daughter Cosima in Bayreuth, and irritated Wagner with his new-found religious fervour. In his last piano works he adopted a totally new, modern style which his contemporaries found incomprehensible. Liszt was the most important figure of musical Romanticism, influencing not only his own age but also the following century.

Until recently, Liszt's posthumous reputation has not been high; his lifestyle has distracted attention from his music. Frequent modern performances of the symphonies and symphonic poems, as well as the work of such pianists as Leslie Howard, Alfred Brendel, and Mikhail Rudy, have revealed a more thoughtful and serious composer.

Works ORCHESTRAL 13 symphonic poems for orchestra, including *Les Préludes* (1848), two piano concertos in A (1839, revised 1849–61) and E♭ (1849, revised 1853, 1856), *Totentanz* (1849, revised 1853, 1859), *Faust* and *Dante* symphonies (1854–57 and 1856).

VOCAL AND ORGAN oratorio *Christus* (1862–66), a number of other choral works; 55 songs; fugue on B.A.C.H., fantasy (1885) and fugue on *Ad nos, ad salutarem undam* and a few other organ works.

PIANO a vast number of piano compositions, including twelve *Études d'exécution transcendante* (1851), sonata in B minor (1853), three volumes of *Années de pèlerinage* (1855–77), two *Légendes*, *Liebesträume* (three nocturnes, originally songs),

20 Hungarian Rhapsodies; innumerable transcriptions for piano including operatic pieces, symphonies, waltzes, and songs.

Litaniae Lauretanae (Latin 'Litanies of Loreto') litany sung in honour of the Virgin Mary in the Roman Church, dating probably from the 13th century. It has its own ➤ **plainsong** melody, but has also been set by composers, including Giovanni da Palestrina, Orlande de Lassus, and Mozart.

litany a supplicatory chant consisting of a series of petitions with an infrequently changing response to each. The best-known litanies in the Roman Church are the Litany of the Saints, sung on Holy Saturday and during Rogationtide, and the 13th-century ➤ *Litaniae Lauretanae*. The reformed churches have also adopted the litany, excluding references to the saints, as in Thomas Cranmer's litany, still used in the Anglican Church.

Literes, Antonio (1673–1747) Spanish bass viol player and composer. He was a member of the royal band in Madrid from 1693. He is often confused with his son, a well-known organist, who was also called Antonio.

Works *STAGE* operas *Júpiter y Danae*, *Los elementos*, *Dido y Eneas*; zarzuela *Coronis*.

CHURCH MUSIC 14 psalm settings; eight Magnificat settings.

Litolff, Henry (Charles) (1818–1891) Anglo-Alsatian composer, pianist, and publisher. He travelled widely as a concert pianist until 1851, and produced his finest opera, *Les Templiers*, in Brussels, Belgium, in 1886.

His father was Alsatian, his mother English. As a boy of 13 he became a pupil of Ignaz Moscheles for piano, made his first appearance in 1832, and at 17 left for France, having married against his parents' wishes. He was a concert pianist until 1851, when he acquired a music publishing business in Brunswick, Germany, marrying as his second wife the widow of the former owner. But he soon left his adopted son Theodor Litolff in charge and settled in Paris, where later he married again, a comtesse de la Rochefoucauld.

Works *OPERA Les Templiers* (1886) and *Héloïse et Abelard* (1872).

ORATORIO Ruth and Boaz.

ORCHESTRAL AND CHAMBER five piano concertos including no. 4 (1852) with the popular Scherzo, violin concerto; overture *Robespierre* and others; chamber music; piano works.

'Little Russian' Symphony Tchaikovsky's second symphony in C minor, Op. 17, also called the 'Ukrainian' Symphony, composed in 1872 and first performed in Moscow, Russia, on 18 February 1873.

Little Slave Girl, The, Swedish *Den lilla slavinnan* opera by Bernhard Crusell (libretto by the composer), first produced in Stockholm, Sweden, on 18 February 1824.

liturgical drama a medieval church representation of Bible and other stories. It originated, probably in France, in a 10th-century trope to the Introit for Easter Day, which takes the form of a dialogue for the Angel and the Marys at the sepulchre. In the second half of the century it was transferred to Matins. The music was originally an extension of plainsong but in course of time came to consist of original compositions. Later subjects treated include the Walk to Emmaus, the Nativity, Epiphany, the Massacre of the Innocents, Old Testament stories, and the lives of the saints. The texts were generally in Latin but sometimes also in the vernacular.

liturgy in the Christian church, any written, authorized version of a service for public worship, especially the Roman Catholic Mass.

Its development over the centuries has had a direct impact on music and composition, because until the Renaissance the church had a near monopoly in the West on skilled musicians and composers, whose work therefore catered to the service.

lituus (Latin) the Roman cavalry trumpet. In the 18th century the term was occasionally used to mean 'horn'.

Liuzzi, Fernando (1884–1940) Italian musicologist and composer. He studied with Guido Fano and later with Max Reger and Felix Mottl in Munich, Germany. He became professor of harmony at the Conservatories of Parma and of Florence, Italy, successively, and professor of music history at Rome University 1927–28. He edited Italian *laudi* (sacred songs) and arranged performances of Orazio Vecchi's *L'Amfiparnaso* (Florence, 1938) and of Sophocles' *Oedipus Rex* with Andrea Gabrieli's music (Rome, 1937). He wrote books on the *laudi*, on Italian musicians in France, a volume of critical studies *Estetica della musica*, and also numerous learned articles.

Livietta e Tracollo intermezzo by Giovanni Pergolesi (libretto by T Mariani), first produced at the Teatro San Bartolommeo, Naples, between the acts of Pergolesi's serious opera *Adriano in Siria*, on 25 October 1734. It tells how Livietta encourages the petty thief and trickster Tracallo to reform.

Livre pour quatuor work in six movements for string quartet by Pierre Boulez, composed 1948–49 and first performed in Donaueschingen and Darmstadt, Germany, 1955–62. It was revised as *Livre pour cordes*, for string orchestra, and performed in Brighton, England, on 8 December 1969, conducted by Boulez.

Lloyd, George (1913–1998) English composer. His father wrote the libretti for his three operas, the first of which was produced in Penzance, Cornwall, in 1934 and the second at the Royal Opera House, Covent Garden, London, in 1938.

He studied violin with Albert Sammons and composition with Harry Farjeon. He was severely wounded in World War II.

Works OPERA *Iernin* (1934), *The Serf* (1938), and *John Socman* (1951).

ORCHESTRAL twelve symphonies (1932–88); four piano concertos; two violin concertos.

CHORAL *Symphonic Mass* for chorus and orchestra (1992).

Lloyd or **Floyd, John (c.1475–1523)** English composer. He sang at the funeral of Henry VIII's infant son Prince Henry in 1511 and was present at the Field of the Cloth of Gold in 1520.

Lloyd, Jonathan (1948–) English composer. He studied with Edwin Roxburgh 1965–69 at the Royal College of Music, London, and worked with Tristram Cary at the electronic studio there. Later he studied with Henri Pousseur and György Ligeti. He has worked as a street musician and was composer-in-residence at Dartington College 1978–79.

Works ORCHESTRAL *Cantique* for small orchestra (1968), *Fantasy* for violin and orchestra (1980), viola concerto (1980), *Rhapsody* for cello and orchestra (1982), five symphonies (1983–89), *Wa Wa Mozart* for piano and orchestra (1991), *There* for guitar and strings (1991), *Tolerance* for orchestra (1993).

VOCAL AND ORCHESTRAL *Everthing Returns* for soprano and orchestra (1978), *Toward the Whitening Dawn* for chorus and chamber orchestra (1980), *If I Could Turn You On* for soprano and chamber orchestra (1981), Mass for six voices (1983), *Revelation* for eight voices (1990).

CHAMBER *John's Journal* for saxophone and piano (1980), *Three Dances*, *Waiting for Gozo* (1980), *Won't it Ever be Morning*, for ensemble (1980–82), two string quintets (1982), *Almeida Dances* for clarinet, piano, and string quartet (1986).

Lloyd Webber, Andrew (1948–) English composer and theatre owner. His early musicals, with lyrics by Tim Rice, include *Joseph and the Amazing Technicolor Dreamcoat* (1968), *Jesus Christ Superstar* (1971), and *Evita* (1978). He also wrote the hugely successful *Cats* (1981), based on T S Eliot's *Old Possum's Book of Practical Cats*, *Starlight Express* (1984), *The Phantom of the Opera* (1986), *Aspects of Love* (1989), and *The Beautiful Game* (2000). His company, The Really Useful Group, owns 13 London theatres.

Other works include *Variations for Cello* (1978), written for his cellist brother Julian Lloyd Webber

(1951–), and a *Requiem Mass* (1985). He was knighted in 1992 and received a life peerage in 1997.

Lobe, Johann Christian (1797–1881) German flautist, composer, and writer on music. He wrote five operas, which were produced at Weimar, Germany, where he was a member of the court orchestra.

He studied at the expense of the Grand Duchess of Weimar, Maria Pavlovna, appeared as a solo flautist at Leipzig in 1811, and then joined the court orchestra at Weimar, where his operas were produced. He left in 1842 and four years later became editor of the *Allgemeine Musikalische Zeitung* in Leipzig; he also published several books on music.

Works OPERA *Wittekind* (1819), *Die Flibustier* (1829), *Die Fürstin von Granada* (1833), *Der rote Domino* (1835), and *König und Pächter* (1844).

ORCHESTRAL AND CHAMBER two symphonies, overtures; piano quartets.

Lobgesang symphonic cantata by Mendelssohn; see ➤ **Hymn of Praise**.

Lobkowitz, (Prince) Joseph Franz Maximilian (1772–1816) Bohemian aristocrat and patron of music, resident in Vienna, Austria; he had sole direction of the Viennese theatres from 1807. He commissioned Haydn's string quartets Op. 77 and was a co-sponsor of *The Creation* and *The Seasons*. The Eroica Symphony was first performed in his house, and Beethoven dedicated the quartets Op. 18 and fifth and sixth symphony, the Triple Concerto, the string quartet Op. 74, and *An die ferne Geliebte* to him.

Lobo, Alonso (c.1555–1617) Spanish composer. He was a choirboy at Seville Cathedral and assistant to the maestro de capilla from 1591; in 1604 he became maestro de capilla there himself. He was influenced by Giovanni da Palestrina, Tomás de Victoria, and Francisco Guerrero.

Works *Liber Primus Missarum* (1602), containing six Masses and seven motets; Credo romano, three passions, Lamentations, psalms, hymns.

Lobo or **Lopez** or **Lupus, Duarte (1565–1646)** Portuguese composer. He was widely known as a composer of polyphonic church music, which he published in six books.

He studied under Manuel Mendes (1547–1605) at Evora and later became choirmaster there. Afterwards he went to Lisbon with an appointment to the Royal Hospital and became maestro di cappella at the cathedral about 1590.

Works Masses, offices for the dead, canticles, motets, and much other church music.

Locatelli, Pietro (1695–1764) Italian violinist and composer. After travelling widely and establishing a reputation as a virtuoso, he settled in

Amsterdam, the Netherlands, in 1729, where he established public concerts.

He was a pupil of Arcangelo Corelli in Rome.

Works a set of twelve concerti grossi, Op. 1, and solo concertos; sonatas; studies, caprices and other pieces for violin.

Locke or **Lock, Matthew (c.1622–1677)** English composer. He is remembered for the music he wrote for masques such as James Shirley's *Cupid and Death* (1653), and his incidental and vocal music for plays, notably *Psyche* (1675). He was a vigorous and acrimonious defender of 'modern music', writing in 1666 a pamphlet defending his church music and in 1672 opening a controversy with Thomas ➔ **Salmon**. Purcell wrote an elegy on his death.

He was a choirboy at Exeter Cathedral under Edward Gibbons. In 1648 he visited the Netherlands, and having returned to London collaborated in Shirley's masque *Cupid and Death* performed before the Portuguese ambassador in 1653. In 1656 he wrote the *Little Consort* for viols in three parts for William Wake's pupils and the same year he was one of the composers who took part in the setting of William Davenant's *The Siege of Rhodes* (1656). He was Composer in Ordinary to the King and for Charles II's coronation in 1661 he wrote instrumental music for the procession. In 1663, having turned Roman Catholic, he became organist to Queen Catherine.

Works STAGE operas Davenant's *The Siege of Rhodes* (with Coleman, Cooke, Hudson, and H Lawes, 1656) and *Psyche* (with G B Draghi, 1675); masque, Shirley's *Cupid and Death* (with C Gibbons, 1653); incidental music to Stapylton's *The Stepmother*, Shakespeare's *Macbeth* (altered by Davenant and containing material from Middleton's *The Witch*), and for Shadwell's version of Shakespeare's *The Tempest* (1674); song in Durfey's *The Fool turned Critic*.

OTHER Kyrie, Credo, anthems, Latin hymns; consorts for viols in three and four parts; songs in three parts, duets; songs for one voice with accompaniment.

loco (Italian 'place') in music, a term used to counteract previous notation ('8ve') calling for the performance of music at an octave higher or lower than normal; it indicates that the music is to return to its normal 'place' on the stave.

Loder, Edward (James) (1813–1865) English composer. He first learnt music from his father, John David Loder (1788–1846), a violinist and music publisher, and in 1826–28 studied with Ferdinand Ries in Frankfurt, Germany. After a second period of study there he settled in London and was induced by Arnold to set an opera, *Nourjahad*, for the New England Opera House, under which name the Lyceum Theatre opened

with it in 1834. He was theatre conductor in London and later in Manchester. About 1856 he began to suffer from a disease of the brain.

Works OPERA AND PLAYS WITH MUSIC *Nourjahad* (1834), *The Dice of Death* (1835), *Francis I* (a concoction from his songs), *The Foresters* (1838), *The Deerstalkers* (1841), *The Night Dancers* (1846), *Robin Goodfellow* (1848), *The Sultana*, *The Young Guard*, *Raymond and Agnes*; masque *The Island of Calypso* (1852).

OTHER string quartets; numerous songs, including *12 Sacred Songs*, and *The Brooklet* (a translation of Wilhelm Müller's *Wohin* set by Schubert in *Die schöne Müllerin*).

Loder, Kate (Fanny) (1825–1904) English pianist and composer. She wrote chamber music and an opera, *L'elisir d'amore*. She was a cousin of Edward Loder.

She studied at the Royal Academy of Music in London, where she later became professor of harmony. She made her first appearance in 1844, when she played Mendelssohn's G minor concerto. The first performance in England of Brahms's Requiem took place at her house on 7 July 1871, the accompaniment being played on the piano by herself and Cipriani Potter.

Works the opera *L'elisir d'amore*, and other pieces.

Lodoïska opera by Luigi Cherubini (libretto by C F Fillette-Loraux), first produced at the Théâtre Feydau, Paris, France, on 18 July 1791. It tells how the evil Count Dourlinski imprisons Lodoïska in order to force her to agree to marry him. Count Floreski rescues her with the help of some Tatar warriors.

The opera of the same title by Rodolphe Kreutzer (libretto by J C B Dejaure) was first produced at the Comédie-Italienne, Paris, on 1 August 1791.

Lodoiska opera by Johann Mayr (libretto by F Gonella), first produced at the Teatro Le Fenice, Venice, Italy, on 26 January 1796. The plot is similar to that of ➔ *Lodoïska*, but Lodoiska is imprisoned by a Count Boleslao and rescued by a Lovinski.

Lodoletta opera by Pietro Mascagni (libretto by G Forzano, after Ouida), first produced at the Teatro Costanzi, Rome, Italy, on 30 April 1917. It tells the story of a Dutch flower seller who follows a poet to Paris but dies of cold when she gets there.

Loeffler, Charles Martin (Tornow) (1861–1935) Alsatian-born US composer, a US citizen from 1887. He went to the USA in 1881, and played in Frank Damrosch's orchestra, in quartets, and with touring companies. In 1882 he joined the Boston Symphony Orchestra, where he remained, sharing the first desk with the leader, until 1903.

Before Alsace was lost to France in the 1870–71 war, Loeffler, whose father was an agricultural chemist and an author who wrote under the name of 'Tornow', was taken to Smela, near Kiev, Russia, and it was there that he was first given violin lessons. The family later moved to Debreczin in Hungary and about 1873 to Switzerland. There he decided to become a violinist and went to Berlin, Germany, to study with Eduard Rappoldi, Friedrich Kiel, Woldemar Bargiel, and lastly Joseph Joachim. Later he had a period of study with Joseph Massart and Ernest Guiraud in Paris, France, joined the Pasdeloup Orchestra and that of a wealthy amateur, where he remained until his emigration to the USA in 1881.

Works the psalm 'By the Waters of Babylon' for women's voices and instruments, *Beat! Beat! Beat! Drums!* (from Whitman's 'Drum Taps', 1917) for male voices and orchestra, *Evocation* for women's voices and orchestra; chamber music.

Loewe, (Johann) Carl (Gottfried) (1796–1869) German composer. He is remembered chiefly for his songs and settings of narrative poems such as 'Archibald Douglas' and 'Tom the Rhymer'.

He was a choirboy at Cöthen, and in 1809 went to the grammar school at Halle. Encouraged by Jérôme Bonaparte, then king of Westphalia, he devoted himself to composition, to further studies, to the learning of French and Italian and later, at Halle University, the study of theology. Jérôme's flight in 1813 deprived him of his income, but he managed to make a living and in 1820 became professor and cantor at Stettin, and was appointed music director and organist in 1821. He visited Vienna, Austria, in 1844, London, England, in 1847, Sweden and Norway in 1851, and France in 1857. In 1864 he suffered from a six-week coma and was asked to resign in 1866, when he went to live in Kiel, Germany. He died there after a similar attack.

Works OPERA *Die Alpenhütte* (1816), *Rudolf der Deutsche* (1825), *Malekadhel* (after Scott's *The Talisman*, 1832), *Neckerein* (1833), *Die drei Wünsche* (1834), *Emmy* (after Scott's *Kenilworth*, 1842).

ORATORIOS *Die Zerstörung Jerusalems* (1829), *Palestrina* (1841), *Hiob, Die Auferweckung des Lazarus* (1863), and twelve others.

OTHER symphonies; concertos; piano solos and duets; numerous songs and ballads, including Goethe's 'Erlkönig', Fontane's German versions of 'Archibald Douglas', 'Tom the Rhymer'.

Loewe, Frederick (1904–1988) German-born US composer. He worked on Broadway from the 1930s and began a collaboration with the lyricist Alan Jay Lerner in 1942. Their joint successes include *Brigadoon* (1947), *Paint Your Wagon* (1951), *My Fair Lady* (1956), *Gigi* (1958), and *Camelot* (1960).

Born in Berlin, the son of an operatic tenor, he studied under Ferruccio Busoni, and in 1924 went with his father to the USA.

Loewenstern, Matthaeus (Apelles) von (1594–1648) German poet and composer. He probably studied at the University of Frankfurt-an-der-Oder. Having been schoolmaster and cantor at Leobschütz, he entered the service of the Duke of Oels-Bernstadt.

Works choruses for Opitz's tragedy *Judith*; Latin and German motets; sacred concertos; book of 30 sacred songs to words of his own entitled *Frühlings-Mayen*.

Logroscino, Nicola (1698–after 1765) Italian composer. He was chiefly a composer of opera buffa (comic opera), though his first known opera was not written until 1738.

He was a pupil at the Conservatorio di Santa Maria de Loreto 1714–27, and held an organ post in Conza 1728–31. From 1747 he taught counterpoint at the Conservatory in Palermo.

Works OPERA *L'inganno per inganno* (1738), *L'inganno felice* (1739), *Ciommetella correvata* (1744), *Il governadore* (1747), *Giunio Bruto* (1748), *Leandro, Li zite, Don Paduano, La Griselda* (1752), *Le finte magie* (1756), and many others.

CHORAL AND CHURCH MUSIC oratorio *La spedizione di Giosué* (1763), two settings of the *Stabat Mater*, and other church music.

Lohengrin opera by Richard Wagner (libretto by the composer), first produced at the Court Theatre, Weimar, Germany, by Franz Liszt on 28 August 1850. The story tells how Elsa marries the knight Lohengrin but loses him after asking his name and dies of grief when he leaves her.

Lohet, Simon (c.1550–1611) German organist and composer. He was appointed organist to the court of Württemberg at Stuttgart in 1571.

Works pieces in fugal style, canzoni, and hymn-tune fantasies for organ.

lombardi alla prima crociata, I, The Lombards at the First Crusade opera by Giuseppe Verdi (libretto by T Solera, founded on a romance by T Grossi), first produced at La Scala, Milan, Italy, on 11 February 1843. It tells how, taken prisoner by the Muslims, Griselda falls in love with her captor Oronte. They resolve to run away together, but he dies in battle, and she returns to the victorious Christians.

London College of Music school founded in 1887, mainly for part-time students. It now caters for around 300 full-time students.

London Pianoforte School name given to a group of composer-pianists working in London,

England, at the turn of the 19th century. They pioneered the Romantic style of keyboard playing, based on a ➤ **legato** touch, and began to develop a more complex harmonic language that ultimately replaced the classical style. Composers of the London Pianoforte School include Muzio ➤ **Clementi**, Jan ➤ **Dussek**, John Field, and Johann ➤ **Cramer**.

London Symphony Haydn's symphony no. 104, in D major (no. 12 of the 'Salomon' symphonies), written for performance in London, England, in 1795.

London Symphony, A the second symphony by Ralph Vaughan Williams, composed in 1912 and first performed in London, England, on 27 March 1914; a revised version was performed at the Queen's Hall, London, on 4 May 1920.

long the name of a note value in medieval ➤ **mensural notation**, half the value of the ➤ **large** and equal to either two or three ➤ **breves**.

Long Christmas Dinner, The, German *Der Lange Weihnachtsmahl* opera in one act by Paul Hindemith (libretto by Thornton Wilder), first produced in Mannheim, Germany, on 17 December 1961; it was first produced in English at the Juilliard School, New York, in 1963. Its subject is 90 Christmas dinners over the four generations of a family.

Longueval, Antoine de (1507–22) French composer. He was a singer in the royal chapel, and wrote three motets, a chanson, and a Passion, formerly attributed to Jacob Obrecht, based on all four gospels. Very little is known about his life.

Loqueville, Richard de (died 1418) French composer. He was in the service of Duke Robert of Bavaria in 1410 and *maître de chant* at Cambrai Cathedral from 1413 until his death. He wrote church music and chansons in the Burgundian style of his day. He probably taught Guillaume Dufay.

Loreley opera by Max Bruch (libretto by E Geibel, originally written for Felix Mendelssohn), first produced in Mannheim, Germany, on 14 June 1863. It tells how Leonore falls in love with Count Otto, unaware of his imminent marriage to the Countess Bertha. When she discovers the deception she sells her soul in exchange for beauty. Otto then rejects Bertha in favour of Leonore, but Bertha dies of grief, Otto then commits suicide, and evil spirits claim Leonore.

Felix Mendelssohn left an unfinished opera on the libretto by Geibel. Only the first-act finale, an *Ave Maria*, and a chorus of vintners exist.

See also ➤ **Lurline**.

Lorenz, Alfred (Ottokar) (1868–1939) Austrian conductor and writer on music. After various other appointments, he became a conductor at Coburg-Gotha in 1898, but retired, took a degree in 1922, and became a lecturer at Munich University in 1923 and professor in 1926. He edited Richard Wagner's literary works and Carl Maria von Weber's early operas, and wrote several books on the form of Wagner's music dramas, on the history of Western music and on Alessandro Scarlatti's early operas.

Lorenzani, Paolo (1640–1713) Italian composer. He spent much of his life in France, where, as director of music to Queen Marie-Thérèse, he was influential in popularizing Italian music. After his death in 1683, his influence declined and he returned to Italy in 1694.

He was a pupil of Orazio Benevoli in Rome. In 1675 he went to Sicily and became maestro di cappella at the cathedral of Messina. In 1678 the French viceroy, Marshal de Vivonne, persuaded him to go to Paris, where he was one of the superintendents of the queen's music 1679–83. After her death he became maître de chapelle at the Theatine monastery, where he wrote motets. His opera *Orontée* was produced at Chantilly in 1688 by order of the Prince de Condé. In 1694 he returned to Rome as maestro di cappella of the Papal chapel.

Works the operas *Nicandro e Fileno* (1681) and *Orontée* (1688); motets and Magnificats; cantatas; Italian and French airs.

Lortzing, (Gustav) Albert (1801–1851) German composer, singer, conductor, and librettist. Although not well known outside Germany, such operas as *Der Wildschütz* (1842) and *Undine* (1845) occupy in his homeland a similar position enjoyed by the works of Gilbert and Sullivan in Britain.

He had some lessons with C F Rungenhagen in Berlin as a child, but since his parents were travelling actors, he had to obtain his general and musical education as best he could. He learnt the piano, violin, and cello and studied such theoretical works as he could find. He married in 1823 and found it difficult to make a living in a travelling opera company. His first stage work, *Ali Pascha von Janina*, was produced in Münster in 1828 and repeated in Cologne, Detmold, and Osnabrück. In 1833–34 he was able to lead a more settled life, being engaged as a tenor and actor at the Leipzig municipal theatre. The first two comic operas he wrote there were very successful, and so was his adaptation from August von Kotzebue, *Der Wildschütz*, in 1842, when he gave up acting. Two short terms as a conductor at Leipzig and Vienna, Austria, were unsuccessful. He had a large family by this time and fell upon more and more difficult times. The conductorship at a suburban theatre in Berlin in 1850 merely humiliated him without doing much to relieve the situation.

Works OPERA *Die beiden Schützen* (1837), *Zar und Zimmermann* (1837), *Hans Sachs* (1840), *Casanova, Der Wildschütz* (after Kotzebue, 1842), *Undine* (after de La Motte Fouqué, 1845), *Der Waffenschmied* (1846), *Zum Grossadmiral, Rolandsknappen* (1849), *Regina*, and others; operettas *Ali Pascha von Janina* (1824, produced 1828), *Die Opernprobe oder Die vornehmen Dilettanten* (1851).

INCIDENTAL MUSIC for plays including Goethe's *Faust*, Grabbe's *Don Juan und Faust* (1829), Scribe's *Yelva*; plays with music *Der Pole und sein Kind* (1832), *Der Weihnachtsabend* (1832), *Szenen aus Mozarts Leben* (with music adapted from Mozart, 1832).

OTHER oratorio *Die Himmelfahrt Christi* (1828); part songs, songs.

Lotario opera by Handel (librettist unknown, based on Antonio Salvi's *Adelaide*, not, as Burney says, on Matteo Noris's *Berengario*), first produced at the King's Theatre, Haymarket, London, England, on 2 December 1729. It describes strife in 10th-century Italy as Queen Adelaide's husband is killed by Berengario, who wants her to marry his son Idelberto. Held prisoner, she appeals to King Lotario of Germany, who defeats Berengario and rescues Adelaide.

Lothar, Mark (1902–1985) German composer. He studied at the Berlin Musikhochschule with Franz Schreker (composition), Paul Juon (harmony), and Rudolf Krasselt (conducting). Later he had lessons with Ermanno Wolf-Ferrari and others. After appointments as director of music at two Berlin theatres, he was in charge of the music at the Bavarian Staatstheater in Munich 1945–55.

Works STAGE operas *Tyll* (1928), *Lord Spleen* (after Ben Jonson's *Epicoene*, 1930), *Münchhausen* (1933), *Schneider Wibbol* (Berlin, 1938), *Rappelkopf* (Munich, 1958), *Der Widerspenstige Heilige* (Munich, 1968); incidental music for Eichendorff's *Die Freier* and other plays.

OTHER *Narrenmesse* for male chorus; *Orchesterstücke* and suite for orchestra; serenade for chamber orchestra; music for film and radio; piano trio; piano pieces; songs.

Lottchen am Hofe, *Lottie at Court* opera by Johann Hiller (libretto by C F Weisse after Carlo Goldoni and Charles-Simon Favart), first produced in Leipzig, Germany, on 24 April 1767.

Lotti, Antonio (c.1667–1740) Italian composer. His operas and church music spanned the late baroque and early classical styles.

He was a pupil of his father and of Giovanni Legrenzi in Venice. Appointed singer at St Mark's in 1687, he rose to become second organist in 1692, first organist in 1704, and finally maestro di cappella in 1736. He produced his first opera, *Il trion-*

fo dell' innocenza, in Venice in 1692 (*Giustino*, 1683, commonly ascribed to him, is by Legrenzi). He visited Dresden, Germany, 1717–19 as an opera composer, but after his return to Italy devoted himself entirely to church music.

Works OPERA *Porsenna* (1713), *Irene Augusta* (1713), *Polidoro* (1714), *Alessandro Severo*, *Constantino* (for Vienna, 1716, with Fux and Caldara), *Giove in Argo* (1717), *Ascanio, Teofane* (1719), and others.

OTHER oratorios *Il voto crudele* (1712), *L'umilità coronata in Esther* (1714), *Gioa, Giuditta*; Masses, Requiems, Misereres, motets, and other church music.

Louise opera by Gustave Charpentier (libretto by the composer), first produced at the Opéra-Comique, Paris, France, on 2 February 1900. It tells the story of how Louise joins her lover Julien against her parents' wishes.

loure (French) originally a special type of ➤ **bagpipe**, found especially in Normandy, France; later the name of a dance in fairly slow 6/4 time.

Lourié, Arthur (Vincent) (1892–1966) Russian-born US composer of French descent. He studied for a short time at the St Petersburg Conservatory, but was self-taught later. He was appointed director of the music section of the Ministry of Public Instruction in 1918, but left in 1921. He settled first in France, then, from 1941, in the USA.

Works STAGE operas *A Feast in Time of Plague* (after Pushkin, 1935), and *The Blackamoor of Peter the Great* (1961); ballet *Le Masque de neige* and others.

ORCHESTRAL two symphonies.

VOCAL AND INSTRUMENTAL *Sonate liturgique* for orchestra, piano, and chorus, *Ave Maria, Salve Regina* and other church music, *Regina coeli* for contralto, oboe, and trumpet (1915), *Improperium* for baritone, four violins, and double bass (1923), *Canzona di Dante* for chorus and strings, Japanese Suite for voice and orchestra.

CHAMBER three string quartets, sonata for violin and double bass, three piano sonatinas.

SONG-CYCLES *Elysium* (Pushkin, 1918) and *Alphabet* (A Tolstoy).

Love for Three Oranges, The, Russian **Liubov k trem Apelsinam** opera by Sergey Prokofiev (libretto by the composer, based on Carlo Gozzi's comedy *Fiaba dell' amore delle tre melarancie*), first produced in French translation at the Auditorium, Chicago, USA, on 30 December 1921. The March from it has become popular. In an imaginary realm the prince's melancholy is cured by the jester Truffaldino. Enraged, Fata Morgana (who was plotting against the prince) casts a spell by which the prince becomes obsessed by three oranges. But the oranges contain princesses, one of whom the prince marries.

Love in a Village opera by Thomas Arne (libretto by Isaac Bickerstaffe), first produced at Covent Garden, London, England, on 8 December 1762. It is partly a ballad opera and partly a pasticcio, Arne having introduced popular songs and airs by Handel, Baldassare Galuppi, Francesco Geminiani, and others.

Love of the Three Kings opera by Italo Montemezzi; see ➤ *amore dei tre re, L'.*

Löwe, Ferdinand (1865–1925) Austrian conductor. He studied at the Vienna Conservatory and taught there 1884–97. From 1896 to 1898 he conducted the Wiener Singakademie, and from 1900 to 1904 the Musik-Gesellschaft concerts. He held further posts in Munich, Budapest, and Berlin, and was director of the Vienna Academy of Music from 1919 to 1922. He championed the symphonies of Anton Bruckner, in spurious editions.

Lowinsky, Edward (E)lias (1908–1985) German-born US musicologist. He studied in Stuttgart and Heidelberg, and became a US citizen in 1947. He taught at Queens College, New York, 1947–56, Berkeley 1956–61, and at the University of Chicago. He was editor of the series *Monuments of Renaissance Music* (1964–77). Josquin Des Prez, Orlande de Lassus, Adriaan Willaert, and Nicolas Gombert featured prominently in his research.

Lualdi, Adriano (1885–1971) Italian composer and music critic. He was critic to the *Secolo* in Milan and in 1936 to the *Giornale d'Italia* in Rome. He later became director of the Naples Conservatory. He was a political conservative and supporter of Mussolini.

He studied with Ermanno Wolf-Ferrari in Venice.

Works STAGE operas *Le nozze di Haura* (1908; staged 1943), *La figlia del rè* (1922), *Le furie del Arlecchino* (1915), *Il diavolo nel campanile* (after Poe, 1925), *La Granceola* (1932); ballet *Lumawig e la Saetia.*

ORCHESTRAL *La leggenda del vecchio marinaio*, *Suite adriatica*, colonial rhapsody *Africa*, three folk tunes *Samnium* for orchestra.

SOLO VOICE AND ORCHESTRA *Sire Halewyn* for soprano and orchestra, *La rosa di Saron* for tenor and orchestra.

CHAMBER string quartet in E major; violin and piano sonata.

OTHER choral pieces; passacaglia for organ; songs and other pieces.

Lucia di Lammermoor opera by Gaetano Donizetti (libretto by Salvatore Cammarano, based on Walter Scott's *The Bride of Lammermoor*), first produced at the Teatro San Carlo, Naples, Italy,

on 26 September 1835. In the story, Lucia loves the family enemy Edgardo, but her brother Enrico forces her to marry Arturo. When Edgardo finds out, Lucia goes mad and kills Arturo. Edgardo commits suicide from grief.

Lucier, Alvin (1931–) US composer. His *Music for Solo Performer* (1965) uses amplified brain signals in harmony with percussion instruments. In 1966 he founded the Sonic Arts Union (with Gordon Mumma and Robert Ashley), for the performance of electronic music.

He studied at Yale University 1950–54, and at Brandeis 1958–60, becoming choral director there 1962–70. He was professor at Wesleyan University 1970–84.

Works *Vespers* (1969), *The Queen of the South* with closed circuit TV system (1972), *Bird and Person Dying* (1975), *Shape of Sounds from the Board* for piano (1979), sound installation (1983), *Serenade* for 13 winds and pure wave oscillator (1985), *Music for Men, Women and Reflecting Walls* (1986), *Salmon River Valley Songs* (1986), *Fidelio-trio* (1988), *Navigations* for string quartet (1991).

Lucio Papiro opera by Antonio Caldara (libretto by A Zeno), first produced in Vienna, Austria, on 4 November 1719.

The opera of the same title by Johann Hasse (libretto by Zeno) was first produced before the court in Dresden, Germany, on 18 January 1742.

Lucio Silla opera by Mozart (libretto by G de Gamerra, with alterations by Pietro Metastasio), first produced at the Teatro Regio Ducal, Milan, Italy, on 26 December 1772.

It is also the title of an opera by Johann Christian Bach (libretto as above), first produced before the court in Mannheim, Germany, on 4 November 1774. The story tells how the banished Cecilio returns to Rome to try to rescue his fiancée Giunia from the dictator Sulla. Cecilio, after failing in an assassination attempt, is condemned to die by Sulla, but the dictator shows compassion when Giunia declares her love.

Lucio Vero opera by Carlo Pollarolo (libretto by A Zeno), first produced at the Teatro San Giovanni Crisostomo, Venice, Italy, in 1700.

The opera of the same title by Antonio Sacchini (libretto as above) was first produced at the Teatro San Carlo, Naples, Italy, on 4 November 1764.

Lucrezia Borgia opera by Gaetano Donizetti (libretto by Felice Romani, based on Victor Hugo's tragedy), first produced at La Scala, Milan, Italy, on 26 December 1833. It tells how Gennaro, unknowingly the son of Lucrezia Borgia, defaces her family crest with his friends. To avenge her honour, Lucrezia intends to poison his friends, but not Gennaro himself, who she knows is her son. The plot misfires and he dies as well.

Ludford, Nicholas (c.1485–c.1557) English composer. He wrote seven festal Masses, motets, a Magnificat, and a unique set of seven Masses for the daily Mass of Our Lady. He was long active at the Royal Chapel of St Stephen, Westminster, London.

Ludovic opera by Ferdinand Hérold, left unfinished and completed by Jacques Halévy (libretto by J H V de Saint-Georges); it was first produced at the Opéra-Comique, Paris, France, on 16 May 1833. Chopin wrote piano variations on an air from it, Op. 12.

Ludwig, Friedrich (1872–1930) German musicologist. His comprehensive studies of 13th- and 14th-century music remain indispensable.

He studied at Marburg and Strasbourg universities. He became a lecturer at Strasbourg in 1905 and professor at Göttingen in 1911, where he was later appointed rector.

Ludwig II (1845–1886) King of Bavaria from 1864, when he succeeded his father Maximilian II. He supported Austria during the Austro-Prussian War of 1866, but brought Bavaria into the Franco-Prussian War as Prussia's ally and in 1871 offered the German crown to the king of Prussia. He was the composer Richard Wagner's patron and built the Bayreuth theatre for him. Declared insane in 1886, he drowned himself soon after.

Luening, Otto (1900–1996) US composer. He studied in Munich, Germany, and in Zürich, Switzerland, with Philipp Jarnach, and privately with Ferruccio Busoni. He was appointed to Columbia University in 1949, and in 1951 began a series of pioneering compositions for instruments and tape, some in partnership with Vladimir Ussachevsky (*Incantation*, 1952; *A Poem in Cycles and Bells*, 1954). In 1959 he became co-director, with Milton Babbitt and Ussachevsky, of the Columbia-Princeton Electronic Music Center. He taught at the Juilliard School, New York, 1971–73.

Works OPERA *Evangeline* (1928–33, produced New York, 1948).

ORCHESTRAL flute concertino (1923), *Symphonic Fantasias* I–IX (1924–88), *Kentucky Concerto* (1951), *Wisconsin Symphony* (1975), *Potawatomi Legends* for chamber orchestra (1980).

CHAMBER three string quartets (1919–28), many chamber suites and sonatas for violin, flute, and cello, *Green Mountain Evening* for six instruments (1988).

ELECTRONIC *Rhapsodic Variations*, with Ussachevsky (1954).

Luigini, Alexandre (Clément Léon Joseph) (1850–1906) French violinist, conductor, and composer. He studied at the Paris Conservatory, became leader at the Grand Théâtre of Lyon in 1869, and its conductor in 1877. In 1897 he became conductor of the Opéra-Comique in Paris.

Works OPERA *Faublas* (after Louvet de Couvray, produced 1881) and *Les Caprices de Margot* (produced 1877).

BALLET *Ballet égyptien* (1875).

OTHER cantata *Gloria victis*, *Ballet russe*, *Carnaval turc*, and other light works for orchestra.

Luisa Miller opera by Giuseppe Verdi (libretto by Salvatore Cammarano, based on Schiller's drama *Kabale und Liebe*), first produced at the Teatro San Carlo, Naples, Italy, on 8 December 1849. It tells the story of Luisa, who loves Rodolfo but is forced to declare love for Wurm in exchange for the release of her father, Miller, who has been imprisoned by Count Walther. Feeling betrayed, Rodolfo poisons Luisa and himself before learning the truth.

Lully, Jean-Baptiste (1632–1687), adopted name of **Giovanni Battista Lulli** French composer of Italian origin. He was court composer to Louis XIV of France. He composed music for the ballet and for Molière's plays, and established French opera with such works as *Alceste* (1674) and *Armide et Rénaud* (1686). He was also a ballet dancer.

The son of a miller, he had little education and learnt to play the guitar and violin without much guidance. At first he joined a group of strolling players, but in 1646 was discovered by the Chevalier de Guise and taken to France. There he entered the household of Mlle de Montpensier, the king's cousin, as a scullion. When she found that he was musical she made him a personal servant and leader of her string band. In 1652 he passed into the service of Louis XIV, who was then 14. Lully became a ballet dancer, a violinist in the king's '24 violins', and a composer. In 1658 he began to compose ballets of his own, having contributed to some since 1653 in which the king himself danced. In 1661 he became a French citizen and Composer to the King's Chamber Music and in 1662 Music Master to the royal family. He continued to enjoy royal protection, in spite of his open homosexual activity, which at that time was punishable by death.

His first opera, *Cadmus et Hermione*, appeared in 1673, when he obtained a royal patent granting him the monopoly of operatic production and annulling a previous patent given to Pierre Perrin and Robert Cambert. The Académie Royale de Musique, as the Opéra was first called, was opened in 1672, with a pastiche from earlier works of his, *Les Festes de l'Amour et de Bacchus*. Most of his operas were written in collaboration with Philippe Quinault, and most of the ballets with Molière. His last complete opera was *Acis et Galatée* (1686); by this time he had transformed French operatic style, developing the formal French overture and introducing a more expressive and melodic recitative accompanied by the orchestra, which replaced the former recitative with harpsichord accompaniment. In 1687 he injured his foot with the staff with which he conducted a Te Deum to celebrate the king's recovery, and died of blood poisoning. His opera *Achille et Polyxène*, left unfinished, was completed by Pascal Colasse.

Works OPERA *Alceste* (1674), *Thésée* (1675), *Atys* (1676), *Isis* (1677), *Psyché* (1678), *Persée* (1682), *Amadis de Gaule* (1684), *Armide et Rénaud* (1686).

COMEDY-BALLET all with Molière, including *Le Sicilien* (1667), *Les Amants magnifiques* (1670), and *Le Bourgeois Gentilhomme* (1670).

BALLET (some possibly by Boësset and others) *Ballet de Xerxès* (for Pier Francesco Cavalli's opera, 1660), *Ballet des saisons* (1661), *Ballet des Muses* (1666), *Ballet de Flore* (1669), *Le Triomphe de l'amour* (1681), *Le Temple de la paix* (1685).

CHURCH MUSIC *Miserere* (1644), *Plaude laetare* (1668), Te Deum (1677), *De profundis* (1683), motets for double chorus.

Lulu unfinished opera by Alban Berg (libretto by the composer), based on Frank Wedekind's plays *Erdgeist* and *Die Büchse der Pandora*). Acts 1 and 2 and a fragment of 3 were produced in Zürich, Switzerland, on 2 June 1937. The third act was realized by Friedrich Cerha and the first complete performance was given in Paris, France, on 24 February 1979, conducted by Pierre Boulez. In the story, the femme fatale Lulu leaves a trail of corpses but is killed by Jack the Ripper.

Lumsdaine, David (1931–) Australian-born British composer. Educated in Sydney, Australia, he moved to London, England, in 1952 and studied with Mátyás Seiber at the Royal Academy of Music. In 1970 he was appointed lecturer at Durham University, and founded an electronic studio there.

Works ORCHESTRAL *Episodes* (1969) and *Shoalhaven* (1982) for orchestra, *Mandala II* (1969) and *III* for chamber orchestra, *Mandala V* (1988) for orchestra.

VOCAL *Easter Fresco* for soprano and ensemble (1966).

CHAMBER *Mandala IV* for string quartet (1983), *Round Dance* for sitar, tabla, flute, cello, and piano (1989).

lunga pausa (Italian 'long pause') in musical notation, indicating a long ➜ rest.

Lupo, Thomas English composer and player of stringed instruments. His father Joseph (died 1616), his uncle Ambrose (died 1591), and his son Theophilus (lived. 1628–42) are also known as composers, but Thomas is distinguished by his pavanas and fantasies for viol consort, particularly in five and six voices.

Lurline opera by Vincent Wallace (libretto by E Fitzball), first produced at the Royal Opera House, Covent Garden, London, England, on 23 February 1860. The subject is that of the German legend of the Loreley.

lusingando or **lusinghiero (Italian 'wheedling', 'coaxing')** a musical direction to perform a piece or passage in a charming, alluring manner.

Lusitano, Vicente (died after 1553) Portuguese music theorist and composer. He was known as Vicente de Olivença in Portugal, but was called Lusitano ('the Portuguese') in Rome, Italy, where he settled about 1550. In 1551 he had a dispute with Nicola Vicentino, which was settled in his favour, with Ghiselin Danckerts and Bartolomeo Escobedo as judges. He published a treatise on cantus firmus in 1553.

Works motets, *Epigrammata*, and other pieces.

Lustigen Weiber von Windsor, Die, The Merry Wives of Windsor comic opera by Otto Nicolai (libretto by S H Mosenthal, after Shakespeare), first produced at the Berlin Opera, Germany, on 9 March 1849. It is a German version of Falstaff's amorous adventures.

Lustige Witwe, Die, The Merry Widow operetta by Franz Lehár (libretto by V Léon and L Stein), first produced at the Theater an der Wien, Vienna, Austria, on 30 December 1905. In the story, Baron Zeta wants Count Danilo to marry the widow Hanna Glawari for her money, but the two fall genuinely in love, although they hide their feelings at first.

lute member of a family of plucked stringed musical instruments of the 14th–18th centuries, including the mandore, theorbo, and chitarrone. Lutes are pear-shaped with up to seven courses of strings (single or double), plucked with the fingers. Music for lutes is written in special notation called ➜ **tablature** and chords are played simultaneously, not arpeggiated as for guitar. Modern lutenists include Julian Bream and Anthony Rooley.

Lutes are descendants of earlier Eastern instruments. In Western use, members of the lute family were used both as solo instruments and for vocal accompaniment, and were often played in addition to, or instead of, keyboard instruments in larger ensembles and in opera.

The notation of lute music, tablature, uses a stave made up of six lines rather than the normal five and letters rather than notes. Of the 13 or 14 strings on a lute, six can be held down against the keyboard like a guitar, whilst the remainder are bass notes which are played by the thumb. The six lines on the stave represent the six strings. The letters of the alphabet indicate which fret the string must be held down against. The bass notes are shown by letters and numbers, and curved lines across the top of the stave are used to represent the rhythm.

The open strings typical of the lute during the 16th century.

lute-harpsichord musical instrument made for Johann Sebastian Bach in 1740, called *Lautenclavicymbel*, with gut strings and a keyboard.

luthier in music, a term which originally meant a lute-maker and later, by transference, came to indicate a maker of string instruments in general.

Lutosławski, Witold (1913–1994) Polish composer and conductor. His output includes three symphonies, *Paroles tissées/Teased Words* (1965) for tenor and chamber orchestra, dedicated to the singer Peter Pears, and *Chain I* for orchestra (1981). For 30 years he conducted most of the world's leading orchestras in his own compositions, and was greatly influential both within and beyond his native land.

His early major compositions, such as *Variations on a Theme of Paganini* (1941) for two pianos and *First Symphony* (1941–47), drew some criticism from the communist government. After 1956, under a more liberal regime, he adopted avant-garde techniques, including improvisatory and ➤ **aleatoric** (chance) forms, in *Venetian Games* (1961).

Lutosławski was born in Warsaw while it was still part of the Russian Empire. He spent part of his early childhood in Moscow – the family moved there in 1915 to escape from the German Army – where his father was arrested by the Bolsheviks and summarily executed in 1918. He returned to Warsaw and began piano and violin lessons. From the age of 15 he also studied composition with Witold Maliszewski, who was teaching at the Warsaw Conservatory. At the same time he studied mathematics at Warsaw University. Military service in 1937 and World War II interrupted his career.

His *First Symphony* occupied him on and off 1941–47, but it was condemned at its first performance in 1949. He had made no concessions either to the Nazis or to the Stalinist regime. Only his 'functional' music – film and theatre music or pieces based on folk melodies – received a hearing.

In his 'serious' music he worked to produce a new musical language based on 12-note harmony, first revealed in his *Musique funèbre* (1958). He

was taken with the idea of aleatoric operations in 1960 after hearing music by the US composer John Cage. *Venetian Games* was the first piece in which he used this technique, after which came the *String Quartet* (1964), *Livre pour orchèstre* (1968), the *Cello Concerto* (1970), and many other compositions.

Lutosławski was sensitive to poetry, and also composed vocal works, including *Les Espaces du sommeil/Spaces of Sleep* (1975) and *Chantefleurs et chantefables* (1990), the latter to verses by the French surrealist poet Robert Denos.

Works ORCHESTRAL four symphonies (1941–92), *Concerto for Orchestra* (1954), *Venetian Games* for small orchestra (1961), cello concerto (1970), *Mi-parti* for orchestra (1976), concerto for oboe, harp, and chamber orchestra (1982), *Chain I* for chamber orchestra (1981), *Chain II* for violin and orchestra (1984), *Chain III* (1986), piano concerto (1988).

VOCAL *Paroles tissées* for tenor and chamber orchestra (1965), *Les Espaces du sommeil* for baritone and orchestra (1975), *Chantefleurs et chantefables* for soprano and orchestra (1990).

CHAMBER string quartet (1964), *Grave* for cello and piano (1981), *Variations on a Theme of Paganini* for two pianos (1941).

Lutyens, (Agnes) Elizabeth (1906–1983) English composer. Her works, using the twelve-tone system, are expressive and tightly organized, and include chamber music, stage, and orchestral works. Her choral and vocal works include a setting of the Austrian philosopher Ludwig Wittgenstein's *Tractatus* and a cantata *The Tears of Night* (1971). She also composed much film and incidental music.

The youngest daughter of the architect Sir Edwin Lutyens, she married the BBC director of music Edward Clark. In a lecture at Dartington in the 1950s she coined the term 'cowpat music' to describe the work of those early 20th-century English composers who had turned to pictorial pastoralism in their music. Her works include the opera *Infidelio* (1956) and *Fleur du silence* for tenor and ensemble (1980). Her autobiography *A Goldfish Bowl* was published in 1973.

She studied viola and composition at the Royal College of Music in London, the latter with Harold Darke, and later with Caussade at the École Normale de Musique in Paris, France.

Works OPERA *Infidelio* (1956, produced 1973) and *Time Off? – Not a Ghost of a Chance!* (1967–68, produced 1972).

BALLET *The Birthday of the Infanta* (after Oscar Wilde, 1932).

CHORAL chamber cantata *Winter the Huntsman* (Osbert Sitwell), *Bienfaits de la lune* (Baudelaire), and other choral works.

ORCHESTRAL three symphonic preludes (1942), *Pe-*

tite Suite, *Divertissement*, viola concerto, *Lyric Piece* for violin and orchestra.

CHAMBER six chamber concertos (1939–48), twelve string quartets (1938–82), string trio, *Suite gauloise* for wind octet, *Aptote* for solo violin (1948), sonata for solo viola.

VOICES AND INSTRUMENTS *O saisons, o châteaux* (Rimbaud, 1946), and other works for voice and chamber ensemble, including *And Suddenly it's Evening* for tenor and 11 instruments (1967), *Essence of our Happiness* for tenor and ensemble (1968), *Vision of Youth* (1970), *Dirge for the Proud World* (1971), *The Tears of Night* (1971), *Elegy for the Flowers* (1978), two *Cantatas* (1979), *Echoes* (1979), *Fleur du silence* for tenor and ensemble (1980), *Mine Eyes, My Bread, My Spede* for tenor and string quartet (1980); songs.

OTHER piano music, suite for organ.

Luyton, Karel (c.1556–1620) Flemish organist and composer. He was in the service of the emperor Maximilian II in Prague, Bohemia, in 1576, and when Maximilian died, was appointed to the emperor Rudolf II in the same capacity. He succeeded Philippe de Monte as court composer from 1603.

Works Masses, motets, Lamentations, *Sacrae cantiones*; Italian madrigals; *Fuga suavissima* and *Ricercare* for organ.

Luzzaschi, Luzzasco (c.1545–1607) Italian organist and composer. He wrote some sacred works, but his madrigals are his best-known compositions. His skilfully composed five-part madrigals were his most popular works; the later ones show an increased use of homophony.

Luzzaschi was a pupil of Cipriano de Rore at Ferrara and in 1561 became a singer at the Este court there. In 1564 he became court organist, and was also active as a composer and teacher; Girolamo Frescobaldi was one of his organ pupils. By 1570 he was directing the duke's chamber music, and by 1576 was his organist and maestro di cappella. He was also organist at Ferrara Cathedral and the Accademia della Morte. Here he composed madrigals for the celebrated 'singing ladies' of Ferrara, a group of virtuoso singers who performed for private audiences. His *Madrigali per cantare, et sonare a 1–3 soprani* (1601) contains some of these pieces with their fully notated keyboard accompaniments, which were long kept secret. From 1597 Luzzaschi served Cardinal Pietro Aldobrandini, who controlled Ferrara when the city passed to the papacy.

Works motets, *Sacrae cantiones*; madrigals; organ music, and other pieces. His *Madrigali per cantare et sonare* (1601) are for three voices and have keyboard accompaniments.

Lvov, Aleksey Feodorovich (1798–1870) Russian composer. He studied with his father, Feodor Lvov, an authority on church music and folk song, who succeeded Dmitri Bortniansky as director of the Imperial Chapel in 1825. His son, who rose to high rank in the army and became adjutant to Nicholas I, succeeded him there 1837–61. He was a good violinist and founded a string quartet at St Petersburg. He became deaf and retired in 1867.

Works OPERA *Bianca e Gualtiero* (1844), *Undine* (after Fouqué, 1847), and *The Bailiff* (1854).

OTHER much church music; violin concerto; fantasy *The Duel* for violin and cello; Russian Imperial hymn 'God save the Tsar' (1833), quoted by Tchaikovsky in his *1812 Overture*.

Lyadov, Anatol Russian composer; see Anatol ➤ **Liadov**.

Lydian mode in music, one of the church ➤ **modes**, a scale F–E centred around and beginning on F, which uses only notes of the C major scale. It is also a scale of ancient Greece, the equivalent of the modern major scale.

lyra one of two different musical instruments: either an alternative spelling of ➤ **lira**, or a percussion instrument with tuned steel bars or plates which are played with hammers, similar to the ➤ **Stahlspiel**, used in English military bands and made for them in the shape of a lyre.

lyra viol or **lero viol** or **leero viol** or **viol lyra way** musical instrument, a small bass ➤ **viol**, tuned in various ways and played from a tablature (the form of notation used for lute music). It was in use in England around 1650–1700.

lyre stringed musical instrument of great antiquity. It consists of a hollow soundbox with two curved arms extended upwards to a crosspiece to which four to ten strings are attached. It is played with a plectrum or the fingers. It originated in Asia, and was widespread in ancient Greece and Egypt.

Tuned to a given ➤ **mode**, it provided a pitch guide for vocal melody and embellishment.

lyre-guitar or **Apollo lyre** six-stringed musical instrument produced in France near the end of the 18th century, built to suggest the shape of the ancient Greek lyre, but with a fretted fingerboard.

lyrical in music, of melodic, songful quality.

Lyric Suite work for string quartet in six movements by Alban Berg, composed 1925–26 and first performed in Vienna, Austria, on 8 January 1927. Movements 2, 3, and 4 were arranged for string orchestra and first performed in Berlin, Germany, on 31 January 1929, conducted by Jascha Horenstein. Berg quotes from *Tristan* and Alexander von Zemlinsky's *Lyric Symphony* and bases the work's note row on the name of Hanna

Robettin-Fuchs, with whom he had an affair. An alternative vocal finale, using a translation of Charles Baudelaire's 'De profundis clamavi' by Stefan George, was first performed in New York, USA, on 1 November 1979.

Lyrische Symphonie, **Lyric Symphony** work by Alexander von Zemlinsky in seven movements for soprano, baritone, and orchestra (text by Rabindranath Tagore in a German translation by the composer). It was composed 1922–23 and first performed in Prague, in the present-day Czech Republic, on 4 June 1924, conducted by Zemlinsky (two days later Zemlinsky conducted the first performance of Arnold Schoenberg's *Erwartung*). The format of the *Lyric Symphony* is modelled on Gustav Mahler's *Das Lied von der Erde*, although the content is Zemlinsky's own.

lyzarden or **lyzardyne** or **lizard** or **lysard** in music, an old English name for the bass cornett or corno torto, the predecessor of the ➔ serpent, which came into use in the 17th century.

Macbeth incidental music by Locke for Davenant's version of Shakespeare's play, produced in London at the Dorset Gardens Theatre, summer 1674. There were later productions with music by D Purcell, Eccles, Leveridge.

Opera by Bloch (libretto by E Fleg, after Shakespeare), produced at the Paris Opéra-Comique, 30 November 1910.

Opera by Collingwood (libretto by composer, chosen from Shakespeare), produced at Sadler's Wells, London, 12 April 1934.

Opera by Verdi (libretto by Francesco Maria Piave and A Maffei, after Shakespeare), produced at the Teatro della Pergola, Florence, 14 March 1847; revised version (French libretto by C Nuitter and A Beaumont) produced at the Théâtre Lyrique, Paris, 21 April 1865. Lady Macbeth takes centre stage in the Italian version.

Overture by Spohr, Op. 75.

Symphonic poem by Richard Strauss, Op. 23, composed 1886–87, revised 1890, first performed at Weimar, 13 September 1890.

McBride, Robert (1911–) US composer. He studied and took the Bachelor of Music at Arizona University; he obtained the Guggenheim Fellowship in 1937. Later he joined the faculty of Bennington College.

Works *BALLET Show Piece.*

ORCHESTRAL Mexican Rhapsody (1934) and *Prelude to a Tragedy.*

CHAMBER fugato for 25 instruments, *Workout* for 15 instruments (1936); prelude and fugue for string quartet; sonata *Depression* for violin and piano, *Workout* for oboe and piano, *Swing Music* for clarinet and piano (1938); dance suite for piano, *Lament for the Parking Problem* for trumpet, horn and trombone (1968).

McCabe, John (1939–) English composer and pianist. As a pianist he often performed the sonatas of Joseph ➔ **Haydn**. His own compositions include much orchestral and chamber music. He was director of the London College of Music 1983–90.

He studied at Manchester University, the Royal Manchester College of Music, and the Munich Hochschule für Musik. He became visiting professor of composition at the Royal Academy of Music, London, in 1995.

Works *OPERA The Play of Mother Courage* (1974) and *The Lion, the Witch and the Wardrobe* (1969).

BALLET Mary, Queen of Scots (1976) and *Don Juan* (1973).

ORCHESTRAL three symphonies (1965, 1971, 1978), *Variations on a theme of Hartmann* (1964), *The Chagall Windows* (1974), *The Shadow of Light* (1979); concerto for orchestra (1982), three piano concertos (1966, 1970, 1976), two violin concertos (1959, 1980); *Notturni ed Alba* for soprano and orchestra (1970), *Stabat Mater* for soprano, chorus, and orchestra (1976).

OTHER three string quartets (1960, 1972, 1979); piano and organ music, songs.

MacCunn, Hamish (1868–1916) Scottish composer and conductor. His overture *Cior Mhor* was performed at the Crystal Palace, London, when he was 17 years old. After 1890 he conducted the Carl Rosa Opera Company for some time, and also conducted Edward German's light operas at the Savoy Theatre, London.

He studied with Parry and Stanford at the Royal College of Music in London. In 1889 he married a daughter of the painter John Pettie.

Works *OPERA Jeanie Deans* (after Scott, 1894), *Diarmid* (1897), and *Breast of Light* (unfinished); light opera, including *The Golden Girl* (1905) and *Prue*; music for *The Masque of War and Peace* and *Pageant of Darkness and Light.*

CANTATAS The Moss Rose (1885), *Lord Ullin's Daughter* (Thomas Campbell, 1888), *The Lay of the Last Minstrel* (after Scott), *Bonny Kilmeny* (James Hogg), *The Cameronian's Dream* (James Hyslop, 1890), *Queen Hynde of Caledon* (Hogg), *The Death of Parcy Reed, The Wreck of the Hesperus* (Longfellow, 1905), and others.

OTHER Psalm 8 for chorus and organ; overture *The Land of the Mountain and the Flood*; ballads 'The Ship o' the Fiend' and 'The Dowie Dens o' Yarrow', three descriptive pieces *Highland Memories* for orchestra; three Romantic pieces for cello and piano (1914).

MacDermot, Galt (1928–   ) US composer. He wrote the rock musical *Hair* (1967; filmed 1979), with lyrics by Gerome Ragni and James Rado. Featuring popular songs such as 'Aquarius' and 'Let the Sun Shine In', it challenged conventional attitudes about sex, drugs, and the war in Vietnam.

In the UK, the musical opened in London in 1968; stage censorship ended on the same day.

MacDowell, Edward (Alexander) (1860–1908) US Romantic composer. While his music is essentially European-Romantic, he also flirted with American nationalistic materials in works such as the *Indian Suite* (1895). He was at his best with short, lyrical piano pieces, such as 'To a Wild Rose' from *Woodland Sketches* (1896). The most popular US composer of his era, he succeeded both in ambitious works, such as the *Piano Concerto No. 2* (1889), and in parlour pieces for piano.

MacDowell was born in New York, New York. After learning the piano at home, he went to the Paris Conservatory, Paris, France, in 1876, where he studied piano under Marmontel and theory under Savard. Afterwards he worked with Louis Ehlert at Wiesbaden in 1878, and the following year entered the Frankfurt Conservatory, where Raff taught him composition. In 1881 he became piano professor at the Darmstadt Conservatory, and in 1882 was invited by Liszt to play his first piano concerto at Zürich. Returning to the USA for good in 1888, he lived and worked in Boston, Massachusetts, and then headed Columbia University's new department of music (1896–1904), and was awarded an honorary doctorate in music by Princeton University. In 1904 he began to suffer from mental illness which afflicted him until his death. His widow established the MacDowell Colony at their farm in Peterborough, New Hampshire, to serve as a summer residence for artists in various fields.

Works ORCHESTRAL symphonic poems *Hamlet and Ophelia* (after Shakespeare, 1885), *Lancelot and Elaine*, *Lamia* (after Keats, 1889); two suites (no. 2 *Indian*) for orchestra; two piano concertos (1882, 1889); six orchestral works.

PIANO 26 Op. nos of piano solos, including four sonatas, two *Modern Suites*, 24 studies, *Woodland Sketches*, *Sea Pieces*, *Fireside Tales*, *New England Idylls*, also two books of technical exercises; two sets of pieces for piano duet.

OTHER 42 songs; 26 part songs.

Macfarren, George (Alexander) (1813–1887) English composer and educationist. He edited works by Purcell and Handel and was principal of the Royal College of Music, London from 1876.

A pupil of C Lucas from 1827, he entered the Royal Academy of Music in 1829 and became a professor there in 1834 and principal in 1876. In 1845 he married the German contralto and translator Natalia Andrae (1828–1916). In the 1870s his eyesight began to fail and he eventually became blind, but he continued to work at composition and to teach.

Works OPERA *The Devil's Opera* (1838), *The Adventures of Don Quixote* (after Cervantes, 1846), *King Charles II* (1849), *Robin Hood* (1860), *Jessy Lea* (1863), *She Stoops to Conquer* (after Goldsmith, 1864), *The Soldier's Legacy*, *Helvellyn*, masque *Freya's Gift*; oratorios *St John the Baptist* (1873), *The Resurrection* (1876), *Joseph* (1877), *King David*.

OTHER cantatas *Emblematical Tribute on the Queen's Marriage* (1840), *The Sleeper Awakened*, *Lenora*, *May Day*, *Christmas*, *The Lady of the Lake* (after Scott, 1876); much church music; symphony in F minor and seven others (1831–74), overtures to Shakespeare's *Hamlet*, *Romeo and Juliet*, and *The Merchant of Venice*, Schiller's *Don Carlos* (1842), overture *Chevy Chase* and other orchestral works; violin concerto; five string quartets and other chamber music; sonatas for various instruments.

MacGregor, Joanna (1959–   ) English pianist and composer. She has written music for theatre, radio, and television. In 1993 she gave the premiere of Birtwistle's *Antiphonies*, under Boulez, and has performed other modern repertory by Berio, Xenakis, Ligeti, and Takemitsu.

She studied at Cambridge with Hugh Wood, at the Royal Academy of Music in London, and with Van Cliburn in Texas. She made her London debut in 1985 and has since appeared with all the leading British orchestras. She gave the first performance of Wood's Concerto at the 1991 London Promenade Concerts and returned in 1993 for Messiaen's *Turangalîla-Symphonie*. She founded the Contemporary Music platform in London 1991–93.

McGuire, Eddie (1948–   ), born **Edward McGuire** Scottish composer. He studied at the Royal Academy of Music 1966–70 and in Stockholm as a pupil of Swedish composer Ingvar ➤ Lidholm. He has played flute with the Scottish folk group The Whistlebinkies since 1973. His music has been performed at the Edinburgh Festival and London Promenade concerts. Recent works include *A Glasgow Symphony* (1990) and *A Trombone Concerto* (1991).

Works OPERA *The Loving of Etain* (1990) and *Cullercoats* (1993).

BALLET *Peter Pan* (1989) and *The Spirit of Flight* (1991).

ORCHESTRAL *Calgacus* (1977), guitar concerto (1989), *A Glasgow Symphony* (1990), *Scottish Dances* (1990), *A Trombone Concerto* (1991), and *Symphonies of Scots Songs* (1992).

OTHER *Symphonies of Trains* (1992), *Sidesteps* (1992), and *Zephyr* (1993) for ensemble; *Loonscapes* (1983) and *The Web* (1989) for soprano and ensemble; *Elegy* for piano trio (1990), *Eastern Echoes* (1991) and *Fountain of Tears* (1992) for flute and guitar, *Remembrance* for oboe trio (1993); piano music.

Machaut, Guillaume de (1300–1377) French poet and composer. Born in Champagne, he was in the service of John of Bohemia for 30 years and, later, of King John the Good of France. He gave the ballade and rondo forms a new individuality and ensured their lasting popularity. His *Messe de Nostre Dame* (c.1360), written for Reims Cathedral, is an early masterpiece of *ars nova*, 'new (musical) art', exploiting unusual rhythmic complexities.

Machover, Tod (1953–) US composer and cellist. He studied with Dallapiccola in Florence and with Elliott Carter at the Juilliard School, New York. He was director of musical research at ➔ IRCAM, Paris 1980–85. In 1985 he was appointed director of Experimental Media Facility, Media Laboratory at the Massachusetts Institute of Technology.

Works concerto for amplified guitar and ensemble (1978), *Nature's Breach* (1985), and *Descres* (1985–89), computer-generated opera *Valis* (first performance Paris, 2 December 1987) and *Epithalamion* (1990) for vocal soloists, 25 players and live and recorded electronics.

Mackenzie, Alexander (Campbell) (1847–1935) Scottish composer. He composed prolifically in all genres, perhaps his most notable works being the operas *Colomba* (1883), *The Cricket on the Hearth* (1914) and *The Eve of St John* (1924), and the oratorio *The Rose of Sharon* (1884). He published his autobiography, *A Musician's Narrative*, in 1927.

Born in Edinburgh, Mackenzie studied in Germany and later at the Royal Academy of Music, London, of which, after 14 years as a violinist and teacher at Edinburgh and some years at Florence, he was principal 1888–1924. He was also conductor of the Philharmonic Society 1892–99, and president of the International Musical Society 1908–12. In 1923 he received the Royal Philharmonic Society's gold medal.

Works OPERA *Colomba* (1883), *The Troubadour* (1886), *The Cricket on the Hearth* (after Dickens, 1914), and *The Eve of St John* (1924); incidental music for *Marmion* and *Ravenswood* (plays based on Scott), Shakespeare's *Coriolanus*, Byron's 'Manfred', and Barrie's *The Little Minister*. ORATORIOS *The Rose of Sharon* (1884), *Bethlehem* (1894), *The Temptation* (after Milton, 1914). CANTATAS *The Bride*, *Jason*, *The Story of Sayid*, *The Witch's Daughter*, *The Sun-God's Return*.

ORCHESTRAL *The Cottar's Saturday Night* (Burns) for chorus and orchestra (1888); suite, Scottish Rhapsody, Canadian Rhapsody, ballad 'La Belle Dame sans merci' (after Keats, 1883), 'Tam o' Shanter' (after Burns), overtures *Cervantes* (1877), *Twelfth Night* (Shakespeare), *Britannia*, and *Youth*, *Sport and Loyalty* for orchestra; concerto, Scottish Concerto (1897), suite and *Pibroch* suite for violin and orchestra.

CHAMBER string quartet (1875); piano quartet, piano trio; violin and piano pieces.

OTHER organ and piano music; songs; part songs.

MacMillan, James (1959–) Scottish composer. In works such as *The Confessions of Isobel Gowdie*, premiered at the London Promenade concerts in 1990, he has forsaken modern orthodoxies for a more popular approach.

He studied at Edinburgh University and at Durham with John Casken. He was composer-in-residence at Maxwell Davies's Magnus Festival in 1989. He has taught at the Royal Scottish Academy from 1990.

Works OPERA the chamber opera *Tourist Variations* (1991); opera *Inès de Castro* (1993); music theatre *Busqueda* (1988) and *Visitatio Sepulchri* (1993).

ORCHESTRAL *Into the Ferment* for ensemble and orchestra (1988), *Tryst* for orchestra (1989), *The Berserking*, piano concerto (1990), *Sinfonietta* (1991), *Veni, Veni Emmanuel*, percussion concerto for Evelyn Glennie (1992), *Epiclesis*, trumpet concerto (1993), *VS* for orchestra (1993).

CHAMBER *Tuireadh (Requiem)* for clarinet and string quartet (1991), *Scots Song* for soprano and chamber quintet (1991).

OTHER music for band, choral pieces and piano music.

Maçon, Le, The Mason opera by Auber (libretto by Scribe and G Delavigne), produced by the Opéra-Comique, Paris, on 3 May 1825.

Maconchy, Elizabeth (1907–1994) English composer of Irish descent. Several of her works were performed abroad and she had particular success in Belgium and eastern Europe. She composed a great deal of chamber music, including a remarkable series of thirteen string quartets, and three one-act operas, *The Sofa* (1957), *The Departure* (1961), and *The Three Strangers* (1967).

She was born at Broxbourne, Hertfordshire. She studied composition under Vaughan Williams and Charles Wood, and piano under Arthur Alexander at the Royal College of Music in London. Later she went to Prague on a Blumenthal scholarship, where she studied under Karel Jirák in Prague. She married William LeFanu, who translated poems by the Greek poet Anacreon for her. She was awarded *The Daily Telegraph* medal for chamber music in 1933, and a medal for distinguished service to chamber music from the Worshipful Company of Musicians in 1970. Her *And Death Shall Have No Dominion*, for chorus and brass, was performed at the Three Choirs Festival in 1969. The composer Nicola ➤ LeFanu is her daughter.

Works OPERA *The Sofa* (1957), *The Departure* (1961), and *The Three Strangers* (1967): performed as a trilogy at Middlesbrough 1977.

BALLET *Great Agrippa* (from Hofmann's 'Shock-headed Peter') and *The Little Red Shoes* (after Andersen).

CHORAL two motets for double chorus (Donne); *The Leaden Echo and the Golden Echo* (Gerard Manley Hopkins) for chorus and chamber orchestra (1978).

ORCHESTRAL symphony and suites for orchestra *The Land* (on a poem by Vita Sackville-West) and *Puck*; piano concerto (1930), violin concerto (1963), concertino for clarinet; *Samson at the Gates of Gaza* for voice and orchestra; Sinfonietta (1976), *Little Symphony* (1981), *Music for Strings* (1983).

CHAMBER 13 string quartets (1933–85), string trio, *Prelude*, *Interlude* and *Fugue* for two violins.

OTHER song-cycle *The Garland* (Anacreon).

McPhee, Colin (1901–1964) Canadian-born US composer. His studies with Edgard Varèse much influenced his own music, as did his research into Balinese music 1934–36. His best-known work, *Tabuh-tabuhan* for two pianos and orchestra (1936), uses a combination of Balinese and Western orchestral instruments.

He studied with Gustav Strube (1867–1953) at the Peabody Conservatory, Baltimore, and graduated in 1921. He then studied piano with Arthur Friedheim (1859–1932) at the Canadian Academy of Music, where he played a piano concerto of his own in 1924. Next he studied composition in Paris with Paul le Flem and piano with Isidore Philipp (1863–1958). From 1934 to 1939 he spent much time in Bali and Mexico. He also wrote a number of books on Bali and its music, including *Music in Bali* (1966).

Works ORCHESTRAL three symphonies (1955, 1957, 1962); concerto for piano and eight wind instruments (1928), *Tabuh-tabuhan* for two pianos and orchestra (1936), four *Iroquois Dances* for orchestra.

PIANO *Balinese Ceremonial Music* for two pianos (1942), and other piano music.

Macque, Giovanni de (c. 1551–1614) Flemish composer. He was a pupil of Philippe de Monte. He went to Italy, living in Rome 1576–82, and at Naples from 1586, where he was choirmaster of the royal chapel from 1594. He wrote 14 volumes of madrigals and *madrigaletti*. His other works include motets and keyboard music.

Madama Butterfly opera by Puccini (libretto by Giacosa and L Illica, based on David Belasco's dramatic version of a story by John Luther Long), produced at La Scala, Milan, on 17 February 1904. US naval officer Pinkerton marries Madam Butterfly while visiting Japan. After fathering a son, he abandons her for an American wife. Japanese codes of honour require that Madam Butterfly commits suicide.

Madame Sans-Gêne opera by Giordano (libretto by R Simoni after the play by Sardou and Moreau), first produced at the Metropolitan Opera, New York, on 25 January 1915, conducted by Toscanini. Laundress Caterina marries Sergeant Lefèbre and becomes Duchess of Danzig after promotion following the French Revolution. Chastised for her common behaviour, Caterina is summoned before Napoleon, a former washing customer, who forgives her.

Maddalena opera in one act by Prokofiev (libretto by composer after M Lieven); 1911–13, first performed by the BBC on 25 March 1979. It was orchestrated by E Downes and conducted by him. Maddalena's husband Genaro and lover Stenio kill each other in a struggle.

Mademoiselle Fifi opera by Cui (libretto in Russian, based on Maupassant's story). It was first produced in Moscow on 15 December 1903.

Maderna, Bruno (1920–1973) Italian composer and conductor. He collaborated with Luciano Berio in setting up an electronic studio in Milan in 1954. His compositions combine aleatoric and graphic techniques (see ➤ aleatory music, ➤ graph notation) with an elegance of sound. They include a pioneering work for live and prerecorded flute, *Musica su due dimensioni* (1952), numerous concertos, and *Hyperion* (1964), a 'mobile opera', consisting of a number of composed scenes that may be combined in several ways.

Maderna was born at Venice. He studied violin and piano, and composition with Alessandro Bustini at the Academy of St Cecilia in Rome, and then took composition and conducting lessons with Malipiero and Scherchen. He conducted throughout Europe, specializing in modern music. In 1954 he founded the Milan Radio Studio di Fonologia Musicale with Berio, pioneering Italian electronic music with *Divertimento*, *Notturno*, *Continuo*, and *Le Rire*. He visited the USA in 1965, conducting Nono's *Intolleranza* at Boston and concerts in New York and Chicago.

Works STAGE *Hyperion*, composite theatre work (performed Venice 1964).

ORCHESTRAL concertos for piano, two pianos, flute, oboe; *Introduzione e Passacaglia* for orchestra (1947); *Musica su due Dimensioni* for flute, percussion and electronic tape (1952–58).

INSTRUMENTAL including *Composizione in tre tempi, Improvisizione I, II, Serenata I, II* for 11 and 13 instruments (1946–57); *Studi per il Processo di Franz Kafka* for speaker, soprano and chamber orchestra (1949).

ELECTRONIC including *Notturno, Syntaxis, Continuo, Dimensioni.*

Madetoja, Leevi (Antti) (1887–1947) Finnish conductor, critic, and composer. He conducted the Helsinki orchestra 1912–14, and afterwards that of Viborg. In 1916 he became a music critic at Helsinki and teacher at the Conservatory there, and began teaching at Helsinki University in 1926. Madetoja was born at Uleaaborg. He studied at the Conservatory of his native town, then with Järnefelt and Sibelius at Helsinki, and afterwards with d'Indy in Paris and Fuchs in Vienna.

Works OPERA *Pohjalaisia* (1924) and *Juha* (1935).

ORCHESTRAL three symphonies (1916, 1918, 1926), symphonic poems and overtures.

VOCAL *Stabat Mater*; eight cantatas.

CHAMBER piano trio, violin and piano sonata; *Lyric Suite* for cello and piano.

OTHER piano pieces; songs; ballets.

Madonna of Winter and Spring work for orchestra and electronics by Jonathan Harvey. It was first performed in London on 27 August 1986, conducted by Peter Eötvös.

madrigal form of secular song in four or five parts, usually sung without instrumental accompaniment. It originated in 14th-century Italy. Madrigal composers include Andrea Gabrieli, Monteverdi, Thomas Morley, and Orlando Gibbons.

madrigal comedy a sequence of ➔ madrigals in a quasi-dramatic form. The most famous but not the earliest example is Orazio Vecchi's *L'Amfiparnaso*, and similar works of his are *La selva di varie ricreazioni/The Forest of Multifarious Delights, Il convito musicale/The Musical Banquet* and *Le veglie di Siena/The Vigils of Siena*. A similar work, Simone Balsamino's *Novellette*, based on Tasso's *Aminta*, appeared the same year as ➔ *L'Amfiparnaso* (1594), but there were earlier ones, notably Striggio's *Il cicalamento delle donne al bucato/The Cackling of Women at the Wash*, and later Vecchi was imitated by Banchieri and others.

Maelzel, Johann Nepomuk (1772–1838) German inventor. His name is invariably linked to the ➔ metronome. He did not invent the machine, but appropriated the idea, developing it in 1814. He settled in Vienna in 1792 and invented various mechanical instruments. In 1808 he was appointed court mechanician there. Later he lived in Paris and from 1826 in the USA. Beethoven's *Battle of Victoria* was originally written for Mael-

zel's 'Panharmonicon' and the second movement of the eighth symphony imitates the ticking of the metronome. The 'Panharmonicon', first exhibited in Vienna in 1804, was an automatic instrument operated by weights acting on cylinders. Maelzel finished a new version of the 'Panharmonicon' in 1812.

maestoso (Italian 'majestic, dignified') Italian term used in musical notation. When used as part of a tempo marking, for example *allegro maestoso*, it modifies it, directing the performer to maintain a dignified character.

maestro (Italian 'master') title given to a distinguished musician, whether composer, performer, or teacher.

maestro al cembalo (Italian 'master at the harpsichord') in the late 17th and 18th centuries, the harpsichord player who not only played continuo in the orchestra but also acted as assistant to the conductor and helped to coach singers.

maestro di cappella (Italian 'chapel master') Italian equivalent of ➔ Kapellmeister.

Magalhães, Filippe de (c. 1571–1652) Portuguese composer. He studied with Manuel Mendes (1547–1605) at Evora. He was maestro de capilla of the Misericordia at Lisbon and from 1614 of the royal chapel there under the Spanish king Philip III.

Works Masses, canticles to the Blessed Virgin, chants.

Magelone Romances a cycle of 15 songs by Brahms, settings of poems from Ludwig Tieck's *Die schöne Magelone/Story of the Fair Magelone*, Op. 33, composed 1861–66.

maggiore (Italian 'major key') term used in musical notation, sometimes explicitly stated at a point in a composition where the major key returns after a prolonged section in the minor, especially in variations, to prevent the performer from overlooking the change of key.

Magic Flute, The opera by Mozart; see ➔ Zauberflöte.

Magic Fountain, The opera by Delius (libretto by composer and J Bell); composed 1894–95, first performed by the British Broadcasting Corporation (BBC), and broadcast on 20 November 1977. The conductor was Del March. Explorer Solano seeks a magic fountain with native Indian lover Watawa as a guide. Although she has sworn revenge on white men, she falls in love with him, but both die when they drink the fountain's poisonous water.

Magic Opal, The opera by Albéniz (libretto by A Law), produced in London at the Lyric Theatre on 19 January 1893.

magic opera a species of opera not unlike the English pantomime, popular particularly on the Viennese stage at the end of the 18th and opening of the 19th centuries, where it was called *Zauberoper*. It consisted of dialogue and musical numbers, had a fairy-tale subject with incidents of low comedy, and contained numerous scenic effects. The outstanding example is Mozart's *Zauberflöte*; others are Müller's *Zauberzither*, Wranitzky's *Oberon*, Süssmayr's *Spiegel von Arkadien*, and Schubert's *Zauberharfe*.

Magnard, (Lucien Denis Gabriel) Albéric (1865–1914) French composer. His masterpieces, the operas *Guercoeur* and *Berenice*, owe something in their structure to the example of Wagner, but also reveal an individual visionary lyricism.

Magnard studied at the Paris Conservatory and in 1888 became a private pupil of d'Indy. As the son of Francis Magnard, editor of *Le Figaro*, he was comfortably off and never held any official posts. He retired to Baron, in Picardy, to devote himself to composition, published his works himself, and never took any trouble to have them performed, though some were brought out by enthusiastic friends. During the very first days of World War I he shot two German soldiers from his window and was killed by a sniper. His house, including several of his manuscripts, was burnt down.

Works OPERA *Yolande* (1891, destroyed), *Guercœur* (partly destroyed 1900; performed 1931), and *Bérénice*.

ORCHESTRAL four symphonies (1890, 1893, 1896, 1913); *Suite dans le style ancien*; *Chant funèbre*; overture *Hymne à la Justice* and *Hymne à Vénus* (1904).

CHAMBER string quartet (1903), piano trio, piano and wind quintet; violin and piano sonata, cello and piano sonata.

OTHER piano pieces; songs.

Magnetton (German 'magnet tone') electrophonic instrument invented by Stelzhammer of Vienna in 1933. It produces its notes by means of electromagnets and is capable of imitating various instruments.

Magnificat in the New Testament, the song of praise sung by Mary, the mother of Jesus, on her visit to her cousin Elizabeth shortly after the Annunciation. It is used in the liturgy of some Christian churches in the form of a ➤ **canticle** based on text from St Luke's gospel 1:46–55 ('My soul doth magnify the Lord ...'). It is sung at Roman Catholic vespers and Anglican evensong, either in ➤ **plainsong** or to a composer's setting, as in works by Monteverdi, Johann Sebastian Bach, Palestrina, and Vaughan Williams.

Mahillon, Victor (1841–1924) Belgian music scholar, son of the instrument maker Charles Mahillon (1813–87). He studied at the Brussels Conservatory, where he became curator of the museum of musical instruments. He wrote on acoustics and instruments.

Mahler, Alma (1879–1964), born **Alma Schindler** Austrian pianist and composer of lieder (songs). She was the daughter of the artist Anton Schindler and abandoned composing when she married the composer Gustav Mahler in 1902. After Mahler's death she lived with the architect Walter Gropius; their daughter Manon's death inspired Berg's *Violin Concerto*. She later married the writer Franz Werfel.

Mahler, Gustav (1860–1911) Austrian composer and conductor. He composed nine large-scale symphonies incorporating folk music and pastoral imagery, with many using voices, including *Symphony No 2, the 'Resurrection'* (1884–86). He revised it in 1893–96, but left a tenth unfinished. He also composed orchestral lieder (songs) including *Das Lied von der Erde/ The Song of the Earth* (1909) and *Kindertotenlieder/Dead Children's Songs* (1901–04).

The second movement of his *Resurrection* symphony, based on a *ländler* (folk dance in three time), is reinterpreted in stream-of-consciousness mode by Luciano Berio in *Sinfonia* (1968), into which Berio inserts a history of musical references from J S Bach to Stockhausen. The *Adagietto* slow movement from *Symphony No 5* provided a perfect foil for Luchino Visconti's film *Death in Venice* (1971).

Mahler was born in Bohemia (now the Czech Republic), the son of a distillery manager. He showed great talent as a pianist in his childhood. In 1875 he entered the Vienna Conservatory. His piano professor, Julius Epstein, advised him to study composition and conducting. After leaving the conservatory in 1878 he wrote the first version of his cantata *Das klagende Lied* (1878–80). His conducting career began in the summer of 1880 in Hall, Upper Austria. Posts followed at theatres in Ljubljana in 1881 and Olmütz in 1882. While in Kassel, 1883–85, he wrote the *Lieder eines fahrenden Gesellen* and began the thematically related first symphony. In 1885 he was conductor at the Prague Opera, where he gave performances of the operas by Mozart and Wagner, which were to form the basis of his repertory; his conducting was already noted for its precision of ensemble and the individuality and flexibility of tempi. At Leipzig, 1886–88, he was second conductor to Arthur Nikisch; his completion of Carl Weber's sketches for *Die drei Pintos* was premiered in 1888. While at Budapest, 1888–89, he led the unsuccessful first performance of his first symphony.

Mahler was chief conductor of the Hamburg Opera in 1891–97. While there he furthered his reputation for inspiring high standards of theatrical, as well as musical, performance, and in 1892 he took the company to London, for the first Covent Garden performances of Wagner's *Ring*. In December 1895 he led the first performance in Berlin of his *Resurrection* symphony (1887–94), achieving his first success as a composer; in the same year his brother committed suicide, one of several family tragedies. In 1897 Mahler converted from Judaism to Roman Catholicism specifically in order to gain appointment as director of the Vienna Court Opera. Over the next ten years he established a magnificent company of singing actors and, most notably, with the help of the stage designer Alfred Roller, mounted influential productions that sought to harmonize all aspects of stage and musical experience. He succeeded Hans Richter as conductor of the Vienna Philharmonic Orchestra in 1898 but, largely as a result of his autocratic methods, he departed in 1901. Various intrigues at the Opera led to his resignation in 1907. During his years in Vienna Mahler wrote his symphonies nos 4–8 near a villa on the Wörthersee in Carinthia. In the trilogy of purely instrumental symphonies (nos 5, 6, and 7), nos 5 and 7 suggest a progression from doubt and darkness to an optimistic conclusion; no. 6 is classically proportioned and ends with three enormous hammer blows. The massive choral 8th symphony, known as the '*Symphony of a Thousand*', ends with a Goethe setting in which human suffering is transformed in a universal acclamation.

In 1902 he married Alma Schindler; through her teacher, Alexander Zemlinsky, he met the composer Arnold Schoenberg. Their friendship is reflected in the complex polyphony and extreme chromaticism of Mahler's later music and Schoenberg's early work. The *Kindertotenlieder/Dead Children's Songs* (1901–04) is the first of several works which integrate vocal music of emotional intensity with sympathetic woodwind accompaniments. This style finds its culmination in *Das Lied von der Erde*, which was begun in the year that saw the death of Mahler's daughter Maria, aged four. On 1 January 1908 he made his debut as principal conductor of the Metropolitan Opera House, New York; due to artistic and personal differences his tenure there and with the New York Philharmonic Society was brief. In 1910 he led the triumphant Munich first performance of his eighth symphony, and the following year returned to Europe for the last time, mortally ill with a bacterial infection of the blood. Mahler's music took many years to gain acceptance (four of the symphonies were not heard in Britain until after 1945) but he is now widely acknowledged as one of the founders of 20th-century music.

Works SYMPHONIES ten symphonies; all except the last two were premiered by Mahler: no. 1 in D (1883–88, first performance Budapest, 20 November 1889); no. 2 in C minor, *Resurrection* with soprano, mezzo, and chorus in finale (text by composer and Friedrich Klopstock; 1887–94, first performance Berlin, 13 December 1895); no. 3 in D minor with alto, womens' and boys' voices (texts from Friedrich Nietzsche and *Des Knaben Wunderhorn*; 1893–96, first performance Krefeld, 9 June 1902); no. 4 in G with soprano in the finale (1899–1901, first performance Munich, 25 November 1901); no. 5 in C sharp minor (1901–02, first performance Cologne, 18 October 1904); no. 6 in A minor (1903–06, first performance Essen, 27 April 1906); no. 7 in E minor (1904–06, first performance Prague, 19 September 1908); no. 8 in E flat, '*Symphony of a Thousand*', with soloists, adults' and boys' choruses (text 9th-century hymn *Veni creator spiritus* in first movement and from Goethe's *Faust* part II in second; 1906, first performance Munich, 12 September 1910); no. 9 in D (1908–09, first performance Vienna, 26 June 1912, conductor Walter); no. 10 in F sharp minor was incomplete at Mahler's death: performing version by Deryck Cooke given in London, 13 August 1964.

OTHER cantata *Das klagende Lied* (1878–80); song-cycles *Lieder eines fahrenden Gesellen* (1884), *Kindertotenlieder/Dead Children's Songs* (1901–04), three books of early songs, five songs to words by Rückert, many other songs, including settings from *Des Knaben Wunderhorn*, *Das Lied von der Erde*, symphony for mezzo and tenor solo and orchestra (1907–09).

Maid of Orleans, The, Russian **Orleanskaya Dieva** opera by Tchaikovsky (libretto by composer, based on V A Zhukovsky's translation of Schiller's drama), produced in St Petersburg on 25 February 1881. Joan of Arc leads the French to miraculous victories over the English, but her father Thibault denounces her as a sorceress. She runs away and is captured by the English, who burn her at the stake.

main droite or **M.D. (French 'right hand')** see ➔ **R.H.**

main gauche or **M.G. (French 'left hand')** see ➔ **L.H.**

Mainzer Umzug work by Hindemith for soloists, chorus, and orchestra; composed in 1962, and first performed in Mainz on 23 June 1962, conducted by the composer.

maître de chapelle French term for ➔ **Kapellmeister.**

maîtrise (French 'mastership') former French name for the whole establishment of the choir at cathedrals and collegiate churches, including not only all that appertained to their performance in church, but also their accommodation and maintenance. The maîtrises were actually schools of music.

Majo, Gian Francesco di (1732–1770) Italian composer. He was a pupil of his father, Giuseppe di Majo (1697–1771), maestro di cappella at the court at Naples, and later of Padre Martini in Bologna. He was appointed second organist at court in 1750, but lived chiefly as an opera composer.

Works OPERA 20 including *Ricimero, rè dei Goti* (1758), *Astrea Placata* (1760), *Cajo Fabricio*, *Ifigenia in Tauride* (1764), *Eumene* (unfinished at his death, completed by Errichelli and Insanguine).

ORATORIOS eight including *La passione di Gesù Cristo* (1780).

OTHER five Masses and other church music; cantatas.

major in music, one of the two important ➔ scales (the other being minor) of the tonal system. The main characteristic of the major scale is the major third between the first and third degrees (or notes) of the scale. A major key is one based on the major scale. See ➔ major interval.

major interval in music, the interval between the key note (tonic) and a higher note from the same major scale. Seconds, thirds, sixths, and sevenths can all be major (or minor) intervals, but fourths, fifths, and octaves are called perfect intervals, in both major and minor keys. If the upper note of the major interval is flattened (or the lower note is sharpened) it becomes a minor interval. If the upper note of a major interval is sharpened (or the lower note is flattened) it becomes an augmented interval. If the upper note of a minor seventh is flattened (or the lower note is sharpened) it becomes a diminished seventh (which is equivalent to a major sixth).

Major, minor, and augmented thirds and sixths.

Makropoulos Case, The, Czech **Věc Makropulos** opera by Janáček (libretto based on Karel Čapek's play), produced in Brno on 18 December 1926. Elena searches with the help and hindrance of lawyers Kolenatý and Prus for the magic document that has prolonged her life for 300 years. She longs for death and young Kristina

burns the paper after it is found.

malagueña a Spanish dance, named after the town of Málaga, in moderate to fast ➔ triple time (3/8 or 3/4). It can refer to several varieties: an 18th-century dance related to the ➔ fandango, an older kind of dance based on a ➔ chaconne, with a repeating accompaniment of four harmonies and an improvised melody, or a kind of freely formed emotional song. An example of a stylized malagueña can be found in Albéniz's *Iberia* (1909).

Maldere, Pierre van (1729–1768) Belgian violinist and composer. He travelled as a virtuoso 1752–58, visiting Dublin, Paris, and Vienna. On his return to Brussels he entered the service of the Duke of Lorraine. He was director of the Brussels Opera 1763–66.

Works OPERA *Le Déguisement pastoral* (1756), *Les Précautions inutiles* (1760), *La Bagarre* (1763), and others.

OTHER symphonies; concertos; sonatas.

male alto in singing, an artificial extension of the highest male-voice register, produced by ➔ falsetto, used in Anglican church choirs and in male-voice quartets and choral societies, particularly in glees and part songs.

***Malheurs d'Orphée, Les**, The Miseries of Orpheus* opera by Milhaud (libretto by A Lunel), produced at the Théâtre de La Monnaie in Brussels on 7 May 1926. Peasant Orphée cannot cure the illness of gypsy Euridice and is killed by her sisters.

Malipiero, Gian Francesco (1882–1973) Italian composer and editor of Monteverdi and Vivaldi. His own works, influenced by Stravinsky and Debussy, include operas in a neoclassical style, based on Shakespeare's *Julius Caesar* (1934–35) and *Antony and Cleopatra* (1936–37).

Malipiero was born in Venice. In 1898 he began studying violin at the Vienna Conservatory, but on failing an examination turned to composition, returning to Venice in 1899. He graduated from the Bologna Liceo Musicale in 1904. In 1913 he went to Paris, where he attended the first performance of Stravinsky's *The Rite of Spring*. He was professor of composition at Parma University 1921–23 and director of the Liceo Musicale Benedetto Marcello, Venice 1939–53. He edited the complete edition of Monteverdi's works, as well as many of Vivaldi's.

Works STAGE operas *Sette canzoni* (1919), *Torneo notturno* (1931), *La favola del figlio cambiato* (libretto by Pirandello, 1934), *Ecuba*, *I capricci di Callot* (after E T A Hoffmann, 1941), *Venere Prigionera* (1955), *Uno dei dieci* (1971); ballet *Pantea* (1919).

ORATORIOS *San Francesco d'Assisi*, *La cena*, *La passione* (1935); eight string quartets

(1920–64); including *Rispetti e strambotti, Stornelli e ballate*, and *Canzoni alla madrigalesca*.

ORCHESTRAL *Impressioni dal vero* (three sets, 1913), *Sinfonia in quattro tempi come le quattro stagioni* (1933), *Sinfonia elegiaca*, *Sinfonie delle campane*, and eight others (1946–69); six piano concertos (1934–58), two violin concertos, cello concerto.

Malipiero, Riccardo (1914–2003) Italian composer, nephew of Francesco ➤ **Malipiero**. He studied at Milan and Turin and with his uncle in Venice. His early compositions are neoclassical in spirit; he turned to serialism in 1945.

Works OPERA *Minnie la Candida* (1942), *La Donna è mobile* (1957) and *Battano alla Porta* (1962).

ORCHESTRAL three piano concertos (1937–61), two cello concertos (1938, 1957); three symphonies (1949–59), *Cadencias* for orchestra (1964), *Mirages* for orchestra (1966); *Ombre* for orchestra (1986).

CHAMBER three string quartets (1941, 1954, 1960), piano quintet (1957), *Cassazione* for string sextet (1967).

OTHER Requiem (1975); piano music.

Malko, Nikolai (Andreievich) (1883–1961) Russian conductor. He studied at St Petersburg with Nikolai Rimsky-Korsakov, Alexander Glazunov, and Nikolai Tcherepnin, and at Karlsruhe with Felix Mottl. After teaching in Moscow and Leningrad, he became conductor of the Leningrad Philharmonic Orchestra in 1926 and gave the first performances of Shostakovich's first and second symphonies, but left Russia in 1928 for Denmark and the USA. He was conductor of the Yorkshire Symphony Orchestra 1954–56 and was appointed conductor of the Sydney Symphony Orchestra in 1957.

Mallarmé, Stéphane (1842–1898) French poet. His works inspired Pierre ➤ **Boulez** (➤ *Pli selon pli* and ➤ *Improvisation sur Mallarmé*), Claude ➤ **Debussy** (➤ *Prélude à l'Après-midi d'un faune*), Paul ➤ **Hindemith** (➤ *Herodiade*), and Maurice ➤ **Ravel**.

Mamelles de Tirésias, Les, The Breasts of Tiresias *opéra bouffe* in two acts by Poulenc (libretto by G Apollinaire), produced at the Opéra-Comique in Paris on 3 June 1947. Thérèse, tired of her monotonous life as a wife, becomes a man, Tirésias. Meanwhile her husband takes on the duty of producing children – over 40,000 in one day.

Ma Mère l'Oye, Mother Goose suite by Ravel, written for piano duet in 1908 and published in 1910, scored for orchestra and produced as a ballet. It was performed at the Paris Opéra on 11 March 1915 with scenary by Louis Laloy and choreography by L Staats. The movements are based

on tales by Perrault: 1. *Pavan of the Sleeping Beauty*; 2. *Hop-o'-my-Thumb*; 3. *Little Ugly, Empress of the Pagodas*; 4. *Colloquy between the Beauty and the Beast*; 5. *The Fairy Garden*.

Manchester group group of musicians who studied together at the Royal Northern College of Music in the early 1950s (then the Royal Manchester College of Music). These were the composers Peter Maxwell ➤ **Davies**, Harrison Birtwistle, and Alexander Goehr, and the pianist John ➤ **Ogdon**. As the New Music Manchester they undertook many performances of contemporary music.

Manchicourt, Pierre de (c.1510–1564) Flemish composer. He worked at Tournai 1539–45, Arras around 1555, and Antwerp from 1557. In 1561 he took charge of the Flemish choir of Philip II in Madrid.

Works Masses, motets; chansons.

Mancini, Henry (1924–1994) US composer. A four-time Academy Award winner for film music, he wrote and conducted the music for more than 80 films. His tunes include the song 'Moon River' from *Breakfast at Tiffany's* (1961) and the theme to *The Pink Panther* (1963) and its numerous sequels.

Mancini was born in Cleveland, Ohio, learned flute and piano, and began arranging music while in his teens. World War II interrupted his studies at the Juilliard School of Music in New York.

He became an arranger for the post-war Glenn Miller Orchestra and worked on the film *The Glenn Miller Story* (1954). One of his most striking early scores was the jazz-tinged music for Orson Welles's film *Touch of Evil* (1958), and he achieved wider attention with the music for the TV series *Peter Gunn* (1958–60). He later scored all the films of Blake Edwards, maker of the *Pink Panther* series, and accepted TV assignments as well as features.

Mancini was also a prolific recording artist, collecting 20 Grammy awards and six gold albums. On television, he appeared on a half-hour musical series, *Mancini Generation*, as well as in numerous specials, and his concerts were popular around the world. At the time of his death he was collaborating with Leslie Bricusse (1931–) on a stage version of the film *Victor-Victoria* (1982), for which they provided music and lyrics.

Mancinus, Thomas (1550–c.1612), born **Thomas Mencken** German composer. He was cantor at the cathedral school of Schwerin, 1572–76, tenor at court in Berlin, 1579–81, and then in the service of the Duke of Brunswick at Wolfenbüttel.

Works Passions according to St Matthew and St John; Latin and German motets and madrigals; secular German songs for several voices.

mandolin plucked string instrument which flourished 1600–1800. It has four to six pairs of strings (courses) and is tuned like a violin. The fingerboard is fretted to regulate intonation. It takes its name from its almond-shaped body (Italian *mandorla*, 'almond'). Vivaldi composed two concertos for the mandolin in about 1736.

The Neapolitan mandolin, a different instrument which appeared about 1750, is played with a plectrum and has metal strings. Composers for the Neapolitan mandolin include Beethoven, Hummel, Schoenberg, and Stravinsky in *Agon* (1955–57).

mandore small, plucked string instrument of the ➔ lute family.

Mandragola, La, The Mandrake opera by Castelnuovo-Tedesco (libretto based on Machiavelli's comedy), produced at the Teatro La Fenice in Venice, Italy, on 4 May 1926. Callimaco sleeps with the beautiful Lucrezia after Ligurio arranges a supposed magic potion to cure her infertility.

Mandyczewski, Eusebius (1857–1929) Romanian-born Austrian musicologist. He studied at the Vienna Conservatory. In 1887 he became keeper of the archives of the Vienna Philharmonic Society and in 1897 professor at the Conservatory. He co-edited the complete Schubert and Brahms editions, and Haydn's works (later abandoned).

Manfred incidental music for Byron's drama by Schumann, Op. 115, composed 1849. The first concert performance of the overture was given at the Gewandhaus in Leipzig in March 1852 and the whole was produced with Byron's play at Weimar on 13 June 1852.

Symphony by Tchaikovsky, Op. 58, based on the same play 1885, first performed in Moscow on 6 April 1886.

Manfredini, Francesco Onofrio (1684–1762) Italian composer. His 43 published instrumental works including a set of twelve 'Concertini', chamber sonatas (1704), twelve *Sinfonie da chiesa* (1709), and six sonatas were published in London in 1764.

He studied with Torelli and Perti in Bologna and held appointments in Ferrara and Monaco before returning to Pistoia by 1727, as maestro di cappella at St Philip's Cathedral. Four oratorios date from his return to Pistoia.

Manfredini, Vincenzo (1737–1799) Italian theorist and composer, son of Francesco ➔ Manfredini. After study with his father he went to Moscow in 1758. He became maestro di cappella at the court of St Petersburg's Italian opera company in 1762; until he was superseded by Galuppi he wrote operas for Catherine II. After his return to Italy in 1769 he became a teacher and writer on

music, notably *Regole armoniche, o sieno Precetti ragionati* (1775). His compositions include settings of Metastasio's *Semiramide* (1760), *Olimpiade* (1762), and *Artaserse* (1772), as well as six symphonies and six string quartets.

Männergesangverein (German 'men's singing-association') male-voice choral society.

Mannheim School a group of composers associated with the Electoral court at Mannheim in the mid-18th century. Under the leadership of Johann ➔ Stamitz the court orchestra became the most famous of the time, establishing a completely new style of playing, and placing particular emphasis on dynamic contrasts, *crescendo*, and *diminuendo*. The Mannheim composers (in addition to Stamitz), Franz Richter, Ignaz ➔ Holzbauer, Franz ➔ Beck and (Johann) Christian ➔ Cannabich, made notable contributions to the early development of the symphony, and also influenced later composers such as Mozart and Beethoven.

Manns, August (Friedrich) (1825–1907) German-born British conductor. He began popular Saturday concerts in London in 1856, giving early performances of music by Schubert, Schumann, Wagner, and Berlioz, and conducting the Handel Festival 1883–1900.

At first a cellist and violinist in various bands and orchestras in Germany, he later became a bandmaster. He went to London as subconductor at Crystal Palace in 1854, becoming full conductor in 1855, when he enlarged the orchestra.

mano destra or **M.D. (Italian 'right hand')** see ➔ R.H.

Manon opera by Massenet (libretto by H Meilhac and P Gille, based on Prévost's novel *Manon Lescaut*), produced at the Opéra-Comique in Paris on 19 January 1884. Manon and Des Grieux fall in love and elope, but De Brétigny persuades Manon to go with him instead. The distraught Des Grieux plans to become a priest, but Manon returns and they are reunited. She is arrested, accused of prostitution, and sentenced to transportation. She dies in Des Grieux's arms.

Manon Lescaut ballet by Halévy (scenario by Scribe, based on Prévost's novel, choreography by Jean-Pierre Aumer), produced at the Paris Opéra on 3 May 1830.

Opera by Auber (libretto by Scribe, based on Prévost's novel), produced at the Opéra-Comique in Paris on 23 February 1856.

Opera by Puccini (libretto, in Italian, by M Praga, D Oliva and L Illica, based on Prévost's novel), produced at the Teatro Regio, Turin, on 1 February 1893. Manon and Des Grieux elope, thwarting the schemes of Geronte, who wants her for himself. Later Manon lives with Geronte, but on seeing Des Grieux returns to him. In revenge, Geronte has her arrested. She is deported to America, where she dies in Des Grieux's arms.

mano sinistra or **M.S. (Italian 'left hand')** see ➤ L.H.

Manru opera by Paderewski (libretto by A Nossig after J I Kraszewski's 1843 novel *The Cabin behind the Wood*); composed 1892–1901, produced in Dresden on 29 May 1901. Ulana marries young gypsy Manru, but loses him to Asa when he returns to his people.

Mantra work by Stockhausen for two amplified pianos; composed 1969–70 and first performed in Donaueschingen on 18 October 1970. Pianists also play woodblock and bells, while they contemplate the Indian word *mantra*, or mystical repetition.

manual in music, any of the keyboards of a multikeyboard instrument played by the hands. A harpsichord often has two manuals and an organ has up to four (➤ **great organ,** ➤ **swell organ,** ➤ **choir organ,** and ➤ **solo organ**). The pedal keyboard (pedalboard) of the organ is not a manual.

Manuel Venegas unfinished opera by H Wolf (libretto by M Hoernes, based on Alarcón's *El niño de la bola*), begun 1897. Fragments were performed in Munich on 1 March 1903.

Manzoni, Giacomo (1932–) Italian composer. His music has featured in festivals at Berlin, Osaka, Prague, and Warsaw. He published a book on Schoenberg in 1975.

He studied at the Milan Conservatory and taught there 1962–69; he also taught at the Bologna Conservatory 1964–74, before returning to Milan.

Works OPERA *La Sentenza* (1960), *Atemtod* (1965; given by Abbado in the 1965 Salzburg Festival), *Per Massimiliano Robespierre* (1975), and *Doktor Faustus* (after Thomas Mann, 1985).

ORCHESTRAL *Masse: Omaggio a Edgard Varèse* for piano and orchestra (1977), *Il deserto cresce*, after Nietzsche, for chorus and orchestra (1992).

CHAMBER *Ten Poems of Emily Dickinson* for soprano, string quartet, strings, and harp (1988); string quartet (1971).

Manzoni Requiem name sometimes given to Verdi's Requiem, composed in 1873 for the anniversary of the death of Alessandro Manzoni, on which it was first performed in Milan at the church of San Marco on 22 May 1874; the performance was repeated at La Scala on 25 May. The 'Libera me' is adapted from that contributed by Verdi to the collective Requiem he suggested should be written by various Italian composers on the death of Rossini in 1868, a plan which did not materialize. That the 'Libera me' was not merely taken over as it stood is proved by the fact that it contains allusions to material occurring earlier in the Manzoni Requiem. The 'Lachrymosa' is derived from the prison scene in the first version of *Don Carlos* (1867).

Manzuoli, Giovanni (c. 1720–c. 1780) Italian castrato soprano. He made his Italian debut in Florence in 1731. Later he visited Madrid, London, and Vienna. In 1763 he sang in the first performance of Gluck's *Trionfo di Clelia* (Bologna) and in 1765 was in London to create the title role in Johann Christian Bach's *Adriano in Siria*. He retired in 1771, after creating Ascanio in Mozart's serenata *Ascanio in Alba*.

Maometto Secondo, Mahomet II opera by Rossini (libretto by C della Valle, Duke of Ventignano), produced in Naples at the Teatro San Carlo on 3 December 1820. A French version entitled *Le Siège de Corinthe*, was produced in Paris on 9 October 1826. Muslim warrior Maometto falls for Anna, but she prefers Calbo, and dies in his defence.

maqam, Turkish **makam** melodic ➤ **mode,** used as a basis for improvisation or composition in Arab and Turkish musics. See ➤ **taqsim** and ➤ **dastgah.**

maraca Latin American percussion instrument consisting of a hollow gourd partly filled with dry seeds or beans (although today modern materials are often used) which rattle when shaken. They are usually played in pairs, with one being held in each hand. Traditionally they form part of the rhythm section of Latin American bands. Classical composers who have used maracas include Sergey Prokofiev in *Romeo and Juliet* (1935).

Marais, Marin (1656–1728) French bass viol player, known as a virtuoso player, and composer. He was a pupil of Sainte-Colombe (died c.1691–1701) at the Sainte-Chapelle, and later became a member of the royal band and the orchestra at the Paris Opéra, where he studied composition under Lully and cooperated with him in the performance of operas. In 1725 he retired to devote himself to gardening, but continued to teach. He added a seventh string to the bass viol, and wrote five collections of bass viol pieces (1686–1725).

Works OPERA *Idylle dramatique*, *Alcide* (1693), and *Pantomime des pages* (both with Lully's son Louis), *Ariane et Bacchus* (1696), *Alcyone* (1706), *Sémélé* (1709).

OTHER *Te Deum*; concertos for violin and bass; trios for flute, violin, and bass; pieces for one and two viols; *La Gamme* pieces for violin, viol, and harpsichord.

Maratona ballet by Henze (scenario by Luchino Visconti); composed 1956, produced Berlin, 24 September 1957.

Marbeck, John English composer and writer; see John ➤ **Merbecke.**

Marcabru or **Marcabrun (lived c. 1130–50)** Provençal ➤ **troubadour.** He was one of the earliest of the troubadours, a Gascon of humble origins (tradition has it that he was a foundling). Many of his poems are in a satirical, moralizing, and realist vein that contrasts sharply with the conventional treatment of courtly love characteristic of many later troubadours. The most famous of his four surviving songs with tunes is the semi-religious 'Pax in nomine Domini'. One of his best-known poems deals with the crusade against the Moors in Spain.

marcato (Italian 'marked, accentuated') a musical direction indicating that a piece or movement is to be played in a decided, energetic manner, so that a part is to be brought out strongly above the accompaniment or surrounding parts in a passage.

Marcello, Benedetto (1686–1739) Italian violinist, composer, and author. His masterpiece is the *Estro poetico-armonico* (1724–26), a musical setting of the first 50 psalms as paraphrased into Italian by Girolamo Giustiniani. As well as composing, he wrote the libretto for Giovanni Maria Ruggieri's (fl. 1690–1720) opera *Arato in Sparta*, and in 1720 published the important satire on contemporary opera *Il teatro alla moda*.

He was born at Venice. A pupil of Gasparini and Lotti, he combined his musical interests with a career in law and the civil service. He also wrote canzoni in the madrigal style, instrumental concertos, an oratorio, and an opera. His brother Alessandro (1669–1747) wrote cantatas and concertos.

Works OPERA AND SERENATAS *La fede riconosciuta, Arianna,* and others.

ORATORIOS *Il pianto e il riso delle quattro stagioni* (1731), *Giuditta, Gioaz* (1726), *Il trionfo della poesia e della musica* (1733).

OTHER Masses, Misereres, and other church music; *Estro poetico-armonico,* settings of 50 psalm-paraphrases by G A Giustiniani; concertos, sonatas for various instruments.

march, Italian **marcia** in music, a piece originally intended to accompany marching soldiers or other people in procession, using a regular and repeated drum rhythm. One of the earliest known forms of music, marches are usually in duple time (2/4) or quadruple (or common) time (4/4), with a strongly marked beat and regular phrasing. There are various types, named according to their tempo: the funeral march, slow march, quick march, and, occasionally, double-quick march. The earliest examples of the march in art music are found in the work of Jean-Baptiste Lully and Françoise Couperin in the 17th century. The march has been used ever since, from Mozart operas as in *Die Zauberflöte/The Magic Flute* (1791), to Beethoven's *Eroica* symphony (1804), to Elgar's *Pomp and Circumstance Marches* (1901).

Marchand de Venise, Le, The Merchant of Venice opera by Hahn (libretto by M Zamaçoïs, after Shakespeare), produced at the Paris Opéra on 25 March 1935.

Marchettus (lived 13th–14th centuries) Italian music theorist. He lived at Cesena and Verona at some time and was in the service of Rainier, Prince of Monaco. He wrote a treatise on the division of the scale and two more on notation, which aroused much opposition.

Marching Song opera by Benjamin Frankel (libretto by H Keller, after John Whiting's play); composed 1972–73 and left in short score at Frankel's death. First performed, in edition by Buxton Orr, BBC 3 October 1983.

marcia in music, Italian term for ➤ **march.**

Marenzio, Luca (c. 1553–1599) Italian singer and composer. He is the most important of the Italian madrigalists, having written over 400. His madrigals were introduced into England through music editor Nicholas Yonge's (died 1619) *Musica transalpina* in 1588 and he was in correspondence with Dowland in 1595.

Born at Coccaglio, near Brescia, Marenzio studied with Giovanni Contino (1513–1574), organist at Brescia Cathedral, and published his first work in 1581. Soon afterwards he went to Rome, where he served cardinal Cristoforo Madruzzo from around 1574 until 1578, when he became maestro di cappella to cardinal d'Este until 1586. During this time he published many madrigals, and began to gain an international reputation as a composer. In 1588 he entered the service of Ferdinando de' Medici and in 1589 contributed two *intermeddi* for wedding festivities in Florence. Later that year he returned to Rome, where he was employed by Virginio Orsini, Duke of Bracciano, until 1593. His next patron, Cardinal Cinzio Aldobrandini, recommended Marenzio as music director to the king of Poland. He was in Warsaw during 1596–98, at the court of Sigismondo (Zygmunt) III of Poland. About 1599, however, he returned to Rome and became organist at the papal chapel.

Marenzio published 18 books of madrigals for 4–10 voices (1580–99), as well as five books of villanelles and two books of motets. Many of the madrigals he wrote before 1587 are settings of pastoral texts whose authors include the poet Petrarch; these were widely imitated in Europe, and in England by Thomas Morley. As he grew older, Marenzio's madrigals became increasingly serious in tone, with melancholy texts and more dissonance and chromaticism in the music.

Works Mass, motets, *Sacri concenti*; over 400 madrigals, *Villanelle ed arie alla napolitana* (five volumes).

Mareuil, Arnaut de (1170–1200) Provençal ➔ **troubadour**. About 25 of his lyric poems remain, mostly love poems, and some others including the earliest known Provençal verse epistles.

He was born in Mareuil-sur-Belle, in the Dordogne.

Margherita d'Anjou opera by Meyerbeer (libretto in Italian, by F Romani, based on a play by R C G de Pixérécourt), produced at La Scala, Milan, on 14 November 1820.

Margot-la-Rouge opera in one act by Delius (libretto by B Gaston-Danville); composed 1901–02, vocal score by Ravel in 1902. It was unperformed in Delius' lifetime but part of the score was used in the *Idyll* of 1930. Given an orchestration by Eric Fenby by the BBC on 21 February 1982; the Delius orchestration was then discovered and first performed in St Louis on 17 June 1983. Old flame Thibault is accidentally killed by Margot's new lover when he lunges at her during an argument. Margot then kills her lover and is arrested.

Maria di Rohan opera by Donizetti (libretto by S Cammarano), produced in Vienna at the Kärntnertor-theater on 5 June 1843. The Count of Chalais fights a duel to avenge an insult to Maria, wife of the duc de Chevreuse. Chalais, Maria's former lover, writes her a passionate letter, which is intercepted and delivered to Chevreuse. Chalais kills himself.

Maria di Rudenz opera by Donizetti (libretto by S Cammarano), produced at the Teatro La Fenice, Venice, on 30 January 1838. Maria elopes with Corrado, but he prefers her heiress sister, Matilde. Maria stabs Matilde and, unable to move Corrado, dies of wounds previously inflicted by him.

Maria Stuarda opera in two acts by Donizetti (libretto by G Bardari, after A Maffei's translation of Schiller's *Maria Stuart*), produced at La Scala, Milan, on 30 December 1835. While in rehearsal at Naples the opera was banned by the King; Donizetti used much of the music in a different work, *Buondelmonte*, which was premiered in Naples on 18 October 1834. *Maria Stuarda* was not staged in London until 1966 and in New York, 1972. Leicester intercedes on behalf of the imprisoned Mary, but Elizabeth is jealous of the two and signs Mary's death warrant.

Maria Theresa Symphony name given to Haydn's symphony no. 48 in C major, supposedly composed for a visit of the Empress Maria Theresa to Eszterháza in 1773.

Maria Tudor opera by Gomes (libretto by M Praga, based on Victor Hugo's tragedy), produced at La Scala, Milan, on 27 March 1879. Giovanna, fiancée of Gilberto, is seduced by the disguised Count Fabiano, who is Queen Mary's lover. In a jealous rage Mary arrests both Gilberto and Fabiano. Calling for Fabiano's execution, she intends secretly to substitute Gilberto in his place, but Don Gilberto allows his rival to die instead.

Mariazell Mass the familiar name of Joseph ➔ **Haydn's** C major Mass originally entitled *Missa Cellensis*. Composed in 1782 for Anton Liebe von Kreutzner, who on his ennoblement wished to make a votive offering at the Marian shrine at Mariazell.

Marienleben, Das, The Life of Mary cycle of 15 songs for soprano and piano by Hindemith (texts by Rainer Maria Rilke); composed 1922–23 and first performed in Frankfurt on 15 October 1923. It was revised 1936–48 and performed in Hanover on 3 November 1948. Six of the songs were arranged for soprano and orchestra 1938–48.

Mariés de la Tour Eiffel, Les, The Wedded Pair of the Eiffel Tower ballet by five of ➔ **Les Six**: Auric, Honegger, Milhaud, Poulenc, and Tailleferre (scenario by Jean Cocteau), produced at the Théâtre des Champs-Élysées, Paris, on 18 June 1921.

Mariette, Auguste Edouard (Mariette Bey) (1821–1881) French Egyptologist and founder of the museum at Cairo. He outlined the libretto for Verdi's *Aida*, drafted in French by C du Locle and written in Italian by Ghislanzoni.

marimba musical instrument with wooden bars like a ➔ **xylophone**, but much larger and with a larger range and much lower pitch. The instrument has metal tubes under the keys that both amplify and sustain the sound.

The marimba became very popular in the late 20th century, with many international virtuosos such as Scottish player Evelyn Glennie taking the instrument to new levels of artistry as a solo instrument.

marimba gongs percussion instrument similar to the ➔ **marimba**, but with metal plates instead of wooden strips to produce the notes.

Marin, José (1619–1699) Spanish tenor and composer. He sang in the Encarnación convent at Madrid in his younger years, then became a highwayman and a priest. He fled to Rome after committing murder, and was imprisoned, but at the end of his life had a great reputation as a musician.

Works songs with continuo, songs with guitar accompaniment.

Marini, Biagio (c.1587–1663) Italian composer and violinist. He was employed successively as a violinist at Venice, as music director at the church of Sant' Eufemia at Brescia, at the courts of Parma and Munich, and at Düsseldorf, Ferrara, and Milan.

Works psalms, vespers, and other church music; symphonies; sonatas, dances, and other pieces for string instruments, vocal and instrumental chamber music, madrigals, canzonets, sacred songs, and other pieces for several voices.

Marino Faliero opera by Donizetti (libretto by E Bidera, based on Byron's drama), produced at the Théâtre Italien, Paris, on 12 March 1835. The Doge of Venice, Faliero, is first betrayed by his unfaithful wife Elena, then executed after engaging in a political conspiracy.

Maritana opera by Vincent Wallace (libretto by E Fitzball, based on the play *Don César de Bazan* by A P d'Ennery and P F Dumanoir), produced at the Drury Lane Theatre, London, on 15 November 1845.

Markevich, Igor (1912–1983) Russian-born Italian conductor and composer. He was conductor of the Lamoureux Orchestra, Paris 1958–61, and of the Monte Carlo Orchestra from 1967.

His parents emigrated and lived in Switzerland, but he went to Paris at the age of 15 and studied composition under Nadia Boulanger. His austere ballet *L'Envol d'Icare/The Flight of Icarus* (1932) influenced Bartók. Early in his career he was a protégé of Diaghilev, and was one of his lovers. He became an Italian citizen during the war years. After World War II he concentrated on conducting, specializing in Russian and French composers 1880–1950.

Works BALLET *Rébus* (1931) and *L'Envoi d'Icare* (1932).

VOCAL cantata *Le Paradis Perdu/Paradise Lost* 1933–35 to words by Milton (performed London, 1935) and others, *Cantique d'Amour, Nouvel Age*, cantata for soprano and male-voice chorus (Jean Cocteau).

ORCHESTRAL *Hymnes*, concerto grosso and sinfonietta for orchestra; concerto and partita for piano and orchestra; *Galop* for small orchestra; psalm for soprano and orchestra.

OTHER serenade for violin, clarinet, and bassoon.

Marmontel, Jean François (1723–1799) French author. He was librettist for Rameau, Grétry, Piccinni, Cherubini, and others. He was

a defender of Piccinni against Gluck and author of an 'Essai sur les révolutions de la musique en France' (1777).

See ➤ *Acante et Céphise* (Rameau); ➤ *Antigone* (Zingarelli); ➤ *Atys* (Piccinni); ➤ *Céphale et Procris* (Grétry); ➤ *Clari, or The Maid of Milan* (Bishop, from *Laurette*); ➤ *Démophoon* (Cherubini); ➤ *Didon* (Piccinni); ➤ *Guirlande, La, ou Les fleurs enchantées* (Rameau); ➤ *Rameau* (*Lysis et Délie*; *Les Sybarites*); ➤ *Zémire et Azore* (Grétry); ➤ *Zemire und Azor* (Spohr).

Mârouf, savetier du Caire, Mârouf, the Cobbler of Cairo opera by Rabaud (libretto by L Népoty, based on a story in the *Arabian Nights*), produced at the Opéra-Comique, Paris, on 15 May 1914. Mârouf escapes wife, marries Sultan's daughter, and steals his treasure.

Marpurg, Friedrich Wilhelm (1718–1795) German theorist and writer on music. From 1749 he lived mainly in Berlin, where he began a music weekly, *Der critische Musicus an der Spree*. This was followed by other critical and theoretical writings, including a notable preface to the second edition of Bach's *Kunst der Fuge*, treatises on subjects including fugue, thorough bass, and keyboard playing.

In Paris as secretary to General Bodenburg about 1746 he met, among others, Voltaire and Rameau, and was influenced by the latter's theories. He also composed some songs and keyboard music.

Marriage of Figaro opera by Mozart; see *Le* ➤ *Nozze di Figaro*.

Marriage, The, Russian ***Zhenitba*** unfinished opera by Mussorgsky (libretto taken from Gogol's comedy, composed 1864. It was never performed in Mussorgsky's lifetime, but was produced with piano accompaniment in St Petersburg on 1 April 1909, and with orchestra in Petrograd on 26 October 1917 with Mussorgsky's *Sorochintsy Fair*. Podkolesin hires a marriage broker in pursuit of Agafya.

Comic opera by Martinů (libretto by composer, after Gogol); composed 1952, first performed NBC TV, New York, on 7 February 1953.

Marschner, Heinrich (August) (1795–1861) German composer. He wrote 13 operas, including *Hans Heiling* 1833, and is regarded as the most important German opera composer between Weber and Wagner.

As a boy he played the piano, sang soprano, and composed tentatively without much instruction. In 1813 he was sent to Leipzig to study law, but met Johann Rochlitz, who induced him to take up music. In 1816 he went to Vienna and Pressburg with a Hungarian, Count de Varkony, and settled in Pressburg, where he composed several operas. In 1823 he became assistant conductor to Weber and Francesco Morlacchi at Dresden. In 1827 he became conductor of the Leipzig theatre and from 1831 to 1859 court conductor at Hanover. He married four times.

Works OPERA *Saidar, Heinrich IV und Aubigné* (1820), *Der Kyffhäuserberg* (1822), *Der Holzdieb* (1825), *Lucretia, Der Vampyr* (1828), *Der Templer und die Jüdin* (after Scott's *Ivanhoe*, 1829), *Des Falkners Braut* (1832), *Hans Heiling* (1833), *Der Bäbu* (1838), *Das Schloss am Aetna, Kaiser Adolf von Nassau* (1845), *Austin, Sangeskönig Hiarne* (1863).

OTHER incidental music to Kleist's *Prinz Friedrich von Homburg* and other plays; overture on 'God Save the King' and other orchestral works; malevoice choruses; sonatas; songs.

Marseillaise, La French national anthem; the words and music were composed in 1792 as a revolutionary song by the army officer Claude Joseph Rouget de Lisle (1760–1836).

Marsh, John (1752–1828) English amateur composer. He practised as a lawyer until 1783, when a legacy enabled him to retire and devote his time to music, in which he was largely self-taught. He conducted concerts in Chichester and elsewhere, and composed some notable symphonies, as well as concertos, chamber music, and keyboard music.

Marsh, Roger (1949–) English composer. He studied at York University with Bernard Rands and has been lecturer there from 1988.

Works MUSIC THEATRE *Cass* (1970) and *Calypso* (1974); *Not a Soul but Ourselves*, for four amplified voices (1977), *Point to Point* for ensemble (1981); *Samson* (1984), *Love on the Rocks* (1989).

ORCHESTRAL *The Song of Abigail* for soprano and orchestra (1985); *Dying for it*, for ensemble (1987); *The Big Bang* (1989); *Stepping Out* for orchestra (1990).

Marteau sans maître, Le, The hammer without a master work by Pierre ➜ **Boulez** for mezzo-soprano, flute, guitar, vibraphone, xylorimba, viola, and percussion; composed 1952–54, revised 1957; first performed Baden-Baden, 18 June 1955, conductor Rosbaud.

martellato (Italian 'hammered') in musical notation, percussive, with sharp attacks and detached articulation. The term usually appears in compositions for strings or for piano.

Martelli, Henri (1895–1980) French composer. He studied at the Paris Conservatory under Widor and others.

Works OPERA *La Chanson de Roland* (1921–23; performed 1967), incidental music.

ORCHESTRAL three symphonies (1953–57), symphonic poem *Sur la vie de Jeanne d'Arc, Bas-*

reliefs assyriens and concerto for orchestra; piano concerto.

OTHER two string quartets; string quintet; piano pieces; songs.

Martha, oder Der Markt von Richmond, Martha, or The Market at Richmond comic opera by Flotow (libretto by F W Riese, pseudonym 'W Friedrich', based on a ballet-pantomime, *Lady Henriette, ou La Servante de Greenwich*, by J H V de Saint-Georges, produced in Paris on 21 February 1844, with music by F Burgmüller and Deldevez), produced in Vienna at the Kärntnertortheater on 25 November 1847. Lady Harriet and maid Nancy disguise themselves and meet two young farmers, Plumkett and Lyonel, at a country fair. They fall in love, and complications of differing social class are resolved when Lyonel turns out to be of noble blood.

martin in singing, a baritone voice of exceptional range. It is named after the French singer Jean Blaise Martin (1768–1837), who specialized in comic roles in operas by Dalaryac, Boieldieu, and Méhul.

Martin, Frank (1890–1974) Swiss composer, pianist, and harpsichordist. His works are characterized by delicate colouring in instrumentation and an expressive quality combined in later works with a loosely interpreted ➜ **twelve-tone system**. Composing for both large- and small-scale forces, from orchestra to chamber music, his best-known works are the operas *Der Sturm/ The Tempest* (1956) and *Monsieur de Pourceaugnac* (1962).

He was born in Geneva, studied there with Joseph Lauber, and in 1928 became professor at the Institut Jaques-Dalcroze. In 1946 he settled in Amsterdam, where he remained even after his appointment as professor of composition at the Cologne Conservatoire. Martin was among the most distinguished composers of his generation.

Works STAGE opera *The Tempest* (Shakespeare, 1956), *Monsieur de Pourceaugnac* (1963); *Six Monologues from 'Jedermann'* (after Hofmannsthal, 1943), ballet *Die blaue Blume*; incidental music for Sophocles' *Oedipus Coloneus* and *Oedipus Rex* and Shakespeare's *Romeo and Juliet*.

CHORAL Mass for double chorus, oratorios *In terra pax* (1945), *Golgotha* (1948); *Le Mystère de la Nativité* (1957–59).

ORCHESTRAL symphonic suite *Rhythmes, Esquisse*, symphony for orchestra; *Petite Symphonie concertante* for harp, harpsichord, piano, and strings (1945); piano concerto, violin concerto (1951), cello concerto (1966); *Cornet* (Rilke) for contralto and orchestra.

CHAMBER Piano quintet, rhapsody for string quintet, string quartet, string trio, piano trio on Irish tunes; *Le vin herbé* for twelve voices, strings, and piano (on the subject of Tristram and Yseult, from Joseph Bédier, 1938–41); two violin and piano sontatas.

Martinez, Marianne (1744–1812) Austrian composer and keyboard player of Spanish descent. She was the daughter of the master of ceremonies to the pope's nuncio in Vienna. Her teachers were Metastasio, Porpora, and Haydn.

Works ORATORIOS *Isacco* (1782) and *Santa Elena al Calvario.*

OTHER psalms translated by Metastasio, Mass, motets, cantatas; symphonies; overtures; concertos; sonatas.

Martini, Giovanni Battista or **Giambattista**, known as **Padre Martini (1706–1784)** Italian priest, theorist, teacher, and composer. As the most famous teacher and theorist of his time he attracted many distinguished pupils, including Mozart, and corresponded with musicians throughout Europe. His most important works are *Storia della musica*, the unfinished history of music in three volumes 1757–81, and *Saggio di contrappunto*, a treatise on counterpoint 1773–75.

He was born at Bologna, and received a thorough education from his father and others in violin, harpsichord, singing, and composition. He entered the Franciscan Order in 1721, was ordained priest in 1729, and was appointed maestro di cappella of San Francesco, Bologna in 1725, after which he rarely left his home town. He collected a vast musical and scientific library, and was a prolific composer of sacred vocal music.

Works about 1,500 works, with about 1,000 canons.

ORATORIOS *L'assunzione di Salomone* (1734), *San Pietro, Il sacrificio d'Abramo.*

OTHER about 32 Masses, motets, psalm settings and other church music; stage works; keyboard works.

Martini, Jean Paul Egide (1741–1816), adopted name of **Johann Paul Aegidius Schwartzendorf** German organist and composer. He settled in France in 1760 and wrote the first of his 13 operas in 1771. He also wrote the song 'Plaisir d'amour'.

He adopted the name of Martini on settling in Nancy as a music teacher in 1760. He was in the service of the Duke of Lorraine (the former King Stanislaus of Poland) at Lunéville 1761–64; he then went to Paris, where he wrote military music and produced his first opera in 1771. After three years' absence during the Revolution, he returned to Paris in 1794 to become one of the inspectors of the Conservatory in 1795 and professor of composition in 1800. At the Restoration in 1814 he was appointed superintendent of the court music.

Works OPERA *L'Amoureux de quinze ans* (1771), *Le Fermier cru sourd* (1772), *Le Rendezvous nocturne* (1773), *Henry IV* (1774), *Le Droit du Seigneur, L'Amant sylphe* (1783), *Sapho, Annette et Lubin* (1789), *Ziméo*, and others.

CHURCH MUSIC two Masses, two Requiems, Te Deum, psalm settings and other church music.

OTHER cantata for the marriage of Napoleon and Marie-Louise; chamber music; marches and other pieces for military band; songs including 'Plaisir d'amour'.

Martino, Donald (1931–2005) US composer. He studied with Bacon, Babbitt, and Sessions in the USA, and with Dallapiccola in Florence. He was professor of composition at the New England Conservatory of Music 1969–79, and Harvard from 1983. His works often feature his own instrument, the clarinet: quartet for clarinet and strings (1957); concerto for wind quintet (1964); B,A,B,B,I,T,T for clarinet (1966); cello concerto (1972); *Paradiso Choruses*, oratorio after Dante (1974); Triple Concerto for three clarinets and orchestra (1977); string quartet (1983).

Martinů, Bohuslav Jan (1890–1959) Czech composer. He settled in New York after the Nazi occupation of Czechoslovakia in 1939. His music is voluble, richly expressive, and has great vitality. His works include the operas *Julietta* (1937) and *The Greek Passion* (1959), symphonies, and chamber music.

He studied violin at the Prague Conservatory 1906–13 while playing in the Prague Philharmonic Orchestra. In 1922 he took composition lessons with Joseph Suk at the Prague Conservatory and studied with Albert Roussel in Paris 1923–24, and wrote works influenced by jazz and neoclassicism. Operas with Czech subjects followed during the 1930s, and after arriving in the USA as a refugee in 1941 he confined himself largely to instrumental music. He remained in the USA until 1946, when he became professor of composition at Prague Conservatory, returning to the USA in 1948, where he taught at Princeton and the Berkshire Music Center. He chose not to return to Czechoslovakia after the communist takeover in 1948, and lived in Switzerland from 1957. His music is often neoclassical in style, enriched with Czech folk song melody, and with an emphasis on rhythm and counterpoint.

Works OPERA *Julietta* (1938); *The Greek Passion* (1961).

BALLET La revue de cuisine, *Špaliček*.

CHORAL *Bouquet of Flowers, Field Mass* for solo voices, chorus, and orchestra; *The Epic of Gilgamesh*, oratorio (1955).

ORCHESTRAL six symphonies (1942–53); concerto for double string orchestra, piano, and timpani (1938), tone poem *The Frescoes of Piero della Francesca* (1955), *Sinfonietta giocosa, Memorial to Lidice* (1943), *Tre Ricercari*; five piano concertos (1934–57), two violin concertos, two cello concertos, oboe concerto and various other works for instruments and orchestra.

CHAMBER two piano quintets (1933, 1944), nonet for wind and strings, and much other chamber music; three cello and piano sonatas; *Ritournelles*, and other pieces for piano.

Martín y Soler, Vicente (1754–1806) Spanish composer. He travelled widely, producing operas in Italy, Russia, and Vienna, notably *Una cosa rara* (1786), written in collaboration with the librettist Lorenzo da Ponte.

He was born at Valencia, and was a chorister there. He made his debut as an opera composer in Madrid in 1776, then went to Italy, where he probably studied with Padre Martini, and produced operas successfully in Naples, Turin, and Venice. In Vienna, 1785–88, he composed three operas on libretti by da Ponte, the most successful of which, *Una cosa rara* (1786), for a time eclipsed Mozart's *Marriage of Figaro*; Mozart quotes from it in the supper scene in *Don Giovanni*. Apart from a visit to London 1794–95, he lived from 1788 in St Petersburg, in the service of the Russian court.

Works OPERA *Ifigenia in Aulide* (1779), *Ipermestra*, *Andromaca* (1780), *Astartea*, *Partenope*, *L'amor geloso* (1782), *In amor si vuol destrezza* (*L'accorta cameriera*, 1782), *Vologeso*, *Le burle per amore* (1784), *La vedova spiritosa*, *Il burbero di buon cuore* (1786), *Una cosa rara, o Bellezza ed onestà* (1786), *L'arbore di Diana* (1787), *Gore Bogatyr Kosometovich* (1789), *Melomania* (Russian), *Fedul and his Children* (Russian; libretti of these three by Catherine II), *Il castello d'Atlante* (1791), *La scuola de' maritati* (1795), *L'isola del piacere* (1795), *Le nozze de contadini spagnuoli*, *La festa del villaggio* (1798).

OTHER prologue *La Dora festeggiante* for *Vologeso*; several ballets; church music; cantatas *La deità benefica* and *Il sogno*; canzonets; canons.

Martland, Steve (1959–) English composer. His music eschews classical principles and aspires to 'street cred'. *Babi Yar* for orchestra (1983), had a joint first performance with the Royal Liverpool Philharmonic Orchestra and the St Louis Symphony Orchestra.

He studied with Louis Andriessen at the Hague and with Gunther Schuller at Tanglewood in 1984.

Works *Lotta continua* for orchestra and jazz band (1981); *Orc* for horn and chamber orchestra (1984); *Crossing the Border* for strings (1991); *Remembering Lennon* for seven players (1981); *American Invention* for 13 players (1985); *Patrol* for string quartet (1991); *Terra Firma* for five voices and video (1989); *The Perfect Act* for amplified ensemble and voice (1991); piano pieces and tape items.

Martucci, Giuseppe (1856–1909) Italian pianist, conductor, and composer. He travelled widely as a pianist, founded the Quartetto Napoletano for the cultivation of chamber music, and became an orchestral conductor. In 1888 he produced the first Italian performance of Wagner's *Tristan* at Bologna.

He was first taught by his father, a bandmaster, and appeared as a pianist in his childhood. He then studied at the Naples Conservatory 1867–72, and became professor there in 1874. In 1886 he was appointed director of the Liceo Musicale at Bologna and there produced *Tristan* in 1888. In 1902 he returned to Naples as director of the Conservatory.

Works ORATORIO *Samuele*.

ORCHESTRAL two symphonies, *4 piccoli pezzi* for orchestra; piano concertos in D minor, B♭ minor (1878, 1885).

CHAMBER piano quintet, two piano trios; cello and piano sonata; various instrumental pieces; variations and fantasy for two pianos.

OTHER songs, 'Pagine sparse', 'Due sogni', and others.

Martyrdom of St Magnus, The chamber opera in nine scenes by Peter Maxwell Davies (libretto by composer, from 'Magnus' by George Mackay Brown), produced at Kirkwall, Orkney, on 18 June 1977. Orkney's patron saint murdered by Hakon, Earl of Orkney.

Martyre de Saint Sébastien, Le, The Martyrdom of St Sebastian incidental music by Debussy for the mystery play, written in French, by G d'Annunzio, composed for solo voices, chorus, and orchestra in 1911, first performed Paris, Théâtre du Châtelet, 22 May 1911, in five acts.

Martyrs, Les opera by Donizetti (libretto by Scribe, based on Corneille's *Polyeucte*), produced at the Paris Opéra on 10 April 1840. See also ➤ **Poliuto**.

Marx, Adolph Bernard (1795–1866) German musicologist and composer. He studied law, but gave it up for music, to which he devoted himself in Berlin, where in 1824 he founded the *Berliner Allgemeine Musikalische Zeitung*. In 1830 he became professor of music and in 1850 founded a music school with Kullak and Stern (later Stern Conservatory). He wrote books on the history of music, teaching, on Gluck, Handel, Beethoven, composition, and tone-painting.

Works OPERA *Jery und Bätely* (Goethe, 1824); melodrama *Die Rache wartet*.

ORATORIOS *Johannes der Täufer*, *Moses* (1841), *Nahid und Omar*.

OTHER instrumental works.

Marx, Joseph (1882–1964) Austrian composer. He studied in Vienna and in 1922 became director of the Academy of Music there in succession to Ferdinand Löwe. From 1947 he was professor at Graz University.

Works ORCHESTRAL *Autumn Symphony* (1921); *Symphonic Night Music*, *Spring Music* for orchestra; romantic concerto for piano and orchestra.

OTHER several choral pieces; three string quartets, piano quartet, fantasy for piano trio; violin and piano sonata, cello and piano sonata; c.120 songs.

Marx, Karl (1897–1985) German composer. He studied natural science at first, but met Carl Orff during World War I and later studied music with him. He was appointed professor of the Munich Academy in 1924 and was conductor of the Bach Society there in 1928. From 1939 to 1945 he taught at Graz Conservatory, becoming professor in 1944, and in 1946 he became professor at the Hochschule für Musik in Stuttgart. He was much occupied with school music.

Works ORCHESTRAL a passacaglia for orchestra (1932); concertos for piano, violin, two violins, viola, and flute.

CHAMBER divertimento for wind instruments (1934), string quartet and other chamber music; various choral works and songs, some to words by Rilke.

marziale Italian musical term; 'martial, warlike'.

Masagniello furioso oder Die neapolitanische Fischer-Empörung, *Masagniello enraged, or The Neapolitan Fisherman's Revolt* opera by Keiser (libretto by Barthold Feind), produced at the Theater beim Gänsemarkt, Hamburg, on June 1706. Masagniello leads his people against unfair taxes, but goes mad and is killed.

Masaniello opera by Auber; see ➤ *Muette de Portici*.

Mascagni, Pietro (1863–1945) Italian composer. His one-act opera *Cavalleria rusticana/Rustic Chivalry* was first produced in Rome in 1890 in the new verismo or realistic style.

He was born at Livorno; his father, a baker, wished him to study law, but he managed to take lessons in secret at the Istituto Cherubini. On being discovered, he was adopted by an uncle, and soon reconciled with his father by having two works performed at the Istituto. Later, Count Florestano de Larderel paid for his further musical education at the Milan Conservatory, where Ponchielli was among his masters. Not wishing to apply himself to solid study, he ran away with a travelling opera company. After many wanderings and a marriage that forced him to settle at Cerignola near Foggia to make a precarious living by teaching the piano and conducting the local band, he won the first prize in

an operatic competition with *Cavalleria rusticana* in 1889, and after its production in Rome the following year, he began to accumulate a great fortune, though his many later operas never repeated its success. Besides operas, he wrote some occasional works, cantatas, and the incidental music for Hall Caine's *The Eternal City*, produced in London in 1902. He became a member of the Italian Academy in 1929.

Works OPERA *Cavalleria rusticana* (1890), *L'amico Fritz* (1891), *I Rantzau* (both based on Erckmann-Chatrian), *Guglielmo Ratcliff* (after Heine, 1895), *Silvano*, *Zanetto* (1896), *Iris*, *Le maschere*, *Amica* (1905), *Isabeau* (1911), *Parisina* (d'Annunzio), *Lodoletta* (1917), *Il piccolo Marat* (1921), *Pinotta*, *Nerone* (1935); operetta *Si*.

OTHER incidental music for Hall Caine's *The Eternal City*; *Kyrie*, Requiem in memory of King Humbert; cantata for Leopardi centenary (1898), setting of Italian translation of Schiller's 'Ode to Joy' for chorus and orchestra, cantata *In Filanda*; symphony in C minor, symphonic poem for a film *Rapsodia satanica* (1917).

mascherata (Italian 'masquerade') type of 16th-century ➤ **villanella**, sung at masked balls or during fancy-dress processions.

Maschere, Le opera by Mascagni (libretto by L Illica), produced Genoa, Milan, Rome, Turin, Venice and Verona, 17 January 1901. Rosaura wishes to marry Florindo but her father Pantalone lines up Captain Spaventa for her.

Maschinist Hopkins opera by Max Brand (libretto by composer), produced in Duisburg on 13 April 1929. The opera pre-figures several dramatic themes in Berg's *Lulu* and was widely performed in Europe before the rise of the Nazis. The first complete post-war performance was by the BBC in London on 9 February 1986. Hopkins saves his factory from closure by Bill, who has murdered his wife's first husband. Hopkins blackmails Bill, who seeks to destroy his enemy's shop, but he falls into the machinery and is killed.

masculine cadence in music, a ➤ **cadence**, or full close; the final note or chord of which falls on a strong accented beat of a bar.

mask see ➤ **masque**.

Maskarade opera by Nielsen (libretto by V Andersen after a play by Holberg); composed 1904–06, first performed in Copenhagen on 11 November 1906. Leander meets his future wife at a masked ball.

Mask of Orpheus, The opera by Birtwistle (libretto by P Zinovieff), composed 1973–84, produced at the Coliseum, London, on 21 May 1986. The main characters in legend are seen from three different viewpoints: person, hero, and myth.

Mask of Time, The oratorio by Tippett in two parts for soloists, chorus, and orchestra; composed 1981–83, first performed in Boston on 5 April 1984, conducted by Colin Davis.

Masnadieri, I, The Brigands opera by Verdi (libretto by A Maffei, based on Schiller's drama *Die Räuber*), produced at Her Majesty's Theatre, London, on 22 July 1847. It is the only opera commissioned by London from Verdi. Jenny Lind and Lablache appeared in it. Carlo joins a band of robbers after betrayal by his brother, Francesco, and disinheritance by his father, Massimiliano. Carlo seeks revenge against Francesco and in the process kills the orphan Amalia.

Mason, Benedict (1954–) English composer. His highly eclectic and allusive music includes *Playing Away*, premiered in Munich in 1994, which was alleged to be the first opera to be based on football.

He studied with Peter Maxwell Davies, and with Pousseur in Liège. He has won several international prizes, including the Siemens Stiftungpreis in 1992.

Works ENSEMBLE *Lighthouses of England and Wales* for orchestra (1987) and *Concerto for the Viola Section* (1990); *The Hinterstoisser Traverse* for twelve players (1986), *Nodding Trilliums and Curved Line Angles* for four solo percussion and 15 players (1990).

VOCAL *Chaplin Operas* for mezzo, baritone, and 22 players (1988), *Seven Self-Referential Songs and Realistic Virelais* for soprano and 16 players (1990), *Oil and Petrol Marks on a Wet Road are sometimes held to be spots where a rainbow stood*, for 16 voices (1987).

ELECTRONIC *Six Rilke Songs* (1991), *Animals and the Origins of the Dance* (1992) and *Colour and Information* (1993).

OTHER two string quartets (1987, 1993); six Etudes for piano (1988).

masque spectacular court entertainment with a fantastic or mythological theme in which music, dance, and extravagant costumes and scenic design figured larger than plot. Originating in Italy, where members of the court actively participated in the performances, the masque reached its height of popularity at the English court between 1600 and 1640, with the collaboration of Ben Jonson as writer and Inigo Jones as stage designer. John Milton also wrote masque verses. Composers included Thomas ➤ Campion, John Coperario, Henry Lawes, William ➤ Byrd, and Henry Purcell.

The masque had great influence on the development of ballet and opera, and the elaborate frame in which it was performed developed into the proscenium arch.

Masques et bergamasques music by Fauré, Op. 112, for an entertainment by René Fauchois produced in Monte Carlo on 10 April 1919; and at the Opéra-Comique, Paris, on 4 March 1920, with a Watteau setting. It included an overture and three dances, newly composed, as well as the Pavane, Op. 50, of 1887 and an orchestral version of the Verlaine song 'Clair de Lune', Op. 46 no. 2, of the same year, in which the words 'masques et bergamasques' occur.

Mass in music, a setting of the music for the main service of the Roman Catholic Church. The items of the Mass are sung in Latin and fall into two groups: the **Ordinary** (the items of the Mass are invariable, regardless of day or season) consists of the *Kyrie, Gloria, Credo, Sanctus* with *Benedictus*, and *Agnus Dei*; the **Proper** (the items of the Mass are 'proper' to the day or season) consists of additional matter namely the Introit, Gradual, Alleluia or Tract, Offertory, and Communion). A notable example of the Ordinary of the Mass is J S Bach's *Mass in B Minor* (about 1748).

The medieval practice of writing the movements of a Mass on plainsong melodies, sung by the tenor, was soon extended to the employment of secular tunes. *L'Homme armé* on the continent and *The Western Wind* in England, for example, were especially favoured for this purpose. In the course of the 16th century, however, more and more composers wrote wholly original Masses, though the practice of borrowing material from motets or *chansons* was also common. Even in later times the treatment of the Mass remained essentially polyphonic, though not necessarily throughout. Certain portions, 'Et vitam venturi saeculi' at the end of the Credo, were almost always set as fugues. Major examples are Wolfgang Amadeus Mozart's *Requiem* (1791), Ludwig van Beethoven's *Missa solemnis* (1819–22), and György Ligeti's *Requiem* (1963–65).

Massé, Victor, actually **Félix Marie (1822–1884)** French composer. He studied at the Paris Conservatory, where Halévy was his composition master, and gained the Prix de Rome in 1844. He travelled in Italy and Germany after his stay in Rome; in 1860 he became chorus-master at the Paris Opéra and in 1866 professor of composition at the Conservatory.

Works OPERA AND OPERETTAS *La Chambre gothique* (1849), *La Chanteuse violée* (1850), *Galathée* (1852), *Les Noces de Jeannette* (1853), *La Reine Topaze* (1856), *Le Cousin de Marivaux* (1857), *La Fiancée du Diable, Miss Fauvette, Les Saisons, La Fée Carabosse, Mariette la promise* (1862), *La Mule de Pedro* (1863), *Fior d'Aliza* (after Lamartine, 1866), *Le Fils du brigadier* (1867), *Paul et Virginie* (after Saint-Pierre), *La favorita e la schiava, Les Chaises à porteurs, Le Prix de famille, Une*

Loi somptuaire, *Les Enfants de Perrette*, *La Petite Sœur d'Achille*, *La Trouvaille* (composed 1873), *Une Nuit de Cléopâtre* (1885).

OTHER *Messe solennelle*; cantata *Le Rénégat*; songs.

Massenet, Jules Emile Frédéric (1842–1912) French composer of operas. His work is characterized by prominent roles for females, sincerity, and sentimentality. Notable works are *Manon* (1884), *Le Cid* (1885), and *Thaïs* (1894); among other works is the orchestral suite *Scènes pittoresques* (1874). He was professor of composition at the Paris Conservatory 1878–96.

His long and successful career included no fewer than 27 operas, mainly for the Paris Opéra and Opéra-Comique, and the Monte Carlo Opera. There have been revivals of some of his lesser-known works since the 1980s.

Massenet was born at Montaud, St Etienne, and entered the Paris Conservatory at the age of 11, studying composition with A Thomas and winning the Prix de Rome in 1863. On his return from Rome in 1866 he married a piano pupil and had his first opera, *La Grand'tante*, produced at the Opéra-Comique the next year. He achieved his first major success with the opera *Le Roi de Lahore* (1877), indulging a current taste for the exotic and oriental. Similar success came with *Hérodiade* (Brussels, 1881) but lasting fame came with *Manon*, premiered at Paris in 1884, in which Massenet indulged to the full the lifelong sympathy he felt for his central female characters. In *Werther* (1892), the lyrical impulse is balanced with a strong dramatic flair. Later operas such as *Cendrillon*, *Grisélidis*, *Chérubin*, and *Don Quichotte* have found recognition as a result of recent revivals.

Works OPERA *Don César de Bazan* (1872), *Le Roi de Lahore* (1877), *Hérodiade* (1881), *Manon* (after Prévost, 1884), *Le Cid* (after Corneille, 1885), *Esclarmonde* (1889), *Le Mage*, *Werther* (after Goethe, 1892), *Le Portrait de Manon*, *La Navarraise* (1894), *Sapho* (after Daudet), *Cendrillon* (1899), *Grisélidis* (1901), *Le jongleur de Notre-Dame* (1902), *Thaïs* (1894), (both after A France), *Chérubin* (1905), *Ariane* (1906), *Thérèse* (1907), *Bacchus*, *Don Quichotte* (after Cervantes, 1910), *Roma*, *Panurge* (after Rabelais), *Cléopâtre* (1914), *Amadis* (composed 1895; produced 1922).

BALLET *Le Carillon*, *La Cigale*, *Espada*.

ORATORIOS *Marie-Magdeleine* (1873), *Eve* (1875), *La Vierge*, *La Terre promise* (1900).

CANTATAS *David Rizzio*, *Narcisse*, *Biblis*.

OTHER 13 orchestral works including *Scènes pittoresques* (1874), *Scènes napolitaines* (1876), and three other similar suites, symphonic poem *Visions*; incidental music to Leconte de Lisle's *Les Erynnies*, Racine's *Phèdre*, and other plays; piano

concerto, fantasy for cello and orchestra; about 200 songs; duets; choruses.

mässig German musical term; 'moderate'.

Massimilla Doni opera by Schoeck (libretto by A Rüeger, based on Balzac's novel), produced in Dresden on 2 March 1937. Massimilla falls for Emilio in this Venetian fable, set at La Fenice opera house. The subplot balances the artistic virtues of technique versus passion.

Mass in B minor setting of the Latin Mass by J S ➤ Bach. The work begins in B minor, but as a whole centres on D major; it was not composed in one piece, however, but in four sections, some of them intended for separate performance.

The *Kyrie* and *Gloria* (constituting in themselves a complete Lutheran short Mass) were written in 1733, and used to support Bach's application for the title of Court Composer to the Elector of Saxony. The *Symbolum Nicenum* (Creed) was written about 1748, the *Sanctus* in 1724, and, finally, the movements from *Osanna* to *Dona nobis pacem* about 1748. Several of the movements were adapted from earlier works, such as church cantatas nos 11, 12, 29, 46, 120, and 171 and the secular cantata *Preise dein Glücke*.

Mass of Life, A setting of words from Nietzsche's *Also sprach Zarathustra* for solo voices, chorus, and orchestra by Delius, composed 1904–05, produced (second part only in German) at the Munich Music Festival in 1908; the first complete performance (in English) was in London on 7 June 1909, conducted by Thomas Beecham.

Master of the King's/Queen's Music(k) honorary appointment to the British royal household, the holder composing appropriate music for state occasions. The first was Nicholas Lanier, appointed by Charles I in 1626; later appointments have included Edward Elgar and Arthur Bliss. The present holder, Peter Maxwell ➤ Davies, was appointed in 2004.

Master Peter's Puppet Show marionette opera by Manuel de Falla; see ➤ *Retablo de Maese Pedro*.

mastersinger English for ➤ Meistersinger.

Mastersingers of Nuremberg, The music drama by Richard Wagner; see ➤ *Meistersinger von Nürnberg*.

Mathias, William (1934–1992) Welsh composer and pianist. He studied at the Royal Academy of Music with Lennox Berkeley and Peter Katin. He was lecturer at University College of North Wales 1959–68, and professor from 1970.

Works OPERA *The Servants* (1980).

ORCHESTRAL *Divertimento* for strings (1958), Concerto for Orchestra (1966), three symphonies

(1966, 1983, 1991), *Dance Variations* for orchestra (1977); concertos for piano (1955, 1961, 1968), harp (1970), clarinet (1975), horn (1982); *In Arcadia* for orchestra (1992); *This Worldes Joie* for soloists, chorus, and orchestra (1974); *Lux Eterna* for soloists, chorus, organ, and orchestra (1982), *Let us now praise famous men* for chorus and orchestra (1984).

CHAMBER two violin sonatas, wind quintet, two piano sonatas (1964, 1979), two string quartets (1968, 1982).

Mathis der Maler, Matthew the Painter opera by Paul ➤ Hindemith (libretto by composer), produced in Zürich on 28 May 1938. The painter of the title is Matthias Grünewald (15th–16th centuries).

The plot of the opera – in which Grünewald sides with peasants against the Church authorities, but retreats into his art after witnessing the cruel reality of life – was a thinly disguised metaphor for Hindemith's own struggles against the Nazis. The political climate was too dangerous for Hindemith to have a performance staged in Germany, however he wrote the *Symphony: Mathis der Maler* using material from the opera; it was performed in Berlin on 12 March 1934, conducted by Wilhelm Furtwängler. The three movements are based on an extant triptych by Grünewald: they are entitled *Engelkonzert/Concert of Angels*, *Grablegung/Entombment*, and *Versuchung des heiligen Antonius/The Temptation of St Anthony*.

Matilde di Shabran, ossia Bellezza e cuor di ferro, Matilde of Shabran or Beauty and Heart of Iron opera by Rossini (libretto by J Ferretti), produced at the Teatro Apollo, Rome, on 24 February 1821. Corradino orders poet Isidoro to murder Matilde for supposedly allowing his enemy Edoardo to escape from the dungeon. When Matilde's innocence is proved, Corradino resolves to commit suicide, but is prevented by Edoardo and his father Raimondo.

Matin, Le, Le Midi, Le Soir et la Tempête, Morning, Noon, Evening and Storm the original titles of Haydn's symphonies Nos 6 in D major, 7 in C major, and 8 in G major, composed in 1761.

matins the first Roman Catholic office (or non-Eucharistic service) of the day. It is also used by the Anglican Church to refer to Morning Prayer.

Matrimonio segreto, Il, The Clandestine Marriage opera by Cimarosa (libretto by G Bertati, based on G Colman and D Garrick's play of that name), produced at the Burgtheater, Vienna, on 7 February 1792. Geronimo wants to marry his daughter Elisetta to Count Robinson, but the Count prefers her sister, Caroline, who is already secretly married to Paolino. The marriage is revealed and the Count settles for Elisetta.

Mattei, Stanislao (1750–1825) Italian priest, theorist, and composer. He was a pupil of Padre Martini, whom he succeeded as maestro di cappella at the church of San Francesco in Bologna, and later at San Petronio. From 1804 he was professor at the newly founded Liceo Filarmonico; his pupils included Rossini and Donizetti. He wrote a treatise on playing from figured bass.

Works eight Masses and other church music; a Passion; intermezzo *La bottega del libraio*.

Mattheson, Johann (1681–1764) German writer on music, organist, and composer. Among his many writings on music the most important are *Der vollkommene Capellmeister* (1739), *Grundlage einer Ehrenpforte* (1740), and a treatise on thorough bass.

From the age of nine he sang at the Hamburg Opera, and there produced his first opera in 1699. He became friendly with Handel in 1703 and went with him to Lübeck as a candidate to succeed Buxtehude; but both declined on learning that marriage to Buxtehude's daughter was a condition of the post. After some years as a tutor, then as secretary to the English Legation, he was appointed minor canon and music director at Hamburg Cathedral in 1715, but had to resign in 1728 because of his deafness.

Works OPERA *Die Pleiades* (1699); *Die unglückselige Cleopatra* (1704), *Henrico IV*, *Boris Goudenow* (1710), and *Nero* (1723).

OTHER 24 oratorios and cantatas; trio sonatas; keyboard music.

Matthews, Colin (1946–) English composer. He studied at Nottingham University and taught at Sussex University 1972–77. He worked with Deryck Cooke on the performing version of Mahler's tenth symphony and edited and issued several early works by Britten, whose assistant he was 1974–76. His output includes several *Sonatas* for orchestra; *Night's Mask* (1984), for soprano and chamber orchestra; and ... *through the glass* (1994), for ensemble.

He is the brother of English composer David ➤ Matthews.

Works ORCHESTRAL two *Sonatas* for orchestra (1975, 1980), cello concerto (1984), *Night's Mask* for soprano and chamber orchestra (1984).

CHAMBER *Ceres* for nine players (1972), *Rainbow Studies* for piano and four wind (1978), three string quartets (1979, 1982, 1993), oboe quartet (1981).

VOCAL *Five Sonnets: to Orpheus* (texts by Rilke) for tenor and harp (1976), *Shadows in the Water* for tenor and piano (1978); *A Rose at Christmas* for unaccompanied voices (1992).

Matthews, David (1943–) English composer. He is the brother of Colin ➤ Matthews, with whom he collaborated, with Deryck Cooke, on the performing version of Mahler's tenth symphony. He graduated in Classics from Nottingham University, and worked as an assistant to Benjamin Britten 1966–69. He published a biography of Tippett in 1980.

Works ORCHESTRAL four symphonies (1975, 1979, 1985, 1990); *In The Dark Time* for orchestra (1985); *Chaconne* for orchestra (1987); *The Music of Dawn* for orchestra (1990); *A Vision and a Journey* for orchestra (1993); oboe concerto (1992); violin concerto (1982); *September Music* for small orchestra (1979); *Serenade* for chamber orchestra (1982).

VOCAL three songs for soprano and orchestra (1971).

CHAMBER six string quartets (1970–90), *Songs and Dances of Mourning* for cello (1976), clarinet quartet (1984), Variations for Strings (1986), *Cantiga* for soprano and ensemble (1988).

Matthisson, Friedrich von (1761–1831) German poet. He is remembered chiefly for Beethoven's setting of his 'Adelaide'; Franz ➔ **Schubert** set 26 of his poems.

Matthus, Siegfried (1934–) German composer. His music is in a conservative idiom and includes the operas *Der letzte Schuss* (1967), *Noch ein Löffel Gift, Liebling?* (1972), *Omphale* (1976), *Judith* (1984), *Die Weise von Liebe des Cornets Christoph Rilke* (1984), *Graf Mirabeau* (1988), and *Desdemona und ihrer Schwestern* (1992).

He studied in East Berlin during the 1950s, with Wagner-Régeny and Hanns Eisler. In 1964 he was appointed composer-in-residence at the Komische Oper Berlin.

Works ORCHESTRAL three symphonies (1969, 1976, 1993), concerto for orchestra (1963), concertos for violin (1968), piano (1970), cello (1975), flute (1978), oboe (1985), and triangle (1985).

VOCAL Vocal Symphony for soprano, baritone, two choruses, and orchestra (1967), *Holofernes Portrait* for baritone and orchestra (1981).

CHAMBER *Wem ich zu gefallen suche* for tenor, baritone, and piano (1987); two octets (1970, 1989), string quartet (1972).

Mauduit, Jacques (1557–1627) French lutenist and composer. He was, like his father before him, registrar to the courts of justice in Paris, but became famous as a musician. In 1588 he saved the manuscripts of his Huguenot friend Claude Le Jeune from destruction by Catholic soldiers, though he was himself a Catholic.

In 1581 he won first prize at the annual Puy de Musique at Evreux, and he was associated with Jean-Antoine de Baïf (1532–1589) in his experiments with *musique mesurée*, though after Baïf's death he relaxed the rigid subordination of music to verbal rhythm in his settings of verse.

Works Requiem on the death of the poet Ronsard (1585), motets, chansons, chansonnettes mesurées for four voices, and other pieces.

Maunder, John Henry (1858–1920) English composer and organist. His oratorio *The Martyrs* was performed in Oxford in 1894 and his church cantata *From Olivet to Calvary* (1904) was popular for many years.

He studied at the Royal Academy of Music and later played the organ in various London churches. He first wrote operettas, including *The Superior Sex* and *Daisy Dingle* (1885), but then turned to sacred music.

Má Vlast, My Country cycle of six symphonic poems by Bedřich ➔ **Smetana**, composed 1874–79 and containing programme works on various aspects of Czech history and geography: 1. *Vyšehrad/The Citadel of Prague*; 2. *Vltava/The River*; 3. *Šárka/The Czech Amazon*; 4. *From Bohemia's Woods and Fields*; 5. *Tabor/The City*; 6. *Blaník/The Mountain*.

Mavra opera in one act by Stravinsky (libretto in Russian, by B Koshno, based on Pushkin's *The Little House at Kolomna*), produced in French translation by J Larmanjat at the Paris Opéra on 3 June 1922. 'Mavra' is Parasha's lover Vasilly, a hussar disguised as a cook in her mother's house. However, Mavra is discovered shaving, and her true identity is revealed.

Maw, Nicholas (1935–) English composer. His music is largely traditional in character. He studied with Lennox Berkeley at the Royal Academy of Music 1955–58 and with Nadia Boulanger in Paris 1958–59. He has taught at Cambridge University 1966–70 and at Yale, and currently teaches in New York. Important works include *Scenes and Arias* (1962) and *Odyssey*, a massive orchestral work composed 1973–89.

Works STAGE comic operas *One Man Show* (1964) and *The Rising of the Moon* (1970).

ORCHESTRAL *Morning Music* for orchestra (1982); *Spring Music* for orchestra (1983); *Sonata Notturno* for cello and strings (1985); *Odyssey* for orchestra (1972–85); *The World in the Evening* for orchestra (1988); *Little concert* for oboe, two horns, and strings (1988); *Shahnama* for orchestra (1992); *Life Studies* for 15 solo strings (1973–76).

CHORAL AND VOCAL Requiem for soprano and contralto soloists, women's chorus, string trio, and string orchestra; *Nocturne* for mezzo-soprano and orchestra (1958); *Scenes and Arias* for solo voices and orchestra (1962); *La Vita Nuova* for soprano and chamber ensemble (1979).

CHAMBER Sonata for strings and two horns (1967); Chamber Music for flute, clarinet, horn, bassoon, and piano (1962); two string quartets

(1965, 1982); *Music of Memory* for guitar (1989).

Maximilien opera by Milhaud (libretto by A Lunel, translated from a German libretto by R S Hoffmann, based on Franz Werfel's play, *Juarez und Maximilian*), produced at the Paris Opéra on 4 January 1932. It chronicles the misfortunes of the Habsburg monarch in a Mexican war.

Maxwell Davies, Peter English composer and conductor; see Peter Maxwell ➤ **Davies**.

Mayer, Robert (1879–1985) German-born British philanthropist. He founded the Robert Mayer Concerts for Children and the Transatlantic Foundation Anglo-American Scholarships. KCVO 1979.

Maynard, John (1577–after 1614) English lutenist and composer. He was connected with the school of St Julian in Hertfordshire, and at some time in the service of Lady Joan Thynne at Cause Castle in Shropshire.

Works INSTRUMENTAL pavanes and galliards for the lute; an organ piece; lessons for lute and bass viol and for lyra-viol; twelve songs *The XII Wonders of the World*, describing various characters, for voice, lute, and viola da gamba.

May Night, Russian **Maïskaya Notch** opera by Rimsky-Korsakov (libretto by composer, based on a story by Gogol), produced in St Petersburg on 21 January 1880. Levko's wedding to Hanna is made possible by help from water sprites.

Mayone, Ascanio (c.1565–1627) Italian composer. He studied with Jean de Macque in Naples, was appointed organist at the Annunziata, Naples, in 1593 and maestro di cappella there from 1621.

Works INSTRUMENTAL solo and chamber instrumental music. His two volumes of keyboard music, *Capricci per sonar* (1603, 1609) contain canzonas and toccatas in an advanced idiom.

OTHER madrigals.

Mayrhofer, Johann (1787–1836) Austrian poet. The composer Franz ➤ **Schubert** set 47 of his poems and used his libretto for the operetta ➤ *Die Freunde von Salamanka/The Friends of Salamanca*.

Mayseder, Joseph (1789–1863) Austrian violinist and composer. He first appeared in Vienna in 1800, and later held several important appointments, including that of chamber musician to the emperor.

Works CHORAL Mass.

CHAMBER three violin concertos; eight string quartets; five string quintets; piano trios and other chamber music; violin duets; piano pieces and studies for violin.

Mazas, Jacques (Féréol) (1782–1849) French violinist and composer. He appeared with a violin concerto written for him by Auber, travelled widely, lived in Paris 1829–37, and was director of the music school at Cambrai 1837–41.

He studied under Pierre Baillot at the Paris Conservatory.

Works OPERA *Le Kiosque* (1842).

ORCHESTRAL two violin concertos.

CHAMBER string quartets; violin duets; many violin pieces.

Mazeppa opera by Tchaikovsky (libretto by composer and V P Burenin, based on Pushkin's *Poltava*), produced at the Bolshoi Theatre, Moscow, on 15 February 1884. Mazeppa demands to take Judge Kochubey's daughter Maria as his wife. Kochubey denounces Mazeppa as a separatist but the Tsar does not believe him. Mazeppa has Kochubey executed and Maria goes insane.

Symphonic poem by Liszt, composed in 1854 on Victor Hugo's poem and on the basis of one of the *Grandes Etudes pour le piano* of c.1838 and their new version, the *Etudes d'exécution transcendante* of 1851, first performed at Weimar on 16 April 1854.

mazurka any of a family of traditional Polish dances from the 16th century, characterized by foot-stamping and heel-clicking, together with a turning movement. The music for the mazurka is in triple time (3/4), with dotted rhythms and the accentuation of weak beats, on which phrases also begin and end. It is found at a variety of speeds, but is usually not as fast as the waltz, which is also formally a more rigid dance than the mazurka. During the 18th and 19th centuries, it spread throughout Europe and was made famous by Chopin's approximately 60 works in the genre. Other composers of the mazurka include Karol Szymanowski, Glinka, and Mussorgsky.

Mazzocchi, Domenico (1592–1665) Italian composer. His music has some of the earliest printed ➤ **dynamics**, including 'crescendo' and 'diminuendo'.

He was in the service of the Aldobrandini Borghese family for 20 years.

Works STAGE the opera *La catena d'Adone* (1626); oratorios *Querimonia di S Maria Maddalena*, *Il martirio dei Santi Abbundia ed Abbundanzio* (1641).

OTHER *Musiche sacre*; madrigals; *Dialoghi e sonetti*.

Mazzocchi, Virgilio (1597–1646) Italian composer, brother of Domenico ➤ **Mazzocchi**. He was maestro di cappella at St John Lateran in Rome, 1628–29, and then at St Peter's until his death.

Works OPERA *Chi soffre speri* (with Marazzoli, 1637) and *L'innocenza difesa* (1641).

VOCAL psalms for double chorus; *Sacri flores* for two–four voices.

mbira term used in the singular to describe several types of large gourd-resonated lamellophones throughout southeastern Africa, especially Zimbabwe. Tuned metal strips are attached to a soundboard and amplified by a gourd or box resonator. Also known to non-Africans as a 'finger piano', 'thumb piano', or 'hand piano'.

Meale, Richard (1932–) Australian composer. He studied as a pianist at New South Wales Conservatory. His later music has been influenced by Boulez, Messiaen, and Indonesian music.

Works OPERA *Voss* (1979–86) and *Mer de Glace* (1986–91).

ORCHESTRAL *Images* for orchestra (1966), *Clouds Now and Then* for orchestra (1969); *Viridian* for strings (1979); Symphony (1994).

CHAMBER flute sonata (1960), wind quintet (1970), two string quartets (1974, 1980).

meantone in music, a tuning system which was a common technique used for keyboard instruments before ➤ **equal temperament** came into general use. It provided for the pure intonation of the key of C major and those lying near it at the expense of the more extreme sharp and flat keys, which is the reason why remote keys were rarely used in keyboard works, before the adoption of equal temperament. There was, for example, a pure F sharp and B flat, but these notes were out of tune when used as G flat or A sharp.

Meares, Richard (lived 17th–18th centuries) family of English instrument makers. **Richard** Meares (died c.1722) made lutes, viols, and other string instruments in London in the second half of the 17th century.

He was succeeded by his son, also named **Richard** (died c.1743), who enlarged his father's business, by selling not only instruments, but music books and cutlery, and he began to publish music around 1714, including several operas by George Handel, such as *Radamisto* (1720).

measure in music, US term for ➤ **bar**.

Medea play with music (melodrama) by Jiří Benda (text by F W Gotter), produced in Leipzig on 1 May 1775. The plot is based on the Greek myth: Medea takes revenge on treacherous husband Jason by killing their children and his lover, Creusa.

Medea in Corinto opera (*melodramma tragico*) by Mayr (libretto by F Romani); produced at the Teatro San Carlo, Naples, on 28 November 1813. Medea takes revenge on treacherous husband Jason by killing their children and his lover, Creusa.

Médecin malgré lui, Le, Doctor against his Will opera by Gounod (libretto, a small alteration of Molière's comedy by composer, J Barbier and Michel Carré), produced Paris, Théâtre Lyrique, 15 January 1858. Doctor Sganarelle helps Lucinde escape the attentions of a rich suitor and elope with lover Léandre.

Médée opera by Marc-Antoine Charpentier (libretto by T Corneille), produced at the Paris Opéra on 4 December 1693.

Opera by Cherubini (libretto by F B Hoffmann), produced at the Théâtre Feydeau, Paris, on 13 March 1797. Abandoned by Jason, Medea poisons his new wife and kills their two sons.

Opera by Milhaud (libretto by Madeleine Milhaud, the composer's wife), produced in the Flemish translation at Antwerp on 7 October 1939.

medesimo tempo (Italian 'same time') a musical direction indicating that a change of metre does not imply a change of pace. The more usual term is *l'istesso tempo* (formerly *lo stesso tempo*).

mediant in music, the third note (or degree) of the ➤ **diatonic scale**, for example E in the C major scale. A chord of the mediant is a ➤ **triad** (chord of three notes) built upon the mediant note.

Medium, The opera in two acts by Menotti (libretto by the composer), produced at Columbia University, New York, on 8 May 1946. A fraudulent medium, Baba, accidentally kills her mute assistant Toby, believing him to be a genuine ghost.

Medtner or **Metner, Nikolai Karlovich (1880–1951)** Russian composer. His music is almost wholly confined to piano works (including three concertos and twelve sonatas) and to songs, but he also wrote three sonatas and three Nocturnes for violin and piano, and at the end of his life he produced a Quintet for strings and piano. Characteristic titles are *Improvisations*, *Dithyrambs*, *Fairy Tales*, and *Novels*.

Medtner was born in Moscow. He studied piano under Vassily Safonov at the Moscow Conservatory, won the Rubinstein Prize there, and toured Europe as a pianist 1901–02, becoming professor at the Conservatory for a year on his return. He then retired to devote himself to composition. After the Revolution he taught at a school in Moscow and in 1921 went on another tour in the West, but found himself unable to return. He settled in Paris for a time and later in London, where he died.

As a keyboard composer he is as important, and in his way as characteristic, as Chopin or Schumann. His numerous songs are deeply felt and tasteful, with piano parts as important as those for the voice. For their words he relied largely upon Russian and German poets, including Pushkin, Tyutchev, Goethe, and Heine. Sponsored by the Maharajah of Mysore, he made gramophone recordings of many of his own works, including all three concertos.

Works PIANO three piano concertos (1914–43); piano quintet; three sonatas and three nocturnes for violin and piano; twelve piano sonatas and a great number of pieces for piano including *Fairy Tales* Op. 8, 9, 14, 20, 26, 34, 35, 42, 48, 51, *Forgotten Melodies* Op. 38–40, *Dithyrambs, Novels, Lyric Fragments, Improvisations, Hymns in Praise of Toil*, and others; *Russian Dance* and *Knight-Errant* for two pianos; sonata-vocalise for voice and piano.

VOCAL 17 Op. nos of songs to words by Pushkin, Tiutchev, Goethe, Heine, Nietzsche, and others.

Meeresstille und Glückliche Fahrt, Calm Sea and Prosperous Voyage two poems by Goethe, set by Beethoven as a cantata for chorus and orchestra in 1815, Op. 112, and dedicated to the poet; and used by Mendelssohn as the subject for a concert overture, Op. 27, in 1828. Elgar quotes from the latter in the romance of the 'Enigma' Variations.

Mefistofele opera by Boito (libretto by composer, based on Goethe's *Faust*), produced at La Scala, Milan, on 5 March 1868. Faust gains a moment of happiness but loses Margherita after accidentally poisoning her mother. Faust repents and eludes Mephistopheles.

Méhul, Etienne Nicolas (1763–1817) French composer. *Euphrosine* (1790) established him as an opera composer, after which he became one of the most notable composers of the Revolution, his greatest success being *Joseph* (1807).

He became an organist in his home town at the age of ten, and went to Paris in 1778, where Gluck encouraged him to write for the stage. He took piano lessons from Edelmann, and supported himself by teaching until the success of the operas *Euphrosine* (1790) and *Stratonice* (1792). On the foundation of the Conservatory in 1795 he became one of its inspectors. His overture *Le jeune Henri* and operas *Uthal* and *Joseph* are notable for their novel instrumental effects.

Works OPERA *Euphrosine et Coradin, ou Le tyran corrigé* (1790), *Cora, Stratonice* (1792), *Le jeune sage et le vieux fou* (1793), *Horatius Coclès, Mélidore et Phrosine* (1794), *La caverne, Doria, Le jeune Henri* (1797), *Le Pont de Lodi* (1797), *Adrien, Ariodant* (1799), *Epicure* (with Cherubini), *Bion, L'irato, ou L'emporté* (1801), *Une Folie, Le trésor supposé* (1802), *Joanna, Héléna* (1803), *Le baiser et la quittance* (with Kreutzer, Boieldieu, and Isouard, 1803), *L'Heureux malgré lui, Les deux aveugles de Tolède* (1806), *Uthal* (without violins), *Gabrielle d'Estrés, Joseph* (1807), *Les Amazones, Le Prince Troubadour* (1813), *L'Oriflamme* (with Paer, Berton, and Kreutzer,

1814), *La journée aux aventures* (1816), *Valentine de Milan* (unfinished; completed by his nephew Louis Joseph Daussoigne-Méhul, lived 1790–1875).

BALLET *Le jugement de Paris* (with additions from Haydn and Pleyel), *La dansomanie* (1800), *Daphnis et Pandrose* (1803), *Persée et Andromède* (1810)

OTHER incidental music to Joseph Chénier's *Timoléon*; Mass for the coronation of Napoleon I (not performed); cantatas *Chanson de Roland, Chant lyrique* (for the unveiling of Napoleon's statue at the Institut); patriotic songs 'Chant national du 14 juillet', 'Chant du départ', 'Chant de retour'; symphony; two piano sonatas.

Mei, Girolamo (1519–1594) Italian music theorist. His four surviving works include the *Discorso sopra la musica antica e moderna/ Discourse on ancient and modern music*, published at Venice in 1602.

Meistersinger (German 'master singer') one of a group of German lyric poets, singers, and musicians of the 14th–16th centuries, who formed guilds for the revival of minstrelsy. Hans ➤ Sachs was a Meistersinger, and Wagner's opera *Die Meistersinger von Nürnberg/The Mastersingers of Nuremberg* (1868) depicts the tradition.

Meistersinger von Nürnberg, Die, The Mastersingers of Nuremberg music drama by Richard ➤ Wagner (libretto by composer), produced at the Court Theatre, Munich, on 21 June 1868. The work is inspired by the ➤ Meistersinger tradition: in the plot Walter wins Eva in a song contest, but only after tempering his passion with the wisdom of Hans Sachs.

Mel, Rinaldo del (c.1554–c.1598) Flemish composer. After serving at the Portuguese court, he went to Rome in 1580, where he entered the service of Cardinal Gabriele Paleotti (1522–97) and may have studied under Palestrina. He was at Liège (1587–91), in the household of Ernst, Duke of Bavaria, but he rejoined Paleotti at Bologna, who appointed him maestro di cappella at Magliano Cathedral.

Works CHORAL motets, *Sacrae Cantiones*, a Litany; twelve volumes of *madrigaletti* and spiritual madrigals.

Melartin, Erkki (1875–1937) Finnish composer. He studied at the Helsinki Conservatory, Wegelius being his composition master, and later in Germany. He became professor of composition at the Conservatory in 1901, and conductor at Viipuri 1908–10. He was director of the Conservatory 1911–22.

Works STAGE the opera *Aino* (1907); ballet *Sininen helmi*.

ORCHESTRAL eight symphonies (1902–24), five or-

The melodic minor scale on E.

chestral suites, symphonic poems; violin concerto.

CHAMBER four string quartets; violin and piano sonatas; piano sonata and c.400 pieces.

OTHER c.300 songs.

melisma (from Greek 'song'; plural *melismata*) an ornament: in plainsong a group of notes sung to a single syllable; in modern music any short passage of a decorative nature.

melodic minor scale in music, one of the minor scales where the sixth and seventh notes are raised by a semitone when the scale is played ascending, and lowered (returned to their original positions) when played descending. It is so called because its notes are likely to be used when creating melodies as it is much easier to sing than the harmonic minor scale.

mélodie (French 'a melody or tune') in music, a term now generally current in French as an exact equivalent of the English ➤ song or the German ➤ Lied.

melodrama play or film with romantic and sensational plot elements, often concerned with crime, vice, or catastrophe. Originally a melodrama was a play with an accompaniment of music contributing to the dramatic effect. It became popular in the late 18th century, due to works like *Pygmalion* (1770), with pieces written by the French philosopher Jean-Jacques Rousseau. The early melodramas used extravagant theatrical effects to heighten violent emotions and actions artificially. By the end of the 19th century, melodrama had become a popular genre of stage play.

In melodramas of the 18th century there was no direct correlation between the free rhythm of the actor's voice and the music which was played in strict metre. In addition to self-contained melodramas, some operas of the period included scenes of this style, as in the grave-digging scene in Beethoven's *Fidelio* (1805). Schoenberg developed the genre in his *Pierrot lunaire* (1912), by the inclusion of semi-musical speech called ➤ Sprechgesang (German 'speech-song').

Beginning with the early work of Goethe and ➤ Schiller, melodrama was popularized in France by Pixérécourt (1773–1844), whose *L'Enfant de mystère* was first introduced to England in an unauthorized translation by Thomas Holcroft as *A Tale of Mystery* (1802). Melodramas were frequently played against a Gothic background of mountains or ruined castles.

melodramma (Italian 'music drama') term for 'opera' current in Italy from the end of the 18th century onwards. See ➤ melodrama.

melody (Greek *melos* 'song') in music, a recognizable series of notes of different pitches played or sung one after the other. It could also be described as the tune. Melody is one of the three main elements of music, along with ➤ rhythm and ➤ harmony. In Western music a melody is usually formed from the notes of a ➤ scale or ➤ mode. A melody, with or without ➤ accompaniment, may be a complete piece on its own – such as a simple song. In classical music it is more often used as a ➤ theme within a longer piece of music.

melodic structure Melody is often seen as an element in music that is distinct from ➤ harmony and ➤ rhythm. However, in Western music the three are mostly interdependent. For example, phrases within a melody can often be analysed as a series of notes that imply chords, and thus a harmonic structure; and rhythmic ideas (or motifs) may help to shape the structure of the melody. Other factors, such as the ascending or descending phrases, or the width of intervals between notes in the melody, can greatly change its quality.

harmonic structure The harmony that is implied by a melody, whether in the form of an accompaniment or not, helps to give the melody a distinctive character and establish its ➤ key. It arouses an expectation in the listener that certain conventions will be followed, but it is often the breaking of these conventions that makes a melody interesting. It is largely the implied harmonic or key structure that creates the mood of a melody. For example, a melody will have a very different 'feel' according to whether it is in a major or minor key, or there can be a greater or lesser build-up of tension depending on how far from its 'home' (tonic) key it has moved (modulated).

rhythmic elements It might be thought that the ➤ pitch of the notes of a melody would be its main distinguishing feature, but this is very often not the case. Rhythmic patterns and ➤ tempo can also be an important part of the melody, to the extent that some melodies can be recognized just by their rhythm.

aesthetics of melody What makes 'a good tune' has been a matter of much debate throughout the history of music, each age having its own views on the subject. As musical tastes have changed, so each generation has criticized the next for its lack of melodic beauty. Similarly, music from cultures unfamiliar to the listener is often described as 'tuneless'. As with any branch of aesthetics, there are no hard-and-fast rules for creating a memorable or beautiful melody, but attempts are still made to analyse those elements that make for a good melodic structure.

Melusine overture by Felix Mendelssohn; see ➜ *Schöne Melusine*.

membranophone one of the four main classes of musical instrument used in the original ➜ **Sachs-Hornbostel system**, the others being ➜ **idiophone**, ➜ **aerophone**, and ➜ **chordophone**. In instruments which are membranophones, the sound emanates from the vibration of a tight membrane such as the skin on a side drum. Included in this class of instruments are many percussion instruments of the drum type.

Mendelssohn (-Bartholdy), Fanny (Cäcilie) (1805–1847) German pianist and composer. She was encouraged in composition by her family but published very few of her 500 works, most of them piano pieces and Lieder (songs), which have enjoyed a revival. She was the sister of Felix ➜ **Mendelssohn**.

She studied with Marie Bigot in Paris and C F Zelter in Berlin. She was the focal point of her Berlin Salon in the 1830s and played her brother's first piano concerto in public in 1838. Her D minor piano trio of 1846 does not suffer from comparison with the early works of her brother.

Mendelssohn (-Bartholdy), (Jakob Ludwig) Felix (1809–1847) German composer, also a pianist and conductor. His music has the lightness and charm of classical music, applied to Romantic and descriptive subjects. Among his best-known works are *A Midsummer Night's Dream* (1826); the *Fingal's Cave* overture (1830–32); and five symphonies, which include the 'Reformation' (1832), the 'Italian' (1833), and the 'Scottish' (1842). He was involved in promoting the revival of interest in Johann Sebastian Bach's music.

Mendelssohn was the son of the banker Abraham Mendelssohn and grandson of the Jewish philosopher Moses Mendelssohn. His branch of the family converted to Christianity and moved to Berlin in 1812. At the age of six he had piano lessons from his mother and at seven from Marie Bigot in Paris. In 1817, back in Berlin, he learnt composition from Carl Zelter, whose friend Johann Wolfgang von Goethe he visited at Weimar in 1821. Before that, in 1818, aged nine, he appeared at a public chamber concert, and before he was 13 he had written many works, including the piano quartet Op. 1.

His father was wealthy enough to enable him to conduct a private orchestra, and he wrote his first symphony at 15, afterwards writing 13 symphonies for strings. By 1825 he had ready the short

opera *Camacho's Wedding*, produced at the family's expense in 1827. Also in 1825 he wrote his first masterpiece, the Octet for strings. At 17 he had written the overture to Shakespeare's *A Midsummer Night's Dream* (1826; the rest of the incidental music followed in 1842). In 1829 he gave the first performance since the composer's time of J S Bach's then forgotten *St Matthew Passion* at the Vocal Academy and paid the first of his ten visits to England. While there he conducted the Philharmonic Society in London, and took a holiday in Scotland, where he gathered impressions for the *Hebrides* overture and the 'Scottish' symphony, which he worked on in Italy during 1830–31. He finished the 'Italian' symphony in 1833, the year he conducted the Lower Rhine Festival at Düsseldorf, where he was engaged to stay as general music director. He left for Leipzig, where he was appointed 'official' conductor of the Gewandhaus concerts in 1835.

During a visit to Frankfurt he met Cécile Jeanrenaud, whom he married in March 1837. In September of the same year he conducted *St Paul* at the Birmingham Festival. In 1841 he left for Berlin, having been appointed director of the music section of the Academy of Arts, and there provided incidental music for several classical plays in Greek, English, and French. He returned to Leipzig late in 1842 and founded the conservatory there in November, opening it in April 1843. He was still living in Berlin, but resumed his conductorship at Leipzig in 1845, conducting the premiere of his most popular work, the violin concerto. But he was in poor health, and his visit to England to conduct *Elijah* at the Birmingham Festival on 26 August 1846 was his last but one. The death of his sister Fanny in the spring of 1847 greatly depressed him, and he went to Switzerland too ill to do any work, returning to Leipzig in September completely exhausted.

Mendelssohn's music is most highly valued for its combination of Romantic qualities with a sure sense of form. Much of his best music, including the octet (1825), the first five string quartets, *St Paul*, and the 'Italian' symphony were written while he was in his teens or twenties. Exhaustion through frail health and overwork prevented him from meeting his full potential, although such late works as the violin concerto and *Elijah* (1833) are among his best.

Works OPERA several; incidental music to Shakespeare's *A Midsummer Night's Dream* (1843).

ORATORIOS *St Paul* (1836) and *Elijah* (1846); Goethe's *Erste Walpurgisnacht* for solo voices, chorus, and orchestra.

ORCHESTRAL 13 symphonies for strings (1821–23), five symphonies, including A minor 'Scottish' (1842), A 'Italian' (1833), D 'Reformation' (1832); four concert overtures, *A Midsummer Night's Dream* (1826), *Fingal's Cave* (1830–32), *The Fair*

Melusine (1833), *Ruy Blas* (1839); two concertos and three shorter works for piano and orchestra; violin concerto in E minor.

CHAMBER MUSIC including six string quartets, two string quintets, string octet in E♭ Op. 20 (1825); two piano trios, in D minor Op. 49 (1839) and C minor Op. 66 (1845).

KEYBOARD AND SONGS a large amount of piano music including 48 *Lieder ohne Worte/Songs without words*; six sonatas, and other pieces for organ; over 80 songs; twelve sets of vocal duets and part songs.

Mendès, Catulle (1841–1909) French poet, novelist, playwright, and librettist. He was one of *Les Parnassiens*, and founded *La Revue fantaisiste* in 1861. His poems include *Philoméla* 1864, *Poésies* 1876, 1885, and 1892, *Hesperus* 1872, and *La Grive des vignes* 1895. He also wrote plays, novels, and critical works, such as *Richard Wagner* (1886), *L'Art au théâtre* (1897–1900), and *Le Mouvement poétique français de 1867 à 1900* (1903).

Mendès wrote libretti for several composers, including Chabrier, Messager, Pierné, Pessard, Massenet, and Debussy. Debussy's work, *Rodrigue et Chimène*, was never finished. He married Judith Gautier (1850–1917), with whom he visited Richard Wagner at Triebschen in Switzerland in 1869. She had an affair with Wagner seven years later at Bayreuth, during the first production of the *Ring*.

Mendès's plays include *Médée* (1898) and *Glatigny* (1906), and his novels *Mephistophela* (1890) and *La Maison de la vieille* (1894).

See also ➤ **Bruneau** (*Chansons à danser and Lieds de France*), *Gwendoline* (➤ **Chabrier**), ➤ **d'Indy** (*Médée*), ➤ **Leroux** (*Reine Fiammette*).

Mengelberg, Willem (1871–1951) Dutch conductor. In 1895 he was appointed conductor of the Concertgebouw Orchestra in Amsterdam. He made it one of the finest orchestras in Europe, giving early performances of works by Strauss and Mahler, including the first complete cycle of Mahler's symphonies at Amsterdam in 1920. However, he fell under a cloud when he openly declared his sympathy with Nazi rule during World War II, and went into exile in Switzerland.

He studied at Cologne, became conductor at Lucerne in 1891, and in 1895 was appointed conductor of the Concertgebouw Orchestra. In 1933 he was appointed professor of music at Utrecht University.

Mennin, Peter (1923–1983) US composer. He studied at the Eastman School and taught composition at the Juilliard School, New York, 1947–58. He was president at the latter from 1962.

Works ORCHESTRAL nine symphonies (1942–81),

Sinfonia for chamber orchestra (1947), *Fantasia* for strings (1948), violin concerto (1950), Concertato, *Moby Dick* (1952), cello concerto (first performance New York, 1956, with Leonard Rose), piano concerto (1958), *Cantata de Virtute*, based on *The Pied Piper of Hamelin* (1969), Symphonic Movements (1971), *Reflections of Emily*, to texts by Emily Dickinson (1979), flute concerto (1982).

CHAMBER two string quartets (1941, 1951), piano sonata (1963).

meno (Italian 'less') term used in musical notation, as in *meno mosso* ('less moved'), meaning slower.

Menotti, Gian Carlo (1911–) Italian-born US composer. He created small-scale realist operas in tonal idiom, including *The Medium* (1946), *The Telephone* (1947), *The Consul* (1950; Pulitzer Prize), *Amahl and the Night Visitors* (1951; the first opera to be written for television), and *The Saint of Bleecker Street* (1954). He also wrote orchestral and chamber music.

Later operas include *Goya* (1986), written for Placido Domingo, and *The Singing Child* (1993). Menotti's later vocal works include *Jacob's Prayer* (1997); *Gloria*, written as part of a composite Mass celebrating the 1995 Nobel Peace Prize; *For the Death of Orpheus* (1990); and *Llama de Amor Viva* (1991).

Menotti was born in Cadegliano, Italy. He went to Philadelphia in 1928 and studied with Rosario Scalero at the Curtis Institute there. He wrote libretti for his own operas and for Barber's *Vanessa* and *A Hand of Bridge*. His first great success was *The Medium* (1946), a sensational one-act opera, followed by the one-act comedy *The Telephone* (1947); but most striking of all, if musically no more refined, was the full-length *The Consul*, produced in New York in 1950 and in London in 1951. It won the Pulitzer Prize and the New York Drama Critics Circle award as the best musical play of the year in 1954. In 1958 he founded the Festival of Two Worlds at Spoleto, Italy. In 1977 Spoleto USA was founded in Charleston, South Carolina, which Menotti led until 1993 when he became director of the Rome Opera. In his operas he has attempted to introduce some popular elements, including values derived from the Broadway musical.

Works OPERA *Amelia goes to the Ball* (1937), *The Medium* (1946), *The Telephone* (1947), *The Consul* (1950), *Amahl and the Night Visitors* (1951), *The Saint of Bleecker Street* (1954), *Maria Golovin* (1958), *Le dernier sauvage* (1963), *Martin's Lie* (1964), *Help, Help, the Globolinks!* (1968), *The Hero* (1976), *The Most Important Man* (1971), *Tamu-Tamu* (1973), *La Loca* (1979), *A Bride from Pluto* (1982), *Goya* (1986), *The Wedding* (1988), *The Singing Child* (1993); radio opera *The Old Maid and the Thief* (1939).

OTHER symphonic poem *Apocalypse* (1951); *Pastorale* for piano and string orchestra, two piano concertos, violin concerto (1952); four pieces for string quartet, *Trio for a Housewarming Party* for flute, cello, and piano; *Poemetti*, piano pieces for children; pieces for carillon; symphony *The Halcyon* (1976).

VOCAL WORK *Jacob's Prayer* (1997).

mensurable music medieval measured or measurable music which can be grouped according to regular successions of beats, as distinct from ➤ plainsong, which has no measured rhythmic pulse.

mensural notation the musical notation which, as distinct from ➤ modal notation, came into use during the 13th century and for the first time began to indicate the exact value of notes and rests by its symbols.

menuet (French, diminutive of *menu*, 'small') French 17th century dance. See ➤ minuet.

Menuetto in music, term used by German composers of the 18th century to label their ➤ minuets under the impression that they were using an Italian term. The correct Italian is *minuetto*, the German *Menuett*.

Mer, La, The Sea three symphonic sketches by Debussy, *De l'aube à midi sur la mer*, *Jeux de vagues*, and *Dialogue du vent et de la mer*, composed 1903–05, first performed in Paris on 15 October 1905.

Merbecke or **Marbeck, John (c.1505–c.1585)** English composer and writer. He compiled *The Booke of Common Praier Noted* (1550), the first musical setting of an Anglican prayer book. He was lay clerk and organist at St George's Chapel, Windsor from 1531. In 1543 he was arrested and in 1544 tried and condemned for heresy as a Calvinist, but he was pardoned and allowed to retain his office.

His concordance of the English Bible, the first complete edition, was published in 1550. After Edward VI's accession, Merbecke compiled *The Booke of Common Praier Noted*. It was the first book of its kind, and used adaptations of plainsong in addition to music written by Merbecke himself. Merbecke's other surviving works are a large-scale Mass, two motets, and an anthem.

Works VOCAL Mass and two motets (probably early); carol 'A Virgine and Mother'; *The Booke of Common Praier Noted* [set to notes] (1550, first version authorized by Edward VI).

Mercadante, (Giuseppe) Saverio (Raffaele) (1795–1870) Italian composer. He wrote about 60 operas, the most successful of which, *Il giuramento* (1837) and *La Vestale* (1840), have a strong dramatic purpose and seriousness of style that influenced Verdi.

He studied under Niccolò Zingarelli at the Collegio di San Sebastiano at Naples and, having learnt the flute and violin, became leader of the orchestra there. On being dismissed he began to earn his living as a stage composer, producing his first opera at the San Carlo theatre in 1819. After several successes in Italy he won favour in Vienna, visited Spain 1827–29, and in 1833 succeeded Pietro Generali as maestro di cappella at Novara Cathedral. In 1840 he became director of the Naples Conservatory. While at Novara he lost an eye and in 1862 became totally blind.

Works OPERA about 60, including *Violenza e costanza* (1820), *Elisa e Claudio* (1821), *Caritea, regina di Spagna* (1826), *Gabriella di Vergy* (1828), *I Normanni a Parigi*, *I briganti*, *Il giuramento* (1837), *I due illustri rivali* (1838), *Elena da Feltre*, *Il bravo* (1839), *La Vestale* (1840), *Leonora*, *Gli Orazi ed i Curiazi* (1846), *Virginia*.

VOCAL 20 Masses, motets, psalms, and other pieces; cantata *L'apoteosi d'Ercole* and others; songs.

Mercury nickname of Joseph Haydn's symphony no. 43, in E flat major, composed c.1771.

Merikanto, Aarre (1893–1958) Finnish composer. His opera *Juha* (1922) has been successfully revived, suggesting an individual style that recalls Janáček.

He studied with Max Reger and others at Leipzig and with Sergey Vasilenko at Moscow. He later became professor at the Helsinki Conservatory.

Works STAGE the opera *Juha* (1922, staged 1963); ballet *The Abduction of Kylliki* (on a subject from the *Kalevala*).

ORCHESTRAL three symphonies (1916, 1918, 1953), variations and fugue and several suites for orchestra; four violin concertos (1916–54), three piano concertos, two cello concertos, concerto for violin, clarinet, horn, and strings.

OTHER partita for woodwind and harp; choral works; folk-song arrangements.

Merlo, Alessandro (1530–after 1594), also known as **Alessandro Romano** or **Alessandro della Viola** Italian tenor-bass, violist, and composer. He was a pupil of Willaert and Rore, and singer in the Papal Chapel in Rome.

Works motets; madrigals, *Canzoni alla Napolitana*, *villanelle*.

Merope opera by Gasparini (libretto by A Zeno), produced Venice, Teatro San Cassiano, 26 December 1711. Polyphontes overthrows King Cresphontes, executing him and two of his three sons. Aepytus escapes and, after growing up, kills Polyphontus and becomes the rightful king.

Also settings by Jommelli (1741) and Graun (1756).

Merry Widow, The opera by Franz Lehár; see
→ **Lustige Witwe**.

Merry Wives of Windsor see → **Falstaff**, → **Lustigen Weiber von Windsor**, and → **Sir John in Love**.

Mersenne, Marin (1588–1648) French monk, mathematician, philosopher, and music theorist. His treatises include the two-volume *Harmonie universelle*, published at Paris in 1636–37, with a section on instruments, 'Questions harmoniques de la nature des sons'.

Educated at Le Mans and La Flèche, he became a Minorite friar, and was ordained in 1612. He taught philosophy at Nevers and then studied mathematics and music in Paris, where his colleagues included Descartes and the elder Pascal. He corresponded with scholars in England, Holland, and Italy, the last of which he visited three times.

Merulo, Claudio (1533–1604), adopted name of **Claudio Merlotti** Italian organist, teacher, and composer. Famous in his lifetime for his organ playing, he is best known today for his keyboard music.

He was appointed organist at Brescia in 1556 and second organist at St Mark's, Venice, in 1557, advancing to first organist in 1564. In 1584 he left Venice, visited the court of Mantua, and became organist to the ducal chapel at Parma.

Works STAGE intermezzi for Dolce's *Le Troiane* (1566) and Cornelio Frangipani's *La tragedia* (1574).

VOCAL AND KEYBOARD Masses, motets, *Sacrae Cantiones*, Litanies; madrigals; toccatas and ricercari for organ.

messa di voce (Italian 'setting or placing of the voice') in music, sustained singing of notes or phrase. **Messa** may also mean a crescendo followed by a diminuendo on a single breath.

Messager, André Charles Prosper (1853–1929) French composer and conductor. As well as composing light operas, such as *La Béarnaise* (1885) and *Véronique* (1898), he was noted as a conductor of Mozart and Wagner, and also as a pianist.

He studied at Niedermeyer's school in Paris, under Fauré and Saint-Saëns. In 1876 he won prizes for a symphony and a cantata and in 1883 produced a completion of an operetta *François les Bas-bleus* left unfinished by Firmin Bernicat. He became conductor of the Opéra-Comique and in 1898 its general director. He was artistic director at Covent Garden, London 1901–06 and joint director of the Paris Opéra 1901–13. His wife was the Irish composer Hope Temple (Dotie Davies, 1859–1938), who had been a pupil of his. In 1902 he conducted the first performance of Debussy's *Pelléas et Mélisande*.

Works OPERA AND OPERETTAS *La fauvette du Temple*,

La Béarnaise (1885), *Le bourgeois de Calais* (1887), *Isoline* (1888), *Le mari de la reine* (1889), *La Basoche* (1890), *Madame Chrysanthème* (after Pierre Loti's novel, 1893), *Miss Dollar*, *Mirette*, *Le chevalier d'Harmental* (1896), *Les p'tites Michu* (1897), *Véronique* (1898), *Les dragons de l'impératrice* (1905), *Fortunio*, *Béatrice* (1914), *Monsieur Beaucaire* (in English, 1919), *La petite fonctionnaire* (1921), *L'amour masqué*, *Passionnement* (1926), *Coup de roulis*.

OTHER ballets *Les deux pigeons* (1886), *Scaramouche* (1891), *Le chevalier aux fleurs* (1897), *Une aventure de la Guimard* (1900) and others; instrumental pieces; piano duets; songs.

Messe solennelle see → **Missa solemnis**.

Messiaen, Olivier Eugène Prosper Charles (1908–1992) French composer, organist, and teacher. His music is mystical in character, vividly coloured, and incorporates transcriptions of birdsong. Among his works are the *Quartet for the End of Time* (1941), the large-scale *Turangalîla Symphony* (1949), and solo organ and piano pieces. As a teacher at the Paris Conservatoire from 1942, he influenced three generations of composers.

His theories of melody, harmony, and rhythm, drawing on medieval and oriental music, have inspired contemporary composers such as Boulez and Stockhausen.

He was born in Avignon, and spent most of his life in Paris, where he was appointed organist at La Trinité church in 1931. He was a devout Christian.

Messiah oratorio by George → **Handel** (words selected from the Bible by Charles Jennens), performed at the Music Hall in Fishamble Street, Dublin, on 13 April 1742; the first performance in England was at Covent Garden, London, on 23 March 1743. It includes the famous 'Hallelujah Chorus'. The title of the work is simply *Messiah*, not *The Messiah*, as it is frequently called.

Messidor opera by Bruneau (libretto by Emile Zola), produced at the Paris Opéra on 19 February 1897. Bruneau had already written operas on subjects from Zola's works (*L'Attaque du moulin* and *Le Rêve*), but this was the first for which Zola himself wrote the libretto.

mesto (Italian 'mournful, sad') term used in musical notation.

Metamorphosen study in C minor for 23 solo strings by Richard → **Strauss**; composed in 1945 in response to the wartime devastation of Europe, in particular the destruction of the opera houses, in which his works were performed throughout World War II. It was dedicated to Paul Sacher and the Collegium Musicum and first performed in Zurich on 25 January 1946.

Metamorphoses after Ovid, Six (*Pan, Phaeton, Niobe, Bacchus, Narcissus, Arethusa.*) Work for solo oboe by Britten; composed in 1951 and first performed at Thorpeness on 14 June 1951.

metamorphosis the transformation of theme or motif, especially rhythmically while the same notes are retained, as for example the *idée fixe* of Berlioz, the themes in Liszt's symphonic poems, or the *Leitmotive* in Wagner's musical dramas.

metaphor aria see ➤ parable aria.

Metastasio (1698–1782), pen-name of **Pietro Armando Dominico Trapassi** Italian poet and librettist. In 1730 he became court poet to Charles VI in Vienna. Acknowledged as the leading librettist of his day, he created 18th-century Italian ➤ opera seria (serious opera). His chief dramatic works are *Didone abbandonata, Catone in Utica, Olimpiade,* and *La clemenza di Tito.* Among the composers who used his work were Scarlatti, Handel, J C Bach, Mozart, and Gluck. He also wrote some beautiful canzonette.

Born in Rome, the son of poor parents, he was adopted by the scholar Giovanni Vincenzo Gravina (1664–1718), from whom he acquired his knowledge of Latin and the classics.

metre in music, refers to the number and value of the beats in a bar of music. It is also known as **time**. Metre is different from rhythm in that it is regular (although the number can change as in the additive metres of African music and the works of Olivier Messiaen), whereas rhythm is irregular.

The metre or time of the music may be: **duple**, two beats to a bar; **triple**, three beats to a bar; **quadruple**, four beats to a bar; or indeed any other number such as eleven in Bulgarian folk music.

Time may also be **simple** or **compound**. In simple time each beat is a whole note (not dotted) that can be divided by two. For example, in 4/4 (simple quadruple time) there are four crotchet beats to a bar and each beat can be divided into two quavers. In compound time each beat is a dotted note that can be divided by three. For example, in 6/8 (compound duple time) there are two dotted crotchet beats to a bar; each beat can be divided into three quavers.

In music, the numerical sign for time is known as a **time signature**. This is always found at the beginning of the music and consists of two numbers shown as a fraction of a **semibreve**. The upper number is the number of beats in a bar and the lower number the type of beat. For example, 2/2 means two minim (half-note) beats to the bar; 3/4 means three crotchet (quarter-note) beats to the bar; and 6/8 means two beats each of three quavers (eighth notes).

metronome clockwork device, invented by Johann Mälzel in 1814, using a sliding weight to regulate the speed of a pendulum to assist in setting tempo, particularly in music. It is now largely superseded by silent digital display devices.

Metropolitan Opera Company foremost opera company in the USA, founded in 1883 in New York City. The Metropolitan Opera House (opened in 1883) was demolished in 1966, and the company moved to the new Metropolitan Opera House at the Lincoln Center.

Meyer, Ernst Hermann (1905–1988) German musicologist and composer. He studied in Berlin and Heidelberg. He lived in London from 1933 to 1948, when he was appointed professor of music sociology at the Humbolt University, Berlin. His books include studies of 17th-century instrumental music and English chamber music from the Middle Ages to Purcell.

Works the opera *Reiter der Nacht* (1973); film and chamber music.

Meyer, Leonard B(unce) (1918–) US theorist and aesthetician. He studied at Columbia University and the University of Chicago, and taught at the University of Chicago (1961) and the University of Pennsylvania (1975). His books include *Emotion and Meaning in Music* (1956) and (with Grosvenor Cooper) *The Rhythmic Structure of Music* (1960).

Meyerbeer, Giacomo (1791–1864), adopted name of **Jakob Liebmann Meyer Beer** German composer. His spectacular operas include *Robert le Diable* (1831) and *Les Huguenots* (1836). From 1826 he lived mainly in Paris, returning to Berlin after 1842 as musical director of the Royal Opera.

His father Herz Beer, a banker, gave him every facility to develop his precocious gifts. He was at first trained as a pianist and had some lessons from Clementi during the latter's stay in Berlin. He played in public at the age of seven, but afterwards studied theory and composition under Carl Zelter, Bernhard Weber, and Georg Vogler, and in 1810 moved to the latter's house at Darmstadt, where he was a fellow student with Carl Maria von Weber. His first opera was produced at Munich in 1812 and the second at Stuttgart in 1813. He then went to Vienna and, hearing Hummel play, he retired for further piano studies, after which he appeared again as a virtuoso.

On Salieri's advice he went to Italy in 1815 to study vocal writing, and produced his first Italian opera at Padua in 1817. In 1823 he tried his luck in Berlin, but without much success, and having produced *Il crociato* at Venice in 1824, went to Paris for its first performance there in 1826. He settled and spent much time there for the rest of his life. He wrote no new work between 1824 and

1831, among the reasons being his father's death, his marriage, and the loss of two children. In 1831 *Robert le Diable* made him sensationally fashionable in Paris. This opera, followed by *Les Huguenots* and *Le Prophète* established Meyerbeer as a master of the French grand opera, with ingredients including strong local colour, a sure sense of history, novel instrumental effects, and extended ballets. In 1842 the King of Prussia appointed him general music director in Berlin. He visited Vienna and London in 1847 and the latter again in 1862, when he represented German music at the Great Exhibition. His health began to fail about 1850, and one of his most evocative operas, *L'Africaine*, was left uncompleted at his death.

Works OPERA *Jephthas Gelübde* (1812), *Alimelek, oder Die beiden Kalifen, Romilda e Costanza* (1817), *Semiramide riconosciuta* (1819), *Emma di Resburgo* (1819), *Margherita d'Anjou* (1820), *L'esule di Granata, Das Brandenburger Tor, Il crociato in Egitto* (1824), *Robert le Diable* (1831), *Les Huguenots* (1836), *Ein Feldlager in Schlesin* (1844), *Le Prophète* (1849), *L'Etoile du Nord* (1854), *Le Pardon de Ploërmel (Dinorah), L'Africaine* (1865), *Judith* (unfinished).

OTHER monodrama *Thevelindens Liebe*; incidental music to Michael Beer's (his brother's) drama *Struensee*, Blaze de Bury's *Jeunesse de Goethe*, and Aeschylus' *Eumenides*; masque *Das Hoffest von Ferrara*; ballet *Der Fischer und das Milchmädchen* (1810); oratorio *Gott und die Natur* (1811); *Stabat Mater*, Te Deum, psalms, and other church music; several cantatas, including two for the Schiller centenary, 1859, seven sacred cantatas (Klopstock) for unaccompanied chorus; March for unaccompanied chorus, three Torch Dances, Coronation March, *Overture in the Form of a March* for the London Exhibition; piano works; songs.

Meyerowitz, Jan (1913–1998) German-born US composer. He studied in Berlin with Zemlinsky and Rome with Respighi. He moved to the USA in 1946, and became a US citizen in 1951.

Works OPERA *The Barrier* (1950), *Eastward in Eden* (1951), *Esther* (1957), *Godfather Death* (1961), *Winterballade* (1967).

ORCHESTRAL *Silesian Symphony* (1957), oboe concerto (1963), six pieces for orchestra (1967).

OTHER Cantatas on texts by Emily Dickinson, Cummings and Herrick; chamber music.

mezzo- or **mezza- (Italian 'half')** in music, term used to indicate medium range or intensity, as in mezzo-soprano, mezzo forte (mf), and so on. The short form 'mezzo' stands for ➤ **mezzo-soprano**.

mezzo forte or **mf (Italian 'medium strong')** in music, notation indicating a volume less loud than ➤ **forte**, but louder than ➤ **mezzo piano**.

mezzo piano or **mp (Italian 'medium soft')** in music, notation indicating a volume louder than ➤ **piano**, but softer than ➤ **mezzo forte**.

mezzo-soprano female singing voice with an approximate range of A4–F5, between contralto and soprano. It is commonly abbreviated to just 'mezzo'.

Janet Baker is a well-known British mezzo-soprano.

mf in music, abbreviation of ➤ **mezzo forte**.

Mi the old name for the note E (➤ **solmization**), still used in Latin countries, and in tonic sol-fa the mediant note in any key, represented by the symbol m, pronounced Me.

Miaskovsky, Nikolai Yakovlevich (1881–1950) Russian composer. His compositions include 27 symphonies and 13 string quartets. Although he was denounced in 1948 with Prokofiev and others for 'formalism', his music is in a tonal, conservative idiom.

He was the son of a Russian military engineer stationed in Poland, whence the family moved successively to Orenburg, Kazan, and Nizhniy-Novgorod, where Miaskovsky joined the cadet corps. Intended to follow his father's career, he did not finally take to music until 1907, when he resigned his commission, though he had composed many piano preludes, studied with Glière and Krizhanovsky. He entered the St Petersburg Conservatory in 1906 where he studied with Rimsky-Korsakov, Liadov, and Wihtol. In 1914–17 he fought on the Austrian front and was badly wounded; in 1921 he became composition professor at the Moscow Conservatory.

Works ORATORIO *Kirov is with us*.

ORCHESTRAL 27 symphonies (1908–50), two sinfoniettas, symphonic poems *Silence* (after Poe) and *Alastor* (after Shelley), serenade and *Lyric Concertino* for small orchestra; violin concerto (1938); cello concertino (1945); *Salutatory Overture* on Stalin's 60th birthday (1939).

CHAMBER 13 string quartets (1913–49); two cello and piano sonatas; nine piano sonatas.

OTHER piano pieces; 13 Op. nos. of songs.

Michael, Tobias (1592–1657) German composer, son of Roger Michael. He studied as a boy chorister under his father in the Dresden court chapel and became music director at Sondershausen in 1619. In 1631 he succeeded Schein as cantor of St Thomas's Church at Leipzig.

Works CHORAL *Musikalische Seelenlust* containing sacred madrigals for voices and sacred concertos for voices and instruments (1634–37); other church music.

Mi contra Fa in music, medieval designation of the ➤ **tritone** (the forbidden interval of the augmented fourth), the Mi being the mediant of the hard ➤ **hexachord** beginning on G.

microphone receiver which turns sound into electrical signals. The signals, transmitted and amplified, can also be used for radio, television, or recording purposes, or in theatres and public halls for the relaying of speech, song, and taped sound to amplifiers placed at various points of the building.

microtone in music, any precisely determined division of the octave smaller than a semitone.

Examples of quarter-tone divisions are heard in the violin solo parts of Béla Bartók's *Violin Concerto No 2* (1937–38), Alban Berg's *Chamber Concerto* (1923–25), and Pierre Boulez's cantata *Le Visage nuptial/The Bridal Countenance* (1946 rev. 1950–51). The Czech composer Alois ➤ **Hába** and Mexican Julián ➤ **Carrillo** composed in smaller divisions, and since 1984 Karlheinz ➤ **Stockhausen** has developed notations of up to 16ths of a tone for basset horn and flute, for example in *Xi* (1986) for basset horn.

Normally microtones belong in the domain of expressive pitch variation in acoustic music, being difficult to notate and perform precisely because most instruments other than the voice or violin family are designed to produce tempered pitches, or have fixed frets or keys. When played against a ➤ **drone**, however, they become more clearly quantifiable as audible ➤ **beat frequencies**. Conversely, electronic music is virtually unlimited in the extent and precision to which it can break down the octave.

middle C white note, C4, at the centre of the piano keyboard, indicating the division between left- and right-hand regions and between the treble and bass staves of printed music. Middle C is also the pitch indicated by a C clef, for example, for viola.

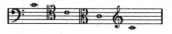

Middle C in bass, tenor, alto, and treble clefs.

middleground see ➤ **structural level.**

MIDI, acronym for Musical Instrument Digital Interface manufacturers' standard allowing different pieces of digital music equipment used in composing and recording to be freely connected.

The information-sending device (any electronic instrument) is called a controller, and the reading device (such as a computer) the sequencer. Pitch, dynamics, decay rate, and stereo position can all be transmitted via the interface. A computer with a MIDI interface can input and store the sounds produced by the connected instruments, and can then manipulate these sounds in many different ways. For example, a single keystroke may change the key of an entire composition. Even a full written score for the composition may be automatically produced, with software capable of producing this in 'real time', as the instrument is played.

Midsummer Marriage, The opera by Tippett (libretto by composer), produced at Covent Garden, London, on 27 January 1955. Spiritually-minded Mark and Jenifer are matched by more down-to-earth Jack and Bella in magical initiation ceremonies.

Midsummer Night's Dream, A incidental music by Mendelssohn to Shakespeare's play. Overture composed in the summer of 1826 first performed in Stettin in February 1827; the rest of the music was composed in 1842 and used for a stage production at Potsdam on 14 October 1843.

Opera by Britten (libretto from Shakespeare), produced at the Jubilee Hall, Aldeburgh, on 11 June 1960. Lovers, fairies, and rustics intermingle in an enchanted forest.

'Mighty Five' or **Mighty Handful** Russian group of composers; see The ➤ **Five.**

Mignon opera by Ambroise Thomas (libretto by J Barbier and Michel Carré, based on Goethe's *Wilhelm Meister*), produced at the Opéra-Comique, Paris, on 17 November 1866. Gypsy girl Mignon falls for Wilhelm Meister, who seems more interested in the actress Philine. After later nursing Mignon, who is injured in a fire, Wilhelm affirms his love. Mignon turns out to be the long-lost Spirata, daughter of the Lord in whose house she recuperates.

Mignone, Francisco (1897–1986) Brazilian composer. He studied at São Paulo Conservatory and later in Milan, and in 1929 became professor at the National Conservatory in Rio de Janeiro.

Works STAGE the operas *O contratador dos diamantes* (1924), *El jayon/L'innocente* (1927); ballet *Maracatú de Chico-Rei* (1933).

OTHER clarinet and bassoon concertos; orchestral music; songs, and other pieces.

Migot, Georges (Elbert) (1891–1976) French composer. He studied with various masters, including Widor, and made a speciality of medieval music. In 1917 he made himself known in Paris by giving a concert of his own, and, holding no official post, he relied on his own efforts to keep before the public.

Works STAGE the opera *Le Rossignol en amour* (1926); ballets *La Fête de la bergère* (1924), *Le Paravent de laque*, *Les Aveux et les promesses*.

VOCAL Psalm 19 for chorus and orchestra, *The Sermon on the Mount* for solo voices, chorus, organ and strings.

OTHER 13 symphonies (1919–67), *Les Agrestides*, *Trois Guirlandes sonores* for strings; *La Jungle* for organ and orchestra; *Le Livre des danseries* for violin, flute and piano and other chamber music; songs.

Mihalovici, Marcel (1898–1985) Romanian composer. He studied with d'Indy in Paris and joined a group of advanced French and Russian composers there after World War I. He was married to the pianist Monique ➤ Haas.

Works BALLET *Karagueuz* (1926), *Divertissement*, and others.

ORCHESTRAL *Cortège des divinités infernales* (from the opera), *Introduction au mouvement*, *Notturno* and fantasy for orchestra.

CHAMBER three string quartets (1923, 1931, 1946); string trio; violin and piano sonata, sonatina for oboe and piano.

OTHER *L'Intransigeant Pluton* (1928).

Mikado, The or **The Town of Titipu** operetta by Sullivan (libretto by W S Gilbert), first produced in London, at the Savoy Theatre on 14 March 1885. Nanki-Poo loves Yum-Yum, against the Mikado's wishes. However, she must marry Ko-Ko, the Lord High Executioner. The lovers marry and escape decapitation.

Mikołaj z Krakowa (lived 16th century) Polish organist and composer; see ➤ Nicolaus de Cracovia.

Mikrokosmos, Microcosm a set of 153 small piano pieces by Bartók, arranged in progressive order of technical difficulty and published in six volumes, setting the player various problems of modern technique, each piece being written on a particular principle or system (special rhythms, time-signatures, chords, intervals, atonal or bitonal combinations), composed 1926–37 and published in 1940.

Milán, Luis (c.1500–after 1561) Spanish vihuelist and composer. His works were all published in *El Maestro* (1536), the earliest surviving vihuela collection. They include fantasies and pavans for vihuela, Spanish and Portuguese *villancicos*, Spanish ballads, and Italian sonnets for voice and vihuela. He was one of the first composers to write tempo indications.

He was the son of a nobleman, Don Luis de Milán. He visited Italy and Portugal.

Milanese Chant see ➤ Ambrosian Chant.

Milford, Robin (Humphrey) (1903–1959) English composer. He was educated at Rugby and studied music at the Royal College of Music, where his masters were Holst, Vaughan Williams, and R O Morris.

Works ORATORIO *A Prophet in the Land*.

VOCAL cantata *Wind*, *Rain and Sunshine*, *Bemerton Cantatas*, *Five Songs of Escape* for unaccompanied chorus.

ORCHESTRAL symphony, concerto grosso, double fugue; violin concerto, *The Dark Thrush* (on Hardy's poem) for violin and small orchestra.

VOCAL AND KEYBOARD *Two Easter Meditations* for organ; piano works; songs; part songs.

Milhaud, Darius (1892–1974) French composer and pianist. A member of the group of composers known as ➤ Les Six, he was extremely prolific in a variety of styles and genres, influenced by jazz, the rhythms of Latin America, and electronic composition. He is noted for his use of ➤ polytonality (the simultaneous existence of two or more keys), as in the *Saudades do Brasil* (1921) for orchestra and *L'homme et son désir* (1918). A pastoral element also runs through many of his works, as in his first string quartet (1912) and six chamber symphonies (1917–22). His Jewish ancestry is evident in the cantata *Ani maamiu* written for the Festival of Israel (1973). Other works include the operas *Christophe Colombe/ Christopher Columbus* (1928) and *Bolívar* (1943), and the jazz ballet *La création du monde* (1923).

He studied violin and composition at the Paris Conservatory from 1909, under Gédalge, Widor, and d'Indy. His teachers also included Dukas. He was attaché to the French Legation at Rio de Janeiro 1917–19, and there he met Paul Claudel, who collaborated frequently with him as a librettist. In 1922 he was represented for the first time at the festival of the International Society for Contemporary Music. In 1940 he went to the USA as professor of music at Mills College, California, and in 1947 became professor of composition at the National Conservatory in Paris.

Works STAGE operas include *Christophe Colomb* (1930); ballets *L'homme et son désir* (1918), *Le bœuf sur le toit* (1919), *La création du monde* (1923); incidental music for *Oreste* translated from Aeschylus (*Agamemnon*, *Les Choëphores*, and *Les Euménides*, 1917–22).

ORCHESTRAL works include twelve symphonies for large orchestra (1940–62), *Suite provençale* (1937), *Saudades do Brazil*; *Ballade*, *Le carnaval d'Aix* (1926), *Concertino de printemps* for violin and orchestra (1934).

CHAMBER 18 string quartets (1912–62), wind quintet *La cheminée du Roi René* (1939); sonatas and sonatinas for many instruments; six piano works including *Printemps* (two volumes), *Saudades do Brazil* (two volumes, 1920–21); suite *Scaramouche* (1939) for two pianos.

SOLO VOCAL AND CHORAL 14 books of songs including *Poèmes juifs*, *Catalogue des fleurs* for voice and chamber orchestra (1920); *Liturgie Comtadine* (1933), *Service Sacré* (1947).

military band musical band attached to military regiments and used by them for their ceremonial occasions, but also often engaged to play for the entertainment of the general public, for example in parks, or at the seaside. It generally includes woodwind, brass, and percussion.

'Military' Symphony Haydn's symphony no. 100 in G major (no. 8 of the 'Salomon' symphonies), composed for London in 1794; so called because of the trumpet call and percussion effects found in the second movement.

Millico, Giuseppe (1737–1802) Italian castrato soprano and composer. He was discovered by Gluck, in whose *Le feste d'Apollo* he sang at Parma in 1769. Engaged by the imperial opera in Vienna, he sang the following year in the first performance of Gluck's *Paride ed Elena*. He later visited London, Paris, and Berlin, and from 1780 lived in Naples.

Works OPERA *La pietà d'amore* (published 1782), *La Zelinda, Ipermestra, Le Cinesi* (1780); cantata *Angelica e Medoro* (with Cimarosa).

Millöcker, Karl (1842–1899) Austrian composer and conductor. After studying at the Vienna Conservatory, he became a conductor at Graz in 1864 and at the Harmonietheater in Vienna in 1866. In 1869 he was appointed conductor at the Theater an der Wien in Vienna, and produced operettas for it.

Works OPERATTAS *Der tote Gast* (1865), *Die beiden Binder, Diana* (1867), *Die Fraueninsel, Ein Abenteuer in Wien* (1873), *Das verwunschene Schloss* (1878), *Gräfin Dubarry* (1879), *Apajune der Wassermann, Der Bettelstudent* (1882), *Der Feldprediger* (1884), *Der Vice-Admiral, Die sieben Schwaben* (1887), *Der arme Jonathan* (1890), *Das Sonntagskind* (1892), *Gasparone*, and many others.

OTHER numerous piano pieces.

Mills, Charles (1914–1982) US composer. He studied with a six-year scholarship under Copland, Sessions, and Roy Harris, two years with each, and later devoted himself entirely to composition.

Works music for solo dance *John Brown*.

ORCHESTRAL five symphonies (1940–80), slow movement for string orchestra; concertino for flute and orchestra, prelude for flute and strings.

VOCAL Festival Overture for chorus and orchestra; *Ars poetica* for unaccompanied chorus (1940).

CHAMBER chamber symphony for eleven instruments (1939), chamber concerto for ten instruments, chamber concertino for woodwind quintet, five string quartets (1939–59), piano trio in D minor, sonatas for cello, violin, and piano.

Milner, Anthony (1925–2002) English composer. He taught at Morley College, London, 1947–62, and was then appointed to the Royal College of Music. He was appointed lecturer at King's College, London, in 1965 and Senior Lec-

turer at Goldsmiths College in 1971. He became principal lecturer at Goldsmiths College in 1974 and at the Royal College of Music in 1980.

He studied piano with Herbert Fryer (1877–1957) and composition with R O Morris and later with Mátyás Seiber.

Works ORCHESTRAL three symphonies (1972, 1978, 1986), *Sinfonia Pasquale* for string orchestra, *April Prologue* for orchestra; chamber symphony (1968), concerto for symphonic wind band (1979), concerto for strings (1982); *The Song of Akhenaten* for soprano and chamber orchestra (1954).

CHURCH MUSIC canatas *Salutatio Angelica* (1948), *The City of Desolation* (1955), *St Francis, The Water and the Fire* (1961), *Emmanuel Cantata* (1975); Mass for *a cappella* chorus (1951).

CHAMBER string quartet (1975), oboe quartet, wind quintet; songs; piano sonata (1989).

Milton opera by Spontini (libretto by V J E de Jouy and M Dieulafoy), produced at the Opéra-Comique, Paris, on 27 November 1804. A second Milton was planned by Spontini in 1838, when he visited England in the summer to study the environment. It was to be entitled *Miltons Tod und Busse für den Königsmord/Milton's Death and Expiation for the King's Murder* (libretto by E Raupach), but turned into *Das verlorene Paradies/Paradise Lost*; it remained unfinished.

Milton, John (c.1563–1647) English composer, father of John Milton the poet. He is said to have received a gold medal from a Polish prince for an In Nomine in 40 parts.

He was educated at Christ Church, Oxford. After being cast out by his father as a Protestant, he went to London, and in 1600 became a member of the Scriveners' Company, marrying Sarah Jeffrey about that time. Having made a fair fortune as a scribe, he retired to Horton in Buckinghamshire in 1632, but after his wife's death moved to Reading about 1640. In 1643 he returned to London, where he lived with his son John.

Works VOCAL various sacred pieces for several voices; madrigal contribution to *The Triumphes of Oriana*, four vocal pieces contributed to Leighton's *Teares or Lamentacions*; two tunes for Ravenscroft's Psalter; five fancies for viols.

Mines of Sulphur, The opera by Richard Rodney Bennett (libretto by Beverley Cross), produced at the Sadler's Wells Theatre, London, on 24 February 1965, conducted by Colin Davis. Plague-carrying actors punish Boconnion, deserter and murderer.

minim, US **half note** in music, a note value, half the duration of a ➤ semibreve. It is written as an empty white note-head with a stem. It is the basic unit of beat for the following metres: 2/2, 4/2, and cut time (➤ alla breve).

minimalism movement in abstract art and music towards extremely simplified composition. Minimal art developed in the USA in the 1950s in reaction to abstract expressionism, rejecting its emotive approach in favour of impersonality and elemental, usually geometric, shapes. It has found its fullest expression in sculpture, notably in the work of Carl Andre, who employs industrial materials in modular compositions. In music, from the 1960s and 1970s, it manifested itself in large-scale statements, usually tonal or even diatonic, and highly repetitive, based on a few 'minimal' musical ideas. Major minimalist composers are Steve ➤ **Reich** and Philip ➤ **Glass**.

Minimalism inspired a wealth of writing on art theory, in particular popular aesthetics, and extended its influence into poetry and dance.

Minimalism was the first significant art movement to have been established entirely by US-born artists. The term developed from a comment by US art critic Barbara Rose, who described the artworks as being pared down to the 'minimum'.

Minimalist art removes all representational imagery or similarity to the subject, and works on the belief that art should be like mathematics – rational, simple, and clear – not complicated by personal, social, moral, and philosophical values. Artworks are, therefore, without metaphor, imagery, or meaning. Paintings are often geometric in style, featuring grid systems and single, unified images. Evidence of an artist's personal touch, such as brushstrokes, is also removed in an attempt to make art that bridges the gap between a work of inspiration and an everyday object.

Despite its apparent restrictions, minimal art varies greatly in style from the monochrome (one-colour) paintings of Agnes Martin, to Carl Andre's horizontal structures of stacked beams. Minimalism has also set new goals in art, particularly in sculpture, by attempting to remove the spatial illusions that give artworks space, depth, or perspective.

Leading minimalist artists include Carl Andre, Dan Flavin, Donald Judd, Sol LeWitt, Richard Serra, and Frank Stella.

Minnesinger (German 'love-singer') any of a group of 12th- to 14th-century German lyric poets and musicians. They represent a continuation of the French ➤ **troubadour** tradition, their songs dealing mainly with the theme of courtly love, but their musical and literary styles diverged. Many were of noble birth, unlike the later ➤ **Meistersingers** (German 'master singers') who were from the middle classes. Dietmar von Aist, Friedrich von Hausen, Heinrich von Morungen, Reinmar, and Walther von der Vogelweide were well-known Minnesingers.

minor one of the two predominant scales (the other being major) of the tonal system. There are three forms of the minor scale: the ➤ **harmonic minor**, the ➤ **melodic minor**, and the less commonly used natural minor.

minore (Italian 'minor') in music, a word often used as a warning to a performer in the course of a composition which is predominantly in a major key.

minor intervals in music, ➤ **seconds**, ➤ **thirds**, ➤ **sixths**, and ➤ **sevenths** which are a semitone smaller than the corresponding major intervals.

Minor and major seconds and sevenths.

Minotaur, The ballet in one act by Elliott Carter; composed in 1947 and produced in New York on 26 March 1947.

minstrel professional entertainer of any kind, but particularly a musician, in the 12th–17th centuries. Most common in the Middle Ages, minstrels were usually in the service of a court or of a member of the aristocracy. In the 19th century, a minstrel was one of a group of white entertainers popular in the USA who painted their faces black and impersonated a stereotype of the music and humour of workers from the Southern plantations.

minuet French country dance in three time adapted as a European courtly dance of the 17th century. The music was later used as the third movement of a classical four-movement symphony where its gentle rhythm provides a foil to the slow second movement and fast final movement.

minuetto the correct Italian name for the ➤ **minuet** (not 'menuetto').

'Minute' Waltz the nickname sometimes given to Chopin's Waltz in D flat major, Op. 64 no. 1.

'Miracle, The' nickname of Joseph Haydn's symphony no. 96, in D major (no. 4 of the 'Salomon' symphonies), written for London in 1791. The name is due to the story that a chandelier fell from the ceiling at the first performance, when the audience miraculously escaped injury; but in fact the accident occurred at the first performance of symphony no. 102 in B flat major (1794–95).

Miracle in the Gorbals ballet by Bliss (scenario by M Benthall, choreography by Robert Helpmann), produced in London at the Prince's Theatre on 26 October 1944.

Miracles of our Lady cycle of four one-act operas by Martinů: *The Wise and Foolish Virgins* (libretto by V Nezval after 12th-century French text); *Little Mariken of Nijmegen* (libretto by H Gheon after 15th-century Flemish legend); *The Nativity* (libretto by composer after Moravian folk texts); *The Legend of Sister Pasqualina* (libretto by composer after poem by J Zeyer and folk texts). Composed 1933–34, first performed in Brno, Czechoslovakia, on 23 February 1935.

Miraculous Mandarin, The, Hungarian **A csodálatos mandarin** ballet in one act by Béla ➤ **Bartók** (scenario by M Lengyel), 1918–19, produced in Cologne on 27 November 1926. The Mandarin of the title is mugged by a prostitute and her gang, but he cannot die until he is sexually united with the woman who has attempted to murder him.

An orchestral suite derived from the music was performed in Budapest on 15 October 1928, conducted by Ernst von Dohnányi.

Mireille opera by Gounod (libretto by Michel Carré, based on the poem 'Mirèio' by F Mistral), produced at the Théâtre Lyrique, Paris, on 19 March 1864. Vincent and Mireille love each other, but they are opposed by her father, who favours the advances of bull-tamer Ourrais. Ourrais injures Vincent and is drowned by water spirits. Mireille undertakes a pilgrimage to see Vincent and dies of exhaustion in his arms.

mirliton toy musical instrument similar to the eunuch flute, also known as ➤ **kazoo** in England.

Miroirs set of five piano pieces by Ravel; composed in 1905, and first performed in Paris on 6 January 1906: *Noctuelles*, *Oiseaux tristes*, *Une barque sur l'océan* (orchestral version, first performed Paris, 3 February 1907), *Alborada del gracioso* (orchestral version first performed in Paris on 17 May 1919), *La Vallée des Cloches*.

mirror canon or **mirror fugue** a ➤ canon or ➤ fugue in which two or more voices are inverted so that the intervals appear simultaneously upside down as well as right side up, looking on paper like a mirror image of each other.

Miserere (from Latin Miserere mei, Deus, 'Have mercy on me, Lord') in music, title of a work using the text of Psalm 51, *Miserere mei, Deus* ... (Latin 'have mercy upon me, O God ...'). It is sung (often in ➤ plainsong) during the Roman Catholic office (or non-Eucharistic service) of Lauds, at sunrise, during the week preceding Easter Sunday. Simple polyphonic settings of the text have been made by early composers such as Josquin Des Prez and Gregorio Allegri (the work of the latter is famous for its embellishments and popular with modern audiences). Later composers have set *Misereres*, including Giuseppe Verdi in the opera *Il trovatore* (1852).

Miserly Knight, The, Russian **Skupoy ritsar'** opera in three scenes by Rachmaninov (libretto by the composer, after Pushkin, 1903–05), produced at the Bolshoi, Moscow, on 24 January 1906. A poor son and his penny-pinching father have money problems.

Missa Latin term for ➤ Mass.

Missa parodia (Latin 'parody Mass') term arising from a mistaken conjunction of the words *Missa* and *parodia* which occur separately on the title-page of a Mass by the 16th-century composer Jacques Paix. His Mass is described as 'Parodia mottetae Domine da nobis auxilium', that is, it is based on material from the motet cited. Neither in this work nor in any other are the words *Missa* and *parodia* joined together. Many 15th- and 16th-century Mass cycles were based on material from a motet or polyphonic song, usually named in the title.

Missa pro defunctis (Latin 'Mass for the dead') see ➤ requiem.

Missa solemnis or **Missa solennis (Latin 'solemn Mass')** title sometimes used by composers for a Mass of a particularly festive or elaborate kind, such as Beethoven's Op. 123. Schubert also used it, and it occurs in French as *Messe solennelle* (Gounod). The title is now used particularly for Beethoven's work, composed 1818–23; first performed in St Petersburg on 7 April 1824. Three sections were given in Vienna on 7 May 1824, in the concert with the first performance of the Choral Symphony.

Miss Julie opera by Ned Rorem (libretto by K Elmslie after Strindberg), produced in New York on 5 November 1965. The daughter of the house seduces a servant.

Opera by William Alwyn (libretto by the composer, after Strindberg); composed 1961–76, first performed by the BBC on 16 July 1977.

misura (Italian 'measure, time') musical term; thus *senza misura*, 'without time, not strictly in time'. Also the Italian term for 'bar'.

Mitridate Eupatore, Il, **Mithridates Eupator** opera by Alessandro Scarlatti (libretto by G F Roberti), produced in Venice at the Teatro San Giovanni Grisostomo, Carnival in 1707. Mitridate gains revenge after his mother, Stratonica, murders his father, Pontos.

Mitridate, Rè di Ponto, Mithridates, King of Pontus opera by Mozart (libretto by V A Cigna-Santi, based on a tragedy by Racine), produced at the Teatro Regio Ducal, Milan, on 26 December 1770. Brothers Sifare and Farnace love Aspasia, the fiancée of Mithridates. Mithridates is reported killed in battle, but returns and learns of the infidelity. Mortally wounded, however, he gives his blessing to Sifare's and Aspasia's union.

mixer in sound recording, equipment that allows an engineer to set a different volume level for each individual sound track so that solos can be highlighted and loud instruments can be kept from dominating softer ones. Multimedia systems that allow recording generally include similar, though not as sophisticated, functions through software. This is useful in applications such as adding background music to a scene where two people are talking and it is important to hear the voices clearly over the music.

Mixolydian mode in music, one of the ➔ church modes, the mode or scale G to F centred around and beginning on G, that uses only notes of the C major scale. It was originally a scale of ancient Greece equivalent to the white notes of a piano from B to A.

mixture in music, an organ stop, controlling at least two rows of very high-pitched pipes. It is not used alone, but in conjunction with lower-pitched pipes in order to enrich the tone quality of a pre-existing combination of stops.

Mlada opera-ballet commissioned from Borodin, Cui, Mussorgsky, and Rimsky-Korsakov by the Russian Imperial Theatres in 1782, but never completed (libretto by V A Krilov).

Opera by Rimsky-Korsakov (libretto as above), produced in St Petersburg on 1 November 1892. Voyslava has poisoned rival Mlada, the bride of Prince Yaromir. Using magic to try to seduce him, Voyslava is foiled by Mlada's ghost. Yaromir dreams of the murder and kills Voyslava, before joining Mlada's heavenly spirit.

Mládí, Youth suite for wind sextet in four movements by Janáček, first performed in Brno on 21 October 1924, by professors of the Brno Conservatory.

mobile in music, a piece consisting of sections, the order of which may be varied at will or according to rules of association, so named after the example of Alexander Calder's mobile sculpture. Examples include Henri Pousseur's *Mobile* for two pianos (1956–58), and *Mobile for Shakespeare* (1959) by Roman Haubenstock-Ramati. See also ➔ aleatory music.

mock trumpet early English name for the ➔ clarinet, a musical instrument.

modal notation a form of notation in use for vocal music in the 12th and early 13th centuries, where the rhythm was determined not by the shapes of individual notes but by the various types of ➔ ligature in which they were combined according to one or other of the ➔ rhythmic modes.

mode in music, an ancient or exotic scale of five or more pitches to the octave, often identified with a particular emotion, ritual function, time, or season, to which music is composed or improvised.

mode of limited transposition system of ➔ modes developed by Olivier ➔ Messiaen. These modes may be transposed only a limited number of times, after which the original notes reappear. The modes are fundamental to Messiaen's harmonic language.

moderato (Italian 'moderate') in musical notation, term indicating a tempo between ➔ andante (walking pace) and ➔ allegro (lively).

modulation in music, movement from one ➔ key to another. In classical dance music, modulation is a guide to phrasing rhythm to the step pattern.

Electronic modulation of live or prerecorded instrumental sound is also used to create unusual timbres, as in ➔ Stockhausen's *Mixtur* (1964–67) for instrumental groups and ring modulation.

Moeran, E(rnest) J(ohn) (1894–1950) English composer. His music belongs to the English pastoral tradition, Delius being among his major influences. His works include two sets of choral songs with Old English words, two rhapsodies, a symphony and other orchestral works, a violin concerto, a cello concerto for his wife, Peers Coetmore (whom he married in 1945), chamber and piano music, many songs, and arrangements of folk songs.

He was born in Heston, Middlesex, and lived in Norfolk in his childhood, where his father was a clergyman. He was educated at Uppingham School and later studied music at the Royal College of Music in London. After serving in World War I he continued his studies with John Ireland. In 1923 he came to public notice with a concert of his works given in London, but after some years spent there he retired to Herefordshire.

Works VOCAL *Nocturne* for baritone, chorus, and orchestra (1934), *Songs of Springtime* and suite *Phyllida and Corydon* for unaccompanied chorus (both 1934), *Blue-eyed Spring* for baritone and chorus; song cycle *Ludlow Town* (texts by Housman) for baritone and piano (1920); seven *Poems of James Joyce* for baritone and piano (1929), and other pieces; madrigals, part songs, and folk-song arrangements.

ORCHESTRAL Sinfonietta, two rhapsodies, symphonic impression *In the Mountain Country* for orchestra (1921), two pieces for small orchestra *Whythorne's Shadow* (1931) and *Lonely Waters* (1932), symphony in G minor (1934–37); concertos for piano, violin, and cello (1942–45).

CHAMBER string quartet in A minor, string trio in G major, piano trio in D major, sonata for two violins, violin and piano sonata in E minor.

OTHER Magnificat and Nunc Dimittis, Te Deum and Jubilate, two anthems.

Moeschinger, Albert (1897–1985) Swiss composer. He studied at Bern, Leipzig, and Munich, in the latter place under Courvoisier. In 1927 he settled at Bern as professor, but in 1943 he retired to Saas Fee, Ct Valais, and later to Ascona.

Works ORCHESTRAL five symphonies, including *Symphonie à la gloire de ...* and suite for orchestra, variations on a theme by Purcell for strings and percussion, divertimento for strings, *Fantasia 1944* for chamber orchestra; five piano concertos, violin concerto.

VOCAL the motet *Gottes Pfad*; cantatas *Angelus Silesius*, *Tag unseres Volks*; *Das Posthorn* for male chorus and orchestra; Mass for chorus and organ (1943); part songs and other choral works.

CHAMBER six string quartets, piano quintet, six wind trios.

Moffat, Alfred (1866–1950) Scottish composer and editor. He studied in Berlin, where he worked for a time. He settled in London in the 1890s and edited a large collection of early string music, including many English and French works, also several volumes of Scottish, Welsh, and Irish folk songs.

Moïse, Moses opera by Rossini, French version of *Mosè in Egitto* (libretto by G L Balochi and V J E de Jouy), produced at the Paris Opéra on 26 March 1827. See ➤ *Mosè in Egitto* for plot synopsis.

Moldenhauer, Hans (1906–1987) US musicologist. He studied with Rosbaud in Mainz and was active as a *répétiteur* and conductor in different European cities. In 1939 he went to the USA, where after further studies he became director and then president of the Spokane Conservatory (WA) and lecturer at the University of Washington. Moldenhauer's most important contribution to scholarship was his recovery of a large number of Webern manuscripts and documents, including some previously unknown works, and their publication. Books on Webern include *The Death of Anton Webern, A Drama in Documents* (1961) and *Anton Webern: Chronicle of his Life and Work* (1978). He became blind in 1980.

Molière, Jean-Baptiste Poquelin (1622–1673) French dramatist. Associated works and composers include ➤ *Ariadne auf Náxos* (*Bourgeois Gentilhomme*, Richard Strauss); ➤ *Bourgeois*

gentilhomme, Le (Richard Strauss); Marc-Antoine ➤ **Charpentier** (*Comtesse d'Escarbagnas* and *Malade imaginaire*); ➤ **Fêtes de l'Amour et de Bacchus, Les** (Lully); ➤ **Galuppi** (*Vertuouse ridicole*); ➤ **Grétry** (*Amphitryon*); Rolf Liebermann (1910–99) (*School for Wives*); ➤ **Lully** (*Mariage forcé*; *Amour médicin, Princesse d'Elide, Sicilien, George Dandin, M de Pourceaugnac, Amants magnifiques* and *Bourgeois Gentilhomme*); ➤ **Médecin malgré lui, Le** (Gounod); Virgilio Mortari (*Scuola delle mogli*); Henry ➤ **Purcell** (*Female Virtuosos*); J B Quinault (*Bourgeois Gentilhomme* and *Princesse d'Elide*); Erwin ➤ **Schulhoff** (*Bourgeois Gentilhomme*); ➤ **Shaporin** (*Tartuffe*); ➤ **Franchetti** (*Signor di Pourceaugnac*); ➤ **Szymanowski** (*Bourgeois Gentilhomme*); Rudolf Wagner-Régeny (*Sganarelle*); Ermanno ➤ **Wolf-Ferrari** (*Amor medico*).

moll (German 'soft') in music, German equivalent to 'minor' when referring to ➤ key, as in 'B *moll*' (B minor).

It is the opposite of *dur* ('hard','major').

Molter, Johann Melchoir (1696–1765) German composer. He is known today for having written 170 symphonies (strictly, sinfonias). He also wrote 66 concertos, including six for clarinet, and a Passion.

He was Kapellmeister at the court at Karlsruhe, where he was responsible for opera production 1722–33. After a time as director of church music at Eisenach 1734–41 he returned to Karlsruhe. He made several visits to Italy.

molto (Italian 'much','very') term used in musical notation, as in *allegro molto*, 'very quickly'.

Moments musicals the title, which in correct French should be *Moments musicaux*, of Schubert's six piano pieces Op. 94, written 1823–28.

Mompou, Federico (1893–1987) Spanish pianist and composer. He studied at the Barcelona Conservatory and later in Paris, where Isidore Philipp (1863–1958) was his piano master and Marcel Samuel-Rousseau (1882–1955) taught him composition. He lived at Barcelona again 1914–21, then settled in Paris, returning to Barcelona in 1941.

Works PIANO 6 *Impresiones intimas* (1911–14), *Scènes d'enfants* (1915–18), *Suburqis*, three *Pessebres* (1914–17), *Canço i dansa, Cants magics, Fêtes lointaines, Six Charmes* (1920–21), *Dialogues, Three Variations* (1921), *Dix Préludes* (1927–51).

SONGS 'L'hora grisa', 'Cançoneta incerta', 'Quatre Mélodies', 'Le Nuage', 'Trois Comptines'.

Mond, Der, The Moon opera by Orff (libretto by composer after Grimm), produced in Munich on 5 February 1939. Four boys steal the moon and hang it on a lamp. When they grow old and die, its light wakes the dead, before the moon is returned to the sky.

Mondo alla roversa, Il, o sia Le donne che comandano, The World Upside Down, or Women in Command opera by Galuppi (libretto by Goldoni), produced at the Teatro San Cassiano, Venice, on 14 November 1750.

Mondo della luna, Il, The World of the Moon opera by Galuppi (libretto by Goldoni), produced at the Teatro San Moisè, Venice, on 29 January 1750.

Opera by Haydn (libretto as above), produced at Eszterháza on 3 August 1777. Old Bonafede refuses to allow the marriage of his daughters Clarice and Flaminia to Ecclitico and Ernesto, but is duped into consent in his moonscape garden.

Mondonville, Jean Joseph (Cassanea) de (1711–1772) French violinist and composer. During the *Guerre des Bouffons* in 1752 he was chosen as the representative of the French National school, opposing the Italians under the patronage of Mme de Pompadour.

His parents were aristocrats in reduced circumstances, but he succeeded in studying the violin. He settled in Paris in 1733, made his name as a violinist and composer, and appeared at the Concert Spirituel in 1737, for which he wrote motets until 1770. In 1744 he became superintendent of the royal chapel and was director of the Concert Spirituel 1755–62.

Works OPERA AND OPERA-BALLET *Isbé* (1742), *Le Carnaval du Parnasse* (1749), *Titon et l'Aurore* (1753), *Daphnis et Alcimaduro* (in Provençal, 1754), *Les Fêtes de Paphos* (1758), *Thésée, Psyché* (1762), *Erigone, Vénus et Adonis, Les Projets de l'Amour*.

ORATORIOS *Les Israélites au Mont Oreb* (1758), *Les Fureurs de Saül* (1758), *Les Titans*.

OTHER the *Privilège du Roi* set as a cantata; trio sonatas for two violins or flutes and bass; sonatas including *Les Sons harmoniques* for violin and bass; sonatas and pieces for harpsichord with violin or voice; harpsichord works including *Pièces de clavecin en sonates*; organ pieces.

Moniuszko, Stanisław (1819–1872) Polish composer. He founded a national Polish school of opera in many respects comparable to that of Glinka in Russia. The opera *Halka* (1848) became his most famous, in fact the classic Polish folk opera.

After studying at home, he went to Berlin 1837–39 as a pupil of Carl Rungenhagen. On his return he became an organist at Wilno, where he taught, conducted, and produced a one-act operetta in 1839. After several more works that remained unperformed he produced *The Lottery* at Warsaw in 1846. He produced *Halka* there in 1848 (a revised version was produced in 1858). In 1858 he became conductor at the Warsaw Opera

and later professor at the Conservatory. Moniuszko also wrote six Masses, a Requiem, secular choral works, orchestral pieces, two string quartets, and about 400 songs.

Works OPERA *Halka* (performed 1848, revised 1857), *Flis, Hrabina/The Countess* (1860), *Verbum nobile* (1860), *Straszny Dwór/The Haunted Mansion* (1865), *Paria, Beata* (1872).

ORCHESTRAL overture *Bajka* (*Fairy Tale*).

INCIDENTAL MUSIC for Shakespeare's *Hamlet* and *Merry Wives of Windsor* and other plays.

VOCAL cantatas *Spectres, Crimean Sonnets,* and others; seven Masses (1850–74), Litanies and other church music; 270 songs, including ballads by Adam Mickiewicz.

Monk, Meredith (Jane) (1942–) Peruvian-born US composer and singer. She studied at Sarah Lawrence College in Bronxville, New York, and has appeared worldwide from 1978 with her vocal group Appearances. Her compositions are closely related to her work as an avant-garde performance artist. Her opera *Atlas* was given at Houston, Texas, in 1991.

Works ELECTRONIC *A Raw Recital* for voice and electric organ (1970); *Engine Steps* for tape collage (1983); *Book of Days* for 25 voices, synthesizer, and piano (1985).

OTHER *Quarry*, opera for 38 voices and ensemble (1976); *Cat Song* for voice (1988); *Waltz* for two pianos (1988).

Monn, Matthias Georg (1717–1750) Austrian composer and organist. His symphony in D major of 1740 is the earliest dated symphony to have four movements with a minuet in third place.

After being a chorister at Klosterneuburg, near Vienna, he was, from about 1738, organist of the Karlskirche in Vienna.

Works ORCHESTRAL 21 symphonies; ten partitas for string orchestra; seven harpsichord concertos, including one arranged by Schoenberg for cello and orchestra (1933).

OTHER six string quartets; keyboard music; church music.

Monna Vanna opera by Février (libretto Maeterlinck's play with alterations), produced at the Paris Opéra on 13 January 1909.

Opera by Rachmaninov (libretto as above); composed (one act) in 1907, and first performed (concert) at Saratoga, New York, on 11 August 1984. Monna Vanna's husband Guido, commander of besieged Pisa, is suspicious of the help given to relieve the town.

monochord (Greek 'one string') in music, an ancient scientific instrument consisting of a single string stretched over a soundbox which is graduated to allow the adjustment of a movable bridge. The monochord is used to demonstrate the existence of ➔ **harmonics**, and the proportional relations of ➔ **intervals**.

monocorde (Italian *monocordo* 'single string') musical direction used in violin music where the composer wishes a passage to be played on one string.

monodrama a musical stage work for a single singer, an opera with a cast of one, as for example Meyerbeer's *Tevelindens Liebe*, Gomis's *Sensibilidad y prudencia*, or Schoenberg's *Erwartung*. See also ➔ *Lélio* (Berlioz).

monody in music, declamation by an accompanied solo voice, used at the turn of the 16th and 17th centuries.

monophonic music in a single melodic part, without harmony, as distinct from homophonic, which is melodic music accompanied by harmony, or polyphonic, which is music in a number of melodic parts moving simultaneously.

monothematic in musical analysis, describing a composition based on a single theme. In the 18th century Haydn experimented with the technique: several finales of his symphonies are composed monothematically. Composers of the 19th century were also interested in the idea, sometimes involving it as a means of creating coherent ➔ **cyclic form**. Schubert's *Fantasia* ('Wanderer') (1822) may be argued to approach monothematicism, as may Liszt's Sonata in B minor for piano 1854, which presents themes derived from possibly a single ➔ **motif**. Some compositions using the ➔ **twelve-tone system** have another type of monothematic construction, in which only one twelve-note row is manipulated in the work.

Monsigny, Pierre-Alexandre (1729–1817) French composer. His first opera was produced in 1759, and his association with Sedaine as librettist soon consolidated his success. After *Félix* (1777), at the height of his fame, he wrote no more. He lost his fortune during the Revolution, but was given an annuity by the Opéra-Comique.

He studied the violin in his youth, but after the death of his father took an official position in Paris in order to support his family. A performance of *La serva padrona* in 1754 re-awakened his musical interests, and he took composition lessons from Pietro Gianotti (died 1765), double-bass player and author.

Works OPERA AND OPÉRAS-COMIQUES *Les Aveux indiscrets* (1759), *Le Maître en droit* (1760), *Le Cadi dupé* (1761), *On ne s'avise jamais de tout*, *Le Roi et le fermier* (1762), *Rose et Colas* (1764), *Aline, reine de Golconde* (1766), *L'Isle sonnante* (after Rabelais), *Le Déserteur* (1769), *Le Faucon* (1771), *La Belle Arsène* (1775), *Félix, ou L'enfant trouvé* (1777), and others.

Montag aus Licht, Monday from 'Light' opera in three acts by Stockhausen (libretto by composer), produced at La Scala, Milan, on 7 May 1988. The inaugural opera of Stockhausen's *Licht* cycle, but the third to be composed, it celebrates 'Eve's Day'; the three acts are titled *Eve's First Birth*, *Eve's Second Birth*, and *Eve's Magic*.

Montagnana, Domenico (c. 1690–1750) Italian violin-maker. Possibly a pupil of Antonio Stradivari, he worked first at Cremona, and set up a workshop in Venice in 1721.

Montague, Stephen (1943–) US composer. He moved to London in 1975 and toured widely with Philip Mead from 1985 in a piano duo. He was co-founder of the Electro-Acoustic Music Association of Great Britain, and his music has been featured at the Warsaw, Paris, and Edinburgh Festivals and at the John Cage Festival, London.

He studied at Florida State and Ohio State Universities, USA.

Works BALLET *Median* (1984) and *The Montague Stomp* (1984).

ORCHESTRAL *At the White Edge of Phrygia* for chamber orchestra (1983), *Prologue* for orchestra (1984), piano concerto (1988).

VOCAL *Varshavjan Spring* for chorus and chamber orchestra (1973–80), *Sotto Voce* for chorus and electronics (1976), *Boom-box Virelai* for four male voices (1993).

OTHER two string quartets (1989, 1992); keyboard music and electronic pieces.

Monte, Philippe de (1521–1603) Flemish composer. He was a prolific polyphonist; about 40 of his Masses, 300 motets, 45 chansons, and over 1,100 madrigals survive. Among his friends were the composers Roland de Lassus and William ➔ **Byrd**. Monte's secular music enjoyed widespread popularity, as the distribution of his publications and manuscripts testifies.

Monte was born in Malines, and went to Italy while still young. He served the Pinelli family in Naples (1542–51) as singer, teacher, and composer. In 1554 he left Naples and went to the Netherlands. He was in England (1554–55) as a member of the choir of Philip II of Spain, when he met William Byrd and his family; by 1558 he had returned to Italy. In 1568 he went to Vienna as Kapellmeister to the Emperor Maximilian II, after whose death in 1576 he followed the next emperor, Rudolf II, to Prague. He served the emperor for the rest of his life, and was made a canon of Cambrai Cathedral, but did not reside there.

Many of his Masses are based on motets by contemporary composers. His madrigal settings follow the text closely (most of the texts are by contemporary pastoral poets such as Guarini);

his later madrigals are simpler in form and increasingly homophonous.

Works VOCAL around 40 Masses, motets; over 30 books of madrigals, including 1,073 secular and 144 spiritual works. His motet *Super Flumina Babylonis* was sent to Byrd in 1583, to which the latter responded with *Quomodo Cantabimus* in 1584.

Montéclair, Michel (Pinolet) de (1667–1737) French composer, theorist, and teacher. He studied music as a chorister at Langres Cathedral; later he sang in other churches, and went to Italy in the service of the Prince de Vaudémont. After 1702 he settled in Paris and played the double bass in the Opéra orchestra from 1707 until his death.

Works OPERA AND OPERA-BALLET *Les Festes de l'été* (1716) and *Jephté* (1732); ballet music for C F Pollaroli's opera *Ascanio*.

OTHER chamber music, cantatas, and sacred music.

Montemezzi, Italo (1875–1952) Italian composer. He learnt the piano as a child, then went to Milan to be trained for engineering, but wished to take up music. He entered the Conservatory with some difficulty, but obtained a diploma there in 1900. After the production of his first opera in 1905 he was able to give all his time to composition. From 1939 to 1949 he was in the USA, after which he returned to Italy.

Works OPERA *Giovanni Gallurese* (1905), *Hellera* (1909), *L'amore dei tre re* (1913), *La Nave* (d'Annunzio, 1918), *La notte di Zoraima* (1931), *La principessa lontana* (after Rostand's *Princesse lointaine*, 1931).

ORCHESTRAL *The Song of Songs* for chorus or orchestra; symphonic poem *Paolo e Virginia* (after Saint-Pierre).

OTHER elegy for cello and piano.

Monteux, Pierre (1875–1964) French conductor. Ravel's *Daphnis and Chloe* and Stravinsky's *The Rite of Spring* were first performed under his direction. He conducted Diaghilev's Ballets Russes 1911–14 and 1917, and the San Francisco Symphony Orchestra 1935–52.

Monteverdi, Claudio Giovanni Antonio (1567–1643) Italian composer. He contributed to the development of the opera with *La favola d'Orfeo/The Legend of Orpheus* (1607) and *L'incoronazione di Poppea/The Coronation of Poppea* (1642). He also wrote madrigals, motets, and sacred music, notably the *Vespers* (1610).

Born in Cremona, he was in the service of the Duke of Mantua about 1591–1612, and was director of music at St Mark's Cathedral, Venice, from 1613. He was the first to use an orchestra and to reveal the dramatic possibilities of the operatic form. His first opera *Orfeo/Orpheus* was produced for the carnival at Mantua in 1607.

Monteverdi was the son of a doctor. He was a chorister at Cremona Cathedral and a pupil of Marcantonio Ingegneri. He then became an organist and viol player and in 1583, aged 16, published sacred madrigals. About 1591 he entered the service of the Duke of Mantua, Vincenzo Gonzaga, as a viol player and singer, and there married the harpist Claudia Cataneo. He was in Gonzaga's retinue in the war against the Turks on the Danube and again in Flanders in 1599. He probably heard Jacopo Peri's *Euridice* at Florence in 1600, and in 1602 was made music master to the court of Mantua. His wife died in 1607 after a long illness, and in the same year Monteverdi finished his first opera, *La favola d'Orfeo/The Legend of Orpheus*. It remains the earliest opera to be regularly performed today. His next opera, *Arianna* (1608), now lost except for the famous 'Lament', made him widely famous. Meanwhile Monteverdi had written his first five books of madrigals, which are also important in the development of this form. In 1610 he dedicated his collection of church music, the *Vespers*, to Pope Paul V. From the opening chorus, based on the Toccata of *Orfeo*, and through to the concluding Magnificat, it can be seen that music is now being written for public performance and not just for private use.

When Francesco Gonzaga succeeded his brother to the dukedom in 1612, he quarrelled with Monteverdi, who left for Cremona to wait for a new appointment. This came from Venice in 1613, where he was was appointed maestro to St Mark's Cathedral, the most coveted church appointment in northern Italy. He remained there until his death, adding church music of great splendour to his previous output. He had by this time written much church music and numerous madrigals. His church music makes very effective use of the architecture of St Mark's, using separate groups of instruments and singers to exploit its antiphonal effects. The nine books of madrigals develop from the small-scale pieces of 1587 to the hugely extended forms in Book 8 of 1638. In 1630 he took holy orders after escaping the plague at Venice. In 1639 the second public opera theatre in Venice, the Teatro dei SS Giovanni e Paolo, was opened with Monteverdi's *Adone*, and *Arianna* was revived the same year when the Teatro di San Moisè was opened in Venice. Two further operas survive from this period: *Il ritorno d'Ulisse in patria* (1641), and his last opera *L'incoronazione di Poppea/The Coronation of Poppea* (1642), widely performed today in an increasing variety of editions. Monteverdi's work in this genre was highly important and influential in establishing opera during this early period. More broadly, Monteverdi was a key figure in providing the drive for change in which secular music and music for the general public became increasingly important.

Works OPERA *Orfeo/Orpheus* (1607), *Arianna* (lost except the 'Lament', 1608), *Il combattimento di Tancredi e Clorinda* (after Tasso, 1624), *Il ritorno d'Ulisse in patria* (1640), *L'incoronazione di Poppea/The Coronation of Poppea* (1642), and about a dozen lost stage works.

BALLET *Ballo delle ingrate* (1608) and *Tirsi e Clori* (1619).

VOCAL Masses, Magnificats, and psalms; *Vespers* (1610), *Sancta Maria* for voice and eight instruments; 40 sacred madrigals; 21 *canzonette* for three voices; nine books of secular madrigals containing 250, including Book VIII, *Madrigali guerrieri e amorosi/Madrigals of love and war*; 26 madrigals published in various collections; 25 *Scherzi musicali* for one to three voices (1607).

Montezuma opera by Roger Sessions (libretto by G A Borgese); composed 1941–63, produced in west Berlin on 19 April 1964.

Montsalvatge (Bassols), Xavier (1912–2002) Catalan composer. He studied with Enrique Morera and Jaime Pahissa at the Barcelona Conservatory, winning the Pedrell Prize in 1936.

Works OPERA AND BALLET the opera *El gato con botas* (1947); four ballets.

ORCHESTRAL *Sinfonia mediterranea* (1949); *Concerto breve* for piano and orchestra (1956), *Poema concertante* for violin and orchestra; orchestral suite *Calidoscopo*.

OTHER string quartet (1952); songs.

Monumentum pro Gesualdo di Venosa ad CD annum three madrigals recomposed in 1960 by Igor Stravinsky for twelve wind instruments and strings to celebrate the 400th anniversary of Gesualdo's birth. First performed in Venice on 27 September 1960. The madrigals are *Asciugate i belli occhi*, *Ma tu, cagion di quella* and *Belta poi che t'assenti*.

mood, Latin **modus** in music, the relationship between the long and the breve in ➤ mensural notation.

Moog, Bob (1934–2005), born **Robert Moog** US engineer who developed the first synthesizers widely used in popular music. Moog is also known for building ➤ theremins, electronic instruments that musicians play by moving their hands between two antennae. In 1978 he founded Big Briar Music in Asheville, North Carolina, changing the name to Moog Music in 2002. See also ➤ Moog synthesizer. In 1996 his company announced a ➤ MIDI interface for theremins.

Moog synthesizer any of a family of inexpensive analogue ➤ synthesizers developed in 1963 by Robert ➤ Moog (1934–2005), incorporating transistorized electronics and voltage control, which brought electronic music synthesis within the reach of composers, performers, and academic institutions. A Moog-designed ➤ theremin featured in the Beach Boys' hit 'Good Vibrations' (1966).

Moonlight Sonata nickname of Beethoven's piano sonata in C sharp minor, Op. 27 no. 2, probably due to a description of the first movement by the critic Johann Rellstab.

Moore, Douglas (Stuart) (1893–1969) US composer. He studied at Yale University and with Horatio Parker, Bloch, d'Indy, Tournemire, and Nadia Boulanger. He served in the US Navy in World War I, was an organist and lecturer at Cleveland 1921–25, and taught at Columbia University in New York 1926–62.

Works STAGE The operas *The Devil and Daniel Webster* (1939), *The Ballad of Baby Doe* (1956), and *Carrie Nation* (1966); operetta *The Headless Horseman* (1936); chamber opera *White Wings* (1935).

VOCAL motet *Dedication* for six voices, *Simon Legree* for male chorus, *Perhaps to dream* for female chorus.

ORCHESTRAL *A Symphony of Autumn*, *Overture on an American Tune*, *Pageant of P T Barnum* (1924), *Moby Dick* (after Herman Melville), *In Memoriam*, symphony in A for orchestra (1945).

CHAMBER string quartet; sonata and *Down East* suite for violin and piano; wind quintet, clarinet quintet.

Moore, Jerrold Northrop (1934–   ) US musicologist. He studied at Yale and was curator of sound recordings there 1961–70. He resided in England from 1970. He became an authority on British composer Edward Elgar, co-editing the *Elgar Complete Edition* and publishing *Elgar: a Life in Photographs* (1974), *Spirit of England: Edward Elgar in his World* (1984), and *Edward Elgar: A Creative Life* (1984). He also edited Elgar's letters.

He also wrote *Sound Revolutions: A Biography of Fred Gaisberg, Founding Father of Commercial Sound Recording* (1999), and – in a departure from his field of musicology – *F. L. Griggs, 1876–1938: The Architecture of Dreams* (2000).

Moore, Thomas (1779–1852) Irish poet. From about 1802 he began to publish songs with words and occasionally music by himself, and between 1807 and 1834 he produced collections of Irish tunes with new words of his own. He also produced, in 1811, an opera *M P, or The Blue Stocking* with music by himself and C E Horn. He wrote the tune as well as the words of 'The Last Rose of Summer', used by Flotow in *Martha*. For works used by composers, see W S ➤ Bennett (*Paradise and the Peri*); Frederic ➤ Clay (*Lalla Rookh*); ➤ Feramors (A Rubinstein); ➤ Paradise

and the Peri (Schumann); ➤ **Spontini** (*Nurmahal and Lalla Rookh*).

Morales, Cristóbal (c.1500–1553) Spanish composer. He wrote many masses and motets which rank him among the finest contrapuntists of his time. Palestrina based a mass on his motet *O Sacrum Convivium.*

He studied at Seville under the cathedral maestro de capilla Fernández de Castilleja. He was maestro de capilla at Avila 1526–30, and some time later went to Rome, where he was ordained a priest and became cantor in the Pontifical Chapel in 1535. In 1545 he was given leave to visit Spain, but did not return, remaining as maestro de capilla at Toledo and Málaga, and serving in the household of the Duke of Arcos at Marchena.

Works CHORAL 21 Masses, 16 Magnificats, 91 motets, Lamentations and other church music; cantatas for the peace conference at Nice (1538) and for Ippolito d'Este; madrigals.

Moran, Robert (1937–) US composer. His music has embraced random choice techniques, minimalism, and multiple synthesizers. His *Smell Piece for Mills College* (1967) was intended to burn down his alma mater and was followed by the chamber opera *Let's Build a Nut House* (1969).

He studied in Vienna, and with Berio and Milhaud at Mills College. He has performed throughout the USA and Europe as a pianist, and has lectured widely. He directed the West Coast Music Ensemble and taught at the San Francisco Conservatory. His environment piece *Hitler: Geschichten aus der Zukunft* (1981) was too much for the Germans who commissioned it, and was promptly banned; the succeeding *Erlöser*, a music drama in two acts, depicts the rantings of a dying Wagner. A collaboration with Philip Glass on the opera *The Juniper Tree* (1985) prompted a conversion to synthesizer-inspired Romanticism: *Desert of Roses* (1992) is based on the *Beauty and the Beast* story, while *From the Towers of the Moon* (1992) is prompted by an ancient Japanese legend. *The Dracula Diary* (1994) suggested a return to anarchism.

Moravia, Hieronymus de (lived 13th century) Music theorist, probably a Dominican friar living in Paris. His *Tractatus de Musica* is a comprehensive compilation dealing mainly with plainsong, with an extensive tonary attached.

mordent in music, a specific type of ➤ ornamentation which consists of the rapid alternation (usually only once) of the written note with the note a semitone or whole-tone below it. It begins on the beat rather than before it.

Mörder, Hoffnung der Frauen, Murderer, the Hope of Women opera in one act by Hindemith

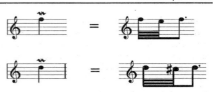

The notation for mordents on D and F, and the approximate execution of each.

(libretto by Oskar Kokoschka); composed 1919, first performed in Stuttgart on 4 June 1921, conducted by Fritz Busch. It tells of a sado-erotic meeting of a Man and a Woman.

Moreau, Jean-Baptiste (1656–1733) French composer. He learnt music as a boy chorister at Angers Cathedral and composed motets as a youth. He was appointed choirmaster at the cathedral of Langres (where he married), and later at Dijon. He went to Paris during the 1680s and found his way into the court, for which he began to write stage pieces. In 1688 he was commissioned to write music for Racine's *Esther* for performance at the young ladies' academy of Saint-Cyr. This earned him a pension for life and an appointment at Saint-Cyr jointly with the organist Nivers and later with Clérambault. He remained under the patronage of the king and Mme de Maintenon. He taught both singing and composition: among his pupils for the former were his daughter Claude-Marie Moreau, and for the latter Clérambault, Dandrieu, and Montéclair.

Works CHURCH MUSIC Requiem, motet *In exitu Israel* (1691), *Cantiques spirituels* (Racine), Te Deum for the king's recovery (1687) and other.

OTHER stage divertissements including *Les Bergers de Marly*; chorus for Racine's *Athalie* (1691); *Idylle sur la naissance de Notre Seigneur*; drinking songs.

morendo (Italian 'dying') in musical notation, becoming softer.

Moresca Moorish dance of remote antiquity, first introduced by the Moors into Spain and popular all over Europe by the 15th–16th centuries. Allied to the English Morris Dance, 'morys' being an English variant of 'Moorish'; at any rate one of the latter's features – bells or jingles tied to the legs – belonged to the Moresca also.

Morhange, Charles Henri Valentin French piano virtuoso and composer; see ➤ **Alkan.**

Mörike, Eduard (1804–1875) German poet and novelist. His *Gedichte* are, for the most part, simple but exquisite lyrics, graceful in style and original in conception. He is at his best in love or nature poems, based on his inner experiences. He also wrote short stories, the best known being *Idylle vom Bodensee* (1846) and *Mozart auf der*

Reise nach Prag (1856), as well as an autobiographical novel *Maler Nolten* (1832).

His works inspired Othmar ➤ **Schoeck** (songs); Heinrich ➤ **Sutermeister** (*Jorinde*); Max ➤ **Trapp** (*Letzte König von Orplid*). Two songs were set by Brahms, three by Schumann, and 57 (including four early) by Wolf.

He was born in Ludwigsburg, studied theology, and from 1834 was a Protestant pastor, retiring 1843. He was appointed professor of literature at the Katharinenstift, Stuttgart, an office he held for 16 years.

Morley, Thomas (c.1557–c.1602) English composer. He wrote consort music, madrigals, and airs including the lute song 'It was a lover and his lass' for Shakespeare's play *As You Like It* (1599). He edited a collection of Italian madrigals *The Triumphs of Oriana* (1601), and published an influential keyboard tutor *A Plaine and Easie Introduction to Practicall Musicke* (1597). He was also organist at St Paul's Cathedral, London.

Morning Heroes symphony for orator, chorus, and orchestra by Arthur Bliss (words by Homer, Li-Tai-Po, Whitman, Robert Nichols and Wilfred Owen), first performed at the Norwich Festival on 6 October 1930.

Moross, Jerome (1913–1983) US composer. He studied at Juilliard and worked in Hollywood from 1940. He is best known for ballets and ballet-operas: *Paul Bunyan* (1934), *American Patterns* (1937), *Susannah and the Elders* (1940), *The Eccentricities of Davy Crockett* (1946), *The Golden Apple* (1952), *Sorry, Wrong Number* (composed 1983).

Morris, R(eginald) O(wen) (1886–1948) English teacher and composer. He was educated at Harrow, New College, Oxford, and the Royal College of Music in London, where he later became professor of counterpoint and composition. In 1926 he was appointed to a similar post at the Curtis Institute at Philadelphia, but soon returned to England. His books include *Contrapuntal Technique in the 16th Century*, *Foundations of Practical Harmony and Counterpoint*, *The Structure of Music*.

Works ORCHESTRAL symphony in D major; violin concerto in G minor, *Concerto piccolo* for two violins and strings.

CHAMBER fantasy for string quartet, motets for string quartet.

OTHER songs with quartet accompaniment.

Morris dance old English folk dance, deriving its name from the Moorish *Moresca* (old English 'morys', 'Moorish'), introduced into England about the 15th century. It partook of a pageant in character and was danced in various kinds of fancy dress, with jingles tied to the dancers' legs.

In some districts elements of the Sword Dance were introduced into it. The music, a great variety of tunes, was played by a pipe and tabor, or more rarely by a bagpipe or violin.

Mors et Vita, Death and Life oratorio by Gounod, a sequel to *The Redemption*, produced at the Birmingham Festival on 26 August 1885.

Morton, Robert (c.1430–c.1476) English singer and composer. He composed French chansons, of which two were among the most popular of their day. He was employed at the court of Burgundy (1457–76), under Philip the Good and Charles the Bold.

Moscheles, Ignaz (1794–1870) Bohemian pianist and composer. He composed about 140 Opus numbers, including piano concertos, sonatas, chamber music, and studies for the piano. He was a gifted improviser and introduced some innovations in piano playing later developed by the Liszt school. His correspondence with Mendelssohn was published in 1888, and an English translation of a biography by his wife in 1873.

He was born in Prague, and studied under Dionys Weber at the Conservatory there. He played a concerto in public at the age of 14. He was sent to Vienna and there took lessons in counterpoint from Johann Albrechtsberger and composition from Salieri. He made Beethoven's acquaintance when he arranged the vocal score of *Fidelio* in 1814. He then began to travel widely, and in 1821 appeared in Holland, Paris, and London. In 1824 he taught Mendelssohn in Berlin and became his lifelong friend; in 1826 he married Charlotte Embden at Hamburg and settled permanently in London as a teacher and soloist, and became one of the directors of the Philharmonic Society. In 1832 he conducted the first performance there of Beethoven's *Missa solemnis*. In 1846 he went to Leipzig at Mendelssohn's invitation to become first piano professor at the new conservatory.

Works ORCHESTRAL symphony in C (1829); eight piano concertos (1819–38), including G minor and *Concerto pathétique*.

PIANO a great number of piano works including *Sonate mélancolique*, *Characteristic Studies*, *Allegro di bravura* and numerous sonatas, variations, fantasies, studies, and other pieces; *Hommage à Händel* for two pianos.

Mosè in Egitto, Moses in Egypt opera by Rossini (libretto by A L Tottola), first performed at the Teatro San Carlo, Naples, on 5 March 1818. Moses frees the Israelites in Egypt and parts the Red Sea on the way home.

See also ➤ **Moïse**.

Moser, Hans Joachim (1889–1967) German singer, musicologist, and composer. He studied with his father, Andreas Moser (1859–1925), who was a violinist and also wrote on music, including a biography of Joachim. He was later educated at Berlin, Marburg, and Leipzig, and became professor of musicology at Halle, Heidelberg, and later Berlin. His literary works include a history of German music, studies of medieval string music, Luther's songs, German song, and biographies of Hofhaimer, Schütz, and Bach.

Moses und Aron, Moses and Aaron opera in two acts by Schoenberg (the projected third act was never composed; libretto by the composer), first performed (concert) in Hamburg on 12 March 1954; produced in Zurich on 6 June 1957 (music composed 1930–32). Moses and his brother Aaron bring God's message to the people, but the Israelites cannot understand Moses' abstract ideas. Aaron leads an orgy around the Golden Calf, but Moses interrupts with the Tablets of the Law.

Mosonyi, Mihály (1815–1870), adopted name of **Michael Brand** Hungarian composer. He studied at Pozsony (now Bratislava) and was music master to a noble family 1835–42, then settled at Budapest. He changed his German name of Brand in 1859, when he began to aim at writing Hungarian national music.

Works OPERA *Kaiser Max auf der Martinswand* (composed 1857), *The Fair Ilonka* (1861), and *Almos* (1862), both in Hungarian.

CHORAL three Masses.

ORCHESTRAL symphonies, symphonic poems *Mourning for Széchényi* and *Festival Music* and other orchestral works.

PIANO AND SONGS 20 piano pieces in the Hungarian manner; 25 Hungarian folk-song arrangements.

mosso (Italian 'moved') term used in musical notation, as in *più mosso* ('more moved'), meaning faster.

Mossolov, Aleksandr Vassilevich (1900–1973) Russian pianist and composer. His family, which cultivated various branches of art, moved to Moscow in 1904 and in 1921 he entered the Conservatory there, studying under Glière until 1925. He travelled much as a pianist and to study folk music in central Asia.

Works OPERA *The Dam*, *The Hero* (1928), *The Signal* (1941).

CANTATAS *Sphinx* (Oscar Wilde) and *Kirghiz Rhapsody*.

ORCHESTRAL six symphonies (1929–50); *Turcomanian Suite* and *Uzbek Dance* for orchestra; two piano concertos (1927, 1935), violin concerto, harp concerto, two cello concertos.

BALLET *The Factory* (1927) with realistic sound effects, including a shaken metal sheet, also performed as a concert item with the title *The Iron Foundry* (*Music of Machines*).

CHAMBER string quartet, *Dance Suite* for piano trio; viola and piano sonata.

VOCAL songs to words by Pushkin, Lermontov, and Blok; massed choruses, battle songs.

motet sacred, polyphonic music for unaccompanied voices in a form that originated in 13th-century Europe.

Mother Goose suite and ballet by Maurice Ravel; see ➤ *Ma Mère l'Oye*.

Mother of Us All, The opera by Virgil Thomson (libretto by G Stein), produced in New York at the Brander Matthews Theatre, Columbia University, on 7 May 1947.

motif or **motive** in music, a group of at least two notes forming an intelligible, characteristic figure, which through repetition and development forms a foundation for larger figures and themes; one of the most basic units of composition. Often, a single motif will serve as the building block for a variety of themes and accompaniment figures.

Beethoven was one of the greatest masters of motivic composition. The first movement of his Fifth Symphony (1808) is a famous example of the constant recurrence of the four-note motif which forms the first four notes of the piece. Throughout the 19th century, composers relied on motifs to provide compositional coherence in an era in which traditional large-scale structures such as ➤ **sonata form** were beginning to lose their relevance. Motifs continued to be an essential compositional tool to early 20th-century artists, including Arnold Schoenberg and Igor Stravinsky. Since the evolution of chance procedures and other avant-garde techniques introduced in the 1950s, many composers have abandoned the motif, but it still remains a vital part of composition. See: ➤ **motivic analysis**; ➤ **developing variation**; ➤ **musical idea**.

motion in music, the succession of notes of different pitch. The word is used only with an adjectival qualification: **conjunct motion**, a single part moving by steps of adjoining notes; **contrary motion**, two or more parts moving together in different directions; **disjunct motion**, a single part moving by larger than stepwise intervals; **oblique motion**, one part moving when another stands still; and **similar motion**, two or more parts moving together in the same direction.

motivic analysis method of analysing a piece of music according to its important constituent motives. The method identifies ways in which motives are transformed or developed, and links melodies which contain identical or similar motives. A motive which is linked to all the other motivic material of a piece may be called the fundamental motive. The method is equally applicable to tonal and non-tonal music, but limited by having little to say concerning harmonic features of a work. See: Arnold ➤ **Schoenberg**; Hans ➤ **Keller**; ➤ **developing variation**; ➤ **musical idea**.

moto (Italian 'motion') term used in musical notation, as in *andante con moto* ('andante with motion'), meaning faster than the usual ➤ **andante** tempo.

moto perpetuo (Italian 'perpetual motion') musical form; see ➤ **perpetuum mobile**.

motoric rhythm in music, a 20th-century term for rhythm based on one specific note value (quavers, for example), usually in order to sustain or generate energy. ➤ **Ostinatos** (repeating melodic or rhythmic figures) often form motoric rhythms, as in Igor Stravinsky's *The Rite of Spring* (1913).

Mottl, Felix (Josef) (1856–1911) Austrian conductor and composer. He studied at a choir school and at the Conservatory in Vienna, became conductor of the Wagner Society there and in 1876 was engaged by Richard Wagner to conduct the music on the stage in the production of the *Ring*; he gave *Tristan* and *Parsifal* at Bayreuth in 1886. In 1881–1903 he was conductor at the ducal court of Karlsruhe, where he directed the symphonic concerts and the opera, producing many unfamiliar works including the first performance of all five acts of *Les Troyens* (1890). From 1903 he was conductor in Munich. He collapsed while conducting *Tristan* and died shortly after.

Works STAGE operas *Agnes Bernauer* (after Hebbel), *Rama* and *Fürst und Sänger*; festival play *Eberstein*; music for O J Bierbaum's play *Pan im Busch*.

OTHER string quartet (1904); songs.

motto in music, a short and well-defined theme usually occurring at the opening of a composition and used again during its course, in its first form or altered, in the manner of a quotation or an allusion to some definite idea. The opening themes in Tchaikovsky's fourth and fifth symphonies are familiar examples.

Mount of Olives, The oratorio by Beethoven; see ➤ **Christus am Oelberg**.

Mouret, Jean Joseph (1682–1738) French composer. He entered the service of the Duchess of Maine in Paris about 1707 and in 1714 began to write for the stage. He was director of the Concert Spirituel 1728–34, also for a time conductor of the Comédie-Italienne. In 1736 he became insane and was taken to the psychiatric hospital of Charenton.

Works OPERA AND OPERA-BALLET *Les Festes de Thalie*, *Ragonde*, *Ariane* (1717), *Les Amours des dieux* (1727), *Le Triomphe des sens* (1732), and others.

ORCHESTRAL two *Suites de Symphonies*, 47 divertissements for orchestra; two books of *Concerts de chambre*; fanfares.

VOCAL Mass, two books of motets; cantatas *Cantatilles*.

Mourning Symphony symphony by Jopseph Haydn; see ➤ *Trauer-Sinfonie*.

Moussorgsky Russian composer; see Modest ➤ **Mussorgsky**.

mouth organ any of a family of small portable free-reed wind instruments originating in Eastern and South Asia. The compact **harmonica**, or European mouth organ, developed by Charles Wheatstone in 1829, has tuned metal free reeds of variable length contained in a narrow rectangular box and is played by blowing and sucking air while moving the instrument from side to side through the lips.

As the **mouth harp**, the mouth organ is a staple instrument in country and western music. As a melody instrument it achieved concert status through the virtuosity of Larry Adler. All mouth organs bend in pitch in response to variation in pressure of the player's breath.

The Chinese sheng, Japanese sho, and Laotian khen are examples of early mouth organs. These older forms consist of a bundle of up to 17 pitch pipes connected at the base to a common wind chamber and mouthpiece, and played by closing finger holes in the pipes that are to sound, forcing air to escape through the free reeds and creating a variable harmony. There are interesting resemblances with the medieval regal, also a portable free-reed instrument, but incorporating Western refinements of a keyboard and bellows.

Mouton, Jean (c.1459–1522) French composer. He was in the service of Louis XII and François I, and became canon of Thérouanne, which he left probably on its being taken by the English in 1513, and afterwards of the collegiate church of Saint-Quentin.

He was a pupil of Josquin Desprez.

Works CHORAL Fourteen Masses, 110 motets, psalms, *Alleluia* and *In illo tempore* for Easter, *Noe, noe, psallite* for Christmas, and other pieces.

mouvement (French 'tempo, pace') movement of a sonata, symphony.

Mouvements de cœur seven songs for bass and piano in memory of Chopin (poems by Louise de Vilmorin): 1. *Prélude*: Henri Sauguet; 2. *Mazurka*: Francis Poulenc; 3. *Valse*: Georges Auric; 4. *Scherzo Impromptu*: Jean Françaix; 5. *Étude*: Léo Preger; 6. *Ballade* (*Nocturne*): Darius Milhaud; 7. *Postlude, Polonaise*: Sauguet.

movable doh in music, the ➤ **tonic** or keynote in the tonic sol-fa system which shifts the tonal centre at each modulation into another key instead of prescribing accidentals.

movement in music, a self-contained composition of specific character, usually a constituent piece of a ➤ **suite**, ➤ **symphony**, or similar work, with its own tempo, distinct from that of the other movements.

Movements work for piano and orchestra by Stravinsky; composed 1958–59, first performed in New York on 10 January 1960, with Marchgit Weber, who commissioned the score.

Mozarabic chant one of the important branches of early Latin chant, also called Visigothic, and used in central and southern Spain during the Middle Ages. Liturgically it is associated with the Gallican and Ambrosian rites, pre-dating that of Rome and showing similarities with Eastern liturgies. Its music is found in manuscripts of the 8th–11th centuries, but mostly in undecipherable neumes. Only a few melodies survive in readable form. Roman chant and rite were imposed everywhere by 1076 except in Toledo, and in spite of the attempted revival under Cardinal Francisco de Cisneros (c.1500), little of the musical tradition has been preserved.

Mozart, (Johann Georg) Leopold (1719–1787) Austrian violinist and composer. He was the father of the composer Wolfgang Amadeus ➤ **Mozart**. His important violin tutor, *Versuch einer gründlichen Violinschule*, was published in 1756.

He was educated at the Jesuit college in Augsburg and at Salzburg University, turned entirely to music in 1739, and first held a post with Count Thurn-Valsassina und Taxis. In 1743 he entered the service of the Archbishop of Salzburg, rising to become court composer in 1757 and vice-Kapellmeister in 1763. In 1747 he married Anna Maria Pertl; of their seven children the only two to survive were Maria Anna and Wolfgang Amadeus.

Works ORCHESTRAL symphonies; divertimenti and descriptive pieces for orchestra including 'Musical sleigh-ride', 'Toy Symphony', and other pieces; concertos for various instruments.

OTHER chamber music, sonatas for violin; church music.

Mozart, (Johann Chrysostom) Wolfgang Amadeus (1756–1791) Austrian composer and performer who was a child prodigy and an adult virtuoso. He was trained by his father, **Leopold Mozart** (1719–1787). From an early age he composed prolifically, and his works include 27 piano concertos, 23 string quartets, 35 violin sonatas, and 41 symphonies including the E♭ K543, G minor K550, and C major K551 ('Jupiter') sym-

phonies, all three being composed in 1788. His operas include *Idomeneo* (1780), *Entführung aus dem Serail/The Abduction from the Seraglio* (1782), *Le nozze di Figaro/The Marriage of Figaro* (1786), *Don Giovanni* (1787), *Così fan tutte/Thus Do All Women* (1790), and *Die Zauberflöte/The Magic Flute* (1791). Together with the work of Joseph Haydn, Mozart's music marks the height of the classical age in its purity of melody and form.

His works were catalogued chronologically in 1862 by the musicologist Ludwig von Köchel (1800–1877) whose system of numbering – giving each work a 'Köchel number' – for example, K354 – remains in use in modified form.

Mozart showed early signs of talent, learnt the harpsichord from the age of three or four, and began to compose under his father's supervision when he was five. With his sister (then aged 11) he was taken to Munich in 1762, then to Vienna, where they played at court. Encouraged by their success, Leopold Mozart set out with the children the following year on a longer tour, which took them first through southern Germany, on to Brussels, and to Paris, where they arrived in November 1763. They appeared at court at Versailles, and four sonatas for violin and harpsichord by Mozart were published in Paris. Moving on to London in April 1764, they played before the royal family and made a sensation in public concerts.

In London Mozart was befriended by Johann Christian Bach, three of whose sonatas he arranged as piano concertos, and who also influenced the symphonies and other pieces he wrote at the time. They left for Holland in July 1765, and after several stops on the journey through France and Switzerland returned to Salzburg in November 1766. The next months were spent in study and composition, but in September 1767 the whole family went to Vienna. There Mozart composed his first Mass (C minor, K139) and produced the Singspiel, *Bastien und Bastienne*. Returning to Salzburg in January 1769, Mozart had barely a year at home before setting out with his father on an extended tour of Italy; in Rome he wrote down Gregorio Allegri's *Miserere* from memory, in Bologna he took lessons from Padre Martini and gained election to the Philharmonic Society with a contrapuntal exercise, and in Milan he produced the opera *Mitridate* with great success in December 1770.

Two further visits to Italy followed, both to Milan, for the performance of the serenata *Ascanio in Alba* in October 1771, and the opera *Lucio Silla* in December 1772. At the performance of *Ascanio*, Johann Hasse is alleged to have said 'This boy will cause us all to be forgotten'. Apart from short visits to Vienna, in 1773, and Munich, in 1775 for the production of *La finta giardiniera* (1775), most of the next five years was spent in

Salzburg, his longest period at home since infancy. In September 1777, in company with his mother, he embarked on a lengthy journey that took them via Mannheim to Paris, where his mother died in July 1778. The main object of this trip was to find suitable employment, but being unsuccessful, Mozart returned in January 1779 to the post of court organist at Salzburg, which he did not enjoy. One of his finest instrumental works, the *Sinfonia concertante* (K364), was written later that year.

His opera seria *Idomeneo* was produced in Munich in January 1781, but later the same year, on a visit to Vienna with the household of the archbishop of Salzburg, he gave up his post to settle in Vienna as a freelance, living by teaching and playing in concerts. His German opera *Die Entführung aus dem Serail/The Abduction from the Seraglio* was produced in July 1782, and the next month he married Constanze Weber. At the height of his fame as a pianist, between 1782 and 1786, he composed many concertos for his own use, but thereafter there followed increasing financial worries, which his appointment in 1787 as court composer on the death of Christoph Willibald von Gluck did little to ease. The first of three operas using a libretto by the Italian poet Lorenzo da Ponte, *Le Nozze di Figaro/The Marriage of Figaro*, was produced in 1786, followed by *Don Giovanni* for Prague, in 1787, and *Così fan tutte/Thus Do All Women* in 1790. In these works Mozart brought opera to new heights of musical ingenuity, dramatic truth, and brilliance of expression. For almost the first time opera characters are recognizable human beings, rather than stock types.

In 1788 he wrote his last three symphonies, which are his most famous. Assimilating all he had learned from Joseph Haydn and others, he took standard forms and gave them new meaning. A visit to Berlin with Prince Lichnowsky in 1789 took him through Leipzig, where he discussed Bach's music with Doles, Bach's successor, and in 1790 he made a fruitless journey to Frankfurt, hoping to earn money as a pianist. After several lean years, 1791 was one of overwork, which must have contributed to his early death; in addition to the last piano concerto (K595), the clarinet concerto (K622), and several smaller works, he composed the operas *La Clemenza di Tito* (produced in Prague for the coronation of Emperor Leopold II), and *Die Zauberflöte/The Magic Flute* (1791, produced in Vienna). The Requiem remained unfinished at Mozart's death, and was completed later by his pupil Franz Süssmayr.

While Mozart was not a great innovator in the manner of Haydn and Beethoven, he set creative standards in a wide variety of forms to which later composers could only aspire.

Works OPERA *Idomeneo, rè di Creta* (1781), *Die Entführung aus dem Serail* (1782), *Le nozze di Figaro* (1786), *Don Giovanni* (1787), *Così fan tutte/Thus Do All Women* (1790), *Die Zauberflöte/The Magic Flute* (1791), *La Clemenza di Tito* (1791).

BALLET *Les petits riens/Sweet Nothings* (1778).

CHURCH MUSIC including Motet, *Exsultate, jubilate* for soprano, organ, and orchestra, (K165, 1773), *Kyrie* in D minor (K341, 1781), Mass in C, *Coronation* (K317, 1779), *Vesperae solennes de confessore* (K339, 1780), Mass in C minor, unfinished (K427, 1783), Motet, *Ave verum corpus* (K618, 1791), Requiem Mass in D minor, unfinished (K626, 1791).

SYMPHONIES (41; nos 1–24 composed 1764–73), no. 25 in G minor (K183, 1773), no. 29 in A (K201, 1774), no. 31 in D, *Paris* (K297, 1778), no. 34 in C (K338, 1780), no. 35 in D, *Haffner* (K385, 1782), no. 36 in C, *Linz* (K425, 1783), no. 38 in D, *Prague* (K504, 1786), no. 39 in E♭ (K543, 1788), no. 40 in G minor (K550, 1788), no. 41 in C, *Jupiter* (K551, 1788). Other music for orchestra includes: Divertimenti in D (K136, 1772), in B♭ (K137, 1772), in F (K138, 1772), in B♭ (K287, 1777), in D (K334, 1779–80); Serenades in D, *Serenata Notturna* (K239, 1776), in D, *Haffner* (K250, 1776), in D, for four orchestras (K286, 1777), in D, *Posthorn* (K320, 1779), in B♭ for 13 wind instruments (K361, 1781), in E♭ for eight wind instruments (K375, 1781), in C minor for eight wind instruments (K388, 1782 or 83), in G for strings, *Eine kleine Nachtmusik* (K525, 1787); *Mauerische Trauermusik/Masonic Funeral Music* (K477, 1785).

CONCERTOS 27 for piano, including no. 9 in E♭ (K271, 1777), no. 14 in E♭ (K449, 1784), no. 15 in B♭ (K450, 1784), no. 16 in D (K451, 1784), no. 17 in G (K453, 1784), no. 18 in B♭ (K456, 1784), no. 19 in F (K459, 1784), no. 20 in D minor (K466, 1785), no. 21 in C (K467, 1785), no. 22 in E♭ (K482, 1785), no. 23 in A (K488, 1786), no. 24 in C minor (K491, 1786), no. 25 in C (K503, 1786), no. 26 in D, *Coronation* (K537, 1788), no. 27 in B♭ (K595, 1791); five for violin, including no. 3 in G (K216, 1775), no. 4 in D (K218, 1775), no. 5 in A (K219, 1775); Sinfonia Concertante for violin, viola, and orchestra (K364, 1779); for bassoon in B♭ (K191, 1774); for flute in G (K313, 1778); for oboe in C (K314, 1778); for flute and harp in C (K299, 1778); for clarinet in A (K622, 1791); Sinfonia Concertante in E♭ for oboe, clarinet, horn, and bassoon (K297b, 1778, judged as spurious by some scholars); four for horn (1782–87).

CHAMBER MUSIC 23 string quartets, nos 1–13 (1770–73), nos 14–19 dedicated to Haydn (1782–85) in G (K387), in D minor (K421), in E♭ (K428), in B♭ (K458, *The Hunt*), in A (K464), in C (K465, *Dissonance*), no. 20 in D, *Hoffmeister*

(K499, 1786), nos 21–23 dedicated to King of Prussia (1789–90) in D (K575), in B♭ (K589), in F (K590); six string quintets, including no. 3 in C (K515, 1787), no. 4 in G minor (K516, 1787), no. 5 in D (K593, 1790), no. 6 in B♭ (K614, 1791); string trio in B♭, *Divertimento* (K563, 1788); five piano trios; two piano quartets in G minor (K478, 1785), in B♭ (K493, 1786); oboe quartet (K370, 1781); horn quintet (K407, 1782); quintet for piano and wind (K452, 1784); clarinet quintet (K581, 1789); clarinet trio in E♭ (K498, 1786); 17 piano sonatas, including no. 8 in A minor (K310, 1778), no. 9 in D (K311, 1777), nos 10–13 in C, A, and F (K330–333, 1781–84), no. 14 in C minor (K457, 1784), no. 15 in C (K545, 1788), no. 16 in B♭ (K570, 1789), no. 17 in D (K576, 1789); sonata in D for two pianos (K448, 1781); 35 sonatas for violin and piano, nos 1–16 composed 1762–66; no. 17 and nos 18–23 in 1778; nos 24–35 from 1781–78. Variations for piano, Fantasia in D minor (K397, 1782 or 1786–87), Fantasia in C minor (K475, 1785), Rondo in A minor (K511, 1787).

SOLO SONGS AND LIEDER including 'Die Zufriedenheit' (K349), 'Oiseaux, si tous les ans' (K307), 'Der Zauberer' (K472), 'Das Veilchen' (K476), 'Als Luise' (K520), 'Abendempfindung' (K523), 'Das Traumbild' (K530), 'Sehnsucht nach dem Frühlinge/Longing for Spring' (K596).

Mozart and Salieri opera by Rimsky-Korsakov (libretto Pushkin's dramatic poem, set as it stands), produced in Moscow on 7 December 1898. It tells a now discredited story (though still believed by some) that Salieri poisoned Mozart.

Mozartiana Tchaikovsky's fourth suite for orchestra, Op. 61, composed in 1887. It consists of four works by Mozart scored for orchestra by Tchaikovsky: jig and minuet for piano, K475 and 355; motet *Ave, verum corpus*, K618, and variations on a theme from *La rencontre imprévue* by Gluck for piano, K455. First performed in Moscow on 26 November 1887.

mp in music, abbreviation of ➤ mezzo piano.

Mravinsky, Evgeny (1903–1988) Russian conductor. He often conducted the stage works of Tchaikovsky, and orchestral music by Bartók and Stravinsky.

He studied at the Leningrad Conservatory and was conductor of the Leningrad Philharmonic Orchestra from 1938. Active on behalf of Soviet music, he gave the first performances of Shostakovich's symphonies nos 5, 6, 8, 9, and 10. He conducted the first performance of Prokofiev's sixth symphony at Leningrad in 1947.

mridangam elongated barrel drum with two tuned heads. Found in various sizes as an accompaniment to art-music throughout India. Known as *mrdang* or *phakvaj* in northern India, where it is also used in devotional temple music, and *mrdanga* or *khol* in eastern India.

Muck, Carl (1859–1940) German conductor. He was noted for his performances of Bruckner's symphonies. He gave the first Russian performances of Wagner's *Ring* in 1889.

He studied at Heidelberg University and at Leipzig University and Conservatory. In 1880 he began a career as a pianist, but became a conductor at Salzburg, Brno, and Graz in succession, at Prague in 1886, and finally at the Royal Opera, Berlin, in 1892. He gave the first Russian performance of the *Ring* in 1889, and conducted Wagner in London and from 1901 at Bayreuth (*Parsifal* until 1930), also the Philharmonic concerts in Vienna. From 1906 to 1918, with an interruption, he conducted the Boston Symphony Orchestra. Arrested as an enemy alien in 1918, he returned to Europe after World War I and conducted in Hamburg 1922–33.

Mudd, Thomas (1560–after 1619) English composer. He went to St Paul's School in London and in 1578 to Cambridge as a sizar for the sons of London mercers.

Works services, anthems; dances for three viols.

Muette de Portici, La, The Dumb Girl of Portici opera by Auber (libretto by Scribe and Delavigne), produced at the Paris Opéra on 29 February 1828. Carafa's *Masaniello*, on the same subject, had been produced at the Opéra-Comique two months earlier. Auber's work is often called *Masaniello*. The seduction of his sister Fenella inspires Masaniello to lead a peasants' revolt against the Spanish viceroy and his son Alphonse. Horrified by the waste of life, however, Masaniello shows mercy to the nobles and as a result is poisoned by his compatriots.

Muffat, Georg (1653–1704) Austrian organist and composer. In 1678 he was appointed organist to the Archbishop of Salzburg, and after visiting Vienna and Rome went to Passau to become organist to the bishop in 1690.

He studied in Paris, with Lully or members of his school.

Works KEYBOARD *Apparatus musico-organisticus* for organ (twelve toccatas, chaconne, and passacaglia, 1690), *Suaviores harmoniae* (1695), two volumes for harpsichord.

OTHER the chamber sonatas *Armonico tributo* (1682), *Auserlesene mit Ernst und Lust gemengte Instrumental-Musik*.

Muldowney, Dominic (1952–) English composer. He studied with Jonathan Harvey at Southampton and with Birtwistle in London. In 1975 he was appointed assistant music director to Harrison Birtwistle at the Royal National Theatre,

London, succeeding as director in 1981. His output includes music for many National Theatre productions; a realization of The ➤ *Beggar's Opera* (1982), and concertos for percussion, oboe, and trumpet (1991, 1991, 1993).

Works STAGE *Macbeth*, ballet music (1979); a realization of *The Beggar's Opera* (1982); five *Theatre Poems*, after Brecht (1981).

ORCHESTRAL piano concerto (1983); saxophone concerto (1984); violin concerto (1989); concertos for percussion (1991), oboe (1991), and trumpet (1993).

OTHER ENSEMBLE *An Heavyweight Dirge* for soloists and chamber ensemble (1971); *Driftwood to the Flow* for 18 strings (1972); *Music at Chartres* for 16 instruments (1973); *Love music for Bathsheba Everdene and Gabriel Oak* for chamber ensemble (1974); *Double Helix* for eight players (1977); *The Duration of Exile* for mezzo and chamber ensemble (1982); *The Duration of Exile* for mezzo and ensemble (1983); sinfonietta (1986); *Ars subtilior* for tape and ensemble (1987).

CHAMBER two string quartets (1973 and 1980).

PIANO *The Ginger Tree* for piano (1989), *Klavier-Hammer* for one or more pianos (1973).

Mulè, Giuseppe (1855–1951) Italian cellist and composer. He studied Sicilian folk song and found that its roots went back to Greek music; he wrote much incidental music for the performance of Greek plays at Syracuse.

He studied at the Palermo Conservatory, of which he was director 1922–25, when he became director of the Santa Cecilia Conservatory in Rome. He also became secretary to the fascist syndicate of musicians.

Works STAGE operas *La Baronessa di Carini* (1912), *Al lupo*, *La monacella della fontana* (1923), *Dafni* (1928), *Liolà* (on Pirandello's play, 1935), *Taormina*; music for Greek plays: Aeschylus' *Choephori*, *Seven against Thebes*, Euripides' *Bacchae*, *Medea*, *The Cyclops*, *Hippolytus*, *Iphigenia in Aulis*, *Iphigenia in Tauris*, Sophocles' *Antigone*; incidental music for Corradini's *Giulio Cesare*; oratorio *Il cieco di Gerico* (1910).

ORCHESTRAL symphonic poems *Sicilia canora* and *Vendemmia*.

OTHER *Tre canti siciliani* for voice and orchestra; string quartet; violin and cello pieces.

Müller, Wilhelm (1794–1827) German poet. His poems were set by the composer Franz ➤ Schubert in the song cycles *Die ➤ Schöne Müllerin* and ➤ *Winterreise*.

multiphonics in music, a technique of ➤ overblowing a woodwind instrument combined with unorthodox fingering to produce a complex dissonance. Composers who use multiphonics include Luciano Berio and Heinz Holliger, and the

technique is also used by jazz saxophonists.

Mumma, Gordon (1935–) US composer. In 1957 he cofounded Space Theatre, giving performances with computerized electronics. He worked at an electronic studio, Ann Arbour, from 1958, and at the Merce Cunningham Dance Company from 1968. His works involve use of computer techniques, called cybersonics, and include *Sinfonia* for twelve instruments (1960), *Le Corbusier* (1965), *Mesa* (1966), and *Ambivex* (1972).

Munch, Charles (1891–1968) conductor and violinist. Conductor of the Boston Symphony (1949–62), Munch was known for allowing his players room to express themselves, producing warm and musical performances.

Munch was born in Strasbourg, France. After a long career as a violinist, he made his conducting debut in Paris in 1932 and three years later organized his own orchestra there. After conducting the Boston Symphony, he organized the Orchestre de Paris; he died on tour with that group in Virginia.

Mundy, John (c.1555–1630) English organist and composer. He studied under his father, William Mundy, became a Gentleman of the Chapel Royal in London, and succeeded Marbeck as one of the organists of St George's Chapel, Windsor, about 1585.

Works VOCAL anthems, *Songs and Psalmes* for three to five voices; madrigals (one in *The Triumphes of Oriana*).

OTHER virginal pieces including the 'Weather' fantasia.

Munrow, David (1942–1976) English early music specialist and wind-instrument player. He founded the Early Music Consort in 1967 and taught at Leicester University and the Royal Academy of Music, London. He gave numerous performances of medieval and Renaissance music and was a frequent broadcaster. He published *Instruments of the Middle Ages and Renaissance* in 1976. He died by suicide.

Murail, Tristan (1947–) French composer. He co-founded the Groupe de L'Itinéraire, to promote performances of music which combine electronic and traditional instruments. He has taught computer music at the Institut de Recherche et de Coordination Acoustique/Musique (➤ IRCAM) and the Paris Conservatory.

He studied with Messiaen at the Paris Conservatory.

Works ORCHESTRAL AND ENSEMBLE *Couleur de mer* for ensemble (1969); *Altitude 8000* for orchestra (1970); *Cosmos privé* for orchestra (1973); *Les nuages de Magellan* for ondes Martenot and ensemble (1973); *Sables* for orchestra (1974); *Mém-*

oire/Erosion for horn and nine players (1976); *Désintégrations* for 17 players and tape (1983); *Sillages* for orchestra (1985); *Les sept paroles du Christ en Croix* for orchestra (1986–89).

CHAMBER *Vues aeriennes* for horn, violin, cello, and piano (1988); *Le fou à pattes bleues* for flute and piano (1990).

Murino, Aegidius de (lived 14th century) Music theorist and composer of uncertain nationality. He may possibly be the 'Egidius Anglicus' of the Manuscript Chantilly (1047). His treatise *Tractatus de diversis figuris* is about note-forms and motet composition. Two motets and one chanson also survive.

Muris, Johannes de (c.1300–c.1350) French mathematician, astronomer, and music theorist. He lived for some time in Paris and worked there as a mathematician and astronomer. The most notable of the music treatises attributed to him is the *Ars novae musicae* (1319).

murky bass an 18th-century term of unknown origin for a bass played in broken octaves on keyboard instruments.

Murrill, Herbert (Henry John) (1909–1952) English composer. He studied at the Royal Academy of Music in London and at Worcester College, Oxford. After holding various organist's posts from 1926, he became professor of composition at the Royal Academy of Music in 1933, joined the music staff of the British Broadcasting Corporation (BBC) in 1936 and became Head of Music in 1950.

Works OPERA *Man in Cage* (1930).

ORCHESTRAL three hornpipes for orchestra; two concertos and three pieces for cello and orchestra.

CHAMBER string quartet and other chamber music.

Murschhauser, Franz Xaver Anton (1663–1738) Alsatian composer. He was a pupil of Kerl at Munich, where he became Kapellmeister at the church of Our Lady. In 1721, by a remark made in his treatise on composition, 'Academia musicopoetica', he came into conflict with Johann Mattheson.

Works ORGAN organ books *Octitonium novum organum*, *Prototypon longobreve organicum*, *Opus organicum tripartitum* (1696).

OTHER *Vespertinus latriae* for four voices and strings (1700).

Muset, Colin (lived 12th century) French trouvère (see → troubadour) and jongleur. The poems of 15 and the music of eight of his songs have survived.

musette small French → bagpipes; also a dance movement and character piece, imitating the music of a bagpipe, with its → drone accompaniment. Musette sections are often found in classical suites, as the trio to a gavotte. A modern 'musette' is found in Schoenberg's *Suite for Piano* (1921).

Musgrave, Thea (1928–   ) Scottish composer. Her music, in a conservative modern idiom, includes concertos, chamber music, and operas, such as *Mary, Queen of Scots* (1977), and *Harriet, the Woman Called Moses* (1985). Later works include the opera *Simón Bolívar* (1993), the bass clarinet concerto *Autumn Sonata* (1995), and the orchestral piece *Phoenix Rising* (1998). Her opera *Pontalba: A Louisiana Legacy* (2003) places the struggle of its heroine in the larger historical context of the Louisiana Purchase and the forging of the young USA.

She studied at Edinburgh University and with Nadia Boulanger in Paris 1950–54; her *Cantata for a Summer's Day* dates from this period. After 1953 she felt the influence of Schoenberg's 12-note method, which is seen in a number of works up until the Sinfonia of 1963. After this she gradually, particularly under the influence of US composer Charles → Ives, wrote with greater freedom of dramatic gesture, as in the clarinet concerto (1968), in which the soloist moves around the various groups of the orchestra in performance. She lectured at London University from 1959 to 1965, and at the University of California from 1970. As Distinguished Professor at Queens College, City University of New York 1987–2002, she guided and interacted with many new and gifted young student composers. Her music has employed serial and improvisatory techniques. She was awarded a CBE in 2002.

Works OPERA *The Abbot of Drimock* (1955), *The Decision* (1967), *The Voice of Ariadne* (1974), *Mary, Queen of Scots* (1977), *A Christmas Carol* (1979), *An Occurrence at Owl Creek Bridge* (1981), *Harriet, the Woman Called Moses* (1985), *Simón Bolívar* (1993), *Pontalba, A Louisiana Legacy* (2003).

ORCHESTRAL *Scottish Dance Suite* for orchestra, *Divertimento* for string orchestra, *Perspectives* for small orchestra; three chamber concertos for various instruments, Concerto for Orchestra (1967), *Peripateia* for orchestra (1981), *The Seasons* (1988) and *Rainbow* (1990) for orchestra.

VOCAL *Triptych* for tenor and orchestra; *The Five Ages of Man* for chorus and orchestra; songs.

CHAMBER string quartet (1958); two piano sonatas.

music art of combining sounds into a structured form, usually according to conventional patterns and for an aesthetic (artistic) purpose. Music is generally divided into different genres or styles such as → classical music, → jazz, → pop music, country, and so on.

The Greek word *mousikē* covered all the arts presided over by the Muses. The various civilizations of the ancient and modern world developed their own musical systems. Eastern music recognizes smaller changes of pitch than does mainstream Western music (with the exception of much 20th-century contemporary art music) and also differs from Western music in that the absence, until recently, of written notation ruled out the composition of major developed works, though these are created through improvisation using melodic and rhythmic patterns governed by particular modes and formal devices. Such improvisations (as in the Indian ➤ raga) can last up to 70 minutes, interpreted by virtuosos.

Middle Ages The documented history of Western music since classical times begins with the liturgical music of the medieval Catholic Church, descended from Greek and Hebrew roots. The four modes (derived from ancient Greek models), to which the words of the liturgy were chanted were first set in order by St Ambrose in 384. St Gregory the Great added four more to the original Ambrosian modes, and this system forms the basis of Gregorian ➤ plainsong, still used in the Roman Catholic Church. The organ was introduced in the 8th century, and in the 9th century, music using a very primitive form of harmony began to be used in churches, with notation gradually developing towards its present form.

In the 11th century ➤ counterpoint was introduced, notably at the monastery of St Martial, Limoges, France, and in the late 12th century at Notre-Dame in Paris (by Léonin and Perotin). In the late Middle Ages the Provençal and French ➤ troubadours and court composers, such as Guillaume de Machaut, developed a secular music, developed from church and folk music (see also ➤ Minnesingers).

15th and 16th centuries Europe saw the growth of contrapuntal or polyphonic music. One of the earliest composers was the English musician John Dunstable, whose works inspired the French composer Guillaume Dufay, founder of the Flemish school. Its members included Dufay's pupil Joannes Okeghem and the Renaissance composer Josquin Desprez. Other major composers of this era were Giovanni Pierluigi da Palestrina from Italy, Orlande de Lassus from Flanders, Tomás Luis de Victoria from Spain, and Thomas Tallis and William Byrd from England. ➤ Madrigals were developed in Italy by members of the Flemish school and later by native composers, including Giovanni Gabrieli. They were written during the Elizabethan age in England by such composers as Thomas Morley, Orlando Gibbons, and Thomas Weelkes. Notable composers of organ music were Antonio de Cabezon in Spain and Andrea Gabrieli in Italy.

17th century The Florentine Academy (Camerata), a group of artists and writers, aimed to revive the principles of Greek tragedy. This led to the invention of dramatic recitative and the beginning of opera. Claudio Monteverdi was an early operatic composer; by the end of the century the form had evolved further in the hands of Alessandro Scarlatti in Italy and Jean-Baptiste Lully in France. In England the outstanding composer of the period was Henry Purcell. ➤ Oratorio was developed in Italy by Giacomo Carissimi; in Germany, Heinrich Schütz produced a new form of sacred music.

18th century The early part of the century was dominated by Johann Sebastian Bach and George Frideric Handel. Bach was a master of harmony and counterpoint. Handel is renowned for his dramatic oratorios. In France, their most important contemporaries were François Couperin in keyboard music and Jean-Philippe Rameau in grand opera and ballet; the later operas of Christoph Willibald von Gluck, with their emphasis on dramatic expression, saw a return to the principles of Monteverdi. The modern orchestra grew out of various movements of the mid-1700s, notably that led by Johann Stamitz at Mannheim. Bach's sons C P E Bach and J C Bach reacted against contrapuntal forms and developed sonata form, the basis of the classical sonata, quartet, and symphony. In these types of composition, mastery of style was achieved by the Viennese composers Joseph Haydn and Wolfgang Amadeus Mozart. With Ludwig van Beethoven, music assumed new structural form and growth in expressive function, with his late works providing the basis of Romanticism and even modernism.

19th century Romantic music, represented in its early stages by Carl Weber, Franz Schubert, Robert Schumann, Felix Mendelssohn, and Frédéric Chopin, tended to be more 'subjective' in emotional content. Orchestral colour was increasingly exploited – most notably by Hector Berlioz – and harmony became more chromatic. Nationalism became more important at this time, as seen in the intense Polish nationalism of Frédéric Chopin; the use of Hungarian folk music by Franz Liszt; the works of the Russians Nikolai Rimsky-Korsakov, Alexander Borodin, Modest Mussorgsky, and, less typically, Pyotr Il'yich Tchaikovsky; the works of the Czechs Antonín Dvořák and Bedřich Smetana; the Norwegian Edvard Grieg; and the Spaniards Isaac Albéniz, Enrique Granados, and Manuel de Falla. Revolutionary changes were brought about by Richard Wagner in the field of opera creating a new genre of music theatre, although the traditional structure of the Italian style continued in the work of Gioacchino Rossini, Giuseppe Verdi, and Giacomo Puccini. Wagner's contemporary

Johannes Brahms stood for classical discipline of form combined with Romantic feeling. The Belgian César Franck, with a newly chromatic language, also renewed the tradition of polyphonic writing.

20th century Around 1900 a reaction against Romanticism was found in the Impressionism of Claude Debussy and Maurice Ravel, and the exotic chromaticism of Igor Stravinsky and Alexander Skriabin. In Austria and Germany, the tradition of Anton Bruckner, Gustav Mahler, and Richard Strauss was developed in the new world of atonal, then serial expressionism by Arnold Schoenberg, Alban Berg, and Anton Webern.

After World War I neoclassicism, represented by Igor Stravinsky, Sergei Prokofiev, and Paul Hindemith, attempted to restore 18th-century principles of objectivity while combining classical harmony with colouristic dissonance. More forward-looking composers such as Edgard Varèse began using the orchestra to produce blocks of sound to be played off against each other, anticipating later figures such as György Ligeti, Harrison Birtwistle, and Olivier Messiaen. In Paris, composers such as Debussy and Ravel radically altered the use of consonance and form, while composers further from the cosmopolitan centres of Europe, such as Edward Elgar, Frederick Delius, and Jean Sibelius, took the Romantic symphonic tradition forward by extending other parameters than harmony, Sibelius using modernist formal development together with a Romantic harmonic language. The rise of radio and recorded media created a new mass market for classical and Romantic music, but one which was initially resistant to music by contemporary composers. Organizations such as the International Society for Contemporary Music became increasingly responsible for ensuring that new music continued to be publicly performed. Interest in English folk music was revived by the work of Gustav Holst and Ralph Vaughan Williams.

Among other important contemporary composers are Béla Bartók and Zoltán Kodály in Hungary; Olivier Messiaen in France; Luigi Dallapiccola and Luciano Berio in Italy; Dmitri Shostakovich in Russia; and Arthur Bliss, Aaron Copland, Edmund Rubbra, William Walton, Samuel Barber, Benjamin Britten, and Michael Tippett in England and the USA.

modern developments The second half of the 20th century saw dramatic changes in the nature of composition, with many new techniques such as those developed from medieval and biological or natural processes by composers such as Harrison Birtwistle, and the immense complexity and ultra-expression of Brian Ferneyhough. The recording studio has helped in the development of ➤ **musique concrète**, based on recorded natural

sounds, and ➤ **electronic music**, in which sounds are generated electrically. These developments meant that music could be created as a finished object without the need for interpretation by live performers. Chance music, promoted by John ➤ **Cage**, introduced the idea of a music designed to provoke unforeseen results and thereby make new connections; ➤ **aleatory music**, developed by Karlheinz ➤ **Stockhausen**, introduced performers to freedom of choice from a range of options, and in Poland, Witold Lutosławski took this further to create immense controlled complexity in sound, while allowing performers much freedom to play naturally. Further initiatives by Stockhausen introduced new musical sounds and compositional techniques, often combining electronic and live performances. Since the 1960s the computer has become a focus of attention for developments in the synthesis of musical tones, and also in the automation of compositional techniques, most notably at Stanford University and MIT in the USA, and at IRCAM in Paris.

musica ficta (Latin 'feigned music') in music of the Middle Ages, the theory of nondiatonic notes (those notes not normally present in a simple C major scale). B flat was the first nondiatonic note allowed, in order to avoid the ➤ **tritone** B–F. Other notes later became sharpened or flattened for similar reasons. Musica ficta also introduced nondiatonic notes in order to create a semitone between the ➤ **leading note** (seventh note of a scale) and ➤ **tonic** (first note of a scale). For example, when the tonic is G the leading note F must become F sharp in order to have the desired semitone.

Musica ficta was not always written using ➤ **accidentals** (sharp, flat, or natural signs); rather it required precise knowledge by the performer of correct theory and practice.

musica figurata (Latin and Italian 'figured or decorated music') in music, ornamentation of ➤ **plainsong** by auxiliary notes or the addition of a ➤ **descant** sung against a fundamental melody.

musical 20th-century form of dramatic musical performance, combining elements of song, dance, and the spoken word, often characterized by lavish staging and large casts. It developed from the operettas and musical comedies of the 19th century.

operetta The operetta is a light-hearted entertainment with extensive musical content: Jacques Offenbach, Johann Strauss, Franz Lehár, and Gilbert and Sullivan all composed operettas.

musical comedy The musical comedy is an anglicization of the French *opéra bouffe*, of which the first was *A Gaiety Girl* (1893), mounted by George Edwardes (1852–1915) at the Gaiety Theatre, London. Typical musical comedies of the 1920s were *Rose Marie* (1924) by Rudolf Friml (1879–1972); *The Student Prince* (1924) and *The Desert Song* (1926), both by Sigmund Romberg (1887–1951); and *No, No, Nanette* (1925) by Vincent Youmans (1898–1946). The 1930s and 1940s were an era of sophisticated musical comedies with many filmed examples and a strong US presence (Irving Berlin, Jerome Kern, Cole Porter, and George Gershwin). In England Noël Coward and Ivor Novello also wrote musicals.

musical In 1943 Rodgers and Hammerstein's *Oklahoma!* introduced an integration of plot and music, which was developed in Lerner and Loewe's *My Fair Lady* (1956) and Leonard Bernstein's *West Side Story* (1957). Sandy Wilson's *The Boy Friend* (1953) revived the British musical and was followed by hits such as Lionel Bart's *Oliver!* (1960). Musicals began to branch into religious and political themes with *Oh, What a Lovely War* (1963), produced by Joan Littlewood and Charles Chiltern, and the Andrew Lloyd Webber musicals *Jesus Christ Superstar* (1971) and *Evita* (1978). Another category of musical, substituting a theme for conventional plotting, includes Stephen Sondheim's *Company* (1970), Hamlisch and Kleban's *A Chorus Line* (1975), and Lloyd Webber's *Cats* (1981), using verses by T S Eliot. In the 1980s, 19th-century melodrama was popular; for example, *Les Misérables* (first London performance 1985) and *The Phantom of the Opera* (1986).

musical box toy musical instrument made in various shapes of decorative boxes and containing a cylinder with pins which, turning round by clockwork, twangs the teeth of a metal comb producing the notes of a musical scale. The pins are arranged so as to make the pattern of a piece of music. Several sets of pins can be set in the barrel, only one touching the teeth at a time, a choice of more than one piece being thus capable of being produced by the simple device of shifting the barrel slightly sideways. The musical box industry is traditionally centred in Switzerland.

musical idea term associated with Arnold ➤ Schoenberg, who used it to describe the initial musical impulse behind a work. Sometimes the term refers to a single musical motive, which he termed the fundamental motive, and sometimes to a more abstract concept of which the fundamental motive is a single instance. In any case, it is the musical idea which gives a work both its unique character and its organic unity. See ➤ motivic analysis.

musical instrument digital interface manufacturers' standard for digital music equipment; see ➤ MIDI.

Musical Offering work by J S Bach; see ➤ *Musikalische Opfer*.

musical saw musical instrument made from a hand saw. The handle is clasped between the knees with the top of the blade held in one hand so that it forms an S curve. A cello bow is played with the other hand across the back edge of the blade to produce an eerie wailing sound. The pitch is altered by varying the curvature of the blade. Composers include George ➤ **Crumb**.

musical science the ancient Greeks distinguished between **musical sound** as an indicator of Pythagorean concepts of number relation and **musical influences** on human (and animal) behaviour, as recounted in the Orpheus legend.

In general, musical science has sought to rationalize ➤ **pitch**, first into ➤ **modes**, then into ➤ **scales** and ➤ **temperament**, and to quantify ➤ **timbre**, to account for differences between sounds of the same pitch. To this end it has evolved a standard division of the ➤ **octave** allowing for the development of Western ➤ **tonality**, a universal notation for pitch, and keyboard instruments for conducting experiments in tonal relations, all of which prefigure recent digital technologies of information storage and retrieval.

The art of music has developed and adapted the discoveries of musical science for the purposes of artistic expression. The emotional power of music lies in its ability to transcend language and appeal directly to subconscious associations of ➤ **melody**, ➤ **rhythm**, ➤ **dynamics**, and ➤ **tempo**.

musical snuffbox kind of musical box made especially in the 18th century, with a double bottom concealing a mechanical music apparatus beneath its normal contents.

musica recta (Latin 'orthodox music') term used in the 14th and 15th centuries to mean the notes of the ➤ **gamut** as projected by the three kinds of ➤ **hexachord**, that is, the white-note scale from G to E but including B flat as well as B natural (or, with a key signature of one flat, including E flat as well as E natural, and so on). Since this was the normal scale, the note B could be sung either flat or natural without special indications. This concept is important for editorial accidentals and ➤ **musica ficta**: where there is an alternative, *musica recta* should be operated before *musica ficta*.

musica reservata (Latin 'reserved music') 16th-century term applied to music intended for connoisseurs and private occasions, particularly vocal music that faithfully interpreted the words.

music drama alternative term for ➤ **opera** used by composers, notably Richard ➤ **Wagner**, who felt that the older term implies methods and forms for which they had no use.

music hall British light theatrical entertainment, in which singers, dancers, comedians, and acrobats perform in 'turns'. The music hall's heyday was at the beginning of the 20th century, with such artistes as Marie Lloyd, Harry Lauder, and George Formby. The US equivalent is vaudeville.

Many performers had a song with which they were associated, such as Albert Chevalier (1861–1923) ('My Old Dutch'), or a character 'trademark', such as Vesta Tilley's immaculate masculine outfit as Burlington Bertie. Later stars of music hall included Sir George Robey, Gracie Fields, the Crazy Gang, Ted Ray, and the US comedian Danny Kaye.

history Music hall originated in the 17th century, when tavern keepers acquired the organs that the Puritans had banished from churches. On certain nights organ music was played, and this resulted in a weekly entertainment known as the 'free and easy'. Certain theatres in London and the provinces then began to specialize in variety entertainment. With the advent of radio and television, music hall declined, but in the 1960s and 1970s there was a revival in working men's clubs and in pubs.

Music Makers, The ode for contralto solo, chorus, and orchestra by Elgar, Op. 69 (poem by Arthur O'Shaughnessy), first performed at the Birmingham Festival on 1 October 1912. The work contains a number of quotations from earlier works by Elgar.

musicology the academic study of music, including music history, music analysis, music aesthetics, and ➔ performance practice. All areas of music fall under the category of musicology except composition, performance studies, and practical music teaching (pedagogy).

music theatre staged performance of vocal music that deliberately challenges, in style and subject matter, traditional operatic pretensions.

Drawing on English music hall and European cabaret and *Singspiel* traditions, it flourished during the Depression of the 1920s and 1930s as working-class opera, for example the Brecht—Weill *Die Dreigroschenoper/The Threepenny Opera* (1928); in the USA as socially conscious musical, for example Gershwin's *Porgy and Bess* (1935); and on film, in René Clair's *Sous les toits de Paris/Under the Roofs of Paris* (1930, music composed by Raoul Moretti) and *À nous la liberté/Freedom for Us* (1931, music by Georges Auric).

In the 1960s and 1970s in Britain the composers Alexander Goehr, Harrison Birtwistle, and Peter Maxwell ➔ Davies wrote several important music theatre pieces, and Birtwistle and Maxwell Davies formed the Pierrot Players (later called The Fires of London) to extend the music theatre repertory. Other composers addressing a mood of social unrest in the years after 1968 include Henze (*Essay on Pigs*, 1968), Berio (*Recital I*, 1972), and Ligeti (*Le Grand Macabre/The Great Macabre*, 1978).

Since 1970 music theatre has emerged as a favoured idiom for short-term community music projects produced by outreach departments of civic arts centres and opera houses.

Musikalische Opfer, Das, The Musical Offering a late work by Bach (BWV 1079) containing two *ricercari*, a fugue in canon, nine canons, and a sonata for flute, violin, and continuo, all based on a theme given to Bach by Frederick II of Prussia during the composer's visit to Potsdam in 1747.

musikalischer Spass, Ein, *A Musical Joke* a work in four movements for two horns and strings by Mozart, K522 (composed June 1787), sometimes also known by such names as 'The Village Band'. But the joke is not at the expense of rustic performers; the work is a parody of a symphony by an incompetent composer.

musique concrète (French 'concrete music') music created by reworking natural sounds recorded on disk or tape. It was developed in 1948 by Pierre ➔ Schaeffer and Pierre ➔ Henry in the drama studios of Paris Radio. The term was used to differentiate the process from ➔ electronic music, which used synthesized tones and sounds. From the mid-1950s the two techniques were usually combined, and the term is now purely historic.

musique mesurée (French 'measured music') method of setting words to music cultivated in 16th-century France by Jean Antoine de Baïf, Claude ➔ Le Jeune, Jacques ➔ Mauduit, and others. The metrical rhythm of the words was based on classical scansion and the musical rhythm followed this exactly, long syllables being set to long notes, and short syllables to short notes.

Mussorgsky, Modest Petrovich (1839–1881) Russian composer. He was a member of the group of five composers ('The ➔ Five'). His opera masterpiece *Boris Godunov* (1869, revised 1871–72) touched a political nerve and employed realistic transcriptions of speech patterns. Many of his works, including *Pictures at an Exhibition* (1874) for piano, were 'revised' and orchestrated by others, including Rimsky-Korsakov, Ravel, and Shostakovich, and some have only recently been restored to their original harsh beauty.

Mussorgsky, born in Karevo (Pskov, Russia), resigned his commission in the army in 1858 to concentrate on music while working as a government clerk. He was influenced by both folk music and literature. Among his other works are the incomplete operas *Khovanshchina* and *Sorochintsy Fair*, the orchestral *Night on the Bare Mountain* (1867), and many songs. He died in poverty, from alcoholism.

The son of well-to-do landowners, Mussorgsky was sent to St Petersburg at the age of ten to prepare for a military school, which he entered in 1852. He joined a regiment in 1856 and he did not seriously think of a music career until he met the composers Dargomizhsky and Balakirev in 1857 and began to study under the latter. He resigned his commission in 1858, but never studied systematically. His family's fortune waned after the liberation of the serfs in 1861, but he was in sympathy with that movement and content to live on the small pay he obtained for a position in the civil service. He finished *Boris Godunov* in its first form in 1869, but it was rejected by the Imperial Opera and he recast it 1871–72, this second version being produced in 1874. It gained wide popularity in an orchestration by Rimsky-Korsakov, but Mussorgsky's original is now more often preferred. He sank into ever more acute poverty and ruined his health with drink, but between 1872 and 1880 managed to complete most of his historical opera, *Khovanshchina*.

Works OPERA *Salammbô* (after Flaubert, unfinished, 1863–66), *The Marriage* (Gogol, unfinished, 1868, produced 1909), *Boris Godunov* (after Pushkin, 1869, revised 1872), *Khovanshchina* (1886), *Sorochintsy Fair* (after Gogol, unfinished, 1874–80); an act for a collective opera, *Mlada* (with Borodin, Cui, and Rimsky-Korsakov, afterwards used for other works).

ORCHESTRAL *Night on the Bare Mountain* for orchestra (later used in *Mlada* [with chorus] and further revised) and three small orchestral pieces; suite *Pictures at an Exhibition* (1874) and twelve small pieces for piano.

OTHER four Russian folk songs for male chorus; over 60 songs including cycles *The Nursery* (1870), *Sunless*, and *Songs and Dances of Death* (1875–77).

Mustafà, Domenico (1829–1912) Italian castrato and composer. He was the last male soprano of the Sistine Chapel, which he entered in 1848. He was later maestro di cappella there until 1902, when he was succeeded by Lorenzo Perosi.

Works CHURCH MUSIC *Miserere*, *Tu es Petrus*, *Dies irae* for seven voices, *Laudate*, and other church music.

Mustel organ keyboard reed instrument invented by Victor Mustel (1815–90) of Paris. It is of the ➤ harmonium type, but contains some improvements, including a device by which the top and bottom halves of the keyboard can be separately controlled for dynamic expression.

muta (Italian 'change') musical direction used in scores where a change is to be made between instruments (such as A and B flat clarinet or different horn crooks) or in tunings (such as kettledrums, strings of instruments of the violin family temporarily tuned to abnormal notes). The plural is *mutano*.

mutation in music, an organ ➤ stop which produces a ➤ pitch other than the normal wavelength pitch (8 ft) or one related by octave (16 ft, 4 ft, 2 ft, or 1 ft). For example, a Quint stop (2⅔ ft) produces a pitch an octave and a fifth higher than the depressed key (for example the C4 key sounds at G5). Other mutation stops sound higher by two octaves and a third, by two octaves and a fifth, or by two octaves and a flat seventh. They are not played alone, but with other stops which sound their proper notes.

mute in music, any device used to dampen the vibration of an instrument and so affect the tone. Orchestral strings apply a form of clamp to the bridge – the change is used to dramatic effect by Bartók in the opening bars of *Music for Strings, Percussion, and Celesta* (1936). Brass instruments use the hand or a plug of metal or cardboard inserted in the bell.

Although the word implies a reduction of volume, a variety of mutes used in big band jazz are used principally to vary the quality of tone, as in Stravinsky's *Ebony Concerto* (1945).

Müthel, Johann Gottfried (1728–1788) German organist, harpsichordist, and composer. He was appointed court organist to the Duke of Mecklenburg-Schwerin in 1747. On leave of absence to study in 1750 he visited Johann Sebastian Bach in Leipzig just before he died. He also visited Johann Altnikol in Naumburg, C P E Bach in Berlin, and Telemann in Hamburg.

He was a pupil of Adolph Kunzen (1720–81) in Lübeck. From 1755 he was an organist in Riga.

Works concertos, sonatas, and miscellaneous pieces for harpsichord.

Muzak proprietary name for ➤ piped music.

Muzen Siciliens, Die*, *The Muses of Sicily concerto by Henze for chorus, two pianos, wind, and percussion (text from Virgil's *Eclogues*), first performed in Berlin on 20 September 1966.

Muzio Scevola, Il*, *Mucius Scaevola opera by Filippo Mattei (or Amadei), Giovanni Bononcini, and Handel (libretto by P A Rolli), produced in London at the King's Theatre, Haymarket, on 15 April 1721.

Myaskovsky, Nikolay Russian composer; see Nikolai ➤ Miaskovsky.

My Country cycle of symphonic poems by Bedřich Smetana; see ➤ *Má Vlast*.

Mysliveček, Josef (1737–1781) Bohemian composer. Between 1767 and 1780 he wrote about 30 operas, most to texts by Metastasio, for the principal theatres in Italy. His oratorio *Abrame ed Isacco* (1776) was admired by Mozart.

He studied organ and composition in Prague, and published there in 1760 a set of symphonies named after the first six months of the year. In 1763 he went to study with Giovanni Battista Pescetti in Venice, and a year later produced his first opera in Parma. He also visited Munich, where he met Mozart in 1777 (they had already met in 1772).

Works OPERA *Medea* (1764), *Il Bellerofonte* (1767), *Farnace*, *Demofoonte* (1769), *Ezio*, *Il Demetrio* (1773), and others.

ORATORIOS *Abramo ed Isacco* (1776) and three others.

OTHER symphonies; concertos; chamber music; church music.

Mystic Trumpeter, The scena for soprano and orchestra by Holst (text by Whitman, 1904), first performed London, 29 June 1905. Revised 1912 and performed London, 25 January 1913.

Nabokov, Nikolai (1903–1978) Russian-born US composer. He studied in Berlin and Stuttgart. He became attached to Diaghilev's Russian Ballet in the 1920s, and later settled in the USA.

Works OPERA AND STAGE MUSIC operas *The Holy Devil* (1958) and *Love's Labour Lost* (1973); ballets *Ode on seeing the Aurora Borealis* (1928), *Union Pacific* (1934), *Don Quixote* (1965); incidental music to a dramatic version of Milton's *Samson Agonistes*.

ORCHESTRAL AND CHORAL symphony *Sinfonia biblica* for orchestra; piano concerto (1932); three symphonies (1930–68); cantata *Collectionneur d'échos* for soprano, bass, chorus, and percussion; six poems of Anna Akhmatova for soprano and orchestra (1966).

Nabucco, Nebuchadnezzar opera by Verdi (libretto by T Solera), produced at La Scala in Milan, Italy, on 9 March 1842. In the story, Nabucco's supposed daughter, Abigaille, who is actually an adopted slave, attempts to seize power.

Nachtanz (German 'after-dance') quicker dance following a slower one, often with the same music in different rhythm. Prevalent in the 15th–16th centuries, the dance frequently consisted of the ➤ **galliard** in triple time, which is more lively, following the more stately ➤ **pavane** in double time.

Nacht in Venedig, Eine*, *A Night in Venice operetta by Johann Strauss, Jr, (libretto by F Zell and R Genée), produced in Berlin at the Städtisches Theater on 3 October 1883. It was written for the opening of that theatre. Its first Vienna performance was at the Theater an der Wien on 9 October 1883. In the story, the elderly Delaqua wants to marry his ward, but has double competition.

Nachtlager von Granada, Das*, *The Night-Camp at Granada opera by Conradin Kreutzer (libretto by K J B von Braunthal, based on a play by Friedrich Kind). It was first produced in Vienna at the Josefstadt Theatre on 13 January 1834. In the story, the crown prince of Spain helps Gabriela unite with Gomez.

Nachtmusik (German 'night piece') see ➤ nocturne.

Nachtstücke und Arien*, *Nocturnes and Arias work by Hans Werner Henze for soprano and orchestra (text by Ingeborg Bachmann). It was first performed in Donaueschingen on 20 October 1957, and was conducted by Rosbaud.

Nägeli, Hans Georg (1773–1836) Swiss composer, teacher, and publisher. In 1803 he began to publish a series entitled *Répertoire des clavecinistes* and included in it Beethoven's sonatas Op. 31 nos 1 and 2, adding four bars to the former, much to the composer's annoyance.

He studied at Zürich and Bern and began to publish music at Zürich in 1792. He established the *Schweizerbund* choral society, which soon formed branches, and reformed music teaching in schools on the lines of Pestalozzi's education system. He also wrote on music education and lectured on music in Switzerland and Germany. He wrote 15 books of popular songs, including *Freut euch des Lebens* and *Lied vom Rhein*.

Works CHURCH MUSIC AND SOLO church and school music; toccatas and other piano pieces.

Naich, Hubert (c.1513–after 1546) Flemish composer. He lived in Rome, where he was a member of the Accademia degli Amici. He published a book of madrigals there about 1540.

nail violin or **nail fiddle** or **nail harmonica** 18th-century musical instrument, invented by Johann Wilde, a German violinist living at St Petersburg, Russia. It had a semicircular soundboard studded with nails along the rounded edge, which were scraped with a bow.

Naïs pastoral-héroïque by Jean-Philippe Rameau (libretto by L de Cahusac). It was composed for the peace of Aix-la-Chapelle and was produced at the Opéra in Paris on 22 April 1749. The suitors of Naïs are overwhelmed by Neptune.

Naissance de la lyre, La*, *The Birth of the Lyre lyric opera in one act by Albert Roussel (libretto by Théodore Reinach, after Sophocles). It was first produced in Paris at the Opéra on 1 July

1925, with choreography by Nijinska. Symphonic fragments in six movements were conducted by Paray in a performance in Paris on 13 November 1927.

nakers (from Arabic through old French *na-caires*) Old English name for the ➤ timpani or kettledrums, which were then much smaller and therefore higher in pitch, and could not have their tuning altered. In cavalry regiments they were played on horseback, hung on either side of the horse's neck.

Namensfeier, Name Celebration concert overture by Beethoven, Op. 115, in C major. It was composed in 1814 in Vienna and performed at the Redoutensaal on 25 December 1815, conducted by the composer. The name-day was that of the Austrian emperor, which happened to coincide with the completion of the work; it was not composed specially for that occasion.

Namouna ballet by Edouard Lalo (scenario by Charles Nuitter; choreographed by Marius Petipa), produced in Paris at the Opéra on 6 March 1882.

Nancarrow, Conlon (1912–1997) US composer. Using a player-piano as a form of synthesizer, punching the rolls by hand, he experimented with mathematically derived combinations of rhythm and tempo in *37 Studies for Piano-Player* (1950–68), works of a hypnotic persistence that aroused the admiration of a younger generation of minimalist composers.

He studied at the Cincinnati College-Conservatory 1929–32 and later with Slonimsky and Sessions in Boston. After involvement in the Spanish Civil War he lived in Mexico 1940–81. His music is notated by perforating piano player rolls, although it has been played by other means – the string quartet no. 3 was given its first performance in 1988 by the Arditti Quartet.

Works CHAMBER AND SOLO *Blues and Prelude* for piano (1935), *Toccata* for violin and piano (1935), septet (1940), sonatina for piano (1940); trio for clarinet, bassoon, and piano (1943); suite for orchestra (1943); three string quartets.

Nanino, Giovanni Bernardino (c. 1560–1623) Italian composer. He studied under his brother, Giovanni Maria Nanino, went to Rome, and was maestro di cappella at the church of San Luigi de' Francesi 1591–1608, and later at that of San Lorenzo in Damaso. He made early use of the basso continuo (a harmonic accompaniment with a bass line, prevalent in 17th-century baroque music).

Works CHURCH MUSIC motets, psalms, and other church music, some with organ accompaniment.
CHAMBER AND VOCAL five-part madrigals.

Napolitana a light song for several voices, allied to the ➤ villanella (an Italian part song set to rustic words) and cultivated at Naples especially in the 16th and 17th centuries.

Nápravník, Eduard Franzevich (1839–1916) Czech composer and conductor. As principal conductor of the Mariinsky Theatre, St Petersburg, he gave the first performance of Mussorgsky's opera *Boris Godunov* in 1874.

He studied music precariously as a child, being the son of a poor teacher, and was left an orphan and destitute in 1853, but succeeded in entering the Organ School in Prague, where he studied with Kittel and others, and became an assistant teacher. In 1861 he went to St Petersburg as conductor of Prince Yusupov's private orchestra, became organist and assistant conductor at the Imperial theatres in 1863, second conductor in 1867, and chief conductor, succeeding Liadov, in 1869, holding the post until his death; he gave the first performances of *Boris Godunov*, five operas by Tchaikovsky, including *The Maid of Orleans*, *Mazepa*, and *The Queen of Spades*, and five by Rimsky-Korsakov, including *May Night*, *The Snow Maiden*, and *Christmas Eve*. He also conducted concerts of the Russian Music Society.

Works OPERA AND STAGE MUSIC operas *The Nizhniy-Novgorodians* (1868), *Harold* (1886), *Dubrovsky* (1895), and *Francesca da Rimini* (on Stephen Phillips's play, 1902); incidental music for Alexei Tolstoy's play *Don Juan* (1892).

ORCHESTRAL AND CHORAL ballads for voices and orchestra *The Voyevode*, *The Cossack*, and *Tamara* (after Lermontov); four symphonies (1860–79), no. 3 *The Demon* (after Lermontov), suite; *Solemn Overture*; marches and national dances for orchestra; concerto and fantasy on Russian themes for piano and orchestra; fantasy and suite for violin and orchestra.

CHAMBER three string quartets (1873–78), string quintet (1897), two piano trios, piano quartet, violin and piano sonata, two suites for cello and piano; string instrument and piano pieces.

naqqara kettledrum of the Islamic world, the Caucasus, and Central Asia. It is used in military, religious, and ceremonial music. Made of silver, copper, brass, wood, or pottery the naqqara are usually played in pairs with the skin drum heads tuned at different pitches and beaten with a stick.

Narciso, Narcissus opera by Domenico Scarlatti (libretto by C S Capece), produced in Rome at the private theatre of Queen Maria Casimira of Poland on 20 January 1714, under the title of *Amor d'un' ombra*. It was performed in London on 31 May 1720, with additional music by Thomas Roseingrave, under the new title.

Nasolini, Sebastiano (c.1768–c.1816) Italian composer. He was a pupil of Ferdinando Bertoni in Venice, and in 1787 was appointed *maestro al cembalo* at the opera in Trieste, and 1788–90 maestro di cappella of the cathedral there. From 1790 he devoted himself to opera composition.

Works OPERA *Nitteti* (1788), *Andromaca* (1790), *La morte di Cleopatra* (1791), *Eugenia* (1792), *Le feste d'Iside* (1794), *Merope*, *La morte di Mitridate* (1796), *Il medico di Lucca* (1797), *Gli umori contrari* (1798), *Il ritorno di Serse* (1816).

national anthem patriotic song for official occasions. In Britain 'God Save the King/Queen' has been accepted as the national anthem since 1745, although both music and words are of much earlier origin. The US national anthem, 'The Star-Spangled Banner', was written in 1814 by Francis Scott ➔ Key and was adopted officially in 1931. The German anthem 'Deutschland über Alles/Germany before Everything' is sung to music by Joseph Haydn. The French national anthem, the ➔ 'Marseillaise', dates from 1792.

Countries within the Commonwealth retain 'God Save the King/Queen' as the 'royal anthem', adopting their own anthem as a mark of independence. These include 'Advance Australia Fair' (1974–76) and from 1984 'O Canada', written in 1882 and adopted gradually through popular usage. The anthem of united Europe is Schiller's 'Ode to Joy' set by Beethoven in his Ninth Symphony.

nationalism in music, the development by 19th-century composers of a musical style that would express the characteristics of their own country. They did this by including tunes from their nation's folk music, and taking scenes from their country's history, legends, and folk tales, as a basis for their compositions. Nationalism was encouraged by governments in the early 20th century for propaganda purposes in times of war and political tension. Composers of nationalist music include Bedřich ➔ Smetana, Jean ➔ Sibelius, Edvard ➔ Grieg, Antonín ➔ Dvořák, Carl ➔ Nielsen, Zoltán ➔ Kodály, Aaron Copland, Edward Elgar, Dmitri ➔ Shostakovich, and Stephen ➔ Foster.

Nattiez, Jean-Jacques (1945–) Canadian musicologist. As director of the Groupe de Recherches en Sémiologie Musicale at the University of Montréal from 1974, he is important for developing the use of semiotics in musical analysis, as first expounded in his book *Fondements d'une sémiologie musicale* (1975).

natural, symbol ♮ in music, a sign placed in front of a note, cancelling a previous sharp or flat. A **natural trumpet** or **horn** is an instrument without valves, and can therefore only play natural harmonics.

naturale (Italian 'natural') musical direction indicating that a voice or instrument, after performing a passage in some unusual way (such as *mezza voce* or muted), is to return to its normal manner.

Naumann, Johann Gottlieb (1741–1801) German composer. At the age of 16 he accompanied the Swedish violinist Wesström to Hamburg, then to Italy, where he studied with Tartini, Hasse, and Padre Martini. He produced his first opera in Venice in 1763, and the following year was appointed to the court at Dresden as second composer of church music. He revisited Italy to produce operas 1765–68 and 1772–74, and in 1776 became kapellmeister in Dresden, where, apart from visits to Stockholm, Copenhagen, and Berlin, he remained till his death. His opera *Gustav Vasa* was revived in Stockholm in 1991.

Works OPERA *Achille in Sciro* (1767), *La clemenza di Tito* (1769), *Solimano*, *Armida*, *Ipermestra*; *Amphion* (1778), *Cora och Alonzo* (1782), *Gustaf Vasa* (1786; all three in Swedish); *Orpheus og Euridice* (in Danish, 1786), *Protesilao* (with Reichardt), *La dama soldato* (1790), *Aci e Galatea* (1801), and others.

CHURCH MUSIC AND ORATORIOS 21 Masses, other church music, 13 oratorios.

Navarraise, La, *The Girl of Navarre* opera by Massenet (libretto by J Claretie and H Cain, based on the former's story *La Cigarette*). Produced in London at Covent Garden on 20 June 1894, the opera is about the girl Anita's attempts to win a dowry by assassinating a military leader.

Navarro, Juan (c.1530–1580) Spanish composer. He was highly regarded as a polyphonist, and his church music was popular in Spain, Portugal, and Mexico for some time.

After the death of Cristóbal Morales in 1553 he competed unsuccessfully for the post of maestro di cappella at Málaga Cathedral, but he later obtained a similar post in Salamanca. He visited Rome in 1590, where his nephew Fernando Navarro Salazar arranged for the publication of some of his church music.

Works CHURCH MUSIC AND OTHER psalms, hymns, Magnificats, madrigals, and other pieces.

Naylor, Bernard (1907–1986) English composer, conductor, and organist. He studied at the Royal College of Music in London with Vaughan Williams and Holst; he conducted in Winnipeg and Montréal from 1932, and settled in Canada in 1959.

Works ORCHESTRAL twelve motets in two sets (1949, 1952); *The Annunciation according to St Luke* for soloists, chorus, and orchestra (1949); *Variations* for orchestra (1960); string trio (1960); *Stabat Mater* (1961); *The Nymph and the Faun* for mezzo and ensemble (text by Marvell,

1965); *Three Sacred Pieces* for chorus and orchestra (1971).

Naylor, Edward (Woodall) (1867–1934) English organist, musicologist, and composer. He studied at Cambridge and the Royal College of Music in London, and after two appointments as organist there he returned to Cambridge in 1897 to become organist at Emmanuel College, taking the doctorate in music degree at the university. He lectured and wrote on music, publishing a book on *Shakespeare and Music*.

Works OPERA *The Angelus* (produced at Covent Garden, 1909).

ORCHESTRAL AND OTHER cantata *Arthur the King* (1902); part songs; piano trio in D major.

Neapolitan sixth a chord consisting of a minor third and a minor sixth on the subdominant of the key, which came into vogue in the 17th century. It occurs most often in a cadential progression in a minor key.

The Neapolitan sixth in an A minor cadence.

Neapolitan Songs, Five, German **Fünf neapolitanische Lieder** work by Hans Werner Henze for baritone and orchestra (to an anonymous 17th-century text). It was first performed in Frankfurt on 26 May 1956, with Fischer-Dieskau.

Nebra, José (Melchor de) (1702–1768) Spanish organist and composer. He wrote religious and secular works for the stage. In 1751, he was made vice-maestro di cappella at the royal chapel in Madrid under Francesco Corselli (c.1702–1778), who neglected his duties for the composition of Italian operas. By 1757, Nebra had completely reorganized the court music.

He became organist at the Convent of the Descalzas Reales in Madrid and principal organist at the royal chapel in 1724. After the destruction of the library there in the fire of 24 December 1734, he and Antonio Literes Carrión (1673–1747)

were commissioned to replace the lost church music and to restore what had survived. In 1758, he composed a Requiem (*Pro defunctis*) for eight voices, flute, and strings for the funeral of Queen Barbara of Braganza, who had been Domenico Scarlatti's patroness.

Works STAGE AND CHURCH MUSIC 57 stage works; Requiem, Miserere, psalms, and other church music; villancico for four voices.

neck on a stringed musical instrument, the narrow piece of wood which projects from the ➤ soundbox, supporting the ➤ fingerboard. At its end is the peg box, which secures the strings.

Neefe, Christian Gottlob (1748–1798) German conductor and composer. He studied in Leipzig under Hiller, whom he succeeded as conductor of a touring opera company in 1776. He settled in Bonn in 1779, where he was appointed court organist three years later. Beethoven was his pupil from the age of 11. The French occupation of Bonn in 1794 cost him his post, and from 1796 he was music director of the Bossann theatre company in Dessau.

Works OPERA AND STAGE MUSIC operas *Die Apotheke* (1771), *Adelheid von Veltheim*, *Amors Guckkasten* (1772), *Die Einsprüche* (1772), *Heinrich und Lyda* (1776), *Sophonisbe*, *Zemire und Azor* (1776), and others; incidental music for Shakespeare's *Macbeth*.

OTHER church music, chamber music.

Neel, Boyd (1905–1981) English conductor. He founded the Boyd Neel String Orchestra in 1933 and gave the first performance of Britten's *Variations on a Theme of Frank Bridge* at Salzburg in 1937. The orchestra was renamed Philomusica of London in 1957. He was dean of Toronto Conservatory 1953–70.

Neidhart von Reuental (c.1180–c.1240) German Minnesinger (a poet and singer about courtly love in the 12th–14th centuries). A younger contemporary of Walther von der Vogelweide, his music survived in print during the Renaissance. Several of his songs are preserved; many others are attributed to him.

He went on a crusade 1217–19 and settled in Austria on his return.

neighbour-note or **neighbouring harmony** note in a melodic line which is not harmonized, and which moves by step away from a harmonized note, or by step onto a harmonized note, or away and then back again. In voice-leading analysis, a neighbouring harmony is one in which a neighbour-note is harmonized, this harmony being subordinate to the main harmony. See also ➤ passing notes, ➤ prolongation.

Nelson Mass the name given to Haydn's Mass in D minor, composed in 1798. The fanfares in the

Benedictus are said to commemorate Nelson's victory in the battle of the Nile, but Haydn cannot have heard the news of the battle until after the Mass was finished. His own title was *Missa in angustiis*. It was first performed in Eisenstadt on 23 September 1798.

Nenna, Pomponio (c.1550–before 1613) Italian composer. He lived mainly at Naples and taught Gesualdo, Prince of Venosa (1594–99). He moved to Rome about 1608.

Works CHURCH MUSIC AND OTHER two books of responsories, nine books of madrigals.

neo-Bechstein piano electrophonic piano invented by Vierling of Berlin 1928–33 and further developed by Franco and Nernst, producing its notes by the conversion of electrical waves into audible sounds.

neoclassical in 20th-century music, term describing a deliberate combination of baroque or classical forms such as ➤ **sonata form**, ➤ **fugue**, and so on, and modern harmony, for example Sergey Prokofiev's ➤ *'Classical' Symphony no. 1* (1916–17), Igor Stravinsky's ballet *Apollo* (1927–28), and Busoni's opera *Doktor Faust* (1916–24).

neomodal modern music using new derivations from the ancient ➤ **modes**, harmonized, transposed, or otherwise altered.

Nero or **Néron** opera by Rubinstein (libretto, in French, by Jules Barbier). It was first produced, in German, in Hamburg at the Municipal Theatre on 1 November 1879.
See also ➤ *Nerone*.

Nerone, Nero opera by Boito (libretto by composer), begun in 1879, but left unfinished at Boito's death in 1918. Produced and edited by Tommasini and A Toscanini in Milan at La Scala on 1 May 1924, the opera is about the conflict between corrupt Romans and spiritual Christians as the city burns.

Nessler, Viktor (Ernst) (1841–1890) German composer. He was well known for his opera *Der Trompeter von Säckingen* (1884), which was often conducted by Mahler.

He studied theology at Strasbourg, but took to music and produced a French opera there in 1864. He then went to Leipzig, where he became a choral and afterwards an operatic conductor.

Works OPERA *Fleurette* (1864), *Die Hochzeitreise*, *Dornröschens Brautfahrt* (1867), *Nachtwächter und Student*, *Am Alexandertag*, *Irmingard* (1876), *Der Rattenfänger von Hameln* (1879), *Der wilde Jäger* (1881), *Der Trompeter von Säckingen* (after Scheffel's poem, 1884), *Otto der Schütz* (1886), *Die Rose von Strassburg* (1890).

OTHER part songs.

Neues vom Tage, **News of the Day** opera by Hindemith (libretto by M Schiffer), produced in Berlin at the Kroll Opera on 8 June 1929, conducted by Klemperer. The opera was condemned by Goebbels in 1934: 'in their eagerness to make a sensation atonal musicians exhibit naked women in the bathtub on stage in the most obscene situations'. (Exactly 50 years later Peter Hall's wife, Maria Ewing, took a nude bath in the Glyndebourne production of *Poppea*.)

Neukomm, Sigismund von (1778–1858) Austrian composer. As a chorister at Salzburg Cathedral he was a pupil of Michael Haydn, who in 1798 sent him to J Haydn in Vienna. In 1806 he went to Sweden and Russia, becoming conductor at the Tsar's German theatre in St Petersburg. He returned to Vienna in 1809 and went to live in Paris soon after, succeeding Dussek in 1812 as pianist to Talleyrand. From 1816 to 1821 he was maestro di cappella to Pedro I of Brazil, with whom he returned to Lisbon, after the revolution, afterwards travelling with Talleyrand. In 1829 he visited London, meeting Mendelssohn, and lived there and alternately in Paris for the rest of his life.

Works OPERA *Alexander in Indien* (1804), *Niobé* (1809), and others.

CHURCH MUSIC 48 Masses and Requiem for Louis XVI.

ORATORIOS *Mount Sinai*, *David*, and six others.

OTHER incidental music for Schiller's *Braut von Messina* (1805); songs.

Neumann, František (1874–1929) Czech composer and conductor. He conducted the first performances of Janáček's *Káta Kabanová*, *The Cunning Little Vixen*, *Šárka*, and *The Makropoulos Case*.

He started in a commercial and military career, but went to study music at the Leipzig Conservatory. After filling various chorus-master's and conductor's posts at German and Czech theatres, he went to Brno as chief conductor at the National Theatre.

Works OPERA *Idalka*, *Die Brautwerbung* (1901), *Liebelei* (on Schnitzler's play, 1910), *Herbststurm* (1919), *Beatrice Caracci* (1922).

STAGE MUSIC melodrama *Pan*; ballets *In Pleasant Pastures*, *The Peri*, *Pierrot*.

ORCHESTRAL symphonic poem *Infernal Dance*, suite *The Sunken Bell*, *Moravian Rhapsody*, overtures for orchestra.

OTHER octet, piano trio choruses, songs, Masses, and motets.

Neumark, Georg (1621–1681) German poet and musician. In 1657 he published a collection of sacred and secular songs, *Musikalischepoetischer Lustwald*; some were set to music by himself, including the hymn 'Wer nur den lieben Gott lässt walten'.

neumes signs in Eastern chant and Western ➤ **plainsong** (and in some medieval songbooks) indicating the single notes or groups of notes to which each syllable was to be sung. Originally not set on staves, but merely marked above the words and showing neither precise length nor exact pitch, they served as reminders of tunes already known to the singers.

New England Holidays unnumbered symphony by Ives, composed 1904–13. The work includes *Washington's birthday, Decoration Day, The Fourth of July,* and *Thanksgiving.* It was first performed in New York on 10 January 1931, and was conducted by Slonimsky.

Newlin, Dika (1923–) US musicologist and composer. Her writings include studies of Bruckner, Mahler, and Schoenberg; also translations, particularly of Schoenberg's writings: *Schoenberg Remembered: Diaries and Recollections, 1938–76* (1980).

She studied privately with Sessions and Schoenberg and then taught at Western Maryland College and Syracuse University. In 1952 she established a music department at Drew University, New Jersey. She has also composed for various media, especially chamber music.

Newman, John Henry (1801–1890) English theologian and poet. The composer Edward Elgar set his poem *The* ➤ **Dream of Gerontius.**

New Music, German **Die Neue Musik** term invented to describe the atonal and serial music of the ➤ **Second Viennese School** (Arnold Schoenberg, Alban Berg, and Anton Webern) and their followers. The term is used by Webern in the title of his autobiographical manifesto, *The Path to the New Music,* and especially by the critics Theodor ➤ **Adorno** and Carl ➤ **Dahlhaus.**

'New World' Symphony Dvořák's Ninth Symphony in E minor, Op. 95, with the subtitle *From the New World,* because it was written in the USA. Composed in 1893, it was first performed at the New York Philharmonic Society on 16 December 1893.

New Year opera in three acts by Michael Tippett (libretto by composer), produced in Houston on 5 October 1989. In the story, the neurotic psychologist Jo Ann finds the time-traveller Pelegrin and true love. He teaches her how to be independent before leaving again for the future.

nexus set see ➤ **set complex.**

ngoni plucked lute of the Manding peoples of West Africa. Commonly found with three strings, the ngoni is played exclusively by men from the professional musicians' caste and is used to accompany praise-singing and historical narrative.

Nibelungenlied, Song of the Nibelung ancient Teutonic epic in the Middle High German dialect. It has been the inspiration for many composers, including Heinrich ➤ **Dorn** (*Nibelungen*); Felix ➤ **Draeseke** (*Gudrun*); Ernest ➤ **Reyer** (➤ **Sigurd**) and, most famously, Richard ➤ **Wagner's** massive opera cycle *Der* ➤ **Ring des Nibelungen.**

Nibelung's Ring, The trilogy of music dramas with a prologue, by Richard Wagner; see ➤ **Ring des Nibelungen.**

Niccolini, Giuseppe (1762–1842) Italian composer. He was at first very successful in opera, but was eventually driven from the stage by Rossini. He was maestro di cappella at Piacenza Cathedral from 1819.

He studied under Giacomo Insanguine at the Conservatorio di Sant' Onofrio, Naples.

Works OPERA *I baccanti di Roma* (1801), *Traiano in Dacia* (1807), *Coriolano* (1808), and about 40 others.

OTHER Masses and other church music.

Nicholson, George (1949–) English composer, whose music is largely for chamber groups. He studied with Bernard Rands and David Blake.

Works CHAMBER AND VOCAL Overture for seven winds (1976), *Recycle* for eleven instruments (1976), *The Arrival of the Poet in the City,* melodrama for actor and seven instruments (1983), chamber concerto (1980), brass quintet (1977), *Aubade* for soprano and five instruments (1981), *Movements* for seven instruments (1983), *Stilleven* for five instruments (1985), *Blisworth Tunnel Blues* for soprano and ensemble (1986), *Sea-Change* for 14 strings (1988), cello concerto (1990), flute concerto (1993).

Nicholson, Richard (died 1639) English organist and composer. In 1595 he became choirmaster and organist at Magdalen College, Oxford, took a degree in music in 1596, and became the first professor of music there in 1627.

Works VOCAL anthems; madrigals, including one in *The Triumphes of Oriana;* 'dialogue' (or song cycle) 'Joane, quoth John' for three voices.

OTHER music for viols.

Nicodé, Jean Louis (1853–1919) German-Polish conductor and composer. He is known for his symphonic poems and song cycles.

In 1856 his family moved to Berlin, where Nicodé studied, first under his father and from 1869 at the Neue Akademie der Tonkunst. Afterwards he taught there and arranged concerts at which he appeared as pianist, toured in the Balkans with Désirée Artot and, in 1878, became professor at the Dresden Conservatory. From

1885 he devoted himself to conducting and composition.

Works ORCHESTRAL AND CHORAL symphonic ode *Das Meer* for solo voices, male chorus, orchestra, and organ (1889); symphonic poems *Maria Stuart* (after Schiller, 1880), *Die Jagd nach dem Glück, Gloria*; symphonic variations for orchestra; romance for violin and orchestra; cello and piano sonata; sonata and numerous pieces for piano; songs, including the cycle *Dem Andenken an Amarantha* (1886); male-voice choruses.

Nicolai, (Carl) Otto (Ehrenfried) (1810–1849) German composer and conductor. In 1847 he was appointed director of the cathedral choir and the Court Opera in Berlin, where he died of a stroke, two months after the production of his *Merry Wives of Windsor*; after initial rejection, this soon became his most popular opera, and is still often heard in Germany.

He studied the piano as a child, but was so unhappy at home that in 1826 he ran away and was sent to Berlin by a patron the following year for study under Carl Zelter and Bernhard Klein. In 1833 another patron sent him to Rome as organist in the Prussian Embassy chapel, and there he studied under Giuseppe Baini. He returned there after a year at the Kärntnertortheater in Vienna 1837–38. He became court kapellmeister in Vienna in 1841 and founded the Philharmonic concerts there in 1842.

Works OPERA *Enrico II* (later *Rosmonda d'Inghilterra*, 1839), *Il templario* (1840), *Odoardo e Gildippe*, *Il proscritto* (later *Die Heimkehr des Verbannten*, 1841), *Die lustigen Weiber von Windsor* (after Shakespeare, 1849).

CHURCH MUSIC AND OTHER Mass for Frederick William IV of Prussia, Requiem, Te Deum; Symphonic Festival Overture on 'Ein' feste Burg' for the jubilee of Königsberg University.

Nicolaus de Cracovia (lived 16th century), Polish **Mikołaj z Krakowa** Polish organist and composer. He was in the service of the royal court, and wrote organ music that is included in two manuscripts: that of Jan of Lublin (1537–48) and the Kraków Tablature (1548).

Nielsen, Carl August (1865–1931) Danish composer. His works combine an outward formal strictness with an inner waywardness of tonality and structure, best exemplified by his six programmatic symphonies 1892–1925.

Being poor as a youth, he joined a military band at the age of 14, but at 18 succeeded in entering the Copenhagen Conservatory as a pupil of Niels Gade. In 1891 he entered the royal orchestra and was its conductor 1908–14. He also became conductor of the Music Society and director of the Conservatory.

He was one of the most remarkable late Romantic symphonists, combining traditional forms with a new and original approach to tonality; the first symphony is an example of progressive tonality, ending in a different key to the initial one. Later symphonies developed a complex, rhythmically driven polyphony. The third symphony, *Espansiva*, is the first of these great works in which thematic formation is achieved within closely controlled forms. In the fifth symphony, chaos is threatened by a side drummer who is instructed to obliterate the rest of the orchestra; order is restored in a triumphant conclusion.

Works OPERA AND STAGE MUSIC operas *Saul og David* (1902), *Maskarade* (after Holberg, 1906); incidental music for Oehlenschäger's *Aladdin*, and many other plays.

ORCHESTRAL AND CHORAL *Hymnus Amoris* for chorus and orchestra (1897); *Springtime on Fyn* for soloists, chorus, and orchestra (1922); *Hymn to Art* for vocal soloists and wind instruments (1929); three motets for unaccompanied chorus; six symphonies: 1. in G minor (1892); 2. *The Four Temperaments* (1902); 3. *Espansiva* (1911); 4. *The Inextinguishable* (1916); 5. (1922); 6. *Sinfonia semplice* (1925); symphonic rhapsody *Saga-Dream* for orchestra; violin concerto (1911); flute concerto (1926); rhapsody *An Imaginary Journey to the Faroes* (1927); clarinet concerto (1928).

CHAMBER AND SOLO four string quartets (1887–1919), two string quintets, wind quintet (1922), and other chamber music; two violin and piano sonatas; *Commotio* for organ (1931); suites and other piano works; incidental music on Danish texts.

Nielsen, Hans (c.1580–c.1626) Danish lutenist and composer. After learning music as a choirboy in the royal chapel at Copenhagen, he studied with Giovanni Gabrieli at Venice 1599–1606, and with the English lutenist Richard Howett at Wolfenbüttel 1606–08. After that he was lutenist at the Danish court until 1611, when he was dismissed and went to Heidelberg University. In 1623, he was appointed vice-director of the royal chapel in succession to Mogens Pedersøn.

Nielsen, Riccardo (1908–1982) Italian composer of Scandinavian descent. He studied at the Liceo Musicale of Bologna and at Salzburg, and was influenced by Alfredo Casella.

Works STAGE the monodrama *L'Incubo* (1948), radio opera *La via di Colombo* (1953), incidental music for *Maria ed il Nazzareno*.

ORCHESTRAL psalms for male voices and orchestra (1941), concerto for orchestra (1936), two symphonies (1933, 1935), capriccio and *Sinfonia concertante* for piano and orchestra, violin concerto (1932), divertimento for bassoon, trumpet, violin, viola, and cello; trio for oboe, bassoon, and horn (1934); Adagio and Allegro for cello and eleven instruments.

SONATAS sonatas for violin and piano and cello and piano; *Musica* for two pianos (1939); sonata and 'ricercare'.

OTHER chorale and toccata on Bach for piano; *Laude di Jacopone da Todi* and *Tre satire di Giusti* for voice and piano.

niente (Italian 'nothing') musical term generally used in connection with *quasi* ('so to speak', 'almost') when extreme softness of tone is required.

Nigg, Serge (1924–) French composer. He studied under Messiaen at the Paris Conservatory, but in 1946 adopted the 12-note technique under the influence of Leibowitz, who he in turn came to disagree with two years later.

Works DRAMATIC the melodrama *Perséphone* (1942).

ORCHESTRAL symphonic movement *Timour* for orchestra (1944); *La Mort d'Arthus* for voice and orchestra; concerto *Concertino* for piano, wind and percussion; *Jérôme Bosch-Symphonie* (1960); variations for piano and ten instruments; two piano concertos (1954, 1971).

OTHER sonata and *Fantaisie* for piano.

Night at the Chinese Opera, A opera in three acts by Judith Weir (libretto by composer, based in part on Chi-Chun-Hsiang's *The Chao Family Orphan*). It was produced in Cheltenham at the Everyman Theatre on 8 July 1987. In the story, Chao Liu is in exile after the invasion by Kublai Khan, but after an earthquake interrupts a play which runs parallel to the course of his life, he is arrested. Although the play ends happily, Chao is executed.

Nightingale, The, Russian **Soloveg** opera by Stravinsky (libretto by composer and S N Mitusov, from Hans Andersen's fairy tale) about a dying emperor who is revived by the sound of the nightingale. It was first produced at the Paris Opéra on 26 May 1914 and was revived in the form of a ballet (choreography by Leonid Massin) at the same venue on 2 February 1920.

Night on the Bare Mountain a work in various forms by Mussorgsky, more properly called *St John's Night on the Bare Mountain*, based on the incident of the witches' sabbath in Gogol's story 'St John's Eve'. It was first composed as a symphonic poem for orchestra 1866–67 and later used in a version for chorus and orchestra called *Night on Mount Triglav* in 1872, as part of the opera *Mlada* commissioned from Mussorgsky, Borodin, Cui, and Rimsky-Korsakov, but never completed. The revised version of this is used as the introduction to Act III of the unfinished opera *Sorotchinsty Fair* (1875). This last version was revised and arranged as an orchestral piece by Rimsky-Korsakov after Mussorgsky's death.

Nights in the Gardens of Spain symphonic impressions for piano and orchestra by Falla. See ➤ *Noches en los jardines de España*.

Nikisch, Arthur (1855–1922) Austro-Hungarian conductor. He conducted the first performance of Bruckner's seventh symphony in 1884, and in 1913 conducted Wagner's *Ring* at Covent Garden, London.

He studied in Vienna and played violin in the court orchestra 1874–77. He was conductor at the Leipzig Opera 1878–89. Subsequent posts included the Boston Symphony Orchestra 1889–93, Budapest Opera 1893–95, Leipzig Gewandhaus from 1895, and the Berlin Philharmonic Orchestra.

Nilsson, Bo (1937–) Swedish composer. Largely self-taught, he has belonged to the younger generation of avant-garde composers.

Works ORCHESTRAL AND VOICE *Songs on the Death of Children* for soprano and small orchestra, *Autumn Song* for baritone and orchestra (1985), *Vagues pour Madame Curie* for soprano and orchestra (1993).

CHAMBER *Moments of Time* for ten wind instruments, *Frequencies* for chamber ensemble, *A Prodigal Son* for contralto, alto flute, and chamber ensemble; *Reactions* for percussion quartet (1960), *Quantities* for piano, *Attraktionen* for string quartet (1968), *Madonna* for mezzo and ensemble (1977), piano quintet (1979).

OTHER *Wendepunkt* for brass and electronics (1981), *Audiograms* for electronic generators.

Nin (y Castellanos), Joaquín (1878–1949) Spanish pianist, musicologist, and composer. He edited much old Spanish music and wrote three books.

He studied in Barcelona and in Paris, where in 1906 he became piano professor at the Schola Cantorum. After short periods in Berlin and Cuba, he settled in Brussels and later in Paris again.

Works DRAMATIC the mimodrama *L'Autre*, ballet *L'Écharpe bleue*.

OTHER violin pieces, piano works, songs.

Nina, o sia la pazza per amore, Nina, or the Lunatic from Love opera by ➤ Paisiello (libretto by Giuseppe Carpani, with additions by G B Lorenzi, based on the French libretto by B J Marsollier). It was first produced in Naples at the Caserta Palace, for the visit of Queen Maria Carolina of Sicily on 25 June 1789. Its first public performance was at the Teatro Fiorentino in Naples in 1790. In the story, Nina is engaged to Lindoro, but her father cancels the wedding plans when a rich suitor arrives. Lindoro fights a duel with him and is shot. Nina goes mad, but recovers her sanity when he revives.

ninth in music, an interval that is a whole tone larger than an octave (major ninth) or a semitone larger (minor ninth).

Major and minor ninths.

Ninth Symphony symphony by Beethoven. See ➤ 'Choral Symphony'.

Nivers, Guillaume (Gabriel) (c.1631–1714) French organist, harpsichordist, theorist, and composer. He was a pupil of Chambonnières in Paris and organist of the church of Saint-Sulpice in 1654. He was also appointed organist to the king in 1678 and music master to the queen. He wrote a treatise on singing and other theoretical works, and composed motets and other church music.

Nixon in China opera in two acts by John Adams (libretto by Alice Goodman), produced in Houston at the Grand Opera on 22 October 1987. In the story, the media-conscious Dick and his wife Pat are impressed by Chairman Mao. Nixon is portrayed as a superficial character, in contrast to the revolutionary Mao.

Nobilissima visione dance legend (ballet) in six scenes by Hindemith (choreography by composer and Massine) about the story of St Francis. It was produced at Drury Lane, London, on 21 July 1938. The orchestral suite in three movements was performed in Venice on 13 September 1938.

Noces, Les, The Wedding ballet by Igor ➤ Stravinsky (choreographed by Bronislava Nijinska), and produced at the Théâtre Lyrique, Paris on 13 June 1923. The work is scored for chorus (Russian words), four pianos, and percussion.

Noches en los jardines de España, Nights in the Gardens of Spain symphonic impressions for piano and orchestra by Falla, composed 1909–15. There are three movements: 1. *En el Generalife*; 2. *Danza lejanya/Dance in the distance*); 3. *En los jardines de la Sierra de Córdoba*. It was first perfomed in Madrid on 9 April 1916.

nocturne in music, a reflective character piece, often for piano, introduced by John Field (1782–1837) and adopted by Frédéric ➤ Chopin.

Nocturne song cycle for tenor, seven obbligato ('obliged') instruments, and strings by Britten (texts by Shelley, Tennyson, Coleridge, Middleton, Wordsworth, Owen, Keats, and Shakespeare). It was first performed in Leeds on 16 October 1958, with the English tenor Peter Pears.

Nocturnes three orchestral pieces by Debussy – *Nuages*, *Fêtes*, and *Sirènes*, the last with female chorus. Composed 1893–99, the pieces were first performed in Paris on 9 December 1900 (nos 1 and 2) and on 27 October 1901 in their complete form.

node (from Latin *nodus*, 'knot') in music, the point in a vibrating string at which the vibration becomes cut into segments.

Nola, Domenico da (Joan Domenico del Giovane) (c.1510–1592) Italian composer. He was maestro di cappella of the church of the Annunciation at Naples 1563–88. He composed motets, madrigals, and *villanelle*.

nonet in music, an ensemble of nine instruments, or a composition written for such a group. The standard instrumentation is a string quartet (two violins, viola, and cello) augmented by flute, oboe, clarinet, bassoon, and French horn; a famous example is by Louis Spohr (1813).

Non nobis Domine a canon for voices, probably by William ➤ Byrd, often sung in England for 'grace' after public dinners. It is a riddle canon capable of being sung with the entries in various positions and also in inversion (the mirror image of a melody used in counterpoint).

Nono, Luigi (1924–1990) Italian composer. He wrote attenuated pointillist works such as *Il canto sospeso/Suspended Song* (1955–56) for soloists, chorus, and orchestra, in which influences of Webern and Gabrieli are applied to issues of social conscience. After the opera *Intolleranza/Intolerance* (1960) his style became more richly expressionist, and his causes more overtly polemical.

Born in Venice, he abandoned law for music, and studied with Bruno Maderna and with Hermann Scherchen, who conducted his *Polifonia-monodiaritmica* at Darmstadt in 1951. His work was initially performed principally in Germany, and developed from serialism, in the manner of Schoenberg (whose daughter he married), to more politically committed works. Nono's earlier output included numerous orchestral works, but after *La fabbrica illuminata/The Illuminated Factory* in 1964, he concentrated exclusively on the electronic-vocal medium.

Works OPERA the opera-oratorio *Intolleranza* (1961), the opera *Al gran sole carico d'amore* (1974).

ORCHESTRAL *Variazioni canoniche* (on a theme of Schoenberg's from *Ode to Napoleon*), *Due espressioni*, *Diario polacco '58*; *Canti* for 13 instruments, *Incontri* for 24 instruments.

CHORAL *Il canto sospeso* (1956), *La Victoire de Guernica*, *Epitaph 1 for F Garcia Lorca*, *Cori di Didone*; cantata *Sul ponte di Hiroshima* for soprano and tenor and orchestra (1962); *La fabbrica illuminata* for mezzo and electronic tape; *Epitaphs II & III for F Garcia Lorca* II for flute, strings, and percussion (II), and for speaker, speaking chorus, and orchestra (III).

ELECTRONIC AND OTHER electronic music, including *Omaggio a Emilio Vedova* (1960) and *Sofferte onde serene* (1976); *Quando stanno morendo* for voices and ensemble (1982).

Noonday Witch, The, Czech **Polednice** symphonic poem by Dvořák, Op. 108. It was composed in 1896 and first performed on 21 November 1896, in London.

Nordgren, Pehr Henrik (1944–   ) Finnish composer. He studied at Helsinki and Tokyo universities, and was interested in traditional Japanese music.

Works ORCHESTRAL orchestral series *Euphone I-IV* (1967–81); three violin concertos (1969, 1977, 1981), three viola concertos (1970, 1979, 1986), two symphonies (1974, 1989), two cello concertos (1980, 1983).

CHAMBER the chamber opera *The Black Monk* (1981), five string quartets (1967–86), piano quintet (1978), piano trio (1983).

Nordheim, Arne (1931–   ) Norwegian composer. He studied in Oslo and with Vagn Holmboe (1909–1996) in Copenhagen. He was active as a performer and as a composer of electronic music from 1968.

Works BALLET AND DRAMATIC three ballets, including *Ariadne* (1977), *The Tempest* (1979), *The End of Time* (1981); musical play for TV *Favola* (1965).

ELECTRONIC MUSIC *Colorazione* (1968), *Pace* (1970), and *Osaka-Music* (1970).

ORCHESTRAL *Tenebrae* for cello and orchestra (1982), *Varder* for trumpet and orchestra (1986).

CHAMBER AND CHORAL *Be Not Afeared* for soprano, baritone, and ensemble (1978); *Rendezvous* for strings (1987); other chamber and choral music.

Norgård, Per (1932–   ) Danish composer. He studied with Vagn Holmboe (1909–1996) and Nadia Boulanger (1887–1979), and taught at Aarhus in Denmark from 1965. An early influence was Sibelius. Norgård later turned to 'infinite' serialism, ➤ **pointillism**, and graphic notation.

Works OPERA *The Labyrinth* (1967), *Gilgamesh* (1973), *Siddharta* (1983), *The Divine Tivoli* (1983).

ORCHESTRAL four symphonies (1954–81); *Illuminationi* for orchestra (1984); cello concerto (1985), violin concerto *Helle Nacht* (1987); *Pastorale* for strings (1988).

ENSEMBLE *Spaces of Time* for piano and ensemble (1991), *Scintillation* for instruments (1993), seven string quartets (1958–93).

Norma opera by Vincenzo ➤ **Bellini** (libretto by Felice Romani, based on L A Soumet's tragedy), produced in Milan at La Scala on 26 December 1831. In the story, the Druid priestess Norma still loves the Roman consul Pollione after he abandons her for another priestess, Adalgisa. However, jealousy and rivalry result in the deaths of both Norma and Pollione.

North Country Sketches work for orchestra in four movements by Frederick Delius. It was composed 1913–14, and first performed (conducted by Beecham) in London on 10 May 1915.

Nose, The opera by Shostakovich (libretto by A Preis, A Zamyatin, G Yonin, and composer, after a short story by Gogol). The story concerns the disappearance of a nose belonging to a government official and the opera was described by contemporary Russian critics as an example of bourgeois decadence. Barber Ivan discovers a nose in his morning bread; Major Kovalyov wakes up missing his nose. The nose later appears running aound in human size and treating everyone with contempt, as the police inspector chases it. Eventually it is caught and returned to Kovalyov. Composed 1927–28, first performed Leningrad, Maly Theatre, 12 January 1930.

nota cambiata (Italian 'changed note') in music, term used in two senses in the analysis of 16th-century polyphony. In one sense, nota cambiata refers to a dissonant passing note (note joining two notes a third apart) on the beat. In a second sense, the term refers to a curling figure (also called 'changing note group') in which a dissonant passing note (not on the beat) leads to a note a third lower, which then rises one step.

A nota cambiata as a simple passing note (1) and as a changing note group (2).

notation system of signs and symbols for writing music, either for performers to read from, or to make a permanent record. Early systems of music notation were developed by the ancient Sumerians, by the Chinese in the 3rd century BC, and later by the ancient Greeks and Romans for their music dramas. The Greeks were the first to name the notes of the ➤ **scale** with letters of the alphabet.

A form of notation using signs called ➤ **neumes** appeared in Europe in the Middle Ages as a means of writing down ➤ **plainsong**. These graphic signs showed the rise and fall of the notes of a ➤ **melody**, but did not give a precise placing of ➤ **pitch** or ➤ **rhythm**. The system of using notes on a ➤ **stave** or staff of horizontal lines first appeared in the 11th century, and was invented by an Italian monk, ➤ **Guido of Arezzo** (c.991–after 1033).

Modern music notation uses a stave of five lines, with a ➤ **clef** to show the exact pitch of the notes on it. The position of a note on the stave represents its pitch, and the shape of the note and its 'tail' indicate its duration in time. Other signs and words can be added to the written music to show the ➤ **tempo**, ➤ **dynamics** (how loudly or softly the music should be played), and how the music should be played – for example ➤ **legato** (smoothly) or ➤ **staccato** (each note short and separate).

the need for music notation The vast majority of music belongs to some form of oral/aural tradition, and has never been written down. It is generally passed from one performer to another by repetition and memory, and consequently, like the game 'Chinese whispers', changes its character through the ages. The need for a more reliable system for instructing performers and recording music for posterity was felt very early in the history of music. Unfortunately, the lack of written records makes it difficult for us to know much about the music of ancient cultures, and what we do know usually comes from verbal rather than musical sources, from examination of the instruments played, and from texts about playing technique.

early systems It is likely that music notation developed alongside written language, and that the ancient Sumerians and Egyptians devised symbols to accompany the system of hand signs they used, indicating the pitch and shape of the melody by a sort of 'conducting'; certainly the Chinese had a quite sophisticated system of notation as early as the 3rd century BC. These early systems consisted of either symbols to represent separate vocal syllables – a form of ➤ **solmization** – or signs and instructions for playing specific instruments – a form of ➤ **tablature**. The use of letters of the alphabet to name notes of the scale dates back to ancient Greece and possibly earlier, and was well established by 500 BC, when letter-names were given to the ➤ **diatonic scale**, and inflections of a semitone or even a quartertone could be expressed by rotation of the letter symbols. This system seems to have been devel-

oped more for the study of ➤ **acoustics** than as an aid to performance or to make a permanent record of specific pieces of music.

neumic notation It was not until the 7th century that a notation was developed for recording pieces of music with some degree of accuracy. As the medieval Church had a virtual monopoly on written learning, it is not surprising that it was here that modern music notation had its beginnings. The chants of plainsong had been until then an oral/aural tradition, but to the medieval mind this was not a satisfactory state of affairs; some means of writing down the plainchant melodies for performance and posterity had to be found. As this was a purely vocal tradition, the first symbols derived from written language, and resembled acute and grave accents representing the rise and fall of the melody. These signs, known as neumes, developed into a complex system in which an individual neume could represent a single note or as many as four notes in a particular sequence. The neumic system gave a very graphic indication of the shape of a melody, but the addition of a horizontal line removed its main drawback by fixing an absolute pitch as a point of reference.

the stave Guido of Arezzo further improved the system of notating plainsong in the first half of the 11th century. As well as inventing his own version of solmization, using the syllables *ut*, *re*, *mi*, etc in conjunction with a set of mnemonics related to the joints of the fingers (the 'Guidonian hand'), he also suggested the use of a stave of four horizontal lines, which would not only provide a pitch reference, but would also graphically represent relative pitch by the vertical placing of notes on its lines and spaces. He is also credited with the invention of the clef, further refining the accuracy of the system.

Guido's innovations were, however, all concerned with notating pitch, and it was not until the 13th century that any systematic reform of rhythmic notation was achieved. The first to tackle this was Franco of Cologne, who codified and rationalized the existing system, and established the relationships between different note values. A system similar to present-day rhythmic notation had evolved from this by the middle of the 15th century, but based on triple rather than duple divisions.

the modern system By about 1700 the modern system of notation, using a stave of five lines as opposed to the four used in plainsong, had become firmly established. It almost completely replaced solmization and tablature, although some forms of solmization, such as the ➤ **tonic sol-fa**, are still used today, especially in vocal music and as a teaching aid, and tablature has remained in use by lutenists and guitarists. Despite its drawbacks, particularly in notating non-diatonic pitches and complex rhythms, conventional modern notation is also being used outside Western art music: music of previously aural/oral traditions is being transcribed, and even classical traditions such as Chinese music now make use of Western notation.

innovations The history of music notation is one of continual evolution, and the 20th century was no exception. As composers have found new means of expression, they have developed new means of writing them down. Methods of indicating microtones, intervals less than a semitone, were found early in the century, and symbols borrowed from mathematics have been used to notate complex rhythmic relationships. Some composers, such as John ➤ Cage and Karlheinz ➤ Stockhausen, virtually abandoned conventional notation in favour of graphic representations or even passages of text; others, such as Pierre ➤ Boulez and Luciano ➤ Berio, have attempted to refine it and improve its accuracy. There have even been attempts, particularly in the first half of the century, to invent completely new systems such as Klavarscribo, but these have not been enthusiastically received.

note in music, the written symbol indicating pitch and duration, the sound of which is a tone.

note row in music, another term for ➤ tone row.

Notker Labeo (950–1022), also known as **Teutonicus** German monk. He lived at the monastery of St Gall and wrote on music and other subjects, including a short treatise in Old High German on the measurement of organ pipes.

Notre-Dame opera by Franz Schmidt (libretto by composer and L Wilk, after Hugo's novel *Notre-Dame de Paris*). The opera was composed 1902–04 and was produced in Vienna on 1 April 1914. The well-known *Intermezzo* was performed in Vienna on 6 December 1903.

notturno (Italian 'night piece') 18th-century forerunner of the ➤ nocturne, not then a single lyrical instrumental piece, but a composition in several movements similar to the serenade or the ➤ divertimento. In the 19th century the notturno became simply the Italian equivalent of the nocturne, as in Mendelssohn's *Midsummer Night's Dream* music.

Novae de Infinito Laudes*, *New Praises of the Infinite cantata by Hans Werner Henze for soloists, chorus, and orchestra (text by Giordano Bruno, the Italian astronomer burnt at the stake by the Inquisition). Composed in 1962, the cantata was first performed in Venice on 24 April 1963, with the vocal talents of Peter Pears, Dietrich Fischer-Dieskau, Kerstin Meyer, and Elisabeth Söderström.

Novak, Jan (1921–1984) Czech composer. He studied at the Brno Conservatory 1940–46 and at the Prague Academy. He was influenced at first by the neoclassicism of Martinů, with whom he studied in New York, but then turned to jazz and serialism.

Works ENSEMBLE *Orpheus et Eurydice* for soprano, viola d'amore, and piano (1971).

ORCHESTRAL AND CHORAL concerto for two pianos (1955), *Philharmonic Dances* for orchestra (1956), *Variations on a theme of Martinů* for orchestra (1959), *Dodo*, oratorio (1967), *Ludi Concertantes* for 18 instruments (1981), *Symphonia bipartita* (1983).

Novák, Vitězslav (1870–1949) Czech composer. He made a career as a distinguished teacher of composition and in 1909 was appointed professor at the Prague Conservatory. After World War I, which restored his country's independence, he became professor of the 'Master School' and was its director 1919–22.

He was the son of a doctor, but lost his father early and had to support the family by teaching. While studying law at Prague University he attended the Conservatory, studying piano with Jiránek and composition with Dvořák, who persuaded him to devote himself wholly to music. His first works were published with the help of Brahms.

Works OPERA *The Imp of Zvíkov* (1915), *A Night at Karlstein* (1916), *The Lantern* (1923), *The Grandfather's Will* (1926), *The Wood Nymph*.

BALLET *Signorina Gioventù, Nikotina*.

ORCHESTRAL AND CHORAL cantatas *The Storm* and *The Spectre's Bride*; choral ballads; symphony dedicated to Stalin after the liberation of Prague (1945); symphonic poems *In the Tatra, Eternal Longing, Toman and the Wood Nymph, De profundis* (1941); overtures *The Corsair* (after Byron), *Maryša, Lady Godiva*; serenade for small orchestra; piano concerto (1895).

ENSEMBLE two string quartets, two piano trios, piano quartet, piano quintet, *Sonata eroica, Manfred* (ballad after Byron), *Songs of Winter Nights, Pan, Exoticon*, six sonatinas, *Youth* (children's pieces), other pieces for piano.

SONGS song cycles *Gypsy Songs, Melancholy, In the Valley of a New Kingdom, Melancholy Songs of Love, Nocturnes, Eroticon*, and other songs; part songs.

Novelletten (German 'short stories') category title used by Schumann for his eight piano pieces, Op. 21, composed in 1838, and also for no. 9 of the *Bunte Blätter* for piano, Op. 99.

Novello, Vincent (1781–1861) English publisher, organist, editor, and composer of Italian origin. He established the firm Novello and Co. in London in 1811, originally to publish sacred music in order to facilitate his duties as a choirmaster. He later published the music of Purcell, Mozart, Haydn, and Beethoven. He also composed church music and cantatas.

He was the father of the soprano Clara Novello (1818–1908) and he handed the firm to his eldest son Alfred (1810–1896).

November Woods a symphonic poem by Arnold Bax, composed in 1917. It was first performed in Manchester by the Hallé Orchestra on 18 November 1920.

Novotný, Jaroslav (1886–1918) Czech composer. He studied in Prague, joined the Austrian army during World War I, and was a prisoner in Russia, where he wrote much in camp; he was released but was killed near the end of the war fighting on the other side with the Czech legion.

Works ENSEMBLE string quartet, piano sonata.

CHORAL choruses; song cycles *The Eternal Wedding* and *Ballads of the Soul*.

Nowak, Leopold (1904–1991) Austrian musicologist. He wrote books on Haydn (published 1951) and Bruckner (published 1947, 1973); in 1945 he succeeded Robert ➔ **Haas** as editor of the complete works of Bruckner.

He studied in Vienna and was professor at the University there 1932–73. He was director of the music division at the Vienna National Library 1946–69.

Nowowiejski, Feliks (1877–1946) Polish composer and conductor. He studied in Berlin, at Regensburg in Bavaria, where he studied church music, and afterwards in France, Belgium, and Italy. In 1909, he returned to Poland, conducting the Kraków Music Society until 1914. In 1919, he became professor of organ at the Poznań Conservatory, where he conducted orchestral concerts.

Works OPERA AND BALLET operas *Baltic Legend* (1924), *The Mountain Goblin*; opera-ballet *Leluja*; ballets *Tatra*, *Polish Wedding*.

ORCHESTRAL Masses, motets, and psalms; oratorios *Quo vadis?* (1907), *Beatum scelus*, *Missa pro pace*; cantata *Upper Silesian Folk Scene*; symphonic poems *Beatrix*, *Nina*, overture *Polish Wooing*, *The Prodigal Son*, *Jerusalem*; nine symphonies.

Noyes Fludde opera in one act by Benjamin Britten (text from the Chester miracle play). It is based on the biblical story of Noah's flood; the setting makes much use of children's voices. The opera was first produced at Orford in Suffolk on 18 June 1958.

Nozze d'Ercole e d'Ebe, Le, The Nuptials of Hercules and Hebe opera by Christoph Willibald von Gluck. It was produced at Pillnitz, near Dresden, at the double wedding of Max Joseph, Elector of Bavaria, and Maria Anna, Princess of

Saxony, and Frederick Christian, Prince of Saxony, and Maria Antonia Walpurgis, Princess of Bavaria, on 29 June 1747.

Opera by Porpora (libretto as above), produced in Venice on 18 February 1744.

Nozze di Figaro, Le, The Marriage of Figaro opera by Mozart (libretto by Lorenzo da Ponte, based on Beaumarchais's comedy *La Folle Journée, ou Le Mariage de Figaro*). The story concerns Figaro and Susanna, who are to be married, but first Figaro is pursued by the elderly Marcellina (who turns out to be his mother), and Susanna must evade the eager Count Almaviva. All the characters must disentangle themselves from a web of mistaken identities. The opera was produced in Vienna, at the Burgtheater on 1 May 1786.

Nozze di Teti e di Peleo, Le, The Nuptials of Thetis and Peleus opera by Cavalli (libretto by O Persiani), produced in Venice at the Teatro San Cassiano, probably on 24 January 1639. In the story, Thetis and Peleus are to marry, but Aeolus (Peleus' father) opposes the match because he believes Jupiter has seduced Thetis. Pluto sends Discord to interrupt the lovers before the marriage proceeds.

Nuits d'été, Les, Summer Nights six songs by Hector Berlioz (poems by Théophile Gautier), composed 1840–41 for mezzo-soprano or tenor and piano. The work was revised for voice and orchestra in 1843 (no. 4) and 1856. The six songs are: 1. *Villanelle*; 2. *Le spectre de la rose*; 3. *Sur les lagunes*; 4. *Absence*; 5. *Au cimetière*; 6. *L'île inconnue*.

Nuitter, Charles (Louis Étienne) (1828–1899), born **Charles Truinet** French librettist and writer on music. A lawyer at first, he later devoted himself to the writing and translation of libretti and of books on opera. In 1865 he became archivist of the Paris Opéra.

Nunc Dimittis (from Latin Nunc dimittis servum tuum, 'Now dismiss thy servant') a musical setting of St Luke's *Song of Simeon* ('Lord, now lettest thou thy servant depart in peace'). It is sung at Roman Catholic compline (the last service of the day) and Anglican evensong, either in ➔ **plainsong** or to a composer's polyphonic setting. It is often linked compositionally with the Anglican ➔ **Magnificat**.

Nursery, The song cycle by ➔ **Mussorgsky** (words by composer), composed 1868–72. The songs include: 1. *With Nurse*; 2. *In the Corner*; 3. *The Cockchafer*; 4. *With the Doll*; 5. *Going to sleep*; 6. *On the Hobby-Horse*; 7. *The Cat 'Sailor'*.

Nursery Suite orchestral suite in seven movements by Elgar. Dedicated to the then Duchess of York and her daughters Princess Elizabeth and Princess Margaret Rose, it was first performed as a concert in London's Queen's Hall on 20 August 1931. The movements are: 1. *Aubade*; 2. *The Serious Doll*; 3. *Busy-ness*; 4. *The Sad Doll*; 5. *The Waggon (passes)*; 6. *The Mercy Doll*; 7. *Dreaming*; 8. *Envoi*.

Nusch-Nuschi, Das opera in one act for Burmese marionettes by Hindemith (libretto by F Blei). It was composed in 1920 and produced in Stuttgart on 4 June 1921; its conductor Fritz Busch claimed to be shocked by satirical references to Wagner's ➔ **Tristan**. The castration of an Oriental philanderer is accompanied by a quotation from King Marke's music: '*Mir − dies?*' ('This − to me?').

nut on a stringed musical instrument, the ridge at one end of the ➔ **fingerboard**, next to the peg box, which raises the strings from the surface of the fingerboard. On some instruments, such as the ➔ **ukulele**, there is a movable nut, which raises the pitch of the entire instrument.

A nut is also the part of a bow which secures the horsehair at the heel and, by incorporating a screw mechanism, allows the tension of the hairs to be adjusted.

Nutcracker, Casse-Noisette well-known ballet by Tchaikovsky (choreography by Lev Ivanovich Ivanov, based on a tale by E T A Hoffmann). It was first produced in St Petersburg, at the Mariinsky Theatre on 18 December 1892.

Nyman, Michael (1944–) English composer. His highly stylized music is characterized by processes of gradual modification by repetition of complex musical formulae (known as minimalism). His compositions include scores for the English film-maker Peter Greenaway and the New Zealand film-maker Jane Campion (*The Piano*, 1992); a chamber opera, *The Man Who Mistook His Wife for a Hat* (1989); and three string quartets.

He studied at the Royal Academy of Music in London and at King's College, London. In 1974 he published *Experimental Music − Cage and Beyond*, but his music has followed more populist paths, drawing on a wide range of influences, including post-minimalism, rock and roll, Stravinsky, and Mozart; examples are: *I'll Stake my*

Cremona to a Jew's Trump (1983), and *Letters, Riddles and Writs* (TV opera for the 1991 bicentenary). He is widely known through his Peter Greenaway film scores: *The Draughtsman's Contract* (1982), *The Cook, the Thief, his Wife and her Lover* (1989), and *Prospero's Books* (1991). He formed the Michael Nyman Band for the performance of an eclectic range of pieces, for example *Piano Concerto* (1993).

Nystedt, Knut (1915–) Norwegian composer. In 1950 he founded the Norwegian Soloists' Choir and conducted it 1951–90, giving many performances of modern works.

After studying at the Oslo Conservatory and with Copland in the USA, he worked as a church organist from 1938, and as a conductor with the Oslo Philharmonic Orchestra from 1945.

Works CHORAL AND OPERA *Christmas Opera with Crown and Star* (1971); church opera *Song of Solomon* (1989); *Lucis Creator Optime* for soloists, chorus, and orchestra (1968); *Four Grieg Romances* for a cappella chorus (1992).

OTHER *Sinfonia del Mare* (1983); five string quartets (1938–88).

Nystroem, Gösta (1890–1966) Swedish composer and painter. He was the son of a headmaster who taught him music and painting, which he afterwards studied at Stockholm, Copenhagen, and Paris, where Vincent d'Indy and Leonid Sabaneiev were among his masters for composition. He lived in Paris for twelve years and came under the influence of Picasso, Braque, Chirico, and other modern painters. After further studies in Italy and Spain, he settled at Göteborg and in 1933 became music critic of the *Göteborgs Handelstidning*.

Works STAGE MUSIC ballet-pantomime *Maskerade*; incidental music to various plays, including Shakespeare's *Merchant of Venice* and *The Tempest*.

ORCHESTRAL four symphonies: *Sinfonia breve, Sinfonia espressiva, Sinfonia del mare, Sinfonia Shakespeariana*; symphonic poems *The Arctic Sea, The Tower of Babel*; *Lyric Suite and Festival Overture* for orchestra; *Concerto grosso* for string orchestra; violin concerto; viola concerto; *Sinfonia concertante* for cello and orchestra.

OTHER piano suites and pieces; songs.

o in music, abbreviation for ➤ **open string**, marked over a note in music for a string player; or an indication that a harmonic is to be played (see ➤ **harmonics**).

obbligato (Italian 'obligatory') in musical notation, indicating that an instrument or voice is essential and not to be omitted. However, some composers have used this term with the opposite meaning in mind: that an instrument or voice may be omitted if so desired. Generally, the older the notation, the more likely it is that obbligato retains its original meaning of an 'obliged', essential part.

Oberon, König der Elfen*, *Oberon, King of the Fairies opera by Paul ➤ Wranitzky (libretto by Ludwig Gieseke, based on Wieland's poem and F S Seyler's libretto *Hüon und Amande*). It was produced in Vienna at the Theater auf der Wieden on 7 November 1789.

Oberon, or The Elf King's Oath opera by Weber (libretto by James Robinson Planché, based on Wieland's poem and further back on the medieval French romance *Huon de Bordeaux*). It was produced in London at Covent Garden on 12 April 1826. The opera is about Oberon, King of the Elves, and his queen, Titania, who resolve to stay apart until they find a human couple who stay faithful in the face of adversity. Sir Huon and Rieza face a series of tests, restoring the elves' faith in love.

obertas or **oberek** Polish folk dance performed in figures by couples following a leader. The music is in 3/4 time, not unlike that of the ➤ **mazurka** but livelier in character.

Oberto, Conte di San Bonifacio opera by Verdi (libretto by A Piazza, altered by B Merelli and T Solera), Verdi's first opera, produced at La Scala in Milan on 17 November 1839. The story concerns Count Ricardo, who is to marry Cuniza. But after learning of his earlier affair with Leonora, Cuniza demands that he marry Leonora instead. Oberto, Leonora's father, is killed in a duel with Ricardo, who, stricken with guilt, leaves the country, while Leonora enters a convent.

Oberwerk in music, German for ➤ **swell organ**, the second manual (keyboard) of an organ.

oboe double-reed woodwind instrument with a conical bore and moderately flared bell, descended from the ➤ **shawm**. It is one of the four instruments that make up the woodwind section of the orchestra. The oboe was developed by the Hotteterre family of instrument makers in about 1700 and was played in the court ensemble of Louis XIV of France. Pitched in C, with a normal range of about two and a half octaves, it has a reedy and penetrating tone. This is why it is used at the beginning of concerts to sound the note A for the other players to tune their instruments. Oboe concertos have been composed by Antonio Vivaldi, Tomaso Albinoni, Richard Strauss, Bohuslav Martinu, and others. Heinz Holliger is a modern virtuoso oboist and important composer.

The oboe's most important close relative is the ➤ **cor anglais**, which sounds a fifth lower. Alto variants ➤ **oboe d'amore** (a minor third lower) and ➤ **oboe da caccia** (a fifth lower) are heard in the work of Johann Sebastian Bach and other 18th-century composers. They were replaced by the cor anglais in the modern orchestra. The rarely heard ➤ **heckelphone** is a baritone relative.

The compass of the oboe.

oboe da caccia (Italian 'hunting oboe') an oboe tuned a fifth lower and transposing a fifth down (see ➤ **transposing instrument**). Its parts in early music are now generally played on the cor anglais, whose pitch is the same.

oboe d'amore (Italian 'love oboe') an oboe tuned a minor third lower and transposing a minor third down. (See also ➤ **transposing instrument**.)

Obrecht, Jacob (c. 1450–1505) Flemish composer. His mostly polyphonic sacred music (which in style predates that of Josquin Desprez) centred on the Mass. He was innovative, developing borrowed material, and using a secular fixed ➔ *cantus firmus* in his *Missa super Maria zart*. He also wrote motets and secular works.

He was born at Bergen-op-Zoom and studied at Louvain University. He directed the singers at Utrecht 1476–78, Bergen-op-Zoom 1479–84, then at Cambrai, at Bruges in 1486 and 1490, and elsewhere in the Low Countries. He was obliged to resign in 1500, and after a spell at Antwerp 1501–02 went to Italy for his health. He had already spent six months at the ducal court of Ferrara in 1487–88 and returned there in 1504 as head of Ercole d'Este's choir, only to die of plague the following year.

Works CHURCH AND SECULAR MUSIC 27 Masses, including *Fortuna desperata*, *Maria zart*, and *Sub tuum praesidium*; motets; chansons.

Obukhov, Nikolai (1892–1954) Russian composer. He was a pupil of Nikolai ➔ **Tcherepnin** and Maksimilian Osseievich ➔ **Steinberg** at the St Petersburg Conservatory. He settled in Paris in 1918 and made further studies with Ravel and others. He experimented with a 12-note system.

Works mystery *Le Livre de la vie*, *Poèmes liturgiques*.

Oca del Cairo, L', The Goose of Cairo unfinished opera by Mozart (libretto by G B Varesco). It was first produced in a version completed with other Mozartian fragments (libretto by V Wilder) in Paris on 6 June 1867. A new version by Virgilio Mortari (libretto by L Cavicchioli) was produced in Salzburg on 22 August 1936, and another by Hans Redlich in London, at Sadler's Wells on 30 May 1940.

ocarina early musical instrument of the flute type with finger-holes, roughly pear-shaped, with a mouthpiece protruding like a fish's fin, and usually made of terracotta.

Occasional Oratorio oratorio by Handel (libretto from Milton's *Psalms*, probably completed by Morell), composed to celebrate the suppression of the Jacobite rebellion. It was produced in London at Covent Garden on 14 February 1746.

occasione fa il ladro, L', Opportunity makes a Thief opera by ➔ **Rossini** (libretto by L Prividali). It was produced in Venice at the Teatro San Moisè on 24 November 1812.

Oceanides, The or **Aliottaret** symphonic poem by Sibelius, Op. 73. Composed in 1914, it was first performed in Norfolk, Connecticut, on 4 June 1914, conducted by Sibelius himself.

Ockeghem or **Okeghem** or **Ockenheim** or **Hoquegan, Jean d'** or **Johannes (c.1421–c.1497)** Flemish composer of church music. His works include the antiphon *Alma Redemptoris Mater* and the richly contrapuntal *Missa Prolationum/Prolation Mass*, employing complex canonic imitation in multiple parts at different levels. He was court composer to Charles VII, Louis XI, and Charles VIII of France.

He was a chorister at Antwerp Cathedral until 1444, was in the service of Charles, Duke of Bourbon at Moulins 1446–48, and in the service of the French court from about 1452, where he became the first maître de chapelle. Louis XI appointed him treasurer of Saint-Martin at Tours, where he lived during the latter part of his life, though he visited Spain in 1469.

Works CHURCH AND SECULAR MUSIC ten Masses, including *Ecce ancilla Domini*, *L'homme armé*, and *Mi-mi*; motets; French chansons.

Octandre work by Edgard ➔ **Varèse** for eight instruments (wind septet and double bass). Composed in 1923, it was first performed in New York on 13 January 1924. It is named after octandrous plants, which have eight stamens.

octatonic scale eight-note scale in alternating tone and semitone steps.

One of the earliest composers to make consistent use of this scale was Nikolai ➔ **Rimsky-Korsakov**. His pupil, Igor ➔ **Stravinsky**, also used the scale, as have a number of other 20th-century composers.

The repetitive nature of the internal structure of the scale means that it has no sense of a keynote or tonic, and the scale has a limited number of transpositions. Olivier ➔ **Messiaen** used the octatonic scale as one of his ➔ **modes of limited transposition**.

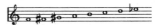

An octatonic scale.

octave in music, a span of eight notes as measured on the white notes of a piano keyboard. It corresponds to the consonance of first and second harmonics.

octet an ensemble of any eight instruments, or the music written for such a group. The most common combination of instruments is the string octet for four violins, two violas, and two cellos, as in ➔ **Mendelssohn**'s String Octet in E♭ (1830). ➔ **Stravinsky** wrote an octet in 1923 for a wind ensemble. A mixture of strings and winds is also possible, as in ➔ **Schubert**'s Octet in F (1824), scored for two violins, viola, cello, double bass, clarinet, bassoon, and horn.

octo bass musical instrument, a three-stringed double bass of huge size invented in 1849 by Jean-Baptiste Vuillaume in Paris. It was capable of playing extremely low notes, but its strings were so thick and heavy that they had to be stopped by means of levers and pedals. It was very unwieldy and never became widely used.

8ve lower _____ **(loco)**

The opening strings of the octo bass.

ode in music, a composition, usually vocal, of a dedicatory character. The form of such works varies considerably, reflecting the poetry, but they may appear in several sections with alternating solos and choruses.

Ode Work for orchestra by Stravinsky, composed in 1943. It was first performed in Boston on 8 October 1943, conducted by Serge Koussevitzky.

Ode for St Cecilia's Day setting by Handel of John ➔ Dryden's poem. It was produced in London at the Theatre in Lincoln's Inn Fields, on 22 November 1739.

Odes for St Cecilia's Day odes by Purcell. These are: 1. *Laudate Ceciliam* (1683); 2. *Welcome to all the pleasures* (Fishburn; 1683); 3. *Hail, bright Cecilia* (Brady; 1692); 4. *Raise, raise the voice*.

Ode to Napoleon Buonaparte work by Arnold ➔ Schoenberg for string quartet, piano, and reciter (text by Byron), composed in 1942. A version with string orchestra was performed in New York, on 24 November 1944, conducted by Rodziński.

Ode to the West Wind work for cello and orchestra by Hans Werner ➔ Henze (after Percy Bysshe Shelley's poem). Composed in 1953, it was first performed in Bielefeld, Germany, on 30 April 1954.

Odington, Walter de, or **Walter of Evesham (1298–1316)** English monk, musician, and astronomer. He entered the Benedictine monastery at Evesham in England and wrote the treatise *Summa de speculatione musice*.

odzmek a Slovak dance in quick 2/4 time with a more moderately paced middle section. The ninth of Antonín ➔ Dvořák's *Slavonic Dances* for piano duet is an odzmek.

Œdipe à Colone, **Oedipus at Coloneus** opera by Antonio ➔ Sacchini (libretto by Nicolas François Guillard, after Sophocles). Originally produced in Versailles, at court, on 4 January 1786, the opera's first Paris performance was on 1 February 1787 at the Opéra. In the story, Polynices engages Theseus to help drive his brother Eteocles from the usurped throne of Thebes, but he feels guilty about having driven his father Oedipus away in earlier years. Polynices seeks reconciliation with

his father even at the price of relinquishing his claim to the throne.

Oedipus auf Kolonos incidental music by ➔ Mendelssohn for Sophocles' tragedy, Op. 93, for male chorus and orchestra. It was first produced at Potsdam on 1 November 1845.

Oedipus der Tyrann musical play after Sophocles by Carl ➔ Orff, produced in Stuttgart on 11 December 1959.

Oedipus Rex stage oratorio by ➔ Stravinsky (libretto in Latin by J Daniélou and translated from French by Jean Cocteau, after Sophocles). The parts are sung in costume but without action, and the words are in Latin in order not to distract the ordinary listener by verbal associations. In the story, Oedipus unknowingly kills his father, King Laius, and marries his mother, Jocasta. When the truth is revealed to him, he blinds himself in remorse.

It was first produced in Paris at the Théâtre Sarah Bernhardt, on 30 May 1927, but its first stage performance was at the Staatsoper in Vienna, on 23 February 1928.

Oedipus Tyrannus incidental music by ➔ Mendelssohn for Sophocles' tragedy. It was never performed and is now lost.

Incidental music for Sophocles' tragedy by Charles Villiers Stanford, produced in Cambridge 22–26 November 1887.

Oedipus und die Sphinx unfinished opera by ➔ Varèse (text by Hofmannsthal). It was composed 1909–13, but the manuscript is lost.

oeuvre (French 'work') in music, alternative term for ➔ Opus.

Offenbach, Jacques (1819–1880), adopted name of **Jakob Levy Eberst** French composer. He wrote light opera, initially for presentation at the Bouffes Parisiens. Among his works are *Orphée aux enfers/Orpheus in the Underworld* (1858, revised 1874), *La belle Hélène* (1864), and *Les contes d'Hoffmann/The Tales of Hoffmann* (1881).

Offenbach was born at Cologne, where his father was cantor at the synagogue. He was sent to Paris early in his youth, studying at the Conservatory 1833–37, perfecting himself in playing the cello, and then playing in the orchestra of the Opéra-Comique even before he left the Conservatory. In 1850 he became conductor at the Théâtre Français. In 1853 he produced his first operettas and during a quarter of a century he turned out nearly 100 light stage pieces. In 1855 he took over the management of the Théâtre Comte and renamed it the Bouffes Parisiens. This lasted until 1861, after which he had no theatre of his own until 1873, when he managed the Théâtre de la Gaîté until 1875. In 1876–77 he was in the USA, but returned to Paris, where he had some of his greatest successes. He was also popular abroad, and such works as *La belle Hélène*, *La vie parisienne*, and *La Périchole* helped establish musical comedy as a significant form, leading to Johann Strauss, Sullivan, and the great Broadway musicals. His only large-scale opera, *Les contes d'Hoffmann*, occupied him for many years, but he left it not quite finished at his death, and it was revised and partly scored by Guiraud.

Works OPERA opera *Les contes d'Hoffmann* (1881), *The Goldsmith of Toledo* (after a tale by E T A Hoffmann), a pasticcio of various operettas; 89 operettas, including *Barbe-bleue* (1866), *Bata-clan* (1855), *La belle Hélène* (1864), *Chanson de Fortunio*, *Le Docteur Ox* (after Jules Verne), *La Fille du tambour-major* (1879), *La Foire de Saint-Laurent*, *Geneviève de Brabant* (1859), *La Grande-Duchesse de Gérolstein* (1867), *L'Île de Tulipatan*, *La Jolie Parfumeuse*, *Madame Favart*, *Orphée aux enfers* (1858), *La Périchole* (1874), *Princesse de Trébizonde*, *Robinson Crusoe* (after Defoe, 1867), *Vert-Vert*, *La Vie Parisienne* (1866), *Voyage dans la lune* (after Verne), *Whittington and his Cat* (1874), *Le Corsaire noir* (1919).

STAGE ballet *Le Papillon*; incidental music for Barrière's *Le Gascon* and Sardou's *La Haine*.

OTHER cello concerto.

Offertory the fourth part of the Roman Catholic Mass Proper, in which the bread and wine are placed on the altar, preceding the Credo and Communion. In musical terms, a psalm in the form of a ✦ **plainsong** was originally sung, but composers including ✦ **Palestrina** and Lassus have written polyphonic works for the Offertory. The term is also used in other denominations of the Christian church.

Offrandes work by ✦ **Varèse** for soprano and chamber ensemble (texts by V Huidobro and J J Tablada). Composed in 1921, it was first performed in New York, on 23 April 1922.

Offrandes oubliées, Les, The Forgotten Offerings work for orchestra in three parts by ✦ **Messiaen**. It was composed in 1930 and first performed in Paris, on 19 February 1931.

Ogdon, John Andrew Howard (1937–1989) English pianist and composer. A contemporary of Alexander Goehr and Peter Maxwell Davies at Manchester University, he won early recognition at the Moscow Tchaikovsky Piano Competition in 1962 and went on to become an ebullient champion of neglected virtuoso repertoire by Alkan, Bartók, Busoni, and Sorabji.

For a number of years unable to perform as a result of depression, he recovered to make a successful return to the concert hall shortly before his death.

Ohana, Maurice (1914–1992) English composer of Moroccan descent. He studied in Barcelona, at Rome, and at the Schola Cantorum in Paris. His music belongs to the avant-garde school of his time.

Works OPERA operas *Chanson de Toile* (1969) and *La Celestine* (1987), opera for marionettes *Autodafé* (1972).

BALLET *Prométhée* (1956), *Paso*.

ORCHESTRAL *Les Représentations de Tanit* and *Suite pour un Mimodrame* for small orchestra; guitar concerto; concertino for trumpet; piano concerto (1981); *Etudes*; *Choréographiques* for percussion; piano music; choral music, film music.

Oiseau de feu, L' ballet by Igor Stravinsky; see ✦ **Firebird, The**.

Oiseaux exotiques, Exotic birds work by Olivier ✦ **Messiaen** for piano, eleven wind instruments, and seven percussion. It was composed 1955–56, and first performed in Paris on 10 March 1956.

Okeland, Robert (lived 16th century) English composer. He was a member of Eton College 1532–34, and of the Chapel Royal 1547–48. Much of his music is preserved in the 'Gyffard' partbooks, which date from about 1555.

Olav Trygvason unfinished opera by ✦ **Grieg** (libretto by Bjørnson); there are three scenes only. It was performed in concert form in Christiania (now Oslo), Norway, on 19 October 1889, but it was never staged in Grieg's lifetime. It was first staged in Christiania in 1908.

Oldham, Arthur (William) (1926–2003) English composer. He was, for a time, music director at the Mercury Theatre and to the Ballet Rambert, but later devoted himself wholly to composition.

He studied composition with Herbert Howells and piano with Kathleen Long at the Royal College of Music in London; he also studied privately with Britten.

Works BALLET AND DRAMATIC four ballets, including *Bonne-Bouche* (1952); incidental music for Ronald Duncan's *This Way to the Tomb*.

CHORAL AND ORCHESTRAL six anthems; orchestral music, including Sinfonietta for wind band (1974).

OTHER violin and piano sonata, songs.

Olimpiade, L', The Olympiad libretto by ✦ **Metastasio**, probably the most frequently composed work by Metastasio or by any other librettist. The story concerns Megacles, who loves Aristaea, and is to compete in the Olympics under the name of his friend, Lycidas. He then learns that Aristaea is to be the prize for the winner. Torn between duty and love, Megacles chooses duty, but after a few twists all ends happily.

Opera by ✈ **Caldara**, produced in Vienna on 28 August 1733. Other settings of the libretto include those by ✈ **Vivaldi** (Venice, 1734); Pergolesi (Rome, 1735); ✈ **Galuppi** (Milan, 1747); ✈ **Hasse** (Dresden, 1756); ✈ **Traetta** (Verona, 1758); ✈ **Jommelli** (Stuttgart, 1761); ✈ **Sacchini** (Padua, 1763); and ✈ **Cimarosa** (Vicenza, 1784). There are at least 30 other settings of this libretto.

***Olimpia vendicata**, Olympia revenged* opera by Alessandro ✈ **Scarlatti** (libretto by Aurelio Aureli). It was first produced in Naples at the Palazzo Reale, on 23 December 1685.

oliphant (from Old English *olifaunt* 'elephant') musical instrument, a bugle-like horn made of an elephant's tusk, often beautifully carved. It was formerly used for signalling and hunting.

Oliver, Stephen (1950–1992) English composer. He studied electronic music with Robert Sherlaw Johnson at Oxford. The best known of his many operas and theatre pieces is *Tom Jones*, after Fielding, produced in Snape, Newcastle, and London in 1976. He was a popular teacher and broadcaster.

Works OPERA AND STAGE MUSIC *Perseverance* (1974), *Bad Times* (1975), *The Great McPorridge Disaster* (1976), *The Duchess of Malfi* (1971–77), *The Dreaming of the Bones* (1979), *Nicholas Nickelby* (1980), *Blondel* (1983), *Britannia Preserv'd* (1984), *Timon of Athens* (1991).

Oliveros, Pauline (1932–   ) US composer. Her works employ live electronics and scenic effects, often guided by meditation.

She worked at the San Francisco Tape Music Center 1961–67 and has taught electronic music at San Diego from 1967.

Works OPERA, CHORAL, AND VOCAL ceremonial opera *Crow Two* (1974); *King Kong Sings Along* for chorus (1977); *The New Sound Meditation* for voices (1989); *Midnight Operas* for chorus (1992); *Nzinga, the Queen King* music theatre (1993).

ELECTRONIC AND ENSEMBLE *To Valerie Solonis and Marilyn Monroe in recognition of their desperation* (1970); *Phantom Fathom* for mixed-media (1972); *1,000 Acres* for string quartet (1972); *The Yellow River Map*, meditation (1977); *Gone with the Wind* for ensembles (1980); *The Wheel of Times* for string quartet and electronics (1982); *Portraits* for brass quintet (1989); *Listening for Life* electronic (1991).

Olympians, The opera by Arthur Bliss (libretto by J B Priestley), produced in London at Covent Garden on 29 September 1949. In the story, rich Lavatte has arranged for his daughter Madeleine to marry an old nobleman, but she falls in love with the young poet Hector. After the appearance of Greek gods, Lavatte is foiled and the lovers are united.

Olympie opera by Gaspare ✈ **Spontini** (libretto by M Dieulafoy and C Brifaut, based on Voltaire's tragedy). It was first produced at the Opéra in Paris on 22 December 1819.

ombra di Don Giovanni, L', Don Juan's Shade opera by ✈ **Alfano** (libretto by E Moschino). First produced in Milan at La Scala on 2 April 1914, the opera was later revised as *Don Giovanni de Mañara* at Florence on 28 May 1941.

ondes Martenot (French 'Martenot waves') electronic musical instrument invented by Maurice Martenot (1898–1980), a French musician, teacher, and writer who first demonstrated his invention in 1928 at the Paris Opéra. A melody of considerable range and voicelike timbre is produced by sliding a contact along a conductive ribbon, the left hand controlling the tone colour.

In addition to inspiring works from Messiaen, Varèse, Jolivet, and others, the instrument has been in regular demand among composers of film and radio incidental music.

On Hearing the First Cuckoo in Spring one of two pieces for small orchestra by Frederick Delius (the other being *Summer Night on the River*, 1911) composed in 1912. It was first performed at the Leipzig Gewandhaus on 2 October 1913. The cuckoo call is heard unobtrusively on the clarinet and the main theme is a Norwegian folk song, *In Ole Dale*, previously used by Grieg, arranged for piano in *Norske Folkeviser*, Op. 66 (no. 14).

Onslow, (André) George or **Georges (Louis) (1784–1853)** French composer of English descent. He settled at Clermont-Ferrand as a country squire, held regular chamber music practices there, studied the cello, and went for two years to Vienna to study composition.

He was the grandson of the first Lord Onslow. While living in London for some years as a young man, he studied piano with Nicolas Hüllmandel, Jan Dussek, and Johann Baptist Cramer. In the 1820s, wishing to write operas, he made further studies with Antonin Reicha in Paris, where he lived alternatively.

Works OPERA *L'alcade de la Vega* (1824), *Le Colporteur* (1827), *Le Duc de Guise* (1837).

ORCHESTRAL AND CHAMBER four symphonies, three string quartets, 34 string quintets, two piano sextets, piano septet, nonet for strings and wind, six piano trios; violin and piano and cello and piano sonatas; sonatas for piano duet; piano pieces.

On Wenlock Edge song cycle for tenor, piano, and string quartet by Vaughan Williams (text by A E Housman), first performed in London on 15 November 1909. A version with string orchestra was performed in London on 24 January 1924.

Op. in music, an abbreviation for ➤ **Opus**.

open in music, organ pipes whose upper end is left open and which, unlike the stopped pipes, produce notes corresponding to their full length.

open notes on wind instruments, the notes produced naturally as harmonics as distinct from stopped notes produced by valves, keys, or other mechanical means, or by the hand in horn playing.

open string the string of a musical instrument played without the finger touching it, allowing it to vibrate along its entire length. This is notated by an 'o' above the note. The open strings of the violin are: G3, D4, A4, and E5; of the viola: C3, G3, D4, and A4; of the cello: C2, G2, D3, and A3; and of the double bass: E1, A1, D2, and G2.

opera dramatic musical work in which singing takes the place of speech. In opera, the music accompanying the action is the main element, although dancing and spectacular staging may also play their parts. Opera originated in late 16th-century Florence when the musical declamation, lyrical monologues, and choruses of classical Greek drama, were reproduced in the style of that time.

early development One of the earliest opera composers was Jacopo Peri, whose *Euridice* influenced Claudio Monteverdi, the first great master of the operatic form. Initially solely a court entertainment, opera soon became popular, and in 1637 the first public opera house was opened in Venice. It spread to other Italian towns, to Paris (about 1645), and to Vienna and Germany, where it remained Italian at the courts but became partly German at Hamburg from about 1680.

In the later 17th century the aria, designed to show off the skill of the singer, became very important, overshadowing the dramatic element of the opera. Composers of this type of opera included Pier Cavalli, Pietro Antonio Cesti, and Alessandro Scarlatti. In France, opera was developed by Jean-Baptiste Lully and Jean-Philippe Rameau, and in England by Henry Purcell, but the Italian style retained its ascendancy, as exemplified by George Frideric Handel.

Comic opera (*opera buffa*) was developed in Italy by such composers as Giovanni Battista Pergolesi, while in England *The Beggar's Opera* (1728) by John Gay started the vogue of the **ballad opera**, using popular tunes and spoken dialogue. *Singspiel* was the German equivalent (although its music was newly composed). A lessening of artificiality began with Christoph Willibald von Gluck, who insisted on the pre-eminence of the dramatic over the purely vocal element. Wolfgang

Mozart learned much from Gluck in writing his serious operas, but also excelled in Italian opera buffa (comic opera). In works such as *The Magic Flute* (1791), he laid the foundations of a purely German-language opera, using the *Singspiel* as a basis. This line was continued by Ludwig van Beethoven in *Fidelio* (1805) and by the work of Carl Weber, who introduced the Romantic style for the first time in opera.

developments into the 19th century The Italian tradition, which placed the main stress on vocal display and melodic smoothness (bel canto), continued unbroken into the 19th century in the operas of Gioacchino Rossini, Gaetano Donizetti, and Vincenzo Bellini. It is in the Romantic operas of Weber and Giacomo Meyerbeer that the work of Richard Wagner has its roots. Dominating the operatic scene of his time, Wagner created, in his 'music-dramas', a new art form. He completely transformed the 19th-century idea of opera by 'through-composing' entire acts and providing formal clarity by the use of particular themes associated with each character. In Italy, the later work of Giuseppe Verdi contained a lot of Wagner's techniques, while still keeping the vocal clarity and good melodies of the Italian style. This tradition was continued by Giacomo Puccini. In French opera in the mid-19th century, represented by such composers as Léo Delibes, Charles Gounod, Camille Saint-Saëns, and Jules Massenet, the drama continued to be subservient to the music. Comic opera (*opéra comique*), as represented in the works of André Gréry and, later, Daniel Auber, became a popular genre in Paris. More serious artistic ideals were put into practice by Hector Berlioz in *The Trojans* (1856–58), but the value of his work was largely unrecognized in his own time.

George Bizet's *Carmen* began a trend towards realism in opera. His lead was followed in Italy by Pietro Mascagni, Ruggiero Leoncavallo, and Puccini. Claude Debussy's *Pelléas et Mélisande* (1902) was a reaction against the over-emphatic emotionalism of Wagnerian opera. National operatic styles were developed in Russia by Mikhail Glinka, Nikolai Rimsky-Korsakov, Modest Mussorgsky, Aleksander Borodin, and Pyotr Il'yich Tchaikovsky, and in Bohemia (now the Czech Republic) by Bedřich Smetana and, later, Antonín Dvořák and, most importantly, Leoš Janáček. Several composers of light opera emerged, including Arthur Sullivan, Franz Lehár, Jacques Offenbach, and Johann Strauss.

20th-century opera In the 20th century the Viennese school produced an outstanding opera in Alban Berg's *Wozzeck* (1925), and the Romanticism of Wagner was revived by Richard Strauss in *Der Rosenkavalier*. Other 20th-century composers of opera include George Gershwin, Leonard Bernstein, and John Adams in the USA; Roberto

Gerhard, Michael Tippett, Benjamin Britten, and Harrison Birtwistle in the UK; Arnold Schoenberg, Paul Hindemith, and Hans Henze in Germany; Luigi Dallapiccola and Goffreddo Petrassi in Italy; and the Soviet composers Sergey Prokofiev and Dmitri Shostakovich. The operatic form has developed in many different directions, for example, towards oratorio in Igor Stravinsky's *Oedipus Rex* (1925), and towards cabaret and music-theatre, as represented by the works of Kurt Weill.

opera-ballet a combination of opera and ballet originating in 17th-century France and there called *opéra-ballet* from the beginning.

opéra bouffe (French 'comic opera', derived from Italian *opera buffa*) a type of French comic opera, or rather operetta, lighter in tone and sometimes flimsier in musical workmanship than an ➔ *opéra comique*. See also ➔ opera buffa.

opera buffa, French **opera bouffe (Italian 'comic opera')** type of humorous opera with characters taken from everyday life. The form began as a musical intermezzo in the 18th century and was then adopted in Italy and France for complete operas. An example is Rossini's *The Barber of Seville*.

opéra comique (French 'comic opera') opera that includes text to be spoken, not sung; Bizet's *Carmen* is an example. Of the two Paris opera houses in the 18th and 19th centuries, the Opéra (which aimed at setting a grand style) allowed no spoken dialogue, whereas the Opéra Comique did. The ➔ operetta is derived from this form.

Opera Factory UK opera company founded in 1981 under the umbrella of the English National Opera; in 1991 it became resident at the Queen Elizabeth Hall, South Bank, London. It had an iconoclastic approach to classic operas and performed several new works. Its director was David Freeman (1952–). The company's last performances took place in May 1998.

opera seria (Italian 'serious opera') type of opera distinct from opera buffa, or humorous opera. Common in the 17th and 18th centuries, it tended to treat classical subjects in a formal style, with most of the singing being by solo voices. Examples include many of Handel's operas based on mythological subjects.

operetta light form of opera, with music, dance, and spoken dialogue. The story line is romantic and sentimental, often employing farce and parody. Its origins lie in the 19th-century *opéra comique* and it is intended to amuse. Examples of operetta are Jacques Offenbach's *Orphée aux enfers/Orpheus in the Underworld* (1858), Johann Strauss' *Die Fledermaus/The Flittermouse*

(1874), and Gilbert and Sullivan's *The Pirates of Penzance* (1879) and *The Mikado* (1885).

Opernball, Der, *The Ball at the Opera House* operetta by Richard ➔ Heuberger (libretto by V Léon and H von Waldberg), which was produced in Vienna at the Theater an der Wien on 5 January 1898. The story concerns mistaken identity at a ball, as Angèle and Margeurite test the fidelity of husbands Paul and Georges.

ophicleide in music, an obsolete brass instrument of the bugle family. It was a development of the ➔ serpent, patented by Halary in Paris in 1821, and was played with fingered keys and a cup-shaped mouthpiece. Although there were alto, bass, and double bass variants, only the bass model, with its compass of about three octaves, was commonly used, until superseded by the bass tuba. It was used in military bands and in the orchestral scores of composers including Berlioz, Verdi, and Wagner.

Opieński, Henryk (1870–1942) Polish musicologist, composer, and conductor. He edited Chopin's letters and wrote on him, Paderewski, and Polish music in general.

He studied piano with Paderewski, composition with Vincent d'Indy at the Schola Cantorum in Paris, and conducting and musicology with Arthur Nikisch and Hugo Riemann at Leipzig. He formed a vocal society at Lausanne in 1918 and lived in Switzerland until his death, except when he was director of the Poznań Conservatory 1920–26.

Works OPERA AND STAGE operas *Maria* (Malczewski, 1904), and *Jacob the Lutenist* (1918); incidental music for Calderón's *El principe constante*.

CHORAL AND ORCHESTRAL oratorio *The Prodigal Son*; cantata *Mickiewicz*; symphonic poems *Zymunt August i Barbara* and *Lilla Weneda*.

CHAMBER string quartet; instrumental pieces; songs.

Op. posth. abbreviation for ➔ Opus posthumous.

Opus or **Op. (Latin 'work')** in music, a prefix, used with a figure, to indicate the numbering of a composer's works, usually in chronological order.

It was at first a publisher's rather than a composer's device and in the early 18th century was used only for instrumental composers. Later in that century it began to become more general, being used for Haydn but not for Mozart, and from Beethoven onward it began to be used regularly, though the number of an Opus is not necessarily a guide to the date of its composition.

Opus posthumous a work of which the existence became known after the composer's death.

oratorio dramatic, musical setting of religious texts, scored for orchestra, chorus, and solo voices. Originally it was acted out with scenery and costumes, but gradually it became more commonly performed as a concert. Its origins lie in the *Laude spirituali* performed by St Philip Neri's Oratory in Rome in the 16th century, followed by the first definitive oratorio in the 17th century by Cavalieri. The form reached perfection in such works as Johann Sebastian Bach's *Christmas Oratorio* (performed 1734–35), and George Handel's *Messiah* (1742).

The term is sometimes applied to secular music drama in which there is little or no stage action, as in Igor Stravinsky's *Oedipus Rex* (1925–27) and Olivier Messiaen's *St François d'Assise* (1975–83). In the earliest oratorios there was often an element of ritual and spatial dramatization, and Bach himself introduced audience participation with the chorales of his *St Matthew Passion* (1727 or 1729). In 1993 Jonathan Miller reintroduced simple actions to a London performance of Bach's *St John Passion* (1724) with telling effect.

Orazi ed i Curiazi, Gli, The Horatii and the Curiatii opera by Domenico ➤ **Cimarosa** (libretto by A S Sografi), produced in Venice at the Teatro La Fenice on 26 December 1796. The story concerns two families, the Horatius family of Rome and the Curiatius family of Alba, who are traditional enemies. Curiatius' betrothal to Horatia brings the families together. However, Rome and Alba go to battle and Curiatius is killed by Horatia's brother, Marcus, who then kills Horatia for not rejoicing with him.

Opera by Saverio ➤ **Mercadante** (libretto by Salvatore Cammarano), produced in Naples at the Teatro San Carlo on 10 November 1846.

orchestra large group of musicians playing together on different instruments. In Western music, an orchestra is usually based on the bowed, stringed instruments of the violin family, to which is usually added the woodwind, brass, and percussion sections. The number of players per section and the instruments used may vary according to the needs of the composer.

history The term was originally used in Greek theatre for the semicircular space in front of the stage, and was adopted in 17th-century Italy to refer first to the space in front of the stage where musicians sat, and later to the musicians themselves.

Western instruments In the 17th century, the orchestra was a chance combination of whatever instruments might be available. For a while, viols and violins were played alongside each other but gradually the viols were dropped in preference to the superior projection quality and versatility of the violin, violas, and cellos.

By the beginning of the 18th century, the string section had developed into a self-contained unit usually divided into two groups of violins (first and second), violas, cellos, and double basses. Other instruments were also added when needed, singly or in pairs, mostly flutes, oboes, bassoons, and horns. A continuo keyboard player was also a part of the orchestra, building up the chords from a bass-line to fill out the harmonies. The woodwind section became standardized by the end of the 18th century. It now contained pairs of flutes, oboes, clarinets, and bassoons, to which were later added piccolo, ➤ **cor anglais**, bass clarinet, and double bassoon. At that time, two timpani and two horns were also standard, and two trumpets were occasionally added.

During the 19th century, the brass section was gradually expanded to include four horns, three trumpets, three trombones, and tuba. To the percussion section a third timpano was added, and from Turkey came the bass drum, side drum, cymbals, and triangle. One or more harps became common and, to maintain balance, the number of string instruments to each part was increased. Other instruments used in the orchestra include xylophone, ➤ **celesta**, ➤ **glockenspiel**, piano (which replaced the harpsichord in the late 18th century), and organ.

In the 20th century, composers often preferred smaller groupings of instruments, sometimes in unconventional combinations. The orchestra used to be conducted by means of a violin bow, but by Felix Mendelssohn's time the baton took over.

non-Western ensembles The term may also be applied to non-Western ensembles such as the Indonesian ➤ **gamelan** orchestra, founded on families of percussion instruments, mainly tuned gongs and bells.

orchestration scoring of a composition for orchestra; the choice of instruments of a score expanded for orchestra (often by another hand). A work may be written for piano, then transferred to an orchestral score.

Ordonez or **Ordoñez, Carlo d' (1734–1786)** Austrian composer and violinist who was a major influence in the developing instrumental style of the years 1750–75. For most of his life he worked as a government administrator in Vienna.

Works OPERA two operas.
ORCHESTRAL AND CHAMBER over 70 symphonies, over 30 string quartets, other chamber music.

ordre in music, an old French name for the ➤ **suite**.

Orel, Alfred (1889–1967) Austrian musicologist. A lawyer and civil servant at first, he studied music with Adler when nearly 30. He was later appointed professor at Vienna University and head of the music department of the municipal library. He wrote works on Bruckner and co-edited with Robert ➤ **Haas** the edition of the original versions of Bruckner's works.

Oresteia trilogy of short operas by Sergey Ivanovich ➤ **Taneiev** (libretto by A A Venkstern, after Aeschylus). Scenes depict the Greek myths *Agamemnon*, *Choephorae/The Libation Bearers*, and *Eumenides/The Furies*. *Oresteia* was first produced in St Petersburg on 29 October 1895.

Orestes opera by Felix ➤ **Weingartner** (libretto by composer, after Aeschylus). It was produced in Leipzig on 15 February 1902.

Opera by Křenek. See ➤ *Leben des Orest*.

Orfeide, L' cycle of operas by Francesco ➤ **Malipiero** (libretto by composer). There are three cycles: I. *La morte delle maschere/The Death of the Maskers*; II. *Sette canzoni/Seven Songs*, produced in French translation at the Paris Opéra on 10 July 1920; and III. *L'Orfeo, ossia l'ottava canzone/Orpheus, or the Eighth Song*. The cycle was first produced in complete form, in German translation, on 30 October 1925, in Düsseldorf.

Orfeo opera by Claudio Monteverdi; see ➤ *Favola d'Orfeo, La*.

Orfeo, L', *Orpheus* opera by Luigi ➤ **Rossi** (libretto by F Buti), produced in Paris at the Palais Royal on 2 March 1647.

Orfeo ed Euridice, *Orpheus and Eurydice* opera by Ferdinando ➤ **Bertoni** (libretto by Raniero da Calzabigi, written for Christoph Willibald von Gluck), which tells the story of Orpheus descending into Hades to bring back his deceased Eurydice. It was produced at the Teatro San Benedetto, Venice, on 3 January 1776.

Opera by Christoph Willibald von Gluck (libretto as above), produced at the Burgtheater, Vienna, on 5 October 1762. (For the French version, see ➤ *Orphée et Eurydice*.)

Orff, Carl (1895–1982) German composer. An individual stylist, his work is characterized by sharp dissonances and percussion. Among his compositions are the cantata ➤ *Carmina Burana* (1937) and the opera *Antigone* (1949).

He studied at Munich and became professor of composition at the Günther School there. He was also a conductor and editor of early music, notably the operas of Monteverdi. His early success with *Carmina Burana*, founded on rhythmic ostinati (persistently repeating rhythms) and appealing vocal melody, was not repeated in later works.

Works OPERA AND STAGE MUSIC eleven operas and musical plays, including *Carmina Burana* (settings of medieval poetry, 1937), *Die Kluge* (1943), *Catulli Carmina*, *Antigonae* and *Oedipus*

der Tyrann (after Sophocles, 1949, 1959); *Trionfo di Afrodite* (1953), *Prometheus* (1966), *De temporum fine comoedia* (1973), ballet *Der Feuerfarbene*; incidental music for Shakespeare's *Midsummer Night's Dream* (first version composed to replace Mendelssohn's music, banned by the Nazis, 1939–62).

OTHER *Schulwerk* for combinations of popular instruments and similar compositions intended for use by amateurs; cantata *Des Turmes Auferstehung*.

organ oldest of the keyboard instruments, in which sound is produced when a depressed key opens a valve, allowing compressed air to pass through a single pipe or a series of pipes. The number of pipes may vary according to the size of the instrument. Apart from its continued use in serious compositions and for church music, the organ has been adapted for light entertainment.

Only one note is sounded by each pipe. The pipes are lined up in ranks or rows, and are brought into play ('speak') by a stop operated from the console by the player. An organ is made up of different manuals (keyboards) that control separate divisions of the organ, each with its own pipes and stops. These separate manuals are the great, swell, choir, solo, echo, and pedal organs, and are controlled by the player's hands and feet. By various groupings and subdivisions of the above, the organ is capable of a wide variety of timbre and volume.

history The organ developed from the panpipes and hydraulis (water organ), and is mentioned in writings that date from the 3rd century BC. The first development of the organ was the supply of compressed air from bellows. Organs were imported to France from Byzantium in the 8th and 9th centuries, and then manufactured in Europe. The replacing of the old drawslides by the key system dates from the 11th–13th centuries and the first chromatic keyboard dates from 1361. Later a keyboard of pedals, played by the feet, was added to control the largest bass pipes. The number of pipes, ranging from 9.8m/32ft down to a fraction of an inch, was enormously increased, and they were made in a growing variety of shapes from different materials, and with different speaking mechanisms, each range being controlled by stops that could bring it into action or shut it off at the player's will. The number of manuals (hand keyboards) increased to three or more, which meant that a greater number of stops drawn before the performance could be controlled and varied.

From the late 19th century the bellows, formerly worked by hand, were operated mechanically and devices were invented that could bring into action whole ranges of stops in various combinations. Expression was added by swell pedals producing crescendo (increasing loudness) and diminuendo (decreasing loudness). These are the only means that the player has to vary the timbre either in strength or in quality, the keyboard not responding to changes of touch like a piano.

The electric tone-wheel organ was invented in 1934 by US engineer Laurens Hammond (1895–1973). Other types of electric organ were developed in the 1960s. Electrically controlled organs substitute electrical impulses and relays for some of the air-pressure controls. These, such as the Hammond and Wurlitzer organs, built during the 1930s for the large cinemas of the period, include many special sound effects as well as colour displays. In electronic organs the notes are produced by electronic oscillators and are amplified at will.

organology branch of musicology which is concerned with the systematic study and classification of musical instruments, their history, design, fabrication, and taxonomy. Canon Francis Galpin's *Old English Instruments of Music* (1910) was one of the first works to attempt to deal with musical instruments systematically. The scholarly society formed in 1945 in his name – the Galpin Society – is a focus for British organologists. Its counterpart in the USA is the American Musical Instrument Society (formed in 1974).

organo pieno or **(pro) organo pieno (Italian 'full organ')** musical direction indicating that an organ passage is to be played with the use of the full extent of the instrument's power, or in earlier music, with a substantial body of ➤ tone.

organ-point (from German *Orgelpunkt*) another term, used mainly in the USA, for ➤ pedal point.

organ stop a set of organ pipes that sound together; also the knob or mechanism that operates such a set of pipes. See ➤ stop.

organum in music, a form of early medieval harmony in which voices move in parallel fourths or fifths.

Orione, o sia Diana vendicata, Orion, or Diana Avenged opera by Johann Christian Bach (libretto by G G Bottarelli), Bach's first opera for London. It was produced at the King's Theatre, London, on 19 February 1763.

Orlandi, Santi (died 1619) Italian composer. He was maestro di cappella to Ferdinando Gonzaga at Florence and succeeded Monteverdi as maestro di cappella to the Gonzaga family at Mantua in 1612.

Works OPERA AND CHAMBER the opera *Gli amori di Aci e Galatea* (performed in Mantua, March

1617), five books of madrigals, and other pieces.

***Orlando*, Roland** opera by ➤ Handel (libretto by G Braccioli, based on Ariosto's *Orlando furioso*), produced at the King's Theatre in London on 27 January 1733. In the story, the knight Orlando falls in love with Angelica, but she does not return his feelings because she already loves Medoro. When Orlando discovers this he goes mad, until the magician Zoroastra (or Astolfo in the Vivaldi version) restores his reason. Orlando then blesses Angelica and Medoro's union.

Orlando Furioso opera by ➤ Vivaldi (libretto by G B Braccioli), produced in Venice at the Teatro Sant'Angelo in 1727.

Orlando Paladino opera (*dramma eroicomico*) by Franz Joseph ➤ Haydn (libretto by C F Badini and N Porta), produced in Eszterháza on 6 December 1779. The story is similar to that of *Orlando*, but here Orlando is already mad when the curtain goes up, his senses are restored by the sorceress Alcina, and the additional character Rodomonte appears, also in love with Angelica.

Ormandy, Eugene (1899–1985), adopted name of **Jenö Ormandy Blau** Hungarian-born US conductor. He was music director of the Philadelphia Orchestra 1936–80. Originally a violin virtuoso, he championed the composers Rachmaninov and Shostakovich.

Ormindo opera by Francesco ➤ Cavalli (libretto by G Faustini), produced in 1644 at the Teatro San Cassiano, Venice. The story takes place in North Africa. Ormindo has fallen in love with Erisbe, who is married to King Hariadeno (Ormindo's long-lost father). When Hariadeno learns of the couple's planned escape, he captures them and is about to execute them, before relenting and allowing Erisbe to join Ormindo. The opera was revived in 1967 in a new version by Raymond Leppard, at Glyndebourne in East Sussex.

ornamentation in music, notes that are additional to the main notes of a melody. They are used to 'ornament' or decorate a melody, or to accent a structural feature such as the end of a phrase. They are indicated by special signs, or by small notes printed among the melody notes. Examples of ornaments are the ➤ turn, the ➤ trill, the ➤ appoggiatura, the ➤ arpeggio, and the ➤ mordent.

Throughout musical history until at least the early 19th century there were many pieces in which the performer was expected to add ornamental details. Shorthand signs for the simpler ornaments are found at least from the early 16th century (though there are traces of them much earlier in the chant repertory). They were catalogued in elaborate systems described in detailed tables from the 17th century and had their heyday in the first half of the 18th century. Since the early 19th century, performers have tended not to add their own improvised ornaments, but (with the exception of the trill) rely instead on the embellishments written out by the composer.

See also ➔ acciaccatura, ➔ cadenza, ➔ plica, ➔ tremolo, ➔ vibrato.

Ornithoparcus, Andreas (born c.1490) German music scholar. He was the author of the Latin treatise *Musicae activae micrologus* in 1517, which was translated into English by John Dowland in 1609.

He studied at Tübingen University, travelled in many countries, and taught at Wittenberg University.

Orontea opera by Antonio ➔ **Cesti** (libretto by G A Ciognini), Cesti's first opera, which has been successfully revived in modern editions. The story concerns Orontea, Queen of Egypt, who falls in love with a lowly painter, Alidoro. There is stiff opposition to her wedding plans, but all is resolved when it turns out that Alidoro is of noble birth. The opera was first produced in 1649 at the Teatro dei Apostoli, Venice.

It was later revised (libretto by G F Apolloni) and produced at the Teatro di Sala at Innsbruck, on 19 February 1656.

orpharion early musical instrument of the ➔ **cittern** type. It had six or seven pairs of strings played with a plectrum (a device for plucking a stringed instrument).

Orphée aux enfers, Orpheus in the Underworld operetta by Jacques ➔ **Offenbach** (libretto by Hector Crémieux and Ludovic Halévy), produced at the Bouffes Parisiens in Paris on 21 October 1858. The operetta is a spoof on the original ➔ *Orpheus*: Orpheus is delighted at the prospect of freedom when Eurydice dies, and arrives in Hades to reclaim her only because Public Opinion forces him to.

Orphée et Eurydice opera by Christoph Willibald von ➔ **Gluck** (libretto by P L Moline, translated from Raniero da Calzabigi's *Orfeo ed Euridice*). Produced in Paris in August 1774, it is a revised version of Gluck's first setting in 1762. See ➔ *Orfeo ed Euridice* for a plot synopsis.

Orphéon French male-voice choral society similar to the German *Liedertafel*.

Orpheus ballet by Stravinsky (choreographed by George Balanchine) produced in New York, 29 April 1948.

Opera by Reinhard ➔ **Keiser** (libretto by F C Bressand). Part I: *Die sterbende Eurydice* was produced in Brunswick in 1699. Part II: *Die verwandelte Leyer des Orpheus* was produced in Hamburg in 1709.

Symphonic poem by Liszt, composed 1853–54 and first performed as an introduction to Christoph Willibald von Gluck's *Orfeo* at Weimar on 16 February 1854, with closing music on the same themes after the opera.

See ➔ *Favola d'Orfeo, La*; ➔ *Malheurs d'Orphée*; ➔ *Orfeide, L'*; ➔ *Orfeo*; ➔ *Orfeo ed Euridice*; ➔ *Orphée aux enfers*; ➔ *Orpheus*; ➔ *Orpheus og Euridice*; ➔ *Orpheus und Eurydike*.

Orpheus ballet in two acts by Hans Werner ➔ **Henze** (scenario by Edward Bond), produced in Stuttgart on 17 March 1979.

The suite for ballet, *Apollo triofante*, was performed at Gelsenkirchen, on 1 September 1980. The *Arias of Orpheus* for guitar, harp, harpsichord, and strings was performed in Chicago, on 25 November 1981. *Dramatic Scenes from Orpheus* for large orchestra was performed in two parts: no. 2 in Zurich on 6 January 1981, and no. 1 in Frankfurt on 12 September 1982. A concert version of the ballet was performed in Cologne on 4 March 1983.

Orpheus Britannicus a collection of vocal music by Purcell begun soon after Purcell's death by Henry Playford, who published a first volume in 1698 and a second in 1702. It is also a collection of Purcell's songs published by John Walsh in 1735.

Orpheus og Euridice opera by Johann Gottlieb ➔ **Naumann** (libretto by C D Biehl, based on Raniero da Calzabigi). Produced in Copenhagen on 21 January 1786, it was the first grand opera on a Danish libretto. See ➔ *Orfeo ed Euridice* for a plot synopsis.

Orpheus und Eurydike opera by Ernst ➔ **Krenek** (libretto by Oskar Kokoschka) produced in Kassel, Germany, on 27 November 1926. The story is a psychoanalytical rendering of the Greek myth.

Orr, Buxton (Daeblitz) (1924–1997) Scottish composer and conductor. He conducted the London Jazz Composers' Orchestra 1970–80 and the Guildhall New Music Ensemble 1975–91. In 1983, he completed Benjamin ➔ **Frankel**'s opera *Marching Song* for a posthumous first performance.

He studied with Frankel 1952–55 and wrote film and theatre music until 1961.

Works OPERA AND STAGE opera *The Wager* (1962); music theatre *Ring in the New* (1986).

ORCHESTRAL AND ENSEMBLE *A Celtic Suite* for strings (1968); trombone concerto, with brass band (1971); *Sinfonia Ricercante* (1988); *Refrains VI* for chamber orchestra (1992).

Orr, C(harles) W(ilfred) (1893–1976) English composer. He was educated at Cheltenham College. He suffered much from ill-health in his youth and did not begin to study music at the Guildhall School of Music and Drama in London until 1917. He lived most of his life quietly at

Painswick, Gloucestershire, and never held any official musical posts; but he did war work in London during World War II.

Works ORCHESTRAL AND SONGS *A Cotswold Hill Tune* for string orchestra; numerous songs, especially settings of A E Housman, D G Rossetti, and James Joyce.

Orr, Robin (1909–2006) Scottish composer. He studied at the Royal College of Music in London and with Edward J Dent at Cambridge, also with Alfredo Casella at Siena and Nadia Boulanger in Paris. From 1938 to 1956 he was organist and director of studies at St John's College, Cambridge. He was professor of music at Glasgow University 1956–64, and at Cambridge 1964–76. He was chair of the Scottish Opera 1962–76, and director of the Welsh National Opera 1971–83.

Works OPERA *Full Circle* (1968), *Hermiston* (1975), *On the Razzle* (1988).

ORCHESTRAL three symphonies (1965, 1971, 1978); *Sinfonietta Helvetia* (1990).

CHAMBER divertimento for chamber orchestra; three Latin psalms for voice and string quartet; string quintet (1971); sonatina for violin and piano; violin sonata; viola sonata; piano pieces; songs.

Ortiz, Diego (c.1510–c.1570) Spanish composer. He went to Naples in 1555 to become maestro di cappella to the viceroy, the Duke of Alva. While there, he worked with many other Spanish musicians, including Francisco de Salinas. He wrote an important treatise on ornamentation in viol music, the *Trattado de Glosas*, published in two editions (Spanish and Italian) at Rome in 1553.

Works CHAMBER motets; variations for bass viol.

Orto, Marbrianus de (c.1460–1529), adopted name of **Marbrianus Dujardin** Flemish singer and composer. He changed his name when he went to Rome, where he was a singer in the papal chapel 1484–94, with Josquin Desprez. Early in the 16th century he became chaplain and singer at the court of Philip the Fair of Burgundy.

Works CHURCH AND OTHER Masses, motets, and other church music; chansons.

Osborne, Nigel (1948–) English composer. He is best known for his vivid and iconoclastic stage works, which include the operas *The Electrification of the Soviet Union* (1986) and *Sarajevo* (1994). He studied at Oxford with Egon Wellesz and Kenneth ➤ **Leighton** and in Poland with Witold Rodziński. He lectured at Nottingham University from 1978.

Works ORCHESTRAL AND CHORAL *Byzantine Epigrams* for chorus (1969); cantata *Seven Words* (1971); *Charivari* for orchestra (1973); *Concert Piece* for cello and orchestra (1977); *Gnostic Passion* for 36 voices (1980); flute concerto (1980);

Sinfonia for orchestra (1982); violin concerto (1990); *The Sun of Venice* for orchestra (1991).

CHAMBER AND ENSEMBLE *Chansonnier* for chamber ensemble (1975); *I am Goya* for baritone and instruments (1977); *In Camera* for 13 instruments (1979); *The Cage* for tenor and ensemble (1981); *Alba* for mezzo, instruments, and tape (1984); *Zansa* for ensemble (1985); *Pornography* for mezzo and ensemble (1985); *Esquisse I and II* for strings (1987–88).

OPERA *The Electrification of the Soviet Union* (1986), *Terrible Mouth* (1992), *Sarajevo* (1994).

oscillator in music, an electrical generator used to convert electricity into sound. It produces an oscillating current that may be heard as sound when played at a frequency between 16 Hz and 20,000 Hz and attached to an amplifier and loudspeakers. Different types of tone produced by an oscillator include ➤ **sine waves** and ➤ **saw-toothed waves.**

ossia (Italian, from *O sia,* 'or else') in musical notation, an indication of an alternative version of a given passage. It often appears during a technically difficult passage, providing a simpler version for less proficient performers.

Ossian semi-mythical Gaelic bard whose works, allegedly translated by James Macpherson (1736–1796), influenced the early Romantic movement. Ossian's works were in fact by Macpherson, drawing on ancient sources. Franz ➤ **Schubert** set nine Ossian songs 1815–17.

ostinato (Italian 'obstinate') musical pattern that is continuously repeated during a section or throughout a complete piece of music. The repeating idea may be a rhythmic pattern, part of a tune, or a complete melody.

Ostinati play an important role in Igor ➤ **Stravinsky's** *The Rite of Spring* (1913), Maurice Ravel's *Boléro* (1928), and Carl ➤ **Orff's** *Carmina Burana* (1937). Ostinato-like structures are also important in Balinese ➤ **gamelan** (percussion ensemble). In the 1960s, tape-loop recycling of fragments of melody and sound was a starting point for the minimalism of Terry Riley, Steve Reich, Philip Glass, and John Adams.

Ostrovsky, Alexander Nikolaevich (1823–1886) Russian dramatist. He was a founder of the modern Russian theatre. He dealt satirically with the manners of the merchant class in numerous plays, for example *The Bankrupt* or *It's All in the Family* (1849). His best-known play is a family tragedy, *The Storm* (1860). His fairy-tale play *The Snow Maiden* (1873) inspired the composers Tchaikovsky and Rimsky-Korsakov.

For influences on the works of composers, see Rimsky-Korsakov (➤ **Snow Maiden, The**); ➤ **Tchaikovsky** (*Snegurotchka*); Nikolai ➤ **Tcherepnin** (*Pov-*

erty no Crime); and Tchaikovsky (➔ **Voyevoda**).

Osud, Fate opera in three scenes by ➔ **Janáček** (libretto by composer and F Bartosova) composed 1903–04 and first performed on the Brno Radio on 18 September 1934. In the story, the composer Živný is reunited with his former mistress Míla, but she and her insane mother are killed in a fall.

Otello opera by Verdi (libretto by Arrigo Boito, after Shakespeare), produced at La Scala in Milan on 5 February 1887. The plot concerns Otello, who, driven by the evil Iago, murders his wife Desdemona in a jealous rage, and commits suicide.

Otello, ossia Il Moro di Venezia, Othello, or The Moor of Venice opera by ➔ **Rossini** (libretto by M F B di Salsa, after Shakespeare). It was first produced at the Teatro Fondo, Naples, on 4 December 1816.

Othello concert overture by ➔ Dvořák, Op. 93, referring to Shakespeare's tragedy. It was composed in 1892 and forms, with *Amid Nature* and *Carnival*, a cycle with thematic connections originally called *Nature, Life and Love*.

See ➔ *Otello*.

ottavino (Italian from *ottava* 'octave') musical instrument, the octave flute usually known as the ➔ **piccolo**.

Otto, Stephan (1603–1656) German composer. He studied at Freiberg under Christoph Demantius, and after an appointment at Augsburg became cantor at his home town in 1632 and at Schandau in 1639. Andreas Hammerschmidt was among his pupils.

Works CHAMBER AND VOCAL *Kronen-Krönlein*, a collection of sacred vocal pieces in a mixed motet and madrigal style, for three–eight voices; setting of Luther's hymn 'Ein' feste Burg' for 19 voices.

Ottone, rè di Germania, Otho, King of Germany opera by ➔ **Handel** (libretto by Nicola Francesco Haym), produced at the King's Theatre, Haymarket, London, on 12 January 1723. In the story, Otto defeats an attempted revolt by Adalberto and is united with his promised bride, Teofane.

Our Hunting Fathers song cycle for high voice and orchestra by Benjamin Britten (text by W H Auden), first performed at Norwich on 25 September 1936, and conducted by Britten.

Ours, L', The Bear nickname of Joseph ➔ Haydn's symphony no. 82 in C major, composed for Paris in 1786.

overblowing in music, a technique of exciting higher harmonics in a wind instrument by increasing air pressure at the mouthpiece, causing it to sound an octave (second harmonic) or twelfth (third harmonic) higher.

The note in an ascending scale at which a player switches to overblowing is called the **break point**. For instruments of the clarinet family, which overblow at the twelfth, the break point is relatively unstable and difficult to control. Overblowing may occur in organ pipes if the air pressure is too great, but safety-valve devices can prevent this.

overspun string in musical instruments of the violin family and also those of the piano, a string that consists of a central wire around which another wire is spun. Strings manufactured in this way are thicker without losing their flexibility, and are used to produce the lower notes.

overstrung in music, method of manufacture of modern pianos, in which the bass strings cross diagonally over the strings of higher-pitched notes, in order to secure greater length in the strings, thereby improving tone quality.

overtones in music, tones of the harmonic series, excluding the first harmonic (fundamental), which determine the tone quality or ➔ **timbre** of an instrument.

overture in music, the opening piece of a concert or opera. It has two roles: settling the audience before the main music starts, and allowing the conductor and musicians to become acquainted with the acoustics of a concert auditorium. See also ➔ **prelude**.

The use of an overture in opera began during the 17th century; the 'Italian' overture consisting of two quick movements separated by a slow one, and the 'French' of a quick movement between two in slower tempo.

ovvero (Italian 'or rather, or else') in music, an early word for ➔ **ossia**. It is also found in front of second, alternative titles of works.

Owen Wingrave opera in two acts by Benjamin Britten (libretto by Myfanwy Piper after Henry James). It was first performed for BBC TV on 16 May 1971 and later produced at Covent Garden, London, on 10 May 1973. In the story, pacifist Owen Wingrave drops out of Spencer Coyle's military school. His family is disgusted. Fellow student Lechmere drives Owen to spend the night in a haunted room; a family prophecy comes true and Owen is found dead.

Oxford Elegy, An work by Vaughan Williams for speaker, small chorus, and orchestra (text from Matthew Arnold, *The Scholar Gipsy* and *Thyrsis*). It was first performed privately at Dorking, in Surrey, on 20 November 1949; its first public performance was at Queen's College, Oxford, on 19 June 1952.

Oxford Symphony name given to ➤ Haydn's symphony no. 92 in G major, composed in 1788. It was not written for Oxford, but received its title after it was performed there in July 1791, when Haydn was given an honorary degree.

Ox Minuet, German **Die Ochsenmenuette** a *singspiel* by ➤ Seyfried, produced in Vienna in 1823, with music arranged from compositions by Haydn. It was based on two earlier French works, *Le Menuet de bœuf, ou Une Leçon de Haydn* (1805) and *Haydn, ou le Menuet du bœuf* (1812). The title is sometimes mistakenly thought to be the nickname of one of Haydn's minuets.

p in music, abbreviation for the instruction ➔ **piano.**

Pace, Pietro (1559–1622), also known as (Latin) **Pacius** Italian composer. He was organist at Pesaro in 1597 and of the Santa Casa at Loreto 1591–92 and 1611–22.

Works CHURCH MUSIC AND ORCHESTRAL music for Ignazio Bracci's *L'ilarocosmo, ovvero Il mondo lieto* (performed 1621); Magnificats, motets (with accompaniment), other church music.

OTHER *Arie spirituali*, madrigals with and without accompaniment.

Pacelli, Asprilio (1570–1623) Italian composer. He was choirmaster of the German College 1592–1602, and later at the Vatican basilica in Rome until 1602, when he went to the court of Sigismund III of Poland at Warsaw, succeeding Luca ➔ **Marenzio.**

Works CHURCH MUSIC AND CHAMBER motets, psalms, *Sacrae cantiones*; madrigals.

Pachelbel, Johann (1653–1706) German organist and composer. Due to the great popularity of his *Canon and Gigue* in D major for three violins and continuo, he is today known to many people only by this work. However, he was a leading progressive composer of keyboard and religious works, influencing Johann Sebastian Bach.

He studied under Heinrich Schwemmer at home and, after holding brief appointments at Altdorf and Regensburg, went to Vienna in about 1671–72. Between 1677 and 1695 he was organist successively at Eisenach, Erfurt, Stuttgart, and Gotha, and in 1695 was appointed organist at St Sebaldus' Church at Nuremberg. He was one of the most important composers before J S Bach.

Works CHURCH MUSIC, VOCAL, AND CHORAL vocal music, arias, motets, sacred concertos (cantatas), eleven Magnificat settings, 94 organ fugues on the Magnificat, organ variations and preludes on chorales.

OTHER suites for two violins, *Canon and Gigue* for three violins, *Musikalisches Ergötzen*, six sets of variations for harpsichord *Hexachordum Apollinis* (1699).

Pachelbel, Wilhelm Hieronymus (1686–1764) German organist and composer, son and pupil of Johann ➔ **Pachelbel.** He was organist at St Sebaldus' Church, Nuremberg, from 1719. He wrote organ and harpsichord music.

Pacific 231 symphonic movement by Arthur ➔ **Honegger.** It was named after a railway engine and depicts its start and progress, not merely realistically, but, the composer claims, 'lyrically'. It was first performed in Paris at a Koussevitsky concert, on 8 May 1924.

Pacini, Giovanni (1796–1867) Italian composer. He studied first under his father, a famous tenor, and later at Bologna and Venice. At the age of 17 he produced his first opera at Venice. He became maestro di cappella to Napoleon's widow, the Empress Marie Louise, and in 1834 settled at Viareggio, where he opened a music school, later transferred to Lucca. For this he wrote some theoretical treatises.

Works OPERA *Annetta e Lucindo* (1813), *La sacerdotessa d'Irminsul* (1820), *La schiava in Bagdad* (1820), *La Gioventù di Enrico V* (after Shakespeare's *Henry IV*, 1820), *L'ultimo giorno di Pompei* (not based on Bulwer-Lytton, 1825), *Gli Arabi nelle Gallie* (1827), *Saffo* (1840), *Medea* (1843), *Lorenzino de' Medici* (1845), *La regina di Cipro*, *Il saltimbanco*, *Ivanhoe* (after Scott, 1832) and over 60 others.

OTHER incidental music for Sophocles' *Oedipus Rex*; Masses, oratorios, cantata for Dante anniversary and others; six string quartets (c.1860).

Pacius, Fredrik (1809–1891) German-born Finnish violinist and composer. He was a violinist in the court orchestra at Stockholm 1828–34, then became a music teacher at Helsinki University. He remained in the Finnish capital, established orchestral concerts there in 1845, and became professor of music at the university in 1860.

He studied with Louis Spohr and Moritz Hauptmann at Kassel.

Works OPERA AND STAGE the operas *Kung Karls Jakt* (1852) and *Loreley* (1887); incidental music for Topelius's *Princess of Cyprus* (1860).

OTHER violin concerto; cantatas; songs, including 'Suomis Saang' and 'Vaart Land', both adapted as Finnish national anthems.

Paderewski, Ignacy Jan (1860–1941) Polish pianist, composer, and politician. After his debut in Vienna in 1887, he became celebrated in Europe and the USA as an interpreter of the piano music of Chopin and as composer of the *Polish Fantasy* (1893) for piano and orchestra and the *'Polonia' Symphony* (1903–09).

He studied at the Warsaw Conservatory and went on his first concert tour in 1877. After teaching 1878–81 at the Conservatory he went to Berlin for further study, finishing with Leschetizky in Vienna and reappearing there and in Paris in 1887. He soon became established as one of the leading virtuosi of the day. In 1890, he paid his first visit to England and in 1891 to the USA. His opera *Manru* was premiered at Dresden in 1901 and performed at the New York Metropolitan Opera the following year.

During World War I he helped organize the Polish army in France; in 1919 he became prime minister of the newly independent Poland, which he represented at the Peace Conference, but continuing opposition forced him to resign the same year. He resumed a musical career in 1922 and supervised a complete edition of Chopin's music 1936–38. He was made president of the Polish National Council in Paris in 1940, and died in New York.

Works OPERA AND ORCHESTRAL opera *Manru* (1901), symphony in B minor (1903–09), concerto in A minor (1888), *Polish Fantasy* for piano and orchestra.

OTHER violin and piano sonata; sonata in E♭ minor and many other piano works; songs.

Padlock, The opera by Charles Dibdin (libretto by Isaac Bickerstaffe, based on a story by Cervantes, 'El celoso extremeño'), produced at the Drury Lane Theatre, London, on 3 October 1768. The story concerns Old Don Diego, who hopes to marry young Leonora and locks her in the house. Young Leander, however, climbs the wall and woos her.

Padmâvatî opera-ballet by Albert ➤ Roussel (libretto in French by Louis Laloy), produced at the Paris Opéra on 1 June 1923. In the story, the Sultan Aladdin encircles Chitor with his army and sues for peace, but when he sees Queen Padmâvatî and is struck by her beauty, he demands her in return for not destroying the city. King Ratan-Sen offers her, so Padmâvatî stabs him before joining him on the funeral pyre.

Padua, Bartolino da (lived 14th–15th centuries) Italian composer. He wrote madrigals and *ballate* (ballads) in the Italian ➤ ars nova style.

Paer, Ferdinando (1771–1839) Italian composer. He was a prolific and popular composer of operas. His works, which included *Griselda* (1798), *Camilla* (1799), and *Le maître de chapelle* (1821), were performed in Italy, Austria, Germany, and France.

He was born at Parma, and studied there with Gasparo Ghiretti. At the age of 20 he became a conductor at Venice. Having married the singer Francesca Riccardi, he was invited to Vienna in 1798, where she was engaged at the court opera. There he produced *Camilla* in 1799. In 1803 he went to Dresden, remaining there as an opera conductor until 1806, and producing *Leonora*, a setting of an Italian version of Gaveaux's opera on which Beethoven later based his *Fidelio*. In 1807, after accompanying Napoleon to Warsaw and Posen, he was appointed his maître de chapelle and settled in Paris.

Works OPERA *Circe* (1792), *Il tempo fa giustizia a tutti* (1792), *Il nuovo Figaro* (after Beaumarchais' *Mariage de Figaro*, 1794), *Il matrimonio improvviso*, *Idomeneo* (1794), *Eroe e Leandro* (1794), *L'intrigo amoroso*, *Il principe di Taranto*, *Camilla, o Il sotterraneo* (1799), *La sonnambula* (1800), *Achille, Leonora, o L'amore conjugale* (1804), *Sofonisba, Numa Pompilio* (1808), *Agnese di Fitz-Henry* (1809), *Didone abbandonata* (1810), *Le maître de chapelle* (1821), *La Marquise de Brinvilliers* (with Auber, Batton, Berton, Blangini, Boieldieu, Carafa, Cherubini, and Hérold, 1831), and over 20 others.

OTHER oratorios *Il santo sepolcro* and *La passione*; Masses and motets; about twelve cantatas (Italian, French and German); Bacchanalian symphony for orchestra; Bridal March for the wedding of Napoleon and Joséphine.

Paganini, Niccolò (1782–1840) Italian violinist and composer. He was a concert soloist from the age of nine. A prodigious technician, he drew on folk and gypsy idioms to create the modern repertoire of virtuoso techniques.

His dissolute appearance, wild love life, and amazing powers of expression, even on a single string, fostered rumours of his being in league with the devil. His compositions include six concertos and various sonatas and variations for violin and orchestra, sonatas for violin and guitar, and guitar quartets.

Paganini's father taught him to play the guitar and violin. He afterwards studied with the theatre violinist Antonio Cervetto and the cathedral maestro di cappella Giacomo Costa. As a composer he profited by the advice of Francesco Gnecco, and in 1795 his father sent him to the violinist Alessandro Rolla at Parma. While there he also studied composition with Gasparo Ghiretti, and in 1797 made his first professional tour, winning early acclaim for his technical virtuosity and flamboyant platform personality. After that he became increasingly famous, travelled widely, beginning with Vienna and Paris 1828–31, and in the latter year went to England for the first time. In 1834, he invited Berlioz in Paris to write a concert work for viola; *Harold en Italie* was the result, but he never played it.

Works ORCHESTRAL six violin concertos (1815–30; Op. 7 with the *Rondo alla campanella*); variations (including one on 'God save the King') and concert pieces for violin and orchestra.

CHAMBER three string quartets with a guitar part; twelve sonatas for violin and guitar; 24 *capricci* (studies) for violin solo.

Paganini Rhapsody work by Sergei ➔ **Rachmaninov** for piano and orchestra; see ➔ *Rhapsody on a Theme of Paganini*.

Paganini Studies a set of six studies for piano by Franz ➔ **Liszt**, transcribed from the 19th-century virtuoso violinist Niccolò ➔ **Paganini**'s violin *capricci* (except no. 3 which is another version of *La Campanella*). The studies were dedicated to Clara Schumann. There is an original version, *Études d'exécution transcendante d'après Paganini*, written in 1838, and a revised version, *Grandes Études de Paganini*, written in 1851.

Two sets of studies for piano (six in each) by Robert ➔ **Schumann** on themes from Paganini's violin *capricci* (studies): Op. 3 was written in 1832, and Op. 10 was written in 1833.

Paganini Variations two sets of studies for piano in variation form by Johannes ➔ **Brahms**, Op. 35, composed in 1866, on a theme in A minor from the 19th-century virtuoso violinist Niccolò ➔ **Paganini**'s violin *capricci* (studies).

Two other well-known works – Sergei Rachmaninov's ➔ *Rhapsody on a Theme of Paganini* and Witold Lutosławski's ➔ *Variations on a Theme of Paganini* – use the same theme as Brahms' work and are frequently referred to as *Paganini Variations*.

Pagliacci, Players opera by Leoncavallo (libretto by composer), produced in Milan at the Teatro dal Verme, on 21 May 1892. The story involves a group of actors. Tonio reveals Nedda's lover (Silvio) to her husband Canio. During a play which reflects their real-life situation, Canio stabs his wife and then Silvio.

Paik, Nam June (1932–2006) Korean composer, sculptor, and performance artist who is regarded as the founder of video art. He moved to the USA in 1964. Originally part of the Fluxus movement (an experimental arts group), Paik became a major influence on numerous forms of late 20th-century avant-garde music and art. Performance of his music involved such activities as a topless cellist using Paik's spine as a finger-board; in *Variations on a Theme of Saint-Saëns*, the pianist plays 'The Swan' while the cellist immerses herself in an oil drum. As a video artist he was distinguished for his inventive use of technology, incorporating the equipment as sculptural objects; in *My Faust* (1989–91), for example, Paik represented intent through video images screened from 13 television monitors set up as the Stations of the Cross, the installation enforcing, deepening, and expanding the meaning of the images depicted.

Using irony and wit, Paik's work pushes the boundaries of video as a fine art medium, as well as promoting technological advancement; his *TV Bra for Living Sculpture* (1969), in which the cellist Charlotte Moorman wore a bra made from two tiny television sets, is a prime example. Other avante-garde compositions include *Hommage à John Cage* (1959), in which two pianos are totally destroyed, *Performable Music* (1965), with directions for the performer's forearm to be cut with a razor, and the music *Symphony for Twenty Rooms* (1961), *Opera Sextronique* (1967), and *Young Penis Symphony* (1970). The *Earthquake Symphony* of 1971 concludes with an appropriate finale.

Paik was born in Seoul, and studied music, art history, and philosophy at the University of Tokyo. He moved to Germany to study music history at the University of Munich. He was also taught and influenced by the US composer and avant-garde artist John ➔ **Cage** during this period. Fluxus, a multi-disciplinary artistic movement with an aesthetic of spontaneous, expressive minimilism, was emerging in Europe at that time, having started in New York in the 1960s. Paik joined the movement, performing in several experimental concerts where objects and sound were employed as artistic media. In 1964 Paik moved to New York City, and began to exploit video as an artistic medium. He moved to Los Angeles in 1970, and taught media studies at the California Institute of Arts.

Paine, John Knowles (1839–1906) US organist, composer, and teacher. He studied at home and at the Hochschule für Musik in Berlin, gave organ recitals in Germany, and returned to the USA in 1861. He became instructor of music at Harvard University in 1862, assistant professor in 1872, and full professor in 1875. In 1890 he was awarded an honorary doctorate in music by Yale University.

Works OPERA AND STAGE opera *Azara* (produced in Leipzig, 1901); incidental music for Sophocles' *Oedipus Tyrannus* and Aristophanes' *Birds*.

CHORAL AND ORCHESTRAL oratorio *St Peter* (1872); cantatas *A Song of Promise* (1888), *Phoebus arise* (William Drummond), *The Realm of Fancy* (Keats, 1882), *The Nativity* (Milton); symphony in C minor (1875) and A major (*Spring*, 1880); symphonic poems *An Island Fantasy* and *The Tempest* (after Shakespeare); overture for Shakespeare's *As You Like It*.

CHAMBER string quartet, piano trio; violin and piano sonata; instrumental pieces.

OTHER Mass in D (1867).

Paisiello, Giovanni (1740–1816) Italian composer. He wrote about 100 operas, including *Il barbiere di Siviglia/Barber of Seville* (1782), which was very successful until it was displaced by Rossini's opera of the same name.

He was born at Taranto. He studied first with Franceso Durante, and later with Cotumacci and Abos at the Conservatorio Sant' Onofrio in Naples 1754–63, and there wrote his first oratorios and church music. With *Il ciarlone* in 1764, however, he began his successful career as a composer of ➔ opera buffa, and over the next 20 years produced many works in Modena, Naples, and Venice. While in the service of the Russian court at St Petersburg 1776–84, he wrote his most famous opera, *Il barbiere di Siviglia* (after Beaumarchais' *Le Barbier de Séville*) in 1782, which held the stage until Rossini's setting of the same story in 1816. Back in Naples, he was appointed maestro di cappella and court composer to Ferdinand IV. Summoned to Paris as music director of Napoleon's household in 1802, he remained only a year before returning to his old post in Naples. Modern revivals of such operas as *Il barbiere di Siviglia, Nina,* and *Il Ré Teodoro in Venezia* reveal a composer of real charm and vivacity.

Works OPERA about 100, including *Il ciarlone* (after Goldoni's *La pupilla,* 1764), I *Francesi brillanti, Demetrio* (1765), *Le finte Contesse* (1760), *L'idolo cinese, Socrate immaginario* (1775), *La serva padrona, Il barbiere di Siviglia* (after Beaumarchais, 1782), *Il mondo della luna* (1782), *Il Rè Teodoro in Venezia* (1784), *L'Antigono* (1785), *Nina, ossia La pazza per amore, La molinara* (1789), *Proserpine* (1803), and others.

CHORAL oratorios, including *La Passione di Gesù Cristo, Christus* (1783).

OTHER cantatas; Masses, two Requiems, *Miserere,* and other church music; symphonies; concertos; six string quartets, twelve piano quartets; keyboard music.

Paix, Jakob (1556–after 1623) German composer. He wrote German songs and Latin church music, but his chief work was his collection of keyboard music, published in 1583, which included original compositions as well as highly ornamented arrangements of songs and motets.

He was organist at Lauingen, Swabia 1576–1601, and court organist at Neuburg an der Donau 1601–17.

Palester, Roman (1907–1989) Polish composer. He studied at Lviv and under Kazimierz Sikorski in Warsaw. For some years he lived in Paris, but he later settled in Warsaw. During the 1939–45 war he was imprisoned by the Germans.

Works OPERA AND BALLET the opera *The Living Stones* (1941); ballets *Song of the Earth* (1937) and *The End of the World.*

ORCHESTRAL incidental and film music, five symphonies (1935–72), symphonic suite, *Symphonic Music* (1931), *Wedding Celebration, Musique polonaise,* variations (overture) and other orchestral works, *Concertino* for saxophone, piano concerto.

ENSEMBLE *Divertimento* for six instruments, three string quartets (1932–43), sonatinas for three clarinets and for violin and cello, sonata for two violins and piano.

CHURCH MUSIC Requiem (1948), Psalm for solo voices, chorus, and orchestra.

Palestrina opera by Hans ➔ Pfitzner (libretto by composer), produced in Munich on 12 June 1917. The plot concerns the composition of of 16th-century Italian composer Giovanni ➔ Palestrina's *Missa Papae Marcelli,* which the composer undertakes only after long deliberation. In the end the Mass is performed and the Pope is greatly moved.

Palestrina, Giovanni Pierluigi da (c.1525–1594) Italian composer. He wrote secular and sacred choral music, and is regarded as the outstanding exponent of Renaissance ➔ counterpoint. Apart from motets and madrigals, he also wrote 105 Masses, including *Missa Papae Marcelli.*

Paliashvili, Zakharia Petrovich (1871–1933) Georgian composer. He studied at the Moscow Conservatory under Taneiev, later taught at Tiflis, conducted the orchestra there, and made excursions into eastern Georgia to study its folk music, on which his work is based.

Works OPERA *Abessalom and Eteri* (1919), *Twilight* (1923), *Latavra.*

OTHER choral works; folk song arrangements.

palindrome in music, a piece constructed the same backwards as forwards, more or less loosely, as with the prelude and postlude in Paul ➔ Hindemith's *Ludus tonalis,* and his one-act opera *Hin und zurück.* Other examples are Act III of Alban Berg's ➔ *Lulu* or Béla ➔ Bartók's fifth string quartet. The procedure is that of *recte et retro* or *rovescio,* in which a second entry brings in the tune sung or played backwards, but on a larger scale.

Pallavicino, Benedetto (1551–1601) Italian composer. He was in the service of the Duke of Mantua from 1582, and succeeded Giaches de

Wert as maestro di cappella there in 1596, but retired to the monastery of Camaldoli in Tuscany in 1601.

Works CHURCH AND CHAMBER MUSIC Masses, psalms, and other church music; ten volumes of madrigals.

Pallavicino or **Pallavicini, Carlo (c.1630–1688)** Italian composer. He lived at Salò, married Giulia Rossi at Padua and settled there, producing operas between 1666 and 1687 at Venice, where he also lived for a time. In 1667–73 he was at the Saxon court at Dresden; first as assistant and later as first music director. In 1674 he was back at Venice, but was recalled to Dresden in 1685 to reorganize the Italian opera.

Works OPERA *Demetrio* (1666), *Diocletiano* (1674), *Enea in Italia* (1675), *Vespasiano* (1678), *Nerone, Le amazoni nell' isole fortunate* (1779), *Messalina* (1679), *Bassiano, overro Il maggior impossible* (1682), *Penelope la casta* (1685), *Massimo Puppieno, Didone delirante* (1686), *L'amazone corsara, La Gerusalemme liberata* (after Tasso, 1687), *Antiope* (finished by Strungk, 1689), and nine others.

OTHER a Mass and an oratorio; arias and canzoni with instruments; string fantasies.

Palmer, Robert (1915–) US composer. He studied at the Eastman School of Music at Rochester, New York, where he took degrees in 1938–39, also privately with Roy Harris. In 1943 he became an assistant professor of music at Cornell University, Ithaca, New York. He retired in 1980.

Works ORCHESTRAL the ballet *Irish Legend* with chamber orchestra; symphony, elegy *K. 19* (1945), and concerto for orchestra; concerto for chamber orchestra (1940), piano concerto (1970); *Abraham Lincoln Walks at Midnight* (Vachel Lindsay) for chorus and orchestra (1948).

CHAMBER four string quartets (1939–60), two piano quartets (1947, 1974), two string trios; concerto for flute, violin, clarinet, English horn, and bassoon; viola and piano sonata; sonata for two pianos; sonata and three preludes for piano.

Palmgren, Selim (1878–1951) Finnish pianist, composer, and conductor. He was professor of composition at the Eastman School of Music at Rochester, New York 1923–26 and from 1936 at the Sibelius Academy in Helsinki, where he died. His works include operas, incidental music, choral works, five piano concertos, and numerous piano pieces.

He studied at the Helsinki Conservatory, where his teachers included Martin Wegelius (1846–1906), and later with Conrad Ansorge (1862–1930) in Germany and Ferruccio Busoni in Italy. On his return he became conductor of the Finnish Students' Choral Society and later of the Music Society at Turku. He also frequently

appeared as a pianist. He married the singer Minna Talvik in 1930, and toured Europe and the USA with her.

Works OPERA AND STAGE operas *Daniel Hjort* (1910) and *Peter Schlemihl* (after Chamisso); incidental music to Kyösti's *Tukhimo* (*Cinderella*).

OTHER choral works; five piano concertos (II. *The River*; III. *Metamorphoses*; IV. *April*); numerous piano pieces.

Palotta, Matteo (c.1688–1758) Italian composer, priest, and music scholar. He wrote treatises on ➔ **solmization** and the rhythmic modes and composed Masses, motets, and other church music.

He studied at Naples and returned to Sicily after being ordained, but was appointed one of the court composers in Vienna in 1733.

Paminger, Leonhard (1495–1567) Austrian composer. He became a Lutheran and published religious pamphlets and a series of motets for the Lutheran year.

He was educated at the monastery of St Nicholas at Passau, then studied in Vienna, but returned to Passau in 1513 to become a teacher and later secretary at the monastery.

Works CHURCH MUSIC Latin motets, German hymns, psalms, and other pieces.

Pammelia the first part of a collection of canons, rounds, and catches published by Thomas ➔ **Ravenscroft** in London, England, in 1609. The second part of the collection is ➔ ***Deuteromelia***.

panchromaticism in music, extreme ➔ **chromaticism**, in which all twelve tones are used equally frequently. Such music might be described as 'one degree less than atonal', that is, very chromatic but still with some sense of a tonic. The term is associated particularly with Arnold ➔ **Schoenberg**'s ultra-chromatic, but pre-serial, compositions.

pandoura (from Greek; also from Arabic *tanbur* 'tamboura') string instrument of the lute type with a long neck and a small body, surviving in various forms only in the Balkans, Turkey, Egypt, and the East.

panpipes or **syrinx** musical wind instrument consisting of a set of unpierced pipes in cane, clay, or other material, graded by length to provide a scale of pitches when blown across their opening. Invented according to legend in ancient Greece by the god Pan, the pipes flourish in the folk-music traditions of South America, Eastern Europe, and Japan. They produce a notably pure tone with a breathy onset.

The title instrument of Mozart's opera *The Magic Flute* (1791) is a set of pitch pipes, played by the character Papageno and symbolizing innocent pastoral humanity.

pantaleon string percussion instrument of the ➤ **dulcimer** type invented by Pantaleon Hebenstreit in the 18th century and named after him by Louis XIV.

pantomime (from Greek 'all-imitating') properly, a play in dumbshow, but in England since the 18th century a popular stage entertainment with music, deriving from the Italian *commedia dell'arte*. It is still based, even if remotely, on fairy-tales, but it has lost the Harlequinade which used to be an indispensable supplement and has become a spectacular extravaganza, often introducing songs popular at the time. Also a term used in 20th century for mimed episodes in ballet (Maurice Ravel, *Daphnis et Chloe*), or ballet as a whole (Béla Bartók, *Miraculous Mandarin*).

pantonality in music, alternative name for ➤ **a-tonality**. The term was coined by Arnold Schoenberg, who wanted to convey a type of tonality that embraces all keys simultaneously, in preference to 'atonality', which he felt implies a negative tonality.

Panufnik, Andrzej (1914–1991) Polish-born composer and conductor. His music is based on the dramatic interplay of symbolic motifs.

Panufnik was a pupil of the Austrian composer and conductor Felix Weingartner. He also studied with Kazimierz Sikorski at the Warsaw Conservatory and received a diploma in 1936. Some of his music was destroyed in the bombardment of Warsaw. He came to Britain in 1954 and became a British citizen in 1961. He was conductor of the Birmingham Symphony Orchestra 1957–59.

Works BALLET *Miss Julie* (produced in Stuttgart, 1970).

ORCHESTRAL film music, Psalm 145 for chorus and orchestra; nine symphonies, including *Rustica* (1948), *Elegaica* (1957), *Sacra* (1963), *Sfere* (1975), *Mistica* (1977), *Votiva* (1981), no. 9, *Sinfonia di Speranza* (1986), no. 10 (1988, revised in 1990); symphonic variations; two symphonic studies, 'Tragic Overture' and 'Heroic Overture'; trumpet concerto, piano concerto (1972), bassoon concerto (1985).

CHAMBER *Harmony* for chamber orchestra (1989); piano trio; two string quartets (1976, 1980).

OTHER five Polish folk songs for treble voices, two flutes, two clarinets, and bass clarinet; preludes, mazurkas, and other works for piano.

Pan Voyevoda opera by Rimsky-Korsakov (libretto by I F Tiumenev). A rarely performed story of love and revenge set in 17th-century Poland, the opera was first produced at St Petersburg, Russia, on 16 October 1904.

Paolo e Francesca opera by Luigi Mancinelli (libretto by A Colautti, after Dante), produced in Bologna, Italy, at the Teatro Comunale, on 11 November 1907.

Paolo e Virginia opera by Pietro Carlo Guglielmi (libretto by Giovanni Diodati, based on Bernardin de Saint-Pierre's novel), produced in Naples, Italy, at the Teatro Fiorentino, on 2 January 1817.

Papandopulo, Boris (1906–1991) Croatian composer and conductor. He studied at Zagreb and Vienna, and became choral and orchestral conductor at Zagreb, returning there after teaching at the Music School of Split 1935–38. He later worked as an opera conductor.

Works OPERA AND BALLET operas *The Sun Flower* (1942), *Amphitryon* (1940), and *Rona*; ballet *Gold* (1930).

CHORAL AND ORCHESTRAL oratorio *The Torments of Our Lord Jesus Christ* for unaccompanied chorus (1935), *Laudamus* for solo voices, chorus, and orchestra; *Croatian Mass* for soloists and chorus; two symphonies (1933, 1945); symphonic picture *The Overflowing*; two piano concertos.

CHAMBER AND OTHER five string quartets (1927–70) and other chamber music, piano music, songs.

Papillons, Butterflies set of short piano pieces by Robert Schumann, Op. 2. It has been suggested that this work might be a kind of preliminary sketch for Schumann's larger suite of piano pieces, *Carnaval*. The finale of *Papillons* suggests the end of a ball in the early morning, with a clock striking six and a quotation of the *Grossvatertanz* ('grandfather's dance'), which also appears in *Carnaval*. There is a further connection between the two works: the opening of *Papillons* is quoted in *Carnaval*'s *Florestan* piece.

The first part of Op. 2 was composed (before Op. 1) in 1829; the end was composed in 1831.

parable aria or **metaphor aria** or German **Gleichnisarie** in music, a type of mainly operatic ➤ **aria** in which certain abstract conceptions are illustrated by concrete ideas resembling them — fidelity by a rock in a stormy sea, love by cooing turtle-doves, and so on. The form was cultivated in the early 18th century, especially by Apostolo Zeno and ➤ **Metastasio** in their libretti. Examples of parable arias are 'As when the dove' in Handel's ➤ **Acis and Galatea**, and 'Come scoglio/Like a rock' in Mozart's *Così fan tutte* which is both verbally and musically a parody of the type. The music of a parable aria was usually illustrative of the image chosen by the librettist.

Parabosco, Girolamo (1520 or 1524–1557) Italian composer and organist. He was well known for improvisations on the organ. He published two pieces in the miscellaneous collection of instrumental music *Musica Nova* (1540).

He studied with Adrian Willaert in Venice. In 1551, he succeeded Jachet Buus as first organist at St Mark's, Venice, a post which he held until his death.

Parade ballet in one act by Erik ➤ **Satie** (scenario by Jean Cocteau), produced in Paris at the Théâtre de Châtelet, on 18 May 1917, with Diaghilev's Ballets Russes (curtain, décor and costumes by Pablo Picasso, conductor Ernest Ansermet). A suite for piano (for four hands in six movements) was published from the ballet in 1917.

paradigmatic analysis see ➤ semiotic analysis.

Paradise and the Peri, German **Das Paradies und die Peri** a setting for solo voices, chorus, and orchestra of one of the poems in Thomas Moore's *Lalla Rookh*, translated into German with alterations, by Robert Schumann, Op. 50. The composition was first contemplated in 1841, begun in February 1843, and first performed in Leipzig, on 4 December 1843.

Paradise Lost opera, 'sacra rappresentazione', by Krzysztof ➤ **Penderecki** (libretto by Christopher Fry after Milton), produced in Chicago, at the Lyric Opera, on 29 November 1978.

parallel motion in music, two or more parts in ➤ counterpoint moving up or down, in which the interval between each part does not change.

Paray, Paul (Charles) (1886–1979) French conductor and composer. He studied with Xavier Leroux and others at the Paris Conservatory and took the Prix de Rome in 1911. Returning to Paris from imprisonment during World War I, he became assistant and later successor to Chevillard, whose concerts he continued to conduct until 1933, when he succeeded Gabriel ➤ **Pierné** as conductor of the Colonne Orchestra. In 1952 he became conductor of the Detroit Symphony Orchestra, remaining there until 1963.

Works ORATORIOS *Jeanne d'Arc* (1931), Mass for the 500th anniversary of the death of Joan of Arc (revised version of oratorio, 1956).

BALLET *Artémis troublée* (1922).

ORCHESTRAL AND CHAMBER symphony in C major, fantasy for piano and orchestra, string quartet, violin and piano sonata.

Pardon de Ploërmel, Le opera by Giacomo ➤ **Meyerbeer** (libretto by Jules Barbier and Michel Carré), produced in Paris, at the Opéra-Comique, on 4 April 1859. The work is also known as *Dinorah*. In the story, Dinorah has gone mad after losing her husband Hoël during a storm on their wedding day. A year later Hoël returns, seeking a buried treasure, but he does not recognize her. After saving her from drowning, Hoël realizes who she is and Dinorah recovers.

Paride ed Elena, **Paris and Helen** opera by Christoph Willibald von ➤ **Gluck** (libretto by Ra-

niero da Calzabigi), produced in Vienna, at the Burgtheater, on 3 November 1770. In the story, Paris finds Helen more beautiful than the gods and takes her back to Troy, but Athena warns that their joy will not last.

Parisina opera by Gaetano Donizetti (libretto by Felice Romani, based on Byron's poem) produced in Florence, at the Teatro della Pergola, on 17 March 1833. The story concerns Parisina, wife of Duke Azzo, who falls in love with Ugo. Azzo forces her confession when she murmurs Ugo's name in her sleep, then executes Ugo, despite the revelation that Ugo is his long-lost son.

Opera by Pietro Mascagni (libretto by Gabriel d'Annunzio), produced in Milan, at La Scala, on 15 December 1913.

Paris Symphonies set of six symphonies by Joseph ➤ **Haydn** commissioned by the Concert de la Loge Olympique in Paris. The six works include: no. 82 in C major (*L'Ours/The Bear*) (1786); no. 83 in G minor (*La Poule/The Hen*) (1785); no. 84 in E flat major (1786); no. 85 in B flat major (*La Reine/The Queen*) (1785–86); no. 86 in D major (1786); and no. 87 in A major (1785).

'Paris' Symphony Mozart's symphony in D, K297, written in Paris for performance at the Concert Spirituel in 1778. After the first performance Mozart replaced the slow movement by another.

Paris: The Song of a Great City nocturne for orchestra by Frederick Delius, composed in 1898 and dedicated to Hans Haym, who gave the first performance at Elberfeld, Germany, in 1902. It was given by Ferruccio Busoni in Berlin on 15 November 1902.

Its first British performance was at Liverpool, on 11 January 1908, conducted by Beecham.

Parker, Horatio (William) (1863–1919) US organist and composer. He held several church organist's posts in Boston and New York, and wrote choral music.

He studied at Boston and Munich, where he was a pupil of Joseph Rheinberger. In 1884 he returned to New York and became an organist and choirmaster. He also taught at the National Conservatory, directed by Dvořák. Later he became organist at Trinity Church, Boston, and, in 1894, professor of music at Yale University. He visited England several times for performances of his works at music festivals and to receive an honorary doctorate from Cambridge University in 1902.

Works OPERA operas *Mona* (1912) and *Fairyland* (1915).

CHORAL oratorios *Hora novissima* (1893), *The Legend of St Christopher* (1897), *Morven and the Grail* (1915); cantatas, including *The Holy Child*

(1893), *The Dream of Mary* (1918); choral ballads.

OTHER church services; symphony in C major (1885), overtures, and other orchestral works; organ concerto; string quartet in F major (1885); organ sonata; piano pieces; songs.

parlando or **parlante (Italian 'speaking')** musical direction indicating, in instrumental music, that a passage is to be performed in a 'speaking' manner, expressively but not sustained or 'sung'; in vocal music, that the tone is to be reduced to something approximating to speech.

parody Mass see ➔ Missa parodia.

Paroles tissées, Woven Words work for tenor, strings, harp, piano, and percussion by Witold Lutosławski (text by J F Chabrun); commissioned by Peter Pears, who gave the first performance at the Aldeburgh Festival, on 20 June 1965.

Parry, (Charles) Hubert (Hastings) (1848–1918) English composer. His works include songs, motets, and the setting of Milton's 'Blest Pair of Sirens' and Blake's 'Jerusalem'.

He studied at Oxford with George Macfarren and William Sterndale Bennett. He did not make his mark in public until his piano concerto was played by Edward Dannreuther at the Crystal Palace at Sydenham Hill, London, in 1880, and his choral scenes from Shelley's 'Prometheus Unbound' appeared at the Gloucester Festival the same year. He was awarded honorary doctorates by Cambridge University in 1883, Oxford University in 1884, and Dublin University in 1891. After examining for London University and teaching at the Royal College of Music, London, he succeeded George Grove as director of the latter in 1894, remaining until his death. He was professor of music at Oxford 1900–08. He wrote several books on music, including a study of Bach and a volume of the *Oxford History of Music*.

Works STAGE opera *Guinevere* (1885–86); incidental music to Aristophanes' *The Birds*, *The Frogs* (1891), *The Clouds* (1905), and *The Acharnians* (1914).

CHORAL WITH ORCHESTRA oratorio *Job*; six motets, four *Songs of Farewell*, and two other motets for chorus; scenes from Shelley's 'Prometheus Unbound' (1880), ode 'Blest Pair of Sirens' (Milton, 1887), 'L'Allegro ed il penseroso' (Milton), 'Jerusalem' (Blake) for chorus.

ORCHESTRAL five symphonies (1878–1912), *Lady Radnor's Suite* (1894), *An English Suite* for string orchestra (1921).

CHAMBER AND SONGS nonet for wind instruments, four piano trios; sonatas for violin and piano, and cello and piano; organ and piano music; over 100 songs, including 74 in twelve books of *English Lyrics* (1885–1920).

Parsifal music drama, or *Bühnenweihfestspiel* ('sacred festival drama'), by Richard Wagner (libretto by composer), produced in Bayreuth at the Wagner Festival Theatre, on 26 July 1882. In the story, Parsifal recovers the sacred spear from the evil magician Klingsor and returns to the Kingdom of the Grail to heal the wounded Amfortas. The 'wild woman' Kundry, whom Parsifal had met earlier, is also redeemed but then dies.

Parsons, John (c.1575–1623) English composer. He wrote a burial service, which Purcell used in 1685 for the funeral of Charles II.

He became parish clerk and organist at St Margaret's Church, Westminster, England, in 1616, and, in 1621, organist and choirmaster of Westminster Abbey.

part music written for a performer (instrumental or voice) in a piece of music; for example, the flute part, violin part, or soprano part. In a large composition, the score and parts would include the ➔ full score (showing all the parts on each page) and the separate parts for the players and/or singers. A part, or ➔ voice, can also be an independent line of a contrapuntal work, for example a fugue in four parts.

A large-scale section of a composition is also called a part, for example Part I of Edward Elgar's *Dream of Gerontius* (1900).

Pärt, Arvo (1935–) Estonian composer. He adopted serial techniques early in his career, later shifted to aleatorism, and finally settled for minimalism and sacred music. His *Nekrolog* (1960) for orchestra was dedicated to the victims of the Holocaust.

He graduated from the Tallinn Conservatory in 1963 and settled in West Berlin in 1982.

Works CHORAL WITH ORCHESTRA oratorio *Stride of the World* (1960); *St John Passion* (1981).

ORCHESTRAL three symphonies (1964, 1966, 1971); *Pro et Contra* for cello and orchestra (1964); cello concerto (1981); concerto for violin, cello, and chamber orchestra (performed in London, 1981).

ENSEMBLE *Cantus in Memory of Britten* for strings and glockenspiel (1977); *Arbos* for seven instruments (1977); *Wenn Bach Bienen gezüchtet hätte/If Bach had been a bee-keeper*, two versions for harpsichord and ensemble (1978, 1980).

CHURCH MUSIC Te Deum (1985), *Seven Magnificat Antiphons* (1988), *Magnificat* (1989), *Miserere* (1989), *Beatus Petronius* for two choruses and two organs (1990), *The Beatitudes* for chorus and organ (1990), *Berlin Mass* (1991).

Partch, Harry (1901–1974) US composer. Largely self-taught, he experimented with microtonal scales and new instrumental designs.

Works CHORAL AND VOICE WITH INSTRUMENTS *Eight Hitch-hiker Inscriptions from a California Highway Railing* and *US Highball, a Musical Account* *of a Transcontinental Hobo Trip* for chorus and instruments (1944); *The Letter, a Depression Message from a Hobo Friend* for voices and instruments (1944).

DRAMATIC music drama *Oedipus* (1952); dance satire *The Bewitched* (1957); music tragedy *Revelation in the Courthouse Park*; *Water, Water*, an American ritual (1962).

Part du diable, La, **The Devil's Share** opera by Daniel Auber (libretto by Scribe), produced in Paris at the Opéra-Comique, on 16 January 1843. The work is sometimes called *Carlo Broschi*, the real name of Farinelli, who is the chief character, sung by a soprano.

Partenope opera by Handel (libretto by S Stampiglia), produced in London at the King's Theatre, Haymarket, on 24 February 1730. The story concerns the couples Partenope and Armindo, and Rosmira and Arsace, who are united after complications of betrayal, jealousy, and false identity.

Opera by Johann Hasse (libretto by Metastasio), produced in Vienna at the Burgtheater, on 9 September 1767.

Parthenia (Greek 'Maidenhood') punning title of a collection published in 1611 of pieces for the ➤ virginals composed by William ➤ Byrd, John Bull, and Orlando ➤ Gibbons. The collection was engraved in standard notation and was aimed at a new market of domestic amateur keyboard musicians.

Parthenia inviolata companion volume to a 17th-century music collection, ➤ *Parthenia*, containing 20 pieces for ➤ virginals and bass viol.

Parthia in music, a variant spelling of the German *Partie* for ➤ suite, used by Haydn and Beethoven among others. See also ➤ partita.

partials see ➤ harmonics.

partita in music, a set of classical ➤ variations, or more often a ➤ suite.

Partos, Ödön (1907–1977) Hungarian-Israeli composer. He studied violin with Jeno Hubay and composition with Zoltán ➤ Kodály. He led various orchestras in Lucerne, Berlin, and Budapest between 1925 and 1936, and from 1938 played viola with the Israel Philharmonic Orchestra.

Works ORCHESTRAL *Yis Kor (In Memoriam)* for viola and string orchestra (1947); *Song of Praise* for viola and orchestra (1949); symphonic fantasy *En Gev* (1952); *Phantasy on Yemeni Themes* for chorus and orchestra; *Images* for orchestra (1960).

CHAMBER *Fuses* for viola and chamber orchestra (1970); *Arabesque* for oboe and chamber orchestra (1975); two string quartets (1932, 1960).

part song technically, any song composed for a number of vocal parts, often used to describe ➤ madrigals, but generally referring to songs of homophonic texture, that is, where the melody is sung in the top voice and the other voices provide harmonic accompaniment. Part song is associated with 19th-century choral works by composers including Robert Schumann, Hubert Parry, and Edward Elgar.

part-writing in musical composition, the blending of each individual ➤ voice (independent line) into a coherent whole; the successful application of ➤ counterpoint to a composition.

Pasatieri, Thomas (1945–) US composer. He studied at the Juilliard School in New York and with Darius ➤ Milhaud in Aspen, Colorado. He has avoided the avant garde and remained faithful to a *bel canto* style, emphasizing perfect technique and beautiful tone.

Works OPERA *The Widow* (Aspen, 1965); *La Divina* (New York, 1966); *Padrevia* (Brooklyn, 1967); *Calvary* (Seattle, 1971); *The Trial of Mary Lincoln* (Boston, 1972); *Black Widow* (Seattle, 1972); *The Seagull* (Houston, 1974); *Signor Deluso* (Greenway, Virginia, 1974); *The Penitentes* (Aspen, 1974); *Ines de Castro* (Baltimore, 1976); *Washington Square* (Detroit, 1976); *Maria Elena* (Tuscon, 1983); *Three Sisters* (Columbus, OH, 1986).

Pasdeloup, Jules (Etienne) (1819–1887) French conductor. He founded the Société des Jeunes Artistes du Conservatoire in 1851, and the Concerts Pasdeloup in 1861, at which he produced many works previously unknown in France, including music by Wagner and Schumann. In 1868 he founded the Société des Oratories, and joined the Théâtre Lyrique the same year. He studied at the Paris Conservatory.

Pashchenko, Andrey Filipovich (1883–1972) Russian composer. He entered the St Petersburg Conservatory in 1914, after receiving private musical instruction, and studied composition under Maksimilian Steinberg and Joseph Wihtol. He was active as teacher and music organizer, but devoted most of his time to composition. During World War II he remained at Leningrad throughout the siege.

Works OPERA *The Revolt of the Eagles* (1925), *Emperor Maximilian* (1927), *The Black Cliff* (1931), *The Pompadours* (after Saltikov-Shtchedrin's story, 1939), *The Stubborn Bride* (1956), *Radda and Loyko* (after Gorki's story *Makar Tchudra*, 1957).

ORATORIOS *The Liberation of Prometheus*, *Lenin*.

ORCHESTRAL film music; Requiem in memory of the heroes of the great war; 15 symphonies (1915–70); *Solemn Polonaise*; *Festive Overture*; symphonic poems *The Giants* and *The Bacchantes*; scherzo *Harlequin and Columbine*; suite in the Classical Style; *Legend* for orchestra.

OTHER three pieces for a band of folk instruments; nine string quartets; songs.

Pasquali, Niccolò (c.1718–1757) Italian violinist and composer. He wrote treatises on thorough bass and harpsichord playing.

He settled at Edinburgh, Scotland in about 1740, lived in Dublin 1748–51, then returned to Edinburgh, visiting London in 1752.

Works OPERA AND STAGE opera *The Enraged Musician* (1753); masque *The Triumph of Hibernia*; dirge in Shakespeare's *Romeo and Juliet*.

ORATORIOS *Noah* and *David*.

ORCHESTRAL AND ENSEMBLE twelve overtures for (or with) horns; sonatas for violin or two violins and bass.

OTHER songs contributed to various collections.

Pasquini, Bernardo (1637–1710) Italian harpsichordist, organist, and composer. His *Accademia per musica* was performed at the Roman palace of Queen Christina of Sweden in 1687 to celebrate the accession of James II, with Arcangelo Corelli leading a string orchestra of 150 players.

He studied with Loreto Vittori and Antonio Cesti. As a young man he settled in Rome and became organist of the church of Santa Maria Maggiore.

Works OPERA *La donna ancora è fedele* (1676), *Dov' è amore e pietà* (1679), *La forza d'amore*, and eleven others.

CHAMBER 13 sonatas and other works for harpsichord.

passacaglia Spanish dance form in three time that evolved into an instrumental form constructed over a ➤ **ground bass**, or cyclically repeating bass line. Dramatic tension is created by the juxtaposition of a developing melody and an unchanging background.

An example is Benjamin Britten's disturbing setting of Tennyson's poem 'The Kraken' in *Nocturne* (1958).

passage in music, a non-technical term referring to a length of music of unfixed duration, but usually a short section, which is characterized by a single melodic or textural feature.

passage work in music, a textural piece characterized by fast running notes that are technically difficult, and in the case of the 19th-century repertory, often 'showy'.

passaggio in music, a term similar to ➤ **passage**, but used in more specialized senses for modulations (that is, passing from key to key) and for florid vocal or instrumental decorations.

passamezzo (Italian, probably a corruption of *passo e mezzo* 'pace and a half') brisk dance of the late 16th and early 17th centuries, popular not only in Italy but throughout Europe. Its name is probably due to the fact that it was a more lively form of the ➤ **pavane**. It consisted basically of variations on a ground bass. The **passamezzo antico** was in the minor key, the **passamezzo moderno** in the major key. See ➤ **romanesca**.

passepied old French dance in triple time (3/4), less strict than a minuet, featured in classical opera and the French ➤ **suite**.

Passereau (1533–55) French composer. His chansons, some humorous, some obscene, were published by Pierre Attaignant and others at various times between 1529 and 1572. The best known of them, 'Il est bel et bon', was arranged for organ by Girolamo Cavazzoni.

passing notes in music, notes joining two notes a third apart, by conjunct motion; they are therefore always approached and quitted by step. They do not form part of the harmony. An unaccented passing note falls on a strong beat, creating a momentary dissonance.

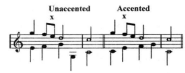

Accented and unaccented passing notes.

Passione, La, The Passion name given to ➤ **Haydn**'s symphony no. 49 in F minor, composed in 1768.

Passion music music depicting the gospel story of Christ's Passion. Passion music evolved from the medieval recitation, which was sung, as it still is, by three singers with different vocal ranges. The singer representing the Evangelist had a medium range, Christus a low range, and the singer responsible for the other characters and the crowd (*turba*) a high range. By the 15th century, the *turba* began to be entrusted to a vocal ensemble, and in the course of the 16th century the whole text was sung in a polyphonic setting. In the 17th century, Lutheran composers introduced recitative, chorales, and instrumental accompaniment. In the early 18th century, the inclusion of arias set to non-Biblical words turned the Lutheran Passion into an ➤ **oratorio**, indistinguishable in form from opera. Johann Sebastian Bach's two surviving Passions belong to this category.

Pasterwiz, Georg (1730–1803) Austrian monk, organist, and composer. He studied at Kremsmünster Abbey, where he was ordained priest in

1755, and with Johann Eberlin at Salzburg. He was choirmaster at the abbey 1767–82, but later lived chiefly in Vienna.

Works OPERA *Samson* (1775).

CHURCH MUSIC 14 Masses, Requiem.

OTHER numerous fugues and other pieces for keyboard instruments.

pasticcio (Italian 'pie' or 'pasty') stage entertainment with music drawn from existing works by one or more composers and words written to fit the music. It was particularly popular in the 18th century.

pastoral a light-hearted English madrigal with words of a pastoral character. See ➤ **pastorale**.

Pastoral anthology by Arthur Bliss for mezzo-soprano, chorus, flute, drums, and strings (using words by Theocritus, Poliziano, Ben Jonson, John Fletcher, and Robert Nichols). It was first performed in London, on 8 May 1929.

pastorale type of 17th-century opera, or opera-ballet, with recitatives, airs (verse songs), and choruses. It was often produced on festive occasions and treated pastoral subjects in a courtly and artificial manner, often allegorically. Its origin was the pastoral drama of the 16th century. In later times the term pastorale has been often used as a title for all kinds of compositions of a pastoral character.

Pastorale, La, called *La Pastorale d'Issy* opera by Robert Cambert (libretto by Pierre Perrin), produced at Issy near Paris, in April 1659. It has long been regarded as the first French opera.

'Pastoral' Sonata nickname for Beethoven's piano sonata in D major, Op. 28, composed in 1801 and dedicated to Joseph Edler von Sonnenfels. The nickname was not Beethoven's own, but was invented later by the Hamburg publisher Cranz. It suits only the finale.

Pastoral Symphony symphony by Ludwig van ➤ Beethoven, no. 6, in F major, Op. 68, composed 1807–08 and first performed at Vienna, on 22 December 1808. The title-page bears Beethoven's own heading of *Symphonie pastorale*, and on the first violin part is the inscription, 'Pastoral-Sinfonie oder Erinnerung an das Landleben (mehr Ausdruck der Empfindung als Mahlerey)/ Pastoral Symphony or Recollection of Country Life (Expression of Emotion rather than Painting)'.

Pastoral Symphony, A third symphony by Vaughan Williams, for orchestra with a soprano voice (without words). Composed in 1920, it was first performed in London at Queen's Hall, on 26 January 1922, conducted by Adrian Boult.

pastor fido, Il, *The Faithful Shepherd* opera by Handel (libretto by Giacomo Rossi after Guarini's pastoral play), produced in London, at the Queen's Theatre, Haymarket, on 22 November 1712.

pastourelle in music, a medieval pastoral song.

Pathétique Sonata, French *Grande sonate pathétique* Beethoven's piano sonata in C minor, Op. 13, composed c.1798 and dedicated to Prince Carl von Lichnowsky. The title (in French) is, exceptionally, Beethoven's own.

Pathétique Symphony Tchaikovsky's sixth symphony, in B minor, Op. 74, composed in 1893 and first performed under the composer, at St Petersburg, on 28 October 1893. The title 'Tragic Symphony' was suggested by the composer's brother Modest, but rejected by Tchaikovsky, who afterwards agreed to the adjective 'Pathétique'.

Patience, or Bunthorne's Bride operetta by Sullivan (libretto by W S Gilbert), produced in London, at the Opéra-Comique, on 25 April 1881. The story concerns the poets Bunthorne and Grosvenor, who are rivals for Patience, the milkmaid.

Patiño, Carlos (died 1675) Spanish composer. He was in the service of John IV of Portugal early in the 17th century and in 1633 became choirmaster in the royal chapel at Madrid.

Works CHURCH MUSIC Masses, Benedictus for the funeral of Philip II (1599), and other church music.

OTHER incidental music for plays; villancicos (songs).

Patrie overture by George Bizet (though not for Sardou's play of that name), composed in 1873 and first performed at Paris, on 15 February 1874.

Patterson, Paul (1947–) English composer. He studied with Richard Rodney Bennett and at the Royal Academy of Music, London, where he became director of electronic studies in 1975.

Works ORCHESTRAL AND ENSEMBLE wind quintet (1967); trumpet concerto (1969); *Concertante* (1969); *Piccola Sinfonia* (1971); horn concerto (1971); *Fiesta Sinfonica* (1972); concerto for clarinet and strings (1976); *Cracovian Counterpoints* for 14 instruments (1977); Concerto for Orchestra (1981); *Sinfonia* for strings (1982).

CHORAL WITH ORCHESTRA Requiem for chorus and orchestra (1975); *Canterbury Psalms* for chorus and orchestra (1981); *Mass of the Sea* for soloists, chorus, and orchestra (1984).

patter song type of song, usually comic, the effect of which depends on a rapid, syllabic delivery of the words to quick music. Many familiar examples occur in Arthur Sullivan's operettas.

Pauke (German) German name for the ➤ **timpani**.

Paukenmesse, Kettledrum Mass name given to ➤ Haydn's Mass in C major, which was composed in 1796 and performed at Vienna, on 26 December 1796. The reason for the unusually prominent timpani, especially in the *Agnus Dei*, is suggested by Haydn's own title, *Missa in tempore belli/Mass in time of war*.

Paukenschlag, in full **Symphonie mit dem Paukenschlag, 'Symphony with the Drum-beat'** another name for Joseph Haydn's ➤ **'Surprise' Symphony**.

Paukenwirbel, in full **Sinfonie mit dem Paukenwirbel** German name for Joseph Haydn's ➤ **'Drum-Roll' Symphony**.

Paul Bunyan choral operetta in two acts and a prologue by Benjamin Britten (libretto by W H Auden), produced at Columbia University, New York, on 5 May 1941. The plot, based on American colonists' tall tales of a giant lumberjack named Paul Bunyan, has strong Christian overtones and reflected both Britten and Auden's desire to be accepted in the USA; the music also gently parodies US music from blues to Aaron Copland.

Paulus the German title of Felix Mendelssohn's oratorio ➤ **St Paul**.

Paulus, Stephen (Harrison) (1949–) US composer. He is best known for his operas. He studied at the University of Minnesota with Dominick Argento and founded the Minnesota Composers' Forum in 1973. He was composer-in-residence with the Minnesota Orchestra 1983–87, and with the Atlanta Symphony Orchestra 1987–91.

Works OPERA *The Village Singer* (1979), *The Postman Always Rings Twice* (1981), *The Woodlanders* (1985), *Harmoonia* (1991).

ORCHESTRAL *Concerto for Orchestra* (1983), *Symphony in Three Movements* (1985), violin concerto (1987), *Symphony for Strings* (1989).

CHORAL *So Hallow'd is the Time* for soloists, chorus and orchestra.

CHAMBER two string quartets.

Paumann, Conrad (c.1410–1473) German composer and organist. He travelled widely through France, Italy, Germany, and Austria as an organist and is believed to have invented a form of lute ➤ **tablature**. His treatise, *Fundamentum organisandi/Principles of Composition* (1452), gives examples of the ornamentation of chant, with keyboard arrangements of chants and secular melodies.

Paumann was born in Nuremberg. Blind from birth, he was educated by the Grundherr family of Nuremberg, learnt the organ and composition, and was organist at St Sebald's Church in the 1440s. In 1450 he was appointed organist to Duke Albrecht III of Bavaria at Munich, and retained the post for the rest of his life. Few of his compositions survive, probably because he could not write them down.

Works ORGAN MUSIC AND SONGS organ arrangement of monophonic (without harmony) and polyphonic pieces; the German song 'Wiplich figur'.

Paumgartner, Bernhard (1887–1971) Austrian musicologist and composer. He studied first with his parents, the critic Hans Paumgartner and the singer Rosa Paumgartner (born Papier), and afterwards with Bruno Walter. He was director of the Mozarteum at Salzburg 1917–38, and was one of the organizers of the Salzburg festivals; his editions of Mozart's *Idomeneo* and Emilio de' Cavalieri's *Rappresentazione* were produced there in 1956 and 1968. He wrote mainly on Mozart.

Works OPERA *Das heisse Eisen* (after Hans Sachs), *Die Höhle von Salamanca* (after Cervantes, 1923), *Rossini in Neapel* (1935), *Aus dem Leben eines Taugenichts* (after Eichendorff's novel).

STAGE MUSIC ballet *Pagoden*; incidental music to Shakespeare's *King Lear* and *Twelfth Night* (on old English tunes), Goethe's *Faust*, and Gozzi's *Turandot*.

OTHER music for chorus and for orchestra; songs.

pause in music, the prolongation of a note, chord, or rest beyond its normal value, indicated by the fermata sign. In the 18th-century concerto it is regularly placed over the $\frac{6}{4}$ chord which precedes the cadenza. In a *da capo* it marks the point at which the piece ends after repetition of the first section. In the German chorale or in works based on it, the pause marks the end of each line and is to be ignored in performance.

Pause del silenzio, Pauses of Silence seven symphonic expressions by Francesco ➤ **Malipiero**, produced at Augusteo, Rome, on 27 January 1918.

Pauvre matelot, Le, The Poor Sailor opera by Darius ➤ **Milhaud** (libretto by Cocteau), produced at the Opéra-Comique, Paris, on 16 December 1927. In the story, a sailor returns home to his wife, but passes himself off as a friend of her husband. He tells her that the sailor is a prisoner. When he spends the night in her house, the wife kills him (still not realizing his true identity) in order to take his money and free her husband.

pavane or **pavan** a slow, stately court dance in double time, of Paduan origin, especially popular in Italy and France in the 16th and 17th centuries. Music composed for or derived from the pavane is often coupled with that composed for a ➤ **gal-**

A pavane in A minor by Byrd.

liard. Composers of the pavane include John Dowland and Willliam Byrd, and more recently Maurice Ravel, whose *Pavane pour une infante défunte/Pavane for a Dead Infanta* for piano (1899) was orchestrated in 1905.

Pavane pour une infante défunte, Pavan for a dead Infanta piano piece by Maurice ➤ **Ravel** composed in 1899. It was first performed in Paris, on 5 April 1902. An orchestral version was first performed in Paris, on 25 December 1910, conducted by Casella; it is this version which is more commonly heard today.

Pavesi, Stefano (1779–1850) Italian composer. He studied at the Conservatorio dei Turchini, in Naples 1795–99, and became very popular as a composer of operas, including *La festa della rosa* (1808), *Fenella* (1831), and *Ser Marcantonio* (1810).

Payne, Anthony (1936–   ) English composer and critic. He studied at Durham University 1958–61, and worked as a music critic for the *Daily Telegraph* from 1965. He has written on Schoenberg and British composers.

Works CHORAL *Phoenix Mass* for chorus and brass (1965–72); song cycle *First Sight of her and After* for 16 voices (texts by Hardy, 1975).

ORCHESTRAL Concerto for Orchestra (1975); *Songs and Dances* for strings (1984); *Half Heard in the Stillness* for orchestra (1987); *Time's Arrow* for orchestra (1990).

CHAMBER *Sonatas and Ricercars* for wind quintet (1971); *The World's Winter* for soprano and eight instruments (text by Tennyson, 1976); string quartet (1978); *Spring's Shining Wake* for chamber orchestra (1981); *Sea-Change* septet (1988); *Symphonies of Wind and Rain* for ensemble (1993).

Paz, Juan Carlos (1901–1972) Argentine composer. He studied in Buenos Aires and was one of the founders of the Group Renovación of progressive composers in 1929. He also founded a society for the performance of new music.

Works ORCHESTRAL incidental music for Ibsen's *Julian the Emperor*, *Canto de Navidad*, *Movimiento sinfónico*.

OTHER chamber and instrumental music.

Peacock Variations variations on a Hungarian folk song by Zoltán ➤ **Kodály**, composed 1938–39 to celebrate the 50th anniversary of the Concert-

gebouw Orchestra. It was first performed at Amsterdam, on 23 November 1939, and conducted by Willem Mengelberg.

Pearsall, Robert (Lucas) (1795–1856) English composer and barrister. He composed choral works, madrigals, and church music.

He studied law and became a barrister in 1821, though he had already composed by that time. In 1825, he settled at Mainz, devoting himself entirely to music. Another year in England, 1829–30, was his last, except for visits; he settled in Germany for good, although he inherited a property at Willsbridge, Gloucestershire, in 1836. He sold this and bought Wartensee Castle on Lake Constance.

Works CHURCH MUSIC church music (Anglican and Roman Catholic), Requiem (1853–56).

CHORAL AND VOCAL overture and chorus for Shakespeare's *Macbeth*, madrigals, part songs.

Peasant a Rogue, The, Czech **Selma Sedlák** comic opera by ➤ **Dvořák** (libretto by J O Veselý), produced in Prague at the Czech Theatre, on 27 January 1878. The story is similar to that of ➤ **Le Nozze di Figaro**. A Prince wants to seduce Bětuška, who already loves Jeník; the Princess helps to stop her husband's attempted exploits by dressing up as Bětuška.

Peasant Cantata or **Mer hahn en neue Oberkeet/We have a new magistracy** secular cantata by Bach for solo voices, chorus, and orchestra, composed in 1742, to words in Saxon dialect. The music is noticeably rustic and comes as near to the manner of folk song as anything Bach ever wrote.

Pêcheurs de perles, Les, The Pearl Fishers opera by George ➤ **Bizet** (libretto by E Cormon and Michel Carré), produced at the Théâtre Lyrique, Paris, on 30 September 1863. In the story, Leila, once the love of both Zurga and Nadir, returns to the men's village as a priestess of Brahma. She provokes Zurga's jealousy by seeing Nadir; Zurga orders them both to be put to death, but allows them to escape at the last moment.

ped. abbreviation used in the notation of piano music to indicate the use of the sustaining pedal. (The use of the soft pedal is indicated by the words *una corda* (one string), which is abbreviated to *u.c.*) The abbreviation also occurs in organ music written on two staves, to indicate which notes or passages are to be played on the pedals.

pedal a sustained note in a polyphonic composition, generally but not always in the bass. It often occurs at the climax of a ➤ **fugue**, above which the harmony changes in order to create tension.

See also ➤ **pedals**.

pedal board in an ➤ **organ**, the keyboard of pedals.

Pedalflügel (German 'pedal (grand) piano') German name for the pedal ➤ **piano**.

pedal harp the ordinary ➤ **harp** in current use, as distinct from the chromatic harp.

pedal notes the fundamental notes of trombones and other brass wind instruments, the normal compass of which consists of the upper ➤ **harmonics**.

pedal piano ➤ **piano** specially constructed with a keyboard of pedals and used mainly for organ practice at home. Very little music was written expressly for it, except by ➤ **Schumann**.

pedal point in organ and piano music, a bass note that is sustained or continually repeated beneath changing harmonies. It is also a long-held bass note in orchestral music, as in the symphonies of Jean ➤ **Sibelius**.

pedals in certain musical instruments, mechanical devices which require manipulation by the feet. Pedals may actually produce notes, as in the organ; they may be a means of obtaining certain effects of tone, as in the sustaining and soft piano pedals; or they may be used to alter the length, and thus the tuning, of strings, as in the harp.

Pedrell, Carlos (1878–1941) Uruguayan composer of Spanish descent. He studied at Montevideo, with his uncle Felipe ➤ **Pedrell** at Barcelona 1898–1900, and then with Vincent d'Indy and Bréville at the Schola Cantorum in Paris. In 1906 he went to Buenos Aires, where he held various official music posts and founded the Sociedad Nacional de Música in 1915. In 1921, he settled in Paris.

Works OPERA operas *Ardid de amor* (1917) and *Cuento de abril*.

BALLET *Alleluia* (1936).

ORCHESTRAL *Une Nuit de Schéhérazade* (1908), *Danza y canción de Aixa* (1910), *En el estrado de Beatriz*, *Fantasia Argentina*, *Ouverture catalane*.

OTHER choruses; songs with orchestra and with piano.

Pedrell, Felipe (1841–1922) Spanish composer and musicologist. He was the leader of the Spanish nationalist movement in composition and

also became a famous scholar in the domain of old Spanish church music and folk music, much of which he edited. He was the uncle of Carlos ➤ **Pedrell**.

Pedrell was almost wholly self-taught, but learnt much as a chorister at Tortosa Cathedral. He first published music in 1871 and had his first opera, *El ultimo Abencerraje*, produced at Barcelona in 1874. From that time he taught music history and aesthetics at the Madrid Conservatory, but settled at Barcelona in 1894, where he worked for the revival of old and the spread of new Spanish music. He edited the complete works of Tomás de Victoria and a collection of early Spanish church music, early stage and organ music, and other pieces.

Among his later operas, *Los Pirineos* (1902), *La Celestina* (1903), and *El Comte Arnau* (1921) are the most important; he also wrote incidental music for *King Lear*. His many pupils included Manuel de Falla, Enrique Granados, and Roberto Gerhard.

Works OPERA *El último Abencerraje* (after Chateaubriand, 1868), *Quasimodo* (on Victor Hugo's *Notre-Dame de Paris*, 1875), *Cleopatra* (1881), *Los Pirineos* (1902), *La Celestina* (1903), *El Conde Arnau* (1904), *Visión de Randa*; four early light operas.

ORCHESTRAL incidental music for Shakespeare's *King Lear*; symphonic poems.

CHURCH MUSIC Mass, Requiem, and Te Deum.

OTHER cantatas, chamber music, string quartet, piano music, songs.

Peel, John (1776–1854) English yeoman (independent farmer). He is the hero of the song 'D'ye ken John Peel', said to have been written in about 1829 by his friend John Woodcock Graves to a folk tune, 'Bonnie Annie'. It was the regimental march of the Border Regiment.

Peer Gynt incidental music for Ibsen's drama by Edvard ➤ **Grieg**, produced at Christiania, on 24 February 1876. Grieg afterwards arranged two orchestral suites from it: Op. 46 and Op. 55.

Opera by Werner ➤ **Egk** (libretto by composer), produced in Berlin on 24 November 1938, and admired by Hitler.

Peerson, Martin (c.1572–1651) English organist and composer. He took a music degree at Oxford in 1613 and was soon afterwards appointed organist and choirmaster at St Paul's Cathedral in London.

Works CHURCH MUSIC contributions to Leighton's *Teares and Lamentacions* and Ravenscroft's psalter, other church music.

CHAMBER airs and dialogues for voices; *Mottects or Grave Chamber Musique* (on sonnets from Fulke Greville's 'Caelica') for voices and instruments (1630); fancies and almains for viols;

pieces for virginal; *Private Musick* (1620).

Peeters, Flor (1903–1986) Belgian organist and composer. He toured widely as a recitalist and edited several collections of early organ music. He held teaching posts at the Lemmens Institute, Mechlin, and at the conservatories of Ghent, Tilburg, and Antwerp; he was director of the latter 1952–68.

He studied at Mechlin and with Marcel Dupré and Charles Tournemire at Paris. In 1925 he was appointed organist of Mechlin Cathedral.

Works CHURCH AND SECULAR MUSIC eight Masses, Te Deum, organ concerto, piano concerto, concerto for organ and piano; about 200 organ works; chamber music, piano works; songs.

Peire d'Auvergne (lived c.1140–80) French ✦ troubadour, from the Clermont region. He entered the Church but broke his vows and wandered from court to court, dying penitent. Some 25 of his poems remain. He was one of the first troubadours to write on religious subjects and was also perhaps the originator of the hermetic style known as *trobar clus*.

Peking Opera (Chinese *Ching-chu*) the most famous type of regional theatre in China, dating from 1790. A simple stage design contrasts with complex costumery, make-up, and acting. Peking Opera consists of dialogue sections and singing with orchestral accompaniment (dominated by Chinese 'fiddles', such as the *erhu*, and the *pipa* plucked lute). There are well over 1,000 items in the repertory which fall into two categories: the *wen* (civilian) portraying love stories or social matters; and the *wu*, the military exploits of heroes or brigands.

Pèlerins de le Mecque opera by Christoph Willibald von Gluck; see ✦ **Rencontre imprévue, La**.

Pelléas et Mélisande incidental music by Gabriel ✦ **Fauré** for Maurice Maeterlinck's play of the same name. It was first produced in London at the Prince of Wales Theatre, on 21 June 1898.

Opera by Claude ✦ **Debussy** (libretto from Maeterlinck's play, slightly altered), produced at the Opéra-Comique, Paris, on 30 April 1902. In the story, married to Golaud, Mélisande falls in love with Pelléas. Golaud soon becomes jealous, and the lovers realize the futility of their situation. After their last meeting, Pelléas is killed by Golaud, and later Mélisande dies, having borne Golaud a child.

Symphonic poem after Maeterlinck by Arnold ✦ **Schoenberg**, Op. 5, composed in 1902 and first performed at Vienna, on 26 January 1905.

Incidental music, an orchestral suite in nine movements, by ✦ **Sibelius**, Op. 46, composed in 1905 and produced at Helsinki on 17 March 1905.

Pellegrini, Vincenzo (died 1640) Italian cleric and composer. He was a canon at Pesaro from 1594 and maestro di cappella at Milan Cathedral 1611–31.

Works CHURCH AND SECULAR MUSIC Masses and other church music; organ canzonets; instrumental pieces in three–four parts; secular canzonets for voices.

Penderecki, Krzysztof (1933–) Polish composer. His expressionist works, such as the *Threnody for the Victims of Hiroshima* (1961) for strings, use cluster and percussion effects. He later turned to religious subjects and a more orthodox style, as in the *Magnificat* (1974) and the *Polish Requiem* (1980–83). His opera *The Black Mask* (1986) uncovered a new vein of surreal humour.

His early music made use of aleatory techniques (see ✦ **aleatory music**) and microtonal clusters developed by Iannis Xenakis (1922–2001) and Witold ✦ **Lutosławski**. Belonging at one time to the avant-garde, he dramatically changed style during the 1970s and began writing in a 19th-century orchestral style with occasional surface dissonance (a form of Neo-Romanticism). He gained great commercial success with these later works.

Works OPERA *The Devils of Loudun* (1969), *Paradise Lost* (1978), *Die schwarze Maske* (1986), *Ubu Rex* (1991).

CHORAL AND ORCHESTRAL *St Luke Passion* for speaker, two soloists, chorus, and orchestra (1963–66); *Stabat Mater* and *Psalms of David* for chorus and orchestra (1963, 1958); *Emanations* for two string orchestras (1958); *Anaclasis* for strings and percussion (1960); *Threnody for the Victims of Hiroshima* for 52 strings (1960); *De natura sonoris* for orchestra (1966); *Dies Irae* for soloists, chorus, and orchestra (1967); *Utrenja* for soloists, chorus, and orchestra (1969–71); two cello concertos (1972, 1982); two symphonies (1973, 1980); *Canticum canticorum* (1972); *Magnificat* (1974); *Polish Requiem* (1980–1983); *Songs of Cherubim* and *Veni Creator* for chorus (1986–87); *Passacaglia* (1988) and *Adagio* (1989) for orchestra; violin concerto (1977); *Te Deum* (1979); Viola concerto (1983).

ENSEMBLE *Fluorescences* for chamber ensemble (1961), *Der Unterbrochene Gedanke* for string quartet (1988), two string quartets (1960, 1968).

Penelope opera by Baldassare ✦ **Galuppi** (libretto by Paolo Rolli), produced in London, at the King's Theatre, Haymarket, on 12 December 1741.

See also ✦ **Circe and Penelope**.

Pénélope opera by Gabriel ✦ **Fauré** (libretto by René Fauchois), produced at Monte Carlo, on 4 March 1913. Its first Paris performance was at the Théâtre des Champs-Elysées, on 10 May 1913.

Other operas on the Penelope myth include those by ➤ **Monteverdi** (*Il ritorno di Ulisse*, 1641), ➤ **Scarlatti** (1696), Piccinni (1785), Cimarosa (1795), and Liebermann (1954).

penillion old form of Welsh song accompanied by the harp which was improvised (often the words as well as the music) as a ➤ **counterpoint** or descant (and improvised melody sung above the basic melody) to the harp part. It is still cultivated, but now tends to rely on tradition rather than improvisation.

Penna, Lorenzo (1613–1693) Italian monk and composer. He wrote treatises on counterpoint and figured bass, including *Primi albori musicali* (1672), in three volumes.

He entered the Carmelite order at Bologna in 1630 and, in 1672, became maestro di cappella at the Carmelite church of Parma. He was also a professor of theology.

Works CHURCH AND SECULAR MUSIC Masses and other church music; *correnti francesi* for four instruments.

Penny for a Song opera by Richard Rodney Bennett (libretto by C Graham from John Whiting's play), produced in London, at Sadler's Wells, on 31 October 1967. The story is set in 19th-century England. Sir Timothy Bellboys is concerned that his country is vulnerable to invasion, and comedy arises as the local militia is mistaken for an for an assault force.

penny whistle small and rudimentary wind instrument, a pipe of the ➤ **fife** or ➤ **recorder** type, also known as a 'tin whistle'. It is played vertically and has a small range of treble notes controlled by six finger holes.

pentatone (from Greek 'five notes') another name for the ➤ **pentatonic scale**.

pentatonic scale in music, a scale consisting of five notes. The most common pentatonic scale is made up of the notes that are equivalent to the black notes of the piano. Found as early as 2000 BC, the pentatonic scale is common in folk music from many countries. Some examples include the Scottish tune 'Auld Lang Syne' and the African American tune 'Swing Low, Sweet Chariot'.

Penthesilea opera by Othmar ➤ **Schoeck** (libretto by composer, based on Heinrich von Kleist's drama), produced at Dresden on 8 January 1927. In the story, Achilles falls in love with the Amazon Queen Penthesilea, whom he has defeated in combat. When she recovers from her wounds, she becomes deranged and kills Achilles. After coming to her senses she commits suicide.

Also, a symphonic poem on the same story by Hugo ➤ **Wolf**, composed 1883–85.

Pentland, Barbara (1912–2000) Canadian composer. She studied in Paris, at the Juilliard School, New York, and with Aaron Copland at Tanglewood Music Center in Massachusetts. She taught at the University of British Columbia 1949–63.

Works ORCHESTRAL four symphonies (1945–59), piano and organ concertos, *Variations Concertantes* (1970), *Res Musica* for string orchestra (1975).

CHAMBER five string quartets (1945–85), *Horizons* for piano (1985), *Ice Age* for soprano and piano (1986), *Intrade and Canzona* for recorder quartet (1988).

OTHER *Disasters of the Sun* for mezzo, instruments, and tape (1976).

Pepita Jiménez opera by Isaac ➤ **Albéniz** (libretto, in English, by F B Money-Coutts, based on a story by Juan Valera). It was first produced in Spanish, at the Liceo, Barcelona, on 5 January 1896. The story concerns the rich young widow Pepita, who has many suitors, but falls in love only with Don Luis. The priest warns her against this, but despite adversity the two are eventually brought together.

Pepping, Ernst (1901–1981) German composer. He studied at the Hochschule für Musik in Berlin and devoted himself chiefly to the cultivation of Protestant church music, being appointed professor at the Kirchenmusikschule at Spandau in 1947.

Works CHURCH MUSIC setting of the 90th Psalm; unaccompanied motets; a Te Deum; *Spandauer Chorbuch* (20 volumes for the whole ecclesiastical year), including vocal pieces for two–six voices (1934–38).

OTHER three symphonies (1939–44), piano concerto (1951), two organ concertos, four piano sonatas, chamber music, songs.

Pepusch, Johann Christoph (1667–1752) German composer. He settled in England in about 1700 and contributed to John Gay's ballad operas *The Beggar's Opera* and *Polly*.

Pepusch was appointed to the Prussian court at the age of 14. After emigrating to Holland, he went to England about 1700, and settled in London for the rest of his life. He married Margherita de l'Epine in 1718.

Works OPERA AND STAGE recitatives and songs for the pasticcio opera *Thomyris* (1707), and probably others; incidental music for Colley Cibber's *Myrtillo* (1715); music for masques *Apollo and Daphne* (1716), *The Death of Dido* (1716), *The Union of the Sister Arts*, *Venus and Adonis* (1715); dramatic ode for the Peace of Utrecht; overture for *The Beggar's Opera* and arrangements for it and its sequel, *Polly*, and another ballad opera, *The Wedding* (1729).

An example from Bach's Art of Fugue *in which the second voice enters by inversion,* per arsin et thesin.

CHURCH AND SECULAR MUSIC services, anthems, and Latin motets; cantatas (to words by John Hughes), including *Alexis* and others; odes; concertos; sonatas.

per arsin et thesin (Latin 'by rise and fall') musical direction indicating imitation by contrary motion; one part goes up where the other goes down.

percussion term used in harmony for the actual occurrence of a discord (a combination of notes jarring to the ear), after its ➤ **preparation** and before its ➤ **resolution.**

percussion instrument musical instrument played by being struck with the hand or a beater, crashed, shaken, or scraped. Percussion instruments can be divided into those that can be tuned to produce a sound of definite pitch, such as the timpani, tubular bells, glockenspiel, xylophone, and piano, and those of indefinite pitch, including the bass drum, tambourine, triangle, cymbals, castanets, and gong.

The **timpano** is a large hemispherical bowl of metal with a membrane stretched across the rim, affixed and tuned by screwtaps or with a pedal mechanism; **tubular** or **orchestral bells** are vertically suspended on a frame and struck at the top end with mallets. These instruments were often used by Witold Lutosławski in his orchestral works; the **glockenspiel** is a small keyboard of aluminium alloy keys played with small beaters; the **xylophone** has hardwood, rather than metal, bars, and is played using hard-headed beaters to give a distinctive 'pop' to the sound.

The **snare drum** is a shallow double-sided drum on the underside of which gut coils or metal springs are secured by a clamp, and which rattle against the underside when the drum is beaten, while the **bass drum** produces the loudest sound (unpitched) in the orchestra; the **tambourine** has a wooden hoop with a membrane stretched across it, and has metal discs suspended in the rim to make a jangling sound; a **triangle** is formed from a suspended triangular-shaped steel bar, played by striking it with a separate bar of steel – the sound produced can be clearly perceived even when played against a full orchestra; **cymbals** are two brass dishes struck together; **castanets** are two hollow shells of wood struck together; and the **gong** is a suspended disc of metal struck with a soft hammer.

perdendosi (Italian 'losing itself') musical direction indicating that the sound of a note or passage is to become gradually weaker until it fades away.

Perez, Davide (1711–1778) Spanish composer. He was maestro di cappella to Prince Naselli at Palermo and, in 1752, went to Lisbon, where he became attached to the royal chapel and the new opera house, which opened in 1755. He composed many operas to libretti by Metastasio.

He studied at the Conservatorio di Santa Maria di Loreto at Naples and produced his first opera, *La nemica amante,* in 1735.

Works OPERA many operas, including *Siroe* (1740), *I travestimenti amorosi* (1740), *L'eroismo di Scipione* (1741), *Astartea* (1743), *Medea* (1744), *L'isola incantata, La clemenza di Tito* (1749), *Semiramide* (1750), *Alessandro nell' Indie* (1755), *Demetrio* (1766), *Demofoonte, Soimano* (1757), *Il ritorno di Ulisse in Itaca* (1774).

ORATORIO *Il martirio di San Bartolomeo.*

OTHER *Mattutino de' morti,* Masses, and other church music; other pieces.

Perfect Fool, The opera by Gustav ➤ **Holst** (libretto by composer), produced at Covent Garden, London, on 14 May 1923. The story concerns a mother who tries (with help from the Wizard) to marry her son, the Fool, to the Princess, who falls in love with him after other suitors fail to attract her. The opera ends with a comic wedding.

perfect intervals in music, ➤ **intervals** that do not possess alternative major and minor forms, but become augmented or diminished by being enlarged or reduced by a semitone, such as fourths, fifths, and octaves; also their repetitions beyond the octave, that is, 11ths and so on.

perfect pitch in music, alternative term for ➤ absolute pitch.

performance practice the study of how music was performed in the age in which it was written. A discipline associated with the ➤ authenticity movement, it was first applied to music written in the ➤ baroque period and earlier, and subsequently also to that of the ➤ classical period. Recent academic interest in early recordings of the 20th century has led to the expansion of performance practice to embrace music of any period before the present day.

Pergolesi, Giovanni Battista (1710–1736) Italian composer. He wrote Masses, a *Stabat Mater* and other church music, secular cantatas, oratorios, some instrumental works, and nine operas, three of which, including *La serva padrona*, are comic intermezzi to be performed between the acts of a serious opera. His music is most often heard today through the pieces which Stravinsky selected for *Pulcinella*.

His parents were poor, and he seems to have been sent to Naples in 1725 to study at the Conservatorio dei Poveri di Gesù Cristo, under the patronage of Marchese Pianetti. His teachers there were Gaetano Greco, Leonardo Vinci, and Francesco Durante. His earliest works were sacred pieces, but he made his debut as a composer for the stage in 1731, and two years later produced the comic intermezzo *La serva padrona* (performed between the acts of his serious opera *Il prigionier superbo*), which was to be decisive in the history of opera buffa.

In 1732, he became maestro di cappella to the Prince of Stigliano at Naples, for whom he wrote cantatas and chamber music, and entered the service of the Duke of Maddaloni about 1734, but returned to Naples the next year, becoming organist to the court. In February 1736, he retired on grounds of ill health to the Capuchin monastery in Pozzuoli, where he completed his last work, the *Stabat Mater*, just before his death. Much music attributed to him after his death is now known to be by other composers, but his output is nevertheless astonishing for a composer who suffered from ill-health and died of tuberculosis at the age of 26. Recent revivals of his operas reveal a resourceful and engaging composer.

Works OPERA the operas *Salustia* (1732), *Il prigionier superbo* (1733), *Adriano in Siria* (1734), *L'Olimpiade* (1735), *Lo frate 'nnamorato* (1732), *Flaminio* (1735); intermezzi *La serva padrona*, *Livietta e Tracollo* (1737).

ORATORIOS *La morte di S Giuseppe* (1731), *La Conversione di S Guglielmo d'Acquitania* (1731), *La morte d'Abel*, and others.

CHURCH MUSIC Masses, *Stabat Mater* for soprano and alto soloists and strings (1736), settings of *Salve Regina* (1736), and other church music.

OTHER chamber music, keyboard music, and other pieces. There are also many other works attributed to Pergolesi which are of doubtful authenticity.

Peri, Jacopo (1561–1633) Italian composer who lived in Florence in the service of the Medici. His experimental melodic opera *Euridice* (1600) established the opera form and influenced Monteverdi. His first opera, *Dafne* (1597), believed to be the earliest opera, is now lost.

Peri was a pupil of Cristoforo Malvezzi, then became a canon at the church of San Lorenzo at Florence. He was attached to the Medici court from about 1588, and was later appointed their maestro di cappella and chamberlain. He became a member of the progressive artists grouped round Count Giovanni Bardi, with the composers Giulio Caccini, Jacopo Corsi, and Vincenzo Galilei, and the poet Ottavio Rinuccini. In their endeavour to revive Greek drama with the kind of music they imagined to be genuinely Greek, they stumbled on the invention of opera. They discarded counterpoint in favour of melody and expressive harmony. Peri, with Caccini, experimented in musical declamation to a suitable accompaniment, and they thus became the earliest composers of recitative. They may also be considered the world's first operatic composers.

Works OPERA AND STAGE *Dafne* (1598), *Euridice* (1600), *Tetide* (1608), *Adone* (1611); tournament with music *La precedenza delle dame* (1625); parts of operas (with others), including *La guerra d'amore* and *Flora* (with Gagliano); several ballets.

VOCAL *Lamento d'Iole* for soprano and instruments, madrigals, sonnets, and arias in *Songbook* (1609).

Péri, La ballet by Paul Abraham ➤ Dukas, produced at the Théâtre du Châtelet, Paris, on 22 April 1912.

Périchole, La operetta by Jacques ➤ Offenbach (libretto by Henri Meilhac and Ludovic Halévy, based on Prosper Mérimée's comedy *Le Carrosse du Saint-Sacrement*), produced at the Théâtre des Variétés, Paris, on 6 October 1868. In the story, the Viceroy of Peru, Don Andrès, takes on poor Périchole as a chambermaid. Her lover Piguillo agrees unwittingly to marry her, and much confusion ensues when they recognize each other.

périgourdine French country dance from the region of Périgord, known to musicians from at least the 18th century. Its music is in 6/8 time.

period in musical analysis, one of the basic structural units of melody, consisting of a pair of phrases, the first often ending with an 'imperfect cadence' ('half close'), the second often ending with a 'perfect cadence' ('full close').

Perle, George (1915–) US composer and theorist. His studies have centred on the Second Viennese School and his books include *Twelve-tone tonality* (1977). He taught at Queens College, New York, 1961–84. His teachers included Ernst Krenek.

Works ORCHESTRAL *Three Movements* for orchestra (1960), cello concerto (1966), *A Short Symphony* (first performance 1980), piano concerto (1990).

CHAMBER three wind quintets (1956–67), eight string quartets (1938–88).

Perle du Brésil, La, The Pearl of Brazil opera by Félicien ➔ David (libretto by J J Gabriel and S Saint-Etienne), produced at the Théâtre Lyrique, Paris, on 22 November 1851.

Perosi, Lorenzo (1872–1956) Italian priest and composer. He studied at Milan and Ratisbon, in Bavaria, and among other appointments became choirmaster at St Mark's, Venice, in 1894, and music director of the Sistine Chapel in Rome, in 1898. In 1905, he was nominated perpetual master of the Pontifical Chapel.

Works SACRED AND SECULAR MUSIC 33 Masses, four Requiems, *Stabat Mater*, a Te Deum, and much other church music; organ works.

ORATORIOS *The Transfiguration* (1898), *The Raising of Lazarus* (1898), *The Resurrection*, *Moses*, *Leo the Great*, *The Last Judgment* (1904).

ORCHESTRAL ten planned symphonies on the names of Italian cities, including *Il sogno interpretato; Florence, Rome, Venice* and *Bologna*.

Perotinus   Magnus   (c.1160–c.1205   or c.1225), French **Pérotin** French composer and scholar. He was maître de chapelle of the church of the Blessed Virgin Mary (later Notre-Dame Cathedral). He is said to have revised Leoninus' *Liber organi de graduali* and composed organa (see ➔ organum) in as many as four parts. His best known organa are on the Christmas and St Stephen's Day Graduals (1198, 1199).

perpetual canon in music, a ➔ canon in which each part begins again as soon as it is finished, the other parts being at that moment at other stages of their progress. Since even a perpetual canon must finish sooner or later, however, it is broken off at a point agreed to by the performers.

perpetuum mobile (Latin 'perpetually in motion') a piece of music in which there is a rapid and repetitive figuration of notes, especially as part of the accompaniment. It is similar to ➔ motoric rhythm.

Perrin, Pierre (c.1620–1675) French author. He wrote libretti for operas by Robert ➔ Cambert and others.

He preceded Jean-Baptiste Lully 1669–72 in holding the patent for the management of the Académie de Musique (Opéra) in Paris.

Persée, Perseus opera by Jean-Baptiste ➔ Lully (libretto by Quinault), produced at the Paris Opéra on 18 April 1682. In the story, Perseus and Andromeda are in love, but she must marry Phineas. Perseus then proves his love in a series of tests and battles.

Perséphone melodrama for the stage or concert-room by Stravinsky (libretto by André Gide), produced at the Paris Opéra on 30 April 1934. The melodrama comprises three scenes about the mythical Persephone, who is raped by Pluto. Stravinsky, however, introduces the idea of self-sacrifice into the plot, so that the myth becomes similar to a Christian parable.

Persichetti, Vincent (1915–1987) US composer. His *Lincoln Address* of 1973 was scheduled for first performance at Richard Nixon's inauguration in Washington, DC; the performance was postponed owing to an allusion to the Vietnam War.

He studied piano with Alberto Jonás (1868–1943) and Olga Samaroff (1882–1948), composition with Paul Nordoff (1909–77) and Roy Harris, and conducting with Fritz Reiner. He taught composition at the Philadelphia Conservatory 1942–48, then taught at the Juilliard School, New York .

Works OPERA AND STAGE the operas *Parable XX* (1976) and *Sibyl* (1984); ballet *King Lear*.

ORCHESTRAL nine symphonies (1942–71); 14 serenades for different instrumental groups; *The Hollow Men* for trumpet and string orchestra; piano concerto.

CHAMBER two piano quintets, four string quartets (1939–72), twelve piano sonatas, six piano sonatinas; vocal music.

Perti, Giacomo (Antonio) (1661–1756) Italian composer. He studied with his uncle Lorenzo Perti, a priest at San Petronio at Bologna, and later with Petronio Franceschini. After visits to Venice and Modena in the 1680s, he became maestro di cappella at San Pietro at Bologna in 1690, and of San Petronio in 1696.

Works OPERA *Oreste* (1685), *Marzio Coriolano*, *L'incoronazione di Dario* (1686), *Teodora*, *Il furio Camillo* (1692), *Pompeo*, *Nerone fatto Cesare* (1710), *Penelope la casta* (1696), *Fausta*, *Rodelinda* (1710), *Lucio Vero* (1717), and 17 others.

CHURCH MUSIC Masses, including *Missa solemnis* for solo voices, chorus, and orchestra; four Passion oratorios; motets, and other pieces.

SECULAR ORATORIOS several, including *Abramo* (1683).

pes (Latin 'foot') in medieval English music, the lowest part of a vocal composition in several parts, particularly one that consists of a recurrent figure, as in the 13th-century English round 'Sumer is icumen in'.

pesante (Italian 'heavy, weighty') musical direction indicating that a passage is to be played very firmly. In the 19th century and later, the term often implied a slight ➤ *ritenuto* (an immediate reduction of speed).

Pescatrici, Le, The Fisher Girls opera by Ferdinando ➤ **Bertoni** (libretto by Goldoni), produced at the Teatro San Samuele, Venice, on 26 December 1751.

Opera by ➤ **Haydn** (libretto as above), produced at Eszterháza, Hungary, in September 1770. In the story, Prince Lindoro must discover who the heiress of Benvento is. Both Nerina and Lesbina claim to be the princess, but their lovers Burlotto and Frisellino foil their plans. Eurilda is revealed as the true heiress.

Pescetti, Giovanni Battista (c.1704–1766) Italian composer. He produced his first opera, *Nerone detronato*, in Venice in 1725. He lived in London 1737–45, and was for a time music director of the Covent Garden and King's theatres.

He studied with Antonio Lotti. After his return to Italy, his last opera was produced at Padua in 1761. He was appointed second organist at St Mark's, Venice, in 1762.

Works OPERA *Gli odi delusi del sangue* (1728), *Dorinda* (1729, both with Galuppi), *Demetrio* (1732), *Diana ed Endimione* (1739), *La conquista del vello d'oro*, *Tamerlano* (with Cocchi, 1754), and about 20 others.

OTHER the oratorio *Gionata*, church music, harpsichord sonatas.

Peter and the Wolf symphonic tale for narrator and orchestra by ➤ **Prokofiev** (text by composer), Op. 67. It was composed in 1936 and first performed at Moscow on 2 May 1936.

Peter Grimes opera by Benjamin Britten (libretto by M Slater, based on part of George Crabbe's poem 'The Borough'), produced in London at Sadler's Wells, on 7 June 1945. In the story, the fisherman Peter Grimes is accused of murder when his apprentices keep dying. Only Ellen Orford has faith in him, but that is not enough to stop the villagers from hounding him until he drowns himself.

Peter Ibbetson opera by Deems Taylor (libretto by composer and C Collier, based on George du Maurier's novel), produced at the New York Metropolitan Opera, on 7 February 1931.

Peter Schmoll und seine Nachbarn, Peter Schmoll and his Neighbours opera by ➤ Weber (libretto by J Türk, based on a novel by Carl Gottlob Cramer), produced Augsburg, March 1803.

Peterson-Berger, Wilhelm (1867–1942) Swedish composer. He wrote music criticism 1896–1930 and was stage manager of the Stockholm Opera 1908–10. He translated Wagner's *Tristan und Isolde* and was influenced by Wagner in his own stage works. His *Arnljot* (1910) is a national opera which has frequently been revived.

He studied at the Stockholm Conservatory 1886–89, and in Dresden with Hermann Kretzschmar (1848–1924).

Works ORCHESTRAL AND CHAMBER five symphonies (1889–1933), violin concerto (1928), 100 piano pieces, including *Frösöblomster* (1896); song collection *Svensk lyrik*.

Petite messe solennelle, Little Solemn Mass Mass setting by Gioacchino ➤ **Rossini** for soloists, chorus, two pianos, and harmonium. It was composed in 1863 and first performed at Paris on 14 March 1864.

The setting was arranged with full orchestra in 1867 and first performed in Paris, on 24 February 1869.

Petites Liturgies de la Presence Divine, Trois choral work by Olivier Messiaen; see ➤ *Trois Petites Liturgies de la Présence Divine*.

Petite Symphonie Concertante work by Frank ➤ **Martin** for harp, harpsichord, piano, and double string orchestra. It was composed 1944–45 and first performed at Zurich, on 17 May 1946. A version with full orchestra in place of solo instruments, *Symphonie Concertante*, was produced in 1946.

Petits Riens, Les, The Little Nothings ballet by Mozart, K299b (choreographed by Jean Noverre), written in Paris and produced there, at the Opéra, on 11 June 1778.

Petrarch (1304–1374), born Francesco Petrarca Italian poet. Three of his sonnets were set as songs by Franz ➤ **Schubert** in translations by August Wilhelm von Schlegel, and there are three *Sonetti di Petrarca* in Franz ➤ Liszt's ➤ *Années de Pèlerinage/Years of Pilgrimage* for piano, arranged in 1846 from earlier settings of the poems for voice and piano. Many settings by Italian 16th–17th-century madrigalists.

Petrassi, Goffredo (1904–2003) Italian composer. His music made individual use of 12-note methods. Though mainly an instrumentalist, his big choral works, *Psalm IX* (1934), *Coro di morti* (1940), and *Noche oscura* (1950), were of prime importance.

He was born at Zagarolo, near Rome, and learnt

music as a child in the singing-school of the church of San Salvatore in Lauro at Rome. He only began to study music systematically at the age of 21, when he entered the Conservatorio di Santa Cecilia, winning composition and organ prizes there. He came under the influence of Alfredo Casella and Paul Hindemith, and in 1933 made his composition debut with a performance of his orchestral Partita at the Augusteo, which was later given at the International Society for Contemporary Music festival in Amsterdam. In 1939 he became professor of composition at his former school. He continued as a brilliant orchestral composer (writing seven concertos for orchestra) in the neoclassical idiom until the early 1950s. Eventually his style became outmoded, but in the late 1950s he renewed his prominence with a succession of smaller instrumental works in an avant-garde idiom.

Works OPERA AND STAGE the operas *Il Cordovano* (1949) and *La morte dell'aria* (1950); ballet *Il ritratto di Don Chisciotte* (after Cervantes, 1947); incidental music for A Aniante's play *Carmen*.

CHORAL AND VOICE *Psalm IX* for chorus and orchestra; *Il coro dei morti* and *Noche oscura* for chorus (1940); *Magnificat* for voice and orchestra (1940); Partita, Passacaglia, concertos, and concert overture for orchestra (1933–72).

CHAMBER *Tre Cori* for chamber orchestra; piano concerto; *Lamento d'Arianna* (Rinuccini) for voice and chamber orchestra (1936); *Introduzione ed Allegro* for violin and eleven instruments (1933); *Sinfonia, Siciliana e Fuga* for string quartet; *Preludio, Aria e Finale* for cello and piano; toccata for piano; *Siciliana e Marcetta* for piano duet; song cycle *Colori del tempo*, and other songs.

Petrić, Ivo (1931–) Slovenian composer. He studied at the Ljubljana Academy. His early music was neoclassical in inspiration; he later employed aleatory techniques and tone clusters.

Works ORCHESTRAL three symphonies (1954, 1957, 1960), Concerto Grosso (1955), Concertante music (1962), *Dialogues Concertantes* for cello and orchestra (1972), *Three Images* for violin and orchestra (1973) *Fresque Symphonique* (1973).

CHAMBER three wind quintets, chamber concerto (1966), *Quatuor 69* for string quartet.

Petridis, Petro (1892–1977) Greek composer. He studied at Constantinople and in Paris.

Works STAGE the opera *Zemfyra* (1923–25), ballet.

ORCHESTRAL five symphonies (1928–51), dramatic symphony *Digenis Afrikas*, Greek and Ionian Suites, Elegiac Overture, *Prelude, Aria and Fugue* for orchestra; two piano concertos, cello concerto, concerto grosso for wind instruments, violin concerto (1977).

CHAMBER piano trio; two *Modal Suites* for piano; songs.

Petrus de Cruce (lived c.1290) Composer, possibly from Amiens (in northeastern France). His mensural theory is expounded in the works of Robert de Handlo and John Hanboys. Two motets from the Montpellier manuscript can be assigned to him, on the authority of the *Speculum Musicum* by Jacobus of Liège.

Petrushka ballet by ➤ Stravinsky (scenario by composer and Alexander Benois; choreography by Mikhail Fokin), produced at the Théâtre du Châtelet, Paris, on 13 June 1911. A new version in four parts with 15 movements was written in 1946.

Petrželka, Vilém (1889–1967) Czech composer. He studied with Novák in Prague and Janáček at Brno, became a conductor at Pardubice and in 1919 went to Brno as professor at the Conservatory.

Works ORCHESTRAL the symphonic drama *Sailor Nicholas* (1928), *Hymn to the Sun* for chorus and orchestra, symphony (1956), *Eternal Return*, two suites, dramatic overture for orchestra.

CHAMBER five string quartets (1909–15), fantasy and suite for string quartet, sonata and *Intimate Hours* for violin and piano, piano pieces, songs, part songs.

Pettersson, Gustaf Allan (1911–1980) Swedish composer. He is best known for the 16 symphonies he wrote 1950–80, which were influenced by Mahler.

He was born at Stockholm and studied at Stockholm Academy. After playing viola in a local orchestra 1940–51 he studied with Arthur Honegger and René Leibowitz in Paris. In the 1960s he was crippled by rheumatoid arthritis, but was able to continue composing.

Works ORCHESTRAL three concertos for string orchestra (1949–57), violin concerto (1977); *Vox humana*, 18 songs for vocal soloists, chorus, and strings (texts by American Indians, 1974).

CHAMBER seven sonatas for two violins (1952).

petto (Italian 'chest') musical term; hence *voce di petto*, 'chest voice'.

Pevernage, André (1543–1591) Flemish composer. After holding an appointment at Courtrai 1565–85, he moved to Antwerp about 1587 and became choirmaster at the cathedral, holding the post until his death. Apart from cultivating church music, he held weekly concerts at his house.

Works CHURCH AND SECULAR MUSIC *Cantiones sacrae* and other church music; madrigals and five volumes of chansons; ode to St Cecilia.

pezzo, plural **pezzi** Italian word for a piece of music.

Pfeifertag, Der, The Piper's Day opera by Max von Schillings (libretto by F von Sporck), produced at Schwerin, Germany, on 26 November 1899.

Pfitzner, Hans (1869–1949) German composer and conductor. After the success of his opera *Palestrina* in 1917 he devoted himself mainly to composition, but wrote many essays and pamphlets attacking modern music, especially ➤ **Busoni**, and defending Romantic and Germanic ideals.

Pfitzner grew up in Frankfurt, where his father, a violinist, was music director of the municipal theatre. He studied piano with James Kwast (1852–1927) and composition with Iwan Knorr at the Frankfurt Conservatory. In 1893 he gave a first concert of his own works in Berlin, and after some teaching and conducting appointments he became professor at the Stern Conservatory there in 1897, and first conductor at the Theater des Westens in 1903. He also conducted the Kaim Orchestra at Munich and the Opera at Strasbourg. He was a political conservative and wrote *Krakauer Begrüssung* in honour of Hans Frank, the Nazi governor of Poland.

Works OPERA AND STAGE the operas *Der arme Heinrich* (1895), *Die Rose vom Liebesgarten* (1901), *Christelflein* (1906), *Palestrina* (1917), *Das Herz* (1931); incidental music to Ibsen's *Feast at Solhaug* (1890) and Kleist's *Käthchen von Heilbronn* (1905).

CHORAL WITH ORCHESTRA cantatas *Von deutscher Seele* (Eichendorff, 1922), *Das dunkle Reich* (1930), and others; ballads and songs for voice and orchestra.

ORCHESTRAL three symphonies, scherzo for orchestra, piano concerto (1921), violin concerto (1923), two cello concertos (1935–44).

CHAMBER four string quartets (1886–1942), piano quintet, piano trio, violin and piano sonata, cello and piano sonata, sextet (1945), 106 Lieder (1884–1931).

Phaedra dramatic ➤ **cantata** for mezzo-soprano and orchestra by Benjamin Britten (text by R Lowell, after Racine's *Phèdre*). Composed in 1975, it was first performed at Aldeburgh, on 16 June 1976, with the English mezzo-soprano Janet Baker.

Phaéton opera by Jean-Baptiste Lully (libretto by Philippe Quinault), produced at Versailles on 9 January 1683 and first performed at Paris on 27 April of that same year. The story concerns Phaéton, who abandons his love Théone and wants Princess Libya. He rides recklessly around the sky in a chariot until Jupiter strikes him down with a thunderbolt.

Symphonic poem by Camille ➤ **Saint-Saëns**, first performed at Paris on 7 December 1873.

phagotus (Italian *fagotto* 'faggot, bundle') musical instrument developed from the Serbian bagpipe by Afranio Albonese of Pavia early in the 16th century. It consisted of two pipes like those of an organ, supplied with wind from hand bellows, and with a variable pitch produced by fingering on holes.

phantasy musical form; see ➤ fantasia.

Philémon et Baucis opera by Charles Gounod (libretto by Jules Barbier and Michel Carré, after Ovid), produced at the Théâtre Lyrique, Paris, on 18 February 1860. In the story, the elderly Philemon and Baucis are rewarded by Jupiter: he restores their youth. But the god falls in love with Baucis, and she requests old age again to dampen his amorous enthusiasm.

Philemon und Baucis, oder Jupiters Reise auf der Erde, Philemon and Baucis, or Jupiter's Journey to Earth marionette opera by ➤ Haydn (libretto by G K Pfeffel), produced at the palace Eszterháza, Hungary, on 2 September 1773. In the story, Jupiter restores life to Narcissa and her lover Aret, the dead son of Philemon and Baucis, after the god finds shelter in the parents' home. He transforms the hut into a temple and Philemon and Baucis into priests.

Philharmonic Society group of people organized for the advancement of music; the term is derived from Greek 'love of harmony'. The Royal Philharmonic Society was founded in London in 1813 by the pianist Johann Baptist Cramer (1771–1858) for the purpose of improving musical standards by means of orchestral concerts organized on a subscription basis. Another Philharmonic Society was founded in New York in 1842.

Philips, Peter (1561–1628) English organist and composer. He was famous as an organist throughout the Netherlands and was probably the best-known English composer in northern Europe. His collections of madrigals and motets are Roman in style, with Italianate word painting and polyphony; they were reprinted many times in Antwerp.

Philips sang in the choir of St Paul's Cathedral as a boy. He left England in 1582, probably because he was a Roman Catholic; he was received in Rome at the English College, where he became organist. He travelled in Italy and Spain, settled at Antwerp in 1590, and became a canon at the collegiate church of Soignies. In 1585, he entered the service of Lord Thomas Paget and spent five years travelling through Italy, Spain, and France. He settled in Brussels in 1589, and on Paget's death in 1590 moved to Antwerp. In 1593, returning from a visit to hear Jan Sweelinck play in Amsterdam, he was arrested on suspicion of being involved in a plot to assassinate Queen Elizabeth I; he was released. In 1597, he entered the household of the Archduke Albert in Brussels; he was appointed organist at the royal chapel there in 1611, and remained there until the Archduke's death in 1621. He was then appointed chaplain of the church of Saint-Germain at Tirlemont and in about 1623 became canon of Béthune, but may not have resided at either place.

Some of Philips' large output of keyboard music is preserved in the Fitzwilliam Virginal Book. It belongs to the English tradition, with the most inventive pieces being based on madrigals.

Works CHURCH MUSIC Masses, 106 motets published in *Paradisus sacris cantionibus* (Antwerp, 1628), hymns, *Sacrae cantiones*.

CHAMBER madrigals; fantasies, pavanes, and galliards for various instruments; organ and virginal pieces.

Phillips, Peter (1953–) English choral director. With the Tallis Scholars, he has won renown for recordings of such works as Gesualdo's *Tenebrae Responsories*, *Missa Pastores* by Clemens non Papa, Byrd's *Great Service* and three Masses, the English anthems of Tallis, and the Masses of Josquin Desprez and Palestrina.

After studying at St John's College, Oxford, he founded the Tallis Scholars in 1978. They have given many concerts in Britain, Australia (Byrd's five-part Mass at the Sydney Opera House), and the USA (from 1988). They made their London Proms debut in 1988, with Victoria's Requiem, and toured the Far East in 1991. Phillips is the author of *English Sacred Music, 1549–1649* (1991).

Philosopher, The nickname of Joseph ➤ Haydn's symphony, no. 22 in E flat major, composed in 1764 and containing, unusually for the time, two ➤ cor anglais (large oboe) parts.

Philtre, Le, **The Love Potion** opera by Daniel ➤ Auber (libretto by Scribe), produced at the Opéra, Paris, on 20 April 1831. See also ➤ *Elisir d'amore, L'*.

Phinot or **Finot, Dominique (c.1510–c.1555)** French composer. He was associated with the courts of Urbino and Pesaro in Italy and wrote many motets and chansons.

Phoebus and Pan secular cantata by Johann Sebastian Bach; see ➤ *Streit zwischen Phöbus und Pan*.

phrase in music, one of the most basic structural units of ➤ melody. It consists of a group of notes that give the impression of belonging together. There is no fixed length for a phrase, but the most usual is four bars. In the 19th century, some composers, such as Beethoven, Chopin, Liszt, and Wagner, also favoured much longer phrases, with composers such as Hadyn and Mozart using 11- and 13- bar phrases in order to upset the formal balance. The notes to be included in a phrase are usually indicated by a ➤ **slur** (a curved line drawn above or below the notes) and are performed ➤ **legato** (smoothly and continuously) unless otherwise directed.

Phrygian cadence in music, a cadence widely used in the late 17th and early 18th centuries, particularly to mark a transition from one movement to another. This transition – transposed into any key that was required – was not always harmonically obvious; it was common practice to use it at the end of a slow middle movement in a minor key in order to lead into a final movement in a major key. In Bach's Third Brandenburg Concerto it is used by itself without any middle movement at all.

The cadence owes its name to the fact that in the Phrygian mode (E-E), the sixth degree of the scale (D) was not sharpened by ➤ *musica ficta*, since this would have resulted in an augmented sixth with the note F, and altering F to F♯ would have destroyed the character of the mode. This cadence was so firmly established that it survived the disappearance of the rhythmic ➤ **modes** and acquired the flavour of a kind of imperfect cadence on the dominant of A minor.

Phrygian mode the third ecclesiastical ➤ **mode**, represented on the piano by the scale beginning with the note E played on the white notes.

physharmonica small reed organ invented by Anton Hackel of Vienna in 1818; a forerunner of the ➤ **harmonium**.

piacevole (Italian 'pleasing, agreeable') term used in musical notation; similar to ➤ **dolce**.

Pia de' Tolomei opera by Gaetano ➤ **Donizetti** (libretto by Salvatore Cammarano), produced at the Teatro Apollo, Venice, on 18 February 1837. In the story, Ghino is infatuated by his sister-in-law Pia, but denounces her as unfaithful when she does not succumb. Her husband Nello imprisons her and poisons her after mistaking her brother Rodrigo for a lover. Ghino confesses, but it is too late.

pianissimo or **pp (Italian 'very soft')** musical direction rarely written out in full, but indicated by the sign pp or a multiplication thereof.

piano or **pianoforte**; originally **fortepiano** keyboard instrument. The sound is produced when a depressed key strikes the strings with a felt-covered hammer, causing them to vibrate. It is therefore a form of mechanized ➤ **dulcimer**, a percussion instrument. It is different from the earlier ➤ **harpsichord**, a mechanized harp, where the strings are plucked. The piano is capable of a wide range of dynamics from soft (Italian *piano*) to loud (Italian *forte*), hence its name. The first piano was built in 1704 and introduced in 1709 by Bartolommeo Cristofori, a harpsichord maker from Padua. It uses a clever mechanism to make the keyboard touch-sensitive. Extensively developed during the 18th century, the piano became popular among many composers, although it was not until 1768 that Johann Christian ➤ Bach gave one of the first public recitals on the instrument.

Further improvements in the keyboard action and tone were made by makers such as Broadwood, Erard, and Graf. This and the rapid expansion of published music by Joseph Haydn, Ludwig van Beethoven, Franz Schubert, and especially the musical innovations of late Romantics such as Franz Liszt, Frédéric Chopin, and Johannes Brahms, led to the development of the powerfully resonant concert grand piano, such as the modern Steinway, and the mass production of smaller upright pianos for the home.

piano or **p (Italian 'soft')** in musical notation, a direction to play softly.

pianoforte, formerly **fortepiano (Italian 'soft-loud')** another name for the ➤ piano.

Pianola trademark for a type of ➤ player piano.

piano-organ or **handle-piano** mechanical instrument similar to the barrel organ in the shape of an upright piano, producing its notes in the same way by a studded cylinder, but from strings struck by hammers instead of pipes.

It was widely used by street musicians in the larger English cities in the late 19th and early 20th centuries, especially in London. It was often wrongly called the 'barrel organ' and even more incorrectly the 'hurdy-gurdy'.

piano quartet ➤ quartet of piano and three other instruments (usually violin, viola, and cello), or the music written for such an ensemble. The earliest examples played today are those by ➤ Mozart (K478 and K493). The quartet of Beethoven (Op. 16) and three quartets of Brahms (Op. 25, Op. 26, Op. 60) are also well-known.

piano quintet ➤ quintet of piano and four other instruments (usually a string quartet), or the music written for such an ensemble, as in those by Johannes Brahms, Edward Elgar, and Dmitri Shostakovich; Robert Schubert's famous 'Trout' Quintet is for piano, violin, viola, cello, and double bass.

piano score in music, a reduction of an orchestral or vocal score to two staves of music to be played on the piano.

piano trio in music, a group of three players made up of piano, violin, and cello. The term also refers to the music written for such a group. Composers who wrote piano trios include Jo-

seph Haydn, Wolfgang Amadeus Mozart, Ludwig van Beethoven (the 'Ghost' trio and the 'Archduke' trio), Johannes Brahms, Franz Schubert, Antonín Dvořák, Maurice Ravel, and Dmitri Shostakovich (piano trio no. 2, in E minor).

Piave, Francesco Maria (1810–1876) Italian librettist. He collaborated largely with ➤ Verdi, most notably *La Traviata* and *Rigoletto*. He also wrote libretti for Pacini and ➤ Mercadante, though not for Ponchielli, as has been stated elsewhere.

He studied briefly for the priesthood and for a time earned subsistence from a publisher. A collaboration with Verdi began in 1844 with *Ernani*. Other libretti for Verdi were *I due Foscari*, *Macbeth*, *Il corsaro*, *Stiffelio*, *Simon Boccanegra*, *Aroldo*, and *La Forza del Destino*. An abandoned project, *Allan Cameron*, was taken up with Pacini and produced in Venice in 1848. In the same year Piave's libretto for Mercadante's *La schiava Saracena/The Saracen Slave-Girl* was produced in Milan.

Picander German poet and cantata librettist; see Christian Friedrich ➤ Henrici.

Piccinni, Niccolò (1728–1800) Italian composer. He wrote over 120 operas, using many of Metastasio's libretti, and was a significant figure in the development of both French and Italian opera.

He studied at the Conservatorio di Sant' Onofrio at Naples, where he was taught by Leonardo Leo and Francesco Durante. He produced his first opera at Naples in 1754. It was well received and was soon followed by other operas, both comic and serious. In 1756 he married the singer Vincenza Sibilia, his pupil. In 1760, his opera *La buona figliuola*, based on Richardson's novel *Pamela*, was an enormous success in Rome. He enjoyed some years of success there before being ousted by his former pupil Pasquale Anfossi and returning to Naples in 1773.

In 1776 he was invited to Paris, where he was at first in great difficulties but was helped by the author Jean Marmontel, who taught him French and wrote the libretto of his first French opera, *Roland* (1778). He was pitted against Christoph Willibald von ➤ Gluck by partisans who liked to have something to quarrel about. The feud between the Gluckists and Piccinnists – in which the composers themselves took no part – reached its height when, in 1781, Piccinni set the libretto of *Iphigénie en Tauride*, which had already been used by Gluck.

At the Revolution he left for Italy, visited Venice, and then returned home to Naples, where he was placed under close surveillance and lived in great poverty. In 1798 he at last succeeded in returning to Paris. After a period of comparative affluence, he again fell into poverty, was relieved by a gift from Napoleon and an inspector's post at the Conservatory, but became paralysed and finally died in distress.

His son Luigi (1766–1827) and his grandson Louis-Alexandre (1779–1850) were both composers. The former wrote operas for Paris and Stockholm, the latter ballets and melodramas for the Paris theatres.

Works OPERA about 120, including *Le donne dispettose* (1754), *Le Gelosie, Zenobia* (1756), *Alessandro nell' Indie* (two versions), *Madama Arrighetta* (1758), *La buona figliuola, La buona figliuola maritata* (both after Richardson's *Pamela*, 1760, 1761), *Il cavaliere per amore* (1762), *Le contadine bizarre, Gli stravaganti* (1764), *L'Olimpiade* (1761), *I viaggiatori* (1775), *La pescatrice* (1766), *Le finte gemelle, Vittorina* (Goldoni), *Roland, Atys, Iphigénie en Tauride* (1781), *Didon* (1783), *Le Faux Lord* (1783), *Pénélope, Endymion* (1784).

OTHER oratorio *Jonathan* and three others; Mass, psalms, and other church music.

Piccola musica notturna, Little night Music work for orchestra by Luigi→ **Dallapiccola**, first performed in Hanover on 7 June 1954. It was arranged for eight instruments in 1961.

piccolo woodwind instrument, the smallest member of the → **flute** family, with a brilliant and penetrating tone. It sounds an octave higher than the flute, and for this reason is sometimes known as the *ottavino* (Italian, 'octave'). Antonio Vivaldi composed three concertos for the piccolo, and it can also be heard in the first movement of Sergey Prokofiev's *Lieutenant Kijé* (1934).

Picco pipe woodwind instrument of the → recorder or → flageolet type which became fashionable in England on being introduced to London in 1856 by a Sardinian player named Picco.

Pichl, Wenzel (1741–1805) Bohemian violinist and composer. He was admired by Luigi Cherubini and Adalbert Gyrowetz, and Haydn performed his quartets at Eszterháza.

He studied in Prague and in 1765 became violinist and vice-director of music (under Karl Dittersdorf) to the Bishop of Grosswardein. In 1769 he moved to Vienna and thence to Milan in the service of the Archduke Ferdinand, remaining in Italy until his return to Vienna in 1796.

Works OPERA according to Pichl's own catalogue, twelve operas, including four Latin operas (1765–76), four opera buffa, *Der Krieg* (1776), and Italian arrangements of French operas.

ORCHESTRAL AND CHAMBER MUSIC over 30 Masses; 89 symphonies; about 30 concertos; 172 quartets, 21 quintets, and other pieces; 148 pieces for baryton (euphonium).

Pictures at an Exhibition, German **Bilder einer Ausstellung** suite of piano pieces by → **Mussorgsky**, composed in 1874 in memory of the painter and architect Victor Alexandrovich Hartmann (died 1873). The work illustrates pictures and designs by Hartman shown at a memorial exhibition organized by Vladimir Vassilevich Stassov. Orchestral versions of the suite have been made by Henry J Wood, Stokowski, and Walter Goehr, as well as a brass band arrangement by Elgar Howarth. The most frequently heard version, however, is the orchestration by Maurice Ravel which is so well-known that it is a common mistake to assume that Ravel wrote the original piece.

The Ravel orchestration was first performed at the Paris Opéra, on 19 October 1922, conducted by Koussevitzky.

pieno (Italian 'full') musical direction used especially in organ music in combination, *organo pieno*, meaning either that a figured bass is to be filled with ample harmony or that the instrument is to be played with full registration.

Pierné, (Henri Constant) Gabriel (1863–1937) French composer and conductor. His numerous ballets include *Cydalise et le chèvre-pied/Cydalise and the Satyr* (1923), containing the 'Entry of the Little Fauns'. As a conductor he gave many important first performances, including Debussy's *Khamma* in 1924 and *La Boîte à joujoux* in 1923.

He studied at the Paris Conservatory and won the Prix de Rome in 1882. In 1890 he succeeded César Franck as organist of the church of Sainte-Clotilde, became second conductor of Edouard Colonne's orchestra in 1903, and at Colonne's death in 1910 succeeded him as chief conductor.

Works OPERA AND STAGE the operas *Les Elfes, Pandore, La coupe enchantée* (after La Fontaine, 1905), *La nuit de Noël, Vendée, La fille de Tabarin, On ne badine pas avec l'amour* (after Musset, 1910), *Fragonard, Sophie Arnould* (1927); ballets, pantomimes, and incidental music.

OTHER oratorios, suites for orchestra, piano quintet, piano trio, songs.

Pierrot lunaire, Moonstruck Pierrot song-cycle by Arnold → **Schoenberg** for female voice and chamber ensemble, Op. 21, consisting of 21 poems by Albert Giraud translated into German by Otto Erich Hartleben. It was composed in 1912 and first performed in Berlin, on 16 October 1912. The treatment of the voice-part is one of the outstanding examples of the use of → **Sprechgesang** ('Speechsong' – a hybrid of pure song and speech), and the piece is generally held to be one of the key works of the early 20th century.

The 21 poems are arranged in three sections: 1. *Mondestrunken, Colombine, Der Dandy, Eine blasse Wäscherin, Valse de Chopin, Madonna, Der*

Kranke Mond; 2. *Die Nacht, Gebet an Pierrot, Raub, Rote Messe, Galgenlied, Enthauptung, Die Kreuze*; 3. *Heimweh, Gemeinheit, Parodie, Der Mondfleck, Serenade, Heimfahrt, O alter Duft.* The work was commissioned by Albertine Zehme; it was soon admired by composers as different as Puccini and Stravinsky, but wider public success did not come until a performance in Berlin on 5 January 1924, with Marie Gutheil-Schoder and Gregor Piatigorsky (cello), Artur Schnabel (piano), and Fritz Stiedry (conductor).

Pierson, Henry Hugh or **Heinrich Hugo (1815–1873)**, born **Henry Hugh Pearson** English-born German composer. Educated at Harrow and Cambridge, he studied music with Thomas Attwood and Corfe, and interrupted a medical course to continue music studies at Leipzig, where he met Mendelssohn, Schumann, and others. He became Reid Professor of Music at Edinburgh in 1844 in succession to Henry Bishop, but soon resigned and returned to Germany, where he remained, married Caroline Leonhardt, and changed the spelling of his name.

Works OPERA the operas *Der Elfensieg* (1845), *Leila* (1848), and *Contarini* (composed in 1853, produced in 1872), *Fenice* (1883); incidental music to Goethe's *Faust* (Part II).

ORATORIO *Jerusalem* (1852).

ORCHESTRAL *Macbeth* symphony (1859); overtures to Shakespeare's *Twelfth Night, Julius Caesar*, and *Romeo and Juliet* (1874); funeral march for *Hamlet* (1859).

OTHER numerous songs; part songs.

Piéton, Loyset (died after 1545) French composer. He wrote Masses, motets, psalms, and chansons; his work was published in Lyon and Venice.

He has often been confused with Compère, since both are usually called only by their first names.

pietoso (Italian, from *pietà,* **'pity')** in musical direction, pityingly, compassionately.

pietra del paragone, La, The Touchstone opera by Rossini (libretto by I Romanelli), produced in Milan at La Scala, on 26 September 1812. The story unfolds as Count Asdrubale and Marchesina Clarice meet at a party and their affections grow. Each tests the other's sincerity with the help of disguises and they are finally united.

piffaro (Italian 'fife') small flute-like pipe, also a shepherd's pipe similar to the oboe or bagpipe. It was often played in Italian cities, especially Rome and Naples, at Christmas time, by pipers from the hills.

They seem to have played tunes like that of the second section of Bach's *Christmas Oratorio* or the 'Pastoral Symphony' in Handel's *Messiah*, which bears the word 'pifa' in the manuscript, evidently in reference to the piffaro.

Pigheaded Peasants, The, Czech **Tvrdé Palice** opera by Dvořák (libretto J Stolba), produced at the Czech Theatre, Prague, on 2 October 1881. In the story, the widower Vávra and the widow Říhová decide their children, Toník and Lenka, should marry. Knowing their children to be stubborn, the two use reverse psychology to coax them together.

Pijper, Willem (1894–1947) Dutch composer. He was influenced by the contemporary French school on the one hand, and by Mahler on the other. Despite obvious difficulty in reconciling these influences, he became the most important Dutch composer of his generation. His works include the operatic cantata *Halewijn* (1934), music for plays by Sophocles, Euripides, and Shakespeare, three symphonies, concertos, chamber music, sonatas for various instruments, piano music, and songs.

He studied with Johan Wagenaar and was appointed professor of composition at the Amsterdam Conservatory in 1925. He was director of the Rotterdam Conservatory from 1930 until his death.

Works OPERA the opera *Halewijn* (1933); incidental music for Euripides' *The Cyclops* and *The Bacchantes* (1924), Sophocles' *Antigone*, and Shakespeare's *Tempest* (1930).

ORCHESTRAL three symphonies, six symphonic epigrams for orchestra, piano concerto (1927), violin concerto, cello concerto.

CHAMBER five string quartets (1914–46), two piano trios, sextet for wind and piano, violin and piano sonatas, piano music.

OTHER choruses, songs.

Pilgrim's Progress, The opera by Vaughan Williams (libretto by the composer after Bunyan), produced at Covent Garden, London, on 26 April 1951. It incorporates most of the composer's one-act opera *The Shepherds of the Delectable Mountains* (produced at the Royal College of Music in London, on 11 July 1922). The story concerns the journey of the Pilgrim as he faces many trials on his way to the Celestial City.

Pilkington, Francis (c.1570–1638) English composer. Upon taking his degree in music at Oxford in 1595, he was soon after appointed as singer at Chester Cathedral where he remained to his death, becoming a minor canon in 1612.

Works CHORAL AND VOICE anthems, including one in Leighton's *Teares or Lamentacions*; madrigals; pastorals for three–six voices.

OTHER lute pieces, songs to the lute.

Pimmalione, Pygmalion opera by Luigi ➔ **Cherubini** (libretto by S Vestris), produced at the palace of the Tuileries, Paris, at Napoleon's private theatre, for which it was written, on 30 November 1809.

Pimpinone three intermezzos by Tomaso Albinoni (libretto by P Pariati), produced with the opera *Astarto* in Venice, in 1708. As with Pergolesi's *La serva padrona*, the intermezzo is now better known than the *opera seria* for which it was intended to provide light relief. In the story, Vespetta persuades elderly Pimpinone to employ her as a servant. She then makes him promise to marry her, after which she seeks pleasure elsewhere.

Intermezzo by Georg Philipp Telemann, produced at Hamburg in 1725.

Pincherle, Marc (1888–1974) French musicologist. He was professor at the Ecole Normale de Musique in Paris and edited successively *Le Monde musical* and *Musique*. His works include studies of Corelli, Vivaldi, the violin, and violin music.

Pinello di Gherardi, Giovanni Battista (c.1544–1587) Italian composer. After an appointment at Vicenza Cathedral he went to Innsbruck in the 1570s as musician to the archduke, to the Imperial Chapel in Prague soon afterwards, and to the Saxon court at Dresden in 1580 in succession to Antonio Scandello, but was dismissed because of differences with other musicians, and returned to Prague.

Works motets, German Magnificats and other church music; madrigals and *canzone napoletane*; part songs.

Pinkham, Daniel (1923–   ) US composer, organist, and conductor. He studied with Walter Piston at Harvard and with Nadia Boulanger in Paris. He was music director of King's Chapel, Boston, from 1958.

Works OPERA the chamber opera *The Garden of Artemis* (an arrangement of *The Beggar's Opera*, 1956).

ORCHESTRAL four symphonies, two violin concertos, concerto piccolo (1989).

CHURCH MUSIC *Wedding* and *Christmas Cantatas*, *Requiem* and *St Mark Passion* (1965), *Daniel in the Lion's Den* (1972), *The Passion of Judas* (1976), *A Curse, a Lament and a Vision* for chorus and piano (1984), *Getting to Heaven* for soprano and chorus (1987).

piobaireachd Scots Gaelic term meaning *piping*. Its Anglicized form *pibroch* denotes a specific category of music for the Scottish Highland pipes.

pipa four-string, plucked ➤ lute with a pear-shaped soundbox, found in China and Korea. Used as a solo or ensemble instrument in a variety of genres, it arrived in China from Central Asia during the Northern Wei dynasty.

pipe small woodwind instrument popular in the 13th century. A ➤ whistle flute played only with the left hand, it freed the right hand to play the traditional accompanying drum, the tabor.

'Pipe' is also a generic term used to describe the hollow cylinder or cone of woodwind and brass instruments in which air vibrates to generate sound; or one of many tubes which make up some musical instruments, as in an organ pipe or panpipes.

pipe and tabor combination of two early musical instruments: a small pipe of the recorder type, but held with one hand only while the other beats the tabor, a small drum without snares hung round the player's shoulder or waist. The instruments have been revived for folk-dancing.

piped music, proprietary name **Muzak** music recorded to strict psychological criteria for transmission in a variety of work environments in order to improve occupier or customer morale.

Pipelare, Matthaeus (lived 15th–16th centuries) Flemish composer. He wrote Masses, motets, and secular works to French and Dutch texts. His motet *Memorare mater Christi* commemorates the seven sorrows of the Virgin Mary. In 1498 he became master of the choristers at 's-Hertogenbosch.

Pique-Dame German title of Pyotr Tchaikovsky's opera *The Queen of Spades/Pikovaya Dama*.

Pirame et Thisbé, Pyramus and Thisbe opera by Rebel and Francœur (libretto by J L I de La Serre), produced at the Opéra, Paris, on 17 October 1726. The story begins as Pyramus and Thisbe decide to run away together. Thisbe arrives at the rendezvous first but runs away when she sees a wounded lion. Pyramus arrives and, seeing the blood, believes Thisbe has been eaten. He stabs himself; she returns to find him and does likewise.

Pirata, Il, The Pirate opera by Vincenzo Bellini (libretto by Felice Romani), produced in Milan at La Scala, on 27 October 1827. In the story, Ernesto has forced Imogene to marry him despite her love for Gualtiero, who in desperation turns to piracy. When Gualtiero is shipwrecked near Ernesto's castle, the lovers meet, but their joy is short lived: Gualtiero kills Ernesto and is sentenced to death.

Pirates of Penzance, The, or The Slave of Duty operetta by Arthur Sullivan (libretto by W S Gilbert), produced at the Bijou Theatre in Paignton, Devon, on 30 December 1879. A pirated performance was given at New York's Fifth Avenue Theatre, on 31 December 1879, and the first London performance, at the Opéra-Comique, was given on 3 April 1880. The story is about Frederic, who is mistakenly apprenticed to some pirates but intends to turn in the outlaws when he comes of age. He discovers, however, that he was born on 29 February in a leap year and is consequently not yet 21; he must remain an apprentice.

Pirro, André (1869–1943) French musicologist. He studied law and literature in Paris and at the same time picked up as much musical education as he could, attending the organ classes of César Auguste Franck and Charles-Marie Widor. In 1912, he succeeded Rolland as professor of music history at the Sorbonne. His books include studies of Schütz, Buxtehude, Bach (general and organ works), the French clavecinists, Descartes and music, and early German church and secular music.

In 1896 he became professor and a director of the newly-opened Schola Cantorum. In 1904, he began to lecture at the Ecole des Hautes Etudes Sociales, Paris.

Pirro e Demetrio, Pyrrhus and Demetrius opera by Alessandro Scarlatti (libretto by A Morselli), produced at the Teatro San Bartolommeo in Naples, probably on 28 January 1694.

Pirrotta, Nino (1908–1998) Italian musicologist. His major studies were of 14th-century Italian music, including the *ars nova* and 17th-century Italian opera.

He studied at the conservatories of Palermo and Florence, and later was librarian of the Santa Cecilia Conservatory in Rome 1948–56. From 1956 to 1972, he was a professor at Harvard and then at Rome 1972–83.

Pisendel, Johann Georg (1687–1755) German violinist and composer. He studied with Vivaldi in Venice, and wrote concertos and pieces for the violin.

He was a choirboy at the chapel of the Margrave of Ansbach, and while there studied the violin under Giuseppe Torelli and theory under Francesco Pistocchi. After studying at Leipzig University he went to Dresden to enter the service of the king of Poland there in 1712, travelled widely with the king, became concert master in 1728 on the death of Jean Baptiste Volumier, and led the opera orchestra under Johann Hasse.

Pisk, Paul A(madeus) (1893–1990) Austrian-born US musicologist and composer. He edited early music including Masses by Jacobus Gallus, and wrote on modern music and the Second Viennese School.

He studied under Adler at Vienna University and composition with Schreker and Schoenberg. After conducting at various German theatres, he returned to Vienna, conducting and broadcasting, and became director of the music depart-

ment of the Volkshochschule, but left for the USA in 1936 and became professor of musicology at the University of Texas. In 1963, he joined the staff of Washington University, St Louis; he retired in 1973 and moved to Los Angeles.

Works STAGE MUSIC the monodrama *Schattenseite* (1931); ballet *Der grosse Regenmacher* (1927); cantata *Die neue Stadt* (1926).

ORCHESTRAL Requiem for baritone and orchestra; partita for orchestra, suite for small orchestra; *Bucolic Suite* for strings; and other orchestral works.

CHAMBER string quartet and other chamber music; piano music; songs with organ.

piston on a brass musical instrument, a valve which alters the length of tubing through which air vibrates, changing the pitch. The first valve lowers the pitch a whole tone, the second a semitone, the third three semitones. Most orchestral brass instruments today employ three valves, but sometimes a fourth is added.

Piston, Walter Hamor (1894–1976) US composer and teacher. His music follows European neoclassical models, often favouring contrapuntal textures; his works include eight symphonies, a number of concertos, chamber music, the orchestral suite *Three New England Sketches* (1959), and the ballet *The Incredible Flutist* (1938). He wrote a number of textbooks, including *Harmony* in 1941 and *Orchestration* in 1955.

Piston was born in Rockland, Maine. After studying at Harvard University, and in Paris with Nadia Boulanger, he returned to the USA and taught at Harvard 1926–60. He was well regarded as a teacher; his pupils included Leonard Bernstein. Piston's music is clear and finely disciplined, and has some affinities with ➤ Stravinsky's neoclassical work.

Works ORCHESTRAL the ballet *The Incredible Flutist* (1938); eight symphonies (1937–65); suite, concerto, Symphonic Piece, Prelude and Fugue for orchestra; concertino for piano and chamber orchestra (1937), clarinet concertino, two violin concertos (1939, 1960).

CHAMBER five string quartets (1933–62), piano trio, three pieces for flute, clarinet, and bassoon; violin and piano sonata, flute and piano sonata, suite for oboe and piano, partita for violin, viola, and organ.

CHORAL *Carnival Song* for male chorus and brass instruments.

pitch in music, the technical term used to describe how high or low a note is. It depends on the frequency (number of vibrations per second) of the sound, which is measured in hertz (Hz). Pitch also refers to the standard to which instruments are tuned. Nowadays the internationally agreed-upon pitch is the A above middle C (A4 or a'), which has a frequency of 440 Hz (vibrations per second). This is often known as ✦ **concert pitch**.

Pitch can now be measured accurately by electronic tuning devices. These are beginning to replace the traditional tuning fork, but it is still normal practice for orchestras to tune to an oboe playing A4.

absolute pitch (also called perfect pitch) is the ability to name any note heard, or to sing any note asked for. It is now considered to be learned at a very young age through exposure to a well-tuned instrument. A person who has perfect pitch does not necessarily have any other musical ability. Perfect pitch is not particularly rare and many musicians have it.

For any musical note, the pitch is determined by what the ear perceives as its fundamental frequency. In stringed instruments this depends on the length, tension, and composition of the vibrating string, and in wind instruments on the length of the tube. Some instruments, mainly in the percussion family, are of indefinite pitch and are referred to as 'untuned' instruments. In organ terminology, ranks of pipes are classified in wavelength pitch, such as 4-foot, 8-foot, or 16-foot, according to the octave range in which they fall.

The internationally-recognized standard pitch of 440 Hz at A above middle C was set in 1955 by the International Organization for Standardization, and ended centuries of confusion, although in the 1990s some orchestras and ensembles used 441 Hz and 442 Hz to give a bright sound in contrast to the normal 440 Hz. Before 1955 pitch had varied at different times and from country to country, from 410 Hz to 480 Hz. The general trend had been for a gradual rise in standard pitch, often encouraged by wind-instrument makers anxious to achieve a more brilliant sound. This meant that music in the newer pitch sometimes became too high for singers, and also required many of the stringed instruments designed for the old, lower pitch to be modified. Nearly all the great stringed instruments made by Antonio Stradivari, Joseph Guarneri, and the Amati family were converted to accommodate the new pitch. At times two pitches were in use, the higher for orchestral performances and the lower 'classical' or 'French' pitch for church and purely vocal music. This French pitch, known also as 'diapason normal', had A4 or a' at 435 Hz and was fixed in Paris in 1849.

pitch-class set or **pc set** group of notes considered entirely from the point of view of their pitch classes; that is, independently of their tonal function, the octave in which they occur, the order in which they occur, or the number of occurrences of each pitch in the set. By convention, pitch clas-

ses are numbered from 0 to 11, with 0=C natural/B sharp, 1=C sharp/D flat and so on. Pitch-class sets are labelled with two digits, the first indicating the number of pitches in the set, and the second the number of the set in the list of all possible sets. For example, the pitches C, E, and G (0, 4, and 7) form the set 3–11. If transpositions and inversions of sets are considered to be equivalent to one another, the twelve chromatic notes can form a total of only 234 distinct pitch-class sets. Pitch-class set analysis describes music entirely in terms of the pitch-class sets identifiable in a piece and the relationships between these sets, and is principally used in the analysis of atonal music. See Allen ✦ **Forte**; ✦ **set complex**; ✦ **subset/superset**; ✦ **similarity relation**.

Pitoni, Giuseppe Ottavio (1657–1743) Italian composer. He wrote large quantities of church music, including a 16-part *Dixit Dominus* that is still sung at St Peter's, Rome, in Holy Week. He also wrote on the history and theory of music.

He studied with Pompeo Natale from an early age, and became a chorister at the churches of San Giovanni dei Fiorentini and Santi Apostoli in Rome, where he was a pupil of Foggia. After church posts in Monterotondo and Assisi he became maestro di cappella at Rieti (in western Italy) in 1676, and from the next year to his death at the Collegio San Marco in Rome, later also at the Lateran and St Peter's.

Works CHURCH MUSIC over 250 Masses, 780 psalm settings, Magnificats, motets, Litanies, and two Passions.

pittore parigino, Il, The Parisian Painter opera by Domenico Cimarosa (libretto by G Petrosellini), produced in Rome at the Teatro Valle, on 4 January 1781. The story concerns Eurilla, who must marry Baron Cricca if she is to receive her inheritance. However, she falls in love with Crotignac, a painter. After first choosing money, Eurilla changes her mind and decides on Crotignac.

più (Italian 'more') term used in musical notation, as in *più mosso* ('more moved', 'faster') or *più lento* ('slower').

pluttosto (Italian 'somewhat, rather') word used with musical directions where the composer wishes to make sure that an indication of tempo or expression is obeyed in moderation.

Pixérécourt, René Charles Guilbert de (1773–1844) French dramatist and librettist, biographer of the composer ✦ **Dalayrac**, and author of melodramas with music. See ✦ ***Margherita d'Anjou*** by Meyerbeer.

Pixis, Johann Peter (1788–1874) German pianist and composer. He lived in Paris for several years, and acquired a reputation as a gifted pianist and piano teacher.

He studied with his father, Friedrich Wilhelm Pixis (c.1760–c.1810), and began to appear as a pianist with his brother Friedrich Wilhelm Pixis (1786–1842), a violinist. He settled in Munich in 1809 and in Paris in 1823, where he became a noted piano teacher. In 1845, he bought a villa at Baden-Baden and continued to train pupils there. He adopted and trained the singer Franzilla Göhringer (born 1816); she created the title role in Pacini's opera *Saffo* in 1840.

Works OPERA *Almazinde* (1820), *Bibiana* (1829), and *Die Sprache des Herzens* (1836).

PIANO MUSIC piano concertos, sonatas, and other pieces.

Pizzetti, Ildebrando (1880–1968) Italian composer. He is remarkable as a composer of serious, heroic, rather austere operas, for which he wrote his own libretti, except for the first, *Fedra* (produced in 1915), which is by Gabriele d'Annunzio. He also wrote incidental music for plays, film music, choral and orchestral works, chamber music, and songs.

Pizzetti was born at Parma. The son of a piano teacher, he studied at Parma Conservatory 1895–1901. In 1908 he was appointed professor of harmony and counterpoint at the Istituto Musicale at Florence, of which he became director in 1917. In 1924 he was appointed director of the Conservatory Giuseppe Verdi, Milan, and in 1936 he succeeded Ottorino Respighi as professor of advanced composition at the Accademia di Santa Cecilia in Rome.

Works STAGE operas *Fedra* (1915), *Debora e Jaele* (1922), *Lo straniero*, *Fra Gherardo* (1928), *Ifigenia* (radio opera, 1950), *Assassinio nella cattedrale* (after T S Eliot, 1958); incidental music for *La Nave* and *La Pisanella* (both by d'Annunzio).

ORCHESTRAL WORKS three symphonic preludes for Sophocles' *Oedipus Rex* and *Coloneus* (1903), *Concerto dell' estate* (1928), *Rondo veneziano* (1929).

CHORUS AND ORCHESTRA *Missa di Requiem* (1922) and *De profundis* for unaccompanied chorus (1937); *Due compositioni corali* (1961); *Cantico di gloria* (1966).

CHAMBER two string quartets (1906, 1933), piano trio; sonatas for violin and piano and for cello and piano; songs, including *Due Poesie di Ungaretti* for baritone and piano trio, three with string quartet, and 21 with piano, including *I Pastori* and *Altre cinque liriche*.

pizzicato (Italian 'pinched') in music, an instruction to string players to pluck the strings with the fingers instead of using the bow. It is frequently abbreviated to 'pizz'.

Good examples of pizzicato are in the *Pizzicato Polka* (1870) by Johann Strauss II and Josef Strauss, and in the 'Playful Pizzicato' of Benjamin Britten's *Simple Symphony* (1933–34).

pizzicato tremolando (Italian 'pinched and trembling') musical effect in which the orchestra strings play chords by thrumming the strings both ways across with the fingers of the right hand. It was first used by Edward Elgar in the cadenza of his violin concerto.

plainchant type of medieval church music; see ➤ plainsong.

plainsong or **plainchant** traditional single-line chant melodies used for singing the texts of the Christian church. Plainsong was first adopted by Ambrose, Bishop of Milan, and then by Pope Gregory in the 6th century, the latter being referred to as ➤ Gregorian chant. It is properly sung in unison, without harmony and with no definitely measured rhythms. Its groupings of notes have, however, a strongly rhythmic character, but it resembles the free rhythm of prose, whereas that of measured music is comparable to the rhythm of verse. The old ➤ notation on a stave of four lines, with square or diamond-shaped notes and ligatures, is still used for plainsong.

plainte (French 'complaint') lament or memorial piece, which can be either vocal or instrumental.

Plamenac, Dragan (1895–1983) US musicologist of Croatian origin. He studied law at the University of Zagreb, then composition with Schreker, musicology with Adler in Vienna and with Pirro in Paris, taking his doctorate in 1925. In 1939 he went to the USA, becoming Professor of Musicology at the University of Illinois in 1955. He published a number of studies of pre-classical music and edited the works of Johannes Okeghem.

Planché, James Robinson (1796–1880) English dramatist, librettist, and critic. He was popular in his own day for his burlesques, such as *The Island of Jewels* (1849). He introduced historically accurate costume and accessories to the theatre, and helped to change the law governing theatrical copyright after one of his plays had been plagiarized. He wrote a number of libretti including *Maid Marian* for Henry Bishop, *Oberon* for Carl Weber, and *The Surrender of Calais*, intended for Mendelssohn and later offered to H Smart, who left it unfinished.

He was an expert on heraldry, with the title Rouge Croix Pursuivant of Arms (1854) and Somerset Herald (1866) at the Heralds' College. His *History of British Costume* was published in 1834.

Planets, The suite by Holst for orchestra with organ and (in the final section) female chorus.

The suite includes: 1. *Mars, the Bringer of War*; 2. *Venus, the Bringer of Peace*; 3. *Mercury, the Winged Messenger*; 4. *Jupiter, the Bringer of Jollity*; 5. *Saturn, the Bringer of Old Age*; 6. *Uranus, the Magician*; 7. *Neptune, the Mystic*. The idea of writing music on the planets was not new: Buxtehude wrote a harpsichord suite on them, but Holst dealt with them from the astrological aspect.

It was first performed privately at the Queen's Hall, London, on 29 September 1918; its first public performance was in London, on 15 November 1920.

Planquette, (Jean) Robert (1848–1903) French composer. He studied briefly at the Paris Conservatory and then wrote songs that were performed at café-concerts. From this he passed on to operettas, the fourth of which, *Les cloches de Corneville* (1877), was immensely successful.

Works OPERETTAS *Valet de cœur*, *Le serment de Mme Grégoire*, *Paille d'avoine* (1874), *Les cloches de Corneville* (1877), *Le Chevalier Gaston* (1879), *Les Voltigeurs de la 32me* (*The Old Guard*), *La Cantinière*, *Rip van Winkle* (after Washington Irving, 1882), *Nell Gwynne* (1884), *La cremaillère*, *Surcouf* (*Paul Jones*), *Capitaine Thérèse*, *La cocarce tricolore*, *Le talisman*, *Panurge* (after Rabelais, 1895), *Mam'zelle Quat' Sous* (1897), and *Le Paradis de Mahomed* (produced in 1906).

Platée, Plataea comédie-ballet by Jean-Philippe Rameau (libretto by J Autreau and A J V d'Orville), produced at Versailles, at court, on 31 March 1745. Its first Paris performance was at the Opéra on 4 February 1749. In the story, Jupiter decides to cure Juno's constant jealousy: he woos the ugly but vain marsh-nymph Plataea, knowing that when Juno discovers Jupiter's new lover is ugly, she will realize how groundless her jealousy is. Juno appears just in time to stop the wedding, to Plataea's rage.

Plato (c.428 BC–c.348 BC) Greek philosopher. He outlined a system of 'harmony', as understood by the Greeks, in *Timaeus* and discussed the nature of the ➜ modes, from their supposed moral aspect, in *The Republic*.

Platti, Giovanni (1697–1763) Italian harpsichordist and composer. He made important contributions towards the development of a modern style of keyboard music. Little is known of his life, but from 1722 he was a composer and teacher in the service of the archiepiscopal court in Würzburg.

Works CHURCH MUSIC six Masses and other church music.

CHORAL MUSIC oratorios, cantatas, and other choral pieces.

CHAMBER sonatas for flute, and for cello; concertos and sonatas for harpsichord and other keyboard music.

player piano mechanical piano designed to reproduce key actions recorded on a perforated paper roll. The hammers are made to touch the strings not by action of the hand on the keyboard but by air pressure. This is regulated by a roll of perforated paper running over a series of slits corresponding with the musical scale and releasing the air only where the holes momentarily pass over the slits. The mechanism is set in motion by pedals like those of a harmonium.

Dynamics were at first controlled by the action of the players' hands, more or less roughly according to their skill, but they were later reproduced mechanically exactly as played by the recording artist. Debussy, Mahler, Grainger, and Stravinsky recorded their own works on piano roll. The concert *Duo-Art* reproducing piano encoded such detailed information that audiences were unable to distinguish a live performance from a reproduced performance. However, without a player, the player piano became simply a playback device for recordings, in which role it was superseded by the gramophone. In the 1950s–70s the US composer Conlon ➜ Nancarrow realized the instrument's potential for playing pieces that no human player could encompass – with strictly controlled tempo fluctuations, or extremely large numbers of notes – and produced his *Etudes for player piano*.

In 1986 the Viennese firm Bösendorfer produced an instrument which, it is claimed, can reproduce every nuance of a performance. Optical sensors scan the keys, hammers, and pedals 800 times per second and the registered information is fed into a computer. It is stored on tape or disk and can be relayed back to the piano for 'performance'.

plectrum in music, a device for plucking a string instrument. For a guitar or lute, it may be worn on the finger, as a substitute fingernail; others are held between two fingers, for example to play the mandolin. The harpsichord employs mechanical plectra of quill or leather to pluck the strings.

Most plectra are hard, but soft felt plectra are also used to ease abrasion of the ball of the finger. A plucked sound can be simulated on a synthesizer by programming an instantaneous or rapid onset, followed by a rapid decay and longer reverberation.

plein jeu (French 'full play') in musical direction, the French equivalent of ➜ organo pieno)

Pleyel, Camille (1788–1855) French piano maker, publisher, and pianist. He succeeded his father, Ignaz Joseph ➜ Pleyel, in the family's piano-making business in 1824 and associated himself with Friedrich Kalkbrenner. He was the husband of the French pianist Marie Moke.

He studied music with his father and Jan Dus-

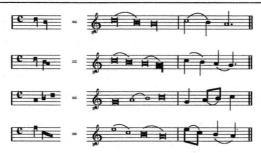

Various plicas (left) with literal and modern equivalents (right).

sek and published some piano pieces.

Pleyel, Ignaz Joseph (1757–1831) Austrian pianist, piano maker, and composer. After travelling widely as a conductor and kapellmeister (court music director), and composing a large number of popular pieces, he settled in Paris as a music publisher and in 1807 opened a piano factory. His son, Camille Pleyel (1788–1855), succeeded him in the family business.

He studied with Johann Baptist Vanhal and Joseph Haydn, and in 1777 became kapellmeister to Count Erdödy, who gave him leave for further study in Rome. In 1783, he moved to Strasbourg as vice-kapellmeister, succeeding Franz Xaver Richter as kapellmeister in 1789. Three years later he visited London as conductor of a rival series of concerts to those given by Johann Peter Salomon and Haydn. He settled in Paris in 1795, and in 1807 founded his piano factory.

Works OPERA *Die Fee Urgele* (produced at Eszterháza, 1776) and *Ifigenia en Aulide* (produced at Naples, 1785).

ORCHESTRAL AND ENSEMBLE 29 symphonies, five *sinfonie concertanti*, concertos; 45 string quartets, and much other chamber music.

plica (medieval Latin *plicare* 'to fold') an ornamental passing note indicated in medieval notation by a vertical stroke at the side of the note. Its length was determined by the length of the stroke, its pitch by the context. According to theorists, the plica should be sung with a kind of quavering in the throat, but its convenience as an abbreviation led to its frequent employment as a substitute for a written note.

Pli selon pli work for soprano and orchestra (based on sonnets by Stéphane Mallarmé) in five parts by Pierre ➤ Boulez. It was first performed at Donaueschingen on 20 October 1962.

Plummer, John (c.1410–c.1484) English composer. His surviving works consist of four antiphons for two and four voices, a Mass, *Omnipotens Pater*, and a Mass fragment.

He was a clerk of the Chapel Royal by 1441 and in 1444 became the first official master of its children. In about 1458 he became verger at St George's Chapel, Windsor, while continuing as a member of the Chapel Royal; he held the Windsor post until 1484.

pneuma (Greek 'breath') vocal ornament in ➤ plainsong, inserting long cadential phrases on the syllables of certain words, notably 'Alleluia'. The pneuma were also called by the Latin name of *jubili*, and they developed later into tropes (interpolations) and sequences. It is sometimes written *neuma*, by confusion with the word for a ➤ neume.

Pocahontas ballet by Elliott Carter, composed 1936–39 and first produced in New York on 24 May 1939. Pocahontas (1595–1617) was an American Indian princess who befriended the early settlers in America.

poco (Italian 'little') term used in musical notation, as in *poco crescendo* ('getting a little louder') or *crescendo poco a poco* ('getting louder little by little').

Poème de l'amour et de la mer, Poem of love and of the sea work for mezzo-soprano and orchestra by Ernest ➤ Chausson (text by M Bouchor), composed 1882–90 and revised in 1893. The work's three sections are *La fleur des eaux*, *Interlude*, and *La mort de l'amour* (with the closing section *Le temps de lilas*).

Poèmes pour Mi, Poems for Mi cycle of nine songs for soprano and piano by Messiaen (texts by composer), for his wife. It was first performed in Paris on 28 April 1937. An orchestral version was performed in Paris in 1946, conducted by Désormière. Mi was the composer's name for his first wife.

Poem of Ecstasy, Russian ***Poema ekstasa*** work for orchestra by Aleksandr ➤ Skriabin, composed 1905–08. It was first performed at New York, on 10 December 1908, and its first Russian performance was at St Petersburg, on 1 February 1909.

Poet's Echo, The cycle of six songs for high voice and piano by Benjamin Britten (texts by Pushkin), first performed in Moscow on 2 December 1965, with the soprano Galina Vishnevskaya and the conductor Rostropovich.

Pohjola's Daughter symphonic poem by Sibelius, Op. 49, composed in 1906 and based on an incident in the Finnish poem 'Kalevala'. It was first performed at St Petersburg on 29 December 1906.

poi (Italian 'then') term used in musical directions where some music section is to follow another in a way not made immediately obvious by the notation; for instance, after a repeat of an earlier section, *poi la coda* or *e poi la coda*.

pointillism in music, a form of 1950s ➤ serialism in which melody and harmony were replaced by complexes of isolated tones. Pointillism was inspired by Anton ➤ Webern and adopted by Olivier ➤ Messiaen, Pierre ➤ Boulez, Luigi ➤ Nono, Karlheinz ➤ Stockhausen, and Igor ➤ Stravinsky.

Although not strictly serial, the music of Iannis ➤ Xenakis and John ➤ Cage at this time was also pointillist in texture.

pointing in music, the distribution of the syllables of the Psalms in Anglican chant according to the verbal rhythm.

Poise, (Jean Alexandre) Ferdinand (1828–1892) French composer. He studied with Adam and others at the Paris Conservatory and in 1853 produced his first opera.

Works OPERA *Bonsoir Voisin* (1853), *Les Charmeurs* (1855), *Polichinelle* (1856), *Le Roi Don Pèdre*, *Le Jardinier galant* (1861), *Les Absents*, *Corricolo* (1868), *Les Trois Souhaits* (1861), *La Surprise de l'amour* (after Marivaux), *L'Amour médecin* (after Molière, 1880), *Les Deux Billets*, *Joli Gilles*, *Carmosine* (after Musset, produced in 1928); the oratorio *Cécile* (1888).

Poisoned Kiss, The or **The Empress and the Necromancer** opera by Vaughan Williams (libretto by Evelyn Sharp), produced at the Cambridge Arts Theatre, on 12 May 1936. Much of the score is a satire on various musical styles. The story concerns the magician Dipsacus, who long ago was abandoned by one-time love Persicaria. He plans revenge: to kill her son Amaryllus with a poisoned kiss from his daughter Tormentilla. But Amaryllus has the antidote and they all live happily ever after.

polacca (Italian 'polonaise') musical term often used more loosely for pieces with ➤ polonaise (Polish dance music in 3/4 time) rhythm, but not necessarily in polonaise form, in which case they are more aptly designated as *alla polacca*.

Polifemo opera by Giovanni Bononcini (libretto by Attilo Ariosti), produced at the Lietzenburg Palace, Berlin, in the summer of 1702.

poliphant or **polyphone** string instrument of the ➤ lute or ➤ cittern type but with anything from 25 to 40 strings, invented around 1600 by Daniel Farrant and played by Queen Elizabeth I.

'Polish' Symphony Tchaikovsky's third symphony, in D major, Op. 29, finished in August 1875 and produced at Moscow, on 19 November 1875. The finale is in ➤ polonaise rhythm.

Poliuto opera by Gaetano Donizetti (libretto devised by A Nourrit and written by Salvatore Cammarano, based on Corneille's tragedy *Polyeucte*). Though finished in 1838 for production at Naples, the opera was forbidden by censor; it was later produced in French as *Les Martyrs* (translation by Scribe) at the Opéra, Paris, on 1 April 1840. The story is set in 3rd-century Armenia. Poliuto is converted to Christianity, but is captured by Callistene, the high priest of Jupiter. His wife Paolina cannot convince him to renounce his faith, and joins him in death.

polka Bohemian dance in quick duple time (2/4). Originating in the 19th century, it became popular throughout Europe. The basic step is a hop followed by three short steps. The polka spread with German immigrants to the USA, becoming a style of Texas country music. It was also used by European composers, including Bedřich Smetana in *The Bartered Bride* (1866) and *Bohemian Dances* (1878), Antonín Dvořák, and others.

From about 1830 it became fashionable in European society.

Pollarolo, Antonio (1676–1746) Italian composer. He was a pupil of his father, Carlo ➤ Pollarolo. He became assistant maestro di cappella at St Mark's, Venice, in 1723, and maestro di cappella in 1740.

Works OPERA *Aristeo*, *Leucippo e Teonoe*, *Cosroe*, *I tre voti*, and ten others.

OTHER church music.

Pollarolo, Carlo Francesco (1653–1723) Italian organist and composer. He was a popular composer of operas in his day, writing over 80 in all, though only about 20 have survived. He was the father of Antonio ➤ Pollarolo.

He was taught by Giovanni Legrenzi at Venice, becoming a singer at St Mark's there in 1665, second organist in 1690, and assistant maestro di cappella in 1692. He was director of music at the Conservatorio degli Incurabili from 1696.

Works OPERA *Roderico* (1686), *La forza dela virtù* (1693), *Ottone* (1694), *Faramondo*, *Semiramide* (1713), *Marsia deluso*, *Ariodante* (1716), *Le pazzie degli amanti*, *Gl'inganni felici*, *Santa Genuinda* (with Violone and A Scarlatti, 1694), and many others, though most are lost.

OTHER twelve oratorios, organ music.

polonaise Polish dance in stately 3/4 time that was common in 18th-century Europe. The composer Frédéric ➤ Chopin developed the polonaise as a pianistic form.

Polonia symphonic prelude for orchestra by Edward Elgar, Op. 76, written for a concert given for the Polish Relief Fund, in London, on 6 July 1915. It was dedicated to ➤ Paderewski, and contains a quotation from his *Polish Fantasy*, as well as one from Chopin and the Polish National Anthem.

Polyeucte opera by Charles Gounod (libretto by Jules Barbier and Michel Carré, based on Corneille's drama). It was first produced at the Opéra, Paris, on 7 October 1878.

See also ➤ *Poliuto*.

polyphone alternative name for the ➤ poliphant, a musical instrument.

polyphony in music, when two or more lines of melody combine so that they fit well together. ➤ Counterpoint is another word that has a similar meaning.

Polyphony is also the ability of a synthesizer to play more than one note at a time. If the synthesizer can produce more than one type of sound – for example, a flute and a guitar – simultaneously, it is **multi-timbral**.

polyrhythm in music, a combination of different rhythmic formations.

polytonality in music, an overlapping of multiple parts in different keys, associated in particular with Darius ➤ Milhaud, whose miniature *Serenade* for orchestra (1917–22) combines up to six major keys. Two keys superimposed is bitonality.

The effect is akin to multiplexing, allowing the ear to fasten on any one line at will, but the combination effect is less coherent.

Pomo d'Oro, Il, The Golden Apple opera by Antonio ➤ Cesti (libretto by F Sbarra), produced in 1667 at the Carnival, in Vienna, for the wedding of the Emperor Leopold I and the Infanta Margherita of Spain. It was reputed to be the most expensive opera production ever mounted. In the story, Discord throws a golden apple, inscribed 'to the most beautiful', to Juno, Athena, and Venus. Paris judges Venus the most beautiful after she offers him Helen. There is disarray amongst the goddesses until Jupiter puts an end to the bickering.

Pomone opera by Robert Cambert (libretto by Pierre Perrin), produced at the Paris Opéra on 3 March 1671.

Pomp and Circumstance five military marches by Edward Elgar, Op. 39, originally intended as a set of six. The first contains, as a trio, the tune afterwards used in the *Coronation Ode* to the words 'Land of hope and glory'. The title of the set comes from *Othello*: 'pride, pomp and circumstance of glorious war'. Nos 1–4 were composed 1901–07, and No 5 in 1930.

pomposo (Italian 'pompous, stately') musical direction used for music of a sumptuous character.

Ponce, Manuel (1882–1948) Mexican composer. He is best known for his guitar music, performed by Segovia and others.

He learnt music from his sister at first, became cathedral organist at Aguas Calientes, and at 14 composed a gavotte which was later made famous by the dancer Argentina. He entered the National Conservatory at Mexico City and in 1905 went to Europe for further study with Enrico Bossi at Bologna and Martin Krause in Berlin. In 1906, he returned home and became professor at the National Conservatory. He lived in Havana 1915–18 and at the age of 43 went to Paris to take a composition course with Paul Dukas.

Works ORCHESTRAL symphonic triptych *Chapultepec* (1929), *Canto y danza de los antiguos Mexicanos* (1933), *Poema elegiaco*, *Ferial* for orchestra (1940); piano concerto; violin concerto (1943); concerto for guitar and chamber orchestra (1941); three Tagore songs with orchestra.

CHAMBER *Sonata en duo* for violin and viola, two Mexican Rhapsodies and many other piano works, numerous songs.

Ponchielli, Amilcare (1834–1886) Italian composer. His masterpiece, *La Gioconda*, based on Victor Hugo's play *Angelo*, was produced at La Scala, Milan, in 1876; its inspired melody and strong dramatic characterization established him as a worthy successor to Verdi.

Ponchielli was born near Cremona. He studied at the Milan Conservatory 1843–54 and produced his first opera, based on Manzoni's famous novel *I promessi sposi*, at Cremona in 1856. In 1881 he was appointed maestro di cappella at Bergamo Cathedral.

Works OPERA *I promessi sposi* (1856), *La Savoiarda* (1861), *Roderico* (1863), *Bertrand de Born*, *Il parlatore eterno* (1873), *I Lituani* (Aldona), *Gioconda* (after Hugo's *Angelo*, 1876), *Il figliuol prodigo* (1880), *Marion Delorme* (on Hugo's play, 1885), *I Mori di Valenza* (unfinished; produced in 1914).

BALLET *Le due gemelle* and *Clarina*.

CANTATAS cantatas for the reception of the remains of Donizetti and Mayr at Bergamo and in memory of Garibaldi.

Poniatowski, Rotondo (1816–1873) Polish composer and tenor. He studied at the Liceo Musicale at Florence and under Ceccherini. He sang at the Teatro della Pergola there and produced his first opera there in 1839, singing the title part. After the 1848 Revolution he settled in Paris, but after the Franco-Prussian war he followed Napoleon III to England, in 1871.

Works OPERA *Giovanni da Procida* (1838), *Don Desiderio* (1840), *Ruy Blas* (after Hugo), *Bonifazio de' Geremei* (*I Lambertazzi*, 1843), *Malek Adel* (1846), *Esmeralda* (after Hugo's *Notre-Dame de Paris*, 1847), *La sposa d'Abido* (after Byron's *Bride of Abydos*), *Pierre de Médicis* (1860), *Gelmina* (1872), and others.

OTHER Mass in F major.

Ponte, Lorenzo da Italian poet and librettist. See Lorenzo ➤ **Da Ponte**.

ponticello (Italian 'little bridge') in string instruments, the bridge over which the strings are stretched to keep clear of the body of the instrument. The direction *sul ponticello*, 'on the bridge', indicates that the bow is to be drawn close to the bridge, which results in a peculiar nasal tone.

pont-neuf (French 'new bridge') satirical song of the 18th century similar to the ➤ **vaudeville**, sung in public mainly on the Pont-Neuf in Paris.

Poole, Geoffrey (1949–) English composer. He studied at Southampton University with Jonathan Harvey and with Goehr at Leeds, and he was senior lecturer at Manchester University from 1989. He received commissions from the Hallé Orchestra and London Sinfonietta.

Works CHAMBER *Fragments* for strings (1974); *Crow Tyrannosaurus* for soprano and ensemble (1975); *Chamber Concerto* (1979); *Machaut-Layers* for voice and ensemble (1980); *Sailing with Archangels* for wind band (1990); two string quartets (1983, 1990); *In Beauty May I Walk* vocal duo with strings (1990); *The Magnification of the Virgin* for female consort and twelve instruments (1992).

ORCHESTRAL AND CHORAL *Visions* for orchestra (1975); music theatre *Biggs v Stomp does it again and again…* (1981); symphonic poem *The Net and Aphrodite* (1982); *Cummings Choruses* (1985); oratorio *Blackbird* (1993).

Poot, Marcel (1901–1988) Belgian composer. He became interested early in film, radio, and jazz music, and in 1935 founded the group known as Les Synthétistes.

He studied at the Brussels Conservatory. In 1930 he won the Rubens Prize and went to Paris to study with Paul Abraham Dukas. On his return he held several teaching posts, including at the Brussels Conservatory, of which he became director in 1949.

Works OPERA AND STAGE the operas *Het Ingebeeld Eiland* (1925), *Het Vrouwtje van Stavoren* (1928), and *Moretus* (1944); ballets *Paris in verlegengheid* (1925) and *Pygmalion* (1951).

CHORAL AND ORCHESTRAL oratorios *Le Dit du routier* and *Icaros*; six symphonies (1929–78) and other orchestral works.

OTHER chamber music and other pieces.

Pope, Alexander (1688–1744) English poet. His works inspired Handel's ➤ *Acis and Galatea*, ➤ *Jephtha*, and ➤ *Semele*.

pop music any contemporary music not categorizable as jazz or classical. Pop music contains strong rhythms of African origin, simple harmonic structures often repeated to strophic melodies, and the use of electrically amplified instruments. Pop music generically includes the areas of rock, country and western, rhythm and blues, soul, and others. Pop became distinct from folk music with the development of sound-recording techniques; electronic amplification and other technological innovations have played a large part in the creation of new styles. The traditional format is a song of roughly three minutes with verse, chorus, and middle eight bars.

history Before 1920 the singer Al Jolson was one of the first recording stars. Ragtime was still popular. In the 1920s, in the USA Paul Whiteman and his orchestra played jazz that could be danced to, country singer Jimmie Rodgers reached a new record-buying public, and the ➤ **blues** were flourishing; in the UK popular singers included Al Bowlly, born in Mozambique. The 1930s saw crooner Bing Crosby and vocal groups such as the Andrews Sisters as alternatives to swing bands. Rhythm and blues evolved in the USA in the 1940s, while Frank Sinatra was a teen idol and Glenn Miller played dance music. The UK preferred such singers as Vera Lynn.

1950s In the USA in the early 1950s doo-wop group vocalizing preceded rockabilly, the earliest form of rock and roll with its folk roots still in evidence. The main rock and roll singers at this time were Elvis Presley, Little Richard, Chuck Berry, and the Everly Brothers, and US records were dominating the charts. At the end of the 1950s the Motown label made its first impact with hits by the Miracles and Marvelettes, and a dance craze, 'the twist', enjoyed a brief popularity.

1960s In 1962, the Beatles emerged as leaders of the new 'beat' groups and, while restoring the excitement of early rock, introduced a new element of sophistication. British rhythm and blues developed from 1963, the main groups being The Animals and The Rolling Stones. Bob Dylan's mature, poetic songwriting achieved commercial success, although British groups largely dominated the US charts. Psychedelic rock grew in popularity on both sides of the Atlantic with groups such as The Doors and Pink Floyd. Jimi Hendrix produced a new and exciting improvisational rhythm and blues which achieved world success, paving the way for the later popularity of such 'heavy' rock groups as Led Zeppelin. Frank Zappa's Mothers of Invention fused elements of jazz, symphonic, and avant-garde classical music. Conventional pop during this time relied on gospel-derived soul music, and Motown groups including The Supremes and The Four Tops.

1970s By the end of 1971, after the disbandment of the Beatles, and the deaths of Jimi Hendrix, Janis Joplin, and Jim Morrison of The Doors, it seemed that pop music was changing dramatically. The first half of the decade produced glam rock, most notably by David Bowie, heavy metal, and disco. Reggae music from Jamaica also gained wide popularity. From 1976 punk was highly successful, a harsh and aggressive style best demonstrated by the Sex Pistols and The Clash. The US term New Wave included bands not entirely within the punk idiom, such as Talking Heads and Elvis Costello.

1980s Dance music developed regional US variants, most notably hip-hop in New York and house in Chicago. Live audiences grew, leading to 'stadium rock' (U2, Bruce Springsteen) and increasingly elaborate stage performances (Michael Jackson, Prince, and Madonna). An interest in world music sparked new fusions.

1990s Rap, hard rock, and heavy metal were the main genres in the USA at the start of the decade. On the UK indie scene, guitar and dance music were increasingly merged, notably by Manchester bands including the Stone Roses and the Happy Mondays, who followed on from the original and musically innovative Smiths. Minimalist techno dance music gained popularity; in UK clubs **jungle** crossed this with reggae. Grunge music emerged from Seattle, Washington, with bands including Nirvana. The mid-1990s saw a revived interest in British bands, centred on groups such as Oasis and Blur; Portishead and other English groups pioneered **trip-hop**. The late 1990s saw a continuation of the popularity of a large range of pop music genres, including **hip-hop**, by artists such as Lauryn Hill, **rap** and **R & B** (rhythm and blues), with US artists such as Dr Dre and Macy Gray finding an audience in the USA and the UK. Artists who merged country with pop, such as Garth Brooks and Shania Twain, achieved great commercial success. Aimed at a young audience, commercial pop music became increasingly popular, and UK groups such as Take That, the Spice Girls, Boyzone, and Westlife, as well as US artists such as Britney Spears, gained success.

recent developments Computer-based distribution of music has played an important role since the turn of the century, with bands such as Arctic Monkeys gaining popularity through this route. Rock bands including Coldplay, the Kaiser Chiefs and Franz Ferdinand have been popular in the UK, while the US scene has been dominated by rap and hip-hop artists such as Eminem and 50 Cent.

Porgy and Bess classic US folk opera written in 1935 by George and Ira Gershwin, based on the novel *Porgy* (1925) by DuBose Heyward, a story of the black residents of Catfish Row in Charleston, South Carolina.

Poro, rè dell' Indie, Porus, King of the Indies opera by Handel (librettist unknown, altered from Metastasio's *Alessandro nell' Indie*), produced in London, at the King's Theatre, Haymarket, on 2 February 1731. In the story, Porus faces defeat at the hands of Alexander the Great, fearing especially that he will lose his love, Cleophis, to the invader. Jealousy and passion ensue before Alexander realizes the depth of feeling between Porus and Cleophis, and blesses their union.

Porpora, Nicola Antonio (1686–1768) Italian composer and singing teacher. His works are chiefly vocal pieces, and include about 50 operas, as well as cantatas and oratorios. He travelled extensively in Europe as a teacher and conductor.

Porpora was born at Naples, and studied there under Gaetano Greco and his assistants, M Giordano and O Campanile at the Conservatorio dei Poveri di Gesù Cristo, where his first opera, *Agrippina*, was produced in 1708. At first maestro di cappella to the Imperial Commandant in Naples, Prince Philip of Hesse-Darmstadt, Porpora was appointed singing teacher at the Conservatorio di Sant' Onofrio there in 1715, and ten years later became maestro at the Conservatorio degli Incurabili in Venice.

Among his pupils were the castrati singers Farinelli and Caffarelli, and, briefly, the composer Johann Hasse. Travelling as an opera conductor, he rivalled Handel in London 1733–36 and Hasse in Dresden 1748–52. In Vienna, Haydn was his pupil-valet. Porpora finally returned to Naples in 1760; he taught for a year at the Conservatorio di Sant' Onofrio, but after that fell on hard times and died in extreme poverty.

Works OPERA about 50 operas, including *Basilio* (1713), *Berenice* (1718), *Flavio Anicio Olibrio*, *Faramondo* (1719), *Eumene*, *Amare per regnare* (1723), *Semiramide* (1724), *Semiramide riconosciuta*, *L'Imeneo* (1726), *Adelaide, Siface, Mitridate* (1730), *Annibale* (1731), *Il trionfo di Camilla, Arianna* (1733), *Temistocle* (1743), *Filandro*.

CHORAL ten oratorios, including *Il martirio di Santa Eugenia* (1721); cantatas; Masses, motets,

duets on the Passion and other church music.
OTHER violin sonatas, keyboard music.

Porta, Costanzo (c.1529–1601) Italian monk and composer. He was a pupil of Adrian Willaert at Venice. He took holy orders and became choirmaster at Osimo near Ancona 1552–64, then went to Padua to take up a similar post at the Cappella Antoniana, the church of the Minorite order to which he belonged. He left for a time to work at Ravenna 1567–74, then at Loreto 1574–80. He returned to Ravenna and lived there 1580–89.

Works CHURCH MUSIC 15 Masses, 200 motets, psalms, hymns, introits, and other church music.
CHAMBER MUSIC five books of madrigals (1555–86).

Porta, Giovanni (c.1690–1755) Italian composer. He worked in Rome 1706–16 in the service of Cardinal Ottoboni, then at the Conservatorio della pietà in Venice. He also visited London, where his opera *Numitore* was produced in 1720. From 1736 to his death he was kapellmeister to the court in Munich.

Works OPERA over 30 operas, including *Arianna* (1723), *Antigono* (1724), *Ulisse* (1725), and *Semiramide* (1733).
CHORAL oratorios, cantatas, 19 Masses and other church music.

portamento (Italian 'carrying') in singing and on string instruments, an expressive device in which one note is 'carried' to the next by a slide, without an interruption of tone production. It is sometimes indicated by a ➔ slur connecting the two notes, but is usually freely interpreted by a performer. It was used more frequently in the first half of the 20th century and earlier, when musical expression was more pronounced.

portative organ small organ with a single keyboard and one range of pipes, which can be carried, placed on a table, or suspended from the shoulder by a strap. It is often represented in medieval and Renaissance paintings.

portato (Italian 'carried') in music, a type of articulation midway between ➔ staccato (detached) and ➔ legato (tied). It is indicated by a ➔ slur over the notes, each of which is marked by a staccato dot.

Porter, Andrew (1928–) English music critic and scholar. He is noted for his research on Verdi and has prepared for performance much material for *Don Carlos* which Verdi discarded at the first production in 1867. He also worked on several translations of Verdi's libretti. His translation of Wagner's *Ring* was heard at the Coliseum, London, in 1973, and his version of the *Parsifal* libretto was also given there in 1986. He has been a critic for the *Observer* since 1992.

He studied at Oxford University and worked for various newspapers and journals from 1949, editing the *Musical Times* 1960–67. Five volumes of his criticism were published 1974–91.

Porter, (William) Quincy (1897–1966) US composer. He studied at Yale University and School of Music with Horatio Parker and D S Smith, later with Ernest Bloch and with Vincent d'Indy in Paris. He taught extensively; at the Cleveland Institute of Music for two periods during 1922–32, at Vassar College in Poughkeepsie, New York, 1932–38, and at the New England Conservatory in Boston from 1938. He also played viola in various string quartets.

Works ORCHESTRAL incidental music for Shakespeare's *Antony and Cleopatra* (1934) and T S Eliot's *Sweeney Agonistes* (1933); the symphony *Poem and Dance* for orchestra; *Ukrainian Suite* for strings (1925); *Dance in Three Time* for chamber orchestra (1937); viola concerto, harpsichord concerto (1959), concerto for two pianos.
CHAMBER three Greek Mimes for voices, string quartet, and percussion; nine string quartets (1923–58); two violin and piano sonatas, suite for viola solo.

Porter, Walter (c.1588–1659) English composer. He became a Gentleman of the Chapel Royal in London in 1617. At some time, probably earlier, he was a pupil of the Italian composer Monteverdi. In 1639, he became choirmaster at Westminster Abbey and when the choral service was suppressed in 1644, he came under the patronage of Sir Edward Spencer.

Works VOCAL motets for two voices and instruments; psalms (George Sandys' paraphrases) for two voices and organ; madrigals and airs for voices and instruments (published 1632).

Portinaro, Francesco (c.1520–after 1578) Italian composer. He was associated with the Accademia degli Elevati at Padua in 1557, and later with the d'Este family at Ferrara and Tivoli. His three books of motets and six of madrigals were published at Venice.

Portman, Richard (died c.1655) English organist and composer. He was a pupil of Orlando Gibbons, and succeeded Thomas Day as organist of Westminster Abbey, London, in 1633. Like Walter ➔ Porter, who was choirmaster, he lost his post with the suppression of the choral service in 1644 and became a music teacher.

Works CHORAL services, anthems; *Dialogue of the Prodigal Son* for two voices and chorus, meditation; *The Soules Life, exercising itself in the sweet fields of divine meditation*.
OTHER harpsichord music, and other pieces.

Portsmouth Point concert overture by William Turner Walton, inspired by Rowlandson's drawing and first performed at the International Society for Contemporary Music (ISCM) Festival,

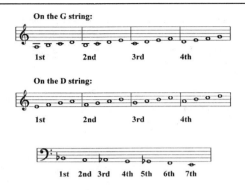

On the G string:

1st   2nd   3rd   4th

On the D string:

1st   2nd   3rd   4th

1st 2nd 3rd   4th 5th   6th   7th

Various positions on a string instrument (top and centre) and on the trombone (bottom).

Zurich, on 22 June 1926.

Portugal, Marcus Antonio da Fonseca (1762–1830), Italian **Portogallo** Portuguese composer. He wrote about 50 operas, both Portuguese and Italian. He was court music director at Lisbon, followed the court when it moved to Brazil in 1810, and continued to enjoy success as a composer at Rio de Janeiro.

He was educated at the Patriarchal Seminary at Lisbon, where later he became cantor and organist, and learnt music from Joño de Sousa Carvalho. He was also a theatre conductor and in 1785 produced his first stage work. In 1792, he went to Naples and began to write Italian operas in great numbers. In 1800, he returned to Lisbon to become director of the San Carlos Theatre, where he continued to write for the stage. In 1807, the French invasion drove the court to Brazil, and he followed it in 1810, but was unable to return with it in 1821, being incapacitated by a stroke.

Works OPERA 22 Portuguese operas, including *Licença pastoril, A Castanheira*; about 40 Italian operas, including *La confusione nata della somiglianza* (1793), *Demofoonte* (1794), *Lo spazzacamino principe*, *La donna di genio volubile* (1796), *Fernando nel Messico* (1799), *Alceste, La morte di Semiramide* (1801), *Non irritare le donne, L'oro non compra amore* (1804), *Il trionfo di Clelia* (1802), *Il diavolo a quattro, La pazza giornata* (on Beaumarchais's *La Folle Journée* [*Figaro*, 1799]).

CHORAL church music; cantata *La speranza*; songs.

Posaune German name for the ➤ **trombone**, a musical instrument.

positif (French 'choir organ') French name for the third manual (keyboard) of an ➤ **organ.**

position in harmony in music, the spacing of a chord. For example, 'root position' indicates that the ➤ **root** of the chord is in the bass; 'open-position harmony' indicates a chord in which the notes are spread out, as opposed to 'closed-position harmony', in which every note of the harmony is filled within an octave.

position in music, on a stringed instrument, one of a few specific areas on the ➤ **fingerboard** where the left hand is placed in order for the player to find a set of notes. On the trombone, 'position' refers to the placement of the slide for playing different notes.

In violin positions, first position is furthest away, nearest to the ➤ **scroll** end of the fingerboard. Second and third position are closer in, nearer to the body of the instrument.

positive organ in music, a small chamber ➤ **organ.**

posthorn brass instrument akin to the bugle rather than the horn, used by postillions (coachmen) in the 18th and early 19th centuries. It has no valves and can therefore produce only the natural harmonics, which are coarse and penetrating in tone.

The posthorn is hardly ever used in serious music, but Johann Sebastian Bach imitated it on the harpsichord in his ➤ **capriccio** on his brother's departure, and Mozart scored parts for two in his *German Dances* K605 and in his *Posthorn Serenade* K320.

Postillon de Lonjumeau, Le, The Coachman of Lonjumeau opera by Adolphe Charles Adam (libretto by A de Leuven and L L Brunswick), produced in Paris at the Opéra-Comique, on 13 October 1836. The story is about the coachman Chapelou, who abandons his bride, Madeleine, to join the Paris Opéra. Meeting her ten years later, he does not recognize her, and asks her to marry him; then she reveals her identity.

postlude or **postludium** in music, a composition intended as the final piece, especially an organ piece played after a service. It is the opposite of a ➤ **prelude**.

postmodernism in music, a style of composition in which the composer draws on the influence of a variety of musical periods and styles. The term is used specifically to describe the music of certain 20th-century composers. Igor ➤ **Stravinsky** was the first great postmodernist, working in neoclassical and serial styles, as well as a more traditional, yet progressive Russian style. Postmodernism began to blossom after the period of ➤ **integral serialism** in the 1950s, when composers reacted against the rigid restrictions imposed by that technique (of fixing the parameters of every compositional component: pitch, rhythm, dynamics, duration, and so on). Contemporary postmodernist composers include Peter Maxwell ➤ **Davies**, who writes in a wide range of styles, influenced by elements of music from the 16th-century masters right through to the modern techniques of the ➤ **twelve-tone system**.

Poston, Elizabeth (1905–1987) English composer. She was a student at the Royal College of Music in London and studied piano with Harold Samuel. In 1925 she published seven songs and her prize work, a violin and piano sonata, was broadcast in 1927. From 1940 to 1945 she was director of music in the foreign service of the British Broadcasting Corporation (BBC).

Works ORCHESTRAL AND CHORAL music for radio productions; choral music.

OTHER songs.

pot-pourri (French 'rotten pot') in music, a medley of themes from various musical works, especially operas or operettas. The term is identical to the Spanish *olla podrida*.

Potter (Philip) Cipriani (Hambley) (1792–1871) English pianist and composer. He had a reputation as a fine pianist. His compositions were largely instrumental.

He studied under Thomas Attwood, John Callcott, and William Crotch, and had finishing piano lessons from Joseph Woelfl 1805–10. He became an associate of the Philharmonic Society on its foundation in 1813 and a member when he reached majority. In 1816 he wrote an overture for it, also playing the piano there that year in a sextet of his own. In 1817 he went to Vienna, where he studied with Aloys Förster and met Beethoven. After visiting Germany and Italy he returned to London in 1821, became professor of piano at the Royal Academy of Music the next year, and became principal in succession to Crotch in 1832, but resigned in 1859. In 1855, Wagner conducted one of his symphonies with the Philharmonic Society.

Works ORCHESTRAL nine symphonies (1819–34), four overtures for orchestra; three piano concertos (1832–35), Concertante for cello and orchestra; three piano trios, sextet for piano and strings.

CHORAL WITH ORCHESTRA cantata *Medora e Corrado*, Ode to Harmony.

CHAMBER horn and piano sonata, duo for violin and piano, two sonatas, *The Enigma* ('Variations in the style of five eminent artists', 1825), and other music for piano, songs.

Pougin, (François Auguste) Arthur (Eugène Paroisse-) (1834–1921) French musicologist. He had little general education, but studied violin with Delphin Alard and theory with Réber at the Paris Conservatory. After working at various theatres as a violinist and conductor, he began to write biographical articles on 18th-century French musicians and gradually made his way by writing for papers, contributing to dictionaries, and writing music criticism. He wrote biographies of Verdi, Campra, Meyerbeer, Vincent Wallace, Bellini, Rossini, Auber, Adam, Etienne Méhul, and studies of French music history.

Poule, La, The Hen the nickname of a symphony by Haydn, no. 83, in G minor (no. 2 of the 'Paris' symphonies), composed in 1786.

Poulenc, Francis Jean Marcel (1899–1963) French composer and pianist. A self-taught composer of witty and irreverent music, he was a member of the group of French composers known as ➤ **Les Six**. Among his many works are the operas *Les Mamelles de Tirésias/The Breasts of Tiresias* (1947) and *Dialogues des Carmélites/Dialogues of the Carmelites* (1957), and the ballet *Les Biches/The Little Darlings* (1923).

Poulenc was born in Paris. He received a classical education, and took piano lessons from Ricardo Viñes. When he was called up for war service in 1918 he had already written one or two works under the influence of Erik Satie, and on being demobilized he joined the group of 'Les Six' with Auric, Durey, Honegger, Milhaud, and Tailleferre, and thus came for a time under the influence of Jean Cocteau, notably with his three songs *Cocardes* in 1919. A commission from Diaghilev led to the ballet score *Les Biches*, influenced by the neoclassical brilliance of Stravinsky but also containing Poulenc's characteristic wit, charm, and melancholy. Similar traits are found in his great series of songs 1919–60, settings of poems by Apollinaire, Ronsard, Eluard, Colette, and Vilmorin.

Works STAGE opera *Dialogues des Carmélites* (1957); comic opera *Les Mamelles de Tirésias* (libretto by Guillaume Apollinaire, 1947), monodrama *La voix humaine* (1959).

CHORAL Mass in G minor (1937) and cantata *Figure humaine* (Paul Eluard); choruses (unaccompanied), *Gloria* (1959).

ORCHESTRAL *Concert champêtre* for harpsichord and orchestra (1928), concerto in D minor for two pianos and orchestra (1932), organ concerto (1938); piano concerto (1949).

CHAMBER much music for wind instruments, including trio for oboe, bassoon, and piano (1926); also violin and piano and cello and piano sonatas (1943, 1948).

PIANO *Mouvements perpétuels* (1918), *Nocturnes* (1929–38), and other pieces.

SONGS 'Tel jour, telle nuit' (1937), 'Fiançailles pour rire' (1939), and other songs.

poussé (French 'pushed') in the playing of string instruments, the upstroke of the bow, as opposed to the *tiré* ('drawn'), the downstroke.

Pousseur, Henri (1929–) Belgian composer. His works investigate computer and aleatory techniques, influenced by Luciano Berio and Stockhausen. He was strongly influenced by post-Webernian ➤ serialism, one of his earliest works being *Quintet in Memory of Webern*. His later music makes use of open forms, where the performer has freedom to decide the order of the musical material (for example, *Mobile* for two pianos and *Caracteres* for piano solo).

Pousseur was born at Malmedy, in eastern Belgium. He studied at Brussels Conservatory and took private composition lessons from André Souris and Pierre Boulez. In 1958 he founded a studio for electronic music in Brussels. He lectured at Darmstadt 1957–67, Cologne, and the State University of New York, Buffalo, 1966–69. He was appointed professor of composition at Liège Conservatory in 1971.

Works STAGE the operas *Votre Faust* (1969) and *Die Erprobung des Petrus Hebraïcus* (1974); *Schoenbergs Gegenwart* for actors, singers, and instruments (1974); chamber opera *Leçons d'enfer* (1991).

CHAMBER *Trois Chants sacrés* for soprano and string trio; *Symphonies* for 15 solo instruments; *Modes* for string quartet; quintet to the memory of Webern (1955); *Répons* for seven musicians (1960); *Mobile* for two pianos.

ORCHESTRAL *Couleurs croisées* for orchestra (1967); *L'effacement du Prince Igor* for orchestra (1971); *Chronique illustrée* for baritone and orchestra (1976); *Nuits des Nuits* for orchestra (1985).

ELECTRONIC WITH VOICE AND ORCHESTRA *Seismographs* for magnetic tape; *Scambi* for tape (1957); *Rimes pour différentes sources sonores* for orchestra and tape (1959); *Portrait de Votre Faust* for soloists, instruments, and tape (1966); *Système des paraboles*, seven tape studies (1972); *Agonie* for voices and electronics (1981); *Déclarations d'Orage* for soloists, tape, and orchestra (1989).

Powell, Mel (1923–1998) US composer. He played piano in dance bands, and later studied with Johann Wagenaar, Ernst Toch, and Paul Hindemith. He founded an electronic music studio at Yale in 1960. He was Dean of Music at the California Institute of Arts 1969–75.

Works ORCHESTRAL *Stanzas* for orchestra (1957); the concerto *Duplicates* for two pianos and orchestra (1990). *Setting* for cello and orchestra.

CHAMBER *Filigree Setting* for string quartet (1959); string quartet (1982).

ELECTRONIC *Immobiles* 1–5 for tape and orchestra (1967–69); *Computer Prelude* (1988).

Power, Leonel (c.1375–1445) English composer and theorist. He wrote a treatise on the singing of descant (a high-pitched line for one or more sopranos added above the normal soprano melody of a hymn tune) and composed Masses, including *Alma redemptoris*, motets, and other church music.

Powers, Anthony (1953–) English composer. He studied at Oxford University, in Paris with Nadia Boulanger, and at York University with David Blake. He has taught at Dartington College of Arts and Exeter University, both in Devon.

Works VOICE WITH INSTRUMENTS *Souvenirs de voyage* for soprano and piano (1979), *The Winter Festival*, for mezzo and nine instruments (1985).

CHAMBER *Another Part of the Island* for ensemble (1980); *Chamber Concerto* (1984); *Music for Strings* (1984); *Vespers* for 21 solo strings (1986); two piano sonatas (1983, 1986); string quartet (1987); 2nd string quartet (1991).

STAGE opera *The Search for the Simorgh* (1981); music theatre *A Sussex Carol* (1982).

ORCHESTRAL *Stone, Water, Stars* for orchestra (1987); Horn concerto (1989); Cello concerto (1990).

praeludium see ➤ prelude.

'Prague' Symphony Mozart's symphony in D major, K504, composed in Vienna in December 1786 and performed in Prague, on 19 January 1787, during a visit for the production there of *Le nozze di Figaro*.

Pralltriller in musical ornamentation, the rapid repetition of a note, with a note a degree higher in between.

Pré aux clercs, Le, *The Scholars' Meadow* opera by Ferdinand Hérold (libretto by F A E de Planard), produced a the Opéra-Comique, Paris, on 15 December 1832. In the story, King Henry of Navarre wants Isabelle, a friend of Queen Marguerite, to marry Comminge even though she loves Mergy. Marguerite arranges for the couple's escape and attends their wedding, then Mergy kills Comminge in a duel.

The notation for pralltrillers on F and G, and the approximate notation of each.

Preciosa play with music by Weber (libretto by P A Wolff, based on Cervantes's story *La Gitanella*), produced in Berlin at the Opera House on 15 March 1821.

precipitando (Italian 'precipitately') musical direction indicating that an *accelerando* (gradual increase in speed) is to be made to increase in pace very rapidly.

prelude in music, a composition intended as the preface to further music, especially preceding a ➤ **fugue**, forming the opening piece of a ➤ **suite**, or setting the mood for a stage work, as in Richard Wagner's *Lohengrin*. As used by Frédéric Chopin, a prelude is a short self-contained piano work.

A prelude is often rhetorical in style, mixing fast runs and sustained chords. It thereby allows the musicians to form an aural picture of the sound quality of the auditorium. In orchestra concerts the ➤ **overture** fulfils a similar role.

Prélude à l'Après-midi d'un faune, Prelude to 'The Afternoon of a Faun' an orchestral piece by ➤ **Debussy** intended as a musical introduction to Stéphane Mallarmé's poem of that name, composed 1892–94 and first performed in Paris, at the Société Nationale, on 23 December 1894.

Ballet on this work (choreographed by Vaslav Nizhinsky), produced at the Théâtre du Châtelet, Paris, on 29 May 1912.

Préludes two sets of piano pieces, twelve in each, by Debussy, composed 1910–13. The second set includes quotes from the folk song 'Au clair de la lune' (7), 'God save the King' (9), and a few notes of the *Marseillaise* (12).

The first set includes: 1. *Danseuses de Delphes/ Dancing Women of Delphi*; 2. *Voiles/Sails*; 3. *Le Vent dans la plaine/The wind in the plain*; 4. *Les Sons et les parfums tournent dans l'air du soir/ Sounds and scents whirl in the evening air* (a quotation from Baudelaire); 5. *Les Collines d'Anacapri/The hills of Anacapri*; 6. *Des Pas sur la neige/ Footprints in the snow*; 7. *Ce qu'a vu le vent d'Ouest/What the West Wind saw*; 8. *La Fille aux cheveux de lin/The Flaxen-haired Girl* (based on a Scottish song by Leconte de Lisle); 9. *La Sérénade interrompue/The interrupted serenade*; 10. *La Cathédrale engloutie/The Submerged Cathedral* (on the old Breton tale of the sunken city of Ys);

11. *La Danse de Puck/Puck's Dance* (after Shakespeare's *Midsummer Night's Dream*); 12. *Minstrels* ('music-hall artists, not troubadours').

The second set includes: 1. *Brouillards/Mists*; 2. *Feuilles mortes/Dead Leaves*; 3. *La Puerta del Vino* (a gate at Granada); 4. *Les Fées sont d'exquises danseuses/The Fairies are exquisite Dancers*; 5. *Bruyères/Heather*; 6. *General Lavine-eccentric* (a music-hall character); 7. *La Terrasse des audiences du clair de lune/The Terrace of the Moonlight Audiences* (a reference to an account of George V's Durbar in 1912; the piece contains a quotation of the folk song 'Au clair de la lune'); 8. *Ondine* (Water-spirit maiden of 19th-century story); 9. *Hommage à S Pickwick Esq., PPMPC* (after Dickens; the piece quotes *God save the King* in the bass); 10. *Canope* (a Canopic jar holding the ashes of a dead lover); 11. *Les Tierces alternées/Alternating Thirds*; 12. *Feux d'artifice/ Fireworks* (quoting a few notes of the *Marseillaise* at the end).

Préludes, Les symphonic poem by Liszt, composed in 1848, revised in the early 1850s, and first performed at Weimar on 28 February 1854. The title is taken from a poem by Alphonse Lamartine, with which, in fact, the music has no connection.

preparation in harmony, term used for a ➤ **chord**, one note of which will create a dissonance in the chord that follows.

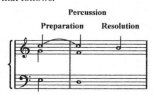

In this example the top voice (C) is prepared for dissonance and resolution.

prepared piano piano altered in such a way as to produce a different ➤ **timbre** or special effects. The concept was introduced by Henry ➤ **Cowell**; John ➤ **Cage** developed and popularized the technique, producing novel sounds by placing objects on the strings, as in his *Bacchanale* (1940).

prestissimo (Italian 'extremely fast') term used in musical notation, at the greatest possible speed; faster than ➤ **presto**.

presto (Italian 'quick') in music, a tempo marking meaning very quick. 'Prestissimo' means extremely fast.

Preston, Thomas (died c.1563) English composer. He was probably organist and master of the choristers, Magdalen College, Oxford, and is recorded as having played at Windsor Chapel in 1558 and 1559. He wrote a large amount of organ music for the Latin rite, including the Proper of the Mass for Easter Day (incomplete).

Prêtre, Georges (1924–) French conductor. He studied at Douai (south of Lille) and in Paris, making his debut in 1946 at the Paris Opéra-Comique; he was music director there 1956–59. He made his London debut in 1961 and his New York Metropolitan Opera debut in 1964. He made frequent performances and recordings with Maria Callas. In 1959, he conducted the first performance of Francis Poulenc's *La voix humaine*.

Preussisches Märchen, Prussian Tales ballet-opera by Boris ➤ **Blacher** (libretto by H von Cramer). It was composed in 1949 and produced at Berlin, on 23 September 1952.

Prévost d'Exiles, Antoine François (1697–1763) French novelist whose works, particularly *Manot Lescaut*, formed the basis for several musical works, inlcuding Hans Werner Henze's ➤ **Boulevard Solitude**, Jules Massenet's ➤ **Manon**, and operas by Jacques Halévy, Daniel Auber, and Giacomo Puccini (all entitled ➤ **Manon Lescaut**).

Prey, Claude (1925–) French composer. He wrote the chamber opera *Le coeur révelateur* in 1962, after Poe's *The Tell-Tale Heart*, and is best known for the operas *Les liaisons dangereuses* (1974) and *Le rouge et le noir* (1989). He studied with Milhaud and Messiaen at the Paris Conservatory.

Works STAGE chamber opera *Le coeur révelateur* (after Poe's *The Tell-Tale Heart*, 1962); the operas *Les liaisons dangereuses* (1974) and *Le rouge et le noir* (1989); *La grand mère française* (1976); *Lunedi bleue* (1982), *Pauline* (1983), and *Sommaire Soleil* (1990).

Price, Curtis (Alexander) (1945–) US musicologist. He became professor at King's College, London, in 1988, and principal of the Royal Academy of Music in 1995. Early English stage music has been at the centre of his studies; he published *Henry Purcell and the London Stage* in 1984 and edited *Dido and Aeneas* in 1986. Other titles include *Italian Opera and Arson in Late 18th-Century London* (1989) and *The Early Baroque Era* (editor, 1993). He studied at Harvard 1968–74 and taught at Washington University, St Louis, 1974–81. In 2005 he was made an honorary KBE.

prick-song written, as opposed to improvised, music. In the 15th to 18th centuries, the verb 'to prick' was used to mean 'to write notes'.

Prigione di Edimburgo, La, *Edinburgh Gaol* opera by Federico Ricci (libretto by Giacomo Rossi, based on Scribe and Planard's *Prison d'Edimbourg* and, further back, on Scott's *Heart of Midlothian*), produced at Trieste, Italy, on 13 March 1838.

Prigioniero, Il, *The Prisoner* opera (prologue and one act) by Luigi ➤ **Dallapiccola** (libretto by composer after De L'Isle Adam and C de Coster); composed 1944–48 and first performed on Turin Radio, on 4 December 1949. Produced Florence, 20 May 1950. The story is set during the era of the Inquisition in Spain. The Prisoner finds hope in a comforting Gaoler. One day the cell is left open and he finds his way to freedom, only to be caught by the Grand Inquisitor.

prima donna (Italian 'first lady') strictly, the singer of the principal female role in an opera.
By the 19th century the term had entered non-musical vocabulary to describe an arrogant and histrionic person, either male or female.

primary tone in music, the first note of the ➤ fundamental line.

prima volta (Italian 'first time') in musical notation, indicating a passage at the end of a section, before a repeat sign, to be substituted with the *seconda volta* ('second time') passage at the same point during the repeat.

primo (Italian 'first') in musical notation, word often written over the top part in piano duets, the bottom one being *secondo*; the word also appears in orchestral scores where the composer wishes to make sure that a passage is played by only the first of a pair or groups of similar instruments.

primo uomo (Italian 'first man') singer of the leading male soprano part in an opera or the leading male soprano in an opera company in the 18th century.

Prince Igor, Russian *Kniaz Igor* opera by Aleksandr Borodin (libretto by composer, based on a sketch by Vladimir Stassov), composed between 1871 and 1887 and left unfinished at Borodin's death in the latter year. It was completed and scored by Rimsky-Korsakov and Glazunov, and produced at St Petersburg, on 4 November 1890. In the story, Prince Igor and son Vladimir are taken prisoner by the Polovtsi. Khan Konchak treats his prisoners well, blessing the union of his daughter Konchakovna with Vladimir. Igor escapes and is welcomed home.

Prince of the Pagodas, The ballet by Benjamin Britten (choreography by John Cranko), produced in London at Covent Garden, on 1 January 1957.

Princesse de Navarre, La comédie-ballet by Jean-Philippe Rameau (libretto by Voltaire), produced at Versailles, on 23 February 1745, to celebrate the wedding of the Dauphin with Maria Teresa of Spain. In the story, Princess Constance escapes from the King of Castile and hides with Don Morillo, evading the amorous pursuit of the Duke of Foix.

Princesse jaune, La, The Yellow Princess opera by Saint-Saëns (libretto by L Gallet), produced at the Opéra-Comique, Paris, on 12 June 1872. The story concerns Kornélis, who loves everything Japanese. He imagines he is in Japan, but then realizes that he loves his Dutch girlfriend Léna more than his fantasy.

Princess Ida or **Castle Adamant** operetta by Arthur Sullivan (libretto by W S Gilbert, a parody of Tennyson's *Princess*), produced in London at the Savoy Theatre, on 5 January 1884. The story concerns Prince Hiarion's marriage to Princess Ida, which was arranged a long time ago, but she has since spurned all men and founded a university for women. She eventually falls in love with him.

principal in an ➤ organ, an open ➤ **diapason** stop. The term is derived from the German *Prinzipal* to denote a neutral stop, in contrast with the variety of other, more colourful, diapason stops. Also, in early music, the word refers to the lowest trumpet part, in which high and florid notes were not demanded. In modern terminology, a principal is the leading player of any group of orchestral instruments.

principal subject in music, the main, first theme of a piece in ➤ **sonata form** or ➤ **rondo** form. It is usually the first important theme to appear, doing so in the ➤ **tonic** key.

Prinz von Homburg, Der opera by Hans Werner Henze (libretto by Ingeborg Bachmann, after Heinrich von Kleist), produced at the Staatsoper, Hamburg, on 22 May 1960. In the story, the Prince is lost in a fantasy world with his beloved Princess at its centre. As a result, he ignores battle orders and is condemned to death. Offered his freedom after Princess Natalie intervenes, he still prefers an honourable death, but the Elector shows mercy in the end.

Prise de Troie, La opera by Hector Berlioz; see ➤ **Troyens, Les**.

Prisoner in the Caucasus, The or **Russian Kavkasky Plennik** opera by César Antonovich Cui (libretto by V A Krilov, based on Pushkin's poem), produced at St Petersburg on 16 February 1883.

Pritchard, John (1921–1989) English conductor. He was music director of the London Philharmonic Orchestra 1962–66, and the BBC Symphony Orchestra from 1981. He conducted the first performances of Benjamin Britten's *Gloriana* and Michael Tippett's *Midsummer Marriage* at Covent Garden, and *King Priam* with the company at Coventry in 1962.

Pritchard studied in Italy and went to Glyndebourne, England, in 1947, where he gave three Mozart operas in 1951 and was music director 1969–77. He was principal conductor of the Cologne Opera from 1978. He made his US debut in 1953 with the Pittsburgh Symphony Orchestra, and his New York Metropolitan Opera debut in 1971.

Prodaná Nevěstá opera by Bedřich Smetana; see ➤ **Bartered Bride**.

Prod'homme, J(acques) G(abriel) (1871–1956) French musicologist. He founded the French section of the Société Internationale de Musicologie and wrote several works on Beethoven and Berlioz, and also works on Mozart, Schubert, and Wagner.

He studied in Germany and lived at Munich 1897–1900, where he founded a periodical. After his return to Paris he founded the French section of the Société Internationale de Musicologie, became its secretary, and performed various other music administrative functions, succeeding Bouvert in 1931 as librarian and archivist at the Opéra.

Prodigal Son, The church parable by Benjamin Britten (libretto by William Plomer), produced at Orford in Suffolk, England, on 10 June 1968, and conducted by Britten himself. The story depicts the biblical parable of the prodigal son. In the country, the father of two sons gives his younger son an inheritance, which is squandered during a moral decline in the city. The son repents and is reconciled with his family on his return home.

Ballet by Prokofiev (*L'Enfant prodigue*), composed in 1928 and first performed in Paris, on 21 May 1929, by the Ballets Russes (scenario by B Kokno, choreography by George Balanchine, décor by Georges Roualt; conductor Prokofiev).

See ➤ *Enfant prodigue* by Claude Debussy.

programme music instrumental music that interprets a story, depicts a scene or painting, or illustrates a literary or philosophical idea. The term was first used by Franz ➤ **Liszt** in the 19th century, when programme music was especially popular with composers of Romantic music (see ➤ **Romanticism**), but there had been a great deal of descriptive music before then. Examples include Antonio Vivaldi's *Four Seasons* concertos (1725), Ludwig van Beethoven's *Eroica* and *Pastoral* symphonies (1803 and 1808), Felix Mendelssohn's *Hebrides Overture* ('Fingal's Cave', 1830), and the ➤ **symphonic poems** of Liszt and Richard Strauss.

narrative and descriptive music Liszt coined the

phrase 'programme music' in the mid-19th century, originally using it for music that is introduced by a 'programme' and expresses (rather than describes) a poetic idea. Nowadays it is applied to any purely instrumental music based on a literary, pictorial, historical, biographical, autobiographical, or any other extramusical subject, as opposed to ➤ **absolute music** – music with a purely abstract meaning. The programmatic element can be as vague as simply having a descriptive title given to it by the composer to set the mood, or a much more detailed depiction of a scene or story. Often, however, it is impossible to tell the difference between the depiction of a scene and the composer's reaction to it.

early programme music Musical descriptions of actions and events have existed from the earliest times. One of the first developments of real programme music came in Elizabethan England with composers for the ➤ **virginal**, whose music is often very descriptive. Titles such as Giles Farnaby's *Dream*, and Doctor Bull's *Myself* and *Up Tails All* are typical. This tradition was continued well into the 18th century by the music of the French harpsichordists, notably François Couperin and Jean-Philippe Rameau, and German composers such as Johann Kuhnau, whose *Biblical Sonatas* are programme music similar to that of Liszt – each one is introduced by a summary of what the music depicts.

popular subjects One of the first popular forms was battle music, using musical sounds to depict the sounds of battle, an early example being Clement Janequin's ➤ **chanson** *La Bataille* (1529). The tradition continued with pieces for harpsichord such as William Byrd's *The Battell*, through to the 19th century with Beethoven's *Battle Symphony* (written for a mechanical orchestra) and Pyotr Tchaikovsky's *1812 Overture* (1880). Another popular subject has been the description of nature in one form or another. Vivaldi's *Four Seasons* (1725), Beethoven's *Pastoral Symphony* (1808), and Claude Debussy's *La Mer/The Sea* (1905) are perhaps the best-known examples.

symphonic poems In the 19th century, composers such as Hector Berlioz took Beethoven's idea of the symphony a stage further, developing the Romantic programme symphony. Despite its basically classical form and abstract tradition, the symphony provided a framework into which the Romantic composers could put all kinds of extramusical ideas. Berlioz's use of an *idée fixe* (fixed idea) to depict characters in his *Harold in Italy* symphony (1834) and *Symphonie Fantastique* (1830–31) paved the way for the development of the ➤ **symphonic poem** and its use of Richard Wagner's ➤ **leitmotif**. The symphonic poem became very popular as a form in the latter half of the 19th century and was particularly favoured by

Liszt and Richard Strauss. In the 20th century, programme music became less popular for a while with the rise of neoclassicism and serialism, and was even looked down upon as less 'serious' than absolute music, but its appeal to the general public has never been in doubt.

links with other arts Because programme music attempts to convey an extramusical idea, it very often has links with other artistic disciplines, and its inspiration may come from sources such as literature or painting. Particularly during the Romantic period, music looked outside its traditional forms for inspiration – as personal expression had become the goal of the artist, the classical notion of abstract formal beauty had become outdated – and increasingly turned to the other arts. In Britain and Germany the literary tradition has been a significant source of inspiration, while in France and Italy it is more likely to be painting and sculpture.

progression logical movement of two or more chords in succession, either harmonically, with all the notes moving simultaneously, or polyphonically, with each one being part of a continuously moving horizontal melodic line.

Prohaska, Carl (1869–1927) Austrian composer. He studied piano with d'Albert and composition with Mandyczewski and Herzogenberg, being also befriended by Brahms. He taught at the Strasbourg Conservatory 1894–95 and conducted the Warsaw Philharmonic Orchestra 1901–05. In 1908, he became professor at the Conservatory of the Vienna Philharmonic Society.

Works OPERA *Madeleine Guimara* (1930).

CHORAL oratorio *Frühlingsfeier* (1913); motet *Aus dem Buch Hiob*; *Lebensmesse, Der Feind, Infanterie*, and other choral works.

ORCHESTRAL variations on a theme from Rousseau's *Devin du village*, symphonic prelude to Anzengruber's *Das vierte Gebot*, symphonic fantasy, serenade, passacaglia and fugue for orchestra.

CHAMBER string quartet, string quintet, piano trio; sonata and *Allegro con spirito* for violin and piano; songs, duets.

Prokofiev, Sergey Sergeyevich (1891–1953) Russian composer. His music includes operas such as *The Love for Three Oranges* (after Carlo Gozzi, 1921); ballets for Sergei Diaghilev, including *Romeo and Juliet* (1935); seven symphonies including the *Classical Symphony* (1916–17); music for film, including Sergei Eisenstein's *Alexander Nevsky* (1938); piano and violin concertos; songs and cantatas (for example, that composed for the 30th anniversary of the October Revolution); and *Peter and the Wolf* (1936) for children, to his own libretto after a Russian folk tale.

Prokofiev was essentially a classicist in his use of form, but his large and varied output shows great lyricism, humour, and skill. His music in his earlier years has a hard brilliance, but his later works show a mellowing and maturity of style. Born near Ekaterinoslav (now Dnipropetrovs'k), he studied at St Petersburg under Nikolai Rimsky-Korsakov and achieved fame as a pianist. He left Russia in 1918 and lived for some time in the USA and in Paris, but returned in 1927 and again in 1935.

Prokofiev began to compose almost before he could write, and tried his hand at an opera at the age of nine. He was sent to Glière for lessons, wrote twelve piano pieces in 1902 as well as a symphony for piano duet, and at age 12 set Pushkin's play *A Feast in Time of Plague* as an opera. At the St Petersburg Conservatory, which he left in 1914, he studied piano with Anna Essipova, composition with Rimsky-Korsakov and Anatol Liadov, and conducting with Nikolai Tcherepnin. By that time he had written many works, including the first piano concerto, which won the Rubinstein Prize. He then set to work on a ballet commission for Sergei Diaghilev that became the *Scythian Suite* for orchestra.

In 1918 he left Russia, living in the UK, France, Japan, and the USA before returning to Russia. The opera *The Love for Three Oranges* was produced at Chicago in 1921, and the next year he went to live in Paris and became connected with Diaghilev's Ballets Russes (Russian Ballet), which produced several of his works. The visionary opera *The Fiery Angel* was completed in 1923 but not staged until 1955. Limited opportunities in the West caused him to return to Russia.

In 1936 he settled in Moscow. He was persuaded by the Soviet government to make his style more simple and popular; this is very noticeable in such works as *Peter and the Wolf* and the quantities of film music he wrote there. However, the cantata from the film music for *Alexander Nevsky* is one of his most powerful scores. Two years later he began his great patriotic opera *War and Peace*, and the victory in the war against Hitler was celebrated with one of his finest scores, the exuberant and expansive 5th symphony. Like many other Soviet composers, he was severely criticized in the Zhdanov censures, in 1948, for formalism (the separation of form from content). Ironically, after enduring years of Stalinist oppression, he died on the same day as Stalin.

Works OPERA *The Love for Three Oranges* (after Carlo Gozzi, 1921), *The Fiery Angel* (1919–27, produced 1955), *War and Peace* (after Tolstoy, 1941–52, produced 1953).

BALLET *The Buffoon* (1921), *Le pas d'acier* (1927), *L'enfant prodigue*, *Romeo and Juliet* (after Shakespeare, 1938), *Cinderella* (1945).

ORCHESTRAL includes *Classical Symphony* (1921) and six other symphonies (1924–52); film music for *Lieutenant Kijé* (1934), *Ivan the Terrible*; five piano concertos (1911–32), two violin concertos (1917, 1935).

CHAMBER two string quartets (1930, 1941), sonata for two violins, sonatas in D major and F minor for violin and piano (1944, 1946).

PIANO AND SONGS nine piano sonatas, about 25 other Op. nos of piano pieces, including *Visions fugitives*; eight sets of songs (one without words, one to words by Pushkin).

CHORAL *Alexander Nevsky* (1939).

prolation system of proportional timing in Renaissance music, relating shifts in tempo to harmonic ratios, for example 1:2, 2:3, and so on.

prolongation in voice-leading analysis, the technique by which a composer 'prolongs' a single harmony over a span of time by making other chords in the passage subordinate to the one being prolonged. The prolonged harmony is said to operate at a deeper structural level than the subordinate harmonies, and may itself be a part of a larger prolongation at a still deeper level. The term may also be used of structural melodic notes rather than harmonies. See ➤ **structural harmony**; ➤ **fundamental line**.

promenade concert originally a concert where the audience was free to promenade (walk about) while the music was playing, now in the UK the name of any one of an annual BBC series (the 'Proms') at the Royal Albert Hall, London, at which part of the audience stands. They were originated by English conductor Henry Wood in 1895.

promessi sposi, I, The Betrothed opera by Amilcare Ponchielli (libretto by E Praga based on Manzoni's novel), produced at Cremona on 30 August 1856. In the story, Renzo and Lucia are to marry but the wedding is interrupted by Don Rodrigo. Having sought refuge in a convent, Lucia is kidnapped by L'Innominato, but she escapes, and takes holy orders. When at last she meets Renzo again her vows are dissolved and the wedding takes place.

Prométhée, Prometheus open-air spectacle by Fauré (libretto by Jacques Lorrain and Ferdinand Hérold, based on Aeschylus), produced at Béziers, Arènes, on 27 August 1900. Its first Paris performance took place at the Hippodrome on 5 December 1907.

Prometheus ballet by Beethoven. See ➤ *Geschöpfe des Prometheus, Die*.

Symphonic poem by Liszt, composed in 1850 as an overture to the choruses from Herder's *Prometheus*. It was first performed at Weimar on 28 August 1850 and was revised in 1855.

Opera by Carl Orff (libretto by composer after Aeschylus) produced at Stuttgart on 24 March 1968.

Prometheus, the Poem of Fire symphonic work for piano and orchestra by Aleksandr ➤ **Skriabin**, first performed in Moscow on 15 March 1911. The score contains a part for an instrument projecting coloured lights, called *Tastiera per luce*, which was, however, never perfected.

Prometheus Unbound setting of Shelley's poem for solo voices, chorus, and orchestra by Hubert Parry, performed at the Gloucester Festival in 1880.

Prophète, Le opera by Giacomo Meyerbeer (libretto by Scribe), produced at the Paris Opéra on 16 April 1849. In the story, John's wedding to Berthe is thwarted by Count Oberthal, when he kidnaps John's mother, Fidès. Later John is hailed as a prophet king, and Berthe, horrified, stabs herself. Imperial troops enter John's palace and he detonates himself along with the forces of order.

Prophetess, The or **The History of Dioclesian** music by Henry Purcell for the play adapted from Beaumont and Fletcher by Thomas Betterton, produced in London at the Dorset Gardens Theatre, in spring 1690. Pepusch wrote new music for its revival at the Lincoln's Inn Fields Theatre, London, on 28 November 1724.

proportion in music, the mathematical relationship between the numbers of vibrations of different notes, which are exactly in tune with each other when the ratios between these vibrations are mathematically correct. For instance, a perfect fifth stands in the relation of 2:3 in the number of vibrations of its two notes. The term proportion was also used in early music to designate the rhythmic relationships between one time-signature and another.

Proscritto, Il, The Outlaw opera by Otto Nicolai (libretto, originally written for Verdi, by Giacomo Rossi), produced at La Scala, Milan, on 13 March 1841.

prose in music, another name, chiefly French, for the ➤ **sequence** (in the medieval sense of an ornamental interpolation into the music of the Mass). After the 9th century, words began to be added to the sequences, and this is the reason for them being called proses, since the texts were not originally in verse.

Proserpine opera by Jean-Baptiste Lully (libretto by Quinault), produced at Saint-Germain on 3 February 1680 and first performed in Paris on 15 November that same year. The story concerns Attis and Proserpina, who are in love. But jealous Cyane arranges for Pluto to abduct Proserpine. Attis commits suicide and Cyane confesses her plot. In the end, Mercury and Jupiter restore the couple.

Opera by Giovanni Paisiello (libretto by Quinault, revised by Nicolas François Guillard), produced at the Opéra, Paris, on 29 March 1803. It was Paisiello's only French opera.

Prout, Ebenezer (1835–1909) English theorist and composer. In 1876, he became professor at the National Training-School for Music in London and three years later at the Royal Academy of Music. He wrote a number of books on harmony, counterpoint, form, and orchestration, and composed cantatas, symphonies, organ concertos, and chamber music.

He studied piano and organ, and began his career as an organist and piano teacher, and, later, became a music editor and critic.

Prozess, Der, The Trial opera by Gottfried von Einem (libretto by Blacher and H von Cramer, after Kafka), produced at Salzburg on 17 August 1953. The story begins as Joseph K is charged with an unspecified crime. The plot documents his feelings of helplessness and paranoia before being taken to execution.

Prunières, Henry (1886–1942) French musicologist and editor. He studied with Rolland at the Sorbonne, founded the *Revue musicale* in 1920, and was appointed editor of the complete edition of Jean-Baptiste Lully's works. He wrote books on Lully, Monteverdi, Cavalli, French and Italian opera and ballet, and also a history of music (unfinished).

Pruslin, Stephen (Lawrence) (1940–) US pianist and librettist. He studied at Princeton until 1963; piano with Eduard Steuermann. He moved to London in 1964 and gave his debut recital at the Purcell Room in 1970. He wrote libretti for Birtwistle's *Monodrama* (1967) and *Punch and Judy* (1968). He cofounded Fires of London 1970, premiered the Maxwell Davies piano sonata and collaborated with him on music for *The Devils*. He made concert appearances with the London Sinfonietta, BBC Symphony Orchestra, and Royal Philharmonic.

'Prussian' Quartets a set of three string quartets by Mozart, composed 1789–90 and dedicated to the cello-playing King Frederick William II of Prussia. The quartets K575 in D, K589 in B flat, K590 in F are the first three of an intended set of six. All have prominent cello parts.

psalm sacred poem or song of praise. The Book of Psalms in the Old Testament is divided into five books containing 150 psalms, traditionally ascribed to David, the second king of Israel. In the Christian church they may be sung antiphonally in ➤ **plainsong** or set by individual composers to music in a great variety of styles, from Josquin Desprez's *De profundis* to Igor Stravinsky's *Symphony of Psalms* (1930).

Psalmus Hungaricus work by Zoltán ➤ Kodály for tenor, chorus, and orchestra, based on the Psalm 55, first performed in Budapest, 19 November 1923.

psaltery musical instrument, triangular in shape and with strings stretched across its frame harpwise, played with the bare fingers or with a plectrum. It became obsolete during the 17th century.

Pskovitianka, The Maid of Pskov; or Ivan the Terrible opera by Rimsky-Korsakov (libretto by composer based on a play by L A Mey), produced St Petersburg, 13 January 1873. Revived with a new prologue-opera, *Boyarina Vera Sheloga*, Moscow, 27 December 1898. Ivan the Terrible destroys Novgorod but spares nearby Pskov when he discovers his daughter Olga is there. Tucha, who has not heard of the ceasefire, leads a force against Ivan and Olga is killed in the crossfire.

Psyche opera by Locke (libretto by Shadwell), produced London, Dorset Gardens Theatre, 27 February 1675. Princess Psyche suffers the evil plots of her sisters Cidippe and Aglaura, who are jealous of her beauty. Venus, also jealous, arranges with Apollo for Psyche to marry a serpent, but Cupid saves her.

Psyché opera by Jean-Baptiste Lully (libretto by Thomas Corneille and Bernard le Bovier de Fontenelle), produced at the Opéra, Paris, on 19 April 1678. See ➤ *Psyche* for a plot synopsis.

Suite by César Auguste Franck for orchestra with choral interpolations, composed 1887–88 and first performed at the Société National, Paris, on 10 March 1888.

Puccini, Giacomo (Antonio Domenico Michele Secondo Maria) (1858–1924) Italian opera composer. His music shows a strong gift for melody and dramatic effect and his operas combine exotic plots with elements of *verismo* (realism). They include *Manon Lescaut* (1893), *La Bohème* (1896), *Tosca* (1900), *Madama Butterfly* (1904), and the unfinished *Turandot* (1926).

Puccini was born in Lucca, the fifth in a line of musicians and composers. (The earlier members of the family were Giacomo Puccini (1712–1781), his son Antonio Puccini (1747–1832), his grandson Domenico Puccini (1771–1815), and his great-grandson Michele Puccini (1813–1864).) Although his father died early, Puccini was given a musical education by his uncle, and at the age of 19 was organist and choirmaster at the church of San Martino and had written a motet. In 1880 his mother managed with the aid of a grant from the queen to send him to the Milan Conservatory,

where he studied composition first under Antonio Bazzini (1818–1897) and later under Amilcare Ponchielli. Here he wrote a *Capriccio sinfonico* for orchestra. Ponchielli urged him to take part in a competition for a one-act opera advertised by the music publisher Sonzogno, and he wrote *Le Villi*; but the prize was won by Pietro Mascagni's *Cavalleria rusticana*. *Le Villi*, however, was produced at Milan in 1884, and as a result Ricordi commissioned him to write a second opera, *Edgar* in 1889. It failed, but Puccini had his first great success with *Manon Lescaut* at Turin in 1893; *La Bohème* was produced in the same city in 1896. His first *verismo* opera, *Tosca*, confirmed his stature: the combination of natural melody, a sure dramatic sense, and unerring aptness of orchestral colouring have made it his most enduring piece.

His successes made him immensely wealthy and he bought an estate at Torre del Lago near Lucca, where he lived with Elvira Bonturi, who had left her husband for him, but whom he was unable to marry until much later, when she became a widow. Their life together was marked by scandal in 1909 when their servant committed suicide after Elvira accused her of having a sexual relationship with Puccini. The following year *La fanciulla del West/The Golden Girl of the West* was produced at the New York Metropolitan Opera House. If this opera, and *La rondine* (1917), represent a decline in Puccini's career, his final work, *Turandot*, unites some of the elements that most fired his imagination: physical passion, cruelty, strong sentiment, and oriental flavour. In the last years of his life he suffered from cancer of the throat and died after an operation undergone at Brussels.

Puccini was the dominant figure in Italian music in his time; and his operas, which combine the sensuous melody of Verdi with the richness of modern Impressionist harmony, are exceedingly popular.

Works OPERA *Le Villi* (1884), *Edgar* (1889), *Manon Lescaut* (1893), *La Bohème* (1896), *Tosca* (1900), *Madama Butterfly* (1904), *La fanciulla del West* (1910), *La rondine* (1917), *Trittico*, *Il tabarro*, *Suor Angelica*, *Gianni Schicchi* (1918), *Turandot* (unfinished, completed by Alfano, 1926).

ORCHESTRAL AND CHORAL *Scherzo sinfonico* for orchestra (later used in *La Bohème*); cantata *Juno*; a Mass and a motet *Inno a Roma* for chorus.

OTHER two minuets for strings.

Puits d'amour, Le, The Well of Love opera by Michael Balfe (libretto by Scribe and A de Leuven), produced at the Opéra-Comique, Paris, on 20 April 1843. It was Balfe's first French opera.

Pujol, Juan (c.1573–1626) Spanish priest and composer. He was maestro di cappella at Tarragona 1593–95, Saragossa Cathedral 1595–1612, and Barcelona 1612–26.

Works CHURCH MUSIC 13 Masses, 74 psalms, nine motets, nine Passions and other church music. OTHER songs.

Pulcinella ballet by Stravinsky with music adapted from Giovanni Pergolesi and others (choreography by Massin). It was first produced in Paris at the Opéra on 15 May 1920. The settings were designed by Picasso.

An orchestral suite was performed at Boston on 22 December 1922.

Pullois, Jean (c.1420–1478) Flemish composer. His output consists mainly of songs but also includes some sacred music. He is important as one of the few named composers active during Guillaume ➜ **Dufay**'s middle years.

He was a singer in the Burgundian court chapel until 1463, then was choirmaster at Antwerp 1444–47. He sang at the papal chapel in Rome 1447–68. His single Mass cycle may really be the work of an English composer.

pulse in music, a basic unit of rhythm and metre. See ➜ **beat**.

Punch and Judy opera in one act by Harrison Birtwistle (libretto by Stephen Pruslin), produced at Aldeburgh on 8 June 1968, and conducted by Atherton. A revised version was produced in London on 3 March 1970. The plot follows the murderous Punch, who stabs Judy and sets out on a quest for Pretty Polly, eventually winning her favour after hanging Jack Ketch.

punta (Italian 'point') term used in musical notation, as in *a punta d'arco* ('at the point of the bow'), instructing a string player to use only the tip of the bow as opposed to the heel (the end which is held by the player's hand).

Purcell, Daniel (c.1663–1717) English organist and composer. He finished the opera *The Indian Queen*, which his brother Henry ➜ **Purcell** had left unfinished at his death. After a busy career writing music for plays, he became organist of St Andrew's Church, Holborn, London, in 1713.

He was a choirboy in the Chapel Royal and was organist at Magdalen College, Oxford, 1688–95. He then went to London and added music to *The Indian Queen*.

Works STAGE music for *Brutus of Alba* (1696), Cibber's *Love's Last Shift* and *Love makes a Man* (1700), Durfey's *Cynthia and Endymion* (1696), Lacy's *Sawny the Scot* (based on Shakespeare's *Taming of the Shrew*, 1698), Steele's *Funeral and Tender Husband* (1705), Farquhar's *The Beaux' Stratagem* (1707), *The Inconstant* and (with Leveridge) *The Constant Couple* (1699), Vanbrugh's *The Relapse* and (with Finger) *The Pilgrim* (1701), music for Congreve's *Judgment of Paris* (third prize in competition with Eccles, Finger, and

Weldon, 1700), an adaptation of Shakespeare's *Macbeth* (1704), and many others.

CHAMBER sonatas for violin and bass, and for flute and bass; sonatas for trumpet and strings; cantatas for one voice.

OTHER odes, including odes for St Cecilia's Day; church music.

Purcell, Henry (c.1659–1695) English baroque composer. His works include the opera *Dido and Aeneas* (1689) and music for John Dryden's *King Arthur* (1691) and *The Fairy Queen* (1692). He wrote more than 500 works, ranging from secular operas and incidental music for plays to cantatas and church music.

Born at Westminster, he became a chorister at the Chapel Royal, and subsequently was a pupil of Dr John Blow. In 1677 he was appointed composer to the Chapel Royal, and, in 1679, organist at Westminster Abbey. As composer to the king, Purcell set odes and anthems to music.

Puritani di Scozia, I, The Puritans of Scotland opera by Vincenzo Bellini (libretto by C Pepoli, based on a play by Jaques Ancelot and X B Saintine, *Têtes rondes et cavaliers*, and farther back on Scott's *Old Mortality*), produced in Paris at the Théâtre Italien on 25 January 1835.

Puschmann, Adam Zacharias (1532–1600) German master singer. He was a pupil of Hans Sachs at Nuremberg 1566–60. He wrote about 200 meisterlieder (master-songs), and in 1574 published a treatise on master-singing, containing songs of his own, as well as by Sachs, Behaim, and others.

Pushkin, Aleksandr Sergeyevich (1790–1837) Russian poet, dramatist, and novelist. Two contrasting pieces by Pushkin are great works of literature in themselves and also form the basis of the two finest Russian compositions of the 19th century: *Eugene Onegin* and *Boris Godunov*.

Dating from 1825, *Boris Godunov* is a huge historical drama, which drew an appropriate response from Mussorgsky in 1869. If the wide political panorama of Pushkin's *Boris*, within the context of a gradually unfolding personal drama, suggests the influence of Shakespeare, then the presence of Byron in the verse novel *Eugene Onegin* (1828) is even more strongly felt. The figure of the sardonic outsider attracted Tchaikovsky for his opera of 1879. Here, as in other works of Pushkin, a composer was inspired by the poet's fluent naturalness of language and vivid imagery. Pushkin's huge range encompassed nationalist fairy tale, and his *Ruslan and Ludmilla* of 1820 was the inspiration for Glinka's opera of 1842. Rimsky-Korsakov was also attracted by Pushkin's fantasy, setting *The Tale of Tsar Saltan* (1831) in 1900 and *The Golden Cockerel* (1834) in 1909. Other major settings of Pushkin include Dargomizhsky's *Stone Guest* of 1872 (the poet's version of the Don Juan legend) and Tchaikovsky's *The Queen of Spades*, setting Pushkin's *Conte* of 1830 in 1890. The continued theme in his work of exile from society was personally familiar to Pushkin, and he was banished from Moscow for six years for political dissent. In 1837 he was shot dead in a duel.

Pyamour, John (died 1431) English composer who wrote primarily church music. He was a member of the Chapel Royal 1420–21 and of the chapel of the Duke of Bedford in 1427.

Pycard (lived c.1410) French composer. His music, represented in the Old Hall manuscript, is remarkable for its extensive use of canon. He served in John of Gaunt's household in the 1390s.

Pygmalion *acte de ballet* by Jean-Philippe Rameau (libretto by B de Savot, after A H de La Motte), produced at the Opéra, Paris, on 27 August 1748. In the story, the sculptor Pygmalion falls in love with his statue. After it comes to life he must teach it how to move gracefully.

Pygott, Richard (c.1485–1552) English composer. He was in Wolsey's private chapel in 1517 as Master of the Children and in 1533 became a Gentleman of the Chapel Royal. Later he was given a living allowance at Coggeshall monastery in Essex and a canonry at Tamworth, but lost some of the benefits at the dissolution of the monasteries. Henry VIII, however, and after him Edward VI, retained his services.

Works CHURCH MUSIC Masses, motets, *Salve Regina*; carols and other pieces.

Pythagoras (lived 6th century BC) Greek philosopher. He contributed to the science of music by working out by mathematics the intervals of the scale according to the number of vibrations to each note and by helping to systematize the tetrachords (scales of four notes). Aesthetically, he developed the theory of the 'harmony of the spheres'.

qin plucked ➤ **zither** of the Han Chinese consisting of a shallow, oblong, lacquered wooden box, with a curved wooden soundboard, no bridges or frets, and seven silk strings stretched along the length of the instrument and tied onto mother of pearl studs. Experts agree on its origins around the 14th and 15th centuries. It has an abundance of lore and anecdotes attached to it.

quadrille square dance for four or more couples, or the music for the dance, which alternates between two and four beats in a bar.

quadruple counterpoint in music, ➤ **counterpoint** in which four parts are reversible. See also ➤ **triple counterpoint**.

quadruplet in music, a group of four notes to be played in the time of three. It is indicated by a ➤ **slur** over the four notes with the number '4' written above. It usually occurs in compound time (metre in which each beat divides into three units).

Quagliati, Paolo (c.1555–1628) Italian composer. He was organist at the church of Santa Maria Maggiore in Rome from 1601. For the wedding of Carlo Gesualdo's daughter, Isabella, in 1623 he wrote a collection of instrumental pieces, entitled *La sfera armoniosa*.

Works CHORAL the dramatic cantata *Carro di fedeltà d'amore* (1806); motets; spiritual and secular madrigals and canzonets.

OTHER organ and harpsichord works.

Quantz, Johann Joachim (1697–1773) German flautist and composer. He composed 300 flute concertos, but is best remembered for writing the treatise 'Versuch einer Anweisung die Flöte traversiere zu spielen/On Playing the Transverse Flute' in 1752. He improved the flute's adaptability by adding the second key and devising a sliding tuning mechanism.

As a boy he learned several instruments, and studied composition with Jan Zelenka in Vienna in 1717. The following year he was appointed oboist to the court of August II in Dresden and Warsaw, but later turned to the flute, studying under Pierre-Gabriel Buffardin (1690–1768). After travels in Italy, France, and England he returned to Dresden, becoming first flautist to the court, until he entered the service of Frederick II of Prussia in 1741. He was the king's flute teacher and wrote for him over 500 works for flute.

Works ORCHESTRAL AND OTHER about 300 concertos and about 200 other works for flute.

OTHER hymns on poems by Gellert.

quartal harmony harmonic theory (a theory about the formation of chords and their interrelation), expounded by Yasser and others, which bases the harmonic system on the intervals of the fourth, instead of the third which decisively determines major or minor tonalities.

quarter tone in music, an interval half that of a ➤ **semitone**. A kind of ➤ **microtone**, it is the smallest conventional interval, commonly used in Western music by 20th-century composers such as Pierre ➤ **Boulez** and Karlheinz ➤ **Stockhausen**.

Quarter tones were known to the Greeks and were apparently used in early ➤ **plainsong** but soon came to be abandoned and were not revived in Eastern music until the 20th century. The chief exponent of quarter-tone music is Alois ➤ **Hába**; others, such as Béla ➤ **Bartók** and Ernest Bloch, have used the device, but not systematically.

quartet ensemble of four musicians, or the music written for such a group. The most common type of quartet is the ➤ **string quartet**.

Quartettsatz (German 'quartet movement') name given to the first movement of Franz Schubert's unfinished string quartet in C minor, composed in December 1820 (D703) and not performed until 1 March 1867, in Vienna. The work was clearly intended to be completed, for Schubert wrote 41 bars of a slow movement in A flat major.

quasi (Latin 'as if') apparently but not actually; also used in musical notation, as in *sonata quasi fantasia* ('sonata in the manner of a fantasia').

Quatorze Juillet, Le, The Fourteenth of July play by Romain ➤ **Rolland**, forming part of the trilogy *Le Théâtre de la Révolution* with *Danton* and *Les*

Loups. It was published and performed c.1900–02, and collectively published in 1909. It was produced in the open air at the Arènes de Lutèce, Paris, on 14 July 1936, with music by Auric, Honegger, Ibert, Koechlin, Lazarus, Milhaud, and Roussel.

Quattro pezzi sacri, Four Sacred Pieces four works for chorus and orchestra by Verdi: *Ave Maria*, *Lauda alla Vergine Maria*, *Te Deum*, and *Stabat Mater*, composed 1888–97. The last three pieces were performed in Paris on 7 April 1898.

quattro rusteghi, I, The Four Boors opera by Ermanno Wolf-Ferrari (libretto by G Pizzolato, based on Goldoni's comedy), produced at Munich, Germany, on 19 March 1906. The opera was produced in England as *The School for Fathers* at Sadler's Wells, London, on 7 June 1946. In the story, Lunardo and Maurizio decide their children, Lucieta and Filipeto, should marry. Having forbidden the couple to meet before the wedding, the parents are foiled when Filipeto manages to meet Lucieta in disguise and they immediately fall in love.

quatuor French word for ➤ quartet.

Quatuor pour la fin du temps, Quartet For the End of Time work by ➤ Messiaen for piano, clarinet, violin, and cello; it was composed in 1940 in a Silesian prisoner-of-war camp and was first performed on 15 January 1941.

quaver, US **eighth note** in music, a note value one-eighth the duration of a ➤ semibreve. It is written as a filled black note-head with a stem and flag (tail).

Queen Mary's Funeral Music music by Purcell for the Westminster Abbey funeral of Mary, wife of William III, in 1695. The sequence includes music written three years earlier for Shadwell's play *The Libertine*. Other sections were given at Purcell's own funeral in November 1695.

Queen of Cornwall, The opera by Rutland Boughton (libretto from Thomas Hardy's play, with alterations), produced at Glastonbury on 21 August 1924. The subject is Tristram and Iseult.

Queen of Golconda, The, Swedish **Drottningen av Golconda** opera by Franz Adolf Berwald (libretto by composer after J B C Vial and E G F de Favieres) composed in 1864 and first performed at Stockholm on 3 April 1968. In the story, Aline, the widowed Queen of Golconda, and Saint Phar meet after years of separation. Revolutionary disturbances delay only temporarily the couple's union.

Queen of Sheba opera by Karoly Goldmark. See ➤ Königin von Saba, Die ; ➤ Reine de Saba, La.

Queen of Spades, The, Pikovaya Dama opera by Tchaikovsky (libretto by M I Tchaikovsky, Tchaikovsky's brother, based on Pushkin's story) produced at St Petersburg on 19 December 1890. The story concerns Hermann, who tries to find the secret of playing cards through the old Countess. She dies but her ghost reveals the winning combination to him. But after rejecting Lisa, the Countess's grand-daughter, Hermann loses everything at the gambling table when his necessary ace turns out to be the queen of spades instead.

Quentin Durward opera by François Gevaert (libretto by E Cormon and Michel Carré, based on Scott's novel), produced at the Opéra-Comique, Paris, on 25 March 1858.

Querflöte German name for the transverse ➤ flute.

Quest, The ballet by William Walton (choreography by Frederick Ashton, based on Spenser's *Faerie Queene*), produced in 1943 by the Sadler's Wells Ballet, London.

Quilter, Roger Cuthbert (1877–1953) English composer. He wrote song settings of Shakespeare and Alfred Lord Tennyson, including 'Now Sleeps the Crimson Petal' (1904), and others, as well as incidental music, such as *A Children's Overture* (1920), and chamber music.

Quilter was born at Brighton and educated at Eton. He studied music with Iwan Knorr at Frankfurt. He never held any official musical posts. His works include a light opera, incidental music for Shakespeare's *As You Like It*, and the children's fairy-play *Where the Rainbow Ends*. His songs are especially and deservedly well known. His artless melodic invention has a refined and distinctive harmonic support and outweighs limitations of manner.

Works STAGE opera *Julia* (produced Covent Garden, 1936), radio opera *The Blue Boar*; incidental music for Shakespeare's *As You Like It* (1922) and the children's fairy-play *Where the Rainbow ends* (1911).

ORCHESTRAL *Children's Overture* on nursery tunes, *Three English Dances* for orchestra (1910), serenade.

SONGS song-cycle *To Julia* (Herrick, 1906), songs to words by Shakespeare, Tennyson, and others.

Quinault, Philippe (1635–1688) French poet, librettist, and dramatist. He wrote libretti for many works by Jean-Baptiste ➤ Lully.

See ➤ Alceste (Lully); ➤ Amadis (Lully); ➤ Armida (Mysliveček); ➤ Armide (Gluck and Lully); ➤ Atys (Lully and Piccinni); ➤ Cadmus et Hermione (Lully); ➤ Fêtes de l'Amour (Lully); ➤ Isis (Lully); ➤ Lully (*Églogue de Versailles*); ➤ Persée (Lully); ➤ Phaéton (Lully); ➤ Proserpine (Lully and Paisiello); ➔ *Roland* (Lully and Piccinni); ➔ *Thésée* (Lully).

quint or **great quint** in music, an ➔ organ stop of 5⅓ ft, transposing a fifth upwards.

quinta falsa (Latin 'false fifth') in music, another name for the ➔ tritone when it appears as a diminished fifth, not an augmented fourth.

quinte in music, word used for the interval of the fifth. It was formerly also the name of a string instrument of the viol family, the tenor viol with five strings, and later of the viola, another French name of which was ➔ taille.

quintet ensemble of five musicians, or the music written for such a group. A common type of quintet is the piano quintet, which often consists of a ➔ string quartet and piano.

quinton 19th-century name for a hybrid string instrument, half ➔ viol and half ➔ violin.

quintuplet in music, a group of five notes to be played (usually) in the time of four. It is indicated by a ➔ slur over the five notes with the number '5' written above it.

quintus (Latin 'the fifth') in early music, the fifth part in a ➔ polyphonic composition for five or more voices. It was so called because its range was always equal to that of one of the other parts, so that it could not be described as *cantus, altus, tenor* or *bassus.*

quire the old English spelling of ➔ choir.

quiterne French and old English name for the ➔ cittern, a musical instrument.

quodlibet (Latin *quod libet*, 'as it pleases') composition made up of a medley of tunes, usually familiar songs, in polyphonic combinations. Jacob ➔ Obrecht's *Missa diversorum tenorum* is an elaborate quodlibet, introducing the melodies of *chansons* by 15th-century composers. A more familiar example is the quodlibet at the end of Bach's *Goldberg Variations*. The Spanish term for a quodlibet was *ensalada.*

quotation in music, the use of short passages in musical works taken from other music by the same composer or by another.
Examples of auto-quotations include:
Brahms, *Regenlied* in finale of G major violin sonata;
Elgar, a number of themes from earlier works in *The Music Makers*; demons' chorus from *The Dream of Gerontius* in *The Fourth of August* (as a theme for the enemy);
Mozart, 'Non più andrai' from *Figaro* in second-act finale of *Don Giovanni*;
Prokofiev, March from *The Love for Three Oranges* in ballet *Cinderella*;

Puccini, 'Mimi' theme from *La Bohème* in *Il tabarro*;
Rimsky-Korsakov, theme from *Pskovitianka* (*Ivan the Terrible*) in *The Tsar's Bride* (referring to Ivan);
Saint-Saëns, theme from *Danse macabre* in *Fossils* section of *Le Carnaval des animaux*;
Schumann, opening of *Papillons*, Op. 1, in *Florestan* piece in *Carnaval*, Op. 9;
Shostakovich, themes from tenth symphony and first cello concerto in eighth string quartet (1960);
Smetana, theme associated with the Vyšehrad citadel of Prague in the first symphonic poem of *Má Vlast* and referring to in the later one entitled *Vltava*;
Strauss, theme from *Guntram* in 'Childhood' section of *Tod und Verklärung*; a number of themes from earlier works in the 'Hero's Works' section of *Heldenleben* and in the dinner music in the *Bourgeois Gentilhomme* incidental music; *Ariadne auf Náxos* in *Capriccio*; transfiguration theme from *Tod und Verklärung* in *Im Abendrot* ('Last Songs');
Vaughan Williams, theme from *Hugh the Drover* in violin concerto;
Wagner, two themes from *Tristan* in *Meistersinger*, III. i; swan motive from *Lohengrin* in *Parsifal*, I; themes from *Siegfried* in *Siegfried Idyll* (some going back to a projected string quartet);
Wolf, song, 'In dem Schatten meiner Locken' from *Spanish Song-Book* in opera *Der Corregidor*, I.

Examples of quotations from a different composer's work include:
Bartók, Nazi march theme from Shostakovich's seventh symphony in Concerto for Orchestra;
Beethoven's 'Song of Thanksgiving' in the third piano concerto (both composers had just recovered from illness);
Bax, theme from Wagner's *Tristan* in symphonic poem *Tintagel*; passage from Elgar's violin concerto, in G major string quartet dedicated to Elgar;
Beethoven, 'Notte e giorno faticar' from Mozart's *Don Giovanni* in Variations on a theme by Diabelli, Op. 120;
Berg, themes from Wagner's *Tristan* and Zemlinsky's *Lyric Symphony* in Lyric Suite for string quartet; Bach chorale *Es ist genug* in violin concerto;
Berio, scherzo from Mahler's second symphony and other items in *Sinfonia*;
Brahms, 'Batti, batti' from Mozart's *Don Giovanni* in song *Liebe und Frühling*, Op. 3 no. 2;
Bréville, 'Tarnhelm' motive from Wagner's *Ring* in *Portraits de Maîtres* for piano, indicating a transformation between the pieces imitating various composers;
Britten, theme from Wagner's *Tristan* in *Albert Herring*;

Chabrier, Serenade from Mozart's *Don Giovanni* in song *Ballade des gros dindons*;

Charpentier, theme from Wagner's *Ring* in *Louise*, II;

Chopin, air from Rossini's *Gazza ladra* in Polonaise in B minor dedicated to Kolberg (1826);

Debussy, theme from Wagner's *Tristan* in *Golliwogg's Cake-Walk* (*Children's Corner*);

Elgar, theme from Mendelssohn's overture *Calm Sea and Prosperous Voyage* in 'Enigma' Variations (*Romance*); Chopin's G minor nocturne and Paderewski's *Polish Fantasy* for piano and orchestra in symphonic prelude *Polonia*;

Falla, opening motive from Beethoven's fifth symphony ('Fate knocking at the door') in ballet *The Three-cornered Hat*;

Fibich, various themes from Mozart's *Don Giovanni* in opera *Hedy* (based on Byron's *Don Juan*);

Křenek, Mendelssohn's *Spring Song* in incidental music for Goethe's *Triumph der Empfindsamkeit*;

Mahler, theme from Charpentier's *Louise* and Hunding's motive from Wagner's *Ring* in the first movement of the ninth symphony; prelude to scene 3 of *Boris Godunov* in *Der Einsame im Herbst* (*Das Lied von der Erde*);

Mozart, tunes from Martín y Soler's *Una cosa rara* and Sarti's *Fra due litiganti* in second act finale of *Don Giovanni*;

Mussorgsky, Handel's 'See the conquering hero' and themes by Famitsin and from Serov's opera *Rogenda* in satirical song *The Peep-Show*; sea motive from Rimsky-Korsakov's *Sadko* in song *The Classicist*;

Offenbach, 'Notte e giorno faticar' from Mozart's *Don Giovanni* in *Tales of Hoffmann*, prologue; 'Che farò' from Christoph Willibald von Gluck's *Orfeo* in *Orphée aux enfers*;

Rimsky-Korsakov, themes from Mozart's *Requiem* in opera *Mozart and Salieri*;

Saint-Saëns, themes from overture to Offenbach's *Orphée aux enfers* in *Tortoises* section of *Le Carnaval des animaux* (because Orpheus's lute was made of tortoise-shell); also Berlioz's *Danse des Sylphes* in *Elephants* and a phrase from Rossini's *Barber of Seville* in *Fossils* in the same work;

Schumann, theme from Beethoven's *An die ferne Geliebte* in *Carnaval*, Op. 9 (written while Schumann was separated from Clara Wieck); aria from Heinrich Marschner's *Der Templer und die Jüdin* in finale of *Etudes symphoniques*, Op. 13;

Shostakovich, overture from Rossini's *William Tell* and the fate motif from Wagner's *Ring*, in the 15th symphony;

Strauss, Denza's song *Funiculi, funiculá* in symphony *Aus Musicien* (under the impression that it was an Italian folk song); giants' motive in Wagner's *Ring* in *Feuersnot*; Wagner's Rhinemaidens' theme in dinner music (salmon) of Strauss's *Bourgeois gentilhomme* (*Ariadne*, first version); themes by Bull, Legrenzi, Monteverdi and Peerson in *Die schweigsame Frau*; fragment from funeral march in Beethoven's 'Eroica' symphony in *Metamorphosen* for strings;

Stravinsky, waltz by Lanner (played on a barrelorgan) in ballet *Petrushka*; themes from Tchaikovsky's piano music and songs in ballet *The Fairy's Kiss*/*Le Baiser de la fée*;

Tchaikovsky, song from Grétry's *Richard, Cœur de Lion* in *The Queen of Spades*;

Vaughan Williams, opening theme from Debussy's *L'Après-midi d'un faune* in incidental music for Aristophanes' *Wasps*;

Wagner, *Di tanti palpiti*, from Rossini's *Tancredi*, parodied in the tailor's episode in *Meistersinger*, III.

Walton, two themes from Rossini's *William Tell* overture in *Facade* (*Swiss Yodelling Song*); theme from Rossini's *Tancredi* overture in *Scapino* overture.

Also numerous examples of quotations from earlier works in the music of contemporary composers – Kagel, Holloway, and Stockhausen (*Beethausen, Op. 1970, von Stockhoven*).

Quo vadis? opera by Nouguès (libretto by H Cain, based on Henryk Sienkiewicz's novel of the same name), produced at Nice, France, on 9 February 1909.

r the supertonic note, pronounced 'Ray', in any key in tonic sol-fa notation, the system of musical notation without staves and notes and based on the old syllabic system of Do (Ut), Re, Mi, and so on.

Rabaud, Henri (Benjamin) (1873–1949)

French composer. He wrote six operas, including *Mârouf, savetier du Caire* (1914), which was his most successful. He also wrote music for films, and was director of the Paris Conservatory 1920–41.

He studied under his father, the cellist Hippolyte Rabaud (1839–1900), and with André Gédalge and Massenet at the Paris Conservatory, where he won the Prix de Rome in 1894. After his stay in Rome he visited Vienna and travelled elsewhere, and after his return to Paris he became harmony professor at the Conservatory and conductor at the Opéra. In 1920 he succeeded Fauré as director of the Conservatory, and was in turn succeeded in that post by Claude Delvincourt in 1941.

Works OPERA AND STAGE *La fille de Roland* (1904), *Le premier glaive* (1907), *Mârouf, savetier du Caire* (1914), *L'appel de la mer* (after Synge's play *Riders to the Sea*, 1924), *Rolande et les mauvais garçons* (1934); incidental music for Shakespeare's *Merchant of Venice* and *Antony and Cleopatra* (1917).

MUSIC FOR FILM *Joueurs d'échecs* and *Le miracle des loups*.

ORCHESTRAL AND CHORAL Psalm 4 for chorus, two symphonies, symphonic poem *Andromède, La procession nocturne* (after Lenau's 'Faust' (1899), *Le sacrifice d'Isaac, La flûte de Pan, Divertissement grec, Divertissement sur des airs russes, Poème sur le livre de Job*.

CHAMBER string quartet; songs.

Rachmaninov, Sergei Vasilevich (1873–1943)

Russian composer, conductor, and pianist. After the 1917 Revolution he emigrated to the USA. His music is melodious and emotional and includes operas, such as *Francesca da Rimini* (1906), three symphonies, four piano concertos, piano pieces, and songs. Among his other works are the *Prelude in C-Sharp Minor* (1892) and *Rhapsody on a Theme of Paganini* (1934) for piano and orchestra.

Rachmaninov was the son of a captain in the Imperial Guards and the descendant of a wealthy and noble family. The family fortune was gravely impaired during his childhood and his parents separated in 1882, Rachmaninov living with his mother in St Petersburg. There he took music lessons at the Conservatory in a desultory way until Alexander Siloti, who was his cousin, advised his mother to send him to Moscow to study under Nikolai Sverev. He went to the Moscow Conservatory and lived in Sverev's house for four years; later he went to live with his aunt, whose daughter, Natalia Satin, he later married. He wrote the one-act opera *Aleko* while still a student, and the piano pieces Op. 3, containing the popular C♯ minor prelude, at the age of 19. In 1895 he wrote his first symphony and in 1898 was invited by the Philharmonic Society in London to appear as a pianist and to conduct his orchestral fantasy *The Rock*. In 1905–06 he became conductor of the Imperial Grand Opera at Moscow and in 1909 visited the USA for the first time, writing the third piano concerto for the occasion and playing it himself. He had by this time become one of the finest pianists of the time and he remained pre-eminent in that respect throughout his life.

He lived in Moscow again 1910–17 and conducted the Philharmonic concerts there 1911–13. During World War I he played much for charity, and at the death of Aleksandr Skriabin, who had been his fellow-pupil under Anton Arensky, he decided to make a tour playing that composer's works only. From that time on he became a much-travelled pianist, and finding himself out of sympathy with the Revolution in Russia, he took the opportunity of a concert journey to Scandinavia in 1917 to leave his country forever. He lived in Paris for a time and then spent most of the rest of his life in the USA, touring there each year from January to April and visiting Europe as pianist in October and November, spending some of the summer months at a small property he had acquired on Lake Lucerne in

Switzerland.

Rachmaninov's reputation with the public has always been secure, although his frequently dark and emotional music has had some harsh words from the critics: the exceptionally tall Rachmaninov was summed up by the diminutive Stravinsky as 'six-and-a-half feet of sheer misery'.

Works STAGE opera *Aleko* (1893), *The Miserly Knight* (1906), *Francesca da Rimini* (1906), *Monna Vanna* (1907; performed Philadelphia, 1985).

CHORAL choral symphony *The Bells* (Poe) for solo voices, chorus, and orchestra (1913); cantata *The Spring*; *Liturgy of St John Chrysostom* (1910), and Vesper Mass; three Russian folk songs and chorus.

ORCHESTRAL piano concertos (1890–1926) and *Rhapsody on a Theme of Paganini* for piano and orchestra (1934); three symphonies (1895, 1907, 1936), fantasy *The Rock*, *Caprice Bohémien*, and symphonic poem *The Isle of the Dead* (after Böcklin's picture) for orchestra (1909); *Symphonic Dances* (1940).

CHAMBER AND SOLO MUSIC *Elegiac Trio* for violin, cello, and piano (1893), string quintet and piano trio (unpub); cello and piano sonata, two pieces for violin and piano, and two for cello and piano; a dozen works for piano solo, including two sonatas, variations on themes by Chopin (1903) and Corelli (1931), and 57 smaller pieces (preludes, *Etudes-Tableaux*, and others); four works for two pianos; 77 songs.

Racine, Jean Baptiste (1639–1699) French poet and dramatist. He was an exponent of the classical tragedy in French drama, taking his subjects from Greek mythology and observing the rules of classical Greek drama. Many choral and operatic works, by such names as Handel, Gluck, and Mendelssohn, were based on his dramas.

See ➤ *Andromaque* (Grétry); ➤ *Athalie* (Mendelssohn and others); ➤ *Boieldieu* (*Athalie*); ➤ *Esther* (Handel); ➤ *Fauré* (*Cantique*); ➤ *Ifigenia in Aulide* (Graun); ➤ *Iphigénie en Aulide* (Gluck); ➤ *Lully* (*Idylle sur la paix*); ➤ *Massenet* (*Phèdre* incidental music); ➤ *Mitridate, Rè di Ponto* (Mozart); ➤ *Moreau* (*Cantiques spiritueles*, *Esther* and *Athalie*); ➤ *Roseingrave* (*Phaedra and Hippolytus*); ➤ *Rossini* (*Ermione*); ➤ *Saint-Saëns* (*Andromaque*); ➤ *Vogler* (*Athalie*).

rackett or **racket** or **ranket** or **sausage bassoon** ingenious Renaissance double-reed woodwind musical instrument incorporating a ninefold straight tube packed into a 22 cm/9 in compact cylinder. It emits a strong, rasping tone extending to F1 in double-bassoon range.

Radamisto opera by Handel (libretto by Nicola Francesco Haym, after Tacitus), produced in London at the King's Theatre, Haymarket, on 27 April 1720. In the story, the tyrant King Tiridate lusts after Zenobia, wife of Prince Radamisto, sending armies to conquer his rival. When Zenobia opts to die with her husband rather than yield to Tiridate, news arrives of a revolt in the tyrant's army and the married couple are saved.

Radcliffe, Philip (FitzHugh) (1905–1986) English scholar, author, and composer. He was educated at Charterhouse and King's College, Cambridge, and was a university lecturer in music at Cambridge 1947–72. His compositions include chamber music, part songs, and songs. He also wrote a book on Mendelssohn, and contributed chapters on the Scarlattis, Corelli, and Vivaldi to *The Heritage of Music*.

Radnai, Miklós (1892–1935) Hungarian composer. He studied at Budapest and Munich and was a professor at the Budapest Conservatory 1919–25, and later director of the Opera there.

Works OPERA AND STAGE the opera *The Former Lovers*; ballet *The Infanta's Birthday* (after Wilde, 1918).

ORCHESTRAL AND CHAMBER Hungarian Symphony, *Mosaic* suite, five poems, *Fairy Tale*, and *Orcan the Hero* for orchestra; piano trio; instrumental sonatas; piano works; songs.

Raff, (Joseph) Joachim (1822–1882) Swiss composer. He is best known for such single symphonies as *Im Walde* and *Frühlingsklänge/Voices of Spring*, suggesting Alpine imagery tinged by German Romanticism.

He studied to become a schoolmaster, but took to music and in 1843 had some works published on Mendelssohn's recommendation. He met Liszt, and at Cologne in 1846 Mendelssohn, who invited him to become his pupil at Leipzig but died before this was done. He then wrote criticism at Cologne, studied further at Stuttgart, and in 1850 settled at Weimar to be near Liszt. In 1856 he went to Wiesbaden, where he wrote incidental music for a drama by Wilhelm Genast and married his daughter Doris, an actor. In 1877 he became director of the Hoch Conservatory at Frankfurt.

Works OPERA AND STAGE operas, including *König Alfred* (1851) and *Dame Kobold* (on Calderón's *Dama duende*, 1870); incidental music for Genast's *Bernhard von Weimar* and other plays.

CHORAL oratorio *Weltende* and other choral works.

ORCHESTRAL eleven symphonies, including programme symphony *An das Vaterland*, *Im Walde*, *Lenore* (on Bürger's ballad), *Gelebt, gestrebt …*, *In den Alpen*, *Frühlingsklange*, *Im Sommer*, *Zur Herbstzeit*, *Der Winter* (unfinished), two suites, and three overtures for orchestra; sinfonietta for wind instruments; concerto, suite, and *Ode au printemps* for piano and orchestra; two violin concertos, cello concerto.

CHAMBER eight string quartets, string sextets, string octet, four piano trios, two piano quartets, piano quintet; five violin and piano sonatas; numerous piano works; violin pieces.

raga (Sanskrit *rāga* 'tone' or 'colour') in ➤ Indian music, a scale of notes and style of ornament for music associated with a particular mood or time of day; the equivalent term in rhythm is ➤ tala. A choice of raga and tala forms the basis of improvised music; however, a written composition may also be based on (and called) a raga.

ragtime US form of syncopated dance music of African-American origin and coming into fashion c.1910; it was the forerunner of jazz and swing. By far the best known composer of ragtime was Scott Joplin, whose *Maple Leaf Rag* was the first instrumental sheet music to sell a million copies.

Ragtime Work by Igor ➤ Stravinsky for eleven instruments, composed in 1918 and first performed in London on 27 April 1920, conducted by Arthur Bliss.

Raimbaut d'Orange (died 1173), also known as **Raimbaut de Vaqueiras** French count of Orange, Provence, and an eminent ➤ troubadour. Some 40 of his poems remain (including about 30 love songs). He was an outstanding practitioner of the hermetic style known as *trobar clus*.

He travelled widely with Guillaume des Baux, Prince of Orange, and the Marquis Boniface of Montferrat. He died in Thessaloniki, Greece.

Raimondi, Pietro (1786–1853) Italian composer. He studied at the Conservatorio di Pietà de' Turchini at Naples and wandered all over Italy in great poverty until he succeeded in producing an opera at Genoa in 1807. He produced operas at Rome, Milan, Naples, and in Sicily until 1824, and was director of the royal theatres there until 1832, when he became professor of composition at the Palermo Conservatory. In 1852 he was appointed maestro di cappella at St Peter's in Rome in succession to Francesco Basili.

Works OPERA the operas *Le bizzarrie d'amore* (1807), *Il ventaglio*, and 60 others, including a serious and a comic opera which could be performed together; 21 ballets.

CHORAL eight oratorios, including the trilogy *Giuseppe* (including *Putifar*, *Farao*, and *Giacobbe*, performable separately or simultaneously); Masses, Requiems, psalms, and other church music, much of it in very numerous parts; vocal fugues, one in 64 parts and including others in four parts, four of which could be sung together in 16 parts.

Raindrop Prelude piano prelude by Frédéric ➤ Chopin in D flat major, Op. 28, no. 15, written at Valdemosa, Majorca, in 1838. It is said to have been suggested by the dripping of raindrops from the roof; hence the continuously repeated A flat = G sharp, which is the dominant both of the main key and of the C sharp minor middle section.

Rainier, Priaulx (1903–1986) South African composer. She studied at Cape Town and after 1920, at the Royal Academy of Music in London, and lastly with Nadia Boulanger in Paris. In 1942, she was appointed professor at the Royal Academy of Music, London.

Works CHORAL *Archaic Songs* for chorus.

ORCHESTRAL ballet suite for orchestra (1950), *Sinfonia da camera* for strings (1947); *Incantation* for clarinet and orchestra; cello concerto (1964); *Aequora Lunae* for orchestra (1967); *Ploërmel* for winds and percussion (1973); violin concerto (1977), concertante for oboe, clarinet, and orchestra (1981).

CHAMBER string quartet (1939), viola and piano sonata, piano works, songs.

Raitio, Väinö (1891–1945) Finnish composer. He studied the piano with his mother, and later composition with Erkki Melartin and Furuhjelm, and with Ilyinsky in Moscow 1916–17. He taught composition at Viipuri 1932–38, but settled at Helsinki and devoted himself entirely to composition.

Works OPERA AND STAGE the operas *Jephtha's Daughter* (1931), *Princess Cecilia* (1936), and three others; ballet *Waterspout* (1929).

ORCHESTRAL symphonies, ten symphonic poems; piano concerto, concerto for violin and cello (1936), poem for cello and orchestra (1915).

CHAMBER string quartet, piano quintet; violin and piano sonata; songs.

Rakastava, The Lover three songs for male chorus a capella by Sibelius, Op. 14: *The Lover*, *The Path of the Beloved*, and *Good night*. Composed in 1893, they were first performed at Helsinki on 28 April 1894. A version for male chorus and strings was written that same year. In 1911, another version was rewritten for strings, triangle, and timpani.

Rake's Progress, The opera by Stravinsky (libretto by W H Auden and Chester Kallman, based on Hogarth), produced in Venice on 11 September 1951. The story begins as Tom Rakewell inherits a fortune and leaves his sweetheart Anne. Nick Shadow corrupts and ruins him, finally demanding his soul. Tom evades Nick, but loses his reason before dying.

Rakhmaninov alternative spelling for Russian composer Sergei ➤ Rachmaninov.

Rákóczy March Hungarian national tune named after Prince Ferencz Rákóczy, the leader of the revolt against Austria 1703–11. The Hungarian March in Hector Berlioz's *Damnation of Faust* is an orchestral arrangement of it and Franz ➤ **Liszt**'s 15th *Hungarian Rhapsody* for piano is based on it. Liszt also made a symphonic arrangement for orchestra and himself transcribed this for piano duet. The origin of the tune is unknown.

rallentando or **rall. (Italian 'slowing down')** in musical notation, indicating a gradual reduction in the speed of a passage; synonymous with ritardando.

Rameau, Jean-Philippe (1683–1764) French organist and composer. His *Traité de l'harmonie/ Treatise on Harmony* (1722) established academic rules for harmonic progression, and his varied works include keyboard and vocal music and many operas, such as *Castor and Pollux* (1737).

Ramis de Pareja, Bartolome (c.1440–after 1491) Spanish theorist and composer. He wrote a theoretical work in which he devised a way of tuning the ➤ **monochord** and wrote church music.

After lecturing at Salamanca he went to Italy, living at Bologna 1480–82 and later in Rome.

Ramler, Karl Wilhelm (1725–1798) German poet. His works inspired Johann Christoph Friedrich ➤ **Bach** (*Tod Jesu*) and ➤ **Telemann** (*Tod Jesu* and *Auferstehung Christi*), and Georg ➤ **Vogler** (*Ino*), among others.

Rands, Bernard (1935–) English composer. His music uses electronic techniques and is strongly influenced by ➤ **Berio**.

He studied at University College of North Wales, Bangor, and then in Italy with Roman Vlad and Luigi Dallapiccola. He lectured at Bangor 1961–70, and at York University 1970–76. In 1976 he moved to the USA and taught at the universities of California and Boston.

Works ENSEMBLE *Refractions* for 24 performers; *Actions for Six* for flute, viola, cello, harp, and two percussion players (1963); *Quartet Music* for piano quartet; *Four Compositions* for violin and piano; *Espressione IV* for two pianos; *Three Aspects* for piano; *Formants* for harp (1965); *As All Get Out* for chamber ensemble (1972); *... in the receding mist ...* for ensemble (1988).

ORCHESTRAL *Agenda* for orchestra (1970); *Canti del Sole* for tenor and orchestra (won a Pulitzer Prize in 1984); *Ceremonial I* and *II* for orchestra (1985–86); *Serenata 85*; *Hiraeth* for cello and orchestra (1987); *Body and Shadow* for orchestra (1988).

Ranz des Vaches Swiss cowherds' song or ➤ **alphorn** signal by which the cattle are called in June from the valleys to the mountain pastures. There are many different tunes, varying according to the cantons or even districts. They are metrically

very irregular and use only the natural notes of the alphorn. In classical music versions are heard in Gioacchino ➤ **Rossini**'s *William Tell* overture, Beethoven's ➤ *Pastoral Symphony* (link between last two movements), and the *Scène aux champs* in Hector Berlioz's ➤ *Symphonie fantastique*.

Rape of Lucretia, The opera by Benjamin Britten (libretto by Ronald Duncan, based on Livy, Shakespeare, and Obey's *Viol de Lucrèce*), produced at Glyndebourne in East Sussex, England, on 12 July 1946. The story is set in ancient Rome, where Lucretia is reckoned to be the only chaste woman. Prince Tarquinius sets out to test this, arriving at her house and asking for a bed for the night. While Lucretia sleeps, Tarquinius appears in her bedroom and kisses her. At first Lucretia responds, believing it to be her husband, but soon she realizes the awful truth. The next morning she is overcome by shame and stabs herself.

Raphael, Günther (1903–1960) German composer. In his early 20s he succeeded in having works published, played by the Busch quartet, and conducted by Wilhelm Furtwängler among others. He was professor at the Leipzig Conservatory 1926–34, resigning after the Nazis banned his music; after World War II he taught at Duisburg Conservatory 1949–53, and from 1957 at the Cologne Musikhochschule.

He studied under his father, a church organist, and later with Max Trapp and Robert Kahn at the Berlin Hochschule für Musik.

Works SACRED CHORAL MUSIC Requiem (1928), Te Deum (1930), cantata *Vater unser* (1945); 16 motets, Psalm 104 and other unaccompanied sacred choral works.

ORCHESTRAL five symphonies (1926–53), sinfonietta, *Theme, Variations and Rondo*, divertimento, *Smetana Suite* for orchestra; two violin concertos (1921, 1960), organ concerto (1936).

CHAMBER chamber concerto for cello with wind and strings, much other chamber music; organ and piano works.

Rapimento di Cefalo, Il, The Abduction of Cephalus opera by Giulio Caccini (libretto by Gabriello Chiabrera), produced at the Palazzo Vecchio, Florence, on 9 October 1600. In the story, Aurora (Dawn) seduces Cephalus, and as a result of her preoccupation, Night remains over the world. Jupiter has Cupid find Dawn and bring her back to illuminate the Earth.

Rappresentazione di anima e di corpo, Representation of Soul and Body a dramatic allegory, music by Emilio de' Cavalieri with words by Manni, produced in Rome, at the oratory of St Philip Neri, in February in 1600.

Rapsodie espagnole, Spanish Rhapsody orchestral work by Maurice Ravel in a Spanish manner as cultivated by a typically French composer with a strong taste for and leanings towards Spanish music. Composed in 1907, it was first performed at Paris on 15 March 1908.

rasch (German 'quick') term used in musical notation.

Raselius, Andreas (c.1563–1602), born Andreas Rasel German clergyman, theorist, and composer. He wrote a treatise on the ➤ hexachord, set hymn and psalm tunes in five parts, and composed German motets.

He studied at the Lutheran University of Heidelberg, became cantor at Regensburg 1584–1600, and was then music director to the Elector Palatine at Heidelberg.

Rasumovsky Quartets Beethoven's three string quartets, Op. 59 in F major, E minor, and C major. They were composed in 1806 and dedicated to the Russian ambassador to Vienna, Count (later Prince) Andrey Kiryllovich Rasumovsky (1752–1836), by whose domestic quartet, led by Schuppanzigh, they were first performed. The first two quartets contain Russian themes.

rataplan (French onomatopoeic; English 'rub-a-dub') word imitating the sound of the side-drum and used for music pieces, especially in opera, of a military-march character.

Ratcliff opera by Volkmar Andreae (libretto taken from Heine's tragedy *William Ratcliff*), produced at Duisburg, in Germany, on 25 May 1914.

Rathaus, Karol (1895–1954) Polish-born US composer. He studied with Franz Schreker in Vienna and followed him to Berlin when Schreker became director of the Hochschule für Musik, where Rathaus taught 1925–33. In 1934 he took refuge in London from the Nazi regime and later settled in the USA, becoming a US citizen in 1946.

Works OPERA AND STAGE the opera *Strange Soil* (1930); ballets *The Last Pierrot* (1927), and *Lion amoureux* (1937); incidental music to Shakespeare's *Merchant of Venice*, Gutzkow's *Uriel Acosta*, Hebbel's *Herodes und Mariamne*.

ORCHESTRAL three symphonies (1921–43), overture, serenade, suites, *Four Dance Pieces*, *Kontrapunktisches Triptychon* (1934), *Jacob's Dream*, *Polonaise symphonique* for orchestra; concertino for piano and orchestra; suite for violin and orchestra.

CHAMBER *Little Prelude* for trumpet and strings; five string quartets; two trios for violin, clarinet, and piano.

OTHER film music, including *The Brothers Karamazov* (1931) and *The Dictator* (1934); choral works.

Ratswahlkantate cantata by Bach (BWV 71), *Gott ist mein König*, written for the election of the town council of Mühlhausen on 4 February 1708 and performed on that day in St Mary's Church. Bach was at the time organist of St Blasius'.

rattle noise-producing toy, a ratchet, occasionally used as a percussion instrument in the modern orchestra.

Ratto di Proserpina, Il, The Rape of Proserpine opera by Peter Winter (libretto by Lorenzo da Ponte), produced in London at the King's Theatre, Haymarket, on 3 May 1804.

Rauchfangkehrer, Der, The Chimney-Sweep singspiel by Antonio Salieri (libretto by L von Auenbrugger), produced at the Burgtheater, Vienna, on 30 April 1781. In the story, Volpino, the chimney-sweep, tricks Herr von Bär and von Wölf into giving him a dowry for his fiancée Lisel. Bär and Wölf become engaged to the mother and daughter of the house.

rauschpfeife medieval windcap double-reed woodwind instrument in soprano or sopranino range, of wide bore and having a powerful reedy tone. It has been revived in recent years for use in Renaissance ➤ broken consorts and as a folk instrument.

Rautavaara, Einojuhani (1928–) Finnish composer. His music embraces a wide variety of idioms, including neoclassicism, ➤ serialism, and jazz.

He studied at the Sibelius Academy in Helsinki, at the Juilliard School in New York, and with Sessions and Copland at Tanglewood Music Center in Massachusetts. He was professor at the Sibelius Academy 1976–90.

Works OPERA AND STAGE *The Mine* (1963), *Apollo and Marsyas* (1973), *Marjatta the Lowly Maiden* (1977), *Thomas* (1985), *Vincent* (based on the life of Van Gogh, 1990).

ORCHESTRAL seven symphonies; concertos for cello, piano, and violin.

Ravel, (Joseph) Maurice (1875–1937) French composer and pianist. His work is characterized by its sensuousness, exotic harmonics, and dazzling orchestral effects. His opera *L'enfant et les sortilèges* (1924) illustrates most of the various styles that influenced him at different times. Other works include the piano pieces *Pavane pour une infante défunte/Pavane for a Dead Infanta* (1899) and *Jeux d'eau/Waterfall* (1901), and the ballets *Daphnis et Chloë* (1912) and *Boléro* (1928).

Ravel's father was of Swiss and his mother of Basque descent; they moved to Paris in the year of his birth. Ravel entered the Paris Conservatory in 1889, studying piano with Eugene Anthiôme and later with Charles Wilfrid de Bériot, also theory under Emile Pessard from 1891. He composed a good deal and in 1897 passed to Fauré's class for composition and to that of André Gédalge for counterpoint. In 1899 the Société Nationale performed his overture *Shéhérazade* (unconnected with the later song-cycle) and the *Pavane pour une infante défunte* in the original piano version. In 1905 the Paris Conservatory rejected his Prix de Rome submission. This provoked a scandal that led to the resignation of the director. Two of his finest works, the string quartet (1903) and the piano piece *Miroirs* (1905), date from the same period. In these pieces, as in others, Ravel's indebtedness to the Impressionists, as well as a concentration on minute detail, may be seen. In 1908 he set a new standard of piano writing with *Gaspard de la nuit*.

During the next ten years he wrote some of his best works. His first great public success came in 1911, when the Opéra-Comique brought out *L'heure espagnole*, and the second in 1912, when Diaghilev's Ballets Russes (Russian Ballet) produced *Daphnis et Chloé*. In this work Ravel displays his mastery of colourful orchestration, combining instruments in a subtle, ever-changing way.

During World War I he served in an ambulance corps at the front, but had to leave owing to ill-health in 1917. Although physically weakened, he produced such successful post-war works as *La valse*, a sinister work depicting a Viennese ballroom at the end of an era, the almost neobaroque *Le tombeau de Couperin*, and *L'enfant et les sortilèges*, an opera on the theme of childhood. He scornfully remarked of his *Boléro*, 'There's not a note of music in it', but was grateful for its popular success. His last large-scale works were the piano concerto in G and concerto for piano left hand. He made a great reputation and a comfortable living without ever holding an official musical post. In the 1920s he visited London more than once with great success and in 1928 received an honorary doctorate from Oxford University. A car accident in 1933 marked the beginning of a long illness, and he died after a brain operation.

Works *STAGE* opera *L'heure espagnole* (1911); opera-ballet *L'enfant et les sortilèges* (1925), ballet *Daphnis et Chloé* (1912), also *La valse* (composed 1919–20; first performance as ballet, 1928).

ORCHESTRAL works include *Rapsodie espagnole* for orchestra (1908), *Boléro* (1928); concerto for piano and orchestra (1929–31); piano concerto for the left hand with orchestra (1930); several orchestrations of piano works.

CHAMBER string quartet (1903), *Introduction et Allegro* for harp, flute, clarinet, and string quartet (1905); piano trio in A minor (1914); sonata for violin and cello (1922), sonata for violin and

piano.

PIANO 15 piano works including five *Miroirs* (1905), *Gaspard de la nuit* (three pieces after Louis Bertrand's prose poems, 1908), suite *Le tombeau de Couperin* (1917).

SONGS 29 songs including the cycles *Shéhérazade* (1903); *Chansons madécasses* for voice, flute, cello, and piano (1926); three part songs.

Ravenscroft, Thomas (c.1582–c.1633) English composer. He was a chorister at St Paul's Cathedral under Edward Pearce, took a degree in music at Cambridge University in 1607, and was music master at Christ's Hospital 1618–22.

Works *VOCAL* anthems, 55 of the 105 hymn-tune settings contained in his Psalter; madrigals: some of the four-part songs *The Pleasures of Five Usuall Recreations* in his treatise on notation *A Briefe Discourse* (1614) are by himself; some of the rounds and catches in the collections *Pammelia* (1609), *Deuteromelia* (1609), and *Melismata* (1611) are probably of his own composing.

Rawsthorne, Alan (1905–1971) English composer. He devoted all his time to composition and produced a comparatively small number of distinctive and highly finished works. His output includes three string quartets (1940, 1954, 1965) and sonatas for violin, viola (1953), and cello (1949).

After studying dentistry, he turned to music at the age of 20 and studied at the Royal Manchester College of Music 1926–29. He taught at Dartington Hall, Devon, 1932–34; but settled in London in 1935 and married the violinist Jessie Hinchliffe. In 1938 and 1939 he had works performed at the International Society for Contemporary Music festivals in London and Warsaw.

Works *ORCHESTRAL* three symphonies (1950, 1959, 1964), *Symphonic Studies*, overture *Street Corner* for orchestra; two piano concertos, two violin concertos (1948, 1956), concerto for clarinet and strings, cello concerto (1965).

CHAMBER AND VOCAL two string quartets (1954, 1964), Theme and Variations for string quartet (1939), quintet for piano and wind (1963); viola and piano sonata; Theme and Variations for two violins; Sonatina for oboe, flute and piano; two oboe quartets; four Bagatelles for piano; songs 'Away Delights' and 'God Lyaeus' (John Fletcher), *Three French Nursery Songs*.

Ray the supertonic note, pronounced 'Ray' and represented by the symbol r, in any key in tonic sol-fa notation, the system of musical notation without staves and notes and based on the old syllabic system of Do (Ut), Re, Mi, and so on.

Raymonda ballet by Alexander Glazunov (choreography by Marius Petipa), produced at the Mariinsky Theatre in St Petersburg on 19 January 1898.

Raymond ou Le Secret de la Reine, Raymond, or The Queen's Secret; or **Raymond** opera by Ambroise ➤ **Thomas** (libretto by A de Leuven and J B Rosier), produced at the Opéra-Comique, Paris, on 5 June 1851.

'Razor' Quartet, German **Rasiermesser** nickname of Haydn's string quartet in F minor, Op. 55, no. 2, composed in 1788, so called because Haydn is said to have offered the publisher Bland his best quartet in return for a good razor.

RCA Mark II synthesizer pioneer digitally programmable analogue synthesizer developed in 1959 by Harry Olsen and Herbert Belar. It was installed in the joint Columbia-Princeton electronic studio under the direction of US composers Otto ➤ **Luening** and Milton ➤ **Babbitt,** its best-known advocate. It was the first integrated device for pre-programmed synthesis and mixing of electronic and concrete sound materials, employing a punched card control system.

Re the old name for the note D in ➤ **solmization** (the designation of the musical scales by means of syllables). It is still used in Latin countries and in ➤ **tonic sol-fa** notation. The supertonic note in any key, it is represented by the symbol r and is pronounced 'Ray'.

Read, Gardner (1913–2005) US composer. He studied at the Eastman School, with Ildebrando Pizzetti in Italy and Aaron Copland at Tanglewood Music Center in Massachusetts. He was professor at Boston University School for the Arts 1948–78.

Works OPERA *Villon* (1967).

ORCHESTRAL AND CHAMBER MUSIC four symphonies, cello concerto (1945), piano concerto (1977); piano quintet (1945), and other chamber music; organ and piano pieces.

realism in music, a realistic style favouring simpler contemporary themes. Examples are the anvils in Richard ➤ **Wagner's** *Rheingold,* the sheep and wind machine in Richard ➤ **Strauss's** *Don Quixote,* and the nightingale (a gramophone record of the bird's song) in Ottorino ➤ **Respighi's** *Pini di Roma.* A realistic style of Italian opera is known as ➤ **verismo,** in which plots draw away from elaborate traditional mythological or historical subjects.

Strictly realistic representation in music is not easily attainable. Imitations of bells, birds, and similar effects are very frequent, but usually the more musical they are the less they approach realism.

realization in music, the writing out or playing at sight of the harmony from a ➤ **thorough bass;** it may also involve the preparation for performance of an uncompleted or sparsely written score, such as Friedrich Cerha's version of Act 3 of Al-

ban Berg's *Lulu,* or Raymond Leppard's popular and imaginative versions of Venetian opera.

In the music of the 18th century and earlier, continuo lines were written in a shorthand that needs realization, often taking account of extremely refined skills cultivated in the baroque era. Up to the end of the 18th century many works were written in the expectation that the soloists would improvise and embellish, often quite elaborately.

Before about 1700, composers often did not specify the ensembles to be used, and it is a complex business devising an ensemble appropriate to the style and techniques of the music. Beyond that, there could be a good argument for believing that an historically accurate reconstruction would be insufficient for present-day audiences; and there is a considerable history – going back to the early 19th century – of recasting earlier works to make them more acceptable to later conditions.

rebec(k) early string instrument of the violin type and of Arab origin, the ancestor of the violin family, though its shape is more like that of the mandolin, which is probably one of its descendants. It has three gut strings and is played with a bow. In France it survived until the 18th century, but only as a street instrument.

It is descended from the Arab rabab, a one- or two-stringed bowed fiddle still popular throughout the Arab world.

Rebelo, João Soares or **João Lourenço (1609–1661)** Portuguese composer. He was a fellow student of King John IV, who made him a nobleman on his accession in 1646.

Works CHURCH MUSIC psalms, Magnificat, Lamentations, Miserere, St Matthew Passion, Requiem, and other pieces.

Rebikov, Vladimir Ivanovich (1866–1920) Russian composer. He was the most advanced, if by no means the strongest or most important, Russian composer of his generation, using many unconventional devices (including whole-tone scales) and evolving an idiom of his own. His short piano and vocal pieces are his most characteristic work, and include a number of dramatic *melomimiki* (or *mélominiques,* small-scale works in an expressionist style).

He was born in Krasnoyarsk, Siberia, and studied at Moscow and Berlin. He later settled in southern Russia and founded music societies at Odessa and Kishinev. Some of his stage works are described as 'musico-psychological' or 'music-copsycholographic' dramas, among them his opera *The Christmas Tree* (1903).

Works STAGE the operas and dramatic scenes *The Storm* (1894), *The Christmas Tree* (1903), *Thea, The Woman with the Dagger* (based on Schnitzler's play, 1911), *Alpha and Omega* (1911), *The Abyss* (after Andreiev), *Narcissus* (after Ovid's *Metamorphoses*, 1913), *Fables* (after Krilov); ballet *Snow-White*.

ORCHESTRAL AND CHAMBER suites for orchestra and string orchestra; numerous sets of piano pieces, including *Rêveries d'automne* (1897), *Mélomimiques*, *Aspirer et attendre*, *Chansons blanches* (on the white keys).

recapitulation in music, the section of ➤ **sonata form** following the development section, in which the themes are presented in a manner similar or identical to the exposition, except that any material which was originally presented in the ➤ **dominant** or any other key, appears in the ➤ **tonic** key. A 'false' recapitulation was used at times by Beethoven and 19th-century composers either to present an additional development of musical ideas or to present temporarily the main themes in a key other than the tonic, as in the first movement of Beethoven's Sonata No. 3 (1795).

reception theory or **reception history** the study of the history of a piece of music after the date of its composition. This may take the form of studying the performance history of the work; or the reactions of audiences, both at its original performance and subsequently; or the writings of critics and scholars. The term is taken from German-speaking scholarship (where it is called *Rezeptionsgeschichte*), and treats pieces of music as historical phenomena which therefore change over time. This is in contrast to other forms of music history, which have tended to view pieces as unchanging, autonomous entities. Reception studies have become very influential in English-speaking scholarship in recent years. See Carl ➤ **Dahlhaus.**

***Re Cervo, Il*, The Stag King** revision made in 1962 by Hans Werner Henze of his 1955 opera ➤ *König Hirsch*; first performed in Kassel, Germany, on 10 March 1963.

recherché (French 'searched out') French equivalent of *ricercato*, from which the ➤ **ricercare** is derived; Beethoven still used this old term, as meaning strict fugal writing, in his *Great Fugue* for string quartet, Op. 133, in which he called a fugue 'tantôt libre, tantôt recherchée'.

récit 17th-century musical term for an accompanying solo, such as a vocal aria, an organ piece with a solo stop, and so on.

recital musical performance, usually with a miscellaneous programme, given by a single performer or by one singing or playing an instrument with a piano accompanist.

recitative declamatory, speechlike style of singing used in opera and oratorio. It rises and falls according to the meaning of the text and follows the rhythms and inflections of natural speech. A form of sung narration, it is used to carry the plot of the work forward. It is usually sparingly accompanied by harpsichord or organ.

recitativo stromentato (Italian 'instrumentated recitative') ➤ **recitative** accompaniment. The term is often used as a synonym for *recitativo accompagnato* (with a plain orchestral accompaniment), though it previously implied a more independent instrumental participation.

recorder any of a widespread range of woodwind instruments of the ➤ **whistle** type which flourished in ➤ **consort** ensembles in the Renaissance and baroque eras, along with viol consorts, as an instrumental medium for polyphonic music. Unlike the flute, the recorder is held vertically and blown into through a mouthpiece in which the air is diverted by an obstructive block called the 'fipple' and produces a milder tone than that of the flute. A modern consort may include a sopranino in F5, soprano (descant) in C4, alto (treble) in F3, tenor in C3, bass in F2, and great bass in C2.

Early Renaissance recorders are of fairly wide bore and penetrating tone; late Renaissance and baroque instruments are ➤ **fipple flutes** of narrower bore and sweet to brilliant tone. The solo recorder remained a popular solo instrument into the 18th century, and the revival of popular interest in recorder-playing after 1920, largely through the efforts of Arnold Dolmetsch, led to its wide adoption as a musical instrument for schools. Present-day makers have taken advantage of exotic hardwoods such as grenadilla to make instruments of brighter and stronger tone for concert soloists, and have also created hypothetical additions to existing consorts.

recte et retro or Italian **al rovescio (Latin 'right way and backwards')** in music, a form of ➤ **canon**, in which a second entry brings in the tune sung or played backwards. Recte et retro is similar to ➤ **cancrizans.**

Redemption, The English oratorio by Charles Gounod (words compiled by the composer), produced at the Birmingham Festival, England, in 1882.

Redlich, Hans (Ferdinand) (1903–1968) Austrian-born British musicologist. He specialized in Monteverdi, several of whose works he edited, including the *Vespers* of 1610 and *L'Incoronazione di Poppea*, and on whom he wrote two books (1932 and 1949, English edition 1952). He also wrote on modern music including a book on Alban Berg.

He studied at the Universities of Vienna, Munich, and Frankfurt. In 1925–29 he was opera conductor at Mainz, but in 1939 he took refuge in England. From 1955 to 1962 he was lecturer at Edinburgh University and in 1962 was appointed professor at Manchester University.

redoute (French, used also in German, and derived from Italian *ridotto*) a kind of public ball, particularly in the 18th century but carrying on into the 19th century in Austria and Germany, where dancers gathered haphazardly from all classes of society, usually at assembly halls called *Redoutensäle* in Germany. Composers of note, especially in Vienna, often wrote dances for redoutes.

reduction an arrangement, especially from a complex to a simpler score, such as an opera 'reduced' to a vocal score or an orchestral work arranged for piano.

reed instrument any of a class of wind instruments that uses a single or double flexible reed made of cane, metal, or plastic. The reed vibrates under pressure within an airtight enclosure (the mouth, ➤ **windcap**, bellows, or airbag as in bagpipes) and acts as a valve to let pulses of pressurized air into a tubular resonator (the body of the instrument). Single-reed instruments, where the reed vibrates against the material of the instrument, include clarinets and saxophones; double-reeds, where the reeds vibrate against each other, include oboes, shawms, bagpipes, and bassoons. A ➤ **free-reed instrument** has a reed, usually of metal, that is fixed at one end and free to vibrate in a slot at the other, such as accordions, mouth organs, and harmoniums.

Most reed instruments use finger holes to alter the pitch, and can be overblown (see ➤ **overblowing**) by the player increasing the tension of the lips to give a note an octave or twelfth higher. They have a very large dynamic and tonal range, and are more efficient than whistles in converting energy to sound in the tenor and bass registers.

reel a Scottish, Irish, and Scandinavian dance, either of Celtic or Scandinavian origin. It is performed with the dancers standing face to face and the music is in quick 2/4 or 4/4, occasionally 6/8, time and divided into regular eight-bar phrases. A musical characteristic of many reels is a drop into the triad of the subdominant unprepared by modulation.

Reese, Gustave (1899–1977) US musicologist. He was associate editor of *The Music Quarterly*, became editor on the death of Carl Engel in 1944, but resigned in 1945. His work includes the books *Music in the Middle Ages* and *Music in the Renaissance*.

He studied at New York University and became lecturer in music there in 1927 and professor in 1955.

Reeve, William (1757–1815) English composer. He was composer at Covent Garden and in 1802 part-owner of Sadler's Wells Theatre. In one of his more popular pieces, *The Caravan* (1803), a child was rescued from a tank of water by a well-trained dog; the music of his theatre pieces failed to gain as much attention.

He studied with Richardson, the organist at St James's Church, Westminster, and was organist at Totnes, Devon, 1781–83. After various engagements at London theatres, he joined the Covent Garden chorus, and there was asked to complete the ballet-pantomime *Oscar and Malvina* (after ➤ **Ossian**) left unfinished by William Shield in 1791 on account of differences with the management.

Works STAGE MUSIC *The Apparition* (1794), *Merry Sherwood* (1795), *Harlequin and Oberon* (1796), *Harlequin and Quixote* (after Cervantes), *Joan of Arc* (1798), *Paul and Virginia* (with Mazzinghi, based on Saint-Pierre, 1800), *Rokeby Castle* (1813), and many others (some with Braham, Davy, Mazzinghi or Moorehead); music for Sadler's Wells pantomimes.

Refice, Licinio (1883–1954) Italian composer. His two operas combined religious sentiments with post-*verismo* Romantic expression and were promoted by the Vatican.

He became professor of church music at the Scuola Pontifica in Rome in 1910 and in 1911 conductor at the church of Santa Maria Maggiore.

Works OPERA *Cecilia* (1934) and *Margherita da Cortona* (1938).

CHURCH MUSIC 40 Masses, motets, Requiem, *Stabat Mater*, and other church music.

CHORAL two oratorios, three sacred cantatas, three choral symphonies, poems.

'Reformation' Symphony Mendelssohn's fifth symphony, Op. 107, in D minor, composed in 1830 for the tercentenary of the Augsburg Confession. It was not performed there owing to Roman Catholic opposition, but was produced in Berlin in November 1832.

refrain in music, a recurrent strain in a song, returning with the same words at the beginning, middle or end of each verse with music which may or may not be derived from the first strain.

regal portable reed organ powered by bellows, said to have been invented about 1460 by Heinrich Traxdorff of Nuremberg in Germany, and current in Europe until the 17th century. A modern version is used in Indian popular music.

Reger, (Johann Baptist Joseph) Max(imilian) (1873–1916) German composer, pianist, and professor at the Leipzig Conservatory from 1907. A master of the fugue, with the ability to control tightly the form and harmonic direction of his compositions, Reger is sometimes regarded as the greatest composer for organ since Johann Sebastian Bach. His works embody a particular blend of contrapuntal ingenuity and Romantic sentimentality, and include symphonic poems, sonatas, Romantic character pieces, and orchestral variations and fugues on themes by Beethoven, Mozart, and other less well known composers.

Reger was a master of counterpoint, integrating 19th-century chromatic developments into his works. He first learnt music from his mother and at the age of 13 he became organist at the Catholic church of Weiden in Bavaria, where his parents had moved in 1874. After three years there Heinrich Reimann was consulted about his gifts and invited him to become his pupil at Sondershausen. Reger went there in 1890 and the next year followed his master to Wiesbaden, where he soon became a teacher at the Conservatory. A period divided between hard work and dissipation led to a serious breakdown, and he lived with his parents at Weiden again 1899–1901, writing vast quantities of music, including many more pieces for organ.

In 1901 he went to Munich in the hope of making his way as a composer, but posing as a progressive while being in reality a conservative, he made enemies all round and had some success only with his piano playing. The *Sinfonietta* for orchestra was a failure at its Berlin premiere, although it is now recognized as one of his most attractive works. He began to tour Germany and also visited Prague and Vienna, and gradually his work became known; he also made a reputation as a remarkable composition teacher. In 1907 he settled at Leipzig as music director to the University and professor at the Conservatory, soon resigning the former post as uncongenial, but retaining the latter for the rest of his life. In 1911 he became conductor of the ducal orchestra at Meiningen, with which he went on tour, but this came to an end in 1914, when he went to live at Jena, travelling to Leipzig each week to carry out his duties at the Conservatory.

Works ORCHESTRAL variations on themes by Johann Adam Hiller (1907) and by Mozart (1914), Romantic Suite (1912), four tone poems (on pictures by Böcklin) for orchestra (1913); piano concerto (1910), violin concerto (1908).

CHAMBER clarinet quintet; seven violin and piano sonatas, three clarinet and piano sonatas.

ORGAN two sonatas, two suites, Fantasy and Fugue on B.A.C.H., Variations and Fugue on original theme, Introduction, Passacaglia and Fugue, and other pieces.

PIANO AND SONGS Variations and Fugue on theme by Bach (1904) and numerous smaller works for piano, piano duets; many songs including *Schlichte Weisen*; part songs.

Regino of Prüm (c.842–915) German Benedictine monk and music historian, canonist, and theorist. He was abbot of Prüm 892–99. He is believed to have been the first to arrange ➤ **antiphons** and responsories according to their mode in a *tonarius* (a liturgical book containing antiphones and responsories of the Office and the Mass, arranged according to the eight psalm tones of the Gregorian chant). The first comprehensive tonary surviving after the Metz tonary of 870, the *Octo toni de musicae artis* is one of the most comprehensive plainchant sources in existence.

Regis, Jean (c.1430–c.1495) Flemish composer. He wrote two Masses, including one on *L'Homme armé*, songs in parts, eight motets, and other pieces.

He was choirmaster at Antwerp Cathedral and was Dufay's secretary at Cambrai in the 1440s. He went about 1451 to Soignies, and remained there.

register in music, a set of organ pipes, controlled by one stop, used in ➤ **registration** to produce a characteristic combination of tone and dynamics. Also, a certain vocal or instrumental range of pitches, often associated with a characteristic timbre, for example, the ➤ **chalumeau** register of a clarinet or the ➤ **head voice** register of a singer.

registration in music, in organ and harpsichord playing, the selection of stops (levers affecting the tone qualities and power of the instrument) to be used, either prescribed by a composer or left to the player's taste.

Regnart, François (c.1540–c.1600) Flemish composer. He learnt music at Tournai Cathedral and studied at Douai University.

Works CHORAL AND VOICE motets, chansons, *Poésies de Ronsard et autres* for four–five voices.

Regnart, Jacques (c.1539–1599) Flemish composer, brother of François ➤ **Regnart**. His two other brothers, Charles and Paschasius, contributed motets to a collection in which François and Jacques also appeared. The collection was edited by a fifth brother, Augustin, a canon at Lille.

He went to Vienna and Prague as a pupil to the Imperial chapel at an early age, became a tenor there in the 1560s, and in the 1570s was choirmaster and vice-kapellmeister. In 1585–96 he was in the service of the Archduke Ferdinand at Innsbruck, but lived in Prague for the last five years of his life.

Works CHURCH MUSIC 37 Masses, 195 motets.

SONGS *canzone italiane* and German songs for five voices.

Reich, Steve (1936–), born **Stephen Michael Reich** US composer. His minimalist music employs simple patterns carefully superimposed and modified to highlight constantly changing melodies and rhythms; examples are *Phase Patterns* for four electronic organs (1970), *Music for Mallet Instruments, Voices, and Organ* (1973), and *Music for Percussion and Keyboards* (1984).

Reich was a pupil of Luciano ➤ **Berio** and Darius ➤ **Milhaud**. In 1966, he founded the ensemble Steve Reich and Musicians, and began to study African, Balinese, and Hebrew music. He became a leading light of the minimalist school of composers, abandoning orthodox notions of harmony and counterpoint in favour of repeated phrases which typically evolve only gradually over time. His works have had much success in Europe and the USA. His other compositions include *The Cave* (1993) and *City Life* (1994).

Works ENSEMBLE *Pitch Charts* for instrumental ensemble (1963); *Music for Piano and Tapes* (1964); *It's Gonna Rain* for tape (1965); *My Name Is* with audience participation (1967); *Pulse Music* (1969); *Drumming* for eight small tuned drums, three marimbas, three glockenspiels, two female voices and piccolo (1971); *Clapping Music* (1972); *Music for Pieces of Wood* (1973); *Music for 18 Musicians* (1975); Octet (1979); *Tehillim* Hebrew psalms (1981); *Vermont Counterpoint* for eleven flutes (1982); *Different Trains* for string quartet and tape (1988); *Sextet* (1985); *New York Counterpoint* for clarinet and tape (1985).

ORCHESTRAL AND STAGE *The Desert Music* for 24 amplified voices and orchestra (1984); *Impact* dance (1985); *Three Movements* (1986) and *The Four Sections* (1987) for orchestra; music theatre *The Cave* (1989–93); *City Life* (1995).

Reicha, Antonín (1770–1836) Czech-born French theorist, teacher, and composer. After working in Bonn 1787–94, where he was friendly with Beethoven, he travelled widely in Europe, settling finally in Paris where he spent the rest of his life. He wrote much experimental music and tried many orchestral innovations but only his more conventional works were published in his lifetime. His compositions include eight operas, two symphonies, three concertos and much piano and chamber music, especially for wind quintet.

He was born in Prague, and studied at Wallerstein, Bavaria, under his uncle Joseph Reicha (1746–1795), from whose wife he learnt French. In 1785 he went to Bonn with his uncle, who became music director there and worked at the electoral court, where he got to know Beethoven. He taught music in Hamburg 1794–99, and had some success as a composer in Paris 1799–1802, but then went to Vienna, where he remained until 1808 and was patronized by the empress. He spent the rest of his life in Paris and became pro-

fessor at the Conservatory in 1818, where his pupils included Berlioz, Franck, and Gounod.

He produced five books on music theory, providing a progressive course to a high compositional and aesthetic level; these were internationally successful.

Works OPERA *Godefroid de Montfort* (1796), *Ouboualdi, ou Les Français en Egypte* (1798), *Cagliostro* (with Dourlen, 1810), *Natalie* (1816), *Sapho*.

ORCHESTRAL 16 symphonies, *Scènes musiciennes* for orchestra.

CHAMBER 20 string quartets, six string quintets, Diecetto and Octet for strings and wind, 24 wind quintets, six string trios, duets for violins and for flutes; twelve violin and piano sonatas; piano sonatas and pieces.

Reichardt, Johann Friedrich (1752–1814) German composer. His output consists chiefly of vocal works, including about 1,500 songs; he was a forerunner of Schubert in song composition. His work is notable for a wide range of literary influences, including Goethe, Shakespeare, Sophocles, Schiller, Milton, and even Metastasio. He also wrote several books on music.

He studied at Königsberg University and picked up a rather haphazard musical education. He travelled widely 1771–74 and published his experiences in *Vertraute Breife*. After working as a civil servant at Königsberg, he obtained the post of music director at the Prussian court in 1776, lived at Berlin and Potsdam, produced operas, and in 1783 founded a Concert Spirituel. He also published collections of music and musical criticism. After the death of Frederick II he made himself disliked more and more and in 1793 he was dismissed, ostensibly for his sympathy with the French Revolution. He retired to Giebichenstein in 1794, only briefly holding a post at the court of Jérôme Bonaparte at Kassel in Germany in 1808.

He married Juliane Benda (1752–1783), a singer, pianist, and composer, daughter of the composer Franz Benda, and had a daughter, Louise (1780–1826), who became a singer and also wrote songs.

Works OPERA AND STAGE *Hänschen und Gretchen* (1772), *Amors Guekkasten* (1773), *Cephalus und Procris* (1777), *Le feste galanti, Claudine von Villa Bella* (Goethe, 1789), *Erwin und Elmire* (Goethe, 1793), *L'Olimpiade* (Metastasio, 1791), *Tamerlan* (in French), *Jery und Bätely* (Goethe), *Der Taucher* (after Schiller's ballad, 1811), *Brenno, Die Geisterinsel* (after Shakespeare's *Tempest*, 1798), and about twelve others; incidental music to Shakespeare's *Macbeth* (1795), several plays by Goethe and Kotzebue's *Die Kreuzfahrer*.

CHORAL cantatas *Ariadne auf Náxos, Ino* (1779), *Morning Hymn* (Milton, translated by Herder) and others.

OTHER instrumental works, about 1,500 songs.

Reichenau, Berno of (died 1048) German Benedictine monk and music theorist. He was first a monk at Prüm, and abbot of Reichenau from 1008. He compiled a *tonarius*, dealing with the organization of the church chants into 'tones' – eight modes of the Gregorian chant.

Reigen (German for 'roundelay') German musical term.

Reimann, Aribert (1936–) German composer and pianist. Many of his works are inspired by literature; his best-known work is the opera *Lear* (1978), after Shakespeare's *King Lear*.

He studied with Boris Blacher in Berlin. His early music uses serial technique, but he renounced this kind of composition in 1967, turning to literary sources for a musical starting point, including Shakespeare, Strindberg, Kafka (*Das Schloss*), Euripides (*Troades*), Günther Grass, Byron, Edgar Allan Poe, and even Sylvia Plath. He gave frequent recitals and made recordings with Dietrich Fischer-Dieskau until his retirement in 1992.

Works OPERA AND STAGE the operas *Traumspiel* (after Strindberg's *Dream Play*, 1965), *Melusine* (1971), *Gespenstersonate* (after Strindberg's *Ghost Sonata*, 1984), *Troades* (1986), and *Das Schloss* (1991); the ballet *Stoffreste* (1957, revised as *Die Vogelscheuchen/The Scarecrows*, 1970).

ORCHESTRAL two piano concertos (1961, 1972), cello concerto (1959), *Totentanze* for baritone and orchestra (1960), *Hölderlin-Fragmente* for soprano and orchestra (1963), *Inane* monologue for soprano and orchestra (1969), Requiem *Wolkenloses Christfest/Cloudless Christmas* for baritone, cello, and orchestra (1974); the symphony *Lear* for baritone and orchestra (1980), *Chacun sa Chimère* for soprano, mezzo, baritone, and orchestra (1982); *Apocalyptic Fragment* for mezzo, piano, and orchestra (1987); *I Fragmente* for orchestra (1988); concerto for violin, cello, and orchestra (1989); nine pieces for orchestra (1994).

CHAMBER AND VOCAL trio for violin, viola, and cello (1987); *Shine and Dark* for baritone and piano (1990); *Lines* for soprano and 14 instruments (after Shelley, 1973); *Unrevealed* for baritone and string quartet (1980).

Reinach, Théodore (1860–1928) French archaeologist and historian. He wrote several works on Greek music and of the libretti of Maurice Emmanuel's *Salamine* (after Aeschylus' *Persae*) and Roussel's *La Naissance de la lyre*.

Re in ascolto, Un, A Listening King opera by Luciano Berio (libretto by I Calvin) produced at Salzburg on 7 August 1984, and conducted by Maazel. In the story, the ageing Prospero holds auditions for a new theatre production, but is dissatisfied until he hears the female protagonist.

Reincken, Johann Adam (1623–1722), German **Jan Adams Reinken** German organist and composer. After studying with Heinrich Scheidemann 1654–57, he became his assistant at the church of St Catherine at Hamburg in 1658, and succeeded him as organist in 1663, remaining in the post until his death. Bach walked from Lüneburg as a youth and later came from Cöthen to hear him play.

Works CHORAL AND ORGAN chorale preludes, toccatas, fugues, and other pieces for organ; *Hortus musicus* for two violins, viola da gamba, and bass (published Hamburg, 1687); keyboard pieces.

Reinecke, Carl (Heinrich Carsten) (1824–1910) German pianist, composer, and conductor. He was conductor of the Gewandhaus concerts and professor of composition at the Leipzig Conservatory from 1860.

He settled in Leipzig in 1843. He was pianist to the Danish court 1846–48, and visited Copenhagen several times.

Works CHORAL fairy-tale cantatas for female voices *Schneewittchen, Dornröschen, Aschenbrödel*, and others.

ORCHESTRAL AND INSTRUMENTAL three symphonies 1870–95), overtures *Dame Kobold* (Calderón's *Dama duende*), *Aladdin, Friedensfeier, Zenobia* and other orchestral works; four piano concertos (1879–1900), concertos for violin, for cello, for flute, and for harp.

CHAMBER AND VOCAL five string quartets, wind octet, seven piano trios and other chamber music; three piano sonatas and many pieces, including sonatinas; songs.

Reine de Saba, La, The Queen of Sheba opera by Charles Gounod (libretto by Jules Barbier and Michel Carré), produced at the Paris Opéra on 28 February 1862. The story concerns King Solomon, who wants to marry Balkis, Queen of Sheba, but she loves the King's architect Adoniram. They plan to elope but Adoniram is killed as they escape.

Reine (de France), La, The Queen of France nickname of Joseph ➤ Haydn's symphony No. 85 in B flat major, composed for Paris 1785–86.

Reinthaler, Karl (Martin) (1822–1896) German composer and conductor. He became cathedral organist and choral conductor at Bremen in 1858. He conducted the first performance of Brahms's German Requiem, in 1868.

After some early music training he went to Berlin to study theology, but turned to music, studying under A B Marx. With a grant from Frederick William IV he then studied further in Paris and Italy; in 1825 he joined the staff of the Cologne Conservatory.

Works OPERA *Edda* (1875), *Das Käthchen von Heilbronn* (after Heinrich von Kleist, 1881).

CHORAL oratorio *Jephtha* (1856), cantata *In der Wüste*, hymns and other church music.

OTHER symphonies; part songs.

réjouissance (French 'enjoyment') in music, sprightly movement sometimes found as one of the accessory pieces in early baroque ➤ **suites**.

relative in music, term describing the connection between major and minor keys which bear the same ➤ **key signature**. The relative major's ➤ **tonic** note is three semitones higher than that of the relative minor. For example, C major is the relative major of A minor, and B minor is the relative minor of D major.

Re Lear, King Lear opera by Italian librettist Alberto Ghislanzoni (libretto by composer based on Shakespeare), produced in Rome at the Teatro Reale on 24 June 1937.

For Verdi's opera and a plot synopsis see ➤ *King Lear*.

Reliquie (German, from Latin 'the relic') nickname sometimes given to Schubert's unfinished C major piano sonata begun in 1825, of which only the first and slow movements were completed. The fragmentary minuet and finale have been completed by Ludwig Stark, by Ernst Křenek, and by Willi Rehberg.

Rellstab, (Heinrich Friedrich) Ludwig (1799–1860) German critic, novelist, and poet, son of the publisher and critic Johann Karl Friedrich Rellstab (1759–1813). He studied with Ludwig Berger and Bernhard Klein, and followed his father as music critic of the *Vossische Zeitung* and edited the periodical *Iris im Gebiete der Tonkunst* 1830–42. He was imprisoned for satirizing Henriette Sontag's devotion to Rossini's operas and attacking Gaspare Spontini. His books include various musical studies and several novels on musical themes. Schubert set ten of his poems to music, including *Ständchen*. See ➤ **Schwanengesang**.

Remigius of Auxerre (c.841–c.908), also known as **Remy of Auxerre** or **Remigius Autissiodorensis** Benedictine monk and music theorist. His music theory takes the form of a commentary on Martianus ➤ **Capella**, especially as concerns notation. He was at the monastery of St Germain in Auxerre 861–883 or 893; afterwards he worked at Rheims. At the end of his life he also taught in Paris; Odo de Cluny was amongst his pupils.

Renard burlesque by Stravinsky, composed 1915–16 and first performed at Paris on 18 May 1922. In the performance, a vixen cajoles a cock out of a tree, but it is saved by the cat; during a second attempt the vixen is killed by the cat and a ram.

Rencontre imprévue, La, The Unforeseen Meeting opera by Christoph Willibald von Gluck (libretto by L H Dancourt, based on a vaudeville by Lesage and d'Orneval), Later known as *Les* ➤ **Pèlerins de le Mecque**/*The Pilgrims to Mecca*, the opera was first produced at the Burgtheater in Vienna on 7 January 1764. In the story, Ali seeks his bride, the Princess Rezia, kidnapped by pirates and desired by an amorous sultan. See also ➤ *Incontro Improvviso, L'* (Haydn).

Re pastore, Il, The Shepherd King opera by Austrian composer Giuseppe Bonno (libretto by Metastasio), produced in Vienna at the Schönbrunn Palace, on 13 May 1751. The story concerns the shepherd Amyntas who is revealed to be the heir of Sidon but is willing to give up the throne to marry Elisa. King Alexander of Macedonia allows him both a crown and a wedding.

Opera by Christoph Willibald von Gluck (libretto as above), produced at the Burgtheater, Vienna, on 8 December 1756.

Opera by Mozart (libretto as above), produced in Salzburg on 23 April 1775.

repeat in music, the restatement of a section of a composition, not written out a second time, but indicated by repeat signs. In music of the 18th century, the expositions of movements in sonata form are nearly always marked for repetition. See also ➤ **reprise**.

Repeat signs.

répétiteur (French 'coach') a musician who coaches opera singers in learning their parts, and may also run rehearsals, usually playing a ➤ **reduction** at the piano. Many conductors of opera first began their careers as répétiteurs.

Répons work by Pierre Boulez for chamber orchestra and six solo instruments and computer. It was composed and first performed in Donaueschingen, Germany, in 1981, and was later revised in London, on 18 June 1982.

reprise in music, a repeat of previous material, usually following an intervening and contrasting section. In ➤ **sonata form** the term has two meanings: usually it is synonymous with ➤ **recapitulation**, but in early sonatas in which a double bar precedes the development it may refer to a repeat of the ➤ **exposition**, as in sonatas by C P E Bach. In ➤ **rondo** form the term denotes the recurring main theme. In the ➤ **binary form** composition of 17th-century France, the term denotes the second section, as in dance movements in the suites of Jean-Henri D'Anglebert (1635–1691).

Requiem (from Latin *Requiem aeternam dona eis, Domine*, 'Give them eternal rest, O Lord') in the Roman Catholic Church, a Mass for the dead. Musical settings include those by Palestrina, Mozart, Berlioz, Verdi, Fauré, and Britten.

Requiem Requiem by Brahms; see ➤ *German Requiem*.

Requiem by Verdi; see ➤ *Manzoni Requiem*.

Requiem Canticles work by Igor ➤ Stravinsky for mezzo-soprano, bass, chorus, and orchestra. It was composed 1965–66 and first performed at Princeton, New Jersey, on 8 October 1966. It was Stravinsky's last major work.

Requiem for Rossini a Mass for the Dead planned by Verdi for performance in memory of Rossini's death in 1868, his suggestion being that each portion should be written by a different Italian composer of eminence. He himself composed the 'Libera me' in 1869, and the other contributors were Bazzini, Cagnoni, Coccia, Mabellini, Pedrotti, Petrella, and Ricci. Mercadante was also invited, but was unable to comply on account of blindness and infirmity. The work was never performed and the composers all withdrew their contributions. Verdi's was later used, with some alterations, for the ➤ *Manzoni Requiem* of 1873–74.

rescue opera a type of French opera, the libretto of which is based on plots, often taken from true happenings (the words *fait historique* sometimes appear in the subtitle), in which the hero or heroine is saved after fearful trials and tribulations. The taste for such works arose during the French Revolution. The most familiar examples are Luigi Cherubini's *Les Deux Journées* and Beethoven's *Fidelio*, both with libretti by Bouilly. The latter work was based on a German translation of *Léonore* written for Gaveaux.

resin alternative name for ➤ *rosin*.

resolution in music, a progression from a dissonant harmony to a less dissonant or consonant harmony. For example, in an ➤ **appoggiatura** (a form of melodic ornament), the dissonant melodic note resolves by moving a step lower, thus creating a consonant harmony. Resolving dissonance by moving a step lower is the traditional classical method. During the 19th century composers used other kinds of resolution more frequently than before, such as moving a step higher or sometimes incorporating a leap. Composers of the 20th century often do not require a dissonance to be resolved.

Respighi, Elsa (1894–1996), born **Elsa Olivieri-Sangiacomo** Italian singer and composer. She was a pupil of Ottorino ➤ Respighi at the Accademia di Santa Cecilia in Rome and married

him in 1919. She finished the orchestration of his opera *Lucrezia* and wrote three of her own. She also wrote choral works, a symphonic poem, a dance suite for orchestra, songs from the *Rubáiyát of Omar Khayyám*, and many other pieces.

Respighi, Ottorino (1879–1936) Italian composer. His works include the symphonic poems *Fontane di Roma/The Fountains of Rome* (1917) and *Pini di Roma/The Pines of Rome* (incorporating the recorded song of a nightingale, 1924), operas, and chamber music. He was a student of Rimsky-Korsakov.

respond in music, a type of church chant; see ➤ **responsory**.

response a type of ➤ **antiphony** used in the churches of the Anglican communion, in which the congregation replies to the ➤ **plainsong** chants of the priest; in Reformed churches, it refers to a short piece sung by the choir following a prayer. In this context the response often consists of a repeated 'amen'.

responsorial psalmody in music, a type of church chant; see ➤ **responsory**.

responsory, Latin **responsorium** in music, church chant involving the response by a choir to a verse sung by soloists, also called *respond*. Originally this would have taken the form of a response by the congregation to the leader or *cantor*. In the 9th century, it became an elaborate musical form demanding trained soloists and choir. The Gradual, Alleluia, and (for a time) the Offertory of the Mass were responsorial chants.

The most important responsoria in the Offices were the *responsoria prolixa*, sung at Matins. Like those of the Mass, they became a vehicle for polyphonic settings, the polyphony being reserved for the soloists' portions of the chant. When choral polyphony became the norm in the mid-15th century, the procedure was frequently, though not invariably, reversed. Late 16th-century settings, such as those by Tomás Victoria for Holy Week, assign the entire text to the polyphonic choir.

rest in music, a silence, or the notation indicating a silence.

Resurrection opera by Franco ➤ **Alfano**; see ➤ *Risurrezione*.

'Resurrection' Symphony symphony by Gustav ➤ **Mahler**, no. 2 in C minor, for soprano, mezzo-soprano, chorus, and orchestra. It was composed 1888–94 and revised in 1910. The finale is a setting of Friedrich Klopstock's chorale *Aufersteh'n/Resurrection*. The work was written partly as a statement of Mahler's conversion to Roman Catholicism; he strongly felt that his Jewish origin was preventing him from gaining

Breve	Semibreve	Minim	Crotchet	Quaver	Semiquaver	Demisemiquaver
∎	▬	▬	𝄽 or 𝄾	𝄾	𝄿	𝅀

The symbols for various rests. For the crotchet, modern notation favours the left-hand one of the two alternatives.

widespread acceptance. Mahler conducted its first performance in Berlin, on 13 December 1895.

Retablo de Maese Pedro, El, Master Peter's Puppet Show marionette opera by Manuel de Falla (libretto by composer based on a chapter from Cervantes' *Don Quixote*). Produced in Seville on 23 March 1923 in concert form; its first stage performance was in Paris on 25 June 1923. The story concerns the knight Gayferos, who, with the bumbling help of Don Quixote, rescues his wife Melisendra from the Moors.

retardation in music, a term sometimes used for a suspension which resolves upwards.

Re Teodoro in Venezia, Il, Theodore at Venice opera by Giovanni Paisiello (libretto by Giambattista Casti), produced at the Burgtheater in Vienna on 23 August 1784. In the story, the deposed King Teodoro hides from creditors in Venice. He falls in love with Lisetta, but she is united with Sandrino, and Teodoro ends up in debtors' prison.

Réti, Rudolf (1885–1957) Austrian composer, pianist, critic, and musical analyst. A champion of new music from the first, he gave the first performance of Schoenberg's Op. 11 piano pieces and was one of the founders of the International Society for Contemporary Music in 1922.

He studied at the Vienna Conservatory and emigrated to the USA in 1938. He wrote *The Thematic Process in Music* and *Tonality, Atonality and Pantonality.*

Works OPERA AND STAGE the opera *Ivan and the Drum* (after Tolstoy), the opera-ballet *David and Goliath.*

ORCHESTRAL AND CHORAL *The Dead Mourn the Living, Three Allegories* for orchestra (1953); two piano concertos; *The Greatest of All* for chorus and orchestra.

CHAMBER string quartet, piano pieces, songs.

retrograde in music, term describing a process in which the order of notes is reversed. It is used as a basic technique in 20th-century ➔ serialism, in addition to ➔ inversion. However, it also occurs in music of the Middle Ages, as a form of musical riddle, the first known example dating from the 13th century. Haydn used retrograde motion in the third movement of his Symphony no. 47 in G (1772), as did Beethoven in the final fugue of his piano sonata *Hammerklavier* (1818).

retrograde motion see ➔ cancrizans and ➔ recte et retro.

Reubke, Julius (1834–1858) German composer and pianist. The son of the organ builder Adolf Reubke (1805–75), he studied under Liszt at Weimar.

Works MUSIC FOR ORGAN AND KEYBOARD organ sonata *The 94th Psalm* (1857), sonata (1857), pieces for piano.

OTHER songs and other pieces.

Reutter, (Johann Adam Karl) Georg (junior) (1708–1772) Austrian organist and composer. He held several posts as kapellmeister (music director) in Vienna, both at court and at St Stephen's Cathedral.

He studied under his father Georg Reutter and with Antonio Caldara, was appointed court composer at Vienna in 1731, and in 1738 succeeded his father as chief kapellmeister of St Stephen's Cathedral, where Haydn was his pupil as a chorister. He was second court kapellmeister from 1747, first from 1751. He held these posts, in plurality with that at St Stephen's, to the detriment of the younger generation of composers, including Christoph Willibald von Gluck and Haydn. Music at the cathedral also suffered during this period, but this was at least partly due to budget cuts at the time. He was ennobled in 1740.

Works OPERA about 40, including *Archidamia* (1727), *La forza dell' amicizia* (with Caldara, 1728), *Alessandro il Grande* (1732), *Dafne* (1734), and *Il sacrifizio in Aulide* (1735).

ORATORIOS *Abel, La Betulia liberata* (1734), *Gioas.*

CHURCH MUSIC 81 Masses; six Requiems; 126 motets, and much other church music.

OTHER symphonies, serenades, chamber music, keyboard music.

Rêve, Le, The Dream opera by Alfred Bruneau (libretto by L Gallet, based on Emil Zola's novel), produced at the Opéra-Comique, Paris, on 18 June 1891.

Reveil des oiseaux, Awakening of the birds works by Messiaen for piano and orchestra, first performed in Donaueschingen on 11 October 1953, and conducted by Rosbaud.

Revelation and Fall work for soprano and 16 instruments by Maxwell Davies (text by Georg Trakl). Composed in 1965, it was first performed in London on 26 February 1968, and conducted by Davies.

Revisor, Der opera in five acts by Werner Egk (libretto by composer after Gogol's story *The Government Inspector*). It was first produced at Schwetzingen on 9 May 1957. In the story, the minor civil servant Chlestakov is mistaken for a government inspector by corrupt town officials and takes advantage of the situation to woo the mayor's daughter.

Revolutionary Etude the nickname of Chopin's étude in C minor, Op. 10 no. 12, for piano, written at Stuttgart in September 1831, when, on his way to Paris, he heard of the fall of Warsaw to the Russians, which marked the end of the November Uprising.

Revueltas, Silvestre (1899–1940) Mexican violinist and composer. His music has great vigour and rhythmic power. His best-known work, *Sensemaya*, is an orchestral depiction of a snake-killing ritual.

He studied at Mexico City and at St Edward's College, Austin, Texas, USA; he also studied composition with Felix Borowski at Chicago. He was appointed at Mexico City as violinist 1920–22, but continued to study the instrument under P Kochansky and Otakar Ševčik (1922–26). Later he gave recitals of modern music with Carlos Chávez as pianist, and after some theatre appointments joined the Orquesta Sinfónica at Mexico City as Chávez's assistant conductor 1929–35. He also became professor at the Conservatory there.

Works FILM MUSIC music for numerous films: *Cuauhnahuac, Esquinas* (1930), *Ventanas, Alcancías* (1932), *Colorines, Planos* (1934), *Caminos, Janitzio, homenaje á García Lorca, El renacuajo paseador, Sensemayá*, and other pieces for orchestra.

CHAMBER AND VOCAL toccata for violin and small orchestra; two string quartets (1930, 1931); *Feria* for string quartet; pieces for violin and piano; *Siete canciones* and other songs.

Reyer, Ernest (1823–1909), adopted name of **Louis Etienne Rey** French composer. He also worked as a music critic, becoming a champion of Wagner and the new French school. His operas *Sigurd* and *Salammbô* show inevitable indebtedness to Wagner but also reveal a Gallic charm and vitality.

He studied music at the Free School of Music at Marseille, but showed no exceptional promise. At the age of 16 he was sent to live with an uncle at Algiers. There he began to compose songs and other pieces, and in 1847 succeeded in having a Mass performed at the cathedral. In 1848 he went to Paris and studied with his aunt, the composer Louise Farrenc. He met Flaubert and Gautier, with whom he shared an interest in oriental subjects, and they provided him with subjects for his

works. He became a critic in the 1850s and in 1871 succeeded Joseph d'Ortigue as music critic to the *Journal des débats*.

Works OPERA AND STAGE operas *Maître Wolfram* (1854), *La Statue* (1861), *Erostrate, Sigurd* (on the Nibelung Saga, 1884), *Salammbô* (after Flaubert, 1890); ballet-pantomime *Sacountala* (after Malidasa, 1858).

ORCHESTRAL AND CHORAL symphonic ode *Le Sélam* (words by Gautier), dramatic cantata *Victoire, L'Hymne du Rhin* for soprano, chorus, and orchestra (1865); hymn *L'Union des Arts*; *Ave Maria, Salve Regina*, and *O Salutaris*; *La Madeleine au désert* for baritone and orchestra (1874); male-voice choruses.

OTHER piano pieces, songs.

Reynolds, Roger (1934–   ) US composer. His music makes use of electronics, synthesized sounds, and graphic notation. He won a Pulitzer Prize in 1989 for *Whispers out of Time*.

He studied at the University of Michigan, founded avant-garde festivals there, and was director of the Center for Music Experiment at San Diego, California, 1971–77.

Works STAGE *The Emperor of Ice Cream* (1962), *A Ritual for 23 Performers* (1971), and incidental music for *The Tempest* (1980).

ORCHESTRAL AND CHAMBER *Graffiti* (1964), and *Threshold* (1967) for orchestra; *Between* for chamber orchestra and electronics (1968); *Archipelago* for chamber orchestra and computer (1982); *Whispers out of Time* for string orchestra (1988); chamber and vocal music.

Rezniček, E(mil) N(ikolaus) von (1860–1945) Austrian composer and conductor. He held several conducting posts and composed light operas. His most successful work was the opera *Donna Diana* (1894).

He studied law at Graz, but at 22, when he was already married to Milka Thurn, a relation of Felix Weingartner's, he went to Leipzig to study at the Conservatory with Carl Reinecke and Salomon Jadassohn (1831–1902). He gained stage experience as a theatre conductor in various towns and finally became a military conductor at Prague, where *Donna Diana* was premiered in 1894. From 1896 to 1899 he was successively court conductor at Weimar and Mannheim. In 1906 he was appointed professor at the Klindworth-Scharwenka Conservatory in Berlin, where he founded a chamber orchestra, and later conducted the Warsaw Opera 1907–08 and the Komische Oper, Berlin 1908–11. He taught at the Hochschule für Musik in Berlin 1920–26.

Works OPERA *Die Jungfrau von Orleans* (after Schiller, 1887), *Satanella, Emmerich Fortunat* (1889), *Donna Diana* (after Moreto, 1894), *Till Eulenspiegel* (1902), *Ritter Blaubart, Holofernes* (after Hebbel's *Judith*, 1923), *Satuala, Spiel oder*

Ernst (1930), *Der Gondoliere des Dogen* (1931); incidental music for Strindberg's *Dream Play*.

CHORAL AND ORCHESTRAL Mass in F major, Requiem in D minor, *Vater unser* for chorus (1919); four symphonies, including *Schlemihl* (after Chamisso), *Tragic*, and *Ironic*; two symphonic suites, Comedy and Idyllic Overtures, fugue in C♯ minor for orchestra; serenata for strings; violin concerto (1925), Introduction and Valse-Caprice for violin and orchestra; *Ruhm und Ewigkeit* (Nietzsche) for tenor and orchestra.

CHAMBER three string quartets (1921–32).

rf or **rfz** in music, abbreviation for ➤ **rinforzando**, a sudden accentuation of a short phrase.

R.H. in musical notation, abbreviation for **right hand**, directing a pianist to use the right hand. This is usually in order to facilitate a technically difficult passage, dividing the notes between both hands. It can also be notated in French or Italian as M.D. (*main droite* or *mano destra*, respectively). The opposite is L.H. ('left hand').

Rhapsodie a setting of a fragment from Johann Goethe's *Harzreise im Winter* by Johannes ➤ **Brahms** for contralto solo, male chorus, and orchestra , Op. 53. It was composed in 1869 and first performed at Jena on 3 March 1870. In English the piece is frequently called the *Alto Rhapsody*.

rhapsody in music, an instrumental ➤ **fantasia**, often based on folk melodies, such as Franz Liszt's *Hungarian Rhapsodies* (1853–54).

In ancient Greece, **rhapsodes** were a class of reciters of epic poems, especially those of Homer, who performed at festivals. The title means 'stitchers of songs'.

Rhapsody in Blue work for piano and orchestra by Gershwin, composed in January 1924 and orchestrated by Grofé. First perfomed at New York on 12 February 1924, with Gershwin and Paul Whiteman band. A version for symphony orchestra in 1942 was one of the earliest orchestral works to integrate jazz elements to a large extent.

Rhapsody on a Theme of Paganini or **Paganini Rhapsody**, **Paganini Variations** work by Sergei ➤ **Rachmaninov** for piano and orchestra. The work is actually a set of variations, composed in 1934 and first performed in Baltimore on 7 November 1934. The piece is frequently referred to as the *Paganini Rhapsody* or *Paganini Variations*.

The theme, in A minor, from the 19th-century virtuoso violinist Niccolò ➤ **Paganini**'s *capricci* (studies) for unaccompanied violin, is the same as that used by Johannes Brahms and Witold Lutosłaski for their respective ➤ **Paganini Variations**.

Rheinberger, Joseph (Gabriel) (1839–1901) German organist, teacher, and composer. Although successful in his lifetime in a wide variety of genres he is largely known today for his demanding organ works.

He was so precociously gifted that he was appointed organist at his local parish church at the age of seven. After some lessons at Feldkirch, he went to the Munich Conservatory 1850–54, and continued to study with Franz Lachner on leaving, supporting himself by teaching, and in 1859 became piano professor at the Conservatory. He also worked for a time at the Court Opera, and became a church organist and choral conductor. When the Conservatory was reorganized by Bülow in 1867, he was appointed organ and composition professor. In 1877, he became director of the court church music in succession to Franz Wüllner.

Works OPERA AND STAGE the operas *Die sieben Raben* (1869), *Der Türmers Töchterlein* (1873), and *Das Zauberwort*; incidental music for Calderón's *Mágico prodigioso*; overtures to Shakespeare's *Taming of the Shrew* and Schiller's *Demetrius*.

CHURCH MUSIC numerous Masses, three Requiems, *Stabat Mater*, motets.

CHORAL cantatas and choral ballads.

ORCHESTRAL symphonies *Wallenstein* (after Schiller) and 'Florentine', *Academic (fugal) Overture* for orchestra; two organ concertos, piano concerto.

CHAMBER three string quartets, two piano trios, piano quintet, piano quartet, string quintet; sonatas for violin and piano, cello and piano, horn and piano.

ORGAN 20 organ sonatas and many other organ works, including 22 trios, twelve *Meditations* and 24 fughettes.

OTHER numerous piano works, songs, part songs.

Rheingold, Das, **The Rhinegold** opera by Richard ➤ **Wagner**, the first of the cycle of music dramas ➤ **Ring des Nibelungen**.

In the story, the dwarf Alberich steals the magic Rheingold from the Rhinemaidens and forges an all-powerful ring. Wotan, chief of the gods, steals Alberich's hoard, including the ring, in order to pay the giants Fasolt and Fafner for building the gods' palace Valhalla.

'Rhenish' Symphony the name of Schumann's third symphony, in E flat major, Op. 97, begun after a Rhine excursion in September 1850. The fourth of the five movements is said to be an impression of Cologne Cathedral. It was first performed in Düsseldorf on 6 February 1851.

rhythm in music, the way that sounds of varying length and stress (or ➤ **accent**) are grouped together in patterns. It is one of the three most important elements of music, together with ➤ **melody** and ➤ **harmony**.

Rhythmic modes as represented by poetic stresses (left), medieval notation (middle), and modern notation (right).

rhythmic modes in music, one of the classification of the rhythms of medieval music; six patterns were used, corresponding to poetic rhythms.

Riccardo I, rè d'Inghilterra, Richard I, King of England opera by Handel (libretto by Paolo Rolli), produced at the King's Theatre, Haymarket, London, on 11 November 1727. The story concerns King Richard I as he conquers Cyprus and marries Costanza after defeating jealous Isaac Comnenus, governor of the island.

Ricci, Federico (1809–1877) Italian composer. He studied with Vincenzo Bellini and Zingarelli at the Naples Conservatory. In 1835 he produced his first opera with his brother Luigi Ricci at Naples and the first of his own at Venice. After several stage successes he was music director at the Imperial theatres in St Petersburg 1853–69.

Works OPERA *Monsieur de Chalumeaux* (1835), *La prigione d'Edimburgo* (on Scott's *Heart of Midlothian*, 1838), *Un duello sotto Richelieu* (1839), *Luigi Rolla e Michelangelo* (1841), *Corrado d'Altamura, Vallombra, Isabella de' Medici* (1845), *Estella di Murcia* (1846), *Griselda, I due ritratti, Il marito e l'amante* (1852), *Il paniere d'amore, Una Folie à Rome, Le Docteur rose,* and four others in collaboration with Luigi Ricci.

OTHER two Masses; cantata for the marriage of Victor Emmanuel; songs.

Ricci, Luigi (1805–1859) Italian composer, brother of Federico ➜ **Ricci**. He studied under Zingarelli at the Naples Conservatory, where he and Vincenzo Bellini became sub-professors in 1819. His first opera was produced there in 1823. In 1835, after a number of successful productions, he became conductor of the Opera and music director of the cathedral at Trieste. His attempt at a

setting of *Le nozze di Figaro* (Milan, 1838) was a failure, and he moved with his twin-sister mistresses, Francesca and Ludmilla Stolz, to Odessa. He married Ludmilla in 1849 and wrote an opera for the sisters but was confined in an asylum in 1859, having become hopelessly insane.

Works OPERA *L'impresario in angustie* (1823), *Il diavolo condannato* (1826), *Il Colombo, L'orfanella di Ginevra* (1829), *Chiara di Rosemberg, Il nuovo Figaro* (1832), *Un avventura di Scaramuccia* (1834), *Gli esposti (Eran due ed or son tre), Chi dura vince, Chiara di Montalbano* (1835), *La Serva e l'ussaro, Le nozze di Figaro* (after Beaumarchais, 1838), *Il birraio di Preston* (1847), *La festa di Piedigrotta, Il diavolo a quattro* (1859); and 14 others, including four in collaboration with Federico Ricci: *Il colonello* (1835), *Il disertore per amore* (1836), *L'amante di richiamo* (1846), and *Crispino e la comare* (1850).

OTHER church music, song-books *Mes Loisirs* and *Les Inspirations du thé.*

Ricciardo e Zoraide opera by Rossini (libretto by M F B di Salsa), produced at the Teatro San Carlo, Naples, on 3 December 1818. The story concerns Zoraide, daughter of Prince Ircano. She falls in love with Christian Knight Ricciardo, but the tyrant Agorante also has designs on her. The couple are captured by Agorante but are saved following a revolt.

Riccio, (Antonio) Teodoro (c.1540–after 1599) Italian composer. After holding the post of choirmaster at a church at Brescia, he was appointed music director by the Margrave of Brandenburg-Ansbach. He settled there and followed the margrave to Königsberg in 1579, having become a Lutheran, and returned to Ansbach with his patron in 1586. Johann Eccard served under him there from 1581 and succeeded him at his death.

Works CHURCH AND SECULAR MUSIC motets and other church music; madrigals, *Canzoni alla napoletana*; some of his canzonas are based on themes by Gabrieli.

ricercare (Italian 'researched') in music, an abstract composition, usually contrapuntal, exploring tonal and intervallic structural relationships, as in Johann Sebastian Bach's several examples from *The Musical Offering* (1747).

Richafort, Jean (c.1480–c.1547) Flemish composer and pupil of Josquin Desprez. He was choirmaster at the church of Saint-Gilles at Bruges in the 1540s. He wrote Masses, motets, and chansons. Palestrina wrote a parody Mass on his four-part motet *Quem dicunt homines*.

Richard Cœur-de-Lion opera by André Grétry (libretto by Michel-Jean Sedaine), produced at the Comédie-Italienne, Paris, on 21 July 1784. Beethoven wrote piano variations on one of its songs,'Une fièvre brûlante' (1795). The story concerns Blondel, squire to King Richard, who discovers that his master is held prisoner in Linz castle in northern Austria. He captures the castle governor Florestan and rescues Richard, reuniting him with his love Marguerita.

Richard (I) the Lion-Heart (1157–1199), French **Cœur-de-Lion** King of England and French trouvère. He was the son of Henry II and his mother was Eleanor of Aquitaine. She introduced the art of the Troubadours to the north of France and thus established the school of the Trouvères to which Richard belonged both as poet and as musician.

According to legend another trouvère, Blondel de Nesle, discovered his place of imprisonment in Austria in 1192, when he is said to have sung outside the castle of Dürenstein and to have been answered by Richard in song from within, a fanciful story which furnished the plot for André ➔ Grétry's opera *Richard Cœur-de-Lion*.

Richardson, Ferdinand(o) (c.1558–1618), born **Ferdinand Heybourne** English composer and pupil of Thomas Tallis. He was Groom of the Privy Chamber, 1587–1611. He composed virginal pieces.

Richardson, Vaughan (c. 1670–1729) English organist and composer. He was chorister in the Chapel Royal, and was appointed organist of Winchester Cathedral in 1692.

Works CHURCH MUSIC services, anthems O Lord God of my salvation, O how amiable and others; Song in Praise of St Cecilia (1700); Entertainment for the Peace of Ryswick (1697).

VOCAL songs for one–three voices with instruments.

Richter, Hans (1843–1916) Austro-Hungarian conductor. He conducted the first performance of Wagner's *Ring* at Bayreuth in 1876, and was conductor of the Hallé Orchestra, Manchester, 1900–11. He gave the first performances of Brahms' second and third symphonies, Bruckner's first, third, fourth, and eighth symphonies, and Elgar's *Enigma Variations* and first symphony. By his unfailing industry over a long period, Richter set new standards for career conductors to follow.

He studied in Vienna, where he played horn at the Kärntnertortheater 1862–66. As assistant to Wagner, he conducted operas at Budapest and Vienna. He organized and played the trumpet in the private premiere of the *Siegfried Idyll* at Triebschen in 1870, and was the first to conduct Wagner's *Ring* at Bayreuth in 1876. He conducted at the Birmingham Festival 1885–1909, including the 1900 first performance of *The Dream of Gerontius*, and conducted much in London 1877–1910, notably the first *Ring* cycles in English, at Covent Garden in 1908. At Drury Lane he gave the British premieres of *Tristan* and *Die Meistersinger* in 1882.

ricochet (French 'rebound') type of ➔ staccato in violin music, produced by letting the bow bounce on the strings, whereas in ordinary *staccato* it remains on the string and is moved in rapid jerks.

riddle canon in music, a form of ➔ canon written in a single part with no indication where the subsequent entries of the parts are to occur, the performer being left to guess how the music fits by solving a riddle.

Riders to the Sea opera by Vaughan Williams (libretto Synge's play), produced at the Royal College of Music, London, on 1 December 1937. Its first public performance was at the Arts Theatre, Cambridge, on 22 February 1938. The opera opens as the body of Maurya's drowned son Michael is identified. Later, her remaining son Bartley also dies at sea.

Ridout, Alan (1934–1996) English composer. He studied with Gordon Jacob and Herbert Howells at the Royal College of Music; he was professor there 1961–84.

Works CHURCH MUSIC The Boy from the Catacombs (1965), The Children's Crusade (1968), Creation (1973), Wenceslas (1978) and The White Doe (1987).

OTHER opera The Pardoner's Tale (1971), Christmas Oratorio, eight Cantatas, eight symphonies and 13 concertinos with strings (1975–79).

Riegger, Wallingford (1885–1961) US composer. He wrote several ballet scores in the 1930s, but later composed in an atonal idiom.

He studied in New York and Berlin, with Percy Goetschius (1853–1943), Edgar Stillman-Kelley, Max Bruch, and others. After conducting in Germany, he returned to the USA, where he held various teaching appointments.

Works ORCHESTRAL AND CHAMBER *La Belle Dame sans merci* (Keats) for four voices and chamber orchestra (1924); four symphonies (1943–57); *Dichotomy* and *Scherzo* for chamber orchestra; *Study in Sonority* for ten violins; two string quartets (1939, 1948), piano trio, *Divertissement* for harp, flute, and cello, three Canons for woodwind and other chamber music; Suite for solo flute.

OTHER *American Polonaise–Triple Jazz* (1922), Rhapsody, Fantasy and Fugue (1955), Lyric Suite, two Dance Suites, Canon and Fugue, and other pieces for orchestra, various works for dancers.

Riemann, (Karl Wilhelm Julius) Hugo (1849–1919) German musicologist. Among his many publications are a *Musiklexikon* (1882), *Handbuch der Musikgeschichte* (1904), *Opernhandbuch* (1887), works on notation, harmony, phrasing, and history. He edited many standard works and also composed mainly teaching pieces for piano.

He studied law at Berlin and Tübingen, and music at the Leipzig Conservatory. He later became lecturer at the university there, 1878–80 and again in 1895 until 1901, when he became professor.

Rienzi, der Letzte der Tribunen, **Rienzi, the Last of the Tribunes** opera in five acts by Wagner (first called *Cola Rienzi*) (libretto by composer based on Bulwer-Lytton's novel and, further back, on Mary Russell Mitford's play), produced at Dresden on 20 October 1842. In the story, Rienzi, proclaimed tribune of Rome, faces assassination plots from the noblemen led by Orsini and Colonna, whose son Adriano loves Rienzi's sister Irene. After his opponents are killed Rienzi is excommunicated by papal allies of Colonna. He is abandoned by all except Irene, who remains loyal to the end. As the siblings are stoned by the people, Adriano tries to rescue Irene but all three are killed as the burning building collapses.

Ries, Ferdinand (1784–1838) German pianist, violinist, and composer. He studied piano with Beethoven 1802–04. He later lived in London for several years, where he acted as Beethoven's agent in dealings with music publishers. Back in Germany, he was involved with F Wegeler in writing a biography of Beethoven.

He was taught piano and violin by his father, Franz Anton Ries (1755–1846), who also taught Beethoven, and studied cello with B Romberg. After a short course in composition with Peter Winter at Munich in 1801, he went to Vienna that year, and studied piano with Beethoven and composition with Albrechtsberger, and became pianist to Counts Browne and Lichnowsky. Later he lived by turns in Paris, Vienna, Kassel, Stockholm, and St Petersburg. In 1813–24 he lived in London, where he married an Englishwoman and played, taught, and composed. He bought a property at Godesberg, near Bonn, but in 1826 went to live at Frankfurt, where he returned again after two years as a conductor at Aachen, 1834–36. He conducted several of the Lower Rhine Festivals.

Works OPERA *Die Räuberbraut* (1828), *Liska* (*The Sorceress*, 1831), and *Eine Nacht auf dem Libanon* (1834); oratorios *Der Sieg des Glaubens* and *Die Könige Israels*

OTHER eight symphonies, four overtures; eight piano concertos; 26 string quartets; eight string quintets, three piano quartets, five piano trios, octet, septet, and other chamber music; 20 duets for violin and piano; ten sonatas and many other works for piano.

Rieti, Vittorio (1898–1994) Italian-born US composer. He studied with Frugatta at Milan and Respighi in Rome, but destroyed all his works written up to 1920. In 1939 he became a US citizen.

Works OPERA AND STAGE opera *Teresa nel bosco* (1934); ballets *Noah's Ark* (1922), *Barabau* (1925), *Waltz Academy, The Sleep-walker, Robinson and Friday* (after Defoe, 1924), and *David's Triumph* (1937); incidental music for Pierre Corneille's *L'Illusion comique* and Giraudoux's *Electre*.

ORCHESTRAL seven symphonies (1929–77); *Notturno* for strings; concerto for wind instruments and orchestra; violin concerto, harpsichord concerto, three piano concertos (1926, 1937, 1955); two cello concertos.

CHAMBER *Madrigal* for twelve instruments (1927), partita for flute, oboe, string quartet, and harpsichord; sonata for flute, oboe, bassoon and piano; *Second Avenue Waltzes* for two pianos, piano pieces.

Rifkin, Joshua (1944–) US musicologist, conductor, and pianist. He is known for bringing Scott Joplin's piano rags to popular attention. He has researched Renaissance and baroque music, and has given authentic performances, including a recording of the B minor Mass without full-scale chorus.

He studied at the Juilliard School in New York and at Princeton, and with Stockhausen at Darmstadt, Germany. He conducted Bach's *St Matthew Passion* at the 1994 London Promenade Concerts.

rigadoon, French **rigaudon** French country dance; see ➔ **rigaudon**.

rigaudon lively French country dance in two time, in four-bar phrases (like a square dance), the music for which was revived by Edvard ➤ **Grieg** in the *Holberg Suite* in 1884. The dance dates to the 17th century at the latest, and is thought to be derived from the French south (Provence or Languedoc).

Rigoletto opera by Verdi (libretto by Francesco Maria Piave, based on Victor Hugo's play *Le Roi s'amuse*), produced at the Teatro la Fenice, Venice, on 11 March 1851. In the story, Rigoletto's daughter Gilda is abducted by the Duke of Mantua, who has designs on her. Rigoletto rescues her, but by now she loves the Duke. Rigoletto arranges his murder, but Gilda substitutes herself instead.

Rihm, Wolfgang (1952–) German composer. He studied in Karlsruhe and with Stockhausen and Wolfgang Fortner.

Works OPERA *Faust and Yorick* (1976), *Harlekin* (1977), *Jacob Lenz* (1979), *Die Hamletmaschine* (1986), *Oedipus* (1987), *Die Eroberung von Mexico* (1992).

ORCHESTRAL three symphonies (1966–77, no. 3 to texts by Nietzsche and Rimbaud); *Dis-kontur* and *Sub-kontur* for orchestra (1974–75); concerto *Cuts and Dissolves* for 29 players (1976); *Tutuguri* series of seven works for various instrumental combinations inspired by Paul Claudel (1981); *Monodram* for cello and orchestra (1983); *Kein firmament* for 14 players; *Fusées* for orchestra (1984); *Dämmerung* for orchestra (1985); *Dunkles Spiel* for chamber orchestra (1990); *Umfassung* for orchestra in two groups (1990).

CHORAL AND VOICE WITH ORCHESTRA *Ein Imaginäres Requiem* for soloists, chorus, and orchestra (1976); *Konzertarie* for soprano and orchestra (based on a telegram sent by Ludwig II to Wagner, 1976); *Abgesangsszene* nos 1–5 for voice and orchestra (1979–81); *Lenz-Fragmente* and five songs for soprano and orchestra (1980); *Dies* for soloists, chorus, and orchestra (1984); *Anderer Schatten* (ditto, 1985); *Mein Tod, Requiem in memoriam Jane S* for soprano and orchestra (1989); *Frau/Stimme* for soprano and orchestra (1989); *Départ* for chorus, narrator, and 22 players (1988); *Geheimer Block* for voice and orchestra (1989); *Engel* for two male voices and 20 instruments (1989).

CHAMBER *Cantus firmus* for 14 players (1990), *Ricercare* for ensemble (1990), *Etude pour Séraphin* for eight brass instruments and six percussion players (1992); eight string quartets (1968–88); *Deploration* for flute, cello, and percussion (1973); *Erscheinung* sketch after Schubert for nine strings (1978), *Nature Morte* for 13 strings (1980); *Fremde Szene* for piano trio (1983); solo songs and music for piano and for organ.

Riisager, Knudåge (1897–1974) Danish composer. He studied political economy at Copenhagen University, but later turned to music, studying composition with Peder Gram and Otto Malling, later with Albert Roussel and Le Flem in Paris, and finally with Hermann Grabner at Leipzig.

Works STAGE opera *Susanne* (1950); ballets *Benzin* (1930), *Cocktail Party*, and *Slaraffenland* (*Land of Cockaigne*, 1942); incidental music to Johannes Jensen's fairy play *Darduse*.

ORCHESTRAL five symphonies (1925–50), variations *Poème mécanique*, *Jabiru T – DOXC*, and overture to Holberg's *Erasmus Montanus* for orchestra; concerto for trumpet and strings.

CHAMBER six string quartets (1918–43), sonata for flute, clarinet, violin, and cello; serenade for flute, violin, and cello; violin and piano sonata; sonata and various pieces for piano; songs.

OTHER choral works.

Riley, Terry (1935–) US composer and saxophonist. He belongs to the minimalist school of composers. His works involve repeated patterns and series, and contain freedom for improvisation. He studied at Berkeley, California, and since 1970 has been influenced by Indian music.

Works ENSEMBLE *Spectra* for six instruments (1959); string trio (1965); *Keyboard Studies* (1965); *Poppy Nogood and the Phantom Band* for saxophone, tape, and electronics (1968); *Rainbow in Curved Air* (1970); *Sunrise of the Planetary Dream Collector* and *The Medicine Wheel* (works which reflect his interest in astrology) for string quartet (1981, 1983); the cycle *Salome Dances for Peace* (formed from five of his nine string quartets, 1988).

BALLET *Genesis '70*.

Rilke, Rainer Maria (1875–1926) Austrian poet and writer who inspired many choral works and songs by such composers as Hindemith and Webern.

See Conrad ➤ **Beck** (*Lyric Cantata*); ➤ **Burkhard** (*Song Cycle*); Lukas ➤ **Foss** (*Parable of Death*); ➤ *Marienleben* (Hindemith); Karl ➤ **Marx** (choruses and songs); ➤ **Webern** (songs); ➤ **Weill** (songs with orchestra).

Rimsky-Korsakov, Nikolai Andreievich (1844–1908) Russian composer. He composed many operas and works for orchestra; he also wrote an influential text on orchestration. His opera *The Golden Cockerel* (1907) was a satirical attack on tyranny that was banned until 1909. He also completed works by other composers, for example, Modest Mussorgsky's *Boris Godunov* (1868–69).

Works OPERA several, including *The Maid of Pskov* (1873), *The Snow Maiden* (1882), *Mozart and Salieri* (1898), and *The Golden Cockerel* (1907).

ORCHESTRAL symphonic poem *Sadko* (1867), programme symphony *Antar* (1869), and the symphonic suite *Shéhérazade* (1888).

Rinaldo cantata for tenor solo, male chorus, and orchestra by Brahms, Op. 50, on a ballad by Goethe, performed at Vienna on 28 February 1869.

Opera by Handel (libretto by Giacomo Rossi, from a sketch based on Tasso by Aaron Hill), produced at the Queen's Theatre, Haymarket, London, on 24 February 1711. It was Handel's first London opera. The story begins as the knight Rinaldo prepares for victory over Saracen king Argante. The heathen temporarily avoids defeat by enlisting the help of the sorceress Armida in abducting Almirena, Rinaldo's love. But Rinaldo saves her; Argante and Armida flee.

Rinaldo di Capua (c.1705–c.1780) Italian composer. He wrote more than 30 operas, the first of which was produced in Rome in 1737. Only fragments of his music survive.

Some of his operas appeared in Florence and Venice, and in 1752–53 the *Bouffons* in Paris performed his *La donna superba* and *La zingara*. His last opera seria was written in 1758, after which he devoted himself to comic opera. Charles Burney found him living in poor circumstances in Rome in 1770, after which nothing is known of him.

Works OPERA over 30, including *Ciro riconosciuto* (1737), *Vologeso, rè de' Parti* (1739), *Mario in Numidia* (1749), *Adriano in Siria* (1758).

ORCHESTRAL intermezzi *Il bravo burlato*, *La donna superba* (1738), *La zingara*, *Le donne ridicole* (1759), *I finti pazzi per amore* (1770), and others.

CHORAL *Cantata per la natività della Beata Vergine* (1755), and other pieces.

rinforzando or **rf** or **rfz (Italian 'reinforcing')** in musical notation, indicating a sudden accent on a single note or short phrase or group of notes. It differs slightly from ➤ **sforzando**, which applies to only one note per marking.

Ring des Nibelungen, Der, The Nibelung's Ring trilogy of music dramas, with a prologue, by Richard ➤ **Wagner** (libretto by composer, based on the *Nibelungenlied/Song of the Nibelung*).

Das ➤ **Rheingold**/*The Rhinegold*, produced at the Court Opera, Munich, on 22 September 1869.

Die ➤ **Walküre**/*The Valkyrie*, produced at the Court Opera, Munich, on 26 June 1870.

➤ **Siegfried**, produced at the Wagner Festival Theatre, Bayreuth, on 16 June 1876.

➤ **Götterdämmerung**/*The Twilight of the Gods*, produced at the Wagner Festival Theatre, Bayreuth, on 17 August 1876.

The whole cycle was produced at the Wagner Festival Theatre, Bayreuth, 13–17 August 1876.

ripieno (Italian 'replenished, supplementary') in music of the 17th and 18th centuries, term describing the full complement of players, as opposed to a ➤ **concertante** (group of instrumental soloists). It is used especially in the context of the ➤ **concerto grosso**, designating the full orchestra, but it may be used to describe other music which exploits the textural contrast of a different number of players, as in Bach's *St Matthew Passion* (1729).

ripresa (Italian 're-taking, repetition') in music, a refrain, especially in the 14th-century Italian ➤ **ballata** (verse song).

Riquier, Guiraut (c.1230–c.1300) French troubadour and the last great exponent of the art. Of his many song-tunes, 48 are extant.

Rising of the Moon, The opera by Nicholas ➤ **Maw** (libretto by Beverly Cross and composer), produced at Glyndebourne in East Sussex, England, on 19 July 1970. The story concerns Cornet Beaumont, a new officer of the 31st Lancers, who undergoes a series of initiation tests that results in his regiment's withdrawal from Ireland and leaves admirer Cathleen without Beaumont.

rispetto a type of old Italian improvised folk poem of six to ten (usually eight) inter-rhyming lines, sung to popular tunes.

Ristori, Giovanni Alberto (1692–1753) Italian composer. He wrote opera and choral works. He was director of the Polish chapel in Dresden in 1718, and became vice-kapellmeister to the court, under Hasse, in 1750.

His first opera was produced in Venice in 1713, but two years later he moved to Dresden with his father, director of an Italian theatrical company. Ristori himself became music director of the company in 1717.

Works OPERA around 20, including *Calandro* (1726), *Don Chisciotte* (1727), *Le fate* (1736), *Didone* (produced Covent Garden, 1737), *Temistocle* (1738), *I lamenti di Orfeo* (1749).

CHORAL three oratorios; 15 cantatas; 15 Masses, three Requiems, motets and other church music.

Risurrezione, Resurrection opera by ➤ **Alfano** (libretto by C Hanau, based on Tolstoy's novel), produced at the Teatro Vittorio Emanuele, Turin, on 30 November 1914. In the story, Katiusha and Dmitri become lovers and she becomes pregnant. He abandons her and she is sent to Siberia, convicted as a prostitute. Dmitri follows her but she rejects him, favouring another prisoner, Simouson, instead.

rit. in musical notation, abbreviation for ➤ **ritardando** (Italian 'slowing'); less commonly for ➤ **ritenuto** (Italian 'held back').

Rita opera in one act by Gaetano Donizetti (libretto by G Vaez). Composed in 1841, it was first performed (posthumously) at the Opéra-Comique, Paris, on 7 May 1860. In the story, Rita dominates her weak husband Peppe until ex-husband Gaspar arrives and shows Peppe how to stand up to her.

ritardando or **rit. (Italian 'slowing')** in musical notation, gradually getting slower; synonymous with rallentando.

ritenuto or **riten.** or **rit. (Italian 'held back')** in musical notation, the immediate reduction of speed, as opposed to a gradual change as with ritardando and rallentando.

Rite of Spring, The, French **Le Sacre du printemps** ballet by Igor ➤ Stravinsky (scenario by composer and Nikolay Roerich, choreographed by Nijinsky), produced as *Le Sacre du printemps* at the Théâtre des Champs-Élysées, Paris, on 29 May 1913. The ballet caused much controversy on the first night – by some accounts a riot – due to the ferociousness of the music.

ritmo di battute (Italian 'rhythm of ... beats') in music, term indicating that the metrical scheme of a piece or movement is to be accented in groups of as many bars as may be shown in this direction between the second and third word. It is used in the Scherzo of Beethoven's Ninth Symphony, where the metre changes between *ritmo di tre battute* and *ritmo di quattro battute*.

ritornello (Italian 'a little return') in music, a repeating section: in the 14th and 15th centuries, it was the refrain at the end of each ➤ madrigal verse, the music being treated separately from the previous material, often including a change of metre. In 17th-century opera and song, a ritornello was an instrumental conclusion or refrain added to the end of an aria or song; in the classical period (1750–1820) it was used in concerto composition, denoting the return of the full orchestra (or 'tutti') after a solo passage.

ritorno d'Ulisse in patria, Il, Ulysses' Return to his Country opera by Monteverdi (libretto by G Badoaro), produced at the Teatro San Cassiano, Venice, in February 1641. The story concerns Ulysses, who, with the help of the goddess Minerva, finds his way back home to Penelope his wife. Dressed as a beggar, he slays her suitors. Juno and Jupiter restore his identity and Ulysses wins back Penelope.

Ritual Dances four dances for chorus and orchestra in Michael Tippett's opera *The Midsummer Marriage*: *The Earth in Autumn*, *The Waters in Winter*, *The Air in Spring*, *Fire in Summer*. Often heard as a concert work, it was first performed at Basel on 13 February 1953 – two years

before its first production as an opera, at Covent Garden.

Rituel in memoriam Bruno Maderna work for orchestra by Pierre ➤ Boulez, written in memory of the Italian composer Bruno ➤ Maderna and first performed at London on 2 April 1975, conducted by Boulez.

Roberday, François (1624–1680) French organist and composer. He held appointments as a goldsmith under Queen Anne of Austria and Queen Marie-Thérèse, and was one of Lully's teachers.
  Works ORGAN *Fugues et Caprices*.

Robert le Diable, Robert the Devil opera by Giacomo Meyerbeer (libretto by Scribe), produced at the Paris Opéra on 21 November 1831. In the story, Bertram, the Duke Robert's father, is a demon and must repossess his son's soul by midnight. Robert is searching for his love Isabelle, and Bertram tries to lead him astray with offers of help. Alice, Robert's foster sister, saves his soul and helps reunite him with Isabelle, as Bertram returns to Hell.

Roberto Devereux, Conte d'Essex opera by Gaetano Donizetti (libretto by Salvatore Cammarano, based on Jacques Ancelot's tragedy *Elisabeth d'Angleterre*), produced at the Teatro San Carlo, Naples, on 2 October 1837. The story concerns Robert Devereux, who wears Queen Elizabeth's ring, which guarantees him protection. But he tears it off for love of Sarah, wife of the Duke of Nottingham.
  Opera by Saverio Mercadante (libretto by Felice Romani, based on Corneille's *Comte d'Essex*), produced at La Scala, Milan, on 10 March 1833.

Robertson, Alec (1892–1982) English musicologist. He was in charge of the music talks for the British Broadcasting Corporation (BBC) Home Service from 1940. His books include *The Interpretation of Plainchant*, *Art and Religion*, *Dvořák*, and *Requiem: Music of Mourning and Consolation*.
  He studied at the Royal Academy of Music in London and became an organist and choirmaster in 1913. After serving in World War I, he lectured at the London County Coucil evening institutes and in 1920 became lecturer and later head of the Gramophone company's education department. He lived in Rome for four years to study plainsong, before joining the BBC.

Robin et Marion, Le Jeu de, The Play of Robin and Marion a pastoral play with monophonic (without harmony) music by Adam de la Halle, written in Naples between 1283 and his death in 1286 or 1287.

Robinson, John (1682–1762) English organist and composer. He was chorister in the Chapel Royal, and became organist of St Lawrence, Jewry, and St Magnus, London Bridge. In 1727 he succeeded Croft as organist of Westminster Abbey. In 1716 he married William Turner's daughter Ann (died 1741), a singer at the Italian Opera.
Works Double Chant in E♭ major.

Robinson Crusoé operetta by Jacques ➤ **Offenbach** (libretto by E Cormon and Hector Crémieux, based distantly on Defoe's novel), produced at the Opéra-Comique, Paris, on 23 November 1867. Robinson meets Vendredi (Man Friday) and his friends in a farcical plot on the desert island.

Rocca, Lodovico (1895–1986) Italian composer. He was a pupil of Orefice and was appointed director of the Turin Conservatory in 1940.
Works OPERA *La morte di Frine*, *La corona del rè Gaulo*, *Il Dibuk* (1934), *In terra di leggenda* (1933), *Monte Ivnor* (1939) and *L'uragano* (1952).
ORCHESTRAL symphonic poems *Contrasti*, *Aurora di morte*, *L'alba del malato* (1922), and *La foresta delle Samodive* (1921); *La cella azzurra*, *Chiaroscuri*, and *Interludio epico* for orchestra.
OTHER chamber music.

Rochberg, George (1918–2005) US composer. He wrote in a serial idiom until 1964, when a family tragedy inspired a change of heart. Such works as the *Sacred Song of Reconciliation* (1970) and the *Transcendental Varieties* for strings (1975) have embraced tonality once more.
He studied composition with Georg Szell and L Manes (1899–1964) in New York, and then at the Curtis Institute of Music, Philadelphia, with Rosario Scalero (1870–1954) and Menotti. In 1950 he was awarded a Fulbright Fellowship and, in 1956, a Guggenheim Fellowship. He taught at the Curtis Institute 1948–54 and was professor of music at Pennsylvania University 1968–83.
Works OPERA *The Confidence Man* (after Melville, 1982).
ORCHESTRAL symphonic poem *Night Music*, six symphonies (1958–87), *Time-Span* (1960), *Waltz Serenade*, *Sinfonia Fantasia*, *Imago Mundé* (1975); violin concerto (1974), oboe concerto (1983).
CHAMBER *Cantio Sacra* for chamber orchestra, seven string quartets (1952–79), clarinet sonata, fantasia for violin and piano, two piano sonatas.

Roche, Jerome (1942–1994) English musicologist. Early Italian music was at the centre of his research and he published books on ➤ **Palestrina** (1971), the Italian madrigal (1972), and Lassus (1982).
He studied at Cambridge University 1959–67, and was lecturer at Durham from 1967. With his

wife Elizabeth he edited the *Dictionary of Early Music, from the Troubadours to Monteverdi* (1981). He was also author of *North Italian Church Music in the Age of Monteverdi* (1984) and *The Flower of Italian Madrigals* (1988).

Rochlitz, Johann Friedrich (1769–1842) German music critic and poet. He studied under Doles at the St Thomas's School, Leipzig, and later theology at the university. In 1798 he founded the *Allgemeine Musikalische Zeitung*, which he edited until 1818. He also composed and wrote libretti and poems, three of which were set by Franz Schubert; others were set by Carl Weber and Louis Spohr.

rococo in music, a highly florid and decorative style of the 18th century. It was first associated with the music of François ➤ **Couperin** and is applicable to much music until the period of Mozart, Haydn, and C P E Bach.

Rodelinda opera by Handel (libretto by Antonio Salvi, adapted by Nicola Francesco Haym), produced at the King's Theatre, Haymarket, London, on 13 February 1725. In the story, Rodelinda, wife of the usurped King Bertarido, agrees to marry Grimoaldo to save her son Flavio. Bertarido returns to see Rodelinda and is captured. Unolfo rescues him, and Bertarido kills the rebel Garibaldo before assuming the role of king again.

Rodelinda, regina de' Longobardi opera by German composer Karl Graun (libretto by G G Bottarelli, altered from Antonio Salvi), produced at court in Berlin on 13 December 1741. The plot is similar to that of ➤ **Rodelinda**.

Rodgers, Richard Charles (1902–1979) US composer. He collaborated with librettist Lorenz Hart (1895–1943) on songs like 'Blue Moon' (1934) and musicals like *On Your Toes* (1936). With Oscar Hammerstein II, he wrote many musicals, including *Oklahoma!* (1943), *South Pacific* (1949), *The King and I* (1951), and *The Sound of Music* (1959).

Rodio, Rocco (c.1535–shortly after 1615) Italian composer. He wrote church music (including ten Masses), madrigals, and instrumental music, and a treatise, *Regole di Musica*, which was published at Naples in 1600 but is now known only from its second and third editions (1609 and 1626), edited by his pupil Giovanni Battista Olifante.

Rodrigo opera in three acts by Handel (libretto after Francesco Silvani's *Il duello d'Amore e di Vendetta*), produced at the Teatro del Cocomero, Florence, in 1707. The opera was revived, with recently discovered Act 3 material, by the Handel Opera Society in 1985. The story concerns Rodrigo, who gains the throne of Aragon by murder but eventually abdicates.

Rodrigo, Joaquín (1901–1999) Spanish composer. His works are filled with Spanish folklore or ambience, as in the well-known *Concierto de Aranjuez* (1939) or the *Concerto heroico* (1943). He has always composed in a conservative, lucid neoclassical style that is less adventurous than Manuel de ➤ **Falla** but nevertheless as effective and colourful.

He was born at Sagunto in Valencia. He was blind from the age of three, but persevered in studying music and in 1927 he went to Paris as a pupil of Dukas. He returned to Spain in 1933 and again, after travels in Europe, in 1936, settling in Madrid in 1939.

Works ORCHESTRAL *Ausencias de Dulcinea* for bass, four sopranos, and orchestra; Heroic concerto and other works for orchestra; 'Aranjuez' concerto for guitar (1939), 'Summer' concerto for violin (1944), *Concierto en modo galante* for cello (1949), *Concierto Serenada* for harp (1954), *Fantasia para un gentil hombre* for guitar and orchestra (1954), *Concierto andaluz* for four guitars and orchestra (1967), *Concierto Pastoral* for flute (1978), *Concierto como um divertimento* for cello (1981), *Concierto para una fiesta* for guitar (1982).

OTHER pieces for solo guitar, and songs.

Rodríguez de Hita, Antonio (c.1724–1787) Spanish composer. In collaboration with the poet Ramón de la Cruz he made important contributions to Spanish opera. He was maestro di cappella of Palencia Cathedral in northern Spain and, from 1757, of the Convent of the Incarnation in Madrid.

Works OPERA *Briseida* (1768), *Las segadoras de Vallecas* (1768), *Las labradoras de Murcia* (1769).

OTHER hymns for four and eight voices.

Roger-Ducasse, Jean (Jules Aimable) (1873–1954) French composer. He was appointed inspector of singing in the Paris city schools in 1909 and succeeded Paul Dukas as composition professor at the Paris Conservatory in 1935. He studied at the Paris Conservatory, where he was a composition pupil of Fauré.

Works STAGE the opera *Cantegril* (1931), mimed drama *Orphée* (1914).

CHORAL WITH ORCHESTRA *Au Jardin de Marguerite* (1905) and *Ulysse et les Sirènes* for voices and orchestra; motets and secular vocal works, including *Sur quelques vers de Virgile* and *Madrigal sur des vers de Molière*. *Le joli jeu de furet*, *Prélude d'un ballet*, *Nocturne de printemps* (1920), *Epithalame*, *Poème symphonique sur le nom de Fauré*; *Variations plaisantes* for harp and orchestra.

OTHER piano works, instrumental pieces, songs.

Rogers, Benjamin (1614–1698) English organist and composer. He held organist's posts at Windsor, Dublin, and Oxford, and wrote the *Hymnus Eucharisticus*, which is still sung at the top of the tower of Magdalen College, Oxford, at 5am on 1 May each year.

He learnt music from his father, Peter Rogers, a lay-clerk at St George's Chapel, Windsor, and from the organist, Nathaniel Giles. He became himself a lay-clerk, but in 1639 went to Dublin as organist of Christ Church Cathedral. He returned to Windsor in 1641, but in 1644 the choir was disbanded and he taught music privately. He received a music degree from Cambridge University in 1658, and a PhD from Oxford in 1669, where he had become organist and choirmaster at Magdalen College in 1664. He was dismissed for musical and other irregularities in 1685, but was given a pension.

Works CHURCH AND SECULAR MUSIC services and anthems, *Hymnus Eucharisticus*; instrumental pieces; organ works.

Rogers, Bernard (1893–1968) US composer. He studied at the New York Institute of Musical Art and with Bloch at Cleveland. He gained several prizes and distinctions and for a time was a music journalist. In 1938 he became professor of composition at the Eastman School of Music at Rochester, New York.

Works OPERA *The Marriage of Aude* (1931), *The Warrior* (1947), *The Veil* and *The Nightingale* (1940).

CHORAL cantatas *The Raising of Lazarus* and *The Exodus*, *Passion* with organ accompaniment.

OTHER five symphonies (1926–59), overture *The Faithful*, *Three Eastern Dances*, *Two American Frescoes*, *Four Fairy Tales*, *The Supper at Emmaeus* (1937), *The Colours of War*, *The Dance of Salome* (1940), *The Song of the Nightingale*, *The Plains*, *The Sailors of Toulon*, *Invasion* and *Characters from Hans Andersen* for orchestra; soliloquies for flute and strings and bassoon and strings, fantasy for flute, viola, and orchestra; *Pastorale* for eleven instruments, string quartet; *Music for an Industrial Film* for two pianos; songs.

Rogowski, Ludomir (Michał) (1881–1954) Polish composer. He studied at the Warsaw Conservatory and with Reimann and Nikisch at Leipzig. On his return to Poland he founded a symphony orchestra at Wilno. He later lived in Paris 1914–21, and withdrew to a monastery in modern-day Croatia in 1926.

Works OPERA AND STAGE the operas *Tamara* (after Lermontov, 1918) and *Prince Marco* (1930); film opera *Un Grand Chagrin de la Petite Ondine* (1920); ballets *St John's Eve* and *Fairy Tale* (1923).

ORCHESTRAL seven symphonies (1926–51); suites *Pictures of my Daughter*, *The Seasons*, *Les Sour-*

ires,Villafranca, Phantasmagoria (1920), *Sporting Scene, Fantasy Pictures* for orchestra.

CHAMBER MUSIC AND SONGS quartet for four cellos, suites for six and nine instruments, instrumental pieces, piano works, choral songs with and without accompaniment.

Roi Arthus, Le, *King Arthur* opera by Chausson (libretto by composer). It was written 1886–95, under the influence of Wagner's *Tristan*, and was produced at theThéâtre de la Monnaie, Brussels, on 30 November 1903. In the story, Mordred betrays Lancelot's affair with Guinevere to King Arthur. Arthur battles his knight, killing him, and Guinevere strangles herself.

Roi David, Le dramatic Psalm by Arthur ➔ Honegger (libretto by R Morax), produced at the open-air Théâtre du Jorat, Mézières, Switzerland, on 11 June 1921.

Roi de Lahore, Le, **The King of Lahore** opera by Jules Massenet (libretto by L Gallet), produced at the Paris Opéra on 27 April 1877. The story, in an exotic setting, concerns the Hindu priestess Sîtâ, who is loved by both King and the evil Scindia.

Roi d'Ys, Le opera by Edouard Lalo (libretto by E Blau), produced at the Opéra-Comique, Paris, on 7 May 1888. Ys is the submerged city of Debussy's piano prelude *La Cathédrale engloutie*. In the story, Margared, daughter of the King of Ys, breaks off her engagement to Karnac when she sees her childhood love Mylio. But Mylio now loves her sister Rozenn. Margared joins forces with Karnac for revenge; she sacrifices herself as she opens the sluices, flooding the city.

Roi l'a dit, Le, **The King has said it** opera by Léo Delibes (libretto by E Gondinet), produced at the Opéra-Comique, Paris, on 24 May 1873. The story concerns the Marquis di Moncontour presenting the young Benoit to the King as his own son. Benoit feigns death during a duel to prevent his true identity from being revealed.

Roi malgré lui, Le, **King against his Will** opera by Emmanuel Chabrier (libretto by E de Najac and P Burani, based on a comedy by Jacques Ancelot), produced at the Opéra-Comique, Paris, on 18 May 1887. In the story, King Henri of Poland faces a conspiracy to remove him from the throne, led by Count Laski. At Laski's ball the King attends in disguise, escaping detection. King Henri returns to the throne after the plot fails.

Roland opera by Jean-Baptiste Lully (libretto by Quinault). Produced at the Versailles court on 8 January 1685, its first Paris performance was on 8 March 1685.

Roland-Manuel, Alexis (1891–1966), adopted name of **Roland Alexis Manuel Lévy** French

composer and critic. He wrote much criticism and books on Ravel and Falla.

He studied with Roussel at the Schola Cantorum in Paris, and with Ravel. In 1947, he became a professor at the Paris Conservatory.

Works STAGE the operas *Isabelle et Pantalon* (1920), *Le diable amoureux* (1932); ballets *Le tournoi singulier, L'écran des jeunes filles, Elvire* (on music by Domenico Scarlatti) (1936).

ORCHESTRAL film music *L'ami Fritz* (after Erckmann-Chatrian) *La Bandéra* and others; oratorio *Jeanne d'Arc*; symphonic poems *Le harem du vice-roi, Tempo di ballo* (1924); suite *Pena de Francia* for orchestra; suite in the Spanish style for harpsichord, oboe, bassoon, and trumpet.

OTHER string trio, part songs, songs.

roll in music, a very rapid succession of notes on drums produced by quick alternating strokes of the two sticks.

Rolland, Romain (1866–1944) French musicologist and author. He also contributed essays on music to various periodicals and wrote plays and other literary works. His works include books on Handel and Beethoven, on early opera, *Musiciens d'autrefois, Musiciens d'aujourd'hui, Voyage musical au pays du passé*, and the ten-volume novel *Jean-Christophe* (1904–12), with a musician as hero. He was awarded the Nobel Prize for Literature in 1915.

He had a first-rate general education and devoted himself to music and other artistic studies. In 1901 he became president of the music section of the Ecole des Hautes Etudes Sociales, Paris, and lectured on music first at the Ecole Normale Supérieure and from 1903 at the Sorbonne, Paris. From 1913 he lived in Switzerland, having retired owing to bad health. He returned to France in 1938 in order not to evade the war, was interned in a concentration camp by the Germans, and was released only when he was mortally ill.

Rolle, Johann Heinrich (1716–1785) German organist and composer. He was taught by his father, Christian Friedrich Rolle (1681–1751), and was appointed organist of St Peter's, Magdeburg, at the age of 17. After legal studies in Leipzig he entered the service of Frederick II of Prussia 1741, but returned to Magdeburg in 1746 as organist of St John's. He succeeded his father as municipal music director in 1752.

Works CHORAL over 20 dramatic oratorios, including *David und Jonathan* (1766), *Der Tod Abels Saul* (1770); Passion oratorios; cantatas and numerous other church works.

OTHER instrumental music, songs.

Roma orchestral suite by George Bizet, composed 1866–68 and first performed at Paris in 1869.

Roman, Johan Helmich (1694–1758) Swedish composer. He was a pupil of his father, who was leader of the court orchestra in Stockholm, and entered royal service in 1711. In England from 1714, he studied with Attilo Ariosti and Johann Pepusch and was in the service of the Duke of Newcastle. Returning to Stockholm, he became vice-kapellmeister in 1721, then kapellmeister in 1729. He toured England, France, and Italy 1735–37, became a member of the Swedish Academy in 1740, and retired in 1745.

Works CHORAL Mass, motets, psalms, festival cantatas.

ORCHESTRAL 21 symphonies, six overtures, concertos, over 20 violin sonatas, twelve sonatas for flute, viola da gamba, and harpsichord.

SOLO *Assaggio* for solo violin, and other pieces.

romance a piece or song of a 'romantic' nature, usually moderate in tempo and emotional in style. There is no prescribed form, but as a rule it is fairly short and in the character of a song. In France, single-voice songs were called *romances* from about the end of the 18th century onward until recently, and the term is still in use, though the more general term now is *mélodie*.

romanesca in music, originally the melody of a 16th-century Spanish song with a simple bass, used as a theme for ➤ **variations**.

A simple form of the romanesca starting on C.

Romani, Felice (1788–1865) Italian librettist and poet. His first libretti were for Simone Mayr (*Medea in Corinto*, 1813). He soon began a collaboration with Rossini and wrote *Aureliano in Palmira* and *Il Turco in Musicia*. For Gaetano Donizetti he wrote *L'Elisir d'amore* (1832) and *Anna Bolena* (1835). His most important work was for Bellini: *Il Pirata* (1827), *I Capuleti* (1830), *La Sonnambula*, *Norma* (1831), and *Beatrice di Tenda* (1833). His only libretto for Verdi was *Un Giorno di Regno* (1840).

Romanticism in music, the period from about 1810 to around 1910 – that is, after the classical period. Classical composers had tried to create a balance between expression and formal structure; Romantic composers altered this balance by applying more freedom to the form and structure of their music, and using deeper, more intense expressions of moods, feelings, and emotions. An increased interest in literature, nature, the supernatural, and love, along with nationalistic feelings and the idea of the musician as visionary artist and hero (virtuoso) all added to the development of Romanticism. The move-

ment reached its height in the late 19th century, as in the works of Robert ➤ **Schumann** and Richard ➤ **Wagner**.

With the emphasis on imagination and vision, the formal structure was stretched to accommodate a wider range of keys and sudden changes between them, and dynamic and instrumental timbres were also used. Harmonies became richer, dissonance was more freely used, and modulation played a more important role. Fantasy and imagination were important to the Romantic style. Composers were often widely read and were inspired by poems, novels, plays, and paintings. There was a large increase in the orchestra at this time, both in the number of instruments and in their range of pitches and timbres. The symphony, concerto, and opera were all written on a larger scale and an interest in ➤ **programme music** led to the development of a new musical form, the ➤ **symphonic poem**. At the opposite end of the scale, composers also wrote extended, virtuosic works for just one or two musicians. These included much work for piano (which was a favourite instrument), and a large number of songs. Virtuoso instrumental players were becoming increasingly popular and the virtuoso composer-performer was a much admired musician. Great examples of these are Niccolò Paganini and Franz Liszt. A strong move towards ➤ **nationalism** developed as composers reacted against the powerful German influences by developing a musical style that expressed the characteristics of their own country. They did this by including tunes from their nation's folk music, and taking scenes from their country's history, legends, and folk tales, as a basis for their compositions.

Romantic Symphony nickname of a symphony by Anton ➤ **Bruckner**, no. 4 in E flat. The first version was composed in 1874 and first performed at Linz on 20 September 1875. A version with a new scherzo and revised finale was performed at Vienna on 20 February 1881, conducted by Hans Richter.

Romanze (German 'romance') see ➤ romance.

Romberg, Andreas (Jakob) (1767–1821) German violinist and composer. He was a pupil of his father, Gerhard Heinrich Romberg (1745–1819). He appeared in string duets with his cousin Bernhard Romberg at the age of seven and at 17 played at the Concert Spirituel in Paris. In 1790 he joined the electoral orchestra in Bonn and in 1793–96 he was in Italy, Spain, and Portugal with Bernhard, whom he joined again in Paris in 1800 after visits to Vienna and Hamburg. He returned to Hamburg, where he married and remained for 15 years, after which he became court music director at Gotha.

Works OPERA *Don Mendoce, ou Le Tuteur portugais* (with Bernhard Romberg), *Das blaue Ungeheuer* (composed 1793), *Der Rabe* (1794), *Die Ruinen zu Paluzzi* (1811), *Die Grossmut des Scipio* (1816) and others.

CHORAL WITH ORCHESTRA Te Deum, Magnificat, psalms and other church music; setting of Schiller's *Lied von der Glocke* for solo voices, chorus, and orchestra; other cantatas *The Transient and the Eternal*, *The Harmony of the Spheres*, *The Power of Song*.

OTHER six symphonies and Toy Symphony; string quartets and quintets.

Romberg, Bernhard (1767–1841) German cellist and composer, cousin of Andreas ➤ Romberg. He was a pupil of his father, Anton Romberg, and appeared at the age of seven with his cousin and in Paris at 14.

He was in the electoral orchestra at Bonn 1790–93, together with Andreas, Beethoven, Reicha, and Ferdinand Ries; then, until 1796, he was in Italy, Spain, and Portugal with Andreas. After visits to Vienna and Hamburg he taught the cello at the Paris Conservatory 1801–03, and 1804–06 he was cellist in the royal orchestra in Berlin, where he was court music director 1815–19. He retired to Hamburg in 1819 after a tour in Russia. He also visited London, Paris, Vienna, St Petersburg, and Moscow.

Works OPERA *Don Mendoce, ou le tuteur portugais* (with Andreas Romberg), *Die wiedergefundene Statue* (after Gozzi, composed 1792), *Der Schiffbruch*, *Alma*, *Ulysses und Circe* (1807), *Rittertreue*.

ORCHESTRAL AND CHAMBER ten cello concertos, concerto for two cello, funeral symphony for Queen Louise of Prussia, 11 string quartets, piano quartets and other chamber music, cello pieces.

Romberg, Siegmund (1887–1951) Hungarian-born US composer. In 1909 he went to the USA as an engineer, but later began composing with great success.

He studied at the University of Bucharest and then in Vienna with Richard Heuberger.

Works OPERETTAS *Blossom Time* (after music by Schubert, 1921), *The Rose of Stamboul*, *The Student Prince* (1924), *The Desert Song* (1926).

Romeo and Juliet fantasy overture by Tchaikovsky, based on Shakespeare's tragedy. It was first performed at Moscow on 16 March 1870, and was revised in October of that same year.

Ballet by Prokofiev, first performed at Brno on 30 December 1938.

See also ➤ Giulietta e Romeo, ➤ Capuleti e i Montecchi, I.

Roméo et Juliette opera by Charles Gounod (libretto by Jules Barbier and Michel Carré, after Shakespeare), produced at the Théâtre Lyrique,

Paris, on 27 April 1867. The story is similar to Shakespeare: the lovers Romeo and Juliet cannot escape the feud between their families, the Montagues and the Capulets, and die for their love.

Symphony by Berlioz, Op. 17, for solo voices, chorus, and orchestra, based on Shakespeare's tragedy and composed in 1839. It was first performed at the Paris Conservatory on 24 November 1839.

Romeo und Julia opera by Heinrich Sutermeister (libretto by composer, after Shakespeare), produced at Dresden on 13 April 1940. See ➤ *Roméo et Juliette* for a plot synopsis.

Opera by Boris Blacher (libretto as above), composed in 1943 and first produced at Salzburg on 9 August 1950.

Romeo und Julia auf dem Dorfe opera by Frederick Delius; see A ➤ *Village Romeo and Juliet*.

Romeo und Julie opera by Jiří Benda (libretto by F W Gotter). The first opera to be based on Shakespeare's tragedy, it was produced at court in Gotha on 25 September 1776. See ➤ *Roméo et Juliette* for a plot synopsis.

Romero, Mateo (c.1575–1647), also known as **Maestro Capitán** Spanish singer, composer, and priest. He composed motets and other church music, as well as songs.

He joined the Flemish section of the royal chapel at Madrid in 1594; he was a pupil of Philippe Rogier, whom he succeeded as maestro de cappella in 1598. He was ordained priest in 1609 and retired with a pension in 1633, but was sent on a musical mission to Portugal in 1638.

Works CHORAL AND VOCAL motets and other church music; secular songs for three and four voices, including settings of poems by Lope de Vega.

Romilda e Costanza opera by Giacomo Meyerbeer (libretto by Giacomo Rossi), produced at Padua on 19 July 1817.

rondeau in music, a medieval song with a refrain; also, by analogy, in the 17th and 18th centuries an instrumental piece in which one section recurs. See ➤ rondo.

rondeña a Spanish folk song, a type of Andalusia, resembling the ➤ fandango, with words in stanzas of four lines of eight syllables.

Rondine, La, **The Swallow** operetta by Puccini (libretto by G Adami, translated from the German of A M Willner and H Reichert), produced at Monte Carlo on 27 March 1917. It was originally intended to be set to the German words for the Carl Theater in Vienna, but this fell through because Italy was at war with Austria. In the story, Prunier, a poet, convinces Magda of the power of love. She meets Ruggero, who falls in love with her; but she abandons him to return to

Rambaldo, leaving him devastated.

rondo or **rondeau** musical form where the main theme keeps recurring with contrasting sections in between (ABACADA). The A section is always in the tonic key, while the contrasting section (or episode) is in a related key. The rondo is often lively in character and is a popular final movement of a sonata, concerto, or symphony.

root in music, in a chord, the ➔ **tonic** note from which the other notes are derived. For example, in a chord consisting of any spacing or arrangement of the notes C–E–G, C is always the root. A chord is considered to be in 'root position' when the root is the lowest voice or part, usually in the bass.

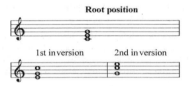

A chord in root position on C. The second diagram shows its first and second inversions. According to this theory, which takes no account of the different functions of chords, a four-note chord has three possible inversions, and so on.

Rore, Cipriano de (c.1516–1565) Flemish composer. He spent much of his life in Italy, where he was a prolific composer of madrigals and sacred music. He wrote 125 madrigals, most of which are contained in the ten books he published 1542–46. His works made a strong impression on Monteverdi.

He studied under Adrian Willaert at Venice, where he was a singer at St Mark's, and began to publish madrigals in 1542. He left Venice about 1550 to enter the service of Duke Ercole II d'Este at Ferrara. In 1558, he visited his parents at Antwerp and the court of Margaret of Parma, governor of the Netherlands, at Brussels, into the service of whose husband, Ottavio Farnese, Duke of Parma, he passed in 1561. In 1563 he succeeded Willaert as maestro di cappella of St Mark's, Venice, but returned to Parma the following year.

Rore's parody Masses and motets follow the style of the previous generation, but it is for his madrigals that he is chiefly remembered. He set many of Petrarch's texts in his earlier madrigals; in the later ones he became more aware of sensitive treatment of the text.

Works CHURCH AND SECULAR MUSIC five Masses, 65 motets, one Passion and other church music; 125 madrigals; instrumental fantasies and ricercari, and other pieces.

Rorem, Ned (1923–) US composer. He studied at the Curtis Institute and Juilliard School, New York. He has held academic posts at the Universities of Buffalo and Utah, and at the Curtis Institute (from 1980).

Works OPERA *A Childhood Miracle* (1955), *The Robbers* (1958), *Miss Julie* (1965), and *Hearing* (1976).

ORCHESTRAL three symphonies (1950, 1956, 1958); three piano concertos (1950, 1969, 1992); *Eagles* for orchestra (1958); Double concerto for violin, cello, and orchestra (1979); symphonic suite *Sunday Morning* (1981); *String Symphony* (1985); organ concerto (1985); violin concerto (1985); cor anglais concerto (1993).

CHORAL *The Poet's Requiem* for soprano, chorus, and orchestra (1957); *Whitman Cantata* (1983); *An American Oratorio* (1984); *Homer* for chorus and eight instruments (1986).

SONGS songs and song cycles, including *Flight for Heaven*, *King Midas*, *Poems of Love and the Rain*, *War Scenes*, *Women's Voices*, and *After Long Silence*.

OTHER septet *Scenes from Childhood* (1985); *Diversions*, brass quintet (1989); church music; keyboard pieces.

Rosalia in music, the usual name for the real ➔ **sequence**: repeating a phrase higher or lower, not within the scale of the same key, as in the **tonal** sequence, but by so changing the key that its steps retain exactly the same succession of whole tones and semitones. The name derives from an Italian popular song, 'Rosalia, mia cara', in which this device occurs.

Rosamond opera by Thomas Arne (libretto by Joseph Addison), produced at the Theatre in Lincoln's Inn Fields, London, on 7 March 1733.

Opera by Clayton (libretto as above), produced at the Drury Lane Theatre, London, on 4 March 1707. In the story, Queen Eleanor, wife of King Henry, discovers his mistress Rosamond and forces her to drink a bowl of poison. When Henry repents, she reveals the liquid was not lethal, and that Rosamond has become a nun.

Rosamunde incidental music by Schubert for a play by Helmina von Chézy, *Rosamunde, Prinzessin von Cypern*, produced at the Theater an der Wien, Vienna, on 20 December 1823. The music consists of three entr'actes, two ballet tunes, a romance for contralto, a chorus of spirits, a shepherd's melody and shepherds' chorus, and a hunting-chorus. No overture was specially written for the piece. At the first performance, the overture to the opera *Alfonso und Estrella* was used; later, the overture to the melodrama *Die Zauberharfe* was published as the *Rosamunde* overture and is still so played.

A rosalia in which the first two bars are repeated a whole tone higher.

rose or **knot** the ornamental fretwork sound hole of many flat-bellied string instruments of the lute and guitar type; also of dulcimers, harpsichords, and similar instruments, sometimes serving as the makers' trademark.

Rose et Colas opera by Monsigny (libretto by Michel-Jean Sedaine), produced at the Comédie-Italienne, Paris, on 8 March 1764.

Roseingrave (lived 17th–18th centuries) English family of musicians:

Daniel (c.1650–1727), organist and composer. He was educated in music as a chorister in the Chapel Royal in London. From 1679 to 1698 he was successively organist of Gloucester, Winchester, and Salisbury Cathedrals, and was then appointed to St Patrick's and Christ Church Cathedrals, Dublin.

Thomas (1688–1766), organist and composer, son of Daniel. He was a pupil of his father at Dublin, where he was educated at Trinity College. In 1710 he went to Italy where he met Alessandro and Domenico Scarlatti, making great friends with the latter and travelling with him. He went to London before 1720, when he produced Domenico Scarlatti's opera *Narcisco* with interpolations of his own. In 1725 he was appointed organist of St George's Church in Hanover Square. He retired in 1741 and moved to Dublin, living probably with his nephew William Roseingrave.

His works include the opera *Phaedra and Hippolytus* (on Edmund Smith's play based on Racine, 1753); services and anthems; organ voluntaries and fugues; suites for harpsichord and an introductory piece for his edition of Scarlatti's sonatas; twelve solos for flute and harpsichord; twelve Italian cantatas (1735).

Ralph (c.1695–1747), composer, brother of Thomas. He studied with his father, who petitioned for him to succeed him as organist of St Patrick's Cathedral, Dublin, in 1719; but he was appointed vicar-choral and not organist until 1726. He also became organist of Christ Church Cathedral on his father's death. He wrote services and anthems.

Rosen, Charles (1927–) US pianist and musicologist. He is well known for his thoughtful interpretations of Bach, Beethoven, and modern music, including Carter, Schoenberg, and Boulez. His books include *The Classical Style* (1971), *Schoenberg* (1975), and *Sonata Forms* (1980).

He graduated from Princeton University, New Jersey, with an arts degree in 1949, and made his debut as a pianist at New York in 1951. He has taught in New York and at Berkeley, California.

Rosenkavalier, Der, The Rose Cavalier opera by Richard Strauss (libretto by Hugo von Hofmannsthal), produced at the Royal Opera, Dresden, on 26 January 1911. In the story, Octavian, the young lover of the Marschallin, bears a silver rose to Sophie, the proposed betrothed of the loutish Ochs. When he meets her Octavian falls in love and conspires to end the arranged marriage, exposing Ochs as a philanderer. The Marschallin, although unhappy, gives Octavian and Sophie her blessing.

Rosenmüller, Johann (c.1619–1684) German composer. He was a prolific and popular composer of both sacred and secular works, and was influential in introducing Italian-style music to Germany.

He studied at Leipzig University and in 1642 became assistant master at St Thomas's School there, studying music with the cantor, Tobias Michael, and acting as his deputy when Michael became infirm. He was marked out for the succession and in 1651 became organist of St Nicholas's Church; but in 1655 was imprisoned for homosexual offences with his choirboys. He escaped to Hamburg and later fled to Venice, where he settled and was influenced as a composer by the local style. There J P Krieger became his pupil. In 1674 he was recalled to Germany by an appointment to the court of Duke Anton Ulrich of Brunswick, at Wolfenbüttel.

Works CHURCH AND SECULAR MUSIC Masses, motets, vesper psalms and Lamentations, Latin and German motets, *Kernsprüche* for three–seven voices and instruments, German motets and cantatas, hymns, hymn by Albinus 'Straf mich nicht'; *Sonata da camera* for five instruments, sonatas for two–five instruments, suites of instrumental dances.

Rose of Castille, The opera by Michael Balfe (libretto by A G Harris and E Falconer, based on a French libretto, *Le Muletier de Tolède*, by A P d'Ennery and Clairville, set by Adolphe Charles Adam and produced in 1854). It was produced at the Lyceum Theatre, London, on 29 October 1857.

Rose of Persia, The or **The Story-Teller and the Slave** operetta by Sullivan (libretto by B Hood), produced at the Savoy Theatre, London, on 29 November 1899.

Rose vom Liebesgarten, Die opera by Pfitzner (libretto by J Grun), composed 1897–1900 and produced at Elberfeld in Germany, on 9 November 1901. The story begins during the celebration of spring, when the fairy queen Minneleide is abducted by the Night Sorceror. Siegnot, who loves her, is killed while rescuing her but is restored to life.

rosin resin, refined from distilled oil of turpentine. Used by makers of musical instruments and performers, it is applied to the hairs of the bow of a string instrument. By increasing the friction between bow and strings, it helps the strings to vibrate when the bow is drawn across them.

Rosina ballad opera by William Shield (libretto by F Brooke, based on an episode in Thomson's *Seasons* and Favart's *Les Moissonneurs* with Egidio Duni's music), produced at Covent Garden, London, on 31 December 1782. The story concerns Rosina, who is the object of both Mr Belville's and Captain Belville's attentions. After the Captain tries to abduct her, Mr Belville realizes she loves him and he proposes marriage.

Rosinda opera by Francesco Cavalli (libretto by G Faustini), produced at the Teatro San Apollinaire, Venice, in 1651.

Roslavets, Nikolai Andreievich (1881–1944) Russian composer. He studied music at the Moscow Conservatory under Sergey Vasilenko, and developed his own 12-tone system of composition. Some of his music has been revived, including the violin concerto of 1925, but has not quite lived up to its avant-garde reputation.

Works CHORAL AND ORCHESTRAL cantata *Heaven and Earth* (after Byron, 1912); symphony, violin concerto (1925), two symphonic poems.

CHAMBER five string quartets (no. 3 12-tone), quintet for oboe, two violins, cello, and harp; two piano trios; five violin and piano sonatas; two cello and piano sonatas; many piano pieces; songs.

Rösler, Franz Anton (c.1750–1792) Bohemian composer. Destined for the priesthood, he attended the Jesuit College of Olomouc, but in 1773 entered the service of the Prince of Ottingen as a double bass player and later became conductor. He left for Ludwigslust in 1789 and was court music director there to his death. He wrote under the name of Francesco Antonio Rosetti.

Works OPERA *Das Winterfest der Hirten* (1789).

CHORAL oratorios *Der sterbende Jesus* (1786) and *Jesus in Gethsemane*; Requiem for Mozart (1791).

ORCHESTRAL AND CHAMBER MUSIC 34 symphonies; concertos for piano, violin, flute, oboe, clarinet, and horn; other chamber music; violin sonatas.

Rosmene, La, ovvero L'Infedeltà fedele, Rosmene, or Faithful Faithlessness opera by Alessandro Scarlatti (libretto by G D de Totis),

produced at the Palazzo Reale, Naples, at the Carnival in 1688.

Rosseter, Philip (1567 or 1568–1623) English lutenist and composer. He worked in London and was associated with Robert Jones, Philip Kingham, and Reeve in the theatre life of the capital. From 1609 he worked with Robert Keysar, managing a company of boy actors, known as the Children of Whitefriars (from 1610 the Children of the Queen's Revels). From 1615 the company performed at the Blackfriars theatre. Rosseter published a book of songs to the lute with Thomas Campion; some, if not all, of the words were by Campion and about half of the music was by Rosseter.

Works ENSEMBLE *A Booke of Ayres* with lute, orpheoreon, and bass viol; *Lessons for the Consort* for six instruments by various composers.

Rossi, Luigi (c. 1598–1653) Italian singer and composer. He composed in an elaborate style, and developed the innovations of Monteverdi. His *Orfeo* (1647) was lavishly produced at court; the expense provoked anti-monarchist feeling in the Parisian populace.

He was in the service of Cardinal Barberini in Rome 1641–46. In 1646 he was called to Paris at the instigation of Cardinal Mazarin and the following year produced *Orfeo*, one of the first Italian operas to be performed there. It has been successfully revived in Bloomington, USA, and London (1988, 1990).

Works OPERA AND CHORAL the operas *Il palagio d'Atlante, or Il palazzo incantato, L'Orfeo* (1647); oratorio *Giuseppe, figlio di Giacobbe*, cantatas, and other pieces.

Rossi, Michel Angelo (c. 1600–1656) Italian organist and composer. His opera *Erminia sul Giordano*, to a libretto by Giulio Rospigliosi, later Pope Clement IX, was given in Rome in 1633. He was a pupil of Frescobaldi.

Works OPERA *Erminia sul Giordano* (after Tasso) and *Andromeda* (1638).

OTHER toccatas and *correnti* for organ or harpsichord.

Rossi, Salomone (1570–c. 1630) Italian composer. He worked at the court of Mantua 1587–1628 and enjoyed the privilege of dispensing with the wearing of the yellow badge that stigmatized the Jews in Italy.

Works CHORAL AND VOICE oratorio *Maddalena* (both with Monteverdi and others, 1608, 1617); 28 Hebrew psalms for four–eight voices; madrigals and canzonets.

OTHER instrumental works *Sinfonie e gagliarde* and *Sonate*; music for Guarini's *Idropica*.

Rossignol, Le opera by Igor Stravinsky; see *The* ➔ *Nightingale*.

Rossini, Gioacchino Antonio (1792–1868) Italian composer. His first success was the opera *Tancredi* in 1813. In 1816 his opera buffa (comic opera) *Il barbiere di Siviglia/The Barber of Seville* was produced in Rome. He was the most successful opera composer of his time, producing 20 operas in the period 1815–23. He also created (with Gaetano Donizetti and Vincenzo Bellini) the 19th-century Italian operatic style.

After *Guillaume Tell/William Tell* (1829), Rossini gave up writing opera and his later years were spent in Bologna and Paris. Among the works of this period are the *Stabat Mater* (1842) and the piano music arranged for ballet by Ottorino Respighi as *La boutique fantasque/The Fantastic Toyshop* (1919).

Rossini was born in Pesaro; his father was a horn and trumpet player, his mother an occasional singer. He learnt piano, singing, and harmony at an early age and sang in churches and theatres; at 13 he was employed as an accompanist at the theatre; at 14, when he had already tried his hand at an opera and other works, he entered the Bologna Liceo Musicale, studying counterpoint and cello. In 1808 he won a prize with a cantata and in 1810 had his first comic opera, *La cambiale di matrimonio*, produced at Venice. From that time he went from success to success, beginning with *Tancredi* at Venice in 1813. However, *Il barbiere di Siviglia* was initially a failure when first performed in Rome in 1816. The two sides of Rossini's creative genius were now well established: the wit, liveliness, and elaborate vocal writing of his comic operas and the considerable dramatic power of his serious works, each in its own distinctive musical 'colour'. His huge popular following was consolidated by *Otello* (1816), *La Cenerentola* in 1817 and *Mosè in Egitto* in 1818 (later revised for Paris). *Mosè* was premiered in Naples and was one of six remarkable serious operas produced there in only five years, the others being *Armida*, *Ermione*, *La donna del lago*, *Maometto II*, and *Zelmira*; each of these works has only recently been revived.

His first great foreign success came during a visit to Vienna in 1822; he met Beethoven and saw his own operas achieve greater acclaim with the Viennese than any Austrian work. In the same year he married the Portuguese singer Isabella Colbran; she had already created leading roles in *Elisabetta*, *Otello*, *Mosè in Egitto*, and *Armida*. At Venice in 1823 she sang the title role in Rossini's last opera written for the Italian stage, *Semiramide*. Rossini and his wife went to Paris and to London that year, remaining in England until July 1824 and being well received at court. He wrote a lament for eight voices on the death of the poet Byron.

On returning to Paris, Rossini was appointed director of the Théâtre Italien, where he produced one new work and two revised works, followed by a French comic opera, *Le Comte Ory*, and finally *Guillaume Tell* (1829) at the Opéra. The strain of composing *Guillaume Tell* brought on a prolonged period of ill health; thereafter, although aged only 37, he gave up opera and lived alternately at Bologna and Paris. In the early 1830s he met Olympe Pélissier and entered into a liaison with her. His separation from Isabella was made legal in 1837 and she died in 1845. He married Olympe in August 1846. Serious illness affected him during this period, but he completed the *Stabat Mater* (1832–42). In 1839 he was commissioned to reform the Liceo Musicale at Bologna, where he had once been a pupil. He worked there at intervals until 1848, when he left for Florence, to remain until 1855, leaving Italy for the last time for Paris that year. In his retirement he wrote many small pièces for the entertainment of his friends and in 1863 the *Petite Messe solennelle*; his musical soirées were much sought after by fashionable society and contemporary musicians.

For many years Rossini's comic operas have overshadowed his serious works, but recent productions have helped to produce a more balanced view of his output.

Works OPERA *Tancredi* (1813), *L'Italiana in Algeri* (1813), *Il barbiere di Siviglia/The Barber of Seville* (after Beaumarchais, 1816), *Otello* (last act after Shakespeare, 1816), *La Cenerentola* (1817), *La gazza ladra* (1817), *Armida* (1818), *Mosè in Egitto* (1818), *Semiramide* (1823), *Il viaggio a Reims* (1825), *Le Comte Ory* (1828), *Guillaume Tell* (after Schiller, 1829).

CHURCH MUSIC *Messa di Gloria* (1820), *Stabat Mater* (1842), *Petite Messe solennelle* (1863), and some shorter sacred pieces.

OTHER *Péchés de vieillesse/Sins of Old Age*, small piano pieces, songs, and six string quartets.

Rota, Nino (1911–1979) Italian composer. He studied with Ildebrando Pizzetti, Alfredo Casella, and in the USA. On his return to Milan he obtained a degree with a treatise on the 16th-century Italian composer Gioseffo Zarlino and Italian Renaissance music. In 1950 he was appointed director of the Bari Conservatory.

Works OPERA *Il principe porcaro* (after Hans Andersen, composed 1925), *Ariodante* (1942), *Il capello di paglia di Firenze/The Italian Straw Hat* (1955).

CHORAL oratorio *L'infanzia di San Giovanni Battista*; two Masses.

ORCHESTRAL AND CHAMBER three symphonies (1936–39), serenade and concerto for orchestra; *Invenzioni* for string quartet, quintet for flute, oboe, viola, cello, and harp; *Il presepio* for voice, string quartet, and piano; sonatas for violin and piano, viola and piano, and flute and harp; songs

Liriche di Tagore, Tre liriche infantili; film music.

rote string instrument of the ➔ lyre type, also called rota or rotte, and similar to the crwth. It was in use up to medieval times.

Rouget de Lisle, Claude-Joseph (1760–1836) French army officer. While in Strasbourg 1792, he composed 'La Marseillaise', the French national anthem.

round in music, an alternative name for a ➔ canon, in which voices imitate each other exactly.

rounds dances performed in circles, and tunes intended for such dances.

Rousseau, Jean-Jacques (1712–1778) Swiss-French philosopher, author, and composer. As secretary to the French ambassador in Venice 1743–44, he became acquainted with Italian music, and during the Guerre des Bouffons sided with the Italian party, decrying French music in his controversial essay, 'Lettre sur la musique française' (1753). His most important composition, the one-act *intermède Le Devin du village*, though in French, was supposedly written in tuneful Italian style.

He was a chorister at Annecy Cathedral but had little formal training in music. He went to Paris in 1741, where he presented a paper to the Académie des Sciences advocating a new system of notation (published in 1743 as 'Dissertation sur la musique moderne') and later contributed music articles to Diderot's *Encyclopédie*, which were severely criticized by Rameau for their inaccuracy. In 1767 he published his valuable *Dictionnaire de musique*. The 'monodrama' *Pygmalion* (1770), only two pieces of which were by Rousseau, attempted to found a new form, and in its combination of spoken words and music was the ancestor of the later melodrama. Among his other writings are two essays in support of Christoph Willibald von Gluck.

Works *OPERA AND STAGE* the operas *Iphis et Anaxerète* (1740), *La Découverte du nouveau monde* (1741), *Le Devin du village* (1752), *Daphnis et Chloé* (unfinished); opera-ballet *Les Muses galantes* (1745); monodrama *Pygmalion* (1770).

SONGS about 100, published as *Consolations des misères de ma vie*.

Roussel, Albert (1869–1937) French composer. One of his most popular works is *Le festin de l'araignée/The Spider's Banquet* (1912), in which the hungry arachnid is depicted with appropriate, delicate scoring.

He was educated in Paris for the French navy, but took piano lessons at the same time. He wrote his first compositions while engaged in naval service and voyaging to the East, but resigned in 1893 to devote himself to music, studying with Eugène Gigout and Vincent d'Indy. In 1902 he be-

came professor at the Schola Cantorum, where he had studied. In World War I, he served with the Red Cross and later with the transport service, and in 1918 he retired, broken in health, to Perros-Guirec in Brittany and in 1920 to a villa near Varengeville.

His naval service in the East had a lasting impression on Roussel, colouring his finest work, the opéra-ballet *Padmâvatî* with Indian melodic patterns. Ballet and choral singing are found also in *La naissance de la lyre*, an evocation of ancient Greece. Other characteristics of Roussel's varying style appear in his third symphony, which includes polytonality and vital rhythmic patterns.

Works *STAGE* opera *Padmâvatî* (1923); ballets *Le festin de l'araignée* (1913), *Bacchus et Ariane* (1931).

VOCAL AND ORCHESTRAL four symphonies, 1908–34; *Suite en Fa* (1927); sinfonietta for strings; concertino for cello and orchestra (1936).

CHAMBER AND SONGS serenade for flute, violin, viola, cello, and harp (1925); string trio, trios for violin, clarinet, and piano and for flute, violin, and clarinet; *Joueurs de flûte* for flute and piano; Impromptu for harp; suite, sonatina, and other pieces for piano; songs.

rovescio see ➔ cancrizans.

Rovetta, Giovanni (c.1595–1668) Italian priest and composer. He learnt music as a choirboy at St Mark's, Venice, and in 1623 was appointed a bass in the choir there. He was ordained priest, became vice-maestro di cappella at St Mark's in 1627, and maestro di cappella in succession to Monteverdi in 1644.

Works *CHURCH AND SECULAR MUSIC* Masses, motets, psalms; madrigals.

OPERA Ercole in Lidia (1645) and *Argiope* (1649).

Roxelane, La authentic name of Haydn's symphony no. 63 in C major, composed c. 1777–80, so called apparently after an old French melody used for variations in the slow movement.

Royal Academy of Music, RAM conservatoire of international standing in London, founded in 1822 by John Fane, Lord Burghesh, later 11th Earl of Westmorland. It was granted a royal charter in 1830. Based in Marylebone Road, it provides full-time training leading to performing and academic qualifications. The current principal is Curtis Price.

Royal College of Music, RCM conservatoire of international standing in London, founded in 1882 in Kensington. It provides full-time training leading to performing and academic qualifications. The current principal is Dr Janet Ritterman.

Royal College of Organists college founded in London in 1864, and currently located in Kensington. Towards the end of the 19th century, it was influential in standardization of organ design. It is an important examining body, and also organizes lectures.

The college was originally set up to provide a central organization for the organ profession; to provide an examinations system for the church; to provide opportunities for meetings and lectures; and to promote composition of church music.

Royal Manchester College of Music see ➤ Royal Northern College of Music.

Royal Musical Association a society formed to promote the investigation of all aspects of music. It was founded in London in 1874 as the Musical Association and became 'Royal' in 1944. The Association published the *Proceedings of the RMA* (until 1956–57), and now publishes the *Journal of the RMA* (from 1987), the *RMA Research Chronicle* (from 1961), *RMA Monographs* (from 1985), and initiated *Musica Britannica* in 1951. It holds two conferences each year, one being for research students.

The society awards the Dent medal annually in association with the International Musicological Society to a musicologist of international repute.

Royal Northern College of Music college founded as the Royal Manchester College of Music in Manchester, England, in 1893. Its first principal was Sir Charles Hallé, followed by Adolf Brodsky (1895), J R Forbes (1929), F R Cox (1953) and J Wray (1970–72). In 1972 the college merged with the Northern School of Music to form the current Royal Northern College of Music. Its principal is Edward Gregson.

Royal Opera House Britain's leading opera house, sited at Covent Garden, London.

The original theatre opened in 1732, was destroyed by fire in 1808 and reopened in 1809. It was again destroyed by fire in 1856, and the third and present building dates from 1858. It has been the home of the Royal Opera and the Royal Ballet since 1946. Due to its financial difficulties, it closed in January 1999, reopening in December of the same year after spending £214 million on refurbishment and undergoing financial and managerial restructuring.

Royal Winter Music two sonatas on Shakespearean characters for guitar by Henze: no. 1 (1975–76) was first performed in Berlin on 20 September 1976, with Julian Bream; no. 2 (1979) was first performed in Brussels on 25 November 1980.

Rozkošný, Josef Richard (1833–1913) Czech pianist and composer. He studied in Prague and toured widely as a pianist. Later he had a great success as a popular opera composer.

Works OPERA *Nicholas* (1870), *The Rapids of St John* (1871), *Cinderella* (1885), *Stoja, Zavis of Falkenstein* (1877), *Krakonos* (1889), *The Poacher, Satanella, The Black Lake* (1906).

OTHER piano pieces; songs.

Rózsa, Miklós (1907–1995) Hungarian-born US composer. He wrote music for such films as *The Jungle Book, Spellbound* (1945), and *Ben Hur* (1959).

He studied piano and composition in Leipzig, and in 1932 settled in Paris, achieving success as a composer. In 1935 he moved to London, where he worked in the film industry, and in 1940 settled in Hollywood.

Works ORCHESTRAL *Ballet Hungarica*, symphony (1930), *Scherzo, Theme, Variations and Finale* for orchestra (1933); concert overture, serenade for chamber orchestra; concerto for string orchestra; two violin concertos, viola concerto (1984); film music.

CHAMBER string quartet; piano quintet, trio for violin, viola, and clarinet; and other pieces.

Różycki, Ludomir (1883–1953) Polish conductor and composer. He studied with Noskowski at the Warsaw Conservatory and with Humperdinck in Berlin. In 1912 he became conductor at Lviv, and later lived by turns in Warsaw and Berlin.

Works OPERA AND STAGE the operas *Bolesław the Bold* (1908), *Medusa* (1911), *Eros and Psyche* (1916), *Casanova, Beatrice Cenci* (1926), *The Devil's Mill* (1930); ballet *Pan Twardowski*.

ORCHESTRAL AND CHAMBER symphonic poems *Bolesław the Bold, Anhelli*, and others; prelude *Mona Lisa Gioconda* and ballad for orchestra; piano concerto in G minor; string quartet (1916), piano quintet (1913), piano music, songs.

rubato (from Italian *tempo rubato*, 'rubbed time') in music, a pushing or dragging against the beat for expressive effect.

Rubbra, Edmund (1901–1986) English composer. He studied under the composer Gustav Holst and specialized in contrapuntal writing, as exemplified in his study *Counterpoint* (1960). His compositions include 11 symphonies, chamber music, and songs. In 1948 he became a Roman Catholic and his later music shows the influence of Catholic mysticism.

Rubbra was born in Northampton and studied at Reading University and the Royal College of Music in London, where his teachers included Holst, R O Morris, and Vaughan Williams. He taught at Oxford University 1947–68 and at the Guildhall School of Music, London, from 1961.

Works STAGE AND CHORAL *La Belle Dame sans merci* (Keats) and *The Morning Watch* (Henry Vaughan) for chorus and orchestra; Masses, motets, madrigals, and other choral works.

ORCHESTRAL eleven symphonies (1935–79), *Improvisations on Virginal Pieces by Farnaby* (1939) for orchestra; viola concerto (1953), piano concerto (1956), *Soliloquy* for cello and small orchestra; works for voice and orchestra.

CHAMBER four string quartets (1934–77); three sonatas and sonatina for violin and piano, cello and piano sonata; piano and organ music; songs.

Rubinstein, Anton Grigorievich (1829–1894) Russian pianist and composer. One of the great virtuosos of his day, he did not join the Russian nationalist movement of his contemporaries, The ✦ **Five**. His music follows a more western European style, but although solidly constructed it lacks the imaginative touch of genius. His many compositions include five piano concertos and six symphonies, including the *Ocean* (no. 2); he also wrote 18 operas, of which the best known is *The Demon* (1871, performed in 1875), and oratorios.

Born at Vykhvatinets, Ukraine, Rubinstein learnt the piano from his mother and from a teacher named Villoing at Moscow. He appeared in public at the age of nine and in 1840 went on tour with his teacher, who took him to Paris and placed him under Liszt for further instruction. He afterwards toured in Europe and studied composition with Dehn in Berlin 1844–46. After teaching in Vienna and Pressburg (now Bratislava) he returned to Russia in 1848, becoming chamber virtuoso to the Grand Duchess Helena Pavlovna. From 1854 he made successful tours as a concert pianist, earning a great reputation in Europe and the USA. In 1858 he was appointed imperial music director at St Petersburg, founding the Conservatory there in 1862. As a composer Rubinstein was antagonistic to the Russian nationalists; his compositions are still little known although *The Demon* was successfully revived at the Wexford Festival in 1991.

Works OPERA AND STAGE ORATORIOS *The Demon* (after Lermontov, 1875), *Kalashnikov* (1879), and others.

VOCAL AND ORCHESTRAL Songs and Requiem for Mignon from Goethe's *Wilhelm Meister* for solo voices, chorus, and piano; six symphonies (1850–86): (no. 2 *Ocean*, no. 4 *Dramatic*); five concertos and *Conzertstück* for piano and orchestra (1850–89).

CHAMBER piano and wind quintet, piano quintet and quartet; four sonatas, Theme and Variations and many other works for piano, including *Melody in F*, Op. 3/1; songs.

Rubsamen, Walter H(oward) (1911–1973) US musicologist. He studied at Columbia University, New York, and at Munich University; he later joined the music department of his college and in 1938 became lecturer. In 1955 he became professor at the University of California at Los An-

geles. His works included studies of Pierre de La Rue and of early Italian secular music.

Ruckers (lived 16th–17th centuries) family of Flemish harpsichord makers founded by Hans ✦ **Ruckers** and continued by his sons Joannes (1578–1642) and Andries (1579–c.1645), and their descendants. Their instruments were noted for their engineering precision and matchless tone, and were imitated widely. Many were commissioned for display and featured paintings inside the lid by artists, including Brueghel and Rubens. About 100 instruments made by members of the Ruckers family survive, in both single and two-manual versions.

Ruckers, Hans (c. 1530–1598) Flemish harpsichord and virginal maker. He founded a business at Antwerp in 1584, producing instruments which provided contrast in register and tone. He was succeeded by his two sons (see ✦ **Ruckers**).

Rückert, Friedrich (1788–1866) German poet. His works inspired ✦ *Kindertotenlieder* (Mahler), also five other songs by Mahler for voice and orchestra (*Ich atmet'einen linden Duft*, *Liebst du um Schönheit*, *Blicke mir nicht in die Lieder*, *Ich bin der Welt abhanden gekommen*, *Um Mitternacht*, 1901–03), five songs by Schubert, 18 by Schumann, two by Brahms.

Rückpositiv (German 'back positive') in music, a small ✦ **organ** at the organist's back, to the front of the gallery. From the 15th to the 17th centuries, it was the second main manual (keyboard) of most organs, providing colouristic and contrasting functions.

Ruddigore or ***The Witch's Curse*** operetta by Sullivan (libretto by W S Gilbert), produced at the Savoy Theatre, London, on 22 January 1887. The story concerns Robin, the villainous Sir Ruthven and bad baronet of Ruddigore, who is condemned by a family curse to commit a crime a day.

Ruders, Poul (1949–) Danish composer and organist. He studied at the Copenhagen Conservatory, and has had commissions from the London Sinfonietta and Ensemble Intercontemporain.

Works ORCHESTRAL AND ENSEMBLE *Wind-Drumming* for wind quintet and four percussion (1979); two violin concertos (1981, 1991); two string quartets (1971, 1979); *Manhattan Abstractions* (for the New York Philharmonic Orchestra, 1982); *Thus Saw Saint Joan* for orchestra (1984); *Break Dance* for piano and ensemble (1984); clarinet concerto (1985); *Dramaphonia* for piano and orchestra (1987); *Nightshade* for ensemble (1987); symphony *Himmelhoch Jauchzend-zum Tode betrubt* (1989); *Trapeze* (1992) and *Zenith* (1993) for orchestra; *Anima* cello concerto (1993).

A typical ruggiero in G major.

VOCAL AND OPERA *The City in the Sea* for contralto and orchestra (1990), *The Bells* for soprano and chamber ensemble (1993); opera *Tycho* (after the Danish astronomer who was obliged to replace his nose with a false nose made of silver, 1986).

Rudhyar, Dane, actually **Daniel Chennevière (1895–1985)** French-US composer. He studied in Paris and settled in the USA in 1916, receiving a composition prize in 1920.

Works BALLET *Dance Poem.*

ORCHESTRAL AND CHAMBER symphonic poem *Surge of Fire* (1920), six 'syntonies' for orchestra (1920–59), *Cosmic Cycle* for orchestra (1981); piano music and songs.

Ruffo, Vincenzo (c.1510–1587) Italian male soprano and composer. His sacred music shows the influence of Tridentine (Council of Trent) reforms, which insisted on verbal clarity.

He held the post of maestro di cappella at Verona Cathedral from 1554 and at Milan 1563–72. He occupied a similar post at Pistoia 1574–79, then returned to Milan.

Works CHURCH AND SECULAR MUSIC Masses, motets, Magnificat, psalms, and other church music; madrigals.

Rugby Honegger's second symphonic movement for orchestra, following *Pacific 231* and succeeded by *Mouvement symphonique no. 3.* It is an impression of a game of rugby football. It was first performed at the Orchestre Symphonique, Paris, on 19 October 1928.

ruggiero in music, a simple bass line, first found in the 16th century, which was widely used for variations. It may originally have been a dance, though it is found also in vocal settings. See also ➤ romanesca.

Ruggiero, o vero L'eroica gratitudine, *Ruggiero, or Heroic Gratitude* opera by Hasse (libretto by Metastasio), produced at the Teatro Regio Ducal, Milan, on 16 October 1771. It was Hasse's last opera. The story concerns Rogerus, who is imprisoned by the Greeks after a battle and is rescued by Leone, who is now betrothed to Bradamante, Rogerus's beloved. Rogerus reluctantly accepts the situation, preferring suicide to a fight against Leone. But all resolves happily: Rogerus and Bradamante are reunited.

Ruggles, Carl (1876–1971) US composer. He was an associate, during the 1920s and 1930s, of the experimentalist composers Charles Ives, Edgard Varèse, and Henry Cowell, trying to forge a new direction in music. His instrumental forms were, however, more conservative than those of other composers, as in his best-known work *Sun-Treader* (1932) for orchestra, which, typically, uses elements of ➤ serialism but in a polyphonic texture.

Ruggles studied at Harvard University with John Knowles Paine. Afterwards he conducted the Symphony Orchestra at Winona, Minnesota, for a time. From 1917 he lived in New York, where his music was performed in concerts organized by Varèse. He also associated with Ives and was an early American exponent of atonalism.

Works OPERA *The Sunken Bell* (composed 1912–23).

ORCHESTRAL AND CHAMBER *Men and Angels* (1920): *Men* (destroyed), *Angels* for four trumpets and three trombones (revised 1938); *Men and Mountains* for small orchestra (1924), *Portals* for 13 strings (1925, revised 1929, 1941 and 1953), *Sun-Treader* (1932), *Evocations* for orchestra (1971); concertino for piano and orchestra; *Vox clamans in deserto* for voice and chamber orchestra; *Polyphonic Compositions* for three pianos, *Evocations*, and other works for piano.

Ruins of Athens, The incidental music by Beethoven, Op. 113, for a play by Kotzebue written for the opening of the German theatre at Pest on 9 February 1812. It comprises an overture and eight numbers, including the *Turkish March*, already composed by Beethoven for his piano variations, Op. 76, in 1809.

'Rule, Britannia' a patriotic song by Thomas Arne, now almost a second British national anthem, originally part of the masque *Alfred*, produced on 1 August 1740, at Cliefden (now Cliveden) House near Maidenhead, the residence of Frederick, Prince of Wales.

rule of the octave in music, an 18th-century procedure in the treatment of thorough bass, especially in Italy (*regola dell'ottava*), It provides a series of simple chords of the tonic, dominant, and subdominant for the elementary harmonization of a bass formed by a rising ➤ diatonic scale.

rumba Afro-Cuban traditional secular dance and music genre, rendered by vocals with percussion, providing complex syncopated rhythms. It has a characteristic quick-quick-slow dance movement and a repetitive melody accompanied by an ostinato (persistently repeating) one-bar pattern played on the maracas. The dance emphasizes the hip and shoulder movements rather than the feet and is a model for the mambo, cha cha cha, and other Latin American ballroom dances.

Runswick, Daryl (1946–) English composer. He studied at Cambridge, and later played double bass with the London Sinfonietta 1970–82. He was tenor singer with Electric Phoenix from 1983 and musical director of the Green Light Theatre Company from 1990.

Works CHORAL AND VOCAL rock opera *Taking the Air* (1989), *Lady Lazarus* for amplified female voice (1985), *Patents: Pending* for six solo voices (1988), *Needs Must when the Devil Drives* for voices and electronics (1990).

OTHER *Main-lineing*, clarinet quintet (1991), orchestration of *Aïda* for 24 players (Welsh National Opera 1983); recordings of Berio and Cage with Electric Phoenix.

Ruslan and Ludmila opera by Glinka (libretto by V A Shirkov and C A Bakhturin, based on Pushkin's poem), produced at St Petersburg on 9 December 1842. During her wedding to the knight Ruslan, Ludmila is abducted by the evil dwarf sorceror Chernomor. Ruslan overcomes his magic and saves his bride.

Russalka, The Water-Sprite opera by Dargomizhsky (libretto by composer, from Pushkin's dramatic poem), produced at St Petersburg on 16 May 1856. In the story, Natasha, abandoned by a prince, drowns herself and becomes Queen of the river nymphs who lure men into the water. Her father, the Miller, laments her loss and goes mad, throwing the Prince into the river, where he joins Natasha.

Opera by Dvořák (libretto by Jaroslav Kvapil), produced at the Czech Theatre, Prague, on 31 March 1901.

Russian bassoon musical instrument, a ➔ serpent made in the shape of a bassoon.

'Russian' Quartets or *Gli scherzi* or *Jungfernquartette* one of the nicknames of Haydn's six string quartets, Op. 33, composed in 1781 and dedicated to the Grand Duke of Russia.

Russo, William (1928–2003) US composer. After study in Chicago, he worked with the Stan Kenton Orchestra 1950–54, as a trombonist and composer-arranger. He directed his own orchestra in New York 1958–61 and the London Jazz Orchestra 1962–65.

Works OPERA *Land of Milk and Honey* and *Anti-*

gone (both Chicago, 1967), *A Cabaret Opera* (New York 1970), *Aesop's Fables* (1971), *The Shepherds' Christmas* (1979), *Isabella's Fortune*, *The Pay-Off* (1984) and *Talking to the Sun* (Chicago 1989).

BALLET *The World of Alcina* (1954) and *The Golden Bird* (1984).

OTHER two symphonies (1957–58); music for jazz bands, and rock cantatas; sonata for violin and piano (1986).

Russolo, Luigi (1885–1947) Italian composer. In 1909 he joined the Futurist movement of Marinetti and formulated a music based on noise, about which he published *L'arte dei rumori* in 1916. His Futurist manifesto of 1913 expanded the orchestra to include explosions, clashes, shrieks, screams, and groans. He also invented the Russolophone, which could produce seven different noises in twelve different gradations.

Works ORCHESTRAL *Meeting of the Automobiles and the Aeroplanes*, *Awaking of a City*.

Rustic Wedding, German **Ländliche Hochzeit** symphonic poem by Goldmark, first performed at Vienna on 5 March 1876. It is usually described today as a symphony.

Ruy Blas opera by William Howard Glover (1819–1875) (libretto by composer, based on Victor Hugo's drama), produced at the Covent Garden Theatre, London, on 24 October 1861. In the story, Don Sallustio, seeking revenge against the Queen of Spain, sends his servant Ruy Blas to her court disguised as a nobleman. He rises through the ranks and is exposed later by the Don as a plebeian, thus dishonouring the Queen. But Ruy Blas earns his honour by killing the vengeful villain and drinking poison.

Opera by Marchetti (libretto in Italian, by Carlo d'Ormeville, based on Hugo), produced at La Scala, Milan, on 3 April 1869.

Overture and chorus for Hugo's drama by Mendelssohn, Op. 95 and Op. 77 no. 3, composed for a production at Leipzig on 9 March 1839.

Ruyneman, Daniel (1886–1963) Dutch composer. He experimented with composition and instruments and invented cup-bells with a rich and long-sustained sonority, which he used in several of his works.

He was trained for commerce and was self-taught in music.

Works OPERA *The Brothers Karamazov* (1928).

CHORAL AND VOICE WITH ORCHESTRA psycho-symbolic play *The Clown* with vocal and instrumental orchestra (1915); scena for tenor and orchestra from Kafka's *Der Prozess/The Trial*.

CHAMBER AND ORCHESTRAL two symphonies, partita for strings, *Hieroglyphs* for chamber orchestra; string quartet (1946); sonata in G major and *Klaaglied van een Slaaf* for violin and piano; nine sonatas, three *Pathemologies* and sonatina for piano.

OTHER two Sacred Songs (Tagore) and several other sets.

RV in music, abbreviation of *Ryom Verzeichnis* ('Ryom's Index'). Accompanied by a number, it refers to Peter ➤ Ryom's catalogue of Antonio ➤ Vivaldi's works, and is used in place of the usual ➤ Opus number.

Ryom, Peter (1937–) Danish musicologist. He catalogued Vivaldi's works in *Verzeichnis der Werke Antonio Vivaldis* (1974).

Rzewski, Frederic (Anthony) (1938–) US composer and pianist. From 1960 he worked as a pianist. In 1966 he was co-founder of an electronic music studio at Rome.

He studied at Harvard with Randall Thompson and with Dallapiccola. In the 1960s he taught at the Cologne Hochschule and was professor at the Liège Conservatory (with Henri Pousseur) from 1977. From 1984 he was visiting professor at Yale University.

Works ORCHESTRAL *Zoologischer Garten* (1965); *Spacecraft* (1967); audiodrama *Impersonation* (1966); *Requiem* (1968); *Symphony for Several performers* (1968); *Coming Together* for speaker and instruments (1972).

OTHER *Satyrica* for jazz band (1983); *Machine* for two pianos (1984).

s the dominant note in any key in ➤ **tonic sol-fa** notation, pronounced 'Soh'.

Saariaho, Kaija (1952–) Finnish composer. She has composed orchestral and instrumental music employing computers and electronics.

Saariaho studied at the Helsinki Conservatory 1976–81, and with Brian Ferneyhough and Klaus Huber at Freiburg.

Works ORCHESTRAL theatre and multimedia pieces, including *Study for life* (1980), *Kollisionen* (1984), *Earth* ballet (1991); *Verblendungen* (1984); *Graal Theatre* for violin and orchestra (1994).

ENSEMBLE *Nymphea* (1987), *For the Moon* (1990), *Aer* (1991), *Gates* (1991), *Amers* (1992); *Nocturne* for violin (1994); *Trois rivières* for percussion quartet and electronics (1993).

CHORAL AND VOICE *The Bride* song cycle (1977); *No and Not*, three songs for four female voices and choir (1979); *From the Grammar of Dreams* for two sopranos (1989); *Nuits, Adieux* for four voices and live electronics (1991); *La dame à la licorne* sound installation, with tape (1993).

Sabbatini, Galeazzo (1597–1662) Italian composer. He was maestro di cappella at Pesaro in the 1620s and director of chamber music to the Duke of Mirandola in the 1630s. In 1628 he published a treatise on thorough bass.

Works CHURCH MUSIC masses; motets; two books of *Sacrae faudes* (1637, 1641).

VOCAL madrigals.

Sabbatini, Pietro Paolo (c. 1600–after 1657) Italian composer. He was maestro di cappella of the church of San Luigi de' Francesci in Rome from 1630, and professor of music from 1650, when he published a treatise on thorough bass.

Works SACRED AND SECULAR MUSIC psalms, spiritual songs; *villanelle* and *canzonette* for one to three voices.

Sacchini, Antonio Maria Gaspare (1730–1786) Italian composer. His operas were popular in Germany, England, and France, the most popular being *Oedipe*, which was produced at Versailles in 1786. He also composed sacred

music.

Sacchini studied under Francesco Durante at the Conservatorio Santa Maria di Loreto in Naples, where his intermezzo *Fra Donato* was produced in 1756. He worked first at the Conservatory, but produced his first serious opera, *Andromaca*, in 1761, and three years later gave up teaching to devote himself to composition. After a time in Rome he went to Venice in 1769, where he became director of the Ospedaletto. He visited Germany, and in 1772 went to London, remaining there ten years and producing many operas. Settling in Paris in 1782, he had the support of Marie Antoinette, and there wrote two operas which show the influence of Gluck. But (like Gluck before him) he became unwillingly involved in rivalry with ➤ **Piccinni** and had little success.

Works OPERA about 60 operas, including *Alessandro nell' Indie* (1763), *Semiramide* (1764), *Isola d'amore*, *Il Cidde* (after Corneille), *Armida* (1772), *Tamerlano*, *Perseo* (1774), *Nitetti*, *Montezuma* (1775), *Rosina*, *Dardanus*, *Oedipe à Colone* (1786).

ORCHESTRAL two symphonies.

CHAMBER string quartets; trio sonatas; violin sonatas.

CHURCH MUSIC masses, motets, and other church music.

Sachs, Curt (1881–1959) German musicologist who devised, along with the Austrian scholar Eric von ➤ **Hornbostel**, one of the most widely-used systems for classifying musical instruments. He was the director of the Berlin Museum of Musical Instruments from 1919 and also a professor at Berlin University. His many writings extend not only over the field of musical instruments, but also over many others.

Sachs first studied history of art at Berlin University, graduating in 1904. After some years as an art critic, he studied music with Hermann Kretzschmar and Johannes Wolf, specializing in the history of musical instruments. From 1933 to 1937 he lived in Paris, then moved to New York, where he became a university professor. From 1953 he was professor at Columbia University, New York.

Sachs, Hans (1494–1576) German poet and composer. Working as a master shoemaker in Nuremberg, he composed 4,275 *Meisterlieder/Mastersongs* and figures prominently in Wagner's opera *Die Meistersinger von Nürnberg*.

Sachs–Hornbostel system system devised by the German-born musicologist Curt ➤ **Sachs** and the Austrian scholar Eric von ➤ **Hornbostel**, which has become one of the most widely-utilized systems for classifying musical instruments. The Sachs–Hornbostel System uses a systematic but basic taxonomic method to classify every instrument as belonging to a particular group or 'class', according to the nature of the vibrating agent that produces sound.

Based on an earlier system devised by Victor Mahillon when he classified the instrument collection at the Royal Conservatory in Brussels, the Sachs–Hornbostel System accommodates all instruments and allows museum curators, for example, to classify and arrange musical objects without knowledge of their music, culture, or origin. The four main classes in the system are ➤ **aerophones**, ➤ **idiophones**, ➤ **membranophones**, and ➤ **chordophones**. A further main class – electrophones – was subsequently added. Each of these classes is further sub-divided through a series of more detailed descriptors. Each class of instrument has a number, the numbering system being derived from the Dewey system of library classification.

sackbut musical instrument of the brass family, a precursor of the trombone. It was common from the 14th century and has been revived in early music performance. Four sizes were listed by Praetorius, from alto to great bass. The sackbut has a narrow bell and its sound is dignified and mellow.

Sackman, Nicholas (1950–   ) English composer. He studied with Alexander Goehr at Leeds University in England. In 1990 he became a lecturer at Nottingham University. His orchestral work *Hawthorn* premiered in 1993 at the London Proms.

Works ORCHESTRAL flute concerto (1989); *Hawthorn* for orchestra (1993).

CHAMBER two string quartets (1979, 1991); *Ensembles and Cadenzas* for cello and five players (1972); *Doubles* for two instrumental groups (1978); *Time-Piece* for brass quintet (1983); *Corronach* for seven players (1985); *A Pair of Wings* for three sopranos and ensemble (1973); *And the World – A Wonder Waking* for mezzo-soprano and eight instruments (1981).

Sadko opera by Russian composer ➤ **Rimsky-Korsakov** (libretto by composer and V I Bielsky), which was produced in Moscow on 7 January 1898. The music is partly based on Rimsky-Korsakov's 1867 symphonic poem of the same name, Op. 5. Cast adrift as a sacrifice to the sea gods, the minstrel Sadko weds nymph Volkova before returning to his wife.

Sadler's Wells theatre in Islington, north London, England, built in the 17th century. Originally a music hall, it was developed by Lilian Baylis as a northern annexe to the Old Vic in 1931. For many years it housed the Sadler's Wells Opera Company (relocated to the London Coliseum in 1969 and known as the English National Opera Company from 1974) and the Sadler's Wells Ballet, which later became the Royal Ballet.

saeta an unaccompanied Andalusian folk song sung during a halt in a religious procession.

Sæverud, Harald (1897–1992) Norwegian composer and conductor. He studied first at Bergen and then studied conducting under Clemens Krauss at Berlin. He returned to Bergen as a conductor and received a state pension for composition in 1933.

Works ORCHESTRAL *Minnesota Symphony*; nine symphonies (1916–66); concertos for oboe, cello, violin, and piano; incidental music for Shakespeare's 'Rape of Lucretia' (1935) and Ibsen's *Peer Gynt*.

CHAMBER 50 variations for chamber orchestra; three string quartets (1969, 1975, 1979); piano pieces.

Saffo, Sappho opera by ➤ **Pacini** (libretto by S Cammarano) produced at the Teatro San Carlo in Naples in 1840. Angered by Sappho's song, Alcander (bass) convinces her husband Phaon that she has another lover. Phaon abandons her; she later finds him about to marry Clymene, and overturns the altar. Penitent, Alcander leaps to her death from the Leucadian rock.

'St Anne' Fugue fugue in E flat major at the end of Part III of Bach's *Clavierübung*, so named in England because its subject is identical with the opening of Croft's hymn-tune *St Anne*.

'St Anthony' Variations part of a set of variations, the ➤ **'Haydn' Variations**, by Johannes Brahms.

St Elizabeth oratorio by Franz Liszt; see *Die* ➤ *Legende von der heiligen Elisabeth*.

Saint-Foix, (Marie Olivier) Georges (du Parc Poullain) de, Count (1874–1954) French musicologist. He wrote on various subjects, including Beethoven and Boccherini, but mainly on the classification and analysis of Mozart's works in a large five-volume work, the first two volumes in collaboration with Théodore de ➤ **Wyzewa**.

Saint François d'Assise opera in eight tableaux composed by ➤ **Messiaen** (libretto by composer)

1975–83 and first performed at the Opéra in Paris on 28 November 1983. St Francis heals a leper, preaches to birds, and receives stigmata before his death and resurrection.

St John Passion Bach's setting of the Passion narrative as told in St John's Gospel, for soloists, chorus, and orchestra. With interpolated texts by the German poet ➤ **Brockes** and chorales, the oratorio was first performed in the church of St Nicholas, Leipzig, on 7 April 1724. A second version was given at the church of St Thomas, Leipzig, on 30 March 1725.

St Ludmilla oratorio by Dvořák, Op. 71 composed in 1886, with Czech words by the poet and dramatist Jaroslav Vrchlický.

St Luke Passion work by Polish composer Krzysztof ➤ **Penderecki** for narrator, soloists, choruses, and orchestra. It was first performed in Münster, Germany, on 30 March 1966.

St Matthew Passion Bach's setting of the Passion narrative as told in St Matthew's Gospel, for soloists, chorus, and orchestra. With interpolated texts by the German poet and cantata librettist Picander and chorales, the work was performed in the church of St Thomas, Leipzig, probably on 11 April 1727 and certainly on 15 April 1729.

Sainton, Prosper (Philippe Cathérine) (1813–1890) French violinist and composer. He played at the Société des Concerts and the Opéra in Paris, then travelled widely in Europe and in 1840 became professor at the Toulouse Conservatory. He was the husband of the singer Charlotte Sainton-Dolby.

He studied violin under François Habeneck at the Paris Conservatory. In 1844 he visited London and played under Mendelssohn, returning in 1845 to settle down as a member of the Beethoven Quartet Society, orchestra leader, and teacher.

Works ORCHESTRAL two violin concertos and other solos with orchestra; variations; romances; operatic fantasies; other pieces for violin and piano.

St Paul oratorio by Mendelssohn, Op. 36, first performed in Düsseldorf at the Lower Rhine Festival on 22 May 1836. It was performed in Liverpool, England, on 7 October that same year.

St Paul's Suite work for string orchestra in four movements by ➤ **Holst**. It was composed for St Paul's Girls' school and was performed there in 1913.

Saint-Saëns, (Charles) Camille (1835–1921) French composer, pianist, and organist. Saint-Saëns was a master of technique and a prolific composer. He wrote many lyrical Romantic pieces and symphonic poems. He is well known for the opera *Samson et Dalila* (1877), which was

prohibited on the French stage until 1892, and the uncharacteristic orchestral piece *Le carnaval des animaux/The Carnival of the Animals* (1886), his most popular work.

Saint-Saëns was born in Paris. He began to compose at the age of five and played the piano well at that age. He gave a public recital in 1846 and entered the Conservatory as an organ scholar in 1848, gaining a first prize in 1851, when he entered Halévy's class for composition. He was appointed organist at the church of Saint-Merry in Paris in 1853, at the Madeleine in 1857, and piano professor at the Ecole Niedermeyer in 1861.

His virtuosity at the organ was admired by Liszt, and he promoted performances of Liszt's symphonic poems. His first two symphonies were performed in 1853 and 1859; he played his second piano concerto in 1868 and founded the Société Nationale de Musique with Romain Bussine in 1871; his own symphonic poems *Le Rouet d'Omphale* and *Phaëton* date from this time. One of his most frequently performed works, the first cello concerto in A minor, was composed in 1872; it displays the composer's familiar and conservative French Romantic style together with melodic inventiveness. He played in England several times from 1871 and toured Spain and Portugal in 1880.

The biblical opera *Samson et Dalila*, begun in 1868, was prohibited on the French stage on account of its subject. It was conducted by Liszt at Weimar in 1877 and was allowed in Paris from 1892, the year he received an honorary doctorate from Cambridge University. The massively proportioned 3rd symphony, with organ obbligato, dates from 1886, and his appealing 3rd violin concerto in B minor followed in 1890. Saint-Saëns recognized that its success with the public would lead to neglect of his more important compositions and banned its performance during his lifetime. In 1906 he visited the USA, and again in 1916, when he also travelled to South America.

Works OPERA *Samson et Dalila* (1877); *Henri VIII* (1883).

ORCHESTRAL five symphonies (1886, two unnumbered; no. 3 with organ and piano duet); symphonic poems, including *Le Rouet d'Omphale* (1872), *Danse macabre* (1875) (originally a song); five piano concertos (1858–96); three violin concertos (1858, 1859, 1890); *Introduction et Rondo capriccioso* (1863); two cello concertos (1872, 1902).

CHAMBER *Le carnaval des animaux* for chamber ensemble (1886); two piano trios; septet for piano, strings, and trumpet (1881); sonatas for oboe, clarinet, bassoon, and piano.

KEYBOARD 24 opuses of piano music; seven organ works.

CHORAL the oratorio *Le Déluge*; several cantatas; Requiem (1878), many songs.

Saite (German 'string') term used in musical notation, as in *mit einer Saite* ('with one string') instructing a pianist to use the *una corda* or ➔ **soft pedal**.

Sala, Nicola (1713–1801) Italian composer and theorist. In 1794 he published *Regole del contrappunto prattico/Rules of Practical Counterpoint* in three volumes.

He studied with Nicola Fago and Lionardo Leo at the Conservatorio de' Turchini at Naples, and later became a master there. In 1787 he succeeded Pasquale Cafaro as principal.

Works OPERA *Vologeso* (1737); *Zenobia* (1761); *Merope* (1769); *Demetrio* (1762).

CHORAL the oratorio *Giuditta*.

CHURCH MUSIC Mass, Litany, and other church music; Prologues for the birth of kings of Naples.

Salammbô the title of two 19th-century operas written by different composers. The opera by ➔ **Reyer** (libretto by C duLocle, based on Flaubert's novel) was produced in Brussels at the Théâtre de la Monnaie on 10 February 1890. The unfinished opera by ➔ **Mussorgsky** (libretto by composer, based on Flaubert) was partly composed in the 1860s and a concert performance of the available fragments was given in Milan on 10 November 1980.

The two operas have similar plots initially: Carthaginian princess Salammbô seduces Libyan warrior Mathô, to regain the sacred veil which he has stolen. After this, in Reyer's version, Salammbô commits suicide when ordered to kill Mathô, and he follows her. In Mussorgsky's version, Mathô is imprisoned and brutally killed; Salammbô is horror-stricken and dies.

Salazar, Adolfo (1890–1958) Spanish musicologist and composer. He edited the *Revista Musical Hispano-Americano* 1914–18 and was music critic to *El Sol* in Madrid 1918–36. His books include studies of modern music, Spanish music, symphonies, and ballet.

Salazar studied with Bartolomeo Pérez Casas (1873–1956) and Manuel de Falla, also Maurice Ravel in Paris. After the Spanish Civil War he emigrated to Buenos Aires, then lived in Mexico after 1939.

Works ORCHESTRAL the symphonic poem *Don Juan en los infiernos*; *Paisajes*; *Tres preludios* for orchestra.

CHAMBER string quartet; *Arabia* for piano quintet; violin and piano sonata; piano pieces; *Romancilla* for guitar.

Sales, Pietro Pompeo (c.1729–1797) Italian composer. He was appointed Kapellmeister to the Prince-Bishop of Augsburg in 1756 and served the Electoral Court in Koblenz in the same capacity from 1770. He also travelled in England and Italy in 1776, appearing as a virtuoso gambaplayer.

Works OPERA including *Le nozze di Amore e di Norizia* (1765), *L'Antigono* (1769), *Achille in Sciro*, *Il rè pastore*.

CHORAL AND ORCHESTRAL oratorios, including *Giefte* (1762), *Giuseppe ricognosciuto*, *La Betulia liberata*; two symphonies, concertos; arias; church music.

Salieri, Antonio (1750–1825) Italian composer. He taught Beethoven, Schubert, Hummel, and Liszt, and was the musical rival of Mozart at the emperor's court in Vienna, where he held the position of court composer. It has been suggested, without proof, that he poisoned Mozart.

He studied with his brother Francesco Salieri, a pupil of Giuseppe Tartini. He was orphaned at 15, and his education at the school of San Marco in Venice was taken care of by the Mocenigo family. There he met Florian Gassmann, who took him to Vienna in 1766, saw to his further education, and introduced him at court. On Gassmann's death in 1774, Salieri became court composer and conductor of the Italian opera. He visited Italy 1778–80, where his opera *Europa riconosciuta* was produced at the opening of La Scala, Milan in 1774, and at Paris 1786–87; his *Tarare* of 1787 had sufficient dramatic strength to be ascribed initially to Gluck. From 1788, when he succeeded Giuseppe Bonno as court Kapellmeister, he lived mostly in Vienna. He was conductor of the Tonkünstler Society until 1818, and played the continuo in the first performance of Haydn's *Creation* in 1798. Recent revivals of operas such as *Les Danaides*, *La grotta di Trofonio*, and *Falstaff* show Salieri to be a more resourceful and entertaining composer than his reputation suggests.

Works OPERA about 40, including *Armida* (1771), *La fiera di Venezia* (1772), *La locandiera* (1773), *Europa riconosciuta* (1778), *La scuola de gelosi* (1778), *La dama pastorella*, *Der Rauchfangkehrer* (1781), *Les Danaïdes* (1784), *Tarare*, *Les Horaces* (the last three for Paris), *La grotta di Trofonio* (1785), *Il talismano*, *Palmira, regina di Persia* (1795), *Falstaff* (after Shakespeare, 1799), *Cesare in Farmacusa*, *Angiolina* (1800).

SACRED AND SECULAR MUSIC incidental music to Kotzebue's *Die Hussiten vor Naumburg*; Passion oratorio and others; seven Masses, Requiem, Litanies, and other church music; cantatas including *La riconoscenza* for the 25th anniversary of the Tonkünstler-Societät (1796); three symphonies and *sinfonia concertante*; concertos, serenades, arias, duets, canons, and miscellaneous other small vocal pieces.

Salinas, Francisco de (1513–1590) Spanish organist, theorist, and folk song investigator. In his treatise *De musica libri septem* (1579) he quotes the tunes of many Spanish folk songs.

He was the son of an official in the treasury of Charles V and became blind at the age of ten, whereupon his parents decided to let him study music. He was taken to Rome in 1538, where he met the lutenist Francesco da Milano and became a great admirer of Lassus. In 1558 he became organist to the Duke of Alba, viceroy of Naples, under Diego Ortiz. In 1561 he returned to Spain and became organist at León in 1563 and professor of music at Salamanca University in 1567. There he got to know the poet Luis de León, who wrote a poem on his organ playing.

Sallinen, Aulis (1935–) Finnish composer. He is best known for the strong characterization and sustained dramatic intensity of his operas.

He studied at the Sibelius Academy, Helsinki, and taught there 1963–76. He was the manager of Finnish Radio Symphony Orchestra 1960–70.

Works OPERA AND STAGE *The Horseman* (1975), *The Red Line* (1978), *The King goes forth to France* (1984), *Kullervo* (1992); the ballet *Variations sur Mallarmé* (1968).

ORCHESTRAL six symphonies (1971–90), *Mauermusik* for a German killed at the Berlin Wall (1962), *Metamorphoses* for piano and chamber orchestra (1964), violin concerto (1968), cello concerto (1978), *Dies Irae* for soprano, bass, male chorus, and orchestra (1978); *Chorali* for wind, percussion, harp, and celesta (1970).

CHAMBER five string quartets (1958–82).

salmo (Italian, plural *salmi*) Italian word for a ➤ psalm.

Salmon, Thomas (1648–1706) English clergyman and writer on music. He wrote on notation and temperament. His *Essay on the Advancement of Musick* (1672) involved him in a controversy with the composer Matthew Locke.

Salomé opera by Mariotte (libretto of Oscar Wilde's original play, which was written in French), produced in Lyon, France, on 30 October 1908. Though this opera was composed earlier than Richard Strauss's opera, it was produced later.

Salome opera and ballet of the same name. The opera, by Richard ➤ Strauss (libretto from H Lachmann's German translation of Oscar Wilde's play, which was written in French) was produced in Dresden, at the Royal Opera on 9 December 1905. The story is biblical: spurned by John the Baptist, Salome demands his severed head after performing a seven-veil striptease for lecherous Herod.

The ballet in two acts was composed by Peter Maxwell Davies and choreographed by Flemming Flindt. It was produced in Stockholm on 10 November 1978. The concert suite was performed in London on 6 March 1979.

See ➤ *Tragédie de Salomé, La*.

Salomon, Johann Peter (1745–1815) German violinist, conductor, manager, and composer. He lived in London from 1780, where he arranged concerts. He wrote four French operas and an English one, *Windsor Castle*, for the marriage of the Prince of Wales in 1795, an oratorio *Hiskias*, and violin sonatas.

He studied at Bonn and joined the electoral orchestra in 1758. After a tour in 1765 he became court musician at Rheinsberg to Prince Henry of Prussia, who, however, dissolved his orchestra about 1780, when Salomon went to Paris and thence to London, in 1781, where he settled as concert violinist, quartet player, and conductor. He gave subscription concerts at the Hanover Square Rooms and invited Haydn to London in 1790 and again in 1794, later arranging for smaller forces some of the symphonies which Haydn wrote for London.

'Salomon Symphonies' the twelve symphonies, nos 93–104, written by Haydn 1791–95 for the concerts given by Johann Peter ➤ Salomon in London during Haydn's two visits to England, 1791–92 and 1794–95.

salsa popular music style of Cuban origin which draws on a variety of Latin American and jazz influences. Salsa rhythms are based on Afro-American dances such as the bolero and cha cha cha. Layered polymeters and hemiolas (in which two bars of triple time are articulated in the manner of three bars in duple time) are common, but the distinctive feature underlying the whole structure is the two-bar clave.

An example of a salsa rhythm.

saltando (Italian 'springing, bounding') in music, a manner of playing the violin and other string instruments that makes the bow rebound from the strings.

saltarello energetic Italian dance characterized by jumps (*salti*) and a gradually increasing pace toward the end. Originally a Roman dance in animated 3/4 or 6/8 time, it is similar to the Neapolitan ➤ tarantella, but uses jerky instead of even musical figuration. The best known saltarello is the finale of Mendelssohn's Italian symphony.

In the 16th century, the saltarello was a kind of after-dance in common time, which was also called by the Latin name *proportio* and the German name *Proporz*, the name being due to its using the same music as the first dance (Passamezzo), but with the 'proportions' (time) altered.

Salve Regina (Latin 'Hail, Queen') one of four antiphons (choral music in Greek or Roman liturgy) to the Virgin Mary. Earliest manuscripts date from the 11th century. Its many settings include those by ➤ La Rue, ➤ Josquin, ➤ Obrecht, and ➤ Okeghem, as well as many English composers, in the 15th-century, and six settings by Schubert 1812–24.

Salzburg Festival annual music festival held in the Austrian town where Mozart was born. Although the festival concentrates on the works of Mozart, other composers are also represented. It grew from the first eight Mozart festivals held between 1877 and 1910. The new theatre opened in 1960 and has the largest stage in the world.

Salzman, Eric (1933–) US composer and musicologist. A music critic in New York, he also founded the Quog Music Theater in 1970 and edited *Music Quarterly* from 1984. He often writes for electronic forces, and calls for improvisation in his works. He studied with the composer Jack Beeson and the composer and musicologist Milton Babbitt.

Works *Larynx Music* (1968); *Civilization and its Discontents*, opera (1977).

Samara, Spiro (1863–1917) Greek composer. He studied at Athens, later with Delibes and others at the Paris Conservatory. The Italian publisher Sonzogno procured him his first operatic production at Milan. He subsequently produced other works at Rome, Naples, Florence, Milan, and Genoa, though his success was short-lived. He last appeared at Athens in 1914.

Works OPERA *Flora mirabilis* (1886); *Medgé*; *Lionella* (1891); *La martire*; *La furia domata* after Shakespeare's *Taming of the Shrew* (1895); *Storia d'amore* (1903); *Mademoiselle de Bella-Isle*; *Rhea*; *La guerra in tempo di guerra*; *The Princess of Saxony* (in Greek).

OTHER suite for piano duet; piano pieces; songs.

Samazeuilh, Gustave (Marie Victor Fernand) (1877–1967) French composer and critic. He was a pupil of Ernest Chausson and, after his master's death, of Vincent d'Indy and Paul Abraham ➤ Dukas at the Schola Cantorum. His writings include studies of Rameau and Dukas, translations of Wagner's *Tristan* and Schumann's *Genoveva*, and songs by Wagner and Liszt. He also made piano arrangements of modern French music.

Works ORCHESTRAL *Nuit*; *Naïades au soir*, *Le Sommeil de Canope* for voice and orchestra.

OTHER string quartet.

samba Afro-Brazillian secular music and couple-dance form, spanning the continuum from traditional percussion and vocal-dominated street styles of the Carnival parade to the more popular renditions of the ballroom dance orchestras.

Sammartini, Giovanni Battista (c.1700–1775) Italian composer. He was the most important Italian symphonist of his time, and contributed much towards the founding of a modern style of instrumental music.

Sammartini spent his whole life in Milan as a church musician, and from 1730 was maestro di cappella at the convent of Santa Maria Maddelena. Gluck was his pupil 1737–41, and borrowed material from Sammartini's symphonies for two of his operas.

Works OPERA two operas, including *L'Agrippina, moglie di Tiberio* (1743).

CHORAL two oratorios.

ORCHESTRAL over 80 symphonies; about 15 concertos; six *concerti grossi*.

CHAMBER six string quintets; about 20 quartets; almost 200 trios; other chamber music.

CHURCH MUSIC three Masses; other church music.

sampling in music, a technique of computer synthesis involving the capture by microphone, conversion to digital code, storage, and subsequent manipulation of an acoustic signal.

The sample length is limited by the storage capacity of the sampling device, typically a memory chip. Keyboard transposition of a sampled sound has an effect not unlike varispeeding an analogue tape or disc.

Samson oratorio by Handel, whose libretto by Hamilton is based on Milton's 'Samson Agonistes'. It was first produced at Covent Garden, London, in 18 February 1743.

Samson et Dalila opera by ➤ Saint-Saëns. It was first produced in Weimar, Germany, on 2 December 1877, but was forbidden on the French stage until 1892 on account of its biblical subject. It was first performed at the Opéra in Paris on 23 November 1892. Delilah seduces Samson and betrays the secret of his strength. Later, blinded, he prays for strength and brings down the temple on himself and his Philistine enemies.

Samstag aus Licht, Saturday from Light opera by ➤ Stockhausen, the second of his cycle *Licht*. It was first performed in Milan, Italy, on 25 May 1984. The opera contains four scenes: *Lucifer's Dream*, *Kathinka's Song*, *Lucifer's Dance*, and *Lucifer's Farewell*.

Sánchez de Fuentes y Peláez, Eduardo (1874–1944) Cuban composer and music historian who wrote several books on the history of Cuban folk music.

Works OPERA AND CHORAL five operas, including *Dolorosa* (1910), *Doreya* (1918); operettas and zarzuelas; the oratorio *Novidad*.

ORCHESTRAL the suite *Bocetos cubanos*; a symphonic prelude *Temas del Patio* for orchestra; the vocal habanera *Tú espera.*

Sancho Pança dans son île, Sancho Panza on his Island opera by the French composer Philidor. Its libretto by A A H Poinsinet is based on Cervantes' *Don Quixote.* The opera was first produced at the Comédie-Italienne, Paris, on 8 July 1762.

Sancho Panza opera by ➤ Jaques-Dalcroze based on Cervantes' *Don Quixote.* It was first produced in Geneva on 13 December 1897.

Sancio Panza, governatore dell' isola Barattaria, Sancho Panza, Governor of the Isle of Barataria opera by Italian composer Antonio ➤ Caldara. The libretto by G C Pasquini is based on Cervantes' *Don Quixote.* The opera was first produced at the Burgtheater in Vienna on 27 January 1733.

Sancta Civitas, The Holy City oratorio by English composer Ralph ➤ Vaughan Williams. With words mainly from the Bible, the oratorio for solo voices, chorus, and orchestra was first performed in Oxford on 7 May 1926.

Sancta Susanna opera in one act by German composer Paul ➤ Hindemith. It was composed in 1921 and first produced in Frankfurt on 26 March 1922. The story concerns a sex-obsessed nun who tears the loincloth from a statue of Christ.

Sanctus the fourth chant of the Ordinary of the Roman Mass. Its text is founded on the book of Isaiah (vi. 3) and Matthew's gospel (xxi. 9) and it was incorporated into the Latin liturgy as early as the 6th century in Gaul.

The *Sanctus* was set in polyphony from the 13th century, and became an integral part of all settings of the Ordinary of the Mass. Later settings are more complex: a total of 231 melodies were catalogued in 1962. The earliest known melody is that of Mass XVIII (Vatican edition).

The chant is basically syllabic, forms a natural continuation from the music of the Preface which precedes it, is psalmodic in structure, and its last phrase echoes the *Per omnia saecula saeculorum* formula which occurs three times during the Preface and Canon of the Mass.

Sandberger, Adolf (1864–1943) German musicologist and composer. He was chief editor of the incomplete edition of Lassus and the *Denkmäler der Tonkunst in Bayern*, and his books include studies of the Bavarian court chapel under Lassus, and of Cornelius.

He studied in a number of European centres and in 1894 became lecturer in music at Munich University and was professor there 1900–29, being at the same time curator of the music department of the State Library.

Works OPERA *Ludwig der Springer*; *Der Tod des Kaisers.*

ORCHESTRAL symphonic poem *Viola* based on Shakespeare's *Twelfth Night*; the symphonic prologue *Riccio.*

OTHER chamber music; piano works; songs.

Sanderson or **Saunderson, James (1769–c.1841)** English violinist and composer. He was self-taught and in 1783 obtained an engagement as violinist at the theatre in Sunderland. Later he taught at Shields, became leader at the Newcastle-upon-Tyne theatre in 1787, and at Astley's Amphitheatre, London, in 1788. He began to write stage pieces and in 1793 went as music director and composer to the Royal Circus (Surrey Theatre).

Works ORCHESTRAL stage pieces and pantomimes, including *Harlequin in Ireland*, *Blackbeard*, *Cora*, *Sir Francis Drake*, *The Magic Pipe*, *Hallowe'en*; instrumental interludes for Collin's *Ode to the Passions.*

OTHER violin pieces; many popular songs.

Sandrin, Pierre Regnault (lived 1540s–1560s) French composer. He composed only chansons, of which the majority were published by the music publisher Attaingnant. Franco-Flemish composer Lassus based a Mass on Sandrin's chanson *Doulce memoire.*

He was a member of the royal chapel 1543–60, during which time he also travelled to Italy.

Sanguine Fan, The ballet by Elgar, Op. 81 (scenario by Ina Lowther), composed in 1917. Produced and conducted by Elgar in Chelsea on 20 March 1917, the ballet was not heard again in complete form until a recording in 1973.

Santa Cruz or **Santa Cruz Wilson, Domingo (1899–1987)** Chilean composer, teacher, and critic. He studied at Santiago de Chile and Madrid. In 1918 he founded a Bach Society at Santiago and in 1932 became dean of the Fine Arts Department at the University of Chile and rector of the university from 1948 to 1951.

Works ORCHESTRAL four symphonies (1948–69); five *Piezas brevas* for string orchestra.

CHAMBER three string quartets; three violin and piano pieces; piano works; songs.

Sant 'Alessio, Il opera in prologue and three acts by the Italian composer Landi (libretto by Rospigliosi). It was first produced at the Paluz Barberini, Rome, on 21 February 1632. In the story, Alessio returns home from the Holy Land, resists worldly temptation, and continues his life of renunciation.

Santini, Fortunato (1778–1861) Italian priest, music scholar, and composer. He studied music with Giuseppe Jannaconi and, after being or-

The sarabande from Bach's English Suite, No. 6.

dained in 1801, began to make an immense collection of early music, scoring it from parts in various music libraries. He made friends with Felix Mendelssohn and through him introduced many works by Johann Sebastian Bach into Italy, as well as other German sacred music.

Works CHURCH MUSIC Requiem for eight voices; Masses; other church music.

Santoliquido, Francesco (1883–1971) Italian composer. He studied at the Liceo di Santa Cecilia in Rome and conducted his student work *Crepuscolo sul mare* at Nuremberg in 1909. He produced his first opera at Milan in 1910. He then went to live in the small Arab village of Hammamek in Tunisia, where he studied the local music.

Works OPERA *La favola di Helga* (1910); *Ferhuda* (1918), *L'ignota*; *La porta verde* (1953).

OTHER the mimed drama *La baiadera della maschera gialla* (1917); symphony in F major.

Sapho opera by Gounod (libretto by Emile Augier). It was Gounod's first opera, first produced at the Opéra in Paris on 16 April 1851. For a plot synopsis, see ➔ **Saffo.**

Opera by Massenet (libretto by H Cain and A Bernède, based on Daudet's novel), produced in Paris a the Opéra-Comique on 27 November 1897. The heroine is not the Greek poet Sappho but artist's model Fanny Legrand, who poses as Sappho. She runs away with Jean Gaussin, but he abandons her after hearing of her sordid past. Later he returns to her but she rejects him.

Sappho opera by Hugo Kaun (1863–1932) (libretto by composer, based on the play of the same name by Austrian poet and dramatist Franz Grillparzer). It was first produced in Leipzig on 27 October 1917. See also ➔ **Saffo**; ➔ **Sapho.**

sarabande French 16th-century court dance, also (**saraband**) an English dance form, in moderate three time with a rhythmic emphasis on the second beat, a dance form featured in the classi-

cal music ➔ **suite.**

Sarabande and Cortège two studies for orchestra by ➔ **Busoni** for his opera *Doktor Faust*. They were composed 1918–19 and were first performed in Zurich on 31 March 1919.

sarangi (Hindi dialect) bowed, stringed instrument similar to a fiddle with three main melody strings and many sympathetic strings (30 or more on a concert instrument). The body is usually carved from a single block of wood in a waisted shape. The neck is short and wide with no frets. It is played held upright and the strings are stopped with the fingernails of the left hand. It is used in the folk music of northwestern India and Pakistan, and in the classical music of North India (Hindustani music), where it is used both as an accompaniment to the voice (in ➔ **khyal** and ➔ **thumri** genres) and as a solo concert instrument.

sardana Spanish dance of Catalonia revived in the middle of the 19th century and performed to pipe and drum.

Sarema opera by Zemlinsky (libretto by composer, after Rudolf von Gottschall's play *Die Rose vom Kaukasus*). Composed in 1895 and first produced at the Hofoper in Munich on 10 October 1897, it was Zemlinsky's first opera. In the story, a Circassian heroine is torn between love for a Russian officer and her own country.

Sargent, (Harold) Malcolm (Watts) (1895–1967) English conductor. He was professor at the Royal College of Music from 1923, chief conductor of the BBC Symphony Orchestra 1950–57, and continued as conductor in chief of the annual Henry Wood ➔ **promenade concerts** at the Royal Albert Hall.

He championed Vaughan Williams and Holst and conducted the first performances of Walton's oratorio *Belshazzar's Feast* in 1931 and the opera

Troilus and Cressida in 1954.

Šárka opera by Fibich (libretto by A Schulzová). It was first produced at the Czech Theatre in Prague, on 28 December 1897. The plot concerns the Bohemian Šárka, who leads women against the oppressive Duke Přemsyl and his men; but she falls in love with the warrior Ctirad, eventually betraying her cause to save him. Guilty, she commits suicide.

Opera by Janáček (libretto by Julius Zeyer). Composed 1887–88 and revised 1918 and 1925, its scoring was completed by Osvald Chlubna. It was first produced in Brno, Moravia, on 11 November 1925. It was first performed in the UK as a concert at Edinburgh in 1993.

See also ➤ *Má Vlast*.

sarod long-necked plucked lute used in North Indian (Hindustani) music. The body is hollow and pear-shaped and carved from a single piece of wood. The sarod has eight playing strings (four melody and four for drone and rhythmic punctuation) and about 15 sympathetic strings that run over a polished metal, fretless fingerboard. Some strings have a small metal resonator attached to the upper end of the neck. A popular solo concert instrument, it is usually accompanied by the ➤ **tabla** drum pair.

Sarro or **Sarri, Domenico (1679–1744)** Italian composer. He was a pupil of Francesco ➤ **Durante** at the Conservatorio di Sant' Onofrio in Naples. He became vice-maestro di cappella to the court in 1703. He lost his post in 1707 but returned in 1725, succeeding Mancini as maestro di cappella in 1737.

Works OPERA around 50 operas; opera *Didone abbandonata* the first setting by any composer of a libretto by Metastasio (1724).

CHURCH AND SECULAR MUSIC four oratorios; cantatas; church music; instrumental music.

sarrusophone any of a family of double-reed keyed brass instruments developed in 1856 by a French bandmaster named Sarrus, intended to replace oboes and bassoons in military bands. The double bass instrument is heard in Stravinsky's sacred cantata *Theni* (1958). Its tone is clear and unforced in the bass register.

Sarti, Giuseppe (1729–1802) Italian composer and conductor. As well as holding posts in Italy as an organist and music director, he spent many years in Denmark as an opera conductor. He later went to Russia, where he lived in St Petersburg and produced Russian operas for the court. His best-known works are the operas *Fra due litiganti* (1782) and *Giulio Sabino*.

He studied under Francesco Vallotti in Padua and Padre Martini in Bologna. He was organist of Faenza Cathedral 1748–51, was appointed

music director of the theatre there in 1752, and produced his first opera the same year. In 1753 he went to Copenhagen as conductor of the Mingotti opera company, and two years later was appointed Kapellmeister to the Danish court. He stayed there until 1775, except for three years in Italy 1765–68. He was director of the Ospedaletto Conservatory in Venice 1775–79, and was then appointed maestro di cappella of Milan Cathedral, where Cherubini was his pupil.

In 1784 he became music director to the Russian court. He travelled to St Petersburg via Vienna, where he met Mozart, who quoted the aria 'Come un agnello' from his opera *Fra due litiganti* in the supper scene in *Don Giovanni*. He produced a number of operas in Russia, including *Oleg* on a libretto by the empress, and stayed there until 1802, founding a music school in the Ukraine and becoming director of the Conservatory in St Petersburg in 1793. He then intended to retire in Italy, but died in Berlin on the way.

Works OPERA *Pompeo in Armenia* (1752); *Il rè pastore* (1753); *La giardiniera brillante* (1768); *Farnace*; *Le gelosie villane*; *Fra due litiganti* (1782); *Medonte* (1777); *Giulio Sabino*; *I finti eredi*; *Armida e Rinaldo* (1786); *Oleg* (in Russian, with Pashkevich and Canobbio).

SACRED AND SECULAR MUSIC two Russian oratorios; Requiem for Louis XVI (1793); Masses; Te Deum; other church music; keyboard music.

Sartorius, Paul (1569–1609) German organist and composer. He was organist to the Archduke Maximilian of Austria in 1599 and lived at Nuremberg.

Works CHURCH MUSIC Masses; *Sonetti spirituali* for six voices (1601); motets.

OTHER madrigals; *Neue teutsche Liedlein*.

Sarum Use the liturgy in use at Salisbury, England, before the Reformation. It differs in some respects from that of Rome and widely spread through medieval England until it was abolished in 1547, though it was revived from 1553 to 1559.

Sás (Orchassal), Andrés (1900–1967) Peruvian composer of French-Belgian descent. He studied in Brussels and went to Peru in 1924 as a violin teacher at the National Academy of Music at Lima. He married the Peruvian pianist Lily Rosay and with her founded a private music school in 1929. He made extensive research into Peruvian folklore and frequently used folk tunes in his works.

Works ORCHESTRAL *Himno al sol*; *Himno y danza*; *Poema Indio*; *Rapsodia peruana* for violin and orchestra.

CHAMBER AND VOCAL *Quenas* for voice, flute, and harp; *Sonatina india* for flute and piano; works for violin and piano; piano pieces; songs.

Satie, Erik (Alfred Leslie) (1866–1925) French composer. His piano pieces, such as the three *Gymnopédies* (1888), are precise and tinged with melancholy, and parody romantic expression with surreal commentary. His aesthetic of ironic simplicity, as in the *Messe des pauvres/Poor People's Mass* (1895), acted as a nationalist antidote to the perceived excesses of German Romanticism.

Mentor of the group of composers ➔ **Les Six**, Satie promoted the concept of *musique d'ameublement* ('furniture music'), anticipating the impact of radio. A commission from Diaghilev led to the ballet *Parade* (1917), with instrumentation for siren, typewriter, and steamship whistle, and he invented a new style of film music for René Clair's *Entr'acte* (1924).

His father was a composer and music publisher in Paris and his mother a minor composer of piano pieces under the name of Eugénie Satie-Barnetsche. Satie spent only a year at the Paris Conservatory and later made a precarious living by playing at cafés and writing music for the Montmartre songwriter Hypsa and the music-hall singer Paulette Darty. Through his friendship with Debussy, about 1890, he came into contact with intellectual circles. He also studied at the Schola Cantorum under Vincent d'Indy and Albert Roussel at the age of 40. He continued to publish small piano works under eccentric titles. In later years he came into touch with Jean Cocteau and established a school at Arcueil where he exercised some influence on younger composers including Poulenc, Auric, and Milhaud, leading them away from the late Romantic style influenced by German composers, especially Wagner, towards a terser, more concise and epigrammatic style.

Works STAGE AND CHORAL symphonic drama *Socrate* (1920); ballets, including *Parade* (1917), *Relâche* (1924), *Mercure* (1924).

PIANO piano pieces, including *Trois gymnopédies* (1888), *Trois gnossiennes* (1890), *Sonneries de la rose-croix*, *Trois véritables préludes flasques (pour un chien)*, *Trois embryons desséchés* (1913), *Trois croquis et agaceries d'un gros bonhomme en bois* (1913), *Trois Chapitres tournés en tous sens* (1913), *Avant-dernières pensées*; *Trois morceaux en forme de poire* for piano duet (1903).

OTHER four sets of songs.

Satyagraha opera by Philip Glass based on the life of Gandhi. The title is based on Gandhi's slogan, the two Hindi words *saty*, 'truth', and *agraha*, 'firmness'. Gandhi's early struggles in South Africa are balanced with portraits of Tolstoy, Tagore, and Martin Luther King. The opera is sung in Sanskrit and was first produced in Rotterdam on 5 September 1980.

Satz (German 'setting') in music, a movement of a multimovement work (for example *erster Satz*, 'first movement'); a theme (*Hauptsatz*, 'main theme'); or a style of composition (*Freier Satz*, 'free style').

Sauguet, Henri (1901–1989) French composer and critic. He was a member of Erik Satie's circle. He composed music for the stage and ballet. He is well known for the opera *La chartreuse de Parme* (1939).

After studying piano and organ at Bordeaux, he became a pupil of Joseph Canteloube at Montauban and in 1922 of Charles Koechlin in Paris. Introduced by Milhaud to Satie, he joined the latter's school at Arcueil. In 1936 he succeeded Milhaud as music critic to *Le Jour-Echo de Paris*, and his major work, the opera *La chartreuse de Parme*, followed in 1939.

Works OPERA *La gageure imprévue* (1944), *Les caprices de Marianne* (1954); two operettas, *Le plumet du colonel* (1924), *La contrebasse* (1932).

STAGE MUSIC ballets, including *La charte*, *David*, *La nuit*, *Fastes*, *Les forains*; incidental music for plays, including Molière's *Le Sicilien*, Roger Ferdinand's *Irma*, Pierre Emmanuel's *Les lépreux*.

ORCHESTRAL four symphonies, including *Symphonie expiatoire* (in memory of war victims); three piano concertos.

CHAMBER AND VOCAL *La voyante* for soprano and chamber orchestra; two string quartets (1926, 1948); sonatina for flute and piano; sonata in D major; other works for piano; songs to poems by Tagore; film music.

Saul oratorio by Handel (libretto by Charles Jennens). It was first produced at London's King's Theatre on 16 January 1739.

Saul og David opera in four acts by Carl August Nielsen. It was composed 1898–1901 and first produced and conducted by Nielsen in Copenhagen at the Royal Theatre on 28 November 1902. When David defeats Goliath, Saul becomes jealous and outlaws him. David runs away with Michal, Saul's daughter. Saul commits suicide after losing a battle against the Philistines, and David becomes king.

sausage bassoon alternative name for the ➔ **rackett**, a musical instrument.

Savile, Jeremy (lived 17th century) English composer. He contributed songs to *Select Musicall Ayres and Dialogues* in 1653. His compositions include the part song 'The Waits' and the song 'Here's a health unto His Majesty'.

Sàvitri opera by Holst (libretto by composer, based on an episode in the *Mahabharata*). Though it was first produced in London at Wellington Hall in 1916, its first public performance was at the Lyric Theatre in Hammersmith on 23

June 1921. In the story, death comes to claim the woodman Satyavān, but he is restored when his wife Sāvitri outwits the grim reaper.

Savonarola opera by Charles Villiers Stanford (libretto by Gilbert Abott à Beckett). It was first produced in Germany (translated by Ernst Frank) in Hamburg on 18 April 1884.

saw-toothed wave in music, an electronically generated tone characterized by its abrasive ➤ timbre. It is named after the jagged pattern of its sound wave.

Sawyer, David (1961–) English composer. He directed premieres of works by Mauricio Kagel at the 1983 Huddersfield Festival and was piano soloist in his *Phonophonie* in London in 1987. His own works have been played by the London Sinfonietta and the BBC Symphony Orchestra (at the London Promenade Concerts in 1992) and at the Almeida Festival, London.
He studied at York University and with Kagel in Cologne.

Works ORCHESTRAL AND STAGE MUSIC the chamber opera *The Panic* (1992); *Etudes* for actors and ensemble (1984); *Cat's Eye* (1986), *Take Off* (1987); *Byrnan Wood* for orchestra (1992); *The Memory of Water* (1993).
CHAMBER AND CHORAL *Rhetoric* (1989) for ensemble; *Songs of Love and War* for 24 voices, two harpsichords, and percussion (1990); *The Melancholy of Departure* for piano (1990).

Sax, Adolphe (Antoine-Joseph) (1814–1894) Belgian instrument maker. He made several improvements in wind instruments and established himself in Paris in 1842. His chief inventions are the ➤ saxhorn and the ➤ saxophone.
He studied flute and clarinet at the Brussels Conservatory and worked in the business established in Brussels by his father Charles Joseph Sax (1791–1865), who made wind instruments and produced several inventions, especially in connection with horns and other brass instruments. Adolphe's brother **Alphonse Sax** (1822–1874) made some inventions in connection with the valves of brass instruments and established himself independently in Paris, but did not succeed.

saxhorn family of brass musical instruments played with valves, invented in 1845 by the Belgian Adolphe Sax (1814–1894). It is played with a cup mouthpiece and made in seven different pitches, covering between them a range of some five octaves: soprano in E flat, alto in B flat (both also called flügelhorns), tenor in E flat, baritone in B flat (both also called althorns), bass in B flat (euphonium), bass tuba in E flat (bombardon), and contrabass in B flat. They are rarely used in the orchestra, but are regular constituents of military and brass bands.

saxophone member of a hybrid brass instrument family of conical bore, with a single-reed woodwind mouthpiece and keyworks, invented about 1840 by Belgian instrument-maker Adolphe Sax (1814–1894). Soprano, alto, tenor, and baritone forms remain current. The soprano saxophone is usually straight; the others are characteristically curved back at the mouthpiece and have an upturned bell. Initially a concert instrument of suave tone, the saxophone was incorporated into dance bands of the 1930s and 1940s, and assumed its modern guise as a solo jazz instrument after 1945. It has a voicelike ability to bend a note.

Saxton, Robert (1953–) English composer. He studied with Elisabeth Lutyens, Robin Holloway, Robert Sherlaw Johnson, and Luciano Berio. In 1990 he was appointed head of composition at the Guildhall School of Music and Drama, London.

Works CHAMBER AND VOCAL *La Promenade d'Automne* for soprano and ensemble (1972), *What does the song hope for?* for soprano and ensemble (1974); *Reflections on Narziss and Goldmund* for two chamber groups, harp, and piano (1975); *Canzona* for chamber ensemble (1978); *Processions and Dances* for eleven instruments (1981); *Piccola Musica per Luigi Dallapiccola* for chamber ensemble (1981); *Eloge* for soprano and ensemble (1981).
ORCHESTRAL *Choruses to Apollo* for orchestra (1980); *Traumstadt* for orchestra (1980); *Ring of Eternity* for orchestra (1983); concerto for orchestra (1984); *Circles of Light* for chamber orchestra (1985); viola concerto (1986); *In the Beginning* for orchestra (1987); *Elijah's Violin* for orchestra (1988); concertos for violin (1989); concertos for cello (1993).
OTHER *Psalm: a Song of Ascents* for trumpet and ensemble (1992); piano quintet (1994); symphony for soprano, baritone, and orchestra (1993).

saz Persian and Turkish term meaning 'musical instrument'. The term is also applied to a family of long-necked lutes found in Iran, the Caucasus, southeastern Europe and Asia Minor. Sazi (plural) have a pear-shaped resonator carved from a single piece of wood or fitted together from wooden staves. The neck of the saz is straight with a variable number of tied but movable gut frets.

Scacchi, Marco (c.1602–c.1685) Italian composer and writer on music. He was a pupil of Giovanni Francesco Anerio. In 1628 he was appointed director of music to the court at Warsaw and introduced Italian opera to Warsaw, Gdańsk, and Vilna. He wrote several theoretical tracts. He returned to Italy in 1648.

Works OPERA *Il ratto di Helena*; *Narciso transfor-*

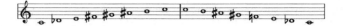

The enigmatic scale on C.

mato; *Armida abbandonata; Enea; Le nozze d'Amore e di Psiche; Circe delusa.*

OTHER oratorio *S Cecilia;* Masses; madrigals.

Scala, La or **Teatro alla Scala** the greatest Italian opera house, established in Milan in 1778. Many of Italy's finest opera composers have written for La Scala, including Puccini, Verdi, and Donizetti.

Scalabrini, Paolo (c.1713–1806) Italian composer. He went to Copenhagen in 1747 as conductor of the Mingotti opera company, and stayed there as music director to the Danish court 1748–53 and again 1775–81, when he retired to Italy. He was among the first to write an opera to Danish words.

Works OPERA Danish operas *Love rewarded, or The Faithful Lovers* (1756), *The Oracle* (1776), *Love without Stockings;* about 20 Italian operas.

CHORAL AND ORCHESTRAL oratorio *Giuseppe riconosciuto;* symphonies.

scala enigmatica (Italian, 'enigmatic scale') in music, Giuseppe ➤ Verdi's term for the curious scale on which he constructed his *Ave Maria* for four voices, composed about 1889.

scale in music, a progression of single notes upwards or downwards in 'steps' (scale originally meant 'ladder'). For example, the most common scale is that of C major, which can be found by playing all the white notes on the keyboard from any C to the next C above or below. A scale is defined by its starting note and may be ➤ major or ➤ minor depending on its arrangement of tones and semitones. A ➤ chromatic scale is made up entirely of semitones. It includes all the notes (black and white) on the keyboard and has no key because there is no fixed starting point.

A ➤ whole-tone scale is a six-note scale and is also indeterminate in key. This scale originated in the South Sea Islands and was used extensively by Claude Debussy. A ➤ diatonic scale has seven notes, while a ➤ pentatonic scale has five.

Scandello, Antonio (1517–1580) Italian composer. He became a Protestant and was music director (Kapellmeister) at the Elector of Saxony's court chapel at Dresden. Both his church music and secular songs combine Italian and German styles for the first time.

He is first heard of as a cornettist in Bergamo in 1541 and was a member of the Saxon court chapel at Dresden in 1553. He often returned to Brescia for visits, as in 1567, when he and his family took refuge there during the plague at Dresden.

Among the court musicians was his brother Angelo Scandello, and also employed at the court was the Italian painter Benedetto Tola, whose daughter Agnese became Scandello's second wife in 1568. In the same year he was appointed Kapellmeister in place of Matthieu Le Maistre, whose assistant he had been for two years. He became involved in quarrels with the German court musicians and the Flemish singers because the Italians received higher pay.

Works CHURCH MUSIC Masses; motets; setting for voices of the Passion and Resurrection narrative according to St John (1561); hymn tunes for several voices; other church music.

CHAMBER AND VOCAL madrigals; epithalamia; *canzoni napoletane* for four voices; sacred and secular German songs for several voices and instruments; lute music.

Scapino comedy-overture by William Turner Walton. It was first performed in Chicago on 3 April 1941.

Scarlatti, (Pietro) Alessandro (Gaspare) (1660–1725) Italian baroque composer. He was maestro di capella at the court of Naples and developed the opera form. He composed more than 100 operas, including *Tigrane* (1715), as well as church music and oratorios.

Scarlatti, (Giuseppe) Domenico (1685–1757) Italian composer. The eldest son of Alessandro ➤ Scarlatti, he lived most of his life in Portugal and Spain in the service of the Queen of Spain. He wrote over 500 sonatas for harpsichord, short pieces in ➤ binary form demonstrating the new freedoms of keyboard composition and inspired by Spanish musical styles. Scarlatti was the most famous harpsichordist of his time, and his music provided the foundation for modern piano technique.

Scarlatti was born in Naples, and was taught by his father. In 1701 he was appointed organist and composer to the court at Naples, where his operas *L'Ottavia restituita al trono* and *Il Giustino* were produced in 1703. Sent by his father to Venice in 1705, he travelled by way of Florence, where he presented himself to Alessandro's patron, Ferdinando de' Medici. In Venice he met Francesco Gasparini, and probably studied with him. Moving to Rome, he is said to have engaged with Handel in a contest in harpsichord and organ playing, arranged by Cardinal Ottoboni. He was maestro di cappella to Queen Maria Casimira of Poland in Rome in 1709–14, and wrote seven operas for her, including *Ambleto/Hamlet.* He was at the Cap-

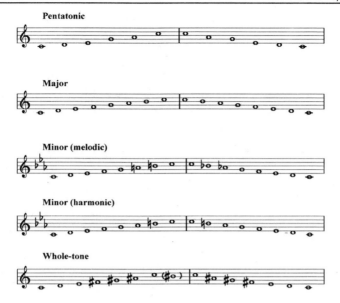

Pentatonic, major, minor, and whole-tone scales on C.

pella Giulia, St Peter's, as assistant maestro from 1713, and as maestro di cappella in 1714–19.

He spent some time at Palermo before going to Lisbon in the service of the Portuguese court. He made intermittent visits to Italy, and in 1729 followed the Portuguese princess Maria Barbara to Madrid on her marriage to the Spanish crown prince. It was for her that he wrote most of his harpsichord music (over 550 'exercises', now called sonatas, which exhibit an original approach to harmony and frequently demand great virtuosity). Harpsichordist Ralph Kirkpatrick's modern edition gives each of these a number prefixed by the letter K.

Works OPERA operas, including *La silvia* (1710), *Tolomeo ed Alessandro* (1711), *L'Orlando* (1711), *Tetide in Sciro*, *Ifigenia in Aulide* (1713), *Ifigenia in Tauride* (1713), *Amor d'un' ombra*, *Ambleto*.

CHAMBER about 600 harpsichord pieces (30 of them published in his lifetime under the title *Esercizi/Exercises*), now commonly called sonatas.

CHORAL church music; cantatas; oratorios.

Scelsi, Giacinto (1905–1988) Italian composer. Under the influence of a visit to Tibet he developed an early form of minimalism, as in *Four pieces, each one on a single note*, for small orchestra in 1961. His *Aion* for orchestra (composed in 1961, first performance in 1985) further evokes virtual stillness.

He studied in Geneva and Vienna and from 1936 was an early exponent of 12-note techniques.

Works ORCHESTRAL AND CHAMBER *Pfhat* and *Konx-Om-Pax* for orchestra (1986); eleven piano suites; five string quartets.

scena (Italian 'stage, scene') in music, subdivision of an act in a dramatic piece. It is also a technical term for operatic solo numbers on a large scale, usually a recitative followed by one or more arialike sections.

scenario the sketch or rough draft for the plot of an opera libretto or for the story of a ballet.

Scenes from Goethe's 'Faust' a setting by Robert ➜ Schumann of a number of scenes from Goethe's drama; see ➜ Szenen aus Goethes 'Faust'.

Scènes Historiques two suites for orchestra by the Finnish composer Jean ➜ Sibelius: no. 1 in three movements (1899, revised 1911) and no. 2 in three movements (1912).

Schachbrett or **Schachtbrett** musical instrument, probably an early form of ➜ harpsichord. It is mentioned in Cersne von Minden's *Minneregeln* of 1404. The name derives from the old Germanic word *Schacht*, meaning spring or quill.

Schadaeus, Abraham (1566–1626) German composer. His *Promptuarium musicum*, a collection of motets, was published in Strasbourg in three parts, in 1611, 1612, and 1613. A *bassus generalis* (continuo) was added by his friend Caspar Vincentius; a fourth part, dated 1617, was entirely by Vincentius.

Schadaeus became *Rektor* of the *Lateinschule*

(grammar school) in Speyer in 1603. Dismissed in 1611, he then held different posts in Upper Lusatia and retired in 1617 in Finsterwalde.

Schaeffer, Pierre (1910–1995) French composer, theorist, writer, and teacher. The son of two musicians, he was educated as a scientist and embarked on a career in telecommunications. In 1941 he founded 'Jeune France', an interdisciplinary arts group which became a focus in French radio for the Resistance movement. In 1948 Schaeffer's experiments in electronic media with this group led to a number of tape compositions which formed the basis of the style known as ➤ **musique concrète** ('concrete music'). He stopped composing in 1960, and devoted his time to a wide range of research and writings. In 1968 he was appointed associate professor at the Paris Conservatoire, where he taught electronic composition. Works are for tape alone.

Schaeffner, André (1895–1980) French musicologist. He studied at the Schola Cantorum in Paris and after 1920 became music critic to various periodicals. His books include studies of Stravinsky and of the origin of musical instruments. In 1929, he became director of the ethnomusicological section of the Musée de l'Homme in Paris.

Schafer, R Murray (1933–) Canadian composer and teacher. His works employ electronics and involve transformation and motivic distortion.

He studied in Toronto and Vienna and worked in England as a journalist.

Works OPERA *Loving/Toi* (staged Toronto, 1978).

CHORAL AND VOICE WITH ORCHESTRA *Minnelieder* for mezzo and wind quintet (1956); *St Jean de Brebeuf* for baritone and orchestra (1961); *Requiems for the Party Girl* for soprano and nine instruments (1966); *From the Tibetan Book of the Dead* for soprano, chorus, and ensemble (1968); *The Son of Heldenleben* after a work by Strauss (1968); *Sappho* for mezzo and ensemble (1970); four string quartets (1970, 1976, 1989, 1988); *In Search of Zoroaster* for male voice, chorus, and percussion (1971); *Adieu, Robert Schumann* for mezzo and orchestra (after Clara Schumann's diaries detailing her husband's madness, 1976); *Apocalypsis* for soloist, chorus, and orchestra (after St John the Divine, 1980).

OTHER flute concerto (1985); series of multimedia theatre pieces, including *The Black Theatre of Hermes* (1989), *The Crown of Ariadne* (1992).

Schäffer, Bogusław (1929–) Polish composer. He studied in Kraków with Artur Malawski and musicology in Warsaw with Zdzisław Jachimecki. For some of his works he has used graphic notation.

Works ORCHESTRAL AND CHAMBER *Scultura* for or-

chestra; *Monosonata* for 24 string instruments; *Topofonica* for 40 instruments; *Equivalenze sonore* for percussion instruments; concerto for harpsichord, percussion, and orchestra; *Four Movements* for piano and orchestra; *Tertium datum* for clavichord and chamber orchestra; ten symphonies (1960–79); three piano concertos (1957, 1967, 1988); two harpsichord concertos (1958, 1961); violin concerto (1963); *Kesukaan* for strings (1978); concertos for guitar (1984), for organ and violin (1984), for flute and harp (1986), for saxophone (1986), for violin and three oboes (1987); six string quartets (1954–73).

OTHER theatre pieces *Miniopera* (1988), *Liebesblicke* (1989).

Schat, Peter (1935–2003) Dutch composer. He became well known as an experimental composer, although he later came under the influence of ➤ **minimalism**.

He studied in Utrecht and The Hague, and then with Mátyás Seiber and Pierre Boulez.

Works ORCHESTRAL *Mosaics* for orchestra; *Cryptogamen* for baritone and orchestra; *Signalement* for six percussion instruments and three double basses; *Improvisations and Symphonies* for wind quintet.

OPERA AND STAGE MUSIC *Labyrinth* for 'musical theatre' with 'happenings' (produced Amsterdam, 1966); circus opera *Houdini* (1976); opera *Symposium* (on the life of Tchaikovsky, 1994).

Schauspieldirektor, Der, The Impresario play with music by Mozart. Its first Vienna performance was at the Kärntnertortheater on 18 February 1786.

Scheherazade song-cycle with orchestra by Maurice Ravel; see ➤ **Shéhérazade** .

Symphonic suite by Nicolai Rimsky-Korsakov. See ➤ **Shahrazad** .

Scheibe, Johann Adolph (1708–1776) German music theorist, critic, and composer. He edited the periodical *Der critische Musikus*, in which he attacked Johann Sebastian Bach.

After studying law at Leipzig University he settled in Hamburg in 1736, where he edited *Der critische Musikus* 1737–40. He was Kapellmeister to the Margrave of Brandenburg-Culmbach 1739–44, and conductor of the court opera in Copenhagen 1744–48.

Works OPERA one opera *Thusnelde* (1749).

CHURCH MUSIC cantatas; Masses; other church music.

OTHER instrumental music; songs.

Scheidt, Samuel (1587–1654) German organist and composer. His influential *Tabulatura nova* for the organ (published in 1624) was printed in score, not in the old German tablature.

He was appointed organist at St Maurice's

Church, Halle, in 1603. He studied under Jan Sweelinck at Amsterdam. He returned to Halle in 1609 and became court organist to the Margrave of Brandenburg, who was Protestant administrator of the archbishopric of Magdeburg. He was appointed Kapellmeister in 1619, but he lost his appointment in 1625 as a result of the Thirty Years' War.

Works CHORAL AND CHURCH MUSIC *Cantiones sacrae* for eight voices; sacred concertos for 2–12 voices with instruments; pavans and galliards for 4–5 voices; *Liebliche Krafft-Blümlein* for two voices and instruments; organ accompaniments for or transcriptions of 100 hymns and psalms.

ORGAN MUSIC *Tabulatura nova* containing a great variety of organ pieces in three volumes.

Schein, Johann Hermann (1586–1630) German composer. His music is influenced by Lutheran chorales and by the latest expressive techniques of the early Italian madrigalists.

After the death of his father, a Lutheran pastor, he went to Dresden as a choirboy in the court chapel in 1599, to the grammar-school at Schulpforta in 1603, and to Leipzig University in 1607. In 1615 he was appointed Kapellmeister at the court of Weimar and in 1616 succeeded Seth Calvisius as cantor at St Thomas's School, Leipzig, remaining there until his death.

Works SACRED AND SECULAR MUSIC *Cantiones sacrae* for 5–12 voices; two volumes of sacred concertos for 3–5 voices with instruments; *Fontana d'Israel* containing biblical words set for 4–5 voices and instruments; *Cantional* hymn-book with about 80 tunes of his own; wedding and funeral cantatas.

SONGS songs for five voices, including *Venus-Kränzlein, Studenten-Schmaus, Diletti pastorali*; instrumental dances *Banchetto musicale*; songs with instruments *Musica boscareccia*.

Schelomo Hebrew rhapsody for cello and orchestra by the Swiss-born US composer Ernest Bloch, based on the Book of Ecclesiastes. It was composed in 1916 and first performed in New York on 3 May 1917.

Schenk, Johann Baptist (1753–1836) Austrian composer. A pupil of Georg Wagenseil 1774–77, he made his public debut as an opera composer in 1785. Beethoven was his pupil in 1793, and he was also a friend of Mozart and Schubert.

Works SINGSPIELE *Die Weinlese* (1785); *Die Weihnacht auf dem Lande* (1786); *Achmet und Almanzine*; *Der Dorfbarbier* (1796); *Die Jagd*; *Der Fassbinder* (1802).

CHURCH MUSIC Masses; cantatas *Die Huldigung* and *Der Mai*.

OTHER ten symphonies; four harp concertos; five string quartets and trios; songs.

Schenker, Heinrich (1868–1935) Polish-Austrian theorist. His literary works, including *Neue musikalische Theorien und Phantasien* and *Das Meisterwerk in der Musik*, laid down his detailed analytical methods.

He studied with Bruckner at the Vienna Conservatory and on Brahms's recommendation published some early compositions. He taught a number of pupils privately.

Scherchen, Hermann (1891–1966) German conductor. He collaborated with ➤ Schoenberg 1911–12, and in 1919 founded the journal *Melos* to promote contemporary music. He moved to Switzerland in 1933, and was active as a conductor and teacher. He wrote two texts, *Handbook of Conducting* and *The Nature of Music*. During the 1950s he founded a music publishing house, Ars Viva Verlag, and an electronic studio at Gravesano.

Scherchen-Hsiao, Tona (1938–) Swiss-born French composer. She studied with her father, Hermann ➤ Scherchen, with Hans Werner ➤ Henze at Salzburg, with ➤ Messiaen in Paris 1963–65, and with György Sándor ➤ Ligeti in Vienna.

Works ORCHESTRAL *Shen* for six percussion (1968); *Khouang* for orchestra (1968); *Tao* for contralto and orchestra (1971); *Vague Tao* for orchestra (1975); *L'Invitation au voyage* for chamber orchestra (1977); *L'illegitime* for orchestra and tape (1986).

CHAMBER *Ziguidor* for wind quintet (1977); *Tzing* for brass quintet (1979).

ELECTRONIC AND MIXED-MEDIA *Un cadre univers ouvert* (1985); *Space Flight* for tape (1987); *Fuite* for low voice and ensemble (1987).

Schering, Arnold (1877–1941) German musicologist. His books include studies of the early violin concerto, the development of the oratorio and sonata, the performance of early music, early organ music, and chamber music. He also made a series of attempts to prove that Beethoven's sonatas and quartets are based on Shakespeare's plays and other dramatic works.

He studied at Leipzig University, where he became a lecturer in 1907 and later professor of music. From 1909 he also lectured at the Conservatory. In 1920, he became professor at Halle University and in 1928 at Berlin University.

scherzando (Italian 'playful, humorous, skittish') musical direction written by composers over passages intended to be performed in that manner. It may also be used as an adjective in tempo directions, such as *allegretto scherzando*.

Scherzi, Gli, The Jokes one of the nicknames of ➤ Haydn's six string quartets, Op. 33, composed in 1781. Also known as the *Russian* quartets or *Jungfernquartette*.

Scherz, list und rache, **Jest, Cunning and Revenge** operetta by Max ➤ Bruch (libretto by Goethe), produced in Cologne on 14 January 1858.
For other settings, see ➤ Goethe.

scherzo (Italian 'joke') in music, a lively piece, usually in rapid triple (3/4) time; often used for the third movement of a symphony, sonata, or quartet as a substitute for the statelier ➤ minuet and ➤ trio.

Schicksalslied, **Song of Destiny** a setting by Brahms for chorus and orchestra of a poem in Hölderlin's *Hyperion*, Op. 54. It was composed in 1871 and first performed in Karlsruhe, Germany, on 18 October 1871.

Schiedermair, Ludwig (1876–1957) German music scholar. He studied with Adolf ➤ Sandberger and Beer-Walbrunn at Munich, where he took a degree in 1901. After further studies with Hugo Riemann and Hermann Kretzschmar in Berlin, he became lecturer at Marburg and in 1914 professor of music at Bonn University. There he became director of the Beethoven Archives. Among his books are bibliographical works on Beethoven and an edition of Mozart's letters with an iconographical volume.

Schikaneder, (Johann Josef) Emanuel (1751–1812) German actor, singer, librettist, playwright, and theatre manager. He was author or part-author with Ludwig Gieseke of the libretto of Mozart's opera *The Magic Flute*, which he produced with himself as Papageno.
He settled in Vienna in 1784. He also wrote libretti for Benedict Schack, Franz Xaver Gerl, Franz Süssmayr, Joseph Woelfl, Ignaz Seyfried, Peter Winter, and others.

Schiller, Johann Christoph Friedrich von (1759–1805) German dramatist, poet, and historian. His works inspired numerous musical settings – Franz Schubert alone set 42 songs to Schiller words. Schiller wrote *Sturm und Drang* ('storm and stress') verse and plays, including the dramatic trilogy *Wallenstein* (1798–99). He was an idealist, and much of his work concerns the aspiration for political freedom and the avoidance of mediocrity.
After the success of his play *Die Räuber/The Robbers* (1781), he completed the tragedies *Die Verschwörung des Fiesko zu Genua/Fiesco, or the Genoese Conspiracy* (his first historical drama) and *Kabale und Liebe/Intrigue and Love* (1783). In 1787 he wrote his more mature blank-verse drama *Don Carlos* and the hymn 'An die Freude/Ode to Joy', later used by ➤ Beethoven in his ninth symphony. As professor of history at Jena from 1789 he completed a history of the Thirty Years' War and developed a close friendship with Goethe, after early antagonism. His essays on

aesthetics include the piece of literary criticism *Über naive und sentimentalische Dichtung/Naive and Sentimental Poetry* (1795–96). Schiller became the foremost German dramatist with his classic dramas *Wallenstein*, *Maria Stuart* (1800), *Die Jungfrau von Orleans/The Maid of Orleans* (1801), and *Wilhelm Tell/William Tell* (1804).
He was born in Marbach on the River Neckar, qualified as a surgeon, and worked for a regiment in Stuttgart. A chance glimpse of Goethe, however, determined him to become a poet. After some early attempts at dramatic writing Schiller completed *Die Räuber*, on the theme of authoritarianism and liberty. It was first performed in Mannheim 1782 and was very successful in France; at home, however, Schiller was imprisoned and forbidden to write any further comedies. He escaped to a village in Thuringia, where he completed his next two works in hiding.
In 1783 he returned to Mannheim, where the director of the Mannheim Theatre made him 'theatre poet'. His position lasted only a year; he then maintained himself precariously by journalism and in 1785 went to Leipzig at the invitation of a friend, Christian Gottfried Körner. There, for the first time, he was happy. He was the centre of a circle of good friends and his ode 'An die Freude' expressed his feelings. He also wrote two novels, *Der Verbrecher aus verlorener Ehre/The Dishonoured Irreclaimable* (1786) and the unfinished *Der Geisterseher/The Ghost-seer, or Apparationist* (1789). His tragedy *Don Carlos* was coldly received and he turned to writing a historical work in 1788 about the Revolt of the Netherlands. This attracted the attention of Goethe, who used his influence to secure for Schiller the position of professor of history at the university of Jena, enabling him to marry Charlotte von Lengefeld in 1790. Despite this gesture, Goethe remained hostile towards Schiller until 1794 when he collaborated in launching the literary magazine *Die Horen* and their lifelong friendship began.
In 1791 Schiller became ill and had to resign his position, but received a pension to continue his historical studies. He completed his *Geschichte des dreissigjährigen Kreiges/History of the Thirty Years' War* (1793), then turned to the study of philosophy, particularly the work of Kant. He acquired a vast philosophical knowledge, which is reflected in his prose works on art and aesthetics, including *Über Anmut und Würde/On Grace and Dignity* and *Briefe über die Ästhetische Erziehung des Menschen/Letters on the Aesthetic Education of Man* (both 1793), and several treatises on tragedy. He concluded this period with *Über naive und sentimentalische Dichtung*. Alongside his academic writing he produced some poetry, including 'Die Götter Griechenlands/The Gods of Greece' and 'Die Künstler/The Artists' and, en-

couraged by Goethe, transformed his philosophical thinking into poetry in such works as 'Das Ideal und das Leben/The Ideal and Life'. 'Das Lied von der Glocke/The Song of the Bell' and his ballads were produced 1795–97.

Goethe and Schiller collaborated on *Die Horen* 1794–97 and the satirical *Xenien* 1796–97, attacking their critics, before Schiller began to write for the stage once again. In this last period he produced his great work *Wallenstein*, the sympathetic *Maria Stuart*, the idealized history *Die Jungfrau von Orleans*, *Die Braut von Messina/The Bride of Messina* (1803) (in ancient Greek style with chorus), and *Wilhelm Tell* (1804). Having suffered ill health since 1791, he died of exhaustion and tuberculosis.

See also ➤ *Bride of Messina, The* (Fibich); ➤ *Briganti, I* (Mercadante); ➤ Bruch (*Lied von der Glocke* and *Macht des Gesanges*); ➤ 'Choral' Symphony (Beethoven); ➤ Costa (*Don Carlos*); ➤ *Don Carlos* (Verdi); ➤ *Giovanna d'Arco* (Verdi); ➤ *Guillaume Tell* (Rossini); ➤ *Ideale* (Liszt); ➤ *Luisa Miller* (Verdi); ➤ *Maid of Orleans, The* (Tchaikovsky); ➤ Mascagni (*Ode to Joy*); ➤ *Masnadieri, I* (Verdi); ➤ Seyfried (*Räuber* and *Jungfrau von Orleans*); ➤ Smetana (*Wallenstein's Camp*); ➤ *Turandot* (Weber); ➤ Vaccai (*Giovanna d'Arco* and *Sposa di Messina*); ➤ Zumsteeg (*Räuber*; *Wallensteins Lager* and *Ritter Toggenburg*).

Schillinger, Joseph (1895–1943) Russian-born US composer and theoretician. He published a number of books on music theory, and also several compositions. George ➤ Gershwin was among his many pupils.

He studied at St Petersburg Conservatory with Alexander ➤ Tcherepnin (Cherepnin), among others, and then taught at Kharkov Music Academy 1918–22, and in Leningrad 1926–28. In 1929 he settled in the USA, teaching a mathematical method of his own.

Works ORCHESTRAL AND SOLO *March of the Orient*; *First Airphonic Suite* for theremin (an early electronic musical instrument), orchestra, and piano; piano pieces.

Schläger (German 'beaters') in musical notation, term used in scores as an abbreviation for percussion. Also, in the singular, a term for a popular song.

Schlaginstrumente (German 'beaten instruments') see ➤ percussion instruments.

Schlagobers (Whipped Cream in Viennese dialect) ballet by Richard Strauss, first produced at the Opera in Vienna on 9 May 1924.

Schlagzither (German 'striking-zither') musical instrument, a zither played by striking the strings with hammers, or rather, a ➤ dulcimer.

Schlegel, August Wilhelm von (1767–1845) German Romantic author and translator of Shakespeare. His 'Über dramatische Kunst und Literatur/Lectures on Dramatic Art and Literature' 1809–11 broke down the formalism of the old classical criteria of literary composition. Friedrich von Schlegel was his brother.

He played a major role in the development of musical aesthetics of the German idealism. Seven poems by Schlegel were set as songs by Schubert. See also ➤ *Fierrabras* (Schubert).

schleppen (German 'to drag') term sometimes used by German composers as a negative imperative, *nicht schleppen*, 'do not drag'.

Schlick, Arnolt (before 1460–after 1521) German organist, composer, and theorist. In 1511, he published his *Spiegel der Orgelmacher und Organisten*, a treatise on organ building and playing. The *Tabulaturen etlicher Lobgesang und Lidlein*, published at Mainz in 1512, was the first printed book of keyboard music to appear in Germany and contained liturgical organ music, lute pieces, and songs with lute.

His early life was spent in Heidelberg, but he subsequently travelled widely: to Frankfurt in 1486, where he played the organ during the festivities for the coronation of Maximilian I; to Holland in 1490; to Strasbourg (many times); to Worms in 1495, where he met Sebastian Virdung; and subsequently to Speyer, Hagenau, and elsewhere. During these journeys he gained an enormous reputation for testing new organs. He also wrote music for the coronation of Charles V in Aachen in 1520. He was blind, probably from infancy.

Schlüssel (German 'key') in music, a ➤ clef.

Schmelzer (von Ehrenruff), Andreas (Anton) (1653–1701) Austrian violinist and composer, the son of Heinrich Schmelzer. He was in the service of the Austrian court 1671–1700.

Works OPERA ballet music for more than 30 of Draghi's operas.

Schmelzer, (Johann) Heinrich (c.1623–1680) Austrian composer. He was chamber musician at the Austrian court in Vienna from 1649, assistant conductor from 1671, and first conductor from 1679. He was the father of Andreas Schmelzer.

Works OPERA AND BALLET ballet music for about 40 operas by Giovanni Battista Draghi and others.

OTHER *Missa nuptialis* and other church music; instrumental sonatas, including the *Sonatae unarum fidium* for violin (1664) and coninuo, the earliest of their kind; trumpet fanfares.

schmetternd (German 'brassy, brazen, clanging') musical term used like the French ➤ cuivré.

Schmid(t), Bernhard the Elder (1535–1592) Composer and poet from Strasbourg. He published a collection of music arranged for organ in two parts: the first contained motets, the second secular songs and dances, published at Strasbourg in 1577.

His son, **Bernhard Schmid(t) the Younger** (1567–1625) was also a composer of organ music.

Schmid(t), Bernhard the Younger (1567–1625) German composer. His collection of organ arrangements, highly ornamented, was published at Strasbourg in 1607. He was the son of Bernhard ➤ Schmidt the Elder.

Schmidt, Bernhard German organ builder; see Bernard ➤ Smith.

Schmidt-Isserstedt, Hans (1900–1973) German conductor. He was director of the Deutsche Oper in Berlin 1942–45 and then chief conductor of the North German Radio Symphony Orchestra.

He studied with Franz Schreker and also at the University of Cologne, graduating in 1923. He began his career at the Wuppertal opera and then conducted at Rostock 1928–31, at Darmstadt 1931–33, and was principal conductor at the Hamburg Staatsoper 1935–42.

Schmieder, Wolfgang (1901–1990) German musicologist. In 1950 he published a thematic catalogue of Johann Sebastian Bach's music, the Bach-Werke-Verzeichnis, which provides standard numbering for the composer's works (preceded by the initials BWV).

After study at Heidelberg, Schmieder was archivist at Breitkopf and Härtel in Leipzig, 1933–42. He was head of the music division at Frankfurt State Library 1946–63.

Schmitt, Florent (1870–1958) French composer. His music shows the influence of Richard Strauss and the French composers Fauré, Debussy, and Massenet. His most successful work is the ballet *La Tragédie de Salome* (revised as a symphonic poem in 1910).

He studied music at Nancy from 1887 and in 1889 was sent to the Paris Conservatory, where he was first a pupil of Dubois and Lavignac and afterwards of Massenet and Fauré for composition. He won the Prix de Rome in 1900 and wrote his first mature works during his three years in Rome. He was director of Lyon Conservatory 1922–24.

Works STAGE MUSIC ballets, including *La tragédie de Salomé* (1907), *Le petit elfe Ferme-l'œil* (1924), *Reflets*, *Ourvasi*, *Oriane et le Prince d'Amour* (1938); incidental music for Shakespeare's *Antony and Cleopatra* (translated by Gide); film music for an adaptation of Flaubert's *Salammbô* (1925).

CHORAL WITH ORCHESTRA Psalm 46 for soprano solo, chorus, organ, and orchestra.

ORCHESTRAL symphonic study *Le palais hanté* (after Poe), symphony (1958), *Trois Rapsodies*, *Ronde burlesque*, *Çancunik*; *Kermesse-Valse*, *Symphonie concertante*, *Suite sans esprit de suite* for orchestra, *Légende* for saxophone and orchestra (1918), *Final* for cello and orchestra.

CHAMBER AND VOCAL piano quintet; *Lied et Scherzo* for double wind quintet; *Andante et Scherzo* for chromatic harp and string quartet; *Suite en Rocaille* for strings, flute, and harp; *Sonatine en trio* for flute, clarinet, and harpsichord (or piano); string quartet (1949); string trio; *Sonate libre* for violin and piano; piano pieces.

Schmittbauer, Joseph Aloys (1718–1809) German composer. A pupil of Jommelli, he was Kapellmeister of Cologne Cathedral 1775–77, and at the court at Karlsruhe from 1777 to his retirement in 1804.

Works OPERA *L'isola disabitata* (1762); *Lindor und Ismene* (1771); *Herkules auf dem Oeta* (1772); *Betrug aus Liebe*.

OTHER much church music; cantatas; symphonies; concertos; chamber music.

Schnabelflöte (German 'beak flute', from French *flûte à bec*) alternative name for the ➤ recorder, a musical instrument.

Schnadahüpfeln (Austrian dialect) folk dances, often sung with words, of the *Ländler* (folk dance in three time) or slow waltz type, which are typical of the Tyrol or other Austrian mountain regions.

Schnebel, Dieter (1930–) German composer and theologian. He has taught religious studies from 1953. Influenced by Kagel and Stockhausen, he has produced such 'non-music' items as music for reading (*mo-no*, 1969), and for conductor only (*Nostalgie*, 1969).

Works ORCHESTRAL *Webern-Variationen* (1972); *Wagner-Idyll* (1980); *Beethoven-Sinfonie* (1985); *Mahler-Momente* (1985); *Sinfonie X* (1987–92).

schnell (German 'fast') term used in musical notation to indicate a rapid tempo, roughly equivalent to ➤ presto.

Schnittke or **Shnitke, Alfred Garriyevich (1934–1998)** Russian composer. He experimented with ➤ integral serialism and unusual instrumental textures, which are characteristically rich with a prominent use of strings, often using quotations and parodies. Among his many works are ... *pianissimo* ... (1969) for orchestra, the oratorio *Nagasaki* (1958), *Sinfonia* (1972), and *Minnesang/Lovesong* (1981) for 48 voices.

He studied in Vienna and at the Moscow Conservatory; and taught at the latter 1961–72. His music often plays on the dichotomy between reality and illusion. For example, his cadenza of the Beethoven violin concerto strikes a sensitive balance between an orderly traditional formula and atonal disintegration. He adopted the term 'polystylism' to describe music which is many-layered and highly allusive.

The operas *Historia von Dr Johann Fausten* and *Gesualdo* were premiered at Hamburg and Vienna respectively in 1995.

Works OPERA *Life with an Idiot* (1992); *Historia von Dr Johann Fausten* (1995); *Gesualdo* (1995).

ORCHESTRAL AND CHORAL eight symphonies: no. 1 (1969–72), no. 2 *St Florian* for small chorus and orchestra (1979), no. 3 (1981), no. 4 for SATB soloists and chamber orchestra (1984), no. 5 *Concerto Grosso*, no. 6 (1992), no. 7 (1993), no. 8 (1994); four violin concertos (1957–82); piano concerto (1960); concerto for piano and strings; five concerti grossi (1977, 1982, 1985, 1988, 1991); two cello concertos (1986, 1990); *Ein Sommernachtstraum* for orchestra (1985); *Epilogue, Peer Gynt* for orchestra and tape (1987); Trio-Sonata (orchestration of string trio, 1987); two oratorios *Nagasaki* (1958) and *Songs of War and Peace* (1959); *Der gelbe Klang* for nine instruments, tape, chorus, and light projection, after Kandinsky; *Requiem* (1975); *Minnesang* (Lovesong) for 48 voices a cappella (1981); *Seid nüchtern und wachet ...* (based on the Faust legend of 1587) for chorus (1983).

CHAMBER two violin sonatas (1963, 1968); three string quartets (1966, 1981, 1984); cello sonata (1978); *Moz-art* for two violins; *Stille Musik* for violin and cello (1979); Septet for flute, two clarinets, and string quartet (1982); string trio (1985); piano quartet (1988); *Moz-art à la Mozart* for eight flutes and harpsichord (1990).

Schobert, Johann (Jean) (c. 1720–1767) German harpsichordist and composer. Mozart arranged one of his sonata movements as the second movement of the concerto K39.

He lived in Paris, and was in the service of the Prince of Conti from about 1720, but died young, with his wife and child, as a result of fungus poisoning.

Works OPERA AND ORCHESTRAL the opéra comique *Le Garde-Chasse et le braconnier*; six harpsichord concertos.

CHAMBER six *Sinfonies* for harpsichord, violin, and two horns; piano quartets (with two violins); piano trios; sonatas for piano and violin; sonatas for harpsichord.

Schoeck, Othmar (1886–1957) Swiss composer. As Switzerland's first major composer, Schoeck cultivated a lush and lyrical postromanticism. He excelled in vocal music of all kinds and wrote many fine song cycles, often with chamber or orchestral accompaniment – for example *Notturno* (1933) and *Lebendig Begraben*

(1947). He also wrote cantatas and several operas.

He was at first undecided whether to follow his father as a painter, but at 17 went to the Zürich Conservatory to study with Friedrich Niggli (1875–1959) and others, finishing with Max Reger at the Leipzig Conservatory. He conducted choral societies at Zürich 1907–17, and remained there when appointed conductor of the St Gall symphony concerts that year. The university conferred an honorary doctorate on him in 1928. His music was successfully performed in Germany during the Nazi era.

Works OPERA *Venus* (after Mérimée, 1922), *Penthesilea* (after Kleist, 1927), *Massimilla Doni* (after Balzac, 1937), *Das Schloss Dürande* (after Eichendorff, 1943).

CHORAL *Der Postillon* (Lenau) for tenor solo, chorus, and orchestra (1909), *Trommelschläge* (Whitman's 'Drum Taps') for chorus and orchestra.

ORCHESTRAL Serenade for small orchestra, pastoral intermezzo *Sommernacht* (after Keller) for strings (1945), suite in A for strings, *Lebendig begraben* (Keller), song-cycle for baritone and orchestra, violin concerto, cello concerto (1947); horn concerto (1951).

CHAMBER AND VOCAL two violin and piano sonatas; song-cycle *Elegie* with chamber orchestra (1923), *Notturno* with string quartet (1933); song-cycles with piano *Wandsbecker Liederbuch* (Matthias Claudius), *Das stille Leuchten* (C F Meyer), and many others.

Schoenberg, Arnold Franz Walter (1874–1951), born **Arnold Franz Walter Schönberg**, Austro-Hungarian composer, a US citizen from 1941. After late Romantic early works such as *Verklärte Nacht/Transfigured Night* (1899) and the *Gurrelieder/Songs of Gurra* (1900–11), he was one of the first composers to use ➔ atonality (absence of key), producing works such as *Pierrot lunaire/Moonstruck Pierrot* (1912) for chamber ensemble and voice, before developing the ➔ twelve-tone system of musical composition.

After 1918, Schoenberg wrote several free-atonal works for chamber ensembles, using classical forms, as well as numerous works for solo piano. He taught at the Berlin State Academy in 1925–33. The twelve-tone system was further developed by his pupils Alban ➔ Berg and Anton ➔ Webern. Driven from Germany by the Nazis, Schoenberg settled in the USA in 1933, where he influenced a generation of US composers. His legacy is still visible internationally in art music, where numerous forms of non-tonal music have now become mainstream in composition. His large collection of essays, published as *Style and Idea*, is set reading at most music colleges worldwide. Later works include the opera *Moses und Aron* (1932–51).

Schöne Melusine, Die, **The Fair Melusina** concert overture by Mendelssohn, Op. 32, composed in 1833 after a performance in Berlin of Conradin Kreutzer's opera *Melusina*, with a libretto by Franz Grillparzer originally written for Beethoven.

Schöne Müllerin, Die, **The Fair Maid of the Mill** song cycle by Schubert (poems by Wilhelm Müller) composed in 1823.
The 17 songs are: 1. 'Das Wandern', 2. 'Wohin?', 3. 'Halt; Danksagung an den Bach', 4. 'Am Feierabend', 5. 'Der Neugierige', 6. 'Ungeduld', 7. 'Morgengrüss', 8. 'Des Müllers Blumen', 9. 'Tränenregen', 10. 'Pause'; 'Mit dem grünen Lautenbande', 11. 'Der Jäger', 12. 'Eifersucht und Stolz', 13. 'Die liebe Farbe', 14. 'Die böse Farbe', 15. 'Trockne Blumen', 16. 'Der Müller und der Bach', and 17. 'Des Baches Wiegenlied'.

Schönzeler, Hans-Hubert (1925–   ) German-born English conductor and musicologist. After study at the New South Wales Conservatorium, he conducted the 20th-Century Ensemble in London 1951–61. He led the Western Australia Symphony Orchestra at Perth from 1967.
An advocate of Bruckner, Schonzeler has written a book on the composer (1970) and recorded the Requiem. He gave the first performance of the original version of the 8th Symphony (1973, BBC) and performed many concerts with the regional BBC orchestras. He became a UK citizen in 1947.

School for Fathers, The opera by Ermanno ➔ **Wolf-Ferrari**; see *I ➔ quattro rusteghi*.

Schoolmaster, The nickname of Joseph Haydn's symphony no. 55 in E flat major, composed 1774.

Schöpfungsmesse, **Creation Mass** the nickname of Joseph Haydn's Mass in B flat major of 1801, where a theme from his famous cantata *The Creation* is used in the *Qui tollis* section.

Schottisch (German 'Scottish') ballroom dance fashionable in the 19th century, introduced to England 1848, not identical with the *Écossaise*. In England it is usually called by its plural, *Schottische*. The music is in 2/4 time, much like that of the polka, but played more slowly.

Schrade, Leo (1903–1964) German musicologist. He studied at several German universities and taught at Königsberg University 1929–32 and at Bonn University from 1932 to 1937, when he left Germany and settled in the USA. He taught at Yale University 1938–58, becoming professor in 1948. From 1958 he was professor at Basel University. His studies ranged widely over medieval, Renaissance and baroque music, and included a book on Monteverdi and editions of the works

of Philippe de Vitry, Machaut, Landini, and other 14th-century composers.

Schreker, Franz (1878–1934) Austrian composer, conductor, and teacher. He conducted the first performance of Schoenberg's *Gurrelieder* in 1913. His operas were late Romantic in expression and popular in the 1920s; first performances were conducted by Otto Klemperer (at Cologne) and Bruno Walter (at Munich).
He studied under Fuchs in Vienna, and founded the Philharmonic Choir there in 1911. He taught at the Imperial Academy of Music until his appointment as director of the Academy of Music in Berlin in 1920; he was forced by the Nazis to resign in 1933.
Works OPERA *Flammen* (1902), *Der ferne Klang* (1912), *Die Gezeichneten* (1918), *Der Schatzgräber* (1920), *Irrelohe* (1924), *Christophorus* (1924–29; produced 1978); pantomime *Der Geburtstag der Infantin* (after Wilde, 1908; reworked as *Spanisches Fest*, 1927).
ORCHESTRAL Chamber symphony for 23 solo instruments (1917; also in version for full orchestra, as Sinfonietta), *Kleine Suite* for small orchestra (1931).
VOCAL *Zwei lyrische Gesänge* for voice and orchestra to poems by Whitman (1929); 43 Lieder to texts by Heyse, Tolstoy, and Scherenberg (1895–1916).

Schroeter, Leonhard (c.1540–c.1595) German composer. He succeeded Gallus Dressler as cantor of Magdeburg Cathedral in 1564.
Works SACRED MUSIC German Te Deum for double choir (1584), *Hymni sacri* for four–five voices, *Weihnachts-Liedlein* for several voices. (1587).

Schröter, Johann Samuel (c.1752–1788) German pianist and composer. He settled in England, and succeeded J C Bach as music master to Queen Charlotte in 1782. He wrote chiefly keyboard music, including some of the earliest pieces written for the piano.
He was taught by his father, the oboist Johann Friedrich Schröter, and made his debut as a pianist in Leipzig in 1767. In 1772 he went on tour with his father and sister Corona Schröter to Holland and England, where he appeared at one of the Bach-Abel concerts.
It was his widow with whom Haydn had an autumnal affair during his first visit to London; Haydn made copies of her letters to him.
Works WORKS FOR KEYBOARD concertos, sonatas, and other pieces; piano quintets and trios.

Schubert, Franz Peter (1797–1828) Austrian composer. His ten symphonies include the incomplete eighth in B minor (the 'Unfinished') (1822) and the 'Great' in C major (1825). He wrote chamber and piano music, including the *Trout Quintet*, and over 600 lieder (songs) combining the Romantic expression of emotion with pure melody. They include the cycles *Die schöne Müllerin/The Beautiful Maid of the Mill* (1823) and *Die Winterreise/The Winter Journey* (1827).

Schubert was born in Vienna, the son of a schoolmaster. He began to learn the piano and violin at an early age and received lessons from Michael Holzer at the age of nine, also learning organ and counterpoint. He entered the choir school in the Imperial Chapel in 1808, played violin in the orchestra there, and sometimes conducted as deputy. At 13 he wrote a fantasy for piano duet and sketched other works, and in 1811 composed his first song. He played viola in the string quartet at home. His mother died in 1812 and his father married again in 1813. In the same year Schubert wrote his first symphony and left the choir school, continuing studies under Antonio Salieri. At 17 he became assistant teacher in his father's school, but disliked teaching; composed the G major Mass, the second and third symphonies and several dramatic pieces. In 1814 he allegedly sold his overcoat in order to buy a ticket for the revival of Beethoven's opera *Fidelio*. His own first opera, *Des Teufels Lustschloss*, was written in the same year. Like all his stage works, it was unsuccessful, but he also composed at this time his first great song, 'Gretchen am Spinnrade'. The following year he wrote almost 150 songs. In 1816 he left the school and joined his friend Schober in rooms, gathering a circle of literary and artistic, rather than musical, friends around him. In 1817 he met the singer Michael Vogl, who took a great interest in his songs and succeeded in getting his play with music *Die Zwillingsbrüder/The Twin Brothers* produced in June 1820.

By this time he had written some of his finest instrumental works, including the 4th and 5th symphonies, the sonatinas for violin and piano, and the *Trout Quintet*. His reputation grew beyond his own circle, but publishers failed to recognize him until his friends had 20 songs published at their own expense in 1821. (Most of his large-scale works were unpublished during his lifetime, however.) His mastery of various instrumental genres is demonstrated in the 'Unfinished' symphony and 'Wanderer' Fantasy for piano of 1822; the last three string quartets, in A minor, D minor ('Death and the Maiden'), and G, followed in 1824 and 1826. His 9th symphony of 1825 is one of the most carefully crafted and consistently inspired works of its kind ever written.

Schubert lived in Vienna all his life, except for some summer excursions and two visits to Hungary as domestic musician to the Esterházy family on their country estate at Zséliz, in 1818 and 1824. He never held an official appointment, but earned enough casually to lead a modest Bohemian existence. His output was phenomenal. He

died from typhoid, his condition having been weakened by syphilis.

Works OPERA AND SINGSPIELE (some incomplete) *Der Spiegelritter* (1811–12, first performed on Swiss radio in 1949), *Des Teufels Lustschloss* (1813–15, first performance Vienna, 1879), *Adrast* (1817–19, first performance Vienna, 1868), *Der vierjährige Posten* (1815, first performance Dresden, 1896), *Fernando* (1815, first performance Vienna, 1905), *Claudine von Villa Bella* (1815, first performance Vienna, 1913), *Die Freunde von Salamanka* (1815, first performance Halle, 1928), *Die Burgschaft* (1816, first performance Vienna, 1908), *Die Zwillingsbrüder* (1819, first performance Vienna, 1820), *Alfonso und Estrella* (1821–22, first performance Weimar, 1854), *Die Verschworenen* (1823, first performance Vienna, 1861), *Fierrabras* (1823, first performance Karlsruhe, 1897); also melodrama *Die Zauberharfe* (1820, first performance Vienna, 1820) and incidental music for *Rosamunde, Fürstin von Zypern* (1823, first performance Vienna, 1823).

CHORAL WITH ORCHESTRA church music including five Masses, in F, G, C, A♭, and E♭ (1814–28); *Deutsche Messe* (1827), oratorio *Lazarus* (unfinished, 1820), six settings of the *Salve regina* (1812–24).

WORKS FOR VOICE WITH AND WITHOUT ACCOMPANIMENT *Frühlingsgesang* (1822), *Gesang der Geister über den Wassern* (1817, second version with orchestra 1821), *Gondelfahrer* (1824), *Miriams Siegesgesang* (1828), and *Ständchen* (1827).

ORCHESTRAL nine symphonies: no. 1 in D (1813), no. 2 in B♭ (1815), no. 3 in D (1815), no. 4 in C minor (1816), no. 5 in B♭ (1816), no. 6 in C (1818), no. 7 in E (1821, sketches, unscored); no. 8 in B minor ('Unfinished', 1822), no. 9 in C ('Great', 1825); two overtures in the Italian style (1817, 1819); five German Dances (1813, also in scoring by Webern); Rondo in A for violin and orchestra (1816).

CHAMBER 15 string quartets: nos 1–7 (1812–14), no. 8 in B♭ (1814, D112), no. 9 in G minor (1815, D173), no. 10 in E♭ (1813, D87), no. 11 in E (1816, D353), no. 12 in C minor (*Quartettsatz*, 1820, D703), no. 13 in A minor (1824, D804), no. 14 in D minor (*Der Tod und das Mädchen/Death and the Maiden*, 1824, D810), no. 15 in G (1826, D887); Octet in F for string quartet, double bass, clarinet, bassoon, and horn (1824, D803); string quintet in C (1828, D956); piano quintet in A (*Die Forelle/The Trout*, 1819, D667); piano trios in B♭ (1827, D898) and E♭ (1827, D929) for piano and violin; sonata in A (1817, D574); three sonatinas in D, A minor, and G minor (1816, D384, D385 and D408); *Rondo brillant* in B minor (1826, D895); Fantasia in C (based on song 'Sei mir gegrüsst', 1827, D934).

WORKS FOR PIANO *Divertissement à la hongroise* (D818), Fantasia in F minor (D940), sonata in B♭

(D617) and sonata in C, Grand Duo (D813), all for four hands; 21 piano sonatas: nos 1–12 (1815–19), some unfinished, no. 13 in A (D664), no. 14 in A minor (D784), no. 15 in C (D840), no. 16 in A minor (D845), no. 17 in D (D850), no. 18 in G (D894), no. 19 in C minor (D958), no. 20 in A (D959), no. 21 in B♭ (D960); Fantasia in C, based on the song 'Der Wanderer' (D760); eight impromptus in two sets: in C minor, E♭, G♭, and A♭ (D899), in F minor, A♭, B♭, F minor (D935); three Klavierstücke, in E♭ minor, E♭, and C (D946); six *Moments Musicaux*, in C, A♭, F minor, C♯ minor, F minor, and A♭ (1823–28, D780); two sets of waltzes, D145 and D365.

SONGS three cycles, *Die schöne Müllerin* (1823), *Die Winterreise* (1827), and *Schwanengesang* (1828). Some of the best known of more than 600 Lieder are 'Abendstern' (Mayrhofer, 1824), 'Die Allmacht' (Pyrker, 1825), 'Am Bach im Frühling' (Schober, 1816), 'An den Mond' (Goethe, 1815), 'An die Entfernte' (Goethe, 1822), 'An die Musik' (Schober, 1817), 'An Schwager Kronos' (Goethe, 1816), 'An Sylvia' (Shakespeare, 1826), 'Auf dem Wasser zu singen' (Stolberg, 1823), 'Auf der Donau' (Mayrhofer, 1817), 'Auflösung' (Mayrhofer, 1824), 'Ave Maria' (Scott, translated by Storck, 1825), 'Bei dir allein' (Seidl, 1826), 'Delphine' (Schütz, 1825), 'Du bist die Ruh' (Rückert, 1823), 'Der Einsame' (Lappe, 1825), 'Erlkönig' (Goethe, 1815), 'Der Fischer' (Goethe, 1815), 'Fischerweise' (Schlechta, 1826), 'Die Forelle' (Schubart, 1817), 'Frühlingsglaube' (Uhland, 1820), 'Ganymed' (Goethe, 1817), 'Die Götter Griechenlands' (Schiller, 1819), 'Gretchen am Spinnrade' (Goethe, 1814), 'Gruppe aus dem Tartarus' (1817), '3 Harfenspieler Lieder' (Goethe, 1816), 'Heidenröslein' (Goethe, 1815), 'Der Hirt auf dem Felsen' with clarinet obbligato (Müller, 1828), 'Horch, horch die Lerch' (Shakespeare, 1826), 'Im Frühling' (Schulze, 1826), 'Die junge Nonne' (Craigher, 1825), 'Lachen und Weinen' (Rückert, 1823), 'Liebhaber in aller Gestalten' (Goethe, 1817), 'Der Musensohn' (Goethe, 1822), 'Nacht und Träume' (Collin, 1822), 'Nur wer die Sehnsucht kennt' (Goethe, five versions), 'Prometheus' (Goethe, 1819), 'Sei mir gegrüsst' (Rückert, 1822), 'Die Sterne' (Leitner, 1828), 'Der Tod und das Mädchen' (Claudius, 1817), 'Dem Unendlichen' (Klopstock, 1815), 'Der Wanderer' (Lübeck, 1816), 'Wanderers Nachtlied' (Goethe, 1822), 'Der Zwerg' (Collin, 1822).

Schuch, Willi (1900–1986) Swiss musicologist. He studied under Courvoisier and Sandberger at Munich and Ernst Kurth at Bern, where he took a doctor's degree in 1927. He became a critic at Zurich, and from 1930 to 1944 he taught at the Zurich Conservatory. His works include studies of Schütz, Swiss folk and early music, and Schoeck. In 1976 he published the first volume

in the authorized biography of Richard Strauss.

Schuhplattler Bavarian country dance with music in moderate 3/4 time similar to that of the *Ländler* (folk dance in three time). The dancers are men only and they strike their palms on their knees and soles.

Schulhoff, Erwin (1894–1942) Czech pianist and composer. Recent performances of his opera *Flammen/Flames* (1928) suggest a powerful assimilation of a wide range of contemporary influences, including jazz and microtonality (using divisions of the octave smaller than a semitone).

He studied at the conservatories of Prague, Vienna, Leipzig, and Cologne. As a communist in Nazi-ruled Czechoslovakia, he sought refuge in Soviet citizenship, but after the 1941 invasion of Russia he was arrested, and died in a concentration camp.

Works OPERA AND STAGE the opera *Flames*; ballets *Ogelala* and *Moonstruck*; incidental music to Molière's *Bourgeois gentilhomme*.

ORCHESTRAL AND CHAMBER two symphonies; piano concerto; chamber music; piano works.

Schuloper (German 'school opera') German work of the 20th century with a didactic (instructional) purpose. It is the same as a ➔ **Lehrstück** (a type of educational music drama) but is invariably intended for the stage.

Schulz, Johann Abraham Peter (1747–1800) German composer, conductor, and musicologist. He travelled widely in Europe and held musical posts in Poland, Berlin, and Copenhagen. He also wrote a number of theoretical works, including a treatise on harmony, on which he collaborated with his teacher, Johann Kirnberger.

He travelled in Austria, Italy, and France in 1768, and after holding a post in Poland returned in 1773 to Berlin, where he collaborated with Kirnberger and contributed to Johann Georg Sulzer's (1720–79) encyclopaedia *Allgemeine Theorie der schönen Künste* (1771–74). He was conductor at the French theatre in Berlin 1776–78, was court composer to Prince Heinrich of Prussia at Rheinsberg 1780–87, then worked at the Danish court in Copenhagen until his return to Germany in 1795.

Works OPERA AND STAGE (in French) *Clarisse, La Fée Urgèle* (after Voltaire, 1782), *Le barbier de Séville* (after Beaumarchais, 1786), and *Aline, reine de Golconde* (1787); (in Danish) *The Harvest Home* (1790), *The Entry* (1793), and *Peter's Wedding*; German melodrama *Minona*; incidental music for Racine's *Athalie* and other plays.

SACRED AND SECULAR MUSIC *Christi Tod, Maria und Johannes*, and other sacred works; chamber music, *Lieder im Volkston* and many other songs.

Schulz-Beuthen, Heinrich (1838–1915) German composer. He studied at the Leipzig Conservatory, taught at Zurich 1866–80, at Dresden 1880–93, in Vienna 1893–95, and at the Dresden Conservatory from 1895.

Works OPERA *Aschenbrödel* (text by Mathilde Wesendonk, 1879), *Die Verschollene*, and three others.

ORCHESTRAL AND STAGE Christmas play *Die Blume Wunderhold*; eight symphonies (no. 6 on Shakespeare's *King Lear*); symphonic poems on Schiller's *Wilhelm Tell*, on Böcklin's picture 'The Isle of the Dead', on Grillparzer's *Des Meeres und der Liebe Wellen*, and others; two suites; two scenes from Goethe's *Faust*, serenade and other works for orchestra; piano concerto; wind octet, string quintet and trio.

PIANO AND SONGS two sonatas and pieces for piano; numerous songs.

CHORAL Requiem, six Psalms and other choral works.

Schuman, William Howard (1910–1992) US composer and teacher. His music is melodic, if sometimes tempered by ➔ **polytonality**, and often emphasizes ➔ **motoric rhythm** or other intense rhythms, as in *American Festival Overture* (1939). His large-scale conception suits the orchestral medium, for which he has written nine symphonies. He has also written chamber and vocal works.

He studied at Columbia University, USA, and at the Mozarteum, Salzburg, Austria. In 1936 he was appointed teacher at the Columbia University summer school and in 1938 at the Sarah Lawrence College in New York. Later he studied with Roy Harris, and had his first major success when his 3rd symphony was premiered under Stokowski in 1941. In 1945 he succeeded Carl Engel as director of music publications in the music publisher Schirmer in New York and Ernest Hutcheson as president of the Juilliard School of Music, New York. He was director of the Lincoln Center, New York, 1961–69.

Works STAGE baseball opera *The Mighty Casey* (1953); ballets *Choreographic Poem, Undertone, Night Journey*; incidental music for Shakespeare's *Henry VIII*; film music for *Steeltown*; *Judith* (choreographic poem).

CHORAL two secular cantatas for chorus and orchestra; four *Canonic Choruses, Pioneers, Requiescat* (without words), and other pieces for unaccompanied chorus.

ORCHESTRAL ten symphonies (1936–76), overtures *American Festival* and *William Billings*; *Prayer in Time of War* (1943) and *Side-Show* for orchestra; symphony for string orchestra (1943).

OTHER *Newsreel* for military band; piano concerto, violin concerto (1947); four string quartets (1936–50), canon and fugue for piano trio; quartettino for four bassoons; *Three-Score Set* for piano.

Schumann, Clara Josephine (1819–1896), born **Clara Wieck** German pianist and composer. She wrote a *Concerto in A Minor* for piano and orchestra 1835–36, a *Piano Trio* about 1846, and romances for piano. She married Robert ➔ Schumann in 1840 (her father had been his piano teacher). During his life and after his death she was devoted to popularizing his work, appearing frequently in European concert halls.

She was taught by her father, Friedrich Wieck, and made her first public appearance at the age of nine. She gave her own first concert at the Leipzig Gewandhaus on 8 November 1830. In 1837 she was in Vienna for some time. Her engagement to Schumann was violently opposed by her father, but they married after many difficulties on 12 September 1840. She appeared in public less frequently during her married life, but after Schumann's death in 1856 she was obliged to do so continuously and to teach. She went to live in Berlin with her mother, who had married the composer Woldemar Bargiel (1828–1897), but in 1863 she settled at Baden-Baden and in 1878 became chief piano professor at the Hoch Conservatory at Frankfurt.

Works WORKS FOR PIANO piano concerto in A minor; piano trio in G minor; variations on a theme by Robert Schumann and about twelve other Op. nos for piano.

OTHER several sets of songs.

Schumann, Robert Alexander (1810–1856) German composer and writer. His songs and short piano pieces portray states of emotion with great economy. Among his compositions are four symphonies, a violin concerto, a piano concerto, sonatas, and song cycles, such as *Dichterliebe/ Poet's Love* (1840). Mendelssohn championed many of his works.

Schumann was born at Zwickau, Saxony, Germany, the son of a bookseller and publisher. He began to learn the piano from a schoolmaster and organist at the age of 8 and played well by the time he was 11. He studied all the music found at his father's shop, where he also developed a literary taste. He played at school concerts and private houses, and made such progress in improvisation and composition that in 1825 Weber was approached to teach him, but could not, being busy preparing *Oberon* for London and expecting to go there. Schumann's father died in 1826, and in 1828 he was sent to Leipzig University to study law. There he met Friedrich Wieck, from whom he took piano lessons, and first met his daughter Clara. He neglected his legal studies, as he did again when, in 1829, he moved to Heidelberg University. There he came under the influence of Anton Friedrich Justus

Thibaut (1772–1840), a legal scholar and amateur musician who, with his book *Über Reinheit der Tonkunst* (1825), made a major contribution to aesthetics and to Cecilian reforms later in the century. Back at Leipzig in 1830, Schumann lodged at Wieck's house, wrote his first published works (Op. 1 and 7), and the next year went to the St Thomas cantor, Christian Weinlig, for instruction, but left him for the younger Heinrich Dorn. In 1832 he permanently injured his hand with a mechanical contrivance he had invented for finger-development and thus had to give up a pianist's career for that of a composer.

With a circle of young intellectuals (calling themselves the 'Davidsbündler') he founded the *Neue Zeitschrift für Musik* in 1834. Apart from the *Allgemeine Musikalische Zeitung* (Leipzig, 1798/9–1848), this was the most comprehensive and innovative musical journal, championing the improvement of music in Germany and promoting Romantic creativeness. He fell in love with Ernestine von Fricken in 1834, but the engagement was broken off in the following year, during which he wrote his first great keyboard work, *Carnaval*. In 1836 Wieck's daughter Clara, already a remarkable pianist, was 17 and she and Schumann fell in love. Some of his feelings were expressed in the C major Fantasy for piano, which also quotes from Beethoven's *An die ferne Geliebte/To the Distant Beloved*. Clara's father violently opposed the match and in 1839 they took legal proceedings against him; he failed to yield, but they married on 12 September 1840, the day before she came of age.

Now followed the most prolific period of Schumann's creative life: the 'Spring' symphony of 1841 seems to symbolize artistic as well as natural growth and the same fervent, vital impulse informs the song cycles *Dichterliebe* and *Liederkreis* (Op. 24, Op. 39), the string quartets Op. 41, and the Piano Quintet, all of this same period. The first, rhapsodic movement of the Piano Concerto also dates from this time (1841–42); the last two movements were added in 1845. In 1843 Schumann suffered a crisis of mental exhaustion and he had a more serious breakdown after a tour in Russia with Clara in 1844, at the end of which year they settled at Dresden. Although his nervous complaint grew more marked after periods of recovery, in 1850 he accepted the conductorship at Düsseldorf, including subscription concerts, choral practices, and church music, a post for which he proved quite unfit.

In spite of his personal problems Schumann completed in 1850 the most exuberant and accomplished of all his orchestral works, the 3rd symphony in E♭, which celebrates the Rhineland, the flowing of the Rhine itself, and Cologne cathedral. The committee at Düsseldorf tactfully suggested his resignation in 1852, but with Clara's injudicious support he obstinately refused to withdraw. Signs of a mental collapse grew more and more alarming and his creative work progressively less convincing, and in February 1854 he threw himself into the Rhine. On being rescued he was sent at his own request to a private asylum at Endenich, where he died more than two years later.

Schumann's works of all genres tend towards the lyrical qualities found most obviously in his songs; although the spontaneity and melodic naturalness of his piano music and Lieder have rightly been praised, his chamber and orchestral music shows similar qualities, although on a larger scale. One of his most attractive features is the essentially private nature of his genius. The quintessential Romantic, his personal experiences, and in particular his love for Clara, found expression in his music. His inward-looking personality is reflected in the musical cryptograms of many of his works.

Works STAGE opera *Genoveva* (1850); incidental music to Byron's 'Manfred' (1852); 15 works for chorus and orchestra with or without solo voices, including *Requiem für Mignon* and scenes from Goethe's *Faust* (1844–53).

ORCHESTRAL four symphonies (1841, 1846, 1850, 1841 revised 1851); *Overture, Scherzo and Finale*; concertos for piano, violin, and cello (1841–45, 1853, 1850); *Concertstück* for four horns and orchestra (1849).

CHAMBER three string quartets, Op. 41 nos 1–3 (1842), three piano trios, piano quartet (1842), piano quartet, *Fantasiestücke* and *Märchenerzählungen* for piano trio (the latter with clarinet and viola).

PIANO 36 Op. nos of piano music including *Papillons* (1831), *Davidsbündlertänze* (1837), *Carnaval* (1835), three sonatas, *Etudes symphoniques* (1837), *Kinderscenen* (1838), *Kreisleriana* (1838), *Humoreske, Nachtstücke, Faschingsschwank aus Wien* (1840), *Waldscenen*.

SONGS 35 Op. nos of songs (some containing numerous pieces), including the cycles *Frauenliebe und -leben* (1840) and *Dichterliebe* (1840), also *Liederkreis* (Heine and Eichendorff, 1840) and *Myrthen*; 14 Op. nos of part songs.

Schuricht, Carl (1880–1967) German conductor. He studied with Humperdinck and Reger. He conducted many early performances of Debussy, Schoenberg, and Stravinsky. From 1944 he was guest conductor with leading orchestras and in London was heard in the standard repertory with the London Symphony Orchestra. He toured the USA with the Vienna Philharmonic Orchestra in 1956 and, in 1957, appeared with the Chicago Symphony Orchestra and the Boston Symphony Orchestra.

Schurmann, Gerard (1928–) British composer. Born in Dutch Indonesia, he went to England in 1941 and studied at the Royal College of Music in London; but he was largely self-taught.

Works ENSEMBLE AND CHAMBER wind quintet (1963, revised 1976), two string quartets, flute sonatina (1968), piano quartet (first performance Cheltenham, 1986), *Contrasts* for piano (1973).

ORCHESTRAL *Variants* for orchestra (1970), *Six Studies of Francis Bacon* for orchestra (1968), piano concerto (1973), violin concerto (1978).

CHORAL WITH ORCHESTRA *The Double Heart*, cantata (1976); *Piers Plowman* for soloists, chorus, and orchestra (1980).

Schusterfleck (German 'cobbler's patch') in music, a playful German description of a technical device, especially the ➤ **rosalia**, used as an easy subterfuge in composition. Beethoven called Diabelli's waltz, on which he wrote the variations Op. 120, a Schusterfleck.

Schütz, Heinrich (1585–1672) German early baroque composer. He was musical director to the Elector of Saxony from 1614. His works include *The Seven Words of Christ* (about 1660), *Musicalische Exequien* (1636), and the *Deutsche Magnificat/German Magnificat* (1671). He increased the range and scope of instrumental and choral ➤ **polyphony** and was an important precursor of Johann Sebastian Bach.

Schütz was born at Köstritz in Saxony. He learnt music as a choirboy in the chapel of the Landgrave of Hesse-Kassel, and studied law at Marburg University and music under Giovanni Gabrieli at Venice, 1609–12. He returned to Kassel as court organist, but left for Dresden in 1614 with an appointment as music director to the Elector Johann Georg of Saxony. He did much there to establish the fashion for Italian music and musicians, but although he had written Italian madrigals at Venice, he set his own works to German or Latin words, notably the 26 *Psalmen Davids* of 1619. In 1627 he wrote the first German opera, *Dafne*, on a translation of Rinuccini's libretto by Martin Opitz, for the marriage of the elector's daughter to the Landgrave of Hesse-Darmstadt.

After the death of his wife in 1628 he again went to Italy in 1629, where he learnt about the newly established form of opera from Monteverdi. In 1633, the economic depression that followed the Thirty Years' War having disrupted the running of the Dresden court chapel, he obtained leave to go to Copenhagen, and he spent the years until 1641 there and at other courts. Returning to Dresden, he did not succeed in reorganizing the court music satisfactorily until the later 1640s. In the 1650s he became much dissatisfied with the new tendencies among the Italian court musicians and had many quarrels with Giovanni Bon-

tempi, but did not succeed in obtaining his release, and after some improvements later on he remained at the Saxon court for the rest of his life. Schütz was the most important of Bach's German predecessors, uniting the lyric and dramatic elements of Venetian vocal style with German polyphony.

Works OPERA *Dafne* (1627, lost), *Orpheus und Euridice* (1638, lost).

SACRED AND SECULAR MUSIC motets, *Cantiones sacrae*, psalms, *Symphoniae Sacrae* (1629, 1647, 1650), concertos for voices and instruments, *Geistliche Concerte* (1636, 1639); Christmas (1664), Passion, and Resurrection oratorios; *The Seven Words of Christ*; Italian madrigals; *Exequien* (funeral pieces) for six–eight voices, Elegy on the death of the electress of Saxony.

Schuyt, Cornelis (1557–1616) Flemish composer. He held a succession of organ appointments in the Netherlands. He published several books of madrigals and a book of instrumental pieces.

He travelled to Italy to study music, returning to the Netherlands in 1581.

Schwanda the Bagpiper opera by Jaromír Weinberger; see ➤ **Švanda Dudák**.

Schwanenberg or **Schwanenberger, Johann Gottfried (1740–1804)** German composer. After studying with Johann Hasse, he was appointed court conductor at Brunswick in 1762.

Works OPERA *Romeo e Giulia* (after Shakespeare, 1776), *Adriano in Siria* (1762), *Solimano* (1762), *Zenobia*, and about ten others.

OTHER symphonies; piano concertos; piano sonatas.

Schwanendreher, Der, *The Swan-Turner* concerto after German folk songs for viola and small orchestra by Hindemith, composed in 1935 and first performed in Amsterdam on 14 November 1935, conducted by Mengelberg. The title alludes to the cooking of swans by turning them on a spit.

Schwanengesang, *Swan Song* song cycle by Schubert, containing the last songs written by the composer in 1828, including seven settings of Rellstab, six of Heine (his only settings of that poet), and Seidl's 'Pigeon Post/Die Taubenpost'. The idea of a cycle was not Schubert's, but that of the publisher, as was the title, which was invented as an allusion to Schubert's death; the inclusion of Seidl's song was also the publisher's afterthought. The songs are 'Liebesbotschaft', 'Kriegers Ahnung', 'Frühlingssehnsucht', 'Ständchen', 'Aufenthalt', 'In der Ferne', 'Abschied', 'Der Atlas','Ihr Bild','Das Fischermädchen','Die Stadt', 'Am Meer','Der Doppelgänger', and 'Die Taubenpost'.

Schwarz, Boris (1906–1983) US musicologist, violinist, and conductor. He studied with Flesch and Thibaud in Berlin and Paris; after a 1920 debut he performed widely in Europe, settling in the USA in 1936. He held various academic posts in New York from 1941 and made a special study of Soviet music.

Schwarz, Rudolf (1905–1994) Austrian-born English conductor. He survived a concentration camp in World War II and went to Sweden in 1945 and then England, where he became conductor of the Bournemouth Symphony Orchestra 1947–51, the City of Birmingham Symphony Orchestra 1951–57, the BBC Symphony Orchestra 1957–62, and the Northern Sinfonia Orchestra 1964–73.

He studied piano and violin, playing viola in the Vienna Philharmonic Orchestra. In 1923 he became an assistant conductor at the Düsseldorf Opera and from 1927 to 1933 conductor at the Karlsruhe Opera, after which he became music director of the Jewish Cultural Union in Berlin until 1941, when he was sent to Belsen concentration camp.

Schwarze Maske, Die, The Black Mask opera by Penderecki (libretto by composer after Gerhart Hauptmann), produced at Salzburg, Austria, on 15 August 1986. The story concerns the hysterical Benigna, who suspects that a party-crasher is her former seducer Johnson, an escaped African-American slave.

Schweigsame Frau, Die, The Silent Woman opera by Richard Strauss (libretto by Stefan Zweig, based on Ben Jonson's *Epicoene*), produced in Dresden on 24 June 1935. The story begins as Henry returns home to his uncle, Sir Morosus, who hates music and noise. Henry hopes to receive an inheritance, but is instead disowned because he has joined a band of singers. He gets revenge, tricking Morosus into marriage with 'Timida', the noisy Aminta in disguise.

Schwertsik, Kurt (1935–) Austrian composer. With Friedrich Cerha he founded the ensemble *Die Reihe* in 1958, for the performance of new music. He has reacted against the contemporary avant garde.

He studied at the Vienna Academy 1949–57. In 1978 he began teaching at the Vienna Conservatory.

Works OPERA AND STAGE operas *Der lange Weg zur Grossen Mauer* (1975) and *Das Märchen von Fanferlieschen Schönefusschen* (1982); ballets *Walzerträume* (1976) and *Macbeth* (1988).

ORCHESTRAL AND VOCAL *Draculas Haus und Hofmusik* for strings (1968); *Symphonie in MoB-Stil* (1971; association with H K Gruber); violin concerto (1977); *Starker Tobak* for soprano and seven instruments (1983); *Verwandlungsmusik* for or-

chestra (1983); concerto for trombone (1988); Double bass concerto (1989).

Schwindl, Friedrich (1737–1786) Dutch or German violinist, flautist, harpsichordist, and composer. He wrote over 30 symphonies, and belonged to the Mannheim School.

He was at The Hague when Charles Burney stayed there in 1770, later at Geneva and Mulhouse, and finally at Karlsruhe as music director to the Margrave of Baden.

Works OPERA *Das Liebesgrab* and *Die drei Pächter.*

OTHER Mass in E♭; over 30 symphonies; quartets, trios.

Sciarrino, Salvatore (1947–) Italian composer. He is best known for his operas, which take an irreverent view of the conventions of the genre, filtering familiar myths through a surreal sensibility.

He studied electronic music at Rome in 1969 and began teaching at the Milan Conservatory in 1974.

Works OPERA *Amore e Psyche* (1973), *Aspern* (1978), *Vanitas* (1981), *Lohengrin 'azione invisible'* (1983), *Perseo e Andromeda* (1991).

ORCHESTRAL *Sonata da camera* for orchestra (1971), variations for cello and orchestra (1974), *Clair de Lune* for piano and orchestra (1975), *Kindertotenlied* for soprano, tenor, and chamber orchestra (1978), two string quintets (1976, 1977), violin concerto (1985), two piano trios (1975, 1986).

Scimone, Claudio (1934–) Italian conductor and musicologist. After study with Franco Ferrara, he founded the ensemble I Solisti Veneti. He has toured throughout Europe and the USA performing 18th-century repertory and modern Italian works and has made many recordings.

Scimone was a teacher of the Verona Conservatory 1967–74, and director at Padua from 1983. He has issued an edition of Rossini's works and recorded the opera *Zelmira* (1990). Other recordings include Vivaldi's *Orlando Furioso* and *La Cetra* by Marcello. He conducted *Il barbiere di Seviglia* at Caracalla in 1992.

Scipione, Scipio opera by Handel (libretto by Paolo Rolli, based on Zeno's *Scipione nelle Spagne*), produced at the King's Theatre, Haymarket, London, on 12 March 1726. In the story, Roman pro-consul Scipio successfully besieges New Carthage and falls in love with Berenice, a Spanish captive. But she loves Luceius, who is captured trying to rescue her. Scipio releases the couple after being impressed by the depth of Berenice's love.

Scipione Affricano opera by Cavalli (libretto by Minato), produced at the Teatro San Giovanni e

The Scotch snap in the upper voice of a passage from Handel's Alcina.

Paolo, Venice, on 9 February 1664. The plot is similar to ➜ *Scipio*, with the addition of a sub-plot involving the efforts of King Syphax to rescue his abducted wife, Sophonisba.

scordatura (Italian 'mistuning') in music, tuning of the violin or other string instruments temporarily to other intervals than the normal tuning, for the purpose of facilitating the playing of chords with certain intervals or altering the instrument's tone-quality. The music is still written as for the normal tuning (and fingering), so that the instrument becomes to that extent a transposing instrument (see ➜ **transposition**).

There are many examples of scordatura in the violin works of Biber; also a famous passage for solo violin in Mahler's Fourth symphony.

score complete copy of a piece of music in manuscript or printed form. A **full score** shows all the lines of music for each instrument playing in a composition. The music is arranged on the page according to the four sections of the orchestra: woodwind, brass, percussion, and strings. It is usually printed on large paper for easy reading, such as for a conductor's score. A **short score** is a reduced or condensed version of a piece of music, such as a full score, into a few staves of music (usually two). It also refers to a composer's 'sketch', which contains the outlines of the instrumentation he will expand later. A **piano score** is a reduction of an orchestral or vocal score to two staves of music to be played on the piano. A **miniature** or **study score** is a full score reduced to notebook size.

scoring see ➜ orchestration.

Scotch snap or **Scots catch** in music, the technical name for rhythmic figures inverting the order of dotted notes, the short note coming first instead of last. Its name in England is due to the fact that the Scotch snap is a feature in the Scottish strathspey (folk dance). It was popular in Italy in the 17th and 18th centuries and was called by German writers the 'Lombardy rhythm'.

Scott, Cyril (Meir) (1879–1970) English composer and poet. During the Edwardian era he was known as 'the English Debussy' on account of his harmonic lushness. In 1913, Alma Mahler, the composer's widow, invited him to Vienna,

where he gave some performances. During World War I some of his works were produced in England and in 1925 the opera *The Alchemist* was performed, in German, at Essen.

He played the piano and began to compose as a child. He studied under Humperdinck and Knorr at the Hoch Conservatory, Frankfurt, 1892–93 and 1895–98. In 1898 he settled at Liverpool as a pianist and gave some lessons, and soon after the turn of the century he began to become known as a composer in London, having some works performed and a number of songs and piano pieces published.

Later he wrote prose prolifically on subjects connected with yoga and philosophy. He wrote two autobiographies, *My Years of Indiscretion* (1924), and *Bone of Contention* (1969).

Works OPERA AND STAGE opera *The Alchemist* (1917); ballet *The Incompetent Apothecary* (1923).

ORCHESTRAL AND CHORAL *La Belle Dame sans merci* (Keats), *Nativity Hymn* (Milton), *Let us now praise famous men* for chorus and orchestra (1935); two symphonies, piano concerto, violin concerto.

OTHER three string quartets; piano music, songs.

Scott, Marion M(argaret) (1877–1953) English musicologist. She studied at the Royal College of Music in London, 1896–1904, with which she afterwards remained associated as secretary of the Royal College of Music Union and editor of the *Royal College of Music Magazine*. She wrote criticism for various periodicals and many articles, notably on Haydn, in whose work she specialized. She also contributed a volume on Beethoven to the Master Musicians Series (1934).

Scott, Walter (1771–1832) Scottish poet and novelist. Celtic romance, a popular subject in the 19th century, was celebrated by Scott in his narrative poems, which were successful in translation throughout Europe. Turning later to the novel, often based on English history, he met with similar success. On a visit to Paris in 1826 Scott attended a pastiche of his *Ivanhoe* (1820) with music by Rossini; more faithful versions of the story were composed by Marschner (*Der Templer und die Jüdin*, 1829) and Sullivan (1891). The first major Italian setting of Scott was Rossini's *La donna del lago* (1819) based on the poem of 1810, *The Lady of the Lake*. This was followed by Donizetti's *Elisabetta al castelio di Kenilworth* (1829) and the most successful setting of Scott, *Lucia di Lammermoor* (1835) based on *The Bride of Lammermoor* (1819). Notable French music derived from Scott includes the *Waverley* and *Rob Roy* overtures of Berlioz (1828, 1832) and Bizet's unjustly neglected opera *La Jolie fille de Perth* (1867), after Scott's *The Fair Maid of Perth*, 1828.

settings
The Bride of Lammermoor: **Adam** (*Le Caleb de Walter Scott*, 1827), **Carafa** (*Le nozze di Lammermoor*, 1829), **Donizetti** (*Lucia di Lammermoor*, 1835).

The Fair Maid of Perth: **Bizet** (*La Jolie Fille de Perth*, 1867).

The Heart of Midlothian: **Bishop** (1819), **Carafa** (*La Prison d'Edimbourg*, 1833), **F. Ricci** (*La prigione d'Edimburgo*, 1838).

Ivanhoe: **Marschner** (*Der Templer und die Jüdin*, 1829), **Nicolai** (*Il Templario*, 1840), **Pacini** (1832), **Sullivan** (1891).

Kenilworth: **Auber** (*Leicester*, 1823), **Donizetti** (*Elizabetta al castello di Kenilworth*, 1829).

The Lady of the Lake: **Bishop** (*The Knight of Snowdoun*, 1811), **Rossini** (*La donna del lago*, 1819).

Rob Roy: **Flotow** (1836).

The Italian: **Adam** (*Richard en Palestine*, 1844), **Balfe** (1874), **Bishop** (1826), **Pacini** (*Il Talismano*, *La terza crociata in Palestina*, 1829).

Also: overtures by **Berlioz**, *Rob Roy* (1832) and *Waverley* (1828), and eight songs by **Schubert** in German translation.

Scottish Fantasy work for violin and orchestra in four movements by Max ➤ **Bruch**, based on Scottish folk songs. It was composed 1879–80 and dedicated to Pablo Sarasate, who gave the first performance in Hamburg in 1880.

Scottish Symphony symphony by Felix ➤ **Mendelssohn**, no. 3 in A minor and major, Op. 56, begun in Italy in 1831 and finished in Berlin on 20 January 1842. It was first performed at the Gewandhaus, Leipzig, on 3 March 1842.

Scriabin see ➤ Skriabin.

Scribe, Eugène (1791–1861) French playwright and librettist. He supplied many of the libretti for the most successful French operas of the 19th century, in particular the Parisian grand operas of Meyerbeer.

Associated works and composers include ➤ *Adriana Lecouvreur* (Cilea); ➤ *Africaine, L'* (Meyerbeer); ➤ *Ali Baba, ou Les Quarante Voleurs* (Cherubini); ➤ *Ballo in maschera, Un* (Verdi); ➤ *Chalet, Le* (Adam); ➤ *Cheval de bronze, Le* (Auber); ➤ *Comte Ory, Le* (Rossini); ➤ *Dame blanche, La* (Boieldieu); ➤ *Diamants de la Couronne, Les* (Auber); ➤ *Domino*

noir (Auber); ➤ *Dom Sébastien, Roi de Portugal* (Donizetti); ➤ *Elisir d'amore, L'* (ditto); ➤ *Etoile du Nord, L'* (Meyerbeer); ➤ *Favorite, La* (Donizetti); ➤ *Fra Diavolo, ou L'Hôtellerie de Terracine* (Auber); ➤ *Gustave III, ou Le Bal masqué* (ditto); ➤ *Huguenots, Les* (Meyerbeer); ➤ *Juive, La* (Halévy); ➤ *Leicester, ou Le Château de Kenilworth* (Auber); ➤ *Lortzing* (*Yelva*); ➤ *Maçon, Le* (Auber); ➤ *Manon Lescaut* (Auber); ➤ *Martyrs, Les* (Donizetti); ➤ *Muette de Portici, La* (Auber); ➤ *Philtre, Le* (Auber); ➤ *Prophète, Le* (Meyerbeer); ➤ *Robert le Diable* (Meyerbeer); A Schmitt (*Trilby*); Giacomo Setaccioli (*Adrienne Lecouvreur*); ➤ **Shebalin** (*Glass of Water*); ➤ *Vêpres siciliennes, Les* (Verdi).

scroll in music, the decorative, curved part of an instrument of the violin family, situated at the end of the fingerboard, away from the body of the instrument.

Sculthorpe, Peter (1929–) Australian composer. He studied at Melbourne University Conservatory and at Oxford University. In 1963 he became a lecturer at Sydney University.

Works OPERA AND STAGE opera *Rites of Passage* (1971–73), theatre music *Tatea* (1988).

ORCHESTRAL AND ENSEMBLE *Sun Music I* for orchestra; *Irkanda IV* for strings and percussion; *Sun Music II* for chorus and percussion (1969); *Mangrove* for orchestra (1979); piano concerto (1983).

CHAMBER two sonatas for strings (1983, 1988); twelve string quartets (1947–88), string trio, piano trio; sonata for viola and percussion; piano sonatina.

Scylla et Glaucus opera by Jean-Marie ➤ **Leclair** (libretto by d'Albaret), produced at the Paris Opéra on 4 October 1746. The plot describes Glaucus in pursuit of the nymph Scylla. Glaucus asks Circe for help but the jealous sorceress turns Scylla into the rock which accompanies the whirlpool Charybdis.

Sea Drift setting of a poem by Walt Whitman for baritone solo, chorus, and orchestra by Frederick Delius, composed in 1903. It was performed in German at the Essen Music Festival on 24 May 1906, and in English at the Sheffield Festival on 7 October 1908.

Sea Interludes concert work by Benjamin Britten; see ➤ *Four Sea Interludes*.

Seal Woman, The opera by Granville Ransome Bantock (libretto by Marjorie Kennedy Fraser), produced at the Repertory Theatre, Birmingham, England, on 27 September 1924. A Celtic folk opera, it contains many traditional Hebridean tunes.

Sea Pictures song cycle for contralto and orchestra by Elgar, Op. 37. It was first performed at the Norwich Festival, England, on 5 October 1899, with Clara Butt. The song cycle includes: 1. 'Sea Slumber Song' (Roden Noel); 2. 'In Haven' (Alice Elgar); 3. 'Sabbath Morning at Sea' (Elizabeth Barrett Browning); 4. 'Where Corals lie' (Richard Garnett); 5. 'The Swimmer' (A L Gordon).

Searle, Humphrey (1915–1982) English composer and writer on music. After studying with the serialist composer Anton Webern, he later employed 12-note methods extensively in his own music. He was a professor at the Royal College of Music 1965–77.

He was educated at Winchester College and Oxford University, and studied music with John Ireland at the Royal College of Music in London and in Vienna under Webern. In 1938 he joined the BBC, then served in the army 1940–46, and in 1947 became honorary secretary to the International Society for Contemporary Music.

Works OPERA AND STAGE operas *The Diary of a Madman* (after Gogol, 1958), *The Photo of the Colonel* (after Ionesco, 1964), *Hamlet* (Shakespeare, 1968); ballets *The Great Peacock*, *Dualities*; *Gold Coast Customs* and *The Shadow of Cain* (Edith Sitwell) and *The Riverrun* (James Joyce) for speakers, chorus, and orchestra; *Jerusalem* for speaker, tenor, chorus, and orchestra (1970).

ORCHESTRAL AND CHAMBER five symphonies (1953–64), two suites and *Highland Reel* for orchestra; two nocturnes and two suites for chamber orchestra; piano concerto; *Intermezzo* for chamber ensemble, quintet for horn and strings; quartet for violin, viola, clarinet, and bassoon; sonata, *Vigil* and *Ballad* for piano; two Housman songs.

Seasons, The ballet by Aleksandr ➤ **Glazunov** (choreography by Petipa), produced at the Mariinsky Theatre, St Petersburg, on 20 February 1900.

Oratorio (*Die Jahreszeiten*) by Haydn (German words by Gottfried van Swieten, based on Thomson's poem), composed 1798–1801. It was produced at the Schwarzenberg Palace, Vienna, on 24 April 1801.

Sea Symphony, A the first symphony by Vaughan Williams, for solo voices, chorus, and orchestra (words by Walt Whitman). It was first performed at the Leeds Festival on 12 October 1910.

Sebastiani, Claudius (died 1565) German music theorist. He held organist's posts at Fribourg and Metz, but is famous particularly for his treatise *Bellum Musicale/The Musical War*, published at Strasbourg in 1563.

Sebastiani, Johann (1622–1683) German composer. He went to Königsberg about 1650, where he became cantor in 1661 and was music director at the electoral church 1663–79. He wrote a

Passion for voices and strings, with chorales included in a Passion setting for the first time. He probably studied in Italy.

Works SACRED AND SECULAR MUSIC Passion for voices and strings; sacred concertos for voices and instruments and other church music; wedding and funeral cantatas; sacred and secular songs *Parnass-Blumen*.

sec (French 'dry') musical term used by some French composers, especially Debussy, where a note or chord is to be struck and released again abruptly without any richness of tone.

secco (Italian 'dry') in music, an abbreviation for *recitativo secco*, a 19th-century musical term for a type of ➤ **recitative** accompanied by a keyboard instrument, played from figured bass. It is also used in a similar manner to the French ➤ **sec**.

Sechter, Simon (1788–1867) Bohemian-Austrian theorist, organist, and composer. When the Italian musician Domenico Dragonetti was in Vienna in 1809, Sechter wrote piano accompaniments for his double bass concertos. In 1825 he succeeded Voříšek as court organist, and in 1850 became a professor at the Vienna Conservatory.

He settled in Vienna in 1804 and continued his studies there. In 1812 he became a teacher of piano and singing at the Institute for the Blind. He wrote several theoretical works.

Works OPERA *Ali Hitsch-Hatsch* (1844).

CHURCH MUSIC Masses, Requiem, and other church music.

CHORAL oratorios and cantatas; choruses from Schiller's *Braut von Messina*.

OTHER chorale preludes, fugues, and other pieces for organ; variations, fugues, and other works for piano.

second in music, an interval of two diatonic notes. A second is an 'imperfect interval' (having 'major' and 'minor' variants). A major second consists of two semitones (for example, C–D). A minor second consists of one semitone (C–D♭).

Maj	Min	Augmented

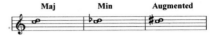

Major, minor, and augmented seconds.

secondo (Italian 'second') in music, the part of the second player in a piano duet, that of the first being called *primo*. The term is used also as an adjective, applied to the second player of a pair or a group, as in *clarinetto secondo*.

Second Viennese School name given to a group of composers (namely Arnold ➤ **Schoenberg**, Alban ➤ **Berg**, and Anton ➤ **Webern**), working in Vienna during the first years of the 20th century, who developed ➔ **atonality** in its early stages and became the foremost proponents of Schoenberg's ➔ **twelve-tone system.**

Secret, The, Czech *Tajemstvi* opera by Smetana (libretto by E Krásnohorská), produced in Prague at the Czech Theatre, on 18 September 1878. The story concerns Kalina and Róza, who are finally united when Kalina discovers a secret passage leading to his beloved's house. In a subplot, Blaženka and Vít make public their secret love.

Sedaine, Michel Jean (1719–1797) French playwright and librettist. See ➔ **Aucassin et Nicolette** (Grétry); ➔ **Grétry** (*Raoul Barbe-bleue*); ➔ **Guillaume Tell** (Grétry); ➔ **Jagd, Die** (J A Hiller); ➔ **Richard Cœur-de-Lion** (Grétry).

Seeger, Charles (Louis) (1886–1979) US conductor, teacher, and composer. After conducting at the Cologne Opera in 1910, he was professor of music at California University 1912–19, and from 1958 he was engaged in research there. He wrote books on theory and ethnomusicology. He studied at Harvard University.

Works MUSIC FOR STAGE masques *Derdra* and *The Queen's Masque*.

ORCHESTRAL AND CHAMBER overture *Shadowy Waters* for orchestra; chamber music; violin and piano sonata; numerous songs.

Segerstam, Leif (1944–) Finnish conductor and composer. He was principal conductor of the Austrian Radio Orchestra 1975–82, of the Finnish Radio Symphony Orchestra 1977–87, and of the Danish Radio Symphony Orchestra from 1989.

He studied at the Sibelius Academy, Helsinki, and the Juilliard School, New York. He was conductor of the Finnish National Opera, then the Stockholm Royal Opera 1965–72, and the Deutsche Oper, Berlin, 1971–73. He made his Salzburg Festival debut in 1971 with *Die Entführung*.

Works ORCHESTRAL Divertimento for strings (1963), *Concerto Serioso* for violin and orchestra (1967), two piano concertos (1978, 1981), 16 symphonies (1977–90), six cello concertos, eight violin concertos, many works for orchestra under the title *Orchestral Diary Sheets*; *Song of Experience* (after Blake and Auden) for soprano and orchestra (1971).

ENSEMBLE 26 string quartets (1962–82), two piano trios (1976–77), three string trios (1977–78), 22 Episodes for various instrumental combinations (1978–81).

Segni, Giulio (Giulio da Modena) (1498–1561) Italian composer. He composed three *ricercari à 4* (published in *Musica Nova* in 1540) and other instrumental works.

After a short period as organist of St Mark's,

Venice, 1530–33, he entered the service of Pope Clement VII.

segreto di Susanna, Il, **Susanna's Secret** opera by Wolf-Ferrari (libretto by E Golisciani), produced (in German translation) at the Court Opera in Munich, by Max Kalbeck, on 4 December 1909. In the story, Susanna is a secret smoker and her jealous husband, Count Gil, suspects she has been harbouring a lover because of her mysterious disappearances (to the tobacconist's).

segue (Italian 'follows') in music, an indication, like *attacca*, that a piece, number, or section is to be played or sung immediately after another one. In manuscripts the word is sometimes used instead of *VS* (*volti subito*) where a blank space is left at the bottom of a page to avoid turning over during the performance of what follows on the next.

seguidilla Spanish dance dating back to at least the 16th century and first heard of in La Mancha, though it is possibly of earlier Moorish origin. The original form was the *seguidilla manchega*, but when the dance spread throughout Spain others developed: the *seguidilla bolero*, slow and stately, and the *seguidilla gitana*, slow and sentimental. The seguidilla is usually played on guitars, often with castanet accompaniment and sometimes with violin or flute. Frequently popular verses are sung to the seguidilla consisting of *coplas*, 'couplets' of three lines, followed by *estribillos*, 'refrains' of three lines.

Seiber, Mátyás (1905–1960) Hungarian-born British composer, conductor, and cellist. Influences in his music range from Bartók and Schoenberg to jazz. He is best known for his cantata *Ulysses* (1947), based on a chapter from James Joyce's novel.

He was born in Budapest, and studied with Kodály at the Budapest Academy of Music 1919–24. After travelling abroad, including North and South America; he taught 1928–33 in the newly established jazz class at the Hoch Conservatory in Frankfurt. He also played cello in a string quartet there and conducted a theatre orchestra and a workers' chorus. In 1935 he settled in London as a choral conductor and film composer, and joined the teaching staff at Morley College.

Works OPERA AND DRAMA opera *Eva plays with Dolls* (1934); two operettas; incidental music for plays; film and radio music.

CHORAL *Missa brevis* for unaccompanied chorus; cantata *Ulysses* (Joyce, 1947).

ORCHESTRAL two Besardo Suites (from 16th-century lute tablatures), *Transylvanian Rhapsody* for orchestra.

CHAMBER *Pastorale and concertante* for violin and strings (1944), *Notturno* for horn and strings; concertino for clarinet and strings; four Greek songs for voice and strings; three string quartets (1924, 1935, 1951), wind sextet, quintet for clarinet and strings, duo for violin and cello; fantasy for cello and piano, violin pieces.

OTHER piano works; songs, choruses, folk-song arrangements.

Seidl, Anton (1850–1898) Hungarian-born German conductor. He conducted the first US performances of Wagner's operas *Tristan*, *Die Meistersinger*, and *The Ring*, and the first performance of Dvořák's 'New World' symphony (1893).

He studied at the Leipzig Conservatory from 1870 and two years later went to Bayreuth as Wagner's assistant. After a period as conductor at the Leipzig Opera, 1879–82, he toured and conducted German opera at the Metropolitan Opera House in New York from 1885 to his death.

Selle, Thomas (1599–1663) German composer. He held various rector's and cantor's posts at Heide, Wesselburen, and Itzehoe, and finally at the Johanneum in Hamburg from 1641. His large output includes sacred and secular music.

Works SACRED AND SECULAR MUSIC Passion music including the St John Passion (1641), the first Passion to include instrumental interludes; motets, sacred concertos; madrigals; sacred and secular songs.

Semele opera-oratorio by Handel, performed at Covent Garden, London, on 10 February 1744. The libretto by Congreve (with anonymous alterations) was originally intended for an opera. The story concerns Semele, who aspires to immortality. But the jealous Juno tricks her into being consumed by the fire of her lover, Jupiter. The opera was revived at Covent Garden in 1982.

semibreve, US **whole note** in music, a note value four times the duration of a ➤ crotchet. It is written as an empty white note-head without a stem. Once the shortest-value note of medieval notation, it is now one of the longest commonly used.

semi-chorus group of singers detached from a chorus for the purpose of obtaining antiphonal (responsive) effects or changes of tone-colour. It does not often literally consist of half the voices, but is more usually a much smaller contingent.

semicroma Italian term for ➤ semiquaver.

semiotic analysis method of analysing music according to theories of meaning drawn from linguistics. In practice, the musical work is divided up ('segmented') into units which are then grouped into similar classes or paradigms; the relationships between these paradigms within and outside the work in question are then explored. There is no single technique of semiotic analysis; the method is distinguished by the desire to treat

music as a structured, communicative form, and by the attempt to define the nature of musical meaning and relate it to meaning in other art forms.

semiquaver, US **16th note** in music, a note value one-quarter the duration of a ➤ crotchet. It is written as a filled black note-head with a stem and two flags (tails).

Semiramide, Semiramis opera by Rossini (libretto by Giacomo Rossi, based on Voltaire's tragedy) produced at the Teatro La Fenice, Venice, on 3 February 1823. In the story, the Queen of Babylon, Semiramide, murders her husband but dies at the hand of Arsace, her long-lost and unrecognized son.

Semiramide riconosciuta, Semiramis Recognized opera by Gluck (libretto by Pietro Metastasio), produced at the Burgtheater, Vienna, on 14 May 1748. Other settings include those by Vinci (Rome, 1729) and Hasse (Venice, 1744). The story concerns Semiramide, who rules Assyria disguised as a man, and eventually marries her former lover Scitalce after complications involving princess Tamiri and her suitors.

semiseria (Italian 'half-serious') in music, term used for a hybrid between ➤ opera seria ('serious opera') and ➤ opera buffa ('humorous opera').

semitone or **half tone** or **half step** the smallest interval normally used in traditional Western music. The octave is divided into twelve semitones.

semplice (Italian 'simple') in musical notation, a term indicating unaffected expression, without extremes.

Senallié or **Senaillé, Jean Baptiste (1687–1730)** French violinist and composer. He was a member of the French king Louis XIV's string orchestra, known as the '24 Violons du Roi'. He spent some time in Italy, and was one of the first composers to combine the French and Italian styles in his violin sonatas.

He studied under his father, Jean Senallié, who was a member of the royal orchestra, and with his father's colleague there, Queversin. Later he studied with Tomaso Vitali at Modena, where he was appointed to the ducal court, and then with Giovanni Antonio Piani (1678–c.1757). He returned to Paris in 1720 and received an appointment at court under the regent, the Duke of Orleans, later confirmed under Louis XV.

Works WORKS FOR VIOLIN about 50 sonatas for unaccompanied violin; violin sonatas with bass; pieces for violin and harpsichord.

Senfl, Ludwig (c.1486–c.1542) Swiss composer. He made imaginative arrangements of traditional German melodies, ranging from chordal

An example of a sequence from Handel's Acis and Galatea.

harmonization to canons, and is regarded as the most important German-speaking composer of motets and songs during the Reformation.

He studied under Henricus ➤ **Isaac** in Vienna and sang 1496–1513 in the *Hofkapelle* of Maximilian I in Vienna, Augsburg, and Constance. He worked with Isaac in copying a large amount of music which was later published as part of Isaac's *Choralis constantinus* (1550–55), a task Ludwig Senfl completed around 1520. In 1513 he succeeded Isaac as kapellmeister to Emperor Maximilian I, holding the post until the emperor's death in 1519. In 1520 he went to Augsburg and in 1523 to Munich, where he settled as first musician at the ducal court of Wilhelm of Bavaria. In 1530 he was in correspondence with Martin Luther.

Works CHURCH AND SECULAR MUSIC seven Masses, Magnificats, motets, and other church music; odes by Horace for voices; about 250 German songs.

Senilov, Vladimir Alekseievich (1875–1918) Russian composer. He initially studied law, but went to Leipzig for musical studies under Riemann. He later worked under Glazunov and Rimsky-Korsakov at the St Petersburg Conservatory.

Works OPERA *Vassily Buslaiev* and *Hippolytus* (after Euripides), music action *George the Bold*.

ORCHESTRAL symphony in D major, overture *In Autumn*; symphonic poems *The Wild Geese* (after Maupassant), *The Mtsyrs* (after Lermontov), *Pan*, *The Scythians*, *Variations on a Chant of the Old Believers* for orchestra.

CHORAL AND VOICE WITH ORCHESTRA *Chole forsaken* for voice and orchestra; cantata *John of Damascus*.

CHAMBER three string quartets; poems for cello and piano; scherzo for flute and piano.

sensible (French noun, or *note sensible*) in musical notation, a ➤ **leading note.**

senza (Italian 'without') term used in musical notation, as in *senza tempo* ('without tempo'), meaning playing in a free tempo, or *senza sordino* ('without mute'), meaning, on a bowed string instrument, playing without the mute or, on a piano, using the ➤ **sustaining pedal**, to release the dampers.

septet an ensemble of seven musicians, or the music written for such a group. For example, Beethoven's Septet in E (1823) is scored for violin, viola, cello, double bass, horn, clarinet, and bassoon.

Sept Haï-kaï work by Olivier Messiaen for piano, 13 wind instruments, xylophone, marimba, four percussion instruments, and eight violins. Composed in 1962, it was first performed in Paris on 30 October 1963.

septuplet or **septimole** a group of seven notes to be fitted into a beat or other time-unit, usually four or six, in which its number is irregular.

sequence in music, a device allowing key ➤ **modulation** favoured by early keyboard composers in which a phrase is repeated sequentially, each time transposing to a different key.

Serafin, Tullio (1878–1968) Italian conductor. He is chiefly remembered for his performances of Italian Romantic operas, especially those of Donizetti and Bellini. He also conducted the first performances of several new works by US composers at the Metropolitan Opera House, New York.

He studied at the Milan Conservatory and made his debut at Ferrara in 1900. In 1909 he became conductor at La Scala, Milan, and gave the Italian premieres of *Der Rosenkavalier* and *Oberon*. He conducted *La Bohème*, *Carmen*, and *La Gioconda* at Covent Garden, London, in 1907, returning in 1931 for *Falstaff*, *Fedra*, *La forza del destino*, and *La Traviata*. From 1924 he was one of the chief conductors at the New York Metropolitan Opera, where he conducted the first performances of operas by Deems Taylor, Louis Gruenberg, and Howard Hanson with the US first performances of *Turandot* and *Simon Boccanegra*. He returned to Italy in 1935, where he worked mostly in Milan and Rome, conducting operas by Pizzetti, Alfano, Berg, and Britten. He also appeared in Paris and London, conducting *Lucia* at Covent Garden in 1959.

Serafino (lived 17th–18th centuries) family of Italian violin makers. **Santo Serafino** worked in Udine in northeastern Italy around 1678–98, and then in Venice until around 1735. His nephew, **Giorgio Serafino** also worked in Venice in the 18th century.

serenade musical piece for chamber orchestra or wind instruments in several movements, originally intended for informal evening entertainment, such as Mozart's *Eine kleine Nachtmusik/ A Little Night Music*.

Serenade work for violin, percussion, and strings by Leonard Bernstein, after Plato's *Symposium*, first performed in Venice on 12

September 1954, with Isaac Stern.

Serenade for Tenor, Horn, and Strings song cycle by Britten (texts by Cotton, Tennyson, Blake, Jonson, and Keats, all on the theme of night). It was first performed in London on 15 October 1943, with Dennis Brain and Peter Pears.

Serenaden, Die cantata by Hindemith for soprano, oboe, viola, and cello (texts by A Licht, Johann Gleim, Ludwig Tieck, Joseph von Eichendorff, J W Meinhold, and S A Mahlmann), first performed at Winterthur, Switzerland, on 15 April 1925.

Serenade to Music work by Vaughan Williams for 16 solo voices and orchestra (text from *The Merchant of Venice*); composed in 1938 for the jubilee of Henry Wood and conducted by him in London on 5 October 1938. A version for orchestra was performed in London on 10 February 1940, conducted by Wood.

serenata (Italian for 'serenade') musical term used (in English) for 18th-century works, often of an occasional or congratulatory type, either produced on the stage as small topical and allegorical operas or at concerts (and even then sometimes in costume) in the manner of a secular cantata.

seria (Italian 'serious') see ➤ opera seria.

serialism in music, a later form of the ➤ twelve-tone system of composition, invented by Arnold ➤ Schoenberg, and hinted at in the later works of Max ➤ Reger.

It usually refers to post-1950 compositions in which elements of the music were brought under the same type of control as pitch in twelve-tone music. The ➤ tone row (the order in which the composer decides to arrange the twelve notes) can be expressed as numbers (a ➤ series) which can then be used to control parameters such as dynamics, rhythm, and attack.

In its extreme form, known as ➤ integral serialism, every parameter of a piece is controlled by one series: a classic example of this is Olivier Messiaen's *Quatre Etudes du Rythm*. Other major works using serialism include Jean Barraqué's monumental sonata for piano and Anton Webern's symphony Op. 21.

series in music, the numerical expression of note orders of a ➤ tone row, related to a starting ➤ pitch of 1. The US composer Milton ➤ Babbitt introduced a convention of numbering a series as intervals from zero (unison with the starting note) to a maximum of eleven half-steps or semitones.

Serly, Tibor (1901–1978) Hungarian-born US composer. He worked as a violinist and conductor in the USA. He completed the last bars of Bartók's 3rd piano concerto and, in 1945, made a

version of Bartók's viola concerto from the surviving sketches.

After being taken to the USA as a child in 1905 and becoming a citizen in 1911, he returned to Budapest 1922–24 to study with Bartók and Kodály. On his return to the USA he played the violin with the Philadelphia Orchestra 1928–35. He played with the National Broadcasting Company Symphony Orchestra under Toscanini and befriended Bartók when he arrived in New York as a refugee.

Sermisy, Claudin de (c.1490–1562), called **'Claudin'** French composer. He was master of the choristers at the French royal chapel, and wrote about 110 sacred works, including motets, Masses, and a Passion. His reputation, however, both during his lifetime and since, has rested on his chansons, of which about 175 survive. They have attractive melodies and are simpler and more homophonic and syllabic in style than those of his contemporaries. Many of them were arranged by other composers for a variety of vocal and instrumental forces.

He was attached to the Sainte-Chapelle in Paris 1508–14. In 1515 he became a singer in the royal chapel just before Louis XII's death, and in the same year his choir competed with the Papal choir before Leo X; he later succeeded Antoine de Longueval as master of the choristers. In 1520, with François I, he met the English king Henry VIII at the Field of the Cloth of Gold. A similar meeting followed in 1532 at Boulogne; and on both occasions the French and English choirs sang together. In 1533 he was made a canon of the Sainte-Chapelle, with a living and a substantial salary attached to it; but his duties there were light and he remained in the royal chapel, with which, under François I, he visited Bologna.

Works CHURCH AND SECULAR MUSIC eleven Masses, motets; about 175 chansons for several voices.

Serocki, Kazimierz (1922–1981) Polish composer. He appeared in Europe as a pianist 1950–52, but later devoted himself to composition in a modernist idiom, including aleatory (random) devices.

He studied at Łódź and later with Nadia Boulanger 1947–48.

Works ORCHESTRAL AND CHORAL two symphonies (1952, 1953; second for soprano, baritone, chorus, and orchestra), *Triptych* for orchestra; piano concerto, trombone concerto; *Symphonic Frescoes* (1963); *Dramatic Story* for orchestra (1971); five pieces for orchestra (1976); choral music.

ENSEMBLE *Episodes* for strings and three percussion groups, *Segmenti* for chamber ensemble and percussion (1960); *Ad Libitum*, *Pianophonie* for piano and electronics (1978); chamber music.

Serov, Aleksandr Nikolaievich (1820–1871) Russian composer and critic. He greatly admired Wagner, and disliked the Russian nationalist composers. Among his own compositions, the operas *Judith* (1863) and *Rogneda* (1865) were highly successful, and had a pronounced effect on later composers.

He studied law, but found time to cultivate music, which eventually, after a career as a civil servant, he took up professionally. He studied cello and theory from around 1840 and began an opera on Shakespeare's *Merry Wives of Windsor* in 1843, but was reduced to taking a correspondence course of musical instruction when transferred to Simferopol. He became a music critic and in 1858, when he returned from a visit to Germany as an ardent admirer of Wagner, he began to attack the Russian nationalist school of composers, but found a powerful opponent in Vladimir Stasov. He was over 40 when he began his first opera. When he died from heart disease, he had just begun a fourth opera, based on Gogol's *Christmas Eve Revels*.

He married the composer Valentina Semionovna Bergman (1846–1927), who wrote some operas of her own, including *Uriel Acosta* (based on Gutzkow's play).

Works OPERA AND STAGE *Judith* (1863), *Rogneda* (1865), *The Power of Evil* (after Ostrovsky's play; orchestration finished by Soloviev, 1871); incidental music to Nikolai Pavlovich Zhandr's tragedy *Nero*.

CHURCH AND SECULAR MUSIC *Stabat Mater* and *Ave Maria*; *Gopak*, *Dance of the Zaporogue Cossacks*, and other orchestral works.

serpent keyed tubular brass or wooden musical instrument of the cornett family, played with a cup mouthpiece, originating in the 16th century, probably in France. It has a distinctive S-shape (resembling a serpent, hence its name) and became popular as a church and military band instrument. It was superseded in the 19th century by the ➔ **ophicleide** and tuba, but has seen a revival in the 20th century as a result of the ➔ **authenticity** movement.

Serse, **Xerxes** opera by Handel (libretto by N Minato, altered), produced at the King's Theatre, Haymarket, London, on 15 April 1738. It contains the famous so-called *Largo*, the aria whose original title was 'Ombra mai fù/Shade never was'. The original libretto was that for Cavalli's *Xerse* (1654). In the story, King Xerxes of Persia falls in love with Romilda, who is in love with Arsamene. After complications, the lovers are allowed to marry when Amastre, who was earlier jilted by Xerxes, arrives to reclaim him.

serva padrona, La, **The Maid as Mistress** intermezzo by Paisiello (libretto by G A Federico),

produced at the Hermitage in St Petersburg, at court, on 10 September 1781. The story concerns Serpina, who tricks her master Uberto into marriage, when she threatens to run away with a soldier. The soldier is, in fact, the servant Vespone in disguise.

Intermezzo by Pergolesi (libretto as above), produced at the Teatro San Bartolommeo, Naples, between the acts of Pergolesi's serious opera *Il prigionier superbo*, on 28 August 1733.

service in music, term implying the setting of those parts of the services of the Anglican Church which lend themselves to musical treatment, that is, the Morning Prayer, Evening Prayer (➔ **Magnificat** and Nunc dimittis), and Communion.

Servilia opera in five acts by Rimsky-Korsakov (libretto by composer, based on a play by L A Mey), produced at St Petersburg on 14 October 1902. In the story, the daughter of a Neronian senator converts to Christianity and provides an example for many noble Romans.

sesquialtera in musical notation, short for *pars sesquialtera*, 'a quantity $1\frac{1}{2}$ times as much'; in mensural notation (the notation indicating the exact value of notes) the proportion is 3:2. See also ➔ **proportion**.

Sessions, Roger Huntington (1896–1985) US composer. His international modernist style secured a US platform for serious German influences, including Hindemith and Schoenberg, and offered an alternative to the lightweight, fashionable modernism of Milhaud and Paris. An able symphonist, his works include *The Black Maskers* (incidental music, 1923), eight symphonies, and *Concerto for Orchestra* (1971).

Born in Brooklyn, New York, he attended Harvard and Yale universities, then studied under Ernest Bloch. In 1917–21 he taught at Smith College, Northampton, Massachusetts, and was head of the theoretical department of the Cleveland Institute of Music 1921–25. He lived in Italy and Germany 1925–33. He became a leading teacher of composition, serving on the faculties of Boston University, Princeton University 1935–44 and 1953–65, the University of California at Berkeley, and the Juilliard School, New York 1965–85.

Works ORCHESTRAL AND CHAMBER nine symphonies (1927–80), three dirges for orchestra; violin concerto (1940), piano concerto, concerto for orchestra (1981); two string quartets (1935, 1951), piano trio; sonata and three chorale preludes for organ; two sonatas and pieces for piano; songs to words by James Joyce and others.

set in music, the old English name for a suite. Also a series, normally of pitches but also of rhythms or other musical parameters, used in the composition of a piece. See also ➔ **serialism**.

set complex in ➔ **pitch-class set** analysis, a group of sets related to each other by being subsets or supersets of a single 'nexus set'.

***Sette canzoni*, Seven Songs** opera by Malipiero (libretto by composer). The French version was produced by Henry Prunières at the Paris Opéra on 10 July 1920. Part II of the operatic cycle *L'Orfeide* is a series of contrasting moral and emotional principles, drawn from the composer's own life.

Settle, Elkanah (1648–1724) English poet and dramatist who contributed to many works. See Jeremiah ➔ **Clarke** (*World in the Moon*, with Daniel Purcell); ➔ *Fairy Queen* (Purcell); Gottfried ➔ **Finger** (*Virgin Prophetess*).

seventh in music, an ➔ **interval** of seven diatonic notes. A seventh is an 'imperfect interval' (having 'major' and 'minor' variants). A major seventh consists of eleven semitones (for example, C–B natural). A minor seventh consists of ten semitones (C–B flat).

Major, minor, and diminished sevenths.

'Seven, They are Seven' Akkadian Incantation for tenor, chorus, and orchestra by Prokofiev, Op. 30 (text by K Balmont), composed 1917–18, first performed in Paris on 29 May 1924, conducted by Koussevitzky.

Seven Words of the Saviour on the Cross, The or ***The Seven Last Words*** orchestral work by Haydn consisting of seven slow movements, commissioned by Cádiz Cathedral in 1785 as musical meditations for a three-hour service on Good Friday. The work was later arranged by Haydn for string quartet (Op. 51, 1787) and as a choral work (1796).

Oratorio by Schütz (*The Seven Words of Christ*) (words from the four Gospels plus two verses of a chorale), composed in 1645.

Séverac, (Joseph Marie) Déodat de (1873–1921) French composer. He studied at the Toulouse Conservatory and with Magnard and d'Indy at the Schola Cantorum, Paris. He returned to the south of France and devoted himself entirely to composition, neither his health nor his taste permitting him to hold any official position.

Works OPERA AND STAGE opera *Le Cœur du moulin* (1909); ballet *La Fête des vendanges*; incidental music for Sicard's *Héliogabale* and for Verhae-

ren's *Hélène de Sparte*.

CHORAL AND CHURCH MUSIC *Ave, verum corpus* and other church music; *Chant de vacances* for chorus.

OTHER string quintet; 19 songs to poems by Ronsard, Verlaine, Maeterlinck, and Poe.

sevillana Andalusian folk song type similar to the seguidilla, a 16th-century Spanish dance, and originally confined to Seville.

sextet an ensemble of six musicians, or music written for such a group. Brahms wrote several string sextets.

sextolet in music, a group of six notes, or double triplet, when used in a composition or movement whose time-unit is normally divisible into two, four, or eight note-values.

sextuplet in music, a group of six notes of equal length, played (usually) in the time of four. It is indicated by a ➔ **slur** over the six notes with the number '6' written above.

sextus in old vocal music, the sixth part (voice) in a composition for six or more voices, always equal in compass to one of the voices in a four-part composition: soprano, alto, tenor, or bass.

Seyfried, Ignaz Xaver von (1776–1841) Austrian composer, teacher, and conductor. He conducted and composed music for Schikaneder's theatre at Vienna 1797–1828, and in 1806 he conducted the first revival of Beethoven's opera *Fidelio* there. As a composer he was known for the quantity, rather than the quality, of his output.

Originally intended for a legal career, he turned to music, studying piano with Mozart and Kozeluch, and composition with Albrechtsberger and Winter. From 1797 to 1828 he was conductor and composer to Schikaneder's theatre (from 1801 known as the Theater an der Wien). After his retirement he composed almost exclusively church music. He also edited Albrechtsberger's theoretical works and, in 1832, published an account of Beethoven's studies in figured bass, counterpoint, and composition.

Works OPERA AND SINGSPIELE over 100, including *Der Löwenbrunnen*, *Der Wundermann am Rheinfall* (1799), *Die Ochsenmenuette* (pasticcio arranged from Haydn's works, 1823), *Ahasverus* (arranged from piano works of Mozart); biblical dramas; incidental music to Schiller's *Die Räuber* and *Die Jungfrau von Orleans*, and others.

CHURCH MUSIC about 20 Masses, Requiem, motets, and other church music; *Libera me* for Beethoven's funeral.

Sf. in musical notation, abbreviation for ➔ **sforzando**.

sfogato (Italian 'airy') in musical direction, an indication of a delicate and ethereal performance of certain passages; used sometimes by composers, such as Chopin. Also an adjective, especially *soprano sfogato*, 'light soprano'.

sforzando or **sforzato** or **sf** or **Sfz. (Italian 'forcing')** in musical notation, a sudden accent placed on a single note or chord. Its loudness depends on the surrounding dynamics. For example, if the dynamic marking prior to 'sforzando' is 'piano' (soft), then it is not accented as loudly as if the prior marking were 'forte' (loud).

Sfz. in musical notation, abbreviation for ➤ **sforzando**.

Shahrazad, Sheherazade symphonic suite by Rimsky-Korsakov on the subject of the storyteller in the *Arabian Nights* and of some of the tales, Op. 35. It was finished in the summer of 1888 and produced at St Petersburg, on 3 November 1888. A ballet based on the suite (choreographed by Mikhail Fokin, settings by Leon Bakst) was produced at the Paris Opéra on 4 June 1910. See also ➤ **Shéhérazade** .

shake in music, an alternative name for ➤ **trill**, in which two adjacent notes rapidly alternate.

Shakespeare, William (1564–1616) English poet and dramatist. Among works based on his plays are:

Antony and Cleopatra: ➤ **Barber** (opera, 1966); Rodolphe ➤ **Kreutzer** (ballet, *Amours d'Antoine et de Cléopâtre*, 1808); ➤ **Malipiero** (opera, 1938); ➤ **Prokofiev** (symphonic suite, *Egyptian Nights*, 1934).

As You Like It: ➤ **Veracini** (opera, *Rosalinda*, 1744).

Comedy of Errors: ➤ **Storace** (opera, *Gli equivoci*, 1786).

Coriolanus: Ján Cikker (opera, 1974).

Cymbeline: ➤ **Schubert** (*Hark, hark, the lark*, 1826); ➤ **Zemlinsky** (incidental music, 1914).

Hamlet: Berlioz (*La Mort d'Ophélie* and *Marche funèbre* from *Tristia*, 1848); ➤ **Blacher** (ballet, 1950); Bridge (*There is a willow* for orchestra, 1928); Faccio (opera, 1865); ➤ **Liszt** (symphonic poem, 1858); ➤ **Mercadante** (opera, 1822); ➤ **Searle** (opera, 1967); ➤ **Shostakovich** (incidental music, 1931, and suite, 1932); ➤ **Szokolay** (opera, 1969); ➤ **Tchaikovsky** (fantasy overture, 1888); Ambrose ➤ **Thomas** (opera, 1868); ➤ **Walton** (film music, 1947).

Henry IV, parts 1 and 2: Elgar (*Falstaff*, symphonic study, 1913); ➤ **Holst** (opera, *At the Boar's Head*, 1925); ➤ **Mercadante** (opera, *La gioventù di Enrico V*, 1834); ➤ **Pacini** (opera, as above, 1820).

Henry V: ➤ **Vaughan Williams** (*Thanksgiving for Victory*, 1945); ➤ **Walton** (film music, 1944).

Julius Caesar: ➤ **Klebe** (opera, *Die Ermordrung Cäsars*, 1959); ➤ **Malipiero** (opera, 1936); ➤ **Schumann** (overture, 1851).

King Lear: Berlioz (overture, 1831); Frazzi (opera, *Re Lear*, 1939); ➤ **Ghislanzoni** (opera, ditto, 1937); ➤ **Reimann** (opera, *Lear*, 1978); ➤ **Shostakovich** (incidental music, 1940).

Love's Labour's Lost: Nabokov (opera, 1973).

Macbeth: Bloch (opera, 1910); ➤ **Collingwood** (opera, 1934); ➤ **Strauss** (tone poem, 1890); ➤ **Verdi** (opera, 1847).

Measure for Measure: ➤ **Wagner** (opera, *Das Liebesverbot*, 1836).

Merchant of Venice: ➤ **Castelnuovo-Tedesco** (opera, *Il mercante di Venezia*, 1961); Josef Bohuslav ➤ **Foerster** (opera, *Jessika*, 1905); ➤ **Vaughan Williams** (*Serenade to Music*, 1938).

Merry Wives of Windsor: Adolphe ➤ **Adam** (opera, *Falstaff*, 1856); Balfe (opera, ditto, 1838); Dittersdorf (opera, *Die lustigen Weiber von Windsor und der dicke Hans*, 1796); ➤ **Nicolai** (opera, *Die lustigen Weiber von Windsor*, 1849); ➤ **Salieri** (opera, *Falstaff osia le tre burle*, 1799); ➤ **Vaughan Williams** (opera, *Sir John in Love*, 1929); ➤ **Verdi** (opera, *Falstaff*, 1893).

Midsummer Night's Dream: Britten (opera, 1960); ➤ **Mendelssohn** (incidental music, 1842; overture written 1826); ➤ **Orff** (incidental music, 1939; commissioned under the Nazi régime to replace Mendelssohn's music); ➤ **Purcell** (*The Fairy Queen*, 1692); Elie Siegmeister (opera, *Night of the Moonspell*, 1976).

Much Ado About Nothing: Berlioz (opera, *Béatrice et Bénédict*, 1862); Stanford (opera, 1901).

Othello: ➤ **Blacher** (ballet, *Der Mohr von Venedig*, 1955); ➤ **Dvořák** (overture, 1892); ➤ **Rossini** (opera – last act only after Shakespeare – 1816); ➤ **Verdi** (opera, 1887).

Richard III: ➤ **Smetana** (symphonic poem, 1856); ➤ **Walton** (film music, 1954).

Romeo and Juliet: ➤ **Bellini** (opera, *I Capuleti e i Montecchi*, based on Shakespeare's sources, 1830); Berlioz (dramatic symphony, 1839); ➤ **Blacher** (scenic oratorio, 1947; revised as opera, 1950); ➤ **Gounod** (opera, 1867); ➤ **Malipiero** (opera, 1950); ➤ **Prokofiev** (ballet, 1938); ➤ **Sutermeister** (opera, 1940); ➤ **Tchaikovsky** (Fantasy overture, 1869, revised 1870 and 1880); ➤ **Vaccai** (opera, 1825); ➤ **Zandonai** (opera, 1922); ➤ **Zingarelli** (opera, 1796).

Taming of the Shrew: ➤ **Götz** (opera, *Der Widerspänstigen Zähmung*, 1874); ➤ **Wolf-Ferrari** (opera, *Sly*, 1927).

Tempest: Thomas Arne (incidental music, 1740); Eaton (opera, 1985); Jacques ➤ **Halévy** (opera, *La Tempestà*, 1850); ➤ **Martin** (opera, *Der Sturm*, 1956); ➤ **Sibelius** (incidental music, 1924); ➤ **Sutermeister** (opera, *Die Zauberinsel*, 1942); ➤ **Tchaikovsky** (symphonic fantasy, 1873); John ➤ **Weldon** (incidental music, 1712; formerly attributed to Purcell), ➤ **Winter** (opera, *Der Sturm*, 1798), ➤ **Zumsteeg** (opera, *Die Geisterinsel*, 1798).

Timon of Athens: Antonio ➤ **Draghi**

(1634–1700) (opera, *Timone misantropo*, 1696);
➤ Oliver (opera, 1991).

Troilus and Cressida: ➤ Zillig (opera, 1951).

Twelfth Night: ➤ Smetana (opera, *Viola*, 1874–84, unfinished; produced 1924).

Two Gentlemen of Verona: ➤ Schubert (*An Sylvia*, 1826).

Winter's Tale: Max ➤ Bruch (opera, *Hermione*, 1872), Karoly ➤ Goldmark (opera, *Ein Wintermärchen*, 1908).

shakuhachi end-blown, notched bamboo flute of Japan. The modern version, originating from around the 15th century, has four finger-holes and one thumb-hole. It is used for meditative solos, in ensembles, folk songs, and in modern works by composers worldwide. The shakuhachi is manufactured in a graduated series of sizes a semitone apart; the size used depends on the genre, the other performers/instruments (if any), and the personal preference of the player.

Shankar, Ravi (1920–) Indian composer and virtuoso of the ➤ sitar. He has been influential in making Indian music more popular in the West. He has composed two concertos for sitar and orchestra (1971 and 1981), and film music, including scores for Satyajit Ray's *Pather Panchali* (1955) and Richard Attenborough's *Gandhi* (1982). He also founded music schools in Bombay (now Mumbai), India (1962), and Los Angeles, California (1967).

He worked first with a group of musicians and dancers led by his brother, Uday Shankar (1900–77). He founded the National Orchestra of All-India Radio and was founder-director of the Kinnara School of Music at Bombay in 1962. Other compositions include the opera-ballet *Ghanashyam/A Broken Branch*, which was premiered by the City of Birmingham Touring Opera in 1989.

Shapero, Harold (Samuel) (1920–) US composer and pianist. His music includes elements of jazz and serialism.

He studied with Nicolas Slonimsky at Boston 1936–38 and with Ernst Krenek (1900–1991) and Walter Piston (1894–1976) at Harvard. He was appointed professor of music at Brandeis University in 1952 and founded an electronic music studio there.

Works ORCHESTRA AND ENSEMBLE *Symphony for Classical Orchestra* (1947); *On Green Mountain* for jazz ensemble (1957; version for orchestra 1981); *Studies* for piano and synthesizer (1969).

OTHER *Hebrew Cantata* (1954), piano music, songs.

Shaporin, Yuri Aleksandrovich (1887–1966) Russian composer. He wrote incidental music for many plays and also opera, and co-founded the Great Dramatic Theatre in St Petersburg.

Shaporin was educated at St Petersburg, where he graduated in law at the university. In 1913 he entered the Conservatory there, studying under Sokolov, Steinberg, and Nikolai Tcherepnin. On leaving he became interested in stage music and founded the Great Dramatic Theatre with Gorky and Blok. In 1937 he moved to Moscow.

Works the opera *The Decembrists* (libretto by A N Tolstoy, 1953); incidental music for Shakespeare's *King Lear* and *Comedy of Errors*, Schiller's *Robbers*, Molière's *Tartuffe*, Pushkin's *Boris Godunov*, Beaumarchais' *Marriage of Figaro*, Turgenev's *The Nest of Gentlefolk* (*Liza*), Labiche's *The Playian Straw Hat*; film music including *General Suvarov*; symphonic cantata *On the Kulikov Field* (1939); symphony in E minor, suite *The Flea* for orchestra, two suites for piano; song cycles to words by Pushkin and Tiutchev, and other songs.

sharp, symbol ♯ in music, a sign that tells a player to raise the pitch of a note by one semitone. It can also describe the inaccurate intonation of players when they are playing higher in pitch than they should be.

Sharp, Cecil (James) (1859–1924) English collector and compiler of folk songs and dances. He visited the USA 1916–18 to collect songs in the Appalachian mountains, where many English songs were still preserved in their early form by descendants of 17th-century emigrants. His work ensured that the English folk music revival became established throughout the English-speaking world.

He led a movement to record a threatened folk song tradition for posterity, publishing *English Folk Song* (1907; two volumes).

Cecil Sharp House, the headquarters in London of the English Folk Dance and Song Society, commemorates his work.

He was educated at Uppingham and Clare College, Cambridge. After living in Australia 1889–92, he returned to London and in 1896 became principal of the Hampstead Conservatory. In 1899 he began to collect folk songs and dances; later he joined the Folk Song Society and in 1911 founded the English Folk Dance Society.

shawm member of a family of double-reed conical bore musical instruments of piercing tone. The Renaissance shawm emerged around 1200 as a consort instrument, the reed enclosed by a ➤ windcap. It was a forerunner of the ➤ oboe.

Shchedrin, Rodion (1932–) Russian composer. He studied at the Moscow Conservatory with Yuri Shaporin (1887–1966), graduating in 1955.

Works OPERA AND STAGE the opera *Not for Love Alone* (1961), *Dead Souls* (1976), *Lolita* (1994); ballets *The Little Hump-backed Horse* (1955),

Carmen Suite (1968), and *Anna Karenina* (1972).

ORCHESTRAL AND CHAMBER two symphonies (1958, 1964); Musical Offering for organ and ensemble (1982); three piano concertos; piano quintet, two string quartets, 24 Preludes and Fugue for piano (1963–70).

CHORAL oratorio *Poetoria* for poet, woman's voice, chorus, and orchestra (1968), cantata *Lenin Lives* (1972), songs.

Shebalin, Vissarion Yakovlevich (1902–1963) Russian composer. He was director of the Moscow Conservatory 1942–58, but was sacked after being denounced by Stalinists as a formalist (along with other leading contemporary composers in the USSR).

He was the son of a teacher and received his first musical training at the Omsk School of Music. In 1923 he entered the Moscow Conservatory as a pupil of Nikolai Miaskovsky and stayed there as a professor in 1928, as well as teaching at the Gnessin School of Music.

Works OPERA AND DRAMATIC MUSIC operas *The Taming of the Shrew* (1957), *Sun over the Steppes* (1958), comic opera *The Embassy Bridegroom* (1942); incidental music for Schiller's *Die Räuber* and *Mary Stuart*, Pushkin's *Mozart and Salieri* and *The Stone Guest* (Don Juan), Lermontov's *Masquerade*, Scribe's *A Glass of Water*, and others; film music.

CHORAL AND ORCHESTRAL symphonic cantata *Lenin* for solo voices, chorus, and orchestra; five symphonies (1925–62), two suites and two overtures for orchestra; violin concerto, concertinos for violin and strings and for harp and small orchestra.

CHAMBER nine string quartets (1923–63), string trio; sonatina for violin and viola, suite for solo violin; two piano sonatas and three sonatinas.

OTHER songs (including settings of works by Pushkin and Heine), popular choruses, and war songs.

Sheherazade symphonic suite by Nicolai Rimsky-Korsakov; see ➤ **Shahrazad**.

Shéhérazade song-cycle with orchestra by Ravel (poems by Tristan Klingsor), composed in 1903 on the basis of an unpublished overture of the same name of 1898. There are three songs: 'Asie', 'La Flûte enchantée', and 'L'indifférent'. It was first performed in Paris on 17 May 1904.

Shekhter, Boris Semionovich (1900–1961) Russian composer. He made a close study of Turkmen folk music, and based some of his works on it. He was a pupil of Nikolai Miaskovsky (1881–1950) at the Moscow Conservatory.

Works OPERA *The Year 1905* (with Davidenko, 1935) and *The Son of the People*.

ORCHESTRAL suite *Turkmenia* for orchestra, five symphonies (1929–51, including symphony

Dithyramb for the 20th anniversary of the Russian revolution).

CHAMBER piano concerto; song cycles.

Shepherds of the Delectable Mountains, The opera by Vaughan Williams (libretto by composer, based on Bunyan's *Pilgrim's Progress*), produced in London at the Royal College of Music on 11 July 1922. In the story, a Pilgrim on his way to Celestial City is summoned by a heavenly messenger and is duly anointed by three Shepherds, who assist his journey on the River of Death. See ➤ *Pilgrim's Progress, The*.

shepherd's pipe rustic wind instrument similar to the oboe and the French ➤ **musette**, played with a double reed, like the chanter of a bagpipe, but usually used separately.

Sheppard, John (c.1515–c.1563) English composer. In 1542 he became organist and choirmaster at Magdalen College, Oxford, and later was in Queen Mary's Chapel Royal.

He learnt music as a choirboy at St Paul's Cathedral in London under Thomas Mulliner.

Works CHURCH MUSIC Masses *The Western Wynde*, *The French Masse*, *Be not afraide*, and *Playn Song Mass for a Mene*; 21 Office responds, 18 hymns, motets, two Te Deums, two Magnificats, anthems, and other choral pieces.

Shield, William (1748–1829) English violinist and composer. He embarked on a career as a violinist, but from 1778 produced his own works with great success at London theatres. His most popular piece was the opera *Rosina* (1782).

Orphaned at the age of nine, he was apprenticed to a shipbuilder, but studied music with Charles Avison in Newcastle-upon-Tyne, where he also appeared as a solo violinist and led the subscription concerts from 1763. After engagements in Scarborough and Stockton-on-Tees he went to London as second violin of the Royal Opera orchestra in 1772, becoming principal viola the following year. After the success of his first opera, *The Flitch of Bacon* in 1778, he was appointed composer to Covent Garden Theatre 1778–91 and again 1792–1807. In 1791 he met Haydn in London, and visited France and Italy. Two treatises, on harmony and thorough bass, were published in 1800 and 1817, in which year he was appointed Master of the King's Musick.

Works STAGE over 50 works, including *The Flitch of Bacon* (1778), *Rosina* (1782), *Robin Hood* (1784), *Richard Cœur de Lion* (1786), *The Marriage of Figaro* (after Beaumarchais, 1797), *Aladdin*, *The Woodman* (1791), *The Travellers in Switzerland* (1794), *Netley Abbey, The Italian Villagers*.

CHAMBER string quartets and trios; violin duets; songs.

Shifrin, Seymour J (1926–1979) US composer. His music is known for its chromatic intensity.

He studied with Otto Luening and William Schuman, and taught at Brandeis University, Massachusetts, from 1966.

Works ORCHESTRAL Chamber Symphony (1953), three pieces for orchestra (1958), *Five Last Songs* (1979).

CHAMBER five string quartets (1949–72), piano trio (1974), *A Renaissance Garland* (1975), *The Nick of Time* for ensemble (1978).

Shnitke alternative spelling for Russian composer Alfred Garriyevich ➔ **Schnittke**.

short octave in music, the bottom octave on an old keyboard instrument, where the notes governed by the extreme bottom keys are sometimes not tuned to the ordinary scale, but to a selection of lower notes more likely to be frequently required.

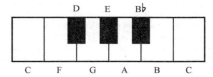

An example of the possible appearance and tuning of a short octave.

short score see ➔ **score**.

Shostakovich, Dmitri Dmitrievich (1906–1975) Russian composer. His music is chromatically tonal/modal, expressive, and sometimes highly dramatic; it was not always to official Soviet taste. He wrote 15 symphonies, chamber and film music, ballets, and operas, the latter including *Lady Macbeth of the Mtsensk District* (first performed in 1934), which was suppressed as being 'too divorced from the proletariat', but revived as *Katerina Izmaylova* in 1963. His symphonies are very highly regarded.

His son Maxim (1938–), a conductor, defected to the West after his father's death.

Shostakovich was born in St Petersburg. He entered the conservatory there in 1919 and studied with Leonid Vladimirovich Nikolaiev, Maximilian Steinberg, and Alexander Glazunov; he left in 1925, having already written a great many works. The first symphony, which dates from that year, was performed in 1926 and later throughout Europe. It quickly established his reputation internationally. He came into conflict with Soviet authority in 1930, when his opera, *The ➔ Nose*, based on a story by Nicolai Gogol, was condemned as bourgeois and decadent. The next, *Lady Macbeth of the Mtsensk District*, produced in 1934, was even more violently attacked in 1936

and had to be withdrawn; his fourth symphony was also withdrawn. It has been claimed that Stalin himself dictated the *Pravda* article entitled 'Chaos instead of Music', in which the composer was attacked for 'petty-bourgeois sensationalism': Stalin had been seated very near the orchestra at a performance of the opera, and had caught the full blast of the brass as they depicted the violent love-making of Sergei and Katerina. Already of a nervous disposition, Shostakovich was shattered by official condemnation. His popular fifth symphony, labelled by a party hack (not the composer himself) as 'A Soviet artist's practical creative reply to just criticism', helped to restore him in official favour, although the deliberately empty speech of the finale may betray the composer's true feelings. Similar deceptions are found in the first movement of the seventh symphony, arising from the siege of Leningrad: the banal march theme suggests Stalinist oppression as much as it does invading Nazis. Other major works include a highly charged cello concerto, and 24 preludes and fugues for solo piano. His string quartets are considered to be some of his greatest work and are often included in musical programmes all over the world.

In his later years he largely adapted his manner to the government's requirements, which in turn became somewhat modified, and established himself as the leading composer of the day, gaining the Stalin Prize with his piano quintet in 1941. With other leading composers he was again denounced in 1948 and did not resume significant composition until 1953, when he wrote his mighty tenth symphony in which the recently deceased Stalin is depicted in a sarcastic scherzo.

Works STAGE AND FILM operas *The Nose* (1927–28; first performed 1930), *Lady Macbeth of the Mtsensk District* (1930–32; first performed 1934); incidental music to several plays including Shakespeare's *Hamlet*, *King Lear*, and *Othello*; music to about 14 films.

ORCHESTRAL 15 symphonies, including no. 1 in F minor (1925), no. 5 in D minor (subtitled *A Soviet Artist's Practical Creative Reply to Just Criticism*, 1937), no. 6 in B minor (1939), no. 7 in C (*Leningrad*, 1941), no. 8 in C minor (1943), no. 10 in E minor (1953), no. 13 in B♭ minor (*Babi Yar*, with bass, bass chorus, and orchestra, 1962), no. 14 for soprano, bass, strings, and percussion (1969), no. 15 in A (1971); two piano concertos (1933, 1957); two violin concertos (1948, 1967); two cello concertos (1959, 1966).

CHAMBER 15 string quartets (1938–74); two piano trios (1923, 1944), piano quintet (1940), sonatas for cello (1934), violin (1968), viola (1975), all with piano.

VOCAL AND PIANO Songs to texts by Pushkin, Shakespeare, Lermontov, Blok, Michelangelo,

Shudi, Burkat (Burkhardt Tschudi)

and Dostoevsky; 24 Preludes and Fugues for piano (1951).

Shudi, Burkat (Burkhardt Tschudi) (1702–1773) Swiss-born English harpsichord maker. He settled in London as a cabinet maker in 1718, joined the harpsichord maker Tabel and set up on his own account in the 1730s.

Sibelius, Jean Julius Christian (1865–1957) Finnish composer. His works include nationalistic symphonic poems such as *En saga* (1893) and *Finlandia* (1900), a violin concerto (1904), and seven symphonies. In 1940 he suddenly ceased composing and spent the rest of his life as a recluse. Restoration of many works to their original state has helped to remove his conservative image and reveal unexpectedly revolutionary features.

Sibelius was the son of a surgeon; he had a classical education, and entered Helsinki University intending to pursue a career in law. He learned piano and violin as a child and tried composing long before he had any instruction. While studying law he took a special course under Martin Wegelius at the conservatory, and in 1885 gave up law altogether to attend the conservatory. He left in 1889 and had a string quartet and a suite for string orchestra performed in public. With a government grant he went to study counterpoint with Albert Becker in Berlin and later orchestration with Robert Fuchs in Vienna, where he also consulted Carl Goldmark. When he returned home he became a passionate nationalist, studying the *Kalevala* (the Finnish national epic poem) and other Finnish literature for subjects for his works, the first being *Kullervo*, performed at Helsinki in 1892. Sibelius had a great success with the work, capturing a popular feeling of protest against foreign, particularly Russian, oppression. Further nationalist sentiments were aroused by the tone poem *Finlandia* in 1899, which became an unofficial national anthem. An annual grant was voted to Sibelius by the Finnish government in 1897 and increased in 1926, and he was thus able to devote himself entirely to composition without having to fill any official or administrative post.

The first symphony, influenced by Tchaikovsky, was premiered in 1899. The second symphony followed in 1902 and is a wholly individual work. Sibelius gradually made his way abroad, but not in every country. Much of his work was published in Germany, but it was not widely performed there. In Britain he became much better known after the performance of the fourth symphony at the Birmingham Festival in 1912. Composed the previous year, it seems to symbolize the view expressed by Sibelius to Gustav Mahler in 1907 that a symphony's justification is the 'profound logic creating a connection between all the mo-

tifs'. The heavily revised fifth symphony of 1915–19 further develops this ideal.

Sibelius conducted the first performance of The *Oceanides* at Norfolk, Connecticut, USA, in 1914, when Yale University conferred a doctoral degree on him. During the Russian Revolution and after World War I there was much unrest in Finland, and Sibelius's country home at Järvenpää was invaded. He spent most of his life there quietly, however, completely devoted to composition. The seventh symphony of 1924, generally considered to be his greatest and most concentrated work, summed up the composer's career, beyond which it was difficult to develop. The conventional four movements are linked thematically into a single unit, lasting 20 minutes, creating an awe-inspiring structure as each idea unfolds and develops over the entire work.

Works STAGE opera *Jungfrun i Tornet/The Maiden in the Tower* (1896); incidental music to Adolf Paul's *King Christian* (1898), Arvid Järnefelt's *Kuolema* (including *Valse triste*, 1903), Maurice Maeterlinck's *Pelléas et Mélisande* (1905), Hjalmar Procopé's *Belshazzar's Feast* (1906), August Strindberg's *Svanevit*, Paul Knudsen's *Scaramouche*, Hofmannsthal's version of *Everyman*, Shakespeare's *Tempest*.

ORCHESTRAL seven symphonies, no. 1 in E minor (1899), no. 2 in D (1902), no. 3 in C (1904–7), no. 4 in A minor (1911), no. 5 in E♭ (1915–19), no. 6 in D minor (1923), no. 7 in C (1924); *Kullervo*, with solo voices and chorus (1892), symphonic poem *En Saga* (1892), *Rakastava* for strings and timpani, Four Legends: *Lemminkäinen and the Maidens of Saari*, *Lemminkäinen in Tuonela*, *The Swan of Tuonela*, *Lemminkäinen's Return* (1895), tone poem *Finlandia* (1899), violin concerto (1903), symphonic fantasy *Pohjola's Daughter* (1906), tone poem *Night-Ride and Sunrise* (1907), tone poem *The Bard* (1913); symphonic poems *The Oceanides* (1914), *Tapiola* (1926), a number of smaller orchestral pieces.

CHAMBER string quartet *Voces intimae* (1909), sonatina and many smaller pieces for violin and piano; *Malinconia* (1901) and two *Serious Pieces* for cello and piano; 18 Op. nos of piano works, including sonata in F major, *Pensées lyriques* (1914), *Kyllikki*, three sonatinas; two organ pieces.

VOCAL *Luonnotar* for soprano and orchestra (1910–13); 85 songs.

Siberia opera by Umberto ➔ Giordano (libretto by Luigi Illica), produced at La Scala, Milan, on 19 December 1903. It was revised in 1921 and produced again in Milan on 5 December 1927. In the story, Vassili is exiled to Siberia for wounding his rival Prince Alexis in a duel. He is joined there by Stephana, and they are both killed trying to escape.

siciliano or **siciliana,** French **sicilienne** a dance of the 17th and 18th centuries which originated in Sicily, Italy. In a relaxed compound time (6/8 or 12/8), it is closely associated with the pastorale. It appears as a slow movement in baroque sonatas, for example in those by Bach, Handel, and Corelli.

Sicilian Vespers opera by Giuseppe Verdi; see *Les* ➔ *vêpres siciliennes.*

sicilienne French term for ➔ siciliano or siciliana.

side drum percussion instrument, see ➔ snare drum.

Sieben Todsünden der Kleinbürger, Die, **The Seven Deadly Sins of the Petit-Bourgeois** ballet with songs by Kurt Weill (libretto by Brecht), produced at Paris on 7 June 1933 and choreographed by George Balanchine.

Siège de Corinthe opera by Gioacchino Rossini; see ➔ **Maometto Secondo.**

Siege of Rhodes, The opera by Matthew Locke, Henry Lawes, H Cooke, Edward Coleman, and Hudson (libretto by William Davenant), produced at Rutland House, London, on September 1656. It was the first English opera; its music is now lost.

Siegfried opera by Wagner, part of the trilogy of music dramas ➔ **Ring des Nibelungen.** The opera was first performed on 16 August 1876. The story concerns Siegfried, who, having been brought up by the dwarf Mime, slays the dragon Fafner and acquires the ring. He confronts the god Wotan, shattering his spear; the end of the gods is near. Although fearless in the face of battle, Siegfried awakens Brünnhilde and is frightened by the prospect of love, before being overcome by its power.

Siegfried Idyll a symphonic piece for small orchestra by Wagner, composed at Triebschen on the Lake of Lucerne in November 1870 and performed on Cosima Wagner's birthday, 25 December, on the staircase of the villa. It was therefore at first entitled *Triebschener Idyll* and called 'Treppenmusik' in the family circle. The thematic material is taken from ➔ *Siegfried,* except the German cradle song 'Schlaf, Kindlein, schlaf', but some of it, even though included in *Siegfried,* dates back to a string quartet of 1864. The musicians had to rehearse in secret, to maintain the element of surprise for Cosima; Hans Richter (six years later to premiere the *Ring* at Bayreuth in Bavaria) practised his trumpet part from a rowing boat in the middle of Lake Lucerne.

Siegl, Otto (1896–1978) Austrian composer, conductor, and violinist. After working as an or-

chestra violinist in Austria, he went to Germany, where he began teaching, and became professor of composition at Cologne Conservatory.

He studied violin with the Austrian composer Egon Kornauth (1891–1959) and composition with Roderich Mojsisovics-Mojsvár (1877–1953) in Vienna. He joined the Vienna Symphony Orchestra as a violinist, worked at the Graz Opera, and then went to Germany. There he became music director at Paderborn, at the same time conducting and teaching at Bielefeld and Essen. In 1933 he became composition professor at the Cologne Conservatory, returning to Vienna in 1948.

Works STAGE fairy opera *Der Wassermann*; music for two puppet plays.

CHORAL oratorios *Das Grosse Halleluja* (Claudius), *Eines Menschen Lied* (1931), *Klingendes Jahr* (1933), *Trostkantate, Mutter Deutschland*; *Missa Mysterium Magnum*; *Verliebte alle Reime* for chorus.

ORCHESTRAL three symphonies, sinfonietta, *Lyrische Tanzmusik, Festliche Ouvertüre, Pastoralouvertüre* (1939), *Concerto grosso antico* (1936), *Galante Abendmusik, Festmusik und Trauermusik* for orchestra; piano concerto (1963), violin concerto.

CHAMBER concerto for string quartet and string orchestra; five string quartets; songs.

signature see ➔ key signature; ➔ time signature.

Signor Bruschino, Il, ossia Il figlio per azzardo, **Mr Bruschino, or The Son by Accident** opera by Rossini (libretto by G M Foppa), produced at the Teatro San Moisè, Venice, in January 1813. In the story, Sofia must marry Bruschino's son, but her lover Florville, disguised as the proposed groom, wins her hand.

Sigtenhorst Meyer, Bernhard van den (1888–1953) Dutch musicologist and composer. He edited works by Jan Pieterszoon Sweelinck (1562–1621) and also wrote books on him. He studied with Zweers, D de Lange and others and later in Paris, afterwards travelling to Java and the Far East. He returned to Amsterdam, but moved to The Hague, where he lived for many years.

Works STAGE incidental music to Tagore's play *The King's Letter.*

CHORAL oratorio *The Temptation of Buddha, Stabat Mater, Hymn to the Sun* (St Francis of Assisi).

OTHER two string quartets; songs.

Sigurd opera by Ernest Reyer (libretto by C du Locle and A Blau, based on the Nibelung Saga), produced at the Théâtre de la Monnaie, Brussels, on 7 January 1884. Its plot is similar to that of *Götterdämmerung.* Sigurd rescues Brunehild under the influence of Hilda's love potion and gives her to King Gunther. However, evil Hagen convinces Gunther that Sigurd and Brunehild are lovers, and Gunther then kills Sigurd. Brunehild throws herself on his funeral pyre.

Siklós, Albert (1878–1942) Hungarian cellist, musicologist, and composer. He studied at the Hungarian Music School in Budapest and appeared as cellist in 1891, as lecturer in 1895, and began to compose seriously in 1896, when he finished a cello concerto, a symphony, and an opera. He held distinguished teaching posts in Budapest and was appointed professor in 1913.

Works STAGE three operas, two ballets.

OTHER choral and a vast number of orchestral works, concertos, chamber and much piano music; ten books of songs.

Sikorski, Kazimierz (1895–1985) Polish composer. In 1936 he was one of the founders of the Society for the Publication of Polish Music. He studied at the Chopin High School in Warsaw and later in Paris. In 1927 he became professor at the Warsaw Conservatory.

His son **Tomasz** (1939–) is a pianist and composer who has written instrumental music in various advanced idioms; he is noted as an early Polish minimalist.

Works CHORAL Psalm 7 for chorus and orchestra.

ORCHESTRAL AND CHAMBER four symphonies (1918–71), symphonic poem for orchestra; three string quartets, string sextet; songs; part songs.

Silbermann (lived 17th–18th centuries) German family of organ builders and harpsichord makers:

Andreas Silbermann (1678–1734), son of the carpenter Michael Silbermann. He worked with Casparini in Görlitz 1797–c.1799. He settled in Strasbourg in 1721 and built the cathedral organ there 1713–16.

Gottfried (1683–1753), the brother of Andreas. At first apprenticed to a bookbinder, he joined his brother in Strasbourg in 1702, staying there till 1710. He then settled in Freiberg, where he built the cathedral organ (1711–14), and died while at work on a new organ for the Dresden court. This organ, for the Katholische Hofkirch in Dresden, was largely destroyed by the British Royal Air Force in 1945. He also built harpsichords and clavichords (one of them commemorated by a piece by C P E Bach entitled 'Farewell to my Silbermann Clavichord'), and was the first German to make pianos, including a grand which may have been used by J S Bach.

Johann Andreas (1712–1783), the son of Andreas. He built 54 organs, including two at Strasbourg and another at Arlesheim Cathedral.

Johann Daniel (1717–1766), the son of Andreas. He worked with his uncle, Gottfried, whose organ at Dresden he finished.

Johann Heinrich (1727–99), the son of Andreas.

He made harpsichords and pianos, some with pedal boards.

Silbersee, Der opera by Kurt Weill (libretto by Georg Kaiser), produced at Erfurt and Magdeburg, Leipzig, 18 February 1933. In the story, Severin, wounded by Olim, joins him in a house by Silver Lake. When they enter a suicide pact, the water freezes over and they escape across the surface to a new life.

Silcher, Friedrich (1789–1860) German composer and conductor. He became a schoolmaster, but in 1815 went to Stuttgart as a conductor and in 1817 to the University of Tübingen in the same capacity. Some of his songs have become folk songs in Germany.

Works CHORAL AND VOICE two hymn-books (three and four voices), collections of songs, some arranged, some composed by himself, including 'Aennchen von Tharau', 'Loreley' (Heine), 'Morgen muss ich fort', 'Zu Strassburg auf der Schanz'.

Silent Woman, The opera by Richard Strauss; see *Die* ➜ *Schweigsame Frau*.

Siloti, Alexander (Ilyich) (1863–1945) Russian pianist and conductor. He studied at the Moscow Conservatory under Pyotr Tchaikovsky, Nikolai Rubinstein, and others, and later with Franz Liszt. He first appeared at Moscow in 1880 and later travelled widely. He left Russia in 1919 and lived in the USA at the end of his life. From 1925 to 1942 he taught at the Juilliard School in New York.

Silvana opera by Weber (libretto by F K Hiemer, altered from Steinsberg's *Waldmädchen*). Produced at Frankfurt on 16 September 1810, this was Weber's second version of *Das Waldmädchen* of 1800. The plot follows Silvana, who is struck dumb after being kidnapped. She eventually revives when she is discovered in the forest by Count Rudolf.

similarity relation in ➜ **pitch-class set** analysis, a method of comparing sets containing the same number of pitches, according to the intervals between the constituent pitches. Maximally similar sets will share many subsets and supersets; maximally dissimilar sets will share no subsets.

simile (Italian 'similar') in musical notation, directing the musician to continue performing a previously notated indication. For example, if the first few bars of a piece are marked ➜ **staccato** (detached) a composer may simply write *simile* rather than continue to mark individual staccato dots.

Simon Boccanegra opera by Verdi (libretto by Francesco Maria Piave, based on a Spanish drama by Gutiérrez), produced at the Teatro La Fenice, Venice, on 12 March 1857. A revised version, with the libretto altered by Boito, was produced at La Scala, Milan, on 24 March 1881. The story concerns the Doge of Venice Boccanegra, who discovers his long-lost illegitimate daughter, Amelia. She loves his enemy, Gabriele Adorno, and he and Boccanegra are reconciled. In the end, Boccanegra dies, poisoned by his jealous courtier, Paolo.

simple intervals in music, any intervals not larger than an octave, those exceeding that width being called ➔ **compound intervals**.

simple time in music, a metre in which each beat divides into two units. For example, 4/4 consists of four beats, each of two quavers.

Simpson, Christopher (c.1605–1669) English viola da gamba player, theorist, and composer. He was employed as a private tutor to the family of Sir Robert Bolles, and wrote many works for solo viol and for viol consorts. His instruction book for the viola da gamba, *The Division-Violist* (1659), was highly successful.

He joined the royalist army under the Duke of Newcastle in 1643 and endured much hardship, but later came under the patronage of Sir Robert Bolles, at whose residences at Scampton and in London he lived in comfort, teaching the children of the family and taking charge of the domestic music-making. He bought a house and farm at Pickering, Yorkshire, but died at one of Sir John Bolles's houses. He wrote another treatise, *The Principles of Practicle Musick* and annotations to Campion's *Art of Descant*.

Works WORKS FOR VIOL AND VIOLA DA GAMBA *Months and Seasons* for a treble and two bass viols, fancies and consorts for viols, suite in three parts for viols, divisions (variations) and pieces for viola da gamba.

Simpson, Robert (Wilfred Levick) (1921–1997) English composer and music critic. He studied privately with ➔ **Howells** and was active in the BBC. He wrote on music, especially that of Bruckner, Nielsen, and Sibelius. His music displays tonal stability and an emphasis on organic unity, influenced by Beethoven and Bruckner. His output includes eleven symphonies and 15 string quartets.

He took a degree in music at Durham University, England, in 1952.

Works ORCHESTRAL AND CHAMBER eleven symphonies (1951–90), *Nielsen Variations* (1986), concertos for violin (1959), piano (1967), flute (1989), and cello; *Variations and Fugue on a theme of Bach* for strings (1991); fantasia for strings; 15 string quartets (1952–91); piano music.

Sinding, Christian August (1856–1941) Norwegian composer. His works include songs and four symphonies, but he is chiefly remembered

for the popular piano piece *Frühlingsrauschen/ Rustle of Spring* (1896). His brothers Otto (1842–1909) and Stephan (1846–1922) were a painter and sculptor respectively.

He studied at Oslo and later, with the Norwegian government's support, went to Germany, continuing his studies at Liepzig, Berlin, and Munich, where he spent many years of his life. For a time he was professor of composition at Rochester, New York.

Works OPERA *The Holy Mountain* (1912).

ORCHESTRAL four symphonies and *Rondo infinito* for orchestra, piano concerto in Db major, three violin concertos (1898, 1901, 1917).

CHAMBER string quartet (1904), piano quintet, piano trio; sonatas and suite for violin and piano; variations for two pianos; suite, studies, and numerous pieces for piano, including the well-known *Frühlingsrauschen/Rustle of Spring*; songs.

sine wave in music, an electronically-generated tone considered to be 'pure' because of its lack of overtones.

sinfonia a symphony. In the early 18th century the sinfonia was simply an instrumental piece in an opera or other vocal work, especially the overture; it is in fact out of the overture that the symphony developed.

Sinfonia work for eight amplified voices and orchestra in five movements by Luciano ➔ **Berio** (1968) which uses collage techniques, particularly the third movement, which quotes the entirety of the Scherzo from Gustav Mahler's second symphony: over this is placed Berio's own music and brief quotations from many other composers including Bach, Brahms, Ravel, Schoenberg, Stravinsky, Berg, and Webern.

Sinfonia Antartica symphony by Ralph ➔ **Vaughan Williams** (his seventh) for soprano, women's chorus and orchestra. Composed 1949–52, it was based on his music for the film *Scott of the Antarctic* (1947–48). It was first performed in Manchester, England, on 14 January 1953, conducted by Barbirolli.

sinfonia concertante work in symphonic form with one or more solo instruments, similar to a concerto. Familiar examples are Mozart's K364 for violin, viola, and orchestra (1779) and Haydn's Op. 84 in B flat for violin, cello, oboe, and bassoon (1792).

Sinfonia da Requiem work for orchestra in three movements by Britten; commissioned to celebrate the 2,600th anniversary of the Imperial Japanese dynasty. The work was rejected for its allusions to the Catholic liturgy. The first performance was conducted by Barbirolli in New York on 29 March 1941 – eight months before Pearl Harbor.

Sinfonia domestica symphony by Richard Strauss; see ➤ *Symphonia domestica*.

Sinfonia Espansiva symphony by Carl ➤ Nielsen, no. 3, Op. 27. It was composed 1910–11 and was first performed in Copenhagen on 30 April 1912, conducted by Nielsen. The slow movement (marked 'pastoral') includes parts for wordless soprano and baritone voices.

It was not performed in public in the UK until 7 May 1962, in London, conducted by Fairfax.

Sinfonia Semplice sub-title of Nielsen's sixth and last symphony, composed 1924–25 and first performed in Copenhagen, on 11 December 1925, conducted by Riccardo Nielsen.

sinfonietta orchestral work that is of a shorter, lighter nature than a ➤ symphony, for example Leoš ➤ Janáček's *Sinfonietta* (1926). It is also the name for a small-scale orchestra specializing in such works, for example the London Sinfonietta.

Singakademie (German 'singing-academy', 'vocal academy') name of certain choral societies in Germany and Austria.

Singspiel (German 'sung play') term originally applied to all opera, later confined to opera with spoken dialogue. Mozart provided the greatest examples with *Die Entführung aus dem Serail/ The Abduction from the Seraglio* (1782) and *Die Zauberflöte/The Magic Flute* (1791). During the 19th and 20th centuries *Singspiel* came to imply a comic or light opera of contemporary manners or ordinary life.

Sinigaglia, Leone (1868–1944) Italian composer. He studied at the Turin Conservatory and with Eusebius Mandyczewski in Vienna. He returned to Turin and settled down to composition and folk-song collecting.

Works ORCHESTRAL suite *Piemonte*, overture to Goldoni's *Le baruffe chiozzote*, *Danze piemontesi* for orchestra (1903); concerto, *Rapsodia piemontese*, and romance for violin and orchestra.

CHAMBER string quartet in D major, concert study and variations on a theme by Brahms for string quartet; sonatas for cello and violin, folk songs.

sino (Italian 'until') in music, a word used in such directions as that indicating a repeat *sin'al fine* (until the end) or *sin'al segno* ... (to the sign ...). It is abbreviated to *sin'* when followed by a vowel.

Sirius work by Stockhausen for soprano, baritone, and ensemble, dedicated to American pioneers and astronauts. It was first performed in Washington, DC, on 18 July 1976.

Sir John in Love opera by Vaughan Williams (libretto selected by composer from Shakespeare's *Merry Wives of Windsor*), produced at the Royal College of Music, London, on 21 March 1929.

Siroe, rè di Persia, **Siroes, King of Persia** libretto by Metastasio.

Opera by Handel, produced at the King's Theatre, Haymarket, London, on 17 February 1728. Settings were also composed by Vinci (Venice, 1726), Hasse (Bologna, 1733), and Pérez (Naples, 1740). The story concerns Siroe, who is passed over by his father Cosroe for succession to the throne. Siroe is accused of treachery but survives the plots of his brother Medarse and Cosroe's mistress Laodice to gain the crown.

sistrum ancient percussion instrument, probably originating in Egypt, played like a rattle. It has a metal frame fitted to a handle and metal bars or loops are loosely hung on the frame and made to strike against it by shaking the instrument.

sitar (Hindi, from Persian seh tar, 'three strings') large long-necked lute used mainly in North Indian (Hindustani) music. The hollow neck is made of wood, and the body is half a hollow gourd with a thin wooden belly. Some instruments have a small gourd resonator attached to the upper end of the neck. The neck has 16 to 24 curved, movable frets made of metal. Modern sitars have six or seven playing strings (five melody and two for drone and rhythmic punctuation) and twelve or more sympathetic strings. The sitar is the best-known solo concert instrument in the tradition, where it is usually accompanied by the ➤ tabla drum pair, and is also well known outside India.

Sitsky, Larry (1934–) Australian composer of Russian descent. He studied at the New South Wales Conservatorium 1951–55, and with Egon Petri, former pupil of Busoni, in San Francisco. He was active as a pianist in the music of Busoni and other major moderns, head of keyboard studies at the Canberra School of Music 1966–78, and of composition from 1981.

Works OPERA *Fall of the House of Usher* (1965), *Lenz* (1972), *Golem* (composed 1980, premiered 1993).

ORCHESTRAL three violin concertos (1971–87), concertos for clarinet (1981), trombone (1982), guitar (1984), and piano (1991).

CHAMBER three string quartets (no. 3 1993) and piano pieces with accompanying electronic effects.

Six, Les group of French 20th-century composers; see ➤ *Les Six*.

sixth in music, an ➤ interval of six diatonic notes. A sixth is an 'imperfect interval' (having 'major' and 'minor' variants). A major sixth consists of nine semitones (for example, C–A). A minor sixth consists of eight semitones (C–A flat).

Major, minor, and augmented sixths; major and minor $\frac{6}{3}$ and $\frac{6}{4}$ chords.

Sjögren, (Johan Gustaf) Emil (1853–1918) Swedish composer. In 1891 he became organist at St John's Church, Stockholm, but devoted most of his time to teaching and composition.

He studied at the Stockholm Conservatory and later in Berlin; he also came under the influence of the Danish composer Peter Lange-Müller (1850–1926) during six months' stay at Meran.

Works ORCHESTRAL AND CHAMBER five violin and piano sonatas; organ works; two piano sonatas, *Erotikon*, *Novellettes*, and numerous other works for piano; songs.

Skalkottas, Nicos (1904–1949) Greek composer. He was Greece's first composer of international stature; only after his death did his vast output begin to be performed. Until 1938 his compositions were influenced by the 12-note method of Schoenberg.

Skalkottas was intended for a career as a concert violinist and studied at the Athens Conservatory and with Economidis. Later he spent twelve years in Germany, where he studied composition with Schoenberg, Weill, and Jarnach. In 1933 he returned to Greece and spent the remainder of his life as an obscure orchestral player, composing in his spare time.

Works STAGE two ballets *The Maid and Death* (1938) and *The Sea* (1949); 36 Greek Dances (1931–6).

ORCHESTRAL *Sinfonietta*, overture *The Return of Ulysses*, two suites for orchestra; concerto and symphony for wind instruments, three piano concertos (1931, 1938, 1939), violin concerto (1938), cello concerto (1938), concerto for violin and viola (1940), concerto for two violins.

CHAMBER four string quartets (1928–40), octet for woodwind quartet and string quartet (1931), four sonatinas for violin and piano (1929–35).

Skilton, Charles Sanford (1868–1941) US composer. He studied at Yale University and in Germany. In 1903 he was appointed Professor of Music at Kansas University and there made a study of American Indian tunes.

Works STAGE the operas *Kalopin* (composed 1927), *The Sun Bride* (1930), *The Day of Gayomair* (composed 1936); incidental music for Sophocles' *Electra* and Barrie's *Mary Rose*.

CHORAL oratorio *The Guardian Angel*, cantatas.

ORCHESTRAL *Primeval Suite* and other suites and overtures for orchestra.

CHAMBER *Two Indian Dances* for string quartet; violin and piano sonata; organ and piano works.

skočná Czech dance in quick 2/4 time in which three-bar phrases are a feature. The 5th, 7th, and 11th of Antonín Dvořák's *Slavonic Dances* for piano duet are in the form of the *skočná*.

Skriabin or **Scriabin, Aleksandr Nikolaievich (1872–1915)** Russian composer and pianist. His visionary tone poems such as *Prometheus* (1911), and symphonies such as *Divine Poem* (1903), employed unusual scales and harmonies.

Škroup, František Jan (1801–1862) Bohemian composer. A song he wrote for the play *Shoemakers' Fair* (1834) later became the Czech national anthem. He also composed the first Czech opera and compiled a six-volume anthology of Czech patriotic songs 1834–44.

He studied law, but was from 1827 second and from 1837–57 first conductor at the National Theatre in Prague. From 1860 he conducted at the Opera of Rotterdam.

Works OPERA AND STAGE the operas *Drátenik* (*The Tinker*, 1826), *The Marriage of Libuša* (1835), *Oldřich and Božena* (1828), *Drahomira* (1848) and some other Czech and German operas; incidental music to Tyl's *Fidlovačka*.

CHAMBER three string quartets and other chamber music; songs.

Skyscrapers ballet by John Carpenter (choreography by Heinrich Kröller), produced by the Russian Ballet in Monte Carlo in 1925. Its first US performance was at the New York Metropolitan Opera on 19 February 1926.

Sleeping Beauty, The, Russian **Spyashchaya krasavitsa** ballet by Tchaikovsky (choreography by Petipa), produced at the Mariinsky Theatre, St Petersburg, on 15 January 1890. A new version, with additional orchestration by Stravinsky and additions to the choreography by Bronislava Nizhinska, was produced at the Alhambra Theatre, London, on 2 November 1921.

sientando in music, the Italian phrase meaning 'gradually decreasing in pace'.

slide in playing string instruments, the technique of passing from one note to another by moving the finger along the string instead of lifting it to make way for another finger. Also, the movable part of the tube of the trombone by which the positions, and therefore the notes, are altered, as well as mechanisms on other wind instruments by which the pitch can be adjusted by a change in the length of the tube.

slit drum not a true drum but a 'percussion tube' made by cutting, burning, or gouging a slit in the wall of a hollowed-out piece of wood (such as a tree trunk). It is used for musical or signalling purposes in cultures from Oceania to Africa.

Slonimsky, Nicolas, originally **Nikolai Slonimsky (1894–1995)** Russian musical author, conductor, and composer. He is best known for editing major reference works such as *Baker's Biographical Dictionary of Musicians*. As a conductor he gave early performances of works by Varèse, Ruggles, Cowell, and Ives.

He studied at the St Petersburg Conservatory and in 1923 settled in the USA, becoming a US citizen in 1931. He compiled the survey *Music since 1900* (1937, revised 1971; supplements 1986 and 1995), and edited *Baker's Biographical Dictionary of Musicians* editions 5, 6, 7, and 8 (1958, 1978, 1985, 1992; editions 7 and 8 with Dennis McIntire).

The opera *Mary Stuart* by his nephew, Sergei Slonimsky (1932–), was produced at the 1986 Edinburgh Festival.

Works *Fragment from Orestes* (Euripides) for orchestra (in quarter-tones); *Studies in Black and White* for piano.

slur in musical notation, a curved line written above or below a group of notes, indicating that all the associated notes are to be played or sung ➤ **legato** (smoothly). If staccato dots appear beneath the slur, then this indicates ➤ **portato**, a form of detached articulation. A slur connecting two notes of the same pitch is called a ➤ **tie**, indicating that the second note is not to be reiterated, but played continuously as one long note.

Sly, Christopher Sly opera by Wolf-Ferrari (libretto by G Forzano, based on the prologue of Shakespeare's *Taming of the Shrew*), produced at La Scala, Milan, on 29 December 1927. In the story, Sly suffers a practical joke: he is made to believe he is an aristocrat suffering from amnesia rather than a poor poet. Dolly, mistress of the Duke of Westmoreland, falls for him, but she cannot save him from a lowly death in the dungeon.

Smalley, Roger (1943–) English composer and pianist. He is an important and uncompromising exponent of the ideas of his former teacher, ➤ **Stockhausen**, and of the avant-garde stance in general. Of his own works, several, including the Missa Brevis (1967), are based on 16th-century models by William Blitheman. He was active with the electronic group Intermodulation 1969–76. Aleatory effects are also present in his music.

He studied at the Royal College of Music with Peter Fricker 1961–65. His study with Stockhausen in Cologne 1965–66 was a formative influence. He began teaching at the University of Western Australia in 1976.

Works CHAMBER septet for soprano and ensemble (text by Cummings, 1963), *Missa Parodia* for ensemble (1967), *Pulses* for 5 × 4 players (1969), *William Derrincourt* for baritone, chorus, and ensemble (1977), string quartet (1979), *Ceremony I* for percussion quartet (1987), *Strung Out* for 13 solo strings (1988).

ORCHESTRAL *Gloria tibi Trinitas* for orchestra (1965), *The Song of the Highest Tower* for soprano, baritone, chorus, and orchestra (texts by Blake and Rimbaud, 1968); *Beat Music* for four electronic instruments and orchestra (1971); *Konzertstück* for violin and orchestra (1980); piano concerto (1985).

OTHER *Zeitebenen* for four players and tape (1973), symphony in one movement (1981), *The Narrow Road to the Deep North*, music theatre (1983).

Smareglia, Antonio (1854–1929) Italian composer. He produced the first of his ten operas at Milan in 1879, but never had any real success, in spite of the good quality of his work. He was able to continue composing due to the support of his patron, the industrialist Carlo Sai, and the conductor Arturo Toscanini.

He was sent to Vienna to study engineering, but on hearing works by the great masters there he left for Milan in 1872 and studied composition under Franco Faccio at the conservatory there. In 1900 he went blind.

Works OPERA *Preziosa* (1879), *Bianca da Cervia* (1882), *Rè Nala* (1887), *Der Vasall von Szigeth* (1889), *Cornelius Schutt* (1893), *Nozze istriane*, *La Falena* (1897), *Oceàna* (1903), *L'Abisso*.

OTHER symphonic poem *Leonore*, songs.

Smetana, Bedřich (1824–1884) Bohemian composer. He established a Czech nationalist style in, for example, the operas *Prodaná Nevěsta/The Bartered Bride* (1866) and *Dalibor* (1868), and the symphonic suite *Má Vlast/My Country* (1875–80). He conducted at the National Theatre of Prague in 1866–74.

Smetana was the son of a brewer. He played piano and violin at a very early age and was soon able to play in the family's string quartet. He was educated in Germany and all his life, in spite of his musical nationalism, spoke and wrote Czech like a foreigner. He was sent to school first in Prague and then at Pilsen. His father opposed a musical career, but eventually allowed him to study music in Prague, though with a very small allowance. In 1844 he obtained the post of music master in Count Thun's family, which helped to support him until 1847. In 1848 he took part in the revolution against Austria, married the pianist Kateřina Kolařová, established a school of music for which Liszt supplied funds, and was recommended by Liszt to the Leipzig publisher Kistner.

In 1856 he went to Göteborg in Sweden, where at first he taught but later became conductor of the new Philharmonic Society and gave piano and chamber-music recitals. He returned to Prague in 1859 because the northern climate did not suit his wife, who died at Dresden on the way back. He married Bettina Ferdinandová in 1860 and returned to Sweden in the autumn, but finally returned to Prague in the spring of 1861. After a long tour in Germany, Holland, and Sweden to raise money, he settled in the Czech capital in 1863 and opened another school of music, this time with distinctly nationalist tendencies, and became conductor of the Hlahol choral society. His work was now becoming thoroughly Czech in character, and he began to produce Czech operas in the national theatre established in 1864, of which he became conductor in 1866.

The nationalist opera *The Brandenburgers in Bohemia* was a success in January 1866, although *Prodaná Nevesta/The Bartered Bride*, for which he is most well known, was a failure in May. In 1872 he began composing his great cycle of symphonic poems, *Má Vlast/My Country*, which is often performed in the Czech Republic at times of national celebration. In 1874 he suddenly became totally deaf, as the result of a syphilitic infection. He still continued to compose operas as well as the string quartet *From my Life*, with its strong autobiographical theme, depicting his love for his first wife and children (all of whom had died by 1859). At the beginning of the last movement, the onset of his deafness is portrayed by a piercing high note on the violin (representing the condition he had, where he could hear a high note in his ear all the time). In 1881 he had his last major success, when his great patriotic festival opera *Libuše* was premiered in Prague. In 1883 he was certified insane and in May 1884 was taken to an asylum, where he died.

Works OPERA *Prodaná Nevesta/The Bartered Bride* (1866), *Dalibor* (1868), *Libuše* (1881), *Two Widows* (1874).

ORCHESTRAL cycle of symphonic poems *Má Vlast/My Country* containing *Vyšehrad*, *Vltava*, *Šárka*, *In the Bohemian Woods and Fields*, *Tábor*, *Blaník* 1872–79).

CHAMBER AND PIANO piano trio in G minor (1855), two string quartets (1876, 1883; the first *From my Life*); 8 Op. nos of piano works and many miscellaneous piano pieces including *Wedding Scenes*, *Scenes from Macbeth*, and Czech dances.

Smirnov, Dmitri (1948–) Russian composer. His music draws on eclectic stylistic sources and is often concerned with refinement of instrumental texture. It includes settings of poems by Blake, Pushkin, Coleridge, and Alexander Blok.

He studied with Edison Denisov at the Moscow Conservatory 1967–72. After the collapse of communism he emigrated to the West, and with his wife Elena Firsova was joint composer-in-residence at Keele University, UK, from 1992.

Works CHAMBER three string quartets (1973, 1985, 1993), two violin sonatas (1969, 1979), piano quintet (1993).

OPERA *Triel* (1983) and *The Lamentations of Thel* (1986).

ORCHESTRAL Symphony no. 1 (*The Seasons*) (1980), two piano concertos (1971, 1978), concerto for violin and 13 strings (1990), cello concerto (1992), *Mozart-Variations* for orchestra (1987).

OTHER *Jacob's Ladder* for 16 players (1990; premiered under Rozhdestvensky in London, 1991).

Smit, Leo (1921–1999) US composer. He was pianist with Balanchine's American Ballet Company 1936–37; he taught at the University College of Los Angeles 1957–63 and was director of the Monday Evening Concerts there.

He studied at the Curtis Institute, Philadelphia, 1930–32, and studied composition with Nicolas Nabokov.

Works OPERA *The Alchemy of Love* (1969; libretto by astronomer Fred Hoyle) and *Magic Water* (1978).

ORCHESTRAL three symphonies (1956, 1965, 1981); piano concerto (1968); *Symphony of Dances and Songs* (1981).

CHAMBER sonata for solo cello (1982); string quartet (1984).

Smith, Bernard (Bernhard Schmidt) (1629–1708), called **'Father Smith'** German organ builder. He settled in England in 1660. His first English organ was at the Chapel Royal in London. He was appointed organist at St Margaret's Church, Westminster, after building the organ there. He also built organs at Durham Cathedral and St Paul's Cathedral, London.

Smith, Carleton Sprague (1905–1994) US critic, musicologist, and flautist. He studied at Harvard University and in Vienna. After a year as critic to the *Boston Transcript*, he became chief librarian of the music section of the New York Public Library and lecturer in history of music at Columbia University. In 1938 he became president of the American Musicological Society.

Smith, John Christopher (1712–1795) German-born English organist and composer. He acted as Handel's amanuensis (artistic assistant) during the composer's blindness.

He was the son of Johann Christoph Schmidt of Ansbach, who went to London as Handel's treasurer and copyist. He studied with Handel, and later with Johann Pepusch and Thomas Rosein-grave. In 1746–48 he travelled on the Continent and in 1754 became organist of the Foundling Hospital, where he conducted annual perfor-mances of the *Messiah* between 1759 and 1768.

Works OPERA *Teraminta, Ulysses* (1733), *Issipile* (1743), *Ciro riconosciuto* (1745), *Dario* (1746), *The Fairies* (from Shakespeare's *Midsummer Night's Dream*, 1755), *The Tempest* (after Shakes-peare, 1756), *Rosalinda* (1740), *The Enchanter, or Love and Magic* (Garrick, 1760).

CHORAL oratorios *David's Lamentation over Saul and Jonathan* (1738), *Paradise Lost* (after Milton, 1758), *Rebecca, Judith* (1758), *Jehoshaphat* (1764), *The Redemption* (1774).

OTHER Burial Service; instrumental works.

Smith, John Stafford (1750–1836) English music scholar and composer. He was one of the first people to undertake the study of early music, and in 1812 published his *Musica Antiqua*, which includes pieces from the 12th century onwards. The tune of his song 'Anacreon in Heaven' was later adopted as the US national anthem, 'The Star-spangled Banner'.

He studied under his father, Martin Smith, who was organist at Gloucester Cathedral. Later he went to London, where he was a chorister in the Chapel Royal and studied under William Boyce and James Nares. He became a Gentleman of the Chapel Royal in 1784, organist of Gloucester Cathedral in 1790, and in 1802 succeeded Arnold as organist of the Chapel Royal. He succeeded Ayrton as Master of the Children in 1805. He as-sisted Hawkins in his *History of Music*.

Works SONGS anthems, glees, catches, canons, madrigals, part songs; songs including 'Anacreon in Heaven' (now 'The Star-spangled Banner').

Smith, Robert (c.1648–1675) English com-poser. He was a chorister at the Chapel Royal in London under Cooke and became Musician in Ordinary to the King on the death of Pelham Humfrey in 1674.

Works STAGE incidental music for numerous plays (some with Staggins and others).

CHAMBER music for strings; harpsichord pieces; songs, duets.

Smith Brindle, Reginald (1917–2003) English composer, teacher, and writer on music. His music is influenced by Berio and Stockhausen and employs electronic techniques. His writings include *Serial Composition* (1966) and *The New Music* (1975).

He studied in Italy with Ildebrando Pizzetti and Dallapiccola and worked for Italian radio (RAI) 1956–61. He was professor at the University of Surrey 1970–85.

Works OPERA the chamber opera *Antigone* (1969). ORCHESTRAL Symphony (1954), *Variations on theme of Dallapiccola* for orchestra (1955), *Extre-mum carmen* for voices and orchestra (1956), *String quartet Music* (1958), *Creation Epic* for or-chestra (1964), *Worlds without End* for speaker, voices, orchestra, and tapes (1973), *The Walls of Jericho* for tuba and tape (1974), *Guitar Cosmos* (1976), *Journey towards Infinity* for orchestra (1987).

Smithers, Don (Le Roy) (1933–) US music historian and trumpeter. He was active as trum-peter and cornet player in various early music groups, including the New York Pro Musica, the Leonhardt Consort, Concentus Musicus Wien, and the Early Music Consort of London. His books include *The Music and History of the Ba-roque Trumpet Before 1721* (1973).

He studied at Columbia University, New York, and at Oxford. He has taught at Syracuse Univer-sity, New York, 1966–75, and at the Hague, Neth-erlands.

smorzando (Italian 'dying') in musical notation, getting gradually softer, dying away. It can also imply some ➔ **ritardando** (slowing down).

Smyth, Ethel Mary (1858–1944) English com-poser. Her works include *Mass in D* (1893) and operas *The Wreckers* (1906) and *The Boatswain's Mate* (1916). In 1911 she was imprisoned as an ad-vocate of women's suffrage.

She studied at the Leipzig Conservatory and then privately there with Heinrich von Herzogen-berg. She had some works performed there and after her return to England one or two appeared in London, including the Mass in 1893. She was encouraged by the conductor Hermann Levi (who had premiered Wagner's *Parsifal* in 1882) to write an opera. *Fantasio* was performed at Wei-mar in 1898 and was taken up three years later by Felix Mottl in Karlsruhe. *Der Wald/The Forest* was premiered at the Royal Opera, Berlin in 1902 and was performed at Covent Garden three months later; the following year it became the first opera by a woman to be shown at the New York Metropolitan Opera. *The Wreckers* was completed in 1904 and premiered at Leipzig in 1906; its 1909 performance in London under Thomas Beecham almost caused the conductor to alter his unflattering opinion of women com-posers.

Smyth lived much abroad, but in 1910 received an honorary PhD from Durham University and about that time joined actively in the movement for women's suffrage. In 1911 when jailed at Hol-loway she led her fellow suffragettes in her song 'March of the Women', conducting them with a government-issue toothbrush. She continued to be fierce in the promotion of her music and in 1916 her most successful opera *The Boatswain's Mate* was premiered in London. After the war she turned increasingly to writing, producing ten entertaining volumes of memoirs, including the autobiographical *Female Pipings in Eden* (1933) and *What Happened Next* (1940). In her later years she lived at Woking in Surrey and, regarding herself as neglected on account of her sex, composed less and less. During her last years she suffered much from deafness and distorted hearing.

Works OPERA *Fantasio* (after Musset, Weimar, 1898), *The Forest* (Berlin, 1902), *The Wreckers* (Leipzig, 1906), *The Boatswain's Mate* (after W W Jacobs, 1916), *Fête galante* (1923), *Entente cordiale* (1925).

CHORAL AND ORCHESTRAL Mass in D major; *The Prison* for solo voices, chorus, and orchestra; overture to Shakespeare's *Antony and Cleopatra*; serenade for orchestra (1890); concerto for violin, horn, and orchestra; three Anacreontic Odes for voice and orchestra.

CHAMBER string quintet, string quartet; sonatas, songs.

Smythe, William (c.1550–c.1600) English composer. He was a minor canon and later master of the choristers (1594–98) at Durham Cathedral. He wrote a number of works for the Anglican church, not to be confused with those by his later namesake, 'William Smith of Durham'.

snare in some types of drum, especially the snare drum, a string of gut, wire, or plastic, stretched over one of the heads. Snares add brilliance to a drum's tone by vibrating against the skin as the drum is struck. If that effect is not required, the snares can be temporarily slackened.

snare drum or **side drum** double-headed drum used in military bands and in orchestras, with skins at both upper and lower ends of the instrument. A snare of catgut string or wire is stretched over the lower skin, to produce a rattling sound when the upper skin is struck by a pair of hard wooden drumsticks. Single strokes on the side drum are ineffective: it is usually made to produce small patterns of repeated notes or more or less prolonged rolls. Its tone is bright and hard, without definite pitch, and it can be muted by relaxing the tension of the snare. There is a famous orchestral snare-drum solo in Carl Nielsen's Fifth symphony.

Snow Maiden, The, Russian *Snegurotchka* opera by Rimsky-Korsakov (libretto by composer, based on a play by Alexander Nikolaevich Ostrovsky), produced at St Petersburg on 10 February 1882. The story concerns the Snow Maiden, who lives among humans but cannot love. She falls for Mizgir and, granted the ability to love by Spring, melts in the sunlight.

Socrate, Socrates symphonic drama by Erik Satie (libretto taken from Victor Cousin's French translation of Plato's *Dialogues*). First produced in Paris on 14 February 1920, it was performed at the festival of the International Society for Contemporary Music (ISCM), Prague, in May 1925.

Söderman, (Johan) August (1832–1876) Swedish composer. He learnt music from his father, a theatre conductor, and at 18 went to Finland as director of music to a Swedish company of musicians. In 1856 he produced his first operetta at Helsinki. After a period of study at Leipzig he was appointed chorus master at the Royal Opera at Stockholm in 1860 and second conductor in 1862.

Works OPERA AND STAGE the operetta *The Devil's First Lesson* (1856) and others; incidental music to Schiller's *Maid of Orleans*, Topelius's *Regina* and other plays.

CHORAL AND VOICE Mass for solo voices, chorus and orchestra; *Swedish Wedding* for female voices, cantatas, and part songs; vocal settings of Bellman's rhapsodies; sacred songs and hymns with organ; ballads and songs for voice and piano.

ORCHESTRAL *Circassian Dance*, concert overture for orchestra.

Sofonisba, La opera by Antonio Caldara (libretto by Francesco Silvani), produced at the Teatro San Giovanni Crisostomo, Venice, in December 1708. In the story, Siface, King of Numidia, is captured by the Romans. His wife Sophonisba joins him, but commits suicide rather than face the humiliation of her chains.

Opera by Gluck (libretto as above, with airs from different libretti by Metastasio), produced at the Teatro Regio Ducal, Milan, on 18 January 1744.

soft pedal or **una corda pedal** on the piano, the left pedal, which reduces volume. On a grand piano this is achieved by moving the position of the hammers so that fewer strings per note are struck. On an upright piano the hammers are moved closer to the strings.

soggetto (Italian 'subject') in music, the subject of a work, especially the subject of a ➔ fugue.

soggetto cavato (Italian 'extracted subject') in the 15th century and afterwards, a vocal theme sung to a melody formed from the vowels of a sentence converted by the composer into musical notes of the ➔ hexachord: a = fa or la, e = re, i = mi, o = do, u = ut.

sogno di Scipione, Il, Scipio's Dream dramatic serenade by Mozart (libretto by Metastasio), produced at Salzburg at the installation of the new archbishop, Hieronymus von Colloredo, on 1 May 1772. In the story, Scipio is faced with two

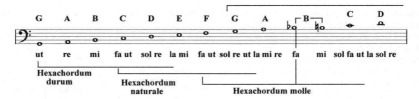

Solmization of the gamut, with different possible readings according to the particular hexachord.

goddesses in a dream. Scipio chooses Constancy rather than Fortune.

Soh the name for the dominant note in any key in ➤ **tonic sol-fa**, the method of teaching music in which notes of a scale are named by syllables (doh, ray, me, etc). Pronounced 'soh', the note is represented by the letter s in notation.

Sohal, Naresh (1939–) Indian composer. He first came to attention with his *Asht Prahar* (1965), performed by the London Philharmonic Orchestra in 1970. *The Wanderer* for baritone, chorus, and orchestra was performed at the 1982 London Promenade Concerts, and *From Gitanjali* by the New York Philharmonic Orchestra under Zubin Mehta in 1985.

He studied with Jeremy Dale Roberts and Alexander Goehr in England.

Works ORCHESTRAL *Indra-Dhanush* for orchestra (1973), *Undulation* for cello (1984), *Tandova Nritya* for orchestra (1984).

OTHER *Inscape* for chorus, flute, and percussion (1979), two brass quintets (1983, 1984).

Sol the old name for the note G (see ➤ **solmization**). It is still used in Latin countries. In tonic sol-fa notation, it is the dominant note in any key represented by the symbol **s**, pronounced 'Soh'.

Soldaten, Die, The Soldiers opera in four acts by Bernd Alois Zimmermann (libretto by composer, after the play by Jakob Lenz, 1776). Composed 1958–60 and revised 1963–64, it was first performed at Cologne on 15 February 1965, conducted by Gielen. The story concerns the moral degradation of Marie: she is at first engaged to Stolzius and then seduced by Baron Desportes and Major Mary. Stolzius poisons himself and Deziortes, and Marie becomes a beggar.

A Vocal Symphony for five soloists and orchestra derived from the opera in 1958; use is made of ballet, mime, *sprechstimme*, electronics, and film. The composer committed suicide in 1970, two years before the first British performance, in Edinburgh.

Soleil des eaux, Le, The Sun of the Waters music by Pierre ➤ **Boulez** for a radio play by René Char in 1948. It was revised as a cantata for sop-

rano, tenor, baritone, and chamber orchestra and first performed at Paris on 18 July 1950. Initially revised with the addition of a chorus and performed at Darmstadt (9 September 1958), it was further revised for soprano and chorus and given in Berlin in 1965.

Soler, Antonio (1729–1783) Spanish organist and composer. He wrote much church music as well as organ concerti and incidental music for plays; but his most celebrated works are probably his many harpsichord sonatas, distinguished successors to those of Domenico Scarlatti, with whom he probably studied 1752–57.

A chorister at Montserrat, he was maestro di cappella at Lleida Cathedral and entered the Escorial monastery in 1752, becoming organist and choirmaster there the following year. His treatise *Llave de la Modulación* was published in 1762.

Works DRAMATIC MUSIC incidental music for plays by Calderón and others.

CHURCH AND SECULAR MUSIC nine Masses, motets, and other church music; 132 villancicos; quintets for organ and strings; organ concertos; 120 harpsichord sonatas.

Solerti, Angelo (1865–1907) Italian musicologist. He wrote several works on the origins of dramatic music in the early 17th century

sol-fa in music, abbreviation for ➤ **tonic sol-fa**, a method of teaching music, usually singing, systematized by John Curwen (1816–1880).

solfège, Italian **solfeggio** an elementary method of teaching sight-reading and of ear-training, practised mainly in France and Italy. The names of the notes ('do, re, mi', and so on) are pronounced while the notes are sung unaccompanied and the intervals have thus to be learnt by ear.

soli in music, a group of solo performers as distinct from the whole vocal or orchestral body employed in a work.

solmization (from Latin *solmisatio*) the designation of the musical scales by means of syllables, similar to modern ➤ **tonic sol-fa**. The notes of the Greek ➤ **tetrachords** were already designated by syllables, but Guido d'Arezzo in the 11th century replaced them by the ➤ **hexachords** and used the

Latin syllables Ut, Re, Mi, Fa, Sol, La for their six notes. Si was added later for the seventh and Ut was replaced by Do in Italy and elsewhere, though it is still largely retained in France.

The syllables were derived from a hymn of the year 770 for the festival of St John the Baptist, the lines of the plainsong of which began on the successive notes of the hexachord: UT *queant laxis*; REsonare *fibris*; MIra *gestorum*; FAmuli *tuorum*; SOLve *polluti*; LAbii *reatum*; *Sancte Ioannes*. The seventh syllable, Si, was derived from the initial letters of the last line. These syllables, as in modern tonic sol-fa with movable Doh, were not immutably fixed to C, D, E, F, G, A, but could be transferred by mutation to other degrees of the scale, so long as the semitone always occurred between Mi and Fa. The so-called 'natural hexachord' beginning on C could thus be changed to the 'hard hexachord' beginning on G, in which case mi-fa corresponded with B–C, or to the 'soft hexachord' beginning on F (see ➤ hexachord).

solo (Italian 'alone') in musical notation, a piece or passage written for one performer. Sometimes this implies an accompaniment provided by another player or players; for instance, Bach's solo cello sonatas are written for unaccompanied cello, but his solo violin concertos are written for a single violinist with orchestral accompaniment.

Solomon oratorio by Handel (libretto probably by Newburgh Hamilton), performed at Covent Garden, London, on 17 March 1749.

solo organ in music, the fourth manual (keyboard) of an organ, characterized by pipes and stops of distinctive tone quality, (resembling individual instruments). Typically, one hand plays a 'solo' on this manual, while the other provides a softer accompaniment on another manual.

Soloviev, Nikolai Feopemptovich (1846–1916) Russian composer and music critic. In 1875 his opera *Vakula the Smith* lost to Tchaikovsky's entry in a competition, but some members of the jury apparently preferred Soloviev's work. He was highly critical of Tchaikovsky as well as the nationalist composers Vladimir Stasov and César Cui.

He began by studying medicine, but turned to music and entered the St Petersburg Conservatory, where his teachers included Nikolai Zaremba (1821–1879). He became a professor there himself in 1874. In 1871 the dying Alexander ➤ Serov charged him with the orchestration of his opera *The Power of Evil*. He was also a critic and collector of folk songs.

Works OPERA *Cordelia* (after Sardou's *La Haine*, 1885), *Vakula the Smith* (on Gogol's *Christmas Eve*, 1875), and *The Cottage of Kolomua*.

CHORAL AND ORCHESTRAL cantata for the bicentenary of Peter the Great; symphonic poem *Russians and Mongols*, a fantasy on a folk song for orchestra.

OTHER piano pieces; songs.

Solti, Georg (1912–1997), born György Stern Hungarian-born British conductor. He was music director at the Royal Opera House, Covent Garden, London 1961–71, and director of the Chicago Symphony Orchestra 1969–91. He was also principal conductor of the London Philharmonic Orchestra 1979–83. He made more than 250 recordings, including 45 operas, throughout his recording career and was honoured with 32 Grammy awards – more than any other artist. He was made a KBE in 1971.

Encouraged to play the piano by his mother, he earned a place at the famous Budapest Liszt Academy at the age of 12. He then worked as an unpaid apprentice *répétiteur* at the State Opera House in Budapest and aided Toscanini in the 1936 and 1937 Salzburg music festivals. As Jews were barred from holding posts at the Budapest Opera, he left for Switzerland in 1939 and remained there throughout the war. At this stage, he was still doing more piano playing than conducting – he won the 1942 Geneva International Piano Competition. However, his determination to conduct eventually paid off and he was given the music directorship at the Bavarian State Opera, Germany (which he held 1946–52), after he had been heard conducting in Munich. Work followed in Frankfurt 1952–60.

Sombrero de tres picos, El, The Three-cornered Hat ballet by Manuel de Falla (scenario by Martínez Sierra, based on Alarcón's story; choreographed by Massin). It was first produced at the Alhambra Theatre, London, on 22 July 1919. The setting and costumes were designed by Picasso.

Somervell, Arthur (1863–1937) English composer and educationist. His songs, especially settings of lyrics from Tennyson's 'Maud', Housman's 'A Shropshire Lad', and Browning's 'James Lee's Wife', are his best-known works. He also composed Masses, choral works, and edited *Songs of the Four Nations* and other folk songs.

He was educated at Uppingham School and King's College, Cambridge, where he studied composition with Stanford. He later went to Kiel and Berlin, to the Royal College of Music in London in 1885, and to Hubert Parry as a private pupil in 1887. In 1894 he became professor at the Royal College of Music. In 1901 he became an inspector of music in schools, which led to an appointment as official inspector of music to the Board of Education, which he resigned in 1928.

Works CHORAL AND ORCHESTRAL Masses in C minor

(1891) and D minor (the latter for male voices, 1907), anthem 'Let all the world', oratorio *The Passion of Christ*; cantatas, including *A Song of Praise*, *The Power of Sound*, *The Forsaken Merman* (Matthew Arnold), *Ode to the Sea*; setting of Wordsworth's 'Intimations of Immortality'.

ORCHESTRAL AND CHAMBER symphony in D minor, *Thalassa* (1912), concerto in G minor and *Concertstück* for violin and orchestra; clarinet quintet; violin and piano sonata; Variations on an Original Theme for two pianos; violin pieces; piano pieces; song cycles *Maud* (Tennyson), *A Shropshire Lad* (A E Housman, 1904).

Somfai, László (1934–   ) Hungarian musicologist. He studied at the Franz Liszt Academy, Budapest, and was appointed professor of musicology there in 1980. He published several works on Haydn: as opera director (1960), his life in contemporary pictures (1966), and on the piano sonatas (1979). He also conducted research on the lives and works of Liszt, Stravinsky, Webern, and Bartók.

Sommeils (French, plural of *sommeil*, 'sleep') quiet airs (verse songs) in old French operas, supposed to induce sleep.

Son and Stranger operetta by Felix Mendelssohn; see ➔ **Heimkehr aus der Fremde**.

sonata (Italian 'sounded') in music, an important type of instrumental composition. Although it can be a piece for a solo player or a small ensemble, it is now commonly used to describe a work for solo piano (piano sonata), or piano and one other instrument (violin sonata – violin and piano; flute sonata – flute and piano). It usually consists of three or four contrasting movements with one or more being in sonata form. The name means that the work is not beholden to a text or existing dance form, but is self-sufficient.

sonata da camera (Italian 'chamber sonata') instrumental work of the late 17th and early 18th centuries of the ➔ **suite** or ➔ **partita** (set of classical variations) type in several movements, mainly in dance forms, but always for more than one instrument, most usually two violins with continuo for bass viol or cello with a keyboard instrument, generally harpsichord. Unlike the ➔ **sonata da chiesa**, the sonata da camera usually had a quick first movement.

sonata da chiesa (Italian 'church sonata') instrumental work of the late 17th and early 18th centuries frequently, though not always, in four movements: slow introduction, fugal ➔ **allegro**, slow ➔ **cantabile** movement, and quick finale. Works of this type were written for more than one instrument, most usually two violins with ➔ **continuo** for bass viol or cello with a keyboard instrument, generally the organ.

sonata form in music, one of the most important forms. The structure divides into three main sections: exposition, development, and recapitulation. It introduced great dramatic possibilities and increased freedom for 18th-century music, which had previously been limited to closed dance routines. It developed initially in the instrumental ➔ **sonata**, from which it took its name, but it is used in many other works besides sonatas. The form does not apply to a whole work but only to one movement of it. It is often associated with the first movement of a work, hence its alternative name of **first movement form**, but this is a misleading term as it can also be found in the second and last movements.

sonata quasi una fantasia (Italian 'sonata in the style of a fantasy') term invented by Beethoven for some of his sonatas in which he began to modify the form freely. The two works of Op. 27 for piano are the first examples.

sonatina in music, a small-scale ➔ **sonata**. Although usually light and relatively easy to play, some 20th-century composers such as Maurice Ravel and Darius Milhaud have written technically demanding works of this kind. Formally, sonatinas often differ from sonatas in having a reduced development (central) section.

Sondheim, Stephen Joshua (1930–   ) US composer and lyricist. He wrote the lyrics for Bernstein's *West Side Story* (1957) and Styne's *Gypsy* (1959). Later he wrote both words and music for such shows as *A Funny Thing Happened on the Way to the Forum* (1962), *Sunday in the Park with George* (1984), and *Into the Woods* (1987).

He studied at Williams College, Massachusetts, and with Milton Babbitt. Other shows for which he wrote words and music include *A Little Night Music* (1972), *Pacific Overtures* (1976), *Sweeney Todd* (1979), *Assassins* (1990), and *Passion* (1994). His musical *Bounce* (2003) was a collaboration with US director Hal Prince.

song a setting of words to music for one or more singers, with or without instrumental accompaniment. Song may be sacred, for example a psalm, motet, or cantata, or secular, for example a folk song or ballad. In verse song, the text changes in mood while the music remains the same; in ➔ **lied** and other forms of art song, the music changes in response to the emotional development of the text.

song cycle sequence of songs related in mood and sung as a group, used by romantic composers such as Franz Schubert, Robert Schumann, and Hugo Wolf.

Songe d'une nuit d'été, Le, The Dream of a Midsummer Night opera by Ambroise Thomas (libretto by J B Rosier and A de Leuven, not based on

Shakespeare's play), produced at the Opéra-Comique, Paris, on 20 April 1850. Shakespeare, Queen Elizabeth I, and Falstaff appear in the work as characters.

song form in music, alternative name for ➤ **ABA form**.

Song of Destiny setting for chorus and orchestra by Johannes Brahms; see ➤ **Schicksalslied**.

Song of the Earth choral symphony by Gustav Mahler; see *Das* ➤ **Lied von der Erde**.

Song of the High Hills, The work by Delius for wordless chorus and orchestra. Composed in 1911, it was first performed in London on 26 February 1920, conducted by Albert Coates.

Song of Triumph work by Johannes Brahms; see ➤ **Triumphlied**.

Songs and Dances of Death song cycle by Modest ➤ **Mussorgsky** (poems by A A Golenishtchev-Kutuzov), composed 1875–77. The cycle includes: 1. *The Peasant's Lullaby*; 2. *Serenade*; 3. *Trepak*; and 4. *The Field Marshal*. It was orchestrated by Dmitri Shostakovich in 1962.

Songs of Farewell work by Delius for chorus and orchestra (text by Walt Whitman). Composed in 1930, it was first performed in London on 21 March 1932, and was conducted by Sargent.

Songs of Sunset work by Frederick Delius for mezzo-soprano, baritone, chorus, and orchestra (text by Ernest Dowson). It was composed 1906–08 and was first performed in London on 16 June 1911, conducted by Thomas Beecham.

Songs of Travel nine songs for voice and piano by Vaughan Williams (texts by Robert Louis Stevenson). The first performance of nos 1–8 took place in London on 2 December 1904, with Hamilton Harty at the piano.

Songs without Words solo piano works by Felix Mendelssohn; see ➤ **Lieder ohne Worte**.

sonnambula, La, The Sleepwalker opera by Bellini (libretto by Felice Romani), produced at the Teatro Carcano, Milan, on 6 March 1831. In the story, Amina is found at night in the bedroom of Count Rodolfo, to the dismay of her betrothed Elvino. Elvino is only placated when Amina's somnambulistic tendencies are revealed.

sonore, Italian **sonoro (French 'sonorous')** in music, an indication that a passage is to be played or sung with full tone.

Sophocles (c.496 BC–405 BC) Greek dramatist. His powerful tragedies inspired ➤ **Antigonae** (Orff); ➤ **Antigone** (incidental music, Mendelssohn; operas, Honegger, Zingarelli); Granville Bantock (*Electra*); ➤ **Elektra** (Richard Strauss);

George ➤ **Enescu** (*Œdipe*); Anselm Hüttenbrenner (*Odipus auf Kolonos*); ➤ **Oedipus auf Kolonos** (Mendelssohn); ➤ **Oedipus Rex** (Stravinsky); ➤ **Oedipus der Tyrann** (Orff); ➤ **Oedipus und die Sphinx** (Varèse); Ildebrando ➤ **Pizzetti** (*Trachiniae, Oedipus Rex* and *Coloneus*); Camille ➤ **Saint-Saëns** (*Antigone*); Niccolò ➤ **Zingarelli** (*Edipo a Colono*).

sopra (Italian 'above') word used in piano music to indicate in passages for crossed hands whether the right is to go above the left or vice versa. See also ➤ **come sopra**.

sopranino term in music describing an instrument of higher range than ➤ **soprano**. An alternative term is **piccolo**.

soprano highest range of the female voice, from around D4 (the D above middle C) to A6. Some operatic roles require the extended upper range of a ➤ **coloratura** soprano, reaching to around F6, for example Kiri Te Kanawa. It is also used before the name of an instrument that sounds in the same range as the soprano voice.

The soprano range has approximately the compass shown, but is often extended further in florid operatic arias requiring dexterity.

soprano clef in musical notation, the C ➤ **clef** in which middle C (C4) is represented by the lowest line of a five-line stave.

The soprano clef.

Sor, (Joseph) Fernando (Macari) (1778–1839) Spanish guitarist and composer. He was educated at the Escolanía at Montserrat, produced his first opera at the age of 19, then went to Paris and in about 1815 went to London, where he played and taught the guitar, returning to Paris in 1823. He wrote an important guitar tutor, which was published in 1830.

Works OPERA AND STAGE *Telemaco nell' isola di Calipso* (1797); eight ballets, including *Cendrillon* (1822), successful in London, Paris, and Moscow. OTHER over 60 guitar pieces and studies.

Sorabji, Kaikhosru Shapurji (1892–1988), adopted name of **Leon Dudley** English Parsee pianist and composer. His piano works are in a complex, late Romantic style and test the endurance of performers and audiences: *Opus clavicembalisticum* lasts for almost three hours and concludes with a passacaglia (Spanish dance form) of 81 variations.

He lived in England all his life. Except for the piano, he was mainly self-taught, but was fortunate in being able to give all his time to musical studies. He performed his own piano works in London, Paris, and Vienna, and also wrote criticism, including a book, *Around Music*. Sorabji premiered the *Opus clavicembalistium* at Glasgow in 1930 but forbade further performances of all his music 1936–76. The pianist Yonty Solomon premiered the 3rd Sonata, and *Opus* was performed at Chicago in 1983.

Works ORCHESTRAL AND CHAMBER two symphonies for orchestra, piano, organ, and chorus (1922, 1951); *Chaleur and Opusculum* for orchestra; eight piano concertos (1915–22), symphonic variations for piano and orchestra; two symphonies for organ; two piano quintets (1920, 1953); five sonatas, *Opus clavicembalisticum, Fantasia Hispanica*, three toccatas, symphony, variations on *Dies irae* for piano; *Trois Poèmes* (Verlaine and Baudelaire), *Fêtes galantes* (Verlaine) for voice and piano.

Sorcerer, The operetta by Sullivan (libretto by W S Gilbert), produced at the Opera Comique, London, on 17 November 1877. The plot is similar to Donizetti's *L'elisir d'amore*, with characters Alexis and Aline, sorcerer John Wellington Wells, and parents Sir Marmaduke and Lady Sangazure.

Sorcerer's Apprentice, The scherzo for orchestra by Paul Dukas; see *L'* ➤ *apprenti sorcier*.

Sordello (c.1200–1270) Italian ➤ troubadour. He came under the protection first of Guillaume de Blacatz, and afterwards of Charles d'Anjou, and wrote in Provençal. He is credited with about 30 love songs, and his lament on the death of Blacatz is notable.

Born in Goito, he first appeared in Florence in a small company of jugglers. He was forced to flee to Provence, France, because of the abduction of Cunizza da Romano.

sordino (Italian 'mute') a ➤ mute, usually of a violin, viola, or cello. In printed music the phrase *con sord.* means 'with the mute in place', while *senza sord.* means 'take the mute off'.

sordune Renaissance ➤ windcap double-reed musical instrument in tenor or bass register, of folded-back conical bore. It is an ancestor of the bassoon.

Soriano, Francesco (c.1549–1621) Italian composer. After a first appointment he went to the court of Mantua 1583–86, and then became maestro di cappella in Rome, by turns at Santa Maria Maggiore, St John Lateran, St Peter's in 1603, and the Cappella Giulia 1603–20.

He was a choirboy at the Church of St John Lateran in Rome and studied with various masters including Giovanni Bernardino Nanino and Palestrina.

Works CHURCH AND SECULAR MUSIC Masses, an arrangement of Palestrina's *Missa Papae Marcelli* for eight voices, motets, psalms, Magnificat, a Passion, and other church music; madrigals.

Sorochíntsy Fair, Russian **Sorochinskaya Yarmarka** unfinished opera by Mussorgsky (libretto by composer, based on Gogol's *Evenings on a Farm near Dakanka*). The composition was begun in 1875, revised by Liadov for concert performance in 1904, and performed in original form at the Comedia Theatre, St Petersburg, on 30 December 1911. In the story, Parasya meets her lover Gritzke at the fair, but her mother objects to their marriage.

Several versions of the opera have been produced by other composers, such as Sakhnovsky (1913), César Cui (with music of his own added, 1917), Nikolai Tcherepnin (in French, 1923), and Vissarion Shebalin (1931).

sortita (Italian from *sortire*, 'to come out') in music, ➤ aria sung by a principal character in an 18th-century opera at his or her first entry on the stage.

Sosarme, rè di Media, Sosarmes, King of the Medes opera by Handel (libretto based on Matteo Noris's *Alfonso primo*), produced at the King's Theatre, Haymarket, London, on 15 February 1732. In the story, Haliate besieges the city controlled by his rebellious son Argone. Melo is announced as Haliate's successor instead of Argone. Sosarme reconciles the rival claimants to throne and weds Elmira.

sostenuto (Italian 'sustained') term used in musical notation, similar to ➤ legato ('tied'). It can also imply a slower speed than the overall tempo marking, similar to ➤ ritenuto.

sostenuto pedal in music, the middle pedal on a grand piano with three pedals (many have only two). When depressed while certain keys are held down, it prevents the dampers of those particular keys from returning to the string until the pedal is released. It allows the hands to play other notes while still sustaining the sound of a previous set of notes.

sotto voce (Italian 'under the voice') in musical notation, term indicating very soft playing or singing.

soubrette (French from Provençal *soubret*, 'coy') in opera, a stock part given to a singer with a light soprano voice. The typical soubrette character is a servant, a young confidante, or a girl connected with the sub-plot.

Examples include Despina in Mozart's *Così fan tutte* and Aennchen in Weber's *Der Freischütz*.

Occasionally the soubrette may assume a principal part, for example, Serpina in Pergolesi's *La Serva padrona* or Susanna in Mozart's *Figaro*.

soundboard in many musical instruments, including the organ, piano, dulcimer, and cimbalom, a resonant wooden part which vibrates with the notes, amplifying the sound.

soundbox or **resonator** in a musical instrument, an enclosed space in which the vibrations of a string or strings are captured and naturally amplified (that is, without electronic amplification). On a member of the string family, it forms the body of the instrument. On a string keyboard instrument the ✦ soundboard forms one surface of the soundbox.

sound-holes the holes in the tables of string instruments, also in the soundboards of harpsichords. In instruments of the violin family they take the shape of f holes or something approximating to them; in keyboard instruments and flat-bellied string instruments such as the guitar, they are usually shaped like a 'rose'.

soundpost in a string musical instrument, a piece of wood inside the body of the instrument which connects the front and back surfaces of the ✦ soundbox. It supports the weight of the bridge and helps to distribute vibrations throughout the instrument.

sourdine, German **Sordun,** Italian **sordone (from French** *sourd,* **'deaf')** in music, a mute (✦ sordino). It is also an instrument of the bassoon type common in the late 16th and early 17th centuries and made in five sizes. It derived its name from the fact that its tone was muffled.

Sousa, John Philip (1854–1932) US bandmaster and composer of marches. He wrote 'The Stars and Stripes Forever' in 1897.

After some years' experience as an orchestra violinist he became master of the US Marine Corps band in 1880; he became known as a brilliant bandmaster. He went on to form the Sousa Band in 1892 and toured internationally with this group until his death. In addition to about 140 stirring marches, including 'The Washington Post' (1889), 'El capitan' (1895), and 'Imperial Edward', he composed operettas, symphonic poems, suites, waltzes, and songs.

Works SONGS 'The Stars and Stripes Forever' (1897), 'The Washington Post' (1889), 'Hands Across the Sea' (1899).

OPERETTAS *The Queen of Hearts* (1885), *El capitan* (1895).

sousaphone large bass ✦ tuba designed to wrap round the player in a circle and having a forward-facing bell. The form was suggested by US bandmaster John Sousa. Today sousaphones are

largely fabricated in lightweight fibreglass.

sousedská Bohemian country dance in slow triple time. The 3rd, 4th, and 16th of Antonín Dvořák's *Slavonic Dances* for piano duet are in the form of a sousedská.

Souster, Tim(othy) Andrew James (1943–1994) English composer. He was co-founder with Roger ✦ Smalley of the group Intermodulation, to explore electronic and aleatory techniques.

He studied at Oxford and Darmstadt and was assistant to Stockhausen in Cologne 1971–73. He worked at King's College, Cambridge, and Keele University.

Works CHAMBER *Songs of the Seasons* for soprano and viola (1965), *Poem in Depression* for soprano and ensemble (1965), *Metropolitan Games* for piano duet (1967), *Titus Groan Music* for wind quintet, tape, and electronics (1969), *Chinese Whispers* for percussion and synthesizers (1970), *Waste Land Music* for saxophone, piano, and organ (1970).

ORCHESTRAL AND CHAMBER *Triple Music* for three orchestras (1970), *Song of an Average City* for small orchestra and tape (1974), *Afghan Amplitudes* for keyboards and synthesizers (1976), trio *Arcane Artefact* (1977), *Driftwood Cortège* for tape (1978), *Sonata* for cello and ensemble (1979), *Equalisation*, brass quintet (1980), *The Transistor Radio of St Narcissus* (1983), *Curtain of Light* for percussion (1984), *Hambledon Hill* for amplified string quartet (1985), trumpet concerto (1986).

souter liedekens (Dutch 'little psalter songs') metrical psalms sung in Holland to popular tunes, translated and provided with appropriate melodies by (probably) Willem van Zuylen van Nyevelt. The first complete collection, printed by Symon Cock at Antwerp in 1540, contained 159 texts: Psalm 119 was in four sections, and the Te Deum and five canticles were included.

✦ Clemens non Papa later arranged the whole collection for three voices, published in Antwerp as the fourth–seventh of Susato's *Musyck Boexken* (little music books) in 1556–57. Ten settings are by Susato himself, perhaps because of Clemens's premature death. The eighth–eleventh books contained another complete setting, the work of Gerhard Mes.

Sowerby, Leo (1895–1968) US composer and pianist. He served as a bandmaster in Europe during World War I and in 1922 won the American Prix de Rome. He was organist of St James's Episcopal Cathedral in Chicago 1927–62.

He studied at the American Conservatory of Chicago, where he later taught. He appeared as a pianist in the USA, England, Italy, and Austria.

Works CHORAL AND ORCHESTRAL oratorio *Christ Re-*

born, cantata *Great is the Lord* and Te Deum for mixed chorus and organ; five symphonies (1921, 1928, 1940, 1947, 1964), suite *From the Northland*, overture *Comes Autumn Time*, *Irish Washerwoman*, *Money Musk*, *Set of Four*, symphonic poem *Prairie, Theme in Yellow* for orchestra.

ORCHESTRAL AND CHAMBER sinfonietta for strings; rhapsody for chamber orchestra; *Sinconata* for jazz orchestra; two piano concertos (1912, 1932), organ concerto, two cello concertos (1917, 1934), violin concerto, ballad *King Estmere* for two pianos and orchestra, *Medieval Poem* for organ and orchestra; two string quartets (1924, 1935), wind quintet, serenade for string quartet; sonata and suite for violin and piano; symphony, sonata and suite for organ.

OTHER *Florida Suite* and other piano works; songs.

space-time notation in music, a form of ➤ graph notation pioneered by Earle ➤ Brown in which notes are individually lengthened to give a precise visualization of relative durations. It involves the performer 'reading time' instead of counting beats, and is useful where musical time is measured chronometrically, as in Stockhausen's instrumental score for the electronic composition *Kontakte/Contacts* (1959–60).

It originates with piano-roll music, which is cut from an original paper roll representing pitches and durations by pencilled lines (see ➤ player piano).

Spagna, la 15th-century ➤ basse danse tune originating in Castile.

Spanisches Liederbuch, **Spanish Song Book** Hugo Wolf's settings of Spanish poems in German translation by Emanuel Geibel and Paul Heyse, composed October 1889–April 1890. There are ten sacred and 34 secular poems in his set.

Spanish Lady, The unfinished opera by Elgar (libretto by B Jackson, based on Ben Jonson's play *The Devil is an Ass*). Begun 1932–33; only a number of sketches are left; arrangements by Percy Young published 1955–56. A performing version of the sketches was made by Dr Young and premiered at Cambridge (University Opera), 24 November, 1994.

špasírka Czech dance in alternating slow and quick 4/8 time. The 13th of Dvořák's *Slavonic Dances* for piano duet is a špasírka.

Spataro, Giovanni (c.1458–1541) Italian composer and theorist. He was involved in a protracted controversy with the theorist Franchino Gafori, against whom two of his printed treatises are directed. He composed a number of sacred works; six motets and one *laude* are extant.

Spataro was a pupil of Ramos de Pareia and corresponded with Pietro Aron. He was maestro di cappella at San Petronio, Bologna, from 1512.

speaker keys extra keys fitted to ➤ reed instruments, to facilitate the production of harmonic notes. Two on the oboe produce octaves (also known as octave keys) and one on the clarinet produces 12ths.

speaking-length in music, that portion of an ➤ organ pipe in which the air vibrates to produce the note.

species in music, the various types of ➤ counterpoint taught in academic contrapuntal instruction.

specification in music, a detailed list of the pipes, stops, keyboards, and mechanisms of an organ given to the builder or used to describe the instrument.

Spectre's Bride, The, Czech **Svatebni košile** (**'The Wedding Shift'**) dramatic cantata by Dvořák, Op. 69 (Czech words by K J Erben). Composed in 1884, it was first performed in England at the Birmingham Festival, in August 1885.

speech-song see ➤ Sprechgesang.

Speziale, Lo, **The Apothecary** opera by Haydn (libretto by Goldoni), produced at Eszterháza, in Hungary, in the autumn of 1768. The story concerns the elderly apothecary Sempronio, who has designs on Griletta. However, she weds young Mengone, his assistant.

spianato (Italian 'smoothed, level') in musical direction, an instruction to play smoothly and evenly.

spiccato (Italian 'articulated') musical direction indicating a special kind of bowing on instruments of the violin family, possible only in rapid passages of notes of equal duration, which are played with the middle of the bow and a loose wrist, allowing the bow to rebound off the strings after each note.

Spiegel von Arkadien, Der, **The Mirror of Arcadia** opera by Süssmayr (libretto by Schikaneder), produced at the Theater auf der Wieden, Vienna, on 14 November 1794. See also ➤ magic opera.

Spieloper (German 'play-opera') type of light German opera of the 19th century, in which the subject is a comedy and the musical numbers are interspersed with dialogue.

Spielwerk und die Prinzessin, Das, **The Musical Box and the Princess** opera by Schreker (libretto by composer). Composed 1909–12, it was first produced at Frankfurt and Vienna on 15 March 1913. In the story, the sound from Meister Florian's musical box intoxicates the Princess, but she is redeemed by a flute-playing wayfarer.

The opera was later revised in one act as a mystery play, *Das Spielwerk*, produced in Munich on 30 October 1920, conducted by Walter.

Spies, Claudio (1925–) Chilean-born US composer. He moved to the USA in 1942 and studied at the New England Conservatory and with Fine and Piston at Harvard. He was appointed Professor of Music at Princeton in 1970. He has written extensively on Stravinsky and conducted the first performance of an early version of *The Wedding*.

Works ORCHESTRAL AND CHAMBER WITH VOICE *Music for a Ballet* for orchestra (1955), *Il Cantico del frate Sole* for baritone and orchestra (1958), *Tempi* for 14 instruments (1962), seven *Enzensberglieder* for baritone and ensemble (1972).

spinet 17th-century domestic keyboard instrument. It has a laterally tapered case with a single manual (keyboard) of up to a three-and-a-half octave range, having a plucking action and single strings. It was the precursor of the ➤ **harpsichord.**

Spinner, Leopold (1906–1980) Polish-born Austrian composer. He settled in England in 1938. His works were influenced by Webern, with whom he studied 1935–38.

Works ORCHESTRAL AND CHAMBER symphony (1934), Passacaglia for chamber orchestra (1936), Concerto for Orchestra (1957); two string quartets (1941, 1952), piano trio (1950), sonatina for cello and piano (1973).

Spirit of England, The three cantatas for soprano solo, chorus, and orchestra by Elgar, Op. 80, *The Fourth of August*, *To Women*, and *For the Fallen* (poems by Laurence Binyon). Composed 1916–17, nos 1 and 2 were performed at London on 7 May 1916, and the cantatas were performed in complete form on 24 November 1917.

spiritoso (Italian 'spirited') musical direction indicating that a composition, movement, or passage is to be performed briskly and energetically.

spiritual an African-American song of the southern states of the USA, with religious words and folk-song tunes. It is one of the chief influences from which jazz and swing have sprung, and the form has influenced many serious US and European composers. The English composer Michael Tippett's oratorio *A Child of our Time* (1939–41) made use of spirituals.

Spitta, (Julius August) Philipp (1841–1894) German musicologist. He was joint editor with Guido Adler and Friedrich Chrysander of the *Vierteljahrsschrift für Musikwissenschaft*, and edited the complete works of Schütz and the organ works of Buxtehude. His chief literary work is his book on Bach in two volumes (1873–80).

He studied at Göttingen University and in 1875 became professor of music history at Berlin University. He also taught the subject at the Hochschule für Musik, of which he became director in 1882.

Spofforth, Reginald (1768 or 1770–1827) English composer. He was a pupil of his uncle Thomas Spofforth, organist of Southwell Minster, and of Benjamin Cooke in London, where he settled. He gained several of the Glee Club's prizes.

Works STAGE farce with music *The Witch of the Wood, or The Nutting Girls* (1796); additions to Salomon's *Windsor Castle* (1795).

SONGS many glees, including 'Hail, smiling morn'.

Spohr, Ludwig (Louis) (1784–1859) German violinist, composer, and conductor. He travelled throughout Europe as a soloist and leader of orchestras, playing with the London Philharmonic Society in 1820. His music reflects his career as a violinist, including 15 violin concertos, chamber music, and 9 symphonies. He was one of the first conductors to use a ➤ **baton.** Spohr's music was widely performed during the 19th century, and he was particularly popular in Victorian England. Today he is known largely through the 8th violin concerto and a few tuneful chamber works.

He first learnt music from his parents, who were both musical, although his father was a physician. They lived at Seesen in his childhood, and he was afterwards taught by two amateurs, but was sent to school and for further studies at Brunswick. He played a violin concerto of his own at a school concert and at 14 went to Hamburg trying to gain a hearing. He failed, but on his return petitioned the duke for assistance and was sent to Franz Eck for lessons. They went to Russia in 1802, where he met Muzio Clementi and John Field. He performed and composed a great deal at that time, returned to Brunswick in 1803, heard Pierre Rode there, and entered the ducal orchestra. In 1804 he visited Berlin and played there with the 13-year-old Meyerbeer. In 1805 he became leader in the Duke of Gotha's orchestra and married the harpist Dorette Scheidler, with whom he toured widely. After producing his third opera at Hamburg in 1811, he visited Vienna in 1812, becoming leader at the Theater an der Wien and staying there until 1815. In 1813 and 1814 he wrote two of his most popular pieces, the nonet and octet; after producing *Faust* in Prague, he travelled in Italy 1816–17 and then became conductor at the Frankfurt opera 1817–19. In 1820 he visited London and Paris for the first time, meeting Luigi Cherubini, Rodolphe Kreutzer, and Giovanni Battista Viotti. After a visit to Dresden he became court music director at Kassel on 1 January 1822, having been recommended for the post by Weber, who had declined it. He remained there for the rest of his life, but continued to travel. In 1831 he finished writing his *Violin School*, in 1834 his wife died, and in 1836 he married the pianist Marianne Pfeiffer. In 1839 he revisited England for the performance of *Cavalry* at the Norwich Festival, and was commissioned to write an English oratorio, *The Fall of Babylon*, for the next festival in 1842, in which year he conducted Wagner's *Flying Dutchman* at Kassel. He was not allowed leave to go to England for the oratorio, but went during his summer vacation in 1843, when he appeared before Queen Victoria and Prince Albert and toured England and Wales. During the 1848 revolutions he showed liberal leanings and so annoyed the elector that he was refused leave of absence. Having taken his vacation without leave, he became involved in a long law-suit, which he lost after four years. In 1852 he adapted *Faust* without recitatives for a production in Italian in London and in 1853 he produced Wagner's *Tannhäuser* at Kassel. He was pensioned off against his will in 1857.

Works STAGE operas *Faust* (1816, revised 1852), *Zemire und Azor* (1819), *Jessonda* (1823); five overtures (including one on Shakespeare's *Macbeth*).

ORCHESTRAL nine symphonies (4. *Die Weihe der Töne*, 1832; 6. Historic Symphony, 1839; 9. *The Seasons*, 1850); 15 violin concertos (8. *In modo d'una scena cantante*, 1816); four clarinet concertos (1812–28).

CHAMBER 33 string quartets (1807–57), eight string quintets, octet for strings and wind (1814), nonet for ditto (1813); sonatas for violin and harp; harp pieces.

Spontini, Gaspare (Luigi Pacifico) (1774–1851) Italian composer and conductor. He produced several operas in Italy, but had little success until 1807, when he produced *La vestale* in Paris. In 1820 he went to Berlin as music director to Frederick William III; his greatest success in this post was the opera *Agnes von Hohenstaufen* (1837). He was hindered throughout his career, however, by his difficult and quarrelsome personality, which led to his dismissal on more than one occasion.

His family intended him for the priesthood, but he ran away to Monte San Vito, where an uncle allowed him to study music. When he had advanced sufficiently, he returned home and was allowed to study at the Conservatorio de' Turchini at Naples from 1791, where his teachers included Nicola Sala and Giacomo Tritto. In 1796 he produced his first opera in Rome, having run away from the Conservatory, but he was readmitted at the intercession of Niccolò Piccinni, from whom

he learnt much. He now produced one opera after another, and in 1798 went to Palermo with the Neapolitan court, which took refuge there and appointed him music director in the place of Domenico Cimarosa, who refused to leave Naples.

In 1803 he left for Paris, where he taught singing and tried his hand at French comic opera, but made his first real success with the serious opera *La vestale* in 1807. He was appointed composer to the Empress Joséphine and in 1810 became director of the Italian opera at the Théâtre de l'Impératrice, giving the first local performance of *Don Giovanni*. In 1812 he was dismissed, but the Bourbon restoration in 1814 reinstated him. He soon sold his post to the soprano Angelica Catalani, however.

In 1820 he was summoned to the court of Frederick William III in Berlin as general music director to the Prussian court. He was not on good terms with the intendant, Count Brühl, though he succeeded in introducing excellent reforms at the court opera; but his success was obscured in 1821 by that of Weber's *Freischütz*, which aroused an appetite for German opera, as distinct from foreign opera set to German words. In 1822–23 he visited Dresden, where he met Weber; he also visited Vienna and Paris. In 1838 he spent the summer in England to study English history and local colour for an opera about the poet Milton, differing from an earlier one, which was never finished. On the king's death in 1840 his position became more and more difficult; this was partly his own fault, for he quarrelled with the new intendant, Count Redern, and became involved in a law-suit, and after much trouble and threatened imprisonment he left Berlin in July 1842. He went to live in Paris, and visited Dresden in 1844 to conduct a performance of *La vestale* rehearsed for him by Wagner. In 1848 he became deaf and returned to his birthplace, founding a music school at Jesi.

In recent years Spontini's operas have enjoyed a limited revival, with performances in Europe of *Fernand Cortez*, *Agnes von Hohenstaufen*, and *Olympie*.

Works OPERA AND STAGE Italian operas, including *I puntigli delle donne* (1796), *Adelina Senese* (1798), *L'eroismo ridicolo*, *Il finto pittore*, *La finta filosofa*, *La fuga in maschera*, and eight others; operas in French and German, including *La petite maison* (1804), *Julie, ou Le pot de fleurs* (1805), *Milton* (in French), *La vestale* (1807), *Fernand Cortez* (1809), *Olympie* (French, revised in German as *Olympia*, 1819), *Pélage, ou Le roi de la paix* (1814), *Nurmahal* (German, after Moore's 'Lalla Rookh', 1821), *Alcidor*, *Agnes von Hohenstaufen* (1837), *Les dieux rivaux* (with Berton, R Kreutzer, and Persuis); festival play with music on Moore's 'Lalla Rookh' (original version of the opera); ballet for Salieri's *Les Danaïdes*.

CHORAL AND VOCAL *Domine salvum fac* and other church music; cantata *L'eccelsa gara* for the victory of Austerlitz, coronation cantata for Nicholas I of Russia; vocal duets and trios; songs with piano or harp; *Sensations douces*.

Sporer, Thomas (c. 1490–1534) German composer. He wrote songs with accompaniment, which were rare at that time, but were cultivated by Henricus Isaac, Paul Hofhaimer, Ludwig Senfl, and others besides Sporer.

Sprechgesang (German 'speech-song') in music, a type of vocal technique, a hybrid of pure song and speech. It consists of recitation on approximate pitches, notated usually by cross-shaped symbols instead of usual notes. Although the pitches are approximate, the rhythm tends to be notated by traditional means. It was first introduced in Engelbert ➤ Humperdinck's melodrama *Königskinder* in 1910. Schoenberg used it in several works, including *Pierrot lunaire* (1912), as did Berg in his operas *Wozzeck* (1920) and *Lulu* (1935).

'Spring' Sonata the familiar nickname given to Beethoven's violin and piano sonata in F major, Op. 24, composed in 1801.

Spring Symphony original name for Robert ➤ Schumann's first symphony, in B flat major, Op. 38, finished in February 1841 and first performed at Leipzig by Felix Mendelssohn, on 31 March 1841.

Choral work by Benjamin Britten, first performed at Amsterdam on 9 July 1949.

sprung rhythm term invented by Gerard Manley Hopkins for displacements of metrical stresses in poetry – not new to his verse, but exploited by him consciously and with great persistence and variety – and transferred to musical terminology by Michael Tippett in the prefatory notes to his second string quartet, where sprung rhythm is used with a deliberation similar to Hopkins's in the finale.

Sprung rhythm may be said to include such devices as ➤ syncopation, transference of stresses to weak beats or by tying notes over bar-lines or beats, the omission of rhythmic units by rests, or the addition of them by triplets.

Squire, W(illiam) Barclay (1855–1927) English musicologist. He published catalogues for the British Museum and the Royal College of Music, edited Purcell's harpsichord music and other works, and, with Fuller-Maitland, the *Fitzwilliam Virginal Book*.

He was educated at Frankfurt and Pembroke College, Cambridge. In 1885 he took charge of the department of printed music in the British Museum. He was also a critic and the author of

the libretto of Standford's opera *The Veiled Prophet*, honorary secretary of the Purcell Society, and one of the honorary secretaries of the International Musical Society.

Stabat Mater medieval Latin sacred poem, probably by Jacopone da Todi, not originally liturgical, but increasingly used for devotional purposes until it was admitted as a sequence to the Roman missal in 1727.

The *Stabat Mater* has been set to music by numerous composers, including Antonín ➤ Dvořák, Joseph ➤ Haydn, Karol ➤ Szymanowski, and Giuseppe ➤ Verdi.

Stabile, Annibale (c.1535–1595) Italian composer. He was a pupil of Giovanni ➤ Palestrina in Rome, where he became maestro di cappella at the Lateran palace. From 1579 to 1590 he held a similar post at the Collegio Germanico there, and in 1591 at the church of Santa Maria Maggiore.

Works CHURCH AND SECULAR MUSIC motets, Litanies and other church music; madrigals.

staccato (Italian 'detached') in music, a term used to describe playing notes in a short, detached manner, rather than legato (smoothly, or 'joined'). Each note is sounded for only part of its written value and this is indicated by a dot placed above or below the note. Staccato gives an upbeat feel to a passage, for example the opening of the scherzo to Beethoven's Symphony no. 6 ('Pastoral', 1808).

Staden, Johann (1581–1634) German organist and composer. He was in the service of the Margrave of Kulmbach and Bayreuth 1603–16, after which he became organist of St Lorenz's Church at Nuremberg and soon afterwards of St Sebald's Church.

Works CHURCH AND SECULAR MUSIC motets for voices alone, motets with instrumental thorough bass, sacred concertos for voices and instruments; *Hauss-Music* for voices and instruments (with German words, 1623–28); sacred and secular songs with continuo for organ or lute; secular songs for four–five voices.

OTHER instrumental pavans, galliards, canzoni.

Stadler, Maximilian (1748–1833) Austrian priest, organist, and composer. He completed some of the unfinished works of his friend Mozart, and his defence of the authenticity of Mozart's Requiem was published at Vienna in 1825.

He studied under Johann Albrechtsberger, and entered the Benedictine monastery of Melk, in Austria, in 1766. He was ordained in 1772, became a prior there in 1784, was appointed abbot of Lilienfeld in 1786, and of Kremsmünster in 1789. In 1796 he settled in Vienna, and after working as a parish priest 1803–15 returned there to devote himself entirely to music.

Works CHURCH MUSIC Masses, two Requiems, Te Deum, three Magnificat settings, and other church music.

CHORAL oratorio *Die Befreyung von Jerusalem* (1811); music for Collin's tragedy *Polyxena* (1811); cantatas, including *Frühlingsfeyer* (Klopstock, 1813).

WORKS FOR KEYBOARD organ sonatas and fugues; piano music.

Staempfli, Edward (1908–2002) Swiss composer. He studied medicine initially, but gave it up for music, which he studied with Jarnach at Cologne and with Paul Dukas in Paris.

Works STAGE ballets *Das Märchen von den zwei Flöten* and *Le Pendu* (1942).

CHORAL AND ORCHESTRAL cantata *Filles de Sion* for solo voices, chorus and orchestra; three symphonies (1938, 1942, 1945), four *Sinfonie concertanti* and other orchestral works; four piano concertos (1932–63), two violin concertos, concerto for two pianos and strings.

CHAMBER music for eleven instruments, concerto for piano and eight instruments, six string quartets (1926–62), quintet for wind, quartet for flute and strings, piano trio, string trio, and other chamber music; piano pieces; songs.

staff in music, alternative name for ➔ stave.

staff notation ordinary musical notation, so called to distinguish it from ➔ tonic sol-fa notation, which does not use ➔ staves and notes.

Staggins, Nicholas (1645–1700) English composer. Charles II appointed him Master of the King's Band in 1674. He advanced to the post of Master of the King's Musick, and was succeeded in it after his death by John Eccles.

He took a degree in music at Cambridge University in 1682, and became professor of music there in 1684.

Works STAGE the masque *Calisto, or The Chaste Nimph* (Crowne); incidental music for Etheredge's *The Man of Mode*, Lee's *Gloriana*, Dryden's *Conquest of Granada* and *Marriage à la Mode*, and Shadwell's *Epsom Wells* (last two with Robert Smith).

OTHER odes for the birthday of William III; songs.

stagione (Italian 'season') musical term used especially for an opera season.

Stahlspiel (German 'steel-play') percussion instrument with tuned steel plates or bars which are played with hammers. It is known in English military bands as a lyra, being made for them in the shape of a lyre. The modern ➔ glockenspiel, being also made of steel bars, and no longer of actual bells, is now to all intents and purposes the same instrument.

Stainer, Jacob (1621–1683) Austrian violin-maker. He learnt his craft at Innsbruck and, probably, with either one of the ➔ Amati family in Cremona or with Vimercati in Venice. He began to work on his own account at Absam around 1640. He died insane, after being accused of Lutheran tendencies.

Stainer, John (1840–1901) English organist and composer. He became organist of St Paul's Cathedral, London, 1872–88 and wrote religious choral works.

He became a choirboy at St Paul's Cathedral at the age of seven and before long was able to deputize at the organ. After working under various masters and receiving an organist's appointment in the City of London, Frederick Ouseley appointed him organist of St Michael's College, Tenbury, in 1856. In 1860 he went to Oxford as an undergraduate at St Edmund Hall and organist to Magdalen College, then succeeded George Elvey (1816–1893) as organist to the University; in 1865 he took a degree in music. In 1872 he returned to London as organist at St Paul's Cathedral. In 1888, having resigned from St Paul's through failing eyesight, he was knighted and in 1889 became professor of music at Oxford. He wrote on music in the Bible, and edited *Early Bodleian Music*, *Dufay and his Contemporaries*, and other books.

Works CHORAL the oratorios *Gideon* (1865) and *The Crucifixion* (1887); *Sevenfold Amen*, services, and anthems; cantatas *The Daughter of Jairus* (1878) and *St Mary Magdalen* (1887).

Stamitz (lived 18th–early 19th centuries) Bohemian family of musicians:

Johann Wenzel Anton (1717–1757), violinist and composer. He entered the service of the Electoral court at Mannheim in 1741, became principal violinist in 1743 and later music director. Under him the orchestra became the most famous in Europe, called by Charles Burney 'an army of generals'. He was the founder and most important member of the Mannheim school of symphonists, which had a profound influence on Mozart's instrumental style.

His works include 74 symphonies (58 extant); concertos for violin, harpsichord, flute, oboe, clarinet; trio sonatas and other chamber music, violin sonatas.

Carl (1745–1801), violinist and composer, son and pupil of Johann. He entered the Mannheim orchestra as second violin in 1762, then went to Strasbourg (1770), Paris, and London, appearing as a virtuoso on the violin and viola d'amore. He continued to travel widely, visiting Prague in 1787 and Russia in 1790, until, in 1794, he settled in Jena as music director to the university.

His works include the operas *Der verliebte Vormund* (1787) and *Dardanus* (1800); about 80 symphonies and *sinfonies concertantes*; concertos; chamber music.

Johann Anton (1750–before 1809), violinist and composer, son and pupil of Johann. In 1770 he went with his brother Carl to Paris, where he settled as violinist in the court orchestra. Rodolphe ➤ **Kreutzer** was his pupil. He wrote twelve symphonies, concertos for violin, viola, flute, and oboe, as well as chamber music.

Ständchen in music, German term for a ➤ serenade.

Standford, Patric (1939–   ), born **John Patric Standford Gledhill** English composer and teacher. He was professor of composition at the Guildhall School of Music and Drama, London, 1967–80, and was director of music at Bretton Hall College, University of Leeds, 1980–93.

He studied with Edmund ➤ **Rubbra** at Guildhall School of Music and Drama and Witold Lutosławski at Dartington.

Works OPERA *Villon* (1972–84).

CHORAL AND ORCHESTRAL five symphonies: no. 1 for orchestra (1972), no. 2 *Christus-Requiem* for soloists, chorus, and orchestra (1972), no. 3 *Towards Paradise* for chorus and orchestra (1973), no. 4 *Taikyoku* for two pianos and six percussion (1976), no. 5 for orchestra (1984); cello concerto (1974), violin concerto (1975), piano concerto (1979), *Rage* for orchestra (1993).

CHURCH AND SECULAR MUSIC Mass for brass and chorus (1980), *Mass of our Lady St Rochas* (1988), *A Messiah Reborn* for soloist, chorus, and orchestra (1992).

OTHER three string quartets (1964, 1973, 1992).

Standfuss, J C (died c.1759) German violinist and composer. At one time a member of G H Koch's opera troupe in Leipzig, he was the first to produce a German ➤ **Singspiel**, in adapting Charles Coffey's (d.1745) *The Devil to Pay* as *Der Teufel ist los* (1752). Coffey's sequel *The Merry Cobbler* was similarly arranged as *Der lustige Schuster* in 1759. His third *Singspiel* was *Der stolze Bauer Jochem Tröbs* (1759).

Stanford, Charles Villiers (1852–1924) Irish composer and teacher, born in Dublin. Stanford was a leading figure in the 19th-century renaissance of British music. His many works include operas such as *Shamus O'Brien* (1896), seven symphonies, chamber music, and church music. Among his pupils were Ralph Vaughan Williams, Gustav Holst, and Frank Bridge.

In 1870 Stanford became a choral scholar at Queens' College, Cambridge, England, and in 1873 organist of Trinity College, where he took classical honours the next year; he was also conductor of the Cambridge University Musical Society. He studied with Carl Reinecke at Leipzig 1874–76 and with Friedrich Kiel in Berlin, and in

1876 Alfred Tennyson suggested him as composer of incidental music for his *Queen Mary*. Stanford received a doctorate from Oxford in 1883 and in 1888 from Cambridge, where he had succeeded George Macfarren as professor of music in 1887. He was also conductor of the Bach Choir in London and professor of composition at the Royal College of Music, where he conducted the orchestral and opera classes. He collected traditional Irish songs and edited an edition of George Petrie's *The Complete Petrie Collection of Irish Music* (1902–1905, three volumes).

Works OPERA *Shamus O'Brien* (after Le Fanu; 1896).

ORCHESTRAL seven symphonies (1876–1911); five Irish rhapsodies (1901–14); cello concerto (1919); clarinet concerto.

CHAMBER two sonatas for cello and piano, clarinet and piano sonata, some smaller instrumental pieces with piano; piano works including sonata, three *Dante Rhapsodies* (1875); eleven organ works including five sonatas.

CHORAL oratorios *The Three Holy Children* (1885), *Eden* (1891), Magnificat; *Stabat Mater*, *The Revenge* (1886), *Songs of the Sea* (1904), *Songs of the Fleet* (1910).

OTHER two psalms, six services, three anthems; 20 op. nos of songs.

Stanley, John (1713–1786) English composer and organist. His works, which include organ ➤ **voluntaries** (solos) and concertos for strings, influenced Handel. He succeeded William Boyce as ➤ **Master of the King's Musick** in 1779.

Stanley was blind from the age of two, but became a pupil of Maurice Greene and later held various organist's appointments in London. In 1759 he joined John Christopher Smith to continue Handel's oratorio concerts, and when Smith retired in 1774, he continued with the younger Thomas Linley.

Works OPERA AND CHORAL opera *Teraminta*; dramatic cantata *The Choice of Hercules*; music for Lloyd's *Arcadia*, or *The Shepherd's Wedding* (1761) and *Tears and Triumphs of Parnassus*, and Southerne's *Oroonoko* (1759); oratorios *Jephtha* (1752), *Zimri* (1760), and *The Fall of Egypt* (1774); twelve cantatas to words by John Hawkins; cantatas and songs for voice and instruments.

ORCHESTRAL six concertos for strings; solos for flute or violin.

Stappen, Crispinus van (c. 1470–1532) Flemish composer. He wrote sacred and secular works, including a *strambotto* in praise of the town of Padua.

He became a singer at the Sainte-Chapelle, Paris, in 1492, and shortly afterwards, until 1507, at the Papal Chapel in Rome. In 1524–25 he was maestro di cappella at the Casa Santa, Loreto. He held a canonry at Cambrai from 1504.

Starer, Robert (1924–2001) Austrian-born US composer. He studied in Vienna, then moved to Jerusalem at the Anschluss. He moved to the USA in 1947, studying at Juilliard School in New York. He taught at Brooklyn College from 1963 to 1991.

Works OPERA AND STAGE operas, including *The Intruder* (1956), *Pantagleize* (1973), *The Last Lover* (1975), and *Apollonia* (1979); ballets *The Dybbuk* (1960), *Samson Agonistes* (1961), *Phaedra* (1962), *The Lady of the House of Sleep* (1968), *Holy Jungle* (1974).

ORCHESTRAL three symphonies (1950–69); three piano concertos (1947, 1953, 1972), concertos for viola (1959), violin and cello (1968), violin (1981), and cello (1988).

OTHER *Voice at Brooklyn* (in seven parts) for soloists, chorus, and orchestra (1980–84); string quartet (1947), two piano sonatas; cantatas on biblical subjects.

Starlight Express, The incidental music by Elgar for a play by V Pearn, after Algernon Blackwood's *A Prisoner from Fairyland*. Composed in 1915, the suite in nine movements, with soprano and bass soloists, was first performed at the Kingsway Theatre, London, on 29 December 1915. The work was very popular as escapist entertainment during the worst days of World War I, but was forgotten until a recent recording.

Starzer, Josef (1726–1787) Austrian composer and violinist. Violinist at the French theatre in Vienna from 1752, he was court composer and leader of the orchestra in St Petersburg 1758–70. Back in Vienna he wrote music for the choreographer Jean-Georges Noverre's ballets and was active in the Tonkünstler-Society, for whose concerts he re-orchestrated Handel's *Judas Maccabeus* in 1779. From 1783 decreasing fitness forced his retirement.

Works SINGSPIEL *Singspiele Die drei Pächter* and *Die Wildschützen*.

BALLET *Roger et Bradamante* (1771), *Adèle de Ponthieu* (1773), *Gli Orazi ed i Curiazi* (all with Noverre), and many others.

CHORAL AND ORCHESTRAL oratorio *La Passione di Gesù Cristo*; symphonies, divertimenti for orchestra; violin concerto.

OTHER chamber music.

Stassov, Vladimir Vassilevich (1824–1906) Russian scholar and art critic. He was the first champion of the Russian nationalist school of composers, writing on César Cui, Mikhail Glinka, Alexsandr Borodin, and Modest Mussorgsky and coining the phrase 'Moguchaya Kuchka' ('Mighty Handful').

Educated at the School of Jurisprudence, he joined the Imperial Public Library in 1845. He studied in Italy from 1851 to 1854, after which he returned to the Library and in 1872 became director of the department of fine arts there.

Statkowski, Roman (1860–1925) Polish composer. He studied with Wladyslaw Zeleński at Warsaw and with Nikolai Soloviev at St Petersburg. On the death of Noskowski in 1909, he was appointed professor of composition at the Warsaw Conservatory.

Works OPERA *Philaenis* (1904) and *Maria* (after Malczewski, 1906).

ORCHESTRAL AND CHAMBER fantasy, polonaise, and other works for orchestra; five string quartets (1896–1929); violin and piano pieces; *Krakowiak* and other works for piano; songs.

stave or **staff** in music, the five parallel, horizontal lines, with spaces in between, on which music is written. The pitch range of the stave is indicated by a ➤ clef.

Steffani, Agostino (1654–1728) Italian diplomat and composer. While he was engaged as music director at Hanover and Düsseldorf, he was sent on various diplomatic missions in Germany, Belgium, and Italy. His most important musical works are about 70 chamber duets – pieces for two singers and continuo; Handel was influenced by them. He also wrote several operas, of which the best known is *Tassilone* (1709).

Steffani learnt music as a choirboy at Padua and was taken to Munich, where he studied music under Johann Kerl at the expense of the Elector Ferdinand Maria. After further studies in Rome 1673–74, he returned to Munich and became court organist in 1675. Having also studied mathematics, philosophy, and theology, he was ordained in 1680. He was made director of the court chamber music, but in 1688 the younger Bernabei was appointed general music director on the death of his father, and Steffani, disappointed in his hopes of obtaining the post, left Munich.

After a visit to Venice he went to the court of Hanover, where the post of music director was offered him, and there he also filled other posts, including diplomatic ones. The philosopher Leibniz, who was also at the court, sent him on a diplomatic mission to various German courts in 1696; in 1698 he was ambassador to Brussels, and on the death of the Elector Ernest Augustus transferred his services to the Elector Palatine at Düsseldorf. In 1706 he was made a nominal bishop. In 1708–09 he was on a diplomatic mission in Italy, where he met Handel, who went into service at the Hanoverian court at his suggestion. His best known opera, *Tassilone*, dates from this time; it unites the Italian and German musical influences which were paramount in Steffani's life. In 1722–25 he lived at Padua and in 1727 he was elected honorary president of the London Academy of Vocal Music. In 1727 he went to Italy for the last time. He died at Frankfurt during a diplomatic visit.

Works OPERA *Marco Aurelio* (1680), *Solone* (1685), *Servio Tullio, Alarico il Baltha* (1687), *Niobe* (1688), *Enrico Leone, La lotta d'Hercole con Achelao* (1689), *La superbia d'Alessandro* (1690), *Orlando generoso* (1691), *Le rivali concordi, La libertà contenta* (1693), *I trionfi del fato* (1695), *Baccanali, Briseide, Arminio, Enea*, and *Tassilone* (1709); *Audacia e rispetto*.

CHURCH AND SECULAR MUSIC motets, vesper psalms for eight voices, *Stabat Mater* for six voices, strings, and organ (1727); *Confitebor* for three voices and strings, and other church music; madrigals; vocal chamber duets with bass; chamber sonatas for two violins, viola, and bass.

Steibelt, Daniel (1765–1823) German composer and pianist. His setting of *Romeo and Juliet* was his most successful work after an initial rejection. It was admired by Berlioz, who may have been influenced by it in his own dramatic symphony.

Steibelt learnt much about keyboard instruments in his childhood, being the son of a harpsichord and piano maker, and studied music with Johann Kirnberger. After serving in the army, he made his first appearance as a pianist and composer in Paris during the late 1780s. At the end of 1796 he visited London, where he remained until 1799 and married an Englishwoman. He visited Hamburg, Dresden, Prague, Berlin, and Vienna, where he met Beethoven, and in 1800 again settled in Paris, but spent as much of his time in London. In 1808 he left for the court at St Petersburg, where he became director of the French Opera on the departure of Boieldieu in 1810.

Works STAGE operas, including *Roméo et Juliette* (after Shakespeare, 1793), *La princesse de Babylone, Cendrillon* (1810), *Sargines*, and *Le jugement de Midas* (unfinished); ballets *Le retour de Zéphyr* (1802), *Le jugement du berger Paris* (1804), *La belle laitière, La fête de l'empereur* (1809); intermezzo *La fête de Mars* (for the victory at Austerlitz); incidental music.

WORKS FOR PIANO eight piano concertos (1796–1820); 50 studies and numerous pieces and transcriptions for piano.

Stein (lived 18th–19th centuries) German family of piano makers: **Johann Andreas** (1728–1792), organ builder and piano maker. He learnt his craft from his father, Johann Georg Stein (1697–1754), worked with Johann Andreas ➜ **Silbermann** in Strasbourg, and settled in Augsburg in 1751. Mozart preferred his pianos above all others. **Maria Anna (Nanette)** (1769–1833), pianist and piano maker, daughter of Johann. She played to Mozart as a child during his visit to Augsburg in 1777, and on her father's death in

1792 carried on the business with her brother, Matthäus, but married Andreas Streicher in 1794 and moved with him to Vienna, where they established a new firm jointly with Matthäus. Later she and her husband became friends of Beethoven. **Matthäus Andreas** (1776–1842), piano maker, son of Johann. He accompanied his sister and her husband to Vienna in 1793 and joined their firm, but established himself independently in 1802. **Andreas Friedrich** (1784–1809), pianist and composer, son of Johann. He went to Vienna as a child with his sister and brother, and studied piano playing and also composition with Albrechtsberger. He appeared in public frequently, especially with Mozart's concertos. His works include three operettas; pantomime *Die Fee Radiante*; violin concerto; piano trio; piano sonata; songs. **Karl Andreas** (1797–1863), composer and piano maker, son of Matthäus. He was a pupil of Förster. He first devoted himself to composition, but later mainly to his father's factory, to which he succeeded. He wrote a comic opera *Die goldene Gans*, two overtures, and two piano concertos.

Stein, Erwin (1885–1958) Austrian musicologist. He was a pupil of Arnold Schoenberg. After conducting at various places, he joined the Universal Edition in Vienna, but settled in London after the Anschluss. He wrote much on Schoenberg.

Steinberg, Maksimilian Osseievich (1883–1946) Russian composer. Stravinsky's *Fireworks* was given its first performance at his wedding in 1908.

He studied at St Petersburg University and Conservatory. He was the pupil (and later son-in-law) of Rimsky-Korsakov, and also studied with Liadov and Glazunov. He became professor at the Leningrad Conservatory.

Works STAGE ballets *Midas* (after Ovid) and *Till Eulenspiegel*; incidental music.

CHORAL AND ORCHESTRAL oratorio *Heaven and Earth* (after Byron); four symphonies (1907, 1909, 1929, 1933); dramatic fantasy on Ibsen's *Brand*, overture to Maeterlinck's *La Princesse Maleine*, and other orchestral works; violin concerto (1946).

OTHER two string quartets; songs, including two Tagore cycles, folk song arrangements.

Steiner, Max(imilian) Raoul Walter (1888–1971) Austrian-born US film composer. With Erich Korngold (1897–1957), he brought the style of Gustav ➜ **Mahler** and Richard ➜ **Strauss** to Hollywood movie scores. He pioneered the use of the ➜ **click-track** for feature films to guarantee absolute coordination of music and film action. His richly sentimental scores include *King Kong* (1934), *Gone With the Wind* (1939), and *Casablanca* (1942).

Steinitz, (Charles) Paul (Joseph) (1909–1988) English organist and conductor. He studied at the Royal College of Music, London, and was church organist in Ashford 1933–42. He founded the South London Bach Society in 1947 (later known as the London Bach Society). With the Steinitz Bach Players (founded in 1969) he gave annual performances in London of the *St Matthew Passion*. He was Professor at the Royal Academy of Music from 1945.

Steinway and Sons company of piano manufacturers founded in New York in 1853 by German-born Heinrich Engelhard Steinweg (later Henry Steinway) (1797–1871). Steinway transformed the 19th-century piano into the modern instrument, introducing 'overstringing' (where the bass strings pass at an angle above some of the higher-pitched strings, thereby enriching the tone quality), larger metal frames that allowed the inclusion of strings of higher tension and better tone quality, and various improvements in the ➔ action. Since Russian pianist and composer Anton ➔ Rubinstein represented the company in the 1870s, most concert artists have preferred the brilliant tone and superior control of Steinway instruments.

stem in musical notation, the vertical stroke attached to the heads of all notes of smaller value than a ➔ semibreve.

Stenhammar, (Karl) Wilhelm (Eugen) (1871–1927) Swedish composer, conductor, and pianist. He became conductor of the royal orchestra at Stockholm and also conductor at Göteborg.

He studied with his father, the composer Per Ulrik Stenhammar (1829–1875), and later with Emil Sjögren and others; he also studied in Berlin.

Works OPERA AND CHORAL opera *Tirfing* (1898); incidental music to plays, including Strindberg's *Ett römspel*, Tagore's *Chitra*; cantata *Sangen*.

ORCHESTRAL AND CHAMBER two symphonies (1903, 1915), serenade in F major for orchestra; two piano concertos (1893–1907); six string quartets (1894–1909); violin and piano sonata; four sonatas and fantasy for piano; part songs including *Sverige*; songs.

Stenka Razin symphonic poem by Aleksandr ➔ Glazunov, Op. 13, composed in 1884 and first performed at St Petersburg in 1885. The work contains the tune of the Volga boatmen's song *Ey ukhnem*.

stentando (Italian 'toiling, labouring') musical direction indicating a dragging delivery of a passage.

Steptoe, Roger (1953–) English composer, pianist, and teacher. He studied at the Royal Academy of Music 1974–77 and was administra-

tor of the International Composer Festivals there 1986–93. He made his debut as a pianist at the Wigmore Hall in 1982.

Works OPERA *The King of Macedon* (1979).

ORCHESTRAL AND CHAMBER symphony (1988), *Sinfonia Concertante* for string trio and strings (1981), concertos for oboe (1982), tuba (1983), clarinet (1989), organ (1990), and cello (1991); two string quartets (1976, 1985) and other chamber music.

CHORAL WITH ORCHESTRA *Winter's Cold Embraces Dye* for soloists, chorus, and orchestra (1985); *Life's Unquiet Dream* for baritone, chorus, and chamber orchestra (1992); choral music and pieces for brass.

Sterndale Bennett English pianist and composer; see William Sterndale ➔ Bennett.

Sternklang, English **Starsound** 'park music' for five electronic groups by Karlheinz ➔ Stockhausen, first performed in Berlin on 5 June 1971.

stesso tempo, lo (Italian, more frequently **l'istesso tempo, 'the same pace')** musical direction; see ➔ istesso tempo, I'.

Stevens, Bernard (1916–1983) English composer. In 1948 he was appointed professor of composition at the Royal College of Music.

He studied at Cambridge with Edward J Dent and C B Rootham and at the Royal College of Music in London with R O Morris. He won the Leverhulme Scholarship and Parry Prize for composition. He served in the army 1940–46.

Works DRAMATIC MUSIC film music.

CHORAL AND ORCHESTRAL cantata *The Harvest of Peace* (1952) and other choral works; symphony *Symphony of Liberation* (1946) and Fugal Overture for orchestra, *Ricercar* and *Sinfonietta* for strings, overture *East and West* for wind band; violin concerto (1946), cello concerto (1952).

CHAMBER string quartet, piano trio, theme and variations for string quartet (1949), *Fantasia* for two violins and piano; violin and piano sonata; piano music; songs.

Stevens, Denis (William) (1922–2004) English musicologist and conductor. He edited the Mulliner Book in *Musica Britannica* and Monteverdi's *Vespers* (1961, revised 1993) and *Orfeo* (1967), and published books on Tomkins and Tudor church music. He was a professor at Columbia University, New York, 1964–74 and he conducted Monteverdi at Salzburg and the London Proms (both in 1967).

He studied at Oxford 1940–42 and 1946–49, and after playing in orchestras was a member of the British Broadcasting Corporation (BBC) music department in London 1950–54. He was cofounder of the Ambrosian Singers.

Stevens, Halsey (1908–1989) US composer, teacher, and writer on music. He is best known for his *Life and Music of Béla Bartók* (1953, revised 1964).

He studied at Syracuse University and with Bloch at Berkeley, 1944. He was chair of the music department at University of California at Los Angeles 1948–76.

Works ORCHESTRAL AND CHAMBER three symphonies (1945–46), three string quartets, three piano sonatas (1933–48).

CHORAL *The Ballad of William Sycamore* for chorus and orchestra (1955), and *Te Deum* for chorus, brass septet, and organ (1967).

Stevens, John (Edgar) (1921–2002) English literary historian and musicologist. He was lecturer in English at Cambridge University in 1952, and professor of Medieval and Renaissance English there in 1978. In addition to his important editions of early English music he is particularly regarded for his books *Music and Poetry in the Early Tudor Court* (1961) and *Words and Music in the Middle Ages* (1986).

Stevens, Risé (1913–   ) US mezzo-soprano. She studied at the Juilliard School, New York, and with Gutheil-Schoder in Vienna. After finding her first successes in Prague, she debuted at the Metropolitan Opera in New York in 1938, where she remained popular for many years, appearing internationally.

She was born in New York City. From 1975 to 1978 she was president of the Mannes College of Music.

Stevenson, Robert M(urrell) (1916–   ) US musicologist. His chief areas of study have been Latin American colonial music and Spanish music; his books include *La Musica en las Catedrales de España durante el siglo do oro* (1992). He has written many articles for *The New Grove's Dictionary of Music and Musicians* (1980).

He studied at Juilliard, Yale, Harvard, and Oxford (with Jack Westrup). He was professor at the University of California at Los Angeles (UCLA) from 1949, and faculty research lecturer from 1981.

Stevenson, Ronald (1928–   ) English composer, pianist, and writer on music. He has made a special study of Busoni: his first piano concerto, *Triptych* (1960), is based on themes from Busoni's *Doktor Faust*.

He studied at the Royal Manchester College of Music and in Italy, and has taught at Edinburgh University.

Works WORKS FOR PIANO *Passacaglia on DSCH*, an 80-minute work for piano (first performance Cape Town, 1963), and *Peter Grimes Fantasia* for piano (1971); piano concerto no. 2 (*The Continents*, 1972).

ORCHESTRAL *Ben Dorain*, choral symphony (1973), violin concerto (The Gypsy, 1973).

CHAMBER *Corroboree for Grainger* for piano and wind ensemble (1987), *St Mary's May Songs* for soprano and strings (1988).

sticcado-pastrole musical instrument, a glass ➤ dulcimer popular in England in the 18th century.

Stierhorn (German 'bull horn') primitive wind instrument, made of a bull's or a cow's horn, sounding a single note of rough quality. Wagner used it for the watchman in *Die Meistersinger von Nürnberg*.

Stiffelio opera by Giuseppe ➤ Verdi (libretto by Francesco Maria Piave), produced at Trieste on 16 November 1850, and revised as *Aroldo* 1856–57. In the story, the Priest Stiffelio forgives the adulterous wife Lina after her father Stankar has killed her lover, Raffaele.

stile rappresentativo (Italian 'representative style') term used by Italian musicians of the new monodic school in the early years of the 17th century to describe the new vocal style of declamatory, ➤ recitative-like dramatic music, which tried to imitate human speech as closely as possible and thus endeavoured to 'represent' dramatic action in a naturalistic way.

Still, William Grant (1895–1978) US composer. His music employs American elements, blues melodies, and American folk songs.

He was educated at Wilberforce University and studied music at Oberlin Conservatory; later he studied with George Chadwick at Boston and with Edgard Varèse. *The Afro-American Symphony* of 1930 was the first by a black US composer to be performed by a major orchestra and the opera *Troubled Island* (1949) was the first premiere given by the newly-formed City Center Opera Company of New York.

Works STAGE operas, including *Blue Steel* (1934), *Troubled Island* (1949), *A Bayou Legend* (1941, first performance 1974), *Highway no. 1* (1942–63), *Costaso* (1949, first performance 1992), *Minette Fontaine* (1958, first performance 1985); ballets *La Guiablesse* (1927) and *Sahdji* (1930).

CHORAL AND ORCHESTRAL *Lenox Avenue* for radio announcer, chorus, and orchestra (1937); five symphonies, including *Afro-American Symphony* (no. 1, 1930), *Africa*, *Poem*, *Phantom Chapel* for strings and other orchestral works.

OTHER *Kaintuck* for piano and orchestra (1935); *From the Black Belt* and *Log Cabin Ballads* for chamber orchestra.

Stimme (German 'voice, part') in music, the human voice, or any ➤ part, vocal or instrumental, in a composition, especially a ➤ polyphonic one; also the copy of an orchestral, vocal, or chamber music part used for performance.

Stimmführung German musical term, meaning ✦ part-writing.

Stimmung, Mood work by Karlheinz ✦ Stockhausen for six amplified voices. It was first performed in Paris on 9 December 1968.

sting old musical term describing the effect of ✦ vibrato in lute playing.

Stobaeus, Johann (1580–1646) German composer and bass. While attending the university at Königsberg, he studied music with Johann Eccard, and, after holding, various minor appointments there, became kapellmeister to the elector of Brandenburg in 1626.

Works SACRED AND SECULAR MUSIC *Cantiones sacrae* for five to ten voices (published 1624), Magnificats for five to six voices, five-part settings of hymn tunes; Prussian Festival Songs for five to eight voices (with Eccard; two volumes, published 1624 and 1644); sacred and secular occasional compositions.

stochastic in music, term used to describe a compositional procedure based on probability theory, where the work's inner details are left to chance (a random sequence of notes), the main outline having been fixed by the composer. Iannis Xenakis introduced this technique to 20th-century composition, relying on computers to generate specific notes, having written a program determining the overall parameters.

stock-and-horn early Scottish musical instrument, similar to the Welsh pibgorn, made of wood or bone fitted with a cow horn. It is played like the chanter of a bagpipe, with a single reed.

It is a different instrument from the stockhorn, which is a forester's horn.

Stockhausen, Karlheinz (1928–) German composer of avant-garde music. He has continued to explore new musical sounds and compositional techniques since the 1950s. His major works include *Gesang der Jünglinge/Song of the Youths* (1956), *Kontakte* (1960) (electronic music), and *Sirius* (1977).

Since 1977 all his works have been part of *Licht/Light*, a cycle of seven musical ceremonies intended for performance on the evenings of a week – these include *Donnerstag* (1980), *Samstag* (1984), *Montag* (1988), and *Dienstag* (1992). Earlier works include *Klavierstücke I–XIV* (1952–85), *Momente* (1961–64), and *Mikrophonie I* (1964). His work has greatly influenced avant-garde composers.

Stockhausen studied at the Cologne Musikhochschule and in Paris with Olivier ✦ Messiaen and Darius ✦ Milhaud. He also learned from the example of Webern, whose tightly controlled brand of ✦ serialism inspired Stockhausen's brief venture into 'integral' serialism (in which all elements of sound – such as pitch, duration, and dynamics – are controlled according to predetermined formulae). Webern's orchestrational technique also influenced Stockhausen's 'group' compositions of the 1950s. From 1953 he worked intensively at German Radio's studio for electronic music at Cologne, influencing contemporaries such as Luciano ✦ Berio and Pierre ✦ Boulez and younger composers such as Tim Souster and Brian Ferneyhough. He is one of the most enterprising of the composers creating electronic music, but has also written music for traditional media. Stockhausen's creative process begins with the premise that all elements of composition can be vigorously controlled, with the progress of a work determined by pre-set acoustic and scientific formulae. In spite of this performers are often allowed a multitude of choices in terms of how they 'read' a score and deploy the equipment at their disposal (the influence of John Cage is evident here).

Works ORCHESTRAL AND CHAMBER *Kreuzspiel* for oboe, clarinet, piano, and three percussion (1951); *Formel* for 29 instruments (1951), *Punkte* for orchestra (1952), *Kontra-Punkte* for ensemble (1952), *Klavierstücke I–XI* (1952–56), *Zeitmasze* for wind quintet (1956), *Gruppen* for three orchestras (1957), *Zyklus* for percussion (1959), *Refrain* for ensemble (1959), *Stop* for instrumental ensemble (1969–73), *Aus den sieben Tagen*, 15 pieces for various instrumental groups (1968); park music *Sternklang* for five groups (1971), *Jubiläum* for orchestra (1977), *Intervall* for piano duo (1972), *Musik im Bauch/Music in the Belly* for six percussion (1975).

ORCHESTRAL AND ELECTRONIC *Kontakte* for piano, percussion, and four-track tape (1960); *Gesang der Jünglinge* for voice and tapes (1956), *Mikrophonie I and II* for electronics (1964–65), *Mixtur* for five orchestras, sine wave generators, and four ring modulators (1964–67); *Telemusik* for four-track tape (1966), *Hymnen* for four-track tape (1967), *Kurzwellen (Short Waves)* for electronics and four short-wave radios (1968), *Spiral* for soloist and short-wave receiver (1969), *Mantra* for two pianos, woodblock, and two ring modulators (1970), *Trans* for orchestra and tape (1971).

CHORAL WITH ORCHESTRA OR ENSEMBLE *Carré* for four choruses and four orchestras (1960), *Momente* for soprano, four choruses, and ensemble (1961–64); *Stimmung* for voices and ensemble (1968), *Atmen gibt das Leben* for chorus (1974).

VOCAL WITH ORCHESTRA OR ENSEMBLE 'Am Himmel wandre ich ...' for soprano and baritone (1972), *Inori* for one/two soloists and orchestra (1974), *Herbstmusik* for four players (1974), *Sirius* for soprano, baritone, and ensemble (1977).

OPERA operas in *Licht* cycle: *Donnerstag* (1981), *Samstag* (1984), *Montag* (1988), *Dienstag* (1992); scenes from *Licht* given as concert pieces: no. 1

Der Jahreslauf for dancers and orchestra (1977); no. 2 *Michaels Reise um die Erde* for trumpet and ensemble (1978); no. 3 *Michaels Jugend* for soprano, tenor, brass instruments, piano, dancers, and tape (1979); no. 4 *Michaels Heimkehr* for soloists, chorus, and orchestra (1979); also *Lucifer's Dream* from *Samstag* (1983).

OTHER *Beethausen, Opus 1970, von Stockhoven* compiled for the Beethoven bicentenary and including fragments of music in quotation and a reading of the Heiligenstadt Testament (developed from *Kurzwellen*).

Stodart (lived 18th–19th centuries) firm of English harpsichord and piano makers. It was founded about 1776 by Robert Stodart, carried on by his son William Stodart, whose employee William Allen invented the metal frame for the piano, and later by his grandson Malcolm Stodart.

Stokem or **Stokhem, Johannes (c.1440–c.1500)** Flemish composer. A few sacred and secular works by him survive, including four chansons printed in Ottaviano Petrucci's *Odhecaton A* (1501).

Stokem was probably born and spent his early life near Liège. He was in the service of Beatrice of Hungary in the early 1480s and a singer in the papal choir 1487–89. He was a friend of the music theorist Johannes ➤ Tinctoris, who sent him portions of his 12th treatise (all that survives) with a letter.

Stoker, Richard (1938–) English composer, conductor, and pianist. He studied in Huddersfield and at the Royal Academy of Music with English composer Lennox Berkeley, and in Paris, France, with the French music teacher Nadia ➤ Boulanger. He taught composition at the Royal Academy of Music 1963–87.

Stoker edited *Composer* magazine 1969–80. He wrote an autobiography, *Open Window – Open Door*, in 1985.

Works OPERA *Johnson Preserv'd* (1967) and *Thérèse Raquin* (after Zola, 1975).

ORCHESTRAL *Petite Suite* (1962) and *Little Symphony* (1969) for orchestra.

CHAMBER three string quartets (1960–69), wind quintet (1963), violin sonata (1964), Sextet (1965), piano trio (1965), Oboe quartet (1970).

Stokowski, Leopold Antoni Stanisław (1882–1977) US conductor. An outstanding innovator, he promoted contemporary music with enthusiasm, was an ardent popularist, and introduced changes in orchestral seating. He cooperated with Bell Telephone Laboratories in early stereophonic recording experiments in the mid-1930s. He was also a major collaborator with Walt Disney in the programming and development of 'Fantasound' optical surround-sound recording

technology for the animated film *Fantasia* (1940).

Stokowski was born in London, the son of a Polish father and an Irish mother. He studied at the Royal College of Music and took a degree in music at Oxford University. In 1900 he became organist at St James's Church, Piccadilly, London, and later studied in Paris and Munich. From 1905 to 1908 he was an organist in New York, and in 1908 a conductor in London; in 1909 he became a conductor of the Cincinnati Symphony Orchestra. As conductor of the Philadelphia Symphony Orchestra he introduced much modern music: he gave the 1926 first performance of *Amériques*, by Varèse, and in 1931 conducted the US premiere of Berg's *Wozzeck*. He also gave the first US performances of Mahler's eighth symphony, *The Rite of Spring*, and the *Gurrelieder*. He was a champion of Rachmaninov, and led the first performances of the 3rd symphony, 4th piano concerto, and *Rhapsody on a Theme of Paganini*. From 1942 to 1944 he conducted the National Broadcasting Company's (NBC) Symphony Orchestra with Toscanini, giving the 1944 first performance of Schoenberg's piano concerto: the NBC terminated his contract after the concert. In 1945 he became music director of the Hollywood Bowl and 1949–50 of the New York Philharmonic Orchestra, taking over the Houston Symphony Orchestra in 1955. In 1962 he formed the American Symphony Orchestra in New York, and in 1965 they gave the first performance of Ives' fourth symphony. In 1940 he won wider fame when he appeared in the cartoon film *Fantasia*.

Stollen (German 'props') in music, the first two stanzas of the songs of the German ➤ Minnesinger and Meistersinger. The song (called a *Bar*) usually had stanzas divided into three sections: two stollen of equal length often sung to the same and always to very similar music called *Aufgesang* ('fore-song') followed by an *Abgesang* ('aftersong') forming a concluding section of unspecified length and with different music.

Stoltzer, Thomas (c.1486–1526) German composer. He became kapellmeister to King Louis of Bohemia and Hungary at Buda, but left after the battle of Mohács in 1526 and took up a post in the service of Duke Albert of Prussia at Königsberg. He drowned in the river Taja.

Works SACRED AND SECULAR MUSIC Latin motets and psalms, Latin hymns for four to five voices, Psalm 37 in Luther's German translation for three to seven voices in motet form, and four others; German sacred and secular songs.

Stolz, Robert (Elisabeth) (1880–1975) Austrian composer and conductor. He wrote about 60 operettas and musicals, the first of which was *Die lustigen Weiber von Wien*, produced in Munich in 1909. He worked in Berlin in the 1920s, writing for early film musicals, and moved to Hollywood in 1940. After returning to Vienna in 1946, he wrote music for ice revues.

His early career was as a pianist; he was conductor at theTheater an der Wien from 1907. He later conducted while in his 90s.

Works OPERETTAS AND MUSICALS about 60, including *Der Favorit* (1916), *Der Tans ins Glück* (1921), *Mädi* (1923), *Wenn die kleinen Veilchen blühen* (1932), *Venus in Seide* (1932), *Der verlorene Walzer* (1933), *Frühling in Prater* (1949), *Trauminsel* (1962).

OTHER about 100 film scores; many individual songs, waltzes, and a funeral march for Hitler, written in anticipation of his death.

Stölzel, Gottfried Heinrich (1690–1749) German composer. He studied at Leipzig University, taught in Breslau 1710–12, and visited Italy 1713–14, meeting Gasparini, Vivaldi, and others. He lived in Prague, Bayreuth, and Gera, and from 1719 was kapellmeister to the court at Gotha.

Works OPERA 22 operas, including *Narcissus* (1711), *Orion* (1712), *Venus und Adonis* (1714).

CHORAL 14 oratorios.

SACRED AND SECULAR MUSIC Masses, motets; Passions; *concerti grossi*; trio sonatas.

Stone Flower, The, Russian **Kamenny Tsvetok** ballet in three acts by Sergey ➤ Prokofiev (scenario by Leonid Lavrovsky and M Mendelson-Prokofieva after a story by P Bazhov). It was composed 1948–53, and produced at the Bolshoi in Moscow, on 12 February 1954.

Stone Guest, The, Russian **Kamenny Gost** opera by Aleksandr ➤ Dargomizhsky (libretto Pushkin's drama, set unaltered). The work was not performed in the composer's lifetime, but was first produced at St Petersburg, on 28 February 1872. In the story, Don Juan dallies with Laura and Donna Anna on the way to Hell.

Stone to Thorn, From work by Peter Maxwell ➤ Davies for mezzo-soprano and ensemble, first performed at Oxford, on 30 June 1971, and conducted by Davies.

stop in music, a knob which controls a ➤ register on an organ or a manual (keyboard) on some harpsichords, enabling the player to alter the instrument's tone quality in various ways. See also ➤ registration.

stopped notes on string instruments, notes produced by shortening the vibrating length of the string with a finger (stopping); on wind instruments, the notes are not produced naturally as harmonics, but by valves, keys, or other mechanical means. In horn playing the hand is used, originally to alter the pitch before the development of valves, but now called for by

composers for their distinctive tone.

stopping in music, an action affecting ➤ pitch: on a string instrument, the shortening of the vibrating length of the string (raising pitch), by pressing the finger onto the string, bringing the string into contact with the fingerboard; on a horn (especially a valveless natural horn), the alteration of pitch and timbre is achieved by blocking the bell to varying degrees, with the hand; in an organ, stopping occurs by the blocking of one end of a pipe, lowering pitch by one octave.

Storace, Stephen (1762–1796) English composer. He wrote operas in Italian and English, including his Mozart-influenced Shakespearean opera *Gli equivoci* (1786), and his most successful English opera *The Pirates* (1792).

He studied at the Conservatorio di Sant' Onofrio in Naples, and in about 1784 went to Vienna, where he produced two operas and became friendly with Mozart. In 1787 he returned to London with his sister, the soprano Anna Storace, and became composer to Sheridan's company at the Drury Lane Theatre. *Gli equivoci* has been successfully revived in London in 1974 and at Wexford in 1992.

Works OPERA AND STAGE the operas *Gli sposi malcontenti* (1785), *Gli equivoci* (after Shakespeare's *Comedy of Errors*, 1786), *La cameriera astuta* (1788), *The Haunted Tower, No Song, No Supper* (1790), *The Siege of Belgrade* (1791), *The Pirates, Dido: Queen of Carthage* (1792), *The Cherokee* (1794), *The Iron Chest* (Colman), *Mahmoud, or The Prince of Persia* (unfinished, completed by Michael Kelly and Ann Storace, produced 1796) and others; ballet *Venus and Adonis*.

Story of a Real Man, The, Russian **Povest' o nastoyashchem cheloveke** opera in four acts by Sergey ➤ Prokofiev (libretto by composer and M Mendelson-Prokofieva), composed 1947–48. Prokofiev sought to gain official favour from Stalin's regime with the story of a heroic legless Soviet aviator, but after private performance in Leningrad, on 3 December 1948, it was not staged until 8 October 1960, at the Bolshoi, Moscow.

Stradella opera by Friedrich von Flotow; see ➤ *Alessandro Stradella*.

Stradella, Alessandro (1644–1682) Italian composer, singer, and violinist. He taught singing in Venice, and wrote operas and oratorios for Rome, Modena, and Genoa. He had numerous love affairs, the last of which led to his assassination.

As he was of noble birth, Stradella was probably educated privately in music. He never held any official posts, and most of what is known of his career seems to be based on legend rather than fact, notably in Friedrich Flotow's opera *Alessandro Stradella* (1844), in which a composer avoids being murdered by a pair of bandits by singing to them of kindness and mercy.

Works OPERA AND STAGE the operas *La forza dell' amor paterno* (1678), *Doriclea*, *Il trespolo tutore balordo* (1679), *Il Floridoro*.

CHORAL motets and other church music; oratorio *San Giovanni Battista* (1675) and others; sacred and secular cantatas.

OTHER serenade *Qual prodigio che io miri* and others; madrigals; concerto for strings.

Stradivari, Antonio (c.1644–1737), Latin **Stradivarius** Italian stringed instrument maker, generally considered the greatest of all violin makers. He produced more than 1,100 instruments from his family workshops, over 600 of which survive; they have achieved the status (and sale-room prices) of works of art.

Stradivari was born at Cremona, served an apprenticeship there with Niccolò ➤ **Amati**, and founded a workshop there in the 1660s. He continually modified the design of his instruments, achieving by 1690 the 'Long Strad'. His finest instruments, including cellos and violas, were produced in the first two decades of the 18th century. The secret of his skill is said to be in the varnish but is probably a combination of fine proportioning and ageing.

His sons Francesco Stradivari (1671–1743) and Omobono Stradivari (1679–1742) carried on the business.

Straeten, Edmond van der (1826–1895) Belgian musicologist. He studied law at Aalst and Ghent, but on returning home cultivated music history. He became secretary to Fétis for the purpose of studying with him, and contributed to his Dictionary. He also acted as critic and wrote books on Flemish music, including *La Musique aux Pays-bas* in eight volumes. He also composed incidental music and a Te Deum.

strambotto a form of verse used by the composers of *frottole* in the 15th–16th centuries. It had eight lines (*ottava rima*), the first six rhyming alternately and the last two consecutively. In the *strambotto siciliano* all eight lines rhyme alternately.

Straniera, La, *The Stranger* opera by Vincenzo ➤ **Bellini** (libretto by Felice Romani), produced at La Scala, Milan, on 14 February 1829. In the story, Arturo, betrothed to Isoletta, becomes infatuated with the veiled stranger, Agnese disguised as Alaide. Arturo seems to kill Agnese's brother Vableburgo, believing him to be a lover; in fact he is only wounded. When it is revealed that Agnese is the Queen of France, Arturo kills himself.

strascinando (Italian 'dragging, slurring') in music, performance direction requiring heavy slurring of the part.

strathspey Scottish folk dance in quick common time, similar to the reel, but with dotted rhythms. The name derives from the strath (valley) of Spey and is first heard of in 1780, though dances of the kind are much older.

Straube, (Montgomery Rufus) Karl (Siegfried) (1873–1950) German organist and conductor. He travelled all over Europe with the choir of St Thomas's, Leipzig. He published many editions of organ and choral music of the past.

He was the son of a German father and an English mother. He studied with his father, an organist and harmonium maker, and with Heinrich Reimann. He was appointed organist of Wesel Cathedral in 1897 and of St Thomas's, Leipzig, in 1902. There he became conductor of the Bach Society in 1903, professor of organ at the Conservatory in 1907, and cantor of St Thomas's in 1918. Leipzig University awarded him an honorary doctorate in 1923.

Straus, Oskar (1870–1954) Austrian composer and conductor. A pupil of Max Bruch, he was chief conductor and composer at the Überbrettl cabaret, becoming a master of light satirical stage pieces. His first major success came in 1907 and 1908, with the operettas *Ein Walzertraum/A Waltz Dream* and *Der tapfere Soldat/ The Chocolate Soldier*.

Straus studied with Hermann Grädener (1844–1929) and Max Bruch in Berlin and became a theatre conductor in various towns, including Bratislava, where he premiered his first operetta, *Der Weise von Cordoba*, in 1895. After *Ein Walzertraum* and *Der tapfere Soldat* he settled in Berlin, in Vienna in 1927, and subsequently in Paris. In 1940 he emigrated to the USA, returning to Europe in 1948.

Works OPERA AND STAGE operas *Die Waise von Cordova* and *Das Tal der Liebe* (1909); operettas, including *Ein Walzertraum/A Waltz Dream* (1907), *Der tapfere Soldat/The Chocolate Soldier* (after Shaw's *Arms and the Man*, 1908), *Love and Laughter* (1913), *The Last Waltz*, *Riquette*.

ORCHESTRAL overture to Grillparzer's *Der Traum ein Leben*, serenade for string orchestra.

Strauss (lived 19th–early 20th centuries) Austrian family of musicians, including Johann (Baptist) Strauss (1804–1849); Johann Strauss (1825–1899); Josef Strauss (1827–1870); and Eduard Strauss (1835–1916).

Johann (Baptist) (1804–1849) was a composer, conductor and violinist. His parents were innkeepers and apprenticed him to a bookbinder, but he learnt the violin and viola and was eventually allowed to study with Austrian composer

Ignaz Seyfried (1776–1841). He played viola in private string quartets and for the Micael Pamer orchestra, and in 1823 joined Viennese musician Joseph Lanner's band, in which he became deputy conductor. In 1825 he and Lanner parted and he began a rival band, for which he wrote dances, especially waltzes, which had by that time become fashionable. By 1837 he had been to Germany, Holland, Belgium, France, and the UK. He added the ➤ quadrille to the music of the Viennese ballrooms, having picked it up in Paris, and made a great hit with the *Radetzky Marsch*. He toured again and was then made conductor of the court balls.

His work includes: 150 waltzes (*Täuberl, Kettenbrücken, Donaulieder Walzer*), 35 quadrilles, 28 galops, 19 marches, 14 polkas.

Johann (1825–1899) was a composer, conductor, and violinist, the son of Johann Baptist. He was not allowed to follow his father's profession, but learnt the violin and studied secretly with Drechsler and others. In 1844 he appeared as conductor at Dommayer's hall in the Heitzing suburb, and his father capitulated. After his father's death he amalgamated his father's orchestra with his own, toured in Austria, Poland, and Germany, and visited St Petersburg. In 1863 he became conductor of the court balls, and directed them until 1872. The previous year his first operetta had been produced at the Theater an der Wien and in 1874 he had his most enduring stage success with *Die Fledermaus*. His greatest popularity was achieved with such waltzes as *Tales from the Vienna Woods* (1868), *The Blue Danube* (1867), *Wiener Blut* (1870), *Roses from the South* (1880), *Frühlingsstimmen* (1883) and the *Emperor Waltz* (1885).

His work includes the operettas *Indigo und die vierzig Räuber* (1871), *Der Karneval in Rom* (1873), *Die Fledermaus* (1874), *Cagliostro in Wien* (1875), *Prinz Methusalem, Blindekuh, Das Spitzentuch der Königin* (1880), *Der lustige Krieg* (1881), *Eine Nacht in Venedig, Der Zigeunerbaron* (1885), *Simplizius* (1887), *Ritter Pázmán, Fürstin Ninetta* (1893), *Jabuka, Waldmeister* (1895), *Die Göttin der Vernunft* (1897); ballet *Aschenbrödel*; *Traumbilder* for orchestra; polkas, galops, and other dances.

Josef (1827–1870) was a composer and conductor, and the son of Johann Baptist. He became an architect at his father's wish, but secretly studied music and during his father's illness conducted his band with success. He then formed his own band and wrote 283 dances for it. He died after a visit to Warsaw, where he injured his hand in a fall on the platform at his last concert.

Eduard (1835–1916) was a composer and conductor, and the son of Johann Baptist. He studied harp and composition and appeared as a conductor in 1862. After 1865 he took his brother

Johann's place at the summer concerts in St Petersburg and in 1870 became conductor of the court balls. He toured much, appearing at the Inventions Exhibition in London in 1885. His works include over 300 dances.

Strauss, Richard (Georg) (1864–1949) German composer and conductor. He followed the German Romantic tradition but had a strongly personal style, characterized by his bold, colourful orchestration. He first wrote tone poems such as *Don Juan* (1889), *Till Eulenspiegel's Merry Pranks* (1895), and *Also sprach Zarathustra/Thus Spake Zarathustra* (1896). He then moved on to opera with *Salome* (1905) and *Elektra* (1909), both of which have elements of polytonality. He reverted to a more traditional style with *Der Rosenkavalier/The Knight of the Rose* (1909–10).

His father, Franz Strauss (1822–1905), was horn player at the Court Opera in Munich. Strauss began to compose at the age of six and at ten wrote his first two published works, the *Festival March* and the serenade for wind instruments. In 1880 he finished a symphony in D minor and the next year his A major string quartet was performed in public. He entered Munich University in 1882, but left in 1883 and went to Berlin for a short period of study, but became assistant conductor to Hans von Bülow at Meiningen very soon after. A member of the orchestra, Alexander Ritter, turned Strauss's classical leanings into admiration for Berlioz, Wagner, and Liszt. In 1885 Bülow resigned and Strauss became first conductor at Meiningen; his first truly characteristic piece, the first horn concerto, had been premiered under Bülow in March. In spring 1886 he visited Italy and afterwards wrote the symphony *Aus Italien*, produced at Munich in spring 1887, when he became sub-conductor at the Opera there. *Macbeth*, his first symphonic poem, was composed that year. In 1889 he became assistant conductor to Lassen at the Weimar Court Opera and gained his first major success with the tone poem *Don Juan*; the famous exuberant opening of the work seems to announce the young composer in all his confidence and technical assurance. In 1891 Cosima Wagner invited him to conduct *Tannhäuser* at Bayreuth.

Under Wagner's influence he wrote his first opera, *Guntram*, most of it during a tour in the Mediterranean undertaken to counteract ill health. It was produced at Weimar in May 1894. The heroine was sung by Pauline de Ahna, whom he married in June, and he was that year appointed conductor of the Berlin Philharmonic Orchestra in succession to Bülow. Although *Guntram* was not a success, in the next five years he composed some of his most popular and enduring tone poems, each one superbly orchestrated and with its own distinctive character: *Till*

Eulenspiegel, Also sprach Zarathustra, Don Quixote, and *Ein Heldenleben*. In 1905 his opera *Salome* was premiered at Dresden; in Vienna, London, and New York it was to have trouble with the censors for its lurid treatment of a Biblical subject. Strauss further collaborated with librettist Hugo von Hofmannstahl in a setting of Sophocles' *Elektra*, in which he was considered wild and dissonant. More general favour was found with *Der Rosenkavalier* in 1911, a comedy set in 18th-century Vienna, with anachronistic waltzes. Strauss had been conductor of the Berlin Royal Opera from 1898 but resigned in 1918 and the following year his masterpiece, *Die Frau ohne Schatten*, was produced in Vienna; the rich allusiveness and symphonic amplitude of the score was a fitting farewell to a world which had all but disappeared in World War I.

Strauss had bought a country house at Garmisch in the Bavarian highlands, and all his later works were written there. After Hofmannsthal's death in 1929 Strauss, who had already written a libretto of his own for the autobiographical *Intermezzo*, produced in 1924 at Dresden, worked with Stefan Zweig on *Die schweigsame Frau* (based on Ben Jonson's *Epicoene*). It was produced at Dresden in 1935 but was quickly withdrawn on a trumped-up excuse because Zweig, as a Jew, had to be boycotted by the Nazi party. Strauss thereupon resigned his appointment as president of the Reichs-Musikkammer and was himself under a cloud for a time, but had long been too important a figure in German musical life to be ignored. He wrote music for the 1936 Berlin Olympic Games and composed four further operas during the Nazi regime. The best known of these is *Capriccio*, although some of Strauss's most attractive music is in the trilogy of operas based on Greek mythology. The *Four Last Songs* were premiered posthumously.

Works OPERA *Salome* (1905), *Elektra* (1909), *Der Rosenkavalier* (1911), *Ariadne auf Náxos* (1912), *Die Frau ohne Schatten* (1919), *Arabella* (1933), *Die schweigsame Frau* (1935), *Capriccio* (1942).

ORCHESTRAL *Don Juan* (1889), *Tod und Verklärung* (1890), *Till Eulenspiegels lustige Streiche* (1895), *Ein Heldenleben* (1899), *Eine Alpensinfonie* (1915); two horn concertos (1885, 1942), oboe concerto (1945); *Metamorphosen* for 23 solo string instruments (1946).

VOCAL *Vier letzte Lieder/Four Last Songs* for soprano and orchestra (1948); 26 Op. nos of songs (about 150).

stravaganza (Italian 'extravagance') musical term sometimes used for a composition of a freakish nature.

Stravinsky, Igor Fyodorovich (1882–1971) Russian composer, later of French (1934) and US (1945) nationality. He studied under Nikolai

➤ Rimsky-Korsakov and wrote the music for the Diaghilev ballets *The Firebird* (1910), *Petrushka* (1911), and *The Rite of Spring* (1913), which were highly controversial at the time for their use of driving rhythms and bi-tonal harmonies. At the first performance of *The Rite of Spring* the audience's reaction caused a riot. His works also include symphonies, concertos (for violin and piano), chamber music, and operas; for example, *The Rake's Progress* (1951) and *The Flood* (1962).

Stravinsky was one of the most important composers of the 20th century, who arguably determined the course of music for the rest of the century more than any other composer. His versatile work ranges from his neoclassical ballet *Pulcinella* (1920) to the choral-orchestral *Symphony of Psalms* (1930). In such works as the *Canticum Sacrum* (1955) and the ballet *Agon* (1953–57), he made use of serial techniques; this was only after the death of Arnold Schoenberg in 1951, as during Schoenberg's lifetime Stravinsky was seen as the main opposition to this technique.

Stravinsky was born near St Petersburg, where his father, Fyodor Stravinsky, was the leading bass at the Imperial Opera. His creative output can be divided into three distinct phases, beginning with Russian nationalism and continuing through neoclassicism to twelve-note technique. In 1903 he met Rimsky-Korsakov at Heidelberg and played him his early compositions, but did not become his pupil until 1907. By this time he had finished a piano sonata, begun a symphony, and married his second cousin, Nadezhda Sulima, in 1906. In 1908 he had the symphony performed and wrote the orchestral piece *Fireworks* for the marriage of Nadia Rimsky-Korsakov and Maximilian Steinberg, and a *Funeral Chant* on Rimsky-Korsakov's death. The performance of the *Fantastic Scherzo* in 1909 attracted the attention of the impresario Sergei Diaghilev, who commissioned Stravinsky to write *The Firebird* for the Ballets Russes. It was produced in Paris in 1910, and Stravinsky began to be known in Western Europe. *Petrushka* followed in 1911 and *The Rite of Spring* in 1913; both were produced in Paris, where the latter provoked much protest and fanatical support. In spite of the wild public protest at its premiere, *The Rite of Spring* was soon successfully performed all over Europe, Russia, and the USA, establishing Stravinsky, with Schoenberg, as the leading avant-garde composer of his time.

In 1914 he settled on Lake Geneva, Switzerland, and in Paris the same year Diaghilev produced the fairy-tale opera-ballet *The Nightingale*. From 1914 Stravinsky became as well known in London as in Paris, and in 1925 made his first tour of the USA. In the inter-war years many of his works were written in the spirit of neoclassicism, beginning with the ballet *Pulcinella* in 1920, based on pieces written by Giovanni Pergolesi (he actually wrote all over Pergolesi's original score), and continuing with the concerto for piano with wind instruments in 1924. *Oedipus Rex*, an opera-oratorio after Sophocles, was premiered in 1927, followed by the classically-inspired ballet *Apollon Musagète* in 1928, the ballet *The Fairy's Kiss* (after Tchaikovsky), *Capriccio* (1929) for piano and orchestra, and the *Symphony of Psalms*, premiered in 1930 under Ernest Ansermet.

In 1937 Stravinsky's ballet *Jeu de Cartes* was produced by George Balanchine at the New York Metropolitan Opera. He settled in Hollywood in 1939, and the following year he conducted the Chicago Symphony Orchestra in his symphony in C. The powerful *Symphony in Three Movements* was premiered by the New York Philharmonic Orchestra in 1946 and in 1948 Balanchine staged the ballet *Orpheus*. A meeting with W H Auden led to the peak of Stravinsky's neoclassical music, the opera *The Rake's Progress* which was premiered at Venice in 1951 and inspired by a series of paintings of the same name by William Hogarth.

Stravinsky had meanwhile met the conductor Robert Craft and under his influence turned towards the serial music of the Second Viennese School. This marks the beginning of the composer's third great period. Interestingly, Stravinsky began fully to explore this kind of music only after its main composer, Arnold Schoenberg, had died. Although the two men lived only a short distance away from each other in Los Angeles, they never met, living in their own entirely separate musical and social circles. The ballet *Agon* (1953–57) and the religious vocal works *Canticum Sacrum* (1955) and *Threni* combine rigorous methods with Stravinsky's familiar creativity. He composed very little after this. His *Requiem Canticles* of 1966 was performed at his funeral in Venice, a city which he regarded as his spiritual home.

He published *Chronicles of my Life* (1936), and (with Robert Craft) *Conversations with Igor Stravinsky* (1959) and *Memories and Commentaries* (1960).

Works STAGE ballets, including *The Firebird* (1910), *Petrushka* (1911), *The Rite of Spring* (1913), *The Soldier's Tale* (dance scene, 1918); *Pulcinella* (ballet with song, 1920), *Les Noces/The Wedding* (Russian choreographic scenes; composed 1914–17 and 1921–23, first performance in 1923), *Apollon Musagète* (1928), *Orpheus* (1948), *Agon* (1953–57); opera-oratorio *Oedipus Rex* (1927); melodrama *Perséphone* (1934); opera *The Rake's Progress* (1951); musical play *The Flood* (1962).

CHORAL *Symphony of Psalms* (1930), *Mass* with double wind quintet (1944–48), *Canticum Sac-*

rum (1955), *Requiem Canticles* (1966).

ORCHESTRAL *Symphonies of Wind Instruments* (1920), Concerto for piano and wind (1924), *Capriccio* for piano and orchestra (1929), Violin concerto in D (1931), Concerto, *Dumbarton Oaks* (1938), *Symphony in C* (1940), *Danses concertantes* (1942), *Symphony in Three movements* (1945), *Ebony concerto* for clarinet and jazz band (1945), Concerto in D for strings (1946).

CHAMBER AND INSTRUMENTAL three Pieces for String Quartet (1914), Octet (1923), *Duo Concertant* for violin and piano (1932), Septet (1952).

Street Scene opera in two acts by Kurt ➤ Weill (libretto by Elmer Rice), produced at the Shubert Theater, Philadelphia, on 16 December 1946. The story is a slice of New York tenement life, as Anne Maurrant is murdered by her jealous husband Frank, and Sam Kaplan fails to make out with Anne's daughter Rose.

The work was also produced in New York in 1947 and in London in 1987, at the Camden Festival.

Streicher German family of piano makers. The Streicher company was founded at Vienna in 1802 by Maria Anna (Nanette) Streicher (daughter of the piano maker Johann Stein). She married in 1794 Johann Andreas Streicher (1761–1833), a music teacher in Vienna, and founded a piano manufactory there after 1794.

Their son Johann Baptist Streicher (1796–1871) succeeded his parents in business, and from him it descended to his son Emil.

Streicher or **Streichinstrumente (German 'strings')** German term for ➤ string instruments.

Streicher, Theodor (1874–1940) Austrian composer, the great-grandson of Johann and Maria ➤ Streicher. He studied in Vienna, Dresden, and Bayreuth.

Works CHORAL WITH ORCHESTRA *Mignons Exequien* for chorus, children's chorus, and orchestra (after Goethe's *Wilhelm Meister*, 1907); *Die Schlacht bei Murten* for chorus and orchestra; *Kleiner Vogel Kolibri* for chamber orchestra; *Um Inez weinten* for soprano and orchestra.

CHAMBER *Die Monologe des Faust* (after Goethe) for string sextet (1912); many songs, including 36 settings from *Des Knaben Wunderhorn*.

Streichzither (German 'stroke-zither') musical instrument, a variety of ➤ zither played with a violin bow instead of being plucked with the fingers or with a plectrum.

Streit zwischen Phöbus und Pan, Der, The Dispute between Phoebus and Pan secular ➤ cantata by Johann Sebastian ➤ Bach, written in 1731 and satirizing Johann Adolf Scheibe, editor of *Der critische Musikus*, in the part of Midas.

strepitoso (Italian 'noisy') musical direction suggesting a forceful and spirited performance, but more often used in the sense of a climax growing in force and speed.

stretta (Italian 'pressure, tightening, squeezing') in music, a passage, usually at the end of a composition, especially an operatic finale, in which the tempo is accelerated either gradually or by sections, creating a climax.

stretto (Italian 'drawn together') in music, in a ➔ fugue, the imitative entry of the subject in different voices, so that each voice begins before the previous statement of the subject has finished. The result is an intensification, appropriate to the close of a fugue. Alternatively, the term indicates the acceleration or intensification of a passage, such as the end of the last movement of Beethoven's Fifth Symphony.

stretto maestrale (Italian 'masterly stretto') ➔ stretto in which the fugal subject not only appears in close, overlapping entries, but is carried through from beginning to end at each entry.

strict counterpoint the traditional name for ➔ counterpoint written according to the rules of the species (type).

Striggio, Alessandro (c.1535–1592) Italian composer, organist, lutenist, and violist. A nobleman from Mantua, he travelled abroad in a diplomatic capacity, visiting England in 1567. He was celebrated as a composer of madrigals and as a virtuoso player of the lira da gamba and viol. His son, the librettist Alessandro ➔ Striggio, was a friend of Monteverdi.

Striggio was in the service of Cosimo de' Medici at Florence 1560–74, collaborating with other composers on contributions to the local *intermedi* (see ➔ intermezzo) for great festivities. His music was admired in Italy and abroad, and in 1568 his 40-part motet, *Ecce beatam lucem*, was performed at the marriage of Duke Albrecht IV of Bavaria. He subsequently visited several European courts, including that of Ferrara in 1584. He returned to Mantua later that year, to the court of Duke Guglielmo Gonzaga. He published seven books of madrigals (1558–97).

Works SACRED AND SECULAR MUSIC Masses, motet in 40 parts for voices and instruments; madrigal comedy *Il cicalamento delle donne al bucato* (1567); intermezzi for performance between the acts of plays; madrigals; various works for voices and instruments in many parts.

Striggio, Alessandro (1573–1630) Italian librettist. He wrote the text of Monteverdi's *Orfeo* and *Tirsi e Clori*. Like his father, Alessandro ➔ Striggio, he also served the Gonzaga family at Mantua.

He was secretary to the Duke of Mantua and a string player at court until 1628.

stringendo (Italian 'tightening') in musical notation, indicating an increase in the tension of a passage by intensifying the tempo, in a manner similar to ➔ accelerando ('quickening').

string instrument musical instrument that produces a sound when a stretched string is made to vibrate. Today the strings are made of gut, metal, and nylon or Pearlon (a plastic). Types of string instruments include: **bowed**, the violin family and viol family; **plucked**, the guitar, ukulele, lute, sitar, harp, banjo, and lyre; **plucked mechanically**, the harpsichord; **struck mechanically**, the piano and clavichord; and **hammered**, the dulcimer.

string quartet ➔ chamber music written for two violins, viola, and cello. The term also refers to the group that performs such a composition. It has always been the most popular of all the types of chamber works and is considered to be the most pure and abstract genre. Important composers for the string quartet include Haydn (more than 80 string quartets), Mozart (27), Schubert (20), Beethoven (17), Bartók (six), and Shostakovich (15). Recent important composers for the string quartet include US composer Elliott Carter (five quartets) and English composer Brian Ferneyhough (four).

String-quartet music began as a decorative, vocal style of viol music but developed into a vigorously instrumental style that used the instruments' expressive potential to the full. The older grouping of solo and accompanying voices was gradually replaced by solo opportunities for each player, a trend that grew in the 19th century when shriller metal strings started to be used.

string quintet ➔ chamber music ensemble consisting of five string instruments – usually two violins, a viola, and two cellos. Luigi ➔ Boccherini wrote many works for the string quintet; the same form was adopted by Schubert for the greatest of his chamber works (1828). Two violins, two violas, and a cello were favoured by Mozart – in four of his finest instrumental pieces – and by Beethoven, Brahms, and Carl Nielsen. Antonín Dvořák's string quintet Op. 77 uses a double bass instead of second viola.

strings in music, the cords, usually of gut (as in the violin family and harps) or wire (as in the lute, violin, and guitar families, and pianos), by means of which the notes are produced on such instruments. The term 'strings' is also used to designate string instruments collectively, especially those of the violin family in the orchestra.

string sextet ➔ chamber music ensemble consisting of two violins, two violas, and two cellos. Pieces written for string sextet include Dvořák's Op. 48, Brahms's Op. 18 and Op. 36, and Schoenberg's *Verklärte Nacht/Transfigured Night* (1899). The prologue to Strauss's *Capriccio* (1940–41) is a string sextet.

string trio in music, the conventional combination of violin, viola, and cello. It is found in one of Mozart's finest works, the Divertimento K563. Haydn and Boccherini had earlier used the combination in occasional works. Beethoven emulated Mozart's example in his trio Op. 3, and his set of three trios Op. 9. After comparative neglect during the Romantic period, notable trios of the 20th century include those of Roussel, Hindemith, Dohnányi, Schoenberg, and Webern.

Strohfiedel (German 'straw fiddle') sixteenth-century percussion instrument similar to the ➤ xylophone.

stromentato (Italian 'instrumented, orchestrated, scored') word associated mainly with ➤ recitative (sung narration, *recitativo stromentato*), where it implies a more or less independent orchestral accompaniment.

Strong, G(eorge) Templeton (1856–1948) US composer. He studied at the Leipzig Conservatory, became a member of the Liszt circle, and was in close touch with Edward Alexander MacDowell while living at Wiesbaden 1886–89. After teaching in Boston in 1891–92, he settled in Switzerland on Lake Geneva, living first at Vevey and later in Geneva.

Works CHORAL WITH ORCHESTRA *Knights and Dryads* for solo voices, chorus, and orchestra; two cantatas for solo voices, male chorus and orchestra.

ORCHESTRAL three symphonies: *Sintram* (after Fouqué, 1888), *In the Mountains* (1886), and *By the Sea*; symphonic poem *Undine* (after Fouqué); two *American Sketches* for violin and orchestra.

CHAMBER *A Village Music-Director* trio for two violins and viola, and other chamber music.

strophic bass in music, an instrumental bass part used without change throughout a series of verses of a song or chorus, the upper parts of which vary at each occurrence; or a similar device in instrumental music.

strophic song in music, the simplest form of song structure, in which each verse of a poem is set to the same music.

Strozzi, Barbara (1619–c.1664) Italian singer and composer. She composed madrigals, cantatas, sacred songs with continuo, duets, ariettas, and other pieces. She studied with Francesco Cavalli, and sang in several of his operas.

She was the adopted daughter of the poet Giulio Strozzi, and sang at the Accademia degli Unisoni, which he established in 1637.

structural cadence see ➤ structural harmony.

structural harmony in ➤ voice-leading analysis, structural harmony that operates at a deeper structural level than the surface or foreground of the music. Voice-leading analysis identifies and distinguishes between 'structural' and 'nonstructural' harmonies in order to describe the harmonic structure of the piece. The terms **structural cadence** and **structural progression** are used to describe the harmonic features at the background level of the piece; the structural cadence is that which closes the ➤ fundamental line.

structural level voice-leading analysis distinguishes between three levels of harmonic structure in music. The **foreground** level consists of the harmonic progressions in the piece itself, ignoring only very local features such as ornamentation of the melodic line or figuration of accompanimental texture. The **middleground** is identified by reducing the foreground to the harmonies which are prolonged over spans of time, ignoring subordinate harmonies such as chromatic chords. Finally, the **background** is the deepest level of harmonic structure, consisting of the simple contrapuntal harmony which underlies the whole piece. It is at the background level that the ➤ fundamental line and ➤ fundamental structure can be identified.

Strungk, Nikolaus Adam (1640–1700) German composer, violinist, and organist. After working as music director at Hanover, Hamburg, and Dresden, he went to Leipzig, where he produced operas. His most successful operas were two of those produced at Hamburg, *Esther* (1680) and *Semiramis* (1681).

He studied under his father, Delphin Strungk, for whom he deputized at the organ at Brunswick from the age of 12. While at Helmstedt University he learnt the violin at Lübeck during vacations. In 1660 he joined the court orchestra at Wolfenbüttel, then at Celle, and in 1665 went to the court of Hanover. After a period at Hamburg from 1678, two visits to Vienna, and one to Italy, he returned to Hanover 1682–86, but in 1688 took up a position at Dresden as chamber organist and second kapellmeister to the Saxon court in succession to Christian Ritter, and in 1692 succeeded Christoph Bernhard (1628–1692) as first kapellmeister. In 1693 he opened an opera house at Leipzig, where he produced his later stage works and where his daughters Philippine and Elisabeth sang.

Works OPERA AND STAGE operas, including *Der glückseligsteigende Sejanus, Der unglücklichfallende Sejanus* (1678), *Esther, Doris* (1680), *Semiramis* (1681), *Nero, Agrippina* (1699); completion of Pallavicini's *L'Antiope*.

CHORAL oratorio *Die Auferstehung Jesu* (1688); *ricercare* on the death of his mother.

CHAMBER sonatas and chaconnes for violin or

viola da gamba; sonatas for two violins and viola and for six strings; airs and dances for recorders.

Strunk, (William) Oliver (1901–1980) US musicologist. He was among the most influential musicological teachers of his generation, but his most important publications concerned Byzantine chant. His *Source Readings in Music History* (1950) remains a classic.

He studied at Cornell University (in New York State) and in Berlin, worked at the Library of Congress from 1928, and taught at Princeton University, New Jersey, 1937–66.

Stuckenschmidt, Hans Heinz (1901–1988) German musicologist. He is an especially well-known writer on 20th-century music, including Schoenberg and the Viennese School; he published biographies of Schoenberg in 1951 and 1978.

He studied piano, violin, and composition in Berlin, and also analysis with Arnold Schoenberg. He held many posts as music critic and from 1948 taught at the Technical University in Berlin, becoming Professor Emeritus in 1967.

study in music, an instrumental piece; see ➤ étude.

stump string instrument of the ➤ cittern type invented around 1600 by Daniel Farrant. The manuscript of the only surviving piece written for it, 'To the Stump by F P', is in Christ Church, Oxford. From it have been inferred various details such as length of strings, number of courses, and compass.

Stumpf, Carl (1848–1936) German music scientist and psychologist. He collaborated with Erich von ➤ Hornbostel in editing the *Beiträge zur Akustik und Musikwissenschaft* and wrote much on the psychological aspects of acoustic phenomena.

He studied at Göttingen University and held professorships at Würzburg, Prague, Halle, Munich, and Berlin from 1893.

Sturgeon, Nicholas (c.1390–1454) English composer. He contributed to the Old Hall Manuscript during the second phase of its existence, when it was in use at the Chapel Royal. Five known works by him survive.

He was a scholar of Winchester College as a child. In 1442, after serving as a clerk of the Chapel Royal, he became a canon of Windsor and precentor of St Paul's Cathedral.

Sturm, Der, The Tempest operas based on Shakespeare's play by Peter ➤ Winter (Munich, 1798) and Frank ➤ Martin (Vienna, 17 June 1956).

Work for chorus and orchestra by Jospeh ➤ Haydn (not based on Shakespeare) composed in 1798 and performed at his concerts in London.

Also commonly used as the title to ➤ Beethoven's piano sonata Op. 31 no. 2 in D minor.

Sturton, Edmund (lived 15th–16th centuries) English composer. He wrote an *Ave Maria* and *Gaude virgo mater*; the latter is in the Eton Choirbook.

subdiapente (from Latin and Greek 'a fifth lower') musical term used especially for canons at the fifth. See ➤ diapente.

subdiatessaron (from Latin and Greek 'a fourth lower') see ➤ diapente.

subdominant in music, the fourth note (or degree) of the ➤ diatonic scale, for example, F in the C major scale. The chord of the subdominant is a ➤ triad built upon the subdominant note.

subito (Italian 'sudden') term used in musical notation, as in *subito piano* ('suddenly soft'), a direction to play softly immediately, without any gradual dynamic change (unlike decrescendo).

subject in music, a principal melody of a work, similar to a ➤ theme. The term is used specifically to describe the main musical ideas of a sonata-form movement, as in first and second subjects. It is also used to describe the opening melody of a ➤ fugue, which appears in imitation in all the voices. A fugue has only one subject, except in double and triple fugues.

submediant in music, the sixth note (or degree) of the ➤ diatonic scale, for example A in the C major scale. The chord of the submediant is a ➤ triad built upon the submediant note.

Subotnick, Morton (1933–) US composer. His works often employ synthesizers. In 1969 he was appointed director of electronic music at the California Institute of Arts, Los Angeles.

He studied at Mills College, California, with Darius Milhaud. He is married to Joan ➤ La Barbara.

Works ELECTRONIC MUSIC *Concert* for wind quintet and electronics, *Angels* for string quartet and electronics (first performance 1984), *The Key to Songs* for chamber orchestra and synthesizer (1985), *All my Hummingbirds have Alibis* for flute, cello, midi piano, mallets, and computer (1991).

ORCHESTRAL *Music for 12 Elevators*, *Silver Apples of the Moon* (1967), *Before the Butterfly* for orchestra (1975); music drama *The Double Life of Amphibians*; *In Two Worlds* saxophone concerto (1988), *And the Butterflies Began to Sing* (1988); incidental music for plays by Brecht and Beckett.

subsemitonium (Latin 'under-semitone') in music, the old name for the ➤ leading note, especially when used in the ➤ modes by sharpening the seventh of the scale.

subset/superset in ➤ **pitch-class set** analysis, a method of relating sets containing different numbers of pitches. One set is a subset of another, larger set if its pitches can be contained within the second set. For example, the set 3–2 (pitches 0, 1, 3) is a subset of set 4–3 (pitches 0, 1, 3, 4); and also, if transposed up two semitones, of set 4–10 (0, 2, 3, 5). The larger set is called a superset of the smaller. See ➤ **set complex**; ➤ **similarity relation**.

subtonium (Latin 'under-(whole) tone') in music, the old name for the seventh degree of the ➤ **church modes**, except the Lydian (and later the Ionian), so called because it was a whole tone below the final, though it was often sharpened in performance according to the principle of ➤ **musica ficta**.

Suchoň, Eugen (1908–1993) Slovakian composer. His earlier music reflects the style of the Czechoslovakian nationalist composers, while his later works were influenced by ➤ **serialism**.

He studied at Bratislava Conservatory 1927–31, and then in Prague with Vítězslav Novák 1931–33. He taught at the Bratislava Academy of Music 1933–41 and was professor at the State Conservatory 1941–47. From 1947 to 1953 he was professor at the Slovak University and from 1953 at the Pedagogic High School in Bratislava.

Works OPERA *The Whirlpool* (1949) and *Svätopluk* (1960).

OTHER serenades for strings, for wind quintet (1932–33); choral music; piano quartet, piano pieces.

suite in baroque music, a set of contrasting instrumental pieces based on dance forms, known by their French names as allemande, bourrée, courante, gavotte, gigue, minuet, musette, passepied, rigaudon, sarabande, and so on. The term refers in more recent usage to a concert arrangement of set pieces from an extended ballet or stage composition, such as Tchaikovsky's *Nutcracker Suite* (1891–92). Igor Stravinsky's suite from *The Soldier's Tale* (1920) incorporates a tango, waltz, and ragtime.

suivez (French 'follow') in music, a direction used in two senses: either to indicate that one movement of a composition is to follow the preceding one immediately (equivalent to Italian ➤ **attacca**); or to indicate that accompanying parts are to follow a vocal or other solo part moving independently of the prescribed rhythm or tempo (equivalent to Italian ➤ **colla parte**).

Suk, Josef (1874–1935) Czech composer, violinist, and viola player. He studied in Prague with Dvořák, whose daughter he married in 1898. His earlier works are in the style of Dvořák; later he developed a more modern style of his own. Much

of his music was influenced by personal experiences, especially the death of his wife in 1905 (including the piano pieces *About Mother* written for his infant son) and that of Dvořák in 1904. The *Asrael* symphony (1906), in particular, refers to these two deaths.

In 1892 he formed the Bohemian String Quartet with Karel Hofmann, Oscar Nedbal, and Otto Berger, playing second violin. He began to compose early and in 1922 became professor of composition at the Prague Conservatory, of which he was director 1924–26. His work includes symphonies (*Asrael*, 1906), chamber music, choral works, piano pieces, and incidental music for three plays.

Works CHORAL WITH ORCHESTRA Mass in B♭ major, *Epilogue* for baritone solo, women's chorus, and orchestra.

ORCHESTRAL *A Tale* and *Under the Appletrees* for orchestra; Serenade (1892) and meditation on a chorale for string orchestra; fantasy for violin and orchestra (1902), symphony in E major (1899), *Asrael* (1906); symphonic poems *Prague*, *A Summer Tale*, and *Maturity*.

DRAMATIC incidental music for Julius Zeyer's *Radúz and Mahulena* (1898), overture to Shakespeare's *Winter's Tale* (1894).

CHAMBER two string quartets (1896, 1911), piano quartet, piano trio, elegy for violin and cello with string quartet, harmonium, and harp; *Ballade and Serenade* for cello and piano; sets of piano pieces; part songs.

Sullivan, Arthur Seymour (1842–1900) English composer. He wrote operettas in collaboration with William Gilbert, including *HMS Pinafore* (1878), *The Pirates of Penzance* (1879), and *The Mikado* (1885). Their partnership broke down in 1896. Sullivan also composed serious instrumental, choral, and operatic works – for example, the opera *Ivanhoe* (1890) – which he valued more highly than the operettas.

Other Gilbert and Sullivan operettas include *Patience* (which ridiculed the Aesthetic Movement) (1881), *The Yeomen of the Guard* (1888), and *The Gondoliers* (1889).

sul ponticello (Italian 'on the bridge') in music, a direction for bowed string instruments to play a passage very near (not actually on) the ➤ **bridge** to produce a particular nasal and rustling sound. It is usually abbreviated to 'sul pont'.

sul tasto (Italian 'on the touch') in music, a direction for bowed string instruments to play a passage with the bow over the finger-board, a technique which reduces the overtones, producing a thinner, flatter sound.

'Sumer is icumen in','Summer has come' English song in parts, dating from around 1270 and known as the Reading Rota (round). It is a canon for four voices and there are two additional bass voices adding a ➤ **pes** or ground-bass, also in canon. In the manuscript the tune is also provided with Latin words, beginning *Perspice, Christicola,* but the accompanying voices (or pes) merely have 'Sing cuccu nu' in both versions, though the music they sing is actually part of an Easter antiphon (choral music involving the exchange of responses).

Sunless song cycle by Modest ➤ **Mussorgsky** (words by A A Golenishchev-Kutuzov), composed in 1874: 1. *Between four walls;* 2. *Thou didst not know me in the crowd;* 3. *The idle, noisy day is ended;* 4. *Boredom;* 5. *Elegy;* 6. *On the River.*

'Sun' Quartets the nickname of the six string quartets Op. 20 by Joseph ➤ **Haydn,** composed in 1772.

Suor Angelica cycle of operas by Giacomo Puccini; see ➤ *Trittico.*

supertonic in music, the second degree of the major or minor ➤ **scale,** so called because it stands above the tonic (the key note of a scale).

Suppé, Franz von (1819–1895), adopted name of **Francesco Ezechiele Ermenegildo Suppe Demelli** Austrian composer and conductor of Belgian descent. His *Das Pensionat* (1860) was the first successful Viennese operetta in response to the French model. His later works are largely known today outside German-speaking countries through their tuneful overtures.

He showed a talent for composition early, producing a Mass and a comic opera *Der Apfel* at Zara in 1834; but he was sent to Padua University by his father to study medicine. On his father's death, however, he settled in Vienna with his mother. He studied there with Ignaz Xaver von Seyfried and conducted at various Viennese and provincial theatres, including the Josephstadt, Wieden, and Leopoldstadt theatres in Vienna from 1841 until his death.

Works OPERA AND STAGE operettas *Das Mädchen vom Lande* (1847), *Das Pensionat* (1860), *Paragraph 3, Zehn Mädchen und kein Mann* (1862), *Pique Dame/Die Kartenschlägerin* (1862), *Flotte Bursche* (with an overture on students' songs, 1863), *Die schöne Galatee* (1865), *Leichte Kavallerie/Light Cavalry* (1866), *Fatinitza, Boccaccio* (1879), *Donna Juanita* (1880), *Die Afrikareise,* and several others; farces; ballets; incidental music to Elmar's *Dichter und Bauer/Poet and Peasant* (1846), Shakespeare's *Midsummer Night's Dream,* Schiller's *Wallensteins Lager,* and others (more than 200 stage works).

SACRED MUSIC Mass, Requiem (*L'estremo giudizia,* 1855; first British performance, 1984).

surbahar Indian bass lute, a relative of the ➤ **sitar.**

'Surprise' Symphony symphony by Joseph ➤ **Haydn,** no. 94 in G major, composed for London in 1791, so called due to the sudden loud interruption after 16 quiet bars at the beginning of the slow movement. It is known in Germany as *Symphonie mit dem Paukenschlag/Symphony with the Drum-beat.*

Survivor from Warsaw, A work by Arnold ➤ **Schoenberg** for narrator, men's chorus, and orchestra, Op. 46 (text by composer), first performed in Albuquerque, New Mexico, on 4 November 1948.

Surzyński, Józef (1851–1919) Polish priest and composer. He studied at Regensburg and Leipzig, later taking holy orders in Rome. In 1882 he became director of the cathedral choir at Poznań and in 1894 provost at Kościan. He edited the *Monumenta Musices Sacrae in Polonia* and *Musica Ecclesiastica.*

Works SACRED AND SECULAR MUSIC numerous Masses, hymns, and other church music; *Polish Songs of the Catholic Church.*

Susa, Conrad (1935–) US composer. He is best known for his operas: *Transformations* (Minnesota, 1973) is a re-telling of Grimm's *Fairy Tales* and has been widely performed. *Black River: A Wisconsin Idyll* (1975) tells of rural angst in 19th-century America, and *The Love of Don Perlimplin* (1984) draws on 18th-century musical sources.

He studied at the Juilliard School in New York and from 1988 has taught at the San Francisco Conservatory of Music. He was dramaturg of the Eugene O'Neill Center in Connecticut from 1986. He also has composed a symphony, *A Sonnet Voyage* (1963), and choral works including *Dawn Greeting* (1986) and *Earth Song* (1988).

Susanna oratorio by Geroge ➤ **Handel** (libretto anonymous), performed at Covent Garden, London, on 10 February 1749.

Susanna's Secret opera by Ermanno Wolf-Ferrari; see ➤ *Segreto di Susanna, Il.*

Susato, Tielman (c.1500–between 1561 and 1564) Flemish composer, publisher, and editor. He was the outstanding Dutch music publisher of his time. His eleven *Musyck Boexken,* 'little music books', of 1551 contained Dutch songs, dance music, and the *Souter Liedekens* of the composers Clemens non Papa and Gerhard Mes.

He worked in Antwerp from 1529, established his business in 1543, and in 1547 built his own premises 'At the Sign of the Crumhorn'. He also published volumes of Masses, motets, and chansons by the leading composers of his day; many of these include works by himself.

suspension in music, a progression of chords in which one note of a chord is tied over to the next chord, while the other voices move to a new harmony, thereby causing ➤ **dissonance** with the tied note. The dissonance is traditionally resolved by the tied note moving a step lower, to a note consonant with the local harmony.

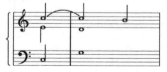

In this example the top voice (note C) is suspended before resolution on note B.

Susskind, Walter (1913–1980) English conductor and pianist of Czech origin. From 1946 to 1952 he was conductor of the Scottish National Orchestra, and from 1954 to 1956 he conducted in Australia. He also conducted the Toronto Symphony Orchestra 1956–65, and in 1968 he took over the St Louis Symphony Orchestra and conducted it until 1975, when he became principal guest conductor with the Cincinnati Symphony Orchestra.

He studied composition with Josef Suk and Alois Hába, conducting with Georg Szell, and making his debut at the German Opera House in Prague in 1932. From 1942 to 1945 he conducted with the Carl Rosa Opera Company and then at Sadler's Wells in 1946. In England he was heard as a piano soloist, and in 1977 gave the first performance in Britain of Alexander von Zemlinsky's *Lyric Symphony.*

Süssmayr, Franz (Xaver) (1766–1803) Austrian composer. He assisted Mozart with the opera *La clemenza di Tito* (probably the recitatives) and completed his unfinished Requiem. In 1792 he became conductor of the Kärntnertortheater.

He was educated at the monastery of Kremsmünster and was a pupil of Salieri and Mozart in Vienna. His completion of Mozart's Requiem has been reviled in recent years by scholars, but it remains the most satisfactory solution to a remaining musical problem.

Works *OPERA AND STAGE* operas *Moses* (1792), *L'incanto superato* (1793), *Der Spiegel von Arkadien* (1794), *Il Turco in Italia* (1794), *Idris und Zenide* (1795), *Die edle Rache, Die Freiwilligen, Der Wildfang* (after Kotzebue), *Der Marktschreier* (1799), *Soliman II* (after Favart, 1799), *Gulnare* (1800), *Phasma*, and others; two ballets.

SACRED AND SECULAR MUSIC Masses and other church music; cantatas *Der Retter in Gelfahr* (1796) and *Der Kampf für den Frieden* (1800).

CHAMBER clarinet concerto; serenades for flute, viola, and horn, and for violin, guitar, and English horn; instrumental pieces.

sustaining pedal or **damper pedal** or **loud pedal** on a piano, the pedal on the right which, when depressed, lifts all the dampers. This allows the notes to continue vibrating after the fingers release the keys. In addition to prolonging the notes played by the fingers, it also enriches the tone quality by allowing other strings to vibrate by means of ➤ **sympathetic resonance**. Used sparingly in 18th-century music, in the 19th century the sustaining pedal was used increasingly to create impressionistic effects.

Sutermeister, Heinrich (1910–1995) Swiss composer. He wrote in a consistently conservative idiom, and is best known as a composer of operas.

He studied philology at Paris and Basel, where he entered the Conservatory, later studying with Courvoisier and Pfitzner at Munich. In 1934 he settled at Bern, at first as operatic coach at the municipal theatre. In 1963 he was appointed professor of composition at the Hochschule für Musik in Hanover.

Works *OPERA AND STAGE* the operas *Romeo und Julia* (1940) and *Die Zauberinsel* (*The Tempest*, 1942) (both based on Shakespeare), *Niobe, Raskolnikov* (on Dostoevsky's *Crime and Punishment*, 1948), *Madame Bovary* (after Flaubert, 1967), *Das Flaschenteufel* (TV, 1971), *Le roi Bérenger* (1985); radio opera *Die schwarze Spinne* (after Jeremias Gotthelf, 1936; produced 1949); ballet *Das Dorfunter dem Gletscher*; Christmas radio play *Die drei Geister* (after Dickens); incidental, film, and radio music.

CHORAL chamber oratorio *Jorinde und Jorindel* (after Mörike); *Baroque Songs* for tenor, women's chorus, and instruments; songs for chorus; *Cantata 1944* for contralto, small chorus, and piano; Requiem (1952) and seven other cantatas.

VOCAL WITH ORCHESTRA *Sieben Liebesbriefe* for tenor and orchestra.

CHAMBER AND ORCHESTRAL divertimento for string orchestra; three piano concertos (1943, 1953, 1962), two cello concertos; three string quartets, string trio, and other chamber music; piano and organ pieces; songs.

Sutton, John (lived 15th century) English composer. He was a fellow of Magdalen College, Oxford, in 1476, and of Eton from 1477 to about 1479. His *Salve regina* for seven voices is in the Eton choirbook.

Švanda Dudák, Schwanda the Bagpiper opera by Jaromír ➤ **Weinberger** (libretto by Miloš Kareš), produced at the Czech Theatre, Prague, on 27 April 1927. In the story, Švanda beguiles Queen Ice Heart with his piping, but finding him already married she orders his execution, and he has to be saved by Babinsky.

Svendsen, Johan (Severin) (1840–1911) Norwegian composer, violinist, and conductor, the greatest Scandinavian conductor of his period. After a career as a virtuoso violinist, he took up composing. He was a friend of Grieg, who admired his orchestrational technique. His style, though Romantic, shows elements of Norwegian folk music. He wrote two symphonies and other orchestral works, as well as chamber and vocal works.

He learnt music from his father, a bandmaster, and at first adopted that profession himself. But, playing several instruments, he joined the orchestra at the Christiania Theatre, began extensive travels in Sweden and Germany in 1861, and studied at the Leipzig Conservatory 1863–67. After travelling in Scandinavia and Scotland in 1867, he settled in Paris in 1868. In 1870–71 he was in Germany again, mainly at Leipzig and Weimar, and taught and conducted at Christiania 1872–77. After visits to Munich, Rome, London, and Paris, he was court conductor at Copenhagen 1883–1908.

Works ORCHESTRAL incidental music to Coppée's *Le Passant* (1869), two symphonies, overture to Bjønson's *Sigurd Slembe*, *Carnaval à Paris*, *Carnaval des artistes norvégiens*, four Norwegian Rhapsodies, legend *Zorahayda*, overture to Shakespeare's *Romeo and Juliet*, and other pieces for orchestra.

CHAMBER violin concerto (1870) and romance, cello concerto (1870); string quartet (1865); string quintet, string octet.

OTHER Marriage Cantata; songs.

Swan Lake, Russian **Lebedinoye ozero** ballet by Pyotr ➔ Tchaikovsky (choreography by Marius Petipa and Lev Ivanovich Ivanov), produced at the Bolshoi Theatre, Moscow, on 4 March 1877.

Swan of Tuonela, The symphonic legend by Jean ➔ Sibelius, Op. 22, one of four on subjects from the *Kalevala*. The work was composed 1893–95, and first performed in Helsinki in 1895.

Swan Song song cycle by Franz Schubert; see ➔ Schwanengesang.

Swayne, Giles (1946–   ) English composer. He studied with Messiaen. In the early 1980s he visited the Gambia and Senegal to study the music of the Jola people.

He studied at Cambridge University and the Royal Academy of Music, and with Messiaen from 1976. He has worked as an opera répétiteur and has taught at Bryanston School, Dorset, and St Paul's Girls' School, London.

Works CHAMBER three string quartets (1971, 1977, 1993), *The Good Morrow*, for mezzo and piano

(to texts by Donne, 1971), *Synthesis* for two pianos (1974), *Missa Tiburtina* (1985), *Into the Light* for seven players (1986), *Tonos* for five players (1987), *Songlines* for flute and guitar (1987), *A Memory of Sky* brass quintet (1989).

ORCHESTRAL *Orlando's Music* for orchestra (1974), *Pentecost-Music* for orchestra (1977), *Song for Hadi* for drums and instruments (1983), symphony for small orchestra (1984), *The Song of Leviathan* for chamber orchestra (1988).

CHORAL *Cry* for 28 amplified solo voices, in which the creation of the world is depicted (1979), *Count-Down* for 16-part chorus and two percussion (1981), *Circle of Silence* for six voices (1991).

OPERA AND STAGE ballet *A World Within* with tape (on the life of the Brontës, 1978); opera *Le nozze di Cherubino* (1984); melodrama *Harmonies of Hell* (1988); children's drama *The Song of the Tortoise* (1992), *The Owl and the Pussycat* for narrator and seven instruments (1993).

Sweelinck, Jan Pieterszoon (1562–1621) Dutch composer, organist, harpsichordist, and teacher. He was the first composer to write an independent part for the pedal keyboard (pedalboard) in organ works, a technique which reached its peak in J S Bach's organ compositions. He taught many of the next generation's organists of the German school.

He studied under his father, **Pieter Sweelinck**, who became organist at the Old Church at Amsterdam in 1566. His father died in 1573 and he succeeded to his post between 1577 and 1580, holding it to his death. His music was influenced by the English virginalists and the Venetian organists. The poet Joost van den Vondel (1587–1679) wrote an epitaph on his death.

Works SACRED AND SECULAR MUSIC four books of psalms for four to eight voices, including three books of *Psalms of David* (1604–14), *Cantiones sacrae* for several voices; organ fantasias, toccatas, and chorale variations; harpsichord pieces; chansons for five voices, *Rimes françoises et italiennes*.

swell device on the harpsichord and organ for the artificial production of ➔ crescendo and ➔ diminuendo, which these instruments are incapable of producing by touch. It takes various forms, the most successful being a contrivance in the form of a slatted blind (hence the name Venetian swell), which, opening and shutting by means of a pedal, increased or reduced the volume of tone.

swell organ in music, the second manual (keyboard) of an organ, characterized by a 'swell' mechanism which can vary the volume given by any combination of stops. The swell organ sometimes has the greatest number of stops and pipes, ranging from a wide variety of flues to a selection of reeds.

Sygar, John (lived 15th century) English composer. He was a singer and chaplain at King's College, Cambridge, 1499–1501 and 1508–15, and contributed a Magnificat (now incomplete) to the Eton Choirbook.

Sylphides, Les ballet with music adapted from Frédéric → Chopin (choreography by Fokin), produced at the Théâtre du Châtelet, Paris, on 2 June 1909.

Sylvia, ou La Nymphe de Diane ballet by Léo → Delibes (scenario by Jules Barbier and Baron de Reinach, choreography by Louis Mérante), produced at the Paris Opéra on 14 June 1876.

sympathetic resonance in music, the physical phenomenon whereby a vibrating string can induce another, initially unmoving, string to vibrate also, without any physical contact. Only strings that are related to others within the harmonic series are subject to sympathetic resonance. For example, a string will cause another, an octave higher, to vibrate by sympathetic resonance because the latter is the first overtone of the former.

sympathetic string a string on a musical instrument which is not plucked, bowed, or hit by a hammer, but sounded by means of → sympathetic resonance. Instruments employing sympathetic strings in order to enrich the timbre include the Hardanger fiddle, viola d'amore, and certain pianos.

symphonia symphony, especially in the earlier sense of any piece of music in which instruments play together in consort; also an early instrument, possibly a kind of bagpipe and, in a later sense, a clavichord. See → sinfonia.

Symphonia domestica, Domestic Symphony symphony by Richard → Strauss, Op. 53, composed in 1903 and first performed in New York, on 31 March 1904. Like his earlier symphonic poem *Heldenleben* (1898), the work is autobiographical, but describes the composer's private life, including love-making and bathing the baby, while the earlier work showed him as a public figure.

Symphonic Metamorphosis on Themes of Carl Maria von Weber work for orchestra by Paul → Hindemith; composed 1940–43 and first performed in New York, on 20 January 1944 (conducted by Rodziński). The four movements use material from → Weber's piano music and the incidental music for a Stuttgart production of Carlo Gozzi's play *Turandot* (1809).

symphonic poem in music, a term originated by Franz → Liszt for his 13 one-movement orchestral works that interpret a story from literature or history, also used by many other composers. Richard Strauss preferred the term 'tone poem'.

symphonic study a term invented by Edward Elgar for his *Falstaff*, probably because it is intended to be as much an outline of Falstaff's character as a description of the events surrounding him. Robert Schumann's *Etudes Symphoniques* (Symphonic Studies) of 1835 consist of a theme and variations for piano solo.

symphonie concertante see → sinfonia concertante.

Symphonie fantastique symphony by Hector Berlioz, Op. 14, composed in 1830. Berlioz gave it a programme arising out of his disappointed love for the actress Harriet Smithson and representing the crazed dreams of a poet crossed in love who has taken opium. The five movements are: 1. *Rêveries-passions/Reveries-Passions*: depicting the emotions when the protagonist first meets his beloved; 2. *Un bal/A Ball*: in which he spots his unobtainable beloved at a ball; 3. *Scène aux champs/Scene in the Country*: in which the artist, alone on a summer's evening, realises she will never be his; 4. *Marche au supplice/March to the Scaffold*: having overdosed on opium, he has a nightmare that he is witnessing his own execution; 5. *Songe d'une nuit de Sabbat/Dream of a Sabbath Night* is the final nightmare: he is buried during a witches' sabbath; the leader of the coven is revealed as his beloved.

The work is particularly famous for its use of a recurring musical theme ('*idée fixe*') to represent the beloved; it becomes progressively more distorted throughout the nightmares.

The work was revised in Italy and first performed in Paris, on 5 December 1830; it was performed with its sequel, *Lélio*, in Paris on 9 December 1832.

Symphonie funèbre et triomphale symphony by Hector Berlioz, Op. 15, for military band, strings, and chorus, composed in 1840 by order of the French government and performed at the tenth anniversary of the 1830 Revolution, in Paris on 28 July 1840.

Symphonie liturgique symphony by Arthur → Honegger composed 1945–46 and dedicated to Charles Munch, who gave the first performance in Zurich on 17 August 1946.

Symphonies of Wind Instruments work by Igor → Stravinsky, dedicated to the memory of Claude Debussy; it was composed in 1920, revised 1945–47, and first performed in London on 10 June 1921 (conducted by → Koussevitzky).

The unusual use of the plural in the title (sym-

Syncopation in a passage from Handel's Water Music. *The second notes of bars 2–5 are syncopated.*

phonies instead of symphony) was explained by Stravinsky as being in its original sense of 'sounding together': much of the interest in the work lies in the different textures generated by varying combinations of instruments.

symphony most important form of composition for the orchestra. It usually consists of four separate but closely related movements, although early works often have three. It developed from the smaller ➔ **sonata** form, the Italian ➔ **overture**, and the ➔ **concerto grosso**.

Haydn established the mature form of the symphony, written in slow, minuet, and allegro movements. Mozart and Beethoven (who replaced the ➔ **minuet** with the ➔ **scherzo**) expanded the form. Further modifications have since taken place, including developments such as the **programme symphony** that 'tells a story' or is descriptive in some way, for example, Hector Berlioz's *Symphonie Fantastique* (1830–31). Other important composers of symphonies include Johannes Brahms, Pyotr Tchaikovsky, Anton Bruckner, Antonín Dvořák, Gustav Mahler, Jean Sibelius, Walter Piston, Sergey Prokofiev, Carl Nielsen, Igor Stravinsky, and Aaron Copland. Important later composers of symphonies include Ralph Vaughan Williams, Dmitri Shostakovich, Witold Lutosławski, and Peter Maxwell Davies.

Symphony in Three Movements work for orchestra by Igor ➔ **Stravinsky**; composed 1942–45 and first performed in New York on 24 January 1946. The outer movements were inspired by Stravinsky's experiences of the war, as viewed from the USA. The central slow movement derives from music for a planned film on St Bernadette.

Symphony of a Thousand name sometimes given to Gustav ➔ **Mahler**'s eighth symphony, in E flat, composed 1906–07. The first performance, in Munich on 12 September 1910, was conducted by Mahler and was the greatest public success of his career. The first movement is a setting on the hymn *Veni creator spiritus* ('Come, Holy Spirit') and the second the closing scene from Goethe's drama *Faust*.

The symphony does not actually require 1,000 performers, but it does not fall far short: the forces include eight vocal soloists, double chorus, boys' chorus, and orchestra with full strings, 20 woodwind, 17 brass instruments, celesta, piano, harmonium, and mandolin. The first US performance was in Philadelphia, on 2 March 1916,

conducted by Stokowski. It was not performed in the UK until 15 April 1930 (London, conductor Wood).

Symphony of Psalms work by Igor ➔ **Stravinsky** for mixed chorus and orchestra; it was written in 1930 to celebrate the 50th anniversary of the Boston Symphony Orchestra, though the first performance was in Brussels on 13 December 1930 (conducted by Ansermet).

synaesthesia the relation of musical sound to the perception of colour. The term applies equally to the theoretical concept and to the actual condition. Some composers have specified colour displays to be performed as part of a musical work (for instance, Skriabin's *Prometheus*, 1913). The composer Olivier ➔ **Messiaen** used a synaesthetic description of modes and harmonies to organize the structure of certain of his works.

syncopation in music, the rhythmic effect of moving the accent on to a beat that is normally unaccented.

synthesis technique of generating sound by artificial means, either by using electronic devices such as oscillators and filters, or by using a computer. See ➔ **electronic music**; ➔ **Fourier transform**.

synthesizer electronic musical device for the simulation of vocal or instrumental ➔ **timbre** (tone quality).

The pipe organ was the first major synthesizer, and allowed a mixture of timbres at the unison or harmonic intervals. Modern electrical synthesizers date from 1904 and the Telharmonium of US inventor Thaddeus Cahill, which used a tone wheel (a programmable oscillator later incorporated in the ➔ **Hammond organ**).

Later synthesizers include the analogue ➔ **trautonium**, ➔ **ondes Martenot**, ➔ **RCA Mark II synthesizer**, ➔ **Moog** (the first electronic synthesizer), ARP, and ➔ **Synthi 100**; and digital Fairlight, Synclavier, Roland, Oberheim, and Yamaha keyboards, and the ➔ **IRCAM 4X series synthesizer**.

types of synthesizer In **preset synthesizers**, the sound of various instruments is produced by a built-in computer-type memory, which triggers all the control settings required to produce the sound of a particular instrument. For example, the 'sawtooth' sound wave produced by a violin is artificially produced by an electrical tone generator, or oscillator, and then fed into an electrical filter that is set to have the resonances characteristic of a violin body.

In **programmable synthesizers** any number of new instrumental or other sounds may be produced as needed by the performer.

Speech synthesizers can break down speech into 128 basic elements (allophones), which are then combined into words and sentences, as in the voices of electronic teaching aids.

Synthi 100 computer-controlled analogue synthesizer developed 1972–75 by Peter Zinovieff (1934–) from his successful EMS briefcase synthesizer. It incorporates a sequencer, which allows the continuous recycling of a series of values applicable to pitch, dynamics, or structural parameters.

Compositions using the Synthi 100 include Henze's *Tristan* (1973) for piano, orchestra, and tape music and Stockhausen's *Sirius* (1975–77) for soloists and tape music.

Syrian chant the earliest of the independent branches of Christian ➤ chant. Its language was the Eastern Aramaic dialect, also called Syriac. Apart from some indecipherable cantillation formulae the music of the early Syrian church has not survived; and it is impossible to say how closely what is sung today resembles it.

In addition to the cantillation (chanting in unison) of the lessons and the singing of psalms, common to all liturgies, a repertory of hymns emerged, anticipating in some cases the forms of Byzantine chant. The *memrâ* was a poetical homily, sung to a recitative formula. The *madráshâ* was a strophic hymn sung by a soloist, with a refrain sung by the choir. The *sogîthâ* was a poem of dramatic character. Lesser forms, inserted between the verses of psalms, are comparable to the *troparion* and *sticheron* of the Byzantine liturgy.

syrinx alternative name for the ➤ panpipe, a musical instrument.

system in music, the number of ➤ staves required for the scoring of a composition, such as two for a piano work, one + two for a song, four for a quartet, and so on, up to any number needed for an orchestral full score. Such a system is connected on the left-hand side of the page by various kinds of braces or brackets; an open space between these shows that the next system begins lower down on the same page.

Szabelski, Bolesław (1896–1979) Polish composer. He studied with Szymanowski and Statkowski at the Warsaw Conservatory, and from 1945 taught composition and organ at the Katowice Conservatory. He embraced the ideals of the Polish avant garde from the late 1950s.

Works ORCHESTRAL five symphonies (1926–68), sinfonietta, *Concerto grosso* for orchestra; concertino and concerto for piano and orchestra.

CHORAL Magnificat for soprano, chorus and orchestra.

CHAMBER two string quartets; piano and organ music.

Szałowski, Antoni (1907–1973) Polish composer. He studied with his father, a violin professor at the Warsaw Conservatory; also piano with two masters and composition with Sikorski. He later studied with Nadia Boulanger in Paris, where he settled and produced works in which local French influences predominated.

Works ORCHESTRAL symphonies, symphonic variations; capriccio and overture for string orchestra; piano concerto (1930); three songs with orchestra.

CHAMBER four string quartets (1928–56); trio for oboe, clarinet, and bassoon; suite for violin and piano; sonatina for clarinet and piano; violin and piano pieces; partita for solo cello; sonata, two sonatinas, and other works for piano.

Szamotulczyk or **Szamotuł, Wacław Z (c.1524–1560)** Polish composer. He wrote much *a cappella* church music, some of which was published by printers Johann Berg 'Montanus' (died 1563) and his partner Ulrich Neuber (died 1571) of Nuremberg.

He studied at Poznań and at Kraków University, and in 1547 became composer to the king. From 1555 he was kapellmeister to Prince Michał Radziwiłł.

Szeligowski, Tadeusz (1896–1963) Polish composer. He studied at Lviv and Kraków, later with Nadia Boulanger in Paris. He taught at Poznań, Lublin, Wilno, and Warsaw. He made special studies of folk-song and early church music and was also influenced in his compositions by French neoclassicism.

Works ORCHESTRAL incidental music for plays, Maeterlinck's *Blue Bird*; two psalms for solo voices, chorus, and orchestra; concerto, *Phantaisie rapsodique*, suite *St Casimir Fair* for orchestra; clarinet concerto, piano concerto.

CHAMBER two string quartets (1929, 1934); *Lithuanian Song* for violin and piano; *Children's Album* for piano; *Green Songs, Flower Allegories*, and other songs.

Szell, Georg (1897–1970) Hungarian-born US conductor and pianist. Szell was one of the last of a generation of conductors who dominated orchestras with iron discipline and sarcastic humour. He conducted at the Berlin Staatsoper 1924–30. In 1939 he settled in the USA, and conducted the Cleveland Philharmonic Orchestra from 1946 until his death. Bartók and Janáček were among the few modern composers in his programmes.

A child prodigy, he studied with Richard Robert (1861–1924) in Vienna, playing a work of his own with the Vienna Symphony Orchestra at the age of 11. He studied composition with Josef Foerster, Eusebius Mandyczewski, and Max Reger, and then, through the influence of Richard Strauss, he obtained a conducting post in Strasbourg, which he held 1917–18, having already made his debut in Berlin in 1914. After further posts in Prague, Darmstadt, and Düsseldorf he was first conductor at the Berlin Staatsoper 1924–30, also teaching at the Berlin Hochschule für Musik 1927–30. From 1930 to 1936 he again conducted in Prague, and took over the Scottish National Orchestra 1937–39.

Szell then went to the USA, where he was guest conductor with the National Braodcasting Company (NBC) Symphony Orchestra 1941–42, and conductor at the New York Metropolitan Opera. His performances of Wagner's works were much admired. From 1942 to 1945, and from 1943 to 1956, he was a frequent guest conductor with the New York Philharmonic Orchestra. In 1946 he became permanent conductor of the Cleveland Philharmonic Orchestra. He conducted *Der Rosenkavalier* at Salzburg in 1949, returning for the first performances of Liebermann's *Penelope* in 1954 and Egk's *Irische Legend* in 1955.

Szenen aus Goethes 'Faust', Scenes from Goethe's 'Faust' a setting of a number of scenes from Goethe's drama for solo voices, chorus, and orchestra by Robert ➔ Schumann. Composition began with a setting of the final chorus in August 1844, and was not completed until the overture was added in 1853.

Szokolay, Sándor (1931–   ) Hungarian composer. He has been influenced by Hungarian national music and by Stravinsky and Orff.

He studied at the Budapest Academy and taught there from 1966.

Works ORCHESTRAL violin concerto (1957), piano concerto (1958), *Déploration*, trumpet concerto (1968).

BALLET *Urban and the Devil* (1958), *The Ballad of Horror* (1960).

CHORAL oratorios, including *Fiery March* (1958), *Ishtar's Descent into Hell* (1960), *Apocalypse* (after Dürer, 1971); Requiem for Poulenc for piano, chorus, and chamber orchestra (1964).

OPERA *Blood Wedding* (after Lorca, 1964), *Ham-* let (1968), *Samson* (1974); radio opera *Deluded Peter* (1978), Passion-opera *Ecce Homo* (1987).

Szymanowski, Karol Maciej (1882–1937) Polish composer. He is regarded as the founder of 20th-century Polish music and the most distinguished Polish composer after Chopin. He wrote piano music, violin concertos, symphonies, and the opera *Król Roger/King Roger* (1918–24), in richly glamorous idiom drawing on national folklore and French Impressionist style. He was director of the Warsaw Conservatory from 1926.

He learnt music privately as a child and composed a set of piano preludes, Op. 1, in 1900. In 1903 he entered the Warsaw Conservatory, studying with Zygmunt Noskowski (1846–1909). At the Lviv Chopin Festival in 1905 he won a first prize with a C minor piano sonata. He lived in Berlin for a time from 1906 and worked on behalf of Polish music. He was initially influenced by Debussy and Richard Strauss, but also created his own lyrical late-Romantic vision, particularly in the 3rd symphony *Song of the Night*, the violin concerto, the *Stabat Mater*, and the opera *King Roger*. His more abstract works such as his piano sonatas and mazurkas embrace more modern techniques within traditional forms, and his masques seem almost improvisatory.

As an aristocrat he lost his property in World War I and was imprisoned in Russia, but escaped to Warsaw, where in 1926 he became professor of composition and director of the State Conservatory. His last years were marred by tuberculosis and he died in a sanatorium in Switzerland.

Works STAGE opera *King Roger* (1926); ballet *Harnasie* (1935).

CHORAL AND ORCHESTRAL four symphonies, including no. 3 for tenor or soprano, male chorus, and orchestra (*Song of the Night*, 1916), *Sinfonia concertante* for piano and orchestra (1932); two violin concertos (1916, 1933); *Hafiz Love Songs* for voice and orchestra; *Stabat Mater* (1926).

CHAMBER two string quartets (1917, 1927); *Masques*, *Métopes*, mazurkas, and many other works for piano; many songs including cycles *Songs of the Infatuated Muezzin* (Jaroslav Iwaszkiewicz), *Słopiewnie* (Julian Tuwim), settings of poems by Kasprowicz.

t the leading note in ➤ **tonic sol-fa** notation, pronounced 'Te'.

Tabarro, Il cycle of operas by Giacomo Puccini; see ➤ **Trittico**.

tabla (Hindi) pair of drums used in North Indian (Hindustani) music both for accompaniment (to vocal, instrumental, and dance performance) and as a solo instrument. The smaller drum, played with the right hand, is barrel-shaped and made of wood. It is tuned to the *Sa* (system tonic). The larger drum, played with the left hand, is kettle-shaped and made of metal or clay. It is lower in pitch but not precisely tuned. The player produces different tones by striking the drum heads in a variety of ways with the fingers; the various strokes are known by mnemonic syllables called *bols*.

tablature in music, an old system of writing down music using symbols representing the fingerboard and strings to show a player's finger positions. It was formerly used for the lute, and nowadays for the guitar and ukulele.

Prior to 1700, tablature protected the status of court lutenists, as the notation could not be interpreted by other instruments, but with the introduction of a universal standard ➤ **notation**, for example in the *Parthenia* in 1611, a collection of pieces for virginal by William Byrd, Doctor Bull, and Orlando Gibbons, the way was open for amateur ➤ **keyboard** instrumentalists to perform music at a level of virtuosity of the professional lutenist.

table in music, the belly of a string instrument; also the sounding board of the harp. In harp playing, *près de la table* is an instruction to play near the sounding board, producing a metallic sound.

Tableau parlant, Le, **The Speaking Picture** opera by Grétry (libretto by L Anseaume), produced at the Comédie-Italienne, Paris, on 20 September 1769. In the story, Isabelle's tutor Cassandre has designs on her after her lover Léandre has been missing for two years, but he returns in time to marry her.

table entertainment English entertainment of the 18th century, only partly musical in character, given by a single performer sitting at a table and telling stories and jokes, giving displays of mimicry, singing songs, and so on. The first table entertainments on record are those of George Alexander Steevens at Dublin in 1752. Dibdin began a series in London in 1789 and continued for 20 years, introducing most of his songs in this way.

tabor small drum with a high, narrow body and small drum-heads, originally made of animal skin, sounding an indefinite pitch and struck with drumsticks. Historically, it was rarely used alone, but accompanied a pipe of a fife or recorder type, similar to the modern tin whistle. The tabor is occasionally used in the modern orchestra to produce a dry, dull, percussive sound, and has been revived for folk-dancing.

Tabor cycle of symphonic poems by Bedřich Smetana; see ➤ **Má Vlast**.

Tabulatur (German 'tablature') musical term similar to the English term ➤ **tablature** in one sense, but also referring to the table of rules for the instruction and guidance of the ➤ **Meistersinger**.

tacet (Latin 'be silent') in written music, a score indication signifying that during a complete movement, or a specific section of a movement, an instrument is not required to play and therefore that no counting of bars will be necessary.

Tacitus, Publius Cornelius (AD 55–c.120) Roman historian. A public orator in Rome, he was consul under Nerva 97–98 and proconsul of Asia 112–113. He wrote histories of the Roman empire, *Annales* and *Historiae*, covering the years 14–68 and 69–97 respectively. He also wrote a *Life of Agricola* in 97 (he married Agricola's daughter in 77) and a description of the Germanic tribes, *Germania* in 98.

His texts form the basis for the libretti of two operas. See ➤ **Incoronazione di Poppea, L'** (Monteverdi) and ➤ **Radamisto** (Handel).

Tafelmusik (German 'table music') music for voices or instruments performed around a table, often as relaxation after a meal. A group or society of singers is called a *Liedertafel*.

Tag des Gerichts, Der, The Day of Judgement oratorio by Telemann (text by C W Alers), composed in 1762.

Tageszeiten, Die, The times of the day song cycle for male chorus and orchestra by Richard Strauss (text by Eichendorff), composed in 1927 and first performed in Vienna on 21 July 1928. The movements are 'Der Morgen', 'Mittagsruh', 'Der Abend', and 'Die Nacht'.
Cantata by Telemann.

Tageweisen (German 'day tunes') songs formerly used in Germany to announce the break of day from church towers or by night watchmen in the streets. They were often folk songs and some have passed into currency as hymns for the Lutheran church.

Taglia, Pietro (lived 16th century) Italian composer. He was active at Milan, and wrote three books of madrigals which were published in 1555, 1557, and 1564.

Tailer or **Taylor, John (died 1569)** English composer. He was master of the choristers at Westminster Abbey from 1561 to 1569. A *Christus resurgens* (Christ Church, Oxford, manuscripts 948–8) may be attributable to him, or to Thomas Taylor, who obtained the BMus at Oxford in 1531.

taille (French 'cut, edge') in music, the tenor part in a vocal and instrumental ensemble, applied particularly in the 17th and 18th centuries to the viola and the *oboe da caccia*.

Tailleferre, Germaine (1892–1983) French composer. She was the only woman member of the group known as ➤ *Les Six*. Her works, though never attaining the popularity of her colleagues', include the opera *Il était un petit navire* (1951), the ballet *Le marchand d'oiseaux* (1923), and several instrumental works.
She studied in Paris and joined Les Six, first appearing as a composer in public in 1920. She lived in the USA 1942–46.
Works OPERA AND STAGE the opera *Il était un petit navire* (1951); ballet *Le marchand d'oiseaux* (1923).
ORCHESTRAL *Pastorale* for small orchestra, piano concerto (1919), ballade for piano and orchestra.
CHAMBER string quartet (1918); two violin and piano sonatas (1921, 1951); *Jeux de plein air* for two pianos (1918); songs.

tail pin or **end pin** in music, an adjustable metal rod protruding from the bottom of a cello or double bass, used to stabilize the instrument on the floor at a height comfortable to the player.

Takemitsu, Toru (1930–1996) Japanese composer. He was mainly self-taught and was initially influenced by Schoenberg, Messiaen, and musique concrète. Like other composers of his generation (such as Ligeti), he was interested in the treatment of texture. His use of the electronic medium is well exemplified in *Relief statique* (1955). He also wrote the music for over 100 films, including *Kwaidan* (1964) and *The Rising Sun* (1993).
He was born in Tokyo, and grew up in China. His family later returned to Japan and he served in the Japanese army in World War II. In 1951 he co-founded an experimental laboratory in Tokyo to examine oriental music and the best in Western techniques.
Works ORCHESTRAL *Requiem* for strings (1957), *Music of Trees* for orchestra (1961), *Textures* for piano and orchestra (1964), *The Dorian Horizon* for 17 strings (1966), *November Steps* for biwa, shakuhachi, and orchestra (1967), *Asterism* for piano and orchestra (1968), *Corona* for 22 strings (1971), *Cassiopea* for percussion and orchestra (1971), *Gemeaux* for oboe, trombone, and two orchestras (1972), *Bouquet of Songs* for marimba and orchestra (1975), *A Flock Descends into the Pentagonal Garden* for orchestra (1977), *Dream Time* for orchestra (1981; ballet version 1983), *Rain Coming* for chamber orchestra (1982), *To the Edge of Dream* for guitar and orchestra (1983), *Star Isle* for orchestra (1984), *Orion and Pleiades* for cello and orchestra (1984), *riverrun* for piano and orchestra (1984), *I hear the water dreaming* for flute and orchestra (1987), *Tree Line* for chamber orchestra (1988), *A String Around Autumn* for viola and orchestra (1989), *Visions* for orchestra (1990), *My Way of Life* for baritone, chorus, and orchestra (1990), *From me flows what you call time* for five percussion and orchestra (1990).
CHAMBER *A Way Alone* for string quartet (1981), series of works for instruments with title *Stanza*, *Entre-temps* for oboe and string quartet (1986); *All in Twilight* for guitar (1987); *Itinerant* for flute (1989); works for tape alone.

Takt (German 'time') term used in musical notation, as in *im Takt* ('in time'). It can also mean 'beat' or 'bar'.

Tal, Josef (1910–) Polish-born Israeli composer. He studied in Berlin with Tiessen and Trapp, settling in Palestine in 1934. In 1937 he became professor of composition and piano at the Jerusalem Conservatory and in 1950 lecturer at the Hebrew University there, also being director of the Conservatory 1948–55.
Works OPERA *Saul at Ein Dor* (1957), *Amnon and Tamar* (1961), *Ashmedai* (1971), *Massada 967* (1973), *Die Versuchung* (1976), *Der Turm* (1987), *Der Garten* (1988), and *Josef* (1993).

CHORAL WITH ORCHESTRA *The Death of Moses*, requiem oratorio for soloists, chorus, and tape (1967).

ORCHESTRAL two symphonies; *Exodus* choreographed poem for orchestra; *Visions* for string orchestra; six piano concertos (1944–70), viola concerto; symphonic cantata *A Mother Rejoices*.

OTHER sonatas for violin, oboe; piano pieces; songs; electronic music.

tala in music, term used to describe the cyclically repeated patterns which form the rhythmic basis of much ➤ **Indian music**, especially as played by a percussion instrument.

Talbot, Michael (Owen) (1943–) English musicologist. He studied at Cambridge and the Royal College of Music, and was appointed professor of music at Liverpool University in 1986. An authority on Venetian music of the 18th century, he published studies of Vivaldi (in the Master Musicians series) and Tomaso Albinoni in *The Venetian Composer and his World* (1994). He was appointed as a fellow of the British Academy in 1990.

talea (Latin 'a cutting') name given to the repeated rhythmic pattern used in isorhythmic ➤ **motets**. See also ➤ **isorhythmic**.

Tales of Hoffmann opera by Jacques Offenbach; see ➤ **Contes d'Hoffmann, Les**.

Talismano, Il unfinished opera by Michael Balfe, completed by George Macfarren (libretto by A Matthison *The Knight of the Leopard*, based on Scott's *Talisman*), produced at Her Majesty's Theatre, London, on 11 June 1874.

talking drum hourglass pressure drum with great tonal flexibility found in many parts of Africa. Used for signalling and for conveying certain features of an unvocalized text, it is incorporated into a variety of West African popular music.

Tallis, Thomas (c.1505–1585) English composer. He was a master of ➤ **counterpoint**, and has become best known for his elaborate and ingenious 40-part motet *Spem in alium* (c.1573). His works also include *Tallis's Canon* ('Glory to thee my God this night') (1567), and a collection of 34 motets, *Cantiones sacrae* (1575), of which 16 are by Tallis and 18 by William Byrd.

Tallis was organist at the Benedictine Priory, Dover, in 1532, and held a post at Waltham Abbey before its dissolution (closure) in 1540. He became a Gentleman of the Chapel Royal in about 1543. He was one of the earliest composers to write for the Anglican liturgy (1547–53) but some of his most ornate music, including the Mass *Puer natus est nobis*, dates from the brief Catholic reign of Mary Tudor (1553–58). In 1557

Queen Mary granted him, jointly with Richard Bowyer, who was Master of the Children in the Chapel Royal, a lease of the manor of Minster, Thanet, and at her death he passed into the service of Elizabeth I, who in 1575 granted him, jointly with Byrd, a patent for the sole right to print music and music paper in English. Two years later, as this was still not profitable, they petitioned for an annual grant, which was approved. The two masters were then joint organists at the Chapel Royal. A tune written for Archbishop Parker's Psalter of 1567 was used by Vaughan Williams in his celebrated *Fantasia* (1910). In his last years Tallis and his wife Joan, whom he had married in about 1552, lived at their own house at Greenwich.

Works CHURCH AND SECULAR MUSIC three Masses, including *Puer natus est nobis* (1554), two Latin Magnificats, two sets of Lamentations for voices, *Tallis's Canon* (1567), about 40 Latin motets, and other pieces, including *Spem in alium* in 40 parts (c.1573); services, psalms, Litanies, about 30 anthems and other English church music; secular vocal pieces; two In Nomines for strings; organ and virginal pieces.

talon in music, the heel (or nut) of the bow of a string instrument.

Tamara symphonic poem by Balakirev based on a poem by Lermontov (sometimes called *Thamar* in English), composed 1866–82 and first performed at the Free School of Music, St Petersburg, in 1882.

A ballet on this work (choreographed by Mikhail Fokine, setting by Leon Bakst) was produced at the Théâtre du Châtelet, Paris, on 20 May 1912.

tambourin (French 'tabor') musical instrument. The *tambourin du Béarn* was a ➤ **zither** with strings sounding only tonic and dominant and struck by a stick. Hence 'tambourin' was used to mean a dance with a drone bass.

tambourine musical percussion instrument of ancient origin, almost unchanged since Roman times, consisting of a shallow frame drum with a single skin and loosely set jingles in the rim which add their noise when the drum skin is struck or rubbed, or sound separately when the instrument is shaken.

tambura Indian long-necked lute instrument used as a drone. Its four strings are tuned by a movable bridge and are strummed separately with the forefinger, always as open strings and never stopped. It provides an accompaniment for such instruments as the ➤ **sitar**. The South Indian version, the *mayuri*, can also be played with a bow.

tamburo (Italian 'drum') term used in musical scores, with various adjectival qualifications, for any kind of drum except the kettledrums, which are called ➤ timpani in Italian.

Tamerlano, Tamburlane opera by Handel (libretto by A Piovene, adapted by Nicola Francesco Haym), produced at the King's Theatre, Haymarket, London, on 31 October 1724. In the story, Tamerlano offers his betrothed, Irene, to ally Andronicus in return for his beloved Asteria, daughter of the captured emperor Bajazet. After feigning cooperation Asteria refuses and is imprisoned; her father takes poison before the original relationships are restored.

Taming of the Shrew, The see ➤ Sly; ➤ Widerspänstigen Zähmung, Der.

tampur three-stringed Caucasian musical instrument of the ➤ lute type, but played with a bow.

tam-tam musical instrument, a large gong originating in China. It has been used in Western music since the 19th century by composers such as Puccini, Stravinsky, and Stockhausen.

Tancrède tragédie-lyrique by Campra (libretto by A Danchet after Tasso), produced at the Opéra, Paris, on 7 November 1702. In the story, Saracen Clorinde saves her crusader lover Tancrèdi from death, but must return to her people. Later Tancrèdi despairs when he kills her in battle, believing that she was the Saracen leader Argante.

The work was revived in Aix-en-Provence, France, in 1986.

Tancredi, Tancred opera by Rossini (libretto by Giacomo Rossi, based on Tasso's *Gerusalemme liberata* and Voltaire's tragedy *Tancrède*). Produced at the Teatro La Fenice, Venice, on 6 February 1813, it was Rossini's first serious opera. In the story, Amenaide, daughter of Argirio, refuses to marry her family's enemy, Orbazzano; she is later accused of aiding the Saracens when her letter to her lover Tancredi is found. He champions her, kills Orbazzano, and leads the Syracusans against the Saracens.

Taneiev, Aleksandr Sergeievich (1850–1918) Russian composer. He entered state service after studies at St Petersburg University, but also studied music there and at Dresden, and came under the influence of the Balakirev circle.

Works OPERA *Cupid's Revenge* (1899) and *The Snowstorm*.

ORCHESTRAL three symphonies (1890, 1903, 1908), symphonic poem *Alesha Popovich*, overture to Shakespeare's *Hamlet*, two suites for orchestra.

CHAMBER three string quartets; pieces for violin and piano and for piano; songs, part songs.

Taneiev, Sergey Ivanovich (1856–1915) Russian composer and pianist, nephew of Aleksandr ➤ Taneiev. He studied composition with Tchaikovsky in Moscow, and after touring as a pianist became director of the Moscow Conservatory in 1885. His works include the operatic trilogy *The Oresteia* (1895). He achieved a major success with his last work, the cantata *At the Reading of a Psalm* (1915).

He studied at the Moscow Conservatory, intending at first to become a pianist, but also studying composition with Tchaikovsky. In 1875 he gave the Moscow first performance of Tchaikovsky's first piano concerto, and completed the original, vocal version of *Romeo and Juliet*. In 1876 he toured Russia, in 1877–78 he visited Paris, and after playing in the Baltic provinces he became professor of orchestration at the Moscow Conservatory. In 1881 he succeeded his former teacher Nikolai Rubinstein as chief professor of piano and in 1885 succeeded Nikolai Albertovich Gubert (Hubert; 1840–1888) as director. He was succeeded by Vassily Safonov in 1889 and concentrated on teaching counterpoint and fugue.

Works OPERA operatic trilogy *Oresteia* (based on Aeschylus, 1895).

CHORAL cantatas, including *John of Damascus* for solo voices, chorus, and orchestra (1884), *At the Reading of a Psalm* (1915).

ORCHESTRAL four symphonies, Overture on Russian Themes for orchestra; concert suite for violin and orchestra.

CHAMBER eleven string quartets, two string trios, piano trio; prelude and fugue for two pianos; about 40 songs to words by Tiutchev and others; part songs.

tañer (Spanish 'to touch') a 16th-century lute prelude, equivalent to a ➤ toccata, with which the strings were 'touched', or tried. Also ➤ tastar.

tangents in music, the screwdriver-shaped pins that strike the wire strings of a ➤ clavichord. The strings continue to sound while the tangents touch them, and their tone can thus approximate a violin's ➤ vibrato by altering the pressure of the finger on the depressed key.

tango dance for couples, the music for which was developed in Argentina during the early 20th century. The dance consists of two long steps followed by two short steps then one long step, using stylized body positions. The music is in moderately slow duple time (2/4) and employs syncopated rhythms. Similar to the ➤ habanera, from which it evolved, the tango consists of two balanced sections, the second usually in the ➤ dominant key or the ➤ relative minor of the first section. William Walton uses a tango in his suite *Façade* (1923).

Tannhäuser und der Sängerkrieg auf der Wartburg, **Tannhäuser and the Singers' Contest at the Wartburg** opera by Wagner (libretto by composer), produced at Dresden on 19 October 1845. It was later revised for Paris, with bacchanale in the first act, and produced at the Opéra on 13 March 1861. The story concerns Tannhäuser, torn between the conflicting demands of carnal Venus and virginal Elisabeth. In the end, Tannhäuser expires before absolution arrives from Rome.

Tansman, Alexandre (1897–1986) Polish-born French composer. He studied at home and then at Warsaw, and in 1919 took two prizes for composition. He settled in Paris, but travelled extensively as pianist and conductor. He married the French pianist Colette Cras.

Works OPERA AND STAGE *La nuit Kurde* (1927), *La toison d'or* (1938); ballets *Sextuor* (1924) and *La grande ville* (1932).

ORCHESTRAL seven symphonies (1925–44), *Sinfonietta* (1925), *Etudes symphoniques*, *Rapsodie polonaise*, and suites for orchestra; two concertos (1925–26) and concertino for piano and orchestra; concertos for viola, violin, and cello (1936, 1937, 1963), and for clarinet (1958).

CHAMBER eight string quartets (1917–56), *Danse de la sorcière* for five wind instruments and piano; *Sonata quasi una fantasia* for violin and piano; flute sonata (1925); five sonatas and other piano works; songs, including 'Stèle in memoriam Igor Stravinsky' (1972).

tape music music composed from tape-recorded material and reproducible only with the aid of audio equipment. It may include acoustic, ➤ **concrete**, or synthesized elements. Tape music can be edited to create juxtaposition effects, composed direct to tape by layer-on-layer addition, and electronically treated and balanced.

Tapiola symphonic poem by Sibelius, Op. 112, composed in 1926 for the Symphonic Society in New York. The title is the old mythological name of Finland, derived from the forest god Tapio, who appears in the *Kalevala*. It was first performed in New York on 26 December 1926.

Tapissier, Johannes (c.1370–1410), adopted name of **Jean de Noyers** French composer. Two Mass movements and an isorhythmic motet by him survive, though records indicate that he was a prominent and prolific composer.

Though he was at the Burgundian court from 1391 to the end of his life, he seems to have been active mainly in Paris.

Tappert, Wilhelm (1830–1907) German music scholar. He wrote numerous musico-literary works, including a *Wagner-Lexikon* (a collection of anti-Wagner reviews) and other works on Wagner, studies of notation, old lute music, and the

settings of Goethe's *Erlkönig* (54).

He studied with Dehn and Theodor Kullak in Berlin and, after eight years as teacher and critic at Glogau (Głogów in modern-day Poland), settled in Berlin in 1866, where he taught at Tausig's piano school. He also wrote piano pieces, including 50 studies for the left hand, and songs.

taqsim, Turkish **taksim**, Greek **taxim** in Arab, Turkish, and Greek music an improvisation in one or more melodic modes, in free-rhythmic style. The performer improvises passages in which the performer realises structurally important degrees of a chosen melodic mode, in an order peculiar to that mode. See also ➤ **maqam**.

tarantella southern Italian dance in very fast compound time (6/8); also a piece of music composed for, or in the rhythm of, this dance. It is commonly believed to be named after the tarantula spider which was (incorrectly) thought to cause tarantism (hysterical ailment), at one time epidemic in the southern Italian town of Taranto, the cure for which was thought to involve wild dancing. The dance became popular during the 19th century, several composers writing tarantellas employing a ➤ **perpetuum mobile** in order to generate intense energy. Examples include those by Chopin, Liszt, and Weber.

Tarare opera by Salieri (libretto by Beaumarchais), produced at the Opéra, Paris, on 8 June 1787. It became known later under the title of *Axur, re d'Ormus* (Italian version by Da Ponte, produced Vienna, Burgtheater, 8 January 1788). In the story, Captain Tarare rescues the abducted wife Astasie from King Atar and stages a successful rebellion.

Taras Bulba rhapsody for orchestra by Janáček (after Gogol). Composed 1915–18, it was first performed at Brno on 9 October 1924 (conducted by František Neumann). The three movements are 'Death of Andrea', 'Death of Ostap', and 'Capture and Death of Taras Bulba'.

tardando (Italian 'delaying') musical direction indicating that a passage is to be played in a lingering manner.

Tarr, Edward H(ankins) (1936–) US trumpeter and musicologist. He studied in Boston, Chicago, and Basel (with Leo Schrade). He founded the Edward Tarr Brass Ensemble in 1967, for performances of Renaissance and baroque music, and edited the complete trumpet works of Torelli. He also plays works by Kagel, Berio, and Stockhausen (*Michaels Reise um die Erde*).

Tartini, Giuseppe (1692–1770) Italian composer and violinist. In 1728 he founded a school of violin playing in Padua. A leading exponent of violin technique, he composed numerous sonatas and concertos for strings, including the *Devil's Trill* sonata, c.1714.

Taruskin, Richard (Filler) (1945–) US musicologist. He has published *Opera and Drama in Russia* (1981) and wrote the articles on Russian composers and operas in *Opera Grove* (four volumes, 1992). He also writes for the *New York Times* and is a critic of the early music movement. He took a PhD at Columbia University, New York, in 1975 and taught there 1973–87. In 1987 he was appointed professor at Berkeley, in California.

Tasso, Torquato (1544–1595) Italian poet. His works and life inspired ➜ **Armida** and ➜ **Armide** (eleven operas on *Gerusalemme liberata*; F ➜ **Caccini**, (*Rinaldo innamorato*); ➜ **Combattimento di Tancredi e Clorinda** (Monteverdi); ➜ **madrigal comedy** (*Aminta*); ➜ **Pizzetti** (*Aminta*); Vincenzo Righini (*Gerusalemme liberata*); ➜ **Rinaldo** (Handel); Michel Angelo ➜ **Rossi** (*Erminia sul Giordano*); ➜ **Tancrède** (Campra); ➜ **Tancredi** (Rossini); ➜ **Torquato Tasso** (Donizetti).

Tasso, lamento e trionfo*, *Tasso's Lament and Triumph symphonic poem by Liszt, based on a poem by Byron. Composed in 1849, it was first performed at Weimar on 28 August 1849, as an overture to Goethe's drama *Torquato Tasso*. It was revised 1850–51, with a new middle section, and performed at Weimar on 19 April 1854.

tastar (Italian *tastare* 'to touch') a 16th-century lute prelude with which the strings were 'touched', or tried. It is equivalent to a ➜ **toccata**. Also ➜ **tañer**.

tastiera per luce (Italian 'keyboard for light') instrument that appears in the score of Skriabin's *Prometheus*, designed to throw differently coloured lights. It was never perfected for practical use.

tasto Italian musical term meaning 'key' (of keyboard instruments); also fingerboard (of string instruments).

tasto solo (Italian 'key alone') musical direction indicating that in a composition with a ➜ **thorough bass** the bass notes are for the moment to be played alone on the keyboard instrument used, without any harmony above them.

Tate, Phyllis Margaret Duncan (1911–1987) English composer. Her works include *Concerto for Saxophone and Strings* (1944), the opera *The Lodger* (1960), based on the story of Jack the Ripper, and *Serenade to Christmas* for soprano, chorus, and orchestra (1972). Her works were generally small in scale, and carefully crafted. She studied composition with Harry Farjeon at the Royal Academy of Music in London 1928–32. Several of her works were performed when she was still a student, and in 1933 her cello concerto was her first work heard at a public concert.

Works OPERA *The Lodger* (1960), *Dark Pilgrimage* (1963), and *Twice in a Blue Moon* (1968); operetta *The Policeman's Serenade* (A P Herbert).

CHORAL *Secular Requiem* for chorus and orchestra (1967), *Serenade to Christmas* for mezzo, chorus, and orchestra (1972), *All the World's a Stage* for chorus and orchestra (1977).

ORCHESTRAL symphony and suite for orchestra, *Valse lointaine* and prelude, interlude, and postlude for chamber orchestra (1941); cello and saxophone concertos (1933, 1944), *Panorama* for string orchestra (1977).

CHAMBER *Divertimento* for string quartet, sonata for clarinet and cello (1947), *Nocturne* (S Keyes) for four voices, string quintet, celesta, and bass clarinet; *London Waits* for two pianos; *Songs of Sundry Natures* on Elizabethan poems for voice and piano, songs to words by Blake, W H Davies, Hardy, Hood, Tennyson, and others, *The Phoenix and the Turtle* for tenor and instrumental ensemble.

Tavener, John Kenneth (1944–) English composer. He has written austere vocal works, including the dramatic cantata *The Whale* (1968) and the opera *Thérèse* (1979). *The Protecting Veil*, composed in 1987 for cello and strings alone, became a best-selling classical recording. Other works include *Vlepondas* for soprano, bass and cello, and *Feast of Feasts* for chorus, both 1996. His *Song for Athene* was played at the funeral of Diana, Princess of Wales.

Tavener studied at the Royal Academy of Music with Lennox Berkeley and David Lumsdaine. He is a member of the Greek Orthodox Church, and draws on Eastern European idioms and Orthodox Christian traditions; he described his chamber opera *Mary of Egypt* (1991), premiered at Aldeburgh Music Festival in 1992, as 'a moving icon'. His composition *Lamentations and Praises* (2002) won a Grammy award. He was knighted in 2000.

Works CHORAL AND VOICE WITH ORCHESTRA AND ENSEMBLE three *Holy Sonnets* for baritone and orchestra (texts by Donne, 1962), dramatic cantata *Cain and Abel* (1965), cantata *The Whale* (1966), *Introit for the Feast of St John Damascene* for soloists, chorus, and orchestra (1968), *In alium* for soprano, orchestra, and tape (1968), *Celtic Requiem* (1969), *Ultimos Ritos* for soloists, speakers, chorus, and orchestra (1969–72), *Coplas* for soloist, chorus, and tape (1970), *Ma fin est mon commencement* for tenor, chorus, brass, and percussion (1972), *Little Requiem for Father Malachy Lynch* (1972), *Requiem for Father Malachy* (1973); *Kyklike kinesis* for soprano, chorus, cello, and orchestra (1977), *Liturgy of St John Chrysostom* for unaccompanied chorus (1978), *Akhma-*

tova: rekviem (1980), *Risen!* for chorus, piano, organ, and orchestra (1980), *Funeral Ikos* for chorus (1981), *Ikon of Light* for chorus and string trio (1984), dramatic cantata *Eis Thanaton* (1987), *Resurrection* for soloists, actors, chorus, and orchestra (1989), *We Shall See Him as he is* for soloists, chorus, and ensemble (1992), *Hymns of Paradise* for bass, chorus, and strings (1993), *The Apocalypse* for soloists, chorus, and orchestra (1994), *Agraphon* for soprano and string orchestra (1995); *Feast of Feasts* and *Prayer to the Holy Trinity* for choir (1995).

STAGE opera *Thérèse* (1973–76; produced 1979), music theatre *Mary of Egypt* (1991).

ORCHESTRAL piano concerto (1963), *The Cappemakers*, *Little Concerto* (1965), *Concerto for Orchestra* (1968), *Palintropos* for piano and orchestra (1977).

CHAMBER *Grandma's Footsteps* for ensemble (1968), *Sappho: Lyrical Fragments* for two sopranos and strings (1980), *Trisagion* for brass quintet (1981); *The Protecting Veil* for cello and strings (1987), *Akathist Of Thanksgiving* (1987), *Ikon of St Seraphini* (1988), *The Repentant Thief* for clarinet and ensemble (1990), *Eternal Memory* for cello and ensemble (1992), *Vlepondas* and *The Hidden Face* (1996).

Taverner opera by Maxwell Davies (libretto by composer), composed 1962–70 and produced at Covent Garden, London, on 12 July 1972. The plot is based on the now discredited story that John Taverner was an agent of Thomas Cromwell dedicated to the persecution of the Catholic Church.

Taverner, John (c. 1495–1545) English organist and composer. He wrote Masses and motets in polyphonic style, showing great contrapuntal skill, but as a Protestant renounced his art. He was imprisoned in 1528 for heresy. He was said to be an agent of Thomas Cromwell and to have assisted in the dissolution (closure) of the monasteries, but this story is now discredited.

Taylor, (Joseph) Deems (1885–1966) US composer and critic. He became music critic to the *New York World* in 1921, but from 1925 devoted himself to composition.

He studied at the Ethical Culture School and went to university in New York. He received piano lessons, but was self-taught in other musical subjects.

Works OPERA AND STAGE *The King's Henchman* (1927), *Peter Ibbetson* (after George du Maurier, 1931), and *Ramuntcho* (after Loti, 1942); incidental music for Thornton Wilder's *Lucrece* and for other plays.

ORCHESTRAL AND CHAMBER symphonic poems *The Siren Song* and *Jurgen* (after James Branch Cabell); suites *Through the Looking-Glass* (after Lewis Carroll) and *Circus Day* (1925); *Lucrece* suite for string quartet.

OTHER choral works.

Tchaikovsky, Pyotr Il'yich (1840–1893) Russian composer. He successfully united Western European influences with native Russian musical material and tradition, and was the first Russian composer to establish a reputation with Western audiences. His strong sense of melody, personal expression, and brilliant orchestration are clear throughout his many Romantic works, which include six symphonies, three piano concertos, a violin concerto, operas (including *Eugene Onegin* (1879)), ballets (including *The Nutcracker* (1892)), orchestral fantasies (including *Romeo and Juliet* (1869)), and chamber and vocal music.

Tchaikovsky's father, an inspector of mines, allowed him to have music lessons from the age of four. The family moved to St Petersburg in 1848; he received more teaching there and in 1850 was sent to the School of Jurisprudence, which he left in 1859 to become a clerk in the Ministry of Justice. He approached music as an amateur, but in 1862 entered the newly opened St Petersburg Conservatory, having already studied with Nikolai Zaremba, and had lessons in orchestration from Anton Rubinstein. Nikolai Rubinstein, having opened a similar conservatory in Moscow, employed him as professor of harmony in 1865, and there he began to compose seriously and professionally. In 1868 he met Mily Alexeyevich ➤ **Balakirev** and his circle of nationalist composers in St Petersburg, but he remained separate from them. In the same year his first symphony *Winter Daydreams* was successfully performed in Moscow; it is a very fresh and youthful work. His first opera *The Voyevoda* was premiered at the Bolshoi Theatre in 1869 and *Romeo and Juliet* in 1870. The second symphony, a distinctly nationalist work, was performed in 1873, and the B♭ minor piano concerto, though at first rejected by Nikolai Rubinstein, was given at Boston by Hans von Bülow in 1875 and given its first Moscow performance later that year by Alexander Taneiev. In 1876 he began a correspondence with Nadezhda von Meck, the widow of a wealthy engineer. She greatly admired his work and made him an allowance so that he could compose without any financial worries, but she never met him face to face. His first important opera, *Vakula the Smith*, was premiered in 1876 and the following year the first of his great ballets, *Swan Lake*, was premiered at the Bolshoi. The hero's name (Siegfried) probably comes from Richard Wagner's *Ring*, which Tchaikovsky had just seen at Bayreuth. Also in 1877 he married Antonina Milyukova; but he was an undeclared homosexual and left her less than a month after the wedding, on the verge of mental collapse. After some months in Switzerland and Italy, he resigned the post at the Moscow Conservatory and lived in the country, wholly devoted to composition. The first of his highly popular symphonies, No. 4 in F minor, was premiered in 1878. *Eugene Onegin* (1879) mirrors some of the recent circumstances of Tchaikovsky's own life; Tatiana writes a hopeful love letter to the reluctant Onegin just as Antonina had done to Tchaikovsky. The brilliant orchestral work the Violin Concerto in D was given at Vienna in 1881, and seven years later he composed one of the most powerful of his symphonies, No. 5 in E minor. In 1888 he made his first international tour as conductor of his own works, which became known in many countries, and the following year he completed the finest of his three ballets, *The Sleeping Beauty*, which was first performed in 1890. In 1890 he had a misunderstanding with Mme von Meck which brought their friendship by correspondence to an end. By that time he was quite able to earn his own living. He visited the USA in 1892 and London in the summer of 1893, when he received an honorary degree from Cambridge University. On his return to Russia he completed his Symphony No. 6 in B Minor (*Pathétique*), which was first performed at St Petersburg in October. This work is now considered to be his masterpiece and shows great maturity and mastery of structure in its gradually unfolding form. Nine days after its performance Tchaikovsky was dead; the cause of death is usually given as cholera, although it has recently been suggested that he took poison at the order of a secret court of honour. The court had been set up to avoid a scandal after allegations of a liaison between him and an aristocrat's nephew. However, the real facts will probably never be known.

Works STAGE the operas *Eugene Onegin* (1879), *Maid of Orleans* (1881), *The Queen of Spades* (1890); ballets *Swan Lake* (1877), *The Sleeping Beauty* (1890), and *The Nutcracker* (1892).

ORCHESTRAL seven symphonies: no. 1 in G minor (*Winter Daydreams*, 1866, revised 1874), no. 2 in C minor (*Little Russian*, 1872, revised 1880), no. 3 in D (*Polish*, 1875), no. 4 in F minor (1878), no. 5 in E minor (1888), no. 6 in B minor (*Pathétique*, 1893), no. 7 in E♭ (unfinished, 1892); *Manfred* symphony (after Byron, 1885); fantasy-overture *Romeo and Juliet* (1869), *Capriccio italien*, Serenade for string orchestra (1880), overture *The Year 1812* (1880); three piano concertos, including no. 1 in B♭ minor (1875), violin concerto (1878), *Variations on a Rococo Theme* for cello and orchestra (1876).

CHAMBER string sextet *Souvenir de Florence* (1887), three string quartets (1871, 1874, 1876), piano trio (1882); 17 Op. nos of piano compositions including *The Seasons*; 13 Op. nos of songs (nearly 100).

Tcherepnin, Alexander (Nikolaievich) (1899–1977), also known as **Aleksandr Cherepnin** Russian-born US composer. He wrote ballets and orchestral and chamber pieces in a neoclassical style.

He was born at St Petersburg and studied under his father, Nikolai ➤ Tcherepnin and Nikolai Aleksandrovich Sokolov (1859–1922), learning the piano from Annette Nikolaevna Essipova (1850–1914). He appeared as a boy pianist and began to publish his works, but in 1921 settled in Paris with his father, studying composition with André Gédalge and piano with Isidore Philipp at the Conservatory. He taught in Paris 1925–38, and from 1949 at De Pauw University in Chicago. He settled in the USA in 1950.

Works OPERA AND STAGE operas *01–01* (after Andreiev, 1928) and *Die Hochzeit der Sobeide* (after Hofmannsthal, 1933); ballets, including *The Frescoes of Ajanta* (1923) and (with Honegger and Harsányi) *Shota Roustaveli*; incidental music for Wilde's *Salome*, Rolland's *L'esprit triomphant*, and Hauptmann's *Hannele*.

CHORAL cantata *Le jeu de la nativité*.

ORCHESTRAL AND CHAMBER four symphonies (1927–58), three pieces for chamber orchestra, six piano concertos (1923–72), *Rapsodie géorgienne* for cello and piano, *Concerto da camera* for flute, violin, and small orchestra; two string quartets (1922, 1926); piano trio; violin and piano sonata, three cello and piano sonatas; sonata, studies and pieces for piano.

Tcherepnin or **Cherepnin, Nikolai (Nikolaievich) (1873–1945)** Russian composer and conductor. He studied with Rimsky-Korsakov and wrote ballets for Diaghilev, including *Armida's Pavilion* (1908). In 1921 he settled in Paris. He was the father of Alexander ➤ Tcherepnin.

He gave up a legal career at the age of 22 and studied at the St Petersburg Conservatory with Rimsky-Korsakov and others. Having appeared as a pianist, in 1901 he became conductor of the Belaiev Symphony Concerts (established in 1885 by music publisher Mitrofan Petrovich Belaiev, 1836–1904), and then began conducting operas at the Mariinsky Theatre. In 1908 he joined Diaghilev and conducted Russian opera and ballet in Paris and elsewhere, remaining with the Ballets Russes until 1914, when he returned to Petrograd, to become director of the Conservatory at Tiflis in 1918.

Works OPERA AND STAGE operas *Vanka the Chancellor* (after Sologub, 1935) and *Poverty no Crime* (after Ostrovsky); ballets *Armida's Pavilion* (1908), *Narcissus* (1911), *A Russian Fairy-Tale*, *The Romance of a Mummy* (after Gautier), *The Masque of the Red Death* (after Poe, 1916), *The Tale of the Princess Ulyba*, *Dionysius*.

ORCHESTRAL AND CHAMBER symphony, sinfonietta,

symphonic poems *Narcissus and Echo* and *The Enchanted Kingdom*; witches' scene from *Macbeth*, suite *The Enchanted Garden* (1904), overture to Rostand's *La princesse lointaine* (1903), six pieces on Pushkin's 'The Golden Fish' for orchestra; piano concerto in C♯ minor (1907), lyric poem for violin and orchestra; string quartet in A minor; piano pieces on Benois's picture-book *The Russian Alphabet* and other piano works; songs.

Te the name for the leading-note in any key in ➔ **tonic sol-fa**, so pronounced, but in notation represented by the symbol **t**.

tedesca or **tedesco (Italian 'German')** musical term; *alla tedesca* means 'in the German manner', but more particularly indicates a piece or movement in rather slow waltz time, in the character of the *Deutscher* or *Ländler*.

Te Deum laudamus, We praise thee, O God Latin hymn or psalm in 'rhythmical prose', possibly by Nicetas of Remesiana (c.400). It is in three sections: a hymn to the Trinity, a hymn to Christ, and a series of prayers. The first part is set to a psalmodic formula ending on G, and the second to a similar formula ending on E. It concludes with a more extended melody in the same mode to the words 'Aeterna fac'. The third part makes further use of these last two melodies.

The Te Deum was set in ➔ **polyphony** during the Middle Ages, especially in England, for voices or organ in alternation with the plainsong. It became a normal part of the Anglican 'Morning Service' and it has also been set in English for occasions of rejoicing (for example, by Handel and Walton). The Latin text has often been set with orchestral accompaniment by composers such as Haydn, Berlioz, Bruckner, and Kodály.

Telemaco, Il, ossia L'isola di Circe, Telemachus, or Circe's Island opera by Gluck (libretto by M Coltellini), produced at the Burgtheater, Vienna, on 30 January 1765. In the story, the Sorceress Circe loves the prisoner Ulysses on her enchanted island. His son Telemachus, also shipwrecked, falls in love with Asteria, Circe's maid (later revealed to be his intended wife). They escape while Circe swears revenge.

Telemann, Georg Philipp (1681–1767) German baroque composer, organist, and conductor. He was the best-known German composer of his time with a contemporary reputation much greater than Johann Sebastian Bach's. His prolific output of concertos for both new and old instruments, including violin, viola da gamba, recorder, flute, oboe, trumpet, horn, and bassoon, represents a methodical and fastidious investigation into the tonal resonances and structure of the new baroque orchestra, research which was

noted by Bach. Other works include 25 operas, numerous sacred cantatas, and instrumental fantasias.

Telemann was born at Magdeburg and educated there and at Hildesheim. He went on to read law at Leipzig University, and seems to have been largely self-taught in music. In Leipzig he founded a student *Collegium musicum* and was appointed organist of the New Church (St Matthew's) in 1704, but the same year moved to Sorau as kapellmeister to Count Promnitz. In the service of the court at Eisenach 1708–12 (kapellmeister from 1709) he made the acquaintance of Johann Sebastian Bach in nearby Weimar. He then worked in Frankfurt until his appointment in 1721 as cantor of the Johanneum (Johanneum Lateinschule, established in the 16th century) and municipal music director in Hamburg, where he stayed for the rest of his life. In 1722, he declined the post of cantor of St Thomas's, Leipzig, and Bach was appointed. He travelled a good deal, several times visiting Berlin, and in 1737 made a successful visit to Paris.

He is famed for his huge output, although some of his instrumental music can sound routine and written to order. His most attractive music is often in his vocal works, notably the operas, oratorios, and cantatas.

Works OPERA about 45 operas (few survive complete), including *Der geduldige Socrates* (1721), *Der neumodische Liebhaber Damon* (1724), *Miriways* (1728), *Pimpinone* (1725), *Emma und Eginhard* (1728).

CHORAL oratorios, including *Die Tageszeiten, Die Auferstehung und Himmelfahrt Christi* (1760), *Der Tag des Gerichts* (1762); Passion oratorios (Brockes and Ramler); 46 liturgical Passions; twelve sets of cantatas for the church's year; motets, psalms.

ORCHESTRAL AND CHAMBER large quantities of instrumental music, including the collection *Musique de table* (Hamburg, 1733); concertos, orchestral suites, trio sonatas, and other chamber music; keyboard music.

Temistocle, Themistocles opera by Nicola ➔ **Porpora** (libretto by Apostolo Zeno), produced in Vienna on 1 October 1718. Opera by Johann Christian Bach (libretto M Verazi, after Metastasio) produced at the Hoftheater, Mannheim, on 5 November 1772. Driven away by the people of Athens, Themistocles seeks refuge in the land of his enemy, Xerxes, King of Persia. Themistocles finds his daughter Aspacia there suffering the advances of Xerxes. When Aspacia would choose suicide rather than marriage to him and when Themistocles would do likewise rather than renounce Greece, Xerxes is impressed by their virtue and makes a happy ending.

temperament in music, a system of tuning ('tempering') whereby the ➤ **intervals** of the scale are made slightly larger or smaller than the 'natural' scale of acoustical theory, to allow for key changes in a piece of music. According to acoustical theory, notes such as D♯ and E♭ are slightly different in pitch. In **equal temperament**, the octave is divided into twelve equal semitones, so that pairs of notes like D♯ and E♭ are adjusted to the same pitch so that the ear ignores the difference and regards it as one or the other depending on context. This is the standard modern tuning for the piano. Owing to the difference being spread across all twelve notes in the octave, one can play in any key with an equal amount of compromise in the tuning. This is especially useful when playing music that modulates from one key to another.

Johann Sebastian Bach composed *The Well-Tempered Clavier*, a sequence of 48 preludes and fugues in every key of the ➤ **chromatic scale** (to be played without any retuning between each one), to demonstrate the versatility of tempered tuning.

Many choirs that sing early music without instrumental accompaniment use 'just intonation', a non-tempered scale where 'real' thirds (D–F♯ not D–F♯/G♭) are used, which, once heard, makes equal temperament sound less clean when heard immediately after. This is possible because Renaissance music does not modulate very suddenly or widely and because adjustments can be made during performance where necessary, due to the flexibility of the voice.

Temperley, Nicholas (1932–) English-born US musicologist. He has published editions of Edward Loder's *Raymond and Agnes* (produced in Cambridge, 1966) and the *Symphonie Fantastique* (in the New Berlioz edition, 1972). He edited collections of *English Songs, 1800–60* (1979), *The Music of the English Parish Church* (two volumes, 1979), and *London Pianoforte School* (20 volumes 1984–87). His completion of Mozart's *L'oca del Cairo* was produced in Illinois in 1991.

He studied at Cambridge 1954–59 and was assistant lecturer there 1961–66; he became professor at the University of Illinois in 1972, and chairman of the musicology division in 1992.

Tempest, The incidental music by Jean ➤ **Sibelius**, Op. 109, composed for a production of William Shakespeare's play at the Theatre Royal, Copenhagen, in 1926. The story concerns Ferdinand, who is shipwrecked on an island with Prospero, Miranda, Ariel and Caliban.

Opera by Zdeněk ➤ **Fibich** (libretto by Jaroslav Vrchlický, based on Shakespeare), produced at the Czech Theatre, Prague, on 1 March 1895.

Symphonic fantasy by Pyotr ➤ **Tchaikovsky**, after Shakespeare. Suggested by Stassov and begun in August 1873, it was first performed in Moscow, 19 December 1873.

Tempest, The, or The Enchanted Island opera adapted from Shakespeare by Thomas Shadwell, with music by Locke, Humfrey, Reggio, James Hart, G B Draghi, and Banister. It was produced at the Dorset Gardens Theatre, London, on 30 April 1674.

Opera adapted from Shakespeare by Shadwell, with music by Weldon (composed c.1712), formerly attributed to Henry Purcell.

Tempestà, La opera by Halévy (libretto by Scribe, originally written in French for Mendelssohn, based on Shakespeare's *Tempest* and translated into Italian). It was first produced at Her Majesty's Theatre, London, on 8 June 1850.

Templario, Il, The Templar opera by Nicolai (libretto by G M Marini, based on Scott's *Ivanhoe*), produced at the Teatro Regio, Turin, Italy, on 11 February 1840.

Templer und die Jüdin, Die, The Templar and the Jewess opera by Marschner (libretto by W A Wohlbrück, based on Scott's *Ivanhoe*), produced in Leipzig on 22 December 1829. In the story, Saxon Rowena and Jewish Rebecca compete for the attention of the knight Ivanhoe. Ivanhoe champions Rebecca after she is accused of witchcraft.

tempo (Italian 'time') in music, the speed at which a piece should be played. One way of indicating the tempo of a piece of music is to give a ➤ **metronome** marking, which states the number of beats per minute; for example, 'crotchet = 60' means that there should be 60 crotchet beats to the minute, that is, one per second. Modern electronic metronomes measure tempo very accurately. Performers sometimes change or even ignore metronome markings, playing at a tempo that suits their interpretation of the music. However, the knowledge of performance practice gained by academic investigation into early music has encouraged performers to pay more attention to original tempo markings.

Music written before the development of precise metronomes could only give a vague idea of speed, and was often notated in a confusing manner. The system of ➤ **time signatures** that was developed during the Renaissance used symbols which, as well as giving the number of beats per bar, gave some indications of speed. In the 17th century, tempo was indicated by Italian words such as 'allegro' (lively), 'presto' (quick), or 'lento' (slow). These words only gave a vague idea of speed to modern musicians, but as the performers of the time dealt only with their contemporary music, norms of tempo were taken as read among most players and composers, although those extending the musical language, such as Ludwig van Beethoven, did have problems as his use of precise markings show. Additionally, descriptive tempo markings have the advantage of indicating mood: for example, 'allegro' not only conveys the idea of quickness, but also brightness; and 'largo' means broad and expansive, but also implies slowness. The expressive qualities of these verbal tempo indications mean that we still use them today, often alongside precise metronome markings.

When Johann ➤ **Maëlzel** developed the metronome in the 19th century, a precise way of describing tempo became possible. The beat of the music could be expressed as the number of beats per minute. For example, 'crotchet = 120', meant 120 crotchet beats to be played per minute. By using electronic metronomes, it is now possible to perform music to a very high degree of accuracy, and this has had a profound effect on performance practice in the late 20th century. Other factors influence the choice of tempo at any one time, and a truly musical interpretation often relies on changes in the underlying tempo throughout a piece, such as 'accelerando' (getting faster), 'ritardando' (getting slower), or 'rubato' (with a beat that is not strictly regular).

tempo giusto (Italian 'strict time') in music, an instruction to play in strict time; that is without ➤ **rubato.**

tempo ordinario (Italian 'common time, ordinary pace') in music, either moderate speed or four beats in a bar (as opposed to *Alla breve*, where there are two beats in a bar).

tempo primo (Italian 'first time'; 'first tempo') musical direction appearing after a change of tempo indicating that the pace first indicated is to be resumed.

Tender Land, The opera by Copland (libretto by H Everett), produced in New York on 1 April 1954 and conducted by Schippers. The orchestral suite was produced in 1956. The story concerns the high-school graduate Laurie, who comes of age when young Martin fails to show up after agreeing to elope with her.

Tenducci, Giusto Ferdinando (1735–1790) Italian castrato soprano and composer. Popular in England as a singer of Handel, he was also heard in his own adaptation of Gluck's *Orfeo*. He published a treatise on singing, composed songs and harpsichord sonatas, and compiled song collections.

Tenducci made his debut in Naples, then went to London in 1758, remaining there, apart from visits to Ireland (1765–68) and Scotland (1768–69), until 1791, when he returned to Italy.

tenor highest range of the adult male singing voice when not using ➤ **falsetto**, approximately C3–A5. It is the preferred voice for operatic heroic roles. Well-known tenors are Luciano Pavarotti and Placido Domingo. It is also used before the name of an instrument that sounds in the same range as the tenor voice, for example tenor saxophone.

The word comes from the Latin *teneo*, 'I hold', because it 'held' the plainsong theme in early polyphony.

The approximate range of the tenor voice.

tenor clef in music, the C ➤ **clef** in which middle C (C4) is represented by the second highest line of the five-line ➤ **stave**. It was used by musicians and singers until the 18th century, but is now used mainly by instruments which read bass clef, except in their higher registers, such as the cello and bassoon.

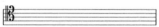

The tenor clef.

tenor cor brass military-band instrument invented around 1860 to provide a better substitute for the horn than had been found in the saxhorn. It is in the circular form of a horn, though half the length, and has valves. It is made in F, with an extra slide to change it to E flat.

tenor drum drum with skin stretched over either end, similar in shape to the side drum and bass drum, but of intermediate size. It produces a duller sound than that of the side drum, having no ➤ **snares**, but gives out clearer notes, though of indefinite pitch, than the bass drum.

tenore robusto (Italian 'robust tenor') one of the categories of operatic singing voices: a ➤ **tenor** capable of sustaining parts of a heroic type; equivalent to the German *Heldentenor*.

tenor horn three-valved brass instrument, often referred to as the E flat horn. It is a modern version of the alto ➤ **saxhorn**, with the bell pointing upwards. It is used in brass bands but not British military bands.

tenoroon early musical instrument of the ➤ **bassoon** type, but smaller and tuned higher than the bassoon.

tenor tuba another name for the ➤ **euphonium**, a musical instrument.

tenor violin early name for the ➤ viola. A small cello, tuned a fifth or a fourth above the normal cello, was sometimes known as a tenor violin.

tenson song of the ➤ troubadour, ➤ trouvère, or ➤ Minnesinger (12th–14th century poet-musicians), the words of which took the form of a dispute.

tenuto (Italian 'held') in musical notation, instruction to hold a note for its full value. In music since the late 18th century, it often also implies that the note should be held beyond its notated value, causing an expressive effect, similar to an ➤ agogic accent.

ternary form basic musical form in three sections (ABA). A^1 contains a musical statement in the tonic key and is complete in itself. B is usually in a new, but related, key and is a contrast to the music of A^1. A^2 is a restatement of the music of A^1. An example of the ternary form is the ➤ minuet and trio. The 18th-century ➤ sonata form is a sophisticated ternary form with an extended middle (development) section. Ternary form can be recognized in popular music by the 'middle-8' or 8-bar middle section preceding the verse and chorus reprise.

Terradellas, Domingo Miguel Bernabe (1713–1751) Spanish composer. He produced his first opera in 1739 in Rome, where he was maestro di cappella at the Spanish church 1743–45. He visited London 1746–47, producing three operas there and in Paris, then returned to Rome.

He studied 1732–38 with Francesco Durante at the Conservatorio dei Poveri di Gesù at Naples, where he composed two oratorios.

Works OPERA *Astarto* (1739), *Gli intrighi delle cantarine*, *Cerere*, *Merope* (1743), *Artaserse*, *Semiramide riconosciuta*, *Mitridate* (1746), *Bellerofonte* (1747), *Imeneo in Atene*, *Didone*, *Sesostri, rè d'Egitto*.

CHORAL oratorios *Giuseppe riconosciuto* (1736) and *Ermenegildo martire*.

OTHER Masses, motets, and other church music.

Terrasse, Claude (Antoine) (1867–1923) French composer and organist. He studied at the Lyon Conservatory, then at Louis Niedermeyer's school in Paris, and afterwards privately with Eugène Gigout. After living obscurely as an organist at Auteuil and a piano teacher at Arcachon, he began to compose and settled in Paris in 1895 as organist of the Trinité.

Works OPERA AND STAGE opera *Pantagruel* (after Rabelais); operettas *La fiancée du scaphandrier*, *Choncette*, *Le Sire de Vergy* (1903), *Monsieur de la Palisse* (1904), *L'ingénu libertin*, *Le coq d'Inde*, *Le mariage de Télémaque* (1910), *Les transatlantiques* (1911), *La petite femme de Loth* (T Bernard), *Les travaux d'Hercule* (1901), *Cartouche* (1912), *Le cochon qui sommeille*, *Faust en ménage*, *Le manoir enchanté*, and several others; incidental music for various comedies; music for Théophile Gautier's and Théodore de Banville's *Matinées poétiques*.

OTHER *Trio bouffe* for strings, *Sérénade bouffe* for piano and strings; songs.

Terry, Charles Sanford (1864–1936) English music historian. He did valuable work for music by writing an authoritative biography of J S Bach (1928) as well as numerous detailed studies of various aspects of his work, and a biography of J C Bach (1929, revised 1967 by H C Robbins Landon). He was appointed professor of history at Aberdeen University, Scotland, in 1903.

terzet, Italian **terzetto** musical composition for three voices or for instruments in three parts.

Teseo, Theseus opera by Handel (libretto by Nicola Francesco Haym), produced at the Queen's Theatre, Haymarket, London, on 10 January 1713. In the story, Teseo, prince of Athens, marries Algilea in spite of interference from the enchantress Medea.

Tessier, Charles (lived c. 1600) French lutenist and composer. He was a *musicien de la chambre du roy* (court composer) to Henri IV and visited England for some time in the 1590s, dedicating a book of chansons to Lady Penelope Rich (the poet Philip Sidney's 'Stella').

Works VOCAL chansons for four to five voices (1597), *Airs et villanelles* for three to five voices (1604), setting of the eighth song in Sidney's *Astrophel and Stella*.

tessitura (Italian 'texture') in music, term indicating the average register of a part (high, middle, low) within the total range of the voice or instrument concerned. It is used specifically to refer to the voice and brass instruments before the invention of valves, when players often specialized in high or low tessituras.

Testament de la Tante Caroline, Le opéra-bouffe by Roussel (libretto by Nino), produced at Olomouc (now in the Czech Republic), on 14 November 1936. The story evolves as Aunt Caroline leaves her fortune to the first of three nieces to produce a male child. Her spinster niece obliges.

testudo (Latin 'tortoise') Latin name for the Greek ➤ lyre, a musical instrument which was often made of tortoiseshell. The name was transferred to the lute in 16th-century Latin.

tetrachord (from Greek 'having four strings') in music, a scale of four notes embracing the interval of a perfect ➤ fourth; a basis for melodic construction in ancient Greek music theory and

20th-century ➔ serial technique.

Teufels Lustschloss, Des, The Devil's Pleasure Palace opera by Schubert (libretto by August von Kotzebue), composed in 1814 but not performed until 1879. The story concerns the Knight Oswald, wife Luitgarde, and squire Robert, who endure a series of trials at the haunted castle of Luitgarde's uncle.

Teutsche see ➔ *Deutsche Tänze*.

texture the vertical density of a musical composition. While the nature of the texture is often one of the main distinguishing features of a work, particularly in 20th-century music, variety of texture is an important component of a work's progression and life in virtually all music.

Thaïs opera by Massenet (libretto by L Gallet, based on the novel by A France), produced at the Paris Opéra on 16 March 1894. It contains the popular *Méditation* as an orchestral interlude. The story concerns the young monk Athanaël, who persuades the courtesan Thaïs to enter a convent but falls in love with her before she dies.

Thalberg, Sigismond (Fortuné François) (1812–1871) Austrian pianist and composer. He travelled widely on concert tours, playing mostly his own compositions. By the 1850s he was pursuing an international career, rivalled only by Liszt as a virtuoso performer.

When he was ten, his father sent him to school in Vienna, where he later studied piano with Hummel and theory with Sechter. He soon played at private parties, appeared at Prince Metternich's house in 1826, and in 1830 made his first tour, in Germany, having by this time begun to publish his compositions. In 1835 he made further studies with Johann Pixis and Friedrich Kalkbrenner in Paris, and in 1836 first appeared in London.

Works OPERA *Florinda* (1851) and *Cristina di Suezia* (1855).

WORKS FOR PIANO piano concerto; piano sonata, studies, nocturnes, romances, and numerous other pieces for piano, operatic fantasies on works by Rossini, Weber, and Verdi, and other transcriptions for piano.

OTHER over 50 German songs.

thalumeau short, thickset double-reed wind instrument, ancestor of the ➔ clarinet. It is also the term used to describe the dark lowest register of clarinet tone.

Thamos, König in Aegypten, Thamos, King of Egypt incidental music by Mozart (K345) to T P von Gebler's play, composed in 1779 (two choruses already in 1773). The work was not produced in Mozart's lifetime except in an adaptation to another play, Plümicke's *Lanassa*.

Theile, Johann (1646–1724) German composer. He was the first composer to contribute to the repertory of the newly opened opera at Hamburg in 1678.

He learnt music as a youth at Magdeburg and Halle, and later studied at Leipzig University, where he took part in the students' performances as singer and viola da gamba player. He then became a pupil of Schütz at Weissenfels, and taught music at Stettin and Lübeck. He was kapellmeister to the Duke of Holstein at Gottorp 1673–75, but fled to Hamburg during the Danish invasion. In 1676 he competed unsuccessfully for the post of cantor at St Thomas's Church, Leipzig. In 1685 he succeeded Rosenmüller as music director at Wolfenbüttel and in 1689 he was appointed to a similar post at Merseburg. In his last years he lived in retirement at his birthplace.

Works OPERA *Adam und Eva* (1678; lost) and *Orontes* (1678; seven arias extant).

CHURCH MUSIC ten Masses, seven Psalms; Passion according to St Matthew, church cantatas.

Theinred of Dover (lived 12th century) English music theorist. His treatise, a study of intervals and proportions, is known only from an early 15th-century copy in the Bodleian Library, Oxford. It includes a diagram of the different forms of alphabetical notation, and a section on the measurement of organ pipes. He was a monk at Dover Priory.

theme in music, a basic melody or musical figure, which often occurs with variations.

Theodora oratorio by Handel (libretto by T Morell), produced at Covent Garden, London, on 16 March 1750.

Theodorakis, Mikis (1925–) Greek composer. He has produced a wide variety of musical compositions, including songs, oratorios, chamber music, ballets, and symphonic works. He also produced film scores, most notably for *Zorba The Greek* (1964), which made him internationally famous, as well as for Costas Gavras' *Z* (1969) and Sidney Lumet's *Serpico* (1973). He also became known for his vocal left-wing politics.

In 1959 his ballet *Antigone* was performed at Covent Garden. His popularity was already growing in the 1960s, before *Zorba the Greek*, when he composed music for the film *Phaedra* (1962), starring Melina Mercouri, and *Elektra* (1962), starring Irena Papas.

He was a member of parliament 1964–67 for the leftist EDA party. In 1967 he was imprisoned during a military coup and in 1970 he was exiled. He returned to Greece in 1974. During the 1980s he became a member of parliament once again, but resigned in 1992.

In 1986 he released *Canto General*, which was based on the poems of the Nobel laureate Odysseas Elitis. In 1992 he composed the *Canto Olympico* for the Olympic Games in Barcelona, and his opera *Hlektra* premiered in 1995. He also composed an opera, *Lysistrath*, for the 2004 Olympic Games in Athens.

Theodorakis detailed his prison experiences in his book *Journals Of Resistance* (1973).

theorbo musical instrument, a bass ➤ lute or archlute developed around 1500 and incorporating dual sets of strings, a set of freely vibrating bass strings for plucking with the thumb in addition to five to seven courses over a fretted fingerboard. It survived to form part of the Italian baroque orchestra from about 1700.

theremin early electronic musical instrument invented by Leon ➤ Theremin in 1922. It is played by the player's hand moving in a magnetic field around a metal loop and rod. It uses ➤ **beat frequency** generation between two high frequency oscillators, one signal of which is fixed, while the other depends on the position of the player's hand in the vicinity of an aerial. Its monophonic sound is voicelike in the soprano register, and trombonelike at a lower pitch. Since the player makes no contact with the instrument, it is difficult to obtain a steady pitch, hence the instrument's wavering quality. Because any position of the hand generates a pitch, the theremin is incapable of detaching notes, so that all intervals are linked together by a wailing ➤ portamento, like that of a siren.

Theremin subsequently invented another instrument shaped like a cello on which notes could be produced detached from each other by means of a cello fingerboard.

Edgard ➤ Varèse incorporated two theremins in *Ecuatorial* (1932–33); it has also featured in film scores such as Bernard ➤ Herrmann's music for the science fiction film *The Day the Earth Stood Still* (1951). A transistorized theremin is heard in the Beach Boys' hit 'Good Vibrations' (1966).

Theremin, Leon (1896–1993) Russian inventor of the ➤ theremin in 1922, a monophonic synthesizer, and of other valve-amplified instruments in the 1930s. Following commercial and public success in the USA and Hollywood, he returned to Russia in 1938 to imprisonment and obscurity. After 1945 he continued acoustic research in Moscow and reappeared at a Stockholm electronic music symposium in 1990.

inventions The theremin was played without being touched by converting the operator's arm movements into musical tones. The instrument could produce a wide range of sounds and was mainly used to make eerie sound effects for films. Theremin also invented an electronic dance platform, called the terpsitone, in which a dancer's movements were converted into musical tones.

Other inventions included a stringless electronic cello, the first syncopated rhythm machine, a colour television system, and a security system which was installed at Sing Sing and Alcatraz prisons in the USA.

life Theremin was educated as a physicist and musician. In 1922 he demonstrated his theremin to the Soviet revolutionary leader Lenin and was sent on a tour which included sell-out concerts in Berlin, Paris, London, and New York. He established a studio in New York, where he lived 1927–38. He was then ordered to return to the USSR and spent time in a Siberian labour camp during the Great Purge carried out by the Soviet leader Stalin against real and imagined enemies. During World War II Theremin worked in a military laboratory, producing a radio-controlled aircraft, tracking systems for ships and submarines, and television systems which are still in use. He also invented a miniature listening device, or 'bug', for the KGB. For this he received the Stalin Prize, First Class, and was allowed to live in Moscow, where he became professor of acoustics at the Moscow Conservatory of Music. He was sacked and his laboratory closed when a chance encounter with a reporter from the *New York Times* resulted in a newspaper article which revealed his earlier imprisonment. He continued his acoustics research, and work aimed at reversing the ageing process, until he died.

Thérèse opera by Massenet (libretto by J Claretie), produced in Monte Carlo, on 7 February 1907. The story concerns Thérèse, who, torn between her husband André and her former love Armand, decides to run away with Armand until André is captured by revolutionaries. She decides to join him at the guillotine.

Opera by John Tavener (libretto by G McLarnon), composed 1973–76 and produced at Covent Garden, London, on 1 October 1979 (conducted by Downes). In the story, the poet Rimbaud guides the spiritual growth of St Thérèse of Lisieux, as she experiences various 20th-century horrors.

Theresienmesse*, *Theresa Mass Mass by Joseph ➤ Haydn in B flat, no. 12, composed in 1799. Despite its name, it seems to have no connection with Maria Theresa, wife of the Emperor Franz II.

Thésée*, *Theseus opera by Jean-Baptiste Lully (libretto by Quinault). Produced at Saint-Germain on 12 January 1675, its first Paris performance was in April 1675. In the story, jealous Medea tries to prevent the union of Theseus and Aegle. She fails when King Aegeus recognizes Theseus as his long-lost son.

thesis (Greek 'lowering') in musical analysis, a term borrowed from Greek poetry, denoting a stressed beat (➤ **downbeat**), usually in comparison with or reference to an arsis, or unstressed beat (**➤ upbeat**). In German usage, 'arsis' and 'thesis' have opposite meanings to the original Greek and English words.

Thespis, or The Gods Grown Old operetta by Sullivan (libretto by W S Gilbert). Produced at the Gaiety Theatre, London, on 26 December 1871, it was Sullivan's first work written in association with Gilbert.

Thétis et Pélée, Thetis and Peleus opera by Colasse (libretto by Bernard le Bovier de Fontenelle), produced at the Paris Opéra on 11 January 1689.

Thibaut IV (1201–1253) French king of Navarre and count of Champagne and Brie. He was a ➤ **trouvère**, and wrote a large quantity of poetry and music in a variety of styles. More than 45 of his songs survive.

third in music, an ➤ **interval** of three diatonic notes.

A third is an 'imperfect interval' (having 'major' and 'minor' variants). A major third consists of four semitones (for example, C–E). A minor third consists of three semitones (C–E♭).

| Maj | Min | Diminished |

Major, minor, and diminished thirds.

Thomas, (Charles Louis) Ambroise (1811–1896) French composer. His operas were written to please contemporary bourgeois Parisian taste; his most successful works, *Mignon* (1866) and *Hamlet* (1868), were written in emulation of Gounod. He also wrote numerous cantatas, part songs, and choral pieces.

He learnt music from his father as a child and in 1828 entered the Paris Conservatory, where he won the Prix de Rome in 1832. He also studied piano privately with Friedrich Kalkbrenner and composition with Lesueur. Soon after his return from Rome he began to win operatic successes in Paris. In 1852 he became professor at the Conservatory and in 1871 succeeded Auber as director.

Works OPERA *La double échelle* (1837), *Le perruquier de la Régence* (1838), *Le panier fleuri* (1839), *Carline* (1840), *Le Comte de Carmagnola*, *Le guerillero* (1842), *Angélique et Médor* (1843), *Mina*, *Le Caïd*, *Le songe d'une nuit d'été* (not Shakespeare, 1850), *Raymond* (1851), *La Tonelli*, *La cour de Célimène* (1855), *Psyché* (1857), *Le carnaval de Venise*, *Le roman d'Elvire* (1860), *Mignon* (after Goethe's *Wilhelm Meister*, 1866), *Gille et Gillotin*, *Hamlet* (after Shakespeare, 1868), *Françoise de Rimini* (after Dante, 1882).

BALLET *La Gipsy* (1839), *Betty* and *La tempête* (1889).

CHORAL *Messe solennelle* (1857), *Messe de Requiem*, motets; cantata *Hermann et Ketty*, cantatas for the unveiling of a Lesueur statue and for the Boieldieu centenary.

OTHER fantasy for piano and orchestra; string quartet, string quintet, piano trio; piano pieces; songs, including six Italian songs, part songs.

Thomas, Arthur Goring (1850–1892) English composer. His music reflects the comfortable, undemanding French style of his time, and includes the operas *Esmeralda* (1883), based on Victor Hugo's *Notre-Dame de Paris*, and *Nadeshda* (1885).

He was educated for the civil service, but later studied music with Emile Durand in Paris and with Sullivan and Prout at the Royal Academy of Music in London. Later he studied orchestration with Max Bruch in Berlin. He began to work on an opera to a libretto by his brother, *Don Braggadocio*, and although he did not finish it, he persevered and eventually received a commission from the Carl Rosa Opera Company. He became insane in 1891.

Works OPERA *The Light of the Harem* (after Thomas Moore), *Esmeralda* (after Hugo's *Notre-Dame de Paris*, 1883), *Nadeshda* (1885), and *The Golden Web*.

CHORAL anthem *Out of the Deep* for soprano, chorus, and orchestra; cantatas *The Sun Worshippers* and *The Swan and the Skylark*.

OTHER *Suite de Ballet* for orchestra; songs, duets.

Thomas and Sally or **The Sailor's Return** opera by Arne (libretto by Isaac Bickerstaffe), produced at Covent Garden, London, on 28 November 1760. In the story, Thomas returns from sea in time to scupper Squire's attempts to woo Sally.

Thomé, Francis, actually **Joseph François Luc (1850–1909)** French composer. He studied at the Paris Conservatory, then became a private teacher of music.

Works OPERA AND STAGE operas *Martin et Frontin* (1877), *Le Caprice de la reine* (1892); operettas *Vieil Air, jeune chanson* (1894), *Le Château de Koenigsberg* (1896), *Le Chaperon rouge* (1900); ballets, including *Endymion et Phœbé*, *La Bulle d'amour* (1898), *La Folie parisienne* (1900); incidental music to plays, including Shakespeare's *Romeo and Juliet*, and mystery *l'Enfant Jésus*.

OTHER *Hymne à la nuit* for chorus; *Simple Aveu* for piano with many arrangements.

Thompson, Randall (1899–1984) US composer. He is chiefly remembered for his choral music and symphonies. He was professor of music at the University of California in 1937, director of the Curtis Institute at Philadelphia in 1939, and a professor at Harvard University from 1948.

He studied at Harvard University, where his teachers included Ernest Bloch. He lived in Rome 1922–25, was assistant professor of music at Wellesley College, and was later appointed to study musical conditions at US colleges.

Works STAGE *Solomon and Balkis* (after Kipling's *Just So Stories*, 1942); incidental music for Labiche's *The Italian Straw Hat*.

ORCHESTRAL three symphonies (1930–49), *Pierrot and Cothurnus* (1923) and *The Piper at the Gates of Dawn* (1924), for orchestra; *Jazz Poem* for piano and orchestra (1928).

CHORAL *Passion according to St Luke*, cantata *The Testament of Freedom*, *Odes of Horace* for unaccompanied chorus, *Rosemary* for women's chorus, *Americana* for mixed chorus and piano.

CHAMBER two string quartets (1941, 1967), *The Wind in the Willows* for string quartet; sonata and suite for piano; songs.

Thomson, Virgil (1896–1989) US composer and critic. His music is notable for a refined absence of expression, his criticism for trenchant matter-of-factness, both at odds with the prevailing US musical culture. He is best known for his opera *Four Saints in Three Acts* (1927–33) to a libretto by Gertrude Stein, and the film scores *The Plow That Broke the Plains* (1936) and *Louisiana Story* (1948).

After studying in France with Nadia ➔ **Boulanger** 1921–22, he was organist at King's Chapel in Boston 1923–24, and returned to Paris 1925–40, mixing with Gertrude Stein and her circle. From 1940 he was music critic to several papers and periodicals in the USA, becoming known for his perceptive views. The most important influences on his music were Satie and the neoclassical Stravinsky.

Works OPERA AND STAGE *Four Saints in Three Acts* (1934), *The Mother of us all* (1947) (libretto by Gertrude Stein), *Byron* (1972); ballet *The Filling-Station*; incidental music for Euripides' *Medea*, Shakespeare's *Hamlet*, and other plays; film music.

ORCHESTRAL two symphonies, suite *The Plough that Broke the Plains* (1936), two *Sentimental Tangoes*, *Portraits*, *Symphony on a Hymn-Tune* (1948), *Sonata da Chiesa* for orchestra.

VOCAL WITH ORCHESTRA OR ENSEMBLE *Oraison funèbre* (Bossuet) for tenor and orchestra; two *Missae breves*, three Psalms for women's voices, *Capital Capitals* (Gertrude Stein) for men's chorus and piano; *Stabat Mater* for soprano and string quartet, *Five Phrases from the Song of Solomon* for soprano and percussion.

CHAMBER two string quartets (1922, 1932), five *Portraits* for four clarinets; *50 Portraits* for violin and piano, sonata for violin and piano; piano music, songs.

Thorne, John (died 1573) English organist, composer, and poet. He was appointed organist of

York Minster in 1542, and worked there in various capacities until two years before his death.

A motet, *Stella Coeli*, was copied by John Baldwin, and another, *Exsultabant Sancti*, survives in organ score. A four-part In Nomine also survives, and there are three poems by him in the same manuscript as Redford's 'Play of Wit and Science' in the British Library and in the 'Paradyse of Daintie Devices' (1576).

thorough bass in music, an alternative term for ➔ **continuo**. 'Thorough' in this case is derived from the old spelling for 'through', meaning the technique is carried out continuously throughout a piece.

Thrane, Waldemar (1790–1828) Norwegian composer. He studied Norwegian folk music and wrote the first Norwegian opera, *Fjeldeventyret/The Mountain Adventure* in 1825, though it was not staged until 1850.

He learnt music at home, his parents being keen amateurs at whose house many musicians met.

Works OPERA *Fjeldeventyret/The Mountain Adventure* (1825).

OTHER overtures for orchestra; choral works, and other pieces.

Three-Cornered Hat ballet by Manuel de Falla and opera by Hugo Wolf; see ➔ **Sombrero de tres picos** and ➔ **Corregidor**.

Three Places in New England work for orchestra by Charles Ives, also known as *Orchestral Set no. 1*, composed 1903–14 and first performed in New York on 10 January 1931 (conducted by Slonimsky). The three movements are: 1. 'The 'St Gaudens' in Boston Common: Colonel Shaw and his Colored Regiment'; 2. 'Putnam's Camp, Redding, Connecticut'; 3. 'The Housatonic at Stockbridge'.

Threni, id est Lamentationes Jeremiae Prophetae work by Igor ➔ **Stravinsky** for soprano, mezzo-soprano, two tenors, two basses, chorus, and orchestra. It was composed 1957–58 and first performed in Venice on 23 September 1958 (conducted by Stravinsky). See also ➔ **Lamentations**.

Threnody for the Victims of Hiroshima work by Krzysztof Penderecki for 52 solo strings, composed 1959–60 and first performed in Warsaw, Poland, on 31 May 1961.

Thuille, Ludwig (1861–1907) Austrian composer. In 1883 he became professor at the Munich school, and there was influenced by Richard Strauss and Alexander Ritter, who wrote the libretto for his first opera, the two later ones being by Otto Julius Bierbaum. Apart from teaching and composition, he also conducted the male-voice choir Liederhort.

He learnt music from his father, an amateur, on whose death he was sent as a choirboy to the

Bach, Cantata 140

The figured bass symbols from Bach's Cantata 140 (a) and a possible realization (b).

monastery of Kremsmünster. At the age of 15 he began to study with Joseph Pembaur in Innsbruck, and in 1879 he went to the Music School at Munich, where Rheinberger was among his masters.

Works OPERA *Theuerdank* (1897), *Lobetanz* (1898), and *Gugeline* (1901).

ORCHESTRAL AND CHORAL *Romantic Overture* (originally for *Theuerdank*) for orchestra; *Weihnaht im Walde* for male chorus, *Traumsommernacht* and *Rosenlied* for female chorus.

CHAMBER piano quintet, sextet for wind and piano; cello and piano sonata; piano pieces; songs.

thump Old English musical term, meaning the plucking of strings (➤ **pizzicato**); also a piece employing *pizzicato*.

thumri (Hindi) vocal genre of North Indian (Hindustani) music in which the text setting (usually in two sections, *sthayi* and *antara*) is used as the basis of extended improvisations intended to draw out the expressive potential of the

(normally romantic) text. Traditionally associated with female courtesan entertainers, it can now be heard sung by singers (of both sexes) specializing in other 'light-' or 'semi-classical' genres, or in ➤ **khyal**.

Thus spake Zarathustra symphonic poem by Richard Strauss; see ➤ **Also sprach Zarathustra**.

tie in musical notation, a ➤ **slur** or curved line connecting two notes of the same pitch (or a group of such notes in a chord), usually over a bar line. It indicates that the second note is not to be reiterated, but played continuously as one long note.

Tiefland, The Lowland opera by d'Albert (libretto by R Lothar, based on a Catalan play, *Terra baixa*, by A Guimerá), produced at the German Theatre, Prague, on 15 November 1903. In the story, Sebastiano marries off his mistress Marta to a simple shepherd, Pedro, who does not realize that he has been dishonoured by marrying her. Later, Pedro learns the truth and strangles Sebastiano when he again stakes a claim on Marta.

tiento in music, a 16th-century type of organ piece similar to the ➤ ricercare.

tierce an early musical term for the interval of the third, major or minor. It survives, however, as the technical term for one of the tones of a church bell, a minor third above the note of the bell.

tierce de Picardie (French 'Picardy third') in music, the major third introduced into the final chord of a composition in a minor key. The major third corresponds to a natural harmonic, the ➤ tierce, but the minor third does not; it was therefore for a long time considered an unsatisfactory ingredient in a concluding chord, if not an actual dissonance, for which reason the tierce de Picardie was often substituted. The origin of the name is not known.

Tigers, The opera by Havergal Brian (libretto by composer, 1916–19, orchestrated 1928–29). The score was lost, but rediscovered in 1977 and given by the BBC on 3 May 1983. The story concerns the comical adventures of an infantry regiment during World War I.

Tigrane, Il*, *Tigranes opera by Gluck (libretto by Francesco Silvani, altered by Goldoni), produced in Crema (in northern Italy) on 26 September 1743. It is also the title of operas by Alessandro Scarlatti (Naples, 1715) and Johann Hasse (Naples, 1729). As a child Tigranes was kidnapped by the Emperor Cyrus from his mother Thonyris. Later he is torn between love for his betrothed, Meroe, and duty. Eventually, all is resolved when Tigranes's true identity is revealed.

Till Eulenspiegels lustige Streiche*, *Till Eulenspiegel's Merry Pranks symphonic poem by Richard Strauss, Op. 28, based on the old Low German folk tale, composed 1894–95 and first performed at Cologne on 5 November 1895.

timbre (French 'tone') in music, the tone colour, or quality of tone, of a particular sound. Different instruments playing a note at the same ➤ pitch have different sound qualities, and it is the timbre that enables the listener to distinguish the sound of, for example, a trumpet from that of a violin. The tone quality of a sound depends on several things, including its waveform, the strength of its ➤ harmonics, and its attack and decay – the 'shape' of the sound. The study of the elements of sound quality is part of the science of ➤ acoustics.

  sound production The characteristic tone quality of any instrument or voice is dependent on a number of factors: the various means of producing sound – for example, vibrating strings or reeds; their methods of excitation – such as plucking, bowing, or blowing; and means of amplification – either mechanical, such as a soundboard, or electrical. These differences have their effect on the waveform, the mixture of ➤ harmonics, and the envelope shape of the sound.

  analysis of waveform By means of an oscilloscope, sounds can be represented visually, and an accurate analysis made of certain of their component parts. Most immediately apparent from these visual representations is the complexity of seemingly simple sounds: picking out the characteristics that distinguish one instrumental colour from another is not easy. Many complex waveforms can be seen as mixtures of pure tones, and in musical sounds as mixtures of harmonics in particular. The two principal parameters of sound – frequency and amplitude – are used in the analysis of timbre to describe the presence and relative strength of the harmonics that make up the sound in its 'steady state', that is, when playing a sustained note. Instruments such as the recorder and flute have tones that are comparatively 'pure', with only a few weak harmonics above the fundamental tone; whereas the double reed instruments such as the bassoon and oboe have complex tones, rich in higher harmonics.

  sound shapes Analysis of a sound in its steady state alone, however, does not completely define its timbre. Equally important is the overall shape of the sound: its starting transient (attack) and envelope shape (the steady state and subsequent decay), which can be studied with the aid of spectrum analysers such as sonagraphs, or real-time analysers. Experiments have shown that recordings of an instrument playing a sustained note, minus its initial attack, are very difficult to identify. Variations of amplitude during the course of a note and the speed with which they occur have a major effect on timbre. A sound may start very quietly and comparatively slowly reach the volume of its sustained tone, as with the flute; or it may begin almost immediately at maximum volume and quickly die away, as does the plucked string of a harpsichord. These changes in amplitude also affect the waveform during the note, as the harmonics may increase or decrease in volume at different rates – thus a note may have a noticeably different timbre at different stages of its production, and even a perceived difference of pitch. There may also be slight variations in frequency in some notes, particularly when some form of ➤ vibrato forms an important part of the timbre.

time in music, an alternative word for ➤ metre or ➤ tempo.

time signature in musical notation, a numerical sign placed after the ➤ clef and ➤ key signature indicating the metre of the music. Consisting usually of two numbers, the upper number represents the number of beats in a bar, the lower number the type of beat, expressed as a fraction of a unit (➔ **semibreve**). Hence 3/4 is three crotchet beats to the bar and 6/8 is two beats each of three quavers; alla breve represents 2/2, or two ➔ **minim** beats to a bar; C (common time) represents 4/4, four crotchet beats to a bar.

Originally dictating a simple metre for a whole piece, since the late 19th century time signatures have become increasingly complex, with many 20th century composers frequently changing time signatures within a piece, and using previously unheard of metres (such as 11/8 or 5/16) to notate complex rhythms.

timpan or **timpe (from Latin** *tympanum*) musical instrument, a kind of ➔ **psaltery** used in the British Isles in medieval times. It had wire strings stretched on a frame, which were plucked by the fingers or a plectrum, later struck with a rod.

timpani or **kettledrums** tuned drums descended from medieval ➔ **nakers** (from Arabic *naqqara*), with a single head of skin stretched over a hemisphere, usually of copper. They produce notes of definite pitch that can be altered by turning screws at the rim of the 'kettle', thus tightening or relaxing the skin. A mechanical device now widely used allows the player to increase or relax the tension (raise or lower the pitch) by means of a pedal. A variety of sticks covered with different materials can be used to produce a harder or softer tone.

Originally used in pairs tuned to the tonic and dominant of the key, timpani began to increase in number in an orchestra. Mechanisms introduced during the 19th century allowed pitch changes to be made during a performance. A normal symphony orchestra will have up to five timpani, ranging in pitch from about B1 to G3. Sometimes greater numbers are required; Hector Berlioz's massive *Requieum Grande Messe des Morts/ High Mass of the Dead* (1837) needs at least 19 timpani, even using modern pedals.

Tinctoris, Johannes (c.1435–c.1511) Franco-Flemish music theorist and composer. He wrote a number of important theoretical works and composed Masses, motets, and chansons. His dictionary of musical terms, *Terminorum Musicae Diffinitorium* (1495), was the first of its kind and defines 299 musical terms.

He was born at Nivelles, and studied both law and theology. He was ordained, and became a canon of Poperinghe. He may have been a singer at Cambrai in 1460, under Guillaume Dufay, and in 1463 was choirmaster at Orléans Cathedral. He went to Italy and from about 1472 was in the service of Ferdinand of Aragon, King of Naples, maintaining connections with the court there for at least the next 15 years. He founded a school

of music and was in the papal chapel at Rome 1484–1500.

Tinctoris is remembered as one of the most important music theorists of his day; he wrote twelve treatises, two of which were printed. His other writings deal with composition, improvisation, the aesthetics of music, and its role in education and religion.

tin whistle or **penny whistle** musical instrument, a small and rudimentary pipe of the ➔ **fife** or ➔ **recorder** type, played vertically and having a small range of high notes controlled by six finger holes.

Tippett, Michael (Kemp) (1905–1998) English composer. With Benjamin Britten, he became the foremost English composer of his generation. His works include the operas *The Midsummer Marriage* (1952), *The Knot Garden* (1970), and *New Year* (1989); four symphonies; *Songs for Ariel* (1962); and choral music, including *The Mask of Time* (1982).

Tippett was born in London. He studied with Charles Wood and R O Morris at the Royal College of Music. He became conductor of educational organizations under the London County Council and music director at Morley College (1940–51), a post formerly held by Gustav Holst. During the war he was a conscientious objector and was imprisoned for refusing to help the war effort by working on the land. His oratorio *A Child of our Time* (1941) was written in response to the persecution of the Jews during the Nazi era. His first major success was with the Concerto for Double String Orchestra (1939); it was followed by the *Fantasia Concertante on a theme of Corelli* (1953). Tippett's early lyrical exuberance reached its peak in the opera *The Midsummer Marriage* and the associated piano concerto (1953–55). A sparer sound was achieved with the opera *King Priam* (1962) and second piano sonata, although by the time of *The Knot Garden* some reconciliation between his two earlier styles was achieved. In this context, his most significant later works are the Triple Concerto, the oratorio *The Mask of Time*, and the fifth string quartet. *The Rose Lake* for orchestra (1994) was announced as his last major work.

He acted as president of the Kent Opera Company (1979–98) and president of the London College of Music (1983–98).

Tippett was very deliberate and highly self-critical, so that his works appeared in slow succession, but always showed closely concentrated craftsmanship and great originality. Amid many contemporaries whose music could be described as static, one gains above all from Tippett's music a sense of movement.

Works OPERA five operas, including *The Midsummer Marriage* (1955), *King Priam* (1962), *The*

Knot Garden (1970).

CHORAL oratorios *A Child of our Time* for soloists, chorus, and orchestra (1939–41), *The Vision of St Augustine* for baritone, chorus, and orchestra (1963–65) and *The Mask of Time* for soloists, chorus, and orchestra (1981–84).

ORCHESTRAL four symphonies (1944, 1957, 1972, 1976), concerto for double string orchestra (1939), concerto for orchestra, *Fantasia concertante* on a theme by Corelli (1953); piano concerto (1953–55), concerto for string trio and orchestra (1979).

CHAMBER AND SOLO VOCAL five string quartets (1935, 1943, 1946, 1979, 1991); four piano sonatas (1938, 1962, 1973, 1979); cantata *Boyhood's End* for tenor and piano (from W H Hudson's *Far Away and Long Ago*, 1943).

tirade (French 'pulling' or 'dragging') in music, an ornamental scale passage between two notes of a melody or two chords.

tirana Spanish dance of Andalusia in 6/8 time, usually danced to guitar music and accompanied by words in four-lined *coplas* ('couplets').

tiré (French 'drawn') in the playing of string instruments, the downstroke of the bow; the opposite of *poussé* ('pushed'), the upstroke.

Tishchenko, Boris (1939–) Russian composer. He studied with Dmitri Shostakovich at the Leningrad Conservatory 1962–65, and taught there from 1965; he was appointed professor in 1986.

Works OPERA AND STAGE opera *The Stolen Sun* (1968), ballets *The Twelve* (1963), *Fly-bee* (1968), and *The Eclipse* (1974).

ORCHESTRAL AND CHAMBER six symphonies (1961–68), piano concerto (1962), two cello concertos, two violin concertos, five string quartets (1957–84), nine piano sonatas (1957–92).

OTHER Akhmatova Requiem (1966); *Garden of Music*, cantata (1987); film music.

Tito Manlio opera by Vivaldi (libretto by M Noris), produced at the Teatro Arciducale, Mantua, carnival in 1720. In the story, Titus Manlius, the Roman Consul, must condemn his son Manlius to death for disobeying orders; but later the two are reconciled.

Tito Vespasiano, ovvero La clemenza di Tito, **Titus Vespasian, or The Clemency of Titus** opera by Caldara (libretto by Metastasio, partly based on Corneille's *Cinna*), produced in Vienna, in 1734.

Opera by Hasse (libretto as above), produced at the Teatro Pubblico, Pesaro, on 24 September 1735.

toccata (from Italian *toccare*, 'to touch') in music, a composition for keyboard instruments,

such as the organ, in which the performer's finger technique is emphasized. This is often done by including passages using features such as arpeggios and elaborate fast runs.

Toch, Ernst (1887–1964) Austrian-born US composer and pianist. After an early modernist phase most of his music was neoclassical in spirit. He is remembered chiefly for his chamber music, symphonies, and film scores.

He studied medicine and philosophy at first and was self-taught in music, but in 1909 was awarded the Frankfurt Mozart prize and studied there under Willy Rehberg, being appointed piano professor at the Mannheim Hochschule für Musik in 1913. He served in World War I, and settled in Berlin in 1929, but emigrated in 1932, going first to the USA, then to London, and settling permanently in the USA in 1934. After teaching in New York for two years, he moved to Hollywood as a film composer and teacher.

Works OPERA AND STAGE operas *Wegwende* (1925), *Die Prinzessin auf der Erbse* (1927), *Egon und Emilie* (1928), *Der Fächer* (1930); incidental music for Euripides' *Bacchantes*, Shakespeare's *As You Like It*, Zweig's *Die Heilige aus USA*, and other plays.

MUSIC FOR RADIO AND FILM radio play *The Garden of Jade* and others; film music for *Catherine the Great*, *The Private Life of Don Juan*, and others.

CHORAL *Passover Service* (1938); cantata *Das Wasser* (1930); *Der Tierkreis* for unaccompanied chorus.

ORCHESTRAL seven symphonies (1949–64), *Bunte Suite*, *Kleine Theater Suite*, *Big Ben*, *Pinocchio* overture (after Collodi's story) for orchestra; *Spiel* for wind band; concerto (1926) and symphony for piano and orchestra.

CHAMBER *Poems to Martha* for baritone and strings; 13 string quartets (1902–53), piano quintet, string trio, divertimento for violin and viola; two violin and piano sonatas; sonata, 50 studies, and about twelve Op. nos of piano pieces.

Tod und das Mädchen, Der, Death and the Maiden song, D531, by Schubert on words by Matthias Claudius, composed in 1817.

The latter part was adapted as a theme for variations in the second movement of his D minor quartet (1824, D810), which is for that reason commonly known by the same name.

Tod und Verklärung, Death and Transfiguration symphonic poem by Richard Strauss, Op. 24, composed 1888–89, and first performed in Eisenach (in central Germany) on 21 June 1890.

Tolomeo, Rè di Egitto, Ptolemy, King of Egypt opera by Handel (libretto by Nicola Francesco Haym), produced at the King's Theatre, Haymarket, London, on 30 April 1728. In the story, Cleopatra favours her younger son Alessandro for succession and exiles Tolomeo to Cyprus, where he is joined by his wife Seleuce. In the end, however, Tolomeo is eventually crowned king of Egypt.

Tomášek or **Tomaschek, Václav Jan Křtitel Wenzel Johann (1774–1850)** Bohemian composer, organist, and pianist. He wrote songs, piano and chamber music, three symphonies, church music, and three operas. His early symphonies followed classical models, while his keyboard works pioneered the type of short lyric piano pieces of the Romantic era. His 13 volumes in this genre were popular all over Europe and directly influenced Schubert. His memoirs provide much information about the musical life of his time.

His father had been reduced to poverty, and he was educated at the expense of two elder brothers. He became a choirboy at the monastery of Jihlava, but left in 1790 to study law and philosophy in Prague. He also studied the great theoretical treatises on music, and any music he could obtain, establishing a reputation as a teacher and composer before the end of the century. Count Bucquoi von Longueval offered him a well-paid post in his household, to which he remained attached even after his marriage to Wilhelmine Ebert in 1823. He often visited Vienna, where he met Beethoven in 1814, and he played his settings of Goethe's poems to the poet at Eger. He published his autobiography in instalments 1845–50.

Works OPERA AND STAGE *Seraphine* (1811) and two not produced; vocal scenes from Goethe's *Faust* and Schiller's *Wallenstein, Maria Stuart,* and *Die Braut von Messina.*

SACRED AND SECULAR MUSIC three Masses, including Coronation Mass (1836), two Requiems, and other church music.

ORCHESTRAL AND CHAMBER three symphonies (1801, 1805, 1807), two piano concertos (1805–06); three string quartets (1792–93), piano trio; five piano sonatas, *Elegie auf eine Rose* (after Hölty), seven sets of *Eclogues* and two of *Dithyrambs* and many other works for piano; numerous songs to words by Goethe, Schiller, and others.

Tomasi, Henri (1901–1971) French composer and conductor. He studied at the Paris Conservatory and in 1927 won the Prix de Rome. On his return from Rome in 1930 he became conductor of the national Radio-Paris. He conducted the Monte Carlo Opera 1946–50. His music has typical French qualities of wit, sophistication, and virtuosic orchestration.

Works STAGE the operas *Don Juan de Mañara* (1956) and *Sampiero Corso* (1956); ballets *La Grisi* (1935), *La Rosière du village* (1936), and *Les Santons* (1938).

ORCHESTRAL symphony *Scènes municipales* (1933), *Chants laotiens* (1934), *Petite Suite médié-vale, Deux Danses cambodgiennes, Danses brésiliennes* for orchestra; capriccio for violin and orchestra; flute concerto (1947), trumpet concerto (1949), viola concerto, saxophone concerto (1951), horn concerto (1955).

CHORAL WITH ORCHESTRA *Ajax* and *Chants de Cyrnos* for chorus and orchestra.

tombeau (French 'tomb[stone]') in music, a commemorative composition, especially in 17th-century French music.

Tombeau de Couperin, Le, *Couperin's Tomb* suite for piano by Maurice ➔ **Ravel** in the form of a classical suite such as François ➔ **Couperin** might have written, but resembling his music in spirit rather than in style, Ravel's idiom being as modern here as in any of his works. It was written 1914–17 and consists of six movements: *Prélude, Fugue, Forlane, Menuet, Rigaudon* and *Toccata*. Ravel orchestrated it in 1919, without the fugue and toccata; the first performance of that version was in Paris on 8 November 1920.

Tom Jones opera by Philidor (libretto by A A H Poinsinet, based on Henry Fielding's novel), produced at the Comédie-Italienne, Paris, on 27 February 1765.

Tommasini, Vincenzo (1878–1950) Italian composer. He travelled a great deal before 1910 and then settled down to compose; his best-known piece is his ballet after Scarlatti, *The Good-Humoured Ladies.*

He studied at the Liceo di Santa Cecilia in Rome and became an associate of the Accademia di Santa Cecilia.

Works STAGE operas *Medea* (1906) and *Uguale Fortuna* (1913); ballet *The Good-Humoured Ladies* (on music by Scarlatti, 1917).

ORCHESTRAL AND CHORAL *Il Carnevale di Venezia* for orchestra (1929), violin concerto (1932); choral works on Dante, Petrarch, and others; overture *Poema erotico* to Calderón's *Life is a Dream,* prelude to Baudelaire's 'Hymne à la beauté', suite *Chiari di luna, Il beato regno, Paesaggi toscani* for orchestra.

CHAMBER three string quartets; violin and piano sonata.

Ton (German 'tone, sound') in its early sense, word used by the German ➔ **Minnesinger** for the words and melody of their songs, and by the ➔ **Meistersinger** for the melody alone. The latter used all kinds of adjectives to differentiate the numerous tunes. Specimens of such names appear in Wagner's *Meistersinger,* where a *Ton* is also called a *Weis* (*Weise,* 'tune').

tonada type of Castilian ballad dating back to the 16th century or possibly earlier.

tonadilla (Spanish, from 'tonada') in music, a stage interlude for a few singers, introduced in the 18th century.

tonale or **tonarium** medieval theoretical work dealing with the arrangement of chants according to their ➤ **mode**, and especially of the ➤ **antiphons** and the choice of psalm-tone to go with them. The earliest known tonale is by Regino of Prüm (c.900).

tonality in music, refers to the major-minor key system. It is also used as the opposite of ➤ **atonality**.

Tondichtung in music, a German tone poem, or ➤ **symphonic poem**.

tone in music, the quality of sound – for instance, different strings of a violin may be able to sound the same note (pitch) given certain fingerings, but each string has a different tone. A tone can also be a ➤ **plainsong** melody; it is also the US term (or **wholetone**) for a note, an interval consisting of two semitones, for example the interval of C–D.

tone colour or **timbre** in music, the term used for the sound of an instrument or voice as regards the peculiar quality produced by it. The term also refers to combinations of such sounds.

tone poem in music, an alternative name for ➤ **symphonic poem**, or a similar piece for smaller forces.

tone row or **note row** in music, alternative term for a ➤ **series**, an order of ➤ **pitches**. The row may be used as a basis for melody or harmony, and in reverse and inverted forms as well as in its original order.

tonguing in music, on a woodwind or brass instrument, the technique used to separate and articulate notes. The flow of wind is interrupted by subtle movements of the tongue, as if pronouncing the letter 't'. In fast passages **double tonguing** ('t-k') or **triple tonguing** ('t-t-k') is possible on certain instruments, especially the flute and brass instruments. **Flutter tonguing**, introduced by Richard Strauss for a trilling effect, consists of an extended rolled 'r'.

tonic in music, the key note of a ➤ **scale** (for example, the note C in the scale of C major), or the 'home key' in a composition (for example, the chord of C major in a composition in the same key).

tonic sol-fa system of musical notation without ➤ **staves** and notes, invented by John Curwen (1816–1880) in the middle of the 19th century on a basis of the principles of ➤ **solmization** and ➤ **solfège**, and once widely used by choral singers, for whom it simplifies the sight-reading of music.

Tonic sol-fa notation is based on the old syllabic system of Do (Ut), Re, Mi, and so on, and takes the following form: d, r, m, f, s, l, t, the names of the notes being Doh, Ray, Me, Fah, Soh, Lah, Te. The substitution of 'Te' for the old 'Si' was made to avoid the duplication of the letter 's' in the abbreviations. The range of voices being limited, upper and lower octaves can be sufficiently indicated by a simple stroke placed behind the letters in a higher or lower position, thus: d' represents the note an octave above d, which in turn is an octave above d͵. Accidentals (sharps and flats) are indicated by the addition of a letter 'a' (ra, ma, etc, or exceptionally 'u' for du) for flats and 'e' (de, re, etc, or exceptionally 'y' for my) for sharps. Accidentals appear comparatively rarely now that the system of the 'movable Doh' has been adopted. This is a system of transposition in which everything is sung from a notation that looks as though the music were always in C major or A minor. The actual key is indicated at the beginning of a piece, so that singers know at once, for example, if the composition is in A major, that their **d** is to be read as A, their **r** as B, and so on. If the piece modulates to another key, a change is indicated, so that, for instance, **d** may become temporarily any other note of the scale; but in major keys it will always remain the ➤ **tonic**, in whatever key the music moves, **s** always the ➤ **dominant**, and **f** always the ➤ **subdominant**. In minor keys **l** will be the tonic, **m** the dominant, **r** the subdominant. (A special syllable, 'ba', is used for the sharp sixth in the melodic minor scale.) Time divisions are indicated by short bar lines, and there are subdivisions between these. The way in which the notes fill these spaces determines their time-values, though there are special signs for dotted notes, triplets, and others. A blank space means a rest, whereas dashes after a note mean that it is to be held beyond the space it occupies over one or more of the following time-divisions.

The merits of tonic sol-fa have always been subject to controversy. Its great defect is that it is insufficient for any general study of music as an art and that it is apt to keep choral singers from expanding their musical experience. Its advantages to instrumental players are very slight, since it is not so much easier to learn than staff notation, nor so flexible in picturing the composer's intentions. For choral singers it has not only the merit of simplicity, but the greater one of teaching them a sense of relative pitch as well as removing all difficulties connected with transposition.

tonos short vocal pieces for several voices sung at the opening of plays in 17th-century Spain.

Tonreihe see ➤ **tone row**.

tonus lascivus

In ex-i-tu Is-ra-el de Ae-gy-pto do-mus Ja-cob de po-pu-lo bar-ba-r o

The two bars of the example are centred on different notes, illustrating the essential quality of tonus peregrinus.

tonus lascivus (Latin 'playful, frolicsome, wanton tone') medieval name for what later became the ➤ **Ionian mode** and the major scale. Though it was not recognized as a church mode at the time, it was often used for secular songs by minstrels and was not unknown in ➤ **plainsong** melodies.

tonus peregrinus (Latin 'foreign tone') ➤ **plainsong** chant which, unlike the eight regular psalm tones, had two reciting notes, one in the first half of the chant and another in the second. For this reason it was described as 'foreign' and was reserved for the psalm 'In exitu Israel/When Israel came out of Egypt'. The melody was also sung in the Lutheran church: Bach used it in his Magnificat and also in the cantata *Meine Seel'erhebt den Herren* (a setting of the German Magnificat).

Toovey, Andrew (1962–) English composer. He studied with Jonathan Harvey, and with Morton Feldman at Dartington. He was director of Ixion from 1987, giving performances of music by Xenakis, Cage, and Ferneyhough.

Works CHAMBER *Winter Solstice* for voice and seven players; *Untitled String Quartet* (1985); *Ate* for chamber ensemble (1986); *Shining* for violin and cello (1987); *String Quartet Music* (1987); *Shimmer Bright* for string trio (1988); *Black Light* for chamber ensemble (1989); *Mozart* for strings (1991).

MUSIC THEATRE *The Spurt of Blood* (1990), *Ubu* (1992) and *The Juniper Tree* (1993).

WORKS FOR PIANO *Artaud* (1986), *Out Jumps Jack Death* (1989), *Down there by the Sea* (1989), and *Embrace* (two pianos, 1990).

Torelli, Giuseppe (1658–1709) Italian composer and violinist. With Arcangelo Corelli he was one of the most important composers in the history of the early concerto.

He played in the orchestra of San Petronio at Bologna 1686–96, then went to Vienna, and was konzertmeister at the court of the Margrave of Brandenburg 1697–99. He returned to Bologna in 1701.

Works ORCHESTRAL *Concerti grossi* (Op. 8, 1709); violin concertos; *sinfonie* (concertos) for trumpet and orchestra.

Torke, Michael (1961–) US composer. His music is highly eclectic, with some popular modern idioms.

He studied at the Eastman School in New York and with Jacob Druckman at Yale University 1984–85.

Works STAGE the opera *The Directions* (1986); ballet *Black and White* (1988).

ORCHESTRAL *Vanada* (1984), *Bright Blue Music* (1985), *Ecstatic Orange* (1986), and *Green* (1986), all for orchestra; *Purple* for orchestra (1987); *Copper* for brass quintet and orchestra (1987); *Bronze* for orchestra (1990); piano concerto (1991); *Run* for orchestra (1992).

CHAMBER *Ceremony of Innocence* (1983) and *The Yellow Pages*, both for flute and ensemble (1984); *Adjustable Wrench* for chamber ensemble (1987); *Rust* for piano and winds (1989); *Mass* for baritone, chorus, and ensemble (1990); *Chalk* for string quartet (1992); *Four Proverbs* for female voice and ensemble (1993).

tornada (Spanish) refrain which is a feature of many old Catalan songs.

Torquato Tasso opera by Donizetti (libretto by J Ferretti), produced at the Teatro Valle, Rome, on 9 September 1833. The story concerns the poet Tasso, who is in love with Eleonore. Her brother, Duke Alfonso, sends him to an asylum for seven years; on his return Eleonore has died and Tasso must seek refuge in his poetry.

Tortelier, Yan Pascal (1947–) French conductor. He was principal of the Ulster Orchestra 1989–92 and the BBC Philharmonic 1992–2002. His orchestration of the Ravel Piano Trio was performed in 1993 and he led London's first performance of Paul ➤ **Hindemith**'s opera *Sancta Susanna* in 1995. He is the son of cellist Paul Tortelier.

Tortelier studied with Nadia ➤ **Boulanger** at the Paris Conservatory and made his debut in 1962, as violinist in the London performance of the Brahms Double Concerto, with his father. He studied conducting with Franco Ferrara and was associate with the Orchestre du Capitole, Toulouse, 1974–83. He led the Royal Philharmonic Orchestra in a London concert in 1978 and the Seattle Symphony Orchestra in 1985.

Torvaldo e Dorliska opera by Rossini (libretto by C Sterbini), produced at the Teatro Valle, Rome, on 26 December 1815. The story concerns the defeated Torvaldo, who returns in disguise to the castle of the Duke of Ordow to rescue Dorliska. Both are imprisoned until the Duke's servants rescue them.

Tosca, La opera by Puccini (libretto by Giacosa and Luigi Illica, based on Sardou's drama), produced at the Teatro Costanzi, Rome, on 14 January 1900. In the story, Tosca commits suicide when she unsuccessfully bargains with lecherous Baron Scarpia for the life of her lover Cavaradossi. Cavaradossi is executed for treason and for harbouring the convict Angelotti.

Toscanini, Arturo (1867–1957) Italian conductor. He made his mark in opera as three-times musical director of La Scala, Milan, 1898–1903, 1906–08, and 1921–29, and subsequently as conductor 1937–54 of the National Broadcasting Company (NBC) Symphony Orchestra, which was established for him by NBC Radio. His wide-ranging repertoire included Debussy and Respighi, and he imparted an Italianate simplicity to Mozart and Beethoven when exaggerated solemnity was the trend in Germany.

Toscanini was born in Parma, Italy. Opposed to the fascist regime, he returned in 1936 to the USA, where he had conducted at the Metropolitan Opera 1908–15. The NBC Symphony Orchestra was formed for him in 1937. He retired in 1954.

Tosi, Pier Francesco (c.1653–1732) Italian castrato, teacher, and composer, son of Giuseppe Tosi (fl.1677–93). He published a book on florid singing (1723), and wrote an oratorio, and cantatas for voice and harpsichord.

He learnt music from his father and travelled much until 1682, when he settled as a singing-master in London. From 1705 to 1711 he was composer at the Imperial court in Vienna. After a further visit to London he finally returned to Italy and was ordained in 1730.

Tosti, (Francesco) Paolo (1846–1916) Italian singing teacher and composer. In 1880 he settled in London as singing teacher to the royal family. His songs were highly popular in his day, and include 'At Vespers', 'Forever', and 'Goodbye'.

He studied at Naples under Saverio Mercadante (1795–1870) and others from 1858 and was appointed a student-teacher, remaining until 1869. During a long illness at home he wrote his first songs. He then went to Rome, where Sgambati helped him to give a concert and Princess Margherita of Savoy (afterwards queen of Italy) appointed him her singing-master. In 1875 he first visited London, returning each year until 1880, where he remained and taught singing to the royal family.

Works songs Italian, English, and French songs, including 'Non m'ama più', 'Lamento d'amore', 'Aprile', 'Vorrei morire', 'Forever', 'Goodbye', 'Mother', 'At Vespers', 'That Day', 'Mattinata', 'Serenata'.

other vocal *Canti popolari abruzzesi* for vocal duet.

Tost Quartets twelve string quartets written by Haydn 1788–90 for the Viennese merchant and violinist Johannes Tost: Op. 54 nos 1–3, Op. 55 nos 1–3, Op. 64 nos 1–6. Tost also commissioned works from Mozart, including the D major string quintet K593.

Toten Augen, Die, The Dead Eyes opera by d'Albert (libretto originally French by M Henry, German translation by H H Ewers), produced in Dresden on 5 March 1916. In the story, the blind Myrtocle is granted her sight by Jesus. When she looks upon the ugliness of her husband Arcesius, however, she decides she would rather remain blind, which she attempts by staring at the sun.

Tote Stadt, Die, The Dead City opera by Korngold (libretto by P Schott, based on Georges Rodenbach's play *Bruges-la-morte*), produced in Hamburg and Cologne on 4 December 1920. In the story, Paul exorcizes the memory of his dead wife Marie when he meets Mariette, who bears a striking resemblance to her. But he strangles his new lover when she insults his faith.

'To the Memory of an Angel', German **Dem Andenken eines Engels** Berg's dedication for his violin concerto, composed in 1935 in memory of Manon Gropius, the daughter of Walter Gropius and Mahler's widow, Alma. The work begins with a musical portrait of Manon and ends with an adagio based on the Bach chorale *Es ist genug*. It was first performed in Barcelona on 19 April 1936, with Louis Krasner and the conductor Hermann Scherchen. It was first performed in London on 1 May 1936 (conductor Webern).

touch in piano playing, the way of approaching the keys to produce the ➤ tone required. The main factor in the player's touch that affects the quality of tone is weight, because of the mechanical action which mediates between the player's hand and the hammers and strings. However, different 'touches' can subtly but directly influence the player's attack and release of each key, thereby causing minute variations of articulation and dynamics which the conscious mind alone would be challenged to achieve. It is these infinitesimal inequalities and inaccuracies that account for subtleties of touch, especially noticeable in passages whose texture invites contrast between several notes played together.

As a verb, up until the early 17th century, touch meant simply to 'sound' an instrument, exactly as *toccare* does in Italian; as a noun ('touch' or 'touche') it was equivalent to ➤ toccata.

Tournal Mass an early 14th-century polyphonic (combining two or more voices or parts) setting of the Ordinary of the Mass, including *Ite missa est*. It is not the work of a single composer, nor is it necessarily from Tournai, Belgium, where the manuscript now is, but it may have been written at least in part in southern France.

Tournemire, Charles (Arnould) (1870–1939)
French composer and organist. Much of his work
is on religious themes, including *L'orgue mys-
tique* (1932), which consists of an organ Mass for
each Sunday of the Church year. In 1898 he succeeded César Franck as organist at the church of
Sainte-Clotilde. Later he became professor of
chamber music at the Paris Conservatory and
travelled much as an organ recitalist in Europe.

He studied under Widor at the Paris Conservatory and later with d'Indy.

Works OPERA *Les dieux sont morts* (1924) and
Nittetis (1905–07).

ORCHESTRAL *Le sang de la sirène* for solo voices,
chorus, and orchestra; eight symphonies.

WORKS FOR KEYBOARD piano quartet, piano trio;
*Pièces symphoniques, Triple Choral, L'orgue mys-
tique* (1932), *Petites fleurs musicales*, and other
organ works; piano pieces.

OTHER songs, other chamber music.

Tourte, François (Xavier) (1747–1835) French
bowmaker. He made great improvements in the
violin bow, especially after 1775. From around
1786 his bows set the pattern for the type of bow
used today.

He learnt his craft from his father and set up in
business with his elder brother, known in literature as Tourte *L'aîné*, probably named Xavier, but
they quarrelled and afterwards worked separately.

Tovey, Donald (Francis) (1875–1940) English
music scholar, pianist, and composer. His music
is classical in form and style; as a pianist he was
for some time in the front rank with his interpretations of Bach, Beethoven, and Brahms. He was
Reid professor of music at Edinburgh University
from 1914, and conducted the Reid orchestral
concerts there. He wrote several books, including six volumes of *Essays in Musical Analysis*,
which were notes for performances by the Reid
Orchestra.

From childhood his knowledge of the musical
classics, his memory, and his contrapuntal skill
were prodigious. At 13 he was a pupil of Hubert
Parry (1848–1918). In 1894, after giving a concert
with Joseph Joachim at Windsor, he went to Balliol College, Oxford, where he studied classics.
He distinguished himself there by brilliant scholarship and by taking a leading part in the university's musical life. He gave piano recitals at St
James's Hall in London 1900–01, and in Berlin
and Vienna 1901–02. In 1914 he was appointed
Reid professor of music at Edinburgh University,
a post he held until his death. His *Essays and Lectures on Music* were edited by H Foss in 1950.

Works STAGE the opera *The Bride of Dionysus*
(1929); incidental music for Maeterlinck's *Agla-
vaine et Sélysette*.

ORCHESTRAL symphony in D major; suite for wind

band; piano concerto (1903), cello concerto
(1935).

OTHER two string quartets; conjectural completion of Bach's *Art of Fugue* (1931).

Tower, Joan (1938–) US composer. Her music
has moved from serial influences to a more impressionistic style.

She studied at Columbia University, New York,
with Otto Luening and founded the Da Capo
Chamber Players in 1969. She taught at Bard College, New York, from 1972, returning in 1988.

Works ENSEMBLE percussion quartet (1963);
Breakfast Rhythms for clarinet and five instruments (1975); *Petroushskates* for ensemble (1980).

ORCHESTRAL *Amazon II* and *Sequoia* for orchestra
(1979, 1981); *Amazon III* for chamber orchestra
(1983); *Music* for cello and orchestra (1984);
piano concerto (1985); clarinet and flute concertos (1988, 1989); Concerto for Orchestra (1991);
violin concerto (1992); *Stepping Stones: A Ballet*,
for orchestra (1993).

Toy Symphony piece by Leopold Mozart (formerly attributed to Haydn) with parts for toy instruments (cuckoo, quail, nightingale). Similar
works have been written by Mendelssohn, Andreas Romberg, and others, most recently Malcolm Arnold.

Traci amanti, I, The Amorous Turks opera by Cimarosa (libretto by G Palomba), produced at the
Teatro Nuovo, Naples, on 19 June 1793.

tract chant with penitential words, sung after
the Gradual in the Mass in Lent (in place of the
Alleluia). Tracts are the only surviving examples
in the regular chants of the Mass of 'direct psalmody', sung without ➤ antiphon or respond. They
occur only in modes two and eight, and it is possible that those of mode two were originally Graduals. Their structure is that of a highly
elaborated psalm-tone. The number of verses
ranges from 2 to 14.

**Traetta, Tommaso (Michele Francesco Saver-
io) (1727–1779)** Italian composer. He was much
influenced by recent innovations of French
opera, in particular the *tragédies lyriques* of Rameau, but also continued the Metastasian tradition of ➤ opera seria. The early comic opera
Buovo d'Antona (1758) and later serious works
have been successfully revived in recent years.

He studied with Nicola Porpora and Francesco
Durante at the Conservatorio di Santa Maria di
Loreto in Naples 1738–48. He first worked as a
composer of church music, but after the success
of *Farnace* in 1751 soon established himself as an
opera composer. He was maestro di cappella and
singing teacher at the court of the Infante Felipe
of Spain in Parma 1758–65, then director of the
Conservatorio dell' Ospedaletto in Venice

1765–68. He then went to St Petersburg as music director at the court of Catherine II of Russia. He returned to Italy in 1775, visited London in 1777, and finally lived in Venice.

Works OPERA over 40, including *Farnace* (1751), *Didone abbandonata* (1757), *Ippolito ed Aricia* (1759), *I Tindaridi* (1760), *Le serve rivali* (1766), *Amore in trappola*, *Antigona* (1772), *Merope* (1776), *Germondo* (1776), *Il cavaliere errante*.

SACRED AND SECULAR MUSIC oratorio *Rex Salomone*; Passion; *Stabat Mater* and other church music.

ORCHESTRAL divertimenti for four orchestras *Le Quattro stagioni e il dodici mesi dell'anno*; sinfonie, and other pieces.

Tragédie de Salomé, La ballet by Florent Schmitt (choreography by Guerra), produced at the Théâtre des Arts, Paris, on 9 November 1907.

tragédie lyrique a 17th–18th-century term for French opera of a serious character, for example Rameau's *Les Boréades* (1764).

Tragic Overture, German **Tragische Ouvertüre** overture by Brahms, Op. 81, composed in 1880 as a companion-piece to the *Academic Festival Overture*, written as an acknowledgment of the honorary degree of doctor of philosophy conferred on him by Breslau University (in Wrocław in modern-day Poland) in 1879. The work was first performed in Vienna on 26 December 1880.

'Tragic' Symphony Schubert's fourth symphony, in C minor, composed in 1816 but not performed publicly until 19 November 1849, in Leipzig. The title was added to the score by the composer.

Tragoedia work for wind quintet, harp, and string quartet by Harrison Birtwistle, composed in 1965.

tranquillo (Italian 'quiet, calm, tranquil') musical term; the adverb, more rarely used as a direction, is *tranquillamente*.

Trans work by Karlheinz Stockhausen for string orchestra, wind, and percussion with tape and light projection. It was first performed in Donaueschingen (then in West Germany), on 16 October 1971.

transcription in music, the arrangement by a composer of a piece by another composer for a different combination of instruments. Liszt and Rachmaninov were famous for their transcriptions for piano, the playing of which required virtuosic skill.

Transfiguration de Notre Seigneur Jésus-Christ, La work in 14 movements for soloists, chorus, and orchestra by Messiaen (texts from the Bible, the Missal, and St Thomas Aquinas). Composed 1965–69, it was first performed in Lisbon, and conducted by Baudo, on 7 June 1969.

transition in music, a passage connecting two sections of a piece. For example, in a ➤ sonata-form movement a transition often connects the first and second subjects (principal melodies). The **retransition** is the transition connecting the development and the ➤ **recapitulation**. Transition is also an alternative name for ➤ **modulation**, especially if the change of keys is abrupt.

transposing instrument musical instrument that does not play at the pitch of its notation, but automatically at a higher or lower pitch. The English horn, clarinet, horn, and trumpet are transposing instruments; the flute, oboe, bassoon, and trombone are not. In brass bands, all the instruments except the bass trombone are transposing instruments.

transposing keyboards in music, contrivances of various sorts to shift the manuals of keyboard instruments so that the music played becomes automatically higher or lower, saving the players from learning to transpose at sight (see ➤ **transposition**). Such keyboards appeared on some organs as early as the 16th century and later on Ruckers harpsichords. Several inventions of the kind were made for the piano late in the 18th century and throughout the 19th century.

transposition in music, performance in a different ➤ **key** from that indicated in the printed music, or the appearance of a theme or motif in an alternative key. A ➤ **transposing instrument** is one that is normally written for in one key and played in another, for example an instrument in B flat, such as a clarinet, sounds a tone lower. An instrument in D sounds a tone higher, while a basset horn or French horn in F sounds a fifth lower than written (all written music is considered as being 'in C').

A passage of music in which one phrase is repeatedly transposed is known as a sequence.

transverse flute the modern ➤ **flute** held horizontally, as distinct from the flutes of the recorder type, which are held vertically.

Trapp, Max (1887–1971) German composer. He studied composition with Juon and piano with Dohnányi at the Berlin Hochschule für Musik, became piano professor there in 1920 and professor of advanced composition in 1924. He also taught at Dortmund. The first performance of his second *Concerto for Orchestra* (1935) was conducted by Furtwängler.

Works STAGE marionette play *Der letzte König von Orplid* (after Mörike); incidental music to Shakespeare's *Timon of Athens*.

ORCHESTRAL seven symphonies, two concertos, two divertimenti, symphonic suite, *Notturno* for orchestra; piano concerto, violin concerto (1926), cello concerto (1937).

This passage from Bach's St John Passion *is transposed from E major to F major.*

CHAMBER two string quartets, piano quintet, three piano quartets; variations for two pianos; sonatina for piano.

traquenard (French 'trap, snare'; also 'racking-pace' [of horses]) a 17th-century dance, the dotted rhythm of which refers to the second sense of the word.

Trauermarsch a German funeral ➤ march.

Trauermusik work for viola and strings in four movements by Hindemith; It was composed on 21 January 1936 in response to the death of George V and performed the next day in London with Hindemith as soloist (conductor Boult).

Trauer-Ode, *Funeral Ode* Bach's cantata no. 198, written on the death of the Electress Christiane Eberhardine of Saxony and performed at the memorial ceremony at Leipzig, on 17 October 1727.

Trauer-Sinfonie, *Mourning Symphony* the nickname of a symphony by Haydn, no. 44, in E minor, composed c.1771.

Trauerwalzer, *Mourning Waltz* the title given by the publisher to Schubert's waltz for piano, Op. 9 no. 2, in 1821, a piece later wrongly attributed to Beethoven. Schubert, who wrote it in 1816, disapproved of the title. The attribution to Beethoven occurred in 1826, when Schott of Mainz brought out a *Sehnsuchtswalzer* (also called *Le Désir*) under his name, although it was a compound of Schubert's piece and Himmel's *Favoritwalzer*.

Traumgörge, Der, *Dreaming George* opera by Zemlinsky (libretto by L Feld), composed 1904–06 and accepted for production at the Vienna Hofoper by Mahler, though it was not performed until 11 October 1980, at Nuremberg. In the story, the idealist Görge abandons his fiancée Grete and takes up with Gertraud, through whom his dreams are eventually realized.

trautonium polyphonic keyboard synthesizer invented in 1928 by German acoustician Friedrich Trautwein (1888–1956) and subsequently developed by Oskar Sala as the *Mixtur-trautonium*. A neoclassical *Concerto for Trautonium and Strings* was composed by Hindemith in 1931, and Richard Strauss included the instrument in his *Japanese Festival Music* (1940).

The instrument remained popular with Hollywood composers until the 1950s.

traversa (Italian 'transverse') abbreviation sometimes used in old musical scores for the transverse flute, the modern ➤ flute played sideways, as distinct from flutes of the recorder type, which are held vertically.

traversière (French 'transverse') French name for the transverse ➤ flute, a musical instrument.

Traviata, La, *The Fallen Woman* opera by Verdi (libretto by Francesco Maria Piave, based on the younger Dumas' *La Dame aux camélias*), produced at the Teatro La Fenice, Venice, on 6 March 1853. In the story, a consumptive courtesan is persuaded by Alfredo's father to renounce her love for the sake of his family's honour. She has an affair with Baron Douphol before Alfredo learns the truth about her actions. The lovers are reconciled before she dies.

Travis, Roy (1922–) US composer. He studied at the Juilliard School and Columbia University (1947–51) and with Milhaud at the Paris Conservatory. He taught first in New York, then at UCLA, where he was a professor from 1968.

Works OPERA *The Passion of Oedipus* (1968) and *The Black Bacchantes* (1982).

CHAMBER string quartet (1958); *Duo Concertante*

for violin and piano (1967); *Barma*, for septet (1968).

ORCHESTRAL *Collage* for orchestra (1968); Piano concerto (1969).

OTHER electronic music pieces (studio at University of California at Los Angeles, from 1969).

treble the highest register of a boy's singing voice (approximately equivalent in range to the ➤ **soprano** voice of a woman), about F4–C6, or the highest-pitched member of a family of instruments, for example the treble viol. The term is also used to refer to the right hand of a piano piece.

The term is derived from the Latin *triplum*, the top part of early three-part motets.

treble clef in music, G ➤ **clef** in which the G above middle C (G4) is represented by the second-lowest line of a five-line stave. Most instruments with a range above middle C use treble clef, including the violin, clarinet, trumpet, and piano (right hand).

The treble clef (a), and the treble clef transposed an octave lower (b).

treble viol musical instrument, the smallest of the normal members of the ➤ **viol** family.

Open strings of the treble viol.

tre corde (Italian 'three strings') musical direction in piano music indicating that after the use of the left pedal (➤ **una corda**) normal playing is to be resumed.

tremolando (Italian 'trembling') musical direction sometimes used instead of the conventional notation for string ➤ **tremolo**, or for a passage to be sung in a tremulous voice.

tremolo in music, a rapidly pulsating tremor on one note, created by rapid movement of the bow on a stringed instrument, or shake of the voice. A buzzing tremolo produced by brass or woodwind instruments is called ➤ **flutter-tongue**.

The effect is exploited to picturesque effect in Rimsky-Korsakov's 'Flight of the Bumble-Bee' interlude from the opera *The Legend of Tsar Saltan* (1900).

tremulant on the ➤ **organ**, a mechanical device operated by a draw stop, for producing ➤ **vibrato**.

trenchmore English country dance 'longways for as many as will', known in the 16th and 17th cen-

The notation of a tremolo on a single note, and between two notes.

turies and introduced into the court and noble houses as a kind of democratic dance in which masters and servants could take part together, temporarily relaxing strict class distinctions.

Trento, Vittorio (1761–1833) Italian composer. He was a pupil of Ferdinando Bertoni (1725–1813). In the last decade of the 18th century he visited London as conductor at the King's Theatre and in 1806 became impresario at Amsterdam, going to Lisbon in the same capacity soon after. After a further visit to London he returned to Venice before his death.

Works OPERA AND STAGE *La finta ammalata, Quanti casi in un giorno* (1801), *Teresa vedova, Ifigenia in Aulide, Climene* (1812) and c.35 others; ballet *Mastino della Scala* and more than 50 others.

CHORAL oratorios *The Deluge, The Maccabees* and others.

trepak Russian dance of Cossack origin in animated 2/4 time.

triad in music, a chord of three notes consisting of a ➤ **root**, ➤ **third**, and ➤ **fifth**. There are four types of triad: major (for example C–E–G), minor (C–E♭–G), augmented (C–E–G♯), and diminished (C–E♭–G♭).

trial French term for a special type of operatic tenor voice of a high, thin, rather nasal quality suited to comic parts. The name is derived from the singer Antoine Trial.

Trial by Jury one-act opera by Sullivan (libretto by W S Gilbert), produced at the Royalty Theatre, London, on 25 March 1875. The story begins when Angelina takes Edwin to court for breach of promise, and the judge proposes to her himself.

triangle small percussion instrument consisting of a thin metal bar bent into the shape of a triangle. Hit by a metal rod, it produces a tinkling tone of high, indefinite pitch. Compositions that call for a prominent triangle part include Liszt's Piano Concerto in E flat (1849; revised 1853, 1856) and the third movement of Brahms' Fourth Symphony (1885).

trihoris or **trihory** or **triori** or **triory** old French dance of Lower Brittany, allied to the ➤ **branle**.

Maj	Min	Augmented	Diminished

Major, minor, augmented, and diminished triads.

trill in music, a rapid oscillation between adjacent notes, also called a **shake**, exploited both for impressionistic effect, as in the opening bars of Béla Bartók's *Piano Concerto No 3* (1945), or to create dramatic tension and ambiguity, as at end of a solo ➔ **cadenza** in a concerto.

trillo del Diavolo, Il, The Devil's Trill Tartini's violin sonata written at Assisi c.1745 and said to have been inspired by a dream in which he bargained with the devil for his soul in return for musical inspiration, the devil playing the violin to him. He related that on waking he immediately wrote down what he had heard, but that the music as written fell far short of the dream devil's performance. The work is in four movements, written for violin and continuo; the famous trill is in the finale. An opera on the story of the sonata was written by Falchi.

Trinity College of Music a school of music in London incorporated in 1875. Famous students include Sir John Barbirolli. Gavin Henderson has been principal since 1993. Together with his predecessor he has helped prevent the college being merged with another institution, and managed to keep it on its current site through the purchase of the lease.

trio in music, an ensemble of three instruments, or the music written fo such a group. It is used for the interlude between repeats of a ➔ **minuet** or ➔ **scherzo**, which was originally for a trio of players.

The most common combination of instruments in a trio is the piano trio, which usually consists of piano, violin, and cello. Famous examples include Beethoven's ➔ **'Archduke' Trio** and Dmitri Shostakovich's *Piano Trio No. 2* in E minor.

Trionfi del fato, I, ovvero Le glorie d'Enea, The Triumphs of Fate, or The Glories of Aeneas opera by Steffani (libretto by O Mauro), produced at the Court Opera, Hanover, in December 1695.

trionfo dell' onore, Il, The Triumph of Honour opera by Alessandro Scarlatti (libretto by F A Tullio), produced at the Teatro dei Fiorentini, Naples, in autumn 1718. Honour wins out in the story, as Flaminio is united with Cornelia and Riccardo with Leonora.

Trionfo di Afrodite, Aphrodite's Triumph concerto scenico by Orff, the second of three works called collectively *Trionfi* (text by composer, after Catullus, Sappho, and Euripides). It was produced at La Scala, Milan, on 14 February 1953 (conductor Karajan).

trionfo di Clelia, Il, Clelia's Triumph opera by Gluck (libretto by Metastasio), produced at the

Various trills and their approximate realizations.

Teatro Comunale, Bologna, on 14 May 1763. Also settings by Hasse (Vienna, 1762) and Jommelli (Lisbon, 1774). The story concerns the Roman noblewoman Clelia, who is captured by the Etruscan king but saves her city with her courage and nobility.

Opera by Jommelli (libretto as above), produced at the Teatro d'Ajuda, Lisbon, on 6 June 1774.

trionfo di Dori, Il, The Triumph of Doris collection of Italian madrigals published by Gardano of Venice in 1592. It contains 29 six-part madrigals on various poems all ending with the line 'Viva la bella Dori', which suggested the similar uniform final line in the English collection modelled on this, *The Triumphes of Oriana*. The composers, all represented by one piece each, include Anerio, Asola, Baccusi, Croce, Giovanni Gabrieli, Gastoldi, Marenzio, Palestrina, Striggio, and Vecchi.

trio sonata most important form of Baroque chamber music. It was usually written for two violins (or viols) to play the melodies, and a cello (or bass viol) to play the continuo bass line. An additional continuo player was also needed to fill in the harmonies on a keyboard instrument (harpsichord or organ), which actually meant that four players were needed. At the end of the 17th century it developed into the *sonata da chiesa* and the *sonata da camera* (see ➤ sonata). Notable examples include those by Françoise Couperin, George Handel, Antonio Vivaldi, Arcangelo Corelli, and Henry Purcell.

tripla in music, old term for triple time in old ➤ **mensurable music**, but also the figure three shown in the time-signature and later, when the device of the triplet came into use, the figure '3' set over a group of notes. It is also a dance in quick triple time.

triple concerto a ➤ concerto with three solo parts, for example Beethoven's concerto for violin, cello, piano, and orchestra, or Michael Tippett's concerto for string trio and orchestra.

triple counterpoint in music, ➤ counterpoint in which three parts are reversible, each being capable of appearing at the top, in the middle, or at the bottom.

triplet in music, a group of three notes of equal length, played in the time of two. It is indicated by a ➤ slur over the three notes with the number '3' written above.

Example of a triplet (bar 2).

triple time in music, a metre in which the bar may be divided into three beats, as in 3/4 and 9/8.

triplum (Latin 'the third') the highest of the original three voices in the ➤ motet; thus it is the origin of the English word ➤ treble.

Tristan work by Henze for piano, tape, and orchestra. Composed in 1973, it was first performed in London on 20 October 1974 (conducted by Davis).

Tristan chord in music, the famously harmonically ambiguous chord which Richard Wagner used in *Tristan und Isolde*. See ➤ augmented sixth chords.

Tristan und Isolde music-drama by Wagner (libretto by composer, based on the Tristram and Iseult legend), produced at the Court Opera, Munich, on 10 June 1865. Tristan and Isolde fall under the spell of a love potion during a journey prior to her marriage with King Mark of Cornwall; Mark's servant Melot mortally wounds Tristan and Isolde sings the famous *Liebestod* over his corpse.

tritone in music, the interval of the diminished fifth, exactly half the octave, and considered in the Middle Ages to be the moral antithesis of the octave's perfect consonance, or 'diabolus in musica' (devil in music). Its prominence during the late 19th and early 20th centuries helped to undermine the remaining foundations of ➤ tonality, as in Debussy's *Prélude à l'après-midi d'un faune* (1894).

The alternative term 'mi contra fa' refers to B in the dominant key of G (do-re-*mi*) in relation to F in the tonic key of C (do-re-mi-*fa*).

Tritonius, Petrus (c.1465–c.1525), German **Peter Treybenreif** Austrian composer and scholar. He wrote music for Horatian odes for four voices, and in 1524 published a hymn book containing the text of about 130 hymns and blank staves for the music to be written on.

He studied at Vienna and Ingolstadt universities and later became a teacher of Latin and music at the cathedral school of Brixen. He later studied at Padua University, and while in Italy he met the Viennese professor Conrad Celtis, who invited him to settle at Vienna. Once there, he joined Celtis's circle and wrote a setting of Horatian odes, which were published in 1507. Ludwig Senfl later took the tenor parts of these as canti firmi for his own settings, and Paul Hofhaimer imitated Tritonius's settings. On the death of Celtis in 1508 Tritonius returned to the Tyrol and became director of the Latin school at Bozen. In 1513 he was in Halle, and in 1521 he retired to Schwaz am Inn.

Works VOCAL AND CHORAL hymns in four parts;

odes by Horace and other Latin poems set in four parts, and other pieces.

Trittico, **Triptych** cycle of three one-act operas by Puccini, produced at the Metropolitan Opera, New York, on 14 December 1918:
Il tabarro/*The Cloak* (libretto by G Adami, based on D Gold's *Houppelande*). Michele kills wife Giorgetta's lover and hides the body under a cloak.
Suor Angelica/*Sister Angelica* (libretto by G Forzano). As convent dweller Angelica is told of the death of her illegitimate son she takes poison and is granted a vision of the Virgin with her child.
Gianni Schicchi (libretto by G Forzano, based on the story of a rogue who is mentioned in Dante's *Divina commedia*). Gianni Schicchi assumes the identity of the rich, recently-deceased Bicose Donati and dictates a will favourable to himself.

Tritto, Giacomo (1733–1824) Italian composer. From around 1760 he wrote over 50 operas. He also wrote treatises on thorough bass and counterpoint. A pupil of Cafaro at the Conservatorio dei Turchini in Naples, he later taught there and in 1806 became co-director (with Paisiello and Fenarolo).
Works OPERA *La fedeltà in amore* (1764), *Il convitato di pietra* (on the Don Giovanni story), *Arminio*, *La canterina*, *Gli Americani* (1802), and *Marco Albinio* (1810).
OTHER Masses and other church music.

Triumphes of Oriana, The English collection of ➔ madrigals written in honour of Queen Elizabeth I, edited by Morley and published in 1601. It was modelled on the Italian collection of *Il ➔ Trionfo di Dori* of 1592 and contains a similar series of different poems all ending with the same line, 'Long live fair Oriana'.
There are 25 pieces by 23 English composers: Bennet, Carlton, Cavendish, Cobbold, Este, Farmer, Edward Gibbons (2), Hilton, Holmes, Hunt, E Johnson, Robert Jones, Kirby, Lisley, Marson, Milton, Morley (2), Mundy, Nicolson, Norcome, T Tomkins, Weelkes, and Wilbye. A madrigal by Bateson intended for the collection arrived too late and was included in his own *First Set of English Madrigals* (1604).

Triumphlied, **Song of Triumph** setting by Brahms of words from the Revelation of St John for eight-part chorus, orchestra, and organ *ad lib*, Op. 55, composed in spring 1871 to celebrate the German victory in the Franco-Prussian war. It was first perfomed at Karlsruhe on 5 June 1872.

Triumph of Neptune, The ballet by Lord Berners (scenario by Sacheverell Sitwell, choreographed by Balanchine), produced at the Lyceum Theatre, London, on 3 December 1926. The settings were based on B Pollock's 'penny plain, two-pence coloured' toy theatre designs.

Triumph of Peace, The masque by James Shirley with music by William Lawes and Simon Ive, produced at the Banqueting House in Whitehall on 3 February (Candlemas) in 1634.

Troades opera by Reimann (libretto based on Werfel's version of Euripides' *The Trojan Women*), produced in Munich, on 7 July 1986.

Troilus and Cressida opera in three acts by Walton (libretto by C Hassall, after Chaucer), produced at Covent Garden, London, on 3 December 1954. It was revived at Covent Garden, London, on 12 November 1976, with Cressida's role altered to mezzo (Janet Baker). In the story, the Trojan Troilus follows Cressida when she accompanies her father Calchas to the Greek camp; although they love each other, she agrees to marry Diomede after she believes Troilus has abandoned her. But all is revealed before Calchas stabs Troilus in a fight and Cressida commits suicide.

Trois Petites Liturgies de la Présence Divine, **Three Little Liturgies of the Divine Presence** work by Messiaen for 18 sopranos, piano, ondes Martenot (an electronic instrument), celesta, vibraphone, three percussion, and strings (text by composer). It was first performed in Paris on 21 April 1945, conducted by Désormière.

tromba da tirarsi (Italian 'trumpet to draw itself [out]') the slide trumpet, a musical instrument of the ➔ trumpet type. It was used in Germany in the 18th century and had the advantage before the invention of valves of being capable of producing more notes than the fundamental harmonics by the temporary changes in the length of the tube, as in the trombone. It never attained a wide currency.

Trombetti, Ascanio (1544–1590) Italian composer. He wrote four books of madrigals 1573–87. From the 1560s he was in the service of the Signoria of Bologna, where he played the cornett. From 1583 he was maestro di cappella at the Church of San Giovanni at Monte.
Works SACRED AND SECULAR MUSIC motets in five to twelve parts for voices and instruments; madrigals for four to five voices, *napolitane* for three voices.

Tromboncino, Bartolomeo (c.1470–after 1534) Italian composer. He was famous as a composer of *frottole* – songs for several singers or for one singer and instruments – he wrote over 170. He enjoyed brief fame for having murdered his adulterous wife in 1499 and was in the service of another adulteress, Lucrezia Borgia, at Ferrara 1502–08.

He was at the ducal court of Mantua 1487–95, then at Venice, Vicenza, Casale, at Mantua again 1501–13, and then at Ferrara.

Works WORKS FOR VOICE lamentations, one motet, and 17 *laude*; over 170 *frottole* for four voices.

trombone brass instrument with a deep cup-shaped mouthpiece and a mainly cylindrical bore that expands into a moderately flared bell. Instead of valves, the trombone has a movable slide: a U-shaped piece of tubing that can be pushed away or pulled towards the player. This lengthens or shortens the sounding length of the tube to create lower or higher-pitched notes. All the notes of the chromatic scale are available by placing the slide in any of seven basic positions, and blowing a harmonic series of notes built upon each basic note. The slide mechanism also makes possible a continuous glissando (slide) in pitch over a span of half an octave.

Descended from the Renaissance ➤ **sackbut**, the tenor and bass trombones are staple instruments of the orchestra and brass band, also of Dixieland and jazz bands, either separately or as a tenor-bass hybrid. The hybrid has a switch that lowers the pitch a fourth from B flat to F.

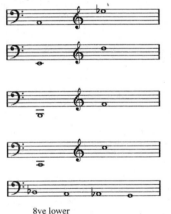

8ve lower

The compass of the alto, tenor, and bass trombones; the compass of the tenor-bass trombone; 'pedal' notes on the trombone.

Trommelbass (German 'drum bass') musical technical term for the notes of a bass part divided up into groups of repeated even quavers, a device used especially in the 18th century to give a kind of artificial animation to music.

Trompeter von Säckingen, Der, The Trumpeter of Säckingen opera by Nessler (libretto by R Bunge, based on Scheffel's poem), produced in Leipzig on 4 May 1884. The opera was very popular in its day and often conducted by Mahler. The story concerns the trumpeter Werner, who loves Maria but her parents prefer Damian, who turns out to be a coward and a simpleton. After being banished, Werner returns to save the Baron from an uprising and is allowed to marry Maria.

tronco (Italian 'truncated, cut off, interrupted') musical direction indicating that a note or chord is to cease abruptly.

trope an interpolation into liturgical chants dating from the 8th or 9th centuries, probably of Byzantine origin. Tropes were at first vocalized as purely musical ornamentations or sung on syllables of certain words, especially 'Alleluia', but later they became so important that special words were newly written for them. Sometimes new words came first and demanded new music; thus the ➤ **sequence**, which began merely as a special kind of trope, developed into a poetical form with musical setting.

Tropen (German 'tropes') musical term used by Josef Hauer for his own version of twelve-note music. He divided the possible combinations of the twelve notes of the ➤ **chromatic scale**, which run into hundreds of millions, into 44 main groups, which he called *Tropen*. The *Tropen* were equivalent to keys in the diatonic system (consisting of the seven notes of any major or minor scale), and a change from one *Trope* to another is equivalent to ➤ **modulation**.

Hauer further divided each row of twelve notes into two halves of six, which form two fundamental chords, whatever the order in which each six may appear.

troppo (Italian 'too much') in musical direction, term often used in the negative: *non troppo*, 'not too much'; or *ma non troppo*, 'but not too much'.

troubadour (French, from Provençal *trobador* [from Latin *tropus*]) poet-musician of Provence and southern France in the 12th–13th centuries. The troubadours originated a type of lyric poetry devoted to themes of courtly love and the idealization of women and to glorifying the chivalric ideals of the period. Little is known of their music, which was passed down orally.

Among the troubadours were Bertran de Born (1140–c.1215), who was mentioned by Dante, Arnaut Daniel, and ➤ **Bernard de Ventadour**. The trouvères were a similar class of poet-musicians active during the same period in northern France and England. The troubadour tradition had a parallel in the German Minnesingers.

The troubadours' poems were usually *poésies courtoises* (courtly poems, mainly love-songs, but also satires and other styles), while *chansons à personnages* (narrative songs) belonged chiefly to the trouvères. Troubadours wrote their own poems and probably composed the tunes as well;

approximately 2,500 troubadour songs have survived, and the melodies of about 280 of these are known. About 2,000 of the trouvères' poems have survived, and most of these have music. The melodies were written down in a notation which showed only the pitch of the notes. The rhythm was either committed to memory or else determined by the poetic metre, a question that has never been solved beyond controversy. It is believed that the songs were accompanied on instruments of the harp or lute type, either by the troubadours and trouvères themselves or by attendants, for many troubadours were not poor wandering musicians but nobles whose audiences were at courts and noble houses.

'Trout' Quintet quintet in A major for violin, viola, cello, double bass, and piano, D667, by Schubert, composed in summer 1819 during an excursion to Upper Austria. The title is so called because the fourth of the five movements is a set of variations on his song *The Trout/Die Forelle*, D550 (1817).

trouvère (French, from old French *trovere* or *troveur*) a poet-musician of northern France in the 12th and 13th centuries. The trouvères cultivated an art similar to that of the ➔ **troubadours** in southern France. The art was encouraged in the north by Eleanor of Aquitaine, who married Louis VII in 1137; about 1,700 melodies have been preserved. The poems include *chansons à personnages* (narrative songs), *poésies courtoises* (courtly poems, mainly love-songs), and crusaders' songs. The notation and manner of performance of the songs was similar to that of the troubadours.

Trovatore, Il, The Troubadour or **The Minstrel** opera by Verdi (libretto by Salvatore Cammarano, based on a Spanish play, *El trovador*, by Antonio Garcia Gutiérrez), produced at the Teatro Apollo, Rome, on 19 February 1853. In the story, Manrico and Count Luna are rivals for the love of Leonora. When Luna is unsuccessful he orders Manrico's execution. Leonora offers her body to the Count in exchange for Manrico's life, but she takes poison before he is freed and Manrico is subsequently killed. It is revealed that he is the Count's brother.

Trowell, Brian (1931–) English musicologist. A professor of music at Oxford University 1988–97, he edited music by Dunstable (joint editor, complete works) and published *The Early Renaissance* (1963), translations and articles on opera. He also published *Elgar's Use of Literature*.

He studied at Cambridge with Thurston Dart and was lecturer at Birmingham University 1957–62. He was director of opera at the Guildhall School of Music and Drama, London,

1963–67, and reader then professor at King's College from 1970.

Troyens, Les, The Trojans opera by Berlioz in two parts (libretto by composer, after Virgil):

La Prise de Troie/The Taking of Troy was produced in Karlsruhe (in German) on 6 December 1890. In the story, Cassandra's warnings are ignored as the departing Greeks leave their wooden horse. Warned by the ghost of Hector, Aeneas escapes the massacre of the Trojans.

Les Troyens à Carthage was produced at the Théâtre-Lyrique, Paris, on 4 November 1863, and later at Karlsruhe (in German) on 7 December 1890 (the first performance of the complete work). In the plot of this second part, Aeneas and Dido, Queen of Carthage, fall in love but he must depart for Italy to found Rome, and as he leaves Dido mounts her funeral pyre. The first performance of the complete work in French was at Brussels on 26 and 27 December 1906.

trumpet brass instrument with a long history. It exists worldwide in a variety of forms and materials. It has a shallow, cup-shaped mouthpiece and a generally cylindrical bore that expands into a moderately flared bell. The sound can be brilliant, penetrating, and of stable pitch, making it useful for signalling and ceremonies. In Medieval times, the trumpet was a 'natural' instrument, consisting of a simple tube with no extra mechanisms. It was therefore only able to produce the 'natural' notes of the harmonic series, depending on the length of its tube. In the early 17th century, valves were introduced, giving access to the full range of notes.

Today the trumpet is valued for its clearly focused, brilliant tone. It makes up part of the brass section in a modern orchestra, where the trumpet in B flat and the trumpet in C are most often played. It is also used in military brass bands and is an important instrument in jazz, where players show off skills using the high harmonics. Famous jazz trumpeters include Louis Armstrong, Bix Beiderbecke, Dizzy Gillespie, and Miles Davis. Other trumpets sometimes used include the bass trumpet, and several smaller trumpets such as those in D and E flat and the piccolo trumpet in B flat.

trumpet marine early string instrument with a single string and thus allied to the monochord, played with a bow. It was used mainly for popular music-making, especially in Germany, but also in convents, as its German name *Nonnengeige*, 'nun's fiddle', indicates. The instrument produced harmonics very easily and, like the old trumpet, often restricted itself to them, its normally produced notes being very poor and coarse in quality.

It was also called *Trummscheit*, 'trumpet wood',

The written compass and actual notes of the B flat trumpet; the actual compass of the trumpet in D.

or *Brummscheit*, 'humming wood', and the Italian and English names connecting it with a trumpet were doubtless due to its penetrating tone. The provenance of the adjective 'marine' is unknown.

trumpet voluntary in the late 17th century, a piece, not for trumpet, but an organ voluntary, the tune of which was played on the trumpet ➔ **stop**. The example still familiar is Jeremiah Clarke's *The Prince of Denmark's March*, which was published in 1700 as a harpsichord piece, but which also occurs in a suite for wind instruments by Clarke.

Tsar and Carpenter opera by Albert Lortzing. See ➔ *Zar und Zimmermann, oder Die zwei Peter.*

Tsar Saltan opera by Nicolai Rimsky-Korsakov. See ➔ *Legend of Tsar Saltan.*

Tsar's Bride, The, **Tsarskaya Nevesta** opera by Rimsky-Korsakov (libretto by I F Tumenev, based on a play by L A Mey), produced at the Imperial Opera, Moscow, on 3 November 1899. In the story, Marfa is chosen by Ivan the Terrible as his bride, but she loves Lykov and is poisoned by a jealous rival. Lykov is beheaded for the crime as Marfa expires.

tuba member of a family of large brass instruments with a conical bore, deep cup-shaped mouthpiece, widely flaring bell, and three to six valves, producing a deep, mellow tone. Tubas were introduced around 1830 as the bass members of the orchestra brass section and the brass band. Despite their size and pitch, they can be surprisingly agile. These qualities have been exploited by composers such as Hector Berlioz, Maurice Ravel, and Vaughan Williams.

Different shapes, sizes, and pitches of tuba exist, including the circular or helicon sousaphone that wraps around the player. Some members of the tuba family are also known as euphonium, bombardon, and sousaphon. The

Wagner tuba is a horn variant.

The orchestral tuba is normally in F (non-transposing) with four valves and this compass.

Tubin, Eduard (1905–1982) Estonian-born Swedish composer. He studied at the Tartu Academy 1924–30 and conducted in Estonia 1931–44, before settling in Sweden.

Works OPERA *Barbara of Tisenhusen* (1969) and *The Priest from Reigi* (1971).

ORCHESTRAL ten symphonies (1934–73), two violin concertos (1942, 1945), balalaika concerto (1964); *Requiem for Fallen Soldiers* (1979).

CHAMBER two violin sonatas (1936, 1949).

tubular bells percussion instrument (approximate range C2–F3), consisting of 18 tuned metal tubes of different lengths, which hang in a frame. They are struck at the top end with a rawhide mallet, and the resonance can be muted with a foot-operated damper. They produce bell effects, used both in orchestral works and opera music.

Tucker, Norman (1910–1978) English administrator and translator. He was joint director at Sadler's Wells, London, 1947–54, and sole director 1954–66. He translated the UK first performances of Janáček's *Káta Kabanová* and *Cunning Little Vixen* (1951, 1961). He also translated *Simon Boccanegra* for its UK first performance (1948), and Verdi's *Don Carlos*.

Tucker studied at Oxford University and the Royal College of Music. He encouraged the careers of such conductors as Charles Mackerras and Colin Davis.

Tucker, William (died 1679) English composer. He was Gentleman of the Chapel Royal in London, and minor canon and precentor of Westminster Abbey from 1660. He wrote services and anthems.

Tuder, John (lived 15th century) English composer. He wrote responsories, lamentations, and the hymn *Gloria, laus*, all of which are included in the Pepys manuscript (c.1465) at Magdalene College, Cambridge. There is a carol by him in the Fayrfax Book (c.1500).

Tunder, Franz (1614–1667) German composer and organist. As organist of St Mary's Church, Lübeck, he greatly improved the church music and also instituted the *Abendmusiken/Evening Music* concerts, which soon became famous beyond the town and were further developed by Dietrich ➔ **Buxtehude**.

In 1632 he was appointed court organist at Gottorf and in 1641 organist of St Mary's, where he preceded Buxtehude, who had to marry his daughter in order to secure the post.

Works church cantatas, sacred arias with strings and organ; chorale variations for organ.

tune colloquial word for melody. 'In tune' denotes accurate intonation, 'out of tune' the opposite. 'To tune' is to adjust the intonation of an instrument.

tuning in music, the adjusting of ➤ **pitch** in instruments to the correct intonation, in order to avoid dissonance. For example, orchestral instruments tune to ➤ **concert pitch** (A4). Keyboard instruments are more difficult to adjust, often requiring a professional tuner.

tuning fork in music, a device for providing a reference pitch, invented in England in 1711. It is made from hardened metal and consists of parallel bars about 10 cm/3–4 in long joined at one end and terminating in a blunt point. When the fork is struck and the point placed on a wooden surface, a pure tone is heard.

There are tuning forks for each musical pitch. A is known as 'concert pitch', since the instruments of the orchestra are tuned to A above middle C.

Turandot incidental music for Schiller's Germany version of Gozzi's play by Weber, Op. 37, composed in 1809 and including the *Overtura cinese/Chinese Overture*, which was composed on a Chinese theme in 1805.

Opera by Busoni (German libretto by composer, based on Gozzi's play), produced at Zurich on 11 May 1917, together with another short opera, *Arlecchino*. The music of *Turandot* was elaborated from incidental music for Max Reinhardt's production of K Vollmöller's version of Gozzi's play, produced at the Deutsches Theater, Berlin, on 27 October 1911.

Opera by Puccini (Italian libretto by G Adami and R Simoni, based on Gozzi's play). It was left unfinished by Puccini and was completed by Alfano and produced at La Scala, Milan, on 25 May 1926. In the story, Calaf saves his head by answering three riddles of cold-hearted Turandot, and eventually wins her love.

Turangalîla-symphonie (Sanskrit turanga, 'time, rhythm'; lîla, 'divine action') work for orchestra in ten movements by Messiaen, with prominent parts for piano solo and the ➤ **ondes Martenot**. Commissioned by Koussevitzky and composed 1946–48, it was first performed in Boston on 2 December 1949, conducted by Bernstein.

The work is the middle of a triptych of works inspired by the Tristan legend; the others are *Harawi* for soprano and piano (1945) and *Cinq Rechants* for unaccompanied chorus.

turca (Italian 'Turkish') in music, word used in the combination *alla turca* ('in the Turkish man-

ner') by Mozart for the finale of the A major piano sonata, K331, and by Beethoven for the *Marcia alla turca* in *The Ruins of Athens*, which is the theme of the piano variations, Op. 76.

Turco in Italia, Il, The Turk in Italy opera by Rossini (libretto by Felice Romani), produced at La Scala, Milan, on 14 August 1814. The story concerns the Turkish Prince Selim, who arrives in Naples and after much confusion is reconciled with his former love, Zaida.

Turina, Joaquín (1882–1949) Spanish composer. He devoted much time to teaching as well as composition and wrote a small treatise expounding his aims in teaching music, *Enciclopedia abreviada de música* (1917). His most successful works are those which employ local Spanish colours, such as *La procesion del Rocio* (1913) and *Danzas fantásticas* (1920).

He studied at Seville and Madrid, and later with Vincent d'Indy at the Schola Cantorum in Paris. He adopted conventional European forms more consistently than his contemporaries Albéniz, Granados, and Falla.

Works STAGE the operas *Margot* (1914) and *Jardin de oriente* (1923) (libretti by Gregorio Martínez Sierra); incidental music for Moreto's *La adúltera penitente* (1917), Martínez Sierra's *Navidad* (1916), and other plays.

ORCHESTRAL *La procesión del Rocio* (1913), *Danzas fantásticas*, *Sinfonía sevillana* (1920), *Ritmos*, and other works for orchestra.

CHAMBER string quartet (1911), piano quintet (1907), *Escena andaluza* for viola, piano, and string quartet; *Poema de una Sanluquena* for violin and piano; suites *Rincones sevillanos* and *Sevilla* and other works for piano; songs.

Turini, Francesco (c.1589–1656) Italian composer. His father Gregorio Turini was ➤ **cornett** player and composer to the Emperor Rudolph II in Prague, but died early, whereupon the emperor sent Turini to Venice and Rome to study music and later made him his chamber organist. He left Prague in 1624 to become cathedral organist at Brescia.

Works CHURCH MUSIC Masses and motets; madrigals, canons.

Türk, Daniel Gottlob (1750–1813) German theorist and composer. He settled at Halle in 1776 and became a central figure in the musical life of the town. He was famous as a teacher, and wrote treatises on organ and clavier playing, thorough bass, and temperament.

He studied under his father and under Gottfried Homilius at Dresden. Later he went to Leipzig University, where he became a pupil and friend of Johann Hiller, who procured him appointments as violinist at the Opera and the orchestral concerts. In 1776 he became organist at

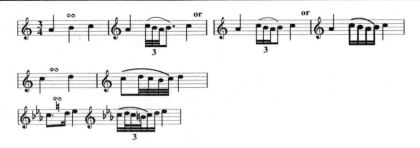

Various turns and their possible executions.

St Ulrich's Church at Halle, in 1779 music director of the university, and in 1787 organist at the Church of Our Lady.

Works OPERA *Pyramus und Thisbe* (1784).

CHORAL cantata *Die Hirten bei der Krippe zu Bethlehem* (1782).

WORKS FOR PIANO piano sonatas and pieces.

turn ornament in musical notation. It initially consisted of the note above the written note, followed by the note itself, then the note below the written note, and finally the note itself. In later performance practice the ornament was preceded with the written note. An **inverted turn** reverses the procedure, with the lower note played first.

Turnage, Mark-Anthony (1960–) English composer. He studied at the Royal College of Music with Oliver ➔ **Knussen** 1974–78, and with Henze and Schuller at Tanglewood in Philadelphia. His music admits a wide range of influences, including popular elements. His opera *Greek*, performed at Munich and Edinburgh in 1988, was a major success, and his other works include a saxophone concerto (1993), and *Three Screaming Popes* (1989), for orchestra.

He was composer-in-association with the City of Birmingham Symphony Orchestra 1989–93; and was featured composer at the 1986 Bath Festival and the 1987 Glasgow Musica Viva.

Works OPERA *Greek* (1988).

ORCHESTRAL *Night Dances* (1982) and *Kind of Blue* (1982); *Ekaya* (1984), *Three Screaming Popes* (1989), *Momentum* (1991), *Drowned Out* (1993); saxophone concerto *Your Rockaby* (1993).

CHAMBER *Let us Sleep Now* for chamber orchestra (1979–82); *After Dark* for wind quintet and string quintet (1983); *Lament for a Hanging Man* for soprano and ensemble (1983); *On all Fours* for ensemble (1985); *One Hand in Brooklyn Heights* for 16 mixed voices, *Release* for eight players (1987); *Kai* for cello and ensemble (1990); *Are you sure?* for string quartet (1991); *Leaving* for soloists, chorus, and ensemble (1991); *Set To* for brass ensemble (1992); *Blood*

on the Floor for ensemble (1994).

Turner, William (1651–1740) English tenor and composer. Most of his works were church music, but he also wrote songs and music for plays.

He was a chorister at Christ Church, Oxford, and later in the Chapel Royal in London, where he joined John Blow and Pelham Humfrey in composing the so-called 'club anthem'. He later became a singer successively at Lincoln Cathedral, St Paul's Cathedral, and Westminster Abbey. He received a PhD in music from Cambridge University in 1696. His youngest daughter, Ann Turner (died 1741), was a singer, and married the organist and composer John Robinson in 1716.

Works SACRED AND SECULAR MUSIC services, anthems (one for Queen Anne's coronation), and other church music.

STAGE masque *Presumptuous Love*; songs for Durfey's *A Fond Husband* (1677) and *Madam Fickle* (1676), Shadwell's *The Libertine* (1675), Settle's *Pastor fido* (1676), and other plays.

OTHER catches, songs.

Turn of the Screw, The opera in a prologue and two acts by Britten (libretto by Myfanwy Piper, after Henry James), produced in Venice on 14 September 1954, and in London, on 6 October 1954. The story begins as the Governess arrives at her new post to find children Flora and Miles in the power of two malevolent ghosts, Quint and Jessil. Eventually the evil spirits are banished, but Miles dies in the process.

Tusch (German 'fanfare') word probably derived from French *touche* and is thus related to the English tucket, a ➔ **flourish** for a trumpet.

tut device used in playing the ➔ **lute**: the damping of a note by a finger not used for stopping.

tutti (Italian 'all') in instrumental works, especially concertos, term used to indicate passages in which the orchestra plays, as opposed to the soloist.

Tveitt, (Nils) Geirr (1908–1981) Norwegian composer and pianist. After studying in Vienna

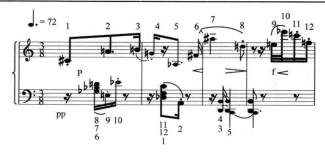

A passage from Schoenberg's 'Waltz' (5 Piano Pieces *op.23); the numbers represent the particular sequence of notes in the tone row.*

and Paris he toured Europe as a pianist. In his compositions he made effective use of Norwegian folk melodies.

Works STAGE the operas *Dragaredokko, Roald Amundsen,* and *Jeppe* (1964); three ballets.

ORCHESTRAL six piano concertos (1930–60), concerto for string quartet and orchestra (1933), violin concerto (1939), two harp concertos, two concertos for hardanger fiddle; four symphonies. CHAMBER two string quartets; 29 piano sonatas.

twelve-tone system or **twelve-note system** method of musical composition invented by Arnold ➜ **Schoenberg** about 1921 in which all twelve notes of the ➜ **chromatic scale** are arranged in a particular order of the composer's choice, without repeating any of the notes. Such an arrangement is called a 'series' or 'tone row'. The initial series may be transposed, divided, and otherwise mutated to provide a complete resource for all melodic and harmonic material in a work.

Twilight of the Gods, The music drama by Richard Wagner, the final part of the ➜ *Ring des Nibelungen* cycle. See ➜ **Götterdämmerung.**

Two Widows, *Dvě Vdovy* opera by Smetana (libretto by E Züngel, based on a French comedy by P J F Mallefille), produced at the Czech Theatre, Prague, on 27 March 1874. The story concerns Anežka, who falls for landowner Ladislav, but as a widow feels she must instead mourn her dead husband. However, when the Widow Karolina feigns a seduction of Ladislav, Anežka finally admits her love.

Tye, Christopher (c.1505–c.1572) English composer and poet. His music shows considerable acquaintance with contemporary continental composers, for example, the Mass for six voices *Euge bone.* He wrote a good deal of verse in his later years.

He became a lay clerk at King's College, Cambridge, in 1537. In 1543 he was appointed choir-

master at Ely Cathedral; he received a PhD in music from Cambridge University in 1545, and from Oxford in 1548. In 1561 he resigned his post at Ely and was succeeded by Robert White. Having been ordained, he accepted the living at Doddington-cum-Marche in the Isle of Ely, and for some time later held two other livings in the neighbourhood; but he had to resign them because of carelessness in the matter of payments due.

Works SACRED AND SECULAR MUSIC Masses, including *Euge bone* and *Western Wind*; motets, services, anthems, *The Actes of the Apostles* for four voices in English (metrical versions dedicated to Edward VI; 1533), In Nomines for instruments.

tyrolienne (French 'Tyrolese') country dance similar to the ➜ **Ländler** or slow waltz, supposed to be native of the mountain regions of the Tyrol. The dance was really an artificial growth introduced into ballets and operas and is loosely based on melodic figurations imitating various forms of yodel. Tyroliennes also became fashionable in the form of piano pieces and songs.

Tyrrell, John (1942–) English musicologist. He studied at Cape Town and Oxford universities. He was lecturer at Nottingham University in 1976, reader in opera studies in 1989, and was on the editorial staff of *New Grove* (1980) and *Opera Grove* (1992) dictionaries, with articles on Janáček and his operas. He published *Káta Kabanová* (1982), *Czech Opera* (1988), *Janáček's Operas: A Documentary Account* (1992), and *Intimate Letters: Janáček's Correspondence with Kamila Stösslova* (1994).

Tyrwhitt, Gerald English composer, painter, and author; see Lord ➜ **Berners.**

tzigane or **tsigane** a gypsy or musician of the bohemian world of Paris. It is also the title of a rhapsody for violin and piano by Maurice Ravel composed in 1924.

UC in piano music, an abbreviation for *una corda*, 'one string', indicating the use of the ➤ **soft pedal**.

Uccellini, Marco (c.1603–1680) Italian composer and violinist. He was master of instrumental music at the ducal court of Modena 1641–62 and maestro di cappella at Modena Cathedral 1647–65. He was then appointed maestro di cappella at the Farnese Court at Parma.

Works STAGE the opera *Gli eventi di Filandro ed Edessa* (1675); ballets *La nave d'Enea* (1673) and *Giove di Elide fulminato* (1677).

OTHER psalms and litanies for voices and instruments; *Composizioni armoniche* and *Sinfonici concerti* for violin and other instruments, *Sinfonie boscareocie* and sonatas for violin and bass.

ud short-necked Arabic lute, the direct ancestor of the European ➤ **lute**, whose name derives from *al 'ud* ('the lute'). Some instruments have frets and some are fretless. The strings are arranged in double courses (in pairs, with each pair tuned in unison). The five course ud is the most common and popular form among performers, and the instrument is used in a great variety of art, folk, and popular music.

See: ➤ **maqam**; ➤ **taqsim**.

Ugarte, Floro M(anuel) (1884–1975) Argentine composer. He studied with Fourdrain in Paris and became a private music teacher on his return in 1913 and professor at the National Conservatory at Buenos Aires 1924. He also became music director of the Teatro Colón, resigning in 1943.

Works OPERA *Saika* (1918) and others.

ORCHESTRAL symphonic poems and suites.

OTHER instrumental pieces.

Ugolini, Vincenzo (c.1580–1638) Italian composer. He was a pupil of Bernardino Nassini. He was maestro di cappella at the church of Santa Maria Maggiore in Rome, 1603–09. He then retired after a severe illness, but in 1610 became maestro di cappella at Benevento Cathedral and returned in 1616 to Rome, where after some other appointments he became Soriano's successor in the Julian Chapel in 1620 and maestro di cappella of San Luigi dei Francesi in 1631, a post he had held 1616–20.

Works VOCAL Masses, motets, psalms and other church music, madrigals.

Ugolino of Orvieto (c.1380–1457) Italian composer and theorist. His *Declaratio musicae discipline* (1435) is mainly a practical handbook for the performing musician of his day.

Uhland, Johann Ludwig (1787–1862) German poet. He was the author of ballads and lyrics in the Romantic tradition.

See also ➤ *Black Knight* (Elgar); ➤ **Humperdinck** (*Glück von Edenhall*); ➤ **Schoeck** (songs); ➤ **Schumann** (*Glück von Edenhall*); Richard ➤ **Strauss** (*Schloss am Meer*).

Uhlig, Theodor (1822–1853) German violinist, composer, and author of theoretical works. He was a pupil of Schneider at Dessau, entered the royal orchestra at Dresden in 1841, and became a close friend of Richard Wagner there. He published articles in Wagner's praise and had an extensive correspondence with him.

ukulele musical instrument, a small four-stringed Hawaiian guitar, of Portuguese origin. It is easy to play; music for ukulele is written in a form of ➤ **tablature** showing finger positions on a chart of the fingerboard.

Ulisse opera by Dallapiccola (libretto by composer, after Homer, 1959–68), produced at the Deutsche Oper, Berlin, on 29 September 1968, conducted by Maazel. The British Broadcasting Corporation (BBC) studio performance was on 20 September 1969. Ulysses meets Princess Nausicaa and recounts his story. He then spends a year with the enchantress Circe before visiting the Sirens and Hades on the way home to his wife Penelope.

Ullmann, Viktor (1898–1944) Austro-Hungarian composer. He was imprisoned in Theresienstadt concentration camp, where he wrote a one-act opera, *Der Kaiser von Atlantis* (1943), about a tyrannical monarch who outlaws death; it was first performed at Amsterdam in 1975. In October 1944 he was transferred to Auschwitz, where he died.

He studied with Schoenberg in Vienna, and was later a theatre conductor at Aussig and a music teacher in Prague.

Works OPERA *Peer Gynt* (after Ibsen), *Der Sturz des Antichrist*, and *Der Kaiser von Atlantis* (1943).

ORCHESTRAL variations and double fugue on a theme by Schoenberg for orchestra.

CHAMBER octet, two string quartets.

Ultimo giorno di Pompei, L', The Last Day of Pompeii opera by Pacini (libretto by Tottola, not founded on Bulwer-Lytton's novel, which was not then published), produced at the Teatro San Carlo, Naples, on 19 November 1825. Rejected by Ottavia, wife of Sallustio, Diomede attempts to revenge himself on her, but all are engulfed by Vesuvius.

Ultimos Ritos, Last Rites oratorio by Tavener for soloists, five speakers, chorus, and orchestra (1972), first performed in Haarlem on 22 June 1974.

Ulysses opera by Keiser (libretto by F M Lersner), produced (in German) in Copenhagen, at court, in November 1722.

Cantata by Seiber for tenor, chorus, and orchestra (text by composer, after Joyce) (1946–47), first performed in London on 27 May 1949.

See also ➜ *Circe and Penelope*.

Umlauf, Ignaz (1746–1796) Austrian composer. He was appointed director of Joseph II's new national *Singspiel* theatre in 1778, the inaugural work being his *Die Bergknappen*.

He became a viola player in the orchestra of the court opera in 1772, and on the foundation of the national *Singspiel* theatre by Joseph II in 1778 became its director. From 1789 he was Salieri's deputy as Kapellmeister of the court chapel. He also took part with Mozart in the performance of Handel's oratorios organized by Gottfried van Swieten. He was the father of Michael ➜ Umlauf.

Works SINGSPIELE *Die Insel der Liebe* (1722), *Die Bergknappen* (1778), *Die Apotheke*, *Die schöne Schusterin oder die pucegefarbenen Schuhe* (1779), *Das Irrlicht* (1782), *Welches ist die beste Nation?*, *Die glücklichen Jäger* (1786), *Die Ringe der Liebe* (sequel to Grétry's *Zémire et Azor*).

OTHER incidental music for *Der Oberamtmann und die Soldaten* (after Calderón); church music.

Umlauf, Michael (1781–1842) Austrian composer and conductor. He was director of music at the court theatres in Vienna. On and after the revival of *Fidelio* in 1814 he assisted Beethoven, who was then too deaf to hear the orchestra, to conduct some of his major works.

He studied under his father, Ignaz ➜ Umlauf, then became a violinist at the Opera and was conductor of the two court theatres 1810–25 and again from 1840.

Works STAGE the opera *Das Wirtshaus in Granada* (1812), play with music *Der Grenadier* (1812); twelve ballets.

OTHER church music; piano sonatas.

una corda (Italian 'one string') in piano music, a direction used to indicate the use of the ➜ **soft pedal**, which so shifts the hammers that they touch only one or two strings for each note, instead of two or three.

Una cosa rara, o sia Bellezza ed onestà, A Rare Thing, or Beauty and Honesty opera by Martin y Soler (libretto by L da Ponte, based on a story by L V de Guevara), produced at the Burgtheater, Vienna, on 17 November 1786. Mozart quotes an air from it in the finale of the second act of *Don Giovanni*. Lilla remains faithful to Lubino in spite of attentions from Don Lisergo, Prince Giovanni, and Corrado.

Unanswered Question the first of Two Contemplations for orchestra by Charles Ives (no. 2 *Central Park in the Dark*). First performed in New York on 11 May 1946 (composed in 1906).

Undine opera by E T A Hoffmann (libretto by the composer), produced in Berlin at the Schauspielhaus on 3 August 1816. Water nymph Undine can gain a soul by marrying a mortal. She meets and falls in love with the knight Huldbrand, but when he changes allegiance to Berthalda, Undine kisses him, drowning him.

Opera by Lortzing (libretto by composer, based on Fouqué), produced in Magdeburg on 21 April 1845. Similar to Hoffmann's version, but Huldebrand is called Hugo von Ringstetten.

Ballet in three acts by Henze (choreographed by Ashton), (1956–57), produced at Covent Garden, London, on 27 October 1958, conducted by Henze, with Fonteyn. *Wedding Music* from the ballet arranged for wind orchestra 1957; two orchestral suites 1958; *Undine, Trois pas des Tritons* for orchestra, performed in Rome on 10 January 1959, conductor Celibidache.

unequal temperament a system of tuning, especially on old keyboard instruments, in which some of the accidentals were treated as sharps according to just intonation and some as flats (for instance, F sharp, not G flat; B flat, not A sharp). An attempt was thus made to make some of the more frequently used keys come nearer to just intonation than is possible in the tempered scale of the modern piano, but the result was also that the more extreme sharp and flat keys were out of tune. This is one of the chief reasons why these keys were rarely used by early composers.

unequal voices in music, term used to describe a composition for several voices which do not lie within the same compass.

'Unfinished' Symphony symphony in B minor by Franz ➤ Schubert, written in October/November 1822. It was planned as a four-movement work, though only the first two movements, and a sketch of the scherzo, survive. In the original *Gesamtausgabe* it is called no. 8, but is more often referred to simply as the 'Unfinished'.

Some authorities believe that the finale was written, but used a year later as the basis of Schubert's B minor Entr'acte in *Rosamunde*. After the Styrian Music Society, through Josef and Anselm Hüttenbrenner, had awarded Schubert their Diploma of Honour in 1823, he promised to send in return 'one of my symphonies at the earliest opportunity'. Later he handed to Josef the score of the two completed movements. Anselm Hüttenbrenner made an arrangement of the work for piano duet in 1853, but made no attempt to get it performed. Johann Herbeck, who gave the first performance in Vienna in December 1865, coaxed the score out of Anselm with a promise to perform one of the latter's own works.

Schubert was the first composer to associate a tragic tone and intense personal feeling with B minor in a substantial symphonic work; in this the 'Unfinished' looks forward to late Romantic works such as Tchaikovsky's 'Pathetique' Symphony and Dvořák's Cello Concerto.

unfolding in ➤ voice-leading analysis, an interval is unfolded if two notes are presented consecutively in the same voice in the music, but can be considered at a deeper structural level to occur simultaneously (that is, to be separate voices within a single harmony). Very often, the interval between the two notes is filled in by passing notes or an arpeggiation.

Unger, (Gustav) Hermann (1886–1958) German composer. He studied in Munich and later with Reger at Meiningen. He taught for more than 30 years in Cologne, and wrote books on Reger and Bruckner, and a treatise on harmony (1946).

Works STAGE the operas *Richmondis* (1928) and *De Zauberhandschuh*; incidental music for Shakespeare's *Tempest*, Kleist's *Penthesilea*, Hofmannsthal's *Der Tor und der Tod*, Hauptmann's *Hannele*, Unruh's *Heinrich aus Andernach* and many other plays.

CHORAL *Der Gott und die Bajadere* (Goethe) and *Old German Songs* for chorus and orchestra.

OTHER two symphonies; chamber music; songs.

unison term used to describe music in which all musicians play or sing the same notes without harmony. Strictly, unison implies that all musi-

cians sound the same pitch in the same octave, but it is also used for the same pitch doubled at the octave.

un poco (Italian 'a little') qualifying musical direction used where any indication of tempo or expression is to be applied in moderation. Often used in the abbreviation form *poco*.

Unterbrochene Opferfest, Das, **The Interrupted Sacrificial Feast** opera by Winter (libretto by F X Huber), produced at the Kärntnertortheater, Vienna, on 14 June 1796. During an Inca sacrifice Elvira and Villacumar unsuccessfully attempt to make Murneg, lover of Myrha, the victim.

upbeat or **anacrusis** or **arsis** in music, at the beginning of certain pieces, one or several notes preceding the first full bar of music; also, the last or the weak beat of a bar, analogous to the upstroke of a conductor's hand. The opposite is downbeat.

up bow in the playing of string instruments, the motion of the bow in the direction from the point to the heel.

Uribe Holguín, Guillermo (1880–1971) Colombian composer. He studied at home and with Vincent d'Indy at the Schola Cantorum in Paris. In 1910 he became director of the National Conservatory at Bogotá, where he founded and conducted symphonic concerts.

Works ORCHESTRAL eleven symphonies (1916–59), *3 Danzas*, *Carnavelesca*, *Marche funèbre*, *Marche de fête*, *Suite típica*, all for orchestra; concert and *Villanesca* for piano and orchestra, two violin concertos.

CHORAL Requiem.

CHAMBER ten string quartets, piano quartet, two piano quintets; five violin and piano sonatas, two cello and piano sonatas.

OTHER piano pieces, including 300 folk dances; songs.

Urio, Francesco Antonio (c.1632–1719 or later) Italian priest and composer. A Franciscan monk, he was maestro di cappella at the church of SS Apostoli in Rome in 1690, seven years later at the Frari church in Venice, and finally from 1715 at S Francesco in Milan.

Works CHORAL Te Deum (once attributed to Handel, who borrowed from it for his *Dettingen Te Deum*, *Saul*, *Israel in Egypt*, and *L'Allegro*); oratorios.

OTHER VOCAL motets and psalms for voices and instruments.

Urtext (German 'original text') an edition of music which tries to capture the original intentions of the composer, minimizing editorial interpretation as much as possible. *Urtext* editions are usually based upon the composer's sketches and manuscripts, as well as original and early editions of the works.

Usper, Francesco (before 1570–1641), adopted name of **Francesco Sponga** Italian priest, organist, and composer. In 1614 he became organist at the Church of San Salvatore at Venice, in 1621 he deputized for Giovanni Battista Grillo (died 1622) as organist at St Mark's, and in 1627 he became principal of the school of St John the Evangelist.

Works CHORAL Masses, motets, psalms for voices with instruments, vesper psalms for four to eight voices and bass, some for double choir; *La battaglia* for voices and instruments, madrigals; *ricercari* and *arie francesi* in four parts.

Ussachevsky, Vladimir (Aleksei) (1911–1990) US composer of Russian parentage. He moved to the USA in 1930 and studied with Hanson at the Eastman School. He was professor at Columbia University, New York, 1964–80, and collaborated with Luening in pioneering the development of electronic music.

Works ELECTRONIC (some with Luening) *Celebration* for string orchestra and electronic valve instruments (1980); *Sonic Contours* for tape (1952), *Incantation* for tape (1953), *Rhapsodic Variations* for orchestra and tape (1954).

CHORAL *Creation Prologue* for four chorus and tape (1961), *Missa brevis* for soprano, chorus and brass (1972).

Ustvolskaya, Galina (1919–   ) Russian composer. Employing the minimum of means, her music has drawn from serialism and from local Russian traditions; but ultimately her style is completely independent: Dmitri Shostakovich commented that he felt under her influence and not the reverse.

Ustvolskaya studied 1939–50 at the Leningrad Conservatory with Shostakovich, and was defended by him when she was criticized by Stalinist authorities.

Works ORCHESTRAL five symphonies: no. 1 for two descant voices and orchestra (1955); no. 2 'True

and Eternal Bliss' for boy speaker and orchestra (1979); no. 3 'Jesus, Messiah, Save Us' with boy speaker (1983); no. 4 'Prayer' with trumpet, tamtam, and piano (1987); no. 5 'Amen' with male speaker (1990).

CHAMBER Trio for clarinet, violin, and piano (1949); Octet (1950); *Composition I–III* (1970–75); six piano sonatas (1947–88).

Ut the old name for the note C, still used in France, but elsewhere replaced by Do. For its origin, see ➤ solmization.

Utendal, Alexander (c.1535–1581) Flemish composer. He learnt music as a choirboy in the Archduke Ferdinand's chapel in Prague, and in 1566 became a singer in his chapel at Innsbruck. In c.1572 he became second Kapellmeister. On the death of Scandello at Dresden in 1580 he was offered the post of Kapellmeister to the Saxon court, but declined it.

Works CHORAL three Masses, motets, *Sacrae cantiones*.

OTHER secular French and German songs.

Uthal opera by Méhul (libretto by J M B B de Saint-Victor, based on Ossian), produced at the Opéra-Comique, Paris, on 17 May 1806. The work is scored without violins. Malvina's husband Uthal deposes her father Larmor as tribal chief: she is torn between love for them both. Larmor's troops defeat Uthal and Malvina joins him in exile before being pardoned.

Utrecht Te Deum and Jubilate work by Handel, composed for the celebration of the Peace of Utrecht and performed in London at St Paul's Cathedral on 7 July 1713.

Utrenja, Morning Service work in two parts by Penderecki, for soloists, choruses, and orchestra: 1. *The Entombment of Christ* (first performed at Altenberg Cathedral on 8 April 1970); 2. *Resurrection of Christ* (first performed at Münster Cathedral on 28 May 1971).

Vaccai, Nicola (1790–1848) Italian composer. Of his 17 operas, only two were successful: *Zadig ed Astartea* and *Giulietta e Romeo* (both 1825). He taught singing and was director of the Milan Conservatory 1838–44. In 1832 he published a well-known singing tutor, *Metodo pratico di cento italiano per camera*.

Vaccai went to school at Pesaro, then studied law in Rome, but at the age of 17 or 18 gave it up for music and studied counterpoint with Giuseppe Jannaconi (also known as Giannacconi or Jannacconi; c.1740–1816). In 1811 he studied with Giovanni Paisiello at Naples and in 1815 produced his first opera there. He then lived at Venice for seven years, produced two operas there, afterwards taught singing at Trieste and Vienna, in 1824 produced two operas at Parma and Turin and in 1825 had his greatest success, at Milan, with *Giuletta e Romeo*, after Shakespeare. In 1829–31 he lived in Paris and afterwards briefly in London, which he visited again 1833–34. In 1838 he succeeded Francesco Basili as director of the Milan Conservatory, retiring to Pesaro in 1844.

Works OPERA *I solitari di Scozia* (1815), *Pietro il grande* (1824), *La pastorella feudataria*, *Giulietta e Romeo*, *Zadig ed Astartea*, *Marco Visconti* (1838), *Giovanna Grey* (1836), *Virginia*, *Giovanna d'Arco* (1827), *La sposa di Messina* (both after Schiller), and others.

SACRED AND SECULAR MUSIC church music; cantata on the death of Malibran and others; *Ariette per camera* for voice and piano.

Vaet, Jacobus (1529–1567) Flemish composer. He was choirmaster to Maximilian, King of Bohemia, in the 1560s and succeeded Jachet Buus as chief music director in Vienna in 1564, when his patron became the Emperor Maximilian II.

Works SACRED AND SECULAR MUSIC Masses, motets, Magnificats, Te Deum for eight voices and other church music; chansons.

vagans (Latin 'wandering, vagrant') in five-part 15th- and 16th-century ➤ polyphonic music, name sometimes given to the fifth part, which duplicates in range one of the basic four voices:

treble, alto, tenor, and bass. The voice required within one *quintus* part-book, though usually a second tenor, may vary from piece to piece; hence, the name *vagans*.

vagrant chord term coined by Arnold Schoenberg (as *vagierender Akkord*) to describe chromatic chords which confuse or lead away from any definite key-centre.

Vaisseau-fantôme, Le, **The Phantom Vessel** opera by French composer Louis Dietsch (libretto by B H Révoil and P H Foucher, founded on Wagner's scenario for *Der* ➤ *fliegende Holländer*/*The Flying Dutchman*), produced at the Paris Opéra on 9 November 1842.

Vakula the Smith, Russian ***Vakula Kuznets*** opera by Tchaikovsky (libretto by Y P Polonsky, based on Gogol's *Christmas Eve*), first produced in St Petersburg, on 6 December 1876; a revised version entitled *Cherevichki*/*The Little Boots* was produced in Moscow, on 31 January 1887. It is also known as *Oxana's Caprices*. At Oxana's request, Vakula flies on the back of the Devil to St Petersburg, to claim from the Tsaritsa a pair of high-heeled leather boots.

Valen, (Olav) Fartein (1887–1952) Norwegian composer. He studied languages at Oslo University, but later entered the Conservatory, finishing his studies with Max Reger at the Hochschule für Musik in Berlin. In 1925–35 he worked in the music department of the library of Oslo University, but then received a government grant for composition.

Works CHORAL three sets of motets and other choral works.

ORCHESTRAL five symphonies (1937–51), *Sonetto di Michelangelo*, *To Hope* (after Keats), *Pastorale*, *Epithalamion*, *Le cimetière marin* (after P Valéry), *La isla en las calmas*, *Ode to Solitude* for orchestra; piano concerto, violin concerto (1940); six works for soprano and orchestra.

CHAMBER two string quartets (1928–31), piano trio, serenade for five wind instruments; violin and piano sonata; two sonatas, variations, and other works for piano; organ music; songs.

Valentini, Giuseppe (c.1680–after 1759) Italian composer. He was in the service of the Grand Duke of Tuscany at Florence from about 1735. His most characteristic music is in his florid violin sonatas.

Works OPERA *La costanza in amore* (1715).

CHORAL oratorios *Absalone* (1705) and *S Alessio* (1733).

ORCHESTRAL AND CHAMBER Concerti grossi; symphony, *Bizarrie*, twelve fantasies, *Idee per camera*, and twelve sonatas for three string instruments and bass; chamber sonatas and *Alletamenti* for violin, cello, and bass.

Valentini, Pier Francesco (c.1570–1654) Italian composer. He was a pupil of Giovanni Maria Nanino in Rome. He was best known for music involving elaborate ➔ **counterpoint**, for example his canon for 96 voices.

Works OPERA (favole/fables) *La mitra* (1620) and *La transformazione di Dafne* (1623).

SACRED AND SECULAR MUSIC motets, litanies, and other church music; *Canzonetti spirituali* and *Musiche spirituali* for the Nativity; madrigals and canons; *canzoni* and arias for one–two voices.

Valkyrie, The, German **Die Walküre** music drama by Richard Wagner, part of the ➔ **Ring des Nibelungen** cycle. See ➔ **Walküre, Die**.

Vallotti, Francesco Antonio (1697–1780) Italian composer and theorist. He became third organist at the basilica of Sant'Antonio at Padua in 1722 and maestro di cappella in 1730. He wrote a learned treatise, 'Della scienza teorica e pratica della moderna musica'.

Works CHURCH MUSIC motets, Requiem for Tartini, and other church music.

Valls, Francisco (1665–1747) Spanish composer. He was controversial in his day for his use of dissonance (a combination of tones displeasing to the ear) in church music, as in the Mass *Scala aretina*, for which he is best known today.

After posts at Mataró and Gerona, Valls moved to Barcelona in 1696; he was maestro de capilla at the cathedral there from 1709. He retired in 1740 to write a treatise called *Mapa armónico*, in which he defended the use of dissonance in sacred music as employed by Spanish composers against the more orthodox views of Alessandro ➔ **Scarlatti**.

Works SACRED AND SECULAR MUSIC Masses, including *Scala aretina* for eleven voices and orchestra (1702), *Regalis* (for the King of Portugal, 1740), and ten others; 22 responsories, 16 Magnificats, twelve psalms, two Misereres, about 35 motets, about 120 *villancicos*.

valse French spelling of ➔ **waltz**.

Valse, La choreographic poem for orchestra by Ravel. Finished in 1920, it was first performed in Paris on 12 December 1920. The work imitates or parodies the style of Johann Strauss's waltzes and has several times served for ballets.

Valses nobles et sentimentales set of waltzes by Maurice ➔ **Ravel**, composed for piano in 1911 and afterwards scored for orchestra. The title is derived from Franz Schubert, who published two sets: *Valses nobles*, D969, and *Valses sentimentales*, D779. Ravel's work was turned into a ballet, *Adélaïde, ou Le Langage des fleurs*, first produced in Paris on 22 April 1912.

valve in brass wind instruments, a mechanism for diverting the air flow through an extension loop, to vary the length and thus the pitch of the instrument. Most valve instruments are of the piston type, but older French horns have rotary valves operated by levers.

Vampyr, Der, The Vampire opera by Lindpaintner (libretto by C M Heigel, based on John William Polidori's story, published in 1819 and thought to be by Byron, and more directly on a French melodrama by Charles Nodier, P F A Carmouche, and A de Jouffroy), produced in Stuttgart on 21 September 1828.

Opera by Heinrich ➔ **Marschner** (libretto by W A Wohlbrück, based on the sources above), produced in Leipzig on 29 March 1828. In the story, the newly created vampire Lord Ruthven must sacrifice three girls to postpone Satan's claim on his soul. Janthe and Emmy fall victim, but Malvina escapes the fangs.

Vanessa opera by Samuel ➔ **Barber** (libretto by Menotti), produced at the Metropolitan Opera, New York, on 15 January 1958. In the story, Vanessa marries Anatol, son of her former lover of the same name, in spite of the fact that her niece Erika is pregnant by him.

Vanhal, Johann Baptist (1739–1813) Bohemian composer. He wrote about 100 symphonies and 100 quartets; his works were performed by Mozart and Haydn.

Vanhal went to Vienna in 1760 and studied there with Karl Dittersdorf; he travelled in Italy 1769–71, and lived on the estate of Count Erdödy in Hungary 1772–80. Back in Vienna, he supported himself as a freelance composer.

Works OPERA two, *Demofoonte* and *Il trionfo di Clelia* (both lost).

CHURCH MUSIC over 50 Masses and much other church music.

ORCHESTRAL AND CHAMBER 70 symphonies; about 100 string quartets; many caprices and programmatic works for keyboard.

Varèse, Edgard Victor Achille Charles (1883–1965) French composer. He left Paris for New York in 1916 where he co-founded the New Symphony Orchestra in 1919 with the French-born US harpist Carlos Salzédo (1885–1961) to promote modern and pre-classical music. His work was experimental and often dissonant, combining electronic sounds with orchestral instruments.

Renouncing the values of ➤ **tonality**, he discovered new resources of musical expression in the percussion sonorities of *Ionisation* (1929–31), the swooping sound of two ➤ **theremins** in *Hyperprism* (1933–34), and the combination of taped and live instrumental sounds in *Déserts* (1950–54).

variation one of the earliest musical forms. A theme or melody is first presented in a straightforward manner and then repeated as often as the composer wishes but each time it is varied in one or more ways. The theme is usually easily recognizable; it may be a popular tune or – as a gesture of respect – the work of a fellow composer; for example, Johannes Brahms's *Variations on a Theme by Haydn* (1873), based on a theme known as the *St Antony Chorale*, although it may also be an original composition. The principle of variations has been used in larger-scale and orchestral works by modern composers, for example Arnold Schoenberg's *Variations for Orchestra* (1928).

Variations on a Theme by Haydn set of variations by Johannes ➤ **Brahms** for orchestra, Op. 56a, or for two pianos, Op. 56b, on a theme called the *St Anthony Chorale* from a Divertimento for wind instruments, attributed formerly to Joseph Haydn, where it is also treated in variation form. The first performance of the orchestral version took place in Vienna, Austria, on 2 November 1873.

Variations on a Theme of Paganini, Polish *Warlacje na temat Paganiniego* work by Witold ➤ **Lutosławski** originally for two pianos (1941), later reworked for piano and orchestra (1978). The familiar theme, in A minor, from the 19th-century virtuoso violinist Niccolò ➤ **Paganini's** *capricci* (studies) for unaccompanied violin, is the same as that used by Johannes Brahms and Sergei Rachmaninov for their respective ➤ *Paganini Variations*.

Variations on a Theme of Frank Bridge work for string orchestra by Benjamin Britten, composed in 1937 for the Boyd Neel Orchestra and performed at Salzburg, on 27 August 1937. The theme is from Frank Bridge's Idyll no. 2 for string quartet.

Varvoglis, Mario (1885–1967) Greek composer. He studied painting at first, then music in Paris with Xavier Leroux and Caussade from

1904 and d'Indy from 1913, having his first successes there. He returned to Greece in 1922, became professor at the Athens Conservatory, and in 1924 at the Hellenic Conservatory, of which he became director with Evangelatos in 1947.

Works STAGE MUSIC the one-act opera *The Afternoon of Love* (1935, produced 1944); classical Greek plays.

ORCHESTRAL AND CHAMBER *Pastoral Suite* (1912), *Meditation*, and incidental music to prelude, chorale, and fugue on BACH for strings; chamber music; piano works; songs.

Vasquez, Juan Spanish composer; see Juan ➤ **Vázquez**.

***Vaterländischer Künstlerverein* (German 'Patriotic Artists' Association')** title of Part II of the variations commissioned by Cappi and Anton Diabelli (1781–1858) of Vienna to be written by Beethoven and others on a waltz by Diabelli. Beethoven eventually wrote 33 variations instead of one, and they were published separately as Part I in 1824, and Part II following with contributions by Czerny, Hummel, Kalkbrenner, Conradin Kreutzer, Liszt (aged 11), Moscheles, Franz Xaver Mozart, the Archduke Rudolph, Schubert, Sechter, and c.40 others.

vaudeville (French) form of light music stage entertainment. In 18th-century France, vaudevilles were at first satirical songs, then songs with words set to popular tunes used in comedies with music (*comédies mêlées de vaudevilles*), as in the English ballad opera (songs specially composed being called *ariettes*). In time vaudevilles in France became songs sung at the end of spoken stage pieces, taken up verse-by-verse by all the characters and sometimes by the chorus, and this device was sometimes introduced into opera in France and elsewhere, as for example at the end of Rousseau's *Devin du village* and Mozart's *Entführung aus dem Serail*. The next step from this was to call a whole light music stage entertainment a vaudeville.

The term has various meanings and is of uncertain origin. The French composer and publisher Adrien Le Roy, in his *Airs de Cour* of 1571, said that such songs were formerly called *voix de ville*, 'town voices'; but the form *vau de Vire* is also known, and may have referred to the valley of Vire in Normandy, the home of Olivier Basselin (c.1400–50), a composer of such songs.

Vaughan Williams, Ralph (1872–1958) English composer. His style was late-Romantic tonal/modal, and his works contain many references to the English countryside through the use of folk themes. Among his works are the orchestral *Fantasia on a Theme by Thomas Tallis* (1910); the opera *Sir John in Love* (1929), featuring the Elizabethan song 'Greensleeves'; and nine symphonies (1909–57).

Vaughan Williams was born at Down Ampney, Gloucestershire, the son of a clergyman. He was educated at Charterhouse School in 1887–90, and Trinity College, Cambridge, 1892–95. The years in between were devoted to study at the Royal College of Music in London, where he returned for another year after Cambridge. He learnt the piano and organ but was always determined to be a composer. On leaving the Royal College of Music in 1896 he became organist at South Lambeth Church in London and saved enough money to gain further experience by study abroad, first at the Akademie der Künste in Berlin, under Max Bruch, and in 1909 with Maurice Ravel in Paris. In 1901 he completed a PhD at Cambridge.

In 1904 he joined the Folk-Song Society (established in 1898) and began to take an active interest in the recovery and study of old country tunes, collecting some in Norfolk. His first public success was with *Toward the Unknown Region* at the Leeds Festival in 1907 and this was followed in 1909 by his first great and characteristic compositions, the *Wasps* overture, the song cycle *On Wenlock Edge*, and *A Sea Symphony* (the first to use a chorus throughout). From 1906 he was editor of the *English Hymnal*, and this resulted in one of his best-loved works, the *Fantasia on a Theme of Thomas Tallis* for strings (1910). The sense of religious wonder evoked by this music was later enhanced in such biblically-inspired works as the masque *Job* (1931) and the opera *The Pilgrim's Progress* (1925–51).

In World War I he served in the army in Macedonia and France. After the war he was appointed professor of composition at the Royal College of Music. The English pastoral tradition was revived in his 3rd symphony, the *Pastoral* (1921), and in the next few years he produced a series of sacred works such as the Mass in G minor, *Sancta Civitas*, and *Benedicite*. His two best-known symphonies, nos 4 and 5, were composed between 1934 and 1943. The last four symphonies continued the composer's spiritual quest, already begun in *The Pilgrim's Progress*. Although Vaughan Williams's compositions are usually considered as pastoral, through the use of folk melodies, he was aware of contemporary musical developments and often included more dissonance in his later works, though in a colouristic, watered-down way.

Works OPERA AND DRAMA *The Pilgrim's Progress* (after Bunyan, begun 1925, premiered 1951); masque *Job* (on Blake's illustrations, 1931); incidental music for Aristophanes' *Wasps* (1909); film music, including *Scott of the Antarctic* (1948).

CHORAL Mass in G minor, Anglican services; (with orchestra) *Toward the Unknown Region* (Whitman), *A Sea Symphony* (no. 1, Whitman, 1903–09), *Five Mystical Songs* (Herbert, 1911), *Flos Campi* (Song of Solomon, 1925), *Five Tudor Portraits* (Skelton, 1935), *Serenade to Music* for 16 solo voices and orchestra (from Shakespeare's *Merchant of Venice*, 1938).

ORCHESTRAL *In the Fen Country*, Fantasia on a Theme by Thomas Tallis for strings (1910), *A London Symphony* (no. 2, 1912–13), *A Pastoral Symphony* (no. 3, 1921), symphonies nos 4–9 (1937, 1943, 1947, 1952, 1955, 1957), *Five Variants of 'Dives and Lazarus'* for strings and harps (1939); *The Lark Ascending* (after Meredith) for violin and orchestra (1914), concerto for oboe and strings (1944), tuba concerto (1954).

CHAMBER AND SONGS *On Wenlock Edge* (Housman) for tenor, string quartet, and piano (1909); many songs, including *Songs of Travel* (Stevenson, 1901–04); ten William Blake songs for high voice and oboe; folk-song arrangements.

Vautor, Thomas (lived early 17th century) English composer. He was educated at Lincoln College, Oxford, where he took the BMus in 1616. He was for many years in the service of Sir George Villiers, father of the later Duke of Buckingham, at Brooksby, and later of his widow at Goadby. He published one book of madrigals (1619–20).

Vázquez, Juan (c.1510–c.1560) Spanish composer. He was maestro di capella at Badajoz Cathedral 1545–50, and was later in the service of Don Antonio de Zuñiga. He was an important exponent of the Spanish song form known as the *villancico*, and also wrote church music.

Vecchi, Lorenzo (1564–1628) Italian composer. He was a pupil at San Petronio at Bologna, where he became maestro di cappella in 1605. He wrote Masses, a Requiem, and other church music.

Vecchi, Orazio (Tiberio) (1550–1605) Italian composer. As well as sacred music, he wrote canzonettes and madrigals, and was celebrated as a composer of entertainments.

Vecchi was born in Modena. He was maestro di cappella at Salò Cathedral from 1581, at Modena from 1584, and at Reggio Emilia in 1586, then became a canon at Correggio and an archdeacon in 1591. Wishing to devote himself to music, he returned to Modena as maestro di cappella in 1593, and then became maestro di cappella at the d'Este court in 1598. He became famous, being summoned to the court of the Emperor Rudolph II at one time and invited to compose music for the king of Poland. In 1604 his pupil Geminiano Capi-Lupi intrigued successfully against him and supplanted him in his post.

His works include *L'Amfiparnaso* comprising 14 madrigals for five voices, with a dramatic plot set to a *commedia dell'arte* text. The characters' parts are not acted, but are sung by concerted voices in the madrigal style.

Works SECULAR AND SACRED MUSIC madrigal comedy *L'Amfiparnaso* (1597); Masses, motets, Lamentations, and other church music; madrigals, canzonets.

Vecchi, Orfeo (c.1550–1604) Italian composer. He was maestro di cappella of the church of Santa Maria della Scala at Milan from c.1590.

Works SACRED AND SECULAR MUSIC Masses, motets, psalms, Magnificats, *Cantiones sacrae*, and other church music; madrigals.

Veilchen, Das, The Violet song by Mozart, K476; it was his only setting of a poem by Goethe, composed on 8 June 1785.

Vejvanovský, Pavel Josef (c.1655–1693) Moravian composer and trumpeter. Many of his Masses, offertories, and motets feature technically fluent parts for trumpets, trombones, and cornets.

He studied at Opava and from 1661 worked at Kroměříž, where he composed and played the trumpet at the court. Much of his music shows the influence of Heinrich Schmelzer and other composers at the court of Emperor Leopold I in Vienna.

Velluti, Giovanni Battista (1780–1861) Italian soprano ➤ castrato (one of the last). He made his first stage appearance at Forlì in 1800, and then appeared in Naples, Milan, and Venice in operas by Guglielmi, Cimarosa, and Mayr. In 1812 he visited Vienna. He created Arsace in Rossini's *Aureliano in Palmira* (Milan, 1813) and Armando in Meyerbeer's *Il crociato in Egitto* (Venice, 1824), and sang the latter role on his first visit to London in 1825.

veloce (Italian 'quick, swift, rapid, fluent') musical direction that does not so much indicate increased speed, though it may include that meaning, as smoothness of rapid figuration.

Vendredis, Les, The Fridays set of pieces for string quartet by Artsibushev, Blumenfeld, Borodin, Glazunov, Kopylov, Liadov, M d'Osten-Sacken, Rimsky-Korsakov, Sokolov, and Wihtol, written for Friday chamber-music reunions in St Petersburg.

Venegas de Henestrosa, Luis (c.1510–c.1557 or later) Spanish composer. He published a book of variations and transcriptions in a special ➤ tablature suitable for keyboard instruments, harp, vihuela, or guitar (*Libro de cifra nueva*, 1557). The notation was later used by Antonio de Cabezón (1510–1566) and Francisco Correa de Arauxo (1576–1654).

venite music based on the text of Psalm 95, *Venite, exultemus Domino* (Latin 'O come let us sing unto the Lord'). It is sung at Anglican ➤ matins, either in ➤ plainsong or to a composed setting. It is used as a prelude to the psalms.

Ventadorn, Bernart de French troubadour. Forty-five of his poems and 19 of his melodies have been preserved.

Vento, Mattia (1735–1776) Italian composer. He produced operas in Rome and Venice, and settled in London in 1763, staging six Italian operas and several ➤ pasticcios there.

Works OPERA *La finta semplice* (1759), *La Egiziana* (1763), *Leucippo* (1764), *Demofoonte*, *Sofonisba* (1766), *La conquista del vello d'orco* (1767), *Artaserse* (1771), *Il bacio* (1776), *La Vestale*.

OTHER cantata *Threnodia augustilia* (Goldsmith) on the death of George III's mother; trio sonatas; violin sonatas; keyboard music; songs.

Venus and Adonis masque by John ➤ Blow (librettist unknown), produced at court in London, c.1682. In the story, Venus persuades Adonis to join the hunt but he returns mortally wounded, gored by a boar.

Vénus et Adonis opera by Desmarets (libretto by Jean Baptiste Rousseau), produced at the Paris Opéra on 17 March 1697.

Vêpres siciliennes, Les, The Sicilian Vespers opera by Verdi (libretto by Scribe and C Duveyrier). Produced at the Opéra, Paris, on 13 June 1855, it was Verdi's first French opera, the only other set to French words being *Don Carlos*. The opera was also produced in Italy, as *Giovanna di Guzman*, at La Scala, Milan, on 4 February 1856, but later was called *I vespri siciliani* there. The story concerns the Sicilians Procida, Hélène, and Henri, who engage in a plot to assassinate Montfort, the French governor of the island. But when Henri learns that Montfort is his father he prevents the murder and Procida and Hélène are arrested. They later are released when Henri reluctantly accepts Montfort as his parent. At Henri's and Hélène's wedding the Sicilians rise and kill Montfort.

Veracini, Francesco Maria (1690–1768) Italian composer and violinist. He travelled widely in Europe, and had operas produced in London. He wrote concertos and about 60 sonatas for violin; his instrumental music was influenced by Arcangelo Corelli and Vivaldi.

Veracini studied with his uncle, Antonio Veracini, and later with Giovanni Maria Casini and Francesco Gasparini in Rome, possibly also with Corelli. He began touring as a virtuoso in 1711, and visited England in 1714. Returning via Germany to Italy, he demonstrated his superiority over Giuseppe Tartini (two years his junior) in a contest in Venice in 1716. The following year he entered the service of the Elector of Saxony in

Dresden, but left for Prague in 1723, then returned to Italy. In 1735 he went again to London, where he produced his first opera, *Adriano in Siria*, followed by several others 1735–44, but as a violinist was overshadowed by Francesco Geminiani. He probably lived in Pisa around 1750–55, then retired to Florence.

Works OPERA AND STAGE the operas *Adriano in Siria* (1753), *La clemenza di Tito* (1737), *Partenio* (1738), *Rosalinda* (after Shakespeare's *As You Like It*, 1744).

CHORAL eight oratorios (music lost); cantatas, including *Nice e Tirsi* (1741) and *Parla al ritratto della amata*.

OTHER violin sonatas; concertos; treatise *Il Erionfo della pratica musicale*.

Vera costanza, La, **True Constancy** opera by Pasquale ✦ **Anfossi** (libretto by F Puttini), produced at the Teatro delle Dame, Rome, on 2 January 1776. Opera by Haydn (libretto as above, altered by P Travaglia), produced at the palace Eszterháza on 25 April 1779. Secretly married to wayward Count Enrico, fisher maid Rosina faces Baroness Irene, who has arrived to arrange a marriage between Rosina and Villoto. Enrico and Rosina are reconciled when he meets their son; the Baroness marries Ernesto.

Vera Sheloga opera by Rimsky-Korsakov. See ✦ **Pskovitianka**.

verbunkos an 18-century Hungarian recruiting dance for soldiers, who performed it in full uniform with swords and spurs. Like the later ✦ **csárdás**, to which it is related, it contained a slow (*lassú*) and quick (*friss*) section. Franz Liszt's *Hungarian Rhapsodies* make use of the dance.

Verdelot, Philippe (c.1470–c.1552) French composer. His sacred music includes two Masses, about 57 motets, and a Magnificat, and was popular throughout Europe, but he was admired chiefly for his nine volumes of madrigals. He was one of the first composers to write madrigals (he was writing them as early as the 1520s), and influenced other madrigalists.

Verdelot was born in northern France. He went to Italy, probably at an early age, and was maestro at the baptistry in Florence 1523–25 and at Florence Cathedral 1523–27.

His motets were parodied by other composers, including Roland de Lassus and Palestrina.

Works SACRED AND SECULAR MUSIC two Masses, about 57 motets; about 100 madrigals, three chansons.

Verdi, Giuseppe Fortunino Francesco (1813–1901) Italian opera composer of the Romantic period. He took his native operatic style to new heights of dramatic expression. In 1842 he wrote the opera *Nabucco*, followed by *Ernani* in 1844 and *Rigoletto* in 1851. Other works include *Il trovatore/The Troubadour* and *La traviata/The Fallen Woman* (both 1853), *Aïda* (1871), and the masterpieces of his old age, *Otello* (1887) and *Falstaff* (1893). His *Requiem* (1874) honoured the poet and novelist Alessandro Manzoni.

Verdi's music is essentially Italian in character, and owes nothing to Wagnerian influences. During the mid-1800s, Verdi became a symbol of Italy's fight for independence from Austria. He often found himself in conflict with the Austrian authorities, who felt that his operas encouraged Italian nationalism.

Verdi was born at Roncole, near Busseto, the son of an innkeeper and grocer. From the age of only three he was taught by the local organist, replacing him as organist at the age of nine. At 11 he was sent to Busseto and went to school there, walking home twice a week to carry out his duties as organist. Barezzi, a friend of Verdi's father at Busseto, took him into his house in 1826, and he learnt much from the cathedral organist Provesi. He had an overture from Rossini's *Il barbiere di Siviglia/The Barber of Seville* performed in 1828, and the next year he wrote a symphony and stood in as deputy for Provesi. In 1831 he was sent to Milan with a scholarship and some financial help from Barezzi, but was rejected by the conservatory as over entrance age. Instead, he studied with Vincenzo Lavigna, the maestro al cembalo at La Scala. When Provesi died in 1833, Verdi tried for the post of cathedral organist, and when it was given to an inferior musician, the Philharmonic Society made him an allowance. In 1836 he married Barezzi's daughter, Margherita, with whom he had two children, but both mother and children died between 1837 and 1840. Meanwhile he had composed his first opera, *Oberto*, produced at La Scala in 1839.

A second (comic) opera, *Un giorno di regno/King for a Day* (1840), was a failure, his wife having died during its composition. Yet *Nabucco*, produced at La Scala in 1842, had a great success; the chorus of the Hebrew slaves was later to provide a rallying cry for the Italian people in their quest for freedom. In the cast of *Nabucco* was the soprano Giuseppina Strepponi. She lived with Verdi from 1848 and in 1859 became his second wife. He now went from strength to strength as an operatic composer, and his fame spread beyond Milan: *Ernani* was produced at Venice in 1844, *I due Foscari/The Two Foscaris* in Rome in 1844, *Alzira* at Naples in 1845, and *Macbeth* at Florence in 1847. Meanwhile *Ernani* had gone to Paris in 1846 and London commissioned *I masnadieri/The Robbers*, which was produced there in 1847.

From 1848 most of Verdi's life was spent at his estate of Sant' Agata near Busseto. *Luisa Miller* (1849) and *Stiffelio* (1850) were the last of his 'galley' operas, in which vigorous drama and strongly expressed emotion are accompanied by some basic orchestration. *Rigoletto*, the first of his great masterpieces, was premiered at Venice in 1851; together with *Il trovatore* and *La traviata* in 1853, it showed how Verdi had become a supreme melody writer. At the same time he showed new refinement of characters and made huge improvements to the orchestra's music. The first version of *Simon Boccanegra* was performed in 1857 and two years later *Un ballo in maschera* was premiered in Rome – it was one of several operas that ran into trouble with the censors. Verdi's support for Italian independence from Austrian rule was sometimes detected in his work.

An opera on Shakespeare's *King Lear*, at which he worked occasionally, was never completed; otherwise all his plans were put into action once they had taken definite shape. France, Russia, and Egypt offered him special commissions and his fame spread all over the world. In 1862 he represented Italy at the International Exhibition in London, and wrote a *Hymn of the Nations*, and in the same year *La forza del destino/The Force of Destiny* was produced at St Petersburg. The potentially sensitive subject of *Don Carlos*, dealing with Spanish oppression of the Netherlands, was performed in Paris in 1867; it is Verdi's most sombre, powerful, and richly varied opera.

Aïda was performed at Cairo in 1871 and the Requiem followed three years later; it was described by the conductor Hans von Bülow as an opera in ecclesiastical garb, and is melodically the most inspired of all Verdi's works. In 1868 he had suggested a Requiem for Rossini, to be written by various Italian composers, but the plan came to nothing. He used his contribution in 1873 for a Requiem commemorating the writer Manzoni. *Otello* was produced at La Scala in 1887, and marked Verdi's greatest public success. After a six-year break from composition, *Falstaff* was given at the same theatre in 1893, when Verdi was in his 80th year. Giuseppina died in 1897 and Verdi was himself growing very weak, but still wrote some sacred pieces for chorus and orchestra in 1895–97.

Verdi is the artistic successor of Donizetti and Bellini, but shows a far greater wealth of passionate feeling, musicianly craftsmanship, and power of enlightening pathos or tragedy by a simple and suggestive spirituality. His musical development was as varied as that of Beethoven; his lyricism was always constant, but his last works show also a rare spirituality, a refinement and religious consciousness, which place him among the foremost composers in the field of sacred, as well as of operatic, music.

Works OPERA *Oberto, Conte di San Bonifacio* (1839), *Un giorno di regno/King for a Day* (1840),

Nabucco (1842), *I Lombardi/The Lombards* (1843), *Ernani* (1844), *I due Foscari/The Two Foscaris* (1844), *Giovanna d'Arco/Joan of Arc* (1845), *Alzira* (1845), *Attila* (1845–46), *Macbeth* (1847), *I masnadieri* (1846–47), *Jérusalem* (French revised version of *I Lombardi*, 1847), *Il corsaro* (1848), *La battaglia di Legnano* (1849), *Luisa Miller* (1849), *Stiffelio* (1850), *Rigoletto* (1851), *Il trovatore/The Troubadour* (1853), *La traviata/The Fallen Woman* (1853), *Les Vêpres siciliennes/The Sicilian Vespers* (1855), *Simon Boccanegra* (1857, revised 1881), *Aroldo* (revision of *Stiffelio*, 1857), *Un ballo in maschera/A Masked Ball* (1859), *La forza del destino/The Force of Destiny* (1862), *Don Carlos* (1867, revised 1884), *Aïda* (1871), *Otello* (1887), *Falstaff* (1893).

CHORAL *Inno delle nazioni* (1862), the Requiem, *Pater noster, Ave Maria, Stabat Mater, Lauda alla Vergine Maria, Te Deum* (1896); *Ave Maria* for soprano and strings.

OTHER 16 songs; one part song; string quartet (1871).

Verdonck, Cornelis (1563–1625) Flemish singer and composer. He was in the service of Cornelius Pruenen, treasurer and later sheriff of Antwerp, until 1598, then, on the death of his patron, he served two of his nephews. He was singer at the royal chapel in Madrid 1584–98.

Works SACRED AND SECULAR MUSIC Magnificat, *Ave gratia plena*, four motets; 21 chansons, 42 madrigals.

Veress, Sándor (1907–1992) Hungarian pianist and composer. He began collecting folk songs in 1929, and settled at Budapest as a teacher of piano and composition and assistant to Bartók at the Scientific Academy of Folk Music.

Veress learnt the piano from his mother and later entered the Budapest Conservatory. He also studied with Bartók and Kodály. In 1929 he studied at the Ethnological Museum in Berlin and began collecting folk songs.

Works STAGE the ballet *The Miraculous Pipe* (1937, produced Rome 1941).

ORCHESTRAL two symphonies (1940, 1953) and divertimento for orchestra; violin concerto (1939); *Hommage à Paul Klee* for orchestra (1952); clarinet concerto (1982); flute concerto (1989); Concerto for two trombones (1989).

CHORAL AND CHAMBER cantata and folk song arranged for unaccompanied chorus; two string quartets (1931, 1937), string trio, trio for oboe, clarinet, and bassoon; violin and piano sonata, cello and piano sonata; two piano sonatas.

Veretti, Antonio (1900–1978) Italian composer. He studied at Bologna and took a diploma, also a newspaper prize in 1927 for the opera *Il medico volante* (after Molière). In 1943 he became director of the Conservatorio della

Gioventù Italiana in Rome and in 1950 of the Pesaro Conservatory.

Works DRAMATIC the opera *Il favorito del re* (1932); ballets *Il galante tiratore* and *Una favola di Andersen* (1934); film music.

CHORAL oratorio *Il figliuol prodigo* (1942), *Sinfonia sacra* for men's chorus and orchestra.

ORCHESTRAL *Sinfonia musiciana* (1929), *Sinfonia epica* (1938), and *Ouverture della Campanella* for orchestra.

verismo (Italian 'realism') term in music referring to opera of 'extravagant realism', particularly Italian late Romantic opera of Leoncavallo, Puccini, and others.

Verklärte Nacht, Transfigured Night string sextet by Schoenberg, Op. 4, composed in September 1899 and first performed at Vienna on 18 March 1902. It was inspired by a poem in Richard Dehmel's *Weib und die Welt*. The work was arranged for string orchestra c.1917, revised in 1942, and given as a ballet, *The Pillar of Fire*, at the New York Metropolitan Opera on 8 April 1942.

Véronique operetta by André ➔ **Messager** (libretto by A Vanloo and G Duval), produced at the Bouffes Parisiens, Paris, on 10 December 1898. In the story, Hélène, disguised as the shopgirl Véronique, meets the man she has arranged to marry, the Viscount Florestan. He falls in love with 'Véronique' and is shocked to meet her as Hélène at the altar, but nevertheless there is a happy ending.

Verschworenen, Die, oder Der häusliche Krieg, The Conspirators, or Domestic Warfare operetta by Schubert (libretto by I F Casteli, based on Aristophanes' *Lysistrata*). It was never performed in Schubert's lifetime, but was first produced in Frankfurt on 29 August 1861. The story involves the wives of crusaders, who attempt to convert their husbands to peace by withdrawing sexual favours.

verse anthem see ➔ **anthem**.

verset, Italian **versetto** in music, a short organ piece, often but not necessarily fugal and frequently incorporating or containing some reference to a given ➔ **plainsong** tune. The name is derived from the former practice in the Roman Catholic service of replacing every other sung verse of psalms, etc, by interludes on the organ to relieve the supposed monotony of plainsong.

Versunkene Glocke, Die opera by German composer Heinrich Zöllner (libretto by composer, based on G Hauptmann's play), produced at the Theater des Westens, Berlin, on 8 July 1899.

See also ➔ *Campana Sommersa, La*.

vertical in music, an adjective applied to the combination of simultaneous sounds, as seen on the page, in contrast to the horizontal appearance of notes in succession.

Vesalii Icones, Images of Vesalius theatre piece by Maxwell Davies for dancer, solo cello, and instrumental ensemble; composed in 1969 and first performed in London on 9 December 1969. The 14 movements are based on anatomical drawings in a treatise (1543) by the physician Andreas Vesalius depicting Christ's Passion and Resurrection.

vespers the seventh of the eight canonical hours in the Catholic Church; also, the seventh Roman Catholic office (or non-Eucharistic service) of the day. It is also used by the Anglican Church to refer to ➔ **evensong**. Claudio Monteverdi and Wolfgang Amadeus Mozart composed notable settings for this service.

The phrase Sicilian Vespers refers to the massacre of the French rulers in Sicily in 1282, signalled by vesper bells on Easter Monday.

Vespri siciliani, I opera by Giuseppe Verdi. See ➔ *Vêpres siciliennes, Les*.

Vestale, La opera by Mercadante (libretto, in Italian, by Salvatore Cammarano), produced at the Teatro San Carlo, Naples, on 10 March 1840.

Opera by Spontini (libretto, in French, by V J E de Jouy, based on Winckelmann's *Monumenti antichi inediti*), produced at the Paris Opéra on 16 January 1807. In the story, the holy fire of vestal virgins becomes extinguished as Julia attempts to elope with former betrothed Lycinius. As she is led to execution, lightning rekindles the flame and she is spared.

Viadana, Lodovico (c.1560–1627), born **Grossi da Viadana** Italian composer. He was a prolific composer, writing mostly vocal church music. His works include 100 *Concerti ecclesiastici* (1602), for one to four voices with organ continuo.

Viadana studied with Costanzo Porta and before 1590 was appointed maestro di cappella at Mantua Cathedral. In 1596 he joined the Franciscan order, became maestro di cappella at Concordia in 1609, and in 1612 at Fano Cathedral. In 1615 he went to live at Piacenza, whence he retired to the Franciscan monastery at Gualtieri.

Works SACRED AND SECULAR MUSIC Masses, psalms, and other church music; 100 *Concerti ecclesiastici* for one to four voices with organ continuo (1602); madrigals, canzonets.

Viaggio a Reims, Il, ossia L'albergo del giglio d'oro, The Journey to Rheims, or the Golden Lily Inn opera by Rossini (libretto by G L Balochi), produced at the Théâtre-Italien, Paris, on 19 June 1825. The opera failed but the music was largely re-used in *Le Comte Ory* (1828). Assorted national types including Lord Sidney, Don Profondo and Belfiore are delayed at the inn of Madame Cortese on the way to a coronation at Rheims.

vibraphone electrophonic percussion instrument resembling a ➤ xylophone but with metal keys. Electrically driven discs spin within resonating tubes under each key to add a tremulant effect that can be controlled in length with a foot pedal.

vibrato in music, a tiny and rapid fluctuation of pitch for dynamic and expressive effect, used mostly by string players and singers. It is different from a ➤ tremolo, which is a rapid fluctuation in intensity (rapid repeating) of the same note.

Vicentino, Nicola (1511–c.1576) Italian composer and theorist. He sought to revive the Greek modes in his madrigals, and invented an instrument he called the *archicembalo*, which could play various microtones.

Vicentino studied with Adrian Willaert at Venice, then entered the service of Ippolito d'Este, cardinal of Ferrara, with whom he went to live in Rome. His treatise *L'antica musica ridotta alla prattica moderna* (1555) involved him in a controversy with Vicente Lusitano in which he was defeated. He returned to Ferrara with his patron and became his maestro di cappella. He wrote madrigals and motets.

Victor, St (died 1177 or 1192), also known as **Adam of St Victor** French monk. In about 1130 he joined the abbey of St Victor near Paris. He wrote sequences composed in pairs of metrically regular three-line stanzas, and was the first important exponent of this type. He apparently composed the melodies of his sequences.

Victoria, Tomás Luis de (1548–1611) Spanish composer. He wrote only sacred music, including 20 Masses, 52 motets, and many other liturgical pieces, and is noted for his expressive settings of the Mass (for example, *Ave regina caelorum*) and other Latin texts.

Victoria sang as a boy at the cathedral of his native Ávila. In 1565 he received a grant from Philip II and went to Rome, where he became a priest and singer at the German College. From 1569 he was employed at the Roman Church of Santa Maria di Monserrato; from 1571 he taught music at the German College, and was choirmaster there from 1573 to about 1577. He was a chaplain at San Girolamo della Carità 1578–85. From 1587 to 1603 he was chaplain to the dowager empress María, Philip II's sister and the widow of Maximilian II, at the convent of the Descalzas Reales in Madrid, where the empress lived and her daughter, the Infanta Margaret, became a nun.

On the death of the empress in 1603 he wrote an *Officium defunctorum* (Requiem Mass) for six voices. Victoria is as great a master of ➤ polyphony in the Spanish school as his contemporaries Palestrina, Lassus, and Byrd were in the Italian, Flemish, and English.

Works CHURCH MUSIC 20 Masses (including two Requiems), 18 Magnificats, one Nunc dimittis, nine Lamentations, 25 responsories, 13 antiphons, eight polychoral psalms, 52 motets, 36 hymns, one Litany, two Passions, three Sequences.

Victory opera by Richard Rodney Bennett (libretto by B Cross, after Conrad), produced at Covent Garden, London, on 13 April 1970. The story evolves as the reclusive Heyst is tempted into a fuller life by the chorus girl Lena.

Vida breve, La, Life is Short opera by Falla (libretto in Spanish, by C F Shaw), produced at Nice, in French, translated by P Milliet, on 1 April 1913. In the story, the gypsy Salud hopes to marry Paco but is jilted for Carmela. Salud confronts Paco at the wedding and falls dead.

Vidal, Peire (c.1175–c. 1210) French ➤ troubadour. About 50 of his poems are preserved, twelve with music.

vielle organisée (French 'organed [rather than 'organized'] hurdy-gurdy'; Italian *lira organizzata*) musical instrument, a ➤ hurdy-gurdy (*vielle*) into which are incorporated one or two sets (stops) or organ pipes. These can be made to sound separately or together, or shut off at will.

Haydn wrote five concertos for two of these instruments.

Vienna State Opera the greatest Austrian opera house and company, originally known as the Vienna Court Opera. There have been various theatres associated with the company, from the Theater bei der Hofburg in 1748 to the most recent theatre, rebuilt in 1955. The company reached its height in the 1890s when Gustav ➤ Mahler was its principal conductor.

Vie parisienne, La, Life in Paris operetta by Offenbach (libretto by Henri Meilhac and Ludovic Halévy), produced at the Théâtre du Palais-Royal, Paris, on 31 October 1866. The story concerns Bobinet and Gardefeu, who trick Swedish aristocrats on tour in Paris by posing as guests in the Grand Hôtel. Gardefeu pursues the Baroness while her husband is too preoccupied with other women to notice.

Vier ernste Gesänge, Four Serious Songs settings by Brahms for baritone and piano of words from the Bible, Op. 121, composed in May 1896. The corresponding passages in English are 'One thing befalleth', 'So I returned', 'O death, how bitter is thy sting', 'Though I speak with the tongues of men and of angels'.

Vierjährige Posten, Der, The Four Years' Sentry comic opera by Schubert (libretto by T Körner). Composed in 1815, it was never performed in Schubert's lifetime but was produced at the Dresden Opera on 23 September 1896. The story is about an abandoned French soldier who is in trouble for desertion with the returning army, after a four-year dalliance with a village girl.

Vier letzte Lieder sequence of songs by Richard Strauss. See ➤ *Four Last Songs.*

Vierne, Louis (1870–1937) French organist and composer. He studied with Franck and Widor at the Paris Conservatory. He became assistant organist to Widor and succeeded him as organist at the church of Saint-Sulpice and later became organist at Notre-Dame, where he died at the console.

Works SACRED AND SECULAR MUSIC *Messe solennelle* for chorus and two organs; symphonies; string quartets; sonatas for violin and piano and cello and piano; six symphonies (1899–1930) 24 *Pièces en style libre*, 24 *Pièces de fantaisie*, and other works for organ.

Vieuxtemps, Henry (1820–1881) Belgian violinist and composer. He was admired for his virtuosity in playing his own works and those of other composers. He is remembered for his seven violin concertos and several short pieces for violin. He taught at the St Petersburg and Brussels Conservatories.

Vieuxtemps learnt the violin at home and at the age of six was able to play a concerto by Rode. At seven he was taken on tour by his father; Charles Bériot heard him and offered to teach him at Brussels. In 1828 he performed in Paris, and in 1833 he went on tour in Germany and Austria, remaining in Vienna to study counterpoint with Simon Sechter. In 1834 he first visited London, where he met Paganini, and the following year he studied composition with Antonin Reicha in Paris. He afterwards travelled long and extensively in Europe and in 1844 went to the USA. In 1845 he married the Viennese pianist Josephine Eder. In 1846–52 he was violin professor at the St Petersburg Conservatory. In 1871–73 he taught at the Brussels Conservatory; he suffered a stroke in 1873, and finally resigned in 1879.

Works ORCHESTRAL AND ENSEMBLE seven violin concertos, *Fantaisie-Caprice*, *Ballade et Polonaise*, and other pieces for violin and orchestra; violin and piano sonata; cadenzas for Beethoven's violin concerto.

vihuela Spanish plucked-string instrument, approximately guitar-shaped but strung like a ➤ lute with six paired courses and normally ten frets. The name, used for any stringed instrument with a flat back, appears in the 13th century, and as early as the 14th century there is a distinction between the *vihuela de arco* (bowed vihuela) and the *vihuela de peñola* (plectrum vihuela) which, with the development of finger-plucking, became the *vihuela de mano*. It seems likely that the *vihuela de arco* evolved into the viol at the end of the 15th century.

The vihuela's repertory appears mainly in seven printed anthologies of the 16th century, starting with Luis Milan's *El maestro* (1536), Luis de Narváez's *Delphin de música* (1538), and Alonso Mudarra's *Tres libros* (1546). Some pieces in these volumes appear also in French lute collections, and there is little technical difference between lute and vihuela music except that the vihuela, with its small body and long neck, was able to be played in higher positions than the lute, as exploited particularly in the collections of Valderrábano (1547) and Fuenllana (1554).

Vilar, José Teodor (1836–1905) Spanish composer and conductor. Returning to Barcelona from his studies in Paris in 1863, he became conductor at one of the minor theatres in Barcelona, and later at the principal theatre. He also did much teaching.

He studied with the cathedral organist Ramón Vilanova (1801–1870) at Barcelona and in 1859 went to Paris to study piano with Henri Herz and composition with François Bazin (1816–1878) and Jacques Halévy.

Works MUSICALS zarzuelas, including *La romería de Recaseéns* (1867), *L'ultim rey de Magnolia* (1868), *Los pescadores de San Pol* (1869), *Una prometensa* (1870), *La rambla de las flores* (1870), *Pot més que pinta* (1870), *La lluna en un cove*, *L'esca del pecat* (1871), *La torre del amore* (1871).

Village Romeo and Juliet, A opera in prologue and three acts by Delius (libretto by composer, after Keller's *Leute von Seldwyla*), produced at the Komische Oper, Berlin, on 21 February 1907. In the story, Sali and Vreli are encouraged by the Dark Fiddler to leave their warring fathers. They wander to an inn, the Paradise Garden, before committing *liebestod* ('love-death') by sinking a boat on the river.

Villa-Lobos, Heitor (1887–1959) Brazilian composer and conductor. He absorbed Russian and French influences in the 1920s to create neobaroque works in Brazilian style, using native colours and rhythms. His gift for melody is displayed in the 'Chôros' (serenades) series (1920–29) for various ensembles, and the series of nine *Bachianas Brasileiras* (1930–45), treated in the manner of Bach. His other works include guitar and piano solos, chamber music, choral works, film scores, operas, and twelve symphonies.

After studying the cello for a while, Villa-Lobos became a pianist and for some time toured as a concert artist. In 1912 he began to explore his country's folk music and in 1915 gave the first concert devoted to his own works at Rio de Janeiro. A government grant enabled him to live in Paris for a few years from 1923, but on his return he did much useful work as a conductor and music educationist, being appointed director of music education for the schools in the capital in 1930. In 1929 he published a book on Brazilian folk music, *Alma de Brasil*.

Works STAGE operas *Izath* (1914, concert performance 1940), *Yerma* (1956, produced 1971); musical comedy *Magdalena* (1948); ballet *Uirapuru*.

CHORAL AND ORCHESTRAL oratorio *Vidapura*; 14 works entitled *Chôros* cast in a new form and consisting of four for orchestra, one for piano and orchestra, one for two pianos and orchestra, two for chorus and orchestra, and six for various combinations and solo instruments (1920–28); orchestral works, including symphonic poem *Amazonas*, *Bachianas Brasileiras* (nine suites in the spirit of Bach, 1930–44), twelve symphonies (1916–57); five piano concertos, two cello concertos, harp concerto.

CHAMBER nonet for wind, harp, percussion, and chorus, quintet for wind instruments (1923); 17 string quartets (1915–58), three string trios (1911–18); four sonata-fantasies for violin and piano (1912–23); a very large number of piano works; songs.

villancico in music, a type of verse with a refrain and a complex rhyme-scheme; also, the music to which such poems were set. At first they were tunes without harmony, later pieces similar to madrigals. The term sometimes refers to a composition for solo voices, strings, and organ to sacred words, especially connected with the Nativity.

villanella (Italian 'country girl') Italian part song (song for a number of vocal parts) of the middle 16th to the early 17th centuries, set to rustic words and light in character.

Villanella rapita, La, The Ravished Country Girl opera by Bianchi (libretto by G Bertati, based on J M Favart's *Le Caprice amoureux*), produced at the Teatro San Moisè, Venice, in 1783. Mozart wrote an additional quartet and a trio for the Vienna performance, on 25 November 1785. In the story, Mandina is abducted by the Count before her wedding to Pippo. Her father Biaggio and her betrothed rescue her after questioning her allegiance, and welcome her back to the village.

villanelle in French music, a vocal setting of a poem of a form consisting of stanzas of three lines, the first and third lines of the opening stanza being repeated alternately as the third line of the succeeding stanzas. The best-known example is the first song of Hector Berlioz's cycle *Les Nuits d'été/Summer Nights*. A villanelle is not the equivalent of the Italian ➤ villanella or the Spanish ➤ villancico.

Villi, Le, The Witches opera by Puccini (libretto by F Fontana), produced at the Teatro dal Verme, Milan, on 31 May 1884. In the story, Roberto abandons his betrothed, Anna, who dies of grief. When he later returns, Anna's ghost haunts him with other ghosts of jilted girls, dancing with him until he dies.

vina Indian plucked string instrument in a variety of forms, including the ➤ sitar, combining features of a ➤ zither and ➤ lute and consisting of a fretted or unfretted fingerboard overlaying dual resonant chambers. It has ➤ sympathetic strings, giving a shimmering tone.

Vinaccesi, Benedetto (c.1670–c.1719) Italian composer. He was maestro di cappella to Prince Ferdinand Gonzaga di Castiglione in 1687, and was appointed second organist at St Mark's, Venice, in 1704.

Works OPERA two (lost).

CHORAL AND CHURCH MUSIC four oratorios (only *Susanna* (1694) extant); motets and other church music.

CHAMBER six *Suonate da camera* and twelve *Sonate da chiesa* for two violins and continuo.

Vincentius, Caspar (c.1580–1624) Flemish composer and organist. He provided a *bassus generalis* to the three volumes of Abraham Schadaeus's *Promptuarium Musicum*, and in 1617 added a fourth volume of his own. He also wrote a continuo part for Lassus's *Magnum Opus Musicum*.

Vincentius was a choirboy at the Imperial chapel in Vienna 1595–97. While serving as town organist at Speyer, about 1602–15, he met Schadaeus. He later held appointments at Worms and, from 1618 until his death, at Würzburg.

Vinci, Leonardo (c.1690–1730) Italian composer. He wrote chiefly for the stage, and composed eleven comedies before progressing to opera seria (Italian, 'serious opera'), of which he wrote more than 20. His most successful opera was his last, *Artaserse* (1730).

Vinci studied with Gaetano Greco at the Conservatorio dei Poveri di Gesù Cristo in Naples. From 1919 he established himself as a composer of Neapolitan dialect *commedie musicali*, and produced his first opera seria in 1722. Appointed as acting maestro di cappella at court in 1725, he was from 1728 also maestro at his old Conservatory, where his pupils included the composer Pergolesi.

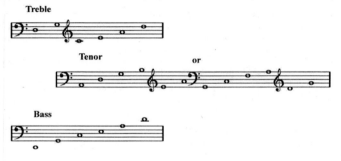

The open strings of the treble, tenor, and bass viols.

Works OPERA AND STAGE commedie musicali, including *Lo cecato fauzo* (1719, lost), *Le zite 'n galera* (1722); opera seria, including *Silla dittatore* (1723), *L'Astianatte* (1725), *Siroe* (1726), *La caduta dei Decemviri* (1727), *Artaserse* (1730), and 19 others.

OTHER six cantatas; chamber music.

Vingt regards sur l'Enfant Jésus work for piano in 20 sections by Messiaen; composed in 1944 and first performed at Paris on 26 March 1945, by Yvonne Loriod.

viol member of a Renaissance family of bowed six-stringed musical instruments with flat backs, fretted fingerboards, and narrow shoulders that flourished particularly in England about 1540–1700, before their role was taken by the violins. Normally performing as an ensemble or consort, their repertoire is a development of ➤ **madrigal** style with idiomatic decoration.

The three principal instruments, treble, tenor, and bass, are played upright, resting on the leg (da gamba), and produce a transparent, harmonious sound. The smaller instruments are rested on the knee, not held under the chin. Tuning is largely in fourths, like a guitar. The double bass viol or **violone**, used in baroque orchestras as bass-line support to the harpsichord or organ, became the model for the present-day ➤ **double bass**.

Viola unfinished opera by Smetana (libretto by E Krasnohorská, on Shakespeare's *Twelfth Night*), begun in 1883.

viola bowed, string instrument, the second largest member of the ➤ **violin family**. It is also one of the instruments that form the string quartet, where its traditional role is to provide harmonies. It is played tucked under the chin, like the violin, and its four strings are tuned to C3, G3, D4, and A5. With its dark, vibrant tone, it is often used for music of a reflective character, as in Igor Stravinsky's *Elegy* (1944) or Benjamin Britten's *Lachrymae* (1950). Concertos have been written for the viola by composers such as George Telemann,

Hector Berlioz, William Walton, Paul Hindemith, and Béla Bartók.

The open strings of the viola.

viola alta (Italian 'high viola') musical instrument, an exceptionally large ➤ **viola** designed by Hermann Ritter and made by Hörlein of Würzburg in the 1870s for use in the orchestra at the Wagner festivals at Bayreuth. In 1898 a fifth string was added, tuned to the E of the highest violin string.

viola bastarda (Italian 'bastard viol') Italian name for the ➤ **lyra viol**, called *bastarda* because it was midway in size between the tenor viol and the bass viol.

viola da braccio (Italian 'arm viol') generic name for members of the ➤ **violin family** in the 16th and early 17th centuries, since the smaller instruments were played on the arm and not, as was the case with the viola da gamba family, on or between the legs. Since the cello was the bass of the family it was known, illogically, as *bassa viola da braccio*. The treble instrument came to be known exclusively by the diminutive *violino*, and *viola da braccio* was reserved for the alto or tenor, shortened to *viola* in Italy and corrupted into *Bratsche* in Germany.

viola da gamba (Italian 'leg viol') generic name for the members of the ➤ **viol** family, all of which, small or large, are played on or between the legs. Unlike the violin family they have flat backs, sloping shoulders, six strings, and frets. The smaller instruments of the family gradually went out of use in the course of the 17th century, but the bass was retained as a solo instrument and for ➤ **conti-nuo** playing. Hence in the 18th century viola da gamba normally means the bass viol. Examples of its use are Johann Sebastian Bach's three sonatas with harpsichord and the obbligatos in the *St*

Matthew Passion. All the members of the family have been successfully revived in modern times.

viola d'amore (Italian 'love viol') musical instrument, a member of the ➤ viol family, though without frets and not *da gamba* ('on the leg') but played under the chin. More substantial than the modern viola, it has seven bowed strings as well as seven ➤ sympathetic strings. It was most popular during the baroque period, but was used occasionally by 19th-century composers, including Giacomo Meyerbeer and Berlioz. It has been revived in the context of the 20th-century ➤ authenticity movement.

In the 17th century, viola d'amore referred to a violin with wire strings.

viola da spalla (Italian 'shoulder viola') musical instrument, a portable ➤ cello used mainly by wandering musicians in the 17th and 18th centuries, held by a shoulder strap; also, an alternative name for the cello.

viola di bordone (Italian 'drone viol') alternative name for the ➤ baryton, a musical instrument.

viola pomposa bowed string instrument of the ➤ violin family, very rarely used. It seems to have had five strings, the lower four tuned as on the viola and the fifth tuned to the E of the violin.

violet the English name sometimes given to the ➤ viola d'amore, a musical instrument.

violetta marina (Italian 'little marine viol') special type of viol, allied to the ➤ viola d'amore, having ➤ sympathetic strings.

violetta piccola (Italian 'small little viol') early name for the treble ➤ viol and the ➤ violin.

violin bowed, string instrument, the smallest and highest pitched (treble) of the violin family. Its four strings are tuned in fifths to G3, D4, A5, and E5. It is usually played tucked between the shoulder and left side of the chin. The right hand draws the bow across a string causing it to vibrate and produce a note.

evolution The violin developed gradually during the 16th century from a variety of fiddle types. It was perfected by three families of makers – Amati, Stradivari, and Guarneri – working in Cremona in Northern Italy around 1670–1710. Designed without frets and with a complex body curvature to radiate sound, its voicelike tone and extended range produced a solo instrument with great versatility and expression. Together with the viola and cello, it laid the foundation of the modern orchestra.

Today's violin has not changed in form since that time, but in the late 18th century aspects of the design were modified to produce a bigger sound and greater projection for the concert hall and to allow for growing virtuoso expression.

These include a lengthened fingerboard, an angled neck, and larger-sized basebar and soundpost.

repertoire The repertoire for solo violin is greater than that for most other instruments (except for piano and organ). Composers include Vivaldi, Tartini, Johann Sebastian Bach, Mozart, Beethoven, Brahms, Mendelssohn, Paganini, Elgar, Berg, Bartók, Carter, Lutosławski, Ferneyhough, and Dutilleux.

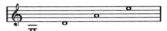

The open strings of the violin.

violin family family of bowed stringed instruments developed in 17th-century Italy, which eventually superseded the viols and formed the basis of the modern orchestra. There are four instruments: violin, viola, cello (or violoncello), and the double bass which is descended from the bass viol (or violone).

violino piccolo (Italian 'little violin') small string instrument of the ➤ violin family with four strings. It stands a fourth or a minor third above the violin in pitch.

The open strings of the violino piccolo.

Violins of St Jacques, The opera by Australian composer Malcolm Williamson (libretto by Warren Chappell), produced at Sadler's Wells, London, on 29 November 1966.

violoncello full name of the ➤ cello.

The open strings of the violoncello.

violoncello piccolo musical instrument, a small ➤ cello on which the playing of high passages was easier than on the normal cello.

A familiar example of its use is the obbligato (Italian, 'obligatory') in Johann Sebastian Bach's aria 'Mein gläubiges Herze/My heart ever faithful' in the cantata no. 68, *Also hat Gott die Welt geliebt/God so loved the world*.

violon d'amour (French 'love violin') musical instrument, the member of the modern string family corresponding to the ➤ **viola d'amore** of the viol family, used in the 18th century, but now obsolete. It had five strings and six ➤ **sympathetic strings**, not touched by the bow but vibrating with those actually played.

The open strings of the violon d'amour.

violone musical instrument, the double bass of the ➤ **viol** family, similar to the bass viol but larger, with six strings similarly tuned an octave lower. The name was also applied to the double bass of the violin family.

violotta modern string instrument of the ➤ **violin** family, invented by Alfred Stelzner (died 1906) of Dresden. It has four strings tuned so as to stand in pitch between the viola and the cello.

The open strings of the violotta.

Viotti, Giovanni Battista (1755–1824) Italian violinist and composer. He was the most important violinist of his day, encompassing both the earlier Italian tradition of Corelli and the beginnings of the 19th-century French Romantic school. He is best known for his 29 violin concertos. After a successful stay in Paris 1782–92, where he was violinist to Marie Antoinette and founded an opera house, he settled in London, where he became manager of the King's Theatre in 1797.

After studying with Gaetano Pugnani, Viotti joined the court orchestra at Turin in 1775, but obtained leave of absence in 1780 to go on tour with Pugnani. He visited Switzerland, Dresden, Berlin, Warsaw, and St Petersburg, and in 1782 arrived in Paris, where he stayed for ten years. He played at the concert spirituel, was solo violinist to Marie Antoinette at Versailles 1784–86, conducted some concerts of the Loge Olympique (for which Haydn wrote his 'Paris' symphonies), and from 1788 was involved in the foundation of a new opera company at the Théâtre de Monsieur. In 1792 he went to London, where he played in Salomon's concerts and became acting manager and leader of the orchestra at the King's Theatre opera, but was forced to leave England for political reasons in 1798, and lived near Hamburg, writing an autobiographical sketch. Returning to London in 1801, he withdrew almost completely from music and entered the wine trade, but twice visited Paris (in 1802 and 1814) and in 1819 became director of the Opéra there, finally returning to London in 1823.

Works WORKS FOR VIOLIN 29 violin concertos (c.1782–c.1805); two *Symphonies concertantes* for two violins and orchestra; 15 string quartets (c.1783–1817); 21 string trios for two violins and cello; violin duos, sonatas, and other pieces.

OTHER six piano sonatas.

Virdung, Sebastian (c. 1465–c. 1511) German cleric and writer on music. He studied at Heidelberg University. He sang, and then was kapellmeister at the Palatine court chapel in Heidelberg, and in 1507 became succentor at Konstanz Cathedral. In 1511 he published at Basel his book on musical instruments, *Musica getutscht und ausgezogen*, dedicated to the Bishop of Strasbourg.

virelai (French, from *virer*, 'to turn', and *lai*, 'a song') type of medieval French song with a refrain before and after each verse.

virginal plucked stringed keyboard instrument of the 16th and 17th centuries, often called 'virginals' or 'a pair of virginals' in England, where the term was applied to any quilled keyboard instrument well into the 17th century. The virginal is rectangular or polygonal in shape and is distinguished from the ➤ **harpsichord** and ➤ **spinet** by its strings being set at right angles to the keys, rather than parallel with them.

The most likely explanation of the name is that the instrument was often played by girls. There are several manuscript collections of virginal music by English composers, including *The Fitzwilliam Virginal Book*, *My Ladye Nevells Booke*, *Will Forster's Book*, *Benjamin Cosyn's Book*, and *Elizabeth Rogers's Book*.

Visée, Robert de (c.1660–c.1725) French lutenist, guitarist, and composer. He was guitar and theorbo (a large lute with long bass strings) player to the dauphin and chamber musician to the king from near the end of the 17th century to 1720.

Works WORKS FOR GUITAR AND LUTE two books of guitar pieces, and one of pieces for lute and theorbo.

Vision of St Augustine, The work by Michael Tippett for baritone, chorus, and orchestra (text in Latin). It was composed 1963–65, and first performed in London on 19 January 1966, with Dietrich Fischer-Dieskau.

Visions de l'Amen suite by Olivier ➤ **Messiaen** in seven movements for two pianos; composed in 1943 and first performed in Paris on 10 May 1943, by Messiaen and his wife, Yvonne Loriod.

Visions Fugitives 20 pieces for piano by Prokofiev. Composed 1915–17, they were first performed at Petrograd on 15 April 1918, by the composer.

Vitali, Giovanni Battista (1632–1692) Italian viol player and composer. In 1673 he became maestro di cappella of the Santissimo Rosario, and in 1674 he went to Modena as vice-maestro of the ducal chapel. His oratorio on the execution of the English Duke of Monmouth was produced there in 1686, the year after Monmouth's execution.

Vitali was a pupil of Maurizio Cazzati, maestro di cappella of San Petronio at Bologna, where Vitali himself was a string player and singer from 1658.

Works SACRED AND SECULAR MUSIC psalms for two to five voices and instruments; oratorios *Il Giono* and *L'ambitione debellata overo La Caduta di Monmouth*; ten cantatas.

OTHER numerous dances for several instruments; sonatas for two violins and continuo and others for various instrumental combinations.

Vitali, Tomaso (Antonio) (1663–1745) Italian violinist and composer. He was best known for his instrumental music; notably trio sonatas and a celebrated ➜ **chaconne** for violin and keyboard (which has recently come into doubt regarding Vitali's authorship of it).

Vitali was taught by his father, Giovanni Battista ➜ **Vitali**, and was later a member of the court chapel at Modena under him. He taught the violin to distinguished pupils, including Evaristo Dall'Abaco and Jean Baptiste Senallié.

Works CHAMBER sonatas for two violins and continuo.

Vitry, Philippe de (1291–1361) French composer, poet, and theorist. One of the masters of ➜ **ars nova**, his works are characterized by contrapuntal intricacy. He wrote four treatises on *ars nova* and some of his motets survive today.

vivace (Italian 'lively') term used in musical notation, as in *allegro vivace* ('fast and lively').

Vivaldi, Antonio Lucio (1678–1741) Italian Baroque composer, violinist, and conductor. One of the most prolific composers of his day, he was particularly influential through his concertos, several of which were transcribed by Johann Sebastian Bach. He wrote 23 symphonies, 75 sonatas; over 400 concertos, including *The Four Seasons* (1725) for violin and orchestra; over 40 operas; and much sacred music. His work was largely neglected until the 1930s.

Vivaldi was born at Venice. He was taught by his father Giovanni Battista Vivaldi, a violinist at St Mark's Cathedral, and possibly also by the composer Giovanni Legrenzi. He entered the church in 1693 and was ordained priest in 1703 (being commonly known as *il prete rosso*, 'the red [-haired] priest'). Later he came into conflict with church authorities for keeping a mistress. He was associated 1703–40 with a girls' orphan-age, the Conservatorio dell' Ospedale della Pietà in Venice, for which he wrote oratorios and instrumental music, even sending manuscripts by post during his frequent absences. His first opera, *Ottone in Villa* was produced in Vicenza in 1713, and was followed by many others in Venice, Florence, Munich, Parma, and Milan. He was in Mantua in 1720–23 as *maestro di cappella da camera* to the Margrave Philip of Hesse-Darmstadt, wrote *The Four Seasons* about 1725, and toured Europe in 1729–33, but little is known of his extensive travels throughout his career. He returned to Venice in 1739, but his popularity was declining, and two years later he died in poverty in Vienna. Vivaldi's real importance lies in some 450 concertos for various solo instruments and combinations of instruments, the majority being of the violin family, but also woodwind and rare instruments such as the piccolo, ➜ **viola d'amore**, and mandolin; he also wrote 73 sonatas for one and two violins and for cello.

Works OPERA about 21 extant, including *Tito Manlio* (1720), *Ercole* (1723), *Orlando furioso* (1727); Latin oratorio *Juditha Triumphans* and others.

SACRED VOCAL including Gloria (two settings), *Salve regina* (3), *Stabat mater*.

INSTRUMENTAL over 230 violin concertos (including *The Four Seasons* (1725), nos 1–4 of *Il cimento dell'armonia e dell'invenzione*, Op. 8), about 120 solo concertos (for bassoon, cello, oboe, flute, oboe d'amore, recorder, and mandolin), over 40 double concertos (about 24 for violins, three for two oboes), over 30 ensemble concertos (instruments included clarinets, horns, theorbos, and timpani), nearly 60 string orchestra concertos (without soloists), and over 20 concertos for solo ensemble (without string ripieno, 'full complement'); about 90 solo and trio sonatas.

vivo (Italian 'lively, animated') term used in musical notation, equivalent to ➜ **vivace** but more rarely used.

Vlad, Roman (1919–) Romanian-born Italian composer. He is the author of books on Dallapiccola and Stravinsky. He studied at the Cernaui Conservatory but in 1938 settled in Rome, where he finished studies under Casella.

Works DRAMATIC MUSIC radio opera *Il dottore di vetro* (1959), ballets *La strada sul caffè* (1945) and *La dama delle camelie* (after Dumas); film music.

CHORAL *De profundis* for soprano, chorus, and orchestra.

INSTRUMENTAL *Divertimento* for eleven instruments; *Studi dodecafonici* for piano.

Vladigerov, Pancho (1899–1978) Bulgarian composer. He studied with Juon and Georg Schumann in Berlin and at the Sofia Conservatory.

Works STAGE opera *Tsar Kaloyan* (1936); incidental music for Strindberg's *A Dream Play*.

INSTRUMENTAL Bulgarian rhapsody *Vardar*; two violin concertos (1921, 1968); piano concerto; piano trio; violin and piano sonata; piano pieces; songs.

Vltava, The River the second of six symphonic poems by Bedřich Smetana; see ➤ **Má Vlast**.

vocalise in music, a concert work for voice without words, sung on one or more vowels, usually 'ah', which is sustainable over the widest range and allows an open tone. Examples include Rachmaninov's *Vocalise for Soprano and Orchestra* (1912, revised 1915) and Villa-Lobos' *Bachianas Brasileiras No 5* (1938–45).

Electric instruments such as the ➤ **theremin** and ➤ **ondes Martenot** are employed in the manner of a vocalise, with the added advantages of amplification and extended range.

voce (Italian 'voice') term used in musical notation, as in *colla voce* ('with the voice'), directing an accompanist to follow carefully a singer's changes of tempo.

Vogel, (Johannes) Emil (Eduard Bernhard) (1859–1908) German music scholar. He studied at Berlin University and privately. In 1883 he went to Italy as assistant to F X Haberl on his edition on Palestrina. From 1893 to 1901 he was librarian of the Musikbibliothek Peters and editor of the Peters *Jahrbuch*.

Vogel, Vladimir Rudolfovich (1896–1984) Swiss composer of German and Russian descent. He studied in Russia, and later with Tiessen and Busoni in Berlin; he settled in Switzerland in 1933. From the time of his violin concerto (1937) he wrote serial music, striving to maintain clarity in his writing and to emphasize the less dissonant (tonally displeasing) aspects of his 12-note rows.

Works CHORAL cantatas *Wagadú's Untergang* for solo voices, chorus, speaking chorus and five saxophones (1930); *Thyl Claes* (after *Till Eulenspiegel*, 1938–45).

INSTRUMENTAL *Sinfonia fugata*, four studies, *Devise, Tripartita* for orchestra; violin concerto (1937), cello concerto (1955); *Komposition* and *Etude Toccata* for piano.

Vogelhändler, Der, The Bird Dealer operetta by Austrian composer Carl Zeller (libretto by M West and L Held), produced at the Theater an der Wien, Vienna, on 10 January 1891. The story unfolds when the village postmistress Christel attempts to secure a job for her birdseller boyfriend Adam. A case of mistaken identity causes complications eventually resolved with the couple's reconciliation.

Vogelweide, Walther von der (c.1170–c.1230) German poet, ➤ **Minnesinger**, and composer. He was in service at the court of Duke Leopold V in Vienna, then led a wandering life in Germany and after 1220 probably lived at an estate given to him at Würzburg. Only a few of his tunes have survived. He appears as a character in Wagner's *Tannhäuser*.

He was a pupil of Reinmar von Hagenau in Austria.

Vogler, Georg Joseph (1749–1814), also known as **Abbé Vogler** German composer, teacher, and theorist. He studied in Italy and became music director to the courts of Mannheim, Munich, Stockholm, and Darmstadt. He was a notable teacher; his pupils included Weber, Meyerbeer, and Crusell, and he wrote a number of theoretical works.

Vogler was the son of an instrument maker and violinist. He studied theology at Würzburg and Bamberg universities, went to Mannheim in 1771, becoming court chaplain the following year, and in 1773 received a scholarship from the Elector to go to Italy. He studied with Padre Martini in Bologna and Palotti in Padua, and in 1775 returned to Mannheim as vice-kapellmeister. Mozart met him there in 1778 and disliked him. When the electoral court moved to Munich in 1778 Vogler at first remained in Mannheim, but later followed, becoming kapellmeister in 1784. He was kapellmeister to the Swedish court in Stockholm 1786–99, but was able to travel extensively, going as far afield as North Africa and Greece. After leaving Stockholm he lived successively in Copenhagen, Berlin, Prague, Vienna, and Munich, until in 1807 he was appointed kapellmeister to the Grand Duke of Hesse-Darmstadt. His opera *Gustav Adolph och Ebba Brahe* has been revived at Drottningholm.

Works SINGSPIELE *Albert III von Bayern* (1781), *Erwin und Elmire* (1781, Goethe).

OPERA AND STAGE operas, including *La Kermesse* (1783), *Castore e Polluce* (1787), *Gustav Adolph och Ebba Brahe* (1788), *Samori* (1804); operetta *Der Kaufmann von Smyrna* (1771); ballet *Jäger-Ballet* (1772); incidental music to Shakespeare's *Hamlet* (1779); choruses for Racine's *Athalie* and Skjöldebrand's *Hermann von Unna*.

SACRED AND SECULAR MUSIC Masses, seven Requiems, motets, psalms, and other church music; cantata *Ino* (Ramler).

INSTRUMENTAL symphonies; several piano variations for piano and orchestra; piano trios and much other chamber music; piano and violin sonatas; piano sonatas and variations; six sonatas for two pianos.

voice in music, the human singing voice. Sound is produced by forcing air from the lungs through the larynx and making the vocal cords vibrate.

The ➤ **pitch** of the sound can be altered by tightening or loosening the muscles of the larynx, and the sound is amplified and modified by the mouth and nasal cavities.

The term 'voice' is also used to refer to the separate parts of a piece of music – even when they are played rather than sung. It is especially used when talking about the separate lines in ➤ **counterpoint**, such as a ➤ **fugue** in four voices.

There are several categories of singing voice, which depend on how high or low the performer normally sings. Female singers are usually classified as either ➤ **soprano** (the highest voice), ➤ **contralto** (often shortened to 'alto', the lowest female voice), or ➤ **mezzo-soprano** (a medium-high voice). Boys whose voices have not yet broken sing in the same range as the female voices, but are referred to as ➤ **trebles** and altos, rather than sopranos and contraltos. The main categories of men's voices are ➤ **tenor** (the highest male voice), ➤ **bass** (the lowest), ➤ **baritone** (between the two), and ➤ **countertenor** (above the tenor range). Some men can use ➤ **falsetto**, a sort of false high voice, to sing in the countertenor, alto, and even soprano ranges.

acoustics of the voice The human voice produces sound in the same way as a ➤ **free-reed instrument**, set in motion by air from the lungs being expelled under pressure by contraction of the diaphragm. The sound source is a set of vocal folds (two strips of cartilage stretched across the larynx at the back of the throat). These act as a flexible valve controlling the escape of air as a series of pulses, creating a sound rich in ➤ **harmonics**. The pitch of this sound can be varied by tension or relaxation of the larynx. The ➤ **timbre** of the voice is created by the resonances of the mouth and nasal cavities, and can be varied by changing the shape of the mouth and throat to produce the different vowel and consonant sounds.

vocal registers Until recently, theorists divided the voice into different registers, known as the ➤ **chest voice**, throat voice, and ➤ **head voice**, based on what was believed to be the physiological source of voice production. These terms are now used more as a description of tonal quality. They are the equivalent of the low, medium, and high portions of a singer's range, felt rather than produced in those parts of the body. The term 'head voice' was probably used in early music to describe falsetto. Modern vocal registers are classified mainly by the vocal range and gender of the singer.

voices in counterpoint Western art music has its roots in medieval church music, which was a purely vocal form. As ➤ **polyphony** developed in the late Middle Ages, each line of music was referred to as a 'voice', a practice that continued even when describing the parts of an instrumental piece. The term refers not only to the separate instruments or singers in an ensemble, but also to the lines of a contrapuntal work. So, for example, a fugue in four voices may be written for four separate instruments (or singers), but is just as likely to be for a keyboard instrument such as the organ or harpsichord.

voice-leading generally in harmony, the method by which the composer creates continuity within each strand of a harmonic texture; so that in instrumental music, each note of a chord is regarded as part of a separate 'voice', which must lead logically to the next note in that voice within the next chord. The term is now used more specifically to describe analytical techniques which reduce the harmonic structure of music to its contrapuntal outlines, identifying the principles of voice-leading underlying even the most outwardly complex passages.

Voice-leading analysis was originally developed to describe tonal works, especially those of the Austro-German tradition from Bach to Brahms; however, its principles have in recent years also been widely applied to pre-tonal, post-tonal, and non-Germanic repertoires. See Heinrich ➤ **Schenker**.

Voice of Ariadne, The opera by Thea Musgrave (libretto by A Elguera, after Henry James's *The Last of the Valerii*). Composed 1972–73, it was first performed at Aldeburgh on 11 June 1974. In the story, Count Valerio becomes obsessed with an excavated statue of Ariadne, neglecting his wife, until the Countess merges her voice with that of the goddess.

Voices work by Hans Werner ➤ **Henze** for mezzo-soprano, tenor, and instrumental ensemble. Composed in 1973, the work was first performed in London on 4 January 1974. It includes 22 settings based on texts by Ho Chi Minh (*Prison Song*), E Fried, Brecht, M Enzensberger, and others.

voices in music, the parts in a polyphonic composition, even those for instruments. See ➤ **voice**.

voice-to-MIDI converter microphone that sends human vocal input to a synthesizer. This system of singing to run a synthesizer does not work well unless the singer has perfect pitch, so it is not commonly used.

voicing in the construction of an ➤ **organ**, the production of particular qualities of tone by mechanical means, and more particularly the control of the tone of a whole range of pipes governed by a single stop in such a way that the tone-colour is exactly the same throughout.

The term also refers to regulating the mechanism of a piano so that its response to the player is even across the range: the response to the player's touch may be made quite 'heavy' and resistant, or 'light' like a hair-trigger. Also, in piano playing, voicing can be the emphasis of one voice over another simultaneously played note, usually in order to create a singing effect.

voix céleste (French 'heavenly voice') in an ➤ organ, an 8-ft stop with two pipes to each note, one tuned slightly sharper than the other, so that they produce a quivering effect.

Voix Humaine, La, The Human Voice tragédie lyrique (monodrama) by Francis ➤ Poulenc (libretto by Jean Cocteau), produced at the Opéra-Comique, Paris, on 6 February 1959. The story concerns a jilted woman in a fruitless telephone conversation with her lover; she eventually strangles herself with the flex.

Volans, Kevin (1949–) South African composer. His music combines avant-garde techniques with native African idioms. The opera *The Man Who Strides the Wind* was performed at the 1993 Almeida Festival in London.

He studied with Kagel and Stockhausen at Cologne. He was composer-in-residence at Princeton University in 1992.

Works OPERA *The Man Who Strides the Wind* (1993).

ORCHESTRAL AND ENSEMBLE *Chevron* (1989) and *One Hundred Frames* (1991) for orchestra; *White Man Sleeps* for two harpsichords, viola da gamba, and percussion (1982), four string quartets: no. 1 *White Man Sleeps* (1986), no. 2 *Hunting: Gathering* (1987), no. 3 *The Songlines* (1988); no. 4 *The Ramanujan Notebook* (1990); *She Who Sleeps with a small blanket* for percussion (1986); *Kneel my Dance* for two pianos (1985, six pianos, 1992); *Cicada* for two pianos (1994); electronic music.

Volkmann, (Friedrich) Robert (1815–1883) German composer. He spent much of his life teaching music in Budapest, where he became professor of composition at the Hungarian National Music Academy in 1875. As a composer he was influenced by Schumann and Mendelssohn.

Volkmann was taught music by his father, who was a schoolmaster and cantor, and another local musician taught him to play string instruments. In 1836 he went to Leipzig for further study, and was a private music tutor in Prague 1839–41. He lived and taught at Budapest 1841–54 and Vienna 1854–75, then returned to Budapest as professor of composition at the National Music Academy.

Works CHURCH MUSIC two Masses for male voices.

ORCHESTRAL incidental music for Shakespeare's *Richard III*, two symphonies, three serenades, Festival Overture for orchestra; *Concertstück* for piano and orchestra; cello concerto.

ENSEMBLE six string quartets, two piano trios and other chamber music; two sonatinas for violin

and piano; violin and piano pieces; cello and piano pieces.

WORKS FOR PIANO sonata and about 20 other Op. nos for piano; several piano duet works.

OTHER nine Op. nos of songs.

Volkonsky, Andrei Mikhailovich (1933–) Russian composer. He is a modernist among Russian composers, using a form of the 12-note system. Discouraged from composing by the Soviet authorities, he emigrated to Israel in 1973.

Volkonsky studied piano with Dinu Lipatti and composition with Nadia Boulanger in Paris. In 1948 he went to Moscow to study with Yuri Shaporin.

Works CHORAL AND VOCAL cantata *The Image of the World* (1953); *The Laments of Shchaza* for soprano and chamber orchestra.

INSTRUMENTAL concerto for orchestra (1954); piano quintet (1954); viola sonata.

Volkslied (German 'folksong') popular German song. Although Germany possesses a treasury of old folk songs, many of which became hymns for the Lutheran church, the term Volkslied no longer exclusively or even principally designates them: what Germans now mean by Volkslied is a type of popular song, such as Friedrich Silcher's *Loreley*, the composers of which are known (which is not the case with genuine folk songs), and which have passed into general currency.

volkstümlich (German adj. from *Volkstum,*'folk matters, folklore') word used in Germany to describe popular music that has become or is likely to become part of the nation's musical heritage, without actually belonging to traditional folk music.

Volo di Notte, Night Flight opera in one act by Dallapiccola (libretto by the composer, after St-Exupéry), produced at Florence on 18 May 1940. The story concerns the airfield director Rivière, who is a pioneer in promoting night flights during the 1930s. His stubborn insistence is partially responsible for the death of Simona Fabien's pilot husband, whose plane runs out of fuel.

volta (Italian 'time, turn, jump') word used in such musical directions as *prima volta* ('first time'), *seconda volta* ('second time'), *ancora una volta* ('once again'). It is also the name of an old dance including a characteristic jump. See also ➤ lavolta.

voluntary in music, a generic term for a quasi-improvisatory composition of the 16th century, but more specifically a piece for solo organ played at the beginning or end of a church service. As the name suggests, the organ voluntary is often free in style, and may be improvised. During the 16th century voluntaries were usually short contrapuntal pieces, without a ➤ cantus fir mus ('fixed melody'). In the 17th and 18th centuries they developed a more secular style, incorporating elements of the suite, sonata, toccata, and even the operatic aria. Composers of voluntaries include Henry Purcell, John Blow, and Samuel Wesley.

Vom Fischer un syner Fru, **The Fisherman and his Wife** dramatic cantata by Schoeck (libretto by composer, after Philipp Otto Runge, after Grimm). Composed 1928–30, it was produced at the Staatsoper in Dresden on 3 October 1930 and conducted by Busch. In the story, a Fisherman catches a turbot which turns out to be a prince under a spell. The Fisher's wife expects a series of wishes to be fulfilled.

Von deutscher Seele romantic cantata by Pfitzner for soloists, chorus, and orchestra (text after Eichendorff). It was composed in 1921 and first performed in Berlin on 27 January 1922.

Von Heute auf Morgen, **From Today until Tomorrow** opera in one act by Schoenberg (libretto by 'Max Blonda', the composer's wife Gertrud). First produced at Frankfurt on 1 February 1930, the opera concerns a husband and wife, who quarrel over supposed lovers and are then reconciled, in a 12-tone conversation piece.

von Karajan, Herbert Austrian conductor. See ➤ **Karajan**, Herbert von.

Voříšek, Jan Václav (1791–1825) Bohemian composer and organist. He became pianist and conductor to the Philharmonic Society at Vienna in 1818 and court organist in 1823. He was an important contemporary and admirer of Beethoven and was a successful composer in a wide variety of genres.

He was taught by his father, who was a schoolmaster, and later by Václav Jan Tomášek (1774–1850). He went to Vienna in 1813 and when Johann Nepomuk Hummel (1778–1837) left Vienna for Stuttgart in 1816, he recommended Voříšek as piano teacher to all his pupils.

Works SACRED AND SECULAR MUSIC church music, including Mass (1824); symphony; duet for cello and piano; divertissement for two pianos; piano works.

Voyevoda opera by Tchaikovsky (libretto by composer and Alexander Ostrovsky, based on a play by the latter), produced at Moscow on 11 February 1869. In the story, an elderly Voyevoda (provincial governor) attempts to wed the sister of his betrothed but is thwarted by a replacement governor.

Voz or **Vos, Laurent de (1533–1580)** Flemish composer. He worked at Antwerp Cathedral and was appointed music director and choirmaster at Cambrai Cathedral by the archbishop Louis de Berlaymont. When the latter's place was usurped by Baron d'Inchy, Voz composed a motet compiled from words from the Psalms in such a way as to attack Inchy, who had Voz hanged without trial. He was the brother of the painter Marten de Vos.

Works SACRED AND SECULAR MUSIC motets, chansons.

Vrchlický, Jaroslav (1853–1912), pseudonym of **Emil Frída** Czech poet and playwright. Works based on his writings include Dvořák (opera ➤ **Armida** and oratorio *St Ludmilla*); ➤ **Fibich** (operatic trilogy *Hippodamia* and melodramas *Haakon* and *Queen Emma*); J B Forster (melodramas *The Three Riders* and *The Legend of St Julia*); ➤ **Janáček** (choral work *Amarus*); ➤ **Novák** (opera *A Night at Karlstein*).

Vrieslander, Otto (1880–1950) German musicologist and composer. As a musicologist he was a pupil of Heinrich Schenker (1868–1935), whose unfinished *Harmonielehre* he completed. He also wrote on C P E Bach and edited some of his works.

He studied at the Cologne Conservatory, settled at Munich in 1906, and went to live at Locarno in Switzerland in 1920.

Works SONGS songs from *Des Knaben Wunderhorn* (on Giraud's 'Pierrot lunaire', 1904) and to words by Goethe, Keller, and Theodor Storm.

VS (Italian *volti subito*, 'turn at once') in musical notation, term often written at the foot of a right-hand page in manuscript music as an indication that a quick turn is necessary in order to be ready for what follows on the next page.

Vučković, Vojislav (1910–1942) Yugoslav composer, musicologist, and conductor. He studied in Prague and became professor and conductor at Belgrade. He was murdered by the Nazi police.

Works CHORAL AND VOICE several choral compositions; two songs for soprano and wind instruments.

INSTRUMENTAL two symphonies, three symphonic poems; string quartet.

Vuillaume, Jean-Baptiste (1798–1875) French violin and cello maker, who established himself independently in Paris from 1828.

Vulpius, Melchior (c.1570–1615) German composer and writer on music. He became cantor at Weimar in 1602 and remained there until his death. He harmonized many hymn tunes by other composers and wrote a treatise, *Musicae compendium* (1608).

Works SACRED AND SECULAR MUSIC *Sacrae cantiones* for five–eight voices, canticles, hymns for four–five voices, and other sacred music; *St Matthew Passion* (1613).

vuota (Italian 'void, empty') musical direction to string players to play a note or notes on an open string. It is also the equivalent of GP, 'general pause', a moment when all players are silent.

Vyšehrad, The Citadel of Prague the first of six symphonic poems by Bedřich Smetana; see ➤ *Má Vlast*.

Wächterlieder (German 'watchmen's songs') songs formerly used in Germany by night watchmen in the streets to announce the hours and by fire-watchers on church towers to proclaim festival days. They were often folk songs and some have passed into currency as hymns for the Lutheran Church.

Wacław z Szamotuł Polish composer; see Wacław ➔ Szamotulczyk.

Wadsworth, Stephen (1953–) US stage director, librettist, and translator. He directed operas by Monteverdi with Skylight Opera, Milwaukee, from 1982. He wrote the libretto for Bernstein's *A Quiet Place* (1983) and directed it in Milan and Vienna. Productions for Seattle Opera include *Jenůfa* and Gluck's *Orphée*; *Fidelio* and *Clemenza di Tito* for Scottish Opera, 1991. He directed *Die Entführung* in San Francisco in 1990. His debut at Covent Garden, London, was in 1992, when he directed *Alcina*; he also translated operas by Handel.

Waffenschmied (von Worms), Der, The Armourer (of Worms) opera by Lortzing (libretto by the composer, based on F J W Ziegler's comedy *Liebhaber und Nebenbuhler in einer Person*), produced in Vienna at the Theater an der Wien on 31 May 1846. Weigl's opera *Il rivale di se stesso/His own Rival*, produced in Milan in 1808, was based on the same play. Marie, daughter of armourer Stadinger, is wooed by Count Liebenau in his own person and, successfully, as an apprentice smith, Conrad. Marie's father Hans Stadinger opposes the match but eventually gives in.

Wagenaar, Bernard (1894–1971) Dutch-born US composer. He studied with his father, Johan ➔ Wagenaar, and at the Utrecht Conservatory and learnt the violin and keyboard instruments. In 1921 he settled in New York, joined the New York Philharmonic Orchestra, and from 1927 taught at the Juilliard Graduate School there.

Works OPERA the chamber opera *Pieces of Eight* (1944).

ORCHESTRAL four symphonies (1926–46), sinfonietta, divertimento, *Feuilleton* for orchestra; violin concerto, triple concerto for flute, harp, and cello (1935).

CHAMBER three string quartets (1932–60), concertino for eight instruments; violin and piano sonata, sonatina for cello; three Chinese songs for voice, flute, harp, and piano; piano sonata.

OTHER Eclogue for organ; including settings of Edna St Vincent Millay.

Wagenaar, Johan (1862–1941) Dutch composer. He wrote operas and orchestral pieces, and was noted for his orchestration. He taught at the conservatories of Utrecht and The Hague. He was the father of US composer Bernard ➔ Wagenaar.

He studied with Rijk (Richard) Hol (1825–1904) and with Heinrich von Herzogenberg in Berlin. He succeeded Hol as organist at Utrecht Cathedral in 1888 and became director of the conservatory there in 1904. He also conducted a choral society. In 1919 he became director of the Royal Conservatory at The Hague, retiring in 1937 in favour of Sem Dresden.

Works OPERA *The Doge of Venice* (1901), *El Cid* (after Corneille, 1916), and *Jupiter amans* (1925).

ORCHESTRAL overtures to Shakespeare's *Taming of the Shrew*, Goldoni's *Philosophical Princess*, Kleist's *Amphitryon*, and Rostand's *Cyrano de Bergerac* (1905), overture *Saul and David* (1906), funeral march and waltz suite for orchestra.

CHORAL fantasy on Dutch folk songs for male chorus and orchestra.

OTHER violin and piano pieces; piano pieces; songs.

Wagenseil, Georg Christoph (1715–1777) Austrian composer. He was also organist to the dowager Empress Elisabeth Christine 1741–50, and was appointed music master to the Empress Maria Theresa and her daughters. Mozart, at the age of six, played at court a concerto by Wagenseil, who turned pages for him.

He studied in Vienna with Johann Fux and others and in 1735 was recommended for a court scholarship, becoming court composer in 1739.

Works OPERA *Ariodante* (1745), *Le cacciatrici*

amanti (1755), and about ten others (six to libretti by Metastasio).

ORATORIOS *La rendenzione* and *Gioas, rè di Giuda* (both 1735).

ORCHESTRAL symphonies; keyboard concertos.

CHORAL nearly 20 Masses, Requiem, motets, and other church music.

OTHER divertimenti for solo keyboard.

Wagenseil, Johann Christoph (1633–1708)
German historian and librarian. He wrote a treatise on the art of the Meistersinger, published in 1697, which served Richard Wagner as a source for *Die Meistersinger.*

Wagner, (Wilhelm) Richard (1813–1883)
German opera composer. He revolutionized the 19th-century idea of opera, seeing it as a wholly new art form in which musical, poetic, and scenic elements should come together through such devices as the ➤ leitmotif. His operas include *Tannhäuser* (1845), *Lohengrin* (1850), and *Tristan und Isolde* (1865). In 1872 he founded the Festival Theatre in Bayreuth; his masterpiece *Der Ring des Nibelungen/The Ring of the Nibelung*, a sequence of four operas, was first performed there in 1876. His last work, *Parsifal*, was produced in 1882.

Wagner's early career was as director of the Magdeburg Theatre, where he unsuccessfully produced his first opera *Das Liebesverbot/Forbidden Love* (1836). He lived in Paris in 1839–42 and conducted the Dresden Opera House in 1842–48. He fled Germany to escape arrest for his part in the 1848 revolution, but in 1861 was allowed to return. He won the favour of Ludwig II of Bavaria in 1864 and was thus able to set up the Festival Theatre. The Bayreuth tradition was continued by his wife Cosima (1837–1930; Franz Liszt's daughter), whom he married after her divorce from Hans von ➤ Bülow; by his son Siegfried Wagner (1869–1930), a composer of operas such as *Der Bärenhäuter*; and by later descendants.

Wagner's father was a clerk to the Leipzig city police; he died six months after Wagner's birth. Wagner's mother moved to Dresden and married the actor and painter Ludwig Geyer in 1815, who in turn died in 1821. Wagner learnt the piano but tried to read vocal scores of operas instead of practising and also learnt about opera from two elder sisters who were both stage singers. He wrote poems and a tragedy at the age of about 13, and at 14 went to school at Leipzig, to where the family had returned. There he heard Beethoven's works and tried to imitate them in compositions of his own.

In 1830 Heinrich Dorn conducted Wagner's overture *Columbus* in the theatre, but it was received with scorn as a very crude work. He then studied harmony and counterpoint with Christian Weinlig at St Thomas's School and entered the university in 1831. He became chorus master at the theatre of Würzburg in 1833 and gained much valuable theatrical experience. He wrote two more operas and held a series of posts at Magdeburg, Königsberg, and Riga.

In November 1836 Wagner married Minna Planer (1809–1866), who was an actress. In 1839 he decided to go to Paris by sea. The very stormy voyage took Wagner and his wife three and a half weeks, and was the inspiration for *Der fliegende Holländer/The Flying Dutchman* (1843). Until April 1842 their time in Paris was spent in wretched poverty, but Wagner, in such time as he could spare from hack work, had managed to finish both *Rienzi* and *Der fliegende Holländer*, the former of which had been accepted by Dresden and was produced there in October 1842. *Rienzi* finds Wagner attempting the contemporary grand opera of Giacomo Meyerbeer, a composer he affected to despise. The opera was Wagner's first major success with the public and was followed a few months later by *Der fliegende Holländer*. Although less immediately popular it shows for the first time Wagner's individual voice as a composer; the evocation of stormy seas and the sense of impending doom are particularly effective.

In 1843 Wagner was appointed second conductor at the court opera. *Tannhäuser* was finished in April 1845 and produced in October. The lifelong theme of the conflict between sacred and profane love is used very powerfully in this opera. The spiritual side of the issue was portrayed in *Lohengrin* (1845–48). Wagner showed sympathy with the liberal ideas of the French Revolution, and gradually became a political agitator. A warrant for his arrest was issued in 1849. He fled to Franz Liszt in Weimar and then on to Switzerland. Liszt performed *Lohengrin* in Weimar in 1850, and began a Wagner movement in Germany. Wagner was unable to attend performances because of the threat of being arrested. He worked in Zürich on the libretti and music for the *Ring des Nibelungen* cycle. The text was completed by 1853 and Wagner began composing the prologue *Das Rheingold* in the same year. The music of the first scene, set at the bottom of the Rhine River, shows the composer's genius for creating convincing sound worlds.

Composition of the *Ring* was interrupted by work on *Tristan und Isolde*, written under the influence of Mathilde Wesendonck, the wife of a friend and benefactor, with whom he fell deeply in love. In 1858 Minna confronted Wagner and Mathilde; the latter decided to stay with her husband, and Wagner went to Venice and later to Lucerne, where *Tristan* was finished in August 1859. In 1860 a revised version of *Tannhäuser*, with a ballet, was commissioned by the Paris Opéra. Wagner complied so far as his artistic conscience would let him. It was not enough for the patrons, and they made sure the work failed disastrously. Wagner next went to Vienna, where *Lohengrin* and *Der fliegende Holländer* were successfully performed. He returned to Paris and began work on *Die Meistersinger von Nürnberg/The Mastersingers of Nuremberg*. He moved again to Vienna and stayed there until March 1864, when he was pursued by his creditors and threatened with imprisonment. At the critical moment he was invited by Ludwig II of Bavaria to join his court at Munich as friend and artistic adviser, and he made sure that Hans von Bülow was appointed conductor. Bülow's wife, Cosima and Wagner soon fell deeply in love. This created a scandal that was fully exploited by his enemies, the courtiers and officials who feared his influence on the youthful and idealistic king. Soon after the production of *Tristan* in June 1865, Wagner had to go into exile once more. *Tristan* was an immensely influential work, and an enduringly great piece of music in its own right. Wagner extended chromaticism and modulatory devices to new heights in this opera in order to portray the love of his leading characters, a love that transcends all human passion by its awareness of mortality: the belief that fulfilment can be found only in death.

Tristan's opposite is found in *Die Meistersinger von Nürnberg* (first performed in 1868), a partly autobiographical comedy in which a romantic hero and a profound poet combine to confound their enemies. While composing *Meistersinger*, Wagner moved to Tribschen on Lake Lucerne in Switzerland, where Cosima joined him in March 1866. Bülow divorced her in 1870 and she married Wagner, whose first wife, Minna, had died in January 1866. After the production of *Die Meistersinger* on 21 June 1868 at Munich, Wagner quietly continued work on the *Ring* cycle, dropped so many years before, and planned a festival theatre to be erected by subscription at Bayreuth in Bavaria. The family took a house there in 1874; rehearsals began the following year, and the four works were performed in August 1876. (*Das Rheingold* and *Die Walküre* had already been given in Munich, against Wagner's wishes, in 1869–70.) Although Wagner was dissatisfied with some aspects of the Bayreuth *Ring*, his genius as a composer and dramatist was justified. The immensely complex musical and moral strands of the *Ring* are brought together in the final opera, *Götterdämmerung* (1876); drama on a vast scale is matched by a constantly allusive orchestral accompaniment through the use of leitmotifs. Wagner's creative testament came with *Parsifal* in which his idea of the *Gesamtkunstwerk* ('complete art work'), was further refined. Wagner was heavily influenced by the ideas expounded in the book *The World as Will and Idea* by the German philosopher Arthur Schopenhauer.

By the time of his death in 1883 Wagner's influence had already spread throughout the musical world and far beyond; his belief in music drama as a combination of all the arts represents his idea of Romantic philosophy. In recent times, his influence can particularly be seen in film.

Works OPERA *Die Hochzeit* (unfinished), *Die Feen* (composed 1833; produced 1888), *Das Liebesverbot* (1836), *Rienzi* (1842), *Der fliegende Holländer/The Flying Dutchman* (1843), *Tannhäuser* (1845), *Lohengrin* (1850), *Tristan und Isolde* (1865), *Die Meistersinger von Nürnberg/The Mastersingers of Nuremberg* (1868), *Der Ring des Nibelungen/The Ring of the Nibelung*, comprising *Das Rheingold* (1853–54), *Die Walküre* (1870), *Siegfried* (1876) and *Götterdämmerung* (1876), *Parsifal* (1882).

ORCHESTRAL symphonies, nine concert overtures (two unpublished), including *Eine Faust Ouvertüre* (after Goethe), three marches for orchestra, *Siegfried Idyll* for small orchestra (1870); several choral works.

SONGS seven from Goethe's *Faust*, five poems by Mathilde Wesendonck (1857–58) and six settings of French poems.

Wagner, Siegfried (Helferich Richard) (1869–1930) German composer and conductor. He was the son of Richard ➤ Wagner. Although intended to become an architect, he studied music with Engelbert Humperdinck and Julius Kniese (1848–1905), and gained much experience by assisting at the Wagner festival performances at Bayreuth, some of which he conducted after 1896. When his mother, Cosima, became too old to manage the affairs of the theatre, he took its direction in hand in 1909.

Works OPERA *Der Bärenhäuter* (1899), *Herzog Wildfang* (1901), *Der Kobold* (1904), *Bruder Lustig* (1905), *Sternengebot* (1908), *Banadietrich* (1910), *An allem ist Hütchen schuld* (1917), *Schwarzschwanenreich* (1918), *Sonnenflammen* (1918), *Der Schmied von Marienburg* (1923), *Der Friedensengel* (1926), *Der Heidenkönig* (1933), and two others not performed or published.

ORCHESTRAL symphonic poem *Sehnsucht*; violin concerto, flute concerto.

Wagner tuba brass wind instrument devised by Wagner for his opera cycle *Der Ring des Nibelungen/The Nibelung's Ring*. The two tenor tubas are not unlike the euphonium, but have funnel-shaped mouthpieces.

Waisenhaus, Das, The Orphanage opera by Weigl (libretto by G F Treitschke), produced in Vienna at the Kärntnertortheater on 4 October 1808.

waits originally the keepers of town gates, in the 15th–16th centuries, salaried bands employed to

The compass of tenor and bass Wagner tubas.

play at various functions, afterwards amateur singers and players performing outside the houses of the wealthier citizens for rewards in money and refreshment at Christmas.

Waldhorn (German 'forest horn') German name for the ➤ horn without valves, producing only the natural harmonics, like the Italian *corno da caccia*.

Brahms's Horn Trio Op. 40 was written for the waldhorn.

Waldmädchen, Das, The Woodland Maid opera by Weber (libretto by C F von Steinsberg), produced in Freiberg, Saxony, on 23 November 1800. Early version of *Silvana*; only two fragments survive.

'Waldstein' Sonata Beethoven's piano sonata in C major, Op. 53, composed in 1804, so called (not by Beethoven) because it is dedicated to Ferdinand Waldstein.

Waldteufel (1837–1915), adopted name of **(Charles) Emile Lévy** French composer and pianist who studied at the Paris Conservatory. He joined a piano factory and was later appointed pianist to the Empress Eugénie. He had great success as a composer of waltzes.

Works many hundreds of waltzes and other dances, including a waltz on Chabrier's *España*.

Walküre, Die, The Valkyrie opera by Richard ➤ Wagner, part of the cycle of music dramas *Der* ➤ *Ring des Nibelungen*.

The plot continues where *Das Rheingold/The Rhinegold* ends, as siblings Sieglinde and Siegmund meet and fall in love. The Valkyrie, Brünnhilde, disobeys Wotan by attempting to allow Siegmund to escape death; she helps Sieglinde to escape to bear her child, the future Siegfried. Wotan punishes Brünnhilde by sending her to sleep, surrounded by a ring of fire.

Wallace, (William) Vincent (1812–1865) Irish composer. He established himself internationally as a pianist and violinist on tours that included Europe, Australia, and North and South America. He used the musical influences from the places he visited in his own compositions, such as the highly successful opera *Maritana* (1845), with its Spanish and gypsy elements.

He studied with his father, a bandleader and bassoon player who moved to Dublin, where Wallace played the organ and violin in public as a boy. In 1831 he married Isabella Kelly, but they separated in 1835 (in New York in 1850 he met the pianist Hélène Stoepel, with whom he lived and had two sons). In 1834 he appeared in Dublin with a violin concerto of his own. He was in Australia and elsewhere abroad 1835–45, then went to London and was induced to compose *Maritana*. After a successful operatic career, including a visit to South America in 1849 and 14 years in Germany, a commission from the Paris Opéra (which he was unable to finish owing to failing eyesight), and another visit to South and North America 1850–53, his health broke down and he was ordered to the Pyrenees, where he died.

Works OPERA *Maritana* (1845), *Matilda of Hungary* (1847), *Lurline* (1860), *The Maid of Zürich* (unpublished), *The Ambler Witch* (1861), *Love's Triumph* (1862), *The Desert Flower* (1863), *Estrella* (unfinished); unperformed operettas *Gulnare*, *Olga*.

OTHER cantata *Maypole*; violin concerto; piano music.

Wallace, William (1860–1940) Scottish music author and composer. He was educated at Edinburgh and Glasgow Universities and in Vienna as an eye specialist. He began to practise in 1888, but gave up his profession for music except during World War I. In 1889 he entered the Royal Academy of Music in London for a brief course in composition, and later he became successively secretary and trustee of the Philharmonic Society. His books include *The Threshold of Music* (1908), *The Musical Faculty* (1914), *Richard Wagner as He Lived* (1925), and *Liszt, Wagner and the Princess* (1927).

Works OPERA *Brassolis*.

ORCHESTRAL symphony *Koheleth* for chorus and orchestra, symphony *The Creation*; symphonic poems *The Passing of Beatrice* (after Dante's *Paradiso*, 1892), *Anvil or Hammer* (after Goethe's *Koptisches Lied*), *Sister Helen* (after D G Rossetti), *To the New Country*, *Sir William Wallace*, *Villon*; suite *The Lady from the Sea* (after Ibsen); symphonic prelude to Aeschylus' *Eumenides*.

OTHER cantatas, chamber music, and songs.

Wallenstein three symphonic poems by d'Indy, Op. 12, after Schiller's dramatic trilogy, composed 1873–79: 1. *Le Camp de Wallenstein*; 2. *Max et Thécla* (first called *Piccolomini*); 3. *La Mort de Wallenstein*. First complete performance Paris, 26 February 1888.

Wally, La opera by Catalani (libretto by L Illica, based on W von Hillern's novel *Die Geyer-Wally*), produced at La Scala, Milan, on 20 January 1892. Wally is intended for Gellner but she loves Hagenbach, and after complications and reconciliation, they die together in an avalanche. Championed by Toscanini, who named his daughter Wally.

Walpurga or **Walpurgis, Maria Antonia (1724–1780)** German composer. She was a member of the Arcadian Academy in Rome under the name of Ermelinda Talèa Pastorella Arcada (pseudonym ETPA). She was the daughter of the Elector of Bavaria (afterwards Emperor Charles VII). She studied with Giovanni Ferrandini, Nicola Porpora, and Johann Hasse; she married Frederick Christian, electoral prince of Saxony.

Works OPERA *Il trionfo della fedeltà* (with additional music by Hasse, 1754) and *Talestri, regina della Amazoni* (1760).

Walsh, John (1665 or 1666–1736) English music publisher and instrument maker. He founded his publishing house in London in about 1690, and in 1692 became instrument maker to King William III. He published much of Handel's music.

Walter, Bruno (1876–1962), born **Bruno Walter Schlesinger** German conductor and pianist. He excelled in the works of Mozart and of Romantic composers, especially Mahler, of whose *Lied von der Erde* and ninth symphony he gave the first performances in 1911 and 1912. As a pianist he accompanied many of the famous singers of his time, including Lotte Lehmann and Kathleen Ferrier, and also appeared as soloist in Mozart's concertos. He published a study of Mahler, an autobiography (*Theme and Variations*), and three volumes of essays.

Walter studied at Stern Conservatory in Berlin and made his first appearance as a conductor at Cologne in 1894. After appointments as an opera conductor at Hamburg (under Mahler), Breslau, Pressburg, Riga, Berlin, and Vienna (1901–12) he was director of the Munich Opera 1913–22. He conducted the first performances of Pfitzner's *Palestrina* (1917) and Schreker's *Das Spielwerk* (1920). He was director of the Städtische Oper, Berlin 1925–33, and of the Gewandhaus concerts in Leipzig 1929–33, in succession to Furtwängler. He first appeared in England in 1909 and was the regular conductor of the German seasons at Covent Garden 1924–31 (productions included *Figaro* and *Rosenkavalier*). He was also active during this period as conductor at the Salzburg festival. He was compelled to leave Germany in 1933 and was artistic director of the Vienna Opera 1936–38. After the Anschluss he emigrated to France in 1938 and to the USA in 1939, where he lived until his death. From 1941 he conducted frequently at the Metropolitan Opera House, New York, (debut with *Fidelio*; also *Don Giovanni* in first season). From 1946 he returned to Europe as

a guest conductor; he appeared at the 1947 Edinburgh Festival.

Waltershausen, Hermann Wolfgang (Sartorius) Freiherr von (1882–1954) German composer and music author. He studied at Strasbourg, lost his right arm and foot in an accident, but learnt to play the piano and conduct with the left hand. He further studied at Munich from 1901 and attended Sandberger's lectures at the university. He founded a music school in 1917, and in 1920 became professor at the Munich State Academy of Music, being appointed director in 1922. His books include works on musical style, opera, and Richard Strauss.

Works OPERA *Else Klapperzehen* (1909), *Oberst Chabert* (after Balzac, 1912), *Richardis* (1915), *Die Rauensteiner Hochzeit* (1919), *Die Gräfin von Tolosa* (composed 1938).

ORCHESTRAL *Apocalyptic Symphona, Hero und Leander*, Partita on three Hymn-tunes, comedy overture; *Passions- und Auferstehungsmusik* for orchestra; *Krippenmusik* for harpsichord and chamber orchestra.

OTHER piano works; songs.

Walther, Johann Gottfried (1684–1748) German composer, organist, and lexicographer. He studied under Johann Bernhard Bach (1676–1749) at Erfurt, where in 1702 he became organist at St Thomas's Church. In 1707 he was appointed town organist at Weimar, where he was in close touch with Johann Sebastian Bach, to whom he was related. He published a *Musicalisches Lexicon* in 1732.

Works much organ music, including preludes and fugues and chorale variations; concertos by other composers arranged for solo harpsichord.

Walton, William Turner (1902–1983) English composer. Among his works are *Facade* (1923), a series of instrumental pieces designed to be played in conjunction with the recitation of surrealist poems by Edith Sitwell; the oratorio *Belshazzar's Feast* (1931); and *Variations on a Theme by Hindemith* (1963).

Walton showed great talent as a child and was sent to Christ Church Cathedral, Oxford, as a chorister, later becoming an undergraduate at Christ Church. He had some composition lessons from the organist Hugh Allen, but after the age of 16 was self-taught, though he later received advice from Ferruccio Busoni and others. In 1923 he appeared for the first time at the International Society for Contemporary Music festival, at Salzburg, where his spiky first string quartet was performed. He settled in London and was in close touch with the literary Sitwell family: Edith, Osbert, and Sacheverell. Their association led to *Facade*, for reciter and ensemble, whose 1923 premiere provoked an uproar. Paul Hindemith was the soloist in Walton's first widely successful work, the viola concerto of 1929, and two years later the aggressively mannered cantata *Belshazzar's Feast* was premiered at Leeds.

In 1934 his symphony in B♭ minor was performed in London before it was completed (the finale was added the next year). In 1938 he went to the USA to talk with the violinist Jascha Heifetz about the solo part of the violin concerto, which is dedicated to him. As in the viola concerto and the First Symphony, the best of contemporary continental influences, including Igor Stravinsky, Francis Poulenc, and Sergey Prokofiev can be heard here. A more Romanticlike style is evident in the post-war works, beginning with the opera for Covent Garden, *Troilus and Cressida* (1948–54), and continuing with the cello concerto for Piatigorsky (1956).

Works DRAMATIC operas *Troilus and Cressida* (after Chaucer, 1954, revised 1976) and *The Bear* (after Chekhov, 1967); film music for *As You Like It, Henry V,* and *Hamlet* (Shakespeare), *The First of the Few* (including *Spitfire* prelude and fugue).

VOCAL *Facade* for reciter and instrumental ensemble (E Sitwell, 1923); oratorio *Belshazzar's Feast* (Bible, arranged by O Sitwell, 1931); *A Song for the Lord Mayor's Table* for soprano and orchestra or piano (1962).

ORCHESTRAL overtures *Portsmouth Point* (on Rowlandson's drawing) and *Scapino*, two symphonies (1931–35 and 1960), Coronation Marches *Crown Imperial* and *Orb and Sceptre* (1937 and 1953), viola concerto (1929), violin concerto (1939), cello concerto (1956), *Variations on a Theme by Hindemith* (1963), *Improvisations on an Impromptu of Benjamin Britten* (1969), Sonata for Strings (from string quartet of 1947, 1971), *Bagatelles* for guitar (1971).

waltz ballroom dance in moderate triple time (3/4) that developed in Germany and Austria during the late 18th century from the Austrian *Ländler* (traditional peasants' country dance). Associated particularly with Vienna and the ➔ **Strauss** family, whose works include *The Blue Danube* and *The Emperor Waltz*, and has remained popular up to the present day. Well-known composers of waltzes who use the waltz as a base for works include Frédéric Chopin, Johannes Brahms, and Maurice Ravel.

Waltz Dream operetta by Oskar ➔ **Straus**; see ➔ *Walzertraum*.

Walzertraum, Ein, A Waltz Dream operetta by Oscar Straus (libretto by F Dörmann and L Jacobson), produced at the Karl Theatre, Vienna, on 2 March 1907. Newly married Lieutenant Niki abandons wife Helene to go to a ball on his wedding night. There he falls in love with Franzi, who teaches Helene how to win back Niki's heart.

Wand, Günter (1912–2002) German conductor and composer. After study in Cologne he held posts at Wuppertal and Detmold. He conducted at the Cologne Opera 1939–44 and was musical director there 1945–48. He was responsible for the Gürzenich concerts, Cologne, 1946–74, giving frequent performances of Ligeti, Varèse, and Schoenberg. London debut 1951 (with the London Symphony Orchestra at Covent Garden). He conducted the Bern Symphony Orchestra from 1974 and has been principal conductor of the Nord-Deutsche Rundfunk Symphony Orchestra (Hamburg) 1982–91.

'Wanderer' Fantasy Schubert's fantasy in C major for piano, D760, composed in November 1822. It is so called because it contains material from his song 'The Wanderer' (1816).

Wand of Youth, The two orchestral suites by Elgar, Opp. 1a and b, which are based on music he wrote for a play in his childhood (1869). Revised and scored in the present form in 1907; first performed in London on 14 December 1907, conducted by Henry Wood.

Wannenmacher, Johannes (c.1485–1551) Swiss priest and composer. He wrote vocal pieces, of which 26 survive.

Wannenmacher was appointed cantor of the collegiate foundation of St Vincent at Bern in 1510, but left in 1514 after a dispute and went to Germany as canon and cantor at Freiburg, Baden. After a brief return to Switzerland in 1519, when he went to Sion (Valais), he went back to Freiburg, but having come under the influence of the Swiss religious reformer Ulrich Zwingli, he embraced Protestantism in 1530, was tortured and banished, returned to Bern and, finding no employment there, became town clerk at Interlaken.

Works Psalm 137 for three to six voices, motets; German sacred and secular songs.

War and Peace, Russian *Voyna I mir* opera by Prokofiev (libretto by M Mendelson, based on Tolstoy's novel), performed in concert in Moscow on 17 October 1944; produced in Leningrad on 12 June 1946 (first eight of 13 scenes only). Revised 1941–52, in eleven scenes, and produced in Florence on 26 May 1953, conducted by Rodzinski. The first seven scenes concern Peace, with the love of Andrei and Natasha, and the last six War, with Napoleon's capture of Moscow.

Ward, John (1571–1638) English composer. He wrote madrigals and church music. He was in the service of Sir Henry Fanshawe, Remembrancer of the Exchequer, at Ware Park, Hertfordshire, and in London.

Works services and 22 verse anthems; madrigals; fantasies for viols.

Warlock, Peter (1894–1930), pen-name of **Philip Arnold Heseltine** English composer. His style was influenced by the music of the Elizabethan age and by that of Delius. His works include the orchestral suite *Capriol* (1926), based on 16th-century dances, and the song cycle *The Curlew* (1920–22). His works of musical theory and criticism were published under his real name.

Warlock was educated at Eton, and was later influenced by Delius and van Dieren. He founded the *Sackbut*, a combative music paper, wrote numerous articles, edited early English music, especially of the lutenist school, and published books on the English ayre, Delius, and (with Cecil Gray) Gesualdo. His music reflects the extreme mood swings of his personality; he died by suicide.

Works ORCHESTRAL *Capriol* suite for full or string orchestra on dances from Arbeau's *Orchésographie* (1926); *An Old Song* (1917) and *Serenade* for string orchestra.

CHORAL *Three Dirges by Webster* (1925) and other choral works.

VOCAL *The Curlew* for tenor, flute, English horn, and string quartet (1921), *Corpus Christi* and *Sorrow's Lullaby* (1927).

OTHER over 100 songs, many on Elizabethan and Jacobean poems.

Warrack, Guy (Douglas Hamilton) (1900–1986) Scottish composer and conductor. He studied at Oxford and with Boult and Vaughan Williams at the Royal College of Music and taught there 1925–35. He made his debut as conductor in London, in 1925, and conducted the British Broadcasting Corporation (BBC) Scottish Orchestra 1936–45 and the Sadler's Wells Ballet 1948–51. He wrote music for various documentary films, including the official film of the 1953 coronation.

War Requiem choral work by Britten, Op. 66 (text of the Requiem Mass, together with poems by Wilfred Owen). It was first performed at Coventry Cathedral on 30 May 1962.

Wasps, The incidental music for Aristophanes' comedy by Vaughan Williams, first performed in Cambridge, in Greek, by undergraduates, on 26 November 1909; the orchestral suite was performed in London on 23 July 1912.

Water Music a set of instrumental pieces by Handel, first performed in London, in 1715, on a boat following the royal barge on the Thames. The music is said to have reconciled George I to Handel after the latter's desertion from the court of Hanover, but the story is doubtful.

Watkins, Michael Blake (1948–) English composer. He studied with Elisabeth Lutyens and Richard Rodney Bennett 1966–75.

Works ORCHESTRAL *Double Concerto* for oboe, guitar, and orchestra (1973); *Youth's Dream and Time's Truth* for tenor, trumpet, harp, and strings (1973); *Concertante* for eleven players (1973), horn concerto (1974); violin concerto (1977); *The Spirit of the Universe* for soprano and ensemble (1978); *Sinfonietta* (1982); concertos for trumpet (1988) and cello (1992).

CHAMBER oboe quartet (1984); string quartet (1979).

Watson, Thomas (c.1557–1592) English scholar and amateur musician. He published in 1590 *The First Sett of Italian Madrigalls Englished*, the successor of Nicholas Yonge's *Musica Transalpina* (1588), and with it the foundation of the native English school of madrigalists.

Waverley overture by Berlioz, Op. 1b, inspired by Walter Scott, first performed in Paris on 26 May 1828.

Webber, Andrew Lloyd English composer of musicals; see ➤ **Lloyd Webber**.

Weber, Bernhard Christian (1712–1758) German organist and composer. It was long claimed that he anticipated Bach by writing a set of preludes and fugues for keyboard in all the keys, entitled *Das wohltemperierte Clavier*, but he was actually an imitator, the work, wrongly dated 1689 (23 years before his birth), being in fact written in 1743. He was appointed organist at Tennstedt in 1732.

Weber, Carl Maria Friedrich Ernst von (1786–1826) German composer. He established the German Romantic school of opera with *Der Freischütz/The Marksman* (1821) and *Euryanthe* (1823). He was Kapellmeister (chief conductor) at Breslau in 1804–06, Prague in 1813–16, and Dresden in 1816. He died during a visit to London, where he produced his opera *Oberon* (1826), written for the Covent Garden Theatre.

Weber was taken about the country in his childhood and received little education, but his father, anxious to make a prodigy of him, taught him all the music he knew. When at last they settled at Salzburg, the ten-year-old Weber became a pupil of Michael Haydn (brother of Joseph). After his mother's death in 1798 he was taken to Vienna and Munich. There he studied under Giovanni Valesi and Johann Kalcher, and at 13 was a good enough pianist to appear at concerts. By 1800 he had written a good deal of youthful music and learned lithography with the Austrian engraver Alois Senefelder; but the wandering life was resumed and he continued his studies with the aid of theory books.

At Augsburg in 1803 his opera *Peter Schmoll und seine Nachbarn* was produced. In Vienna again in 1803–04, he studied for a time with Georg Vogler, who recommended him for a conductorship at Breslau, where he went in the autumn of 1804. In 1806 he became domestic musician to Duke Eugen of Württemberg, and later became a private secretary to the Duke's younger brother Ludwig. Weber settled at Stuttgart in 1807, but led a rather frivolous life there and incurred the displeasure of the king, his patron's elder brother. In 1810 he was banished from the kingdom on a trumped-up charge and went to Mannheim and later to Darmstadt, where he resumed his studies with Vogler more seriously. His brilliant works for clarinet and orchestra (two concertos and a concertino) date from 1811; the clarinet quintet followed four years later.

After much travelling he secured the conductorship at the German theatre in Prague in 1813. In 1816 he was appointed conductor of the Dresden court opera, where he did much to establish German opera in the face of the strong opposition of Morlacchi and other Italians. In 1817 he married the opera singer Caroline Brandt, and took her to Dresden after a concert tour. In 1821 his most famous opera, *Der Freischütz/The Marksman*, was produced in Berlin. It was immediately recognized throughout Germany as helping to establish a truly national style. *Euryanthe* followed in Vienna in 1823, and marked a major development with the way in which spoken dialogue, traditional in German opera, was replaced by continuously composed music. In 1824, Covent Garden commissioned an English opera from him, and he took English lessons to make a success of *Oberon*. He suffered badly from a severe disease of the throat and felt unfit to visit London, but in order to keep his family from want he took the risk in February 1826, visiting Paris on the way. He arrived in London in March, conducted works of his own at a Philharmonic concert, and produced *Oberon* in April. Although ill with tuberculosis, he still conducted the following performances and appeared at several concerts. Utterly worn out early in June, he made preparations for a hasty return home but died during the night at the house of his host, George Smart.

In spite of his early death Weber created a body of work that forms an important foundation of 19th-century German Romanticism. Richard Wagner and Gustav Mahler were particularly indebted to him.

Works STAGE operas *Der Freischütz/The Marksman* (1821), *Euryanthe* (1823), *Oberon* (1826).

ORCHESTRAL two symphonies (1807); 22 works for solo instruments and orchestra, including two piano concertos (1810–12), *Concertstück* for piano and orchestra (1821), concertino for clarinet and orchestra (1811), two concertos for clarinet and one for bassoon (all 1811).

INSTRUMENTAL quintet for clarinet, two violins, viola and cello (1815), trio for flute, cello, and piano (1819); 27 piano works including four sonatas (1812–22), *Aufforderung zum Tanz/Invitation to the Dance*.

Weber, (Jacob) Gottfried (1779–1839) German composer and theorist. He pursued a lawyer's profession at Mannheim (1804), Mainz (1812), and Darmstadt (1818). In 1810 his family provided refuge for their namesakes, Carl Maria von Weber and his father, after the former's banishment from Stuttgart, and they formed a music and cultural society. Weber wrote a number of theoretical books.

Works CHORAL three Masses and other church music.

OTHER instrumental sonatas and pieces; songs with piano and guitar.

Webern, Anton (Friedrich Wilhelm von) (1883–1945) Austrian composer. He wrote spare, enigmatic miniatures combining a pastoral poetic with severe structural rigour. A Renaissance musical scholar, he became a pupil of Arnold ➔ **Schoenberg**, whose 12-tone system he reinterpreted as abstract design in works such as the *Concerto for Nine Instruments* (1931–34) and the *Second Cantata* (1941–43). His constructivist aesthetic influenced the post-war generation of advanced composers.

Webern studied musicology with Guido Adler and took a doctorate at Vienna University in 1906. He studied compoition with Schoenberg. His first major work was the Passacaglia for orchestra, written with an awareness of the example of Brahms; it was followed by the Five Movements for string quartet, which exhibit some of Weber's later epigrammatic style. Song settings of Schoenberg's favourite poet, Stefan George, are Webern's first excursions into atonality. He conducted for a time at German provincial theatres and in Prague. After World War I he settled near Vienna and devoted himself to teaching and composition, though he still conducted, especially the modern performances of the Verein für Musikalische Privataufführungen and the workers' symphony concerts. He adopted Schoenberg's 12-note method of composition in the *Three Traditional Rhymes* of 1925. In succeeding works, such as the string trio, the symphony Op. 21, and the concerto Op. 24, Webern adopted ever more rigidly controlled methods; he was also influenced there by the Renaissance composer Heinrich Isaac.

His death was the result of a misunderstanding (he was shot by a US soldier). Although almost entirely unrecognized during his lifetime, Webern's music has proved very influential since his death: it introduced new concepts of sound, rhythm, and quasi-mathematical organization. It is almost as much through his work as through Schoenberg's that the 12-tone system came to

The subject of Bach's 'Wedge' Fugue, BWV 548.ii.

find so wide an acceptance; Webern's serial technique was stricter than Schoenberg's and Berg's, and later composers have capitalized on its rigour in their development of integral serialism (in which rhythm, dynamics, and even timbre are serialized). Among composers who have been particularly influenced by Webern are Stravinsky (from the early 1950s), Stockhausen, and Boulez.

Works ORCHESTRAL Six Pieces Op. 6 (1909, revised 1928), Five Pieces Op. 10 (1911–13, first performance 1926), Five Movements arranged for string orchestra from Five Movements for string quartet (1928–29), symphony Op. 21 (1928), Variations Op. 30 (1940).

VOCAL *Entflieht auf leichten Kähnen* for unaccompanied chorus Op. 2 (1908, first performance 1927), two songs for chorus and ensemble Op. 19 (texts by Goethe, 1926), *Das Augenlicht* for chorus and orchestra Op. 26 (1935), Cantata no. 1 for soprano, chorus, and orchestra (1938–9), Cantata no. 2 for soprano, bass, chorus, and orchestra (1941–3, first performance 1950); two sets of five songs for voice and piano opp. 3 and 4 (texts by George, 1909), two songs for voice and ensemble Op. 8 (texts by Rilke, 1910), four songs for voice and piano Op. 12 (1915–17), four songs for voice and orchestra Op. 13 (1914–18), six songs for voice and instruments (texts by Trakl, 1919–21), *Five Sacred Songs* for voice and instruments Op. 15 (1917–22), five canons on Latin texts for voice, clarinet, and bass clarinet Op. 16 (1923–24, first performance New York , 1951), *Three Traditional Rhymes* for voice and instruments Op. 17 (1925, first performance New York , 1952), three songs for voice, clarinet, and guitar Op. 18 (1925, first performance Los Angeles, 1954), three songs for voice and piano Op. 23 (1934), three songs for voice and piano Op. 25 (1934).

INSTRUMENTAL Five Movements for string quartet Op. 5 (1909), six Bagatelles for string quartet Op. 9 (1911–13), *Three Little Pieces* for cello and piano Op. 11 (1914), string trio Op. 20 (1927), concerto for nine instruments Op. 24 (1934), string quartet Op. 28 (1938), variations for piano Op. 27 (1936).

We Come to the River opera ('actions for music') by Henze (libretto by E Bond); composed 1974–76, produced London, Covent Garden, 12 July 1976. After a battle, the General sentences the Deserter to be shot; he later finds the condemned man's wife trying to survive amongst the corpses. Realizing the misery he has caused, the General refuses orders and is sent to a mental asylum where the inmates imagine a river carries them to freedom.

Wedding, The ballet by Igor Stravinsky; see *Les* → *Noces*.

Wedekind, Frank (1864–1918) German dramatist. He was a forerunner of expressionism with *Frühlings Erwachen/The Awakening of Spring* (1891), and *Der Erdgeist/The Earth Spirit* (1895) and its sequel *Der Marquis von Keith. Die Büchse der Pandora/Pandora's Box* (1904) was the source for Berg's opera *Lulu*.

See also → **Ettinger** (*Frühlingserwachen*) and → *Lulu*.

'Wedge' Fugue Bach's E minor organ fugue, BWV 548.ii, so called because of the progressively widening intervals of its subject.

Weelkes, Thomas (c.1576–1623) English composer. He wrote ten Anglican services and around 40 anthems, including 'When David heard'. He was also one of the most significant madrigalists of his time, contributing *As Vesta was from Latmos Hill Descending* to the *Triumphs of Oriana* (1601).

Weelkes was in the service of George Phillpot at Compton near Winchester in his early years and then that of Edward Darcye, Groom of the Privy Chamber. In 1598 he was appointed organist at Winchester College, in 1601 he became organist and choirmaster at Chichester Cathedral, and in 1602 was awarded a degree in music at Oxford University. His career at Chichester was turbulent: he received repeated reprimands for unruliness, drunkenness, and neglect of duty, and was dismissed in 1617. He later resumed the post, but died during a visit to London.

Weelkes published almost 100 madrigals, often for four, five, and six voices; they demonstrate his intricate style, fine counterpoint, and brilliant imagery.

Works VOCAL services and numerous anthems; three books of madrigals, *Ayeres or Phantasticke Spirites* for three voices (1608), two vocal pieces contributed to Leighton's *Teares or Lamentacions*.

INSTRUMENTAL three In Nomines for four to five viols and other pieces for five viols.

Weerbeke, Gaspar van (c.1445–c.1517) Flemish composer and singer. Of his works, about eight Masses, 28 motets, and several other liturgical works survive. Five of his Masses were published by the Venetian printer and publisher Ottaviano Petrucci.

Weerbeke took holy orders at Tournai and went to Italy in the 1470s, becoming maestro di cappella at Milan Cathedral and a singer in the service of the Sforza family at the ducal court. He was in Rome as a singer at the papal chapel 1481–89, but in 1488 produced music for allegorical plays given at the marriage of Galeazzo Sforza, Duke of Milan, to Isabella of Aragon. He returned to the Sforza court in 1489. From 1495 he spent two years as a singer in the court choir of Philip the Handsome, Archduke of Austria and Duke of Burgundy. He returned to Rome in 1500, where he again sang in the papal choir. He is last heard of as a canon at St Maria ad Gradus in Mainz.

Works CHORAL eight Masses, 28 motets, *Stabat Mater*, and other church music.

Weigl, Karl (1881–1949) Austrian composer. He studied musicology at Vienna University, worked as assistant conductor under Mahler at the Vienna Opera, became a teacher at the New Vienna Conservatory in 1918 and later lecturer at the university. He settled in the USA in 1938, becoming an American citizen in 1943 and teaching successively at Hartford, Brooklyn and Boston.

Works CANTATA *Weltfeier* for solo voices, chorus, orchestra and organ.

INSTRUMENTAL six symphonies (1908–47); various concertos.

CHAMBER eight string quartets (1903–49); cello and piano sonata.

VOCAL songs with piano and with chamber accompaniment.

Weihe des Hauses, Die, The Consecration of the House overture by Beethoven, Op. 124, written in 1822 for the opening of the Josefstadt Theatre in Vienna, and performed there on 3 October that year.

Weill, Kurt Julian (1900–1950) German composer; a US citizen from 1943. He wrote chamber and orchestral music and collaborated with Bertolt Brecht on operas such as *Die Dreigroschenoper/The Threepenny Opera* (1928) and *Aufstieg und Fall der Stadt Mahagonny/The Rise and Fall of the City of Mahagonny* (1929), both of which attacked social corruption. *Mahagonny*, which satirized US frontier values, caused a riot at its premiere in Leipzig. He tried to develop a new form of ➔ music theatre, using subjects that were currently important, and the simplest musical means. In 1933 he left Germany, and from 1935 was in the USA, where he wrote a number of successful scores for Broadway, among them the antiwar musical *Johnny Johnson* (1936), *Knickerbocker Holiday* (1938) (including the often covered 'September Song'), and *Street Scene* (1947), based on an Elmer Rice play set in the Depression.

His musical *Love Life* (1948), with lyrics by Alan Jay Lerner, describes a typical US couple over a period of 150 years of US history, and expresses Weill's mixture of fascination and repulsion towards the 'American Dream'.

Weill was born in Dessau, where his father was a cantor. He studied locally at first, and later with Engelbert Humperdinck in Berlin. At the age of 19 he was appointed conductor at a small opera house, but after a year of conducting he decided to return to Berlin to study composition under Ferruccio Busoni. He had his first stage success at the age of 26 when his first opera, *Der Protagonist/The Protagonist*, was produced at Dresden. Also at 26, he married the singer Lotte Lenya, who performed many of his songs. His collaboration with Bertolt Brecht on a modern version of John Gay's *Beggar's Opera/Die Dreigroschenoper* (1928) was a huge success, but in 1933 the Nazi regime condemned his works as both Jewish and decadent, and he left Germany. Official opinion also disapproved of Weill's effective use of jazz in his stage works, and there was further suspicion of the sharp social satire in *Die Dreigroschenoper*. He visited London in 1935 for the production of *A Kingdom for a Cow*, an English version of an earlier operetta, but went the same year to settle in the USA. Among the US writers who collaborated with Weill on musicals for Broadway were Ogden Nash and Maxwell Anderson. In 1949 he wrote *Lost in the Stars*, a musical tragedy based on Alan Paton's novel *Cry, the Beloved Country*, and he was planning a folk opera based on Mark Twain's *Huckleberry Finn* when he died suddenly of a heart attack.

Works STAGE (several on libretti by Bertolt Brecht) *Der Protagonist/The Protagonist* (1926), *Der Silbersee* (1933), *Der Zar lässt sich photographieren* (libretto by G Kaiser), *Royal Palace* (1927), *Die Dreigroschenoper/The Threepenny Opera* (1928), *Happy End* (1929), *Aufstieg und Fall der Stadt Mahagonny/The Rise and Fall of the City of Mahagonny* (1929), *Der Jasager* (1930), *Die Bürgschaft*, *A Kingdom for a Cow* (1935), *Johnny Johnson* (1936), *Knickerbocker Holiday* (1938), *The Firebrand of Florence* (1945), *Down in the Valley* (1948), *Street Scene* (1947), *Love Life* (1948), *Lost in the Stars* (1949); ballet *Die sieben Todsünden/Anna Anna* (1933).

CHORAL WITH ORCHESTRA Biblical music drama *The Eternal Road*; cantatas *Der neue Orpheus* and *Der Lindberghflug* (1929).

ORCHESTRAL two symphonies (1921, 1933), *Fantasia, Passacaglia und Hymnus, Divertimento* and *Quodlibet* for orchestra; concerto for violin and wind band (1924).

OTHER two string quartets (1919, 1923); works for voices and chamber orchestra, songs (Rilke) with orchestra.

Wein, Der, The Wine concert aria by Berg (text by Baudelaire, in German translation by S George); composed in 1929 and first performed at Königsberg on 4 June 1930, conducted by Scherchen.

Weinberger, Jaromír (1896–1967) Czech composer. He was professor of composition at the Conservatory of Ithaca, New York 1922–26; he later returned to Europe to conduct and teach. His best-known work, the folk-opera *Schvanda the Bagpiper* was premiered at Prague in 1927. His four later operas did not repeat its success, but the orchestral variations on 'Under the Spreading Chestnut Tree' (1939) made a momentary hit.

Weinberger studied with Hoffmeister and Kricka in Prague and with Reger in Germany. He settled in the USA in 1938.

Works DRAMATIC the operas *Shvanda the Bagpiper* (1927), *The Beloved Voice* (1931), *The Outcasts of Poker Flat* (after Bret Harte, 1932), and *Wallenstein* (after Schiller); pantomime *The Abduction of Eveline*; incidental music for Shakespeare's and other plays.

ORCHESTRAL variations on the English song, 'Under the Spreading Chestnut Tree' for piano and orchestra (1939), *Lincoln Symphony*, *Czech Rhapsody* for orchestra.

OTHER works for organ, piano, violin.

Weiner, Leó (1885–1960) Hungarian composer. He studied at the National Academy of Music in Budapest, where he became a professor in 1908.

Works STAGE ballet on and incidental music for Vörösmarty's *Csongor and Tünde* (1916).

ORCHESTRAL three divertimentos (1934–49), scherzo, serenade, and humoresque *Carnival* for orchestra; *Pastoral, Fantasy and Fugue* for strings; two violin concertos.

CHAMBER three string quartets (1906–38), string trio; two violin and piano sonatas; piano works.

Weingartner, (Paul) Felix (1863–1942) Austrian conductor and composer. He was noted as a conductor of the classical repertoire, and especially of the works of Schubert and Beethoven. He wrote seven symphonies and several operas. His writings include books on conducting and on Beethoven's symphonies.

Weingartner studied at Graz, at the Leipzig Conservatory, and under Liszt at Weimar, where he produced his first opera in 1884. He became conductor at Königsberg, Gdańsk, Hamburg, and Mannheim before 1891, when he was appointed conductor of the Court Opera in Berlin and conductor of the symphony concerts. In 1898 he left for Munich to become conductor of the Kaim orchestra and in 1908 succeeded Mahler as chief conductor at the Vienna Hofoper. He resigned in 1911 but conducted Vienna Philharmonic Or-

chestra concerts until 1927 and continued to conduct throughout Europe and the USA, notably in the symphonies of Beethoven. At Covent Garden he conducted Wagner's *Tannhäuser* and *Parsifal* in 1939. The last years of his life he spent, still actively, in Switzerland, especially at Basel.

Works OPERA *Sakuntala* (after Kalidasa, 1884), *Malawika* (1886), *Genesius*, *Orestes* trilogy (after Aeschylus, 1902), *Kain und Abel* (1914), *Dame Kobold* (after Calderón), *Die Dorfschule*, *Meister Andrea*, *Der Apostat*.

INCIDENTAL MUSIC incidental music for Shakespeare's *Tempest* and Goethe's *Faust*.

ORCHESTRAL seven symphonies (1899–1937), symphonic poem *King Lear* (after Shakespeare).

OTHER three string quartets; songs.

Weinlig, Christian Theodor (1780–1842) German theorist and composer. He was a pupil of his uncle, Christian Ehregott Weinlig (1743–1813), cantor of the Kreuzschule at Dresden. He succeeded Schicht as cantor of St Thomas's School at Leipzig in 1823. Clara Schumann and Richard Wagner were his pupils for a short time. He wrote a treatise on fugue. His compositions include an oratorio, two German Magnificats and church cantatas.

Weir, Judith (1954–) Scottish composer. She studied with John Tavener and worked with computer music at the Massachusetts Institute of Technology in 1973. Later she studied with Robin Holloway at Cambridge. Her compositions include *A Night at The Chinese Opera* (1987); *The Art of Touching the Keyboard* (1983), for piano; and *The Bagpiper's String Trio* (1985).

Works OPERA *The Black Spider* (1985), *A Night at The Chinese Opera* (1987), *The Vanishing Bridegroom* (1990), and *Blond Eckbert* (1994).

ORCHESTRAL orchestral pieces *Wunderhorn* (1979), *The Ride Over Lake Constance* (1984), *Variations on 'Summer is icumen in'* (1987), *Music Untangled* (1992), *Heroic Strokes of the Bow* (1992).

CHORAL *Heaven Ablaze in his Breast* for chorus, two pianos, and eight dancers (1989).

ENSEMBLE re-compositions of Mozart's *Il sogno di Scipione* (1991) and Monteverdi's *Il Combattimento di Tancredi e Clorinda* (1992).

OTHER chamber music; songs and keyboard pieces.

Weis, Flemming (1898–1981) Danish composer. A member of a musical family, he began to compose as a child. In 1916 he entered the Copenhagen Conservatory and in 1920 finished studies at Leipzig. He was active on behalf of contemporary music and also as a music critic.

Works CHORAL *The Promised Land* for chorus and orchestra.

ORCHESTRAL two symphonies (1942, 1948), symphonic overture and *In temporis vernalis* for orchestra.

ENSEMBLE *Introduction grave* for piano and strings.

CHAMBER four string quartets (1922–77) and other chamber music; sonatas for various instruments.

OTHER suite and sonatina for piano; songs.

Weisgall, Hugo David (1912–1997) Czech-born US composer. His family settled in the USA in 1920. He studied at the Peabody Conservatory, Baltimore, and later with Sessions in New York and R Scalero at the Curtis Institute in Philadelphia. He taught at the Juilliard School 1957–68. His music admitted a wide range of influences (including neoclassical and serial) and his operas were particularly successful.

Works OPERA *Night* (1932), *Lillith* (1934), *The Tenor* (1952), *Six Characters in Search of an Author* (after Pirandello, 1959), *Athaliah* (1964), *Nine Rivers from Jordan* (1968), *The 100 Nights* (1976), *The Gardens of Adonis* (1992, composed 1959), *Esther* (1994).

BALLET *Quest, One Thing is Certain, Outpost.*

ORCHESTRAL overture in F major for orchestra.

OTHER choral music; songs.

Weismann, Julius (1879–1950) German composer. He gained Nazi favour by accepting a commission to compose music for *A Midsummer Night's Dream* which was intended to replace Mendelssohn's; his *Die pfiffige Magd* (1939) was performed throughout Germany during the war years.

Weismann studied at Munich, then with Heinrich von Herzogenberg in Berlin, and again at Munich with Ludwig Thuille.

Works OPERA *Schwanenweiss* (1923), *Traumspiel* (1925), *Gespenstersonate* (all after Strindberg), *Leonce und Lena* (G Büchner, 1924), *Landsknechte*, *Regina del Lago* (1928), *Die pfiffige Magd* (after Holberg, 1939).

ORCHESTRAL three symphonies, three pieces for orchestra, three sinfoniettas; four violin concertos, three piano concertos, cello concerto.

CHAMBER eleven string quartets (1905–47), three piano trios (1908–21); sonata for violin solo, five violin sonatas, two cello sonatas, variations for oboe and piano.

OTHER choral works; variations for two pianos; seven Op. nos of piano pieces; 15 Op. nos of songs.

Weiss, Adolph (1891–1971) US composer of German parentage. He studied piano, violin, and bassoon, and at the age of 16 played first bassoon with the Russian Symphony Orchestra of New York and then in the New York Philharmonic Orchestra under Mahler. He then studied composition at Columbia University with C Ryb-

ner and later with Schoenberg in Vienna. He later worked with various California orchestras.

Works ORCHESTRAL *I Segreti* (1923) and *American Life* (1928) for orchestra; theme and variations for orchestra; trumpet concerto.

CHORAL *The Libation Bearers*, choreographed cantata for soloists, chorus, and orchestra.

CHAMBER three string quartets (1925–32).

OTHER music for wind instruments; songs; piano music.

Weiss, Sylvius Leopold (1686–1750) German lutenist and composer. He was both a virtuoso player and a prolific composer, writing nearly 600 pieces of music for solo lute, including over 70 partitas. He also wrote sonatas and concertos for combinations of instruments including the lute.

Weiss was in the service of the Polish Prince Alexander Sobieski, with whom he went to Rome about 1708, later at the courts of Hesse-Kassel, Düsseldorf, and from 1718 at Dresden, where he worked with Lotti, Hasse, Porpora, Hebenstreit, Pisendel, and others; he was sent to Vienna with a visiting Saxon orchestra that year. In 1723 he played in Prague with Quantz and H Graun in Fux's coronation opera *Costanza e fortezza*.

welcome-odes or **welcome-songs** cantatas by Henry ➔ Purcell for the return to London of Charles II and James II on various occasions. One, of 1682, is addressed to James as Duke of York, before his accession.

Weldon, George (1906–1963) English conductor. He studied at the Royal College of Music with Malcolm Sargent, and conducted various provincial orchestras, in 1943 becoming conductor of the City of Birmingham Symphony Orchestra (CBSO), a post he held until 1951; he was later assistant conductor of the Hallé Orchestra under Barbirolli.

Weldon, John (1676–1736) English organist and composer. He held various organist's posts in Oxford and London, and in 1700 won first prize for his setting of Congreve's masque *The Judgment of Paris* against John Eccles, Gottfried Finger, and Daniel Purcell.

Weldon was educated at Eton, where he studied music under the college organist John Walton; he later became a pupil of Purcell in London. In 1694 he was appointed organist of New College, Oxford. In 1701 he became a Gentleman of the Chapel Royal and in 1708 organist there on the death of John Blow; he also became organist of St Bride's and in 1714 of St Martin-in-the-Fields.

Works DRAMATIC masque *The Judgment of Paris* (1701); music for *The Tempest* (about 1712), songs for Cibber's *She would and she would not* and other plays.

OTHER anthems; songs.

Wellesz, Egon Joseph (1885–1974) Austrian-born British composer and musicologist. He taught at Vienna University 1913–38, specializing in the history of Byzantine, Renaissance, and modern music. He moved to England in 1938 and lectured at Oxford from 1943. His compositions include operas such as *Alkestis* (1924); symphonies, notably the Fifth (1957); ballet music; and a series of string quartets.

Wellesz studied with Schoenberg and Bruno Walter in Vienna, and also musicology with Guido Adler at the university there, receiving a PhD in 1908. In 1913 he became a lecturer in music history in Vienna and was professor 1930–38.

He edited and wrote books on Byzantine music, and published works on Schoenberg, Cavalli and the Venetian opera, and the modern orchestra. In 1932 he received an honorary PhD from Oxford University and in 1938 he settled there, becoming a lecturer in 1943 and Reader 1948–56. He was a member of the editorial board of the *New Oxford History of Music* and editor of volume I and one of the editions of *Monumenta Musicae Byzantinae*. His books include *A History of Byzantine Music* and *Eastern Elements in Western Chant*.

Works OPERA *Alkestis* (Hofmannsthal, 1924) and *Die Bacchantinnen* (after Euripides, 1931), *Incognita* (on Congreve's story, 1951).

VOCAL AND ORCHESTRA nine symphonies (1945–71), symphonic suite *Prosperos Beschwörungen* (after Shakespeare's *Tempest*, 1938), violin concerto; three Masses.

CHAMBER AND INSTRUMENTAL *The Leaden Echo and the Golden Echo* (G M Hopkins) for soprano, clarinet, viola, cello and piano (1944); nine string quartets (1911–66); octet; solo sonatas for violin, cello, oboe, clarinet; piano pieces; songs.

Well-tempered Clavier see ➤ *Wohltemperierte Clavier, Das*.

Werfel, Franz (1890–1945) Austrian poet, dramatist, and novelist. He was a leading expressionist. His works include the poem 'Der Weltfreund der Gerichtstag/The Day of Judgment' (1919); the plays *Juarez und Maximilian* (1924) and *Das Reich Gottes in Böhmen/The Kingdom of God in Bohemia* (1930); and the novels *Verdi* (1924) and *Das Lied von Bernadette/The Song of Bernadette* (1941).

Born in Prague, he lived in Germany, Austria, and France, and in 1940 escaped from a French concentration camp to the USA, where he died. In 1929 he married Alma Mahler, widow of the composer Gustav Mahler.

In addition to his novel based on Giuseppe ➤ Verdi's life, he translated many of the composer's operas, including *La Forza del Destino/The Force of Destiny* and *Don Carlos*. His own writings inspired many other composers, including Darius Milhaud's opera ➤ *Maximilien*, Aribert Reimann's ➤ *Troades*, and Ernst Krenek's cantata ➤ *Zwingburg*.

Werle, Lars Johan (1926–2001) Swedish composer. He studied at Uppsala University with Bäck and taught at the National School of Music in Stockholm. He is best known for his technically varied output of operas: *Dream about Thérèse* (1964), *The Journey* (1969), *Tintomara* (1973), *A Midsummer Night's Dream* (1985), *Lionardo* (1988), *The Painting: An Afternoon at the Prado* (1990), double-bill *Hercules* and *Väntarna* (1995).

Werner, Gregor Joseph (1693–1766) Austrian composer. He was appointed music director to the Esterházy family in 1728; Haydn became his assistant there in 1761 and succeeded him five years later. Shortly before his death Werner reported to Prince Nikolaus von Esterházy on Haydn's alleged laziness and ineptitude.

Works CHORAL over 20 Masses, three Requiems and other church music; 18 oratorios.

ORCHESTRAL symphony.

CHAMBER string quartet, six introductions and fugues for string quartet (published by Haydn); sonatas and other pieces for two violins and bass.

Werrecore, Matthias Hermann (died c. 1574) Flemish composer. In 1522 he succeeded Franchino Gafori as maestro di cappella of Milan Cathedral.

Works VOCAL motets for five voices, four-part song on the battles of Bicocca and Pavia, in which Francesco Sforza gained the mastery of Milan.

Wert, Giaches de (1535–1596) Flemish composer. He was music director at the ducal court of Mantua from the early 1560s until 1595. He was a prolific composer, and wrote over 150 sacred vocal pieces, but his most celebrated compositions are his madrigals. He published 16 books of madrigals and other secular works, and had a great influence on his successors, especially Monteverdi.

Wert was sent to Italy as a choirboy when a small child, to sing at the court of the Marchese della Padulla at Avellino near Naples. At age nine he entered the service of Count Alfonso Gonzaga as a member of the choir of the Novellara at Reggio. He began to publish madrigals towards the end of the 1550s and about 1560 went into service at the ducal court of Mantua under Guglielmo Gonzaga. He was also attached to the Church of Santa Barbara, where he succeeded Giovanni Contina as maestro di cappella in 1565. In 1566 he accompanied the duke to Augsburg and there declined an offer from the Emperor Maximilian II. In 1567 he visited Venice with the court and later Ferrara under Alfonso (II) d'Este. About that time he suffered much from the intrigues of the Italian musicians, who disliked him as a foreigner, and in 1570 one of them, Agostino Bonvicino, was dismissed for a love affair with Wert's wife. In 1580 he and his family were given the freedom of the city of Mantua in perpetuity.

His madrigals often had high-quality texts, and were declamatory in style and with the three upper voices frequently emphasized; they were written for virtuoso court singers, particularly the *concerto delle donne* or 'singing ladies' of Ferrara.

Works VOCAL motets, eleven books of madrigals for five voices (1558–95), one for four voices, canzonets, villanelle.

Werther opera by Massenet (libretto by E Blau, P Milliet and G Hartmann, based on Goethe's novel), produced in German, at the Vienna Opera on 16 February 1892, conducted by Jahn; the first Paris performance was at the Opéra-Comique on 16 January 1893. Charlotte promised her dead mother that she would marry Albert, but Werther falls in love with her. Unable to reconcile himself to the situation, Werther shoots himself, dying in her arms.

Wesendonck Lieder five songs for voice and piano by Wagner (texts by Mathilde Wesendonck (1828–1902), with whom the composer was in love); composed in Zurich, 1857–58. Usually heard in orchestral arrangement by Felix Mottl. Titles are 1. 'Der Engel'; 2. 'Stehe still'; 3. 'Im Treibhaus'; 4. 'Schmerzen'; 5. 'Träume'. Nos 3 and 5 were studies for *Tristan*, also written under the influence of Mathilde Wesendonck.

Wesley, Charles (1757–1834) English organist and composer. He was a pupil of Kelway and Boyce in London and later organist at various churches and chapels. He also appeared in public as harpsichordist.

Works ORCHESTRAL incidental music for Mason's *Caractacus*; concerto grosso; six organ or harpsichord concertos.

CHAMBER six string quartets (1776).

OTHER anthems, hymns, harpsichord pieces; songs.

Wesley, Samuel (1766–1837) English organist, composer, and conductor, regarded as the best organist of his day. He was brother of Charles ➤ Wesley, and nephew of John Wesley (the founder of Methodism). He did much to spread a knowledge of Bach in England, and edited some of his works. He conducted the Birmingham Festival in 1811, lectured at the Royal Institution, and gave frequent organ recitals.

Like his brother he showed precocious musical gifts at a very early age. At the age of six he was taught by the organist of the church of St James, in Barton, Bristol, England. At age eight he finished the oratorio *Ruth*, and soon after appeared at the organ as a prodigy. In 1787 a fall left him

with a recurrent illness, ending his career. He wrote many masses, motets, anthems (including *In exitu Israel*), and also secular music.

Works ORATORIOS *Ruth* (1744) and *The Death of Abel* (1799).

CHORAL four masses, numerous Latin and English anthems, including *In exitu Israel*, *Exultate Deo*, *Dixit Dominus*, *All go unto one place*, *Behold how good*, *Hear, O thou shepherd* (some with organ), Morning and Evening Service in F major and other church music; *Ode on St Cecilia's Day*.

ORCHESTRAL four symphonies (1784–1802), and five overtures; organ and violin concertos.

CHAMBER two string quartets and other chamber music.

OTHER opera fugues, voluntaries; numerous piano works; glees, songs, and duets.

Wesley, Samuel Sebastian (1810–1876) English organist and composer, illegitimate son of Samuel ➤ Wesley. He was a pupil of his father and choirboy in the Chapel Royal from 1820. In 1826 he became organist of Hereford Cathedral, and in 1835 (when he married) of Exeter Cathedral; he was organist of Leeds Parish Church 1842–1849, of Winchester Cathedral 1849–1865, and then, until his death, of Gloucester Cathedral. He was awarded a doctorate in music at Oxford in 1839, and became organ professor at the Royal Academy of Music in London in 1850. He continued his father's promotion of Bach's music and conducted the St Mathew Passion at Gloucester (Three Choirs Festival) in 1871.

Works CHORAL five services, 24 anthems, two settings of *By the waters of Babylon* with soprano and with contralto solo, chants and hymn tunes; *Ode to Labour* and *The Praise of Music*.

OTHER organ works; three glees; nine songs (two with cello *ad lib*); piano pieces.

Westrup, Jack (Allan) (1904–1975) English musicologist, critic, composer, and conductor. He was educated at Dulwich College and Balliol College, Oxford, where as an undergraduate he edited Monteverdi's *Orfeo* and *Incoronazione di Poppea* for performance by the Oxford University Opera Club. He taught classics at Dulwich College 1928–34, and was an assistant music critic on the *Daily Telegraph* 1934–40. From 1941 to 1944 he was lecturer in music at King's College, Newcastle-upon-Tyne, 1944–46 professor of music at Birmingham University and 1947–71 professor at Oxford. He conducted *Idomeneo* and *Les Troyens*, the first performance of E Wellesz's *Incognita* and the first UK performance of *Hans Heiling* and *L'Enfant et les sortilèges*. He was chairman of the editorial board of the *New Oxford History of Music* and editor of the sixth volume thereof; he was also editor of *Music and Letters* from 1959. Other literary work includes a book on Purcell and the fourth and fifth editions of the *Everyman Dictionary of Music* (1962 and 1971).

Works CHORAL motet *When Israel came out of Egypt* for unaccompanied double chorus.

ORCHESTRAL passacaglia for orchestra.

VOCAL part song *Weathers*; three Shakespeare songs.

Wheatstone, Charles (1802–1875) English physicist and inventor. With William Cooke, he patented a railway telegraph in 1837, and, developing an idea of Samuel Christie (1784–1865), devised the **Wheatstone bridge**, an electrical network for measuring resistance. He also invented the concertina.

In 1834 Wheatstone made the first determination of the velocity of electricity along a wire. He also improved on early versions of the dynamo so that current was generated continuously. He was knighted in 1868.

Wheatstone was born in Gloucester and joined the family business making musical instruments. His work in acoustics led to his appointment as professor of experimental physics at King's College, London, in 1834, a position he retained for the rest of his life.

In 1827 Wheatstone invented a device called the kaleidophone, which visually demonstrated the vibration of sounding surfaces by causing an illuminated spot to vibrate and produce curves by the persistence of vision. He went on to investigate the transmission of sound in instruments and discovered modes of vibration in air columns in 1832 and vibrating plates in 1833.

Wheatstone showed in 1835 that spectra produced by spark discharges from metal electrodes have different lines and colours formed by different electrodes. He predicted correctly that with development, spectroscopy would become a technique for the analysis of elements.

In 1860, he demonstrated how the visual combination of two similar pictures in a stereoscope gives an illusion of three dimensions.

When Lilacs Last in the Dooryard Bloom'd US Requiem for mezzo-soprano, baritone, chorus, and orchestra by Paul ➤ Hindemith (text by Walt Whitman); first performed in New York on 14 May 1946, conducted by Robert Shaw. The piece was written in memory of Franklin D Roosevelt and the US war dead.

Whettam, Graham (Dudley) (1927–   ) English composer. Largely self-taught, he writes in a fairly conservative style: more honoured abroad then in his own country, he has published his works himself from 1970.

Works DRAMATIC the opera *The Chef who Wanted to Rule the World* (1969), ballet *The Masque of the Red Death* (after Poe, 1968).

ORCHESTRAL concertos for oboe, clarinet, and violin; four symphonies, *Sinfonietta stravagante* (1964), Sinfonia concertante (1966); *Hymnos* for strings (1978); *An English Suite* for orchestra (1984), Ballade for violin and orchestra (1988).

CHAMBER two oboe quartets (1960, 1973), three string quartets (1967, 1978, 1980), horn trio (1976), concerto for ten wind (1979).

CHORAL *A Mass for Canterbury* (1986).

OTHER songs; music for brass band and for organ.

whistle any of a class of wind instruments including recorders, flutes, organ pipes, and panpipes, that uses a rigid edge as an aerofoil to split the air flow, giving a characteristic 'chuff' onset to the tone. Among the most ancient and widespread of musical instruments, whistles produce a relatively pure tone and simple waveform.

Most whistles relying on human breath are soprano or higher in pitch range; those of lower pitch such as organ pipes are usually powered by bellows. Some whistles are of single pitch, others have finger holes to vary the pitch and may be overblown to sound an octave or twelfth higher.

Whitbroke, William (lived 16th century) English cleric and composer. He was educated at Cardinal College (later Christ Church), Oxford, where he was ordained in 1529. In 1531 he was appointed sub-dean at St Paul's Cathedral in London and soon afterwards also vicar of All Saints' Church at Stanton, Suffolk, where he may have retired on leaving St Paul's in 1535.

Works CHORAL Mass for four voices, Magnificat, and other church music.

White or **Whyte, Robert (c.1538–1574)** English composer. He was choirmaster at Ely, Chester, and Westminster Abbey, and wrote church music including psalm motets, anthems, and Lamentations.

White was probably the son of a London organ builder, also named Robert White, and took a degree in music at Cambridge University in 1560. In 1561 he succeeded Tye as choirmaster at Ely Cathedral. He married Tye's daughter Ellen in 1565 and left Ely in 1566 (he was succeeded by John Farrant) to become choirmaster of Chester Cathedral until about 1570, when he went to London to take up a similar post at Westminster Abbey. Along with nearly all his family, he succumbed to the plague of 1574.

Works CHORAL 19 Latin motets; English anthems.

OTHER In Nomines for viols; hexachord fantasia for keyboard.

whithorn or **May-horn** early English musical instrument of the ➤ oboe type, made of willow bark with a double reed of material from the same tree. It was formerly used in Oxfordshire for the Whit-Monday hunt.

Whitman, Walt(er) (1819–1892) US poet. See ➤ **Brian** (*For Valour*); ➤ **Carpenter** (*Sea Drift*); ➤ **Carter** (*Warble for Lilac Time*); Coleridge-Taylor (*Sea Drift*); ➤ **Converse** (*Mystic Trumpeter* and *Night and Day*); R Harris (suite); Harty (*Mystic Trumpeter*); ➤ **Henze** (chamber cantata); ➤ **Holst** (*Ode to Death*); ➤ **Loeffler** (*Beat! Beat! Drums!*); ➤ '**Morning Heroes**' (Bliss); ➤ **Mystic Trumpeter** (Holst); ➤ **Schoeck** (*Trommelschläge*); ➤ **Sea Drift** (Delius); ➤ **Sea Symphony** (Vaughan Williams); ➤ **Vaughan Williams** (*Toward the Unknown Region*); ➤ **When Lilacs Last in the Dooryard Bloom'd** (Hindemith).

Who is Silvia? song by Schubert from Shakespeare's *Two Gentlemen of Verona*, translated by E von Bauernfeld as *An Silvia* and composed in 1826.

whole tone in music, an interval consisting of two ➤ **semitones**, for example the interval of C–D.

whole-tone scale in music, a scale consisting of six whole tones per octave. There are only two possible variants: the scale including the notes C–D–E–F♯–G♯–A♯ and the scale including the notes D♭–E♭–F–G–A–B. In Western music the whole-tone scale became popular with Impressionist composers, including Debussy, partly because having no semitones or perfect intervals within the scale, it has no sense of tonic.

The two possible whole-tone scales.

Whyte, Robert English composer; see Robert ➤ White.

Whythorne, Thomas (1528–1596) English composer. He travelled in Italy and elsewhere in Europe, and published his first book of music, *Songes* for several voices, in 1571, and his second, a book of duets, in 1590; the second volume contains the earlier printed English instrumental music. His autobiography, written around 1576, was published in 1961.

Works VOCAL psalms and secular songs for two to five voices or solo voice with instruments.

Widerspänstigen Zähmung, Der, The Taming of the Shrew opera by Götz (libretto by J V Widmann, after Shakespeare), produced at Mannheim on 11 October 1874. Before Lucentio and Bianca can wed, Petruchio must tame Katherine.

Widor, Charles-Marie (-Jean-Albert) (1844–1937) French composer and organist. He created the solo organ symphony, which in effect treats the instrument itself as an orchestra of variously coloured pipes and ➤ **stops**. He wrote ten such symphonies; the famous *Toccata* (c.1880) is the finale of his Fifth Symphony. He also wrote songs, concertos, ballets, and operas.

Widor was born at Lyon and studied under his father, who was an organist there. Later he studied with Lemmens and Fétis in Brussels. In 1870 he became organist of the church of Saint-Sulpice in Paris, and in 1890 succeeded Franck as organ professor at the Paris Conservatory. He succeeded Dubois as professor of composition in 1896.

Works DRAMATIC operas *Maître Ambros* (1886), *Les pêcheurs de Saint-Jean* (1905), *Nerto* (after Mistral); ballet *La Korrigane*; pantomime *Jeanne d'Arc*; incidental music to *Conte d'Avril* (adaptation of Shakespeare's *Twelfth Night*) and Coppée's *Les Jacobites*.

CHORAL Mass for double chorus and two organs, Psalm 112 for chorus, orchestra, and organ.

ORCHESTRAL two symphonies (1870, 1886), symphonic poem *Une nuit de Valpurgis*; symphony for organ and orchestra, two concertos for piano (1876 and 1906) and one for cello (1882).

CHAMBER piano quintet, piano trio; violin and piano sonata, suite for flute and piano; six duets for piano and organ.

OTHER ten symphonies (1876–1900) and pieces for organ; piano works; songs.

Wieck, Clara German pianist and composer; see Clara ➤ Schumann.

Wiegenlied (German 'cradle song') title often given by German composers to vocal lullabies or to instrumental pieces in their manner.

Wieniawski, Henryk (1835–1880) Polish violinist and composer. He travelled widely, studying in Paris, then settling in St Petersburg, and later teaching in Brussels. He was a celebrated violinist and composed spirited Romantic pieces for the violin, notably his second violin concerto in D minor.

Wieniawski was sent to the Paris Conservatory at the age of eight, and in 1846 made his first tour, in Poland and Russia. From 1850 he travelled with his brother Józef and in 1860 was appointed solo violinist to the Tsar, living in St Petersburg most of his time until 1872, when he toured the USA with Anton Rubinstein. In 1875 he succeeded Henry Vieuxtemps as first violin professor at the Brussels Conservatory. Towards the end of his life he travelled again, in spite of serious ill-health which caused his sudden death in Russia.

Works ORCHESTRAL two violin concertos (1853, 1862).

OTHER *Souvenir de Moscou*, *Le carnaval russe*, *Légende* and numerous other pieces, fantasies and studies for violin.

Wihtol, Joseph (1863–1948) Latvian composer. He studied with Rimsky-Korsakov and others at the St Petersburg Conservatory; in 1886 he returned to Latvia and took an important share in its musical independence as a separate nation, becoming director of the National Opera at Riga and director of the Latvian Conservatory.

Works DRAMATIC music for fairy play *King Brussubard.*

ORCHESTRAL symphonies, symphonic poem *The Feast of Ligo*, Latvian overture *Spriditis*, dramatic overture for orchestra; fantasy on Latvian folksongs for cello and orchestra.

Wilby, Philip (1949–   ) English composer. He studied at Oxford University and with Herbert Howells. He was appointed lecturer at Leeds University in 1972.

Works ORCHESTRAL *Voyaging*, symphony (1991); Mozart reconstructions include concerto for violin and piano K315f and concerto for string trio and orchestra K320e.

CHORAL *Trinity Service* for chorus and organ (1992).

OTHER *Laudibus in Sanctis* for wind band (1993); chamber and keyboard music.

Wilbye, John (1574–1638) English composer. He was not only one of the first English composers to write madrigals, but also one of the finest. Among his most characteristic works are the popular madrigals 'Draw on Sweet Night' and 'Sweet honey sucking bees' (both 1609).

Wilbye was born at Diss, Norfolk, where his father was a tanner and landowner. Wilbye was patronized by the Cornwallis family at Brome Hall near Diss. In about 1595 he went into the service of their son-in-law, Sir Thomas Kytson, at Hengrave Hall near Bury St Edmunds, and was frequently in London with the family. After the death of his patron he remained in the service of Kytson's widow, Lady Elizabeth Kytson, who died in 1628, whereupon he went to Colchester to join the household of her daughter, Lady Rivers. He never married and was well-to-do, having been granted the lease of a sheep farm by Kyston and gradually acquiring property at Diss, Bury St Edmunds, and elsewhere.

Wilbye was influenced by Morley and Ferrabosco. He published two books of madrigals (1598 and 1609), the second of which is generally regarded as one of the greatest English madrigal collections. It contains 'Draw on sweet Night', which uses major and minor tonalities to depict deep melancholy.

Works VOCAL two sacred vocal pieces contributed to Leighton's *Teares or Lamentacions*; two books of 64 madrigals (1598, 1609), madrigal 'The Lady Oriana' contributed to *The Triumphes of Oriana.*

OTHER five sacred works; three fantasies for viols (incomplete), lute lessons (lost).

***Wildschütz, Der, oder Die Stimme der Natur,
The Poacher, or The Voice of Nature*** opera by Lortzing (libretto by composer, based on a play by Kotzebue), produced in Leipzig on 31 December 1842. Schoolmaster Baculus shoots a buck on the estate of the Count of Eberbach and his betrothed, young Grhen, offers to intercede for him. But knowing his philandering reputation, the Count's sister (Baroness Freimann) impersonates Grhen instead. After disguise and confusion, a happy ending.

Wilkinson, Robert (c.1450–c.1515) English composer. He composed two settings of *Salve Regina* for five and nine voices, a *Credo in Deum/Jesus autem* for 13 voices in canon, and four incomplete works. All are in the Eton Choirbook.

Wilkinson, Thomas (1579–96) English composer. He may have been a singer at King's College, Cambridge, and he contributed three anthems to Myriell's *Tristitiae remedium* in 1616.

Works services, twelve verse anthems, three pavans for viols.

Willaert, Adrian (c.1490–1562) Flemish composer. One of the most prolific and influential musicians of the mid-16th century, he was one of the earliest composers of madrigals, though his most important works are his motets. He also had a great influence on church music, broadening its character and achieving effect by a wide use of chromatic scales.

Willaert was trained in law but studied music with Jean Mouton in Paris. In 1515 he became a singer in the household of Cardinal Ippolito d'Este; his extensive travels with the cardinal included visits to Rome, Ferrara, and Esztergom, and a two-year stay in Hungary. On the cardinal's death in 1520 Willaert transferred to the service of Duke Alfonso I d'Este. In 1527 he became maestro di cappella at St Mark's, Venice, where his pupils included Cipriano de Rore, Nicola Vicentino, Andrea Gabrieli, Gioseffe Zarlino, and Costanzo Porta. He revisited Flanders in 1542 and 1556–57.

Willaert's works include a large quantity of church music, as well as many madrigals, chansons, villanelles, and some instrumental pieces. *Salmi spezzati* (1550) contains music for double choirs and set a tradition for polychoral music in St Mark's. His most important work is the collection of motets and madrigals, *Musica nova*, published in 1559, though probably written much earlier.

Works Masses, hymns, psalms, motets, madrigals, chansons, and instrumental ensemble pieces.

William Ratcliff opera by Cui (libretto by A N Pleshtcheiev, based on Heine's drama), produced in St Petersburg on 26 February 1869. Betty's jealous husband MacGregor kills her lover Edward Ratcliffe; Betty dies soon afterwards. Edward's son William is haunted by their ghosts until multiple deaths appease the ghosts.

See also ➤ *Guglielmo Ratcliff*.

Williams, Grace (Mary) (1906–1977) Welsh composer. She was educated at Cardiff University, where she took a degre in music in 1926; she also studied with Vaughan Williams at the Royal College of Music 1926–30 and with Egon Wellesz in Vienna 1930–31.

Works OPERA *The Parlour* (1961).

VOICE AND ORCHESTRA *Hymn of Praise (Gogonedawg Arglwydd*, from the 12th-century Black Book of Carmarthen) for chorus and orchestra (1939); two psalms for soprano and orchestra, *The Song of Mary* (Magnificat) for soprano and orchestra.

ORCHESTRAL Welsh overture *Hen Walia*, legend *Rhiannon, Fantasy on Welsh Nursery Rhymes*, symphonic impressions *Owen Glendower* (after Shakespeare's *Henry IV*), *Penillion* (1955); violin concerto (1950); *Sinfonia concertante* for piano and orchestra (1941); elegy and *Sea Sketches* for string orchestra.

OTHER songs to words by Herrick, Byron, Belloc, D H Lawrence, and others; arrangements of Welsh folk songs.

Williamson, Malcolm (Benjamin Graham Christopher) (1931–2003) Australian composer, pianist, and organist. Williamson studied with Eugene Goossens at the Sydney Conservatory and with Elisabeth ➤ **Lutyens** in London, where he settled in 1953, and became an organist. His works include operas such as *Our Man in Havana* (1963), two symphonies, and chamber music. He was appointed ➤ **Master of the Queen's Musick** in 1975.

His music draws on a wide range of influences, moving from an awareness of the avant garde to a more popular style, and includes several operas, a ballet *The Display*, concertos, church music, and dramatic works for children.

Works OPERA *English Eccentrics* (1964), *Our Man in Havana* (1965), *The Violins of St Jacques* (1966), *Lucky Peter's Journey* (1969).

ORCHESTRAL concerto for organ and orchestra, four piano concertos (1957–94), violin concerto (1965), seven symphonies (1957–84); *Santiago de Espada*, overture for orchestra.

CHORAL *Mass of Christ the King*, for soloists, chorus, and orchestra (1975–78); *Mass of St Etheldreda* (1990), *A Year of Birds* for soprano and orchestra (1995).

OTHER chamber music; piano and organ works.

Wilm, (Peter) Nikolai von (1834–1911) Latvian composer. He studied at the Leipzig Conser-

vatory. In 1857 he became second conductor at the Riga municipal theatre and in 1860 went to St Petersburg as professor at the Nikolai Institute. He lived at Dresden 1875–78 and then at Wiesbaden.

Works CHORAL motets.

CHAMBER string quartet, string sextet; two sonatas and two suites for violin and piano, sonata for cello and piano.

OTHER numerous piano pieces; songs; part songs.

Wilson, John (1595–1674) English lutenist, singer, and composer. He was a musician at the court of Charles I, and wrote many songs, including songs for plays. During the Commonwealth he lived in Oxfordshire and was professor of music at Oxford University, returning to London after the Restoration.

Wilson contributed, possibly with Coperario and Lanier, to *The Maske of Flowers*, performed at Whitehall in 1614. He became one of the king's musicians in 1635 and moved to Oxford with the court during the Civil War. In 1645 he took a PhD in music there, and soon afterwards was in private service in Oxfordshire. He was professor of music at Oxford University 1656–61, then returned to London to be at or near the restored court and succeeded Henry Lawes as a Gentleman of the Chapel Royal in 1662.

Works VOCAL songs for *The Maske of Flowers*; anthem *Hearken, O God*; *Psalterium Carolinum* for three voices and continuo; elegy on the death of William Lawes; *Cheerful Ayres* for three voices; airs and dialogues with lute; songs including Shakespeare's 'Take, O take those lips away' and 'Lawn as white as driven snow'; catches.

Wilson, Thomas (Brendan) (1927–2001) US-born Scottish composer. He studied at Glasgow University and lectured there from 1927. His works employed serial technique and include the operas *The Charcoal Burners* (1968) and *Confessions of a Justified Sinner* (1976).

Works ORCHESTRAL four symphonies (1956, 1965, 1982, 1988), *Touchstone*, 'portrait for orchestra' (1967), concerto for orchestra (1967), piano concerto (1984), chamber concerto (1986), viola concerto (1987), chamber symphony (1990), violin concerto (1993).

CHAMBER four string quartets, piano trio (1966), cello sonata (1973).

CHORAL three Masses, Te Deum, and other church music.

PIANO piano sonata and sonatina.

windcap in music, a cylindrical cover protecting the double reed of a ➤ **woodwind** instrument, such as the ➤ **crumhorn** or ➤ **shawm**. It prevents the player's lips from making direct contact with the reeds and forms a secure airtight container, ensuring consistency of air pressure and tone. In omitting the windcap, baroque instruments introduced a new aesthetic of controlled variability of tone for expressive effect.

wind machine or **aeoliphone** stage device for creating sound effects. It is a barrel covered with silk, the friction of which on being turned produces a sound like a whistling wind.

It was used by Richard Strauss in *Don Quixote*, by Ravel in *Daphnis et Chloé*, by Vaughan Williams in *Sinfonia antartica* and by Tippett in his fourth symphony.

Winter, Peter (von) (1754–1825) German composer. He wrote over 40 works for the stage, including *Das Labyrinth* (1798), a sequel to Mozart's *Magic Flute*. His later works are mainly church music.

Winter played as a boy in the court orchestra at Mannheim, where he was a pupil of Georg Vogler and met Mozart in 1778. He moved with the court to Munich, but went to Vienna 1780–81 and studied with Salieri. On his return to Munich he produced the first of his many operas, *Helena und Paris*, and became vice-Kapellmeister to the court in 1787 and Kapellmeister in 1798, but was periodically absent on tour.

Works OPERA *Helena und Paris* (1782), *Der Bettelstudent* (1785), *I fratelli rivali* (1793), *Das unterbrochene Opferfest* (1796), *Das Labyrinth* (sequel to Mozart's *Magic Flute*, 1798), *Maria von Montelban* (1800), *Tamerlan* (1802), *La grotta di Calipso* (1803), *Il trionfo dell'amor fraterno*, *Il ratto di Proserpina* (1804), *Zaira*, *Colmal* (1809), *Maometto II* (1817), *Scherz, List und Rache* and *Jery und Bätely* (both libretti by Goethe), and about 20 others.

BALLET *Heinrich IV* (1779), *Inez de Castro*, *La mort d'Hector* and six others.

ORATORIOS *Der Sterbende Jesus*, *La Betulia liberata*, and others.

CHORAL Masses and other church music; cantata *Timoteo, o Gli effetti della musica* and others.

ORCHESTRAL three symphonies, *Schlachtsymphonie* and overtures; concerted pieces for various instruments.

OTHER songs, part songs.

Winter Journey song cycle by Franz ➤ Schubert; see ➤ *Winterreise*.

Wintermärchen, Ein, *A Winter's Tale* opera by Goldmark (libretto by A M Willner, after Shakespeare), produced at the Vienna Opera on 2 January 1908.

Winterreise, *The Winter Journey* song cycle by Schubert, based on poems by Wilhelm Müller. It falls into two parts, composed in February 1827 and October 1827 respectively.

The 24 songs are 1. 'Gute Nacht'; 2. 'Die Wetter-fahne'; 3. 'Gefrorne Tränen'; 4. 'Erstarrung'; 5. 'Der Lindenbaum'; 6. 'Wasserflut'; 7. 'Auf dem Flusse'; 8. 'Rückblick'; 9. 'Irrlicht'; 10. 'Rast'; 11. 'Frühlingstraum'; 12. 'Einsamkeit'; 13. 'Die Post'; 14. 'Der greise Kopf'; 15. 'Die Krähe'; 16. 'Letzte Hoffnung'; 17. 'Im Dorfe'; 18. 'Der stürmische Morgen'; 19. 'Täuschung'; 20. 'Der Wegweiser'; 21. 'Das Wirtshaus'; 22. 'Mut'; 23. 'Die Nebensonnen'; 24. 'Der Leiermann'.

'Winter Wind' Study the nickname sometimes given to Chopin's piano Study in A minor, Op. 25 no. 11.

Winter Words song cycle by Benjamin Britten to poems by Thomas Hardy for high voice and piano; first performed at Harewood House, Leeds, on 8 October 1953, by Peter Pears. The titles of the songs are: 1. 'At Day-close in November'; 2. 'Midnight on the Great Western'; 3. 'Wagtail and Baby'; 4. 'The Little Old Table'; 5. 'The Choirmaster's Burial'; 6. 'Proud Songsters'; 7. 'At the Railway Station'; 8. 'Before Life and After'.

Wipo or **Wigbert (c.995–c.1050)** German poet and priest, who ended his life as a hermit. He is the alleged author (and perhaps adaptor of the music) of the sequence *Victimae paschali*.

Wirén, Dag (Ivar) (1905–1986) Swedish composer and critic. He studied at the Stockholm Conservatory; in 1932 he received a stage grant and continued his studies with Leonid Sabaneiev in Paris. On his return he became a music critic at Stockholm.

Works ORCHESTRAL five symphonies (1932–64), sinfonietta; serenade for strings; cello concerto, violin concerto, piano concerto.

CHAMBER five string quartets (1930–70), two piano trios, two sonatinas for cello and piano.

OTHER piano pieces; songs.

Wise, Michael (c.1647–1687) English organist and composer. He held various organist's and choirmaster's positions in London, Windsor, and Salisbury, and wrote church music, especially anthems with fine parts for treble voices.

Wise was a choirboy at the Chapel Royal in London in 1660. In 1663 he became a lay-clerk at St George's Chapel, Windsor, and in 1668 organist and choirmaster of Salisbury Cathedral. He was appointed a Gentleman of the Chapel Royal in 1676, but retained his post at Salisbury until 1685. At the time of the coronation of James II he was suspended from the Chapel Royal, probably because of characteristically difficult conduct. In 1687 he became almoner and choirmaster at St Paul's Cathedral in London, but continued to visit Salisbury, where his wife had remained. After a dispute with her at night he left the house and was killed in a quarrel with a watchman.

Works CHORAL services and anthems (including *The Ways of Zion Mourn*).

OTHER songs and catches.

Wishart, Peter (1921–1984) English composer. He studied with Nadia Boulanger and at Birmingham University and was a lecturer there 1950–59. He later taught at King's College, London (1972–77), and was professor at Reading University 1977–84. His music was influenced by Stravinsky and Orff.

Works OPERA *Two in the Bush* (1956), *The Captive* (1960), *The Clandestine Marriage* (1971) and *Clytemnestra* (1973).

BALLET *Beowulf* and *Persephone* (1957).

ORCHESTRAL two symphonies (1953, 1973), two violin concertos (1951, 1968), concerto for orchestra (1957).

CHORAL Te Deum (1952) and much other choral music.

CHAMBER string quartet (1954); organ sonata.

Wohltemperierte Clavier, Das, The Well-tempered Clavier two sets of preludes and fugues by Bach for keyboard (not exclusively clavichord, as has sometimes been inferred from a misunderstanding of the title), finished in 1722 and 1744 respectively. Each set consists of a cycle of 24 preludes and fugues in all the major and minor keys in ascending order. The two books together are commonly known in England as 'The 48'. See also ➔ **Weber** (Bernhard Christian).

wolf in music, a technical term for a jarring sound produced between certain intervals on keyboard instruments tuned in ➔ **meantone** temperament or on string instruments by defective vibration on a certain note or notes.

Wolf, Hugo (Filipp Jakob) (1860–1903) Austrian composer. He wrote more than 250 *lieder* (songs), including the *Mörike-Lieder/Mörike Songs* (1888) and the two-volume *Italienisches Liederbuch/Italian Songbook* (1892, 1896).

Wolf brought a new concentration and tragic eloquence to the art of lieder, seeking to enhance the dramatic and emotional potential of the poetry he set by establishing an equal partnership between singer and pianist. Among his other works are the opera *Der Corregidor/The Magistrate* (1895) and orchestral works, such as *Italian Serenade* (1892).

His father, a leather merchant, encouraged his early gifts by teaching him piano and violin. He entered the Vienna Conservatory in 1875, but left it the following year, preferring to pick up his own instruction where he could. From 1877, his father having incurred great financial losses, he was obliged to earn his own living by teaching. He often lived in great poverty, but was befriended by various musical families; the conductors Franz Schalk and Felix Mottl took a professional

interest in him. In 1881 he was engaged as second conductor at Salzburg under Carl Muck, but was found to be temperamentally so unfitted for the post that the engagement was terminated within three months. He was music critic for the Vienna *Salonblatt* 1884–87, but here again he offended many people by his irascibility and intolerance (which saw no fault in Wagner and no good in Brahms). Meanwhile his masterful song settings of Mörike and Eichendorff won him wide recognition. However, he had contracted syphilis, and in 1897 became insane. He was sent to a sanatorium. Discharged as cured in 1898, he had a relapse after becoming involved in a quarrel with Mahler at the Vienna Opera, and was taken to an asylum in a hopeless condition at the end of the year, remaining there until his death.

Works DRAMATIC the operas *Der Corregidor* (1896) and *Manuel Venegas* (unfinished); incidental music to Ibsen's *The Feast at Solhaug* (1891).

SONGS 48 early songs, 53 songs to words by Mörike (1888); 20 to words by Eichendorff (1880–88), 51 to words by Goethe (1888–89), *Italienisches Liederbuch* (46 songs, 1892, 1896), *Spanisches Liederbuch* (44 songs, 1889–90), 31 songs to words by various poets, including six by G Keller and three sonnets by Michelangelo (1897); six part songs.

ORCHESTRAL symphonic poem *Penthesilea* (after Kleist, 1883).

CHAMBER *Italian Serenade* for string quartet in D minor (1880).

OTHER VOCAL *Christnacht* for solo voices, chorus, and orchestra, *Elfenlied* from Shakespeare's *Midsummer Night's Dream* for soprano, chorus, and orchestra (1890), *Der Feuerreiter* and *Dem Vaterland* for chorus and orchestra.

Wolf, Johannes (1869–1947) German musicologist. He studied with Spitta in Berlin and took a doctor's degree at Leipzig in 1893. In 1908 he became professor of music at Berlin University and in 1915 librarian of the music section of the Prussian State Library, where he succeeded Altmann as director in 1928. He specialized in and wrote on early music, treatises, and notations.

Wolff, Christian (1934–) French-born US composer. His music makes use of a strictly mathematical basis, particularly with regard to rhythms and rests, while also including chance elements.

Wolff went to the USA in 1941. He studied with Cage, and also studied classical languages at Harvard University, obtaining a doctorate, and becoming a lecturer there in classics in 1962.

Works CHAMBER *Nine* for nine instruments (1951), *For six or seven players*, *Summer* for string quartet, *In Between Pieces* for three players, *For five or ten Players* (1962), *For one, two or three*

people, septet for any instruments (1964), *For Pianist, For Piano I, II, Duo for Pianists I and II, Duet I* for piano (four hands), *Duet II* for horn and piano.
CHORAL *You Blew It* for chorus (1971).

Wolf-Ferrari, Ermanno (1876–1948) Italian composer. His operas include *Il segreto di Susanna/Susanna's Secret* (1909) and the realistic tragedy *I gioielli di Madonna/The Jewels of the Madonna* (1911).

He was sent to Rome to study art by his German father, who was a painter. However, he turned to music and studied with Joseph Rheinberger at Munich. In 1899 he sent his oratorio to Venice and succeeded in having it performed, and in 1900 he brought out his first opera, after which his stage successes were frequently repeated. Many of his operas were first produced in Germany, including several that sought to evoke the spirit of 18th-century Venetian comedy. In 1902–12 he was director of the Liceo Benedetto Marcello at Venice.

Works OPERA *Cenerentola* (1900), *Le donne curiose* (1903), *I quattro rusteghi* (1906), *Il segreto di Susanna* (1909), *I gioielli della Madonna* (1911), *Amor medico* (after Molière, 1913), *Gli amanti sposi* (1925), *Das Himmelskleid* (1927), *Sly* (after Shakespeare's *Taming of the Shrew*, 1927), *La vedova scaltra* (1931), *Il campiello* (1936), *La dama boba* (after Lope de Vega, 1939), *Gli dei a Tebe* (1943).
CANTATAS *La Sulamita* and *La vita nuova* (after Dante, 1903).
ORCHESTRAL violin concerto, chamber symphony for strings, woodwind, piano, and horn (1901).
CHAMBER piano quintet, piano trio, two violin and piano sonatas.
OTHER organ pieces; cello pieces; *Rispetti* for soprano and piano.

Wolfram von Eschenbach (c.1170–c.1220) German Minnesinger. He took part in a singing contest at Wartburg in 1207. Seven lyric poems by him survive, without music, though two tunes are ascribed to him. He wrote an epic, *Parzival*, which was the principal source for Wagner's *Parsifal*. He appears as a character in Wagner's earlier opera, *Tannhäuser*.

Wolkenstein, Oswald von (c.1377–1445) Austrian Minnesinger and politician. He travelled much, reputedly even as far as Asia and Africa. From 1415 he was in the service of King (later Emperor) Sigismund and was sent to Spain and Portugal on diplomatic missions. In 1421–27 he involved himself in much strife and was twice imprisoned in his endeavour to extend his land by encroaching on that of his neighbours. Although he sang of courtly love, he enjoyed a long adulterous affair.

Works songs on themes such as love, spring, and travel, for one–three voices (to his own words).

Wolpe, Stefan (1902–1972) US composer. He studied with Paul Juon and Schreker in Franz Berlin and in 1933–34 with Webern, then went to Palestine and in 1938 settled in the USA.

Works OPERA *Schöne Geschichten* and *Zeus und Elida*.
BALLET *The Man from Midian* (1942).
ORCHESTRAL symphonies, symphony for 21 instruments (1956), Passacaglia and two Fugues for orchestra.
CANTATAS *The Passion of Man, On the Education of Man, About Sport* (1932), *Unnamed Lands, Israel and his Land*.
OTHER chamber music.

Wolzogen, Ernst von (1855–1934) German writer. He studied at the Universities of Strasbourg and Leipzig. With Otto Julius Bierbaum and Frank Wedekind he established the satirical cabaret *Das Überbrettl* in Berlin in 1901, for which Alexander von Zemlinsky, Oskar Straus and Arnold Schoenberg provided some of the music. The cabaret lasted two successful years, before finally closing. He was the author of the libretto of Richard Strauss's *Feuersnot*.

Woman's Love and Life song cycle by Robert Schumann; see ➤ *Frauenliebe und -leben*.

Wood, Charles (1886–1926) Irish music scholar, teacher, and composer. He taught at the Royal College of Music in London from 1883 and at Cambridge University from 1897. As a composer he is remembered for his church music.

Wood learnt music from the organist of Armagh Cathedral, where his father was a lay vicar, and studied at the Royal College of Music in London 1883–87, becoming professor there in 1888. He conducted the University Music Society at Cambridge 1888–94, and took a doctorate in music there in 1894. In 1897 he became music lecturer to the University and in 1924 succeeded Charles Stanford as professor of music.

Works STAGE opera *The Pickwick Papers* (after Dickens, 1922); incidental music to Euripides' *Ion* and *Iphigenia in Tauris*.
ORCHESTRAL AND VOCAL *Ode to the West Wind* (1890) and *The Song of the Tempest* for solo voices, chorus, and orchestra (performed 1902); *Ode on Music* (Swinburne, 1894), *Ode on Time* (Milton, 1898), *Dirge for Two Veterans* (Whitman), *Ballad of Dundee* for chorus and orchestra (performed 1904); *Passion according to St Mark* (1921).
CHAMBER eight string quartets.

Wood, Haydn (1882–1959) British composer. A violinist, he wrote a violin concerto among other works, and is known for his songs, which include 'Roses of Picardy', associated with World War I.

Having appeared as a child prodigy, Wood studied violin with Enrique Fernández Arbós (1863–1939) and composition with Charles Villiers Stanford at the Royal College of Music in London; he also studied violin with César Thomson in Brussels.

Works CANTATA *Lochinvar* (from Scott's 'Marmion').

ORCHESTRAL rhapsodies, overtures, picturesque suites, variations, and other works for orchestra; concertos for violin and for piano.

CHAMBER fantasy string quartet.

OTHER instrumental pieces; over 200 songs.

Wood, Henry Joseph (1869–1944) English conductor. From 1895 until his death, he conducted the London Promenade Concerts, now named after him. He promoted a national interest in music and encouraged many young composers. As a composer he is remembered for the *Fantasia on British Sea Songs* (1905), which ends each Promenade season.

Wood was a talented child, especially as an organist, and gave recitals and held church appointments as a boy. He studied at the Royal Academy of Music and in 1889 had his first experience as a conductor, and toured as an opera conductor for the next few years; he conducted the British premiere of *Eugene Onegin* in 1892. In 1895 he was engaged by Robert Newman to take charge of the Promenade Concerts at the newly built Queen's Hall, and he remained in charge of them for 50 years, until the end of his life, celebrating their half-centenary just before his death. He began modestly with popular programmes, but soon included many of the latest foreign and English novelties as they appeared; gave the first performance of Schoenberg's *Five Orchestral Pieces* in 1912 and first British performances of Mahler's first, fourth, seventh, and eighth symphonies. He conducted further performances of music by Bartók, Strauss, Sibelius, and Skriabin. He also conducted many music festivals and gave the first performances of works by Delius and Vaughan Williams (*Serenade to Music*, 1938). In 1898 he married the Russian soprano Olga Urussov (who died in 1909) and in 1911 Muriel Greatorex.

Wood, Hugh (1932–) English composer. He studied composition with A Milner, I Hamilton, and Seiber. He taught at Morley College 1959–62, at Liverpool University 1971–73, and at Cambridge University from 1976.

Works ORCHESTRAL *Scenes from Comus* for soprano, tenor, and orchestra (1965); cello concerto (1969), chamber concerto (1971), violin concerto (1972), symphony (1982), piano concerto (1991).

CHAMBER four string quartets (1959–93), quintet for clarinet, horn, and piano trio (1967), piano trio (1984), horn trio (1989).

SONGS to texts by Logue, Hughes, Muir, and Neruda.

wood chimes musical instrument of the Tay people of central Vietnam (Nguyen) and now common throughout Vietnam. It consists of differing lengths of hanging bamboo that are struck with a stick.

Wooden Prince, The, Hungarian *A fából faragott királyfi* ballet in one act by Bartók (scenario by Bela Balazs); composed 1914–16, produced in Budapest on 12 May 1917, conducted by Tango. Orchestral suite (1931) performed in Budapest on 23 November 1931, conducted by Ernö Dohnányi.

Woodson, Thomas (lived 16th–17th centuries) English composer. In 1581 he became a member of the Chapel Royal, his place being taken by William West in 1605. He composed 40 canonic settings of the plainsong *Miserere* for keyboard, only 20 of which survive.

woodwind musical instrument from which sound is produced by blowing into a tube, causing the air within to vibrate. These instruments were originally made of wood but are now more commonly made of metal. The saxophone, made of metal, is an honorary woodwind instrument because it is related to the clarinet. The flute, clarinet, oboe, and bassoon make up the normal woodwind section of an orchestra.

Woodwind instruments divide into two groups: **reed instruments**, and those **without a reed**. In a reed instrument, the air enters the instrument through an opening with a single vibrating reed, or double reeds. This group includes clarinet, oboe, cor anglais, saxophone, and bassoon. In instruments without a reed, the air enters through a blowhole. This group includes flute, piccolo, and recorder.

In both cases, different notes are produced by covering the holes along the instrument, which changes the length of the air column in the tube. A short air column gives a high note, and a long air column gives a low note.

There is an enormous variety of woodwind instruments throughout the world.

Wooldridge, H(arry) E(llis) (1845–1917) English painter and music scholar. He was Slade Professor of Fine Arts at Oxford 1895–1904, but made a special study of medieval music. His chief works were the first two volumes of the *Oxford History of Music*.

Woolrich, John (1954–) English composer who studied with Edward Cowie at Lancaster. He has taught at Durham, the Guildhall School of Music in London, Dartington, and Reading. *The Ghost in the Machine* for orchestra was performed at the 1990 Promenade Concerts, London.

Works ORCHESTRAL *The Barber's Timepiece* (1986), and *The Theatre Represents a Garden: Night* for orchestra (1991); *It is Midnight, Dr Schweitzer* for strings (1992).

CHAMBER *Quick Steps*, wind octet (1990); *The Death of King Renaud*, string quintet (1992).

OTHER ensemble pieces and songs.

Wordsworth, William B(rocklesby) (1908–1988) English composer. He did not begin to study music seriously until he was 20, and in 1935 became a pupil of Donald Tovey. During World War II he took to farming, but after that devoted himself entirely to composition. He was a direct descendant of the poet's brother.

Works ORATORIO *Dies Domini* (1944).

ORCHESTRA AND CHORUS *The Houseless Dead* (D H Lawrence) for baritone chorus and orchestra, *Hymn of Dedication* (Chesterton) for chorus and orchestra.

ORCHESTRAL eight symphonies (1944–86), theme and variations, *Three Pastoral Sketches* for orchestra, *Sinfonia* and *Canzone and Ballade* for strings; piano concerto, cello concerto.

CHAMBER six string quartets (1941–64); string trio; two sonatas for violin and piano, two sonatas for cello and piano; sonata and suite for piano.

OTHER three hymn-tune preludes for organ; *Four Sacred Sonnets* (Donne, 1944) and other songs; rounds for several voices.

Worgan, John (1724–1790) English organist and composer. He became famous as an organ recitalist and was organist at Vauxhall Gardens.

Worgan was a pupil of Thomas Roseingrave. In about 1749 he was appointed organist of the church of St Andrew Undershaft and succeeded his brother James Worgan (c.1715–1753), as organist of Vauxhall Gardens about 1751. He remained attached to Vauxhall Gardens as a composer until 1761, and again 1770–74. He was awarded a PhD in music in 1775.

Works ORATORIOS *The Chief of Maon, Hannah* (1764), *Manasseh* (1766) and *Gioas* (unfinished).

CHORAL anthem for a victory, psalm-tunes; serenata *The Royal Voyage*, dirge in memory of Frederick, Prince of Wales; ode on the rebellion of 1745.

OTHER organ pieces; harpsichord lessons; glees; songs.

working-out or **development** the second section of a movement in sonata form; see ➤ **development**.

Worldes Blis work for orchestra by Peter Maxwell Davies, first performed in London on 28 August 1968; although not well received by older members of the Promenade audience, the work established Davies with the younger set as a leading composer.

Woytowicz, Bolesław (1899–1980) Polish pianist and composer. He began by studying mathematics and philosophy at Kiev University and law at Warsaw University, but turned to the piano, which he studied at the Chopin High School at Warsaw, where he later became a teacher. He next took to composition, studying first with Felicjan Szopski (1865–1939) and Witold Maliszewski (1873–1939), and in 1930 with Nadia Boulanger in Paris.

Works ORCHESTRAL concertino, concert suite, *Poème funèbre* on the death of Piłsudski, three symphonies (1926–63), variations in the form of a symphony for orchestra; piano concerto.

CHAMBER two string quartets, trio for flute, clarinet, and bassoon, *Cradle Song* for soprano, clarinet, bassoon, and harp (1931).

PIANO variations and other works for piano.

Wozzeck opera by Alban Berg (libretto by composer, from G Büchner's drama of 1836), produced at the Berlin Opera on 14 December 1925. A jealous soldier Wozzeck knifes his mistress Marie after she is seduced by the Drum Major and he is taunted by the Captain and Doctor. Insane, he drowns himself.

Opera by M Gurlitt (libretto as above), produced in Bremen on 22 April 1926.

Wranitzky, Paul (1756–1808) Moravian violinist and composer. In the 1780s he was in the service of Count Esterházy (not to be confused with Prince Esterházy, Haydn's employer) and in about 1790 became leader of the court opera orchestra in Vienna. He was the brother of Anton Wranitzky.

He studied with J M Kraus and Haydn in Vienna.

Works OPERA AND SINGSPIELE including *Oberon, König der Elfen* (1789), *Das Fest der Lazzaroni* (1794), *Der Schreiner* (1799).

BALLET DIVERTISSEMENTS *Das Waldmädchen* (1796), *Die Weinlese* (1794), *Zemire und Azore, Das Urteil von Paris* (1801).

ORCHESTRAL 51 symphonies.

CHAMBER about 100 string quartets and quintets; piano quartets; violin sonatas and large numbers of other instrumental works.

OTHER over 200 canons; vocal duets and trios; church music.

wrest in music, the old English term for a tuning-key, from the verb meaning to twist or wrench. The tuning-pins of the piano are still called wrest-pins and the board into which they are inserted is the wrest-plank.

Wuorinen, Charles (1938–) US composer, conductor, and pianist. His early works are tonal but he was later influenced by Varèse, Babbitt, and serial technique. He studied at Columbia University, and taught there 1964–71.

Works ORCHESTRAL three symphonies (1958–59), four chamber concertos (1957–59), *Evolutio transcripta* for orchestra (1961), two piano concertos (1966, 1974), *Contrafactum* for orchestra (1969), concerto for amplified violin and orchestra (1971), *Percussion Symphony* (1976), *Bamboula Squared* for orchestra (1983), Concerto for saxophone quartet and orchestra (1993), *The Mission of Virgil* for orchestra (1993).

CHAMBER *Dr Faustus Lights the Light* for narrator and instruments (1957), octet (1962), string trio (1968), chamber concerto (1970), wind quintet (1977), horn trio (1981), three string quartets (1971, 1979, 1987), saxophone quartet (1992).

VOICE AND ENSEMBLE *Symphonia sacra* for vocal soloists and instrumental ensemble (1961), *The Prayer of Jonah* for voices and string quintet (1962).

OTHER masque *The Politics of Harmony* (1967), 'baroque burlesque' *The Whore of Babylon* (1975); *The Celestial Sphere*, sacred oratorio for chorus and orchestra (1979); electronic music.

Wurlitzer trademark for a large pipe ➤ **organ** that was often installed in the huge cinemas of the 1930s (Compton was another make). Such organs were equipped with percussive and other special effects, and had many keyboards, pedals, and stops. A musician would play before the start of the film or between films.

In the early 1960s the US manufacturer Wurlitzer introduced an electric piano in which vibrating metal reeds produced the note or signal sent to the amplifier.

Wyk, Arnold van (1916–1983) South African composer. He began to learn the piano at the age of 12 and, after working in an insurance office at Cape Town, entered Stellenbosch University in 1936. In 1937 he was commissioned to write music for the centenary of the Voortrekkers and in 1938 he went to live in London, having gained the Performing Rights Society's scholarship. He studied composition with Theodore Holland and piano with Harold Craxton at the Royal Academy of Music, joined the British Broadcasting Corporation (BBC) for a short time, and later devoted himself to composition.

Works ORCHESTRAL two symphonies (1944, 1952), suite for small orchestra on African tunes *Southern Cross* (1943); *Saudade* for violin and orchestra.

CHAMBER string quartets, five elegies for string quartet (1941).

OTHER three improvisations on a Dutch folksong for piano duet.

Wylde, John (lived c.1425–50) English music theorist, precentor of Waltham Abbey, near London. He wrote a summary of Guido d'Arezzo's theoretical work, entitled *Musica Gwydonis monachi*. This stands at the head of a collection compiled by him (British Library, Lansdowne MS 763) which later belonged to Tallis, whose signature it bears.

Wynne, David (1900–1983) Welsh composer. He worked as a coalminer during adolescence and studied at University College, Cardiff, from 1925. He was active in the promotion of Welsh music.

Works OPERA *Jack and Jill* (1975) and *Night and Cold Peace* (1979).

ORCHESTRAL five symphonies (1952–80), two rhapsody concertos, *Octade* for orchestra (1978).

CHAMBER five string quartets (1944–80); sextet for piano and orchestra (1977).

OTHER song cycles and choral music.

Wyzewa, Théodore de (1862–1917), originally **Wyzewski** French musicologist of Polish parentage. He lived in France from 1869. In 1884 he founded the *Revue Wagnérienne* with Edouard Dujardin and in 1901 the Société Mozart with Boschot. He became a political and literary journalist, but his chief work is his study of Mozart, of which he completed two volumes in collaboration with Georges de Saint-Foix. He was a friend of Renoir and Mallarmé.

Xenakis, Iannis (1922–2001) Romanian-born French composer of Greek parentage. He evolved a method of 'stochastic' composition using the mathematics of chance and probability and also employing computers. Compositions such as *Metastasis/After Change* (1953–54) for 61 players apply stochastic principles – for example, describing particle motion in fluids – to the composition of densely textured effects in which change is perceived globally. Later works, including a setting of the *Oresteia* (1965–66) for choir and ensemble, drew on Greek mythology.

Xenakis was born at Braila, Romania. He studied music in Paris, France, 1947–51 while practising as an engineering draughtsman for French architect Le Corbusier. He studied with Honegger, Milhaud, and Messiaen. He published *Formalized Music: Thought and Mathematics in Composition* in 1972. His ideas have exercised considerable influence on other composers.

Works THEATRE MUSIC *The Bacchae* (1993).

ORCHESTRAL AND ENSEMBLE *Metastasis* for orchestra (1954), *Pithoprakta* for string orchestra (1956), *Achorripsis* for 21 instruments (1957), *Polytope* for small orchestra (1967), *Synaphai* for piano and orchestra (1969), *Noomena* for orchestra (1975), *Keqrops* for piano and orchestra (1986), *Tracées* for orchestra (1987), *Tuorakemsu* for orchestra (1990), *Dox-Orkh* for violin and 89 players (1991).

ELECTRONIC COMPOSITIONS *Diamorphosis* (1958), *Orient-Occident* (1960); ballets *Kraanerg* for orchestra and tape (1969) and *Antikhton* (1971).

OTHER *Morsima-Amorsima* (1) for four players (1956–62), (2) for ten players (1962).

CHORAL WITH ORCHESTRA OR ENSEMBLE *Oresteia* for chorus and chamber ensemble (1966), *Chants des Soleils* (1983), *Idmen A* for chorus and percussion quartet (1985), *Idmen B* for chorus and percussion sextet (1986), *Knephas* for unaccompanied chorus (1990).

CHAMBER *Syrmos* for 18 strings (1959), *Akrata* for 16 wind (1965), *Atrées* (1962), *Anaktoria* (1969), *Auroura* (1971), *Phlegra* (1975), *Retours-Windungen* (1976), *Tetras* for string quartet (1983), *Thallein* for 14 players (1984), *Palimpsest* for piano and ensemble (1982), *Jalons* for 15 players (1986), *Akea* piano quartet (1986), *Waarg* for 13 players (1988), *Okho* for three players (1989), *Epicycle* for cello and twelve players (1989), *Akanthos* for soprano and ensemble (1977).

Xerse or **Xerxes** opera by Cavalli (libretto by N Minato), produced at the Teatro dei Santi Giovanni e Paolo, Venice, on 12 January 1654.

Opera by Handel. See ➤ *Serse*.

xylophone musical ➤ **percussion instrument** of African and Indonesian origin. It consists of a series of hardwood bars of varying lengths, each with its own distinct pitch, arranged in a similar way to a piano. Beneath each bar is a metal tube resonator that helps to enrich and sustain the sound. It is usually played with hard beaters to produce a hard, bright, penetrating sound, or soft beaters for a mellower sound. It first appeared as an orchestral instrument in Charles Camille Saint-Saëns's *Danse macabre* in 1874, illustrating dancing skeletons, and can also be heard in 'Fossils' from *The Carnival of Animals* (1887).

xylorimba percussion instrument, a small ➤ **marimba** made in the USA.

Yansons or **Jansons, Arvid (1914–1984)** Latvian conductor. He debuted at the Riga Opera in 1944. He conducted the Leningrad Philharmonic Orchestra from 1952, and was chief guest conductor with the Hallé Orchestra from 1964. His son is Marriss Jansons.

Yan Tan Tethera opera by Harrison Birtwistle (text by Tony Harrison), written 1983–84 for television and first performed in London on 5 August 1986. In the story, the shepherd Alan arouses the jealousies of Caleb Raven, who causes Alan's wife Hannah and their twins to be imprisoned. They are released after seven years.

Year 1812, The festival overture by Tchaikovsky, Op. 49. It was written for the commemoration of the 70th anniversary of Napoleon's retreat from Moscow and was first performed during the Moscow Arts and Industrial Exhibition, on 20 August 1882, at the consecration of the Cathedral of the Redeemer in the Kremlin.

Yellow Cake Review, The work by Maxwell Davies for singers and piano (text by composer), which describes the threat to the Orkneys posed by uranium mining. It was first performed at Kirkwall, in the Orkney Islands, Scotland, on 21 June 1980.

Yeomen of the Guard, The or **The Merryman and his Maid** operetta by Sullivan (libretto by W S Gilbert), produced at the Savoy Theatre, London, on 3 October 1888.

yodel elaborate form of song in Switzerland, Tyrol, and Styria, usually sung by men in ➔ **falsetto**, with rapid changes to chest voice (the lower register of the human voice). The song is very free in rhythm and metre and uses, as a rule, the restricted scale of the natural harmonics of instruments like the alphorn. The yodel is thus very probably derived or copied from the ➔ **ranz des vaches**.

Yorkshire Feast Song, The ode or cantata by Purcell (words by Thomas Durfey), 'Of old when heroes', for two altos, tenor, two basses, five-part chorus, recorders, oboes, trumpets, and strings.

It was written in 1690 for the annual reunion of Yorkshiremen in London, intended to be held that year on 14 February but postponed to 27 March owing to parliamentary elections.

Young, La Monte (1935–) US composer. He studied at the University of California, Los Angeles 1956–57, and at Berkeley 1957–60. In 1959 he also studied with Stockhausen, and then lectured on guerrilla warfare at the New York School for Social Research.

Works ORCHESTRAL *The Tortoise Droning Selected Pitches from the Holy Numbers for the Two Black Tigers, the Green Tiger and the Hermit* (1964); *The Tortoise Recalling the Drone of the Holy Numbers as they were Revealed in the Dreams of the Whirlwind and the Obsidian Gong; Illuminated by the Sawmill, the Green Sawtooth Ocelot and the High-Tension Line Stepdown Transformer* both for voice, gong, and strings (1964); *Orchestral Dreams* (1984).

OTHER piano music, including the six-hour *Well-Timed Piano* (1964).

Young Apollo work by Benjamin Britten for piano, string quartet, and string orchestra (1939). It was first performed in Toronto on 27 August 1939, but was withdrawn until 1979.

Yradier, Sebastian (1809–1865) Spanish composer. He was in Paris for a time as singing-master to the Empress Eugénie and later lived in Cuba for some years. He wrote popular Spanish songs, including 'La Paloma' and the melody which formed the basis of the habañera in Bizet's *Carmen*.

Ysaÿe, Eugène-Auguste (1858–1931) Belgian violinist, conductor, and composer. One of the greatest and most individual virtuosos of his day, he toured as a soloist and conductor throughout Europe and America. Although he never studied composition formally, he mastered writing in a Romantic style.

He studied with his father, Nicolas Ysaÿe, then at the Liège Conservatory, and later with Henryk Wieniawski and Henry Vieuxtemps. Having already appeared in public in 1865, he played at

Pauline Lucca's concerts at Cologne and Aachen, where he met Ferdinand Hiller and Joseph Joachim, and later, at Frankfurt, he came into touch with Joachim Raff and Clara Schumann. He was based in Paris 1883–86, becoming close to Debussy, Fauré, and Saint-Saëns. In 1886 he formed the Ysaÿe Quartet, and premiered Debussy's quartet in 1893. He was violin professor at the Brussels Conservatory 1886–98, and founded and conducted orchestral concerts in the Belgian capital. He toured extensively, first visiting England in 1889 and the USA in 1894, playing the Beethoven Concerto with the New York Philharmonic Orchestra. Admired everywhere for his skill and musicianship, he often performed the Franck Sonata dedicated to him and the Elgar Concerto. He conducted the Cincinnati Symphony Orchestra 1918–22.

Works OPERA *Piére li Houîeu* (in Walloon dialect, 1931).

OTHER eight violin concertos; *Poème élégiaque*, mazurkas, and other pieces for violin and piano.

Yun, Isang (1917–1995) Korean-born German composer. He studied in Korea and Japan, and with Blacher and Rufer in Berlin. An espousal of serial techniques (methods of composition based on the ➤ twelve-tone system) led to the withdrawal of works written before 1959. In 1967 he was kidnapped from West Berlin by South Korean agents and charged with sedition. After release, he taught at the Hochschule für Musik, Berlin, 1970–85.

Works STAGE operas *Der Traum des Liu-Tung* (1965), *Die Witwe des Schmetterlings* (1967), *Geisterliebe* (1971), *Sim Tjong* (1972).

ORCHESTRAL *Colloides sonores* for string orchestra (1961), *Dimensionen* for orchestra (1971).

CONCERTOS cello (1976), flute (1977).

SYMPHONIES no. 1 (1983), no. 2 (1984), no. 3 (1985), no. 4 'Singing in the Dark' (1986), no. 5 for baritone and orchestra (1987).

CHORAL WITH ORCHESTRA cycle *Om Mani padame hum* for soprano, baritone, chorus, and orchestra (1964); *Der weise Mann* for baritone, chorus, and small orchestra (1977).

CHAMBER four string quartets, piano trio (1975), *Pièce concertante* for chamber ensemble (1977), flute quartet (1988).

Yvain, Maurice (Pierre Paul) (1891–1965) French composer. His studies at the Paris Conservatory were interrupted by army service during World War I. Resuming his studies after the war, he devoted his whole attention to the composition of operettas, the first of which, *Ta bouche*, was an immediate success in 1922. It was followed by many others, as well as a ballet, *Vent* (1937).

Zacara or **Zacar** or **Zacharie (lived 14th–15th centuries)** Either of two composers active in Italy during the late 14th and early 15th centuries: the works of **Antonio Zacara** of Teramo (fl.1391–c.1420) are found in manuscripts from many parts of Europe and were evidently very influential; they include Mass movements and Italian and French songs. **Nicola Zacharie** of Brindisi (fl.1420–1434) was a singer in the papal chapel 1420–24 and again in 1434; he also sang in Florence. His works include perhaps only one Italian song, motets, and one Mass movement.

Zacconi, Lodovico (1555–1627) Italian priest and music theorist. He wrote a four-volume treatise on figured chant, *Prattica di musica* (1592–1622).

Zacconi went to live at Venice, joined the monastic order of St Augustine, and was maestro di cappella at its church. In 1593, at the invitation of the Archduke Charles, he went to Vienna, where he became court music director and remained until 1619, when he returned to Venice.

Zach, Jan (1699–1773) Bohemian organist and composer. He worked as a violinist and organist in Prague, where he came under the influence of ➔ **Cernohorský**. He later left for Germany, and in 1745 was appointed kapellmeister to the Electoral court in Mainz. He was dismissed c.1757 and spent the rest of his life travelling, without permanent employment.

Works SACRED AND SECULAR MUSIC 33 Masses, three Requiems; *Stabat Mater* and other church music; symphonies and partitas for orchestra; chamber music; organ music.

Zadok the Priest first of four anthems composed 1727 by Handel for the coronation of George II, and given at all subsequent coronations.

Zaide unfinished opera by Mozart (libretto in German, by J A Schachtner). Begun in 1779, it was first produced in Frankfurt on 27 January 1886. In the story, Sultan Soliman's favourite Zaide escapes with the prisoner Gomatz but they are recaptured.

Zaïs ballet *héroïque* in a prologue and four acts by Rameau (libretto by L de Cahusac), produced at the Paris Opéra on 29 February 1748. In the story, the spirit Zaïs sacrifices magic powers for the love of the shepherdess Zélide, but they are restored by spirit-ruler Oromases.

Zampa, ou La Fiancée de marbre, Zampa, or The Marble Betrothed opera by Ferdinand ➔ **Hérold** (libretto by A H J Mélesville), produced at the Opéra-Comique, Paris, on 3 May 1831. In the story, the wedding of Camille and Alphonse is interrupted by the pirate Zampa, the older brother of Alphonse. Before Zampa can force Camille to marry him the statue of his former bride Alice kills him.

Zandonai, Riccardo (1883–1944) Italian composer. His greatest success was with the verismo (extravagant) opera *Francesca da Rimini* in 1914, which is still performed in Europe and at the New York Metropolitan Opera House.

Zandonai studied at Roveredo and later at the Liceo Musicale of Pesaro, where Mascagni was director. He left in 1902 and at Milan met the librettist Arrigo Boito, who introduced him to the publisher Giulio Ricordi, by whom his first opera was commissioned.

Works OPERA *Il grillo sul focolare* (after Dickens' *Cricket on the Hearth*, 1908), *Conchita* (after Louÿs's *La Femme et le pantin*, 1911), *Melenis* (1912), *La via della finestra, Francesca da Rimini* (on d'Annunzio's play, 1914), *Giulietta e Romeo* (after Shakespeare, 1922), *I cavalieri di Ekebù* (after Selma Lagerlöf, 1925), *Giuliano* (1928), *La farsa amorosa* (1933), *Una partitia*.

ORCHESTRAL AND CHORAL film music for *Princess Tarakanova*; Requiem (1915), *Pater noster* for chorus, organ, and orchestra; *Ballata eroica, Fra gli alberghi delle Dolomiti, Quadri di Segantini* (1931), *Rapsodia trentina*, overture *Colombina* for orchestra; *Concerto romantico* for violin and orchestra (1919); serenade and *Concerto andaluso* for cello and orchestra.

OTHER string quartet; songs.

Zarathustra symphonic poem by Richard Strauss. See ➔ **Also sprach Zarathustra**.

Zar Lässt sich Photographieren, Der, The Tsar Has His Photograph Taken opera in one act by Kurt Weill (libretto by Kaiser), produced at Leipzig on 18 February 1928. The story concerns an amorous Tsar, who flirts at a Parisian photo studio with a would-be assassin.

Zarlino, Gioseffo (1517–1590) Italian music theorist and composer. In his theories he discussed modes and intervals, and also looked back to classical models, seeking to summarize and develop the musical theory of the Greeks. He wrote two large treatises, the three-volume *Istitutioni armoniche* (1558) and *Dimostrationi armoniche* (1571). He was attacked for these by Vincenzo Galilei, whereupon he issued another volume, *Sopplimenti musicali* (1588); a fourth, non-musical volume, was added to the complete edition later.

Born in Chioggia, Zarlino was educated by Franciscan monks and joined the order in 1521. In 1536 he was a singer at Chioggia Cathedral. He studied theology and received minor orders in 1539 (when he became organist at the cathedral), but was learned also in philosophy, sciences, and languages. He settled in Venice in 1541, became a fellow student with Cipriano de Rore under Adrian Willaert, and in 1565 became first maestro di cappella at St Mark's. In 1583 he was offered the bishopric of Chioggia, but declined it, preferring to remain at St Mark's.

Zarlino wrote motets and madrigals, but was chiefly a theorist. *Le istitutioni harmoniche* caused Willaert's methods of contrapuntal writing to become models of the style.

Works SACRED AND SECULAR MUSIC Mass for the foundation of the Church of Santa Maria della Salute and other church music; pageant for the victory of Lepanto.

Zar und Zimmermann, oder Die zwei Peter, Tsar and Carpenter, or the Two Peters opera by Albert ➤ **Lortzing** (libretto by composer, based on a French play by A H J Mélesville, J T Merle and E Cantiran de Boirie), produced at Leipzig on 22 December 1837. In the story, Tsar Peter the Great is in disguise in a foreign shipyard. But he is confused with a deserter, Peter Ivanov, whom he befriends. See also ➤ *Borgomastro di Saardam*.

zarzuela Spanish musical theatre form combining song, dance, and speech, named after La Zarzuela, the royal country house where it was first developed. It originated as an amusement for royalty in the 17th century and found an early exponent in the playwright Calderón. Often satirical, zarzuela gained renewed popularity in the 20th century with the works of Frederico Moreno Tórroba (1891–1982).

Tórroba's *La Chulapona*, staged at the 1989 Edinburgh Festival, was claimed to be the first zarzuela to be seen in Britain.

Zauberflöte, Die, The Magic Flute opera by Mozart (libretto by Emanuel Schikaneder, with the aid of K L Giesecke), produced at the Theater auf der Wieden, Vienna, on 30 September 1791. Peter Winter's opera *Das Labyrinth* is a sequel to it. There is also an unfinished libretto by Goethe intended for a sequel. In the story, Prince Tamino and Pamina undergo the trials of their love while the birdcatcher Papageno finds a mate.

Zauberharfe, Die, The Magic Harp ➤ magic opera by Schubert (libretto by G E von Hofmann), produced at the Theater an der Wien, Vienna, on 19 August 1820.

Zauberoper see ➤ magic opera.

Zauberzither, Die, oder Caspar der Fagottist, The Magic Zither, or Jasper the Bassoonist Singspiel by Wenzel Müller, produced at the Leopoldstadt Theatre, Vienna, on 8 June 1791. The plot shows close resemblances to that of Schikaneder's libretto for Mozart's *Zauberflöte*, which may have been borrowed from it or based on the same source.

Zazà opera in four acts by Ruggero ➤ **Leoncavallo** (libretto by composer, after play by Simon and Berton). It was produced at the Teatro Lirica, Milan, on 10 November 1900. The story concerns the music hall singer Zazà, who returns to Cascart after learning that her current lover, Milio Dufresne, is a married man.

Zdravitsa, Hail to Stalin cantata for chorus and orchestra on folk texts by Prokofiev, Op. 85. It was composed in 1939 and was first performed in Moscow on 21 December 1939.

The first British performance for the British Broadcasting Corporation (BBC) was on 21 December 1944, conducted by Boult: the performance had been scheduled for a Prom concert in August 1944 but was cancelled owing to the threat of bombardment.

Zedda, Alberto (1928–) Italian conductor and musicologist. He studied with Giulini in Milan and made his debut in 1956. He conducted at the Deutsche Oper Berlin 1961–63 and New York City Opera from 1963, and led revivals of Rossini's *Ermione* and *Maometto II* in Europe and the USA. Zedda made his Covent Garden debut in 1975. He was co-editor with Philip Gossett of the Rossini complete edition, and artistic director of La Scala from 1992.

Zeitmasze work by Karlheinz Stockhausen for flute, oboe, horn, clarinet, and bassoon; composed 1955–56 and first performed in Paris on 15 December 1956, conducted by Pierre Boulez.

Zelenka, Jan Dismas (1679–1745) Bohemian composer. He wrote lightweight orchestral works, trio sonatas, and solemn religious works, including Magnificats in D (1725) and C (1727). He worked at the court of Dresden and became director of church music in 1735. His compositions were rediscovered in the 1970s. He is best known today for his bold and adventurous instrumental music, including *Hippocondrie* (1723).

Zelenka studied at Prague, was double bass player in the court band at Dresden from 1710, and in 1716 went to Vienna to study under Johann Fux. After this he went to Italy but returned to Dresden to collaborate with Heinichen, whom he succeeded as director of church music in 1735.

Works SACRED AND SECULAR MUSIC Latin *Melodrama de Sancto Wenceslao* (1723); oratorios *I penitenti al sepolcro* (1736), *Il serpente di bronzo* (1730), and *Gesù al Calvario* (1735); 20 Masses, motets, psalms, and other church music; Latin cantatas.

Zeleński, Władysław (1837–1921) Polish teacher and composer. He studied at Prague University and later in Paris. He became professor at the Warsaw Conservatory in 1872 and director of the Kraków Conservatory in 1881.

Works OPERA *Konrad Wallenrod* (1885), *Goplana* (1896), *Janek* (1900), *Balladyna*, and *An Old Story* (1907).

CHURCH MUSIC Masses and motets; cantatas.

ORCHESTRAL two symphonies (1871, 1912), *Woodland Echoes*, concert overture *In the Tatra*, and other orchestral works; piano concerto.

CHAMBER four string quartets, piano quartet, variations for string quartet, sextet for strings and piano, piano trio; violin and piano sonata; piano pieces.

Zeller, Carl (Johann Adam) (1842–1898) Austrian composer. He made his career in the civil service but was continuously active as a composer.

He was a chorister in the Imperial Chapel in Vienna and studied law at the university. He also had counterpoint lessons from Simon Sechter.

Works OPERETTAS *Der Vogelhändler* (1891), *Der Obersteiger* (1894), *Der Vagabund* (1886), and many others.

Zelmira opera by Rossini (libretto by A L Tottola, based on a French tragedy by Dormont de Belloy), produced at the Teatro San Carlo, Naples, on 16 February 1822. In the story, Zelmira is rescued by her returning husband, Ilo, Prince of Troy, after the usurper Antenore and Leucippo accuse her of killing her father Polidoro. She has, in fact, kept Polidoro safe from the treacherous Antenore.

Zelter, Carl Friedrich (1758–1832) German conductor, teacher, and composer. He taught at the Berlin Sinakademie from 1800, where he did much to revive interest in Johann Sebastian Bach's music, and founded the Royal Institute of Church Music in 1822. He was a personal friend of Goethe, many of whose poems he set. He wrote principally songs, also church music, cantatas, and instrumental music.

Having completed his training as a master mason, Zelter joined his father's firm, and abandoned the trade completely only in 1815, but meanwhile was active as a musician. He studied with Schultz and Fasch, and succeeded the latter as conductor of the Berlin Singakademie in 1800. In 1809 he founded the Berliner Liedertafel, in the same year became professor at the academy, and in 1822 founded the Royal Institute of Church Music. Among his pupils were Nicolai, Loewe, Meyerbeer, and Mendelssohn, whose plans to revive Bach's St Matthew Passion in 1829 he at first opposed but later approved. He rejected Schubert's Lieder.

Zémire et Azore opera by Grétry (libretto by Marmontel), produced at court, in Fontainbleau, on 9 November 1771. Its first Paris performance was at the Théâtre Italien on 16 December 1771. The story concerns Prince Azor, who has been transformed into an ugly beast until he is loved by a woman. Zémire offers herself as a sacrifice to him to save her father Sandor. Of course she eventually falls in love and Azor is restored.

Zemire und Azor opera by Spohr (libretto by J J Ihlee, based on that by Marmontel), produced in Frankfurt on 4 April 1819. The familiar song 'Rose, softly blooming' is in this work. For a plot synopsis, see ➤ *Zémire et Azore*.

Zemlinsky, Alexander von (1871–1942) Austrian composer and conductor. He gave the first performance of Schoenberg's monodrama *Erwartung* in 1924. He taught Schoenberg and married his sister, but his personal ties with Schoenberg scarcely influenced his own music; he started composing in a classical style and later was drawn to the progressive, late-Romantic style of Mahler, Strauss, and even Schreker.

Zemlinsky studied at the Vienna Conservatory. He became conductor at the Vienna Volksoper in 1906 and at the Hofoper in 1908. Later he went to Prague, where he conducted the German Opera and the 1924 first performance of Schoenberg's *Erwartung*. He was one of the conductors at the Berlin State Opera and at the Kroll Opera 1927–31, where he gave the first Berlin performance of *Erwartung*. He returned to Vienna in 193. and later emigrated to the USA.

Works OPERA AND STAGE operas, including *Sarem.* (1897), *Es war einmal* (1900), *Kleider machen Leute* (Keller, 1908, produced 1922), *Eine florentinische Tragödie*, *Der Zwerg* (both after Wilde

1917, 1922), *Der Kreidekreis* (after Klabund, 1933), *Der Traumgörge* (1906, produced 1980), *Der König Kandaules* (c.1935, produced 1996); ballet *Das gläserne Herz* (after Hofmannsthal, 1903); incidental music for *Cymbeline* (1914).

ORCHESTRAL two symphonies (1892, 1897), suite for orchestra (1894), *Die Seejungfrau* for orchestra (1903), sinfonietta (1934), *Lyric Symphony* for soprano, baritone, and orchestra (1923), *Symphonische Gesänge* for voice and orchestra (1926).

CHAMBER string quintet (1895), trio for clarinet, cello, and piano (1895), four string quartets (1895–1936); lieder to texts by Heine and Eichendorff.

Zender, Hans (1936–) German conductor and composer. He worked at opera houses in Freiburg, Bonn, and Kiel, and was music director of Hamburg Opera 1984–87 (principal conductor from 1977). In 1987 he became conductor of the Netherlands Radio Chamber Orchestra.

Zender studied at Frankfurt and Freiburg, and in Rome under Bernd Alois Zimmermann, whose works he has frequently conducted. He conducted *Parsifal* at Bayreuth in 1975 and *Fidelio* at Brussels Opera in 1989.

Works OPERA *Stephen Climax* (1986).

ORCHESTRAL piano concerto (1956), *Zeitströme* for orchestra (1974).

CHORAL AND VOICE cantata *Der Mann von La Mancha* for voices and Moog synthesizer (1969), *Continuum* and *Fragments* for chorus, *Cantos I–V* for voices and instruments.

OTHER electronic works.

Zeno, Apostolo (1668–1750) Italian poet and librettist. For operas on his libretti, see ➤ *Ambleto* (Gasparini and Domenico Scarlatti); ➤ *Faramondo* (Handel); ➤ *Ifigenia in Aulide* (Caldara); ➤ *Lucio Papiro* (Caldara and Hasse); ➤ *Merope* (Gasparini, Jommelli, and Terradellas); ➤ *Scipione* (Handel); ➤ *Temistocle* (Porpora and Johann Christian Bach).

Ziani, Marc'Antonio (1653–1715) Italian composer. He was maestro di cappella at the church of Santa Barbara and conductor at the theatre at Mantua in 1686. He went to Vienna, where he became vice-music director in 1700 and first music director in 1711.

Works OPERA *Alessandro magno in Sidone* (1679), *Damira placata* (1680), *Meleagro* (1706), *Chilonida* (1709), and 41 others.

SACRED AND SECULAR MUSIC Masses, motets and other church music; oratorios, cantatas.

Ziani, Pietro Andrea (1620–1684) Italian composer, uncle of Marc'Antonio ➤ *Ziani*. He was organist at Venice, then at Santa Maria Maggiore, Bergamo. He visited Vienna and Dresden in 1660–67, and became organist at St Mark's, Venice, in succession to Cavalli in 1669. He went to Naples on failing to be appointed maestro di cappella in 1676, becoming a teacher at the Conservatorio di Sant' Onofrio and, in 1680, royal maestro di cappella.

Works OPERA *Le fortune di Rodope e di Damira* (1657), *L'Antigona delusa da Alceste* (1660), and 21 others.

SACRED AND SECULAR MUSIC Masses, psalms, oratorios; instrumental sonatas; organ pieces.

Zich, Otakar (1879–1934) Czech composer. He was at first a secondary schoolmaster, but took a degree at the University of Brno and was appointed professor of aesthetics there. He also collected folk songs.

Works OPERA *The Painter's Whim* (1910), *The Sin* (1922), and *Les Précieuses ridicules* (after Molière, 1926).

CHORAL AND VOCAL *The Ill-Fated Marriage* and *Polka Rides* for chorus and orchestra; songs.

Zieleński, Mikołaj (1550–1615) Polish organist and composer. He composed offertories and communions for the service of the whole year. He was in the service of the archbishop of Gniezno 1608–15 and studied with Andrea Gabrieli in Italy.

Zigeunerbaron, Der, The Gypsy Baron operetta by Johann Strauss, Jr (libretto by I Schnitzer, based on another by M Jókai founded on his own story *Saffi*). It was produced at the Theater an der Wien, Vienna on 24 October 1885. After returning from exile, Sándor Barinkay finds family lands occupied by gypsies but falls for Sáffi, a gypsy princess in disguise.

Zillig, Winfried (1905–1963) German composer and conductor. He studied with Schoenberg in Vienna and from 1927 to 1928 was assistant to Kleiber at the Berlin Staatsoper. From 1928 to 1947 he conducted in various German theatres, becoming director of music at the radio station, first in Frankfurt and then in Hamburg. He also made a performing version of Schoenberg's unfinished oratorio *Die Jakobsleiter* (performed in Vienna, 1961).

Works OPERA *Die Windesbraut* (1941), *Troilus und Cressida* (1951), *Das Opfer*, TV opera *Bauernpassion* (1955), radio opera *Die Verlobung von St Domingo* (1956).

OTHER violin and cello concertos; four serenades for various instrumental groups; choral music; songs.

Zimmerman, Franklin B(ershir) (1923–) US musicologist. He studied in California, USA, and at Oxford, where his teachers included Egon Wellesz and Jack Westrup. He has taught at New York University, Dartmouth College, and the universities of Kentucky and Pennsylvania. He is best known for his research on baroque music and Henry Purcell. His Purcell thematic catalogue (1963) gives the definitive numbering for the composer's works.

Zimmermann, Bernd Alois (1918–1970) German composer. He is widely known for his expressionist opera *Die Soldaten*, which employs film, electronics, mime, and other avant-garde effects.

Zimmerman studied music in Cologne with Heinrich Lemacher (1891–1966) and Philipp Jarnach. He also studied linguistics and philosophy at the Universities of Bonn, Cologne, and Berlin. He taught at Cologne University 1950–52 and at the Hochschule für Musik in Cologne from 1958. He committed suicide.

Works STAGE the opera *Die Soldaten* (1965); ballets *Kontraste* (1953) and *Alagoana* (1955).

ORCHESTRAL symphonies; concertos for violin, oboe, and cello; concerto for string orchestra (1948); *Photoptosis* prelude for orchestra (1968), *Stille und Umkehr* sketches for orchestra (1970).

OTHER cantata *Lob der Torheit* (1948), *Die Soldaten*, vocal symphony from opera (1959); *Requiem for a Young Poet* (1969).

Zimmermann, Udo (1943–) German composer. He founded the Studio for New Music at Dresden in 1974, and has worked in experimental music there. In 1970 he was appointed composer and producer at the Dresden Opera; in 1976 he became director of the Studio Neue Musik concerts at Dresden; and in 1990 became intendant of the Leipzig Opera.

Works OPERA *Die Weisse Rose* (1967), *Die zweite Entscheidung* (1970), *Levins Mühle* (1973), *Der Schuh und die fliegende Prinzessin* (1975), *Die Wundersame Schustersfrau* (1982).

ORCHESTRAL *Music for Strings* (1967), *Sieh, meine Augen* for chamber orchestra (1970), *Mutazioni* for orchestra (1972); *Choreographieren nach Edgar Degas* for 21 instruments (1974).

CHORAL cantata *Der Mensch* for soprano and 13 instruments (1969), *Psalm der Nacht* for chorus, percussion, and organ (1973), *Pax questousa* for five soloists, three choruses, and orchestra (1980).

Zingara, La, **The Gypsy Girl** intermezzo by Rinaldo di Gapua, produced at the Académie Royale de Musique on 19 June 1753. The story involves the gypsy Nisa, who, assisted by her brother Tagliaborsi, tricks the rich miser Calcante into marrying her.

Zingarelli, Niccolò Antonio (1752–1837) Italian composer. He wrote 37 operas, chiefly on serious and mythological themes; the best-known of these is *Giulietta e Romeo* (1796). In 1793 he was appointed to the first of several church posts, and after 1804 devoted himself to writing large quantities of church music.

Zingarelli studied at the Conservatorio Santa Maria di Loreto in Naples, where his intermezzo *I quattro pazzi* was produced in 1768. In 1772 he left the Conservatory and at first worked as an organist, but with *Montezuma*, produced at Naples in 1781, he began his career as an opera composer. From 1785 to 1803 he produced works in all the main Italian cities and also in Paris. He was appointed maestro di cappella at the cathedral in Milan in 1793, at Loreto in 1794, and in 1804 succeeded Pietro Alessandro Guglielmi at St Peter's, Rome. From about this time he devoted himself chiefly to church music. He became director of the Real Collegio di Musica in Naples in 1813, and maestro di cappella of the cathedral there in 1816. Bellini and Mercadante were among his pupils.

Works OPERA 37, including *Montezuma* (1781), *Armida* (1786), *Antigono*, *Ifigenia in Aulide* (1787), *Antigone* (1790), *Il mercato di Monfregoso* (1792), *Artaserse*, *Quinto Fabio*, *Gli Orazi e Curazi*, *Giulietta e Romeo* (after Shakespeare, 1796), *Andromeda*, *La morte di Mitridate* (1797), *I veri amici* (1798), *Il ratto delle Sabine* (1799), *Edipo a Colono* (after Sophocles, 1802), *Berenice, regina d'Armenia*.

CHORAL oratorios *La Passione* (1787), *Gerusalemme distrutta* (1812), *La modificazione di Gerusalemme*, and others; many cantatas; 23 Masses, Requiems, and other church music, including 55 Magnificats; canon for eight voices; *partimenti* and *solfeggi* for vocal exercise.

zingaresa or **zingarese** words used to describe music in, or supposed to be in, a gypsy manner; for instance, the finale of Brahms's violin concerto. The adjective is used in the form of 'alla zingarese'.

Zingari, Gli, **The Gypsies** opera by Ruggero ➤ **Leoncavallo** (libretto by E Cavacchioli and G Emanuel, after Pushkin), produced at the Hippodrome, London, on 16 September 1912.

Zipoli, Domenico (1688–1726) Italian composer. He studied with Alessandro Scarlatti in Naples and Bernardo Pasquini in Rome, where he became organist of the Jesuit church in 1715. He entered the Jesuit Order and in 1717 went to South America as a missionary.

Works SACRED AND SECULAR MUSIC three oratorios (music lost); church music; keyboard music (two volumes of *Sonate d'intavolatura*, published 1716).

zither member of a family of musical instruments consisting of one or more strings stretched over a resonating frame or soundbox, played horizontally. The modern concert zither has up to 45 strings of which five, passing over frets, are plucked with a ➤ **plectrum** for melody, and the remainder are plucked with the fingers for harmonic accompaniment.

Simple stick-and-board zithers are widespread in Africa; in India the ➤ **vina** represents a developed form of stick zither, while in Indonesia and the Far East versions of the **long zither** prevail. Tuning is by movable bridges and the long zither is played with a plectrum, producing an intense tone of sharp attack.

Zopfstil (German 'pigtail style') in music, derogatory term sometimes applied to the formal courtly style of the later 18th century.

zoppa (Italian 'limp') in music, a strong accent on a second note off the beat or a long note following a short one, as in the ➤ **Scotch snap**. The motion of a musical piece in such a rhythm is called 'alla zoppa'.

Zoraida di Granata opera seria ('serious opera') by Donizetti (libretto by B Merelli after F Gonzales), produced at the Teatro Argentina, Rome, on 28 January 1822. In the story, Almuzir murders the king and hopes to marry his daughter Zoraide. But he is defeated in combat by Knight Abenamet.

Zoroastre opera by Rameau (libretto by L de Cahusac) produced at the Paris Opéra on 5 December 1749. The story takes place following the death of the Bactrian King. The High Priest Abramane seizes power, enlisting the help of Princess Erinice. Zoroastre is banished and his beloved Amélite is dragged away to be tormented by demons. Later, Zoroastre returns to free his people, defeating the evil powers of Abramane and marrying Amélite.

Zumsteeg, Johann Rudolf (1760–1802) German composer. His extended ballads were especially influential, some later being used as models by Schubert.

Zumsteeg was a fellow-pupil and friend of the playwright Schiller at the Karlschule in Stuttgart. In 1781 he entered the service of the Stuttgart court as a cellist, becoming Konzertmeister in 1792.

Works OPERA AND STAGE operas, including *Das Tartarische Gesetz* (1780), *Le delizie campestri, o Ippolito e Atricia* (1782), *Armida* (1785), *Die Geisterinsel* (after *The Tempest*, 1798), *Das Pfauenfest* and others; melodrama *Tamira*; incidental music to *Hamlet* (1785), *Macbeth*, Schiller's *Die Räuber*, and other plays.

CHORAL AND VOCAL cantatas; Masses and other church music; songs and ballads *Lenore* (Bürger), *Colma* (Ossian), *Die Büssende, Ritter Toggenburg* (Schiller), *Die Entführung*.

OTHER ten cello concertos (1777–92).

Zusammenschlag (German 'hit together') see ➤ **acciaccatura** or ➤ **mordent**.

Zweig, Stefan (1881–1942) Austrian novelist and dramatist. He collaborated with Strauss from 1932; *Die schweigsame Frau* was produced at Dresden (1935) but soon proscribed because of Zweig's Jewish ancestry. Zweig intended to write the libretto for Strauss's *Friedenstag*, suggested to him by Joseph Gregor, but because the Nazi régime made Zweig's appearance on any German stage impossible after 1935, this was afterwards undertaken by Gregor himself. See also ➤ *Schweigsame Frau, Die* (Richard Strauss); ➤ **Toch** (*Heilige aus USA*).

Zwerg, Der, The Dwarf opera in one act by Alexander von ➤ **Zemlinsky** (libretto by G C Klaren, after Wilde's *The Birthday of the Infanta*). Composed 1920–21, it was first performed in Cologne on 28 May 1922, conducted by Klemperer. The story concerns a Dwarf, given to the Spanish Infanta as a birthday present. She toys with him as he declares his love for her. When the Dwarf sees his reflection in a mirror he is horrified by his ugliness and dies of a broken heart.

At Edinburgh and at Covent Garden the work has been given in a production by the Hamburg Opera, under the new title *The Birthday of the Infanta*, with new libretto by A Dresen.

Zwilich, Ellen Taaffe (1939–) US composer. Her music is basically tonal in idiom, sometimes recalling minimalist or late Romantic precedents. Her *Symposium* for orchestra was conducted by Boulez in 1974, and her First Symphony won a Pulitzer Prize in 1983.

Zwilich studied at Florida State University and with Ivan Galamian in New York. She played violin in the American Symphony Orchestra under Stokowski and studied further at the Juilliard School in New York, and with Sessions and Carter.

Works ORCHESTRAL *Symbolom* for orchestra (1988), Symphony no. 2 'Cello' (1985) and no. 3 (1992, commissioned by the New York Philharmonic Orchestra); concertos for trombone (1988), flute (1990), oboe (1990), bassoon (1992), horn (1993), and trumpet (1994).

OTHER choral and solo vocal music; chamber pieces, including the Double Quartet for strings (1984) and Quintet for clarinet and strings (1990).

Zwillingsbrüder, Die, The Twin Brothers play with music by Schubert (libretto by G E von Hofmann), produced at the Kärntnertortheater, Vienna, on 14 June 1820. The story concerns the betrothal of Anton and Lieschen, which is complicated by the prior claim of Franz Spiers and the reappearance of his missing twin brother Friedrich.

Zwingburg scenic cantata by Ernst ➤ **Krenek** (libretto by Franz Werfel). Composed in 1922 and first performed at the Staatsoper, Berlin, on 21 October 1924, it was Krenek's first work for the stage. The story is about a tyrannical overlord who is overthrown in a coup, but new masters establish the same regime.

Zwischenspiel in music, German term meaning ➤ interlude.

Zyklus work for percussion by Karlheinz Stockhausen, involving random choice and improvisation. The work was first performed at Darmstadt on 25 August 1959.

Żywny, Wojciech (1756–1842) Polish piano teacher and composer. He studied with Jan Kuchar and worked at the Polish court of Stanisław August during the 1780s. He later moved to Warsaw and was Frédérick Chopin's piano teacher 1816–22. His works include piano pieces, overtures, and songs.

Chronology

Dates marked 'fp' correspond to the date of first performance, while those marked 'pub.' indicate the publication date. Unlabelled dates are those of composition.

	1360	*Messe de Nostre Dame* (Machaut)
	1364	Mass for the Coronation of Charles V of France (Machaut)
	1365	*Voir-dit* (Machaut)
Guillaume de Machaut dies (77)	1377	
Guillaume Dufay born (–1474)	c.1400	
	1436	*Nuper rosarum flores* (Dufay)
Josquin Des Pres born (–1521)	c.1440	
Guillaume Dufay dies (c.74)	1474	
	1502	First book of Masses (Josquin Des Pres)
Thomas Tallis born (–1585)	c.1505	
	1512	Second book of Masses (Josquin Des Pres)
	1516	Third book of Masses (Josquin Des Pres)
Josquin Des Pres dies (c.81)	1521	
Giovanni Pierluigi Palestrina born (–1594)	c.1525	
Orlande de Lassus born (–1594)	c.1532	
William Byrd born (–1623)	c.1543	
	1554	First book of Masses (Palestrina) pub. *Puer natus est nobis* (Tallis)
	1555	*Missa Papae Marcelli* (Palestrina)
Claudio Monteverdi born (–1643)	1567	
	1573	*Spem in Alium* (Tallis)
	1575	*Cantiones sacrae* (Byrd & Tallis) pub.
	1580	*Laudi spirituali* (Palestrina)
Thomas Tallis dies (c.80)	1585	
	1589	*Songes of Sundrie Natures* (Byrd) *Cantiones sacrae*, Book 1 (Byrd)
	1591	*Cantiones sacrae*, Book 2 (Byrd)
Orlando di Lassus dies (c.64) Giovanni Pierluigi Palestrina dies (c.69)	1594	
	1607	*Gradualia* (Byrd)
	1611	*Parthenia, or the Maidenhead of the First Music that was Ever Printed for Virginals* (Gibbons, Byrd & Bull)
William Byrd dies (c.80)	1623	
	1624	*Il combattimento di Tancredi e Clorinda* (Monteverdi) fp
Jean-Baptiste Lully born (–1687)	1632	
	1642	*L'Incoronazione di Poppea* (Monteverdi) fp
Claudio Monteverdi dies (76)	1643	
Henry Purcell born (–1695)	c.1659	
	1663	*Le Mariage forcé* (Lully)
	1669	*Monsieur de Pourceaugnac* (Lully) fp

	1670	*Le Bourgeois Gentilhomme* (Lully) fp
	1673	*Cadmus and Hermione* (Lully)
	1674	*Alceste* (Lully) fp
Antonio Vivaldi born (–1741)	1678	*Psyché* (Lully) fp
	1681	*Le Triomphe de l'Amour* (Lully) fp
Jean Philippe Rameau born (–1764)	1683	*Phaëton* (Lully) fp
George Frideric Handel born (–1759)	1685	
Johann Sebastian Bach born (–1750)		
Domenico Scarlatti born (–1757)		
	1686	*Armide and Renaud* (Lully) fp
Jean-Baptiste Lully dies (54)	1687	
	1689	*Dido and Aeneas* (Purcell) fp
	1692	*The Fairy Queen* (Purcell)
		Ode for St Cecilia's Day (Purcell)
Henry Purcell dies (c.36)	1695	*Elegy on the Death of Queen Mary* (Purcell)
		The Indian Queen (Purcell) fp
	1708	*Gloria in D* (Vivaldi)
	1711	*Rinaldo* (Handel) fp
	1712	*Harmonic Inspiration* (Vivaldi) pub.
Christoph Willibald von Gluck born (–1787)	1714	
	1717	*Water Music* (Handel)
	1720	Partita in D minor for solo violin (Bach)
	1721	*The Brandenburg Concertos* (Bach)
	1722	*French Suites* (Bach)
		The Well-tempered Klavier (Bach)
	1723	*St John Passion* (Bach)
	1725	*The Four Seasons* (Vivaldi) pub.
		Easter Oratorio (Bach)
	1729	*St Matthew Passion* (Bach)
	1731	*German Suites* (Bach)
Franz Joseph Haydn born (–1809)	1732	*Acis and Galatea* (Handel) fp
	1733	*Hippolyte et Aricie* (Rameau) fp
	1734	*Christmas Oratorio* (Bach)
	1735	*Italian Concerto* (Bach)
		Les Indes Galantes (Rameau) fp
	1737	*Castor et Pollux* (Rameau) fp
	1739	*Dardanus* (Rameau) fp
		Israel in Egypt (Handel) fp
Antonio Vivaldi dies (63)	1741	
	1742	*Goldberg Variations* (Bach)
		Messiah (Handel) fp
	1744	*Semele* (Handel) fp
	1747	*The Musical Offering* (Bach)
		Judas Maccabaeus (Handel) fp
	1748	Mass in B minor (Bach)
	1749	*Die Kunst der Fuge* (Bach)
		Zoroastre (Rameau) fp
		Music for the Royal Fireworks (Handel)
Johann Sebastian Bach dies (65)	1750	
	1752	*Jeptha* (Handel)

Wolfgang Amadeus Mozart born (–1791)	1756	
Domenico Scarlatti dies (71)	1757	
George Frideric Handel dies (74)	1759	
	1761	Minuet and Trio in G for solo piano (K 1) (Mozart)
	1762	*Orfeo ed Eridice* (Gluck) fp
	1763	*Abaris* (Rameau) fp
Jean Philippe Rameau dies (81)	1764	Symphonies No. 21, No. 22, the *Philosopher*, and No. 23 (Haydn)
	1765	Symphony No. 5 (K 22) (Mozart)
	1768	*Missa brevis* in G (K 49) (Mozart)
	1769	Mass in C (K 66), the *Pater Domenicus* (Mozart)
		Symphony No. 48, *Maria Theresa* (Haydn)
Ludwig van Beethoven born (–1827)	1770	*Mitridate, Rè di Ponto* (Mozart) fp
	1771	*Grosse Orgelmesse* (Haydn)
	1772	String Quartets No. 2 (K 155) and No. 3 (K 156) (Mozart)
		Symphony No. 45, the *Farewell* (Haydn)
	1773	*Exultate, jubilate* (K 165) (Mozart)
	1774	*Iphigénie en Aulide* (Gluck)
	1777	Piano Concerto No. 9 (K 271) (Mozart)
	1778	Symphony No. 31 (K 297), the *Paris* (Mozart)
		Flute Concertos No. 1 (K 313) and No. 2 (K 314) (Mozart)
		Symphony No. 53, the *Imperial* (Haydn)
	1779	Mass in C (No. 16) (K 317), the *Coronation* (Mozart)
		Iphigenia en Tauride (Gluck) fp
	1781	*Russian* (or *Maiden*) String Quartets (Haydn)
		Idomeneo (Mozart)
	1782	Symphony No. 35 (K 385), the *Haffner* (Mozart)
	1783	Symphony No. 36 (K 425), the *Linz* (Mozart)
	1785	String Quartets Nos. 14 to 19, the *Haydn Quartets*
		Piano Concertos No. 20 (K 466), No. 21 (K 467), and No. 22 (K 482) (Mozart)
		The Seven Last Words of Our Saviour on the Cross (Haydn)
Carl Maria von Weber born (–1826)	1786	*Le Nozze di Figaro* (Mozart) fp
		Symphony No. 38 (K 504), the *Prague* (Mozart)
		String Quartet No. 20 (K 499), the *Hoffmeister* (Mozart)
Christoph Willibald von Gluck dies (73)	1787	*Don Giovanni* (Mozart) fp
		String Quintet No. 3 (K 515) (Mozart)
	1788	Symphonies No. 39 (K 543), No. 40 (K 550), and No. 41 (K 551), the *Jupiter* (Mozart)
	1789	Piano Sonatas No. 16 (K 570) and No. 17 (K 576) (Mozart)
		Symphony No. 92, the *Oxford* (Haydn)

	1790	*Così fan tutte* (Mozart) fp
		String Quartets Nos. 21 to 23, the *King of Prussia Quartets* (Mozart)
Wolfgang Amadeus Mozart dies (35)	1791	*Die Zauberflöte* (Mozart) fp
Giacomo Meyerbeer born (–1864)		Clarinet Concerto in A major (K 622) (Mozart)
		Requiem Mass (K 626) (unfinished) (Mozart)
Gioacchino Rossini born (–1868)	1792	
	1794	Symphony No. 100, the *Military*, and No. 101, the *Clock* (Haydn)
	1795	Symphony No. 103, the *Drum Roll*, and No. 104, the *London* (Haydn)
Franz Schubert born (–1828)	1797	
Gaetano Donizetti born (–1848)		
	1798	*The Creation* (Haydn)
	1799	*Pathétique* Piano Sonata No. 8 (op. 13) (Beethoven)
Vincenzo Bellini born (–1835)	1801	Mass No. 13 in B flat, *The Creation Mass* (Haydn)
		The Seasons (Haydn)
		Moonlight Piano Sonata No. 2 (op. 27) (Beethoven)
	1802	*Seven Bagatelles* (op. 33) (Beethoven)
Hector Berlioz born (–1869)	1803	*Kreutzer Sonata* in A major (op. 47) (Beethoven)
		String Quartet No. 83 (op. 103) (Haydn)
	1804	*Eroica* Symphony No. 3 (op. 55) (Beethoven)
		Waldstein Piano Sonata No. 21 (op. 53) (Beethoven)
	1805	*Fidelio* (Beethoven) fp
		Appassionata Piano Sonata No. 23 (op. 57) (Beethoven)
	1806	Violin Concerto in D (op. 61) (Beethoven)
		Piano Concerto No. 4 in G (op. 58) (Beethoven)
		Rasumovsky Quartets (op. 59) (Beethoven)
	1807	Mass in C major (op. 86) (Beethoven)
	1808	Symphony No. 5 in C minor (op. 67) (Beethoven)
		Pastoral Symphony No. 6 in F (op. 68) (Beethoven)
		Cello Sonata in A major (op. 69) (Beethoven)
Franz Joseph Haydn dies (77)	1809	*Emperor* Piano Concerto No. 5 in E flat (op. 73) (Beethoven)
Felix-Bartholdy Mendelssohn born (–1847)		String Quartet No. 10, the *Harp Quartet* (op. 74) (Beethoven)
Frédéric Chopin born (–1849)	1810	*Egmont* (op. 84) (Beethoven)
Robert Schumann born (–1856)		
Franz Liszt born (–1886)	1811	*Archduke* Piano Trio in B flat (op. 97) (Beethoven)
	1812	Symphony No. 7 in A (op. 92) (Beethoven)
		Symphony No. 8 in F (op. 93) (Beethoven)

Richard Wagner born (–1883)	1813	*Tancredi* (Rossini) fp
Giuseppe Fortunio Francesco Verdi born (–1901)		
	1816	*The Barber of Seville* (Rossini) fp
	1817	*The Thieving Magpie* (Rossini) fp
Charles François Gounod born (–1893)	1818	*Hammerklavier* Piano Sonata No. 29 (op. 106) (Beethoven)
		Moses in Egypt (Rossini) fp
	1821	*Der Freischütz* (Weber) fp
César(-Auguste) Franck born (–1890)	1822	*Missa Solemnis* (op. 123) (Beethoven)
	1823	*Choral* Symphony No. 9 in D minor (op. 125) (Beethoven)
		Variations on a Waltz by Diabelli (op. 120) (Beethoven)
		Euryanthe (Weber) fp
Bedrich Smetana born (–1884)	1824	
Josef Anton Bruckner born (–1896)		
	1825	String Quartets No. 12 (op. 130) and No. 15 (op. 132) (Beethoven)
Carl Maria von Weber dies (39)	1826	String Quartets No. 13 (op. 130), No. 14 (op. 131), and No. 16 (op. 135) (Beethoven)
		Elvida (Donizetti) fp
		Oberon (Weber) fp
		A Midsummer Night's Dream (Mendelssohn)
Ludwig van Beethoven dies (56)	1827	*Il pirata* (Bellini) fp
Franz Schubert dies (31)	1828	*Count Ory* (Rossini) fp
		Impromptus (Schubert)
	1829	*William Tell* (Rossini) fp
	1830	*Symphonie fantastique* (Berlioz)
		Abegg Variations (op. 1) (Schumann)
	1831	*La sonnambula* (Bellini) fp
		Norma (Bellini) fp
		Robert le Diable (Meyerbeer) fp
	1832	*L'Elisir d'amore* (Donizetti) fp
Johannes Brahms born (–1897)	1833	Symphony No. 4 (op. 90), the *Italian* (Mendelssohn)
Alexander Porfiryevich Borodin born (–1887)		
	1834	*Harold en Italie* (Berlioz)
Vincenzo Bellini dies (33)	1835	*Lucia di Lammermoor* (Donizetti) fp
(Charles-)Camille Saint-Saëns born (–1921)		
	1836	*Les Hugenots* (Meyerbeer) fp
Mily Alexeyevich Balakirev born (–1910)	1837	*Requiem*, op. 5 (Berlioz)
Georges (Alexandre César Léopold) Bizet born (–1875)	1838	*Benvenuto Cellini* (Berlioz) fp
		Kinderscenen (op. 15) (Schumann)
Modest Petrovich Mussorgsky born (–1881)	1839	*Roméo et Juliette* (Berlioz)
Pyotr Il'yich Tchaikovsky born (–1893)	1840	*La fille du régiment* (Donizetti) fp
		Liederkreise (Schumann)
		Dichterliebe (op. 48) (Schumann)
		Frauenliebe und -leben (op. 42) (Schumann)

Anton Dvořák born (–1904)	1841	Symphony No. 1 (op. 38), the *Früling* (Schumann)
Jules Massenet born (–1912)	1842	Symphony No. 3 (op. 56), the *Scottish* (Mendelssohn)
Arthur Seymour Sullivan born (–1900)		*Stabat Mater* (Rossini)
		Nabucco (Verdi)
Edvard Grieg born (–1907)	1843	*Don Pasquale* (Donizetti) fp
		Die fliegende Holländer (Wagner)
Nikolai Andreievich Rimsky-Korsakov born (–1908)	1844	
Gabriel (Urbain) Fauré born (–1924)	1845	*Tannhäuser* (Wagner)
	1846	*The Damnation of Faust* (op. 24) (Berlioz)
		Elijah (op. 70) (Mendelssohn) fp
		Sonetti del Petrarca (Liszt)
		Symphony No. 2 (op. 61) (Schumann)
Felix-Bartholdy Mendelssohn dies (38)	1847	
(Charles) Hubert (Hastings) Parry born (–1918)	1848	*Les Préludes* (Liszt)
Gaetano Donizetti dies (50)		
Frédéric Chopin dies (39)	1849	*Le Prophete* (Meyerbeer) fp
		Totentanz (Liszt) revised
		Manfred (Schumann)
	1850	*Te Deum* (op. 22) (Berlioz)
		Symphony No. 3 (op. 97), the *Rhenish* (Schumann)
		Lohengrin (Wagner) fp
	1851	Symphony No. 4 (op. 120) (Schumann)
		Rigoletto (Verdi)
Charles Villiers Stanford born (–1924)	1852	
	1853	*Il Trovatore* (Verdi) fp
		La Traviata (Verdi) fp
Leoš Janáček born (–1928)	1854	*L'enfance du Christ* (op. 25) (Berlioz)
	1855	*Sicilian Vespers* (Verdi) fp
Robert Schumann dies (46)	1856	*Dante Symphony* (Liszt)
Edward Elgar born (–1934)	1857	
Giacomo Puccini born (–1924)	1858	*Les Troyens* (Berlioz)
		Piano Concerto No. 1 (op. 15) (Brahms)
	1859	*A Masked Ball* (Verdi) fp
Gustav Mahler born (–1911)	1860	
	1861	*Mephisto Waltz* No. 1 (Liszt)
Claude Debussy born (–1918)	1862	*Béatrice et Bénédict* (Berlioz) fp
Frederick Delius born (–1934)		*Die Legende von der heilige Elisabeth* (Liszt)
	1863	*Les pêcheurs de perles* (Bizet) fp
Giacomo Meyerbeer dies (73)	1864	
Richard Strauss born (–1949)		
Carl Nielsen born (–1931)	1865	*Rákóczy March* (Liszt)
Jean Sibelius born (–1957)		*Tristan and Isolde* (Wagner) fp
Ferruccio Busoni born (–1924)	1866	*The Bartered Bride* (Smetana)
Erik Satie born (–1926)		
Enrique Granados born (–1916)	1867	Symphony No. 1 (Borodin)
		Roméo et Juliette (Gounod) fp

		Night on a Bare Mountain (Mussorgsky)
		Don Carlos (Verdi) fp
Gioacchino Rossini dies (76)	1868	Piano Concerto (op. 16) (Grieg)
		Ein deutsche Requiem (Brahms)
		Die Meistersinger von Nürnberg (Wagner)
Hector Berlioz dies (65)	1869	*Die Walküre* (Wagner) fp
		Romeo and Juliet (Tchaikovsky)
	1871	*Jeux d'enfants* (piano) (Bizet)
		Aïda (Verdi) fp
Ralph Vaughan Williams born (–1958)	1872	*L'Arlésienne* (Bizet)
		Symphony No. 2 (Bruckner)
		Boris Godunov (Mussorgsky) fp
Sergey Vasilevich Rachmaninov born (–1943)	1873	Symphony No. 3 (Bruckner)
Arnold Schoenberg born (–1951)	1874	*Pictures at an Exhibition* (Mussorgsky)
Gustav Holst born (–1934)		*Requiem* (Verdi)
Charles Ives born (–1954)		
Maurice Ravel born (–1937)	1875	*Carmen* (Bizet) fp
Georges (Alexandre César Léopold) Bizet dies (36)		*Danse macabre* (Saint-Saëns)
Manuel de Falla born (–1946)	1876	*Les Eolides* (Franck)
		Symphony No. 2 (Borodin)
		Symphony No. 1 (Brahms)
		Symphony No. 5 (Bruckner)
		Götterdammerung (Wagner) fp
		Siegfried (Wagner) fp
	1877	*Swan Lake* (Tchaikovsky) fp
		Samson and Delilah (Saint-Saëns)
		Stabat Mater (Dvořák)
	1878	Violin Concerto No. 1 (op. 77) (Brahms)
		HMS Pinafore (Sullivan) fp
		Symphony No. 4 (op. 36) (Tchaikovsky)
		Violin Concerto (Tchaikovsky)
	1879	*Les Béatitudes* (Franck)
		Violin Sonata No. 1 (op. 78) (Brahams)
		Má Vlast (Smetana)
		The Pirates of Penzance (Sullivan) fp
		Eugene Onegin (Tchaikovsky) fp
	1880	*In the Steppes of Central Asia* (Borodin)
		Symphony No. 6 (Dvořák)
		Serenade for Strings (op. 48) (Tchaikovsky)
Modest Petrovich Mussorgsky dies (42)	1881	Piano Concerto No. 2 (op. 83) (Brahms)
Béla Bartók born (–1945)		*Academic Festival Overture* (op. 80) (Brahms)
		Tragic Overture (op. 81) (Brahms)
Zoltán Kodály born (–1967)	1882	*Le chasseur maudit* (Franck)
Karol Szymanowski born (–1937)		*The Snow Maiden* (Rimsky-Korsakov) fp
Igor Stravinsky born (–1971)		*Parsifal* (Wagner) fp
Richard Wagner dies (69)	1883	Symphony No. 3 (Brahms)
Anton Webern born (–1945)		*Mephisto Waltz* No. 3 (Liszt)
		Symphony No. 7 (Bruckner)

Bedrich Smetana dies	1884	*Canterbury Pilgrims* (Stanford) fp
		Symphony No. 1 (Mahler)
		Te Deum (Bruckner)
Alban Berg born (–1935)	1885	Symphonic Variations (Franck)
		Symphony No. 4 (Brahms)
		Symphony No. 7 (Dvořák)
		Mephisto Waltz No. 4 (Liszt)
		20 Hungarian Rhapsodies (Liszt)
		The Mikado (Sullivan)
Franz Liszt dies (74)	1886	*Carnival of the Animals* (Saint-Saëns)
		Aus Italien (R Strauss)
Alexander Porfiryevich Borodin dies (53)	1887	Symphony No. 8 (Bruckner)
		Ruddigore (Sullivan) fp
		Concerto for Violin and Cello (op. 102) (Brahms)
	1888	*Judith* (Parry)
		Trois gymnopédies (Satie)
		Symphony in D minor (Franck)
		Scheherazade (Rimsky-Korsakov)
		Symphony No. 5 (op. 64) (Tchaikovsky)
		The Yeomen of the Guard (Sullivan)
	1889	*The Gondoliers* (Sullivan)
César(-Auguste) Franck dies (67)	1890	*Prince Igor* (Borodin) fp
Bohuslav Martinu born (–1959)		*Requiem* (Fauré)
		The Queen of Spades (Tchaikovsky) fp
		The Sleeping Beauty (Tchaikovsky) fp
		Tod und Verklärung (R Strauss)
Sergey Sergeyevich Prokofiev born (–1953)	1891	
Darius Milhaud born (–1974)	1892	*Job* (Parry)
		Nutcracker (Tchaikovsky) fp
Charles François Gounod dies (75)	1893	Symphony No. 9, *From the New World* (Dvořák)
Pyotr Il'yich Tchaikovsky dies (53)		String Quartet in F major (op. 96), *American* (Dvořák)
		Karelia Suite (Sibelius)
		Falstaff (Verdi) fp
		Symphony No. 6, the *Pathétique* (op. 74) (Tchaikovsky)
	1894	*Lady Radnor's Suite* (Parry)
		Symphony No. 2, the *Resurrection* (Mahler)
		Symphony No. 9 (Bruckner)
Paul Hindemith born (– 1963)	1895	*Till Eulenspiegel* (R Strauss)
Josef Anton Bruckner dies (72)	1896	*Vier ernste Gesänge* (op. 121) (Brahms)
		La Bohème (Puccini) fp
		Also sprach Zarathustra (Strauss)
Johannes Brahms dies (63)	1897	
George Gershwin born (–1937)	1898	
Francis Poulenc born (–1963)	1899	*The Tsar's Bride* (Rimsky-Korsakov) fp
		Des Knaben Wunderhorn (Mahler)
		Enigma Variations (Elgar)

Aaron Copland born (–1990)	1900	Symphony No. 4 (Mahler)
Arthur Seymour Sullivan dies (58)		*The Dream of Gerontius* (Elgar)
		Tosca (Puccini) fp
		Finlandia (Sibelius)
Giuseppe Fortunio Francesco Verdi dies (87)	1901	*Cockaigne* (Elgar)
		Rusalka (Dvořák) fp
		Piano Concerto No. 2 (Rachmaninov)
William Walton born (–1983)	1902	Symphony No. 5 (Mahler)
		Pelléas et Mélisande (Debussy) fp
		Symphony No. 2 (Sibelius)
	1903	*Trois morceaux en forme de poire* (Satie)
		Symphonia Domestica (R Strauss)
Anton Dvořák dies (62)	1904	Symphony No. 6 (Mahler)
		Kindertotenlieder (Mahler)
		L'ille joyeuse (Debussy)
		Jenufa (Janáček) fp
		Madame Butterfly (Puccini)
		Symphony No. 3, *The Camp Meeting* (Ives)
Michael Tippett born (–1998)	1905	*La mer* (Debussy)
		Introduction and Allegro for Strings (Elgar)
		Symphony No. 7 (Mahler)
		Salome (Strauss)
		String Quartet (Webern)
Dmitri Shostakovitch born (–1975)	1906	*Central Park in the Dark in the Good Old Summertime* (Ives)
		Maskarade (C A Nielsen) fp
Edvard Grieg dies (64)	1907	Symphony No. 8 (Mahler)
		Symphony No. 3 (Sibelius)
Nikolai Andreievich Rimsky-Korsakov dies (64)	1908	Symphony No. 1 (Elgar)
Olivier Messiaen born (–1992)		*The Unanswered Question* (Ives)
	1909	*Das Lied von der Erde* (Mahler)
		Symphony No. 3 (Rachmaninov)
		Piano Concerto No. 3 (Rachmaninov)
		Erwartung (Schoenberg)
		Elektra (Strauss)
		On Wenlock Edge (Vaughan Williams)
Mily Alexeyevich Balakirev dies (73)	1910	*Fantasia contrappuntistica* (Busoni)
		Préludes I (Debussy)
		Symphonies No. 9 and No. 10 (Mahler)
		La fanciulla del West (Puccini)
		Litany of St John Chrysostom (Rachmaninov)
		Pavane pour une infante défunte (Ravel)
		The Firebird (Stravinsky)
		Fantasia on a Theme of Thomas Tallis (Vaughan Williams)
Gustav Mahler dies (50)	1911	Symphony No. 3, *The Camp Meeting* (Ives)
		Symphony No. 3, *Expansive Symphony* (C A Nielsen)

		Ma mère l'oye (Ravel)
		Gurrelieder (Schoenberg)
		Symphony No. 4 (Sibelius)
		Der Rosenkavalier (Strauss)
		Petrushka (Stravinsky)
		On Hearing the First Cuckoo in Spring (Delius)
Jules Massenet dies (70)	1912	*Images* (Debussy)
		Daphnis et Chloé (Ravel) fp
		Valses nobles et sentimentales (Ravel)
		Pierrot Lunaire (Schoenberg)
		14 Songs (op. 34) (Rachmaninov)
		Ariadne auf Naxos (R Strauss)
Witold Lutosławski born (–1994)	1913	*Altenberglieder* (Berg) fp
Benjamin Britten born (–1976)		*Indianische Fantasie* (Busoni)
		The Rite of Spring (Stravinsky)
		Préludes II (Debussy)
		St Paul's Suite (Holst)
		New England Holidays (Ives)
		The Bells (Rachmaninov)
	1914	*Three Pieces for Orchestra* (op. 6) (Berg)
	1915	*Indianische Tagebuch II* (Busoni)
		Symphony No. 5 (Sibelius)
		An Alpine Symphony (R Strauss)
Enrique Granados dies (48)	1916	*Jerusalem* (Parry)
		Nights in the Gardens of Spain (de Falla)
		The Planets (Holst)
		Symphony No. 4, the *Inextinguishable* (Nielsen)
	1917	*Parade* (Satie) fp
		Arlecchino (Busoni) fp
		Violin Sonata (Debussy)
Claude Debussy dies (55)	1918	*Duke Bluebeard's Castle* (Bartók) fp
Leonard Bernstein born (–1990)		*Taras Bulba* (Janáček)
(Charles) Hubert (Hastings) Parry dies (70)		*Il trittico* (Puccini)
	1919	*The Three-Cornered Hat* (de Falla)
		Le tombeau de Couperin (Ravel)
		Die Frau ohne Schatten (R Strauss)
	1920	*Le tombeau de Claude Debussy* (Ravel)
		La Valse (Ravel)
(Charles-)Camille Saint-Saëns dies (86)	1921	*Káta Kabanova* (Janáček) fp
		Love for Three Oranges (Prokofiev) fp
		Faust (Walton)
		Symphony No. 1, the *Classical* (Prokofiev)
György Ligeti born	1923	*Psalmus Hungaricus* (Kodály)
Charles Villiers Stanford dies (71)	1924	*Rhapsody in Blue* (Gershwin)
Feruccio Busoni dies (58)		*The Cunning Little Vixen* (Janáček) fp
Gabriel (Urbain) Fauré dies (79)		
Giacomo Puccini dies (66)		

Pierre Boulez born	1925	*Wozzeck* (Berg) fp
Luciano Berio born (–2003)		Piano Concerto (Gershwin)
Erik Satie dies (59)		
	1926	*The Miraculous Mandarin* (Bartók) fp
		Lyric Suite (Berg)
		Król Roger (Szymanowski)
		Glagolitic Mass (Janáček)
		The Makropoulos Case (Janáček) fp
		Háry János (Kodály) fp
		Turandot (Puccini)
	1927	*Oedipus Rex* (Stravinsky)
Leoš Janáček dies (74)	1928	String Quartet No. 4 (Bartók)
Karlheinz Stockhausen born		Symphony for chamber orchestra (op. 21) (Webern)
		An American in Paris (Gershwin)
		Boléro (Ravel)
	1930	*From the House of the Dead* (Janáček)
		Piano Concerto for the Left Hand (Ravel)
		Symphony of Psalms (Stravinsky)
Carl Nielsen dies (66)	1931	Piano Concerto No. 2 (Bartók)
		Harnasie (Szymanowski)
		Piano Concerto in G (Ravel)
		Belshazzar's Feast (Walton)
	1932	*Sinfonietta* (Britten)
Krysztof Penderecki born	1933	*Hungarian Sketches* (Bartók)
		A Simple Symphony (op. 2) (Britten)
Edward Elgar dies (76)	1934	String Quartet No. 5 (Bartók)
Gustav Holst dies (59)		*Matthis der Maler* (Hindemith)
Frederick Delius dies (71)		*Rhapsody on a Theme of Paganini* (Rachmaninov)
Harrison Birtwistle born		
Peter Maxwell Davies born		
Alban Berg dies (50)	1935	Violin Concerto (Berg)
		Porgy and Bess (Gershwin) fp
		Die schweigsame Frau (R Strauss)
		Symphony No. 1 (Walton)
	1936	*Music for Strings, Percussion, and Celeste* (Bartók)
		Divertimento for Strings (Bartók)
		Poèmes pour Mi (Messiaen)
		Dona nobis pacem (Vaughan Williams)
George Gershwin dies (38)	1937	*Lulu* (Berg) fp
Maurice Ravel dies (62)		*Variations on a Theme by Frank Bridge* (Britten)
Karol Szymanowski dies (54)		
	1938	Violin Concerto No. 2 (Bartók)
		String Quartet (op. 28) (Webern)
		Piano Concerto (op. 13) (Britten)
		Mathis de Maler (Hindemith) fp
		Romeo and Juliet (Prokofiev)

	1939	*Billy the Kid* (Copland) fp
		String Quartet No. 6 (Bartók)
		Violin Concerto (Walton)
	1940	*Sinfonia da Requiem* (op. 20) (Britten)
	1941	*Quartet for the End of Time* (Messiaen)
		A Child of Our Time (Tippett)
	1942	*Rodeo* (Copland)
		Fanfare for the Common Man (Copland)
		Hymn to St Cecilia (Britten)
Sergey Vasilevich Rachmaninov dies (69)	1943	*Serenade* (Britten)
	1944	*Concerto for Orchestra* (Bartók)
		Symphony No. 1, *Jeremiah* (Bernstein)
		On the Town (Bernstein) fp
		Appalachian Spring (Copland)
		Vingt regards sur l'enfant Jésus (Messiaen)
		Symphony No. 5 (Prokofiev)
Anton Webern dies (61)	1945	Piano Concerto No. 3 (Bartók)
Béla Bartók dies (64)		*Peter Grimes* (Britten) fp
		Violin Concerto No. 1 (Prokofiev)
Manuel de Falla dies (69)	1946	*Young Person's Guide to the Orchestra* (Britten)
	1947	*Albert Herring* (Britten) fp
	1948	*Calligrammes* (Poulenc)
		Four Last Songs (Strauss)
		A Survivor from Warsaw (Schoenberg) fp
Richard Strauss dies (85)	1949	Symphony No. 2, *The Age of Anxiety* (Bernstein) fp
		Turangalila Symphony (Messiaen) fp
Arnold Schoenberg dies (76)	1951	*Billy Budd* (Britten) fp
		The Rake's Progress (Stravinksy)
Sergey Sergeyevich Prokofiev dies (61)	1953	*Gloriana* (Britten) fp
		Fantasia Concertante on a Theme by Corelli (Tippett)
Charles Ives dies (79)	1954	*Serenade* (Bernstein)
		The Turn of the Screw (Britten)
		Concerto for Orchestra (Messiaen)
		Troilus and Cressida (Walton) fp
	1955	*Le marteau sans maître* (Boulez)
	1956	*Candide* (Bernstein) fp
Jean Sibelius dies (91)	1957	*West Side Story* (Bernstein) fp
		The Prince of the Pagodas (Britten) fp
		Moses and Aaron (Schoenberg) fp
		Les dialogues des Carmélites (Poulenc)
Ralph Vaughan Williams dies (85)	1958	*Threni* (Stravinsky)
Bohuslav Martinu dies (68)	1959	
	1960	*Circles* (Berio)
		A Midsummer Night's Dream (Britten) fp
		Kontakte (Stockhausen)
		Symphony No. 2 (Walton)
	1961	*Atmosphères* (Ligeti)

	Gry weneckie (Lutosławksi)
	Magnificat and Nunc Dimittis (Tippett)
	War Requiem (Britten)
1962	*Poème symphonique* (Ligeti)
	Pli selon pli (Boulez)
	King Priam (Walton) fp
Francis Poulenc dies (64)	1963	Symphony No. 3, *Kaddish* (Bernstein)
Paul Hindemith dies (68)		Cello Symphony (Britten)
	1965	*Chichester Psalms* (Bernstein)
		Paroles tissées (Lutosławski)
	1966	*St Luke Passion* (Penderecki)
Zoltán Kodály dies (84)	1967	*Antechrist* (Davies)
		Symphony No. 2 (Lutosławksi)
		Hymnen (Stockhausen)
	1969	*Eight Songs for a Mad King* (Davies)
		La transfiguration de notre Seigneur Jésus Christ (Messiaen)
		The Devils of Loudon (Penderecki) fp
Igor Stravinsky dies (88)	1971	*Trans* (Stockhausen)
	1972	*Recital I (for Cathy)* (Berio)
		Symphony No. 3 (Tippett)
		Taverner (Davies) fp
	1973	*Clocks and Clouds* (Ligeti)
		Death in Venice (Britten) fp
Darius Milhaud dies (81)	1974	*San Francisco Polyphony* (Ligeti)
Dmitri Shostakovitch dies (68)	1975	*Rituel in memoriam Bruno Maderna* (Boulez)
Benjamin Britten dies (63)	1976	*Coro* (Berio)
	1978	*Paradise Lost* (Penderecki)
		Le Grand Macabre (Ligeti)
	1980	*The Lighthouse* (Davies) fp
		Notations (Boulez)
	1981	*Répons* (Boulez)
		Donnerstag aus Licht (Stockhausen)
	1982	*The Mask of Time* (Tippett)
William Walton dies (80)	1983	*Into the Labyrinth* (Davies)
		Symphony No. 3 (Lutosławski)
	1984	*Polish Requiem* (Penderecki) fp
		Un re in ascolto (Berio) fp
	1986	*Die schwarze Maske* (Penderecki) fp
	1988	Concerto for Piano and Orchestra (Ligeti)
	1989	*New Year* (Tippett) fp
Aaron Copland dies (90)	1990	Concerto for violin and orchestra (Ligeti)
Leonard Bernstein dies (72)		
Olivier Messiaen dies (83)	1992	
	1993	*Strathclyde Concerto* No. 8 (Davies)
Witold Lutosławski dies (81)	1994	Symphony No. 5 (Davies)
	1996	*Outis* (Berio) fp
Michael Tippett dies (93)	1998	*Exody* (Birtwistle) fp
	2000	*The Last Supper* (Birtwistle) fp
Luciano Berio dies (77)	2003